# 125 YEARS

**Star Tribune**

*125 years of history in the making*

LIBRARY OF CONGRESS CATALOG CARD NUMBER
92-62497

Star Tribune

COWLES MEDIA COMPANY

*the*

**STAR TRIBUNE HAS CHANGED A GREAT DEAL OVER THE PAST 125 YEARS BUT ITS PURPOSE HAS REMAINED THE SAME:**

**TO ENRICH THE SHARED LIFE OF THE COMMUNITY BY BEING THE AREA'S LEADING PROVIDER OF INFORMATION THAT PEOPLE VALUE.**

**THE BOOK IS DEDICATED TO ALL THE PEOPLE WHO HAVE HELPED THE STAR TRIBUNE FULFILL THAT PURPOSE DURING ITS FIRST 125 YEARS OF PUBLISHING.**

Joel R Kramer

**JOEL R. KRAMER**
**PUBLISHER AND PRESIDENT**
**STAR TRIBUNE**
**A DIVISION OF COWLES MEDIA COMPANY**

# *the*

STAR TRIBUNE CELEBRATED ITS 125TH ANNIVERSARY MAY 25, 1992.

THE FOLLOWING PAGES PROVIDE A LOOK AT HOW MINNEAPOLIS AND ST. PAUL, MINNESOTA, AND THE REST OF THE WORLD HAVE CHANGED SINCE THE FIRST EDITION WAS PUBLISHED IN 1867.

THESE FRONT PAGES PROVIDE SNAPSHOTS OF HISTORY. THEY ARE NOT A STUDIED EVALUATION AS FOUND IN HISTORY BOOKS—BUT RATHER, AS THE NEWS APPEARED TO READERS. NEWS EVENTS REPORTED AS ACCURATELY AS POSSIBLE AT THE TIME, WITH THE INFORMATION AVAILABLE.

FRONT PAGES FURNISH US WITH THE IMPORTANT TOPICS OF THE DAY. THE GRIPPING. THE SENSATIONAL. THE EVENTS THAT RIVET A NATION. A WORLD. BUT THEY ALSO LET US GLIMPSE AT THE LESS IMPORTANT EVENTS. THE FADS. THE FASHIONS. THE FRIVOLOUS.

FINALLY, FRONT PAGES SERVE TO REMIND US OF WHO WE WERE AND WHO WE HAVE BECOME. IN WHAT WAYS WE HAVE MOVED AHEAD, REMAINED THE SAME, BECOME SIDETRACKED OR MOVED BACKWARD.

WE HOPE YOU FIND YOUR JOURNEY THROUGH 125 YEARS OF HISTORY FASCINATING. AND REMEMBER, TODAY'S NEWSPAPERS BECOME TOMORROW'S HISTORY.

# 1867~1869

**Minneapolis Tribune,**
*Issued Daily, Tri-Weekly and Weekly,*
BY THE
**TRIBUNE PRINTING CO.**

Daily delivered in the city, per year ... [illegible]
Daily by mail, per year ... [illegible]
Tri-weekly, per year ... [illegible]
Weekly, per year ... [illegible]

# Minneapolis Daily Tribune.

VOL. 1. MINNEAPOLIS, MINNESOTA, SATURDAY MORNING, MAY 25, 1867. NO. 1.





THE lines being down most all day yesterday, we are without the greater part of our dispatches. No one can regret this accident more than ourselves.

### TELEGRAPHIC SUMMARY.

THE fire in New York City on the evening of the 23d inst. was the work of an incendiary. Loss, $30,000. Insured.

THE Union League Club of New York have acted on Horace Greeley's action in bailing Jeff Davis. They condemn the action but refuse to censure.

A number of Catholic prelates left New York, yesterday, for Rome. Among the presents to the Pope was $50,000 in gold from the Catholics of Cincinnati, Ohio.

SECRETARY SEWARD has signified his willingness to interfere with the English Government, in behalf of the Fenian, McClure.

IN consequence of the stringency of the money market, Govenor [illegible], of South Carolina, is going to issue an order staying the collection of debts indefinitely.

THE bombarding of the city of Mexico is still progressing, and great distress prevails in consequence.

MAXIMILIAN, it is said, wishes to surrender but is prevented.

THE demand for flour from San Francisco continues.

A MAN at Boston has sued his brother for $10,000 for alleged slanderous words used in a letter to their sister.

OWING to a memorable interview with Ben. Wood, Hon. John Morrisey does not appear in the income returns this year.

ONE of the new mechanical toys in Paris is a boat with a rower. This rower exactly imitates the movements of a real man, and works a pair of sculls with great energy. At times he seems fatigued, and anon quickens his movements and makes a rapid spurt for a short distance.

THE profits of steel manufacture are enormous. For instance, an iron bar worth $5, worked into horse-shoes, is worth $10 50; made into needles it represents $355; in the shape of pen-knife blades it brings $3,285, and refined and drawn into balance springs for watches, stands for $250,000.

THE colored people of Ohio have called a State Convention to meet in Columbus on the 3d day of July next. The object of the Convention is to ascertain how the colored people can best assist in having the word white stricken from the Constitution of that State.

THE income returns in [illegible] show a great falling off from last year, which is attributed to the depression of business. What else could it be attributed to after allowing for the increased exemptions? The three largest returns are [illegible] Washington, $31,501; J. S. Bailey, $[illegible], and C. M. Buchanan, $[illegible].

THE House tunnel has received another appropriation of [illegible] from the Massachusetts Legislature. A [illegible] pose of the great [illegible] has cost $22,[illegible] and [illegible] forty-five years to complete it. The bores have gone [illegible] distance through the mountain, and has cost $[illegible].

THE dogs belonging to some [illegible] Virginia sportsmen killed a flock of [illegible] sheep the other day, and the owners had to pay $[illegible]. The other day a dog got to the sheep-fold of [illegible], near Quincy, Illinois, and destroyed [illegible] worth of his South Down sheep.

THE Louisiana *Journal* says that a hen crossed between Shanghai and Brahma, belonging to Mr. John J. Arthur, of that vicinity, has *laid* several eggs within the past few weeks which are peculiar. At first appearance one would conclude that they were goose eggs, being about that size, but upon breaking the outside shell another egg is discovered within, the size of an ordinary hen egg, having a smooth hard shell and complete in every particular. The outside egg has its white and yellow also. Mr. Arthur intends to place some of these eggs under a setting hen and see what result comes forth.

### Crop Prospects in Other States

PENNSYLVANIA.

From the Clarion (Penn.) Democrat.

We have conversed with a large number of farmers from various parts of the country during the past week, and they all state that the crops look unusually promising. The cold and wet weather has kept back the sowing of oats and preparing of corn ground, but the wheat and rye, though not so large as it sometimes is at this season, yet it is well set on the ground, and not injured by the winter; and with a good season the harvest will be truly glorious. The late frosts have not greatly injured the fruit, and there is a good prospect for a large yield, particularly of apples.

MICHIGAN.

Michigan papers speak of the coming crop in the most encouraging terms. The number of acres sown is large.

OHIO.

The twenty counties in Ohio, with but a few trifling exceptions, the wheat looks well, and give evidence of a good yield, though the breadth of land sown is less than we would wish.

INDIANA.

The same number of counties in Indiana do not give quite so fair a showing, yet the prospect is good for a fair crop, and should the season prove good the yield will be large.

MISSOURI.

The St. Louis *Democrat* has reports from a large number of counties in that State. The universal testimony is that wheat never looked more promising than it does the present season. The St. Louis *Dispatch* [illegible] coming crop [illegible]

[illegible]

# TELEGRAPHIC NEWS

## Horace Greeley and the Union League.

THEY CONDEMN THE ACTION BUT REFUSE TO CENSURE THE ACTOR.

Departure of Catholic Prelates for Rome.

STRINGENCY OF THE SOUTHERN MONEY MARKET.

The Collection of Debts Indefinitely Postponed.

The Bombardment of the City of Mexico.

### NEW YORK.

NEW YORK, May 24.—The fire last evening at No. 30 Harrison street, occupied by Dempsey & Horton, as a cotton warehouse, was evidently the work of an incendiary. Loss, $30,000, which is insured.

THE UNION LEAGUE AND HORACE GREELEY.

At a special meeting of the Union League Club held last evening for the purpose of taking into consideration the recent action of Horace Greeley, member of the organization, resolutions of censure were presented and rejected. A substitute finally passed condemning the bailing of Jeff. Davis, but deeming it improper for the Club to stigmatize a member for any such act.

THE EXCISE LAW.

Receipts thus far received for excise licenses are $925,000.

JEROME PARK.

Jerome Park opened brilliantly yesterday. The first and second races were won by the filly Ruthless and colt Monday. The third by the filly Redwing.

CATHOLICS FOR ROME.

A number of Catholic ecclesiastics departed yesterday for Rome to attend the assembly of Prelates of the church to celebrate the 18th anniversary of the martyrdom of Peter. Many of the Priests have presents for the Pope, and money to relieve his present difficulties. Among the presents was a silver model of the yacht Henrietta, carrying a cargo of $50,000 in gold pieces, presented by the Catholics of Cincinnati, Ohio.

### WASHINGTON.

SECRETARY SEWARD AND THE FENIANS.

NEW YORK, May 25.—The *Herald's* Washington special says Secretary Seward has signified his willingness to intervene with the English Government in behalf of Fenian McClure, who so gallantly withstood the English cavalry in Ireland.

MONEY MATTERS AT THE SOUTH.

It is reported that in consequence of the stringency of money matters in his district, Orr intends to issue a general order staying the collection of debts for an indefinite period.

### MEXICO.

THE BOMBARDMENT.

NEW YORK, May 24.—The *Herald's* [illegible] of Mexico dated May [illegible], says a bombardment is going on there. The city is in a fearful condition. No later advices. [illegible] Forced loans of men and money [illegible] made by Marquez. Provisions are scarce. Diplomatic corps suspended relations with Imperial authorities on account of alleged partiality towards Americans. Rumored surrender of Queretaro, untrue. Maximilian being desirous of surrendering, but was prevented by Mejia and Marquez, who virtually hold him as a prisoner in their midst. A complete embargo was laid on the capital and every communication outside in any directions. No mails were received or departed for three months, except by private couriers. Business is completely paralized in consequence of the outside seige.

### PENNSYLVANIA.

A SINKING STEAMER.

PHILADELPHIA, May 23.—The Santiago de Cuba has eight feet of water in her holds, and pumps work badly. If a storm comes on she will be a total loss.

### CALIFORNIA.

LOSS BY THE LATE FIRE.

SAN FRANCISCO, May 23.—The estimated loss by the burning of Price & Co's furniture rooms is $130,000.

The demand, from New York, for flour continues.

### RECONSTRUCTION.

Strong Republican Organizations in North and South Carolina—Rebel Anxiety for the Removal of General Sheridan.

Special Dispatch to the Chicago Tribune.

WASHINGTON, May 21.—It has been ascertained that there is a secret political Union organization of great strength in the eastern part of North Carolina and upper part of South Carolina, with smaller memberships in other parts of those States. There are branches or divisions in nearly every precinct of many counties. The members are all white persons, and pledged to oppose the return to power of those who favored rebellion. Parties apparently well informed on the order numbers a majority of the white voters in the western half of North Carolina, and will mostly vote the Republican ticket.

The New Orleans Conservatives are still urging on the President the removal of General Sheridan. They complain that he is unnecessarily severe. King Cutler is now trying to induce Mr. Johnson to put General [illegible] in command. [illegible]

[illegible]

WASHINGTON, May 21.—There seems [illegible]

quiry is ordered to convene here to investigate the disturbance on the 14th instant.

Colonel Shepherd issues an order this evening retaining all the present policemen. The city government will not be disturbed. The military only takes cognizance of particular cases.

CHARLESTON, May 21.—Gen. Sickles has issued an order prohibiting the distillation of spirits from grain in the Second Military District. Offenders are declared liable to punishment by military commissions. The reasons assigned for the order are the scarcity of food in Carolina, the defrauding of the Government of large revenue, etc.

### THE EIGHT-HOUR MOVEMENT.

Convention of Workingmen from Different Parts of the State.

The Position Occupied by the friends of the Movement in Illinois.

Address to the Workingmen of the United States.

From the Chicago Tribune.

A Convention of delegates from the workingmen of this State assembled on Monday morning in the Trades' Assembly Hall, No. 155 Clark street. About forty delegates were present from Chicago, and places in the interior of the State.

Mr. Cameron, of Chicago, Mr. J. P. Ellacott, of Peoria, and Mr. P. Corcoran, of Amboy, were constituted a committee to draw up an address to the workingmen of the United States, setting forth the position occupied by the workingmen of this State. The committee presented the following:

FELLOW CITIZENS—As most of you are aware, at the recent session of the Illinois Legislature, a bill was passed making eight hours a legal day's work for all employees engaged by the day. Previous to its passage, both political parties—Democratic and Republican—had expressed, through town, county and State Conventions, their sympathy with, and belief in, the necessity and beneficial operation of such an enactment. In fact, so general and unreserved was the encouragement given, that little or no opposition was anticipated when the law went into practical operation. No sooner, however, were their partisan purposes accomplished, and the fact developed that the workingmen were in earnest, and determined to avail themselves of its benefits, than a preconcerted and persistent effort was developed to defeat them in such endeavor. Papers and politicians, who had heralded its benefits and advocated its adoption, when the eventful 1st of May arrived, were among the first to ridicule its passage and denounce its defenders. Not content with misrepresenting its objects, and slandering those whom it sought to benefit, the peaceable, law-abiding citizens of Illinois were branded as rioters and incendiary vagabonds. The inconsiderate action of a few misguided men was cited as conclusive evidence that all were alike implicated and responsible, and that these results were the legitimate fruits of the Eight Hour Law.

These slanders, however, were intended for effect in other states. They did not and could not mislead those who knew the falsity of the charges. It was doubtless expected that by publishing them a feeling of opposition among employers in the other localities would be aroused, and consequently a pressure brought to bear to prevent, if possible, the Governors of New York and Pennsylvania from attaching their signatures to similar laws passed by their respective Legislatures. That other States would then hesitate to endorse a movement fraught with such injurious consequences to the material welfare of the country and the brunt of the contest being confined to a few of the Western States, they would be unable to secure the continued observance of the law.

But all such intentions have been signally frustrated, and instead of disheartening they have only rekindled and renewed the enthusiasm of the workingmen of Illinois. Fighting for a principle which commended itself to the endorsement of every intelligent man, a principle, too, which is destined to triumph over all opposition, covert or avowed, they now appeal with confidence to the support and sympathy of their co-laborers in other sections of the country. They know, fellow-citizens, that the eyes of the world are now turned upon this struggle; that they lead the vanguard in this glorious reform, and with a faith that never falters and a hope that never dies, they are determined at all hazards and under all circumstances to secure and maintain the fruits of their victory. They know also that success in Illinois means success in New York, success in Wisconsin, and in fact success in every State in the American Union; while they also realize that defeat at this time implies a postponement, if not a defeat, in all those States which have enacted a law similar to that enacted by their own Legislature.

After struggling for three weeks, they now appeal to their brethren throughout the length and breadth of a common country to come forward and sustain them, and in so doing they feel assured they shall not appeal in vain. After due deliberation it has been determined to dispatch duly accredited and trustworthy agents to every State, who are authorized to receive all moneys collected for their support. All disbursements will be made under the supervision of the Finance Committee, who will give a close and personal attention to all applications for relief, so that the wants of none but the needy and deserving will be supplied.

In conclusion, they beg to assure you that in spite of all calumnies and assertions to the contrary, the workingmen of Illinois are determined to secure the recognition and adoption of the eight-hour principle; that the word "surrender" has no location in their vocabulary. They know that to falter is to yield, to compromise is to betray, and thus realizing the importance of their position, seem to prove recreant to their trust. Come, then, brothers, to the rescue, aid them in this important crisis in their history and yours—and we pledge the honor of the men of the Prairie State that any assistance required by you from them in the future, will be given by a willing and unstinted hand.

A. C. CAMERON, Chicago.
J. P. ELLACOTT, Peoria.
P. CORCORAN, Amboy.

The report of the committee was concurred in.

The Convention then adjourned till this morning without transacting any further business of importance.

—The first railroad was chartered in Connecticut in 1832. Now there are 617 miles of road finished in the State, and 127 miles of double track. The number of passengers carried by all the roads during the year was 1,660,[illegible]. Gross earnings of the past year, $5,[illegible]. [illegible]

### THE BURNING OF THE MERCHANTS' HOTEL.

A Young Lady Believed to Have Perished in the Flames.

The Second Victim of the Conflagration.

From the Chicago Tribune.

Most of our readers, in whose memory is still fresh the fact of the destruction by fire of the Merchants' Hotel, on the corner of State and Washington streets, on the morning of the 4th of the present month, will readily recall the particulars concerning the sad fate of the late Mr. R. A. Cook, of Joliet, who perished in the flames during that memorable conflagration.

When the facts connected with the lamentable occurrence were made known through these columns, and all suspense was ended by the discovery of the bruised and blackened remains where the deceased had been a victim to the devouring element, all breathed freer and thanked a kind Providence that it had been no worse; that no more lives had been sacrificed.

And yet this was not all. It was yesterday ascertained that there was a second victim, and, as if to make the case still more painful, that this victim was a young, fair and accomplished woman. About two weeks before the burning of the hotel, Miss Annie Dean, a young lady residing in Hamilton, Canada West, left her home for the purpose of coming to this city. On her way hither she stopped a few days in Detroit and then came on, arriving in this city but two days before the fire occurred. It was known that she was in the hotel, occupying her room, on the night before the breaking out of the conflagration. Since then nothing whatever has been seen or heard of her.

On Tuesday a young lady came to this city for the purpose of making inquiries relative to the whereabouts of Miss Dean. This young lady stopped at the St. Cloud Hotel, and at once began her investigations. All her efforts to learn anything of her missing friend since the night preceding the fire have been fruitless, and all hope has been abandoned, no doubt being entertained that the ashes of the missing young lady are mingled with the ruins of the hotel.

Miss Dean was a young lady of about twenty-three years of age. She was the only daughter of a widowed mother, and her sole support. She came to this city with the object of obtaining a situation as a teacher. She is described as having been a young lady of rare accomplishments and unusual attractiveness.

### STATE NEWS.

POTATOES are retailing at two dollars a bushel. The all-absorbing question will soon be, "have we a potato among us."—*Faribault Republican.*

THEY have been asking that question here for some time past, and the popular belief is that we have not one of that specie among us.—*Owatonna Journal.*

THAT question has been asked here and answered in the negative long ago. Echo answers "any time."

THE Owatonna *Journal* in speaking of the reported destitution on our frontier says:

"Our fellow townsman, Wm. Pepper, has recently returned from Jackson and Martin counties, where he has been buying cattle. He informs us that the accounts of destitution in those counties are overdrawn, or, in other words the greatest amount of destitution is found in those families who depend on hunting and fishing for a livelihood, and pay no attention to tilling the soil. He says those families who have been there four or five years are in many instances worse off than the new comers.

ONE of the latest things in the way of amusements that we have heard of is a "Sheep Shearing Festival." The Mantorville *Express* announces that the Dodge County Wool Growers' Association will hold a Festival at Mantorville on Saturday, May 25, 1867, commencing at 10 A. M. Premiums as directed by the Committee. Wool growers, please bring on your sheep. All good shearers are cordially invited to attend and give us a specimen of their skill. By order of the Committee."

While there, he was requested by the Pessler family to state, and have put in print, that the public is being humbugged by those who are traveling about the country with their children, whose arms and legs were frozen off in 1866. They informed Mr. P. that they never received a cent from the funds thus contributed, and that they do not wish their names connected any longer with such measures. They are very grateful to those who have sent donations direct and hope any one who has ought to give, will not place it in the hands of any pretended agent. We hope the press will notice this matter.

SUDDEN DEATH.—We are informed that Mr. Joseph Driesback, an old resident of our county, died very suddenly about two weeks since. Mr. D. had [illegible]

[illegible]

### Lumber Items.

Since our last we are enabled to note the following lumber items: On Thursday the propeller Ella went out with a raft of twelve strings of logs in charge of John Parker. Sold by L. E. Torinus to W. G. Clark and H. S. Parker & Co., St. Louis.

On the same day the Minnesota left with a tow of five rafts, as follows:

One 14-string raft of logs sold by David Cover, consigned to B. Hershey, Muscatine—Synoel Register, Pilot.

Eleven strings of logs sold by David Cover, consigned to H. S. Parker & Co., St. Louis—Henry Perry, Pilot.

Ten strings logs sold by David Cover, consigned to W. Clark & Co., St. Louis—Stephen Rhoads, Pilot.

Ten strings logs sold by David Cover, consigned to Hill & Co., Burlington—E. A. Dunham, Pilot.

Eight strings sawed lumber sold by E. D. Whiting, consigned to Morrison & Co., St. Louis—Dan Smith Pilot.

The Minnie Will, Capt. C. G. Bradley, returned on Saturday, having made a trip to Clinton, Iowa, with a raft for W. J. Young & Co.

Thirteen rafts have left here this spring up to date.

The amount of logs on hand at this time—including those in the various mill-booms and the St. Croix Boom Corporation—is about seventeen million feet.

At latest accounts the water on the Upper St. Croix and tributaries was steadily falling, and the drives on the various streams were being abandoned. The drives off Lower Snake River have reached Clam[illegible] Dam, and are awaiting a sufficient head of water to sluice the logs into the St. Croix. The drives on Apple River are getting along slowly, but will undoubtedly get in, as the water is controlled by a succession of dams and can be made available when needed.

It is thought that the rains of the past few days—if they extended to the northern streams—will add materially to the present stage of water.—*St. Croix Messenger.*

A large raft of lumber, containing 800,000 feet, belonging to Schulenburg, Boeckler & Co., of St. Louis, was totally demolished on the forenoon of the 8th, by coming in contact with the piers of the Rock Island Bridge. The Grey Eagle, a boat belonging to the company, succeeded in saving and landing a large portion of the raft. Damage unknown. No lives lost.—*Winona Republican.*

This is a raft from this city, and we believe was in charge of Harry Wheeler.—*Stillwater Messenger.*

MUSKEGON INCOMES.—Our lumbering friends over the lake have been putting money in their purses during the past year, as witness the following report in the Muskegon (Wis.) *News* of incomes returned at that place:

Henry Bradley, $18,045; George Arms, $7,000; Chaney Davis, $9,500; Henry H. Getty, $10,630; C. H. Hackley, $20,891; Edwin Hackley, $5,486; James H. Hackley, $6,576; Charles T. Hills, $10,425; J. McGorden, $9,207; L. G. Mason, $7,000; O. P. Pillsbury, $6,914; E. Stevens, $11,619; J. H. Swan, $5,155; T. Turnbull, $5,000.

LUMBER PROSPECTS.—We have had conversations with several persons interested in lumbering operations in this county, and from these we learn that the amount of lumber that will be run out of the Muskegon and White rivers this season will be very large—much larger than that of any preceding season since the commencement of the lumbering business on these streams. It is stated by the perfectly informed on the subject, that the logs on White river will yield rather more than one hundred million feet of lumber. The Muskegon river will run out to market this year about one hundred and eighty million feet. Much depends upon the supply of water in the small streams during the next month. Many logs are put into creeks which will require a good stage of water to continue for some time in order to float them all out. The late snow, and the weather continuing cold, its [illegible] are considered as likely to cause a gradual and continued rise of all the streams, which is what we all desire, and will be the greatest blessing Providence can send to Muskegon county this year.—*Muskegon News.* (Wisconsin.)

A correspondent of the Polk County *Press*, Wisconsin, writing from Black River, says:

The amount of pine cut on this stream the past winter is double that of any previous season.

It is estimated that not less than 225,000,000 feet of logs were in Black River at the time the ice broke up this Spring. As matters now stand, it looks to us that not over 50,000,000 of this will be manufactured in this State. The remainder will be run to Iowa, Illinois and Missouri, to be manufactured. Such a policy is killing to this part of the State, but your correspondent can see no remedy for it. He devoutly wishes he could. At the rate they have been cutting the past two years, it will not take ten years to "gobble" all the pine in this part of the State. Such a loss will be serious to Jackson and Clark counties.

### Insurance Decision.

From the Freeport (Ill.) Journal.

The case of the Winnebago Insurance Company vs. Samuel Chamberlain, which was tried some days ago in the Circuit Court, was decided yesterday by Judge Sheldon in favor of the company. [illegible]

[illegible]

WIND MILLS.—Messrs. Lea & Hardenburg have entered into a contract with G. A. Relard, to manufacture his patent "self-regulating wind power," of which mention was made a few days since.

### MONETARY.

Minneapolis Money Market.

[illegible]

### MINNEAPOLIS MARKETS.

MINNEAPOLIS, May 24, 1867.

Grain Market. [illegible]

Cattle Market—Live Weight. [illegible]

Wool Market. [illegible]

Produce Market—Retail. [illegible]

Woodenware Market. [illegible]

Hard Wood Market. [illegible]

Lumber Market. [illegible]

# The Minneapolis Daily Tri[bune]

Imperfect Page

VOL. 1. MINNEAPOLIS, MINNESOTA, TUESDAY MORNING, MARCH 17, 1868.

## Minneapolis Tribune,

*Issued Daily, Tri-Weekly and Weekly,*

BY THE

TRIBUNE PRINTING CO.

| | |
|---|---|
| Daily delivered in the city, per year | $12 00 |
| Daily by mail, per year | 10 00 |
| Tri-weekly, per year | 6 00 |
| Weekly, per year | 2 00 |

RATES OF ADVERTISING.

| | One square. | Each add. square. |
|---|---|---|
| One time | $0 75 | $0 [illegible] |
| Three times | 1 50 | [illegible] |
| Six days | 2 00 | [illegible] |
| Two weeks | 3 50 | [illegible] |
| Three weeks | 5 00 | [illegible] |
| One month | 5 50 | [illegible] |
| Two months | 10 00 | [illegible] |
| Three months | 12 50 | [illegible] |
| Six months | 18 00 | [illegible] |
| Twelve months | 25 00 | 12 50 |

### Republican City Convention.

A Republican Convention will be held at Harrison Hall, in the city of Minneapolis, on Thursday, the 2d day of April, 1868, at 2 o'clock P. M., for the purpose of nominating candidates for the municipal election, to be held on Tuesday, the 7th day of April, 1868. The nominations to be made at such convention, are:

A candidate for Mayor.
A candidate for Treasurer.
A candidate for Comptroller.

The Convention will be composed of twenty-five delegates, to be chosen by the several wards, which will be represented as follows:

First ward, by five delegates.
Second ward, by seven delegates.
Third ward, by eight delegates.
Fourth ward, by five delegates.

The ward committees are requested to call ward caucuses, to be held on the evening of Wednesday, the 1st day of April, to elect the above named delegates; also to nominate candidates for one Alderman in each ward, in place of the following named officers, whose terms will expire:

First ward, in place of Frank L. Morse.
Second ward, in place of H. G. Harrison.
Third ward, in place of G. A. Brackett.
Fourth ward, in place of Isaac Atwater.

GEO. H. KEITH, Chairman.
J. M. SHAW,
C. D. DAVISON,
Republican City Committee.

THE lines were down again last evening so that we are without our full complement of dispatches this morning.

### Call for a "Citizens' Convention"—The Management of the Tribune

Our surmise, in Sunday morning's TRIBUNE, that the democracy would attempt their old trick of a "citizen's convention" and a "no-party" ticket in the city election, proved correct. Late Saturday night, after the article referred to had been written, a call signed by some score or more of citizens, "irrespective of party," was brought to us for publication. As the TRIBUNE claims to be a straight-out party journal, we of course refused to give aid and comfort to any mongrel scheme of the kind, devised solely to divide and disintegrate the republican party of this city. The late hour at which it was received precluded comment; and as we understand that the republicans who signed it, under a misapprehension of its character, have since withdrawn from the movement, and resolved to take part in the regular republican convention, and support the regular republican ticket, we should probably have passed it over in silence, had not some sore headed individual, unable to conceal his chagrin, written the following tissue of misrepresentations concerning the matter to the St. Paul Dispatch. We cheerfully give this delectable epistle a larger circulation among our citizens than it could be expected to obtain in any other way, and thank the author for affording the much desired opportunity of contradicting certain assertions which have been, and are made with respect to the management of this journal.

Special Correspondence St. Paul Dispatch.

MINNEAPOLIS, March 16.

Our city has been considerably stirred up within a few days on political matters, caused by the near approach of our municipal election. Our present city officers were elected on a citizen's ticket last year, and nearly all are republicans. All have given entire satisfaction, and it is the almost unanimous wish of our business men that they be retained in office. But not so with a few politicians, who, for certain reasons, are very anxious to defeat Mayor Morrison for re-election.

Now our worthy mayor is a very popular officer, and though he is the staunchest of republicans, he is the choice of a large portion of the Democrats. Before any party call was issued, a citizen call was circulated among our business men, and in a very few hours one hundred and fifty names were obtained, and these were worthy republicans, and comprised three fourths of the business interest of our city. This call was taken to the TRIBUNE office Saturday evening, and *they refused to publish it, either gratuitously or as an advertisement.*

The secret of this opposition of the TRIBUNE is found in the fact that its proprietor, or rather chief owner, is W. D. Washburn, and he, supposing that the citizens' call was intended as a move to ensure the re-election of Mr. Morrison, decided to "take the bull by the horns" at once, by refusing to publish the citizens' call, and publishing a republican call in its place. The animus of the TRIBUNE will be at once appreciated, in the fact that Mr. Washburn and Mr. Morrison are aspirants for congressional honors, and the contest between the two gentlemen is inaugurated by Mr. Washburne by directly insulting a large part of our staunchest republicans.

The refusal to publish the citizens' call is all the more contemptible from the fact that many of our citizens, both republicans and democrats, own small amounts of stock in the TRIBUNE PRINTING COMPANY upon which they never expect to receive any dividends, or see any portion of the principal. But Mr. Washburn evidently intends to run it to advance his own interests without regard to the wishes of our people, or the welfare of our city. How well he will succeed time will tell, but it is my impression that the road to Washington is not the one Mr. Washburn has started on.

VINDEX.

It is not true that Mr. W. D. Washburn is the chief owner of the TRIBUNE establishment, or that he exercises any part in its management, other than that which his position as one of the board of directors gives him. Mr. Washburn does not now, and never did, own a controlling interest in the stock of the TRIBUNE Company. It is true that he owns a quantity of stock, and that he is a member of the Board of Directors; but this does not give him the right to dictate the policy of the TRIBUNE, any more than it gives the same right to any other stockholder or director. The TRIBUNE is controlled, primarily, by a Board of seven Directors elected annually by the stockholders, and they have entrusted the management of this journal to gentlemen whom they deem abundantly qualified for the task, and who are directly responsible to the Board for their conduct of its affairs. We have reason to believe that their management has so far given satisfaction to the Board, and they have no fear but that the Board will sustain them in their recent refusal to give aid and comfort to a scheme to disrupt and demoralize the republican organization of this city.

After having said so much, it would seem unnecessary to deny that Mr. Washburn dictated the course of the TRIBUNE in refusing to publish the "citizens' call," or that he had any previous knowledge of the course the TRIBUNE intended to pursue. Yet, in order to leave no room for cavil, we will explicitly state such to be the fact. He had no more to do with it than the editor of the Dispatch, or the man in the moon.

So far as the TRIBUNE is concerned, this "citizens' call" business has nothing to do with the congressional contest. Our only motive, as stated above, was to preserve the republican organization of this city intact, and prevent, if possible, the disastrous bolting operations which have afflicted the party here in former years. So far as the present incumbent for mayor is concerned, the TRIBUNE cherishes no hostility towards him. If he is renominated by a straight republican convention, the TRIBUNE will heartily support him, as it will support any other regular nominee of the party. But this journal will not, in the presence of an overwhelming national contest between the two great political parties, contribute to the weakening of ourselves and the strengthening of our opponents, by supporting a "citizens' candidate," whose election would certainly be heralded as a great "democratic victory."

### The Impeachment Trial.

The question in respect to giving the president time to prepare his defence was finally settled by accepting Senator Conkling's amendment requiring Mr. Johnson to file his answer on Monday the 23d inst., and an order was accordingly entered to that effect. The following is the vote on Mr. Conkling's amendment:

AYES—Anthony, Cameron, Cattell, Chandler, Cole, Conkling, Conness, Corbett, Drake, Edmunds, Ferry, Fessenden, Fowler, Frelinghuysen, Grimes, Harlan, Henderson, Howard, Howe, Morgan, Morrill (Me.), Morrill (Vt.), Morton, Patterson, (N. H.) Pomeroy, Ramsey, Ross, Sherman, Sprague, Stewart, Sumner, Thayer, Tipton, Trumbull, Van Winkle, Wiley, Williams, Wilson and Yates—40.

NAYS—Bayard, Buckalew, Davis, Dixon, Hendricks, Johnson, McCreery, Patterson, (Tenn.), Saulsbury and Vickers—10.

The decision finally reached will, we doubt not, give universal satisfaction to loyal men. A week is ample time for Mr. Johnson to prepare his defence, and the country can afford to give so much. But the people will rigidly insist that there be no further delay.

### Very Suggestive.

The Boston Traveler, speaking of the "Grand Army of the Republic," and the building occupied as its headquarters at Washington, says: "Within 'musket-shot of Willard's Hotel and 'the treasury quilding at Washington, 'and so near the white house, that a '*sharpshooter with a long range rifle* '*might throw a bullet through the brain* 'of a traitor standing on its steps, there 'stands a modest brick building, which 'is a great annoyance to President 'Johnson as was Mordecai, the Jew, to 'Haman of old, because it is a distinct 'and daily intimation that his authority is not everywhere acknowledged."

It is well that there should be so near Mr. Johnson's end of the avenue a perpetual reminder of the power and will of the loyal people to crush treason and anihilate traitors.

THE La Crosse Democrat denounces the scheme of paying the national debt in greenbacks, saying there is very little difference between that and payment in gold. "The true democrats," says Pomeroy, "will come forward, on the grand and invincible issue of repudiation, and win the victory for the people and the country—for true liberty and equal rights." Brick is only a step or two in advance of Pendleton. Pendleton's theory must lead, ultimately, to repudiation.

### CIVIL RIGHTS.

#### First Case of Murder Tried Under the Bill in this State—The Party Convicted.

From the Louisville Journal, March 6.

In the United States circuit court yesterday, William Bell, colored, was convicted of the murder of Tony Cundiff, colored, after a trial of three days' duration. He was committed to jail to await the sentence of the court. This is the first case of murder yet tried in Kentucky under the civil rights bill. It is destined to occasion no little judicial agitation. The prisoner's consel have intimated their purpose of appealing to the supreme court, in order to test the constitutionality of the act of congress. It will be remembered by our readers that at the last May term of the court here, Associate Justice Swayne, of the United States Supreme Court, then presiding, declared the bill constitutional, in the case of Rhodes, Stuart and Vickers, indicted for burglary and robbery.

The facts of the murder for which Bell was convicted were as follows: In October, 1866, Bell was coming from the fair at Owensboro, and when about six miles back of town, he met the deceased, Tony Cundiff, Wm. Mc Farland and Lewis Johnson, who had been out squirrel hunting. Cundiff had a Springfield rifle, which Bell demanded two or three times, and being refused, he drew a pistol and shot Cundiff, killing him instantly. He then fled, but was captured by the military authorities and sent to this city. On arraignment before Commissioner Ballard, the accused was held to answer the charge of murder. At the May term, 1866, of the United States circuit court, he was indicted for murder, and the trial postponed until the following October term. The jury not agreeing, they were discharged, and the case was again continued until the present term, when Bell was convicted of murder, the penalty for which is death. On behalf of the defense, three white men appeared as witnesses, and for the prosecution two negroes and one white. The former testified that Cundiff drew his gun upon Bell as if he intended to shoot him, when he immediately fired the fatal shot; while the witnesses on the other side state positively that no one except themselves, Cundiff and Bell were present or within sight of the altercation, and that the witnesses for the accused came up half an hour after the shooting.

General W. T. Ward, of this city, and Judge Stewart, of Owensboro, appeared for the defense, and Colonel B. H Bristow, United States District Attorney for the prosecution.

### Court of Impeachment.

#### SECOND DAY'S SESSION

##### Interesting Proceedings.

From the Chicago Tribune.

WASHINGTON, March 13.

IMPEACHMENT PROCEEDINGS—THE SCENES IN AND ABOUT THE CAPITOL BUILDING.

The actual scene in the senate to-day was far less impressive than when the managers presented the articles of impeachment, though the occasion has excited more general interest. This arose, in a great measure, from the fact that while only a thousand could gain admission into the senate wing, a great many thousands in the district were anxious to be present. A large force of policemen were on duty in and around the capitol.

PRECAUTIONS.

At an early hour the senate wing was closed, and all the holes and corridors of the building were continually inspected. The detective force had information of a character which caused great caution. No trouble, however, was anticipated, as such dispositions were made as would meet any contingencies which might arise.

OPENING OF THE COURT.

Precisely at one o'clock, Mr. Wade vacated the chair for the chief justice who took it and directed the sergeant at-arms to make the proclamation, which though now so familiar to the country, still sounds strange and solemn. The command to keep silence seemed to press like a weight upon all who heard, and the quiet of the chamber was significant of the authority which stood behind it.

THE READING OF THE JOURNAL

attracted general attention, from some of its formal terms, rather than its matter. Among them, for instance, the following: "The United States against Andrew Johnson, President thereof."

While the reading of the journal was in progress, the Managers appeared at the outer door of the senate, and waited there till it was finished. Back of them was about one-fourth of the house who did not wait for the formal entrance of the house itself. Mr. Stevens was not able to walk in. The formal announcement of Managers took place, the chief justice invited them forward to their seats at the table, when such senators present as were absent at the last sitting were severally sworn.

THE RETURN.

The sergeant at arms then gave notice that he had served the summons heretofore issued by the senate upon Andrew Johnson at his usual place of abode, and made oath to his statement.

THE ACCUSED CALLED TO ANSWER.

That almost every circumstance of the trial is without precedent, has already become an old story, and yet, as these successfully arise they fix the attention of all. The marked one to-day was made in response to the order of the chief justice directing the sergeant at arms to call the accused, when this officer rose and went through the usual legal form, as follows:

"Andrew Johnson, President of the United States! Andrew Johnson, President of the United States! Appear and answer to the articles of impeachment, exhibited against you by the House of Representatives of the United States."

THE PRESIDENT'S COUNSEL.

This was succeded by a general quiet, and all eyes were turned to the doors leading towards the president's room, as if Mr. Johnson would possibly appear in person. Instead, after a few moments delay, three of his counsel came in, walking slowly and with dignified bearing. First, Stanberry, tall and slim, and bending forward as is his manner. Next, Judge Curtiss, short in comparison to the former, thick set, and with none of the marks of age upon him; and last, Judge Nelson, of Tennessee, whom few knew anything about, of medium weight and proportion, and quite gray. Stanberry sat at the head of the table as leader of the counsel, Curtiss next, and Nelson third in order.

HOUSE MANAGERS.

At the head of the table of house managers sat Bingham, facing the president's counsel. To his left along the table were Boutwell, Wilson and Stevens, in the order named, and on his right, Messrs. Logan, Williams and Butler. The latter had come in late, and at a time and in a manner that, had those witnessing it been in a place of amusement instead, there would have been a perfect roar of laughter. Just as the sergeant-at-arms had concluded the call "Andrew Johnson, President of the United States," Butler hastily entered the front door of the senate chamber and stood alone at the bar, while the sergeant-at-arms finished. Most of the audience failed to notice his entry till their eyes turned from the desk to see if the president would indeed answer in person. When the well-known form of Butler met their gaze, the transition from gravity to merriment was sudden and extremely ludicrous.

ARRIVAL OF REPRESENTATIVES.

At this point the speaker of the house, accompanied by his officers and followed by a majority of the members appeared at the bar. There was a moment's hesitation in recognizing the body, as so many had come in advance, no one expected a formal appearance. Mr. Washburne, of Illinois, however, advancing to the bar, called out in an undertone heard all over the chamber—"Where's the sergeant-at-arms?" Of course this attracted official notice as well as the notice of all present, and the house was formally received.

REPLY OF THE PRESIDENT'S COUNSEL.

The chief justice then directed the counsel of the president to put in their reply to the articles, whereupon Mr. Stanberry exhibited authority for himself and his associates to appear for the president, and, in his name, announced the names of the counsel, to-wit: Henry Stanberry, J. S. Black, Wm. M. Evarts, B. S. Curtiss and Thos. A. Nelson, and asked for forty days in which to answer.

ARGUMENT ON THE MOTION FOR DELAY.

This request Mr. Stanberry supported in a mild and dinified speech. Mr. Bingham, on the part of the managers, in some brief remarks, maintained that, under the rule adopted, the plea must be entered and the trial proceed. Judge Curtiss followed on the part of the president, urging strongly that the interpretation put upon the rule by the managers was not correct. To this Mr. Wilson, of Iowa, further replied, on the part of the managers, and expressed surprise that so able a counsel should construe the rule as they had done. Up to this time the speeches on both sides had been dignified, courteous and moderate in tone and manner. Each speaker had been closely watched and followed, and the impression made was quite apparent. It was no new thing to watch with pride the bearing of the greater part of those who composed the house managers, but there was a general curiosity in remarking the president's counsel. At first Stanberry made a good impression, though Curtiss evidently was better received, but when Stanbery spoke a second time there was an impatient manner and excited tone and style of remark strangely suggestive of sundry ugly passages in the president's veto messages and other communications which have heretofore been attributed to other pens than that of the attorney general. There was an uneasy feeling over a large part of the audience, as it began to look as if a needless delay in trial would yet be secured by the president's party, and this feeling was somewhat strengthened by an order submitted by Mr. Edmunds, as a substitute for the president's request, as the feeling had been quite general that the senate would not grant over ten days. Upon this, Gov. Morton immediately moved that the senate retire to consult, and a vote without a full and free interchange of opinion was avoided.

THE COURT IN CONSULTATION.

The senate retired to the Marble Room, and was absent about two hours and ten minutes. At the consultation the Chief Justice presided, but did not vote. Most of those present expressed their views briefly. It soon became evident that the republicans were not only willing, but desirous, to give the president all the time that could properly be asked, yet there was no disposition on the part of any to yield a single day merely for delay. The democrats were a unit in favor of the full forty days asked for, but in this no republican gave them the support of a vote. The first vote taken was upon a proposition to require an answer one week from to-day, the 20th, which was carried by four majority, a number of republicans being absent. Afterwards it was urged that little could be gained by beginning so late in the week, and the vote was reconsidered by the majority in order to change to a day earlier in the week. The opinion then was somewhat divided between Monday, the 23d, and Wednesday, the 25. The proposition for the latter day was, after a short debate, withdrawn, and Monday, the 23d, fixed, by nearly the entire republican vote.

THE COURT RETURN.

At ten minutes after four the court returned to the chamber. The managers, who had also been in consultation, and the counsel for the defense, who had retired to a private room, had preceded the court.

Chief Justice Chase announced the decision reached, when Mr. Bingham, on the part of the managers, moved that the trial be ordered to begin immediately after the managers should file an answer to the president's response. Upon this the first vote approaching a test occurred, and while it should be distinctly understood that most of the republicans voting were actuated alone by the opinion that it would be more in accordance with all the proprieties to grant a little longer time, the vote was also regarded as so dividing the senate as to show that those voting in the affirmative may be relied upon as men determined that the matter of impeachment shall move on promptly. It will be noticed that among them are the names of senators whom malicious persons have attempted to injure by statements that they could not be relied upon in a close vote.

It will be noticed that Mr. Wade did not vote. He was present throughout. On the contrary, Mr. Patterson, of Tennessee, the president's son-in-law, voted in all cases; his conduct exciting general comment, considering the fact of Mr. Wade's constant refusal to vote.

Mr. Sherman, of Ohio, next made a proposition that the trial should begin on the 6th of April. Mr. Wilson, of Massachusetts, wanted to fix the 1st of April, but subsequently withdrew to allow the proposition of Senator Conkling to be entertained, that unless the senate should order otherwise for cause shown, the trial should proceed whenever the managers should respond to the president's answer. Mr. Butler was put forward by the managers to oppose the motion of Mr. Sherman, and a number of points were thoroughly appreciated by the Republicans; among them, his keen argument for the great strength of the articles drawn, from the fact that such able lawyers as the president had retained asked for forty days in which to prepare a formal answer. After a short response from Mr. Nelson, which impressed the hearers rather favorably, so far as voice and action were concerned the proposition of Senator Conkling passed by a party vote, with the addition of Mr. Van Winkle, of West Virginia, the vote standing forty to ten. With this result the republicans are well pleased, and the misgivings which some felt during the earlier part of the day have entirely disappeared this evening, and general confidence and satisfaction prevails.

A LIVELY SCENE.

While the senate was out for consultation, a lively scene was presented on the floor, in the galleries and in all the lobbies and halls of the senate wing. Little groups of both parties gathered on the floor, a general visiting took place among those who remained in the galleries, while the halls were filled with promenaders and the hum of voices throughout the entire wing was incessant. Lunches were being indulged in on all sides, and Thad. Stevens refreshed himself with a dozen raw oysters served on the Managers' table, with the usual dish of crackers. The whole appearance was for a time more like a great festival than the grave occasion which all recognized it to be. Such relief was absolutely needed after the hours of almost painful attention given by every one.

—Andrew Lawson, a faithful member of the First Presbyterian church, Newburgh, fell dead at the close of an exhortation in a prayer meeting Sunday afternoon. By a singular coincidence, before he attempted to sit down, he told of a fellow Christian whom he had known in his younger days, who, in a certain meeting that he had attended, was powerfully impressed with the conviction that unless he should offer prayer there he would suddenly die before he left the house. Hardly had Mr. Lawson finished the narration of this incident when he was noticed to labor with difficulty in his speech, and sank down in his seat. He soon died.

—The baggage masters at the depots of the New York Central railroad are required to collect twenty five cents for each piece of baggage left by passengers and put into the baggage room of the company. This is one of the latest orders.

## TELEGRAPHIC NEWS

### WASHINGTON NEWS

### THE PRESIDENT SURPRISED.

### The Trial to Proceed on the 23d.

### HE EXPECTS THIRTY DAYS DELAY

### Stanberry Indignant and Talks of Abandoning the Case.

### IMPEACHMENT A FOREGONE CONCLUSION.

### Provision in Case of Vacancy in the Office of Chief Justice.

PRESIDENT SURPRISED.

WASHINGTON, March 16.—The decision of the court of impeachment declining to allow the time asked for by the president to prepare his case surprises that individual and his friends. They were very confident and had been led to believe that from twenty-five to thirty days would be granted, and are terribly chagrined and anxious at being brought up with the short time of a week.

SATISFIED.

The action on the part of the court making the trial commence on next Monday, satisfies the president and his counsel that but little favor can be expected from that body, and there will be no delay in the trial.

IMPEACHMENT CERTAIN.

The decided vote against postponement has caused the president's friends in both houses to give it up. They now say that his occupancy of the white house is only a question of time, and that time they consider short.

STANBERRY INDIGNANT.

Mr. Stanberry reflects the sentiments of the president more closely than any other of his counsel, and he is terribly indignant. He is very bold in his declarations, and states that if time is not allowed he will abandon the case.

THE OTHER COUNSEL.

The course that the other members of the counsel will pursue has not been indicated, but the course of Stanberry gives rise to the rumor again that all will abandon the case, and that the president will resign.

WHO SUCCEEDS THE CHIEF JUSTICE.

It appears that under the constitution there is no provision for filling the office of chief justice in case of sickness or death of that officer, who is the only person that can preside at the trial of the president.

Mr. Elliot has prepared a bill to supply the deficiency, making the next senior justice chief justice until another can be provided. This bill will be pressed and passed in a day or two.

MILITARY ORGANIZATIONS.

Information has been received from General George H. Thomas, stating that there are military organizations on foot in Tennessee, for what purpose be is not informed.

Similar information has been received from various parts of Virginia and North Carolina.

General Grant has ordered the military commanders in those departments to keep a very close watch on their movements.

TRIAL TO PROCEED.

The impeachment court will meet on the 23d, and the trial will proceed without delay.

### GENERAL ITEMS.

—Dr. Holland has recently lost a brother.

—Philadelphia proposes music for its public schools.

—Chicago is to have a two million dollar depot—the finest in the world.

—Doves' wings on the shoulders are now worn by the nobility of Paris.

—Some fool wants to know if there was ever an eclipse of the honeymoon.

—Another one wants to sail across the Atlantic in a twenty-five foot boat.

—The Astor estate is valued by one who professes to know, at about $144,000,000.

—The piling for the custom house at San Francisco cost $200,000.

—An eel weighing fourteen pounds, and four feet nine inches in length, is exhibited in New Bedford, Mass.

—The new American publications for February amounted to 126, or more than four per day.

—At a dance in honor of a newly married pair at Norwich, Conn., Sunday evening, the party got drunk, the bridegroom was whipped, and the bride received a black eye.

—The Mansfield (O.) Herald learns that a man named Jordan, living near Londonville, drank a pint of whisky and pepper one day last week, to break an attack of fever and ague, with which he was troubled. The fever was "broken," but its sudden stopping killed him.

—A French father has made a discovery which is likely to do away with bad boys entirely. In case a youth of seven has been "cutting up," father simply says: "John, you have been a bad boy to-day. I shall take a year from your age. You are now no more than six years old." The boy at once behaves well in order to get the year restored.

—A man about fifty years of age, while playing cards with three other persons, at a tavern in Bethany, Conn., on Saturday night, was noticed suddenly to straighten out his body and gradually slip out of his chair on the floor. The next moment he was taken up a corpse, having expired without speaking a word or receiving a moment's warning.

—It is estimated that Louisville has more attorneys at law, according to its population, than any other city in the country.

—Ten thousand dollars' worth of gold bearing bonds, which were abstracted from a gentleman's pocket in Boston, in the year 1861, whose was forged in their negotiation, have just been recovered by detectives. It is thought that about $500,000 worth of other bonds of various descriptions, which have been stolen from bankers and others, may, from information furnished the assistant treasurer, be recovered.

—Two good natured Irishmen, on a certain occasion, occupied the same bed. In the morning one of them inquired of the other: "Dennis, did you hear the thunder last night?" "No, Pat, did it really thunder?" "Yes, it thundered as if hiven and airth had come together." "Why in the divil, then, didn't ye wake me, for ye know I can't sleep when it thunders."

—Girls, do you want to get married, and do you want good husbands? If so, cease to act like fools. Don't take pride in saying that you never did housework, never cooked a pair of chickens, never made a bed, and so on. Don't turn up your pretty noses at honest industry. Never tell your friends that you are not obliged to work. When you go shopping, never take your mother with you to "carry the bundle."

—Hiram Smith, an eccentric old bachelor at Chester, Mass., is having his sepulchre hewn in a large rock in that town. He pays a man $700 to do the work, and by the stipulations the cave is to be seven feet long, four wide, and four deep, and after the coffin is put in, the aperture will be sealed up with a marble slab and cement. Smith says he doesn't want mud to get round his bones; he means to have a dry place for them. The scheme is an old fancy of his.

—Mr. Rogers has cast in plaster his new work which he calls the "Council of War." This group is composed of three figures, Lincoln, Grant, and Stanton, of whom faithful portraits are given. Mr. Lincoln is represented sitting in an easy posture, holding in his hand a map; General Grant stands a little on one side, and has placed his finger upon some point to which he seems to direct the attention of Mr. Stanton, who is rubbing the dust from his glasses—a familiar habit with the secretary when he is thinking hard. These three figures are modeled with an anatomical accuracy.

MARRIED.

In Rochester, Minn., on the 11th inst., by Rev. A. Fuller, Mr. J. J. CASSEDAY, of Minneapolis, and Miss EMMA J. STAFFORD, of Rochester. No cards.

DIED.

In Minneapolis, on the 12th inst., of consumption, SIDNEY PRATT, of Brandon, Vermont, aged 25 years.

Funeral at Congregational Church, to-day (Tuesday), March 17th, at 2 o'clock P. M.

SEE what Gale & Co. say this morning—last column, 4th page—as to Houses, Lots, Lands, and every kind of Insurance.



LOST—In St. Anthony (on or near Third street), on Thursday, March [illegible], a PITCH FURK [illegible]. The finder will be suitably rewarded by leaving the same at the Episcopal Parsonage, St. Anthony, or at the People's Store, Minneapolis. mar15



A POCKET DIARY FOR 1868, picked up in the street, can be had by the owner, by calling at this office and paying for this advertisement.

A BRASS KEY, picked up opposite First National Hotel, can be had by paying for this notice.

# The Minneapolis Daily Tribune.

VOL. II. MINNEAPOLIS, MINNESOTA, TUESDAY MORNING, MAY 11, 1869. NO.

**Minneapolis Tribune,**

*Issued Daily, Tri-Weekly and Weekly,*
BY THE
**TRIBUNE PRINTING CO.**

Daily delivered in the city, per year.....$12 00
Daily by mail, per year.....10 00
Tri-weekly, per year.....6 00
Weekly, per year.....1 50

### The Permanency of the River Grain Route.

The idea is entertained by some, that the new movement to ship the grain of the Northwest by river via New Orleans to New York and Europe, is the result of a special effort on the part of St. Louis and New Orleans, and will subside as soon as the enthusiasm of those cities has exhausted itself.

This idea is erroneous. The new grain movement is the result of an universal demand by western producers for cheaper freight, and of the energy and foresight of leading business men in making available the splendid natural channel of the Mississippi to meet this demand. During the past few years, nearly the entire industrial enterprise of the country has been directed towards the construction of railroads. In the general intensity and earnestness in opening artificial routes, the natural channels of transportation have been neglected and fallen greatly into disuse. The tendency has been to sacrifice everything to speed, and hence the railroads have to so great an extent superseded water routes. But the progress of consolidation and monopoly in railroads, and the steadily increasing burden of freight tariffs, have aroused public attention to the necessity of competing lines. Railroads are necessities, and of incalculable value in developing the resources of a country, but they need to be held in check by competition. Powerful railroad combinations which can hold communities at their mercy by the imposition of burdensome charges for carrying, which can eat up the entire profit of the producer, and ruinously enhance the cost of everything he consumes, by exhorbitant tariffs, are to be dreaded, and the only effectual defense against such is to oppose water routes against rail.

This is the secret of the river movement, and hence it must be permanent. The reasons which have stimulated the special efforts to inaugurate it, will always exist, and will lead to special efforts to continue it, if need be. But aside from this, natural causes must insure the maintenance of the river route, and secure it an ever increasing volume of business, after it is once fairly started. People have but to take their eyes off from the absorbing pursuit of railroads and direct them towards the river, to immediately perceive what has apparently been forgotten, the immense importance of the great highway which nature has provided, and to begin again to avail themselves of it for transporting their produce and receiving their supplies, as they did at an early day before railroads were built in the Mississippi valley.

It is idle to suppose that railroads can ever compete with a magnificent river like the Mississippi for the carrying of heavy freight and freight the speedy delivery of which is not of greater importance than the cost of transportation. Here is the river, a natural highway, requiring no investment of capital in its construction, no outlay for repairs, no taxations for special franchises or privileges. A steamer which will carry as much grain as seventy trains of cars, can be built for less than the cost of one locomotive, and can be run at less expense. The difference in the comparative cost of operating the two routes is too great for the railroads ever to overcome. Even now, with the river transportation lines not fully organized, a bushel of wheat can be shipped from Minneapolis via New Orleans to New York for 37 cents, while it cannot be shipped via Chicago for much less than 60 cents. The Chicago folks may reduce their charges for elevating, &c., to a mere nothing, and still the odds will remain so largely in favor of the river route as to defy competition.

Still farther beyond competition is the direct route to Europe via the river. St. Louis can ship grain to Liverpool for 26 cents per bushel. How much western grain, designed for a foreign market, will seek an outlet via an eastern port under these conditions? The trade with Europe via southern ports will grow with the progress of the river movement.

We do not expect to see railroads ruined, nor the building of them stopped, by the re-opening of the river route. There will be business enough for all, at reasonable tariffs, as the resources of the country develope, and the rapidity of their development will be hastened by competing routes. The "river movement" is the beginning of a work of reform to endure for all time, and the inauguration of a new and grand era in the material progress of the West.

---

THE CHINESE threaten to "go back on" the treaties negotiated a year ago by Mr. Burlingame with our government and several European governments, looking to the freer opening of the celestial world to commerce and western civilization. The concessions made by Mr. Burlingame are too much for the Oriental stomach, and in order to counteract their effect, they have commenced murdering and driving out Americans and Europeans, in order to avert the flood of progress which threatens to overwhelm them. This sort of thing won't do. John Chinaman must be made to toe the mark and abide by his treaties. A few gunboats wanted for the Chinese.

---

THE Chicago Times thinks that J. Russell Jones, of Illinois, whose nomination as minister to Belgium the senate refused to confirm, will shortly be appointed to that position.

### Finished.

At about 2 o'clock yesterday afternoon, the last blow was struck, and the last spike was driven home through the last rail into the last tie of the Pacific Road, and the great work was finished. All the telegraph wires throughout the country were put in connection, and the wire conducted down to the track, so that the last click of the hammer was distinctly heard throughout the Union—at the same instant in New York and San Francisco, Boston and New Orleans, Chicago and Minneapolis! This incident, to the imaginative mind, seems even more wonderful than the prodigious enterprise of which it marks the completion. In Chicago, New York, and other cities, the fire alarm telegraphs were connected with the main wire, and the city bells all rung simultaneously with the final strokes of the hammer.

An idea of the importance attached to the completion of this enterprise throughout the great cities of the Union, may be gathered from the perusal of our dispatches describing the numerous celebrations of the event. There is sufficient ground for rejoicing, but still it is to be feared that the Pacific Road is only completed in a Pickwickian sense. If half the reports are to be believed, a very large portion will have to be rebuilt before it can be relied on as perfectly safe and trustworthy and according to contract. Trains can, however, for the present, at least, run through uninterrupted from ocean to ocean, and that is glory enough for one day.

---

The official statement of the condition of the public debt on the last day of April, as published in our telegraphic columns a few days ago, contained a few slight errors. The correct figures show that the public debt decreased $6,300,000 during the month of April, that the amount of coin in the treasury was $92,000,000, the coin certificates amounted to $16,000,000 and the currency to $7,000,000. A sum of $3,206,796 was paid as interest in advance, while the debt bearing coin interest footed up $2,107,878,700 and the debt bearing currency interest $67,240,000. This statement affords gratifying assurance of the advance which has been made towards the ultimate extinction, during the past month, of the national debt, as well as of the vast financial resources of the country.

---

—A Washington special to the Chicago Tribune says:

"General Hancock has such a high opinion of himself that he thinks that he has been slighted in being assigned to the command of the department of the northwest, with headquarters at St. Paul, and has protested to the president against the order of assignment. People here who know what Hancock's conduct was toward Grant last summer and fall, think the president has shown great magnanimity in giving him so important a command."

The above is unjust to Hancock. Anybody would have a right to complain of being banished to so dreary a locality as St. Paul. We do not know what Gen. Hancock's conduct towards Gen. Grant last summer and fall was, but it must have been very offensive to warrant and receive such a punishment as that sought to be inflicted!

---

POLITICAL CONVENTIONS.—The following political conventions have been called: Kentucky Republican State Convention at Lexington, May 27. New York State Temperance Convention at Syracuse, June 1. Pennsylvania Republican State Convention at Philadelphia, June 29. Maine Republican State Convention at Bangor, June 24. Pennsylvania Democratic State Convention at Harrisburg, July 14. California Republican State Convention at Sacramento, July 21.

---

The New York Sun has the following:

"The Hon. Ignatius Donnelly will be an independent candidate for Governor of Minnesota at the next election."

We wonder where the Sun gets its information.

## FOREIGN.

*BY OCEAN TELEGRAPH.*

GREAT BRITAIN.

LONDON, May 10.—In the house of commons to-day, Mr. Fortescue, chief secretary for Ireland, in reply to an inquiry of Lord John Manners, said her majesty's ministers were already considering the best means of increasing the powers of the lord lieutenant of Ireland for the more effectual suppression of outrages in that country.

SOUTHAMPTON, May 10.—The steamship Weser, from New York, has arrived.

FRANCE.

The Emperor visited the horticultural exhibition at Chartres, yesterday. He was received by the mayor, who delivered an address. The Emperor made a short speech in reply. He recalled the visit he made to Chartres, when he was president. He then referred to the coming elections and invited all men of all parties to aid in the advancement of the cause of liberal progress by choosing as their representatives men worthy of such a mission.

## CUBA.

HAVANA, May 10.—Captain General Dulce, with the volunteers who accompanied him has returned from his visit to Matanzas. Fighting is reported going on near Nuevitas. No particulars to hand.

The U. S. sloop of war Saratoga arrived to-day.

The Havana press praise the American authorities for their prompt action in detaining the steamer Quaker City.

No important news has been received to-day from the interior. Details of the fighting around Nuevitas are still wanting.

RAILROAD.

KNOXVILLE, May 10.—A large number of delegates, composed of prominent citizens of Knoxville, leave to-morrow for Cincinnati to represent the interests of East Tennessee in the Cincinnati, Knoxville and Charleston railroad.

TWO MEN DROWNED.

MEMPHIS, May 10.—A pleasure boat containing eleven persons was drawn under a coal barge lying off the Arkansas shore last evening. Messrs. Garkey & Miller, well known doctors, Burrel Adams, Miller Sorms, and a negro man, were drowned. The bodies have not been found.

## TELEGRAPHIC NEWS

### Washington News.

The Cuban Question

Discharge of Government Workmen.

THE COMPLETION OF THE PACIFIC RAILROAD.

*Grand Celebrations of the Event.*

The Free Trade League Resolve, &c.

Important Legal Decision by Chief Justice Chase.

*ENCOURAGING REVENUE PROSPECTS.*

South Carolina Cotton Crop Injured.

THE RIVER GRAIN TRADE.

New York Legislature Adjourned.

Fire in Paterson, New Jersey.

CUBA.

Attempt to Bribe the Patriots to Leave the Island.

## WASHINGTON.

THE REPORTED CUBAN EXPEDITIONS.

WASHINGTON, May 9.—The Spanish minister has repeatedly, within the last two months, reported to the secretary of state that expeditions were fitting out in this country for the Cuban service, but he did not produce the evidence. The secretary, however, directed inquiries to be made; when it was ascertained there were no facts upon which to found proceedings. The proper officers have been instructed to exercise due vigilance to prevent a violation of the neutrality laws, which the government assured the Spanish minister would be enforced.

APPOINTMENT.

The president to-day appointed Jas. H. Wheeler consul at Port Mahon.

REVENUE MATTERS.

Receipts from internal revenue sources for the present month have been comparatively heavy, averaging about $500,000 per day. Receipts from customs also continue heavy, and indications of large revenue from that branch of the service for the present month are good. Coin balance in the treasury is now quite $87,000,000, which is increased $20,000,000 by coin certificates.

INDIAN AGENTS.

The war department order assigning army officers to duty as Indian agents was not promulgated to-day as had been expected, some changes in the personnel having been determined on.

On return of commissioner Delano several additional supervisors of internal revenue will be appointed.

IMPORTANT FROM CUBA.

The government to-day received advices direct from the insurrectionary portion of Cuba, giving information as to movements in that quarter. Parties here in the interest of Cuba state that there are now in the Cuban army 25,000 men, 2,500 of whom are Americans and that about 3,000 of the latter nationality have recently been added to the number. It is said by representatives of the revolutionary army in Washington, that success would be placed beyond a doubt if the United States would encourage the belligerent rights of those who are striving to effect the independence of Cuba, and in that case men and money already promised would be furnished in abundance.

SAN DOMINGO.

Mr. Fabens, the confidential agent of the San Domingo government, recently had an interview with Secretary Fish. The subject of annexation will receive official consideration at an early day. Parties interested in the annexation movement furnish an extract from Prof. Gabb, who says he has prospected 200 square miles of gold bearing territory, surpassing in richness any known portion of California and Australia.

NAVAL.

A short time ago, Admiral Farragut was tendered the post at New York, but having declined it, Rear Admiral Stringham was to-day appointed to the position.

TROTTING.

Patchen of Baltimore won the $500 purse to-day on the National Course. Mile heats, best three in five. Mountain Maid of Philadelphia won the first heat; time 2:28½. Star of the West, of Chicago, second time 2:27½. Patchen won the 4th, 5th and 6th heats; time 2:34½, 2:31 and 2:33. Warsaw was withdrawn after the 1st heat.

THE PUBLIC TYPOGRAPHISTS.

A large number of employees of the government printing office have been dismissed. Thirty-six were notified to-day that for reasons sufficient to the congressional printer, their services were no longer required. A colored compositor, the first ever employed in the government printing office, was assigned to a case to-day.

WASHINGTON NAVY EMPLOYEES.

All the master workmen at the Washington Navy Yard are to be removed, and candidates for succession to their places have been before an examination committee.

THE INDIAN OFFICE.

Very little excepting mere routine business has been transacted at the Indian bureau during the past ten days, owing to the absence of Commissioner Parker.

INTERIOR CHIEF CLERKSHIP.

Secretary Cox has appointed George T. Metcalf, of Ohio, chief clerk of the interior department.

COLORED "PRESSURE."

Two or three delegations from Alexandria, Va., have called to see the president within the past few days, having in view the disposition of the federal offices in that city. There is an anxiety among the colored citizens there to have persons of their own race appointed.

## THE EAST.

THE SPANISH OUTRAGES ON AMERICAN COMMERCE.

NEW YORK, May 10.—A Washington dispatch says the secretary of the navy called the attention of Admiral Hoff, commanding the North Atlantic squadron, now in Cuban waters to the fact that armed Spanish vessels are in the habit of searching American merchantmen, not only in Spanish waters, but also in the neutral waters of Mexico. The department directs that the admiral keep a vigilant watch hereafter and prevent such infractions of international law, and advises him, that his duties are to protect, not only American citizens, but vessels as well. He is also ordered to prevent American war vessels from searching merchant vessels, it being their duty to protect American trade, and not molest it.

CUBAN INTELLIGENCE.

It is said that the captain general of Cuba attempted to bribe the leading patriots to leave the island, and Gen. Cespedes has been offered a free pass for his family and $2,000 if he would abandon Cuba. Gen Felix Figueroid, one of those who rose with the original force last October and who since proved himself a very useful soldier, was offered $3,000. These propositions are made through citizens by the captain general.

Several citizens, suspected of patriotic sympathy, have been taken from Santiago de Cuba late at night, by order of Dulce, and murdered.

A DOUBLE HOMICIDE.

NEW YORK, May 10.—Last evening a man named George McNury got into an altercation with a man named Peter Ellinger, in front of a boarding house in Wallace street, and stabbed him in the abdomen and side, inflicting probably fatal injuries. Louis Busta, a friend of Ellinger, interfered, when McNury stabbed him also, cutting his heart in two, and causing instant death. No provocation for the assault appears to have existed. Officers are in search of McNury.

THE RELEASED FENIANS.

Colonels Warren and Castello, the released fenians, arrived yesterday.

ACQUITTED.

BALTIMORE, May 10.—The trial of Martha J. Carnes, accused of the homicide of Nicholas McCorma, at Jarrettsville, resulted in a verdict of not guilty.

HOFFMAN'S VETOES SUSTAINED.

The numerous vetoes of Gov. Hoffman was sustained in the legislature to-day. Final adjournment expected to-night.

COAL MINERS' STRIKE.

MAUCH CHUNK, Pa., May 10.—A strike in the coal region commenced to-day, and work is entirely suspended in Lehigh and Schuylkill region. Nothing has been received from Wilkesbarre, but it is supposed the same state of affairs exists there.

GRANT INVITED TO PEACE JUBILEE.

BOSTON, May 10.—Mayor Shurtliff, and other members of the city government, left for Washington to-night as a special committee to invite President Grant to attend a peace jubilee.

THE PACIFIC CELEBRATION IN NEW YORK.

NEW YORK, May 10.—News was received this afternoon of the completion of the Pacific Railroad. One hundred guns were fired in the city hall park, and mayor Hall forwarded a congratulatory message to the mayor of San Francisco. A commemorative celebration had previously been held in Trinity Church, at which a telegram was forwarded by the chamber of commerce to a similar body at San Francisco was read and an address delivered by Rev. Dr. Vinton. After prayer and reading of a portion of the Episcopal service, the organ pealed and chimes rung as the congregation left the church.

Flags on City Hall and many public and private building were displayed all day in honor of the great event.

Dispatches from Washington, Philadelphia, and many other places report much enthusiasm over the news. The bell of Independence Hall at Philadelphia was especially brought into use to commemorate the completion of the continental railroad, and the scene there generally was more enthusiastic than any since Lee's surrender.

AID TO THE CUBANS.

Report says that on Saturday afternoon a vessel laden with war material for the Cuban insurgents sailed from one of the piers in East river, where she has been lying some weeks unnoticed. It is also said a large number of recruits embarked on a tug at Jersey City and were transferred at Sandy Hook to the war vessel. The authorities and Cubans are both very reticent on the subject. Recruiting is stopped at the principal Cuban headquarters, though it is understood that men are still enlisted at the branch office. The expedition alluded to above is said to be composed of emigrants who enlisted at Castle Garden.

District Attorney Pierrepont has received two letters from the state department directing energetic measures to enforce the neutrality laws and punish violators thereof, and particularly calling his attention to the case of the Quaker City.

ARRIVED.

NEW YORK, May 10.—Steamers Westphalia, from Hamburg via Havre 1st, and Queen from Liverpool arrived to-day.

ASSOCIATED PRESS ELECTION.

UTICA, N. Y., May 10.—The annual meeting and election for officers of the Associated Press of the state of New York, will be held at the Metropolitan city of New York, at 11 o'clock in the morning, Wednesday, 19th inst.

CURIOUS DIVORCE CASE.

NEW YORK, May 10.—A curious divorce case was before the supreme court to-day. Mrs. Kinzier asked for divorce from her husband on the ground that a former divorce obtained in Illinois from a former husband, Mr. Pomeroy, was obtained by collusion and while both were residents of Massachusetts, and therefore invalid, and therefore she was the legal wife of Pomeroy. The court held that the divorce was valid, both parties having submitted to the judgement of the Illinois tribunal.

AFTER THE FILLIBUSTERS.

A Washington special says orders were telegraphed to-day to the federal officials at New Orleans, to look sharp after certain Cuban expeditions said to be fitting out in that port.

REVENUE FRAUDS.

Judge Benedict to-day charged the grand jury in the United States Circuit Court in reference to revenue frauds in this city, and more particularly drawback frauds, involving many government officials in forged papers to the amount of $700,000. It was said by the judge to be the duty of the grand jury to indict all, poor or rich, guilty of fraud on the revenue.

RECOVERED.

The police to-day received by letter, post-marked Elmira, New York, $11,000 worth of shares in the Eureka Mining Company of Polk county, Tennessee, which were stolen from the safe of Small, Wood and Hitchcock, Beaver street, on the night of the 3d.

WM. E. NELSON

was to-day chosen president of the stock exchange, as consolidated by the admission of the open board.

MISSIONARY CONVENTION.

NEWARK, May 10.—The Protestant Episcopal Board of Missions opened their spring meeting in Trinity Church this morning. Rev. Dr. Haight, of New York, presided in the absence of the Bishop. The attendance was very small. The agency system was discussed by Rev. Dr. Rudder, of Philadelphia, and others. In the evening, at Grace Church, Dr. Tyng stated the progress of domestic missions, and urged increased force, and Dr. Rudder spoke on the necessity of co-operation of churchmen for the success of the missions.

LEGISLATIVE.

ALBANY, May 10.—The legislature adjourned sine die at midnight. The city and county tax levies for New York over which there has been quite a fight, finally passed with $1,800,000 cut out of the former and $600,000 from the latter.

FREE TRADE LEAGUE.

NEW YORK, May 10.—A meeting of the American Free Trade League was held at Cooper Institute to-night, at which many of its prominent members were present. Howard Potter called the assemblage to order, and David Dudley Field presided. Addresses were delivered by Wm. Cullen Bryant and Edward Atkinson, and the following resolution was adopted:

*Resolved*, That in the opening of the great Pacific railroad to-day, connecting New York and San Francisco, we recognize a pledge not only for one country, one constitution, and one destiny, with a due regard to the revenue of the present, but of trade with all countries and all continents.

DISASTROUS FIRE.

The Murray silk mills, owned by Ryle & Co., at Paterson, New Jersey, took fire this afternoon and were entirely destroyed. Loss $550,000; no insurance. About a dozen tenement houses adjoining, occupied by some mill operatives, were also burned to the ground. The flames communicated to the Catholic church near by, but fortunately were extinguished before great damage was done. The fire originated in Morris' rag shop, next to the mill, and it is thought was caused by spontaneous combustion. A large number of employees are houseless and thrown out of employment.

## THE WEST.

THE G. A. R.

CINCINNATI, May 10.—A large number of distinguished officers have signified their intention to attend the national encampment army republic meeting in this city Wednesday. Gen. John A. Logan will deliver an address at the reception Wednesday night. Banquet will be at the Spencer House, Thursday night. On Friday, a steamboat excursion will be made to North Bend, tomb of Gen. Harrison. Headquarters will be at the Spencer House.

Delegates to the national encampment, Grandy Army of the Republic, are expected to report at headquarters at the Spencer House, to be assigned lodgings.

SUICIDED.

G. A. Mensel, of Delaware, Indiana, committed suicide on Saturday evening by taking hydracyanic acid. He commenced to write the cause of the act, but did not complete the settlement.

BURNED TO DEATH.

A little girl, the daughter of Natvair Mosnio, of Dayton, was burned to death in that place on Saturday by her clothes taking fire.

CONTRABAND LIQUORS.

ST. LOUIS, May 10.—More seizures of contraband coffee and sugar were made by U. S. revenue officers this morning. It is said that 3,500 sacks coffee, 500 bags pepper and several hundred boxes of sugar have been sent from New Orleans, on none of which has the duty been paid.

EMBEZZLER.

Leopold Hallerman, a clerk of Murdock and Dixon, was arrested to-day, charged with embezzling between two and three thousand dollars from that firm.

TOW BOAT SUNK—LOSS OF LIFE.

About 11 o'clock last night the old tow boat Grey Eagle sprung a leak and capsized near Stag Island, in the Mississippi river, about 75 miles above here, and Patrick Hall, the pilot, and Henry Clerges and James Sams, raftsmen, are supposed to have been drowned. The boat was going up the river with a party of raftsmen and hands on board, all of whom, and the crew, lost everything they had.

THE PACIFIC CELEBRATION IN CHICAGO.

CHICAGO, May 10.—The celebration of the completion of the great interstate railway connection to-day, was the most successful affair of the kind that ever took place in Chicago, and probably in the west. It was entirely impromptu and therefore almost every man, woman and child in the city did their part towards making it a success. The procession was unique in appearance and immense in length, the lowest estimate putting it down at 7 miles. Every merchant, every trader, every drayman, every milkman every express company had his or their business wagon in the line and generally filled with boxes supposed to contain goods directed to merchants in every city and town between here and China. Brigham Young seemed to be by far the largest consignee, as about every one of 3,000 or 4,000 business wagons had one or more packages marked to his address. Almost every wagon bore some pleasant motto or device got up for the occasion. Just before the procession moved every tug in the river or lake front, over fifty in number, opened their whistles and set up a scream which seemed to awake echoes from the other side of Lake Michigan.

Shortly after this the court house sounded its tintinabulations, announcing that the last spike in the last rail was being driven home, and then the procession moved and continued to move until 6 o'clock, when it dispersed.

During the moving of the procession Vice President Colfax received the following dispatch:

PROMONTORY SUMMIT, UTAH,
May 10.

Hon. Schuyler Colfax, Vice President:

The rails were connected to-day. The prophecy of Benton to-day is a fact. This is the way to India!

(Signed) G. M. DODGE,
JOHN DUFF,
SIDNEY DILLON,
T. C. DURANT.

This evening Vice-president Colfax, Lieutenant Governor Bross and others, addressed a large audience at Library Hall, in which they spoke eloquently of the great era which this day marks in the history of our country.

During the evening there was also a general indulgence in fire works, bonfires, illuminations, &c.

FIRE IN QUINCY.

The residence of Rev. Henry Rowenthal Labbie, of the Jewish Church, at Quincy, Illinois, was totally destroyed by fire last night. The Synagogue adjoining, was also badly damaged. Loss from $5,000 to $6,000.

FREIGHT REDUCTION.

The Union Pacific railroad announces to-day a reduction on freight between Omaha and Cheyenne of 40 cents per 100 lbs on 1st, 2d and 3d class freight.

PROSPECTIVE COMPLETION.

The Chicago, Rock Island and Pacific railroad will be completed to Omaha day after to-morrow. This will open a sharp competition between the North Western and Rock Island roads for the Pacific railroad freight.

COMMERCIAL.

ST. LOUIS, May 10.—At a meeting of the board of directors of the Merchants' Exchange to-day, the president of that body was instructed to appoint twenty-four members as delegates to the commercial convention to be held at New Orleans on the 24th inst.

Over 70,000 bushels of wheat were received to-day from the upper Mississippi.

It is announced that a contract was concluded on Saturday for one hundred thousand bushels of No. 2 wheat at points above Rock Island, at a price which will lay it down in Liverpool, its destination, at $1.42 per bushel. It will be shipped via New Orleans.

COUNTERFEITER.

Edward W. Wise pleaded guilty in the United States court to-day to dealing in counterfeit money and plates, and was sentenced to ten years in the penitentiary.

STEAMBOAT LOSS.

Information has been received here that the steamer John D. Perry was burned at Duvall's Bluffs, Ark., two or three days ago. She was valued at $15,000. Insured for $10,000.

The Grey Eagle, which capsized last night, was valued at $6,000.

THE GOLDEN SPIKE.

The fire alarm bells in this city were struck at six minutes to 2 o'clock this afternoon, the response to the blows of the hammer which drove the last spike on the Union Pacific railroad. Quite a crowd assembled at the telegraph office, and much interest was manifested on the occasion. Everybody is rejoiced at the completion of the grandest enterprise ever accomplished by mortal hands.

A METHODIST CHURCH.

The corner stone of the new Centenary Methodist Episcopal Church was laid to-day with appropriate and imposing ceremonies. Several bishops and quite a number of ministers were present.

## CALIFORNIA.

PACIFIC R. R. CELEBRATION.

SAN FRANCISCO, May 10.—The celebration to-day was the greatest occasion ever known in San Francisco. The procession was immense, business suspended, bells rung and salutes fired from all the guns in the harbor. Sacramento, also, in honor of the event, celebrated in a most magnificent manner.

*(Continued on Fourth Page.)*

MARRIED.

In this city, May 9th, by Rev. H. N. Herrick, Mr. SAMUEL H. ADAMS and Miss HATTIE FITZGERALD, both of Minneapolis.

DIED.

In North Minneapolis, May 9th, 1869, Mrs. MARGARET L. CLARK, wife of Amos T. Clark, aged 35 years.

Funeral at the Freewill Baptist Church, Wednesday afternoon at 2 o'clock.

In Minneapolis, on the 10th inst., ANNA A., only daughter of R. J. and E. A. Derby, aged 1 year 3 months and 10 days.

Funeral services at the Methodist Church, Wednesday afternoon at 2 o'clock. Friends are invited to attend.

---

See what Gale & Co. say this morning—last column, 4th page—as to Houses, Lots, Lands, and every kind of Insurance.

## New Advertisements.



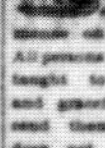

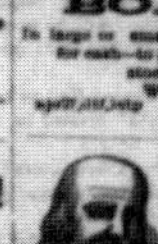

# The Minneapolis Daily Tribune.

VOL. 3. MINNEAPOLIS, MINNESOTA SUNDAY MORNING, NOVEMBER 21, 1869. NO. 155



**The Minneapolis Tribune**

*Issued Daily, Tri-Weekly and Weekly,*

AT THE

**TRIBUNE PRINTING CO.**

| | |
|---|---|
| Delivered in the city, per year | $12 00 |
| Daily by mail, per year | 10 00 |
| Tri-weekly, per year | 6 00 |
| Weekly, per year | 2 00 |

**Sunday, November 21, 1869.**


☞ Communications on subjects of public interest are solicited. All communications must be accompanied by the name of the author, to guard against imposition.


☞ FOR EDITORIALS ON LEADING TOPICS, SEE SECOND PAGE.


AT the Church of the Immaculate Conception, New York, recently, the sacrament of confirmation was conferred upon seven hundred and seventy candidates, male and female, by the Right Rev. Bishop Lynch, D. D., of Charleston, S. C.

THE Waseca News says that for any town to become permanently prosperous, manufactories must be encouraged and fostered. We must be producers as well as consumers, and keep in circulation at home money, which now goes to enrich foreign manufacturers.

SENSATIONAL — PROBABLY. — The New York papers state that a very powerful naval force has been despatched to the Bay of Samana, which is to be used as if it were a possession of the United States, without waiting for the ratification by the senate of the treaty reported to have been made for the cession of certain parts of the dominion of the Dominican.

ONE of the speakers at a recent Equal Rights meeting in Brooklyn, is a lady of rare beauty who has had three husbands, and been twice divorced, and is now the wife of a gentleman much older than herself. She thinks "every woman should be pecuniarily independent, and she trusted that the time would come when no woman would be compelled to marry for a home." We think it would be very well if every man, also, could be independent, and no one mean enough to marry for money—but none of us will, we fear, live to see that day. In the mean time, if the fair oratress should become a widow, she will not probably be at any loss for admirers, or be necessitated to wait very long for number four.

LAWS REGARDING MARRIAGE. — Judge Barnard, of New York, has recently decided where a marriage may be binding where there has been no civil service. In the case before him, according to the report in the World, the man had told the woman, no third party being present, that he would live with her as her husband, and had placed a ring upon her finger, telling her, in effect, that this was marriage enough; he had taken rooms for her as his wife, had in that character presented her to others, and had lived for several years with her as her husband, and children had been born to them. Lately he had informed her that the connection between them was to be broken off, had deserted her, and married another woman. Judge Barnard decides that in effect, the parties were married, and that the absence of a civil or religious ceremony cannot be held to invalidate the contract entered into between the two and acknowledged by both in such an unmistakable way.

### Old Times Renewed.

The absence of telegraphic dispatches the last few days, and the necessity of making up a paper without them, brings up the recollections of editorial life thirty years ago, when such things were unknown. The newspaper of that day was as different from that of the present, as a canoe is from a steamboat, and there was about the same difference in the expenses. The arrival from New York of the "steamboat mail" via Providence, in Boston, was then the great event of the day, and created more excitement than do the dozen or more railroad trains which are now required between the two cities to accommodate the vastly increased travel. The smartest of the newspapers then, were very tame affairs compared with the slowest of the present day. When express riders came into vogue, the people opened their eyes very wide at the reckless prodigality of publishers, and thought the extreme of enterprise had been reached. The "little black pony," whose effigy appeared daily in the New York Journal of Commerce, was a great and distinguished character in those days—quite equal, in his notoriety to "Dexter" and "Gen. Butler" now. In those days editing a paper did not mean, as it now does, perpetual work, such as no man will be able to endure for any length of time unless his heart is in it, and he really loves the profession. There is no end to the work which may be profitably bestowed upon a metropolitan daily like the Tribune, the Times, or the Herald—and if any man thinks it a small or easy job to make up even a provincial daily so as to give reasonable satisfaction to its readers, we have only to say, as Mr. Lincoln did to one who criticised his administration, we wish they would undertake to "run the machine for a month."

### American Industry and Ingenuity.

A statement in a Sheffield (English) paper, goes into an elaborate statement of the reasons why Sheffield cutlery is being superseded in this country by goods of American manufacture, the upshot of the whole appearing to be, that superior ingenuity and enterprise, a better knowledge of the market, and more extensive use of machinery, especially in the getting up of table cutlery, has at last driven the foreign article almost out of our markets.

One reason given in this connection—quoting the English writer—is, "the superior finish, and bolder, larger, and stronger style of the American goods as compared with those formerly sent from Sheffield. Instead of competing with Sheffield for sharpness, the American manufacturers struck out a novel course, offering bold, perfect goods, at a high price at first, and relying on the demand for a better grade of goods to carry them through."

Now scanning the above with care does it not contain a hint such as made good use of by our cotton manufacturers especially, might be of vast service to themselves and the country at large? Suppose that right alongside of the cotton fields they would afford to take a bolder course; would put into their fabrics more of the raw material, making thereby a stronger and better article, as, paying no cost of carriage or commission they could afford to do, how long would it be before goods thus gotten up on a bold and liberal scale would run out the "sleazy," trifling goods now filling every market, the world over. We are glad to chronicle the success of Americans in competition with English manufacturers in almost any field. Let us hope that as the nation advances along the pathway of improvement, we may have occasion to note other triumphs in mechanical and manufacturing industries.

### "John Chinaman."

We print in another part of this paper a very interesting article from the Atlantic for December, by Albert D. Richardson, the well known traveller and correspondent, in which he treats of the question of Chinese immigration. We surely need not tell our readers at this late day, of the brutal manner in which the Chinese have been treated in California—how they have been denied all protection for life or property, and made the sport of cruel and debased men, who, if their conduct in this regard is a fair sample of their general characters, are unfit to be outside the walls of a penitentiary. It is one of the anomalies of this case, that those who have been foremost in this infamous business were not to the manor born, but came to this country to escape oppression, and are now only too prompt to quadruple upon others the wrongs from which they themselves fled. The history of the Irish masses in this country is not calculated to inspire that respect and sympathy which it should be the object of good citizens to deserve. Coming here, as a general thing, rough and uneducated, in too many cases they have aspired, before they could read our laws or understand them, to inaugurate a reign of violence, as a short road to the gratification of their peculiar ideas as to what constitutes freedom. They were at heart quite as bitter and hateful towards the negroes as they now are towards the Chinese, and, if unchecked, would have carried their brutality to an equal extent—but the negroes had more friends than the Chinese, and hence were better protected. Something, it is true, is to be said for them, on the ground that centuries of oppression at home have unfitted them to receive coolly and with discretion the full-blown privileges of American citizenship—but surely there should be a power somewhere to curb their tendency to cruelty to other nationalities, quite as much entitled as they themselves are to the care and protection of the government.

The question of the expediency of encouraging Chinese immigration is one thing, and that of protecting those who come, whether invited or not, is another. It is our national boast that we offer an asylum to the oppressed of the whole world, and the spread eagle eloquence with which we have plumed ourselves on the fact, never seemed to contemplate that we should surrender to one class of immigrants the right to maltreat others, or to say who shall or who shall not, avail themselves of the privilege. Our true policy is to welcome all who come with honest intentions to better their own condition, and to aid us in developing the country—but to surrender to none exclusive privileges, or the right to enforce their peculiar views with the fist or the bludgeon. "Order is heaven's first law," and order by and under the law is as much a necessity to the State as breath is to the individual. It was bad enough to found our government on the declaration that all men were created equal, and keep four millions of men in slavery. Under the guidance of Heaven that plague spot is wiped out; —but we shall be very little the gainer in character or reputation, if we offset the virtue of giving the negro his rights when we could no longer keep them from him, by taking away those of the Chinese, and allowing them to be subjected to a system of cruelty, not even mitigated by the pecuniary interest which the master had in preserving the life and usefulness of the slave. We do not find this disposition to "rush things" on the part of the Germans, Swedes or Norwegians, and wherever it does exist, the good of society, in which the disorganizers themselves have as deep an interest as any body else, requires that it should be met and put down.

### Delay of the Mails.

We are informed by our obliging city Postmaster, Col. Aldrich, that besides the failure of the Eastern mail yesterday, the result of a snow blockade around and beyond Chicago, he has ascertained by telegraphing, that the mail which should be due here to-day, will not be here until to-morrow—Monday evening. The Southern mail is also behind, in like manner; so that without any fault of our own climate here, we are embargoed as a consequence of the bad weather further South.

In view of this, and apart from a talk about the mails—the exemption from snow, is certainly most marked. So far in the season—to be exact about it—we have not had snow enough to hide the ground. If the snow fall at any time had been measured upon a smooth slab of marble, we do not believe it would have measured the quarter of an inch, so that with this remarkable condition of things, we have also escaped the terrible winter gales which seem to have made themselves badly felt no further off than Chicago within the past few days. Truly we should be thankful for all this.

### OUR OWN STATE.

—Kasson is organizing a brass band.

—Wheat in Glencoe is bringing 43 cents per bushel.

—A new cemetery has just been platted in Mankato.

—Blue Earth county paid teachers last year $13,357.45.

—They are raising the War Eagle sunk at Hudson, and she is probably afloat to-day.

—The blacking is killing cattle in Faribault county.

—Company E, of the Ninth, are to have a re-union in Mankato on Thursday next.

—A bulk barge with 7,000 bushels of wheat was sunk by the ice at Red Wing, Friday evening.

—Mrs. Cochlin, an old woman of Brownsville, lately attempted suicide by cutting her throat with a razor.

—Trains have crossed the Minnineopa bridge and the work is fast nearing Lake Crystal.

—F. Juenger, of New Haven, in Olmsted county, raised on four acres 190 bushels of Fife wheat—over 45 bushels per acre.

—Northfield gave Cobb 190 votes, and the prohibitionists have written it at the top of their banner list.

—Wednesday the mercury in Kasson sunk down to zero; ugh! Kasson is too near Chicago for comfort.

—Hay on the Superior shore is $40 per ton, and fears are entertained that, from failure to ship hay by the lake, cattle will suffer during the winter for food.

—A mile of railroad track is laid on Rice Point, Superior shore, and a new engine properly christened "J. C. Jackson," is making regular trips—with a gravel train.

—At the sale of school lands at Glencoe last week, the prices paid were from $5 to $7, and the amount realized was $17,303.75, of which $5,000 was paid down.

—Hiram L. Post, formerly of Webster, N. Y., and educated at Genesee College, has been secured for the principal of the Winona high school.

—George Holcomb was seriously and probably fatally injured by being caught in the gearing of a threshing machine, on Monday, at Pinto, in Carver county. He was clearing up around the machine.

—Somebody sawed down the poles of the telegraph line along the Central road, on Thursday night. A stretch of half a mile between Westcott's and Rosemount was thus broken.

—Lorenzo Rist, of Nicollet, was oiling a threshing machine and his glove being caught by the gearing, his arm was pulled into the cylinder and stripped to the bone of nearly all its flesh.

—The Indian name from which the cognomen of Red Wing is literalized is Hhoo-pa-hoo-doo-ta, meaning Wing of Scarlet, and was borne by a dead and gone Dakotah chief. Red Wing is not dead, however.

—The Le Roy merchants have formed an association for the purpose of buying wheat on the assumption that wheat buyers allow themselves too large a margin. They have taken a sure way to find out.

—Douglas county has $149,500 worth of stock, an increase of $51,759 since the assessment of last year. This shows material prosperity equal to any other portion of the frontier, at least.

—A warehouse, Houseman's Hall, and Mr. Houseman's residence, in Winona, were destroyed by fire on Friday morning. The origin of the fire is unknown. The buildings were valued at $9,000, and insured for $4,000.

—An engine for a saw mill on the Snake at Pine City, half way to Duluth, was shipped upon the Superior road one day last week. It was built at Fond du Lac, Wis. The mill belongs to J. S. Ferson, of Oshkosh, and will commence work early in the spring.

—A young man from Austin, in St. Paul, met a dining room girl. They were acquainted in an hour, fairly in love in two hours, engaged in three hours and in six hours were married and on their way to Austin.

—A man whose wheat was graded No. 2 instead of No. 1, took umbrage and showed his appreciation of the act, and his despise his disposition by whipping the Rochester inspector. It did not however, make any change in the quality of his grain.

—Waseca has not yet attained to the dignity of a police force, and having a law abiding community does not need it, but is arranging for the support of a night watchman to guard against fires, and thereby sets a good example to other villages.

—John N. Hall and J. W. Horn have been elected to fill vacancies in the board of directors of the Minnesota & Northwestern railroad. The filling of a third vacancy was postponed until the annual meeting for election which takes place next February.

—Fred. Boehner and his wife, of Olmsted, raised and harvested seventy-five acres of grain, the past season. From these acres they obtained 1,250 bushels of wheat, 1,000 bushels of oats, and sixty-four bushels of barley. He and his wife did all the labor except a portion of the threshing. They are not likely to starve.

—A German taking a load of dried meat—"all flesh is grass"; consequently dried grass is dried meat—to market at La Crosse, set it afire by dropping fire from his pipe, and only had time, by dint of extraordinary exertions, to release his team from the danger of roasting. The Teuton philosophically hitched on to the charred wagon, fixed his old pipe again and started for another load.

—A painful accident happened near Lewiston Station, in Dover, on Tuesday afternoon, by which a young man, named David Ebert lost his left arm. While engaged in oiling the machine, the loose sleeve of his coat caught in the side gearing of the machine, and in an instant his left hand and half the forearm was ground to pieces by the iron cog wheels. By a desperate effort he tore himself away, actually separating himself from the crushed arm, which was instantly drawn into the machine.

—On Sunday last, the Dodge County Republican says, Frank Hyde, Clara Dearborn, Eva Hyde and Emma Remington, each about 12 years of age, were out riding, accompanied by a terrier dog. When near the Haught plum grove, about 5 miles from Kasson, the dog started a deer, and chased him into a jungle of logs and brush, and there nabbed him by the neck and threw him down. Master Frank and the girls returned to the spot, and with strings tied the animal, drew him forth from his retreat, and loaded him into the wagon. Judge Remington met them at the old Howard mill, where he killed and dressed the animal. He was four years old, or buck with ponderous horns—and his carcass, undressed, weighed 175 pounds.

#### RELIGIOUS.

—The corresponding secretary of the Freeborn county Sunday School Society extends a fraternal invitation to pastors and superintendents of Sunday Schools in adjoining counties to meet with them in convention on the 3d and 4th of December.—Albert Lea.

—The State convention of the Young Men's Christian Association will be held in Rochester this week commencing at 2 p. m. on Thursday. It is expected that the State Christian Convention, which convenes in the same city on the 23d will have so completed its business in time to join in the deliberations of the Y. M. C. A.

—The Sabbath school convention of Houston county convened in the Presbyterian church in Caledonia on Thursday evening last. Friday morning, after the hour of prayer and conference, the convention effected a permanent organization by electing the following officers: President, D. P. Temple; vice presidents, Rev. D. M. Smith, and W. F. A. Graves; secretary, A. H. Reding; executive committee, John McNelly, D. L. Buell, and John H. Smith. A deep interest was manifested by those present, and all seemed resolved to go forth with renewed zeal in the Sabbath school work. The next convention will be held in the Methodist church in Caledonia on the third Tuesday in May, 1870.

### ITEMS.

—Indiana has raised much sorghum this year.

—New York is to have a new public market at a cost of $1,000,000.

—If the poor-house has any terrors for you, never buy what you don't need.

—Cassius M. Clay, late United States Minister to Russia, has arrived in New York.

—Indiana college students have been making money by gathering hickory nuts.

—Southern churches have been investing in organs.

—There is a very loud call for an increased supply of small change at New Orleans.

—One boiler and engine is to heat and do the hoisting for a whole block of buildings in Cincinnati.

—Mark Twain has a new lecture, which he calls, "Our Fellow Savages, the Sandwich Islanders."

—Sir Morton Peto, formerly the "railroad king" in England, is to try his fortune again at railroading in Hungary.

—Pius IX usually devotes two hours daily to his secretary who reads the newspapers to him.

—Three thousand acres in the very heart of Louisville, Ky., are claimed by the heirs of one John Campbell.

—New glass works have been completed at Detroit, Mich., on the site of those destroyed by fire last winter.

—The Empress Eugenie has purchased the ground adjoining Mount David, where it is supposed the Virgin Mary is buried.

—There are thirty slate quarries in Leigh county, Pennsylvania, worth two million dollars.

—The poet Burns is popular in Germany. He has been twice translated—by Freiligrath (partially) and by Adolf Laun.

—Ohio must show 3,000,000 inhabitants in order to retain her representation in Congress at the next apportionment.

—A man died in St. John's, New Brunswick, the other day, whose life was insured for the sum of $280,000.

—David Kendall, Past Grand Master of the Grand Lodge of the Independent Order of Odd Fellows, of California, died a few days ago.

—They are trying to get up a wickedest man sensation in Chicago, but there is too much competition as to who shall be the man.

—Henry Ward Beecher's income will be twenty one thousand dollars the coming year. It was twenty-eight thousand last year.

—An Indiana girl succeeded in committing a thousand Bible verses to memory, and then she laid ill of brain fever for three months.

—The Samana Bay purchase is not yet consummated. The matter has to be settled by congress, as the president has no right to buy territory without the consent of congress.

—The grand lodge of Free Masons of Alabama has resolved to establish an institution for the benefit of the indigent orphans of deceased master Masons, where they can be clothed, fed, educated, and cared for generally.

—Anna Garmiha, a young girl at Kieff in Russia, rescued, recently, seven children from a burning house which none of the firemen dared to enter. The Emperor, upon hearing of her heroism, sent her a thousand silver roubles, and the Empress presented her with a valuable necklace.

—Oil was first noticed about Bear River City, Wyoming territory, about eighteen months ago, and so far about thirteen thousand acres of oil lands have been pre-empted, a new town has been laid out, and many lots sold. The prospect is said to be great, and old Pennsylvania oil men, it is said, intend investigating and investing.

—Eugene Sue was denied burial in consecrated ground by the Catholic clergy, but his grave is cared for by a wealthy hotel keeper of Geneva, who owns land in Savoy. This enthusiastic admirer of the great French novelist pays a gardener three hundred francs a year to keep the grave in order and on the 3d of August, the anniversary of Sue's death, he causes the grave to be beautifully decked with flowers and garlands.

—Secretary Seward's friends here have private advices to the effect that his reported illness was not of a serious character, and that he has probably resumed his travels ere this. He has suffered severely from neuralgia and gout in his limbs, brought on by exposure, and at one time he was seriously threatened with an attack of the same disease in his stomach, which might have proved fatal, but at the latest dates the prospects for his immediate recovery were favorable.—*Washington Chronicle.*

### Killing Fish with Giant Powder.

From the Virginia City (Nevada) Enterprise.

A few days since we copied an item from the Carson Appeal in regard to killing fish with Giant powder. Yesterday we had a conversation with a gentleman who had some experience at this kind of fishing. He says that while stopping at the Warm Springs, near Genoa, last week, he several times went out with parties of gentlemen to blast trout out of the Carson river. The way they practise this new mode of fishing is as follows: They take a cartridge of Giant powder weighing about a quarter of a pound, insert into it a fuse properly capped, about six inches in length, then lighting the fuse the cartridge is thrown into any deep hole supposed to contain trout or other fish. After the cartridge has been thrown into the water, smoke and bubbles of gas are seen to rise to the surface, then in a few seconds comes the explosion—a dull, heavy report. The surface of the water is seen to bulge up, and the ground can be felt to shake for fifteen or twenty feet back from the water. Immediately after the explosion all the fish that happened to be within a circle of twenty-five or thirty feet of the spot where the cartridge fell, come to the surface either killed outright or so badly stunned that it is some minutes before they recover. Our informant says that with two cartridges he saw over fifty pounds of fish killed, counting trout, whitefish and chubs. In places, after a blast the whole surface of the water would be covered with minnows, from an inch to three or four inches in length. At Elko they are practising the same style of fishing, only that out there they tie the cartridge to the end of a long pole and thrust it into the water, holding it until the explosion occurs. This is the most destructive mode of fishing we have ever heard of—it is a regular wholesale slaughter of great and small, good and bad. Should the practice gain ground, it will be necessary for the legislature to put a stop to it by an act making it a criminal offense to fish with Giant powder. Parties have already been talking of trying this blasting process in Lake Tahoe, where by using large cartridges they expect to bring up hundreds of trout at a single shot.

### A Shrewd Paris Detective.

Paris papers tell a detective story. A legacy of 500,000 francs was recently left to a lady who had long lived with her daughter in extreme poverty. Unfortunately this suddenly enriched couple were nowhere to be found, and the affair was put into the hands of a young detective. He asked for fourteen days to prosecute the search. At the end of that time he had been unsuccessful, and he begged for fourteen days more. Still he was apparently no nearer his object, and he requested that the time might be extended to a month. When this period had expired, and he presented himself, unaccompanied by any one, before his superior, the latter upbraided him with his inefficiency. It was obvious, the indignant official remarked, that he did not sufficiently know his business. "Very well, my dear sir," was the calm reply, "but I have now to inform you that I have been eight days married to the daughter of the lady I have been searching for, and I shall now thank you to hand over the 500,000 francs, which are the property of my mother-in-law."

## BY TELEGRAPH.

THE ELECTION IN NEW YORK.

The Egyptio-Turkish Disagreements.

What a Democratic Victory Costs.

And the Dancers that Paid the Piper.

OPENING OF THE SUEZ CANAL.

SPECULATIONS AS TO ITS SUCCESS

THE INAUGURATION FLEET ARRIVED

Only One Line Working to Chicago.

PROBABLE REDUCTION OF TAXES.

A BUILDING FALLS IN ST. LOUIS.

Several Persons Buried in the Ruins.

Vessels Driven Ashore on Lake Michigan

Eight Lives Lost From One Schooner.

Railroad Cars Blown Off the Track on the Harlem.

A FIRE IN BROOKLYN, NEW YORK.

A Family Leaps from the Third Story.

Terrific Gales on the Atlantic Coast.

AN INDIAN WAR IN TEXAS.

### WASHINGTON.

Special to Minneapolis Tribune.

BOUTWELL.

WASHINGTON, Nov. 20.—Secretary Boutwell is in Massachusetts, finishing his report.

SENATOR SHERMAN

arrived here yesterday.

TREASURER SPINNER

has recovered from his illness, and returned to duty.

MORRILL,

of Maine, will probably succeed Fessenden as chairman of the appropriation committee.

CRAGIN,

of New Hampshire, will probably succeed Grimes, on the naval committee.

WORLD'S FAIR.

One hundred and fifty thousand dollars has been subscribed by citizens of Washington, for the proposed world's fair.

The receipts of the custom house to Nov. 8th were $29,242.45.

The investigation by the treasury department into the alleged frauds of the American and National Bank Note companies of New York, is concluded. The treasury department has no idea that any fraud exists. The amount short, which is only about six hundred dollars, is claimed to have been lost.

The republican state committee of Virginia have called a state convention at Richmond, on Wednesday next, to devise the best manner of building up the party, and as to what course to pursue towards the so-called Walker wing.

The favorable aspect of the internal revenue and custom collections during November indicate a further reduction in the national debt of ten millions.

Senator Morton expresses an opinion that congress will reduce the tax on sugar, tea, coffee, salt and all articles the tax on which falls most heavily upon the poorer classes.

INDIAN TROUBLES.

Information has been received from San Antonio, Texas, Nov 17th, that Capt. Trainer has arrived from the frontier and reports that Gen. McKenzie sent 200 cavalry, under Maj. Bacon and Lt. Bean, who met on the Upper Brazos 400 hostile savages coming down on the frontier from the reservation. After two days fighting the Indians fled leaving forty dead and many more wounded. The camp, horses and provisions were all taken. Captain Hooker is badly wounded and eight men hurt, none killed.

Receipts fractional currency for week, $1,097,000; shipments, $42,000; amount destroyed, $550,993.

### THE EAST.

Special to Minneapolis Tribune.

COMMEMORATIVE.

NEW YORK, Nov. 20.—It is proposed to erect a monument to the memory of Geo. Peabody.

TURKEY AND EGYPT.

Cable telegrams say the impending troubles between the sultan and Khedive are strengthening. Turkish and Egyptian agents are contracting for a large quantity of arms. It is rumored that the Turkish agent is negotiating with the Spanish consul for the purchase of 20 gunboats.

WHAT IT COST.

The Times says the late election cost Tammany ring $900,000. The torchlight procession cost $120,000. The democratic candidates, including Mayor Hall, contributing 20 per cent. of their salaries, and others even more; the senatorial candidates paying $25,000 each, excepting two who paid $50,000.

THE OFFICIAL VOTE

of the state of New York gives Nelson, secretary of state, 20,253 majority over Sigel, and Ellis for comptroller 25,691 over Greeley.

THE HORNET.

The investigation into the case of Captain Higgins, shows that the coal put aboard the Hornet was unfit for use, and completely vindicates his course in putting into Wilmington.

EUGENIE.

Cabel telegrams announce the arrival of the empress at Ismalia.

THE CANAL.

The enthusiasm over the opening of the Suez canal is immense. The London Shipping Gazette comments as follows: "Whether the points of difficulty remaining to be overcome here or there before the canal can be available for vessels of the largest tonnage, is merely a question of detail to be determined by the construction of the canal. As far as we are concerned, we can only point to the fact that the French engineers have redeemed their promise. The canal is open and is a magnificent success.

A dispatch dated Ismalia, Nov. 19, evening, says the inauguration fleet has arrived at Bitter Lake and anchored there for the night. The fleet will reach the Red Sea to-morrow.

CARS BLOWN OFF THE TRACK.

NEW YORK, Nov. 19.—A train of cars on Harlem railroad was thrown from the track yesterday, near Boston Corners, by a heavy gale. The express, baggage and two passenger cars were hurled from the bank a distance of 75 feet. Casualties were slight being one boy killed and several persons more or less injured.

CONSUL GRIGGS.

NEW YORK, Nov. 20.—A private letter from Jamaica, dated October 5th, states that Consul Griggs declares that the report of his speech at the Cuban banquet, as represented by the Jamaica papers is incorrect. Mr. Griggs asserts that he simply expressed his belief that Cuba would secure her freedom, and that in his opinion, judging from the existing state of public feeling in America, one of the first acts of congress would probably be the recognition of Cuban rights. He denies having uttered the sentiments attributed to him, what he really did say having a very different application.

VANDERBILT'S TESTIMONY.

The examination of Cornelius Vanderbilt in the suit of the Erie railway vs. Mr. Vanderbilt, on a charge of having defrauded the Erie railroad company out of $5,000,000, was taken to-day.

A FIRE

broke out this morning in the white lead works of Pierce, Anderson & Douglas, Brooklyn. It was the same building in which, a few years since, a fire occurred by which five firemen lost their lives. Thos. Wallace, with his wife and child, occupied the upper part of


*Continued on Fourth Page.*


#### MARRIED.

In this city, on the 18th inst., by Rev. J. F. Chaffee, JAMES A. DENNIS to SARAH E. BUTLER, both of Minneapolis.




See Wants—For Sale—For Rent and Legal Notices on Third Page.

# 1870～1879

# Minneapolis Daily Tribune.

VOL. V. MINNEAPOLIS, MINNESOTA: TUESDAY MORNING, OCTOBER 10, 1871. NO. 118.

**The Minneapolis Tribune**

A REPUBLICAN JOURNAL,

PUBLISHED

Daily, Tri-Weekly and Weekly,

BY THE

TRIBUNE PRINTING COMPANY.

Terms of Subscription:

POSITIVELY—No paper will be sent unless paid for in advance, and all papers will be promptly stopped at expiration of time paid for.

DAILY TRIBUNE.

| | |
|---|---|
| One Year by Mail | $13.00 |
| Less than three months, per month | 1.00 |
| By Carrier, per month | 1.00 |

TRI-WEEKLY TRIBUNE.

One Year........ $6.00 | Six Months..... $3.00

WEEKLY TRIBUNE.

One Year........ $2.00 | Six Months..... $1.00

**The circulation of the TRIBUNE in Minneapolis and St. Anthony is larger than all other daily papers combined. Its circulation in this county and in Northern Minnesota is much larger than any other daily paper. These are facts well known to advertisers.**

TUESDAY, OCTOBER 10, 1871.

### The Great Fire.

The great fire in Chicago has sent a thrill of terror through the entire Northwest. It was a terrible calamity—its extent can hardly be estimated in figures. The TRIBUNE is the only paper in Minnesota, so far as we have seen, which has given anything like a full and accurate account of it, obtained by telegraph exclusively to us. Our special reporters and special facilities for getting news, with the enterprise of the paper, has enabled us to give the only satisfactory report which our people have had. This is another of the many evidences of the truth of what is claimed for the TRIBUNE—that it is the most enterprising paper west of Chicago, and the paper for the people; containing the latest and most reliable news. Our extras yesterday contained full reports. No other paper which has reached us does.

But about the fire. We can hardly realize its great extent. The business center of the great city lying in ashes—a loss of millions, and perhaps billions of money. So large, indeed, that we fear the insurance companies, as a general thing, will be unable to bear the loss that will fall upon them. The risks in Chicago were something enormous in the part of the city destroyed. Indeed, the city may be said to have been essentially wiped out by a single conflagration; so disastrous has been the blow that we fear the means from insurance will not be forthcoming to even partially build up this great and remarkable city. Still, we have faith to believe that it will arise out of its ashes and again shine forth as the wonder of the world in point of enterprise and energy. It will take many years to regain what has been lost in the way of dollars and business. But the men who have once built up this city of near three hundred and fifty thousand inhabitants, out of limited means, can again build it up to what it was, and continue it on to the accomplishment of its wonderful destiny.

The calamity is not only local to Chicago, but extends to every part of the great Northwest and to the entire country. The pulsations that come from Chicago as a center extended to all parts of the United States, and all sections will sympathize with it in this hour of distress. We hope to see measures taken that will result in Minneapolis sending its mite in the way of contribution to the suffering thousands. Who will take the lead?

BY a late Missouri decision it is held that life insurance policies issued in favor of a wife on the life of her husband, are not exempt from execution, whether the company has an existence in that or another State, when the contract is made in that State, if the amount of the annual premium exceeds three hundred dollars. Commenting upon this rather startling decision, the *Democrat* thinks that the next Legislature should pass an act securing this exemption to the widow and children of a deceased subject of a life policy, and the dictates of humanity would seem to urge such an enactment. In nearly all other States of the Union such policies are relieved from the liability of execution.

UNDER the administration of Dr. Chronik, a Jewish congregation in Chicago will take the new departure contemplated by the liberal Hebrews and hereafter observe the first day of the week instead of Saturday for their Sabbath. They have adopted the new Berlin Prayer Book. There is a wide spread disposition on the part of the Jews in the United States to make this sensible innovation upon old customs.

THE New York yachtsmen have finally spunked up sufficiently to make a firm decision regarding terms of the race with Ashbury's English yacht "Livonia." They say now that he must take the New York course or none at all. Heretofore he has been permitted to dictate his own terms.

THEY fire cannon every morning and evening at Vicksburg to purify the atmosphere. Better come to Minnesota where no artificial means are required.

THE earlier reports from the Great Fire will be found on the second page of this morning's TRIBUNE.

On the 1st inst., the residence of Thos. Jennings, of North Ridge, Houston county, was burned. The older members of the family had gone to Brownsville to witness the Catholic church ceremonies, leaving two small children [illegible] a fire from which a broom ignited and communicated the flames to some clothing and then to the house. Loss $2,000.

THE inquest upon the body of Mr. Burton Edsall, of Chicago, who was shot in his house on Friday morning, was not ended at latest dates. None of the evidence offered goes to establish the theory of suicide.

# TELEGRAPHIC!

By Northwestern Line.

## THE CHICAGO FIRE!

### ONE HUNDRED AND SEVENTY PRISONERS IN THE JAIL ROASTED ALIVE.

GREAT LOSS OF LIFE—HUNDREDS ROASTED ALIVE AND CRUSHED TO DEATH IN THE JAM.

Confusion and Terror Reign

Hundreds of Lives Lost.

A SCENE OF CONFUSION

A Territory Six Miles in Extent Each way in Ruins.

FIRE DEPARTMENT AND POLICE POWERLESS.

THE FIRE BY NIGHT.

The City and Citizens Desolate.

Further of the Wisconsin Fires.

A Panic at Oshkosh.

PESHTIGO BURNED.

SIXTY OR SEVENTY LIVES SACRIFICED.

[Our special reporter in Chicago sends us the following further startling particulars of the fire. It is still raging. The rain has not reached the city, though clouds were gathering at last reports.—ED.]

*Special to Minneapolis Tribune.*

CHICAGO, Monday, Oct. 9, 3:30 P. M.—Contrary to the hope I expressed in my previous dispatch, the fire is spreading in every direction, and our own fire department, assisted by that of St. Louis, and the interior cities of Illinois, Michigan, Indiana and Wisconsin engaged in fighting the flames seem powerless to save the city. All that portion of the city enclosed by North Water street, Jefferson and Lake is already destroyed, or in flames.

Water has no perceptible effect on the conflagration. The Pittsburg, Fort Wayne & Chicago depot, and all the sections of the city south and west of Madison street as far out from the river as Sangamon, thence south to Sixteenth street on the west side, are in ashes.

The streets are literally packed with wagon loads of furniture and valuables saved from the burned buildings. The loss of life is very great. As yet, no estimate as to numbers can be made.

All the prisoners in the county jail, numbering about one hundred and seventy, were roasted alive. The jail was located in the basement of the Court House, which was destroyed on Sunday night.

On the north side a large portion of the entire city is flames, and cannot be saved. The city is one entire blaze from 12th st., on the south side, to Erie street, on the north side, a distance of a mile and a half from the river on the north, and three miles and upwards in the extent, and is rapidly spreading in all directions. The firemen are exhausted, discouraged, and find the fire is entirely beyond their control.

To [illegible] all the [illegible] of the [illegible] in flames and hundreds of lives of sailors and others engaged thereabout have been lost and hundreds are still in extreme peril. The sight beggars description.

Thousands of people fill the streets and are rushing from the threatened quarters, fleeing for their lives. Many men, women, and children have been crushed to death, and have been run down by panic stricken horses.

The police are powerless to preserve order, and all is in a state of confusion and dismay.

The Chicago Dock, Nelson, Munger, Armour & Wheeler and Galena elevators are burned to the ground.

Farwell Hall, Briggs House, Field, Leiter & Co., Farwell & Co., and the Drake block, *Tribune* building, Post office, water works, gas works, all gone.

Thousands are leaving the city for shelter.

Assistance from all surrounding towns is coming.

Business is entirely suspended.

All communications from the East are destroyed.

A heavy wind is blowing from the south and everything in the direction of the wind is destined to destruction. Everything within two and three miles of the Court-house east, west, north and south, is reduced to ashes. It is terrible beyond description. No one can get on the south side from Twelfth street.

The fact is the entire business part of Chicago is now one vast mass of smoking ruins. Thousands of merchants and business men who yesterday were worth their thousands are to-day reduced to beggary.

Thieves and robbers, unawed by the terror by which they are surrounded, are pursuing their villainous avocations and plundering that which the more merciful flames had left untouched.

Intense alarm agitates the minds of all in view of the horrors which the ruined city, destined to utter darkness by the destruction of the gas works, will experience to-night.

Children hopelessly separated from their parents, and members of families who are rendered homeless and paupers by this awful visitation, roam about the smoke choked streets, unheeded in the general gloom and distress.

The blackened pavements are strewn with silks and the rich furnishings of wardrobe and parlor, and the destruction of valuables is immense and appalling.

LAST NIGHT.

*Special to Minneapolis Tribune.*

CHICAGO, Oct. 9, Eve., 9 P. M.—The scene of the great fire by night is, if possible, more appalling and awe-inspiring than during the day. The conflagration has spread northward to a point beyond Erie street, and in that direction the city is flooded by a supernatural light, while on the west and south where the advance of the fiery destroyer does not present so solid a front, here and there great tongues of flames shoot upward, casting a lurid light upon the surrounding darkness and presenting a strange contrast to the pitchy darkness in which the city is enveloped by the burning of the gas works. Scenes of terror are upon every side, and groups of men, women and children gather upon the blackened streets, their faces wearing an expression of terrified dismay and each one having his story to whisper of some harrowing incident of the great fire. Women and children pass up and down the streets bewailing the loss of husbands and parents who have either perished in the flames or become separated in the confusion and tumult that prevails everywhere. Many children thus cast out into the cold, devastated streets, have been cared for by the police and charitable citizens, but in the confusion and terror of the night many tender little ones must go uncared for. The scene at the Court House, in the basement of which one hundred and seventy prisoners were roasted alive, is described by those who were in the vicinity as most agonizingly heartrending. But few of the prisoners were confined for important offences, there being only about a dozen State cases in the jail. Many of them had been locked in their cells for the night, and their shrieks as their writhing bodies felt the hot embrace of the flames were most agonizing, while a few who had been allowed to remain in the corridors climbed upon the bars at the windows, crying in tones of piteous agony for aid, but the structure was already enwrapped in one great sheet of flame, and no human aid could reach them. Finally, as their destined shroud of leaping fire came closer upon them and the iron bars to which they clung seared their hands and felt like molten lead, they were seen to dash their heads in mad desperation against the bars, until finally they would sink back bleeding and exhausted, soon to be buried in the debris of fallen walls and smoking ruins.

LATER AND BETTER.

THE JAIL PRISONERS ESCAPED

[What appears under this heading, although relating to the earlier situation in Chicago, was transmitted from Milwaukee after telegraphic communication with the burning city was cut off. The fact that they left before the court house, Briggs House, etc., burned, leaves a doubt as to the correctness of the report. It is to be hoped the prisoners were released and saved the terrible death indicated in our earlier dispatch.—ED.]

MILWAUKEE, Oct. 9—9:30 P. M.—Messrs. C. D. Gibberson and O. A. Gurley, of Cleveland, the latter a telegraph operator, were at the Briggs Sunday night and reached this city today. They report that the prisoners in the jail were not burned. When the fire reached the court house and escape was no longer possible, they were released by the turnkey, 180 in number. The Briggs House and Metropolitan were burned at 3 A. M. Those who had friends were almost the last ones out. They had retired at 12 o'clock, when the fire was a mile and a half distant, without fear for their own safety. In two and a half hours this vast distance had been swept over, and they were awakened to escape. One aged man, a large property holder, whose name is forgotten by our informant, dropped dead on the street from the excitement, which probably produced heart disease.

The wounded in private houses and hospitals were taken out and bundled into express wagons and driven off. Whisky was plenty; many firemen, police and citizens were under influence of it. The firemen and others had no water to drink but river water or that brought a long distance from the lake.

The splendid Catholic church on South Canal street was burned and the walls fell in within 40 minutes after it took fire. The Sherman House burned at 2½ o'clock A. M., the fire walls, iron shutters and slate roof being no more protection than paper. At the *Times* office the files were saved, considerable quantities of type on galleys and cases. Violent explosions throughout the night and morning were heard in all parts of the burning districts—doubtless gas meters, powder in small quantities, &c. Rumors of killed were general and in the vaguest terms; no names or localities given with certainty.

Monday morning, as the smoke lifted once or twice over the ruins, the only blackened wall left standing was that of the water works.

MILWAUKEE, Oct. 9, 10 P. M.—All communication with Chicago is cut off during the last half hour. At 9:30 P. M., communication was had by telegraph with the Chicago & Northwestern freight depot telegraph office, and the fire was then reported to be raging on the north side with unabated fury, though some progress had been made in staying the progress of the flames in their southern course. A building burning here and there, however, indicated that the fire was not yet entirely under subjection. On the west side no flames were to be seen, and it was believed the devastation would extend no farther in that direction.

THE WEST.

FIRE IN OSHKOSH.

OSHKOSH, Wis., Oct. 9.—A fire broke out this morning in the north part of the city. The Chicago & Northwestern depot, together with some other buildings are destroyed, and at this time, 9 A. M., is still burning.

DENIAL.

MILWAUKEE, Oct. 9.—The report of the destruction of the Chicago and Northwestern railway station at Oshkosh is without foundation. The operator at Burnett Junction telegraphs that he is still in communication with Oshkosh, and that the depot was not destroyed. A gentleman who left Oshkosh at 4 o'clock this (Monday) morning, and reached here at 11:25, informs us that the flames on marshes south of the city were running high when he left the depot, and covered an area of two or three miles in length between the railroad track and the river, and the wind was blowing a gale. The fire started Saturday two miles this side of Winneconne and had reached to half or quarter of a mile of Oshkosh. The city was in a state of excitement and the people turning out to arrest the progress of the conflagration.

MILWAUKEE.

The Mayor of Milwaukee has ordered all saloons closed at nine o'clock during the present crisis. It has been raining here quite briskly at intervals since six o'clock this evening.

WISCONSIN.

BURNETT JUNCTION, Wis., Oct. 9.—The thirty men reported burned at Peshtigo became surrounded in a mill, and being unable to escape, were literally roasted alive. There have also been found hands, boots, hair &c., in an abandoned camp in the woods, which indicates a still further loss of life. The man who brought the news is a repairer of the Chicago & Northwestern railroad line.

He says the deer crowded the road at some points to such an extent that they had to fight their way through them. The camps of Dunlap and Elmore, railroad contractors, have been burned.

Telegraphic communication is destroyed north of Green Bay.

FT. HOWARD, Wis., Oct. 9.—Passengers by the Escanaba boat report that the town of Peshtigo, which is situated in the belt of big woods, is entirely consumed by the great fires raging in that section, and that 60 to 70 persons perished in the flames.

### STATE NEWS.

Work is progressing on the railroad bridges at Winona and Hastings.——On November 3d the Literary Society of the Y. M. C. Association and the Sons of Temperance will give a big treat at Red Wing, the profits to be devoted to furnishing their new hall.——Wheat $1.08 at Red Wing, last advices.——The residence of Mr. Cheney, near Zumbrota, was destroyed by fire on Tuesday last. No cause assigned.——Red Wing's steam fire engine has arrived.——John Gill, of Pine Island, set fire to his stables and barns by carelessly lighting his pipe.——Ahneman, his wife and children got overturned from a carriage at Pine Island and he and his wife were badly injured.——A little girl at Belvidere had her leg broken by a cow.——The Duluth weekly *Tribune* has reappeared in a new dress and presents a very neat and handsome appearance. It is an excellent paper and we are glad to note its complete restoration.——The Blue Earth City *Mail* is a new paper, Morris H. Stevens, publisher.——A 400-pound black bear was hunted down by the people of Elmira, Olmsted county, last Sunday night.——Ice men are discontinuing their visits to customers.——The St. Paul & Sioux City railroad received at Mankato, in September, 1,440,740 pounds of freight, and forwarded 1,923,340 pounds. On the Winona road 1,250,300 pounds were received, and 752,540 forwarded.——The Democratic convention for the first judicial district was held at Hastings on Thursday. W. W. Phelps, of Red Wing, was nominated for Judge.——The Canadians of Duluth are about forming a benevolent society.——The Sault canal will not be closed until December 1.——The Duluth *Tribune* denounces the Bolters' convention as without a shadow of excuse.——The Star Hotel and a dwelling house near by, in Duluth, have been burned through the carelessness of a servant girl.——Duluth is to have iron works.——The State board of equalization, recently sitting at St. Paul, has made changes of assessments in Carver, Dodge, Faribault, Fillmore, Freeborn, Mower, Olmsted, Rice, Steele, Winona and Wright counties. Ramsey and other counties have not made returns. The board adjourned till Tuesday next to hear from counties delinquent in their returns. Bank stock is to be assessed at the uniform rate of 65 cents on the dollar.——The sale of [illegible] page of the pine lands of the State took place at the office of the Auditor in St. Paul, on Monday. About thirty-five bidders were present. No retainer was demanded by the Auditor, except in cases where it was evident there was competition or in which the bid was made to keep other parties from cutting.——J. D. Cahoon, a restaurateur of Austin, has eloped with his brother's wife.——The Wright county fair, at Monticello on Wednesday, Thursday and Friday last, was not very largely attended by reason of the prairie fires, which kept many at home protecting their property. The local paper says Col. Stevens' address, Friday afternoon, "was well received. It was brief, pithy, practical, and to the point."——Edward Gibbons, a soldier from one of the frontier posts, was robbed on Saturday evening at the Rogers House, St. Paul, of the sum of $280 and a valuable silver watch by a comrade named Thomas H. Dryden, with whom he had been drinking during the day. Dryden was arrested at the depot, where he was awaiting the departure of the eastern train, and $80 of the money found upon him. Venison receipts at Sauk Centre are large; meat is cheap.——The house of James Duncan, Grove township, Stearns county, was burned on the 29th ult. The furniture in the upper rooms was also destroyed.——Right of way for the St. Paul & Pacific railroad extension is being granted by property owners through the Sauk Valley.——Townships 121, 122, 123 and 124, from range 36 inclusive, to the western boundary of the State, have been transferred from St. Cloud to the Litchfield Land District. Applications will be received after the 9th inst.——Mr. Murray of Manannah shot a bear, seven and a half feet long, which it is estimated would have weighed 700 pounds had it been fat.

New Goods! New Goods! New Goods! New Goods!

New Goods! New Goods! New Goods! New Goods!

AT

# DODD & ANKENY'S

OPPOSITE NICOLLET HOUSE.

SIGN OF "BIG RED BOOT."

JANNEYS & MOLES'

## Hardware and Stove

DEALERS,

## 10 Centre Block,

NICOLLET STREET,

SECOND DOOR ABOVE POST OFFICE.

GLASS. GLASS.

# R. S. PEASE'S

WHOLESALE AND RETAIL

## GLASS ESTABLISHMENT!!

WARNER'S BLOCK,

OPPOSITE NICOLLET.

THIS

IS OUR

SPACE.

REAL ESTATE.

M. P. HAWKINS. O. P. HAWKINS.

## HAWKINS BROS.,

Real Estate Agents,

HARRISON BLOCK.

OFFER FOR SALE:

RESIDENCE LOTS.

121-337 5 Good Lots on Morrison-ave., each $[illegible]. 337 4 Lots on Buffalo and Burnett-sts., $1,[illegible]. 472 20 Lots in Eliot's Addition, each $225, half cash, balance on long time at 10 per cent. *These Lots are the cheapest in the city.* 467 2½-acre Lots on 9th, near Helen-st., *Cheap.* 473 66x110 feet on 7th-st., $1,250. 443 50x165 feet on Hennepin-ave., $1,300. 440 ½-Acre Lot on 4th-st., near "Merritt's," $1,150. 485 Full ½-Acre lot on Hennepin-ave., $1,800.

BUSINESS LOTS.

| | | |
|---|---|---|
| 469 | A choice Lot on Hennepin-ave., per ft., | $125 |
| 437 | 3 Good Lots on Washington-ave., " | $125 |
| 374 | 6 " " " " | $100 |
| 507 | 2 Lots on Washington-ave., " | $250 |
| 507 | 1 Lot " " | $200 |
| 509 | 2 Lots on Nicollet-st., " | $200 |
| 510 | 2 " " " | $100 |

Suburban Property.

355 5 Acres near Fair Ground, $1,200. 401 9 Acres on Portland ave., $7,500. 412 10 Acres on Chicago-ave., $2,000. 444 Sand-to-Acre Lots on Hennepin-ave. extended, at $200 per acre—half cash. 500 5 Acres on Morrison-ave extended, $8,000. 483 3 Acres near Fair Ground gates (a Bargain), $1,500.

RESIDENCES.

[illegible]

Farms & Farming Lands

[illegible]

Wild Lands in nearly every County in the State. march6-1ply

FRENCH LANGUAGE.

Prof. C. FABROT,

FROM PARIS,

INSTRUCTOR OF FRENCH at "Norwood Young Ladies' Seminary," St. Paul.

Instructor of French at the "University of Minnesota."

Instructor of French at "Minneapolis and St. Paul Business Colleges."

Is now ready to give Instruction in French to the Ladies and Gentlemen of Minneapolis and St. Anthony.

Apply at Minneapolis Business College on Fridays and Saturdays from 3 to 7 P. M.

Apply at the University on Fridays and Saturdays from [illegible], or address

PROF. C. FABROT,

P. O. Box 988, Minneapolis.

## New Advertisements

REPORT

Of the condition of the

### First National Bank

AT MINNEAPOLIS,

In the State of Minnesota, at the close of business, Oct. 2d, 1871.

RESOURCES.

[illegible]

LIABILITIES.

[illegible]

STATE OF MINNESOTA, } ss. COUNTY OF HENNEPIN. }

I, Jacob K. Sidle, President of the First National Bank of Minneapolis, do solemnly swear that the above statement is true, to the best of my knowledge and belief.

J. K. SIDLE, President.

Subscribed and sworn to before me, this 9th day of October, 1871.

J. S. HURD, Notary Public, Minnesota.

Correct—Attest:
E. B. AMES, JOHN MARTIN, J. K. SIDLE, } Directors.

SITUATION WANTED—Wanted

A Place to Work for Board and Go to School

During the winter, by a young man of steady habits. Please address

W. H. PETERSON, Minneapolis.

PENCE OPERA HOUSE.

SHERMAN'S

CIRCUMFOREANUS.

C. P. Sherman, Manager and Proprietor.

SIX NIGHTS ONLY, COMMENCING

Monday Evening, October 9th.

ENGAGEMENT OF

THE GREAT NICKLE,

Who will present each evening a choice selection of his Illusions, Wonders and Miracles. 100 Presents will be given away every night.

Admission, 25 cents; reserved seats, 50 cents. Matinee Saturday afternoon.

HARRY WESTON, Business Agent.

COW LOST—A dark brown fat

COW.

With a white star in the forehead, the points of the horns coming close together, and very worn at the base of the horns.

KENN & GLASBRENER, Pacific Meat Market, Washington-ave.

See what Gale & Co. say this morning—last column, fourth page—as to Houses, Lots, Lands, and every kind of Insurance.

MARRIED.

SECOMBE—CROSBY—In Milford, N. H., by the Rev. Mr. Freeman, C. C. Secombe, of Minneapolis, to Miss Annabel F. Crosby, daughter of Capt. Frederic Crosby, of Milford.

DIED.

[illegible]—At her home in the town of Richfield, near this city, after an illness of several years, Mrs. Anna [illegible], wife of Charles [illegible]. Philadelphia papers please copy.

REAL ESTATE.

REAL ESTATE

Headquarters!

THE PLACE FOR BARGAINS!

## CHOWEN, BRYANT & BARTLETT'S

AGENCY

JOHNSTON'S BLOCK,

Opposite Nicollet House.

Houses! Lots! Lands! Farms!

Suburban Tracts, &c., &c.

Call and Examine Our List.

UNITED STATES LIFE INSURANCE COMPANY, of New York.

[illegible]

Jno. Potts Brown & Son,

Agents for the State of Minnesota.

OFFICE—No. 7 Johnston's Block. MINNEAPOLIS, Sept 5 1871.

CROCKERY-WARE

A FULL STOCK AT

SHUMAN & THOMPSON'S,

Merchant's Block, WASHINGTON AVE.

HENNEPIN COUNTY SAVINGS BANK,

MINNEAPOLIS, MINN.

Number 7 Centre Block, Hennepin Avenue.

Organized under the act of 1867, which provides for $25,000 Bonds to be deposited with the State Auditor for security of depositors.

CAPITAL, $75,000.

President, E. S. JONES. Cashier, J. E. BELL.

TRUSTEES

E. S. JONES, J. E. BELL, D. C. BELL, S. A. HARRIS.

Receives savings deposits of all sums from $1 to $2,000 and allows interest at 7 per cent. [illegible]

GENERAL BANKING BUSINESS DONE.

Open Saturday evenings from 5 to 8.

## DIRECTORY

OF

MINNEAPOLIS

AND

ST. ANTHONY,

1871-72,

For Sale and ready for delivery to Subscribers and Advertisers at TRIBUNE Counting Room.

LOTS FOR SALE.

Desirable corner Lots for sale. Three lots on the corner of 10th and Russell-sts. Two Lots on corner of 5th and Russell. 80 feet on corner of 4th and Russell. Apply to the owner at office in Harrison Block.

S. H. MATTISON.

Instruction on the Piano Forte.

Mr. E. L. RIPLEY has located himself in this city for the purpose of giving Instruction on the Piano Forte. [illegible]

Mr. R. has permission to refer to the following gentlemen: Hon. W. D. Washburn, Dr. P. L. Hatch, Wm. W. Eastman, Paris Gibson. Orders left at J. B. Elliot's Music Store will receive attention.

BEST

New Buckwheat Flour!

In the City.

Five Cents Per Pound,

AT CASH GROCERY, 134 Hennepin-ave.

OFFICE OF STREET COMMISSIONER OF THE CITY OF MINNEAPOLIS, HENNEPIN CO., MINN., October 5, 1871.

[illegible]

H. H. CORSON, Street Commissioner.

OFFICE OF THE STREET COMMISSIONER OF THE CITY OF MINNEAPOLIS, HENNEPIN CO., MINN., Minneapolis, Sept. 26, 1871.

[illegible]

H. H. CORSON, Street Commissioner.

"OLD PAPERS FOR SALE AT THIS OFFICE.

# D. WYLIE & CO.,

Plumbers, Steam & Gas Fitters.

We keep a full stock of PLUMBING MATERIAL,

GAS PIPE FITTINGS,

Chandeliers, Brackets, Cut Glass Globes, Pumps, Hose, Engine Trimmings, &c.,

Which we will Sell at Manufacturers' Prices.

Orders Solicited for Work and Satisfaction Guaranteed. Agents for OHIO STONE PIPE CO.

Salesroom and Shop, WASHINGTON AVENUE, Near Minnetonka Street.

## PLUMBING.

STEAM AND GAS PIPING.

LOW PRESSURE STEAM HEATING

For Private and Public Buildings.

Green House Heating,

PIPE FIXTURES, PUMPS, HOSE, &c., &c.,

All Kinds at Lowest Prices.

WRIGHT'S PATENT BUCKET PLUNGER PUMP—THE PREMIUM PUMP. Boiler, Engines, &c.

Minneapolis Steam, Gas and Water Pipe Co.

ALL WORK AND STOCK WARRANTED. [illegible], Manager.

HAVING PURCHASED OF

CLAPP, WATSON & COON

THEIR ENTIRE STOCK OF

## CLOTHS, FLANNELS and YARNS,

[illegible]

Serviceable Goods for Boys' and Men's Wear,

WHOLESALE OR RETAIL.

SALESROOM. - - - At the Falls,

Adjoining the Minneapolis Woolen Mill.

C. K CLAPP.

ATTENTION

CALLED TO THE

New Firm.

JOHN H. ARNELL, President. A. C. MURPHY, Sec'y, & Treas.

## TRADES MF'G. CO.,

HARNESS

AND

COLLARS,

77 Nicollet-st., Minneapolis.

[illegible]

The New Draw Feed

WHEELER & WILSON

SEWING MACHINES.

WONDERFUL IMPROVEMENTS have been made in the machine within the past few months. [illegible]

It is the Best Machine before the Public.

Arthur Farrar & Co.,

Wholesale and Retail Dealers,

58 THIRD STREET, ST. PAUL.

Minneapolis Office, 8 Nicollet Block.

Agents Wanted Throughout the State.

L. H. SMITH, Business Manager.

REAL ESTATE BROKER.

Parties having

Real Estate

For Sale, or wishing to Purchase, will find it to their advantage to call on the undersigned at my office in the Pence Opera House.

JOHN S. WALKER.

Wesley Neill,

No. 23 Washington-ave.,

Has a full line of

STAPLE & FANCY GROCERIES.

Choice B[illegible]r always on [illegible]d.

JOBTURNING.

The undersigned has opened an establishment for all kinds of

WOOD TURNING.

and solicits the attention of Builders and others in want of work in that line. Shop in MORRISON'S PLANING MILL, at the Falls Platform.

HERMAN TROCKE.

FOR RENT.

The whole or a part of a

NEW HOUSE.

On Nicollet Island. For further particulars inquire on the premises.

MRS. E. C. VALENTINE.

GARNISHEE SUMMONS—District Court—at TRIBUNE OFFICE.

YOUNG MEN'S

Christian Association.

[illegible]

Minneapolis and Duluth

RAILROAD.

Passenger and Freight Notice!

On and after

Wednesday, August 30th, 1771,

All Trains of this Railroad will arrive and depart from the new

Second-Street Depot.

All Local and Through Freights will be received at the same Depot, and forwarded without delay.

W. W. HUNGERFORD, Superintendent.

The Secret Monitor.

PRICE FIFTY CTS.,

(Under seal to any address.)

This is a new and well written book of three hundred pages, upon the anatomy and physiology of the urinary and genital organs, in health and disease. Eight fine plates and one hundred and ten wood engravings. [illegible]

The Galenic

INSTITUTE

Office Removed to 98 Third st., one door above Metropolitan Hotel,

St. Paul, Minn.

Incorporated for the cure of all diseases of the Urinary and Genital Organs of both Sexes.

Medicines sent to any part of the country free from exposure. Address,

GALENIC INSTITUTE, St. Paul, Minn.

J. S. Pillsbury & Co

Wholesale and Retail Dealers in

ENGLISH AND AMERICAN

Heavy & Shelf Hardware,

LEATHER AND RUBBER BELTING,

Mill and Circular Saws, Files, Iron, Steel, Nails, Window Glass, &c.,

MINNEAPOLIS, - - - MINN.

Agents for Fairbanks' Standard Scales.

State National Bank.

CAPITAL, . $100,000.

Surplus, $25,000.

NICOLLET HOUSE, CORNER WASHINGTON AVE. AND NICOLLET ST.

R. J. BALDWIN

Cashier

DIRECTORS:

[illegible]

DRY

Black Walnut

FOR SALE BY

L. C. BISBEE.

BUILDER

Minnetonka Street, near Washington Avenue.

F. B. LONG

Architect

Pence's Building, Wash. Ave., Minneapolis.

# The Minneapolis Daily Tribune.

VOL. VI. [Stewart & Co., oldest Shoe firm in Minneapolis, Largest Stock and Lowest Possible Prices.] MINNEAPOLIS, MINNESOTA: FRIDAY MORNING, NOVEMBER 1, 1872. [Stewart—Boots, Shoes, Gloves & Mittens, Muscatine & Tipton, Iowa, & Minneapolis, Minn.] NO. 129

## NEWS OF THE DAY.

We publish in our telegraphic columns today further particulars of the burning of the steamer Missouri and the loss of almost all on board, including seven ladies and as many children. The details are heartrending, and it looks as though what might have proved an insignificant fire became a terrible disaster, owing to bad management.

Our London dispatches state that two British naval officers have immortalized themselves by swimming across the Hellespont (otherwise known as the Dardenelles or Strait of Gallipoli) from Abydos, the narrowest part of the Strait. The feat was frequently accomplished by Leander and afterwards by Lord Byron. Now, let some young Minneapolitan swim across the Mississippi either just above or just below the apron, and get his name in the papers.

Shortly before three o'clock on Tuesday afternoon a fire broke out in the Dubuque Lumber Company's mills, in that city, which, before it could be checked, had destroyed over 1,000,000 feet of lumber, valued at more than $60,000. The pile of lumber in which the fire originated was more than a hundred rods in length, and as dry as tinder. The Fire Department were soon on the spot, but the difficulty in gaining a position with the steamers where they could reach the fire was so great that nearly an hour passed before they were in readiness for action. The slough, which was filled with floating logs, offered the only approach to the fire, and ...

## THE N. P. R. R.

Return of the Executive Committee.

### What Has Been Done.

## AMERICAN MISSIONS.

### Grant's Indian Policy.

### Shot His Neighbor.

### Fatal Frenzies.

## TAMMANY RING.

Motion to Dismiss Indictments Denied.

MAYOR HALL'S TRIAL.

Judge Brady's Charge—"Dangerous Species of Evidence."

WOMEN DESIRING TO VOTE.

McCunn's Will.—Miscellaneous Court and General News.

### The Ring Indictments.

### Sentenced.

### Escape of Prisoners.

## MISSOURI DISASTER.

Particulars of the Burning of the Steamer.

A TERRIBLE SCENE.

Bad Management and Bad News Generally.

### Further Particulars.

## FOREIGN.

Floods, Proclamations and Impeachments.

THE COUNTRY REFORM BILL.

KU KLUX KU KLUXED.

King William Dissolves the Diet and Appeals to the Country.

### Reform Rejected.

### Aqua.

### Persona.

### Impeachment.

### Floods.

## EQUUS MORBUS.

Four Lady Victims Reported Yesterday.

THE MALADY ABATING.

Effects on Car Lines, Politics and Business.

### A Good Effect.

### All Along the Lines.

### Certificates of Deposit.

### A Sensible Negro.

### MARKETS BY TELEGRAPH.

### FINANCIAL.

### COMMERCIAL.

### Vermont Officers.

### Death.



OLD EXCHANGES FOR SALE AT THIS OFFICE.

OLD EXCHANGES FOR SALE AT THIS OFFICE.

Athenaeum

# The Minneapolis Daily Tribune.

VOL. VI. [Stewart & Co., oldest Shoe firm in Minneapolis, Largest Stock and Lowest Possible Price. MINNEAPOLIS, MINNESOTA: SATURDAY MORNING, JANUARY 11, 1873. Leave Your Measure with Stewart's Foreman. You need not take Boots unless they Fit.] NO. 182

## The Minneapolis Tribune

SATURDAY, JANUARY 11, 1873.

We need not explain every typographical error the next day after it happens, but we were particularly aggravated by that gifted compositor who, when we wrote "ought," made us say "out." Of course he meant to spell it "ort."

Our special from New York this morning gives some interesting details of the rearrest of that notorious trio—Blood, Woodhull and Claflin. It seems the indictment this time is based upon the republication of the very article for which the former arrests were made.

In the Legislature yesterday Mr. Demeules, of Hennepin, introduced a joint resolution asking the Minnesota Members of Congress to use their influence in favor of the passage of the Holman bill, giving soldiers and sailors land bounty. The resolution was made the special order for Tuesday next.

Governor Austin deserves credit for firmly resisting the temptation to indulge in a political harangue on reconstruction, the late election, our foreign affairs, &c., into which so many Governors fall in their annual Opportunity. His message is quite a model of conciseness, containing scarcely a superfluous word.

We think the Republican party which has hitherto sustained Pinchbeck, have an elephant on their hands, that will trouble them to get rid of.—*Pioneer*.

Not at all. In six months the Louisiana Democrats will be running him for Congress. They know how to utilize all the elephants that the Republicans turn loose.

We cordially second the suggestion of the Governor to the Legislature to memorialize Congress to donate the military reservation at Fort Snelling to Minnesota for the benefit of the State University. The experiment of the Government in trying to sell it was not a very brilliant one; but we should not wonder if it could give it away without much difficulty. And it certainly could not go to a nobler purpose.

The Chicago *Times* says that Professor Morse will lecture there in "the Star Course." He ought to be familiar with stars by this time. [illegible]

[illegible]

## FROZEN TO DEATH.

### The Terrible Work of the Great Storm.

### APPALLING LIST OF VICTIMS ALREADY.

### Men, Women and Children in the Icy Tomb.

### Teams Found Frozen Dead in all Directions.

### Fate of their Drivers too Easily Surmised.

### The Struggles of the Railroads With the Snow.

### No Such Terrible Storm Ever Known Before in Minnesota.

#### Frozen to Death.

*Special Dispatch to the Minneapolis Tribune.*

LITCHFIELD, Jan. 10.—Two farmers named Pat. Condon and Flynn, the latter known as "Wild Mick," left this place Tuesday on their way homeward. Not reaching their destination according to the expectation of their families, the latter felt grave apprehensions as to their safety. Up to last night nothing had been seen or heard from them. This morning a general search was instituted and both the missing men found lying in the snow-drifts, only three miles from town. Condon was quite dead, but Flynn, who was more covered with snow, was yet alive, but so badly frozen that he will lose both arms. [illegible]

#### More and Worse.

[illegible]

#### And Worse Yet.

[illegible]

#### On the Railroads.

[illegible]

#### The Moderoc—Hard Nuts to Crack.

[illegible]

#### A Shipwreck.

[illegible]

## NEW YORK.

### That Nice Trio—Woodhull, Blood and Claflin.

### Vic.'s Lecture at Cooper's and How They Caught Her.

### A Full Jury List Obtained in Tweed's Case.

### The Center Street Holocaust—The Coroner's Jury.

### Consecration—Temperance—Miscellaneous.

#### Blood-Woodhull-Claflin.

*Special Correspondence of the Minneapolis Tribune.*

NEW YORK, Jan. 10.—The irrefutable Woodhull-Claflin family are again before the New York public. Yesterday afternoon Col. Blood, husband of Mrs. Woodhull, was arrested on a warrant issued from the United States courts, charging him with circulating obscene literature. He was taken to Ludlow street jail. Orders for arrest were also out for Blood's [illegible]

[illegible]

#### FROM CHICAGO.

#### Two Robberies—A Boiler Explosion—Woolen Mills Burned—Snow.

[illegible]

## WASHINGTON.

### The Persecution of the Jews of Roumania.

### The Intervention Demanded from Austria.

### Note from the Austrian Foreign Minister.

### The Goat Island Trouble—Postal—Miscellaneous.

#### Goat Island.

WASHINGTON, Jan. 10.—Chief of Engineers Humphreys reports to the Secretary of War that certain portions of Goat Island can be relinquished by the government to accommodate the wants of commerce without materially impairing the power of the coast defenses projected for that island. Twenty-eight acres can thus be relinquished. Neither will there be any injury to the harbor of San Francisco by the erection of railroad or other bridges connecting with the shore at Oakland. The Pacific Coast Board of Engineers, headed by Gen. Alexander, say in their report to Gen. Humphreys, that the whole of Yerba Buena Island should be retained by the government for the defense of the harbor and city of San Francisco, and that the effect of approaching the island by a bridge of piles or by a causeway would [illegible]

[illegible]

#### Louisiana Affairs.

[illegible]



## THE DEAD EMPEROR.

### The Grief of His Faithful and Stricken Wife.

### Scenes and Incidents of His Last Moments.

### How the News was Received in the Army.

### Spirit of the Paris Press vs. People.

### The Empress will Declare Herself Regent.

#### Scenes and Opinions.

LONDON, Jan. 10.—The Empress Eugenie and all the household of Chiselhurst were present at the bedside of Napoleon when he died. [illegible]

[illegible]

#### In Paris.

[illegible]

#### S. S. A.

BUFFALO, Jan. 10.—Susan B. Anthony was brought before Judge Hall in the United States Court to-day, in charge of the Deputy United States Marshal on a writ of habeas corpus. After consultation between the counsel, the hearing of the case was postponed till the 21st inst., at the Court to be held at Albany.

#### MARRIED.

[illegible]

## New Advertisements.



REPORT

of the condition of the

First National Bank

OF MINNEAPOLIS, MINN.

[illegible]

REPORT

of the condition of the

STATE NATIONAL BANK

OF MINNEAPOLIS.

[illegible]



ELEVENTH STREET.

In the matter of the laying out, extending and opening Eleventh Street in the city of Minneapolis.

[illegible]

Dated January 10, 1873.

THOMAS HALE WILLIAMS, City Clerk.

he Minneapolis Tribune.

FRIDAY, JULY 7.

old in New York, $1.11⅞.

robabilities to-day for the upper Mississippi: idedly high temperature, with southerly to terly winds; stationary or falling barometer; weather, but with severe local storms in the tern portion of Wisconsin.

heat—In New York, No. 1 $1.20@1.30; No. 2 3¾. Milwaukee, No. 1 at $1.13¾; No. 2 at 2¾. Minneapolis, No. 1 at $1.01@1.02; No. 2 1@95c. Chicago, No. 2 $1.02.

The county convention will be held morrow at Brackett's Hall at 11 A. M.

John D. Defrees, of Indiana, a promrt politician and the head of the eral movement in that state in 1872, out for Hayes and Wheeler.

Gen. Rosser believes that Gen. Cusfell early in the fight of the 25th , and that had he not, the fate of detachment would have been ferent.

Although there will be no contest at caucus to-night, everybody being Dr. Butler, nevertheless it is a good for every good Republican to atd every primary meeting of the ty.

Gen. Custer was thirty-six years old the 9th of last December. He was rigadier General at twenty-three, and wenty-five was the most successful alry general in the Union army.

Republicans should not forget the ting of the Hayes and Wheeler b at Brackett's Hall on Saturday ht. The attendance of the members all other Republicans is desired. meeting will be addressed by a nber of able speakers.

Judge David Davis, of the United es Supreme Bench, much talked of re the St. Louis convention as the rk horse" on the Democratic course, announced his purpose to support yes and Wheeler. He knows the lidates and can form an intelligent gment as to which is best adapted is cherished work of reform.

Tammany Hall, within which Samuel Tilden learned his political lessons, done more to corrupt the political als of the American people, and to urage election frauds, than any r or perhaps all other influences bined. When the people look to cause of corruption for its remedy with a view to the wiping out of cause.

During the past six years the Demoe county of Ramsey has had the ressman from the Third District our years. It now claims him for additional period of four years, h would give it that official for t out of a consecutive period of ears. We submit to the Republiof the Third District that this is modest demand, and would not fair division of party honors. nepin, the leading Republican ty of the District, has had the esentative for the past two years, justly demands to have him for the term.

Tilden and Tweed worked together rry New York for Seymour in 1868. as carried by the grossest frauds ever disgraced an election in this y other country. The money by h that campaign was carried ugh, was mainly furnished by d and his associates, out of the million dollars stolen from the city building and furnishing the new house. Tweed is a fugitive from ce, the sheriff who permitted his e is protected in his office by the rnor of the Empire State, and Mr. n is a Presidential candidate makhe canvass entirely upon his spotcharacter and his distinguished tation as a reformer.

he massacre of Gen. Custer's com1 by the Indians under Sitting Bull his confederate chiefs on the Little Horn river should arouse the govent to the importance of the war ressing in that region. The powforce encountered by that gallant, officer, shows that the savages are ughly prepared for hostilities, and oo powerful to be overcome by the nt command of General Terry. an, no doubt, by keeping his com1 intact, repulse any attack made him, or acting on the offensive, t the savages whenever he succeeds riking them. But the war can not uccessfully terminated in that way. Indians will avoid his large force, reserve their strength for the ghter of scouting parties and dements. There is an imperative and for a sufficient number of s in that region to enable their ion into several detachments each l to the entire force of the Indians. hat means they can be forced to , and in no other. It is cruel to ce the veteran officers and soldiers e army to the fate which bethe Seventh cavalry. If the rnment means war, let it institute in a manner that will save reckless e of life, and teach the savages a needed lesson. Up to this time campaign has been a disgraceful and a shame to the nation. In weeks the government could reall the force necessary to enable push forward an aggressive re that in a month would n the crushing out of the savages. uld save waste of life, and while uld increase the expenses for a months would in the long run a great saving to the government. humanity and economy appeal in lf of a vigorous prosecution of so long as war is necessary; and believe it is in this case. Indians can only be made rb their murdering propensities o respect the rights of the whites the frontiers, by understanding f they do not, they will have counter an army against which can have no hope of success. If nce understand that to be the y of the government, Indian wars oon become things of the past. ng small detachments of troops rrass them without power to der destroy them, is simply feeding insatiable thirst for blood.


# The Minneapolis Tribune.

VOL. X. MINNEAPOLIS, FRIDAY EVENING, JULY 7, 1876. NO. 31.



THE MINNEAPOLIS TRIBUNE

THE DAILY TRIBUNE is published every evening (Sundays excepted) for circulation by Carriers, newsmen, and the Mail:

Per Month, by Carrier.........................$ 75
Per Year, by mail.............................9 00

THE WEEKLY PIONEER-PRESS AND TRIBUNE will be sent to weekly subscribers upon the following terms: Per year, one copy, $2.00; five copies, $9.50; ten copies, $16.00; twenty copies, $30.00; thirty copies, $42.00.

Subscriptions payable invariably in advance. Address "THE TRIBUNE," Minneapolis, Minn.


## FIRST EDITION.

3:00 O'CLOCK, P. M.

## CUSTER'S DEFEAT.

### Gen. Terry's "Confidential" Report to Gen. Sheridan—The Dead General Erred.

### The Plan of Battle as Proposed by Terry and Concurred In by Custer.

### In Plain Language, the Brave Custer "Disobeyed Orders" and Paid the Penalty.

### Terry, Too, Thinks He Acted Under a Misapprehension, and Thought the Indians Running Away.

### The Commanding Officer Does not Propose to Give up the War, but Move On.

### He Will Take a Rest, However, and Would be Glad of Any Reinforcements.

### Not an Overly Enthusiastic Contribution.

Official Dispatches.

THE WOUNDED.

CHICAGO, July 7.—The following are the official dispatches so far received at Gen. Sheridan's headquarters:

CAMP ON YELLOWSTONE, NEAR MOUTH OF BIG HORN, July 2.—On the evening of the 28th, we commenced moving down with the wounded, but were able to get on but four miles, as our hand-litters did not answer the purpose; the mule litters did excellently well, but they were insufficient in number. The 29th, therefore, was spent in making a full supply of them. In the evening of the 29th we started again, and at 2 A. M. the wounded were placed on the steamer at the mouth of the Little Big Horn. On the afternoon of the 30th they were brought down to the depot on the Yellowstone. I will send them to-morrow, by steamer, to Fort Lincoln, and with them one of my aids, Capt. E. W. Smith, who will be able to answer any questions you may desire to ask. I have brought down the troops to the same point. They arrived to-night. They need refitting, particularly in the matter of transportation before we start again, and although I had on the steamer a good supply of subsistence and forage, there are other things we need, and I should hesitate to trust the boat again in the Big Horn. Col. Sheridan's dispatch informing me of the reported gathering of Indians on the Rose Bud reached me after I came down here. I hear nothing of Gen. Crook's movements. At least one hundred horses are needed to remount the cavalrymen now here.

[Signed.] ALFRED H. TERRY, Brig. Gen.

GEN. TERRY'S CONFIDENTIAL EXPLANATION [Confidential.]

CAMP YELLOWSTONE RIVER, NEAR THE MOUTH OF THE BIG HORN, July 2.—I think I owe it to myself to put you more fully in possession of the facts of the late operations, and while at the mouth of the Rosebud I submitted my plan to General Gibbon and to Gen. Custer. They approved it heartily. It was that Custer with his whole regiment should move up the Rosebud till he should meet a trail which Reno had discovered a few days before, but that he should not follow it directly to the Little Big Horn, but that he should send scouts over it and keep his main force further to the south so as to prevent the Indians from stepping in between himself and the mountains. He was also to examine the headwaters of Millocka creek as he passed it and send me word of what he found there. A scout was furnished him for the purpose of crossing the country to me. We calculated it would take Gibbon's column until the 26th to reach the mouth of the Little Big Horn, and that the wide sweeping which I had proposed Custer should make would require so much time that Gibbon's command would be able to cooperate with him in attacking any Indians that might be found on the stream. I asked Custer how long his marches would be. He said they would be at first about 30 miles a day. Measurements were made and calculations based on that rate of progress. I talked with him about his strength, and at one time suggested that perhaps it would be better for me to take Gibbon's cavalry and go with him. To this suggestion he replied that he would prefer his own regiment alone; as much could be done with it as with the two combined. He expressed the utmost confidence that he had all the force that he should need.

AND I SHARED HIS CONFIDENCE.

The plan adopted was the only one which promised to bring the infantry into action and I desired to make sure of things by getting up every available man. I offered Custer the battery of gatling guns, but he declined it saying that it might embarrass him, and he was strong enough without it. The movements proposed by Gen. Gibbons' column were carried out to the letter, and had the attack been deferred until it came up, I cannot doubt but we should have been successful. The Indians evidently nerved themselves for a stand. I learn from Capt. Benton that on the 22d the cavalry marched twelve miles, on the 23d twenty-five miles from 5 A. M. to 8 P. M., on the 24th 45 miles, ten miles further; then, after resting, but without unsaddling, 23 miles to the battle field. The proposed route was taken, but as soon as the trail was discovered it was followed. I cannot learn that any examination of Tullocka creek was made. I do not tell you this to cast

ANY REFLECTION UPON CUSTER,

for whatever errors he may have committed he has paid the penalty, and you cannot regard this loss more than I do, but I feel that our plan must have been successful had it been carried out, and I desire you to know the facts in the action itself. So far as I can make out Custer acted under a misapprehension; he thought, I am confident, that the Indians were running, and for fear that they might get away he attacked them without getting all his men up, and divided his command so that they were beaten in detail. I do not at all propose to give the thing up here, but I think that my troops require a little rest, and in view of the strength which the Indians have displayed, I propose to bring up what little reinforcements I can get. I should be glad of any that you can send me. I can take two companies of infantry from Powder River, and there are a few recruits and detailed men whom I can get for the cavalry. I ought to have a larger mounted force than I now have, but this I fear cannot be obtained. I hear nothing from Gen. Crook's operations. If I could hear I should be able to form plans for the future much more intelligently.

[Signed] A. H. TERRY, Brigadier General, Commanding

## SHERIDAN SPEAKS.

### The Truth Is, Our Army is Too Weak for the Business Required of It.

### Extermination of the Indians a Possible Alternative.

NEW YORK, July 7.—Gen. Sheridan, conversing with a reporter on the Custer massacre, said that the truth was the army was not made to carry out the purposes of the government in the Indian country by reason of its weakness. "I have," he said, "sent every man I could spare into that region, even taking troops from Laramie and Salt Lake. The government, in its wisdom, directs the doing of certain things in these regions; it directs an expedition like this of Terry's, an expedition necessary for the development of that country. We do the best we can with our material, but we are in no condition to do the work required of us." In answer to the question, what are the reasons for this campaign, Gen. Sheridan says they are doing this at the special request of the Indian Department. It does not originate with the war department at all. Our purpose is to drive these Indians who are of the very wildest and most savage sort known, onto the reservation. You can say that "We will do it now or exterminate them."

### If True, What Might Happen.

LONDON, July 7.—The Vienna correspondent of The Times, reviewing the military revolution, says if the reports of Turkish victory at Saitschar prove true, and if the success is properly taken advantage of, might place the eastern half of Servia in the hands of the Turks.

## JACOB'S HARD LOT.

### He Pays $10,000 Fine, and Plays Checkers Six Months.

CHICAGO, July 7.—Jacob Rehm, ex-chief of the police in this city, and against whom the grand jury found an indictment last winter for complicity in the whisky frauds, was to-day sentenced to pay a fine of $10,000 and to be imprisoned in jail for six months.

## THE CROPS.

### How They Stand in Ohio, Illinois, Kentucky and Tennessee.

CINCINNATI, July 7.—Crop reports from 238 points in Ohio, Indiana, Illinois, Kentucky and Tennessee, were telegraphed to The Gazette last night. From these reports it appears that the season, thus far, has been very propitious for growing most kinds of grain, but just as the harvest approaches there is threatened disaster from continued rain. In Kentucky fears of the destruction of a portion of the crops from this cause is entertained. As the crops now stand, the wheat crop promises a yield of oats less than an average crop, corn unusually large crop; hay in abundance, but rank and weedy; wheat suffering considerably from ravages of weevil.

The Turks are becoming badly demoralized on the Servian border.

## THE MARKETS.

### Gold $1.11 7-8—Flour Without Decided Change—Wheat Generally Lower

## FINANCIAL.

### New York.

NEW YORK, July 7.

MONEY—No loans, 2 ₩ cent. bid. Sterling exchange, 4 88¾@4 90¾.

GOLD—$1.11⅞.

BONDS—Governments dull and steady. State bonds are dull and nominal.

STOCKS—Dull and steady.

MISCELLANEOUS—Western Union Telegraph, 70¾; Atlantic & Pacific Telegraph, 18¾; Pacific Mail, 26¾.

EXPRESS—Adams, 109¾; Wells & Fargo, 89¾; American, 58; United States, 75.

RAILWAYS—New York Central 108¾; Erie 14¾; Erie, preferred 20; Harlem, 137¾; preferred 133; Michigan Central 52; Union Pacific stocks 63; Panama 133; Lake Shore 50¾; Illinois Central 97; Cleveland & Pittsburg, 93¾; Northwestern, 42¾; Northwestern preferred 60¾; Cleveland, Columbus & Cincinnati 43; Rock Island 109; St. Paul, 40¾; St. Paul preferred, 70¾; Wabash, 2¾; Wabash preferred, 3; Fort Wayne, 102¾; Ohio & Mississippi, 16¾; Atlantic & Pacific preferred, 102¾; Missouri Pacific 7; Burlington & Quincy, 114; Hannibal & St. Jo, 11.

## COMMERCIAL.

### Minneapolis.

MINNEAPOLIS, July 7.

GRAIN—Wheat, No 1 at 99@1 00; No. 2 at 91@95c; No. 3 at 65c.

RECEIPTS—Wheat 68 cars, flour 1, lumber 2, merchandise 26, wood 2, coal 14, staves 2, agricultural implements 4, machinery 3, cement 1, wool 1, live stock 3, railroad iron 1.

SHIPMENTS—Flour 96 cars, lumber 71, bran 8, merchandise 24, feed 2, agricultural implements 2, machinery 1, live stock 4, linseed oil 1.

### Milwaukee.

MILWAUKEE, July 7.

GRAIN—Wheat, unsettled; No. 1 at 1 13¾; No. 1 hard 1 20; No. 2 at 1 02¾ cash; seller August at 1 03¾; seller September 1 05¾. No. 3 at 88¾c; receipts, 73,800 bushels; shipments, 24,300. Corn, steady; 46c for No. 2. Oats, steady; at 29¾c for No. 2. Rye, steady; 68c for No. 1. Barley, nominal; at 70c for No. 2.

### Chicago.

CHICAGO, July 7.

GRAIN—Wheat, quiet and lower; 1 02 for cash and seller July; 1 03⅝ for seller August; 1 03⅞ for September. Corn, quiet; at 46¾@47c seller July 47¾@47¾c for August; 47@48c seller September. Oats, quiet and easier; 29¾c cash, July and seller August. Barley, nominally 58c cash or seller July; new offered at 77c for September. Rye dull, 65@66c.

### New York.

NEW YORK, July 7.

COTTON—Declining; 11¾c middling uplands.

FLOUR—Quiet, without important change; receipts, 21,000 barrels; sales, 12,000 barrels; quotations unchanged, very moderate inquiry.

GRAIN—Wheat, is in buyers favor; receipts, 74,000 bushels; sales, 55,000 bushels; No. 3 Chicago, 95@1 00; No. 3 Milwaukee, 1 00@1 05; No. 2 Chicago, 1 10@1 14; No. 2 Milwaukee 1 14¾; No. 1 spring, 1 20@1 25; winter red western, 1 10; amber western, 1 20@1 30; white western, 1 25@1 40. Rye, quiet; receipts, 19,000 bushels. Corn, without decided change; receipts, 154,000 bushels; sales, 43,000 bushels; 55@60c new western mixed. Barley, dull and nominal. Oats, dull and drooping; receipts, 38,000 bushels; sales, 28,000 bushels; 33@41c mixed western and state; 35@41c for white do.

PROVISIONS—Pork, firmer; 100 bbls. new mess at 20 10@20 15 cash. Beef, dull. Cut meats, western dull. Lard, heavy; 100 tierces 11 60@11 62¾ for steam.

WHISKY—1 12¾

GROCERIES—Sugar, firm.

PETROLEUM—Crude, 9c; refined, 15¾@16c.

LEATHER—Firm.

WOOL—Quiet and firm.

### St. Louis.

ST. LOUIS, July 7.

FLOUR—Firmer for medium grades fall, 4 00@4 75.

GRAIN—Wheat, dull and easier; No. 2 fall 1 37 cash; 1 33 bid seller July; sales at 1 24@1 26 for August; No. 3 fall at 1 16 bid; No. 4 fall, 96c bid. Corn, lower; 43c for cash, 42¾c bid at the close; 43c for July; 44¾c for August. Oats, steady; at 29¾c for cash. Rye quiet, 64c bid.

WHISKY—Unchanged, 1 11.

PROVISIONS—Pork, better; jobbing at 20 50 for cash. Dry salt meats held higher, no sales. Bacon advancing, 9c, 11¾@11¾c, 11¾@12c. Lard, nominal.

HOGS—Firmer; yorkers, at 6 40; bacon, 6 70@6 20; butchers, 6 30@6 40.

## SECOND EDITION.

4:30 O'CLOCK P. M.

## WAR!

### A Conference Between Gen. Sherman, the President and the Secretary of War.

### The Subject Matter for Consideration an Indian War—A Call for Troops.

### Paddock Introduces a Bill in the Senate Authorizing the Acceptance of Volunteers.

### The President to Have the Authority Anyhow.

A Council of War.

SHERMAN, CAMERON AND GRANT.

WASHINGTON, July 7.—Gen. Sherman has been telegraphed to by Secretary Cameron, who arrived this morning. Sherman will leave Philadelphia to-day for this city. It is probable upon the arrival of Gen. Sherman there will be an immediate conference between the President, Secretary of War and the General upon the subject of an Indian war.

Senator Paddock introduced the following bill in the Senate to-day, and gave notice would to-morrow try to call up the bill for action:

A WAR BILL.

Be it enacted, &c., that the president, if he deems it necessary, be, and hereby is, authorized to accept the services of volunteers from the state of Nebraska and territories of Wyoming, Colorado, Dakota or Utah, or either of them, to be employed as part of the army of the United States against the tribe of hostile Sioux in the northwest, who have for years defied the authority of the government, and by whose hands recently several hundred soldiers and citizens of the United States have been slaughtered; provided that not more than five regiments of cavalry and infantry, or both, shall be accepted, and that the term of service shall not extend beyond nine months from the date of enlistment.

THE FOLLOWING DISPATCH

was received at the war department:

To Gen. E. D. Townsend, Adjutant General:

Capt. Smith, of Gen. Terry's staff, telegraphs from Bismarck as follows: General Custer, Capts. Custer, Keogh, Yates and Cook, Lieutenants Smith, McIntosch, Calhoun, Hodgson, Reilly, Porter, Sturgis and Crittenden killed. Lieutenant Harrington and Assistant Surgeon Lord missing. Two hundred and sixty-one dead have been found and fifty-two wounded brought away.

## MORRILL IN.

### He Takes the Oath as Secretary of the Treasury To-Day.

WASHINGTON, July 7.—Senator Morrill took the oath of office as Secretary of the Treasury, this afternoon at the executive mansion. Judge Whylie administered the oat.

## COAL OIL FOOLISHNESS.

### A Man Horribly Burns Himself for His Pains.

PHILADELPHIA, July 7.—Joseph Daly, 76 years old, residing on Mervine street, attempted to kindle a fire this morning by pouring coal oil into the stove. An explosion took place, and the unfortunate man was horribly burned about the head and face, the flesh coming off the bones in some places. His recovery is very doubtful.

## NEGRO CUT UP.

### And Stored Away in an Ash Barrel.

WASHINGTON, July 7.—A colored man named Turpin was killed here on the 4th. His head was severed from his body, and the body cut up and then thrown into an ash pile. A woman with whom he lived has disappeared. She is supposed to be the murderess.

### Gone to the Wall.

NEW YORK, July 7.—A. A. Selover, a well known Wall street operator, has filed a petition in bankruptcy. Total liabilities $660,000, of which $535,000 is partially secured.

## OUT IN THE CENTENNIAL STATE.

### The Pastoral Friend on the Climate of Colorado, the Beauty of Denver, and the Grandeur of Things Generally.

(No. 2.)

COLORADO, SPRINGS, June 27.

The climate here is delightful. At midday the heat is very great, and the sun reflected from the white sandy streets is painful, but by five o'clock in the afternoon the wind rises, and the heated air cools quickly, so that the evenings and nights are delicious.

Last Sabbath was one of the most perfect days I ever saw, clear, cool and sweet-aired. The atmosphere was so light one could scarcely realize whether in the body or out, and the mountains stood out clear against the sky, showing every rugged seam. The fifty miles to Long's Peak seemed, through the clear air, but an hour's walk, and the foot hills, twelve miles away, seemed close against the town, while the white snow on the mountain side looked as near almost as if lying

IN ONE'S OWN DOOR YARD.

As I went into the pleasant Congregational Church of Denver, beautiful flowers on table, pulpit and brackets back of the pulpit greeted my eyes, strange flowers all of them to me, brought in from some mountain excursion the day before. A large vase before the pulpit was filled with the blossoms of the "soap weed," an aristocratic looking plant despite its plebean name, which grows all over the plains, the roots of which, in water, are said to produce a suds like soap, with which the Mexicans wash silks and flanels beautifully.

As near as I can locate this plant it belongs to the Yucca family. As there is yet nothing in book form on the flora of Colorado I cannot name many of the flowers, but they are very beautiful. Two weeks ago the cattle on the plains were literally grazing in rose fields, fields covered with primroses—so-called here, but unlike anything of that name in the states—a low plant spreading like our portulacca and full of large pink and white single roses. The blossoms of the cactus family are very varied and showy, and there is a royal looking poppy now covering the plains with great white blossoms.

DENVER

is a very pleasant and thifty looking city. The houses are mostly built of red brick and the streets well shaded with cottonwood trees, the only tree which can thrive in this almost rainless country. The water, turned aside from the Platte river in the mountains into a canal, obtains force enough to run through the ditches at each side of the streets, and thus by irrigation the trees are kept alive. Clear, sweet drinking water is brought through pipes into most of the houses. Many of the yards have quite nice looking grass, kept alive with great care and constant sprinkling. The water is brought into the yards by hose from the water works, and twenty dollars a season gives one the privilege of sprinkling his grass from 5 to 10 A. M., and from 5 to 10 P. M. But woe betide him if he or the good wife forget, and the water is seen running out of time.

A SEVERE LOOKING IRISHMAN,

with an ugly iron bar appears and turns off the water, and no more comes in the house or yard till pardon is asked or a fine paid at headquarters. On last washing day one hostess forgot to turn the water from off the grass at ten in the morning, and the severe Irishman promptly put in his appearance. Neither tears nor sighs availed—we were thirsty but there was no water—dusty, but no water; the kettle on the stove was empty; the hot water boiler at once lost its contents—the clothes waited for the rinsing. There was nothing for us but to wait till our host could take the long walk to ask for pardon. Then came the Irishman and the bar and again the cool waters gushed forth.

But the beauty of Denver, unlike its water, is free to all. I realized this last night, as I watched the sun sinking behind the mountains, gilding every tip and rocky gorge, and then in an instant transforming them into glistening gold. The sunset was soon over, but the glory was still there, and no hand could shut it off—the glory

OF THE EVERLASTING HILLS.

From Denver we came down on the narrow gauge, or pony railroad, as it is called, to Colorado Springs, a pretty village set at the foot of Pike's Peak. Here, too, are the irrigating ditches, beside which the cottonwood trees grow in all the streets. Smaller ditches are turned aside from them into the yards and gardens, and every man has a right to turn by a ditch the water into his own garden, even if it be at the expense of his neighbor's garden.

If Colorado could exchange some of her grand mountains for some of Minnesota's ten thousand lakes, either country would be perfect. It is better as it is, else, perhaps, the inhabitants of each would have less reason to look away to that better country, even the Heavenly one. F. L. M.

### The Fourth in Constantinople.

CONSTANTINOPLE, July 7.—The American colony enthusiastically honored the Fourth. Horatio Maynard, American minister, presided, read the Declaration of Independence and made a speech

### Admissions to the Centennial.

PHILADELPHIA, July 7.—The admissions to the Centennial exposition yesterday numbered 52,040, of which 46,051 were paid. The whole number of visitors since the opening has been 1,962,054.

### A Strong Point.

BERLIN, July 7.—Much importance is attached to the fact that the Roman Catholics of Bosnia have protested against the annexation of the province to Servia.

### The Admissions this Week.

PHILADELPHIA, July 6.—Even Centennial guards, it seems, will exaggerate sometimes. They were all out of their heads on yesterday, and when they said that there were 150,000 persons on the grounds they showed their want of respect for Washington's little hatchet. The never-lying figures tell us that on Monday the exhibition had 58,000 visitors, and only a little over 56,000 on the Fourth. To-day's admissions were about the same as yesterday's, with a fair sprinkling of dead-heads, but the number of admissions with free tickets is greatly overstated. Each dead-head ticket will admit only one on the same day, but the holder can get a return check every time he goes out.

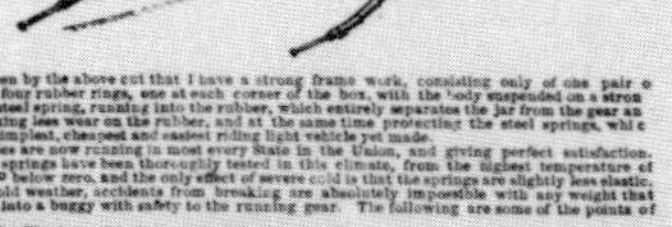

The Minneapolis Tribune.
FRIDAY, SEPTEMBER 1.

GOLD—$1.09½.
MONEY—7 ℘ cent. bid.

Probabilities to-day for the upper Mississippi—high barometer, falling temperature, northwest to northeast winds and clear or partly cloudy weather with rain areas.

The publisher of the Budstikken is sensitive.

The Indian commissioners have arrived at Cheyenne.

Gov. Pillsbury is taking hold of the grasshoppers with vim.

The coal break in New York is appreciated by the consumers.

Capt. C. L. Snyder is elsewhere suggested as a candidate for the Legislature. Ticket not named.

The eleventh of this month Maine will raise her Republican finger and indicate which way the Union will go.

Carl Schurz spoke at Cincinnati last evening, to as many people as could crowd into the Robinson Opera House.

It may be that Crook and Terry cannot whip the Indians. The old recipe for cooking a hare started out thus, "first catch the hare."

California elects state officers next Wednesday. With Senator Booth's following all right the Republicans expect a good round majority.

Vermont next Tuesday expects to increase her Republican majority of 20,325. Last year there was only one Democrat in the State Senate.

The telegraph lines east of La Cross are "mixed" this afternoon, and indifferent about the transmission of news or anything else in the line of dispatches.

Gov. Hayes is a lot-owner in Omaha, and Council Bluffs across the river is red-hot with the green-eyed monster. C. B. is afraid Omaha will become the National Capital.

The appointment of S. C. Gale, Esq., to a place on the State Normal School board is as wise a thing as Gov. Pillsbury has done. Mr. Gale knows something about schools, and has some eminently practical ideas of how they should be managed. He is a fit man for the place.

Gov. Seymour cannot accept. He is in earnest this time. Who will be the man? Our answer would depend upon the character of the state central committee. If it is strongly Tilden, he might be Marble or Hewitt. If a representative party committee, then Clarkson N. Potter, M. C., would be the choice.

Prof. Gray's new book "Darwiniana," (essays and reviews pertaining to Darwinism) is on our desk as a favor from Appleton & Co., publishers. It is a work creating a good deal of interest, as Prof. Gray is a Darwinian "in his own fashion." S. M. Williams has the work for sale in this city. Also, from Appleton we acknowledge the receipt of "Illustrated Lessons in Our Language," by Quackenboss, and the "Universal Metric System."

A speculative friend, and "a very intimate" one, gossips to a Chicago Inter-Ocean correspondent in Columbus, Ohio, about "the probable formation of Hayes' cabinet in the event of his success." He says Blaine will be offered the choice of cabinet positions; Morrill may continue as Secretary of Treasury, though it is not improbable that Conkling or Bristow will be substituted. Morton can be Secretary of War or Minister to England. An unknown gentleman, residing in New York, may be invited to fill Robeson's shoes. Attorney General Taft can stay and will be asked to. Ex-Gov. Noyes, of Ohio, stands a chance of a cabinet position and can have a place abroad. Even Logan might be called and Bob Ingersoll will not be overlooked. Here we will add a communication from a local cabinet maker. All his names are good ones:

Editor Evening Tribune.

I see in your paper of yesterday an extract from The Baltimore Gazette stating that in the event of Tilden's election he would call around him some of the best men in the country for his cabinet, and naming Charles Francis Adams for secretary of state, Horatio Seymour secretary of the treasury, Mr. Curtin secretary of war, C. A. Dana secretary of the interior, &c. Passing over the objectionable characteristics of most of these men, and the unfitness of all except the first for the offices to which they are assigned, allow me to suggest that Gov. Hayes if he is elected, will undoubtedly select men of equal standing and of better fitness. Take, for instance, Geo. William Curtis, for Secretary of State, Benjamin H. Bristow, Secretary of the Treasury, John F. Hartranft, Secretary of War, John A. Kasson or William Windom, Secretary of the Interior, etc. Does any man doubt that these men would make a good cabinet, and besides, they are loyal to the core?

REFORM REPUBLICAN.

Minneapolis, Sept. 1.

### An Independent Opinion of Tilden.

Gen. Banks in New York Graphic.

"Have you any conception that Mr. Tilden would make an efficient President?"

"No, sir. There is nothing in his life, his countenance, or his profession to make him a President of such a people as ours in possibly troublous times. An attorney, one who has leaned on a client or a cause all his life, is not a man of original magistracy and authority. The elements of soldier, governor, lawyer, and legislator in Mr. Hayes, his striking face, power of silence and sternness, and unblemished life, will make him our modern ruler in this new period of America."

### Strait Has Enough.

Hon. H. B. Strait claims that he is sure of forty-nine votes on the first ballot. Only forty-five are necessary.

# Minneapolis Tribune.

VOL. X. MINNEAPOLIS, FRIDAY EVENING, SEPTEMBER 1, 1876 NO. 77.

THE MINNEAPOLIS TRIBUNE

THE DAILY TRIBUNE is published every evening (Sundays excepted) for circulation by carriers, newsmen, and the Mail:

Per Month, by Carrier .......... $ 75
Per Year, by mail .......... 9 00

THE WEEKLY PIONEER-PRESS AND TRIBUNE will be sent to weekly subscribers upon the following terms: Per year, one copy, $2.00; five copies, $9.50; ten copies, $16.00; twenty copies, $30.00; thirty copies, $42.00.

Subscriptions payable invariably in advance. Address "THE TRIBUNE," Minneapolis, Minn.

## SEYMOUR'S HEALTH.

### His Physician Positively Forbids His Acceptance of Any Office.

### He has so Informed His Saratoga Admirers.

NEW YORK, Sept. 1.—The Herald publishes an interview with ex-Governor Seymour this morning, in which the Governor says: "Yesterday morning I received a letter from Dr. Churchill, one of my physicians, forbidding me making any mental or physical effort, and declaring that the acceptance of this or any other public position would be detrimental if it did not prevent my ultimate recovery. In view of these facts it will be impossible for me to accept the nomination, and I so informed the gentlemen from Saratoga when they waited upon me this morning requesting my acceptance."

### Grasshoppers Flying Off.

OMAHA, Sept. 1.—A heavy northwest wind since yesterday has carried off nearly all the grasshoppers. It is impossible as yet to state what the damage done by them will amount to, but it is thought it will not amount to as much as predicted. The river has risen three inches in the last twenty-four hours.

### The Chess Prizes.

PHILADELPHIA, Sept. 1.—The international chess tournament is closed. Mason wins the first prize; Judd, second; Bird, third; Elson and Davidson divide the fourth and fifth prizes, and Roberts wins the sixth.

## TILDEN'S FRAUD.

### How Much is Legally Established Against Him.

New York Times.

On the 29th of December, 1863, Mr. Tilden made an income tax return, under oath, in which he said that his total income from all sources for the year 1862 amounted to only $7,118, and on that amount his tax was paid. But on the 5th of August, 1876, Mr. Tilden made another deposition under oath, in the form of an answer to the suit of the St. Louis, Alton and Terre Haute Railroad, in which he said that on the 17th of October, 1862, he was paid for professional services by the bondholders of that road the sum of $19,000, and that on November 7, 1862, he was paid a further sum of $10,000. On the assumption (which is of course a preposterous one) that these two fees represented Mr. Tilden's sole professional income for 1862, it may be argued that he was legally entitled to make certain deductions for taxes, repairs, etc., which would reduce his taxable income to the amount given in his deposition. But we have Mr. Tilden's own testimony that in 1863 he was unable to figure out the deductions allowed by law at more than $6,552, and we have his further testimony under oath that he admitted an annual income of about $15,000 from dividends and interest on investments. By way of completing this part of the case against Mr. Tilden, we may add a new item of his income, of which we can produce legal evidence, viz: the receipt on June 14th, 1862, of $5,000 from the Cumberland Coal and Iron Company. Keeping, then, strictly within the evidence which can be proved to the satisfaction of a court of law, we have the following case against Mr. Tilden in relation to his income of 1862:

| | |
|---|---|
| Fees from Terre Haute railroad | $29,000 |
| Dividends and interest | 15,000 |
| Cumberland Coal and Iron Company | 5,000 |
| Total | $48,000 |
| Deduct expenses, taxes, etc. | 6,552 |
| Net proved income | $31,448 |
| Net income stated under oath | 7,118 |
| *Income fraudulently concealed* | $24,330 |

We need hardly say that the case against Mr. Tilden, when it comes to be fully investigated, will prove very much stronger than this. A man who made five millions of dollars in fifteen years must have reckoned his annual income by hundreds of thousands. But, without going beyond demonstrated facts, we have shown that in 1863 Samuel J. Tilden evaded payment of his just proportion of income tax by perjury.

### Another Tragic Scene on the Union Pacific.

A few days ago an account was published of a gambler being taken from a sleeping car on the Union Pacific railroad at midnight and carried away with a rope around his neck. Now the Omaha Herald tells of a stabbing affray on the same road. On the 19th Mr. Winney, a passenger from San Francisco, was assaulted by a crazy Italian, who stabbed him twice with a dagger. The Herald says:

The Italian stood at the door of the coach, and just as Mr. Winney passed him, he sprang upon him with a keen stiletto in his right hand, and with his left he grasped Winney's forehead, pulled his head back and made a terrible thrust at his throat. Winney was the more powerful man and forced his head back, but caught the descending knife in the cheek, just below the left eye, the keen, double edged blade penetrating clear through the cheek bone and coming out inside the mouth. The murderous Italian wrenched the knife from the wound, and the terrified victim, tearing himself from his grasp, started to run through the car, but was followed by the Italian and another blow given with the fearful weapon, which penetrated the back of the head just below the crown, the point of the blade protruding above the left ear. Winney succeeded in finally shaking off his murderous enemy and getting through the door, and sprang off the coach with the blood streaming from his wounds. It was all accomplished so quickly that the terrified passengers had not time to interfere. When the assassin saw his victim escape him he became furious with rage, and turned like a thirsty tiger upon the passengers in the coach, his long knife dripping with blood, but before he could injure any one else his arms were pinioned to his side and the dangerous weapon taken from his bloody hands, and he was given over to the authorities at Fremont. Mr. Winney was taken on board the train at his own request, his wound staunched so far as possible, and brought to Omaha for treatment. No explanation is given for the conduct of the Italian other than that he was crazy and was starting to "run a muck." Winney is not dangerously injured, and since his wounds have been carefully dressed he is out of all danger.

### Russell, Butler's Opponent.

St. Paul Dispatch.

Ben Butler's opponent in the canvass for the Republican nomination for Congress in the Lowell, Massachusetts, District, is Wm. A. Russell, a member of the firm of Averill, Russell & Carpenter, paper manufacturers, of this city. Mr. Russell resides at Lawrence, where he has extensive paper mills. He is very wealthy, and his character is irreproachable. The contest is a pretty vigorous one, with the chances apparently in favor of Butler. It is stated that Butler will run independent if he fails to secure the nomination, in which case the Republican vote will be divided and a Democrat elected.

### The Stewart Affair.

Cincinnati Gazette.

The house of A. T. Stewart & Co., in which the genius of its founder is now so sorely missed, has announced a new move. This is a Chicago branch. Many will understand by this an effort to work off an old stock of goods under a new title. This game has been tried before by other men, full as clever as Judge Hilton and William Libby. Hilton has been at Saratoga Springs assisting to manage the great hotel. In the meantime the will case has been appealed, and a dreary litigation is before him. Mrs. Stewart went to Europe to escape the inundation of begging letters, but she will soon return to resume her troubles. The grand palace is now only tenanted by a family of servants, and it is doubtful if the widow reside in it again, unless it is to be a member of Judge Hilton's family. In fact, the palatial mansion is almost as lonely as Stewart's tomb in St. Mark's churchyard. It is a grand mausoleum of death. Not only the will case, but other litigation is bequeathed to the unenviable heirs. The levy for rent on the tenant of the Metropolitan hotel is under contest, and a recent decision has been made against the landlord. Under these circumstances it is not surprising that the firm needs a new way of working off their stock. Would it not be a good thing for them to go into liquidation?

### The Only Answer of Tilden's Defenders.

N. Y. Times.

To these grave accusations of perjury and fraud there has been given but one reply. It is that the $20,000 received from the Terre Haute railroad in 1862 represented the earning of several years, and was therefore not all chargeable to the income of that year. The answer totally fails to meet the case. 1. Because half the fee was actually earned in 1862. 2. Because there were half a dozen like fees received in 1862, of which the Cumberland Coal Company's was one; and, 3. Because the law has been clearly and repeatedly declared to be—by Judge Blatchford, among others, so lately as March last—that the taxable income of a given year is represented by the money actually received in that year, no matter when it was earned. The ignorance of the law displayed by Mr. Tilden's apologists in the press may be real or feigned, that ignorance neither is nor was shared by Mr. Tilden himself.

### A Shot at Prof. Huxley.

Buffalo Cor. N. Y. Tribune.

There is a solitary exception to the cordiality with which Buffalo has received her scientific guests. The following paragraph appears in the last number of The Orbit, a religious newspaper issued in this city, and understood to be the organ of the Right Rev. A. Cleveland Coxe, bishop of the diocese of Western New York:

"We regret to see those who 'profess and call themselves Christians' going out of their way to pay attentions to Prof. Huxley, the molecule philosopher. Mr. Huxley has gone out of his way to insult the Christian faith and the civilization of evangelized nations. As a scientist he might deserve a high position, but as a gratuitous assailant of revelation he has forfeited his claim to the respect of believers. An intellectual suicide who talks of laws and systems while he recognizes no law-giver and rejects an intelligent Creator, demands our pity; but it is only the fool that says in his heart 'there is no God;' it is the dictate of propriety to leave consummate folly to find society with itself."

The paragraph has excited much remark in this city. Few are found to agree with the Bishop's views, and several clergymen were among those who joined in the attentions to Prof. Huxley.

### Little Tiltons.

A Hulmesville (Pa.) paper says that a few days ago two nicely-dressed boys, accompanied by a young girl, passed through Newportville, Bucks county, and stopping at Everett's store, asked for accommodations for the night. Thinking they were tramps this was refused, when they passed on, and soon after applied at James Wilkinson's, in Bensalem, and were taken in. It turned out that they were very respectable persons, who had walked on a banter of their parents from Long Branch, and were on their way to Philadelphia. The young lady was the daughter of Theodore Tilton, and the lads were cousins of hers, named Richards. They had plenty of money, and were well clothed and provided for. The object was to prove that they could accomplish the journey in four days on foot, without stopping at a hotel for accommodations. They were very intelligent and agreeable companions. One night, in New Jersey, they were refused lodgings, so the boys made a tent out of their traveling shawls, and the girl was guarded through the night, the boys taking turns in watching the camp.

### A Horrible Sight for Children.

The McGrath family of Jersey City, father, mother and seven children, lived on the fourth floor of a tenement. The tragedy of Friday evening, briefly mentioned by the telegraph, is in substance thus described by the children: Thomas McGrath found his wife drunk when he came home from work in the evening. He remonstrated with her about her condition. Finding she would not listen to him, he went in search of Father Smith, pastor of the Roman Catholic church of St. Paul's of the Cross, on Jersey City Heights, and returned with him. Father Smith, after talking with the woman, went away, and McGrath lay down and went to sleep. At 11 P. M. he woke up, and asked his wife for ten cents to buy his breakfast with in the morning. She refused to give it to him. The rest of the story is best told by the children, who saw the whole affair. They say that McGrath had a lamp in his hand, and that the woman threw a shoe at McGrath and it broke it. Mrs. McGrath then picked up a carbine standing in the room, and pointed it at her husband, who snatched it from her before she could pull the trigger. He beat her with it until they got into a desperate struggle by the window. The last the children saw of the figh was when the woman lay on the floor beneath the window, while the man struck her with the musket. Some one came running up stairs a few moments after this, and, knocking at the door, said there was a man lying on the ground under the window. He said he thought it was McGrath. Mrs. McGrath replied that she did not care and that he could lie there as long as he pleased.

The police were informed. McGrath was found under the window on the street and was removed to St. Francis Hospital. The doctor said that his injuries had not been caused by the fall but by wounds inflicted by a weapon like the carbine. His skull was crushed, his legs were broken and his eyes were badly cut. The woman was also badly injured during the struggle, and was removed to St. Francis Hospital. Her right wrist and leg are broken, her head is cut, and her condition is very critical. There is small hope of her recovery.

## THE MARKETS.

### COMMERCIAL.

#### Minneapolis.

MINNEAPOLIS, Sept. 1.

GRAIN—Wheat, No. 1 at 95c; old No. 2 at 90c.
RECEIPTS—Wheat 49 cars, lumber 9, merchandise 25, staves 2, flax seed 1, barley 1, brick 1, cement 1, live stock 1.
SHIPMENTS—Flour 24 cars, lumber 45, bran 5, merchandise 15, hides 2, ice 1.

#### Milwaukee.

MILWAUKEE, Sept. 1

GRAIN—Wheat, unsettled; No. 1 at 140; No. 1 hard 1 16; No. 2 at 99½c for cash; 99½c seller September; 99½c for seller October; No. 3, 85c. Barley, nominal; 87c for cash; 87½c seller September.
FREIGHTS—Dull; 1½c to Buffalo; 5½c to Oswego.

#### Chicago.

CHICAGO, Sept. 1.

GRAIN—Wheat, steady; 94½c for September; 95½c seller October. Corn steady; 41½c for seller September; 41½c for seller October. Oats are unchanged.

### MARRIED.

MOORE—LEFFINGWELL—Aug. 30, in Plymouth Church, Minneapolis, by Rev. Mr. Simmon, Mr. CAMPBELL S. MOORE, of Minneapolis, and Miss EMILY O. LEFFINGWELL, of New Haven, Conn.

YOUNG—KEW—In this city, at the residence of Mr. Silas Moffit, Aug. 31st, by Rev. A. J. Davis, Mr. JAMES YOUNG, of Fillmore county, and Miss EMMA KEW, of Hennepin county, Minn.

### DIED.

GRUTSCH—DOMINICK GRUTSCH. Born in Tyrole, Austria, March 15th, 1860.
Funeral on Sunday, at 2 P. M.

# Minneapolis Tribune.

VOL. X. MINNEAPOLIS, THURSDAY EVENING, SEPTEMBER 7, 1876. NO. 82.

**The Minneapolis Tribune.**

THURSDAY, SEPTEMBER 7.

Gold in New York, $1.09⅞.
Money, 1½@3 ℘ cent.
Exchange, long 4.86, short 4.87½.
Government bonds dull but better.

Wheat—In Milwaukee, No. 1 at $1.10; No. 2 at $1.01½. Minneapolis, No. 1 at 95c; No. 2 at 90c. Chicago, No. 2 at 94½c; New York, No. 2 $1.06.

Probabilities to-day for the upper Mississippi—falling followed by rising barometer, southerly winds, shift to northerly, with cooler, cloudy or rainy weather.

Things are Strait down in the second district.

Reports from private sources satisfy us that Wisconsin is good for 10,000 majority for Hayes and Wheeler.

The Connecticut Democracy have nominated Richard D. Hubbard for Governor. The election comes off next spring.

Terry and Crook are still hunting for Sitting Bull. If the latter gentleman meant to be seen he would probably hunt them.

The annual convention of the Minnesota State Temperance Association has been in session for the past two days at Owatonna.

The voters of New York will indignantly resent the attempt to make them vote to thrust the chief magistracy of their state upon a man who scornfully rejects the honor.

The World in speaking of the means by which Seymour was nominated, says: "The trick was disgraceful and disgusting." The strong hand of Boss Tweed is needed to manage the boys of Tammany and keep them in the traces.

The statue of Lafayette, given by the French government as an expression of its good will towards the people of the United States, was unveiled in Union Square, New York yesterday. Statues of Washington and Lincoln also adorn the square.

Gov. Hayes is not willing to lie even for a day, under the charge of having made dishonest returns of his property for purposes of taxation. Honest men are always sensitive to aspersions of that character. By the way, Mr. Tilden has not yet explained that income return.

Alex. H. Stephens, that relic of ante-bellum times, has been nominated for re-election to Congress by the Democrats of the Augusta, Ga., district. He first entered Congress in 1843, is the oldest member dating from original entry into that body, excepting Fernando Wood, who was first elected in 1841.

What has Hayes done for the cause of reform during his three terms as Governor of Ohio? asks a Democratic exchange. We answer that it is quite as creditable to preside over a state so pure in its administration as to be proof against the plunderings of a ring of thieves, as it is to first help thieves into power, and when they are discovered in their crimes, lend a hand to turn them out.

The following reductions have been made in the indebtedness of the nation by the present administration:

| | |
|---|---|
| From March 4, 1869, to June 30, 1869, the close of the fiscal year | $34,460,779 43 |
| For fiscal year ending June 30, 1870 | 102,613,680 84 |
| " " " " 1871 | 94,327,764 84 |
| " " " " 1872 | 100,524,491 28 |
| " " " " 1873 | 43,667,630 05 |
| " " " " 1874 | 4,730,472 41 |
| " " " " 1875 | 14,399,514 84 |
| " " " " 1876 | 29,249,381 33 |
| July 1 to September 1, 1876 | 4,257,403 86 |
| Debt of the United States, including accrued interest thereon, less cash in the treasury, March 1, 1869 | 2,525,463,260 01 |
| September 1, 1876 | 2,095,181,941 14 |
| Decrease | 430,281,318 87 |
| Decrease in the annual interest charge during the past seven and a half years | $31,253,541 46 |

The New York World insists that the best course for the Empire State Democracy to pursue in their muddle over a gubernatorial candidate is to make Seymour run whether he is willing or not. It advises the party to vote for him, and flies his name as its candidate. It says "the public reasons for electing him Governor are overwhelming, and it is the right of the public to choose its own servants, unwilling though they may be to take service." Such a candidate would be likely to awaken *great* enthusiasm.

The reports from Turkey indicate that blind infatuation is still working out the decree of destiny. The English demand for an armistice is to be rejected. Austria has taken England's place as the bottle holder of the Porte. The new Sultan has confidence in the military prowess of his subjects. The latter are full of enthusiasm. Their appetite for blood and rapine was whetted by their sickening slaughter of Christians in Bulgaria. So the old moslem car, rotten with age and loaded with crime, jogs along its way for the time, but its time is coming. The swift-winged messenger of vengeance is abroad, and will soon overtake it.

Mr. Thacher, in addressing the Second District Congressional Convention at Red Wing, yesterday, after his defeat by Major Strait, characterized the occasion as his own funeral. From what we know of that gentleman we are inclined to think him mistaken. He was defeated this year it is true, but congressional elections come around quite frequently, and if his friends stand by the ticket this year we shall not be surprised to find him an exceedingly lively corpse next time. Oh! no, General! there will be no funeral, unless the seeds of death are planted about the ides of November. Keep things Straight this year, and the Republicans of the Second District will see that if any one is likely have a funeral [illegible] it will not be yours.

## KUKLUX.

### Eight Highwaymen this P. M. Attacked the First National Bank of Northfield.

### The Cashier, Mr. Heywood, Killed, and Mr. Bunker, Clerk, Wounded.

**Two of the Robbers Killed—Citizens in Pursuit of the Rest.**

**Intense Excitement Among the People.**

Special to Tribune.

NORTHFIELD, Minn., Sept. 7.—About 2:30 this afternoon the First National bank of this city was attacked by eight mounted highwaymen, and the cashier, Mr. Heywood, was killed, and Mr. Bunker, clerk, was wounded.

Two of the robbers were killed and the rest escaped. There is a large party of citizens in pursuit of them. The excitement is intense.

The robbers were last seen crossing the railroad track at Dundas on the way to the Big Woods.

MONEY TAKEN.

All the money taken was what was in the teller's drawer, which was not large.

MR. C. S. BUNKER,

the teller who was wounded, was formerly an employe of this office, and worked at his trade as a printer in The St Anthony Democrat office and also in St. Paul. His mother and sisters still reside in that city. He was educated at Carleton college, Northfield, and afterwards became identified with the First National bank.

[Northfield has telegraphed to this city and St. Paul for officers to pursue the villains.]

## RIOT.

**Black Republicans Fight it out With White and Black Democrats—Charleston, South Carolina, the Scene.**

Serious Riot.

CHARLESTON, S. C., Sept. 7.—A serious riot occurred late last night between colored Republicans on one side and colored Democrats and white men on the other; pistols were freely used on both sides; the rioters held King street, the main thoroughfare, from midnight until sunrise, breaking windows, robbing stores, and attacking and beating indiscriminately every white man who showed his face. Several of those shot are in a critical condition. Intense excitement prevails.

RIOTOUS PROCEEDINGS

of the strikers on the Cambahee are renewed, and the situation is regarded as serious.

## PISTOL POLITICS.

**The Republicans Raise a Campaign Pole—the Democrats Pull It Down—Several Men Shot.**

KINGSTON, N. Y., Sept. 7.—The Republican Campaign Club, of this city went to Stony Hollow yesterday to raise a pole. After the pole was raised the opposition pulled it down, which was the signal for a general scrimmage.

Stones were thrown and pistols fired, and it is reported several men were shot, one of whom is dead. Several members of the Republican Club from this city received severe wounds from stones, and one a pistol shot on the side of his head.

## MASSACRES.

**Living Men Torn to Pieces and Bodies Torn From the Graves and Defiled**

SHANGHAI, Aug. 15.—The report of the massacre in Ningkushfu is fully confirmed; The Roman Catholic church was destroyed, the officiating priest tortured and killed, his assistant torn in pieces; dead bodies were taken from graves and defiled, and a hundred of the congregation slain; the French minister is taking active steps to secure punishment of the guilty parties, among whom are numerous officials of rank.

Several other assaults and murders of Christians have followed. Forty buildings were destroyed; damage to property estimated at $60,000.

## SLAUGHTERED.

**Fifteen Hundred Egyptian Troops Have Been Massacred.**

NEW YORK, Sept. 7.—A Paris correspondent telegraphs a fresh disaster has befallen the Egyptian arms in Abyssinia. Fifteen hundred troops, with their commander, Rahibe Pasha, have been massacred. The Abyssinians afterwards proceeded to Massacros, which they seized. The garrison and government officers escaped on board some ships which happened to be in the port, and arrived safely at Suez. The Egyptian government is contemplating revenge and sending fresh troops to the scene of action. The cavalry and artillery are also being reorganized.

## PHILADELPHIA.

**The Inventors' Congress—The Rowing Prizes—The Centennial Commission.**

Inventors' Congress.

PHILADELPHIA, Sept. 7.—A Congress of the inventors connected with the U. S. Patent Association was inaugurated at the hall of the Franklin Institute, on Seventh street, above Chestnut. The object of the meeting is the improvement of the patent system and the formation of an international association having reference to greater uniformity in the system of the world. There were about twenty-five gentlemen present, including Hon. J. M. Thatcher, ex-U. S. patent commissioner, Prof. Hedrick, of the U. S. patent office, W. C. Dodge of Washington, and John S. Perry of Albany.

THE PRIZES

rowed for in the professional races on the Schuylkill course will be awarded as follows: To the Thames four, $2,500.

THE U. S. CENTENNIAL COMMISSION

assembled in the rear department of Judges' Hall at half past 10 o'clock this morning, President Hawley in the chair. The calling of the roll showed that twenty-four states and territories were represented—just a quorum and no more.

The business of the session was opened by reading the report of the executive committee. This document was quite voluminous, detailing all the questions discussed by the committee and acts performed by them since the former meetings of the commission.

## SCIENTIFIC BRUISING.

**The Goss-Allen Battle this Forenoon in Kentucky, With a Military Interference.**

**The Covington Light Guards do Gallant Service, But a New Ring is Formed.**

**Goss Gets the Bunged Eyes and the Principal Punishment.**

**He Also Wins the Fight in One Hour and Fifty-two Minutes.**

**Technical Reading for the Local Sports.**

Hurrah for the Home Guards.

THE FIGHT STOPPED.

CINCINNATI, Sept. 7.—The fight was stopped at the end of the seventh round by the militia.

PLACE OF THE FIGHT.

The point chosen for the fight between Allen and Goss is a clover field near Walton, Ky., on Louisville Short Line R. R., eighteen miles from Cincinnati. The crowd in attendance is somewhere near 500. Goss and Allen take their places in the ring at 7 o'clock; the fight begins at 7:40.

GOSS WORST PUNISHED.

Bulletin—Goss was the worst punished of the two men at the end of the seventh round. First blood and first knock down for Allen. The prospect is that the fight will be renewed in another place.

GOSS FIRST

stepped into the middle of the ring.

First round—Both men spar cautiously, Goss falling into Allen's corner. The sparring is getting tiresome for the crowd. First blood for Allen, and a clinch and a fall with Goss on top. Time, 7 minutes.

Second round—Allen strikes Goss on the lips and slightly staggers him. Goss has given Allen some heavy body blows. Goss' mouth is bleeding. A fall for Allen.

Third round—Close fighting, Allen winning. At this point the militia appeared, but the fighting still goes on.

Fourth round—Exchanges fast and heavy; Allen by a terrible blow on Goss' neck knocked him down. Time, nine minutes.

Fifth round—After considerable sparring, Allen struck out and fell short of Goss' face; in return he received a blow in the stomach; this did not appear to worry Allen, and he returned heavily on Goss' body and a fearful one on damaged eye; Goss retaliated, and after a sharp half arm fighting Goss went down to avoid punishment.

Sixth round—Both men promptly to the scratch, Allen leading off, getting in on Goss' face; he repeated this, getting in another blow on Goss' damaged eye; Allen finally fights Goss down.

Seventh round—When time was called the Covington Light Guards appeared, and the fight ceased.

WILL FIGHT IT OUT.

Capt Frank Wood, with the Covington Light Guards, reached a point north of Walton at 7 o'clock, having been carried past the fighting-ground by the conductor. Capt. Wood stopped the train three miles past the point, and the militia marched back, arriving at 8 o'clock. W. G. Lobban, aid to the Governor, sent for Eph Holland and advised him that the fight immediately cease. Holland stated that he was a law-abiding man, opposed to bloodshed, and accordingly stopped the fight after seven rounds had been fought. Holland declares he will make the men fight out the fight before they reach Cincinnati to-night. Neither of the men was much punished.

**Later.**

A SECOND RING.

CINCINNATI, Sept. 7.—After being dispersed by the militia, a second ring was formed a short distance below Walton, in Boone county. The sheriff was present, but hadn't sufficient posse to interfere.

Eighth round—Goss threw Allen, though the former was severely punished.

Ninth round—Goss forced fighting, Allen finished the round for himself with heavy blows on Goss' face.

Tenth round—Heavy blows exchanged, Goss forced on ropes; fighters were parted by seconds.

Eleventh round—Goss led the fighting, the hardest fighting was in this round.

Twelfth round—Both of Goss' eyes badly swollen. Allen knocks Goss down.

Thirteenth round—Terrific blow on Goss' mouth; Goss on his knees.

Fourteenth round—Goss threw Allen by clinch. Foul claimed; not allowed.

Fifteenth round—Heavy close fighting; both badly punished.

Sixteenth round—In chasing Allen about the ring Goss slips and falls.

Seventeenth round—Goss knocked over the ropes.

Eighteenth round—Goss plants a stinger on Allen's body. Close fighting. Foul claimed by Goss, but not allowed.

Nineteenth round—Goss slips and falls. Close fighting.

Twentieth round—Both fall.

Twenty-first round—Close fighting. Goss falls, and is struck by Allen while on his knees. Foul claimed and allowed.

The fight was decided in favor of Goss at 11:50 A. M.

Allen shows little or no injury about the face. Goss was terribly beaten—almost blind. Time of fight one hour and fifty-two minutes.

ALLEN ARRESTED.

CINCINNATI, Sept. 7.—Two trains from the fight to-day arrived at Newport, were stopped by the authorities and Allen was arrested.

**A Divy.**

NEW YORK, Sept. 7.—The Western Union Telegraph Company has declared a quarterly dividend of one and one-half per cent.

## TEMPERANCE.

**A Grand Mass Meeting at Harrison Hall Last Evening.**

**This Meeting the Forerunner of What is to Follow.**

**The Meetings to be Continued all Winter.**

Pursuant to announcement, a mass temperance convention was held in Harrison Hall last evening, which is the forerunner of a series of meetings to be held every Wednesday evening during the coming winter, and, if sufficient interest is manifested, they may be carried on till the good work the temperance people are interested in is accomplished.

A large audience was present, and the indications are that the meetings will be very interesting.

The meeting was called to order by Dr. Stanton, who stated that they were disappointed in not having the Jubilee Singers present; they had faithfully promised to be present, and no doubt would appear before the close of the meeting. The first and most important thing was to thank the Lord for his kindness and mercy to the friends present, and to ask His assistance in making the undertaking a success. Therefore they would, in His praise, sing the familiar hymn "Before Jehovah's Awful Throne." After this the Rev. J. W. Martin, of the Seventh Street M. E. church, delivered a very impressive prayer.

OBJECT OF THE MEETING.

Dr. Stanton then stated that many might be ignorant of the object in thus calling together the people. The object was in no manner connected with politics, and he wanted this distinctly understood. But the great object was, with the assistance of God, to promote the cause of temperance. The meeting was called for the purpose of giving the people an opportunity to indulge in liberal thought. But they must not mistake it for a Liberal League meeting. They did not come together for the purpose of talking party politics but to talk of temperance. They want to get all the light possible on the subject, and by a free discussion help the cause along, and by all working in a harmonious, friendly way, much good may be accomplished towards the great object in view, *i. e.*, the total annihilation of the Rum Fiend. To carry on the great work they proposed to hold weekly meetings to discuss the best means of promoting the welfare of the cause.

THE SPEAKERS.

The Rev. D. Cobb was introduced and delivered an interesting address that contained many new and important points on the subject under discussion. He gave them some important advice in regard to the position they should hold, the methods to employ to accomplish the great aim for which they were working and the manner in which they should do the work. Also, of the obstacles they had to contend with, and the encouragements that were in their favor, closing with the thought that the day would come when intemperance will be done away with. Like Hell Gate in the East river, New York, where for years they have been at work to improve navigation at an enormous expense, we are putting down our dinamite ammunition so that when it is touched off the world will feel the upheaval from one end of the globe to the other.

Mr. H. Lawrence made an apology for the absence of the Jubilee Singers, stating that they had repeatedly promised to be on hand, but had failed to appear, and that he had been informed they were attending a wedding. At future meetings the people might be sure of what was advertised.

A short address was delivered by the Rev. E. M. Williams on the subject of temperance, in which he took a hearty interest. A stranger next spoke, and in a few words told of his experience. How a few months since, by the help of God and some friends at the Centennial Coffee House he was taken from the gutter and furnished with good clothes, and a situation obtained, where he was doing well and would always work in the interest of the temperance cause.

Miss Alice Neal also delivered a recitation in an admirable manner.

The convention then adjourned to meet next Wednesday evening.

## POSTAL PECULATIONS

**The Reports of the Irregularities in the St. Paul Post Office Only too True.**

The rumors of the arrest of two employees in the St. Paul post office for robbing the mails, which reached this city yesterday and were briefly alluded to, prove only too true. Mr. Chas. C. Kelly, whose arrest was made on Tuesday night, and Mr. John C. Terry, Jr., superintendent of carriers, arrested yesterday morning, had a preliminary hearing before Commissioner Cardozo yesterday, and were each bound over in five thousand dollars bail. It appears that the complaints of missing money and letters have been coming in for some time, and since June detectives have been engaged in endeavoring to trace the peculations to the proper persons. Suspicion at last rested on the two young men named, and on Tuesday night one of the detectives secreted himself in the post office, saw Kelly open the safe, take out a package of letters, retire to a water closet, where, through a previously prepared hole, he was seen to open the letters and abstract the money. He was caught in the very act. The proof against Terry is, that there was found his person money previously marked and enclosed in decoy letters—money that he produced from his pockets on demand of the detectives and Dr. Day. The arrests have created no small amount of sensation in St. Paul, where the young men are well known, unusually popular, and splendidly connected. The Masonic relief association has been the chief sufferer by the depredations of the letter pilferer.

Quite an amusing joke was perpetrated Wednesday night at the suspension bridge. The unfinished abutments at the west end of the bridge were converted into a fort, and for guns some large smoke stacks were borrowed, probably in the owner's absence. The guns, four in number, were brought to bear on the road leading from the bridge, and were, indeed, formidable-looking instruments of destruction. Over the first was placed the standard, which was a banner of white bearing the painting of an Indian—probably Sitting Bull. Said redskin held in the left hand his bow and arrow and in the right a tomahawk. One foot rested on a keg of powder, the head being labeled "P. P. and N. P. R. R. C. R." A large sign over the center of the front side of the "fort" bore the following inscription: "Fort Pizzle. In time of Peace prepare for War!"

**Canadian Fires.**

HOTELS BURNED.

TORONTO, Sept. 7.—A fire in Streetsville, early yesterday morning, burned the Telegraph and Globe hotels, also two men who had been carousing in the stable and started the fire.

TAKEN ON SUSPICION.

ST. HYACINTHE, Sept. 7.—A man named Blanchett and several others have been arrested on suspicion of having set fire to their premises to obtain the insurance, thereby causing a disastrous conflagration on Sunday last.

**Insurgents Increasing.**

BELGRADE, Sept. 7.—The insurgents in Bosnia are increasing in numbers. The Turkish forces are confined to the extreme north and south.

**Altogether Too True.**

LONDON, Sept. 6.—The Standard's correspondent says: Seven Russian medical officers who have arrived from Alexinatz confirm the worst accounts of Friday's disaster. They say the Servians do not hold any position at Alexinatz, and confirm the report of the Turkish advance on Belgrade by way of Kragujevatz, on the south east of Montenegro. The Turks cannonaded the whole line from Padgoritza to Sprise on Tuesday, creating the impression that the battle was progressing there. This proves to have been a feint, with the object of diverting the attention of the Montenegrins from Medun, which place they are investing, the Turks desiring to revictual it; they have not succeeded yet, and they must drive the Montenegrins from cliffs 1,800 feet high on either side of the gap in which Medun lies, before they can revictual. The result of the fighting in the northwest is still unknown.

**Death for the Mollies.**

HARRISBURG, Pa., Sept. 7.—Gov. Hartranft has issued death warrants for the execution of Thomas Munley, James Carroll, James Boyle, Hugh McGeaghan and Roorty, the Molly Maguires who were recently convicted in Schuylkill county of murder in the first degree. The execution takes place Oct. 1.

**Bank Failure.**

HARRISBURG, Pa., Sept. 7.—The City Bank of this city has suspended; liabilities $350,000, though the assets will entirely cover that amount. The majority of the depositors are laboring men and women.

Sam Cary classes Nebraska and California as the only northern states that Tilden can possibly carry—a mighty doubtful possibility in Nebraska's case.



## THE MARKETS.

### COMMERCIAL.

**Minneapolis.**

MINNEAPOLIS, Sept. 7.

GRAIN—Wheat, No. 1 at 95c; old No. 2 at 90c.
RECEIPTS—Wheat 20 cars, lumber 3, merchandise 22, wood 5, coal 4, staves 3, hoop poles 1, flax seed 1, brick 1, lime 2, live stock 2, pig iron 1.
SHIPMENTS—Flour 40 cars, lumber 57, bran 8, merchandise 16, oats 1, hides 1, staves 1.

**Milwaukee.**

MILWAUKEE, Sept. 7.

GRAIN—Wheat, unsettled; No. 1 at 1 10; No. 1 hard 1 16; No. 2 at 1 01⅜ for cash; 1 01⅜ seller October; 1 00⅞ for November; No. 3, 90¾c; receipts, 40,200 bushels; shipments, 13,600 bushels. Corn, steady; 42½c for No. 2. Oats, firm; 32c for No. 2. Rye, quiet; 64c for No. 1. Barley, steady; 80c for No. 2.

**Chicago.**

CHICAGO, Sept. 7.

GRAIN—Wheat unsettled and generally lower; 96¾c for cash; 96⅜c seller October. Corn, firm; 43⅜c for cash; 43⅜c seller October. Oats, stronger; 32½c for cash and for October. Barley firmer, 72⅜c.

**New York**

NEW YORK, Sept. 7.

COTTON—Quiet, 11 9-16c for middling uplands.
FLOUR—Quiet, and generally without decided change; receipts, 15,000 barrels; sales, 11,000 barrels; 4 20@4 60 extra state; 4 40@4 75 for hoop.
GRAIN—Wheat quiet and unchanged; receipts 22,000 bushels; sales, 45,000 bushels; 1 05@1 06 for No. 2 Chicago; 1 17 for old amber Michigan in store.

**Sixth Ward Caucus.**

There will be a Caucus of the Republican voters of the Sixth Ward held at Harmonia Hall, THURSDAY EVENING, September 7th, at 8 o'clock, for the purpose of electing Ten Delegates to represent the Ward at the County and District Conventions to be held at Brackett's Hall, September 13th, 1876.

O. J. EVANS,
Chairman Ward Committee.

## MARRIED.

MERRILL—KEITH—At the residence of the bride's father in this city, Sept. 6, by Rev. H. N. Herrick, Mr. EUGENE A. MERRILL and Miss ADDIE M. KEITH, both of Minneapolis.

## ADVERTISED LETTERS.

LIST OF LETTERS unclaimed in the Post Office at Minneapolis, Hennepin county, Minnesota, September 7th, 1876.

To obtain any of these letters the applicant must call for "Advertised Letters," giving the date of this list, and pay one cent for advertising.

If not called for within one month they will be sent to the Dead Letter Office.

LADIES' LIST.

| | |
|---|---|
| Brockway, Mrs Stella | Jones, Mrs Lydia F |
| Bourgois, Miss Delia | Johnson, Miss Anna M |
| Barnes, Olive Mrs | Johnson, Miss Anna |
| Baldwin, Miss Nannie | King, Mrs Annie E |
| Craig, Miss Annie | Krager, Miss Lina |
| Cattson, Mrs Maria | Lingen, Martha E—2 |
| Delony, Mrs E J | Neilsen, Lina Eva |
| Fouske, Miss Annie | Neunsiger, Lizzie |
| Gamain, Mrs Mattie | Ray, Mrs Mary |
| Gamble, Mrs | Rice, Mrs L |
| Goodrich, Mary A | Rolf, Mrs Francis |
| Griswold, Miss Nettie D | Squire, Mrs Sarah |
| Hutchins, Mrs Louisa | Scott, Mrs Mary |
| Hunt, J B, Mrs | Seargeant, Mrs L L |
| Howe, Mrs Mary A | Watson, Mrs E K |
| Honstain, Mrs Ann | Wesley, Mrs Louisa |
| Harris, Miss Louisa | Williams, Miss Elizabeth |
| Ingalls, I F | Wright, Mrs Carrie |

GENTLEMEN'S LIST.

| | |
|---|---|
| Armstrong, Patrick | McMurray, Geo W |
| Bears, A E | McPherson, Peter |
| Bull, Johnathan & Bro | Northrup, Frank |
| Bronlis, T G | Nygaard, L J |
| Chapin, A L & Co | Ostvolden, Nils N |
| Cassidy, David | Putnam, Chas B |
| Collom, G H | Pelletiesi, J |
| Caarl, H O | Pribble T |
| Carlander, N N | Rojgely, Rev B |
| Choate, H | Rivers, Frank |
| Cyr, S J | Redding, Frank |
| Connell, T | Robinson, Jabe |
| Dickerson, Fred | Smith, D Wilmot |
| Dalin, F | Simpson, David |
| Doyle, Jno | Shields, Edward |
| Dinneen, Patrick | Spring, E A |
| Erickson, August | Siggelkow, F |
| Eriksen, P | Smith, J M |
| Hubbard, Frank | Stassl, Joseph |
| Herring, H F | Sandberg, J |
| Heald, Mark | Stone, M M |
| Honsog, N | Sinn, Peter |
| Johnson, A B | Schmid, Robert |
| Jameson, Henry | Smith, R W |
| Kelley, H H | Sharlock, Thos |
| Lovejoy, D P | Torad, Chas |
| Lee, Frank | Willich, Arnold |
| Lee, Tommie | Wilson, Frank H |
| McReynolds, Geo A F | Zimmerman, August |
| Mattson, C G | |

GEORGE H. KEITH, P. M.

**THE MINNEAPOLIS TRIBUNE**

THE DAILY TRIBUNE is published every evening (Sundays excepted) for circulation by Carriers, newsmen, and the Mail:

Per Month, by Carrier ........ $ 75
Per Year, by mail ........ 9 00

THE WEEKLY PIONEER-PRESS AND TRIBUNE will be sent to weekly subscribers upon the following terms: Per year, one copy, $2.00; five copies, $9.00; ten copies, $16.00; twenty copies, $30.00; thirty copies, $42.00.

Subscriptions payable invariably in advance. Address "THE TRIBUNE," Minneapolis, Minn.

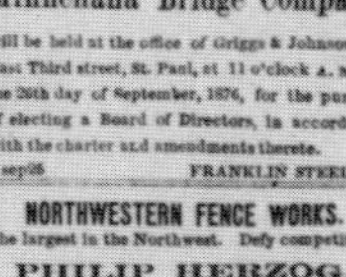

# Evening Journal.

VOL. I.--NO. 14. MINNEAPOLIS, MINN., WEDNESDAY, DECEMBER 11, 1878. THREE CENTS






## CONDENSED TELEGRAMS.

The committee appointed to investigate the charges of bribery against Congressman Brentano, of Chicago, at his own request, in connection with the passage of the district government bill, last season, met this morning and heard several witnesses. None of them knew anything of the charges and did not believe them. The attempt is being made to prove that the First National bank and other New York interests, who own District of Columbia bonds, bribed the District commissioner; but the report is believed to be without foundation.

Senator Conklin's Committee on Commerce met to-day, and the New York custom house nominations were taken up. Conkling has given no indications of the course he will pursue regarding these nominations, and there is great curiosity to see what he will do. His friends are divided in opinion—one of them, a senator and member of the committee, this morning asserting very positively that Conkling will oppose the confirmation of Merritt and others as actively as he did last winter.

Samuel Hayes, the friend of Secretary Schurz, whose appointment as postmaster at St. Louis, in place of Chauncey Filley last summer, created some political agitation—principally because Filley was removed because of his activity in politics.

Buckner's bill, to retire the national bank circulation, was to have been considered to-day in the house, but was crowded out by the diplomatic appropriation bills.

If, Devins insists upon leaving the Cabinet, the president will appoint him to fill the vacancy caused by the death of Circut-Judge Shepley.

Mr. Garfield declares that any more attempts to arouse sectional prejudice will be overthrown and condemned by his countrymen.

The Potter Committee decided to send a Sub-Committee to New Orleans to continue the investigation of the cipher dispatches.

The attempt to impeach Judge Blodgett, promises to be a failure.



### *The Earth not a True Globe.*

Our planet is not a true globe, because of its former plastic condition before the formation and cooling of the surface. When the globe was soft it was more or less yielding, and then the rotation of the earth to which I have referred, tended to drive off, as it were, the matter in the equatorial regions; so that the distance through the center of the earth between the two surfaces as far as possible removed from the pole of rotation, or those parts of the earth which the imaginary axis comes through, is rather greater than the distance between the two points where the two axis comes to the surface. The reason of that fact, and that it must have been so, has been beautifully established by several experiments. That the earth was once hotter than it is now is therefore proved, both by the irregularities of its surface, and by its shape as a whole. We must not imagine, however, there has been but one change. The minor irregularities are all gradually changing by inner energies and the action of air and water, and it may be that even the largest ones are young compared with the age of the planet's surface. Nor does the change end here; the equatorial protuberence itself may but after all mark a point in a great cycle of change, which has compelled the earth to rotate now about one axis and now about another. Mathematicians consider it highly probable that the axis of the earth may have been in ancient times very differently situated to what it is at present, and, indeed, that "it might have gradually shifted to 10, 20, 30, 40 or more degrees, without at any time any perceptible disturbance of either land or water." Thus it appears that nature prevents catastrophes, by the very hugeness of the scale on which she works.



—A French scientific authority states that the ordinary rate of man's walking is four feet per second; of a good horse, in harness, twelve; of a reindeer in a sledge on the ice, twenty-six; of an English race horse, forty-three; of a hare, eighty-eight; of a good sailing ship, fourteen; and of the wind, eighty-two.

### Words of Wisdom.

Very few diseases are so mortal as the fear of death.

All human virtues increase and strengthen by the experience of them.

Relations always take the greatest liberties, and frequently give the least assistance.

Avoid tedious circumlocution in language. Words, like cannon-balls, should go straight to their mark.

We trouble life by the care of death, and death by the care of life; the one torments, the other frights us.

Modern education too often covers the fingers with rings, and at the same time cuts the sinews of the wrists.

The remembrance of a beloved mother becomes the shadow of all our actions; it either goes before or follows.

Our own hands are heaven's favorite instruments for supplying us with the necessaries and luxuries of life.

All men look to happiness in the future. To every eye heaven and earth seem to embrace in the distance.

There are stone bridges in China three and four miles long, and an arch of the incredible span of six hundred feet.

The law should be to the sword what the handle is to the hatchet; it should direct the stroke and temper the force.

Talk of fame and romance—all the glory and adventure in the world are not worth one hour of domestic bliss.

It is dangerous for one to climb his family-tree too high, for he is very apt to get among dead and decayed branches.

Value the friendship of him who stands by you in the storm; swarms of insects will surround you in the sunshine.

We hate to see a boy wrth the manners of an old man; we hate worse to see an old man with the manners of a boy.

Love cannot fully admit the feeling that the beloved object may die; all passions feel their object to be as eternal as themselves.

The man who violently hates or ardently loves, cannot avoid being in some degree a slave to the person detested or adored.

### *Deception of the Senses.*

The deception of the senses are well-nigh as marked as their limitations; indeed, are a part of their limitations. Reid, the metaphysician, argues elaborately that the so-called deceptions of the senses are rather mistakes of judgment in regard to the impressions made on the nerves of special sense. Such argument is needless, since all the convictions that we acquire through the senses—the truth as well as errors—are the products of judgment. It is not the eye, but the brain behind the eye, that sees. The impressions made on the retina do not of themselves carry thoughts to the mind, any more than the impression on the photographer's plate carries thought to the instrument behind it. The eye is an instrument through which the brain sees—the telescope and microscope of the mind. Of itself the eye is as incompetent to see as is the telescope to discover a new planet, or the microscope to detect a humble organism.

The eye is the astronomer and microscopist that discovers; it is the brain that sees through the doors opened by the eye. Conceptions and misconceptions, obtained through the sense of vision, are alike products of the brain rather than the seeing apparatus. In scientific strictness our senses neither teach nor deceive us.

### Brudder Gardner's Opinion.

Some fokes hab got the impresshun dat de man wot does de mos' whoopin' and yellin' and attracks de mos' attenshun am de chap wot makes de bigger' pile o' cash, but doan' you belieb it! De empty wood waggin makes five times de noise dat de costly kerridge does. De burdock takes up ten times de room dat de tulip does, but de tulip hez de bulge on de burdock when it comes down to market value. De modest man hez all de bizness chances dat de forward man hez; he keeps on gainin' de respect ob de woruld, and bimeby he crawls to de top ob de hen coop, while de blowhard roll inter de ditch. Modesty am its own reward. It am capital in de bank; it am fust mortgage on improved real estate; it am a purty fa'r sort o' religun. Stan back! Doan' try to git dar befo' all de rest. Doan' be shootin' off dem moufs for de simple sake of usin' up yer spar' time. As de poet says:

' De big sunflour may rise above
De modest 'tater vine,
And brag about its Sunday clothes.
An' put on airs so fine;
But when de winter howls around;
An' the snow lies at de doah,
De big sunflower, oh! whar am he—
De 'tater hez de floah."

—Any farmer that has a small pond or lake on his farm, or a never-failing spring, so situated that by damming up the gully or hollow below it, a pond can be formed, may make an acre or two thus located the most profitable part of his premises, by stocking the water with fish. This can now be done with little expense through any of the State Fish Commissioners.



—We have heard of men's making a hole in the ice to be baptized. They always have to break the ice before they can get married.

# Evening Journal.

VOL. I.--NO. 131. MINNEAPOLIS, MINN., SATURDAY, APRIL 26, 1879. TWO CENTS.

**Evening Journal.**

Published every afternoon (Sunday excepted), for general circulation, by the

EVENING JOURNAL CO.

(C. H. STEVENS & F. E. CURTIS.)

By carrier, per month, in advance........$ 30
By carrier, per month, if not in advance. 40
By mail, per year, in advance.............. 3 00

All communications should be addressed to the EVENING JOURNAL CO., Room 3, Brackett's Block, Minneapolis, Minn.



### Drill Club.

A Templar drill club was organized last night by the Knights Templar of Darius and Zion commanderies, with a membership of about thirty. The following officers were elected:

President—William Lochren.
Vice-President—John I. Black.
Captain-general—C. McC. Reeve.
Senior Warden—F. L. Smith.
Junior Warden—Ed. McDermott.
Secretary—A. A. Ames.
Treasurer—H. M. Kent.
Executive Committee — C. T. Hobart, M. P. Hayes and M. B. Koon.

The object of this organization is to enable the Sir Knights to become proficient in Knights Templar drill and tactics. The next meeting of the club will be held on Monday evening at the Asylum of Zion Commandery. All Sir Knights in the city are cordially invited to place their names upon the rolls and nearly forty have signified their intention of joining.



### LAST CALL.

One more entertainment by the Gale-Leib troupe to-night, at Association Hall, and H. M. S. Pinafore will weigh anchor and sail from Minneapolis. Among the many ships which are cruising about the world, that above mentioned is the finest. The favorable reception with which they met last week, and the way the tickets are going, indicate that they are appreciated.

Bean, Wales & Co. have just received a new and elegant assortment of teachers' Bibles. Call and examine.

This is the last opportunity that people will have to see Gale's incomparable Pinafore. The sale of tickets indicate a good house.

The usual Sunday afternoon Y. M. C. A. meeting will be omitted to-morrow afternoon, in order to unite with the four o'clock union services at Plymouth church.

### FLANNEL SUITING.

Middlesex standard indigo suiting. A very fine piece of goods, selling cheap at Wm. P. Cady's, 109 south Washington av.

## NEGRO MOVEMENT.

### Meeting of Colored Men in this City.

### Formation of Plans for Helping their Brethren.

A meeting of the colored men of the city was held last night in Good Templar's Hall, to consider by what means they could best obtain and send aid to the colored men of the south in their efforts to get to the north and west, and particularly to help those who are in Kansas now. The meeting was called to order by the President, and the minutes of last meeting were read and accepted, and the reports of the committees were heard. Some very able speeches were made during the course of the evening, notably by Rev. Mr. Simons and Messrs. Sterrett and Hillyer, and many facts of a most startling nature were brought out. Instances were brought up, where credible witnesses had seen and knew of their own knowledge that negroes in the south were persecuted, and in many instances killed; that the same stocks, and whipping posts in use before the war were used for the same purposes to-day, and the negro had no means of redress. As a general thing the negro in the south rents a small farm, and pays for it about $10 per acre, and this for land that is only worth about $20 per acre. Not having any capital of his own, he is obliged to buy goods on credit and pays for them two or three prices. Hence the importance of the "cross roads" store keeper. As the following scale of prices may be of interest, we insert them to show under what disadvantages the negro labors under. A bushel of corn costs $2. A plug of tobacco 50 cents. Molasses $1.50 a gallon and plows and other implements treble the price we are accustomed to pay for them. Under these circumstances what can the poor negro do except emigrate? The following resolutions were offered and adopted by a unanimous vote:

WHEREAS, By the right of might there were held in servile bondage in the southern states of this Union about four millions of human beings deprived of all human rights save that of life; and

WHEREAS, A kind and beneficient Providence, through and by the means of a rebellion brought about the freedom of this people, and an acknowledgment of their claims to humanity—and by the endorsement of a majority of the people of these states, those people were declared to be citizens of the United States; and,

WHEREAS, Those rights have been abridged and in many cases totally denied, and when redress was sought and rights applied for, said people have been shot, butchered, burned, and property destroyed; and since these terrible afflictions, will indefinitely continue, these people have fled from their blood thirsty enemies to seek new homes in the western territories; and,

WHEREAS, From previous condition they are poor and penniless, and much suffering and want exists—even cases of starvation—and their wail has gone up to God and humanity for aid, therefore be it

*Resolved*, That we have heard their cry, and will respond as far as lies in our power.

*Resolved*, That we call on all christian and charitably disposed people to help us aid them. That we give an entertainment in some prominent locality, to consist of speeches, music, and refreshments; the proceeds from such entertaiment to be forwarded to the governor of Kansas for the relief of these suffering people.

The different committees then made their reports. The committee on invitations reported that they had canvassed the town, and some of our most prominent men had promised to attend their meeting and do all in their power to further the good cause, among others Gov. Pillsbury and Eugene Wilson.

Some discussion was then indulged in regarding the merits of various halls, and a committee was appointed to look into the matter. A collection of $10 was taken up, and refreshment and soliciting committees appointed and also one that should endeavor to induce railroad officials to transport all clothes, etc, raised for the emigrants in Kansas free of charge when a motion to adjourn was made and carried. A mass meeting and entertainment will soon be held and all people who are interested in this most righteous cause will have an opportunity of placing themselves on record as to how much they feel for suffering humanity.

## Telegraphic Sparks.

J. F. Roberts committed suicide near Eau Claire, Wis., yesterday, by jumping into a well.

A dispatch from Safed Tang says according to trustworthy information from Cabul, Mahamed Hasham, son-in-law of Shere Ali, now the only avowed claimant to Yakoob Khan's throne, is endeavoring to excite insurrection, and has opened negotiations with England.

A correspondent in Berlin states there are twenty freetrade mechanics and petitions to one or the other side, but the government is obdurate.

Rev. J. G. Bleckley hung himself in his barn near Beloit, Wis., Wednesday.

John Colbert, of Hancock, who was indicted by the last grand jury, for assault with intent to do great bodily harm, has surrendered himself into the hands of Sheriff Du Toit last week, and was immediately bailed for his appearance at the next term of court.

On Thursday last the barn of Samuel Carson, at Le Sueur Center, caught fire and burned, including a lot of hay and grain, and his house was saved only through untiring effort.

Mira Knapp, of Kenosha, Wis., convicted of shooting Edward Bain, was sentenced to two years in the penitentiary. A new trial was refused.

Thousands of political prisoners, most of them arrested only on suspicion, are being sent from St. Petersburg to Golos and the penitentiaries of the empire.

A boiler in the Milwaukee Washington avenue tunnel exploded yesterday, severely scalding the engineer and stoker, and doing considerable damage.

The Breckenridge Free Press says settlers are rapidly taking up claims on the Fort Abercrombie reservation, though it is not yet formerly opened for settlement.



### "A Sad Accident."

Editor Evening Journal.

Again has this community been startled by the accounts in the daily press under the above heading. Little did I think when writing the article for your paper last week that there should be another such a case in our midst, following so closely upon the heels of the last. But it almost seems, at times, that society had formed a systematic combination for the extermination and annihilation of numberless thousands of unwitting and innocent men, simply because they are wage slaves. Two come so closely together that we hardly cease talking of the one before another attracts attention, and calls for sympathy.

This last case, however, should call out more serious consideration than people are generally wont to give to the common "Sad Accident." A short time after the mill explosion last May the city authorities ordered the walls of this mill (the Ankeny) torn down, and partial plans were made for so doing. The property soon after passing into other hands, the new owners threatened to get out an injunction against prosecutors of the work, and our keen-sighted and economical city officers ordered it stopped, since which time until lately it has remained as the fire left it—a menace to passers-by and liable to tumble to the ground any moment. Passing by this man-trap on Sunday last, I remarked to a friend that were any one killed in attempting to bolster up those shaky walls, the owners could hardly be looked upon as little else than murderers. Certain it is, that they are criminals—by either carelessness or greediness. Money is not such a god that a man's life is nothing—even though he be poor. Look you at the value placed upon life in this last case. I am credibly informed that $1,000 or $1,500 would have blown down the old walls and replaced them with new ones. Was not poor Farrell's life worth more to the community than such a paltry sum? Then let not the salvation of money be the first consideration, but rather that of life.

In this last case the city authorities are more to blame than any one else. After the city engineer declared those premises unsafe it was the duty of those in authority to see that it was removed, even though a hundred injunctions had been pointed at them.

That fundamental law of the land, that every man shall be protected in "life, liberty and the pursuit of happiness" has, so far as the wage-worker is concerned, been most fearfully and sadly violated in the last decade or two. But more anon.

‡



## TO-DAY'S MARKETS.

[TELEGRAPHIC REPORT.]

Below are the markets in detail, reported specially for the JOURNAL by G. D. ROGERS, Commission Merchant, City Hall.

LIVERPOOL.

Wheat—Quiet; firm.

LONDON.

Wheat—Cargoes firm: Consols, 98⅜@98½.

NEW YORK.

Wheat—No. 2, $1.01; No. 3, 91c.

CHICAGO.

Wheat—No. 2, 88⅝c; No. 3, 78c; May 89⅞@90c; June, 90⅞@91⅛c.
Receipts, 64,559 bushels; shipments, 156,-832 bushels.
Corn—May 33⅜@33c; June, 35@35½c.
Receipts, 98,519 bushels; shipments, 302,325 bushels.
Oats—May, 24⅛c; June, 25c.
Rye—April, 47c; May, 48c.
Barley—No. 2, 67; No. 3, 44c.
Pork—May, $945@9.52½; June, $9.55@9.67½.
Lard—May, $6.00@6.05; June, $6.07½@6.12½.
Hogs—$3.20@3.74; receipts, 5,000.

MILWAUKEE.

Wheat—Hard, 99¼c; No. 1, 94¼c; No. 2, 88⅝c; No. 3, 76½c; No. 4, 72 @ 73c; rejected, 67c; May 88⅞ @89½c; June, 90⅞@90⅛.
Receipts, 33,690 shipments, 46,117 bushels.

MINNEAPOLIS.

Wheat—No. 1, 88; No. 2, 80c; No. 3, 68c; No. 4, 60.
Corn—No. 2, 30@34c.
Oats—No. 1, 30@31c; No. 2, 27@29c.

NEW YORK, CLOSING.

Wheat—Inactive and firm.

CHICAGO, CLOSING.

Wheat—May, 89⅝c; June, 91.
Corn—33⅛c May; 35 June.
Pork—$9.52½ May; $9.62½ June.

MILWAUKEE, CLOSING.

Wheat—89⅛c May; 91c June.

## CONGRESSIONAL.

[The following is a synopsis of the more important proceedings yesterday.—ED.]

SENATE.

Mr. Windom asked the democrats if the United States had a right to punish armed men who came to the polls for the expressed and avowed purpose of preventing free exercise of the right of suffrage at an election for members of congress. Eaton replied for the democrats that no law had been passed to allow it, and he would never ask for such a law. A resolution declaring that no union soldier should be removed except for cause, and that no confederate soldier should take the place of a union soldier, was defeated by a party vote. Mr. Edmunds proposed an amendment which recognized the validity of providing by law for the presence of an armed power of the United States to repress violence at the polls, either at federal or state elections. This amendment was laid on the table. Falling to pass any amendments, the bill was passed by a strict party vote. When the enrolled bill was brought in, Thurman, as president pro tem, applied his signature below that of Randall, and the bill was conveyed to the executive mansion to await the president's approval.

HOUSE.

Consideration of the legislative appropriation bill was continued. Mr. Thomas characterized the proposed repeal as a conspiracy to secure a democratic majority at the next election at all hazards. Mr. Hooker thought that instead of it being a question of keeping away troops from the polls, it was a question as to whether or not the southern people were liable to be indicted for murder and arson. Springer quoted the English house as authority that the house has the sole right to determine on a supply bill. Ewing closed the debate on the democratic side, and said that republicans had seized upon the pending legislation as a protest for the inauguration of the presidential campaign on an issue of sectional hate and distrust. He then proceeded to argue upon the unconstitutionality of the election laws, when the house adjourned.

### IMMUNITY.

[Special to the Journal.]

BOSTON, April 26.—In the supreme court the jury in the case of George W. Frost against the New York and New England railroad company, has rendered a verdict of $2,000 for the plaintiff.



## BY TELEGRAPH.

### Will the President Veto the Army Bill?

### Russian Political Prisoners Sent to Jail.

### French and English Men-of-War On Short Notice.

### A Methodist Minister Turns Catholic.

### The Bank of France Shows an Increase.

### WHISKEY CASES.

[Special to the Journal.]

SPRINGFIELD, ILL. April 26.—The case of Mills and Steams of Boston who are indicted for complicity in the Pekin and Peoria whiskey ring, has been brought up. The case will be continued further on motion made by the district attorney to enable him to procure an important witness.

### HUSBAND ROBBED.

[Special to the Journal.]

HARRISBURG, Pa., April 27.—Thomas N. Oliver, husband of the "widow Oliver," has just been robbed in this city. He was en route for Cincinnati from Washington. The thieves were arrested.

### AMERICAN HOPES.

[Special to the Journal.]

LONDON, April 26.—Hanlan, the American sculler, is suffering from pains in his head. Hawdon his English antagonist is in excellent condition.

### PRESBYTERIANS.

[Special to the Journal.]

LONDON, April 25.— The Synod of the Presbpterian church of England has resolved to appoint Dr. Patton of Chicago to the chair of apologetical theology in the Presbyterian College of London.

### LEGISLATIVE BILL.

[Special to the Journal.]

WASHINGTON, April 26.—The debate on the legislative bill closed in the house at two o'clock to-day. Hoar made a most amusing speech and Garfield's amendment was rejected. This causes no surprise.

### TURNED CHTHOLIC.

[Special to the Journal.]

WASHINGTON, April 26.—Rev. A J. Faust a Methodist minister has been deposed by that church and has joined the Catholics. This causes much comment in church circles. His friends believe him honest.

### FRANCE'S BANK.

[Special to the Journal.]

PARIS, April 16.—The weekly statement of the bank of France, shows an increase in specie since last week of over 23,000,000 francs. This is regarded by financiers as a most favorable omen.

### EGYPTIAN ACTION.

[Special to the Journal.]

LONDON, April 26.—French and English men of war are ordered to be ready to start for Alexandria at a moment's notice. This decision causes intense feeling here, as it shows a disposition to back up the forthcoming diplomatic note.

### PEDESTRIANISM.

[Special to the Journal.]

LONDON, April 26.—At 2 o'clock the score in the walking match stood Brown 506, Hazard 477, Corkey 458, and Weston 430 miles. The race is now a surety for Brown.

### PRISON TROUBLES.

[Special to the Journal.]

INDIANAPOLIS, April 26.—The northern state prison directorship difficulty is in process of settlement in the civil court here. The case was forced to a trial, but is regarded as most unfortunate. The outcome is uncertain.

### ATTEMPTED MURDER.

[Special to the Journal.]

CHICAGO, April 26.—Gray has been indicted for attempted murder. The indictment is the cause of much excitement here, friends thinking that the evidence is not sufficiently strong to warrant any such proceeding; but the action gives satisfaction to the community at large.

### TURKISH ESTIMATE.

[Special to the Journal.]

LONDON, April 26.—The porte estimates that 200,000 men are necessary for the successful occupation of Roumelia, but this estimate is thought to be too large here.

### TRIAL OF REGICIDES.

[Special to the Journal.]

ST. PETERSBURG, April 26.—The government proposes to approach the other powers with proposals for the establishment of an international court for the trial of regicides.

### ARMY BILL.

[Special to the Journal.]

WASHINGTON, April 26.—The army bill has reached the president, and his intentions towards it are unknown. Great curiosity prevails. His friends expect a veto.

### POLITICAL PRISONERS.

[Special to the Journal.]

BERLIN, April 26.—Thousands of political prisoners are being sent from St. Petersburg to the prisons in the center and west end of the Russian empire. Most of them are arrested on suspicion.

# 1880~1889

# The Tribune.

VOL. XIV MINNEAPOLIS, MINNESOTA, WEDNESDAY MORNING, MARCH 2, 1881. NO. 290




## THE NEWS IN BRIEF.

### THE WEATHER.

The following shows the temperature at the hours named, as indicated by the thermometer at the drug store of Gray & Hoffin, 110 Washington avenue south:
[illegible]
* Indicates above zero; - below zero.

### Indications for To-Day.

For the upper Mississippi and lower Missouri valleys: Cloudy or partly cloudy weather with occasional snows, northwesterly winds, rising barometer preceded in the southeastern portion by southeast [illegible] winds and falling barometer, lower temperature in latter, stationary or higher temperature in first district.

### THE MARKETS.

The Minneapolis produce market is without a single feature of special interest. Of most articles the receipts are reduced, to the minimum and of course trade is limited. In some instances prices are temporarily advanced above the normal value as is the case with eggs, but a few days of good weather will remedy such inequalities. Wheat rules firm at 92c for No. 1; 80c for No. 2; 74c for No. 3. Choice hard wheat, suitable for seed, brings 10c above these quotations if delivered at the mills. Flour, steady; baker's, $4.50@5.25; fancy, $6.50@7.25. Other millstuff, firm; bran, $9.00@9.50; coarse grain, scarce. Fine butter, unchanged; choice creamery, 20@25c; dairy, 20@23c; roll, 14@18c. Eggs sold to-day at 25@28c, owing to the scarcity. Dressed hogs, 7@7¼c for good to choice lots, fresh killed. Provisions, weak. Mess pork, 25c lower; $15.50@15.75. Hides, steady; green salted, 8@8½c. Lumber rules firm, but no active movement is noted.

### IN GENERAL.

Gov. Washburn is rapidly recovering.

Ex-Governor Bradford, of Maryland, is dead.

The boiler-makers of Chicago struck yesterday for higher wages.

The Chicago House, at Sioux City, burned yesterday. Loss, $5,000.

As finally passed, the river and harbor bill appropriates $11,141,800.

The Gardner House, Chicago, has been sold to Cleveland parties for a quarter of a million dollars.

The deficiency bill, the last of the general appropriation bills, was reported to the house yesterday.

The appropriation bills passed and awaiting final action, appropriate in the aggregate $191,280,186.

The river and harbor bill as finally passed carried with it all the Minnesota items added by the senate committee.

The public debt was decreased $11,843,155 in February. A pretty good record for the closing month of the outgoing administration.

Secretary Sherman informed his subordinates that his administration would close Thursday, that he might take his seat in the senate on Friday.

During the existence of the present administration the public debt has been decreased $208,824,730, and the annual interest charge $17,537,708.

The senate yesterday discharged its foreign relations committee from further consideration of all bills and resolutions relating to inter-oceanic transit.

Among the house bills passed by the senate yesterday was that to open a portion of the Fort Ridgely military reservation to homestead and timber-culture entry.

The "arms bill," or the bill authorizing search for deadly weapons in private houses and elsewhere in Great Britain, was introduced and passed in the house yesterday.

President and Mrs. Hayes will leave Washington Saturday evening for Cleveland, where they will remain a few days, go thence to Columbus and and from there to Fremont.

Detailed accounts of the battle in Transvaal show that the English were fairly beaten, and that the fight ended in a rout. The most moderate estimates place the British losses at 300 killed and wounded.

The house yesterday, by a vote of yeas 98, nays 145, refused to consider the apportionment bill. This vote would seem to indicate the purpose of the house not to further consider that measure at this session.

At Detroit yesterday the prosecution rested, and Tobias Ochsner was called as the first witness for the defense. According to his own statement he made no heroic effort to save his wife and babes from their awful fate.

Mr. E. P. Smith, member of the Chicago board of trade, on retiring Sunday night placed a roll of bills containing $2,000, with his diamond pin, in his pillow-case. During the night he was chloroformed and robbed.

### Snow in Michigan.

Special Telegram to The Tribune.

GRAND RAPIDS, March 1.—The snow-storms in this section have been frequent, and a foot of snow has fallen during the past week. Railroads have been blockaded, and in some instances trains have been abandoned. The great depth of snow in the woods has been a serious drawback to lumbering operations, as men and teams have been unable to accomplish as much as they otherwise would.

### Gov. Washburn.

Special Telegram to The Tribune.

LA CROSSE, Wis., March 1.—Gov. Washburn is much better to-day, and will soon be able to resume his attention to business. An impression seems to prevail that Gov. Washburn's illness is such that he could not go to Washington if elected senator, but the facts do not justify such an opinion. He is rapidly recovering, and has long been beyond danger.

### Minnesota Creditors at Milwaukee.

Special Telegram to The Tribune.

MILWAUKEE, March 1.—The prospect that the state of Minnesota will come up to the scratch and pay its repudiated bonds causes considerable rejoicing in Milwaukee. Daniel Wells, jr., owns these bonds to the amount of $70,000; O. D. Nash $18,000, and Selah Chamberlain $1,000,000.

### Freight-House and Car-Shops at Dubuque.

Special Telegram to The Tribune.

DUBUQUE, Ia., March 1.—This city has voted to ratify the action of the city council in donating a tract of land valued at $40,000 to the Chicago Milwaukee & St. Paul Railroad for a depot, freight-house and car-shops.

### Sale of a Hotel.

Special Telegram to The Tribune.

CHICAGO, March 1.—The Gardner House, in this city, has been bought by Cobb & Bradley, of Cleveland, for a quarter of a million dollars.

### Hotel Burned at Sioux City.

Special Telegram to The Tribune.

SIOUX CITY, March 1.—The Chicago House burned this morning. Loss $5,000; insured in three Hartford companies for half the value.

## IN ASHES.

The State Capitol in St. Paul Burned Last Evening.

The Structure Totally Destroyed, with Many Valuable Records.

Over Eleven Thousand Books of the State Library Burned.

The Valuable Collection of the Academy of Sciences Lost.

The Building Valued at $80,000—Other Losses Beyond Estimation.

Narrow Escape from a Far More Terrible Disaster.

Both Bodies in Session when the Fire Broke Out.

Scenes of Great Excitement—Members Escaping by Windows.

Cause of the Fire Unknown—Hints at Incendiarism.

An Extra Session Made Necessary—Scenes and Incidents.

Arrangements for the Meeting of the Two Houses To-day.

### A CINDERED CAPITOL.

Special Telegram to The Tribune.

ST. PAUL, March 1.—The burning of the state capitol building last evening, upon the very eve of the close of the legislative session, is a misfortune the extent of which cannot at this time be fully appreciated. The calamity is so sudden a one, and the excitement which followed the escape of at least 300 people by a single stairway, from a building suddenly, mysteriously and almost entirely enveloped in flames, is so intense that the coolest reporter cannot measure the calamity.

THE FIRE BROKE OUT

at about a quarter past 9 o'clock. Both branches of the legislature were busy with the immense amount of work which had accumulated, and the galleries and lobbies were crowded with an unusually large number of people. The senate was busily grinding away at house bills, and had almost completed that order, and the attendance in that branch was large in anticipation of reaching the bond bill, the amendments to which had to be concurred in by that branch. With a suddenness which is beyond description, and almost beyond appreciation, the members of both branches were apprised of the fact that

THE BUILDING WAS ON FIRE;

that the flames threatened to shut off escape by the only stairway with which the building is supplied, and that an appalling calamity stared at the lowest estimate 300 people in the face. The scene in the senate, where THE TRIBUNE reporter was on duty, was an exciting one, and not soon to be forgotten. The lieutenant-governor was in the chair, and the secretary calling bills upon their third reading, the sawdust memorial just having been reached. The senators were variously occupied in their seats, or lounging about in the smoking-room, when some one burst into the room and shouted "fire!" and

A PERFECT PANDEMONIUM OF SHOUTS

followed. The alarm needed no further proof than was apparent to every person in the room. Through the windows at the back of the gallery it was evident that a great sheet of flame held possession of the hallway or corridor into which the main and only stairway leads. There was a grand rush for the doors, the lieutenant-governor, with admirable coolness, attempting to allay the excitement, which only rose the higher as a body of senators attempted to escape by the door, only to be

BEATEN BACK BY FLAME,

and a cloud of black smoke that threatened to shut off that escape. Brave men blanched with fear. A thousand thoughts rushed through excited minds, and the distance from the windows to the ground was measured with anxious eyes. "Shut the doors!" "Shut the doors!" "Don't make a draft!" "Act like men!" yelled the excited crowd, who rushed about the room measuring every possible mode of escape. "Some one should

MOVE TO ADJOURN,"

shouted the secretary, and Senator Crooks made the motion, which was put and responded to with an unanimity of sentiment not usually encountered. The doors were closed, but a second attempt revealed the fact that the cloud of smoke had raised somehow, and a pell-mell dash was made for the stairs, down which the members of the house and the spectators in the gallery were already passing. Meanwhile some of the occupants of the senate chamber, among them Senators Pillsbury, Officer, Miller, Assistant Clerk Wedge and The Globe and TRIBUNE reporters had escaped by the window to the veranda at the east end of the building, where they were engaged in

YELLING LUSTILY

for ladders and ropes. The escape was none too soon, for before the last person had left the room a great cloud of flame enveloped the dome of the building, had spread through the tinder-box mansard-roof and great cinders were dropping through the ventilator into the center of the senate chamber, where a fire was kindled in the carpet. A few of the senators had the presence of mind to save their effects, nearly all of them bundled into their wraps, and the clerks with admirable coolness and presence of mind

SECURED ALL THEIR RECORDS,

the bills in the pigeon-holes of their desks and everything of value upon which they could lay their hands. They were the last to leave the room, carrying with them the uncompleted legislation, the fruit of months of consideration. Several intrepid members returned by the window later and secured other of their effects, but less than three minutes had elapsed before all the upper portion of the building was enveloped in flames and the structure was doomed.

THE SCENE IN THE HOUSE

was even more exciting. The first premonition of danger was the dropping of fire into the gallery, a shout from the resort of the *vox populi* of Fire! and the bursting into the room of a cloud of black, sickening and forbidding smoke. Two hundred persons rose as one individual, Mr. Rice, who was in the chair, deserting his seat unceremoniously. Those who first attempted it, believed escape by the long narrow hall, more than one hundred feet in length, presented to them what appeared to be

AN INSURMOUNTABLE BARRIER.

Mr. Denny, with more coolness than some others, jumped to the speaker's desk and cautioned the crowd to go, but to do it with discretion and coolness; that the passage was open; but an unknown influence suddenly, and for a brief interval, cleared the hall of smoke, and the mass of humanity, among whom were a number of ladies, poured down the hall an excited, eager and unmanageable crowd. Miraculously no one was hurt, and every person escaped, though more than one occupant of the room counted the cost of a leap for life through the window, and philosophically made up his mind that a great danger was to be met. The scene was

TRAGIC AND HUMOROUS,

and never to be forgotten by the eye-witnesses of it. Men, usually calm, dashed wildly about the room, a thousand terrible fancies flashing through their brains. Only one member, Mr. Schmidt, of Washington county, concluded to jump rather than brave an uncertain battle with the flames, and dropped from one of the windows into a snowbank, with only a few unimportant bruises. The clerks, appreciating their responsibility, gathered together the records and carried them to place of safety. Speaker Fletcher, with an eye to the danger that threatened the younger pages, took them

UNDER HIS PERSONAL CARE,

and dragged them with him out of the building. The spectacle which met the eye of the crowd as they escaped into the free air of safety was a building, the roof of which was almost entirely enveloped in flames, and the dome of which was a great beacon of light, spreading a lurid glare over the entire city.

THE ORIGIN OF THE FIRE

is wrapped in some mystery. There were no premonitory evidences of the fire. When it was first discovered it seemed to have gained full sway throughout the range of the entire French roof. It seemed to have gained more headway in the dome of the building, and is variously ascribed to the explosion of gas in that part of the building and to an incendiary. The janitors hold to the latter theory. There was no gas lit or lights of any kind in the garrets, which are apparently nearly ten feet in heighth in the center, and extending over the entire building, a structure nearly 300 feet in length, and of a width ranging from 50 to 150 feet. Half an hour had not elapsed before the whole second story was enveloped.

THE LOSS.

The loss is beyond estimation. The structure was worth not less than $80,000, and contained the accumulation of years, which cannot be replaced. On the first or ground floor the valuables were placed in the vaults or removed from the building, the carpets in some of the rooms even being removed. The most serious loss, undoubtedly, is the state library, which contained 12,580 volumes, many of which cannot be replaced. Less than 1,000 of the entire number were saved. The money value of the library was probably $75,000, but it does not express the real value of the property. The treasury vault contained $2,190,000 of state and Missouri bonds, besides other valuable property, and towards this receptacle the

FIRST STREAMS WERE TURNED

and were not permitted to cease. The state's property is probably safe. The insurance department across the hall was supplied with a vault, and the secretary of state's room and the auditor's department, with a like safe depository, and nearly all other departments with safes. Such property as could be placed in these receptacles is probably safe, but as soon as it was evident that the lower floor could be entered with safety a steady stream of men were engaging in carring away the contents of the building. The records of the supreme court clerk's office were carried out, and when last seen by THE TRIBUNE reporter were dumped on the snow in front of the burning building. Secretary Williams, of

THE HISTORICAL SOCIETY,

took personal supervision of the removal of the valuable and not-to-be replaced articles in his department, which were carried to the Universalist church, opposite the capitol. Nearly everything not securely deposited in the vault was removed. The Academy of Sciences, which occupied a room in the basement beyond that of the Historical Society, did not fare so well. In the confusion the key to the room was lost, and before the door could be broken open the smoke drove back the workers. A very valuable collection of natural curiosities is therefore lost. The reports of the departments, the accumulation of years in the state department, were stored in the basement also, and

ARE ALL DESTROYED,

and so far as could be learned many valuable documents in the adjutant-general's office. The state officials have confidence in their respective vaults preserving the essential documents in their stands, so that the record of government may be maintained without serious interruption. But the disaster precipitates

AN EXTRA SESSION

of the legislature, although steps were taken promptly during the evening by the mayor and lieutenant-governor and speaker for the legislature to resume its session this morning in the new market building, which will at once be placed in readiness for occupancy. The senate is to meet this morning in the municipal court room in that structure, and the house of representatives in another apartment, known as Market Hall. The various departments of state are to be distributed throughout the first floors, in the stalls, fully separated by glass partitions. It is a fortunate fact that a building so well fitted for the purpose created by the necessity is not yet occupied, and is so near completion. The clerks of the two branches were busily engaged last evening in

STRAIGHTENING OUT THEIR RECORDS,

preparatory to the resumption of business to-day, but it is not anticipated that much will be accomplished, with only another working-day and business in a chaotic condition. There is but one opinion and that is that the government will promptly call an extra session, that provision may be made for temporary quarters for the state departments, and for rebuilding the present structure or some new one. The fire department battled bravely with the flames, but the streams were not many in number nor of notable power. They made no impression whatever, apparently, on the flames, which licked up the combustible interior of the building, leaving the stark walls at 2 o'clock this morning lit up with the embers of the fire. Crowds of people assembled during the progress of the fire. Later in the evening the persons who were in the building when the fire broke out, principally excited solons, gathered in groups and recited their narrow escapes and incidents of

A MEMORABLE NIGHT,

which threatened to be crowded with horror and tragic events. "I had made up my mind," said Col. L. L. Baxter, "that my time had come, and said as much to Mr. Dunn. I've been in tight places before, but never in one that seemed to threaten so sure a fate as that for a few minutes." The eight or ten ladies in the hall of the house of representatives, were almost frantic in their fear and were calmed with difficulty. Senator Hinds promptly took into his care the single lady in the senate chamber, who was engaged in conversation with him when the alarm was first given, and led her in safety out of the building. They were among the first to brave the flames in the hallway.

A number of the members in their haste to escape from the building left their hats and coats, and though some of them were searching for the lost garments among a number taken out by the ladder brigade, numbers will measure their chief loss in this direction. The only insurance on any of the property that has been discovered is that of $10,000 in the London, Liverpool & Globe, placed against the policy of the state upon the library. It will be but

A DROP IN THE BUCKET

in replacing the property. It has been for years, as was developed at the time of the fire at St. Peter, the theory that the state can best afford to insure its own property. The subject of placing insurance on the capitol building was broached recently in one of the legislative committees, but did not meet with favor or approval. Unity church, the Lutheran church, Judge Palmer's residence and other contiguous buildings were made storehouses during the early evening, but at this writing, 1 o'clock, a force of men are engaged in removing the department records and furniture into the market house, where some of the officials expect to be prepared for business at the regular hour. The halls were being made in readiness for the assembling of the two branches of the legislature at 10 o'clock. Among the books discovered to have been saved from the library are a set of old English reports, among the most valuable in the collection.

A HEROIC EFFORT

was made by Chas. Chappel, the one-armed janitor of the capitol building, to save more of this collection, the value of which he was quick to appreciate, and he lingered in the room until a burning timber fell, striking him on the head. He left then, but carried under his single arm all the books he could conveniently and successfully grasp. Gov. Pillsbury who was not in the city last evening, but he had a conversation by telephone with Mayor Dawson, of this city, who promptly tendered the market house, and whom he desired to proceed and make whatever arrangement for the resumption of business as his judgment and generosity dictated. For some unaccountable reason the bond bill was

LINKED WITH THE HINTS AT INCENDIARISM,

but the theory is thoroughly preposterous. Had any designing person desired to wipe out at this stage that portion of the minutes the work could have been more thoroughly accomplished after the bodies had adjourned for the night. But Secretary Jennison, appreciating the importance of that bill, made it the object of his special attention in his effort to save. The most reasonable theory of the fire is that some careless person dropped in the space between the ceiling and dome

A LIGHTED CIGAR,

that started a fire among the cobwebbed rafters of the old and thoroughly seasoned tinder-box. The place is not accessible to the general public, and Jefferson Davis Hudson, the very much eulogized flag-raiser, elected through the efforts of W. D. Rice, has been almost the only person to pass through that part of the building to the dome. He was up there, it is stated, about an hour before the fire broke out, and alleges that he discovered no evidence of fire, and professes total ignorance of its cause. The rapidity of its spread is one of the mysterious features of the disaster, and had there been an explosion, of which there was no evidence, the conflagration might be attributed to escaping gas accumulating in that unventilated part of the building, and igniting; but the generally-accepted theory is that the fire was

INCENDIARY IN CHARACTER,

and near as can be stated was ignited over the senate chamber, if it was not set in more than one place, with what intent beyond cussedness no person can say. Access to the attic and dome was through the gallery of the senate chamber.

Among the valuables known to have been lost was the large painting, belonging to Mrs. Loomans, of St. Anthony Falls in 1821, which had been deposited in the senate chamber. The picture of Gen. Sherman, also in that part of the building, was burned. The life-size picture of Gen. Thomas that hung in the house of representatives was saved. Mrs. Loomans's picture was a rare one, and cannot be replaced.

At 2 o'clock this morning the fire is simply smouldering, and a force of men is engaged in establishing the departments of state in the market house.

# Daily Minnesota Tribune.

VOL. XVII. MINNEAPOLIS, FRIDAY, MAY 25, 1883. NO. 3




## BROOKLYN'S BRIDGE.

PRESENTED TO THE TWIN CITIES YESTERDAY.

**Crowded Streets, Gaily-Decked Buildings, Imposing Military Array, Presence of Prominent People and Great Enthusiasm Mark the Event—A General Holiday—Completion of One of the Largest, Most Perfect and Most Costly Structures in the World.**

NEW YORK, May 24.—Today was a gala day in Brooklyn. Throughout the city there appeared to be a general surrender of business to sight seeing and to celebration. The main business avenues, the heights, and many streets clear out into the suburbs are decked most gaily with flags, bunting and flowers for the bridal with the city over the river. Public buildings, private houses, street cars, wagons and trucks fly the colors of all nations in honour of the opening of the big bridge. On every hand preparations are being made for the illumination tonight. Great satisfaction is expressed among the people of Brooklyn at the completion of the work from which so much is expected for their city. Venders of bridge souvenirs were about in hundreds, and found ready sale for their wares. Enterprising merchants took the opportunity of advertising their wares on the backs of pictures of the Brooklyn bridge. Fulton street from the farthest end to the river front, is gay with colors. The decoration of the Academy of Music occupies a small army of men. It is being prepared for the reception tonight. All through Columbia Heights and the streets opening into that fashionable neighborhood decoration is very general, and the effect handsome. The houses of

COL. ROEBLING,

chief engineer of the bridge, and Mayor Lowe of Brooklyn are decked with flowers and bunting, and the coat-of-arms of New York and Brooklyn. The invalid engineer will receive the President and mayor, and in the evening, for a brief hour, the public. The colonel is feeling better today, but is too weak to leave his house and share in the ceremonies at large. From the towers of the great bridge national flags wave, and the span across the river is dotted with flags from one end to the other. From early morning crowds began to gather at the end where the speech making takes place. In the harbor flags flew from all shipping. The war vessels Tennessee, Vandelia, Kearsarge and Yantic lie in a row off Governor's island, floating the national colors. The navy yards, and all ships along the New York and Brooklyn water front are decked with bunting. In New York business is partly suspended. Most of the exchanges closed at noon, and many business places suspended work for the afternoon. Flags flew from municipal and other buildings in City Hall Park, and from business places. Along Broadway and other streets, and from many private residences, the houses along the route of the procession are decked with colors. At the New York end of the bridge workmen have been busy all morning putting

THE FINISHING TOUCHES

to the decorations. The picket fence in front of the bridge has been removed and a strong force of police guards the approaches. Crowds began to gather early and waited with great patience the arrival of the procession and the beginning of the ceremonies. Nearly all vehicles except street cars are prevented from passing below streets near the bridge and at noon the street cars were stopped.

THE SEVENTH REGIMENT

National Guards state of New York, Col. Emmons Clark, commanding, detailed as the military escort for the occasion, assembled at the armory this morning in full uniform. A guard of 20 was detailed to march on either side of the President's carriage. The command marched down Park and Fifth avenue to the Fifth Avenue Hotel, the President's quarters, where it was drawn up on the sidewalk. The route was lined with people. On Madison Square it was estimated that 10,000 people were gathered. The President and invited guests occupied carriages which were drawn up in line on the south side of the hotel. In the first carriage were President Arthur and Mayor Edson. In other carriages were Secretaries Freelinghuysen and Folger, Postmaster-General Gresham, Secretary Chandler, Atty.-Gen. Brewster, Marshal McMichael of the District of Columbia, Allen Arthur, T. J. Phillips, Surrogate Rollins, Gov. Cleveland, Gov. Ludlow of New Jersey, Gov. Fairbanks of Vermont, Gens. Stryker and Slocum, Gov. Littlefield of Rhode Island, the staff of Gov. Cleveland, Gen. Carr and staff, Collector Robertson, Congressman Cox, Hon. Wm. Windom and Speaker Keifer, state senators and the Peruvian minister. A committee representing the Brooklyn bridge trustees escorted the President and cabinet to the carriages. When the carriages passed 7th regiment the command presented arms. The military then broke into column and marched down Fifth avenue and Broadway to City Hall Park, where the members of common council received the President and cabinet.

THE PROCESSION

of Brooklyn officials and trustees, escorted by the 23rd regiment, arrived at the station at 1 o'clock. The regiment passed up on the anchorage, where it took up its position. Mrs. Roebling, wife of the invalid chief engineer, and her party, arrived afterward in 25 carriages, and at 1:30 P. M. Bishop Littlejohn and his assistants in their robes. Way was made for them with great difficulty, through the crowd that already filled every foot of space in the station. Hundreds turned away without getting seats. A salute announcing that the priests had arrived at the New York tower was fired by war vessels in the harbor and forts. At 2:16 P. M. the yards of the men-of-war were manned, and 15 minutes later cannonading from Fort Green and the navy yards announced the arrival of the procession at Brooklyn tower, where Mayor Lowe received it. On account of the great crowd much difficulty was experienced by the mayor and officials in obtaining passage way to the platform. At the conclusion of prayer by Bishop Littlejohn, J. S. F. Stranahan, who presided, introduced the acting president of the board of trustees, who finally presented the bridge to the people of New York and Brooklyn, through their respective mayors, and each made a speech of acceptance. Congressman Hewitt also made an address, and Rev. Dr. Storrs delivered the oration. Levy succeeded in giving on his cornet the "Star Spangled Banner," "Hail Columbia" and "Yankee Doodle."

BIG FRAUDS.

[Special Telegram to the Tribune.]

HISTORY OF TRANSACTIONS.

NEW YORK, May 24.—Among the most interesting features connected with the history of the bridge is the record of fraud in the financial management. The story of the frauds is too long to repeat, but a specimen may be exhibited. Kingsley, of Brooklyn, was a prime mover in the affair and his supporters were Boss Tweed and Henry C. Murphy. It was chiefly through Tweed's unblushing bribery and that of New York aldermen that they voted to authorize the controller to issue bonds to the amount of $15,500,000 for the benefit of the bridge. In the next place the management made an arrangement between the board of directors and Kingsley by which Kingsley was to receive a standing commission of 15 per cent. on all purchases made for the bridge. By a series of investigations it was discovered that the total expenditure up to September, 1882, for all materials of which the bridge was composed, came inside of $4,000,000—the difference between this amount and $15,500,000 being the balance which the taxpayers of New York and Brooklyn needlessly invested in the structure. It further appeared that $2,118,136 had been paid for granite to four or five firms, all of them more or less directly connected with the original authors of the enterprise, and nearly all contracts being let to bidders whose offers were in excess of those rejected.

THROUGH THIS FAVORITISM

in throwing out the lowest bids, $13,465, was wasted. The same state of affairs reigned in the management of contracts for iron, wire and steel cables, with the variation that the contracts were let to the same parties under different names. Masonry materials, principally furnished by John Roach & Son, amounted to $514,967, forming a part of $2,000,000 paid out for work. So it goes to the end of the book, speculations in timber, overcharges in limestone contracts, jobbing in bonds, mysteries in pay rolls, expensive figure heads, unconsidered trifles of a few thousand dollars, etc. The office furniture cost $9000, and would be dear at $500. The general account was a marvel of ingenuity, and it was said at one time that everyone who ever had anything to do with the Brooklyn bridge building "put in his thumb and pulled out a plum, denying um."

THE ENGINEERS.

COL. ROEBLING.

Col. Roebling, chief engineer of this great structure, is the son of the late John A. Roebling, the author of the first plans of the Brooklyn bridge, and who met his death by an accident. He was born in Butler county, Pa., in 1831, and graduated from the Troy Polytechnic Institute in 1857. He aided his father in the construction of the Allegheny suspension bridge, and on the outbreak of the war served with distinction in the 6th New York artillery, gaining three brevets for gallant conduct. He resigned in January, 1865, to assist his father on the Cincinnati and Covington bridge. Subsequently he spent a year in Europe studying pneumatic foundations and steel manufacture, and to his careful supervision and superior engineering skill, the successful completion of the East river bridge is largely attributable.

COL. W. H. PAINE,

assistant engineer, owing to the illness of his chief, has practically had charge of the work. He is a native of New Hampshire but came as a lad to Wisconsin and grew up to manhood in Sheyboygan. He had only a common school education, but taught himself engineering, having a remarkable aptitude for mathematics and great ingenuity as an inventor. A substitute for the old-fashioned surveyor's chain, now in general use, is his invention. Early after the beginning of the work on the Brooklyn bridge he made some important improvements in the mode of manufacturing wire, by which its strength and durability are much increased. He was also the inventor, if we mistake not, of the so-called grip cars first used in San Francisco, and now in use in Chicago. Early in the war he became attached to the engineer corps of the army of the Potomac, and was on the staff of all its commanders from Bull's Run to Appomatox, rendering invaluable service by his skill, courage and fidelity. He surveyed the country in advance of the army lines, and most of the maps in such works as Swinton's "History of the Army of the Potomac," Greeley's "American Conflict," etc., are drawn by him. At the close of the war he was offered a permanent position in the engineer corps of the regular army, but declined it and has since resided in New York.

TOLL TO BE CHARGED.

The following schedule of fares has been agreed upon by the board of trustees

| | Ct |
|---|---|
| Foot passengers | 1 |
| Car fare | 5 |
| Horse and man | 5 |
| Horse and vehicle | 10 |
| Two horses and vehicle | 20 |
| Every horse beyond two | 5 |
| Neat cattle, each | 5 |
| Sheep and hogs, each | 2 |

A BOLD ROBBERY.

**An Express Messenger in Cleveland Robbed of $10,000—Murdered for Money—The Day's Crimes.**

CLEVELAND, O., May 24.—The United States Express Company's money carrier, Alexander Granger, received sundry packages of money and other valuables from the east-bound Lake Shore train at the Union depot this morning, and put them in a buggy standing outside. Somebody from the ice room called to him, and no one being in sight he stepped a little way from the vehicle to ascertain who called. On returning, he drove to the express company's main office and there discovered that two bags, similar to the company's pouches, but filled with brown paper, had been substituted for the two containing the money. It is supposed the robbery had been carefully planned by experts and executed at a moment when the messenger's attention was diverted. The missing pouches are said to contain in the neighborhood of $15,000, in 30 packages, of remittance from railroad stations on the Lake Shore road between Chicago and Toledo to headquarters. The amount cannot be definitely known for some days. Much of the remittances are thought to be in bank checks and certificates of deposits. Andrew Leland of the Lake Shore thinks the railroad remittances in the pouches exceed $10,000 in money, though there might not be more than $2000. No clue yet to the robbers.

Deliberately Shot.

ST. LOUIS, May 24.—The body of a man named W. L. Howard, with four bullet holes in it, was found in the woods near Nevada, Mo., last Sunday. Yesterday a dissolute character, known as Bill Fox, was arrested on suspicion of having committed the deed, and on being closely pressed acknowledged the act. His story shows that he deliberately lured Howard into the woods, shot him in cold blood, and then robbed the body of $40. It is plainly evident that murder was committed solely for plunder. Fox was indicted and will have a speedy trial. Howard is highly connected.

Captain Rand and mate of the Thomas Pender of Philadelphia, have been convicted of violating the neutrality laws by carrying arms and immigrants to Hayti.

## THE TORNADO'S WORK

A CYCLONE IN HOWELL COUNTY, MISSOURI.

**The Town of Moody Entirely Destroyed and the Surrounding Country Laid Waste—A Boiler Explosion at Bismarck Kills Three Men—Destructive Fires at Chicago and Fond du Lac.**

ST. LOUIS, May 24.—Information is just received that a heavy wind and rain storm swept through Howell county, Mo., last Friday and Saturday, doing very great damage to farms and other property. Part of Howell valley is flooded. Bridges and embankments on the Kansas City, Springfield & Memphis railroad are swept away or damaged, delaying trains several days. The little town of Moody is destroyed, every house in it being blown down. McKelsey was severely injured and several others badly hurt. Farms in that vicinity also suffered very severely. The houses and outbuildings of H. Hall, M. A. Greenstreet, G. W. Trow and others were blown down and fences scattered over the country. Information also comes from Maries county that the tornado swept entirely across it, making a path 100 yards wide, leveling forests, and sweeping the ground of everything in its way. The largest farm in the county, that of James Crissen, which is three miles long, lost all its buildings, and the family barely saved their lives by rushing into the cellar of the milkhouse. A horse was picked up and carried a quarter of a mile. The houses and barns of John Wilder, Jack Nelson and John Hughes were destroyed. Mrs. Hughes' arm was broken. Farms on Maries creek were unfenced but the houses spared. A turtle 11 inches in diameter was scooped out of the creek and dropped in Vienna, three miles distant. The farms of Gillespie and Mrs. Norris were swept clean of everything. In Miller county the storm was also very severe. A dozen farms in the neighborhood of Iberia were ruined and the school house torn to pieces.

A Terrible Boiler Explosion.

[Special Telegram to the Tribune.]

BISMARCK, Dak., May 24.—About 11 o'clock this morning a terrible explosion occurred of a large boiler at Bly & Grandberry's brickyard, resulting in the death of three men and seriously injuring four or five others. The engine house is a complete wreck, being blown to atoms. John Larsen, the engineer, and a carpenter named James Cullett were instantly killed. The body of Larson was carried over 200 feet over the top of sheds and thrown against a wood pile and was torn to shreds. The body of Cullett was also badly mangled and carried some distance by the force of the explosion. Charles Cullett, a son of James, lived about two hours after the accident. His body was badly crushed. Although several others are more or less severely hurt, their injuries will not prove fatal. The boiler was torn in a thousand pieces and scattered for yards around. The cause of the accident is not known, but it is supposed to be the carelessness of the engineer. The loss is not yet known, but will probably reach $6000. The yard had been but just opened. The accident casts a gloom over the entire city.

Tales of Distress.

PORT HURON, May 24.—Joe Smith, seaman of the barge William Raynor, which was towed in last night by tug Champion, says the storm stove a hole in the vessel on Sunday, and the steward had to cover it with canvas. The storm struck at 3 o'clock Sunday pouring off the sand beach. The steward of the Germania was saved by a tow line. Every sea went over 30 feet from crest to trough of the wave. The men worked the pumps 40 hours, as she was part full of water before the blow commenced. He stayed on board until two miles of Sanilac, when he got off in a yawl. Levy Andrus, a Port Huron cook, went overboard three times, but was saved. Charles Wheeler, a sailor on the barge Wyoming, which was towed in at 3 o'clock this morning, says he broke loose from the Germania tow on Monday morning. The storm struck 20 miles above Sand Beach. After the line parted he headed across the lake and lashed the wheel: then drifted sidewise to a point on the Canadian shore, where he anchored and laid until Thursday morning, about 20 miles above the light house. He shipped nothing but a full load, and the crew are all O K. They will pump out the barge here.

A Flour Mill in Flames.

[Special Telegram to the Tribune.]

FOND DU LAC, Wis., May 24.—At 1 o'clock tonight the West Branch flouring mill was totally destroyed by fire. The mill was located in the outside of the city and was owned by Boynton & Severy, the former being a Waupun capitalist. Both water and steam power was used and a run of stone. The mill was valued at $12,000, and the grain, flour, etc., burned, will make the total loss $15,000. There was only $5000 insurance, $2000 of which is in the Millers' Mutual of this state. The fire was discovered by a fisherman and started in the second or top story in some unaccountable manner. The mill was the oldest flouring mill in this section of the state, having been built 30 years ago by Mr. Seymour.

Fire in Chicago.

CHICAGO, May 24.—A fire is now in progress on Eighteenth and Canal streets. Three alarms were given and a large part of the fire department called to the scene. Definite particulars are not yet obtainable, but it is reported that the Wall House and planing mill of Louis Hutt are destroyed. The loss is estimated at $100,000.

National Railway Exposition.

CHICAGO, May 24.—The national exposition of railway appliances was thrown open to the public tonight. The opening exercises included prayer by Prof. David Swing, an address of welcome by Mayor Harrison, an address by Hon. Elihu B. Washburne, the introduction of veteran locomotive builders and engineers by Vice-President A. French, and closing with "God Save the Queen, Our Compliments to Victoria's Birthday." A large number of people thronged the building.

Virginia Election.

RICHMOND, May 24.—There were county elections throughout the state today. In many counties the contest between Readjusters and Democrats was quite spirited, but the returns tonight do not give sufficient data to base calculations as to losses or gains on either side.

Where Was Ben?

BOSTON, May 24.—The veto investigating committee made a report to the House, which divided on party lines. All the Republicans hold that the Governor was absent from the commonwealth from Feb. 28 to March 2.

# Daily Minnesota Tribune.

VOL. XVII. MINNEAPOLIS. TUESDAY, AUGUST 21. 1883. NO. 73




## THE NEWS IN BRIEF.

A religious riot is reported in Scotland.

Rat Portage had a $100,000 fire Sunday morning.

Secretary Folger has extended his trip to Lake Superior.

The famous Porter Rifles of Memphis are "doing" Chicago.

The trial of Frank James began yesterday at Gallatin, Mo.

At Alexandria there were 37 deaths on Sunday from cholera.

The province of Ontario was visited by a severe storm yesterday.

The Florida ship canal will be 137½ miles long and cost $46,000,000.

Arguments in the Hill investigation case are being filed by counsel.

Queen Victoria goes to Balmoral Friday. Her health is much improved.

Secretary Chandler is taking a cruise of indefinite length on the Talapoosa.

Striking operators all over the country are rapidly applying for reinstatement.

The result of second ballots in France, Sunday, shows additional Republican gains.

Dr. Marvin Green, president of the Western Union, has returned from his journey abroad.

Silas Merchant of Cleveland, O., has failed. Liabilities, about $100,000; assets, $150,000.

At the Pensacola navy yard eight cases of yellow fever and three deaths from the disease are reported.

The President was the first person to send a message over the Western Union line to Yellowstone Park.

Berlin was exercised yesterday over the christening of the second son of Prince William of Prussia.

The French ambassador left Pekin, China, in great haste, fearing expulsion if he remained until hostilities commenced.

Nine oil tanks, several stills and a large amount of valuable machinery were destroyed by fire at Franklin, Pa., yesterday.

Cetewayo wants Queen Victoria to make a full inquiry into the treatment he has received at the hands of her majesty's subjects.

Shaw, British missionary in Madagascar, who was imprisoned by the French there on the charge of concealing two Havas, has been released.

A heavy gale at Agate bay, Sunday morning, did considerable damage to shipping, and will cause considerable delay to harbor improvements.

The report in circulation Saturday that there was a crisis in the Egyptian cabinet, and Riaz Pasha would form a new ministry, proves to have been without foundation.

An Alexandria correspondent says if the British troops should be withdrawn from Egypt no European family would remain in the country a week after their departure.

Madrid newspapers are discussing the expediency of forming an alliance of Spain, Austria and Germany, in order to check the influence of French democracy in Spanish politics.

The estimate of leather in vats at the seven Maine tanneries belonging to W. F. Shaw & Bros., is 3000 tons, which, if finished and sold in market, would bring $125,000.

Prince Nikita, ruler of Montenegro, was received at Constantinople with high honors by the Sultan, who has conferred the imperial order of Osmania upon his princely visitor.

C. W. Clement, shoe manufacturer, recently failed with liabilities of a large amount in consequence of the suspension of Shaw & Bros., proposes to his creditors payment in merchandise of the indebtedness, mainly in long time notes at 3 per cent. interest.

### ARTHUR AND SHERIDAN.

**Notes From the Journey of the President Across the Continent—A Thoroughly Enjoyable Trip.**

CAMP TETON, Aug. 18, via Fort Washakie, Wyo., Aug. 20.—Promptly at 6:30 this morning we mounted our horses, not without longing, lingering looks behind, and rode away from Camp Arthur. Our course was in a westerly direction along the north side of the Gros Ventre river. The air was clear and bracing, and the day as fine as any with which we had been favored since we set out from Fort Washakie. The trail was beset with few of those difficulties with which our fortnights, trials in the wilderness has made us so familiar. Indeed, in the absence of timber, rocky side hills, steep ascents and pitches, the ride would have seemed somewhat monotonous, but for single features which actually glorified it. We had climbed to the summit of Long Hill, about five miles from Camp Arthur, when there suddenly burst upon our view the grandest sights we ever witnessed. Below us, covered with grass and flowers, was a lovely valley, many miles in extent, through which was winding its way the river on whose banks we had just encamped. Along the whole westerly edge of this valley, with no intervening foothills to obstruct the view toward the magnificent Teton mountains, their snowy summits piercing the air 8000 feet above the spot on which we stood in reverent admiration, and 14,000 feet above the level of the sea. It was the voice of every member of the party that that sight alone fully repaid all the prices of the march. We are encamped on the Teton basin, on the bank of the Gros Ventre. The locality, aside from the splendid views of mountains which it affords, is our least attractive camp. The river at this point has an excellent reputation as a trout stream, but the wind has been blowing at too many miles an hour to permit much success in angling. It has been powerful enough to break the ridge pole of our mess tent, but fortunately not beyond repair. We are all in excellent health and thoroughly enjoying the trip.

**Western Union Extension.**

NEW YORK, Aug. 20.—The Western Union line has been completed to Cinnabar, Montana, fifty miles south of Livingston, on the Northern Pacific railway, from which point messages to Hot Springs Hotel, Yellowstone Park, are delivered free by pony express. The President and party were first to use the lines.

Dr. Norvin Green, president of the Western Union company, is at his office today after several months' trip abroad. The doctor was warmly welcomed by the officers and employes of the company. The trip has been of great benefit to his health, which he declares is better than before for many years.

**Found Floating**

BALTIMORE, Aug. 20.—The body of Capt. Wm. T. Howell, assistant quartermaster of the United States army (retired), was found floating in the dock on Locust Point today. Sundry papers relating to business were found in his pocket.

## BURNING BENZINE.

**DISASTROUS OIL FIRE IN PENNSYLVANIA.**

**Nine Tanks, Several Stills and a Large Amount of Machinery Destroyed—Damage to Shipping in Agate Bay by a Gale—Heavy Fire at Rat Portage—Divers Disasters at Various Points.**

**AN OIL FIRE.**

GREAT DESTRUCTION.

FRANKLIN, Pa., Aug. 20.—A fire broke out in the still department of the Eclipse Lubricating Refinery last night, and before it was got under control destroyed a large part of the works. The fire started in a 1100-barrel benzine still, that exploded with great force, scattering the oil in all directions. The fire departments of both Oil City and Franklin worked for upward of six hours before they made any headway against the flames. Nine tanks, a number of stills, and a large amount of valuable machinery was lost. The larger part of the works was saved. No estimate can safely be put on the amount of damage as yet. The Eclipse was the largest lubricating refinery in the world, and the part destroyed will be immediately restored, four hundred men being now at work on the ruins. It belongs to the Standard Oil Company.

ANOTHER ONE.

OIL CITY, Pa., Aug. 20.—A Derrick special from Garfield, Warren county, says lightning struck the Kennedy Oil Company's warehouse and barrel tank at 4 o'clock this evening and 100 barrels of oil were destroyed.

**Big Blaze at Rat Portage.**

Special Telegram to the Tribune.

WINNIPEG, Aug. 20.—Word has just reached the city of a serious conflagration at Rat Portage. The Rainy River Lumber Company's lumber mill of which Hugh Sutherland is managing director, burned to the ground on Sunday morning at 2 o'clock. The fire is supposed to be the work of an incendiary. The loss is fully $100,000. The engine and boilers are the only salvage. Insurance, $30,000, divided among the following companies: Imperial Commercial, Union, London, Liverpool and Globe, Citizens, Phoenix of London, Queen, Western, British America, Phoenix of Brooklyn and Northern. About 300 men are out of employment. One million feet of lumber in the yard escaped. The mill was only in operation two months and was the finest mill in the North-west.

**Other Fires.**

DULUTH, Aug. 20.—About 2 o'clock yesterday morning a small two-story building on East Superior street, known as the English Club house, was burned. It was occupied as a saloon. The fire company was on hand and prevented a spread of flames.

KEENE, N. H., Aug. 20.—A fire this morning in the Cheshire House block burned the entire block of wooden stores attached to the hotel on Roxbury Street. Losses aggregate $25,000.

DENTON, N. J., Aug. 20.—A dispatch from Lambertville, says McDowell & Son's large paper mill at that place was almost entirely destroyed by fire yesterday morning. The loss will probably exceed $25,000. Insurance $10,000. Forty men are thrown out of employment.

RICHMOND, Me., Aug. 20.—The Lincoln house and stables, owned by J. L. Robinson, burned this morning with contents. Guests narrowly escaped. Several horses burned. Loss $10,000.

OSHKOSH, Aug. 20.—The sash, door and blind factory owned by Williamson, Libbey & Co., burned this evening. Loss $35,000; insurance $22,000. The factory was filled with stock. The fire originated in the mill and within a minute after the alarm was given was all in flames.

**SEVERE STORMS.**

DISASTERS IN AGATE BAY.

Special Telegram to the Tribune.

DULUTH, Minn., Aug. 20.—The strong northwest wind which was blowing Saturday night did considerable damage at Agate Bay, as that harbor has very little protection from storms from that direction. About 2 o'clock yesterday morning the seas were running very high, and it was almost impossible for any craft lying there to live. The tug Ella G. Stone, owned by the Duluth & Iron Range Railway Company, was driven on rocks and a hole stove in her side. It was with the utmost difficulty that she was kept from sinking. Upham & Williams' dredge, which was down there to do some dredging, sank in 15 feet of water. A scow loaded with lumber, belonging to Peyton, Kimball & Barber, was completely wrecked and the lumber lost. Several small boats were driven on shore and more or less damaged. The watchman on the dredge in endeavoring to save her had his leg broken. The storm will give the harbor improvements at Agate Bay quite a set back.

IN MANITOBA.

Special Telegram to the Tribune.

WINNIPEG, Aug. 20.—The most severe rain storm, accompanied by thunder and lightning, that probably ever visited the northwest, occurred here yesterday. The wind attained a velocity of 40 miles an hour. A number of buildings were blown down in the suburbs, and strong buildings in the centre of the city shook to their centre. Main street and other thoroughfares were filled with sign boards and flying debris. The spire of the new Knox Church, in course of erection, was blown down. The damage is considerable. Fears are entertained regarding the fine crops just ready for harvest, and shipping on Lake Superior. It poured steadily for about 24 hours, during which time two inches of rain fell, as registered at St. John's observatory. The streets were flooded, but the ground was so dry that the water was quickly absorbed. Telegrams just received from different parts of the province report crops slightly injured, but they will recover from the effects. Late sown grain will be greatly benefited by the rain.

IN DAKOTA.

Special Telegram to the Tribune.

NIAGARA, Dak., Aug. 20.—Two or three days of 104-in-the-shade weather resulted in a severe hail storm south of this place Sunday morning about 4 o'clock. The storm traveled from the southern edge of Devil's lake northeast, crossing the western extension of the Manitoba about half way between the Palace and Larimore, then followed the Turtle river north of Larimore. The wheat belt is stripped on Forest river and in Elk valley. A severe wind followed the storm, but has gone down today many shanties are destroyed.

IN CANADA.

TORONTO, Aug. 20.—A terrific rain storm, accompanied by thunder and lightning, visited the northwest part of Ontario yesterday. At Listowel water was two feet deep in the streets. Several buildings and bridges were carried away, and the destruction of property is generally very great. At Wingham the river rose 12 feet. The roadway, bridge and track were washed away, and the country roads covered with four feet of water. Large quantities of standing grain were destroyed.

**LESSER CASUALITIES.**

**Narrow Escape from Cremation.**

HURON, Dak., Aug.—A telegram from Athol says that Mr. Seeilow, living near that town, lost his house this afternoon by fire. Mr. Seeilow, Mrs. Dallman and her son, 4 years old, were in the house trying to remove the furniture when the roof fell in upon them. When they escaped all three were horribly burned about the head, face and back. Mr Seeilow ran to the river and extinguished the flames, but the others were unable to do so. All three are in a critical condition.

**Drowned.**

Special Telegram to the Tribune.

DEVIL'S LAKE, Dak., Aug 20.—William McCulloch, aged 23, son of J. McCulloch of Rice's, Minn., and lately from Yellowstone park, and who for several weeks has been camped with a young friend, A. Adsit of Fargo, was drowned Friday morning near Thompson's Landing, five miles south of Devil's lake. He was taken with cramps while trying to recover a duck which he had shot. The body is not recovered.

**Accidents to Masons.**

SAN FRANCISCO, Aug. 20.—Several accidents are reported in the conclave procession today. Three standard bearers fainted from exhaustion, and Sir Alexander Weed, aide to the grand commander of California, was thrown from his horse and both legs broken.

## POST-STRIKE PARAGRAPHS.

**Steady Stream of Applicants for Reinstatement—Continuing the Congressional Inquiry.**

NEW YORK, Aug. 20.—Supt. Humestone of the Western Union Telegraph Company was busy this morning receiving applications for re-employment from striking operators. About 100 male operators have been taken back since the strike ended. Five more were employed this morning. Sixty ladies went on the strike and only 20 were taken back. It is expected that 25 more will be taken this week. All the linemen who apply for reinstatement are met with the answer that "their places are filled." Nearly all branch offices are open this morning. Jay Gould has expressed great satisfaction with Gen. Eckert's management during the strike and the success resulting from it. It is expected the company will be able to find positions for nearly all the strikers within a couple of weeks. It is emphatically denied that there is any disposition on the part of the company to punish the strikers by refusing them employment.

**Continuing the Inquiry.**

NEW YORK, Aug. 20.—The sub-committee on education and labor resumed its sessions this morning. The first witness examined was Mrs. Charlotte Smith of Washington, president of the Woman's National League. This organization, witness stated, was formed in Washington a year ago in consequence of a refusal of Secretary Teller to employ women in the department under his control. The membership now includes women in every branch of industry throughout the country. Mrs. Smith said among the female telegraph operators many were in a condition of want, and pecuniary distress forced them to surrender in the strike. Mrs. Smith promised to furnish the committee with statistics in regard to women workers in this country.

A. H. Seymour, a telegraph operator of 30 years' experience, who testified last week, was recalled. He favored the establishment of a government telegraph system under control of civil service reform rules, or else the adoption of a law similar to the one adopted in Pennsylvania in 1873, prohibiting the lease or consolidation by one telegraph company of any competing line. Witness cited figures to show the progress in telegraphic business in England since it came under the control of the government. He claimed that all additional facilities were obtained from new inventions and thereby benefited the public, while in this country they only benefited a corporation. He then gave a list of the number of telegraph companies absorbed by the Western Union, and claimed to show by figures the capital stock of that company was greatly inflated.

W. H. Foster, a member of the typographical Union, Cincinnati, testified in regard to the condition of the laboring class in that city. One of the great advantages, he thought, in legalizing trades unions would be that a system arbitration would be thus made compulsory, and the number of strikes diminished. He did not believe the socialistic element prevailed throughout the West, although many trades union men had those views.

**A Sensational Rumor.**

PITTSBURG, Pa., Aug. 20.—A sensational story, to the effect that the failure of the telegraphers strike had resulted in the formation of an alliance between telegraphers, printers and locomotive engineers, and that as soon as an organization is perfected a strike would be ordered, was circulated tonight, but careful inquiry failed to trace it to any reliable source. A number of prominent members of the Telegraphers' Brotherhood were seen and all pronounced it entirely without foundation.

**Flocking Back.**

TOLEDO, Ohio, Aug 20.—The Toledo Assembly of Telegraphers' Brotherhood did not receive official notice of the failure of the strike until Saturday night, and yesterday nearly all members filed applications for reinstatement with the Western Union. Six of the twenty operators were reinstated today, and when all applications have been passed upon probably one half of those who went out will be given employment.

DETROIT, Aug. 20.—Six striking operators were reinstated in the Western Union office here today, making eight altogether.

**Opposition Telegraph.**

ALBANY, N. Y., Aug. 20.—The National Telegraph Company was incorporated today. The capital stock is fixed at $25,000, with provisions that it may be increased to $10,000,000. The stockholders are Calvin Brice, Lima, O.; Frank A. Worcester, Brooklyn; John W. Simpson, Herbert L. Terrill, Walter Katte and James E. Childs, New York.

**Percheron Stallions.**

NEW YORK, Aug. 20.—The steamer Holland, from Havre, brought 180 Percheron stallions. This is the largest shipment of grown stallions ever imported from Europe. Not a single animal was lost on the voyage. All were shipped to the farm of their owner, W. Dunham, of Wayne, Ill., via the New York Central railway tonight.

**Northern Pacific.**

WASHINGTON, Aug. 20.—The secretary of the interior was today informed that a section of 75 miles of the Northern Pacific railway uniting the two ends near Mullans tunnel has been completed. The company has requested the appointment of a commission to examine and report on this section of the road.

# The Minneapolis Daily Tribune.

VOLUME XIX. MONDAY MORNING, SEPTEMBER 15, 1885.—TWELVE PAGES. NO. 127.


## THE NEWS.

### The Weather.

OFFICE OF CHIEF SIGNAL OFFICER, WASHINGTON, D. C., Sept. 14, 9 p. m.—Observations taken at the same moment of time at all stations:

| STATIONS. | Bar. | Ther. | Rain fall | Weath. |
|---|---|---|---|---|
| Minneapolis | 29.91 | 58 | .. | Clear |
| La Crosse | 29.91 | 61 | .. | Clear |
| Bismarck | 30.00 | 56 | .. | Clear |
| Fort Garry | 29.81 | 63 | .01 | Cloudy |
| Minnedosa | 29.82 | 50 | .. | Cloudy |
| Moorhead | 29.92 | 55 | .. | Clear |
| St. Vincent | 29.86 | 52 | .. | Cloudy |
| Fort Buford | 29.97 | 54 | .. | Clear |
| Fort Custer | 29.96 | 64 | .. | Clear |
| Helena | 29.94 | 61 | .. | Clear |
| Huron, Dak | 30.02 | 56 | .. | Clear |
| Duluth | 29.80 | 58 | .. | Clear |
| Omaha | 30.16 | 62 | .. | Clear |
| New Orleans | 30.01 | 80 | .. | Fair |
| Cincinnati | 29.98 | 69 | .. | Clear |
| Memphis | 30.01 | 77 | .. | Fair |
| Pittsburgh | 29.91 | 70 | .. | Clear |
| Buffalo | 29.83 | 70 | .. | Clear |
| Albany | 29.84 | 50 | .. | Clear |
| Toledo | 29.91 | 72 | .. | Clear |
| Alpena | 29.82 | 56 | .. | Clear |
| Chicago | 29.95 | 67 | .. | Clear |
| Davenport | 30.10 | 65 | .. | Clear |
| St. Louis | 30.09 | 75 | .. | Clear |
| Leavenworth | 30.07 | 75 | .. | Clear |
| Yankton | 30.05 | 56 | .. | Clear |
| Cheyenne | 30.02 | 56 | .. | Clear |
| Denver | 30.01 | 65 | .. | Clear |
| Toronto | 29.81 | 65 | .. | Foggy |
| Salt Lake | 30.12 | 68 | .. | Clear |
| New York | 29.87 | 74 | .. | Fair |
| Boston | 29.80 | 72 | .. | Clear |

P. F. LYONS,
Sergeant, Signal Corps, United States Army.

INDICATIONS.

For the Upper Mississippi valley—Fair weather, variable winds; stationary temperature.

For the Missouri valley—Fair weather; variable winds, becoming southerly; stationary temperature.

### Miscellaneous.

Cholera is on the decrease in Spain.

Freeland won the big race at Brighton Beach yesterday.

John L. Sullivan was fined $1 and costs for playing base ball on Sunday.

[illegible]

### Northwest.

[illegible]

### CRIME AND CASUALTY.

[illegible]

## WASHINGTON.

### The Centennial of Temperance Work to be Celebrated Next Sunday.

### A Great Demand for "Pointers" on the Forthcoming Official Crop Report.

### A Mistaken Idea Prevalent as to the Effect of the Special Delivery Service.

### A Story About Bob Toombs—The Silver Question — The Public Printer.

[SPECIAL DISPATCH TO THE TRIBUNE.]

WASHINGTON, Sept. 14.—Many public men are so credulous and such poor readers of human nature as to be readily imposed upon. People who associate much with men in high offices here soon come to the conclusion that these officials are only trained in politics, and are often called to their positions by simple freaks of fortune.

General Robert Brank Vance, of North Carolina, although 58 years old, a graduate from Cincinnati and European colleges, and having served through the war on the confederate side with distinction, reaching the rank of brigadier general, afterward serving in various local offices, then going into congress for twelve years, and now being commissioner of patents, is probably one of the most credulous men who has ever figured prominently and who has paid very dearly for it. [illegible]

... this means that the information generally finds its way to the public. I never allow the confidential papers in my charge to go to the proof room."

### New Postmasters.

WASHINGTON, Sept. 14.—The postmaster general today appointed the following fourth-class postmasters:

In Pennsylvania—At Luzerne, Leeba Matthews; Smyrnia, E. M. Townsend; [illegible]

[illegible]

### A War Story.

[SPECIAL DISPATCH TO THE TRIBUNE.]

WASHINGTON, Sept. 14.—An old soldier here tells a good war story on General Bob Toombs, of Georgia. During the fight at Antietam, he says, General Toombs was retreating with his brigade through Crampton's Gap, and his horse fell and threw the general. In falling he was buried on some dead men, covering him with blood. Some of his men rushed to take charge of the general, who was supposed to be severely wounded. He was carefully lifted from the ground and placed upon his horse, being supported on either side by two of his faithful soldiers, whilst still another held his horse, then led it. They had proceeded but a short distance when General Stewart met them, and in his jocular way hailed them.

"Hello, Bob Toombs," said he, "what's the matter with you?"

"Severely wounded," answered the Georgia general, dishearteningly.

General Stewart called his surgeons and they searched for the wounds. What was their astonishment to find none, and to learn that the blood came from those Toombs fell upon!

### Alleged Influence.

[illegible]

### Does Not Believe It.

[illegible]

### Cattle and Hogs.

[illegible]

### Lucky Creditors.

[illegible]

### "A Reason on Compulsion? No!"

[illegible]

### A Big Trouble.

[illegible]

### Crop Reports.

[illegible]

### Silver Coinage.

[illegible]

### The Special Delivery System.

[illegible]

### Sovereign Santos.

[illegible]

### Georgia Crops.

[illegible]

## ST. PAUL'S DAY.

### Twenty Thousand People Witness the Best Racing of the Week.

### Presentation Exercises—Speeches by Governor Hubbard, President Clark and Mayor Rice.

### The Races the Best of the Week, and the Interest Great.

### The Fair Closes Today—A Fairly Successful Meeting—Closing Scenes—Notes.

The weather was fair, the sun shone bright and the sky was blue yesterday. Nature smiled and the fair was a success. The attendance was large and the attractions excellent. The exercises attending the formal presentation of the fair grounds to the state passed off very pleasantly, the speeches made having the merit of pith and brevity. The chief attractions, however, were the races, and they proved to be the best of the week, and were witnessed by a crowd that was only limited by the space available for a good view. The horse various and cattle-sheds were thronged during the day by curious groups, and the lucky animals, decked with the ribbons of bonny blue, were [illegible]

[illegible]

### The Races.

[illegible]

### The Day's Events.

[illegible]

### The Presentation.

[illegible]

It was evident that First Call had got into a class a few seconds above his speed. On the first quarter he went into the air but quickly settled, and rapidly gaining was soon on an even footing with Silver Leaf. They had a neck and neck race until they went out of sight, and all looked with earnest until they should appear at the three-quarter pole. Silver Leaf came into view first and was leading by about one-half a length. Both came to the wire at a good clip and Silver Leaf won, with First Call on her wheels. Time, 2:29½.

[illegible]

STALLION RACE.

The next event was the stallion race, and the entries were Von Arnim, Silas Wright and Fearnaught. [illegible]

First Heat—The horses were sent off together, Silas Wright having the pole, and Von Arnim on the outside. The former broke on the first turn and fell behind. Von Arnim pushed to the front, and, scoring on the outside, came in and took the pole, leading to the half by two open lengths. Fearnaught was about the same distance behind him and Silas Wright was an equal distance in the rear of Fearnaught. On their reappearance from behind the hill the same positions were observed. The pace home was fast, but Von Arnim came in an easy winner by an open length. Fearnaught second, and Silas Wright third. Time, 2:31½.

It was noticed that when Von Arnim had scored the first time he was lame in the off fore leg, and when he came in at the finish of the first heat this was noticed still more. This lameness was not observed afterwards, but it signified what a gamey horse he was to make such speed with the disadvantage he was laboring under.

Second Heat—Little time was spent in scoring, the horses coming down well together and were sent off on even terms. Silas Wright repeated his dancing act at the first turn and fell behind for several lengths. Von Arnim took the lead when a short distance from the pole, and when Silas Wright broke Fearnaught went into second place and had a sharp contest with Von Arnim for the lead. [illegible]

[illegible]

# The Minneapolis Sunday Tribune.

VOLUME XIX. SUNDAY MORNING, JANUARY 31, 1886.—TWENTY PAGES. NO. 265.

## THE NEWS.

**Minneapolis.**

The Thistle curling club lost a game to St. Paul, 66 to 57.

Canton Minnesota, No. 1, Patriarchal Militant, installed officers.

N. P. Lind lectured to the Scandinavian workingmen's union.

Rev. H. G. Dewitt begins revival work at the Central Baptist Church.

The Norwegian temperance society enjoyed a social at Peterson's hall.

The permit for the $500,000 postoffice building was taken out last Monday.

The Prohibitionists selected 70 delegates for the convention at St. Paul, Tuesday.

Dr. A. Ames will be high chief marshal of the parade at the ice palace excursion.

Joseph Strasser has sued Fred. Harriman and Chas. Silentine to recover $5,000 damages.

Col. O. B. Skinner organized a camp of Sons of Veterans at Hunt's Hall, Wednesday evening.

Helen A. Peck has brought action against John A. McLean and Robt. McNeider to recover $10,000.

There is a plan to form a new church as an off shoot of Plymouth, with Rev. Dr. Hutchins as pastor.

Albert Shock, of Chicago, was awarded the TRIBUNE's championship medal for winning the six day bicycle race.

The firm of Dale, Barnes, Morse & Co., dissolvers today, to be succeeded by the firm of Barnes, Hinger, Dale & Co.

President Cyrus Northrop, of the State University, addressed the teachers' meeting on the need of using good English.

Judge Young has decided the suit of the Farmers Loan & Trust company against the Minneapolis Engine and Machine Works in favor of the plaintiff.

**St. Paul.**

The carnival opening tomorrow.

Gov. Hubbard has gone to Washington, D. C.

The temperature will fall today several degrees.

The program for Monday's opening is now complete.

Fifty-two pupils have been admitted to the high school.

"Uncle Tom's Cabin" again, three days this week.

Gen. R. W. Johnson will take the part of the ice king.

The list of premiums for all the races is published today.

There are about five different carnival clubs now organized.

King Borealis will reach St. Paul in a refrigerator car, by way of Manitoba, next Tuesday.

Rees Moores has commenced a suit against John O'Connor for slander, claiming $5,000 as damages.

Charles F. Tabor wants $10,000 from the city on account of a broken leg, caused by a defective sidewalk.

**Northwest.**

Red Wing has organized a new board of trade.

A pontoon bridge company has been organized at Winona.

A man named Thomas Nelson was seriously injured by the cars near Hastings.

Albert Lea is raiding her gambling dens, and proposes to stop the practice in her limits.

C. Goebel, a wealthy farmer of Alden, drew $500 from a bank and went out riding with a stranger, who robbed him of it.

Des Moines is stirred up by Dr. Kennedy, of that place, who has issued a fourteen page pamphlet charging Oil Inspector B. H. Blanchard with malfeasance in office.

Michael Hart was killed in a planing mill near Eau Claire, Wis., by a board flying from an edger, hitting him in the stomach. He leaves a wife and two children and had relatives in Minneapolis.

**Washington.**

Cleveland is endorsed by the Democratic Senators in his refusal to furnish information to the Senate concerning removals.

A bill will be introduced in the House by Wilson, of West Virginia, to classify the work and pay of all government employes.

The authorities have been notified of the outbreak of a revolution on the isthmus of Panama, but little credence is given to the report.

The house committee on public lands has a large amount of work on hand and much pressure is brought to bear in the matter of opening public lands to settlement.

The attempt of Chicago to absorb the Fifth supervising district by Chicago is rousing the whole Northwest and a stubborn fight is being made by the Northwestern interests.

Now that a few appropriations have gone through the house for appropriations for public buildings in the larger cities, congressmen are flooded by petitions from constituents to secure appropriations for insignificant towns.

**Foreign.**

The Spanish budget shows a large deficit.

Mr. Gladstone goes to Osborne tomorrow.

The Bal de L'Opera at Berlin was a splendid affair.

Twenty of the Aveyron rioters have been arrested.

The terms of the Franco-Malagasy treaty are published.

There is some talk of King George of Greece abdicating his throne.

Polish merchants propose to boycott German manufacturers in retaliation for the expulsions.

The President of Liberia explains why the negotions for a reciprocity treaty with the United States came to nothing.

**Miscellaneous.**

Pittsburgh is investigating charges of corruption in her common councils.

The grand jury just discharged in Salt Lake City indicted 45 Mormons.

The explosion of a boiler known to be unsafe at Breckenridge, Mo., killed two men and badly crippled a third.

A desperate shooting affray took place near Dallas, Tex., in which three persons were killed and several badly hurt.

The attention of the government has been called to Chicago's lake front, which is, it is alleged, being ruined by the railroads.

The ocean steamers Servia and Nordland collided in the East river, New York. The latter was badly broken up. No one hurt.

The Knights of Labor say that the boycotting of the Mallory Company will commence next week, and the public can know what to expect.

Ex-Gov. W. S. Brown, of Tennessee, is dead. He was 76 years old. Ex minister to Russia in 1850 and prominent in diplomatic and national politics before the war.

Chicago Anarchists have threatened to block up the building in which a fancy dress ball is to be given should any of the costumes caricature them.

Mr. Lawrence Barrett will, at the Star Theater, Monday, assume the title roll in the first production in New York of an English version of Victor Hugo's tragedy "Hernani."

The Chapman block, a four-story iron, brick and stone building, its contents and a number of small buildings adjoining were also burned. Loss $25,000. Insurance unknown.

## GOTHAM GOSSIP.

### ACTORS WHO ARE THE ADORATION OF SILLY WOMEN.

**Impertinent Club Men Who Make Insulting Remarks About Passers-by—Morosini's Daughter at the Opera—Incidents at the Stock Exchange.**

[SPECIAL CORRESPONDENCE OF THE TRIBUNE.]

NEW YORK, Jan. 28.—So long as it is denied to us to stand aside and see ourselves go past, we are compelled to confine our observations to others' pedestrianism. It was while I was thus engaged, inside the window of a Broadway hotel, that the Rev. Dr. Collier and the Rev. Dr. Deems went by arm in arm. They are known to fame and acquainted with clerical dignity; and yet the man who had risen

by his own able efforts from the obscurity of the forge to the conspicuousness of a metropolitan pulpit had an aspect of inebriety, while the one who had come to a not less foremost position among the clergy of New York, the spiritual adviser of Commodore Vanderbilt and pastor of a prosperous independent congregation, was in appearance worse off. If an instantaneous camera had been leveled instantly at the pair, the picture would have answered for a representation of two jolly old convivialists. Of course, they were sober, and their semblance to drunkenness was due to a slippery sidewalk; but the likeness was comically remarkable, and what if they had been jolly politicians, sociable lawyers or larking merchants? The spectator would probably have concluded them drunk, and never thought of the icy spot that they were sprawling over.

Standing in the next window, at that same time, were four professional beauties. Are women, then, permitted to lounge in the hotel corridors? O, no. These exhibits of loveliness were actors. The girls who go to the theatres must have their idols, and the four just now on dramatic pedestals happened to gather together. They were a good-looking quartette, though no halos were visible around their heads and they would have attracted no especial attention if deprived of mimic heroism. In three instances they had the additional advantage of London birth, enunciation and manners, which is a great deal in the estimation of the New York doter on juvenile actors. There was Kyrle

Bellew, the new leader of the Wallack company, resembling Henry Irving a little, with his smooth face, rather long hair and stiff attitudinization. Bellew has bad legs, and is not virile, but the girls are inclined to adore him. Two fellows, on whose upper lips the exigencies of the stage had left moustaches undisturbed, and who resembled each other except that one was brunette and the other blonde, were Robert Mantell, who was playing Loris in town to the Fedora of Fanny Davenport, and Herbert Kelcey, at present the first juvenile at the Madison Square. I will not tell which of them, if he had raised his hat, would have revealed the shocking fact that, unwigged in life, he was semi-bald; but I feel bound to write the fact that every man of the four has a wife to prevent him from reciprocating the affection of the fair auditor. The close shaven young fellow, with the fur-bordered overcoat of a minstrel, was the inevitable Henry E. Dixey, than whom no actor ever got half so much flattery undeserved. A good mimic and a graceful dancer, he has gone deeper into the hearts of feminine New York than Booth or Salvini. The consequences of so much admiration are curious. Dixey's saunter down Broadway makes the commotion of a circus entry; his advent in a barroom collects a crowd, who await—often not in vain—for him to cut a caper; and on the stage he is funny in his monopoly. Every other performer is inert while Dixey is speaking or moving. If he drops a hat, cane or other object, in his frequent juggling of such articles, whoever happens to be next to him picks it up and hands it to him. The language of the burlesque has from time to time been altered to laud him at every possible point. It is altogether an exhibition of individual supremacy in a company that provides special diversion to the expert observer.

The demeanor of persons consciously under scrutiny, as they go along the street, can nowhere be more strikingly seen than in Fifth avenue, where the windows of the Union club overlook the promenade. The gazers are members of that famously fashioned body, and the gazed at are the girls

who walk by. Since the noted disturbance over a wanton comment on Mrs. Paran Stevens and her daughter, made by one window-bean and resented by another, and resulting in the expulsion of both, fashionable belles have commonly avoided that particular corner, as though a yellow flag of pestilence hung on it; but the windows are full of men every afternoon, though the sophisticated among the passers by are not, as a general rule, from the wealthy or polite grades of feminine society. They are apt to have either the sauciness of open audacity, or an assumed shyness equally a challenge to admiration. Thus it happens that one section of our finest avenue is used for exhibitions alike shameful to those who show themselves and those whom they show to.

In a box at the Metropolitan Opera House the other night, sat a young woman at whom all the glasses in the place were focused, at one time or another during the evening. She knew it too, and was placidly happy under the ordeal. She sat to the front of her two companions, dressed like them in an evening costume, and she was second to few belles in the audience for bright prettiness of face or outward indications of refinement. She was Victoria Morosini,

the banker's daughter, noted for her elopement with the family coachman. She had for weeks been singing in a comic opera, but illness had disabled her voice, and she is now on the retired list to recuperate for an ensuing production. Identified by many and pointed out by them to the rest, she got more interested attention from fashion's exemplars than any other auditor. I noticed that Jay Gould watched her a great deal from his own box, and it was said that he had never before seen her, although she was the child of his partner in the [illegible] of Conner & Co. Very unsociable [illegible] Gould, and his acquaintance with Victoria indicated nothing in particular. Young George [illegible] went to her box and chatted awhile with her. The box in which she sat was one of those sold night by night, and not a stockholder's; and it is probable that it was provided for her by the manager to whom she is engaged, for the sake of the advertisement resulting from being seen there. That was to be inferred from the fact that her two associates were comic opera actresses. She bore herself composedly and modestly. I presume her salary is a hundred dollars a week; but her husband, Schilling, still works for twelve as a street car conductor.

The whim of intensely fashionable society now is to give dinners at a dozen houses prior to a dance, in which the guests are gathered together from the various places of banquet. Thus the pleasures of the table are obtained in the homes of the nabobs, with the delights of a semi public ball added in the same night, and somethink akin to a new sensation is obtained by the blase class. They are telling in these circulars of an incident of three at

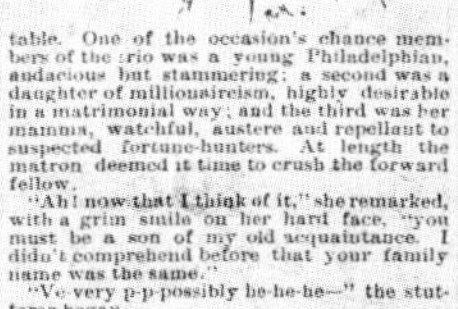

table. One of the occasion's chance members of the trio was a young Philadelphian, audacious but stammering; a second was a daughter of millionaireism, highly desirable in a matrimonial way; and the third was her mamma, watchful, austere and repellant to suspected fortune-hunters. At length the matron deemed it time to crush the forward fellow.

"Ah! now that I think of it," she remarked, with a grim smile on her hard face, "you must be a son of my old acquaintance. I didn't comprehend before that your family name was the same."

"Ve-very p-p-possibly he-he-he—" the stutterer began.

"Yes, you must be his son," the cruel crusher interrupted, "he had exactly your amusing conversational manner."

The chill was so quick and utter that the poor chap's next gulp of cold champagne tasted hot.

The most unsophisticated of brides was one who snuggled up against her rural husband as they stood in the visitors, balcony of the Stock Exchange, the other afternoon. Her garb as well as her manner betrayed her honeymoon condition, and she soon became an object of regard to the mob of brokers on the floor below. Their din and commotion of business were no more, probably than she had read of, and was prepared to see; but neither she nor her verdant spouse knew it when hallooing over stocks changed to hurrahs for her, and three times three—yes, nine times nine—were vociferously cheered for the unconscious bride, who took it all for regular proceedings. The girl distinguished no personality in the cheering, and when they gazed up at her she supposed they were looking at a big clock that hung behind the gallery.

"They seem to be anxious to see what time it is," she remarked to her partner.

"I rather guess," he responded, the truth at length dawning on him, "that it's time for us to go."

The scenes in the Stock Exchange during the recent daily battles between the bulls and the bears have frequently had an old-time liveliness. Five hundred operators are a fair average of the assemblages. The busiest hour is apt to be 2:15 p. m., for at that time the brokers, purple of visage, and punctuating each shout with a shake of the fist at the chairman, remind him that delivery time has come. The day's transactions are then preliminarily adjusted. White-haired old men and dapper youngsters make outcry together, and above the hubbub sound the whacks of a heavy ivory mallet of the chairman. Finally there is a tremendous bang on the desk, and the brokers set up an exultant yell in unison, as they turn to go to the various parts of the hall marked "Lake Shore," "Erie," Western Union," and so on. The little pillars thus labelled are the centers of dealings in the specified stocks. Forty minutes more of noisy words and violent gesticulation remain, and the appearances indicate an altercation that is likely at any moment to break into a riot. The exclamations return from the high ceiling in echoes, mixing the treble of the dudish boy, whose rich father has bought for him a $30,000 seat in the exchange, and the resonant baritone of the mature operator, whose voice has had long cultivation in Wall street. All the racket means business, though the casual visitor may not understand it, and it is only occasional that foolery is indulged in. Thousands of dollars are expressed in a shout, and a shake of a fist has a fortune in it. This continues from 10 in the morning until a gong, at 3 in the afternoon, rings with a sound that would have been the pride of the Chinese generation 1,000 years ago. KANDER.

### A GREAT WESTERN CITY.

When Bishop Berkeley wrote "Westward the Star of Empire takes its way" it was a prophecy. Today it is a fact. We have before us the New Year's issue of the Minnesota TRIBUNE, of 32 pages, 24 by 18 inches each, which is the size of its daily issue. They cover a resume of the year's doings in Minneapolis, with a great deal of other interesting information, indicating the wonderfully rapid progress in wealth and population of that inland city. Minneapolis, as many of our readers know, the capital of Hennepin county, Minnesota, is seated on both sides of the Mississippi river, at the Falls of St. Anthony, one of the greatest water powers in the United States and a prime factor in the growth of the city, owing to the numerous great flouring and planing mills built there to take advantage of the immense motive power furnished by the water of the falls. The growth of Minneapolis has been something quite marvelous, nearly if not quite equal, of late years to the annual growth of Chicago. In new buildings erected or begun in 1885 the approximation is very close. The value of those put up that year in Chicago being estimated at about $19,000,000, and in Minneapolis, a city one-third of the size, at $9,715,010. Its growth in population is not less striking. In 1880 the census put the population at 46,887. At a census taken last June the population had increased to 129,200, and the TRIBUNE now estimates that at the opening of the present year it has reached 140,000. The relative amount of business done in Minneapolis in 1885 is put at $125,500,000, as against $100,500,000 in 1884, and $87,500,000 in 1883. Fifty miles of streets were also graded in 1885, as against 11 miles in 1884. As a wheat market Minneapolis now stands first in the United States. Its receipts for 1885 were 32,470,000 bushels, as against 19,300,000 in Chicago, and 25,500,000 in New York. Three hundred and [illegible] million feet of lumber were sawed at the mills in Minneapolis last year. Its manufacture of flour footed up 5,100,962 barrels, a decline of 800,000 barrels as compared with 1884, but an increase of 500,000 over 1883, the difference last year being attributed to "the protracted closing of the mills while the new canal was in progress." The economical administration of the affairs of the city is shown in the fact that the tax levy for the present year is only 20 mills on the $100. By a wise provision also the city is prohibited from exceeding the 5 per cent limit on the assessed value of property, and has thus far kept well below that prudent limit. But if the city authorities are economical the citizens themselves have been liberal. They have subscribed from a quarter of a million to $300,000 toward a Minneapolis exposition of art and industries, have built or begun on a charitable basis a number of hospitals and asylums, and have founded a conservatory of music, "with an accomplished faculty of 15 members. Railroads are also finding an important centre in Minneapolis. A year ago it had three competing Eastern lines; today there are six, with another soon to be built. But," says the TRIBUNE, with commendable local pride, "these railroads do no not make us tributary to Chicago any more than Chicago is tributary to us, for we have made a declaration of independence and constitute a free, equal and sovereign commercial metropolis." And a metropolis this progressive American city is destined to be. The grain fields of the United States have been gradually moving westward and northwestward, and the railroads in those regions are bringing to Minneapolis, as to a focus, a large part of their products. We here in the central states know very little about the growth of great Western cities on the upper Mississippi and beyond, nor of the intense activity which is giving the West a preponderating influence in national affairs. —Baltimore Sun.

**Groton Grist.**

[SPECIAL DISPATCH TO THE TRIBUNE.]

GROTON, Dak., Jan. 30.—The saloon keepers here are jubilant tonight over the fact of their lawyer having quashed the indictment against them for keeping gambling rooms. The jury was found to contain an alien who had never disavowed the laws against the American hog; and another whose name was said to be Williams but was found to be Wilson. They have been in session about a week and several indictments have been found. Judge Church adjourned court for ten days to allow time to extricate themselves from the difficulty.—Bath, a small village west of here, has let the contract for a new Methodist Church, to be built early in the spring at a cost of $2,180.—Sixteen carpenters are busily at work rebuilding the Putman elevator; blizzards not taken into consideration.—Groton, with its population made up so widely from the East, has not an individual with the prefix "Hon." attached to his name, nor a plug hat in the city.—The farmers have formed an alliance and have resolved upon downing monopolies. At present they are all aglow with enthusiasm, but we fear it will result like the once popular grange movement: it will lose its warmth before it reaches the monopoly.

**Faribault Facts.**

[SPECIAL DISPATCH TO THE TRIBUNE.]

FARIBAULT, Jan. 30.—Rev. Sylvester Clark, of Bridgeport, Conn., has accepted the chair of ecclesiastical history in the Seabury Divinity School, and will come to Faribault at once to enter upon his duties.—The Chicago, Milwaukee & St. Paul railroad will sell round trip tickets to the carnival from Faribault, including a ticket for the ice palace, at $2.80. —There will be a special meeting of Michael Cook Post, 123, G. A. R., on Thursday evening, Feb. 4, to consider matters pertaining to the encampment to be held here.—The Dan Morris Sullivan combination will give an entertainment styled "The Mirror of Ireland," in Hill's Opera house for three evenings beginning on Thursday evening, Feb. 4.—The next meeting of the Faribault city council will be held on Monday evening, Feb. 8.



## FIRE AND WATER.

### THE ICE PALACE AT ST. PAUL DESTROYED BY THE FLAMES.

**Great Excitement Among the Citizens of the Saintly City—The Structure to be at Once Rebuilt.**

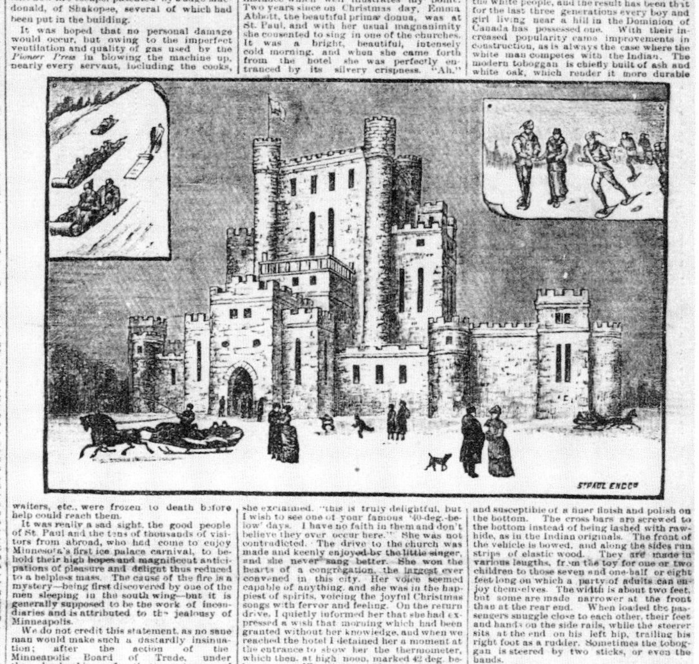

Special Dispatch to the Chicago Mail.

At 4 o'clock this morning the magnificent ice palace at St. Paul was reduced to ashes, being burned to the ground floor. A little before the hour named, smoke and flames were seen to issue from the south wing of the castle, and though the fire alarms were turned on at once, and the fire department soon upon the spot, the grand and imposing structure was doomed. At first it was feared that several workmen who slept in the north and south wings had perished, but were soon found mingling with the general crowd, having made an easy exit by means of the excellent new fire escape, patented by Judge Macdonald, of Shakopee, several of which had been put in the building.

It was hoped that no personal damage would occur, but owing to the imperfect ventilation and quality of gas used by the *Pioneer Press* in blowing the machine up, nearly every servant, including the cooks, waiters, etc., were frozen to death before help could reach them.

It was really a sad sight, the good people of St. Paul and the tens of thousands of visitors from abroad, who had come to enjoy Minnesota's first ice palace carnival, to behold their high hopes and magnificent anticipations of pleasure and delight thus reduced to a helpless mass. The cause of the fire is a mystery—being first discovered by one of the men sleeping in the south wing—but it is generally supposed to be the work of incendiaries and is attributed to the jealousy of Minneapolis.

We do not credit this statement, as no sane man would make such a dastardly insinuation; after the action of the Minneapolis Board of Trade, under the leadership of that prince of generosity, the Hon. D. Blakely, and the sublime efforts of the laundrymen at the dictation of W. E. Steele, Esq.

The good people of St. Paul had better look nearer home, for the cause of this their greatest earthly sorrow.—It was rumored last week that a band of Comanche Indians from the Northwest territory were lurking in the vicinity of the Ice Palace. Little notice had been taken of the fact, as these Indians are scarcely distinguishable from Joe Wheelock or Fred Driscoll of St. Paul, or Dave Blakely and Will Burwell of Minneapolis, when any of these gentlemen appear on the toboggan slides in their full Egyptian dress. Hence the people did not recognize the fact that the hostile Indians were in their midst until the terrible disaster had actually occurred.

Later—4:15 a. m. It is just learned that the chief of the Comanches, the Great Ice Snorter of the Northwest, has been captured by Mayor Rice, and Pat Kelly, after a most desperate struggle on snow shoes.

Later, 4:20 a. m.—The Chief of the Comanche, the G. I. S. O. T. N. W., has confessed. He says that this dastardly deed was conceived as long ago as last spring, and was inspired by the outrageous letters of Johnstone, late city editor of the *Pioneer Press*, written during the Riel rebellion, when "Johnstone was the only correspondent in the field," and was writing 10-column letters in an exaggerated form to the *Pioneer Press* about matters which had appeared correctly in the TRIBUNE and *Globe* more than one month before.

The Indians held a council of war, and resolved to be revenged against the *Pioneer Press* for these horrible letters of Johnstone, and believing that nothing lay so near the hearts of Joe Wheelock and Driscoll as this Ice Palace, they resolved to destroy it.

Later—4:35 a. m.—It is now believed that the confession of the Comanche chief is false, as old Uncle Fairchild reported to the chamber of commerce that soon after the fire was discovered, and while the northern walls were in a roaring sheet of flames, old Bill King and A. Jay Blethen were seen skulking away in a toboggan drawn by a pair of Tom Lowry's mules and driven by a Washington street car driver, going in the direction of the state fair grounds.

Later, 4:40 a. m.—It is now ascertained, upon the most reliable authority, that Bill King arrived home last night at 11:43 p. m., and can prove an alibi, but there is no such escape for Blethen, for newspaper men are always out all night.

Later.—4:45 a. m. It is now believed that the destruction of the ice palace is due to natural cause; both, Judge Ames and Col. Campe, having smiled in the palace just before it was completed. The smile was heard in Shakopee. Later; 4:48½ a. m. The palace was insured against fire for $2,000,000 and as the insurance agents all live in St. Paul, they have agreed to erect a new and more substantial ice palace, and complete the same by Monday at at 3 p. m., and have given bond so to do. There is great rejoicing among the people, and Blethen and Cal King have been released on their own recognizance. Greater crowds will be in attendance than if the accident had not occurred, as the new palace will be built next to the ruins of the old, which will stand as a living curiosity, it being the only ice palace which was ever destroyed by fire.

Inasmuch as the fire, given in detail above, will in no wise interfere with the carnival to be holden from Monday, Feb. 1, to Sunday night, Feb. 14, great pleasure is taken in reproducing the history and causes which lead the good people of St. Paul to erect the Ice Palace, and to prepare for the first ice carnival ever held in the United States. The cut herewith presented is a perfect picture of the Ice Palace, now just completed.

**History of the Palace.**

It appears eminently proper that the city with the saintly name should usher in the Lenten season by a grand carnival. The word "carnival" signifies "farewell to flesh," and is from the Latin words carno (flesh) and vale (farewell). The season selected for holding the St. Paul festival, is perhaps the most beautiful of the winter in our charming climate. It is a time when bright, clear, cold weather is almost a certainty, and a period when the demands of business are not so urgent as to prevent any from participating in the festivities.

One of the principal objects of holding this festival, to which the world is invited, is to correct the wrong impressions, too generally held, that St. Paul and Minnesota are a hyperborean region where existence is a burden during the winter months. Hundreds of thousands of tourists and pleasure-seekers visit this locality during the summer, and the fame of our fair and fertile country is world-wide. They then secure a fresh supply of health and a grand buoyancy of spirits, but return to their Eastern or Southern homes to sacrifice their gain to the damp coldness which pervades their own districts. It is desired that such good people should learn of the charms of the antipodes of our seasons, for we are satisfied that after one trial of the gloriously exhilarating effect of our Minnesota climate, they will become regular winter visitors.

Many people think that during the cold season here none dare venture into the open air. Nothing could be further from the truth. In fact there is something irresistibly enticing in the crisp, pure air, the gleaming sunshine and the soft moonlight, and it would be as impossible to refrain from the enjoyment of a bright winter day as to forswear the charms of the warm summer day with its sweet air, its flowers and its birds. Perhaps the most delightful days of winter are those when the mercury seeks the forties, for then the properly clad person moves as if by inspiration. I remember one particular instance which well illustrates my point: Two years since on Christmas day, Emma Abbott, the beautiful prima donna, was at St. Paul, and with her usual magnanimity she consented to sing in one of the churches. It was a bright, beautiful, intensely cold morning, and when she came forth from the hotel she was perfectly entranced by its silvery crispness. "Ah," she exclaimed, "this is truly delightful, but I wish to see one of your famous '40-deg.-below' days. I have no faith in them and don't believe they ever occur here." She was not contradicted. The drive to the church was made and keenly enjoyed by the little singer, and she never sang better. She won the hearts of a congregation, the largest ever convened in this city. Her voice seemed capable of anything, and she was in the happiest of spirits, voicing the joyful Christmas songs with fervor and feeling. On the return drive, I quietly informed her that she had expressed a wish that morning which had been granted without her knowledge, and when we reached the hotel I detained her a moment at the entrance to show her the thermometer, which then, at high noon, marked 42 deg. below zero. "Why," she said, "can it be possible! If I had known that it was so cold I should have worn 20 more wraps, and should not have been able to sing a note!"

St. Paul is most admirably located for winter sports, its lofty bluffs affording the most excellent opportunities for extensive slides for toboggans or sleds; while snowshoers will find the most perfect trails for the exercise of their pastime, off into the country or around the encircling hills. For curling, skating and polo rinks, a smooth glare of ice will be freshly produced each morning. To those enamored of the excitement of spinning along behind fast nags, the spacious surface of the river and the broad outlying avenues afford splendid courses of regulation length.

The association will offer over 50 prizes to competing clubs and athletes in all the various games. These prizes will consist of gold and silver medals, cups, badges and money. Several international contests will take place during the carnival.

**The Ice Palace.**

The first ice palace of which we find mention was built by order of Empress Anna, of Russia, near the river Neva, in 1741. It was 56 feet in length, 18 in depth, and 21 in height, the pallisading being 87 feet in length by 36 feet in depth. In 1754, when Empress Elizabeth held a winter feast, an ice palace of much greater proportions was builded on the Neva. The idea was introduced into America by the enterprising citizens of Montreal, in 1883, and a palace was erected on a park adjoining the Winsor Hotel. In 1884, another palace, more ornate than the first, was built, and on the last week in January, 1885, a grand carnival was held there with a still more elaborate ice edifice as the central attraction.

The happy suggestion of a St. Paul newspaper man—Mr. George Thompson, of the *Dispatch*—to arrange a carnival for and build an ice palace in that city, was eagerly seized by active, enterprising citizens, and no time was lost in formulating a plan. While, of course, the city hopes to be benefited by the festival, it is intended to give the people of the Northwest, South and Southwest, an opportunity to enjoy such glorious winter recreations as the people of the East have revelled in for several years.

One of the first acts of the organization which was formed was to engage the services of those skillful architects and builders—the Messrs. Hutchinson, of Montreal—who had erected the three palaces in their own city. Late in November Mr. J. H. Hutchinson arrived in St. Paul, bringing plans for an ice palace which, with a few modifications, were adopted. The structure 140 in length by 120 feet in width, with a grand, massive, central tower attaining an altitude of 100 feet. This tower is provided with battlements and embrasures, and the architecture throughout is of the pure mediæval type. The main tower is defended by an outwork about 32 feet in height, with battlements and towers at the angles. The outer walls are 20 inches thick and the central tower 40 inches, and something over 20,000 blocks of ice are required in its construction. The interior will be lighted by night by about 50 large electric lights, and on the occasion of the "storming of the palace" by the army of uniformed snowshoers, various colored lights will be burned within, and immense quantities of fireworks will be discharged from the towers and battlements, producing an effect indescribably magnificent. There are four grand entrances to the palace, through which spectators pass to the labyrinth of apartments, viewing the magical effect of the solid crystal walls, and refreshing themselves at the various booths from which appropriate eatables and beverages are dispensed.

**The Carnival Park.**

The ice palace is located in the very heart of the city, and a better site for the convenience of all could not possibly have been devised. Central park is the latest of the breathing places acquired by the city, and it is appropriately named. It is bounded by Thirteenth street on the south, a boulevard avenue on the north, by Robert street on the east, and by Cedar street on the west. It is 500 feet north and south, and 765 feet east and west. In the center and across the park, from east to west, the palace stands. Adjoining the public park on either side, vacant blocks have been secured and added to form the grand Carnival Park, making a total area of about eight acres.

On the thoroughfares bounding the park proper, on the east and west, are toboggan-ing slides for children, the incline from the bluff at the back being sufficient and safe. A portion of the block of land at the east end is devoted to curling rinks, and on the west is a spacious skating rink. The horse cars from the Union depot pass within two blocks of the Carnival Park on three sides.

**Toboggans and Tobogganing.**

This is a novel and exhilerating sport, and one in which all classes, sexes and ages can participate. The toboggan, which has for many years afforded the means for a popular pastime in Canada, was originally used by Indians for transporting game, etc., through the forests of the Province of Quebec. Sometimes they were hauled by the Indians or their squaws, but oftener by dogs, driven tandem. The primitive toboggan was made of poplar and elder about one-eighth of an inch thick and of different lengths, according to the requirements of the occasion. However, they were rarely more than 15 inches wide, and by their lightness and broad bottom surface they were enabled to run over deep snow without sinking. The Indians used them not only as a means of transportation, but also of sport when a clear hill lay in their course.

Gradually the toboggan was recognized by the white people, and the result has been that for the last three generations every boy and girl living near a hill in the Dominion of Canada has possessed one. With their increased popularity came improvements in construction, as is always the case where the white man competes with the Indian. The modern toboggan is chiefly built of ash and white oak, which render it more durable and susceptible of a finer finish and polish on the bottom. The cross bars are screwed to the bottom instead of being lashed with rawhide, as in the Indian originals. The front of the vehicle is bowed, and along the sides run strips of elastic wood. They are made in various lengths, from the toy for one or two children to those seven and one-half or eight feet long on which a party of adults can enjoy themselves. The width is about two feet, but some are made narrower at the front than at the rear end. When loaded the passengers snuggle close to each other, their feet and hands on the side rails, while the steerer sits at the end on his left hip, trailing his right foot as a rudder. Sometimes the toboggan is steered by two sticks, or even the hands.

**Snow Shoes and Snow Shoeing.**

The snow shoe is of course a near relative of the toboggan, as the Indians found it necessary to devise some means of supporting themselves as well as their burdens over the light snow. The shoe is constructed of some elastic wood which is bent in the form of an ellipse, the two ends joined behind and extending quite a distance behind to form the "trail." Across the frame is woven raw buckskin, which, being put on in a damp state, shrinks and forms a firm, tough net work. A little in front of the center of the net is a hole which affords opportunity for bending the toes. Across the foot, just above the big toe joint, a buckskin thong is passed, and this is brought back, crossed on the instep and firmly tied at the ankle. Thus the back of the foot is entirely free from the shoe, which is lifted only by the toes, the "trail" always remaining on the snow. Snow shoes vary greatly in size, according to the use for which they are required. The regulation club shoe has a frame about 2½ feet long and 12 inches wide, and the front end is turned up. Shoes for surveyors, lumbermen and packers are much larger, reaching even five feet in length, and being correspondingly wide. Moccasins must be worn with snow shoes. No other foot gear will answer the purpose.

**Curling.**

This, which is known as the "roaring game," has for centuries been a favorite with the sturdy sons of Scotia, and a most exciting game it is. The game is entirely new to this part of the country, and while we cannot here set down the complete rules that govern the game, we will give a general idea. The game is played in what are known as "rinks" each one being 42 yards long and five yards wide. There are four players and two "skips" to each side. The game is played with circular stones, highly polished on the bottom and having a handle on the top. The weights of the stones are not more than 50 pounds and not less than 30 pounds, and must not have a greater circumference than 36 inches, nor a height less than one-eighth of its circumference. The object is to slide the stones to or as near the "Tee," or center, of the large circle as possible, and it is the ambition of each player to displace his antagonist's stone in gaining a better position. The "skips" are to keep the ice swept clean and have the exclusive regulation and direction of the game of their respective parties; and if one of the players, may select in what part of the game he will play. There is usually an umpire to each game.

### THE CASTLE COMPLETED.

**Everything Will Be in Readiness on the Opening Day.**

The ice castle is ready. Block by block its translucent walls have been reared until the bastions of the central tower are over 100 feet from the ground, frowning with all the cold sternness of the feudal architecture of the Norman conquerors' time, upon an ingenuity of pellucid battlements, parapets, moats and turrets below. Everybody has seen the ice palace in imagination, and a detailed description of it would be superfluous. Its courts, its halls, its towers and wings have all been pictured vividly. Contractors Hutchinson and Brodie were determined to complete their work in time, and as the time for finishing approached they increased their working force until the numbered in their employ over 2,000 men, as well as over 60 teams and wagons. Nothing now remains but a few finishing touches.

CENTRAL PARK.

The carnival grounds are not yet in a fit condition. The park of evergreens has been planted, the numerous toboggan slides constructed and iced, the booths established on all sides, and the rinks flooded. But the small pieces of ice and a deal of rubbish, caused by the construction of the palace, still remains. Today will probably be devoted to cleaning up and preparing the curling and skating rinks and slides. A magnificent arch of evergreens has been constructed at the entrance to the grounds. This it is intended to illuminate. Near by are saloons and restaurants with almost

# The Minneapolis Daily Tribune.

VOLUME XX. NO. 23. THURSDAY MORNING, JUNE 3, 1886. PRICE: DAILY, THREE CENTS; SUNDAY, FIVE CENTS.

## THE NEWS.

**Minneapolis.**

Commencement at the university.

The State University alumni held their annual meeting.

Auditor McDonald criticised public fund depositories.

More [illegible] fever reported in the vicinity of the Franklin school.

Rev. A. S. Boyum, president of the Hauge's synod, submitted his report.

The Central Park Chautauqua Circle was entertained by Mr. and Mrs. Robt. D. Russell.

Amusements—"The Old Homestead" at the Grand Opera House; "Rosedale" at the Pence Opera House; "The Turtle Boy" at Dime Museum.

**St. Paul.**

Minneapolis and St. Paul today.

Stanley E. Dean pleads not guilty and will fight.

The Loyal Legion gave a banquet in honor to Gen. Ruger.

The 1st regiment will go into camp at White Bear in July.

The trial of criminal cases has begun in the district court.

The New Yorkers mix poor grades with Duluth No. 1 hard wheat and ship it to Dublin.

The third annual sale of trotting bred stock by Minnesota breeders took place at the state fair grounds.

**Northwest.**

Burglars got in their work at Eau Claire.

The Kempfer trial is in progress at Fergus Falls.

The Eau Claire city council and mayor had their regular row.

Blanche Nutter, living near Eau Claire, committed suicide.

The Otter Tail County Alliance is in session at Battle Lake, Minn.

The Grand Lodge, I. O. O. F., in session at Faribault elected officers.

The Presbyterians are having a great time in the trip throughout the Northwest.

W. P. Allen, of Dubuque, has been elected grand master of the Iowa grand lodge.

Mrs. Andrew Werdemeyer, of Hudson, while temporarily insane, attempted suicide.

The Dakota Republican Central committee has been called to meet at Aberdeen, June 22.

Dr. Corson, of Bismarck, arrested on the charge of setting fire to the Sheridan House, was discharged.

Sparks has issued another order which will retard the settlement and growth of the Missouri river country west of Aberdeen.

**Washington.**

It is now Mrs. Cleveland.

The President has vetoed three more pension bills.

Senator Cullom has a new constitutional amendment.

It is understood that Manning is going to Hot Springs.

Sparks has issued another order making more trouble for settlers.

Senator Hale introduced in the Senate a bill making the impeding or obstruction of railroads except by legal process a crime punishable by fine and imprisonment.

Comptroller Durham, of the treasury department, has rendered a decision in which he holds that under the act of June 15, 1880, the double minimum excess paid for land should be returned to the original purchaser and not to the transferee where transfer was made after the passage of the act.

**Miscellaneous.**

The Milwaukee grand jury has indicted a number of Anarchists.

The Chicago grand jury has returned 34 additional indictments.

Most was sentenced to the penitentiary for one year and fined $500.

Powderly wants the Amalgamated Association to join the Knights of Labor.

Canada has reduced the export duty on pine logs from $3 to $2 per 100 feet.

Hottentot, Jaubert, Billy Gilmore and Burr Oak were the Latonia winners.

The second annual convention of the National Association of Stove Manufacturers is in session at Cleveland.

Duke of Westmoreland, Buckston, Inspector B. Stone Deck, Edgefield and Referee were the winners at Jerome Park.

It has been ascertained that Hoke's shortage to the Merchants' National Bank of Peoria, is $103,000 and that $75,000 was taken by Hoke when it was known as the Merchants' bank.

### A Tough Experience.

CHICAGO, Ill., June 2.—At the entrance to the harbor tonight, sunk in the middle of the channel, with her rail several inches beneath the surface of the stream is the steam barge Swallow. She arrived here this evening after passing through a terrible experience in the lake, nearly resulting fatally to her crew of 14. When about 40 miles from Muskegon, Monday, heavily freighted with lumber and making for Chicago, she was suddenly thrown on her beam ends by a frightful squall that came with so little warning as to barely allow time to take in sail. At the same time the deck load of lumber shifted, and a huge sea struck her. The vessel instantly filled with water, her fires went out, and in less than a minute she was a helpless wreck, drifting at the mercy of the wind and sea. When the deck load shifted, three members of the crew were hurled into the lake. Fortunately the barge was driving broadside toward them and they succeeded in pulling themselves aboard. Three deck hands asleep in the forecastle were flooded out of their bunks and narrowly escaped drowning. The cooks, who were asleep in a room off the cabin, had to be dragged on deck through a hole cut in a panel of their door. Capt. Flagsted gathered the crew upon the quarter deck, where they remained while the wreck drifted about all night, all day Tuesday and until 1 o'clock this morning momentarily expecting a gale that would break the barge to pieces and send all hands to the bottom. The steam barge Funbar met her just as the crew were beginning to despair, and towed her to Chicago. She sunk as she was entering the river.

### MAINE DEMOCRATS.

BANGOR, Me., June 2.—The Democratic state convention in session here this afternoon passed a resolution of sympathy with Mr. Gladstone in his Home Rule struggle, and nominated Col. Clark S. Edwards, of Bethel, for governor by acclamation.

The platform eulogizes labor. Industrial worth, not wealth, is pronounced the emblem of individual greatness. It affirms that government has been established for the benefit of labor, while the pure end of legislation is to secure to labor the just rewards of its effort. A law establishing 10 hours for a day's labor is demanded, the passage of a bill prohibiting child labor is called for; arraigns the Republican party for defeating the 10-hour bill in the legislature in 1885, and for giving away in congress the public lands to corporations and monopolies; demands that the federal government shall protect American fishermen in all their just rights at all hazards; endorses the administration of President Cleveland and pledges the earnest support of the Democrat party. The principles of the Chicago platform of 1884 are reaffirmed. Adjourned.

### TROUBLE FEARED.

AUSTIN, Tex., June 2.—Capt. George Schmitt, of the state rangers, who has been stationed at Laredo since the riot of last April, is in this city making arrangements with Gov. Ireland and the adjutant-general for military in anticipation of another outbreak. Schmitt says that proceedings have been instituted to oust the marshal and sheriff from office for the part they took in the late riot, and that trouble is sure to follow when this is accomplished.

## NORTHWEST NEWS.

### Sparks Issues Another Order to Further Annoy Settlers.

### The Eau Claire City Council and Mayor Have Another Parrot and Monkey Time.

### A Miscellaneous Mixture of Poisons Taken with Suicidal Intent.

### Dr. Corson on Trial at Bismarck for Arson Honorably Discharged—Burglars.

[SPECIAL DISPATCH TO THE TRIBUNE.]

DULUTH, June 2.—The following telegram was received at the United States land office here today:

"WASHINGTON, D. C., June 2.—Allow no more preemption, desert land or tree culture filings or entries until further notice. Circular by mail.

[Signed.] SPARKS."

This action is in view of the probable repeal of these laws, and is said at Washington to have the approval of Secretary Lamar, and would practically close the Duluth land office for new business permanently. Only homestead entries would affect titles to large tracts of pine land in the neighborhood, and holdings of settlers are the only preemption filings affected by the order at this office. Register Marble when seen by the Minneapolis TRIBUNE representative in regard to the matter, said he had not seen the telegram, and was very much surprised at the news. He could not understand it, and as he had not seen the telegram could give no definite opinion. The general expression of land men seen in regard to the matter is that it shows on Sparks's part a decided lack of knowledge in the premises. Evidently from the evidence he intends to follow out the bill that has been introduced in congress in regard to land claims, to repeal the preemption, timber culture and desert land acts and to so amend the homestead law as require a three years' residence on the land. Congress has not yet passed this law. Mr. Sparks seems to have done so himself and to have taken the matter as far as possible, out of the hands of congress.

**Still at Loggerheads.**

[SPECIAL DISPATCH TO THE TRIBUNE.]

EAU CLAIRE, Wis., June 2.—War broke out afresh tonight in the council at the first meeting since the return of Mayor Griswell from Canada. During the mayor's absence the council elected the standing committees, which the mayor claims power to appoint, asserting the new rules were adopted by fraud. Tonight one of the committees which the mayor had appointed in opposition to the council, made a report and tried to supersede the committee on the same subject elected by the council. A long and heated war of words ensued. One of the old aldermen moved to refer the subject to a proper committee created by the council. The mayor refused to put the motion and refused to entertain the appeal. The wrangle continued an hour, the crowd breaking in with applause of the mayor, who moved his gavel and became highly excited, and shut off debate arbitrarily. Finally Ald. McDonough offered a resolution ordering the clerk to give all bills which came into his hands to the committees elected by the council May 11, and to no other persons. The mayor refused to put the resolution to a vote, declaring all action of the council in his absence in electing committees was fraud and all illegal.

McDonough appealed from the decision of the chair, and pleaded to have the appeal put to the council, which the mayor refused. Thereupon the old aldermen called loudly on Ald. Frawley, president of the council, to put the question on McDonough's resolution. Frawley rose to do so. The mayor ordered the policemen in the chamber to arrest President Frawley. [illegible]

[illegible]

**Stillwater News.**

[illegible]

**Workingmen's Convention.**

[illegible]

**Court at Mankato.**

[illegible]

**Building and Loan Association.**

[illegible]

dollars was loaned at from 3? to 4? per cent premium.

**Hawkeye Matters.**

[SPECIAL DISPATCH TO THE TRIBUNE.]

DES MOINES, Iowa, June 2.—The Masonic grand lodge today elected W. P. Allen, of Dubuque, grand master; F. M. Howe, S. ? G. W.; Sidney Smith, J. G. W.; Geo. S. Murphy, grand treasurer; T. S. Parvin, grand secretary. Allen has been custodian of work for a generation and is a wealthy druggist. Parvin many years ago was grand master and has ever since been secretary. The next grand lodge will meet at Davenport, Iowa.

The Electric Medical Association met today, with about 40 delegates attending, two or three being ladies. Twenty-one recent graduates were elected members. Dr. Harris, of Grinnell, delivered the president's address. Those expecting to be physicians ought to be physically and mentally robust and imbued with a high respect for law and morality. He spoke in the kindest terms of Pasteur and manifested a very liberal spirit generally. He urged the society to lay aside personal differences and invite the national society to meet in Iowa next year.

In the impeachment court today Hutchin's resolution disapproving of vacation salary snatching was defeated by the following, offered by Woolson:

Resolved, That it is the sense of the senate that the manager manager shall act as he deems proper and in accordance with his own judgment of the law and facts in the case as not accepting compensation for the period of time or any part thereof intervening during the administration of the senate; 126 voted for the substitute and 13 against.

Andrew Watts was placed on the witness stand by the managers. He had examined the Waverly bank, for Brown, and had reported it insolvent. Afterward he had written Brown the bank might possible be rescued. Soon after he became its cashier, but soon quit. His evidence was slightly in Brown's favor on an important article.

**Duluth Doings.**

[SPECIAL DISPATCH TO THE TRIBUNE.]

DULUTH, June 2.—The strike among the iron ore handlers at Two Harbors, near Duluth, is over and all but a few men returned to work.—The Duluth iron range saw mill hands also struck and the mills instantly shut down, it having been in operation partially to give the men employment, there being no pressing work.—Over 5,000 tons of iron ore was loaded on vessels today at Two Harbors on deck, which shows conclusively the death of the strike.

Company K, 2d regiment, to the number of 47 men, assembled tonight at the armory for annual state inspection by Gen King. Until six months ago the company was in a disorganized state, and when the present captain took hold of them was in bad shape. They were surprised, therefore, when Drill Inspector and Gen. King said: "When I was here last year, May 1, at the inspection of your company, I stated that you were the best drilled company of the 2d regiment. Now I say that there are only two companies in the national guard of the state that excel in drill and general excellence, and if you keep on as you began you will soon be able to cope with Company D, the crack company of the West." The members of the company feel highly complimented by the inspector's remarks, as well they may. The company goes to New Ulm the last of the week to attend encampment.

**Took Poison.**

EAU CLAIRE, Wis., June 2.—Blanche Nutter, a pretty girl, aged 16, living with a sister and widowed mother at Truax Prairie, just west of the city, took Paris green yesterday. She was found in great agony. She said she wanted to die because her mother ill-treated her, and kept her at home and would not let her go out to parties with young men. She had also swallowed from a bottle of tincture of iron. This morning she was thought to be dying. She had previously tried to kill herself by eating matches and swallowing aconite, saleratus and a bottle of horse medicine which she found in the barn. Her mother is a school teacher, of a highly respected family.

**Got the Boodle.**

EAU CLAIRE, Wis., June 2.—Burglars at 3 o'clock this morning blew open the safe in Syverson's store, on the north side, with giant powder. The explosion blew a safe door 30 feet smashed out windows, and completely wrecked the interior of the store, doing a damage of $500. The burglars got away with $25 cash and $600 notes and securities. The home of Charles Tello was robbed of $50 by burglars. Another residence and jewelry store was also broken into, but nothing was taken. There is no clew to the burglars.

**Alliances in Session.**

[SPECIAL DISPATCH TO THE TRIBUNE.]

BATTLE LAKE, June 2.—The Otter Tail County Alliance began its annual meeting here today. There are 34 alliances, represented by over 100 delegates, coming from every part of the county. They are discussing the question of binding twine and taking action on various matters of interest to the farmers. Thus far the only thing done has been the appointment of the committees and the election of the officers, the old ones all being re-elected. It is possible that they will nominate a legislative ticket tomorrow, although there is some doubt about it, as there is a division of sentiments. The platform will be adopted before the meeting adjourns.

**The Kempfer Trial.**

[SPECIAL DISPATCH TO THE TRIBUNE.]

FERGUS FALLS, June 2.—In the Kempfer murder trial today, the state introduced testimony proving the fatal nature of Smith's wounds. The deposition by Smith before his death, was to the effect that Kempfer called him names, and Smith hit him with his fist; then Kempfer shot him; that he did not draw his revolver till Kempfer had shot twice. Testimony was given that Kempfer had made threats against different persons. The defendants attorney said they expected to prove that Smith was the aggressor, and that Kempfer, blind with blood and in a dazed condition, drew his revolver to defend himself.

**Officers Elected.**

[SPECIAL DISPATCH TO THE TRIBUNE.]

FARIBAULT, June 2.—At a session held this afternoon the following officers of the Grand lodge were elected: S. J. Jones, grand master, Kasson; H. C. Miller, deputy grand master, St. Peter; J. C. Cockburn, grand warden, Minneapolis; Sherwood Hough, grand secretary and treasurer, St. Paul; H. J. Strauss, grand reporter, two years, St. Paul; C. C. Hurd, grand reporter, one year, Minneapolis; G. S. Gowdy, grand chaplain, Albert Lea; Chas. Lambert, grand marshal, St. Paul; G. M. Green, grand conductor, Amboy; G. A. Gross, grand guardian, Fergus Falls; E. Thermer, grand herald, Owatonna.

**Discharged.**

[SPECIAL DISPATCH TO THE TRIBUNE.]

BISMARCK, Dak., June 2.—The examination of Dr. Dr. Carroll Carson, which has been in progress [illegible]

**Gov. Rusk Unwell.**

[illegible]

**Attempted Suicide.**

[illegible]

**Met with a Band.**

[illegible]

**Dakota Republicans.**

WATERTOWN, Dak., June 2.—Hon. A. C. Mellette, chairman of the Republican territorial central committee has just called a meeting of the committee at Aberdeen June 22, the second day of the editorial association meeting there. The time and place of the Republican territorial convention will be decided on. Other business of importance to the party will also be considered.

**Burglars.**

[SPECIAL DISPATCH TO THE TRIBUNE.]

EAU CLAIRE, Wis., June 2.—At 3 o'clock this morning burglars blew out the door of Casper Syverson's safe and wrecked the inside of the store, doing $500 damage. The burglars secured $25 in money and notes and securities amounting to $600 and made good their escape. The interior of the store was completely devastated, and the glass broken from all the windows.

**The Presbyterians.**

DEVIL'S LAKE, Dak., June 2.—One hundred and fifty commissioners to the recent general assembly at Minneapolis, arrived here this morning, by special train. After breakfasting they took the steamer Minnie to Fort Totten, visiting Sullis Hill and the Sioux Indian agency, and left Devils Lake on the return trip at 12:30. A military parade was had at Fort Totten under command of Maj. Bacon.

**Iowa Masons.**

DES MOINES, Iowa, June 2.—At the Masonic Grand Lodge this morning, W. P. Allen, of Dubuque, for many years custodian of work and past senior grand warden, was elected grand master. Next year the grand lodge meets at Davenport.

**Want Ten Hours.**

[SPECIAL DISPATCH TO THE TRIBUNE.]

EAU CLAIRE, Wis., June 2.—The Knights of Labor have a committee of 12 at work on the matter of trying to induce the Valley Lumber Company to run its saw mill 10 hours instead of 11 per day. The president of the company has thus far declined to hold any communication with the Knights.

**Postoffice Robbed.**

[SPECIAL DISPATCH TO THE TRIBUNE.]

NEW RICHMOND, Wis., June 2.—Last night our postoffice was entered by burglars, who found an easy entrance through the window in the rear of the office. They blew open the safe, but were poorly paid for the job, as there was but $10 or $12 in it.

**Sudden Death.**

[SPECIAL DISPATCH TO THE TRIBUNE.]

NORA SPRINGS, Iowa, June 2.—Mrs. Henry Gast, the wife of a German farmer near here, died last night under very suspicious circumstances, and rumors of foul play are plenty. An investigation will be held.

**At Owatonna.**

[SPECIAL DISPATCH TO THE TRIBUNE.]

OWATONNA, June 2.—The June term of the district court was called to order by Judge Buckham, at Gauser's Hall, yesterday. The calendar is a small one, most of the large cases being settled before they were called.—Hon. G. A. Pillsbury and party were escorted to the train by our citizens and a band after the corner stone exercises yesterday, and three hearty cheers were given the gentlemen as the train pulled out.

**Fire Near Northfield.**

[SPECIAL DISPATCH TO THE TRIBUNE.]

NORTHFIELD, June 2.—Samuel Johnson's house, situated six miles east of this city, was destroyed by fire Tuesday morning. Loss, $2,000; insured for $600.—The bodies of William Alber's little daughter and hired man, drowned in Union lake Sunday afternoon, have been recovered and the funeral services were held this morning.

**Damphool Sparks.**

[SPECIAL DISPATCH TO THE TRIBUNE.]

ABERDEEN, Dak., June 2.—The officials of the United States land office here received special orders from Commissioner Sparks by telegraph today to receive no more entries or filing on preemptions timber cultures or desert land. This will seriously retard the settlement and growth of the Missouri river country west of here, which is being rapidly settled up this year.

### KELLY'S FUNERAL.

NEW YORK, June 2.—Arrangements for John Kelly's funeral were completed this afternoon. A requiem mass will be celebrated in the Cathedral at 10 a. m. on Saturday. Archbishop Corrigan will be the celebrant, assisted by Mgr. Farley. Mgr. Preston will deliver the sermon. Throughout the day prominent citizens called at or sent cards to the house. Telegrams of condolence came from all over the country. The board of aldermen today adopted resolutions paying tribute to the memory of Mr. Kelly, and calling on all public offices to be closed on the day of the funeral and flags on all municipal buildings be displayed at half-mast, and request that the same mark of respect be observed from all public buildings in the city and on the shipping in the harbor. The board then adjourned as a mark of respect. The Tammany society and the Tammany committee on organization held meetings tonight. At the former a large number of members attended. Resolutions of regret were adopted. These recited the sorrow felt by the society and the grief felt by the individual members at the demise of their chief; praised the purity of his life, which, during a period of lax political morals, gave him the title of "the honest;" spoke of his loyalty to the country, devotion to party, faithfulness to friendship, magnanimity toward his enemies and the irreproachableness of his private character; sketched the persevering struggles of his life from boyhood up; recited his services to the city, and ordered a copy of the tributes sent to the family. The committee on organization selected Friday night as the time for holding the memorial meeting, and appointed a committee to arrange therefor.

Recorder Smythe told how Mr. Kelly was satisfied that his end was coming, and how he expressed the hope that when death arrived all mankind would feel kind toward him.

Mr. Kelly desired no ostentatious burial. The recorder confirmed the general report that Mr. Kelly died "peacefully, manfully, and like a Christian."

### G. A. R. REUNION.

INDIANAPOLIS, Ind., June 2.—The Grand Army reunion and camp fire, in connection with the opening of the new City Hall, reached its climax today and tonight. Gen. Logan arrived this morning and Gen. Sherman reached the city this afternoon. The latter was met by the local military and Grand Army posts, and entering a carriage with Gen. Logan was escorted to his hotel. The generals were roundly cheered along the route and at University Park the carriage was bombarded with flowers by the thousands of school children, whose offerings were so numerous as to overflow the vehicle. At the camp fire tonight the program comprised speeches by Gen. Sherman, Gen. Logan, Commander Burdette, of the G. A. R.; Senator Harrison, Gen. Gibson, ex-Secretary of the Navy Thompson and others. The intervals between speeches were filled by patriotic songs, rendered by a large orchestra and a chorus of 600 voices, and scenes of almost frantic enthusiasm were of frequent occurrence.

In the course of his speech Gen. Sherman said: "I am told some of the good people of Indianapolis expressed surprise that I did not come to the funeral of vice-President Hendricks, and though it may be out of place, I am willing to explain that I did certainly intend to come, for Mr. Hendricks was always courteous and friendly to the old soldiers. The moment I heard of his death I concluded to attend his funeral and waited for some sort of an invitation, but none came. I then obtained the published notice prescribing the order of the procession, who should compose it, and in it no place was assigned to the army or navy, so that had I come to Indianapolis I would have been left out."

### THE RUSSIAN BUGBEAR.

ST. PETERSBURG, Russia, June 2.—The *Novoe Vremya* states that the Shah of Persia has refused the proposal from Turkey to join in an universal mussulman alliance. The paper further declares that in the text of his refusal the Shah used the following language: "My friend Russia will not allow anybody to attack me."

Advices from Teheran say the Persian ministry gave a banquet to Neurui Pasha, who mooted an alliance between Turkey, Persia and Russia, and who, in advocating the proposal attributed all the recent misfortunes of Persia and Turkey to "their common enemy, England."

LONDON, June 2.—Dispatches from Constantinople state that the military and naval activity of Russia is looked upon by the Porte as ominous. Turkey is alarmed by them. It is also said that the Sultan is leaning upon Germany for support in case of emergency.

**Manning Going to Hot Springs.**

WASHINGTON, D. C. June 2.—It's understood that Secretary and Mrs. Manning will leave Washington Saturday afternoon for Hot Springs where they will probably remain about a month.

## THE WEDDING.

### The White House Now Has a Mistress to Grace and Adorn It.

### Cleveland and Miss Folsom Married in the Presence of Near Friends and Relatives.

### The Executive Mansion Brilliantly Decorated for the Occasion.

### List of the Guests and Costumes of the Ladies—Cleveland's Bridal Gift.

[SPECIAL DISPATCH TO THE TRIBUNE.]

WASHINGTON, D. C., June 2.—At half-past six o'clock this evening a large crowd of people moved about immediately in front of the White House in eager expectation of seeing somebody or something in connection with the President's marriage. Their curiosity was gratified by slow degrees. At that hour members of the Marine band were arriving and only those who had been in the house all day, were present. Five minutes later Secretary Lamar's carriage drove up. There was an almost deathly silence without and within. The ceremony was to take place in ten minutes, and only one of seven members of the cabinet present. The swelling crowd of spectators began to grow nervous. They feared there would be a disarrangement and disappointment. On came the spectators by pairs, trios, squads, crowds. The assembly numbers 1,000 people on the outside of the Executive Mansion. They move around speaking in low tones, but they are not permitted to enter under the portico in front and leading to the main entrance. The air is warm, sky clear, and the sun is beginning to sink out of sight behind the hills. It is eight minutes to 7 o'clock when up dashes a carriage. In it are Postmaster General and Mrs. Vilas. Scarcely do they alight before another carriage rushes up. A large, smooth-faced man jumps out and the carriage drives on. It is Mr. Bissell, President Cleveland's old law partner. In rapid succession and in the order named carriages containing Secretaries Bayard, Whitney and Manning, the latter two with their wives, arrive. Secretary Manning enters the White House at six minutes to 7 o'clock. His wife and his office messenger assist him to walk, his recent illness having had a telling effect upon him. All are now present and the little flutter caused by arrivals has quieted. The crowd outside listens and gazes as one man. Scarcely a noise is heard anywhere. Members of the Marine band, with their bright sashed uniforms, trimmed in gold, peep out of windows which are almost filled with palms and ferns, arranged very effectually to shut out of view the interior of the house while having the windows raised. It is 6 minutes to 7. The main door opens and out walks a French coiffeur and his wife. They have arranged the toilets of Mr. Cleveland and Miss Folsom. Some one pulls down the blinds at the President's room upstairs and immediately the gas is turned down in Miss Folsom's room. A perfect glare of gas is flashed upon the whole lower portion of the house, and inside there is a scene equal to the grandeur of a royal palace on the occasion of a marriage of a crowned head. It is 7 o'clock. There is a rustle inside. The band begins Mendelssohn's grand wedding march. One minute later the music closes. Grover Cleveland and Frances Folsom stand before Dr. Sunderland in the blue room. Surrounding them are about 30 guests. The picture is extremely beautiful. Five minutes later it is Mr. and Mrs. Cleveland, and they are receiving congratulations. The cannon at Fort Meyer, the navy yard and arsenal begin to belch forth the announcement of the culmination of the event. Bells ring and the people disperse from the center of attraction. So a President was married.

The grounds of the White House were surrounded by newspaper men, anxious to get a glimpse of the wedding party as they left for their honeymoon trip. The President had determined to make his departure as inconspicuous as possible, and with this end in view every precaution was taken to throw reporters off the scent. Still the corps were not to be outwitted. Between them they guarded every gate, and upwards of 50 coupes, hacks and cabs were scattered around the grounds. It was thought that the most likely place of exit would be by the Sixteenth street gate. Several carriages, closely covered, came out this way, but the President's landau was not among them. He left by the opposite gate, on the principle that the farthest way around is the nearest way to the depot. He was closely followed by a carriage in which were several newspaper men, who saw him proceed to the outskirts of the city to the Baltimore & Ohio "Y," where they met a special train sent over from Baltimore, which did not enter the city depot. The train consisted of a baggage car, President Garrett's private coach and one empty passenger coach put on to steady the train. In the Garrett coach were the President, and his bride and their destination is Deer Park, Md., where for one week they will try love in Robert Garrett's cottage. At the expiration of that time they will return to Washington and a reception will be arranged.

Col. Lamont was sitting in the east room at 11 p. m. The guests had departed, the colonel was happy. Everything went off in excellent shape. He said the President went through the ceremony like a veteran and the bride did not show a sign of nervousness.

**"Were There Many Presents?"**

"Yes, quite a number; only the President's presents to his bride will be public, however. That was a diamond necklace. Many have not yet been opened. Many congratulatory telegrams were received. Queen Victoria sent a greeting this morning. I have received about 500 dispatches, but have not had time to open them."

"Many applications for wedding cakes?"

"Hundreds of them. They come in person, sent by mail and today I have had a number of requests by telegraph.

**Other White House Weddings.**

WASHINGTON, D. C., June 2.—Other weddings there have been at the White House, eight in all, but never before today has the highest dignitary in the land bowed his head within its historic walls to receive the blessing of the church on his union in the holy bond of matrimony. From the very dawn of the wedding day the city seemed alive to the approaching event. Little knots of idlers talked it over on the sidewalks in front of hotels, sedate matrons gossipped as they passed along the streets and bevies of laughing girls chatted and speculated about the coming momentous ceremony. If there is truth in the ancient adage a happy bride will reign in the White House, for, though the day opened with a gray and cheerless sky and shadows resting on the earth, yet as it grew older the elements seemed to relent little by little and the sun forced his rays through unwilling clouds until his broad beams fell in generous abundance on the soft green sward of the trim park encompassing the White House, bringing out in bright relief the simple, yet stately white columns of the time-honored home of Presidents, crystalizing in prismatic hues the sparkling sprays of the fountains, and cresting with gold the foliage of the trees. Many were the curious glances that sought to pierce the draped windows, and numberless were the comments and speculations of the loiterers who gathered early in the afternoon within the grounds. Little or nothing in the appearance of the mansion or its surroundings indicated to the casual passers-by that the much-talked-of event was at hand. The still and murky haze of the early afternoon had now wholly given place to a clear sky and warm southerly breezes, while yellow slanting sunbeams filtered through the foliage of the park and made flickering pictures on the velvety turf. The great fountain did its best to attract attention, spurting its cooling spray to the verge of its granite basin, and flowering shrubs and ferns of tropical green filled the marginal gaps in the picture. Seats in the park across the avenue were occupied by fawn-clad maidens, while half the young lovers in town, moved by the common sympathy which stirs the romantic feelings of the 60,000,000, took the winding walks in the line of their evening promenade and speculated upon the emotions which are supposed to fill the hearts of bride and groom. On the walks near the White House the assemblage was thoroughly democratic, and ragged urchins and slip shod colored girls jostled natty young gentlemen and ladies in silk attire. The gates were left wide open, and by 6 o'clock the crowd had swollen to several hundreds, and a score or more of newspaper men held a point of vantage alongside the portico. The successive arrivals of the guests were watched with interest and their names whispered by the more knowing of their companions. Suddenly the strains of the "Wedding March" floated through the open windows, and there was a general exclamation from the outside crowd, "The service has begun." Then there came a tantalizing hush within the walls, which soon ended by the strains of the bridal chorus from "Lohengrin," and it was thereby known that the ceremony was over. One by one the lights sprang up at the windows and the great burners on the portico cast their effulgence over the [illegible]. The scene resembled a summer night [illegible] and the crowd gave itself up to the enjoyment of the delightful music. With short intermissions the fine orchestra rendered the following selections: Bolero, "I O son la Rosa," by Marianna; "Invitation a la Valse," Weber; "Spring Song," Mendelssohn; romance, "Bright Star of Hope," Robandi, and "Mosaic Delsree," Strauss.

[illegible] keep you only unto her so long as you both shall live?"

The groom (firmly)—"I do."

Dr. Sunderland—Frances, do you take this man whom you hold by the hand, to be your lawful wedded husband, to live together after God's ordinance in the holy state of wedlock? Do you promise to love, honor, comfort and keep him in sickness and in health, in joy and in sorrow, and forsaking all others, keep you only unto him so long as you both shall live?"

The bride responded in a low but clear voice, "I do."

"In token of the same let the wedding ring be passed." (The groom placed the ring on the bride's finger.)

Dr. Sunderland (solemnly)—For as much as Grover and Frances have here agreed and covenanted to live together after God's ordinance, in the holy state of wedlock, and confirmed the same by giving and taking a wedding ring, now, therefore, in the presence of this company, in the name of the Father, and of the Son and of the Holy Ghost, I pronounce and declare that they are husband and wife, and what God hath joined together let no man put asunder."

The Rev. Mr. Cleveland then pronounced the following benediction:

"God the Father, the Son and God the Holy Ghost, bless, preserve and keep you. The Lord mercifully fill you with all temporal and all spiritual blessings and grant that you may so live together in this world that in the world to come you may have life everlasting. Amen."

"HEAR THE MERRY WEDDING BELLS, HAPPY BELLS!"

THE TRIBUNE takes a pardonable pride in placing before its large constituency this morning, the only authorized—as one might say official—portrait of the President's bride yet published. It is from a photograph of Miss Folsom taken on her departure for her European trip, and is pronounced by her intimate friends simply perfect. An artist's proof was submitted to the President, eliciting the following reply:

WASHINGTON, D. C., June 2.—To the Editor of the TRIBUNE, Minneapolis, Minn.: I am directed by His Excellency, the President, to acknowledge the receipt of the engraving of the bride-elect, Miss Folsom, and to say for him that he never saw anything like it before. Please send 15 copies of the TRIBUNE wrapped ready for mailing. By order of the President,

DAN'L LAMONT, Secretary.

**The Wedding Guests.**

About 6:30 o'clock the wedding guests began to arrive, their carriages rolling up to the main door of the mansion through the great iron gates on Pennsylvania avenue. The first arrival was Secretary Lamar at 6:37. He was closely followed by Rev. Dr. Sunderland and wife, and during the next few minutes there came in quick succession Postmaster-General Vilas and wife, Mr. Henry S. Bissell, Secretary and Mrs. Endicott, Secretary Bayard, Secretary and Mrs. Whitney and Secretary Manning and his wife. Removing their wraps in the state dining room, the guests proceeded to the [illegible]

**Those Present.**

[illegible]

**The Ceremony.**

[illegible]

**Congratulations.**

At the conclusion of the ceremony, Mrs. Folsom showing traces of deep emotion, was the first to tender her congratulations to the newly married pair. She was followed by Miss Cleveland, the Rev. Mr. Cleveland and the other relatives and friends in turn. While the congratulations were in progress the band, under the leadership of Prof. Sousa, performed the bridal chorus and march from "Lohengrin," and to this music the President and his wife led the way into the stately east room. The adornments of this noble hall were in keeping with its majestic proportions, and its ample space and brilliant illumination afforded an opportunity for a fitting display of the ladies' toilets. The bride wore an enchanting wedding dress of ivory satin, simply garnished on the high corsage [illegible]

**"The Toilets."**

[illegible]

**The Decorations.**

[illegible]

**Interwoven in Immortelles.**

[illegible]

# The Minneapolis Tribune.

VOLUME XXI. NO. 248. SATURDAY MORNING, JANUARY 14, 1888.—TWELVE PAGES. PRICE, THREE CENTS. (ON THE TRAINS, FIVE CENTS.)

## THE NEWS.

**Minneapolis.**

Nineteen deeds aggregated $36,293.

A reception at the Westminster Church parlors.

The State Horticultural society meet next week.

Rev. Francis Tiffany's lecture before the Fine Arts society.

Charles Foster and Minnie Stahl were married at police court.

The Northwestern Ski club contested for the championship.

The McCurdy-Whittaker bicycle affair still agitating the people.

Ellen M. McCoy made application for a divorce from Arnold W. McCoy.

The G. A. R. posts commenced arrangements for receiving delegates to the state encampment.

**St. Paul.**

A $1,000 fire in the Minnesota Bank building.

Prisoners attempt to escape from the county jail.

The Grand Lodge A. F. & A. M. concluded their business yesterday.

Gov. McGill suspended Ole A. Boe, county treasurer of Becker county.

The committee on streets transacted routine business at their meeting last evening.

Fourteen deeds with considerations aggregating $50,120 were filed with the register of deeds yesterday.

The state board of charities and corrections issue an important statement of expenses for service in state institutions.

**Northwest.**

Sioux City had a big fire.

Henry Schmidt was hanged at West Union, Iowa.

The school book question will be investigated by a committee from the Iowa legislature.

Clark's smelter and Colusa copper mines at Butte have been sold to a Boston syndicate.

**Washington.**

## AFTER HIS SCALP.

### Disgruntled Democrats Said to Desire Cleveland's Defeat.

### The So-Called Conspiracy Denied by Friends of Those Implicated.

### Free Trade Organs Want Sabin Read Out of the Party.

### Randall Said to Be Smothering an Obnoxious Resolution in Committee.

#### A QUEER STORY.

**Rumor That Several Prominent Democrats are Working to Defeat Cleveland's Renomination for President.**

[SPECIAL DISPATCH TO THE TRIBUNE.]

WASHINGTON, Jan. 13—A story has been in circulation for a day or two to the effect that Sam Randall, Senator McPherson, of New Jersey; Senator Joe Brown, of Georgia; Congressman Foran, of Ohio; and one or two other well-known protectionist democrats, were organizing a conspiracy for the purpose of defeating the re-nomination of President Cleveland. The story was given an air of plausibility, because when the President sent his message to congress it met with disfavor at the hands of these gentlemen, one or two of them, especially

the idea indicated in the Hewitt bill. The editor of the American Wool Reporter said the bone of contention, which is prolonging the conference, is carpet wools. The question is not whether the duty shall be removed from this class of wools, but whether or not it shall be increased. The manufacture of carpets in the United States has in the last five years nearly, if not quite, doubled, and, of course, there has been a corresponding increase of this class of wool, a kind that cannot be profitably raised in this country.

## DISASTROUS FIRE.

### Several Fine Business Houses in Indianapolis Burned Down.

### The Losses, Roughly Estimated, Approximate One Million Dollars.

### Detroit and Several Other Places Visited by Costly Fires.

### Capture of the Man Who Swindled Residents of the City of Mexico of $30,000.

#### A CONFLAGRATION.

**Several Valuable Business Structures in Indianapolis Destroyed by Fire—The Loss Estimated at $750,000 to $1,000,000.**

INDIANAPOLIS, Ind., Jan. 13.—What promises at this hour (12:30 a. m.) to prove the most destructive fire ever known in this city broke out tonight at 11 o'clock. At that hour an alarm called a portion of the fire department to South Meridian and Maryland streets, in the wholesale district. The fire, as now stated, was first discovered in the rear part of D. P. Erwin & Co.'s dry goods house. Other alarms brought more engines and hose companies, but their efforts are without avail, and the flames are spreading rapidly to the north of Erwin's, and by 12 o'clock both

an agent of Henry E. Abbey and selling bogus tickets to Patti performances.

A reply was received from Gen. Ceballos today asking that the prisoner be held, and saying that extradition proceedings would be begun at once. This prisoner has a remarkable record. When he was arrested he was entering the office of a lawyer whom he had retained to defend him in a suit brought by several foreign houses who accuse him of having swindled them out of large sums of money in a speculation concerning some patent that has no existence. The man is known to the European police as Morton, Coster and Montgomery, in various places. He declares that he is of English birth and of a good family. He is highly educated and speaks five languages. He graduated from an English university and almost immediately got into a gambling scrape. He drifted to the continent, and at the time of the Franco-Prussian war was an editor on a Parisian paper and was one of the three editors who were permitted by the Prussian authorities to leave Paris through the intervention of United States Minister Washburne. Then he conceived the scheme of collecting money for the suffering Parisians. He proceeded to London, showed forged credentials to the lord mayor, and received a check for £1,000 from that official. Presently the Queen and Prince of Wales inaugurated a subscription list. For this he was imprisoned for a year. While in prison he poured oil on his clothing and set it on fire. He was badly burned, and served the remainder of his term in the prison hospital. On his release he joined forces with one Kerr, who conducted a swindling publication which pretended to give "tips" on sporting events. The pair began swinding right and left. Finally the Countess De Goncault of a French province, who had lost £35,000 through the rascals, secured their exposure and sentence to 15 years' imprisonment each. Incidentally it was shown that several Scotland yard detectives were in with them, and the force was reorganized as the result. Bourton served half his time and got out on a ticket-of-leave. In 1886 he escaped punishment for selling fraudulent news in Brussels. Next he worked the Patti scheme and he was here when arrested for the purpose of suing a bank because it refused to pay over to him the proceeds of the sales of fraudulent bonds in Switzerland. He also threatened libel suits against some of the newspapers which published the story.

#### STABBED AN OFFICER.

## SELDOM EQUALED.

### The Recent Blizzard the Worst [illegible] Witnessed in Many Years.

### Though No Snow Is Falling the Wind Still Blows with Hurricanic Velocity.

### Ineffectual Efforts of Railroad Companies to Run Trains.

### Several People Frozen to Death Within Sight of Their Own Homes—Notes.

#### DAKOTA.

**Huron.**

[SPECIAL DISPATCH TO THE TRIBUNE.]

HURON, Dak., Jan. 13.—The storm Thursday was the most severe known here. At 6 o'clock Thursday morning it was 20 above; at 1 in the afternoon 17 below. This morning it was 28 below. At 11:40 Thursday forenoon the velocity of the wind was 12 miles an hour from the south. At 11:42 it was 24 miles, coming from the west. At 11:45 it was 45 miles an hour. At 11:47 it was 48 from the west. Two minutes later it shifted to the northwest and at 12:15 was blowing 57 miles per hour, continuing till 1 p. m. At 1:30 it was 60 miles an hour. From that till Friday morning the wind averaged

pecting to return, but there is no trace of them yet. As the weather was mild early in the morning many persons were undoubtedly caught out in the storm, which came down from the northwest without warning, a perfect, howling, blinding blizzard. Railroads are all completely blocked. No trains are expected for several days.

**Watertown.**

[SPECIAL DISPATCH TO THE TRIBUNE.]

WATERTOWN, Dak., Jan. 13.—Yesterday's storm subsided during the night, leaving a desolate scene to meet one's gaze as today opened. Business is at a standstill. Great drifts of snow blockade the streets, Oak street, the principal business thoroughfare, worst of all. Grave fears are entertained for the safety of many farmers who left town just preceding the commencement of the storm. The blockaded condition of the roads and the extreme cold has hindered reports from the country reaching here yet. The mercury went down 36 below during the night and has kept in the vicinity of 30 below all day. Light snow is falling tonight. The wind northwest; at 7 p. m. it was 28 below.

**Mitchell.**

[SPECIAL DISPATCH TO THE TRIBUNE.]

MITCHELL, Dak., Jan. 13.—One of the most blinding snowstorms ever witnessed raged in this section yesterday. It is feared that many persons have been overtaken by it, as the morning was mild.

The oldest resident in this section never saw a blizzard which equaled in severity that of yesterday and last night. It is reported that a trackman in the Omaha road perished.

Geo. F. Allen and boy, living three miles from Mitchell, were out getting a load of hay, when the storm overtook them and the boy was frozen to death and Allen's feet and arms were badly frozen.

**St. Lawrence.**

[SPECIAL DISPATCH TO THE TRIBUNE.]

ST. LAWRENCE, Dak., Jan. 13.—The worst blizzard for years has prevailed in this section for the past 36 hours, the mercury this morning being 30 below. Trains from all directions are suspended. Snow is piled from three to five feet deep and packed very hard. J. W. Gossloe, living two miles north, lost his way going from his house to the barn across the road, to feed his stock. His mit-

# The Minneapolis Tribune.



VOLUME XXII. NO. 124. TUESDAY MORNING, SEPTEMBER 11, 1888. PRICE FIVE CENTS.

## LARGEST SINCE '66.

**That Describes the Size of the Republican Majority in Maine.**

**The Pine Tree State Sounds the Death Knell of the Democracy and in No Uncertain Tones.**

**Protection Was the Standard and About It Workingmen Rallied by the Thousands.**

**Telegrams from Mr. Blaine and Chairman Manley—Now for November Sixth.**

AUGUSTA, Me., Sept. 10.—[Special]—The returns from the polling places today have surprised everybody, including Mr. Blaine and the whole Republican party, while the Democrats have been fairly overwhelmed by the tide of defeat which has swept over the state. Not only have the Republicans carried the state, but from the latest returns it looks as though their plurality was larger than in any year since 1866. It is a pronounced protection victory. No other issue was thought of. The power of the administration was brought to bear upon the election, and a most desperate effort made by the party workers and leaders to cut down the Republican plurality. For years the Democrats ascribed the splendid Republican victories in Maine to the power of the federal office holders and their money. In this contest the Democrats have controlled the entire federal patronage in the state and made a determined standup fight. The Republicans have met them squarely on their own grounds and swept the state from Kittery to Quoddy Head. They had the aid of Mr. Blaine's powerful arm, and the wool growers of Somerset and Franklin counties, the lumbermen of the Penobscot and Kennebec, the lime workers of Knox, the potato growers of Aroostook and in fact thousands of working men whose interests were jeopardized by the Mills bill, which directly attacked the industries of the state. The workingmen rallied to the support of the Republican ticket. The en masse Republican gains have been greater in the manufacturing districts, which have always been Democratic strongholds, than in places less affected by the proposed tariff reduction. In view of the fact that the Democratic party was better equipped than ever before and that they made the fight on national issues, the pronounced Republican gains cannot but affect in a great degree the success of the free trade party in the national election. Prominent Democrats in this city concede that today's election is a terrible blow to the President's chances of success.

### THIS TELLS THE STORY.

**Interesting Reading to Republicans and Democrats.**

PORTLAND, Me., Sept. 10.—Androscoggin county elects the full Republican ticket. In Knox county the Republicans probably elect all county officers except register of probate.

In Washington county the Republicans elect all county officers by 1,200 majority, and seven out of 10 representatives.

In Lincoln county the entire Republican ticket is elected, and the Republicans elect four out of six representatives.

The Republicans carry Somerset county by over 1,500 plurality, electing one Republican senator and seven of the eight representatives. There is a gain of 1,100 in plurality over 1886.

Waldo county elects the entire Republican ticket by about 300 majority, except sheriff, and elects four Republican representatives out of seven.

Large Republican gains are reported in Hancock county, which will give an estimated majority of 1,000, electing the full county ticket. The entire nine representative districts have elected Republicans.

Returns thus far received from York county indicate a majority for the Republican county ticket of 1,000. Two years ago the majority was less than 10. Reed's majority in this county will be the largest he has ever received. Republicans elect 12 out of 15 representatives.

One hundred and ninety towns give the Republicans 48,323; Democrats, 36,261; Prohibition, 1,554; scattering, 852; against in 1886 Republicans, 41,092; Democrats, 33,077; Prohibition, 2,140; scattering, 28; plurality, 12,672, against 8,015, gain 4,057.

Thirty-seven towns and cities in the First district give Reed (Rep.), 15,548; Emery (Dem.), 13,005; Reed's plurality, 2,543. The same towns in 1886 gave Reed 1,375 plurality. If this gain continues in the same ratio in the remaining towns Reed's plurality will be 2,700.

There are 507 towns and plantations in Maine. Of these, returns have been received from 241 which give Burleigh (Rep.), 56,019; Putnam (Dem.), 41,646; Cushing (Prohib.), 1,774; scattering, 957. The same towns in 1886 gave the Republicans 48,160; Democrats, 39,095; Prohibition, 2,442; scattering, 28. Burleigh's plurality, 14,373, against 10,065 in 1886. Republican gain, 4,138.

The 266 towns to hear from gave in 1886—Republicans, 20,861; Democrats, 17,194; Prohibition, 1,426.

If the same ratio of gain and loss is maintained the final vote will stand: Republican, 80,252; Democrat, 60,445; Prohibition, 2,810; scattering, 957; total, 144,164, with a plurality for the Republicans of 19,807.

In 1884 the total vote stood: Republicans, 78,699; Democratic, 58,954; Republican plurality, 19,745. The labor vote this year is included in the scattering but evidently some of the scattering should be assigned to the Prohibition vote. The Presidential vote in 1884 was smaller than the gubernatorial vote in the aggregate, but there was a slightly larger plurality, viz: 20,084. The legislature in 1886 stood, Republican senators 27, Democratic 4; Republican representatives 122, Democratic 27; Prohibition and Independent 1 each. The Republicans will gain in the House and in the Senate. The four representatives to congress are elected with increased majority.

### LARGEST SINCE '66.

**Mr. Blaine Explains the Size of the Majority.**

AUGUSTA, Me., Sept. 10.—Mr. Blaine has telegraphed Gen. Harrison as follows:

Returns up to 9 o'clock indicate that the Republican candidate will have more than 20,000 majority over the Democratic candidate—the largest majority since 1866. The Prohibition vote falls off everywhere.

Chairman Manley has sent the following telegram:

To Hon. M. S. Quay, Chairman Republican National Committee, New York: We have carried the state by a plurality of 20,000. Have chosen the entire delegation in congress. Reeds majority will reach 2,500. The majorities for Dingley, Boutelle and Milliken will exceed 4,700 respectively. We have chosen every senator, and nearly or quite four-fifths of the representatives in our legislature, and have carried every county in the state on the popular vote.

A large body of citizens headed by a band tendered Gov.-Elect Burleigh a serenade this evening, to which he responded in a brief speech. The procession then called at Mr. Blaine's residence, and in response he also made a congratulatory speech.

### A FEW POINTERS.

**Offices That Were Filled, and the Vote Two Years Ago.**

PORTLAND, Me., Sept. 10.—[Special]—The Maine biennial election occurred today, when a Governor, four congressmen, 31 state senators and 151 state representatives were chosen, as well as county officers in 16 counties. The last legislature stood: Senators—Republicans, 27; Democrats, 46. Representatives—Republicans, 122; Democrats, 27; Prohibition, 1; Independent, 1.

In 1886 the Republican plurality for Governor was 13,702. In the congressional districts the pluralities were:

In the First district, 1,168; Dingley, Second district, 6,218; Milliken, Third district, 5,211; Boutelle, Fourth district, 3,715. In 1884 the Republican plurality for Governor was 19,745; for President, 20,064.

The Republican congressmen were all candidates for re-election, and all but the first district were considered Republican without question. A strong contest was made in the First district, Wm. Emery, of Alfred, being the Democratic nominee. There were four candidates for Governor, E. C. Burleigh, of Bangor, late state treasurer, Republican; Wm. L. Putnam, of Portland, late fishery treaty commissioner, Democratic; V. R. Cushing, Bangor, Prohibition, and H. Simmons, of Rockland, Labor. The vote of each party in 1886 stood: Republican, 68,991; Democratic, 55,299; Prohibition, 3,868.

#### Dingley All Right.

LEWISTON, Me., Sept. 10.—Dingley, Republican, is elected to congress in the Second district by nearly 5,000 plurality over Allen, Democratic, and 3,500 majority over all, a Republican gain of about 1,000 over his majority of 1886.

Dingley runs ahead of his ticket in most of the towns of his district.

## ROBBED TOO OFTEN.

**A Quietus Put Upon an Organized Gang of Iowa Burglars Who Broke into the Hazelton Postoffice.**

**A Human Life Sacrificed in a Quarrel Over a Worthless Cur—Suicide at Sauk Center.**

OELWEIN, Iowa, Sept. 10.—[Special]—At about 12 o'clock last night five burglars entered the store of O. Tuttle, also containing the postoffice, at Hazleton. While there they were discovered by a young man who saw them light a match. He immediately gave the alarm and a posse of citizens was organized. They caught two of the five, and by placing ropes around their necks made them confess to an organized plot to rob Hazleton, Oelwein, Waterloo and other points. The officers secured one of the burglars at Fairbank today and another here. There is still one at large, but he is likely to be captured. Those caught are all young men from 20 to 30 years of age. The first two were caught by Mr. Tuttle, who heard the noise, and he knocked them down. They gave the others away. These same persons are supposed to be implicated in the cracking of the safe in the same place two weeks ago. The names of the thieves, as given by first two captured, are David Martin, John Morris, John Williams and Frank Wyre, the latter being still at large. They claim to all belong to Clinton, Iowa.

#### To Escape His Wives.

ST. LOUIS, Mo., Sept. 10.—[Special]—An actor named Samuel Drake, who has been playing with the Negrotto comedy company, is supposed to have committed suicide at Sehrfield, Mo., to escape the vengeance of his wives, who were after him for bigamy. His victims are said to be Miss Bullard, the daughter of a Louisiana judge, now a resident of St. Louis; Miss Kate Robertson, of Indianapolis; Miss Mary Dolincourt, of Quincy, Ill., and a Holden, Kan., girl, who was his last wife.

#### Because of a Worthless Cur.

WHEELING, W. Va., Sept. 10.—A worthless cur was the cause of a cold-blooded murder at a cabin near here yesterday. George Taber and Robert Oley were at work for a farmer, Oley living at Taber's house in Slipping Creek. Mrs. Taber asked her husband to put Oley's dog out of the house. Taber did so, and Oley resented the treatment of the cur and shot Taber dead. The murdered man leaves an invalid wife and five children. Oley is in jail.

#### Took His Own Life.

SAUK CENTER, Sept. 10.—[Special]—John Cummings, a young man of about 28, and a shoemaker by trade, committed suicide by hanging this afternoon. He was found hanging to a beam in S. Bendleman's barn, on whose farm he had just begun work. Temporary insanity is thought to have been the cause.

#### Alleges Criminal Assault.

FERGUS FALLS, Sept. 10.—[Special]—Mary Jacobson, a girl in the employ of S. A. Austin, in the town of Buse, claims that the hired man, named George Hart, criminally assaulted her on Sunday while Mr. Austin's people were at church. Deputy Sheriff Johnson has gone to make the arrest and the hearing will occur tomorrow.

#### To Strangle Himself.

DULUTH, Sept. 10.—[Special]—An unknown man was arrested last night for drunkenness and this afternoon was found hanging by his neck to the cell door, nearly dead. He had attempted suicide by strangulation. At present he is alive, but in a precarious condition.

#### They Wanted Foot-Wear.

GRAND FORKS, Dak., Sept. 10.—[Special]—Burglars last night broke into the shoe store of E. C. Florence and stole $200 worth of the best shoes in the stock. The police are hard on their track and hope to capture them.

### AT INDIANAPOLIS.

**Jubilation Over the Good News from Maine.**

INDIANAPOLIS, Ind., Sept. 10.—The lights burned until a late hour tonight at Republican headquarters, in the New Denison, and also at Gen. Harrison's residence, the occasion being the interest taken in the Maine elections. Gen. Harrison and his household usually retire about 10 o'clock, but early in the evening telegrams began to reach the general, giving prospects of heavy Republican gains. From time to time a few friends dropped in to inquire the latest news from Maine; and the cordial good humor of Gen. Harrison indicated that the tenor of his bulletins were of an agreeable character. His friends, however, were far more elated than the general himself, who took matters very quietly.

Early in the evening a telegram was received from Joseph Manley, stating that the prospects were good for a majority of 15,000. Telegrams from Mr. Blaine also predicted a big Republican victory.

## MANY THOUSANDS.

**A Quarter of a Million Visitors Already in Columbus.**

**Train After Train Still Arriving Loaded with Excursionists and Thousands to Come.**

**Commander-in-Chief Rea and Party on the Ground—His Probable Successor.**

**A Pretty Presentation by Miss Nellie Sheridan—A Sons of Veterans Campfire.**

COLUMBUS, O., Sept. 10.—The week of the 22d annual encampment of the Grand Army of the Republic has arrived and Columbus is ready for it. For many weeks preparations have been actively under way, and the immense crowds that are pouring into the city on every train and from every part of the country find flags, streamers, arches, Grand Army and other veteran organization emblems on every hand. Reports from Chicago and many other points are to the effect that the crowds increased so greatly and crowded so much that the sale of tickets had to be temporarily discontinued. Ohio posts are arriving at all hours in great numbers, many of them being present almost in a body. Davenport, Iowa, posts have arrived, and were followed by the post from Newport, Ky. This morning early departments from Colorado, Missouri, Iowa, Kansas, Wisconsin, Minnesota and Maryland arrived, many of the trains being gaily decorated and bearing inscriptions in praise of home towns or concerning old army matters.

During the afternoon Miss Nellie Sheridan, of Somerset, O., who is the niece of the late Gen. Phil Sheridan, presented to the Sheridan battalion of Perry county, O., in a neat speech from the grand reviewing stand, a beautiful little silk flag, which had been made expressly for them for the aged mother of gallant "Little Phil."

Delegations continued to arrive during the evening from all directions and with the old veterans were hundreds and thousands of friends. Every train, and long ones were coming every few minutes, was crowded to overflowing and emptied its load into the packed union depot from which the posts marched up town, led by their drum corps, while the other visitors sought quarters.

At a late estimate there are close to a quarter of a million strangers in the city tonight. Quarters have been provided for the Loyal Legion, the Women's Relief Corps, the Sons of Veterans and other kindred organizations. The survivors of the famous Andrews raid are arriving and will hold a reunion.

Commander-in-Chief Rea and staff arrived soon after noon and are being entertained by Mrs. Dennison, wife of the ex-Governor.

The fight has already begun for the holding of the next encampment and Indianapolis and Milwaukee are pressing their respective claims.

Among those who have been already mentioned as candidates for commander-in-chief are Judge Veasey, of Vermont; Gen. John Palmer, of New York; Gen. William Warner, of Missouri; Hon. John C. Linehan, of New Hampshire; Gen. M. M. Curtiss, of New York; Gov. Alger, of Michigan; Col. Sexton, of Illinois, and Gen. Goblan, of Pennsylvania.

Among the delegations this evening was one of 15 members of the Grand Army from Atlanta, Ga. The association of naval veterans, which was organized in January, 1887, had its second regular meeting tonight, T. L. Johnson, of Chicago, presiding. A series of resolutions were adopted expressing the sentiment of the association. They ask for increased pensions for veterans of the navy, advocate the placing of a distinctly naval monument in Washington, request that the Grand Army ritual be so amended as to recognize the navy and ask that Joseph Hadfield, of New York, who is at the head of their association, be made junior vice-commander of the Grand Army of the Republic.

The various states and territories almost without exception are already well represented, and new delegates are coming in on every train. Just outside of town there are seven trains with 100 carloads of excursionists waiting to unload. Word from Pittsburgh is to the effect that there, as at Chicago, the supply of cars is limited, and it has been found necessary to stop the sale of excursion tickets. Such a rush is almost unprecedented, but the Columbus people seem to be anxious to welcome and entertain all who come, however great the crowd.

Three long trains tonight brought in posts, delegations and visitors from California, Oregon and Washington Territory, the parties having enjoyed a long but pleasant journey. Colorado, Dakota, Minnesota, Iowa, Missouri, Wisconsin, Michigan, Illinois, Indiana—in fact all the Western and Northwestern states and territories, are already well represented, while the Eastern and Southern states, in some cases, have their largest portion of members yet to report.

The Loyal Legion held an enjoyable impromptu banquet and social time at the American House this evening, at which music was furnished by the Modoc Glee Club, of Topeka, Kan., and speeches were made by Gens. Fairchild and Belknap.

An informal reception was tendered Gen. W. T. Sherman tonight at the residence of his sister-in-law, Mrs. C. F. Steele, on East Broad street. The Alleghany City band serenaded him and thousands of veterans blocked the street in their eager attempt to get near and shake their old leader by the hand. Among those at the reception were Gov. Rusk, of Wisconsin, Mrs. Gen. Logan and Senator Warner Miller, of New York.

At the big tent, which is said to have a seating capacity of 10,000; over 6,000 persons attended the reception and camp fire of the Sons of Veterans. It was a reception by that organization to the Grand Army of the Republic and the Women's Relief Corps of the United States. On behalf of the Sons of Veterans of the United States, Mr. Brown, of Dayton, O., welcomed the other organizations in a neat speech in which he briefly reviewed the growth of the Sons of Veterans, until it today reaches into 31 states and territories and number over 70,000 men among its members.

Commander-in-Chief Rea responded in a speech which was at once congratulatory and complimentary. Ex-President Hayes was one of the other speakers of the evening and eloquently spoke of the scenes of war which the members of this organization represent to the great satisfaction of the immense crowd. Gen. Gibson and others also spoke.

#### Convictions of Mormons.

SALT LAKE CITY, Utah, Sept. 10.—[Special]—According to the report of United States District Attorney Peers, just forwarded to Washington, there have been 11 convictions for unlawful cohabitation under the laws of 1862 and 1882; total convictions for unlawful cohabitation under the laws of 1882, 497; total conviction for adultery under the laws of 1887-8; total conviction for fornication under the laws of 1887-8. The total fines and costs collected to date for violations of these laws amount to $44,000.

#### Lord Stanley Satisfied.

MORONTO, Ont., Sept. 10.—Governor-General and Lady Stanley arrived here today. This afternoon Lord Stanley, expressing his disappointment at the rejection of the fisheries treaty, said:

I may say that it is a source of great satisfaction to see the confident strength with which the dominion, relying on the goodness of her own motives and the goodness of her own course, is able to maintain an attitude of quiet and dignified observance, and is able to feel certain that the volume of her trade is increasing as it does from day to day.

#### Went Down on Lake Huron.

CHICAGO, Ill., Sept. 10.—[Special]—A telegram from Port Huron this afternoon states that the schooner Cheney Ames has foundered in Lake Huron and that all hands went to the bottom with her. The news was reported by the captain of the schooner Oliver Mitchell, which was in company with the Ames at the time of the disaster. No further particulars have been received. Both the Ames and the Mitchell were bound down the lakes from Chicago with grain. The Ames is owned by Capt. P. Meyers, of Chicago, and her crew is composed of Chicago men. Capt. Myers is here visiting his family, having left his son in command of the vessel.

#### Mason Renominated.

CHICAGO, Ill., Sept. 10.—Congressman William E. Mason was renominated by the Republicans of the Third district this morning.

## THE LAST SAD RITES.

**Impressive Funeral Services over the Late Lester Wallack in New York.**

**Snapper Garrison Tired of a Living Death—Originators of New Dances.**

NEW YORK, Sept. 10.—[Special]—The funeral of Lester Wallack took place today. Behind the coffin, as it was borne from the train, came Mrs. Wallack, supported on either side by her two sons, Arthur and Harold. She was very feeble, and before she got to her carriage, fainted. She was placed in one of the carriages in waiting, where she recovered. Mr. and Mrs. Chas. Wallack followed. The procession then proceeded to the church. There was a large crowd at the church, but no one was admitted until the actors and actresses who came had been seated.

Among the professional people present were: Mrs. Barney Williams, Miss Amy Lee, Thos. Jefferson, W. J. Scanlan and Mrs. Edward Harrington. The church was crowded and the yard outside had quite a number waiting to see the procession.

Miss Laura Moore sang "Angels Ever Bright and Fair," from Handel. Miss Marion Manola sang "Nearer My God to Thee," and at the request of Mrs. Wallace, the choir chanted, "Lord, Abide with Me." After the service the cortege returned to the Grand Central depot, and the remains were taken to Woodlawn for interment.

James Fogarty, the peddler who was stabbed in the eye with an umbrella, died in the hospital today without regaining consciousness. In hopes of saving him it had been decided to pull out the umbrella tip. It was a simple operation, but required strength. While the others held the man's head, Dr. Bird seized the projecting end of the umbrella tip with a pair of forceps, and, after several long, hard pulls, drew it from bone and brain. But little blood followed. He died within two hours after the operation. There is no clue to the murderer.

Snapper Garrison, the jockey, has decided to ride no more after Nov. 1, when his contract with the Haggin stable will expire. His reason for retiring is his objection to the privations of training. He says:

A heavy weight jockey has to undergo a living death in training to ride at the present weights. I eat only one meal a day, and that after my day's work is done. I take a Turkish bath daily in a sickening hot room. I walk six miles and run two every day in heavy sweaters. I come in covered with perspiration and on the hottest day am packed away in blankets. I don't want any more of it. I shall have a stable of my own next year.

The annual convention of the American Society of Professors and Dancing, which is now in session in this city, will consider tomorrow afternoon the subject of the new dances. Each originator of a new dance will then present to the convention an analysis of every step and movement. He will be required also to play the music accompanying the new dance, and to illustrate the method of execution before the convention. If the new dance proves acceptable to the professors the society seal is stamped upon the work and the originators name is emblazoned upon the records of the association. The difficulties attendant upon the attainment of such endorsement by a dancing master are as numerous as the obstacles which a young novelist surmounts in securing the recognition of the leading publishers.

Myles Flynn, 62 years old, and his son got drunk yesterday and quarrelled. The son stabbed his father several times and fled down the fire escape. This morning old Flynn died. Young Flynn is in custody.

A gentleman who refused to give his name entered the mayor's office today and left his check for $12,000 for the relief of the yellow fever sufferers at Jacksonville.

J. Colby Drew, of Lynn, Mass., this morning gave himself up, stating that he was a forger to the amount of $18,000 or $20,000. He has had charge of the financial matters for W. F. Monroe, grocer, and has secured notes in blank signed by Monroe and then forged the names of endorsers and obtained the money at high rates of interest. Most of the parties who held the paper are Lynn men.

Daniel Bennett, who was murderously assaulted in his home at Jersey City, was in a refreshing sleep this evening. The physicians fear that his sight and hearing will be impaired, if his mind, indeed, is not permanently affected. Six of the best officers are working on the case. During today several attempts were made to question the sufferer at moments when his mind was clear. He always wrote in a legible hand the word "whir, whir." The wife and other members of the family at Grahamville could not be notified by telegraph of the assault.

A Hartford, Conn., dispatch says: Mrs. Stowe reached home this evening. For the first time in several days she was able to sleep peacefully, which she did during nearly the entire trip. Her condition is still critical but not hopeless.

## A DUEL OF WORDS.

**Bitter Personalities Between Senators Morgan and Mitchell.**

**One Calls the Other a Liar, and Drunkenness in the Senate Chamber Is the Counter-Charge.**

**An Anxiety Displayed by Many Senators to Reconsider the Chinese Exclusion Bill.**

**A Democratic House Scheme That Will Not Work—Reporting the Appropriation Bills.**

WASHINGTON, D. C., Sept. 10.—[Special]—Discussion of the Chinese exclusion bill occupied most of the time of the Senate this afternoon, and led to the passage of bitter personalities between Senators Morgan and Mitchell. The Senate adjourned without action on the bill, leaving it just where it was last Friday at the time of adjournment—passed, but with a motion pending to reconsider the vote by which it was passed.

Mr. Morgan introduced a bill appropriating $276,000 to compensate Chinese subjects in the United States for losses and injuries received at the hands of lawless men. He then addressed the Senate in explanation and support of the bill, and on the subject of the pending bill for the absolute exclusion of the Chinese.

As China in the pending treaty had expressed a desire to prohibit emigration of Chinese laborers to the United States, this government had the right and ought to exclude Chinese laborers by law and not wait to do it by treaties. The treaty ought to be withdrawn and the bill now pending should be amended so as to provide for compensating the Chinese sufferers and then passed.

In the course of his remarks and in reply to a question from Mr. Mitchell, Mr. Morgan said he believed that the Chinese government, knowing the record of Mr. Harrison, was holding back the treaty until after the November elections, believing that if Harrison was elected his administration would be favorable to Chinese immigration.

Here Mr. Mitchell remarked that he did not believe that a solitary mind in the United States of America honestly believed any such thing.

Mr. Morgan thought Mr. Mitchell very flippant with the use of the word "honestly." "I have just stated that I believe it," he added, and asked, "Does the senator undertake to say that I do not believe it?"

"I do not believe that the senator does believe it," said Mr. Mitchell.

Mr. Morgan then exclaimed indignantly: "I will not be interrupted by a man of your character in the impeachment of my honesty," and Mr. Mitchell observed so far as his character was concerned, he was willing to parallel it with that of the senator from Alabama, "either here or elsewhere."

Mr. Morgan then went on to discuss the Chinese exclusion bill. At the close of his speech the bill he introduced was referred to the committee on foreign relations.

Mr. Mitchell said he was not surprised in view of the inconsistent and contradictory record of the senator from Alabama, on the Chinese question, that when interrupted by a perfectly proper question he should lose his temper and fly off into a rage. He added:

Mr. Morgan had heretofore denounced various propositions looking to the exclusion of Chinese, and had insisted all along that this was a question to be settled by diplomacy. He had referred to measures like the pending bill as the "Colorado idea," "the Oregon idea" or "the Pacific coast idea," or as being brought forward by demagogues for party purposes; but "Lo and behold," when a Democratic house passed a Chinese exclusion bill, even without reference to a committee, the senator flopped, jumped clear over the fence, turned around and declares himself in favor of that bill, and absolutely voted for it. A senator with that kind of a record is not in a position to question the sincerity of senators as Mr. Morgan had done. Without any provocation whatever, Mr. Morgan had resorted to personalities and violated the rules of the Senate by referring to his (Mr. Mitchell's) character.

In closing his remarks, Mr. Mitchell said:

Whatever I may have done in all my life which I ought not to have done, I can say to the senator from Alabama that there is one thing which I never have done, and that is, I have never since I have been a member of this body, come into the Senate chamber, full of whisky, disgracing myself and disgracing the Senate.

Mr. Morgan sat quietly in his seat and made no reply.

The heated, unparliamentary and personal expressions used in the debate by Senators Morgan and Mitchell have, upon reflection and upon the counsel of mutual friends, been stricken from the congressional record.

### TOO HASTY.

**Senators Anxious to Reconsider the Chinese Bill.**

WASHINGTON, D. C., Sept. 10.—[Special]—In the Senate today the House retaliation bill was presented and referred, and the Chinese exclusion bill taken up. Mr. Sherman spoke in favor of Mr. Blair's motion to reconsider the vote by which the bill was passed last Friday, and urged the Senate to let the bill stand where it is, until it could be definitely learned whether the treaty had been or would be ratified. He was free to say that if Great Britain were to act towards the United States as the bill proposed to act towards China, he would without hesitation vote for a declaration of war.

The conference reports on the fortifications bill and on the army appropriation bill were presented, and after brief explanations by Messrs. Allison and Plumb, were adopted.

Mr. George, resuming the discussion of the Chinese bill, said he agreed with the views expressed by Mr. Sherman, and declared that if it had not been for the pending presidential election, such an unseemly contest between the two sides of the chamber to get ahead in the race would not have occurred.

Mr. Evarts urged a reference of the bill to the foreign relations committee.

The people agreed with senators on each side that Chinese immigration must be stopped, but they did not desire the Senate to assume an attitude toward a great and friendly nation which was inconsistent with the relations of good neighbors.

Mr. Wilson, of Iowa, spoke in favor of reconsidering the vote.

Mr. Jones, of Nevada, obtained the floor, and on his motion the Senate, at 4:15 p. m., adjourned without any action on the bill.

### A SCHEME OF THE HOUSE

**To Shift the Responsibility for a Prolonged Session Elsewhere.**

WASHINGTON, D. C., Sept. 10.—As a matter of policy and with a view to placing upon the Senate the responsibility for further prolongation of the current session of congress, the Democrats in the House have determined to hasten final action upon the remaining appropriation bills, so far as it lays in their power. The adoption of the conference report upon the fortifications appropriation bill today marked the inauguration of this policy. The bill was finally disposed of as far as the House is concerned without a word of debate although it embodies the Sayres proposition of an appropriation of $1,500,000 for steel forgings which was originally a subject of strong opposition. The sundry civil and army appropriation bills will be pushed through this week and there will remain of the regular annual appropriation bills only the general deficiency bill which is expected to be returned to the House by the end of this week or the beginning of next week.

A call for a Democratic caucus to be held Thursday is being circulated. The object is to secure uniformity of action upon pending business; to give expression to the wishes of the majority relative to final adjournment or a recess, and to discuss the expediency of attacking the trusts as prop[osed] by the bills introduced by Mr. Breckenridge. Meanwhile it is improbable that a meeting of the ways and means committee will be called until the caucus has outlined the wishes of the Democratic side of the House.

#### To Restrict Naturalization.

WASHINGTON, D. C., Sept. 10.—The bill introduced by Representative Oates today to amend the naturalization laws provides among other things that no alien who has ever been legally convicted of any infamous crime or misdemeanor involving moral turpitude, or who has immigrated to the United States in violation of the laws thereof, or who cannot speak the English language and read the constitution of the United States in English, or who is a polygamist, anarchist, socialist or communist, or belongs to any association of such, shall be naturalized or adjudged by any court to be a citizen of the United States or of any state; nor shall any alien be naturalized who has not continuously for six years next preceding such adjudication resided within the United States.

#### Using Up the Surplus.

WASHINGTON, D. C., Sept. 10.—The heavy purchase of United States bonds last week caused a marked decline in the treasury surplus, which fell from $110,000,000 last Monday to $103,950,000, as stated on the treasurer's statement today. The discrepancy between this amount and the surplus as stated in the President's letter of acceptance ($130,000,000) is probably due to the fact that the President includes about $25,000,000 of fractional coin on hand as part of the surplus, while the treasury accounts don't.

## A FATAL COLLISION.

**A Freight Crashes into a Heavily Loaded Train of G. A. R. Excursionists in Ohio.**

**Four Persons Killed Outright and a Score or More Injured, Some Fatally.**

CLEVELAND, O., Sept. 10.—The fourth section of train No. 5, west bound on the New York, Pennsylvania & Ohio road, carrying G. A. R. veterans from Youngstown and vicinity to the national encampment at Columbus, was wrecked at 1 o'clock this afternoon at Rittman, a small station three miles west of Wadsworth, O. The train consisted of nine cars. The connecting rod of the locomotive drawing the special broke near Rittman, and after much difficulty the train was stopped on a curve. While waiting for repairs to be made, freight train No. 37, which had been following the special, thundered down the heavy grade at the rate of 25 miles an hour and, although warning was given, it was impossible to avert the collision. The locomotive of the freight plunged into the rear coach of the special, wrecking four cars, two of them being completely demolished. The excursionists had notice of the impending danger, and all succeeded in getting out of the cars before the crash came, but as they hurried down the embankment the wrecked coaches rolled down upon them, killing four persons outright and injuring 25 others more or less seriously. The names of the killed are:

BARNEY BOLINGER, Galatia, O., engineer of the freight, who jumped against the bank and fell back under the wheels of his own engine, his head being cut off.

WILLIAM COCHRAN, Caledonia, O., brakeman of freight train, killed outright.

JOHN SHOOK, Youngstown.

SAMUEL BRAUE, Youngstown.

Among the injured were Miss Iva Tucker, Austin, Iowa, seriously hurt internally, and Miss Given, Canfield, O. Both of these are reported to have since died, though the reports are not yet confirmed.

The others who were injured are:

Charles Hogle, Youngstown, leg broken; Daniel MacFadden, Youngstown, back injured; Thomas Marland, Youngstown, both legs injured; Mrs. Sarah Marvin, Youngstown, injured internally; Chris. Deibio, Youngstown, injured about the head; Mrs. D. Callahan, Youngstown, injured in the breast; Mrs. J. L. Botsford, Youngstown, leg injured; Miss Jones, Youngstown, injured in side and foot; Mr. Snyder, Youngstown, injured in side; Mrs. Dr. Hughes, Berlin Centre, O., injured in side; Dr. J. T. Cessna, Canfield, O., injured in leg and side; Mrs. Hugh Manchester, Canfield, O., both legs broken; Jonas Neff, Austintown, O., injured in head and legs; Eli Neff, Austintown, O., head injured; L. Nixon, New Lisbon, O., injured in head, leg and breast; John Gault, Jackson, O., seriously injured; Mrs. McFarland, Coitsville, O., slightly hurt; Mrs. Wilson, Sharon, Pa., wife of the postmaster, injured in back and hip and will die; P. Gerhardt, Galion, O., cut in the face; Wm. Ladt, leg broken; Mrs. A. Wilson, seriously injured and will probably die.

The injured were taken to farm houses and to the nearest station, where surgical attention was given them. The accident is believed to have been unavoidable as a flagman was sent out to stop the freight.

#### Augusta Flooded.

AUGUSTA, Ga., Sept. 10.—Heavy rains Sunday along the Savannah valley caused the river to rise rapidly last night and this morning. Three inches of rainfall from 1 o'clock Sunday morning until last night. The city is covered with water in many places to a depth of several feet. All mills are stopped on account of high water.

#### Virginia Stormed.

NORFOLK, Va., Sept. 10.—A destructive rain and wind storm swept over parts of Nansemond, Isle of Wight and Southampton counties today, destroying standing crops and blowing down trees and farm buildings. E. T. Cross, a prominent farmer of Nansemond county, was killed by a falling tree while fishing in his mill pond.

#### Shot in the Lungs.

EAU CLAIRE, Wis., Sept. 10.—[Special]—While three boys were shooting at a target with a rifle, Edward Thompson, one of them, was accidentally shot in the lungs. He cannot recover.

#### Attacked by a Bull.

KINNICKINNIC, Wis., Sept. 10.—[Special]—Mr. James Gray, a farmer living here, barely escaped being killed by a ferocious bull. His face was torn open and his back badly injured.

#### Many Lives Lost.

CITY OF MEXICO, Sept. 10.—Advices from Orizaba state that the rivers and creeks have overflowed their banks. Houses have been thrown down and many lives lost.

#### Killed by the Cars.

ASHLAND, Wis., Sept. 10.—[Special]—The body of Louie Noie, a saw mill employe, was found this morning on the railroad track near Bad river.

## A FATAL DISEASE.

**The Small Pox Obtains a Start in the Town of Sacred Heart.**

**It Was Introduced by an Immigrant and Thirty-Seven Persons Have Been Exposed to the Contagion.**

**At Least One-Half of the Indians at Lower Brule Agency Ready to Sign the Treaty.**

**The Dakota Women's Christian Temperance Union Passes a Budget of Resolutions and Adjourns.**

SACRED HEART, Sept. 10.—[Special]—An emigrant named Orford, living two miles from here, is very sick with the smallpox. No doctor was called until the ninth day of the woman's sickness. Thirty-seven people have been exposed and Dr. Welch, of this place, and Dr. Brown, of Minneapolis, who was sent here by C. N. Hewitt, secretary of the state board of health, are taking vigorous steps to stop it from spreading. The people are badly frightened and very indignant that a doctor was not called to attend the case sooner.

### THE W. C. T. U. CONVENTION.

**Dakota Women Commend Prohibition and the Press.**

FARGO, Dak., Sept. 10.—[Special]—The W. C. T. U. convention concluded its labors today. The following officers were elected: Mrs. H. M. Barber, Fargo, president; Miss Ada Kinnear, corresponding secretary; Mrs. D. M. Myer, Vermillion recording secretary; Mrs. M. E. Kline, Mitchell, treasurer; Mrs. Hager, of Miller, Mrs. Van Velsor, of Yankton, and Mrs. Williams, of Mitchell, executive committee. Yankton was chosen as the next place of meeting. Resolutions were adopted commending the Blair educational bill; the immediate and total abolition of the internal revenue tax; commending the work of the national social purity department for its efforts in behalf of the white slaves of the northwoods, and the efforts of the press on behalf of the slave girls of shops and factories, urging co-operation on the part of school officers, parents the teachers, to check immorality in the public schools, to prevent the circulation of obscene literature and other aids to vice; believing that in the Prohibition party there is hope of the final overthrow of the drink traffic; demanding the ballot for women; denouncing the Washington Territory court decision against woman suffrage as in the interest of the whisky traffic, and denouncing the Methodist church for refusing women a voice in church government.

### THEY'LL SIGN PROMPTLY.

**Spotted Horse Makes a Good Speech in Favor of the Treaty.**

LOWER BRULE AGENCY, Dak., Sept. 10.—[Special]—A number of councils were held by the Indians here yesterday, and both the friends of the bill and those opposed were well represented. The best speech of the day was by Spotted Horse, a policeman, who made a very hitting and forcible speech in favor of the bill. He finished by saying:

We have violated more of our obligations than the government has, and now that the Great Father kindly extends us his hand and offers us all these things we should take it.

Spotted Horse is very popular with all classes of the Indians, and his speech will help the case wonderfully. By Saturday the commission expect to complete their labors at this agency, and they will then leave for Cheyenne, where they expect to obtain many more signatures. It is estimated that 150 out of 300 Indians at this agency will promptly sign as the commissioners call for signatures.

#### Cleaned Out the "Bank."

DULUTH, Sept. 10.—[Special]—Wing Foo, a recently arrived celestial from San Francisco, tackled a game of public hazard here yesterday. From the start his winnings were large, until at a late hour the funds were drawn from other games running in the same house, and the bank declared itself "broke." A large portion of the Chinese population are tonight emulating Wing Foo.

#### A Sudden Death at Beloit.

BELOIT, Wis., Sept. 10.—[Special]—The landlord of the Grand Hotel, Andrew S. Robinson, died here very suddenly at midnight last night. He attended to business until an hour before his death. He had been prominent as a hotel keeper at Janesville and Waukesha, Wis., but came here directly from California. The remains will be buried at Black River Falls.

#### A Diphtheria Epidemic.

MONTEVIDEO, Sept. 10.—[Special]—Diphtheria is raging in the town of Kragero, Chippewa county, on the east side of Lac qui Parle lake. Fourteen deaths are already reported, five of which are from the family of Thomas Anderson, a prominent Scandinavian farmer in that vicinity. The disease, thus far, is confined to a very small territory.

#### A Divorce and a Judgment.

GRAND FORKS, Dak., Sept. 10.—[Special]—In the district court, Judge McConnell presiding, Mrs. Loretta Tanner was granted an absolute divorce from Cornelius Tanner. In the case of the First National Bank vs. H. G. Stone judgment was entered against the defendant for $188.

#### Saloon Men Tremble.

GRAND FORKS, Dak., Sept. 10.—[Special]—The saloon men are quaking in their boots through fear that Judge Marcou may take some action against them for violating his injunctions, enjoining them from selling liquor. The citizens, generally, are indignant at the action of some of the saloonists.

#### Presented with a Flag.

CEDAR RAPIDS, Iowa, Sept. 10.—[Special]—The 400 state militia men of the First regiment who have been in camp here for a week were surprised today with the presentation of a fine regimental flag by the citizens of Cedar Rapids through Mayor Mullally, Col. Davis responding happily.

#### Teachers of the Young Idea.

PLAINVIEW, Sept. 10.—[Special]—The fall term of school commenced this morning with instructors as follows: Principal, J. A. Van Dyke; grammar department, Miss Amy B. French; A intermediate, Miss Minnie Fisk; B intermediate, Miss Kitty Montgomery; primary, Miss Ab[illegible] E. Redding.

#### Candidates for County Offices.

WATERTOWN, Dak., Sept. 10.—[Special]—The Republican county convention today nominated the following candidates: For treasurer, F. P. Phillips; register, G. R. Williams; auditor, F. H. Adams; superintendent of schools, Frank Crane; attorney, J. R. Mettetie; judge, E. A. Gove.

#### Occupied Their Church.

WATERLOO, Iowa, Sept. 10.—[Special]—The Congregational society of this city occupied their elegant new church for the first time yesterday. Rev. J. A. Adams, of Eldora, was present and assisted the pastor, Rev. Stevenson, in the exercises.

# 1890~1899

# The Minneapolis Tribune.

VOL. XXIV. NO. 34. TUESDAY MORNING, JUNE 17, 1890. PRICE: FIVE CENTS.


## ALL IN A NUTSHELL.

### News of the Day Boiled Down for Hasty Perusal.

**The Weather.**

WASHINGTON, June 16, 8 p. m.—Forecast until 8 a. m. Tuesday—For Minnesota, North and South Dakota—Fair, warmer, except stationary temperature in eastern portions of Minnesota and Nebraska; variable winds, becoming southerly.

WAR DEPARTMENT, Signal Service, United States Army, meteorological reports received at 6:41 p. m., local time; at 8 p. m., 75th meridian time. Observations taken at the same moment of time at all stations.

| Stations. | Barometer height. | Exposed. | Direction of wind. | Rainfall in last 12 hours. | State of weather. |
|---|---|---|---|---|---|
| Cairo | 30.04 | 78 | S W | ...... | Cloudy |
| Detroit | 30.04 | 76 | SE | ...... | Cloudy |
| Chicago | 30.02 | 72 | SE | ...... | Pt Cloudy |
| Duluth | 29.92 | 60 | E | .04 | Pt Cloudy |
| Minneapolis | 29.90 | 74 | S W | .98 | Cloudless |
| La Crosse | 29.94 | 76 | W | .06 | Pt Cloudy |
| Davenport | 30.00 | 80 | C'm | ...... | Cloudy |
| Des Moines | 29.94 | 78 | W | ...... | Pt Cloudy |
| Dubuque | 30.00 | 74 | S W | ...... | Cloudy |
| Keokuk | 29.98 | 78 | C'm | .08 | Cloudy |
| St. Louis | 30.04 | 84 | S W | ...... | Cloudy |
| Kansas City | 29.94 | 82 | S | ...... | Pt Cloudy |
| Omaha | 30.00 | 80 | N W | .02 | Pt Cloudy |
| Huron | 29.96 | 68 | N | ...... | Cloudless |
| Cincinnati | 30.10 | 72 | N | .78 | Rain |
| Moorhead | 29.94 | 72 | N W | .40 | Cloudless |
| St. Vincent | 29.98 | 76 | W | ...... | Pt Cloudy |
| Bismarck | 29.96 | 68 | S W | .01 | Cloudless |
| Ft. Buford | 29.82 | 76 | S W | ...... | Pt Cloudy |
| Ft. Assinaboine | 29.74 | 72 | S W | ...... | Cloudy |
| Ft. Custer | 29.78 | 74 | SE | ...... | Pt Cloudy |
| Helena | 29.84 | 84 | S W | .02 | Pt Cloudy |
| Rapid City | 29.90 | 70 | E | ...... | Cloudy |
| Cheyenne | 29.96 | 66 | S W | ...... | Cloudy |
| North Platte | 30.00 | 70 | SE | ...... | Pt Cloudy |
| Denver | 29.88 | 72 | S | T | Cloudy |
| Cleveland | 30.06 | 76 | N E | ...... | Pt Cloudy |
| Dodge City | 29.82 | 84 | E | ...... | Pt Cloudy |
| Milwaukee | 30.02 | 62 | E | ...... | Cloudless |
| Sault Ste. Marie | 29.98 | 66 | SE | ...... | Pt Cloudy |
| Winnipeg | 29.80 | 70 | N W | ...... | Pt Cloudy |
| Qu'Appelle | 29.76 | 66 | N | ...... | Pt Cloudy |
| Minnedosa | 29.78 | 66 | N W | ...... | Cloudless |
| Swift Current | 29.68 | 70 | C'm | T | Pt Cloudy |
| Calgary | 29.70 | 64 | SE | .22 | Rain |
| Medicine Hat | 29.60 | 64 | C'm | ...... | Cloudy |
| Ft. Sully | 29.90 | 74 | E | ...... | Pt Cloudy |

Local Forecast—For St. Paul, Minneapolis and vicinity: Fair, warmer weather.

P. F. LYONS,
Sergeant Signal Corps, U. S. Army.

**Ocean Steamers.**

HAVRE, June 16.—The steamer La Bourgogne arrived here this morning.

SOUTHAMPTON, June 16.—Arrived: Elder, from New York for Bremen.

GLASGOW June 16.—Arrived: State of Nevada, from New York.

**The City.**

The bank clearings were $904,723.83.

Twenty-one real estate transfers aggregated $101,307.

The Minneapolis Retail Grocers association elected officers.

Yesterday's building permits numbered 14 and aggregated $3,615.

Minneapolis temperance societies will unite in a mass meeting June 27.

Enumerators are still hustling for those who have not been censused.

**St. Paul.**

The chamber of commerce demands an enforcement of the Sunday closing laws.

Delegates were nominated to the state and district convention by the Prohibitionists.

At the meeting of the executive committee of the Farmers' alliance it was decided to call a convention July 16.

The June term of the United States circuit court opened and three decisions were filed by Judges Shiras and Nelson.

**Northwest.**

Thomas Bryant, a 16-year-old boy, is on trial at Butte for the murder of his mother.

Ignatius Donnelly administers a roast to certain members of the Fifth district Farmers' Alliance.

Judge Shiras, in his decision in the Des Moines river land cases, makes some suggestions to the United States.

**Washington.**

Several land decisions were rendered.

Senator Allison spoke on the silver bill.

A house Republican caucus was held last night.

It is expected the house will be ready to adjourn the first week in July.

Provisions of the national election bill as framed by the house Republican caucus.

The changes made in the house tariff bill by the senate finance committee are unimportant.

**The Markets.**

A great many decayed strawberries were in the markets yesterday that did not pay enough to cover freight.

Cattle were in good demand at the Twin City stock yards when of good quality, with no request for inferior animals.

The leading business feature Monday was the break in wheat that brought prices down to 87½c for July delivery and left them 2c below the opening.

**Miscellaneous.**

Senator Washburn is interviewed in New York.

Count Tolstoi is out in an article defending his latest book.

Over 30 lives were lost in a mine explosion at Dunbar, Pa.

At Buffalo, N. Y., Ed Smith whipped Jim Daly, of Philadelphia.

Secretary Blaine writes a letter denying that he is opposed to free sugar.

The wholesale liquor dealers of New York and vicinity are moving against the whisky trust.

## WASHBURN INTERVIEWED.

**The Minnesota Senator Discusses Silver and the Tariff.**

NEW YORK, June 16.—[Special.]—Senator Washburn, of Minnesota, was at the Fifth Avenue Hotel today and chatted with a reporter about the work of the senate. He said: "Some kind of a silver bill will, in my judgment, pass. I think the Jones bill will probably pass, containing substantially the same provisions as when it came from the finance committee. I think an effort will be made to amend the bill so as to permit free coinage, and discussion on that point will occupy some time. Whether the amendment will pass I cannot say, but I hope not. The treasury notes provided for in the bill should be made legal tender and probably may be. Silver and gold certificates are not legal tender, but as soon as they are presented at the treasury their value is paid in coin. In the Jones bill treasury notes are paid out for silver bullion. Why not make these notes legal tender? They represent the government's I owe you and the collateral is in the treasury vaults."

"Do you think the McKinley tariff bill will soon pass?"

"It will pass, but when, I cannot say. We may be kept at Washington until August working on it. Some changes will undoubtedly be made in the bill, but what they will be I cannot guess."

The Indian government has granted a company a subsidy of one-half a lac of rupees annually for 10 years, and one lac annually for a further period of 10 years, to construct railways from Sibia to Kalia.

## A BELGIAN BLUFF.

### Iron for the New Court House at Minneapolis.

### Astounding Offer Made by a Firm of Foreigners.

### They Agree to Cut Pittsburgh Prices 25 Per Cent.

### Interviews With Leading Iron Makers of the Country.

PITTSBURGH, June 16.—[Special.]—There has been a decided sensation created among Pittsburgh iron and steel manufacturers by the offer of a Belgian firm to supply the structural iron necessary for the new court house at Minneapolis 25 per cent cheaper than it could be furnished by Pittsburgh manufacturers. The contract is a large one, $3,000,000 being the estimated cost, and it has attracted the attention of many of the large structural manufacturers throughout the country. Of course the trend of opinion among manufacturers here is that if the Belgian iron firm can make good its offer, the present tariff is insufficient, and the reduction in the metal schedule of a quarter of a cent per pound for structural beams and channel iron, proposed by the McKinley bill, will result in allowing the Belgian manufacturers to carry off most of the contracts for structural iron. The manufacturers seem refused to believe that the offer had been made.

At the Belgian consulate, however, the genuineness of the offer was confirmed, and it was further learned that the consul in Pittsburgh had been notified by the Belgian firm of its intentions. He said that already the Belgians had secured contracts for structural iron at Houston and Austin, Tex., and when the offer was made for the Minneapolis court house he had no doubt that the foreign manufacturers were prepared to make good their claim.

A. M. Byers, the well known iron and steel manufacturer said: "I think the offer is too radical. If the Belgian firm had offered to supply the iron, say 5 or 6 per cent cheaper than could be done here I should entertain but little doubt that they could do it, but 25 per cent difference is too much. It is possible that the Belgian manufacturers may have some means of evading the straight schedule and have the iron imported at a lower rate."

A member of Carnegie, Phillips & Co., the largest structural iron manufacturers of Pittsburgh, said: "The ruling price of beams and channels today is $3.10 per 100 pounds, and of angles, $2.15. I am convinced that the Belgian firm cannot undersell these prices 25 per cent. They charged $3.25 for the iron which was furnished for the contract at Austin, Tex., and since that time wages and other items of cost have advanced in the foreign markets fully 17 per cent. Under those circumstances I hardly see how they can compete for the Minneapolis contract. If the firm does import the structural iron, however, it will undoubtedly be a dangerous blow to American industries."

When the reporter spoke of the offer to a number of the delegates to the Amalgamated Association of Iron and Steel Workers' convention, they were very greatly surprised. Delegate Charles Killon, of Illinois, who is employed in a structural mill, said: "There are three men employed in the mill where I work, who came from near Aix-le-Bains. They stated that the wages paid in the Belgian's mill were nearly 39 per cent lower than those in Pittsburgh, and in the present time of alleged high wages in Belgium the advance is not within 25 per cent of the wages paid here. Under such circumstances I am not at all surprised at the offer made. Pile on the tariff I say."

James Nutt, trustee of the Amalgamated association, said: "If the Belgian iron firm is able to make such a sweeping cut and pay the present duty, what it will not be able to do when the senate gets through cutting the McKinley bill to pieces? It is certainly an astonishing offer, however. After what the Belgian mills did in Texas, there can be but little doubt that the firm is prepared to undertake the contract."

## SOMETHING OF A SLUGGER.

**Ed Smith, of Denver, Makes a Chopping Block of Jim Daly, of Philadelphia.**

BUFFALO, N. Y., June 16.—Ed. Smith, of Denver, and Jim Daly, of Philadelphia, fought seven rounds here tonight before the Arlington club. Daly was seconded by Tom Manning, of St. Paul, and Steve Brodie, of New York; Smith was backed by Mike Cleary and Wm. Muldoon. Daly weighed 185 pounds and Smith 178, though the latter looked heavier. Prof. James Connors, of the Buffalo Athletic club, was referee. The match was for a purse of $1,500.

In the first round Smith led and Daly tried for the wind, but did not reach. After good in-fighting, Smith got the best of it, scored a push down before the round closed.

The second round was give and take. Smith struck the harder blows and seemed to have Daly at his mercy. He planted a right-hander on Daly's mug that dazed him.

In the third round it was clearly apparent that Daly was over-matched. Daly clinched to avoid punishment. He was knocked down and lay several moments before his seconds could get him to his feet again.

Fourth Round—Smith forced Daly at the outset into his corner and into his chair, where he sat powerless. Then Smith let him get up and walked to the center so that he could knock him down. He repeated this before Daly was fairly on his feet. Cries of foul were heard and the referee warned Smith. Smith scored a third knock-down and would have got another if Daly had got up in time.

In the fifth round Smith sent Daly to grass five times.

In the sixth round Daly was again knocked down and pasted until the close of the round. Smith struck more blows, which were alleged to be foul.

In the seventh Daly was knocked down repeatedly, and finally when Smith refused to break away at the referee's order, Daly's seconds tried to claim the fight on a foul for their man, but the referee disallowed it and Daly failing to come to the center, gave the fight and purse to Smith. Time of fight, 28 minutes.

**Waived Its Rights.**

WINNIPEG, Man., June 16.—[Special.]—At a meeting of the executive committee of the Minnesota and Winnipeg Rowing association, held here last night, it was decided to waive the rights of the city for the regatta this year, in favor of Duluth, in view of the important regatta arranged by the Duluth club the 21st of July, and the fact that the Mississippi Amateur association holds its regatta at the same city at the same time.

**TAKE YOUR CHOICE.**

**An Expert Opinion on the Chances for Landing a Big Race.**

NEW YORK, June, 17.—The Tribune's racing reporter in today's issue says:

Of all the horses that will run Tenny and Prince Royal must certainly be considered the most thoroughly seasoned by public racing, and no doubt each of them is just on edge. But the private work of Salvator and Firenzi, and the public gallop of Raceland in a walkover, have shown such indisputable form that these three horses, although perhaps not quite up to the concert pitch that they would have reached after two or three races, not too hard, but just hard enough, must be considered at least reasonably satisfactory. Prince Royal will probably be used to make the pace for Raceland, and if he runs the first mile in 1:40, which he can do if pushed, it is not likely that Proctor Knott, Come-to-Taw, Loantaka, Cassius, St. Luke, Montague, English Lady, Quesal or Tea Tray will be in the way of any of the heavyweights in the last quarter mile in the decisive rush up the home stretch. But, whether Prince Royal makes the pace or not, the pace will undoubtedly be hot. Such horses as Loantaka and Cassius can never afford to lie back for a yard. They will go out, even if Prince Royal should not, and they will run the first mile in the liveliest sort of fashion. If Prince Royal goes out with them he will kill them both, or any other horses except the famous four, Raceland, Salvator, Firenzi and Tenny, in the first mile. Possibly Longstreet might be in the vicinity at the head of the home stretch, but it is doubtful. In carefully considering the circumstances bearing on the situation, it seems to me that Raceland, Salvator, Firenzi and Tenny will settle the first money between them, and these four may make one of the closest and most splendid finishes ever seen on a race course. It is difficult indeed to select the winner from these four. I will not attempt to do it, leaving my readers to make their choice for themselves, contenting myself with this single suggestion that if it should rain before the race, the chances of Raceland will be much improved by heavy, wet going, but that it must not be forgotten that Salvator, Tenny and Firenzi can also run well in mud.

**Football Tonight.**

The first of the final series of games for the Shaw cup comes off tonight on the grounds at Thirteenth street and Vine place, the contesting teams being the Thistles, champions of '88 and '89, and the Rangers. play begins at 7 p. m. prompt. Alex. McCullough, of St. Paul, referee. Both teams are confident of success, the Thistles especially so after their brilliant victory of seven goals to nothing over the St. Pauls last Friday evening. A grand and exciting game is sure to result. Should the weather be favorable, there will be the largest crowd ever seen at a football match in the Northwest. The following are the teams:

Thistles—Goal, J. B. Henry; backs, K. Henry (captain) and D. Pringle; half backs, D. McMillan, Wm. Pringle and Geo. Logan; forwards, Geo. Anderson, Andrew Pringle, John McKendrick, J. McFarlane and Jas. McKendrick.

Rangers—Goal, A. L. Seavey; backs, J. Ratcliffe and W. London; half backs, Andrew Gray, J. Cochrane and P. Cochrane; forwards, G. H. Broadhurst, Cal Martin, W. J. Wix, R. H. Teeple (captain) and John Emslie.

**Proctor Knott Hurt.**

NEW YORK, June 16.—[Special.]—It was rumored at Brighton Beach this afternoon that Scraggin Brothers' Proctor Knott hurt his foot with a nail and together with his stable companion, English Lady, will be returned to Chicago tomorrow without facing the starter for the suburban.

**Sporting Notes.**

The Minneapolis club returned last night.

Carroll has been able to assume his place in the field.

Tim Hurst will umpire the Minneapolis-St. Paul series.

Esterquest has not yet joined the team and will probably not do so.

O'Day's finger is getting better. He will be able to play again in a few days.

Milwaukee is playing good ball. Sioux City dropped three to the brewers.

Minneapolis and St. Paul will play the first of a series of three games on the home grounds today.

The boys say they had a pleasant time on their trip. They won six out of ten games, which is a pretty record on the home ground, much less at homes of the ssailing clubs.

Joe Miller said last night that if St. Paul could play ball, Denver would have been in second place. "But we'll soon get to the front again," said he, as the reporter handed him a fresh cigar.

The Golden Gate Athletic club will give a purse of $3,000 for a finish glove contest according to "Police Gazette" rules, between Jake Kilrain and Ed. Smith, of Denver. The battle to take place in September.

The California Athletic club offer a purse of $1,500 for Fitzsimmons, of New Zealand, and Jack Dempsey to fight for in August. Fitzsimmons agrees to fight Dempsey for the purse, and if he refuses he will challenge the winner of the Young Mitchell and La Blanche fight which takes place on the 27th. Billy Murphy, of Australia, has postponed his departure to fight Larkin, the New Jersey champion, for $1,000 and the "Police Gazette" championship belt.

### CABLEGRAMS.

Lord Hartington writes that the amendments which the government has accepted remove the objections to the licensing bill.

Price Dondukoff Korsakoff has retired from the governorship of the Caucasus, and Gen. Cheremeteff has been appointed to succeed him.

The telegraph conference, owing to the difficulty experienced in defining what constitutes a press telegram, has abandoned the discussion of the subject.

Count Colliglote, Italian consul at Rangoon, replaces Sig. Rajnotti as consul at Chicago, the latter having been retired. Jones Thomas has been appointed consular agent at Newport.

The London Chronicle advises English traders to have patience and trust to the American's own objections to the new tariff for its repeal. The bill, it says was promoted by a small party of wealthy American manufacturers.

The St. Petersburg police have discovered a widespread conspiracy against the czar's life. The imperial palace at Gatchina is undermined. The guards at all the palaces have been doubled. Several arrests have been made.

The National, Allan, Wilson, British India, Peninsula and Oriental and other steamship companies, after a long fight, have secured the right of discharging their own vessels at London independently of the dock companies.

In the house of commons last evening Mr. Shaw-Lefevre's amendment to the licensing bill to postpone the purchasing of licenses until the passage of an act transferring the licensing power to the county councils was rejected under cloture—232 to 199.

The Nihilist arrested at Paris some time ago are still detained, pending an inquiry into the prisoner Reinstein's assertion that an agent provocateur sent by the Third Section at St. Petersburg is residing in the avenue Friedland, and has visited him daily for weeks past.

The Spanish government announced in the senate today that it had not been proved that the disease now prevailing at Puebla de Rugat is Asiatic cholera, and there was no cause for alarm. It was further stated that the board of health had sent a deputation to Valencia and had taken sanitary measures to prevent the spread of the disease.

M. Roche, French minister of commerce, in opening the council of commerce today, said that France, from 1892, would have the fixing of the tariffs in her own hands. The whole country, he said, had agreed to terminate existing treaties, but had not agreed as to the course to be pursued thereafter, so the council must seek a solution of the question.

In the reichstag committee on the army bill yesterday, Herr Richter's motion to determine the peace effective annually was rejected by a vote of 17 to 9. Herr Richter's motion to reduce the time of service two years was also rejected, 18 to 10. The first paragraph of the bill was adopted in its original form by a vote of 17 to 11. The remaining paragraphs were agreed to and the entire bill was passed.

## IN VERY FAIR SHAPE

### Northwestern Measures That Have Not Yet Passed the House.

### A Number Liable to Be Called Up Any Day and Passed.

### The House Will Be Ready to Adjourn Early in July.

### How Business Has Been Rushed by Speaker Reed's Rulings.

WASHINGTON, June 16.—[Special.]—As legislation for the Northwest stands today in the house, there are bills in committee of the whole and liable to be brought up any day for a vote as follows: For public buildings at St. Paul, Mankato, Red Wing, Helena and Butte City, Mont., and Deadwood, S. D.; to authorize the secretary of the interior to negotiate with the Turtle Mountain band of Chippewa Indians for a cession of the reservation; to establish customs district consist of North and South Dakota; to ratify and confirm an agreement with the Sisseton and Wahpeton bands of Dakota and Sioux Indians; to make appropriations for improving St. Mary's river and Hay Lake channel, to reimburse South Dakota for expenses incurred in holding the constitutional convention of 1885; to authorize the secretary of the interior to survey and mark the seventh standard parallel between North and South Dakota; to reimburse North Dakota for expenses incurred in holding the constitutional convention in July and August, 1889; to authorize the secretary of the interior to ascertain damages resulting to any person who had settled upon Crow Creek and Winnebago reservation, S. Dak., between Feb. 25, 1885, and April 17, 1885; to enable the secretary of the interior to carry out an act for the relief and civilization of the Chippewa Indians in Minnesota; granting buildings and one section of land at Ft. Sisseton to South Dakota for the use of the militia of the state and to provide for the disposal of the remaining portion of said reservation; creating an additional land office in North Dakota.

The following bills are in the house calendar: Authorizing Aberdeen, S. D., to purchase certain lands; to amend an act to authorize foot and carriage or railroad bridges across the Mississippi river at St. Paul; to authorize the Duluth, Red Wing & Southern Railroad company to construct a bridge across the Mississippi at or near Red Wing and to establish it as a post road; to amend the act authorizing the construction of a bridge across the Red River of the North; to construct a wagon bridge across the Missouri river between Pierre, in Hughes county, and Stanley county, S. D.; to authorize the construction of a bridge across the Missouri river between Chamberlain, in Brule county, and Lyman county, S. D.; to authorize the construction of a bridge across the Mississippi river at Winona; granting right of way to the Red Lake & Western Railway and Navigation company across Red Lake reservation.

**REGARDING ADJOURNMENT.**

**The House Will Be Ready to Quit Early in Next Month.**

WASHINGTON, June 16.—[Special.]—Owing to Speaker Reed's rulings, business before the house for the first time in legislative history of the country, is far ahead of the senate. There are really but two important measures before it, the Indian appropriation and deficiency bills. Both of these could easily be passed inside of 10 days if necessary, when an adjournment could be effected by the first of July. Mr. Reed said some time since that the House would be ready to adjourn so that he could eat his Fourth of July dinner in Portland and so it could, but the earliest time suggested at which the senate will be in condition to adjourn is the first of August, while many senators set the day much later. In fact, there is really nothing for the House to do but pass a federal election law and the preliminary steps in that direction will be taken in tonight's caucus.

**NATIONAL ELECTION BILL.**

**Principal Features of the Measures Framed by House Republicans.**

WASHINGTON, June 16.—The national election bill, as framed by the house Republican caucus committee, has just been printed. The principal features of the measure are as follows: Chief supervisors of elections in judicial districts are charged with the execution of the law which is to apply to federal elections in cities of 20,000 inhabitants or upward, and in entire congressional districts exclusive of such cities, upon application to the supervisor of 100 voters, or in counties or parishes forming a part of a congressional district, upon application from 50 voters.

The supervisors are required to make—in towns of 20,000 people and upwards—a thorough house-to-house canvass before election to inform voters upon inquiry where and in what box to deposit their ballots, and to scrutinize naturalizations. In canvassing the votes the state laws are to govern, except that all ballots are to be counted by 10s first by an inspector of election and second by a supervisor, the local election officers and the supervisors keeping separate tally sheets, which are to be compared and the result publicly announced. Ballots deposited in the wrong box are to be counted. Returns are to be made by the supervisors in duplicate to the clerks of the United States circuit courts and to the chief supervisor, who is to tabulate and refer them to the United States board of canvassers of the congressional vote, which is to be appointed by the United States circuit court and consisting of three citizens of the state and persons of good repute, not more than two of whom are to be of the same political party. The board is to convene on Nov. 15 each even year and is to declare and certify the result of the election and send one return to the clerk of the house of representatives, one to the governor of the state and one to the proper chief supervisor of elections.

The clerk of the house is to place upon the roll of members-elect the names of the persons declared elected by the United States canvassers, in case there is a difference in the result reached by them and by the state election officers.

**Land Decisions.**

WASHINGTON, June 16.—[Special.]—Assistant Secretary Chandler has today affirmed some important decisions of the land office, over which there has been no inconsiderable contention, among which are the following: Mathias Quam vs. Charles Brown, involving Brown's homestead entry at Grand Forks, N. D.; also Otte Brikson vs. Duncan McDonald, involving the latter's homestead entry at Grand Forks; and Neil C. E. Jorgensen, holding for cancellation his pre-emption entry at Mitchell, S. D.

**HOLD A CAUCUS.**

**Republican Members of the House Consider the National Election Bill.**

WASHINGTON, June 16.—The Republicans of the house were called together in caucus tonight to receive the report of the caucus committee upon the national election bill. This measure, which was completed last Saturday and printed, was laid before the caucus, and, to save the two hours that would have been consumed in its reading, Mr. Lodge briefly and concisely stated the substance of its provisions. Apparently some opposition yet remained to these features of the bill providing for a United States canvassing board in the election districts composed of three citizens of good repute and for the use of the certificates of these boards in the preparation of the roll of members-elect of the house. This took form in the shape of an amendment to the bill proposed by Representative Frank, of Missouri, by the terms of which the canvassing boards are to be composed of the United States chief supervisor, the clerk of the United States district court and the United States marshal for the district, and by reverting to the terms of the original Rowell bill so as to provide that in case of conflicting state and Federal returns, the clerk of the house shall omit the names of both parties from the roll of members.

After some discussion this amendment was rejected and the entire bill was approved as it came from the caucus committee, some few suggestions being made in the line of perfection of detail and removal of possible complexity and ambiguity which the committee was empowered to incorporate in the bill if it should see fit. There was every disposition to secure speedy action upon the bill in the house and it is expected that it will be reported from the committee and provision made by the committee on rules for its consideration before the end of the week.

Having disposed of this subject, the caucus next turned its attention to the McComas-anti-gerrymandering bill. This was discussed at some length. Before the vote was taken many members had left the hall, so that the result, which was the defeat of the bill by a vote of 22 to 26, was unsatisfactory to its friends, who hold that it could not fairly be regarded as an indication of the feeling of the entire party, and they will probably make another effort to have consideration of the bill at a subsequent caucus.

**COMING TO A CLOSE.**

**The Tariff Bill in the Senate—Mr. McKinley Says the Changes Are Unimportant.**

WASHINGTON, July 16.—Printed copies of the tariff bill as amended by the Republican members of the senate finance committee up to Saturday night, were laid before the sub-committee today. It included the sugar and tobacco schedules, and copies of these were given today to Senator Carlisle, representing the minority. Several changes were made today and this will probably be the case every day until the bill gets into the senate. It is expected that the sub-committee will be able to report the measure Wednesday or Thursday. Mr. McKinley said that the changes made in the house bill by the finance committee are comparatively few and unimportant.

Senator Carlisle says he has not yet begun work on the report to be submitted by the minority and that he will not do so until the entire bill has been placed in his hands. This need not delay the report of the bill to the senate by the majority, he says, as the minority will ask leave to present its views at a subsequent date.

**The Baneful Traffic.**

WASHINGTON, June 16.—[Special.]—A large number of religious bodies are reaffirming their determination to use their utmost endeavor for the speedy abolition and certain overthrow of the liquor traffic. Senator Pierce today presented resolutions unanimously adopted by the North Dakota Baptist association, embracing 27 churches, convened at Larimore, June 4 and 5, in which their representatives in congress are urged to insist upon such enactments as will guarantee to North Dakota and every state in the Union the right to enforce a prohibitory law enacted by a majority vote of the people or by legislative enactment. Senator Moody presented the petition of citizens of Codington, Grant, Harrison, Charles and Hughes counties, South Dakota, praying for the passage of what is known as the Pickler bill.

**Postal Changes.**

WASHINGTON, June 16.—[Special.]—A new postoffice has just been established at Bullan, Polk county, Minnesota, Jesse P. Bullan postmaster; also new office at Armington, Cascade county, Mont., William C. McQueen postmaster.

**Pension Examining Surgeons.**

WASHINGTON, June 16.—[Special.]—Doctors W. B. Parsons and E. A. Crane were today appointed by commissioner of pensions members of examining board at Missoula, Mont.

**Capital Gravities.**

The secretary of the navy yesterday directed the award of the contract for the 8,150 ton armored cruiser to William Cramp & Sons, of Philadelphia, at their bid of $2,985,000, and the contract for the 5,500 ton cruiser, No. 6, to the Union Iron Works, of San Francisco, on the department's plans and specifications at their bid of $1,796,000.

The senate committee on commerce yesterday completed consideration of the river and harbor appropriation bill. It was decided to omit, for the present at least, the appropriations for the improvement of Hay Lake channel and St. Mary canal (about $1,000,000 altogether) for the reason that senate bills making those appropriations are now pending in the house.

The president yesterday transmitted to congress a communication from the secretary of the interior relating to the destruction by fires carelessly kindled or left, of the timber upon the public lands. The president expresses the opinion that if proper penalties were imposed by law and a few convictions thereunder secured, much waste of the forests would be prevented.

Senator Blair prepared two amendments to the silver bill yesterday. One is to strike out all the enacting clause and insert a section directing the secretary of the treasury, under the provisions of the act of 1878, to purchase silver bullion at the market price thereof and coin $4,000,000 monthly. The other amendment provides that there shall be no legal tender in the United States except gold silver coin.

Representative Butterworth, of Ohio, yesterday presented in the house a resolution providing for the meeting of the house of representatives on July 4 at 11 o'clock and for the setting apart of the day to the celebration by suitable exercises, of the adoption and promulgation of the declaration of independence. It also provides for the presence and participation of the senate in the exercises, for an invitation to the society of the Sons of the American Revolution to be present, and for a committee of nine members of the house to make suitable arrangements for the occasion.

### CRIMES AND ACCIDENTS.

An unsuccessful attempt was made to burn a New York tenement house.

John Love and Thomas Duckworth, of Pilcolia, Mo., have been arrested, charged with conspiracy to deprive the postmaster of the receipts of the office.

At San Antonio, Tex., an 18-year-old boy was killed by James Stevens, a negro policeman.

The Tacoma cracker factory was destroyed by fire. Loss, $32,000.

Eyraud, the famous French murderer, has been turned over to the French detectives by the Spanish authorities.

A call has been issued for a non-partisan meeting by ministers and business men of New York city.

Lionel Burnell, the original Little Lord Fauntleroy, is slowly dying.

## DEADLY FIRE DAMP.

### Another Terrible Disaster Reported From the Keystone State.

### An Explosion in the Hill Farm Mines, Near Dunbar.

### Over Thirty Lives Are Snuffed Out in an Instant.

### An Awful Fire Now Raging in the Heart of the Mine.

DUNBAR, Pa., June 16.—This morning at 11:10, a sullen, shivering roar shook the lowly miners' dwellings on Hill farm, Fayette county, near this place, and hundreds of affrighted persons, who knew the sound too well, feared another mine disaster, and they reasoned far too well. In a moment the fearful news had spread that the Hill Farm mines, owned by Philadelphia parties, had exploded. The low browed hill from which the slope entered shook from mouth to pit, and the score of miners' houses lining the fatal hill shook for a moment, and then poured out their frenzied inmates by the hundreds. A rush was made to the mouth of the pit, but ingress was impossible, as smoke in dense volumes was issuing forth. Fifty-two miners had gone to work this morning, and were in the slope when the explosion occurred. Of these 52, 18 were in the left heading, and 34 in the right heading. Those in the left heading got out all right. The retreat of the others was cut off, and not one escaped. Their names are:

JOSEPH BRIGNER, married.
RICHARD BRIGNER.
MILT FARLEY, married.
BARNEY MAUST.
EMANUEL MAUST.
PAT COURTNEY, aged 40, married.
GEORGE COURTNEY, son, aged 17.
J. W. MITCHELL, aged 40, married.
JOSEPH BIGLEY, aged 30, wife and two children.
PETER EAGAN, aged 44, married.
ROBERT MCGILL, single.
MARTIN CAVENE, single.
JOHN COPE, married.
ANDREW COPE, son.
PATRICK DEVLIN, married.
JOHN DELANEY, married.
JOHN JOY, married.
JOHN DEVANNEY.
DAVID DAVIS, married.
THOMAS DAVIS, son.
PATRICK CAHILL, married.
WM. CAHILL.
PATRICK COURTNEY, married.
JOHN COURTNEY, son.
JACK MITCHELL, married.
DAN SMITH, married.
DANIEL SHEARN, single.
WILLIAM HAYES, aged 19.
JAMES MCLEARY, married.
THOMAS MCLEARY, married.
ELMER DENNY, single.
PETER MCGOUGH, single.

At 7 o'clock this morning the gang turned in at the mines, the smaller gang drifted off to the left, while the larger, some 35 in number, drifted to the right and descended some 800 feet from the surface, and at least a mile from the opening. These two drifts are connected, but the connection is from the main stem some half mile from the entrance. The mine, it seems, had been somewhat troubled with water and an air shaft had been drilled from the surface to the juncture of the right and left shafts where the water seemed to be most abundant. As the miners marched off from this point they knew that an air hole had been drilled there that had not yet been broken into the mine, but they did not know that the shaft was to be broken into today, this shaft, by the way, being a six-inch hole. A miner named Kerwin had been left in the right drift near where that branch joined the mine's exit and in the course of his labors broke into the perpendicular shaft. The moment this was broken into a flood of water gushed out, and Kerwin and a man named Landy, standing by, yelled out for some one to save the men in the right drift, as the water poured down the hill in a stream and he feared they would drown. Young David Hayes, who had seen the affair, leaped forward at the call, and turned down the left drift in a deluge of water to warn his endangered comrades below. Just as he passed the air shaft that had been broken into, the rush of waters had changed to the ugly roar of a fluid which blanched the cheeks of the men who stood behind and towards the light.

The flow of water had changed to a deadly volume of fire damp, and as young Hayes swung by the shaft a flash of blazing light slid through the shaft from end to end it seemed. The daring youth carried an open burning miner's lamp in his hat, and he had hardly taken a step beyond the roaring shaft when the spark ignited a reservoir of the deadly fluid fire damp that had already accumulated and he sank a corpse 10 feet toward the men who he had hoped to save and the men who he had certainly doomed. In an instant an unquenchable fire sprang up in the nine-foot vein, just between the main entrance and on the right drift, forever shutting off the 32 men imprisoned there.

Poor old David Hayes, the father of the mistaken hero, driven mad by the fate of his son, dashed into the sulphurous smoke, and strangling fire damp, only to fall blindly beside his son, and to be drawn out an hour later, with James Shearn, both recognized only by their wives.

The fire, fanned by the air from the main drift, and from the fatal shaft itself, soon sprung into an awful conflagration. Pat Kelly, who was driving a mule car near the place at the time says the explosion seemed nothing, but the blinding, strangling smoke and gas followed like a fiend to the very door of the shaft and poured out after him, ascended to the top, and waved a black flag of woe and distress of this hitherto prosperous mining region.

**THE RAILS SPREAD.**

**A Burlington Passenger Train Ditched Near Council Bluffs.**

COUNCIL BLUFFS, Iowa, June 16.—The Chicago, Burlington & Quincy train, due here at 9:40 this morning, was ditched five miles east of here by the spreading of the rails and a number of passengers injured. The following are those most seriously injured:

JUDGE REED, Red Oak, Iowa, judge of the district court, badly bruised.
HANNAH ANDERSON, Salt Lake, badly bruised.
J. B. HILL, Augusta, Ill., badly bruised.
A. H. LAREN, Red Oak, Iowa.
MRS. HANNAH DAVIS, Red Oak, Iowa.

Several others were slightly injured.

United States District Attorney Miller was on the train, but escaped with a shaking up.

**QUEER BUSINESS.**

**Startling Message Left by a Young Girl Who Disappears.**

MILWAUKEE, June 16.—[Special.]—"Come immediately, or you will never see me alive," was the message telegraphed tonight by a beautiful woman, who gave her name as Florence Clark, to J. M. Underwood, at Room 23 Harlow block, Marquette, Mich. Miss Clark has been at the Windsor Hotel since last Friday. Yesterday evening she was visited by a fine looking and well dressed man, with whom she walked about the street. At 11 o'clock this morning she left the hotel, leaving a note with instruction that if she did not return by noon the accompanying telegram which read as above should be sent. The hotel clerk held the telegram until late tonight, when it was sent, the girl having failed to put in an appearance. She was a slender blonde of great beauty, and left in her room a large trunk. The police are searching for her in every direction.

**Dr. Hoenes Arrested.**

MILWAUKEE, June 16.—[Special.]—Dr. Andrew Hoenes, in whose office Anna Aulacher died Saturday night, is under arrest, awaiting the action of the coroner's jury. It is generally believed that the girl's death resulted from an attempted abortion.

## HASTINGS' GRADUATES.

**High School Commencement—Republican Convention—Other Items.**

HASTINGS, Minn., June 16.—[Special.]—The graduating exercises of the class of '90, held at the court house, were very pleasant and entertaining. The class was one of the largest in the history of the school. The following are the names of the graduates: Charles A. Reed, Rose A. Simmons, Mary H. Pringle, Katherine W. Kranz, Blanche A. Mace, Louise Todd, Kate M. Canning, John H. Plum, Frances L. Beltz, Emma M. Speakes, Posy A. Follett, Bertha C. Harnish, Elizabeth O. Schwech, Florence J. McNamara, Frank L. Greiner.

The Republican county convention will be held in Farmington on Saturday, June 28. The Republican congressional convention of the Third district will be held in Glencoe on Wednesday.

The 24th annual meeting of the Dakota County Sunday School association will be held at McKinley chapel, near Castle Rock Station, on Tuesday and Wednesday, 24th and 25th insts.

Miss Pauline Matthews, late of this city, was married to Harold P. Wood, of St. Paul, at Portland, Ore., on the 3d inst. They will make St. Paul their future home.

The funeral of the late Fred Scharch took place from the Presbyterian church yesterday afternoon, under the auspices of Dakota Lodge No. 7, A. F. and A. M., of which he was an old and respected member. An appropriate sermon was delivered by the Rev. R. M. Donaldson. It was one of the largest funerals ever witnessed in Hastings.

**Northwest Specials.**

At West Point, Iowa, the residences of C. C. Nacke and Henry Reuther were struck by lightning and several persons stunned.

Joe. Woodrack, son of the postmaster at Gregg, Johnson county, Iowa, was seized with cramps while bathing yesterday and drowned before assistance could reach him.

During the fierce storm of Saturday the massive steeple of St. Mary's Catholic church at Ft. Madison was blown down, crashing through the roof and wrecking a new $2,500 pipe organ.

At Plymouth, a small town in Jefferson county, Neb., Michael Doyle quarreled with Andrew Potter and attempted to shoot him, but struck and fatally wounded a bystander named Shook. Doyle was arrested.

At Aitkin, Albert Casey, about 8 years old, while at play near Mud river, fell in the river near a jam of logs, and the current drew the boy under the logs. He was taken out in about 10 minutes, and everything possible was done to restore him to life, but without avail.

The formal opening of the new Masonic temple at Fargo occurred last evening with reception to the grand officers of the state, followed by a magnificent banquet and ball. The fraternity claim they have the most elegant and complete suite of rooms in the Northwest, and the most complete in the world in a city the size of Fargo.

The trial of Jos. Quan, a desperado who shot and almost killed a merchant while burglarizing his house, began at Des Moines yesterday and a sensation was created when one of the jurors made a statement that Lewis Foley, a pal of the defendant, had offered him $100 to prevent a conviction. Foley was arrested for contempt and for jury bribing and put under heavy bonds.

Oscar Peterson, an employe in a livery stable here in Kasson is accused of an attempt to rape Bertha Crumpt, a servant girl in the employ of W. B. Shaver, editor of the Dodge County Republican. Peterson invited the girl out for a ride. In his efforts to accomplish his purpose, he tore the clothing off the girl. The team was frightened by the girl's screams for help and ran away, but were stopped without causing much damage. Peterson skipped and officers are in pursuit.

The outgoing train on the Montana Union, bound for Garrison met with an accident which resulted in the death of Engineer Wm. Hooker. The train was about half way between Butte place and Silver Bow and was running at a good rate of speed when the engineer suddenly threw the side bar upon the right side. That ponderous piece followed the motion of the driver and crashed through the cab with terrific force, stripping one side entirely from the engine. It caught Hooker, in passing, and threw him from the cab and clear off the train. When picked up Hooker was still breathing, but death came to his relief in a very few minutes.

## EYRAUD EXTRADITED.

**The Famous French Murderer Starts for His Native Land.**

HAVANA, June 16.—Michel Eyraud, the Frenchman who was arrested here May 20 for the murder in Paris on July 26, 1889, of M. Gouffe, a court functionary, was turned over to the French detectives, MM. Gaillarde and Soudani, today. At an early hour the Spanish police entered the cell in which Eyraud was confined. When the prisoner knew the cause of the visit he was surprised, but offered no resistance. He was manacled and conducted to the wharf, where the steamer Lafayette was lying and was there given in charge of the French officers, with whom he conversed freely. He frequently wept and complained of the harshness of the press, which, he said, had no right to judge him until he had been tried. During a conversation with a reporter he said: "You may say you have seen me manacled, but nothing else." After this remark it was noticed that the prisoner appeared more cheerful and he laughed several times. He said he would go quietly to Paris, but it is the impression of all who have come in contact with him since he was arrested here that if he is condemned to death he will adopt every means he can to take his own life. The Lafayette, with the prisoner on board, sailed for St. Nazaire this forenoon.

## THE ILLINOIS MURDER.

**Ella Cordell's Friends Likely to Avenge Her Cruel Death.**

MACOMB, Ill., June 16.—The village of Industry is terribly excited over the revelations in the case of Ella Cordell, who met her death because of criminal malpractice in Keokuk and whose remains were thrown into the river by her slayer. Two public indignation meetings were held yesterday. The investigating committees were ordered to continue their work. Feeling runs so high as to threaten mob violence to the young man who is accused of responsibility for Miss Cordell's death.

**TOLD IN A LINE.**

British sealers have received instructions to cruise in Behring sea and lively times may be expected by the middle of July.

A slight earthquake shock was felt at Cushing, Quebec.

The strike of the New York cloak makers is spreading.

The Roman Catholic diocese of Omaha and Cheyenne have been consolidated under Bishop Burke.

Thomas W. Phillips, the millionaire oil operator of Newcastle, Pa., has sold his extensive interests in the oil field of Glade Run, Butler county, to the Forest oil company. The consideration was private.

Switchmen on all the roads centering in Cleveland are on a strike. They demand Chicago scale.

FULL PARTICULARS
Of the Indian Outbreak in North Dakota will be found in
TODAY'S TRIBUNE.

# The Minneapolis Tribune.

THE TRIBUNE
Spares no expense in [illegible] the News. See its co[illegible]
THIS M[illegible]

VOL. XXIV. NO. 191. TUESDAY MORNING, NOVEMBER 18, 1890. PRICE: FIVE C[illegible]



## ALL IN A NUTSHELL.

News of the Day Boiled Down for Hasty Perusal.

**The Weather.**

WASHINGTON, Nov. 17, 8 p. m.—Forecast for 24 hours—For Iowa—Fair, no change in temperature, except slightly warmer in eastern portion; southeasterly winds.

For Minnesota, North and South Dakota—Fair; cooler; northwesterly winds.

For Wisconsin—Fair, preceded by rain in Eastern Wisconsin; slightly warmer, except stationary temperature in western portions; variable winds.

WAR DEPARTMENT, SIGNAL SERVICE, U. S. ARMY.—Meteorological reports received at 8:15 p. m., local time; at 8 p. m. 75th meridian time. Observations taken at the same moment of time at all stations.

| Stations. | Barom. | Ther. |
| --- | --- | --- |
| [illegible] | [illegible] | [illegible] |

Local forecast for Minneapolis, St. Paul and vicinity—Fair weather; no decided change in temperature.

**Ocean Steamers.**

NEW YORK, Nov. 17.—Arrived: La Normandie, Havre.

GLASGOW, Nov. 17.—Arrived: State of Pennsylvania, from New York.

LIVERPOOL, Nov. 17.—Arrived: Italy, New York.

SOUTHAMPTON, Nov. 17.—Arrived: Werra, New York.

NEW YORK, Nov. 17.—Arrived: Alaska, Liverpool; Normandie, Havre.

HAMBURG, Nov. 17.—Arrived: Wieland, from New York.

**The City.**

The board of trade met.

The bank clearings were $1,[illegible].37.

A lumberman was nearly victimized for $50.

Several large central properties are about to be sold.

Corporal James Tanner lectured at the Lyceum Theater.

Young Doyle's death was shown to be a clear case of suicide.

The Minneapolis Brewing syndicate will erect its new brewery at once.

The Jobbers' association refused to adopt the grain certificate scheme.

A St. Paul woman deserted her husband two weeks after her marriage.

E. S. Waters gave a stereopticon lecture before the History class.

The fair of the United Scandinavian Singers closed at Normanna Hall.

The Congregational, Baptist, Methodist and Presbyterian ministers met.

**St. Paul.**

Bank clearings were $1,[illegible].

Nicholas Kill was placed on trial for murder.

Mrs. Singer was arrested for shooting her husband.

Emma Juch began rehearsing for singing at the May festival.

The Chamber of Commerce discussed the subject of parks.

Judge Collins, of the supreme court, handed down five decisions.

The state federation of labor will hold a state meeting Dec. 14.

**Northwest.**

Mandan is terrorized over the reported Indian uprising.

[illegible]

**Railroads.**

[illegible]

**Markets.**

[illegible]

**Miscellaneous.**

The North River bank will not resume.

Randall & Wierum, New York brokers, suspended.

It is rumored that Parnell will marry Mrs. O'Shea.

The National W. C. T. U. re-elected their old officers.

A serious railroad accident occurred at Kansas City.

English banks raise a guarantee fund of £15,000,000 for Baring Bros.

[illegible]

The London jury found Parnell guilty of adultery, and the court divorced Capt. O'Shea.

**HE WAS TOUGH.**

BIRMINGHAM, Ala., Nov. 17.—This afternoon at Cropwell, 30 miles from here on the Coosa river, Jack Drennen, an employe at Wilder & Hull's sawmill, fell on the saw and his head was cut through from the crown down to midway of the nose. The saw cut out clots of brain. Drennen did not lose consciousness, and three hours afterwards was still alive and talking clearly. He is about 60 years of age.

## THE GIDDY WHIRL.

English Banks to Guarantee Baring Bros. £15,000,000.

Randall & Wierum, New York Brokers, Obliged to Suspend.

Rumor That the Manhattan Bank Borrowed a Million.

List of the Stocks Which Albert H. Smith "Raised."

LONDON, Nov. 17.—After the official close, business on the stock exchange had a decidedly better tendency, prices rallying from the worst points, but still leaving a general decline for the day. Speculative dealings were scarce, few venturing to operate in view of the uncertain and critical condition of the market. Some good investment business greatly assisted to modify the depression and street dealings on late continental telegrams were chiefly purchased by investors who had been attracted by the low level of the quotations. The leading feature of the day has been a further fall in river plate stock, Uruguays dropping 5 to 6, and Argentines 2 to 4. The fall in silver influenced a decline in rupee paper of 1½, while American railroad securities fell off ½ to 2½ and Mexican railroads declined 1½.

The banks supporting the Barings now propose to guarantee the whole £15,000,000 of acceptances. The management of Baring Bros. is expected to go into commission. Lord Revelstoke, the head of the firm, and a director of the Bank of England, withdraws as chief, although he will continue to advise the other members of the firm. The other partners are John Baring, also a director of the Bank of England, the Brewers Guinness, Mr. Hodgson, a director of the Royal Exchange Assurance corporation; Mr. Hallsed, of the Marine Assurance company; Mr. Gair, of the Union Marine Assurance company; Henry Baring, half brother of Lord Northbrook, and Henry Mildmay, all men of solid financial repute.

LONDON, Nov. 17.—It is stated that the guarantee fund raised for the Barings amounts so far to £14,000,000. Telegrams are being constantly received from home and foreign houses offering help.

**ANOTHER SUSPENSION.**

**Randall & Wierum, Brokers, Obliged to Close Their Doors.**

NEW YORK, Nov. 17.—At 10:30 a. m. today Randall & Wierum, brokers, announced their suspension on the stock exchange. Mr. Randall, of Randall & Wierum, is lying critically ill at home. [illegible]

[illegible]

**THIS LOOKS BAD.**

**The Manhattan Bank Borrows a Million from the Clearing House.**

[illegible]

**WILL NOT RESUME.**

**The North River Bank Compelled to Remain Closed.**

[illegible]

**AT PARIS AND BERLIN.**

**A Depression in Stocks and an Unsettled Feeling.**

[illegible]

**FEVERISH BUT STRONGER.**

**Philadelphia Bankers Think the Worst Is Over.**

PHILADELPHIA, Nov. 17.—The market here opened feverish, but stronger. Money was in good demand, but the banks and trust companies were not anxious to lend, as today they are calling in their loans for adjustment. Prices fluctuated from a half a dollar, but on the whole held firmly. Pennsylvania opened at 48⅝c, and by 11 o'clock had declined to 48⅜c. Reading opened at 14½c, and declined to 14 7-16c. Lehigh Valley opened at 48½c, and held firm. Lehigh Navigation declined from 49¼c to 47½c asked. There is no great excitement here, and the general opinion in financial circles seems to be that the worst is over.

**The Times' View.**

LONDON, Nov. 18.—The Times says that Russia had given notice to the Barings of the withdrawal in three installments of £1,500,000 of Russian funds, the first installment to be due about the middle of December and the second in January. The whole of Russia's deposit of £2,440,000 is therefore still with the Barings. The latter decided to ask for assistance, not on account of Russia's action, but on a review of the whole position. At a meeting of stock bank stockholders at the bank of England, the governor of the latter institution in a letter promised assistance whenever needed. In event of a pinch country bankers are withdrawing their balances. A meeting of country bankers to be held shortly will probably tend to allay the [illegible] current of anxiety. The Baring's share in the Buenos Ayres Water and Drainage syndicate is 1,000,000 pounds. Their responsibility also extends to the liabilities of other members of the syndicate in the event of their failure to meet their engagements. The report that a meeting has been held at which a scheme was devised to prop Argentine credit is declared to be untrue.

**Aid for Baring Bros.**

LONDON, Nov. 17.—Three leading Scotch banks have subscribed £250,000 each for the Baring guarantee fund. The scope of the fund and the period over which it will extend are still undefined. The details will be settled according to circumstances. A committee of leading financial houses has been formed to investigate the condition of the Argentine republic's finances. There is an unconfirmed rumor that the Argentine financial agency will be transferred from the Barings to the Rothschilds, in which case the debt of the republic will be reconstructed and consolidated. Country bankers are drawing large sums from London, causing a continued pressure on the Bank of England. The third installment of £1,000,000 has not yet arrived from Paris.

**All Safe in London.**

BALTIMORE, Md., Nov. 17.—Kidder, Peabody & Co. telegraphed C. Morton Stewart, the Baltimore agent of Baring Bros., as follows: "We are in position to state positively that all is safe in London, all drafts and bills will be duly honored and everything go on as before. You may circulate this statement freely."

## HERE IS THE LIST.

**The Stocks Which Naughty Mr. Smith Hypothecated.**

NEW YORK, Nov. 17.—Inspector Byrnes tonight furnished a full list of the shares of "raised" stocks upon which Albert H. Smith hypothecated with the brokerage firm of Mills, Robeson & Smith, and by them deposited with other institutions. The list is as follows:

Nassau Bank, Brooklyn, 4 shares Illinois Central, raised to 90 shares; Central Trust Company, 5 shares St. Paul preferred, raised to 90; Mechanics Bank, 5 shares Illinois Central, raised to 90; Atlantic Trust company, 4 Lake Shore, raised to 90; Lincoln National Bank, 8 Illinois Central, raised to 90; United States Trust company, 4 St. Paul preferred, raised to 90; Fourth National Bank, 8 Lake Shore, raised to 90; Leather Manufacturers bank, [illegible] St. Louis & San Francisco, raised to 90; [illegible] National bank, [illegible] St. Paul preferred, raised to [illegible]; Washington Trust company, 5 Illinois Central, raised to 90; Phenix National bank, 9 Delaware & Hudson, raised to 90; Union Trust company, 4 Illinois Central, raised to 90; American Loan & Trust company, [illegible]

[illegible]

## THROUGH A BRIDGE.

**Four Killed, Four Injured and Five Missing is the Record.**

KANSAS CITY, Mo., Nov. 17.—At 6:25 this morning a freight train of six cars and the engine of the Kansas City, Wyandotte & Northwestern railway, just entering the city, [illegible]

[illegible]

**KILLED.**

[illegible]

## THE W. C. T. U.

**They Re-Elect the Old Officers—Miscellaneous Business.**

ATLANTA, Ga., Nov. 17.—The W. C. T. U. re-elected all the old officers as follows: President, Frances E. Willard; Mrs. Caroline E. Buell, corresponding secretary; Mrs. Mary A. Woodbridge, recording secretary; Miss Pugh, treasurer. Resolutions endorsing Senator Blair and urging his re-election were introduced and created a little excitement. An effort was made to have that part referring to his re-election stricken out, but finally the matter went to the committee on resolutions. The board of trustees, of what is known as the Asheville donation, by a vote to accept the donation of Mr. Miller, of Skylands, of 20 acres of land adjoining the Vanderbilt property at Asheville, upon which a large temperance tabernacle is to be erected. Reports on [illegible] work were made by Dean Wright, Mrs. J. K. Barney, of the prison department; the Misses [illegible] Smith, of Maryland, and Mrs. Saul and Mother Maher, of the railroad department; Mrs. Hammer, on parlor meetings, and Mrs. Nichols, on the work at county fairs. This evening receptions were tendered the delegates at the governor's mansion and at Good Templars' Hall.

## OH, MR. PARNELL!

The Jury Says You and Mrs. O'Shea Committed Adultery,

Whereupon the Court Promptly Divorced the Captain.

It Is Reported That Parnell and Mrs. O'Shea Will Marry.

Dublin People Stoutly Affirm Their Champion's Innocence.

LONDON, Nov. 17.—The trial of the O'Shea divorce case was resumed in the divorce court this morning before Justice Butt and the special jury. The petitioner presented further evidence to prove the charges he makes against his wife and Mr. Parnell. The first witness called was a servant who had worked at the O'Shea house at Eltham at the time O'Shea claims Parnell was paying clandestine visits to his wife. She testified that Mrs. O'Shea and Parnell were on one occasion locked in the drawing room. Mrs. O'Shea afterwards explained that the locking of the door was essential to the safety of Mr. Parnell, as a number of members of secret societies were prowling about the vicinity. She also told the witness to deny that Parnell visited the house.

[illegible]

**HE WILL MARRY.**

**Reports Rife That Mrs. O'Shea Will Become Mrs. Parnell.**

[illegible]

**THE TALK OF LONDON.**

**The Famous Divorce Case Is the Leading Topic of the Day.**

[illegible]

**WILL DISPUTE THE WILL.**

[illegible]

... will be heard at the next sittings. Gen. Wood is sustained by other relatives in the contest.

**Scoring Parnell.**

LONDON, Nov. 17.—The provincial newspapers join in a chorus of denunciation of Mr. Parnell. The Dundee Advertiser (Gladstonian) says that the spectacle of Parnell's sneaking out of back doors and sliding down fire-escapes is contemptible and pitiable, and that he ought for a time to retire to private life, as the Liberal party will prevent any further attempt to brazen it out. Gladstonian papers in many cases advise temporary self-effacement. The London Daily Chronicle says: "It is deplorable that he should have wrecked his career and destroyed his public usefulness merely to gratify a guilty passion. How can Catholic Ireland retain such a leader? The middle-class electors in England will certainly resist any appeal, even by Mr. Gladstone, to support the party led by Mr. Parnell."

**The Standard's Satire.**

LONDON, Nov. 18.—The Standard, commenting on the O'Shea divorce case, says: Mr. Parnell seems to have been actuated by no desire to save the lady's reputation. All sorts of shabby, pitiful devices were adopted to avoid detection by the husband. The whole story is low, disreputable and disgraceful, with no redeeming feature, and nothing to justify the indulgence which has some time been extended to public men who have known how to invest their vices with a glamour of the grand. All Gladstonians will court moral destruction if they continue even in political intimacy with Mr. Parnell."

**Parnell Will Retire.**

LONDON, Nov. 18.—The Times says: The whole squalid apparatus of misleading letters, disguises, aliases and sudden flights make a story of dull and ignoble infidelity, untouched, so far as can be seen by a single flash of passion. If, as it appears, Mr. Parnell intends to remain the leader of his party, he will place the Gladstonians in a grievous dilemma. The Standard understands that Mr. Parnell has definitely intimated his intention to retain the leadership of the Irish party. It is expected that the Irish bishops will protest if he does not retire.

**Press Comment.**

LONDON, Nov. 18.—The Daily News says: The Unionists appear to hope that the discredit that has deservedly fallen on Parnell [illegible]

[illegible]

## APPLYING THE CURE.

**Description of the Application of Koch's Remedy.**

[illegible]

## KESSLER OWNS BUTTE.

**He Did Last Night After He Whipped La Blanche, the Marine.**

[illegible]

## ANSWERED DEATH'S CALL.

[illegible]

**TO IMPROVE THE MISSISSIPPI.**

[illegible]

**GRANT AT GETTYSBURG.**

[illegible]

**SMALL BUT SUFFICIENT.**

[illegible]

## THE WAR WHOOP.

It Is Liable to Be Heard at Any Time in North Dakota.

The People of Mandan Are Terrorized at the Outlook.

Gov. Miller to the Rescue With Arms and Ammunition.

The Army Officers Think There Is Little Danger of an Outbreak.

MANDAN, N. D., Nov. 17.—[Special.]—Settlers from every direction come in, reporting insults received from predatory bands of Indians armed to the teeth, who make circles around the tops of their heads. Citizens of Mandan have practically no arms, and are helpless. During the day the entire community was terrorized. They have been looking for aid from the government, expecting Indians to come upon them every hour, and no help or sign of help comes. Tonight two Indians went into a hardware store and called for ammunition. The storekeeper asked what they wanted it for and they said to shoot white men, and they drew imaginary scalping knives around their heads. A settler named Ardena comes from 10 miles [illegible]

[illegible]

**LATER.**

[illegible]

**GOV. MILLER TO THE RESCUE.**

[illegible]

**PRECAUTION NECESSARY.**

[illegible]

**WILL COME IN DECEMBER.**

[illegible]

... an almost total collapse of [illegible] the Indian prophets and tha[illegible] then resume their peace[illegible] Gen. Ruger is making a to[illegible] to the Sioux nations, and [illegible] ceeded in pacifying the w[illegible] Gen. Ruger will remain wi[illegible] dians during the winter [illegible] department advised as to th[illegible] intentions.

**GEN. MILES' [illegible]**

**He Claims That the Repo[illegible] break Are Exag[illegible]**

CHICAGO, Nov. 17.—Gen. [illegible] accompanied by Asst. Adj[illegible] turned from St. Louis this [illegible] Miles was in consultation w[illegible] War Proctor about the all[illegible] break in the Northwest. He [illegible]

[illegible]

**THE MARSHAL APPEALED TO.**

**Mandan Telegraphs the U. S. Official to Render Assistance.**

FARGO, N. D., Nov. 17.—[Special.]—[illegible] there around Mandan seem considerably [illegible] tated over what they term an Indian in[illegible] rection, and a dispatch was received to[illegible] calling upon A. F. Price, United States M[illegible] shal, for aid. No action was taken by [illegible] deputy marshal in charge, as according [illegible] his understanding the war depart[illegible] should be called on before a marshal [illegible]

[illegible]

**DANCING IS FAVORED.**

[illegible]

**THE ADJUTANT GE[illegible]**

[illegible]

**GREAT EXCITE[illegible]**

[illegible]

**THE CRAZE DESCRIBED.**

[illegible]

# THE MINNEAPOLIS JOURNAL.

PRICE TWO CENTS. | SATURDAY EVENING, FEBRUARY 14, 1891. | FIVE O'CLOCK



## RING OUT THE OLD

### Donnelly Bids Goodbye to the Old Combine Today.

### THE SAGE AND HOMPE HAVE A ROW

### And It Bids Fair to Upset the Combine Entirely.

### DONNELLY BEATEN BY 27 TO 17

### A Number of Alliance Men Desert Him on a Personal Issue—The Precedence of Railroad Bills.

A petition out of the usual line was sent up by Senator John Day Smith, when the senate convened this morning. It came from a number of the inmates of the Minnesota Soldiers' Home, and petitioned the legislature to pass a law prohibiting the trustees of the home from confiscating a portion of their pensions received from the government. The petition went to the committee on soldiers' home.

On motion of Mr. Stevens the concurrent resolution protesting against the passage of the Minnesota Boom Company bill now before the United States senate, was placed on general orders for Monday. Senator Stevens said that the motion was made at the request of Senator Burklandt.

Then an inky cloud hovered over the Alliance camp. The rain of internal dissension poured down for five minutes. It appears that several days ago Senator Hompe offered a resolution seeking to make a radical change in the railroad laws, and yesterday Senator Donnelly presented a measure seeking to amend the constitution, also with a view to making revolutionary changes in the government of railroads. The railroad committe, of which Mr. Donnelly is chairman, has been delaying action on Mr. Hompe's measure, but yesterday, an hour after the bill was introduced, the railroad committee held a meeting and reported back favorably Mr. Donnelly's constitutional amendment bill. This morning Senator Hompe moved that S. F. 200, his bill amending the railroad laws of 1887, be called from the railroad committee and referred to the committee of the whole. He said that the chairman of the railroad committee was favoring his own measures and delaying action on bills presented by the senators.

Mr. Donnelly offered an explanation. "There is a vast difference between his bill and the one we recommended to pass yesterday," said he. "I merely wanted to get action on some important measure before the railroad lobbies commenced to swarm into this city, and so the committee by a vote of eight to two recommended my proposed amendment. It is well known that the last senate railroad committee greatly retarded railroad legislation. It had a brevet member—a railroad official who is now vice president of a railroad, I believe, and I am told that at one time when a bill was called up a member of the committee joyously remarked that if the bill was passed it would not be constitutional, because the brevet member was not present when the bill was being considered. The attack of the gentleman from Otter Tail county on me is not justified. It was due from him as an Alliance member to confer with me as another Alliance member, and the president of the organization, on the matter before attacking me. I could have expected it from the Republicans, but must confess it discourteous from one of my own party."

Mr. Hompe retorted: "It was due the chairman of the railroad committee, as an Alliance member, to confer with me as another Alliance member, before giving his bill precedence over mine. I am not here as a railroad senator, or lobbyist, and propose to have my measures receive courteous treatment."

Things were getting warm. The sage arose and heatedly remarked:

"I will say that if the senator is not a railroad lobbyist, he is pursuing very much the same course as a lobbyist for railroads would. I met him at a caucus of the Alliance and Democratic members last night, sat beside him three hours, and he never mentioned anything about this matter. This morning, without a note of warning, he makes this motion—an indirect attack upon me—an attack which will carry joy to the hearts of all enemies of the people. I will say in conclusion that if I have anything to say regarding any bill in the committee I go to the chairman and say it, and without letting every one know it."

A vote on Mr. Hompe's motion to recall his bill from the committee on railroads and refer to the committee of the whole was then taken, resulting in its adoption, as follows:

Ayes—Allen, Ayers, Barr, Burkhardt, Conestorp, Dougherty, Davis, Day, Deans, Dedon, Erickson, Glader, Grinnell, Gudeman, Hammer, Hompe, Kiester, Lienau, Peterson J. W., Peterson L. D., Sanborn, Smith E. R., Smith J. D., Stevens, Stockton, Streissguth, Tawney—27.

Nays—Bell, Eoeshert, Brown, Craig, Donnelly, Geissel, Grafe, Keller, Kelly, LaDue, McHale, March, Mayo, Morse, O'Brien, Phillips, Probstfield—17.

Messrs. Hompe and Dedon, voting aye with the Republicans, are Alliance men. All voting in the negative were Democrats and Alliance men.

As soon as the vote was announced and the motion declared carried, Mr. Donnelly arose and said:

"I give the bill back to the senate and congratulate it upon the termination of one combine and the beginning of another."

Senator Bell presented a measure amending the several sections regulating the practice of pharmacy in this state. By its provision no one but a registered pharmacist may dispense drugs or poison. The pharmacist must be a graduate in medicine. Any one in the business prior to March 5, 1885, is entitled to a certificate of a dispensing pharmacist. A graduate in pharmacy must have had four years experience in drug stores where prescriptions have been compounded before he can obtain a certificate.

Senator Barr offered a measure authorizing the refunding to purchasers at tax sales amounts paid by them on state school, indemnity schools, agricultural college, state university or internal improvement lands in cases where the land have been forfeited by reason of the taxes on the same not being paid, or because the payments on the same were not made at the proper time.

A bill introduced by Senator Sanborn seeks to reimburse Jasper N. Searles, for money expended in his senatorial election contest, to the extent of $891.42.

Senator Probstfield fathered a bill providing for the appointment and election of another judge in the Fourteenth judicial district.

The senate then resolved itself into committee of the whole with Mr. Hompe in the chair. The committee arose after recommending the passage of several bills and agreeing to report progress on Senator Tawney's bill to allow administrators of estates to name the papers in which their probate notices shall be published, after which the senate adjourned until 10 o'clock Monday.

The senate yesterday afternoon recommended the passage of Senator Stevens' bill to amend the constitution; by its provisions municipalities may, if they choose, exempt property of manufacturing concerns, not exceeding $100,000 for a single corporation, from municipal taxation for a period not to exceed 20 years.

#### TRYING TO DOWN ERIC OLSON

##### A Resolution in the House to Oust Him—The Morning's Business.

J. J. Furlong, chairman of the judiciary committee, with blood in his eye, arose in his might this morning and "wanted to know, you know." The Alliance man was not present yesterday when Matt Gallagher's resolution was passed recalling the Greer telephone bill from the committee within 24 hours. Mr. Gallagher was not present this morning, but it was averred in his behalf that the resolution was withdrawn. Mr. Furlong seemed satisfied with the explanation although the journal did not show that such a disposition had been made of the resolution, nor did the members generally have any idea that Mr. Gallagher had withdrawn his ukase.

The report of the railroad committee, which recommended that the automatic car coupler bill be accepted with amendments, chief of which being that the measure would not become operative until 1898, aroused the ire of Mr. Stockwell. In his three-minute talk he showed that he favored the present bill and would be satisfied with none other, but Speaker Champlin said that the bill would be placed in general orders when it might be discussed, so Mr. Stockwell stemmed the tide of his firey eloquence and took his seat with gentle resignation.

Lomen, of Ramsey, then sat on the appointment of Eric Olson as clerk of the prison and reformatory committee. His resolution provided that the appointment of the blond-bearded Eric be declared "illegal and void." Olson was appointed by Speaker Champlin, who had yielded to the importunities of Olson's friends. An attempt was made to lay the resolution on the table, but it was lost, and then Mr. Lomen took advantage of his opportunity to explain his resolution.

He said that it was not a reflection upon the speaker, nor did party policy inspire it. The Ramsey man called his fellow legislators' attention to house rule 62, and said that in that section, the only one bearing upon the case at issue—the authority of the speaker to appoint a clerk of the prison committee—was not adverted to. Mr. Lomen' explanation was technical rather than sensational, but he hinted that there was no necessity for appointing a clerk for that committee. A desultory debate for and against the resolution followed, but at the end of a 10 minutes forensic flight, notice of debate was given. Thompson A, introduced a resolution which was adopted. It provided that the railroad commissioners be requested to furnish the house a statement showing the amount of land now held by the various railroad companies, granted to them by the state or the United States, to aid in their construction.

An avalanche of bills followed, and buried the house for the next half hour. Mr. McGuire introduced a measure which on the surface looks radical, to say the least. The provisions of the bill are these: Any person or corporation holding a franchise or charter shall make a yearly statement of the actual value of the plant; cost of operating expenses etc. If the receipts amount to a sum greater than just sufficient to pay the legal rate of interest, then it shall be the duty of the railroad commissioners in state matters and of aldermen in the city affairs, to fix the charges to just cover the sum necessary to pay legal rate. The railway commissioners or aldermen shall investigate and see that no exhorbitant salaries are paid, and that the people's interests are fully protected. If a false statement is made the president, auditor and bookkeeper will be deemed guilty of a misdemeanor and imprisoned for not less than 30 days nor more than two years, and the corporation concerned will forfeit its charter.

The bill is an inconsistent botch. There is no provision made as to whom the corporations shall report, nor does the saving clause "on conviction" precede the clause relating to the offender's punishment. The little effort of the Lac qui Parle statesman will probably sleep its last long sleep in the corporation committee.

At noon recess was taken.

Mr. Feig this morning sent up a resolution to have the Duluth & Winnipeg bill taken from the railroad committee, to which it was referred yesterday and sent to the committee on public lands. The resolution was adopted.

The railway committee of the house visited Minneapolis to inspect the bridge of the Minneapolis & Eastern railroad this afternoon. The party left St. Paul at 2:30.

The house met at 2 o'clock with only a bare quorum. A budget of bills was presented and then the house adjourned until 3 o'clock Monday afternoon.

#### A TEXT BOOK COMMISSION

##### An Attempt Will Be Made to Protect Public School Patrons.

A. Thompson's bill creating a state text book commission and a county board of education is that recommended by the state teachers' association. It require the superintendent of public instruction in November, 1891, and every fifth year thereafter, to draw ballots for members of the state text book commission. Eligible members are the presidents of the normal schools, city superintendents of St. Paul and Minneapolis, superintendents of high schools and county superintendents. The state commission will select all text books and make contracts with the publisher, who will supply every county ordering the same. The county board will be made up of the county superintendent, chairman of the board of county commissioners, superintendent of state high school returning the largest number of scholars entitled to apportionment during the previous year, and one teacher. The county board will select from the list of books approved by the state text book commission one book or one series of books on each subject pursued in the public schools of the county, below the state high school, and the books so chosen shall be used to the exclusion of any other book or series of books, for five years. It is the duty of the county commissioners of each county to provide a method of purchase, distribution and sale of text books. The state text commissioners receive no compensation.

##### Jim Smith is Busy.

James Smith is a very busy man these days. The delegation has appointed him a committee of one to receive all reports for or against an extension of the patrol limits. These he is having filed and he will formally present them when the matter comes to the official notice of the local delegation. This morning a large delegation headed by Rev. R. T. Cross, and Messrs. Metcalf, Perkins and Granger waited upon Mr. Smith and presented a petition against extension in behalf of the Tenth and Third wards. The petition is signed by residents in the section between 20th and 34th avs N.

##### The Street Railway Bills.

Thomas Lowry will probably do his "time and the wind up" with the legislature very shortly; at least insofar as it concerns the two bills now before the statesmen which affect the interests of the Twin City street railway systems. Senator McMillan's no seat no fare bill has already received the taut indorsement of the senate committee on incorporations with the exception of Senator Stevens. Senator McMillan's friends claim that he is growing restive and that the friends and opponents of the bill will have their last shy at it in committee meeting next week, when it will then come before the senate. Matt Gallager's amendment to his "3-cent fare" bill will be presented in the house by Tuesday at the latest. The amendment, as THE JOURNAL has already stated, is in effect that the street railway company shall be required to sell eight tickets for 25 cents during certain hours of the morning and evening.

##### John Day Indorses Penney.

R. L. Penney is indorsed. Senator John Day Smith this forenoon declared that he would support Mr. Penney's amendments to the execution law. The salient feature of the Penney bill is the clause which provides that all executions shall take place within the walls of the Stillwater penitentiary. Senator Smith said:

"I endeavored to get that feature incorporated into my bill two years ago, but was unable to do so as it met with so much opposition from the various county sheriffs. Each county claimed that it was able to take care of its own criminals, and could conduct its own executions. Mr. Penney's amendment will give the sheriff about $100 for his services as executioner, while if I remember aright Sheriff Ege received $500 for hanging the Barretts. Of course the interested sheriffs would not relish a curtailment of their fees, but if every execution took place at Stillwater it would rob them of local interest and therefore in my opinion the bill should be indorsed."

##### Railway Magnates Talk.

The railroad committee of the house held a public meeting in the Representative hall last night, many prominent railroad men being present. Judge Howe, of the Omaha, and Vice President Ripley, of the Milwaukee, addressed the committee at great length, and cited the disastrous condition of affairs in Iowa, where a law substantially similar to the proposed Currier bill provisions was in operation.

##### Duluth is Next.

The chances are that the legislature will go on another junket to Duluth next Saturday, remaining over Sunday.

##### Solonia.

The senate investigating committee will probably hold its next meeting in St. Paul Tuesday.

The senate and house committee of the state legislature on penal institutions paid a visit to the reform school, near Macalester, yesterday morning, and remained nearly all day inspecting the premises and buildings.

M. W. Meagher, the Minneapolis attorney, will shortly have introduced in the house a bill providing for the reorganization of the state bureau of immigration. It will provide that the Governor shall appoint a commissioner of immigration, who shall hold office for two years, and that this commissioner shall furnish information to intending immigrants or intending investors.

## TO PREVENT DELAYS

### Important Track and Bridge Improvements by the Union Depot Company.

The Minneapolis Union Depot Company is about to enter upon important improvements above the Union station, the principal of which will be the building of a double-track iron bridge over the Mississippi at the point now covered by the single track wooden bridge, which affords the only outlet to the East Side for the big freight traffic carried on. the building of this bridge will carry with it important changes in the track system above the station. At present tedious delays are experienced by trains due to cross the bridge to the island because of the necessary waiting in the narrow cut at 4th av N. When the new bridge is built, the tracks will be entirely changed. The bridge over the tracks at 1st av N, which formerly gave access to the old Camp & Walker mill, will be removed, as the railroad company owns all of the property between the tracks and the river, thus making it unnecessary to have a crossing at this point. The removal of the end piers of this bridge will give opportunity for a straightening of the tracks to 4th av, guaranteeing greater safety for trains and affording better yard facilities.

The railroad engineers have devised a plan whereby trains bound for the East side will approach the bridge on a curve directly from the depot, so that there will be no more backing of trains into the 4th av cut and long delays. A change is being made in the St. Louis track which is on the West Side. This is being moved one track to the westward, a deal having been made with the depot company satisfactory to both sides. This will afford another track in the yard. Some of the preliminary work is now going on.

#### POOR OLD ST. PAUL

##### Her Finances Are Certainly in a Very Unfortunate Condition.

The suit—mention of which was made in THE JOURNAL yesterday—instituted by the Mutual Life Insurance Company, of New York, against the city of St. Paul, bids fair to become one of the most notable cases in the history of that much distressed municipality. The action which was begun yesterday, is to recover $90,000 on three certificates of indebtedness against the city and the board of education of the city, one for $35,000, dated Nov. 6, 1889; one for $35,000, dated Nov. 27, 1889, and the third for $20,000, dated Feb. 5, 1890, all bearing 7 per cent interest.

The certificates were presented for payment and refused. When asked about the matter, City Treasurer Reis said that the certificates were legally due, but that he had refused to pay them when matured because he had no funds in the treasury. The mutual company, which brought the suit, had previously held overdue certificates, but had never threatened suit. He could not explain why they should do so at this time. Mr. Reis said that the finance committee of the board of education was making efforts to raise the $90,000 in order to redeem these certificates. The same committee is trying ing to raise $40,000 with which to pay the salaries of the school teachers of the city for the month of January. It is claimed that there will be no money available with which to pay the claims of the gas company before April and the money received for licenses is being rapidly eaten up in paying salaries.

#### MOODY RETIRES

##### He Leaves the Field to the Score of Other Men of Ambition.

Special to The Journal.

HURON, S. D., Feb. 14.—Senator Moody was here this afternoon on his way to Washington. He abandons the senatorial contest and leaves the field to the score of other aspirants. He believes Republicans will yet succeed, although the chances are not encouraging. The visit of Speaker Seward to Illinois is believed to be in the interest of the combination between the Independents of South Dakota and the Democrats of Illinois, and is strongly denounced by the members of both parties here this afternoon.

##### A Driver's Mishap.

Wm. Roy, driver on a 1st av electric motor, accidentally fell off his car last night, near 31st st, and was a few moments afterwards picked up unconscious. One of the wire doors at the side was out of place, and he had probably removed it, and, leaning out, been hit by a center pole.

## A GLIB WITNESS

### Leo Heilpern Explains Matters Very Smoothly on the Stand.

### HE ACCUSES ZEIDLER DIRECTLY

### Says the Mill Manager Was Speculating in Wheat.

### THE TROUBLE WITH THE BANK

### It Bobs Up During His Evidence—Heilpern's Interview With Zeidler on His Return from Texas.

Leo Heilpern was on the witness stand this morning, explaining the bad looking condition of the books of the Columbia mill. He was well under way and talked very glibly indeed. He had his explanation all in line, wanted to tell it just his own way and was not desirous of any suggestions from his lawyers in the matter. When Capt. Hart interrupted him he would argue quite persistently as to what he should and what he should not tell. In a somewhat disconnected manner he explained that the books were always kept under the personal supervision of Mr. Zeidler. The bookkeeping was on a very peculiar and loose system. Moreover, everyone when he wanted an advance on salary would go to the cash drawer and help themself, leaving a slip. Mr. Zeidler had told him to stop it, but Mr. Zeidler himself was the first to disobey the order. Mr. Zeidler, he said, was carrying on a personal business himself and that business was speculating in wheat. For this purpose he overdrew his account in large amounts. At one time this amounted to $10,000. It sometimes exceeded this considerably. Mr. Zeidler had kept his account suspended for some time, but had at last had it transferred to a bills receivable account, thus straightening up matters.

Leo was full of charges against the manager of the mill, but was kept in check by his own attorney. At last he became too rambling and his attorney was obliged to take to questions.

"You heard the testimony of Mr. Fossen concerning the drafts that came in and were sent to the bank and currency returned on them?"

"Fossen went every day to the bank with the drafts. Mr. Zeidler gave me separate drafts to cash from the wholesale business and I would give them to Mr. Fossen, explaining that the cash from my business was to be kept separate from that which was to go to Mr. Zeidler. When he came back with the money I would put my cash in the drawer and the cash for Mr. Zeidler I would turn over to him."

"Have you any account of money thus turned over to Mr. Zeidler?"

Yes, the witness had. It was in a big book on the table. He got it and read the amounts and dates.

"Now, I understand those were checks and drafts belonging to the wholesale business and were taken to the bank and cashed, and the money brought back to the office?"

"Yes."

"Now, when Mr. Fossen said all this money went into the cash drawer, you say he was mistaken?"

"Yes, sir, he was. That money went to Mr. Zeidler."

"During August and September?"

"Yes, sir."

"What was put down on the books to show it to a third person in case both you and Mr. Zeidler should die?"

"Mr. Zeidler told me to keep that account suspended so nothing went down on the books." Then the letters were taken up.

"What have you to say in regard to these letters? They are your own work and you have the right to explain what you meant in in them."

"Well, each letter has a separate explanation."

Mr. Thian began arranging the letters and Capt. Hart, in the interval drew a statement from Leo that he had not been to Mr. Grygia's office in a year, and did not know where it was. Mr. Grygia had said the confession was at his office.

The letter to Mrs. Willman was presented. Leo said he referred to Mr. Grygia because of having told him of placing the house in his wife's name.

Next the letter to Mr. Willman, written the next day, was placed in Leo's hands, and he said that what he said about speculation in wheat was all a fabrication. He really had never speculated in wheat in his life. He merely made that an excuse for his leaving town, as he did not like to talk to his best friends of his domestic difficulties. Had he known the matter was going to the mill he would have been more careful.

The letter to Mr. Zeidler was next taken up. It was translated by Leo who said that he said he expected no "favor" and not that he expected no "mercy." Mr. Hart asked him in succession what he meant by their "fixing the bail," "he would make it all right," etc., but the questions were objected to and the court sustained them.

Next Leo told of his talk with Mr. Zeidler at the city hall when he came back with Mr. Hoy. J. B. Bassett was at first in the room with them, but was sent out by Mr. Zeidler.

He asked the manager what the charges were against him. He saw in the Globe that it was $3,000, in THE JOURNAL that it was $70,000, and in the Tribune that it was $47,000. Now, what was the amount? Mr. Zeidler said that he did not know; they had not yet gone over the books.

Mr. Zeidler then asked him if he could say that the National Bank of Commerce had no right to pay the checks sent to them by the mill.

"I want to have it understood right here," said the state's attorney, jumping to his feet, "that we are not going to try a civil suit between the Bank of Commerce and the Columbia Mill Company.

The court allowed witness to go on. Leo said Mr. Zeidler told him that if he could testify that the bank had not the right to pay the checks they might withdraw the charges against him. He had answered that he could give no such testimony, and the conversation had closed. Here the witness was turned over for cross-examination.

In regard to Grygia, Heilpern explained that they had been avowed enemies for a year and that Grygia had told him in presence of witnesses that he was henceforth to consider him as an enemy. The witness thought Grygia was trying to do him up.

In regard to the keys he testified that Mr. Zeidler and Mr. Rupter each turned in a key to the drawer. Afterward a slip in Zeidler's hand writing was put in the drawer, and he tried the key which the manager had given him, and it did not fit the drawer at all. He drew the conclusion that Mr. Zeidler still held a key to the drawer.

He had a theory to answer Mr. Donaldson's in regard to the condition of the books. It was in effect to shift the responsibility upon Mr. Zeidler. That gentleman, Leo said, did not wish his name to appear in the petty cash book so he would put in slips for the money he took out and the slips would count as money. Mr. Zeidler, he said, told him to enter it as charges on the cash book and refer it in the journal in the same manner, thus explaining the expert's two-negatives-make-one-affirmative theory, the only difference being that Mr. Zeidler and not Leo was made the responsible party. The fact that Mr. Zeidler's slips and the figures on the books corresponded was considered significant by the defense. Heilpern was then turned over to Mr. Thain and cross-examined for some time before noon, when an adjournment was taken until Monday at 10 o'clock. Another day will probably wind up the trial.

Capt. Hart and Mr. Longbrake were very much pleased with their client as a witness, and in fact he made a very good showing. He was not nervous or hesitating, but had an explanation for everything, and wanted to talk. As Mr. Longbrake put it, if he was lying he was a very clever liar.

## A CLUMSY SCHEDULE

### The Western Association Committee Is Way Off.

### SO ANOTHER WILL BE DRAWN UP

### The Boston Association Wants Duke, But Can't Get Him—Sioux City After Jantzen.

Special to The Journal.

CHICAGO, Feb. 14.—Nothing was accomplished at the meeting of the Western association yesterday. The schedule committee reported as ordered and stirred up endless confusion. The examination of the document offered showed that one club was scheduled to play in three different cities on the same date, and that another was required to travel 1,200 miles in one night. Then it dawned upon the delegates that the schedule was worthless, and it was decided to appoint a new committee. Rowe, of Lincoln; Watkins, of St. Paul, and Brandt, of Omaha, were named, and they will report today with a new schedule. A strong fight for a Fourth of July game was made for Milwaukee by Manager Cushman, who claimed the Cream City had not been accorded that fat privilege for three years.

Arthur Irwin, of the Boston association, wants Duke, of Minneapolis. He carries a fat check for the desired release of the Flour City twirler, but Baron Hach is not likely to accept it. Jantzen, released by Milwaukee, is sought by Sioux City, and, if signed, will play first base.

The new committee appointed to prepare a schedule for the Western association were hard at work all the morning, but have made but little progress and do not expect to complete their labors until this evening. Meanwhile the association is expectantly waiting. The northern clubs insist upon opening games in their own localities and the southern element makes similar demands, while every club appears to have issued an ultimatum that it will play the holiday games in its own town and nowhere else. In trying to please everybody the committee has more work on its hands than it bargained for, but a strenuous effort will be made to get through today.

## CONGRESSES OF BRAINS

### The World's Brainiest People to Get Together at the World's Fair.

CHICAGO, Feb. 14.—The world's congress auxiliary of the world's fair, after three month's work, have just completed and laid before the directory a comprehensive plan for a series of international congresses during the exposition. The co-operation of distinguished men in politics, science, religion, education, moral and social reforms, literature, law and the artistic and learned professions has been enlisted. The work outlined is on the broadest scale and congresses of representatives of all the branches indicated have been provided for. It is the intention to bring to Chicago not merely a few distinguished people, but a large number of cultivated and intelligent persons from all parts of the world.

## WHO CAN HE BE?

### Independents at Pierre Will Support a Republican Dark Horse.

Special to The Journal.

PIERRE, S. D., Feb. 14.—The harmonious action of the Republican caucus last night in agreeing to support unanimously any Republican who could secure the Independent votes, is already bearing fruit. Stirling's followers have received assurance from several Independents that they will support a Republican whose name has already been mentioned, but which, for prudential reasons, is withheld. Conservative Republicans believe victory is yet possible.

A telegram has been received here from a member of the Illinois senate that Palmer refuses to countenance the proposed senatorial deal between the South Dakota and Illinois fusionists.

The 38th joint ballot, 138 voting, gave Sterling, 64; Kyle, 58; Tripp, 14; Campbell, 1; Cross, 1. Sheafe voted for Kyle, Converse for Sterling and Bowell for Cross. Necessary to elect, 70 votes.

The senate today passed the senate bills making valid a conveyance of the homestead by the husband and wife by separate instruments; abolishing county courts, providing clauses in notes, making them payable in any particular kind of money; making the board of railroad commissioners consist of one commissioner, at a salary of $2,000 and expenses for clerk and office. In the house, Bach presented a petition from citizens of Turner county favoring the abolition of the grand jury. Over a dozen bills were introduced.

#### SOUTH DAKOTA RELIEF

##### Those Who Have Been Aided Now Ready to Help Others.

THE JOURNAL is in receipt of a letter from Mrs. J. F. Jordan, of Howard, S. D., transmitting by express $7.85, the balance on hand from the fund raised last year for relief of those needing help at Howard and vicinity, and asking that it be sent to those at Hecla, S. D., who are appealing through THE JOURNAL for assistance. Mrs. Jordan also wishes THE JOURNAL to say that the relief committee at Howard has some clothing that they will be glad to turn over to the needy at Hecla if the Hecla people will indicate what they want, and how it should be sent.

Mrs. Jordan's money donation and her letter will be forwarded to R. H. Newton, at 36 Washington av S, who has been interesting himself in the Hecla case.

##### Confederate Soldiers Can Vote.

TOPEKA, Kan., Feb. 14.—The house, without an opposing vote, has passed a bill removing political disabilities from all persons who volunteered their services against the government in the war of the rebellion. The constitution debars volunteer confederate soldiers from the right to vote or hold office, and this bill is expected to remove these constitutional bars.

##### South St Paul Live Stock.

Special to The Journal.

SOUTH ST. PAUL, Feb. 14.—Receipts—550 hogs, 60 cattle, 1 calf, 20 sheep. Hogs—5c higher; quality common to fairly good; all sold at $3.15@3.40. Cattle—Strong on good butcher stuff and feeders; 2 oxen brought $3. We quote: Steers, $3.50 @ 4; cows, $2@2.60; common cows, $1@2; bulls, $1@2; milch cows $15@20; calves $3.00@3.75; stockers, $1.75@2.25; feeders, $2@2.75; butcher's steers, $2.75@3.50; sheep, steady sales of light muttons at $4 and tail end lots at $3. We quote—muttons $3.75@4.50; good to choice lambs $4@4.50; feeders $3.50@4; stockers and common $2@3.75.

## HIS LAST TRENCH



### Death Proves Too Strong a Victor For Gen. Sherman.

### THE END COMES AT 1:50 O'CLOCK

### It Was Momentarily Expected Since Early Morning.

### ALL THE FAMILY AT THE BEDSIDE

### Gen. Slocum to Have Charge of the Funeral—the Burial Will Occur at St. Louis—Universal Mourning.

NEW YORK, Feb. 14.—Gen. Sherman died at 1:50 p. m.

During the morning, as the hours passed, every inquirer who called at the general's house was told that all hope had been abandoned, that his relatives and attendants were merely waiting for the end and endeavoring to make his last hours as free from suffering as possible. Among those who called was Cyrus W. Field, who was driven to the house in his carriage. After he had learned the sad tidings he still lingered around. Soon after, Mrs. U. S. Grant drove up to the house. Thomas Ewing, Jr., descended the steps from the house to her carriage, and told her of the condition of her husband's old companion in arms. Shortly after noon, Secretary Barrett was asked if another bulletin was not to be issued. He replied that it had been decided to issue no more bulletins. No change except the last great change of death was considered possible, and that was looked for to come at any moment. Gen. Sherman was still breathing, but no more could be said of him. As on the preceding days, since it became known that Gen. Sherman lay at death's door, knots of people gathered in the street near his home and, after inquiring as to his condition, lingered there, talking to each other in low tones of the dying soldier.

At 1:50 p. m. a servant came out of the house and told the policemen on guard that the end had come and that the general had at last surrendered. Some doubt as to the authenticity of the report was expressed, but the officer said it was official. None of the family came from the house. Word was sent to young Mr. Sherman, who returned the message that he would not be able to give out anything about the death of his father for two or three hours. From Secretary Barrett it was learned that Gen. Sherman had remained unconscious to the last, dying with no visible pain.

The general passed away without speaking to any member of his family who were gathered about the bed. The four daughters were present and his son, P. T. Sherman, and Senator Sherman, and also the attending physician. Secretary Barrett and other friends were in the room below. At five minutes before 2, Private Secretary Barrett went around to the Western Union office and sent a number of dispatches to Washington. In the dispatches he announced the hour of death as 1:50 p. m.

The end came peacefully and quietly at 1:50 o'clock, while the general lay unconscious, surrounded by all the members of his family except Thomas Ewing Sherman, who is now on the ocean on his way to this country. There was just a slight quiver of the muscles of the face, the old soldier ceased to breathe and all was over. Although all hope had been abandoned for hours, the shock was great to the mourning friends who were at the bedside, and for many minutes no one left the room. They hung over the deathbed, weeping and gazing on the stilled face, so dear to them. Then young Sherman left the house and his appearance, even before he spoke a word, was the signal to those who were without, that all was over. He hastened to the telegraph office around the corner, but the reporters were before him and before he had reached it, the news of the general's death was spreading far and wide over the wires throughout the country. Shortly after Secretary Barrett reached the telegraph office and sent messages announcing the general's death to President Harrison, Secretary of State Blaine, Secretary of War Proctor, Mrs. Rusk, and many others. He could not restrain his tears. "He died like a babe falling asleep," he said. "There was no suffering, no pain. After 10 o'clock he lay motionless and nothing but the slightest respiration showed that he was living. Before noontime all had agreed that death was merely a question of minutes. The arrangements for the funeral" concluded Mr. Barrett, "are in charge of Gen. Henry W. Slocum. The interment will probably be made in Calvary cemetery, St. Louis, where his wife and other members of his family are interred."

The funeral services over the remains of the general will take place on Thursday from his late residence, although it may be deferred if his son does not arrive on that day from Europe on the Majestic. Thursday evening the body will be taken to St. Louis in a special train of three cars. It will be in charge of Gen. Schofield, and will be accompanied by a delegation from Post Lafayette G. A. R., of this city. Gen. O. O. Howard will have charge of the remains while being conveyed from the house to the depot. A special boat will be in waiting at the foot of 23d st to convey the remains to the Pennsylvania depot. Undertaker Wigger arrived at the house at 2:55 and took charge of the body.

#### SHERMAN AT FORT SNELLING

##### Stationed There When It Was a Less Desirable Post Than Now.

Soon after his graduation from West Point, General, then Second Lieutenant, Sherman, was ordered to Fort Snelling, and was stationed there for several months, occupying quarters in the old stone barracks along the south side of the old parade ground. His experience at that time was not more eventful than that of several other junior officers by whom an order transferring them to an Eastern post was regarded as a special dispensation of Providence, on account of the lonesomeness and remoteness of their station at that time.

The second memorable visit of Gen. Sherman to the Northwest occurred very soon after the close of the war, and partook of the nature of an ovation. Gen. W. S. Hancock, who was then in command of the department of Dakota, with headquarters at St. Paul, entertained him, but could not, even if he had so desired, monopolize his society, inasmuch as every man desired to do him honor. The trip was undertaken for the purpose of inspecting the forts in the Northwest and hence was fruitful of military receptions as well as pleasant social reunions. One unfortunate 2d lieutenant had occasion to remember the general's visit for many years, and possibly has never forgiven him a rebuke which was publicly administered upon the occasion of a formal military reception and inspection. The young gentleman in question had decked himself in all the panoply of war, but in his desire to make a stunning appearance, had allowed his tailor to adorn the dress coat with more aigullettes than the regulations called for. Gen. Sherman's eagle eye took in the situation at a glance, and he pointedly said, "Mr. ——, I should be pleased to see you in your uniform."

Gen. Sherman was present as an invited guest at the celebration in this city of the bi-centennial anniversary of the discovery of the Falls of St. Anthony, and was one of the speakers on that occasion.

William Tecumseh Sherman, the hero of the great march through Georgia, which has been called the "rapier thrust" that gave the rebellion its quietus, was born in Lancaster, O., Feb. 8, 1820. The family was originally from Essex, England, and came to this country in 1634. The father of Gen. Sherman was a lawyer who went West from Connecticut in 1810 and married Mary Hoyt. They had 11 children, of whom William was the sixth, and John Sherman, the statesman, the eighth.

William T. Sherman was adopted by Thomas Ewing and attended school at Lancaster until 1836. In July of that year he was sent as a cadet to West Point where he was graduated in 1840 sixth in a class of 42. George H. Thomas was his classmate. As a cadet he was earnest, high-spirited, honorable and outspoken.

July 1, 1840 he was commissioned as 2nd lieutenant in the 3d artillery and sent to Florida to take part in the Indian war. In 1841, he was made first lieutenant. In 1843 he studied law "to make himself a more efficient soldier." In 1846 he was sent around Cape Horn with troops that were stationed in California under Gen. Stephen W. Kearney. He returned in 1850, and at Washington married Miss Ellen Boyle Ewing, daughter of his old foster father, then secretary of the interior. He resigned his commission as captain in 1853, he was appointed manager of a branch bank in San Francisco. In 1857 he returned East to St. Louis, then lived in New York a year as agent for a St. Louis firm. In 1858-9 he was a lawyer at Leavenworth, Kan. When the war broke out he was president of the 5th st railroad in St. Louis.

On the war he took what were considered extreme views. He regarded President Lincoln's call for 75,000 volunteers as trifling with a serious matter. He declared that the rising of the secessionists was not a mob to be put down by the posse comitatus, but a war to be fought out by armies. His promotion was rapid, and he made a splendid soldier under Grant. The march through Georgia is too well known to be told again now.

Upon the appointment of Grant to be general of the army, on July 25, 1866, Sherman was appointed Lieutenant General; and when Grant became President in 1869, Sherman succeeded him as General. In 1871-2 he made a professional tour of Europe and was everywhere received with the greatest honors. At his own request he was placed on the retired list on Feb. 8, 1884. He was given the honorary degree of L. L. D. from Dartmouth, Yale, Harvard and Princeton.

He was a thorough organizer and a rapid and forceful writer. In personal appearance he was a typical soldier, tall and erect, dark hazel eyes, head large and well formed. His features showed strong purpose, resolution and grim gravity. His association with his friends and comrades was exceedingly cordial, and his affection for those allied to him was as tender as a woman's. He published his own memoirs in two volumes in 1875.

## 'TWILL PAY TO CATCH HIM

### A $1,000 Reward for the Apprehension of Flett's Murderer.

The Northwestern Elevator Company has offered a reward of $500 for the capture and conviction of the murderer of J. B. Flett, their agent at Arthur, N. D., and the other elevator companies of Minneapolis have added $500 to this amount, making a total reward of $1,000, which amount will be paid on the capture and conviction of the murderer.

It has been stated in some papers that James Remington, the probable murderer, had lost the first point of the forefinger on the right hand; but the information of the company is that it is the first two joints of the first finger of the left hand. The Minneapolis police know little of Remington, though it appears he was hack driver here for some time.

#### Gov. Burke After Fleet.

Special to The Journal.

BISMARCK, N. D., Feb. 14.—Gov. Burke has just offered a state reward of $500 for the arrest of murderer of James T. Fleet, the Arthur elevator agent.

## THE EIGHT-HOUR BATTLE

### A Long but Indecisive Debate in the Council.

The principal thing discussed by the council yesterday was Ald. Rand's eight-hour resolution, and after a long array of speeches, continuing until dark, the question was referred back, without action, to the special committee for further investigation. The majority report of the committee yesterday was for 10 hours a day and $1,75 pay, but the minority report was for eight hours straight, without naming pay.

The police committee presented a report authorizing the mayor to appointed the sidewalk inspector, but providing that his salary shall be paid out of the general fund. Ald. Lovell said the council should have the appointment, if that officer is to be paid by the city, but if the mayor appoints him his pay should come from the police fund. He therefore moved to defer action. The office had been created for the purpose of giving the city attorney a constable to summon witnesses and secure evidence. The inspector had caused some complaint because there was too much of police authority about him. Action was deferred.

Ald. Bradish's ordinance, regulating the weighing of coal and providing for the appointment of deputy weighers, was read a first time and referred to the committee on roads and bridges. Heretofore the weighing has been done by employes of the fuel companies, but the ordinance proposes that the weighing shall be done hereafter by the agents of the city.

A stir was occasioned by an attempt of Ald. Woodward to substitute the name of A. C. Swift for that of Geo. R. Chipman as a commissioner in a street opening case. This did not suit Ald. Bradish, because it amended his report, and the council voted to retain Mr. Chipman by a decided majority.

The aldermen and city officials will leave for Montreal on Monday evening.

The city engineer was directed to prepare plans for bridging the Hastings & Dakota tracks in such manner as to be most advantageous to contiguous property.

#### LAX PRISON DISCIPLINE

##### Additional Testimony Before the Committee on Prison Investigation.

Special to The Journal.

STILLWATER, Feb. 14.—Before leaving for St. Paul last night, the senate committee on state prison investigation examined several witnesses, whose testimony brought out the fact of the lax discipline of former wardens. The convicts would work when they chose, and when chided by the guards replied by violent abuse. Deputy Warden Lemon has a collection of burglars' tools and odds and ends made by the convicts during working hours, that is eloquent evidence of the watchfulness over them. The prison committee of the legislature is expected here this afternoon to report on necessary appropriations for the institution.

#### FORT DODGE TO COUNCIL BLUFFS

##### Proposed Extension of the Fort Dodge & Mason City Road.

Special to The Journal.

FORT DODGE, Iowa, Feb. 14.—Reliable information received here today develops the fact that at a recent meeting of the directors of the Mason City & Fort Dodge railroad, held at St. Paul, it was decided to extend the road from Fort Dodge to Council Bluffs at once. Surveyors will be sent out from this city within two weeks. It is understood that this move is made with a view of bringing the Winona & Southwestern people to terms.

The deputy collector at Roche, Wash., is charged with attempting to move the subport of entry from that place.

## WHY, ASKS ROYER

### The Ex-Agent Wants to Know Why He Was Bounced.

### APPROPRIATIONS FOR INDIANS

### Senator Pettigrew's Chances of Securing a $50,000 Slice.

### COPYRIGHT BILL AMENDMENTS LOST

### The Senate Disagrees with the Committee—Vilas's Credentials—The St. Louis Bridge Matter.

Special to The Journal.

WASHINGTON, Feb. 14.—D. Royer, recently removed from the position of Indian agent at Pine Ridge, saw the secretary of the interior this morning and made an appointment for an interview on Monday morning, when he will make inquiry and be answered concerning the cause of his removal.

Vice President Morton laid before the senate today the credentials of Senator-elect Vilas, of Wisconsin, and Senator Davis introduced the resolutions of the board of trade at Mankato, adverse to the free coinage of silver, also petitions from James McKey & Co., Noyes Bros. and other St. Paul business men, praying for the passage of the Torrey bankruptcy bill. Senator Pettigrew reported favorably from the committee on Indian affairs an amendment to the Indian appropriation bill, appropriating $2,202,000, of which $50,000 shall become immediately available for the purpose of carrying out the agreement with the Wahpeton and Sisseton Indians, Dec. 1, 1889. This report places the matter where Senator Pettigrew can demand consideration, and probably secure the passage of the bill.

Representative Haugen, of Wisconsin, this morning called from the speaker's table and secured the passage of the St. Louis river bridge bill, which recently passed the senate.

Senator Pierce has found Congressman-elect Johnson. He claims that he has not been out of the city, but was seeing the sights in his own good company.

Congressman Dunnell has received numerous remonstrances against the Minnesota Boom Company bill from St. Louis business men and others.

#### THE COPYRIGHT BILL

##### All the Amendments to It Are Voted Down in Bulk.

WASHINGTON, Feb. 14.—The copyright bill was reported from the committee of the whole to the senate today. All the committee amendments were voted on in bulk and were disagreed to. Yeas 29; nays 31.

##### A Bridge for South St. Paul.

WASHINGTON, Feb. 14.—In the senate today the vice president announced the appointment of Messrs. Manderson and Walthall as members of the board of visitors at the annual examination of the cadets at West Point military academy, and of Messrs. Chandler and Harris in a similar capacity at the Annapolis naval academy. Among the bills reported and placed on the calendar were house bills authorizing the construction of bridges across the Red river at Alexandria, La., and across the Mississippi at South St. Paul, Minn.

##### Announced by the President.

WASHINGTON, Feb. 14.—The President this afternoon sent a message to congress announcing Gen. Sherman's death and eloquently eulogizing the deceased soldier.

##### Capital Cullings.

Application for permission to organize has been made by the Citizens' National bank of Wahpeton, N. D.

Senator Pettigrew secured from the Indian committee a favorable report upon the Sisseton and Wahpeton bill.

The census bureau announces the population of the state of Arkansas by races as follows: White, 816,517; colored, 311,227; Indians, 304; Chinese, 131; total 1,128,179.

Minnesota pensions granted yesterday: Original—Philip F. Milnor, Israel B. Felton, John Quinn, Frederick B. Frost, Madison B. McCollum, Robert B. Fulton, Albert Cowin, John Sinclar, Swen Hassler, William Tillack, Franklin W. White. Increase—Philip Phaling. Original widows, etc.—(Special act), Agnes R. widow of Pearson C. Rice; Anna L., widow of John P. Johnson.

## RESUBMISSION WINS

### The North Dakota Senate Concurs with the House.

Specials to The Journal.

BISMARCK, N. D., Feb. 14.—The senate today considered the concurrent resolution of the house on resubmission of prohibition and concurred in it by a vote of 16 ayes, 15 nays.

#### TOWN TALK

The bank clearings today were $737,932.04.

Take your lunch at the Model. Try it, 15 3d st S.

Rogers' knives, forks and spoons; jobbers' prices. Elliot, 251 Nicollet av.

Lowest prices on pianos at Haines, Foster & Waldo's, 43 4th st S, upstairs.

It is reported that F. Weyerhauser will build a saw mill in Minneapolis.

Londonberry Lithia water at Jos. R. Hofflin & Co.'s drug store, corner Washington and 1st av S.

People's Live Stock Insurance Company furnish veterinary services free to Minneapolis customers.

"Muncie Gift," injured on ice yesterday, was insured with the People's Live Stock Insurance Company.

Five per cent paid on six months deposits. Two per cent, subject to check. Title Insurance & Trust Company.

It costs $1 per week to join our watch club. You soon get a watch and don't feel it. Elliott, 251 Nicollet av.

Herbert Conner, the artist, has rented his picture, "Consolation," to George Sawyer, at the Merchants, on Nicollet av.

Artistic watch repairing, jewelry made to order, diamonds reset. Only artist workmen employed. Elliot, 251 Nicollet av.

Cut prices on diamonds. We have more than we wish to carry, and can save dollars on reliable goods. Elliot, 251 Nicollet av.

It was not the Buffalo Scales Company, but another company which offered $55,000 for the Daniels patent scales invented by a Minneapolitan.

Following sums now ready for real estate city loans: $4,000, $4,000, $3,000, $3,000, $1,500, $1,500, $1,200, $1,000, $600. No delay. Wm. Peet, Jr., Boston block.

Novels and magazines of all kinds, as well as daily papers, funny papers, scientific, electrical, sporting and story papers at the Century News and Book Store, 8 3d st S.

The prizes offered to the boy and girl selling greatest number of tickets for the operetta of "Red Ridinghood," are a pair of fine skates for the boy and a string of gold beads for the girl.

W. G. Hollis was unanimously re-elected secretary of the Northwestern Lumbermen's Association, at the last meeting of the board of directors, and his salary placed at $2,000. J. H. Queal was also invested with the authority of the office of treasurer.

# The Minneapolis Tribune.

VOL. XXVIII. NO. 111. MINNEAPOLIS, MINN., MONDAY MORNING, SEPTEMBER 3, 1894. PRICE: FIVE CENTS.




# A CYCLONE OF WIND AND FIRE!

### Northern Minnesota and Wisconsin Bathed in a Sea of Flame and Hundreds of Human Lives Are Sacrificed to the Insatiable Greed of the Red Demon As He Stalks Through the Pine Forests on His Mission of Death.

## TWO HUNDRED DEAD AT HINCKLEY

### The Awful Story of the Destruction of the Town and the Appalling Loss of Life Graphically Told by Correspondents of the Tribune.

#### Flames From the Surrounding Forest Sweep Down Upon the Village, and Being Caught by a Cyclone, Dance in Ghoulish Glee, Leaving Hundreds of Charred Corpses in Their Wake.

A cyclone of wind and fire swept over thousands of acres in northern Minnesota and Wisconsin Saturday afternoon. Hundreds of tons of combustible material in its awful path was swallowed up in flames.

The total loss of life will never be definitely known. There were scattered throughout the woods settlers, clearings and lumber camps, with their watchmen, and many people were [illegible] burned whose bodies were completely destroyed, and will never be found.

**NUMBER OF THE DEAD:**

| | |
|---|---|
| Hinckley | 200 |
| Sandstone | 46 |
| Sandstone Junction | 25 |
| Pokegama | 25 |
| Skunk Lake | 29 |
| Miscellaneous | 30 |
| Total | 355 |

## SANDSTONE

### Forty-Seven Dead Bodies Lying Uncovered in the Morning Sun.

#### The People Who Are Left Are Subsisting on Potatoes and Carrots

#### Twenty Dead Bodies at Kettle River Junction—Homeless Ones at Mission Creek.

## BURNING OF THE DULUTH "LIMITED"

### While the Train Is on Fire From One End to the Other the Passengers Make Their Escape Into a Marsh, and Lying Down in the Water, Save Their Lives.

#### Ten or a Dozen, However, Jump From the Coaches Into the Sea of Roaring Flame and Are Burned to Death—Thrilling Story of a Mad Race With the Fiery Flames.

Continued on Third Page.

16 PAGES **THE MINNEAPOLIS JOURNAL.** 16 PAGES

PRICE TWO CENTS. WEDNESDAY EVENING, DECEMBER 11, 1895. FIVE O'CLOCK

# QUITE A TOWN

**St. Louis People Begin to Think They Have a City There.**

**THE CO[illegible] PREPARATIONS**

**The President Expec[illegible] Back Frida[illegible] or Saturday.**

**SENATE IN SESSION TODAY**

**But the House Still Waits for Mr. Reed to Make Up the Committee List.**

Washington, Dec. 11.—The main details of the Republican national convention at St. Louis on June 16 next were perfected at a meeting today of the subcommittee appointed last night to take charge of arrangements. Messrs. Kerens and Thompson, representing St. Louis, were present at the meeting, and gave assurances that the plans proposed would be speedily executed. The committee agreed that the seating arrangements of the St. Louis exposition building needed remodelling. At present the rostrum is at one end of a vast hall, so that people at the other end are too far away to hear what is going on. It was decided to have the rostrum placed midway and at one side of the hall, with the seats of delegates arranged accordingly. A diagram of the change is to be completed by the St. Louis people by the time of the subcommittee's reassembling. It will show the central arrangement, and will designate the seats of each state delegation. The alterations of the building probably will cost $15,000.

The question of alloting tickets brought out much animated discussion. The exposition building accommodates 15,000 people, but these limits are expected to be severely taxed. It is understood that an understanding was reached that the St. Louis local committee would not control more than 3,000 tickets, and that of these 500 should go to veterans of the war and 500 to distinguished guests. The national committee, it is understood, will control the balance of the tickets, as well as retaining a supervisory authority over the 3,000 tickets going to St. Louis.

The subcommittee adjourned to meet in St. Louis the latter part of January, the date to be announced thereafter. They will personally inspect the hall and all other features of the convention.

Chairman Carter expects to issue the formal call for the national convention within the next day or two. It is imperative that it is issued by the 15th inst., in order to give full six months notice for the election of delegates to the convention.

The excitement attending the national committee meetings has subsided now that most of the committeemen and delegations representing cities have gone home. The jubilant St. Louis party left on a special train at 12:30 today for New York city, where they will have quarters at the Waldorf hotel.

The friends of Gov. McKinley will close their quarters at the Arlington today and thereafter will have permanent rooms at the Hotel Cochrane, in this city, with Chairman Grosvenor, vice-chairman, and an executive committee of five persons in general charge.

**HEATWOLE DENIES**

**That He Is Hustling for a Committee Place.**

Special to The Journal.

Washington, Dec. 11.—Joel P. Heatwole emphatically denies today that the rumor circulated recently, here and in Minnesota, that he is working hard to secure the assignment on the house committee on foreign affairs, is true. He still asserts that he is not pressing his claim upon Mr. Reed for any committee assignment, and proposes, so far as he is concerned, that Mr. Reed do exactly as he likes.

If Mr. Heatwole is not making any bid for a good committee assignment, he differs materially from any of his colleagues from Minnesota.

The majority, if not all of them, Mr. Heatwole excepted by his own statements, are making an energetic fight to secure good places. Mr. Fletcher is too old in politics not to pull wires in his own interest to secure an excellent committee assignment if he can. Mr. Tawney has also been in politics too long not to endeavor to further his own interests.

Mr. Eddy is a very modest gentleman, but it is probably true, also, that he is doing all in his power to secure a committee assignment which would enable him to be of benefit to his constituents.

Towne and McCleary are also hustling, and if they fail to succeed in getting what they want it will not be due to any lack of energy. Mr. Heatwole, therefore, may be more shrewd than his colleagues in not endeavoring, as he states, to influence Speaker Reed in any way regarding his personal interest. He said today:

"I saw Speaker Reed and told him of the Third district and expressed a desire to be placed where I could do the people of the district the most good. I have not made a campaign to secure a place on any particular committee."

**IN THE SENATE**

**The Committees and Their Appropriation Bills.**

Washington, Dec. 11.—Mr. Mitchell (Dem., Wis.) introduced a joint resolution today for the purchase of a statute of Victor Hugo for the congressional library. On motion of Mr. Harris (Dem., Tenn.) a resolution was passed calling upon the secretary of war for copies of all papers relating to the railroads seized and operated by the government from 1861-65 in order to furnish information for an adjustment of the government claims against Tennessee.

Mr. Dubois (Rep., Idaho) then called up his amendment to the senate rules for the distribution of the various appropriation bills to the committees especially interested in the subject dealt with.

**SECTION 30 CASE**

**A Hearing Set in Washington for Jan. 27.**

Special to The Journal.

Washington, Dec. 11.—Attorney John C. Judge, representing Minnesota in the famous section 30 case, appeared before Commissioner Lamourex today and urged an immediate hearing. Attorneys for the other side were not ready, however, and Commissioner Lamourex fixed the date for hearing here for Jan. 27. Judge will return to Minneapolis tonight.

WALLACE HAS SCRUPLES.

Ottawa, Ont., Dec. 11.—Hon. Clarke Wallace, controller of customs in the dominion cabinet, has resigned because he cannot approve of the course which the government has adopted in its attitude toward the Manitoba school question. Wallace is grand master of the Orange grand lodge of British North Americ

AN EFFECTIVE REMEDY

How Uncle Sam might save our minis ter to England from some of the evil effects of the mouth disease.

# WHAT'S THE INSIDE

**Esoteric Meaning of the Choice of St. Louis.**

**IT WORRIES THE POLITICIANS**

**Some of the Hunters for Mystery Try to See the Hands of Platt and Quay.**

Special to The Journal.

Washington, Dec. 11.—The selection of St. Louis for the Republican national convention next year was received favorably in some quarters today and in others unfavorably. Of course, the representatives of San Francisco, Chicago and Pittsburg are disappointed. The men who were also back of the booms of several Republican presidential aspirants are also not entirely satisfied. St. Louis may be able to handle the convention successfully next year, but if it is able to meet all the requirements it will do much more than the Southern metropolis was able to do when the Democratic convention was held there in 1888.

There is a good deal of politics in connection with the action of the Republican committee this year. It is still believed that for certain reasons best known to themselves, ex-Senator Platt, Senator Quay, of Pennsylvania; and Gen. Clarkson, of Iowa, succeeded in having St. Louis named. It will probably be known later just what their purpose was in influencing the members of the committee to make this selection.

There is a good deal of bitterness displayed among the friends of many presidential candidates today, and, while they are not talking for publication, they believe that there was a deep-laid plot on the part of Platt, Quay and Clarkson in the interest of themselves personally; and by this it is meant that they propose, unless within the next few months their plans are checkmated, to name the ticket that will be selected by the convention.

The Northwestern members of the national committee have very little to say regarding the outcome. It is believed, however, that Committeeman Evans is of the opinion that, in choosing St. Louis, the committee made the best possible selection. He carried out his promise to the San Francisco people in casting his vote for the Pacific coast metropolis, and, after discovering that there was no hope for that town to win, he believed it to be for the best interests of the Republican party that the convention go to the Missouri metropolis. It may be several weeks yet before the inside facts regarding the choice of St. Louis come to the surface. Meantime the politicians who were defeated in pressing the claims of other cities are indulging in a good deal of speculation regarding the maneuvers of Messrs. Platt and Quay from behind the scenes.

**REED STILL PUZZLED**

**Having Much Trouble in Making Up Committees.**

Washington, Dec. 11.—There seems to be no possibility now that the committees of the house will be announced this week and the house may adjourn tomorrow until Monday. Speaker Reed has experienced more difficulty than was anticipated in making up the membership of committees owing to his lack of personal acquaintance with the new members, of whom there are 163. From a source close to the speaker the information is given out today that the committees will probably not be announced until the latter part of next week, just before the Christmas holidays.

**PRESIDENTIAL DUCKS**

**Will Be Brought Back to Washington Friday.**

Washington, Dec. 11.—The president is expected to return to Washington Friday or Saturday. At present the Viola is lying in the sound, back of Cape Hatteras. Notice of the approach of the prevailing stiff blow was served upon her skipper in due season and the boat was placed in a sheltered anchorage, where she lies in perfect safety, and the only outward effect of the blow is to make the shooting uncomfortable for the time.

**Scattering of the Politicians.**

Special to The Journal.

Washington, Dec. 11.—National Committeeman Robt. G. Evans, of Minnesota, leaves here tonight for New York. T. E. Byrnes and the other Minnesota politicians who came here to attend the national convention, will leave for home tomorrow. Secretary Dowling, of the National League of Republican Clubs, will also leave here tonight for New York.

THE GOLD RESERVE.

Washington, Dec. 11.—Today's statement of the condition of the treasury shows: Available cash balance, $174,812,581; gold reserve, $76,-534,607.

# TRAGIC!

**A Heartrending Scene at the Cemetery This Afternoon.**

**The Half Crazed Mother's Words by the Bier of Her Son.**

At the simple burial services over the remains of Harry Hayward, at 2 o'clock, this afternoon, at Lakewood cemetery, there occurred one of the most tragic incidents of the many which have marked the course of his trial and execution. The ceremony was held in the little chapel at the cemetery, over the vault in which the body will rest until spring, and was attended by a very few friends and the members of the family, Adry included. At the services, Rev. M. D. Shutter officiated.

After the words of scripture and prayer from Dr. Shutter, Mrs. Hayward desired to place some flowers on the casket and, supported by her son Dr. Thaddeus and her husband, advanced to do so. When she walked around the head of the coffin, strewing carnations as she did so. When she had distributed her flowers and had arrived at the right hand side of the bier she hesitated. In response to a signal from her, Thaddeus and her husband loosened their support of her and she stood alone. To everyone's surprise she raised her clenched hands and broke forth in a low moaning tone.

"Poor, dear Harry! Poor, dear Harry!

"My baby boy! My dear baby boy!

"God has forgiven him! God has forgiven him!

"Poor, dear Harry! Poor, dear Harry!

"Be a brave mother, be brave and strong! The chains bind me, but they can't chain my soul! I come again!

"Poor, dear Harry! Poor, dear Harry! My baby boy!"

With this the mother half turned and started towards where Adry sat. Thaddeus and Mr. Hayward caught her, but she pushed forward, and they followed, still supporting her. In front of Adry she stopped, and, lifting his face in her hands, said:

"Tell him I've forgiven him, mother." Her reproachful tones echoed in the silent room. Seemingly half crazed, the bereaved mother turned from her elder boy to where her youngest, her darling, lay, but Mr. Hayward, Thaddeus and Adry persuaded her to turn back, and as she did so she fell fainting into the seat near by.

The few present were deeply impressed by Mrs. Hayward's outburst of sorrow, but most affecting of all was her approach to Adry and her words to him as though Harry were speaking.

"Tell him I've forgiven him, mother."

The decorations at the service were very simple, Ernest Goodsell bringing some lilies and friends sending some roses. The only other flowers were the pink carnations the mother herself dropped on her son's coffin.

**MONOPOLIES!**

**The French Legislators Get After Them.**

Paris, Dec. 11.—In the chamber of deputies today the war budget was discussed, and a resolution was adopted inviting the government to prosecute those who have been engaged in cornering leather. The minister of war, M. Cavignaic, admitted that there had been a rise in the price of leather, and intimated his intention to inquire if the operations of the American Trust was responsible for it. He added that if it was proved that a leather ring existed in France, the general had power to deal with it. M. Marcel-Habert called attention to the monopoly of wheat, and urged that the law be applied to defeat its objects.

**PINGREE WINS**

**The Mayor Vs. the Detroit Fire Commission.**

Detroit, Dec. 11.—The damage suit of James F. Tryon, secretary of the fire commission, against Mayor Pingree, was decided by the jury today, who found "no cause for action."

Mayor Pingree had Secretary Tryon, Chief Elliott and Commissioner Goodfellow arrested on a charge of conspiracy in having refused his honor access to the department records.

All three officials brought suit for damages. Goodfellow's suit has been continued until the next term of court, and Elliott's withdrawn.

A CIGARETTE CRUSADE.

Special to The Journal.

Neenah, Wis., Dec. 11.—Residents here have drafted a petition to President Hewitt, of the Northwestern road, protesting against the smoking of cigarettes in baggage rooms and news-stan[illegible]

# MEETS A FELON'S DEATH

## A DEGENERATE

**Harry Hayward's Skull Was Queer in Several Ways.**

**It Possesses at Least Three of Lombroso's Four "Stigmata."**

**The Interesting and Significant Results of the Autopsy This Morning.**

**The Obsequies at Lakewood This Afternoon Pass off Quietly.**

The specialists who examined and measured Harry Hayward's skull and brain have not completed all their calculations yet; but so far as they have gone they have found three of the four abnormalities or stima which, according to Prof. Caesaro Lombroso, the distinguished Italian authority, invariably characterize the "degenerate" or "delinquent" man. These three stigma are pronounced a symmetry of skull, brain and face; the protrusion of the front teeth, and the narrow and sharply arched palate. The calculations made from the measurements of the skull which will determine the facial and nasal angles, which are of great importance in detecting degenerates, have not yet been made. The capacity of the cranial cavity, also depending on calculations from the measurements taken, has not yet been determined, but the weight of the brain was found—55 ounces—considerably more than was expected from an ocular examination. The doctors say that, on the whole, it is a very fair brain, the chief peculiarity being the slight development of the frontal lobes. But to counterbalance this fact, the other portions of the brain were found to be highly developed. What deficiencies, if any, there may be in the brain, are so subtle in their nature that neither the knife nor the microscope is capable of revealing them.

After the black robed figure had dangled at the end of the hemp for a half hour or so and the witnesses to the execution had looked over the object, N. F. Warner and his assistant, Charles Johnson, pushed their way into the cellroom bearing between them a long black casket. Resting this on a pair of stools they raised the body a few inches, while Coroner Kistler cut the rope, releasing the body, which was at once lifted into the casket.

The black cap was not removed, and the crowds which surged into the room received but little gratification for their struggles. Speedily the narrow house, with its contents, was carried outside, the policemen breaking a path through the crowd to the undertaker's wagon.

When the driver had received his load, he whipped up his horses and was soon at Warner's morgue, where the body was divested of the black cap, robe, and all clothing. In this condition it lay on the slab until the doctors arrived for the autopsy.

Shortly after 8 o'clock this morning the physicians who were to superintend and witness the measurement of the skull and brain were worming their way through the thickly packed crowd that blocked the entrance to N. F. Warner's morgue in their frantic but unavailing effort to reach the slab where lay Harry Hayward's corpse.

They came rather slowly, but in due time there were a half score on hand, and they proceeded with the preliminaries of their task, which seemed so gruesome to the uninitiated, but from which the medical men plainly anticipated much scientific benefit.

When the party bent its steps to the rear room, in which the splendidly moulded form was stretched on an embalming table, the following well-known physicians and specialists were present: Drs. W. A. Jones, Haldor Sneve, Frank Burton, G. G. Eitel and C. J. Ringnell, of Minneapolis; Charles Wheaton, John Fulton, J. A. Quinn and McNamara, St. Paul; H. A. Tomlinson, of the St. Peter asylum.

Their first work before opening the skull was to take the outside measurements of the skull and face. Drs. Jones, Eitel and Tomlinson made the measurements according to a diagram supplied by Dr. Sneve, who noted the various figures. A small, fine steel tape was used and the process was very slow and tedious to the spectators who had managed to gain entrance; but the doctors were all attention and heard the various measurements with interest, nodding approval and uttering noncommittal "hum-hums." The figures were all given in centimeters, and when the doctors have time they will try to ascertain in what respects Harry Hayward's head is abnormal or deficient. The measurements are as follows:

| Measurement of Skull— | Centimeters |
|---|---|
| Circumference of skull | 58.0 |
| Breadth over most prominent parietal bone | 15.2 |
| Breadth, ear to ear | 36.5 |
| Length occiput to ophryon | 33.5 |
| Length from extremety of ear to alveolar border, right side | 15.3 |
| Same, left side | 16.0 |
| Nasal index, right, length, 1.5; breadth | 1.0 |
| Nasal index, left, length, 1; breadth | 0.6 |
| Nasion to middle ear, right side | 15.6 |
| Nasion to middle ear, left side | 14.6 |
| Nasion to abcolor border | 9.0 |
| Ophryon to occiput, right side | 30.6 |
| Ophryon to occiput, left side | 28.4 |
| From the jaw around highest part of head | 69.0 |
| Jaw angle to chin, right side | 12.5 |
| Jaw angle to chin, left side | 12.0 |
| From jaw angle to jaw angle | 34.0 |
| From jaw angles over chin | 36.0 |

The doctors had very little to say when the figures were all tabulated, but every one agreed that the measurements indicated a most abnormal form and size of skull.

After this, Drs. Eitel and Burton took a plaster paris cast of the face and head, an operation which was eagerly watched.

According to Dr. Sneve's notes on the autopsy, Hayward's body was well nourished. Rigor mortis was well marked six hours after death. The scapl was eight millimeters in thickness and adhered closely to the skull. The temporal muscles were so large as to cause surprise. The temporal fossae, or cavities, were very deep and three centimeters long. The frontal fossae were shallow. The mastoid processes were noticed to be unusually large, but the occiput was not as well developed. The bones were much corrugated. The temporal bones were very thick, while they are usually very thin.

The head and brain were small in proportion to the size of the body. The forehead was narrow and very receding, but the head was particularly wide on a line drawn through the ears. The brain appeared to be small—more than that the doctors would not say. One of them took it away, and when it has been sufficiently hardened it will be weighed, measured and examined microscopically, and then from these data deductions will be drawn. Dr. Jones would say nothing except that the irregularities of shape, size and form of the skull were due to a congenital defect.

Goodsell and Dr. Hayward witnessed the whole autopsy, which was conducted by Doctors W. A. Jones, G. G. Eitel, Haldor Sneve and H. A. Tomlinson.

**AT THE MORGUE**

**The Preparations for the Funeral Services.**

Hayward's attire for the tomb is his broadcloth evening dress, which he wore at so may social events before his sensational arrest. The coat, vest and trousers are, of course, of fashionable cut, the former being faced with silk. A pretty white silk tie and spotless white collar hides the hideous furrow in his neck.

Harry as a corpse looks very presentable. The face, with the exception of a discolored swelling of the right eye, was

Continued on Sixth Page.

## "I STAND PAT"

**Harry Hayward's Last Words Savor of the Gaming Table.**

**He Proves to Be the Coolest Man at His Execution.**

**Addressing the Spectators in a Perfectly Easy, Conversational Style.**

**He Dies in 13 Minutes Without a Sound or Struggle.**

Harry T. Hayward, for instigating the murder of Catherine Ging on Dec. 3, 1894, was hung this morning at the Hennepin county jail. The drop fell at precisely 12 minutes past 2 o'clock, and in 13 minutes the prisoner was pronounced dead by County Physician Frank Burton.

The keynote of his life, phrased in the slang of the gambling cult, to which the blunting of his moral sensibilities was undoubtedly due:

"Pull her tight; I'll stand pat."

These were Harry Hayward's last words. They were uttered as the fatal noose was being adjusted about his throat. No sign of a tremor in voice or body no, the slightest blanching of the face betrayed the fact that the man knew that eternity was less than five minutes away.

"A d—d long time to wait for a railroad train," Hayward said a few days ago when it was announced to him that the time of the execution had been set. Indeed, it was a long time. He went to death as he might have gone to a railroad train. He had no more fear of the end than he had conception of right or wrong. But his dogged determination to die game, once formed, was a crushing burden to carry; not on account of fear, but because of repeated efforts of many advisers to break through his stoicism and find somewhere a true man.

That is why it was a long time to wait.

Harry Hayward was the coolest man at his own execution.

He was the coolest man who ever faced certain death for three days and then died as he had expected to. There was no bravado about it. Nowhere about the most trifling details of his deportment was there the slightest indication that anything was assumed. There was no heroic show of stoicism, no apparent effort to keep firm; in fact, nothing that could be called firmness. The prisoner, except for the gruesome surroundings, might have been standing in the foyer of a theater, greeting his friends as they passed by.

About 15 minutes before the entrance of the procession of death, Deputy Otto Langum had gone into one of the second tier cells, which opened at a level with the rear of the scaffold, and had gone back toward the prisoner's quarters bearing a mysterious black cloth bundle, just of a comfortable size to fit under his arm. In the meantime, a hush had fallen over the little knot of spectators, as Winn Brackett, Sheriff Chapel, of Ramsey county, and Warden Wolfer, of the state penitentiary, ascended the scaffold. It was supposed that the entrance of this party marked the near approach of the death march.

Hours seemed to pass and still no sign from the other section of the jail. The one gas jet had been turned off and the room was illuminated only by a locomotive headlight, suspended at the opposite side of the apartment from the gallows, about four feet above the level of the scaffold. The huge cone of light, intercepted by the gallows, cast a distorted shadow of the engine of death in horrid detail upon the rough, whitewashed stone wall behind. Two nooses there were; one swung off behind the right-hand side support, and the other thrown up over the cross-beam. Both were of five-eighths manilla rope, and so hung that when down two feet of the length lay upon the trap. The former had been tested the night before, with a 300-pound bag of sand, and found to hold.

And now Deputy Otto Langum, who had been here and there looking after various details, appeared upon the scaffold. He nodded to the three gentlemen already upon the platform and then proceeded to take a well worn bar of soap from the top of the cell block. First one noose and then the other was carefully soaped to insure speedy and certain action. This done he took a piece of chalk and, finding the spot on the drop directly under the place where the rope was attached to the gallows beam, he made two small circles to indicate where the feet of the man to be executed should be. A chalk line drawn around the outside of the trap door so that none of the officers might be deceived in the dim light by the close joint was the last thing to be done, and the gallows was ready for its deadly work.

As these deliberate preparations progressed, even those among the spectators who had felt little of the horror of the occasion, began to experience a change. Those little details, the soaping of the nooces, the chalk spots on the floor, and, finally, the trial drop to make sure that the trap was in perfect order, accentuated the feeling that death was near at hand. Men talked in whispers. A little diversion was caused by a brief visit to the room by John Day Smith, Hayward's former attorney and an opponent of the hanging, but as the quarter hour bells rang Phil Megaarden ascended the scaffold and all knew that the time had come.

"Gentlemen," said Phil, "at the entrance of the procession all will remove their hats and there must be no demonstration on the part of any one. There must be no smoking."

A rustle of compliance followed and Phil disappeared. Hearts began to thump loud. A cordon of policemen filed into the room and enclosed a little passageway between the door and the scaffold steps. Hearts began to thump louder and faces loooked more ghastly than ever in that gruesome half light. Even the whisperings ceased as the door was thrown wide open and from the cell block, the sound of an inarticulate yell floated through, ending with "He's all right." Then came three cheers for somebody.

It was awful. A man convicted of a most fiendish crime on his way to death with such a demonstration!

A shudder ran through the little audience and almost before the echoes of the cheer had died away, Sheriff Holmberg, the head of the procession to the gallows, appeared in the door. The prisoner, between Deputies Bright and Anderson, followed, and Phil Megaarden came last.

Harry Hayward entered the death chamber with the same easy swinging stride which was one of his marked characteristics. He wore a long gown of black China silk with sleeves and gathered full into the neck. On his head was the black cap which was to hide the contortions of his face in the death struggle. It was a large cylinder of stiffened silk, the shape of a rimless stovepipe hat, and had a large flap which turned up in front, and projecting at the sides near the top, gave the general effect of the headgear popularly attributed to Napoleon. His costume was not grotesque, because Hayward wore it as gracefully as though it had been a dress suit of the latest cut. With a "Good evening, gentlemen," the last syllable very clearly enunciated, he bowed his way into the room with the deputies hanging to his arms in an almost perfunctory manner. His arms were placed wrist to elbow behind his back and securely strapped, and in

The Scene on the Gallows.

FOUR EDITIONS DAILY.

# The Minneapolis Tribune.

FOUR EDITIONS DAILY.

VOL. XXXI. NO. 265 — MINNEAPOLIS, MINN., WEDNESDAY, FEBRUARY 16, 1898. — PRICE ONE CENT

# THEIR CAMPAIGN OPENS!

*Question of Fusion Confronting People's Party Men.*

## SAGE AND HIS PROXY

*Bitter Fight Today Is Among the Possibilities.*

The fight between the fusion element and the mid-roaders to be taken up at the meeting of the state central committee of the Populists today, is growing warm, and it now promises to be almost a draw. A great deal depends upon what action the committee takes upon a proxy which is said to be in the possession of Ignatius Donnelly, who is not himself a member of the committee. If Mr. Donnelly is admitted, the committee may stand even upon the proposition of an early convention. But as Mr. Donnelly has no say as to his own standing upon the committee, it is probable that he may be turned down.

Last night the fusionists were all in a flutter. They had heard that Chairman Gibbs was coquetting with the mid-roaders, and they also heard that he was to have a conference with Donnelly and his cohorts. In order to head off this meeting Mr. Gibbs was sent out to dine last evening with Senator Butler, with the understanding that he was to return in time to confer with Messrs. Bowler, Lynch and others at the West Hotel at 8:30 o'clock. Messrs. Gibbs and Butler returned at the appointed time, but the former gentleman slipped away, and kept his appointment with the mid-roaders. When this was known as a fact, no time was lost in sending a committee after the recreant chairman to bring him back to the West Hotel. The committee went direct to the Windsor and found their worst suspicions verified. Gibbs was there, and so was Donnelly. What happened then no one knows save those present, but the committee soon returned to the West with Mr. Gibbs in their company.

This feeling of suspicion towards Chairman Gibbs is very pronounced among the adherents of fusion, and they make no bones of classifying the chairman among the mid-roaders, although they hope he may be brought to see the error of his ways and act with them.

The state central committee is composed of 21 members, or three from each congressional district, and of that number the fusionists admit that the following nine gentlemen are mid-roaders: T. J. Meighen, A. F. Rudolph, H. A. Swain, H. V. Poore, E. W. Bonham, J. W. Lyndard, David Cochran, Louis Hansen, Chris. Johnson. Inasmuch as this strength of the mid-roaders is admitted by their opponents, it is more than possible that there are others who may be added to the list. One of the committee is out of the state, and that leaves the committee but 20 members. Thus it can be seen that if Ignatius Donnelly is admitted upon a proxy it would give the mid-road element 10 votes, or one-half the committee.

This plain statement of the standing of the committee shows that if Mr. Donnelly is admitted today it will only be after the hottest kind of a fight.

THE STARS ARRIVE.

Senators Marion Butler and Frederic Dubois arrived yesterday over the Wisconsin Central, instead of the St. Louis road, as had been arranged by the local reception committee, and in consequence there was a repetition of the fiasco which attended the arrival of Mr. Bryan last month, though the local people were not at all to blame in the matter, there being a misunderstanding that could not be corrected in time. Consequently the two men wended their way to the West hotel unattended, and were seated at the breakfast table when the committee discovered their whereabouts.

It seems that the local reception committee was not at fault. They had sent word to the visitors, enclosing transportation over the St. Louis road, but the letter must have miscarried. Messrs. Butler and Dubois say they knew nothing of the arrangements made for their reception, and were therefore not disappointed when they arrived in the city and were unattended to the hotel.

The local reception committee, consisting of Maj. J. H. Bowler, E. S. Corser, J. M. Owen, E. B. Lynch, L. D. Brown, W. K. Dobbyn, W. O. Long and M. P. Hobart, were at the St. Louis depot at the appointed time. When the train arrived and it was evident that the expected guests were not aboard, they immediately went to the depot of the Great Western, where they met Gen. J. B. Weaver, of Iowa, and with him repaired to the West Hotel. When they arrived at the hotel they discovered that their other guests were already on hand and their souls were made glad in consequence.

The three distinguished guests were assigned to Rooms 370, 372 and 374, and during the early morning hours many of the local and visiting friends called and paid their respects.

The coming of William Jennings Bryan, which had been announced by a press dispatch, was freely discussed, but was not believed by the party leaders, inasmuch as Mr. Bryan had not been invited to participate. At a late hour no word had been received from Bryan, and his coming was not considered a possibility. A story was current that the local silver Republicans had taken it upon themselves to ask Mr. Bryan to be present, but could not be verified. The Populists were chary of touching upon the subject, as it was generally considered by them to be something which it would be good politics for them to avoid, because, as they stated, of the appearance it would give of turning the demonstration into a Democratic gathering. They would not wire to Lincoln to discover the truth of the report, saying that if Mr. Bryan did come it would be so much to the good and a dispensation of Providence. But if he did not come they would have nothing with which to reproach themselves. Senator Butler declared that he knew nothing of any attempt to secure Bryan's presence, and Mr. Dubois expressed equal ignorance. Therefore, if the young Nebraskan does arrive this morning, it will be not because of any invitation received from those having charge of the meeting.

A telegram was received from John Lind last evening saying that he could not be present, but it had a postscript saying that he would wire again this morning, and might be in the city in time for the evening meetings. Accordingly the committee will leave his name upon the program.

Mr. Dubois also received a telegram from Congressman Hartman, dated Washington, in which he stated that his physician had promised to get him to Chicago Wednesday morning, and that he would wire from there today. It is thought he will be present.

After Messrs. Butler, Weaver, and Dubois had breakfasted they were taken in charge by School Inspector W. K. Hicks, and in company with Messrs. Dobbyn and Lynch were taken in carriages to the South Side high school, where each of the three addressed the scholars briefly.

In introducing Senator Butler to the scholars, Mr. Hicks called attention to the extreme youth of the gentleman from North Carolina. Though but 34 years of age, Senator Butler occupies the proud position of a senator of the United States, having broken into that body at the earliest possible age.

Senator Butler took up this remark in commencing his remarks to the scholars. He said that the reason he had been able to break into the senate at such an early age was because he had received an educational training at just such a place as the one in which he then stood. After graduating from the schools of his state he had been a teacher for three years, and he therefore took great interest in all that pertained to educational matters. He recalled his own youth. Until he was 12 years old he had never attended school, having been born on a farm and living there until he went away to attend school. His early education he owed to his mother, and in view of his own experience he could see the importance of educating the mothers of future generations. "If you have to neglect either the boys or the girls in that respect," said he, "by all means neglect the boys. With well educated mothers the boys will not suffer."

Before his election to the United States senate he had served several terms in the legislature of North Carolina, and his first vote had been cast for the establishment of practical training in the schools of his native state, where the schools are not so far advanced as in the state of Minnesota, if he could judge from his surroundings. He would return to North Carolina with a message of cheer to the educational forces of that state from Minnesota.

GEN. WEAVER FOLLOWS.

Gen. J. B. Weaver followed with a few remarks, and then Mr. Hicks introduced Senator Dubois, who caught the undivided attention of his youthful audience when he stated that he had been catcher in the old Yale ball team. That statement was enough to start the applause, and when he touched upon football matters the uproar increased. The speaker contended that athletics were desirable in an educational institution, and that excellence in athletics meant excellence in every other way. He spoke of his recent tour in China and Japan and of the latter country especially, where he had visited many of their schools and was surprised to find that English was being taught in the public schools, and in fact was the only foreign language taught there.

When the visit to the South Side school was concluded the entire party, with the exception of Mr. Dubois, paid a similar visit to the Central High school, where Gen. Weaver and Senator Butler again entertained the scholars with a few remarks.

Mr. Dubois pleaded that he was somewhat weary and returned immediately to his rooms at the West.

During the afternoon the spacious parlors at the West were thrown open to the general public, and the distinguished visitors received all who presented themselves.

Last evening Senator Butler was entertained at dinner by W. O. Long, at 11 East Seventeenth street, where he met about a dozen North Carolina people who are now residents of Minneapolis.

All the visitors are enthusiastic as to the future, and they are solidly and undoubtedly in favor of a fusion of all the forces opposing the Republican party in the campaign this year. On this point there seems to be no difference of opinion among them. Senator Butler is non-committal in speaking about political matters, and Mr. Dubois declares that he is out of politics so far as he is concerned personally, although he is greatly interested in forwarding the cause of the white metal in the United States. Since his retirement from the United States senate he has purchased a cattle ranch at Blackfoot, Idaho, and says he cannot afford to neglect business for the sake of politics.

Quite a number of Populists prominent in Minnesota are also on the ground, and are almost unanimous in favor of the plan of fusion which is to be the object of the meeting.

PLANS FOR TODAY.

The arrangements for today's meetings are unchanged from yesterday's announcements in The Tribune. The meeting of the general committees will be called to order at 9 o'clock at Labor Temple by Chairman Gibbs. This meeting will be open to all, and will be addressed by Senator Butler. The senator will also read and talk upon an address sent out from Washington yesterday by the national committee, which appears in another column.

At 2 o'clock the state central committee is scheduled to meet at the Windsor hotel, and it is expected that this meeting will be executive. It is here that the real fight will come off, and if possible the fusionists will make it open to all that their opponents may be placed on record. At least, that is what they say.

At 10:45 Senator Butler and ex-Senator Dubois are expected to address the students at the state university.

The exposition meeting will open at 7 o'clock, and the doors will be thrown open at 6. The speakers will be Chairman Butler, Senator Dubois, Gen. Weaver, John Lind, Senator Ringdahl. If Congressman Hartman is present he will also be called upon.

At the conclusion of Senator Butler's address he will be immediately driven to Harmonia hall, where the banquet is to be held, and that function will commence at 9 o'clock sharp.

Arrangements have been made whereby ample street car service to and from the Exposition building is assured, and cars will also cover the city until 1 o'clock in order to accommodate those who may wish to remain late at the banquet.

Chairman Gibbs last evening said to The Tribune that the prospects for harmonious action today were, in his opinion, very bright. He expected that the committee would decide to call the state convention at a reasonably early date, though he hardly thought the question of fusion should cut much figure in that connection. Fusion was a matter which should properly be entrusted to the state convention for action, and he hoped that his colleagues would see the matter in that light and act accordingly.

## IS NOW TOO BUSY

**C. C. Shane Declines the "Polite Invitation" of the Ohio Senate Bribery Investigating Committee to Visit Ohio.**

NEW YORK, Feb. 16.—C. C. Shayne, of this city who was summoned by the Ohio senate bribery investigation committee to appear before that committee tonight, has sent the following telegram to Newman H. Burke, chairman of the committee. "Engagements until after the London fur sales in March will prevent me from accepting your kind invitation. If, however, you desire a chapter for your Ohio political history, I refer you to my statements already published in the leading journals; or you can send a committee here, to whom every courtesy will be extended.

C. C. SHANE.

Mr. Shayne was jointly summoned with Senator Hanna, Major Dick and Major Rathbone.

**Hanged.**

SENATOBIA, Miss., Feb. 16.—In the presence of 4,000 spectators at noon yesterday George Washington Edwards, colored, was hanged here for the murder of Roxie Williams. The crime, a peculiarly atrocious one, was committed in July, 1896. The killing was done with a shotgun in a room occupied by the Williams woman, whose head was completely torn away by the load of lead.

*Addresses Are Issued to the Various Silver Parties.*

## FUSION IS ADVOCATED

*Keynote for the Coming Campaign Is Sounded.*

WASHINGTON, Feb. 15.—The addresses on behalf of the Democratic, Populist and silver Republican parties, which are the result of the conferences which have been in progress among the leaders of these parties at the capital for the past few weeks, were issued last night. They seek to unite the members of three parties in the future elections upon the financial issue as the question of paramount importance and are separate appeals to each of the parties to consolidate all along the line for this purpose.

The address to Populists is as follows:

"The conspiracy of gold and monopoly is nearing its culmination. Every advance it has made during the past 25 years has been by adroit and stealthy processes. These would have been impossible if it had not had its agents and confederates holding positions of public trust in the legislative, executive and judicial branches of the government. Neither the beneficiaries nor the tools of this conspiracy have any particular politics. In name the last administration was Democratic. The present administration is called Republican, but it has ingloriously practiced and defended the perfidious policies of its predecessor.

"At length the selfish and brutal interests behind this conspiracy deem themselves strong enough to dispense with the caution and duplicity hitherto necessary to their success. The administration boldly avows its endorsement of their scheme against the liberty and prosperity of the people. Within a few weeks it has formulated and sent to congress a bill, the leading purpose of which is, in the words of the secretary of the treasury: 'To commit the country more thoroughly to the gold standard.'

"This country has, during the past 24 years, suffered enough of the blighting effect of the gold standard, so far as fraudulent legislation and executive usurpation have been able to establish it. It is now boldly proposed to legalize what has been done in defiance of law and to use the power secured by false pretenses from a long suffering and the trustful people to put upon this infamous design the stamp of alleged popular authorization.

"In the pursuit of this purpose of committing the country more thoroughly to the gold standard the plan of this administration, as of the last, is to retire the greenbacks and other non-interest bearing paper money of the government, to issue interest burdened gold bonds and to increase the powers, privileges and profits of national banks. This achievement would turn over the duty of supplying the people's money, the very life blood of business to a selfish, heartless and irresponsible foreign gold syndicate and its American agents and allies.

FOREIGN SYNDICATE CONTROLS.

"It must be remembered also that this foreign gold syndicate and its allies have, with the connivance if not the assistance of our government, captured and today control every instrument of commerce in the nation. In framing the constitution our patriotic forefathers, with zealous cares, with prophetic wisdom, provided that commerce should be regulated by congress; but this tremendous power has been abdicated by congress in favor of the gold trust and the banking ring. Money is the first great instrument of commerce, but the [illegible]

MILLIONAIRES AT THE HELM.

[illegible]

Continued on Fourth Page.

# GOOD BY DE LOME

*The Late Spanish Minister Will Sail Today.*

## MADRID PEOPLE ANGRY

*Bitterly Opposed to an Apology Being Offered.*

NEW YORK, Feb. 16.—Senor Dupuy de Lome arrived in this city last night en route for Madrid. All efforts to get an interview with him or any of his party proved futile, and efforts last evening to locate him at the leading hotels were unsuccessful.

WASHINGTON, D. C., Feb. 16.—The late Spanish minister, Dupuy de Lome, accompanied by Mme. De Lome, their two sons and a Spanish valet, left Washington at 4 o'clock yesterday afternoon for New York, whence they sail tomorrow for Liverpool. A large delegation from the diplomatic corps, accompanied by their wives, gave a hearty au revoir at the station to their late associate. Quite a crowd was attracted by the gathering but further than the ex-minister's departure, the meeting was undemonstrative.

Senor Dubosc, the Spanish charge d'affaires, was busy at the legation office yesterday with an extended communication just received from Madrid. These did not relate to the recent incident. The legation is now turning its attention to other subjects, mainly to the new commercial treaty between Spain and the United States. Up to last evening, Mr. Dubosc had not been officially advised of the appointment of Senor Luis y Polo Bernabe as minister at Washington. He is well known among the officials here, coming from a family of diplomates and having had an extended diplomatic service himself.

It is thought that the fact that he was chief of the commercial section of the foreign office accounts for his choice, as this position has given him a hand in the commercial negotiations now approaching the final state.

Up to a late hour last night the state department had no additional word from Minister Woodford. As matters stand, the only further action to be expected from Spain is a disavowal of sentiments to be expressed by Dupuy de Lome concerning President McKinley, but this, if made, will come as a voluntary courtesy.

CONDEMNED IN STRONG TERMS.

**Spanish Cabinet Ministers Do Not Approve of De Lome's Letter.**

NEW YORK, Feb. 16.—In conversation with a Madrid correspondent of the Herald last night one of the cabinet ministers said: "You may say openly, as coming from Senor Sagasta and from each of us, that we entirely condemn, in the most absolute manner, Senor De Lome's letter. We are ashamed, grieved and sorry thereat. The ministers feel more aggrieved than President McKinley can possibly be. We are honest men who have been placed in a false position by a fool."

In reply to further questions the minister said: "Canalejas' journey was absolutely private and in no way possible did we trust or use him."

The Washington correspondent of the Herald says that the announcement from Madrid that the Spanish ministry has decided to reply in a fitting manner to Minister Woodford's representations in regard to the De Lome letter is highly satisfactory to administration officials.

No one is more pleased over the matter than the president. He has never doubted from the first that Spain would repudiate the action of its minister. His only concern has been that the delay in closing the incident might lead to some outburst in congress which would cause embarrassment to the administration before the Spanish government had had an opportunity to make a satisfactory response.

GOMEZ IS EXULTANT.

**He Asserts That the Insurgent Cause Is Gaining.**

NEW YORK, Feb. 15.—T. Estrada Palma, head of the Cuban junta, has received a letter from Gen. Maximo Gomez, commander-in-chief of the Cuban army, dated at Mayajagua, Feb. 2. It says in part:

"Our forces have been very active since the promulgation of autonomy by the Spanish government. We see in it Spain's weakness and feel now more sanguine of our success than ever before. Autonomy has had the advantage to rid us of some of the undesirable elements in our ranks. We trust it may serve to still purge our army of men of the ilk of Masso Parra, Cuervo and other Majases. Col. Armando Sanchez Agramonte, with 300 men, attacked a Spanish convoy three days ago and captured thirty pack mules, with ammunition and a regimental strong box with $18,000. The Spanish commander and fifteen privates were killed in the first charge."

THEY PREFER WAR.

**Spanish Populace Indignant Over the Alleged De Lome Apology.**

(By Cable to The Tribune.)

LONDON, Feb. 15.—A special from Madrid says the populace of that city is greatly enraged owing to the belief that the Spanish cabinet has apologized to the United States. The populace, the dispatch adds, is bitterly opposed to such a course and exceedingly hostile to the government and may make a demonstration. In conclusion the dispatch says:

"The people prefer war to an apology, thinking that Spain will suffer the least thereby, as war would be exceedingly disastrous to the large commerce of the United States."

**An "Amazon" Captured.**

HAVANA, Feb. 16.—It is announced in Spanish circles that Senorita Isabel Rubio, who is described as an amazon, was captured after being wounded, in a skirmish between a detachment of Spanish troops and some insurgents in the province of Pinar Del Rio.

Spanish reports say Gen. Nario, operating in the Contra Maestre district with 900 Spanish infantry, 153 cavalrymen and two guns, during the last five days, has destroyed the camp of the insurgent general, Calixto Garcia.

## WRECKAGE PICKED UP

**FURTHER EVIDENCE OF THE LOSS OF THE CLARA NEVADA.**

**The Owners of the Steamer However, Are Slow to Believe She Was Burned.**

SEATTLE, Feb. 16.—No further news has been received concerning the reported loss of the Clara Nevada in Alaskan water. Owing to the many conflicting rumors hopes for her safety have not yet been abandoned. On account of the remoteness of the scene of the reported disaster, it is impossible to get anything authentic. Unless some unexpected steamer arrives no definite news is expected before next Thursday.

The latest report was the one brought down by the steamer Excelsior, which arrived yesterday. Capt. Donnellson said that just before he left Juneau, the steamer Coleman arrived and reported that wreckage and bedding marked "Hassler" had been washed ashore at Seward. He said: "The Clara Nevada was formerly a government vessel known as the Hassler, and I have no doubt that she is at the bottom of the sea."

The Excelsior arrived at Juneau five hours after the steamer Rosalie, which reported passing the Clara Nevada.

# CRUISER MAINE A TOTAL WRECK

## The United States Warship Blown Up in Havana Harbor by an Explosion Which Shook the Whole City.

## OVER ONE HUNDRED ARE KILLED!

### The Cause of the Disaster Is Not Definitely Known—Great Excitement Prevails in Havana.

HAVANA, Feb. 16.—At a quarter of 10 o'clock last evening a terrible explosion took place on board the United States cruiser Maine in Havana harbor. Many were killed or wounded. All the boats of the Spanish cruiser Alfonso XIII. are assisting.

As yet the cause of the explosion is not known. The wounded sailors of the Maine are unable to explain it. It is believed that the cruiser is totally destroyed.

The explosion shook the whole city. The windows were broken in all the houses.

The correspondent of the Associated Press says he has conversed with several of the wounded sailors and understands from them that the explosion took place while they were asleep, so that they can give no particulars as to the cause.

Later—The wildest consternation prevails in Havana. The wharves are crowded with thousands of people. It is believed that the explosion occurred in a small powder magazine. At a quarter of eleven, what remains of the Maine is still burning.

Capt. Sigsbee and the other officers have been saved. It is estimated that over one hundred of the crew were killed, but it is impossible as yet to give exact details.

Paymaster Charles W. Littlefield, who is given in the list of officers on the Maine, has recently been replaced by Paymaster Ryan. Littlefield is now in Washington.

The Havana firemen are giving aid, tending carefully to the wounded as they are brought on shore. It is a terrible sight. General Solano and the other generals have been ordered by Capt. Gen. Blanco to take steps to help the Maine's crew in every possible way. The correspondent of the Associated Press has been near the Maine in one of the boats of the cruiser Alfonso XII., and seen others of the wounded who corroborate the statement of those first interviewed that they were already asleep when the explosion occurred.

Capt. Sigsbee says the explosion occurred in the bow of the vessel. He received a wound in the head. Orders were given to the other officers to save themselves as best they could. The latter, who were literally thrown from their bunks in their night clothing, gave the necessary orders. They showed great self-possession and heroism.

The first theory was that there had been a preliminary explosion in the Santa Barbara (magazine) with powder or dynamite below the water.

Admiral Manterola believes that the first explosion was of a grenade shell that was buried over the navy yard.

LEARNED AT WASHINGTON.

**Capt. Sigsbee Wires Further Particulars of the Disaster.**

WASHINGTON, D. C., Feb. 16.—The secretary of the navy received the following telegram from Capt. Sigsbee:

"Maine blown up in Havana harbor, nine forty, and destroyed. Many wounded and many more killed and drowned. Wounded and others on board Spanish man-of-war and Ward line steamer. Send lighthouse tenders from Key West for crew and few pieces of equipment still above (water). No one had other clothes than those upon him.

"Public opinion should be suspended till further report. All officers believed to be saved. Jenkins and Merritt not yet accounted for. Many Spanish officers including representatives of General Blanco now with me and express sympathy.

(Signed.) "SIGSBEE."

The officers referred to in the above dispatch are Lieut. Friend W. Jenkins and Assistant Engineer Drawing R. Merritt.

From the wording of the dispatch the navy department think it possible that they were on shore at the time of the accident.

The secretary of the navy received another dispatch from Key West at the same time with the above, but its contents were not made public.

The orders for the lighthouse tenders were at once sent to Key West in [illegible] language, thus avoiding the delay that would have arisen from the use of cipher.

Secretary Long received Capt. Sigsbee's dispatch but a few minutes before the Associated Press dispatches from Havana were handed to him. He received the news with apparent calm, and his first act was to comply with Capt. Sigsbee's request that assistance be sent from Key West. He immediately wired Capt. Forsythe at Key West to proceed with the naval tender Fern to Havana harbor.

Secretary Long then sent for Captain Dickens and the two discussed Capt. Sigsbee's brief telegram. No other naval officers were present and besides the secretary and Captain Dickins the naval colony here is ignorant of this disaster, the greatest which has befallen the American navy since the disaster at Apia many years ago. The secretary is inclined to believe that most of the officers of the Maine were on shore at the time of the accident, as it was still early in the night. While neither the secretary nor Capt. Dickens are inclined to discuss probable causes of the accident several suggestions were ventured upon. They believe that it may have been caused by a fire in the bunkers, heating the bulkhead near a magazine, or that an accident may

Continued on Fifth Page.

United States Cruiser Maine, which was blown up in Havana Harbor last night.

## LEAGUE TURNED DOWN

**The Republicans Win a Decisive Victory in the Pittsburg Municipal Election.**

PITTSBURG, Feb. 16.—The municipal election here yesterday resulted in a decided victory for the Republicans, notwithstanding the division in their ranks caused by the municipal league or reform ticket. The latter ticket, according to returns at midnight, elected but one councilman, that of Hop Berger in the 20th ward. George H. Stengel, the present league councilman from the 20th ward on whom the principal fight was made, was defeated.

**Peter Maher Gets the Decision.**

PHILADELPHIA, Feb. 16.—Peter Maher defeated "Thunderbolt" Smith last night in the third round. The match was for six rounds.

FOUR EDITIONS DAILY. **The Minneapolis Tribune.** FOUR EDITIONS DAILY.

VOL. XXXII. NO. 37 MINNEAPOLIS, MINN., MONDAY, JULY 4 1898. PRICE ONE CENT EXCEPT ON TRAINS

# A GLORIOUS VICTORY

HURRAH!

VICTORY!
VICTORY IS OURS!

HURRAH!

## Cervera's Fleet in Santiago Harbor Destroyed by Sampson's Warships.

WASHINGTON, D. C., July 4.---The following cable dispatch is given out at the White House:

"Playa del Este, July 3.---The destruction of Cervera's fleet is confirmed.

Signed ALLEN, Lieutenant-Colonel."

## The Spanish Army Must Comply With Shafter's Demand to Surrender.

WASHINGTON, D. C., July 4.---The following statement is given out at the White House:

"Gen. Shafter telegraphs: Playa del Este, July 3.---Early this morning I sent a demand for the immediate surrender of Santiago, threatening to bombard the city. I believe the place will be surrendered."

### SPECIAL TO THE TRIBUNE.

NEW YORK, July 4.—A Washington special to the New York World says: Admiral Sampson is the hero of Santiago. He has turned defeat into a glorious victory. His warships yesterday morning sailed into Santiago harbor, and after a short engagement destroyed Cervera's fleet.

Secretary of War Alger confirmed this statement at midnight. He had been at the executive mansion for some hours in the hope of obtaining something more definite, but has not yet been successful. As he was leaving he said the dispatch was received from the operator in the cable station, who sent on authority of a United States captain in the regular army.

Secretary Alger stated that accordihg to his advices Admiral Sampson steamed up to the city and anchored. Word was then sent to Gen. Shafter, who demanded the immediate surrender of the city, threatening that unless this was immediately complied with the American ships would immediately bombard the city.

In order that non-combatants might be removed, the Spanish were given until Monday morning to comply with the request. It is believed the Vesuvius, protected by an armored ship, steamed into the entrance of the bay, deliberately attacked each fort and silenced it.

There is a general belief among naval officers that the mines in Santiago were not properly looked after by the Spanish, and were rendered useless by barnacles and sea growth.

The president, upon reading the dispatch, took it to Mrs. McKinley. She was as gratified as the president. BAXTER.

### Sent by the Associated Press.

WASHINGTON, D. C., July 4.—Glorious news from Cuba affords the American people just reason for an enthusiastic celebration of this, the nation's natal day.

Admiral Sampson has accomplished the work which he was directed to perform when he left Key West for the southern coast of Cuba. He was ordered to find and destroy Cevera's fleet. Several weeks ago Commodore Schley located the fleet in the bay of Santiago. Yesterday, after being bottled helpless in the harbor for weeks, the fleet was destroyed. Nothing now remains of the Spanish squadron but shattered and burning hulks.

In addition to the splendid work accomplished by Admiral Sampson, Gen. Shafter, in command of the land forces before Santiago, had so far progressed in the carrying out of his plans for the reduction of the city that at 10:30 yesterday morning he demanded the immediate surrender of the Spanish forces. At 4:30 yesterday afternoon Gen. Shafter's demand had not been complied with, so far as the war officials here were able to ascertain. That the demand will be complied with, however, Gen. Shafter fully believes, and that the stars and stripes will on this Fourth of July be raised over the former capital of Cuba is regarded as practically certain.

Shortly after 12 o'clock this morning Assistant Secretary of Navy Allen left the White House hastily, and going directly to the department posted the following upon the department bulletin board:

"Gen. Shafter telegraphs:

"Pelaya del Este, July 3.—Early this morning I sent a demand for the immediate surrender of Santiago, threatening to bombard the city. I believe the place will be surrendered."

(This contradicts the report that Gen. Shafter has fallen back.)

The following dispatch was received at the war department: "Playa del Este, July 3.—Siboney office confirms statement that all the Spanish fleet except one warship destroyed and burning on the beach. It was witnessed by Capt. Smith, who told the operator there was no doubt of its correctness. (Signed) ALLEN, Signal Office."

The information contained in the above statement was received early in the evening, but was not announced officially until several hours later. As a result of its receipt, however, a conference of prominent officials was held at the White House immediately.

Details of the destruction of Cervera's fleet have not been received at this writing by either the war or navy departments. Whether Sampson's ships entered the harbor and there attacked and annihilated the Spanish squadron, or whether Cervera made a desperate dash past the sunken Merrimac to the ocean beyond, in the hope that he might be able to save at least a part of his fleet, has not been officially ascertained.

The information was discussed in all its phases. The news sent by both Gen. Shafter and Lieut. Col. Allen was received with intense satisfaction. It was taken to indicate not only that Admiral Sampson had accomplished magnificently the task to which he had been set, but it also clearly proved that Gen. Shafter was in a much stronger position than the war officials had been led to believe he held.

One of the officials who attended the conference said after the news had been officially announced that it very materially modified the seriousness of the situation. The destruction of the fleet, which was not confirmed until a few minutes before the news was given to the public, removes by far the most serious obstacle to the occupation of Santiago by the American land forces.

FOUR EDITIONS DAILY. **The Minneapolis Tribune.** TWELVE PAGES.

VOL. XXXII. NO. 77. MINNEAPOLIS, MINN., SATURDAY, AUGUST 13, 1898. PRICE ONE CENT

# PEACE PROTOCOL SIGNED AT LAST

## *Secretary Day and M. Cambon Affix Their Signatures to the Document.*

## *Closing Chapter of the Three Months' War Was Full of Interest.*

(Sent by the Associated Press.)

WASHINGTON, Aug. 13.—With simplicity in keeping with Republican institutions, the war which has raged between Spain and the United States for a period of three months and twenty-two days was quietly terminated at 4:23 o'clock yesterday afternoon when Secretary Day for the United States and M. Cambon for Spain, in the presence of President McKinley signed a protocol, which will form the basis of a definite treaty of peace. It is but simple justice to our sister republic of France to record the fact that to her good office this speedy termination of a war that might have run on indefinitely was brought about, and the president himself deemed that action on the part of the French government as worthy of his special praise.

The closing chapter of events that led up to the signature of the protocol and the cessation of hostilities was full of interest. There were rumors in the early morning that over night the French embassy had received the long expected final instructions from Madrid, but these upon inquiry proved groundless as it was not until half past twelve that the message began to come from Madrid in small lots. The state department was soon advised of the fact that the message was under transmission, but as it was evident that it would be long and that its reception would occupy much time, the secretary of state left the state department for his luncheon.

**SECRETARY DAY IS NOTIFIED.**

At 2:45 o'clock Secretary Thiebaut, of the French embassy, appeared at the state department to inform Secretary Day that the ambassador was in full possession of the note; was fully empowered to sign the protocol for Spain, and only waited the pleasure of the state department. He intimated that the ambassador would be pleased to have the final ceremony conducted in the presence of President McKinley, where the negotiations were begun. Leaving the secretary of the embassy in his own office, Secretary Day made a short visit to the White House to learn the president's wishes in the matter. The latter immediately consented to accept the suggestion, and Mr. Thiebaut hastened to inform the principal that the president would receive him at the White House at 4 o'clock.

At the appointed hour a driving rain storm prevailed obliging all the parties to resort to carriages or transportation to the White House. Secretary Day came first with a large portfolio under his arm enclosing copies of the protocol of the, proclamation to be issued by the president stopping hostilities, and some other necessary papers.

He was accompanied by Assistant Secretary Moore, Second Assistant Secretary Adee and Third Assistant Secretary Cridler. They went immediately into the cabinet room, where the president sat in waiting. He had invited to be present Assistant Secretaries Bruden and Corteliou and Lieut. Col. Montgomery.

**M. CAMBON ARRIVES AT THE WHITE HOUSE.**

When Ambassador Cambon reached the White House it was just 3:55 o'clock, five minutes in advance of the appointed hour. The rain was still violent and the ambassador abandoned his usual custom of alighting at the outer gates of the executive grounds. He was driven under the porte cochere, passing through a cordon of newspaper men before he and Secretary Thiebaut were ushered inside. They went direct to the library adjoining the cabinet room on the upper floor. At 4:05 they were announced to the waiting party in the cabinet room and were ushered into their presence. After an exchange of diplomatic courtesies, unnecessary loss of time did not occur and Assistant Secretary of State Gridler, on the part of the United States and First Secretary Thiebaut on the part of Spain, retired to a window when there was a critical formal examination of the protocol.

This inspection had all the outward formalities of a document of this importance. It was prepared in duplicate at the state department, one copy to b retained by the United States government and the other to become the property of Spain. The text is handsomely engrossed in a running old English script.

Each copy of the protocol is arranged in double column, French and English, standing alongside for easy comparison as to the exactness of translation. The two copies are alike, except that the one held by this government has the English text in the first column and the signature of Secretary Day ahead of that of M. Cambon, while the copy transmitted to Spain has French in the first column and the signature of M. Cambon ahead of that of Secretary Day.

The protocol sent to Spain was accompanied by the credentials issued by President McKinley, especially empowering the secretary of state to affix his signature to this document. The authorization was brief and in typewriting, save for the president's characteristic bold signature. Later the American copy of the protocol will be accompanied by the written credentials of the Spanish government sent to M. Cambon, and bearing the signature of Queen Christina.

The cable dispatch received by M. Cambon today conferred full authority to sign the protocol, and stated that the written authorization

(Continued on Second Page.)

## PRESIDENT McKINLEY'S PROCLAMATION.

(Sent by the Associated Press.)

**By the president of the United States of America:**

**A PROCLAMATION.**

**Whereas, by a protocol concluded and signed Aug. 12, 1898, by William R. Day, secretary of state of the United States, and his Excellency Jules Cambon, ambassador extraordinary and plenipotentiary of the republic of France, at Washington, respectively representing for this purpose the government of the United States and the government of Spain, the United States and Spain, have formally agreed upon the terms on which negotiations for the establishment of peace between the two countries shall be undertaken; and**

**Whereas, it is in said protocol agreed that upon its conclusion and signature hostilities between the two countries shall be suspended, and that notice to that effect shall be given as soon as possible by each government to the commanders of its military and naval forces:**

**Now, therefore, I, William McKinley, president of the United States, do in accordance with the stipulations of the protocol declare and proclaim on the part of the United States, a suspension of hostilities, and do hereby command that orders be immediately given through the proper channels to the commanders of the military and naval forces of the United States to abstain from all acts inconsistent with this proclamation.**

**In witness whereof, I have hereunto set my hand and caused the seal of the United States to be affixed.**

**Done at the City of Washington, this 12th day of August, in the year of Our Lord one thousand eight hundred and ninety-eight, and of the independence of the United States the one hundred and twenty-third.**

**WILLIAM McKINLEY.**

**By the president, William R. Day, secretary of state.**

# ORDERS ISSUED

### *Naval and Military Commanders Cease Hostilities.*

### *All Notified of the Signing of the Protocol.*

(Sent by the Associated Press.)

WASHINGTON, Aug. 13.—In accordance with the proclamation issued by the president, suspending hostilities, orders were issued last evening to the naval commanders at the several stations in the United States, Cuba and the Philippines, carrying into effect the directions of the proclamation. The navy department not only transmitted the president's proclamation in full to the several commanders-in-chief, but also directions as to the disposition of their vessels. The following orders are in that sense self-explanatory:

**NAVY DEPARTMENT, WASHINGTON, Aug. 12.—Sampson, Santiago—Suspend all hostilities. Blockade of Cuba and Porto Rico is raised. Howell ordered to assemble vessels at Key West. Proceed with New York, Brooklyn, Indiana, Oregon, Iowa and Massachusetts to Tompkinsville. Place monitors in safe harbor in Porto Rico. Watson transfers his flag to Newark and will remain at Guantanamo. Assemble all cruisers in safe harbors. Order marines north in Resolute.**

**(Signed.) ALLEN,**
**Acting Secretary Navy Department.**

**WASHINGTON, Aug. 12.—Remy, Key West—In accordance with the president's proclamation telegraphed you, suspend immediately all hostilities. Commence withdrawal of vessels from blockade. Order blockading vessels in Cuban waters to assemble at Key West.**

**(Signed.) ALLEN,**
**Acting Secretary.**

The orders to Gen. Merritt of suspension were as follows:

**Adjutant-General's Office, Washington, Aug. 12, 1898.—Merritt, Manila: The president directs all military operations against the enemy be suspended. Peace negotiations are nearing completion, a protocol having just been signed by representatives of the two countries. You will inform the commanders of the Spanish forces in the Philippines of these instructions. Further orders will follow. Acknowledge receipt.**

**By order of the secretary of war,**
**H. C. CORBIN,**
**Adjutant-General.**

The order sent to Gen. Miles and Gen. Shafter were identical with the above save as to name.

The notification to Admiral Dewey was not made public, but Assistant Secretary Allen stated that besides being put in possession of the president's proclamation he was ordered to cease hostilities and raise the blockade of Manila.

In compliance with the orders sent, Admiral Sampson and Commodore Remy will each send a vessel around the coast of Cuba to notify the blockading squadron that the blockade has been raised. Admiral Schley being on the Brooklyn and included in the orders to that vessel will come north with her.

**SHAFTER REPLIES.**

**The First to Acknowledge Receipt of Peace Orders.**

(Sent by the Associated Press.)

WASHINGTON, Aug. 13.—At 11 o'clock last night Adjt.-Gen. Corbin received from Gen. Shafter an acknowledgement of the receipt by him of the proclamation of the president. Up to midnight no reply had been received from Gen. Miles, it having been impossible to get into communication with him.

All of the corps commanders of the army were notified of the suspension of hostilities. In response to the notification sent to Gen. Fitzhugh Lee, the former consul-general at Havana wired the war department:

"Thanks. The seventh corps has ceased firing. Unofficial."

It is well understood that Gen. Lee's command was being reserved for the attack upon Havana if the necessity for one should arise. As an official of the war department expressed it last night, "It was a bit of sarcasm of fate that Lee did not have a part in the active operations in Cuba or Porto Rico."

The text of Gen. Shafter's reply follows:

SANTIAGO, Cuba, Aug. 12, 1898.—Adjutant-General, Washington: Telegram received. Message as to peace negotiations being about concluded. Will notify Spanish at Holguin by courier tomorrow and Manzanillo and Cienfuegos by wire and will try to get Havana. Will also notify all Cuban forces I can reach.

(Signed.) SHAFTER.

# TERMS OF PROTOCOL

### *Spain Loses All Western Hemisphere Possessions.*

### *Details Will Be Attended to by Two Commissions.*

(Sent by the Associated Press.)

WASHINGTON, Aug. 13.—The terms of the protocol, signed yesterday afternoon by Secretary Day, on behalf of the United States, and M. Cambon, on behalf of Spain, and as handed to the press by Secretary Day, are as follows:

**1. That Spain will relinquish all claim of sovereignty over and title to Cuba.**

**2. That Porto Rico and other Spanish islands in the West Indies and an island in the Ladrones to be selected by the United States, shall be ceded to the latter.**

**3. That the United States will occupy and hold the city, bay and harbor of Manila, pending the conclusion of a treaty of peace, which shall determine the control, disposition and government of the Philippines.**

**4. That Cuba, Porto Rico and other Spanish islands in the West Indies shall be immediately evacuated and that commissioners, to be appointed within ten days, shall, within thirty days from the signing of the protocol, meet at Havana and San Juan, respectively, to arrange and execute the details of the evacuation.**

**5. That the United States and Spain will each appoint not more than five peace commissioners to negotiate and conclude a treaty of peace. The commissioners are to meet at Paris not later than the 1st of October.**

**6. On the signing of the protocol, hostilities will be suspended, and notice to that effect will be given as soon as possible by each government to the commanders of its military and naval officers.**

**Camp at Knoxville.**

KNOXVILLE, Tenn., Aug. 13.—Brig.-Gen. McKee is here to inspect a camp site for his troops, the second division of the first army corps, to be removed here from Chickamauga. Lieut. Way, of Grigsby's rough riders, is also here and has selected a camp for 1,000 cavalry, which will later be sent here.

# GREAT RELIEF

### *Spanish Press Pleased With McKinley's Action.*

### *Feared a Convocation of the Cortes at Once.*

(By Cable to The Tribune.)

MADRID, Aug. 13.—Midnight—The protocol will be published simultaneously in the official gazettes here and in Washington. The papers discuss the situation quietly and great relief is felt in government and court circles that President McKinley has not demanded a convocation of the cortes to approve the peace preliminaries. The cortes will now not be summoned until autumn, by which time it is expected that the agitation of the extremists will have cooled down and the country have become more inclined to accept accomplished facts.

The commission to meet in the West Indies will be composed, it is understood, of military officers, and it is believed here that this commission will pave the way for commercial treaties and for a recognition by the United States or Cuba of a portion of the Cuban debt.

The suggestion that Senor Moret, former minister of the colonies, may preside over the Paris commission is not very popular. Various names are mentioned in connection with the commission's personnel, but nothing has yet been settled as to this.

Senor Sagasta has again assured the queen regent that he does not fear Carlist trouble and the Carlists themselves appear to recognize that the country is not in the temper that would support a Carlist rising. They are speculating on the return of the discontented repatriated army, hoping for mischief there.

The government has decided to withdraw its prohibition of wheat export from and after next Monday.

**M. CAMBON'S COMPETENCY.**

**A Question Which President McKinley Did Not Make Prominent.**

(By Cable to The Tribune.)

LONDON, Aug. 13.—The Madrid correspondent of the Times, confirming the earlier statements that the text of the protocol was only received Thursday evening, says: "Some difficulty arose in the cabinet council over the competency of M. Cambon to sign the protocol. As it is quite certain that the cortes will ratify the treaty, President McKinley acted wisely in not giving undue prominence to this question.

"There is no conceivable doubt that Senor Sagasta will get the requisite sanction for concluding peace. Whether he will ask for it in one or two installments is a question of parliamentary strategy. A member of the cabinet assures me that it has not yet been decided."

**ONE BRIGHT FEATURE.**

**Liberal Finds It in the Peace Proposition.**

(By Cable to The Tribune.)

MADRID, Aug. 13.—The Liberal thinks the only bright feature of the peace treaty is the immediate suspension of hostilities, "so that our unhappy soldiers will no longer have to die without knowing wherefor."

Continuing the Liberal congratulates the country upon the fact that the war is ended "though Spanish rule in America is completely terminated. We reserve the right to criticise the protocol when freedom is restored to the press."

In conclusion the Liberal says: "Those who pretend that the events of the last three years were simply accidents which do not affect Spanish history are deceiving themselves."

**Auxiliary Navy Going.**

WASHINGTON, Aug. 13.—The navy department yesterday issued orders detaching all naval officers from the Mangrove, the lighthouse vessel, which has been in service at Key West, and will turn it back to the treasury department. Four revenue cutters on the Pacific coast also have been turned back to the treasury department. The treasury department desires the Mangrove for use along the coast. The navy department when peace is declared will return all treasury vessels. The action in regard to the Mangrove is really the beginning of the dismemberment of the auxiliary navy.



**THERE IS NO OTHER DAILY PAPER PUBLISHED IN THIS TERRITORY WHOSE CIRCULATION EQUALS THAT OF**



**The Minneapolis Tribune.**

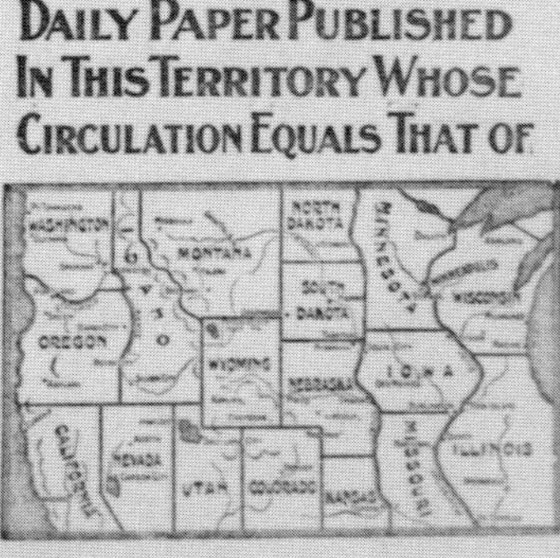

# 1900 ~ 1909

SIXTEEN PAGES

# The Minneapolis Tribune.

CITY EDITION

VOL. XXXV. NO. 106. MINNEAPOLIS, MINN., SATURDAY, SEPTEMBER 7, 1901. PRICE ONE CENT EXCEPT ON TRAINS

# WILLIAM M'KINLEY, PRESIDENT OF THE UNITED STATES STRICKEN BY ASSASSIN'S BULLET IN CITY OF BUFFALO

## The Dastardly Deed Committed in the Temple of Music, While the Chief Executive Was Greeting the People.

## Fred Nieman, or Leon Czolgosz, the Assassin, Arrested on the Spot and Hurried Into a Buffalo Lockup.

Associated Press Dispatch.

**BUFFALO, Sept. 7.—The president's physician issued the following bulletin at 1 o'clock this morning:**

**"The president is free from pain and resting well. Temperature, 100.2; pulse, 130; respiration, 24.**

**BUFFALO, Sept. 7.—At 3 a. m. the following bulletin was issued from the sick room:**

**"The president continues to rest well. Temperature, 101.6; pulse, 110; respiration, 24.**

Associated Press Dispatch.

BUFFALO, Sept. 7.—Just a brief 24 hours ago the newspapers of the city blazoned forth in all the pomp of headline type, "The Proudest Day in Buffalo's History." Last night, in sombre type, surrounded by gruesome borders of black, the same newspapers were telling in funereal tones to a horrified populace the deplorable details of "The Blackest Day in the History of Buffalo."

President McKinley, the nation's chief executive, and the city's honored guest, lies prostrate, suffering the pangs inflicted by the bullet of a cowardly assassin, while his life hangs in the balance.

Out on Delaware avenue, at the home of John G. Milburn, president of the Pan-American exposition, with tearful face, heart torn by conflicting hopes and fears, sits the faithful wife, whose devotion is known to all the nation.

It was a few moments after 4 p. m., while President McKinley was holding a public reception in the great Temple of Music on the Pan-American grounds, that the cowardly attack was made, with what success time alone can tell.

### PRESIDENT SMILED AND BOWED.

BUFFALO, Sept. 7.—President McKinley was shot and severely wounded by a would-be assassin, while holding a reception in the Temple of Music at the Pan-American a few minutes after 4 o'clock yesterday afternoon. One shot took effect in the right breast, the other in the abdomen. The first is not of a serious nature, and the bullet has been extracted. The latter pierced the abdominal wall, and has been located.

The president, though well guarded by United States secret service detectives, was fully exposed to such an attack as occurred. He stood at the edge of the raised dais, upon which stands the great pipe organ, at the east side of the magnificent structure. Throngs of people crowded in at the various entrances to gaze upon their executive, perchance to clasp his hand, and then fight their way out in the good-natured mob that every minute swelled and multiplied at the points of ingress and egress to the building.

The president was in a cheerful mood and was enjoying to the full the hearty evidences of good will which everywhere met his gaze. Upon his right stood John G. Milburn, of Buffalo, president of the Pan-American exposition, chatting with the president and introducing to him especially persons of note who approached. Upon the president's left stood Mr. Cortelyou.

It was shortly after 4 p. m. when one of the throng which surrounded the presidential party, a medium-sized man of ordinary appearance and plainly dressed in black, approached as if to greet the president. Both Secretary Cortelyou and President Milburn noticed that the man's hand was swathed in a bandage or handkerchief. Reports of bystanders differ as to which hand. He worked his way amid the stream of people up to the edge of the dais, until he was within two feet of the president.

### PRESIDENT M'KINLEY SHOT.

President McKinley smiled, bowed and extended his hand in that spirit of geniality the American people so well know, when suddenly the sharp crack of a revolver rang out loud and clear above the hum of voices, the shuffling of myriad feet and vibrating waves of applause that ever and anon swept here and there over the assemblage.

There was an instant of almost complete silence. The president stood stock still, a look of hesitancy, almost of bewilderment on his face. Then he retreated a step, while a pallor began to steal over his features. The multitude, only partially aware that something serious had happened, paused in surprise, while necks were craned and all eyes turned to the rostrum where a great tragedy was being enacted.

Then came a commotion. With the leap of a tiger three men threw themselves forward, as with one impulse, and sprang toward the would-be assassin. Two of them were United States secret service men, who were on the lookout, and whose duty it was to guard against just such a calamity as had here befallen the president and the nation.

The third was a bystander, a negro, who had only an instant previously grasped in his dusky hand the hand of the president. As one man the trio hurled themselves upon the president's assailant. In a twinkling he was borne to the ground, his weapon was wrested from his grasp, and strong arms pinioned him down.

Then the multitude which thronged the edifice began to come to a realizing sense of the awfulness of the scene o. which they had been unwilling witnesses.

A murmur arose, spread and swelled to a hum of confusion, then grew to a babel of sounds, and later to a pandemonium of noises.

The crowds that a moment before had stood mute and motionless, as in bewildered ignorance of the enormity of the thing, now with a single impulse surged forward toward the stage of the horrid drama, while a hoarse cry welled up from a thousand throats and a thousand men charged forward to lay hands upon the perpetrator of the deadly crime.

### THE CONFUSION TERRIBLE.

For a moment the confusion was terrible. The crowd surged forward regardless

(Continued on Page Two, Sixth Column.)

## Vice President Roosevelt Shocked

Special Dispatch to The Minneapolis Tribune.

BURLINGTON, Vt., Sept. 7.—Vice President Roosevelt received his first news of the attempted assassination of the president through a press dispatch. He said:

"I am so inexpressibly shocked, horrified and grieved that I cannot find words in which to express myself."

The vice president started at once for Buffalo with Senator Proctor on the Elfrida, going by way of Burlington. He will reach Buffalo today. Pending the hurried preparations for his departure, a bulletin was received announcing that President McKinley was resting quietly, the bullet having been removed from the stomach. Another bulletin announced his probable recovery. On the receipt of this Vice President Roosevelt sent this word to those assembled outside:

"Like all other people, and like the whole world, you will be overjoyed to hear the good news."

Senator Proctor made the announcement and men, women and children burst into tears. A later bulletin was received stating that the president was resting quietly and that the chances were favorable for his recovery. "Good," exclaimed the vice president, and his face lighted up. He showed his pleasure by eagerly announcing the good news to the assembly.

The vice president then left immediately on the yacht Elfrida, owned by W. Seward Webb, and came to this city as quickly as possible, having directed that all messages should be held for him here. The yacht was to have gone to Arrow Point, where a special train was waiting for the vice presidential party. The train was sent on to Burlington and was there when the yacht came into the harbor at 8:15. President Clement, of the Rutland, placed a train at the disposal of the vice president and made arrangements to take him on it to the scene of the tragedy. Col. Roosevelt was asked at the wharf for a statement for publication and said:

"I am so inexpressibly grieved, shocked and horrified that I can say nothing."

He boarded the train and left for Buffalo.

## THE SAD NEWS BROKEN TO MRS. McKINLEY.

Associated Press Dispatch.

BUFFALO, N. Y., Sept. 7.—Immediately the president was cared for at the exposition grounds, Director General W. I. Buchanan started for the Milburn residence to forestall any information that might reach there by telephone or otherwise. Very luckily he was first to arrive with the information. The Niagara Falls trip had tired Mrs. McKinley, and on returning to the Milburn residence she took leave of her nieces, the Misses Barter, and the president's niece, Miss Duncan, as well as their hostess, Mrs. Milburn, and went to her room to rest.

Mr. Buchanan broke the news as gently as possible to the nieces, and consulted with them, and Mrs. Milburn as to the best course to pursue in breaking the news to Mrs. McKinley. It was finally decided that on her awakening or shortly thereafter, Mr. Buchanan should break the news to her, if, in the meantime her physician, Dr. Rixey, had not arrived.

Mrs. McKinley awoke from her sleep at about 5:30 o'clock. She was feeling splendidly, she said, and at once took up her crocheting, which, as is well known, is one of her favorite diversions.

Immediately on Mr. Buchanan's arrival at the Milburn home he had telephonic communication therewith cut off, for already there had been several calls, and he decided on this as the wisest course., lest Mrs. McKinley, hearing the continued ringing of the telephone bell, might inquire what it meant.

While the light of day remained, Mrs. McKinley continued with her chrocheting, keeping to her room. When it became dusk and the president had not arrived, she began to feel anxious concerning him.

"I wonder why he does not come?" she asked one of her nieces.

There was no clock in Mrs. McKinley's room, and when it was 7 o'clock she had no idea it was so late, and this was when she began to feel anxious concerning her husband, for he was due to return to Mr. Milburn's house about 6 o'clock.

At 7 o'clock Dr. Rixey arrived at the Milburn residence. He had been driven hurriedly down Delaware avenue in an open carriage. As he came up Mr. Buchanan was out on the lawn conversing with a reporter.

"Do you know," said Mr. Buchanan, "I had a sort of premonition of this? Since early morning I had been extremely nervous, and feared that something might go wrong. Our trip to the Falls was uneventful, but what an awful sad ending to our day!"

At 7:20 o'clock Dr. Rixey came out of the house accompanied by Col. Webb Hayes, a son of former President Hayes, who is a friend of President McKinley. They entered a carriage and returned to the exposition hospital.

After Dr. Rixey had gone, Director General Buchanan said that the doctor had broken the news in a most gentle manner to Mrs. McKinley. He said she stood it bravely, though considerably affected.

If it was possible to bring him to her she wanted it done. Dr. Rixey assured her that the president could be brought with safety from the exposition grounds, and when he left Mr. Milburn's it was to complete all arrangements for the removal of the president.

A big force of regular patrolmen was assigned to the Milburn residence.

At 7:30 Secretary of Agriculture Wilson and Miss Wilson called, and were admitted to the Milburn residence.

## At the Milburn Home at 3:30 This Morning.

*(Special Dispatch to the Minneapolis Tribune.)*

**Telegraph station, Milburn residence barn, 2:30 a. m.**—All is now quiet about the home of the president of the Pan American Exposition which has now become famous.

At the nearby street corner the electric light casts its glow on four policemen guarding the rope which bars entrance to Delaware Avenue, Buffalo's most beautiful and fashionable residence street and at the north end of the block two more policemen stand in lonely vigil. The house stands second from the corner and is embowered in trees. At the gate watch two policemen and one guards the rear.

All lights in house burn low except in front parlor, which has been converted into business office by Secretary Cortelyou and corps of assistants. On the opposite side of the hall is the drawing room and it is used to receive callers. In the dining room refreshments are set for the tired watchers.

The large front room upstairs is occupied by Mrs. McKinley and to the rear is that containing the stricken president. Opening from this is a sitting room occupied by the physicians, one of whom sits constantly by the sufferer's side. The other ladies of the president's party occupy rooms adjacent to Mrs. McKinley, who has one of them with her.

In the stable two telegraph companies have had offices in operation since 10 o'clock last night, while telephones in neighboring houses have been secured by newspaper representatives. During the early evening members of the diplomatic corps and many state commissioners came.

A score of reporters flit about the shadows on the lawn watching every move of those within, the doors and windows being open to relieve the closeness of the still atmosphere.

All speak in whispers and doff their hats when approaching the door to receive bulletins and pick up bits of news.

With the sad silence, the moon in cloudless sky, the soft footfall of the patrolmen, lends a weirdness to the scene. The wires are kept busy by the clerical force receiving and sending messages to Washington and elsewhere, requiring two operators at each office.

Senator Hanna and other officials have arranged for wire connections to their hotels, and will be summoned if the patient gets any worse.

## 48 HOURS WILL TELL THE STORY.

*SPECIAL DISPATCH TO THE MINNEAPOLIS TRIBUNE.*

BUFFALO, N. Y., Sept. 7—12:30 a. m. The doctors say it will require 48 hours to definitely determine the president's condition. At this hour, he is improving steadily and unless peritonitis sets in, which seems, unlikely, he is expected to recover rapidly, his splendid physical condition and fighting ability being greatly in his favor.

Senator Hanna and Secretary Wilson have just left President's bedside. Senator said to the Tribune's correspondent that the President's pulse was better, and that he was steadily improving and hoped to get some rest.

## Mrs. McKinley at Bedside

Special Dispatch to The Minneapolis Tribune.

BUFFALO, N. Y., Sept. 7.—Just after the doctors had completed the operation, Dr. Rixey went to the Milburn residence and broke the news to Mrs. McKinley. After the first shock she rallied and has since borne up bravely under the terrible affliction. The president arrived at the house at 8 o'clock and was conveyed to a second story room. He bore the trip well.

At 9 o'clock a bulletin by the five doctors said that if his present condition prevailed he would recover.

Many police surround the Milburn home, keeping back the crowds of citizens. The parlor has been turned into an executive office, with Secretary Cortelyou in charge. The yard is full of reporters.

Gov. Odell, Secretary Wilson, President Milburn, Director General Buchanan, and Bishop Walker are in attendance.

Messrs. Hanna, Secretaries Root, Hitchcock, Postmaster General Smith and Vice President Roosevelt are en route here.

Thousands of messages of sympathy are pouring in, a wire having been run to the house.

The diplomatic corps met last night and decided to remain in the city until a decided change for the better or worse occurs, and passed resolutions of deep and sincere sympathy.

Mrs. McKinley has been twice at the bedside of the president, who remains cheerful, though suffering severe pain in consequence of the operation. She is bearing up like a heroine and she and the president are deeply affected by the sympathy of the people.

The streets for squares about the police station, where Nieman is confined, are full of people. All reserve police are on duty. Conservative men deprecate ideas of lynching and the police have the situation in hand.

Secretary Root has wired the commandant of the 14th infantry at Fort Porter, to place a guard at the Milburn house and hold his men in readiness in case of a riot down town.

### Hanna En Route.

Associated Press Dispatch.

CLEVELAND, Sept. 6.—The fast mail over the Lake Shore was stopped at a suburban station this afternoon to permit Senator Hanna to go aboard en route to Buffalo, where he is due at 10 o'clock tonight.

## Statement From One of the Attending Surgeons

Special Dispatch to The Minneapolis Tribune.

BUFFALO, Sept. 7.—Dr. Edward Wallace Lee, formerly medical director of Omaha exposition, assisted at the operation on President McKinley. He said:

"I was called to the Emergency hospital at 4:20 o'clock. The president was then on the operating table and seemed to be suffering little pain. We waited for Drs. Park and Mann, and upon consultation decided that an operation was necessary. I told the president and he said:

"Gentlemen, do what seems best and necessary."

"Dr. Mann then made an incision of the abdominal cavity four inches long. We examined the stomach and found that the bullet, a 32 or 38 calibre size, had passed entirely through the stomach and its contents, being discharged into the abdominal cavity.

"The two holes in the stomach were stitched and the intestines and the entire abdominal cavity were thoroughly cleansed, when we again sewed up the incision.

"The operation lasted for two hours and a half. The operation is a delicate one. Inflammation is the most serious complication that can set in.

## President Anticipated Much Pleasure at Expo.

Special Dispatch to The Minneapolis Tribune.

CHICAGO, Sept. 7.—The home of Lafayette McWilliams, whose wife is a schoolmate and first cousin of Mrs. McKinley and where the president and wife have been frequent guests during their visits to Chicago, was pervaded with a spirit of sorrow when the news of the attempt on the president's life was received. Mrs. McWilliams was almost prostrated for a time after she learned the news from her husband who left his office in the New York Life building immediately on receiving a telegram, and hurried to his home.

Only two weeks ago Mr. and Mrs. McWilliams on their return trip from Europe, visited Mr. and Mrs. McKinley at their Canton home. At that time, says Mr. McWilliams, the president was looking unusually well and anticipating with great pleasure his visit to the Pan-American exposition. He had been preparing his speech which received so hearty a reception and made known to Mr. McWilliams his program after he should leave the exposition.

Immediately on leaving Buffalo the president was to have gone to Cleveland to visit an old time friend and schoolmate, Myron T. Herrick. According to his schedule Mr. McKinley was also looking forward to a few days stay at Senator Hanna's home in Cleveland.

## Senator Hanna in Tears

Associated Press Dispatch.

CLEVELAND, Sept. 6.—Senator Hanna said: "I cannot say anything about it. To think that such a thing should happen to such a splendid man as Mr. McKinley, on such an occasion, and such a time, is awful. He never had fear of danger from that source. Of course, I never talked to him upon such a subject, but I know he never even dreamed of anything like this happening. I cannot be interviewed upon this; it is too awful."

To a reporter he exclaimed: "What is this great country coming to when such men as Lincoln, Garfield and McKinley fall by the bullet of assassins?

"I shall hurry to the bedside of the president as rapidly as the train will take me. I only hope that he is not seriously injured, but I am afraid that my hopes will be in vain. I do want to reach the president before he dies, if he is going to die. Nobody can be safe from the work of an insane man, it seems. It is terrible."

As the senator boarded a car tears were streaming down his face.

### Assassin Identified.

Associated Press Dispatch.

BUFFALO, N. Y., Sept. 6.—The police have just learned that the real name of the would be assassin is Leon Czolgosz. He was born in Detroit and came here from Cleveland.

## The Wounded President Taken to Emergency Hospital, Where Surgeons Make a Hasty Examination.

## Though the Injuries Are Very Serious, the Physicians Hold Out Hopes of the Recovery of Mr. McKinley.

Special Dispatch to The Minneapolis Tribune.

**BUFFALO, Sept. 7.—1:50 a. m.—Dr. Rixey says the president is doing finely, and will have a good night, as he suffers no pain.**

**2 a. m.—Secretary Cortelyou has just reported that Mrs. McKinley secured some sleep and is greatly encouraged by report of the doctors.**

Special Dispatch to The Minneapolis Tribune.

BUFFALO, Sept. 7.—William McKinley, twenty-sixth president of the United States was shot in the Temple of Music at 4 o'clock yesterday afternoon. He had just began to shake hands with the people who were filing in front of him. The great building was packed with people and at intervals cheers for the president went up. The president was standing in his usual attitude at public receptions, a smile on his face, one hand across his breast and the other extended to where the people were pressing to him. He had just patted the head of a pretty child that had been lifted to him, had spoken a pleasant word to the child's mother, and was extending his hand to greet the next in line, when two shots rang out.

The president fell down abruptly in the chair behind him and there was a struggle immediately before him. Those about had thrown themselves upon the assassin and were tussling with him.

That was all most of the crowd in the great building saw. Those who were back of the president saw a great deal more.

They saw a small dark, well dressed young man, with what seemed to be a bandage about his right hand extend his left to the president, and as he reached to take it the supposed bandage fell, there was the gleam of a weapon, a flash of fire, and the smile on the president's face disappeared.

A negro shouted and threw himself before the dark man, but before he could close, the second shot was fired.

The president's hand fell and he dropped back into the chair.

There was a moment's pause, when the only action in the great chamber was the silent struggle in front of the wounded executive.

Then a woman shrieked:

### "HE'S SHOT THE PRESIDENT."

Those near Mr. McKinley surged to him. Those beside the stand fell upon the man with the revolver. There was little noise, just a muffle of blows that fell too thickly to do much hurt, and a scuffling and growling of men who meant to kill.

The very intent and unanimity of the purpose to have the life of the man who had shot the nation's head saved him. Too many were striking at him with fists and feet for it to be possible for any serious blow to reach him. The pressure of the crowd was so great that he could not even move, else he would have been stamped to death then and there.

The man who was the object of all this hate made neither defense nor outcry.

The confusion was only for a moment. The police awoke to the situation in an instant, and in a solid phalanx wedged their way to the squirming nucleus of the writhing crowd. Officials, detectives and plain people were tossed aside. A policeman got a hand on the collar of the president's assailant and jerked him from the rush of the people that were still about him.

In another moment he was swallowed up in a solid block of policemen, upon which the surging waves of frenzied people broke in vain. In this way the man was dragged out of the main hall and imprisoned in an adjoining room. When the door of that room slammed behind him the crowd surged to where the president was. A line of police had been thrown before him that kept the people back. While his physician, who reached his side within three minutes from the time of the shooting, was given room.

In the body of the hall there was terrible confusion. Women were fainting or falling into hysterics, and being allowed to lie where they fell. Men were shouting:

### "HE'S DEAD! HE'S DEAD! HE'S DEAD! OH, MY, GOD!"

"It was only hysterical women's cries, but the crowd took it to be inspired, and in a moment a thousand people had echoed it.

A level headed policeman of those about the president realized where the cry might lead the crowd, and answered it.

"No!" shouted this giant, with a voice like a clap of thunder. "The doctor says he'll live!"

That stilled the excitement and checked the riot. There was intense silence while the little knot of men bent over the president, and the doctor did the simple things that were required in advance of the surgical operations that were to be done.

Both bullets had struck the president—one in the center of the breast, and the other in the groin or lower abdomen.

When the president was shot he fell into the arms of Detective Gerry, who he coolly asked:

"Am I shot?"

Gerry unbuttoned the president's vest, and seeing blood, replied: "I fear you are, Mr. President."

### FIRED THROUGH A HANDKERCHIEF.

The would-be assasin fired through the handkerchief which concealed the weapon. Detective Ireland was only two feet away when the shot was fired. He immediately jumped upon Neiman and forced him to the ground. Instantly 20 men sprang to his assistance.

A doctor jumped to the president's side and with one rip tore the president's shirt open. Dr. Rixey examined him hastily.

Hardly five minutes had elapsed from the shooting, and in that time all danger of

## Diagram of the Locality Where the President Was Shot.

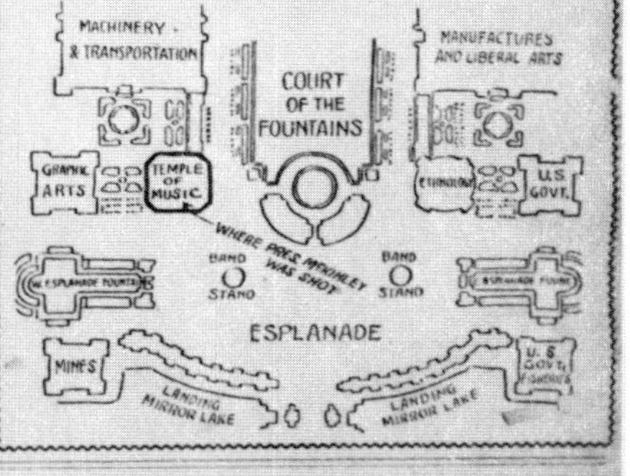


## THE ASSASSIN'S CONFESSION.

BUFFALO, Sept. 7.—Leon Czolgosz, the accused and self-confessed assassin, has signed a confession, covering six pages of foolscap, which states that he is an anarchist, and that he became an enthusiastic member of that body through the influence of Emma Goldman, whose writings he had read and whose lectures he had listened to. He denies having any confederate, and says he decided on the act three days ago, and bought the revolver with which the act was committed in Buffalo.

He has seven brothers and sisters in Cleveland, and the Cleveland directory has the names of about that number living on Hoemer street and Ackland avenue, which adjoins. Some of them are butchers, and others in different trades. He is now detained at police headquarters pending the result of the president's injuries.

Czolgosz does not appear in the least degree uneasy or penitent for his action. He says he was induced by his attention to Emma Goldman's lectures and writings to decide that the present form of government in this country was all wrong, and he thought the best way to end it was by killing the president. He shows no sign of insanity, but is very reticent about much of his career. While acknowledging himself an anarchist, he does not state to what branch of the organization he belongs.

FAIR AND CONTINUED COLD TONIGHT AND WEDNESDAY

# THE MINNEAPOLIS JOURNAL.

PRICE TWO CENTS. TUESDAY EVENING, FEBRUARY 9, 1904. 16 PAGES—FIVE O'CLOCK.



# Three Russian Ships Disabled by Jap Torpedoes

## CIVIC PROBLEMS NOW CONFRONT BALTIMORE

### Citizens Awake to Find the Entire Business District a Mass of Smouldering Ruins-- No Fatalities Reported.

**City Is Under Military Control and There Has Been No Looting—Fire Was Unique in That History Affords no Parallel to a Calamity So Costly in Property and So Fortunately Free from Loss of Life or Limb—For the First Time in 27 Hours Some of Baltimore's Fire Fighters Secure a Little Rest.**

**FIRE FACTS IN LITTLE**

Insurance men place loss at $125,000,000.

Outside fire fighters leave for home.

Federal troops withdrawn — City orderly.

Valuable securities in vaults of financial institutions unharmed by flames.

Mayor MacLane says a greater Baltimore will rise to replace the old.

Area of fire was 140 acres.

Militia is still on guard and there has been no looting.

Baltimore, Feb. 9.—Baltimore will now enter undauntedly upon the task of resurrection. Another and more beautiful city will rise from the ruins and we shall make of this calamity a future blessing.

We are staggered by the terrible blow, but we are not discouraged, and every energy of the city as a municipality, and its citizens as private individuals, will be devoted to a rehabilitation that will not only prove the stuff we are made of, but will be a monument to the American spirit.

—MAYOR MacLANE.

**INSURANCE ESTIMATE OF LOSSES.**

Baltimore, Feb. 9.—After a meeting of the representatives of insurance companies to-day, it was announced that they estimate the loss at $125,000,000, with insurance to the amount of $90,000,000.

Baltimore, Feb. 9.—With the great fire which ate up property variously estimated from $25,000,000 to $150,000,000 slowly burned itself out, Baltimore awoke this morning to face the grave questions of civic and municipal readjustment. Confronting the mayor and his associates of the city government are the problems of aid, the acceptance or refusal of generous offers of assistance from every section of the country, the policing of the vast burned district where lies buried untold treasure in warped vaults and safes and all the hundred minor things that follow a calamity so stupendous that it is not even yet fully realized.

With admirable promptness all the important phases of the situation have already been provided for. To relieve banks and citizens from the embarrassment of financial transactions the next seven days have been declared legal holidays in the commonwealth of Maryland.

**MILITIAMEN ON GUARD.**

Three regiments of state militia are on duty and Troop A of the state cavalry also has been called into service. So thoroly is the policing of the city now systematized that the big force of federal troops yesterday ordered here to assist the national guard was not needed, and after a conference with Brigadier General Riggs, Major General Corbin has returned to New York, and it is not probable that a single federal soldier will be retained in Baltimore.

The city is orderly and but one man is under arrest for an offense directly connected with the fire.

**NO FATALITIES IN FIRE.**

Probably never before has there been a fire of such magnitude absolutely without loss of life and so remarkably free from accidents. The only person seriously injured was Jacob Inglefritz, a volunteer fireman of York, Pa., who was unconscious when taken to the hospital. A report arose that he was dead. He soon revived, however, and was reported this morning to be suffering only from a broken leg and minor injuries.

In this respect, as in many others, the great blaze that had the city in its grasp for twenty-seven terror-full hours, is unique. History affords no parallel to a calamity so costly in property and so fortunately free from loss of life or limb.

Bright and early, in spite of the fact of his long tour of duty, Mayor MacLane was at his office this morning holding conferences with the other city and state officials, and Governor Warfield was also on hand.

To-day dawned cold and clear and lacking wind. There was a decided fall in temperature during the night and by early morning the full gutters of the fire district and the flooded streets were turned to ice. The cold, however, is not intense enough to cause suffering among the police, soldiers and firemen on duty. The absence of wind is a godsend for thousands of feet of tottering walls would surely tumble in a strong breeze and add greatly to the peril of the men whose duty calls them in the danger zone.

Baltimore is not under martial law. General Riggs terms the condition "military control," but in no way have the civil authorities been superceded. Military and civil authorities are working together.

**FIRE FIGHTERS GET REST.**

One-half of the local fire companies were ordered to their quarters at 1

(Continued on Second Page.)

**WAR NEWS IN A NUTSHELL**

Japan scores the first naval victory.

Russian cruiser Pallada sunk by Japanese torpedo. Battleships Retvisan and Czarevitch badly damaged. They are out of it for this war.

Japan is landing troops at Fusan and Pen Yan, in Korea, preparatory to open attack.

Movement is protected by fleet stationed between Chi-fu and the Yalu river.

Japanese minister in London says night torpedo attacks will continue against Russian fleet while it remains outside Port Arthur.

Russian torpedo flotilla icebound in interior of Port Arthur harbor.

Russian warships in the far east number 94, including eight battleships, sixteen cruisers, seven gunboats and fifty-six torpedo boat destroyers and torpedo boats.

Secretary Hay proposes that the powers join in a demand for the recognition of Chinese neutrality and integrity by belligerent nations.

Formal statement by Russia gives the Muscovite version of the diplomatic negotiations.

Japan's note shows that the independence of Korea and the integrity of China were the points in dispute.

## UNITED STATES TAKES ACTION

### State Department Initiates Movement Among Powers Which Is Designed to Guarantee the Integrity of Chinese Territory.

Washington, Feb. 9.—Secretary Hay has addressed an identical note to a number of European powers, to ascertain if they are willing to join in a notice to Russia and Japan that during hostilities, and thereafter, the neutrality and integrity of China must be recognized.

Details of the note are not obtainable in advance of the receipt of replies.

It is known, however, that exchanges already have taken place which justify the state department in expecting favorable responses.

The matter has created a great sensation in diplomatic circles here.

**UNITED STATES SHIPS ORDERED TO CHINA.**

Orders will be cabled to-day to Rear Admiral Evans to send his cruiser squadron, consisting of the Alliance, New Orleans, Raleigh and Cincinnati, from Subig bay to some point in Chinese waters, yet to be determined, to observe the naval operations.

Admiral Evans is expected to keep the battleship squadron in Philippine waters thruout the period of hostilities between Russia and Japan. This decision was reached at the cabinet meeting to-day, after long consideration.

It has been definitely settled that the cruiser squadron will not go to Port Arthur.

## JAPAN STRIKES HARD— CATCHES RUSS NAPPING

### Four of Mikado's Torpedo Boats Start Things at Port Arthur by Sinking One and Disable Two Russian Ships.

ADMIRAL ALEXIEFF.
Who wired the Czar admitting the Japanese Success at Port Arthur.

**Russian Bourse Near Panic.**

St. Petersburg, Feb. 9.—The effect on the bourse where, it was rumored, the full extent of the fighting at Port Arthur had been made public and that the engagement was still progressing, was that a panic seemed inevitable. The market had no support, imperial 4s falling another point. Lottery bonds were quoted at 36 roubles and bank stocks at 26.

**Russian Cruiser Sails.**

Odessa, Feb. 9.—The Russian volunteer cruiser Tampoy sailed to-day with a full cargo for the far east. The Russia steamers Kieff and Vladimir are starting for the far east this week.

### Admiral Alexieff in Official Message to Czar Admits Disaster at Port Arthur.

### Two of the Three Boats Disabled are the Finest Russia Has in the East

### Chi-Fu Dispatch Says the Naval Battle Is Still Going On Furiously.

**Beyond question the Japanese have scored a great naval victory off Port Arthur in the first encounter of the war. The news of the battle thus far is mostly from Russian sources. Dispatches that have filtered thru St. Petersburg admit enough to show that a staggering blow has been dealt to the Russian navy. An impartial version of the affair will probably make the disaster to Russian arms worse. The St. Petersburg report that eleven Japanese warships were sunk has been authoritatively denied.**

Port Arthur, Feb. 9.—Japanese torpedo boats attacked the Russian fleet here last night and three of the Russian ships were badly damaged. The Japanese, who thus scored the first success of the war, escaped undamaged.

Martial law has been proclaimed here.

**ALEXIEFF ADMITS THE DISASTER.**

St. Petersburg, Feb. 9.—Admiral Alexieff's official report of the early attack by the Japanese is as follows:

"I most respectfully inform your majesty that at or about midnight of Feb. 8, nine Japanese torpedo boats made a sudden attack by means of mines upon the Russian squadron in the outer roads of the fortress of Port Arthur, in which the battleships Retvisan and Czarevitch and the cruiser Pallada were damaged. An inspection is being made to ascertain the character of the damage. Details are following for your majesty."

**THE NAVAL BATTLE IS STILL ON.**

Chifu, China, Feb. 9.—The Japanese fleet attacked Port Arthur at midnight on Monday.. Two Russian battleships and one Russian cruiser were disabled by torpedoes.

The battle is being continued this morning at a range of three miles. There has been no further damage.

**THREE OF RUSSIA'S FINEST DISABLED.**

The Russian battleship Retvisan was built by the Cramps at Philadelphia. She is of 12,700 tons displacement, has 16,000 indicated

**BIRDSEYE VIEW OF THE SEAT OF THE WAR**

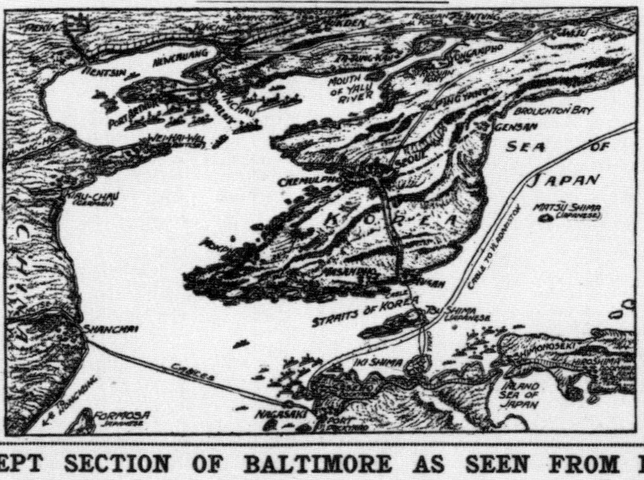


## THE FIRE SWEPT SECTION OF BALTIMORE AS SEEN FROM FEDERAL HILL

**The Fire Started at a Point Indic ated by X and Swept Thru the Heart of the City Until the City Hall Was Reached. There It Turned Toward the Harbor and Reached the Wharves of the Transportation Companies Indicated by O.**

1—Wharves of Bay Line Transportation Co. 2—Fidelity Trust Building. 3—Equitable Building. 4—Postoffice. 5—City Hall. 6—C. A. Gambrill Flour Mill. 7—The "Old Shot Tower." 8—Wharves of Merchants' and Miners' Transportation Company.

—Photo by W. E. Bateman, Minneapolis.

FAIR TONIGHT AND TUESDAY; WARMER TUESDAY

# THE MINNEAPOLIS JOURNAL.

PRICE TWO CENTS. MONDAY EVENING, AUGUST 22, 1904. 16 PAGES—FIVE O'CLOCK.



# NEARLY A SCORE DEAD; UNTOLD DAMAGE DONE BY TWISTING TERROR THAT FALLS IN NIGHT

## STORM'S PATH LAY THRU VERY HEART OF STRICKEN CITY

### MOWED A SWATH LAKES TO RIVER

**The Twister Passed Thru the Most Populous District of the City.**

**HUNDREDS OF HOMES ARE SAVED BY TREES**

**Early Rain Drove People to Cover, Thus Preventing Many Casualties.**

Entering Minneapolis from the direction of Lake Calhoun and rushing furiously toward the northeast, a tornado, accompanied by a downpour of rain which resembled a cloudburst, and a violent, blinding electrical display, ripped its way across the city Saturday evening. It uprooted and splintered thousands of giant trees, stripped off portions of roofs and knocked down scores of chimneys and pinnacles in the residence section, and destroyed thousands of dollars worth of plate glass and other property in the retail district. Near the Tenth avenue S bridge it crossed the river, passed lightly over Southeast Minneapolis, continued with accelerating speed thru St. Anthony Park, and then, turning, swept into and out of St. Paul, doing great damage there.

But one person was killed in Minneapolis, and he not by the wind, but by the lightning and in a location removed from the track of the storm. The injured number only seven. The property loss, while mounting, perhaps, into the hundreds of thousands of dollars, appears small in the face of the devastation.

**Rain a Godsend.**

There is an explanation for each of these remarkable records. Rain fell for more than an hour before the tornado struck the city. The inclement weather kept thousands indoors who otherwise would have been in the streets.

Had the usual Saturday night crowds been in the downtown streets when the storm came, the loss of life undoubtedly would have been heavy, for huge stone cornices were knocked from office and store buildings, glass from a thousand broken windows went crashing to the sidewalks, and signs were wrenched from their fastings and hurled thru the air.

Out among the residences and churches trees and telephone poles fell, the latter carrying with them tangled masses of deadly live wires. But they did not kill and maim because people were within doors.

**Trees Saved Homes.**

To the trees is due credit for the small amount of damage to houses. The wind, sweeping along at one time at the rate of two miles a minute, rushed at magnificent stone houses or frail frame dwellings, threatening to raze them or to wrest them from their foundations.

But tall, sturdy oaks, or elms, or poplars, or basswood trees stood guard in the yards. They let the wind split from them their spreading limbs or rip their big roots up out of the ground and send the natural giants crashing to earth—and saved the homes and the families within. That this service of the trees was performed is shown by the fact that where there were none, as along Cedar avenue between Fifth and Franklin, houses like those which stood unharmed in other places were badly wrecked.

**Before the Blow.**

The afternoon had been bright and warm. Clouds flecked the sky at 4 o'clock, and an hour later the sun was obscured. By 6 the appearance of things portended a thunderstorm, and this came about 6:30. The downpour was heavy, and about 7:30 the rain was falling in sheets. Then came hail, and the little white balls of ice danced on sills and porches. Suddenly there was a gust of wind which made pedestrians try to make two hands perform the work of a dozen, holding onto umbrellas that wanted to soar and hats which wouldn't stay on. Then the wind shifted and umbrellas pushed hard against the north wind, became light as a feather and tried to float away. Many of them did. A moment later umbrellas were useless. Persons in the streets gave up hope of reaching home and broke for a place of shelter, splashing blindly thru rain and mud.

**Family Scares.**

At home, meanwhile, there was a general scurrying to close all windows and doors. Then followed the roar and hiss of the wind, with now and then the crash of a falling tree or pole nearby, or the rumbling of brick or stone as a chimney or portion of wall fell and bounded over the roof.

Families were gathered together in groups, and there was much hugging and kissing and some weeping. Cellars were sought, even by many who lived in big brick houses. When the wind subsided and tenants peered out thru the windows between the blinding flashes of lightning which still continued, or timorously poked their noses out of half-opened doors, there was much wondering and many voluble disquisitions on the marvelous escapes everybody realized they had had.

**Course of the Storm.**

Evidently the wind, after sweeping over the territory this side of Waconia, crossed the Calhoun and Harriet district without doing much damage, altho clipping off a tree here or a part of a roof there just to let the residents know it had been there, came into Minneapolis proper at about

Continued on Second Page.

### PANIC REIGNED IN THE STORES

**Shoppers Who Sought Shelter from Rain Had a Terrifying Experience.**

**The Glass Block Suffers Severely—Skylight Lifted from Guaranty Building.**

Unreasoning panic possessed the business district when the storm broke. The heavy rain preceding the fierce wind had driven the throngs of Saturday night shoppers to seek shelter in the stores. When the thunder and lightning increased and the tornado precipitated a pandimonium of crashing awnings and jingling glass grim terror reigned.

All thru the buisness district yesterday temporary repairs were being made while curious thousands stood agape at the work of the wind. Broken glass represented the principal direct damage by the storm, but the soaking of costly good will bring the total loss in the business district up to a quarter of a million dollars.

Somehow the storm seemed to reach its culmination at Sixth street and Nicollet avenue and Donaldson's Glass block suffered most severely. L. S. Donaldson roughly estimates the damage at $100,000.

**A Scene of Terror.**

The Glass Block was the shelter sought by scores of shoppers who waited for the rain to stop.

Suddenly there was a terrific creaking and a crash of breaking timbers as the wooden structure in front of the corner entrance was torn from its moorings and swept across Sixth street. The fearsome crash of breaking glass hurled against steel and wooden obstructions followed and the awful situation suddenly dawned upon the refugees. There was a mad rush away from the danger point and toward the back of the store. Children cried, women screamed, and several of them fainted; men called hoarsely trying to keep some semblance of order, and, high above all sound of human fear and distress, and drowning it, surged the roar of the mighty storm.

Like egg shells, half-inch plate-glass windows crashed inward, and their powdered and broken fragments were hurled thru the air. Seventy-five of them in all were broken, and to add to the terror and the danger, 145 panes out of the 162 in the skylight were shattered and hurled down thru the store onto the cases and the floor beneath.

In one wall of spray, broken glass, pieces of wood and odds and ends of drygoods, the storm rolled thru the store and broke against the cowering masses of humanity. It was a fearful experience and one never to be forgotten by those who participated in it.

**Some Wonderful Escapes.**

The young lady who presided at the umbrella counter, near the corner entrance to the store, was simply showered with broken glass from the windows, which broke near her, but she escaped without a single scratch.

Miss Eckhart, who works at the lace counter, was considerably cut and bruised and had to be assisted home. Miss Bradshaw, a clerk at the underwear counter, was cut about the face and hands by flying glass, but not seriously enough to prevent her from being on duty today.

John Lindsay, clerk at the dressgoods counter, stepped on some broken glass, and yesterday appeared with a bandaged pedal extremity and walked only with the use of a cane. Other slight injuries were sustained by persons whose names have not been learned.

As in all crises there were some odd attempts to gain safety. One of the employees locked himself in the vault in a maddened effort to escape. Another one is said to have crawled into the cold-air shaft, while several men in the crowd which had sought shelter in the store, are said to have trampled over and even upon the prostrate bodies of children in their eagerness to get out of danger's way.

On the other hand, there were heroic acts, and one of them is related of a young man named Johnson, an employee in the office. When the storm in all its fury struck the building every member of the office force except Johnson thought discretion the better part of valor, and made the most of the opportunity to escape. This young man, however, had his employer's interest in mind, and instead of running, he opened a drawer, pulled out a six-shooter, and, with weapon in hand, stood guard over the cash drawer until the storm had abated and order had been secured out of chaos.

**L. S. Donaldson's Account.**

"It was terrific and no mistake," said L. S. Donaldson to a Journal reporter yesterday afternoon as he stopped for a moment from his strenuous labor of superintending the straightening out process. "I was in the office when it all happened. It did not last long but while it did it was bad enough for anyone. There was a panic, but considering the situation, I think everyone behaved very well.

"Our damage is a thing we cannot estimate at present, but at a rough guess I would place the figure at $100,000. The principal loss will come on the fourth and fifth floors, where the linen storerooms are, and on the ground floor. The Nicollet avenue windows on the two top floors were nearly all broken and what with the water and the dust hurled from the roofs of the buildings across the street the goods have sustained heavy damage.

"You may call that just a blow if you want to, but some of the freaks

Continued on Second Page.

## A TYPICAL MINNETONKA WRECK

MAPLE HEIGHTS INN, PHELPS ISLAND, A BEAUTIFUL COLONIAL BUILDING, WHICH HAS LOST ITS GABLED ROOF AND THE ENTABLATURE ON ITS CORINTHIAN COLUMNS.

—Photo by E. G. Mozart.

### ST. PAUL HIT BY 180-MILE WIND

**The Storm There Was Even More Severe Than in Minneapolis.**

**The Tivoli Theater Collapses and the High Bridge Is Wrecked.**

St. Paul is emerging from the devastating effects of one of the worst storms in its history, and one which wrought even more general damage than that which visited Minneapolis at the same time Saturday evening.

Notwithstanding the fact that the tornado swept the saintly city at the terrific rate of 180 miles an hour and left a path of wreckage in its wake, the greatest loss will have to be borne by the city and the damage sustained by the various business houses and individuals is not sufficient to interfere with the regular operation of business today.

The storm area was comparatively small. Mendota, Fort Snelling, South St. Paul and Como Park escaped without scarcely any damage, while the

Continued on Second Page.

### CITY IS PULLED OUT OF THE PAST

**Hundreds of Men, Working Day and Night, Reinstate Conveniences.**

**Street Railway and Telegraph and Telephone Lines Again in Order.**

Electrical workers are bringing Minneapolis up to date again. Hundreds of men have toiled unceasingly since the storm removing the wrack of wires and debris.

Without telephone or street railway service, cut off from all communication with the outside world, and with trains unable to enter the city, temporarily Minneapolis seemed half a century behind the times as a result of Saturday evening's blow. The absence of wire communication made it almost impossible to estimate the damage with any accuracy for some time after the storm. In the absence of streetcars, efforts were made by many who desired to investigate, to secure livery rigs. But the livery owners feared live wires and would not permit their animals to

Continued on Second Page.

### THREE ARE DEAD AT ST. LOUIS PARK

**Western Suburbs Suffer Severely From the Fury of the Wind.**

**Manufacturing Plants Wrecked and the Financial Loss Is Heavy.**

Three persons were killed Saturday night at St. Louis Park by the storm and much property loss resulted both in St. Louis Park and Hopkins. The dead are:

AUGUST OHDE, a saloonkeeper, 30 years old.

ANNIE HADE, a 6-year-old girl.

JOHN HEDGER, a 6-year-old boy.

Ohde was killed by the collapse of his saloon building, while the family were safely housed in the cellar. Annie Hade was killed by the cave-in of the house after her father had been knocked senseless while trying to protect his wife and four children. John Hedger was also a victim of the wind.

At St. Louis Park the buildings of the Minnesota Sugar company were

Continued on Sixth Page.

## AWFUL RECORD OF THE BIG STORM

### THE DEAD.

**AT MINNEAPOLIS.**

Richard Hilgedick, aged 24.

**AT WACONIA.**

Gustaf Moy, aged 42.
Mary Moy, aged 40.
Freddie Moy, aged 4.
Hubert Lohmar, aged 79.

**AT ST. PAUL.**

Loran F. Hohanson, aged 22.
George Kveton, aged 17.
Viola Robertson, aged 12.

**AT DALLAS, WIS.**

Mrs. Calvin Thompson, aged 62.

**AT ST. LOUIS PARK.**

Albert Ohde, aged 30.
Annie Hade, aged 6.
John Hedger, aged 6.

**AT GLENCOE, MINN.**

Mary O'Donnell, aged 13.
Anthony O'Donnell's Daughter, aged 7.
Frederick Gross.
Mother of Frederick Gross.

**AT BRYANT, S. D.**

Mrs. H. S. Hilling.

**AT WILLOW LAKES, S. D.**

—— Erickson, farmer.

### THE INJURED.

**AT MINNEAPOLIS.**

Charles Wilson, 620 Hoag avenue; leg broken.
A. A. Brault, Regal Shoe company; cut by glass.
J. White, Regal Shoe company; cut by glass.
Miss Bradshaw, Glass Block; face cut by glass.
Miss Eckart, Glass Block; face cut by glass.
Charles Gifford, Plymouth Clothing house; cut by glass.
Mrs. P. S. Pauline, Jones-Harrison Home; badly bruised.
George Blown, 3336 Clinton avenue; broken toe.
Thomas Dushey, Minneapolis hotel; burned by hot grease in overturned sandwich wagon.
Francis G. Jigger, 415½ Main street NE; contusion of ankle and broken leg.

**AT ST. PAUL.**

Andrew Lundby, 948 Payne avenue; skull fractured by falling debris.
F. E. Ford, 5 Crocus place; burned about head by live wire.
James Devery, 463 North street; foot cut and bruised.
Roy Smith, Bradley and Minnehaha streets; ill in bed; may die from shock.
John Rogan, York and Edgerton streets; seriously cut about the head.
Mrs. Robert Younger, 612 Lafayette avenue; injured by collapsing house.
Sister at House of Good Shepherd; injured by falling dormitory.
Little girl at House of Good Shepherd; injured by falling dormitory.
F. C. Schultz, driver of laundry wagon; thrown from rig and bruised.
George Hobrecker, 1463 Charles street; badly bruised about body.
Edward Hobrecker, 1463 Charles street; badly bruised about body.
Harry Gammons, 66 Fairchild avenue; head cut by falling roof.
Lena Hoffman, Woodward street and Monroe place; feet cut and back injured.
Barney Hoffman, Woodward street and Monroe place; cut on face and body bruised.
Peter Schweigel, Willus and East Seventh streets; side injured.
August Holt, Chiaago City; face cut by glass in Sandell's saloon, 182 East Seventh street.
Mrs. A. V. Fisher, 336 East Seventh street; back injured by falling debris.
F. S. Hass, 631 Bronson street; left arm badly cut.
Theodore Schweitzer, address not given; blown into Lafayette bridge; bruised.
Olaf Hansen, 936 Forrest street; hit on head by arc lamp and knocked unconscious.
James Dougherty, Omaha brakeman; blown from top of car and badly bruised.
Charles Strong, machinist; caught in collapse of East St. Paul roundhouse.
George Le Claire, 338 South Wabasha; cut by falling glass.
Theresa Kempf, actress, Tivoli theater; hurt by falling timbers.
Sadie Kenny, actress, Tivoli theater; arms cut, head bruised.
David Berlin, waiter, Tivoli theater; arm cut.
Polly O'Neill, actress, Tivoli theater; hip and body bruised.
Warren Whitney, piano player, Tivoli theater; cut and bruised; knocked unconscious.
Kittie Ransom, actress, Tivoli theater; hit by falling timbers and knocked unconscious.
Annie Scott, actress, Tivoli theater; bruised about head and shoulders.
John Hammond, Fort Snelling; hit by falling timbers at Tivoli theater.
Peter Smith, bartender, Tivoli theater; shoulder dislocated; seriously bruised.
Michael Egan, popcorn man; cut by falling glass.
John Hayden, 410 East Lucy street; head cut.
Bert Hayden, 410 East Lucy street; serious contusions.
Unknown boy, injured by live wire at Rice street and Como avenue.
Walter Sanborn, 384 Bedford street; burned by live wire.
Joseph Hansen, Cook street; struck by electric light pole.

**AT WACONIA.**

—— Moy, hit by falling timbers.
Albert Kohler, bruised by falling timbers; serious.
—— Winser, injured in collapse of residence; serious.
Mrs. —— Winser, wife of former; caught in falling house; serious.
—— Nelson, hit by falling bricks and badly bruised.
Mrs. —— Nelson, his wife; hit by falling brick; badly bruised.
George Roussopoulos, St. Paul; hit by falling bricks from destroyed residence.
Mrs. George Roussopoulos, St. Paul; hit by falling bricks.

**AT ST. LOUIS PARK.**

Charles Peterson, forehead cut and arm broken.
Frank Hade, struck by flying beam.
Frank Hade, Jr., rib broken.
Sophie Hade, internally injured; may die.
Nels Nelson, head cut; condition serious.
Mrs. Nels Nelson, nose broken and spine injured.
Julius Nygard, struck by lightning; will live.
Rasmus Nelson, broken arm.
—— Nelson, daughter of Rasmus; crushed by falling beams; serious.

**AT SPRING PARK.**

William Peterson, Minneapolis Dry Goods company; leg broken.
William K. Simmons, 2631 Bryant avenue S; leg broken.
Mrs. William K. Simmons, 2631 Bryant avenue S; five ribs broken.

**AT HOPKINS.**

John Picha, struck by falling timbers; may die.

## FOUR ARE KILLED IN STORM WHICH SWEEPS WACONIA

### SEVEN DEAD AT COUNTRY POINTS

**Four Perished Near Glencoe, Two in South Dakota and One in Wisconsin.**

**Willow Lakes, S. D., Wrecked by a Tornado—Heavy Losses Over a Wide District.**

Glencoe, Minn., Aug. 22.—A tornado struck the township of Rich Valley and Bergen Saturday night about 8 o'clock killing four persons: Mary O'Donnell, aged 13, daughter of Patrick O'Donnell; the 7-year-old daughter of Anthony O'Donnell and Frederick Gross and his mother.

Thousands of acres of grain and many barns, houses and sheds were destroyed. The most complete wreck were the houses, barns, granaries and grain stacks of William Gayland, Anthony O'Donnell and Herman Tekur. Many others sustained heavy losses.

The storm extended over the entire county. The greatest damage was confined to a section ten miles long and a mile wide. The windstorm was followed by hail and a terrific rain lasting an hour or more. Large groves of heavy timber were leveled to the ground.

Corn was completely stripped and beaten into the ground. Hundreds of grain stacks were scattered broadcast and are no better than straw.

Fred Howes' house, barn and all outbuildings were destroyed. Two horses were killed. One horse was picked up bodily and carried thirty rods and thrown into an old strawstack.

Oscar Howes' buildings were swept away and his crops heavily damaged.

Matthew Basts' buildings and crops are all lost.

Mrs. Ed Currans lost her house and barn and had two horses killed.

Charles Zanke's house was swept away and Gotlieb Pullman's barn and crops were literally destroyed. John H. Beneke lost his house and windmill. William Matthew's barn collapsed into kindlingwood. No damage was done in Glencoe.

**STILLWATER SUFFERS**

**Loss to Lumber and Other Interests Estimated at $100,000.**

Stillwater, Minn., Aug. 22.—The damage by the storm in the neighborhood of this city will exceed $100,000. The damage was heavy on the St. Croix and at South Stillwater. Scores of log rafts were broken loose and formed a jam across the lake. Many of the logs drifted down the stream. David Tozer and William Sauntry are the heaviest losers in this respect.

The immense lumberyard of David Tozer at South Stillwater suffered heavily, piles being strewn about. The smokestack of the Eclipse sawmill was blown down. The large box factory of William Kaiser was unroofed. The Oak Park wagon bridge was partly wrecked. Telegraph and telephone communication in all directions was cut off.

**WOMAN KILLED**

**Home of the Thompsons at Dallas, Wis., Wrecked by Storm.**

Barron, Wis., Aug. 22.—A severe storm accompanied with hail, wind and lightning, swept this county. Around the village of Dallas, twelve miles south, the storm assumed cyclonic form. Much property was damaged. The home of Calvin Thompson, at Dallas, was wrecked and Mrs. Thompson, aged 62, was instantly killed and a son injured.

The main portion of the house was carried forty rods. A planing mill was unroofed. The large barn of K. Espesteh was nearly demolished.

The property loss will reach several thousand dollars.

**WILLOW LAKES HARD HIT**

**One Man Killed and the Town All but in Ruins.**

Special to The Journal.

Clark, S. D., Aug. 22.—A tornado struck Willow Lakes, destroying almost the entire town, and also buildings in the vicinity.

One man, a farmer by the name of Erickson, living a mile west of Willow Lakes, was killed. He was in his barn, which was demolished. His house was carried about twenty feet.

Six or seven persons in Willow Lakes were injured, but none fatally. Nearly all store buildings, the churches, the schoolhouse, railway station and a majority of the dwellinghouses are more or less wrecks—some totally demolished.

A heavy hailstorm visited the section near Willow Lakes, it being reported that stones of enormous size fell.

add Clark S D story D head nw storms

—¼—¼—¼—¼—¼

Willow Lakes is on the Huron-Benson division of the Great Northern railroad, thirty miles north of Huron, in the heart of a purely agricultural region of the prairie district of South Dakota.

Before the storm it boasted of a bank, a weekly paper, a hotel, creamery, three churches and four elevators and was a thriving place.

**SUMMIT IN ITS PATH**

**Several Persons Injured and Buildings and Crops Destroyed.**

Special to The Journal.

Summit, S. D., Aug. 22.—A severe windstorm, accompanied by hail, passed over this section Saturday night. In some localities the storm seemed to be a tornado and did much damage. Several good houses and barns were completely demolished and several persons were injured.

Continued on Second Page.

### FATHER, MOTHER AND BABY DEAD

**Gustaf Moy Family Sorely Smitten—Only Survivor May Die.**

**FREAKISH TORNADO RAZES MANY HOMES**

**Terrorized Village Folk Unable to Explain How They Escaped.**

Tempestuous wind and rain mingled in a twisting, tearing and uprooting onslaught which nearly wiped Waconia from the earth Saturday night. The tremendous forces which worked disaster in Minneapolis and St. Paul seemed to center over the little German village and summer resort, fourteen miles beyond Excelsior on the St. Louis road. Yet the people of Waconia, waking gradually from their daze, are thankful.

Nearly every one of the houses which, nestling together on the shores of Clearwater lake, make the picturesque towns, shows evidence of the wind's fury. The lashing of the tail of the funnel cloud and the flaying of the torrents of rain and hail, killed four persons, destroyed the town hall, stores, churches and private homes, and whipped the crops into shreds.

Lying in the gutters in the pelting rain, clinging to the green sward, clutching the timbers of the Coney Island boat, or blindly groping their way among creaking and rending timbers, the terrified people, one and all, prayed for life to be spared.

Death visited two families. From one was removed the father, mother and baby boy; from another the aged father.

**Family Killed Outright.**

Gustaf Moy, his wife and child, were killed outright. The seriously injured are Freddie Moy, who was brought last night to St. Barnabas hospital, and Mr. and Mrs. Winser. The funeral of the Moy family will be held Tuesday. Today their bodies lie in the little brick schoolhouse.

**Baby Terribly Crushed.**

As the twister left the village it whirled a neighbor's barn thru the kitchen of the four-room house where the Moy family were sitting.

The investigation of the Carver county coroner, Dr. J. E. Soper of Norwood, showed that Gustaf Moy had a surely fatal injury to the back of his head from flying debris and his ribs were crushed. Mary Moy, his wife, was struck by a scantling, 2 by 6 inches and 12 feet long, across the forehead and her eyes, crushing the skull. Freddie Moy, the baby, was found to have had an injury in the occipital region. Cruel cuts were dealt his head, and one little leg was crushed.

**Other Moy Boy May Die.**

One member of the Moy family remains. A boy 12 years old, who was immediately assumed as a charge by the town of Waconia. Unconscious from a blow at the base of the brain, producing a probable clot, he was placed on a cot last night and taken the long drive to the station. Here he was removed to the baggage car of the night train and removed to St. Barnabas hospital as patient of Dr. W. E. Rochford. As yet the boy does not know he has suddenly been made alone in the world.

**Killed by Shock.**

Hubert Lohmar, the fourth to die, was an aged farmer, living over two miles from town. His house was destroyed, and examination, failing to develop signs of injury, it is supposed he died from the shock of the storm's impact. He was the father of John Lohmar, 1514 Dupont avenue N.

**Man Blown Seven Blocks.**

Almost miraculous seem the escapes of many. Twenty-five young people stood in the little railroad station for protection from the storm. When one wall was blown down, all walked out uninjured.

A boatload bound for Coney Island was thrown ashore by lofty waves two minutes before the storm broke.

A young man was blown seven blocks and escaped uninjured. House after house was blown down.

A hardware store was wrecked, but the seven inmates of the second story rooms, taking hold of hands after the manner of the Alpine climbers, pulled one another from the falling ruins.

Notable deeds of bravery arising from the circumstances of the storm will go down in history of Waconia also. Doctors braved the elements to attend the injured. Men and women dared many things to rescue their beloved, all amid the roar, the creaking, tearing Gatling gunlike sound of the twisting storm cloud.

**Crowds' Narrow Escape.**

The two clouds which apparently collided and together did the damage at Waconia, appeared about half-past seven, Saturday. The night train from Minneapolis had just arrived. One busload had started for the boatlanding and about twenty-five of the passengers and townspeople waited for the second load. For five minutes a peculiar rumbling sound was heard, and finally everybody on the platform crowded into the station for protection against the imminent breaking of the storm.

As the height of the whirl struck the tinderbox of the building, the wall toward the rails bulged out and the people inside rushed over across the tracks and hid in the ditch. Almost at the instant the station fell with a crash.

**Minneapolitans In It.**

Many Minneapolis and St. Paul peo-

Continued on Second Page.

The Minneapolis Tribune

VOL. XXXVIII., NO. 208. — MINNEAPOLIS, MINN., TUESDAY, JANUARY 3, 1905. — PRICE ONE CENT EXCEPT ON TRAINS

# PORT ARTHUR FALLS OF EXHAUSTION

## BELIEVE RUSSIANS WILL ATTEMPT A RECAPTURE

**CZAR'S REPRESENTATIVES IN EUROPEAN CAPITALS STATE THAT SURRENDER OF PORT ARTHUR WILL BE FRESH INCENTIVE TO RUSSIANS, AND THAT ATTEMPT WILL BE MADE IN THE SPRING TO RETRIEVE SITUATION.**

## NO AMMUNITION IN THE FORTRESS

**Brave Russians Had Nothing With Which To Return Fire of the Japanese.**

### STARVATION AT HAND

**This, With Exhaustion and Nerve Strain Had Reduced Garrison To Helplessness.**

### [illegible] WAS FIRM

**General Refused To Surrender, Even When He Knew Defeat Was Certainly His Portion.**

CHE FOO, Jan. 2. (Midnight)—Commander Kartzow of the Russian torpedo boat destroyer Vlastni, in an interview with the Associated Press correspondent last night said:

"Port Arthur falls of exhaustion—exhaustion not only of ammunition but of men.

"The remnant of the garrison left had been doing the work of heroes for five days and five nights, but yesterday they reached the limit of human endurance.

"In the casemates of the forts one saw everywhere faces black with starvation, exhaustion and nerve strain. You spoke to them, but they did not give answer only staring dumbly."

FORTS WITHOUT AMMUNITION.

"The lack of ammunition alone would not have suggested the seeking of terms. Scant ammunition had long been common in the fortress and during the past month many of the forts had nothing with which to return the fire of the enemy, the Russians in the casemates not firing once to the more than 200 shots sent by the Japanese.

"When the assault came they repulsed the enemy with bayonets. But the men themselves having existed for three months on reduced rations, were so worn that it is marvelous they stood the final strain so long.

"Yesterday Gen. Stoessel would still fight. His wound, which was received early in the siege, had been bothering him, but his determination to fight while one man stood had not been diminished.

"'But we cannot fight,' said his generals. 'Our men cannot move. They sleep standing. They cannot see the bayonets at their breasts. We can order, but they cannot obey.'

"'Then you generals fight,' said Stoessel, clenching his fists.

WON OVER BY SUBORDINANTS.

"He seemed fanatical on the subject, but finally he was brought to see reason by the insistence of his subordinates Admirals Lochinsky and Wiren, Generals Smyrnoff and Fock and many others, sometimes with broken voices, urged the step which all dreaded so long.

"I am sure Port Arthur would have sought terms a month ago had it not been for Gen. Stoessel, who, with bulldog tenacity steadily refused to permit such action to be taken. He had told his emperor that he would never surrender, and he meant to keep his word.

"The greatest loss suffered by Port Arthur occurred a fortnight ago when Maj. Gen. Kondratenko was killed. Officers and men alike regarded him as the brightest star in Port Arthur's firmament. When his death became known the fall in the spirits of the soldiers was plainly visible.

"Gen. Kondratenko was seated in the casemate of a certain fort discussing with seven other officers the best way of countermining against the Japanese when an eleven inch shell burst, killing everybody in the casemate.

"Gen. Nogi has taken Port Arthur with his artillery and his tunnels. His rifle bullets were seldom found to be of any use.

TERRIFIC BOMBARDMENT.

"We constantly endured a bombardment fiercer than any in history. The Japanese periodically assaulted, and then, if repulsed, they calmly resumed their bombardments.

"We who came here today do not know the terms of surrender suggested by Gen. Stoessel to Gen. Nogi nor the answer to them, having left Port Arthur even before the messenger has been dispatched.

"The general impression however, is that Stoessel has proposed that the army shall go free and that he alone be made a prisoner. Even that concession seemed to wrench out the sturdy old man's heart.

"Whether or not the negotiations terminate in an agreement on terms of surrender it is certain that Port Arthur is doomed, as you say the Associated Press predicted two months ago.

"We still have some ammunition and some guns on Liaoti mountain, but that mountain is not adapted for the best defense from the land side, and the Japanese would find its capture easier than the other tasks they have attempted. Tiger's Tail peninsula has to be similarly viewed, and Golden Hill has been without ammunition for three months.

"Since reaching Che Foo I have seen that attempts have been made to make it appear that Stoessel alone wishes to surrender, and other generals desiring to continue the fight. This is a lie and it is based solely on personal dislike of Stoessel.

HELD BY BAYONETS ALONE.

"It is a simple story. Had the ammunition held out the fortress would have held out indefinitely. For months we held Port Arthur by bayonets alone, until

Continued on Page 2, Fourth Col.

LONDON, Jan. 3.—The capitulation of Port Arthur was the sensation of London yesterday. It was the one topic of discussion, from the street corners, where groups were sheltered from the driving snow to the comfortable clubs, the legations and the residences and offices of cabinet ministers.

Everywhere the utmost admiration was expressed for the defenders and the attacking army, and the probability that Gen. Nogi has made concessions to the gallant Gen. Stoessel is received with much satisfaction.

The announcement of the fall of the Russian stronghold created little surprise in official and diplomatic circles where it had been discounted by recent events. It was known as early as last October that, notwithstanding the brave showing in the official dispatches, Stoessel's resources were nearly at an end.

EFFECT OF THE SURRENDER.

Nowhere, not even at the Russian embassy, was there a doubt concerning the generosity of the Japanese in arrangement of the final terms.

In diplomatic circles the main question was that of the effect of the surrender. The concensus of opinion was that it might tend in the direction of peace, but none dared venture to say that peace is in sight.

It is believed it will do no more than to bring out suggestions from foreign governments.

At the foreign office it was stated that the British government's attitude is unchanged that while peace is most desirable affairs have not reached a stage where any foreign power could hope to offer its good offices with the assurance that it would be considered a friendly act by either of the belligerents.

At the Russian embassy the same spirit of determination to prosecute the war to the bitter end was expressed. In fact, it was confidently stated that Russia would only regard the surrender of Port Arthur in the light of a fresh incentive and would spare no efforts for its recapture.

First Secretary Poklewsky-Koziel, in the absence of Ambassador Benkendorff, gave voice to the sentiment that the fortress would only serve to unite all Russia in the determination to put forth her whole strength in the spring with a view to retrieving the situation.

The general tone at the Russian embassy formed a striking contrast to the cheerfulness and activity prevailing at the Japanese legation. Minister Hayashi was the recipient during the day of hundreds of telegrams of congratulation from all parts of Great Britain and other countries and official dispatches confirming the news from Tokio were received at frequent intervals.

MINISTER HAYASHI TALKS.

Minister Hayashi was interviewed but declined to discuss the probability of peace negotiations. He said, however:

"The fall of Port Arthur will at any rate end the horrible slaughter in one part of the theatre of war, and I sincerely hope that in some way it will facilitate final peace. This depends on Russia and not on us. It may strengthen the determination of Russia to continue the war at all costs. Its effect on Japan, however, cannot be doubted. Our fleet is free and the release of the besieging army gives us increased forces available for service elsewhere. Our base becomes more severe than ever."

Speaking of Gen. Stoessel, Minister Hayashi said:

"The surrender will in no way diminish the glory belonging to him or his men for their splendid defence."

Baron Suyematsu, son-in-law of Marquis Ito, and former Japanese minister of the interior, said:

"Now that we have again got Port Arthur we will not allow any other power to hold it after we have beaten Russia, and I am now more than ever confident that Japan will be victorious. I do not expect the fall of Port Arthur will make much difference with the progress of the war, though Japan will undoubtedly be in a better position."

In British naval circles the prevailing opinion is that the recall of the Russian second Pacific squadron has now become an absolute necessity.

**Count Cassini's Opinion.**

WASHINGTON, Jan. 2.—Although he had no official news regarding the surrender of Port Arthur Count Cassini, the Russian ambassador, had no hesitation in reiterating what he has repeatedly announced that the loss of Port Arthur would not have the slightest effect on Russia's determination to fight to the end.

**Military Honors For Stoessel.**

TOKIO, Jan. 2—2:20 p. m.—Marshal Yamagata, chief of general staff, under orders from the emperor, has dispatched the following cablegram to Gen. Nogi:

"When I respectfully informed his majesty of Gen. Stoessel's proposal for capitulation, his majesty was pleased to state that Gen. Stoessel has rendered commendable services to his country in the midst of difficulties, and it is his majesty's wish that military honors be shown to him."

THE WEATHER.

**Minnesota Forecast—Fair Tuesday; warmer in west and north portions; Wednesday, fair, variable winds.**

Minneapolis, Jan. 2.

| | |
|---|---|
| Maximum temperature | 34 |
| Minimum temperature | 11 |
| Daily range of temperature | 23 |
| Mean temperature | 22 |

## FIRE DESTROYS RUSSIA'S VESSELS

**Battleships Retvisan and Poltava and Cruiser Pallada Burning —Sevastopol Blown Up.**

CHE FOO, Jan. 3.—Advices reaching Che Foo say that the Russian battleships Retvisan and Poltava and the protected cruiser Pallada caught fire Monday morning and are still burning and that in the afternoon the Russians blew up the battleship Sevastopol.

CHE FOO, Jan. 2.—Noon.—Capt. Kartzow, commanding the torpedo boat destroyer Vlastni, which put into the harbor this morning from Port Arthur, says the Japanese expected to enter Port Arthur Tuesday.

The Russians yesterday blew up two of their own forts near the railway and completed the destruction of the cruiser Bayan. The destroyers Smirli and Boikai also left Port Arthur yesterday. Their fate is unknown.

Port Arthur is described by later arrivals as a living hell.

The hospitals are said to be nearly all destroyed.

### THE SIEGE OF PORT ARTHUR.

| | | |
|---|---|---|
| Began | | May 27, 1904, with Battle of Nanshan |
| Ended | | Jan. 1, 1905 |
| Russian Commanders | Army | General Stoessel. |
| | Navy | Admirals Alexieff, Stark, Makaroff, Wiren. |
| Japanese Commanders | Army | General Nogi |
| | Navy | Admiral Togo |
| Strength of Armies | Japanese | Original army 75,000 |
| | Russian | 40,000 soldiers and marines |
| Losses | Japanese army | About 70,000 men |
| | Russian army | About 20,000 to 30,000 |
| Losses | Japanese Navy | One battleship, several cruisers and torpedo boats. |
| | Russian Navy | Whole fleet put out of action |

## STOESSEL FIGHTS UNTIL RESOURCES ARE DRAINED

## CAPITULATION TERMS DECIDED

BULLETIN

PARIS, Jan. 3.—A Che Foo dispatch to the Temps says the officers of the Russian torpedo boat destroyers, which have arrived there, report that the entire town of Port Arthur has been destroyed, including the hospitals in the northwest section.

BULLETIN

ST. PETERSBURG, Jan. 3.—Late yesterday the report of the death of Gen. Fock was denied. It was admitted that he was wounded but it was stated that the report of his death had not yet been confirmed.

BULLETIN

CHE FOO, Jan. 3.—9 a. m.—This morning two Russian torpedo launches from Port Arthur arrived here. There are seven Japanese torpedo boat destroyers in the harbor.

The Japanese protected cruiser Akitsushima and the torpedo boat destroyers Asashio, Yugiro and Shirakumo are guarding the harbor tonight.

It is now believed there will be no trouble as the Russians are seemingly sincere in the disarmament of their destroyers.

BULLETIN.

CHE FOO, Jan. 3, 10:20 a. m.—A third Russian launch has just arrived from Port Arthur. Four of the Japanese torpedo boat destroyers have departed.

Chinese report having heard heavy firing last night.

BULLETIN.

WASHINGTON, Jan. 3.—A dispatch received at the Russian embassy from St. Petersburg announces the death at Port Arthur of General Kondratenko, commander of the Russian artillery at Port Arthur.

BULLETIN.

TOKIO, Jan. 2.—The Russian and Japanese commissioners appointed to arrange the terms of the capitulation of the Russian forces at Port Arthur signed the compact of surrender at 9:45 o'clock last night.

### RUSSIANS AGREE TO ALL ENEMY'S STIPULATIONS

**CONDITIONS OF SURRENDER. IT IS ANTICIPATED. ARE SUCH AS AN HONORABLE SOLDIER MAY ACCEPT FROM A BRAVE AND VICTORIOUS ENEMY — BOTH ARMIES SUSPEND HOSTILITIES.**

RUSSIAN CAPITULATION ANNOUNCED.

TOKIO, Jan. 2, 10 p. m.—The text of Gen. Nogi's telegram announcing the capitulation of the Russian forces at Port Arthur is as follows:

The plenipotentiaries of both parties concluded their negotiations today at 4:30 o'clock. The Russian commissioners accepted on the whole the conditions stipulated by us and consented to capitulate. The document has been prepared and signatures are now being affixed. Simultaneously with the conclusion of negotiations both armies suspend hostilities. It is expected that the Japanese army will enter the city of Port Arthur tomorrow.

**Port Arthur, whose hills have for months run red with the blood of the bravest of two warlike nations, has at last succumbed to the fiercer tenacity of the Japanese attack.**

**Gen. Stoessel has been stubborn in carrying out the will of his sovereign, watching the attacking army gain, until to hold out longer would be a crime against humanity.**

**The conditions of the surrender are not yet known but in all quarters it is anticipated that they are such as an honorable soldier may accept from a brave and victorious enemy.**

**At 9:45 o'clock last night the commissioners completed the signing of the capitulation agreement. Both armies had suspended hostilities five hours earlier. The city of Port Arthur will be occupied by the Japanese today.**

The authorities at St. Petersburg, in the absence of direct official news from Gen. Stoessel that Port Arthur has surrendered, have not permitted the news to become public.

Emperor Nicholas is in the south of Russia, and his ministers are for the time being in the dark as to what dispatches have been sent to him from the front.

TOKIO IS SCENE OF REJOICING.

Tokio was the scene of rejoicing, people of all ranks finding in the outcome compensation for all the sacrifice of life and money that was entailed in the ten months' siege.

To what extent the fall of Port Arthur will make for a restoration of peace is an open question. There is an encouraging note in the expression by Baron Hayashi, Japanese minister at London, of the "hope that in some way it will facilitate peace." Though the Pacific note is perhaps lost in the later words of the minister which call attention to the fact that the besieging army will now be free to go north where it will be an offset to the reinforcements Gen. Kuropatkin had received from Russia since the battle of Shakhe.

The spirit of the Russians may be judged by the statement of the secretary of the embassy at London that the campaign will be renewed with fresh vigor in the spring and that the nation will not be content to permit Port Arthur to remain in the hands of the Japanese.

Both in Paris and London the impression that Admiral Rojestvensky's squadron, which started from Libau for the far east three months ago, will have to retrace its way home as adherence to the original plans would invite disaster without probability of executing a junction with the warships at present in the harbor of Vladivostok.

MAY DISPUTE JAPAN'S OCCUPANCY.

That Japan may not be permitted to retain possession of Port Arthur without dispute is shown in the fact that Paris newspapers are already reviving the claim made in 1901 that the holding of that position commanding the eastern seas by the Japanese would be a menace to European powers.

There is an expectation in diplomatic circles in St. Petersburg that some one of the powers may make a tender of friendly offices and the intimation is conveyed that the United States may take the initiative.

Should this be the case it could only be upon assurances from both the warring powers that the tender would be received by them in good part.

Early yesterday two Russian torpedo launches arrived at Che Foo and there were then seven Japanese torpedo boat destroyers in the harbor. Later in the morning four of these departed.

Russian officers who have reached Che Foo relate that the Port Arthur garrison was completely worn out by five days of continuous fighting, that the supply of food was about exhausted and that the limit of resistance had been reached when General Stoessel made his offer of capitulation.

At 9 o'clock Sunday night Gen. Nogi, commanding the Japanese army of investment, received from the Russian Gen. Stoessel a note saying that he found further resistance useless and asking for a meeting to arrange terms of capitulation.

The note was simple and direct and the Japanese general immediately named commissioners to confer with representatives of the Russian commander. They met at noon yesterday to arrange the conditions of surrender.

HONORS FOR VANQUISHED.

The emperor of Japan himself, through the chief of the imperial staff, has given public his expression that "Gen. Stoessel has rendered commendable service to his country in the midst of difficulties" and that it is his wish "that military honors be shown him."

A dispatch from Tokio quotes military opinion as believing that the entire garrison will be allowed to march out under arms and may be sent to Russia on parole.

Late dispatches from Japan have shown that the gallant defence of Stoessel and his men has nowhere been given a finer appreciation than in the land of his foes, and it more than likely

## SCENE OF JAPANESE VICTORY

The tremendous natural obstacles which the Japanese have so bravely overcome are plainly indicated in the above topographical map of Port Arthur, Russia's Far Eastern fortress, which has been so tenaciously and skillfully held by Gen. Stoessel and his men for eight long months.

FIRST CHAPTERS OF
THE CZAR'S SPY,
A Thrilling Story of the Russian Secret Service in this issue

# The Minneapolis Tribune

THE WEATHER.
Minnesota Forecast—Snow and Colder Wednesday, High Northwest Winds, Thursday fair and warmer.
Maximum ........................ 34
Minimum ........................ 28

VOL. XXXIX., NO. 172. MINNEAPOLIS, MINN., WEDNESDAY, NOVEMBER 29, 1905. PRICE ONE CENT. EXCEPT ST. PAUL AND ON TRAINS.

## CRUSHED

Root Shatters Hopes of the Residents of Isle of Pines.

CUBA CONTROLS THE TERRITORY

In Communication, Secretary Defines the Government's Position.

NO CHANCE FOR ANNEXATION

United States, By Treaty, Has No Substantial Claim to Isle.

WASHINGTON, Nov. 29.—The administration yesterday dashed the hopes of the little band of American colonists on the Isle of Pines, who have been working toward the separation of the island from Cuba and its inclusion in the United States, when Secretary Root, after consultation with the president, made public the text of a letter which he had addressed to Charles Raynard, president of the American club of the Isle of Pines, defining the attitude of the United States government towards the proposed formation of a territorial government in the island as a part of the United States.

The secretary was most pointed in the statements in his letter, which is as follows:

"I have received your letter of Oct. 25, in which you say: 'Kindly advise me at your earliest convenience the necessary procedure to esablish a territorial form of government for the Isle of Pines, West Indies, U. S. A.'

PROCEEDING UNDER ERROR.

"It is no part of the duty of the secretary of state to give advice upon such subjects. I think it proper, however, to answer your inquiry so far as it may be necessary to remove an error under which you appear to rest concerning the status of the Isle of Pines and your rights as residents of that island.

"There is no procedure by which you and your associates can lawfully establish a territorial government in that island. The island is lawfully subject to the control and government of the republic of Cuba and you and your associates are bound to render obedience to the laws of that country so long as you remain in the island.

"If you fail in that obedience you will be justly liable to prosecution in the Cuban courts and to such punishment as may be provided by the laws of Cuba for such offense as you commit.

"You are not likely to have any greater power in the future. The treaty now pending before the senate, if approved by that body, will relinquish all claim of the United States to the Isle of Pines. In my judgment the United States has no substantial claim to the Isle of Pines. The treaty merely accords to Cuba what is hers in accordance with international law and justice.

ISLE OF PINES PART OF CUBA.

"At the time of the treaty of peace, which ended the war between the United States and Spain, the Isle of Pines was and has been for several centuries a part of Cuba. I have no doubt whatever that it continues to be a part of Cuba, and that it is not and never has been territory of the United States.

"This is the view with which President Roosevelt authorized the pending treaty and Mr. Hay signed it and I expect to urge its confirmation. Nor would the rejection of the pending treaty put an end to the control of Cuba over the island. A treaty directly contrary to the one now pending would be necessary to do that, and there is not the slightest possibility of such a treaty being made.

"You may be quite sure that Cuba will never consent to give up the Isle of Pines, and that the United States will never try to compel her to give it up against her will.

"Very respectfully,
"ELIHU ROOT."

### MAYOR McCLELLAN AIDS HEARST

**Ballot Boxes Will Now Be Opened For Recount.**

NEW YORK, Nov. 29.—Mayor McClellan yesterday gave his aid to the efforts of William R. Hearst to have the ballot boxes in New York's recent mayoralty election opened and the ballots recounted.

He announced that he had directed Alton B. Parker, his attorney, not to appeal from the decision of the supreme court yesterday, which ordered five ballot boxes to be opened.

It was announced Monday night that members of the Tammany Hall law committee, after a conference at Mr. Parker's office, had decided to appeal from this order and that this appeal would delay the opening of the boxes at least until next week Wednesday.

The formal orders directing how the ballot boxes are to be opened, were issued yesterday by Justice Amend.

The orders direct the inspectors of election to report at the supreme court on Dec. 1 and recount and canvass the ballots.

The ballots to be recounted come from the First, Second, Fourth and Sixth assembly districts.

**Another Illegal Gotham Voter.**

NEW YORK, Nov. 29.—George Ackerman, 23 years old, and convicted of illegal voting at the recent city and county elections, was sentenced to the Elmira reformatory for not less than fourteen months. He pleaded guilty to voting twice.

### ST. PAUL IS OFF FOR PACIFIC

**Chicago, Milwaukee Directors Will Spend $50,000,000.**

NEW YORK, Nov. 29.—At a special meeting of directors of the Chicago, Milwauke and St. Paul raielway company yesterday the board formally authorized the building of the St. Paul extension to the Pacific coast, from Evarts, S. D., to Seattle and Tacoma.

It was specified in the official announcement that the work of construction is to begin forthwith.

It is estimated that the cost will be about $50,000,000.

## MAYOR JOHNSON WINS

VICTORY IN FIGHT FOR THREE-CENT FARES.

**Supreme Court of Ohio Hands Down Final and Important Decision in Favor of Cleveland's Energetic Democratic Chief Executive.**

COLUMBUS, Ohio, Nov. 29.—By a decision of the supreme court yesterday, Mayor Tom L. Johnson, of Cleveland, wins a victory in his fight for three-cent fares.

On one ground or another all the other franchise ordinances granted by the Cleveland city council, proposing three-cent fares, have been set aside by the courts in litigation inspired by the opposition companies.

The court yesterday reversed the judgment of the circuit court of Cuyahoga county in the case of the Forest City Railway company and E. A. Greene vs. W. J. Day, and dismissed the petition of the plaintiff below. This is final.

The franchise given in Dennison avenue to the Forest City Railway company and Greene provides for three-cent fares.

Day, a property owner, presumably in the interest of the opposition companies, enjoined the company from acting under it on the ground that it was not legally granted.

## MARKS NEW EPOCH IN AUSTRIAN HISTORY

**Francis Joseph's Subjects Make Known to Crown Their Imperial Demand For Equal Suffrage—"It Will Be Done," Declares Emperor.**

VIENNA, Nov. 29.—Yesterday marked a new epoch in Austrian history, for the Austrian people throughout the entire land made known to the crown their imperial demand for equal suffrage, and even as this demand was being voiced the crown, through Premier Baron Gautch Von Frankenthurn, in parliament was assuring the people that its will would be done.

The premier promised to bring in by the end of February a bill providing for a full and free universal equal and direct suffrage.

SERIES OF DEMONSTRATIONS.

The people made known their demand by a series of monster demonstrations in all the principal cities and towns of the country.

From only one town, Austerlitz, are serious disorders reported. There the troops fired on disorderly demonstrators, killing two and wounding thirty. Otherwise the demonstrations were characterized by the maintenance of order and dignity.

Hundreds of thousands of men paraded yesterday, thus emphasizing their demand for political freedom. Such a demonstration was never before witnessed in Austria. The most impressive feature of the whole day in Vienna was found in the fact that not a single voice was raised, as the masses marched silently but earnestly and with unmistakable determination.

Parliament opened at eleven o'clock and at noon Premier Baron Gautch von Frankenthurn announced the granting of suffrage to the people. Between ten a. m. and three p. m. fully 175,000 men and women marched past the parliament building each person wearing on the arm a red cloth band bearing words imperatively demanding the granting of equal suffrage.

The demonstrators turned out in much larger numbers than had been expected and the day's occurrence has made a deep and serious impression upon the country at large. The premier's words in particular relating to suffrage made a good impression, particularly upon the Germans, who are gratified because of the governmental promise to protect the various nationalities composing the population of the empire.

In this they see an assurance of the continuance of their national predominance. The next election to the chamber of deputies will take place next year, probably during the summer.

AUSTERLITZ, Austria, Nov. 29.—A mob of Czech workmen, during a suffrage demonstration here yesterday, broke into a sugar refinery.

Gendarmes fired on the mob, wounding twenty-seven of the workmen, many of them seriously.

### ROOSEVELT SENDS GREETINGS

**King Haakon Receives Cablegram From President.**

CHRISTIANIA, Nov. 29.—King Haakon yesterday received the following cablegram from President Roosevelt:

"I appreciate your majesty's announcement that you have taken possession of the royal power and on my own behalf and that of my countrymen I offer cordial wishes for your personal welfare and the happiness and prosperity of the Norwegian people."

King Haakon and Queen Maud yesterday visited the warships of the powers and lunched with Prince Henry of Prussia.

### KEPT HER PROMISE

**Mankato Girl Deserts Lover at Doors of Church to Become a Nun.**

(Special Dispatch to The Tribune.)

ST. PETER, Minn., Nov. 29.—A determination formed in her girlhood to enter a convent and dedicate her life to charity and mercy has caused Miss Emma Oster, a young woman of Mankato, to renounce her lover at the very doors of the church. When a small child, Miss Oster frequently told her parents she intended to become a nun, and she was firm in her resolution until three years ago. Then she began receiving the attentions of a young man, and it was thought that her early ambitions were forgotten.

Last winter their engagement was announced and she offered no objections to preparations for her marriage, which was to have taken place this week.

Together they went to a Catholic priest to arrange for the publication of their bans, but once inside the doors of the parish house, the attitude of the bride-to-be suddenly changed and she informed her lover that she would never wed.

All his pleadings have failed to shake her determination and she will take the veil.

## FOOTBALL

Columbia College Takes Radical Action and Has Abolished Game.

ASSOCIATION TO BE DISBANDED

Recommendation Made That Sport Be Prohibited at University.

COMMITTEE'S ACTION IS FINAL

"Harmful to Academic Standing and Dangerous to Human Life."

NEW YORK, Nov. 29.—Columbia university has abolished the game of football as at present played, as one of the sports in which students of the university will be permitted to engage.

The action was taken at a meeting of the Columbia university committee on students organizations, held yesterday at the university at which were present the members of the committee, Prof. Lord, chairman, Prof. Mitchell and Prof. Odell, and also President Butler, and Dean Kirchvey and Prof. Bogert, the two latter former chairmen of the committee. The following preamble and resolutions were adopted:

"Under the authority conferred by the university council on student organizations 'to supervise and control all student organizations, athletic and other, which in any way represent the university before the public,' it is,

LAST DAY OF YEAR THE LIMIT.

"Resolved, that from and after Dec. 30, 1905, the football association of Columbia university shall be disbanded, before which date all its accounts shall be settled to the satisfaction of the comptroller of student organizations.

"Resolved, that in the opinion of this committee the present game of football shall be abolished and the committee respectfully recommend to the university council that the game be prohibited at Columbia university."

The action of this committee is final. The students are not permitted to play without the consent of the committee and if they do so they render themselves liable to expulsion.

Prof. Lord said, after the meeting of the committee:

"The reasons for this action need no explanation. They must be present to the mind of everyone acquainted with the game as now played. Only by such radical action can the university and college life be rid of an obsession which, it is believed, has become as burdensome to the great mass of students as it has proved itself harmful to academic standing and dangerous to human life."

**President Northrop Opposes.**

"I think that is going entirely too far," said President Cyrus Northrop of the university of Minnesota last night, when asked for an expression of opinion regarding the action of Columbia university in abolishing football as a college sport.

"I am not in favor of the elimination of football from college sports," Dr. Northrop continued. "On the contrary, I am very strongly in favor of its retention. There is no question but that changes should be made in the game as played at present. In my opinion, the rules can be so amended as to make the plays more open, more punting and end runs and fewer mass formations and scrimmages.

"Therein lies the chief danger of brutality or the foul play. What should be done is to make the game one of skill rather than a contest in which brute strength is the principal element. But the complete abandonment of football as a college sport is, to my mind, entirely too severe a penalty to impose."

**Chicago's Head Would See Change.**

CHICAGO, Nov. 29.—Prof. Harry Pratt Judson, acting president of the university of Chicago, when informed of the action taken by Columbia university against the present style of college football, said:

"That's a very interesting action, indeed. My personal opinion is that unless intercollegiate football is modified the game will have to be abolished, but I trust this will not be necessary and that the necessary reforms controlling the sport will be brought about without detracting from the interest of the game. Football is too good a sport to be entirely abolished from the American colleges and the drastic action taken last night by Columbia university will undoubtedly be the inauguration of a movement which will ultimately result in such a modification of the game as to eliminate any danger to the players that may now exist."

### WHAT WILL TAKE THE PLACE OF FOOTBALL

NEW YORK, Nov. 29.—Almost at the hour when the body of young Harold Moore, the Union college student who was killed in a football game with the University of New York team last Saturday, was being laid to rest in Ogdensburg yesterday, the faculty of the University of New York took definite action looking to the abolishment of the game of football as it now is played.

Every college, whose football team has played against New York university since 1885, when the latter's team was organized, has been invited to take part in a conference to fully consider and finally dispose of the future of the game.

With the call for the conference went the announcement that the New York university delegates will support a resolution that the present game of football ought to be abolished.

NINETEEN COLLEGES INVITED.

The colleges invited to the conference, nineteen in number, are: Union, Syracuse, Hamilton, Wesleyan, Lehigh, Rutgers, Trinity, Haverford, Rensselaer, Stevens, West Point, Princeton, Columbia, Fordham, Ursinus, Lafayette, Rochester, Amherst and Swarthmore.

The invitation which was sent to each of the colleges suggests the following questions for consideration:

"Ought the present game of football to be abolished? If not, what steps should be taken to secure its thorough reform? If abolished, what game or games may be possible in its place?"

Each college or university is invited to send a representative of its faculty and a representative of its athletic organization, making a possible membership of forty.

### AMERICAN EVANGELISTS CLOSE BRITISH MEETINGS

LIVERPOOL, Nov. 29.—Ten thousand persons gathered in Tournament hall here last night to bid farewell to Rev. Torrey and Charles M. Alexander, the American evangelists, at the close of their successful revival movement in the United Kingdom.

This movement has covered a period of three years, during which nearly 100,000 converts were made.

## *MICHIGAN-CHICAGO GAME TO BE DUPLICATED HERE*

**Weather conditions permitting, The Tribune's famous gridiron across Fourth street will be used for displaying the returns of the Chicago-Michigan football game the afternoon of Thanksgiving day.**

**Special North American Company wires will run direct from the football field at Chicago to The Tribune building, and every play will be telegraphed as soon as made.**

**The plays will be announced through a megaphone, in addition to the moving ball.**

BUT—
How much of a gain is he likely to make?

# MOST TERRIFIC GALE SWEEPS GREAT LAKES

## FRIGHTFUL

Lighthouse Keeper Tells a Thrilling Tale of Awful Experiences.

FINALLY RESCUED BY LIFE-SAVERS

Mountainous Wave Breaks Entire Wall in Home—Grabs Stanchion.

MILWAUKEE, Nov. 29.—The fiercest windstorm in many years prevailed on the Great Lakes Monday night and yesterday, causing much damage to shipping and other property.

Lake Michigan on this shore was a mass of foam while the water was driven high on the beach and against the clay banks south and north of Milwaukee.

The gale on the lake was imperilled by a wind which reached a velocity of forty-five miles an hour, but on Lake Superior the storm approximated a hurricane, racing at over sixty miles an hour. On the most northern lake the storm was accompanied by snow, making navigation more perilous than ever.

The entire Lake Superior country is buried under snow.

GOVERNMENT LIGHTHOUSE BATTERED.

The government lighthouse and fog signal building at the end of the Milwaukee breakwater pier was battered by the high seas and the assistant keeper, William Foster rescued with difficulty by the life-saving crew.

Mr. Foster told a thrilling story of his experiences, which, he says, will always be retained in his memory as among the most frightful of his life.

"Because I saw that the sea was going to be bad," said he. "I went off to the breakwater about 2 o'clock in the afternoon, although my time to go on duty was not until 6 o'clock. As soon as I arrived at the house I told Emil Tews, the man whom I relieve, that he had better go ashore before the seas got any higher.

"From that time on," continued he, "the sea steadily became worse. In all my experiences on the lakes—fifteen years—I never saw the like before. About 5 o'clock the sea began breaking over the house and the thunder of the waves was something awful. I busied myself with making things safe and in keeping a full head of steam on with no thought of any particular danger to myself, although it was evident that the storm was all the time growing fiercer.

PRESENCE OF MIND SAVES LIFE.

"It was about 7:20 when as I stood at the east window, looking out on the lake, I saw a particularly large wave coming which I saw was certain to hit the house. Involuntarily I grabbed hold of the stanchion, and it is to that act that I owe my life. The wave struck the house with full force breaking in the entire east wall, carrying away with it all the windows and doors and bursting open the door on the west side. I was carried along with the wave, out of doors and it was only the beam I clung to that stayed my progress and thus saved me from being swept away.

"We had an understanding," said Mr. Foster, referring to the manner in which he was to attract the attention of the life-saving crew, "that if at any time I wanted them to come out to me I was to swing a lantern over my head.

"Slowly crawling back into the house, all the time keeping a secure hold on something, I got to where the lantern was suspended, lighted it and went back to the west side of the house, where I swung it in the manner indicated. It was but a short time when I saw a boat put out from the station and knew that help was on the way."

Mr. Foster says that while he was waiting for the crew to get to him the minutes dragged like hours and it seemed that the house would surely be swept away before he could be rescued. Before he left the building it had been partially turned around, the boilers had been shifted and the pipes broken.

SEAS SWEEP OVER HARBOR PIERS.

While the life-saving crew were attempting to get to the breakwater to rescue Mr. Foster, the seas were sweeping completely over the harbor piers and it was with the greatest difficulty that the crew were able to get outside the piers.

As soon as Foster's danger was seen, Captain Ingar Olson ordered out the crew. The heavy sea and wind made the trip a perilous one. The end of the pier finally was reached and Foster was rescued with difficulty. Battling the waves which threatened every moment to overturn them, the live-savers brought their little boat in safety to the quarters on Jones' island.

The big steamer Appomattox, coal laden, which went ashore seven miles north of this city several weeks ago and later abandoned, was battered to pieces by the intensity of the waves. The boat broke into three pieces. Bow and stern were washed away and driven upon the shore. The hulk was left lying about 200 feet from shore, after it had been washed in a bit nearer from where the vessel stranded.

Wreckage strews the shore of the lake from Lake Park to Whitefish bay. Timbers and portions of the decking of the vessel have been scattered along the beach, although the greater part of the wreck is scattered along Lake Park.

WORST BLIZZARD SINCE 1872.

Superior reports a blizzard the like of which has not been experienced since 1872. Several feet of snow fell, prostrating street railway service and demolishing wires of all kinds.

The steel freighter Crescent City, driven by a seventy-mile gale which rendered her engines powerless, was driven on the rocks at Lakewood, twelve miles from the entrance of Duluth harbor. The crew got off in safety.

Port Washington, thirty miles north of Milwaukee, reports that the steamer D. C. Whitney, coal laden, ran ashore during the gale. The vessel belongs to the Gilchrist fleet of Cleveland.

The Milwaukee life-saving crew went to the rescue and this afternoon took off the crew in safety. Two Milwaukee tugs also went to the scene and will endeavor to release the vessel.

Ashland and Washburn, Wis., report an extraordinary snowfall, rendering train service irregular. Considerable damage was done to dock property and lumber and coal piles at Menominee, Mich.

Mackinaw City reports that the straits experienced one of the worst storms ever known. The weather there is at the freezing point.

## MICHIGAN IS SUFFERING

UNUSUALLY HEAVY SNOWFALL IS REPORTED THROUGHOUT STATE

**Greatest Damage Report From Lake Huron, As Result of Gale Is at Alpena—40 to 60-Mile Wind Sweeps Throughout Territory.**

DETROIT, Nov. 29.—Lake Superior from Duluth to the Soo, the upper peninsula of Michigan, the upper ends of Lakes Huron and Michigan and the northen counties of lower Michigan, were swept Monday night and yesterday by a terrific wind and snow storm.

Marquette reports an unusually heavy snowfal for this time of year, with drifts so high that train and traction service is impeded and greatly delayed. Tremendous seas are running on Lake Superior off Marquette harbor and more than a dozen vessels are riding out the gale inside the breakwater there. Many wires are down between Marquette and the north and communication was demoralized for the large part of the day.

GREATEST DAMAGE AT ALPENA.

The greatest damage report from Lake Huron as a result of the gale is at Alpena.

The waterlogged barge Harvey Bissell, which was tied at a dock, was torn to pieces by the gale, the barge Vinland broke away from her consort and is aground and the small passenger and freight steamer City of Holland went on the rocks while trying to make the harbor at Rogers City.

The passengers and crew were taken from the steamer in safety by a crew from shore. Docks and other waterside property sustained heavy damage at Alpena. Much damage was also done on Thunder Bay island, where the weather station and watch house were surrounded with water and the northern portion of the island was submerged.

More than a dozen vessels are in shelter at Port Huron at the lower end of Lake Huron. One small schooner, the J. M. Spaulding, bound down from Rogers City, was unable to make the harbor yesterday and went on the beach near Fort Gratiot. The crew of four men reached shore safely in their yawl boat.

Ludington reports a forty-mile gale sweeping the upper end of Lake Michigan yesterday afternoon and no boats leaving the harbor but the Pere Marquette ferry steamers.

Thousands of dollars' damage was done to waterside property at Menominee and along the west shore of Green Bay. The straits of Mackinaw were lashed during the day by the worst gale in years, the wind reaching forty-eight miles an hour, accompanied by a heavy snow which made the air thick.

CANADIAN STEAMER BEACHED.

From Fort William, Ont., on the north shore of Lake Superior, comes news of the beaching of the Canadian steamer Rosemount inside of the Welcome island. The Rosemount, it is understood, is not greatly damaged and her crew are understood to be in little danger.

The steamer Argo which went ashore off Holland last Friday was driven further on the beach by yesterday's gale which was so heavy that it was impossible to proceed with wrecking operations on the steamer.

The storm warnings on the lower lakes, which have been up for the past twenty-four hours, were ordered down at 6 o'clock last night.

Although the wind was high on the lower lakes Monday night and yesterday, it was not accompanied by the heavy snow which prevailed on the upper lakes.

There was no snow south of Harbor Beach on Lake Huron. From Alpena north to the upper peninsula above Lake Superior, from five inches to a foot of snow were reported early last evening.

The steamer, Jim Jeffries, which left Alpena Monday night with the barges Moffatt and E. T. Judd in tow, returned to that port last night without her barges and with one spar and her deck load of lumber gone. The barges broke away in the storm.

## LIVES LOST

Three Big Steamers Driven Ashore Near Duluth Lighthouse.

CREW MEMBERS PERISH IN WATERS

Boats Fast Being Pounded to Pieces—One Already a Total Wreck.

**DULUTH, Minn., Nov. 29.—One life lost, three others believed to have perished and the big ore carrier Mataafa, of the Pittsburg Steamship company, wrecked tells a tale of the most thrilling and spectacular marine disaster at the head of the lakes in recent years.**

**The steamer is resting in fifteen feet of water within one hundred yards of the shore while its crew of twenty-seven members are being subjected to the fury of the wind and waves until daylight comes. After going on the bottom three of the crew who were aft made the journey to the fore part of the craft followed by a fourth, who retreated after having been washed off the deck and nearly into the lake.**

**He caught a projection, however and crawled back to the deck, thence to the boat's stern. The tragic spectacle was witnessed by three thousand spectators on shore who raised their hats and shouted lustily when they saw him regain apparent safety.**

**Efforts to rescue the crew were practically abandoned at midnight by the life-saving crew. The night was bitter cold, a northeast wind blew at the rate of sixty-five miles an hour and a heavy snowstorm made it impossible to work to any advantage.**

**Three times lines were shot out to the stranded craft but the men on board failed to reach them and so were left to their fate. In the morning it is believed the sea will have abated sufficiently to permit of the use of life saving boats which was utterly impossible last night.**

**At the moment the boat struck the canal pier one of the crew was seen to make a jump for it, but he was carried into the sea by the stiff gale. Three others just behind him were seen no more by those on shore, but it could not be determined whether they were jostled off the boat or retreated. At any rate they were not seen again by those on shore.**

**Huddled in the pilot house are held to be most of the crew and it is believed that they will be saved by morning, providing the gale does not increase.**

**Aft are four men, however, and if they are saved it will be little short of miraculous as they have been subjected to the bitter elements all afternoon and night.**

DULUTH, Minn., Nov. 29.—In one of the most terrific gales of the history of navigation on the great lakes, even surpassing in fury the terrible storm of last September, in which so many men lost their lives in the vicinity of the Apostle islands, three big lake steamers were yesterday driven ashore within sight of the lighthouse at the Duluth entrance to the local harbor, and several members of the crew of one of the boats, the Mataafa, are believed to have perished.

The wrecks are the Crescent City and the Mataafa, of the Pittsburg Steamship company, and the R. W. England, owned by the England Transportation company, of Cleveland. As soon as the interrupted telegraphic communication with other lake ports is resumed, it is expected that further reports of wrecks will be received, for the storm is thought to have been a record-breaking one.

For thirteen consecutive hours, between 11 o'clock Monday night and 12 o'clock yesterday, the velocity of the wind averaged sixty miles an hour.

BOATS ARE TOTAL WRECKS.

The Mataafa is being slowly pounded to pieces. The crew of the Crescent City escaped, but the boat is a total wreck. Captain R. W. England is the only man who left the England. The vessel is lying on the sand, and is in no danger of going to pieces.

The captain was taken off by the life saving crew with the help of a breeches buoy. The sailors will remain on the boat until today. Unless the wind abates before morning the Mataafa will be a total loss.

The Mataafa's accident was the most unfortunate of the three. She struck the north pier of the harbor entrance while making her way into the harbor, and was unable to get through the canal. She swung around and ran aground just north of the pier, where she is now being raked by the waves, every one of which dashed completely over her.

The accident occurred shortly before 2 o'clock. The Mataafa left here at 5 o'clock last night with the Nasmyth in tow. She was captained by R. F. Humble. The storm was so severe that she was forced to turn back. As she came up the lake with her tow, a large crowd flocked around the piers to watch her entrance.

A mile or two out in the lake she left the Nasmyth which immediately anchored and came on alone, endeavoring to make the entry, as the Ellwood and the Pope had done a few hours earlier, but the lateral roll of the waves threw her starboard and she struck the north pier fairly on end, almost squarely with her nose, which was badly battered as a result of the collision.

WAVES MOUNTAINOUS IN HEIGHT.

A moment later she veered off slightly with her bow headed between the canal piers. She had swung quartering to the waves, however, and was unable to proceed more than a few yards. At the entrance the waves were almost mountainous in height and great clouds of water kept sweeping the laboring vessel from stem to stern.

It soon became evident that she would be unable to make the harbor. At this point an effort was made to turn her out into Lake Superior again, but the attempt was in vain. As her prow headed toward the lake again she turned almost completely around with her nose toward the shore. She cleared the pier and went on the beach broadside.

The anchors were thrown out immediately. Every wave sweeps completely over the boat. There, with thousands of people watching them, almost within a stone's throw, and unable to do anything, the poor fellows huddled in the

TODAY'S SPORTING NEWS WILL BE FOUND ON PAGE 16.

FAIR AND [illegible] TONIGHT AND THURSDAY.



# THE MINNEAPOLIS JOURNAL.





PRICE TWO CENTS. | WEDNESDAY EVENING, APRIL 18, 1906. | 22 PAGES—FIVE O'CLOCK.

# HORROR OF EARTHQUAKE AND FIRE IN SAN FRANCISCO—HUNDREDS DEAD

## PRESIDENT SCORES IMMUNITY DECISION

### "Miscarriage of Justice," Declares President in Message Regarding the Packers' Cases.

Washington, April 18.—In a special message delivered to congress today, President Roosevelt declares that the result of the recent trial of the beef packers in Chicago was a "miscarriage of justice" and that the interpretation placed by Judge J. Otis Humphrey on the will of congress "is such as to make that will absolutely abortive."

The message, which is most sensational in character, is based largely on a letter to the president from Attorney General Moody, in which the attorney general reviews the proceedings of the case of the government against the beef packers. The president says it is clear that no criticism attaches to Commissioner Garfield, as what he did was in pursuance of a duty imposed on him by congress.

**Scores Judge Humphrey.**

He refers sharply, however, to the decision of Judge Humphrey, saying that congress could not have foreseen such a decision and that he can hardly believe that the ruling of Judge Humphrey will be followed by other judges. He declared that such interpretation of the law as that placed on it by Judge Humphrey "comes measurably near making the law a farce," and he recommends that congress pass a declaratory act stating its real intention.

The president also requests congress to confer upon the government, by statute, the same right of appeal, in criminal cases which the defendant now enjoys, where the merits of the case have not been determined.

The full text of the message follows:

**Defends Garfield.**

I submit herewith a letter of the attorney general, enclosing a statement of the proceedings by the United States against the individuals and corporations commonly known as the "beef packers," and commenting upon the decision of District Judge Humphrey. The result has been a miscarriage of justice.

It clearly appears from the letter of the attorney general that no criticism whatever attaches to Commissioner Garfield; what he did was in strict accordance with the law and in pursuance of a duty imposed on him by congress could not be avoided, and of course congress, in passing the Martin resolution, could not possibly have foreseen the decision of Judge Humphrey.

But this interpretation by Judge Humphrey of the will of the congress, as expressed in legislation, is such as to make that will absolutely abortive. Unfortunately there is grave doubt whether the government has the right of appeal from this decision of the district judge.

The case well illustrates the desirability of conferring upon the government the same right of appeal in criminal cases on questions of law which the defendant now has, in all cases where the defendant had not been put in jeopardy by a trial upon the merits of the charge made against him.

The laws of many of the states, and the law of the District of Columbia recently enacted by the congress, give the government the right of appeal. A general law of the character indicated should certainly be enacted.

**Wants General Interpretation.**

Furthermore it is very desirable to enact a law declaring the true construction of the existing legislation so far as it affects immunity.

I can hardly believe that the ruling of Judge Murphy will be followed by other judges, but if it should be followed the result would be either completely to nullify very much, and possibly the major part of the good to be obtained from the interstate commerce law and from the law creating the bureau of corporations in the department of commerce and labor, or else frequently to obstruct an appeal to the criminal laws by the department of justice.

There seems to be no good reason why the department of justice, the department of commerce and labor and the interstate commerce commission each should not, for the common good, proceed within its own powers without undue interference with the functions of the other.

It is of course necessary, under the consti-

Continued on 2d Page, 6th Column.

## SHOCK IS WIDESPREAD

Washington, April 18.—The San Francisco earthquake has reached across the entire continent. The seismograph at the weather bureau here showed such a violent agitation about 8:30 o'clock this morning that the pen passed off the recording sheet. The instrument at 12 o'clock was still under vibration, showing that the earthquake has not ceased.

**Conflagration in Berkeley.**

New York, April 18.—The Western Union received a report that a serious fire is burning in Berkeley, where the state university is located. The report came from Pinola, a station ten miles out of San Francisco, and the nearest point to the latter city which the company has been able to reach up the time of this dispatch. Berkeley is between Pinola and San Francisco.

At the offices of the St. Louis & San Francisco railroad in this city a message was received from the company's agent in Nevada, saying that the earthquake shock was severely felt thruout Nevada and that all wires were thrown down west of Reno.

**Shock Severe in Sacramento.**

Sacramento, Cal., April 18.—The severest earthquake felt in this city in many years occurred at 5:13 o'clock this morning. Buildings rocked like cradles. Many clocks stopped.

No serious damage was done. A few cracks were discovered in the stone postoffice building. Slight damage was done to some brick buildings.

Chimneys and water tanks were shaken down at Suisan, Solano county, and at Tracy, San Joaquin county.

**Machine Shop Wrecked.**

San Francisco, April 18.—The Santa Fe roundhouse and machine shop at Point Richmond, across the bay, have collapsed.

The earthquake was not seriously felt at other points along the coast so far as can be ascertained.

## EASTERNERS ARE SAFE

**San Francisco, April 18.—For the benefit of the eastern people who have friends visiting in San Francisco, it is safe to say that they are not injured, as the loss of life was confined to the cheap lodginghouses and the wholesale districts.**

**All persons in the larger hotels escaped, and most of their effects have been removed and are out of the way of the fire peril.**

## LATE BULLETINS.

**PALACE HOTEL BURNING.**

**San Francisco, April 18.—The Palace hotel is now on fire. Other buildings on fire are the Claus Spreckels structure, seventeen stories high; the Phelan building and the O'Farrell store.**

## The Costly City Hall at San Francisco Which Is Now a Huge Mass of Debris

This Beautiful $7,000,000 Building, Razed by the Earthquake.

MARKET ST, PRINCIPAL THOROFARE, SCENE OF HEAVIEST LOSS

To the Left in the Foreground Is the Palace Hotel, now Intact; in the Background Is the Sixteen-Story Building of the San Francisco Call (Destroyed), and Between the Palace and the Call Buildings Is the Examiner Building, also Destroyed. Across the Street from the Call Building Stood the Home of the Chronicle, While in the Foreground on the right Are the Telegraph Offices and the Associated Press Building, Which Were Badly Racked. This View Is Looking Up Market Street from Montgomery Street, Away from the Bay.

## The Buildings in San Francisco That Have Been Razed or Racked

**CITY HALL**, cost $7,000,000, in ruins.

**VALENCIA HOTEL**, between Seventeenth and Eighteenth streets, on Valencia, topples into street. Seventy-five buried.

**KINGSLEY HOTEL**, Seventh street, between Howard and Mission, collapses, burying between seventy-five and eighty persons. Ruins burning.

**LIPMAN DRY GOODS**, Twenty-second and Mission, burned.

**EPISCOPAL CHURCH**, Eleventh street, badly damaged.

**CALL BUILDING**, Third and Market, practically ruined.

**EXAMINER BUILDING**, Third and Market, practically ruined.

**WESTERN UNION BUILDING**, Kearney street, badly wrecked.

**PALACE HOTEL**—Badly shaken. Now in path of flames.

**ST. FRANCIS HOTEL**—Badly shaken. Interior damaged.

**EMPIRE BUILDING**, Oakland, collapses. Five dead in ruins.

**GORE BLOCK**, Market and Pine; burned.

**PACIFIC STATES TELEPHONE COMPANY'S BUILDING**, New Montgomery street; destroyed.

**RIALTO BUILDING**, Mission and Market; destroyed.

**MUTUAL LIFE BUILDING**, California and Sansome; destroyed.

**NATOMA BUILDING**, Second and Market; destroyed.

**POSTAL BUILDING**—Destroyed.

**LICK HOUSE**—Badly damaged.

**HOBART BUILDING**—Destroyed.

**STUDEBAKER BUILDING**, Tenth and Market; badly damaged.

**HALL OF JUSTICE**—Tottering and expected to fall.

**MAJESTIC THEATER**—Destroyed.

**POSTOFFICE**—Collapsed.

**FISH MARKET**, Clay and Merchants street; burning.

**GRAND OPERAHOUSE**—Ten-story building adjoining Third and Mission streets; afire and doomed.

## MANY FROM THIS CITY IN FRISCO

### Anxious Hearts in Minneapolis, and No One Able to Get Tidings of Friends.

Great anxiety and extreme nervous apprehensiveness were evident at the Chamber of Commerce and in the local hotels and cafes, where friends of Minneapolis people now on the Pacific coast crowded around the bulletin boards and the tickers, reading with suppressed emotion the news of the earthquake. The telegraph offices were besieged with inquirers and numerous messages were filed for San Francisco and other southern California points despite the knowledge of inability to secure prompt connection.

Call after call came in on The Journal telephones, and anxious voices begged information as to the extent of the catastrophe. The Journal bore the first news to Minneapolis people in an early extra, copies of which were eagerly bought up, and succeeding extra editions of The Journal were in insistent demand.

**Minneapolis People There.**

Many Minneapolis people are in the west, but the tide of tourists flows to southern California rather than to San Francisco. Still, many of the travelers from this city are known to have included San Francisco in their itinerary.

T. B. Walker's sons and daughters, Mr. and Mrs. Willis Walker and Mr. and Mrs. Clinton Walker, and their families are near San Francisco. They live in Piedmont, and hopes are entertained that theirs is one of the districts which has escaped the ravages of the earthquake.

Mr. Walker returned only yesterday from San Francisco. In speaking of the earthquake he said:

"During my visits in San Francisco shocks and minor earthquakes have been frequent occurrences, and I remember one evening, a year ago last December, when I was giving an address before the Y. M. C. A., in San Francisco, we experienced a shock which scattered the furniture about the hall and created terrible confusion. I was obliged to discontinue my address for almost an hour. We are in hopes that the members of our families are safe, as they are in Piedmont, one of the outlying residential districts, which was only severely shaken up."

C. A. Smith, who is traveling on the coast with Hugh Bellas of New York, is supposed to have been in San Francisco, but no news has reached here from the two men.

E. P. Wells of the Wells & Dickey company, is one of the Minneapolis men who was last heard of from San Francisco. Mr. Wells is accompanied by Mrs. Wells.

J. H. Queal of the firm of J. H. Queal & Co., Minneapolis, with offices in the Sheare building, San Francisco, is in that city with Mrs. Queal. Mrs. John Lind and daughter are also in Berkeley or San Francisco, and former Governor Lind has received no news from them. Mrs. Charles Elliott Thompson, a former Minneapolis girl, is visiting this month in San Francisco. Mr. Thompson is the son of B. N. Thompson of this city, and has lived on the coast the past year.

**Anxiously Awaiting News.**

Mrs. W. K. Pennell of 3036 Clinton avenue is anxiously awaiting news from her father, M. T. Smith, who resides on Folsom street, twenty minutes' ride from the Palace hotel. An aunt of Mrs. Pennell and a nephew live next door to her father.

Dr. and Mrs. F. E. Westbrook of the University of Minnesota have cousins, Mr. and Mrs. John Robertson, who make their home in San Francisco; they were residents of Minneapolis for several years.

Miss Helen Fifield, formerly of the South Side high school, is a Minneapolis resident now in San Francisco. Miss Florence Sylvester, a cousin of Mrs. Frank N. Stacy, Mrs. George M. Eddy, and Mrs. D. Draper Dayton and a niece of N. H. Winchell and Mrs. E. D. Brann of this city, is a student at the medical college of the state university, Berkeley, and lives on Washington street, San Francisco. Her mother, Mrs. A. H. Sylvester, has been spending the past two months in Pasadena. Mr. and Mrs. L. B. Davenport and Miss K. Lind, former residents of Minneapolis, also live now in San Francisco.

Miss Rachel Beard is a student at Leland Stanford university. Mr. and Mrs. Frank Hamilton are residents of San Francisco. Mrs. Hamilton was Miss Pauline Kruger of Minneapolis.

Major John Bigelow of Hennepin avenue, whose wife and daughter, Mrs. Bigelow and Mrs. Gardner-Hodson, are visiting their relative, Mrs. Dodge, at her home, 2015 Franklin street, San Francisco.

Dr. George H. Martin, formerly of Minneapolis, and brother of Arthur Martin at the Palace hotel, of the Chamber of Commerce, has resided at the Palace hotel in San Francisco for several years past. Nothing has been heard from him to this time. George B. Douglas of Cedar Rapids, Iowa, who is a brother of Walter D. Douglas, the Minneapolis capitalist, came up with Mrs. Douglas from Santa Barbara to San Francisco preparatory to starting east, and they were to have left San Francisco today.

Mrs. W. H. Chambers, wife of the manager of the Peavey Elevator company, was to leave San Francisco today. With her were J. W. Chambers and wife of Des Moines, Iowa, father and mother of Mr. Chambers. They were at the Hamilton hotel, which is on Market street, just off Ellis, and near the center of destruction. W. H. Chambers left San Francisco a week ago and is in Minneapolis.

**Scores of Messages.**

Scores of messages were filed here for Salt Lake City in hope of intercepting travelers or drawing some encouragement, but nothing was obtainable.

A number of prominent Minneapolis people were in California until recently, some in San Francisco. A week ago there were thirty Minneapolis transients on the hotel registers, but most of them left and some are already home. C. M. Harrington and wife, Dan Raymond, James S. Bell and J. S. Bell, Jr., and wife, General George B. Wilson and S. T. McKnight were there recently, but all are home now. Mrs. B. H. Morgan and daughter are at Los Angeles.

St. Paul people now in San Francisco, and not heard from to this time are Charles Northrop, Mr. and Mrs. George H. Hallowell, Dr. Frank Carpenter and wife and Mrs. Pepper, mother of Mrs. Hallowell and Mrs. Carpenter.

The Misses Susan and Anna Christian of Minneapolis were in San Francisco yesterday en route to Honolulu, and were to have sailed today.

## SEES TIDAL WAVE PERIL

**Rochester, N. Y., April 18.—"Another and even a graver disaster than the earthquake threatens San Francisco. A tidal wave would not be an unlooked-for accompaniment to the present seismic disturbances," said Professor H. L. Fairchild of the University of Rochester today. "Much of San Francisco is only twelve feet above tidewater, and this fact renders it particularly liable to destruction in such an event."**

## HEART OF CITY LIES IN RUINS: LOSS APPALLING

### Horror Grows as Fire Continues the Awful Work of Destruction Begun by the Earthquake.

### Many Dead and Dying in the Debris—Best Business District a Scene of Desolation.

**1,000 MAY BE DEAD.**

**San Francisco, April 18.—(3 p.m.)—At this hour it is estimated that the earthquake and fire have cost 1,000 lives, with twice as many injured. The financial loss already done will foot into the scores of millions.**

**The dead are being carted from the destroyed buildings in dozens in the lodginghouse district. The city is full of injured.**

**Thousands are fleeing from the city. All means of transportation are cut off.**

**San Francisco, April 18.—By earthquake and by fire San Francisco was today the scene of most appalling disaster.**

**Hundreds of lives have been lost and the value of the property destroyed will mount well up into the millions.**

**With the terror still gripping the populace, with bursted gas mains adding to the fierceness of the fire now raging in the debris and with the water supply cut off, it is as yet impossible to give an adequate estimate of the calamity. But it is one which has set at naught all organized agencies for averting or minimizing catastrophes to life and property.**

**Thruout the entire business district of the city there is hardly a building that is not razed or racked almost beyond repair. In the heaps of flaming debris there are known to be hundreds of human bodies.**

**MARKET STREET DEVASTATED.**

**Market street, the pride of the city and its best business thorofare, is the scene of the worst desolation. The sky-scraping Call building, sixteen stories high, is racked and burning; the city hall is a mass of ruins; the great retail stores are in heaps, or are tottering, while the fear of another shock impeis people to keep away from that portion of the city where high buildings line the streets.**

**Thus has San Francisco paid the penalty for forgetting the wisdom of its founders, who lived in fear of the earthquake and who decreed that in their time the city should be one of low, light structures.**

**Heavy as is the loss of life, it would have been still more heartrending had not the disaster come at an early hour when the streets were deserted except by those who had lingered long at their night work or had come down town early to begin the labor of the day.**

**WHOLE CITY TREMBLES.**

**It was at 5:10 a.m. that the first sickening tremor came, speedily followed by the rolling and rocking of the ground.**

**This shock was felt over a large area and was equally severe thruout the city, but the damage was largely confined to that district where business buildings of stone and brick construction lined the streets in heavy masses. The lower part of Market street is on made ground reclaimed from the bay, and it was here that the worst effects of the shock were felt, tho the $7,000,000 city hall, at Sixteenth street, which was razed, was fully a mile and a half from the bay.**

**As huge masses of masonry crashed down into the streets, yawning chasms opened in the ground and chaos came in the twinkling of an eye. Not more than a minute from the first hard shock the aspect of the stricken district was changed. But this was not all. The terror of fire was to be added to the horror of the earthquake. Except along the bay within range of streams from the firetugs there was no protection against the fire, which was soon raging in the ruins, for the watermains had been destroyed by the heaving of the ground. Screams from the wrecked buildings told the awful story of those who had escaped death by the shock only to die prisoned by heavy timbers, while those of their fellowmen who dared to traverse the death-lined streets were powerless to help.**

**Hour by hour the horror grew as the fire worked its way up Market street and racked buildings toppled over or were blown up with dynamite to stay the progress of the flames.**

**DETAILS OF THE DISASTER**

**Bulletins Tell the Story of the Awful Calamity Which Has Come Upon San Francisco.**

San Francisco, April 18.—The postoffice has entirely collapsed.

The fish market at Clay and Merchant streets has collapsed.

Chief of Police Sullivan and his wife have been badly injured.

The Grand operahouse is now aflame and doomed.

The ten-story building at Third and Mission streets, adjoining the Grand operahouse is apparently doomed, as are other big buildings between the theater and St. Patrick's church.

**Gas Works Blown Up.**

The gas works, south of Market street, have been blown up and started another big fire in that section of the city.

A portion of the Mission, several miles from the business section of the city, is in flames.

The fire began at Twenty-second street and is rapidly moving eastward. Should the wind increase, it may sweep the entire southern section of the city.

**Five Killed in Oakland.**

In Oakland five persons were killed by the collapse of the Empire building.

The Gore block, at the junction of Market and Pine streets, is in flames and probably will be a total loss.

Mayor Schmitz, Chief of Police Dinan and General Funston, commander of the department of the Pacific, met this morning and General Funston called all the available troops for service if necessary in the emergency.

The board of supervisors will meet immediately to take measures for relief and protection of the sufferers by disaster.

Chief of Fire Department Sullivan is lying in a very precarious condition.

**Morgue Overfilled.**

Twenty-one bodies have been taken to the morgue, which cannot accommodate any more.

Mayor Schmidt established headquarters at the hall of justice and has appointed a relief committee of fifty prominent citizens.

The military are patrolling the streets, guarding the banks and other establishments. They have received orders to shoot anyone on sight detected in theft.

Fire has started in the sixteen-story Call building on Third street, and is now burning fiercely in the interior of the building, but as yet has not spread beyond the fourth floor. The building is also threatened on the Market street side, only one structure separating it from the flames, which swept everything on the south side of Market street from Fourth almost to Third.

The end of the eleven-story Monadnock building, now nearing completion, has fallen out, and the flames threaten to cause great fire loss. The front of the Monadnock was badly cracked by the earthquake.

**Palace Hotel Still Stands.**

Altho flames are raging on all sides

Continued on 2d Page. 2d Column.

HOME EDITION

# THE MINNEAPOLIS JOURNAL.

GENERALLY FAIR TONIGHT AND TUESDAY.

HOME EDITION

16 PAGES—FIVE O'CLOCK. MONDAY EVENING, OCTOBER 22, 1906. PRICE ONE CENT IN MINNEAPOLIS.



## NATION MAY FORCE PRESIDENT TO RUN

**Leaders Believe Popular Sentiment, by 1908, Will Be Insurmountable.**

**THIRD TERM OBJECTION COINED BY ROOSEVELT**

**Present Term Really Is First to Which He Was Elected.**

By W. W. Jermane.

Washington, Oct. 22.—The liveliest political subject in Washington just now is as to whether President Roosevelt will accept renomination under any circumstances. Three months ago this question was promptly and emphatically answered in the negative by every man who stood in a close relation to the president. Now it is different. It is the firm conviction of three-fourths of the leaders of the republican party that popular sentiment will so shape itself before the national convention of 1908 as to amount to a call to duty upon the president.

Even Mr. Roosevelt's closest political friends admit there are circumstances under which he or any other man would be compelled, as a matter of public duty, to accept. Leading republicans do not take the ''third term'' proposition as seriously as the president does. The president himself conceived and published the idea that his present term is his second term.

**Really His First Term.**

As a matter of fact, strictly speaking, it is his first term to which the people have elected him. But the question of a second or a third term is not figuring prominently as a reason for the president's accepting or declining the nomination. The real question is, can the president, who has created by his own aggressive policies an unusual situation in his party, refuse to carry out the work he has so well begun? It is apparent now that many of the reforms which the president has suggested and some which have already begun, or will have been started before the convention meets in 1908, will not be perfected at the end of his present term of office.

Senator Elkins, who was not in accord with the president in the matter of railroad rate legislation, made the statement a few days ago that the president will be his own successor. He said the people would demand it and the president would be forced to accept as a matter of public duty. Representative Babcock, who was in Washington a few days ago, was asked by a friend what he thought about the next nominee for president.

**Cannot Decline, He Says.**

''I have believed for six months,'' said Mr. Babcock, who is an unusually far-sighted politician, ''that the president will be renominated. He will be renominated under circumstances which will not admit of his declining. His policies have been such that a situation has been created which no other candidate we could name could so well meet. I know it is distasteful to the president to have the leaders of his party speculate on the possibility of his accepting another nomination. I hesitate, therefore, to express an opinion for publication, but the conditions ought to be patent to any one. The people will demand the president's renomination, and how can he decline it? I believe he would be elected by a much more pronounced popular majority than was given to him in 1904.''

This is the expression of the stalwart wing of the republican party in Wisconsin. The other wing goes even a little farther. Senator La Follette says that Roosevelt is the only republican mentioned who can be elected in 1908.

**Root, Taft and Shaw Inactive.**

It is significant that men like Root, Taft, and even Shaw, who have been mentioned as presidential candidates, have taken no steps to build an organization. Secretary Shaw has recently given his friends an impression that his presidential candidacy is out of commission. Mr. Shaw has said privately to friends that he believed popular sentiment would compel the president to accept renomination.

It will be remembered that Uncle Joe Cannon, who is very close to the president, promptly arrested a movement begun in his own behalf and declared from the platform in the Maine campaign ''that stranger things might happen than the re-election of President Roosevelt.''

A situation may be presented in the fall elections soon to occur that will make the president's nomination imperative. If the election in New York should indicate that the radical forces of society are likely to endanger the election of a republican president in 1908 the republicans would turn to President Roosevelt as one who would be certain of re-election. Every candidate for office on a republican ticket would be anxious to have at the head of the national ticket in 1908 a leader who could insure victory. This element alone would have much to do with shaping sentiment in the next national convention.

**To Check Hearst Peril.**

If Hearst should be elected governor of New York he would be a formidable candidate for the democratic nomination for president. He would probably be able to nominate himself just as he did in New York. He would at once become a menace to the business interests.

Leading republicans here do not believe that they could afford to take any risks by nominating for president a candidate against whom any charge of corporate affiliation or interest could be brought. They would be looking for a vote-getter. One of the president's closest friends said today that he could imagine one condition under which the president would yield to the unanimous call of his party and that would be to save the country from Hearstism. ''It would be the delight of Mr. Roosevelt's life to trim Hearst,'' said he.

While the national convention is nearly two years away the chances are that popular sentiment will be sufficiently crystallized one year from now to indicate beyond a doubt just who the candidate of each political party will be. Political events move rapidly these days and sentiment is quick to anticipate political conventions.

**More Reforms Due.**

In the next session of congress the president will recommend many reforms. He will outline his inheritance

Continued on 2d Page, 6th Column.

## EDISON TRIUMPHS; FINDS RARE POWER

***'Wizzard' Declares He Has Invented Long-Sought Storage Battery.***

***Horses Will Be Driven into Obscurity by Discovery, He Says.***

Journal Special Service.

New York, Oct. 22.—Thomas A. Edison has accomplished a surprise for the world. He has worked out successfully the problem of cheap power. He promises to put on the market within six months a new storage bettery which will enable every man to travel in his own private carriage at about the cost of carfare. Without danger, without breakdowns, without cost, almost, a carriage, once supplied with the new power for $200, will travel without repairs for fifteen years for 100,000 miles if necessary, says ''the wizard.''

Mr. Edison reiterates the declaration that he has invented a storage battery which will solve the problem of congested traffic in the big cities of the world as soon as he can manufacture enough of the batteries. He is erecting two large factory buildings, now nearly completed, and is installing in them new machinery especially for the manufacture of the motor battery.

**Horse to Be a Curiosity.**

''In fifteen years from now the horse will be a curiosity; we shall be paying 50 cents to look at him in sideshows,'' said Mr. Edison to an interviewer.

''Last year you were sure that you had solved this problem?'' he was reminded.

''Yes, last year I was sure,'' replied Mr. Edison, ''but now I am dead sure. There is a difference between the two. It's one thing, for instance, to be sure and another thing to be —Wall street sure.

''I never believed that nature, so prolific of resources, could provide only lead as material ingredient of the battery,'' said Mr. Edison. ''I have always found her ready for any emergency, and based on this confidence that she has never betrayed, I communed diligently with her. One day I discovered that nickel rust was as good as lead. Then I thought I had accomplished the task.''

**Cobalt a Lucky Find.**

But he hadn't, to the satisfaction of his commercial instinct. The question of the weight of the battery was most important, as was that of its durability.

Nickel rust failed, other things failed, everything the ingenious Edison, with his trained, scientific mind could conceive, failed.

''Then I tried cobalt,'' he said, and punctuated the statement with a broad smile.

''And it worked?''

''It certainly did, but cobalt, being one of the rare metals, the problem was not solved. I scoured the country to find cobalt and discovered lots of it in Canada, in Wisconsin, in Oregon and in Kentucky. Then I knew that I was all right.''

### MESSAGES 5 YEARS ON WAY

**Buoys Contain Notes from the Baldwin-Zeigler Expedition.**

Buffalo, Oct. 22.—Two buoy messages, set adrift near Franz Josefland by the Baldwin-Zeigler polar expedition in1901 have been found and forwarded to Evlyn B. Baldwin, the founder of the expedition, who is now in this city. The messages were picked up on July 10, 1906, on Moffen island by Captain Strenerson of the whaler Gottfreid.

The messages are typewritten on film paper and show the effects of their journey in the Arctic sea. The messages were an appeal for a supply of coal, the lack of which forced the expedition to turn back.

### OIL KING'S LIPS SEALED

**Rockefeller Refuses to Discuss Verdict Against Standard Oil.**

Journal Special Service.

Cleveland, Oct. 22.—John D. Rockefeller said yesterday that his present unexpected return to his Forest Hill home in Cleveland was in no way influenced by the recent legal troubles of the Standard Oil company at Findlay.

When asked what view he took of the verdict and what he thought its future results would be, Rockefeller replied:

''Of course I have my own opinion regarding that verdict and I feel confident that my opinion on that subject coincides with that of a great many people, but I don't care to express my views on the matter publicly as I am sure it would not be proper for me to criticize the court.''

### FAILURES FOLLOW SLUMP

**Two New York Firms Go Down when Stocks Break.**

New York, Oct. 22.—The suspension of P. T. White, a heavy trader, was announced on the Consolidated Stock exchange today. Under the rules, Mr. White will have twenty-four hours to fulfill his contracts.

The failure of J. W. Henning, an operator on the New York Stock exchange, was announced on the floor of the exchange today.

Nearly all of Mr. Henning's business was confined to New York city interests, and it is not believed that the failure will affect any large out-of-town accounts. The failure is believed to have resulted from overtrading in the heavy slump in the market late last week.

### UNSEEN ASSASSIN KILLS 2

**Fires Thru Window, Slays Widow—Posse Chases Suspect.**

Cole Camp, Mo., Oct. 22.—While Mrs. Alice Winemiller, a widow, was sitting with her five children in their home near here last night, shots were fired thru a window and Mrs. Winemiller was instantly killed. Her son, aged 14, was badly wounded.

Felix Crawford, a neighbor who heard the firing and hurried to the scene, was shot and died two hours later. Crawford's son-in-law, J. A. Long, is charged with having done the shooting, using a shotgun. A posse headed by the sheriff is scouring the Pettis county hills searching for Long.

### HAS FAMED BATTERY

THOMAS A. EDISON,
Who Announces that He Has Invented a Cheap Storage Battery that Promises the Revolution in Transportation He Hoped to Make Possible.

## BUTTE CHILDREN BECOME BANDITS

**Two Take Watch and Money from a Lad of 13 at Point of a Revolver.**

Special to The Journal.

Butte, Mont., Oct. 22.—Apparently, the ''Amalgamated Order of Holdups,'' which has been doing a landoffice business in Butte and vicinity for several months, has reduced the age limit and taken into its ranks a few children.

At any rate, Arthur Hornberg, the 13-year-old son of M. A. P. Hornberg, a well-known business man, was held up last night by a pair of youthful bandits who had a revolver almost as big as they were.

The young desperadoes conducted things in a decidedly workmanlike manner, not even forgetting to tell young Hornberg to ''skidoo'' after they had rifled his pockets.

Hornberg says he was returning to his home about 8:30 when two boys on the other side of the street called upon him to come over to them.

''I did not do it at first,'' said young Hornberg, ''and one of them pulled out a big, blue-looking gun and pointed it at me. It was a real pistol all right. Neither of them wore masks, but I did not know either of them. After they held me up and took my watch and money, a girl living near by said she heard them quarreling over a division of the spoils and also saw their revolver.''

### RICH ORE IN GREENLAND

**Expedition Reports Discovery of Vast Deposits of Copper.**

Journal Special Service.

Stockholm, Oct. 22.—The last expedition dispatched by M. Bernburg, Copehagen merchant, to make mineralogical researches in Greenland has just returned. It reports the discovery of vast deposits of copper ore at Alanjarmanak, which it is believed may prove the richest and best in the world.

## WHOLE HEMISPHERE SWEPT BY STORMS

**Worst Blizzard Since 1892 Rages in the Rocky Mountain Region.**

**Ruin in Salvador and Honduras After Hurricane—Snow in Minnesota.**

ALL RECORDS BROKEN.

Washington, Oct. 22.—Practically the entire western hemisphere has been swept by storms of more or less severity within the last few days, the blizzard in the Rocky mountain region completing a record that has not been equaled in the memory of the oldest inhabitants.

Where there have not been destructive winds rain has fallen, giving the whole nation a taste of inconvenience.

Denver, Oct. 22.—The storm thruout the Rocky mountain region which began here with rain, changing to snow Friday, subsided this morning. It is said to have been the worst snowstorm in this vicinity since 1892. There was more than a foot of snow on the level, and the melted snow measured one and eight-tenths inches. The temperature generally fell to 20 degrees.

Locally but little damage was done, but sheepmen in Wyoming, Colorado and New Mexico, it is believed, will suffer heavy losses, as they were unprepared for such severe weather.

There are hundreds of tons of sugar beets and thousands of barrels of apples still in the open in northern Colorado, and should the cold continue the damage will be great. Telegraphic service thruout the west is badly hampered and trains indefinitely late.

**Snow Reaches Kansas.**

Ellis, Kan., Oct. 22.— Colorado's snowstorm is passing east, and prevailed today in western Kansas. Passengers reaching here this morning on belated east-bound trains report a heavy snowstorm in progress between Ellis and Denver some points assuming the proportions of a blizzard with from four inches to one foot of snow on the ground. The temperature is moderate, however.

**Storm Smites Ogden.**

Ogden, Utah, Oct. 22.—One man was killed and $100,000 in property was destroyed by a heavy wind storm that swept over this section last night and today. William Gibbs was struck by a flying plank and killed.

The Catholic church was badly damaged and other large buildings suffered.

Trains between Ogden and Salt Lake have been stalled since early last night.

**Fire as Storm Rages.**

Salt Lake City, Utah, Oct. 22.—For the last thirty-two hours this city and vicinity has been swept by a windstorm of unparalleled severity. In addition to three serious accidents to persons, property over a wide area has been devastated, a fire fanned by a high wind has destroyed the plant of the Utah Packing company, causing a loss of about $250,000.

Ruined buildings, fallen chimneys, broken windows, loosened signs and toppled trees thruout this and adjoining towns are the most common souvenirs of the storm and form, in the aggregate, an immense source of loss.

**Two Are Injured.**

The wind attained a maximum velocity of fifty-two miles an hour at 9 o'clock Saturday night and 4 and 6 o'clock Sunday morning. For hours afterward it maintained an average speed of thirty-eight miles.

Captain W. G. Cahoon and Driver

Continued on 2d Page, 4th Column.

### FROM SENATE TO JAIL

J. R. BURTON,
Former United States Senator, Who Enters Jail Today to Serve a Term of Six Month for Wrongful Conduct While a Senator.

## JAIL DOORS OPEN TO ADMIT BURTON

**Former United States Senator Surrenders and Will Serve Six Months' Term.**

St. Louis, Oct. 22.—Former United States Senator J. R. Burton of Kansas, accompanied by his wife and niece, arrived this morning from his home at Abilene and surrendered, preparatory to serving his sentence of six mouths in the Ironton, Mo., jail.

Apparently Mr. Burton has changed little since he was tried and convicted a year ago in the federal court here of having accepted $2,500 for services rendered the Rialto Grain & Security company of St. Louis before the post-office department at Washington in a fraud order proceeding.

As he stepped from the train this morning he said:

''I am feeling very well, exceedingly well, under the circumstances. Perhaps the trees, the bluffs and nature generally look sweeter to me this morning than they shall for some time, but I don't let myself think about that. I expect to go to Ironton today and begin the life that is laid out for me.''

**Proud of Her Husband.**

After taking breakfast at the Union station, the former senator went to the offices of his attorney, F. W. Lehmann, and preparations were begun for the official surrender to the United States marshal.

Mrs. Burton maintained her composure remarkably well. ''I never was more proud of my husband than at this moment when he is on his way to jail,'' she declared at the Union station. ''I know who our friends are and I intend to be friendly to them, but I shall reserve the right to say who shall be my friends.''

**THREE BOXCAR THIEVES SENTENCED.**

Special to The Journal.

Red Wing, Minn., Oct. 22.—Frank Kelly, Frank Rush and Ed Jennison, boxcar burglars, were sentenced to one year in state's prison by Judge Williston today.

## FIVE BANDITS HOLD CITIZENS AT BAY

***Over 300 Shots Fired in Battle with Bank Cracksmen at Sawyer, N. D.***

***Stray Bullet Strikes a Farmer—Others Have Narrow Escapes.***

***Bank's Loss Is $4,500—A Posse Hurriedly Organized for Pursuit.***

Special to The Journal.

Minot, N. D., Oct. 22.—After keeping at bay a crowd of citizens for more than an hour and firing over three hundred shots, five masked bandits secured $4,500 from the Sawyer State bank at Sawyer, twenty miles southeast of Minot, at 1 o'clock this morning. They also took several hundred dollars' worth of clothing, revolvers and ammunition from Sigerstrom's general store and Brackett's hardware store.

**Farmer Wounded.**

A farmer who was driving to town was hit in the head with a bullet, but will probably recover. His wagon box was filled with bullet holes and several citizens had narrow escapes.

The burglars began work about 1 o'clock and several citizens were awakened by the first explosion. On arriving at the bank they were met with a fusilade of bullets coming from several directions.

**Attack Well Organized.**

More citizens gathered, but owing to lack of organization they were repulsed. The burglars had a man at each corner of the bank building, while a fifth man worked at the safe. Nine explosions were required to open the safe.

The burglars rode out of town on horseback, firing in all directions as they went. Several shots were fired by the citizens, but none took effect. A posse was quickly organized and is now in pursuit of the bandits.

**Sheriff Joins the Chase.**

The authorities at Sawyer got a good view of the robbers and expect to apprehend them in a short time. Sheriff John J. Lee of Minot has started out with a crew to assist in the search.

## REBATE HUNTERS IN SESSION HERE

**Federal Grand Jury Met Today with Definite Work Laid Out.**

Rigid investigation on infractions of the anti-rebate clauses of the new railroad law began at 2 p.m. today before a specially called grand jury in the federal building. After a charge by Judge William Lochren of the United States court the jury was locked into its room with Bailiff Sherman S. Smith at the door. Witnesses who had been summoned for today were admitted one by one as the investigation proceeded under direction of C. C. Houpt, United States district attorney. The investigation will last a week.

It has been stated almost authoritatively that the district attorney knows pretty well what he has to do and witnesses and jurymen will have definite work from the start. On the other hand an examination of the list of witnesses goes to show that the general subject of rebates is to be burrowed into, rather than any specific violations of the law. This is shown from the fact that each railroad running into the twin cities will furnish its quota of witnesses. In some instances they are from the executive circles and at other times from the clerical ranks.

**Three Jurors Late.**

Proceedings were postponed several hours today by the non-arrival of three jurors. These men had been delayed by train connections and Judge Lochren said that inasmuch as the number present was so near the minimum limit he would postpone his charge until 2 o'clock.

F. A. Durfee of Reading, W. E. Beerse of Hastings and Edwin Whiting of Bolton were the delinquents. The jury appears to be above the average of the federal panel and it is apparent from a physiognomological study that a fair consideration of the evidence to be offered by the government may be expected.

Proceedings are under the direct charge of C. C. Houpt, the district attorney. It is prophesied that, to avoid such failures as were exemplified in the last interstate commerce case called here will be avoided in this district by leaving the prosecution of the future rate investigations in the hands of Mr. Houpt. Paul A. Ewart, assistant district attorney, will aid Mr. Houpt, who will be somewhat handicapped by the opening of the Mankato term of court with five jury cases and the consequent absence of the first assistant, Mark Dickey. Extra assistance will be given, however, by H. B. Duncan of Chicago, special agent of the department of justice.

One of the principal witnesses for the government will be S. H. Smith of Washington, rate clerk for the interstate commerce commission. Among the other witnesses reported as summoned are:

S. C. Stickney, general manager of the Great Western road at St. Paul.

J. Martin, Minneapolis grain man.

James De Veau, Minneapolis grain man.

L. A. Robinson, controller of the Omaha at St. Paul.

Joseph Gaskell, secretary and assistant treasurer of the St. Louis road.

E. O. Eckhart, local freight agent of the St. Louis.

S. G. Palmer, Minneapolis fruit merchant.

John M. McCaulay, chief clerk claims department of the St. Louis road at Minneapolis.

F. E. Draper, auditor of the Great Northern at St. Paul.

H. A. Kimball, assistant general freight agent of the Great Northern at St. Paul.

S. W. Patton, clerk St. Louis road at Minneapolis.

E. B. Ober, general freight agent of the Omaha road at St. Paul.

L. T. Jamme, secretary of the Chamber of Commerce at Minneapolis.

George T. Huey, assistant general freight agent of the Wisconsin Central at Minneapolis.

John T. Conley, assistant general freight agent of the Milwaukee road at Minneapolis.

Paul B. Seevers, general claim agent of the St. Louis road at Minneapolis.

Two of the Minneapolis members of the grand jury are members of the Minneapolis Real Estate board, and are not supposed to have any railroad experience. They are R. D. Cone of R. D. Cone & Co., and James B. Sutherland, treasurer of the David C. Bell Investment company.

**State Well Represented.**

The complete grand jury list is as follows:

Walter Peet, Wolverton; John Falkner, Pine City; Robert D. Cone, 3116 First avenue S, Minneapolis; G. E. McKay, Redwood Falls; Christ Anderson, Little Sauk; Bert M. Wheeler, Duluth; S. Running, Alexandria; F. A. Durfee, Reading; O. N. Lundberg, Duluth; James Hurley, Pine City; William Laabs, Le Sueur; W. C. Davis, Cleveland; E. E. Price, Milaca; Joseph P. Davis, Pine City; W. E. Beerse, Hastings; F. W. Winters, Wayzata; Edwin Whiting, Bolton; Martin McDonough, 460 St. Peter street, St. Paul; George H. Deans, Forreston; Charles Bruer, Morris; George W. Hall, 2701 Fremont avenue N, Minneapolis; James B. Sutherland, 1819 Dupont avenue S, Minneapolis; John Tesch, Long Prairie.

### KING OPENS PARLIAMENT

**Haakon Speaks Hopefully of Future of Norway.**

Christiania, Oct. 22.—The newly elected parliament was opened today by King Haakon in the presence of Queen Maud and the diplomatic corps. The king, who read his speech from the throne, said he rejoiced at the ''great good will shown by foreign countries towards our fatherland since the establishment of its independence,'' and spoke hopefully of Norway's future prospects. He said that trade was improving, making reductions in taxation in the next budget, and congratulated the country on the fact that the budget of 1907-1908 showed a surplus.

### MANIACS SLEEP ON FLOOR

**Governor Magoon Finds Deplorable Conditions in Cuban Asylum.**

Havana, Oct. 22.—Governor Magoon, as a result of the deplorable condition of things which he has discovered at the national asylum for insane, has ordered the immediate repair of the old and the erection of new buildings.

The governor found that while hundreds of patients were sleeping on the floor, the management saved $5,000 from the food account, which Mr. Magoon has ordered applied to the immediate purchase of bedding and clothing.

Tho the Cuban congress appropriated a sum of money for the improvement of the condition of the inmates of the asylum, for some unknown reason the money was not expended. The governor ordered an investigation.

### FIND INSURANCE TOO HIGH

**Indiana Investigators Declare Premiums Are in Excess of Needs.**

Indianapolis, Ind., Oct. 22.—A special committee appointed by the governor, which has been investigating the office of the auditor of state for a year with special reference to mutual and stock life insurance companies, today submitted its report to Governor Hanley. The general conclusions of the committee are that the cost of life insurance to the public is too high. The present maximum premiums for insurance are so much in excess of needs as to permit of extravagant management of companies, theft of their funds, division of profits and other great abuses without rendering the companies insolvent.

### WIFE SLAYER SURRENDERS

**Arkansas Man Cheats Mob by Giving Up to Police.**

Arkansas City, Kan., Oct. 22.—John C. Moore, the policeman who yesterday shot and killed his wife on the street as she was returning from church and who escaped with a posse in pursuit, bent upon lynching him, surrendered today to a justice of the peace at the latter's home on the outskirts of the city, on the promise of protection. He was taken secretly to Wichita today and placed in jail there for safe keeping.

### SHIP SINKS; 180 PERISH

**Russian Coasting Vessel Strikes Floating Mine and Founders.**

London, Oct. 22.—A dispatch received here from Vladivostok by Lloyd's agency says the Russian wooden coasting steamer Warjagin struck a floating mine and foundered on Oct. 20. Some of her passengers and crew were saved, but 180 persons were drowned.

Another message received by a news agency says two hundred passengers perished on board the Warjagin, only one being saved.

### BALLOONS AND AUTOS RACE

**Airships Sail from Pittsfield, Pursued by Three Cars.**

Pittsfield, Mass., Oct. 22.—Two balloons, the Centaur and Eagle, made an ascension here today to participate in the race originally planned for Saturday last, but postponed on account of unfavorable weather. Three automobiles also started in the pursuit race with the airships.

The balloons headed northwest. The sky was overcast.

### U. S. S. MINNESOTA IS READY

**Powerful New Battleship May Get Standardization Trial Tomorrow.**

Rockland, Me., Oct. 22.—The new battleship Minnesota arrived today from Newport News. She will be given a standardization trial tomorrow or Wednesday over the Owls Head course.

A LONG-PROMISED RIDE.
The Man Beneath—It will be ready to go very soon now.

# The Minneapolis Evening Tribune

VOL. XLI., NO. 131. | MINNEAPOLIS, MINNESOTA, FRIDAY, OCTOBER 18, 1907. | FIVE O'CLOCK EDITION PRICE ONE CENT

## SOLVENT

### Clearing House Reports the Mercantile Bank in Satisfactory Condition.

### HEADS OF SEVERAL HOUSES CONFER

Rumor That Heinze Institution Has $500,000 Unnegotiable Securities.

### PRICES ON STOCK MARKET GO DOWN

General Depression Down List—Copper Sold in Large Blocks.

NEW YORK, Oct. 18.—Precipitate declines to the lowest prices of the year in the stock market followed a meeting of the clearing house committee today, sentiment on the stock market being disturbed by rumors as to the proceedings of the committee.

Statements were made by several of those who participated in the conference to the effect that except for possible changes in the personnel of the management of other banks than the Mercantile National, the situation was satisfactory.

IN GOOD CONDITION.

All of those present at the clearing house agreed, however, that the examination of the affairs of the Mercantile National bank had shown that institution to be absolutely solvent with its capital stock unimpaired.

It was said also that rumors as to other banks were unfounded, that today's meeting of the Clearing House had shown that all of New York City's institutions were fully able to meet their obligations and that except for the possible changes in the officers and boards of directors of one or two other institutions the situation was satisfactory.

OPENED BETTER.

The stock market opened with a better tone than had been expected and held rather well until after the Clearing House meeting, when rumors as to the discussion of that meeting became a disturbing factor.

Under this influence prices began to drop rapidly and it seemed that there was little or no buying power in the market.

At first the metal stocks suffered more sharply, but a little later the railroads, especially Union Pacific, Reading and St. Paul fell away on heavy selling to the lowest prices of the year. In some instances the quotations for stocks were the lowest since 1893.

The solvency of the Mercantile National bank, as reported by President Nash of the Corn Exchange bank last night, was reaffirmed.

From outside sources, however, it is learned that about three-fourths of the [illegible]

SITUATION UNDER CONTROL.

[illegible]

IN STOCK MARKET.

[illegible]

### OLD BANKING HOUSE IN TEXAS GOES TO WALL

HOUSTON, Texas, Oct. 18.—The private bank of T. W. House, made a general assignment after banking hours yesterday [illegible]

Another Failure in Hamburg.

[illegible]

Boilermakers Enjoined.

[illegible]

AMBASSADOR TOWER DESIRES TO RETIRE

BERLIN, Oct. 18.—The American ambassador, Mr. Tower, has written President Roosevelt asking that he be permitted to retire from the diplomatic service next spring. [illegible]

## BOY KILLS SELF ON CHURCH PLATFORM

### SWEETHEART IN AUDIENCE AT TIME OF ACT.

Says "Good-bye, Eva," Then Blows Out His Brains.

SENSATIONAL ENDING TO EVANGELIST MEETING AT SEATTLE—YOUTH WAS ENGAGED.

SEATTLE, Wash., Oct. 18.—With the words "Good-by, Eva," Edward Neil Kelly, a young workman, drew a revolver and fired a bullet through his head on the platform of the Apostolic Faith church here last night. The girl he referred to was sitting in the audience within 10 feet of the young man when he fired the fatal shot.

Kelly died at the hospital half an hour later.

Kelly, who was 19 years old, met Eva Nesterson, a 15-year-old school girl, at evangelist meetings held here in the early part of September and a week ago they became engaged. They were to be married on Thanksgiving day.

As one of the speakers at the church finished testifying "in foreign tongues," which is part of the belief of this creed, Kelly arose with the words:

"It is my turn next." He then started singing, "The fire of heavenly love is burning in my soul."

As the last words were finished he drew a gun, turned toward the girl, said "good-by" and fired the fatal shot.

## STRIKE TIES UP TUGS

### COASTWISE STEAMERS LAY IDLE IN THE EAST.

Engineers on Thirty Boats Demand Helpers—Controversy May Involve All Carriers on Middle Atlantic Seaboard.

NEW YORK, Oct. 18.—Thirty large coastwise tugs are idle in the waters of New York city, Baltimore, Philadelphia and Boston because the two engineers on each boat refuse to work unless a third engineer is employed to help them. [illegible]

## DRAINAGE THEME AT BIG MEETING

### BALTIMORE GATHERING OF NATIONAL INTEREST.

Several Cabinet Officials to Speak Before Convention.

SENATOR CLAPP, CONG. STEENERSON AND CAPT. BARNARD TO REPRESENT MINNESOTA.

[illegible]

The interest shown by the interior and agricultural departments indicates that the bill for federal drainage appropriations will have liberal support in congress this winter.

The drainage convention will be held at a date shortly before the opening of congress and within an hour's ride of Washington, and it is expected that there will be a strong representation on hand from among members of congress who are interested in the drainage bill.

## FOUR ARE KILLED IN STREET CAR CRASH

### Head-On Collision Between Two Chattanooga Trolleys—Ten Seriously Hurt—Both Motormen Are Dead—Confusion of Signals Cause of Tragedy.

CHATTANOOGA, Tenn., Oct. 18.—Four persons are dead, 10 are in the hospital and more than a score were more or less injured in a headon collision of two Sherman Heights street cars on Arizona avenue, near the city limits, today.

Confusion of signals is said to have been the cause of the accident. Both cars were running at a rapid rate into a dip in the track when the crash came.

The incoming car was heavily loaded with persons on their way to work in the city, and most of those killed and injured were on this car.

Both motormen were killed instantly.

The dead:

Motorman Ed Parker.

Motorman Will Pennington.

Will E. Smith, a meat dealer.

—— Cleveland, negro.

Fatally injured:

J. K. Brice, Payne, Mich., both legs mashed off and amputated. Will probably die.

The collision occurred during a heavy fog.

## PRISONER KILLS SELF

### Yukon Official, Charged With $40,000 Theft From Mails, Takes Poison.

VANCOUVER, B. C., Oct. 18.—George Kincaid, head foreman of the public works department in Yukon territory, [illegible]

Porto Rico Wants Guard.

[illegible]

## ROOSEVELT KILLS BEAR

### After Long Chase President Lands Big Bruin in Thicket.

### ANIMAL IS OF THE BLACK VARIETY

Success Comes After a Day of Hard Work on the Trails.

### NEW DOGS GREAT HELP IN SEARCH

Party Now Plans to Make a Brilliant Finish of Hunt.

NEW ORLEANS, La., Oct. 18.—News of the killing of a big black bear by President Roosevelt in the canebrakes near Bear Lake, La., reached New Orleans today in a telegram to John M. Parker, one of the gentlemen who invited the president to hunt in the state and who himself was a member of the hunting party until business required his returning to New Orleans several days ago.

The telegram to Mr. Parker was signed by Leo Shield, another member of the party, and read as follows:

"President Roosevelt killed a great, big bear. Went into thicket after him."

No particulars were stated in the telegram, but Mr. Parker surmised that the president got his bear late yesterday. Two days ago several trails were struck, but only once did the dogs come upon the bears and then it became necessary for a negro hunter in the party to kill the bear immediately in order to save the dogs.

It was announced yesterday that the president had started out early, and that, with fresh and better dogs, trails had been struck in the morning and were being followed in a lively manner.

STAMBOUL, La., Oct. 18.—The president killed a bear late yesterday afternoon. Few details of the president's bear killing are known except that it took place late yesterday afternoon after he and other hunters with him had followed the dogs in the chase through the jungles for four hours.

A BRILLIANT FINISH.

The beast was a female of the black variety and was beyond the average size. The fact that she was secured at all is attributed to the staying qualities of the new dogs.

The news was brought in by a courier, who arrived from Bear Lake this morning.

The exploit has given heart to the camp and the hunters are now out again with renewed vigor in the hope of making a brilliant finish.

## Balloon and Aeronaut Which Won Prize Trophy

Who guided balloon on the record-breaking trip.

ARMY BALLOON No. 10, WHICH WON FAMOUS CUP.

## THREE KILLED IN PHILADELPHIA RIOT

PHILADELPHIA, Oct. 18.—A fight between two Chinese in Chinatown this afternoon developed into a riot, the rival Tong societies taking sides.

Pistols and knives were freely used in the crowded quarters and it is reported that three of the participants were killed.

The police reserves from the tenderloin districts were hastily summoned and had great difficulty in quieting the crowds.

### MORE COAL TRUST INDICTMENTS

Forty-five Additional Defendants Named in Government's Suit

PHILADELPHIA, Pa., Oct. 18.—In an amended bill filed by the attorneys for the government in the equity proceedings against the alleged anthracite coal trust, 45 additional defendants are named.

All the new defendants were mentioned in the answers filed by the original defendants and are named in the amended bill on the ground that they were connected with the previously named coal roads and mining companies by certain financial transactions and coal purchase contracts.

## ARMY BALLOON IS STILL UP IN AIR

### CHANDLER AND McCOY MAY BREAK RECORD.

Equal Time of Lieut. Lahm, Made in Winning Bennett Cup.

DROP MESSAGE WHILE TRAVELING OVER HILLSBORO, OHIO STARTED 4:10 P. M. THURSDAY

YANKEES WIN CUP.

**ST. LOUIS, Oct. 18.—It was announced at the Aero club of St. Louis that Aeronauts McCoy and Chandler had won the Lahm cup for long-distance flight, having, when they passed over Gallipolis, Ohio, beaten the record of 402 miles established by Lieut. Lahm last year as the international contest record.**

CHICAGO, Oct. 18.—The following dispatch was received this morning by the Associated Press:

Leesburg, O., Oct. 18.—This message is dropped from the balloon signal corps, No. 10, at 6 o'clock a. m., Oct. 18, over Hillsboro, traveling fast southeast. —Chandler and McCoy.

Hillsboro and Leesburg are in the same county in Ohio and the Chandler-McCoy balloon left St. Louis at 4:10 yesterday afternoon.

ST. LOUIS, Mo., Oct. 18.—The message dropped from the United States signal corps balloon, No. 10, by Aeronauts James McCoy and Capt. Charles DeF. Chandler and telegraphed to the Associated Press at Chicago from Leesburg, O., by the finder, shows that the balloon in 13 hours and 50 minutes covered a distance measuring 350 miles on a straight line.

LIEUT. LAHM'S RECORD.

The international record established by Lieut. Lahm last year in Europe was 402 miles on a straight line, winning for him the James Gordon Bennett cup. [illegible]

PASSES OVER JACKSON, OHIO.

[illegible]

HAWLEY BACK TO EARTH.

[illegible]

## DANISH BOAT IS WRECKED; 20 DROWN

### Steamer, Engaged in Trading Between Denmark and England, Strikes Rock Off Castle Point, Near Scotland—Life Boat Has a Narrow Escape.

LONDON, Oct. 18.—The Danish steamer, Alfred Erlandsen, has been wrecked on the rocks off Castle Point, near Stabb's Head, Scotland. She went ashore during a gale last night and twenty of her crew were drowned. [illegible]

### SUPPORTS SWEDISH CHALLENGE.

Prince Gustavus Aids in Movement to Build Yacht Challenger.

[illegible]

## GIVE UP

### Downturn in Wheat Continues and Bulls Seem to Have Surrendered.

### GRAIN ON SALE IN LARGE CHUNKS

Nobody Has the Courage to Stand Under Avalanche of Selling Orders.

### WORLD MARKETS ALL DROP LOWER

European Centers as Demoralized During Day as Domestic Trading Points.

The downturn in wheat continued today, and from all indications the bulls have surrendered to the bears. Early there was a show of resistance to the onslaught, but wheat was for sale in large chunks and nobody felt emboldened to stand under the avalanche of selling orders that came into the pit in a steadily increasing volume.

INTERNATIONAL MARKETS LOW.

The international markets were all lower, with European centers as demoralized as the domestic trading points. A sharp break of a cent in the local market at the opening and a full recovery inside of 10 minutes raised the hopes of the bulls that the worst was over. It was as elusive as the rainbow, however, and on the second charge of the bear brigade prices melted away as fast as the ticker could record the trades. [illegible]

WHO CARRIED ON WAR?

[illegible]

Chicago Wheat Again Drops.

[illegible]

### REACTION HARMLESS SAYS D. R. FORGAN

INTERESTING STATEMENT RELATIVE TO FINANCIAL SITUATION.

Present Conditions No Parallel—Country Banks Great Relief.

MONEY TO SUPPORT COUNTRY—DEPRESSION NOT TO BE COMPARED WITH THAT OF 1893.

[illegible]

HAS NO PARALLEL.

[illegible]

FELT MORE CLEARLY.

[illegible]

## Remarkable Career of Man Now at Head of Gotham Traction System

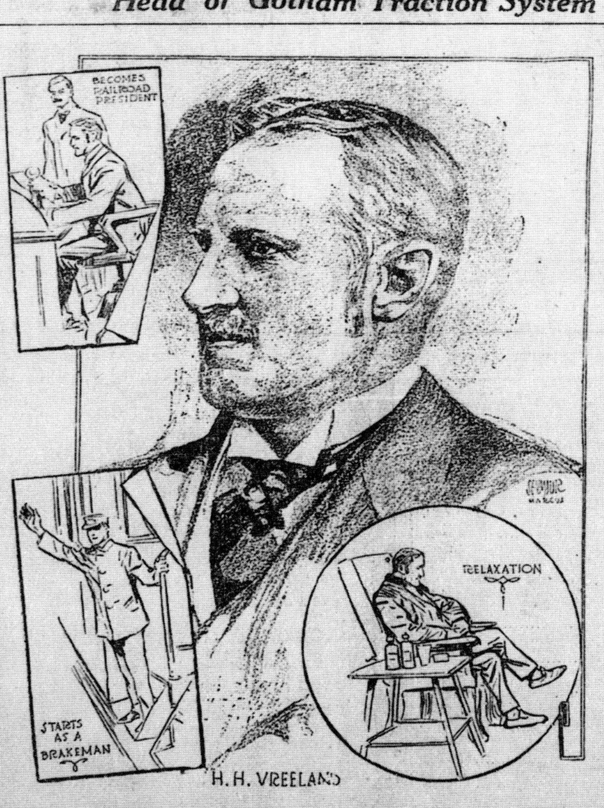


NEW YORK, Oct. 18.—(Special.)—In the topsy turvy tumbling of affairs brought up on the public service commission's investigation of the interborough-Metropolitan, there is no phase of more human interest than the effect it has had upon the life story of H. H. Vreeland. [illegible]

# The Minneapolis Sunday Tribune

VOL. XLII, NO. 89. MINNEAPOLIS, MINNESOTA, SUNDAY, SEPTEMBER 6, 1908. PRICE FIVE CENTS

# 10,000 MADE HOMELESS BY FOREST FIRES NORTHERN MINNESOTA TOWNS IN ASHES

## WORLD'S AUTO MILE RECORD IS LOWERED BY DePALMA

### Terrific Speed Is Reached in Race

Youthful Driver Sends Car Over Circular Track in 51 Seconds.

Defeats Christie, Former High Man, in Sensational Run.

Last Day of State Fair Affords Exciting Sport for Visitors.

Ralph De Palma in his giant-powered Fiat cyclone, chopped a full second off the world's automobile record for one mile on a circular tract at the Minnesota State Fair yesterday. He made the mile in 51 seconds flat, in the most sensational event of the entire fair week.

De Palma's thrilling battle with Father Time was by far the biggest feature of the afternoon's program of automobile events and when it was announced that De Palma had broken Walter Christie's world's record of 52 seconds, there occurred a scene not unlike the pandemonium 30,000 lunatics would have created had they been herded together in one inclosure. The tremendous crowd went wild.

FAILED TWICE.

Walter Christie, in his famous "front drive" car of 120 horse power, took a couple of turns at the record, first going against his own record of 52 seconds for the mile and later making another try after De Palma's sensational figures.

Neither time was Christie able to accomplish his desire. Disheartened after his first attempt, which preceded De Palma's wonderful mile, yet he announced that he would make another attempt.

Christie's first mile was reeled off in 52¼ seconds and on his next trial he made 52¼ seconds. His efforts were received with much enthusiasm. The crowd admired the man's gameness and applauded his zeal, but was for De Palma every minute after the speed merchants had whirled several fast miles for practice. De Palma seemed to handle his car with more skill than Christie.

LOOKED FOR "THRILLER."

Thrilling scenes were predicted by knowing ones in the match race between De Palma and Christie. It was run off after the time trials and was for the best two out of three heats, each heat three miles. Whispers were spread about that the men were out for blood and each intended to drive his car to the very limit; that the racers could neither one afford to lose, and that the contest was bound to be the most exciting match ever held in the Twin Cities.

De Palma won the first two heats handily. In the second heat it seemed as if he might have run away from Christie but deliberately slowed up and allowed the defeated racer to draw nearer. The time for the first heat was 3:14, and for the second 3:01 4-5.

WAS INSPIRING SIGHT.

The exhibition of the great racing machines fairly flying around the track was a sight to set one's blood a-tingling. The Christie car spouted tongues of flame and the incessant "crack-crack" of the throbbing and thudding engines tinged the race with interest of such intensity that its reflection could easily be seen in any eager face of the thousands craned to see the drivers turning into the stretch.

Two motor cycle races and several minor automobile contests were on the program and while some proved not too exciting, others were as thrilling in their finishes as one could well wish for.

The track was in fairly good shape for the big events, but even after the water cart had made a couple of miles in fast time, the big racers tossed clouds of dust in their wake and begrimed innocent spectators as well as the famous drivers.

CROWD CAME EARLY.

The crowd began to flock into the grandstand and bleachers at an early hour. The people came thick and they came fast. Gatemen had all they could do to handle the throng as it poured into the enclosure and anxious spectators pushed and scrambled over one another for advantageous seats.

Hundreds of automobiles, crammed with merry parties, were packed in the quarter stretch. Stand boxes were filled, and for the most part with gay crowds of social leaders of St. Paul and Minneapolis. Many of the smart sets of the two cities gave parties for the races and several informal gatherings were made up on the spur of the moment. Business men, too, took a half holiday to see the races.

By 2 o'clock the place was a humming, buzzing flurry of human voices, chugging engines, blaring music from the band stand and shrill, sharp cries from lemonade and program vendors. Soprano voices mingled equally with the deep bass in forecasting the races and deciding beforehand what was to come.

The paddock was choked with a whirling mob of men and women, almost fighting for choice spots next the rail. Many of the more venturesome crowded onto the track, but a force of policemen from both cities rapidly chased them back behind the railing and away from any possible danger.

A perfect day added the sauce to the meal of intense excitement prepared for the delectation of the thousands. The sun was hot and the sky cloudless, but a splendid breeze cooled warm cheeks while the lemonade man did the business for parched and dusty throats.

**A complete account of the automobile races at the State Fair track yesterday will be found on page 20 of this issue.**

### Today's Contents
The Sunday Tribune.





### Fair Breaks All Previous Gate Records

State Exposition Ranks Ahead of All in America.

Total of Nearly 330,000 Persons Visit the Grounds During Week.

Minnesota's Greatest Exhibition Closes the Forty Ninth Annual Show.

STATE FAIR STATISTICS.

| | 1907 | 1908 |
|---|---|---|
| Monday | 82,049 | 28,632 |
| Tuesday | 30,913 | 82,666 |
| Wednesday | 47,099 | 66,922 |
| Thursday | 57,086 | 63,042 |
| Friday | 35,995 | 61,612 |
| Saturday | 32,536 | *37,000 |
| Totals | 286,678 | 329,274 |

*Estimated.

Grand Stand Attendance.

| | 1907 | 1908 |
|---|---|---|
| Monday | 46,239 | 19,979 |
| Tuesday | 11,565 | 27,940 |
| Wednesday | 13,790 | 30,627 |
| Thursday | 23,314 | 26,090 |
| Friday | 9,332 | 27,640 |
| Saturday | 13,368 | *20,000 |
| Totals | 120,668 | 132,276 |

*Estimated.

Cash Receipts.

| | 1907 | 1908 |
|---|---|---|
| Monday | $43,548.00 | $19,400 |
| Tuesday | $15,063.65 | $32,350 |
| Wednesday | $18,600.25 | $35,300 |
| Thursday | $26,858.15 | $31,088 |
| Friday | $14,216.35 | $29,700 |
| Saturday | $13,058.90 | *$27,000 |
| Totals | $131,337.10 | $174,788 |

*Estimated.

Minnesota's biggest and best state fair ended last night in a blaze of glory, after winning the title of champion of champion state fairs. The conditions were perfect for the closing day. The weather was ideal and the attractions were never better.

Although the figures are still incomplete, it is known that the attendance this year will exceed that of last by from 37,000 to 48,000. The money receipts of the fair will show a corresponding increase.

This phenomenal attendance places the total at about 329,274 and places the Minnesota State Fair at the head of all state fairs. For several years the fair has been the best in the United States, and it is almost certain that the attendance will enable the state to take away the laurels of the Toronto fair, which went to the top of all last fall with a total attendance of 320,000.

The actual attendance of the first five days is given in the foregoing table. The estimate of 37,000 for yesterday is conservative. Up to 6 o'clock last evening the turnstiles had registered 32,346. There is no doubt but the night attendance and the motorists who are not included in the turnstile figures will boost the day's mark to 37,000, and probably 40,000 or more.

The exact attendance and receipts will not be known until this evening. The army of employes were working hard last night and today the exact figures will be ready for publication. The most conservative admit that the Minnesota State Fair is now entitled to first place.

MANAGEMENT DID WELL.

B. F. Nelson, president of the State Fair association, and all other officials are entitled to great credit for the successful manner in which they have conducted the fair.

Not only was the fair the biggest in point of attendance in America, but it was also one of the very best in point of attractions. The management deserves credit for the high class entertainments provided. Without exception all of the attractions were clean and instructive. The horse show and hippodrome in the Livestock pavilion is one of the best attractions of the kind ever held west of Chicago.

Not only the kings and queens of the animal world were presented for the inspection of the masses, but there were vaudeville attractions of the highest order. The hippodrome was probably the best card on the grounds.

A close second was the historic spectacle, "Fort Ridgely in '62." Three hundred Sioux Indians from the Sisseton agency in North Dakota and 600 persons from the Twin Cities took part in this stupendous production. In novelty of conception and vividness of presentation the "show" was most interesting.

The program of horse and automobile

(Continued on Page 10, Column 3.)

THE WEATHER.

**Minnesota Forecast—Fair Sunday, slightly cooler in south portion; Monday fair, fresh west and northwest winds.**

Minneapolis, Sept. 5.

| | |
|---|---|
| Maximum temperature | 92 |
| Minimum temperature | 64 |
| Range of temperature | 28 |
| Mean temperature | 78 |

### Gov. Johnson Orders Militia To Chisholm

Word was received early this morning by Governor Johnson that thieves were making away with goods that had been saved from the burning buildings of Chisholm. He immedi[illegible]dered Company M of the Third regiment, M. N. G., stationed at Hibbing, to proceed to the ruined city.

### BAYFIELD, WIS., STILL BURNING

Loss Reached $200,000, but Wind Was Becoming Favorable to Fire Fighters.

BAYFIELD, Wis., Sept. 6.—Bayfield industries suffered losses estimated last night at $200,000 by fire and the flames were still raging though the blaze was being confined within an area of about ten blocks. The heaviest sufferers are the Wachmuth Lumber Co., the Stearns Lumber Co., of Odanah, the Jacob Johnson Fish Co. and the Bayfield Ice Co.

The fire broke out yesterday afternoon and is supposed to have been caused by a spark from a planing mill. The departments of Washburn, 12 miles away, and of Ashland, 21 miles distant, were appealed to, each responding with an engine sent here by special train.

Late last night the flames were still burning, but fortunately the wind came from the northeast, a direction which materially aided the fire fighters.

### Thinks Shot Fired Inside the House

Domestic Tells of Talk With Rustin After the Shooting.

OMAHA, Neb., Sept. 6.—(Special.)—Anna Dineen, the maid at the home of Dr. Frederick Rustin, who was killed at his home Tuesday night, yesterday admitted that she talked with Rustin while he was lying on the hallway in his home before he lapsed into unconsciousness.

"He told me he had been shot, but was not suffering great pain," said Miss Dineen. "I asked him who shot him, but his answer was not intelligible. I did not hear any shot fired and was awakened by Mrs. Rustin's voice at the foot of the stairs. When I came down, she was trying to get somebody on the telephone. I have no idea who fired the shot."

Mrs. R. E. Archer declared she heard a woman scream just after the shot was fired. She was awake at the time and looked across the street to the Rustin home not over 75 feet away, but did not see anybody on the porch. She thinks the shot was fired inside the house.

Relatives of Mrs. Abbie Rice, who is held pending the inquest, began flocking in yesterday. Her father was the first to visit her and talked two hours with his daughter. County Attorney English says the case is still very mysterious but believes he will be able to place the blame in the right place.

## People Flee Before Onrushing Flames; Property Loss Will Reach Millions

Town of Chisholm, Minn., Completely Razed With Loss Estimated at Over $2,000,000.

Ashawa and Many Mining Centers Devastated—Bayfield, Wis., Still Burning—Several Other Towns and Hamlets in This State Surrounded by Flames and Their Total Destruction Seems Probable.

BULLETIN.
By Associated Press.

DULUTH, Minn., Sept. 6.—Thousands of acres of agricultural lands and millions of feet of standing timber were laid waste, one towns was wiped out, three more towns may have been destroyed, several mining locations were burned and at least 10,000 people are homeless as the result of forest fires, which swept through many districts in Northern Wisconsin and Northern Minnesota yesterday afternoon and last night.

Chisholm, Minn., 90 miles north of Duluth was completely destroyed. The only building standing is the new $125,000 high school.

Nashwauk, Minn., 50 miles northwest of Duluth, was surrounded by flames and the outskirts of the town were burning.

Buhl, Minn., 12 miles east of Chisholm, was cut-off from the world by the fires that were bearing down on the town.

Wrenshall, 25 miles northwest of Duluth, faced a wall of flames that was sweeping toward the village. It appeared to be doomed. Several small settlements in Douglas county, Wisconsin, were burned and forest fires were sweeping the northern part of the county. A fire at Bayfield, Wis., damaged buildings to the extent of $75,000.

One fatality is believed to have occurred. May Fisher, a woman at Chisholm, was intoxicated and would not leave the city, and she is believed to have perished.

HIBBING, Minn., Sept. 6.—(Special.)—Forest fires swooped down upon the town of Chisholm, four miles from this city, at 6 o'clock last evening, and nothing but mouldering ruins marked its site two hours later.

Citizens fought the flames until human endurance could no longer withstand the rush of smoke and heat, then they were forced to retreat to this city, leaving behind their all for the flames to feed upon.

Three trainloads of the refugees were hurried to Virginia. Those not fortunate enough to get away by rail hurried to places of apparent safety by team and on foot, some vainly endeavoring to save various articles of value.

The retreat was a pitiful spectacle. Men, women and children, fear and consternation on their faces, the latter with eyes bloodshot from weeping and the sickening clouds of smoke, rushed frantically hither and thither in a mad stampede for shelter.

The wind howled over the tree tops, driving the tongues of flames into the city, and the outskirts were wrapped in flames about 6 o'clock. Building after building fell a prey to the onrush, until every structure had been leveled. Then the fire again jumped into the dry forest and continued on in unabated fury.

LOSS IN THE MILLIONS.

The total loss at midnight was estimated at $2,000,000, with every indication that before morning this figure would be greatly increased.

The mining locations of Shenando, population 2,000; Hartley, 1,000, and Pillsbury, 1,000, were completely destroyed, immediately following the destruction of Chisholm.

Lodge halls, churches and homes of Hibbing were thrown open to the refugees, even while the citizens were, themselves, packing up the more valuable of their chattels with a view to forsaking their own city, should the flames approach much closer. At midnight the advance guard of fire was not more than a mile distant and the fire fighters had been utterly unable to check the onslaught at any point, but a little later the wind shifted and the town was safe, for a while at least.

The saloons here were ordered closed by the mayor, and as a result of a mass meeting 20 men were sworn in as special policemen to keep order and prevent any attempt at looting.

Calls were sent to Virginia and Duluth for fire fighters and fire apparatus, and special trains were ordered out at once at both places.

The railroad bridge on the Great Northern between here and Chisholm burned out early in the evening, thus cutting off rail connection in that direction.

BEFORE FLAMES TOWNS FALL

*By Associated Press.*

DULUTH, Minn., Sept. 6.—Forest fires which have been burning for three days closed on several towns and small settlements near Duluth yesterday afternoon, wiping them out, rendering several thousand people homeless, destroying property valued at several million dollars and sweeping over cut-over lands in many counties in Northern Wisconsin and Northern Minnesota.

Chisholm, Minn., a town of 4,000 people on the Mesaba Iron range, 90 miles north of Duluth, was completely wiped out.

Hibbing, Minn., five miles from Chisholm, was surrounded by forest fires last night and the city was in danger until the wind shifted. The entire northern portion of Douglas county, Wis., was on fire and several small settlements have been destroyed. Renshaw, a village 25 miles west of Duluth, was surrounded by fires early last night, and there was no hope for the town. Hundreds of farmers have been driven from their homes by the flames and as passage along the roadway was difficult owing to the dense smoke and the heat of the burning forests, it is believed that some lives may have been lost, although none has been reported. A fire at Bayfield, Wis., starting in a lumber yard, damaged two docks and the lumber company's property to the extent of $700,000.

FEARED NO DANGER.

The most destructive of the many forest fires was that which embraced Chisholm in its fiery grip and completely destroyed it. For three days the dry woods have been on fire west and north of the town and small bush fires were reported to the eastward. Gradually these closed in upon the doomed town, but no danger was felt by the citizens as the town is protected on the east by Long Year lake, a small body of water, and there are many mining locations to the west, in

*FIRE SITUATION BRIEFLY TOLD*

**COMPLETELY DESTROYED**—Chisholm, population 8,000; Shenando, mining location, population 2,000; Hartley, mining location, population 1,000; Pillsbury, mining location, population 1,000; Bayfield, Wis., population 2,000.

**ESTIMATED LOSS**—In Chisholm $2,000,000; total loss unknown.

**THREATENED**—Towns of Hibbing, population 15,000; Nashwauk, population 10,000; Buhl, population 800.

**REFUGEES**—Pouring into Hibbing and Duluth from Chisholm and smaller settlements burned out.

**HELP**—Sent to Chisholm and Hibbing from Virginia and call made upon Duluth for fire fighters and operators.

**WEATHER**—Very windy at midnight no sign of rain.

### *Bulletins.*

HIBBING, Minn., Sept. 6.—(Special)—2 a. m.—If the powder houses of the Oliver Mining company (a part of the U. S. Steel corporation) escape the flames it is regarded that the safety of Hibbing is assured. The powder houses are situated about a mile from the town. If these catch fire however, the town will be doomed.

The St. Paul mines at Keewatin, 12 miles north of here, suffered by fire. The loss is not known.

Buhl, in St. Louis county, 20 miles north of here, is threatened.

Ashawa, on the Duluth & Winnipeg line, containing 1,000 inhabitants, has been destroyed.

DULUTH, Minn., Sept. 6.—(Special.)—It is reported here this morning that Virginia, Eveleth, Mountain Iron, Biwabik and many other range towns are now in danger from forest fires.

HIBBING, Minn., Sept. 6.—(Special.)—Five thousand fire refugees from Chisholm, Minn., left Hibbing last night at 11 o'clock in a special train of 15 coaches for Duluth over the Duluth, Missabe & Northern railroad. These people constitute the majority of the fire refugees from Chisholm, that could not be accommodated in Hibbing.

HIBBING, Minn., Sept. 6—(Special.)—At midnight fires were menacing the outlying districts of this city, and the streets were filled with anxious citizens, hundreds of whom have prepared to take the early morning train for Duluth. The train leaves Hibbing at 7 o'clock. The night was spent by many in packing their most valuable belongings, and general preparation to desert their homes if necessary.

HIBBING, Minn., Sept. 6—(Special.)—A courier reached here this morning at 1 o'clock and reported that the wagon road between this city and Chisholm is the avenue of escape for at least two hundred people, and that most of them are on foot.

## RAWSON SKETCHES OFFICIALS AT AUTOMOBILE RACES

De Palma in his Flat Cyclone didn't touch only once or twice around. Asa Paine Got awful cranky. Uncle Louis Koch stopped his watch alright. Dr. Dutton started and stopped. Stewart Elliott's machine acted up. Leonard Zengal just kept going. L. A. Wood kept time. Walter Christie flew alright, but not quite fast enough.

# The Minneapolis Tribune

VOL. XLII., NO. 93. MINNEAPOLIS, MINNESOTA, THURSDAY, SEPTEMBER 10, 1908. PRICE ONE CENT IN MINNEAPOLIS.


# MINNESOTA TOWNS SAVED BY HEROIC BATTLES WITH FLAMES

## NEW WORLD'S AEROPLANE RECORDS SET BY WRIGHT AT FORT MEYER, VA.

### Makes 2 Flights of One Hour Each

And Another in Which Two Men Ride in the Air Six Minutes.

Success of Official Trials Before Army Board Is Thus Assured.

Aerial Navigation Now Regarded Only a Matter of Development.

WASHINGTON, Sept. 10.—Orville Wright, in three phenomenal flights at Fort Meyer yesterday established new aeroplane records that not only assure the success of the official trials before the army board, but indicate that aerial flight is now only a matter of development.

War on land and sea will find in the aeroplane a valuable means of reconnaissance and possible carnage.

**Yesterday's time and distance will be accepted as official by the Aero Club of America, as Augustus Post, its secretary, already has approved them.**

**Two flights of approximately one hour each, another flight in which two men where whirled through the air for upwards of six minutes, were the achievements of the Wright Brothers aeroplane yesterday.**

**That these flights, record-breaking as they were, will even be surpassed by Orville Wright during his trials at Fort Meyer is confidently predicted.**

**The first flight, made yesterday morning in which the machine circled the drill grounds at the fort 57 times in 57 minutes and 31 seconds was surpassed last last evening when a flight of 62 minutes and 15 seconds was made.**

Not satisfied with breaking all distance and time records for a heavier-than-air flying machine, Mr. Wright took Lieut. Frank P. Lahm, the aeronaut of the signal corps, for a spin around the drill grounds, and making a new record for a two-man flight.

All this happened so quickly and unostentatiously that the spectators, among whom were members of the cabinet and high officers of the army and navy, could hardly realize that history had been made and that a new era in the progress of the civilized world was begun.

CROWD QUICKLY GATHERS.

The morning flight was witnessed by only a handful of enthusiasts, but the news spread so rapidly that fully a thousand people gathered on the military reservation across the Potomac from the national capitol to see the afternoon event.

At 5:16 as the sun was disappearing below the Virginia horizon, the latest invention of man to challenge the laws of nature, rose grandly into space and sailed over the greensward of the drill ground.

Higher and higher it rose, turned at a slight angle as the aviator brought it around at the far side of the field, and raced along at increasing speed. There was hardly a quiver of the aeroplane in the first few rounds of the field. Mr. Wright evidently having the steering apparatus well in hand.

AT NAVIGATOR'S WILL.

Rising and lowering at will, the sight of the man-built bird was impressive.

Round after round the machine traveled on cutting short turns, shooting along the stretches and presenting somewhat the appearance of an automobile racing about an imaginary course in the air.

The navigator paid little heed to anything but his levers for warping the surface of the planes and controlling the planes which control the altitude of the craft.

He seemed oblivious to the crowd below until having broken the record of 57 minutes and 31 seconds established by him yesterday morning, the crowd raised a cheer that told him of his new achievement. Then Mr. Wright waved his acknowledgments.

Before the flight was begun a watch was tied to the seat next to Wright and when a little later he saw that he had stayed aloft for over an hour, the time required in order for him to fulfill his contract with the government, he made for "mother earth."

BACK TO EARTH.

Swooping down in a sort of "bump the bumps fashion" the machine bore down in the direction of the crowd, which quickly scattered, fearing that the aeroplane would run them down. Raising a cloud of dust as it slid along on the skids, the aeroplane, which weighs nearly 1,000 pounds, came to a stop within 20 feet of the crowd.

As Mr. Wright stepped from the seat and removed his goggles he was greeted with lusty cheers. At the same time a letter from his brother Wilbur, who has been making flights at LeMans, France, was handed to him. Mr. Wright smiled as he broke the seal. It was the first letter he had received from his brother for nearly two weeks, and it seemed to interest him more than the record-breaking flight he had just completed.

CHEER "WIZARD OF AIR."

Lieutenant Selfridge, who repaired the first successful aeroplane of the aerial investigation, talked with Mr. Wright. Enthusiasts from every walk of life gath-

(Continued on Page 10, Column 1.)

### Orville Wright's Aeroplane

WASHINGTON, Sept. 10.—By his wonderful flight at Fort Myer yesterday, Orville Wright practically doubled the best official records ever made by heavier-than-air machines. It was only on Sunday last that Leon De La Grange, president of the Aviation club of France, established a new world's record up to that time by remaining in the air 29 minutes 54 seconds. He circled the field at Issy, near Paris, 15½ times and covered a distance of 15¼ miles.

Monday De La Grange, after installing a fuel tank of increased capacity on his machine, made a flight of 31 minutes, but the record was not allowed to stand, three minutes being deducted on account of the machine having touched the ground while making the first round of the field.

### AEROPLANE RECORDS.

The best aeroplane record (unofficial) prior to Wednesday's flights by Orville Wright was by Wilbur Wright at Dayton, O., Oct. 5, 1905, when he flew 24 1-5 miles in 38 minutes and 20 seconds.

Other official records are: Oct. 23, 1906—Santos Dumont, 27.34 yards at Bagatelle, France.

Nov. 12, 1906—Santos Dumont, 240.5 yards at Bagatelle, France.

Nov. 12, 1906—Henry Farman, 843 yards at Issy-Les-Molineux.

Jan. 11, 1908—Henry Farman, 1,200 yards in one minute and 55 seconds.

Jan. 13, 1908—Henry Farman won the Deutsch Arch Deacon prize of $10,000 by making a circular flight of 1,093.6 yards at Issy-Les-Molineux, in 1 minute and 28 seconds.

March 21, 1908—Henry Farman, 1 mile and 431 yards in 2 minutes and 15 seconds.

April 11, 1908—Leon DeLagrange, 2 miles and 172 yards in 6 minutes and 15 seconds at Issy-Les-Molineaux.

May 14, 1908—Wilbur Wright, 6 miles in 7 minutes and 40 seconds (unofficial) at Kill Devil hill.

May 22, 1908—Henry Farman, 3 miles, no time recorded, at Ghent.

May 27, 1908—Leon De Lagrange, miles in 4 minutes at Rome, Italy.

May 30, 1908—Leon De Lagrange, 7.9 miles in 15 minutes and 26 seconds at Rome.

June 29, 1908—M. Bleriot flew 100 yards with a monoplane in France.

July 4, 1908—Glenn H. Curtiss flew 1 mile in aeroplane June at Hammond Springs, N. Y., and won Scientific American trophy.

July 7, 1908—Henry Farman won Armonaud prize of $2,000 in flight of 12 miles in 12 minutes and 20 seconds, France.

Sept. 5, 1908—Wilbur Wright, 15 miles in 20 minutes, Lemans, France.

Sept. 6, 1908—M. De Lagrange, 24 miles in 29 minutes and 55 seconds at Paris (unofficial).

## "Uncle Boston" Smith, Evangelist, Is Dead

Baptist Worker Known in All Sections of the Country.

Familiar and Affectionate Figure to School Children.

Suddenly overcome by an attack of apoplexy in his home yesterday afternoon, Boston W. Smith, a well known evangelist, lay down on a lounge at his home, 2309 James street north, and a few minutes later was found dead by his wife. Mr. Smith, who was familiarly called "Uncle Boston," had carried the gospel to every corner of the United States and his work as an evangelist and disseminator of religious propaganda had made him more or less famous throughout the country.

He had recently been connected with the American Baptists Publication society and distributed books and pamphlets of the Baptist religion in every quarter. "Uncle Boston" was a bright and witty speaker and was always a welcome visitor in the Baptist churches of the towns he visited on his rounds.

RAISED $2,000 EASILY.

An example of the ease with which Mr. Smith's eloquence brought forth golden harvests was witnessed only last Sunday at the Fourth Baptist church, Minneapolis, where Mr. Smith did his last real work. He essayed to raise $600 to pay off a church obligation and so worked up his audience into a frenzy of benevolence that $2,000 was gotten almost like finding it.

Mr. Smith was born in England 55 years ago. At an early age he came to Alton, Ill., where he engaged in business which he soon abandoned to enter the evangelistic work of the Baptist church. Twenty-five years ago he came to Minnesota on the invitation of prominent members of the Baptist church, and since that time he has been actively engaged in missionary and Sunday school work throughout the Northwest.

He was intimately associated with evangelistic work of different kinds in the Twin Cities, and to school children "Uncle Boston" was a familiar and affectionate figure. For a number of years he was superintendent of the chapel car work of the Baptist church in Minneapolis, and in this capacity preached in many remote parts of the state where no regular churches had been erected. He became connected with the American Baptists' Publication society four years ago and was associated with that organization at the time of his death.

DID ALL KINDS OF WORK.

Mr. Smith confined himself to no particular branch of evangelistic work. He preached, taught Sunday school, and did much to build churches and schools. Some weeks ago he was a prominent figure at the "Flower Day" celebrations which were held at the Chicago Avenue Baptist church, the object of which was to interest the children of that locality in the cultivation of flowers.

Mr. Smith is survived by a widow and six children, Alfred H., Hills, Houghton, Elizabeth, Miriam and Mrs. C. F. Wyant, all of whom reside in Minneapolis.

The funeral will be held tomorrow at 3 p. m., from the Fourth Baptist church, Eighteenth avenue north and Dupont. Interment will be at Lakewood cemetery.

## Led Lynching Mob and Is Glad of it

Former U. S. Senator W. V. Sullivan Credited With This Attitude.

MEMPHIS, Sept. 10.—A special from Oxford, Miss., quotes former U. S. Senator W. V. Sullivan as follows with references to the lynching Tuesday night:

"I led the mob which lynched Nelse Patton, and I'm proud of it. I directed every movement of the mob, and I did everything I could to see that he was lynched.

"Cut a white woman's throat! And a negro! Of course I wanted him lynched.

"I saw the body dangling from a tree this morning and I'm glad of it.

"When I heard of this horrible crime, I started to work immediately to get a mob. I did all I could to raise one. I was at the jail last night, and I heard Judge Roane advise against lynching. I got up immediately after and urged the mob to lynch Patton.

"I aroused the mob and directed them to storm the jail.

"I had my revolver but did not use it. I gave it to a deputy sheriff and told him: 'Shoot Patton and shoot to kill.'

"He used the revolver and shot. I suppose the bullets from my gun were some of those that killed the negro.

"I don't care what investigation is made, or what are the consequences. I am willing to stand them.

"I wouldn't mind standing the consequences any time for lynching a man who cut a white woman's throat. I will lead a mob in such a case any time."

### ARMY OFFICER WANTS TO WED, BUT CAN'T SECURE LEAVE

Three Times Dr. Clayton Appeals to War Department for Vacation.

COLUMBUS, O., Sept. 10.—(Special.)—Denied a leave of absence, though he has explained to the war department that invitations for his wedding in Poughkeepsie, Sept. 19, have been issued, Dr. Eben Clayton, first lieutenant of the medical reserve corps U. S. A., threatens to resign from the army. He is stationed in the Columbus barracks in the absence of another surgeon and his applications for a 30-day leave and later for a 10-day leave have been rejected.

Clayton has made a third application, setting forth that he is to marry Miss Lucy Lovell Atwater, daughter of Edward Atwater, president of two Poughkeepsie banks, and that he must be given permission to attend the wedding. "I'll quit if I don't get my leave," he declared yesterday.

### THE WEATHER.

**Minnesota Forecast — Fair Thursday, showers at night or Friday, cooler Friday; fresh southwest to west winds.**

| | |
|---|---|
| Maximum temperature | 85 |
| Minimum temperature | 69 |
| Range of temperature | 16 |
| Mean temperature | 77 |

Dies at Age of 113.

TOPEKA, Kan., Sept. 10.—Mrs. Sallie Ruthford died here yesterday at the age of 113 years. She was born in Middleton, Ky., in 1795, and had never experienced a week's sickness in her life.

### ASIATIC CHOLERA IN ST. PETERSBURG

ST. PETERSBURG, Sept. 10.—The fact that Asiatic cholera exists in St. Petersburg has been established beyond doubt. The body of the woman who died in this city Tuesday, supposedly from this disease, has been examined and the bacilli of cholera found.

The present weather conditions are favorable to the spread of the disease, and the authorities are making preparations for a rapid increase in the number of cases.

Six suspected cases are now in hospitals.

## Humanity's Appeal Gets Most Generous Response

### $20,194.50 Sum Already Given

Minneapolis Citizens Pour in Money for Fire Sufferers.

Monster Benefit Planned by Theatrical Men for Sept. 18.

Persons in Every Walk of Life Make Some Sacrifice.

Contributions for the $50,000 fund that Minneapolis citizens will give to the fire sufferers of the iron range continue to roll into the collection box of Perry Harrison, treasurer, with such rapidity he was able to do nothing yesterday afternoon but count the money.

From 2 o'clock until 5 p. m. the various committees reported receipts amounting to $2,092. This money was received principally from the implement men of the city. The total subscription received is now $20,194.50.

Pursuant to the call of Theodore L. Hayes, chairman of the committee on theaters the Associate Theater Managers of Minneapolis met at the office of Lac Stafford in the Metropolitan Opera House building yesterday afternoon.

Nearly all of the local amusement places were represented and it was the unanimous desire that theaters contribute their share to the worthy movement by the giving of a monster benefit to be participated in by the attractions from the different theaters.

L. N. Scott and La Stafford donated the use of the Metropolitan Opera House for Friday afternoon, Sept. 18, which was selected as the date for a benefit.

The Roosevelt club through Merrill Bartlett has been invited to co-operate with the managers in giving this event and will consider the matter at a meeting to be held at its club rooms at noon today. Mr. Bartlett voiced the opinion that the Roosevelt boys would undoubtedly co-operate and would furnish an important part of the program of the benefit occasion.

POLICE AND FIREMEN TO AID.

It was decided that the disposal of tickets be left to the police and fire departments. Colonel F. T. Corriston and Chief J. R. Canterbury expressed their willingness to co-operate in this movement, which action received the hearty consent and approval of Mayor J. C. Haynes.

It is proposed to give a mixed program with acts and features from all of the different theaters and will undoubtedly offer one of the strongest entertainments of the kind that has ever been given locally. G. E. Raymond of the Orpheum will act as stage manager and Oscar Apfel, stage director of the new Lyric theater, will assist him.

The disposal of boxes will be left to the city council and Commercial club. It is aimed to have absolutely no expense in connection with this event. The Minneapolis Musicians' association, through Felix McIver, secretary, has an-

(Continued on Page 10, Column 3.)

SUBSCRIPTIONS TO THE MESABA RANGE FIRE SUFFERERS' RELIEF FUND.

Sept. 9—

| | |
|---|---|
| Previously Reported | $10,211.00 |
| Shevlin-Carpenter Co. | $1,000.00 |
| R. M. Bennett | 1,000.00 |
| T. B. Walker | 1,000.00 |
| Carpenter-Lamb Co. | 500.00 |
| A. T. and R. R. Rand | 500.00 |
| L. S. Donaldson Co. | 250.00 |
| W. S. Nott Company | 200.00 |
| Minneapolis Drug Co. | 200.00 |
| Patterson & Stevenson Co. | 100.00 |
| Rogers Lumber Co. | 100.00 |
| E. Pennington | 100.00 |
| G. H. Warren | 100.00 |
| C. D. Dorr | 50.00 |
| William Gardner | 50.00 |
| Hood & Penney | 50.00 |
| Wingate Co. | 25.00 |
| Cohen, Atwater & Shaw | 25.00 |
| C. M. Loring | 25.00 |
| Office Clerk District Court | 25.00 |
| W. V. Newlin | 10.00 |
| C. W. Van Tuyl | 10.00 |
| D. D. Webster | 10.00 |
| S. W. Morris | 5.00 |
| Cash | 5.00 |
| Cash | 5.00 |
| Cash | 5.00 |
| A. C. Hickman | 5.00 |
| Gloria Branch, International Sunshine Society | 5.00 |
| J. H. Davis | 5.00 |
| E. B. Johnson | 5.00 |
| Geo. H. Drake | 5.00 |
| H. O. Juve | 2.50 |
| Mrs. Harriet B. Warton | 2.00 |
| Cash | 2.00 |
| Dr. W. H. Aurand | 2.00 |
| N. J. Almquist | 1.00 |
| Cash | 1.00 |
| A. L. Bail | 1.00 |
| James Murphy | 1.00 |
| Cash | 2.00 |
| Deere & Webber Co. | 500.00 |
| Stenographer | 2.00 |
| Cash | 10.00 |
| George Harrison | 10.00 |
| Bardwell, Robinson Co. | 150.00 |
| A. D. Thompson Drug Co. | 10.00 |
| Mpls. Stamp & Stencil Co. | 10.00 |
| Northrup, King & Co. | 30.00 |
| New England Furniture Co. | 250.00 |
| Boutell Bros. | 150.00 |
| Cash | 3.00 |
| S. H. Franklin Co. | 10.00 |
| James E. Mehan | 2.00 |
| F. W. Little | 25.00 |
| Stevens & Stevens | 5.00 |
| C. G. Ireys Elevator Co. | 15.00 |
| Great Northern Impl. Co. | 200.00 |
| Lindsay Bros. | 100.00 |
| Huber Bros. Mfg. Co. | 5.00 |
| Bradley, Clark & Co. | 20.00 |
| Minneapolis Iron Store Co. | 100.00 |
| La Crosse Implement Co. | 50.00 |
| Racine Sattley Mfg. Co. | 50.00 |
| Dean & Co. | 100.00 |
| Emerson-Newton Imp. Co. | 50.00 |
| Empire Cream Separator Co. | 10.00 |
| Waterbury Implement Co. | 10.00 |
| Stoughton Wagon Co. | 5.00 |
| L. B. Wood | 10.00 |
| Huber Manufacturing Co. | 5.00 |
| Cash | 5.00 |
| S. W. Turner | 5.00 |
| Fred. A. Richter | 5.00 |
| M. G. Truman | 5.00 |
| George R. Smith | 10.00 |
| Chute Realty Co. | 25.00 |
| H. Poller | 5.00 |
| E. L. Matthews | 10.00 |
| Pence Automobile Co. | 50.00 |
| William H. Eustis | 50.00 |
| TOTAL | $20,194.50 |

SOMETHING REVEALED BY THE LIGHT OF THE FLAMES.

## Elements Aid Man in Checking Range Fires

Less Wind and Some Rain Reported in Several Sections, Making Late Reports From Menaced Districts More Hopeful—Hibbing Passed All Danger—Grand Marais Is Safe.

### Fires Near Towns of Eveleth and Virginia

BULLETIN.

DULUTH, Minn., Sept. 10.—(Special.)—Bovey, Coleraine, Buhl, Nashwauk and Mountain Iron were threatened by fires all day yesterday, but when the wind went down late in the afternoon the danger was passed for the present.

One hundred and fifty thousand ties owned by the Detroit Tie company were burned near Susie Island, on the north shore of Laake Superior.

BULLETIN.

EVELETH, Minn., Sept. 10.—(Special.)—Forest fires approached this city from the north yesterday to within half a mile. The city met the danger heroically, employing 200 men to fight the flames. The battle with the fire started at noon and the fire was kept under control.

BULLETIN.

EVELETH, Minn., Sept. 10.—Virginia, a town of about 8,000 inhabitants, which seemed doomed by the forest fires last night, was reported at midnight to be temporarily out of danger.

A strong north wind, which seemed destined to blow the fire into the city, changed to the east. If it continues in this direction the city will be saved.

People are praying for rain.

At the nearest point the fire is now but three miles from Virginia. Another change in the wind may spell the doom of the entire village.

Five separate gangs, composed of 50 men each, are now fighting the flames in this vicinity. A property damage of over $1,000,000 would result in the destruction of the Virginia Lumber company's plant alone. Telephone service was repaired late yesterday connecting Virginia with the outside world.

The fire had reached Mountain Iron, a small town near Virginia, yesterday afternoon, and one store building was burned.

Late reports from there last night stated that no further damage had been done and that with reinforced protection the town would probably be saved.

(BY A STAFF CORRESPONDENT.)

HIBBING, Minn., Sept. 10.—(Special.)—Rain! Blessed, pattering water from the clouds and the remaining towns and villages of the iron ranges of Northern Minnesota spared by the licking tongues of flames from the forest fires of the last week or more was the encouraging feature of the reports last night.

The rain, however, was not reported at Eveleth or Virginia.

RAIN IN MANY PLACES.

Early last evening rain in sufficient quantities to halt the spread of the forest fires fell at certain points on the Mesaba range.

This, together with a decided lessening of the wind and the precautions in the way of clearing and back fires carried on around all settlements, and the fact that much of the inflammable growth is now gone, removes the anxiety which has hung heavy on the hearts of the people on the Mesaba range.

At Eveleth, while the city is not in immediate danger, the fires are apt to rekindle and sweep the town. The same is true at Virginia.

As a result of the favorable turn in the condition of the elements, optimism filled the reports from the north country last night.

At Nashwauk, the town is surrounded by a wide strip formed by the clearing and back firing of the citizens. Buhl, which was threatened as late as yesterday morning, is now out of danger, and with Aurora the same condition exists.

SNOWBALL STILL ON MAP.

Snowball, which was reported entirely destroyed Tuesday, did not suffer to the extent at first supposed. It was only the outskirts of the village which was burned, the central portion remaining intact. About half the town still stands. The flames there have died out.

Reports from Hibbing were somewhat exaggerated, also, in that the suburb of Brooklyn did not suffer, although, by one of the many freaks of the fiery onslaught, the flames approached within a few feet of the village.

Grand Marias is out of danger. The tongue of flame which stretched in the direction of the little town, breathing its heat into the faces of the terror-stricken inhabitants, has subsided, and the people at least breath free.

But between the cities which momentarily feared devastation for days, there is now only a barren waste—miles and miles of burned-over ground, whereupon there is not a living thing, and from which every trace of civilization's progress has been completely obliterated.

Here and there over this expanse are burning piles, smouldering ruins, and in other spots little flames still crawl over the ground.

At the Mahoning location the only serious fire was yesterday afternoon about two miles west of Hibbing, but four locomotives and 200 men worked on the blaze and it is expected will have it entirely subdued by this morning.

The relief committee is doing heroic work. Clothing is the one thing most needed. About three-fourths of Chisholm is destroyed, leaving about 6,500 persons homeless. The relief men are providing meals free to the refugees. Forty-two houses are all that remain standing in a city which before possessed accommodation for 8,000 inhabitants.

REFUGEES IN TENTS.

Tents have been pitched back of the schoolhouse at Chisholm, where the women and children are being cared for until better accommodations can be provided.

The railroads are taking people away from the burned district free of charge, but there are very few who elect to go. In spite of the hardships which must be endured before the situation is normal again, the spirit of rising above their misfortune fills the unfortunate victims, and they mean to "stick it out" and start anew the moment opportunity offers.

### Grand Marais Is Safe From Fire

Subsidence of Wind Quiets Circling Flames—Relief Boat There.

DULUTH, Minn., Sept. 10.—After being menaced for days by forest fires that were creeping up in a wide semi-circle upon the helpless village, 100 miles from Duluth, Grand Marais, is reported to be safe.

The wind which had been driving the huge front of the flames for hours toward the threatened village subsided Tuesday night and in the morning a fresh breeze carried the menace in the opposite direction.

The steamer Easton of the Booth line returned yesterday from a trip up the north shore bringing in the news that for a time at least, Grand Marais is not in danger of being wiped out by fire.

The subsidence of the wind has quieted the circling flames and only in a few places near the town are there serious conflagrations.

A strong wind blowing toward the lake would once more imperil the town.

The Easton made the Grand Marais port about five o'clock yesterday morning. She met the United States training ship Gopher with Adjutant General Wood on board in command of a relief expedition ordered out by Governor Johnson at 9 o'clock in the forenoon.

Captain Smith, of the Easton, said that there were no fires within half a mile of Grand Marais, when the ship made port.

The citizens were much relieved over the change in wind conditions and expressed the belief that they were safe. They realize, however, that continuous dry weather and strong winds blowing toward the lake will again jeopardize the town.

A big fire is burning in the timber around Split Rock, a few miles from Grand Marais, and at many points on the North shore Captain Smith, reported that these flames can be seen from the shore.

Maple Grove, two miles from Grand Marais, had a desperate fight with the fire that threatened Grand Marais with destruction, but finally warded off the danger.

Grand Marais was covered with a dense smoke pall yesterday when the Easton left the town. There was no wind and the smoke that came from the conflagration near the town hung over the place like a canopy.

### Save Marble By a Hard Battle

Citizens Fight Onrushing Flames and Prevent Disaster.

DULUTH, Minn., Sept. 10.—(Special.)—Yesterday's feature of the great battle of numerous Mesaba range towns against the encroachments of forest fires was easily the fight that the people of the new town of Marble, on the Alborn branch of the Duluth, Missabe and Northern road, put up. It is a village of 600 inhabitants, and the town is surrounded with timber and underbrush, and when a wall of flame burst through the woods from the southeast yesterday the town was right in the track of the devouring element.

Had the village been taken unawares the place would now be a heap of ashes. But the destruction of Chisholm has put every range town on its guard, and fire fighting apparatus is kept constantly on hand.

The people of Marble have considered themselves outside of the fire scene on the range, but new fires are springing up here and there all the time, and yesterday it was Marble's turn to fight for existence.

Of the population of Marble there are about 400 men and 300 women and children. When it was seen that the fire was sure to sweep the town away unless it was checked in some manner, an alarm was sent out to the headquarters

# THE MINNEAPOLIS JOURNAL



24 PAGES—HOME EDITION. WEATHER—Fair and slightly warmer tonight and Wednesday. TUESDAY EVENING, SEPTEMBER 7, 1909. PRICE ONE CENT IN MINNEAPOLIS.

## COLUMBUS SCHOOL ORDERED CLOSED

**Two Members of the Board Act in Mae Snow Case.**

**PRINCIPAL REPORTS; SENDS PUPILS HOME**

**The Hearing Before Judge Booth Now Set for Saturday.**

Miss Mae Snow, deposed and reinstated principal of the Columbus school, found her school building closed when she reported today for the opening of the school year. A notice was on the door. It said that the school would not be opened until further notice. It suggested a perusal of the daily papers. It was written on an envelope of the board of education and was signed by Superintendent of Schools C. M. Jordan.

George H. Elwell, president of the school board, says he knew nothing of the closing of the school until a late hour this morning. He was found in the office of Fred B. Chute.

Mr. Chute said that he and Wallace G. Nye are responsible for the closing of the school, and also for a special delivery letter sent by Dr. Jordan to Miss Snow telling her that the school would not open just now.

Mr. Elwell was asked: "Do you mean that Mr. Chute and Mr. Nye had the school closed and Miss Snow notified without any consultation with the president of the board?"

"That appears to be the case," said Mr. Elwell.

**Casually Mentioned.**

The school board met at 3 p.m. today. The closing of the Columbus school was not the special matter to be discussed, but it was discussed, and to the point.

Mr. Chute explained the action of himself and Mr. Nye as follows:

"I can explain it, and in a very few words. The court's restraining order prevents the board from doing anything to remove Miss Mae Snow from the school system or to prevent her from acting as principal of the Columbus school. That meant that while a majority of the board thought she ought to be dismissed, she nevertheless would have the right to open that school. In consultation with the special attorney for the board and with Judge Brooks, who issued the restraining order, it was thought best, so as not to injure the rights of either side, to close the school until the hearing could be had. The court realized that the hearing was too late, and gave Miss Snow to understand that if she wished, he would advance the date of the hearing. The hearing has been set for Saturday. The attorney for the board will now see the judge and try to advance the hearing to as early a date as possible. The court gave permission to close the school."

**Only Two Acted.**

"When did the board take this action?" Mr. Chute was asked.

"The board did not take action," replied Mr. Chute.

"Who did it?"

"Mr. Nye and myself," said Mr. Chute.

"Did you instruct Dr. Jordan to notify Miss Snow and to close the school?"

"Yes."

"Did the other members of the board know about it?"

"I think they all know about it now," said Mr. Chute.

President Elwell happened to be in Mr. Chute's office at the moment.

"It is news to me," said Mr. Elwell. "I have only just heard about it. No; I haven't anything to say. I can't talk now. It appears that this was done without consulting others. The matter will certainly come up at this afternoon's meeting of the board."

**Children Sent Home.**

Miss Snow received Dr. Jordan's letter, but, nevertheless, presented herself at the school. It is said to have been closed and locked, and Miss Snow is understood to have been unsuccessful in her search for the janitor. Neither of the other teachers was present. They are said to have been transferred elsewhere. The children were on hand, standing around. After a vain effort to effect an entrance, Miss Snow dismissed the children and sent them home.

Dr. Jordan was not in his office at the city hall all morning. Clerk Hugh Marchbank, when asked for an explanation of the non-opening of the Columbus school, said it was news to him. Mr. Chute said later that he supposed it was news to most of the members of the board, too.

Mr. Nye said he knew the school was closed.

"It was closed at the order of the teachers' committee," he said. "Mr. Chute is chairman of that committee. No, I am not on that committee."

"The Columbus school is closed on order of the teachers' committee," he repeated. "That's all I have to say."

### SEVEN CARS GO INTO RAVINE

**Only One Passenger on Burlington's Express Is Hurt.**

St. Joseph, Mo., Sept. 7.—The Burlington express, No. 22, southbound, ran into a washout four miles south of St. Joseph this morning. Seven coaches left the track and five of them rolled into the ravine. Only one person was hurt, an unknown man, whose foot was sprained.

### MISS STEWART IS PRINCESS

**Austrian Emperor Creates Title for Miguel's Bride in Her Own Name.**

Special to The Journal.

Vienna, Sept. 7.—The emperor has created Miss Anita Stewart a princess in her own right, thus removing any difficulty of etiquet which might have been raised at the exclusive Austrian court following her marriage. Prince Miguel has just been here to visit the emperor and to thank him for the honor conferred on Miss Stewart.

### MRS. BARCLAY DROPS FIGHT

**"Incubator Baby's" Possession Conceded to Mrs. Bleakley.**

Kansas City, Mo., Sept. 7.—The fight for the possession of Marian Bleakley, the "incubator baby," is at an end. So declared John H. Atwood in the circuit court here today when he, on behalf of Mrs. James G. Barclay, withdrew the habeas corpus suit brought to prevent the return of the child to Mrs. J. J. Bleakley, from whose home little Marian was kidnapped.

### TELEGRAMS FROM THE PEARY EXPEDITION

Philadelphia, Sept. 7.—The following telegram was received here today:

Indian Harbor, Via Cape Ray, N. F. Sept. 7.

Henry G. Bryant, Land Title building, Philadelphia.

"The pole is ours, thank you.

"—Peary."

New York, Sept. 7.—Captain R. A. Bartlett of the Roosevelt telegraphed to a friend in this city from Indian Harbor as follows: "It is accomplished. Kind regards to all."

New York, Sept. 7.—A second message from Commander Peary was received by Albert L. Bridgman, secretary of the Peary Arctic club, early today. In this message Commander Peary requested Mr. Bridgman to notify the geographical societies throughout the world that the Peary Arctic club expedition had reached the north pole. The message was dated at Indian Harbor, Labrador.

New York, Sept. 7.—General Thomas Hubbard, president of the Peary Arctic club, today received the following message from Commander Peary:

"Indian Harbor, via Cape Ray, N. F., Sept. 6.—Thanks to your assistance the 300 years' search of north pole is ended. Pole occupied by club's expedition April 6. Roosevelt returns uninjured. —Peary."

In response General Hubbard sent the following cablegram to the explorer:

"New York, Sept. 7.—Commander Robert E. Peary, Indian Harbor, via Cape Ray: Your cable gives me the best news I have had this century. Congratulations and best wishes."

Freeport, Me., Sept. 7.—Confirmation of Peary's success was received here in a telegram from D. B. McMillan, who accompanied Peary. The message, sent to McMillan's sister, Mrs. W. C. Fogg, the local postmistress, follows:

"Indian Harbor, Sept. 6, 1909.
Mrs. W. C. Fogg, Freeport, Me.: Arrived safe. Pole on board. Best year of my life. —Ben."

Worcester, Mass., Sept. 7.—Dr. D. W. Abercrombie, principal of Worcester academy, received the following dispatch:

"Indian Harbor, Sept. 6, 1909.—Dr. D. W. Abercrombie, Worcester academy, Worcester, Mass.: Top of the earth reached at last. Greetings to faculty and boys.

"—D. B. McMillan.

Donald B. McMillan was an instructor in mathematics and physical training at the academy until the close of the school last year, when he was granted a leave of absence of two years to go with the Peary expedition to the north pole.

## SUSPECT HELD FOR MURDER OF DOCTOR

**Moorhead Physician Is Hurled From Bicycle and Clubbed to Death.**

Special to The Journal.

Moorhead, Minn., Sept. 7.—While on his way home from a professional call at 11:20 o'clock last evening, Dr. Thrond S. Egge, one of the most prominent physicians in this part of the state, was hurled from his bicycle and was brutally murdered by a maniac or an enemy with a huge club. Frank Keathman of Fargo, with whom the doctor was known to have had trouble yesterday, was arrested at his home at an early hour today as a suspect in the murder.

It is alleged that Egge had a wrestling match in a saloon early last evening and that Egge threw Keathman, which so enraged the defeated man that he waited near Egge's home. It is said that there were blood spots on the prisoner's clothing. An inquest over the physician's remains will be held tonight.

**Clubbed to Death.**

Dr. Egge had just reached the intersection of Sixth street and Second avenue when his assailant stepped from behind a tree and knocked him to the street. He was within one hundred feet of his own home, and it is thought that the slayer had hidden near by for several hours waiting for his return. The doctor's watch was stolen and his pockets rifled, but it is believed that he was not murdered for the purpose of robbery, but that this was done to cover up the real motive of the crime. His murderer struck the physician again and again and then raced like a madman down the street, hitting trees as he passed with a big bludgeon that he still carried.

A. J. Wright of Moorhead saw the man rush down the street and states that he acted like a maniac. A few moments later Harry Larson and his brother, residents of Moorhead, while on their way home, stumbled over the body. They at once notified neighbors and the police were summoned, but Dr. Egge was dead before the officers arrived. His head had been beaten out of all resemblance to its original form.

**Keathman Is Arrested.**

The police at once swore in deputies who searched the neighborhood, and at 2 a.m. Frank Keathman was arrested at his home in Fargo. Keathman, who is a carpenter, was in bed at the time, and is reported to have been under the influence of liquor. In his clothes $7 or $8 was found. Keathman, up to the present time, has remained silent and has refused to make any statement.

Dr. Egge was a prominent Norwegian physician and had lived in Moorhead for nearly twenty years. He was married about six years ago and leaves a wife and two small children. Although at first it was believed, from the peculiar actions of the slayer that he was a maniac, another theory—that of murder for revenge with robbery to cover up the motive—is more generally accepted. Dr. Egge, however, was exceedingly popular in the city and was not a man who had enemies.

The weapon with which Dr. Egge was killed was the kingbolt of a wagon, belonging to John Lamb, a fuel man. It had been returned after the crime, and is covered with human hair and human blood. It is reported that an old row had existed between Egge and Keithman for several years.

### MOVING PICTURE ACTORS STRIKE.

Chicago, Sept. 7.—A strike of 250 actors and actresses employed at moving picture shows here marks a demand for $25 weekly for single acts and $50 for doubles. No playhouses were closed, but a general strike, involving 2,300 players, is threatened unless the demand is met.

## WATERS OF LAKE RUSH ON DENVER

**Great Jefferson Dam Breaks, Releasing Deluge That Imperils City.**

**MEXICAN TOWN OF 6,000 IS REPORTED DESTROYED**

**Heavy Loss of Life Feared in Settlements Along Gulf of Mexico.**

Denver, Sept. 7.—The great dam at Jefferson lake, fifty miles south of Denver, broke early today, and a deluge is rushing toward this city.

It is expected that the water will reach here late this afternoon.

Men on horseback are riding along the Platte river, warning residents of the lowlands to seek safety in the hills.

**Flood Raids Towns; Many Die.**

Tampico, Mex., Sept. 7.—An overflow of the Soto la Marina river, which empties into the Gulf of Mexico, five miles north of Tampico, has caused an enormous destruction of property and great loss of life, according to messages for relief which were received here today from points in that section.

It is stated that the town of Soto la Marina, with a population of 6,000, was destroyed.

**Americans Suffer.**

The homes of a large number of American colonists, mostly from Missouri and Kansas, who lived near Soto la Marina, were washed away. Several persons are missing.

The loss of life at Soto la Marina and other towns in the path of the overflow was heavy.

The towns of Palo Alto, Abasolo and Jiminez were some of the larger places from which reports of loss of life have been received.

Provisions will be sent from here to the relief of the destitute people.

## PESTERED WITH CHICKENS

**FERGUS FALLS FARMER APPEALS FOR PROTECTION FROM PRAIRIE HENS.**

Joseph Jackman, a farmer living near Fergus Falls, threatens to sue the state of Minnesota for damages as a result of injuries done the grain on his farm by prairie chickens.

Of course Mr. Jackman couldn't really sue the state, for the state is immune from damage suits; but he thinks he has cause for complaint, and he states his position in a letter to Governor John A. Johnson. The letter, mailed a week ago, was received in the governor's office today. As today is the first day of the chicken season, Harvey Grimmer, the governor's executive clerk, is of the opinion that the onslaught of chickens on the Jackman grain have been repulsed with a great loss of life on the chicken side.

Mr. Jackman's letter to the governor follows:

"Dear Governor: I am in trouble about what to do with six or seven flocks of prairie chickens that are destroying my grain. I can't shoot them off, as it is against the law to shoot them, and I understand that they belong to the state. Now, I don't want the state to turn loose its property on my farm to destroy my grain any more than I want one of my neighbors to turn loose his property on my farm.

"I should like to know if the state is liable for damages done by its property, the same as private individuals. The game warden has appointed deputies to keep me from shooting the chickens until the gun club season comes, and all the dudes from the Pacific to the Atlantic can turn loose and shoot the chickens raised on my farm.

"If I have raised six or seven coveys of chickens, who do they belong to—me or the state?"

### COOK'S BROTHER ISN'T EXCITED

**Theodore Gets News; Says He Expected It, and Returns to Bed.**

Special to The Journal.

Callicoon, N. Y., Sept. 7.—This town is Dr. Frederick A. Cook's birthplace. Its reception of the recent news again brings up the adage, "a prophet is not without honor," etc.

On last Tuesday evening the same train which brought the papers to Callicoon telling of the discovery of the pole by Dr. Cook also had on board a party of summer vacationists from New York.

In the excitement attendant upon the arrival of these visitors and their getting started by hired conveyances for the mountain hotels in the vicinity, the story regarding Dr. Cook practically was overlooked at the time.

But later, at 9 p.m. that night, W. J. Young of Young's fancy bazar and general store, also hay and feed, thought to himself that Dr. Cook's brother, Theodore Cook, might be interested in hearing the news, so he went to the telephone and called him up.

Theodore answered in the following language:

"Hello."

Mr. Young said to him:

"Well, Theodore, Fred has got there."

"Got where?" asked Mr. Cook.

"To the pole," said Mr. Young, glancing at the copy of the New York paper which he then held in his hand to refresh his memory.

"There is a dispatch from Copenhagen, which is up in that section, saying that Fred has found the pole."

"Well, It's nothing more than I expected all along," replied Mr. Cook. "Fred told me that's what he was going to do when he started. But I'm obliged to you, Will, for calling me up and telling me, and if that's all, I guess I'll be going back to bed now."

### "FARTHEST NORTH"

| Year. | Explorer. | Deg. | Min. |
|---|---|---|---|
| 1553 | Willoughby and Chandler | 64 | 32 |
| 1594 | Barnts | 77 | .. |
| 1598 | Ryp and Heemskerck | 79 | 49 |
| 1607 | Hudson | 80 | 23 |
| 1827 | Parry | 82 | 45 |
| 1895 | Nansen | 86 | 14 |
| 1906 | Peary | 87 | 6 |
| 1908 | Cook | 90 | .. |
| 1909 | Peary | 90 | .. |

SEEIN' THINGS.
Uncle Sam—Two poles; and I haven't had a drop!

## HARRIMAN WEAK; HAS HIGH FEVER

**Attack of Indigestion Leaves Financier in Critical Condition.**

Arden, N. Y., Sept. 7.—All the alarming rumors regarding the condition of E. H. Harriman have been revived, following his relapse of Sunday night.

From the best information obtainable today, however, it was believed that the attack that caused a hurry call for a New York nurse and probably two nurses was a temporary sickness caused by a sudden change of temperature or an indiscretion in diet, which the sick man in his weakened condition was unable to throw off.

Dr. W. G. Lyle, Mr. Harriman's private physician, calls the attack "acute indigestion." In a statement last night he said that his patient was better.

It was said today that although the progress of Mr. Harriman's latest attack has been at once arrested, his temperature remains high and he is exceedingly weak. The best information is that he is in bed, and although no confirmation of the report has yet been obtained from the house, little doubt exists here that there are other physicians attending him besides Dr. Lyle.

Talk of an operation has been revived, but there is nothing definite to support such a rumor.

**Odell Is Alarmed.**

Former Governor Benjamin B. Odell came from his home in Newburg today and was taken up on the inclined railway to the Harriman house.

Mr. Odell told a passenger on the train that Mr. Harriman was a "very sick man."

The former governor had long been a close personal friend of Mr. Harriman. It is believed from the early hour at which Mr. Odell left home that he was summoned to Arden last night.

It is said that the party now at the Harriman house includes former Governor Odell; Robert E. Gerry, Harriman's son-in-law; Dr. Lyle and two other physicians, all the members of his immediate family, and several nurses.

**Inquirers Referred to Doctor.**

New York, Sept. 7.—At the Union Pacific offices no direct information concerning Mr. Harriman's condition was obtainable.

"I shall have to refer all inquiries to Dr. Lyle," said Judge Lovett. "It is true that Mr. Harriman had another attack of indigestion, but I understand he is feeling much better this morning."

Representatives of the Harriman banking interests were with Judge Lovett during the morning, but it was declared that no significance was to be attached to this.

### HARRIMAN RAILS SLUMP

**Decline Is Followed by Waiting Attitude in Wall Street.**

New York, Sept. 7.—An opening break of 5¼ points in Union Pacific, 3¾ in Southern Pacific, 3⅛ in New Central, 2⅜ in Reading and 1 to 1⅞ in most other active speculative stocks showed the great anxiety caused in stock market circles by the reports of a relapse suffered by E. H. Harriman, while the stock exchange was closed for a three days' holiday.

### MARRIED FIFTY-FIVE YEARS

Dr. and Mrs. Jabez Brooks yesterday celebrated the fifty-fifth anniversary of their wedding. There was no formal function, simply an informal gathering of the children of the aged couple who dropped in for dinner and to congratulate their parents.

Dr. Brooks was for many years, until last year, professor of Greek in the academic department of the University of Minnesota. Despite his 87 years, he is still active of mind and body.

Among those who called yesterday at the Brooks residence, 1708 Laurel avenue, to pay their respects, were Mr. and Mrs. E. T. Sykes. Mr. Sykes is supervisor of the Minneapolis waterworks.

## SACK SEEN IN AUTO

**HEAD AND LIMBS OF GIRL ARE FOUND AND MAY CLEAR MYSTERY.**

**BODY IS IDENTIFIED.**

**Detroit, Mich., Sept. 7.—The dismembered body of the murdered girl found in Ecorse creek this afternoon was identified as that of Miss Mable Millman of Ann Arbor, Mich., who came here a week ago to visit friends.**

Detroit, Mich., Sept. 7.—The head and arms of a young woman were found today enclosed in a sack in Ecorse creek, under the Jefferson avenue bridge.

The face was in such a fair state of preservation that identification of the torso of the young woman, which was discovered sewed in a similar sack in the creek, should prove easy.

The authorities this afternoon began a search to find a farmer who is said to have seen an automobile from Detroit speeding toward the Ecorse creek bridge two weeks ago carrying a well-dressed man and a dirty and heavy-looking sack.

## CZAR TO LEAVE TONIGHT

**IMPERIAL FAMILY ON WAY TO CRIMEA WILL STOP AT BORKI.**

St. Petersburg, Sept. 7.—Emperor Nicholas and the members of the imperial family will leave St. Petersburg tonight for Crimea.

The celebration at Moscow and other cities on the way has been abandoned on account of the empress' weakness and nervousness. The only important halt before reaching Sevastopol will be at Borki, in southern Russia, where Emperor Nicholas, his father, and other members of the imperial family, narrowly escaped death in a railroad accident in 1888. Religious services will be held in the memorial church at Borki.

At Sevastopol there is to be an official reception and a review of the Black sea fleet. After this the imperial family will go to the palace at Livadia to remain about one month.

Emperor Nicholas' departure will delay the presentation of W. W. Rockhill, the new American ambassador, who is expected here about Sept. 15. John W. Riddle, the retiring ambassador, will leave here tomorrow without seeing the emperor in farewell audience. He will meet Mr. Rockhill in Berlin.

### DARES SISTER TO SHOOT; DEAD

**Lad, Aged 8, Living Near Bagley, Minn., Is Accidentally Killed.**

Duluth, Sept. 7.—Playfully daring his 14-year-old sister to shoot when she pointed a gun at him cost Elling Gulbranson, aged 8, his life today. He lies at his home near Bagley, Minn., with the top of his head shot off. The children were playing with a double-barreled shotgun which neither supposed to be loaded. His sister is prostrated over the tragedy.

### "BLIND PIGS" SMASHED

Memphis, Mo., Sept. 7.—Farmers and temperance people of the town met in the public square today; marched into all "blind pigs" in Memphis; smashed bottles, barrels and kegs, and poured hundreds of dollars' worth of liquor on the ground.

The temperance people brought legal action against the jointkeepers but no convictions were had at the August term of court, which has just adjourned.

At 8 a.m. today a number of farmers appeared on the street and were joined by a number of local temperance people. Then their smashing crusade began.

BERLIN.—The official statistics for the second quarter of 1909 show that 1,051 dogs have been slaughtered for food under government inspection, and 5,785 horses.

## SIOUX FALLS MAN SLAIN IN FIGHT

**Shot and Killed by Brother of Daughter's Suitor—Two Jailed.**

Special to The Journal.

Sioux Falls, S. D., Sept. 7.—Because he interfered with the love affairs of his daughter, George Hurd of this city was the victim of a murder at an early hour today, being shot and killed by a brother of the girl's suitor. Charles Radford, the slayer, and his brother, Eugene, have surrendered to the police. They claim self-defense.

Eugene Radford came to the city several months ago from his home at Franklyn, Ill., and his brother arrived last Friday. Eugene had been a friend of Miss Hurd for some time, despite her father's objection, and last evening the brothers accompanied Miss Hurd and her aunt to the carnival grounds and the local park, returning about 1:30 a.m.

Soon after arriving, they assert that they were attacked by Hurd and another man, both of whom were armed with clubs. In response to calls for assistance from his brother, Charles Radford was personally attacked by Hurd, who is said to have beaten him with a club. The two men clinched and Charles Radford fell to the ground with Hurd on top of him. The prisoner stated that he fought until he believed that both would be killed, when he drew a revolver and shot twice at his assailant, killing him. One bullet struck Hurd over the right eye and the other hit him in the neck, death resulting in a few moments.

Charles Radford explains the fact that he was armed by stating that both brothers intended leaving this week for the west and that he had a large sum of money in his pocket for the proposed trip and wished to be able to defend himself if attacked by robbers.

### REFUND OF MILLION ORDERED

**Interstate Commerce Commission Decides Yellow Pine Rate Case.**

Washington, Sept. 7.—An order involving approximately a million dollars in reparation was issued today by the interstate commerce commission. It included claims in what is known as the Central Yellow Pine association territory—Louisiana, Mississippi and western Alabama—and involves a refunding of amounts paid by a large number of shippers of yellow pine lumber from the territory to points in other states on which an overcharge of 2 cents a hundred pounds was collected by various railroads.

### MOORS SUFFER REVERSE

**Decisive Battle Soon May Bring Spanish Campaign to an End.**

Melilla, Sept. 7.—Fifteen hundred Moors suffered a severe reverse yesterday in an attack on the column of General Aguelera, who was marching to Sokelarb when attacked. The loss to the Moors was unusually heavy.

A decisive battle and the end of the campaign is expected within the next few days, as the Moors are anxious to strike a blow before the arrival of the 11,000 reinforcements that are preparing to leave Spain under the command of General Fernando Alvarez de Solomayer.

### ENGLISH-GERMAN WAR?

**Lord Northcliffe Believes Clash Will Come Within a Few Years.**

Winnipeg, Man., Sept. 7.—Lord Northcliffe, owner of the London Times, in an interview here today, predicted war between Germany and Great Britain. He said in the Krupp gun works alone 100,000 men are working night and day and on Sundays preparing for war.

"Many persons now say that Germany will fight Great Britain in the near future, and some have mentioned the year 1912," said Lord Northcliffe.

FORT WORTH, TEXAS.—Sixteen candidates for the governorship of Texas, all democrats, addressed Labor day crowds in various cities.

## PEARY TO CLAIM POLAR DISCOVERY

**London Message Says Commander Will Assert He Saw North Pole First.**

**EXPLORING EXPEDITIONS RACED BACK TO FRONTIER**

**Arctic Club Prepares to Seek World's Recognition for Second Claimant.**

**PEARY FIRST?**

London, Sept. 7.—The Reuter Telegram company publishes a dispatch from St. Johns, N. F., in which it is said that Commander Peary claims that he was the first man to reach the north pole.

News of Dr. Cook on Page 18.

New York, Sept. 7.—Announcement by Commander Peary that he has discovered the north pole rivets the attention of the entire civilized world.

Whatever question of priority may exist between the claims of Commander Peary and Dr. Cook, there can be no doubt that to the United States belongs the unquestionable credit and lasting renown of discovering the north pole. The remarkable coincidence of two American announcements of such a colossal achievement coming within five days, after centuries of fruitless endeavor, constitutes one of the most remarkable coincidents in history. The question of priority in reaching the pole now absorbs attention in this country and Europe. That Peary will claim to be the first discoverer appears to be definitely assured from the following:

First—Formal announcement has been telegraphed from Indian Harbor, Labrador, to all principal American and geographical societies of all nations, including Japan and Brazil, specifically announcing that "the north pole was discovered April 6 by the Peary Arctic club expedition under command of Commander Peary."

Second—A London dispatch received from St. Johns, Newfoundland, states that Commander Peary claims that he was the first man to reach the north pole. Aside from the question of priority, Commander Peary's announcement of reaching the pole appears to be accepted throughout the United States and the world at large by scientists as well as the general public, and there is an absence of the doubt and skepticism which greeted the Cook announcement. There is, however, apparent reserve of judgement on the question of priority between the two explorers.

Dr. Cook, in an interview at Copenhagen today, says he is the "first to shout 'hurrah for Peary.' If he has telegraphed an announcement that he has reached the pole, then it is true, and I congratulate him."

Dr. Cook also states that he does not want any controversy.

No further word direct from Peary has been received today, nor can there be any further word from him until he reaches Chateau Bay, Labrador, tonight or tomorrow. The world continues to be stirred with excitement and admiration for the achievement by which America has solved the problem of centuries.

Special to The Journal.

New York, Sept. 7.—Persons here who know the Arctic zone and Commander Robert Edwin Peary said today that without a doubt during the last month or six weeks the dome of the world, up in the narrowing circles, had been a race course of which the low hanging polar sun had marked the start and the first slender tip of the telegraph wire in the northernmost frontier of civilization, the goal.

Down this swelling curve of the earth's shoulder hastened the two racers for the prize of the world's adulation—Dr. Frederick A. Cook, perhaps unconscious that his rival behind him was pressing him so closely, and Commander Peary, fully aware that there was a man somewhere ahead of him who was going to put in the claim of the pole's discovery and receive the fruits of praise.

Dr. Cook won the dash for civilization by just five days. At Lerwick, in the Shetland Islands, he found the coveted cable end on Wednesday last and through it caught the world's ear.

Yesterday Peary got his message on the wire at Indian Harbor, away up on the northeast coast of Labrador—the same message as that which Cook had sent thrumming through the wire on Sept. 1.

**"Glory Enough for All."**

Two men dashed for the pole. Two dashed for the lands of men below. The dash for the pole was made with the energy of inspiration; that for the kindlier climes was urged by sternest rivalry and the great worth of fame.

Perhaps, said these intimates of Peary today, he struggled harder to get back to civilization ahead of Dr. Cook than he did to reach the goal of his twenty years' effort.

Peary's messages, coming as the very echo of Cook's thrilling story of his own dash into the arctic night, have set the whole world tingling as with a galvanic shock. They have demonstrated beyond all possibility of a doubt that the pole has been discovered—and by an American. Whether Cook or Peary is entitled to the greater credit is now not a matter of controversy. The words of Admiral Schley after the battle of Santiago bay are now applicable to the polar imbroglio, "The United States has won. There is glory enough for all."

Commander Peary's cablegrams reveal the enactment of a remarkable drama within confines of the eighty-eighth northern parallel, which, up to the time of Cook's appearance, had never been crossed by a living being.

**Trace of Visit Gone.**

Within a period of one year two white men, muffled deep in furs and leading gaunt cavalcades of dogs and Eskimos, had gone creeping, crawling, sliding through the polar night toward that spot "as big as a 25-cent piece," which is the geographical "top of the earth." Here, for the space of a few hours, each had paused, awed and terrified, beneath a sky in whose zenith gleamed the polar star.

Nearly a year passed between the first visit and the second. The flag which the first white man had planted in the frozen sea flaunted its brief interval in the boreal gales and then, torn to shreds by flying snow and ice, fell and was buried deep beneath the drifts.

The summer sun, corkscrewing up from the east, beat down upon the spot

Continued on Page Twelve.

# 1970~1979

# THE MINNEAPOLIS JOURNAL



14 PAGES—HOME EDITION. MINNEAPOLIS WEATHER—Fair tonight and Sunday; warmer Sunday. SATURDAY EVENING, MAY 7, 1910. PRICE ONE CENT IN MINNEAPOLIS.


## WORKS OF ART IN ENDLESS STREAM

**Antique Articles Furnished in Inexhaustible Quantity by Italian Shops.**

**ONLY EXPERTS ABLE TO PICK OUT THE GENUINE**

**Remarkable Supply Casts Suspicion as to the Truth of Representations.**

By William E. Curtis.
Correspondence of The Journal.

Florence, April 4.—One would expect that the consular returns from such places as Naples, Florence and Genoa would show very large exports of paintings, statuary and other works of art to the United States, since the tariff on such articles was removed in the Aldrich act last summer. But Mr. Crowninshield, the American consul at Naples, told me that he had not had any invoices of that sort brought to him; Mr. Smith, the consul at Genoa, said that he had certified to but one shipment, and that was a painting worth only $75, and Mr. Quay, the consul at Florence, said that the number of invoices from that office had not been any larger than before art was placed on the free list.

About half a million dollars' worth of antique furniture, curios, picture frames, wool carvings and similar articles, representing the art industries, are shipped annually from Florence to the United States, and about a quarter of million dollars' worth from Venice. The greater part of it is furniture from the palaces of those two cities, and that source of supply seems inexhaustible. Without including the antique furniture that has been sent from Florence and Venice to other countries, the amount that has gone to the United States already would furnish every palace in Italy, and the supply still seems to hold out.

**Supply of Antiques Inexhaustible.**

There are 160 shops in Venice where such articles are sold, and 122 in Florence. Some of these shops are very large, and they are crowded with beautiful old pieces of oak and black walnut, upholstered in leather and brocades of the fifteenth and sixteenth centuries; mantels and chests, picture frames of all sizes, marble ornaments for the garden, the courtyard and the drawing room, busts, benches, baptismal fonts, well curbs, seats, columns which are supposed to have once supported the ceilings of palaces and churches; fragments of altars, wainscoting, ceilings, doors and window frames and everything that anybody can conceive of, made of wood, iron, silver or stone.

All of these articles are represented to be genuine, and no doubt many of them are. It is difficult for anyone but an experienced expert to decide, and the only ground for suspicion is the unreasonable abundance, for at the rate they are shipped to all countries of Europe, as well as to the United States, one would think that the supply must have been exhausted years ago.

The most difficult class of articles to judge are rugs, and very few persons can tell the old from the new. Mr. Nesbitt, the rug buyer of Carson, Pirie, Scott & Co. of Chicago, who has had long experience, says the only way he can pick out an antique rug is by the smell, and he could not define that evidence so that anyone else could profit by it.

**Government Prevents Export.**

The Italian government for many years has had a very stringent law prohibiting the shipment of works of art from this country. This law provides that the government shall have an option to purchase every article of this sort that is offered for sale, and whenever anyone purchases a painting or a piece of sculpture, a piece of wood carving, or object of that sort, it must be sent for the inspection of a board of commissioners who are supposed to know all about such things.

This commission reports the case to the minister of education, who decides, upon their recommendation, whether the interests of Italy will be injured if the article in question is sent out of the country. The government has the first option for the purchase, and if it does not exercise that option it may either permit or forbid the shipment. In case of a permit, either the seller or the buyer must pay a duty of 6 per cent upon the appraised value, the proceeds of which support the art commission.

**Smuggled Across Border.**

Sometimes the government absolutely refuses either to buy or to permit valuable works of art to be shipped out of the country, but there are many ways of evading the law and that is the reason why so few articles of value appear in the record of exports from Italy. They are smuggled to Paris in various ways, by passengers on railway trains and steamers with their luggage.

Pictures and statuary are concealed in sacks of rice, barrels of beans and various other packages where the customs inspectors would not look for them. The four famous portraits by Velasquez, which were recently sold in the United States for $500,000, are said to have been sent from Genoa to Paris, concealed in the upholstery of furniture, but nobody knows whether that story is true or not. The smugglers know a hundred different ways of getting things over the frontier.

**Census of All Works of Art.**

In order to prevent this smuggling, the government has had a census made of all the valuable works of art in Italy, both in public and private galleries, in churches and in other places, and that list is tabooed; that is, the owners of pictures, statuary and other objects which are so recorded, are absolutely prohibited from selling them or allowing them to leave Italian territory. But the government is practically powerless to enforce the law. If a man who owns a valuable picture is hard up and needs the money, he can mortgage his picture at the bank; the bank will keep it until the note matures, and if the debt is not paid, it can foreclose and sell the property like any other collateral. And the government cannot prohibit the purchaser from taking the picture away if he chooses to do so.

Sometimes the commissions in the different cities catch a work of art that has remained unknown. For example, Marshall Cutler of Florence told me the other day about an American tourist who picked up a picture by an unknown artist which had no ap-

Continued on 2d Page, 3d Column.

## PUBLICITY BILL TO GO BEFORE SENATE

**It Is Amended So as Not to Require Publication Before Election.**

Washington, May 7.—The senate committee on privileges and elections today voted to report the campaign publicity bill. It was amended so as not to require publication in advance of elections.

**CLARK MAY RETIRE**

**No Lack of Aldermanic Candidates in Eighth, However.**

Alderman E. W. Clark of the eighth ward, it was said by friends today, will not be a candidate for renomination. The lines are being drawn for quite a contest in the ward, and it is said that Mr. Clark is willing to quit if there is a prospect of a good man taking his place. When seen today the alderman said he had not told his intentions yet.

W. W. Rowell of 3224 Second avenue S has filed for the republican nomination, making the third candidate in the field, Frank Haywood and Robert H. Saxton being already candidates. Mr. Rowell is a pioneer grain man and is now secretary of the United Commercial Travelers.

J. F. Conroy, member of the legislature, filed yesterday for the republican nomination for alderman of the ninth ward.

**HIDDEN WEAPONS DANGEROUS**

**Colored Man Held to Grand Jury for Carrying Revolver.**

That it is a serious offense to carry a revolver concealed on the person in Minneapolis was realized by Calvin Butler in Judge C. L. Smith's court today.

Butler was held to the grand jury in $50 bonds. He is the colored man who, Thursday night, became involved in a quarrel with a conductor of a Lyndale and Grand streetcar. Some one noticed that his right hip pocket bulged, and a policeman was called.

The evidence convinced Judge Smith that Butler did have the revolver. The offense is a gross misdemeanor.

"It is what should be done," said W. M. Nash, assistant county attorney, who was prosecuting the case. "There have been too many murders that might have been avoided if the murdered did not have a revolver in his pocket."

**NEW KING LOSES SUBJECT**

**George V. Renounced Almost at Hour of Succession.**

James Henry Rapelje of Minneapolis is the first man on record to renounce allegiance to George V., new king of England.

Almost at the moment the king was taking his oath of office Rapelje went to the clerk of the district court and declared his intention to become an American citizen. There the name of George V. was substituted in the oath for the name of Edward VII and Rapelje went away with his papers.

Rapelje is an accountant at the Beaufort hotel. He came from Canada. The last man in Minneapolis to renounce allegiance to Edward VII. was William J. Smith, formerly of Manchester, Eng. He lives at 320 Seventh avenue S.

**REDEEMS HIS PROPERTY**

**Farmer Pays 3 Cents Tax and 27 Cents Costs and Penalty.**

Joseph Glockner of Crystal Lake township had to pay 900 per cent penalty on his personal taxes today to rescue the statement from the sheriff. With this penalty his taxes amounted to 30 cents.

The original assessment on his property was 3 cents and the amount was so small he overlooked it. He received a notice from the sheriff yesterday asking him to pay or the van would have to be sent out.

To save the county a losing trip he and Mrs. Glockner came to town today and paid the taxes. There was a penalty of 1 cent, a clerk's fee of 25 cents, and a sheriff's penalty of 1 cent.

**PATROLMAN SUSPENDED**

**Revolver Borrowed for Inspection Gets Officer in Trouble.**

Patrolman John Ward of the fourth precinct police station is suspended for twenty days by order of Chief of Police Frank T. Corriston.

Ward, according to Chief Corriston, displayed a handsome and well-kept revolver at police inspection several days ago. The chief complimented the officer on the weapon.

"But later I learned that the gun was borrowed for the occasion," said the chief. "So I suspended Ward. He must show me a revolver of his own that will stand inspection."

**WASHINGTON MAY BE ORATOR**

**Macalester College Considers Negro Leader for Commencement Speaker.**

Booker T. Washington may be the commencement orator at Macalester college. The board of trustees has been in correspondence with several national figures, but it appears likely that the negro leader will be invited. The exercises will be June 8 at the Central Presbyterian church, St. Paul. On account of the commencement being the twenty-fifth of the college, the program is to be unusually elaborate. The graduating class will be the largest in the institution's history.

**GOVERNOR POWERLESS**

**Under Ruling, Cannot Make St. Paul Police Stop Dice Gambling.**

Attorney General George T. Simpson has advised Governor A. O. Eberhart that he has no power to compel the St. Paul police department to stop dice gambling. The complaint of Mrs. Russell R. Dorr, which was made to the governor, was referred to the legal department, and on this ruling Governor Eberhart will drop the matter.

**DUNN IS UNDECIDED**

**Princeton Man May Not Attend Republican Convention.**

A state republican convention without R. C. Dunn of Princeton would be a novelty, but in a statement at the state capitol today Mr. Dunn said he might forego that pleasure this time. He does not know whether he will run for the legislature or not as has been reported in some quarters.

**ARMOUR WINS IN NEW JERSEY**

Trenton, N. J., May 7.—Governor J. Franklin Fort today refused the request of Prosecutor Garvin of Hudson county, for a requisition on the governor of Illinois for the extradition of J. Ogden Armour, a director of the National Packing company, who is under indictment in Hudson county on a charge of conspiracy to unlawfully enhance the cost of meat.

## CASH IS FOUND IN STEWART'S OFFICE

**Administrators and County Treasurer Discover $500 in Old Purses and Boxes.**

**MUSTY DEEDS AND LEASES ARE COVERED WITH DUST**

**Old Executor in Feeble Health—Strain Telling on Him.**

Tucked away in pocketbooks and boxes in odd corners of the vault in the office of the late Levi M. Stewart, millionaire real estate operator, with vault door unlocked, was found yesterday more than $500 in bills and currency. The money was found yesterday by Henry C. Hanke, county treasurer, who with Charles H. Morse, executor, L. W. Collins and Paul J. Thompson, special administrators, J. H. Winchester, legatee, and Albert Hall, attorney, conducted a preliminary examination at the office of Mr. Stewart in the Kasota building.

Mr. Stewart had not entered his offices on the second floor of the Kasota building since last November, when his illness became serious. He had conducted his business from his home across the street, although he had occasionally sent L. A. Gordon to his office for papers and documents.

**All Dust Covered.**

When the men who are handling the estate of Mr. Stewart entered the offices yesterday they found dust covering everything. They went first to the office safe, which is in the middle room on the Hennepin avenue side of the building. Mr. Stewart occupied six rooms. Four of them are lined with bookcases filled with books.

Mr. Gordon, who knew the combination of the safe, unlocked the safe. In the safe were found about forty leases, covering Mr. Stewart's Minneapolis holdings, thousands of receipts, deeds and other documents, and a wooden box. In the box was $25 in small silver and a piece of a gold watch chain. The bulk of the silver was in quarters and fifty-cent pieces. The leases were not minutely examined, but a cursory examination convinced Mr. Hanke and the other men that Mr. Stewart's holdings were more extensive than was originally believed.

**Money Tucked Away.**

It was in the vault that the officials found evidence of the eccentricities of Mr. Stewart. The vault was unlocked. Tucked away on shelves were three pocketbooks and several boxes, each containing money. In the pocketbooks were bills, in the boxes silver. There was nothing in pockets or boxes to indicate that the money was intended for any specific purpose.

In the vault was also found the big ledger in which Mr. Stewart kept his accounts. The ledger and the money were locked in the county strong box after the officials were convinced they had left no money or documents of value in the office.

Among the things found in the Stewart office were two bottles of grape juice, a box of collars and two shirts.

**Officially Locked.**

At the conclusion of the examination, the offices were locked and the keys delivered to the special administrators. The work of inventorying the estate will not begin until the return from the east of John H. Winchester, the nephew, who left for Corrina, Me., with his uncle's body last night.

On the basis of values of the Stewart property of which he has knowledge, Henry C. Hanke, county treasurer, expects the state will receive $150,000 inheritance tax. Mr. Hanke believes he has a record of all the real property Mr. Stewart owned, and by doubling the assessed value he finds the estate to be worth between $3,000,000 and $4,000,000. Mr. Stewart's requirement that lessees of his property pay the taxes through himself enabled the county to keep track of all the real estate. The only exception to the Stewart rule in regard to taxes is said to have been in the lease to W. L. Harris and in leases made within the last few months.

**Inheritance Tax Heavy.**

Legatees of the Stewart estate, except D. D. Stewart, will pay 1½ per cent on their legacies after $10,000 has been deducted from the amount of each bequest. The Minnesota inheritance law exempts the first $10,000 of legacies. It places a tax of 1½ per cent on bequests up to $50,000; 3 per cent between $50,000 and $100,000, and 5 per cent on more than $100,000.

If the Stewart inheritance tax is $150,000, it will be three times the amount paid by the Lowry estate. The John Martin estate was about $2,000,000, and the Sarah Brown estate $150,000.

The inheritance tax must be paid within a year after the death of the testator, and 7 per cent interest is added if there is delay. The money becomes part of the state tax fund.

**Sets Day for Hearing.**

Judge of Probate George R. Smith has set May 31 as the day for the preliminary hearing, when appraisers will be named if the will is admitted to probate.

In company with Charles H. Morse, one of the executors, Mr. Gordon, G. B. Loomis and Mr. Winchester late yesterday inspected several of the real estate holdings of Mr. Stewart.

**Body Taken East.**

The body of Mr. Stewart was taken east last night for burial at Corinna, Me. J. H. Winchester, the nephew who came west for the purpose, and Mrs. L. A. Gordon, one of Mr. Stewart's attendants for the last five months, accompanied the body. At the train also were Mr. and Miss Gordon. The body had been removed early from the house and placed in a baggage car on the 6:45 Milwaukee train. No ceremonies were observed at the house. E. S. Pattee and Mrs. W. S. Pattee, cousins of Mr. Stewart, were at the house when the body was removed.

**STEWART'S HEIR ENFEEBLED**

**Aged Maine Lawyer Unable to Stand Trip to Minneapolis.**

Special to The Journal.

St. Albans, Me., May 7.—Sitting in an armchair in the library of his palatial home and showing evidence that the death of his brother in Minneapolis had affected him greatly,

Continued on 2d Page, 5th Column.

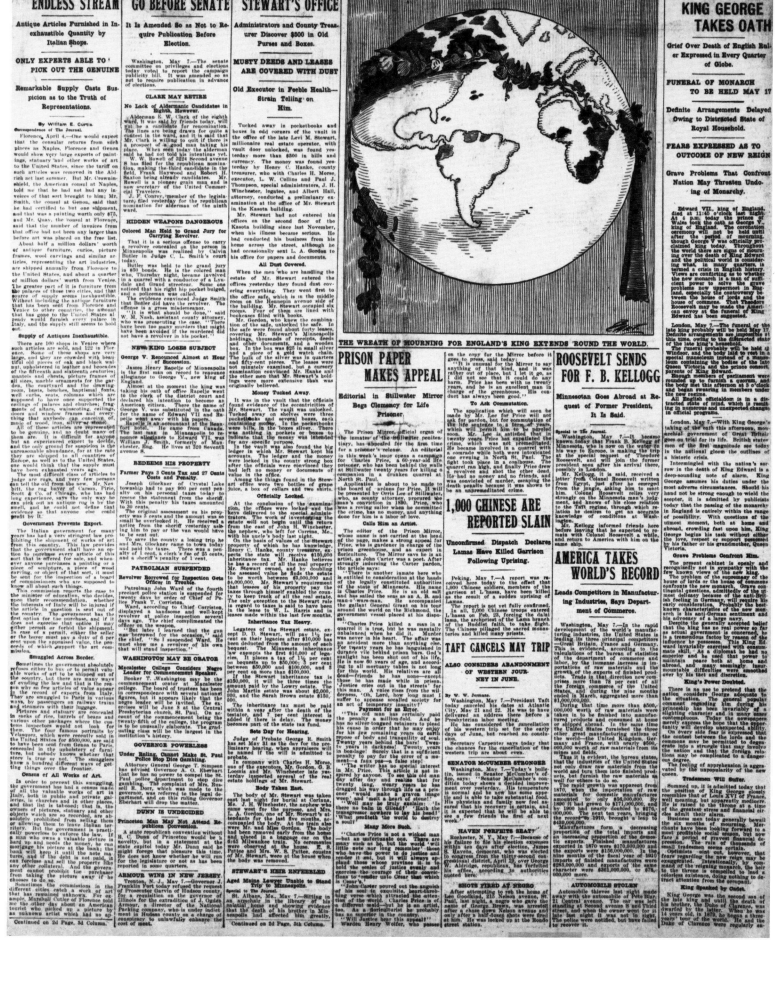

THE WREATH OF MOURNING FOR ENGLAND'S KING EXTENDS 'ROUND THE WORLD.

## PRISON PAPER MAKES APPEAL

**Editorial in Stillwater Mirror Begs Clemency for Life Prisoner.**

The Prison Mirror, official organ of the inmates of the Stillwater penitentiary, has appealed for the first time for a prisoner's release. An editorial in this week's issue opens a campaign for Charles Price, a 60-year-old life prisoner, who has been behind the walls at Stillwater twenty years for killing a companion in a drunken quarrel at North St. Paul.

Application is about to be made to the board of pardons for Price. It will be presented by Orris Lee of Stillwater, who, as county attorney, procured the man's conviction in 1890. Price, who was a roving sailor when he committed the crime, has no money, and anything done for him is a labor of love.

**Calls Him an Artist.**

The editor of the Prison Mirror, whose name is not carried at the head of the page, makes a strong appeal for Price, who is gardener in charge of the prison greenhouse, and an expert in floriculture. The Mirror says he is an artist, as John Carter was a poet. After strongly indorsing the Carter pardon, the article says:

"There is another inmate here who is entitled to consideration at the hands of the legally constituted authorities of the state of Minnesota. His name is Charles Price. He is an old salt and has sailed the seas as an A. B. and man-o'-wars-man. He accompanied the gallant General Grant on his tour around the world on the Richmond, the government vessel placed at his disposal.

"Charles Price killed a man in a quarrel it is true, but he was mentally unbalanced when he did it. Murder was never in his heart. The affair was an accident more than anything else. For twenty years he has languished in durance vile behind prison bars. God's sunlight has been shut out of his life. He is now 60 years of age, and according to all mortuary tables is not long for this world. His relatives are all dead—friends he has none—except those he has made while in prison. 'Justice cries out in the streets' for this man. A voice rises from the wilderness, 'Oh, Lord, how long must I suffer to appease socalled society for an act of temporary insanity?'

**Payment for an Error.**

"This old man has certainly paid the penalty a million-fold. And he has no silver-tongued retainers to plead his cause in order that he may enjoy for his few remaining years on earth repose of body and tranquility of soul. Twenty years behind the bars! Twenty years in darkness! Twenty years in bondage! Surely that is a sufficient penalty to pay for the error of a moment—a faux pas—a false step!

"The writer has no special interest in Mr. Price. This article is not inspired by anyone. To see this old man day after day and realize that for twenty long, weary years he has dragged his way through life as a prisoner 'would make a graven image weep' and 'melt a heart of stone!'

"Well may he truly exclaim: 'Is there no balm in Gilead?' 'Hath the transgressor nowhere to lay his head?' 'What profiteth the world to destroy a soul?'

**Many More Such.**

"Charles Price is not a wicked man—but an unfortunate one. There are many such as he, but the world 'will little note nor long remember' those who have the power to do justice and render it not, but it will always applaud those whose province it is to hold the scales of justice evenly and exercise the courage of their convictions to 'render unto Cesar that which is Cesar's.'

"John Carter poured out the anguish of his soul in exquisite, heart-throbbing verse which attracted the attention of the world. Charles Price is of a different mold—but he is an artist, too. As a floriculturist he probably has no superior in the country.

"Will Justice hear this appeal?"

Warden Henry Wolfer, who passes on the copy for the Mirror before it goes to press, said today:

"It is unusual for the Mirror to say anything of that kind, and it was rather out of place, but I let it go, as I did not see that it could do any harm. Price has been with us twenty years, and he is an excellent man in charge of the greenhouse. His conduct has always been good."

**To Ask Commutation.**

The application which will soon be made by Mr. Lee for Price will not ask for pardon, but for commutation of the life sentence to a term of years, which will permit him to be paroled soon. Mr. Lee is satisfied that in twenty years Price has expatiated the crime, which was not premeditated. He became involved in a quarrel with a comrade while both were intoxicated one evening in North St. Paul. The fight took place in a coalhouse. The quarrel ran high, and finally Price drew a revolver and shot the other dead. He had no money and no friends, and was convicted of murder, escaping the death penalty because it was shown to be an unpremeditated crime.

## 1,000 CHINESE ARE REPORTED SLAIN

**Unconfirmed Dispatch Declares Lamas Have Killed Garrison Following Uprising.**

Peking, May 7.—A report was received here today to the effect that 1,000 Chinese soldiers, members of the garrison at L'hassa, have been killed as the result of a sudden uprising of Lamas.

The report is not yet fully confirmed. In all, 2,000 Chinese troops entered L'hassa on Feb. 23, forcing the dalai lama, the archpriest of the Lama branch of the Buddist faith, to take flight. The Chinese pillaged the sacred monasteries and killed many priests.

## TAFT CANCELS MAY TRIP

**ALSO CONSIDERS ABANDONMENT OF WESTERN JOURNEY IN JUNE.**

By W. W. Jermane.

Washington, May 7.—President Taft today canceled his dates at Atlantic City, May 21 and 22. He was to have delivered an address there before a Presbyterian labor meeting.

He has considered the cancellation of his western trip set for the early days of June, but reached no conclusion.

Secretary Carpenter says today that the chances for the cancellation of the western trip are about even.

**SENATOR McCUMBER STRONGER**

Washington, May 7.—Today's bulletin, issued in Senator McCumber's office, says: "Senator McCumber's condition today shows a decided improvement over yesterday. His temperature is normal and he now has some appetite and is able to take substantial food. His physician and family now feel assured that his recovery is certain, and it is expected that he will be able to see a few friends the first of next week."

**HAVEN FORFEITS SEAT?**

Rochester, N. Y., May 7.—Because of his failure to file his election expenses within ten days after election, James S. Havens, democrat, who was elected to congress from the thirty-second congressional district, April 19, over George W. Aldridge, republican, has forfeited his office, according to authorities quoted here.

**SHOTS FIRED AT NEGRO**

After attempting to rob the home of Leo Goodkind, 215 Nelson avenue, St. Paul, last night, a negro who gave the name of George Brown, was arrested after a chase down Nelson avenue and only after a half-dozen shots were fired at him. He was locked up at the Rondo street station.

## ROOSEVELT SENDS FOR F. B. KELLOGG

**Minnesotan Goes Abroad at Request of Former President, It Is Said.**

Special to The Journal.

Washington, May 7.—It became known today that Frank B. Kellogg of Minnesota, who is now on the water on his way to Europe, is making the trip at the special request of Theodore Roosevelt, and will join the former president soon after his arrival there, possibly in London.

Mr. Kellogg, it is said, received a letter from Colonel Roosevelt written from Egypt, just after he emerged from the jungle, asking him to meet him. Colonel Roosevelt relies very strongly on the Minnesota man's judgment, and knows of his close relation to the Taft regime, through which relation he desires to get an accurate knowledge of conditions at Washington.

Mr. Kellogg informed friends here before leaving that he expected to remain with Colonel Roosevelt a while, and return to America with him on the same ship.

## AMERICA TAKES WORLD'S RECORD

**Leads Competitors in Manufacturing Industries, Says Department of Commerce.**

Washington, May 7.—In the rapid development of the world's manufacturing industries, the United States is leading its three principal competitors—Great Britain, France and Germany. This is evidenced, according to the calculations of the bureau of statistics of the department of commerce and labor, by the immense increase in importations of raw materials and the growth of the exports of finished products. Trade in that direction now comprises more than 78 per cent of all the foreign commerce of the United States, and during the nine months ended in March, aggregated more than $1,000,000,000.

During that time more than $500,000,000 worth of raw materials were taken in to be finished into manufactured products and consumed at home or shipped abroad. In the same time the United States furnished the three other great manufacturing nations of the world—the United Kingdom, Germany and France, with nearly $500,000,000 worth of raw materials from its mines and fields.

Thus it is evident, the bureau states, that the industries of the United States not only draw raw materials from the world and turn them into finished products, but furnish the raw materials as well for others to do so.

The rapid growth was apparent from 1870, when the importation of raw materials for domestic manufactures amounted to only $56,000,000. By 1890 it had grown to $171,000,000, and by 1900 had nearly doubled to $276,000,000. The next ten years, bringing the record to 1910, brought a leap to $439,000,000.

Manufactures form a decreasing proportion of the total imports and an increasing proportion of the domestic exports. Finished manufactures exported in 1870 were $170,000,000 and the exports were $156,000,000. In the nine months of the fiscal year of 1910 imports of finished manufactures were $283,000,000 and exports of the same character were $361,000,000, or $78,000,000 more.

**AUTOMOBILE STOLEN**

Automobile thieves last night made away with the automobile of Pete Blair, 21 Central avenue. The car was left standing at Second avenue S and Third street, and when the owner went for it late last night it was not in sight. The police were notified, but have failed to recover it.

## EDWARD DEAD; KING GEORGE TAKES OATH

**Grief Over Death of English Ruler Expressed in Every Quarter of Globe.**

**FUNERAL OF MONARCH TO BE HELD MAY 17**

**Definite Arrangements Delayed Owing to Distracted State of Royal Household.**

**FEARS EXPRESSED AS TO OUTCOME OF NEW REIGN**

**Grave Problems That Confront Nation May Threaten Undoing of Monarchy.**

Edward VII., king of England, died at 11:40 o'clock last night. At 4 p.m. today the prince of Wales took the oath as George V., king of England. The coronation ceremony will not be held until after the period of mourning, though George V was officially proclaimed king today. Throughout the world there are signs of mourning over the death of King Edward and the political world is considering what, in many quarters, is termed a crisis in English history. Views are conflicting as to whether the new monarch is a man of sufficient power to solve the grave problems now uppermost in England, especially the controversy between the house of lords and the house of commons. That Theodore Roosevelt may be made the American envoy at the funeral of King Edward has been suggested.

London, May 7.—The funeral of the late king probably will be held May 17. Definite arrangements are impossible at this time, owing to the distracted state of the late king's household.

The funeral probably will be held at Windsor, and the body laid to rest in a special mausoleum instead of a mausoleum containing the bodies of the late Queen Victoria and the prince consort, parents of King Edward.

Enough members of parliament were rounded up to furnish a quorum, and the body met this afternoon at 3 o'clock and began swearing in members under the new regime.

All English officialdom is in a distracted state of mind, which is resulting in numerous and unexpected changes in official programs.

London, May 7.—With King George's taking of the oath this afternoon, monarchial government of Great Britain goes on trial for its life. British statesmen of the first magnitude see today in the national gloom the outlines of a historic crisis.

Intermingled with the nation's sorrow in the death of King Edward is a deep-sounding note of alarm. King George assumes his duties under the most adverse circumstances. Should his hand not be strong enough to wield the scepter, it is admitted by publicists today that the passing of the monarchy in England is entirely within the range of possibility. With questions of the utmost moment, both at home and abroad, crowding fast upon him, King George begins his task without either the love, respect or support possessed by his father or his grandmother, Queen Victoria.

**Grave Problems Confront Him.**

The present cabinet is openly and recognizedly not in sympathy with the few known views of the new king.

The problem of the supremacy of the house of lords or the house of commons confronts the new monarch. Grave continental questions, admittedly of the utmost delicacy because of the anti-British feeling in Germany, will require his early consideration. Probably the best known characteristics of the new monarch is his anti-German sentiment and his advocacy of a large navy.

Despite the generally accepted belief that the king has no real power so far as actual government is concerned, he is a tremendous factor by reason of the influence he possesses. This King Edward invariably exercised with consummate skill. As a diplomat he had no superior and he used that power to maintain peace both at home and abroad, and many seemingly insurmountable difficulties were smoothed over by his tact and discretion.

**King's Power Doubted.**

There is no use to pretend that the nation considers George adequate to the situation. The general popular comment regarding him during his princeship has been invariably of a slighting character and in many cases contemptuous. Today the newspapers merely express the hope that the opportunity will develop unexpected ability.

On every side fear is expressed that the contest between the lords and the commons may be permitted to degenerate into a struggle that may involve the nation and that the foreign relations may be complicated to a dangerous degree.

The feeling of apprehension is aggravated by the unpopularity of the new queen.

**Tradesmen Will Suffer.**

Summed up, it is admitted today that the position of King George closely resembles that of Louis XVI of France, well meaning, but apparently mediocre. He is raised to the throne at a time of the greatest stress and financial circles admit their alarm.

Business men today generally bewail the six months of mourning. Merchants have been looking forward to a most profitable social season, but now face a period of gravest financial depression. The ruin of thousands of small tradesmen seems certain.

Optimists point out, however, that fears regarding the new reign may be exaggerated. Intentionally, by command of the reigning monarch, the heir to the throne is compelled to lead a colorless existence, doing nothing to detract attention from the occupant.

**King Spanked by Cadet.**

King George was the second son of the late king and until the death of his brother, the Duke of Clarence, was dwarfed by the latter. When he was 14 years old, in 1879, he began a three-years' tour of the world. He and the Duke of Clarence were regularly an-

# THE MINNEAPOLIS JOURNAL



20 PAGES—HOME EDITION. MINNEAPOLIS WEATHER—Fair tonight and Tuesday; cooler Tuesday. MONDAY EVENING, OCTOBER 10, 1910. PRICE ONE CENT IN MINNEAPOLIS.

## SULTAN'S LIBRARY QUEER COLLECTION

**Trade Catalogs Mixed With French Novels on Abdul Hamid's Bookshelves.**

**TURKEY TO ARRANGE MORE VALUABLE WORKS**

**Ancient Manuscripts Are Found Among Dusty Volumes in Constantinople.**

By William E. Curtis.
Correspondence of The Minneapolis Journal.

Constantinople, Sept. 5.—The privilege of searching the libraries of the mosques of Constantinople has long been coveted by the scholars of the world, because they are supposed to contain many ancient manuscripts of unique value and interest by Arabic, Persian, Greek, Latin, Egyptian and Byzantine scholars and historians, but very few originals of literary merit are likely to be found there.

Constantinople has never been renowned for its scholars or literary men. It never had a university until recently. The ancient city of Khiva, far away to the northeast, beyond the Caspian sea and the deserts of central Asia, was a literary center when Constantinople was the political capital of the world. Samarkand, Bokhara and the cities of Asia Minor were centers of learning and theological controversy when the thoughts of Constantinople were absorbed in military and political affairs.

Practically all of the literary treasures in the libraries of this city are the loot of a score of conquered nations. Most of them, when brought home from the wars, were dumped at the mosques and other places without arrangement and generally without any appreciation of their value of knowledge of their contents. Several of the sultans had an appreciation of literary merit and encouraged science and art, but this encouragement has never been continuous. More of them have been iconoclasts, like the Caliph Omar, who used the books of the great library at Alexandria, the greatest of its period, to heat the waters for the public baths.

**Valuable Books Neglected.**

Many of the manuscripts of the Alexandrian library were stolen, and some of them doubtless found their way to Constantinople. There were colonies of Greek and Roman scholars all along the coast of the Black sea, particularly at Trebizond and in the Crimea. Palestine was once rich in lore. Damascus, Antioch, Ephesus, Armenia and several cities of Persia and Turkestan were well blessed with wise men, authors, philosophers, theologians, mathematicians, poets and essayists, and were the seats of colleges and universities.

Nobody knows much about the libraries of Constantinople, however; none of them have ever been catalogued; few of them have even been consulted. The books are piled up on their sides in shelves and covered with the dust of ages. The Mohammmedan priests who have charge of them are usually illiterate men and look upon learning with superstition. They can give no information concerning the volumes in their charge. Only occasionally, when some scholar from Germany, England or Italy comes here, with sufficient patience and persistence to break through the restrictions that have protected these collections has anything of interest ever been brought to light.

**Ancient Manuscripts Found.**

These unknown collections, however, are believed to contain early copies of the gospel, of the Greek poets, of the Egyptian geographers, the Phenecian astrologers and other ancient tomes, and probably within a short time we will be able to learn something about them. The lost books of Livy are supposed to be in a collection of ancient manuscripts at what is called the topcapon or Cannongate of the Seraglio, the ancient residence of the Turkish sultans.

About fifteen years ago Dr. Amenius Vambery, a Hungarian author, writer and scholar of note, who somehow or other made himself popular with Abdul Hamid, obtained permission to examine the cannongate collection, and spent several weeks there. He afterward persuaded the sultan to let him take back to Hungary a number of historical manuscripts which were brought to Constantinople as loot from Budapest, after the Turkish army sacked that city in the middle ages. As it was strictly a personal matter between the sultan and Dr. Vambrey, there is no record of what the latter carried away.

Several years ago an enterprising Russian scholar found his way into the same library and secured a very early manuscript copy of the Hexateuch, the first six books of the Bible. The manuscript was sent to the Russian institute at St. Petersburg, where it is now being edited for publication.

Arthur Evans of London also got an opportunity to look over the books at the Cannongate a few months ago, and found a manuscript of great historical interests. It was a life of Mohamed II, by Critobolus, a Greek author, who accepted service under that sultan and became a sort of Boswell for him. His work is especially important because he was the only Greek writer of importance in that period who belonged to the Mohammedan faith and had an opportunity of consulting the Mohammedan authorities.

**Libraries Looted of Treasures.**

There is a strong impression that the libraries at all the mosques have been looted of their treasures from time to time, because the opportunity has not been lacking, and they have never been properly protected. No one has been responsible for the library at that most famous of all mosques, St. Sophia, which must have been very important at one time but is now only a collection of bound manuscripts, not more than three or four hundred in number, in the custody of a fanatical old priest. They have been kicked around the mosque and could easily have been looted by anyone who was able to gain the confidence of the custodian. But all the libraries are amply protected now, and the world of book lovers will soon have accurate information about them.

D. S. Mahmoud Bey, who has been recently appointed inspector general of libraries, tells me that there are forty-five distinct collections of books in the mosques and medresses of Constantinople, but all of them have been badly kept and are usually regarded as of

Continued on Twelfth Page, 7th column.

## SHERIFF'S PATROL AT MINNETONKA

**Property at Lake to Be Protected by Deputies During Winter Months.**

Lake Minnetonka's shores are to be patroled regularly this winter by sheriff's deputies in a determined effort to protect the property of lake dwellers from vandals and thieves. A plan for the policing of the lake is being outlined by Sheriff Otto S. Langum and the work at the lake will begin in about a month.

Thousands of dollars' worth of property has been stolen every winter for years past from the summer homes at the lake. Care takers have been employed in many communities, but hundreds of houses have been ransacked. In many cases the thieves have lived in the houses for days at a time and conducted their campaigns in the neighborhood. The only constables on the lake are at Excelsior and Wayzata and arrests have been few and far between.

Sheriff Langum feels that the time has come when he would be warranted in assigning one or more deputies to the work of protecting the property of lake residents. He plans to establish headquarters at some point on the lake and to have his men at the lake make a thorough study of the situation, patrol the lake shores regularly and keep in constant touch with the sheriff's office in Minneapolis.

### SUES TO REMOVE TRACKS

**City Begins Legal Proceedings in Kenwood Matter.**

Legal proceedings were today instituted by the city to compel removal of the Minneapolis & St. Louis spur track across West Twenty-first street in the Kenwood district. This is the track laid in 1908 to furnish facilities for an icehouse. Permission to maintain the track is rescinded in an ordinance passed at the last meeting of the council which has just been published.

"We will serve notice on the railroad company today asking the removal of the Twenty-first street track," said City Attorney Frank Healy today, while reading the official publication of the ordinance, which delayed action last week. The Twenty-first street track will be the first matter to be disposed of. We will move later in the other, the Franklin avenue crossing, but will wait a few days before beginning the proceedings."

### ANDERSON TO SPEAK

**Will Address Minneapolis Publicity Club at Luncheon, Oct. 19.**

Sidney A. Anderson of Lanesboro, Minn., the young attorney who wrested the congressional nomination from James A. Tawney in the first district, will be the speaker at the next noonday luncheon of the Minnesota Publicity club, Oct. 19. His subject will be "Publicity, Political and Otherwise."

President W. L. Harris says that the invitation was extended to Mr. Anderson without any political motive. "Mr. Anderson is the type of young man in politics that is attracting public notice," said Mr. Harris today, "and his success is a demonstration of good publicity work. For that reason we decided we would like to hear from him."

### SCIENTIST ENTERTAINED

Dr. L. O. Howard of Washington, secretary of the American Association for the Advancement of Science, was entertained at luncheon in the directors' room of the Commercial club today by the executive committee of the Minneapolis organization. Plans for the entertainment of the national meeting to be held in Minneapolis Dec. 27 to Jan. 1 were discussed and Dr. Howard told something of the program being arranged for the meeting. Those attending the luncheon were T. B. Walker, W. F. Decker, T. B. Chute, Professors H. F. Nachtrieb, E. M. Freeman, Dean F. J. Wulling, E. E. Nicholson, F. W. Washburn and F. E. Clements. Dr. Howard said the attendance on the national meeting this year promised to be large.

## FOR FIRE RELIEF

By virtue of my position as president of the State Red Cross society, in view of the dire needs of citizens of the northern part of this state who have suffered from recent forest fires, I hereby call upon the people of Minnesota to respond at once with contributions of money, provisions and clothing, to be distributed to the needy under the direction of this society.

Such contributions will be received by Kenneth Clark, St. Paul, treasurer of the State Red Cross society, and F. M. Prince, Minneapolis, acting as assistant state treasurer, and I hereby designate the mayors of the towns and cities of the state to act as collectors of this fund in their respective localities.

Prompt and generous response is imperative as the reports from the afflicted districts indicate that the need is great and will continue for months.

Given under my hand and seal this 9th day of October, 1910.
—Adolph O. Eberhart, Governor.

## MURDER CHARGED AGAINST DEITZ

**Coroner's Jury at Winter Blames Father, Wife and Son for Death.**

Correspondence of The Journal.

Hayward, Wis., Oct. 10.—John Deitz, his wife and his eldest son, Leslie, are all to be charged with murder in the first degree in connection with the killing of Deputy Oscar Harp. News of the verdict at the coroner's jury at Winter reached here shortly after noon. It was to the effect that Harp came to his death from a bullet fired either by Deitz, Mrs. Deitz or Leslie.

The hearing of the family will be conducted late today.

Deitz's wound is slight. The physician who dressed it today says it is only a flesh wound under the left thumb. Deitz put in his day complaining of the steam heat, to which he is unaccustomed. Clarence does not appear in sympathy with his father, and did not want to see him. Leslie continues defiant. Mrs. Deitz is in good health, though bitter. The children are kept in the residence part of the jail, cared for by Mrs. Michael Madden. They probably will be sent to their maternal grandfather at Rice Lake.

It is said by the authorities that if the charge of murder against Deitz fails he will be tried on the other charges, including that of assault with intent to murder Bert Horel. It is thought that Harp's death may be placed on Deitz by a consideration of the attendant circumstances.

### HARP'S FUNERAL TODAY

Winter, Wis., Oct. 10.—The coroner's jury today returned a verdict that Oscar Harp came to his death at the hands either of John F. Deitz, Mrs. Deitz or Leslie Deitz. Coroner W. F. Buck conducted the inquest before Justice W. H. Noyes.

Harp, who was found dead on the Cameron Dam battlefield late Saturday, will be buried late today, and all Winter will turn out for the funeral. Harp was 32 years old. He was born in Knapp, Wis., moved lated to Elmwood, married in 1897, and came to Winter in 1905. He was employed in a sawmill and was popular in the town. Mrs. Harp has partly recovered from the shock of her husband's death.

The coroner's jury found that the bullet that killed Harp must have been fired from the Deitz barn.

Everything is quiet today on the Deitz farm. Deputies Louis Lambert, William Fortier and Chester Colpitch are there taking care of the Deitz cows and the Deitz dogs. Colpitch is one of the men who was wounded. His ear was torn by a bullet, but the wound is not serious.

The closing scenes of the Deitz tragedy have made Deputy Sheriff Fred Thorbin a popular idol, and a movement has been started to make him sheriff. He is not a candidate for the place, but friends and admirers have started a petition in his behalf and predict they will have the necessary names very shortly.

## SPRING WHEAT QUALITY HIGH

**Estimated at 94.1 Per Cent, as Compared With 86.2 in 1909.**

Washington, Oct. 10.—The production of spring wheat, as estimated by the crop-reporting board for 1910, was 233,475,000 bushels, compared with 290,823,000 bushels in 1909, the yield per acre being 11.8 bushels, compared with 15.8 in 1909 and 13.7 the ten-year average. The quality was 94.1 per cent, compared with 86.2, the ten-year average.

The production of all wheat for 1910 was 691,769,000 bushels, compared with 737,189,000 bushels in 1909, the yield per acre being 14.2 bushels, compared with 15.8 in 1909 and 14.1 the ten-year average. The quality was 93.1 per cent.

The corn crop was 80.3 per cent of a normal on Oct. 1, or at time of harvest, as compared with 73.8 a year ago and 78.4, the ten-year average, according to the crop-reporting board of the department of agriculture.

## LUMBER YARDS SAVED

**MINNEAPOLIS FIRM RECEIVES INFORMATION REGARDING BEAUDETTE FIRE.**

Among the Minneapolis concerns interested along the Rainy River is the T. M. Pattridge Lumber company, which has suffered some loss, but has no accurate information.

Word was received today that the company's cedar yard in Beaudette was saved, but no one can explain what is regard as a phenomenon of the fire, which took all surrounding property. The company had a lot of cedar poles and ties at Pitt, but cannot learn how much has been destroyed.

George B. Partridge, a son of President T. M. Partridge and manager of the yard in Beaudette, like all the other residents of the city, had to flee for his life last Friday night. He saved nothing. Mr. Partridge returned to Beaudette Saturday and was surprised to find the yards safe.

### BICKNELL TO TAKE CHARGE

**Red Cross Director Will Come From Washington to Minnesota Fires.**

Earnest P. Bicknell, national director of the Red Cross society, located at Washington, today telegraphed Governor A. O. Eberhart that he will arrive in the twin cities Wednesday, and following an interview with the governor, will go to the scene of the northern Minnesota fires, and personally take charge of the Red Cross relief work. He says in his telegram that the news dispatches indicate a serious fire, requiring immediate relief.

A PICTURE IT MIGHT BE WELL TO HANG ON THE WALLS OF THE STATE CAPITOL.

# FLAMES ALONG BORDER STILL RAGE UNCHECKED

## TOWNS ENGULFED; MILLIONS LOST

**Fire Rangers Mustering Men to Fight Flames—Roosevelt Seeks Aid.**

**RAINY RIVER ON FIRE; ENTIRE TOWN MAY BURN**

**Blaze Sweeps Over a District Eighty-five Miles in Length—Spreading Rapidly.**

Special to The Journal.

Warroad, Minn., Oct. 10.—The fire zone covers a district 85 miles in length, from Gravel pit spur, west of here, to Stratton, Ont., and thirty miles in width, including all the territory between Red Lake, Minn., and the Lake of the Woods in the north. The fire is spreading rapidly in all directions.

One prominent lumberman stated that the loss will be about $6,000 a square mile, and as practically 3,000 square miles have been burned over the loss will be many millions.

The state of Minnesota is sparing no expense in fighting the flames, and has given instructions to the fire rangers to muster all the men they can possibly get.

**Roosevelt Appeals for Help.**

The town of Roosevelt, Minn., has sent an appeal for help to Rosseau, Minn., all the other available towns having been appealed to, and fifty fire fighters left from there last night for the scene of the fires. However, it is expected they will be of little use, as no human power can extinguish the raging walls of flames which are sweeping the country. No effort is being made to stop the flames where there is a thick growth of moss and even where there is no moss it is necessary to dig trenches very wide and deep. It is said that near Roosevelt one of these trenches was dug for twenty-five miles in length.

**Brands Carried for Miles.**

When the fire once gains headway it shoots like a whirlwind through the air, scattering sparks and flying embers in all directions. J. Simmons, sawmill owner at Roosevelt, said that one of these whirlwinds carried a piece of burning bark high in the air for a mile or more and set fire to his timber limit.

A son of Mr. Simmons, with his wife and family, would have been burned to death, only for the fact that they jumped into a well and there remained until the fire had gone past. Practically every railroad bridge between here and Pinewood, along the Canadian Northern railway, has been burned and trains consequently cannot get through.

**Rainy River Partly on Fire.**

Rainy River, Ont., Oct. 10.—The town of Rainy River is on fire from the International brigade to Sixth street, a distance of over half a mile, and it is feared the entire town will be destroyed. In the burned area, was the Rat Portage Lumber company's mill, one of the finest in western Canada, costing $350,000 to build. This was destroyed as well as the company's yards, containing 10,000,000 feet of lumber. The western Canada Flour mills, stave mills and fifty odd residences were destroyed.

All available hose and fire-fighting apparatus is in use, and appeals for assistance have been sent to towns in a large radius.

**More Losses Near Beaudette.**

The fine new plankmill of the Engler company, half a mile west of Beaudette, was burned Sunday, after escaping the flames which destroyed Beaudette early Saturday.

The women and children in Rainy River are packing, and many have already taken refuge on the steamers Five Roses, Empress and Wapiti, ready to leave should the wind change or the situation become too precarious.

All bridges are down between Gravel Pit Spur and Pinewood, and passengers have been obliged to return to either Winnipeg or Fort Francis. Yesterday, when the wheat train went through the trestle, a trainload of refugees had a narrow escape. It was traveling close behind the freight and was stopped on the very brink of the bridge.

**Many Pitiful Scenes.**

People who arrived from Beaudette while that town was burning to the ground tell of pitiful scenes while the population was waiting for a train. The piteous pleas of the women, mingled with the cries of the children and the oaths of the men, left impressions on their memory which will never be forgotten. As the train pulled in there was a wild scramble for places, many of them forgetting they were human beings, and pushing the helpless from their way. So crowded was the trainload of refugees that no one was allowed to carry anything, and the fifty odd cars of the train were so packed that many were obliged to get on the roofs of the cars.

**Seek Refuge in River.**

At Spooner several hundred rushed for safety to the Shevlin-Mathieu Milling company's buildings, relying on the efforts of the company's fire-fighting service to save them from being burned like rats in a trap.

Others rushed waist deep into the river, men carrying their wives or children out and dipping them into the water to stop the scorching of their clothes.

The agony these people suffered was intense, for the heat was so great that buildings several hundred yards from the flames would suddenly burst into fire, starting another blaze to add to the main body of the fire.

**Old Man Dies at Post.**

An old man, a servant of Albert Berg, remained faithful to the last. He refused to leave his master's property while there was any chance of saving it, and perished in the building he was trying to save.

Fully 2,000 persons have lost all they have except for the clothes they wear and many of these literally had the clothing burned off their backs.

Many settlers arriving her are suffer-

Continued on 2d Page, 7th Column.

### DETAILS OF DISASTER.

Towns and Settlements destroyed: Beaudette, Spooner, Swift, Langworth, Tipple, Creek, Graceton, Swift, Gravel, Pitt, Spur, and Cedar Spur. In danger or partly burned: Rainy River, Pinewood, Stratton, Sleemans and many smaller towns.

Estimated dead: From 200 to 1,000.

Bodies found: Sixty.

Known dead: Seventy-five.

Missing: 2,000 some of these supposed to be seeking shelter at various points, but many believed dead).

Hundreds of homesteaders outside the towns, unheard from. Feared they may have perished.

Area covered by fires: 2,550 square miles.

Estimated loss, $4,000 with fires still burning, increasing damage hourly.

### DEATH LIST.

Six unknown residents of Pitt, Minn.

Unidentified woman and baby, homesteader, near Pitt.

Two entire families, one of eight members and one of seven, residents ten miles east of Pitt, recently arrived from Grafton, N. D.

John Tully and five members of family, recently arrived from Fullerton, Neb., burned to death west of Spooner.

One servant of Albert Berg of Spooner.

Four land speculators from Davenport, Iowa, recent arrivals at Beaudette, caught by flames while out for homesteads on south side of Beaudette river.

John Simmons of Red Oak, Iowa, timber ranger, caught by flames on railway track while trying to escape to Rainy River.

Matson Ber~ and five members of his family burned to death on outskirts of Spooner when house was destroyed.

John Rolin and family of eight, from Pitt.

Severt Hagen.

George Weaver.

Charles Baker and Patrick O'Meara, both of Arlington, Minn.

Julius Bratten, homesteader, wife and five children.

——— Cliffen, homesteader, wife, and five children.

Tom Barr, homesteader, living near Pitt.

——— Macumber, wife and six children.

Three unidentified dead along Rapid river.

Matthew Brennan, living near Rapid River.

John Colvin, wife and three children.

J. C. O'Neil, wife and seven children.

Mrs. Pearl Brown's infant child. Mrs. Brown being badly burned.

Julius Bord, wife and children.

Carlo Lorenzo, homesteader.

Walter Ferguson.

Barwick, a homesteader, Mike Beaver, Kate, a woman homesteader, known by her first name only, and three unidentified dead are at Beaudette.

Seven settlers up the Beaudette River and eleven settlers between Rapid River and Beaudette were found dead, lying along a logging road by settlers who escaped the fury of the flames.

Nine dead bodies were seen on the Canadian Northern tracks by women who mounted horses and fled down the railway tracks.

Four unidentified are on the Root house west of Pitt, including one man, two women and a baby.

## RED CROSS WILL COLLECT RELIEF

**Meeting of Civic Organizations Opens Campaign in Behalf of Fire Sufferers.**

Relief through the Red Cross society will be subscribed by Minneapolis citizens for the aid of forest-fire sufferers along the boundary of Minnesota to the north, where several towns have been wiped out and thousands of persons are homeless, to say nothing of the dead.

At the call of Mayor J. C. Haynes, the presidents of the different commercial clubs of Minneapolis, the Publicity club, the Joint Improvement association and the Trades and Labor assembly, met in the mayor's office late today to plan a campaign for relief funds. At the same time, the mayor issued an appeal, calling the attention of Minneapolis people to the necessity for immediate action.

The Mayor's proclamation follows:

**The Mayor's Appeal.**

"Pursuant to action taken at a meeting of representative men of the twin cities, held at the governor's office yesterday, I hereby appeal to the people of this city to contribute to the relief of our fellow citizens in the northern portion of the state, thousands of whom have not only been rendered homeless, but also have suffered the loss of all their worldly possessions by reason of the forest fires, which have recently swept that district and are still raging.

"Many lives have been lost and much suffering has already ensued. Hence the necessity of most generous and prompt relief.

"By common consent of the meeting above referred to the state Red Cross society, with Governor A. O. Eberhart as president and F. M. Prince of this city acting as treasurer, will have charge of all funds and disbursements thereof, together with other forms of relief.

"All contributions should be made directly to F. M. Prince, treasurer, care of the First National bank of this city.

"Judging from the experience of former occasions, I am confident that the people of this city will be most liberal and prompt in their response to this appeal.

—"J. C. Haynes, Mayor."

Dated Oct. 10, 1910.

**Business Men Help.**

A meeting was seld in Governor O. A. Eberhart's office in the capitol yesterday, attended by representative twin city business men, at which time plans to aid the sufferers were discussed. The

Continued on 2d Page, 2d Column.

## KNOWN DEAD ARE 75; ROLL IS GROWING

**Estimates of the Number of Lives Lost Run From a Thousand Down.**

**FINANCIAL LOSS WILL FOOT UP MANY MILLIONS**

**First Relief Train From Bemidji Reaches Beaudette—Martial Law Declared.**

**EIGHT OR TEN TOWNS ARE ALREADY WIPED OUT**

**Survivors and Rescuers Tell of Terrible Scenes in Burning Zone.**

Special to The Journal.

Rainy River, Ont., Oct. 10.—Death-roll estimates of the forest fires which have destroyed several border towns and settlements run all the way from 100 to 500, and even to the appalling total of 1,000. These estimates, however, cannot be considered as more than guesses.

**The Known Dead Number 75.**

The reports from the country districts are slow and the losses in life will not be known for many days. The fires are still burning and nothing like a systematic investigation or attempt at rescue work can be done at this time. It may not be known for weeks just how many have perished in the lonely recesses of the fire-swept forests.

The towns of Beaudette and Spooner are but blackened wastes, and the settlements of Graceton, Langworth, Swift, Pist and Cedar Spur have been wiped out.

The town of Rainy River, on the Canadian side, and many smaller places are in imminent danger of destruction.

Some sixty bodies have been found, and the known dead are seventy-five or more. The missing number 2,000, but the most of them are no doubt safe. Hundreds of homesteaders outside the towns have not been heard from and many of them may have perished. The estimated financial loss is $4,000,000.

**The Worst Feared.**

It is feared that every settler in the district bounded by the Rainy river and Lake of the Woods on the north to twenty-five miles south of Fort Frances, Ont., and from Spooner and Beaudette, Minn., on the east to Warroad, Minn., on the west, who is not accounted for, is dead, as there seems to have been no escape.

For a distance of fifty miles from Beaudette and the Rainy river west to Warroad the woods were a solid mass of fire Sunday.

**Refugees Starving.**

The terrible results of Friday, Saturday and Sunday forest fires are beginning to be realized by the disheartened and homeless thousands. Bodies found along the railway track three miles west of Beaudette were brought here today. There was not a particle of clothing left on any of them save parts of shoes.

It will be days before all the dead can be reached, owing to the dead trees which have fallen over the roads. These will have to be chopped away before wagons can get through. In some instances houses are filled with refugees who are without food but a few miles from town.

**Sixteen Sheltered in Well.**

Matt Hendrickson came in from his claim three and a half miles southwest of Beaudette today and told of thirty persons who were housed in his shack without food.

He says that when the fire struck his place sixteen of them got into a dry well eight feet deep and remained there, nearly suffocating from the heat and smoke until the fire had passed. While the tornado of fire passed over the well it veered to the southeast of his house, which was not burned.

Every other inflammable object on the place was licked up by the flames.

**Seven Bodies in a Clearing.**

Many settlers got into the Rapid river and saved themselves by wading in the water, although even then their faces were blistered by heat. Seven bodies, which are probably those of the Roulin family, were found in a clearing in the woods where they sought safety.

The fire still threatens the few houses along the river in old Beaudette. The Engler company's men gave up hope of saving their property two miles down the river and sent all of their horses to a place of safety. The mill is valued at $250,000 and was only completed last August.

**Rainy River Fighting Hard.**

In Rainy River, 100 deputy fire wardens have been sworn in and divided into groups of ten, have started to fight the fire from all sides. Another wind such as came up Friday would seal the fate of this town.

Tired and worn out, destitute men, women and children roam the streets. The business men of Spooner and Beaudette, however, are showing a fine spirit of hopefulness and as soon as the people are provided for will organize plans to build the two towns as one on a better plan than that of the past.

Mayor Williams of Beaudette called the business men of those towns together on the streets here today and an organization was effected to distribute all possible supplies to the destitute.

**Bemidji Relief Train Arrives.**

A special train arrived on the Minnesota & International railway bearing provisions for Rainy River and the Bemidji company of the Minnesota na-

# The Minneapolis Sunday Tribune

VOL. XLIV., NO. 177. MINNEAPOLIS, MINNESOTA, SUNDAY, MARCH 5, 1911. EIGHTY-SIX PAGES. PRICE FIVE CENTS.

## 4 Per Cent Bond Issue Upheld by Hennepin

### Senate Delegation Goes on Record for Fixed Interest After Study.

### Reasons for Stand Set Forth in Statement Issued Yesterday.

### Advantages in Below Par Scale Declared Manifold in Scope.

All doubt as to how the Hennepin senatorial delegation will act on the bonds asked for by the Minneapolis council and approved by the Hennepin house delegation, was dispelled in a typewritten statement of the senators' position issued after an executive session of the delegation yesterday.

The total bonds asked for will be cut $1,050,000. Of this amount, the graded schools will lose $100,000, the park board $200,000, and maintenance and improvement fund $750,000.

The five Republican senators were present in the offices of Senator Dwinnell, 1217 Plymouth building. They were: Senators Dwinnell, Wallace, Fosseen, Wilson and Ewen.

The house delegation has already passed the school bonds asked for and will attempt to pass under suspended rules the remainder of the bond authorization, either Tuesday or Monday. In no case, it is expected, will they cut the appropriation asked for. This will compel the bills to be sent back to the house, after being passed in their amended form by the senate.

**Bond Values Discussed.**

The house and senate delegations are at loggerheads on another point. The city council and the house delegation want the interest rate raised from four per cent to four and one-half per cent, as it is said they cannot sell them at par at four per cent. The senators say the bonds should retain the four per cent maximum interest rate and offered below par if necessary to dispose of them. They say it is not only a better business proposition but will tend to better the credit of the city and make them more easily salable.

The statement issued by the senatorial delegation follows:

The senate delegation, after a most thorough investigation and after mature deliberation, have decided that the only proper method for the issuance of bonds is to have the interest fixed at four per cent and to limit the price at which the bonds should be sold at 95, or five per cent less than par. The reasons for the position are as follows:

**Reasons for Position.**

First, that the established rule for the sale of municipal bonds provides that the interest shall be fixed at the whole per cent or at the half per cent; in other words our bonds must have a rate of either four per cent or four and one-half per cent. At the present time our bonds can be marketed at approximately par, and, in the past bonds have sold at such a premium that the rate of interest thereon in a few instances has not amounted to more than 3.20 per cent. It is to be hoped that this condition will again arise.

Second, to advertise to the world that we are compelled to go on a four and a half basis is a much more serious reflection upon the credit of the city that it is to permit bonds to be sold at slightly less than par.

Third, bonds sell better in the market at slightly under par than they will sell at an amount considerably in excess of par.

Fourth, if the bonds sell at a considerable amount above par it gives the various boards and commissions a larger sum than they have asked for. For instance four and a half per cent bonds at the present time would sell at about 1.0869 and the sale of $1,000,000 worth of bonds instead of bringing in proceeds of $1,000,000 would produce a fund of $1,086,900.

**Below Par Favored.**

We are told by bond houses, through whom most of the bonds of the city have been negotiated, that it is much easier to sell a bond slightly less than par than it is at a considerable premium; that in fact there would be a difference of about one per cent between the proceeds of bonds sold at a discount and those sold at a premium in favor of those sold at a discount. This is the opinion of all of our local purchasers of bonds and is reinforced by all of the other bond houses with whom we have been able to communicate.

For instance, the Harris Trust & Savings bank of Chicago, the largest bond house in the world, says: "We think it is safe to say that at almost anytime when the 4's would sell readily at par, the 4½'s would not sell at all freely on a four per cent basis and that, for instance instead of getting 1.0869 the bonds would probably have to be sold around 1.07.

A. B. Leach & Co. of Chicago also state: "We have always found it very much easier to interest the investor in a bond at par or at a discount than where his purchase necessitates the payment of a premium. It is generally the custom to get a lower interest for discount bonds than premium bonds. In all the years that we have been in business we have never heard of any city's credit suffering through having sold its bonds below par."

**City's Credit Not Affected.**

N. W. Halsey & Co. of Chicago also say: "If the market is not in a condition to absorb the 4 per cent bonds, the mere fact that these 4 per cent bonds are sold at a discount rather than 4½ per cent bonds being sold at a premium, does not to our mind reflect in any way whatever upon the credit of the city."

This same opinion is held by the Minnesota Loan & Trust company, the Hennepin County Savings Bank, the Northwestern National Bank, the First National Bank and the Wells & Dickey company of this city.

Realizing the very large issue of bonds which may be placed in this city in the near future the delegation believes it absolutely necessary that some provision as to the rate of interest be

(Continued on Page 11, Col. 2.)

### THE WEATHER

**Local Official Forecast.**

Fair.

**Yesterday's Temperatures.**

| | | | |
|---|---|---|---|
| 6 a. m. | 15 | 3 p. m. | 32 |
| 7 a. m. | 14 | 4 p. m. | 32 |
| 8 a. m. | 13 | 5 p. m. | 31 |
| 9 a. m. | 16 | 6 p. m. | 30 |
| 10 a. m. | 18 | 7 p. m. | 29 |
| 11 a. m. | 22 | Maximum | 32 |
| 12 m. | 26 | Minimum | 13 |
| 1 p. m. | 27 | Range | 19 |
| 2 p. m. | 30 | Mean | 22 |

**The Wind.**

The wind yesterday reached a maximum velocity of 17 miles.

**Washington Official Forecast.**

Minnesota—Increasing cloudiness today; rain or snow in west portion; tomorrow rain or snow; colder west portion.

Iowa—Generally fair today; tomorrow unsettled, probably rain; warmer today.

North Dakota—Local snows today and probably tomorrow; colder tomorrow.

South Dakota—Local rains or snow today and probably tomorrow; colder tomorrow; in west portion tonight.

Montana—Unsettled weather, with rain or snow today and probably tomorrow; colder today in west portion.

Upper Michigan—Increasing cloudiness and warmer today; tomorrow rain or snow.

Wisconsin—Generally fair today, rising temperature; tomorrow rain or snow, moderate probably brisk south and east winds.

**General Observations.**

| Station. | A | B | C | Station. | A | B | C |
|---|---|---|---|---|---|---|---|
| Boston | 28 | 32 | .... | Bismarck | 30 | 32 | .... |
| Buffalo | 20 | 28 | .04 | Des Moines | 36 | 40 | .... |
| New York | 32 | 34 | .01 | Duluth | 20 | 24 | .... |
| Wash'ton | 38 | 42 | .... | Huron | 32 | 34 | .... |
| El Paso | 72 | 76 | .... | Kansas C | 44 | 46 | .... |
| Galveston | 66 | 72 | .... | Moorhead | 28 | 28 | .... |
| Jack'ville | 66 | 71 | .... | Omaha | 40 | 44 | .... |
| N Orleans | 66 | 76 | .... | St. Louis | 42 | 46 | .... |
| S Antonio | 72 | 74 | .... | St. Paul | 28 | 34 | .... |
| Alpena | 16 | 20 | .02 | Denver | 50 | 50 | .... |
| Chicago | 28 | 33 | .... | Havre | 24 | 24 | .... |
| Cincinnati | 38 | 46 | .02 | Helena | 34 | 38 | .... |
| Cleveland | 24 | 32 | .... | Salt Lake | 44 | 56 | .02 |
| Detroit | 24 | 34 | .... | L. Angeles | 56 | 66 | .32 |
| Escanaba | 18 | 24 | .... | S Francisco | 50 | 52 | .50 |
| G Rapids | 26 | 30 | .... | San Diego | 58 | 62 | .10 |
| Green B | 26 | 28 | .... | Calgary | 28 | 32 | .... |
| Madison | 26 | 30 | .... | Edmonton | 26 | 30 | .... |
| Marquette | 12 | 16 | .06 | Medicine H | 16 | 32 | .... |
| Memphis | 54 | 60 | .... | M'nnedosa | 16 | 16 | .04 |
| Milwaukee | 26 | 30 | .... | Montreal | 16 | 20 | .... |
| Ste. Marie | 10 | 16 | .... | Winnipeg | 16 | 16 | .... |

A—Temperature at 7 p. m. yesterday.
B—Maximum during last 24 hours.
C—Precipitation during last 24 hours.

### Today's Contents.

The Sunday Tribune today consists of nine sections and 86 pages, as follows:



**Special Features.**

First Section—Editorial; Telegraph News; Minneapolis News; Sunshine Society.

Second Section—Society News; Automobile News; Art; Settlement Work; Women and Their Work; Theaters; Music; Women's Clubs by Mrs. H. N. McKusick.

Third Section — Real Estate; Markets.

**Telegraph News.**

Sixty-first congress ended; Taft issues proclamation calling for extra session to begin April 4 to pass upon reciprocity treaty; tariff board bill strangled by filibuster; Arizona and New Mexico statehood bills not acted upon; Cannon eulogized and delivers valedictory as he steps down and out as speaker; turbulent scenes mark closing hours.

Pacific fleet is ordered to Hawaii to guard island possessions from any hostile movement.

Frank G. Bigelow paroled from Leavenworth federal prison; jokes about life in bastile.

Italian baron who stabbed princess may live to answer for crime; bullet still in his head.

F. M. Richardson, basketball association president, defeats Mayor Thompson for Rochester, Minn., mayoralty nomination after campaign of day.

Territorial legislature in Honolulu may ask federal aid in stamping out cholera epidemic in capital.

**News of the Twin Cities.**

Jerry McCarthy and Peter Jule, two Minneapolis crooks, break jail at Stillwater and escape. Posse is in close pursuit.

Mine lease squabble aired in courts results in lively tilts between opposing counsel—Permanent injunction issued restraining directors from leasing mining property.

Hennepin senatorial delegation, after an investigation and mature deliberation, declare that the only proper method for the issuance of bonds is to have the interest fixed at 4 per cent and to limit the sale price.

Realty in the business section of Minneapolis is declared to be cheaper than in other cities of its class. It is said property offers better investment chances here than in larger cities.

"The Servant in the House" will be put on as a benefit for the Husted family. The play will be given at the Shubert and will be under the auspices of the Associated Charities and Sunshine Society.

A substitute for saloons will be discussed by Rev. James E. Freeman of St. Mark's church at the next meeting of the Publicity club.

Tenants crowd the office in the new Plymouth building before the workmen have finished the rooms. The floor space of the new building is bigger than that of any of the newer ones.

### BOY FLEES TRAINING SCHOOL

**Red Wing Institution "Trusty" Escapes in the Night.**

Red Wing, March 5.—(Special.)—A 20-year old inmate of the boys' department of the state training school escaped from the institution during the night and has not been captured.

He was one of the "trusties" and had been assigned to perform the duties of night fireman at the school.

It is believed his capture and return to the school will be brought about in a few days, as but few make good their escape.

**Twelve-Story Plunge Fatal.**

*By Associated Press.*

Chicago, March 5.—While installing an elevator here yesterday, Charles Lindstrom, 27 years old, plunged 12 stories to his death, in view of his brother, John. Lindstrom's body struck the bottom of the shaft, where the brother was working.

## Cruisers of Pacific Ordered to Hawaii

### Six Armored Boats to Guard Uncle Sam's Possessions in Mid-Ocean.

### Navy Department Not Taking Chances on Being Caught Napping.

### Formidable Showing Hoped to Suppress Any Hostile Power.

(Special to The Sunday Tribune.)

Washington, D. C., March 5.—The whole Pacific fleet, by agreement with the stragetists of the war department, will proceed to the Hawaiian Islands.

This was yesterday's additional development showing that the war and navy departments do not propose to be caught napping in case of an attack on the Hawaiian Islands, where a sudden onslaught, in the opinion of all officials, would be first directed by Japan in case she declared or entered upon a war with the United States. The fact that the whole Pacific fleet in the near future will be stationed at Honolulu is explained as having two objects, both of which are manifestly important and of international significance.

**First: Four or five cruisers of the Pacific fleet will attempt to make landings in places from which the department has reports from the hydrographic officers that landings might be made by vessels of heavy displacement.**

**Second: In addition to this practical experiment, and under the guise of an experiment, the war and navy officials will succeed in having necessarily at Honolulu, four or five armored cruisers. There is no official of the government who will say for publication that these movements are aimed at any particular naval power, friendly or hostile.**

The fact remains, however, that all the moves which have been described bear directly upon the alarming report current in congress and elsewhere that the United States might as well be on guard against a traditionally irresponsible enemy.

Officials of the war department said yesterday that it would be criminal negligence if the United States did not make all the preparation possible to defend Hawaii, both as an educational factor for this country and place in position the best force obtainable, without exciting the irritable temperament of Japan.

**Boats in Fleet.**

The six armored cruisers, components of the Pacific fleet, are:

California (flagship of Read Admiral Thomas), Captain Charles H. Harlow, at San Pedro, Cal.

Maryland, Captain James C. Gilmore, at the navy yard, Bremerton, Washington.

South Dakota, Captain Frank M. Bennett, at San Pedro, Cal.

Second division—Read Admiral William H. H. Sutherland ordered to command.

West Virginia, Captain John N. Orchard, at the navy yard, Bremerton.

Colorado, Captain William A. Gill, at the navy yard, Bremerton.

Pennsylvania, Captain Charles F. Pond, at San Pedro, California.

These do not constitute a first class fleet, but they are an aggregation of first class pawns in the game which it is proposed to play.

### PRESIDENT WILL GO SOUTH

**Recreation Trip to Precede Strenuous Work of Extra Session.**

*By Associated Press.*

Washington, March 5.—During the month's interim between now and the assembling of the extra session of congress, President Taft expects to spend several weeks in the South, most of it in resting up from the strenuous days he has had during the last few months and in getting ready for a possible entire summer in Washington.

## Iron Range Road Planned

### Canadian Northern to Invade the Vermillion Territory—Surveyors at Work.

Duluth, Minn., March 5.—(Special.)—The Canadian Northern road is planning to invade the Vermillion iron range and has a crew of surveyors in the field running line from Cook on the Rainy Lake division to Pine Island and east.

The company's agents are getting data concerning the range with reference to present and prospective tonnage. This data embraces the prospective product of new mines. It is expected that the new line will continue north and east to connect with the old Port Arthur, Duluth & Western road, which is owned by the Canadian Northern and which runs southwest from Port Arthur to near the Minnesota line.

**Capablanca Still in Lead.**

*By Associated Press.*

San Sebastian, March 5.—Adjourned games were played in the International Chess Masters' tournament yesterday, resulting as follows:

Capablanca beat Janowski, Spielman beat Leonhardt, Rubinstein beat Janowski, Vidmar beat Burn, Leonhardt lost to Rubinstein and Duras lost to Spielman. Narozaya and Niemzowitsch drew their game and the Teichmann-Garrasch game was further adjourned. Capablanca still leads the players with a record of 6½ games won and 1½ lost.

**Former Slave, 105, Is Dead.**

*By Associated Press.*

Seattle, March 5.—Mrs. Mary Wray, who was born a slave in Virginia in February, 1807, died here Friday in her 105th year. In her childhood she was sold to John Lovell of Nashville, Tenn., on whose plantation she lived until the close of the war. She helped to cut and haul ties for the first railroad built into Nashville. She leaves two children, aged 82 and 86, in Nashville.

## Banker Leaves Cell; Thanks His Jailers

### Frank G. Bigelow, Paroled From Federal Prison, Goes to Milwaukee.

### Aged Man and Fellow Prisoner Are Escorted From Leavenworth Bastile.

### Smiles Wreath Wisconsin Man's Face—Jokes of Jail Life.

*By Associated Press.*

Leavenworth, Kan., March 5.—"I believe there is little probability of my return and I thank you for your well wishes, I appreciate the treatment I have received while here and hope that the same courtesy will be extended others."

Such were the words of Frank G. Bigelow, the Milwaukee ex-banker, as he left the gate of the government reservation yesterday afternoon, paroled until the termination of his short time sentence, Feb. 20, 1912, when he finally will be discharged as a prisoner under the federal government.

Bigelow, in company with T. G. Hayes, a former banker of Washington, D. C., who was also paroled yesterday, passed through the big gates at the front of the penitentiary and walked the quarter mile to the car station, still in charge of a guard. It was when he shook hands and told the guard good-by that he made the foregoing statement.

Thomas Cogbill, formerly a banker of Seymour, Wis., was also paroled.

A reporter met the two paroled men as they left the guard. Mr. Bigelow refused a cigar, took a piece of tobacco from a well worn pouch, a relic of the years spent in the prison, and conversed freely with the reporter and Hayes.

"I dislike to talk of the experience inside the walls," he said, looking back at the great penitentiary. "But it has been a strange experience. I regret it in one way, but in another it is different. What I will do after I return to my home in Milwaukee I will not say. I don't care to discuss the possibility of returning to active business. I will comply with the clause of the parole law which makes it obligatory for a man to keep busy after he is out, however," said the aged banker, smiling.

**Jokes About Prison Life.**

When the car arrived, the three boarded it, and Bigelow sat in a corner looking out of the window. As the prison passed out of sight, he sighed and turned to Hayes. They talked lightly and joked each other on different experiences in the institution.

"I always had it on you fellows," Bigelow said, as he took his tobacco pouch from his pocket, "my supply of tobacco never ran out," and with similar conversation they continued the ride.

A woman with a small baby got on the car. Bigelow turned to Hayes and the reporter. "I suppose that neither of you has a family?" he asked. "You appear young. It is better for you, Tommy," he said to Hayes, "and neither of you can realize what this means to me," and he smiled at the child. Upon his arrival here Bigelow went directly to the home of M. L. Hacker, former mayor of Leavenworth. There he had dinner and will await the arrival of his son Gordon. The two, according to Bigelow, will go to Milwaukee together.

## Baron, Slayer of Princess, May Be Saved for Law

### Vincenzo Paterno, Who Shot Self After Murder, Probably Will Live.

### Denies He Killed Woman Over Money—Says Love Was the Cause.

*By Associated Press.*

Rome, March 5.—It would seem now that Baron Vincenzo Paterno, the army lieutenant, who stabbed Princess Giulia Trigona Di Sant'Elia, lady-in-waiting, to Queen Helena, to death will live to answer for his crime. The attending physicians believe that the crisis has passed. The fever has decreased and Paterno rested for several hours yesterday.

The bullet, which he fired in an attempt to commit suicide, is still lodged in his skull, but the patient appears not to have been seriously injured. Owing to the improvement in Paterno's condition, the crown prosecutor interrogated him yesterday afternoon for nearly an hour. Paterno took advantage of his condition to answer only what he wished. He repeated often:

"I loved that woman. I loved her too much. She refused to belong to me longer. It made me lose my head."

He insisted on issuing a note denying that he killed the princess for revenge or that he desired to have her money.

Paterno, after waking from a restful sleep yesterday, was asked by a doctor if he desired anything. He answered:

"Yes, cigarets and black coffee," but his request was denied.

### MISSING SON'S BODY FOUND

**Remains of Red Wing Man Missing Four Months in River.**

Red Wing, Minn., March 5.—(Special.)—The body of Charles Miller, son of Mr. and Mrs. W. I. Miller of this city, who had been missing from his home since Nov. 18 last, was found yesterday in the Mississippi river near the city sewer outlet. An officer of the state training school, in search of an escaped inmate, located the body encased in the ice. There were no marks of violence on the body and no inquest will be held. It is believed that he wandered to the river park and fell into the river and was drowned. He was about 30 years old.

**Football Hurts Fatal in Year.**

*By Associated Press.*

Helena, Mont., March 5.—Walter Smith died yesterday at Friday as the result of injuries received in a football contest between the Montana and Utah agricultural colleges a year ago.

## Minneapolis Convicts Escape State Prison

### Jerry McCarthy and Peter Jule Thwart Guards at Stillwater.

### Long Term Men at Large, With Large Posse in Pursuit.

### Closely Woven Human Net Formed—Rewards Posted.

Two well-known Minneapolis crooks escaped from the state prison at Stillwater last night at 8 o'clock and up to an early hour this morning had not been recaptured. One of the men, Jerry McCarthy shot at Patrolman Jonasson Christmas eve in 1909 when the officer attempted to arrest him as a suspicious character. The bullet passed between the arm and the body of the policeman. The other man, Peter Jule, was sent up from Minneapolis last June on a charge of grand larceny. Jule was serving nine years and McCarthy 10 years.

The men made false keys from bits of iron and unlocked their cell doors. They managed to reach the wall undetected and sealed it. Men passing the prison saw them as they dropped from the wall and promptly notified the police department in Stillwater.

As the Stillwater officers ran to the prison the guards discovered the escape. A general alarm was sent out to the wardens, guards and officers and a closely woven human net began a systematic search of the territory surrounding the town. The telephone and telegraph wires were freely used and practically every town within a radius of 50 miles was notified.

A reward of $50 for each convict was posted. It is thought the men crossed the St. Croix river on the ice and made for the Wisconsin woods. Warden Wolfer says the men will be captured inside of a few hours although the daring and clever manner of their escape indicates that they will probably be hard men to capture.

Jule is said by Minneapolis police to have a sweetheart in Minneapolis and they believe he will ultimately come here. Both men are under 30 years of age. Jule is described as being five feet, five inches tall, sallow complexion and weighing about 137 pounds. McCarthy is a little over six feet tall, weighs about 197 pounds, is of light complexion.

## Woman Editor Fights Graft

### Publisher Will Conduct Campaign for Civic Virtue in Indiana Town.

West Hammond, Ind., March 5.—(Special.)—The Searchlight, a semi-weekly newspaper, published by Miss Virginia Brooks, will soon make its appearance and will declare editorially that the editor will continue the publication regardless of expense till corruption is driven out of this city.

Miss Brooks has been making a campaign against graft and other official corruption in this city for two years, and at the last election was a potent factor in changing conditions by driving out some officials and voting in others. She is 22 years old, a property owner and imbued with the spirit of reform.

When Miss Brooks began her campaign her first assaults were made upon gambling, and she forced the local officers to raid gambling houses and arrest gamblers till she has rid the town of them. She has been instrumental in ridding the town of other criminals and now purposes to proceed against delinquent officials and expose those who have gained control of property by questionable means.

### *Girls Leave Factories to Labor on a Farm With Mrs. Belmont*

*By Associated Press.*

New York, March 5.—Mrs. O. H. P. Belmont opened her first class in farming for girls yesterday. Twenty young women, "farmerettes," she calls them, garbed in blue bloomers, broad brimmed hats and boy's shoes, were comfortably ensconced last night in the farmhouse at "Brockett," Mrs. Belmont's 1,000 acre estate on Long Island.

The young women were selected from 600 applicants from New York factories. They will first be instructed thoroughly in household duties upon a farm and with the arrival of "planting time" in the spring, will take up plowing, planting and poultry raising.

Not a man will be on the premises, even to chop wood or tend the horses. The girls will receive $4 a week during their two-month course of instruction and thereafter may purchase small farms from the benefactress if they wish to do so, upon agreement to till the soil themselves.

### LINCOLN MEMORIAL DISCUSSED

**Commission Holds First Meeting—Ideas Are Sought.**

*By Associated Press.*

Washington, March 5.—The Lincoln memorial commission, provided for by the congress which has just adjourned, held its first meeting at the White House yesterday. It decided to ask the National Fine Arts commission to suggest various plans for the proposed memorial to be erected in that city to Abraham Lincoln.

The commission will be asked to take three or four sites in the national capitol and give its opinion as to various forms of memorial which might be appropriate to these places. The amount granted by congress for the memorial was $2,000,000.

**Sailor Ends His Life.**

*By Associated Press.*

Washington, March 5.—Thomas W. Coey, a seaman, committed suicide on board the tug Patuxent, which is with the Atlantic fleet in Guantanamo bay, Cuba, according to a report from Rear Admiral Seaton Schroeder. Coey was a native of Bruce, Wis., where his father now resides.

## 50 Federals Fall in Fight

### Railroad Contractor Reports Victory for Insurrectos in Battle at Corral, Mexico.

**BULLETIN.**

*By Associated Press.*

**El Paso, Texas, March 5.—American Consul Edwards of Juarez yesterday sent a telegram to Secretary of State Knox asking that he make formal demand upon Mexico for the release of Lawrence Converse and Edward Blatt. He adds that he is convinced the two were kidnaped by Mexicans.**

(Special to The Sunday Tribune.)

Nogales, Ariz., March 5.—(Special)—That 50 federals were killed and General Luis Torres of Hermosillio, commanding the first military zone, was captured by the insurrectos in a battle at Corral Thursday, is the report brought here by James Trainer a railroad contractor who arrived from Guaymas.

The battle was fought just outside Corral, the federal force numbering about 150 and the rebels 500. Lookouts posted by the federals were watching the advance of one band of rebels coming up the mountainside, but failed to see two other commands, the federal forces being attacked from three sides simultaneously and surprised by two sections of the rebel force.

## Honolulu May Seek Aid to Fight Cholera Spread

### Territorial Legislature May Ask Federal Assistance to Check the Epidemic.

### Fund Voted to War on Disease—To Enforce Sanitary Regulations.

*By Associated Press.*

Honolulu, March 5.—It is believed the territorial legislature now in session will ask the federal government to take charge of the cholera situation in Honolulu. Two more deaths and three new cases in the last 24 hours brings the total up to 18 cases and 15 deaths, the three persons taken ill yesterday being still alive.

The legislature appropriated $25,000 yesterday as an emergency fund for the board of health with which to handle the epidemic.

The legislature also will pass a bill giving the health authorities full power to enforce sanitary regulations, the present law being ineffective in this emergency.

The opinion is general that the territorial authorities should ask the federal government to take charge of the fight against the cholera and that this alone will prevent a serious situation. The resources of the territory are admittedly inadequate to properly cope with the outbreak, but confidence is expressed that the federal health authorities would quickly stamp out the epidemic. This action, it is declared, also would tend to create confidence in the minds of tourists.

A Japanese daily was closed yesterday as a source of infection. Additional laborers have been put to work cleaning up the city. The United States revenue cutter Thetis is cooperating by keeping Japanese sampans from carrying fish or fresh vegetables from Honolulu to other islands.

## Rochester Mayor Defeated

### F. M. Rihardson, Basketball Leader, Wins Nomination After Day's Campaign.

Rochester, Minn., March 5.—(Special.)—In one of the most startling caucus campaigns ever waged in this city, F. M. Richardson, president of the Rochester Basketball association, defeated Mayor James C. Thompson for the Republican nomination for mayor at the spring election to be held March 14.

Richardson announced his candidacy at 3 p. m. and the largest vote ever polled in a city caucus was registered, Richardson getting 550 votes to Thompson's 278.

Mayor Thompson has held the office but one term and announced his candidacy for re-election two weeks ago and had the entire support of the anti-saloon party.

The fight for mayor promises to be an interesting one, two young Rochester attorneys being pitted against each other. Theodore Schol is the Democratic candidate and Richardson, the Republican.

Both are graduates of the University of Minnesota.

### VETERAN QUITS LEGAL FIGHT

**J. B. Flack Drops Case to Force State Employment Job.**

Duluth, Minn., March 5.—(Special.) The case of J. B. Flack against State Labor Commissioner Houk, in which Mr. Flack declares he was entitled to the appointment of the office of superintendent of the Duluth state employment bureau on the ground that he was an old soldier, was withdrawn yesterday by Mr. Flack's attorney, in district court, when, at a special term of court, Mr. Houk testified that he had never received Mr. Flack's application.

### PUGILIST'S SLAYER IS HELD

**Fractured Skull Fatal to Fighter in Newark Bout.**

*By Associated Press.*

New York, March 5.—Following the death of Angelo Venizona, a pugilist, in Newark, N. J., yesterday from injuries which it is alleged he received during a four-round boxing bout, a charge of manslaughter has been placed against William Kennedy, his opponent. Venizona died of a fractured skull.

**Falling Tree Kills Woodsman.**

Duluth, Minn., March 5.—(Special.)—John Ekenenois of Hibbing, a miner at the Rust property, was killed by the cars on the mine dump yesterday. James B. Atcburch, a woodsman, with no other name, was killed by a falling tree at Camp 7, Alger, Smith & Co.

## Old Congress Dies Amid Tumult; Extra Session Is Called

### Body to Reconvene April 4 to Act on Reciprocity Agreement.

### President Confident Measure Will Not Be Rejected By Bourbons.

### Tariff Board Bill Strangled by House Democratic Filibuster.

### Statehood for Arizona and New Mexico Is Lost in Senate.

### All of Big Appropriation Bills Finally Put Through.

*By Associated Press.*

Washington, March 5.—The Sixty-first congress, heedless of one of the most important legislative tasks set before it, came to an end shortly after noon yesterday. Within the hour following President Taft had issued a proclamation calling the new congress to meet in extraordinary session at noon on Tuesday, April 4.

At that time he will submit for ratification to a house overwhelmingly Democratic and to a senate barely Republican, the reciprocity agreement with Canada. The McCall bill, carrying that agreement into effect and passed by the house, met yesterday at the hands of the old senate the death that had been freely predicted for it.

The president, well warned if not entirely reconciled to the fate in store for the measure, was at the capitol to witness the obsequies. The bill was not allowed at any time to come up in the senate for a moment's consideration.

The permanent tariff board bill, forced to its passage through a reluctant senate at 8:30 o'clock yesterday morning, was hurried over to the house, there to be strangled by a Democratic filibuster. The president, in the room reserved for him in the senate lobby, heard the news with resignation. Congress provided funds to continue the work of the temporary tariff board bill for another year.

**Democrats Name Date.**

It was at the request of the Democrats of the house and senate that President Taft fixed the date of the extra session on April 4. The new Democratic ways and means committee of the house, which is also to act as the new "committee on committees," will meet on Monday to take up its latter duties. A full caucus of all the Democratic members of the new house will not be held until April 12. In the meantime the plans for the extra session will have developed.

There is little doubt now that the Democrats of the house will undertake to revise at least two or three of the schedules of the Payne-Aldrich tariff act, and there is every reason also to believe that these bills will be favorably received in the new senate—the increasing Democratic and insurgent strength in that body giving a majority on the principle of a further revision of the tariff downward.

It is supposed also that so long as the new schedules do not flagrantly violate the policy of protection, President Taft will not withhold his approval of them. He has announced, however, that if a general revision, in violation of the protective policy, should be inaugurated he would not hesitate to use the power of the veto.

**Session May Be Long.**

How long the extra session will last is problematical. While the new congress may promptly ratify the reciprocity agreement, some Democrats are in favor of withholding confirmation until two or three new tariff schedules are ready. If tariff differences should arise between the new house and the senate, the session unquestionably would be a long one.

In this connection, however, the interesting fact was developed yesterday that the president had a constitutional right to bring the session to an end in case the two houses of congress cannot agree upon a time for adjournment. Such action, it is admitted, would be revolutionary and there is thought to be little likelihood that any president would care to invoke the power invested in him by section three, article two of the constitution.

The old congress ended amid scenes of extraordinary excitement and uncertainty. In the house the disorder at times during the closing hours, when the successful filibuster against the tariff board bill was in progress, became almost a riot.

Representative Johnson of Kentucky, glaring angrily at Speaker Cannon, shouted, above the general roar of confusion, a challenge to the effect that but for the speaker's gray hairs he would carry the wordy disagreement to a more serious conclusion.

**Uncle Joe Pugnacious.**

The speaker, his sparse gray hair bristling with rage, declared with a vicious blow of his gavel on the desk, that no member need let his gray hairs be a bar to anything they had to offer. The house stood up and cheered.

In the senate filibuster, conducted by Senator Owen of Oklahoma, threatened the final approval of four of the appropriation measures up to within half an hour of the time set for adjournment. Senators of both parties appealed in vain to Senator Owen to stop talking and let the supply bills go through. The senators said he had set out to talk to death the resolution approving the constitution of New Mexico and conferring upon that territory the last rights of statehood.

So it was that when President Taft arrived at the capitol at 10:30 o'clock to sign the last of the bills rushed through in the closing hours, he found

# The Minneapolis Morning Tribune

VOL. XLV., NO. 222 MINNEAPOLIS, MINNESOTA, FRIDAY, APRIL 19, 1912. PRICE ONE CENT IN MINNEAPOLIS

# CARPATHIA BRINGS 745 TITANIC SURVIVORS TO LAND; 1,601 DROWNED; ALL WOMEN BUT THREE ARE SAVED

## TITANIC'S SIDE WAS RIPPED IN CRASH; HUGE LINER BREAKS AMIDSHIP

## Hundreds Take to Lifeboats; Band Plays as Vessel Sinks

### Passengers First Refused To Believe Leviathan Had Received Mortal Wound—Party Playing Bridge Resumed Game After Hearing of Crash—Crew Routs Sleepers from Berths To Take To Life Boats—Captain Refused to Flee.

### MEN ARE CALM IN FACE OF DANGER

### Distressing Stories Told by Passengers in Lifeboats—Rescued Watch Great Liner Break and Settle—Astor Last Seen Walking With Wife—Great Crowds Pack New York Piers When Carpathia Docks.

**New York Sun Service.**

New York, April 19.—(Special.)—It was the submerged ledge of an iceberg of ordinary proportions that send the White Star liner Titanic more than two miles to the bottom of the Atlantic off the banks of Newfoundland. She was steaming almost ful itilt through a gently swelling sea and under a starlit sky in charge of First Officer Murdock, who, a moment after the collision, surrendered the command to Captain Smith, who went down with her. The captain was washed from the bridge and was seen to make his way back again. He had been urged to get into a lifeboat, but refsed.

**Life Boats Not Filled.**

The lifeboats that were launched were not filled to their capacity. The general feeling aboard the ship, even after the boats had left her sides, was that she would survive her wound and the passengers who were left aboard believed almost up to the last moment that they had a chance for their lives.

The captain and officers behaved with the utmost gallantry and there was perfect order and discipline in the launching of the boats and after all hope had been abandoned for the salvation of the ship or for those who were aboard. Just before she went down she broke her back.

The great liner was plunging through comparatively placid sea on the surface of which there was much slushy ice and here and there a number of comparatively harmless looking floes. The night was clear and stars visible. First Officer Murdock was in charge of the bridge. The first intimation of the presence of iceberg that he received was from the lookout in the crows nest. They were so close upon theh berg at that time that it was pretty near impossible to avoid collision with it.

**Seamanship Fails.**

The first officer did what other unstartled and alert commanders had done under similar conditions, that is he made effort by going full speed ahead on his starboard propeller and reversing his port propeller, simultaneously throwing his helm over, to make a rapid turn and clear the berg.

The manoeuver was not successful. He succeeded in saving his bow from crashing into the ice cliff but nearly the entire length of the underbody of the great ship on the starboard side was ripped.

The speed of the Titanic, estimated to be at least 21 knots, was so terrific that theh knifelike edge of the iceberg's spur protruding under the sea cut through her like a can opener. The shock was almost imperceptible. **The first officer did not apparently realize that the great ship had received her death blow, and none of the passengers it is believed had the slightest** suspicion that anything more than usual minor sea accident had happened.

Hundreds of whom had gone to their beds and were asleep, were unwakened by the vibration.

To illustrate the placidity by which all men regarded the accident it is related that the four who were in the smoking room playing bridge calmly got up from the table, and after walking on deck and looking over the rail, returned to their game. One of them had left his cigar on the card table and while the three others were gazing out on the sea he remarked that he couldn't afford to lose his smoke, returned for his cigar and came out again. The three remained only for a few moments.

**Resumed Card Game.**

They resumed their game under the impression that the ship had stopped for reasons best known to the commander, and not involving any danger to her. The tendency of the whole ship's company, except the men in the engine department, who were made aware of the danger by the inrushing water, was to make light of, and in some instances even to repel the thought of danger to so substantial fabric.

Within a few minutes stewards and other members of the crew were sent around to arouse the people. Some utterly refused to get up. The steward had almost to force the doors of the staterooms to make the people appreciate their peril. Mr. and Mrs. Astor were in their room and saw the ice vision pass by. They had not appreciably felt the gentle shock and supposed that nothing out of the ordinary had happened. They were both dressed and came on deck leisurely. It was not until the ship began to take a heavy list to starboard that a tremor of fear pervaded the passengers.

The crew had been called to clear away the life boats, of which there were twenty, four of which were collapsible. The boats that were lower on the port side of the ship touched water without capsizing. Some of the others lowered to starboard including one collapsible were capsized. All hands in the collapsible boats that pretty soon went to pieces, were rescued by the other boats.

**Boats Get Away Safely.**

Sixteen boats in all got away safely. It was even then the general impression that the ship was all right and there is no doubt that that was the belief of even some of the officers. At the lowering of the boats the officers superintending the lowering of the boats were armed with revolvers, but there was no necessity for using them as there was nothing in the nature of a panic and no men made an effort to get into a boat while the women and children were being put aboard. As the ship began to settle to starboard heeling at an angle of nearly 45 degrees, those who had believed it was all right to stick by the ship began to have doubts and a few jumped into the sea.

They were followed immediately by others and in a few minutes there were scores swimming around. Nearly all of them wore life preservers. One man who had a Pomeranian dog leaped overboard with it and striking a piece of wreckage was badly stunned. He recovered after a few minutes and swam toward one of the lifeboats and was taken aboard.

**Mr. Ismay in Boat.**

Most of the men who were aboard the Carpathia except the members of the crew who manned the boats had jumped into the sea as the Titanic settled. J. Bruce Ismay was one of few who boarded a lifeboat from the deck of the ship. J. Bruce Ismay, according to some of his fellow voyagers, behaved with exceptional gallantry. He took charge of the launching of the lifeboats and went around among the women and children, soothing and encouraging them, and according to one of the rescued on the Carpathia, remarking at intervals, "Don't fear, we will get you into the boats all right."

Nobody seemed to know how Mr. Ismay himself got into a boat, but it was assumed that he wished to make a presentation of the case of the Titanic to his company. He was among those who apparently realized that the splendid ship was doomed.

All hands in the life boats, under instructions from officers and men in charge, were rowed a considerable distance from the ship herself in order to get far away from the possible suction that would follow her foundering. The marvelous thing about her disappearance was so little suction as to be hardly appreciable from the point where the boats were floating. There was ample time to launch all boats before the Titanic went down, as she was two hours and 20 minutes afloat.

So confident were all hands that she had not sustained a mortal wound, that it was not until 12:15 a. m. or 35 minutes after the berg was encountered, that the boats were lowered. Hundreds of the crew and a large majority of the officers, including Captain Smith, stuck to the ship to the very last. **It was evident after there were several** explosions, which doubtless were the boilers blowing up, that she had but a few minutes more of life.

She broke in half amidships and almost simultaneously her after half and her forward half sank. The forward half, vanishing bow first and the other half stern first.

The commotion caused was much less than the horrified watchers in the life boats had expected. They were close enough to the broken ship to see clearly the most grewsome details of the foundering. All the spectators agree that the shattered sections of the ship went down so quietly as to excite wonder.

Like Mr. and Mrs. John Jacob Astor, Mr. and Mrs. Harder occupied a stateroom on the starboard of the ship. They said that they felt a distinct shock and saw ice pass the port. Mr. Harder said that he believed the berg must have been at least as high as the ship. It drifted away from the neighborhood of the accident long before the Carpathia came along and picked up all hands. They were in the life boats they believe until about 5:30 a. m.

Some were scantily clad and suffered exceeding from the cold, but the majority of them were fully dressed. In the darkness about the ship that came shortly after the collision it was impossible for those in the boats to distinguish the identity of any persons who leaped into the sea. It is believed that nearly all cabin passengers who had not gone overboard immediately the boats were launched vanished with the officials and the crew. It is likely Col. Astor was one of this number.

**Last Seen With Wife.**

He was last seen walking arm in arm with his wife on the promenade deck, sweetly oblivious of his danger. When word came from the women and children to be put into the boats, Col. Astor went to the life boat with her.

Some of the stewards who formed part of the lifeboat crew say that after the ship hit the berg the majority of the cabin passengers went back to their staterooms and that it was necessary to route them out and in some instances force life preservers on them. All agree that the engines of the ship were stopped immediately after she had made the ineffectual turn to clear the berg.

The lifeboat crews were made up of stewards, stokers, coal trimmers and ordinary seamen. It is said that the davites were equipped with a new contrivance for the swift launching of the boats, but that the machinery was so complicated and the men so unfamiliar with it that they had trouble in managing it.

The passing of the Carpathia by the health officer, J. J. O'Connell, was a mere formality. The surgeon of the Carpathia attested to the health of the ship's company, and the steamship was released in a few minutes. It was observed by the Sun reporter who boarded her at quarantine and came up with here that the crew of the Titanic and of Carpathia mingled, and that they and the passengers crowded all the stairways and passages of the Cunard boat.

**One Woman Badly Hurt.**

Dr. O'Connell learned from the Carpathia's surgeon that there was only one woman seriously hurt, and she was a second cabin passenger. All the rest seemed to be in good condition.

One of the Titanic's passengers who is familiar with shipbuilding, said that if the berg had not pierced the engine compartment, the ship might have floated for a long time. The longitudinal bulkhead, the doors of which were doubtless closed, kept her port compartments from filling at least long enough to permit the launching of the boats, and but for the explosion of the boilers it is not improbable that she might have been on the water when the Carpathia arrived.

**Associated Press Dispatch**

New York, April 19.—How the White Star liner Titanic, the largest ship afloat, sank off the Grand Banks of New Foundland on Monday morning last, carrying to their death, 1601 of the 2,340 persons aboard, was told to the world in all its awful details for the first time last night with the arrival in New York of the Cunard liner Carpathia, bearing the 745 exhausted survivors of the catastrope.

The great facts that stand out from the chaotic account of the tragedy, these are the most salient:

The death list has been increased rather than decreased. Six persons died after being rescued.

The list of prominent persons lost stands as previously reported.

**Three Women Lost.**

Practically every woman and child, with the exception of those women who refused to leave their husbands, were saved.

The survivors on the life boats saw the lights on the stricken vessel glimmer to the last, heard her band playing and saw the doomed hundreds on her deck and heard their groans and cries when the vessel sank.

Accounts vary as to the extent of the disorder on board.

Not only was the Titanic tearing through the April night to her doom with every ounce of steam crowded on, but she was under orders from the general offices of the line to make all the speed of which she was capable. This was the statement made last night by J. H. Moody, a quartermaster of the vessel and helsman on the night of the disaster. He said the ship was making 21 knots on hour and the officers were striving to live up t othe orders to smash the record.

"It was close to midnight," said Moody, "and I was on the bridge with the second officer who was in command. Suddenly he shouted 'port your helm.' I did so, but it was too late. We struck the submerged portion of the berg."

**Like a Can Opener.**

Of the many accounts given by the passengers most of them agreed that the shock when the Titanic struck the iceberg, although ripping her great sides like a giant can opener, did not greatly jar the entire vessel, for the blow was a glancing one along her side. The accounts also agree substantially that when the passengers were taken off on the lifeboats there was no serious panic, and that many "wished to remain on board the Titanic, believing her to be unsinkable."

**The most distressing stories are those giving the experiences of the** passengers in lifeboats. These tell not only of their own suffering but give the harrowing details of how they saw the great hulk of the Titanic stand on end stern uppermost for many minutes before plunging to the bottom.

As this awful spectacle was witnessed by the groups of survivors in the boats they plainly saw many of those whom they had just left behind leaping from the decks into the water.

To the awful death list of 1,601 six persons were added. One died in the lifeboat which was put off from the liner's side and five subsequently succumbed on the rescue ship Carpathia.

The list of prominent men missing stands as previously reported and the total death list as brought to port last night by the Carpathia is 1,601.

Survivors in the lifeboates huddled in the darkness at a safe distance from the stricken ship and saw her go down.

As to the scene on board when the liner struck, accounts disagree widely. Some maintain that a comparative calm prevailed; others say that wild disorder broke out and that there was a maniacal struggle for the lifeboats. That the liner struck an iceberg as reported by wireless was cnonfirmed by all.

**Sensational rumors told by hysterical passengers who would not give their names, said that Captain Smith had killed himself on the bridge; that the chief engineer had taken his life and that three Italians were shot in the struggle for the boats.**

**These rumors could not be confirmed in the early confusion attendant on the landing of the survivors.**

Ripped from stem to engine room by the great mass of ice she struck amidships, the Titanic's side was laid open. She quickly listed to starboard and a shower of ice fell on to the forecastle deck. Shortly before she sank she broke in two abaft the engine rom and disappeared beneath the water, the expulsion of air caused two explosions which were plainly heard by the survivors adrift. A moment more and the Titanic had gone to her doom with the fated hundreds grouped on the after deck. To the survivors they were visible to teh last and their cries and moans were pitiable.

**Physicians and Nurses.**

Physicians and Nurses went aboard the Carpathia before anyone was allowed to go down the gangplank, but soon after the first-cabin passengers, women predominating, began descending the incline. Some walked unaided. Some were assisted by friends, relatives and nurses and some were on stretches.

Mrs. John Jacob Astor, now a widow, was met by her stepson, Vincent, and her sister, Miss Force. They embraced with tears, hurried to an automobile and drove to the Astor town house.

The 200 and more steerage passengers did not leave the ship until 11 o'clock. They were in a sad condition.

The women were without wraps and th few men there were very little clothing.

A poor Syrian woman who said she was Mrs. Habash, bound for Youngstown, Ohio, carried in her arms a six-year-old girl. The child wore only a light calico dress, was barefooted and bareheaded. This woman had lost her husband and three brothers. "I lost four of my men folks," she cried.

The Titanic's four rescued officers were placed aboard the Red Star liner Lapland for the night. They refused to talk, saying they were under instructions to give no information except to the senate committee.

J. Bruce Ismay, president of the International Mercantile Marine company, owners of the White Star line, who was among the men saved, P. A. S. Franklin, vice president of the White Star line and United States Senator William Alden Smith, chairman of the senate investigating committee held a conference aboard the Carpathia soon after the passengers had come ashore.

**Begin Investigation Today.**

After nearly an hour, Senator Smith came out of the cabin and said he had no authority to subpoena witnesses at this time, but would begin an investigation into the cause of the loss of the Titanic at the Waldorf-Astoria hotel today. He announced that Mr. Ismay had consented to appear at the hearing and that Mr. Franklin and the four surviving officers of the Titanic would appear for examination by the senate committee. He said the course the investigation would follow would be determined after the preliminary hearing.

Senator Smith was questioned as to the speed the Titanic was proceeding at when she crashed into the iceberg. He said be had asked Mr. Ismay but declined to say what Mr. Ismay's reply was.

(Mr. Ismay's statement will be found elsewhere in this paper.)

The arrival of the Carpathia brought a vast multitude of people to the Cunard docks. They filled the vast pier sheds and, overflowing for blocks, crowded the nearby streets in a dense throng. Through it all the rain fell steadily, adding a funeral aspect to the scene.

The landing of the survivors was attended with little excitement, the crowd standing in awed silence as the groups from the ship passed along.

The docking actually began shortly after 9 o'clock and the debarking of passengers was so quickly disposed of by the waiving of the usual formalities that practically everything had been concluded by 10:30 o'clock.

**Crowds Haunt Pier.**

The crowds remained about the pier long after this, however, to get a glimpse of the rescue steamer and to hear the harrowing stories which had been brought back to the ship.

Mr. Ismay after his interview with Senator Smith said that he was desirous of sailing on the Carpathia tomorrow afternoon. The Carpathia is scheduled to said at 4 o'clock. Mr. Ismay assured the senators, however, that he would make a complete statement of the catastrophe and that if he could not finish in time for the sailing he would change his plans.

**TITANIC SEEN IN THE MAKING**

**Minneapolis Man Gets Glimpse of Monster Ship After Launching.**

H. A. Rogers, 3715 First avenue south, is among the few Minneapolis residents who have seen the ill-fated Titanic. Mr. Rogers with his wife and daughter caught a glimpse of the ship while cruising from Ireland, to Scotland last summer.

Speaking of the incident, Mr. Rogers said:

"While crossing the Irish sea the early part of last June, we were fortunate to get a view of the Titanic. The boat was launched about the first of June, and our cruiser in nearing the large ship, was stopped about ten minutes in order to give the passengers a glimpse of it.

"We were told it was to be the largest ship, as well as the finest equipped, in the world. And it certainly was a monster of a boat. Our cruiser, the Viper, looked like a match compared to the Titanic, which looked to be as high as the Syndicate building."

## Titanic Horror Told in Figures.

New York, April 19.—The following tabulation of the passengers and crew on board the Titanic, together with those saved and lost, has been compiled from the figures in the statement issued by the committee of passengers:

Approximate number of passengers aboard:
First class 330; second class 320; third class 750.

* * *

Officers and crew 940. Totals 2,340.

* * *

Number of passengers saved by Carpathia:
First class 210; second class 125; third class 200.

* * *

Total passengers saved 535.

* * *

Members of crew saved: Officers 4; seamen 39; stewards 96; firemen, 71.

* * *

Total members of crew saved 210.

* * *

Total saved passengers and crew 745.

* * *

Total number perished 1,595.

* * *

First and second class cabin passengers 650.

* * *

First and second class passengers saved 335.

* * *

Total cabin passengers lost 315.

## Suction Not Felt Much as Liner Takes Plunge

### H. B. Stephenson of Swedish Legation in Boat But 200 Yards Away.

### Mrs. George Wick and Her Daughter Saved, but Husband Is Lost.

### Waves Dear Ones Farewell as Life Craft Is Lowered Away.

New York, April 19.—H. B. Stephenson, one of the survivors, who it was said is attached to the Swedish legation at Washington, made the following statement.:

"At the time of the collision a Mr. Woolner and myself were seated in the cafe. There was only a slight jar, and we thought nothing of it until we heard the excitement on deck. There was an order issued for all women to come on deck. Woolner and myself went two decks down and saw water water rushing in there. A lifeboat was lowered with several women and children from the steerage and as it passed where I was, I jumped in. I grabbed an oar and assisted the two men in the boat to row away from the steamer. We were about 200 yards away when the Titanic went down. There was hardly any suction. We were picked up about five hours later, suffering from the cold."

Mrs. George D. Wick and daughter, Natalie of Youngstown, Ohio, and the Misses Bonnell, went to an uptown hotel. The four women wore rain coats and were heavily veiled. The husband of Mrs. Dick Wick was lost.

Wm. F. Bonnell, a cousin of the party, made the following statement as coming from Mrs. Wick:

**Thought a Boiler Exploded.**

"When the collision occurred, Mrs. Wick and her husband were in the stateroom. They thought that a boiler had exploded. When they reached the deck, all was confusion. Miss Natalie and the Misses Bonnell were on deck. The four women entered the second lifeboat let down. Mrs. Wick said the boat was not launched for an hour after the collision. Mr. Wick stood at the rail as his wife and daughter were helped into the boat and waved his hand as the party left the Titanic. The last seen of him he was standing on the deck waving a farewell. Mrs. Wick said the party drifted about in the intense cold for five hours before they were picked up. I want to say that Mrs. Wick told me that if the lifeboats had been launched as soon as the captain knew the extent of the damage, every one would have been saved."

Wilson Potter of Philadelphia, who was at the pier to meet his mother, Mrs. Thomas Potter, Jr., one of the survivors, said his mother was unable to make any formal statement, but said she related the story to him as follows:

**Room for 40 More.**

"She told me that she was in the first boat with about 10 others, and that there was plenty of room for 40 more. My mother said she saw Mr. and Mrs. John Jacob Astor standing by the rail and that she called to them to come in the boat, but that they refused, saying it was safe where they were, that there was no danger. The first three or four boats that were launched, my mother said, were hardly filled.

"I saw John S. Thayer, Jr., whom I know, on the pier," continued Mr. Potter, "and he told me that he and his father jumped overboard and clambered aboard a raft, which overturned. That was the last, young Thayer said, that he had seen of his father."

Mrs. Wm. B. Stephenson of Haverford, Pa., who left on the Pennsylvania train for survivors, gave out the following interview:

"I ran upon the deck where I met Mr. Thayer. He informed me that an accident had occurred but said there was no particular reason for panic. Soon afterward, however, he advised me to put on a life preserver. So I went below. When I came back on deck boats were already being lowered. Mrs. Thayer, Mrs. Widener and I were assisted into one. Young Thayer failed to get into any of the boats. He fell overboard and landed alongside the one we were in and drifted away. He was picked up later by another boat after having been in the water for a long time.

"It was terribly cold but none of us suffered any ill effects. Mr. Thayer was not seen again. What became of him I do not know, except when we all met again on the Carpathia, his absence was noted."

**FIRST PERSONS OFF CARPATHIA**

**Dr. H. Frauenthal and Wife Driven Quickly from Pier.**

New York, April 19.—Dr. Henry Frauenthal and his wife of this city were t ehfirst persons off the Carpathia. They were driven off quickly in an automobile without having spoken to anyone. They were following off the ship by a man who said he was James Googht of Philadelphia. Googht said that it was exactly 2:20 a. m. on the 15th when the liner Titanic sank. He says he was thrown bodily into a small boat and it was 5 o'clock that morning when tehy were picked up by the Carpathia.

Googht was met by two brothers and a sister and after he had made this short statement he was driven away.

**Hays Family Hurried to Montreal.**

New York, April 19.—Mrs. Charles M. Hayes, wife of Charles M. Hays, president of the Grand Trunk railway, who went down with the Titanic, and their two daughters, Mrs. Thornton Davidson and Miss Margaret Hays, were hustled from the pier in automobiles last night to the Grand Central station, where they took a special train of two private cars and two coaches for Montreal at 10:30 o'clock.

The Hays family were met at the pier by Mr. Grey, father of Mrs. Hays, Mrs. Hope Scott, a daughter of Mrs. Hays, Howard G. Kelly, chief architect of the Grand Trunk, Dr. J. Alexander Hutchinson of Montreal, who had been Mr. Hays physician for years, and E. H. Fitzhugh, vice president of the Grand Trunk.

**CAMPAIGN FUND LIGHT ASKED**

**Gubernatorial Candidates Asked to Publish Receipts Every Week.**

E. E. Hughes, editor of Farm, Stock and Home, who is identified with the Minnesota Progressive league, has sent letters to the various Republican candidates for governor asking if they would consent to the weekly publication of campaign receipts.

It is said that Lewis C. Spooner of Morris and W. E. Lee of Long Prarie immediately signified their willingness.

Mr. Hughes in his letter said that it was reported that the steel trust, brewers, railroads and various public service corporations were financing the campaign of some of the candidates for governor and he used this report for the basis of his request.

## Mr. and Mrs. Snyder Escape in First Boat From Titanic

### Minneapolis Bridal Couple Were on Deck When Crash Came—Husband Declares That Women Refused to Enter Lifeboats Aftr Looking at Water.

*By Associated Press.*

New York, April 19.—John Pillsbury Snyder of Minneapolis, and his bride of eight weeks, who were first class passengers on the Titanic, went to a hotel when they landed. Mr. Snyder said that when the crash came he and his wife went to the deck, but were told that there was no danger and returned to their stateroom.

Shortly afterwards a steward told them they had better go on deck and they did. Mrs. Snyder, however, complained of the cold and again returned to the stateroom for heavier clothing and came back with it and also her jewel case. Then the people were ordered itno the lift boats.

"But the women," continued Mr. Snyder, "after looking over the rail into the water refused to change their seeming safe position for the more precarious one in a life boat. An officer pleaded, tehn ordered them into the boat. But still they refused to go."

**Escaped in First Boat.**

Mr. Snyder said he and his wife were in the first boat launched and which was full. There was no excitement, only the moaning and quiet sobbing of the women and once in a while an exclamation from a man. He could see the deck plainly and it appeared remarkable to him that nobody was wearing a life preserver.

Gradually the lifeboat floated away until it was fully 500 yards from the Titanic. Then came a loud explosion, followed closely by two others not so resonant.

With the first explosion Mr. Snyder said the side of the stricken ship bulged out and by the bright starlight he could see the nose of the liner dip into the sea. The stern of the boat was raised high into the air, two propellers glistened above the water and the Titanic sank.

## New York Wires Make No Change in Early Report

### Certain Now That Walter D. Douglas, of Minneapolis, Was Lost.

### Mrs. Douglas and Mr. and Mrs. J. P. Snyder, Saved, Say Messages.

### City Breathlessly Grasps for Details of Great Sea Tragedy.

### Business Associate of Victim Refuses to Give Up Hope Until Last.

### Bereaved Widow and Sons Expect to Reach Here on Sunday Morning.

**"Mr. Douglas lost. Mrs. Douglas arrived safely."**

* * *

**"Mr. and Mrs. Snyder have arrived safe and well."**

These two messages, received in Minneapolis last night following the arrival of the Carpathia in New York, brought no change in the reports received earlier by wireless, concerning the fate of the four Minneapolitans who were passengers on the ill-fated Titanic.

The messages were received by relatives and business associates of the parties and came at the same time extra newspaper editions were beginning to flash details of the manner in which the Titanic and its 1,400 souls met their fate. Flashes of news, waited for for days, were read breathlessly on the streets, in clubs and cafes, at theater performances—everywhere that the extras circulated last night, and exclamations over the details and horror of the great disaster were heard on every side.

Mr. and Mrs. T. W. Stevenson, father and mother of Mrs. John Snyder, received a telegram at 10:30 p. m. from C. R. Williams, who had gone to New York to meet Mr. and Mrs. Snyder. It contained no particulars, but its few words further verified reports that the honeymoon couple were safe. The message read: "Mr. and Mrs. Snyder safe and well. Will wire particulars later."

**Stevensons Overjoyed.**

"Of course we are overjoyed that my daughter and her husband are safe," said Mrs. Stevenson last night. "The suspense has been a terrible strain, and we will be so glad when they get home. We are too happy for anything to think they are safe. But we are grieved deeply, as well, over those who have been lost and those who are not receiving good news. We know how to sympathize with them."

George C. Piper, business associate of Walter D. Douglas, received a wire from George Douglas a son, from New York at about one o'clock last night. It said: "Mr Douglas lost. Mrs. Douglas arrived safely," read its brief line.

"I had hoped until the last," said Mr. Piper, "but this message from relatives shatters the last hope. It is a terrible thing."

Hopes that Walter D. Douglas was saved from the wrecked Titanic were at full ebb yesterday among Mr. Douglas' many Minneapolis friends. At the Chamber of Commerce every effort was made to learn what happened to the Minneapolitan when the great steamer floundered. The private telephone wires of numerous grain commissioners, used to constantly carry messages to and from New York since the first news of Mr. Douglas's danger reached Minneapolis, were still laden with queries and unsatisfactory replies. Members of the firm of Piper, Johnson & Case, of which Mr. Douglas was formerly a members, kept by the wires until the last doubt as to his fate had been removed.

**Hoped Until the Last.**

For a time there was hope on the part of Mr. Douglas' relatives and friends that he might have sent a wireless message which was confused. They were sure that he would have communicated with them, if saved. As there were several Douglases in the list of survivors it was hoped also that there might have been a mistake in initials.

All these hopes were dashed last night, however, when wires and long distance telephone messages brought the final message that Mr. Douglas had gone down to a watery grave.

Confirmation of the rescue of Mrs. Walter D. Douglas and the loss of Mr. Douglas reached Mrs. George Douglas, daughter-in-law, at her residence last night in the shape of a telephone message from her husband in New York. That Mrs. Douglas and her maid were safe at the Waldorf and that Mr. Douglas had not been accounted for was the substance of the message. The information was also sent that Mrs. Walter Douglas, with her two sons, George and Edward, and Mrs. Edward Douglas would arrive in Minneapolis Sunday morning.

The telephone message from George Douglas contained the first intimation that Mrs. Walter D. Douglas' maid had been rescued with her, and the information presents an instance in which the life of a husband was surrendered that his wife's maid might live.

Regarding other Northwest passengers on the Titanic, last night's wires from New York also failed to make any change in the previous wireless messages. From definite lists received it was made positive that W. B. Silvey of Duluth, and H. F. **Chaffee of** Amenia, S. D., met the **same fate** as Mr. Douglas. Mrs. Silvey and Miss Constance Willard, also of Duluth, and Mrs. H. F. Chaffee were among the saved.

# The Minneapolis Sunday Tribune

VOL. XLV., NO. 238. MINNEAPOLIS, MINNESOTA, SUNDAY, MAY 5, 1912. 100 PAGES PRICE FIVE CENTS


## Astor Fortune Goes to Youth Not Yet of Age

### Boy First of Family to Do What He Pleases With Money.

### His Father Went to Europe to Arrange for Trust.

### Colonel's Wife Received Cash Settlement of Only $200,000.

### In Division of Estate His Daughter Muriel Receives $15,000,000.

### Will Get Only Half That if There Is a Posthumous Child.

**HOW ASTOR'S MILLIONS WILL BE DIVIDED**

Approximate amounts heirs of John Jacob Astor will inherit:

| | |
|---|---|
| Vincent Astor | $60,000,000 |
| Muriel Astor (if there is no posthumous child) | 15,000,000 |
| Muriel Astor (if there is a posthumous child) | 7,000,000 |
| The expected child of Mrs. John Jacob Astor | 7,500,000 |
| Mrs. John Jacob Astor | Nothing |
| Mrs. Ava Willing Astor | Nothing |

New York, May 5.—With the arrival of Mrs. Ava Willing Astor here last week, and with Mrs. John Jacob Astor approaching motherhood in the Astor home in Fifth avenue, speculation concerning the terms of the Astor will has become intense.

**Climax Approaching.**

One of the great dramas of present-day social life is fast drawing to a climax in that austere Fifth avenue mansion, and its various personages are priming themselves for a final struggle that involves many millions. In the ocean of talk that seethes about them, no one apparently realizes that the denouement is already written.

In spite of many rumors, two facts, obtained through a reliable source, stand out supreme. First, Colonel Astor made no will which is known of in this country since his second marriage; second, whatever will he did leave, and the terms of that are known to only one person, Lewis Cass Ledyard, will not make any appreciable difference in the financial standing of any of the persons concerned.

**80 Per Cent Goes to Vincent.**

The outstanding fact in the question of the Astor inheritance is this: Eighty per cent of the Astor estate is left as it was left to John Jacob Astor by his father, William Astor, goes to Vincent Astor.

The remaining 20 per cent goes to the other children. At present there is but one other child, Muriel, ten years old. Should there be issue from the second wife, this child will share the 20 per cent with Muriel. If the issue is a girl each will have 10 per cent; if the issue is a boy, Muriel will receive less and the boy more.

**With the terms of this bequeathal John Jacob Astor had nothing to do. They were made by his father, William, and have been on file in the Surrogate's office for over forty years, but have never before been published.**

**Terms Set by William Astor.**

The terms of this will of William Astor are such that the only property John Jacob, his son, could bequeath, would be such as he might have acquired by purchase and held separate from the entailed Astor estate which had come down from father to son in lineal succession from the first John Jacob Astor. This may be a relatively small amount; possibly it is larger than any one suspects.

**When William Astor died the estate amounted to approximately $30,000,000. At the present time it amounts to not more than $80,000,000 and is probably about $75,000,000.**

These figures were secured from a representative of the family who will not permit the use of his name, but who is in a position to know the facts.

**Nearly All Entailed.**

Of this seventy-five or eighty millions all but a few millions is in the entailed estate. Thus, Vincent Astor's inheritance will be approximately $60,000,000. If there is no issue from the second marriage, Muriel Astor will receive approximately $15,000,000. If there is issue from the second marriage, she will be obliged to share her fifth equally if the child is a girl and unequally if a boy.

**Therefore, the unborn Astor child is worth, if the startling situation is reduced to cold figures, at least seven and a half millions.**

But this fact, startling in its suggested reality, provocative of apprehension, doubt and mystery, centering the hopes, fears and longings of every branch of the family about the bedside of the second Mrs. Astor, is not so remarkable as the situation in which Vincent Astor is placed.

**The young man is not of age. In five months he will be 21 years old. And he is the first man in the lineal descent of the family who will hold his fortune in fee simple, to do with as he pleases. There will be no trus-**

(Continued on Page 8, Col. 1.)

### THE WEATHER

**Washington Official Forecast.**

Minnesota—Thunder showers today, cooler in west and south portions; tomorrow probably fair, slightly warmer in north portion; brisk to high northeast winds.

Wisconsin—Showers today, cooler in southwest portion; moderate to brisk northeast and east winds; tomorrow probably fair.

Upper Michigan—Showers today and probably tomorrow, brisk east winds.

Montana—Fair in west, rain or snow in east portion today; tomorrow fair, warmer in east portion.

North Dakota—Rain or snow today, colder in north and east portions; tomorrow fair, slightly warmer.

South Dakota—Local rains today, colder in east portion; tomorrow fair, warmer.

Iowa—Thunder showers and cooler today; tomorrow probably fair.

**General Observations.**

| Sta. | A | B | C | Sta. | A | B | C |
|---|---|---|---|---|---|---|---|
| Alpena | 48 | 52 | | J'ksonville | 72 | 82 | .16 |
| Bismarck | 58 | 64 | .24 | Kan. City | 76 | 80 | .22 |
| Boston | 50 | 58 | | Los Angeles | 62 | 72 | |
| Buffalo | 56 | 68 | | Madison | 68 | 78 | .08 |
| Calgary | 54 | 54 | | Marquette | 38 | 40 | .68 |
| Chicago | 62 | 66 | .10 | Memphis | 76 | 78 | |
| Cincinnati | 76 | 84 | .40 | Milwaukee | 52 | 60 | .12 |
| Cleveland | 62 | 72 | | Med. Hat | 48 | 56 | |
| Denver | 50 | 52 | .08 | Minnedosa | 44 | 44 | .16 |
| Detroit | 66 | 68 | | Montreal | 50 | 58 | |
| DesMoines | 74 | 78 | | Moorhead | 58 | 66 | .46 |
| Duluth | 38 | 38 | 1.58 | New York | 54 | 64 | |
| El Paso | 72 | 72 | | N. Orleans | 80 | 86 | |
| Edmonton | 44 | 56 | | Omaha | 68 | 78 | .40 |
| Escanaba | 46 | 46 | .16 | San Antonio | 78 | 80 | .60 |
| Galveston | 74 | 76 | | 'Frisco | 62 | 62 | |
| Gr. Rapids | 66 | 70 | | Ste. Marie | 44 | 50 | .16 |
| Gr. Bay | 46 | 58 | .92 | Salt Lake | 50 | 62 | .22 |
| Havre | 48 | 50 | | St. Louis | 78 | 82 | |
| Helena | 42 | 58 | .40 | Washington | 64 | 74 | |
| Huron | 50 | 70 | .96 | Winnipeg | 48 | 66 | |

A—Temperature at 7 p. m. yesterday.
B—Highest temperature yesterday.
C—Precipitation.

## 15,000 Suffragettes March In Demonstration Parade

### New York Agitators for Ballot Cheered by Thousands Along Line of March.

### Procession Headed by Squad of 50 Women Mounted on Horses.

New York, May 5.—With banners flying and bands playing, "The Boy I Left Behind Me," the great army of suffragettes marched up Fifth avenue yesterday afternoon in the biggest public demonstration of women ever seen in this city. It is estimated that there were more than 15,000 marchers in line.

From Washington Square up Fifth avenue to Fifty-seventh street, and thence to Carnegie Hall, great enthusiastic crowds lined the way; windows, balconies, roofs and sidewalks were filled with admiring and cheering throngs for the women taking the two and half mile walk to demonstrate the earnestness of their appeal for the ballot.

So great were the crowds at Washington Square when the marchers began to gather that the reserves were called out to clear the streets and square for the delegates of the suffragettes assembled there.

Promptly at 5 o'clock, Miss Josephine Beiderhase, grand marshal of the day, sounded the bugle call and the head of the parade moved out from under Washington arch with the procession and assemble of military training.

Ten mounted policemen and ten motorcycle policemen, in charge of Inspector McLuskey proceeded the woman's cavalry troop in charge of Mrs. Charles Edward Noblauch, wearing a gray riding habit with a great green sash with the words in yellow "votes for women."

The 50 women riders smilingly bowed recognition of the cheering avenue onlookers. All wore the three cornered black straw riding hat with suffrage colors, green and white of the Women's Political union under whose management the parade was held.

## Jail Breaker Is Captured

### Appleton Man Jumps Through Plate Glass Window in Effort to Escape.

(Special to The Sunday Tribune.)

Appleton, Wis., May 5.—(Special.)—Max Pansow yesterday made a sensational attempt to gain his liberty. The young man was being held in the local jail on a charge of stealing a suit of clothes and $21 from his roommate. Pansow, with the aid of rope made of blankets, succeeded in making his escape from the jail by sliding down an air shaft to the basement. He then went to his boarding house and wrote his attorney a note telling him he was going to leave town. His attorney notified the police and the young man was captured after an exciting chase in an automobile. Pansow, in one of his efforts to evade the officials, jumped through a plate glass window.

## "Kimmel" Now Remembers

### Tells Startling Story of His Life to Surgeons Who Operated on Him.

*By Associated Press.*

Chicago, May 5.—Memory yesterday returned to the man who claims to be George Kimmel, according to surgeons who operated on the man's skull a few days ago.

The surgeons last night said that the man who claimed to be Kimmel had told them his life story and had made startling statements.

Already a new story of his life, from his own voluntary statements has been patched together and is declared so startling that it is kept secret, pending investigation.

Within 48 hours according to Dr. Loren Wilder, Kimmel, or Andrew White, as he was known for several years, will have recovered sufficiently from the effects of the operation to permit a thorough questioning.

"In voluntary statements, Kimmel told circumstances regarding the attack on him in 1908 which deprived him of his memory, and these are of such a surprising nature that we are making an investigation," said Dr. Wilder.

## DAMAGE IN DULUTH IS HEAVY

### Rain Lasts 48 Hours and Is Accompanied by Gale.

Duluth, Minn., May 5.—During the 24 hours ending at 7 o'clock last evening, 1.58 inches of rain fell in Duluth. Considerable damage was done. Five thousand dollars' damage was done to the retaining wall in the Soo Line passenger terminal yard.

Rising water in the glen section drove numerous people from their dwellings. Basements in all parts of the city were flooded. The rain was accompanied by a gale which reached a maximum velocity of 48 miles an hour.

## President Says Perkins Halted Attack on Trust

### Taft Adds New Chapter to Harvester Case History in Baltimore.

### He Declares That Director Induced Roosevelt to Defer Prosecution.

### Colonel Accused of Desiring to Introduce "Benevolent Despotism."

### Former Chief Executive Is Scored for "Assumption of Virtue."

### White House Occupant Holds Rival Is Treating Him Unfairly.

*By Associated Press.*

Baltimore, May 5.—In the closing speech of a 14-hour campaign trip through Maryland, President Taft last night in this city added a new chapter to the history of the Harvester "trust."

Speaking to a vast audience, Mr. Taft declared that Colonel Roosevelt had prevented the prosecution of that "trust" after George W. Perkins, one of its directors and now a Roosevelt supporter, had asked that the trust be not taken into the courts.

**Mr. Bonaparte "Mistaken."**

The speaker intimated that Charles J. Bonaparte, attorney general under Mr. Roosevelt, had been "mistaken" when he said that he (Mr. Taft) had been present at a cabinet meeting which decided against prosecution. Mr. Taft said that the diary of Herbert Knox Smith, then and now head of the bureau of corporations, proved that at the time referred to he, the speaker, was on a trip around the world.

**Other Points of Attack.**

Mr. Taft's explanation of the Harvester trust muddle was only one of the many points on which he attacked Colonel Roosevelt. He said that his predecessor's attitude towards the trusts showed clearly that he wished to perfect a benevolent "despositsm" that would discriminate between the good and the bad trusts; he pointed out, he asserted, how Mr. Roosevelt had changed from his attitude of regarding his entrance into the presidential race as a calamity to that of being an active campaigner for the renomination, and insisted that Mr. Roosevelt was striving to make this campaign one in which the men who had little should be arrayed against him who had more.

He paralleled the achievements of his administration and the charges which Mr. Roosevelt has made against it, declaring that in his own term in the White House there had been more progressive legislation enacted than in the term of any other president since the Civil war.

**Seven Speeches in Day.**

Mr. Taft's Baltimore speech came at the end of a day that took him over much of the central and southwestern part of Maryland. In all, he made seven speeches, to crowds that were attentive and that cheered him frequently.

For most of the trip he traveled in his private car, but just before turning south, to Baltimore, he motored for 30 miles over dusty roads that added perceptibly to the huskiness of his voice.

In practically all of his early speeches, delivered at Hyattsville, Laurel, Elkton, Aberdeen, Belaire and Havre de Grace, the president brought in the name of Colonel Roosevelt and asked again and again for a "square deal."

The president's Baltimore speech was delivered just before he left for Washington where he will take breakfast and luncheon today before leaving for Cincinnati for a short stay.

In it, he said in part:

**Mr. Taft's Version.**

"The truth about the Harvester trust is that Mr. Bonaparte thought it ought to be prosecuted. Mr. George W. Perkins, who was director in the Harvester trust, then a director in the Steel trust, and also a member of the firm of Morgan & Co., came over to Washington and pleaded with Mr. Herbert Knox Smith of the bureau of corporations not to bring suit.

"Mr. Perkins induced Mr. Smith to make a report to Mr. Roosevelt in which he set forth the fact that the Steel trust and the Harvester trust and the other Morgan interests had attempted to carry out Mr. Roosevelt's idea of publicity and, therefore, they ought not to be subjected to prosecution under the anti-trust law, even though they technically were guilty, threatening that if they were prosecuted they would fight the administration, would give them no more access to their books, and would conduct themselves in opposition to the administration.

**Suit Delay Recommended.**

"The result was that Mr. Smith made a report on Sept. 21 to Mr. Roosevelt in which he detailed this conversation and recommended that no suit be brought until he had made a full investigation of the Harvester trust.

"Before this a report was made by the assistant district attorney of North Dakota and by the district attorney of Minnesota that there was ground for

(Continued on Page 2, Column 5.)

**Excerpts From Address Made by President Taft Before Baltimore Throng**

**Mr. Roosevelt's assumption of virtue is so intense that it is sufficient to purify anything that becomes a supporter of Mr. Roosevelt, even though it be a trust or even though it be a director of a trust contributing to his campaign.**

**He (Mr. Roosevelt) means to introduce a benevolent despotism in which he means to select the trusts which he thinks ought to continue and smash those he thinks ought not to continue.**

**It hardly lies in his mouth, as a matter of the square deal, to charge me with being controlled by special interests and privileges when the record of my administration shows a prosecution of all the trusts without regard to their directors, and without regard to the interests that control them.**

**The criticism that has been made of my administration is that I have been too thorough in the prosecution of trusts. Certainly I have excepted none on account of the pleas of their directors and there are no contributors that I know of who can point to any immunity from prosecution in my administration.**

**If any one should have more than two terms there is no reason why he should not have four or five terms.**

### *Today's Contents.*



## RAILROAD TRACKS WASHED OUT

### Traffic Tied Up On South Shore Line—Freighter Driven Ashore.

*By Associated Press.*

Calumet, Mich., May 5.—The Sturgeon river, in Barga county, overflowed its banks yesterday and carried away a long section of the South Shore railroad tracks. Traffic in the southeast and west was suspended for 24 hours and the only communication with the outside world was by way of Saginaw. Two inches of rain has fallen here in the past two days. The heavy wind yesterday afternoon drove the lake freighter, Agassiz, ashore in Portage lake, near the Osceola stamp mills.

## Women Favor Reducing Bars; Laud Movement

### Members of Clubs to Appear Before Council Committee to Aid Plan.

### Which Saloon to Be Eliminated Is Problem Before Aldermen.

### President Selover Is Expected to Return to City Today.

### Proposition to Be Taken Before Woman's Federated Clubs.

### Councilman Gould Has a Scheme for Weeding Out Buffets.

Clubwomen were not slow to see that the time is propitious for reduction in the saloon roster of Minneapolis, and last night they voiced their approval of the council majority which in the last few days has gone on record for a substantial reduction.

**To Appear Before Council.**

The leader of all the clubwomen of this section of the state promises that she will appear before the special committee which Alderman Hooker will have appointed for the purposes of considering what reduction should be made, how to make it and the license fee to be charged the saloons which survive.

**Other Women Favor Plan.**

Other club women joined her in approval of the proposed council action. Always their first word was one of approval and the next a suggestion that the saloons which have been conducted on an immoral basis be the first to feel the ax.

Such is the disposition everywhere. It seems to be settled that some of the saloons are to go and it is likely that 350 or possibly 300, will be the figure to which they are cut. The present number is 408. There is no unanimity of sentiment toward a radical cut to 200 such as was first mentioned by Alderman Ortquist.

With it apparently a foregone conclusion that there is to be a cut in the number of saloons the unanimous cry is for weeding out the low saloons first. Aldermen, business men and club women agree entirely on this point. Those who are in a position to know, say that in most instances the low saloon will be found to be the saloon which could not do a paying business on a legitimate basis.

**Saloons to Go a Problem.**

But the big problem to which no solution of a definite nature has been offered is that of actually picking the places to go. It is probable that the only active effort toward saloon reduction between now and next Friday night will be confined to seeking a solution of this question. So far as everything else in connection with the saloon reduction movement is concerned, the officials are willing to wait until Mr. Hooker obtains the appointment of his committee Friday night.

It is not believed that there will be the slightest trouble in Mr. Hooker obtaining this committee. President Selover of the city council is known to be an anti-saloon man. He is due to return from Washington today. Early this week Alderman Engen, who has not had opportunity to express his opinion on saloon reduction as yet, will return.

Here is what some of the most prominent club and other women of the city think of the movement for saloon reduction:

"I most certainly favor a movement to reduce the number of saloons in Minneapolis," said Mrs. V. C. Sherman, president of the Fifth district of Federated Women's clubs. "I have discussed the matter with several members of the federation and their views coincide with mine. We expect to consider the proposition thoroughly at our next meeting. It is likely plans will be formulated at this meeting to send a committee to the council to make any helpful suggestions we may see fit. It is gratifying to see some of the best men of our council making a clear stand in favor of saloon reduction."

**Move Called Good Idea.**

"The city council can make no better move than to take immediate action reducing the number of saloons," said Mrs. James Thurston. "One needs only to take a walk through some parts of our down town business district to become convinced that there are too many saloons. Personally, I will do all I can to assist in the movement. Practically all of the women of the city, I believe, feel as I do regarding the proposition."

Mrs. S. A. Stockwell said she highly indorsed the movement to eliminate a number of the saloons. "I believe there are many objectionable bars that could be knocked out very easily," said Mrs. Stockwell, "and it surely would elevate the morals of the city. A reduction in the number of saloons and a stricter enforcement of the law as regards those allowed to remain, undoubtedly would bring results. The Political Economy club, of which I am a member, will discuss the movement at our next meeting. The majority of the members are heartily in favor of reasonable reduction of saloons. I cannot say as to whether we will go before the council, but it is likely we will, if there is anything that we can do."

Mrs. H. L. Day expressed the belief that there are entirely too many saloons in Minneapolis. "I am strongly

(Continued on Page 12, Col. 2.)

## Trolley and Train Collide; Passengers and Crew Hurt

**POLICE ARREST FOUR IN RAID**

**Proprietor and Three Inmates of La Mar Hotel Taken in Custody.**

In a raid on the La Mar hotel, 719 Third street south, last night by Detectives Garvey, Morrissey and Berry, F. G. Beckendorf was arrested on the charge of keeping a disorderly house, and Andrew Kirken, May Burke and Louise Johnson for being inmates of the place.

The raid followed the complaint made to the police by a man refusing to give his name, who said that a woman at the hotel had enticed him into the place and robbed him of $20. No trace of the woman nor the man who had made the complaint could be found when the raid was made.

## Women Narrowly Escape in Flat Building Fire

### Several Persons Overcome by Smoke When Flames Attack Hennepin Apartments.

### Mrs. Barnes and Mrs. Wesley Lose Way in Halls—Janitor Is Hero.

Two women narrowly escaped weath and several persons were overcome by smoke in a fire last night which broke out in a flat building at 1605-1607 Hennepin avenue. A dozen families were driven fro mtheir homes and an estimated loss of $1,500 was caused.

Mrs. B. L. Barnes and Mrs. Mary Wesley, who occupied flats on the third floor, lost their way in the smoke-filled hallways of the second floor after the other occupants had left the building. They were assisted to safety by George Bell, a roomer on the second floor, who rushed up the stairs and led the women down a rear stairway. Firemen assisted women on the second and third floors to the street. The janitor, Otto Nelson, was overcome by smoke while assisting women on the third floor.

The fire started in a closet in the hallway of the flat occupied by Mr. and Mrs. E. B. Mettee, on the first floor. It was discovered by Mrs. H. L. Coons, who, with her husband, occupies a rear flat on the first floor. She notified the other residents of the flat and attempted to put out the blaze, while her husband turned in an alarm.

The damage was confined chiefly to the hallways of the first floor, though considerable damage was done to the flats occupied by E. B. Mettee, Mr. an, Mrs. E. B. Mettee, Mr. and Mrs. Joseph Wylie, Mr. and Mrs. H. L. Coons and Mrs. Henry Fravel.

The loss is covered by insurance. The building is owned by E. P. Kapen.

## Chicagoans Are Beaten by Strike Sympathizers

### Injunctions Fail to Prevent Violence in Circulation of Newspapers.

### Newsboys and Their Customers Attacked—Many Arrests Made.

(Special to The Sunday Tribune.)

Chicago, May 5.—While injunctional orders were issued to prevent violence and interference with the circulation of morning and afternoon newspapers, battles continued yesterday between newsboys and citizens who were attempting to purchase papers, and professional sluggers.

The first injunction to restrain members of the News Delivery and Mail Drivers' union, local No. 706, was issued shortly after midnight, Thursday, by Judge Richard E. Burke, of the superior court.

The injunction was asked for by the Tribune company in then ames of the daily newspapers.

The second injunction, issued yesterday afternoon, was asked by Attorney John J. Symes, representing the Daily News, and was directed specifically to the pressmen, stereotypers and similar unions, to enjoin them from interference with the printing of the daily papers.

Despite the injunctions there was little cessation in the violence that had previously marked the strike against the members of the Publishers' association. Incipient riots were started at several loop corners, but were promptly quelled by the police before any very serious results happened.

**Try to Beat Newsboy.**

Two arrests werem ade at the corner of South Fifth avenue and West Madison street when several professional sluggers attempted to attack and beat a newsboy at that corner. The men arrested, who gave the names of Martin Silver and Emil Creddio, were taken into custody by the police just as they were about to kick Edward Cleary, a newsboy whom they had struck to the ground.

Several bystanders suffered minor injuries in the excitement and scuffle that ensued, but no serious injuries were reported nor were any more arrests made at that time.

Peter Bartzen, Jr., son of Peter Bartzen, president of the county board, was arrested after he had stubbornly refused to obey an order by a policeman to keep moving. Under direct instructions from Captain P. J. Lavin, no loiterers are permitted at any loop corners.

**100 Policemen Patrol Corner.**

Having been warned that there was likely to be serious trouble at the corner of West Madison street and West Fifth avenue, Captain Lavin has detailed nearly 100 policemen permanently to that corner and has also issued orders that two patrol wagons take up a permanent stand there. Police officers with drawn clubs were on every hand to keep crowds moving, and to protect citizens who wished to buy newspapers.

"If we saw this on the vaudeville stage," said one man during the afternoon, "it would be funny. **As soon as a man reaches to his pocket for a penny, a policeman steps to his side to see that he is not molested while making his purchase.** I saw one man protected by three policement with drawn clubs, while he spent a cent. But it isn't funny at all. I also saw one man who bought a paper, slugged after he had left the corner and got into the middle

(Continued on Page 2, Column 4.)

## N.P. Way Freight Hits Street Car; Six Are Injured

### Collision Occurs at Fifteenth Avenue Northeast During Height of Storm.

### Traction Vehicle Ripped Off Trucks—Carried 50 Feet.

### Conductor, Unable to See Train for Storm, Signalled Clear Way.

### Victims Have Miraculous Escape—One in Serious Condition.

### Patrolman Crawls Into the Debris to Aid in Rescue Work.

**Injured in Wreck.**

J. P. Dewey, brakeman, 1008 O'Brien place north; back and shoulder seriously hurt; will recover.

Nels Howe, Lake Benton and New Brighton, a passenger; head, chin and hand painfully cut.

John Mullen fireman, 545 Mississippi street, St. Paul; ankle fractured and back scalded.

Walter Baker, boy passenger, 421 Second street north; back and leg hurt and hand cut.

William Nadeau, engineer 198 Granite street, St. Paul; slight cuts.

E. J. Jonassen, motorman, 3128 Pillsbury avenue south; slight cuts.

Four passengers and the motorman on a First and Central avenue car, the train men, including the engineer, the fireman and brakeman on a Northern Pacific way freight, were injured, and the street car, the engine, tender and two box cars were wrecked in a collision which occurred at the Northern Pacific railroad and the Fifteenth avenue northeast crossing late last night.

**Storm at Its Height.**

The collision took place between 10 and 11 o'clock, when the storm of last night was at its height.

The crossing gates failed to work and the conductor of the street car apparently was unable to see the approaching train, for it is said he signalled his car to proceed.

**Escapes Marvelous.**

That anyone got out of the wreck alive was considered nearly a miracle, for the street car was thrown to one side and carried along for about 50 feet, the engine was thrown off the rails to the other side, disconnecting with the tender, which continued for a short distance on the rails and then turned turtle.

One of the box cars lost its trucks and then was turned at right angles to the track, another continued until it struck the tender, when it also turned upside down. The locomotive itself was a heap of broken iron.

The banks around were plowed up into piles of dirt and smashed timbers, twisted rods, broken glass and jammed freight were piled into an inextricable mass.

**Versions of Wreck Cause.**

There is considerable difference of opinion about the cause of the accident. W. Lawler, the flagman at the crossing, said last night that the gates didn't work; in fact, they had not been in service during the four days he had been on the job. He said he saw the danger and called out, but his voice was drowned and the next thing he knew he was trying to get out of the tower, which was struck by the derailed engine and slewed to one side. He said there was no flagman on the crossing.

The conductor of the street car, William Gilbert, 3111 Pillsbury avenue, stepped off the car as usual when it reached the crossing. Owing to the rain and thunder he was unable to see the approaching train and signalled his car to come on.

**Car Struck in Front.**

The car had just reached the railroad tracks when the engine struck it near the front vestibule with such force that it was carried along for a considerable distance and finally ditched alongside the track, the front trucks being left in a heap near the wreck of one of the box cars. Every window in the car was broken.

After the engine and the tender had "jack-knifed" the engine plowed into the right-hand bank and turned on its side. The fireman, who was shoveling coal into the firebox at the time, was shoved out of the cab by the engineer, who called to him to jump for his life. Both escaped with only slight injuries.

**Steam Envelopes Wreck.**

The tender, which continued on the rails for a short distance, was struck by the following boxcar and upset, the car losing its front trucks and was slewed to the left, the front end being driven into a sandbank for several feet. The car immediately behind it landed on its roof. The other cars—there were 49 of them—broke away and staid on the rails.

Patrolman Violet, who was only a short distance away when the colision occurred, hurried to the assistance of the injured. He said he could see nothing for some time, as the steam and rain enveloped the wreck as in a pall. He crawled on his hands and knees toward the center of the mass of debris and assisted the passengers to extricate themselves. He then called police headquarters and ambulances and patrol wagons were rushed to the

# THE MINNEAPOLIS JOURNAL.

12 PAGES—HOME EDITION. MINNEAPOLIS WEATHER—Fair tonight and Sunday; warmer Sunday. SATURDAY EVENING, OCTOBER 11, 1913. PRICE ONE CENT IN MINNEAPOLIS.


## MACKS GET ONE RUN IN FIRST; 2 IN THE THIRD

### With Their Backs Against the Wall, Giants Stake Hopes on Big Six.

### BUMPER CROWD OUT TO WITNESS CRUCIAL GAME

### Plank Works for Athletics in What May Be Last Contest of Series.

Polo Grounds, New York, Oct. 11.—The New York Giants stood in their last line of entrenchments today and with their big gun, Christy Mathewson, wheeled into action, faced the storming attack of the Philadelphia Athletics, who needed but one more victorious charge to make them world's champions of 1913.

With all his pitching artillery shattered by the Athletics' cannonading, Manager McGraw was forced to send his lone pitching star, Mathewson, to the firing line with only two days' rest. The National league champions have won only one game in the series.

**Another Monster Turnout.**

Thirty-five thousand or more persons, undismayed by the herculean task of the Giants, came out to the Polo grounds to view the battle. The gloomy weather kept the Philadelphia crowd down to a small number, but those enthusiastic few sat behind the Athletics' bench and never missed an opportunity to cheer their team.

With heavy clouds drifting in from seaward, there was a constant fear that rain would end the struggle. Canvas protected the inner playing field from the night's downpour and the groundkeepers had the diamond in shape for smart fielding.

"We may give you a chance to look over two new pitchers today," said big Ira Thomas, the Athletic catcher. "There are Brown and Shawkey, who have yet to show their pitching wares. Either one will give Matty a run and we can use Plank if necessary."

Manager McGraw had little to say, but that little showed that the New York manager was still fighting hard to repulse Mack's brigade.

**McGraw Still Hopeful.**

"We'll be in there fighting until they drag us or the other fellows out," remarked McGraw.

The Giants were the first on the field for a long batting practise. McGraw had told them in the clubhouse that if they expected to make a stand today, they would have to give Mathewson support with their bats. McGraw and Mathewson were the last to come upon the field and the crowd accorded them a loud demonstration, for there was not a fan present who did not realize that it was up to Mathewson to stop the Athletics' rush. The Athletics marched across the field in a body and began to warm up on the side lines by tossing the ball back and forth to each other. One o'clock found nearly every seat in the unreserved stands and bleachers occupied and the crowd was still jamming through the turnstiles at the entrances.

**Matty and Plank Chosen.**

It was announced that Umpire Klem would make the decisions behind the plate while Umpire Egan would take care of the base path work. Umpire Rigler went to left field and Umpire Connolly to right field. Mathewson warmed up with Wilson for the Giants, while Plank and Lapp warmed up for the Athletics.

Mathewson and McLean were announced as the battery for New York. Plank and Schang were announced as the battery for the Athletics.

**FIRST INNING.**

Philadelphia—The crowd gave a big cheer when Mathewson walked out to the hurling hill. Murphy singled on the first ball pitched. Fletcher was barely able to reach it with his ungloved hand. Murphy was forced at second when Matty took Oldring's bunt and tossed to Fletcher. Mathewson made a nice play on the ball. Collins shot a single to right, Oldring easily making third. Oldring scored when Burns caught Baker's sacrifice fly. Burns made a wild throw to the plate, the ball going over McLean's head. Collins went to second on the wild heave. Herzog took McInnis' splash and threw to Doyle who touched out Collins. One run; two hits; one error.

New York—Plank's first pitch was a ball. Schang and Collins had a conference in the pitcher's box. Herzog out on a fly to Murphy. Plank worked coolly and deliberately as if trying to conserve all his energy. Doyle out, Barry to McInnis, on a lightning fielding play in which Barry took the ball on the run behind the pitcher's box. Fletcher went out on a long fly which Oldring took. No runs, no hits, no errors.

**SECOND INNING.**

Philadelphia — Doyle tossed out Strunk at first. Mathewson's big looping drop curve was in fine working order. Barry out on a high fly to Murray. Schang faced Mathewson for the first time in the series. Schang got an infield single which bounded off of Matty's glove. Plank popped out to Herzog. No runs, one hit, no errors.

New York—McGraw made a complaint to Umpire Klem that Plank was shifting his feet from the slab while making his delivery. Umpire Klem apparently did not sustain the claim. Baker threw out Burns at first. Shafer fouled out to McInnis, who caught the ball leaning over the boxes of the grandstand. Murray was thrown out by Plank at first. No runs, no hits; nor errors.

**THIRD INNING.**

Philadelphia—Murphy got his second single to left, the ball going like a rocket between Fletcher and Herzog. Doyle made an error on Oldring's hot grounder, Murphy going to second. Collins out when Merkle took his sacrifice bunt and touched him on the line. Both runners moved up. Murphy scored when Merkle took Baker's smash and threw to the plate. It was a Cincinnati base hit for Baker. Oldring went to third. Oldring scored on McInnis' sacrifice fly to Burns. Baker was held at first. Doyle threw out Strunk at first. Two runs, two hits, one error.

New York—McLean sent up a high fly to Oldring. Merkle line flied to Collins. Barry threw out Mathewson at first. No runs, no hits, no errors.

**FOURTH INNING.**

Philadelphia—Fletcher threw out Barry. Murray took Schang's short fly after a good run. Fletcher caught Plank's fly back of second base. No runs, no hits, no errors.

New York—Herzog went out on three strikes. Doyle out to McInnis unassisted. Fletcher flied out to Strunk. No runs, no hits, no errors.

**FIFTH INNING.**

Philadelphia—Doyle threw out Murphy at first. Doyle also took care of Oldring's grounder and tossed to first. Collins out on a fly to Shafer. No runs, no hits, no errors.

New York—Burns' line flied to McInnis. Shafer walked. He was the first Giant to reach first base in the game. Schang almost caught Shafer napping at first. Plank dropped Murray's pop fly and Shafer went to second. Shafer scored on McLean's single to left. Murray was held at second. A double play ended the inning, when Collins took Merkle's grounded and threw to Barry, forcing McLean at second. Barry then completed the double by throwing out Merkle at first. One run, one hit, one error.

**SIXTH INNING.**

Philadelphia—Baker shot a liner to right for a base. McLean threw out McInnis. It was a sacrifice bunt. Doyle threw out Strunk, Baker going to third. Fletcher threw out Barry at first. Fletcher made a bad throw and Merkle a beautiful stop. No runs, one hit, no errors.

## TODAY'S WORLD SERIES SCORE BY INNINGS

| | 1 | 2 | 3 | 4 | 5 | 6 | 7 | 8 | 9 | 10 | R | H | E |
|---|---|---|---|---|---|---|---|---|---|---|---|---|---|
| PHILADELPHIA | 1 | 0 | 2 | 0 | 0 | 0 | 0 | 0 | | | | | |
| NEW YORK | 0 | 0 | 0 | 0 | 1 | 0 | 0 | | | | | | |

## HERCULES GETS JOB, BUT IT'S FOR WIFE

### Women's Branch of Employment Agency Goal of Muscular Husband.

The man was six feet tall and proportioned like a barrel and he appeared as if Hercules was his middle name and "labor" his peppermint candy. When he leaned over and breathed across the railing upon Miss Florence Burton, manager of the women's department of the Minnesota state free employment bureau, he exhaled like the sigh of a hippopotamus, and when he coughed the papers on a desk ten feet away fluttered like the autumn leaves before a blast from the north.

Miss Burton pointed to the sign and indicated that his place was next door, where the men are given jobs. But he insisted upon remaining and said he knew he was in the right place.

"No, no," he said. "This is the right place."

"But this is the women's department," said Miss Burton.

"Yes, yes," he said. "That's it, that's right."

Then he went to the door, beckoned down the hallway and said, "Hurry up," impatiently.

A small woman, wearing a faded Paisley shawl and a bonnet of the season of 1889, with thin hands, long fingers and big knuckles, came in, haltingly.

"My wife," said the man. "Good woman. Want to get her a job."

Miss Burton almost collapsed. Then she asked the man if he was working.

"No," he said, slowly. "Not yet."

Miss Burton had a job for the woman and the man seemed delighted.

"He said he would go into the men's department and look for a job for himself," Miss Burton said, "but I did not see him enter."

## NORTHWESTERN MEN IN THE NEW POPULAR GOVERNMENT LEAGUE

Washington, Oct. 11.—Several northwestern men besides Senator Clapp are prominent in the proposed popular government league which is to meet here for organization in December. Among the committee of fifty which has the subject in hand are Stiles H. Jones of Minneapolis, secretary of the Voters' league, and Representative James Manahan and Senator Myers of Montana. The organization is intended to be nonpartisan and the men interested in the movement include republicans and democrats who are regarded as progressive as well as members of the progressive party. The object of those interested in the organization is to secure progressive laws for the nation, states and cities.

### CAPTAIN HANKS CELEBRATES

**Cousin of Abraham Lincoln Reaches Ninety-second Milestone.**

Winona, Minn., Oct. 11.—Captain S. B. Hanks of Albany, Ill., one of the veteran Mississippi river pilots, celebrated on Thursday the ninety-second anniversary of his birth. Captain Hanks is a cousin of Abraham Lincoln, his father being a brother of Lincoln's mother, Nancy Hanks. He has the distinction of having served more years on the river than any other steamboat pilot.

### COLD TO BE SHORTLIVED

**Warm, Fair Sunday Is Prediction of Weather Bureau.**

Cold weather which followed fast on the heels of the recent rainstorm is scheduled, according to the weather bureau's prediction, to depart sometime tonight or early tomorrow. A fair, warm Sunday will probably be the result. The coldest point in the thermometer's dropping market was recorded at 6 a.m. today when the quotation was 36 degrees. At noon the mercury and mounted to 49 and a further rise was in order.

### GREEN BAY DRIVER KILLED

Green Bay, Wis., Oct. 11.—W. H. Clark, aged 70, driver employed by a transfer company, was killed today when an automobile driven by E. N. Murphy, son of Albert Murphy, a millionaire, ran into a carriage that he was driving.

## HUERTA DISSOLVES CONGRESS; TAKES REINS AS DICTATOR

### Arrest of 110 Deputies and Display of Force Precedes Action.

### WASHINGTON BELIEVES SITUATION IS CRITICAL

### Holding of Elections Oct. 26 Declared Doubtful—Lind May Be Recalled.

Mexico City, Oct. 11.—Provisional President Huerta's coup last night, whereby he rid himself in a spectacular manner of the legislative bodies of the government and constituted himself dictator of the Mexican republic, has left the city today in a state of tense expectancy.

Both branches of the Mexican national congress were formally declared suspended.

The declaration was made after 110 members of the chamber of deputies had been arrested and lodged in the penitentiary for signing resolutions of warning to General Victoriano Huerta because of the disappearance of the senator for Chiapas, Dr. Belisaro Dominguez.

**New Elections Called.**

A proclamation was issued just before midnight calling for new elections of senators and deputies on Oct. 26, which date is coincident with the presidential election.

The arrests of the 110 deputies followed a demand by President Huerta that the chamber withdraw the resolution, which carried the threat that the deputies would abandon the capitol owing to an alleged lack of guarantees for their personal safety.

Senator Dominguez early in the month made a speech in the senate violently attacking Huerta.

He said the currency of Mexico had depreciated, fields had been neglected and towns razed, and that famine threatened. He added that the situation was due first and foremost to the fact that the Mexican people could not resign themselves to be governed by Huerta.

Before the hour for the regular opening of the session of the chamber the basement and roof of the building had been packed with troops. Scores of police were scattered through the gallery.

**Troops Guard Chamber.**

When the deputies were in their places Minister of the Interior Manuel Garz Aldape entered the chamber.

Simultaneously several hundred fed-

Continued on 2d Page, 4th Column.

## HILL ASKED TO CARRY EASTERN WOMEN WEST TO MARRY FARMERS

Boston, Oct. 11.—So anxious is Miss Caroline Smith, head of the Woman's Trade Board, to send 500 New England women and girls out west to find husbands that she would mail them by way of parcel post if she could. But she cannot, so she asked James J. Hill if he would give the fair brigade free transportation.

"I have letters from Minnesota asking for 500 women to become wives," said Miss Smith today. "The men out there mean business, and the 500 are the kind of women these farmers want. I can't send them by parcel post, so I went to Mr. Hill."

Mr. Hill listened to Miss Smith's request, but went away without committing himself.

## 5 TRAPS AND HOUND FOR GINSENG THIEF

### Galgin Lake Truck Gardener's Gun Scheme Fails to Protect $4,000 Patch.

Three bear traps, two gun traps and a vicious hound will within a week be awaiting the return of the thief who early today escaped a charge of shot when he set off a gun trap in the ginseng patch of Arthur Brackett, who has a twenty-acre truck garden farm near Galpin lake, a few miles from Excelsior, acording to Mr. Brackett today.

A month ago, on a moonlit night, a thief stole 500 ginseng roots, valued at $200. The thief dug the roots at his leisure and picked out the best in the acre and a half planted several years ago. Mr. Brackett values the entire planting at more than $4,000.

Believing the thief would return, Mr. Brackett fastened a loaded shotgun in a fence corner and attached to the trigger a wire, he told Sheriff Otto S. Langum today. The gun pointed along the wire. Early today the gun was discharged. By the time the owner reached the ginseng patch, the thief had fled. No blood was discovered and it is believed the thief escaped injury. Roots to the value of $15 had been stolen.

Brackett notified the sheriff of the theft and declared he will surround the patch with bear traps, gun traps, and buy a hound with a savage disposition.

### COLONEL HICKS TAKES BRIDE

**Veteran Editor Married Today at Oshkosh, Wis.**

Oshkosh, Wis., Oct. 11.—The marriage of Colonel John Hicks, publisher of the Daily Northwestern at Oshkosh, and Miss Mary Agnes Powers, a kindergarten teacher, took place today, the ceremony being performed by Rev. John W. Greenwood, rector of Trinity Episcopal church. Only relatives were present.

PUZZLE PICTURE — WHERE IS THIS MAN FROM?

## LINER BURNED AT SEA IN TERRIFIC GALE; 136 LIVES LOST; 521 RESCUED

The steamship Volturno, which burned in midocean with loss of 136 lives.

### FACTS ABOUT VOLTURNO AND ILL-FATED JOURNEY

**The Volturno was commanded by Captain Francis Inch, who was promoted to captaincy two months ago. He formerly was second officer aboard the liner Campanello of the Uranium line.**

**Indications were that there were no native-born Americans on the steamship Volturno. A nearly complete passenger list, received at New York from Rotterdam, showed that practically all on board were immigrants, mostly bound for Canada.**

**The immigrants aboard the Volturno were composed of Russians, Dalmatians, Poles and a few Germans. Most of them were bound for Canada.**

**The Cunard line has ordered Captain Barr to call at Queenstown, and the Carmania is expected there Sunday night.**

**At the headquarters of the Canadian Northern Royal line, at Toronto, it was stated that the Volturno, while owned by that company, had never been operated by it. The Uranium line had it chartered for seven years and the Canadian Northern merely acted as agents for the Uranium company in Canada.**

**The burning of the Volturno brought sharply to the attention of congress today the fact that the "safety at sea" bill, drawn after the Titanic disaster, has not yet been made a law. It was passed by both branches of congress last year, but was not signed by President Taft and is now "unfinished business" in the senate.**

**The Volturno was valued at $400,000 and was insured for $300,000.**

### MRS. J. J. ANKENY STRICKEN

**Old Resident Suffers Stroke While With Husband and Children.**

Mrs. Catherine Ankeny, wife of John J. Ankeny, 1807 Laurel avenue, died suddenly of paralysis at 11:30 a.m. today. Mrs. Ankeny was 66 years of age. She had lived in Minneapolis since 1869, coming to this city with her husband forty-four years ago. She had been in good health until the time of her death. She suffered a stroke of paralysis while sitting at home and died within a few minutes. With her at the time were her husband and her son, H. W. Ankeny, 1616 West Twenty-fifth street, and her daughter, Mrs. Peter George. Mrs. George A. Cobb of St. Paul, a sister, survives Mrs. Ankeny. Funeral arrangements have not been made.

La Crosse, Wis., Oct. 11.—Alma Rebecca Osborne, a resident of La Crosse and a member of the First Methodist church here for fifty-five years, died today at the age of 95. She was the mother of R. E. Osborne and E. W. Osborne of Minneapolis.

## 4 MINNEAPOLITANS ON ILL-FATED SHIP

### Mrs. Victoria Greilech and Children Believed to Have Been on Burned Volturno.

Four Minneapolis people are believed to have been on board the illfated Volturno, which was destroyed in midocean by fire. They are Mrs. Victoria Greilech, wife of Carl Greilech of Columbia Heights, and their three children, who left St. Petersburg several weeks ago on a trip that was to take them to Warsaw, Poland, thence to Antwerp, where they were to board the Volturno. Nothing has been heard from Mrs. Greilech and her children since they left St. Petersburg, where they were at the time Mr. Greilech sent them their passage tickets for the Volturno, according to M. Zajdel, Uranium line agent in Minneapolis. Mr. Greilech could not be found today.

Mr. Zajdel said today that Mr. Greilech came to him six months ago and purchased tickets for the passage of his wife and three children from Antwerp. They had intended taking an earlier boat, he said, but later changed their plans and wrote to Mr. Greilech of their intention to return on the Volturno. As no word has been received from them since, Mr. Greilech was expecting them on the Volturno and had so told Mr. Zajdel.

In their efforts to ascertain the names of all those on board the Volturno, Uranium agents today are searching for Mr. Greilech, to learn from him if by any chance his family might not have boarded the ship, but Mr. Zajdel said that as Greilech had kept almost constantly in touch with him regarding his family's departure from Europe, there seemed little chance that he had heard anything contrary to the message that informed him of their intended departure.

## TRAFFIC IS RECORD; CONGESTION FEARED

### 500,000 Freight Cars Handled in Minneapolis This Year—Thousands Tied Up in Yards.

Minneapolis is on the verge of traffic congestion as a result of the handling here of the record total of 500,000 freight cars so far this year, and James C. Andrews, chairman of the transportation committee of the traffic division, Minneapolis Civic and Commerce association, today notified Secretary John G. McHugh of the Minneapolis Chamber of Commerce that a situation exists that demands co-operation on the part of shippers, and receivers and the railroads.

The Great Northern road alone has more than 2,000 cars of wheat on hand in its Minneapolis yards, and in the movement of Oct. 7 received switching orders for 633 cars and holding orders for only 226, thus feeling the cumulative effect of daily backing up of the incoming tonnage.

The Milwaukee road has 600 cars undelivered, for which it is waiting switching orders, some of the arrivals dating back into September.

The Northern Pacific has 929 of its cars on the rails of other roads, in the Minneapolis terminals, in the process of switching to mills and elevators.

**Grain Cars Blocked.**

The Minneapolis & St. Louis in the St. Louis Park terminals, the Chicago Great Western in its terminals in the Southeast Minneapolis milling and elevator district and the Soo Line in its North Minneapolis wheat yards and at elevators, have collectively 1,500 cars of grain blocked by the congestion.

The receipt of Mr. Andrews' communication caused much comment at the Chamber of Commerce, because, while it made no reference to Canada as a possible future contributing factor, the probability of free Canadian wheat after the first of the year has been much discussed on 'change. Should the Canadian government act and take off the countervailing duty on wheat, as many grain men believe will be done, western Canada probably would send in thousands of cars of grain to the Minneapolis market.

**Manufacturers May Be Affected.**

The wholesale and manufacturing interests of the city do not figure in Mr. Andrews' statement of the situation, and these interests have to this time been able to get along with reasonable facility. But in the event of a great influx of Canadian grain it is possible that the terminals might get into a state of congestion that would mean a general blockade, especially if winter comes on early and a heavy coal movement develops.

Referring to instances of cars loaded Oct. 1, 2, 3 and 7, and not yet billed out, Mr. Andrews pronounces it "the most reckless use of railroad equipment." "If this is continued," his letter says, "it will not only result in continued congestion in the terminals but it is probable that the railroads will take action and order into public warehouses all cars not billed out within forty-eight hours."

## WIRELESS CALL SUMMONS TEN SHIPS TO SCENE

### Vessels Forced to Stand Idly by in Storm and Watch Disaster.

### MANY HOURS BEFORE ANY VICTIMS ARE TAKEN OFF

### Four Lifeboats, Launched in Huge Waves, Dashed to Pieces.

### SEARCHLIGHTS REVEAL INDESCRIBABLE HORROR

### Carmania Leads Fleet of Steamers in Work of Saving Passengers.

Liverpool, Oct. 11.—One hundred and thirty-six women, children and men lost their lives when the Uranium line steamship Volturno, leased from the Royal line, caught fire in mid-Atlantic on Thursday and burned to the water's edge on Friday.

Ten big liners, led by the Cunarder Carmania, Captain Barr, stood by the stricken ship and battled for many hours in a fierce gale to rescue the passengers and crew, but were able to take off and pick up only 521 persons.

**Rescue Long Delayed.**

While hundreds of passengers aboard the rescue fleet crowded the rails, spellbound with horror, the captains maneuvered in desperate attempts to get alongside the Volturno, but were unable to do so until daybreak Friday.

Captain Barr then ran a lifeboat under the stern of the Volturno and took off eleven passengers. Other captains followed, and the survivors taken from the Volturno as well as those picked up in the only two Volturno lifeboats that got away during the fire were distributed among the rescuing liners.

From Thursday noon the Carmania stood by, helpless, on account of the terrific storm and mountainous waves, until early Friday. The last of the surviving passengers and crew were taken off at 9:30 a.m. Friday. The Carmania was alone with the burning liner until the Grosser Furst and Seidelitz came up about 4 p.m. Thursday. The other seven rescue ships arrived shortly afterward.

**Four Lifeboats Smashed.**

While the Carmania's passengers looked on, frantic and helpless, four lifeboats lowered from the Volturno were smashed against the side of the heavily rolling ship and their passengers, including women and children, were drowned. A broken propeller of the Volturno had so fouled the tackle of the lifeboats that only six could be lowered and only two got away.

As darkness fell, the Carmania kept its powerful searchlights playing on the waters around the burning boat, looking for possible passengers that might have taken to the sea in their desperation. Captain Barr also threw out burning buoys all night to light the ghastly scene. Their light played on the poop of the Volturno and showed plainly the hopeless women, children and men huddled there throughout the night.

At midnight there was some hope aroused when the fire appeared to be dying down. Captain Barr made another attempt to get a boat to the ship, and when this failed he ran the Carmania head-on within 100 feet of the Volturno's stern. It was impossible, though, to get a line aboard the wreck.

The fire broke out fiercely in the after engine room before dawn and when daylight came it was seen that the Volturno was sinking by the head.

The gale had abated by then and lifeboats from the rescue fleet were run alongside the burning liner, taking off the last of the survivors.

**Volturno Sinks.**

The Volturno was abandoned at 9:20 a.m. on Friday and sank a few minutes later.

The 136 missing passengers were burned to death, drowned in the smashed boats or jumped overboard.

About 9 p.m. Thursday a burst of flame lighted the sky and the surging waves for miles around. It was followed by a terrific explosion which sent clouds of sparks and burning fragments high in the air.

It was then that the searchlights of the ships standing by came into play. Several steerage passengers with life belts jumped into the water and were picked up by the Carmania's boats.

**Ten Vessels at Scene.**

The vessels that went to the Volturno's assistance and the survivors they have aboard are: Carmania, 11; La Touraine, 40; Minneapolis, 30; Rappahannock, 19; Czar, 102; Narragansett, 29; Devonian, 59; Kroonland, 90; Grosser Furst, 105; and Seidlitz, 36.

The Volturno sailed from Rotterdam on Oct. 2 for New York by way of Halifax, where it was due to stop next Monday.

Captain Barr of the Carmania received the distress call of the Volturno when seventy-eight miles distant, in latitude 48.25 north, longitude 34.33 west. The Carmania crowded on full steam and with extra stokers made over twenty knots an hour in the teeth of the gale.

When the Carmania reached the

# THE MINNEAPOLIS JOURNAL.

18 PAGES—HOME EDITION | MINNEAPOLIS WEATHER—Fair tonight and Tuesday; slowly rising temperature. | MONDAY EVENING, JUNE 29, 1914. | PRICE ONE CENT IN MINNEAPOLIS.



# CONGRESS MAY INVESTIGATE CHARGE THAT AMERICAN INTERESTS FOSTERED MEXICAN REVOLUTION AND HINDERED WORK OF MEDIATION

## *Correspondence Between Captain Hopkins and H. C. Pierce and With General Carranza*

, 6th May, 1914.

Dear Mr. Pierce:

I thank you for your remittance of the 2nd instant, of $500.00, and regret that you could not, for the moment, make it for $1,000.00, the amount needed. I trust, however, that within the next week or ten days you will be able to let me have the balance, since it is very important for me to have funds at this particular time.

Faithfully yours,

Henry Clay Pierce, Esq.,
25 Broad Street,
New York City.

---

HENRY CLAY PIERCE
25 BROAD STREET
NEW YORK

New York, April 18th, 1914.

S. G. Hopkins, Esq.,
Hibbs Building,
Washington, D. C.

Dear Captain:-

Referring to your letter of the 17th inst. with enclosures: Mr. Richards is in the country this afternoon, but on Monday, he will advise you concerning the references which you have kindly sent. Mr. Vasconcelos was to have seen me today, but he telephoned that he would come in on Monday. He told me the other day he was waiting to receive money from Carranza before going to Canada. The attorney of the Canadian parties told me yesterday that Vasconcelos would be wasting his time to go to Canada, as their representative and the parties to whom Vasconcelos should talk reside in New York, and consequently, I have arranged to have the party come to my office Monday, and if after talking with him it seems best, I will have Vasconcelos meet him.

Yours very truly,
H C Pierce

---

HENRY CLAY PIERCE
25 BROAD STREET
NEW YORK

New York, May 7th, 1914.

S. G. Hopkins, Esq.,
Hibbs Building,
Washington, D. C.

Dear Captain:-

Referring to your letter of May 6th: Yesterday I tried to impress upon Mr. Vasconcelos the necessity for prompt action on the part of his Chief concerning railroad matters.

Mr. G. with our American Tampico refinery and oil field people left Galveston May 5th on Danish Steamer Atlantis for Tampico under arrangements for them to remain on the steamer until safe for them to go ashore for the purpose of protecting and if possible operating our property in Tampico proper and our oil fields at Topila, about 17 miles inland on the Panuco River.

Before Mr. G's departure I requested his views concerning railroad matters in Northern Mexico and quote his telegram in reply as follows:

"Carranza should as soon as possible make a clean sweep of all present directors and officials of the National Railways, including those in New York, and not make the blunder which F. I. Madero and Ernesto Madero made in keeping them in a position to assist the Cientifico party and Lord Cowdray in his secret intrigue against F. I. Madero's constitutional government, which finally resulted in his overthrow and death. There are many good Mexicans competent to serve as directors, and with two good railroad men as President and General Manager the properties are easy to operate and can make good money in anything like peaceable times."

It is not necessary nor desirable to wait until the capture of Saltillo, San Luis Potosi, Tampico and Aguascalientes is accomplished before undertaking the new organization of the National Rys. of Mexico. I have not the pleasure of Mr. Pani's acquaintance, but assuming that he is well fitted for the work in connection with Mr. Vasconcelos, who I am sure understands the situation and requirements, I should think their appointment by Mr. Carranza to investigate and with power to arrange, and their early arrival here, most desirable.

Yours very truly,
H C Pierce

REPRODUCTIONS of ORIGINAL LETTERS from H. C. PIERCE to S. G. HOPKINS, the SIGNATURES HAVING BEEN MADE WITH a RUBBER STAMP. IN the UPPER LEFT HAND CORNER IS a REPRODUCTION of MR. HOPKINS' CARBON COPY of HIS LETTER to MR. PIERCE, REPLYING to the MEMORANDUM FROM MR. PIERCE, FACSIMILE of WHICH IS on PAGE 3

---

, 29th April, 1914.

Dear Mr. Pierce:

I confirm conversation on the telephone of today, and beg to state that reports to the Navy Department indicate continued fighting in the streets of Tampico, but nothing indicates that there has occurred any damage to foreign property. I note that Mr. Galbraith and your other employees at Galveston are to return to Tampico on a Danish steamer, and will wait there until it is safe to land, upon the fall of which city they will go on to Vera Cruz and commence operations in the refineries at that place. * * * * * * * *

I asked you to favor me with a remittance several days ago, and regret that I did not receive one this morning. I presume you must realize that my expenses in conducting the work that I have laid out for me, amount to a great many times my income and I have not, up to the present, felt like calling on Carranza for anything, because my prestige would be so much the greater in the end. I have been pressed with offer after offer of retainers during the last six weeks from various interests in Mexico, but up to the present time I have not accepted one cent from any of them, although I might have done so with perfect propriety, my sole object being to remain absolutely free from entanglements whatsoever, that I might better represent you upon the establishment of the new regime. I do not expect anything extravagant, but in laying the foundation, that I certainly am, for the protection of your interests, I think it is only fair that you should respond with promptness when I need funds, especially so when I am asking only what I require for expenses. I have made such extraordinary sacrifices during the past twelve months, that I feel the necessity for protecting myself in some degree. I had a draft to meet on the 28th instant, but managed to hold it over until tomorrow awaiting your advices. If you have not already sent me a check, I trust that you will give the matter your immediate consideration.

Faithfully yours,

Henry Clay Pierce, Esq.,
New York City.

REPRODUCED FROM S. G. HOPKINS' COPY OF HIS LETTER TO HENRY CLAY PIERCE EXPLAINING HIS RELATIONS WITH THE CONSTITUTIONALISTS

---

P. J. "Jan 14

I have the honor to report to you that I went to New York on the 5th instant to meet Mr. Luis Cabrera and Mr. Roberto V. Pesqueira, for the purpose of having a conference with Mr. Henry Clay Pierce, who as you know was formerly the owner of the Mexican Central Railway and who sold it to the government, in order that the merger might be effected, receiving in exchange bonds and stocks of the National Lines. Mr. Pierce from the time of the merger down to last October was chairman of the Board of Directors of the National Lines in New York. At that time (1908) the government was very desirous of obtaining the benefit of his valuable services and good counsel, because of his long experience in financing railroad organizations and in negotiation with bankers both in Europe and in the United States. As you are aware, however, Mr. Pierce was always considered an enemy by the cientificos as well as by the Porfiristas, the great majority of whom were anxious to enrich themselves at the expense of the National Lines. Had it not been for the confidence which the bankers had in Mr. Pierce's judgment, [illegible] would have robbed the lines in the most outrageous manner.

When I went to Mexico a few days after the arrival of Mr. Madero at the capital, in June, 1911, I spoke to him about changing the board of Directors, and he agreed with me that the cientificos ought to be immediately eliminated, and although he tried to have the personnel of the Board changed, Don Ernesto always found some excuse for not complying with his suggestions. The result was that while Don

- 2 -

Ernesto was forced to make some new appointments on the Board, he not only retained men like Luis Elguero as chairman of the Board but E. N. Brown as President, these two men being, in my opinion, the worst enemies the new government had. Both of these were owners of shares of the Aguila Oil Company and received their orders from Lord Cowdray. At that time Mr. Pierce offered to employ me as a lawyer to make all the trouble I possibly could for these cientificos, and I accepted his offer, exposing their acts to the public, attacking them in every way possible.

This was the beginning of my well known antagonism to the house of Pearson. For this service Mr. Pierce, as I remember, paid me the sum of $2,000 gold. I merely mention this so that you may know how I came to be associated with Mr. Pierce in the campaign against this particular group of malefactors. I gave these details to Mr. Cabrera and informed him that I believed Mr. Pierce would not only give him any information which he might desire about the National Lines, but being vitally interested in them he would give him the best possible advice in respect to the organization and operation of the lines in the northern states as a separate system, apart and distinct from the lines in the possession of the Huerta government.

I thereupon acquainted Mr. Pierce with the purport of the mission of Mr. Cabrera, and he authorized me to bring them to him.

REPRODUCED from MR. HOPKINS' FIRST DRAFT of a LETTER to GENERAL CARRANZA—The "P.J." STANDS for "PREMER JEFE"—FIRST CHIEF

---

Dear Capt—
Best I can do tonight
Hurry [illegible]
HCP
5/2—

H. C. PIERCE TO S. G. HOPKINS

---

## "BIG BUSINESS" OFFERED HUERTA $10,000,000 TO RESIGN, SAYS MEXICAN

### Publication of Letters Revealing Activities of "Constitutionalist Junta" Causes Sensation in Washington.

## SENATE SUBCOMMITTEE LIKELY TO START INQUIRY

### Peace in Mexico Is Believed Impossible Until Foreign Financiers Are Eliminated From Situation.

(Another instalment of the Hopkins-Pierce-Carranza correspondence will be found on page 4.)

Washington, June 29.—"Big business" is to be placed once more on the grill by the United States senate for the purpose of establishing exactly the part it has played in initiating and supporting revolutions in Mexico. This determination has come as the result of the publication of the sensational correspondence between New York financiers and their Washington agents and General Carranza and other constitutionalists. It is also alleged that two months ago financial interests in Wall street offered General Huerta $10,000,000 to resign.

Under the circumstances senate leaders feel there is but one thing to do. That is to set at work anew the subcommittee of the senate foreign relations committee of which Senator William Alden Smith is chairman, and to give it full powers to investigate to the very bottom of one of the greatest international scandals of the age.

Nothing that has occurred recently has aroused such intense interest as the publication of the private correspondence between the Washington junta of the constitutionalists, the moving figure in which is Sherburne G. Hopkins, a Washington attorney; Henry Clay Pierce, the oil man; Charles R. Flint, who has large financial relations with South and Central America; General Carranza, the "supreme chief" of the revolution, and other constitutionalists.

**Oil Interests in Control.**

President Wilson and Secretary Bryan have refused to discuss the revelations, which clearly show that the Standard Oil interests are backing Huerta and are in control of the situation so far as the Mexican railroads and oil interests are concerned, while, on the other hand, the Pierce-Flint interests are supporting Carranza.

In the opinion of everyone here, until the differences between these great interests are composed, the war in Mexico will continue. Peace is impossible until "big business" has been eliminated from the situation.

Mediation at Niagara Falls was doomed to failure, so far as the internal situation of Mexico is concerned. The Waters-Pierce interests could not afford to permit Carranza to participate in the negotiations and to enter in agreement with Huerta as the effect of such an agreement would be to retain the Cowdray or Standard Oil interests in control of the railroads.

**Bombshell to Constitutionalists.**

The expose has acted as a bombshell in the headquarters of the constitutionalists here. The whole matter is expected to be aired in the United States senate. The senators who are not at all surprised at the latest and senatorial developments are Senators Smith, McCumber of North Dakota, Borah of Idaho, Shively of Indiana, Hitchcock of Nebraska and Fall of New Mexico. These men investigated the question "whether any persons, associations or corporations domiciled in or owing allegiance to the United States, have heretofore been, or are now engaged in fomenting, inciting, encouraging or financing rebellion, insurrection or other flagrant disorders in Mexico."

The committee was forced to cease its investigation because of insidious influences which were applied. Senator Smith asked for more money to pay expenses. His request was never granted. Consequently, the inquiry had to be suspended.

**Smith Expressed Opinion.**

It has developed also that when the president, months ago, discussed the Mexican situation with Senator Smith, the latter told him of the underlying causes of the revolutions. The senator also had advised Secretary Bryan of the sensational facts in his possession.

Neither the president nor Secretary Bryan appeared to be interested. The president, however asked Mr. Smith what remedy he would apply.

"Mr. President," responded the Michigan senator, "I would establish a neutral zone along the border states of Mexico in which all foreigners would be safe and which would end incursions by armed men into American territory. But before doing that, I would kick out of the District of Columbia Captain Sherburne G. Hopkins and the constitutionalist junta."

At the time Mr. Smith gave this advice, the president and Mr. Bryan were in friendly relations with the constitutionalist organization here. They have continued such relations. In order to maintain them, the junta employed Charles A. Douglas, an old-time friend of Mr. Bryan. Mr. Douglas still is in this employment and has held frequent conferences with the secretary of state.

**Conclusions Are Supported.**

"The correspondence published is of the highest importance," said Senator Smith today. "It supports the conclusions I arrived at as a result of the investigation we conducted last summer. There is not the slightest doubt that the revolutions in Mexico have been the consequence of a war between rival interests seeking control of the railroads and vast resources of Mexico. The interests behind the constitutionalists are working hand-in-hand with the interests endeavoring to gain control of the transportation in the Central American states. They plan to dominate the rail routes from the Rio Grande to the Panama canal. I am informed that Captain Hopkins when in Mexico, made frequent trips to Guatemala City. President Cabrera of that country is ambitious to be the chief executive of the confederation of Guatemala, Honduras, Nicaragua, Salvador and Costa Rica. He has $20,000,000 deposited, so it is said, in European

## PLAY OF INTERESTS, INTIMATES LIND

### President's Special Envoy Refuses, However, to Discuss Hopkins Letters.

"I do not care to discuss the purported correspondence made public in New York," said John Lind at his office in Minneapolis today. Mr. Lind's name and views attributed to him figure in one of the Hopkins letters. "I have never seen the letters," Mr. Lind continued, "and I have no reason to assume that they are authentic. Persons who will steal letters generally will have no scruples about forging them."

It is Mr. Lind's belief, apparently, that publication of the letters is a sort of last desperate play by the Huerta interests, in an effort to influence public sentiment.

**Refers to Dodson Interview.**

"The St. Paul gentlemen who have been interviewed," said Mr. Lind, "apparently understand the situation in Mexico. That is all I care to say at this time."

Mr. Lind referred especially to the statement of Frank Dodson, a St. Paul capitalist who has large land holdings in Mexico.

**Dodson Gives His Views.**

"There is certainly something to the reports," said Mr. Dodson, commenting on the Hopkins letter disclosures. "Americans in Mexico have known that the Pearson people were backing Huerta in order to get possession of valuable concessions. Lord Cowdray had everything he wanted under Porfirio Diaz. Cowdray's people were enabled to grab whatever concessions they wanted. Madero dragged the skeleton out of the closet when he set up his revolution against the Diaz regime.

**Says Americans Were Protected.**

"If Huerta had been recognized by this country there would have been no chance for the Americans who invested their money in Mexico to save their property. They would have been frozen out by the Pearson interests.

"The oil interests certainly have furthered the revolt. The Americans feel that our people's interests in Mexico must be protected."

A similar statement was made by J. W. Lemon, 1184 Laurel avenue, St. Paul, a bridge engineer, who has spent some time in Mexico.

---

## FOUR "CLUBS" CLOSED, C. D. BRENCK'S CAFE AND OTHERS GIVEN 11 P.M. LID

### Mayor's Order Through Police Forbids Women Admission to Two Places Under Any Circumstances at Any Time.

### Other Places Being Watched, Says Police Chief, Who Declares Four "Clubs" to Close July 15 Mere Devices for Evading Liquor Laws.

Oscar Martinson, chief of police, today gave orders to four cafes that hereafter their doors must be locked and the places vacated on the stroke of 11 p.m., and that in two of them women must not be permitted to enter. Mayor Wallace G. Nye, acting through his police head, at the same time, ordered four "clubs" in the downtown district to close by July 15.

The chief today informed the owners of the Pit cafe, 428 Fourth street S., that it must close at 11 p.m., lifting at the same time the special order that has forced the place to close at 9 p.m. daily for the last week, pending an examination into the character of the business and the persons frequenting the place.

**No Women Admitted.**

Charles D. Brenck, 328 Third street S, and H. B. Trask, 250 Nicollet avenue, were officially informed that their doors must be closed at 11 p.m. and that no women were to be permitted in the future to enter either place. An order requiring a prompt 11 p.m. closing was given to the Court cafe, 310 Fourth street S.

**Four Orders to Close.**

The Army and Navy club in Sixth street S, with a membership of more than 1,000, was ordered closed by the police chief, and similar orders given to the Chauffeurs' club, 14 Fifth street S, the Minneapolis Press Assistants' club, 329 Hennepin avenue, and the Ice Drivers' club at the same address.

**Follows Frequent Complaints.**

For some time past many complaints have been made to the authorities that a large number of the "clubs" in the downtown districts were "blind pigs," pure and simple, and operated only to evade the excise laws.

**Liquor Law Evasion Charged.**

"I am convinced that these clubs just ordered closed," said the chief today, "were organized and run for the purpose of evading the liquor statutes and regulations, and not in any sense social or fraternal organizations, and that they have been run solely for the gain of the one or two men behind them.

**Other Places Watched.**

"And I might say," concluded Mr. Martinson, "that other clubs and cafes are being closely watched."

Mayor Wallace G. Nye declined to discuss the rumor that a dozen or more so-called clubs were to be ordered closed. He referred questioners to Chief Martinson.

**Closed Clubs Submit.**

The managers of the "clubs" ordered to close said today they will make no effort to insist that the police either permit them to operate or close other clubs of the city.

"The mayor has ordered us to close," said Edward Kennedy, manager of the Chauffeurs' club, "and we will abide by the order. The chief has given us until July 15 to get rid of our stock so as to work no unnecessary hardship upon us, and we respect his consideration."

**To Obey Order.**

At the Army and Navy club, Wilford H. Fawcett, the organization's president, was said to be out of town, but those in charge said they had heard of the closing order, and understood that the place would be closed on July 15. The man in charge of the Press Assistants' club and the Ice Wagon Drivers' club, said that they expected to obey the order of the police chief without question.

**Where Money Goes Is Test.**

As the club owners throughout the city understand the chief's position, it is that any club where liquors are dispensed under a government license, and where the receipts of the bar do not go to the general benefit of the club for fraternal or social purposes, but to one or more men as individuals, the spirit and letter of the law are both violated, and the doors of the institutions must close.

## $65,000 SALE AT TWELFTH STREET

The W. L. Harris Realty company today closed a deal with the Nicollet Associates, of which company H. C. Earle is president, for the property at the southeast corner of Marquette avenue and Twelfth street, for $65,000. The corner is unimproved. It has a frontage of 165 feet on Marquette avenue and is 110 feet deep on Twelfth street. W. L. Harris, president of the purchasing company, said that within a reasonable time the property will be improved in line with the general policy by the company for the upbuilding of Marquette avenue.

## TAKEN AT SIOUX CITY IN BANDIT CHASE

### Minneapolis Man, Sought Since Erickson Murder, to Be Brought Back.

Joe Anderson, known also as Eddie Solan and John Wolf, for whom the police have searched since the holdup and murder of John E. Erickson more than a week ago in his store, 1721 East Franklin avenue, has been arrested in Sioux City, Iowa. A Minneapolis detective will go to Sioux City and attempt to bring him back. Anderson was sought as a suspect the day after the shooting, but his friends told the police that he was in Council Bluffs at the time and the matter was dropped. Later the police were told that Anderson was in Minneapolis on the night of the crime. He is said to answer the description of the bearded bandit, but the police today refused to say that they had any case against him. Captain John Galvin said Anderson was one of many suspects and was merely held for investigation.

James Sudmeier, held in the city jail on a charge of leading a holdup in the Milwaukee yards, where twenty men were robbed, was not identified by any of the robbery victims.

Fred Wanberg, 4633 Bloomington avenue, told a story of being attacked by three men and beaten with a hammer when he was found partly conscious near Diamond lake at Portland avenue and Fifty-eighth street. He said he believed the men were tramps and had robbed him. Physicians at the city hospital said today that he was not seriously injured.

**"COTTON FUTURES" BILL PASSES**

Washington, June 29.—By 84 to 21, the house today passed the Lever "cotton futures" bill, regulating speculation in cotton on exchanges.

## RIOTING FOLLOWS ASSASSIN'S CRIME; BOMBS ARE HURLED

### Archduke Francis Ferdinand and Wife of Austria Murdered in Bosnian Capital.

### Death of Heir to Throne Believed Plotted by Servians Who Hated Dual Monarchy.

Serajevo, Bosnia, June 29.—Martial law was proclaimed today, both in the city and the district of Serajevo, in consequence of the assassination yesterday of Archduke Francis Ferdinand heir to the Austrian throne, and his wife, the Duchess of Hohenberg, by a Servian student, Gavrio Princip.

**Bomb Starts Anti-Serb Outbreak.**

A bomb thrown by a youth standing on the corner of the main street of the Bosnian capital, was the signal early today for an anti-Servian outbreak, which the troops found great difficulty in quelling. Later in the day serious rioting by furious mobs occurred on the streets here.

**Servian Dwellings Demolished.**

Scores of Servian business places and dwellings were demolished by pro-Austrian mobs, while preparations were being made to remove the bodies of the assassinated Archduke Franz Ferinand and his consort to Vienna tonight. Police and soldiers charged the rioters ineffectually in several quarters of the city. It is reported that several Servians were killed.

**Slaughter of Serbs Feared.**

Late today the fury of the mobs was increasing and it was believed when the bodies of the Servian assassin's victims are removed from the army hospital there is grave danger of a slaughter of the Serbs by the infuriated Austrians.

**Story of the Tragedy.**

According to the semi-official report of the tragedy, when Gaviro Princip, the young assassin, fired the fatal shots, Field Marshal Oskar Potiorek, governor of Bosnia, was seated in the archduke's motor car. Count Francis von Harrach was standing on the footboard of the car acting as a shield to the occupants, of whom he constituted himself the special bodyguard after the bomb had been thrown a short time before Nedejo Gabrinovics.

**Shots Ring Out.**

The archduke was joking with the count about his precautions, when the reports of several shots rang out.

The aim of the assassin was so true

Continued on 11th Page, 1st Column.

## $2,887.73 RAISED IN 72 HOURS TO GIVE CHILDREN OUTINGS

### Fresh Air Association Gets Hearty Response From Appeal, but Needs More Money.

### Hopes to Send Many Mothers With Babies From City Toil to Rockford Camp.

In seventy-two hours after the Minneapolis Fresh Air Fund and Outing association made its appeal Thursday for financial assistance, $2,887.73 was sent to Treasurer E. W. Decker.

Forty children are now at the association's farm at Rockford, Minn., and it can take care of forty every ten days. How many children who have no opportunity to get an outing the association will be able to take out during the season and how many working women will be able to go, will depend upon how much money is received.

**More Money Is Needed.**

The association needs much more money. Any sum may be sent in and it will be gratefully received.

E. W. Decker, president Northwestern National bank, is the treasurer.

**Wants All to Give Something.**

President F. H. Carpenter asks that all Minneapolis people contribute. Small contributions are acceptable. A dollar sent in will go a long way towards taking a boy or girl out of the shut-in neighborhood into the country.

Following is a supplementary list of contributors: W. H. Bovey, Imperial Elevator Co.; Richard F. Bauman, James Crays, Lydia E. Cargill, A. A. Clothier, Miriam E. Carey (St. Paul), W. R. Calloway, Henry Doerr, J. N. Davis, Anna F. Drew, Williamina Donaldson, G. H. Feetham, Rowland Gilmore (Bemidji), Katharine M. Gibbs, W. D. Hale, P. O. Heide, J. Hartmann, E. P. Inglee, Kendon Manufacturing company, J. A. Latta, H. R. Lyon, Lyman Bros., Fred C. Lawrence, W. A. Lancaster, D. Mackerchar, McClintock-Loomis company, M. J. Murphy, Katharine Patten, Gertrude R. Pettit, Charles S. Pillsbury, F. M. Prince, Joseph Robitshek, B. A. Rose, Maurice L. Rothschild, Gustave Robitshek, C. G. Roosen, J. H. Sargent, Sterling Electric company, E. A. Schneider, The Shevlin company, C. A. Smith, T. W. Stevenson company, David Simon, Town Market Furniture company, Helene B. Tanner, W. M. Todd, The Wingate company, E. W. Wigley (Fairfax), A. D. Walker, Isaac Weil & Sons, Henry Weis-

Continued on 2d Page, 6th Column.

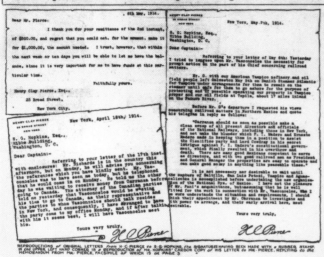

# The Minneapolis Morning Tribune

VOL. XLVII., NO. 228. MINNEAPOLIS, MINNESOTA, MONDAY, AUGUST 3, 1914. PRICE ONE CENT In Twin Cities and Suburbs. Two Cents Elsewhere.


# 100,000 GERMANS ADVANCING ON FRANCE; FOUR GREAT POWERS ENGAGED IN WARFARE

## Germans Invade France, Moving Towards Paris

Movement Is Made Without Formality of Declaration of War.

Unconfirmed Report Says a Detachment of Kaiser's Army Is Repulsed.

Neutral Territory of Luxemburg Is Also Entered By Germans.

Believed Emperor Hopes to Vanquish France Before Russia Is Ready.

Wilhelm Refuses to Answer England as to Respecting Neutrality of Belgium.

*By Associated Press.*

London, August 3.—German forces yesterlay began the invasion of France without, so far as is known, a declaration of war having been made. Two German detachments entered French territory moving in the direction of Paris.

**German Army in France.**

One German force crossed the French frontier near the village of Cirey, betwe.n Nancy and Strassburg, and another German detachment, probably the Twenty-ninth infantry, Saturday night, invaded the Grand Duchy of Luxemburg, neutral territory between Belgium and Germany, and continued its march on the French fortified town of Longwy. A dispatch from Brussels said there was good reason to believe that this force, later in the day, entered France.

**Duplicating Franco-Prussian War.**

The German force which came into Fran.e near Cirey, which is 40 miles from Nancy, is reported to have been repulsed with heavy losses, but this has not yet been confirmed.

Apparently the German army is duplicating the first movement of the Franco-Prussian war. It was on Aug. 2, 1870, that the French and Germans clashed in the first battle of that war at Saarbrucken where the Prince Imperial, under the orders of the emperor, received his famous "Baptism of fire."

It appeared yesterday that Germany is taking the fullest possible advantage of her supposed superiority in rapid mobilization over France.

The plan of the German emperor, according to military observers here, is to vanquish or attempt to vanquish France in the interval before Russia will be able to create serious trouble on her northern frontier. It is supposed that Russian mobilization will take abo.t three weeks.

All telegraphic and telephonic communication between Brussels and Luxemburg has been severed.

**Neutral Territory Invaded.**

By the treaty of London, signed in 1867, the Grand Duchy of Luxemburg was declared neutral territory. Its integrity and independence were guaranteed.

Longwy is a fortified town of France on the Belgium frontier, 40 miles northwest of Metz in Germany.

A train full of German soldiers arrived at the station at Luxemburg during the night. The troops seized the station and the bridges on the Treves and Trois Vierge [illegible]e in order to insure the regular [illegible]ssage of military trains across the Grand Duchy.

**Germans Claim Right.**

After these seizures the soldiers proceeded to the barracks. The major of the Luxemburg volunteers protested against the violation of neutrality, but in reply the Germans asserted that the railway belongs to them and that they have the right to do what they like in Luxemburg.

According to an evening newspaper published at Liege, 20,000 German troops crossed the French frontier this morning near Nancy. They encountered French forces and were repulsed with heavy losses. This news, however, lacks confirmation.

A telephone dispatch from Brussels yesterday said it was reported that Germany had declared war on France and that the French ambassador, Jules Cambon, had left the German capital. This report could not be confirmed.

**French Territory Invaded.**

The French embassy yesterday issued the following statement:

"French territory has been invaded at Cirey and German troops are marching on the fort at Cirey. This act has been committed without a declaration of war. The German ambassador is at present in Paris."

Germany declared today that she was unable to answer the question put by the British ambassador at Berlin as to whether she is prepared to respect the neutrality of Belgium.

This statement appeared in a communication issued by the French embassy

The neutrality of Belgium has been guaranteed by Great Britain and she is bound to protect Belgium for her own safety as Belgium under German rule would be a never ending menace to England.

AUSTRIAN CAVALRY REGIMENT IN MANEUVERS JUST BEFORE WAR AGAINST SERVIA WAS DECLARED

—Copyrighted, 1914, by the International News Service.

## Hopes of Averting Strike on 98 Railroads Brighter

President Confident of Ability to Bring Enginemen and Managers Together.

Latter Asked to Remember What a Calamity to Nation a Walkout Would Be.

Washington, Aug. 3.—Unofficial reports that the managers of the 98 western railroads involved in the threatened strike of 55,000 engineers and firemen will heed President Wilson's plea for peace were current last night among men in close touch with the situation. The president is understood to be confident that a strike will be unnecessary.

**Managers On Carpet.**

The committee of managers to whom the president appealed Saturday is to tell Mr. Wilson this morning whether they will accept the settlement proposed by the federal board of mediation, which suggested the arbitration of wage differences.

The president last night called in Charles P. Neill, former commissioner of labor, and had him take a message to the railroad managers again urging on them the necessity for adopting the proposed plan of settlement.

**Warned Against Calamity.**

The railroad managers were asked to remember that a great calamity might come to the country if a strike is declared by the engineers and firemen, thus holding up the moveme.t of the crops of the West.

## What of Great Britain?

France Agitated Over Plans of Their Ally Across the Channel.

*By Associated Press.*

Paris, Aug. 3.—Most of the Paris news papers have reduced the size of their editions for the sake of economy, the eight-page sheets cutting down to four pages and the four-sheets to two. The Patrie yesterday afternoon printed one small leaflet giving the news of Germany crossing the French frontier.

On every side the questions most agitating the public are what Great Britain will do, where is the British fleet and will a British force be landed on the continent.

The male population is rapidly disappearing from Paris, except those above 45 years of age, and those under 20.

The underground railways probably will stop running today. The great public services—the telephones, telegraphs, railways and mails—are daily becoming less available for public uses.

### THE WEATHER

**Temperatures for the Last 24 Hours.**

| | | | |
|---|---|---|---|
| 2 a. m. | 68 | 4 p. m. | 81 |
| 3 a. m. | 67 | 5 p. m. | 80 |
| 4 a. m. | 66 | 6 p. m. | 78 |
| 5 a. m. | 66 | 7 p. m. | 77 |
| 6 a. m. | 67 | 8 p. m. | 76 |
| 7 a. m. | 69 | 9 p. m. | 75 |
| 8 a. m. | 71 | 10 p. m. | 73 |
| 9 a. m. | 73 | 11 p. m. | 73 |
| 10 a. m. | 78 | Midnight | 70 |
| 11 a. m. | 82 | 1 a. m. | 70 |
| Noon | 80 | Maximum | 83 |
| 1 p. m. | 82 | Minimum | 66 |
| 2 p. m. | 80 | Range | 17 |
| 3 p. m. | 82 | Mean | 74 |

**Humidity.**

Humidity at 7 p. m. was 61 per cent.

**The Wind.**

The wind yesterday attained a velocity of 10 miles; direction, northeast.

**Today's Almanac.**

The sun rose today at 4:32 a. m. and will set at 7:39 p. m. The moon set at 1:32 a. m.

**Washington Official Forecast.**

Minnesota, Upper Michigan and Wisconsin—Generally fair today and tomorrow.

Iowa, Montana, North and South Dakota—Generally fair today and tomorrow.

**General Observations.**

| Sta— | A | B | C | Sta— | A | B | C |
|---|---|---|---|---|---|---|---|
| Alpena | 66 | 74 | | Kan City | 86 | 99 | |
| Bismarck | 78 | 80 | .44 | L. Angeles | 78 | 84 | |
| Boston | 70 | 84 | .06 | [illegible] | 78 | 84 | |
| Buffalo | 68 | 75 | | Marquette | 60 | 64 | .10 |
| Calgary | 80 | 88 | | [illegible] | 82 | 84 | |
| Chicago | 82 | 86 | | Milwaukee | 70 | 80 | |
| Cincinnati | 88 | 90 | | Med Hat | 98 | 100 | |
| Cleveland | 72 | 78 | .04 | Minnedosa | 80 | 86 | |
| Denver | 68 | 80 | .24 | Montreal | 66 | 82 | .02 |
| Detroit | 74 | 80 | .10 | Moorhead | 78 | 80 | |
| D. Moines | 88 | 92 | | New York | 76 | 82 | |
| Duluth | 60 | [illegible] | | N. Orleans | 86 | 94 | |
| El Paso | 88 | 96 | | Omaha | 82 | 86 | .02 |
| Edmonton | 76 | 80 | | S. Antonio | 98 | 98 | |
| Escanaba | 62 | 70 | .12 | San Diego | 70 | 74 | |
| Galveston | 84 | 88 | | S. Francisco | 60 | 62 | |
| G. Rapids | 76 | 84 | | Ste. Marie | 64 | 72 | .11 |
| Green Bay | 70 | 78 | | Salt Lake | 90 | 92 | |
| Havre | 92 | 98 | | St. Louis | 88 | 92 | |
| Helena | 94 | 94 | | Washington | 80 | 88 | |
| Huron | 84 | 88 | .02 | Winnipeg | 78 | 84 | |
| Jacks'ville | 82 | 92 | | Portland | 78 | 84 | |

A—Temperature at 7 p. m. yesterday.
B—Highest temperature yesterday.
C—Precipitation.

## INTERNATIONAL WAR CRISIS OUTLINED IN PARAGRAPHS

One hundred thousand German troops cross the duchy of Luxemburg and are concentrating on the frontier of France. Twenty-five thousand Germans are engaged in constructing earthworks at the concentration point.

* * *

Four European powers, Austro-Hungary, Russia, Germany and France are now actually engaged in warfare. Germany and France appear to be trying to throw the onus of responsibility for a formal declaration of war on each other.

* * *

Great Britain's policy in the crisis will be announced by Premier Asquith today. In the meantime all England is undergoing the greatest suspense it has known in a century.

* * *

Russian forces invade German territory at several points. One patrol is repulsed at a bridge over the Farthe and another destroys the post office at Bilderweitschen.

* * *

Two squadrons of Cossacks are moving toward the frontier of East Prussia.

* * *

London populace remains calm in face of impending war. The decision of the British cabinet regarding the entering of the conflict will be announced today.

* * *

Montenegro mobilizes to assist Servia and is reported as bombarding Cattaro, in Dalmatia.

* * *

Austria is said to be leaving Servia alone for the moment in order to concentrate against Russia.

* * *

British government takes possession of cable service and restricts service.

* * *

Neutral nations concerned as to what will be considered controband articles.

* * *

Sleeping Dutch cities filled with marching troops.

* * *

1,575 miles of frontier to be defended constitutes nations' chief cause of worry.

* * *

French embassy in London protests Against the Germans' occupation of Luxemburg.

* * *

Teuton government held to have violated neutrality act regarding the Grand Duchy.

* * *

Germany declares move was only made to protect railway connected with home system.

* * *

Great Britain calls out naval reserves, indicating readiness to engage in struggle.

* * *

Reports of naval fighting in the North sea indicates that an engagement took place between German and French naval forces.

* * *

Members of French chamber of deputies enlist in the ranks.

* * *

All provincial towns and cities ring with tramp of marching thousands.

* * *

Care of citizens abroad occupies attention of administration.

* * *

French aviator is reported dropping bombs near Nuremburg, Bavaria.

* * *

Further desire of Italy to remain neutral conveyed to United States government.

* * *

President Wilson and Secretary Bryan have planned means for relief of American citizens in war stricken Europe.

* * *

German troops have invaded France and attempting to march toward Paris.

* * *

Germans have invaded Grand Duchy of Luxemburg, a neutral territory, lying between Belgium and Germany.

* * *

English government has assumed control of all wireless telegraphy.

* * *

German troops fire upon and bring down French flying machine near Wesel.

* * *

British and German fleets in Asiatic waters, concentrating at Hong Kong and Tsing Tau respectively.

* * *

Slave parade in streets of Kansas City cheered by Servian sympathizers.

* * *

Treasury officials have made plans to fortify American banks against the possibility of financial trouble, owing to the war in Europe.

* * *

French aviator rammed and destroyed German airship in mid-air, according to London newspaper.

* * *

Steamers loaded with Europe-bound tourists are recalled to New York by wireless.

* * *

Forty-four years ago to a day since French and German forces clashed in Franco-Prussian war.

* * *

Russian Socialists rally to unquestioning support of czar.

* * *

United States ambassador at Berlin is beseiged by Americans who wish to leave country.

* * *

The utmost harmony prevails in the French chamber of deputies and all measures for defense will be voted immediately. Universal indignation for the course Germany has pursued is expressed in every direction in Paris.

AUSTRIA'S DECLARATION OF WAR AGAINST SERVIA HAS NOT TAKEN LITTLE EMPIRE OF BALKANS UNAWARES

—Copyright 1914 b. Underwood & Underwood, N. Y.

Two scenes showing Servians mobilized for the defense of their country. Austria's declaration of war has not taken the Serbs unawares. The soldiers of the little Empire of the Balkans have practically slept on their arms during the past decade, and her men are trained to the minute. The upper photo shows the type of the privates in the Servian army while the lower photo shows the trained-to-the-minute type of officers in command.

## FRANCE AND GERMANY WOULD EACH DODGE RESPONSIBILITY FOR A DECLARATION OF WAR

### BULLETIN

London, Aug. 3.—Germany has sent an ultimatum to Belgium in which she offers an entente provided Belgium facilitates the movements of German troops.

## Germans Bring Down French Flying Machine

Troops Fire Upon Craft Near Wesel—Other Hostile Airships Seen.

Two Men Killed While Trying to Blow Up Railroad Tunnel at Kochem.

*By Associated Press.*

Berlin, Aug. 3.—German troops yesterday fired upon and brought to earth a French flying machine near Wesel.

Saturday night several other hostile air craft were seen in the Rhine provinces. One was observed flying from Keprich in the direction of Andernach, ten miles northwest of Coblenz. Otheds were sighted near Duere flying in the direction of Cologne.

Last night a hotel keeper in Kochem and his son tried to blow up the Prussian state railroad tunnel at Kochem. Their attempt failed and the men were shot and killed.

Wesel, where the aeroplane was destroyed, is about 140 miles from the northeastern frontier of France.

While a train was crossing a bridge at Thorn yesterday a passenger tried to throw a bomb from the window of a coach, probably with the hope of destroying the bridge. He was arrested.

## French Aviator Rams a German Ship in Midair

London Newspaper Tells of a Novel Battle at Outbreak of War.

Berlin Correspondent Says That 2,000,000 Men Are Called to Colors.

*By Associated Press.*

London, Aug. 3.—The Standard publishes a report that a French aviator, Roland Garros, met and engaged a German airship in mid-air, rammed and destroyed it. The Standard fails to give the source of its story.

The Standard's Berlin correspondent sends a message from Boxtel, the Netherlands, that 2,000,000 men have been called to the colors.

Many of the railway lines, says the correspondent, are reserved exclusively for the transport of troops who are being conveyed in open and closed trucks.

The men are in excellent spirits, all of them singing. The authorities have taken over the control of all of the necessaries of life, as well as petrol, all motor cars and most of the horses in the country.

The proclamation of martial law has entirely crushed the socialist opposition. All light houses have shut off their lights.

**At Same Time a State of Actual Warfare is Regarded as Existing Between Teutonic and Gallic Nations—France is Seen as Having Strongest Justification for Declaring War as German Troops Have Already Invaded Her Territory and the Germans are Declared to Have Violated the Treaty of Luxemburg in Sending an Army Across That Duchy.**

## POLICY OF GREAT BRITAIN WILL BE ANNOUNCED TODAY

**England Undergoes Greatest Suspense it has Known in Century—Further Measures for Defense are Taken—Parliament Expected to Pass Today Bill for Loan of $250,000,000 for Defensive Purposes—Suspension of Banking Act Appears Assured—Peace Movement Continues but Finds Little Popular Support.**

### BULLETIN

*By Associated Press.*

**London, Aug. 3.—The Daily Chronicle publishes a rumor that Emperor Francis Joseph of Austria has been assassinated. This has not been confirmed.**

*By Associated Press.*

**Berlin, Aug. 3.—Via Brussels, Aug. 3.—The small cruiser Augsburg has sent the following report to Berlin by wireless.**

**"Am bombarding the naval harbor at Libau and am engaged with the enemy's cruiser. The naval port of Libau is in flames."**

**Libau is one of the principal ports of Russia and is located on the Baltic sea, 100 miles or more north of the German coast. It is fortified and used as an arsenal by the navy.**

**The German protected cruiser Augsburg is of 4,280 tons displacement and her chief armament consists of 12 4.1-inch guns. Her crew aggregates about 400 men.**

*By Associated Press.*

**Paris, Aug. 3.—The Temps this morning prints a dispatch from Montmedy, which reports cannon firing in the direction of Longwy.**

*By Associated Press.*

**Arlon, Belgium, Aug. 3.—According to advices received here, 100,000 German troops are crossing the grand duchy of Luxemburg and concentrating on the French frontier near Liege.**

**Frontier engagements are reported in which the Germans are said to have lost.**

**More than 25,000 men are engaged in digging trenches in front of the German and French positions.**

**The strategical line from Malmedy in Rhenish Prussia to Liege is guarded by military on both the German and Belgian sides.**

*By Associated Press.*

London, Aug. 4.—Four great powers of Europe, Austria-Hungary, Russia, France and Germany, are now engaged in actual warfare, but two of them, Germany and France, not only have not declared war against each other, as far as is known here, but have not even severed diplomatic relations. This is despite the fact that Germany's ultimatum to France has either been ignored or rejected.

The explanation of this would appear to be that Germany and France are each seeking to throw upon the other the onus of beginning the war. In fact, while the nations of Europe are flying at each other's throats, they are vieing with each other in protesting their desire to maintain peace and they repudiate the responsibility for plunging the whole continent into bloodshed.

**Sympathy With France.**

In this curious situation France, according to British opinion, has the strongest justification. She certainly was the last to mobilize and seems to have taken the greatest precautions to avoid frontier collisions.

On the other hand, Germany, in addition to invading French territory without making a formal declaration of war, has violated the neutrality of Luxemburg and declines to give any undertaking to respect Belgian neutrality.

**Diplomacy Fails.**

The efforts of the British ambassador at Berlin to obtain such an undertaking have been waisted. It is difficult to see how Great Britain can avoid being drawn into the conflict to protect Belgian and Dutch neutrality and on this point Premier Asquith's official announcement in parliament today is awaited with intense anxiety, the British public being no longer under any illusions as to the gravity of the crisis, which transcends anything in their experience.

The least observant man in London yesterday could not fail to be impressed with the fact that something tremendous was happening. Short of actual formal mobilization, the British government is taking all necessary steps to meet a situation unprecedented in the nation's history.

**Ovation to Rulers.**

There was a scene of great enthusiasm outside Buckingham Palace last night. A crowd of 5,000 or 6,000 persons gathered before the palace, sang the national anthem and called for King George who, with Queen Mary, appeared on a balcony and bowed in response to cheers given for him and for France.

**Reports of Battles.**

News of the progress of hostilities is vague and conflicting owing to the severe censorship everywhere. Actual German invasions of France occurred at Nancy and Longwy while a battle is reported to have taken place at Nancy. From the Russo-German frontier come reports that Russians invaded Germany near Schwinden.

Servia, the original cause of the upheaval, seems to have almost been lost sight of. The Austrians, according to reports from Nish, have virtually ceased operations against Servia in order to meet the greater danger in Russia.

Montenegro has mobilized to assist Servia and is reported to be bombarding Cattaro, in Dalmatia.

Various rumors are current of naval movements, but none is reliable.

**London Sunday Solemn.**

Sunday was a day of the greatest suspense England has known in a century. For hours the cabinet was in council at Whitehall and the whole country believed it to be wrestling with the question of whether Great Britain should take up arms in support of her partners of the Triple Entente.

No statement was made officially concerning the cabinet's deliberations, except that the premier would make an announcement in the house of commons to[illegible] and the cabinet would hold another meeting in the morning.

The government took three measures for defense yesterday, none of them inconsistent with the policy of remaining outside the conflict, if that should be her policy. The naval reserves and naval marine pensioners were called out by proclamation; the territorials, who had just assembled at the training camps for annual practice, were ordered to their headquarters; the home secretary prohibited flights over the entire kingdom and territorial waters, except by military craft.

**Cable Service Restricted.**

Censors took charge of all the cable offices in the kingdom last night. All code messages were prohibited, even to Australia. Telephone communication with the continent was stopped entirely.

The king issued a proclamation declaring a moratorium for a month, and the suspension of the banking act today appears assured. Parliament prob-

Full Service of UNITED PRESS

# THE MINNEAPOLIS JOURNAL

Full Service of ASSOCIATED PRESS

12 PAGES—HOME EDITION | MINNEAPOLIS WEATHER—Partly cloudy tonight and Sunday; local showers; warmer. | SATURDAY EVENING, AUGUST 15, 1914. | PRICE ONE CENT IN MINNEAPOLIS.



# 300,000 GERMANS BEGIN ADVANCE ON ALLIED ARMIES

## DOUGLAS A. FISKE WRITES OF FLIGHT FROM WAR ZONE

**Glad He Was in Berlin When Trouble Started—Equally Glad to Get Away.**

**MRS. MAURICE ROTHSCHILD ORDERED OUT OF BERLIN**

**Writes of Harrowing Experience Getting Across Border and Escaping to England.**

Stories of hardships endured by Americans in trying to get out of the European war zone and of the excitement at the outbreak of hostilities were received in Minneapolis today by friends bottled up in Europe and waiting passage home. Douglas A. Fiske, president of the Civic and Commerce association writing from the Picadilly hotel in London to Mrs. Fiske, under date of Aug. 3, tells of the furore in Berlin when war was declared and of the strenuous fight he and S. S. Thorpe made to get into England. Mrs. Maurice L. Rothschild, wife of the president of the Palace Clothing company, writes from the Savoy hotel, London, along the same lines. She and her husband and daughter, Teresa, and Mr. and Mrs. David Simon have been touring Europe for several weeks.

**Glad He Was in Berlin.**

"I cabled you this morning I was safe in London," writes Mr. Fiske, "for I feared you might be worried about me on account of the extraordinary things that are taking place in Europe. I wrote you from Berlin that Murt (a brother-in-law, Dr. C. M. Torrance, dentist, at Frankfort-on-the-Main) had come up with me and Sam (S. S. Thorpe) for a few days' outing and visit. Well from the time of our arrival Berlin was in a state of wonderful excitement, but as these matters usually move slowly we felt glad we were there to witness the unusual scenes. The streets were thronged with people all night long, marching and singing their national songs, all done so beautifully and orderly. Then would come along a squad of soldiers and immediately in front of them, back of them and on both sides, the people would fall in and march with them. It was wonderfully inspiring and you couldn't help but admire these wonderful people.

**Begins to Look Serious.**

"It was 3 a.m. before we got in Friday night, or rather Saturday morning, and by that time things looked serious. The Imperator failed to sail and Germany had sent her ultimatum to France and Russia, so Murt decided to leave for home the next morning, Saturday, and left a call for 6:30. I felt no uneasiness and rather enjoyed excitement, so I slept until noon, but Russia had not replied as yet. We took an auto ride and then went to our room for more rest, but the city was in an uproar. We got up about 8 and found the kaiser had ordered mobilization and war had been declared. The Russian ambassador had left the city.

**Met Maurice Rothschild.**

"Then we ran into Maurice Rothschild, who told us we ought to get out of the city at once. We had no tickets and all places on the 10 o'clock had been sold. And also we had had no dinner and our trunks were unpacked. As I still did not favor going, Mr. Thorpe and I went to a hotel and talked it over, and as he was keen on going, we made quick work of packing, paying bills, getting taxis and getting to station. There a wonderful sight met our eyes of struggling humanity trying to get out of town. I really had very little hope of getting away that night. Trunks to be checked were piled mountain high. All of course could not be checked; there was not time. You should have seen your husband fighting for position and investing his marks with a lavish hand. Victory seemed in sight when a great big German diensman took me by the leg and began dragging me and my trunk down from the high counter where my two men had placed it, but a liberal tip to the man having a bright uniform on made my success sure. And my check was issued, but as to ever getting the trunk again that is a different matter.

**Packed Like Sardines.**

"The next great struggle was to get in the train at all. We didn't expect to sit down, so Mr. Thorpe and I decided on a different plan and succeeded in landing a seat, although some French people said we couldn't have it, but we got it just the same. We were congratulating ourselves when a lady gasping for breath came in, said she was ill, so we divided up the same seat with one more. She proved to be an American wife of the Persian minister to the United States. In less than fifteen minutes there were five Persians in our compartment, three children, the diplomat and his wife. They claimed to have a compartment reserved, but remained with us until 2 a.m. At 4 we changed cars and then we did have a merry time. The cars were so crowded we could not get in at either end, so we climbed in the window. About 6 we discovered a seat in a car in the rear and as we did not enjoy standing changed and took part of our baggage there. We left the coach a minute to get the balance of the baggage an hour later, and when we got back no car was there. It was a German one and could not go past the frontier. I finally found my coat, etc., and still had no place to either sit or stand. Again we climbed into the window of another car that had done duty as a diner and here the people were packed in like sardines, standing or sitting on their suitcases. Police of all kinds came continually through the train and it was with a sigh of relief that we passed the frontier into Holland and at 1:30 arrived at Flushing. We immediately went on to the channel boat which takes six or seven hours to cross.

**Boat Stopped by a Shot.**

"It was rumored that if we did not get landed by 8 we would have to stay

Continued on 2d Page, 3d Column.

## German Chancellor Appeals For Fair American Opinion

**Declares Comprehension of Situation Will Throw U. S. Sympathy to Fatherland.**

London, Aug. 15.—(3:05 a.m.)—A Marconi wireless dispatch from official sources at Berlin, dated Friday, gives an interview with the German imperial chancellor, Dr. von Bethmann-Hollweg, who representing the war as a life and death struggle between the Germans and Russians, arising from the assassination of Archduke Ferdinand and his wife, declared that England avails herself of a long awaited opportunity to begin a war for the destruction of commercially prosperous Germany.

"It is with heavy hearts," said the chancellor, "that we see England ranged among our opponents, notwithstanding the close ties of blood and culture between England and Germany. The former placed herself on the side of Russia, whose insatiability and barbaric insolence helped this war in order to humiliate and suppress the German race by Russian Pan-Slavism.

"We expect that the sense of justice of the American people will enable them to comprehend our situation. We invite their opinion as to the one-sided English representations and ask them to examine our point of view in an unprejudiced way.

"The sympathy of the American nation will then lie with German culture and civilization, which is fighting against a half-Asiatic and slightly cultured barbarism."

Chancellor von Bethmann-Hollweg, who asks unprejudiced consideration of Germany's stand.

## OFFER MADE FOR FLEET OF LINERS

**Hamburg-American May Sell Steamships to Sail Under American Flag.**

New York, Aug. 15.—The Hamburg-American line issued a statement today saying it had under consideration offers to purchase some of its steamships in American waters, valued at $20,000,000. The fleet embraces the Vaterland, largest in the world. If sold the vessels would fly the American flag and would be the first big acquisition to the proposed American merchant marine.

The statement of the company says it has always been its policy to dispose of steamers whenever a good opportunity offers, provided they can be spared, and adds that as the war has forced the fleet into temporary idleness and the line now has in American waters steamers worth more than $20,000,000, bona fide offers for the purchase of some of them are being considered. It is not stated what ships the offers cover.

No mention is made as to the identity of the possible purchasers.

## DENIES ADVICE TO HOLD CROPS

Washington, Aug. 15.—Secretary Houston today requested publication of an announcement that department of agriculture had sent no communication or advice whatever to farmers throughout the country counselling them to hold their crops.

## TEACHERS HELD IN SWITZERLAND

Washington, Aug. 15.—The state department was asked today, in a cable from the American minister at Berne, Switzerland, to inform all schools and colleges in the United States that teachers traveling must remain in Switzerland until their transportation back to the United States has been arranged. The minister advises all school boards in this country to take notice of the situation there.

## 5 WOUNDED BY AVIATOR'S BOMBS

Brussels, Aug. 15.—Three bombs were dropped on Namur by a German aviator during the night. Five persons were wounded, three perhaps fatally.

## SUIT FILED TO TEST OIL INSPECTION LAW

**State Brings Action Against Van Tilburg Company Following Refusal to Pay Fees.**

A suit to determine whether the state can collect fees for oil inspection and whether the law on which the position of the state oil inspector was established is valid was begun today in the Hennepin county district court by the state. The suit was filed by Attorney General Lyndon A. Smith against the Van Tilburg Oil company.

The company has declared that oil companies cannot legally be compelled to pay fees and has claimed that the inspection in reality means nothing to the state. The company has refused to pay for the inspection.

The suit alleges that the company has not paid the fees due from June, 1913, to and including February, 1914.

The fees at that time amounted to $1,389, according to the complaint. All points of the statute will be contested as a test. It is the first action ever brought to test the validity of the law.

## WILSON DISAPPROVES OF FLOATING LOANS

**Opposes Plan for American Bankers to Aid Belligerent Countries.**

Washington, Aug. 15.—President Wilson today formally disapproved of the plan for American bankers to float loans in the United States for the benefit of belligerent countries of Europe, but expressed no objections to loans made to neutral countries.

## BEER GAS KILLS MAN IN BIG VAT

Max Lore, 32 years, was overcome by beer gas in one of the curing vats at the Gluck brewery, early today, after he had gone into the vat to clean it, and died before he could call for help. Other workmen, who missed him, found the body later and notified the coroner. Carbon dioxide gas, with which beer is charged, being heavier than air, settles in the empty vats, and it is customary to open traps at the bottom to let the gas out. This had not been done, and the gas was still in the vat when Lore went there today, fellow workers said. Lore lived in Columbia Heights and leaves a wife and two children.

## Today's War Analysis

By J. W. T. MASON.

**GERMANY'S reconnaissances have now explored Belgian territory thirty miles into the interior from Liege, more than half way to Brussels. The curtain behind which the kaiser's skirmishers in force have penetrated forms almost a perpendicular from north to south through Herenthals, Aerschot, Tirlemont and Namur. The first three towns are important railway centers and Namur, guarding the allies' right, is probably by this time better fortified than Liege.**

**Brussels is twenty miles to the rear and about in the center of this line. Somewhere between Brussels and the Herenthals-Aerschot-Tirlemont-Namur curtain, the allies have concentrated their main Belgian forces, while their outposts are trying to check the German efforts to discover the secret.**

**North and west of the Meuse and east of Herenthals-Namur line is now practically frontier territory, except for the Liege forts. It seems probable the great battle, when it begins, will not be in this district, unless some tactical error by the Germans causes the allies to leap forward on the offensive. Otherwise the field doubtless will be within twenty miles east of Brussels.**

**IT IS a principle of modern warfare that victories are won by offensive and not defensive movements. Nevertheless, the allies cannot afford to attempt to turn the tables on Germany and change their defensive attitude in Belgium into an offensive one. The higher strategy must take into consideration Russia's slow mobilization and the tremendous advantage of delaying Germany's western advance.**

**The risk of a victory, of course, is greater than the risk of a drawn battle. The latter, at this stage of the war, would be almost as disastrous to Germany as a defeat, because of the time given to the slow-moving Slavs to draw their lines about the German western frontier. Thus a defensive Belgian campaign for the moment is excellent strategy for the allies.**

**THE news from Diest that the standard of the Death's Head Hussars has been captured confirms the report that the Russian frontier has been denuded of the first line fighters. The headquarters of the Death's Head Hussars is Posen, one of the main centers of the defenses against Russia. The Death's Head Hussars is the kaiser's favorite regiment. It has been given traditionally the motto: "Never Take Prisoners."**

## PANAMA CANAL IS OPENED TO SHIPS OF ALL NATIONS

**Steamship Ancon First Big Vessel to Be Put Through Waterway.**

**OFFICIALS AND INVITED GUESTS CROWD THE BOAT**

**Workers, Given Holiday, Line Banks at Various Points Along Trip.**

Panama, Aug. 15.—The United States war department steamship, Ancon, today made the passage through the Panama canal, and transit through the waterway is now officially open to the traffic of the world.

The Ancon left her berth at Cristobal at 7 a.m. today and made her way to the end of the deep water channel from the Atlantic to the Gatun locks. She went through these locks, which have a lift of eight-five feet, in seventy minutes. She continued through the waterway, from deep water on the Atlantic to deep water on the Pacific side without incident. She is due at the Pacific side at 6 p.m.

The decks of the Ancon were crowded with guests of the government and officials of the canal administration and the republic of Panama. The party included Colonel Goethals, builder of the canal, and governor of the zone; President Porras of Panama, and Captain Hugh Rodman, U. S. N., superintendent of transportation.

In conformity with a proposal made by Colonel Goethals, the peace flag of the American Peace society fluttered from the foremast of the Ancon. Beneath her decks, however, were two huge pieces of artillery which are destined to form an imporant part of the defense of the waterway.

**Boat Glistens With New Paint.**

All the seventy-four regular officers and men aboard the Ancon appeared in spotless white uniforms and the ship itself glistened with new paint over which fluttered signal flags and ensigns.

Invitations to be guests on this first trip had been much coveted and the rails were lined with local canal officials and those of the Panama republic, together with their ladies, as the big steamer backed away from her berth.

**Play "Star-Spangled Banner."**

The Panama national band and the regimental band of the Tenth United States infantry played "The Star-Spangled Banner," and the steamer pulled away, but the music was almost drowned by the whistles of the steamers in the harbor.

To assure unimpeded passage for the Ancon, all of the traffic, including the working boats in Culebra cut, was brought to a standstill from early this morning on.

Several thousand canal workers enjoyed a holiday and they, together with villagers of all types from the surrounding territory, lined the banks at various vantage points.

The Ancon was fully loaded with the regular cargo that she had brought from New York, the freight having been purposely left on board to give the canal a full test with the ship drawing its full depth of water. The Ancon has a complement of seventy-four officers and men and is commanded by Captain G. E. Sukeforth.

**Open to Boats of All Nations.**

With the passage of the Ancon through the canal today the great waterway becomes "free and open to the vessels of commerce and of war of all nations on terms of entire equality," in accordance to the provisions of the Hay-Pauncefote treaty.

Vessels drawing not more than thirty feet of water may now take the passage. It would be possible to put some of the big American dreadnoughts through at any time.

No embarrassment will face the United States should one of the war vessels of the belligerents in the European war seek passage. Strict rules are laid down in the treaty for the perpetual neutralization of the canal, and every detail will be under the direction of Governor Goethals and his staff. Except in cases of absolute necessity, vessels of belligerents must make uninterrupted passage through the canal. They may not coal, revictual or embark or disembark troops in the canal zone, and these provisions also apply to the terminal waters at both ends of the canal within a limit of three miles.

**Can Remain Only 24 Hours.**

Twenty-four hours is the limit of time a belligerent vessel can remain within the canal except in cases of distress, and a vessel of war of one belligerent cannot depart within twenty-four hours from the departure of a vessel of war of another belligerent. All of the plant and establishments that are part of the canal are immune from attack or injury by any belligerents.

The principal work remaining to be done in completing the canal is the deepening and widening of the channel through Culebra cut as well as excavation operations at both approaches.

## WHEAT BELOW DOLLAR MARK

Dollar wheat as a Minneapolis proposition disappeared today. September sold under the dollar line yesterday and closed at 98¾ cents, but December remained above the line, closing yesterday at $1.00½. September opened today at 96¼ cents, was 97 cents at high time, 96@96¼ cents at low time, and closed at 96¾ cents. December opened at 99½ cents to $1, was $1 for high price, 97⅞ cents for low, and closed at 98⅛@98¾ cents.

## BRITISH CAPTURE AUSTRIAN LINER

Alexandria, Egypt, via London, Aug. 15.—12:50 p.m.—The big new Austrian-Lloyd liner Marienbad was captured today by a British warship near here while on the voyage from Bombay to Trieste. The vessel was brought into port.

## War Developments Today

**Reports of the continued advance of the Germans toward Brussels, the march extending through the heart of Belgium on a line extending relatively from Namur to Haelen, and of continued fighting at the Liege fortresses were the chief items of news of the warfare in Europe that winnowed through the sieve of the censor last night.**

**Of the movement of the armies of the Germans and the allies it was stated that it had progressed to a point where it seemed apparent that the first great battle of the war could not long be deferred. A dispatch from Brussels said the concentration of French troops in Belgium was complete and that all the troops that had been expected were in battle order.**

**A German report from in front of Liege said the fortress Pontisse had fallen into the hands of the Germans. Belgians denied this and declared the Germans had suffered heavy losses in the attack.**

**A special dispatch received in London said the Japanese purpose to carry out their treaty obligations with Great Britain and that the Japanese fleet had put to sea to co-operate with the British ships.**

**Greece, it was stated, probably would engage Turkey again should the report that the Ottoman government had purchased the German cruisers Goeben and Breslau prove true.**

**The German cruiser Karlsruhe, after coaling at San Juan, Porto Rico, following her fight with British cruisers, put into the Dutch island of Curacao last Wednesday.**

**The Petit Journal, of Paris, says it learns "on unimpeachable authority" that Japan is resolved to declare war on Germany.**

**A wireless dispatch from Berlin received in London says in an interview "Imperial Chancellor von Bethmann-Hollweg represented the war as a life and death struggle between the Germans and Russians."**

**Paris declares officially that the Saales Pase over the Vosges has been occupied by French troops.**

**Grand Duke Nicholas, of Russia, commander in chief of the army, calls on the Poles to be loyal to Russia and promises them autonomy.**

**The Exchange Telegraph company of London, says 40,000 Austrian troops made a concerted dash on Servia, but were repulsed with heavy casualties.**

**The Belgian general staff reports the position of its army as excellent.**

**Belgian dispatches report two companies of German infantry ambushed by Belgians. Fifty Germans are said to have been killed.**

**Field Marshal Sir John French, commander in chief of the English field army, arrived in Paris.**

**From Rome comes a report of an attempt to reconstruct the league of the Balkan nations with the object of assisting Russia and restraining Turkey.**

**General Otto von Emmich, German commander at Liege, is dead. He has been succeeded by General von der Marwitz.**

## Dispatch Confirms Death of Kaiser's Liege Commander

General Otto Von Emmich.

London, Aug. 15 (3:30 p.m.).—A dispatch from Brussels to the Exchange Telegraph company says the death of General Otto von Emmich, the German commander at Liege, is confirmed. He is to be succeeded by General von der Marwitz. Earlier reports said General von Emmich shot himself after the attack on the Liege forts failed.

General von Emmich was 66 years old. He joined the army as a volunteer in 1866 and was promoted two years later to a lieutenancy. He took part in the Franco-Prussian war in 1870-71. Afterward he was promoted through all the grades until he became major general in 1901. When he was appointed to the command of the tenth army corps he was made a general.

## HUNTINGTONS NOT UNDER ARREST

Washington, Aug. 15.—Archer M. Huntington and family were not arrested in Nuremburg, Germany, the state department was officially advised today by the American consul at Hamburg. The Huntington family, he said is enjoying the fullest liberty in that city.

## BULLETINS

**Washington, Aug. 15.—Germany will permit the cruiser Tennessee, bearing $5,867,000 in gold for Americans, to enter Bremen and will provide trains to take Americans to that port. This government was so advised today. The Tennessee is expected to land in Falmouth late tomorrow.**

**London, Aug. 15.—The sailors, firemen and stewards of the Atlantic Transport line steamer Minnewaska, when about to leave London today with 250 passengers for New York, went on strike and demanded "danger" money. The trouble was arranged and the boat sailed.**

**Meadville, Pa., Aug. 15.—The main plant of the Spirella Corset company, an American concern, at Dusseldorfs, Germany, has been seized by the German government and turned into a hospital, according to private advices received today by President W. W. Kincaid.**

**Berlin, via Rome, Aug. 15.—The German government today notified the governments of France and Belgium that, beginning today, all private citizens interfering in the slightest degree with the advance of the German army will be immediately shot. "If the war thus assumes a brutal character, it will not be the fault of the German nation," the note says.**

**London, Aug. 15.—The Brussels correspondent of the Daily Telegraph wires that among the captured trophies taken by the Belgians in the fighting is the standard of the famous Death's Head Hussars, the kaiser's favorite regiment.**

**London, Aug. 15.—The official press bureau announces: "There are indications that the Germans are moving forward in force in an attempt to turn the allies' extreme left. The artillery of the latter is proving much superior to that of the Germans, while the German infantry has found it impossible to break through the line of the allies. Several bayonet charges have failed."**

**New York, Aug. 15.—The French government has purchased 400,000 bushels of Canadian oats, 300,000 bushels of which are to be shipped from Boston and New York.**

**Washington, Aug. 15.—Legal experts of both the departments of state and justice today were asked by President Wilson to prepare an opinion regarding the authority of the government to censor both wireless and cables.**



## KAISER ORDERS CHIEFTANS TO TAKE BRUSSELS

**Belgians Claim Cavalry Has Momentarily Checked Invaders' March.**

**ALLIES UNITED AND EXCHANGE OFFICERS**

**French Assert They Have Fought Way to Control of Vosges Mountains.**

**WIRELESS ANNOUNCES VICTORY BY GERMANS**

**New York, Aug. 15.—A dispatch from German official sources in Berlin was received here today via Sayville, L. I., wireless as follows:**

**"The seventh French army corps and an army division from Belfont which had invaded upper Alsace were defeated yesterday by German troops near Mulhausen."**

**The dispatch, somewhat mutilated by poor transmission, indicated that French entrenchments were taken at the point of the bayonet.**

Brussels, Aug. 15.—The German advance is checked, at least momentarily. After feeling out the Belgian lines at various points from Diest and Malines, along the Meuse river to Belgian Luxemburg, the German forward movement gave way before wild assaults by Belgian cavalry, which cleared the ground of the Prussian Uhlans. The German infantry remains in its trenches, however, and the heavy masses of reinforcements are being moved forward, slowly and steadily. The German artillery is in position and the long range duel, commenced at daybreak, continues.

**After Allies' Left Wing.**

The German infantry in very heavy force is moving forward in an effort to envelop the extreme left wing of the allied army to the south by east of Antwerp. Officials here believe the German objective is to penetrate the line of the allies and to drive the extreme left back on Antwerp. Up to the present the artillery fire of the allied army has proven very effective.

**War Office Moves Ominous.**

How acute the situation really is is best shown by the shutting down by the war office of news from the front. None is permitted to come through. This is interpreted as meaning that the German infantry is now in touch with the allied forces and that the next forward movement of the Germans must involve the entire armies. When it comes it must of necessity last for several days, as the Germans have 300,000 men of all branches on their front and a reserve admittedly enormous.

**Kaiser Demands Brussels.**

Captured German officers quietly but seriously admit that the German general staff has decreed the complete subjugation of Belgium, including the capture of Brussels at any cost. They also emphasized that the kaiser and his general staff are ready to sacrifice 100,000 men to break the allied line.

**Disconcerted by Opposition.**

The Belgians assert the stubborn defense of Liege has completely disconcerted the German attacking forces. It is claimed that in night attacks in the series of desperate charges against the forts on the left bank of the Meuse entire regiments were again wiped out by the rain of explosives from the forts and that the ground immediately in front of the chief forts was literally covered with dead and wounded. So terrible were the losses, it is said, that German officers and men, made insane by their futile attempt to carry the positions by storm, jumped into the Meuse and were drowned.

**Food Supplies Fail.**

That the German commissary department utterly failed in the test and that this is the chief reason why the general advance was delayed is stated by Belgian officials familiar with the situation. They declare that the officers were so anxious to get their commands to the front that they sacrificed equipment, and that the long trains laden with the food supplies were sidetracked and left behind.

**Men on Short Rations.**

An official Belgian statement dealing with this phase of the situation said that the rations for one entire regiment for a day consisted only of one sausage, a couple of spoonsful of dried peas and a small square of bread per man.

Advices to the war office say German deserters declare that among the wounded in the fighting in Lorraine is General Von Daimling, who is now in the hospital.

**Wounded Pouring In.**

Hundreds of additional wounded are arriving here. Every hospital and public hall is filled and many private houses are being requisitioned. The captured German wounded tell pathetic tales of the slaughter. They declare the Uhlans have lost enormously in nearly every fight.

**Machine Guns Mired.**

The German defeat at Haelen is attributed by the German officers to the failure of the machine guns to operate as had been planned. Those mounted on automobiles proved too heavy for the ground over which they were moved, becoming mired and utterly useless.

**Cavalry Harasses Invaders.**

The Belgian cavalry assumed the offensive today in the region between Tirlemont and Hasselt, attacking a German cavalry column which was reconnoitering toward the former city. In the fighting that followed the Germans

Crisis in the Far East Averted---Page 2
188 Americans Were on Lusitania---Page 2
Italian Press Says Nation Is on War Verge---Page 2
Press Comment on Sinking of Lusitania---Page 2
Transylvania Sails Despite Warning---Page 6
Mrs. Carman Testifies in Own Defense---Page 7
First Cabin Passengers on Lusitania---Page 4.
Barnes-Roosevelt Libel Suit---Page 7
Auto Injures Minneapolitan; Driver Flees, Caught---Page 21

The Minneapolis Morning Tribune

VOL. XLVIII., NO. 142. MINNEAPOLIS, MINNESOTA, SATURDAY, MAY 8, 1915. WEATHER—Minnesota, generally fair today and tomorrow, except showers today Northwest. PRICE ONE CENT In Minneapolis

# HUNDREDS ABOARD LUSITANIA ARE BELIEVED LOST; BIG LINER IS TORPEDOED AND SUNK OFF IRISH COAST

## VESSEL, NOT WARNED, STRUCK TWICE; GOES DOWN IN 15 MINUTES

**Cunarder Which Sailed From New York Last Saturday With More Than 2000 Souls Was on Last Leg of Journey off Old Head Kinsale When Attacked—Passengers at Luncheon.**

## AGENTS OF DESTRUCTION TEAR INTO BOW AND ENGINES

**Life Boats Were Already Swung Out and Provisioned But Time Believed too Brief to Have Rescued Many—Numerous Boats Answer Distress Signal.**

(By Associated Press.)

London, May 8—The Cunard liner Lusitania, which sailed out of New York last Saturday with more than 2,000 souls aboard, lies at the bottom of the ocean off the Irish coast. She was sunk by a German submarine which sent two torpedoes crashing into her side, while the passengers were having luncheon.

How many of the Lusitania's passengers and crew were rescued cannot be told at present, but the official statements from the British Admiralty up to midnight accounted for not more than 400 or 600.

A ship's steward, who landed with others at Queenstown, gave it as his opinion that 900 persons were lost.

**Dead and Wounded Among Landed.**

There were dead and wounded among those brought ashore; some since have died. But not a name of rescued or lost, of dead or injured has yet been listed.

The Lusitania was steaming along about ten miles off Old Head Kinsale, on the last leg of her voyage to Liverpool when about 2 o'clock in the afternoon a submarine suddenly appeared and, so far as all reports go, fired two torpedoes without warning at the steamer. One struck her near the bows, and the other in the engine room. The powerful agents of destruction tore through the vessel's side, causing terrific explosions. Almost immediately volumes of water poured through the openings and the ship listed.

**Passengers Appalled by Attack.**

Boats which were already swung out on the davits, were dropped overboard and were speedily filled with passengers who had been appalled by the desperate attack. A wireless call for help was sent out, and immediately rescue boats of all kinds were sent out from the neighboring points along the coast and Queenstown. But within fifteen minutes, as one survivor estimated, and certainly within half an hour, the Lusitania had disappeared.

Where Great Britain's fastest merchant vessel went down—Old Head Kinsale—is a landmark that has brought joy to many travelers as it always stood as the sign from shore that the perils of the voyage across the Atlantic were at an end.

**Ship That Startled World Is Lost.**

The line, whose boast it has been that it has never lost a passenger in the Atlantic service has now lost the ship that dodged the lurking enemy off Nantucket Light the day after war was declared, and later startled the world by flying the Stars and Stripes.

The British Admiralty is discouraging the publication of surmises and guesses regarding the dead and injured. Even before the crude details are known the British press is asking editorially what the United States will say to this event and how she will hold Germany to the "strict accountability" mentioned in previous diplomatic correspondence.

## Views on Lusitania Sinking Varied Here

Dr. Cyrus Northrop Says "Not Against War Law, but Horrible."

Dr. W. W. Folwell, "Right to Sink Passengers Vessels Seems Doubtful."

C. B. Elliott, "Legal Only If Germany Can Make It So."

The sinking of the Lusitania was variously interpreted in Minneapolis. Dr. Cyrus Northrop, president of the Minnesota Peace society, while saying it was horrible, took a practical view of the incident. "The Lusitania," he said, "was a British ship. Germany is at war with the British. It had given warning that it would sink British merchant vessels and it has done so, and that's all there's to it. I don't know that this action is contrary to the laws of war, but it is horrible, as all war is horrible."

Dr. W. W. Folwell emphasized the point that the sinking of the Lusitania served no purpose toward bringing the war to a close and was, therefore, questionable.

**"Subject to Capture."**

"As a British vessel," he said, "the Lusitania was, I suppose, subject to capture. One must be careful in these times in expressing opinions on the legality of war moves. The right to sink freighters has been conceded, but with passenger vessels the case seems doubtful. The action is outrageous anyhow. It doesn't tend to bring the war to a close and it has been generally held that any war movement that does not tend to such end was questionable."

C. B. Elliott, former justice of the supreme court in the Philippines, began his statement by saying that no one questioned the right of the Germans to sink a British ship. "That is well established," he said, "but before this Lusitania development it had been held the duty of the enemy to take off the crew, and, except in extraordinary circumstances, to take the vessel into a prize court.

**Illegal Move at Present.**

"No one ever has claimed the right before to sink a merchant ship without caring for the passengers. The Germans say they can't do this because of the nature of the attacking ships—submarines—and they are trying to put the burden on passengers to stay at home. At present, this position is illegal. It will become legal only if the Germans can make other nations accept it. Thus far it has not been accepted."

Asked whether the advertisements placed by the Germans in New York newspapers warning prospective travelers to stay at home, would have any bearing on the legality of the sinking of the Lusitania, Judge Elliott said: "None whatever."

**DOCTORS AND NURSES ABOARD**

**112 American Red Cross Workers Were Going to Front.**

Lima, Ohio, May 8.—(Special.)—"I have 12 doctors and more than 100 nurses on board the Lusitania," said Dr. Joseph Hall of Cincinnati, official of the Red Cross Society and member of the Lima State Hospital commission, when he heard of the torpedoing of the big ocean liner here yesterday.

"We were sending them to Europe as relief workers for the Red Cross association," he continued, "and they were to take the places of others who are worn out with the work in the field. I suppose they might just as well die there as on the battlefield somewhere. It's a mighty hard blow, though, for I knew all of them well."

Doctor Hall was in Lima attending a meeting of the hospital commission and going over the big institution on a final inspection tour.

## PARTIAL LIST OF THE LUSITANIA SURVIVORS

(By Associated Press.)

Washington, May 8.—A dispatch to the State Department early today from American Consul Lauriat at Queenstown stated that the total number of survivors of the Lusitania was about 700.

Consul Lauriat's message said:

"Total saved of all nationalities, 700. The following are American survivors of Lusitania. Other names will follow:

"O. S. Grab, Major and Mrs. Pearl and two children; Mrs. Jessie Taft Smith, Charles C. Hardwick, Stuart D. Pearl, Ardray Pearl, Mrs. Stanley L. B. Lines, C. T. Hill, Robert Rankin, Miss Toney, Mrs. William Doherty and infant, Thomas Phillips, William McMadams, J. H. Houghton, John M. Sweeney, Oaden H. Hammond, J. H. Brooks, Charles T. Jeffery, Mrs. C. H. Lund, Arthur Shepperdson, Dr. D. V. Moore, Clinton Bernard, Herbert Light, J. Linnson, Jr., Edith Williams, James J. Leary, Thomas Slidell, Mrs. John Wolfenden, Mrs. Nina Holland, George Kissler, Mrs. Thomas Mesh, George A. Kessler, L. L. McMurray, Robert Kay, R. B. Lockhart, Owen Cannon, Duright C. Harris, Fred S. Judson, Ed M. Collis, R. C. Wright, F. J. Gauntlet, S. N. Knox, Patrick O'Donnell.

(By Associated Press.)

Queenstown, May 8.—Among the survivors here are: A. T. Mathews, Montreal; S. Abramowitz, Miss Catherine Kaye, G. B. Lane, W. G. E. Meyers, J. T. Trimmins, Mrs. A. F. Witherbee, Lady Mackworth, Mrs. Henry Adams, Boston; Samuel Sharp, M. G. Byrne, New York; Emily Davis, Annie Walker, E. Housnell, A. B. Cross, Philip Young, Montreal; W. A. F. Vassar, London; George Steele, Cyrus Crosley, James Parker, R. Colebrook, the Rev. H. C. S. Morris, Mrs. Fish and two children; Miss R. Martin, May Maycock, Violet Henderson, Uno Marderud, T. D. Levin, D. A. Thomas, Cardiff, Wales; T. J. M. Evans, A. R. Clarke, W. G. Burgess, J. H. Charles and daughter, Toronto; Miss Loney, New York; John Herris, Josephine Brandell, F. K. A. Perry, C. G. Mosley, New York; E. J. H. Brooks, New York; A. M. Jeffry, M. Cairns, New York; A. Manley, H. Heath, Miss North, Miss Winter, George Duguid, Daniel Moore, John W. McConnell, Memphis, Tenn.; Miss Sharpe, Miss Conner, H. M. Daly, Patrick Cliffe, James Bohan, Toronto; Mrs. Cyrus Crosley.

London, May 8.—The Cunard company announces among the survivors General Lassiter and son, first cabin; Mrs. Bretherton, second cabin.

## Two Men From Minneapolis on Lusitania List

Sidrel Braddick and George Arthur Booked From This City.

Two Minneapolis men were passengers on the Lusitania when it was blown up and sunk yesterday.

According to B. G. Benson, manager of the Northwestern department of the Cunard Steamship company, Sidrel Braddick and George Arthur, both second class passengers, said they lived in Minneapolis when they engaged passage on the last trip of the Lusitania.

**Employed as Machinist.**

Braddick lived at the Grand apartments, 620 Seventh street south. He left there on April 20. Braddick was said to have been employed as a machinist by the Minneapolis Steel & Machinery company. He claimed to be from Mankato, and made his home at the Grand apartments for two years. According to the proprietor of the apartments he left last month with the intention of returning to Mankato.

Little was known about him at the apartments, as the men with whom he associated left there on his departure. He is said to have a brother who is a pastor in a Wisconsin town. Braddick is unmarried.

**Arthur Not Known Here.**

Practically nothing is known here about George Arthur. He told Mr. Benson that letters addressed to general delivery would reach him.

Other Northwest passengers on the ill-fated steamship were Mrs. Caroline Treverrow, Butte; Henry C. Ashman, Butte; F. J. Milford, Hancock, Mich.

Justus M. Forman of New York, whose name appears among the first-class passengers, is a brother of the late Frank Forman, one of the founders of Forman, Ford & Co. of Minneapolis. Mr. Forman, who is an author, has visited in Minneapolis a number of times.

**DULUTH GIRL PASSENGER ON ILL-FATED STEAMSHIP**

Duluth, Minn., May 8.—(Special.)—Miss Millie Baker, daughter of Mrs. A. Baker of this city was a passenger on the Lusitania. She had been studying music under Madame Guilia Valda in New York and started to Paris to resume her studies under her former instructor, Trabadello.

She was ready to make her debut in grand opera in Madrid when the war broke out. She returned to America only when conditions forced her to leave.

**FORMER SUPERIOR MAN AND WIFE ON SUNKEN LUSITANIA**

Superior, Wis., May 8.—(Special.)—Ogden Hammond, a former Superior realty man, a son of the founder of West Superior, with his wife was a passenger on the Lusitania. The trip was taken to please Mrs. Hammond, member of a wealthy New Jersey family, who insisted on seeing Europe in

(Continued on Page 4, Col. 1.)

STEAMER LUSITANIA, SUNK OFF IRISH COAST ON LAST LEG OF HER VOYAGE

## BULLETINS

Queenstown, May 8—A steward in the first boat which landed here said he feared 900 lives lost by the sinking of the Lusitania.

London, May 8—A Dublin dispatch to the Exchange Telegraph company says that the latest reports indicate a loss of life on the Lusitania at about 1,000.

London, May 8—The Central News says that the number of the Lusitania's passengers who died of injuries while being taken to Queenstown will reach 100.

London, May 8—The Times' Queenstown correspondent says that some of the survivors who have arrived there report that Alfred Gwynne Vanderbilt was drowned.

London, May 8—Captain Turner of the Lusitania was among those saved.

Dublin, May 8—The motorboat Elizabeth has arrived at Kinsale and reports that yesterday afternoon she picked up two life boats containing 79 survivors. The passengers said that owing to her list to port the Lusitaina could not launch many of her life boats.

## Lusitania's Steward Says Few Officers Were Saved

Tug "Storm Cock" Lands About 150 Survivors at Queenstown, Eng.

Queenstown, May 8.—The tug Storm Cock has returned here bringing about 150 survivors of the Lusitania, principally passengers, among whom were many women, several of the crew and one steward.

Describing the experience of the Lusitania, the steward said:

"The passengers were at lunch when a submarine came up and fired two torpedoes which struck the Lusitania on the starboard side, one forward and the other in the engine room. They caused terrific explosions.

"Captain Turner immediately ordered the boats out. The ship began to list badly immediately.

"Ten boats were put into the water and between 400 and 500 passengers entered them. The boat in which I was approached the land with three other boats and we were picked up shortly before 4 o'clock by the Storm Cock.

"I fear that few of the officers were saved. They acted bravely.

"There was only 15 minutes from the time the ship was struck until she foundered, going down bow foremost. It was a dreadful sight."

Two other steamers with survivors are approaching here.

**SURVIVORS IN DEPLORABLE CONDITION; SOME WOUNDED**

Queenstown, May 8.—That there was great confusion aboard the Lusitania after the steamer was torpedoed is evident from the conflicting statements of survivors, some of whom state that she was struck on the starboard side, while others insist that it was upon the port side.

The Dublin Times states that the survivors aboard the tug Storm Cock are all in a deplorable condition and that some of them are wounded.

**GENEVA ONE OF FEW CITIES TO GREET FORMER KHEDIVE**

Geneva, Switzerland, May 8, via Paris—Geneva is one of the few places in Europe where Abbas Hilmi, the former Khedive of Egypt, appears to be welcome. The reason is that this city is the headquarters of the National Egyptian party, headed by Frorid Bey.

## Attitude of U. S. Public Over Sinking of Steamer May Force Quick Action

Probable Loss of Life Among Women and Children Presents New Problem—Incident Held Entirely Different Than That of "The Falaba."

By GEO. F. AUTHIER.

WASHINGTON, May 8—(Special)—Suspending judgment until complete information concerning the sinking of the Lusitania has been obtained, the American government is today facing the gravest responsibility that has confronted it since the outbreak of the European war. Official Washington has been stunned by receipt of news of an event which it feared and anticipated but could not avert. Silence reigns in official circles, but it is the grim sort of silence that indicates a keen realization of the gravity and importance of the situation.

As the details of the sinking of the liner trickled through during the afternoon and evening, there was an apparent tightening of the avenues of communication and officials are as silent as the tomb, expressing no opinion or judgment, but merely waiting.

Shocked by the receipt of the first news of the sinking of the giant liner, government officials felt that the fact that all passengers were saved would in itself absolve this government from responsibility, but as the later information came, carrying with it a story of appalling loss of life, this source of comfort disappeared.

**Secretary of State Silent.**

Not the slightest word indicating what possible attitude this government may take has escaped any official of prominence. The White House and the office of the Secretary of State are places of silence. Senator William J. Stone, chairman of the senate committee on foreign relations, is in Washington, but refused to discuss the case, saying it would be improper to do so until all the facts were known. He said if the incident involved merely the loss of a British owned ship that was a matter which did not involve us materially, but refused to go further pending the receipt of the complete details.

The only inference that could be drawn relative to the possible attitude of the administration was that it would probably urge calmness of judgment on the part of the American people and a suspension of discussion until all the facts are known.

It is significant that information concerning the Lusitania was obtained by the administration quickly. There was none of the delay that has characterized the receipt of official information by the department relative to other cases.

The inference might be drawn that the government may take the view that there are mitigating circumstances from the fact that it was suggested in various places that the liner might have been blown up by an infernal machine in her hold. The suggestion was also offered that extenuating circumstances might be found in the fact that the liner may have carried munitions of war, or carried reservists, or that it was convoyed by British ships of war, an unlikely fact in view of the liner's speed.

**Bound to Stir Public.**

While the compelling nature of the tragedy involved in the loss of life in a passenger list made up of men, women and children, many of them Americans, is bound to stir the American public, the principle involved is not different than that involved in other cases.

The Lusitania was a British owned vessel, her passengers had been warned not to take passage on her, and, according to the German viewpoint, the passengers who have been drowned paid the penalty for their unwillingness to take heed. The same circumstances surrounded the death of Leon C. Thrasher, who lost his life when the Falaba was torpedoed.

The American public has been inclined to take a complacent view of this incident and to follow the lead of the administration in its suggestions of delay and adjustment. But while the principle involved is the same, the fact that women and children were included in the passenger list of the Lusitania and if they have not been drowned were subjected to the danger of death, it is feared is likely to make an impression upon the minds of the American public which will nullify the administration's disposition to adjust and delay.

The opinion is occasionally expressed here that if this government had acted promptly in the case of the Thrasher incident, which has been looked upon as a German "feeler," the present situation might have been avoided.

Aside from the danger of an aroused public opinion which the administration faces today in its ajustment of the present case, it is recognized in diplomatic circles that the American government had already committed itself in a manner which would have made it difficult in any event to avoid a rupture with Germany, or at least a near breaking of friendly relations.

**At Variance With Germany.**

At the time of the establishment of the German zone by means of the submarine blockade, the American government refused to accept the German position. The German government was warned that it would not recognize any abridgement of the rights of American citizens as neutrals, that it would hold Germany "strictly accountable" for the loss of American lives and that it could not regard the violation

(Continued on Page 5. Col. 1.)

## Charles Frohman Among Passengers on Lusitania

New York Theatrical Man Was on Way to Europe to Pick Up War Plays.

(By Associated Press.)

New York, May 8.—Uncertainty as to the fate of Charles Frohman, probably the most widely known theatrical man in the world, who was a passenger on the Lusitania, was the absorbing topic among thousands in the theatrical district last night. Mr. Frohman had gone to Europe with Charles Klein and Justus Miles Forman, playwrights. Mr. Frohman's offices in the Empire Theater building were besieged until a late hour for possible news of him and when told that there was none, the inquirers turned sadly away.

**In Search of Plays.**

Before sailing, Mr. Frohman said he was going to England to look over his theatrical interests and to see if he could find some new war plays for the American stage. Mr. Forman went with him.

Mr. Forman's latest addition to the American stage was the play called "The Hyphen," a play of American patriotism, which elicited much unfavorable comment from citizens of German extraction. Mr. Klein, author of "The Lion and the Mouse," and other successes, was going to Europe on business connected with his enterprises.

**Determined to Sail.**

Members of Mr. Frohman's staff said they had pleaded with him not to sail, but Mr. Frohman answered that business made it imperative that he go at that time.

In German clubs, restaurants, and other places where Germans foregather, the news of the disaster was received quietly and generally without comment.

## Lusitania's Fate Shocks Officials at Washington

Most Serious Situation of War Believed Confronting United States.

President Is Grave as He Peruses Dispatches Bearing on Disaster.

Profound Grief Occasioned by Reports of Heavy Loss of Life.

Feeling Rife That Germans Deliberately Planned Destruction of Ship.

Scores of Warnings Sent Out Are Cited as Direct Proof.

(By Associated Press.)

Washington, May 8.—Destruction of the British liner Lusitania with the loss of many lives shocked officials of the United States government and spread profound grief in the national capital.

Although it was not known how many, if any, of those lost were Americans, the view was general that the most serious situation confronted the American government since the outbreak of the war in Europe.

**U. S. Warning Cited.**

The warning of the United States that Germany would be held to a "strict accountability" for the loss of "American lives," irrespective of whether they were aboard belligerent or neutral vessels when attacked, focused attention of the White House, where President Wilson, until late in the night, read the dispatches with grave interest.

The President made no comment. Officials said facts and circumstances would have to be obtained by careful investigation during the next few days before any announcements could be made by the American government.

The feeling was widespread that if any American lives had been lost the United States, in view of its strong warning to Germany, would be confronted with the necessity of taking steps to safeguard the lives of its citizens on the high seas.

**Climax Reached.**

The sinking of the Lusitania marks the climax of a series of incidents since the announcement of the German war zone decree, concerning which the American government has been silent. It is now predicted that even though it developed that no American lives were lost on the Lusitania, general representations will be made by the United States covering all the cases involved—the death of Leon C. Thresher, an American citizen, when the British steamer Falaba was sunk, the dropping of bombs on the American steamer Cushing, and the attack on the steamer Gulflight, which was wrecked with a loss of three American lives.

The report that the Lusitania was torpedoed without warning created a profound sensation, for it was the first case in which this threatened procedure has been carried out with Americans on board a belligerent vessel.

Aside from the diplomatic questions in the case, which were widely discussed in Washington yesterday, the sinking of the liner brought to light an interesting story of repeated threats and warnings which have reached high officials for several days past of a plan by the German Admiralty to sink the Lusitania for the psychological effect it would have on Great Britain and the terror it might spread among ocean travelers generally.

Information gathered among officials of the government tended to confirm the belief that plans for the destruction of the Lusitania were made several weeks ago. First, the German embassy was instructed to advertise in the leading newspapers of the United States, warning passengers against traveling on belligerent ships.

**Anonymous Warnings Sent.**

Anonymous warnings then were sent to individuals who proposed sailing on the Lusitania.

Most significant of all were letters received here from officials in Germany by private persons stating that the Lusitania surely would be destroyed.

From the day the ship sailed from New York, officials here have received inquiries from many sources almost daily as to the safety of the vessel. One official was told with much positiveness early yesterday that this was the day selected for the destruction of the vessel.

The naval radio station at Arlington has been on the alert for news and from time to time has been reported as having picked up messages saying the vessel was sunk.

**Reports Not Confirmed.**

Inquiry at the navy department each time failed to confirm the reports and they were not circulated because it was feared they would spread unnecessary alarm.

At the German Embassy here, while no comment was made as to whether

# First Armed U. S. Ship Sunk, Minneapolis Man Aboard


# The Minneapolis Morning Tribune

*Fiftieth Year. No. 314.* The Associated Press. MINNEAPOLIS, MINN., TUESDAY, APRIL 3, 1917 The United Press. *Price One Cent* in Minneapolis.


# *Wilson Asks State of War Declaration and 500,000 More Soldiers for Army*

## U.S. Steamer Aztec Is Sunk Near France

Torpedo Hits Armed But Unwarned Boat Squarely Amidships in Dark.

SOME SAVED, BUT MANY ARE REPORTED MISSING

Victim, First to Sail With Guns, Carried Half-Million Cargo.

FIFTEEN OF HER CREW BORN IN UNITED STATES

Heavy Sea Running at Time Hampers Rescue Work By French.

Adolf Hendrickson, a coxswain, who enlisted from the Minneapolis station and gave this city as his residence, was one of the armed guard on the Aztec. Inability to obtain access to the enlistment records here last night prevented learning the man's house address.

**Paris, April 3.—The American steamer Aztec, the first armed U. S. ship to sail from an American port, has been sunk without warning by a submarine near an island off Brest. A French patrol picked up nineteen of the men aboard. Twenty-eight are reported missing. Little hope is entertained that they can be saved, as the steamer was torpedoed at night while a heavy sea was running.**

### AMBASSADOR SHARP NOTIFIED.

**William Graves Sharp, the American ambassador, was informed this afternoon by the French government of the torpedoing of the Aztec and immediately cabled the State department.**

**Representatives of the American government will proceed to Brest to take the deposition of survivors of the disaster.**

### *Believed Aztec Had No Chance to Fight.*

New York, April 3.—The steamship Aztec—first armed American merchant vessel to sail from this side of the Atlantic—was sunk Sunday night by a German submarine off an island near Brest, France. The cable message from the American consul at Brest that brought the news of the ship's sinking to her owners, the Oriental Navigation Co., gave no inkling as to the fate of her crew. An Associated Press dispatch from Paris said, however, that while some of the men were rescued, a number were missing and probably had perished.

The Aztec, under command of Captain Walter O'Brien, was manned by a crew of 39. Seventeen of them, including the captain, were American citizens.

**Americans in Crew.**

The following Americans were among the crew. Their addresses were filed here with the United States shipping commissioner: I. J. Anderson, mate, Brooklyn, N. Y.; G. C. Larkin, third mate, Passaic, N. J.; B. Borjensen, engineer, Brooklyn, N. Y.; Harry Larkin, engineer, West Lynn, Mass.; Herbert Collins, engineer, Wilmington, Del.; Charles L. Bickson, engineer, Brooklyn, N. Y.; Chester T. Long, messman, New York city; Watson Sianey, radio operator, New York city; Charles Kelly, Brooklyn, N. Y.; Julian R. Macomber,


(Continued on page 7, col. 2.)


**MINNESOTA WEATHER.**

**Cloudy today, probably rain in south portion by night; tomorrow partly cloudy and colder.**

## President Denounces German Autocracy's Warring on U.-S. Asks Congress to Provide Forces to Defend Humanity

*President Wilson, addressing the 65th Congress at its war session, holds that the German Autocracy has been at war with the U. S. since February 1. He asked Congress to proclaim war with Germany and to provide means to establish a lasting peace by eliminating Prussianism from existence. The message was spoken yesterday at a joint session of both Houses. The message was referred to the foreign relations committees of both House and Senate and will be acted upon today.*

I have called the Congress into extraordinary session because there are serious, very serious choices of policy to be made and made immediately, which is was neither right nor constitutionally permissible that I should assume the responsibility of making.

On the third of February last I officially laid before you the extraordinary announcement of the Imperial German government that on and after the first day of February it was its purpose to put aside all restraints of law or of humanity and use its submarines to sink every vessel that sought to approach either the ports of Great Britain or Ireland or the western coast of Europe or any of the ports controlled by the enemies of Germany within the Mediterranean.

That had seemed to be the object of the German submarine warfare earlier in the war but since April of last year the Imperial government has somewhat restrained the commanders of its undersea craft in conformity with its promise then given to us that passenger boats should not be sunk and that due warning would be given to all other vessels which its submarines might seek to destroy, when no resistance was offered or escape attempted, and care taken that their crews were given at least a fair chance to save their lives in their open boats.

The precautions taken were meagre and haphazard enough as was proved in distressing instance after instance in the progress of the cruel and unmanly business, but a certain degree of restraint was observed.

### RESTRAINT SWEPT ASIDE.

The new policy has swept every restriction aside. Vessels of every kind, whatever their flag, their character, their cargo, their destination, their errand have been ruthlessly sent to the bottom without warning and without thought of help of mercy for those on board, the vessels of friendly neutrals along with those of belligerents. Even hospital ships and ships carrying relief to the sorely bereaved and stricken people of Belgium, though the latter were provided with safe conduct through the proscribed areas by the German government itself and were distinguished by unmistakable marks of identity have been sunk with the same reckless lack of compassion or principle.

I was for a little while unable to believe that such things would in fact be done by any government that had hitherto subscribed to the humane practices of civilized nations. International law had its origin in the attempt to set up some law, which would be respected and observed upon the seas, where no nation had right of dominion and where lie the free highways of the world. By painful stage after stage has that law been built up with meagre enough results indeed, after all was accomplished that could be accomplished, but always with a clear view, at least, of what the heart and conscience of mankind demanded.

### NO SCRUPLES OF HUMANITY.

This minimum of right the German government has swept aside under the plea of retaliation and necessity, and because it had no weapons which it could use at sea except these which it is impossible to employ as it is employing them without throwing to the winds all scruples of humanity or of respect for the understandings that were supposed to underlie the intercourse of the world.

I am not now thinking of the loss of property involved, immense and serious as that is, but only of the wanton and wholesale destruction of the lives of noncombatants, men, women and children, engaged in pursuits which have always, even in the darkest periods of modern history, been deemed innocent and legitimate. Property can be paid for; the lives of peaceful and innocent people cannot. The present German submarine warfare against commerce is a warfare against mankind. It is a war against all nations. American ships have been sunk, American lives taken, in ways which it has stirred us very deeply to learn, but the people and ships of other neutral and friendly nations have been sunk and overwhelmed in the waters in the same way. There has been no discrimination.

### CHALLENGE TO MANKIND.

The challenge is to all mankind. Each nation must decide for itself how it will meet it. The choice we make for ourselves must be made with a moderation of counsel and a temperateness of judgment befitting our character and our motives as a nation. We must put excited feeling away. Our motive will not be revenge or the victorious assertion of the physical might of the nation, but only the vindication of right, of human right, of which we are only a single champion.

When I addressed the Congress on the twenty-sixth of February last I thought that it would suffice to assert our neutral rights with arms, our right to use the seas against unlawful interference, our right to keep our people safe against unlawful violence. But armed neutrality, it now appears, is impracticable. Because submarines are in effect outlaws when used as the German submarines have been used against merchant shipping, it is impossible to defend ships against their attacks, as the law of nations has assumed that merchantmen would defend themselves against privateers or cruisers, visible craft giving chase upon the open sea. It is common prudence in such circumstances, grim necessity indeed, to endeavor to destroy them before they have shown their own intention. They must be dealt with upon sight, if dealt with at all.

### NEUTRAL RIGHTS DENIED.

The German government denies the right of neutrals to use arms at all within the areas of the sea which it has proscribed, even in the defense of rights which no modern publicist has ever before questioned their right to defend. The intimation is conveyed that the armed guards which we have placed on our merchant ships will be treated as beyond the pale of law and subject to be dealt with as pirates would be. Armed neutrality is ineffectual at best, in such circumstances, and in the face of such pretensions it is worse than ineffectual; it is likely at once to produce what it was meant to prevent; it is practically certain to draw us into the war without either the rights or the effectiveness of belligerents.

There is one choice we cannot make, we are incapable of making. We will not choose the path of submission and suffer the most sacred rights of our nation and our people to be ignored or violated. The wrongs against which we now array ourselves are not common wrongs; they cut to the very roots of human life.

### ASKS WAR DECLARATION.

With a profound sense of the solemn and even tragical character of the step I am taking and of the grave responsibilities which it involves, but in unhesitating obedience to what I deem my constitutional duty, I advise that the Congress declare the recent course of the Imperial government to be in fact nothing less than war against the government and people of the United States; that it formally accept the status of a belligerent which has thus been thrust upon it and that it take immediate steps not only to put the country in a more thorough state of defense, but also to exert all its power and employ all its resources to bring the government of the German empire to terms and end the war.

What this will involve is clear. It will involve the utmost practicable co-operation in counsel and action with the governments now at war with Germany, and, as incident to that, the extension to those governments of the most liberal financial credits, in order that our resources may, so far as possible, be added to theirs. It will involve the organization and mobilization of all the material resources of the country to supply the materials of war and to serve the incidental needs of the nation in the most abundant and yet the most economical and efficient way possible.

### 500,000 MORE MEN ASKED.

It will involve the immediate full equipment of the navy in all respects, but particularly in supplying it with the best means of dealing with the enemy's submarines. It will involve the immediate addition to the armed forces of the United States already provided for by law in case of war of at least 500,000 men, who should, in my opinion, be chosen upon the principle of universal liability to service, and also the authorization of subsequent additional increments of equal force as soon as they may be needed and can be handled in training.

It will involve also, of course, the granting of adequate credits to the government, sustained, I hope, so far as they can equitably be sustained by the present generation, by well conceived taxation. I say sustained so far as may be equitable by taxation because it seems to me that it would be most unwise to base the credits which will now be necessary entirely on money borrowed. It is our duty, I most respectfully urge, to protect our people so far as we may against the very serious hardships and evils which would be likely to arise out of the inflation which would be produced by vast loans.

In carrying out the measures by which these things are to be accomplished we should keep constantly in mind the wisdom of interfering as little as possible in our own preparation and in the equipment of our military with the duty—for it will be a very practical duty—of supplying the nations already at war with Germany with the materials which they can obtain only from us or by our assistance. They are in the field and we should help them in every way to be effective there.

### DEPARTMENTS TO REPORT.

I shall take the liberty of suggesting, through the several executive departments of the government for the consideration of your committees measures for the accomplishment of the several objects I have mentioned. I hope that it will be your pleasure to deal with them as having been framed after very careful thought by the branch of the government upon which the responsibility of conducting the war and safeguarding the nation will most directly fall.

While we do these things, these deeply momentous things, let us be very clear, and make very clear to all the world, what our motives and our objects are. My own thought has not been driven from its habitual and normal course by the unhappy events of the last two months, and I do not believe that the thought of the nation has been altered or clouded by them.

### TO VINDICATE JUSTICE.

I have exactly the same things in mind now that I had in mind when I addressed the Senate on the 22nd day of January, last; the same that I had in mind when I addressed the Congress on the 3rd day of February and on the 26th day of February. Our object now, as then, is to vindicate the principles of peace and the justice in the life of the world as against selfish and autocratic power and to set up amongst the really free and self-governed peoples of the world such a concert of purpose and action as will henceforth insure the observance of those principles; neutrality is no longer feasible or desirable where the peace of the world is involved and the freedom of its peoples, and the menace to that peace and freedom lies in the existence of autocratic governments backed by organized force which is controlled wholly by their will, not by the will of their people. We have seen the last neutrality in such circumstances.

We are at the beginning of an age in which it will be insisted that the same standards of conduct and of responsibility for wrong done shall be observed among nations and their governments that are observed among the individual citizens of civilized states.

### NO QUARREL WITH PEOPLE.

We have no quarrel with the German people. We have no feeling towards them but one of sympathy and friendship. It was not upon their impulse that their government acted upon entering this war. It was not with their previous knowledge or approval.

It was a war determined upon as wars used to be determined on in the old, unhappy days when peoples were nowhere consulted by their rulers and wars were provoked and waged in the interest of dynasties or of little groups of ambitious men who were accustomed to use their fellowmen as pawns and tools.

Self-governed nations do not fill their neighbor states with spies or set the course of intrigue to bring about some critical posture of affairs which will give them an opportunity to strike and make


(Continued on page 2, cols. 3 and 4.)


## *Germany's Course Called a Challenge to All Humanity*

## *"U. S. Must Enter Conflict to Make World Safe for Democracy," Declares Nation's President*

## *JOINT RESOLUTION AUTHORIZES ACTION*

Washington, April 3.—President Wilson last night urged Congress, assembled in joint session, to declare a state of war existing between the United States and Germany. In a dispassionate, but unmeasured denunciation of the course of the German government which he characterized as a challenge to all mankind and a warfare against all nations, the President declared that neutrality no longer was feasible or desirable where the peace of the world was involved; that armed neutrality had become ineffectual enough at best and was likely to produce what it was meant to prevent and urged that congress accept the gauge of battle with all the resources of the nation.

### RESOLUTIONS INTRODUCED.

When the President finished speaking, resolutions to declare a state of war existing were introduced in both houses, referred to appropriate committees and will be debated today. There is no doubt of their passage. The resolution follows:

"Joint resolution declaring that a state of war exists between the Imperial German government and people of the United States and making provision to prosecute the same:

"Whereas, the recent acts of the Imperial German government are acts of war against the government and people of the United States:

"Resolved, by the Senate and House of Representatives of the United States of America in Congress assembled that the state of war between the United States and the Imperial German government which has thus been thrust upon the United States is hereby formally declared; and,

"That the President be, and is hereby authorized and directed to take immediate steps not only to put the country in a thorough state of deefnse but also to exert all of its power and employ all of its resources to carry on war against the Imperial German government, and to bring the conflict to a successful termination."

### PRESIDENT ADVISES WAR.

"I advise that the Congress declare the recent course of the Imperial German government to be in fact nothing less than war against the government and people of the United States," said the President in his address, "that it formally accept the status of belligerent which has thus been thrust upon it and that it takes steps not only to put the country in a more thorough state of defense, but to exert all its power and employ all its resources to bring the government of the German empire to terms and end the war."

The objects of the United States in entering the war, the President said, "were to vindicate the principles of peace and justice against selfish and autocratic power."

### NO CONQUEST SOUGHT.

"Without selfish ends, for conquest or dominion, seeking no indemnities or material compensation for the sacrifices it shall make, the United States must enter the war," he said, "to make the world safe for democracy, as only one of the champions of the rights of mankind, and would be satisfied when those rights were as secure as the faith and freedom of nations would make them."

The address was sent in full to Germany by a German Official news agency for publication in that country.

The text also went to England and a summary of its contents was sent around the world to other nations.

### PRESIDENT'S RECOMMENDATIONS.

To carry on an effective warfare against the German government, which he characterized as a "natural foe to liberty" the President recommended:

Utmost practical co-operation in counsel and action with these governments already at war with Germany.

Extension of liberal financial credits to those governments so that the resource of America may be added so far as possible to theirs.

Organization and mobilization of all the material resources of the country.

Full equipment of the navy, particularly for means of dealing with submarine warfare.

An army of at least 500,000 men, based on the principle of universal liability to service and the authorization of additional increments of 500,000 each as they are needed or can be handled in training.

Raising necessary money for the United States government, so far as possible without borrowing and on the basis of equitable taxation.

**Wouldn't Hold Up Munitions.**

All preparations, the President urged, should be made in such a way as not to check the flow of war supplies to the Allies.

Measures to accomplish these ends, the President told Con-

# OPENING DAY AT STATE FAIR BREAKS ALL RECORDS


# The Minneapolis Morning Tribune

Fifty-first Year. No. 103. United Press. Associated Press. MINNEAPOLIS, MINN., TUESDAY, SEPTEMBER 4, 1917 International News Service. Price One Cent in Minneapolis


# Riga, Abandoned by Russians, Falls Into German Hands

## Initial Crowd at State Fair Totals 116,555

### Attendance Exceeds Estimates—Last High Mark 100,792 in 1912.

### WAR FEATURES DRAW IMMENSE THRONG

### Thousands Jump to Feet and Applaud Tableau "Call to Colors."

A record-breaking crowd—116,555 persons, to be exact—attended the Minnesota State Fair yesterday. This was 23,978 more than were present at last year's opening and biggest day. Before 6 p. m. yesterday's attendance had broken the previous high record, that of Labor day, 1912, when 100,792 admissions were recorded.

The tremendous attendance exceeded estimates, in spite of the fact that fair officials had anticipated an unusual crowd. More than 30,000 persons were estimated to have witnessed last night's patriotic entertainment before the grandstand. Thousands were denied admittance after stand, bleachers and all available space in front of them had been packed.

Correspondingly large attendances were reported at the horse show and other attractions. Some of the large eating houses on the grounds ran out of provisions long before the supper crowd had been taken care of.

In spite of the fact that every street was crowded and every building and booth packed, there was excellent order. The Fair police force reported its troubles for the entire day to be limited to the disappearance of three automobiles. The fire department did not make a run. The hospital on the ground, kept busy treating such slight ailments as headache and bee-stings, reported only two serious accidents.

**Expect 400,000 This Week.**

When President George Atchison of the State Fair board could recover from his surprise over the attendance enough to express his elation, he forecasted an unprecedented attendance for the week.

"Give us the same kind of weather Wednesday, Thursday and Saturday, the automobile days, and the 1917 Fair should have a total of 400,000 persons," he said. The previous high record was approximately 367,000.

War and agriculture's preparations to meet it, was given by Thomas H. Canfield, fair secretary, as a big reason for the unprecedented opening. "Everybody wants to see the soldiers, the military demonstrations and the other wartime features of the program," he said.

If that was the case the big crowd got what it paid for. Last night in "Modern Warfare" the pyrotechnical spectacle before the grandstand it saw in vivid similitude German assault and repulse. Zeppelins and airplanes, illuminated by their own explosives, dropped bombs that wrought cataclysmal destruction upon a realistic-looking Belgian city. War balloons soared through the air, tanks tumbled through the streets, ammunition wagons exploded, shrapnel and heavy artillery shrieked and roared. Detachments of Allied troops, carrying their colors, finally emerged through it all and triumphantly drove the attackers back from the ruins.

Interspersed with all this was the exhibition of the Butt manual of arms, a band concert and drill by the Winnipeg 100th Grenadier Guards band which got enthusiastic receptions.

**Jump to Feet and Applaud.**

The big crowd got a thrill of patriotism at the beginning of the program in the tableaux, "The Call to the Colors." When the spectators saw the symbolic figure of America beckoning to them and two soldiers waving the summoning signal flags they responded as one man, rising from their seats and applauding for many minutes.

The Horse Show, also, was given an especially patriotic color by the appearance of Col. George Leach and other members of the First Minnesota Field artillery whose part in tonight's program was moved forward because of their impending departure for France today.

**Farmers Study Machinery.**

Agriculture's contribution to the war campaign, the maximum production and the greatest possible conservation of

(Continued on Page 2, Col. 4.)

## German Airplanes Visit English Coast

### Bombs Are Dropped at Several Places—No Report of Damages or Loss of Life.

(By Associated Press.)

London, Sept. 4.—German airplanes visited the Southeast coast of England last (Monday) night, dropping bombs at various places according to an official statement issued shortly after midnight. No report of casualties or damage has been received up to the present time.

"Enemy airplanes crossed the Southeast coast at 11 o'clock last night and dropped bombs at various places. No reports of casualties or damage have yet been received.

"A number of our airplanes pursued the enemy."

**MINNESOTA WEATHER.**

Fair today and tomorrow, not much change in temperature.

## *Don't Hoard Sugar But Be Economical, Hoover's Advice*

### No Immediate Fear of Famine in Supply Here—Yield Is Nearly Normal.

(International News Service.)

WASHINGTON, Sept. 4.—"Don't hoard sugar. Be economical in its use, but do not stint the household. There is no immediate prospect of a sugar famine."

This in effect is the suggestion made the United States yesterday by the food administration.

It is not actually a lack of sugar that confronts the government and the people but the question of its distribution, Mr. Hoover announces. After October 1, with good luck, the sugar situation will be practically normal in the United States. The world shortage is small and practically confined to Europe.

The world supply of sugar for the present year is estimated at 18,659,792 tons against an average production before the war of 18,712,997 tons.

## Peace Council Silent Monday

### No Public Meetings Held in Chicago Since Guardsmen's Arrival.

(By Associated Press.)

Chicago, Sept. 4.—Delegates to the People's Council of America for Democracy and Peace made no effort to hold a public meeting yesterday. Several conferences were held at hotels where the delegates are quarterd.

Some of the pacifists attended a labor picnic, having previously said they would make speeches there if permitted to do so. None made an address, but no person would say that they either asked permission to speak or were denied the privilege. A large force of deputy sheriffs was sent to the picnic grounds by Sheriff Traeger, who has been co-operating with Adjutant General Dickson since the arrival of the four companies of national guardsmen from Springfield.

Mayor Thompson by whose instructions the meeting of pacifists was held under police protection was in seclusion throughout the day. Members of the state Council of Defense discussed possibility of action against the mayor for what was regarded as his illegal action in permitting the pacifists meeting to be held in defiance of Governor Lowden's orders.

**Record for Patriotic Relatives.**

Gilbert, Minn., Sept. 4.—The record for patriotic relatives is claimed by Mrs. John Murphy of this village. She has nine brothers and cousins in the British army. Two have been killed and one slightly wounded.

## "Eyes of the World Will Be On You," President's Message to Drafted Men

(International News Service.)

Washington, Sept. 4.—On the eve of their mobilization, President Wilson yesterday addressed a final word to the drafted men who will make up America's first great national army.

The President's greeting follows:

"To the soldiers of the national army:

"You are undertaking a great duty. The heart of the whole country is with you. Everything that you do will be watched with the deepest solicitude not only by those who are near and dear to you, but by the whole nation besides.

"For this great war draws us all together, makes us all comrades, and brothers, as all true Americans felt themselves to be when we first made good our national independence.

"The eyes of the world will be upon you, because you are in some special sense the soldiers of freedom. Let it be your pride, therefore, to show all men not only what good soldiers you are, but also what good men you are, keeping yourselves fit and straight in everything and pure and clean through and through.

"Let us set for ourselves a standard so high that it will be a glory to live up to it and add a new laurel to the crown of America.

"My affectionate confidence goes with you in every battle and every test.

"God keep and guide you."

## Labor Loyalty Pledged Anew

### Official Says Workers Stand Like Stone Wall Behind Government.

(By Associated Press.)

Boston, Sept. 4.—Labor's loyalty to the government in the present war crisis was pledged anew yesterday by James Duncan, vice president of the American Federation of Labor and other speakers at a big labor rally on Boston common. The mass meeting took the place of Labor day parades of other years.

Mr. Duncan, who was a member of the American mission to Russia, was interrupted by cheers when he declared:

"The very large majority of the workers of our country stand as a stone wall back of President Wilson and Congress."

Mayor Curley, Edward McGrady, president of the Boston Central Labor union, and others dwelt at length on the loyalty of labor.

### *Gompers Says Slackers Entitled to No Protection.*

(By Associated Press.)

Erie, Pa., Sept. 4.—Samuel Gompers, president of the American Federation of Labor, declared that persons unwilling to do their full duty in this hour of national peril are not entitled to the protection of the republic, during a Labor day address here yesterday.

"I am a pacifist—that is, I was until President Wilson asked Congress to declare war," said Mr. Gompers. "Now I would betray the great body of workingmen which I represent if I did not urge them to give their last

(Continued on Page 2, Col. 1.)

## *Champ Clark Urges Unqualified Support of U. S. War Moves*

### Declares Government Must Be Sustained Mentally, Morally, Physically, Financially.

(International News Service.)

Monmouth Courthouse, N. J., Sept. 4.—Full support of the government in the war was urged yesterday by Speaker Champ Clark in a Labor day address here.

"No nation will long endure, nor deserve to endure, that does not protect all of its citizens wherever they may be on land or sea," he declared. "We have not degenerated into a race of 'mollycoddles,' as certain pessimists contend, a fact which will be clearly demonstrated in the immediate future. A finer body of young men never went forth to battle than our soldiers now 'swiftly forming in the ranks of war.'

"In this supreme crisis of our affairs—not of ours alone, but the whole world's affairs—it is the duty of every American, male and female, native or naturalized, to support, aid and sustain the government in every manner possible—mentally, morally, physically and financially.

"That is the plain, imperative duty we owe to our ancestors, to ourselves, and above all, to our posterity. I beg to suggest that patriotism does not consist entirely in public speeches, braying bands, flag bedecked parades and vociferous assertions of love of country, but genuine patriotism consists in being thorough-going American citizens, discharging all the various duties of citizenship every day of the year."

## Lowden Hits Pacifists in Labor Day Address

### Freedom of Speech Which Aids Enemy Is Treason, He Says.

(By Associated Press.)

Ottawa, Ill., Sept. 4.—Governor Frank O. Lowden in a Labor day address delivered here yesterday defined freedom of speech and branded as traitors those pacifists who are harassing the government in the prosecution of the war. He said nothing directly in regard to the People's council incident in Chicago.

"I agree with all my heart in freedom of speech," the governor said. "That is one of the things we are fighting for in this war, but civilization has adopted a definition to the effect that it is treason to say anything which will give aid or comfort to the enemy.

"We want peace to come speedily and the only thing to do is to follow Grant's strategy, which is to locate the enemy and strike him hard. Peace must come with honor and not bring peril to our children. I would consider myself a traitor if I did not support the government. There is only one test in time of war; we are either with the government or against it."

**22,000 Harvesters in Canada's Fields.**

Winnipeg, Man., Sept. 4.—More than 22,000 harvesters from Eastern Canada and the United States are at present working in Western Canada's wheat fields. Manitoba has obtained less than one-third of the number, official figures show.

## *Draft Men Allowed Only Few Personal Effects in Camps*

WASHINGTON, Sept. 4.—Drafted men of the first 5 per cent contingent, who will leave tomorrow for mobilization camps, are directed in regulations issued yesterday to take a minimum of civilian clothing and personal belongings.

Toilet articles, towels and handkerchiefs are recommended and no objection will be made to two changes of underclothing, but other articles are frowned upon.

Attention is called to the fact that civilian clothing will be discarded when camp is reached and it was suggested that clothing not worth keeping be worn. The men carry only light hand-baggage on the train, and suitcases and hand bags will not be allowed for permanent use at camp.

## Gopher Gunners to Leave Today

### First Artillery to Entrain for First Lap of Trip to France.

After days of anxious anticipation, the First battalion of the One Hundred and Fifty-first field artillery (First Minnesota Field artillery) will leave Fort Snelling at noon today for Camp Mills, Mineola, Long Island, from whence it will start soon for "somewhere in France" as part of Major General Mann's "Rainbow division."

With men busy all day yesterday loading into the freight and baggage cars the personal and camping equipment of the division, and the small supply wagons and lighter arms, little time will be needed to entrain the men today.

A Minneapolis representative of the American Railway association, in charge of the transportation arrangements, last night did not know the exact time for the leaving of the men. He said, however, the order to move would come some time this morning.

Two special trains of 25 cars each will be required to transport the men and equipment of the First battalion. The "Gopher Gunners" will occupy 25 tourist cars, and the equipment will be carried in 25 freight and baggage cars. The trip to the Eastern point will require four or five days.

The artillery regiment has reached war strength as far as the enlisted personnel is concerned, but Col. Geo. E. Leach said last night the regiment lacked 14 officers. The Central office has been authorized to fill the vacancies by assigning graduates of the first officer's training camp at Fort Snelling, who are now at Camp Dodge, Des Moines, Iowa.

## Strike Rioters Routed at Point of Bayonets

Springfield, Ill., Aug. 4.—Charging with fixed bayonets, Company F, Ninth Illinois infantry, late last night dispersed a mob of more than 1,000 street car strike sympathizers who had wrecked four street cars and were then attacking the headquarters of the railway company. No shots were fired by the soldiers.

**Blast in Boarding House; No One Hurt**

Butte, Mont., Sept. 4.—A dynamite blast was set off on the porch of a miners boarding house in this city yesterday. Twenty persons were asleep in the building but no one was injured. An Austrian is suspected.

## *German Reforms Planned to Meet Views of Wilson*

### Clerical and Socialist Leaders Are Profoundly Impressed by President's Reply to Pope.

(By Associated Press.)

LONDON, Sept. 4.—A Reuter's dispatch from Amsterdam says:

"President Wilson's reply to Pope Benedict's peace proposal has made a profound impression in Germany. Mathias Erzberger, member of the clerical center of the Reichstag, is expected at the next sitting of the main committee to demand immediate introduction of a government responsible to the Reichstag and the abandonment by the government of its plea of inability to act regarding Alsace-Lorraine, to the extent of proposing that the decision regarding the allegiance of these territories shall be left to their inhabitants. It is expected also that he will advocate general disarmament after the war.

"It is considered possible that the Reichstag will be dissolved soon after it reassembles and that general elections will be ordered.

"Dr. Eduard David, Socialist leader, maintains that the Reichstag has constitutional means of enforcing its will and says that new elections, in which soldiers at the front would participate, would result in a crushing defeat of the Pan-Germans and Annexationists."

## State Rocked by First Quake

### Earth Tremors in Several Towns New Experience for Minnesota.

Minnesota experienced its first earthquake yesterday afternoon.

Shocks that lasted for more than 20 seconds were reported at a number of north central towns along the Northern Pacific line between St. Cloud, Little Falls, Brainerd and Staples, but so far as could be learned last night no one was injured. Damage caused by the quakes was slight, for the most part being confined to broken windows and dishes.

The worst shock was reported at Staples. The tremor there began shortly after 3:30 p. m. and continued for nearly half a minute. There virtually the goods stored on shelves in the stores were knocked down and customers had miraculous escapes. Many windows and chimneys were broken there, as well as at Brainerd, Little Falls and other places.

At the Northern Pacific station at Staples all the windows were smashed. The concrete depot platform was cracked in many places.

C. J. Posey, assistant professor of geography and geology at the University of Minnesota, said last night he had never heard of an earthquake in Minnesota. The geological formation of the state is not such as would give rise to such a thing, he said.

A. E. Honstain, 118 Rustic Lodge avenue, Washburn park, was the only person who reported having felt the earthquake. He was lying down at his home and felt a perceptible tremor, his bed springs reacting to an east-to-west movement. His daughter and wife, in an adjoining room, also noted the phenomenon. Mrs. Honstain said that two distinct shocks were noticeable.

## *Millions of Kaisers, Cult of Might Converts, Must Be Crushed, Says Cochin*

(By Associated Press.)

Paris, Sept. 4.—"You ask for my opinion concerning the utterances of Pope Benedict and President Wilson," said Baron Denys Cochin, one of the leaders in parliament of the Catholic party of France to the Associated Press yesterday. "It is certain that those of the Pope," he continued, "have rather the character of a protocol, while those of the President are encyclical, but I do not see why we should oppose them to each other.

"The President desires to end militarism. So does the Pope. But in addition, Mr. Wilson desires the end of the Hohenzollern dynasty which instituted this regime. He makes war less upon the German nation than upon its guilty head. He uses about the same language as that used by the Allies against Napoleon in 1815 after the return from Elba.

**Millions of Hohenzollerns.**

"My notion is quite different. There was only one Napoleon, while there are among the Teutons of the North millions of Hohenzollerns—among the manufacturers and bankers of Prussian cities, among the legions of avid merchants, who, as the advance guard of their armies, fell upon our countries. They are among the Socialist workmen, even, and all of them are animated by the fury of domination. Literary Germany and philosophic Germany, the Kants and Fichtes, prepare the evolution of the state, the cult of might, with their celebrated 'die weltgeschicht ist das weltgericht' (the world's history in the world's tribunal), at once explained and completed by the words 'Deutschland uber alles.' The haughty and aristocratic reform of Luther both prepared and seconded the aberration. 'I am and shall always remain,' said Hegel, 'a pure Lutheran.'

**Kaiser Not Only Offender.**

"As for me, it goes without saying that I shall be delighted with all the vexations that come to Emperor William. To have the power of that man after 25 years of marvelously prosperous reign and to have let loose upon the world a tempest of ruin and death—to have allowed that to be done through weakness or to have done it through arrogance, takes from him all right to any consideration. But I confess that I do not see in the fall of this traditional autocrat and in his being replaced by some other elected autocrat a solution of the European catastrophe. For us that would not be worth another week of the war.

"The President is more happy when he declares the present Germany to be the enemy of four-fifths of the human race. She is their enemy because she wanted to oppress them. Let that people, says the President in high and generous sentiment, resign itself to the acceptance of a regime of equality and no longer seek to dominate all other nations as it is trying to do today—such is the primordial basis of every peace project. There is none other than that, and the desires of the Pope are the same as those of the President.

"Such is the peace we shall have, the peace we owe to the heroes we mourn, the peace of which the liberation of the French provinces of Lorraine and Alsace will be the only acceptable pledges."

## Slavs Fleeing on Open Road to Petrograd

### Forces That Evacuated Big Port Are Burning Everything in Retreat.

### ITALIANS CONTINUE TO PRESS AUSTRIANS HARD

### Haig's Batteries Further Pave Way for New Drive in Flanders.

(By Associated Press.)

Riga, Russia's big port on the Gulf of Riga, is in the hands of the Germans and its garrison and the civilian population are in retreat eastward.

Following up rapidly the advantage they gained in driving the Russians across the Dvina river on both sides of Uxkull last Saturday, the Germans threw bridges across this stream and soon were on the heels of the former defenders, some of whom offered resistance, but others of whom showed the white feather, giving the invaders no trouble in marching up the eastern bank of the Dvina toward Riga, 15 miles distant. Seeing the disaffection and the inability to stem the tides of the advance, the Russian commander ordered an evacuation.

**Retreating Russians Force Capture.**

With the falling back of the Russians from the city proper and the advance of the Germans northward along both sides of the stream, the Russians still defending the western bank around Dahlen, seemingly are in danger of being caught between the two fast moving bodies of the enemy and made prisoner.

The Russians in their retreat from Riga are laying the country in waste, burning villages and farms. Whether the city itself remains intact has not yet been made known, but doubtless the guns in the fortress and the ammunition stores either were moved or destroyed to prevent them falling into the hands of the Germans.

Aside from the strategic value of controlling the Gulf of Riga and of a base nearer the mouth of the Gulf of Finland, at the head of which Petrograd is situated, for the moment it is impossible to see the importance of the German gain, especially with the near approach of winter, when military operations in this northern region are almost impossible.

**Italians Continue Gains.**

On none of the other fronts have there been operations of great moment except in the Austro-Italian theater, where the Italians have made further progress on the Bainsizza plateau and on the Brestovizza valley, and at various points along the line have repulsed fresh counter-attacks launched by the Austrians. Throughout this entire theater violent artillery duels are in progress from Temino to the sea.

Advices to the Italian embassy in Washington are to the effect that along the front of the present offensive the Austrians have lost more than 128,000 men. Reports from Udine, Italy, give the Austrians' losses as one-third of the first line army.

**Haig's New Dash Not Started.**

The batteries of Field Marshal Haig are still pouring an incessant fire against the German trenches in Flanders, but as yet the anticipated new dash by his men to capture them has not started. Doubtless the knocking down of the defenses has not reached the limits which the British commander always requires before he throws his infantrymen into the fray.

On the remainder of the front in the West held by the British there have been the usual trench raiding operations in one of which, south of Monchy-Le-Preux, German dugouts and machine guns were destroyed and some prisoners taken.

Artillery duels which are somewhat violent in the Verdun region are taking place along the front where the French are facing the Germans. No infantry actions of importance have occurred.

### *Great German Flanking Movement Is Foreseen.*

(International News Service.)

Amsterdam, Sept. 4.—Advices reaching here from the Riga front by way of Berlin state that the German commander, Prince Leopold of Bavaria, is using the sector immediately before Dvinsk, 140 miles southeast of Riga, as a pivot for a huge flanking movement, designed to shake the Russian front from Dvinsk southward to Roumania. The whole German front has begun to swing into motion. Strong columns of the German Riga army are moving northeastward along the Riga-Wohnar railway. In several sectors between Riga and Dvinsk Russian troops have crossed the Dina.

### *French Airmen Flying Low Fight With Machine Guns.*

On the French Front in France, Sept. 4.—All day yesterday the Germans tried vainly to dislodge the French from the positions at Hurtebire, captured on Friday night, but their incessant efforts resulted only in increasing their already heavy casualty list. The French, who displayed such dash in their successful attack on this strong point, proved themselves equally the masters in its defense. They submitted to the most vigorous bombardment while consolidating their gains and remain unshaken in morale by the thousands of shells which are continuing tonight to fall on the conquered terrain.

During the operation 200 Germans were captured including seven officers.

The French now occupy the northern edge of the Hurtebise plateau and hold all the observation points.

The French infantry engaged in the victorious attack advanced with irre

## *Minneapolis Day Program at Minnesota State Fair*

### Tuesday, Sept. 4

7 a. m.—Admission gates open.

9 a. m.—Judging of horses begins in Stock Pavilion. Sheep and swine judging continued in Sheep and Swine buildings.

10:00 a. m.—Home sewing demonstration. Woman's Building, one hour.
Expert Red Cross demonstration, first aid to the injured, Woman's Building, one hour.
Demonstration in canning, salting and drying of vegetables and fruits, Woman's Building.
Demonstration by Dudley Crafts Watson, "Painting a Picture," Art Galleries.

10:30 a. m.—Patriotic Program with music, Woman's Committee of Minnesota Public Safety commission, Woman's Building.

11:00 a. m.—Educational Fashion Revue, Woman's Building, two hours.

12:30 p. m.—Public demonstration by judges with reasons for awarding of prizes, canning division, Woman's Building.

1:00 p. m.—Home sewing demonstration, Woman's Building, one hour.
Expert Red Cross demonstration, first aid to the injured, Woman's Building, one hour.
Demonstration in salting, canning and drying of vegetables and fruits, Housewives' Conservation and Safety Council of St. Paul, Woman's Building.

1:15 p. m.—Judging of cattle in Livestock Pavilion. Judging of Hereford and Red Polled cattle concluded. Sheep and swine judging continued in Sheep and Swine buildings.

1:30 p. m.—Program, Equal Franchise League, Institute Hall.

2:00 p. m.—Educational Fashion Revue, Woman's Building, two hours.
Drawing from living and costumed model, by Dudley Crafts Watson, director of Milwaukee Art Institute, in out-of-door studio, Art Galleries.

3:30 p. m.—Red Cross Patriotic Program with music, Institute Hall, one hour.
Art Gallery tour.

4:00 p. m.—Red Cross Patriotic Program with music, Woman's Building, one hour.
Demonstration in canning, salting and drying of vegetables and fruits, Woman's Building.

4:30 p. m.—Expert Red Cross demonstration, first aid to the injured, Woman's Building, one hour.

5 p. m.—Home sewing demonstration, featuring use of dress forms, Woman's Building.
Patriotic Program with music, Woman's Building.

7:00 p. m.—Evening Horse Show, Livestock Pavilion, lasting until 10:30 o'clock.

An entertainment program will be staged before the grandstand from 1:30 p. m. to 10 p. m., with an intermission of one hour between 5:30 p. m. and 6:30 p. m. Music afternoon and evening, Minnesota State Band. Races begin at 2 p. m.

1:30 p. m.—Bugle and Drum Corps, and bag raising, First Minnesota Infantry.

2:50 p. m.—Guard Mount, First Minnesota Infantry.

3:30 p. m.—Lawrence Brown in airplane flights.

5:15 p. m.—Retreat and Parade, First Minnesota Infantry.

**Evening.**

6:30 to 7:30 p. m.—Concert, 100th Grenadier Guards Band, Winnipeg.

7:30 to 7:45 p. m.—Parade, 100th Grenadier Guards Band.

7:45 to 8:00 p. m.—Parade, Minneapolis Working Boys Band.

8:00 to 8:15 p. m.—Butts' Manual Drill, First Minnesota Infantry.

8:15 to 8:20 p. m.—Patriotic Tableaux, "The Call to the Colors."

8:20 to 10:00 p. m.—European Hippodrome and production of the spectacle "Modern Warfare," with a special vaudeville entertainment and fireworks program.

10:00 p. m.—Lawrence Brown, aviator, night flight, with fireworks effect.

# The Minneapolis Morning Tribune

Fifty-first Year. No. 169. Associated Press. United Press. MINNEAPOLIS, MINN., FRIDAY, NOVEMBER 9, 1917 International News Service. Price One Cent in Minneapolis.

# *Russian Warship Bombards Capital; Kerensky Flees*

## Italians Continue Retreat as Foes Cross Livenza

Teutons in Venetia Hard on Heels of Cadorna's Armies.

SEVENTEEN THOUSAND MORE MEN CAPTURED

Berlin Says Prisoners in Drive to Date Total 250,000.

(International News Service.)

London, Nov. 9.—The Teutons have crossed the Livenza, the second Venetian stream on which the Italians were expected to make a stand. Rome conceded yesterday that the Italian retreat westward continues.

"The larger units" said the Italian official bulletin, "are retiring unmolested."

A quarter of a million prisoners had been taken by the Teutons, Berlin announced. Seventeen thousand of Cadorna's troops were cut off and captured on the Tagliamento. The Teutons are hard on the heels of Cadorna's armies. Alarm increased here yesterday for the safety of his forces that fought originally in the Carnic Alps and the Dolomites. The Teuton advance is so swift that it is feared the bulk of these northern Italian armies may have been cut off. The situation on the Trentino front is still stationary.

**Next River Ten Miles Away.**

The next river—the last before Venetia is reached—is the Piava, running parallel with the Livenza at a distance of about 10 miles.

General von Buelow's army, the Teuton center, is driving on relentlessly, continuing to threaten the Italian armies with being split. The retreating front narrows as the armies approach southern Venetia. Stubborn rear guard action are fought by Cadorna's troops. Italian aircraft continue to do valuable work in hampering the pursuing foe. Five Teuton airplanes were brought down within the last 24 hours.

### *Italians Still Retreating Across Venetian Plains.*

*(By Associated Press.)*

There has been no cessation in the retreat of the Italians across the Venetian plains toward the new line of defense on which it is purposed to stand and face the invading Germans and Austro-Hungarians. The larger units of the Italians are falling back without molestation, according to the Rome official communication, but considerable fighting has taken place in the hills of Vittorio and at other points in the north.

The Berlin war office says that on the middle Tagliamento river Italian troops who were still standing out against the invaders were captured. A general and 17,000 additional Italian troops are reported to have been captured, bringing the total prisoners since the retreat from the Isonzo began to more than 250,000, according to Berlin. It is asserted also that in excess of 2,300 guns have fallen into the hands of the Teutonic allies.

Along the line in France and Belgium only artillery duels and raiding operations between the French and

(Continued on Page 2, Col. 2.)

## First Minneapolitan Gives Life in France

Harold M. Barber Dies of Heart Failure Due to Over-Exertion.

Harold M. Barber, 21 years old, son of R. R. Barber, 3045 Humboldt avenue south, died in line of duty on November 5 of acute dilation of the heart, General Pershing advised the War department yesterday. Young Barber was a private in Battery D, 151st Field artillery (First Minnesota Field artillery), and is the first member of a Minneapolis contingent to die while in France.

Darrell Barber, a younger brother, is a member of the same contingent and enlisted at the same time as Harold. Both graduates of West High school.

Harold Barber was well known in Minneapolis as a prominent high school athlete. He played football and baseball on the West High school teams for three years and was also a hockey player. He was graduated from high school in January, 1915, and was president of his class.

Barber enlisted in Battery D on April 13, shortly after the declaration of war. While the contingent was in training at Long Island he was elected captain of the battery football team and practiced at night. Doctors say that overexertion, caused by military training during the daytime and football practice at night, may have been the cause of his death.

Barber is survived by his parents, his brother and his wife, to whom he was married shortly after enlisting. She was formerly Miss Vera Chandler, daughter of Mr. and Mrs. W. A. Chandler, 2024 Emerson avenue south.

### WOUNDED MINNESOTAN ON CANADIAN LIST

Ottawa, Ont., Nov. 9.—Among American names appearing in yesterday's casualty list as wounded is that of G. Anderson, French River, Minn.

**MINNESOTA WEATHER.**

Fair today and tomorrow; not much change in temperature.

## *Doubt Shadows Ohio Prohibition Voting; Wets Again Lead*

Incomplete Official Returns Give Majority of 588 for Liquor.

*(By Associated Press.)*

CINCINNATI, Nov. 9.—At the end of the second day following the prohibition election in Ohio the result of whether the citizens would be subjected to a wet or a dry state was still in doubt, but with complete returns from the 88 counties, 67 of which had turned in official reports, the wets were leading by a majority of 3,643 on the face of the returns.

This figure, however, included a gain of 1,832 wet votes in Hamilton county, officially counted by the board of elections, which had not been reported to the secretary of state yesterday.

An announcement made by Secretary of State Fulton from figures compiled in his office gave the wets a majority of 588. These figures included all except one county and the 1,832 gained in the unofficial vote of Hamilton county.

## Farmers Do War Bit With Record U. S. Corn Crop

66,000,000 Bushels More Grown Than Ever Before, Government Says.

POTATO ESTIMATE SETS NEW RECORD

Poor Weather Spoils 20 Per Cent of Corn of Nation.

Washington, D. C., Nov. 9.—**A summary of preliminary estimates of crop production for the state of Minnesota, as compiled by the Bureau of Crop Estimates, United States Department of Agriculture, is as follows:**

Corn—Production this year, 86,900,000 bushels; last year (December estimate), 84,420,000 bushels.

Wheat—This year, 66,470,000 bushels; last year (December estimate), 27,558,000 bushels.

Oats—This year, 123,025,000 bushels; last year (December estimate), 88,112,000 bushels.

Barley—This year, 35,232,000 bushels; last year (December estimate), 26,125,000 bushels.

Rye—This year 6,435,000 bushels; last year (December estimate), 5,025,000 bushels.

Flaxseed—This year, 2,600,000 bushels; last year (December estimate), 2,338,000 bushels.

Potatoes—This year, 34,500,000 bushels; last year (December estimate), 16,800,000 bushels.

All Hay—This year, 5,197,000 tons; last year (December estimate), 6,384,000 tons.

Apples—This year, 482,000 barrels of 3 bushels; last year (December estimate), 422,000 barrels.

*(By Associated Press.)*

Washington, Nov. 9.—A corn crop, larger by more than 66,000,000 bushels than ever before grown in the history of American agriculture, is the production of the farmers of the United States this year. The Department of Agriculture yesterday in its preliminary estimate of the crop placed the quantity at 3,191,083,000 bushels.

Conditions since the October forecast caused a reduction of about 19,700,000 bushels in the indicated output.

Potatoes also are a record crop with a total of 439,686,000 bushels, but unfavorable weather late in the season caused a reduction of 13,000,000 bushels.

Tobacco production is a record.

**Largest Ever Recorded.**

"The corn crop of 1917 is notable as occupying the largest acreage and producing the largest total crop of record," said a statement of the Department of Agriculture. The yield per acre, however, is not exceptional owing to an unfavorable season, characterized by a late spring, a cold summer which was also too dry over much of the corn belt and early and damaging frosts and freezes, the season being thus shortened at both ends. Thus, unhappily, the bountiful crop contains much corn that did not fully mature, probably in excess of 20 per cent, although most of this had reached the dough state making it useful for silos and early feeding. Corn quality was

(Continued on Page 5, Col. 1.)

## 9,000,000 Men to Tell U. S. If Eligible for War

New Regulation Ordering Personal History Report to Come Next Week.

RADICAL CHANGES IN DRAFT SYSTEM

Married Men to Be Exempt Until Pressure Is Greater.

(International News Service.)

Washington, Nov. 9.—Nine million men will be called upon within the next week to state their personal history in order that their availability for military service may be ascertained.

Secretary of War Baker announced yesterday that the new regulations for classifying the registered men not drawn in the first call have been completed and will be promulgated within a day or two. The revised regulations as they will be made public are radically different in several respects from the tentative list of five classes made public by Provost Marshal General Crowder in his first announcement of the reorganization of the draft system about a month ago.

The principal change, it was indicated yesterday, is the practical determination of the government to place all married men in the non-belligerent class.

Only men whose physical resources or whose family resources would guarantee their dependents a living during their absence will be liable to service in the field. In the overwhelming majority of cases, however, married men will be entirely exempt from military service unless the war should take a turn which would necessitate the mobilization of every able bodied man in the nation—a circumstance not considered by the authorities in the present light of the war situation, serious as it is.

## 21 on U. S. Ship Given Up as Dead

Admiral Sims Cables Hunt for Survivors of Alcedo Is Abandoned.

*(By Associated Press.)*

Washington, Nov. 9.—All hope for the safety of Lieut. John T. Melvin and the 20 enlisted men, reported missing after the torpedoing of the American patrol ship Alcedo, has been abandoned. Vice Admiral Sims cabled the Navy department yesterday that the search for survivors of the Alcedo had been given up and that it was believed most of the missing men had been killed outright by the explosion of the torpedo.

Secretary Daniels authorized this statement:

"The Navy department has received a report from Vice Admiral Sims stating that no trace had been found of the one officer and 20 men reported missing after the sinking of the American patrol vessel Alcedo. Several vessels which were searching for possible survivors have given up the search. It is believed that most of the missing men were killed by the explosion of the torpedo."

The Alcedo, a converted yacht, was torpedoed and sunk by a submarine early Monday morning, being the first American warship to go down since the war began. No details have been made public.

## Federal Agents Seize Wireless Near Norwich

Norwich, Conn., Nov. 9.—A complete wireless receiving outfit has been discovered near here by federal agents, it became known last night, and confiscated by the government. The owner and operator of the outfit was not arrested.

**Convict Slain in Flight.**

Lexington, Ky., Nov. 9.—Seizing a huge lock from a cell door, Calvin Yancy, convict from Christian county, yesterday attempted to beat down Eddyville penitentiary guards and escape. He was shot and killed as he fled.

## *Ministers Condemn Use of Tobacco by Soldiers*

***Minneapolis Pastors Favor Concerted Action to Stop "Great Economic Waste"—Proposed Church Federation Approved.***

Smoking or the use of tobacco by soldiers was condemned at great length yesterday afternoon by the Federation of Minneapolis Ministers at a meeting held at Joyce Memorial M. E. church. The meeting was called to discuss whether Minneapolis should have a federation of churches. After a long discussion on the merits of tobacco using by soldiers and civilians the resolution regarding the federation of churches was adopted by unanimous vote.

**Tobacco Condemned by All Who Spoke.**

None of the ministers who spoke on the subject of tobacco defended it; there was no difference of opinion. All were in favor of concerted action by the churches of Minneapolis on "this great economic waste."

"When the Red Cross sends a package to a soldier it always includes tobacco in some form," said the Rev. J. T. Bergen. "Of course the Red Cross is not a religious organization nor does it profess to be, but by the sending of tobacco to our boys in France they are slowly but surely destroying the morale as well as the morale of the army."

"Last night I returned from Fort Snelling, where I had been visiting some of the soldiers," began the Rev. Stanley Roberts. "When I got into the house I was forced to cleanse my hair and mustache of the cigaret odor,

(Continued on Page 5, Col. 2.)

## Argentine Army Mobilizes; Brazil Fears Trouble

Officials See Renewal of Hostilities Over Old Boundary Dispute.

SCOFF AT EXCUSE OF ACT AGAINST GERMANS

South American Republic Pestered With Work of Foe Propagandists.

*(By Associated Press.)*

Santa Anna De Livramento, Brazil, Nov. 9.—In the midst of its preparation for participation in the war with Germany, Brazil is confronted with a new crisis.

Persistent reports that Argentine is mobilizing at Libres and Santo Tome, near the southern Brazilian frontier, has led to open expectancy of a clash between the two nations.

Officials scoff at Argentine's excuse that the mobilization is precautionary against a German uprising in Brazil and fear a renewal of hostilities over the old boundary dispute concerning the Missiones province, which was settled some years ago by President Cleveland.

The government is maintaining strong forces throughout the affected district and Brazilians are declared to be anxious for action against the Argentine troops.

The municipal authorities believe that the settlement of the general strike which has been in progress here for some time is only temporary and that the Germans are fomenting a new walkout.

The strike just settled was the third to come in quick succession, and, like the other, it greatly interfered with the shipment of foodstuffs and other supplies to the Entente Allies. Officials believe these strikes are part of a revolutionary movement.

Among other internal problems Brazil is faced by a renewal of active propaganda by the monarchists, especially in the Rio Grande de Sul and Porto Alegro districts and which also is active here.

Brazil has prohibited entrance into the country of Uruguayan Germans. It is reported here that a national decree has been issued, suspending the constitutional rights of Germans. The decree is expected to cause a new outburst in the German provinces.

## Woman Sculptor Will Mend Mutilated Faces

War Department Accepts Mrs. Ladd's Services in Eliminating Trace of War Wounds.

*(By Associated Press.)*

New York, Nov. 9.—Mrs. Anna Coleman Ladd, a Boston sculptor, announced yesterday that the War department at Washington had accepted an offer of her services in France in reconstructing the features of soldiers whose faces have been marred by wounds. Mrs. Ladd is the wife of Dr. Maynard Ladd, who now is in France giving special aid to children. She said she would leave for France as soon as orders are issued by the War department.

Mrs. Ladd's plan, which was submitted to Maj. V. P. Blair of the War department is to obtain a photograph of a wounded soldier which was taken before his face was mutilated. A plaster of paris cast of his marred face would then be taken, she explained, from which she would model with clay a cast of his features as shown in the photograph. From the completed cast a copper plate mask, silvered and painted flesh color would be made, which would be held in place in spectacle frames. Major Blair praised the proposal, Mrs. Ladd said, and suggested that the work be extended to the Allies' armies.

## Great Britain Approves Zionist Palestine Plan

*(By Associated Press.)*

London, Nov. 9.—Arthur J. Balfour, secretary of state for foreign affairs, has written the following letter to Lord Rothchild expressing the government's sympathy with the Zionist movement.

"The government views with favor the establishment of Palestine as a national home for the Jewish people and will use its best endeavors to facilitate the achievement of this object, it being clearly understood that nothing will be done that may prejudice the civil or religious rights of existing non-Jewish communities in Palestine."

## First Election Arrests Made in Philadelphia

Philadelphia, Nov. 9.—Frank G. Smith, a Vare-Republican leader, was arrested here yesterday afternoon and held in heavy bail in the first of a series of arrests promised by the town meeting party for irregularities at Tuesday's election. The entire election board of one division was likewise taken into custody.

**Mail Clerks Join A. F. of L.**

Portsmouth, N. H., Nov. 9.—The Railway Mail Clerks association has voted to affiliate with the American Federation of Labor. The result of the recent referendum ballot was announced here last night as 6,827 in favor of joining the federation to 2,072 against.

# Rebels in Complete Control of Petrograd After Battle in Harbor

## Washington Sees Korniloff Now Kerensky's Hope

Expectation New Revolt Will Be Short, Based on Cossack Power.

NO OFFICIAL NEWS REACHED U. S. YET

Feared Much Bloodshed Is Certain Before Order Is Restored.

*(By Associated Press.)*

Washington, Nov. 9.—Discouragement here over the news of the overthrow of the Kerensky government at Petrograd is tempered by the hope that the extreme Radicals who have seized the capital may not be able to extend their control over the army or any considerable part of the country. However, it is feared that much blood must be shed and the nation further demoralized before any power rises above the turmoil strong enough to control the situation.

Both the State department and the Russian embassy still were without official advices last night. Consequently there was no official comment on the situation. It was pointed out that with the telegraph lines and the semi-official news agency at Petrograd in the hands of the Radicals, it would be difficult to learn the true state of affairs.

Whether this control of the channels of information will extend to interference with dispatches, which Ambassador Francis and other diplomatic representatives undoubtedly are seeking to send their government, is not known.

**Korniloff Holds Key.**

The suggestion that the new power at Petrograd may be short-lived is based to an extent upon the fact that the Cossacks, the best military force in Russia, though extremely jealous of their own local liberties, always have been reckoned upon to support a strong conservative government. It was conceived in some quarters that if Kerensky, fleeing from the capital, should be able to bring to his support General Korniloff, the strong man of the Russian army, with his Cossack backers, he might set up a new and stronger government at Moscow, where he could count upon the loyalty of a majority of the large population of that ancient capital.

An obstacle to the success of such a plan is found in the popular belief that General Korniloff, embittered by the treatment he had received at the hands of Kerensky when the latter was vacillating between the Radicals and the Conservatives, might refuse to risk his future further upon such an uncertain leader. Some officials think this compromising by Kerensky was largely responsible for his disaster.

In view of the intensity of the democratic spirit developed in Russia since the overthrow of the czar, it is regarded here as difficult to conceive of the appearance of any other form of government than a republic, yet in diplomatic circles where the peculiarity of the Russian masses is well understood, the opinion is expressed that out of sheer weariness with revolutions and anarchy, the majority of the people might suddenly decide to confide their destinies in a dictator, thereby following the footsteps of the Radicals in the French revolution.

**Winter Would Balk Teutons.**

Recalling that even the Bolshevikis themselves have declared for "a democratic peace," which is opposed to the German idea, it is believed to be hardly possible that on this basis Germany could entertain proposals from the Maximalists for either a peace or an armistice.

It is pointed out, too, that even if the Germans did make a separate peace with the Maximalists, the fact that this party represents only a small section of the Russian people would make it necessary for the Central powers to continue to maintain a large military force on the border to guard against an offensive from the other element. Therefore, it is hoped that the military situation will not change materially for the worse for the Entente powers and America as a result of these latest developments. If any considerable portion of the Russian army can be kept in the trenches, the advent of winter will operate to prevent the German troops who face them from taking advantage of any temporary weakness to start an offensive.

## Virginia Teacher Beaten for Asking Food Pledge

Virginia, Minn., Nov. 9.—Miss Ruth Butler, a Virginia school teacher, was attacked and severely beaten about the face while circulating a Hoover pledge card here yesterday. P. P. Colgrove, superintendent of the local schools, swore out a warrant which caused the arrest of Mrs. Peter Shugel in connection with the affair.

Charles Jacobson, an I. W. W. leader under indictment by the federal grand jury in Chicago, refused to sign a pledge card here and ordered Miss Lillian Shapiro from his home. Jacobson did not purchase Liberty bonds and has received two "death threats" in the last month.

**Half Million Given 'Y' War Work.**

New York, Nov. 9.—The subsidiary companies of the United States Steel corporation yesterday subscribed $[illegible]600 to the new $35,000,000 war fund of the Y. M. C. A.

Military Revolutionary Committee Issues Proclamation Calling for Immediate Peace; Threatens to Arrest All Who Hamper Plans

*POWERFUL HUN FLEET REACHES FINN CAPITAL*

*(By Associated Press.)*

**Petrograd, Nov. 9.—Government forces holding the Winter Palace were compelled to capitulate yesterday morning under the fire of the cruiser Aurora and the cannon of the St. Peter and St. Paul fortress across the Neva river. At 2 o'clock yesterday morning the woman's batallion, which had been defending the Winter Palace, surrendered.**

**The workmen's and soldiers' delegates are in complete control of the city.**

At Sveaborg, the sea fortress protecting the Finnish capital, Helsingfors, a powerful German fleet has arrived. Little or no resistance is looked for from the Finns. Helsingfors taken, a German army could be landed, and with Finnish acquiescence or even support, march northward and take Petrograd by land.

With the utter confusion among Russia's fighting forces, a simultaneous naval drive up the Gulf of Finland would be an easy matter. Marching northward from Petrograd, the Germans, under such a plan, would take Archangel, and the isolation of the Muscovite realm from the west would be complete.

Premier Kerensky has fled. He is reported to be at Luga, 85 miles southwest of Petrograd. At the winter palace, before its capitulation, it was said that the premier had gone to the front.

M. Kishkin, minister of public welfare, to whom Kerensky delegated authority, has been arrested, as have also M. I. Terestchelko, minister of foreign affairs; M. Malyantovitch, minister of justice and M. Nikitin, minister of the interior. An order for Kerensky's arrest has been issued by Maximilists.

**Winter Palace is Besieged.**

Late Wednesday evening, after the government forces had been driven into the winter palace, the palace was besieged and a lively fight of machine guns and rifles began. The cruiser Aurora, which was moored at the Nicolai bridge, moved up within range, firing shrapnel. Meanwhile the guns of the St. Peter and St. Paul fortress opened fire.

The palace stood out under the glare of the searchlights of the cruiser and offered a good target for the guns. The defenders held out for four hours, replying as best they could.

There was spasmodic firing in other parts of the city, but the workmen's and soldiers' troops took every means to protect citizens, who were ordered to their quarters. The bridges and the Nevsky prospect, which early in the afternoon were in the hands of the government forces, were captured and held during the night by the workmen's and soldiers troops.

**Battle Spectacular One.**

The battle at the palace was a spectacular one, armed cars of the revolutionaries swinging into action in front of the palace gates, while ashes from the Neva were followed by the explosion of shells from the guns of the Aurora.

The general congress of workmen's and soldiers' delegates of all Russia is in convention here with 560 delegates in attendance. The chairman declared that the time was propitious for political speeches and the order of business of the congress ordered approved was as follows:

First, organization of power.

Second, peace and war.

Third, a constituent assembly.

The officers elected comprise 14 Maximalists, including Nikolai Lenine, the Radical Socialist leader, and M. Zinovieff, an associate of Lenine and Leon Trotzky, president of the central executive committee of the Petrograd council of workmen's and soldiers' delegates. In addition seven revolutionary Socialists were appointed.

**Immediate Peace Is Plan.**

Of the 560 members of the workmen's and soldiers' congress 250 are Bolsheviki, 150 Socialist revolutionists, 60 Maximalists and 14 of the Maximalist-Internationalist group, six of the Nationalist-Socialist group, three non-party Socialists, the others being independent.

A resolution proposed by the Maximalists that an effort should be made to reach an agreement with the provisional government was voted down.

Vice President Cameneff of the workmen's and soldiers' delegates told the Associated Press yesterday that the object of taking possession of the posts and telegraphs was to thwart any effort the government might make to call troops to the capital.

The Russkia Volia and the Bourse Gazette have been commandeered by the workmen and soldiers' delegates.

A delegation was named to initiate peace negotiations with the other revolutionary and democratic organizations "with a view to taking steps to stop bloodshed."

**Three Proclamations Issued.**

The official news agency made public the following statement:

"The congress of the councils of workmen's and soldiers' delegates of all Russia, which opened Wednesday evening, issued yesterday the three following proclamations:

"To all provincial councils of workmen's and soldiers' and peasants' delegates:

"All power lies in the workmen's and soldiers' delegates. Government commissaries are relieved of their functions. Presidents of the workmen's and soldiers' delegates are to communicate direct with the revolutionary government. All members of agricultural committees who have been arrested are to be set at liberty immediately and the commissioners who arrested them are in turn to be arrested."

The second proclamation follows:

"The death penalty re-established at

## New Slav Power Menace to U. S., Says Russ Envoy

Ambassador Believes Kerensky Government Will Survive Ordeal.

*(By Associated Press.)*

Memphis, Tenn., Nov. 9.—In an address here last night, Boris A. Bakhemetieff, the Russian ambassador, declared that if Russia is to achieve her political freedom the Maximalists who revolted against the Kerensky provisional government at Petrograd must be overthrown. Immediate peace, such as the Maximalists propose, he said, could result only in Russian oppression.

Bakhemetieff announced he had canceled all other speaking engagements and would return to Washington immediately. He said the crisis that has developed in his country demands his presence there.

He expressed the belief that the Kerensky government will survive, and that "we will go on with you and the Allies with this fight for democracy." He declared that the new power that has sprung up in Russia is a menace not only to Russia but to the United States and the Allies.

## Suffrage Pickets Fed by Tube in Hospital

Miss Alice Paul and Comrade Offer No Resistance to Efforts of Physicians.

(International News Service.)

Washington, Nov. 9.—Miss Alice Paul, chairman of the National Woman's party, was fed by means of a tube in the mouth late yesterday by the District of Columbia jail hospital physicians to save her from the results of her hunger strike since Monday.

Miss Rose Winslow of New York, another one of the suffrage picket prisoners, also has been fed by tube. Both had refused food the preceding 72 hours as a part of their attempt to force assent to their demands that milk and eggs be granted all the suffrage prisoners as part of the prison diet, or that they be allowed to buy the eggs and milk.

Dr. James Hannon, physician at the jail, made this statement last night: "Miss Paul was tube-fed at 3 o'clock this afternoon. There is a distinction between that and forcible feeding. Miss Paul swallowed the tube without trouble and without resistance. We were not compelled to use force.

"Miss Rose Winslow has received the same treatment as has Miss Paul. Each will receive through the tube a pint of milk with two eggs, two teaspoonfuls of sugar and a pinch of salt, three times a day."

## Pro-Germans Forced to Quit Public Positions

Billings, Mont., Nov. 9.—In a roundup of alleged pro-Germans and financial slackers here last night, a delegation of citizens headed by the "Third Degree" committee, appointed incident to the Liberty Loan campaign, forced Curtis C. Oehme, a local architect, to resign as a member of the state board of architectural examiners and also forced the resignation of Alderman Herman Schwanz as a member of the city council.

Accompanied by the "Third Degree" committee, Oehme was escorted to a telegraph office, where he wired his resignation to Governor Stewart. Schwanz tendered his resignation at a special meeting of the city council last night. No acts of violence attended the demonstration.

## Austrian Kaiser Honors German Leaders in Italy

*(By Associated Press.)*

Amsterdam, Nov. 9.—A Vienna dispatch says that in recognition of the successes won on the Italian front, Emperor Charles has made General von Korbatin a field marshal, has conferred on Duke Eugene and Field Marshal von Hindenburg the brilliants of the cross of the Military Order of the First Class, with the war decoration, and has awarded to General von Buelow the grand cross of the Order of Leopold, with war decorations.

# The Minneapolis Morning Tribune

Fifty-first Year. No. 232. Associated Press. United Press. MINNEAPOLIS, MINN., FRIDAY, JANUARY 11, 1918 International News Service. Price TWO CENTS

# Woman Suffrage Measure Wins in House, 274 to 136

## Slavs Agree Not to Shift Parleys, One Report Says

At London Hear ...ky Says Failure to ...fer Means War.

BOLSHEVIKI DECREE TO CANCEL NATION'S DEBT

Germans Request Sweden to Act as Go-Between With Allies.

(By Associated Press.)

Amsterdam, Jan. 11.—The Russian delegation at Brest-Litovsk has announced its readiness to continue the peace negotiations at that place, according to the latest information received here.

In this decision the Germans have scored a big victory, as it was the insistence of the Bolsheviki that the meeting place be moved to Stockholm, which recently caused the break in negotiations.

**Another Report Contradictory.**

London, Jan. 11.—Unofficial reports received here concerning the first session of the peace conference at Brest-Litovsk, which was resumed Tuesday with Leon Trotzky, the Bolsheviki foreign minister, at the head of the Russian delegates, say that Trotzky, in a speech insisted on a removal of the conference to Stockholm. Trotzky declared the Russians came to Brest-Litovsk not as the representatives of a conquered country and did not intend to ask for pity, but would continue to act as true revolutionists. He is reported to have told the German and Austrian delegates that if they did not accede to his request they would feel the weight of the voice of the democracies of the Teutonic powers and the weight of arms of the Russian democracy.

**German Reply Evasive.**

The Evening Post asserts that the Germans replied that they did not decline to carry on the peace negotiations, but that they failed to specify where.

The Russian delegation at Brest-Litovsk includes, in addition to Trotzky, who is serving as its president, one woman, Madame Bithenko, a former exile, and M. Joffe, M. Kameneff, M. Pokrovsky and three counselors.

Nikolai Lenine, the Bolsheviki premier, has gone to a Finland sanitarium for several days' rest.

**Bolsheviki Plan to Cancel Debt.**

The Bolsheviki government intends to publish a decree within a few days, canceling the Russian national debt, telegraphs the correspondent at Petrograd of the Manchester Guardian. The correspondent understands the decree will contain these provisions:

First—All loans and treasury bonds held by foreign subjects abroad or in Russia are repudiated.

Second—Loans and treasury bonds held by Russian subjects possessing more than 10,000 rubles in capital are repudiated.

Third—Loans and treasury bonds held by Russian subjects possessing capital in loan scrip or deposits not exceeding 1,000 rubles are to receive 5 per cent interest on the nominal value of the loan, and those possessing 10,000 rubles are to receive 3 per cent.

Fourth—Workmen and peasants holding 100 rubles worth of loans or bonds may sell their holding to the state at 75 per cent of its nominal value. Those holding 600 rubles worth may sell it at 70 per cent of its nominal value.

**Sweden Sought as Intermediary.**

From Petrograd comes a report based on a newspaper statement that representatives of Germany now in Petrograd are seeking to have Sweden act as a means of communication with Great Britain, France and Italy. The German delegations in Petrograd were understood originally to have been charged only with commercial and other similar negotiations outside the realm of major political affairs.

Bulgaria and Russia have concluded a separate peace according to circumstantial advices by way of Switzerland.

If a separate adjustment between these nations has been reached it seems probable that it was because Bulgaria found no difficulty in subscribing to the Bolsheviki formula of no annexations and no indemnities so far as Russia was concerned. Bulgaria has desired no Russian territory seeking her acquisitions from Roumania and Serbia. It was for Serbia's assistance, however, that Russia prepared for war under the old regime, her mobilization after Austria had threatened Serbia being made the occasion for Germany's declaration of war.

**Turkish Proposal Rejected.**

According to yesterday's advices the Bolsheviki have declined to entertain Turkey's peace proposal requesting the Turks to participate in the general peace conference between the Central Powers and Russia.

Meanwhile, fighting continues in central and southwestern Russia between the Bolshevik forces and the Cossacks of General Kaledines and General Dutoff. The latest accounts of these operations indicate that the Bolsheviki for the time being have the upper hand, both Kaledines and Dutoff having been compelled to flee after defeats in battle.

**Dividends Taxable Income.**

Washington, Jan. 11.—Stock dividends will be included in taxable income, the internal revenue bureau announced yesterday, despite the supreme court's decision that dividends are not taxable under the 1913 income tax law.

**MINNESOTA WEATHER.**

Generally fair today, colder in east portion; tomorrow probably unsettled, continued cold.

## Trotzky Will Tell of Aims and Policies of Bolsheviki Exclusively in The Tribune

LEON TROTZKY.

### "The Bolsheviki and World Peace."

THE Minneapolis Tribune is going to give the people of Minneapolis and the Northwest their first authentic information about Leon Trotzky, the dominant figure in Russia today, and aims and purposes of the Bolsheviki.

Trotzky is giving his message to the world in form of a series of articles that constitute the most sensational and striking document of the world war, up to date.

Six months ago Trotzky was living in a New York tenement, working as a journalist to pay off small debts. Today the fate of Russia is in his hands and success of his efforts may work a world revolution, not against any one government but against all governments.

To undertand the war, you must understand Russia. To understand Russia, you must read Trotzky's message.

Trotzky's message will be published in The Minneapolis Tribune, beginning Sunday, January 13, and every morning thereafter until the series is concluded.

You cannot read this epochal story except in The Minneapolis Tribune.

## Prosecution of Men Who Burned Kaiser's Picture Is Frowned On by State

Attorney General Advises Hawley Prosecutor Not to Aid Citizen Whose House Was Entered and Whose Prize Possession Destroyed.

Bewailing the act that his official opportunities of showing patriotism were "only too few," Attorney General Smith late yesterday advised against the prosecution of five Hawley men for breaking into a man's house and destroying a picture of the kaiser and his royal family.

"I do not sympathize with any violations of law," he said, in his formal opinion, "but am of the opinion that at the present time it would not be advisable to bring charges against persons who, through excess of loyalty and zeal, without wisdom, have taken a picture of the kaiser and destroyed it.

**Prosecutor Asks Advice.**

"It is a time when the repression of men who think that a 25-cent picture of the kaiser is worth $100 is more in keeping with American citizenship than is the arrest and trial of persons who have destroyed such pictures."

The opinion followed a request from C. G. Dosland, county attorney of Clay county, for advice as to the advisability of beginning prosecutions demanded by George H. Peters of Hawley against other residents of that town. The complainant's statement, which accompanied the request, involved the well known "John Doe" and Alfred Hagen, Richard Wouters, Donald McDonald, Henry Burrill and Clifford Baske.

**House Entered, Picture Taken.**

Peters' complaint charges his home was entered, through use of a skeleton key, January 4, while his family was away. He also alleges that a picture of the imperial German family was torn from the wall, removed from a glass-covered frame, and later burned in a bonfire on Hawley streets. He placed a valuation of $100 on the picture, and adds that its greatest value was through long association with it. Its intrinsic value, he says, when he obtained it as a premium with a Chicago newspaper, 27 years ago, probably was 25 cents.

## U. S. Packing Probe Will Open in St. Paul Monday

Washington, Jan. 11.—Commissioner Joseph E. Davies and Francis J. Heney, special counsel, left yesterday for St. Paul, Minn., where hearings will begin Monday in the Federal Trade commission's investigation into the meat packing industry. Other Middle Western towns probably will be visited when the St. Paul hearings are concluded.

## No Court Martial; Camp Dodge Record Praised By Baker

War Secretary Thanks Commander for Remarkable Showing of Draft Men.

(By Associated Press.)

Washington, Jan. 11.—Secretary Baker has expressed to the commander of the 352nd infantry regiment, National army, Camp Dodge, Iowa, through Adjutant General McCain, his appreciation of the remarkable record of the command in having had no court martial case or incident requiring court martial proceedings from the time of its organization up to November 24.

The division commander has been authorized to publish the regiment's record in general orders.

Writing to the regimental commander, General McCain said the record "reflects credit upon the drafted men as indicating a high spirit of obedient service."

## American Army, 1,539,506 Men, Baker Reveals

Secretary of War Declares No Other Army Ever Raised So Fast.

'SUBSTANTIAL' FORCE IN FRANCE, HE SAYS

Investigators Surprised to Learn Supply Committee Is No More.

Washington, Jan. 11.—The American army which is to be sent into the battle to make the world safe for democracy is rapidly being formed. In the nine months since the United States declared that a state of war existed with Germany the army has risen from 212,034 officers and men to 1,539,506 officers and men.

This statement was made yesterday by Secretary of War Baker who declared that no other army in the history of the world had ever been raised, equipped or trained so quickly.

The Secretary added that a "substantial" force of Americans already was in France and fit for active service and that full equipment is on hand for every man who will be sent to Europe during 1918.

**Every Phase Outlined.**

Every phase of the War department's preparations for battle against Germany was outlined and defended by Secretary Baker before the Senate military committee. He answered those who have criticised the department during the committee's investigation with the assertion that no army such as that now under the American flag ever had been raised, equipped or trained so quickly and that never before had such provision been made for the comfort and health of an army.

The Secretary read an exhaustive prepared statement when he took the stand and was not interrupted until it was concluded. Then questions began to fly from every side of the committee table, launching a cross-examination that was not concluded at adjournment last night and probably will continue all day today.

**Some Mistakes Admitted.**

Chairman Chamberlain and other committeemen wanted to know particularly about delays in furnishing machine guns and rifles and much attention was devoted to the army's supply purchasing system. Mr. Baker admitted there had been some mistakes and and delays, but declared that all fighting men in France were adequately equipped and armed and all that were sent over would be. He took full responsibility for delay in approving a machine gun, holding that the value of the Browning gun now developed was worth it. He also said the superior weapon obtained by having the British Enfield rifle rechambered for American ammunition compensated for the delay there.

**Committee Abandoned, He Says.**

It was revealed to the surprise of everyone that Mr. Baker had abandoned the system of purchasing army supplies through the supply committee of the Council of National Defense and that the committee had been abolished.

When it was alleged that members of this committee had "sold to the government" the Secretary repeatedly insisted that he did not believe any such thing happened.

Members of the Senate committee were frank in their disapproval of the secret purchasing system of the department. They did not shake Mr. Baker's support of it, however. He insisted that it was essential to guard against publicity concerning plants engaged on war work.

(Secretary Baker's Statement on Page 11.)

## 400 French Women Next Boche Victims

Berlin Will Deport 600 Men, Too, From Alsace-Lorraine as "Reprisal."

(By Associated Press.)

London, Jan. 11.—A German official statement, according to an Amsterdam dispatch to the Central News says:

"As a reprisal for the retention of inhabitants of Alsace-Lorraine against the law of nations, 600 French will be conveyed to Russia from January 6 and, within a few days, 400 French women will be sent to the camp at Holzminden, (Duchy of Brunswick).

On fighting fronts, the infantry is inactive, except for small raiding operations, but artillery duels continue intense on various sectors.

In northern Italy snow has fallen to a depth of from three to five feet, bringing operations to a halt. Movement of supplies to enemy armies in the hills is greatly impeded, and indications at present are that fighting of great intensity will be impossible while the snow lies on the ground.

## Class 1 Men to Fight, Not to Be Staff Officers

Washington, Jan. 11.—Draft men placed in Class 1 will not be given commissions in the noncombatant arms of the service, under a resolution adopted by the war council and approved yesterday by Secretary Baker. It is the announced purpose of the War department to draw fighting men from this class of registrants and the department is said to be determined to prevent further inroads upon the nation's fighting material for staff positions, unless there is a substantial reason for exception in individual cases, due to special qualifications of the men involved.

## Suffrage Cause Also Victorious in House of Lords

LONDON, Jan. 11.—The House of Lords yesterday rejected Lord Loreburn's amendment to the representation of the people's bill, by which it was sought to exclude women from the suffrage. The vote against the amendment was 134 to 69.

Debate had lasted two days.

The debate showed one important convert to the women's cause, in the Bishop of London. But Earl Loreburn, the Marquis of Lansdowne, Baron Finlay and Earl Curzon strongly opposed placing the names of 6,000,000 women on the voting register.

## U. S. Destroyer Routs U-Boat; Saves 3 Ships

American Warship Opens Fire on Enemy Diver at Six Miles.

GERMANY NOW USES SUPER-SUBMARINES

Cruiser Type of Plunger Proves New Terror to Allied Shipping.

(By Associated Press.)

London, Jan. 11.—The submarine warfare has gradually taken on a new phase since the wintry weather set in. Submarines of the so-called cruiser type now are doing most of the sinkings, while the smaller submarines apparently are confining their work largely to mine laying.

The reason for this shifting of German technique is that small submarines are not good surface craft in stormy seas, while the cruiser type has proved wonderfully seaworthy, being actually more manageable than the modern torpedo boat destroyer in heavy weather. These cruiser submarines carry two 5.9 guns and 16 torpedoes and can remain at sea six weeks. The Germans have built a considerable number of these super-submarines since the first one visited American waters, but so many of them have been lost that there are now not more than seven or eight operating. These, however, are manned by the pick of the whole German navy, and their power for harm may be judged from the fact that these seven or eight vessels are able to keep up such a heavy toll of sinkings among Allied shipping.

**Most Sinkings by Gunfire.**

A considerable proportion of the recent sinkings have been accomplished by gunfire. The cruiser submarine guns no longer are of the old type, which folded into the body of the craft when it submerged and had to be unfolded before a U-boat could get into action. The new guns are of a species known technically as "wet guns," being constructed of material which sea water does not harm. They are mounted on stationary platforms. Therefore, they are always ready and can be fired the instant the deck of an emerging boat is above water.

An American torpedo boat destroyer had an encounter with one of these submarine cruisers a few days ago. The German was engaged in sinking three armed merchant men from a range of four miles and had fired about 30 shots when the American destroyer appeared on the horizon, attracted by the sound of the guns.

**Destroyer Opens Fire.**

The destroyer opened fire at six miles with the wonderful American naval guns. The U-boat, however, was lying with decks almost awash and therefore was a most difficult target and as the American drew in toward her at full speed she submerged suddenly. The smoking muzzles of her wet guns disappeared beneath the waves only an instant after their last shots had been fired.

The Americans were unable to destroy the U-boat, but the destroyer escorted two of the three merchantmen

(Continued on Page 2, Col. 3.)

## U. S. Limits Charity Sent Out of Country

Washington, Jan. 11.—The State department and the War board yesterday agreed to limit money sent out of the country for charity to $300,000 a month.

This will affect moneys intended for Palestine, for the Armenians and all similar purposes for which organized funds are sent abroad. They require a government war license.

## Virginia Senate Ratifies Federal Dry Amendment

(By Associated Press.)

Richmond, Va., Jan. 11.—The National prohibition amendment was ratified last night by the Virginia senate by a vote of 30 to 8. A resolution to submit the amendment to a referendum was defeated 28 to 10. It is expected that the house of delegates will vote today.

## Town in Ecuador Wiped Out by Volcano, Report

Guayaquil, Ecuador, Jan. 11.—The volcano of Tunguragua, in Central Ecuador, has been in eruption for several days, emitting showers of stones and ashes. It is reported that the town of Banos, at the foot of the volcano, has been destroyed.

## Exactly Required Number of Votes Cast for Victory

Champions Begin Fight for Favorable Action in Senate; Expect to Force Ballot Before End of Present Session.

ENFRANCHISEMENT IS SEEN IN TWO YEARS BY LEADERS

President's Support of Amendment Credited With Having Prompted "Ayes" From Many Democratic Congressmen.

(By Associated Press.)

Washington, Jan. 11.—Woman suffrage by federal constitutional amendment won in the House last night with exactly the required number of affirmative votes.

While members in their seats and throngs in the galleries waited with eager interest the House adopted by a vote of 274 to 136 a resolution providing for submission to the states of the so-called Susan B. Anthony amendment for national enfranchisement of women.

But for the promise of Speaker Clark to cast his vote from the chair for the resolution if it was needed, the change of a single vote to the opposition would have meant defeat. Republican Leader Mann, who came from a Baltimore hospital where he has been under treatment ever since Congress convened, and Representative Sims of Tennessee, just out of a sick bed and hardly able to walk to his seat, brought the votes which settled the issue.

**Fight Begins in Senate.**

The House hardly had adjourned before the suffrage champions began their fight for favorable action on the Senate side of the capitol. Recent polls there have indicated that the necessary two-thirds vote could not be mustered, but encouraged by the House victory and counting upon the influence of President Wilson who came to their support last night, the suffragists hope to bring the Senate into line so as to have the amendment before state legislatures during the coming year. They feel sure at least of forcing a vote in the Senate before the present session ends.

Advocates of the amendment had been supremely confident of the result in the House after President Wilson advised the members who called upon him Wednesday to support it. They were so confident that the close vote was received with amazement and some of the opponents were almost as much surprised. When the first roll was finished unofficial counts put the result in doubt, and before the speaker could make an announcement there was a demand for a recapitulation. Then the name of member and the way he was recorded was read.

Announcement of the vote was greeted with wild applause and cheering.

Women in the galleries literally fell upon each others' necks, kissing and embracing and shouting "Glory, glory, hallelujah."

The resolution, as adopted, follows:

"Joint resolution proposing an amendment to the Constitution of the United States extending the right of suffrage to women.

"Resolved, By the Senate and House, etc., two-thirds of each house concurring therein, that the following article be proposed to the legislatures of the several states as an amendment to the Constitution of the United States which, when ratified by three-fourths of said legislatures, shall be valid as part of said Constitution, namely:

"Article —. Section 1.—The right of citizens of the United States to vote shall not be denied or abridged by the United States or by any state on account of sex.

"Section 2—Congress shall have power, by appropriate legislation, to enforce the provisions of this article."

**Attempts to Amend Language.**

Every attempt made to amend this language was beaten. Representative Gard of Ohio tried unsuccessfully to put on it the same limitation carried by the resolution for the prohibition constitutional amendment, that it must be ratified by the states within seven years from the date of its submission. Representative Moores of Indiana sought to have a referendum or special convention in each state required. The Gard amendment was rejected 159 to 246 and the Moores amendment 131 to 272.

When the final vote came on the resolution Representative Austin of Tennessee challenged the vote of Representative Dominick of South Carolina, who appeared late in the roll call and said he had not heard his name called. Mr. Dominick told the speaker he was in the hall and listening and did not hear his name called. His vote was then recorded.

The speaker watched the vote, prepared to cast his own into the breach if necessary.

"One more negative vote," he explained afterward, as he chuckled over the victory," would have changed the situation and the amendment resolution would have been lost in which event I would have directed the clerk to call my name and that would have been sufficient to carry it."

**410 Members Voted.**

Of the total membership of 435 there were 410 members who voted. Their line-up follows:

For the resolution, Democrats, 104; Republicans, 165; miscellaneous, 5; total, 274.

Against the resolution, Democrats, 102; Republicans, 33; Progressive, 1; total, 136.

Urgent orders had been given by the leaders to bring in everybody possible. When Representative Mann walked slowly to his accustomed place as leader of the Republicans, applause rang over the house, members from all sides rushed over to him and Speaker Clark broke a precedent by announcing from

## Suffragists Here See Sure Victory for Equal Rights

Confident Next Minnesota Legislature Will Ratify Amendment.

Delighted over the House adoption yesterday of the Susan B. Anthony amendment, Minneapolis Suffragists see certain success for nation-wide equal suffrage. In their opinion, the Senate is practically certain to follow suit, and the necessary majority of states to ratify the amendment. They said work would start at once to obtain Minnesota's endorsement and felt confident it would come at the next session of the Legislature.

Monday Suffragists of the state will celebrate the congressional action. At 12:15 p.m. at state headquarters, 403 Essex building, a luncheon will be held at which representatives of various organizations will be present. Originally this was scheduled for reports on the recent annual meeting of the National American Woman Suffrage association in Washington, but leaders said the event of yesterday would be the chief interest. Workers from all parts of the state are to be present.

**Roster of Speakers.**

Among those who will speak are Mrs. Andreas Ueland, president of the Minnesota Woman Suffrage association; Mrs. D. F. Simpson, president of the Hennepin county Suffrage association; Mrs. Walter H. Thorp, Mrs. A. E. Zonne, Mrs. Milton D. Purdy, Mrs. H. G. Harrison, Mrs. Alfred Merrill, Miss Nellie Merrill, and Miss Hope McDonald of Minneapolis and Mrs. Stiles W. Burr and Mrs. Walter Burr of St. Paul.

"We're terribly pleased over the victory," said Mrs. Ueland last night. "Of course, it was close, but a win is as good as a mile. We're very hopeful about the Senate, and with congressional prestige behind it there is no doubt of the amendment being ratified.

"We shall start plans for organizing Minnesota right away. Our logical program is to concentrate in Minnesota for the next year. When our Legislature has approved the amendment we can go to help other states. There should be no doubt about legislative approval if hard work is done. Minnesota is getting more progressive all the time. The House already is for us and we look for a new Senate that will be more friendly.

**All Feel Very Happy.**

"We feel very happy over the attitude taken by Mr. Wilson. There is no doubt that his position had a great deal to do with the action of the House, nor that it will assure similar action by the Senate."

Mrs. Simpson took the same view.

Women opposed to national suffrage saw a lean victory in the House vote. When Mrs. J. B. Gilfillan, president of the Minnesota Association Opposed to Woman Suffrage, learned that the ballot of a single representative in favor of, instead of against the resolution had pushed the vote to the necessary majority she gave out this statement:

**Opponents See Lean Victory.**

"Either the pickets or the President failed in influence. The amendment should have passed by an effective majority. There must be a strong opposition to the method or the measure if the combined political force of Tammany, Socialism and Pacifism, added to the honest conviction of many people commanded so narrow a majority.

"What will anti-suffragists do? Go on with their quiet and effective war work as a patriotic obligation. It entails, from their point of view, no reward of merit from the government in franchise or sex recognition. Woman suffrage has still a long way to travel. When our soldiers are safely home and the war against autocracy won, anti-suffrage can again logically take up the question of votes for women. But the ultimate result is not yet above the sky line."

**The Latest in Sedition.**

De Kalb Junction, Ill., Jan. 11.—Webster L. Chandler, a wealthy resident of Ogdensburg, was arrested on a train yesterday by a fellow passenger, charged with sedition. Arraigned here, Chandler declared he only characterized William J. Bryan as an "educated fool."

# The Minneapolis Morning Tribune

Fifty-second Year. No. 26. | Associated Press | MINNEAPOLIS, MINN., WEDNESDAY, JUNE 19, 1918 | United Press. | Price TWO CENTS.


# Austrian Offensive Has Broken Down, Says Bonar Law

## Minnesota Delivers Knockout to Townley

*Burnquist's Majority Exceeds 50,000; Wheaton Fast Gaining on Comstock; Pacifist Lundeen Called Home by Great Vote; Caswell's Lead Fading; Frankson, Too, in Danger.*

By George E. Akerson.

The victory of the loyalists of Minnesota and Minneapolis became more striking when late returns on the primary election of Monday piled in last night.

These are some of the high lights in the "never such" primary that are giving loyalists cause for rejoicing:

**Minnesota rebuked, in no uncertain terms, A. C. Townley, boss of the Nonpartisan league, by giving Governor Burnquist a majority of 50,000 votes in more than two-thirds of the precincts already in.**

**Senator Knute Nelson, Minnesota's grand old man, fought by the Nonpartisan league, is renominated over James A. Peterson by a vote of more than four to one.**

**In Minneapolis, J. E. Meyers, drafted by the Republican conference to run for mayor, leads the other nominee, Thoman Van Lear, by 1,200 votes.**

**"Ernie" Lundeen, pacifist congressman, indorsed by the Municipal Townleyites, is eliminated altogether and Walter H. Newton, loyalist, is the Republican nominee for congress in the Fifth district.**

**Lynn Thompson, Socialist member of the Minneapolis school board, is hopelessly lost in his fight to be one of the nominees for sheriff of Hennepin county.**

Late returns showed several surprises. The lead of Judge Willard L. Comstock of Mankato for the Democratic nomination for governor was melting so fast that there were strong possibilities that Fred E. Wheaton of Minneapolis, would be the nominee. In 1,338 out of the 3,119 precincts the vote was: Comstock, 12,188; Wheaton, 10,919.

The Wheaton strength is showing up in the rural sections. Comstock got his first big lead in Ramsey county, where he came out with almost 3,000 to the good. Blue Earth, his home county, gave him 500 majority. Wheaton is gaining steadily.

One of the present office holders will likely have to give way to a Nonpartisan league candidate. Two others are in jeopardy.

**Caswell in Danger.**

Indications last night were that Hermann Mueller of St. Cloud will eliminate Irving A. Caswell, clerk of the state supreme court. In 1,446 precincts the vote for the clerk of court was: Caswell, 63,960; Magnuson, 50,260; Mueller, 60,761.

Returns from 1482 precincts out of the 3119 gave Clifford L. Hilton, 93,276 an Thomas V. Sullivan, 80,487, in the race for attorney general. Hilton's lead included his big lead of 14,000 in Hennepin county. Friends of the attorney general were concerned.

In 1445 precincts, Thomas Frankson, lieutenant governor, is only 10,000 in the lead over Ralph Crane. That lead is expected to dwindle. The vote at midnight was: Frankson, 76,556; Crane, 66,255; Stephens, 39,942.

The total vote on governor in these precincts was: Burnquist, 167,523; Lindbergh, 117,755. Complete returns from 27 counties were included, some of them Nonpartisan league strongholds. Every county was represented with comparatively heavy returns.

**Office Holders in Jeopardy.**

While Governor Burnquist's nomination had been assured by a tremendous majority and Senator Knute Nelson was assured of a four to one vote against James Peterson, there were several of the present state office holders who were placed in jeopardy by late returns.

While returns kept piling up, showing Minnesota's stinging rebuke to Townleyism, A. C. Townley, boss of the Nonpartisan league, was out in North Dakota, insisting that his candidate, Lindbergh, had carried the state.

Townley, speaking at Hillsboro, said: "We have won the election unless big business with its crooked methods counts us out." He spent his time denouncing "Big Biz" and the "kept press."

## 34 Soldiers Hurt When Train Is Wrecked in Texas

Waco, Texas, June 18.—Thirty-four soldiers were injured, five probably fatally, near Selby, Texas, about 15 miles east of Waco, today, when a St. Louis & Southwestern railroad train, carrying troops stationed at Camp McArthur, was wrecked while passing over a wooden bridge. The engineer and two firemen also were probably fatally injured.

## Flier Killed as Mother Reaches Camp on Visit

Fort Worth, Tex., June 18.—Lieut. Joseph Rose, an instructor at Barron field, near here, was killed this afternoon when the airplane in which he was riding with a fellow officer fell. His companion was badly hurt.

Lieutenant Rose's mother was here today from his home at Coatesville, Pa., to visit her son, arriving this morning. She was at the field when the fatal crash occurred.

## Gen. D'Esperey Named Allied Chief in Near East

Athens, Greece, June 18. —General Franchet D'Esperey has been appointed commander-in-chief of the Allied forces in the Near East, in succession to General Guillaumat, who has been made military governor of Paris. General Franchet D'Esperey was given a luncheon today by Premier Venizelos of Greece.

*Eat No Wheat Today.*

MINNESOTA WEATHER — Unsettled today and tomorrow; not much change in temperature.

## U-Boat Failure Proven by Raid on U. S. Coast

**American Naval Headquarters Says Allies Command Seas.**

**Tours by Submarines Far Afield Are Welcomed.**

London, June 18.—Recent operations of German submarines off the Atlantic coast of the United States are declared proof that the U-boat campaign has failed, in a statement issued tonight from the American naval headquarters. The statement says:

"The activity of the German submarine on the American coast is a manifestation of the failure of the enemy's submarine campaign. The enemy has a limited number of submarines and his only chance of employing this available number successfully is to concentrate their operations on the focal points of Allied trade. All shipping which supplies the Allied armies must converge in the areas in the vicinity of England and France.

**Means Less Losses.**

"Every submarine which operates far afield, as off the extensive coast of America, simply means less losses to the Allies, because it is one less submarine where shipping is heavy and therefore harder to protect. If the Allies could in any way influence the enemy they would encourage him to send his submarines to these areas distant from the critical areas.

"Such activities will, of course, result in the loss of some ships—losses undoubtedly will go on until the end of the war. What we are concerned about is whether the losses the enemy inflicts are critical—are more than we can stand. As long as they are kept below the critical stage they could go on indefinitely and not affect the war.

**Situation Held Good.**

"The situation today is that there is sufficient tonnage available to meet the Allied demands and it is constantly growing. At the present rate of concentration it will continue to grow larger even if the submarine losses increased. The enemy's high command knows these basic facts only too well, as is evidenced by their desperate attempts to force a decision on land before the full weight of American intervention can be brought to bear.

"From the enemy press it is evident that these futile submarine raids in remote areas, such as raids on the American coast, the bombardment of Monrovia and the activities in the Azores cannot have any effect on the outcome of the war and are carried on to deceive their own public as to the submarine campaign. The German public is led to believe by cleverly constructed press accounts that their submarines operate at pleasure in all parts of the world. The fact remains that the Allies have command of the seas—subsurface as well as surface."

## Jury Deliberates on Smith Sedition Case

The jury in the A. D. Smith case, out since 2:30 p. m. yesterday, had not reported at 1:30 a. m. today. Smith is on trial before Judge Leary in district court, on a charge of violating the state anti-sedition law. He is alleged to have said that he would like to see the streets of Minneapolis running a foot deep in blood, and to have asserted that "the Gerams are the chosen people of God and should rule the world."

Smith, in testimony given yesterday, admitted that he had threatened to shoot Judge J. F. McGee, but declared that he said so by way of exaggeration, and that he never owned a revolver in his life.

## *Nelson's Home County 'Over Top for Kaiser*

*Peterson Is Given More Votes Than Senator; New Ulm Too.*

While the great bulk of the citizens of Minnesota arose in their might to smite disloyalty on Monday, there were some few communities that went "over the top with the Kaiser."

There are a few communities in Minnesota where loyal citizens are blushing with shame at the record made.

Up in Douglas county, the home of Knute Nelson, Minnesota's grand old man, the loyalists are wearing sack cloth and ashes. For there James A. Peterson, under sentence of four years in the federal penitentiary at Leavenworth for violations of the espionage act, got more votes than the county's most distinguished citizen. The vote was: Nelson, 1,517; Peterson, 1,956. Lindbergh carried the county two to one.

**Gets League's Support.**

The Douglas county vote indicates that the Nonpartisan league was throwing what support it could to the man convicted of disloyalty. Douglas county is said to be the strongest Nonpartisan league county in Minnesota.

The league made no indorsements on the senatorship but constantly made slighting and slurring remarks about the senior senator. It was evident from the league's organs that Nelson was not to the liking of A. C. Townley, boss of the league.

But, Douglas county, with its strong Nonpartisan league leanings, is not the only county in the state where loyalists are ashamed of the vote cast in the primaries.

**New Ulm Too.**

In Brown county, with New Ulm the county seat, the vote for Peterson was surprisingly large. New Ulm itself, the scene of the anti-draft meeting and a place where proGermanism has thrived, gave Peterson a majority over Senator Nelson. Brown county itself reversed the lead but the Peterson vote was much too large to suit the loyal citizens. New Ulm has had one newspaper that has continually printed Nonpartisan league propaganda.

Carver county went strong for Lindbergh and gave Peterson a big vote.

Even right in Hennepin county, where Governor Burnquist received a majority of 20,000, there was one place where James A. Peterson, with his sentence hanging over him, proved preferable to the voters. Corcoran Town, where the Nonpartisan league has been strong, Peterson won out over Senator Nelson.

## Washington Convinced Minnesota Is Loyal

Primary News Pleases Congressmen—Nelson Felicitated on Victory.

By George F. Authier.

Washington, June 18.—News of the primary results in Minnesota has attracted nation-wide attention. In government circles and in Congress comment was general. Senator Knute Nelson was made the recipient of many congratulations all during the day from his fellow senators on account of the splendid tribute accorded the veteran senator.

The significant figure of the primary attaches to the interpretation of Minnesota's attitude on the war. The nomination of Senator Nelson and of Governor Burnquist are looked upon as a positive advertisement on the part of Minnesota that it repudiates those who would have fouled it with the taint of disloyalty. Minnesota in the nomination of Nelson and Burnquist is regarded as having followed the example of Wisconsin in repudiating its disloyal and treasonable elements.

This is especially so in the case of Senator Nelson whose record as a proponent of Americanism in Congress is 100 per cent.

Early news received here indicated the defeat of both Lundeen and Davis. This news was not confirmed this evening, but it brought joy everywhere, more especially in Republican circles which aims to rid itself of those congressmen who have brought discredit upon the Republican organization.

## Secret Gun Plans Found as Spy Suspects Are Held

New York, June 18.—A trunkful of blue prints and plans of airplanes, guns, anti-submarine craft and other data, intended for shipment to Germany via Mexico, according to the police, was seized here today following the arrest of George L. Lindquist and Lee Bert, charged with espionage, and Franz Strohmeier, an Austrian, who was charged with having a revolver and failing to register. A plan of the latest improved Browning machine gun was among the blueprints seized.

A girl of 17, who speaks with a French accent, and who is expected to testify against Lindquist, was brought here from Hartford, and held in connection with the case. The police declared Lindquist and Bert planned to sell the blueprints to Germany.

## American Rail Mission Reported Now in Russia

London, June 18.—Foreign Minister Balfour announced in the House of Commons today that he understood an American mission had arrived in Russia to consider the reorganization of the Russian railways.

"We are willing to co-operate," added Mr. Balfour, "but it is better to leave the question mainly with America."

## Baker Gives O.K. to Draft Age Extension

**Decides Plan Is Only Way to Assure 5,000,000 Victory Army.**

Washington, June 18.—The draft age limits will be extended probably to 18 and 45. Secretary of War Baker has been persuaded that this step is necessary. He announced today that he will approve any change in the selective service act necessary to raise an army of the required size.

American and Allied military leaders now are convinced that the United States must place an army of at least 5,000,000 men in the field, if victory is to be won. This will be possible with the proposed extension of the age limits.

**Baker Won Over to Plan.**

Secretary Baker was won over to the plan at a conference with Provost Marshal General Crowder. The secretary's approval removes the last obstacle in the path of the army general staff's move to bring the proposal before Congress at an early date. It is possible the question will not come up until late in the fall.

The approval of Secretary Baker is taken to indicate a similar attitude by President Wilson. The War department, therefore, is convinced that Congress will enact the necessary legislation without lengthy debate.

General Crowder has favored an extension of the draft age for several months. No official action looking to a revision in the law was taken, however, because Secretary Baker formerly opposed the proposed extension.

**Draft Machinery Ready.**

When General Crowder is called upon for an official opinion, he will recommend that the new limits be from 18 to 45, it is understood. The draft machine has been made ready to take care of the additional task.

Available fighting men under the present age limits are expected to be exhausted about January 1. General Crowder is anxious to avoid inroads on skilled industrial and skilled farm labor and married men.

Including June calls aproximately 1,600,000 draft men have been called to the colors. The July calls will bring this number up to nearly 2,000,000. General Crowder has told the Senate military affairs committee, that the July calls would aggregate 290,000.

**3,000,000 Strong By August.**

With the 2,000,000 draft under arms by the end of July and the 1,000,000 in the regular army and the National Guard, the strength of the American army by August 1 will be 3,000,000 men. Another 1,000,000 men can be furnished by the draft system without necessitating the invasion of the deferred classes. Thus, an army larger than 4,000,000 is impossible without extending the age limits of the draft or invading the deferred classes.

A registration of 10,683,249 between the ages of 31 and 45, both inclusive, is the estimate of General Crowder. From 18 to 20, both inclusive, he would expect to enroll 3,087,063. Ninety-six per cent of the men between 18 and 20 are not married, it is estimated, while 77 per cent of the men between 31 and 45 are believed to be married.

**Could Raise Army to 6,500,000.**

The number of single males between 31 and 45 therefore is expected to be 3,525,472, and between 18 and 20 there should be 2,963,581.

Figuring on a basis of percentage of acceptances in the first registration General Crowder would count on registration of men between 31 and 45 producing 1,389,338 fighting men. The 18 to 20 registration should produce 1,167,947 fighting men.

The total number of fighting men expected therefore, under the proposed age limits would be 2,557,285. With the present available total of 4,000,000 the extension of the draft ages to 18 and 45 would allow for an enlargement of the army to more than 6,500,000 without disturbing the industrial, agricultural or domestic conditions of the country.

## Hindenberg, Mentally Ill, Is in Sanitarium

Geneva, June 18.—The Tribune says it learns from a reliable source that Field Marshal von Hindenburg is suffering from an acute nervous disease and that his mental capacity is much affected and that he is confined in a private sanitarium. The newspaper adds that Hindenburg took no responsible part in the recent offensive on the Western front, the work being chiefly done by General Ludendorff.

## Germans Prepare New Offensive in West, Says Writer

**LONDON, June 18.—The Germans, the Central News correspondent at the front telegraphs, are preparing for a fresh push in the West.**

**He considers as highly significant the intense bombardment of the British and American positions north of Montdidier.**

## *Austrians Upset by Sudden Check of Drive in Italy*

*Foe Counted on Big Gains in Terrain and Booty; Milan Goal.*

(By Associated Press.)

Geneva, June 18.—News from the eastern Swiss frontier indicates that the Austro-Hungarians are surprised and disconcerted at the sudden check of their great offensive against Italy, where much greater gains of territory and booty were expected.

From Lugano comes word that the Austrian objectives include Brescia and eventually, Milan.

The Austrian emperor and his staff are expected to arrive at Trent this week.

**Vienna Socialists Raise Cry.**

Paris, June 18.—Socialist manifestations took place in Vienna yesterday, according to a dispatch received by the Havas agency from Basel, Switzerland.

## Army Lieutenant Who Trained Here Accused of Fraud

**War Contract Plot Is Found to Involve Scores of Men.**

**Secretaries of Several Congressmen Are Among Suspects.**

(By Associated Press.)

Washington, June 18.—The trail of the government's pursuit of illegal profiteers on war contracts today led to the arrest in New York of Lieut. James C. Staley, a reserve army officer, on a charge of accepting money from the Truefit Raincoat company of New York, for a contract which he promised to procure.

The arrest was made by Department of Justice agents who had followed the officer during his inspection of the plant of the raincoat company, whose proprietors acted in co-operation with the government to detect the fraud.

**Trained at Snelling.**

Lieutenant Staley is about 50 years old and came originally from Iowa. He entered a training camp in that state last summer and later was transferred to Fort Snelling, Minnesota, where he was commissioned in August. Subsequently he was trained at the quartermasters' school at Camp Dodge, Iowa, and last December 11 was appointed an inspector in the Quartermaster's department for raincoats and other army rubber goods. He has been stationed in New York most of the time since.

Lieutenant Staley made a complete confession of his part in the transaction, Department of Justice officials said, and gave much valuable information which may lead to the detection of other cases of fraud.

**To Face Court Martial.**

He will be tried by court martial.

The shadow of complicity in the extensive scheme by which commission agents made millions out of government war orders by acting as middlemen in obtaining contracts for manufacturers, today extended to scores of businessmen and attorneys in Washington, New York and other cities and even to a few secretaries of members of Congress. These men, many of of whom were amateurs in the game of soliciting war contracts, promised to use their influence with government officials, army officers or with members of Congress to secure the awarding of contracts to special firms and in turn were to receive compensation if the contracts were landed.

**Some May Not Be Prosecuted.**

A large proportion of these cases, disclosed by correspondence and other documents seized in the simultaneous raids yesterday on offices of several hundred manufacturing plants and forwarded today to the Department of Justice were not prompted by sinister motives, officials believe and prosecution will not follow. Many others, however, appear the result of carefully planned plots to squeeze millions from contractors, who in turn were to add the contingent fees to prices which the government was required to pay.

Secret agents of the Department of Justice, Treasury, War and Navy departments were at work today on new phases of the disclosures in Washington and elsewhere, while a corps of investigators under the direction of Assistant Attorney General Huston Thompson digested the evidence contained in the thousands of seized documents.

**Cabinet Gets Information.**

Attorney General Gregory took the latest information on the raids to the cabinet meeting, and cabinet members and heads of all executive departments making contracts received the attorney general's recommendations, approved by President Wilson for insertion in future contracts of a clause binding the contractor not to pay contingent fees nor to employ middlemen in negotiating a war order.

**Accidentally Kills Himself.**

Birchwood, Wis. June 18.—Frank Thompson today accidentally killed himself by discharging a shotgun which he carried. He had gone into a field to shoot crows when the accident occurred. He is survived by a widow and two children.

## *Americans Bringing Victory, He Asserts*

*First Day's Objectives Still Unattained in Italy After 3 Days of Fighting, House of Commons Is Told.*

London, June 18.—After three days of fighting Austria's great offensive against Italy has failed, Andrew Bonar Law, chancellor of the exchequer, told the House of Commons this afternoon.

In introducing a vote of credit for 500,000,000 pounds, the chancellor gave a review of the general situation.

American troops are flowing to the Western front at such a great rate of speed as to make ultimate victory certain, he declared.

**Italian Offensive Fails.**

Speaking of the military situation, he said:

"The latest phase of this great struggle, is the Austrian offensive in Italy. It is part of an intense offensive which has been carried on along the whole battle front. Our enemies are right in thinking that a great success gained on that front would have been far-reaching perhaps decisive results on the general battle front in France. For that reason the general suspicion that the initiative came from Berlin, rather than from Vienna, I believe to be justified.

"The offensive was launched by a very large number of Austrian divisions. A good deal more than half their total force on that front is engaged in the attack. All I can say today is that after three days of fighting, the attack has failed.

**First Day's Objectives Saved.**

"Our advices from Italian headquarters is that the enemy has not secured in three days the objectives which he had hoped to obtain the first day. And it is also true to say that no offensive of this scale throughout the war has at its initiation secured so little success.

"There is no doubt that our own and the French troops are giving a good account of themselves, and the Italians have been fighting throughout with the highest courage and the most marked tenacity. The Italian higher command has no fear of the result.

"The danger is not over, but the government can express admiration and gratitude to the Italians for the share they have taken in the general struggle."

**Knew German Plans.**

Speaking of the Western front, Mr. Bonar Law said that British and French headquarters knew the positions to which the German divisions were being sent before the commencement of the offensive on March 21. He admitted that the attack had attained an amount of success which had caused the utmost anxiety.

"But," he added, "three months have passed, and although the battle is a continuous one, we can look back upon what has happened with some confidence.

"In this whole campaign the Germans have had before them three great

(Continued on Page 2, Col. 2.)

## Foreign Troops to Train in U. S.

**War Department Will Ask Congress to Provide Funds.**

(By Associated Press.)

Washington, June 18.—Congress is to be asked by the War department for an appropriation to provide training facilities in this country for forces other than American troops. This was learned authoritatively today.

The natural assumption is that any troops to be trained here would come from some one of the nations in the Western hemisphere who have joined the countries at war with Germany. While no arrangements have been discussed looking to that end the department feels that it would be wise to have the funds on hand so as to be in a position to act promptly should another nation consent to the training and equipping of its forces in the United States.

It is reported that the request for the appropriation will be made before the present session of Congress ends.

## Foe Patrols Checked by American Gunners

Accuracy of Fire Almost Annihilates One German Party in Marne Sector.

(By Associated Press.)

With the American Forces on the Marne, June 18.—Several German patrols which attempted last night to aproach the American lines in the Marne sector were smashed by the accuracy of the American machine gun fire. One German patrol was almost wiped out.

Two German prisoners, who, after escaping from a detention camp 100 miles to the rear of the American front six days ago, wandered through woods and bushes and swam rivers in the night time, were captured last night in the American lines. The prisoners said they had traveled with comparative ease until they approached American territory where it became so hot that they could not cross to the German lines.

## Allies Elude Austrian Grip at All Points

**Foe Is Stalled on Plateau and Attacks Repelled Along Piave.**

*Day's War Summary.*

(By Associated Press.)

The Austrian pincers are not closing up on Italy with the precision of last October when they forced back the Italian armies of General Cadora from the Julian Alps to the Piave river and from the northern mountain regions almost to the plains of Venetia. In fact they do not seem to be closing at all.

The upper jaw in the Venetian Alps is stalled under the resistence of the British, French and Italian forces and the nether one seems to lack the force to bring it across the Piave. In the Alps the Austrians have been unable to advance farther since last week. Everywhere from the Asiago plateau sector eastward to the Piave their attacks have quickly been repulsed by the Allied troops who have regained lost terrain, inflicting heavy casualties and taking a considerable number of prisoners.

**Fighting Fierce Along Piave.**

All along the Piave fierce fighting is going on, especially on the Montello plateau and further south from Fossalta to some 20 miles east of Venice.

The Italian war office announces that the enemy everywhere is being held along the Piave. From Vienna comes a variant report. It does not concede to the Allies any gains of ground in the mountain region, saying that all their counter attacks were repulsed. It asserts that the Austrians have gained ground at numerous points on the Piave and that the battle is following its intended course.

In addition the Austrian war office says the number of prisoners taken in the fighting has increased to 30,000 and that 120 guns in addition to mine throwers, machine guns and war material have been captured.

The prisoners taken by the Italians Monday at one point amounted to 1,550 which would bring their total and those of the Allies well in the neighborhood of 5,000.

**Lull Continues In France.**

The infantry operations on the battle front in France continues virtually at a standstill.

The French continue daily to regain ground taken from them in the recent German offensive of the Aisne and also to take prisoners in these enterprises.

Several attempts by the Germans to penetrate the American lines in the Marne sector have been smashed by the American machine gun fire.

### *Battle Increasing in Violence Along Piave.*

(By Associated Press.)

Rome, June 18.—The battle on the mountain sector of the Italian front has died down, but is fiercer from the mountains to the sea, along the Piave river, according to the statement issued by the war office today.

The statement reads:

"The violence of the battle has somewhat decreased along the mountain front but is increasing along the Piave river.

"The third army withstood the powerful efforts of the enemy yesterday. In front of Muserada and at Candelu (on the Piave river) renewed attempts to establish new openings on the right bank of the river were sanguinarily repulsed.

"From Fossalta to Capo Sile the struggle raged without pause."

"On the northern edge of the Montello we strengthened our occupation on the river as far as Pasa Serena.

**Two Attacks Arrested.**

"In the afternoon the enemy from the northeastern salient in the mount delivered two attacks. The first was arrested to the east of a line northeast of Giavera. The second was stopped immediately south of the Sosuro-San Andrea railway.

"In the Grappa region we repulsed enemy attacks and carried out successful raids, taking about 100 prisoners.

"At the end of the Brenta valley and east of the Frenzela valley enemy thrusts were promptly arrested.

"On the eastern margin of the Asiago plateau our troops wrested from the enemy Razea Pizzo and the heights southeast of Sasso, capturing about 200 prisoners.

"Our parties and a French contingent in a strong attack gained ground on the spur of Costalunga and took some prisoners there.

**Vigorous Advances Crushed.**

"Formidable enemy attacks alternated with our counter attacks. At the beginning vigorous advances were crushed by our resistance or arrested by counter offensive actions. The struggle was suspended only late at night.

"The valiant troops of our army were strenuously tried, but the enemy was not able to increase the short depth in the strip of ground within

# The Minneapolis Morning Tribune

Fifty-third Year. No. 24. | Associated Press | MINNEAPOLIS, MINN., MONDAY, JUNE 16, 1919 | United Press. | Price Two Cents in Minneapolis


# American Troops, 3,600 Strong, Cross Mexican Border Into Juarez

# Alcock and Brown in Nonstop Flight Cross Atlantic in 16 Hours

## British Airman Completes History-Making Journey

### Machine Lands at Clifden, Ireland—Fliers Stand Journey Well.

### Make Straight-Away, Clean-Cut Dash for $50,000 Prize.

(By Associated Press.)

London, June 15.—The final goal of all the ambitions which flying men have ventured to dream since the Wright brothers first rose from the earth in a heavier-than-air machine, was realized this morning, when the British officers, Capt. John Alcock and Lieut. Arthur Brown, landed on the Irish coast after the first non-stop flight across the Atlantic ocean.

Their voyage was without accident and without unforeseen incident, so far as can be learned. It was a straight-away clean-cut flight, achieved in 16 hours and 12 minutes—from New Foundland to Clifden, Ireland, a distance of more than 1,900 miles.

**Plane Battles With Fogs.**

But the brief description which comes from the air men at Clifden tells of an adventurous and amazingly hazardous enterprise. Fog and mists hung over the North Atlantic, and the Vickers-Vimy biplane climbed and dove, struggling to extricate herself from the folds of the airplane's worst enemy.

She rose to 11,000 feet, swooped down almost to the surface of the sea and at times the two navigators found themselves flying upside down only ten feet above the water.

Before booming down to earth near the Clifden wireless station Alcock circled the wireless aerials, seeking the best spot to reach the earth but no suitable ground was found, so he chanced it in a bog.

The wireless staff rushed to the aid of the aviators. They found Brown dazed and Alcock temporarily deafened by the force of the impact. As soon as they were able to be escorted to the wireless station they telegraphed the news to their friends, then had breakfast.

"That is the best way to cross the Atlantic," said Lieutenant Brown after he had eaten.

The landing was made at 9:40 a. m. British summer time. In taking the ground the machine struck heavily and the fuselage ploughed into the sand. Neither of the occupants was injured.

**Radio Out of Commission.**

Captain Alcock explained the silence of his radio instrument by saying that the wireless propellor blew off soon after leaving New Foundland.

The Daily Mail's correspondent found Alcock and Brown at Clifden packing their gear into a huge sack. Alcock's face lit up with a smile when he was congratulated by the correspondent. Brown, who was bending over packing, said quietly:

"We didnt' do so badly, did we?"

**Crowd Gasps, Then Cheers.**

Alcock said with a laugh: "I am not at all tired. Brown, however, confessed, "I am a bit fagged out." The correspondent says Brown's eyes were slightly bloodshot, but that otherwise the men looked as if they had not travelled across the ocean.

When the officers, operators and soldiers from the wireless plant rushed toward the machine after it landed, Alcock said:

"This is the Vickers-Vimy machine. We have just come from New Foundland."

The little crowd gasped and then cheered and cheered again. Alcock in telling his story, said among other things:

"We landed in the softest spot in Ireland but I really wonder that we got here with our wireless out of action. Neither of us got much fun out of the flight. It was a job of work."

Brown said: "We are too near it to realize what it is we have done."

Brown was able to take only four readings of the airplane's position, one from the sun, one from the moon, and one from the polar star and one from Vega.

Mists robbed the night of the advantage of the full moon and the wireless apparatus was torn away by the wind soon after the start. So the two young pioneers of the Atlantic flight without a stop were thrown upon their own resources. The skillful navigation which brought the machine near to the center of the Irish coast line was one of the finest features of the flight.

Word came from Clifden this afternoon that the pilot and navigator were leaving for Galway, whence Lieutenant Brown planned to travel by train to London, arriving there Tuesday. Captain Alcock hoped to be able to fly to London in the machine as soon as it could be repaired. It was planned to have him give an exhibition over London, if possible.

**Report to Aero Club.**

The Aero club received a message from Clifden soon after the trans-Atlantic fliers landed, which said that they had completed the flight in 16 hours and 12 minutes. They requested instructions from the club.

In reply the club telegraphed:

"Keep machine intact until observer arrives."

The air ministry said certain marks

(Continued on Page 2, Col. 6.)

### Weather Forecast

MINNESOTA—Partly cloudy today and tomorrow; possibly local thunder storms; not much change in temperature.

### Alcock and Brown Report "Terrible" Journey in Fog and Sleet.

### Found Selves Upside Down Only Ten Feet Above Ocean.

Public Ledger-Minneapolis Tribune Service. Special Cable Dispatch. Copyright, 1919, by Public Ledger Co.

London, June 15.—A Daily Mail interview with Captain John Alcock, given by courtesy to the London Times-Minneapolis Tribune Service, follows:

"We have had a terrible journey and the wonder is that we are here at all. We scarcely saw the sun or moon or stars. For hours we saw none of them. The fog was very dense and at times we had to descend to within 300 feet of the sea.

"For four hours the machine was covered in a sheet of ice carried by frozen sleet. At another time the fog was so dense that the speed indicator did not work and for a few seconds it was very alarming. We looped the loop, I do believe and did a very steep spiral. We did some very comic stunts for I had no sense of horizon. The winds were favorable all the way, northwest and at times southwest.

"We said in New Foundland we would do the trip in 16 hours, but we never thought we should. An hour and a half before we saw land we had no certain idea of where we were, but we believed we were at Galway or thereabouts. Our delight in seeing Eastal island and Turbot island (five miles est of Clifden) was great. The people did not know who we were when we landed and thought we were scouts looking for Alcock. We encountered no unforeseen conditions.

"We did not suffer from the cold or exhaustion except when looking over the side, for then the sleet chewed bits out of our faces. We drank coffee and ate sandwiches and chocolate. The flight has shown that the Atlantic flight is practicable, but I think it should be done, not with an airplane or a Zeppelin, but with a flying boat. We had plenty of reserve fuel left, using only two-thirds of our supply. The only thing that upset me was to see the machine at the end get damaged. From above the bog looked like a lovely field, but the machine sank into it up to the axle and fell over on to her nose.

### *Brown's First Message Is to His Fiancee.*

Public Ledger-Minneapolis Tribune Service. Special Cable Dispatch. Copyright, 1919, by Public Ledger Co.

London, June 15.—Miss Kennedy, who will marry Lieutenant Brown, lives in London at 26 Oakley avenue and her house is decked with flags. She said to your correspondent:

"The suspense of waiting was terrible. I shall sleep sounder tonight. You may be certain I had great confidence in the Vimy machine."

She is a tall, vivacious girl, and wore a cool tennis costume. The first thing Lieutenant Brown did on reaching Ireland was to send her this cablegram from Clifden:

"Landed safely this morning, will be with you very soon."

(Signed.) TEDDY."

Miss Kennedy is the daughter of a major in the Royal Air force. Lieutenant Brown carried as a mascot an American flag given him by Miss Kennedy. They are to tour the world on their honeymoon and will reside in the United States.

### *King George Sends His Congratulations.*

(By Associated Press.)

London, June 15.—King George learned of the success of the flight of Alcock and Brown as he was leaving church at Westminster today. He immediately telegraphed his congratulations to the airmen. Many high officials also sent them messages of greetings.

Major General Sykes, chief of the air staff, on behalf of the King, wired Alcock and Brown as follows:

"It is with pleasure that I have to convey to you the following message I have received from the King:

"'The King is delighted to receive the welcome announcement that Captain Alcock and Lieutenant Brown have landed safely in Ireland after a trans-Atlantic flight.

"'His majesty wishes you to communicate at once with these officers and to convey to them the King's warmest congratulations on the success of their splendid achievement.'"

## Conference Seen on Keymen's Strike

(By Associated Press.)

Atlantic City, June 15.—Frank Morrison, secretary of the American Federation of Labor, announced to national convention delegates tonight that Postmaster General Burleson had promised to give orders which would result in conferences between representatives of the striking commercial telegraphers of the Western Union and Postal companies and representatives of the companies.

**Germans Halt Home-bound Poles.**

Coblenz, June 15.—Eight train loads of General Haller's Polish troops en troute from France to Poland have been halted at Giessen by order of the Berlin government. A shortage of food has arisen among these soldiers.

## Germans Warned Against Opposing Allies' Movements

### Berlin Proclamation Cautions Civilians to Be Good If Troops Advance.

(By Associated Press.)

Coblenz, Thursday, June 12.—A proclamation cautioning civilians to remain in their home towns and refrain from acts of resentment in the event that Allied troops cross the Rhine in force and advance farther into Germany is published in German newspapers in districts opposite Mayence, Coblenz, and Cologne bridgeheads.

The proclamation is a result of reports that civilians in villages over a radius of 90 miles beyond the occupied zones were planning to withdraw, or were moving into the interior of Germany. In some villages opposite Coblenz, burgomasters have ordered district government employes to remain at their posts, even if the Allies should come.

## Peace Change Gives Germany an Added Army

### 200,000 Men for Three Years Allowed by Big Four Concession.

(By Associated Press.)

Paris, June 15.—Germany is to be allowed an army of 200,000 men for three years. This is one of the changes in the peace terms which has been sedulously kept secret.

The reason given for this doubling of the previous number of effectives is the impossibility of adjusting the armies of Austria, Poland, Czecho-Slovakia and other new states proportionately to the previously arranged 100,000 men for Germany.

A general reduction of armaments is to be negotiated immediately.

Germany's admission to the league of nations is fixed for "the near future."

Her admission will enable Germany to bring up for discussion her economic propositions. Germany will be given four months to submit to the Allies proposals dealing with her total indebtedness through reparations, and methods for the payment thereof. She may propose merchandise and labor.

The Allies are to reply within two months.

A plebiscite for Upper Silesia will be taken within six to eighteen months.

A clause deals with the protection by the league of nations of German minorities inhabiting the districts taken from Germany. Another deals with the inter-Allied civil commission, which will administer the left bank of the Rhine occupied by the Allied troops, to which the existing military commission will be subordinated.

### *Germany to Be Handed Peace Answer Today.*

(By Associated Press.)

The stage is set for the closing scenes of the peace congress so far as the Germans are concerned. Within a few hours it is expected the Germans will be told the terms, brought down

(Continued on Page 2, Col. 7.)

## Harry A. Tuttle Is Seriously Ill

### President of North American Telegraph Company at Balsam Lake, Wis.

Harry A. Tuttle, 72 years old, 1710 Dupont avenue south, president and general manager of the North American Telegraph company, is seriously ill at Balsam Lake, Wis., where he went 10 days ago, hoping to regain his health. Advices received last night by A. S. Harris, vice president of the company, from the attending physician declared that he was not expected to survive the night. Mr. Tuttle has been a resident of Minneapolis for 37 years and has been active in the business and social life of the city.

## Pathological Ward Urged for Wilhelm

Berlin, June 15.—Former Emperor William "belongs in the Pathological ward" and is not wanted in Germany, declared Herman Mueller, Majority Socialist leader and whip in the national assembly, in a speech before the Majority Socialist convention today.

Herr Mueller, referring to the rumor that an attempt was to be made to bring about the return of the ex emperor, warned the Prussians said to be interested in such a move, that a majority of the German people would not permit his return. The speaker declared the former ruler was dangerous to the country, and blamed his verbosity for Germany's misfortunes.

Herr Mueller's speech was received with cheers.

**Woman "Slept" 56 Days; Dead.**

Big Sandy, Mont., June 15.—After being unconscious 56 days, Mrs. Levi Stevenson died from what is supposed to have been sleeping sickness. She had been confined to her bed 111 days.

**Disorders in Switzerland.**

Paris, June 15.—Bolshevik and anarchistic disorders are reported from Switzerland. Two persons were killed and 17 wounded, according to official figures in a serious uprising in Zurich.

## Town Flooded, Trains Blocked by Cloudburst

### Marietta Reported Under Four Feet of Water—Without Lights.

### Railroads and Highways in Redwood County Also Tied Up.

### Eleven Minneapolis Persons Hurt as Taxicabs Collide in Downpour.

Damage estimated at thousands of dollars was done to property by cloudbursts yesterday, according to reports received last night from Marietta, in Lac Qui Parle county, and other towns in that district.

The cloudburst struck Marietta at 5 a. m. For half an hour, the water literally tumbled out of the skies. When the rain ceased a large area, including the business and part of the residence sections of the town, was under four feet of water. Hundreds of chickens and pigs were drowned. The corn crop in the county was reported damaged. All day yesterday residents of the town floated along the streets in canoes, rowboats, and on makeshift rafts. The plant of the Interstate Electric Light and Power company, which furnishes light for towns in Lac Qui Parle county and the adjoining district in South Dakota, was put out of commission, and the district was in darkness last night.

**Trains Blocked at Walnut Grove.**

As the result of a cloudburst yesterday afternoon, the Chicago & Northwestern railroad bridge at Walnut Grove, Minn., was washed out and all traffic was tied up. It was impossible to transfer passengers, the National highway being stopped by the overflow of Pell creek, three miles west of Lamberton. Both towns are in Redwood county.

Begining at 3 o'clock, rain fell at 10-minute intervals in Minneapolis all yes-

(Continued on Page 2, Col. 5.)

## Foe Reply to Be Answered by Big Four Today

### Official Summary of German Protests Against Terms Made Public.

(By Associated Press.)

Paris, June 15.—The German reply to the peace treaty submitted at Versailles May 7, maintains that the enemies of Germany have forsaken the peace of justice to which they had pledged themselves in the armistice negotiations for a peace of might.

The reply, an official summary of which was made public today, protests against the proposed terms individually and collectively, and demands a return to the original agreement. It presses for verbal negotiations, and states that Germany expects justice on a basis of equality and reciprocity.

The reply follows the lines of the summary of the German counter proposals given out in Berlin at about the time they were presented.

The document covers 119 pages and includes a governing letter by Count Von Brockdorff-Rantzau under date of May 29, which has been published, and a second section of comments following the main outline of the original draft treaty. Two separate papers on legal and financial questions are included as part of the general reply. Both English and French translations have been furnished in pamphlet form, the former totalling about 60,000 words.

**Detailed Analysis.**

The reply begins with a detailed analysis of the legal basis of peace, alleges a flagrant series of contradictions of this basis and points out that the results would be the complete enslave-

(Continued on Page 3, Col. 3.)

## 19 Drown, 12 Are Missing as River Boat Overturns

### Rescuers Dragging Alabama Stream for Victims, Most of Them Children.

(By Associated Press.)

Tuscaloosa, Ala., June 15.—Nineteen persons, most of them children, are known to have been drowned, while rescue parties, aided by searchlights tonight were dragging the Warrior river near Tuscaloosa for the bodies of 12 others missing from a pleasure party of 55 who were cast into the water late today when a gasoline launch was overturned in midstream.

## Baker's Aides Prepared for Investigation

### House Due to Meet Counter-Offensive By War Department.

Public Ledger-Minneapolis Tribune Service. Copyright, 1919, by Public Ledger Co.

Washington, June 15.—Republicans in the House, hopeful of obtaining campaign material for 1920 from the investigation of the War department by a special committee of 15 members are due to meet a counter-offensive when their attack is launched next week.

Not only has Secretary Baker issued orders that the War department must be ready from top to bottom to meet any inquiry raised by the investigating committee, but there has been prepared at his direction what is considered as the largest business inventory in the world, reciting every fact of the department's work in the war.

Disregarding statements of some members of the House that the inquiry is expected to develop campaign material, Secretary Baker has instructed all of his aides, assistants and bureau chiefs to have every record, paper or account ready for examination by the committee.

**Baker's Position Summarized.**

Secretary Baker's position may be summarized as follows:

"Of course Congress is going to investigate the management of the war. Congress not only should conduct such an investigation, but would be derelict in its duty if it did not investigate. Where billions of dollars have been expended there can be no objection to the most exhaustive sort of investigation and auditing of accounts."

This attitude does not alter the fact that the War department heads are anticipating the investigation as a means of emphasizing before the country, as perhaps nothing else could, that the department did a highly creditable piece of work.

The department is proceeding upon the theory that the best defense is a good offense and the records department is being prepared in a manner, Secretary Baker and his bureau heads believe, that will make it difficult for either the committee, or any individual on the committee, to dig up damaging facts that will to any extent mar the record as a whole.

Some of the most capable officers have been detailed to this work. They have not only been assigned to digging up the facts, but also have been paying attention to the manner of presentation. The data is not to be laid before the investigators in a dreary mass. Rather it is being collated, summarized and captioned in a manner calculated to attract attention and stimulate interest, the attention and interest of the country as well as that of the investigators.

**Huge Invoice Prepared.**

When the investigators get into the department they will discover, among other things, that for their guidance there has been prepared what is said to be easily the greatest inventory in the history of the world.

Some idea of the number of articles which the government accumulated as a result of the war may be gained from the fact that the inventories received in Washington filled 40,600 sheets of paper, the size of an ordinary large letter head, with the typewriting single spaced. To take the inventory required a force in Washington of approximately 100 officers and 400 civilians, while there were 10,000 additional officers and men engaged in the entire operation over the country.

## Education Is Illimitable Burton Tells "U" Graduates

"The aim of American education is to put a person in the process of becoming educated," President Marion Leroy Burton told members of the graduating class of the University of Minnesota and their friends in his address at the annual baccalaureate service in the University armory yesterday afternoon. Three thousand persons were present.

**Never Saw Educated Person.**

"I have never seen an educated person and hope I never shall," President Burton declared. "As for being in the process of becoming educated, a man might be graduated from the best university in America, take all available degrees in the United States and abroad, be the best authority in his field, and yet fail to attain that position, for 'many persons are exposed to an education without catching it.'

"Education still has something to do with intellect, I believe. What are some of the requisites for a person who is in the process of becoming educated? First, acquisition of a broad, liberal foundation for his professional, or technical, career. He should be generally familiar with the whole field of languages and literature, and he should have more than a passing acquaintance with at least one language beyond his native tongue. He should have had sufficient experience with the sciences to know what are the scientific aim and point of view. He should have at least a bowing acquaintance with economics, sociology, history, finance, music, and art. He ought to be able to philosophize—to think, abstractly. One mark of a person of education is the capacity to meet new problems and to think straight through them with clearness. He must have an open, receptive mind, intellectual awareness, power to concentrate.

**Broad Minds Necesary.**

"Class of 1919," he continued, "you won't be doing your part in this world unless you have minds broad, well-grounded, capable of facing facts. You must have the ability to feel correctly.

(Continued on Page 8, Col. 6.)

## Yank Guns Fire Over City Cavalry Surrounds Rebels

### Men Cross to Opposite Side of Rio Grande 10 Minutes After Being Called—Both Cavalry and Infantry Set for Action.

### Brigadier General Erwin Says It Is Not to Be an Invasion of Mexico, but a Plan to Stop Villa's Rebels.

(By Associated Press.)

El Paso, June 16.—The first shrapnel shot from United States army guns was fired over Juarez at 12:30 this morning in the direction of the Juarez race track to dislodge Villistas. A second shot followed in five minutes, which struck near the race track, followed at two-minute intervals from two guns placed near the international bridge on the Mexican side.

(By Associated Press.)

El Paso, Texas, Jne 15.—The Twenty-fourth infantry, fourth battalion, crossed the international border to Juarez at 11 o'clock tonight. The Fifth and Seventh cavalry regiments crossed at three fords east of El Paso.

A battalion of the Eighty-second cavalry crossed east of the stock-yards. There were approximately 3,600 American troops on Mexican soil ten minutes after they were ordered to make the crossing.

Colonel Selar R. H. Tompkins of the Seventh cavalry was in command of the cavalry brigade which crossed at the fords and Col. Hadsell was in command of the infantry. Two armored motor cars rumbled over the bridge at 10:55 p. m., going to Juarez.

Following a signal rocket, the American cavalry near San Lorenzo, Chihuahua, started an enveloping movement to the east and southeast of Juarez, to surround the rebels, who were then in the vicinity of the race track. A second green signal rocket indicated the cavalry were advancing at a charge. Heavy firing by American artillery continues.

**To Prevent Firing on El Paso.**

The reason given at military headquarters for ordering the troops to cross was "to prevent firing from the Mexican side on El Paso."

Brigadier General Erwin refused to comment at the time of the crossing.

He added emphatically that it was not to be an invasion of Mexico, that the situation was fully understood by General Francisco Gonzales and the Carranza officials and that no resistance was anticipated from the Carranza forces which have been fighting in Juarez and "no strong resistance is anticipated from the Villa forces," General Erwin added.

**Troops Patrol Juarez.**

Negro soldiers of the Twenty-fourth infantry were patrolling the principal streets of Juarez after midnight tonight. All Americans without special permits were taken to the bridge and ordered to the American side. Juarez is quiet. No shots have been fired by or at the American soldiers.

Following the killing of one artillery man of the Eighty-second artillery and the serious wounding of another by Mexican snipers tonight, General Erwin ordered 25 expert riflemen to that point to return the snipers fire. The shots which killed the artilleryman were fired before the American artillery began the bombardment of the race track.

**Erwin Issues Statement.**

General Erwin's official statement, issued to the Associated Press stating the cause for the crossing of American trops read: "Upon the affidavits of three reputable citizens of El Paso that the Villistas fired into El Paso, and upon the investigation of the wounding of the Mexican girl (in El Paso) showing she was wounded by a shot fired by Villistas, and, upon investigation by the district inspector of these headquarters it was shown that shots undoubtedly coming from the direction of the Villista forces had been fired into El Paso.

"Further, because of the wounding of several innocent and law abiding persons residing in El Paso, and the wounding of two United States soldiers who, in the discharge of their duty, all of these on June 14 and 15, therefore, under the authority given me in telegrams from the headquarters of the Southern department, June 12, 1918, I ordered troops of my command to cross the border and disperse the Villistas. But, upon no account, were they to undertake an invasion into Mexico.

"As soon as I have accomplished this, and have assured the safety of the citizens in El Paso, then the troops of my command will be withdrawn to the American side of the border."

An unknown woman was shot and killed at 8 o'clock in a street four blocks from the Rio Grande on the American side of the border. This was the first fatality on the American side. Previously five persons had been wounded. Following the wounding of Corporal Edward Reilly, of a motor transport company and Corporal Earl Smith of the Twenty-fourth infantry by stray bullets, General Erwin ordered this port closed and the international bridge was taken over by the military.

No one is permitted to cross to Juarez without a military pass.

A Mexican girl was struck in the leg near her home in the Mexican quarter where bullets fell during the fighting. Bullets also struck hotels and buildings downtown in El Paso.

### *Villa Forces Attack Juarez Early in Day.*

Washington, June 15.—Reports of fighting between rebel and government forces in Juarez, Mexico, were scanned closely today by State and War department officials. The fact that bullets had fallen on the American side of the border, endangering American life and property, led to the belief that some action might be ordered by the government.

At the War department it was reiterated that Major General De Rosey C. Cabell, commanding the border guard, had instructions to deal with the situation as he saw fit.

Dispatches to the State department said no Americans had been killed although stray bullets wounded several in El Paso.

The War department in later dis-

## Villa Rebels Again Hurled Back at Juarez

### Federal Chief Wounded 5 Times in Brilliant Dash With Reinforcements.

(By Associated Press.)

Juarez, Mex., June 15.—Fighting was resumed in Juarez at 4:40 p. m. By 6 o'clock the rifle fire was more general than at any time last night. Federal troops charged the rebels as they advanced down Calle Comercio, the principal business street, repulsing them as they did last night.

This dashing cavalry charge was costly to the federals, however, as Colonel J. Gonzales Escobar, garrison commander and hero of the early morning battle today, was wounded five times and hurried to El Paso for medical treatment.

**Reinforcements Revive Battle.**

Prior to the arrival of the reinforcements the fire had died down to occasional sniping. With their arrival it burst out again and continued for more than 30 minutes with the severity of a desperately fought general engagement.

Slowly, under pressure of superior numbers on the outskirts, the federals were forced back. Down Calle Comercio swept the wave of battle, past the old military headquarters, and into the main business district. It was then that Colonel Escobar appearing from around a corner, charged the rebels with waving saber, shouting to his men as he rode down the rebels who scurried for cover. The coup was successful and the Villa force was driven back across Laredo avenue along Comercio street, Colonel Escobar receiving five wounds as he charged past the customs house.

Starting just 24 hours after Villa first appeared before Juarez last night preparatory to giving battle, the fight tonight swung to the south and was in progress around the abandoned Juarez agricultural college where Villa had his 70 wounded. As the federals were apparently not expecting an attack before dark, the outer line of trenches were thinly manned and it was necessary for the federal troops to withdraw toward the town proper, carrying their machine guns and boxes of Mauser ammunition with them.

Then reinforcements were hurried from the flats to the west of town, where no military activity had yet occurred.

Other reinforcements were marched down the steep hill from Fort Hidalgo and engaged the advancing enemy.

## Reds Will Attempt Labor Conversion

Atlantic City, N. J., June 15.—Indications today were that the small radical element in organized labor intends to make strong efforts this week to convert delegates attending the convention of the American Federation of Labor to less harsh views concerning "Bolshevism."

Delegates with more or less radical ideas, plan to have a lecture on Bolshevism and Russia in a local hall, early in the week.

## Fokker Planning Airplane "Train"

London Times-Minneapolis Tribune Service. Special Cable Dispatch. Copyright 1919 by Public Ledger Co.

London, June 15.—Keenest interest is aroused in aviation circles by a report from The Hague that Herr Fokker, the Dutch inventor of the German battle plane and proprietor of the works that manufactured it, proposes having himself seated in one airplane and towed by another plane. This is the first step toward the creation of an aerial train, the idea being an aerial locomotive with a chain of cars similar to a modern railway train.

# The Minneapolis Morning Tribune

Fifty-third Year. No. 30. | Associated Press. | MINNEAPOLIS, MINN., MONDAY, JUNE 23, 1919 | United Press. | Price Two Cents in Minneapolis


# 200 Are Reported Killed at Fergus Falls By Tornado

# German National Assembly Votes 237---138 to Sign Treaty

## Confidence Expressed in New Government Headed By Herr Bauer

### Offer Communicated to Paris Peace Conference With Reservations Against Responsibility-of-War Clauses.

### All Requests of Germans for Further Alterations Rejected by Allies; Time Limit Expires This Afternoon.

(By Associated Press.)

Berlin, June 22.—Germany will sign the peace treaty of the Allied and associated powers. The National Assembly this afternoon by vote of 237 to 138 decided to sign. The Assembly also voted confidence in the new government of Herr Gustav Sauer, 236 to 89. Sixty-eight members abstained from voting.

On the question of signing five members of the Assembly abstained from voting.

Before the vote of confidence was taken, Premier Bauer declared the government would sign the treaty, but without acknowledging the responsibility of the German people for the war and without accepting the obligations contained in Articles 227 to 230 in the treaty relating to the trial of the former emperor and the extradition of other German personages.

*Weimar Offer Communicated to Allied Peace Conference at Paris.*

(By Associated Press.)

The offer of the National Assembly at Weimar has been communicated to the Peace conference in Paris who have discussed its provisions, including reservations made by the Germans against affixing their signatures to the document while it contains clauses acknowledging the responsibility of the German people for the war and demanding the trial of former emperor William.

All the requests of the Germans for further alterations have been rejected by the Allies, and Germany now must give her acquiescence to the treaty as it stands before the expiration of the time limit this afternoon.

**Troops Are Ready to March.**

All is in readiness on the part of the Allied troops in the occupied areas. More than 500,000 soldiers are concentrated here and are only awaiting the word to march eastward into Germany if the Germans prove obdurate. About 150,000 Americans are included in this force.

On the other hand prepartions are being made at Versailles to hold a session of the Peace conference during the present week at which the Germans may affix their signatures to the treaty in the famous Hall of Mirrors in the Trianon Palace.

*Big Four Received Four Notes From Foe.*

(By Associated Press.)

Paris, June 22.—The council received four notes from the Germans, which are supposed to have been prepared in advance and were held to await advices from Weimar on the result of the meeting of the Assembly. President Wilson went at once to the residence of Premier Lloyd George, where the council took up consideration of the notes.

The Council of Four remained in session until 8 p. m. and then adjourned for dinner. The council met again at 9 o'clock and then decided to reject the German request.

*Count Von Bernstorff Will Affix Signature.*

Public Ledger-Minneapolis Tribune Service.
Special Cable Dispatch.
Copyright, 1919, by Public Ledger Co.

Paris, June 22.—Going by the latest official information which has reached the American delegation from Weimar, one member of the German delegation which will affix his signature to the treaty will be Count von Bernstorff, the ambassador who issued "The Lusitania warnings," and whom President Wilson was compelled to order out of the country because of anti-American propaganda.

It is regarded as certain that Germany's enforced "We surrender" will be transmitted to the Allied governments by 7 o'clock Monday night. The

(Continued on Page 3, Col. 1.)

## Drug Using Grows; Beer Lack Blamed

London Times-Minneapolis Tribune Service.
Special Cable Dispatch.
Copyright, 1919, by Public Ledger Co.

London, June 22.—The report of the London coroner says: "Owing to the present inadequate supply of good wholesome beer and the scarcity and expensiveness of light wines and spirits, many people are taking drugs as palliatives with dire results. The principal drugs used are morphia and heroin."

## New Strike Breaks Out in Hungary

London Times-Minneapolis Tribune Service.
Special Cable Dispatch.
Copyright, 1919, by Public Ledger Co.

Berne, June 22.—Word has been received here from Hungary that a general strike has broken out in Szeged, and disorder reigns in the town. The chief workers were arrested, but this only tended to enlarge the revolution and irritation of the strikers. The police side with the workers and all efforts of the French and the white guards to restore order have failed.

### Weather Forecast.

Minnesota—Generally fair today and tomorrow, except possible showers in extreme east portion today; warmer tomorrow in east portion.

## Girl Gives Life Rescuing Sister From Automobile

### Helen Redden, 10 Years Old, Is Killed in Front of Home on Lyndale.

At the cost of her own life Helen Redden, 10 year old daughter of Mr. and Mrs. E. A. Redden, 1909 Lyndale avenue south, saved the life of her seven year old sister, Lucille, shortly before 11 a. m. yesterday.

The smaller child was playing in the street in front of her home in the path of an automobile driven by Fred H. Stenson, 3202 Sixth street north, and did not see the approaching machine. Her sister perceived the danger and rushed to the rescue. Both girls were struck by the machine, but the elder had succeeded in pushing the smaller child out of danger. She herself was injured under the wheels of the automobile.

J. A. Smith of the Smith Taxicab company carried the injured girl to the Hillcrest hospital where she died a few minutes later, her skull fractured by the blow from the machine. Stenson was arrested by the police and is held pending further investigation of the accident.

## Townley Rule in Finish Fight Before Voters

### Future of Nonpartisan Movement Depends on Referendum Thursday.

By George E. Akerson.

Bismarck, N. D., June 22.—Every method known in politics to line up the voters of North Dakota back to the Townley program is being resorted to in the referendum election campaign, which closes Wednesday.

On Thursday the people will approve or disapprove of seven of the laws, making up the main Townley program.

Scurrying from one end of the state to the other, into every township are "carpet-baggers," Socialists and others of extreme radical views, brought here and placed on the league payroll.

Arthur C. Townley and his chief aides are staking everything on this referendum election. They are spending money like water. Much of it is going to pay the outside Socialists and agitators who come from all parts of the United States.

There is one thing to be said for the Nonpartisan league in North Dakota. It has the organization. It has the money. The opposition is not organized nearly so well. In the fight for American institutions the people are not united in a thorough political organization.

**Measures to Be Voted on.**

These are the measures which are to be referred to the people next Thursday:

1. Industrial Commission Law—This forms the keystone of the public ownership arch. It provides for operation and control of all state industries by a commission of three officers. The governor is the real power since everything must be approved by him before it is valid.

2. The Bank of North Dakota—This measure puts North Dakota into the banking business for the purpose of financing the public ownership experiments.

3. The Administration or Educational Bill—This law wipes out the boards of control, education and regents and places the supervision of the entire public school system, the university and all penal correctional and charitable institutions under one

(Continued on Page 5, Col. 2.)

## "Marriage Contract Like House Lease"

### English Noblewoman Deplores the Frequency and Number of Divorce Actions.

Public Ledger-Minneapolis Tribune Service.
Special Cable Dispatch.
Copyright, 1919, by Public Ledger Co.

London, June 22.—Lady Beecham, wife of Sir Thomas Beecham, director of Covent Garden Operas, in the Weekly Dispatch, says:

"Modern marriage is becoming curiously like a contract to lease a house. At the end of, say three years, when one of the contracting parties desires a change, the agreement is ended and the relationship between landlord and tenant ceases. The break-up of home life by the war has also played an important part.

"When the present disturbance has subsided I believe woman will realize that she cannot have freedom without losing freedom for herself and her children and by this knowledge she will reform her course."

Lady Beecham's remarks were occasioned by the recent surfeit of London divorces, more than 800 cases, many in high life, being called in the divorce court this session.

## Atlantic Flyer Not Wordy Over Honor

London Times-Minneapolis Tribune Service.
Special Cable Dispatch.
Copyright, 1919, by Public Ledger Co.

London, June 22.—Captain Sir John Alcock tells this simple story of what happened to him and Lieutenant Sir A. Whitten Brown at Windsor:

"We were introduced to the Prince of Wales, who shook hands and said how delighted he was to know we had successfully flown across the Atlantic. We then went into one of the drawing rooms and were presented to the king. He shook hands and complimented us. Then we both knelt on one knee and the king touched us on each shoulder with his sword and conferred the titles on us.

"The queen then came in and shook hands, after which the king talked with us for ten minutes, asking us many questions about aviation."

## Kaiser's Youngest Son Buys a Villa

London Times-Minneapolis Tribune Service.
Special Cable Dispatch.
Copyright, 1919, by Public Ledger Co.

Berne, June 22.—Prince Joachim, the youngest son of the ex-kaiser, has bought Villa Favorita in Castagnole, Lugano, at a price of $75,000.

## New York Today Is Temporary "Capital" of "Irish Republic"

Public Ledger-Minneapolis Tribune Service.
Copyright, 1919, by Public Ledger Co.

New York, June 22. — New York city will become tomorrow the temporary "capital" city of Ireland. Instead of the Mansion House in Dublin, where Irish history has been in the making at a furious pace recently, the Waldorf-Astoria hotel will be the physical center of Ireland's hopes and aspirations, and the one spot upon which the eyes of Irish sympathizers the world over will be fixed for some time to come.

For tomorrow Professor Edward de Valera, whom the Nationalists, who recently proclaimed an Irish republic, named as their president, and who has arrived unexpectedly in America, will emerge from the seclusion in which he has been living and, from the suite which has been engaged for him at the Waldorf, will send broadcast to the American people a fervent plea for sympathy in his efforts to win recognition for the Irish republic.

**Presence Discovered.**

Professor de Valera had not planned to disclose himself so soon after his secret voyage across the Atlantic, but the announcement, published exclusively in Saturday's Public Ledger and The Minneapolis Tribune, of his presence in this country, convinced him that secrecy could no longer be maintained, and caused a hurried change in his plans. Hence his determination to summon the newspaper men and publicly and formally declare the purpose of his visit here.

His ultimate objective will be the official recognition of the republic by the United States government.

It was hoped by Irish leaders who had assembled here today in anticipation of meeting Professor de Valera that he would issue a statement which would recompense them for their failure to greet him. Instead, a lengthy statement was issued from the headquarters of the Friends of Irish Freedom, at 280 Broadway, by Henry J. Boland, secretary of the Sinn Fein organization in Ireland, who recently came to this country disguised as a stoker in order to have printed here,

(Continued on Page 10, Col. 5.)

## Minneapolis Struck by Fag End of Storm

### Windows Broken, Trees Uprooted; Many Believed Injured.

### Canoeists on City's Lakes Make Scramble for Shore.

Minneapolis suffered considerable property damage when it was struck at 10:45 o'clock last night by the fag ends of the storm which raged throughout western Minnesota. Plate glass windows were broken, trees were uprotted, lamp posts were snapped off and many persons were injured by flying glass, the police believe, although few were injured seriously enough to be taken to the hospitals. Although there were hundreds of canoeists on the city's lakes when the storm broke, no drownings had been reported.

Plate glass windows were blown in at 314 Fourteenth avenue southeast, and in the establishments of the Stone Piano company at 900 Nicollet avenue, the Campbell Coal company, 900 Marquette avenue, and the Barker Bakery company between Sixth and Seventh streets on Hennepin avenue.

In front of 113 Nineteenth avenue south a big tree was blown down, taking with it a dozen telephone and telegraph wires. At Thirteenth street and Harmon place a large oak tree was uprooted into the street, blocking the passageway into Hennepin avenue.

**No Drownings Reported.**

There were no drownings reported on Minneapolis lakes at 1:30 o'clock this morning. On Lake Calhoun and the Lake of the Isles, 100 canoes were out on the waters when the storm broke but at that time all but three of them had reported to the municipal authorities at Lake Calhoun. Although there were hundreds of canoeists on Lake Harriet it is thought that all got to safety, making for the nearest shores. No drownings had been reported there early this morning.

In an automobile accident at Lyndale and Superior boulevard a telephone post was snapped off close to the ground and a fire hydrant was broken off, flooding Lyndale avenue with water for several blocks.

**Pylons Broken Off.**

At Ninth street and Nicollet two of the pylons erected to hold bunting which was used in welcoming home the 151st field artillery were broken off, crashing across the sidewalk and endangering the persons of numerous pedestrians who were scurrying across the sidewalk in search of shelter.

Throughout Loring park trees were uprooted. Among the largest plate glass windows to be destroyed was one in the Elks' club building, Second avenue south and Seventh street.

## Man Killed By an Unknown; Argued Over Glass of Beer

### Slayer Leaves for Doctor and Escapes—Shooting Occurs at 310 N. Second Street.

An argument over a glass of beer resulted in the shooting of Jean Dilworth, 1005 Nineteenth avenue northeast, at 1 o'clock this morning, by an unidentified man. The shooting took place at the home of J. W. Henkas, Flat 7, 310 North Second street. Dilworth died shortly after being shot.

Four people were in the room at the time, Mr. and Mrs. Henkas, Tom Ryan and the unidentified man had met met Dilworth early in the evening, and taken him to the police, according to the information secured by the police.

The argument started when Dilworth picked up a glass of beer claimed by the unidentified man. After a few words the unknown drew a revolver and shot Dilworth on the right side, the bullet passing through the heart. At first it was thought that the victim was only injured and the unidentified man left for a doctor, managing to make his escape. A few minutes later Dilworth died.

**Forest Fire Rages in Colorado.**

Pueblo, Colo., June 22.—Seven hundred acres of timber have been destroyed in a fire that is sweeping the San Isabel forest reserve near Beulah, 35 miles west of Pueblo.

### *Correspondents Discuss Foreign, Local Subjects*

T. P. O'CONNOR tells in a special cable dispatch to The Minneapolis Tribune how the Irish-American envoys, indictment of Erin's conditions has stirred British. Every effort being made to prevent publication of statements made by Walsh and Dunne. His article appears on page 6.

GEORGE F. AUTHIER tells of movement for reform of rural mail service on page 4.

E. J. DILLON says recent adverse vote against Orlando by the Italian parliament is regarded in Paris as presaging an anti-Ally policy in a special article on page 5.

WILLIAM HOWARD TAFT'S comment on Elihu Root's plan for ratifying the treaty and league covenant "with resolutions" is that Mr. Root has changed his mind. His article is on page 10.

## Air Liners Soon to Supercede Cable, Says British Leader

### Quick Mail and Passenger Service to Bring New Era, Lord Morris Believes.

Public Ledger-Minneapolis Tribune Service.
Special Cable Dispatch.
Copyright, 1919, by Public Ledger Co.

London, June 22.—Lord Morris, the former prime minister of New Foundland, in the Weekly Dispatch, says:

"The time is not far distant when an airplane, flying 200 miles an hour will supercede the cable and the wireless for quick message carrying purposes, for the machine will be able to take to America from the United Kingdom and back thousands of messages at a cost which will render the present expense of cable and wireless a thing of the past. The most important phase of the revolution in social and commercial life, which the aeroplane will achieve like as not, will be the provision of daily mail to such places as New York and Philadelphia from London and Manchester.

"Millions of people, dependent upon the result of the negotiations between the business houses in Great Britain and America will find that industry has entered on a new lease of life once it has become practicable to get prompt reply from the other side of the Atlantic.

"People will write long letters instead of uncomfortably abbreviated cables. The big business men of the two countries will be able to exchange visits with the full assurance that weeks of worry can be wiped away by a 48-hour trip through the air. One's imagination conjures up a certain prospect of the overhead sky traversed by the great passenger lines and the increasingly cosmopolitan character of everybody."

## Winnipeg Mob First to Fire, Mayor Asserts

### Executive Issues Statement on Saturday's Demonstration—City Is Quiet.

(By Associated Press.)

Winnipeg, Man., June 22.—Winnipeg was quiet today after the bloody rioting of yesterday afternoon. The city is not under martial law but federal soldiers still are on duty in the business district to aid and support the civil authorities. Certain defined areas are still guarded by soldiers.

**Mayor Says Strikers Fired First.**

Mayor Charles F. Gray today issued a statement in which he declared that an investigation showed that strikers, and not Royal Northwest Mounted police fired the first shots yesterday. He declared that the riot followed addresses by union men who had made "inflammatory speeches."

Early tonight the soldiers were withdrawn from Main street, and the duty of policing this district was again taken over by returned soldier constables. Traffic is proceeding normally, except for street cars, which, company officials state, will be running tomorrow. Soldiers are held in readiness at barracks.

**Three Seriously Wounded.**

No additional deaths were reported today. Three men who sustained bullet wounds are said to be in a serious condtion. Official records show one death, 14 persons suffered from bullet wounds and upwards of 60 who sustained less serious injuries.

In the past 36 hours 22 foreigners have been arrested. Six were taken last night by the Royal Northwest Mounted police and sent to Kingston, Ont., penitentiary, pending a hearing before a special immigration board of inquiry. The remainder were taken into custory by city police and will be dealt with through the civil courts on deportable charges.

The area patrolled by the soldiers was the scene of the fighting yesterday, and also was the scene of fighting on June 10, when returned soldier constables replaced the dismissed policemen. The district includes two blocks on Main street north of Port-

(Continued on Page 8, Col. 3.)

## Blunder of Underlings Turns Egyptians' Loyalty to Hatred

By William T. Ellis.

Special Correspondent of The Minneapolis Tribune and the New York Herald.
(Copyright, 1919, by the N. Y. Herald Service.)

Cairo, May 22.—Recent events in Egypt have wounded Great Britain in her most sensitive spot, her spirit of sportsmanship and fair play. In a critical hour a considerable number of the British in Egypt have proved to be bad losers and not loyal to their own leader.

Suddenly, within an hour, Cairo's unprecendented festival of jubilation was transformed into scared, scurrying, resentful and murderous minded mob of men and women bent on bitter vengeance. What caused this dramatic change, ending, as by magic, all the rejoicings and celebrations? Nothing less than the collapse, locally, of a glorious British tradition.

The lack of chivalry on the part of many or most British citizens in Cairo has cost their nation more dearly than any man can at present estimate. The historic British reputation for square dealing, which has hitherto been the Empire's supreme asset in the world, is now being blanketed by the swift-flying news that when a great official rectified a stupid government blunder in Egypt his subordinates and nationals refused to play the game and at the sight of a subject people's rejoicings over the good news of British fairness gave way by railings, cursings, violence and killings, finally precipitating a situation which made the latter state of things worse than the first.

Such an incident is not easy to write. By conviction I am essentially pro-British. I have seen her work all over the world, and while criticisms could be written of British manners, the British character, on the whole, has everywhere stood for even-handed justice and integrity of purpose. British rule has meant the substantial welfare and progress of the native peoples, even here in Egypt.

**American Ideals Dominate.**

The new ideals which are coming to dominance in the world are more than American—they are Anglo-Saxon.

(Continued on Page 4, Col. 1.)

## 400 Believed Injured; 600 Homes Wrecked; Trains Rushing Aid

### 50 to 75 Thought Dead in Collapse of Grand Central Hotel; Wind Cuts Wide Path Through City.

### Governor on Way With Troops, Doctors and Nurses; Guard Units Called Out; Airplanes Expected to Help.

A. Larson, a real estate man of Fergus Falls, reached Wendell, Minn., 25 miles from Fergus Falls, at 1:30 a. m. by motorcycle with the first story of the disaster from an identified survivor, according to information received here at 2 a. m. He assisted in the rescue work and then made his way across country.

Larson said he assisted in removing ten bodies from the Grand Central hotel. He said the hotel was wrecked and 40 persons were buried in the debris. The peaceful quiet of a Sunday afternoon was disrupted by a terrific electric storm, he said, accompanied by heavy rain. Citizens were seeking shelter from the rain when the cyclone struck.

The storm swept through the center of the business district along Union avenue, the principal business street, demolishing practically every building for a distance of three blocks and scores of residences on adjacent streets.

The state hospital and two private hospitals, Wright and St. Luke's, were unharmed, he said. The Great Northern depot was wrecked and a score of persons killed or severely injured. He estimated the number of buildings destroyed in Fergus Falls at 100.

More than 200 persons are believed to have been killed in a tornado which swept Fergus Falls and Western Minnesota last night. Four hundred persons are said to have been injured, and hundreds of buildings demolished, in Minnesota's greatest disaster since the forest fires which swept the Northern part of the state last year.

With telegraph and telephone connections disrupted throughout the entire area over which the tornado passed, and no telegraph line standing nearer than [illegible] miles to Fergus Falls, reports from widely scattered localities agreed as to the number of dead and injured.

**Grand Central Hotel Wrecked.**

In the havoc wrought by the wind is the destruction of the Grand Central hotel in Fergus Falls, in the ruins of which 75 persons are thought to be buried; the demolishing of the Northern Pacific passenger and freight station, and the overturning of the Great Northern "Oriental Limited" near Carlisle, where eight coaches filled with passengers were lownb into a ditch.

Latest available reports said that three blocks in the business section of the city had been wiped out.

Relief agencies were at work within a short time after news of the tornado was received in Minneapolis. Governor Burnquist, Adjutant General Rhinow, Major Bellows, and 150 members of the Fourth Minnesota infantry, National guard, left the Great Northern station in Minneapolis for Fergus Falls at 1 a. m. A corps of doctors, 30 nurses, and residents of Fergus Falls were also on the train.

**Four Trains on Way.**

At the same time a railroad wrecking crew left from St. Paul, a second special relief train left for the scene of the disaster by way of Moorhead, and throughout the western section of the state doctors and nurses and supplies were speeding toward Fergus Falls early today.

Civilian agencies also were at work. Mayor Meyers was informed by The Tribune of the disaster and immediately took steps to give aid to the sufferers. Telegrams were filed to the Mayor of Fergus Falls as follows, with instructions to telegraph officials to deliver them at the earliest possible moment:

"Minneapolis offers every assistance we can render. Hope reports of disaster are over-estimated. Await your advice, at your service. J. E. Meyers, Mayor."

The telephone operator at Wahpeton, a town on the North Dakota line, about fifty miles west of Fergus Falls, said that reports there placed the loss of life in Fergus Falls at 200. Seven hundred houses and other buildings were destroyed by the storm or by a fire which followed, doubtless caused by the collapse of buildings in which fires were being used for various purposes.

**Strikes Town in Evening.**

The storm struck Fergus Falls about 7 o'clock. Great Northern train No. 1, the Oriental Limited, west bound from Chicago to Seattle, was blown from the track about 20 miles west of Fergus Falls, but early reports said only one passenger was injured. A girl received a sprained ankle. The passengers were taken to Moorhead.

Brainerd, Minn., residents saw the storm sweeping in a northeastly direction, passing over several towns after its destruction at Fergus Falls, but no other towns in that vicinity reported serious damage.

Train No. 1 was traveling between 30 and 40 miles an hour when the twister struck the baggage car behind the tender when about six miles west of Fergus Falls, throwing seven of the eleven coaches from the rails. The baggage car was torn out of the train and set down about 30 feet from the rails at right angles to them.

The suction also tore out the tracks under this car.

**Several Passengers Bruised.**

Another baggage car, an express car, the smoker and three day coaches kept their momentum and their trucks were piled up where the track had been removed.

The coaches were deposited along

## Officer Injured in Auto Accident

### Captain Cobb, Aiding in Mobilizing Sanitary Corps, Cut by Glass.

Acting as a messenger for Colonel Bellows in mobilizing the sanitary corps of the Fourth Minnesota infantry for aid in the Fergus Falls disaster, Capt. Frederick L. Cobb, 1783 Colfax avenue south, was thrown from the automobile in which he was driving at Lyndale avenue and Superior boulevard at 11 o'clock last night.

He was on his way to the Armory in a taxicab, operated by Edward Hanville, 18 Thirteenth street north and was driving rapidly when to avoid a collision with a touring car owned, according to the police, by F. B. Wells, 2119 Park avenue, the car containing the officer swerved to the right, struck the touring car and careened into a water hydrant and then a telephone pole. The water gushed into the street. Captain Cobb was struck by flying glass and Hanville was also cut on the face and hands. The chauffer was taken to the City hopital. Captain Cobb was unable to take the train which he had planned and was taken home.

Teh wind and rainstorm rendered the drivers of both cars momentarialy blinded, they said.

About the same time a car driven by Earl Warner, 1704 Nicollet avenue, collided at Seventh street and Hennepin avenue with another driven by W. Shelley, 99½ Seventh street, St. Paul. Mrs. Shelley was thrown through the glass windshield and suffered cuts and bruises. She was taken to the City hospital, thence home.

**Lowden Signs Search Bill.**

Springfield, Ill., June 22.—Governor Lowden late today signed the so-called search and seizure bill.

# The Minneapolis Sunday Tribune

Fifty-third Year. No. 36. Associated Press. MINNEAPOLIS, MINN., SUNDAY, JUNE 29, 1919 United Press. 68 Pages. Price Six Cents in Minneapolis


# Wilson Refuses to Lift War-time Prohibition Ban at Present
# Peace Treaty Signed by Germany, Ratification Next Step

## National Assembly Now Looked to by Allies to Take Final Action

### Withdrawal of Blockade Depends on the Teuton Government — Clemenceau Gives Warning on Pact Observance.

### Ceremony of Signing Befitting Sorrows and Sufferings of Five Years Lacking Impressiveness of Expected Pageant.

Summary of the peace treaty as signed at Versailles yesterday, and sidelights on the signing will be found on Pages 6 and 7 of this section.

(By Associated Press.)

Paris, June 28.—President Wilson left Paris for his homeward journey tonight. His train started from the Gare Des Invalides for Brest at 9:45.

Versailles, June 28.—World peace was signed and sealed in the historic Hall of Mirrors at Versailles this afternoon, but under circumstances which somewhat dimmed the expectations of those who had worked and fought during long years of war and months of negotiations for its achievement.

The absence of the Chinese delegates, who at the last moment were unable to reconcile themselves to the Shantung settlement, and left the eastern empire outside the formal purviews of peace, struck the first discordant note in the assembly. A written protest which General Jan Christian Smuts lodged with his signature was another disappointment to the makers of the treaty.

But, bulking larger, was the attitude of Germany and the German plenipotentiaries, which left them as evident from the official program of the day, and from the expression of M. Clemenceau, still outside any formal reconciliation, and made actual restoration to regular relations and intercourse with the Allied nations dependent, not upon the signature of the "preliminaries of the peace" today but upon ratification by the National Assembly.

The Allied note to the German delegation dealing with ratification of the treaty by Germany, was also delivered. It is pointed out in the note, among other things, that withdrawal of the blockade of Germany depends on ratification of the treaty.

#### Clemenceau's Warning.

To M. Clemenceau's stern warning that they would be expected and be held to observe the treaty provisions legally and completely, the German delegates, through Dr. Hainiel Von Haimhausen, replied after returning to the hotel that had they known they would be treated on a different status after signing than the Allied representatives as shown by their separate exit before the general body of the conference they never would have signed.

Under the circumstances the general tone of sentiment in the historic sitting was one rather of relief at the uncontrovertible end of hostilities than of complete and unalloyed satisfaction.

The ceremony came as a dramatic close with the wildly enthusiastic reception of President Wilson, M. Clemenceau and Mr. Lloyd George by the crowds outside the palce, who ignored or disregarded the minor discords of the day. They tore the three statesmen from their escorts and almost carried them bodily in their progress through the chateau grounds, to watch the playing of the fountains—a part of the program which had been planned as a dignified state processional of all the plenipotentiaries.

#### Ceremony Was Quiet.

The ceremony otherwise had been planned deliberately to be befitting the sorrows and sufferings of almost five years and the lack of impressiveness and picturesqueness which many spectators who had expected a magnificent state pageant, complained, was a matter of design, not merely omission.

The actual ceremony was shorter than had been expected, in view of the number of signatures which were to be appended to the treaty and the two accompanying conventions, ending a bare 49 minutes after the hour set for opening. The proceedings were carried out without surface incidents, since the Germans were silent, and the Chinese refused to sign was evident only by the vacant chairs. The sole words to be recorded in the protocol were M. Clemenceau's short opening allocution, with its brief stern warning to the Germans, and his equally terse phrases declaring the ceremony closed.

#### Goose Quills Scratched.

The intervening three quarters of an hour was marked by the scratching of big goose quills or modern steel pens, which most of the delegates preferred, and the steady procession of delegation after delegation to the seats at the three tables, within the enclosures, upon which the documents were placed for signatures.

Contrary to expectations the Germans were called to sign first, and no precedence was given M. Clemenceau, President Wilson or Mr. Lloyd George, who in the peace treaty appear only as members of the respective delegations, and discard the dignities and responsibilities which during the negotiations were summed up in the phrase, "the big three."

These two German delegates arose without a word at M. Clemenceau's

(Continued on Page 2, Col. 2.)

#### Weather Forecast.

MINNESOTA—Generally fair today and tomorrow; somewhat warmer today and in east portion tomorrow.

## New Treaty Only a Scrap of Paper, Berlin Paper Says

### "Vengeance for Disgrace of 1919," Is Appeal of Another Journal.

(By Associated Press.)

Berlin, June 28.—The pan-German Deutch Zeitung prints the following across its front page:

"German honor today will be carried to its grave in the Hall of Mirrors, in which in the glorious year of 1871, the German empire was resurrected in all its splendor. Lest we forget.

"In restless labor the German people will again strive to obtain that place among the nations of the world to which it is entitled. Then vengeance for the disgrace of 1919."

The Tageblatt says: "The German people reject the treaty, which its delegates are signing today, and it does not believe for a single moment that it will endure. Despite the fact that it is written on parchment, it remains a scrap of paper, because it is a mockery of all the laws of reason and morals and the most disgraceful exhibit in the museum of civilization."

## Pact Signing Brings Senate Issue to Head

### Opposition to League Suddenly Crystallizes on Root Proposal.

By George F. Authier.

Washington, June 28.—Signing of the peace treaty at Versailles and the President's statement, which is interpreted as a demand for ratification of the peace treaty without any amendment, has provided a sharp issue. Out of the chaos which has enveloped opposition to the league covenant as it has been framed, united action has suddenly sprung and the Senate will insist upon amendments, or reservations, probably the latter.

The situation developed with kaleidoscopic quickness and, promptly following the President's statement, senators in opposition were declaring themselves. Even Senator Porter J. McCumber of North Dakota, who has been in favor of the league, is now in favor of amendments, and Senators Spencer of Missouri and Capper of Kansas, declared there must be reservations or amendments before the Senate would ratify the treaty.

#### Sentiment Is United.

At no time during the controversy has there been such united sentiment, and the general disposition of both Republican and Democratic objectors to the treaty is to unite, in substance, upon the plan suggested by Senator Elihu Root. Mr. Root is coming to Washington to confer with senators who are in doubt as to whether reservations will safeguard the American rights. It is understood that Senator Root believes "reservations" will be sufficient

(Continued on Page 2, Col. 6.)

## Germans Indicate Plan to Quit Danzig

### Teutons Systematically Seek to Bait Poles Into an Attack.

By Christopher Lumby.

London Times-Minneapolis Tribune Service. Special Cable Dispatch.



Warsaw, June 28.—There is a certain amount of evidence from Danzig and western Prussia to show the Germans are making preparations for evacuation by removing the government stores. Danzig is perfectly calm, but General Below, commanding the area, has declared his intention of keeping troops on the spot until he can hand it over to the Allied forces on the ground that there will certainly be riots if they were withdrawn.

Minor conflicts with the Germans are reported on the Silesian front. There are likely to be sensational rumors of outbreaks of fighting there which should not be too readily believed. The Germans are continuing to do everything in their power to provoke and excite the Poles with a view to causing an explosion and thereby they could not be losers.

One effect of their effort at war is to cause the Poles to withdraw troops from Eastern Galicia to strengthen the covering force on the German frontier and the result is apparent from the success of the last Bolshevist offensive.

## Rotten Egg Hits Von Reuter's Face

(By Associated Press.)

London, June 28.—A dispatch to the Central News from Oswestry, Shropshire, says that Admiral von Reuter, who commanded the German fleet sunk in Scapa Flow, was recognized when he called today at a local bank. He was struck in the face with a rotten egg and was otherwise assaulted.

## Extremity of Law for Tax Dodgers

(By Associated Press.)

Washington, June 28.—Tax dodgers, rich and poor, were promised limit of the law by Commissioner of Internal Revenue Roper in a statement today commenting on the recent conviction in Boston of William A. English and John H. O'Brien, wool merchants, who returned their taxes at $109,000 instead of $1,379,817. Mr. Roper said the government refused to allow English and O'Brien to pay on $1,500,000 to escape prison sentences.

## Sinn Fein Quarters Raided at Dublin

(By Associated Press.)

Dublin, June 28.—Sinn Fein head quarters was raided this afternoon and the building searched by a large force of military.

## City Will Honor Thousand New Citizens Today

### Americanization Day Mass Meeting Will Welcome Adopted Aliens.

### Secretary Lane Sends His Greetings to New Citizens.

With the significance of the day deepened immeasurably by the realization that now indeed the time has come for taking up again the normal development of that American ideal of life, to preserve which for the world we went to war, Minneapolis today celebrates Americanization day.

The signing of the final peace treaty by the defeated foe of America is the world fact that will give tone to the observance of the day. It will make Americanization day peace day as well. It will bring it about that the huge mass meeting of Minneapolis citizenry called for today to express the value that Minneapolis puts on American citizenship shall become a mass meeting in which that citizenry shall dedicate itself to the new citizenship responsibilities that come with peace.

#### 1,000 New Citizens Welcomed.

The mass meeting, which will be held in the Armory, at 3 p. m., will be the city's welcome to the 1,000 men and women of alien birth living in Minneapolis who have this year been received into American citizenship.

Floyd Gibbons, noted war correspondent, will give the principal address. Governor Burnquist and Mayor Meyers will welcome the new Americans into participation in everything that citizenship implies. The meeting, which is under the auspices of the Civic & Commerce association, is the culmination of the first state conference on Americanization, held here this week.

#### Lane Sends Greetings.

Franklin K. Lane, secretary of the interior, has sent his cordial greetings to the foreign-born people of Minneapolis just entering into American citizenship in a letter to Cavour Langdon, president of the Civic & Commerce association.

"To them are freely given," Mr. Lane said, "the rights and privileges, the liberty that millions have died to achieve and retain. Uncounted thousands of foreign-born before them have found in America a fuller measure of life and happiness. I hope these citizens will have the same good fortune. I join you in extending to them the hand of cordial fellowship."

#### Alien Woman and Child, Topic.

The immigrant woman, and the relation of the children of the immigrants to the fathers and especially to the mothers over whom their own more rapid Americanization gives them dominance was the principal topic of the last session of the state Americanization conference yesterday.

California's plan of "home teacher" employed by boards of education under the state's commission of immigration and housing is one plan which cuts

(Continued on Page 7, Col. 3.)

## Peace Links Britain With U. S. in Ideals, King Tells President

### Kinship in Common Sacrifice Makes Nations Brothers, He Declares.

(By Associated Press.)

London, June 28.—King George has sent the following message to President Wilson:

"In this glorious hour when the long struggle of nations for right, justice and freedom is at last crowned by a triumphant peace, I greet you, Mr. President, and the great American people in the name of the British nation.

"At a time when fortune seemed to frown, and the issues of the war trembled in the balance, the American people stretched out the hand of fellowship to those who on this side of the ocean were battling for a righteous cause. Light and hope at once shone brighter in our hearts, and a new day dawned.

"Together we have fought to a happy end; together we lay down our arms in proud consciousnes of valiant deeds nobly done.

"Mr. President, it is on this day one of our happiest thoughts that the American and British people, brothers in arms, will continue forever to be brothers in peace. United before by language, traditions, kinship and ideals there has now been set upon our fellowship the sacred seal of common sacrifice."

## J. Barleycorn Dying Hard; No Mourners

### Glasses Tinkle, "Wealthy Water" Fizzes as Coming Demise Celebrated.

Bulletins from the bedside of John Barleycorn were watched with eager interest in Minneapolis last night.

As it became evident that, although the patient was still alive and possessed the old kick, no hope could be extended that he would survive the night tomorrow, there was no evidence of sadness. The funeral bells tolled not.

On the other hand, there was a merry tinkling of certain well-known glasses. There was a familiar fizz, and a musical gurgling sound, as the city joined in a demonstration almost equalling the most ecstatic of greetings to the New Year.

But not the whole city celebrated thus. Oh no! There were those who watched with glee as President Wilson handed the prostrate patient a backhand wallop that made certain an early end to the sufferings he has undergone so heroically of late.

Customers—seated, standing, leaning upon the bar or upon each other—thronged the saloons and cafes last night. Many dispensers of liquid refreshment refused to mix drinks after 5 p. m., and from then on it slipped down "straight."

There was an enormous demand for bottled goods—but the old relation be-

(Continued on Page 16, Col. 1.)

## Liquor Lid to Be Off After Demobilization, President Declares

### Executive Asserts He Lacks Power to Act While Million Men Are Still in Service.

### Expects to Permit Sale When Soldiers Enrolled for Emergency Are Discharged, He Cables.

(By Associated Press.)

Washington, June 28.—President Wilson has decided he cannot legally lift the war-time prohibition ban before the country goes dry at midnight Monday, but he expects to do so as soon thereafter as his power is made clear by the completion of demobilization.

In a cablegram made public tonight at the White House, the President said he was convinced after consultation with his legal advisers that he had no authority to act at this time.

"When demobilization is completed," he continued "my power to act without congressional intervention will be exercised."

The message expressed no opinion as to the authority of the President, when he raises the ban, to make his action applicable only to beer and wine.

Secretary Tumulty gave out at the White House tonight the following cable from the President:

"I am convinced that the attorney general is right in advising me that I have no legal power at this time in the matter of the ban on liquor. Under the act of November, 1918, my power to take action is restricted. The act provides that 'after June 30, 1919, until the conclusion of the present war and thereafter until the termination of demobilization, the date of which shall be determined and proclaimed by the President, it shall be unlawful, etc.'

#### Demobilization Not Ended.

This law does not specify that the ban shall be lifted with the signing of peace but with the termination of the demobilization of the troops, and I cannot say that that has been accomplished. My information from the War department is that there are still 1,000,000 men in the service under the emergency call. It is clear therefore that the failure of Congress to act upon the suggestion contained in my message of May 20, 1919, asking for a repeal of the act of November 21, 1918, so far as it applies to wines and beer, makes it impossible to act in this matter at this time.

"When demobilization is terminated my power to act without Congressional action will be exercised.

"WOODROW WILSON."

Refusal of President Wilson to act at this time means that the arm of the war-time law will reach out at midnight Monday and close the doors of every liquor establishment on American soil.

Next in public interest to the announcement of the President's comes the question "how soon will the army be demobilized?" There was belief in some quarters tonight that this date would not be long delayed in view of the signing of the treaty, the action of Congress in reducing the size of the army, and the effort of the government to bring back all the troops from abroad just as speedily as possible.

#### May Come This Summer.

The President's emphatic announcement as to what he would do when demobilization "is terminated" was in line with the opinion of the House Judiciary committee members, expressed heretofore, that it did not require Congressional action to authorize him to declare war-time prohibition ended.

This may come, it was pointed out, sooner than most people imagine, and there were predictions tonight that saloons in cities where the sale of liquor now is permitted might be in operation by the end of the summer. They could not operate, however, beyond January 16, 1920, when the constitutional amendment goes into effect.

With all doubt relieved as what the President would or could not do, anti-prohibitionists in the House prepared to make the best fight possible on the general prohibition enforcement bill which was reported out yesterday by the Judiciary committee. It will not be taken up on the floor until after the short holiday recess, which means the government will depend upon present laws for enforcement of the war-time act. Warning has been given that these provide ample penalties and ample means of prosecution.

#### Bill on Floor Tomorrow.

Chairman Volstead of the Judiciary committee, announced that the majority report recommending passage of the enforcement measure would be presented to the House Monday.

In Congress, the only movement was by Representative Hoch, Republican, Kansas, a prohibition advocate who introduced a resolution calling on Secretary Glass for a report as to whether government tax receipts, permits or licenses had been issued, entitling manufacturers or vendors of liquor to continue business after June 30. The measure, introduced without comment, was deferred to a committee.

In attacking the general enforcement bill, Representative Dyer of Missouri declared that the war time act "has no effect or force" because the "war is over" and that "any effort to enforce it will meet with failure in the courts."

He contended also that Congress was without authority to define intoxicating liquor for either enforcement of war-time or constitutional prohibition and that such definition was solely a judicial question.

## Soldier Misses $100 After Ride

Police are looking for an unidentified man who rode in a taxi cab with Bernard J. Coffman of St. Paul, a discharged soldier, last night. Coffman reported that a man who rode with the driver climbed into the rear of the cab. When he alighted, Coffman said, he missed $100. A. Lesard, alleged to have been the driver of the taxi cab, was arrested by John Finlayson, detective, and is being held pending the finding of his companion.

## Berlin Rail Men Defy Union Order

(By Associated Press.)

Berlin, June 28.—The striking railway men in the Berlin district, some 20,000 shop and yard workers, have decided to continue on strike, in spite of the demand of their union that they resume work.

## Grand Palace and Hall Where Memorable Treaty Was Signed

The upper photo is of the Grand Palace at Versailles, at which the peace treaty was signed, while the lower photo is the Hall of Mirrors in which room the Germans affixed their signatures to the memorable document.

# The Minneapolis Morning Tribune

Fifty-third Year. No. 48. | Associated Press. | MINNEAPOLIS, MINN., FRIDAY, JULY 11, 1919 | United Press. | Price Two Cents in Minneapolis

# League Is Practical Necessity for World, Wilson Says

## Wood Absolves Townley of War Program Blame

### Leaguer Credits Self and Lemke for Resolutions Booklet.

### North Dakota Officials Take Stand in Support of Nonpartisans.

### Prominent Twin Cities Men to Be Subpoenaed, Defense Announces.

(By Associated Press.)

Jackson, July 10.—Fred B. Wood of Minneapolis, former North Dakota farmer and a member of the Nonpartisan league's executive committee of three, was the principal witness at the afternoon session of the conspiracy trial of A. C. Townley and Joseph Gilbert, league officials.

Mr. Wood was the first man to join the organization, he said, and has been closely connected with it since 1915.

After a bitter argument, Wood was allowed to testify regarding the drawing of the league's war resolutions at the close of the St. Paul convention in 1917, which have been attacked by the state in this case.

The witness stated that so far as he knew, President Townley had nothing to do with the resolutions.

"William Lemke, also a member of the executive committee, and myself were the only ones who talked at that time about the resolutions," Wood declared.

**Dakota Officials on Stand.**

This witness was preceded on the stand by his son, Lieut. Gov. Howard Wood, of North Dakota. The latter was not permitted to testify regarding a number of Townley speeches not set forth in the indictment or upon which proof has not been offered by the state.

John M. Hagan, commissioner of Agriculture and Labor for North Dakota, was called to testify regarding his views of the loyalty of the speech Townley delivered before the Nonpartisan League convention at St. Paul in September, 1917, but Judge E. C. Dean sustained a state objection against this line of testimony.

**Townley May Be Called.**

The defense announced tonight that Walter Liggett, publicity director for the league, probably would be called tomorrow, and that his testimony would be rather extensive. Townley may be called after Liggett's testimony is concluded.

"You also have been speaker of the House in North Dakota?" Mr. Hoke asked Lieutenant Governor Wood.

"Yes."

"There have been offered in evidence in this case certain resolutions with reference to the attitude of the league toward the war. You are familiar with these resolutions?"

"Yes."

"Do you know where they were first circulated?"

**Objections Block Answers.**

A state objection was sustained.

"[illegible] you say whether or not those resolutions have been indorsed by 50,000 farmers in North Dakota?"

A state objection was sustained.

"I mean prior to the circulation of the resolutions in Minnesota."

The state again objected that the question was immaterial and was sustained.

"Do you know whether these resolutions contain part of the platform

(Continued on Page 6, Col. 1.)

## Contractor Burned in Rescuing Horses

E. Q. Stone, teaming contractor, was painfully burned about the head and body, while attempting to rescue horses from his barn, 2842 Twelfth avenue south, which caught fire shortly before 10:30 o'clock last night. Three of the animals perished in the flames and it was while leading the fourth one from its stall that Mr. Stone suffered his burns. The fire was believed to have started by sparks from a passing locomotive. The loss was estimated at $2,500.

## Planes Will Patrol Whole Mexican Line

San Diego, Cal., July 10.—The Mexican border from the Pacific ocean to the Gulf of Mexico will be patrolled from dawn to dusk by military airplanes traveling at an average height of 4,000 feet, it was announced today by Col. Henry H. Arnold, aeronautical officer of the Western department of the army. The aerial patrol will begin as soon as the squadrons can be organized.

## 4th Division Units Start for America

London Times-Minneapolis Tribune Service. Special Cable Dispatch. Copyright, 1919, by Public Ledger Co.

Coblenz, July 10.—The American Fourth division has sent its first train load of troops for the United States. Other units will follow.

### Weather Forecast

MINNESOTA—Fair and warmer today, tomorrow probably fair and continued warm.

## 3 Motor Policemen Figure in Spills; Each Loses Quarry

### Hallet Misses Brake, Heusler Hits Car Track, Couch Has Header; Speeders Ramble.

Three motorcycle patrolmen figured in three spills late yesterday and in each incident an automobile speeder escaped arrest.

Patrolman Frank Hallet was seriously injured when he toppled from his machine on Sixth street and Third avenue south. At the City hospital it was found his left ankle had been sprained. According to witnesses, Hallet was following a speeder, and when close upon the violator, took his foot off the brake. Hallet plowed into the rear of the pursued automobilist's car. The auto driver continued on his way, not noticing the troubles of the patrolman.

Patrolman George Hensler was dumped from his machine while driving 45 miles an hour up University avenue southeast hill, hot after a St. Paul-bound auto speeder. His front wheel caught in a car track as he was attempting to turn out, and he fell, sliding 20 feet along the pavement.

Patrolman S. A. Couch was bruised in a spill from his machine near police headquarters late in the afternoon. His uniform and machine were damaged. All three patrolmen were assigned to the mounted squad June 1, by Chief Walker.

## R-34 Hits Up 75-Mile Speed on Home Trip

### Super-Dirigible 1,000 Miles From Mineola Last Wireless Shows.

(By Associated Press.)

Washington, July 10.—Aided by a westerly wind that sometimes reached a velocity of nearly 40 miles an hour, the British dirigible R-34 was well out over the Atlantic on the return trip to East Fortune, Scotland. The last message from the airship, received late today by the Navy department, gave her position then as 650 miles from Mineola, L. I., from which she started last midnight.

The dirigible, according to wireless reports received by the Navy department averaged more than 60 miles an hour for the first 15 hours of the return flight, and at times, the speed reached between 75 and 80 miles an hour. The dirigible thus was making better time during the flight to America, and if weather conditions remain favorable naval officers believe Maj. G. H. Scott, commander, and members of the R-34's crew will see British shores early Saturday.

The first word heard from the R-34 after it left American shores this morning, was a radio message sent at 4 a. m. giving the ship's position as 130 miles due east from Long Island. Direct communication was maintained with the Navy department thereafter. At 10 a. m. a message said the dirigible was then making 58 miles an hour, equivalent to about 64 miles. An hour later the R-34 signalled that the wind was becoming stronger and that her speed had reached 80 miles at times.

Telegrams of thanks to American officials were sent today by Major Scott, one to Rear Admiral J. H. Glennon, commandant of the Third naval district, which includes the Mineola field where the R-34 landed on its arrival in this country, thanked the officers and men who assisted in mooring the dirigible. Another was to E. H. Bowie, of the United States weather bureau.

A request was sent to the weather bureau today that weather reports be sent to the R-34 regularly during the trip in order that it might be kept informed of unfavorable weather conditions along the route. Another radio message asked all reports from vessels along the path being followed by the R-34, be wirelessed.

## Korean Women Ask Wilson to Intervene

San Francisco, July 10.—The Korean Women's society of San Francisco sent today an appeal to President Wilson to intervene to protect Korea from "Japanese aggression."

The telegram concluded:

"We beseech you to earnestly consider immediate investigation of the Japanese protectorate over Korea and to help in whatever way you can to rectify the greatest wrong the world knows today."

## Peace Ratification Aug. 15, French Aim

Paris, July 10.—Debate in the Chamber of Deputies on the bill to ratify the peace treaty probably will begin August 1. It is expected that the debate will consume 10 or 12 sessions of the chamber, so that the deputies may ratify the treaty about August 15. The senate will debate ratification during the first 10 days of September.

## Russia Volunteers to Rule Dardanelles

Paris, July 10.—Prince Lvoff, representative of the All-Russian government of Admiral Kolchak, has written to Premier Clemenceau as president of the Peace conference, proposing an international mandate for Constantinople, with Russia represented, and a Russian mandate for the Dardanelles.

## 'Come Home,' German Plea to Ex-Kaiser

### League for Protection of Wilhelm II. Sends Letter of Invitation.

### Cousin of Eitel Friedrich Offers to Go on Trial, Too.

London Times-Minneapolis Tribune Service. Special Cable Dispatch. Copyright, 1919, by Public Ledger Co.

Berlin, July 10.—The central office of the "League of German Men and Women for the Protection of the Personal Freedom and Life of Wilhelm the Second" at Goerlitz, has addressed an open letter to the former kaiser inviting him to return to Germany.

Prince Friedrich Wilhelm of Lippe informs conservative journals that he has addressed the following letter to Prince Eitel Friedrich, second son of the former kaiser:

"Most serene prince, much loved cousin.

"The humiliation to which the enemy powers desire to subject the Prussian royal house cannot but be felt by us members of other German princely houses also as a humiliation. In virtue of this circumstance, I beg your royal highness kindly to dispose of me also for extradition instead of his majesty, your imperial father.

"Your royal highness' obedient cousin,

"Friedrich Wilhelm, Prince zur Lippe."

The same prince has addressed the following appeal to all the princely houses:

"German impotence—due to our nation's disarming itself—granted to our enemies the satisfaction of their revenge which includes their covetous desire for our kaiser when not long ago they envied us. The shame which they wish to inflict upon him touches us also. Shall we stand aside when our kaiser needs that path of suffering? This must not be and cannot be. We German princes who have stood beside him in good times, who followed him in war and peace, wielding the sword which was also his, we will now place ourselves beside him and call out to our enemies, 'Take us for him or with him.'

"This is my call to you, German cousins, let us show that German faithfulness still lives, true to the oath which we took to him for whom so many of our blood at the head of the brothers of

(Continued on Page 2, Col 1.)

## Wrong Train Takes Him 2,000 Miles Off

### Washington Rancher Reaches St. Paul Broke—Thinks He's Home.

Aaron Clixby, 82-year-old rancher of Whatcom, Wash., might have been considerably nearer home had he not carried so large an amount of money when he started on his homeward journey from Seattle a few days ago.

He completed a journey of nearly 2,000 miles, ending in St. Paul last night, going as far away from his destination, as his funds would carry him.

According to the story Clixby told when his wanderings brought him to central police station in St. Paul, he left his ranch in Whatcom a few weeks ago to visit a brother in Seattle. At the end of his visit, he boarded an east-bound Great Northern train without a ticket, believing he was on the way home.

After paying his fare as far as St. Paul, his funds gave out and he got off the train, he said. He then thought himself still in the state of Washington and started to walk to Whatcom, believing that is was just a few miles north.

The police will communicate with his wife and children in Whatcom. Clixby declared last night that besides an 80-acre tract of land, he owns a sailboat plying between Seattle and Portland.

## 1 Day Paris Strike to Tie Up Railways

Paris, July 10.—A general strike lasting 24 hours will begin at 5 a. m. July 21 and terminate at 5 a. m. July 22, according to a statement issued from the labor exchange today. Instructions issued to the railway workers are that all trains in motion at 5 a. m. July 21 must stop at the nearest watering and coaling stations.

**Pessoa Now President.**

Rio Janeiro, July 10.—Congress today proclaimed Dr. Epitachio Pessoa president of the republic for the term ending 1922.

### *State's Crop Outlook Declared Above Average*

Favorable weather should result in a crop yield above the average in Minnesota, according to the estimate of Paul H. Kirk, field agen for the U. S. Bureau of Crop Estimates. This forecast is borne out by reports to The Tribune from every part of the state of excellent prospects in most communities, showing blight to have caused serious injury only in isolated instances. Article and comprehensive tables showing 1918 yields and 1919 estimates for Minnesota and nation on page 13.

## Dr. Mathews Given Post in Universal Training League

Dr. Shailer Mathews.

Chicago, July 10.—Dr. Shailer Mathews of the University of Chicago has been elected a director of the Universal Military Training league, it was announced today. The educator has become a strong advocate of training and discipline, and believes the country should be in a position to defend itself in case of an emergency, the announcement stated.

## Joffre Can't Ride Horse, So Must Sit Out Victory March

### Marshal Not Mounted for Years—No Autos for Monday's Parade.

Public Ledger-Minneapolis Tribune Service. Special Cable Dispatch. Copyright, 1919, by Public Ledger Co.

Paris, July 10.—While politics and army rivalries are blamed for the trouble over Marshal Joffre's place in next Monday's Victory parade, there is a very satisfactory explanation in the fact that the commander who stopped the rush of the Germans on Paris cannot rid a horse well.

The parade will not include any modern paraphernalia of war such as automobiles and hence the difficulty in Joffre taking part in the conduct of military operations. Joffre always rode in an automobile even at reviews of troops. It is recalled that for several days preceding the outbreak of hostilities the famous chief was never mounted.

In view of the circumstances the president of the republic decided the highest honor which could be accorded the commander who saved France would be to have him sit by his side in the tribune of honor where he will in fact review the troops whom he led to victory in the early years of the war.

## Japan's Prosperity During War Shown

London Times-Minneapolis Tribune Service. Special Cable Dispatch. Copyright, 1919, by Public Ledger Co.

London, July 10.—E. T. F. Crowe, commercial counsellor of the British embassy at Tokio, speaking at the London Chamber of Commerce, said that during the war Japan's financial, industrial and commercial position had greatly improved. Japan, he said, had actually reduced her debt, if special exchequer notes were excluded. She had lent to the Allies well over $500,000,000, and had become a creditor instead of a debtor nation. Her total foreign trade, as compared with the latest pre-war period, showed an increase of nearly 400 per cent.

As regards imports into Japan, America had made great inroads into the trade, he said.

## Kellogg to Aid U. S. Unload Railroads

Washington, D. C., July 10.—(Special)—Senator Kellogg of Minnesota has been named one of the sub-committee to formulate a senate program for the return of railroads to private ownership. The sub-committee as announced today by Senator Cummins of the committee on interstate commerce will consist of Senators Cummins of Iowa, Poindexter of Washington, Kellogg of Minnesota, Pomerene of Ohio and Robinson of Arkansas, three Republicans and two Democrats.

## Spectators Injured as Plane Hits Autos

Pontiac, Ill., July 10.—Seven persons were injured, when an army airplane from Chanute field, Rantoul, Ill., fell on several automobiles in which spectators were watching a flight at Kempton today. The plane was wrecked but Lieutenant Greer and a mechanician, escaped with bruises. They said the engine had failed.

**Germans Steal as They Retire.**

Paris, Wednesday, July 9.—The German delegation was requested today by the Peace conference to draw the attention of the German government to the fact that German troops who are withdrawing from the west bank of the Vistula river, Poland, in accordance with the treaty, are carrying off with them the stock and furniture from farms.

## Wilson Seems Confident Pact to Be Ratified

### 'Assumes' Senate Will Approve, in Talk With Newspapermen.

### Goes Into Detail on League—Declares Reservations Dangerous.

By R. T. Small.

Public Ledger-Minneapolis Tribune Service. Copyright, 1919, by Public Ledger Co.

Washington, July 10.—President Wilson granted an informal interview to the Washington correspondents in which he discussed with them a great many details of the treaty with Germany and the league of nations. His talk was far more explicit and informative in a way than was his address to the Senate in which he dealt with his subjects only in a broad, general manner.

The President was in rare good humor and seemed more physically fit than at any time since he entered the White House. Several times during the conversation, which lasted for nearly an hour, he "assumed" the Senate might ratify the treaty and the league of nations, and it could be seen that he was entirely confident in this respect, but not once did he actually say he was sure of the treaty's fate.

**Dodges Leading Questions.**

Nor would the President commit himself definitely as to whether or not he would be satisfied with a ratification of the treaty which would include certain reservations. When pressed on this subject by the correspondents, who were given free rein to ply the President with questions, Mr. Wilson smilingly replied that reservations would constitute a complicated problem. Should the ratifying reservations go so far as to constitute an "if" to any terms of the treaty, the President was sure they would have to be submitted to all of the 25 nations signing the treaty for their consent asked. This would require a great length of time and meanwhile the United States would be in the position of continuing at war with Germany.

But it had been suggested that most of the contemplated reservations by the Senate would be more or les innocuous and "would not require submission to the other countries," the President was told. In answer to this he said there would be no one officially in a position to say the reservations were innocuous. It would be dif

(Continued on Page 9, Col. 1.)

## Peace Makers Aided Reds, French Assert

### Delegates' Interference Repeatedly Saved Collapse in Hungary, Is Charge.

By Dr. E. J. Dillon.

Public Ledger-Minneapolis Tribune Service. Copyright, 1919, by Public Ledger Co.

Paris, July 10.—The French press sharply criticizes the intervention of the Peace conference in Hungary, where Bolshevism was several times on its last legs, but appears always to have been saved by the measures of the Peace delegates. In May the Roumanian premier declared the Bolshevist regime was about to collapse, but the Peace conference ordered the Roumanian troops to hold.

At the beginning of June it was dying of inanition for want of food and military supplies, but the conference issued a note promising to negotiate with Dictator Bela Kun, whereupon his domestic adversaries abandoned the plan of overthrowing the regime.

On June 24 the Hungarian peasantry revolted, and fighting went on in the outskirts of Budapest. A section of the Red army turned against the government, but the conference again interfered, contenting itself with the evacuation of Slovakia, whereupon the Bolshevist troops were withdrawn from that province to reinforce those in Budapest.

One of the principal delegates with whom the Roumanians officially expostulated, is alleged to have said: "You say Bolshevism is profiting by the measures taken, as though that were an irreparable catastrophe. Are you sure Bolshevism is wholly devoid of progressive ideas? Don't you think there is a kernel of good in it, which, however small, is real?"

## Germans Dispatch Ratification Text

Paris, July 10.—The official text of the German National assembly's ratification of the Peace treaty will arrive shortly by a special courier from Weimar, Baron Kurt von Lersner, head of the German peace mission, announced today in a note to Premier Clemenceau. Baron von Lersner asked that the blockade against Germany be raised and that prisoners of war be liberated as soon as possible.

### *Germany and Russia Plan Trade Alliance*

Germany and Soviet Russia are laying plans which will culminate in an industrial and economic alliance with Teuton industry, taking the lead in the rehabilitation of Russia, says a special cable from Berlin on page 5.

America is judged abroad by her countrymen of various callings who visit there, William T. Ellis says in a special article on Page 10.

## Bolsheviki Making Way From Hungary Into Lower Austria

### 5,000 Reported Concentrated, Supposedly to Move Against Vienna.

Basle, July 10.—Detachments of Hungarian Bolsheviki are penetrating lower Austria, according to Vienna dispatches from Vienna. Nearly 5,000 Bolsheviki are concentrated in the region of Altenburg and Neusiedle lake, supposedly with the intention of moving against Vienna and Neustadt.

Paris, July 10.—High tension between the Austrian and the Hungarian governments is indicated in dispatches received today from Vienna and Budapest. The Austrian foreign minister, Dr. Otto Bauer, has demanded the recall from Vienna of the Hungarian minister.

Bela Kun, head of the Hungarian Soviet government, in return has demanded that the campaign against the Hungarian legation at Vienna be stopped. The despatches report that supporters of Bela Kun are entering Austrian territory.

**Bela Kun Protests.**

Basle, Switzerland, July 10.—Bela Kun, Hungarian soviet head, according to a Budapest dispatch has protested to the Austrian government against what he terms a press campaign against the Hungarian legation at Vienna. He asked satisfaction for the official encouragement given the campaign.

## G.O.P. Senators Score Speech, Others Praise

### Democrats Declare Wilson Utterance One of His Greatest.

(By Associated Press.)

Washington, July 10.—President Wilson's address to the Senate transmitting the Peace Treaty, was praised by Democratic leaders as one of his best state papers, but Republican Senators generally were inclined to criticize it. Senator Lodge of Massachusetts, the Republican leader, and Senator Knox, made no comment.

Senator Borah, Republican, Idaho, one of the leading opponents in the Senate of the league of nations, also declined to comment except to say that President Wilson "completely answered" his own argument that the league of nations is a league for peace by his statement that it is "formed as an alliance of war."

Senator Smoot, Republican, Utah, characterized the address as "Another Wilsonian essay, but not quite up to the standard."

**Calls it Come-On Game.**

Senator Harding, Republican, Ohio, said the address was "the appeal of the internationalist and utterly lacking in ringing Americanism." Senator Moses, Republican, New Hampshire, declared the address to be an appropriate description of the league of nations as an international 'come-on' game, and it appears to me that any country that wishes to work the international badger game will find in the league of nations the sliding panel with which to operate."

"It was a fine, comprehensive presentation of the case," said Senator Hitchcock, Democrat, Nebraska; "It was a dispassionate and convincing statement of the reasons that led the representatives of one billion people to agree on its reorganization of the world."

**"Impressive," says McCumber.**

Senator McCumber, Republican, North Dakota, a supporter of the league of nations, said the address was "very impressive."

"The address," said Senator Swanson, democrat, Virginia, "is magnificent, able, eloquent and inspiring. The reasons presented for the ratifica-

(Continued on Page 9, Col. 3.)

## Dutch Spurn Hint to Hold the Prince

Paris, July 10.—The Council of Five today received a reply from Holland regarding the reported escape from the Island of Wieringen of the former German crown prince. The Dutch note, in what was said to be rather curt terms, pointed out that the rumor was unfounded, and expressed surprise at the warning given by the council.

The Dutch government, the reply added, is conscious of international obligations, and must be left free to exercise its sovereignty as it sees fit.

## Four-Year-Old Boy Commits Suicide

Kankakee, Ill., July 10.—"Goodbye Leonard, I'm going to jump in here and drown myself," with that admonition four-year-old Harold Clarke, son of Mr. and Mrs. Paul Clarke, threw himself into 10 feet of water, in the old city quarry today and drowned before help could reach him. His friend was Leonard Holoveck, 5 years old.

## Wives Bring Raises to Bank's Employes

Chicago, July 10.—A premium is placed on matrimony by S. W. Straus & Co., local bankers and brokers, who today announced a cash bonus plan for employes who acquire wives or heirs.

## U. S. Is Leader in a New Era, Senate Is Told

### Nations Look to America for Guidance, President Asserts.

### "Treaty Not Ideal, but Violates No Principle Vitally."

### Executive Declares Practical Statesmen Convinced of Plan's Usefulness.

Text of President Wilson's speech in presenting the peace treaty to the Senate will be found on Page 4.

(By Associated Press.)

Washington, July 10.—The Peace Treaty with its league of nations covenant was laid before the Senate by President Wilson today in an address accounting to the country for his part in the negotiations at Versailles.

The league, declared the President, was born of the conviction of practical statesmen that an international concert had become a world necessity to end the old order and guarantee civilization. He asserted that in such a concert a world looked confidently to America for leadership and added that while the treaty might not be exactly as the American delegation would have written it, no vital principle had been sacrificed by the necessary compromise.

The Senate, already divided in the bitter fight over the league proposal, received the President with cheers and listened to his words in grave silence.

**Cheered as He Finishes.**

When he had concluded there was another burst of cheering until he had passed out of the chamber. Later at his capitol office he talked for an hour with senators who wished to ask about specific features of the treaty. The President discussed freely such subjects as the disposition of Shantung, the German indemnities and Irish freedom.

In his address, however, there was no direct reference to many of the questions around which Senate debate has centered, the President declaring he could not construe details of the treaty in a short address.

He did not directly mention the Monroe doctrine, Shantung or the obligations assumed under article 10 of the league covenant, nor did he allude to the proposal to write reservations into the ratification. He asserted a hope that he would be given opportunity to discuss details later with the whole senate or the Foreign Relations committee.

**Offers Full Services.**

"My services and all the information I possess," he said, "will be at your disposal and at the disposal of your committee on Foreign Relations at any time, either informally or in a session, as you prefer, and I hope that you will not hesitate to make use of them."

American isolation, the President asserted, was ended 20 years ago when the war with Spain put the nation in partial control of Cuba and the Philippines.

"But we have not exploited them," he continued. "We have been their friends and have sought to serve them. There can be no question of our ceasing to be a world power. The only question is whether we can refuse the moral leadership that is offered us, whether we shall accept or reject the confidence of the world.

"The stage is set, the destiny disclosed. It has come about by no plan of our conceiving, but by the hand of God, who has led us into this way. We cannot turn back. We can only go forward with lifted eyes and freshened spirits to follow the vision."

**Practical Necessity.**

Alluding to the skepticism with which the plan for a league of nations was at first received, the president said that as the negotiations proceeded it became apparent to all delegates that such a concert was a "practical necessity demand" by all the peoples of the world." For the United States to reject it, he asserted, "would break the heart of the world."

Pointing out that many minor compromises were necessary to secure the support of all the interested nations, he continued:

"The treaty, as a result, is not exactly what we should have written. It is probably not what any one of the national delegations would have written. But results were worked out which on the whole bear test. I think it will be found that the compromises which were accepted as inevitable nowhere cut to the heart of any principle."

In disregard of precedent, the Senate received the address in open session and afterward ordered that the treaty be published in the Congressional Record and as a public document. The galleries were overflowing and crowds unable to gain admission waited in the rain to cheer the President when he arrived and departed. Many members of the House crowded into the rear of the Senate chamber and most of the members of the Cabinet were seated near the vice president's desk.

**Reads Address Slowly.**

Speaking from the same platform, where 30 months ago he astounded the world with his first declaration for a league of nations, the President read his address slowly and in a clear, quiet voice. His manuscript, typewritten on small pages, he held in his left hand and with his right he punctuated his utterances with an occasional gesture. Before him on the vice president's desk lay the treaty, brought by him in person from Versailles.

There was no attempt at oratory and no applause interrupted him. Nearly every senator was in his seat, and all listened attentively.

In his talks afterward with league supporters the President was said to have discussed at length the Shantung

# 1920~1929

# The Minneapolis Sunday Tribune

Fifty-third Year. No. 232. Associated Press MINNEAPOLIS, MINN., SUNDAY, JANUARY 11, 1920 72 Pages. Price Six Cents in Minneapolis


# "Vacant Seat Berger" Renominated After Second Expulsion

## Hughes Flayed As Lending Aid to Revolution

### New York Assembly Speaker Sends Sharp Reply to Jurist's Criticism.

### Legislators Ones to Determine Socialists' Fitness, Sweet Declares.

### "Patriotic Citizens Should Withhold Judgment," Is Assertion.

*(By Associated Press.)*

New York, Jan. 10.—Suspension of the five Socialist assemblymen was characterized in resolutions adopted by the Young Men's Republican club here today "as a stupid and wanton denial of the fundamental principles of Republican government."

*(By Associated Press.)*

New York, Jan. 10.—The action of the state assembly in suspending the five Socialist members was to determine whether the organizations they represent "advocate methods, or employ tactics" to bring about the overthrow of the government, Thaddeus C. Sweet, speaker of the assembly, declared in a letter to Charles E. Hughes, made public tonight. It was in reply to the former governor's letter condemning the ousting of the Socialist assemblymen.

Every patriotic citizen should withhold judgment, Sweet added, until evidence respecting the Socialist party of America and other organizations had been presented to the judiciary committee of the assembly, before which the suspended Socialists will be "impartially judged" as to their "rights and fitness" to take their seats.

**Aid Given to "Enemy."**

Mr. Sweet declared that criticism of the assembly's action "without full knowledge of the facts in the case, of necessity gives aid and comfort to those elements of our society which seek the destruction of our institutions."

The speaker pointed out that a "sharp line of demarcation was drawn in April, 1917, between Socialism and the Socialist party of America," declaring that "Socialists who placed the honor of their country above their creed" and resigned from the party and have "done their utmost to point out" that the Socialist party, as at present constituted, is un-American."

Referring to the former governor's letter, which urged that all evidence against public officers and private cit-

(Continued on Page 2, Col. 1.)

## Burnquist to Back Wood for President

### Governor Accepts Place on Committee; Statement Cites General's Qualifications.

Governor Burnquist last night came out openly for Leonard Wood for president.

The Governor gave out a formal statement announcing his support of Wood and explaining that he had accepted a place on the Wood committee. Governor Allen of Kansas and Governor Shoop of Colorado are also to be on that committee.

Governor Burnquist's statement, in full, follows:

"In accepting a position on General Wood's committee I wish to say that I am strongly in favor of General Wood for president. From reports and conversations with people of different portions of Minnesota, I am firmly convinced that he is the choice of the Republicans of this state.

"General Wood is the type of man needed for our country at this particular time. His record shows him to be sound and practical. Business efficiency has been one of his strongest characteristics. His experience in different sections of this country and in so many portions of the world has given him the needed insight into domestic and international affairs.

"The executive and military training of General Wood makes him the kind of candidate that these times demand. Nominating him would give to the service men of the nation the recognition they deserve. Opposition to a service man must, of course, be expected from certain elements in the country, but when one can be found with the character, ability and Americanism of General Wood nothing, in my opinion, will so closely unite all our loyal people as his nomination and election."

## Grave Mistake Is Made by Bandit

Twisting a revolver from the hand of a man who attempted to hold him up, Ole P. Olson, city detective, last night placed him under arrest.

Olson was accosted on Washington avenue between Sixth and Seventh avenues south after he had shadowed the man for an hour.

A charge of attempted robbery was placed against the suspect and he will be arraigned in municipal court tomorrow. He is said to be 17 years old by the police.

### Weather Forecast.

MINNESOTA—Fair today and probably tomorrow, somewhat colder in northeast portion today; rising temperature tomorrow.

## *Special Features on World Events by Tribune Writers*

WILLIAM J. McNALLY—Pictures China's open door policy as doomed by the league of nations.

ROBERT T. BARRY tells how Lodge forced a Bryan-Wilson strength showdown on treaty compromise suggestions.

FREDERICK WILE says Japanese trade today exceeds that of any other nation with which America does business.

MOPPING UP BOLSHEVISM is described by Robert Davis, Red Cross envoy to South Russia.

WILLIAM T. ELLIS pictures Bible lands as seething in revolt.

HAND EMBROIDERED stockings are described by Margaret Walter as the latest European novelty.

O. W. FIRKINS gives a review of New York theatrical news.

IRVING BACHELLER condenses Saint Pierre's novel, "Paul and Virginia."

NEWS FROM ABROAD assembled in a page of special cable dispatches.

HOW MINNEAPOLIS funds made Armenian relief work possible revealed by Dr. George E. White.

## Census Evaded By Radicals In Gateway Zone

### Transients, Ignorant of Aim of Count, Fear They Will Be Deported.

Ignorant of the census laws and the purpose for which Uncle Sam is undertaking the nationwide nose count, transients in the Gateway district, especially those of radical leanings, are avoiding enumerators and some, fearing that any information given may lead toward their deportation, are antagonistic, according to Stephen McElnell, enumerator.

One man, who admitted he was a member of the Communist party, not only hesitated before giving Mr. McElnell the necessary data yesterday but even attempted to convert the enumerator to the "cause."

"Men in Gateway rooming houses, especially aliens, think that the government will obtain information concerning them which may be turned over to immigration officers," Mr. McElnell said. "This attitude makes the taking of the census difficult and from the census-takers' viewpoint, the recent deportations came at a wrong time."

Mr. McElnell claims he has met with a few typical "Reds" but that the majority of men in the district are frightened over the census through ignorance. When told that the information is not revealed, they usually submit gracefully to the questioning, he said.

Clerks in the rooming houses are doing more to assure a successful count in the district than anyone else, the enumerator averred. "Their assistance is wonderful and many take upon themselves the voluntary task of filling out blanks for all of the roomers in their hotels," he said.

"And they are the best anti-radical preachers I have ever known. When a so-called 'Red' delivers some of his propaganda, the clerks will take him to task and usually the 'sermon,' intended to be serious, will be regarded as humorous by the listeners."

The congestion in the rooming houses makes the census work especially difficult, Mr. McElnell said. He told how he and another enumerator assembled 150 roomers in one house and how after 10 blanks had been completed, the crowd had disappeared.

## 'Big Policemen' Join in Search as Baby Girls Sob 'Mamma'

### Well-Dressed Woman Deserts Children in Downtown Store.

To please two sobbing baby girls, sisters, the oldest one said, the police department bestirred itself mightily last night.

The mother was sought.

The babes—one of them two years old and the other six months—were left with the matron of a downtown store rest room early in the morning. Their mother had not returned for them at closing time so the police were called.

Sobbing bitterly for "mamma," both fell asleep in the arms of the matron during the afternoon. She fed them and waited. But the mother did not return.

The ride in the police patrol was an adventure for them and they forgot to cry until they found themselves surrounded on all sides by big patrolmen. They went a duet until Mrs. Sarah Schaefer, police matron, snuggled them into a crib in her private quarters. Bowls of milk and bread at 7 p. m. proved an antidote.

In the meantime the police searched the morgue and all city hospitals believing the mother had met with some accident. They could not believe she had deliberately deserted the little ones.

Both are dressed in costly garments. They are robust with good health. The older girl has not learned many words and all she would say to the police was "mamma." Her tiny sister's vocabulary was equally as limited.

Mrs. Schaefer said that if the mother is not found the children will be sent to the Rosedale cottage, 3912 Blaisdell avenue, under the care of the Children's Protective society.

The store matron was unable to give a good rescription of the woman who left the girls with her. She remembered only that she was well dressed and seemed cultured.

The two girls bring the total of foundlings cared for by the police in the last two weeks to four. The latter part of December a baby was deserted in the same store. He is now at the Lymanhurst hospital.

## Civil Commission Replaces War Chiefs After Peace Ratification

### Inter-Allied High Board Assumes Control of Occupied Territory.

*(By Associated Press.)*

Coblenz, Jan. 10.—The Inter-Allied High Commission today issued a proclamation announcing that it is assuming "supreme representation of the Allied governments in the occupied territories" in fulfillment of the terms of the peace treaty. The commission asked the co-operation of German officials and population.

### United States Only Nation at War With Germany.

*(By Associated Press.)*

Paris, Jan. 10.—Ratifications of the treaty of Versailles were exchanged and peace between Germany, France, Great Britain and the other Allied and associated powers with the exception of the United States, became effective at 4:16 o'clock this afternoon.

The outstanding comment tonight on the ceremony is that it leaves the United States the only power which was actively at war with Germany not now on a peace basis. That was the note sounded by Baron Kurt von Lersner, head of the German peace delegation, in a statement to the Associated Press immediately after the ceremony.

"I am naturally happy that peace has finally become effective," Baron von Lersner said. "My great regret is that the United States is the only

(Continued on Page 5, Col. 1.)

## Lawful to Ship, Not Transport Booze, Ruling

### Minneapolis Detective Puts Damper on Last "Wet" Hope.

Uncle Sam, speaking through Congress, says that liquor for private use may be shipped out of Minnesota.

The State of Minnesota, speaking through the attorney general's office says liquor for private use may be shipped out of Minnesota.

The County of Hennepin, speaking through the county attorney's office, says liquor for private use may be shipped out of Minnesota.

But Michael Johannes, detective, of Minneapolis says—"Nix."

Johannes is carrying on a campaign against liquor law violators.

Alfred Jaques, United States district attorney, yesterday said that there is nothing in the Volstead Enforcement act for wartime prohibition which will prohibit shipment of liquor for personal use out of the state, provided there is no violation of the Webb-Kenyon law which prohibits shipment of liquor into dry territory.

But Johannes says not.

"In order to ship liquor out of the state you must carry it to the express office," he admonished. "If you do I'll catch you. You'll be transporting liquor inside the state in carrying it to the express office for shipment. I don't care where the liquor is to go to."

So there you are!

**One Killed in Tunnel Crash.**

Geneva, Jan. 10.—One man was killed in a train collision in the St. Gothard tunnel yesterday, the first accident since the tunnel was constructed. Neglect to signals by one of engine drivers caused the collision.

## Man Sought as 'Red' Alien Surrenders

### John Savchuk of St. Paul Out of Town When Warrant Was Issued.

John Savchuk, St. Paul, is the only alleged alien Communist to surrender to agents of the Department of Justice voluntarily. A warrant for Savchuk was issued at the time of the first raids, but Savchuk was out of town at the time. He returned to St. Paul Friday and gave himself up yesterday. He will be held in custody until bail, which was set at $1,000, is furnished, T. E. Campbell, chief special agent, said last night.

Preliminary deportation hearings for the alleged radicals will be resumed before Charles W. Seaman, immigration inspector, tomorrow, it was announced last night.

The St. Paul Trades and Labor assembly has adopted a resolution asking the release of all "political and industrial prisoners." Copies of the resolution will be forwarded to President Wilson, Attorney General Palmer, Secretary Baker and Samuel Gompers, president of the American Federation of Labor.

## *Hohenzollerns Seek to Know Just Where They'll Get Off At*

*(By Associated Press.)*

Berlin, Jan. 10.—Former Emperor William, says a report from Amsterdam, will call a family conference of the Hohenzollerns after the Peace treaty is ratified. The property question and the future residence of the family will be discussed, according to the report.

## Armistice Is Still Binding, Germans Told

### United States Holds Berlin to Agreement Until Peace Ratified.

*(By Associated Press.)*

Washington, Jan. 10.—Formal notice has been served on Germany by the United States, in connection with the deposit at Paris today of ratifications putting into effect the treaty of Versailles, that conditions of the armistice still govern relations between the United States and Germany.

Announcement of this action was made tonight by the State department in a statement showing that official notification of the exchange had been received. Outlining the situation due to the fact that the United States had not ratified the treaty, it said:

"It is the position of this government that the armistice continues in full force and effect between the United States and Germany, and accordingly the provisions of the armistice agreement of November 11, 1918, as well as the provisions of the extensions of that agreement, remain binding on these two nations." Notice of this was given to the German government by the United States.

The announcement showed that the deposit of ratifications and signing of the proces verbal took place in Paris at 4:16 p. m., and adds:

"The moment at which the first proces verbal was completed marked the moment at which a status of peace was restored between Germany on the one hand and those of the Allied and associated powers, which have completed the necessary formalities of ratification of the treaty of Versailes, on the other."

## Bill to Punish Sedition Acts Passes Senate

### Five Years and $5,000 Fine Provided for Moves to Wreck Nation.

*(By Associated Press.)*

Washington, Jan. 10.—An anti-sedition bill, prescribing severe penalties for acts or propaganda advocating overthrow of the government by force or violence, was passed by the Senate today without a record vote. The measure now goes to the House.

Maximum penalties fixed in the bill are a fine of $5,000 and five years imprisonment, applying to all acts or circulation of literature in furtherance of forcible overthrow of the government. The bill also bars from the mails any matter advocating force or sabotage.

**Mail Censorship Seen.**

Principal attack on the bill was aimed at the mail exclusion section, which opponents declared would confer press censorship power on the Postmaster General. Advocates of the measure, however, denied that the bill would limit constitutional rights of free speech or assemblage.

Under an amendment by Senator Borah, accepted by the Senate, persons against whom this clause is invoked can appeal to federal courts.

The bill prohibits persons from advocating by speech, writing or printing, the forcible overthrow of the United States or all government, or by physical injury to person or property. It also would penalize attempts or acts hindering execution of laws, or federal agents in their duties.

Another section prohibits display of flags, banners or emblems intended to symbolize advocacy of force against the government.

**Jail and Ouster for Aliens.**

Aliens violating the act would be subject to deportation and permanent exclusion after serving the imprisonment period.

The bill, drawn by Senator Sterling, South Dakota, has been heralded as a measure against "Reds." It goes to the House for consideration in connection with sedition legislation being prepared by the House Judiciary committee and in a measure is a substitute for legislation recommended by Attorney General Palmer.

Senator Sterling told the Senate today that the bill did not penalize peaceful agitation looking to changes in the government. This was criticized by Senator McKellar, Democrat, as an alleged weakness. The Tennessee senator declared the bill would not reach dangerous anarchists and other radicals who preach insidious propaganda against the government, suggesting violence, while disclaiming advocacy of force.

### Reports of Revolution in Germany Discounted by Washington.

Public Ledger-Minneapolis Tribune Service. Copyright, 1920, by Public Ledger Co.

Washington, Jan. 10.—Brussels, Copenhagen and London stories reporting a revolution in Germany, the overthrow of the Ebert government, and establishment in its stead of an Independent Socialist regime, are without official confirmation at the State department. Authorities in Washington in intimate touch with German developments expect more than one "revolution" before political affairs at Berlin shake down to a durable level. The Ebert regime, or rather the Noske regime—for President Ebert's redoubtable war minister, Gustav Noske, is the strong man of the administration—is believed by the best judges to be based on shifting sands. It is experimental. It will sustain itself if it can. But, though it has maintained a precarious existence for a year, few persons with knowledge of the internal situation in Germany expect it to be permanent.

The militarists, aided by the irreconcilable junkers, are openly planning and plotting for the re-establishment of an autocratic and Hohenzollern regime, but their schemes are unlikely to be realized. The great business interests, traditionally mistrustful of Socialist domination, are believed to favor a constitutional monarchy on British lines, and this is to be considered the eventual form of government which Germany may adopt.

## Federal Chiefs Search City for Drug Violators

### One Arrest Made Under Harrison Narcotic Act —Ten Places Visited.

Seeking violators of the Harrison narcotic act on information believed furnished by Tony Serpa in New York, operatives of the Internal Revenue department last night searched ten places in Minneapolis and made one arrest.

G. R. Rogers, negro, 212 Eleventh street, is in the county jail, held for action of the government in connection with alleged distribution of drugs in this city. It is said several dollars worth of drugs were confiscated.

The police department co-operated with the revenue agents in making the raids. According to William Forby, government operative, the situation in Minneapolis is considered good. This was borne out by the fact that only a small quantity of habit-forming drugs was taken during the investigation.

In making the investigation in Minneapolis, operatives of the Internal Revenue department visited veritably all of the so-called underworld places, including sections of the Bridge Square district.

Rogers probably will be arraigned before Howard S. Abbott, United States commissioner, tomorrow. No formal charge has been placed against him.

Agents of the department said the investigation probably will continue all of this week.

**Cattleman Killed as Auto Upsets.**

Pueblo, Colo., Jan. 10.—A. W. Landkin, 40, a cattleman of La Veta, Colo., was instantly killed today when an automobile in which he was riding overturned on the highway between Colorado Springs and Pueblo. Landkin formerly lived at Battle Creek, Mich.

## Nay, Nay, Says Bryan, There's No Split in Democratic Ranks

### President and Commoner Differ in Method, That's All, He Avers.

*(By Associated Press.)*

Chicago, Jan. 10.—William Jennings Bryan advocated "free and open discussion where concessions may be asked and given" in the United States Senate in an effort to reach a compromise on the Peace treaty, in an address at the Iroquois club today. Then "if no compromise can be reached, we must asquiesce, for the present, with the Republican majority." He proposed that in that case enough Democratic votes be withdrawn to permit the Republicans a constitutional two-thirds vote by which the treaty and league of nations covenant would be ratified with reservations and allow "the people to pass judgment" at the polls.

Mr. Bryan very emphatically stated that there had been "no split" in the Democratic party, and that such a conclusion should not be 'rawn from addresses of himself and President Wilson at the Jackson day banquet. "The President and I differ in method and not in purpose," he said.

"The President's letter read at Washington," continued Mr. Bryan, contains words open to construction that indicate to me that compromise is possible. The President did well at Paris. He did more there than we could expect any man to do."

Mr. Bryan said his plan of compromise or the alternative of allowing the Republican majority to record its will was "just the simple old American plan of majority rule." "With ratification accomplished," he said, "then we will have peace and the league of nations and we can go to work."

### Bryan Reiterates He's Not Desirous of Filling Shoes of Br'er Wilson

Chicago, Jan. 10.—William Jennings Bryan came out flatfooted tonight in asserting that he is not a candidate for the presidency. That is, he came as near being positive as the "Peerless Leader" ever does at this particular period of a presidential campaign. Referring to his own position in the coming race for the White House, Mr. Bryan said: "I stated at Washington that I am not a candidate for the presidency, and I do not understand the attitude of the newspapers that seek to drag big issues down to the personal level."

What he actually said at Washington on the occasion of the Jackson day banquet was, "I have no favors to ask," which has been variously interpreted.

## All Reported Quiet at International Falls

"Everything quiet" was the report made to Governor Burnquist last night by Maj. William A. Garis, in command of National Guard troops in International Falls.

Reports of strike activities in Gemmel by the I.W.W. was declared exaggerated by Major Garis. He said he found no disorder in the village.

Telephone communication between Gemmel and other Northern Minnesota points was restored yesterday by repair crews. Major Garis said the service was interrupted Friday by a broken cable.

## *House Jeers Voigt Defense of Berger as Loyal Citizen*

Washington, Jan. 10.—(Special.)—During the Victor Berger debate in the House, Representative Voigt, who was the only member to vote to seat Berger the first time, spoke in favor of seating him again today. igt repeated his former arguments, contending that Berger was not a traitor but that, on the contry, he was a "noble, high-minded gentleman," and only a "mild Socialist." Both these contentions brought a chorus of jeers from all parts of the House.

"If you say Berger is a traitor," said Voigt, "then you must say there are 25,000 traitors in his district."

"There are," shouted several members.

"They are not," answered Mr. Voigt, "but they are just as loyal as others," a statement that again brought jeers and shouts of "no" from all sides. Mr. Voigt referred to the lack of law breaking in the Berger district, and said they responded to all calls during the war.

"Judas Iscariot was treasurer of 12 Apostles when he committe the one act of betrayal," interrupted Representative Greene, Republican, of Vermont, a remark which was loudly cheered.

## Philipp Bars Election to Fill Vacancy

### Wisconsin Governor Is Opposed to Expenditure of Money Involved.

Milwaukee, Jan. 10.—(Special.)—With the ousting of Victor L. Berger, Milwaukee Socialist, convicted under the espionage act, from his seat in Congress today for the second time in two months, it became almost certain that 55,000 voters in Berger's district will be forced to go without representation in Congress until after the regular fall elections. Governor E. L. Philipp plainly stated that under no circumstances will he call another special election to fill the vacancy. He asserts that an election will entail too great an expense.

It became known here today that the Socialist party central committee for the Fifth district will not press mandamus proceedings against the Governor to have him call an election. The Berger forces, so close observers say, prefer to let the whole situation drag on until the next general election.

It was learned tonight that the anti-Berger faction in Milwaukee will start at once to prevail on the Ballinger committee to declare H. H. Bodenstab officially elected to Congress. Bodenstab was defeated by Berger in the December special election.

If these efforts are unsuccessful, it is probable that the anti-Berger forces and loyalist element will unite on W. H. Stafford as the Republican candidate in the fall election. Stafford was defeated at the last regular election by Berger for the reason that there was a third candidate, Joseph P. Carney, in the field.

### Bolsheviki, British Plan Exchange of Prisoners

*(By Associated Press.)*

Copenhagen, Jan. 10.—Negotiations between Maxim Litvinoff and James O'Grady, representing the Russian bolshevik and British governments respectively, for an exchange of prisoners, have nearly reached completion. An agreement has been arrived at on all the fundamental points.

## House Rejects Socialist by 328 to 6 Vote

### Milwaukee Committee Says Game Will Continue Until 'Hades Freezes.'

### Mann's Defense of Convicted Congressman Proves Surprise of Debate.

### Nonpartisan Members, in Doubt, Almost Lose Opportunity of Voting.

*(By Associated Press.)*

Milwaukee, Jan. 10.—The Socialist committee of the Fifth Wisconsin congressional district, within a half hour after receiving the news that Victor L. Berger had been excluded from Congress a second time, renominated him.

"We will keep on nominating Berger until Hades freezes over if that un-American aggregation called Congress continues to exclude him," declared a statement issued by the committee.

"We want every person in this country to understand that the voters of the Fifth Wisconsin district know exactly whom they want as their representative in Congress, and we do not propose to let Gillette and his bunch of Wall street fawners dictate to us on the subject.

"Berger is our congressman, and the action of Congress in unseating him a second time only starts the real fight that will not end until every one of the reactionaries who voted in today's disgraceful proceedings has been retired by the ballot to the oblivion they so richly deserve."

### Nonpartisan Members in Doubt About Voting.

**By George F. Authier.**

Washington, Jan. 10.—Victor Berger, Socialist of the Fifth district of Wisconsin (Milwaukee) has again been denied a seat in the Congress of the United States. This rebuke to a man who sat throughout the debate which accompanied the House action today, was administered by a vote of 328 to 6. Among those who voted to seat him was James R. Mann of Illinois, former Republican floor leader and the man who led a large group of Republicans into the unfortunate error of voting in favor of the McLemore resolution, which would have warned Americans off the high seas, and would have surrendered America's protest against the German claim to the right to sink neutrals on the ocean. The others who voted to seat Berger were Representatives Voight of Wisconsin and Harreld of Oklahoma, Republicans, and Griffith, New York; Sherwood, Ohio, and Sisson, Mississippi, Democrats.

As Representative Dallinger expressed it, "if the Fifth district of Wisconsin had elected the kaiser or Von Hindenburg, according to the argument advanced, the Congress would be called upon to seat them, notwithstanding the fact that the Fifth district congressman legislated not only for his own district but for the whole country."

**Mondell Attacks Contentions.**

Mr. Mondell denied the soundness of every point made by Mr. Mann, quoted Section 3 of the Fourteenth amendment to the Constitution, which makes ineligible for federal office any one who has been found guilty of giving aid and comfort to our enemies, and said all arguments to show that Berger was entitled to a seat was "counter to the law and the Constitution," and that members must vote to reject Berger or violate their oath of office.

Mr. Mann, by his act today, is regarded as having forever barred himself from being recognized in the future by his Republican colleagues for the position of leadership. This was a comment heard repeatedly from the lips of scores of prominent Republicans who have been his supporters in the past.

Mr. Mann's speech was made the basis of criticism by other speakers who favored the rejection of Berger, notably that of Representative Eagle, Democrat, of Texas.

"If the argument made by Mr. Mann is sound, the House would be compelled to seat a murderer or a felon if a majority of his district had voted for him," said Mr. Eagle. "It would force the House to seat a man under the constitutional age of 25 years, if his district elected him.

**House Precedents Quoted.**

"A committee appointed by this House patiently heard Mr. Berger's side of this question, and deliberated for four months before making a finding. This finding was submitted to the House and by a vote of 311 to 1 he was rejected because in the time of his country's woe he was a traitor. Nevertheless, because he has constituents un-American enough to approve his position, it is claimed he should be seated. But we cannot seat him if we are true to our convictions and our oath of office."

Mr. Eagle quoted precedents for the action the House was about to take, repeated the charges of hostility to America's cause shown by Berger during the war, and called upon the House to reject him.

Representative Dallinger, Republican of Massachusetts, brought up the resolution to unseat Berger, and led the fight for its adoption. He sought to obtain unanimous consent from the House to allow Berger to make a speech, but this request was the signal for objections from all parts of the floor. Later Representative Sisson, Democrat of Mississippi, made a similar request, and being denied sought to make a motion to the same effect. This was held out of order by Speaker Gillett, on the ground that as Berger was not a member of the House, the rules precluded him from being allowed to speak except by unanimous consent. Mr. Sisson voted against the resolution as a protest

# The Minneapolis Morning Tribune

Fifty-fourth Year. No. 15. | Associated Press | MINNEAPOLIS, MINN., TUESDAY, JUNE 8, 1920 | United Press. | Price Two Cents in Minneapolis

# Sproul Is Hope to Solve Republican Presidential Puzzle

## *Convention Will Open Today With Deadlock for Favorites Unparalleled in Political History*

## Seven St. Paul Men Indicted in Rum Plot Case

### Bill Also Returned Against Winnipeg Merchant—All Named Under Bond.

### Special Federal Grand Jury Will Take Up Nash Case in City Today.

### County Jury to Meet But Will Defer Action, Pending Ouster Decision.

Seven St. Paul men and one man from Winnipeg, Canada, were indicted by the federal grand jury in St. Paul yesterday in the liquor smuggling conspiracy ramification which culminated in the fatal shooting of Jack Burke January 14 during an attempt to unload a carload of whisky in St. Paul.

The men named in the indictments returned in St. Paul are: Edward Holton, Euclid hotel, St. Paul, manager of a taxicab line; Charles Couplin, St. Paul merchant; George Morrison, St. Paul; William G. Gifford and James W. McDonald, St. Paul railroad men; William Ueber, 440 Wabasha street, St. Paul, saloon proprietor; Albert Speices, St. Paul taxicab driver; and Harry Rabinovich, a merchant of Winnipeg.

**All Named Under Bond.**

All of the men named have been arrested and released on bonds. Rabinovich is under $15,000 bond and the others under $5,000 each. They will be arraigned in United States district court Friday, according to Alfred Jaques, United States district attorney.

Twenty other indictments were returned by the federal grand jury, 12 being charges of operating a still, five charges of violating the wartime prohibition act, one embezzlement of United States mails, one larceny and one illegally wearing the uniform of the United States army.

**Grand Jury to Take Up Nash Case.**

A special federal grand jury will convene in Minneapolis at 10 a. m. today to make inquiries into the charges preferred against William M. Nash, until recently Hennepin county attorney, in a formal complaint signed by Alfred Jaques, United States district attorney. The complaint charges Mr. Nash with "conspiring to receive and conceal and facilitate the transportation" of whisky imported from Canada.

These charges were submitted to the federal grand jury called here for the April term, but that grand jury was discharged by Judge Page Morris of the United States district court before

(Continued on Page 6, Col. 2.)

## Secret Martens Case Hearing to Resume

### Bolshevist Minister Expected to Deny He Advocated Overthrow of Government.

Public Ledger-Minneapolis Tribune Service. Copyright, 1920, by Public Ledger Co.

Washington, June 7.—Hearing in the case of Ludwig C. A. K. Martens, Bolshevist ambassador to the United States against whom a deportation warrant has been issued, will be resumed tomorrow before A. B. Shell, immigration inspector. At the session, which like all the others conducted on deportation matters by the Department of Labor, will be in secret, Martens is expected to make his defense against the charge of the Department of Justice that he is an advocate of the overthrow of the government of the United States by force and violence and therefore a violator of the alien deportation act of October 16, 1918.

No agents of the Department of Justice will be present at the hearing, because under the ruling laid down some months ago by Louis F. Post, assistant secretary of labor and director of labor department's deportation policy, justice agents will not be permitted to cross-question Martens.

The case against the Bolshevist envoy consists, as far as can be learned, of his admission, before the Lusk investigating committee, that he was a member of the Russian Communist party, the organization of "Lenin and Trotzky," which affiliated with the Third International of Moscow, favors destruction of all governments, not of soviet structure. Martens is expected to reiterate the denial he recently made at the Senate Red investigation that he is a member of the Russian Communist organization.

## Mystery Car, Still Found in Lonely House

What may have served as a robbers' rendezvous, St. Paul police believe, was raided by St. Paul detectives yesterday when they entered a lonely cottage beyond the north city limits. In the loot found was a touring car answering description of that figuring in Minneapolis bank robberies and the escape of "Big Chris" Dowlin. Two other cars were also found. The raiders reported that they found a still and a barrel of whisky. In a drawer were discovered several hundred dollars' worth of Liberty bonds.

**Weather Forecast**

MINNESOTA—Unsettled but generally fair weather today and tomorrow, not much change in temperature.

## Army Chief Seeks to Leave Service

General John J. Pershing.

(By Associated Press.)

Washington, June 7.—General Pershing wrote Secretary Baker today asking permission to retire from active service "within the next few months." The former commander of the American Expeditionary Forces declared that after the completion of work incident to the recently enacted army reorganization bill his normal duties would require only a portion of his time and therefore he wished to be "free to engage in something more active."

## One Drowned; One Stricken, Toll of Heat

### Hottest Day Fatal for Swimmer Seeking Relief in Mississippi.

Heat in Minneapolis yesterday claimed the life of one man and sent another to a hospital. It was the hottest day of the year, the mercury reaching a maximum of 84 degrees at 5 p. m.

H. O. Ostrom, 30 years old, who rooms at 222½ Washington avenue south, told two companions he was suffering from the heat about 4:30 p. m. and suggested a swim in the Mississippi river. Diving in under the Great Northern bridge below St. Anthony falls Ostrom failed to emerge. Police dragged the river but were unsuccessful in finding the body.

Martin Rogers, Bird Island, Minn., overcome by the heat about 5 p. m. at Marquette avenue and Third street, fainted in the middle of the street and was nearly run over by a street car. He was taken to the General hospital where he recovered and was permitted to leave last night for his home.

Bathing beaches were crowded last night when early swimmers learned the water had warmed to nearly 70 degrees. Calhoun and Glenwood were well patronized for the first time this summer and parks and canoe racks took on a summery appearance.

The weatherman has promised fair weather all day today with not much change in temperature.

## Prima Donna to Fly Alone Across Channel

Cross-Atlantic Newspaper Service—Copyright. Special Cable to Minneapolis Tribune.

London, June 7.—Sophie Braslau, contralto, giving song recitals here, now will fly to Paris alone on a two days' shopping trip, a first time in history event.

## *Saving $15,000,000 From Sunken Liner, Task of Salvage Ship*

Cross-Atlantic Newspaper Service—Copyright. Special Cable to Minneapolis Tribune.

London, June 7.—Equipped with special salvage apparatus that will displace 800 tons an hour of water, mud and wreckage, the British Admiralty salvage ship, Racer, has resumed the task of saving $15,000,000 in gold bullion which went down with the liner Laurentic off the north Irish coast early in 1917. In previous attempts some $5,000,000 was salvaged.

In 1919 divers and marine engineers found that two years of incessant pounding on the ocean bottom had reduced the powerful frame of the liner to a corroding heap of debris. The decks had settled down, one upon another, as a card house collapses. The height of the pile was some 10 feet, covering an area of some hundreds of feet.

As a result of this collapse it took two months to locate the portion of the wreckage containing the gold. In these calculations, such details as the lie of the boats' davits were noted to ascertain which was the fore and aft of the vessel. It finally was decided where the gold lay.

It then became necessary to place rings of explosives on the exposed plates and blast out a section exposing girders and more plates beneath, which in turn, were cut through with explosives. The strong-room of the vessel, 12 feet high, was found collapsed to a height of a few inches.

## Highest Court Sustains Legal Ban on Liquor

### Prohibition Amendment and Volstead Act Declared Constitutional.

### Decision Believed to Invalidate State Laws Favoring Wets.

Analysis of the basis for the decision of the United States Supreme court, holding constitutional the Eighteenth amendment and the Volstead act, is made by by Justices White and McKenna on Page 12.

(By Associated Press.)

Washington, June 7.—The prohibition amendment and the enforcement act were held constitutional by the United States Supreme court today in a unanimous decision. While attorneys for the interests attacking the two measures were granted permission to file motions for re-hearings, the decision was regarded generally as striking a death blow to the hopes of the wets.

**Van Devanter Gives Opinion.**

The court's opinion rendered by Justice Van Devanter, was sweeping. It held the amendment, not only came within the amending powers conferred by the federal Constitution, but was proposed lawfully and now is the law of the land. While recognizing that Congress has limitations in respect to the enforcement of laws regarding beverages, the court held those limits were not transcended in the enactment of the enforcement act restricting alcoholic content to one half of one per cent.

While New York, New Jersey and Wisconsin acts, permitting manufacture and sale of beverages of more than one-half of one per cent alcoholic content, were not involved directly, the decision was interpreted as invalidating them. The court said the first section of the amendment, of its own force, "invalidates any legislative act—whether by Congress, by a state legislature or by a territorial assembly—which authorizes or sanctions what the section prohibits."

Concurrent power, granted by the amendment to federal and state governments to enforce prohibition, the court further held, "does not enable Congress or the several states to defeat or thwart prohibition, but only to enforce it by appropriate means."

The decision of the court was set forth in eleven conclusions covering seven separate proceedings. These proceedings included original suits brought by the state of Rhode Island, directly attacking the constitutionality of the amendment. The conclusions of the court follow.

**Text of the Decision.**

1. The adoption by both Houses of Congress, each by a two-thirds vote, of a joint resolution proposing an amendment to the Constitution sufficiently shows that the proposal was deemed necessary by all who voted for it. An express declaration that they regarded it as necessary is not essential. None of the resolutions whereby prior amendments were proposed contained such a declaration.

2. The two-thirds vote in each house which is required in proposing an amendment is a vote of two-thirds of the membership present assuming the presence of a quorum—and not a vote of two-thirds of entire membership, present and absent.

3. The referendum provisions of state constitutions and statutes cannot be applied, consistently with the constitution of the United States in the ratification or rejection of amendments to it.

4. The prohibition of the manufacture, sale, transportation, importation and exportation of intoxicating

(Continued on Page 6, Col. 1.)

## *35,000 Walk Home; 400 Cars Tied Up 2 Hours*

About 35,000 persons, men and women who had completed their daily toil and those doing downtown shopping became reluctant pedestrians late yesterday afternoon when a steam shovel doing excavating work at First avenue north and Eighth street struck a conduit severing eight power cables which supply power to street cars in the loop district, tying up about 400 cars in the loop district for two hours.

The street car company, during the busy afternoon and evening hours, carries about 75,000 passengers, officials said last night. Many choose to wait than walk to their homes in the outlying sections of the city. Automobilists came to the rescue of hundreds, and nearly every machine coming out of the downtown district carried its portion of "passengers." Sidewalks of streets leading from the business section were crowded with enforced hikers

(Continued on Page 10, Col. 3.)

## England Seeks Guarantees From Soviet Government

Cross-Atlantic Newspaper Service—Copyright. Special Cable to Minneapolis Tribune.

London, June 7.—Conversations of Leonid Krassine with Lloyd George were adjourned until today, it is known, to enable the Soviet representative to obtain from his government three guarantees. The first of these was a guarantee for the release of all British subjects now detained in Russia; the second, that a restoration of trading relations would not be utilized as a means of disseminating Bolshevik propaganda; and third, that there would be no further Bolshevik aggression in the near or middle east.

## Favorite "Dark Horse"

**Governor Sproul, Left, and His Backers.**

Chicago, June 7.—Gov. William C. Sproul of Pennsylvania is regarded as the favorite "dark horse" of the Republican convention. Chief among those who are pushing his candidacy are Mrs. Barclay H. Warburton and William E. Crow of Pennsylvania.

## Convention Without 'Big Chief;' Old Time Leaders Are Minus

### Deadlock of 'Big Three' Is Feature—'Dark Horse' Talk Increasing.

(By Associated Press.)

Chicago, June 7.—The old time leaders unhorsed, and its favorites for presidency deadlocked, the Republican party will begin its national convention here tomorrow under conditions of uncertainty unparalleled in recent political history.

Unbossed and largely unorganized, the delegates were asking one another tonight in what direction they were straying and when a member would arise to lead them out of the wilderness of their own indecision.

Amid the noisy turmoil of convention eve, the only definable trend seemed to be driving Wood, Lowden and Johnson into a deadlock fight which it was recognized everywhere might destroy them all. The old timers reflecting that it is but a step from a deadlocked convention to a stampeded convention wondered what might happen next unless some tried and trusted leader settled himself securely in the saddle. Many were recalling the Chicago convention of 1880 when the favorites were all deserted after a deadlock of 35 ballots and James A. Garfield who had won the convention by a nominating speech was nominated.

**Practical Politicians Talk 'Dark Horse.'**

Talk of a dark horse, in which some of the more experienced practical politicians joined tonight for the first time, began to revolve with an increasing frankness about the disclosures of the Senate's investigation of campaign expenditures. At many scattering conferences those who advocated a dark horse nomination predicated that in the end no man whose name was involved at all in the evidence of the investigating committee could be put before the country as the party's choice.

In the main, however, the leaders, and near leaders, caucused and conferred and brought forth nothing. Even those who held the whip hand over a few delegates here and there seemed unable to get together with the other greater and lesser potential dictators of party policy. The result was a foggy picture of the possibilities of the next few days. It became apparent that unless there was a dramatic and unexpected change the first ballot to be taken Wednesday or Thursday will record votes for between 15 and 20 candidates for the presidency with scarcely more than half enough to nominate in the Wood, Lowden or Johnson column.

**Claims of Big Three Contradicted.**

To what extent the managers for the leading three can hold their delegates in line after an unsuccessful test of strength is a subject of controversy. There are those who contradict the claims of the Wood, Lowden and Johnson whips that their organizations are cohesive enough to stand the strain of failure to nominate on an early ballot.

In any case no one any longer pre-

(Contiued on Page 8, Col. 4.)

## Registration Falls Below Previous Mark

### Total Less Than Half That in Last Election—Another Chance Next Week.

Less than half the number of voters who registered for the last general election registered yesterday, Henry N. Knott, city clerk, estimated when the 210 precincts in Minneapolis closed at 9 p. m. He declared the total would fall under 30,000. Confusion over the new precincts recently established by the City Council caused but little trouble, Mr. Knott said, in nearly every case the difficulty being straightened out easily.

There will be another registration next Monday. Voters not registered yesterday nor at the registration next Monday will be unable to vote at the primaries June 21 unless they are "sworn in" by two freeholders, a cumbersome process, Mr. Knott declared.

The total number of registered voters at the last general election was 70,000 but this was a total of three registration days. Mr. Knott said he was confident that at least as many votes would be cast on June 21 as were cast at the last general election.

## Nonpartisan Sympathizer Beaten, Strangled by Mob

Bismarck, N. D., June 7.—Ambrose Galliger of Bismarck, former sergeant with the American forces, was beaten and strangled by a mob at Richardton, Stark county, Sunday because he professed sympathy with the national Nonpartisan league, according to a story told by Galliger who reach Bismarck this afternoon.

## *Suffrage Is Near Test in Louisiana*

(By Associated Press.)

Baton Rouge, La., June 7.—The Senate passed the federal suffrage amendment to the third reading tonight after heated debate. It will come up for final action Thursday.

Congressman Champ Clark will address a joint session of the general assembly tomorrow and has declared he will urge the Legislature to ratify the amendment.

## Pennsylvanian Gaining Strength on All Fronts

### Thompson Attack on Lowden May Make or Break Him as Candidate—Johnson Abandons Fight for Borah as Chairman.

**By George F. Authier.**

Chicago, June 7.—Two dramatic situations were being outlined today in Chicago in connection with the nomination of the next Republican candidate for president.

One of them is a genuine movement for Governor William C. Sproul of Pennsylvania.

The other was the attack which Mayor William Hale Thompson of Chicago is making upon the candidacy of Governor Frank O. Lowden.

Sproul may furnish the solution to this convention puzzle.

Again, the attack on Governor Lowden may, and probably will, either make the governor the nominee or defeat him utterly.

The Illinois governor's candidacy revolves about this singular situation which has arisen in Illinois politics, a state situation which has become national in scope and which will have a large part in the proceedings.

These two developments are closely connected yet separate, and have ramifications leading all through the convention maze. This paradoxical relationship is a clear index of the puzzling situation which continues to pervade the entire atmosphere of the Republican gathering.

**All Guns Turn on Lowden.**

So far as Governor Lowden is concerned, he remains the high man in the estimation of the delegates. Naturally all guns from opposing candidates are turned on him and he is occupying exactly the exposed position that was held by General Wood a short time ago. It was at this psychological moment that Thompson forces undertook to even up scores with the governor for the failure of Thompson to land the national committeemanship. Seventeen votes controlled by the Chicago city hall crowd leave Lowden on this issue, and announced to the delegates that Lowden is not the solid choice of Illinois.

With the assistance of the Hearst papers, which are apparently doing their best to mess up the Republican situation, the Thompson people plan to make a campaign against Governor Lowden which will have all the features of a ward fight. They will make especial use of the incident in Missouri, where Governor Lowden's managers put money in the hands of men for organization purposes, who failed to use it, and who were later elected delegates.

**Thompson Crowd to Fight.**

The Thompson crowd met today and passed resolutions which they will also present to the national convention, condemning the use of money as it was used in Missouri. This will be a hard nut to crack, for naturally all of the delegates will be glad to vote for that,

(Continued on Page 8, Col. 1.)

## *State Leaders Named, Stage Set for Battle*

(By Associated Press.)

Chicago, June 7.—Among the National committeemen selected in the caucus of various states today are: Alabama, Oliver D. Street; Colorado, Dr. Hubert Work; Delaware, T. Coleman DuPont; Maine, Guy P. Gannett; Massachusetts, John W. Weeks; Nebraska, R. B. Howell, New Hampshire, F. W. Estabrook; New Mexico, H. O. Bursum; North Dakota, Gunder Olson; Ohio, Rudolph K. Hynicka; Pennsylvania, Boies Penrose; Vermont, Earle S. Kinsley; Wyoming, Patrick Sullivan; Illinois, Lawrence Y. Sherman; Wisconsin, Alfred T. Rogers; Florida, George W. Bean; Iowa John T. Adams; Oklahoma, Jacob Hamon; Louisiana, Emile Kuntz.

The Lowden slate of officers was elected without opposition at the caucus of Illinois delegates to the Republican convention. Senator Lawrence Y. Sherman was chosen national committeeman, and L. L. Emmerson chairman of the state delegation. Mayor William Hale Thompson presided and no Thompson slate was introduced.

Everything seems to be set for the opening of the convention tomorrow. The chaplain for the opening day, the Rev. Gardner McWhorter, Episcopalian, Libertyville, Ill., tried out his voice. Speaking in so large a place as the Coliseum was new to him, Dr. McWhorter explained and he wanted to find how loud he would have to pray so everyone could hear.

The labor unions have won their fight with the Republican National committee to keep telegraph wires of the Western Union and Postal Telegraph companies out of the Coliseum during the national Republican convention.

## Shaw Dramatizes Life to Millenium

### Noted English Playwright to Picture Existence 20,000 Years Hence.

Cross-Atlantic Newspaper Service—Copyright. Special Cable to Minneapolis Tribune.

London, June 7.—George Bernard Shaw is completing a trilogy of plays which the veteran English playwright believes will be hailed as among his greatest productions. They deal with the comprehensive subject of the life of man.

The first of the three volumes concerns the Adam and Eve period, the second dwells on the present era and the third depicts man 20,000 years from now, when he discovers immortality.

Humans born as adults are at this stage as inexperienced as infants are today and the early adventures of this infant man present astounding incidents. Shaw has thrown the whole force of his philosophy and satire into his latest work and the British public is keenly awaiting its production.

## *Calling Day, Lowden Visits Wood, They Get Thick, R.S.V.P.*

Chicago, June 7.—Governor Lowden exchanged visits today with candidates for the presidential nomination. Calling first on Major General Wood, he visited headquarters on Presidential Row. General Wood later returned the governor's call and stopped in to shake hands with the other candidates.

## Grand Jury to Sift Bergdoll's Escape

### Inquiry Into Case as It Affects Civilians Ordered By Department of Justice.

Public Ledger-Minneapolis Tribune Service. Copyright, 1920, by Public Ledger Co.

Washington, June 7.—Coincident to the announcement of Secretary Baker that the War department's investigation of the escape of Grover Cleveland Bergdoll had been completed, it became known that inquiry into the case as it involves civilians had been ordered by the Department of Justice and begun by a federal jury in Philadelphia under the direction of Charles McAvoy, district attorney.

Sergeants John O'Hare and Calvin York, army guards from whom Bergdoll escaped while visiting his mother's home in Philadelphia, have been ordered to Philadelphia as witnesses to assist the grand jury investigation. Department of Justice officials propose to push the grand jury inquiry with the utmost vigor sparing no one connected with the escape outside of members of the military service, who will be dealt with by the War department.

It is not unlikely that the grand jury inquiry will go into the arrangements made between the War department and D. C. Gibboney, and Ansell & Bailey, counsel for Bergdoll, to bring the latter to Philadelphia and later to Maryland to hunt for $150,000 he is alleged to have cashed somewhere near Hagerstown.

Secretary Baker's announcement that the investigation of the War department had been completed and transmitted to the Department of Justice for the information of officials engaged in the civilian inquiry made it plain that army men upon whom responsibility might be fixed would be subjected to disciplinary action.

## Longshoremen Strikers Riot; 10 Caught, Fined

Public Ledger-Minneapolis Tribune Service. Copyright, 1920, by Public Ledger Co.

Philadelphia, June 7.—The first rioting in the longshoremen's strike broke out today when strikers, including many negro I. W. W. attempted to prevent unloading of the steamer Osakis at Pier 19, north wharves. A flying squad of mounted police swept down and soon clubs were cracking heads and the mob started to move. The the police fired their pistols into the air and the strikers broke and fled. Ten of the leaders were rounded up in a magistrate's court and fined.

**Archbishop Mannix in America.**

San Francisco, June 7.—The Most Rev. Daniel J. Mannix, archbishop of Melbourne, Australia, arrived here today on his way to Rome. He was greeted by city officials, members of the Catholic church and delegations from Irish societies.

## *Pacific Coast States Renew Anti-Japanese Law Efforts; House Plans Investigation*

(By Associated Press.)

Washington, June 7.—Investigation of the Japanese immigration question will be made on the Pacific coast during the summer months by members of the House Immigration committee.

Representative Johnson, Washington, chairman of the committee, announced late today that at least five members of the committee would conduct the inquiry, which will cover all Pacific coast states and concentrate in California.

Decision was reached at a conference today, between Chairman Johnson and Senator Phelan, Democrat, California. The latter asked the committee investigate the situation, with a view to renewing efforts to pass pending legislation, which would bar all Japanese immigrants from the Pacific coast, and also prohibit Japanese children, born in this country, from acquiring citizenship.

The investigation will be conducted following the primary elections throughout the country, Mr. Johnson said, adding that members would be appointed by telegraph, when it was learned who could serve on the committee.

# The Minneapolis Morning Tribune

Fifty-fourth Year. No. 23. | Associated Press | MINNEAPOLIS, MINN., WEDNESDAY, JUNE 16, 1920 | United Press | Price Two Cents in Minneapolis

# Duluth Mob Hangs 3 Negroes to Avenge Young Girl; 3 Freed By Lynch Law Court Held in Battered Jail

## Aldermen Told City Must End Board System

### Committee of 13 Starts Inquiry Into Health Staff Dismissals.

### City Attorney Rules Council Has Power to Remove Board Members.

### 'Politics' Charge Plays Frequent Part in Opening of Hearing.

Backed by an opinion from C. D. Gould, city attorney, that the City Council has governing authority over city boards, even to the extent of removal of board members, the council special committee of 13 yesterday afternoon took the first step in investigation of the Board of Public Welfare for dismissal of nine health department employes, and the first step in what was hinted as abolition of all boards in the city.

Sharp criticism against the board system of government in Minneapolis was voiced by persons protesting the dismissal action; the City Council was called a "rubber stamp;" and persons attending the hearing were urged by those protesting "to vote men into the Legislature who will favor abolition of the boards." Further, council committee men were notified by George M. Bleecker, attorney, and first civil service commission chairman in Minneapolis, that should the Welfare board refuse to give the nine employes a rehearing, he would seek to bring mandamus proceedings against the board on behalf of the nine who had retained him as attorney.

On motion of Alderman Rudsdil the committeemen voted to adjourn, subject to the call of Chairman Williams, and that Aldermen Kistler and Rendell, council members of the Welfare board, be requested to appear before the committee to explain the board's dismissal action, and their own part in voting for the discharges. The two councilmen are on a fishing trip and probably will not be back until some time next week.

**"Clean Own House First."**

The motion and resultant committee action followed the declaration by Alderman Williams that:

"We ought to clean our own house first."

With the nine employes relieved of their duties yesterday, the civil service commission has certified to the board names of five eligibles, taken from a list of applicants, who have passed civil service examinations successfully for such positions. Four others will be certified later. In the meantime, Dr. F. E. Harrington, health commissioner, said the work of the department will continue unaffected, and inspections will be carried on as usual.

The five who were certified to Doctor Harrington are: Miss Hazel Hamblet, telephone operator, 521 Fourth street northeast, and four public health inspectors, E. C. Mork, 3041 Eleventh avenue south; J. H. Kenney, 2008 Bloomington avenue; R. H. Tenney, 3217 Aldrich avenue south; Bror G. Frykman, 1919 Johnson street northeast.

Answering questions by council members, the city attorney said the board

(Continued on Page 5, Col. 1.)

## Nash Ouster Case Hearing Tomorrow

### Governor Orders Proceedings Against Suspended County Attorney Be Resumed.

Hearings in removal proceedings against William M. Nash, Hennepin county attorney, now under suspension following charges connecting him with the Minneapolis liquor conspiracy, will be resumed at 10 a. m. tomorrow, according to telegraphic orders received last night from Governor Burnquist, who is in Chicago.

Because of arrangements for Mr. Nash's trial in federal court on charges growing out of the same case, it was predicted last night that a further continuance of the proceedings before the Governor will be sought by his attorney.

Governor Burnquist's telegram says he expects to go directly to Northfield from Chicago today to deliver an address at the commencement exercises at Carleton college.

The seven St. Paul men indicted by the St. Paul federal grand jury last week for complicity in the liquor conspiracy case pleaded not guilty when arraigned before Judge Page Morris in United States district court.

## Louisiana House Beats Suffrage By 67 to 44

Baton Rouge, La., June 15.—The proposal to ratify the woman suffrage federal amendment was defeated by the lower House of the State Assembly today 67 to 44. The Senate last week defeated the ratification resolution.

### Weather Forecast

MINNESOTA—Showers today, tomorrow unsettled, not much change in temperature.

## *Minneapolis School Boy of Seven Heir to Vast Estate in Mexico*

### Senora, Driven From Luxury by Rebels, Dies in West, Leaving Large Fortune to Child of Her Only Son.

Down in Mazatlan, Mexico, there's an estate in land and cattle, public utilities and banking securities and a palatial home, once presided over by a redoubtable senora until rebels drove her forth to seek a haven and to find death in San Francisco—and here in Minneapolis, the closely guarded ward of his doting grandparents in an apartment house basement, is a seven year old school boy who's believed to be the heir to this vast fortune.

The next few hours may decide whether Robert Parades, the hero of this international drama of fortune, is to remain the inconspicuous, carefree "Bobby" he is known to his newly made pals at the Douglas school or is to be established in splendor possibly somewhere on the other side of the border as the owner of these great properties.

From Houghton, Mich., there is speeding to Minneapolis, L. Rivera, reputed representative of the Mexican embassy at Washington, D. C.,—though, be sure the grandparents will make certain of his credentials—who is expected to arrive here today to investigate the standing of the little claimant. And from Winnipeg, his mother, Mrs. Irene Parades Newton, will start for here at 4 p. m. today to look after the interests of her son.

"Guard Bobby carefully," the mother telegraphed last night to the grandparents.

A conference of the principals may result tomorrow to decide on what steps to take in seeing that the small boy comes into his own.

The way seems paved for his entrance into fortune's exclusive company for Mexican authorities themselves have instituted the search for the lad which led to Minneapolis after months of effort, and a Mexican justice, one Licenciade Juan Ramon Urbide, of Mazatlan, who has charge of affairs of the estate, has alredy aided the youngster by declaring null and void the claim of a woman, Adela Absolo, who posed as the lawful wife of Jose A. Parades, only son of the wealthy senora and father of "Bobby," who was shot to death during an uprising in Mazatlan.

**Child's Whim to Be Consulted.**

And what plans have this small heir apparent himself made on the eve of impending events? He confided last night that he doesn't mean to be separated from his toys or his grandpar-

(Continued on Page 2, Col. 2.)

### Events of Drama

Events in fortune's drama which may establish "Bobby" Parades as heir to rich Mexican estate at Mazatlan.

1912—Jose A. Parades, only son of Dona Francisca Rojas vuida de Parades, married Miss Irene Robert at Houghton, Mich., as culmination of a college romance. They went to San Francisco.

1913—"Bobby" was born.

1914—Jose A. Parades killed in Mazatlan uprising. Widow brought son to Minneapolis. Places him in custody of her parents, Mr. and Mrs. Dolphis Robert.

Senor Parades' mother fled to San Francisco. Died there September, 1919.

After months of search, L. Rivera, representing Mexican embassy, Washington, D. C., visited Houghton yesterday to gain data on marriage and birth of Bobby. Grandparents were notified. Rivera starts for Minneapolis. Expected here today.

"Bobby's" mother, now Mrs. Irene Parades Newton, Winnipeg, starts for Minneapolis to support son's claim to fortune.

### Bobby Parades Content in Basement Home While Marble Mansion Awaits; Wants to Be With Grandparents.

## Herman Preus Asks Arrest of Frankson Aide

### Brother of Candidate for Governor Charges Criminal Libel in Pamphlet.

A warrant charging George H. Moeller, former state representative and supporter of Thomas Frankson, candidate for governor, with criminal libel will be sworn out today, according to Eugene M. O'Neill, St. Paul city prosecutor.

The complaint upon which the warrant is to be issued was filed yesterday by Herman Preus, brother of J. A. O. Preus, indorsed by the Republican convention for governor.

The charge is the result of a pamphlet said to have been issued by Moeller in the interests of the Frankson candidacy. The pamphlet attacks the war records of the Preus brothers and relatives.

The pamphlet attacks first the record of Mr. Preus himself. Then it names Herman Preus, Paul A. Preus and "two other brothers." Besides, William Preus, a cousin, and A. C. Wiprud, a brother-in-law, are mentioned.

**Complainant Is Law Student.**

Concerning Herman Preus, the pamphlet, which carries the statement that it is issued and circulated by George H. Moeller, says: "Herman Preus, another brother, went into Y.M.C.A. work and thus kept away from the firing line."

Herman Preus, who filed the complaint against Moeller, is to graduate from the law school at the University today. In his complaint he says that he enlisted as an ordinary seaman in the navy and served during the war, coming out as an ensign.

In attacking Paul A. Preus and A. C. Wiprud, the pamphlet says that these two men obtained exemptions because of their connections with the Federal Land bank. It also says that "two other brothers" obtained exemptions because of being "students of theology." The two men, the Rev. O. J. H. Preus and the Rev. J. C. K. Preus, have been ministers in the Nor-

(Continued on Page 9, Col. 1.)

## War Veteran Refuses Job and Rebukes Nonpartisans

St. Peter, Minn., June 15. — Henry Nelson, an ex-service man, now a student at Gustavus Adolphus college in this city, recently was tendered the position of clerk of court of Dickey, N. D., but flatly refused to take the job. In turning down the job, he said: "I do not wish to be affiliated with a political organization which is plundering my state and casting it to the dogs. I fought in France to preserve a democracy and do not propose to be a henchman to A. C. Townley and his mob of Socialists." Nelson served two years in France and was wounded in Chateau Thierry.

## Barragan, Carranza Aide, Escapes Military Guard

Mexico City, June 15.—General Juan Barragan, Carranza's debonair chief of staff, eluded his military guard and escaped today while en route from the military prison to the courthouse in another part of the city. Barragan was to be tried in connection with the murder of Carranza at Tlaxcalantongo.

**Irish Police Inspector Slain.**

Gory, County Wexford, Ireland, June 15.—A police inspector, Captain Wilson, has been shot dead by five armed men. Seven shots were fired at him.

## *$70,000 to Two Cents Is Range of Tax Returns*

### 1,000 Hurry In Assessments on Last Day of Second Quarter.

Nearly 1,000 persons paid $250,000 in income taxes yesterday, the last day for paying the second quarterly installments. A check for $70,000 from a corporation was the maximum received, while two cents from a woman was the minimum.

Other high numbers among checks were $27,000, $17,000 and $12,000. Most of the receipts were in checks, but more than $10,600 was received in cash.

Yesterday was not as high a day as the end of the first quarter when $400,000 was received. Theodore Lentz, chief deputy collector, said that many with small income chose to pay their taxes at the end of the first quarter rather than exercise their right of paying quarterly.

The number of women who paid taxes yesterday was but 5 per cent of the total. The majority of the women paid their taxes in advance, explained Mr. Lentz.

Those who failed to pay the second quarterly installment yesterday have their taxes for the remainder of the year due today, with 5 per cent of the tax added as a fine. This will be increased by 1 per cent a month while the tax is unpaid.

## Slayer of Woman, Insane, Kills Self

### James Whelan, Shell-Shocked War Veteran, Commits Suicide in Jail.

(By Associated Press.)

Marshall, June 15.—James Whelan, ex-service man, who on May 29 killed his cousin, Miss Elizabeth Smith, with a piece of gas pipe, and seriously injured Lyle Shifstead, 15, by beating him with a hammer, committed suicide in county jail here today. His lifeless body was found by the jailer who was bringing his supper at 6 p. m. Yesterday in district court Whelan was adjudged criminally insane and was ordered committed to the state asylum at St. Peter.

"I'm no crazier than any one else and they'll never take me there," Whelan told the jailer after the verdict.

His body will be sent to Denver, Col., where his mother lives, for burial.

Whelan was a veteran of Chateau Thierry and his mental condition was believed to have been brought on by shell shock for which he had been under treatment prior to his discharge from the service.

The murder occurred on the farm of Whelan's uncle, J. S. McGovern, near Marshall. Miss Smith was McGovern's housekeeper. During McGovern's absence from the farm on May 29 Whelan attacked Miss Smith and Shifstead. He claimed they were in league with German spies and trying to "get" him.

## Danish Explorer Plans 5 Year Visit to Esquimaux

Copenhagen, June 15.—Knud Rasmussen, Danish explorer, and Peter Frenchen, his cartographer, are preparing an expedition to visit the northern most American Esquimax. Rasmussen announced today the expedition probably would be the longest one he has ever made. He plans to take provisions enough to last five years, but considers it more likely the trip will last seven. Fourteen men will comprise the party.

## Harding Asked to Open Fair in Minnesota

### Republican Candidate Assured of Largest Audience of Farmers in Country.

Warren G. Harding, Republican presidential nominee, has been invited to make the address on the opening day of the Minnesota state fair this fall. He has been assured of the largest audience of farmers that can be gathered together anywhere in the United States.

An invitation was sent to Senator Harding yesterday by Frank W. Murphy, president of the State Fair and Mr. Murphy left for the East last night to extend the invitation personally.

While word has gone out that Senator Harding has indicated a desire to conduct his campaign along McKinley lines, from his front porch at Marion, Ohio, it has been definitely stated that he will make a few main speeches in various parts of the country.

"Senator Harding has a real message for the farmers of America," said Mr. Murphy, just before departing for the East last night. "No better place for him to deliver that message could be devised than the Minnesota state fair. He will have the greatest agricultural audience ever gathered together anywhere in this country.

"The farmers of the Northwest want to see and hear the Republican nominee for the presidency. Senator Harding knows the problems of the farmers. He has lived on the farm. He has never lost the human touch. As a newspaper publisher in a small city in Ohio he maintained that active interest in the problems of his neighbors which he had acquired in his youth."

"Senator Harding will stand squarely upon the platform adopted by the Republican convention at Chicago. The planks dealing with the agricultural interests of this country are forward looking and hold out hope for the farmers."

Mr. Murphy was Minnesota's member of the resolutions committee in the Chicago convention and made the fight for the agricultural planks which carried the indorsement of the National Farm Bureau federation.

Mr. Murphy believes that Senator Harding and his managers will see the advantage of having him speak at the State Fair.

## Harding Takes Up Work of Campaign.

Public Ledger-Minneapolis Tribune Service.


Washington, June 15.—Senator Warren G. Harding of Ohio, the Republican presidential nominee, said today that

(Continued on Page 7, Col. 4.)

### *The Tribune Wants High School Boys as Election Messengers*

The Tribune will require a large number of special messengers to gather returns for the evening of June 21, the primary election.

High school boys who helped get returns at previous elections and who want to do similar work now are asked to apply at once to the Election Editor, fourth floor, The Tribune building.

As many of the former messengers may not be available, applications will be considered from others. Any high school boy who is a hustler and who wants to serve may apply.

### America Accepts Armenia's Envoy

Garo Pasdermadjian.

Mr. Pasdermadjian, minister from Armenia to the U. S., has been in this country for the past three months, but the Armenian republic was not officially recognized by America until a few days ago.

## Carmen Ask Committee to Decide Stand

### Meeting Tonight Will Determine Course in Street Car Wage Dispute.

Decision as to the course to be followed by Minneapolis street railway trainmen to obtain wage increases and shorter hours will be made tonight, at a meeting of the executive committee of the trainmen, at the Nicollet station.

The meeting tonight follows the protest yesterday of Mayor Meyers against the establishment of a uniform street car fare for Minneapolis and St. Paul through a conference between the street railway committee of the Minneapolis City Council and the St. Paul City Council, and the gathering of the sentiment of the trainmen through meetings at the Minneapolis car stations.

At a meeting of 300 trainmen at the North Side station last night, speakers declared that any compromise on demands already submitted would be impossible, and that if wage increases were not forthcoming by July 1, a strike must be called.

Answering calls for "action," Horace Lowry, president of the company told the men that an increase in wages could not be granted unless the city council would make possible increased revenue. He asked that they exhaust every peaceable means of securing increased revenue without calling a strike. The members of the executive

(Continued on Page 9, Col. 1.)

## Girl's Kin Sought in Elwell Murder

### Kentucky Man Belived to Have Been Slayer of Whist Expert.

(By Associated Press.)

New York, June 15.—District Attorney Swan announced tonight that several detectives had left here for Lexington, Ky., where they hope to arrest the murderer of Joseph B. Elwell, wealthy sportsman and whist expert, who was found shot through the head at his home here last Friday.

"Several detectives left this morning on an excellent trail for Lexington, Ky.," Mr. Swan said. "They are looking for the father or the brother of a girl named Annie, one of whom we believe to be the man who fired the shot. We got the information from an excellent source, but cannot divulge the name of the man who gave it to us.

"We know that Mr. Elwell spent 10 weeks in Lexington up to June 1 when he left there and not because he wanted to."

Asked if the girl is a member of a prominent family in Lexington, he replied, "So far as we know she is."

## State Aid for Fire Heroes Asked of Legislature

Moorhead, Minn., June 15.—Resolutions favoring passage of a bill by the State Legislature making provisions for the care of families of firemen who lost their lives in the line of duty and for firemen disabled while fighting a blaze, were adopted by the forty-eighth annual convention of the Minnesota State Firemen's association in session here today.

**Albanians Continue Alvona Attack.**

Paris, June 15.—Albanian insurgents are continuing their attacks on Alvona, according to a dispatch from Rome to the Temps. The insurgents, however, have been driven back by cannon fire from the Italian warships.

## Troops Rush to Aid of Helpless Police

### 5,000 in Crowd Which Overpowers Guards, Breaks Down Cell Doors and Seizes Doomed Men—Priests Plead for Mercy as Victims Are Given 'Penalty' Imposed By 'Jury.'

### 10 Negroes Spirited to St. Paul.

Duluth, June 16.—(3 a. m.)—While a score of automobiles filled with irate citizens were speeding toward Virginia early this morning intent on finding more guilty negroes, deputy sheriffs spirited 10 blacks from the John Robinson circus at Virginia and are rushing them in automobiles to St. Paul for safe keeping. The autos with the negroes are expected to be lodged in the Ramsey county jail by daylight. Warren E. Green, county attorney of St. Louis county, when notified of the lynchings, said his office would make a thorough investigation to ascertain the leaders of the mob.

Duluth, June 16.—(Wednesday.)—"Lynch law" ruled Duluth last night and held sway until an early hour this morning.

Three negroes, attaches of a circus, arrested for attacking a 17-year-old white girl, were lynched in one of the city's main thoroughfares by a mob of 5,000 persons, which had stormed the police station with bricks and stones, and gained entry after overriding the city's police force.

At midnight the three bodies dangled from a telephone pole in the heart of the city and the mob—satisfied with its night's work—was disbanding.

**Troops Ordered Out.**

Its action was hastened by a report from Minneapolis that Adjutant General Rhinow had dispatched two companies of the state guard from Fort Snelling. The adjutant, at the same time, telegraphed to this city orders for mobilization of a company of Duluth home guards. The train bearing the Fort Snelling troops left St. Paul at 1:30 a. m. today. They were scheduled to arrive here at 6 a. m.

The three negroes lynched were Isaac McGhie, Elmer Jackson and Nate Green, all about 22 years old. They are said to have confessed to the attack on the girl at the circus grounds the night before. The girl's own story, it is said, almost certainly identified them. The victim of the attack is recovering.

**Three Negroes Acquitted.**

Three other negroes—the mob found six in the police station cells—were acquitted by a "lynch law court" held by mob members, and were turned back to the police. Those escaping the mob's noose were Louie Williams, John Thomas and Harry Richardson.

Calls for troops were sent to St. Paul. It appeared, however there would be little use for military aid, as the mob had dwindled greatly soon after midnight, although several hundred persons were still about the police station. The police believed they would experience no further trouble.

But the mob seemed to have turned its attention in another direction.

It was reported that three of four trucks and automobiles, loaded with members of the mob, had started at midnight toward Virginia, where it was said four other Negroes had been arrested in connection with the same case.

The circus was in Virginia today, and it was said eight Negroes were taken into custody there, but only four held.

One report was that the Virginia authorities and John Murpny, Duluth's chief of police, had started back to Duluth with these four suspects before the mob trouble broke out here, but it was understood that the party had been diverted to another city.

**Police Keep Arrest Secret.**

News of the arrest of the negroes was kept secret from the public by the police until this afternoon, although two were arrested last night after the girl had told her story. The subsequent arrest of four other negroes several miles from here, and their arrival at the jail, started subdued discussion among little groups of citizens gathered in the streets. As more facts became known, the street corner groups merged into an angry mob of 2,500 persons in Superior street, Duluth's main thoroughfare.

**Motor Trucks Pressed in Service.**

Motor trucks, loaded with men, dashed up and down the principal streets, the men calling for "volunteers to avenge the wrong done the white girl." They found many recruits who joined the mob.

Demands were made for the negroes' lives. Cries of "Lynch them!" "Burn them!" from hundreds of throats were intermingled with the horrified protests from others against "mob rule." In the end the mob spirit governed and leaders headed the angry throng for police headquarters.

**Crowd Grows to 5,000.**

By the time the mob had reached the police station it was estimated 5,000 persons had assembled. Police attempted to disburse it, but failed.

Self-appointed leaders demanded the negroes from the police. The police refused and renewed attempts to disperse the mob.

"Give 'em to us, or we'll take 'em," was the mob spokesman's reply.

**Police Defy Mob's Demand.**

"You'll have to take them," the police retorted.

Under direction of leaders a systematic collection of planks and stones began. Stones and bricks shattered the windows and drove the police into shelter.

Then the doors were battered down and the mob took possession of the entire building. Every policeman was driven into the streets.

**Cell Doors Broken Down.**

Soon after 10 o'clock the mob had forced its way into the steel-barred main corridor, where the six negroes were imprisoned. Another range of steel doors stood between the jail stormers and their quarry.

"Get an ax or a sledge," was the command. Both were produced. One after another the steel bars were battered and broken and finally the negroes were at the mercy of the mob.

**Fire Hose Turned on Lynchers.**

One excited citizen produced a revolver and attempted to shoot a negro. The pistol was wrenched from his hands before he could fire. There was no other attempt to use firearms.

The retreating police, however, had not given up the fight for the lives of their prisoners. Calls for aid to the fire department brought the city's fire force to the scene. Hose lines were attached to hydrants and streams of water were played on the mob.

**Firemen Are Driven Back.**

This failed to disperse the throng, part of which turned its attention temporarily to the firemen. Four lines of hose were taken from them and, in one of its more amiable moments, the mob enjoyed the scene of the firemen retreating before the streams of their own hose lines trained upon them.

Something of a sense of fairness seemed to permeate the mob atmosphere, however, for no violence was offered either the police or firemen, except that they were roughly handled when they attempted to block the mob's way.

**Trial of Men Is Suggested.**

None of the police was injured severely, and no weapon was used on them.

The same semi-sense of fairness found its way into the police station, where the mob leaders had the six fear-stricken negroes at their mercy.

"Maybe some of these fellows aren't guilty," was the opinion voiced by one leader.

"Let's try them," was a suggestion. It was followed out.

**'Jury' Hears Story of Crime.**

Up to the second floor of the police station the negroes were taken, with the mob surging behind them. The upper corridor of the station was crowded to capacity.

A lynch law court was organized, with a judge and 12 jurors. Order—or as much order as might be expected—prevailed. The negroes, tied hand and foot, were seated in a "prisoners' dock" and the trial proceeded. Two of the mob were named as counsel for the negroes. No attempt was made during the hearing to do any of the prisoners bodily injury.

**Condemned to Death.**

At 11:15 o'clock the trial was ended. Three of the negroes had been "convicted" by the "court," on their own stories, it was said. The other three, the "court" decided, were innocent. In fact, it was reported, the three found

# THE MINNEAPOLIS JOURNAL

THE JOURNAL RECEIVES BY LEASED WIRES THE COMPLETE NEWS REPORTS OF THE CHICAGO TRIBUNE, THE ASSOCIATED PRESS AND THE UNITED PRESS

28 PAGES—HOME EDITION. * WEATHER—Fair tonight and Friday; warmer in west Minnesota. THURSDAY EVENING, AUGUST 26, 1920. PRICE TWO CENTS IN MINNEAPOLIS




# SUFFRAGE NOW IN CONSTITUTION

## SCHOOL SURVEY TO FIND ROOMS FOR 5,000 PUPILS IN MINNEAPOLIS BEGUN

**Temporary Places in Lodges and Clubs, Halls and Churches Sought.**

**RAISING $250,000 FOR PROJECT HELD PROBLEM**

**Alterations by Board Required, Jackson Says—Womrath Favors Portable Buildings.**

A survey of Minneapolsi to find suitable quarters in lodge rooms, commercial club rooms, halls and churches temporarily to relieve the shortage in school housing conditions and to privide accommodations for 5,000 school pupils who otherwise would be on part time schedule, was begun today by George F. Womrath, business superintendent of the board of education, at the direction of the board.

Mr. Womrath has requested The Journal to give widest publicity to the effort of the board to locate temporary rooms throughout the city, each to accommodate from 20 to 40 pupils, the board to provide the desks and suitable school equipment. The sm..llest rooms that can be used, Mr. Womrath said, must contain at least 360 square feet of floor area and from this up to 729 square feet of floor space or more. Every room or building reported to the office of the business superintendent, 305 City hall, will have to be inspected to determine if the quarters will lend themselves to school purposes, Mr. Womrath said.

While the survey is in progress, B. B. Jackson, superintendent of schools, and Mr. Womrath say they are at a loss to suggest how the necessary $250,000 to carry out the program, even if the survey reveals the 120 nesessary temporary rooms, can be raised. Mr. Jackson expressed the opinion it would be difficult, if not impossible, to use a sufficient number of suitable rooms without extensive alteration sto make them comply with state and city legal requirements. At least $100,000 would be needed, Mr. Womrath said, to equip the temporary rooms with ventilating, toilet and other necessary facilities. He said he believed the money might be more advantageously expended in providing well equipped, portable buildings, more accessible, where accommodations could be made for 1,000 pupils.

"The laws of the state have necessitated extensive alterations in more than 100 schoolrooms in Minneapolis schools and those which could not be made to meet the requirements have been abandoned. Fire hazard regulations, also, must be considered.

"The teacher problem would be solved, for already sufficient teachers have signed contracts for part time work."

The schools where the housing conditions are most serious are the Bremer, Calhoun, George Bancroft, Clara Barton, Clinton, Hamilton, Holmes and Irving buildings, while the Lake Harriet, Lincoln, Lowell, Lyndale, Miles Standish, Minnehaha, Pillsbury, Robert Fulton and Simmons schools have insufficient room to accommodate all the pupils propertly, Mr. Jackson said.

**Expense Called Obstacle.**

The expense of equipping the temporary quarters, both the superintendent and the business superintendent agreed, would be one of the obstacles in connection with the board's program suggested in the survey. The money required, they said, would mean a flat loss to the board, the finances of which already are strained.

To equip properly the temporary rooms would entail an expenditure of $90,000 for seats, $5,000 for blackboards, $15,000 for temporary supplies, $9,000 for extra janitor service and $130,000 for plumbing, ventilating equipment and operating the heating plants, according to Mr. Womrath.

"These figures make provision for only six months and do not include a rental item," said Mr. Womrath. "We assume that we will receive some offers for free use, but in the cases of the most desirable store buildings, this rental item must be considered.

"The board now had available $600,000 to be used expressly for new schools, and these funds cannot properly be diverted to other purposes. Two courses are open to the board in the expenditure of this money, one of which is to begin construction of the Northeast Senior and the Bremer Junior high schools, taking the chance that the forthcoming legislature will provide the remainder of the funds necessary to complete the buildings, or a portion of the money could be used to provide portable rooms for the districts in most urgent need because of crowded conditions. The first plan will bring little relief for a year, while the second would have immediate benefits."

Superintendent Jackson said he could see little prospect of finding a solution in the survey.

"Experiences have shown that rooms which would be available for pupils would not meet the legal requirements, with their drastic limitations," said Mr. Jackson. "One of these laws forbids housing school children in rooms which are even partly depressed below the ground surface. Many Sunday school rooms, for that reason, would be barred for use as schoolrooms. Poor lighting of rooms in churches is also a barrier."

Seymour Steadman of Chicago, socialist candidate for vicepresident, who is to be in Minneapolis, Labor day, Sept. 6, today issued a challenge to Governor James M. Cox of Ohio to debate with him that day on the "Fundamental Differences Between the Democratic and Socialist Parties." The challenge was given out from socialist national headquarters in Chicago. The invitation to debate was sent first to Senator Warren G. Harding, but later it was learned that he would not be in Minneapolis until Sept. 8.

## Poles Capture Grodno; Russians To Modify Terms

**Bolsheviki Agree to Withdraw Demand That Poland Arm Workmen's Militia — Soviet Reserves Rushed to Front.**

**London, Aug. 26.—The Russian soviet government replied today to the note of Arthur J. Balfour, lord president of the council, concerning the soviet peace terms to Poland. The soviet government agrees to withdraw its condition that the Poles provide arms for a workmen's militia of 200,000 men in Poland. The Russian delegation in London claims that this concession meets the wishes of the British and Italian governments.**

Paris, Aug. 26.—Polish forces have entered Grodno, according to a dispatch to the Matin today. Grodno, 150 miles northeast of Warsaw, was last reported to be the bolshevik main headquarters. It is a Russian territory. The Russian soviet forces have evacuated Vilna, Lithuania, their former headquarters, and the railway station and public buildings there were occupied by Lithuanians Tuesday night, according to advices reaching the French foreign office today.

Russian soviet reserves are reported being brought up on the southern front in great numbers. According to information in the hands of the Polish general Haller, reserves some distance behind the bolsheviki north front also are reported to be concentrating in great numbers along the Beresina river,

Continued on Page 19.

## Plan 1921 Paving Now, Meagher Asks of Council

**Committee Chairman Offers Resolution to Draw Program by Nov. 1, Following The Journal's Study of Work in Other Cities.**

A resolution calling upon all aldermen to outline proposed 1921 paving projects by November was to be presented to the city council's paving committee when it met late today, Alderman Michael Meagher, chairman, said in advance of the meeting. This proposal for early planning of all 1921 paving follows the series of special articles on the paving situation, published this week in The Journal, which revealed that Minneapolis was about the only important city in the country that does not draw up its approval of street improvement programs a year in advance.

**Nicollet Paving Sought.**

Paving of Nicollet av from Forty-second st to Fifty-second in the 1921 program will be asked by aldermen of the thirteenth ward, Alderman J. T. Kean said today.

"In my opinion we should get to work at once to outline the paving program for 1921," said Alderman Kean, "and put the entire project up to the engineer's office. The paving engineer should be able to give us assurance of the amount of work he can do and the remainder should be let to private contractors. Personally, I am in favor of the contract system for paving, but, realizing the sentiment of other aldermen, I believe next year we should at least give that portion of the work the city engineer cannot do to private contractors."

**Others Plan Far in Advance.**

"The real reason for delayed paving and increase of expense lies in the failure of the council to order paving far in advance," said Alderman Meagher. "If we give the city paving engineer time, he will be in a position to buy the

Continued on Page 19.

## *BUSINESSMEN, IN OVERALLS, ERECT REST STATION*

**North Broadway Tourists' Structure Expected to Be Complete by Night.**

Business and professional men of West Broadway sawed boards, hammered nails and mixed mortar while they erected a new rest station for automobile tourists at Thirty-second av N and West Broadway today. They will complete the building by night, they said.

Attired in working clothes, the businessmen formed in a procession along the street at 7 a.m. today and accompanied by wagons loaded with lumber marched to the site of the new station. There under the direction of carpenters and plumbers they started work on the building and expect to be practically through by tonight. At noon wives of the amateur builders furnished refreshments.

Tonight the workers will celebrate the completion of the station by a band concert, refreshments and probably a dance.

At a recent meeting of the businessmen of West Broadway, it was decided to have the new station in readiness for the automobilists while the State Fair is in progress, hence the concerted action of the residents today, according to C. W. Steffes, editor of the Minneapolis Chronicle, who is chairman of the building committee.

## *Woodbury Assistant Secretary of Navy*

Washington, Aug. 26.—Gordon Woodbury, formerly a member of the New Hampshire legislature, has been appointed assistant secretary of the navy to succeed Franklin D. Roosevelt.

## FULL ELEVATION OF MILWAUKEE TRACKS ASKED; DEPRESSION RULED INFEASIBLE

**Raising Rails in South Minneapolis Favored by Gould and Cappelen.**

**ROAD HELD READY TO MAKE IMPROVEMENT**

**City Attorney and Engineer, in Opinions, Oppose Alderman Bastis' Proposal.**

Complete elevation of the Milwaukee railroad tracks in south Minneapolis, between the Milwaukee station and Twenty-sixth st, is the only remaining solution of a problem that has been under consideration for more than a quarter century, Chairman John Walquist, of the council committee on railroads, said today, following opinions of City Attorney C. D. Gould and City Engineer F. W. Cappelen, holding impracticable a proposal of Alderman A. G. Bastis, socialist, that complete depression be ordered as a means of separation of the grades.

An original plan, providing for 17 foot depression with part elevation, was defeated in the courts in 1916. Recently a modified plan of depression and elevation was defeated in the committee, on opposition by socialist aldermen. This modified plan would have met the objections set forth in the court ruling, Alderman Walquist said.

The Milwaukee railroad, according to F. W. Root, counsel, is ready to elevate the tracks in the district affected.

The opinions of the city attorney and city engineer were submitted to the council today at the request of the committee, following a proposal of Alderman Bastis asking preparation of an ordinance calling for complete depression.

**Sewerage System Split Seen.**

"Such a depression would split the entire sewerage system east and west of the tracks, in two distinct divisions," said Mr. Cappelen, "the portion of the city lying east of the tracks could be used under the depression system, but a great deal of the system on the west side of the tracks, clear to and including Lake st, would have to be entirely rearranged and a new outlet for same be provided for, which would entail a vast sum of money, and in my opinion would be impracticable.

"The grades involved in making provisions for the various sidetracks and spurs now reaching large business interests, as well as the large railroad yards, would be of such a nature that you might call that impractical, too.

"Although the depression work in itself, of course, could be carried out, because of the difficulty involved on account of water and to provide for drainage of same, the cost would be so excessive that, judging rom the verdict in a former suit to compel 17 foot depres-

Continued on Page 19.

## MARCH OR PAY FINE, ORDER TO WORKERS

**Radicals Ruling Several Unions Act to Compel Appearance in "Protest Parade."**

Radicals in control of a number of Minneapolis unions have taken steps to see that more conservative members join in the "injunction protest demonstration" planned for Saturday.

Members of a number of unions are now being notified that they must appear in the demonstration or pay fines to the unions.

The demonstration is to take the form of a parade which will follow four radical labor men who have announced they will go to jail rather than pay fines of $125 each placed against them by Judge W. W. Bardwell of the district court for contempt of court in disregarding an injunction restraining them from participating in a boycott.

I. G. Scott, socialist alderman, today confirmed reports that the Twin City Plasterers union, No. 20, had notified all members that failure to appear in the parade will be punished by a $5 fine. He said he understood other unions had taken similar action. Lynn Thompson, socialist labor organizer, also said some of the unions had ordered all members to march or pay fines.

Plans for the parade were formulated last night at a meeting of the Trades and Labor assembly, at which plans also were made for an attempt to have union men boycott the loop district during the imprisonment of the four men.

## *Sailor Denies Part In Trunk Murder*

Rio de Janeiro, Aug. 26.—Because there is no extradition treaty between the United States and Brazil, the sailor believed to be Eugene Leroy, wanted in connection with the trunk murder mystery of Detroit and New York, will be taken to Buenos Aires, when the British steamer Dryden leaves for that port.

The man, who shipped under the name of Morris Fox, was placed under arrest on the Dryden, at the request of the American authorities, before it reached this port.

He denied any knowledge of the murder.

## *American Fails to Swim British Channel*

Dover, England, Aug. 26.—Henry Sullivan of Lowell, Mass., who started at 8:40 last night in an attempt to swim the English channel from Dover to Calais, was taken from the water 10 miles from the French coast, according to an unconfirmed report received here today.

## *WEALTHIEST AND MOST BEAUTIFUL INDIAN PRINCESS*

—Copyright by Bertram Park.

The Princess Tikka of Kapurthala whose husband is the son and heir of the Maharjah of Kapurthala. Before her marriage she was the Princess Brinda of Jubbal, daughter of the Rajah Kanwur Gambhir. She is said to be the most beautiful as well as the wealthiest princess of India. She was educated in Paris and has often visited England.

## Reputed Owner of Auto Questioned In Hallet Slaying

**Mystery Message Brings Detectives' Action—Fund for Family of Policeman Started by Mayor—Funeral Tomorrow.**

Acting on a mysterious telephone message received by Captain A. C. Jensen at police headquarters early today, and following a conference between him and Captain John J. Galvin, acting chief of police, detectives took into custody a man said to be the owner of the car used by the four bandits who shot and killed Patrolman Frank S. Hallet at 2 a.m. yesterday.

Frank A. Regan, captain of detec-

Continued on Page 19.

## RISE IN LIVING COST HERE THIRD LOWEST

**Minneapolis Increase Since 1917 Only 43.4 Per Cent, U. S. Figures Show.**

Minneapolis, in a list of 10 cities for which figures were given out today by the United States department of labor, has had the third lowest increase in the cost of living since 1917. Among northern cities Minneapolis has had the lowest percentage of increase. The increase in the 10 cities follow:

| City. | Pct. |
|---|---|
| Birmingham | 41.9 |
| New Orleans | 41.9 |
| Minneapolis | 43.4 |
| Richmond, Va. | 42.8 |
| Memphis | 46.4 |
| Atlanta | 46.7 |
| Cincinnati | 47.1 |
| St. Louis | 48.9 |
| Indianapolis | 50.2 |
| Kansas City | 51.0 |

In Minneapolis the largest increase was in clothing, 76.7 per cent, while the smallest was in housing, 10.7 per cent. The percentages of increase in Minneapolis over December, 1917, on different items follow:

| | Dec., 1918. | June, 1919. | Dec., 1919. | June, 1920. |
|---|---|---|---|---|
| Food | 17.71 | 21.44 | 34.10 | 50.0 |
| Clothing | 33.49 | 40.14 | 66.98 | 7.67 |
| Housing | .10 | 2.01 | 7.97 | 10.7 |
| Fuel, light | 14.71 | 13.41 | 22.42 | 36.9 |
| Furnishings | 18.08 | 25.55 | 45.57 | 65.5 |
| Miscellaneous | 12.27 | 15.90 | 25.43 | 31.3 |
| Total | 15.80 | 18.75 | 32.71 | 43.4 |

Figures showing increases from 1914 to 1920 were given out for eight other cities. They range from 96 per cent in San Francisco to 121.5 per cent in Buffalo.



## HARD COAL RETAIL PRICES GO UP 65 CENTS TON IN CITY ON FREIGHT RAISE

**Absorbs Increased Cost of Moving Fuel From Duluth Here, Say Dealers.**

**$1 ADVANCE EXPECTED ON BITUMINOUS PRICES**

**Northwest Is Declared Facing Shortage of Five to Seven Million Tons.**

Increased freight rates struck home in Minneapolis immediately today when retail coal dealers began announcing an increase of 65 cents a ton on anthracite coal deliveries, except for the small amounts of anthracite already on hand. This increase, dealers said, absorbs the increased cost of moving coal from Duluth to Minneapolis. A further increase to absorb the cost of moving coal from the mines to Lake Erie and down the lakes will come when present supplies at the head of the lakes are depleted, dealers said. Bituminous prices are expected to go up about $1.

Exact figures on the movement of coal cars from mines to Lake Erie ports, made public today by the car service section of the interstate commerce commission, shows that 96,720 cars should have been moved since the order became effective one month ago today, and that 88,000 cars have been moved. The average shortage under the specified 4,000 daily cars is 340 cars a day.

Other developments in the coal situation today included:

**With the Cleveland and Toledo civic commercial bodies petitioning the interstate commerce commission for changes in Order No. 10, which would affect the northwest's priority on bituminous coal from Lake Erie, members of the state railroad and warehouse commission were preparing to send a representative to the hearing in Washington Monday. W. H. Groverman, secretary of the Northwest Coal Dock Operators association also will go.**

**The Associated Business Organizations of Minneapolis threw open its quarters in the Builders Exchange building late today for members and the public to hear from Judge J. F. McGee his statement of the present status of the coal industry and the movement of coal into the northwest.**

**Inquiry at Duluth revealed that while 24 vessels are now loading at Lake Erie, afloat on the lakes or discharging at Duluth coal for the northwest, practically no progress has been made toward making up the early season shortage and the northwest is faced with a shortage of 5,000,000 to 7,000,000 tons of soft coal, according to the computation of a capable authority.**

Minneapolis coal dealers today declared that reports from the east that the department of justice is preparing to force lower coal prices applies only to local conditions in the Newport News and Baltimore export trade, where "cost plus" bidding by foreigers has been sending soft coal prices to unprecedented heights.

**No Relief in Sight.**

"If there was 100 per cent car service and the mines were working full time, I should look for a drop in coal prices, but those conditions do not exist and no relief can be foreseen," said W. W. Broughton, president, in Minneapolis, of the Pittsburgh Coal company. "It must also be borne in mind that prices have to go up to cover the increased freight charges effective today. The increase will be between $1.50 and $1.75 on hard coal when its full force is felt, and about $1 on bituminous."

"Even the larger dealers have but a few hundred tons of anthracite on hand and that is all contracted for," said J. A. Campbell, a dealer. "The only coal we can get to sell is that which must be moved into town and on which the higher freight must be paid. Naturally the freight increase must be added. Most dealers are putting the increase into effect today."

**Big Shortage Predicted.**

That there is "no more chance of getting a full supply of coal up the lakes this fall than there is of flying," and that the northwest's shortage will probably be from 5,000,000 to 7,000,000 tons, so far as dock bituminous coal

Continued on Page 2.

## MARTINSON MADE TRUSTY AT PRISON

**Former Sheriff Will Have "Outside" Job Because of Poor Health, Says Warden.**

Leavenworth, Kan., Aug. 26.—Oscar Martinson, former Hennepin county sheriff, who was sentenced to two years in the federal penitentiary here for complicity in the Minneapolis-Winnipeg whisky smuggling case, will be employed as an outside trusty, Warden A. Vanderson announced today.

Martinson arrived here in custody of Deputy United States Marshal McGuire and a Minneapolis detective. He was in good spirits when he entered the prison and declared that he would do his best to become a model prisoner.

Warden Anderson said the former sheriff is in poor health and the outside work is given him so that he may more quickly recover.

While Martinson's term is two years, he will be eligible for parole next May under the one-third rule. Should his prison record be good it is probable that he will be released at that time. With good time off his minimum sentence would expire in November, 1921.

## Wilson, Member of Three Presidents' Cabinets, is Dead

"TAMA JIM" WILSON.

**"Tama Jim," Secretary of Agriculture 15 Years, Introduced Durum Wheat.**

Traer, Iowa, Aug. 26.—"Tama Jim" Wilson, secretary of agriculture in the cabinets of Presidents William B. McKinley, Theodore Roosevelt and William Howard Taft, died at his home here today. He had been in poor health for several months. He was 85 years old.

Mr. Wilson was head of the department of agriculture for 15 years, during which he contributed largely to the phenomenal agricultural development of

Continued on Page 2.

## Suffragists of Minneapolis Plan Fete Saturday

**Homes and Downtown Buildings Will Be Decorated—Whistles to Shriek at Noon—Organizations Arrange Celebrations.**

Minneapolis will celebrate on Saturday the official proclamation of Secretary of State Bainbridge Colby granting women the right to vote. Flags are to float from downtown buildings and from homes, and whistles will shriek at noon. The courthouse chimes also will be rung. As soon as she heard that Secretary of State Bainbridge Colby had issued the suffrage proclamation, Mrs. Andreas Ueland, honorary president of the Minnesota League of Women Voters, sent out word today to the members of the last board of Minnesota Woman Suffrage association and to the county chairmen to celebrate Saturday.

"That talk of the antis about blocking the amendment is just bluff," said Mrs. Ueland. "They can nomore stop wom-

Continued on Page 17.

## Mining Engineers, Headed by Hoover Convene in City

**150 Members of American Institute Conduct Technical Sessions at University—Former Food Chief to Speak at Banquet Tonight.**

Headed by Herbert Hoover, their president, more than 150 members of the American Institute of Mining and Metallurgical Engineers reached Minneapolis at 8:30 today on the Soo line for an all day session in their progressive "Lake Superior meeting." Beginning at 10 a.m. with technical sessions in three of the large auditoriums at the Unievrsity of Minnesota, the most important formal meetings of the week's trip, the engineers were taken to St. Paul at the close of the sessions for luncheon at the Town and Country club. Tonight they will attend a banquet at the Curtis hotel, at which Mr. Hoover, J. E. Spurr, an authority on mining matters; Bradley Stoughton, secretary of the Institute, and Fred B. Snyder will be the speakers. William C. Edgar will be toastmaster.

During early technical sessions, women members of the party were enter-

Continued on Page 19.

## *WELCOME TO AUTO TOURISTS GAINS PRAISE FOR CITY*

**New York Sun Prints Half Page Article—Cincinnati Paper Comments Editorially.**

Automobile tourists, returning to eastern states, are carrying praise for Minneapolis hospitality, according to newspaper comment.

The New York Sun in the issue of Sunday, Aug. 22, devoted a half page to the Minneapolis method of welcoming tourists, illustrating the articles with pictures of the Gateway park and a policeman tagging one of the cars. The Cincinnati Times-Star, editorially praises Minneapolis and Minnesota hospitality to automobile tourists.

Mayor J. E. Meyers' automobile tourist bureau, established at the Gateway park, welcomes all automobile tourists, tags machines and extends all courtesies.

## COLBY PROCLAIMS RATIFICATION OF ACT ENFRANCHISING 17,000,000 WOMEN

**Secretary Signs Tennessee's Ratification After It Is Held Flawless.**

**19th AMENDMENT MADE EFFECTIVE IMMEDIATELY**

**Suffrage Leaders, Absent at Signing Ceremony, Ask That It Be Repeated.**

Washington, Aug. 26.—The right of 17,000,000 American women to the ballot was formally made a part of the constitution of the United States today when Secretary of State Bainbridge Colby proclaimed ratification of the 19th amendment.

**Women Vote in November.**

Proclaiming of the 19th amendment by Mr. Colby makes it effective immediately, and it gives American women the right to cast their vote in the presidential election in November, also in all state and municipal elections.

Secretary Colby announced the proclamation when he arrived at his office today having signed it at 8 a.m. at his home here.

The official certification that Tennessee had become the 36th state to ratify the amendment was taken to his home early today.

**Suffragists Cheer Signing.**

A group of suffrage leaders who had waited until a late hour last night for the arrival of the Tennessee certification were hurriedly summoned to the state department and met Colby.

They cheered when told the last step to make the amendment operative had been taken.

Among them were: Alice Paul, chairman of the National Women's party; Mrs. Abby Scott Baker, Miss Julia Emorty, Baltimore; Dr. Lydia Allen Devilbis of Georgia and Miss Mary Moore Forrest of Massachusetts.

**Certification Held Flawless.**

The Tennessee certification was taken to Secretary Colby's home by Charles L. Cooke, master of ceremonies of the state department. Mr. Colby and Frederick Neilson, state department solicitor, went over it for possible flaws. They found none, it was said.

Suffragists had expected Mr. Colby to make the ceremony of proclaiming the amendment a public one and were evidently disappointed.

**May Repeat Ceremony.**

They requested him to go through theh ceremony again for their benefit and for motion picture men.

Secretary Colby said he would consider going over the ceremony again and went to his office.

The women, however, left the state department without waiting for Mr. Colby's decision. They had a jubilation at their own headquarters a short distance away.

**Suffragists to Continue Vigilance.**

Miss Alice Paul declared that the suffragists will not relax their vigilance until they are sure that no further attempts will be made to take from the women what they have won.

"We are confident that the signature of Secretary of State Colby completes the suffrage struggle in this country," she said. "Despite every obstacle that our opponents could put in our way, women have won the right to equal voice in the affairs of the government."

**Antis Give Up Fight.**

Antisuffragists, who yesterday failed in their attempt to have the District of Columbia supreme court issue an order to restrain Secretary Colby from proclaiming the amendment as law, made no further attempt to prevent issuance of the proclamation.

Efforts will be made, antisuffragist leaders declared, to have the United States supreme court pass on the legality of Tennessee's ratification. Suffrage opponents predicted the court would held that the legislature had not authority to act.

Mrs. Carrie Chapman Catt, president of the National American Woman Suffrage association, was expected to arrive in Washington from Nashville in time for a suffrage jollification to be conducted here tonight in a theater.

## SCRIVER URGED FOR SCHOOL BOARD POST

**Parents and Teachers Association Adopt Resolution Naming East Side Businessman.**

Hiram A. Scriver was urged for election to the vacant post on the Minneapolis school board, in a resolution unanimously adopted by the executive committee of the Parents and Teachers council last night.

Resignation of Professor David Swenson leaves the east side without any representation on the board. Mr. Scriver is an old east side resident, a well known businessman, and long has had a special interest in education, serving as a trustee of Carleton college for years. He was a candidate for the board two years ago and was nominated in the primary, but withdrew in order to simplify the problem at the general election.

The vacancy on the board is to be filled by the city council, which may take the matter up at its meeting tomorrow.

Nicholas Dell, attorney, 706 University av NE, has been indorsed by the Northeast Commercial club, according to letters received from the club by members of the council today, and Asa M. Hunter, insurance man, is another man mentioned for the vacancy, aldermen said.

# The Minneapolis Morning Tribune

Fifty-fourth Year. No. 163. | Associated Press | MINNEAPOLIS, MINN., WEDNESDAY, NOVEMBER 3, 1920 | United Press | Price Two Cents in Minneapolis.

# Republican Landslide Elects Harding
# Preus and Collins Carry Minnesota

## Townley Fails in Attempt to Capture State

### Shipstead Is Defeated By Republican Standard Bearers.

### Hodgson Runs Poor Third in Contest for Governor.

### Socialistic Overtures Fail to Appeal to Minnesota Voters.

**At 2 a. m. today, the returns from 258 precincts out of 3,220 in Minnesota, scattered through 46 counties, gave for governor: Preus, 45,132; Shipstead, 27,699; Hodgson, 9,984.**

**Hennepin county precincts included gave Preus, 9,703; Shipstead, 6,894; Hodgson, 1,285.**

**For attorney general, 127 precincts in 33 counties gave Hilton, 14,124; Sullivan, 6,294; McQuat, 1,260.**

**Harding continued his three to one ratio, 259 precincts in 48 counties giving Harding, 49,028; Cox, 13,564.**

**By George E. Akerson.**

Minnesota has repudiated Townleyism in no uncertain term.

Returns received up to an early hour today indicated that J. A. O. Preus, Republican nominee for governor, and all his associates on the state ticket, have been elected by plualities which are expected to run well over 50,000.

At the same time, Minnesota has gone for Warren G. Harding for president by a plurality which is now estimated will run as high as 150,000.

"The returns indicate that I have been elected governor of Minnesota," said Mr. Preus early this morning. "It is a victory for constitutional government and American ideals over Townleyism and Socialism."

As the returns came in, first from Minneapolis and then from the country districts, it became increasingly evident that Preus, Hilton, Collins and all the other Republicans who have carried on the fight against Townleyism and the kindred "Isms," were going over by big majorities. In no case did the returns upset predictions. In rural precincts where the Nonpartisan league has been strong, Preus made surprising gains.

**Hodgson is Poor Third.**

Laurence C. Hodgson, Democratic nnominee for governor, will be a poor third in the race. Dr. Henrik Shipstead, Townley nominee, is the second man.

The vote for Clifford L. Hilton, attorney-general, was running right along with the Preus vote. The Townleyites made a bitter fight in the effort to gain control of the office of the chief law officer of the state.

**Justice Returns Meager.**

There were not enough returns in on justice of the supreme court to indicate the final result. In the few precincts that did come in Justice Homer B. Dibell, incumbent, was running ahead of George L. Siegel, Townley candidate.

In eight precincts in Minneapolis the vote was Dibell, 1,047; Siegel, 619.

Justice of the supreme court was the last name on the state ballot and consequently the vote on it was the last to be counted.

There were not sufficient returns upon the good roads amendment early today to indicate what action the voters had taken. Returns from scattering districts in Ramsey and Hennepin counties were overwhelmingly in favor of the amendment. In the Twentieth district of the Eighth ward, Minneapolis, there were 821 votes for, 53 against, and 64 blanks. Four precincts in Itasca cast 26 votes for and only 10 against the amendment.

It is true that the strictly rural precincts are still to be heard from. Very few purely rural townships had reported up to 2 a. m. but the vote for the Republican nominees from counties formerly carried by the league indicated that the town vote would be so large that the country cannot overturn it.

Louis L. Collins, "fighting corporal of the 151st," Republican nominee for lieutenant-governor, was running ahead of the ticket in many of the reports received.

From strong Nonpartisan league territory, in the Ninth congressional district, came most encouraging reports for the Republican nominees. It was

(Continued on Page 2, Col. 1.)

**New State Executive**

J. A. O. Preus.

## New Congress Is Republican By Good Lead

### 30 More Votes Indicated in G. O. P. Majority in Lower House.

**By Universal News Service.**

New York, Nov. 2.—The next House of Representatives will have a Republican majority of 75, or an increase of 30 votes over the present Republican majority, according to indications from all quarters tonight. The Republican congressional committee claims a gain of at least two representatives in Massachusetts; two in California, two in Montana and possibly two in Kentucky. In addition gains are expected in Missouri, Michigan and Wisconsin.

In all states where the Republicans now have large delegations in the lower house they have held their own or bettered their standing. Illinois, New York, Iowa, Ohio, Kansas and Indiana all have returned their Republican members and in several instances have increased their strength.

**South Remains Solid.**

Throughout the solid South the Democrats have elected their full ticket without exception. In a number of states Alabama, Georgia, Louisiana, Mississippi and in a number of districts in Texas the Republicans failed to oppose the Democratic candidates for the lower house.

In the border states, however, including Kentucky, Maryland and Tennessee there is every indication of a slight gain for the Republicans. In Massachusetts, Congressman Olney, Democrat, has apparently been defeated by former Lieutenant Governor Frothingham, Republican, while Congressman Phelan, Democrat, has apparently been defeated by Maloney, Republican. Frederick H. Gillett, speaker of the last House, has won with a big majority.

**Gains in Senate.**

The Republicans have made a net gain of eight and possibly 10 in the next Senate, according to a statement by the Republican senatorial com-

(Continued on Page 2, Col. 5.)

### Senators Elected in Doubtful States

California—Shortridge, Republican.
Colorado—Nicholson, Republican.
Connecticut—Brandegee, Republican.
Georgia—Watson, Democrat.
Idaho—Gooding, Republican.
Illinois—McKinley, Republican.
Indiana—Watson, Republican.
Iowa—Cummins, Republican.
Kentucky—Beckham, Democrat.
Missouri—Spencer, Republican.
New Hampshire—Moses, Republican.
New York—Wadsworth, Republican.
Ohio—Willis, Republican.
Oklahoma—Ferris, Democrat.
South Dakota—Norbeck, Republican.
Utah—Smoot, Republican.
Washington—Jones, Republican.
Wisconsin—Lenroot, Republican.

## Fifth Re-elects W. H. Newton By Big Plurality

### Margin Is Largest Ever Given to Congressman in Minnesota.

### 20,000 Lead Over Socialist Opponent Indicated By Returns.

### G. O. P. Winning in First, Second, Third, Fourth, Sixth, Ninth, Tenth.

**At 2 a. m., 34 out of 155 precincts in Fifth district give Newton, 8,134; Thompson, 4,677; Lundeen, 1,784; Dahl, 1,590.**

Walter H. Newton, Republican, has been re-elected congressman from the Fifth district by the largest plurality ever given a congressional candidate in Minnesota.

Returns received up to 2 a. m. indicate that he will have a plurality of more than 20,000. Lynn Thompson, Socialist member of the school board, who is now in the county jail, is running a poor second, and "Ernie" Lundeen, former pacifist congressman, a still poorer third. The vote for T. O. Dahl, Democrat, was very small.

Early this morning reports from 28 of the 155 precincts in the Fifth district gave Newton 6,926, Thompson 3,820, Lundeen 1,525, Dahl 1,259.

**Other G. O. P. Congressmen.**

Returns from other congressional districts indicate that the Republican nominees in the First, Second, Third, Fourth, Sixth, Ninth and Tenth districts will be returned by large majorities.

In the Seventh district, now represented by Andrew J. Volstead, Republican, returns are still too meager to indicate the result. Mr. Volstead was opposed by the Rev. O. J. Kvale, Townley candidate.

In the eighth district, O. J. Larson of Duluth, Republican, was pushing W. L. Carrs, incumbent, but here, too, the returns were not sufficient to indicate the final result.

In the first district, Sydney A. Anderson, incumbent, won easily over Julius J. Reiter, Farmer-Labor candidate, who had the indorsement of the Nonpartisan league.

**Clague Defeats Fuller.**

In the second district, Frank Clague, former judge of the district court, defeated H. A. Fuller, league candidate, without difficulty.

In the third district, Charles R. Davis, veteran congressman, won without any trouble.

Oscar E. Keller of St. Paul, fourth district congressman, was elected over Thomas J. Brady, who ran as a "wringing wet" on the Democratic ticket.

Harold N. Knutson, sixth district congressman, opposed by Charles A. Lindbergh, author of "Why Is Your Country At War?" Townley candidate for governor two years ago, had a hard fight, but his election was deemed certain.

In the ninth district Halvor Steenerson was elected over N. E. Thormodson, Townleyite.

Thomas D. Schall, tenth district congressman, simply ran away from his opponents in Minneapolis and in the seven counties comprising the district.

### Many Wire Harding Birthday Greetings

**By Frederic William Wile.**
Public Ledger-Minneapolis Tribune Service.
Copyright, 1920, by Public Ledger Co.

Marion, Ohio, Nov. 2.—Telegraphic congratulations on his 55th birthday, many of them mingling anticipatory felicitations on his election, reached Senator Harding throughout the day. One of the first messages came from Senator Philander C. Knox at Pittsburgh. It read:

"I send my heartiest congratulations early to avoid the rush."

### Allied Ban Worries Ex-King of Greece

Geneva, Nov. 2.—Former King Constantine is greatly depressed by the report that Great Britain and France, which guaranteed the kingdom of Greece, would refuse, even if the elections were favorable to him, to allow his return to the Greek throne.

## Fusion Nominee Leads Frazier in Dakota Race

### Townley Man Is Running 16,000 Behind O'Connor for Governor.

### Carries Red River Valley By an Overwhelming Majority.

### Ladd, of Fargo, Is Elected United States Senator.

J. F. T. O'Connor, fusion candidate for governor of North Dakota, was leading Governor Lynn J. Frazier, Townley candidate for re-election, by 16,000 votes when one-tenth of the state had been heard from at 2 a. m. today.

The returns were practically all from town and city precincts, however, and no predictions were made in North Dakota on the final outcome. Practically no returns had been heard from the rural precincts of the state.

**Baer Apparently Beaten.**

It was apparent, however, on the returns tabulated, that Congressman John M. Baer of the First district had been defeated by O. B. Burtness of Grand Forks. Baer, a cartoonist for the Nonpartisan league, was the first congressman elected by Townley. He was defeated for the Republican nomination last June and ran again as an independent.

O'Connor has carried practically all of the Red river valley counties.

The returns from western North Dakota were very slow in coming in and no effective tabulations were made.

**O'Connor Ahead Of Langer.**

O'Connor's vote proportionately runs far ahead of the vote given William Langer, anti-Townley candidate, in June. At that time, Langer was defeated by Frazier for the Republican nomination by a small vote.

Dr. E. F. Ladd of Fargo, has been elected United States senator on the basis of early returns.

### State Legislature Results in Doubt

Composition of the State Legislature was still a matter of speculation this morning. In view of the tremendous vote cast throughout the state and the rush made by election boards to get through returns on the national and state officers' tickets, no returns on legislative candidates and county officials were available early today. In Hennepin county not a single return had been reported early today upon candidates for the district bench, judge of probate, clerk of court or board of county commissioners.

### New York Re-elects Unseated Socialists

New York, Nov. 2.—Louis Waldeman and August Claessens, Socialists, who were twice expelled from the New York legislature, were re-elected. Waldeman, from the Eighth Manhattan Assembly district and Claessens from the Seventeenth. Samuel A. DeWitt and Samuel Orr, who also were expelled by the Legislature last winter and when reseated this fall after they had been re-elected in a special election and who subsequently resigned, were again elected from the Third and Fourth Bronx Assembly districts, respectively.

**France to Keep Clear of Greece.**

Paris, Nov. 2.—The French foreign office informed the Associated Press today that France would not interfere in the Greek situation unless former King Constantine attempts to return to Greece. In such case it was added, "France will take such measures as are deemed necessary."

### The Avalanche

Harding carries Carrmonte, Cox's own precinct.

Harding carries, by 300,000 the state of Ohio, of which Cox now is governor.

Harding carries Hyde Park, N. Y., home town of Franklin D. Roosevelt, running mate of Cox.

Harding carries the home district in New York of Charles Murphy, Tammany chieftain.

Harding carries Massachusetts, home state of Senator Lodge, and declared by Cox to be "the basest conspirator in history," by the largest plurality ever given a Presidential candidate in that commonwealth.

Harding carries Pennsylvania by 750,000 plurality.

Harding carries New York by a plurality, estimated at the unprecedented total of one full million.

Harding turns the Wilson majority of 56, achieved in New Hampshire in 1916, into a plurality of 30,000.

Harding carries 2 to 1 Montana, which gave Wilson a plurality of 25,000 in 1916.

Harding sweeps the Wilson League of Nations into the limbo of things forgotten.

Harding, in a word, administers to the Democratic party the most crushing defeat known in American political history.

**The New President**

Warren G. Harding.

## Lenroot Leads By 5,500 Votes in Wisconsin

### 10,000 Majorty Predicted Over Thompson—Blaine Elected Governor.

Milwaukee, Wis., Nov. 2.—With 251 out of 2,413 precincts reported Senator Irvine L. Lenroot is leading James Thompson, his nearest competitor for senator, by 5,500 votes. Starting out with a good lead, Lenroot's margain was cut down by early reports from La Follette districts. As the votes in Milwaukee county were counted, Lenroot again picked up and went into the lead.

The northwestern part of the state, Lenroot's strongest territory, is still to be heard from, and indications are that he will come through with a 10,000 plurality. Dr. Paul S. Reinsch, Democrat, the third candidate, is hopelessly out-distanced.

Lenroot made his campaign on the League of Nations with reservations and the state took kindly to his promises. He also holds his election as a vindication of the part he played in putting over the Esch-Cummins law. The Thompson forces, headed by Senator La Follette, conducted a hot campaign against Lenroot, scoring him for voting for the peace pact and for his part in the Esch-Cummins bill.

John J. Blaine, La Follette man, and Republican candidate, is leading Robert McCoy, Democrat, by a 2 to 1 margin in the race for governor. Blaine's election is assured.

The following congressmen, all Republicans, have been elected: Henry A. Cooper, Edward P. Voight, John H. Nelson, John C. Kleczkar, William H. Stafford, Florian P. Lambert, Joseph D. Beck, Edward P. Browne, David G. Classon, James A. Frear, Adolphus P. Nelson.

### Republicans Lead In Montana Race

Helena, Nov. 2.—Returns from 45 out of 471 precincts in the First congressional district give Watson, Democratic, 2,334; McCormick, Republican, 3,662. Returns from 72 precincts out of 1,011 in the Second district give McCusker, Democratic, 2,245; Riddick, Republican, 5,220.

## Deluge of Votes Swamps Clerks at City's Polls

### Election Officials Find Task of Counting Ballots Strenuous One.

**77 out of 219 precincts in Minneapolis give: Preus 18,93-; Shipstead, 14,586; Hodgson, 2,886.**

**93 out of 210 precincts give: Harding, 26,882; Cox, 9,747; Debs, 6,339.**

**47 out of 210 precincts give: Collins, 9,303; Mallon, 6,397; McDonnell, 1,494.**

**38 out of 210 precincts give: Hilton, 6,337; Sullivan, 4,531; McQuat, 765.**

**13 precincts out of 210 give: Dibell, 2,155; Siegel, 1,106.**

There was such a great outpouring of votes in Minneapolis yesterday that judges and clerks were fairly swamped in their efforts to get the ballots counted.

It was estimated that at least 135,000 votes were cast. Most of this vote was cast long before 6 p. m. Men vied with the women in getting their votes in early.

Warren G. Harding fairly swept the city. In 77 precincts out of 210 the vote on president was: Harding 22,742, Cox 8,146, Debs 5,619.

J. A. O. Preus, Republican nominee for governor, will carry Minneapolis by more than 25,000 plurality, in the opinion of Arch Coleman, chairman of the Hennepin county Republican committee. Louis L. Collins, nominee for lieutenant governor; Clifford L. Hilton, attorney general, and the other candidates on the Republican state ticket were running right along with Mr. Preus.

**Preus Favorite in Eighth.**

The vote in the Eighth and Thirteenth wards was overwhelmingly for Mr. Preus and his associates. In some precincts it ran as high as seven and eight to one.

Dr. Henrik Shipstead, Townley nominee for governor, received a large vote in some of the so-called labor wards. But even in these sections, Mr. Preus had a mighty large vote.

Precincts in strong Shipstead territory were among the first to report and ran up the Shipstead vote. Never, however, did Shipstead come anywhere near the Preus total.

The lead for Corporal Louis L. Col-

(Continued on Page 2, Col. 3.)

## G. O. P. Victory Most Colossal in U. S. Annals

### Lead Larger Than Sweep By Roosevelt in 1904.

### Wilson Pluralities Are Turned Into Republican Avalanche.

### Party Will Control Senate By 8, House By 70.

**By Universal News Service.**

New York, Nov. 2.—The most stupendous political victory in American history was won today by the Republican national ticket when Senator Warren G. Harding was swept into the presidency by a popular plurality far beyond the high water mark established by Theodore Roosevelt in his memorable 1904 triumph over Alton B. Parker.

Incomplete, but absolutely convincing, reports indicate that Governor James M. Cox has suffered a defeat more crushing than even the most sanguine Republican prophet has predicted.

Aside from the 10 states of the solid South, with 114 electoral votes, and possibly Kentucky, the Democratic ticket appeared to have been buried under an overwhelming landslide that erased the word "doubtful" from the political lexicon, and restored to the G. O. P. a dozen or more states that had swung to Wilson in the 1916 overturn.

The nation not alone heeded Senator Harding's plea for an emphatic repudiation of the Wilson League of Nations, and unmistakeable condemnation of the administration's policies, but likewise answered his demand for a Republican Congress to carry out his policies.

**Majority in Senate.**

In the next Senate, the Republicans will have, according to indications, a majority of from six to eight, and in the House of Representatives a lead of nearly 70.

In the states that had been conceded to the Republicans by impartial pre-election observers, there never was the slightest doubt of the result.

In these states Governor Cox failed to hold even the Wilson vote of 1916, while Senator Harding added to the Hughes strength almost the entire enrolment of new voters.

It was this outstanding feature of today's election that enabled the Republicans to carry a Democratic stronghold like New York City by more than 200,000 votes, and roll up in New York state a plurality that may reach 1,000,000.

**Big Sweep in Pennsylvania.**

The same story was told in the figures from Pennsylvania, where the Harding plurality may be 750,000 votes, and in Massachusetts, where it is expected to reach 300,000. New Jersey appeared from incomplete returns to have repudiated the Democratic ticket, which it supported in 1916 by giving Harding a 200,000 lead.

Results in so-called close territory were equally emphatic.

New Hampshire, in which the Democrats had waged a vigorous fight, turned Wilson's plurality of 56 into a plurality of from 15,000 to 30,000 for Harding, according to incomplete returns.

West Virginia's electoral votes, counted as almost certain for the Democratic cause, appear to have swept into the Republican paw, along with Oklahoma's 10, and Missouri's 18, and quite possibly Maryland's eight.

Democratic leaders clung desperately to the hope that the miracle of 1916, when Wilson was returned a winner after Hughes had been granted the election, would be repeated, but early returns from the West gave them little hope.

It had been generally reckoned that Cox, to win, must carry Utah, Arizona, Montana, New Mexico, Indiana, Ohio, Colorado, Nevada, Connecticut, Rhode Island, New Jersey, New Hampshire,

### Home of Texan Who Seconded Nomination of Harding Goes G. O. P.

Brownsville, Tex., Nov. 2—Brownsville, the home of R. B. Creager, who seconded Warren G. Harding's nomination for President in the Chicago convention, went for the Republican candidate today by a majority of 99 votes. Point Isabel, a coast town twenty miles below Brownsville, voted solid for Harding. The Brownsville vote was Harding, 376; Cox, 277.

## Harding Says He Will Pray to Be Made Worthy of Task

Marion, Ohio, Nov. 2.—Senator Harding's statement on being informed of his election said:

"It is all so serious, the obligations are so solemn that instead of exulting I am more given to prayer to God to make me capable of playing my part and that all these calls to responsibility may meet the aspirations and expectations of America and the world.

"I am sure the people who have voted the Republican ticket will understand my feeling that I should make no unstudied statement of policies at this time beyond the expression made throughout the campaign."

Dayton, Ohio, Nov. 2.—"Republican landslide: Harding wins," is the headline in the extra edition of Governor Cox's newspaper, the Dayton News, issued at 10:40 p. m.

The admission of Harding's election by his newspaper, Governor Cox said tonight, did not mean that he conceded his defeat.

"I will make no statement tonight," the governor again declared, "and whatever my paper says, is purely impersonal."

Publication of the New's story, however, was made with the candidate's approval.

## Charter Apparently Ratified; Defeat of Pension System Seen

**At 2 o'clock this morning the vote on Home Rule in 29 precincts was: for, 11,756; against, 3,929. The number who had failed to vote on the question had not been tabulated, but it was small.**

Minneapolis voters apparently went "50-50" on the two city proposals submitted at yesterday's general election. Returns from 15 representative precincts would indicate the home rule charter has been ratified, while early returns on the vote on the proposed pension system for city employes indicates that proposal was turned down. Yesterday's charter referendum was the sixth home rule proposal to be submitted to the people of Minneapolis.

Twenty-two precincts gave a total of 9,356 votes for, 3,135 votes against and 317 blanks on the home rule proposal. In these precincts the total vote in favor of ratification is more than 2,000 in excess of the four-seventh vote required to ratify the charter.

While some of these precincts made no return on the number of blank bal-

(Continued on Page 2, Col. 6.)

# The Minneapolis Sunday Tribune

Fifty-fifth Year. No. 40. | Associated Press. | MINNEAPOLIS, MINN., SUNDAY, JULY 3, 1921. | Public Ledger-Minneapolis Tribune Service. Universal News Service. | Price Six Cents in Minneapolis.

# Georges Fought With Broken Thumb

# Harding Writes Finish to World War

## Radicals Likely to Have Control in New Council

### Socialist Clean-Up of Appointive Offices Looms as Possibility.

### Minority in Conservative Group Refuses to Oppose Townleyites.

### Caucus Divided on Selection of President—Secret Alliance Seen.

The fight to organize the new City Council will be settled on the floor of the Council Tuesday afternoon, with Socialist control and a "cleanup" by the radicals of all appointive offices, with the possible exception of Henry N. Knott, city clerk, looming as possibilities.

This situation was apparent late yesterday when 14 aldermen and aldermen-elect, who owe their positions to the conservative electors of Minneapolis, became hopelessly divided on the selection of a candidate for president of the Council. After a three-hour session, during which time 40 ballots were taken, no selection could be made.

**Members of Minority.**

Four of the aldermen-elect, Edward W. Hawley, Second ward; J. O. Peterson, Fifth ward; O. J. Turner, Seventh ward, and W. C. Buck, Thirteenth ward, and Alderman Claus Mumm, Third ward, apparently refused to vote with the majority of the conservatives in the selection of a president of the Council. Their expressions and attitude during the caucus indicated they are the five who voted for Alderman Buck for president on nearly all of the 40 ballots.

The persistency of the minority in voting for Buck is interpreted by Aldermen John Ryan, J. H. Chase, W. H. Rendell and some other members of the conservative majority, as pointing to some possible agreement of the five with the Socialists, who control 12 votes in the new Council, to elect Buck as president of the Council in exchange for committee appointments for the Socialists and votes of the appointive offices.

**Likely Plan of Socialists.**

The Socialists are reported to be supporting John Shaffer for city engineer, to replace F. W. Cappelen, and Buck also is said to be working for Shaffer's election. Members of the conservative majority said last night this may be one of the trades being negotiated between the group of five and the Socialists to seat Buck as president. In this connection it is said the Socialists also are willing to support Hawley for president, but Hawley told the conservatives at yesterday's caucus that he would not accept the presidency of the Council.

During the caucus of conservative members at the Andrews hotel yesterday, that group voted on various ballots for every one of the 14 members attending in an effort to pick any one man of the group for president, but the minority of five with the exception of two of the 40 ballots, continued to vote for Buck.

**Hawley Minority Spokesman.**

Hawley, as spokesman for the minority group, was asked by the majority what the minority wanted, and he replied that they wanted nothing and would enter into no agreement not to support candidates who solicit or receive Socialist support. Hawley declared the five would vote as they see fit and did not think it necessary to make any agreement to oppose the Socialists in their efforts to gain control of the City Council, appoint the committees and discharge such efficient employes as City Engineer Cappelen and G. L. Fort, city assessor.

If the Socialists do organize the Council and "clean up" appointive officers it will be due entirely to the fact that Hawley, Buck, Peterson, Turner and Mumm have voted with the Socialists, for the majority of the conservative members of the Council declare they will stand pat on their pledge not to vote for any candidate who needs the Socialist votes to assure his election.

**Eight Sign Agreement.**

Eight of the nine members of the majority of the conservatives have signed a written agreement to that effect. These are Aldermen John Ryan, J. H. Chase, Harry H. Downes, John Walquist, A. B. Fruen, W. H. Rendell, George S. Sheffield and John T. Kean. Alderman William A. Currie, who voted against Buck at the caucus, also is expected to sign this agreement. It will not be difficult for the electorate in the conservative wards to know exactly how their representatives in the Council will align themselves at the organization meeting Tuesday, despite the fact that elections will be by secret ballot.

The nine conservatives will caucus again Tuesday just prior to the meet-

(Continued on Page 2, Col. 4.)

Turn to the sport pages for a complete review of the fight.

### Weather Forecast.

MINNESOTA — Thunder showers today and tonight, probably clearing by tomorrow; cooler today except near Lake Superior.

## Way Open for Resuming Diplomatic Relations

### Trading With Enemy Act, Liberty Bond Statute Terminated.

### Formal Peace Proclamation Expected Within Few Days.

### Treaty to Be Negotiated as Next Step to End Technical Strife.

**Raritan, N. J., July 2.—The resolution of Congress declaring war with Germany and Austria-Hungary at an end was signed here late today by President Harding.**

**The President affixed his signature to the measure at 3:10 p. m. Eastern standard time, at the home of Senator Joseph S. Frelinghuysen where he is spending the week-end.**

So that there might be no unnecessary delay in consummation of the long deferred state of peace, the resolution was brought here by special messenger from Washington, where it had been given congressional approval yesterday. The messenger left for the capital again tonight to complete the formalities of the declaration by depositing the document in the archives of the State department.

There was little of the dramatic in the actual ceremony of giving presidential aproval to the measure. Returning here from a luncheon and golf game at the Somerville Hill Country club, the President found the White House messenger, E. W. Smithers, waiting for him on the veranda of the Frelinghuysen house.

### Technical State of War Ended With Signature.

Washington, July 2.—Signing of the resolution declaring a state of peace with Germany and Austria, it was held here, ended today the technical state of war with these powers. There was some difference of opinion among lawyers of the administration and diplomatists as to whether the affixing of the President's signature ended the state of war at the exact moment of signing, or whether the resolution would be held to be in force all of today in the view that such acts might not require taking into consideration fractions of a day.

**Proclamation Expected.**

The view was also expressed by one or two that the state of peace legally would not be considered in effect until the resolution had been deposited in the State department, but almost generally the opinion was held that the state of war was ended today.

The next step, it was pointed out, would be the issuing of the formal peace proclamation which could be expected within a few days. This it was added, would be a mere formality and in its effect would date from today. The proclamation, it was explained, would be by President Harding and signed in additon by Secretary Hughes.

**Treaty Next Step.**

A treaty of peace will then be negotiated, it was said, but the administration is understood not to have developed as yet the steps by which it will undertake such negotiations.

The signing of the resolution, it was added, opens the way for resumption of diplomatic relations between the United States and the former enemy powers, although it has been indicated that the manner in which this will be approached has not been determined.

The issuing of the peace proclamation as of today, it was pointed out, would operate to terminate war-time laws which have not previously been repealed by congressional action. Among the more important are the trading with the enemy act and the Liberty bond act.

### Envoy Exchange Expected Within Next Two Months.

Washington, July 2.—The United States and Germany will exchange ambassadors probably within two months. Negotiations of a treaty of amity and commerce will start as soon as the German ambassador reaches Washington. This was the consensus of opinion in official circles today, following receipt of word that President Harding has signed the peace resolution.

### *Gas Car Hits Train; Four Killed, 3 Hurt*

Harrisburg, Pa., July 2.—Four men were killed and three seriously injured today when a gasoline car on the Cumberland Valley division of the Pennsylvania railroad collided head-on with a freight train at Wilnor, near Green Castle. The accident is said to have been due to fog.

### *Trio Stage $2,700 Holdup in Detroit*

(By Associated Press.)

Detroit, Mich., July 2.—Three armed men held up a messenger of the Hemmeter Cigar company today and robbed him of $2,700, then escaped in an automobile. The messenger was carrying the money from a bank to the company's plant.

## 40,000 Gallons of Oil Explode

### Blast and Fire Wreck Plant at St. Louis Park—Damage Estimated at $25,000.

Forty thousand gallons of crude oil exploded at midnight in the plant of the Republic Creosoting company at St. Louis Park, and the fire following wrecked the building housing the vats. The damage will be about $25,000. Three firemen on duty in the adjacent building were shaken by the explosion, but otherwise unhurt.

The oil let loose with a low, muffled rumble. Neighbors several blocks away were disturbed and on reaching their windows saw flames shooting high in air. The oil did not run from the vats, but burned in three furnaces. A new process being used to separate the oil for creosoting work was blamed as the probable cause.

The blast tore the roof from the building. To guard against possible spreading an engine company from Station No. 8 in Minneapolis was called. A fourth vat adjoining the three that exploded was saved.

### *Bootblacks Battle in Hopkins Streets Over Cut in Prices*

Boot-blackers turned their attention from shoes to eyes yesterday afternoon in Hopkins, when two clans of wellders of the blacking-brush engaged in a battle royal on village streets over the tender question of the right price for a shine.

One group held out for the 15-cent shine, a relic of the World War. Their price cutting rivals insisted that now was the time for deflation of prices and offered the shiniest of shines for a dime.

The battle raged down, up, and down the main thoroughfare of the town, and the cohorts of each side took considerable punishment before Mayor Moore intervened as a self appointed referee.

The mayor admitted that he was strong for price reduction and that he had recently patronized the lower priced artists. He ordered the 15-cent artists to return to their labors and get what business they could without interfering with the return to normaley.

### *Lincoln's Nephew Dies After Struck By Auto*

Springfield, Ill., July 2.—Edward T. Smith, 68 years old, a nephew of Abraham Lincoln, is dead here as a result of injuries received when he was struck by an automobile at one of Springfield's busiest corners. His mother, Mrs. Anne Smith, and Mrs. Lincoln were sisters. His father, C. M. Smith, was known as the "Merchant Prince" of Springfield. It was in the rear of the Smith store that Lincoln wrote his inaugural address.

## The Tribune Fight Staff

ARTHUR BRISBANE, famous editorial writer

J. OGDEN ARMOUR, famous financier.

BILL BRENNAN, heavyweight prize fighter.

REV. JOHN ROACH STRATTON, minister.

HARRY ERTLE, who refereed the fight.

ANDRE GLARNER, Paris sport writer.

NORMAN HAPGOOD, sociologist.

WINNIFRED VAN DUSER, woman writer.

DAMON RUNYON, sport writer.

JACK LAIT, author.

WILLIAM ROCAP, sport writer.

FRANK McCRACKEN, sport writer.

RAYMOND CARROLL, news commentator.

**Turn to the Sport Section of The Sunday Tribune for a full description of the fight from every angle.**

***Monday Morning The Tribune*** **will print the first action pictures of the** ***Dempsey-Carpentier Fight***

## *Injuries Make Georges' Right Hand Useless*

(By Associated Press.)

Manhasset, July 2. — Georges Carpentier broke his right thumb in two places and suffered a bad wrist sprain in the second round of his fight with Jack Dempsey in Jersey City this afternoon. This was reported by Dr. Joseph Connolly of Glen Cover, N. Y., who examined him at his training camp tonight.

Dr. Connolly's report follows:

This is to certify that I examined Georges Carpentier after his fight with Jack Dempsey and found him to be suffering from a compound fracture of the meta-carpal bone of his right thumb and a slight wrist sprain. These injuries have rendered his right hand useless."

He said Carpentier's hand was swollen to three times it normal size.

"We noticed that there was something the matter with Georges' wrist when he came into the dressing room after the fight," said Wilson "but he assured us there was nothing but a sprain. It began paining him on the journey home and the physicians here now said it was broken in two places.

"Georges said he hurt the wrist in the second round when he hit Dempsey on the jaw, but that he did not think he had broken it."

## *5,000 Feminine Fans See Tiger Conquer Panther*

### Women Shrill Victory Cry of Jungle in Brief Reversion to Primitive.

By Winifred Van Duzer. Universal News Service.

Jersey City, N. J., July 2.—The Tiger stood in the bit of jungle clearing here they call the ring. Tawny, smiling, splendid; beast victorious.

At his feet, the panther, head in resin dust.

Five thousand women voices shrilled the victory cry.

Jagged edge on a rolling surface; crackle against roar of the primitive.

For the "greatest battle" waged and won in this shallow saucer of golden pine was no woman's affair. More feminine fans today saw Dempsey, America's own, vanquish Georges, the aspiring Carpentier of France, than have seen the past three championship bouts, all put together. But they were scattering; nearly submerged in the enormity and action of it all.

**Broadway Come to New Show.**

At eight o'clock they stood at the gates with their men, seeking admission. At 2 o'clock a long line of them, released from office and business climbed up under the rim of the saucer, where they made a little tracing of color against interminable black-banded straw sailors.

Down in the shadow of the ring they gathered there; spattering broad bands of color. Swagger sport clothes here; orange, vivid, green. Broadway came to a new show.

Back where the saucer rim began to roll were the boxes: Mrs. Nicholas Longworth, Mrs. Kermit Roosevelt, Mrs. Laimbeer and their families; such as these.

**Rallying Cry of Primitive.**

Coney Island and Newport; the work-a-day, the weary; those who play at the game of life; others with ears almost deadened by centuries of culture to the call of the wild.

All of these rallying to the voice of the primitive. First law to first law; jungle dweller to jungle beast!

A famous psychologist told me that

(Continued on Page 2, Col. 2.)

Turn to the sport pages for a complete review of the fight.

## Dempsey's Iron Attack Beats French Challenger

### Swift Blow to Jaw Fells Frenchman in Fourth Round of Battle of Century—Carpentier Fights On Till Fourth Despite Injury—90,000 Attendance.

Ringside, Jersey City, July 2.—With a broken right hand and a badly sprained wrist, Georges Carpentier, idol of France, fell gallantly before the crashing attack of Jack Dempsey here this afternoon.

The battle of a century ended in the fourth round with the unmarred Dempsey a decisive victor. But tonight thousands who saw the fight, are wondering what might have happened had the Frenchman's hand stayed whole.

The second round, when injury forced him to a weak defensive, saw the Frenchman stagger Dempsey so effectively that the 90,000 spectators had visions of a new world champion. But the iron-jawed American quickly recovered from the blow and resumed his merciless punishment.

After this round, maimed and his confidence shaken by the failure of his famous attack, Carpentier, shifting from the aggressive role he had played throughout, turned to his skill as a boxer to save himself from a rain of crushing blows.

**Knockout Near.**

But everywhere he turned, swings, jabs and uppercuts smote the little challenger on head and body. A clubbing right landing flush on the back of Georges' neck, dazed him. More punishment followed and as the third round ended spectators could see that victory for the American was not far away.

The fourth round opened and Dempsey rushed his opponent to the ropes, waited for an opening and let drive a right to the jaw. Carpentier fell. No one expected to see him rise after that terrific blow. But at the count of nine the Frenchman's invincible spirit brought him to his feet. Helpless, he was an easy mark for the smash that ended the battle.

**Way Paved to Victory.**

Although the knockout punch was a drive to Carpentier's jaw the way to Dempsey's victory had been paved by a continual bombardment of blows which landed on every section of the Frenchman's body. Each swing, jab and uppercut, scored to the stomach, ribs and sides, contributed to the slowing up process of the speedy Carpentier.

In addition, a clubbing right which landed flush on the back of Georges' neck in the third round, played an important part in his defeat. The Frenchman folded over in an attempt to protect his body, left the back of his neck exposed, and Dempsey with the fair target in front of him, drove down a terrific slam to Carpentier's vertebrae.

After the knockout the Frenchman stated in his dressing room that this punch was the cause of his pugilistic downfall. He said that the punch stung his entire physical and mental makeup and he was thereafter unable to carry on any effective attack.

**Remarkable Skill Shown.**

Regardless of just which blow caused the vanquishing of Carpentier, the Frenchman gave a remarkable exhibition of pugilistic skill and gameness against a heavier and more punishing opponent. The favorite when he entered the ring, judging from the amount of cheering he received, he left the arrena with even a greater amount of applause running in his ears. A tribute to an exhibition which in every way verified and upheld a record which had preceded him regarding his boxing ability and danger-defying work during the World war.

Dempsey as the winner ran true to his fighting form.

**Georges Strikes First Blow.**

Although Carpentier struck the first blow of the encounter, a flying left to the head, Dempsey never at any time backed up or showed a disinclination to avoid trading blows with his opponent. While the champion bored in at every opportunity, he devoted as much of his attention as was possible to close in-fighting. Rights and lefts were steadily driven home to Carpentier's body, alternated at times by drivel, jabs.

(Continued on Page 2, Col. 1.)

Turn to the sport pages for a complete review of the fight.

### *Soldier Greets Dempsey as a 'Real Champion.'*

Ringside, Jersey City, July 2.—A soldier of the first division, his fatigue cap cocked on one side of his head, let out a great whoop when the knockout came. From his seat in the last row of five-fiftys he started walking along the chair tops to the ring.

"Gangway for a general," he shouted and the crowd let him pass.

Arrived at the ring, he shook Dempsey's hand. "Atta boy, Jack," he said; "You're a real champion. We're proud of you."

The champion's lips circled into a smile as he acknowledged the greeting.

### *90,000 Witness Fight; Receipts $1,600,000.*

Ringside, Jersey City, July 2.—Announcement was made after the contest was over that 90,000 persons had witnessed the battle, of whom 80,000 had paid admissions. The receipts totaled one million six hundred thousand dollars.

### *England Disappointed Over Georges' Defeat.*

London, July 2.—The victory of Dempsey over Carpentier today caused keen disappointment here, for Carpentier had been a popular favorite with the English. Public interest was no less keen than if he had been an Englishman.

### *Ball Players Desert Diamond to See Fight.*

Jersey City, N. J., July 2.—A double header baseball game between Newark and Jersey City of the International League, was postponed because none of the players reported. Neither did any onlookers. They all went to the big fight.

### *Closest to Fight, But Can't See It.*

Ringside, Jersey City, July 2.—The folks who were closer to the ring than any one else could not see a thing of the fight. They were the wire chiefs, with headquarters under the rings beneath the boxers very feet. They heard the thud of a knockout, but could not tell who won.

### *Dempsey 3 to 1 Favorite in Paris Betting.*

Paris, July 2.—Betting on the fight was brisk this morning with Dempsey a 3½ to 1 favorite. Several large bets were recorded.

### *Bonus Urged for Soldier Who Will Beat Dempsey.*

Tulare, Calif., July 2. — Tulare post of the American Legion today telegraphed State Commander Burton R. Fitts of the Legion, suggesting the raising of a purse of $25,000 for any boxer formerly a member of any of the allied or associated armies, who defeats Jack Dempsey. The post's telegram said: "Tulare post urges you to take a poll of the American Legion regarding raising of a bonus purse of a quarter of a million dollars for the member or former member of any of the allied or associated armies who will whip Dempsey in the ring next year."

### Million Dollar Blaze, Started By Fireworks, Hits California Town

Universal News Service.

Marysville, Calif., July 2.—Twelve city blocks were destroyed by fire here today with an estimated loss of several million dollars. The blaze started from firecrackers exploding in a stable.

Fanned by a high wind the flames leaped across B street, destroying all buildings, including 109 residences.

The Southern Pacific company's trestle leading into the city was burned, cutting off all traffic to the south.

## Paris Stunned By Report of Idol's Defeat

### Crowd, Which Waited to Celebrate Victory, Doubted First Bulletin.

### Thousands Gathered in the Boulevards Long Before Fight Commenced.

### Carpentier's Wife Says He Is Young—Will Know Victory Again.

Public Ledger-Minneapolis Tribune Service. Special Cable Dispatch. Copyright, 1921, by Public Ledger Co.

Paris, July 2.—Madame Carpentier interviewed by the Public Ledger-Minneapolis Tribune correspondent said:

"What can I say? I know no more about it than you. Certainly everything attests that my husband has been vanquished. You find me exceedingly unhappy, but not discouraged.

My husband has the future before him. He is young and will progress and know victory again."

Paris, July 2.—The Gallic cock did not crow on the boulevards tonight.

The dreadful crushing news of Carpentier's defeat arrived promptly at 9 o'clock, before even the street lamps were lit and before those who had confidently lingered too long over dinner could assemble to add their quota of tears to the overflowing cup of popular lamentations.

A crowd resembling that of Armistice day, eagerly waited the news which would proclaim the physical superiority of the Latin over the Anglo-Saxon race and which, moreover, would give an excuse for the wildest outburst of riotous joy ever known in the tempestous annals of the French capital.

**Great Consternation.**

Suddenly a hush of great consternation spread through the throng as if it were the bacillus of some deadly contagion.

White lights lit up the heavens, such was the token that Georges was knocked out. Had it been otherwise the sky was to have been colored a lurid red with joyous flares.

In the midst of the evening excitement, confusion and dismay, Madame Curie arrived from America at Gare St. Lazare with her gram of priceless radium. Besides the baggage master, the only person to greet her was a representative of the Public Ledger-Minneapolis Tribune.

Here is a small lesson in simple proportion.

Long before the result of the fight could possibly have arrived—before probably the champions of the old and new world had changed into fighting togs—thousands had begun to gather under huge screens erected in the immense Place de la Concorde and before billboards prominently displayed in front of the great newspaper offices on the boulevards.

**Only One Sentiment.**

Apart from the few Americans who were almost lost among so dense a concourse, there was only one universally prevailing sentiment.

"Georges, our Georges, must win. One who could beat the English hopes likes Wells and Beckett in one round will surely triumph over even the brawniest and lustiest fighter America could ever hope to produce when he has 12 rounds to go.

"No, no; defeat for Georges is unthinkable, unimaginable, as impossible as the surrender of Paris to the Boches."

When the defeat of Carpentier was signalled the crowds were absolutely dumfounded. They refused to believe the first bulletin telling of Carpentier being knocked out.

**Where Americans Met.**

The chief gathering place of Americans was the Place de la Concorde, where the returns were received blow by blow and given to the crowd in English and French on a huge screen. Dempsey's victory was received by wild cheering by the Americans, who threw their hats in the air, while the French spectators gazed upon the Americans in silence. The Paris newspapers followed the American methods in issuing a series of extras with the receipt of the fight and details.

During the evening there were gigantic crowds on the boulevards awaiting word from Jersey City. Fifty thousand persons gathered in the Place De La Concord to watch the auto club screen where, when the result was flashed on the sheet, it was met with dead silence from the French and by hilarious cheers from the Americans who later flooded Maxim's New York bar, Claridge, and the Mont Matre Joy palaces, keeping up the celebration with champagne suppers until dawn of Sunday.

**National Opera Hears.**

For the first time in history, prize fight returns were communicated to the audience at the national opera, hundreds of Americans in the boxes and loges rising to their feet, cheering wildly for the American victory and interrupting the performance.

From 7 o'clock until 9 p. m., when the result of the battle became known, immense throngs paraded the streets of

(Continued on Page 2, Col. 6.)

Turn to the sport pages for a complete review of the fight.

## *2 Minneapolis Men Drowned, One Prostrated as Heat Wave Breaks*

Two Minneapolis men were drowned in Lake Minnetonka yesterday afternoon, as city crowds flocked to lake homes for the week-end holiday. The drownings swelled the Twin Cities total for the last two days to five.

Harry J. Morey, 2612 Sixth avenue south, assistant district superintendent for Armour & Company, and Andrew Truog, 28 years old, 1023 Twenty-seventh avenue northeast, a mechanic, were yesterday's victims.

Only one heat prostration was reported to police yesterday, when the heat wave which continued through the month of June began to break. The maximum temperature was 89 degrees at 3 p. m. Thundershowers with cooler weather are expected today. Pat Kelly, 109 Second street south, collapsed on the Third avenue bridge late in the afternoon, and was still unconscious at the General hospital last night.

Morey was drowned while bathing with a party of friends on the west shore of Crystal bay, Lake Minnetonka. J. M. O'Shea, 601 Ridgewood avenue, one of the party, said that Morey was suddenly missed after the friends had been bathing for half an hour.

When they started to come in, he said, someone observed that Morey was not with them. They turned back toward the lake just in time to see his hands rise above the water a short distance from shore.

They quickly brought him to the boathouse nearby, and worked for several hours to revive him, without success. Crystal bay physicians who attended him believed that he was not drowned, but died of heart disease after sinking once.

**Fisherman, Other Victim.**

He is survived by a wife and three daughters, three, five and eight years old. Funeral services will be held Tuesday.

Truog was drowned while fishing with

(Continued on Page 2, Col. 8.)

Turn to the sport pages for a complete review of the fight.

# The Minneapolis Morning Tribune

Fifty-fifth Year. No. 197. MINNEAPOLIS, MINN., WEDNESDAY, DECEMBER 7, 1921 Price Two Cents in Minneapolis

# PREUS ORDERS OUT TROOPS

## *Birth of 'Irish Free State' Ends Centuries' Old Fight With Britain*

### Island Is Given the Same Status as Canada and Australia.

### Treaty Must Run Gauntlet of Ulster and Imperial Parliament.

### Clauses in Pact Care for Possible Rejection By Northerners.

*(By Associated Press.)*

London, Dec. 6.—The centuries-old quarrel between England and Ireland was ended, as had been fervently hoped, in the small hours of Tuesday morning by the signature in the premier's cabinet room of "a treaty between Great Britain and Ireland," consisting of 18 articles, giving Ireland the title of the Irish Free State and the same constitutional status as Canada, Australia and other overseas dominations.

The question of allegiance, which up to the last moment threatened to wreck the negotiations, was surmounted by permitting the members of the Irish Parliament to swear allegiance to the constitution of the Irish Free state and "be faithful to his majesty the king."

**Fust Pass Parliament.**

The treaty has yet to run the gauntlet of the Ulster government and of the imperial Parliament. The imperial Parliament has been summoned to meet December 14 and will be opened in state by the king, who has taken the closest personal interest in the Irish negotiations since he practically inspired them when he opened the Ulster Parliament.

Approval by the imperial Parliament is a foregone conclusion, as the government has an overwhelming majority in the House of Commons favoring its Irish policy, and the action of the British representatives in reaching the agreement has already been unanimously indorsed by the cabinet. The position of Ulster is less certain. Evidence comes from Belfast tonight that the treaty will be subjected to the most searching examination before receiving assent, and doubtless many modifications will be proposed.

**King Sends Message.**

King George telegraphed Prime Minister Lloyd George this afternoon the royal congratulations on the reaching of the Irish agreement.

The message read:

"I am overjoyed to hear the splendid news you have just sent me. I congratulate you with all my heart on the successful termination of these difficult and protracted negotiations, which is due to the patience and conciliatory spirit which you have shown throughout, and I am indeed happy in some small way to have contributed by my speech in Belfast to this great achievement."

The king will come to London purposely tomorrow to preside over the privy council to approve the proclamation summoning Parliament, as the constitution requires a six day's notice by royal proclamation.

The treaty was signed by all the members of the British and Irish delegations participating in the negotiations, the Irish delegates signing their Gaelic names.

Ireland is treated as a single entity in the provisions of the treaty, with special clauses providing against the possibility that Ulster should refuse acquiescence in the settlement, in which case the government of Ireland act of 1920 will remain in for so far as the northern parliament is concerned, but with the stipulation that a special commission shall determine new boundaries for northern Ireland.

**Clauses on Religion.**

Provisions also are made for the cooperation of the two parliaments in providing certain safeguards in the event of Ulster remaining out of the new free state. Neither parliament, however, will be permitted under the treaty to make laws endowing any particular religion, or to impose any religious disability.

The treaty looks to Ireland's undertaking in the future, its own coastal defense and provides that Ireland shall in time of war give the British forces necessary harbor and other facilities. It further, by providing against international limitation of armaments, recognizes the Irish Free state's right to maintain its own military defense force.

**Premier Congratulated.**

Premier Lloyd George is the recipient of universal congratulations for having successfully rescued the negotiations from what appeared to be a complete impasse. The general belief, however, is that Lord Birkenhead, who came to the government's rescue when the question of renewal of the Anglo-Japanese treaty had reached a critical stage, is this time responsible for the formula overcoming the allegiance difficulty.

Austen Chamberlain, who is leader of the government in the House of Commons and of the Unionist party, speaking at Birmingham tonight expressed the conviction that before Christmas peace and good will would be established between "the parent races of the British commonwealth," and he appealed with emotion to Northern Ireland to join the new free state.

**Theatrical Effect.**

Theatrical effect was added to the great drama staged in Downing street

(Continued on Page 2, Col. 1.)

## Oath of Allegiance to Be Taken By Irish Free State Parliament

*London, Dec. 6.—The oath to be taken by the members of the Parliament of the Irish Free state is prescribed in the treaty between Great Britain and Ireland as follows:*

I do solemnly swear true faith and allegiance to the Constitution of the Irish Free state as by law established, and that I will be faithful to His Majesty King George V and his heirs and successors by law, in virtue of the common citizenship of Ireland with Great Britain and her adherence to and membership of the group of nations forming the British Commonwealth of nations.

*The text of the treaty as announced last night in London appears on Page 2.*

## *Meighen Swept From Power By Canada Liberal Landslide*

*Canada Premier Who Goes Down to Defeat*

Premier Arthur Meighen.

### Tariff Is Issue in General Elections—Women Vote for First Time.

Ottawa, Dec. 6.—Liberal candidates, on the crest of a landslide, swept the government party headed by Premier Meighen from power in the Canadian general election today.

The Liberals, headed by W. L. Mackenzie King, were running on a tariff reductions platform, while the Meighen party stands for protection.

**Beaten in Home District.**

Premier Meighen was defeated even in his home constituency, Portage La Prairie, Man. His opponent was Harry Leader, Progressive. Seven members of the cabinet were defeated.

With the polls thrown open to them for the first time on the same basis as men, women turned out today in every province to help elect Canada's fourteenth parliament.

At the last election, ballots were distributed to women serving with war forces and certain soldier kin. This year, however, women needed only the electoral qualifications of the other sex.

**Ontario Decides.**

The battle was won and lost in Ontario, the most populous of all the provinces, and long regarded as safe for the government. Of the 62 Ontario seats held by the government when parliament dissolved, the Meighen party retained only 38.

Complete returns were not expected to be available before tomorrow but sufficient information was at hand to show that Mr. King, Liberal chieftain, would have the largest group in the next parliament, and probably a clear majority over all parties. He will thus be called upon by the governor general to form a government.

One surprise of the contest was the poor showing made by the new Progressive party, headed by T. A. Crerar. While sweeping the Western provinces, the Progressives elected only 15 members east of the Great Lakes, according to tonight's showing.

## Fight Renewed Over Roosevelt School's Name

### Board Attacked, Defenders Hooted at Community Mass Meeting.

The opening skirmish of a second struggle to change the name of Roosevelt high school to Nokomis was fought last night at a mass meeting in Simmons school, held against the wishes of the Board of Education.

Attacks on so-called "railroading" tactics of the school board were renewed, the lie was passed and defenders of the present name of the school were hooted and jeered to silence. A resolution, later withdrawn upon solicitation of Lynn Thompson, member of the school board, asked that aldermen of the district fight approval of school budgets until the name of the school was changed to conform with the ideas of the Nokomis District association.

A resolution, seeting forth the views of the organization and a letter, in reply to one from the school board refusing a change in name, were, however, given approval by the gathering.

Throughout the meeting there was wrangling, but the greatest disorder occurred when Harry H. Seff, chairman of the Citizen's Constitutional committee, asked the floor as a "citizen of Minneapolis."

After a vote, Mr. Seff was denied the floor because he was not a resident of the district. He had intended to read a resolution adopted by another group of South Minneapolis residents commending the action of the School board and attacking the Nokomis exponents.

The only defense of the present name of the school was offered by W. D. Bell, who, although connected with several civic organizations in South Minneapolis, made it plain that he was speaking "just as a citizen."

"Changing the name of the school at this time would, I believe, be an insult to the memory of Theodore Roosevelt," Mr. Bell said. "Besides, I understand that the School board intends to name all other new high schools in the city after our presidents."

"It's a malicious lie," F. F. Giroux, 4824 Thirty-first avenue south, declared when he took the floor to refute Mr. Bell's statements as to the policy to be followed in naming of high schools yet to be built.

The name Roosevelt was given the high school by the Board of Education when residents of South Minneapolis appeared at a board meeting and indorsed the name. Other factions in the district took up a fight for "Nokomis" but the board refused to reconsider its action.

About a week ago the name was definitely fixed and a letter forwarded to the Nokomis District association, telling of its action and asking that the association discontinue its campaign. The meeting last night was called against the wishes of the board. A "finish fight" is promised by the association.

## 3 More China Advisors Quit

### Dr. Chung-Hui, of 'Big Three,' Also to Quit Conference, According to Report.

**Universal News Service.**

Washington, Dec. 6.—General Wang-Fu, military adviser to the Chinese delegation, has resigned by direct cable to Peking, saying nothing to Minister Sze, head of the Chinese delegation.

This fact, following the resignation of Dr. Tyau, secretary general of the conference and accompanied by the resignations of Mr. Tzu-Chi and Mr. Ting-Kau, superior advisors, brings the three chief delegates up against the need of deciding quickly; will they stand for the way the Japanese are treating them in the secret committee meetings, or will they take an open stand of protest and possibly of rejection?

When General Wang-Fu ignored Mr. Sze in his resignation he pointed out a criticism prevalent among Chinese, that Mr. Sze is "too easy." He said he resigned because of "conflicting principles." What he meant was that the Chinese delegates did not seem able to cope with the Japanese.

A well grounded report that Dr. Wong Chung-Hui, one of the "big three," had cabled his resignation to Peking was widely circulated tonight. Members of the delegation would neither confirm nor deny the report.

## *Wounded Policeman in Critical Condition*

Patrolman John Moen, who was shot by bandits attempting to rob the Orpheum theater November 28, was reported in critical condition at the General hospital last night. After the shooting, Patrolman Moen appeared to be on the way to a rapid recovery. But yesterday his condition suddenly changed for the worse.

## *100 Persons Are Reported Killed By Oil Tank Blast in Prussia Dynamite Plant*

Berlin, Dec. 6.—It is reported that 100 persons lost their lives today as the result of the explosion of an oil tank in the Nobel dynamite works at Saarlonis, Rhenish, Prussia. The works are burning.

## Senate Rises as Factor in Arms Parley

### Upper House to Be Considered Partner in All World Negotiations.

### Treaty-Ratifying Rights to Be Guarded By Harding and Hughes.

### Sentiment Grows in Favor of Substitute for Anglo-Japanese Pact.

*(By Associated Press.)*

Washington, Dec. 6.—The effort to find an acceptable substitute for the Anglo-Japanese alliance has so diverted the attention of many of the arms delegates as to throw even the question of the naval radio temporarily into the background.

Both the Japanese and British have shown a desire to include the United States in any entente that may replace the alliance, and a tentative treaty draft under consideration by some governments concerned would provide for a quadruple arrangement, also including France.

What may have been the attitude of the American delegates in the behind-the-scenes developments having to do with the proposal remains a mystery.

**Secrecy Maintained.**

Taking the position that no entente suggestion is "formally" before them, the American representatives steadfastly refuse to discuss publicly the possibility of American participation in a political agreement regarding the Far East.

In the absence of an authoritative explanation of the American viewpoint, the impression is gained by the delegates of other powers that the American plenipotentiaries are feeling their way very cautiously, as they seek to ascertain what course would be in accord with American official and public opinion.

Recognizing the Senate's claim to partnership in the shaping of international agreements, Secretary Hughes and his colleagues are said to be solicitous that the sentiment of the treaty ratifying branch of the government, as well as that of the executive, shall be taken into account. How an accurate canvass of Senate opinion could be made in midst of the negotiations, however, presents still another puzzle.

**Recognition of Sen .**

A "gentlemen's agreement," or "understanding," if that diplomatic instrument were used in place of a treaty, would not require Senate confirmation, but President Harding and other administration officials have indicated they do not propose to take steps which senators might regard as ignoring the Senate's claim to participate in international policies.

All these considerations are being weighed carefully by the foreign delegates who desire to have the United States a party to the next Far Eastern concert of nations.

While this phase of the Washington conference is developing, the naval ratio negotiations still are at a standstill while the Japanese delegates wait for word from Tokio. It may be several days before they are in a position to resume the naval discussions. The full committee of the whole on the Far East will meet again tomorrow after a recess of five days and proceed with its discussions of Chinese problems.

## France Adopts Big Sea Budget

### Deputies Favor Appropriation of 844 Million Francs for Additions to Navy.

*(By Associated Press.)*

Paris, Dec. 6.—The Chamber of Deputies today adopted provisionally the naval budget of 844,000,000 francs, which covers the commencement of and progress on three light cruisers, six torpedo boat destroyers, twelve torpedo boats, twelve submarines and one airplane carrier, and later in addition three cruisers and twenty-four submarines.

It developed during the debate that annual construction probably would cost 333,000,000 francs. This would include 50,000,000 francs annually for submarines and coast defense.

Admiral Guepratte, describing France's fleet as almost non-existent, said five of the former German warships, despite the fact that they are antiquated, are France's best units.

France now has about 50 submarines, mostly small and many of them obsolete.

## Harding Pleas Stir Congress to Quick Action

### Important Recommendations in President's Message Taken Up at Once.

### Senate Passes Bill, Donating Supplies of Army to Relief Purposes.

### Finance Committee Starts Work to Hasten Tariff, Debt Measures.

*(By Associated Press.)*

Washington, Dec. 6.—Launching of the new session of Congress was completed today with delivery by President Harding of his opening address at a joint session of the Senate and House, made notable by the presence of delegates to the armament limitation conference.

Proposals for a flexible tariff, adjustable by the President or the tariff commission; for an industrial tribunal and for a constitutional amendment to stop the flood of tax free securities were the President's outstanding statements on domestic affairs.

Turning to the international field the President said of the armament limitation conference that "a most gratifying world accomplishment is not improbable."

He also urged enactment of the measure for funding the Allied debt, proposed food relief for starving Russia, expressed satisfaction over the nation's being at peace and held out promise of aid to the world in war restoration.

**Reception Is Hearty.**

A hearty reception was given the President by what was said to be one of the largest audiences ever jammed into the House chamber.

Presentation later of more detailed views on the shipping situation was promised by the executive, in declaring that he opposed abrogation of commercial treaties provided by the Jones act. Such abrogation, he said, would cause "chaos." A suggestion for a plan of "reimbursement" to ship operators was accepted as an advance statement of his previously announced views as to ship subsidies.

Prompt response came to portions of the President's recommendations. Immediately after the joint session, the Senate passed a bill urged by Secretary Hoover of the Department of Commerce as head of the American relief administration, authorizing donation to the administration of surplus medical and other stores of the army.

**Senate Takes Action.**

Legislation to meet the President's recommendations for a flexible tariff also was proposed immediately by Senator Smoot, Republican, Utah. He introduced amendments to the pending tariff bill, which would authorize the President, by proclamation, to reduce or increase tariff rates based on American valuation. Hearings on the tariff bill will be resumed tomorrow by the Senate finance committee.

In accordance with the President's request for prompt action on the Allied debt funding bill, the Senate finance committee held two meetings today in an effort to get the bill before the Senate immediately.

The President in his message also emphasized need for agricultural relief. He urged improved methods in distribution and marketing of farm products, advocating legislative assistance to cooperative marketing. Railroad freight rates, he added, were subjects of just complaint by farmers.

**Other Recommendations.**

Other recommendations of the President included reclamation and irrigation development, especially of Southern swamp lands, highway improvement, and measures to aid the unemployment situation. He expressed satisfaction over the tax revision law enacted in the extra session, and its billion dollar reduction in the tax draft on the people. Urging economy and efficiency, he declared the budget system "the greatest reformation in government practices since the beginning of the republic."

Party responsibility in government was stressed by the President in what some of his hearers regarded as thinly veiled dislike over the "bloc" system in Congress.

## *Mystery Fire Causes Big Loss at Aberdeen*

Aberdeen, S. D., Dec. 6.—Fire of undetermined origin, believed to have started in the basement of the Buttz drug store, on Main street, caused damage, estimated at from $75,000 to $100,000 tonight, before being brought under control. The Buttz store building was destroyed and the Harms Musical store, next door, badly damaged. Fire was still burning at midnight but under control.



## *Mayor Leach Wins Point in High Dam Fight*

### Induces Hodgson to Place Matter Before St. Paul Council.

### Decision Reached at Meeting of Municipal Corporation.

Mayor Leach's efforts to delay the action of the federal power commission in awarding power rights at the Mississippi high dam were partially successful yesterday, when he persuaded Mayor Hodgson of St. Paul to place the matter of delay befor the St. Paul City Council.

The decision was reached at a meeting in Mayor Leach's office of the Municipal Electric corporation, whose three directors are Mayor Leach, Mayor Hodgson and Fred B. Snyder, president of the University of Minnesota board of regents.

Mayor Hodgson carried out his announced determination to block formal application by the corporation for power rights at the high dam, when he refused to vote with Mr. Snyder and Mayor Leach for the application. Unanimous vote is necessary.

The St. Paul mayor was inclined also to block a resolution asking the federal power commission to delay action on the separate applications of the cities of Minneapolis and St. Paul, and the Northern States Power company.

**Agreement Is Reached.**

After some discussion, however, he agreed to carry over final action on this resolution until next Monday at 3 p. m., when the three directors will meet again in Mayor Leach's office. In the meantime, he consented to Mayor Leach's proposal that both mayors place the matter before the City Councils of the two cities, and ask instructions.

Mayor Leach had stated before the meeting that he did not hope to alter Mayor Hodgson's determination to block the corporation's application for power rights, but that he was fighting to delay the federal commission's award.

Mr. Snyder voted with Mayor Leach in every instance, expressing his belief that delay in this case was the only means of giving full justice to the claims of all the people of Minnesota.

**Hodgson Is Warned.**

Mayor Leach and Mr. Snyder joined in warning Mayor Hodgson and the people of Minnesota that the Northern States Power company was seeking a power monopoly of power privileges in this area, and that such a monopoly would take all rate control out of the hands of the state and the municipilities, by giving the private corporation the excuse that it was operating under federal contract.

Mayor Leach further declared that the time was not far distant when it would be necessary to build sewers around the pool of still water which would be formed at the dam. These sewers would cost at least $2,000,000 for Minneapolis, he said, and at least $1,000,000 for St. Paul.

"If the Northern States Power company gets the power permit, how are you going to explain the situation to your people when you set out to get a bond issue to finance those sewers?" he asked Mayor Hodgson. "The peopde of these two cities will be in no mood to issue large bond issues for such a purpose, when they know that their officials are responsible for turning over the power to a private corporation."

## Grocer Fighting Gunmen Is Shot

### Opens Fire at 'Hands Up' Command, Saving $300; One of Bandit Trio Believed Hit.

In a running gun battle with three holdup men, George J. Thomas, a grocer living at 441 Main street northeast, last night was shot in the shoulder, but saved $300.

Thomas had locked up his grocery store, and was returning to his home when the three robbers drove up in a touring car. Two of them leaped out and ordered him to throw up his hands. In reply he drew a gun and opened fire.

One of the men fired at close range, the bullet striking Thomas in the right shoulder. The two bandits then jumped into the car, and sped down the street. Thomas ran behind, still firing. He said that one of the men appeared to be hit.

The holdup men were believed to have lain in wait for Thomas, expecting to rob him of the day's receipts.

## *Ex-Twin City Woman Nominee for Governor*

Pierre, S. D., Dec. 6.—Miss Alice Lorain Daley, a graduate of the University of Minnesota and a former St. Paul resident, today became South Dakota's first woman nominee for governor. She was indorsed by the Nonpartisan league to head its ticket in the state election. Miss Daley was a Nonpartisan nominee for South Dakota superintendent of schools last year, and is now a faculty member of Madison state normal school. She was one of the few Nonpartisan enthusiasts who went to Jackson, Minn., this fall to see A. C. Townley begin his jail term.

## *Colonel W. C. Sanger, Once War Aide, Dies*

New York, Dec. 6.—Colonel William Cary Sanger, 65, assistant Secretary of War from 1901 to 1902, died here today.

## State Guards Enter Zone of Packer Strike

### South St. Paul and Dakota County Claim Inability to Handle Situation.

### Governor's Decision Made After Talk With Rhinow and Union Man.

### Adjutant General Mobilizes Four Companies of the Sixth Infantry.

With South St. Paul and Dakota county authorities admittedly unable to cope with the strike of packing house employes, Governor Preus by long distance telephone from Washington last night ordered out National Guard troops to take charge of the situation.

Four hundred state guardsmen under personal command of Adjutant General W. F. Rhinow will be in the strike area today. They will be housed in buildings at the Swift and Armour plants and in the adjacent stockyards. Their task will be to open up the picket lines of strikers to permit all workers to come and go without molestation. Peaceful picketing and missionary work by the strikers shall not be interfered with, however, according to the instructions issued by the state's chief executive from Washington.

**Decision Follows Talk.**

The governor's decision was made after long distance telephone conversation with Adjutant General Rhinow, Charles Adams, his secretary, and J. P. McCoy, secretary of the workers' union.

Immediately on receipt of the instructions from Governor Preus, Adjutant General Rhinow ordered mobilization of Companies A, B, C and D of the Sixth infantry of St. Paul and the headquarters companies of the Third battalion of the Sixth infantry of St. Paul Park at the St. Paul Armory last night. Trucks and reconnaisance cars under command of Capt. Fred D. Kenyon of the 151st field artillery, stationed at the Minneapolis Armory, were transferred to St. Paul last night also. Captains of the companies are Bronson West, A company; Carlton Sclaub, B company; A. A. Van Dyke, C company, and Stafford King, D company. Lieut. Albert Noilet is in command of the St. Paul Park unit.

**Others in Readiness.**

While the Rhinow order called for only 400 state troops others are to be held in readiness for immediate call should occasion arise.

Governor Preus issued the following statement in Washington last night relative to his move in calling the troops:

"I have ordered General Rhinow to have on duty in South St. Paul tomorrow (Wednesday) morning the number of national guardsmen necessary to allow those wanting to go to work in the packing plants opportunity to do so without intimidation. Peaceful picketing and missionary work by the strikers shall not be interfered with. Men wanting to go to work in the past twenty-four hours have not been permitted to do so and I have called on the guard to take charge of the situation by reason of that fact."

Informed of the governor's action in calling out the state troops, George Anderson, member of the strike committee, declared that "picket duty will continue just the same."

The decision of the adjutant general to advise calling out state troops came yesterday after striker chiefs had failed to keep an agreement reached at a noon conference of South St. Paul, Dakota county, and state authorities that those who should seek to enter the packing plants should not be molested. A few passed through the picket lines shortly after the agreement was announced, and then again the picket lines closed tight. The comment of J. P. McCoy, secretary of the Meat Cutters and Butcher Workers' local was that the agreement had been that those who wished to pass through could do so if they were not accompanied by police or deputy sheriffs. He said he had not understood that there was to be complete opening of the lines.

**State of Siege.**

On the eve of the governor's order for the dispatch of troops into the strike area last night, "Packingtown" on the banks of the Mississippi lay in a veritable state of siege with the striker campfires glowing in picket duty a stone's throw away.

In the Swift and Armour plants employes were bivouacking for the night lest their departure might make their return through picket lines impossible. For a mile or more, stretching on both sides of the Mississippi and along the Great Western tracks there were striker campfires with men marching back and forth to halt any would-be entrant. The "besieged army" ate all meals in the packing house fortresses, and then as the night wore on retired on cots and chairs and desks turned into improvised beds. At the two plants the earlier hours of the evening were whiled away by card parties, with "cards played at four tables" or more. The besieged retired amidst the after-midnight "mooing" of cattle.

**Guards Face Pickets.**

All through the night hours packing house guards faced strike pickets across the Great Western tracks. The strikers said they would not give up until they had won. Efforts at keeping open the avenues of entrance to the Swift and Armour plants baffled all hopes of Mayor George Kramer of South St. Paul and Sheriff James Dunn of Dakota county for piercing the picket lines.

"It's gotten beyond me," declared the mayor of South St. Paul.

The sheriff completed the day yesterday with a force of 45 deputy sheriffs.

(Continued on Page 14, Col. 1.)

## The Weather.

MINNESOTA—Mostly cloudy today and probably tomorrow; not much change in temperature.

Additional weather on page 13.

# The Minneapolis Morning Tribune

Fifty-fifth Year. No. 260. MINNEAPOLIS, MINN., WEDNESDAY, FEBRUARY 8, 1922 Price Two Cents in Minneapolis.


## Steady Return to Normal Seen by Auto Trade

### Optimism Rules Among Manufacturers Attending Exposition Here.

### Purchasers Declared Plentiful for Automobiles and Tractors.

### Automotive Equipment Day to Be Celebrated at Show Today.

A steady movement toward normal business conditions is under way in the Northwest, according to the opinions of manufacturers who yesterday joined the crowds attending the Twin City National Automotive exposition in the Overland building and the National Tractor and Power Farming show at the Minnesota state fair grounds.

Attendance at the automobile show was officially set at 16,397 yesterday, and more than 10,000 attended the tractor show, a figure which doubles the number of visitors on the first day.

W. L. Day, president of the General Motors Truck company of Pontiac, Mich., reached Minneapolis yesterday, bringing a message of business revival in the motor truck industry.

**Increased Demand for Trucks.**

Trucks were hit hard in 1921. Combined with the general depression felt by business, the truck makers were deprived of a large share of their market when the government released to the states and to the federal departments thousands of trucks purchased for the army. Several manufacturers with limited capital caught by the necessity to unload, sold off their stocks at almost any price with a disorganizing effect on the general market.

These factors, which made 1921 an extremely bad year, have been overcome, according to Mr. Day. The demand since the first of the year has shown a tremendous spurt.

"Trucks shipped in January from our plant on orders from dealers were 42 more than double those of January, 1921," Mr. Day said. "Retail sales reports from dealers showed 126 per cent increase over January, 1921."

**Rock Botton Truck Prices.**

The General Motors Truck company is on a rock bottom price basis, its president declared. Depreciated inventories have been completely written off and the business revival finds the truck end of the General Motors corporation in a strongly intrenched position.

Among the leaders who attended the automobile show yesterday were J. E. Gittins, vice president and general manager of the J. I. Case company, Racine, Wis., manufacturer of automobiles and tractors, and H. B. Harper, sales manager of the Studebaker corporation. Both expressed confidence that another year will see the elimination of most of the present economic difficulties.

As seen by Mr. Gittins, who was at the show yesterday with D. P. Davies, vice president in charge of design and development, the United States has passed the "uncertain stage." He said that the obstacle in the way of a return to normal conditions has been the feeling of uncertainty, to a great extent a psychological factor. He said that within a year industry will have settled down to the normal increase.

"A good deal of this is a matter of thinking right," he said. "And I believe that people are beginning to think right."

**Studebaker Six Leads.**

As seen from the activities of the Studebaker corporation, business conditions are moving towards decided improvement, Mr. Harper said. He pointed out that Studebaker production in January, 1922, was a 200 per cent increase over January, 1921, and that retail sales for January, 1922, throughout the United States were three times retail sales of January, 1921. He added that Studebaker is now building more six-cylinder cars than any other manufacturer in the United States.

"Prospects for 1922 are exceptionally bright," he said. "There has been a 94 per cent increase in retail sales at this show. At the Chicago show 110 cars were sold for immediate Chicago delivery. Retail sales in Detroit in January are larger than any month in 1921 and nearly three times those of January, 1921. Dealers are particularly interested in the Studebaker offerings of three distinct models and 12 body styles."

He said sales at the show through yesterday exceeded those for the corresponding period a year ago.

He added further that, exclusive of the Ford and the Studebaker, the four other largest producers in the United States put out 238,000 less cars in 1921 than in 1920, while the Studebaker increased 13,500.

**Studebaker Dealers Meet Today.**

The Gray company, local dealers for the Studebaker, he said, showed an increase of 27 per cent for 1921 over the total sales for 1920, an increase of 140 per cent in January, 1921, over January, 1920, while December, 1921 sales were double those of December, 1920.

Mr. Harper, who came here from South Bend, Ind., will speak before Northwest dealers of the Studebaker car at a luncheon meeting in Hotel Radisson at 12:30 p. m. today.

Army and Navy day at the show yesterday brought military notables to the show. They included J. M. Wainwright, first assistant secretary of war; Maj. Gen. H. Harries, national commander of the Military Orders of the World War, and Col. L. S. Upton, chief of staff in the Seventh army corps area, headquarters at Fort Crook, Neb., attending the show in place of Gen. Omar Bundy, area commandant, transferred to the Philippines.

**Ford May Visit Show.**

There was talk yesterday that Henry Ford would come to the auto show in

(Continued on Page 13, Col. 3.)

### Weather Forecast.

Minnesota—Cloudy today and tomorrow, possibly snow in north portion tonight, warmer in east portion today; colder tomorrow.

Additional weather on page 25.

## 'Wrinkle Meat' Pneumonia Victim

Ga-Be-Nah-Gewn-Wonc.

## 137-Year-Old Chippewa Indian Dies in North Minnesota Home

### Oldest Man in Country Was Active Until Week Before Death.

Cass Lake, Minn., Feb. 6.—Ga-Be-Nah-Gewn-Wonce, also known as John Smith, a Chippewa Indian reputed to be 137 years old, died here today after a week's illness with pneumonia.

Smith, whose Indian name meant "Wrinkled meat," had been very active in late years. A year ago he became totally blind, but his mind remained clear to the last, and he often recalled the days when he was a scout for the Chippewas in the wars with the Sioux. He also remembered events of the war of 1812. One of his boasts was that he had never fought against the white man.

Up to four years ago he had never visited a big city. His first trip of this kind was to the Twin Cities. Later he visited the Automobile show at Chicago.

A year and a half ago he returned to the north woods of Minnesota to spend his time fishing for sturgeon in Lake of the Woods, in the same waters that he fished more than a century ago.

Ga-Be-Nah-Gewn-Wonce had been married eight times. He had no children and the only survivor is Tom Smith, an adopted son at whose home he died.

The "Old Indian" as he was generally known among the white people, was active until six months ago, since which time he had not been seen outside his adopted son's house. Before that time he had made it a practice to meet all trains entering the village and offer postal cards for sale.

He claimed to have met the Schoolcraft and Cass exploration party which passed through here about 100 years ago, and recalled the changing of the name of the lake, then known as Red Cedar Lake, to Cass Lake, in honor of one of the leaders of the expeditions.

Two years ago he took the central part in moving pictures taken of Indians, called the "Recollections of Ga-be-nah-gewn-wonce," which have been exhibited all over the United States.

Soon after prohibition was put into effect, some bootleggers sold "Old Indian" what they claim to be a quart of whisky, but which proved to be water. "Old Indian" did not say anything, but three years later the same bootleggers purchased a hind quarter of "venison" from him. This turned out to be a portion of an old horse which had just died.

To illustrate his vitality, it is related that seven years ago, when 130 years of age, "Old Indian" was knocked down by a switch engine, while crossing the railroad tracks. His injuries confined him to a hospital for only three weeks after which he suffered no ill effects.

Pagan rites will be omitted at the funeral of John Smith. He will be buried from the Catholic church here, which he joined about eight years ago.

### Texas Steer Runs Wild in Chicago; Killed in Chase Through Streets

Chicago, Feb. 7.—A terrified Texas steer today led a rifle squad from the detective bureau, a chase of two miles through the stockyards district, ran pedestrians into doorway, and charged through a display window in a butcher shop before it was finally shot after automobiles had joined in the chase. A policeman climbed to the top of a fence to shoot the animal which charged so precipitately that the officer saved himself by falling on the other side of the fence.

## Masked Bandits Rob Ye Taverne Guests of $4,000

### Looting Party Lines 75 Guests Against Wall When Raid Begins.

Ten automobile bandits, all masked and each carrying two guns, held up Ye Taverne, road house on Superior boulevard, early today lined 75 guests against the wall and robbed them of at least $4,000 in jewelry and cash.

The raid was staged at 12:30 a. m., while the dancing floor was crowded. The bandits drove up to the front entrance and marched into the place, led by a man believed to have an artificial leg.

"Throw up your hands! Line up against the wall!" he commanded, and as the panic-stricken crowd obeyed he ordered four of the bandits to watch the door.

As the bandits advanced into the room George Gilbert, head waiter, started to resist them. He was beaten on the head and fell. The leader of the gang stooped over and took $75 from his pockets.

**$1,000 Diamond Taken.**

John Kopald, 2627 Nicollet avenue, and Louis Sherman, 615 East Seventeenth street, proprietors, rushed to the aid of Gilbert, but were halted and searched. Kopald was robbed of $200 in cash and a diamond ring valued at $1,000. Sherman lost $60 in cash and a diamond worth $1,000.

Mrs. Kopald, who tried to conceal cash in the register, was forced away from the cage. The register then was robbed of $400. The bandits then turned to the dancers.

**Conceals Ring in Mouth.**

One woman concealed a $1,500 diamond ring in her mouth and pretended to faint. The bandits did not molest her.

Carl G. M. Johnson, 3304 Fourth avenue south, a waiter who came to the assistance of Mrs. Kopald, was struck down. Resistance then ceased.

Among others in the crowd who were robbed were:

H. W. Barger, 1411 La Salle avenue, $25.

C. A. Stewart, 713 University avenue, St. Paul, $175 in cash and diamond valued at $200.

C. A. Estabrook, Chicago, $50 in cash and diamond pin valued at $250.

H. Harris, Curtis hotel, $165 in cash and watch valued at $40.

Martha Hedtke, St. Louis Park, diamond bracelet valued at $200.

Scores of others who were robbed left the Taverne without admitting their losses and refusing to give their names.

**Attack Chinese Cook.**

The bandits left their victims lined against the wall, and went into the kitchen where they attacked the Chinese cook, leaving him unconscious when they backed through the dance hall to the door.

### Chicago Is Allowed Third of State Senate

Springfield, Ill., Feb. 7.—The long fight in the constitutional convention over legislative apportionment ended tonight. By a vote of 76 to 6 the convention adopted a plan which limits Cook county to one-third of the Senate and 57 members and apportions the lower House membership of 153 on a basis of voting population.

### Harding Names Marion Pastor as U. S. Envoy

Washington, Feb. 7.—The Rev. Joseph M. Denning of Marion, Ohio, was nominated by President Harding today to be agent and counsel general at Tangier, Morocco. Mr. Denning is pastor of St. Mary's Catholic church at Marion and has been a lifelong friend of the President.

## Citizens Debate Militarism in Public Schools

### 500 Attend Discussion Arranged By Board of Education.

### Speakers Criticize and Defend Present System of Training.

### Fail to Agree on Advantages to Be Derived From Drills.

The question of retaining voluntary military training in the public schools of Minneapolis was debated under supervision of the Board of Education in the assembly room of the court house yesterday before 500 citizens.

The debate was arranged by the Board of Education in order that the question might be given fullest exploitation by both groups. Members of the board sat as judges and held stop watches on the various speakers. The question to be settled was whether voluntary military training should be abolished in the public schools of Minneapolis. Final action in any event remained with the board.

**Hour to State Case.**

The group opposing any form of military training was given one hour in which to state its case and a 15-minute period for rebuttal. Advocates of retention of the system were given one hour and 15 minutes in which to state their case.

When A. P. Ortquist, president of the board, announced that opponents of military training would be given first right to the floor, Miss Marguerite Wells, representing the League of Women Voters, assumed direction of the argument. She announced the first speaker in opposition to voluntary military training to be Prof. David Swenson, University of Minnesota.

"The question of voluntary military training," Mr. Swenson said, "is not so much of an unmitigated evil as a proposition mixed with good and evil. It has definite military preparedness value. It may be that military training leads to respect for authority, law and order, but I doubt it. Snobbishness and arbitrariness are outgrowths of military training."

**Fail to Show Benefits.**

Dr. F. W. Wittich said he attended a meeting recently in a local high school and was impressed with the scrawniness of many of the boys. He said military training was not helping them physically, from all appearances.

Mrs. Arthur Brin, 2566 West Lake of the Isles boulevard, read the names of numerous organizations which had gone on record as opposed to military training in various forms. She engaged in adramatic appeal for abolition of voluntary military training in the public schools of Minneapolis and won much applause.

Mrs. Ole Knudtson read a resolution adopted recently by the W.C.T.U. in which military training was opposed. She advocated systematic physical train-

(Continued on Page 8, Col. 1.)

## Six Are Dead, 30 Missing in Virginia Fire

### Hotel Guests, With Clothes Burning, Leap From Windows.

(By Associated Press.)

Richmond, Va., Feb. 7.—Six known dead, 30 reported missing or unaccounted for, and 28 known injured, was the toll of a fire which early today started from an undetermined cause in the basement of the Lexington hotel, quickly spread through the four stories of the structure and then spread to other buildings, sweeping half a city block before it was checked. The property loss is estimated at from $250,000 to $500,000.

The known dead are Hirman S. Austin of Fincastle, Va.; M. J. Fox of Williamsport, Pa.; C. M. Thomas, sheriff of Albermarle county, Va., E. T. Cox of Richmond; F. L. Shaw of Richmond, and T. D. Pierier of Yonkers, N. Y. The bodies of the last three were still in the ruins tonight, according to the police.

The flames cut off all exits in the hotel and the guests, many with clothing in flames, jumped from the windows, some landing in life nets but others plunging to the pavements.

At police headquarters tonight a force of men endeavored to check on those unaccounted for, while searchers continued their efforts to locate bodies in the ruins.

Seventy-two guests were registered at the hotel when the fire broke out. The list of the missing tonight included the following: E. T. Carter, U. S. Navy; Frederick Keller, U. S. Navy; Thomas Flagan, Brooklyn, N. Y., and C. C. Eberly, T. W. Crannen, C. W. Hawthorne, T. T. Leftwich, and S. Hamin, whose addresses are unknown.

## U. S. Transport Afire at Sea; Crew Quits Ship; Four Missing

(By Associated Press.)

New York, Feb. 8.—The United States transport Northern Pacific was reported burning off the entrance to Delaware bay in a wireless dispatch received here early today. The message indicated the ship had been abandoned by her crew which had been picked up by vessels that hurried to the scene in response to radio calls for assistance. Four men of the vessel's personnel, however, had not been accounted for.

## U. S. to Save $200,000,000 By Stopping Navy Building Program

(By Associated Press.)

Washington, Feb. 7.—A saving of about $200,000,000 for the United States on the present building program of the navy will result from agreements reached at the limitation of arms conference, the federal reserve board declared in a statement tonight.

High naval officials, however, were of the opinion that the board's estimate was too high as, it was explained, the scrapping of ships now under construction would involve the payment of claims to the builders which might offset a considerable portion of the savings.

Limitation decided upon at the conference will effect immediately, the board declares, savings only in three countries—the United States, England and Japan—whose finances are already in a relatively sound condition.

In France and Italy, however, the board explained no increase in naval armaments had been contemplated so that their immediate problems would not be affected.

"It is particularly important," the board said, "not only that government budgets should be balanced so that short time borrowing may be discontinued, but also that the sum of expenditures should be decreased in order to reduce the tax burden on business.

"In most countries, however, curtailment of taxes seems highly problematical at present. Only in the United States has it been attempted.

## Laughter and Prayers for Dead Mingle at Slain Director's Rites

### Women Faint as Crowd of 30,000 Fights to Enter Cathedral.

(By Associated Press.)

Los Angeles, Feb. 7.—Laughter and screams and prayers marked the funeral here today of William Desmond Taylor, murdered motion picture director.

A crowd of 30,000—almost 10 times as many as could be seated in St. Paul's Episcopal pro-cathedral, fought for admittance and when that was denied to the vast majority, those left on the outside jammed the streets and overflowed Pershing square, a small park. Police were practically helpless in attempts to control the throng which awaited outside the church for the passing cortege to the cemetery.

**Women Faint.**

Many women in the crowd outside fainted. Within the darkened pro-cathedral only one fainted. She was Mabel Normand, attired in deep mourning, who is one of the last to have seen the director alive.

Another within the structure also gave way to hysteria. He was Henry Peavey, Negro houseman employed by Taylor. After the service Douglas MacLean, film actor, took Peavey aside for a whispered conversation. It was observed that MacLean seemed excited.

Tonight it was stated a complaint charging Edward F. Sands, alias Edward Fitz Strathmore with the murder may be issued tomorrow. Sands was formerly Taylor's butler-secretary and a nationwide search is being made for him in connection with robberies of Taylor's apartments.

**Dressed in Uniform.**

Long before the hour set for the services, the pro-cathedral was crowded. The casket, draped with the Union Jack and topped by Taylor's army cap, stood before the altar. Taylor's body was dressed in the uniform of an officer in the British army with which he served during the World war.

Four uniformed and armed veterans of the British forces guarded the casket which was banked with massive floral pieces from friends and fellow workers.

Half of the seats were given over to people of the film colony and half to the general public. On one side of the casket sat members of the Motion Picture Directors' association of which Taylor had been president. Stars and producers were scattered here and there.

**Prayers and Laughter Mingle.**

While the Very Rev. William McCormack, dean of St. Paul's, was reading the burial service and speaking the

(Continued on Page 2, Col. 3.)

## Rescuers Fail to Reach Ship

### Coast Guard Crews Are Turned Back By Sea in Trip to Stranded Steamer.

(By Associated Press.)

Provincetown, Mass., Feb. 7.—The British steamer Thistlemore went aground late today on Peaked Hill bar, four miles north of Highland light, at the tip of Cape Cod. A coast guard crew has gone to the rescue.

Peaked Hill bar is a notorious danger spot for shipping.

The Thistlemore is an oil burner freighter registering 4,146 tons, and is bound from Liverpool to Boston.

The coast guard crews from the Peaked Hill and Mace Point stations were forced to give up attempts to get out to the steamer because of the high seas and ebbing tide. The coast guard cutter Tampa arrived in the vicinity of the Thistlemore early in the evening, but it was considered doubtful whether she could be of any assistance before morning.

### Head of Italy Chamber Refuses Premiership

Rome, Feb. 7.—Enrico De Nicola, president of the Chamber of Deputies, has declined King Victor Emmanuel's invitation to form a new cabinet to succeed the ministry of former Premier Bonomi, it was reported this evening. The king's invitation was extended to Signor De Nicola yesterday. The excessive demands of the various groups for portfolios in the new cabinet was given as Senor De Nicola's reason for declining the invitation.

### Chinese Hens' Eggs Invade Gotham Market

New York, Feb. 7.—Chinese hens' eggs today invaded the New York market. Six thousand cases arrived by way of Vancouver, showing little breakage after a five-weeks' journey. They are smaller than domestic eggs, with harder shells.

### Methods to Extinguish Five-Year-Old Fire in Mine Shaft Are Sought

Wilkes Barre, Pa., Feb. 7.—Methods of extinguishing a fire which has been raging in the Red Ash mine of the Wilkes Barre mountain more than five years were discussed today at a conference called by Seward Button, chief inspector of mines. Several methods of meeting the situation were considered but definite action was postponed.

## Congress Chiefs at White House, Form Program

### Arms Pacts, Bonus, Farm and Ship Legislation Reported Discussed.

(By Associated Press.)

Washington, Feb. 7.—A legislative program, contemplating ratification of the treaties growing out of the arms conference and passage of the tariff, soldier bonus, farm credit and merchant marine bills, with adjournment of Congress about June 1, was said to have been agreed upon at a White House dinner conference tonight, attended by members of the Senate and House steering committees.

It was the understanding that treaties which the President expects to submit to the Senate this week, or as soon as the American delegation can make its report, would be given the right of way in the Senate until such a time ask the tariff bill was reported by the finance committee. The plan then would be to consider the tariff measure and the treaties alternately.

**No Opposition Expected.**

It was said that the President had been assured by senators that there would be little, if any, opposition to the treaties. The President it was added, gave no indication as to whether he will present the treaties to the Senate in person.

The bonus bill was said to have been discussed at the conference but the problem of financing it was not touched upon. Some of the President's callers said they were satisfied to leave this to the majority members of the House ways and means committee and the Senate finance committee.

**Farm Legislation.**

The farm credit legislation contemplated, it was explained, will be drawn with a view to carrying out the recommendations of the special congressional commission which has been inquiring into conditions in agriculture. In its report the committee emphasized the necessity for adopting existing bank facilities to fill the gap so as to extend long-time credits to farmers.

Members of the Senate who attended the conference included Senators Lodge, Massachusetts, the Republican leader; Curtis, Kansas, the Republican whip; McCormick, Illinois; Wadsworth, New York; Fernald, Maine; Kellogg, Minnesota; Frelinghuysen, New Jersey, and France, Maryland.

The House members who attended were Representatives Mondell of Wyoming, Republican leader; Longworth, Ohio; Dunn, New York; Darrow, Pennsylvania; Anderson, Minnesota; Nolan, California, and Green Vermont.

### German Rail Strike Called Off by Men

(By Associated Press.)

Berlin, Feb. 7.—The railway strike has been called off. The strikers' committee late tonight notified Chancellor Wirth that the men would resume work conditionally on the government's assurance that it would refrain from reprisals in the nature of wholesale discharges. The government reserves the right to reprimand the leaders but promised that the regular workers would be reinstated.

### W. M. Empie Elected Mayor of Virginia

Virginia, Minn., Feb. 7.—W. M. Empie was elected mayor at today's election in this village over S. S. Dahl, by a majority of 502 votes. William Brenner defeated J. W. Trimble for treasurer by a majority of 350.

**Trade Association Decision Soon.**

Washington, Feb. 7.—Announcement of the government's attitude toward trade association activities under the recent decision of the Supreme court in the Hardwood Lumber association case may be made in a day or two, Attorney General Daugherty said today.

## Oscar Lindgren Breaks Down Telling of Life

### Admits He Might Have Killed Madelyn La Count in 'Spell.'

### Denies Murder of Dorothy Bowers—Will Be Arraigned Today.

### Expresses Sorrow for Family and Girl Whom He Attacked.

Oscar Lindgren, confessed assailant of Mary Bloke, broke down last night when he discussed events in the last three years of his life.

Almost at the end of 14 hours of questioning he admitted attacking Miss Mary Bloke Monday night, and added that a man in his state of mind might have murdered Madelyn La Count.

He would make no such admission concerning the murder of Dorothy Bowers, although he said it had bothered him. Whenever a pointed question was put to him about either murder he lapsed into a characteristic pose and "could not remember."

**Emotion Shown.**

When he was told that the girl whom he had attacked was recovering in the General hospital, he appeared unconcerned, but last night, after he had been taken to the county jail, he showed emotion.

Sitting with bowed head, a picture of despair, he expressed his sorrow for all that had happened, and once more half admitted connection with the La Count murder.

"I am sorry for the girl," he said. "I am sorry for my wife. I am sorry for my family, my folks. I am sorry for my friends. I am sorry for my neighbors.

**Believed Him Innocent.**

"I am sorry for them because they stuck by me through thick and thin in the La Count trial. They believed I was innocent. Now they know I am guilty.

"I have tried to be and have been a good neighbor. I have tried to be a good friend. Now they know better. I don't want a lawyer. I don't want to see anybody except my wife.

"I am ready to go into court and plead guilty. I don't want any formalities.

"I am tired. I want to sleep."

Lindgren was taken to the county jail at his own request at 6 p. m. yesterday, after having been questioned almost continually since 9 a. m. He had been under a constant fire of questions from 9 o'clock Monday night until 1 a. m. yesterday.

**Arraigned Today.**

He is to be arraigned in municipal court today on a charge of assault with intent to commit rape. The penalty for conviction of this charge is from two to 10 years imprisonment. According to Floyd B. Olson, county attorney, Lindgren has expressed a willingness to waive indictment by the grand jury and go into district court and plead.

Futher questioning in an effort to clear up the La Count and Bowers murders probably will delay this procedure.

"When Lindgren is brought into district court, if the judge sees grounds for the appointment of a sanity commission that probably will be the first proceeding," Mr. Olson said. "If Lindgren is adjudged insane, he can be committed to the asylum at St. Peter."

**Scene of Attack Searched.**

Police and deputy sheriffs searched the vicinity of the attack upon Miss Bloke for blocks yesterday, but were unable to find a weapon. Without this, it was explained, no more serious charge than assault with intent to commit rape can be placed against Lindgren.

All during the hours of questioning Lindgren showed a willingness to talk until a question definitely related to the murders of Madelyn La Count or Dorothy Bowers was asked. Then he would hesitate, rub his hands over his eyes, and mutter:

"I don't remember. I might have done it. I don't remember."

No results were obtained by Mr. Olson and Capt. Frank Brunskill during the four hours of grilling Monday night. At 1 a. m. Lindgren asked to be allowed to sleep and rest his mind.

**Ignorance Professed.**

Brought into the room yesterday at 9 a. m., with Sheriff Earle Brown added to the group, he professed ignorance of the assault of Miss Bloke for several hours. Then memory came to him.

"I remember now," he said. "I remember waiting for a woman. My wife was not at home and I was supposed to meet her downtown. I felt a spell coming on and decided to go out and walk it off.

"I often had sat in the window in my home and watched girls going home from work along the road where I met the girl last night. I left the house and walked over there, and waited for a woman to go by. A man passed me, but I felt no desire to attack him. I seemed to have a desire to make a brutal attack upon a woman."

"What do you mean by a brutal attack?" asked Captain Brunskill.

**Wanted to Grab Woman.**

"I wanted to grab a woman by the throat," replied Lindgren. "I have had the desire before. I have felt the spells coming on in my home, and feared that I would attack my wife. Then I would go away and walk it off."

"Do you remember striking this woman last night?" he was asked.

"Yes, I remember striking her now," he said. "I don't know what I struck her with. She screamed and that brought me out of the spell, I think."

"Do you remember walking behind a tree and washing your hands in the snow?" asked Mr. Olson.

"No, I did not do that."

"But, Oscar, a deputy sheriff found the place where you had scooped up snow to do this," insisted Mr. Olson.

**Incident Recalled.**

Lindgren passed his hands over his face and sat in deep thought.

"Let me see," he said, finally. "Yes, I did do that. I went behind that tree and washed my hands."

"Why?"

"I didn't want anyone to see me with

# The Minneapolis Morning Tribune

*Fifty-fifth Year. No. 274.* MINNEAPOLIS, MINN., WEDNESDAY, FEBRUARY 22, 1922 *Price Two Cents in Minneapolis.*


# 34 KILLED IN ROMA DISASTER

## Lightning Bolt Fires St. Paul Grain Elevator

### Damage Estimated at $65,000 When 16,000 Bushels of Grain Burn.

### Rain, Sleet and Snow Follow in Rapid Succession in Minneapolis.

### Storms General Through Northwest Threaten Serious Traffic Delay.

A bolt of lightning in a freak midwinter thunder storm is believed to have set fire to the Wayne Elevator company's structure, Courtland and Maryland streets, St. Paul, late last night.

Sixteen thousand bushels of grain were destroyed, and the damage to the building and its contents is estimated at $65,000.

The blaze started immediately after a brilliant flash of lightning at the top of the elevators, according to witnesses. The flames quickly ate their way downward, but were quenched before they were able to get to the base.

**Ice Covers City.**

Minneapolis experienced thunder and lightning, rain and sleet and snow and falling temperatures, all within 24 hours yesterday. The sleet, although it coated street car tracks and telegraph and telephone wires with a heavy covering of ice, at midnight last night had failed to interrupt communication or transportation. If the storm continued today, however, street railway and railroad officials said, serious delays are to be expected.

The thunder and lightning, apparent at 11:30 p. m., was followed by gradually falling temperatures and a renewal of the sleet storm which raged all during the afternoon.

**Storms General.**

Conditions similar to those in Minneapolis and St. Paul were reported in almost all Northwest States. Snow accompanied by falling temperatures was reported in Montana, North Dakota, Wisconsin, and Western Canada. Winona, Minn., was buried under a heavy sleet and Green Bay, Wis., endured a heavy snowfall. The same conditions prevailed at Eau Claire, Wis.

Heavy snowfall also was reported in Washington, Oregon and several other western states, but traffic was unaffected. A continued snowfall, rail officials said, probably will result in a heavy delay in trains coming into Minneapolis and St. Paul.

A gale of fine snow, driven by a 40-mile an hour wind off Lake Superior, was reported at Duluth. Street cars struggled to maintain their schedules and were from 20 minutes to one hour late.

Rising temperatures accompanied the thunder and lightning at Wausau, Wis. Several windows in the downtown district were broken by a driving sleet.

## *Quebec Prime Minister Opposes Waterway*

Quebec, Que., Feb. 21.—Unswerving opposition to the proposed international waterway connecting the Great Lakes and the St. Lawrence by a deep canal was expressed tonight by Premier Taschereau of Quebec, speaking at a dinner in honor of Minister of Marine Lapointe. "It is completely proved that the export traffic will not justify the construction of this canal," he said. "All Atlantic ports together are not exporting more than 4,000,000 tons of grain. Mr. Hoover has declared that in 10 years—the time when the canal will be about finished, this country will have no wheat to export."

## *Man, Believed Sands, Held in North Carolina*

Concord, N. C., Feb. 21.—Chief of Police Talbert arrested a man here tonight suspected of being Edward F. Sands, who is wanted in connection with the killing of William Desmond Taylor, the motion picture director, in California. The man held here is said to fit closely the description of Sands. The prisoner throughout a grilling cross-examination by local authorities denied that he was the man wanted or that he had any knowledge of Taylor or Sands.

## *Crowds Block Court to See Mary Pickford*

New York, Feb. 21.—Mary Pickford and Douglas Fairbanks, her husband, today proved so popular in federal court where the diminutive motion picture star is defending a [illegible] suit for commissions, that reserve marshals were called to restrain over-demonstrative crowds. At the adjournment, Mr. Fairbanks, preceded by a phalanx of police and carrying his wife in his arms, strode through an enormous crowd to their automobile.

**Laborer Found Dead.**

A man believed to be Fred Henning, laborer, was found dead beside the steps of the Swartz livery stable, 254 East Eighth street, St. Paul, late yesterday.

### Weather Forecast.

MINNESOTA—Snow today, somewhat colder in west portion, tomorrow unsettled and colder, with snow in east portion.

Additional weather on page (15).

## *Mathilde Defies Rockefeller Edict in Determination to Live Abroad*

Chicago, Feb. 21.—Mathilde McCormick, 16-year-old daughter of Chicago's millionaire harvester magnate, vindicated her father's characterization of her as "a very determined young woman," when she came down flat-footedly today in opposition to John D. Rockefeller's edict that she make her home in America. Mr. Rockefeller voiced his wishes when he consented to his grand-daughter's marriage to Max Oser, 48-year-old Swiss riding master.

"I'll go back to Switzerland to be married, or shortly after my marriage, and make my future home there," Miss Mathilde is reported to have declared.

Mr. Rockefeller has boasted that no members of his family have married European fortune-seekers.

Two years ago Mathilde revealed her feelings for the riding master. Although a number of persons opposed the match, the girl's feeling did not change. Her faithfulness convinced both relatives and friends that her love was no passing fancy.

Dispatches received here from Zurich today reported that Herr Oser is contemplating the sale of his riding academy. Although a man of modest means, he is well educated and at one time was an officer in the Swiss army. He is an accomplished landscape painter. He has never been married.

After the marriage, he plans to take his bride to reside near Montreaux, in French Switzerland.

Emil Burgy, who says he is the cousin of Max Oser, drove up to the McCormick residence today in his flivver to pay his respects to his new "relations," but the butler told him "Mr. McCormick is not receiving visitors today."

"I didn't bring Mama along with me because she is busy with the family washing," he apologized to newspaper men gathered near the McCormick home.

While he was waiting for the butler to come back, Emil looked over the place. "Needs a little paint," he said, speaking from his viewpoint of decorator. "Maybe I can get the job."

When the butler brought back his employer's word, Emil cranked up cheerfully. "Some other time, then," he said. "Nothing stuck up about us. We want 'em to feel at home in the family."

## *Ard Fheis Instructs Leaders to Keep Sinn Fein United*

### Unexpected Harmony of Delegates Surprises Leaders of Both Factions.

*(By Associated Press.)*

Dublin, Feb. 21.—There is a possibility that a split in the Sinn Fein over the Anglo-Irish treaty will be avoided, the Ard Fheis, the national Sinn Fein convention, which met today for the purpose of defining the attitude of the Sinn Fein clubs on the treaty, whether for a free state or a republic, adjourned until tomorrow with instructions to the leaders of the two parties to come together and devise a plan to keep the Sinn Fein organization united.

The unexpected outcome was due to the direct initiative of the meeting in general and was not prompted by the leaders of either side. After Eamon De Valera had presented a resolution pledging adherence to the constitution adopted by the Ard Fheis in 1917, looking to "international recognition of Ireland as an independent republic," and stated his objections to the treaty on republican principles, the debate, unlike the discussion in the Dail Eireann, did not settle down into an examination of the merits and demerits of the treaty.

**Election Delay Suggestion Cheered.**

Arthur Griffith, president of the Dail Eireann, replying to Mr. De Valera, raised no new points; he merely reasserted that the treaty gave Ireland the opportunity [illegible].

Cheers from both sides greeted the suggestion of Father Gaynor, an influential member of the standing committee, composed of both supporters and opponents of the treaty, for a three years' postponement of the elections, and proved that the prevailing sentiment of the convention was for unity in the organization in view of possible eventualities, and that it should not be difficult for Mr. De Valera and Mr. Griffith to reach an arrangement avoiding disruption of the organization on which Ireland, in the case of a breach between the British ministers and Ireland, might be compelled to rely.

**De Valera Urges Delay.**

Mr. De Valera argued that elections at the present time would be unfair because the Irish people would have only the vaguest idea of what they were offered in exchange for the Republic. Michael Collins did his best to meet this objection, and indicated that he did not desire that the elections be rushed, but was unable to give a guarantee against elections.

He pointed out that so long as the elections were delayed, it was open to

(Continued on Page 9, Col. 3.)

### *Washington's Birthday Has Special Meaning to Child Descendants*

If George Washington, first president of the United States, were alive today, four Minneapolis children could call him "Uncle George" and prove their right to the intimacy.

The four children who can trace their lineage back to a sister of George Washington are the children of Mr. and Mrs. C. W. Nye, 2216 Newton avenue south. They are George Louis Nye 3rd, Franklin Lusk Nye, James Lusk Nye and Jane Nye.

If George Washington were living and these children really addressed him by his correct appellation, they would call him "Great Great Great Great Uncle George," for their great great aunt married Joseph Lowell of Ohio, whose grandmother was a sister of George Washington.

The four Nye children, who range in age from 12 to 4, have books to prove this relationship by marriage.

## *Sayre, Missing 'Bond Exchange' Head, Is Indicted*

### 'Broker' Suspect Charged With Writing Checks Without Funds.

C. Gorman Sayre, missing Minneapolis investment promoter, was indicted late yesterday by the Hennepin County grand jury on a charge of checking on a bank in which he had no funds.

The charge was made in connection with a check Sayre gave to C. A. Stockland, 3521 Forty-seventh avenue south, in payment for a $100 Liberty bond. The check later was returned from the bank marked "no funds."

After examining Sayre's correspondence, Floyd B. Olson, county attorney, said that other charges are being considered, which may result in additional indictments, among them embezzlement.

Alleged financial operations include floating stock for an eggless egg company, Mr. Olson said yesterday. The company, which Sayre is alleged to have sponsored, centered its activities in St. Peter, Minn., in 1919, dealt in a chemical subsitute for eggs to be used for cooking purposes. On complaint of Leland Duxbury, investigator for the state securities commission, Sayre was arrested and on May 5, 1919 was indicted on a charge of selling stock without a license. He was fined $100 and costs.

Walter C. Cristoph, 19-year-old office manager of th bond exchange of . hich Sayre was the head, received a second letter from his former employer yesterday. In the letter Sayre is alleged to have stated that he does not consider it's "good business" to return to Minneapolis immediately. The letter bore the mark of Colfax, Wis. The letter has been turned over to the county attorney.

Working on the theory that Sayre is in Chicago, police last night wired lengthy descriptions of the Minneapolis "Ponzi" to authorities of that city and asked them to make a thorough search.

Sayre is under a five year sentence in Ramsey county for abandonment of a minor child. He was placed on probation about two years ago, it was learned yesterday.

## *American Declared in Italy Plane Crash*

London, Feb. 21.—A dispatch to the Central News from Rome says a British airplane, flying across Italy, with an "American industrial magnate" whose name is given as Henry Taynel, has fallen near Venice.

## *One Dead in Riots, Troops Guard Three Textile Strike Areas*

Providence, R. I., Feb. 21.—An early morning riot in Pawtucket, the establishment of National guard units in three troublesome strike centers and a meeting of the state board of mediation and conciliation here were developments in the textile situation in Rhode Island. The Pawtucket riot, in which one strike sympathizer was killed, two critically wounded, and five less seriously hurt by riot gun fire when a crowd came to grips with the police at the Jenckes Spinning company plant, led to the immediate dispatch of four coast artillery companies to the Blackstone Valley city from Providence.

## *New Obregon Ouster Plot Brewing in Texas*

San Antonio, Texas, Feb. 21.—Ramifications of a huge conspiracy aaginst the Obregon government in Torreon and belief that a conference of revolutionists was held in San Antonio yesterday attended by Esteban Cantu were the developments of the Mexican situation today. While every inquiry to locate Cantu failed and no one admits participation in a conference, the rank and file of the old Carranzistas were very much in evidence about hotel lobbies yesterday.

## Pacific Treaty Foes Disarmed by Senate Move

### Irreconcilables' Amendment to Be Adopted to Speed Approval.

### Measure, Taken as Slap at Delegation, Is Declared Innocuous.

### Administration Reveals Inclination to Humor 'Bitter Enders.'

**By George E. Akerson.**

Washington, Feb. 21.—Senate irreconcilables, still desiring to assert themselves, today presented their proposed reservation to the four-power pact, one of the treaties of the Washington conference.

To their surprise, the Senate foreign relations committee indicated its intention to accept the reservation, which is considered innocuous. It is believed that such acceptance will speed early ratification.

**Text of Reservation.**

The following is the text of the reservation to the treaty between the United States, Great Britain, France and Japan, as presented by Senator Brandegee:

"The United States understands that it assumes no obligation either legal or moral to maintain the rights in relation to the insular possessions or insular dominions of any of the other high contracting powers and that the consent of Congress shall be necessary to any adjustment of understanding under Articles One and Two, by which the United States is bound in any way and that there is no obligation either legal or moral to give such consent."

President Harding has indicated that he believes no reservation is necessary to this or any of the other treaties. However, having been a reservationist himself while in the Senate, it is understood that he is not averse to letting the Senate put on some such reservation. The reservation simply voices an understanding which the administration already holds.

**Kellogg Opposes.**

The reservation was presented at a meeting of the foreign relations committee today. Senators Kellogg of Minnesota, McCumber of North Dakota and New of Indiana all opposed it. It received unexpected support from Senator Wadsworth of New York. The treaty may be reported out tomorrow.

Senator Lodge of Massachusetts, chairman of the committee and a member of the American delegation to the conference, took no part in the discussion except to indicate that the reservation would not be opposed.

If the acceptance of this particular reservation speeds up ratification of the treaties, it is considered here that it will be a small price to pay. Furthermore, there is a feeling that some of the irreconcilables must be given some leeway. Men like Senators Hiram W. Johnson and William E. Borah are still anxious to oppose the work of the Washington conference. If their main prop is taken out from under them that much will be gained.

The reservation is taken to be really a reflection upon the American delegation. It is that in effect. Some of the irreconcilables are out to take a slap at Secretary of State Hughes. Some of these men are not yet reconciled to the fact that Mr. Hughes has won the confidence of the American people to a most remarkable degree. They didn't want him appointed to the cabinet in the first place and have been extremely jealous of his growing popularity.

So, by making the reservation to the treaty, the irreconcilables, some of whom are being dubbed the "treaty killers", feel they are not only asserting themselves but casting some odium upon the head of the American delegation.

It is evident, however, that the administration intends to humor the irreconcilables. No one considers the reservation as proposed as dangerous or as impairing the four power pact. The attitude seems to be that if the Senate wants to pass such a reservation the thing to do, in the interests of harmony, is to let it pass it.

President Harding is apparently not going to be so insistent about trying to make the Senate do the thing just exactly as he wants it done.

Debate on the Yap treaty will begin tomorrow. Senator Lodge brought it before the Senate late today, announcing he will make the opening speech.

## *Chinese Laundrymen to Wash Windows and Stop Holdups*

Seven Chinese laundry hold-ups during the last few days have convinced Frank W. Brunskill, captain of detectives, that 50 Oriental laundrymen in Minneapolis must clean the windows of their laundries.

"The dirty windows of most Chinese laundries make them ideal spots for hold-up men to do their work," Captain Brunskill said. "If clean windows prevailed the hold-up men would hesitate before entering the places. I'm going to start a clean-up campaign among the laundrymen."

Harry Kong, proprietor of the O. K. Laundry, 813 Fourth avenue south, joined the ranks of Chinese hold-up victims last night. Two men took $75 from him. Charles Sam, an employe, lost $24.

"The same two men have staged all the laundry hold-ups," Lieutenant Frank Little said.

# *BLIMP WRECK BLAMED ON RUDDER ACCIDENT*

## Three Titanics of Skies Crash in 13 Months

### Greatest Toll of Life Taken in ZR-2 Wreck—Gale Destroyed R-34.

### Six Peace Time Zeppelins Ended Careers in Accidents.

*(By Associated Press.)*

New York, Feb. 21.—The dirigible Roma which was wrecked today at Hampton Roads, was the third big airship to be destroyed in a spectacular mishap in the last 13 months.

On August 24, 1921, the ZR-2, built by the British for purchase by the United States at a cost of $2,000,000 exploded over Hull, England, killing 42, including 16 Americans.

On January 1, 1921, the R-34, which flew from England to Long Island and back in the summer of 1919, the first airship to cross the Atlantic, was wrecked in a gale while tethered outside her airdrome in Howden, England.

**28 Killed by Zeppelin.**

Before the ZR-2 disaster, the greatest number killed in an airship accident in peace times was 28, the toll of the explosion of the German Zeppelin L-2 over the Johannisthal aerodrome on October 17, 1913.

Some of the other airship accidents in which heavy losses of life occurred follow:

July 21, 1919—Ten lost when dirigible exploded at Chicago and fell in flames into the Illinois Trust and savings bank.

July 2, 1912—Five killed at Atlantic City when balloon Akron, in which Melvin Vaniman hoped to cross the Atlantic, exploded shortly after leaving the ground.

September 9, 1913—Fifteen lost in destruction of Zeppelin L-1 off Helgoland.

July 15, 1919—Twelve lost when British airship NS-11 fell into North sea after being struck by lightning.

**Collision in Air.**

June 20, 1914—Nine lost in collision of airship and airplane at Vienna.

Six of the great peace-time dirigibles built by Count Zeppelin, the German aviator, were wrecked in accidents. They were Zeppelins I, II, III, and VI and Deutschlands I and II.

The Germans lost 66 of the 83 dirigibles sent out during the war, 34 of them being accounted for by the Allies and the remaining 32 wrecked.

## M'Cumber Asks Fund for Seeds

### Files $5,000,000 Bill on Heels of House Committee Announcement of Opposition.

From the Washington Bureau of The Minneapolis Tribune.

Washington, Feb. 21. — Following closely upon the heels of an announcement from the House appropriations committee that it would not vote to appropriate money for so-called seed loans to farmers in drought areas, Senator McCumber of North Dakota, presented his bill calling for an appropriation of $5,000,000 for that purpose.

The subcommittee on agriculture in the House appropriations committee has decided not to appropriate money for so-called seed loans. The Department of Agriculture informed the subcommittee that out of the appropriations previously made for such a purpose 13,935 loans has been made and that of that number only 4,124 farmers have paid back the loans to the government. It was pointed out that in all $1,955,000 had been loaned out and that only $607,000 had been paid back, leaving the government holding the sack for $1,348,000.

But Senator McCumber insists that the farmers of the drought stricken regions in North Dakota, his home state need seed loans and he intends to get the money for them if possible. He said that the government had loaned $20,000,000 to help starving Russians and farmers in some parts of North Dakota and Montana needed help just as much. His bill limits the amount any one farmer can borrow to purchase seed to $300. He would also make possible loans for the purchase of feed for live stock.

The House appropriations committee took its action yesterday and will fight to keep out of the final bill any appropriations for such a purpose.

## *French Plane to Try Flight to America*

New York, Feb. 21.—Louis Gaubert, French aviator, before sailing for home today, said he intended to fly back to the United States in a Goliath plane carrying ten passengers, within the next two months. Gaubert predicted he would make a nonstop flight across the Atlantic, in less than 32 hours. The plane, driven by four engines, is nearing completion at the Farman works, France, which is making arrangements for the flight, he said.

## Falling Ship Strikes Power Line; Explodes

### Eleven Survivors Escape Death By Jumping as Dirigible Nears Ground in Fatal 1,000-Foot Plunge at Hampton Roads—Flames Balk Rescuers.

*(By Associated Press.)*

Norfolk, Va., Feb. 21.—Thirty-four men were killed, eight were injured seriously and three were uninjured or only slightly bruised when the giant army airship Roma, with her crew and a number of civilians, totaling 45 in all, aboard, plunged today from a thousand feet or more in the air to the ground at the Hampton Roads naval base.

The accident presumably was caused by a broken rudder, and as the huge dirigible plunged to earth it capsized across a high tension electric line, bursting into a roaring furnace of blazing hydrogen gas.

**Hydrogen Gas Feeds Flames.**

Long after dark tonight the ship was still a mass of flames from end to end of her 410-foot mass.

The fire fed on the million cubic feet of gas which had distended the great bag for the flight and made all attempts at rescue work futile.

Barely a dozen of those aboard were picked up alive and one of these died on the way to the hospital. All who survived the fire escaped by jumping as the ship struck. The others, penned in the hull of the fallen bag, were burned to death.

The flames were finally brought into submission by three fire departments, who fought them with chemicals, and then derricks began picking up the wreckage, which consisted of scarcely more than the aluminum frame work and the six Liberty motors of the once proud ship of the air. Within the wreckage lay the bodies, practically all charred beyond recognition. But before the night had passed 33 bodies had been removed, accounting for the last of those known to have taken flight on the fatal voyage.

**Rudder Slips to Side.**

Accounts of survivors and of eye witnesses as to what had happened appeared to agree tonight that the huge kite-like structure of the stern rudder, itself as large as a bombing plane, had slipped to one side as the Roma drove along a thousand feet above the army base.

She was making a trial flight with a new battery of Liberty motors. They were installed to replace Italian engines brought with her from Italy but which have not proved satisfactory. It was just before 2 p. m. when those below at the army base at Hampton Roads base, their attention caught by the approaching thunder of the six motors, looked up to see the Roma dip down from her straight flight.

**Ship Noses Down.**

They agreed that the rudder seemed to have slipped bodily down and to one side. The ship nosed steeply down and as she came closer it was seen that members of her crew were hurling out sand ballast from the ports in the fragile fabric that formed the covering of the space between her keel and back, the living and operating quarters of the ship. The dipping blunt nose of the bag did not respond. On the ship came, unchecked in her glide earthward head first.

Her commander could not force her the few hundred feet that would have dropped her into the waters of the bay and comparative safety for her people. Below ran the high double wires of the high power electric line. It carries a 2,300 volt current. The Roma's nose, shod with its aluminum guard, thrust into the wires, broke them as the ship flattened to earth and rolled over, and the next moment came the noise of an explosion and the flames burst out along the hull space. There was a rush of men to the rescue from the army post and the navy base beyond.

**Men Seen to Jump.**

Just as the Roma neared the wires two men were seen to leap from high up in her hull. As the stricken, flaming monster writhed in her first death agony 10 more dropped from doors or ports through holes they tore in the fabric sides that enclosed them. Some leaped from the platform where the engines stood, far out from the hull. So swift was the flare of the gas flame that rescuers were driven back as the great bag shriveled in the fierce blaze of the liberated gas. The Roma was a wall of flame a city block long and until the thousands of gallons of chemicals and water had checked the holocaust it was impossible to reach the comrades mangled and dead in that fiery furnace.

The ship left no passenger list behind her when she set out for a brief trial run from Langley. She carried many officers and men as passengers, however, in addition to her operating crew.

**Few Had Chance.**

Officers who knew personally many of the officers and enlisted men were unable to identify a single one of the victims, so badly charred was each—virtually cooked to death in the mass of wreckage when the explosion and mass of flames encompassed them. Only those in the forward part of the operating compartment of the ship had a chance for their lives. Several were injured severely by jumping but three came out practically unhurt and were discharged from the hospital within a few hours after the disaster.

Lieutenant Burt, who with Captain Reed was the principal pilot of the Roma, was one of these. A civilian, Roy Hurley, also escaped unhurt, as did Master Sergeant Reek. Of the 45 who left the Langley field station only 11 survived the accident. Some of these, more dead than alive, lay on their cots at the United States Public Health service hospital with burned and broken limbs swathed in bandages. Some had their faces smeared with cream to relieve them of their intense suffering, while others lay asleep or unconscious with only their closed eyes visible. All who were able to talk were suffering from shock.

**Felt Ship Tilt.**

Albert Flores, who was in the observer's pit on top of the bag, said: "I felt the ship tilt up from the back

## *Official List of Dead, Missing in Roma Disaster*

*Washington, Feb. 21.—An official list of the survivors, dead, and missing in the Roma disaster was received from Langley field by the army air service tonight. The addresses, however, in most cases were unavailable. The list follows:*

**IDENTIFIED DEAD.**

First Lieut. William E. Riley, New York.

**MISSING.**

Major John G. Thornell.
Major Walter W. Zantsmeree.
Captain Dale Mabry.
Captain George D. Watts.
Captain Allen P. McFarland.
Captain ——— Durschmidt.
First Lieut. J. R. Hall.
First Lieut. C. Burns.
First Lieut. Clifford E. Smythe.
First Lieut. Wallace C. Cummings.
First Lieut. Ambrose V. Clinton.
First Lieut. Harold Hine.
Master Sergeant McNally.
Master Sergeant Murray.
Master Sergeant Gorby.
Sergeant Harril.
Sergeant Hillyard.
Sergeant Beal.
Sergeant Yarborough.
Sergeant Ryan.
Sergeant Huffman.
Sergeant Schumacker.
Sergeant Holmes.
Sergeant Heveron.
Private Kingston.
Private Blakley.
Private Thompson.
Private Hill.
Stryker.
Hanson.
O'Laughlin.
Merriman.
Schulenberger.

The last five are names of civilians, all said to have been employes at McCook field.

**SURVIVORS.**

Captain Walter J. Reed, of Scarsdale, N. Y.

Major John D. Reardon, Washington, D. C.

First Lieut. Clarence H. Welch, Papillion, Neb.

Lieut. B. G. Burt, pilot, slightly injured.

Sergeant Harry A. Chapman, St. Joseph, Mo.

Sergeant Virden T. Peek, Terre Haute, Ind. (uninjured).

Sergeant Joseph M. Budenbach, Akron, O.

Corporal Alverto Flores.

Charles D. Worack, McCook Field, Dayton, O.

Ray Hurley, of the National Advisory committee on aeronautics (uninjured).

Walter A. McNair, of the Bureau of Standards, Washington, D. C.

## *T. T. Hudson, Duluth Attorney, Is Dead*

Duluth, Minn., Feb. 21.—T. T. Hudson, 62 years old, prominent Duluth attorney, died today. He had been ill a week. Mr. Hudson came to Duluth in October, 1883, from Geneseo, Ill., with Alfred Jaques, present United States district attorney. He organized the law firm of Jaques & Hudson, which has been in existence since that time.

## *Senate Passes Bill Providing Own Pay*

Washington, Feb. 21.—The legislative bill carrying $12,490,000 for expenses of Congress next year was passed today by the Senate and sent to conference. It was the third of the regular supply measures to get through both branches of Congress.

# The Minneapolis Morning Tribune

Fifty-fifth Year. No. 330. MINNEAPOLIS, MINN., WEDNESDAY, APRIL 19, 1922 Price Two Cents in Minneapolis.

# ALLIES BACK DOWN AT GENOA

## Senate To Lay Tariff Aside for Bonus Measure

### G. O. P. Conference Decides to Sidetrack Revenue Raising Provision.

### Members Vote, 26 to 9, to Pass Soldier Act at This Session.

### Finance Committee Formally Requested to Report Act for Veterans.

(By Associated Press.)

Washington, April 18.—Senate Republicans meeting today in party conference voted, 26 to 9, in favor of the passage of a soldiers' bonus bill at this session of Congress. The finance committee majority was requested in a formal resolution to report such a measure "within a reasonable time," which was construed by some leaders as three or four weeks.

Senator Watson of Indiana, a Republican member of the finance committee, said the bonus bill probably would be taken up in the Senate and put through immediately after it was reported.

**Would Lay Aside Tariff.**

Under the present plan, the tariff bill, which, by a decision of the party conference, is to be called up Thursday "without further delay," would be laid aside temporarily for consideration of the bonus. There was a suggestion that the means of financing the bonus might be provided for in an amendment to the tariff bill.

There is a division of opinion among majority Senate leaders as to whether the Senate could attach a revenue provision to the bonus bill itself, because of the requirement that revenue measures originate in the House. The bonus measure passed by that body carried no means of financing. Aside from the House bill, which was referred to it last month, the Senate committee has before it the bonus legislation, which was recommitted by the Senate last July at the request of President Harding. This likewise has no revenue-raising provision.

**Opposed by Calder.**

Only one member of the finance committee, Senator Calder of New York, voted against the conference resolution, declaring for passage of the bonus. The other eight senators were reported to have been Wadsworth, New York; Edge, New Jersey; Nelson, Minnesota; Weller, Maryland; Newberry, Michigan; Pepper, Pennsylvania; Sterling, South Dakota, and Moses, New Hampshire.

After the return here Thursday of Chairman McCumber of the finance committee, majority members of that committee will meet to determine procedure on the bonus. Representatives of the American Legion and other organizations of veterans of the World war will be heard, possibly late this week.

**McCumber Wants Speed.**

Senator McCumber desires to get the bill before the Senate as soon as possible. He and several others of the majority members are inclined to favor the House bill with its adjusted certificate bank loan provision, but there is considerable opposition to this measure by other committeemen, including Senators Smoot of Utah, Watson of Indiana and Calder.

Before the committee comes to any decision a number of its members plan to discuss the question with President Harding.

The President also has expressed a desire that the tariff bill be given preference and there was some conflict of opinion today at the Capitol as to whether the program of proceeding with the tariff Thursday with a plan to lay it aside later for consideration of the bonus conformed to this view of the Executive.

**Confidence Expressed.**

Republican senators say they anticipate a fight by the Democrats and some Republicans, but confidence was expressed that the bill could be put through at this session of Congress despite the threatened split between the Senate and House on the question of American valuation.

Democratic members of the finance committee continued today with their study of the tariff in preparation for a minority report attacking the measure.

### *Tugs Rescue Liner Stranded on Rocks*

Havana, April 18.—After an hour's effort, eight tugs succeeded in pulling the Ward liner Orizaba off the rocks inside Havana harbor late today. The steamer, inbound from New York, went aground after going wide in attempting to pass the British tramp San Lamberto outward bound. All passengers were transferred safely ashore by launches. The extent of the damage done to the vessel could not be ascertained.

**Weather Forecast.**

MINNESOTA — Cloudy today, probably rain or snow in northeast portion; tomorrow partly cloudy; not much change in temperature.

Additional weather on page (17).

**THERE IS NO SUBSTITUTE FOR CIRCULATION**

The Tribune's Average Sworn Net Paid Circulation for March, 1922:

| DAILY | SUNDAY |
|---|---|
| 120,758 | 169,044 |

## *Reserve Corps Officers Bring Charges Against Pastor Who Opposes Army Drill in Schools*

### *Senate Committee Given Credit for Making 2,057 Changes in Tariff Bill*

Washington, April 18. — Senate clerks with a statistical turn of mind have totalled up the amendments made to the Fordney tariff bill by the Senate finance committee majority. They place the number at 2,057, which is declared to be something of a record in Senate rewriting of a House bill.

### Rev. R. H. Stafford Is Cited for Stand Taken on Military Training.

### Accusations Are Attacked in Protests Filed With War Department.

By George E. Akerson.
Washington Correspondent of The Minneapolis Tribune.

Washington, April 18.—Because the Rev. Russell H. Stafford, pastor of the First Congregational church, Minneapolis, and a chaplain in the reserve corps, United States army, opposed military training in the Minneapolis high schools at a hearing before the school board there, certain reserve officers filed charges against him alleging "conduct unbecoming an officer by allying himself with a questionable element in the community."

REV. R. H. STAFFORD

Vigorous protests against even the consideration of these charges have been lodged with the War department. As a result the whole matter is to be reviewed in order to determine whether or not an attempt is being made to "Prussianize" the reserve corps by "muzzling" its officers. If necessary, the matter will be placed before President Harding.

As a preliminary, there is to be an inquiry and to that end, C. E. Purdy, member of the Minneapolis school board, was today subpoened to come to Washington and give the details of what Mr. Stafford said at the hearing to which brother officers now take exception.

**Reported Expelled From 'Mess.'**

The report here is that some of these reserve officers not satisfied with the filing of the charges against Mr. Stafford, expelled him from the officers "mess." That is something with which the War department has nothing to do. A "mess" is run just like a club and the members can do as they see fit.

It is the charges, which War department attaches here admit do not constitute any violation of existing rules which have caused the real trouble. It is reported here that Mr. Stafford, in

(Continued on Page 8, Col. 2.)

## Prosecutor in Move to Obtain Mooney Pardon

### Governor Stephens Urged to Free Men in Bomb Case.

(By Associated Press.)

San Francisco, April 18.—Another step in the campaign to free Thomas J. Mooney and Warren K. Billings from state prisons, where they are serving life sentences in connection with a bomb explosion here, was taken today when District Attorney Brady addressed a letter to Governor Stephens asking that the men be pardoned.

Brady's action came as the result of his promise in open court several months ago while a phase of the Mooney case was being heard, that he would endeavor to have the governor liberate the men.

In his letter to the governor, Brady said that it was his belief that Mooney and Billings were convicted on perjured evidence and that their continued incarceration is a reflection on justice as it is administered in California. He specifically attacked the testimony of Frank C. Oxman Durkee, a cattle man and John McDonald, leading witness for the prosecution in the bomb cases.

The cases, which became world-famous and prompted a federal investigation on which a plea by President Wilson in Mooney's behalf was based, followed the explosion of a bomb while a preparedness parade was passing on July 22, 1916. Ten people were killed and 40 injured.

Mooney was sentenced to death but the sentence was later commuted to life imprisonment. Two others were tried and acquitted, one of them Mooney's wife, Mrs. Rena Mooney.

"I believe no person who permits himself to analyse the situation," Brady's letter said, "entertains any doubt that Mooney and Billings were convicted on false testimony. The only reason for keeping them in prison is that they are undesirable citizens.

"The situation is one that comes clearly within the purpose of the provision granting the governor power to pardon."

## 1,000 to Seek Missing Pastor

### Posses Seeking Illinois Man Includes National Guard and Legion Members.

(By Associated Press.)

Peoria, Ill., April 18.—A posse of 1,000 persons will leave for East Peoria to make a thorough search tomorrow in the hills for the Rev. W. J. Leach, missing Peoria minister and newspaper writer.

The searching parties will include National Guardsmen, members of the American Legion to which Mr. Leach belonged and citizens.

The most recent clue today came from Sparland, Ill., where a man resembling the pastor was seen Friday night and talked with people in a restaurant about Wisconsin. Rewards for the man now total more than $1,000.

## *Mathilde McCormick Plans to Sail Soon to Marry Max Oser*

(By Associated Press.)

Chicago, April 18.—Miss Mathilde McCormick, daughter of Harold F. McCormick and granddaughter of John D. Rockefeller, will sail for Europe with her father in a month or two and will marry Max Oser, Swiss riding master, in Switzerland, Howard A. Colby, friend of the McCormick family announced today.

Oser, he said, would not come to this country. Asked whether Mr. Rockefeller had consented to the marriage, Mr. Colby said: "Oh, they'll probably win him over." He added, however, that the wedding is "absolutely going through."

### *House Votes to Cut Size of Naval Class*

Washington, April 18.—The House today approved the provision in the naval bill that not to exceed 200 of the 541 members of the Naval academy class to be graduated in June should be commissioned as ensigns. Several efforts were made to save the entire class. An amendment by Representative McClintic, Democrat, Oklahoma, designed to provide commissions for 541 graduates by retiring higher officers now in reserve, was defeated, 95 to 32. Other attempts to change the academy section were thrown out on points of order.

## *Hays Cancels All Picture Contracts Starring Arbuckle*

### Bookings for 10,000 Showings Are Affected By Director's Order.

New York, April 18.—Cancellation of all contracts for the showing of films in which Roscoe C. Arbuckle appears was announced tonight by Will Hays, head of the Motion Picture Producers association. This action, he said, affected nearly 10,000 contracts.

"After consultation with Mr. Nicholas Schenck, representing Mr. Joseph Schenck, the producers, and Mr. Adolph Zukor and Mr. Lasky of the Famous Players-Lasky corporation, the distributors," Mr. Hays statement said, "I will state that at my request they have cancelled all showings and all bookings of the Arbuckle films. They do this that the whole matter may have the consideration that its importance warrants and the action is taken notwithstanding the fact that they had nearly 10,000 contracts in force for the Arbuckle pictures."

When Mr. Zukor was asked if the action of the Producers' association had removed Arbuckle definitely from the list of screen stars, he replied: "We simply left the matter in the hands of Mr. Hays. It is up to him to decide in the future whether it will be proper to re-introduce the Arbuckle pictures."

Mr. Zukor said recently that three Arbuckle feature comedies had been completed before the arrest of the comedian on charges growing out of the death of Miss Virginia Rappe. The producer announced shortly after Arbuckle's acquittal that one of the films would be released as a "test" of public opinion.

### *129 Non-Union Mines Closed, Strikers Claim*

Pittsburgh, April 18.—District offices of the United Mine workers tonight gave out a list of 129 non-union mines in Western Pennsylvania which it was declared, had been closed by union organizers since the coal strike began. There was no statement from operators other than that some of the mines in the list were not closed entirely and that others had been shut down by the business depression. Included in the list were 38 mines of the H. C. Frick Coke company.

### *Landon Leads Race for Mayor of Seattle*

Seattle, Wash., April 18.—With 210 out of the city's 294 precincts heard from in the city primaries here tonight State Senator Daniel Landon was leading the field for mayor with a total of 12,503 votes.

### *Irish Army Barracks Resist Long Attack of Civilian Raiders*

(By Associated Press.)

Dublin, April 18.—According to an official report issued this evening, the Celbridge barracks, now occupied by the Irish Republican army as headquarters for that district of County Kildare, was the scene of a prolonged attack Monday evening. Numerous parties of strangers in civilian clothes arrived in motor cars and for an hour maintained a strong rifle fire against the building. The guard replied to the shots.

## Broken Levee Floods Towns on Mississippi

### Highest Water Stage in History Forecast at New Orleans.

New Orleans, April 18.—The Mississippi river levee which almost surrounds the little town of Bayou Sara, La., 25 miles north of Baton Rouge, broke today and flooded that place and the lower part of St. Francisville, another small town near there.

The break had been anticipated and all residents of the town about 25 persons had moved to higher ground before the crevasse occurred.

Predicting that the Mississippi river would exceed by one foot the highest flood stage ever attained here, Dr. I. M. Cline, forecaster of the New Orleans weather bureau issued a revised forecast today calling for a maximum of 23 feet between May 1 and 10.

The previous record stage which was established in 1912 was 22 feet.

### Boats Carry Voters to Flooded Polls.

Beardstown, Ills., April 18.—With contests in each of the five wards in the city, Beardstown voters paddled to the polls in boats today to cast their ballots in the aldermanic election.

Every boat in the flooded city was commandeered by politicians to transport voters to the polls. One ward worker equipped an automobile with high wagon wheels and used the machine to haul voters through the submerged streets of his ward.

Interest in the election, intense before the flood, was revived today and a much heavier vote than was anticipated was registered.

### Coast Guard Leaves for Beardstown Aid.

Chicago, April 18.—Lieutenant T. A. Malloy of the Chicago coast guard district, announced that he was prepared to leave with 15 men, three power surf boats, a number of skiffs and other equipment for the flooded area near Beardstown, Ill.

Lieutenant Malloy acted upon instructions from Assistant Secretary Clifford of the treasury department at Washington.

All equipment will be loaded on an Illinois Central train, Lieutenant Malloy said, and will be taken as near the flooded area as possible by rail. The men and boats will then strike out for Beardstown by water.

## Worker Burns in Flaming Oil

### Northern States Master Mechanic Sprayed By Electrically Ignited Fluid.

Joseph Rhoades, 628 Aldrich avenue north, master mechanic of the Riverside plant of the Northern States Power company, was probably fatally burned by electricity ignited oil in the plant at Twenty-ninth avenue and Marshall street northeast yesterday.

Rhoades was believed to be dying last night in the Northwestern hospital.

William Shore, 2653 Marshall street northeast, chief engineer at the plant, who went to the rescue when Rhoades was a mass of flames, was seriously burned about the face and hands, but is recovering at his home.

The accident was caused by a short circuit in an oil switch used to start an auxiliary motor. When Rhoades threw in the switch yesterday he was sprayed from head to feet by burning oil.

In an instant his clothing caught fire, and the flames had enveloped his body when Shore dashed to his rescue. The engineer succeeded in closing the switch, and then, with his hands and face severely burned, beat out the flames in Rhoades' clothing. Rhoades had been burned deeply, however, and when he was taken to the hospital physicians pronounced his condition critical.

### *Texas Grocer Flogged for Alleged Immorality*

Texarkana, Texas, April 18.—H. E. Clark, local grocer, was seized by masked men last night as he alighted from a street car, driven by auto into the country and given a flogging. Clark was given a lecture for alleged immorality.

## Aviators Finish Voyage Across Atlantic Ocean

### Portuguese Fliers Reach St. Paul's Rock in Safety.

### Rio Janeiro Citizens Hold Demonstrations Over Success of Flight.

### Last Leg of 900 Miles Is Covered in Fifteen Hours.

(By Associated Press.)

Rio Janeiro, April 18.—Confirmation was received here this evening from Pernambuco by the Correio Manhas that the Portuguese hydro-airplane flying from Portugal to Brazil landed at St. Paul's rocks at 8 o'clock this evening.

The unofficial time of the flight is given as 15 hours. The estimated distance flown is approximately 900 miles, thus making the time of the airplane 60 miles an hour.

Rio Janeiro, with approximately 200,000 Portuguese inhabitants, was a scene of great rejoicing tonight. Plans have been made for a big celebration on the arrival of the aviators at Pernambuco, Bahia and Rio Janeiro.

The government wireless station tonight received a message from the steamer Vauban, saying it had picked up the following radio message from the station at Olinda, near Pernambuco:

"Aviators arrived. Well. Slight damage was sustained by machine in landing."

The message does not indicate whether the hydro-airplane landed in the ocean or at Fernanho Noronha.

### Plane Is Damaged in Landing at Island.

(By Associated Press.)

Pernambuco, Brazil, April 18.—Captains Coutinho and Sacadura, in their flight from the Cape Verde islands for Brazil, arrived at the cliffs of the St. Paul's Rock, just above the equator northwest of the island of Fernando Noronha, at 8 o'clock this evening, Brazilian time.

The hydro-airplane Lusitania experienced slight motor trouble and had to stop at the St. Paul's cliffs.

A later dispatch says the hydro-airplane motor had no trouble, but that the plane was slightly damaged in mooring.

## *Wife of Semenoff Asked to Quit as Red Cross Aide*

### Alleged Misuse of Supplies in Siberia Brought Removal.

Universal News Service.

Washington, April 18.—Madame Gregorie Semenoff, the beautiful young wife of the Cossack leader, now held in New York, was revealed here today as a one-time Red Cross worker. It also was said that her connection with the relief organization was severed under peculiar circumstances.

The information shows that when the Red Cross opened activities in the Chita district of Siberia in 1920, the woman now claiming to be the wife of Semenoff was enlisted to distribute supplies to the war-stricken population. Although she was never officially enrolled as a member of the Red Cross, Madame Semenoff was entrusted with considerable quantities of foodstuffs and medical supplies for distribution to the destitute. These she accepted, it is said, but reports to Red Cross headquarters at Chita indicated that the supplies were not being distributed.

**Aided Husband.**

An investigation was begun, revealing the fact that Madame Semenoff was using the supplies as means of furthering the political ambitions of the Cossack ataman. Madame Semenoff, it is said, distributed the Red Cross supplies only to political adherents of Semenoff.

As soon as this fact was discovered by Red Cross officials in Siberia, Madame Semenoff was immediately removed from the list of volunteer workers and all the Red Cross supplies in her hands were called in. From that time forth, it is said, the Red Cross carefully investigated the records of those volunteering to act for it in and near Chita.

**Perjury Trial Hinted.**

Immigration officials here are making an exhaustive study of the testimony of Mme. Semenoff and the Cossack leader upon admittance into this country. This testimony, upon which their plea for admission was based, discloses startling discrepancies which must be explained, if there is a possibility of trial for perjury.

Examined at different times, Semenoff declared that his "wife" was living in Chita with her mother and sister at the time they were married. Mme. Semenoff's testimony directly contradicted this. She states to immigration examiners that she was living in Chita as the guest of Colonel Radesi; that her family was in Japan, and that she had left an eight months' old child with them. Semenoff testified that his wife did not work, while Mme. Semenoff testified that she was working in staff of General Annafsief in Siberia, at the time of her marriage.

## *Storm Death Toll Increased to 33, With 320 Hurt*

### Reports Are Still Coming In From Districts Isolated By Tornadoes.

### Storms Move Eastward, With Strength Apparently Spent.

(By Associated Press.)

Chicago, April 18.—The terrific storms sweeping eastward across the country, which in some parts of the Central states became tornadoes, resulted in at least 33 persons killed, two missing, 320 injured and several millions of dollars damage to property, according to reports tonight from the stricken areas.

The 320 listed thus far as injured include only those in towns which felt the full effect of the storms. Scores of others in sections which were not in the tornado belts were hurt, and the total is believed to be beyond the 500 mark. In addition several of the injured are in critical condition and may not live.

**Many Sections Isolated.**

Illinois and Indiana were hit hardest, the list of known dead in Illinois being 11, while in Indiana 19 fatalities already have been reported. The Illinois reports are believed to be complete, but there are some areas in Indiana from which no word has been received, all lines of communication being broken.

Two persons were killed in Missouri, while Kansas, Michigan and Ohio sustained heavy property damage.

Tonight the storms still were moving eastward but apparently had spent their full strength, subsiding in most places to snow, rain or hail with winds which while high were not of tornado velocity.

**Hundreds Homeless.**

Tonight hundreds of families were homeless, their houses demolished by the storms, and Red Cross and other relief workers had been rushed into the devastated areas. Telephone and telegraph lines were down in most of the affected regions, so that complete reports of the destruction still were unavailable.

### Indiana Suffers Most From Storm.

Indianapolis, April 18.—Twenty persons are dead, more than 300 injured and a property loss estimated at more than a million dollars, was the toll of tornados which swept western and central Indiana, according to figures received here. It will be several days, however, before the correct figures will be known, owing to the confusion in the stricken areas.

Two persons were killed at Sloan, in Warren county. Two persons were reported missing at Orestes, where three persons are already known to have died in the tornado there late yesterday.

Seven persons were killed at Hedrick, and many were injured seriously. At Williamsport three were killed, while Brook, in Newton county, reported two killed and several injured.

### $1,000,000 Loss Reported in Ohio.

Columbus, Ohio, April 18.—Meager reports from the section in northwestern Ohio visited by last night's storm indicated today that no lives had been lost, although many persons had been slightly injured and many barns and outbuildings had been demolished. Property loss near Lima was estimated roughly at more than $1,000,000.

## *Rail Employes Reject Proposal to Organize Into 'One Big Union'*

(By Associated Press.)

Chicago, April 18.—A proposal to amalgamate all railway workers into one industrial organization, modeled on the "One Big Union" idea, was rejected today by delegates attending the convention of the railway employes department of the American Federation of Labor.

Resolutions adopted declared that the railway workers "have sustained the sound and proven principle of craft organization, with its democracy and complete autonomy for each class of workers, united through affiliation of the international organizations with the American Federation of Labor."

### *Angry Prisoners Pelt Guards With Tincups*

Chicago, April 18.—Solitary confinement imposed upon one of their number angered 250 prisoners in the county jail tonight and resulted in a riotous demonstration that guards had difficulty in ending. Bunks were broken and guards were pelted with tin cups as they went about trying to quiet the prisoners. Fearing that the demonstration might be a part of an effort to effect a jail delivery, armed guards were posted about the building. Hundreds of persons attracted by the din surrounded the building.

### *Carpenters Volunteer to Take Wage Cut*

Billings, Mont., April 18.—Members of the carpenters' union here at a meeting last night voted to take a voluntary cut in pay of $1 a day, effective at once. The former scale was $8 per day. This action follows similar action taken by plumbers, plasterers and bricklayers within the past few weeks, announcement of which was made today.

## Russo-German Treaty Fails to Halt Sessions

### Conference to Continue, Despite Action By Moscow and Berlin.

### Teutons Are Barred From Further Discussions on Soviet Problem.

### Neutral Countries Protest 'Elimination' From the Deliberations.

(By Associated Press.)

Genoa, April 18.—It is not impossible, says the Lavora today, that owing to the complications that have arisen from the Russo-German treaty, Premier Lenin of Soviet Russia may come to Genoa and submit to the conference and to the world the situation in Russia in the interest of reconstruction the necessity for reconstruction of Rusia in the interest of reconstruction of Europe.

(By Associated Press.)

Genoa, April 18.—The representatives of the powers which convened the Genoa conference, together with the little entente, decided tonight after an all-day discussion, to continue the economic conference regardles of the attitude of Germany and Russia.

With Germany debarred from further deliberations with respect to the agreement which the powers hope to conclude with Russia, the conference is tonight in a state of crisis. The Allied powers, sitting with the state of the little entente, have imposed a severe penalty on Germany because of what is termed her violations of the conditions to which she pledged herself in entering the conference.

**Form of Violation.**

This violation took the form of "secretly concluding" a treaty with Russia on the very matters which all the powers had agreed to discuss in common at Genoa.

Notwithstanding the Allies vigorous actions, indications tonight were that the Germans would not bolt the conference, although they had not disclosed what attitude they would adopt.

It was said, however, they were engaged tonight in drafting a reply to a note of the Allies and little entente denying the German's right to participate in the commissions dealing with Russian affairs. The reply will state that the Allies began secret negotiations with the Russians before the Germans did, and, furthermore, that the full conference of 32 powers, and not 11 powers, alone has the right to exclude the Germans.

**Neutrals Protest.**

The neutral countries headed by Denmark, which are not pleased because the small powers have been almost eliminated from the conference by reason of the private sitting of the entente powers, have held several meetings, and have protested against Germany's exclusion from Russian affairs without a full vote of the conference.

Dr. Rathenau, the German foreign secretary, has protested the Allies' action, declaring that the Germans did nothing secret or dishonorable. He asserted that the Allies themselves were preparing a treaty with Russia in secret, after which Germany would be informed of it and would be expected to sign.

The note sent to the German delegation declared that "Germany's act had destroyed the spirit of mutual confidence in indispensible to international co-operation," and informed Germany that she is debarred from further participation in discussion of Russian affairs at the economic conference.

**Meeting Continuous.**

The meeting at which this note was drafted was held at the Villa Raggid, Premier Facta's home, and was continuous with the exception of brief periods for lunch and tea, when more intimate conversations were carried on between the various delegates.

The discussions at the meeting were calm and dignified, although considerable differences of opinion existed. Two groups formed, one led by England and the other by France, while the Italian delegates displayed a conciliatory attitude. Some of the extremists are said to have proposed breaking up the conference, but a majority favored awaiting Moscow's reply to the Allied demands.

According to information from French sources, Mr. Lloyd George emphasized the necesity of adopting a severe attitude toward both Russia and Germany, but especially against Germany, pointing out that Germany had signed the Versailles treaty whereas Russia had not.

**Moderation Favored.**

Signor Schanzer, the Italian foreign minister, favored an attitude of moderation in the interests of the conference. Mr. Lloyd George pleaded that it was no time to display weakness. He counseled sending a note to Germany and Russia declaring they must modify their attitude if they expected to be permitted to discuss Russian affairs at Genoa.

At the evening session there was a discussion as to the advisability of insisting That Germany either revise the treaty with Russia or be expelled from all commissions of the conference.

### Germans Not Uneasy Over Results of Coup.

(By Associated Press.)

Genoa, April 18.—M. Chicherin, head of the Russian delegation, called on Chancellor Wirth and Dr. Walter Rathenau, of the German delegation, at their hotel today while the big and little entente powers were meeting to decide what they would do about the Russo-German treaty, and had a long conference with the Germans, who displayed no uneasiness about the posi-

# GREATEST DAIRY EXPOSITION TO OPEN DOORS TODAY

The Minneapolis Morning Tribune

Fifty-sixth Year. No. 136. MINNEAPOLIS, MINN., SATURDAY, OCTOBER 7, 1922 Price Two Cents in Minneapolis

# U. S. BARS LIQUOR FROM SHIPS

## 'Discard' Twirls 3 to 0 Victory Over Yankees

### John Scott, More 'Never Was' Than 'Has Been,' Sensation of Series.

### McGraw's Choice to Lead Forlorn Hope Outpitches Huggins' Ace.

### 37,620 Fans See Comeback Which Puts Team in 2-0 Lead for Title.

New York, Oct. 6.—(By Associated Press)—A little more than three months ago John William Scott dropped out of the baseball box score and no tears, save possibly his own, were shed. Jack had never ranked with those whose names are passed on. A hard working plodder had just worn out and was expected to fade away. Tonight he is the most talked about man in the United States and his name will live.

John Scott transformed himself today and became an identity by pitching 112 balls that resulted in his team, the New York Giants, defeating the New York Yankees, 3 to 0 in the third game of the world's series, and supplied his club with a two-game lead in the classic, an advantage that has been overcome only once in history.

**'Discard' Gets Chance.**

Nearer to having been a "never was" than a "has been," in cold fact, a discard, a cast off, a useless ball player, Jack Scott was shunted out of the baseball world by the Cincinnati club last July. He had gone to Cincinnati in a trade with Boston last December but didn't make good. His arm was dead. He was through.

A creditable story traveled among the 37,620 fans who occupied every possible bit of space at the Polo grounds today that Scott, after his Cincinnati dismissal, sought a chance with Manager McGraw, who needed pitchers more than any man in the baseball world. But he needed good ones. According to his story, McGraw, desperate, took a chance and had Scott's arm treated by a specialist and it helped some—just "some." Scott won eight out of 10 games but still was rated low.

**McGraw in Distress.**

Today John Joseph McGraw, famed for his decisiveness, instantaneous and permanent, led his team out on the field with his mind open and anxious to be closed. McGraw was in distress. His face betrayed his anxiety as he watched his men go through their practice. Their faces, too, mirrored their manager's feeling. Came the time for the pitchers to get ready—for someone, anyone, to "warm up."

Still McGraw pondered. With the time for a final decision dangerously near, the "Napoleon of baseball" nodded silently to Hugh McQuillan to "warm up." Word was sent to the press box that the assignment had been made and the wires buzzed. Temporarily relieved, the manager watched his selection twirl a few balls. But only for a moment.

**Scott Substituted.**

McGraw didn't like McQuillan's form. He turned to Scott, sitting on the bench, and with the air of a man who is resting all his hopes on a broken reed, ordered him to replace McQuillan. It was almost unprecedented for a manager to change his choice in so important a matter at such a time.

Everyone knew that Waite Hoyt, the "boy wonder," who won two out of three games from the Giants in the 1921 series, striking out 18 men, allowing only 18 hits and yielding only two runs, both unearned, was to pitch for the Yankees. One fan remarked that McGraw virtually was conceding the game, believing Hoyt unbeatable, and had decided not to throw away a man who might win tomorrow.

Jack Scott's record is on the books now. It says there the castoff's pitching was so marvelous that the Giant outfielders made only six putouts—that the Yankees were so thoroughly subdued that 18 out of their 24 out, were of the easy infield variety. Only four hits were made by the Yankees with their touted "murderers row" and only six times did they get a man on first.

**Incarnation of Earnestness.**

On the mound, facing 40,000 pairs of critical eyes, Scott was the incarnation of earnestness, faith and hope, but he never smiled. He remained inscrutably calm and cool. Jack Scott, combined his head and his aging right arm today, and he followed orders. Earl Smith, the catcher, said afterward that every time he called for a high pitch, a high one came. Not once, he said, did Scott fail. He used only a curve ball; he had such remarkable control that always it went where Smith, whose knowledge of the Yankee batters and discerning judgment cannot be overlauded, ordered.

McGraw was voluble in his praise of Scott and Miller Huggins, the beaten and crestfallen mentor of the Yanks, was not remiss.

Though Scott's marvelous pitching stood out today as only the victory of the "under dog" can, two other incidents furnished material for the crowd,

(Continued on Page 28, Col. 1.)

### Weather Forecast

MINNESOTA—Fair today, except showers in extreme east portion, tomorrow fair; not much change in temperature.

Additional weather on page 27.

## Army Aviators Set World's Record With 35-Hour Flight

### Lieutenants Mac Ready and Kelly Land Safely at San Diego.

### Airmen Credit Success to Liberty Motor—'Best in the World.'

San Diego, Calif., Oct. 6.—(By Associated Press)—Lieutenants John A. MacReady and Oakley Kelly, who had been flying over San Diego since 5:56 a. m. yesterday in the great monoplane T-2, landed at Rockwell field soon after 5 p. m. today, having broken all known records for sustained flight in the heavier-than-air flying machine. They were in the air 35 hours, 18 minutes, 30 seconds.

The aviators were well tired out but willing, they said, to have continued their flight except for their desire to reach the ground before darkness should make landing more difficult.

**Aviators Begrimed.**

Captain R. G. Erwin, commandant of Rockwell field, soon after the flight ended gave out the time the aviators had been aloft.

The aviators were begrimed with oil and grease when they stepped from the big machine in which they had remained aloft, circling over the city for virtually two days and a night. That did not stop Mrs. Benjamin MacReady, mother of the aviator, from rushing to greet her son.

She kissed him full on his grimy cheek and when she turned around, smiling gladly, her lips were black with grease and oil.

**Liberty Motor Credited.**

Lieutenant MacReady and Kelly joined in making the following statement: "It was the wonderful Liberty motor which kept us up. There is no question that this flight proves the motor to be the best and most efficient in the world. It is due to the development of army aviation. The primary purpose of the test, it should be said, was to test the motor in the United States army transport T-2, and the result was al' that could be expected.

"We are going to make the flight from San Diego to New York in November and we are confident that we shall be successful."

### Needle Swallowed by Mother Is Found in Her Baby's Shoulder

Stockton, Cal., Oct. 6.—Three years ago Mrs. Frank J. Schwing swallowed a needle two inches long. Charlottee, her 22 months old baby, began to cry yesterday and continued crying, apparently without cause.

Mrs. Schwing investigated the little girl's repeated rubbing of a spot on her left shoulder and felt a foreign body under the skin.

She probed and found the needle and withdrew it. The mother and daughter had never suffered pain from the needle until the girl felt it in her shoulder.

## Armory Levy Killed Before Budget Passes

### Proposed $5,400 Appropriation Voted Down in Council, 11 to 11.

The proposed tax levy of $5,400 for armory maintenance in 1923 was voted down by the city council yesterday, 11 to 11. The radical group voted solidly against a tax levy for this purpose and the conservatives were unanimously in favor of the levy. The remainder of the tax levy budget was adopted unanimously by the council.

The armory commission will hold a special meeting next week to determine what course it will pursue to keep the armory open next year, according to C. A. Bloomquist, one of the commissioners.

**May Not Close Armory.**

"Action of the city council does not mean that the armory is to close if the commission can find funds to keep the building open," Mr. Bloomquist said. "It may be tough sledding to maintain the building from rental receipts alone, but I am confident some way will be found to keep the armory going.

"The state law specifically requires a tax to be levied for armory maintenance, and it may yet be possible to get the armory tax levy spread on the county auditor's books. The commission probably will meet in a few days to decide what course it will follow."

**Budget Is Deadlocked.**

For five minutes yesterday the entire city burget over which the city council has jurisdiction was killed by the deadlock. Then Alderman W. H. Rendell of the conservative group requested that some member of the radical group move for reconsideration. Alderman John Peterson made such a motion, it being carried unanimously.

Alderman Peterson next moved to amend the report of the finance committee by striking out the armory tax levy. This motion carried without a record vote, and the budget exclusive of the armory item was adopted by 22 votes.

**Levy Lost by Tie Vote.**

Alderman Josiah H. Chase then moved that the armory levy be adopted, but this was lost by a tie vote. The roll call showed Aldermen Dunleavy, Lindsten, John Peterson, Gisslen, Voelker, Scott, Guider, Pryts, Beneke Rudsdil and Jenson voting against the armory levy, and Aldermen Chase, Hawley, Mumm, Currie, J. O. Peterson, Walquist, Turner, Rendell, Sheffield, Robb and Buck voting for it. Aldermen Ryan, Fruen and Downes of the conservative group and Alderman Bastis, Socialist, were absent.

When the finance committee report, including the armory levy, was read, Alderman A. R. Gisslen moved that each of the separate levies named in the report be voted on separately. This motion was voted down, 11 to 11.

**Peterson Opens Debate.**

Debate on the armory levy started when Alderman John Peterson moved that the report of the committee be

(Continued on Page 16, Col. 1.)

### Former Record Flight Made in New York.

New York, Oct. 6.—The world's record for sustained flight in a heavier than air flying machine was held by Edward Stinson and Lloyd Bertaud, who on December 30, 1921, remained aloft above Roosevelt field, Mineola, N. Y., for 26 hours 19 minutes and 35 seconds, it was stated today by aviation authorities. Stinson used the all-metal monoplane J. L-6. The previous record was held by two French fliers, Lucien Boussou Troy and Jean Bernard, who in June, 1920, stayed in the air 24 hours 19 minutes and 2 seconds. It was stated that the San Diego flight had probably set a new world's record"

### Ben Hecht Charged in 'Obscene' Book Plot

Chicago, Oct. 6.—Warrants were issued today for the arrest of Ben Hecht, a newspaper feature writer and author, and Wallace Smith, a cartoonist, charging them with conspiracy to send obscene literature by interstate common carrier, the warrants being issued by Lewis F. Mason, United States commissioner. Warrants were also issued for the heads of a publishing firm that printed "Fantazius Mallare," a book written by Hecht and illustrated by Smith and which is the basis for the federal warrants. Bonds for each of the defendants was fixed at $5,000.

### Independent Oil Pays 200 Per Cent Dividend

Okmulgee, Okla., Oct. 6.—Directors of the Independent Oil and Gas company of Okmulgee met here today and declared a 200 per cent stock dividend. A meeting of stockholders will be called for October 20 to vote on increasing the capital from $3,000,000 to $10,000,000.

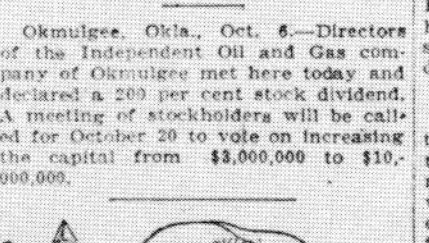

### NationalBankBranches Indorsed by Harding

Washington, Oct. 6.—President Harding cordially indorses the policy of Comptroller of the Currency Crissinger concerning the establishment of branch offices by national banks, it was officially stated today. The administration feels, it was said, that national banks should be permitted to maintain branches wherever branches of state banks are allowed.

### Tchitcherin Cheered on Return to Russia

Moscow, Oct. 6.—(By Associated Press.)—A crowd of diplomats, civilians and soldiers with bands greeted Foreign Minister Tchitcherin at the station today on his arrival here after a six months' absence abroad. During his stay outside of Russia he represented his country at the Genoa conference and later carried on negotiations with other countries.

## Exhibits Ready as Gates Open at Dairy Show

### Activities Today Include Judging and Introduction of 'Healthland.'

### Wisconsin and Michigan Herds Demonstrate Building Up Results.

### Poultry Valued at $250,000 on Display—Car Service Assured.

**Today's Program**

7 a. m.—Gates open.
7:30 a. m.—Boys and girls contests in judging dairy cattle.
Exhibits will be ready for inspection in all buildings and will remain open during the day and evening.
Band concerts during afternoon with announcement of winners and winning butter and cheese exhibits.
7:30 p. m.—Band concert in Hippodrome building.
8 p. m.—Amateur Athletic association track and field meet.

The sixteenth annual National Dairy exposition opens at the Minnesota State Fair grounds at 7 a. m. today with more than 1,000 head of purebred cattle and exhibits valued at $1,000,000, on display.

One hundred thousand dairy enthusiasts, representing almost every state in the Union will attend the show. The first annual National Poultry exposition, which boasts the largest collection of domestic fowls ever assembled, will be offered in connection with the Dairy show.

Late shipments of machinery were placed last night, housing of cattle and poultry was completed and finishing touches were put on the exhibits of dairy products.

**'Healthland' a Fairyland.**

One of the features of the show will be the exhibit "Healthland," which has been arranged to interest adults and children in the benefits of milk drinking. In the exhibit will be found a castle with real knights, a house of gold, a miniature radio station, an art gallery and a theater, where performances will be continuous. Physicians of 11 national health organizations prepared the exhibit. Health talks will be given on Monday, Tuesday, Wednesday and Thursday at 2:30 p. m.

All children attending "Healthland"

(Continued on Page 2, Col. 1.)

## Kellogg Drops Election Drive to Aid Farmers

### Senator Invokes Esch-Cummins Law for Cars to Move Potatoes.

Moorhead, Minn., Oct. 6.—(Special.)—With hundreds of thousands of bushels of potatoes awaiting shipment and at the mercy of the first frost because of an alarming car shortage, Senator Frank B. Kellogg today forgot his campaign for re-election and devoted the entire afternoon and part of the night to an effort to alleviate the situation.

He sent urgent messages to Washington in an attempt to get the sorely needed cars started in the direction of the Red River valley.

One touch of irony connected with the serious situation is the fact that Senator Kellogg has invoked the Esch-Cummins law, a measure that has been roundly condemned by Shipstead adherents to carry relief to this decided Nonpartisan stronghold.

**Tie-Up Causes Low Price.**

Paragraph Fifteen, Section one, of the Esch-Cummins law provides that the Interstate Commerce Commission may order cars about the country at will, regardless of sectional lines, in emergencies. It is upon this provision that Senator Kellogg is relying to accomplish his ends.

Farmers who received as high as $5.50 per bushel for their potatoes in this vicinity three or four years ago, today are offered as little as 10 cents per bushel for their product.

The extremely low price is the result of inability to ship the potatoes, buyers tell the farmers.

Mr. Kellogg today visited several of the leading potato centers and said that at least 10,000 cars are urgently needed on Soo Line points.

**Appeal to Washington.**

His first move was to ask the help of George Huntington, president of that system. He followed this up with messages to the Honorable Charles C. McChord, chairman of the Interstate Commerce commission, in Washington, urging that no time be lost in relieving the situation. In another message, sent tonight, he declared that conditions are far more serious than he realized when sending the first message. The second telegram was written after he had made personal visits to shippers at Hawley, Calloway, Ogama and Westberry, while on his way from Detroit to Moorhead.

## Allies Split on Turk Policy as Kemal Issues Ultimatum

### Nationalist Chief Demands Immediate Evacuation of Thrace.

### Italy Instructs Envoy at Mudania to Support Moslem Claims.

Paris, Oct. 7.—The conference on the Turkish situation between Premier Poincare and Lord Curzon, the British foreign minister, which began last night, was ended shortly after two o'clock this morning. In reply to questions the British foreign minister declared: "I am exhausted, but we have done good work."

M. Politis, the Greek minister of foreign affairs, tonight informed Premier Poincare that he had sent instructions to Greece to stop all further despatching of Greek troops into Thrace.

Constantinople, Oct. 6.—(By Associated Press.)—Although no definite news has yet been received from Mudania, where the Allied representatives have gone again to renew their conference with the envoys of the Turkish Nationalist government, at midnight tonight there was a distinct current of optimism among the Allied diplomats here regarding a possible successful outcome of the negotiations.

This feeling prevailed notwithstanding that the Kemalists today issued an ultimatum to the Allies demanding their consent to Turkish occupation of Thrace, and the previous rejection by the Kemalists of the proposal for the sending of Allied troops and the establishment of an Allied control commission in the province.

**Conferees Return to Mudania.**

The ultimatum regarding the evacuation of Thrace was extended to 6:30 o'clock this evening, and still later to 8 o'clock. Meantime the Allied generals had sailed for Mudania.

According to information from a British source the Angora government has notified the Allied generals that unless it is given formal assurances that Thrace will be handed over to the Turks within a month after the evacuation by the Greek troops tonight the Turkish troops will resume operations against the Greek forces.

Dispatches received during the day from London and Paris seemed to indicate that the French and British governments still were seeking ground for

(Continued on Page 16, Col. 6.)

### Countryside Flees From Driver Pinned Down When Auto Load of Nitro Upsets

Bradford, Pa., Oct. 6.—When an automobile truck carrying 160 quart cans of nitroglycerin went into the ditch near Duke Center today all persons in the vicinity who knew the nature of the machine's load put their hands over their ears and ran. For half an hour the truck driver was pinned under the wreckage before he was cautiously extricated. Surgeons found that he had a fractured arm and was internally injured.

## Old Settlers Fete John Daubney on 103rd Birthday

### 'Uncle John' Steps Briskly From Auto to Attend Party at Stillwater.

"Uncle John" Daubney, Minnesota's oldest man, dropped into Stillwater yesterday to celebrate his 103rd birthday with 68 white-haired men and women, all of them members of the Old Settlers' association of the St. Croix Valley and the Minnesota Territorial Pioneers' association.

Stepping briskly from the automobile which had carried him from his home in Taylors Falls to Stillwater, Uncle John shook hands with his friends, and remarked:

"I feel just as young as I did on my 100th birthday."

Completely ignoring the aid of his cane, he strolled into the dining room of the Stillwater club, took his seat at the head of the table, ate a hearty meal, and arose to exchange banter of Civil war days with his companions. Then, on the arm of the proprietor, he climbed 25 steps to the meeting room above. Finally Adam Marty of Stillwater, the president of the St. Croix Old Settlers association, requested that Uncle John "say a few words."

He arose to his feet with just a trace of stiffness, clasped his hands on the back of the chair, and began:

"Well,—I forget the year I came to Taylors Falls—"

"It was 1845, John," George H. Hazzard of St. Paul put in.

"Oh, yes, so it was, so it was. I came to Taylors Falls from the lead mines at Galena. Came up just to take a ride, and got stuck. And have been here ever since."

"I don't know of anything I could say that would be interesting. Been lumbering some, had a pretty checkered life. Camped out the first four winters driving a tote-team with supplies."

There the story of his life ended. His eyes came back from their far look and settled on the people in the room. Then he lowered himself back to the chair.

Uncle John is the last survivor of the "Forty Niners," membership in which was confined to those who were above 21 years old in 1850. Yesterday was the forty-eighth annual session of the St. Croix Old Settlers association, which meets on Uncle John's birthday.

When it came time to break up the party at a little after 4 p. m., a sudden quiet came over the members. Uncle John arose. Someone proposed that they sing "God Be With You Till We Meet Again." Voices choked, feet stirred uneasily, then they closed in and each shook hands with Uncle John. Several kissed the active veteran of 103 years as he left the room on the arm of his grand-niece, Mrs. George W. Daubney, Taylors Falls.

Wyman X. Folsom of Taylors Falls was elected president of the St. Croix Valley Old Settlers' association, replacing Adam Marty, the retiring 84-year-old president of the association.

## Weston, in 84th Year, Completes 495-Mile Jaunt

### Noted Pedestian Has Completed 92,500 Miles of Walking.

New York, Oct. 6.—Striding through the crowds assembled in City Hall park to watch the world series bulletin boards, Edward Payson Weston, the famous walker, now in his eighty-fourth year, completed today a 495 mile jaunt, begun Labor day, from Buffalo to this city. A brass band preceded the white haired champion into the city hall, where he was received by Murray Hulbert, president of the board of aldermen.

Weston grinned broadly as Mr. Hulbert reminded him of the singular appropriateness of his visit, in view of the recent decision of a Supreme court justice ordering the suspension of the municipal bus system, which, Mr. Hulbert said, would force 200,000 persons to walk to work daily.

The champion's total walking mileage over his long career, today was more than 85,000 miles in this country and 7,500 miles in England.



## Ruling Hits All Craft in Three Mile Dry Zone

### Decision Applies to American Vessels Throughout World.

### Ports Closed to Foreign-Owned Bottoms With Wet Cargoes.

### Decision Follows Parley of Harding, Lasker and Cabinet Chiefs.

Washington, Oct. 6.—(By Associated Press.—All vessels, American and foreign-owned, are prohibited from having liquor on board in American territorial waters under an interpretation of the prohibition amendment and the enforcement act handed down today by the Department of Justice. Moreover, the transportation or sale of intoxicants on American craft, wherever operated, was held to be forbidden.

American territorial waters were construed to include those not only within the three-mile limit of continental United States but also that within the same limit of the Philippines, the Hawaiian Islands, Porto Rico, the Virgin Islands and Alaska. The Panama canal zone is specifically exempted by the statute itself.

**Ruling Effective at Once.**

The sale or transportation of liquor by American ships will cease at once, or as soon as those vessels reach their home ports. The decision will become operative on foreign ships as soon as the necessary regulations can be prepared by the Treasury department.

Court action looking to a final determination of the application of American dry laws to foreign ships entering American ports was foreseen by both Attorney General Daugherty and Chairman Lasker of the Shipping board. Mr. Daugherty said he already had been advised that a case was about to be filed which would bring the issue to the Supreme court.

Chairman Lasker was of the opinion that the first move of foreign lines would be to seek an injunction restraining the government from enforcing the law. The Attorney General said his department would co-operate in every effort to expedite a ruling by the Supreme court.

**White House Parley.**

Publication of the opinion of the Department of Justice followed a White House conference to which President Harding summoned Mr. Daugherty, Secretaries Hughes and Mellon and Chairman Lasker. Various phases of the situation were discussed, including the possible results of enforcement upon the international relations of the United States.

Administration officials explained that there was no course for the executive branch of the government except to enforce the law as interpreted by the legal department. The interpretation was based upon recent decisions of the Supreme court in a case involving the authority of the United States to interfere with the transfer of a liquor cargo from one foreign ship to another in an American port.

**Divided Opinion.**

In a divided opinion the court confirmed the authority of prohibition agents to prevent such a transfer and, in the view of the Attorney General, went so far as to hold that the Eighteenth amendment and the Volstead act repealed a prior existing treaty with Great Britain.

Chairman Lasker predicted that enforcement of the law would operate to an immediate disadvantage of the American merchant marine and would make more necessary enactment of the ship subsidy bill.

An undoubted effect of enforcement, Mr. Lasker said, would be to hamper the board in building up American shipping to the Orient and South America. He expressed Vancouver, B. C., to profit at the expense, particularly of Seattle and Portland, in the Oriental trade and Montreal at the expense of New York in the South American trade. Also he looked for Montreal to gain over New York in the trans-Atlantic trade.

**Lasker Sees Blow To Shipping.**

Irrespective of the decision of the Supreme court, the Shipping board chairman said foreign ships would have an advantage over American lines. As an illustration he said that even if the court should hold that foreign ships might not bring liquor into American territorial waters, they would sell up to the three mile limit on their inward voyage and dump overboard any remaining stocks.

Sales of liquor on Shipping board vessels was based on an opinion of the general counsel of the board, who held that it did not contravene the prohibition laws.

Orders for enforcement of prohibition laws, as construed by Mr. Daugherty, were issued by President Harding late today.

**President Writes, Mellon, Lasker.**

In a letter to Secretary Mellon the President requested that due notice be given to the masters of all privately owned ships operating under the American flag and that regulations for the enforcement as to foreign ships be formulated and that such notice be given to the agents of foreign lines "touching American ports or docking therein as becomes the circumstances and commits us to the full enforcement of the law."

Writing to Mr. Lasker, the executive said the transportation and the service of intoxicating liquors on all ships owned, operated or leased by the Ship-

(Continued on Page 16, Col. 2.)

# The Minneapolis Morning Tribune

Fifty-sixth Year. No. 269. MINNEAPOLIS, MINN., SATURDAY, FEBRUARY 17, 1923 Price Two Cents in Minneapolis.


## Senate Passes DebtSettlement Measure, 70-13

### Congressional Approval of Funding Agreement Is Virtually Complete.

### Bill Is Returned to House for an Adjustment of Amendments.

### Vote Held at Seven o'Clock, After Eight Hours of Bitter Debate.

Washington, Feb. 16.—Congressional approval of the British debt funding settlement virtually was completed tonight when the Senate passed the House funding bill. The vote was 70 to 13.

The bill was returned to the House for adjustment of amendments not relating to the plan for funding the British debt of $4,604,000,000 over a term of 62 years at reduced interest rate, but providing that settlements with other debtor nations must have the approval of Congress instead of the President.

The opposition consisted of four Republicans: Senators Borah of Idaho, France of Maryland, La Follette, Wisconsin, and Norris of Nebraska, and nine Democrats: Ashurst of Arizona, Gerry of Rhode Island, Heflin of Alabama, Hitchcock of Nebraska, McKellar of Tennessee, Reed of Missouri, Trammel of Florida, Walsh of Massachusetts and Walsh of Montana.

**24 Democrats Vote Passage.**

Forty-six Republicans and 24 Democrats voted for passage of the bill. The Republicans were Ball, Brookhart, Bursum, Calder, Cameron, Capper, Colt, Couzens, Curtis, Dillingham, Ernst, Fernald, Frelinghuysen, Gooding, Hale, Harreld Johnson, Jones of Washington, Kellogg, Keyes, Lenroot, Lodge, McCormick, McCumber, McKinley, McLean, McNary, Moses, Nelson, New, Oddie, Page, Phipps, Poindexter, Reed of Pennsylvania, Shortridge, Smoot, Spencer, Stanfield, Sterling, Sutherland, Townsend, Warren, Watson, Weller and Willis.

The Democratic supporters were Bayard, Broussard, Caraway, Dial, Fletcher, George, Glass, Harrison, Jones of New Mexico, King, Myers, Overman, Owen, Pittman, Pomerene, Ransdell, Robinson, Sheppard, Shields, Smith, Stanley, Swanson, Underwood and Williams.

**Vote Follows Day of Debate.**

The vote was not reached until after 7 o'clock and after a continuous session of eight hours and a total of four days of debate. The bill was passed a week ago today by the House after one day's discussion and goes to conference with a certainty of enactment before Congress adjourns. Chairman McCumber of the finance committee, Senator Smoot, Republican, Utah, a member of the finance committee and also of the Allied debt commission, and Senator Williams, Democrat, of Mississippi, were appointed as the conferees of the Senate.

Only two important Senate amendments are in dispute between the Senate and House. These are the amendment of Senator Robinson, Democrat, of Arkansas, providing for approval by Congress instead of the President of funding agreements with other nations and one by Senator Harris, Democrat, of Georgia, providing for appointment of three Democrats on the Allied debt commission. Both were adopted by the Senate without record votes.

**Robinson Amendment Accepted.**

The Robinson amendment was accepted by administration leaders, but they opposed that of Senator Harris and said it would be dropped out in conference if it threatened to delay enactment of the legislation.

The attacks in final debate today as well as in previous discussion centered on the reduced interest provided in the British settlement. This is 3 per cent for the first 10 years and 3½ per cent thereafter. Opponents rallied finally upon the amendment of Senator Hitchcock, Democrat, of Nebraska, proposing that Great Britain should pay the same rate paid by the United States upon its securities, averaged each year.

**Interest Fight Ended.**

This was rejected 51 to 21, and ended the interest fight. Senators Reed, Democrat, of Missouri, and McKellar, Democrat, of Tennessee, prominent among the opposition, refraining from offering similar amendments. Senator Reed said the vote on the Hitchcock amendment made it apparent that the Senate intended to "swallow" the bill as it stood.

Fourteen Democrats and seven Republicans supported the Hitchcock amendment. The Democrats were Senators Ashurst, Broussard, Dial, Gerry, Harrison, Heflin, Hitchcock, McKellar, Reed, of Missouri, Smith, Stanley, Trammell, Walsh, of Massachusetts, and Walsh of Montana. The Republicans were Borah, Brookhart, Couzens, France, Johnson, La Follette and Norris. Eighteen Democrats joined the majority of Republicans in opposing the Hitchcock amendment.

**Advocates Deny Cancellation.**

Opponents of the interest rates in the British funding agreement argued that they constituted a cancellation in part of the British debt and transferred a burden estimated at $1,666,000,000 based on the 4¼ per cent rate on Liberty bonds to the American taxpayer. The advocates of the bill denied that cancellation was involved, declaring the opposition argument "preposterous," and reiterated that the British agreement was fair and the best that could be obtained.

The battle was waged all day before crowded galleries with flights of oratory. Probably the most dramatic speech was by Senator Glass, Democrat, of Virginia, former secretary of the treasury, who painted in vivid colors a picture of the British and Allied services in the war against the common enemy.

### Weather Forecast.

MINNESOTA—Fair today and tomorrow; not much change in temperature.

Additional weather on page 23.

## Splendor Dazzles Excavators as Tut-Ankh-Amen's Tomb Is Pierced

### Sarcophagus of Pharaoh Seen by Human Eyes After 3,000 Years of Darkness; Gilded Canopy Covers Coffin.

Luxor, Egypt, Feb. 16.—(By Associated Press.)—Opening of the mortuary chamber in the tomb of King Tut-Ankh-Amen today showed the sarcophagus of the pharoah to be still in the same position which it was placed by his mourners more than 3,000 years ago.

When the exploring scientists, after removing the delicate seals, broke their way through the masonry of the inner chamber door, they were confronted with splendors which, upon the first cursory examination, appear to surpass even those of the ante-chamber which have held the interest of the entire world.

**Coffin Left Undisturbed.**

The exploring party, headed by Howard Carter, exclaimed with amazement at finding the center chamber, which is about 14 feet square, occupied by an immense gilded canopy, richly inscribed.

The canopy was closed, but there was a door, and the opening of this revealed inside what is undoubtedly Tut-Ankh-Amen's coffin. For the present, however, this was left undisturbed.

A canopy jar, which probably contains the heart and other internal organs of the king was found inside the canopy.

### Carnarvon Pale as He Steps From Burial Chamber.

By H. V. Morton.

Copyright, 1923, by Public Ledger Co.

Luxor, Egypt, Feb. 16.—One of the most wonderful sights ever witnessed by Egyptologists was seen by the excavators of King Tut-Ankh-Amen's tomb today when the inner chamber was opened and they peered into the darkness. Around the great sarcophagus lay a mass of precious objects, vases, urns, statuettes and boxes with the dust of 30 centuries on them.

The lights of the three powerful electric torches flickered like white moons in the pitch darkness, illuminating sections of the painted walls where the weird gods of Egypt were pictured tending the soul of the king on its journey to the shades.

**Carnarvon Enters Chamber.**

Although 20 persons were present there was not a single sound in the dim tomb. The lights focused on the break in the wall leading to the death chamber. Hearts beat fast as the excavator-in-chief was bidden to look at that which no human eye had seen for 3,000 years. No matter how little superstitious a man may be, the act of breaking the rest so carefully guarded through the centuries must cause an emotion which time can never efface. Lord Carnarvon was pale as he stepped slowly into the darkness and was lost in the shadows of ancient Egypt.

This peep into the mummy chamber of the Pharaoh took place amidst great secrecy. Not one tourist was present and no correspondent, not even those favored by the excavators, entered the tomb.

**Impressions of Seals Taken.**

The preparations for opening the chamber began at 8:30 this morning. The impressions of the seals on the inner doorway were taken by Dr. Alan Gardiner and Professor Breasted of Chicago. The glaring electric lights were tested and the last of the timber work made ready.

The mats on which the life sized statues of the king had stood were brought out. The statues themselves had been encased to prevent damage.

The party of 20 arrived at 1:15 for the great event. It included Howard Carter, whose 20 years of work is now crowned with success; Sir William Garvin, Lord Carnarvon, Inspector Engelbrash in charge of antiquities in Upper Egypt; Director General Jacau, of Egyptian Antiquities and Soliman Pasha, Under Secretary for Public Works. Lady Evelyn Herbert, Lord Carnarvon's daughter, was the only woman present.

**Dramatic Suspense.**

The door of the outer chamber was reopened at 1:30. Cane chairs were taken into the tomb for visitors. The men removed their coats because of the stifling heat which they would experience below, and at last the party entered. A dramatic period of suspense and excitement followed. Howard Carter could be heard making a speech to the assembly in the depths of the tomb and there was a sound of handclapping at the close. Then at exactly 12 minutes to two came the first knock on the wall sealing the mummy chamber. Piercing the wall with chisels had begun.

I cannot exaggerate the indescribable weird effect of this knocking within the depths of the earth as it echoed in the still, hot hush of the afternoon through the silent valley which had so long kept its royal secret.

**Hawk Hovers Over Tomb.**

A hawk hovered over the tomb like a spirit of the old gods. "Chip, chip, chip," sounded the chisels incessantly for 20 minutes. Then a native in white pattered up the tomb steps barefooted, carrying the first stones from the wall in the inner chamber. He stacked them against the wall which had been built around the tomb.

Another half hour passed and the stone wall outside grew higher. Then the sound of chiseling ceased and the clear voice of Lady Evelyn Herbert was heard saying, "No, I can't," as some one invited her to tell if she could see anything in the gloom. This was the first sign that those within were able to look into the mummy chamber.

The sound of chisels started again and continued until 20 minutes past 2. A dead silence followed. The mummy chamber had been entered. It had taken 30 centuries to find the pharoah and only 40 minutes to break his rest.

**Carnarvon Worn Out.**

Ten minutes later Lord Carnarvon, deadly white and looking worn out with excitement and the heat of the tomb, walked slowly up the steps and sat down alone.

After a few puffs of a cigaret he re-entered the tomb, at 25 minutes past 4, after more than two hours in the tomb the party straggled up in twos and threes, pale and heated and trying to conceal what they had experienced, but their attempt was unavailing.

At last the news leaked out. Hopes had been realized. From eye witnesses it was learned that when the wall was broken the excavators looked into a high dark room, 14 feet square magnificiently painted with pictures of the gods of the underworld and covered with bands of hieroglyphic inscriptions. The paint was as bright as new and the torchlight flickered on an immense sarcohphpagus standing in center. It was impossible to move the great lid inside of which is another coffin and inside that a third in which it is believed the body of Tut-Ankh-Amen will be found.

**Carter Enters First.**

Mr. Carter went in first, with Lord Carnarvon, the under secretary of state, Lady Evelyn, and M. Lacau fol-

(Continued on Page 2, Column 4.)

### Mussolini to Act as Notary at Marriage of Princess Yolande

Rome, Feb. 16.—(By Associated Press.)—Premier Mussolini by reason of the Italian constitution will act as notary of the crown on the occasion of Princess Yolande's marriage to Capt. Count Calvi di Bergolo to take place this spring. At that time the king will confer on Premier Mussolini the order of the Annunziata, which will make him rank as a cousin to the king.

## Flames Drive Four Families From Building

### Women and Children Escape as Fire Burns Through Roof of Dwelling.

Four families were driven into the street with only a few personal belongings when a fire broke out in the roof of the four-family frame dwelling at 1513-1515 East Twenty-fifth street yesterday afternoon.

The fire had been burning for some time when it was discovered by Mrs. Harvey B. Miller, one of the tenants. Shortly after the women and children who were at home fled, the roof caved in, spreading the fire throughout the second floor.

The second floor was occupied by Mr. and Mrs. Eugene Pidgeon and their 3-year-old son, and Mr. and Mrs. Victor Hillstrom and baby. The first floor was occupied by Mr. and Mrs. Frank Watkins and Mr. and Mrs. Miller.

Both women and children on the second floor and Mrs. Miller were at home, when the latter smelled smoke and went upstairs to investigate. The women found the roof nearly eaten away by a fire in the attic.

The women notified A. Sklute, owner of the house, residing next door at 1511 East Twenty-fifth street, who called the fire department. The women collected what few belongings they could carry and left with the children. Furnishings and interior decorations were almost a total loss, according to an estimate last night. Mr. Sklute estimated damage to the building at $2,500.

## Harding Shifts FrontonBudget for Waterways

### Announces Congress Grant of $56,000,000 Will Be Carried Out.

From the Washington Bureau of The Minneapolis Tribune.

Washington, Feb. 16.—It was disclosed today that President Harding had shifted position relative to his previously announced decision to restrict the army engineers to an expenditure of only $27,000,000 of the $56,000,000 appropriated by Congress for river and harbor improvements. Since the announcement several days ago, the White House has been deluged with telegrams protesting against the curtailment of the expenditure.

Answering one of these telegrams, George B. Christian, secretary to the President, said: "The President directs me to acknowledge your telegram and to say that Congress has the sole power of determining the amount and character of expenditures on rivers and harbors improvement. The administrative government has no choice but to execute the will of Congress."

The changed position of the President assures the carrying on of construction work on the six-foot channel for the Mississippi river during the coming fiscal year as recommended by the engineers. The engineers asked $1,200,000 for the year's program.

## Man Arrested as Gang Leader in $500,000 Schoellkopf Robbery

New York, Feb. 16.—John F. Derby, alias Marshall, of Albany, was arrested tonight as the ring leader of a gang which last New Year's eve, robbed Mrs. Irene Schoellkopf of Buffalo of $500,000 of jewels as she was leaving a midnight watch party at the apartment of Frank Barrett Carman, an actor artist.

He is 29 years old. Detectives declared his arrest meant the solution of the jewel mystery.

The Schoellkopf robbery was one of the most baffling the police ever have had to deal with. Mrs. Schoellkopf, wife of Charles P. Hugo Schoellkopf, a wealthy Buffalo broker, had been one of nine guests at a New Year's eve party at the Carman apartment. She had worn a considerable part of the collection of jewels, reputed worth over a million.

## Submarine Officer Is Detailed for ZR-3

Los Angeles, Calif, Feb. 16.—Lieut. Commander Maurice R. Pierce, commander of the submarne base here, today was ordered to leave March 1 for Lakehurst, N. J., where he will assume command of a naval detachment en route to Germany to take over the ZR-3, a 750-foot airship under construction there for the United States navy.

## Explosion Razes Two Government OfficesinDublin

### Men Who Set Mines Escape—Free State Hotel Is Wrecked in Blast.

Dublin, Feb. 16.—(By Associated Press.)—The land commission offices and the government stationery office in Dublin were blown up this evening.

The mine which caused the explosion was thrust through a window by two men who were observed, but made their escape. Several persons were injured by the detonation. An ambulance man was hurt by a falling beam while searching the ruins of the building for injured persons.

A mine wrecked a large dwelling in the fashionable district, converted into a hotel for men and women supporters of the Free State. The explosion shook a nearby maternity home, where there were 200 women patients. Many became hysterical.

The historic mansion of Sir Bryan Mahon at Mullabondan, County Kildare, was destroyed by incendiaries today. Sir Bryan is a Free State senator. He was formerly commander-in-chief of the British forces in Ireland.

**Neutral Republicans Seek Truce.**

Dublin, Feb. 16.—(By Associated Press.)—The association of neutral members of the Irish Republican army, representing 20,000 members, tonight forwarded to the Free State leaders and the heads of the Republican movement proposals for a truce of a month to permit of the submission of peace negotiations.

## Sentences of Draft Obstructors Upheld

Cincinnati, Feb. 16.—The United States circuit court of appeals late today sustained the decision of the lower courts in sentencing Thomas Hammerschmidt, former Socialist candidate for mayor of Cincinnati; Lotta Burke and 11 others charged with obstructing the selective service law. Hammerschmidt was sentenced to serve 15 months in the federal penitentiary at Atlanta, while Miss Burke was given an equal number of months in the Missouri federal prison for women.

## Man, Horse Drowned Under Load of Bricks

Chicago, Feb. 16.—Weighted with a wagon load of bricks, Theodore J. Bolio was drowned with his horses in the river near the Michigan avenue bridge today. The wagon slipped down an incline on the river bank, dragging horses and driver to the bottom of the river.

## Hardings to Leave for Florida March 5 or 6

Washington, Feb. 16.—President and Mrs. Harding expect to leave Washington for their vacation in Florida, March 5 or 6, it was said at the White House today. A more definite date cannot be announced at present, it was added.

## HouseDemands Facts on Liquor Sent Embassies

### Investigation of Foreign Envoys' Supplies Is Ordered Made.

### Cramton Resolution Puts Action in Hands of Secretary Mellon.

### Representative Charges Diplomats Made Barrooms of Receptions.

Washington, Feb. 16.—An inquiry into the importation of intoxicating liquors by foreign diplomats was ordered today by the House by a vote of 189 to 113.

The inquiry is directed to Secretary Mellon, who already has informed the House judiciary committee that he could "not properly" give out the information which the House now asks for.

The resolution calling on Mr. Mellon for a statement of the amounts of liquor imports for all embassies and legations was introduced recently by Representative Cramton, Republican of Michigan, after publication of statements by police authorities that foreign diplomatic establishments here formed the source of much of the illicit liquor supply in Washington.

**Committee Discharged.**

The resolution had been referred to the judiciary committee, but the House, on Mr. Cramton's motion, today discharged that committee from further consideration of the resolution and then voted to adopt it.

Supporting his resolution, Mr. Cramton read a newspaper article which said that at a recent reception at an embassy a bar-room was established with three bartenders on duty.

"We have felt," he added, "that some embassies have abused their privileges. Certainly they ought not to make barrooms of their receptions."

**Declared to Be 'Funny Page.'**

Representative Britten, Republican of Illinois, declared the article Mr. Cramton had read was from the "funny page" of a newspaper and was "ridiculous."

"There is nothing funny about this situation," Mr. Cramton retorted. "It involves the flaunting of our laws."

He added that he was quoting from the magazine section of a paper, and not the "funny sheets."

Opposing the resolution, Representative Garrett of Tennessee, the Democratic leader, said the manner in which it had been handled was proof of the "blundering incapacity of the Republican majority since the present session began."

**May Regard It As Insult.**

"This resolution," he said, "involves the possibility that it may be regarded as an insult to foreign nations. There is nothing in it that will help the dry cause."

Declaring under the comity between nations, importations assigned to diplomats were admitted without inquiry, Mr. Garrett asked Mr. Cramton what Congress would do with the information after it was furnished.

"This whole thing will only cause friction and irritation," the Democratic leader said.

## Girl, Three, Is BurnedtoDeath

### Child, Playing With Matches While Mother Is Away, Sets Dress Afire.

Pearl Range, 3-year-old daughter of Mr. and Mrs. Edward W. Range, 2734 Queen avenue north, was burned to death yesterday when she set fire to her clothing with a match while her mother was on an errand.

Plans of the father and mother for a birthday celebration for Pearl and her baby sister, Delores, sent the mother to a neighbor's home. Pearl would have been 3 years old tomorrow and Delores will be 1. Mrs. Range mislaid her scissors and needed a pair to cut material for bedclothes for Pearl's doll bed.

The mother was gone only five minutes. Delores was asleep in the front room. She might have been in danger, but the fire was confined to Pearl's dress. Dr. C. A. Hobbs, deputy coroner, reported that the girl was suffocated. The burns, however, would have proved fatal.

Funeral services will be conducted this afternoon from the Quist undertaking rooms, 1008 West Broadway. The Rev. W. T. Christ, pastor of St. Mark's Lutheran church, where Pearl attended Sunday school, will officiate.

## Nevada Senate Passes Dry Enforcement Bill

Carson City, Nev., Feb. 16.—The state Senate today unanimously passed a prohibition bill enforcing state-wide prohibition.



## Hulk of 'Tuscan Prince' Is Found; Crew All Alive

### Men Huddled Under Bow of Steamship Wrecked on Vancouver Coast.

### Dauntless Craft Fight Heavy Atlantic Seas to Aid Sinking Vessels.

Seattle, Wash., Feb. 16.—(By Associated Press.)—The steamship Tuscan Prince, for which intensive search had been made since she flashed two messages of distress, was found this evening, a total wreck, on a small, rocky island near Village Point, Vancouver Island. Her crew of 43 men, suffering severely from exposure, were huddled on the rock at the bow of the ship.

The wreck was found by the United States coast guard cutter Snohomish, after a search lasting more than 24 hours.

Fourteen of the Tuscan Prince's crew were taken aboard the cutter and the others are to be picked up tomorrow. The Snohomish wirelessed that in returning tomorrow after completing rescue of the crew of the Tuscan Prince, she would pick up the crew of the steamship Santa Rita. The Santa Rita men, said to be short of food, have been camped on Carmanah Point, Vancouver Island, since she hit a rock early yesterday while attempting to go to the aid of the steamer Nika, which burned to the water's edge.

### Freighter Feared Lost, After Frantic S. O. S.

New York, Feb. 16.—The daring of the crews of ships seeking to aid sinking and distressed vessels was reported in wireless messages today as ice-coated trans-Atlantic boats brought to port stories of severe storms and suffering.

Four dauntless craft, fighting heavy seas, searched the Atlantic 700 miles off the Virginia Capes for the Italian freighter Moncenisio, reported sinking yesterday with her crew of 36.

**Find No Trace of Ship.**

The steamer Carpiaka, en route to Havre from New Orleans; the tanker John Worthington from Houston to England, and two coast guard cutters sought the Moncenisio but reported at dusk that they had found no trace of her.

Wireless reports from the Moncenisio were reported to have ended with a frantic "S. O. S." yesterday afternoon, and belief was expressed by mariners that she had gone down. Severe cold weather was reported from the rescue ships, and it was doubtful, they said, that the Moncenisio's crew, if in lifeboats, could survive.

**Schooner Found Sinking.**

The schooner Friendship, with a cargo of lumber for New York, was located in a sinking condition today off Oregon Inlet, 90 miles south of Virginia Beach, by the coast guard cutter Manning. The Manning reported that the seas were unusually heavy and that it was impossible to take off the Friendship's crew of seven. The Manning was standing by, however, awaiting the first opportunity for rescue. Captain G. K. Martin of Cales, Maine, commands the Friendship.

**Rum Ship Abandoned.**

The luckless British auxiliary schooner Dorin, which after having escaped from the severe storms off the New England coast, last month, was abandoned off the New Jersey coast and her crew rescued by the Lamport & Holt steamer Vasaria. The Vasaria arrived tonight with the Dorin's men. The Dorin was in the rum trade between the Bahamas and St. Pierre, Miquelon.

Coast guard cutters continued their search for a two-masted schooner reported adrift off Fire island yesterday morning. The schooner, it was reported yesterday, apparently had been abandoned. She had not been found late today.

The steamer Araguaya from Bermuda, her bridge wrecked and forward deck badly damaged, arrived today. Her commander said they had been battered by northwest gales for several days.

## William L. Waldron, Owner of Cleaning Firm, Dies Suddenly

William L. Waldron, head of the Waldron Cleaning company, died suddenly at his home, 1937 Kenwood parkway, yesterday. Death was due to heart disease.

He was active in making arrangements for the Kiwanis district conference, especially the entertainment features. When news of his death reached the conference dinner at the Leamington hotel last night, he was given a tribute of one minute of silence.

Mr. Waldron came to Minneapolis from St. Cloud 35 years ago. For 25 years he had been connected with the dry cleaning business. He was born in Norwood, N. Y., and moved to Minnesota with his parents while a child.

Mr. Waldron was a Mason, a member of Khurum Lodge, A. F. & A. M., Scottish Rite, and of the Mystic Shrine. He also was a member of the Minneapolis Athletic club, the Lafayette club, Kiwanis club and the Interlachen club. He is survived by his wife, a daughter, Virginia, two sons, William L. Waldron Jr., and Laurence D. Waldron, and a brother, Herbert Waldron of Staples.

## Larsen's Successor Named by Lutherans

Chicago, Feb. 16.—Dr. C. H. Schuette of Columbus, Ohio, was elected president of the National Lutheran Council at a meeting of the council here today to choose a successor to the late Dr. Lauritz Larsen of New York. Dr. Schuette is president of the joint synod of Ohio. Dr. G. A. Brandelle, president of Augustana synod of Rock Island, Ill., was elected vice president, succeeding Dr. Schuette, and Dr. Peter Peterson of Chicago will continue as secretary. The council represents about 1,800,000 Lutherans in America.

## French Troops DisarmGerman Police in Essen

### Chief Arrested, Headquarters Seized to Retaliate for Shooting.

### Town Is Center of Brewing Storm as Friction Follows Cafe Brawl.

### Fournier Aids Charge Security Officer Fired First Shot at Troopers.

Copyright, 1923, Universal News Service.

Brussels, Feb. 16.—It is learned from a thoroughly trustworthy source that Germany is now prepared to consider any reasonable proposal for negotiation of the reparations question.

Premier Jaspar of Belgium will see Premier Poincare Monday to try to arrive at a precise understanding of the conditions under which France and Belgium would evacuate the Ruhr.

Essen, Feb. 16.—(By Associated Press)—Essen was the storm center today in the Ruhr, where the friction between the French and the Germans has increased because of Thursday night's shooting of two French soldiers by security police in a cafe brawl.

In retaliation for this shooting, General Fournier ordered a battalion of French infantry to occupy the German police barracks. The chief of police was arrested, all the files and documents at police headquarters were taken by the French and the disarming of the police was begun.

**French Soldiers Shot.**

The shooting of the French soldiers occurred when eight of them, off duty, entered the cafe. The waiters refused to serve them because of the boycott against the French started last Monday night, and fighting immediately began.

A member of the security police appeared at the door of the cafe when the brawl began, and the French contend that he was the first person to begin shooting.

The director of the Essen electric light plant, Herr Buszmann was sentenced by the French courtmartial at Bredeney today to pay a fine of 5,000,000 marks for alleged interference with the French.

On Monday after the taking over by the French of the Kaiserhof hotel, which is the headquarters of General Coste, head of the industrial mission in the Ruhr, the director facilitated the cutting off of the hotel light when the boycott started with the waiters refusing to serve the French.

Oberburgomaster Havenstein of Oberhausen, who was arrested for disregarding French orders, also was tried by the Bredeney courtmartial for disregarding French orders. He was convicted and sentenced to two years' imprisonment.

**Crowds Gather.**

Large crowds gathered outside the building where the courtmartial was held, but the French soldiers on guard prevented close approach to the building. No serious trouble occurred.

General Fournier has notified the burgomaster's office that all Allied soldiers, as well as all Allied civilians are entitled to make purchases in the stores of Essen and to be served in restaurants and cafes, and that any keepers of such places who refuse to sell will run the risk of their places being closed or requisitioned. The Germans claim that the food situation around Bochum is serious.

Delegates from the Brandenburg People's alliance, one of the largest associations in Germany, have been meeting at Bochum with the steel representatives. It was decided at this meeting to transfer 500,000 children into the country, where many hundreds already have been sent. It was stated that the association has nearly 3,000,000 marks which have been subscribed for the benefit of children.

### Essen Vice-Mayor Fined; Sentenced Two Years.

Essen, Feb. 16.—(By Associated Press.)—Vice Lord Mayor Schaef of Essen, who was tried by the Bredeney courtmartial, charged with not supplying automobiles and coal for the troops, contended that the government to which he owed allegiance had forbidden his fulfilling such orders. He was sentenced to two years in jail and a fine of 10 million marks.

### French Presses Prepare to Print German Marks.

Paris, Feb. 16.—(By Associated Press)—France is ready under an agreement with Belgium to set her printing presses at work turning out German marks for use in the Ruhr if the German government starts a financial blockade of the occupied region, the Associated Press was informed tonight on good authority. The original plan to issue an entirely new currency guaranteed by the resources of the Ruhr has been abandoned owing to the numerous complications that would arise with two kinds of money in circulation when the final settlement comes. There have been plenty of marks to meet all requirements in the Ruhr thus far and the French officials are confident that the Germans will not oblige them to resort to the printing of marks on their own accounts.

### Appeal for U. S. Food Supplies Stirs French.

Paris, Feb. 16.—(By Associated Press)—A press dispatch from Washington saying that Dr. Otto Wiedfeldt, German ambassador, was soliciting American assistance to feed 500,000 persons starving in the occupied Ruhr district, caused a wild sensation today in French official circles.

Officials pointed out that a report on food situation in the Ruhr issued eight days ago by Dr. Tuther, burgomaster of Essen and food minister in the Cuno government, stated that the population was provided with wheat and potatoes sufficient to last until March 15.

The burgomasters of Bochum, Duisburg and Gelsenkirchen have refused to accept the establishment of French soup kitchens in their municipalities, it was added, as they said they were well able to take care of themselves.

# The Minneapolis Morning Tribune

Fifty-seventh Year. No. 71. MINNEAPOLIS, MINN., FRIDAY, AUGUST 3, 1923. Price Two Cents in Minneapolis.


# PRESIDENT HARDING DEAD FROM APOPLEXY ATTACK

## COOLIDGE BECOMES PRESIDENT

### Executive Will Take Oath of Office Today

**New Incumbent Has Been Intimately in Touch With All Phases of Administration's Work.**

Plymouth, Vt., Aug. 2.—Calvin Coolidge, vice president of the United States, was notified tonight that through the death of President Harding he succeeded to the President's chair. He will take the oath of office tomorrow morning probably before a federal judge and will then proceed to Washington there to await the arival of the funeral cortege.

The vice president was visibly affected when the news of the death of the President was conveyed to him.

President Coolidge issued the following statement early today:

"Reports have reached me which I fear are correct that President Harding is gone. The world has lost a great and good man. I mourn his loss. He was my chief and my friend.

"It will be my purpose to carry out the policies which he has begun for the service of the American people and for meeting their responsibilities wherever they may arise. For this purpose I shall seek the co-operation of all those who have been associated with the President during his term of office. These who have given their efforts to assist him I wish to remain in office that they may assist me. I have faith that God will direct the destinies of our nation."

President Coolidge sent the following telegram to Mrs. Harding:

"We offer you our deepest sympathy. May God bless you and keep you.

(Signed)
"CALVIN COOLIDGE,
"GRACE COOLIDGE."

A message from Attorney General Daughtery shortly after 11 o'clock to Vice President Coolidge suggested that he take the oath of office immediately as president of the United States.

The attorney general's telegram to Mr. Coolidge said: "I suggest you take steps immediately to take presidential oath."

Mr. and Mrs. Coolidge went to bed at 10:30 and at 12 midnight, W. A. Perkins of Bridgewater, came to the Coolidge house with a telegram and this message was read to John C. Coolidge, the vice president's father. The telegram:

"Palace Hotel, San Francisco, Calif.

"Mr. Calvin Coolidge:

"The President died instantly while conversing with members of his family at 7.30 p. m. The physician's report that death was apparently due to some brain embolism, probably apoplexy."

**Message Signed by Christian.**

The message was signed by George B. Christian, secretary.

The telegram was read to Calvin Coolidge by his father, while the vice president was in bed.

Mr. Coolidge dressed immediately and met reporters in his sitting room at 11:35.

The President has not yet decided when he will leave Plymouth. The vice president received word that he had become President of the United States while he was in a house just across the street from where he was born.

Calvin Coolidge was born on the Fourth of July, 1872, at Plymouth, Vermont. He was reared in a farming country, 12 miles from a railroad, and while his parents were far from rich, they were not poor. Young Coolidge grew up in a practical atmosphere, which though free from privation, was equally distant from luxury. His college education was at Amherst, from which institution he was graduated in 1895. He was known as a good student and in his senior year won a gold medal offered by the Sons of the American Revolution for the best essay on "The War for American Independence." This competition was open to all American colleges. He was always a close student of American history and early had a thorough grasp of its principles. Evidence of this understanding is conspicuous in his official papers and his speeches.

After graduation, he studied law in the office of Hammond & Field, Northampton, Mass. Here, likewise, he was a diligent student, and in 20 months had made such progress that he was admitted to the bar. Already his power of concentration and his mental vigor were apparent.

**Early Success in Law.**

Shortly after his admission to the bar, he opened a law office and soon achieved a local success. His first public office came by appointment. The county clerk of Hampshire county died, and the Supreme court of Massachusetts appointed him to fill the vacancy. When election time came, he refused his party's nomination for the office and resumed his practice of law.

Always possessed of a keen interest in politics, he took politics seriously. To him an office was an occasion of service rather than the fulfillment of a personal ambition. He was constitutionally incapable of playing "cheap" politics. He was totally devoid of the talents of a "mixer" or a "glad hander." Early in life he said "Nothing is worth having from politics unless you get it in the right way."

**Elected Northampton Mayor.**

In 1899 he was elected a member of the Northampton city council. In 1900 and again in 1901 he was chosen city solicitor. In these capacities he was always of a serious mind and a hard-working bent. In 1907 he was elected to the Massachusetts House of Representatives and was re-elected in 1908. His legislative services were interupted by his election as mayor of Northampton. He served in that office two years—1910 and 1911, and made an exceptional record. In view of the present financial condition of the country, it is interesting to recall that as Northampton's mayor he reduced the local tax rate in a year when state taxes were higher than they had ever been. This was regarded at the time as a remarkable achievement, and served to call immedite attention to his accurate knowledge of financial methods and his grasp of economics which are not destructive.

As mayor he familiarized himself with all departmental details; raised school teachers' salaries, reduced the city's debt $90,000, increased the size and efficiency of the police and fire departments, ran the city two years without issuing any bonds for borrowed money. His record as mayor of Northampton is important and significant. It showed at once his fitness for executive office.

**Four Years in State Senate.**

He next served four years in state senate: 1912, 1913, 1914 and 1915. He was president of the senate two years: 1914 and 1915.

His legislative record, in both the house and the senate, is conspicuous for practical legislation and a broad understanding of large problems. In the house he was prominent on the Committee on Banks and Banking. He led in codifying the state banking laws and was prominent also on the judiciary committee. Labor men were favorably interested in his lead in modifying a state law by which court injunctions were issued. It was his speech in its support which secured its acceptance by the house.

As president of the state senate he displayed notable leadership. He presided ably and won the respect of every man in that body. He showed as president notable qualities of judgment and fairness. The senate worked hard under him, and did so enthusiastically. He did not "drive." He led. This phase of his career is significant, because he has always won results by clear force of his logic and by giving wise encouragement. As senate president he demonstrated his power to get results.

**Lieutenant-Governor Three Years.**

He served three years as lieutenant governor: 1916, 1917 and 1918. In this office he maintained a high standard of political honor. He never "played politics," and won statewide esteem. He studied all state problems. It is important to note that he was preparing himself to deal with problems of state affairs. He has always been preparing for anything that might come in the future and is never unprepared.

Massachusetts has an executive council, sometimes called the Governor's Council. While Lieutenant-Governor Mr. Coolidge was chairman of the finance committee of the council. As such he was in contact with all the activities of the state committee on public safety—a war committee—and his approval was necessary for expenditure of public funds. This gave him valuable experience and benefited the state, his judgment being held in great esteem.

**Governor—Boston Police Strike.**

In 1918 he was elected governor and re-elected in November, 1919. His plurality in 1918 was about 17,000. His plurality in 1919 was about 125,000.

It was the issue of "law and order," precipitated by the Boston police strike, which gave Calvin Coolidge his great plurality. It won him support far beyond party lines. The story of the strike is briefly as follows:

The Boston police, demanding several things, but chiefly, increased pay, rearrangement of hours and station house improvements, formed a union among themselves and affiliated with the American Federation of Labor. This was done in defiance of an order from the police commissioner, Edwin U. Curtis. In issuing his order, Commissioner Curtis carried forward the policy of his predecessor in office, the late Stephen O'Meara. Commissioner Curtis suspended 19 patrolmen, said to be officials of the new police union. On the following day, September 9, about three-fourths of the Boston police left their posts. "Struck," they said. It was later labeled "desertion" by Governor Coolidge, and public opin-


(Continued on Page 2, Col. 7.)


**Weather Forecast.**

MINNESOTA—Mostly cloudy today and tomorrow, probably showers and somewhat warmer today; cooler in north portion tomorrow.


Additional weather on page 13.


1865 — Warren G. Harding — 1923

### Harding's Body Will Leave for Home on Special Train

**Guard of Enlisted Men Standing at Attention Will Conduct Remains of President to East by Way of Reno and Chicago.**

San Francisco, Aug. 2.—The body of President Harding will leave San Francisco on a special train at about 7 o'clock Friday evening and go direct to Washington by way of Reno, Ogden, Cheyenne, Omaha and Chicago.

The train will make no stops en route except those necessary for its operation. The body of the President will be borne in the rear car, probably the same in which he made the trip from the capital to the Pacific coast.

The car will be lighted at night and at all times two soldiers and two sailors, a part of a naval and military guard of 16 enlisted men, will stand at attention guarding the casket. The train will carry the presidential party as composed during the trip across the country to Alaska and also General Pershing, Attorney General Daugherty and Mr. and Mrs. E. E. Remsberg and family, Mrs. Remsberg being a sister of the President.

The body will not be taken from the hotel except to go directly to the train and there will be only the very simplest private ceremony at the hotel before it is moved.

### Harding Death Is Severe Blow to Aged Father

**Receives News After Retiring for Night in Marion Home.**

Marion, Ohio, Aug. 2.—Dr. George T. Harding, aged father of the President, is almost prostrated at the death of his son. Just as soon as the news of the President's death reached here a messenger went to the home of the President's father. Dr. Harding had just retired for the night and was only awakened after several minutes.

Miss Abigail Harding and Mrs. Carrie Votaw, sisters of the President, who have been traveling in the East, were located in Washington by Dr. Carl W. Sawyer, son of Brig. Gen. Charles E. Sawyer, personal physician of the President. They wired that they would take the first train to Marion.

**President's Brother Gets News by Radio.**

Columbus, Ohio, Aug. 2.—Dr. George T. Harding of this city received word of the death of his brother, the President, through a neighbor whose home is equipped with radio. He had the message within a few minutes after news of the President's death was flashed from San Francisco.

"Yes, I have heard that brother is dead and I am very sorry," he said when called shortly after the news was flashed.

"It seems too bad that so useful a man had to be taken. That is all I can say."

### MRS. HARDING WITH HUSBAND AS END COMES

**Nation's Leader Dies After Battle Against Pneumonia —U. S. in Mourning.**

**Presidential Headquarters, Palace Hotel, Aug. 2, (By Assd. Press)—President Harding died instantly and without warning tonight at 7:30 o'clock, (9:30 Mpls. time).**

The President was stricken by apoplexy after having almost won his fight against broncho-pneumonia and other complications.

The end came while Mrs. Harding, truly faithful until death, sat by his bedside reading to him.

Two nurses were the only other persons in the room and there was no time for a last word from the nation's leader either to his wife or to the republic he served.

A shudder shook his frame, weakened by seven days of illness and worn by a trip of 7,500 miles from Washington to Alaska and return as far as this city. He collapsed and it was over.

**Mrs. Harding Calls Physicians.**

Mrs. Harding only had time to rush to the door and call, "find Dr. Boone and the others, quick," meaning the physicians. Brigadier General Charles E. Sawyer, personal physician to the President, was in a nearby room but when he hurried into the room medical skill was useless.

Mrs. Harding was as brave and strong after the end as she had been faithful to the end. Although not strong and still affected by her illness of nearly a year ago, she declared she could not break down now and she did not break down in the hour of her greatest grief.

**Funeral Plans Indefinite.**

Arrangements for the funeral of the nation's chief were still indefinite three hours after his passing. Members of the presidential party conferring among themselves but deferring final decision until communication could be established with George B. Christian, Jr., the executive secretary who went to Los Angeles today to deliver an address for the President. It was believed probable that the funeral train would leave San Francisco tomorrow evening, either to Washington or to Marion, Ohio, on the saddest trans-continental trip in the history of the nation.

Until the departure of the train from San Francisco the body of the chief executive will remain at the Palace hotel on the top floor of which he had been since Sunday, when he was brought to the city by the Golden Gate, a sick man.

**Body to Lie in State.**

Conferences were in progress late tonight at which details of the sad trip will be worked out. It generally was believed that the body would be taken to Washington to lie in state in the Capitol rotunda, as have the bodies of several of the 28 presidents who passed before Mr. Harding.

Interment undoubtedly will be at Marion, the small city where Warren G. Harding struggled determinedly forward, first as a newspaper publisher, then as lieutenant governor, and then as United States senator, to the highest office within the gift of the American people.

**President's Last Words.**

"That's good. Go on. Read some more."

These were the last words uttered by President Harding to Mrs. Harding.

Mrs. Harding was at his bedside reading aloud when she paused and looked at the President, according to Alfred Holman, San Francisco publisher, and close personal friend of the President, who visited the sick room a few moments before the end came.

Mr. Holman told interviewers that the President's hand raised as he asked Ms. Harding to continue reading. Instantly the expression changed. He was dead.

Dr. Sawye was alone of all the doctors in the apartment when the climax came. The first was called by Mrs. Harding who then rushed to the door leading into the hotel corridors and commanded an immediate search for the other physicians.

**Bulletin Announces Death.**

The death of the nation's chief executive was announced in these words:

"The President died instantaneously and without warning and while conversing with members of his family at 7:30 p. m. Death

# The Minneapolis Sunday Tribune

*Fifty-seventh Year. No. 101.* (11) MINNEAPOLIS, MINN., SUNDAY, SEPTEMBER 2, 1923 120 Pages. *Price Six Cents in Minneapolis.*

# TOKIO IN FLAMES; MANY DIE

## *ITALIANS SEIZE TWO MORE ISLANDS; ARMY OF 5,000 IS LANDED AT CORFU*

### Greek Cabinet Falls, Is Report From Athens

Paxos and Anti Paxos Occupied by Fleet—Submarine Fires on Ship.

Roman Crowds Cheer Enthusiastically as Troops Embark for Taranto.

Warships Move to Strategic Points—Army Reservists Held in Readiness.

**London, Sept. 2.—(Universal News Service.)—An unconfirmed report from Athens states that the Donates cabinet has fallen and that Zaimis, former minister of public education, has been asked to form a new ministry.**

**Army Landed at Corfu.**

**London, Sept. 1.—Five thousand Italian troops have been landed on Corfu, says an Athens dispatch to the Exchange Telegraph. These soldiers were sent ashore from 15 naval vessels.**

The Italian government is actively engaged in military movements to exact reparations from the Greeks for the killing of the members of the Italian delimitation mission in Greek territory.

In addition to the bombardment and seizure of Corfu, where five thousand Italian soldiers have landed, the Italians have occupied the islands of Paxos and Antipaxos, of the Ionian group, lying to the south of Corfu; Italian warships are moving to strategic points and Italian reservists in various cities have been ordered to hold themselves in readiness for a call to the colors.

Greece has placed her case in the hands of the League of Nations, but the council of the league has postponed discussion of the question until Tuesday next. Meanwhile the Scandinavian and Anglo-Saxon delegates at Geneva have expressed themselves strongly in favor of the league, asserting its full prerogatives conferred on it by the covenant and taking over the settlement of the controversy.

The Italian government is opposed to the controversy going to the League of Nations, asserting that it is a controversy to be settled by Italy and Greece themselves.

### Submarine Fires on Ship; Troops Embark.

Rome, Sept. 1.—An Italian submarine has fired on the Greek steamship Gorgios in the Gulf of Gomentia, according to a dispatch late today from Athens. The Gorgios was slightly damaged, the dispatch said.

Two regiments of infantry, with units of artillery, carbineers, airplane squadrons and sanitary units, embarked today for Taranto. The detachment consisted of the Forty-seventh and Forty-eighth regiments.

Enthusiastic crowds waved farewell to the troops who sang patriotic songs as they marched through the streets.

An official statement on the bombardment of Corfu says:

"The shots from the Italian guns killed or wounded a dozen Greek citizens because the authorities had not removed the population despite warnings from the squadrons.

### Washington Holds Belief War Will Be Averted.

Washinton, Sept. 1.—Belief held in Washington from the first that a solution of the difficulties between Italy and Greece would be reached by peaceful means, was even stronger today as a result of the reports received from European capitals. Official advices, it was said, were similar to those received by the press and were considered hopeful.

Although it was admitted that the situation holds potential dangers, the view generally expressed in diplomatic circles was that an adjustment was in prospect either through the League of Nations or the good offices of some power such as Great Britain. Even if some further military moves were made, it was said that the trouble would in all probability remain localized.

During the day the State department received long dispatches from Rome and Athens which were said to contain nothing not previously published in the press. Among the inquiries received at the department was one from the near East Relief of New York which asked for the latest advices concerning conditions in the affected areas.

### Greece to Defend Self if Necessary.

Athens, Sept. 1.—(By Associated Press.)—Greece will abide by the de-

(Continued on page 2, Col. 2.)

**Weather Forecast.**

Minnesota—Generally fair today and tomorrow; slightly warmer today in southeast portion.

Additional weather on page 7, second news section.

### *London, Fearing Mussolini's Ambition, Waits League Action*

Italy Denies Seizing of Corfu Is Hostile Act, Says Occupation Is Only Provisional, Insists Dispute is 'Private'—Greece Asks Geneva Ruling.

London, Sept. 1.—(By Associated Press.)—The Near Eastern crisis pivoted today upon Geneva, where the council of the League of Nations had fortunately arranged a meeting place before it was known it would be faced by the strongest test of the league's vitality which has yet confronted it. The council went only so far as to adopt a resolution urging moderation upon the Greek and Italian governments until the council could examine the circumstances of the case.

No further belligerent events were reported during the day from reliable sources, although a rumor was current that Italians had landed on the island of Samos, but there has been an active bombardment of diplomatic statements and arguments from Rome and Athens.

**Deny Occupation Is Hostile Act.**

The Italian premier, Mussolini, telegraphed to all the powers and the League of Nations that the Italian occupation of Corfu was a provisional one, and the Italian minister in Athens informed the Greek government that it should not be regarded as a hostile act and advised that Greece should refrain from belligerency, adding that the Italian fleet would leave when Italy's demands had been complied with.

The Italian government asserts strongly that the question is not one of the League of Nations, but concerns only Greece and affects Italy's honor. The Greek government apparently adopts an attitude of helplessness; it says it is in the hands of the League of Nations and will do whatever the league decides it should do. The Greek government also says it is prepared to accept in advance any reparations demanded by the council of ambassadors.

**Protests Against Bombardment.**

Greece has protested to the powers against the bombardment of Corfu and makes the points that the Italians opened fire at 4 o'clock in the afternoon, whereas the second ultimatum was not to expire until 5 o'clock. Greece also makes the point that Corfu was not fortified. The reports of the casualties there vary from 10 killed or wounded to 15 killed.

Italian navy proceeded with the organization of Corfu in a businesslike way. Vice Admiral Simonetti was appointed governor and local police who were willing to serve were drafted into the Italian service. This proceeding is not welcomed with enthusiasm abroad, certainly not in England, for while all comments, official and by the newspapers here, with exceptions on the part of a few Liberal papers, are guarded, there is beneath the surface unmistakable uneasiness regarding Mussolini's ambitions, for the Italian premier is still a man of mystery abroad.

**Mussolini Man of Mystery.**

It is not forgotten in England that about the time of his rise to power he made a speech voicing his belief that Italy's destiny is to play a far more powerful part in the Mediterranean than heretofore.

Opportunity may be knocking so hard on Mussolini's door in the present instance that he may not be able to resist sealing Italy's domination of the Adriatic. That is the apprehension which the Italian coup at Corfu arouses. Mussolini has Italy's ancient enemy in his grasp. Will he let go completely, in response to the wishes of the other powers is a question hardly asked, but hinted. While the British and French papers draw a parallel between today and the events of the summer of 1914, there is determination in this country that no general European war shall result. The British papers express the heartiest good will toward Italy, even those who criticise her leader.

**Avoid Offending Italy.**

France appears alike with England in carefully avoiding any step of even the mildest form of intervention which might offend Italy; their ambassadors have not been instructed to make any representations to the Italian government.

This crisis arose at an opportune time for Italy in one respect. Both Great Britian and France want Italy's support in dealing with the other absorbing difficulty — the settlement of the German reparations; both have good reasons to refrain from making themselves appear cool to Italy or her real ruler. Ripples are visible on the surface of affairs, which is characteristic of European politics in delicate situations and sections of the press in both Paris and London hint that the papers of the two capitals haven't shown an attitude toward Italy as friendly as they might display.

**Downing Street Quiet.**

The precincts of Downing street give no evidence of anything stirring in world diplomacy. The prime minister is spending a vacation at a French watering place and it is said he does not intend to curtail his vacation. Lord Curzon, foreign secretary, is returning tonight from France, it is asserted, according to previous plans.

Significant naval movements are reopened. Lieutenant Colonel Amery, first lord of the admiralty, is proceeding to Malta, which is the British naval base in the Mediterranean, but he is on a tour of inspection, combined with a vacation which he announced several weeks ago.

One of the unusual features of this crisis is the lack of discussion of the crime which brought it about; the crime seems to have been almost forgotten under debate of the far reaching interest it precipitated.

### Coal Receipts at Duluth Show Gain Over 1922

30 Per Cent More Unloaded to Date Than During Entire Season.

Thirty per cent more coal has already been unloaded at the head of the lakes than was received during the entire navigation season last year, it was disclosed Saturday by the issuance of government figures on lake receipts.

Three months of navigation still remain and the total receipts promise to more than double those of last year.

Dock operators at Duluth and Superior said Saturday that the Northwest has no reason to be alarmed over a fuel shortage despite the fact that the hard coal miners are idle and that indications are that they may remain so indefinitely.

**7,501,104 Tons Unloaded.**

So far this season there has been unloaded at the coal docks at Duluth and Superior a total of 7,501,104 tons of hard and soft coal compared with 5,05,296 tons received during the shipping season in 1922.

The hard coal receipts up to Saturday amounted to 902,815 tons. This figure is about one-half of the normal seasonal receipts. At least 250,000 tons of hard coal are available at the lower ports on Lake Erie for shipment to the docks at the Head of the Lakes, it is estimated by dock operators. If this hard coal is brought up the lakes, as the operators believe it will be, the total hard coal receipts for the season would reach 1,152,815 tons.

**Plentiful Supply at Ports.**

Up to the first of this month the receipts of soft coal at the Duluth and Superior docks amounted to 6,598,289 tons. There is a plentiful supply of hard coal waiting to be moved at the Lake Erie ports, the operators say. They are confident that at least 3,500,000 tons more of bituminous coal will be brought to the Head of the Lakes before the lake freezes. That would give the Northwest 10,098,289 tons of soft coal, and would make the 1923 movement of soft coal one of the largest on record because the average yearly receipts of soft coal range from 8,000,000 to 9,500,000 tons.

In July, 282,291 tons of anthracite and 1,835,274 tons of soft coal were received at Duluth and Superior docks. In August 179,170 tons of hard coal and 1,273,341 tons of soft coal were received at these docks.

**Comparison Is Striking.**

The coal situation at the Head of the Lakes on Saturday presented a striking comparison with that of a year ago. On September 1, 1922 there were only 502,570 tons of hard and soft coal on hand, all having been brought up during the season. Of this amount only 10,562 tons of anthracite were on hand.

Even though shipments into the interior are picking up at the coal docks, it was said at Duluth Saturday that the stocks of soft coal are adequate to fill all orders. Cars are reported plentiful and operators look for a heavy movement.

### *Tellegen Engagement to Actress Confirmed*

New York, Sept. 1.—Reports that Lou Tellegen, actor, who was divorced from Geraldine Farrar on June 27, and Miss Lorna Ambler, Australian actress, were engaged to wed were confirmed tonight by Miss Ethel Walker, a friend of Miss Ambler. Miss Walker said Miss Ambler came to America from England in response to a cablegram from Tellegen. The date of the wedding has not been set, Miss Walker said, but she thought likely it would be soon after September 27, when Miss Farrar's divorce from Tellegen will become final.

### *Speaker Gillett Sails for Tour of Europe*

New York, Sept. 1. — Frederick H. Gillett of Massachusetts, speaker of the House of Representatives, sailed today on the George Washington for a six weeks' tour of Europe. He declined to discuss politics.

### *Queen Victoria of Sweden Reported Ill*

Stockholm, Sept. 1.—Queen Victoria of Sweden is ill, it was announced today at the royal palace.

### 18,112 Persons Attend Opening of State Fair

Bad Weather Fails to Dampen Enthusiasm of First Day Visitors.

Dairy and Agricultural Exhibits Prove Center of Interest.

Chairman Urges Mixed Farming in Broadcast Exposition Invitation.

The Minnesota State Fair and Northwest Dairy exposition were attended by 18,112 persons Saturday, despite the bad weather which resulted in the cancellation of the afternoon automobile race program and other outdoor features of the opening day.

The Fair will be closed to the public today.

The attendance was below that of the opening day last year, but, considering the unusually poor weather, officials were satisfied. They were confident that last years' record will be passed before the turnstiles close next Saturday night.

**Children Swell Total.**

Attendance of many children, who were admitted free under 12 years of age, helped to swell the total. About noon the skies cleared temporarily and visitors began to arrive to see the auto races, only to be met with a deluge of rain which put the track into such a poor condition that the races were finally called off shortly before 2 p. m.

The dairy and agricultural exhibits were the center of interest during most of the day and evening. Crowds also visited the Boys' and Girls' club building, where contest work in baking, canning and other projects was in progress. At the Northwest Dairy exposition building, members of the Boys' and Girls' Dairy Calf clubs exhibited their stock. Judging began in the poultry, agriculture, horticulture, and bee culture departments Saturday morning, but no decisions were announced.

**Health Lectures Delivered.**

Children's dental examination clinics, demonstrations, and lectures were held in the Public Health building during the day, and home sewing demonstrations in the Woman's building, while Dudley Crafts Watson, director of the Milwaukee Art institute, conducted gallery tours of the International Art exhibit and gave illustrated lectures. All of these features were well attended, as were the free movies of the dairying industry, shown at various places on the grounds.

The state horseshoe tournament, which was scheduled for 2 p. m., was called off because of the muddy condition of the pitching courts, and will be played off Monday, with events scheduled for that day. The Osman Temple Shrine band, which was to have given a concert before the grandstand at 6:30 p. m. played in the Woman's building instead on account of the rain, and other band concerts scheduled for outside were played in various buildings.

**Livestock Arrives from Iowa.**

Two trains of livestock in palace cars which were due Saturday from the Iowa State fair at Des Moines arrived after midnight, and will be supplemented by two other trainloads from the Wisconsin fair at Milwaukee today. With this complement, a total of more than 900 head of dairy cattle will be on exhibition at the Northwest Dairy exposition during the week, in addition to several hundred beef cattle, and the entries of the Boys' and Girls' Calf clubs.

Jule M. Hannaford, executive chairman of the exposition, formally opened it to the public Saturday morning, and later broadcast an invitation and greet-

(Continued on page 2, Col. 1.)

### Troops Guard Tulsa County From Floggers

Martial Law Becomes Stern Reality as Soldiers Patrol Roads.

Tulsa, Okla., Sept. 1.—Martial law in Tulsa county became a stern and uncompromising reality at noon today, the hour when Governor J. C. Walton's new proclamation governing military rule took effect. At one minute past noon, khaki clad soldiers were in charge of the police department and the county sheriff's office and were giving orders to civil authorities.

With the coming of night the already drab situation took on a more stern aspect. Darkness had barely fallen when army trucks sped over the city to drop small detachments of armed guardsmen at strategic points. Guards were posted at all gateways to the city and began stopping all traffic. Only those able to explain their errands were allowed to pass.

**Soldiers Patrol City.**

A score of military cars loaded with soldiers set out at nightfall on a patrol of both business and residence sections. All persons on the streets after 11:30 o'clock tonight were stopped but those whose work required passage on the street were allowed to go about their business.

Regulations governing the county were issued tonight by Adjutant General B. M. Markham. The order prohibits the sale of arms or ammunition; forbids all assemblages that may tend toward disorder; allows all places of business to remain open during the usual hours and calls on all law abiding citizens to co-operate in the military effort to bring about "the restoration of law and order."

**Civil Authorities Denounced.**

The adjutant general further declared that civil authorities have failed to bring floggers to justice and apparently have been in sympathy with their activities; that the civil authorities have "failed and refused" to co-operate with the military since its investigation was started nearly three weeks ago, and that "certain elements" of the city of Tulsa have opposed the investigation and hindered the military authorities and by so doing have been parties to a "general condition of lawlessness."

That an attempt was made late Friday night to kidnap and whip a woman resident of Tulsa was a current report Saturday. Her identity is not known but it is understood a similar attempt was made two weeks ago, shortly after martial law was declared. For some unexplained reason the would-be floggers failed both times, it was reported.

### Spanish Cabinet Forced to Quit

Opposes Plan Relative to Military Operations in Morocco.

Madrid, Sept. 1.—The Spanish cabinet presented its resignation tonight.

At the cabinet meeting preceding the resignation of the ministers, Miguel Villanueva, minister of finance, voiced strong opposition to the plan submitted by the general staff relative to the military operations in Morocco.

The minister of labor and commerce also sought to convince his colleagues that it was impossible to provide the funds necessary for the operations demanded by the general staff because of the enormous expenditures already made in this connection. The minister of public works, Rafael Gasset, disapproved of the plan because under it he would have to surrender all the funds put at his disposal for the improvement of public works.

Alvarez Valdes and Luis Armminan Albiia are mentoined for the new ministry.

## A New Daily Paper For Minneapolis

Beginning tomorrow, Monday, Sept. 3, the FAST MAIL edition of The Morning Tribune will be sold by newsboys in the city of Minneapolis, every evening excepting Saturday. It will be available throughout the Loop district and at prominent outlying corners at 9 p. m., or shortly after.

The FAST MAIL edition was created to supply Northwest cities and towns with the latest news of the world, six to 24 hours ahead of any other Twin City paper. It now will give Minneapolitans the first **complete** Sports, Markets and other news reports of the day.

The Fast Mail edition places Minneapolis on a parity with other metropolitan centers where 9 o'clock editions of morning papers have become an important unit in the daily news cycle.

New mechanical equipment, including an immense super-speed press, makes it possible for The Tribune to render this service to Minneapolis.

## U. S. Fleet Speeds to Relieve Victims

Number of Dead and Injured Incalculable as Fire, Following Quake, Sweeps Japanese Capital.

**Osaka, Sept. 2.—With the exception of the Shiba road, the whole of Tokio is burning. Part of the Imperial palace at Tokio is reported to be ablaze.**

**San Francisco., Sept. 1.—(By Associated Press.)—At 8:20 o'clock tonight the Radio Corporation received a message from its station at Tomioka which said that 700 persons were reported killed when the 12-story tower at Asakusa fell. Many boats sank in a tidal wave in the Bay of Suruga. Most of the houses at Numazu collapsed, the message said. In Tokio the Imperial railway station was swept by fire and the Imperial theater collapsed. The railway station of Ueno burned. It is rumored that the imperial palace is in danger.**

Washington, Sept. 1.—After communication with President Coolidge, the Navy department tonight ordered the commander of the Asiatic fleet to rush vessels to Yokohama for relief of sufferers from the earthquake in Japan.

Admiral Anderson, commanding the fleet, was instructed to use all possible speed in dispatching the vessels and their commanders to render every aid possible.

**Prince Regent Safe, Says Report.**

San Francisco, Calif., Sept. 1.—(By Associated Press.)—Prince Regent Hirohito and his household are safe, according to a message received here by the Radio corporation tonight from its station at Tomioka.

**Tokio Water System Wrecked.**

San Francisco, Calif., Sept. 1.—(By Associated Press.)—Tokio is afire, many of the buildings of the city have collapsed, the water system is destroyed, the loss of life is heavy, all traffic has been suspended and the flames are spreading to surrounding towns, according to a message received here tonight by the Radio Corporation of America from the superintendent of the company's station at Tomioka.

The Radio corporation tonight received from its station at Tomioka, Japan, a first-hand story of the earthquake and fire in Tokio from a refugee. The refugee said that at the first shock fires broke out at various places in the city.

The flames originated in the Mitsukoshi department store and spread to the metropolitan police board's building and the Imperial theater. These were burned to the ground, as were many other large buildings.

The city, the refugee said, is still in flames and the fire is spreading from Senju to Shinagawa. The flames can be seen seven miles away from Tokio. All railway bridges are destroyed and in many places there is no traffic at all.

The refugee said the number of dead and injured was incalculable.

**Radio Corporation Receives Message.**

The Radio Corporation received a message from a morning paper at Sendai, a large seacoast town about 200 miles north of Tokio, which read:

"Severe earthquake Tokio and vicinity at noon yesterday. Railway stations near Tokio collapsed and no means to reach Tokio. Heavy damage in Tokio. Water system destroyed and many big buildings collapsed with outbreak of fire in various places. Flames spreading toward Asakusa, Kanda, Hongo, Fukagawa and Shitaya. Heavy casualties reported. Rumor afloat that all traffic suspended throughout Tokio. Refugees running all directions.

"Principal buildings burned down are Matuzakaya department store at Ueno; 12 story tower at Asakusa; Mansiebashi railway station at Kaijo; the building occupied by the Peers club, and the Tokio arsenal.

"Many disastrous accidents have been reported, a number of trains running to Tokio have been wrecked during the quake. It also is reported that a severe tidal wave struck the coast at Yokohama. No damage western side of Shizuoka."

**Tokio Modern City.**

Tokio, capital of Japan, with a densely populated area of 40 square miles, is one of the world's largest cities. Conditions in it approximate more nearly both the crowded conditions of Occidental cities and their architectural development than any other of Japan's cities.

Until the restoration, the city was called "Yedo," and it became the capital of Japan only in comparatively recent years, the old capital being Kioto, 200 miles distant. It is perhaps the city of Japan best known to visitors from the Occidental countries, is one of the principal railway centers of the empire. Around it are numerous suburbs and pleasure gardens. The celebrations of the picturesque festivals for which Japan is noted are unusually brilliant in Tokio.

Great numbers of temples, imperial palace buildings, imposing business structures after the western model, modern railway buildings and industrial plants along most modern lines are located in the city.

**Tokio Well Situated.**

On a hill west of the city is the castle of Tokio, scene of the ancient Shogun's palace and several public offices of the old Japan. About it the old Daimos' plantations originally stood, but this area some years ago was given over virtually entire to public offices, barracks, government schools and similar structures, all of stone or brick.

Tokio is well situated on undulated ground on the shore of the Bay of Tokio and is divided into two parts by the River Sumida, emptying into the bay. It is divided into 15 wards and its suburbs into six divisions. The different industries and occupations are, to a degree, segregated to particular districts. The principal thoroughfare is the "Ginza" a wide, brick-paved street with trees on either side.

**Many Disastrous Fires.**

The density of buildings and the light wood and bamboo construction of most of the dwelling houses have made Tokio subject to a number of disastrous fires. Each of these has been seized upon as an opportunity for widening streets and making other improvements.

Of districts in which the flames are reported making headway, Kanda is a ward of the city proper, northeast of the imperial palace, which is in the approximate center of the city; Hongo is in the extreme northern part of the city in the hilly section; Asakusa and Shitaya are contiguous to the first two; Fukagawa is southward of Hungo on ground reclaimed from marshes and is much cut up with canals; and Shinagawa is a suburban town of 21,000 between Yokohama and Tokio.

### Fear Americans in Yokohama Perished.

San Francisco, Sept. 1.—(Universal News Service)—Messages filtering in tonight over broken cables and faltering radio waves carrying the news of a disastrous earthquake that is believed to have shaken all of Japan and converted many of its great cities into smouldering ruins with terrible loss of life.

Definite reports tell of flames sweeping Tokio and its suburbs from end to end, of Yokohama, the silk center of the empire, gutted by the flames that followed the earthquake, and of villages along the coast swept by a tidal wave and fire.

Osaka reported a severe and long sustained quake but little damage, as the center of the violent shake seems to be near Tokio, and the teeming district around it.

**Communication Is Broken.**

Cables to Japan and Manila are broken and meager messages are coming in via China and the South Seas, but indications are that all wire communication and railway traffic has been interrupted near Tokio and Yokohama and no news is available of what lies behind the clouds of smoke that cover the coast.

Japan tonight was cut off practically from the entire world. Except for brief messages from cities on the western edge of the empire, which seems to have been only slightly shaken, there has been no news from the country since a faltering wireless message early today told of Tokio and Yokohama and the country around the capital being a sea of flames and an inferno of destruction.

For a distance of 100 miles in all directions from Tokio, the railway and telegraph lines were wrecked and put out of commission by the quake, and even at Yokusuka, the nearest city to the outside of the fire zone, the destruction was almost complete and many were reported dead.

**Many Cities Destroyed.**

Although only meager reports have reached here of the disaster, due to the broken cables and the interrupted wireless, it is feared that many other Japanese cities besides Yokohama have been buried or burned with a huge loss of life.

Fear is also felt for the more than 1,000 Americans known to have been in Yokohama, which is the silk depot of Japan. Many Americans interested in the silk industry are stationed there, and a number of tourists also were visiting there.

The quake and fire, it is feared, will surpass in its horror that which caused heavy damage and terrible loss of life in the province of Kansu, China, in 1920.

At Gonzales University, at Victoria,

# The Minneapolis Morning Tribune

Fifty-seventh Year. No. 256. MINNEAPOLIS, MINN., MONDAY, FEBRUARY 4, 1924 Price Two Cents in Minneapolis.

# WOODROW WILSON IS DEAD

## Action on Fall's Defiance First in Senate Plan

### Oil Committee to Determine Move Before Hearing Other Witnesses.

### Gregory in Letter to President Denies Knowing of Doheny Fee.

### Declares Testimony Gave First Hint Regarding Connection.

**Washington, Feb. 3.—Albert B. Fall's challenge to the Senate oil committee, in which he disputed the authority of that body to examine him in connection with naval oil leases, resulted today in a decision by the committee to postpone the hearing of all other witnesses until the question of whether Mr. Fall will testify is definitely settled.**

The committee will not meet tomorrow, because Congress will suspend its sessions in memory of Woodrow Wilson. On Tuesday it will assemble, but will adjourn immediately to await action of the Senate on its request for reenactment of the resolution under which it has been proceeding, Mr. Fall having contended the committee's authority had expired.

A number of witnesses summoned in the inquiry are on hand to testify, including Washington brokers whose books have been subpenaed to throw light on stock market operations in oil issues, but these must await until the case of Mr. Fall is disposed of.

**Gregory Explains Position.**

Thomas W. Gregory, attorney general in the Wilson cabinet, who was one of those originally selected by President Coolidge to act as counsel in the government's oil cases, called on the President today and gave him a letter explaining his position, both in respect to possible service in the proceedings and his connection with oil interests. Mr. Gregory said in the letter that in his telephone conversations with the White House prior to the announcement of his appointment, he had no idea that he was accepting appointment or that the President had so construed it.

Mr. Gregory said also that if it had been in his mind at the time of his telephone conversation with Mr. Coolidge that he ever had been employed, directly or indirectly, by E. L. Doheny whose company holds the leases to the California oil reserves, the matter would have ended at once.

President Coolidge confirmed Mr. Gregory's understanding of the telephone conversations had with the White House as to the inferences to be drawn from the conversations.

The conference between the President and Mr. Gregory leaves the way open for the formal submission to Congress of another Democrat as a member of the special oil counsel and the name of former Senator Atlee Pomerene of Ohio will go forward within the next few days.

**Gregory's Letter.**

Mr. Gregory's letter, dated February 2, follows:

"Mr. President: On last Tuesday night when I was in Austin, Texas, you stated to me over the long distance telephone that you wished to employ me in the investigation of the leases of the naval oil reserves.

"You will recall that after expressing my appreciation, I stated that I was not in close touch with the developments in the matter; that nothing occurred to me that would prevent me from serving, but that I would be in Washington Saturday afternoon and would then confer with you on the subject. I had no idea that in saying this I was accepting an appointment or that you so understood it.

"I assumed that that would be decided when we conferred and that in the meantime I would have an opportunity to go through my books and correspondence to see whether in the course of my private practice I had ever had any employments which might stand in the way. It was also my desire before definitely committing myself to confer with Senator Walsh of Montana, who has conducted the investigation of the Senate committee.

"I was very much surprised to read in the Texas newspapers the next morning that I had been appointed, but did not feel at liberty to make any public statement, and consistently declined to do so until I had seen you.

"Of course if it had been in my mind at the time of our telephone conversation that I had been employed by Mr. Doheny, directly or indirectly, or at any time, near or remote, that would have ended the matter at once, because I would have realized that however free from criticism such employment might have been, it would have disqualified me from acting as your counsel on the present occasion.

"I have no recollection of having seen or communicated with Mr. Doheny in my life, and at that time did not recall ever having had any business connection with him or with any company controlled by him.

"I returned to Washington as quickly as possible for the purpose of keeping my engagement with you and arrived here this afternoon.

"Yesterday, while on the train, my attention was called to a statement

(Continued on Page 6, Column 1.)

### Weather Forecast

MINNESOTA—Partly cloudy and colder today; cold wave in east portion, and snow in southeast portion; tomorrow fair and continued cold, strong northerly winds in east portion today.

Additional weather on Page 9.

## *Workmen Rush Installation of Late Auto Show Exhibits*

### The Auto Show Today

9. a. m.—Doors open.
11:25 a. m. — Broadcasting from WLAG auto show branch of talk by Roscoe Saunders, representative of the Iowa Bankers' association.
2:30 to 5:30 p. m. — Dancing to music by Dan Desdune's band.
7:30 p. m.—Broadcasting and dancing.
8:30 p. m.—Style show.
9:30 p. m.—Dancing.
10:00 p. m.—Doors close.

### 15 Freight Cars Unloaded to Complete Display for Today's Visitors.

### Opening Day Attendance Is New Record, Officials Declare.

After an opening Saturday which established a record, everything is ready for the Twin City Automotive exposition to swing into its full stride today. A crew of workmen hustled all night after a delayed train from Chicago arrived with 15 baggage cars filled with automobiles, chassis and accessories. Manager Walter Wilmot announced shortly after midnight that the entire trainload of new exhibits will be "on the floor" at the show when the doors open at 9 a. m. today.

**Building Busy Place.**

The special train brought more than 30 cars, but contrary to expectations, it arrived so late that there was some doubt as to whether the additional exhibits could be unloaded and placed in time for the opening today. After a hasty conference the management decided to recruit special unloading crews and when the train reached the Minnesota Transfer late Sunday it was quickly backed into the Overland building siding where, according to Mr. Wilmot, unloading began "before the train had come to a full stop."

The Overland building was a busy place throughout the night and at midnight the management was assured that everything would be in readiness for the show today.

Although the attendance of 11,284 on Saturday was a record for an automobile show opening day, it failed to surprise the automobile men of the Twin Cities, who are convinced that the present exhibition will bring an unusual response from the public.

Today, men who are leaders in the automobile industry will begin to arrive. Among those expected is Edward S. Jordan, president of the Jordan Motor Car company of Cleveland. He will be guest of honor and principal speaker at a luncheon of the Minneapolis Association of Sales Managers at the Curtis hotel tomorrow. Mr. Jordan's subject will be "The Greatest Industry in the World."

E. V. "Eddie" Rickenbacker, famous World war ace and now president of the Rickenbacker Motor company of Detroit, also is expected today. Telegrams announcing the time of arrival of other leaders in the industry are expected this morning by the management.

**Style Review Tonight.**

Tonight the style review, arranged by E. E. Atkinson & Co., of Minneapolis and St. Paul, will open with 25 professional models and 15 girls who won beauty contests conducted by the Northwest newspapers, showing the latest creations in feminine apparel. A. L. Green, who is in charge of the review, promises women of the Northwest an opportunity to view styles in the manner of the acknowledged fashion centers of the world.

The showing of automobiles is larger than ever, with a greater variety of models on exhibition. The newer cars proved popular particularly those shown for the first time, but the old standing favorites shared the attention of motorists.

The radio show, which is installed on the second floor, with 40 exhibits of equipment, proved popular on the opening day. Programs will be broadcast from the show by WLAG every day and beginning Wednesday the afternoon dance program will be broadcast every afternoon until the end of the show.

## *Automobile Racer Killed in Los Angeles*

Los Angeles, Feb. 3.—Jimmy Craft, automobile racing driver of Detroit, was killed, and Norris Shears, Los Angeles driver, seriously injured, when Shears' car crashed into Craft's machine on a turn during a race here today.

## Coolidge Will Lead Meeting on Credit Plan

### President to Ask Speed on Measure for Relief of Northwest.

By George E. Akerson.
Tribune Staff Correspondent.

Washington, Feb. 3.—President Coolidge tomorrow will take the leadership in an effort to bring about a solution of the temporary ills of the Northwest. The chief executive is expected personally to open the conference of 80 business leaders, farmers, transportation heads, bankers and others who have been called by him to consider means for bringing about relief in the agricultural section.

All arrangements for the conference had been completed tonight, and it is apparent that every means will be put forth to bring action instead of mere discussion. The President seeks quick action. The present program calls for an opening address by the President himself before the conference is turned over to others for guidance. The executive likely will reiterate the things he recently stated in his special message to Congress, when he stressed the necessity for some governmental aid to speed up diversification in the Northwest. He will also likely repeat his pleas for some sort of refundment program, to be backed by private capital, if necessary, and to be aided by the war finance corporation.

The banking situation in the Northwest also will come in for attention.

**Dr. Coulter to Talk.**

Following the address of the President, Herbert Hoover, Secretary of Commerce, will be asked to take charge of the conference, and he will outline the purposes of the meeting. Since every man invited is presumed to know the full situation in the Northwest, no words are to be wasted on that score. Mr. Hoover is expected to ask for quick action.

Dr. John Lee Coulter, president of the North Dakota Agricultural college, has been asked to make a brief address on the situation in which the Northwest finds itself as the result of adherence to the one crop idea.

With these speeches out of the way, those of the President, Secretary Hoover and Dr. Coulter, the conference will get down to real business, and the study of the problems confronting it. The present plan calls for the formation of at least four committees and perhaps more. These committees will be asked then to take up the subjects alloted to them and retire to prepare

(Continued on Page 4, Column 1.)

## *British Premier Sends Sympathy to Mrs. Wilson*

### Calls Former President One of World's Greatest Pioneers.

London, Feb. 3.—(By Associated Press.)—The death of Woodrow Wilson will make a deep impression upon the British people tomorrow, it is not known to the great majority of the people tonight, because Sunday is a day when the English completely put aside their customary week-day interests and forget the newspapers and when the city dwellers make their exodus into the country.

The prime minister, Ramsay Macdonald, gave to The Associated Press the following statement:

"I am deeply grieved to hear of the death of ex-President Wilson, and I know that the whole of the British nation shares my feelings.

"Mr. Wilson had a fine vision of reason and wisdom in leading Europe to peace and security. It was 'the highest for earth'; too high perhaps and he has gone before its fulfillment. But 'There will never be one lost good' and in time to come the people will look back upon him and the part he played, and generous judgment will be easy, because he will be recognized as one of the world's greatest pioneers. I send the sympathies of my government to Mrs. Wilson."

## *H. P. Fletcher Grieved at Wilson Death News*

Brussels, Feb. 3. — (By Associated Press.)—Henry P. Fletcher, United States ambassador to Belgium, was deeply moved by the news of the death of President Wilson.

"Former President Wilson," said Mr. Fletcher, "takes his place immediately among the American immortals. His fame will grow as humanity struggles toward the goal of his high idealism."

## Wilson Exerted Influence on Entire World

### Acclaimed as 'Friend of Humanity' on First Trip to Europe.

### Caused Abandonment of American Policy of Isolation.

### Was Born in Staunton, Va., Dec. 28, 1856, of Scotch-Irish Parentage.

**Washington, Feb. 3.—(By Associated Press.)—Woodrow Wilson was one of the few men who by the progress of events are called upon to exert great influence on the affairs of the whole world. It was under his leadership that the United States abandoned its policy of isolation, became an active participant in European affairs, and, establishing itself as a great military power, ended the deadlock between the Allies and the Central powers, bringing Germany to defeat.**

The first Democrat since Andrew Jackson to serve two consecutive terms as president, Woodrow Wilson's career in office resembled, in some respects, that of his illustrious predecessor, although Jackson was a rough, self-willed soldier, and Wilson an intellectual, "a polished schoolmaster."

No other president ever took such a part in world affairs; no other president ever exercised such an influence upon thrones and cabinets, upon kings and premiers. He began smashing precedents almost immediately upon his induction into office by delivering his addresses in person to Congress and finished by going to Europe to attend the Peace conference.

**Task of Great Magnitude.**

His two ventures to Paris—he went first in December, 1918, and again in March, 1919—were devoted to a task of tremendous magnitude, that of peacemaker to the war weary, yet fearful nations of Europe.

He declared that the United States could no longer hold aloof, that it was a world power and, as such, must take its place at the peace table in the endeavor to help solve the world problems that were pressing for solution. He said the United States sought "no conquered territory," nor inequitable indemnity, but that its sole desire was to restore law and order and help bind up every nation's wounds.

Upon his first trip to Paris he was everywhere acclaimed as "the friend of humanity" and the man who had come to put "an end to all wars." No monarch of ancient times was ever accorded greater laudation or listened to with greater admiration. It seemed as if all Europe hung upon the words that fell from his lips. He was acclaimed as a practical idealist, the representative of a mighty new land, whose people were altruistic and unselfish and who desired to see the devastated world restored to amity and happiness.

**Fourteen Points Presented.**

Before his departure, in an address to Congress, he repeated his famous "fourteen points" which, he said, constituted America's interest in the forthcoming council at Versailles. Presentation of these "points," one of which provided for a League of Nations covenant, precipitated a bitter controversy in Congress which lasted for many months. It engendered such opposition to the president's plans that upon his return to Europe on the second stage of his mission he was less cordially received. Especially was this the case in certain parts of Italy where, because of his attitude on Fiume, his name was hissed. French newspapers also excoriated him and he was de-

(Continued on Page 3, Column 1.)



1856—Woodrow Wilson—1924

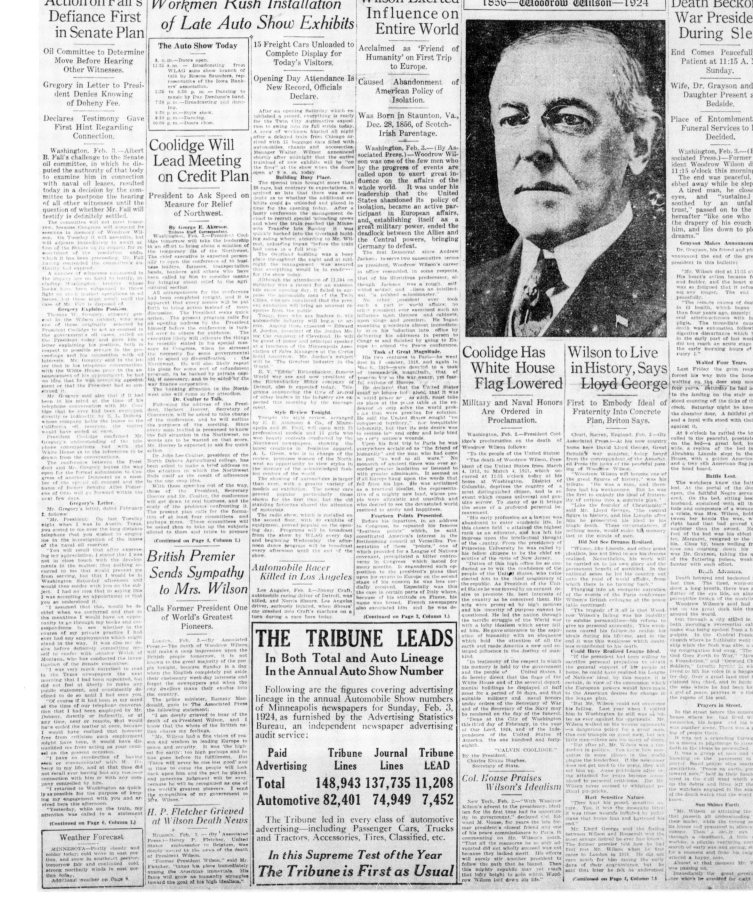

## Coolidge Has White House Flag Lowered

### Military and Naval Honors Are Ordered in Proclamation.

Washington, Feb. 3.—President Coolidge's proclamation on the death of Woodrow Wilson follows:

"To the people of the United States:

"The death of Woodrow Wilson, President of the United States from March 4, 1913, to March 4, 1921, which occurred at 11:15 o'clock today at his home at Washington, District of Columbia, deprives the country of a most distinguished citizen, and is an event which causes universal and genuine sorrow. To many of us it brings the sense of a profound personal bereavement.

"His early profession as a lawyer was abandoned to enter academic life. In this chosen field he attained the highest rank as an educator, and has left his impress upon the intellectual thought of the country. From the presidency of Princeton University he was called by his fellow citizens to be the chief executive of the state of New Jersey.

"Duties of this high office he so conducted as to win the confidence of the people of the United States, who twice elected him to the chief magistracy of the republic. As President of the United States he was moved by an earnest desire to promote the best interests of the country as he conceived them. His acts were prompted by high motives and his sincerity of purpose cannot be questioned. He led the nation through the terrific struggle of the World war with a lofty idealism which never failed him. He gave utterance to the aspiration of humanity with an eloquence which held the attention of all the earth and made America a new and enlarged influence in the destiny of mankind.

"In testimony of the respect in which his memory is held by the government and the people of the United States, I do hereby direct that the flags of the White House and of the several departmental buildings be displayed at half mast for a period of 30 days, and that suitable military and naval honors under orders of the Secretary of War and of the Secretary of the Navy may be rendered on the day of the funeral.

"Done at the City of Washington this third day of February, in the year of Our Lord, 1924, and of the Independence of the United States of America the one hundred and forty-eighth.

"CALVIN COOLIDGE."

By the President,
Charles Evans Hughes,
Secretary of State.

## *Col. House Praises Wilson's Idealism*

New York, Feb. 2.—"With Woodrow Wilson's advent to the presidency, idealism for the first time had its opportunity in government," declared Col. Edward M. House, for years the late former president's closest friend and one of his peace commissioners to Paris, in commenting on Mr. Wilson's death. "That all the measures he so ably advocated did not wholly succeed was not because they lacked merit. His efforts will surely stir another president to follow the path that he blazed. Then this mighty republic may yet reach that lofty height to gain which Woodrow Wilson laid down his life."

## Wilson to Live in History, Says Lloyd George

### First to Embody Ideal of Fraternity Into Concrete Plan, Briton Says.

Churt, Surrey, England, Feb. 3.—(By Associated Press.)—At his new country home here David Lloyd George, Great Britain's war minister, today heard from the correspondent of the Associated Press the news of the peaceful passing of Woodrow Wilson.

"Woodrow Wilson will become one of the great figures of history," was his tribute. "He was a man, and therefore had his weaknesses. But he was the first to embody the ideal of fraternity of nations into a concrete plan."

"Like the founder of Christianity," said Mr. Lloyd George, "the central figure in history, and like Lincoln after him he prosecuted his ideal to his tragic death. These circumstances, if nothing more, would make his memory last in the minds of men.

**Did Not See Dreams Realized.**

"Wilson, like Lincoln, and other great idealists, has not lived to see his dreams realized. Nevertheless, his work will be carried on to his own glory and the permanent benefit of mankind. In the national sense he led his country out onto the road of world affairs, from which there is no turning back."

Plunging into an energetic narration of the events of the Paris conference Wilson's British colleague at the peace table continued:

"The tragedy of it all is that Woodrow Wilson's failing was his inability to subdue personalities—his refusal to give up personal animosity. This weakness caused his failure to realize his ideals during his lifetime, and in the end it was this weakness which doubtless contributed to his death.

**Could Have Realized League Ideal.**

"If the president had been willing to sacrifice personal prejudices to obtain the general support of his people at home, he could have realized his League of Nations' ideal, by this means, it is certain, in view of the concession which the European powers would have made to the American desires for change in the league plan.

"But Mr. Wilson could not overcome his failing. Last year when I visited him in Washington he still was as bitter as ever against his opponents. Mr. Wilson walked on his weaker opponents—a dangerous policy for a great man. One can trample on great men, but not little men—there are too many of them.

"But after all, Mr. Wilson was a tenderfoot in politics. You know how mosquitos in some places in the world plague the tenderfoot. If the newcomer does not get used to the pests, they will eat him up. Some politicians after being attacked for years become innoculated to personal criticisms. But Mr. Wilson never seemed to withstand political pin pricks.

**Hurt Sensitive Nature.**

"They hurt his proud, sensitive nature. Yes, it was the mosquito bites; it was those wounds inflicted by politicians that broke him and hastened his end."

Mr. Lloyd George said the feeling between Wilson and Roosevelt was the most savage hatred he ever had known. The former premier told how he had first met Mr. Wilson when he first came to London in 1918. He did not care much for him during the early days of their acquaintance, but he said that later he felt he understood

(Continued on Page 4, Column 1.)

## Death Beckons War President During Sleep

### End Comes Peacefully to Patient at 11:15 A. M. Sunday.

### Wife, Dr. Grayson and One Daughter Present at Bedside.

### Place of Entombment and Funeral Services to Be Decided.

**Washington, Feb. 3.—(By Associated Press.)—Former President Woodrow Wilson died at 11:15 o'clock this morning.**

**The end was peaceful. Life ebbed away while he slept.**

**A tired man, he closed his eyes, and "sustained and soothed by an unfaltering trust," passed on to the great hereafter "like one who wraps the drapery of his couch about him, and lies down to pleasant dreams."**

**Grayson Makes Announcement.**

Dr. Grayson, his friend and physician, announced the end of the great war president in this bulletin:

"Mr. Wilson died at 11:15 o'clock. His heart's action became feebler and feebler, and the heart muscle was so fatigued that it refused to act any longer. The end came peacefully.

"The remote causes of death lie in ill health, which began more than four years ago, namely: General arterio-sclerosis with haemoplegia. The immediate cause of death was exhaustion following a digestive disturbance which began in the early part of last week but did not reach an acute stage until the early morning hours of February 1."

**Waited Four Years.**

Last Friday the grim reaper had forced his way into the house after waiting on the door step more than four years. Saturday he had advanced to the landing on the stair case and stood counting off the ticks of the great clock. Saturday night he knocked on the chamber door. A faithful physician and a loyal wife stood with their backs against it.

At 9 o'clock he rattled the knob and called to the peaceful, prostrate figure on the bed—a great bed, long and wide, a replica of the bed in which Abraham Lincoln slept in the White House, with a golden American eagle and a tiny silk American flag just over the head board.

**Battle Lost.**

The watchers knew the battle was lost. At the portal of the door, now open, the faithful Negro servant hovered. On the bed, sitting beside her husband, sustained with all the fortitude and composure of a woman facing a crisis, was Mrs. Wilson, holding between her hands the wan, withered, right hand that had proved the pen mightier than the sword. Near the foot of the bed was his eldest daughter, Margaret, resigned to the inevitable. Close by, tears welling from his eyes and coursing down his cheeks, was Dr. Grayson, taking the measure of the fluttering pulses, weaker and fainter with each effort.

**Death Advances.**

Death hovered and beckoned for the last time. The tired, worn-out man drew a long breath, there was a slight flutter of the eye lids, an almost imperceptible twitch of the nostrils.

Woodrow Wilson's soul had drifted out on the great dark tide that runs around the world.

Out through a city stilled in a Sabbath morning's reverential calm, his name was being spoken from a hundred pulpits. In the Central Presbyterian church where he faithfully went to worship while the flesh was able, a choked-up congregation had sung, "The Son of God Goes Forth to War," "How Firm a Foundation," and "Onward Christian Soldiers," favorite hymns in which he loved to lift his voice in a happier, better day. Over a great land that had acclaimed him chief, and in lands across the seas where he had been hailed as a god of peace, prayers were rising for the repose of his soul.

**Prayers in Street.**

In the street before the square brick house where he had lived with his memories, his hopes and his regrets, was another scene. There was a gathering of people there.

It was not a crusading throng come to a mecca in pilgrimage to attest their faith in the ideals he personified.

It was a group of men and women kneeling on the pavement in silent prayer. Small prayer slips bearing the inscription, "Peace on earth, good will toward men," held in their hands, fluttered in the chill wind which swirled up the debris and litter left there by the watchers engaged in the solemnity of the death watch that the world might know.

**Sun Shines Forth.**

"Mr. Wilson is attaining the peace that passeth all understanding," said their leader, while the throng sank to its knees and remained in silence for a minute. Then a sickly sun broke through a cloudbank. A little native warbler, a pilgrim venturing north in search of early sun and spring, stopped for a moment and from his twig aloft uttered a happy note.

Almost at that moment Mr. Wilson was passing on.

Immediately the great government over which he presided for eight years

Markets **THE MINNEAPOLIS JOURNAL** Markets

Associated Press—United Press—Chicago Tribune Foreign Service

36 PAGES—HOME EDITION • WEATHER—Unsettled tonight and Thursday, probably some snow; much colder tonight. WEDNESDAY EVENING, NOVEMBER 5, 1924. PRICE TWO CENTS IN MINNEAPOLIS.

# CHRISTIANSON APPARENTLY ELECTED

# Coolidge Gets Biggest Popular Vote in U. S. History

## LA FOLLETTE RUNS POOR THIRD; LABOR DESERTS SENATOR

**President Given 374 Votes in Electoral College—Majority May Go to 224**

**G. O. P. NOMINEES WIN IN OLDTIME LANDSLIDE**

**Republican National Ticket Sweeps Country With Exception of Solid South**

By ARTHUR SEARS HENNING

Chicago, Nov. 5.—Calvin Coolidge, who was elected president yesterday in an old-time republican landslide, polled 18,000,000 votes, the largest popular vote ever given a presidential candidate in the nation's history.

Senator Robert M. La Follette, radical, who ran a poor third in the presidential race, polled 4,000,000 votes, while John W. Davis, the democratic standard bearer, got twice as many as La Follette, his popular vote being 8,000,000.

**Coolidge Breaks Harding Mark**

Coolidge's record popular vote was 2,000,000 greater than that given the late President Harding four years ago. Davis' popular vote fell 1,000,000 below that of James M. Cox, the democratic standard bearer who got 9,000,000 in 1920.

Despite La Follette's vote of 4,000,000, which approximates that of Theodore Roosevelt when he led the third party movement in 1916, La Follette apparently has only carried one state, Wisconsin, his home.

The heaviest vote in the history of the nation was polled yesterday.

**Coolidge Sweeps Nation**

From Maine to California and from the Canadian border southward across the Mason and Dixon line an avalanche of votes, varying here and there only in degree, swept the republican national ticket to overwhelming victory over the democratic and La Follette third parties combined.

The indications were that the total electoral vote for President Coolidge would be found approximating 379 when the returns are complete. That would give Coolidge the enormous majority of 224 in the electoral college.

**For Coolidge 374.**
**For Davis 139.**
**For La Follette 13.**
**Doubtful 5.**

Outside of the democratic solid south the choice of President Coolidge to succeed himself and of General Charles G. Dawes for vicepresident was almost unanimous and even the traditional stronghold of the Jeffersonians was severely shaken in its political allegiance. While Tennessee, which Harding carried, remained steadfast to democracy this time, Kentucky appeared in the latest returns to have strayed into the republican fold.

Both J. W. Davis, the democratic candidate, and Senator La Follette, leader of the third party, were ignominiously routed. In an election in which the fundamental issue was conservatism vs. radicalism, the result revealed radicalism snowed under and a decided preference registered for that one of the two conservative candidates who had made no compromise with radicalism.

**La Follette Badly Beaten**

La Follette, the apostle of discontent, showed up at the finish with a scant handful of electoral votes, while Mr. Davis, running little better than Cox four years ago, had only a handful outside of the southern block.

Democratic National Chairman Clem Shaver refused to concede defeat even in the face of the abundant testimony of the landslide for Coolidge.

Senator La Follette declined to comment, but his national manager, John M. Nelson, admitted it looked like a landslide for Coolidge, asserting in the same breath that the third party still lives and immediately will begin preparations for the elections of 1926 and 1928.

**Labor Deserts La Follette**

The La Follette candidacy proved a fizzle, not only in the electoral but in the popular vote. Neither the working men, nor the discontented farmers now the German-Americans nor any other of the promised aggregations of disgruntled citizens came through for Battling Bob in anywhere near the numbers expected. The La Follette boom was a dud. In nearly every state where it had been predicted he would run second to Coolidge, Davis ran second and La Follette a poor third.

The "silent vote," on which Davis and La Follette were relying for victory or at least for enough support to cause the projection of the election into congress, turns out to have been cast for "Silent Cal."

The east and the middle west, with the exception of Wisconsin, the only state it now can be said with certainty La Follette carried, were a unit for Coolidge and west of the Mississippi where La Follette was supposed to be supreme it turned out that the taciturn man in the White House was the farmers' fair haired boy.

Throughout the night of tabulations of returns Minnesota and Missouri remained the most important doubtful states, the former being the scene of a hard fought battle between Coolidge and La Follette, the latter being in dispute between Coolidge and Davis. Today the indications were that the President had carried Minnesota and was conceded Missouri.

California went overwhelmingly for Coolidge and Washington was found lashed to the republican chariot after all, making the Pacific coast solid for the G. O. P. Kansas outdid itself in rolling up its Coolidge plurality.

Take it every way you can possibly look at it, the election of Mr. Coolidge constitutes the most extraordinary, the

Continued on Page 2.

**ELECTED IN LANDSLIDE**

CALVIN COOLIDGE

CHARLES G. DAWES

## Brookhart Trails Steck by 6,515; Defeat Predicted

**Democrat Maintains Steady Lead With All but 400 Precincts Out of 2,418 in State Reported**

By Associated Press.

Des Moines, Nov. 5.—The defeat of Senator Smith W. Brookhart, to whom most of Iowa's political leaders had, before the election, conceded a comparatively easy victory, appeared on the face of unofficial returns today to have been accomplished by Daniel F. Steck, an Ottumwa attorney.

Senator Brookhart refused to concede defeat, as also did his campaign manager, L. H. Cook, but republican leaders, including B. B. Burnquist, state central committee chairman, declared the unofficial returns seemed to leave little doubt that Steck had been successuf. Returns from 2,113 precincts out of 2,418 in Iowa for United States senator gave Brookhart (rep.) 379,065; Steck (dem.) 385,580, a lead of 6,515 for Steck. The missing precincts were scattered through two dozen counties, most of which are largely rural. In most of the counties where numerous city precincts were outstanding, Steck had been leading for hours.

The democratic candidate had been more than 5,000 in the lead since midnight and maintaining a steady increase in city as well as rural counties.

Brookhart's followers today regarded Steck's strength as the result of a combination of this "regular" republican faction, which had in the last few weeks appealed to the voters to scratch their ballots in favor of the democratic candidate, and to the strenuous campaign carried on by the democratic leaders.

The unexpected strength of President Coolidge also was believed to have some bearing because of the passive alignment of Brookhart with La Follette and thes enator's renunciation of the heads of his own thicket—Coolidge and Dawes.

All through the night the race was close, the lead at first alternating, then remaining wih Stock through the early morning, with nearly every county report boosting his lead slightly. This seemed to indicate that the rural precincts, always the last to report, were fairly evenly divided—unexpectedly so.

In county after county, where Brookhart has been accustomed to large majorities, Steck either led or trainel closely.

Senator Brookhart aparently lost his own county and his home city. Washington gave Steck a majority in all four wards. Brookhart's own precinct was carried by him by only 12 votes.

### *Senator Walsh Holds Lead in Montana*

Helena, Mont., Nov. 5.—President Coolidge maintained more than a 2 to 1 lead in Montana on the face of returns available early today. In 376 complete and 28 incomplete precincts out of 1,533 in the state, the vote stood:

Coolidge, 28,889; Davis, 13,502, and 21,748 for La Follette.

For the senate, T. J. Walsh, incumbent, had 31,967; Frank Linderman, republican, 27,241.

For governor, Dixon, republican, incumbent, 22,974; J. E. Erickson, democrat, 28,388.

On the basis of the returns, the pluralities of Coolidge and Walsh are put between 12,500 and 13,000 and of Erickson at 10,000.

## WHERE TO FIND OTHER NEWS OF THE ELECTION



## HOW ELECTORAL VOTES WILL GO

| | Coolidge | Davis | La Follette | Doubtful |
|---|---|---|---|---|
| Alabama | .. | 12 | .. | .. |
| Arizona | 3 | .. | .. | .. |
| Arkansas | .. | 9 | .. | .. |
| California | 13 | .. | .. | .. |
| Colorado | 6 | .. | .. | .. |
| Connecticut | 7 | .. | .. | .. |
| Delaware | 3 | .. | .. | .. |
| Florida | .. | 6 | .. | .. |
| Georgia | .. | 14 | .. | .. |
| Idaho | 4 | .. | .. | .. |
| Illinois | 29 | .. | .. | .. |
| Indiana | 15 | .. | .. | .. |
| Iowa | 13 | .. | .. | .. |
| Kansas | 10 | .. | .. | .. |
| Kentucky | 13 | .. | .. | .. |
| Louisiana | .. | 10 | .. | .. |
| Maine | 6 | .. | .. | .. |
| Maryland | 8 | .. | .. | .. |
| Massachusetts | 18 | .. | .. | .. |
| Michigan | 15 | .. | .. | .. |
| Minnesota | 12 | .. | .. | .. |
| Mississippi | .. | 10 | .. | .. |
| Missouri | 18 | .. | .. | .. |
| Montana | 4 | .. | .. | .. |
| Nebraska | 8 | .. | .. | .. |
| Nevada | 3 | .. | .. | .. |
| New Hampshire | 4 | .. | .. | .. |
| New Jersey | 14 | .. | .. | .. |
| New Mexico | .. | 3 | .. | .. |
| New York | 45 | .. | .. | .. |
| North Carolina | .. | 12 | .. | .. |
| North Dakota | .. | .. | .. | 5 |
| Ohio | 24 | .. | .. | .. |
| Oklahoma | .. | 10 | .. | .. |
| Oregon | 5 | .. | .. | .. |
| Pennsylvania | 38 | .. | .. | .. |
| Rhode Island | 5 | .. | .. | .. |
| South Carolina | .. | 9 | .. | .. |
| South Dakota | 5 | .. | .. | .. |
| Tennessee | .. | 12 | .. | .. |
| Texas | .. | 20 | .. | .. |
| Utah | 4 | .. | .. | .. |
| Vermont | 4 | .. | .. | .. |
| Virginia | .. | 12 | .. | .. |
| Washington | 7 | .. | .. | .. |
| West Virginia | 8 | .. | .. | .. |
| Wisconsin | .. | .. | 13 | .. |
| Wyoming | 3 | .. | .. | .. |
| Total | 374 | 139 | 13 | 5 |

## PRESENT SUPREME JUDGES HOLD LEAD

**Vote in 440 Precincts Is Wilson 51,631, Holt 43,742 and Stone 39,776**

Sitting members of the State Supreme Court were leading today on returns from over the state.

The vote on chief justice from 440 precincts gave Chief Justice Samuel B. Wilson 51,631 votes to 39,579 for Judge Albert Johnson.

The same precincts, on associate justices, gave Andrew Holt, 43,742; Royal A. Stone, 39,776; W. A. Anderson, 30,287, and Thomas Fraser, 28,238.

### *Pine Leads Walton, Foe Of Klan in Oklahoma*

By Associated Press.

Oklahoma City, Nov. 5.—Oklahoma followed the solid south into the Davis column in yesterday's election, but apparently the democrats have lost a seat in the United States Senate.

Belated returns increased the democratic presidential candidate's plurality to approximately 25,000 while piling up a majority of almost 90,000 for W. B. Pine, republican senatorial aspirant over J. C. Walton, democrat, former governor, who based his campaign upon an intensive fight on the Ku Klux Klan.

For the second time in its history Oklahoma had seemingly elected a republican to the United States Senate.

### *Davis Congratulates Coolidge on Victory*

Washington, Nov. 5.—John W. Davis today congratulated President Coolidge on his election to the presidency.

"Permit me to congratulate you," Mr. Davis telegraphed, "on your sweeping victory, and to express the hope that your administration may, by its success, insure the welfare of the country."

President Coolidge sent this reply: "Please accept my thanks for your message and my appreciation of the patriotic sentiments you express."

## REPUBLICANS HAVE CHANCE FOR ACTUAL CONGRESS CONTROL

**Apparent Net Gain of 12 in the House and Three or Four in the Senate**

**COLORADO G. O. P. WINS BOTH SEATS IN SENATE**

**Ballot Count Spells General Disaster for Radicals in Both Branches of Congress**

By Associated Press.

New York, Nov. 5.—With returns in from 346 of the 435 congressional districts and 19 of the 34 senatorial contests, uncertainty continued today as to whether the sweep for Coolidge and Dawes would carry with it enough republican gains in the two houses to give the president a full working majority in congress. With 183 republicans and 163 democrats elected to the house the net turnover had been only 12 in favor of the republicans, or five less than normally would enable the majority party representatives to control over opposition by the La Follette bloc. Nine democratic senators were re-elected and 10 republicans with only one upset, that in Kentucky, where Fred M. Sackett, republican, won over Senator A. Owsley Stanley. The republican nominees are leading their democratic opponents in several other states, including Massachusetts, Oklahoma and Delaware.

Washington, Nov. 5.—Control of both houses of congress by administration republicans seems to be in prospect.

The Coolidge landslide made almost a clean sweep in the senatorial election and latest returns indicate that the radical group has been dislodged from power in the senate as well as in the house.

Out of 14 doubtful senatorial contests the republicans appear to have won 12, their victories being more sweeping than any of their managers had dared to predict.

The republicans were running ahead in Colorado, where the seats have been held by, one republican and one democrat.

The surprisingly good showing made by Coolidge in Minnesota indicated a possible gain in Minnesota and the retirement of Senator Magnus Johnson, radical farmer-laborite.

**Brookhart's Defeat Seen**

In addition the wave of sentiment for Coolidge and against the radical republicans seems to have carried to defeat Senator Smith Brookhart (rep., Iowa). With about half of the precincts heard from, D. F. Steck, democratic nominee, was leading by about 5,000. Senator Brookhart, who has been one of the most conspicuous of the La Follette group, had been considered certain of re-election.

The radicals met disaster all along the line.

Of three La Follette senators running for re-election, Senator Norris (rep., Neb.) was the only one whose election was assured.

L. D. Tyson, democratic nominee, won handsomely over H. B. Lindsay, the republican candidate, in Tennessee. Senator A. O. Stanley (dem., Ky.) was defeated by Fred M. Sackett, republican nominee in Kentucky.

**G. O. P. Gains in Colorado**

The two republican victories in Colorado, indicated as likely by early returns, would be among the most important of the election. Senator L. C. Phipps, republican, was leading Senator Adams, democrat, for the long term, while Rice W. Means, republican nominee, was leading Morris Shafroth, the candidate of the democrats for the short term. The La Follette radicals were helping the democrats.

Indicatins are that there may be 52 or 53 republicans in the senate instead of 51 as at present. Forty-nine constitute a majority. Of the republicans, five are counted as consistent La Follette men, while two or three others are in the wobbly class. There will be from 46 to 42 democrats and one or two farmer-labor members.

**Get Control in House**

The incomplete returns showed almost a nominal republican majority in the house definitely elected. A majority requires 218 of the 435 members. It seemed a certainty that final figures would show more than 235 republicans. With this total the regular republicans would barely control after eliminating about 15 La Follette supporters. In view of the heavy Coolidge vote it was considered entirely possible that the republican total might run close to 250. On the basis of partial returns, 155 democrats were definitely elected together with at least two farmer-labor members and one or more socialists.

In the present house there have been 225 republicans, 207 democrats, two farmer-laborites and one socialist. Returns were missing on Minnesota districts, but it was expected that two or more farmer-labor nominees would be elected.

### *Berger Trails Braun For Congressman*

Milwaukee, Nov. 5.—On the basis of unofficial returns and with four precincts missing in the fifth district, Congressman Victor L. Berger (soc.) is trailing E. A. Braun (rep.). The vote at noon was Berger 29,970, Braun 30,029. Three of the missing precincts are in the fifteenth ward, where Braun is making a strong run, and one precinct in the twenty-second ward, in which Braun also is outdistancing Berger.

**TICKET LEADERS' MAJORITIES GROW**

THEODORE CHRISTIANSON

THOMAS D. SCHALL

## LEADING IN STATE

### *State Offices*

Governor—Theodore Christianson (rep.).

United States Senator—Thomas D. Schall (rep.).

Lieutenant Governor—W. I. Nolan (Rep.).

Secretary of State—Mike Holm (rep.).

State Treasurer—Henry Rines (Rep.).

Attorney General—Clifford L. Hilton (rep.).

Railroad and Warehouse Commissioner—Frank W. Natson (rep.).

Chief Justice—Samuel B. Wilson.

Associate Justices—Andrew Holt, Royal A. Stone.

### *Congressional*

First District—Allen J. Furlow (rep.).

Second District—Frank Clague (rep.).

Third District—A. H. Andresen (rep.).

Fourth District—Oscar E. Keller (rep.).

Fifth District—Walter H. Newton (rep.).

Sixth District—Harold Knutson (rep.).

Seventh District—O. J. Kvale (farmer-labor).

Eighth District—Victor Power (rep.)

Ninth District—F. H. Peterson (rep.)

Tenth District—Godfrey G. Goodwin (rep.).

### *Legislature*

Twenty-eighth District—John F. Bowers and Joseph Kozlak.

Twenty-ninth District — Louis Duemke and Wilbur L. Paulson.

Thirtieth District—Frank E. Nimocks and Mabeth Hurd Paige.

Thirty-first District—W. D. Washburn and Sumner T. McKnight.

Thirty-second District—Otto D. Nellermoe and Arthur T. Nelson.

Thirty-third District—W. I. Norton and John E. Stevens.

Thirty-fourth District—Ewin L. MacLean and L. E. Brophey.

Thirty-fifth District—Harry A. Montgomery and Erling Swenson.

### *White Third in Race For Kansas Governor*

By Associated Press.

Topeka, Kan., Nov. 5.—William Allen White, who entered the Kansas gubernatorial race as an independent on an avowed antiklan platform, ran far behind the successful candidate, Ben S. Paulen, republican, and today, with half the state's precincts reported, was trailing Governor Jonathan M. Davis, democrat, by 15,000 votes.

Returns from 1,282 precincts, out of 2,591, gave Paulen 155,783; Davis, 88,049; White, 37,076.

The Emporia editor waged a campaign unique in the annals of American politics. Before the balloting he expressed "fear" that he would be elected, declaring he made the race as a "duty" and preferred his editorial desk to the governor's chair.

## MINNEAPOLIS TURNS DOWN ELEVATOR

**Other Constitutional Amendments Get Big Majorities Here, Returns Indicate**

All proposed amendments to the state constitution except the proposal for state owned grain elevators were given big majorities on the basis of first returns from Minneapolis, where tabulations were complete in 55 districts.

The gasoline tax amendment had the biggest total, 18,356 for it and 5,572 against.

The forest fire prevention amendment counted 14,874 to 6,058, and the reforestation amendment scored heavily with 15,659 to 4,359.

Only the radical grain elevator amendment suffered at the hands of Minneapolis voters. It had 7,967 votes to 10,205 against it.

**STORE ROBBER SENTENCED**

Fergus Falls, Minn., Nov. 5.—Frank White, who entered a plea of guilty to a charge of robbing a store at New York Mills, a village near here, was sentenced to serve a term of from one to 10 years in the state reformatory at St. Cloud.

## G. O. P. Landslide Sends Markets Up, Grain Prices Soar

**Promise of Stability, Combined With Heavy Orders, Boosts May Wheat Over $1.44—Rye Jumps 6 Cents—Oats, Barley Gain**

Spurred by the landslide which ended fears of an election tieup and gave President Coolidge a remarkable victory, grain markets of the nation today made a spectacular upward swing, sending wheat up almost four cents at Minneapolis and carrying other grains with it.

Orders for 2,000,000 bushels of grain furnished additional strength to the market, as December wheat reached $1.39¾ and May wheat went over $1.44. Chicago wheat went up 3 cents.

Rye was strong, jumping close to 6 cents over Monday. Oats and barley made similar gains.

Grain men agreed that the election was the chief impetus to the market gai ntoday, as the success of the republican party's cause was assured, carrrying with it the promise of stability.

## COOLIDGE LEADS BY 20,161 IN N. DAKOTA

**La Follette Camp Says Western Count Will Overcome Margin—Halvorson Holds Edge**

By Associated Press.

Fargo, N. D., Nov. 5.—"President Coolidge will without question carry North Dakota," L. B. Hanna, state Coolidge manager, told the Associated Press today when informed that the president has a lead of 20,161 votes over Senator R. M. La Follette, when 577 of the state's 2,160 precincts had been counted.

"Returns that have come in so far," said Mr. Hanna, show that Coolidge and Dawes will receive North Dakota's five electoral votes. True, the return from the west, the La Follette stronghold, are not in but I am reasonably sure that they will not give the Wisconsin senator a large enough majority to overcome the lead. The help of the earnest people of North Dakota in both the towns and farms has made this wonderful victory possible."

Halvor Halvorsen, democratic candidate for governor, who also received the support of republicans opposed to the Nonpartisan League, clung to his lead over Arthur G. Sorlie, League candidate when 583 precincts out of the state's 2,160 gave him 42,717 and Sorlie 31,820. Sorlie, however, was expected to gain throughout the day as returns from the third congressional district, western North Dakota, his stronghold, came in.

Thomas Hall, republican, continued to lead the way in the second North Dakota congressional race over Gerald P. Nye, progressive. When 100 precincts from the district's 749 had reported, the vote stood: Hall, 6,939; Nye, 4,686. M. C. Freerks, Nonpartisan, was a very poor third, receiving only 33 votes. Hall also led the short term contest to fill the vacancy created by the resignation of Representative George Young, republican. The vote (49 precincts): Hall, 2,012; Nye, 1,516.

**FRAZIER CLAIMS LA FOLLETTE SORLIE WILL CARRY STATE**

Fargo, N. D., Nov. 5.—"Bob La Follette will carry North Dakota by 10,000," Roy Frazier, acting campaign manager for the Wisconsin senator, declared after reading unofficial returns this morning which gave President Coolidge a lead of approximately 20,000 votes when about one-fourth of the state's precincts had been reported.

"I don't care what the early reports are," Mr. Frazier said. "The La Follette strongholds are still to be heard from."

### *Heffelfinger Wins For County Board*

W. W. Heffelfinger was elected county commissioner in the third district over W. C. Robb. With 13 precincts missing, Heffelfinger's total was 29,322; Robb's was 20,990.

With only five precincts missing, A. R. Ferrin had nearly 900 lead over H. R. Chase for county commissioner in the first district. The vote was Chase 9,075, Ferrin 9,954.

## FULL G.O.P. STATE TICKET HOLDS LEAD; SCHALL'S IS 25,000

**Republican Candidate for Governor Piles Up Edge of 40,000 in 1,748 Precincts**

**OTHER NOMINEES GET ALMOST COOLIDGE VOTE**

**Showing of Ticket Leaders Surprises Own Friends—Returns Come Slowly**

By CHARLES B. CHENEY

Theodore Christianson of Dawson apparently has been elected governor of Minnesota, and chances late today favored Thomas D. Schall to defeat Senator Magnus Johnson. With President Coolidge's big Minnesota lead mounting on every new tabulation, the republican state ticket now seems to have been swept through by the "undertow" of republican sentiment.

With nearly half the precincts in the state reported, Mr. Christianson was 40,000 ahead of Floyd B. Olson, his farmer-labor rival.

On a smaller number of precincts, Mr. Schall had 25,000 margin over Senator Johnson.

**Run Surprises Own Friends**

The two candidates, on whom the opposition centered its fire, made runs which surprised many of their own supporters. Instead of their early leads fading away, they continued to mount higher. The Christianson margin now is so large that it does not seem possible for rural returns to wipe it out.

In 1,748 precincts out of 3,607, Mr. Christianson had 259,898 votes to 219,800 for Olson, and 31,070 for Caralos Avery (dem.).

In 303 Hennepin county precincts Christianson has 81,355 to 61,629 for Olson and 4,962 for Carlos Avery (dem.). In 212 precincts in Ramsey county the vote stands: Christianson, 37,328; Olson, 39,253; Avery, 8,002.

**Schall Increases Lead**

Mr. Schall held tenaciously to his lead and increased it as new returns came in.

On 1,739 precincts, Schall had 230,741 to 205,294 for Magnus Johnson and 30,899 for J. J. Farrell, democrat.

The senatorial figures include 311 Hennepin county precincts, giving Schall 84,926; Johnson, 57,766, and Farrell, 6,571. They include 190 Ramsey county precincts, giving Schall, 27,358; Johnson, 31,227, and Farrell, 8,439.

**Other State Officers**

On the minor state offices, the count early this afternoon was:

Lieutenant governor: 840 precincts, Nolan, 117,807; Holmes, 92,491; Schilpin, 15,123.

Secretary of state—682 precincts, Holm, 92,584; Stageberg, 51,022; Halvorson, 8,839.

Treasurer—591 precincts, Rines, 71,269; Berg, 59,593; Reindl, 8,160.

Attorney general—697 precincts, Hilton, 95, 466; Sullivan, 73,009; Bell, 9,683.

Railroad and warehouse commissioner—952 precincts, Matson, 151,210; Smith, 107,831; Lanin, 16,867.

All other republican state candidates are running ahead of Christianson and Schall. Some of them probably will have margins larger than the good round one being piled up for President Coolidge. All of them appear to be safe, including Attorney General Clifford L. Hilton, who ran like a scared deer in Hennepin county and practically broke even in his opponent's county, Ramsey.

**Strength Surprises Opposition**

Schall and Christianson, both "short enders" in the pre-election betting, showed strength that surprised the opposition. Senator Magnus Johnson and Floyd B. Olson, who were confident of success up to last night, today were hoping to overcome the substantial margins of their republican opponents.

Democratic strength, as expected, was almost negligible, but with John W. Davis running ahead of the state ticket.

Returns came in today much more slowly than in past elections, and the count was far from complete 18 hours after the polls closed.

Christianson's showing in both the cities surprised the opposition. He was "doped" to lose St. Paul by a heavy margin, and Floyd Olson's friends expected him to carry his home county, Hennepin. They fought for it desperately.

In Ramsey county 90 precincts give Rines 12,869 for state treasurer, Berg 1,282; Reindl, 3,364. For attorney general, Hilton, 12,507; Sullivan, 13,269; Bell 1,793. On railroad and warehouse Matson, 13,222; Smith, 12,619; Laun, 1,746.

**Coolidge Far Ahead in Hennepin**

Returns compiled late today from 251 Hennepin county precincts out of 348 gave the following totals:

President—Coolidge (rep.), 72,879; Davis (dem.), 8,580; La Follette (ind.), 41,976.

Senator—Schall (rep.), 68,708; Johnson (f.-l.), 46,219; Farrell (dem.), 5,432.

Governor—Christianson (rep.), 67,533; Olson (f.-l.), 49,574; Avery (dem.), 3,932.

Lieutenant Governor—Nolan (rep.), 67,914; Holmes (f.-l.), 41,063; Schilpin (dem.), 5,649.

Secretary of State—Holm (rep.), 74,077; Stageberg (f.-l.), 33,996; Halvorson (dem.), 5,437.

State Treasurer—Rines (rep.), 68,119; Berg (f.-l.), 38,135; Reindl (dem.), 6,087.

Attorney General — Hilton (rep.), 66,749; Sullivan (f.-l.), 41,782; Bell (dem.), 5,361.

### *Rancher Is Stabbed to Death at Voting Place*

Belle Fourche, S. D., Nov. 5.—James Storm, a prominent rancher across the Wyoming border, was stabbed to death at a polling place in Crook county, Wyoming, by William Osgood of New Haven.

The Minneapolis Sunday Tribune

Fifty-eighth Year. No. 176. (11) * * MINNEAPOLIS, MINN., SUNDAY, NOVEMBER 16, 1924 104 Pages. Price Six Cents in Minneapolis.

# EIGHT DIE IN N. W. ACCIDENTS

## Steck Demands Senate Recount Iowa Ballots

### Democrat Will Contest the Apparent Election of Brookhart.

### 'Arrow' Votes to Be Made Basis of Fight for Seat.

### Thousands Were Wrongfully Ruled Out, He Declares.

Des Moines, Nov. 15.—(By Associated Press.)—Ballots thrown out by election judges in numerous Iowa counties and estimated to number into the thousands, may decide who shall be Iowa's junior senator—Smith W. Brookhart or Daniel F. Steck.

These ballots, missing from the official tabulations completed in all counties today, will form the basis of a contest of the recent senatorial election which Steck, the Democratic candidate for Senator Brookhart's seat, announced today would be made when the new Congress convenes next March.

**Many Ballots Thrown Out.**

Steck pointed out in his announcement of the contest that approximately 950,000 votes were cast for presidential candidates on November 4, while the tabulations show less than 900,000 votes for the senatorial candidates. While many voters undoubtedly refrained from expressing their choice for senator, Steck declared he has been advised that "a great many ballots in which the voter attempted to exercise his choice, were not counted by local election boards."

This statement, it was indicated, referred to the numerous ballots discarded under the state election law because they bore arrows pointing to the "x" before Stecks' name and which the Democratic candidate believes the Senate would accept on a recount as ballots bearing merely an emphasis of the voter's intention. Under the state law, the arrows constitute identification marks.

Another class of votes which Steck feels would aid in overcoming the Brookhart majority, were not counted he said because of a misunderstanding of the election laws by precinct judges. These votes were straight Republican ballots except for a scratch for Steck which were not counted it is said, because of a misunderstanding of a recent change in the law relating to the marking of ballots. Many of these ballots it is said, were not counted in Polk county (Des Moines).

**To Determine Will of Voters.**

Steck will institute the contest, he said, to determine definitely the will of the Iowa voters rather than for the purpose of obtaining the Senate seat for himself. The uncounted ballots, he declared, will aggregate many thousands.

Democratic workers in various counties have gathered evidence of error, according to Clyde L. Herring, national committeeman, which is believed sufficient to sustain Steck's contest and open up the question of the validity of Senator Brookhart's election when the new Congress meets.

Senator Brookhart, at his home in Washington, Iowa, issued a statement declaring a recount would strengthen his majority which stands at 750 and claiming that he had been deprived of thousands of votes through failure of election judges to count straight Republican ballots. Several thousand votes were not counted for him in that manner, the senator said.

The total vote as shown by the complete county canvasses tonight, was Brookhart, 447,711; Steck, 446,961.

## *Weeks Approves Two Citations for Wood*

Washington, Nov. 15. — Secretary Weeks announced today approval of two citations for gallantry in action, carrying with them silver stars, awarded by an army board to Major General Leonard Wood, retired, because of incidents in Cuba when he was colonel of the First Volunteer cavalry (the Rough Riders). The specific dates and places mentioned in the citations are Las Guasiamas June 24, 1898, and Santiago, July 1, 1898.

## *Man in Canoe Fails to Cross Channel*

Dover, Eng., Nov. 15.—E. C. Smythe, Toronto, who left Dover yesterday morning in a canoe alone to cross the English channel on his way by canoe to Rome, was caught in bad weather on the channel last night. After great difficulty he reached the South Goodwin lightship, which picked him up. The channel was choppy when Smythe started on his paddling trip, but he faced the situation courageously. He was aiming to land at Calais.

## *ZR-3 Designer Sails to Join U. S. Company*

Bremerhaven, Germany, Nov. 15.—Dr. Karl Arnstein, designer of the ZR-3, sailed today on the George Washington for America where he will become the technical manager of construction for the new Goodyear-Zeppelin company of Akron, Ohio. Dr. Arnstein was accompanied by Dr. Klemper scientific aero-dynamic research worker and eight other experts.

### Weather Forecast.

MINNESOTA—Generally fair today and tomorrow; colder today in northeast portion.

Additional weather on page 7, second news section.

## *'Red' Grange Carried Home on His Shield; Imported Runner Loses on Gopher 'Track'*

### Fans Who Came to See Football's Hero of Heroes Get Surprise.

### Humbled Henchmen Trail Illini's Proud Banners in Dust on Return.

**By Lorena A. Hickok.**

We have met the enemy and he is ours.

On his shield, with injuries that may put him out of the game for the rest of the season, we sent him back to Illinois Saturday night—"Red" Grange the Incomparable, football's hero of heroes.

With him, and also with our respects to the whole sporting world, we dispatched his humbled henchmen, the Invincible Illini, trailing their proud banners in the dust.

Forty thousand football fans, who gathered in the Memorial stadium to see, not a football game, but "Red" Grange in a track meet all by himself, got—with the exception of a thin wedge of Illinois rooters in the south stands—the glorious surprise of their lives Saturday afternoon.

**Upset That 'Makes' Sports.**

It was one of those upsets that "make" sports, one of those little tricks that life carries about in her reticule to woo the bored away from old Father Mississippi.

Tommy Gibbons went 15 rounds with Jack Dempsey and didn't get knocked out. The Senators won the World's series away from the Giants. And Minnesota—the oldtime fighting Minnesota—took "Red" Grange for a 20 to 7 dry cleaning Saturday afternoon.

"Red" Grange didn't get away with any 80-yard runs in Saturday's little field meet, but he put up a gallant performance—a performance that brought the Minnesota rooters to their feet with complimentary cheers as he was led respectfully from the field by a Minnesota player near the end of the third quarter.

For it was "Red" Grange vs. Minnesota—"Red" Grange against a pack of wildcats—"Red" Grange in a fight with a huge, well oiled steam roller—that game.

**Stopped Time and Again.**

Again and again "Red" Grange hugged the ball to his ribs and started one of his famous runs in the game. Again and again he started—and dropped, with three or four Gophers on top of him. Again and again, poised for flight, he sent his famous swift glance over the field and sprinted away toward one of the ends. Again and

(Continued on Page 2, Column 2.)

## Fireman Killed in Flyer Wreck

### Passengers Escape Injury When 'Capitol Limited' Is Badly Jolted.

Weverton, Md., Nov. 15.—(By Associated Press.)—The fireman was killed and four other members of the train crew were injured when the Capitol Limited, the Baltimore & Ohio flyer between Washington and Chicago, was wrecked here late today. None of the passengers is reported to have been injured, although they were badly shaken when the cars tilted to a sharp angle.

The fireman was Harry Griffin and he was reported killed instantly. The engineer, A. L. Ross, was seriously injured, and two mail clerks and a dining car porter were the others injured. Their names could not be learned here.

The train was passing from a westbound to an east-bound track when the wreck occurred. Although railroad officials declined to give an opinion as to the cause, a split switch is believed responsible. The engine and two mail cars left the track and turned over and the coaches of the all-pullman train were tilted to an angle.

Several hours' work is believed necessary before the track can be cleared and meanwhile a special was made up and the passengers transferred and taken to Brunswick.

## *Husband and Minor Bride of Five Days Are Held in Jail*

Mr. and Mrs. Uriah H. Randall, who were married five days ago, were held at the Hennepin county jail Saturday night because Mrs. Randall, who is just 16 years old, is said to have been married without the consent of her parents. Her husband is 22 years old.

The couple came to Minneapolis last Monday, obtained a license, and were married by a minister on Armistice day. Shortly after the ceremony they returned to Mora, the home of the husband, and they were taken into custody there Saturday on a warrant issued in Municipal court of Minneapolis. The bride was Louisa Olive Voss of Marshall, Minn.

The father of Randall told police Saturday night that he had received a letter from his son which said that the girl had obtained the permission of her parents to marry.

**Hunter Shoots Canada Snow Goose.**

Windom, Minn., Nov. 15.—Lee Rowland, a local hunter, brought in just one Canada snow goose after a trip he made for ducks. The goose was a monster, of its kind, measuring six feet from tip to tip of its wings and three feet 10 inches from the tip of bill to tail-end. It weighed 14 pounds.

### Man With Real Hunch Renegs on 20-to-1 Bet as Grid Battle Starts

One of the Hunch Brothers started out to bet on Minnesota.

He met up with an Illinois fan who was perfectly willing to put up $500 to his $25.

The Hunch brother took him on. Then he got to thinking it over.

At 1:55 p. m., standard time, Saturday, he reneged.

Friends please omit flowers.

## New Stadium Presented to 'U' at Dedication

### Bowl Formally Passes Into Possession of Board of Regents.

Minnesota's new $700,000 memorial stadium was officially dedicated Saturday afternoon at the Minnesota-Illinois football game. Thomas F. Wallace, head of the Greater University corporation, presented the stadium to Fred B. Snyder, chairman of the board of regents, at ceremonies between halves of the game. The Greater University corporation is the alumni organization that conducted the campaign for funds and carried through the construction plans.

**Memorial to Soldiers.**

"Acting as the mouthpiece of the 17,256 alumni students, faculty and friends of the university, whose gifts made possible the erection of this stadium, it is my privilege," Mr. Wallace said, "now to present it to the University of Minnesota as a token of their love for their alma mater and as a memorial to all the men and women of this institution who in our country's hour of need unselfishly answered her call.

"As a soldiers' memorial, it is fitting that it should be dedicated by a soldier's creed, and I do now dedicate this stadium as an everlasting memorial to courage, to comradeship, to sacrifice, and as evidence thereof we hereby present to you an engraved deed of the gift of this stadium."

Mr. Snyder said that the stadium is a memorial to the 3,527 University people who served in the World war, 98 of whom died in the service.

**Is a Shrine.**

"It is a shrine," Mr. Snyder said, "to which athletes of renown in days gone by may return to clasp hands, recall victories and defeats, and pledge themselves anew to their alma mater, and an arena where courage, a will to win, fair play, restraint of passion, fortitude in defeat and humility in victory will be taught and always practiced."

The addresses were carried to the stands by loudspeakers and were broadcast by WCCO, the Gold Medal radio station.

## Grain Alcohol Carload Seized

### $30,000 Shipment Is Held Under Heavy Guard at Minnesota Transfer.

A carload of grain alcohol was confiscated by Federal prohibition agents Saturday night at Minnesota transfer. The seizure was made on a tip received from the East, where the stuff was shipped about a week ago.

No arrests had been made at a late hour Saturday night, but the agents intimated that they know who the consignees are.

Captain A. C. Townsend, regional prohibition director, who ordered the seizure, posted a heavy guard around the car for the night, and the alcohol will be stored to-day. The car is believed to contain 3,000 gallons of alcohol, which at bootleg prices would total in value about $30,000.

**25 Missing, 22 Hurt in Ship Blast.**

Helsingfors, Nov. 15.—Twenty-five workmen were missing and believed drowned and 22 were injured today when a steamer carrying 60 workers sank in the harbor here after a boiler explosion.



### Invading Speed King Is Stopped Repeatedly By 'North Woods' Huskies.

### Ripples of Applause After Foes' Touchdown Turn to Cheers for Minnesota.

**By Alexander F. Jones.**

What a tough year this has been on imported runners!

First Papyrus, fed on old ale and Piccadilly oats, comes over to take an awful licking from Zev.

An then Mons. Wertheimer shoots Epinard across to see if he can garner any of the loose nickels the British novelists and the Chauve Souris have left on this side. And the homebreds run past him so fast that the timers were home ruining the evening beef stew before he limped past the stand.

**And Then 'Red' Grange.**

And then "Red" Grange was imported to the Memorial stadium from Champagne. Imported to show 40,000 folks in the north woods how a real runner looks and acts when let loose among eleven dumb and ploding young men.

Forty thousand folks there just to see "Red" Grange run! Forty thousand folks who wouldn't have bet a plugged rouble on Minnesota's chances. Forty thousand folks with their eyes glued on that big "77" on the red-head's back; ready to say "there he goes." Forty thousand folks apologizing for the red sweatered lads and wondering how many touchdowns "Red" would unbosom himself of before the sun sank over the stadium rim.

No Minnesota team ever had to sell itself to a crowd under more uncomfortable conditions in the history of the school

When Grange took that first punt on the bound and returned 15 or 20 yards there were a few murmurs of applause for the ambitious Maroon and Gold boys who downed him. But they were not noisy about it. Just a polite little hand for the incident. Never mind, "Red" would break loose in a minute or two.

**And Then Some Applause.**

And then, with the Minnesota line fighting like wildcats, outcharging the proud Illini, sideswiping its interference, and nailing the fleet "Comet" time after time, a ripple of applause sprang up here and there.

Now comes that neat little dash around end and Mr. Grange is over for the first score of the game.

Groans. A storm of "I told you so's." As Illinos came trotting back for the

(Continued on Page 2, Column 3.)

## *Heroic Flagman Prevents Double Wreck in Florida*

### Stunned and Pinned Under Car, But Recovers, Stops Freight.

Miami, Fla., Nov. 15.—Pinned beneath the body of a dead woman passenger and made almost unconscious by the shock of his fall, A. R. Davis, of New Smyrna, Fla., flagman of the ill-fated Florida east coast train which left the tracks at Wabasso Friday night and took a toll so far of five dead and 17 injured, averted more serious results by freeing himself and successfully flagging a south bound train which was bearing down upon the scene of the wreck.

With but ten minutes to spare the flagman extricated himself, made his way the length of the wreck, obtained signal flares, and flagged the on-coming train.

**Pinned Under Car.**

How the flagman's heroism averted a second tragedy and a possible greater toll of dead and injured is told by W. M. Clemens, managing editor of the Knoxville (Tenn.) Journal, a passenger on board the Miami-bound train.

The flagman, who was standing on the rear of the train when the coach left the track, fell beneath a woman and the two were pinned under the debris of the wrecked car.

Uninjured but stunned by the fall, his first thoughts were of the train, carrying perishables, which entitles it to run on passenger train time, and which at the last station had been reported 10 minutes behind the passenger train.

**Train Flagged in Time.**

It took the flagman six or seven minutes, he told Clemens, to collect his wits and extricate himself from beneath the body of the dead woman. Then, with his flagman's equipment scattered somewhere beneath the wreck, it was necessary for him to run almost the length of the train to obtain other fuses with which to signal the freight train. He dashed back, approximately 250 yards, lighted the flare just in time to stop the coming train from crashing headlong into the derailed passenger coach.

## *Fair Weather Forecast for Most of Week*

Washington, Nov. 15.—The weather bureau today issued the following weather forecast for next week:

Region of Great lakes mostly fair except for rains or snows about the middle of the week. Tempeartures mostly near normal. Upper Mississippi and lower Missouri valleys mostly fair weather with temperatures near normal.

## Mrs. Harding Failing Slowly, Sawyer Says

### Physician Expresses Belief Patient Will Survive Night.

### Despite Sleep During Day, Widow of Late President Is Weaker.

### Report Declares She Took Nourishment—Decline Is Perceptible.

Marion, Ohio, Nov. 15.—(By Associated Press.)—At midnight, Dr. Sawyer issued the following bulletin.

"Mrs. Harding has been comfortable up to midnight. She was stronger and more cheerful."

Marion, O., Nov. 15.—(By Associated Press.)—Mrs. Florence Kling Harding, widow of the late President, seriously ill at White Oaks farm here, is growing weaker each hour, a bulletin issued by Dr. Carl W. Sawyer, her physician, at 8:30 tonight said. The physician, however, expressed the belief that she would survive the night.

"Mrs. Harding has slept most of the day," the bulletin read, "and has also taken a small amount of nourishment. Regardless of this, she is very exhausted and weak tonight. She has failed perceptibly during the day."

### Mrs. Harding Reported to Be Conscious.

Marion, Nov. 15.—(By Universal Service.)—Mrs. Harding is suffering from her old complaint of kidney trouble and complications that have developed in the region of the abdomen.

Mrs. Harding is not unconscious. At Trinity Baptist church, where a centennial celebration is being conducted this week, the large audience today after hearing a tribute paid President Harding by the pastor, Rev. George M. Landis, stood for several minutes in silent prayer for Mrs. Harding's recovery. President Harding was a trustee of Trinity church for many years.

## German Export Tax Is Problem in Dawes Plan

### Germans Greatly Excited Over Decision By U. S. Agent General.

Berlin, Nov. 15.—(By Universal Service.)—Great excitement has been caused in German political and business circles by the letter of Seymour Parker Gilbert, reparations head, the effect of which it is believed here, will decide the fate of the whole Dawes plan.

The letter concerns the export taxes which some foreign countries have placed on imported German goods. Heretofore the German exporter simply deducted the tax from his bill and was indemnified by the German government, the government being credited with a like amount on its reparations payments.

The Gilbert letter notified the finance minister that Seymour Parker Gilbert alone has control of reparation payments and that Germany will no longer be credited with such tax payments if she makes them herself, but that Gilbert will make these payments "until a further decision of the transfer committee" and that only "insofar and to the extent that he is authorized by the transfer committee."

Germans believe that, if the Dawes plan is to be carried out at all, German exports must increase and also that if some countries are permitted to collect ready cash in this way on their own accounts all other countries entitled to reparation payments will also introduce import taxes. In that case the amount of this tax would soon grow far beyond the amount available to the agent general.

The result, it is said, would be that Germany would either be forced to reduce its exports or to pay, through the import tax a larger amount than the maximum provided by the Dawes plan.

In both cases the Germans are convinced that the Dawes plan would break down as it cannot be squared with the export tax. This tax is the main hitch in the French-German trade negotiations. Stresemann's organ Die Zeit believes Gilbert himself will be forced to come out against this tax in order to save the Dawes plan.

## *Week-End Dinners of Mrs. Kellogg Are Popular in London*

London, Nov. 15.—(By Associated Press.)—Among the most brilliant and interesting week-end dinners in diplomatic London are those given by Mrs. Kellogg, wife of the American ambassador.

Socieyt chroniclers say that these Friday and Saturday dinners given by the ambassador's wife last season were much sought after and the announcement that they will be continued this year, has given much satisfaction.

It is said that Mrs. Kellogg quickly recognized the fact that Friday and Saturday were the only days on which hostesses could count on members of parliament accepting invitations and that Saturday was the only evening on which journalists could conveniently dine out. Consequently these parties are said by many to be more intellectually brilliant than any given in London.

### Dean Coffey Is Guest of Coolidge on Week-End Voyage of Mayflower

Washington, Nov. 15. — President and Mrs. Coolidge left in a snowstorm early this afternoon for a week end cruise down the Potomac on the Mayflower.

The guests on the presidential yacht included three members of agricultural conference, which will hold its first meeting on Monday. They were Dean W. C. Coffey of the Minnesota University agricultural school, chairman of the conference; W. M. Jardyne of Kansas and R. W. Thatcher of Geneva, N. Y.

Other guests were David H. Blair, commissioner of internal revenue, and Mrs. Blair; Herbert Pratt of New York, a classmate of Mr. Coolidge, and Mrs. Pratt and Mrs. Frank W. Stearns of Boston.

## War Experts to Aid League's Disarming Plan

### Great Nations Will Appoint Army and Navy Delegates to Rome Meeting.

Geneva, Nov. 15.—(By Associated Press.)—Preparations for the proposed international conference for the reduction of armaments were advanced a step today when the military commissions of the League of Nations selected the countries which will furnish six experts to sit with the special committees which are to help in framing the agenda of the arms conference.

France and Italy will each appoint a military representative, Great Britain and Japan a naval representative each, and Brazil and Spain an air expert. Czecho Slovkia, Sweden and Belgium will each furnish one substitute delegate for each of the above three groups.

The military commission also drew up a preliminary category of military and civil experts, from whom will be chosen the commissions which later will conduct an investigation of the armament situation in Germany and other central powers under the treaty of Versailles.

## *Golden Wedding Club of G.A.R. Is Thinned by Death*

### Annual Reunion Is Touched With Sorrow, Missing Two Couples.

The passing of a year has seen a dwindling in the ranks of the Golden Wedding club of the John A. Rawlings Post of the G. A. R. And so, when the silver-haired members gathered for their annual dinner at the Leamington hotel Saturday night, the reunion was not without a touch of sorrow.

Of eight couples in the club, only four were present. Death had taken two members and two couples were unable to attend. Judge Daniel Fish, a member, died February 9, 1924, and Augustus M. Corey died September 2, 1924. Charles C. Leland was kept away because Mrs. Leland is ill, and Mr. and Mrs. William H. Kellar are in California.

**Club Gathers Again.**

But the four grand army veterans and their wives, all of whom have been married more than 50 years, gathered again about the dinner table. They are: Judge and Mrs. Eli Torrance, who celebrated their fifty-sixth wedding anniversary on September 22; Mr. and Mrs. Alfred M. Shuey, who were married April 28, 1868; former Governor and Mrs. Samuel R. Van Sant, married December 7, 1868, and Major and Mrs. Silas H. Towler, married November 21, 1871.

A table, decorated with flowers of yellows, russets and old golds that blended in the soft candle light, stood out in the center of the dining room. People in the room glanced at the vacant table.

**Walk With Shoulders Erect.**

The couples enered and walked slowly to their places. There was a twinkle in the eye of Judge Torrance. Former Governor Van Sant walked with steady step and with shoulders erect. Their wives smiled graciously. They took their seats at the table and the dinner of memories of more than a half a century of married life was under way.

The annual business meeting of the club was held in the evening in the apartment of Judge Torrance. No minutes of the last meeting had been kept, but newspaper accounts of the two preceeding annual reunions served as the records and were read.

## *Franco-Belgian Rule Over Ruhr Railways Closes at Coblenz*

Coblenz, Germany, Nov. 15.—(By Associated Press.)—The Franco-Belgian regime here will turn over the railroad administration to the Germans at midnight, by order of the Inter-Allied high commission, under the terms of the London Agreement. The commission, however, has provided for a certain amount of military control.

The Script issue by the French and Belgians during the money shortage, it was announced, will be withdrawn.

## Hunting Season Is Blamed for Five Killings

### Three of Deaths Are Caused By Accidental Discharge of Guns.

### Woman Is Fatally Injured When She Jumps From Burning Car.

### Motorcycle Driver Thrown From Machine, Succumbs to Injuries.

Eight were killed and five seriously injured in accidents reported from northwest and western Wisconsin points Saturday.

Five of the deaths resulted from accidental shootings occasioned by the hunting season, and the others in automobile accidents.

At Duluth, John Koskela, 36 years old, resident of East Lake, Aitkin county, died of gunshot wounds suffered near his home. Companions believe that he was mistaken for a deer.

William Koelund, 26 years old, of Hibbing, died at a hospital there of injuries received in an accidental discharge of a shotgun he was cleaning preparatory to going hunting. His death was the first of the hunting season in the Hibbing area.

**Gun Accidentally Discharged.**

From Hiles, Wis., the death of Philip Corbett, 35 years old, was reported. Corbett was fatally wounded when his gun slipped from his hands and was discharged when it hit a stump. He was a resident of Antigo.

William F. Nichol, 52 years old, was mistaken for a deer by a hunter near Owen, Wis., and was fatally wounded.

Gus Peterson, 70 years old, was instantly killed near Shaw, Minn., when the gun of Gus Peterson, a [illegible] year-old man, discharged as he was loading it and sent a bullet into the older Peterson's neck. The two are not related, it was said.

Archie E. Sutton, 28 years old, was killed when his motorcycle skidded in a pile of loose sand on a trunk highway two miles north of Windom.

Jumping from the automobile in which she was riding on her way to Watertown, S. D., from Badger to attend the funeral of a friend, when the car caught fire and flames shot up around her feet, Mrs. Christ Larson was fatally injured. She struck the back of her head on the road and died three hours later of her injuries.

**Woman Killed.**

Mrs. A. J. Becker of Fergus Falls was killed near St. Cloud when the automobile driven by her husband skidded in soft snow and went into the ditch.

Alfred A. Pettit of Meadowlands, was shot through the thigh in a hunting accident. He is at St. Mary's hospital in Duluth in a serious condition.

At Mankato, C. L. Oleson, one of the founders of the National Bank of Commerce, was struck by an automobile while crossing a street, and was seriously injured. The car, according to witnesses, was traveling at an excessive speed.

**Auto Dragged by Train.**

The automobile driven by John J. Long of Stanley, Wis., was dragged 200 feet by a freight train with which it collided and Mr. Long was seriously injured. At the hospital it was announced that his recovery is doubtful.

A. E. Edner of Duluth and Edward Williams of Milepost 43, old Alger-Smith line, are at a Two Harbors hospital as the result of an automobile collision near there. They have a slight chance to recover.

W. Alfred Bjork, a farmer near Willmar, escaped practically uninjured from the collision of his automobile and a passenger train. The train dragged the car over 200 feet but, other than a few minor bruises, Bjork was not hurt by the accident.

### Two Boys Are Injured as Bus Overturns Trucks.

Two boys were injured Saturday afternoon when a motorbus collided with an automobile truck at Sixth avenue south and Ninth street Saturday afternoon. Seven passengers in the bus escaped unhurt.

The boys are Edward Faulkner, 17 years old, 3243 Franklin avenue, and Harry Bussard, 18 years old, 2309 Fifth avenue south. Their truck was overturned in the collision and they were taken to thhe General hospital where they were treated for cuts and bruises. The driver of the bus was Benjamin R. Brewster, 3950 Hayes street northeast.

Charles McNab, 4211 Twenetieth avenue south, was injured when he was struck by an automobile at Cedar avenue and Lake street. His leg was injured and his head cut. Police failed to obtain the name of the driver of the car.

## *Governor Preus Will Speak at Convention*

Jacksonville, Fla., Nov. 15.—(By Associated Press.)—Measures to prevent grade crossing accidents and safeguard state highways, are among discussions on the tentative program of the sixteenth annual governors' conference which will convene here Monday for a two days' session. The visiting executives will be welcomed to Florida by Governor Carey A. Hardee and Governor Preus of Minnesota will make the response.

## *Drouth in Maryland Broken by Snowstorm*

Baltimore, Md., Nov. 15.—A downpour of rain turned into a snowstorm here and throughout western Maryland today. The storm broke a drouth that had lasted more than a month.

# The Minneapolis Morning Tribune

Fifty-eighth Year. No. 346 | MINNEAPOLIS, MINN., TUESDAY, MAY 5, 1925 | Price Two Cents in Minneapolis


# U. S. DEMANDS REAL PEACE

## Gold Standard Bill Passed by British House

### Commons Puts Measure Through Critical Stage Without Division.

### Churchill Refutes Charge of Subservience to United States.

### Policy Beneficial to America Will Also Aid England, He Says.

London, May 4.—(By Associated Press.)—The house of commons, after a comparatively brief debate and without division, tonight passed the second reading of the gold standard bill and agreed to the necessary money resolution for putting into force the government's arrangements for restoring the gold standard.

The house had been extremely anxious to learn the details of the terms of the government's agreement for American credits to protect the Bank of England's gold reserve; hence, the explanation of the bill given by Walter Guinness, financial secretary to the treasury, showing that the country would not be liable for any interest payments unless it became necessary to utilize the American credits, was received with great satisfaction.

**American Credits.**

These credits are for $300,000,000, the first, amounting to $200,000,000, being arranged with the Federal Reserve bank., and the second with the house of Morgan, amounting to $100,000,000. In each case the arrangement is for two years.

The secretary emphasized that any credits raised under the bill must be repaid within two years. He believed there was no fear of a consequent rise in bank rate or a rise in prices, as had been intimated by some of the Labor members. It was the opinion of all the best expert evidence that the difference in price levels between Great Britain and the United States now was so small, if, indeed it existed at all, as to be consistent with the view that Great Britain had reached a stage where its purchasing power was a parity. The government belief was that there would be no serious movement of prices either way from the present level.

**Opposition Is Slight.**

Philip Snowden, who was chancellor of the exchequer in the late Labor cabinet, in moving his amendment for the rejection of the bill on the ground that the proposed action was unduly precipitate and might aggravate the existing condition of unemployment, explained that the Labor party was not opposed to resumption of the gold standard, but that the motive of the Laborites was to fix full responsibility on Mr. Churchill and the government for any adverse results of hasty action.

Sir Robert S. Horn, also a former chancellor of the exchequer, taunted Mr. Snowden with heroically and skilfully playing a double role—that of ex-chancellor, who might again occupy that position, while at the same time adopting the dashing role of leader of financial criticism.

Mr. Churchill wound up the debate. "It had often been said that the gold standard would shackle Great Britain to the United States," he said. He would tell them what it would shackle them too. It would shackle them to a reality for the good of all, and he believed that to be the only basis offering permanent security.

**Favorable to America.**

Mr. Churchill admitted the contention of the opposition that adoption by foreign countries of the gold standard was a great advantage for America, but he argued that it did not follow that because it was an advantage to America it was not also an advantage to England. Again alluding to the charge that England would be shackled to America, the chancellor said that whether Great Britain resumed the gold standard or not, her interests were profoundly involved with those of America; the two great communities were woven together by a thousand ties of trade and finance. England's conditions were bound to be affected by trans-Atlantic conditions; therefore, it was not a question whether the resumption of gold made her dependent on the United States, but whether it made her dependent in an unhealthy or subservent manner. The answer to that question depended on another—was Great Britain stronger on a gold standard, or off it? He believed that the empire would be stronger on gold; so strong, indeed, as to be able to exist side by side in amicable association with even a large economic and financial power without being prejudicially affected. His view was that Great Britain was not dependent on America, but that the interests of the two countries were interdependent.

**World May Benefit.**

It was possible, the chancellor added, that because of the widespread adoption of the gold standard, inert gold in American vaults would gradually become active and serve as a foundation of credit in many parts of the world. If so, there would ensue a slow, healthy and perfectly legitimate expansion of credit all over the world, keeping every one on check by continuous relation to a definite and unchangable standard of value. If gold made its appearance in England in inconvenient quantities all the treasury would need to do would be to float an internal loan, purchase the gold and remit it back to the United States in cancellation of the war debt.

## Three Suspects Hunted in Explosion of Bomb Package in Downtown Office

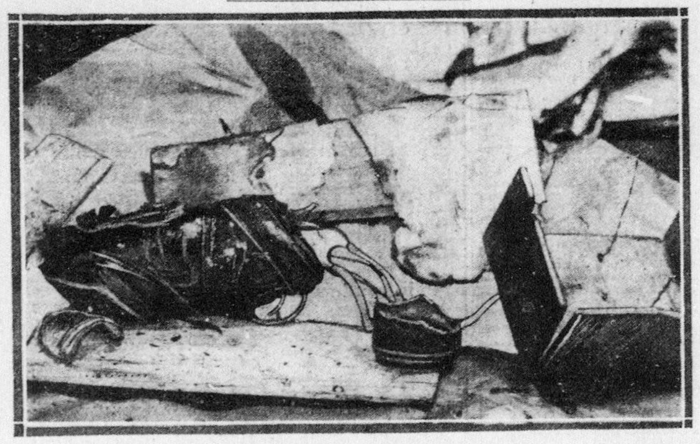

A small pistol, with the barrel sawed off, and a bottle of nitroglycerin taped to the magazine, was the ingenious machine used Monday in an attempt on the life of Edwin H. Chapman, of the United States Fidelity & Guaranty Co., in the Lewis building. When Chapman opened the inner box of a package delivered to him by a messenger boy, a wire pulled the trigger on the pistol, firing a shot into the bottle and discharging the explosive. What remained of the machine, gathered together after the explosion, is shown in the photograph.

### Man and Woman Hurt as Mysterious Box Is Set Off.

### Candy Sent to Intended Victim Is Ordered Analyzed.

The names of three suspects were furnished to police late Monday in their search for the sender of a package which exploded in the hands of Edwin H. Chapman of the United States Fidelity & Guaranty Co. in the Lewis building, shortly before noon. Mr. Chapman and a woman clerk in the office escaped with slight burns.

The package contained a sawed off revolver and a small bottle of some sort of explosive, presumed by police to have been nitroglycerin. The gun was loaded with a blank cartridge and wires were so arranged that when the cover of the box was lifted the cartridge was discharged at the explosive. If the package had been constructed perfectly, and if the bottle contained pure nitroglycerin, the detonation would have set off an explosion which easily would have killed Mr. Chapman and the clerk.

**Messenger Boy in Danger.**

Nitroglycerin is exploded by percussion or heating. Assuming that the explosive was pure nitroglycerin, Alex Webber of St. Paul, the Western Union messenger who carried the package from St. Paul to Mr. Chapman's office, was in constant danger of death. A sudden jolt, or dropping of the package would have been sufficient to set off the nitroglycerin with force enough to kill a carload of people.

While police carried on their investigation of the explosion, postal inspectors and chemists were engaged in analyzing a box of candy which Mr. Chapman received through the mails five days ago. The box was mailed to him in Minneapolis, but when he opened it, he said, he thought "it looked phony," and he put it aside.

The candy box was neatly wrapped and addressed to Mr. Chapman personally. With the candy was this note:

"Just a little token of appreciation for the claim which you settled for me.

Signed "N. E."

The note was written, evidently, by a woman. Mr. Chapman's suspicions were aroused by the fact that the box contained only six pieces of candy, and because he could not remember having handled a claim for any person whose initials corresponded to those in the note.

The package of explosives was received at the Western Union office in St. Paul Monday morning by Miss Lucille McCleary, a clerk. The man who left it she described as "a little less than medium in height, wearing a dark suit. He paid the charge of $$1.50 without question and left immediately.

**Chapman Is Knocked Down**

The messenger reached his destination in Minneapolis shortly before noon. In the office with Mr. Chapman was Mrs. Josephine Smith, 3315 Nicollet avenue, the chief clerk for the company. Chapman removed the outside covering of the package and pried off one of the boards on the inside, when the machine exploded.

Chapman was knocked down by the shock and Mrs. Smith was burned about the face and fell fainting into a chair at the desk. Pieces of the box were scattered about the room.

Chapman is 27 years old, a graduate of the University of Minnesota and lives with his father, E. G. Chapman, 4375 Wooddale avenue. He served as a first lieutenant of infantry during the war.

## *Coast Guards Tune Up Speed Boats to Open Greatest Drive on Liquor Smuggling Fleet*

### Every Boat on Rum Row to Be Watched by Agents Day and Night.

New York, May 4.—By Associated Press.)—War was declared on rum row when Captain W. V. E. Jacobs, divisional commander of the United States coast guard, announced that the entire force of men and vessels under his command tomorrow would launch the largest anti-rum offensive in the history of American prohibition.

Five speedy cutters, six patrol boats and 12 chasers were at the Clifton bay, Staten island base with the supply ship Argus being overhauled for the drive. Engines were tuned up in expectation of speed contests with the more courageous of the whisky buccaneers, and machine guns were put into condition for any emergency.

A part of the plan will be the assignment of one or more coast guard boats to watch each of the floating warehouses on the row every hour. In this manner, the government men believe they will be able to prevent the transfer of stocks into small boats plying between the illicit fleet and the shores of Connecticut, Long Island and New Jersey. This precaution also would prevent the carrying of provisions, water and other supplies to the ships on the rum line by small boats operating from the shore.

Captain J. I. Bryan, in charge of the Staten island unit of the coast guard, said today that 19 members of this unit were in jail on charges involving dishonesty. Department of justice agents, he said, were trailing another former member who landed 1,400 cases of liquor on a Manhattan dock.

As a former boatswain, the man sought is said to have paid the men under him $200 each for their trips from rum row and to have profited personally by many thousands of dollars.

### *Imperial Valley Threatened by Flood*

Calexico, Calif., May 4.—Work crews tonight were rushing train loads of rock to stop a breach in the levees protecting Imperial valley, much of which lies below sea level, from the waters of the Colorado river.

**Jury Gets Campbell Case.**

Great Falls, Mont., May 4.—The case of Gordon Campbell, Montana oil operator, charged with fraudulent use of the mails in the promotion of an oil syndicate was given to the jury in federal court here late today.

## $700,000 Ford Bridge Bond Sale Approved

### Ways and Means Committee Recommends Immediate Marketing.

Sale of $700,000 of Ford bridge bonds at an early date was recommended Monday by the council committee on ways and means.

This plan was decided on after it had been ascertained that some of the surety companies might refuse to bond the contractor if the council went through with its original scheme of taking the money from the city's permanent improvement bond fund and selling Ford bridge bonds only when it became necessary to replenish the permanent improvement fund. To avoid any legal obstacles which might delay construction of the Ford bridge it was decided to recommend sale of the bonds at once.

The city's share of the Ford bridge bonds amounts to $800,000, of which $25,000 already have been sold. The remaining $75,000 will be sold later as needed, it was said.

## Federal Agents File Charges Against Eagles

### Aerie President and Three Others Face Four Complaints Each.

Erick Howe, president of the St. Anthony Aerie of Eagles, and three others, were charged with four violations of the national prohibition act in complaints issued Monday afternoon as a sequel to Sunday's raid at their clubhouse, 119 Fourth street southeast.

Named with Mr. Howe in the complaints are Ed Bliss, 1700 Third avenue north; William Brunskill, Van Dyck hotel; C. H. Wadsworth, 1815 Quincy street northeast, and Albert Johnson, a bartender.

Each of the four are charged with four liquor law violations. The charges are possession of liquor, sale of liquor, operating a nuisance, and complicity in a conspiracy to violate the national prohibition act.

Mr. Hove and Mr. Bliss were arraigned before Howard S. Abbott, United States commissioner, Monday afternoon and released on bonds. Mr. Hove furnished $5,000 bonds, and Bliss $2,000.

Sunday's raid followed several weeks investigation on the part of "under cover" prohibition agents, Maurice Silverman, acting divisional prohibition chief, said Monday. The under cover agents, according to report, became members of the lodge, and through their membership obtained evidence.

Three jugs containing moonshine whisky were found behind the bar in the basement of the club house, Mr. Silverman said. He added that cancelled checks found behind the bar showed that $7,100 had been paid the lodge by the custodian of the bar during April.

Eleven others taken in the raid were questioned Monday and released without charge.



## Bonds to Build Poor House Are Voted by Board

### Funds to Complete Mendota Bridge Also Allowed by County Commission.

Resolutions calling for the issuance of $950,000 worth of bonds to finance the construction of a county poor house at a cost of $250,000 and to complete the construction of the Mendota bridge were adopted by the board of Hennepin county commissioners, Monday afternoon.

Following the sale of the poor house bonds, plans will be drawn for a building to accommodate 200 persons, George H. Mallon, chairman of the board announced. Actual construction will begin in September, he said.

The sale of $600,000 for the completion of the Mendota bridge and five miles of approaches will constitute the final financial step in the construction project. Bonds amounting to $1,800,000 have already been issued. The remaining $100,000 will be used to finance the completion of the Sixth avenue north road project.

Bids for the bonds will be opened by the board on May 25.

## Shepherd Said to Have Carried Medicine Box

### Cousin of 'Millionaire Orphan' Testifies to Habit of Indicted Man.

Chicago, May 4. — (By Associated Press.)—William D. Shepherd, former druggist, charged with the murder of his ward, William Nelson McClintock, was pictured today as going about with a "box of medicine" offering free medication to persons who wished it. Testimony to this effect was offered at the coroner's inquest, which was continued until tomorrow.

Mrs. Maude Eaton Walker of Ottumwa, Iowa, cousin of young McClintock, testified her sister, Mrs. Viola Eaton and her daughter observed, while at Bay View, Texas, that Shepherd administered medicine to Mrs. Emma McClintock, Billy's mother, from a box of medicine he carried around with him.

"My brother, I am told, was ill at Bay View," she said, "and Shepherd offered to give him some medicine, but my sister said 'no' and he said 'no.'"

Dr. Charles Krusemark, former physician to Mrs. McClintock, testified he never had prescribed mercury for Mrs. McClintock. The coroner's analysis showed mercury in deadly quantities in Mrs. McClintock's body.

At the time when it was expected the inquest would be closed, Judge Olson moved the jury be instructed to hold any principals they believed responsible for the death of Billy, his mother or his physician, Dr. Oscar Olson. He asked that the inquest be continued for 30 days.

Mrs. Stella Costigan Carson of Linden, Iowa, who nursed Mrs. McClintock in her last illness, said, in testifying today, that she saw Mrs. Shepherd remove a diamond ring from the finger of Mrs. McClintock soon after the latter died and that later she had seen the same diamond in another setting worn by Mrs. Shepherd.

## *Two Hurt in Sofia Bomb Explosion Die; More Arrests Made*

Sofia, Bulgaria, May 4.—Two additional deaths of persons injured in the recent bomb explosion in the cathedral here occurred today. The men who died were Lieutenant Colonel of Reserves Nicolaeff and Ambulance Colonel Tantcheff. The government has decided to allow the people to circulate in the streets until 9 p. m. A committee of agrarian Communists was discovered today at Pelovdiv. Several men were arrested. The former aviator, Agodd, a trusted friend of the late Premier Stamboulisky was killed while attempting to escape.

## *Death of Three at Liquor Party Puzzles Officials*

### Question Is, What Will Kill Man and Leave Him Bolt Upright.

### Cause in Doubt as Police Consider Poison Rum and Gas Theories.

Some time between 11 o'clock Saturday night and 4 o'clock Sunday afternoon, death descended suddenly and swiftly on three convivial friends at 2206 Twenty-fourth avenue south. What caused their death is still a mystery. A pint bottle containing the dregs of moonshine was found on the table and the police and coroner came to the quick conclusion that deadly liquor had done its fatal work. The three victims were neither of social nor economic consequence and the matter of their taking off was of little official consequence.

The fact that a pint of whisky that is at all drinkable is hardly enough to kill three men gave the police matter for thought. Then, too, the trio were found seated, upright, none of them having slumped into the posture of death. The verdict, unofficial, Sunday night was moonshine. Monday, the coroner investigated and came to the conclusion that the three men, William E. Maher, James Castle and Edward Savage, came to their deaths from gas poisoning. Their lungs showed traces of gas.

**Fourth Man Is Complication.**

But there was even less gas than alcohol. There was some slight escape of gas on the second floor, but no jets were open. It was manifestly impossible for a leaky jet to fill a house so full of gas that three men would die, bolt upright. In addition, Moxie Woolman, who discovered the bodies, found no odor of gas and none of the many persons who went in and out of the house afterward noticed gas.

Joseph Marron added an irrelevant complication by being found speechless from liquor in the back yard of the Maher home. He insisted, however, that his presence was a coincidence; that he had nothing to do with the drinking party inside, but had had one of his own, and by chance had picked out this yard in which to go to sleep, totally oblivious of the grim tragedy within.

There the matter rested Monday night, a matter of official curiosity rather than official investigation. There is no evidence that the deaths were other than accidental, but it is not every day that three men are found dead, seated upright around a bottle. Woolman, who found them, has no theories. His narrative is one of bald unenlightening fact.

**Believed Friends Alive.**

"I knocked at the door at 2206 Twenty-fourth avenue south," he told the police. "No one answered and I walked around to the back of the house. The


Continued on Page 2, Column 3.)


## Means Must Serve Term in Federal Jail

### Former Department of Justice Agent Loses Appeal to Circuit Court.

New York, May 4.—The conviction of Gaston B. Means, former department of justice agent, by a jury last July, on a charge of having conspired to illegally remove liquor from a bonded warehouse, today was affirmed by the United States circuit court of appeals. Means, who has been on bail, was ordered taken into custody that he might begin the two-year term in the federal penitentiary at Atlanta, to which he was sentenced at the time of his conviction. A $10,000 fine also was imposed.

Means also was convicted in a federal court last January of having conspired with Thomas H. Felder, an attorney, to bribe government officials, including former Attorney General Daugherty, to call off prosecution of a large number of defendants in a stock sale mail fraud scheme.

On this conviction Means was sentenced to serve an additional two years at the Atlanta penitentiary and to pay another $10,000 fine.

## *Defense Action by French Troops Brings Calm Along Riffian Front*

Fez, Morrocco, May 4.—(By Associated Press.)—A slight action by the French troops today along the Ouergha river at a point where it was necessary to get food and other supplies to French advance posts which had been surrounded in the first drive by the Riffians, sufficed to bring comparative calm all along the front. These isolated posts had defended themselves single-handed until today when General Colombat sent forward a small column to clear that region.

Abd-El-Krim's forces left 50 dead and lost a number of prisoners and a quantity of supplies. The French losses were insignificant and so far the advanced posts have been able to keep the invaders at a distance with machine guns and three-inch field pieces.

The Riffian forces, however, had slipped between the posts and assembled considerable forces south of the Ouergha river. Although Marshal Lyautey is not yet ready to begin a carefully organized operation to clear out the French zone, it was decided that the tribesmen could not be allowed to proceed farther, and a slight push, it developed, was all that was needed to drive them back.

It is anticipated, however, that the Riffians will return to the attack with reinforcements as there is every indication that Abd-El-Krim is determined to make every effort to get to Fez and so deliver a blow both to the prestige of the French authorities and of the sultan of Morocco.

The bulk of the attacking forces now seem to be assembling in the center of the 60-mile front of the present activities which is called the "Skerbouazou line." This point probably will be the objective of the first French drive. Airplanes have been active the past few days keeping the French headquarters informed of the tribesmen's movements.

## American Loan Policy Outlined by Ambassador

### Houghton Says Maintenance of Financial Aid Rests on Reconstruction.

### Restoration of Good Faith Between Nations Held Essential.

### European Problems Discussed at Traditional Dinner of Pilgrims.


The text of Ambassador Houghton's address is printed on Page Fifteen.


London, May 4.—(By Associated Press.)—Alanson B. Houghton, newly appointed ambassador to the court of St. James, made his bow to a British audience tonight at the traditional dinner of the Pilgrims, which is always the first to welcome a new American representative to London and always the first to receive a full and frank expression of his views on vital matters which affect the relations between the two countries.

It was a night of plain speaking. Ambassador Houghton, in a brief, concise address, told his audience, which included the duke of York, Premier Baldwin and other members of the British cabinet, and some of the most representative men of the realm, that the United States wanted a settlement of Europe's vexing problems, and that unless permanent peace were established in Europe he feared the part the United States had previously played as an interested and sympathetic participant might give way to a lesser role.

In return, Lord Desborough, the chairman, Stanley Baldwin, the prime minister, and former Premier Ramsay MacDonald assured him of the interest in which the people of Great Britain received his pronouncement and laid stress upon their appreciation of the bond between the two nations.

**Exchange of Confidences.**

It was not an occasion of a mere exchange of complimentary remarks between guest and host, but one of closer exchange of confidences, enlivened by humor that sparkled throughout the evening and kept the distinguished company in laughter most of the time.

Mr. Houghton told those assembled that the plain people of America wanted the re-establishment of a real peace—assurance of the return of good faith—in Europe and upon that their participation in the reconstruction of normal conditions largely depended.

Coming as it did from the former American ambassador to Germany following his recent visit to the United States and conferences with President Coolidge, the pronouncement was calculated to create a profound impression upon the statesmen and diplomats gathered to hear the new ambassador. Because of its importance and the authoritative note which it sounded, it was assumed by those trained in diplomacy that he must undoubtedly be voicing the views of the administration at Washington.

**Speech Declared Significant.**

Special significance was attached to the fact that the statement comes at a time when considerable suspicion and distrust of Germany are being voiced in various parts of Europe, particularly France, because of the election to the presidency of Field Marshal von Hindenburg, who is asserted by some to represent those reactionary forces which are inimical to the peace and interest of at least some of the allies.

Interlocked with this idea, it has been commented, may be the fate of the security pact proposed by Germany and warmly seconded by England as a great step toward the re-establishment of real peace. Indeed, there has been some speculation as to whether the effective working of the Dawes plan might be impaired by this fanning of the smouldering fire of distrust.

**Establishment of Peace Essential.**

Whether Ambassador Houghton had any of these things in mind was open to conjecture, but contented himself with making it plain not only that the re-establishment of peace was essential to the continuation of assistance from the United States but that the answer to the question whether there was to be peace must come from the peoples of Europe themselves.

As the guest of honor of the Pilgrims, Mr. Houghton was making his maiden address in the capacity of ambassador to Great Britain. Among the most prominent gathered to welcome him, in addition to Premier Baldwin, to introduce him, were the Duke of York, former Premier MacDonald, the ambassadors from Belgium, Japan, Germany, Portugal and Brazil, the Archbishop of Canterbury, Colonial Secretary Amery, Sir Auckland Geddes, Sir Samuel Hoare, the Earl of Craven and Lord Astor.

**Message From King.**

Lord Desborough, chairman of the Pilgrims, presided at the dinner.

Replying to a loyal message sent him by the Pilgrims, King George telegraphed:

"Please convey to the Pilgrims of Great Britain and their guests assembled this evening my sincere thanks for their message and for the kind reference to my recovery.

"I am glad to have this opportunity of associating myself with the welcome given by them to Mr. Houghton as ambassador for the United States of America."

Premier Baldwin in proposing Ambassador Houghton's health dwelt in a complimentary manner on the ambassador's familiarity with many problems through his previous high diplomatic positions. He then alluded to charges made in London in connection with the restoration of the gold standard about the British people "putting themselves in pawn to America," and remarked on America's faith in this matter.

The prime minister said:

"I wish to say publicly at this dinner that in the men responsible in

**Weather Forecast.**

MINNESOTA—Generally fair and continued cool today and tomorrow. Additional weather on page 15.

# The Minneapolis Morning Tribune

Fifty-ninth Year. No. 59 — MINNEAPOLIS, MINN., WEDNESDAY, JULY 22, 1925 — Price Two Cents in Minneapolis


# SCOPES BATTLE IS STILL ON

## Seven Killed on Crossings in Northwest

### Three Men Lose Lives as Their Car Is Run Down Near Little Falls.

### Two Other Occupants of Machine Escape Injury by Jumping to Safety.

### Four Members of One Family Die in Crash Near Minot, N. D.

Two grade crossing accidents in the northwest Tuesday took a toll of seven dead.

At Little Falls, Minn., three workmen died when a train crashed into their automobile, two companions escaping by leaping from the car as the train bore down on them.

In the second crossing accident, four members of one family, two of them small children, were killed near Minot, N. D.

FRED SEARS, 58, Motley, Minn.
GESLEY OLSON, 15, Randall, Minn.
JOHN GALLUS, 35, Pierz, Minn.

The dead in the Minot accident:
MRS. CLARA KENNEDY, 26, Williston, N. D.
MRS. EDNA KENNEDY, 50, Williston.
LUELLA DORIS, 4, and Floyd, 1 month old, children of Mrs. Clara Kennedy.

### Three Killed, Two Escape at Little Falls, Minn.

Little Falls, Minn., July 21.—Train No. 13 of the Northern Pacific railroad struck an automobile near here at noon today, killing two men instantly and fatally injuring a third, who died three hours later. The dead are Fred Sears, 58 years old, a road contractor; Gesley Olson, 15, Randall, Minn., and John Gallus of Pierz, 35.

Two other occupants of the automobile escaped injury or possibly death, by leaping from the machine just before the engine struck it. They were Lawrence Daugherty of Little Falls, 60 years old, and Leslie Torgeson of Motley, 25 years old.

The men were employed on a road construction job near Randall and were returning to their camp for dinner. The engine struck the automobile squarely and carried it for 80 rods to a bridge, where it was thrown over an embankment. The victims were carried with the machine and were picked up near the bridge.

Gallus was brought to a Little Falls hospital, where he died three hours later. The survivors of the tragedy were unable to describe the details of the accident this afternoon.

### Four in One Family Die in Accident.

Minot, N. D., July 21.—A mother, her daughter and two grandchildren were killed when the automobile in which they were riding was struck by a Great Northern extra passenger train on a grade crossing near Des Lacs early today. The dead are Mrs. Edna Kennedy, 50 years old, Williston; Clara Kennedy, 26, and the latter's two children, Luella Doris, 4, and Floyd, 10 months old. They were en route to Minot where they had planned to make their home.

The automobile was struck in the center, it is apparent, being carried about 1,200 feet by the train, and was nearly demolished. A coroner's jury empaneled by Dr. R. W. Pence, county coroner, viewed the scene of the accident this morning and testimony is to be taken later.

### Trolley Employe Hurt by Passing Automobile

Struck by an automobile, which failed to stop, Harry Wright, 4520 Third avenue south, an employe of the Minneapolis street railway company, was injured Tuesday while welding a track near 422 Fourth street southeast.

James E. Quinlan, 1024 Seventeenth avenue southeast, was arrested later at his home in connection with the accident. Quinlan was held without charge.

Wright was taken to the General hospital, where he was treated for cuts and bruises.

Louis Marks, Granite Falls, Minn., was treated at the General hospital for cuts and bruises following an accident Tuesday when his car skidded into a ditch on the Excelsior boulevard near West Thirty-sixth street.

Mrs. E. Evanston, 2618 Grand avenue south, was injured when an automobile driven by an unidentified man struck the gates as she was boarding a street car at Chicago avenue and East Twenty-ninth street. She was taken to the General hospital where she was treated for bruises of the shoulder. Police are searching for the driver of the car.

In a collision between an automobile driven by Playmart Swanson, 1612 East Franklin avenue, and a Minneapolis-St. Paul street car at Tenth and Washington avenue south, Edward Swanson, brother of Playmart, Morris Kauffman, 2024 Sixteenth avenue south, and Sam Moscovitch, 1915 Eleventh avenue south, were injured. They were taken to the General hospital, where they were treated for bruises and lacerations and later released. The accident occurred when Swanson attempted a left hand turn.

### Weather Forecast

MINNESOTA—Fair today, warmer in west portion; Thursday, unsettled, warmer in south and west portions.

Additional weather on page 15.

## Only Four Days Remain to Complete Legion Fund Quota

With only four days remaining before Minneapolis subscriptions to the American Legion Endowment fund must be forwarded to national headquarters, the city total reached $16,686.17 Tuesday night with the receipt of $1,270, in contributions during the day.

| | |
|---|---|
| Previous Contributions | $15,416.17 |
| Dr. William R. Murray | 25.00 |
| Mrs. Helen S. Winton | 200.00 |
| W. B. & W. G. Jordan | 50.00 |
| Willis K. Nash | 100.00 |
| Robert F. Pack | 100.00 |
| Marsh & McLennan | 25.00 |
| The Dayton Co. | 250.00 |
| H. R. Weesner | 100.00 |
| Mrs. A. E. Elrod | 10.00 |
| Minneapolis Drug Co. | 150.00 |
| City Fire Fighters Union No. 82 | 200.00 |
| Charles I. Fuller | 10.00 |
| McClellan Paper Co. | 25.00 |
| Charles B. Mills | 25.00 |
| Total | $16,686.17 |

Russel Creviston, national adjutant of the American Legion and former Minneapolis man, in a letter received by Irving Fish, Minneapolis chairman, Tuesday, said:

"I know the patriotism of Minneapolis and its devotion to duty. I am confident Minneapolis will do its part and more for the disabled veterans and helpless orphans of veterans through the American Legion Endowment fund.

"I have followed closely the progress of the fund as recorded daily in The Minneapolis Tribune and I want to congratulate you and the legion upon enlisting the aid of The Tribune in setting clearly before the public the real facts.

"As a matter of fact, Minneapolis was the birthplace of the American Legion Endowment fund when the first national conventon of the legion was held in Minneapolis. The work of curing and assisting the thousands of war veterans who today are fighting a losing battle against disease and wounds received in service is the outgrowth of that idea at the Minneapolis convention. The legion, through its 11,000 posts in every part of the country is the only organization capable of dealing with this problem on a nation-wide scale.

"To my mind, after nearly six years' association with the legion this work that the fund will make possible is one of the biggest problems facing the United States. Disabled veterans are dying at the rate of 15 a day. Thousands of children are becoming depenuents through the fact that their fathers gave their lives or health in serving the flag.

"I know that Minneapolis will respond promptly and whole-heartedly to the appeal of the fund. To me personally this will be especially pleasing and fitting, for it would put a golden period to my work as a legion official which started in Minneapolis six years ago."

All Minneapolis contributions must be on the way Saturday night, according to Mr. Fish. Those who desire to contribute may bring or mail their gifts to the American Legion Endowment fund at The Minneapolis Tribune.

## Judges Favor Closed Door in Scandal Trials

### Adopt Rule Giving Court Discretionary Power to Exclude Public.

Rochester, Minn., July 21.—Prior to concluding the annual session today, the District Judges association of Minnesota adopted a new rule providing for the exclusion, at the court's direction, of the general public from court rooms during criminal trials in which testimony of a salacious character is expected.

While the state judges were arraigning some lawyers for alleged impositions upon the bench, members of the Minnesota State Bar association, in another room of the same building, opened their annual convention here late today. Following an eventless 90-minute session the lawyers called it a day and while the jurists were still engaged in discussions, left the building for a heavy program of entertainment, including golf, quoits, dinner and dancing.

**Examination of Talesmen.**

With the object of speeding up trials, a subject which yesterday the judges discussed at length and charged the legislature with ignoring efforts to obtain legislative aid, rules were adopted authorizing courts in civil suits to examine talesmen and curbing delays by counsel to accommodate each other.

The new rule states that the presiding judge shall examine jurors in civil cases, his examination to be followed by such further inquiry by counsel as the judge may deem proper.

**Not Applied in Criminal Cases.**

Following a short debate late today the judges voted down a proposal that they limit to $15 each day in court, fees for expert witnesses. The vote was 12 to 11.

The judges tonight were guests of the Minnesota State Bar association which opened its annual convention today with a supper and dance at the Rochester Country club.

**Would Amend Marriage Law.**

During the bar association's brief session earlier in the day Burt W. Eaton of Rochester, state president, in his address, admonished the lawyers to strengthen their state organization and declared that they should recommend to the legislature that the state's marriage and divorce laws should be amended "for the better protection of society."

### *Ninth District Legion Posts Fill Fund Quota*

Crookston, Minn., July 21.—The 25 posts of the American Legion in the Ninth district have subscribed or oversubscribed their quotas of the $5,000,000 endowment fund being raised by the Legion to take care of the disabled veterans and orphans of veterans. Halstad and Hendrum are among the 11 posts in the state that raised more than double their quotas.

## St. Paul Mayor Delays Signing Bridge Contract

### Wants Signature First of City Comptroller for Ford Span.

Mayor Arthur E. Nelson of St. Paul declined Tuesday to sign the Ford bridge contract and stated that he would refuse to sign it until it had the signature of the St. Paul city comptroller, William F. Scott.

The St. Paul mayor's action, taken at the meeting Tuesday of the bridge commission in the offices of the state highway department, was based upon the St. Paul political situation, he said. His refusal to sign the contract at this time, however, does not mean that a delay in the start of construction of the bridge would result, members of the commission explained.

"The signature of Mr. Scott is necessary to make the contract legal, and he must take the first step," the mayor explained. Other members of the commission were prepared to sign the contract, although the meeting was called especially to discuss terms in the contract with representatives of the Heyworth Construction Co., the bridge builders.

Mr. Scott said Tuesday night in Rochester, N. Y., where he is attending a convention of city comptrollers, that he would sign the contract "as soon as I legally can." He said he expected he could act July 29, when bids for the St. Paul Ford bridge bonds will be

(Continued on Page 2, Column 4.)

### *'Baby' Pursuit Planes at Cheyenne Ahead of 'Mother' Bomber*

Cheyenne, Wyo., July 21.—(By Associated Press.)—Children proved more frisky than their parents even among airplanes today, when six army pursuit airplanes on a flight from Omaha over the western half of the trans-continental air mail route reached the hangers here three hours ahead of their giant "mother ship," a Curtiss bomber.

Tomorrow morning the six pursuit planes fly to Salt Lake City. The bomber will remain here and will escort the pursuit ships on their return flight to Omaha.

The army pursuit planes arrived at the air mail field here at 1:02 p. m., while the huge bomber did not reach its destination until three hours later.

The seven-plane squadron under the command of Major Thomas G. Lanphier, is flying over the trans-continental air mail route in order to ascertain its effectiveness for military use in case of war. The flight of the squadron today was the second day's tour over the air mail route, the airplanes having started from Selfridge field, Mount Clemens, Mich., yesterday morning and landing at Omaha that day.

## Miners Request Hoover, Davis to Intervene

### Cabinet Members Asked to Act to Prevent Soft Coal Strike.

### Government Aid in Checking Abrogation of Wage Pacts Is Sought.

### Anthracite Parley Resumed—Operators Decline to Furnish Data.

Atlantic City, N. J., July 21.—(By Associated Press.)—Bituminous union coal miners here today asked Herbert Hoover, secretary of commerce, and James J. Davis, secretary of labor, to intervene in behalf of the government in the northern West Virginia fields to check abrogation of wage agreements which they said would otherwise force a general strike throughout the country.

Meanwhile the anthracite scale parley was resumed after a three day adjournment. Operators reconsidered their decision to open their books to the hard coal men, as announced Friday, and declined to furnish at this time data on salaries of company heads and officials, which the miners had requested.

**Repudiations of Pacts Alleged.**

The joint telegram asking Secretaries Hoover and Davis "to take a definite position against abrogation of wage contracts by the coal operators of northern West Virginia," was sent by Van A. Bittner here, chief union representative in those fields.

Mr. Bittner also wired protests to John D. Rockefeller, Jr., and Samuel Untermyer, a New York attorney, in which he alleged repudiations of the Jacksonville agreement on the part of the Consolidation Coal company and the Bethlehem Mines corporation, in which the two men respectively are prominent stockholders.

To Mr. Hoover and Mr. Davis, Mr. Bittner said:

**Grievances Are Listed.**

"Several large coal companies in northern West Virginia, among whom are the Bethlehem Mines corporation, a subsidiary of the Bethlehem Steel corporation and the Consolidation Coal company, which is controlled by the Rockefeller and Watson interests, have abrogated their wage contracts with the United Mine Workers of America and are attempting to put into effect a wage reduction approximately 50 per cent.

"Defenseless miners, their wives and little children are being evicted from their homes by these coal companies because the miners will not agree to violate and abrogate the terms of the wage agreement, which is effective until March 31, 1927.

"Hundreds of armed gun men are being employed to intimidate, coerce and force our people to accept this reduction in wages. In the interests of the coal miners and all the people of our country the time has arrived when the government of the United States should take a definite position against abrogation of wage contracts by the coal operators of northern West Virginia."

## GleemansName Gangster as Real Slayer

### Convicted St. Paul Brothers Start Proceedings for New Trial.

Ben and Abe Gleeman of St. Paul, serving life sentences for the murder last February 16, by shooting, of Burton H. Stevens, alleged alcohol runner, have named a Chicago gunman as the real murderer.

This was revealed Tuesday during the progress of a move for retrial of the case in the Ramsey county courts.

The Gleeman brothers, it was learned, have not only charged another man with the murder, but have charged that heads of a "million dollar alcohol ring" are involved, and the case against them was "framed."

The Gleemans, it is said, are prepared to ask a police search for the man they name as the murderer; to ask indictment of two other St. Paul men, who were said to be in an automobile, from which the fatal shots are alleged to have been fired at Stevens; to name the leaders of the "alcohol ring" they declare is involved in the murder, and to ask indictment of these leaders.

They allege, that "hi-jacking" of liquor by Stevens led to the "alcohol ring's" reprisal move which resulted in his death.

The move for a new trial is being conducted by Thomas J. Sullivan, an attorney newly entered in the case as counsel for the brothers.

Mr. Sullivan's first move was to secure consent of Allen M. McGill, assistant Ramsey county attorney, acting for H. H. Peterson, county attorney, for a stay of present supreme court appeal proceedings until August 22.

Mr. Sullivan immediately secured consent of Attorney General C. L. Hilton, and this morning will ask Justice Henry Holte to sign the order, with a view to remanding the case from the supreme court back to the Ramsey county district court, and appealing before Judge R. D. O'Brien for a new trial.

## *French Heroes Lead 150,000 Against Riffians*

### Two Marshals, Five Generals Instill Fresh Morale Into Troops.

### Indications Reported That Rebel Chief Believes Days Are Numbered.

Paris, July 21.—(By Associated Press.)—Two marshals of France, Petain and Lyautey, and five generals, Naulin, Colombat, De Chambrun, Heusch and Bertrand, are leading 150,000 French troops arrayed against Abdi-El-Krim, the rebel war lord in Morocco.

In French sources it was said today that the re-organized military command had caused the Riffian chief to see the handwriting on the wall, and that there are indications that he believes his days as a leader are numbered.

The stupendous offensive across "the land of thirst," of Taza and Ouezzan, with the fertile plains of the sacred city of Fez as the objective, which had been threatening for the past two days, seems momentarily to have been abandoned by the Moors.

**Riffs Spread Propaganda.**

Marshal Petain's presence on the Riff front is declared to have instilled fresh morale into the tired and dejected French troops. Faced by ever increasing French reinforcements, the Riffian chief is endeavoring to raise revolt among all possible tribes as part of his last desperate effort to crush the Christian soldiers who stand between him and Moslem rule in Fez, it was asserted today.

The battle facing Marshall Petain is similar to that which confronted him when he assumed the leadership of the French army in 1917. It is one of the morale of the troops under his command more than of stopping the onslaughts of the enemy.

**Weather Unbearable.**

French official advices from Morocco continue to emphasize a general improvement in the situation. The correspondent of the Temps at the front telegraphs that trains loaded with troops and supplies, passing toward the battle region day and night, have so congested the road that traffic at Tunis was ordered stopped for several days.

"However," the correspondent adds, "The Moors have a strong ally in the climate, which is unbearable to Europeans. The Riffians chose the hottest season for the offensive against the French. None but natives can live in the temperature around Taza, which averages a maximum of 108 degrees Fahrenheit and never is lower than 77."

## *City Folks Shiver as Mercury Does July Fade-away*

### Temperature Drops to 59 Degrees in Minneapolis—38 at Dickinson.

Mid-summer shivers attacked the population of Minneapolis and the entire northwest Tuesday.

The shivers were caused by a drop in temperature to a minimum of 59 degrees at four a. m. Tuesday. The maximum for the day was 71, eight degrees lower than the day previous. A chilly northwest breeze, blowing 20 miles an hour, made the July "cool wave" more penetrating.

**Maximum is 71 Degrees.**

Tuesday's maximum of 71 degrees in Minneapolis was registered at 1 p. m., and from that point the mercury dropped one degree each hour to 63 at midnight.

Dickinson, N. D., shivered the most Tuesday with the minimum temperature at 38 degrees. Pipestone, Minn., temperatures somersaulted from 85 to Monday to 48 degrees Tuesday morning.

Minneapolis bathing beaches were practically deserted Tuesday. Automobile drivers especially doffed their straw hats and put on caps and topcoats. Summer frocks were covered with jackets or sport sweaters.



## Darrow Tells Bryan What He Believes

Dayton, Tenn., July 21.—(By Associated Press.) — Forbidden to examine Clarence Darrow on the witness stand concerning his religious views, William Jennings Bryan late today administered the examination through the medium of a statement. Nine questions were propounded and these were answered shortly afterward by the Scopes defense attorney.

"The questions are as follows:

Mr. Bryan—Do you believe in the existence of God as described in the Bible?

Mr. Darrow—I do not know of any description of God in the Bible. We are informed, in the first part of the Bible, however, that God is a spirit. If Mr. Bryan will describe what he means by God, I probably could tell better whether or not I believe in his God. Mr. Bryan said, in effect, that God is like a man and is fashioned in the image of man. I do not believe in this kind of a God. As to the origin of the universe and who or what is back of it, I do not pretend to know.

Mr. Bryan—Do you believe that the Bible is the revealed will of God, inspired and trustworthy?

Mr. Darrow—I think that there is much that is of value in the Bible. I do not believe it was written or inspired by God. I believe it should be taken like every other kind of book, and that the portions that are sublime are like such portions of any great book—as much inspired as, say, in His image.

Mr. Bryan—Do you believe in the supernatural Christ, foretold in the Old Testament and revealed in the New Testament?

Mr. Darrow—I do not believe that any supernatural Christ was foretold in the Old Testament or revealed in the New Testament. I believe that the Christ prophesied in the Old Testament was a great Jew who should deliver his people from their physical bondage and nothing else.

Mr. Bryan—Do you believe in the miracles recorded in the Old and New Testaments? If you believe in some but not all of them, please name a few of those which you accept and those you reject with the reasons for the same. Do you believe that Christ was conceived of the Holy Ghost and born of the Virgin Mary, as recorded in Matthew and Luke? Do you believe that Christ rose from the dead as described in the four gospels?

Mr. Darrow—I do not believe in miracles. I believe the universe acts and has always acted in accordance with an immutable law, and that whatever may be back of the universe has never violated these laws.

Mr. Bryan—Do you believe in the immortality of the soul?

Mr. Darrow—I have been searching for proof of this all my life, with the same desire to find it that is incident to every living thing, and I have never found any evidence on the subject.

Mr. Bryan—If you believe in evolution, at what point in man's descent from the brute is he endowed with hope and promise of a life beyond the grave?

Mr. Darrow—I have no knowledge on the question of when man first believed in life beyond the grave. I am not at all sure whether many other animals have not the same hope of a future life that man has. The origin of this belief may have arisen in vivid dreams concerning the return of the dead, or, for all I know, from actual evidence of the return of the dead.

"I have never tried to impose my views on religion on any human being," said Mr. Darrow, as he finished his answers. "I have a right to my own views, and I try as hard to protect the right of every other man to his views as I do to protect my own."

## *Unidentified Man, Found Unconscious, Dies in St. Paul*

An unidentified man, about 50 years old, wearing eye glasses bought in Minneapolis, a black mohair suit, and a gray felt hat, was found unconscious shortly before midnight Tuesday at the foot of the Selby tunnel stairs in St. Paul. He died at Ancker hospital half an hour later without regaining consciousness.

A white handkerchief and a package of cigarets were the only contents of his pockets, leading police to the belief that the man had been slugged and robbed. The spot has been the scene of several robberies.

A passerby heard the man's groans and after investigation called the police ambulance.

### *Warrant Out to Bring Ole Olson to Trial*

A bench warrant was issued for Ole Olson, federal prohibition agent, when he failed to appear before Justice Charles Schwarg at Bloomington, Minn., Tuesday night to answer charges of alleged violation of the federal prohibition law. Neither Olson nor his attorney appeared at the hearing Tuesday night. Olson was arrested at Richfield on June 3 by Constable F. W. Renner. A hearing was held June 27 before Justice H. E. Kahler at Richfield, when Olson was granted a change of venue to Bloomington. Federal agents said Tuesday night that Olson was in North Dakota.

## Lawyers Argue After Jury Has Given Verdict

### Bryan, Darrow and Malone State Their Positions on Main Issue.

### Fundamentalist Denies Bigotry—Defense Counsel Rejects Atheism.

### Teacher Is Fined $100 and Appeal to State Supreme Court Begins.

Dayton, Tenn., July 21.—(By Associated Press.)—Although technically the Scopes trial finished today, with the conviction of the defendant, the imposition of a fine of $100, and the commencement of appeal proceedings leading to the state supreme court, the battle did not end with the adjournment of court. Judge John T. Raulston had ordered the testimony of William Jennings Bryan, given the day before, expunged as irrelevant, and Clarance Darrow had had no opportunity to be examined by Mr. Bryan. These opposing counsel, therefore, proceeded to "have their say" in a series of "statements."

**Bryan Opens Battle.**

The first one came from William Jennings Bryan. It brought immediate responses from Clarence Darrow and Dudley Field Malone, representing conflicting religious opinions. The statements set forth these views both as related to the evolutionary and religious phases of the Scopes trial and from their own personal standpoints.

Mr. Bryan asserted that the case had uncovered an "insidious attack upon the authority of the Bible." It termed Clarence Darrow's entrance into the case "most fortunate for the Christian church," and pronounced him the perfect product of evolution in the United States and charged that Mr. Darrow had "slurred the Bible, insulted the court, shown his contempt for everything Christian and everybody identified with Christianity."

**Plans Complete Answer.**

"I shall prepare an answer to Mr. Darrow's charge that I am an ignorant bigot," Mr. Bryan said. "I am not vain enough to think that this compliment—for coming from him, it was a compliment—was intended for me alone. While it was addressed to me, it was intended for all who dare differ from him to the extent of believing in the Bible, the God whom it reveals and the super-natural Christ of whom it tells. I shall answer for all Christians as well as for myself, but I feel that the answer will receive more consideration if it is separated from the proceedings of today."

Mr. Darrow, replying, declared he had not come into the Scopes case until after the entrance of Mr. Bryan, and added that he was "inclined to think that intelligent religionists would like to get rid of Mr. Bryan." He came with the anticipation of being allowed to produce expert testimony, he said.

**Darow Hits Back.**

Darrow's statement follows:

"Mr. Bryan has done me the honor to say that I am the finest product of evolution. I do not believe I am. Mr. Bryan is not the finest product of evolution but he comes under the classification of those who revert to type.

"Perhaps my entrance into this case was unfortunate for the Christian church, but I did not come into it until after Mr. Bryan and which one's entrance was the most unfortunate must be determined by religonists." I am inclined to think that most intelligent religionists would like to get rid of Mr. Bryan.

"I never said I did not believe in a God. I have never been able to satisfy myself of a first cause and as to that I am an agnostic. I am ready to receive light upon the subject from anyone who can give it."

"Mr. Bryan is not the best judge of whether my questions were competent enough to be answered. It is enough to say he answered them in his way in the presence of the court and it is rather interesting that the next morning the court of his own accord struck them from the record. I cannot help wondering why the court helped Mr. Bryan out of his dilemma, especially so early in the morning and before any request had been made in open court."

**Mr. Malone's Opinion.**

"Our objects in coming to Tennessee have been fulfilled," Mr. Malone said. Though Professor Scopes has been convicted, we have made a record filled with reversible error which will, we believe, ultimately declare the Tennessee evolution law unconstitutional. After his examination by Clarence Darrow yesterday no intelligent person in America can believe that Mr. Bryan is an authority on science education or the Bible.

"The life, the sacrifice, the sweet spirit of charity and tolerance, the years of service to the downtrodden which Clarence Darrow has given to his fellowmen, will stand contrast with the arrogant assumption of William Jennings Bryan that he is the predestined representative in the United States of all Christians."

**Trial Ended With Prayer.**

The Scopes evolution trial ended here today with prayer—as it began.

Between the invocation and the benediction, and interspersed with other prayers, lay the record of many stormy scenes; of sharp words and almost as many apologies.

Contending voices which had been raised in protest and exasperation, opposing actors in the legal drama, merged their tones into a grand ensemble and declared as the curtain fell:

"Truth is mighty and will prevail."

After the discord and conflict of eight trial days, harmony at length prevailed when the jury returned its verdict "for the state." Not a voice was raised in disagreement with the judgment, de-

# The Minneapolis Morning Tribune

Sixtieth Year. No. 75. | Thirty-two Pages | MINNEAPOLIS, MINN., SATURDAY, AUGUST 7, 1926 | Price Two Cents in Minneapolis

# EDERLE CONQUERS CHANNEL

## Dark Horse Is Iowa G.O.P.'s Senate Choice

### David W. Stewart, Sioux City Lawyer, Chosen at Des Moines Meet.

### Compromise Candidate Averts Clash Between Cummins and Brookhart Men.

### Democrats Fail to Nominate Candidate—Field Clear to Republicans.

Des Moines, Iowa, Aug. 6.—(By Associated Press.)—Davis W. Stewart, a Sioux City lawyer, and a progressive Republican, is the choice of the Republican party of Iowa for the unfinished United States senate term of the late Senator Albert B. Cummins. He will go before the voters in the November election as the candidate for the short term, while Colonel Smith W. Brookhart, the party's primary nominee, will run for the full six-year term.

Stewart was nominated late this afternoon on the third formal ballot of the party's convention. His selection was hailed on all sides as a happy compromise between the forces of Colonel Brookhart, who sought the short term nomination for their leader and the group of party "regulars" who went into the convention determined to block the Brookhart boom and, if possible, to nominate a man who had stood close to Senator Cummins during the latter's long service.

The unexpected strength of Stewart proved a surprise to all factions working for other candidates. He left his home in Sioux City yesterday with little thought of going before the convention and the Woodbury county delegation launched a boom for him only this morning, more as a complimentary move than in the hope of success.

**Outsider Is Chosen.**

But as the voting progressed and the candidates whose names have been before Iowa voters on numerous occasions in the past, failed to rally the strength anticipated the delegates began looking about for a man that would break what appeared to be an approaching deadlock and Stewart, the outsider and a comparative youngster in Iowa politics, proved to be the man.

Stewart himself was so surprised that he scarcely realized he had stepped into a convention without an organization, except the local support of his own county and defeated men like Brookhart, Burton E. Sweet, former Des Moines; Howard J. Clark, Des congressman; Charles J. Bradshaw of Moines; former Governor N. E. Kendall; Colonel George French of Davenport, Dan Turner, of Corning, and H. O. Weaver of Wapello—all veteran campaigners.

**Managed Coolidge Campaign.**

Stewart, a graduate of the University of Chicago Law school and a former school teacher and athletic coach, now is head of the Sioux City Chamber of Commerce. He has been interested in municipal politics in his home city and managed the Coolidge campaign in the northwestern part of the state in the last national election.

Addressing the convention after his nomination, Stewart declared the Republican party should be the medium through which the midwest should seek desired legislation and predicted that a united effort through that party for economic readjustment would meet with success. If elected he pledged he would support the principles of true Republicanism.

None of Stewart's opponents in the balloting approached the 693 majority necessary for a nomination and when the tide finally turned after one informal or complimentary ballot and three formal ballots, the total rolled up for the Sioux City man was 855.

**Brookhart's Highest 317 1-5.**

Colonel Brookhart's vote mounted only as high as 371 1-5 on the second formal ballot an increase from 368 on the first ballot and from 350 on the complimentary ballot.

Mr. Stewart, who is 39 years old and one of the youngest Iowans to be nominated for public office, said his nomination was one of the big surprises of his life.

"I have always worked hard for what I got," he said. "This was the easiest thing that was ever handed to me. I cannot say how much I appreciate the honor."

Mr. Stewart paved the way for his education in academy, college and university by working at various things that brought him sufficient income to defray all of his expenses. He was born in New Concord, Ohio, June 22, 1887, and attended the public schools of that place. He then attended an academy and Geneva college in Pennsylvania, and later, the University of Chicago, graduating from the law department in 1917.

**Figured in City Politics.**

Coming to Iowa in the summer of 1911, Mr. Stewart located at Cherokee, where he taught in the high school, the subjects of civics and economics, at the same time he acted as athletic director and produced several championship football teams.

In 1913 Mr. Stewart went to Sioux City to reside. For the next few years he was attending summer school and preparing himself for the study of law.

Starting practice in Sioux City after his graduation from law school, Mr. Stewart married Helen Strable of Lemars. They have no children.

His political career began in Sioux

(Continued on Page 2, Column 4.)

### Weather Forecast.

MINNESOTA—Fair today. Sunday probably increasing cloudiness followed by unsettled, not much change in temperature.

### News Index

WASHINGTON.

All arrangements for construction of the tow boats and barges to operate on the upper Mississippi river were completed by the war department. Page 1.

DOMESTIC.

The death of Edward H. Parr at the hands of a madman revealed to his Chicago wife that he had a second wife in Minneapolis. Page 1.

President Coolidge talked politics with Representative Tilson at the old homestead in Plymouth, Vt., and later tried fishing, while Mrs. Coolidge went berry picking. Page 1.

Iowa Democrats voted not to enter a candidate in the short term senatorial race at Des Moines, leaving the field clear for David W. Stewart of Sioux City, an outsider, nominated by the Republicans in convention. Page 1.

Residents abandoned Ashford, Wash., a town in the path of the forest fires, which are growing more serious, forestry officials declared. Page 6.

One flier was killed when his plane crashed at Chanute field, Rantoul, Ill., and two others were injured when their machine fell in an effort to aid the first victim. Page 12.

LOCAL.

Minneapolis detectives expect to leave Seattle Monday, bringing Thomas Johnson back to this city for trial. Page 1.

A 17-year-old baby boy "ran away" from home in northeast Minneapolis to the south side, on the running board of a car, and was unhurt. Page 1.

Trade tourists of the Minneapolis Radio Trade association returned Friday night. Page 4.

The president of the Twin City Railway Business Women's association scored the Union Pacific for announcing it would replace women employes with men. Page 5.

Rate discriminations against Minnesota railroads was charged in a hearing before the railroad and warehouse commission. Page 7.

Many out-of-town pastors will fill Minneapolis pulpits Sunday. Page 8.

The Disabled American Veterans will open their convention today. Page 8.

Fifteen thousand persons attended the annual boys and girls field and track day at the Parade Friday. Page 11.

The Minnesota Linseed Oil Paint Co. will erect a plant for the production of varnish in Minneapolis. Page 14.

Several aldermen expressed the fear that efforts are being made to engage an auditorium manager without the consent of the entire council. Page 15.

FOREIGN.

Gertrude Ederle, 19-year-old American girl, swam the English channel in the record time of 14 hours and 31 minutes. She is the first of her sex to accomplish the feat. Page 1.

A meeting of the ministerial council called by Premier Poincare of France to consider hastening of ratification of debts pacts with the United States and Great Britain was delayed until Monday when opposition developed in parliamentary lobbies. Page 3.

Both sides in the Mexico religious controversy apparently were prepared for an indefinite contest. Page 16.

EDITORIALS.

A Challenge to Cancellationists; Gertrude Ederle Swims the Channel; Yet the Direct Primary Was on the Job; Citing the Records in Proof; Why Latin America Fears Us. Page 18.

SPORTS.

Jimmy Johnston and J. K. Wetherby will clash for the state amateur golf championship at the Country club today. Page 24.

Lester Bolstad of Minneapolis will play Carl F. Kauffmann of Pittsburgh for the national public links golf championship in the finals of the tournament in Buffalo, N. Y., today. Page 24.

Helen Wills received her first setback this season when she was defeated by Elizabeth Ryan in the finals of the Seabright tournament. Page 24.

Ace Hudkins and Stan Loayza, leading contenders for the lightweight championship, fought to a furious draw. Page 24.

The Millers failed to hold a four-run first-inning lead and were defeated by St. Paul in the first game of the intercity series, 9 to 8. Page 25.

Babe Ruth hits his thirty-fifth home run as the Yankees nosed out Cleveland, 8 to 7. Page 25.

The Pirates forged ahead in the National league race with a 5 to 4 victory over Boston while the Reds were dropping their tenth consecutive game to the Giants. Page 25.

MARKETS.

Speculators for the advance regained control of the stock market, featured by broader activity and many gains in prices. Page 26.

Cash wheat was firm on the market here, but futures were quiet to dull during most of the session. Primary receipts dropped 1,000,000 bushels from last week's totals. Page 27.

Low estimates of new exports depressed wheat in Chicago. Page 28.

Cattle and hogs held firm in a light run at South St. Paul. Page 28.

## *Jap Prince Defies Imperial Order to Return From Paris*

Tokio, Aug. 6.—(By Associated Press.)—Prince Higashi-Kuni, husband of Princess Toshiko, youngest daughter of the late Emperor Meiji, is reported to have incurred the displeasure of the imperial household because of disinclinations to return to Japan after residing in Paris more than five years. The prince went to Paris in 1920 to "study tactics."

The princess, with their two children, resides in Tokio. Recently two friends of the prince, said to have been sent to Paris with orders from the imperial household for the absentee to return, reported that his highness liked France so well he was uncertain when he would return to Japan.

The prince, who is 39 years old, is a colonel of infantry. In Paris he is known as Count Higashi.

## Detectives Plan Speedy Return With Johnson

### Minneapolis Operatives Ready to Leave Seattle on Monday.

### Warrant Mailed to Coast Charges Highway Robbery.

### Another Victim of Holdup Identifies Photograph of Erdall Slayer.

Minneapolis police detectives now at Seattle expect to leave Monday for this city, bringing with them Thomas Johnson, self-confessed slayer of Leonard Erdall, who was fatally shot during a holdup on December 19, 1925.

The return trip will be started Monday, provided the warrant issued by the county attorney's office charging Johnson with highway robbery reaches Seattle by that time, and also that Johnson himself does not decide to resist the plan to bring him to Minnesota.

County Attorney Floyd B. Olson mailed the warrant Thursday. It was prepared upon evidence furnished by M. H. Lattimer, manager of the Feltman & Curme shoe store at 215 Nicollet avenue, who identified a photograph of Johnson as being that of the man who had held him up. If this warrant is delayed, it will only mean a day or two of waiting before the date of departure, during which time Johnson will continue to be held on a fugitive from justice warrant which was sworn out in Seattle upon instructions from Minneapolis.

The latest identification of the Johnson photographs was made Friday by Robert A. Merrill, Eau Claire, Wis., former University of Minnesota student, who said he was the engineering student Johnson claimed he had held up and shot. He declared Johnson's story of this holdup was accurate in the main, but gave a different version of his own actions after being shot.

In Johnson's confession, he said that

(Continued on Page 3, Column 5.)

## U. S. Approves Contracts for Barge Fleet

### All Details for Start of Operations Next Spring Completed.

**By George E. Akerson.**

**Washington Correspondent of The Tribune.**

Washington, Aug. 6.—All arrangements for construction of the tow boats and barges to operate on the upper Mississippi river have been completed. Contracts entered into for the building of equipment were given final approval at the war department today.

General T. Q. Ashburn, acting for the Inland Waterways corporation, and A. C. Wiprud of Minneapolis, acting for the Upper Mississippi Barge Line corporation, were in conference during the day. When their work was finished, they announced that all details had been settled satisfactorily and approval given.

A fleet designed especially to fit the river on which it is to be operated will be ready when the navigation season opens next year. Work already has started on some of the equipment. From now on it will be full speed ahead.

**Busines Men Praised.**

Credit was being freely given today to the Minneapolis and St. Paul business men who have labored during the past few months to clear away all of the details necessary in order that actual work might start. Financial houses of Minneapolis were also credited with having done much for river development by the financing of the project.

Mr. Wiprud summed up the work accomplished to date in the following manner:

"We have just completed final arrangements for the construction of tow-boats and barges for the Upper Mississippi Barge Line Co., which the Inland Waterways corporation is to operate, beginning with the opening of navigation on the upper river next spring. Formal contracts have been entered into with the contractors, steel has been ordered and is now being rolled, the first shipment to be in the hands of the contractors next week.

**A Novel Undertaking.**

"This concludes nine months of earnest application on the part of the directors of the barge line company, in co-operation with naval architects and General T. Q. Ashburn, executive in charge of the Inland Waterways corporation, to finance, design and contract for the most modern river fleet ever built. In the selection of the naval architects and engineers the greatest care was used to obtain the best in this field. This is the first time in the history of river navigation that

(Continued on Page 2, Column 2.)

## *Father, Two Children Die When Home Burns*

Morgantown, W. Va., Aug. 6.—(By Associated Press.)—A father and his two small children were fatally burned when their home at Clifton Mills, a small hamlet in Preston county, was destroyed by fire. Word of the fire reached here today. The man, Porter McKinley, died of burns sustained when he tried to rescue the children, 6 and 3 years old. The mother was also burned and was in a serious condition last night.

**19-Year-Old American Girl Who Set Channel Record**

Gertrude Ederle.

## *Baby Sleeps on Running Board in 2-Mile Runaway*

### 17-Months-Old Wanderer, Home Again, Laughs Off Peril With Blink.

A 17-months-old boy, far too young to know the trouble he had caused, "ran away" from home Friday afternoon and covered more than two miles of city streets, across town, before he was found. Then he rewarded his parents with a sleepy blinking of his eyes.

The baby boy is Vernon Solem, son of Mr. and Mrs. Emil Solem, 604 Monroe street northeast.

He was playing in the front yard at 4 p. m. Friday. At 4:05 p. m. he had disappeared. His mother, unable to find him, enlisted the aid of the police department, and a futile but thorough search of the neighborhood was begun.

Three-quarters of an hour later a man stopped a motorist at Tenth avenue and Fourth street south, and asked him what he had on the running board of his car.

"Ain't nothing of mine there," the driver answered.

Nevertheless there was something—a sleeping child stretched precariously on the narrow running board. The pedestrian, not concerning himself with the identity of the driver, gallantly offered to take care of the child. He got the job.

He carried the child to the Riverside police station, deposited it on a desk and was himself allowed to walk off with the charming anonymity of all heroes. Later the child was taken to police headquarters, where he was identified as Vernon by the Solems.

Violet, 3-year-old sister of Vernon, had the only definite information concerning the disappearance. She saw an automobile parked outside in the front of the Solem home shortly before her brother disappeared.

## Chicago Prison Break Averted

### Guards, Acting on Tip, Raid 'Hard-Boiled' Row and Get Shower of Weapons.

Chicago, Aug. 6. — (By Associated Press.)—Another prison break attempt was averted at the county jail tonight when a corps of guards acting on a tip, descended on tier three and seized dozens of improvised weapons.

A double guard had been posted prior to the raid, to prevent the prisoners from disposing of the implements, but the weapons were tossed in a shower at the raiders' feet and ownership of none was discovered.

Spoons whetted to razor edges and a number of saws comprised the assortment which greeted arrival of the guards.

The tier is occupied by the "hardest boiled" of the prisoners. It was reported to authorities that one of the leaders of the plot disclosed tonight was Dan McGeogeheoagan, sentenced to be hanged with Henry "Midget" Fernekes, to the jail wall on "murderers' row."

## *Navy Picks Up SOS From British Vessel*

New York, Aug. 6.—(By Associated Press.)—The naval communications bureau tonight reported the receipt of an SOS call from the steamer Antonio, somewhere off Bermuda. All broadcasting stations were ordered shut out until definite location of the distressed vessel could be established. The Antonio, a British vessel of 3,168 net tons, sailed from Hampton Roads August 3, for St. Vincent, Cape Verde.

**Mexico Gets U. S. Oil Note.**

Mexico City, Aug. 6.—(By Associated Press.)—Ambassador Sheffield has delivered a new United States note with reference to Mexico's petroleum and land laws to the Mexican foreign office, it was learned today from circles close to the foreign office.

## 'Pop' Ederle Sings Way Across Aboard Tug as 'Trudy' Swims

### Father Kept Up a Constant Fire of Encouragement During Voyage.

### Friends on Ship Hang Funny Drawings on Side to Amuse Her.

Dover, England, Aug. 6.—(INS.)—The most excited man aboard the two tugs which accompanied Gertrude Ederle on her channel swim was "Pop" Ederle, her father.

"Pop" insisted on leading all the songs and kept up a constant fire of encouragement for "Trudy" all the way across the channel.

The strains of "Show Me the Way to Go Home," "Animal Crackers" and other popular songs were heard intermingled with the strains of patriotic American anthems as the shore was neared.

"Don't worry, we'll get there yet," shouted Miss Ederle from the water to her father, as they approached the Goodwin light.

"My, it's wet," she commented as the rain began to fall.

There was never any indication of her courage weakening although the weather for this nautical jaunt was enough to discourage the score or more newspaper men aboard the tug Mornie which they chartered to make the trip.

"They'll have to take me out of the water unconscious if I don't make the shore this time," Miss Ederle said when she gazed up through the slapping waves at funny drawings which were suspended over the side of the tug Alsace for her amusement.

Throughout the swim "Pop" kept "Trudy" supplied with lumps of sugar, the sweets being carried to her by Margaret Ederle, Ishaak Helmy and Lillian Cannon who took turns pacing her.

And when the Alsace started back to Gris Nez, the happiest man aboard was "Pop" Ederle.

### Gertrude Family Gets Bulletins on Swim.

Highlands, N. J., Aug. 6.—(INS.)—While Gertrude Ederle battled across the cross-currents of the English channel, her mother, Mrs. Henry Ederle, sat close to a telephone in a summer cottage here, waiting for late bulletins on her daughter's progress. As editions of the New York newspapers reached the street, Miss Helen Ederle, oldest daughter in the family, got a copy, absorbed the latest cable reports on Gertrude and then telephoned the news to her mother. The young brothers and sisters of Gertrude, George, Emma and Henry, were close around their mother.

## Parr Slaying Reveals He Has Second Widow

### Chicago Woman Learns Dead Husband Left Wife in Minneapolis.

Chicago, Aug. 6. — (By Associated Press.)—The chance bullet of a madman's gun has revealed to Erna Johnson Parr that the bond salesman she married last May, now lying dead in Chicago morgue, left another wife.

Edward H. Parr and his bride of less than four months, left their uptown apartment Monday night to go to the theater. On their way home in the crowded street, they were fired upon suddenly by one Fletcher Andrews, who, an examination revealed, was suffering from hallucinations of injury by Parr, who had never met him.

Both were wounded, Parr fatally. He died early yesterday. His name was noted in the newspapers by Mrs. E. H. Parr of Minneapolis, and she wired Chicago police that she had claims to widowhood prior to Erna's.

Erna works in a State street department store. Her brother said today that she met Parr some months ago, and that they were married in May. But officials of the bond company where Parr was a salesman confirmed the existence of the Minneapolis spouse and said Parr had lived there until recently, having been a salesman for Conboy & Co., of Minneapolis, and having later run a brokerage house there under the name of Edward Parr & Co.

Erna, retreating from the Parrs' north side apartment to her brother's home, delayed tonight the funeral plans which she had all but completed, and

(Continued on Page 3, Column 3.)

## *Cardinals' New Wage Scale for Vatican Is Approved by Pope*

Rome, Aug. 6.—(By Associated Press)—Pope Pius has approved a new scale of wages for Vatican officials and employes, drawn up by a special commission of cardinals, whereby their pay will be brought to a figure equalling five times that received before the war. At the same time the Pontiff expressed a desire that the working day of the employes be increased, effective in October. At that time the working day, which seldom amounts to more than three hours actual toil, will be lengthened to five or six hours.

Recently there has been agitation among the Vatican employes for increased pay, some of the gardeners going so far as to declare a strike.

**Duggan Safe in Argentine Port.**

Buenos Aires, Aug. 6.—(By Associated Press.)—La Nacion's Rio Grande do Sul correspondent reports that Bernardo Duggan and his fellow aviators missing since Monday arrived there unexpectedly at noon today.

### Camden Park Singers Celebrate 'Ederle Night' With Pop's Favorites

The conquest of the English channel by Gertrude Ederle was celebrated at Camden park during The Minneapolis Tribune-Park board community singing contest Friday night.

When Harry Anderson, director of the sing, announced that it was "Trudy Ederle" night, he was greeted by cheers. The program thereupon was changed to include the songs that Gertrude's father, "Pop" Ederle, sang from the tug that accompanied his daughter on the swim.

"Show Me the Way to Go Home" and "Animal Crackers," two of "Pop's" favorites, were sung heartily, and the words of "My Bonnie Lies Over the Ocean" were changed to "My Bonnie swam easily over, and touched at the white cliffs of Dover."

Tonight at Van Cleve park, the community singers will try "Oh, Ederle, Gem of the Ocean."

## *Coolidge Lends Ear to Politics at Old Homestead*

### Learns Plans for Eastern Campaign, Airs Mexico Views and Fishes.

Plymouth, Vt., Aug. 6.—(By Associated Press.)—President Coolidge was informed today by Representative Tilson of Connecticut, Republican floor leader in the house, that joint eastern senatorial and congressional campaign headquarters would be opened in New York next week.

Mr. Tilson, who is to open the offices himself, came with Mrs. Tilson from Lake Sunapee, N. H., where he has a camp, and remained for lunch with the President and Mrs. Coolidge at the old homestead where the latter are visiting for a few days.

A number of subjects were said to have been discussed by the President and Mr. Tilson, but the political situation was not taken up in detail. After the eastern campaign offices have been opened, Mr.

Later in the day, the President received newspaper correspondents.

In his behalf and in response to questions, it was said that he had received no reports of any offenses against American citizens in Mexico. The government, it was explained, is interested in any situation like the present one in Mexico only in reference to seeing that its own citizens are cared for. What action the Mexican or any other government may take toward its own citizens, it was emphasized, is purely a domestic matter for that country.

During the afternoon, Mr. and Mrs. Coolidge went calling in Ludlow, 12 miles away. They stopped at the Ludlow Banking & Trust Co., while the President went in and talked with Homer L. Skeels, president, and other officials of the bank.

The Coolidges then went a few miles farther to Proctorsville, a section of Ludlow, where both went to the home of Mrs. Sarah Pollard, aunt of the President on his mother's side, and visited for half an hour.

Mr. Coolidge went with rod and line to Pinney Hollow brook, a quarter of a mile from the Coolidge home. Although he remained for five hours, little luck attended him, and the few trout he caught were so small that he threw them back.

Mrs. Coolidge, in the meantime, went blue berry picking in a neighboring pasture and had better luck, returning in little more than an hour with a pailful.

## Rescuers Near Five in Mine

### Crews Working All Night Expected to Reach Entombed Miners This Morning.

Paducah, Ky., Aug. 6.—(By Associated Press.)—Rescue crews working without let-up tonight to release five miners entombed in the Hudson Zinc & Spar Company's mine near Salem, Ky., 35 miles from here. The miners were trapped 24 hours ago when a great mass of earth slipped through an old cut above an abandoned working. The men were imprisoned on the 150 foot level and 75 feet from the mouth of the mine.

Belief among miners here tonight was that the resucers probably would be able to reach the entombed men by tomorrow morning. No indication has come from the interior of the mine that would give hope that the men still were alive.

## *Two Killed, 56 Hurt, When Engine Blows Up*

Ashtabula, Ohio, Aug. 6.—(By Associated Press.)—Engineer William Coyne and Fireman W. J. Quinn, both of Youngstown, were killed, six men were so badly injured they were taken to a hospital and 50 others suffered lesser injuries when the boiler of a New York Central freight train locomotive exploded here today. The explosion occurred opposite the plant of the American Fork & Hoe Co., where the injured were employed. The injured were cut by flying glass and other debris. Houses nearby were shaken and windows smashed.

## American Girl Swimmer Sets World's Record

### Crosses 19-Mile Stretch of Water in 14 Hours and 31 Minutes.

### First Woman to Accomplish Feat Betters Mark Set by Argentinian.

### Summer Colony Crowds Cheer Victory at End of Long Test.

Kingsdown, Eng., Aug. 6.—(By Associated Press.)—Gertrude Ederle today conquered the English channel.

The 19-year-old New York girl, swimming the grim waters in 14 hours and 31 minutes, thus became the first of her sex to accomplish the feat which has been performed by only five men before her. She left Cape Gris Nez at 7:09 o'clock this morning and landed at Dover at 9:40 o'clock tonight.

Miss Ederle's time for the swim set a world's record, the best previous mark of 16 hours and 33 minutes being that of Tirabocchi, the Argentinean, who swam from Calais to Dover three years ago.

**Strong and Fresh at Finish.**

Miss Ederle walked triumphantly up the beaches between the little village of Kingsdown and Walme Castle, Deal, quite strong and fresh. The last few hundred yards of the swim were watched from the shore by thousands of visitors from all parts of the country sojourning at the seaside resort of Deal, who collected all available material to build a bonfire on the beach to guide the plucky American girl as she neared her goal.

Thus she finished the feat in a flare lighting the coast for miles, since the accompanying tugs burned flares and displayed searchlights.

**Refuses Aid in Landing.**

The swimmer refused all offers of help in landing. Waving all aside, she walked out of the surf unaided, amid tremendous outbursts of cheering which completely drowned the tugboats' sirens. She was so fresh she even wanted to plunge into the sea again to swim back to the boat lying some 200 yards out. But this was not allowed, and she was rowed back to the boat, and helped aboard for the return trip to Cape Gris Nez.

"I am a proud woman," said the victorious swimmer as she paused for a moment on English soil, before she returned in the small boat to the tug Alsace, which accompanied her across the treacherous channel.

The latter part of the swim was accomplished in bad conditions, a stiff breeze churning up heavy seas, and there was a slight rain. The scene as Miss Ederle finished the last few hundred yards was intensely thrilling. The blaze of light enabled the great crowd which gad gathered, mostly women, to watch the swimmer. Their elation over the triumph of one of their sex knew no bounds.

**Log of Channel Swim.**

The log of Miss Ederle's record swim follows:

7:09 a. m.—Entered the water at Cape Gris Nez shouting, "The next time I cross the channel I hope it's by airplane."

7:30 a. m.—One mile out.

8:08 a. m.—Mile and a half out.

10:20 a. m.—Four miles out with water calm.

11:38 a. m.—Seven and a half miles out.

11:55 a. m.—Drank bottle of chicken broth and ate leg of chicken.

12:45 p. m.—Swimming strongly against choppy sea and high gale, ten and a half miles from Dover.

1:20 p. m.—Fighting against wild wind and high waves.

2:00 p. m.—Swimming strongly nine miles from English coast.

3:05 p. m.—Nearing Varne buoy, eight miles off coast.

4:45 p. m.—Two miles from East Goodwin lightship and seven miles from Dover.

6:05 p. m.—Wind growing worse and sea more choppy. Trainer Burgess suggests abandonment of the attempt.

7:10 p. m.—Five miles from Dover with waves mounting higher. Burgess insists that she be taken out of the water. Miss Ederle swims on, shouting "What for?"

7:17 p. m.—Drank cocoa and ate bar of chocolate.

8:20 p. m.—Three miles off coast with storm abating.

9:40 p. m.—Miss Ederle walked up the beach at Kingsdown, the first woman to swim the channel.

**Records of Five Men.**

Miss Ederle's record-breaking swim across the English channel today is the sixth time this turbulent stretch of water has been conquered in something over a half century.

The record of the five previous triumphs, all by men, follow:

August 24-25, 1875, by Captain Matthew Webb of Eastbourne, England, Dover Sands, England, to Sangatte Beach, France. Time, 22 hours, 45 minutes. Estimated distance traveled, 39 miles. (Second attempt.)

September 5-6, 1911, by Thomas W. Burgess of London, England, Dover admiralty pier to Cape Gris Nez, France. Time, 22 hours 35 minutes. Estimated distance traveled, 39 miles. (Nineteenth attempt.)

August 5-6, 1923, by Henry Sullivan of Lowell, Mass., Dover admiralty pier to Cape Griz Nez. Time, 27 hours, 23 minutes. Estimated distance covered, 45 miles. (Third attempt.)

August 11-12, 1923, by Sebastian Tirabocchi of Buenos Aires, an Italian, Cape Gris Nez to Dover Sands, England. Time, 16 hours 23 minutes. Estimated distance traveled, 27 miles. (Third attempt.)

September 8-9, 1923, by Charles Toth of Boston, Cape Gris Nez to Dover Sands. Time, 16 hours 54 minutes. Es-

The Minneapolis Morning Tribune

Sixtieth Year. No. 121. Thirty-six Pages MINNEAPOLIS, MINN., FRIDAY, SEPTEMBER 24, 1926 Price Two Cents in Minneapolis

# TUNNEY DETHRONES DEMPSEY

## Leaders in Nine Cities Welcome Harvest Tour

### Towns Turn Out to Greet 100 Minneapolis Business Men on C. & C. Trip.

### Mutual Interests Stressed in Addresses by Hosts and Visitors.

### Group Returns Home After Ending All Day Journey at Mankato.

By Hilton Hornaday.

Minneapolis carried the message of good will and friendship Thursday to nine prosperous cities and towns in the territory served by the Minneapolis, Northfield & Southern railway between Minneapolis and Mankato.

One hundred business men, on the Civic & Commerce association annual harvest trade tour heard the leading business men of these communities tell of their achievements and then listened to a message of good will from the friendship tourists. They returned to Minneapolis Thursday night.

The mutuality of interests between Minneapolis and the smaller cities and towns was the keynote of the addresses on the tour. The Minneapolis visitors, after an all-day trip, were guests last night of the business men of Mankato at a dinner at the Heinrich hotel. A. R. Kroh of The Minneapolis Tribune, the principal speaker, said that Minneapolis is always eager to extend the hand of fellowship to its neighboring communities. J. E. Brett, president of the Mankato Chamber of Commerce, extended the welcome. M. B. Fritz, president of the Mankato Free Press, was chairman of the reception committee.

**Morristown Turns Out.**

The friendship tourists were given a royal welcome at Morristown, a village of 688 persons. Rice county school children left their studies, marched to the main street and sang "America" for the visitors. The Rev. M. L. Reynolds, pastor of the Baptist church, said Morristown is proud that its jail has been empty for five years, and that the Bible is read in the schools every day. Mayor W. H. Bean headed the reception committee. John Burgess, vice president of the Metropolitan National bank, speaking for the Minneapolis tourists, said that people of Morristown have the spirit of hospitality in their hearts.

**Stop 45 Minutes.**

The harvest special stopped 45 minutes at Waterville. Rain began falling during the march from the station to the business section, but the Minneapolis visitors and the townspeople grouped around the broad porch of the Commercial hotel for a brief program.

Carl W. Jones of The Minneapolis Journal, spoke for the friendship tourists. At Elysian, the speaking program was cancelled because of rain. The Minneapolis visitors paraded to the main street, however, and were greeted by a committee headed by W. K. Wilcox, publisher of The Enterprise, and A. W. Westhaver, the village president. Elysian people distributed big baskets of apples on the special train.

At Madison Lake the address of welcome on behalf of the townspeople was made by the Rev. A. M. Meinder, the mayor. The Catholic Women's guild served a luncheon.

**Lakeville Is First Stop.**

At Lakeville, the first stop, H. J. van Valkenburg, secretary of the Lakeville Commercial club told the business men that Lakeville citizens virtually feel themselves a part of Minneapolis.

"Lakeville ships 40 tons of milk each day to Minneapolis," Mr. van Valkenburg said, "and Lakeville and adjoining communities ship about 8,000 pounds of butter a day to Minneapolis as well as a large quantity of poultry and eggs. We like to feel that after all Lakeville is really a suburb of Minneapolis. Our people use your schools, your theaters and your wonderful parks. We are glad to welcome you and want you to feel that our citizens want most of all a new and greater neighborship."

**Mayor Welcomes Visitors.**

B. E. Eggren, mayor of Lakeville, and George .. Barres, president of the Commercial club, with Mr. van Valkenburg made up the committee which welcomed the trade tourists.

Edward M. Conant of the Northern States Power Co. spoke on behalf of the visiting business men, pointing out that the tour came to Lakeville to spread the gospel of friendly trade relationship, and to let Lakeville know that Minneapolis wants the friendship of its business people.

After the speaking program, the trade emissaries of good will fell in line behind Michael Jalma's American Legion band and marched to the business center, where after a short entertainment program, tourists called personally on the business establishments of the town.

**Schools Dismissed.**

At Northfield the friendship tourists marched two blocks in spite of the downpour of rain. After a band concert Mr. Kroh gave a short talk. The success of the dairy farmers in the vicinity of Northfield, he said, illustrates in a most striking fashion that agriculture can be made profitable when farmers own herds of dairy cows and put into practice crop rotation and diversification.

C. L. Brown, chairman of the welcoming committee of Northfield business men, pointed out that Northfield is rapidly developing into a manufacturing center, and that the territory within a radius of 30 miles has not had a bank failure for years.

### Weather Forecast

MINNESOTA — Partly cloudy to cloudy; colder in east portion today; much colder along Lake Superior; probably snow flurries in north portion; Saturday generally fair and somewhat warmer.

## News Index



## *Six Killed, 18 Injured in French Train Wreck*

Paris, Sept. 23. — (By Associated Press.)—Six persons were killed today when the Lyons express was in a collision just outside the Hericy station of the Paris-Montereau line. Eighteen persons were injured. Although one of those killed was at first reported an American student, the railroad company's announcement said the victim was a British citizen.

## *Beach Life Guards Begin Catalina Swim*

Balboa, Calif., Sept. 23.—(INS.)—Nicholas Sanoff and Robert Foster, beach life guards, plunged into the sea here today in an attempt to swim to Catalina island, 36 miles distant from this point.

## Question of U. S. Entry to World Court Reopens

### Reconsideration by Senate Expected by Washington Officials.

### Geneva Committee Advises Against Full Acceptance of Reservations.

### Adherence to Tribunal Is Likely to Be Impeded by Decision.

Washington, Sept. 23.—(By Associated Press.)—American entry into the World court will have to be reconsidered by the senate in the judgment of a number of informed officials in the capitol, if the member powers adopt the recommendations submitted to them by the Geneva advisory conference on the American reservations.

In the absence of official advices from Geneva any authorized expression of views was lacking, but an undercurrent of feeling was discernable that the whole question of American participation in the work of the court had been greatly complicated.

**Report Merely Advisory.**

Initiative now rests with the powers participating in the Geneva discussion, as the report of the conference, as adopted today, is merely of an advisory character. It recommends to the powers a formula of reply to the inquiry of the Washington government as to whether American signature of the World court protocol on the basis of the reservations attached by the senate would be satisfactory.

The powers are not committed to accept the advice of the Geneva delegates, each being free to formulate whatever reply to Washington it deems best, and the next move expected is the decision of the individual powers on the nature of these replies.

Should the powers accept the advice of the Geneva gathering and transmit identic replies holding that American signature of a supplemental protocol as well as of the original protocol, was necessary, it is said in some quarters that President Coolidge must of necessity submit the new protocol drafted at Geneva to the senate if he believed it desirable that the United States enter the court on that basis.

**New Draft for Senate.**

These observers say he would be without authority to exchange ratifications without further advice and consent of the senate, but whether the administration would take that course, or merely drop the whole matter, was a question on which no official cared to venture a prediction.

However, there apparently was no doubt in any quarter that the supplemental protocol, if submitted to the senate, would mark a renewal of the whole argument as to American entry into the court and defer indefinitely, if not prevent completely, American adherence to that judicial body.

In effect such informal expressions as could be obtained indicate the belief that, regardless of the merits of the questions raised at Geneva as to the

(Continued on Page 4, Column 1.)

## Tornado Rips Huron, Ohio

### Barns Unroofed and Trees Torn Up—Twister Disappears Into Lake Erie.

Sandusky, Ohio, Sept. 23.—(By Associated Press.) — A tornado twisted its way along a 12-mile stretch of Lake Erie near here today, whisked through the center of Huron, nine miles from here, and disappeared into Lake Erie. No fatalities were reported following a checkup of the district. The damage at Huron was placed at between $10,000 and $20,000. Barns were unroofed and trees unrooted in the vicinity. A house was wrecked at Bloomingville and hal fa dozen other homes unroofed.

The tornado was first reported west of Bogart, a small community five miles south of Sandusky shortly after 4:30 o'clock. Farm houses and barns were flattened as the storm passed to the northeast.

The storm as it traveled to the southwest and south of Sandusky followed almost the same path as one or two tornadoes which devastated this region on June 28, 1924, it being reported that several houses badly damaged in the 1924 storm were struck again today.

## *St. Paul Woman Killed by Auto Near Her Home*

Mrs. Daniel M. Vogelgesang, 60 years old, died of injuries received Thursday night when she was struck by an automobile near her home, 913 Randolph street, St. Paul. W. T. Croft, 2276 Otto avenue, St. Paul driver of the automobile, was held by the police pending an investigation of the accident. Two sisters, Mrs. Frances Dertz, 648 Hague avenue, St. Paul, and Sophie Simonds, 10 years old, escaped serious injury when an automobile, driven by the former, skidded through the Oakland hill guard railing at Duke street, St. Paul, Thursday night. Although the car fell over a 50-foot embankment the occupants were but slightly hurt.

**Touchet, French Cardinal, Dies.**

Orleans, France, Sept. 23.—(By Associated Press.)—Cardinal Arturo Touchet, bishop of Orleans, is dead. He was born in Bayeaux, France, November 13, 1848, and was created a cardinal November 16, 1922.

## *School Teacher Relates Escape in Florida Flood*

### Miss Adelaide Marin Was Rescued From Drowning by Brother-in-Law.

### Was Trapped by Hurricane in Sister's Bungalow at Hollywood.

After having been saved from drowning during the Florida hurricane, Miss Adelaide Marin, 23 years old, 3444 Portland avenue, arrived in Minneapolis Thursday from Hollywood, Fla., the first Minneapolis refugee to reach home.

Miss Marin, who left the city one month ago to teach school in Florida, boarded an 18-car train at Hollywood Monday. Without money or ticket, she was missed by trainmen in the jam of refugees until after she had borrowed a pass. The pass carried her to Melbourne, 200 miles north of Hollywood where she wired her father, W. A. Marin, attorney, of her safety and for funds.

Miss Marin was staying with her sister, Mrs. W. E. Watkins in Hollywood, and it was in the Watkins' bungalow that she, with her sister, brother-in-law and the Watkins' 17-month-old boy, was trapped for 12 hours during the hurricane. None of the family suffered injuries.

The Watkins and Miss Marin were attempting to leave the home Saturday when she was caught in a surging flood of ocean water, over five feet deep, and was saved only when Mr. Watkins plunged into the torrent and dragged

(Continued on Page 2, Column 3.)

## *Tunney's Aerial Dash to Stadium Terrorized Tex*

### Rickard Worried for Hour and 26 Minutes as Gene Was in Air.

Philadelphia, Sept. 23.—(By Associated Press.)—Gene Tunney, new king of the heavyweights, threw terror in the stout heart of Tex Rickard this afternoon when he flew from Stroudsburg to Philadelphia, the scene of his coronation. The promoter worried for an hour and 26 minutes, the time Gene was in the air.

Rickard, when informed of Tunney's hop-off, made no secret of his wish that one-half of his championship fighting crew had waited until the title was decided before he took his second lesson in aviation.

**Gene's Second Flight.**

Until today's dash from the training camp Tunney had flown but once. On his arrival in Philadelphia he laughed off the concern his air dash had caused those interested in the financial end of the bout, taking refuge in the trite but expressive: "All's well that ends well."

Stepping into the plane at Stroudsburg, Tunney asked Pilot "Casey" Jones if he had a parachute. When told that he did not but had the assurance of the airplane driver that they would go down together, Tunney laughed and said, "That's enough assurance for me."

Arriving in Philadelphia for the formal weighing in ceremony and physical examination by the medical representative of the Pennsylvania athletic commission, Tunney's heart was found normal. No extra pulse beats had been added by the novel conveyance chosen for the last lap. This bore out the conviction of those in intimate touch with Tunney that he has nerve in plenty but no nerves.

**Has No Nerves.**

King Dempsey, although at that time his crown was still on perfectly straight, was pushed out of the spotlight by his rival's aerial stunt.

Dempsey had no royal air coach and could not make such dramatic entrance. He contented himself with the slower but safer train from Atlantic City to Philadelphia, and had no welcome on his arrival shortly before time for him to enter the ring.

## *Local Enforcement of Prohibition Urged by General Andrews*

Washington, Sept. 23.—(By Associated Press.)—The 22 national prohibition administrators in conference here with Assistant Secretary Andrews of the treasury, were urged today by the dry chief to encourage, as far as possible under state laws, the local enforcement of the prohibition law by county officers.

The general said such a plan was in effect successfully in 40 California counties and that while prohibition prosecutions cost these counties $51,000 in six months, the counties in turn collected $434,000 in fines and penalties.

General Andrews urged administrators to seek similar action by local officers in all states which have prohibition laws permitting it.

## *Jury Will Investigate Fonck's Plane Crash*

Great Neck, N. Y., Sept. 23.—The Nassau county grand jury tomorrow will begin an investigation into the tragedy following the attempt of Captain Rene Fonck, French ace, to fly from New York to Paris, it was learned tonight. Colonel H. E. Hartley, vice president of the Argonauts, sponsors for the flight in which two men were killed, was served with a subpena at his home here, it was announced.

## Florida Storm Region Fights Disease Peril

### Flotilla of Warships Reaches Miami With Fresh Supplies of Serum.

### Rehabilitation Speeded With Efforts to Ward Off Epidemic Threat.

### New Check Shows 365 Known Dead—11 Trapped Five Days Are Rescued.

Miami, Fla., Sept. 23.—(By Associated Press.)—While rehabilitation work went forward rapidly here and in other Florida coast towns and resorts, sanitary conditions resulting from the hurricane assumed a serious aspect and American Red Cross and state officials centered attention on an effort to prevent outbreaks of disease.

As yet no case of typhoid has been reported, but medical men are agreed that conditions were such that an extensive outbreak is possible.

Doctors, sanitation experts and nurses sent from as far off as Chicago, found their staunchest ally in a blazing semi-tropical sun which has glared from virtually cloudless skies ever since the storm passed.

Serums still are being rushed here from many points and inoculation against typhoid and tetanus is proceeding as rapidly as possible.

**Destroyers Bring Serum.**

A flotilla of destroyers came in from Charleston with fresh serum and a representative from the Nashville (Tenn.) Banner arrived by airplane with a cargo of medical supplies and an offer from J. G. Stahlman, managing editor, of as much more as might be requested.

Negro men were conscripted today for cleaning up the city outside the business district, where many streets still are blocked by tangled wreckage. In addition, volunteer workers were called for.

Additional surveys and rechecks made today in the storm devastated southeastern coast of Florida showed 365 known dead, 1,100 injured, probably 500 seriously, in hospitals, and property loss of approximately $165,000,000.

**Death Lists Compiled.**

As compiled by W. H. Combs, in charge of the bureau of missing persons here, Colonel L. S. Lowry, Jr., leader in the rescue work at Moorehaven, the Associated Press, and the Miami Daily News, the deaths by cities and towns were as follows:

Moorehaven 126, Miami and immediate vicinity 109, Hollywood and imme-

(Continued on Page 2, Column 4.)

## Rahn Leaves to Direct Shrine's Florida Relief

### Minneapolis Man Calls at White House After Talk With Red Cross Head.

By George Akerson.
Tribune Washington Correspondent.

Washington, Sept. 23.—A. A. D. Rahn of Minneapolis, appointed by David W. Crosland, imperial pontenate of Mystic Shrine, as relief representative in Florida, left Washington today for the stricken regions.

Before leaving the capital Mr. Rahn conferred with representatives of the national Red Cross. He interviewed Ernest Bicknell, national director of the Red Cross, and then called at the White House. Following his conference with Herbert Hoover yesterday and his interviews today, Mr. Rahn stated that the shrine's relief work would be done through the Red Cross.

"Always, in times of grief and stress such as these," Mr. Rahn said, "it is demonstarted that sectional, religious and group feeling is only superficial and that no sectional, party or religious lines are known to the true type of American when matters get down to rock bottom. Those who have felt alarm over certain tendencies in our present-day life ought to take a lesson from this.

"In the present undertaking, all of us are moved to take immediate measures to provide for our own groups. In behalf of the Shrine, our first act was to send $5,000 to our own people in Florida. Other groups followed the same practice, but, in a large way, all of us, recognizing in the Red Cross an impartial medium for meeting the needs of sufferers of all classes, are turning to that organization. If what we have given is shown to be inadequate our order, for one, will be ready to go to greater lengths.

"The sum of $20,000 is to be turned over immediately to the Red Cross, and the shrine is not asking where it goes, so long as it is applied to general relief work. That is the spirit of other bodies now responding to the appeals from Florida.

"Florida is reminding us that, after all, there is is no room in America for narrowness and bigotry."

## *Grand Rapids Man Heads City Managers*

Colorado Springs, Colo, Sept. 23. — (By Associated Press.)—Fred H. Locke, city manager of Grand Rapids, Iowa, was elected president of the International City Managers' association at the annual meeting here today. Dubuque, Iowa, was selected as the 1927 convention city.

## Challenger Batters Jack Mercilessly to Win Decision

### Gene, Cautiously Sidestepping Onrushes of Champ Early in Fight, Takes Eight of Ten Rounds.

By George A. Barton.
The Tribune's Sports Editor.

Philadelphia, Sept. 23.—Gene Tunney, former Marine and World war hero, proved himself a man of destiny here tonight when he decisively whipped Jack Dempsey and won the world's heavyweight championship in their 10-round fight. There was no question about the result, for Tunney won by such a wide margin that the judges and referee were unanimous in their decision.

Tunney not only outboxed but he out-fought Dempsey all the way and the champion was a terribly beaten battler when the gong finally came to his rescue in the tenth round. His left eye was closed tight and there was a deep gash under his right eye. He was bleeding from the mouth and a tiny stream of blood was dripping from his nose.

Tunney battered Dempsey all over the ring in the tenth round and had him groggy and floundering around from bell to bell during the closing session. Tunney's stiff left jabs to the mouth followed by crushing right handers to the point of the chin shook Dempsey from head to heels and it is doubtful whether he could have weathered the storm much longer.

**Gene Wins Eight Rounds.**

How badly Tunney whipped the champion was shown by our score sheet on which we credited Tunney with eight rounds, Dempsey with one and called one even. Jack carried off the honors in the seventh round, while the second round was even.

The seventh round was the only round in which he looked anything like the fighter who battled his way through the greatest heavyweights of his day—Willard, Firpo, Carpentier, Brennan, Miske, Fulton, "Gunboat" Smith, Jim Flynn and others of lesser consequence. Dempsey started the seventh round with a rush, catching Tunney unawares in his own corner and nearly knocked him through the ropes with a left hook to the jaw and a murderous right-hander to the body. Tunney finally saved himself by clinching and a few moments later broke away and danced along the ropes with Dempsey rushing after him and trying desperately to put over a knockout punch.

**Dempsey Closes In.**

The champion finally closed in on the challenger and nearly upset him with another left hook which landed high on Gene's head. Dempsey tried hard to finish Tunney with another left hook, but Gene saved himself from further damage by retreating from the wild rushes of the enraged and desperate champion. This round and the second, in which Dempsey fought on even terms with Tunney, were the only real flashes of the old Dempsey that the crowd saw during the entire 30 minutes of fighting.

Dempsey shot his bolt in the seventh round and from that time on Tunney won as he pleased. He jabbed Dempsey dizzy with stiff lefts to the mouth and shook him up time and again with heavy right crosses to the chin.

Tunney fought a perfect battle against Dempsey tonight. He knew that Dempsey would be strong and dangerous in the early rounds and he never gave the champion a chance to close in on him and deliver the murderous blows with which he battered so many rivals into s[u]bmission during his spectacular career which started in 1916 and ended tonight.

**Jack Rocked by Blows.**

Tunney met Dempsey's fierce charges throughout with a rapier-like left hand, which he kept in the champion's face throughout. These left-hand stabs to the mouth always were followed by a crushing straight right which not only stopped Jack cold, but set him back on his heels. When Dempsey started his vicious left hook to the chin or to the body, Tunney either pulled back out of range and nailed the "Manassa mauler" with well-directed blows to the mouth, or stepped in close and belted Jack on the chin with right-handed uppercuts that sent the champion's head flying back.

Not only did Tunney give Dempsey a boxing lesson but he thr[i]lled and amazed the crowd by frequently standing toe to toe and trading punches with him.

Although Dempsey was badly whipped tonight, he went down fighting like a true champion. He was the aggressor in every round and regardless of how hard Tunney belted him on the face and body, he continued to tear in for more.

**Jack Seeks Knockout.**

Jack realized after the third round that he had met his match from a standpoint of speed and accurate punching, and made desperate attempts to turn the tide of battle in his favor with a knockout punch. Tunney did not escape unscathed, for Dempsey scored frequently with resounding thumps to the body and jaw. But the former marine quickly shook off the effects of these deadening blows and retaliated by cuffing Jack in a manner entirely new to the latter.

Although Dempsey was far from his former self, nevertheless he was in no way a physical wreck and Tunney is entitled to much credit in beating him. The former champion trained faithfully for the fight, and really was in first class condition.

**Trained Faithfully for Bout.**

Knowing that he would be called upon to fight either Tunney or Wills this summer, Dempsey began active training a year ago. Being a clean living fellow it stands to reason that at the age of 31 he should still possess much of his former effectiveness, especially over such a short route as 10 rounds. In Tunney he met an opponent who had made a close study of his style and devoted several years in planning the best way in which to fight him. The result

### First as Usual

The Tribune, as invariably is the custom, was the first paper on the streets of Minneapolis with its extra announcing the results of the Tunney-Dempsey fight.

Four minutes after the fight was ended Tribune extras were being sold by newsboys.

The presses were running in 2 minutes and 45 seconds after the judges' decision.

In 35 minutes 51,000 papers were dispersed, after which the usual editions were produced.

## *Dempsey Weeps, Wants Another Chance at Title*

### Dethroned King's Mourners Say Gene Promised Return Bout.

Philadelphia, Sept. 23.—(By Associated Press.)—Dethroned as heavyweight champion, Jack Dempsey wept when he reached the seclusion of his hotel room. Only Jerry the Greek, his trainer, and Mike Trant, his companion, were present to comfort him after he had held up en route to the hotel from the sesquicentennial stadium.

Dempsey, his left eye closed, and his right eye cut, was a pathetic figure. He buried his face in his hands for a few seconds, but quickly regained his composure and stretched out on the bed for a rubdown. He went to bed happy in knowing that his wife would join him tomorrow.

**Promised Return Bout.**

Dempsey said he wants another fight with Gene Tunney, his conqueror.

When he rushed to the center of the ring to greet Tunney he asked him for another chance.

Dempsey's handlers said that Tunney had agreed.

Dempsey said he knew that he was licked as early as the eight round, and declared that Gene won fairly.

"I could not seem to get going," he said, "but I have no complaint to offer. I knew I was going to get licked some time, and I am glad I lost the championship to an American.

**Beat All Foreigners.**

"I defeated all the foreigners they could send over after it. I think I have given the public a run for its money every time I started. I licked Firpo, I licked Carpentier. If I had to lose I am glad that a fellow like Tunney won the championship. He is a credit to the sport, a clean, fine fellow.

Dempsey had accepted an invitation to attend a banquet given by the sesquicentennial officials tonight whether he won or lost, but his handlers induced him to break the engagement. He wanted to go anyway, even with the cut over his left eye. Two stitches were required to close the wound.

## *Champs Who Battled in Old Ring Days Awed at Title Purse*

Philadelphia, Sept. 23.—(By Associated Press.)—Jack McAuliffe, old undefeated lightweight champion, who once defended his title in a 75-round fight—London prize ring rules—for a small side bet and before a gallery of 500, was a member of the $1,750,000 crowd that saw Jack Dempsey earn $450,000, and Gene Tunney $200,000 tonight.

"Some people," said Jack, "were born lucky. The rest of us were born right after the Civil war."

Battling Nelson, who almost 20 years ago fought Joe Gans for Tex Rickard, in the premier promoter's first big pugilist venture at Goldfield, Nevada, sat mouth agape for five minutes awed by the spectacle.

## *Niece Dies, Salesman Hurt in Auto Crash*

Miss Anna Olson of Chicago, a nurse, was killed, and O. E. Rooth, 3245 Thirtieth avenue south, her uncle, suffered serious injuries Thursday night when an automobile in which they were riding was struck by a Great Northern train near Floodwood, Minn. Miss Olson died on a train which was carrying her to Duluth.

Mr. Rooth, who travels for the Minneapolis [illegible] Co., received several fractured ribs, a broken arm and body bruises. He was driving Miss Olson to a hospital in Duluth. Peter Rooth, a brother, left for Duluth, where the injured man is in a hospital.

# The Minneapolis Morning Tribune

*Sixtieth Year. No. 160.* Twenty-four Pages MINNEAPOLIS, MINN., MONDAY, NOVEMBER 1 1926 *Price Two Cents in Minneapolis*


# 40,000 GREET QUEEN MARIE

## Candidates to End Campaign Appeals Today

### Three Gubernatorial Aspirants Will Speak at Luncheon.

### Sweeping Republican Victory Is Forecast by Observers.

### Three Constitutional Amendments, Charter Change on Ballots.

The Minnesota political campaign will wind up today with last minute appeals by state and congressional candidates. There will be few meetings, however, and the radio will be used by several aspirants.

Governor Christianson will speak at a luncheon this noon at the Masonic club in Minneapolis, to be given by Zuhrah temple. Judge Alfred Jaques of Duluth, Democratic candidate for governor, and Magnus Johnson, the Farmer-Labor candidate, also will speak at the luncheon.

At 2 p. m. the governor will speak over WCCO, addressing his final message to the voters before the election.

Floyd Olson, candidate for re-election as Hennepin county attorney, will speak over WAMD at 7:30 p. m. today.

The polls will open at 6 a. m. tomorrow and remain open until 9 p. m.

A sweeping Republican victory throughout the state has been freely forecast by Republican observers.

Congressman Walter H. Newton and Godfrey G. Goodwin are expected to win by party leaders. They have conducted their campaigns on the record of national Republican accomplishments and ask to be permitted to continue a constructive program.

In addition to the 10 congressmen from as many districts, seven of which are expected to elect Republicans, a complete slate of state officers will be elected tomorrow, as well as the county officials. Three state constitutional amendments also are to be voted on.

A city charter amendment also is before the people of Minneapolis. It proposes to set the city election coincident with the general election, in the even numbered years, with present officials automatically holding over until the 1928 election.

## Defense Will Open Case for Shepard Today

### First Witness Expected to Take Stand to Deny That Defendant Drove.

The first witness for the defense is expected to take the stand this morning when the trial of Harry Shepard on a third degree murder charge is resumed before Judge Gunnar H. Nordbye.

The state rested late Friday, and A. M. Cary, counsel for Shepard, announced in his opening address to the jury that his witnesses would prove the defendant did not drive the car which killed Mr. and Mrs. F. E. Carlton the morning of Labor day.

Joe Cittadino and Jack Smith, alleged to have been companions of Shepard at the time of the tragedy and indicted as accessories after the fact, will be the principal witnesses for the defense, and one of the two is scheduled to start testimony this morning. George Murphy, indicted with Cittadino and Smith, turned state's witness Friday and charged that Shepard had been at the wheel when his car struck the Carlton couple.

## *Home Folks Plan Reception Election Day for Coolidges*

Northampton, Mass., Oct. 31.—(By Associated Press.)—Plans for a public reception for President and Mrs. Coolidge, when they come home here to vote Tuesday, were made today. Arriving at about 9 a. m. Tuesday, President Coolidge will go at once to the polls under escort of a reception committee of 12 citizens. Then the first citizens of the land will visit their old home on Massasoit street, where Mrs. Coolidge's mother, Mrs. Elmyra Goodhue, will be waiting.

At 10:10 a. m. a public reception will be held, which will last until the presidential party goes to the return train at 11:30.

John Coolidge has three recitation periods at Amherst college on election day, and since he is making particularly close application to his studies this year it was thought he would not be in Northampton to see his parents.

## *Golfer Makes Long Drive; Drops Dead*

Chicago, Oct. 31. — (By Associated Press.)—Robert W. Gibson, 65 years old, an insurance broker, lifted a long drive from the sixteenth tee at Oak Hill golf course and dropped dead. Physicians blamed heart disease.

### Weather Forecast

MINNESOTA—Fair today; colder in east portion; Tuesday increasing cloudiness.

Additional weather forecast on Page 11.

## News Index



## *Body of Navy Stunt Flier Is Found in Sea*

Norfolk, Va., Oct. 31.—(By Associated Press.)—The body of Lieutenant Frank H. Conant, Jr., navy speed and stunt flier, was recovered today from the water in which his plane crashed off Mathews, Va., yesterday afternoon. It was found strapped in the seat of the wrecked plane, the parachute in place and his hand still clutching the control.

## *Lake Boat Makes Port After Striking Reef*

Duluth, Minn., Oct. 31.—(By Associated Press.)—The steamship Thomas Maytham struck a reef off Knife island in a blinding snowstorm on Lake Superior tonight, but managed to get afloat again and reached a dock at Knife river, tying up for the night. The ship's bottom was damaged and it was thought the propellor was lost.

## *Patron, Face Lathered, Tells Police Barber Died*

Chicago, Oct. 31. — (By Associated Press.)—With his face half covered with lather, W. S. Lady dashed into a precinct police station and gasped "something has happened to my barber." The officers found Joseph Gaetno had dropped dead with the razor in his hand.

## *Minneapolis Host to Royal Rumanian Visitors*

Above are pictures of Queen Marie and her family taken on their visit to Minneapolis Sunday. The upper left picture shows Queen Marie being greeted by Mayor Leach upon her arrival at the reception at the Art Institute. Her children, Prince Nicolas and Princess Ileana, are shown to the upper right, coming out of the Union station. Below they are shown in their dusters and caps with John Crosby, who escorted them on a tour of the Washburn-Crosby mills Sunday afternoon.

## Harry Houdini, Magician, Is Dead in Detroit

### Actor Fails to Rally After Second Operation—Was Born in Wisconsin.

Detroit, Mich., Oct. 31.—(By Associated Press.)—Harry Houdini, the magician, died today.

The noted escape artist, whose adeptness at freeing himself from strait-jackets, chains and cells mystified audiences in all parts of the world, died after a second surgical operation had been made to save his life from the effects of peritonitis.

Houdini was operated upon last Monday for appendicitis.

Although it was known the magician was ill when he arrived here eight days ago, the seriousness of his condition was not learned until he collapsed at the end of his opening performance.

**Was Born in Wisconsin.**

Houdini, popularly supposed to be of oriental birth, was born in Wisconsin in 1874, the son of Rabbi Mayer Samuel Weiss. His theatrical name was early acquired through legal procedure.

As one of the outstanding personages of the American stage and leader of magicians, his popularity lasted for a quarter century. Beginning his stage career as a trapeze performer, he toured the world. It was during his journey through Asia that he became interested in mysticism and shifted his role to that of magician.

**Fought to Expose Spiritualism.**

Houdini counted among his audiences the royalty of Europe and Asia. He wrote numerous treatises intended to expose spiritualism as a fraud. His book, "A Magician Among the Spirits," created a furore among professional spiritualists, by its assertion that the practice was "bunk."

One of his public challenges of long standing asserted that he could duplicate or expose any seemingly magic feat was accepted by Raymen Bey, Egyptian mystifier, in August. The Egyptian had created a sensation by remaining in a sealed coffin under water for 19 minutes. "Short breaths and conservation of oxygen," said Houdini, who entered the coffin and stayed there 90 minutes, "did it."

## *Society Girl to Wed Cousin of Late Czar*

New York, Oct. 31.—(By Associated Press.)—Miss Audrey Emery, New York society girl, will be married soon to the Grand Duke Dimitri Constantinovitch, cousin of the late czar of Russia, it was announced in a cablegram from Europe, made public today. Miss Emery now is at Biarritz, France, with her mother, Mrs. Alfred Anson. The Grand Duke Dimitri was once master of horse for the late Czar Nicholas. In 1913 he was announced by imperial ukase as second in succession to the Russian throne.

## Mussolini Is Again Attacked by Assassin

### Premier Unharmed But Mob Kills Youth Who Fired Shot.

Bologna, Italy, Oct. 31.—(By Associated Press.)—An 18-year-old youth, who today attempted to shoot Benito Mussolini, was himself stabbed and beaten to death by an infuriated mob.

Mussolini escaped injury. The assassin's bullet missed passing through the premier's chest by the fraction of an inch. It actually ripped both sides of his coat and cut the sash of the order of St. Maurice and St. Lazarus.

The youth had pressed forward as Mussolini was seated in his automobile on leaving the stadium, where he had attended the congress for the advancement of science, and was ready to fire a second shot. Carabineers and Fascists threw themselves on him as he was in the act of sending a second bullet at the premier.

Within a minute or two of his attack on Il Duce, the body of the youthful assailant was being dragged along, a crumpled and inert mass, by strong armed Fascists, through a screaming, milling sea of humanity to his death. Later at the police station, where the body was taken, 14 knife wounds were found and marks of strangling on his throat.

The premier reached Bologna last night. Early today he opened the Littoriale stadium, an immense structure to be devoted to all branches of sports, and later in the afternoon officiated at the opening of the congress for the advancement of science at the stadium.

At the morning exercises, the Duce was astride a charger. He wore the uniform of commander in chief of the national militia and was hailed vociferously. Advancing to the center of the Littoriale and addressing his beloved black shirts, he souted:

"Black shirts, put on your stirrups. Raise high your rifles, so that the entire world can see that forest of bayonets and feel the pulsations of your determined and invincible hearts."

## *Lloyd Hamilton's Wife Gets Divorce Decree*

Los Angeles, Calif., Oct. 31.—Lloyd Hamilton, motion picture comedian, and Mrs. Ethel Hamilton were divorced yesterday. Mrs. Hamilton brought suit more than a year ago, charging desertion. Hamilton agreed to give Mrs. Hamilton a $15,000 home and $100 a week alimony.

## Prince Takes Informal Tour: Princess Plays Tennis in Rain

### Heir Reveals Liking for Mechanics on Trip Through Flour Mills.

By Edward R. Sammis.

As the Royal Rumanian rolled into Minneapolis Sunday afternoon, and the regal Queen Marie extended an official greeting to an officially silk-hatted reception committee, two very unofficial looking young people slipped quietly away into the crowd.

Prince Nicolas, who would be either a cowboy or a captain of industry if he weren't a prince, and his sister, Princess Ileana, were vacation bent.

To them a few hours in which they might do as they pleased were infinitely more to be prized than governors' and mayors' welcomes, formal receptions and the applause of crowds.

Prince Nicolas wanted to see the flour mills, and the princess wanted, above all things, a game of tennis. So for a few brief hours, they were allowed the infinite privilege of choosing how they should pass their time.

**Visit Flour Mills.**

After an embarrassed moment in front of the crowds at the Union station, they were whisked away in an automobile to the Washburn Crosby mills, where, as the guests of John Crosby and Franklin Crosby, Jr., they were taken through the entire process of flour-making.

Although both of them expressed a keen interest in the milling process, their dominant emotion seemed to be an overwhelming exuberance at being free for a few moments from official routine. The dusters and caps which the party donned as they entered the mill afforded endless amusement to the prince and princess.

"I don't think your cap is very becoming," the prince remarked to his sister. "Can't you fix it some other way?"

"You look like an Apache in yours," the princess replied.

At the top of the mill the giant sifters were put in operation as a demonstration for the prince and princess. Back and forth they sped with dizzying motion.

**Prince Does Charleston.**

Suddenly the prince began to execute a few steps of the charleston.

"It's just the way it makes me feel," he explained.

"It reminds me of our ocean voyage," the princess said.

Prince Nicolas followed closely the technical explanation of the making of flour as expounded to him by Dwight Bell, the master miller of the firm.

But the interest of the princess was more fanciful. She was most impressed

(Continued on Page 2, Column 3.)

### Weather Fails to Dampen Ardor of Ileana, Wins First Set.

By Helen Gage.

"Tennis, no matter what the weather!"

That was the cry that went around the Great Northern station Sunday afternoon as the Princess Ileana of Rumania stepped from her mother's special train into a pouring, icy rainstorm.

Dressed in a squirrel coat, along with a flared skirt, a small brown hat, and low-heeled pumps, the princess smiled at the group who came to meet her, went through the Washburn-Crosby flour mills, and arrived at the Minikahda club in the middle of a cold Minnesota afternoon.

Undaunted, the princess ran through the rain for the shelter of the club, and tried to decide what one did when one wanted to play tennis in one's traveling clothes.

Margaret Crosby, daughter of Mr. and Mrs. John Crosby, who was to be the princesses' opponent in a singles match, solved the problem. There were clothes in the club lockers suitable for tennis. With her charming, frank smile, the princess agreed that life was rosy once more. She appeared in the sodden court attired in a grey pleated

(Continued on Page 2, Column 6.)

## *Mercury Hovers Near Freezing as Rain and Snow Fall Alternately*

Drizzling rains, accompanied by trace of snow, fell intermittently in Minneapolis Sunday, while the mercury hovered above the freezing point and well stoked furnaces roared their answer to the chill north winds.

While the mercury was ineffectually struggling to rise, a chilly rain began to fall about noon, and continued at short intervals throughout the day, driving traffic from the treacherous streets. The mercury was able to make but little headway against the adverse weather conditions, rising only seven degrees from the 31-degree mark set at 1 a. m.

The maximum of 38 degrees was reached at 2 p. m. and the mercury held to the peak until shortly after 5 p. m. Then it began dropping off, until it was back at 32 degrees at midnight. Continuation of cold weather was forecast for today.

## Reception in Twin Cities Is Second to N. Y.

### Crowds Stand in Sleet and Rain to Get Glimpse of Rumanian Ruler.

### Royal Visitor Appears to Enjoy Every Minute of Nine-hour Stay.

### Prince and Princess Tour Mills Donned in Dust Coats and Caps.

By Lorena A. Hickok.

Greeted by the largest crowds that have turned out to see her since she left New York, Queen Marie of Rumania paid a nine-hour visit to the Twin Cities Sunday.

When the handsome and smiling English princess who rules in the Balkans resumed her journey to the west shortly after midnight, she left behind her in Minneapolis and St. Paul more than 40,000 new friends.

It was the Twin Cities' first experience at entertaining a queen, and on the whole they found it exhilarating and pleasing.

**Shake Hands With Queen.**

Some 200 or 300 of those more than 40,000 new friends she acquired here were presented to the queen and shook hands with her. A few of them talked with her for five or 10 minutes.

The rest only had glimpses of her—and most of them after standing for hours in rain and sleet. But they went home satisfied, though damp. They had seen a real queen.

More than 10,000 of them were packed in and around the St. Paul union station when Queen Marie—wearing the gold turban and Callot red coat with sable collar and muff that she wore when she arrived in New York—stepped out of her special train.

Some 25,000 more stood in the wet or sat in automobiles parked every foot of the way between the state capitol and the Minneapolis Institute of Arts.

It was dark and wet when her limousine drew up in front of the Art institute, but, huddled under umbrellas on the broad steps, crouched on window ledges, and filling the sidewalks, nearly 3,000 more awaited here there.

**Presented With Flowers.**

And as many more were milling around the Saint Paul hotel when she arrived there at 7 o'clock for a short rest before going out to the home of Louis W. Hill for dinner.

It was a heavily loaded program that confronted Queen Marie when she entered the Twin Cities Sunday afternoon. But she was not dismayed. She appeared to enjoy every minute of it. If she was tired, she did not show it.

First, she was taken to a raised platform in the St. Paul Union station, while a National guard band played the Rumanian national anthem. There were speeche and flashlights, and she was presented with flowers.

Next, she went to the WCCO broadcasting station in the depot. It was her first visit to a broadcasting station, she said. She produced a battered fountain pen from her mesh bag, wrote out a little speech, and read it in front of the microphone.

In this speech, she invited North Dakota farmers and their wives to come aboard her train today and ride with her across the plains. She suggested that two farmers and their wives board the train at each station and ride with her to the next stop. She wants to discuss agricultural methods with them, face to face and informally.

**Visits Rumanian Church.**

From the broadcasting station she was taken in a big limousine, through streets packed with rain-soaked spectators, to the state capitol, where Governor and Mrs. Theodore Christianson were presented to her by Mayor L. C. Hodgson of St. Paul, who had met her at the train.

From the capitol she went to St. Mary's Rumanian Orthodox church, at 852 Woodbridge street, St. Paul. Standing on a dais under a canopy in the candle-lighted church, whose walls were banked with palms and chrysanthemums, she heard a mass sung. It was a special mass, reserved for royalty.

Next through lines of parked automobiles and mobs of people crowding the curbs, her limousine sped along University avenue to Minneapolis, across the Third avenue bridge, up Nicollet avenue, and to the Art Institute.

Here, Mayor and Mrs. George E. Leach and Mrs. Karl DeLaittre, wife of a former president of the Civic & Commerce association, were first presented. They awaited her in the rotunda.

**Tours Art Galleries.**

She then took Mayor Leach's arm and climbed the long, wide flight of marble stairs to the second floor galleries, where 100 residents of Minneapolis, guests of the board of directors, were presented.

While at the institute she also found time to tour the galleries, talk over the community fund with Sumner T. McKnight and Lyman E. Wakefield. She was also presented with several more bouquets and a beautiful silver fox scarf.

Shortly before 7 o'clock, she got back into her limousine and rode to the Saint Paul hotel.

They drove back over the Lake street bridge. Near the Town and Country club, her car drew up beside a policeman standing in the rain. The queen leaned forward.

"It must be wet out there," she said to him.

"Wet is right," the policeman replied with a grin.

Arriving in St. Paul, the queen rested for a short time, changed into evening dress and went out to the Hill residence for dinner. From the dinner she went to her train.

**Go Through Flour Mills.**

While Queen Marie was going through her strenuous afternoon's program, her son and daughter, Prince

(Continued on Page 2, Column 1.)

# The Minneapolis Morning Tribune

Sixtieth Year. No. 319. Thirty Pages. MINNEAPOLIS, MINN., FRIDAY, APRIL 8, 1927 * * * Price Two Cents in Minneapolis

# SUSPECT SHOT FLEEING RAID

## Hearing Airs Schall Pleas in Rum Cases

### Townsend, Former Northwest Dry Chief, Tells of Requests.

### Says Jacobs Also Asked If Aid Could Be Had for Violator.

### Witness Under Questioning Admits Ill Will Toward Senator.

A. C. Townsend, former northwest prohibition chief, took the stand before the senate investigation committee Thursday night and testified that on two occasions United States Senator Thomas D. Schall asked him about the disposition of liquor cases.

On a third occasion, he said, A. N. Jacobs, in the presence of Schall, spoke to him about another case. This case, he told the committee, he thought was that of Fortunato Peori, whose name was on the list of those who are alleged to have contributed to the Schall campaign fund.

The testimony of Captain Townsend was the first, with the exception of that given by Jacobs, which directly connected Senator Schall with intervention in liquor cases. Townsend appeared at the hearing as an investigating committee witness.

The first case in which the senator intervened, Captain Townsend testified, was that of Rabbi Horowitz. Senator Schall asked him, he said, if he couldn't clear the rabbi and suggested that it would help in the election. Townsend said he replied that to drop prosecution would be in violation of his oath of office, and that Mr. Schall then asked him to do what he could. The rabbi was not prosecuted, Townsend added, because the evidence wasn't sufficient to warrant conviction.

**Tells of Another Case.**

Later, he told the committee, the senator talked to him about Florence Josewich — Fani Terrin case, and asked if prosecution of Miss Josewich could be avoided. Townsend testified that he replied he would have to be bound by the evidence in the case. Miss Josewich, he said, was later cleared of the charge, when it was found that the liquor found in the automobile on her premises belonged to Terrin.

In the Peori case Jacobs told him, the man was a "high-class" Italian and wanted to know if anything could be done. Townsend said he didn't think so because he had been a consistent violator, that he had been caught red-handed and that he intended to prosecute.

Later under the cross-examination of Tom Davis, Townsend admitted that he had been asked to do nothing improper in the Josewich case and in the Peori case and that after his first request to have the rabbi cleared, Schall had suggested nothing that might be construed as improper in the Horowitz case.

**Admits Schall Was Right.**

He admitted that Schall told him the rabbi was not responsible for the sale of the sacramental wine and that Schall only asked him to do what the law afterwards compelled him to do.

Also under the cross-examination Townsend admitted that he felt a certain ill-will toward the senator because of certain circumstances which existed in the prohibition department. To bring out his points, Davis went into the record of the senate contest in Washington several times and sought to corroborate Townsend's testimony with the statements he made at that time.

Other witnesses at the hearings Thursday were Ed Corneaby, who concluded his testimony; S. B. Qvale, former state prohibition director, and Fred A. Dickey, chairman of the Hennepin county Republican committee.

**Dickey's Testimony Short.**

Mr. Dickey was on the stand only a few minutes and he made it clear that his committee did not espouse the candidacy of any particular candidate in the 1924 election, but was out to carry the state ticket with special emphasis on the "big four"—Coolidge, Dawes, Schall and Christianson. He testified that his committee arranged speaking dates for Senator Schall in Hennepin county on several occasions.

S. B. Qvale occupied the stand most of the morning and for a few minutes at the evening hearing. During that time he denied that he had ever made promises of any kind to Jacobs and that at any time he ever agreed with any one to drop liquor prosecutions.

At the opening of the hearing the sergeant-at-arms reported to Senator Blanchard that E. W. Backus and W. H. Oppenheimer, for whom subpenas have been issued were out of the state. Mr. Oppenheimer, he said was in the east and would return Monday, while Mr. Backus was in Ontario. Senator Blanchard said he would wire Mr. Backus that the committee desired his testimony.

At the opening of Thursday's hearing Ed Corneaby took the stand and Mr. Davis questioned him about his visit to Mr. Rhinow's home and then introduced letters to

(Continued on Page 10, Column 1.)

## News Index

WASHINGTON.

Henry L. Stimson was ordered to go to Nicaragua as special representative of President Coolidge. Page 2.

Broadcasting stations obtaining permits to continue after April 24, may expect some shift in frequency allocations. Page 18.

LEGISLATURE.

Two witnesses testified before the legislative committee considering a resolution for an auditing of the state treasurer's office. Page 1.

While the house passed eight crime prevention measures, the senate committee debated provisions in the state crime bureau bill. Page 4.

The senate took steps to insure an early vote on the bill which would increase the salaries of all legislators. Page 6.

The house passed seven bills relative to state taxation. Page 7.

Legislative bills. Page 7.

DOMESTIC.

A boat tender admitted he threw the match which caused destruction of De Pinedo's seaplane at Roosevelt dam. Page 1.

John D. Rockefeller, Jr., termed employer and employe partners and predicted a solution of the labor problem. Page 2.

The United States filed an injunction suit against the alleged potash gang. Page 5.

Railroad officials presented evidence in support of freight rate increases in the middle west at the hearing in Kansas City. Page 6.

Illinois coal miners will invite the operators to a conference. Page 15.

Senator Reed questioned Aaron Sapiro on his dispute with the Minnesota potato co-operative. Page 16.

LOCAL.

A. C. Townsend, former N. W. dry chief, testified Schall asked him to drop charges against dry law violators. Page 1.

Godward made his initial report on city wide paving survey. Page 1.

The Minneapolis Taxpayers' association opposed the Elsberg plan of financing arterial street improvements. Page 3.

Minneapolis Realtors indorsed the proposed amendments to the building code. Page 6.

Parent-Teacher association workers for the organ fund meet today to map solicitations. Page 8.

The school board asked the council to issue $400,000 in bonds for a new vocational school site. Page 8.

General Frank T. Hines, director of the United States veterans' bureau, and other officers, it was announced, will arrive today for the dedication of the new hospital at Fort Snelling Saturday. Page 19.

WOMEN'S ACTIVITIES.

Mrs. A. A. Passer filed as candidate for president of the State Federation of Women's Clubs. Page 11.

Ten schools will present 50 initiates for membership in the Girl Reserves of the Y.W.C.A. Page 12.

Mrs. W. H. Foster accepted the request of the Minnesota Colony of New England Women to run as a candidate for first vice president of the Fifth District Minnesota Federation of Women's Clubs. Page 12.

Social and club news. Page 12.

NORTHWEST.

Gordon Cooper and his wife were held in jail at Wabasha while authorities investigated the story of their 5-weeks-old baby's disappearance. Page 1.

FOREIGN.

An American mining man was slain by Mexicans. Page 1.

EDITORIALS.

A Request Which Should Not Be Refused; A Faithful Steward and a Great Hospital; A Practical Veto of an Impractical Bill; Garrett on McNary-Haugenism; The Lessened Recourse to Strikes. Page 14.

SPORTS.

The revamped Miller baseball team defeated Buffalo, 2 to 1, in the second game of their series. Page 20.

Jack Malone is favored to defeat Haakon Hansen in their 10-round bout at the Kenwood armory tonight. Page 20.

The Bruins and Senators battled to a scoreless tie in the first game of the series for the Stanley hockey cup. Page 20.

Johnny Weissmuller set a new national record in the 220-yard free style swim to defeat George Kojak, youthful rival, in the national A.A.U. championships. Page 20.

The state college swimming tournament will be held at Hamline university today. Page 20.

Joe Deberry and Otis Wicker allowed Cincinnati only one hit apiece and the Louisville Colonels won a 2 to 1 contest. Page 21.

Barton's Sportographs. Page 21.

Ban Johnson returned to his Chicago office and resumed his duties as president of the American league. Page 22.

Forty-one major letters in five sports were voted Gopher athletes at a meeting of the senate committee. Page 22.

The 350 American athletes at the Olympic games will be housed aboard a chartered liner. Page 22.

The state high school championship swimming meet will open in Hibbing today. Page 23.

MARKETS

A raise in the call money checked the opening advance in the stock prices. Page 24.

The price advance was resumed on the New York curb. Page 24.

Heavy rains in the southwest depressed wheat price levels. Page 25.

Buyers failed in their attempts to check cattle price advances at South St. Paul. Page 25.

Trade turned dull in the bond market as the reinvestment demand slackened. Page 26.

Weekly reports of the Federal Reserve banks. Page 26.

## Weather Forecast

MINNESOTA—Snow or rain in north, and rain in south portion; slightly warmer today. Saturday unsettled, warmer near Lake Superior. Additional weather on page 19.

## Arterial Plan for Developing City Drafted

### Godward Takes First Step in Mapping and Classifying Streets.

### 700 of 950 Miles Would Be Put in Residential Zones.

### Engineer Favors Circular Boundary for Loop District.

The first step in the mapping and classification of a $50,000,000 paved-street system for Minneapolis for the next 30 years was recorded Thursday in a report to a committee of the city planning commission by A. C. Godward, city planning engineer. The council has asked for a complete schedule of paving plans, with traffic classifications and routes, on which to predicate expenditures over a term of years.

Faced with the problem of producing a survey of this magnitude, Mr. Godward had been able thus far only to marshal his figures and cost estimates on a city-wide basis, without designation of future heavy traffic, arterial and residential streets. The report was the first verbal one he has made since he became planning engineer.

With 950 miles of streets within the city limits, only 215 miles have been paved, but the cost of this paving has been close to $16,000,000, Mr. Godward said.

"As a result of paving without a street plan, heavy traffic naturally follows the paved streets," he said, "with expensive wear and tear on existing pavement. In the next three or four years, we are faced with nearly 1,000,000 square yards of resurfacing, which will cost approximately $2,000,000."

By carrying out a definite street paving and traffic plan, not all the mileage will have to be covered with heavy pavement. In the 950-mile total, Mr. Godward said 700 miles will be in residential zones requiring from $2 to $2.50 a yard for paving. If this all were paved without regard to traffic routings, and made

(Continued on Page 9, Column 1.)

## Two Held After Mother Charges Theft of Child

### Parents Jailed While Police Investigate Disappearance of Baby.

Lake City, Minn., April 7.—Gordon Cooper and his 19-year-old wife were in the county jail at Wabasha tonight, while authorities investigated the mysterious disappearance of their 5-weeks-old child.

While no charges have been placed against the couple, county officials said they wanted to delve into the circumstances surrounding the disappearance of the child, who, Mrs. Cooper said today was kidnaped by two armed men late Wednesday after she had failed to meet their demands for money.

County Attorney L. R. Lundy took charge of the investigation tonight after the couple were taken to Wabasha late this afternoon by Sheriff D. E. Brown and a deputy.

Mrs. Cooper told officers that she was seized by two men late Wednesday when she went to investigate a noise on the porch. Demanding money, she said, the men took the baby when she told them that she had no cash in the house.

Before departing, according to Mrs. Cooper's story, the men bound her to a chair, but she managed to work her way to a window and reveal her plight to her father-in-law, who was working in the yard. The father-in-law, George Cooper, reported his daughter-in-law's story to the city marshal.

Sheriff Brown, who returned here from Wabasha after lodging the couple in jail, said that investigators of the case were handicapped by lack of clues.

Questioning of several persons, he said, failed to reveal that any one had seen the two men accused by Mrs. Cooper of carrying off her son.

## *N. Y. Audience Sees Hoover Speaking 200 Miles Away*

### Voices and Likenesses of Radio Performers Also Transmitted—Demonstration of Television Hailed as New Scientific Miracle.

New York, April 7.—(By Associated Press.)—Television, a scientists' dream ever since the telephone was invented half a century ago, became an actuality today when Secretary of Commerce Herbert Hoover spoke over the telephone in Washington and was seen as well as heard in the Bell telephone laboratories here.

Not only were Secretary Hoover and a score of others in Washington seen in New York by telephone wire, but a radio program was broadcast over the laboratory's experimental station 3XN at Whippany, N. J. and moving likenesses of the performers as well as the sound of their voices were put on the air and transferred to a screen in this city.

Officials of the American Telephone & Telegraph Co. announced that today's demonstration marked the result of years of research and experimentation and that study would be continued with the purpose of improving television to a higher state of efficiency.

**Admit Improvement Needed.**

They acknowledge that at present the seeming miracle of seeing by wire and wave length was not at a stage where it could be put to such general use as the telephone. The necessary equipment precludes that possibility for some time to come, they said, but the feat of television itself has been accomplished and indications are that "it is likely to have a real place in the world's work of distant communication."

The images of today's speakers in Washington and Whippany were thrown onto both small and large screens. On the screen designed for the telephoner's use solely, the pictures were exceedingly clear, easily recognizable as likenesses of the persons at the other end of communication. On the large screen about one and one-half by three feet, the results were not so clear. Especially was this noticeable when Secretary Hoover's image was transferred from the small screen on which it showed clearly, while he talked with President Walter S. Gifford of the telephone company, to the large screen for the benefit of the half a hundred newspapermen and scientists present at the demonstration.

**Likeness Fades at Times.**

At times during Mr. Hoover's address the likeness on the screen was recognizable, but at others it so faded and rippled as if water were running over it, that it became nothing but a formless shadow. Again at changing moments, only a pair of eyebrows or an ear, or a mouth would be visible as the secretary's voice boomed from the loud speaker.

After Secretary Hoover had addressed the gathering in New York, business associates in the two cities exchanged greetings and those on the New York end viewed the men they were in communication with on the smaller screen.

The first exchange, after the official greetings, passed between Frank B. Noyes, president of The Associated Press, in Washington, and Carl S. Brandebury of the New York office of The Associated Press. The likeness of Mr. Noyes was so clear in New York that the scintillation of light on his spectacles as he moved his head in speaking could be seen plainly.

The next part of the demonstration, it having been conclusively shown that television by telephone wire was an actuality, was the radio program from Whippany. Here again the likenesses of the speakers were thrown on the large screen and were with almost no exception distinct. Newspapermen who spoke after a man and woman entertainer had sung were easily recognized by their associates in New York.

**Basic Principles Given.**

Although the mechanism of television is naturally immensely technical in detail, its basic principles may be compared to those of the telephone. As in the telephone, instruments are used which are electrically sensitive to sound, so now instruments have been devised sensitive in a like way to light.

The subject, as he telephones, is "placidly scanned" by three great photo-electric "eyes," the largest photo-electric cells ever built. The impressions made on these cells are translated into varying intensities of electric current and as such are carried over wire or wave length. At the receiving end, machines have been invented which can turn the varying current back into light and shade and so reproduce the image of the scene scanned by the electric "eyes." More than 15 complete images of the scene are sent over wires or air every second, so that motion of the subject has no more of jerkiness than a moving picture.

The company announced that there is no one inventor of television, many scientists at the laboratories having co-operated in its development, but three men were mentioned as having contributed most to the research which led to the present stage. The three are Herbert E. Ives, son of Frederick E. Ives, inventor of the halftone process of reproduction; Frank Gray and H. M. Stoller.

## *Steers Bring Highest Price in 18 Months*

Kansas City, April 7.—(By Associated Press.)—Fat steers sold at $13.25 a hundred pounds today, the highest price in 18 months on the Kansas City market. A bunch of 50, averaging 1,390 pounds, going at that price were shipped here by William Bowness, Fairfax, Mo., who purchased them on the market here last September at $7.90, when they averaged 1,017 pounds.

## Allied Fleet Mobilizing at Hankow Front

### Ships on Guard as Powers Draft Demands on Cantonese.

Shanghai, China, April 7.—(By Associated Press.)—Police late today surrounded the Soviet consulate here, barring entrance or exit, leading to the belief that a raid of the premises was intended.

Tientsin, April 7.—(By Associated Press.)—Chinese police this afternoon entered the French concession with permission of the consul and searched the Dahlbank and various Soviet trade missions. French police took no direct part in the raid, but maintained order outside.

Washington, April 7.—(By Associated Press.)—Official reports confirming the violation of Russian diplomatic immunity in Peking by police and soldiery vied for attention with the disclosure that a fleet of 21 foreign warships has mobilized at Hankow, Nationalist political capital, at a time when demands for reparations for the Nanking outrages are being drafted for presentation at Hankow.

Minister MacMurray cabled that the Russian embassy raid had followed permission granted the Chinese authorities by the senior diplomat of the Boxer protocol powers, the Dutch minister, for a search of the privately owned Dahlbang and the building of the Chinese Eastern railway adjacent to the embassy compound for evidences of "subversive Soviet agitation."

He added that the Chinese had evidently exceeded this authorization to search private Russian-owned and occupied property and had invaded the barracks in the old compound occupied by the Russian legation guard before the Moscow government waived its special rights under the Boxer protocol.

Of far greater moment as it affects the whole Chinese situation, however, is the course the Moscow government may take as a result of the incident.

The fleet mobilization at Hankow was reported by Consul General Lockhart. His dispatch as made public did not indicate that the concentration of war vessels had any other significance than as reflecting tension over the status of foreigners still prevailing at Hankow.

Four Japanese destroyers reached the city within 48 hours after the rioting of April 3, in the Japanese concession, in which Japanese and Chinese were killed, Lockhart said. There are eight Japanese naval craft, four American, six British, two French and one Italian now at Hankow.

## St. Paul Missionary Missing in Interior.

Peking, China, April 7.—(By Associated Press.)—Dr. C. P. Friberg, a Lutheran missionary of St. Paul, Minn., is missing in northern Honan province. It is feared he has been made captive by bandits.

Dr. Friberg has been in China as a missionary for the past 15 years in behalf of the Augustana synod. His wife and three children are with him in China.

Dr. Friberg, according to synod officials, has served in Honanmu, Honan province, but a recent cable

(Continued on Page 2, Column 4.)

## Intervention by Governor Predicted in Student Strike

Superior, Wis., April 7.—(By Associated Press.)—Becoming more bitter with every passing hour the Superior Central high school student strike of nearly 1,000 students enters its seventh day tomorrow with no sign of settlement or compromise and the prospects are that the matter will be carried to Governor Fred R. Zimmerman for action.

Action to bring the strike controversy before the governor is predicted to follow immediately upon the official filing of the city attorney's report which states that Mayor Fred Baxter has not the legal power to remove the Rev. A. T. Ekblad, chairman of the school board, and Paul H. Spencer, superintendent of schools, from their offices.

Requests for the resignation of the school authorities were served upon the mayor today by a committee of three persons representing citizens' committees organized in each ward to back the striking students in their demands that Miss Lulu Dickinson, discharged teacher, be reinstated by the board.

Forty-four teachers today were endeavoring to organize classes among the 69 students at Central high who have failed to join the strike. Difficulties were also experienced by educational authorities at East high, where according to reports the number of sympathetic strikers has mounted from 50 two days ago to 100 today.

All sides are denying that compromises had been considered and continued firm in their original policies.

Organized labor of Superior is beginning to take an active part in the fight on the school board. The Superior Trades and Labor Assembly is considering a resolution expressing its view.

Paid advertisements have been placed in newspapers by strikers warning against "false" reports that the strike was to end before Monday.

## Attack Made on Treasury Bookkeeping

### System Branded Faulty by Former St. Paul Comptroller.

### Skipton Tells Legislative Committee of Alleged Discrepancies.

### Co-operation by State Auditor Necessary, Two Witnesses Declare.

Two witnesses testified before the joint legislative committee considering a resolution for an audit of the state treasurer's office Monday, one of them recommending that changes be made "with the co-operation of the state auditor's office" in the bookkeeping system of the state and the other stating that he had found discrepancies in the books during an investigation made in 1921.

The two witnesses were E. M. Skipton, former St. Paul city comptroller, who said he had been employed by the state to institute a new system of surveys and records in the state treasurer's office, and George Olson, now a cashier in the treasurer's office, who reported he had found the discrepancies while he was a deputy public examiner.

Mr. Skipton was employed, he told the committee, following the disclosure of cash shortages in the treasurer's office. Walter C. Martin, a former employe, is serving a sentence in Stillwater prison as an outgrowth of the shortages.

"Before any further real improvement can be made in the treasurer's bookkeeping system, the auditor's office must give its heartiest co-operation," Mr. Skipton testified. "It is possible to misappropriate systematically sums of money from the treasurer's office because there is no proper reconciling of warrants by the auditor's office," he explained.

He submitted a lengthy typewritten manuscript detailing the results of his work in improving the bookkeeping system, stating, "If the auditor's office will carry out instructions and verify the warrants paid daily, all discrepancies will be detected at once. A complete revision of the warrant system should be made."

Outlining the findings of his in-

(Continued on Page 11, Column 1.)

## *Boy Admits He Caused Fire on Pinedo's Plane*

### Says It Was Accidental—Flier Scoffs at Anti-Fascist Plot Story.

Phoenix, Ariz., April 7.—(By Associated Press.)—John Thomason, 17 years old, of Phoenix, Ariz., a boat tender at Canyon lake, Arizona, late today signed a statement admitting he was responsible for setting fire to Commander Francesco de Pinedo's seaplane, the Santa Maria, at Roosevelt lake yesterday.

The youth said he was the one who threw the lighted match on the oilcoated waters of the lake near the plane which resulted in the destruction of the ship.

"It was an accident," he said. "I am sorry."

Canyon lake is a few miles below Roosevelt lake, and is used for storing irrigation water.

The statement was obtained after a reporter for The Arizona Republican, who was at Roosevelt dam, had questioned Thomason. Satisfied that the youth was responsible, the reporter had him sign the written statement in the presence of Commander de Pinedo, Roland A. Still, manager of Apache lodge, and John W. Hughes.

The boy who threw the match into the water, bringing to a halt De Pinedo's air tour of four continents, had been sought since yesterday.

Commander de Pinedo said that

(Continued on Page 9, Column 4.)

## *'Big Bill' Warns London to Beware of Crook Invasion*

Chicago, April 7.—(By Associated Press.)—London wants to know whether "Big Bill" Thompson, Chicago's mayor-elect, hates the king of England.

Thompson, whose campaign slogan was "America First," and who mentioned the king in denouncing European interference in American affairs, received a long distance call today. It was from the New York representative of a London newspaper.

"I say," said the voice over the wire, "there is great excitement in London. Is it true that you hate the king of England?"

"No," said his honor-elect, "I don't hate your king, but I want him to stay in England and keep out of our affairs."

"Are you there?" came the anxious query, "look here! Is it true that you hate Englishmen?"

"No," said Thompson, "the best friend I have in the world is Sir Thomas Lipton."

"Extraordinary," said the voice, "but he's an Englishman. But, I say, is it true that your hooligans are on the way to London?"

"If you mean crooks," said Thompson, "they are going to be on their way out of Chicago within 90 days after I'm in office. We have a lot of them, enough to supply a good many cities. Some of them may get as far afield as London. You better cable Scotland Yard to get ready for the invasion."

## *Scalpers Grab Borah-Butler Debate Tickets*

### National G.O.P. Chairman Accepts Bid to Be Honor Guest Tonight.

Boston, April 7.—(By Associated Press.)—The acceptance by Chairman William M. Butler of the Republican national committee of the invitation of the Roosevelt club, Inc., to occupy a place of honor tomorrow night at the debate between Senator William E. Borah and Dr. Nicholas Murray Butler, announced today by President Robert M. Washburn of the club, sets at rest the rumors of party disapproval which have been current for a week.

The talk of the street has been that speculators were obtaining prices for tickets to the debate which match those paid scalpers for such contests as a Harvard-Yale football game.

Speculation as to the political consequences of the impending public discussion of the question of whether the Republican platform should take cognizance of the prohibition issue was started by the information that Frank W. Stearns, intimate friend of President Coolidge, had resigned from the club on the eve of the debate.

While Mr. Washburn offered no explanation of his withdrawal, persons close to him said that it was because of disapproval of the debate. This was followed yesterday by the statement of Morgan Butler, son of the Republican committee chairman, that he was returning two tickets to the debate because he was not interested.

Rumors were also current that party pressure had been brought to bear on the disputants to cause their withdrawal. The rumors apparently were occasioned by the fact that Senator Borah yesterday held a brief conference in Washington with the President. There was nothing to indicate, however, that the debate had been discussed at the conference.

## *Court Orders Return of Whiteman's Boy Banjoist to St. Louis*

New York, April 7.—(By Associated Press.)—From the night clubs of New York to the sidewalks of St. Louis—that's the trip next on the program for "Snowball" Harris, 14-year-old Negro and his banjo. "Snowball" can't play the banjo any more for Paul Whiteman, band leader. Magistrate Flood in West Side court decided today, and agreed to discharge a complaint against "Snowball's" portly employer if he would pay the boy's fare back home where he was "discovered" and hired. "Snowball" was making $100 a week here in a musical show, when the Children's society cited the law against the public performance of a minor.

## *Mrs. Dodge Silent on Marital Affairs*

Honolulu, April 7.—(By Associated Press.) — Mrs. Horace E. Dodge, whose husband is en route here reported to be seeking a reconciliation, refused today to discuss her marital affairs. She would not indicate whether Mr. Dodge had advised her of the purpose of his hurried trip to the island. Mrs. Dodge charged incompatibility in a suit for divorce which she filed against the scion of the motor car family in Detroit in January. The steamer Wilhelmina on which Mr. Dodge is coming here was held up two hours at San Francisco yesterday while he was completing an airplane flight from Los Angeles.

## Deputies' Fire Opens Search for Stolen Furs

### Victim of Bullets Perhaps Fatally Wounded —Two Jailed.

### $6,000 in Raccoon Pelts Recovered in North Side House.

### Skins Identified by Owner of Looted Columbia Heights Store.

Louis Hackel, 819 Twelfth avenue north, was shot, perhaps fatally, by deputy sheriffs, Thursday night when they raided a house at 1501 Washburn avenue north in search of stolen furs. Edmond Grabber and William Hendrickson, who live at the address, and Amanda Annis, 1415½ Washington avenue north, were jailed and racoon pelts valued at $6,000 recovered.

Hackel was taken to General hospital with a dangerous bullet wound in the abdomen, and it was considered doubtful if he would recover. Physicians at the hospital said he was too weak to submit to questioning by the Anoka county attorney.

**Raid Follows Tip.**

The raid followed a tip obtained by the Hennepin county sheriff's office Thursday that racoon pelts, stolen from the tannery of the Superior Fur & Leather Co., in Columbia Heights, April 6, had been taken to the Washburn avenue house. The raiding party included Sheriff U. S. Pratt of Anoka; H. F. Hanson, his deputy; Chief Jake Heller, of the Columbia Heights police and Deputy Sheriffs McGuire, Kittridge and Kramer of Hennepin county.

The officers surrounded the house and were about to demand admittance when Grabber and the Annis woman opened a side door and walked out. At about the same time an automobile parked in front of the house began to move. When the sheriffs called on the driver to halt, Hackel jumped out and ran. He failed to halt when called upon to surrender, and several shots were fired. He dropped after running a block.

**Furs Identified as Stolen.**

The sheriffs said Grabber then admitted that the stolen furs were in the house and led them to the basement, where the pelts were found strung on a line. They were identified as the stolen furs by an official of the Northern Fur Coat Manufacturing Co., for whom they were being treated at the Columbia Heights plant when stolen.

After they had been questioned at the office of the Hennepin county sheriff, Grabber, Hendrickson and Amanda Annis were lodged in the county jail and ordered held without charge.

Hackel, the wounded man, is 31 years old, unmarried and is employed by the park board. He lived at home with his mother.

## U. S. Mining Man Is Slain by Mexicans

### Body of Another American Citizen Found in Rio Grande.

Nogales, Ariz., April 7.—(By Associated Press.)—A dispatch received here today said that Fred Combs, 37 years old, an American connected with the La Dura Mining Co. at La Dura, Mexico, was murdered last Saturday while en route from Esparanza, a railway station, to La Dura, in his automobile. A Chinese cook with him also was slain, the dispatch stated, adding that the murder is attributed to Mexican bandits.

### Body of American Found in Rio Grande.

El Paso, Texas, April 7.—(I.N.S.)—The body of a well-dressed American, found floating in the Rio Grande here recently, will be exhumed in order to attempt identification. Arthur J. Derrick, an Arizonan, believes the body is that of J. Gifford of Clarksville, Ariz., who had been working as an architect in Borger, Texas, recently. Tattoo marks on the man's body correspond with similar markings on Gifford, Derrick said.

### Plot to Kill Mexican Minister Frustrated.

Mexico City, April 7.—(By Associated Press.)—From police sources today came information that a plot to kill Luis Morones, minister of industry, commerce and labor, had been frustrated.

## *Belden Decides Not to Run for Mayor*

George K. Belden, Minneapolis business man and president of the Minneapolis baseball club, has decided not to enter the race for mayor. Mr. Belden left Thursday night for Chicago en route to Louisville, Ky., where he will attend the opening Minneapolis game in the American association series on Tuesday. He will return the middle of next week.

# The Minneapolis Sunday Tribune

Sixtieth Year. No. 363. Ninety-two Pages. MINNEAPOLIS, MINN., SUNDAY, MAY 22, 1927 * * * (11) Price Six Cents in Minneapolis


# LINDBERGH LANDS IN PARIS; SPANS ATLANTIC IN 33 HOURS

## 10,000 Bid for Lindbergh at Auditorium

### Minneapolis Manufacturers Cable Offer for Flier's Appearance.

### Terms Are Accepted 'Lucky' Will Be Here June 11.

### Frenzy of Joy Reigns in City as Victory News Is Received.

n impromptu celebration, followby a "cash offer" to Captain rles A. Lindbergh to come to neapolis and help dedicate the municipal auditorium, resulted urday when news bulletins anced that the Minnesota youth completed his flight to Paris. he offer to participate in the aurium dedication was cabled by Minneapolis Manufacturers' assoion, which promised him $10,000 he can accept. If Captain Lindgh consents, he will be in Minnelis on June 11.

nnouncement of the completion the flight broke the tense extancy of two days of waiting. ince crowds at the theaters ered the news, and at Nicollet t, where several thousand basefans had the bulletin "meganed" to them by the announcer, information brought a shout as ll as those given the player who s in the winning run in the th inning.

**Enthusiastic Cheering.**

t the Shrine ceremonial in the wood armory, there was a demtration of several minutes dura, when a miniature airplane laed "Lindbergh" bobbed across the ge on a wire in front of a backp painted to represent the Atlanocean.

requent comparisons were made ween the celebration of Saturday that on the original Armistice While the celebration Saturwas intense, it was short, and hin a few minutes had quieted wn to broad grins and unlimited nversation about the exploits of e flier.

No sooner had the result been anounced than a number of cableams of congratulation were distched. One of the first was that nt by the Manufacturer's Assoation of Minneapolis:

**Cable $10,000 Offer**

"Congratulations. Minnesota elat. Minneapolis wants you Saturday ne 11. Dedication new auditorium. ll pay you $10,000. Cable anr."

If the invitation is accepted Lindbergh will take the central part of the dedication of the new municipal auditorium.

"Minnesota is proud of you" was the message dispatched by Governor Christianson, who said, in commenting on the exploit:

"I felt from the start he would succeed. There was something in his manner which seemed to make failure impossible. The people of Minnesota have good reasons to be proud of Charles Lindbergh. His exploit will undoubtedly give his name a place in history".

A cablegram of congratulations from Senator Henrik Shipstead to the flier read:

"Congratulations. You are a worthy son of a brave father and Minnesota is proud of you".

Mayor Leach, on behalf of the city congratulations:

"People of Minneapolis congratulate you".

Members of the Minnesota chapter of the National Aeronautics society also cabled their congratulations

"Minnesota flyers proud of you." read the message. "You have been elected to honory membership. All envy your skill and courage. More power to you. Many future happy landings".

Members of the organization had spent the afternoon at the headquarters, 3519 West Calhoun boulevard waiting for news of the flight.

Other cablegrams were sent by Mayor Hodgson of St. Paul; General W. F. Rhinow, Colonel W. A. Welsh, commandant at Fort Snelling postal employes of the state and the St. Paul association.

**Stories Repeated.**

Stories of Lindbergh's exploits were repeated all through Minneapolis Saturday night. One of the incidents brought up was a plane wreck at Glencoe, when young Lindbergh was transporting his father, the late C. A. Lindbergh, then a Farmer-Labor candidate for senator on a speaking campaign trip through the state.

On this occasion the plane had landed on a farm near Glencoe. In trying to take off again, defective control apparatus prevented Lindbergh from clearing a high bank along one side of the roadway. The plane tumbled to the ground, and one of its wings was torn away. Both the father and son were uninjured and continued their trip in an automobile.

### Weather Forecast

Minnesota—Showers today and probably Monday; not much change in temperature.

Additional weather forecast on page 5, second news section.

## Mother Hears News Joyfully; Sends Brief Cable of Congratulation

Detroit, May 21.—(By Associated Press.)—"That's all that matters." In these words Mrs. Evangeline Lodge Lindbergh, mother of Captain Charles Lindbergh, expressed her relief when informed that her intrepid son had arrived safely at Le Bourget flying field, France, after an epochal flight from New York.

Mrs. Lindbergh, who had been waiting silently since the takeoff from New York yesterday morning for the word of her son's safe arrival, allowed herself a few tears of joy and then said:

"I am deeply thankful for his safety and appreciative of the true sympathy expressed by so many people."

Asked whether she had been confident of his success, she countered with:

"I knew if it were possible for any pilot, given a good machine, to make the flight, that he would."

Detroit, Mich., May 21.—(INS.) —Mrs. Evangeline Lindbergh, mother of the "flying fool," tonight cabled her son a brief cablegram of congratulations. The cablegram follows: "Captain Charles Lindbergh, Le Bourget, France. Congratulations from us all. E. LINDBERGH."

## Coolidge Sends Cable Lauding Flier for Feat

### Says 'American People Rejoice With Me at Brilliant Finish.'

Washington, May 21.—(By Associated Press.)—President Coolidge in a congratulatory cablegram to be delivered to Charles A. Lindbergh in Paris, told the trans-Atlantic flier that the "American people rejoice with me at the brilliant termination of your heroic flight."

The message of the President, sent to the American embassy in Paris for transmission to Lindbergh immediately on his arrival, follows:

"The American people rejoice with me at the brilliant termination of your heroic flight. The first nonstop flight of a lone aviator across the Atlantic crowns the record of American aviation and in bringing the greetings of the American people to France you likewise carry the assurance of our admiration of those intrepid Frenchmen, Nungesser and Coli, whose bold spirits first ventured on your exploit and likewise a message of our continued anxiety concerning their fate."

Secretary of State Kellogg also sent a message of congratulation to Lindbergh through the American embassy.

## *Lindbergh, Clad in Ambassador's Pajamas, Talks of Flight; Never Got Sleepy, He Says*

### Too Full of Experiences to Sleep, Flier Sits Up for Chat.

### Encountered 1,000 Miles of Snow and Sleet—Ate Sandwich and Half.

**By Carlyle MacDonald.**

Copyright, 1927, by The New York Times.

Paris, May 22.—Captain Lindbergh was discovered at the American embassy at 2:30 a. m. Sunday, attired in a pair of Ambassador Herrick's pajamas. The aviator sat on edge of the bed and talked of the flight. At the last moment Ambassador Herrick had dismissed the plans of the reception committee, and by unanimous consent took Lindbergh to the embassy in the Place Diena. The staff of American doctors, who had arrived at the field early to administer to an exhausted aviator, found instead a bright-eyed, smiling youth, who refused to be examined, and said:

"Oh, don't bother. I am all right. I'd like to have a bath and a glass of milk—I would feel better then."

The bath was prepared immediately, and in less than five minutes this amazing young man had disrobed in one of the embassy guest rooms, taken his bath, and was out again, drinking a bottle of milk and eating a roll.

**Says 'Don't Worry About Me.'**

"There's no use worrying about me, Mister Ambassador," insisted Lindbergh when Mr. Herrick and members of his staff wanted him to be examined and go to bed immediately. It was apparent the young man was too full of his experience to want sleep and he sat on the bed and chatted with the ambassador, his son and daughter-in-law. By this time the frantic corps of newspapermen who had been chasing the American airman from one false scent to another finally tracked him to the embassy.

In a body they descended upon the ambassador, who received them in the salon and informed them he had just left. Lindbergh who had strict instructions to go to sleep, as Mr. Herrick was talking with the journalists, his son-in-law came downstairs and said Lindbergh had rung and announced he didn't care to go to sleep just yet, and would

(Continued on Page 2, Column 6.)

### *Lindbergh's Own Story in Tribune Tomorrow*

Captain Charles A. Lindbergh was too exhausted after his arrival in Paris late Saturday night, to do more than indicate his experiences during his flight. After he awakes Sunday, he will narrate the full story of his remarkable exploit for readers of Monday's Minneapolis Tribune.

### 'Lucky' Lindbergh

## Little Falls Cuts Loose With Celebration of Slim's Feat

Little Falls, Minn., May 21.—Cheers and tears and prayers of thanksgiving greeted the announcement here that Captain Charles A. Lindbergh, who grew to manhood in this town, had landed safely in France.

Milling crowds jammed the street in front of the local newspaper office all day waiting for the sporadic bulletins that told of the young flier's progress.

When word came that he had reached the coast of France, some of the tenseness was relieved, and from that point on, cheers in increasing volume greeted each announcement.

**Start Wild Celebration.**

Then came the report from the French flying field that he had been sighted. Without waiting for the safe landing of the intrepid airman, the crowd turned loose in wild celebration.

Backslapping and cheers, un-

(Continued on Page 9, Column 1.)

## Plans for Presenting $25,000 to Lindbergh to Be Completed Soon

New York, May 21.—(By Associated Press.)—Arrangements for the payment of Raymond Orteig's $25,000 prize to Charles A. Lindbergh will be made soon at a meeting of the trustees designated by the donor, it was learned tonight.

Paris, May 21.—(By Associated Press.)—Raymond Orteig, whose $25,000 Captain Lindbergh wins for his transatlantic flight, lost his race by train today to get to Lebourget before the aviator. He had been spending a vacation in his old home in the Basque country and started for Lebourget when he heard Lindbergh had started. He had to change trains several times and left Paris for the flying field 15 minutes after Lindbergh had landed.

## Crowds Mow Down Police, Rush to Flier

### Reception Committee Gets Lost as Crowd Carries Flier From Cockpit.

Copyright, 1927, by The New York Times.

Paris, May 21.—"The flying fool" did it. At 20 minutes after 10 tonight, suddenly and softly there slipped out of the darkness a great white airplane as 20,000 pairs of eyes strained at the sky and a second later the lines of soldiers, ranks of policemen, and the stout steel fences went down before a mad rush as irresistible as the tides of the ocean. At almost the instant the plane touched the ground it was surrounded by thousands as willing hands pulled the brave pilot from his seat.

Not since the armistice has there been such a scene here. A frantic and enthusiastic crowd filled the field at Le Bourget, where a few seconds before doubts had followed doubts as the time of the probable arrival announced in the newspapers passed.

The official reception committee got lost in the rush, and silk hats were tumbled into the dust in the terrific rush towards the plane. Lindbergh finally was borne on the shoulders of Frenchmen, who had seized him as the wheels of the "Spirit of St. Louis" touched the ground, into the aviators' clubhouse, while 10,000 wildly shouting people cheered and pushed for a glimpse of him. Renewed cheers went up as Lindbergh appeared at a window, waving the helmet he had worn on his epoch-making flight from America to the French metropolis. The aviator looked pale and strained, but he shoved away the doctors who wished to give him pills and a hypodermic injection.

At Le Bourget field a big automobile was waiting to whirl the weary flier into Paris, where a luxurious

(Continued on Page 8, Column 1.)

## Minnesotan Is Hailed International Hero in Record-Making Hop

### Lone Flier, Driving Over 4,000-Mile Air-Track, Clips Two and a Half Hours From Time Estimates.

### Thousands of Frenchmen Besiege Plane of Ocean Conqueror Delirious With Joy at Epochal Achievement.

**By Associated Press.**

A new epoch in aviation has been inaugurated.

Charles Lindbergh of Little Falls, Minn., landed at Le Bourget, France, at 10:21 Paris time (3:21 Minneapolis), yesterday, in one record-smashing jump from Roosevelt Field, New York.

"Well, here we are," was his greeting to the enthusiasm-maddened crowds.

Unaccompanied, Lindbergh drove his plane, "The Spirit of St. Louis," over the nearly 4,000-mile air track, clipping about two hours and a half off the most optimistic time allowance.

The world imagination was fired by his exploit.

Spontaneous celebrations in scores of cities both here and abroad lasted far into the night; President Coolidge and executives of other nations flashed their congratulations and these were supplemented by thousands from other individuals publicly prominent.

At Detroit, Charles' mother relaxed her steadily maintained attitude of silent confidence and through tears of joy declared his victory was "all that mattered."

## Joy-Mad Throng Hails Conqueror of Atlantic

Paris, May 21.—(By Associated Press.)—Captain Charles A. Lindbergh, the young American aviator who hopped off from New York yesterday morning all alone in his monoplane, arrived in Paris tonight, safe and sound, as everyone hoped he would.

The sandy-haired son of Minnesota dropped down out of the darkness at Le Bourget flying field, a few miles frm Paris, at 10:21 tonight, (3:21 p. m. Minneapolis time), only 33½ hours after leaving Long Island—the first man in history to fly from New York to Paris.

To the young American it was seemingly merely the achievement of an ambition.

To Paris, to France, to America, to the world, his landing tonight made him the greatest of heroes since man made the air a means of travel.

"It wasn't such a bad trip," he said later at the American embassy. "I ran into some snow and ice in the early part, but the rest was not so bad."

"The biggest trouble was staying awake. I went to sleep several times, but was lucky enough to wake myself right away. I was afraid of the sandman all the time."

Computing the distance as 3,800 miles, his speed averaged around 113 miles an hour.

**Gets Supreme Welcome.**

A crowd of at least 25,000 surrounded his plane, the "Spirit of St. Louis," when it came to earth after its epochal voyage from the new world to the old.

The airman was lifted from the seat, where for two days and a night he sat fixed, guiding his plane over land and sea, and for 40 minutes he was hardly able to talk or do anything else, except let himself be carried along by a mass of men made delirious with joy at his achievement.

Never has an aviator of any nation, even king or ruler, had a greater or more spontaneous welcome from the hearts of the common people of France. The very recklessness of his endeavor, as it appeared, appealed to the quick emotional imagination of Frenchmen, and they were quick to respond with everything their hearts could give.

**National Ties Forgotten.**

All ties of nationalism were forgotten by the Le Bourget throng. They saw in Lindbergh only a man who had brilliantly gambled with death—and won. There was regret, of course, for Nungesser and Coli, and regret, too, that the daring Frenchmen had not been the first. But there was no bitterness in their greeting of the American winner.

It was the common people of France who first hailed the intrepid Lindbergh as he emerged from what only yesterday morning he had called his "death chamber". Shortly after 10:10, the roar of his motor, for which they had been waiting for hours, came out of the clear sky to the ears of the multitude. Police lines were swept aside as thousands surged over the field to welcome the man who had won their hearts and had earned immortal fame.

**Crowd Towards Plane.**

"There he is," the cry went up, as the rays of the searchlights gleamed upon the monoplane gracefully descending from the darkness.

Smoothly the airplane, the "Spirit of St. Louis" glided down upon the lighted ground. Even before it had come to a pause a hundred hands caught hold of the wings.

The wheels had scarcely ceased to roll, the propellor had barely come to a stop when Lindbergh, weary-eyed, but smiling, got up from the

### *Log of Flight*

**Minneapolis Time.**

8:52 a. m. (Friday)—Hopped off from Roosevelt field.

7:40 a. m.—Sighted at Halifax, Mass.

10:05 a. m.—Reached Springfield, N. S.

11:30 a. m.—Plane was seen passing over Milford, Nova Scotia.

1:05 p. m.—Sighted over Mulgrave, N. S., on Strait of Canso, separating mainland of Nova Scotia from Cape Breton island.

2:00 p. m.—Left Main-A-Dieu, easternmost tip of Nova Scotia.

3:00 p. m.—Cleared Nova Scotia at Main-A-Dieu, the easternmost tip.

5:15 p. m.—Passed St. Johns, Newfoundland, headed over broad Atlantic.

6:10 a. m. (Saturday) — Reported sighted 500 miles off Irish coast.

11:30 a. m.—Sighted over Smerwick harbor, Ireland.

2:00 p. m.—Passed Bayeux, France.

3:21 p. m. Landed safely in Paris.

## Bellanca Hop Is Off; Flames Menace Plane

### Friends Persuade Chamberlin to Withdraw—Gas Is Ignited.

Roosevelt Field, N. Y., May 21.—(By Associated Press.)—Gasoline spilled from the Bellanca plane as it was being towed across the field, caught fire tonight and for a time threatened the plane with destruction.

The plane was on the way from Roosevelt field to Curtis Field after Clarence Chamberlin had announced indefinite postponement of a hop-off for Paris.

A puddle of gasoline was believed to have been ignited by a cigaret. Firemen, who rushed to the blaze, found the fire had burned itself out. The plane was not damaged.

Chamberlin's hop-off, which had been planned for 8 p. m., was "indefinitely postponed", when friends persuaded him not to make an immediate attempt.

"All right, it's all off," Chamberlin said at length. "It's off indefinitely, and when we do take off it won't be for Paris in all probability."

## *World's Non-Stop Air Record Broken*

Paris, May 21.—(By Associated Press.)—Captain Charles Lindbergh, established a new world's non-stop straight line distance record in his New York to Paris flight. In covering 3,600 miles, he broke the world mark of 3,100 miles set by the two Frenchmen, Coste and Rignot in their Paris to Yask, Persia, flight last October.

## 'Lucky' Lindbergh's Trail in Air Conquest of Atlantic

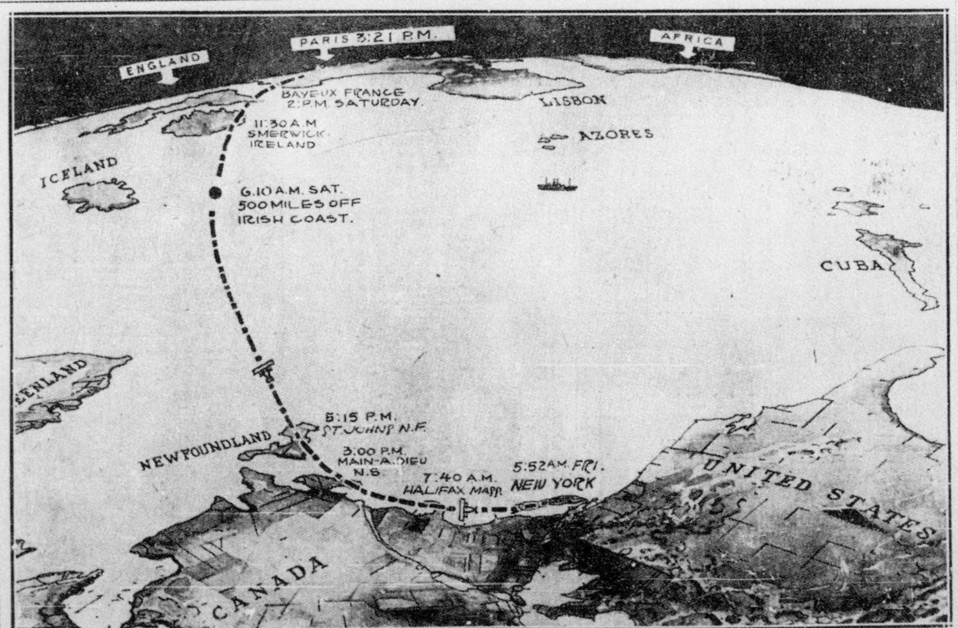


The map shows Captain Lindbergh's course on his New York-Paris flight and the few points at which he was sighted during the hop. Time indicated in the map is Minneapolis central standard time.

# CITY ACCLAIMS LINDBERGH TODAY

The Minneapolis Morning Tribune

Sixty-first Year. No. 91. Twenty Pages. MINNEAPOLIS, MINN., TUESDAY, AUGUST 23, 1927 * * Price Two Cents in Minneapolis

# SACCO AND VANZETTI EXECUTED

## BOY GOLFER LEADS NATIONAL AMATEUR AT 'KAHDA

## Gene Homans Shoots 71 in First Round

### Jersey Youth Carries Off Honors—Finlay Trails With 72.

### Scores Climax Day of Thrills for Thousands at Course.

### Tournament Opened With 300-Yard Drive by Veteran Player.

By Milt Davis.

Youth had its fling at the thirty-first national amateur golf championship Monday when one stripling of 19 scored a 71 for the first 18 holes of qualifying play, and another scored a par 72. Eugene Homans, junior champion of New Jersey, went out in 37 and came in with 34, for the day's record score of 71.

Phillips Finlay of New York made both nines in 36 for a par 72. There is a saying that golf is an old man's sport—and it seemed fair enough until late in the afternoon. For "Mister Par—that sun-baked gent in the weather-beaten knickers, that spavined stalking horse, who has been playing the game ever since they turned the cow pastures into links," was able to snap his fingers at the best of them.

**Dark Horse Comes Through.**

Don Carrick, the Canadian amateur champion, shot a 73; Harrison "Jimmy" Johnston, Minnesota state champion; George V. Rotan, D. Clark Cochran, Max Marston and Arthur Sweet took 74s; Bobby Jones took a 75; George Von Elm, the present titleholder, a 79. So it went.

"Old Man Par," concealed somewhere in the crowd of several thousand who made up the galleries, must have allowed himself a few polite chuckles, as youngsters tried to beat his card—the score, hole by hole, which is supposed to represent perfect golf. At that particular stage of a hectic day, it seemed indeed that golf, as exemplified by the aged "Mister Par," was an old man's game.

Then as a soggy sun was on its way into a decline, Finlay shot the par 72, and a little while afterward came word of Homans' 71, the lowest score of the day. The dark horses had come through.

Youth had come through, the unexpected had happened.

**Bring Day to Climax.**

These scores brought to a climax a day that had been for several thousand persons, who made up the galleries, and even for the players themselves, chiefly a spectacle. It was the big parade that precedes the main show—the match play which is to begin Wednesday. This parade comprised a galaxy of stars, sectional—titleholders, unknowns, officials, caddies and spectators. Up hill and down dale that parade wound. It swept across fairways, scurried through bunkers, trod cautiously on greens, but kept moving, ever moving. It began in the early morning when the grass was still heavy with rain and when heavy clouds threatened to drench the colorful assemblage. It ended at dusk, with the fagged but still eager onlookers following the last twosome to the eighteenth hole. It ended as "Old Man Par" and his croney, "Colonel Bogie" went arm and arm away from the course, shaking their heads sadly and remarking to one another that youth will not be denied.

It was at 8:30 a. m. sharp under a cloud-raked sky that threatened to spill a tubful of rain on each and every person present, the tournament got under way.

Several hundred men and women were pressed against the railing about the first tee, located a short distance from the club house.

James McMahon, executive secretary of the United States Golf association, the organization under whose auspices the championship is being held, paged John Redick, the first man to start out.

**Redick Starts Big Parade.**

Mr. Redick of the Omaha Country club, Omaha, Neb., was on hand. In fact he was impatiently cropping grass with his club before the call came. He is a veteran of many matches and he knew better than to be late.

Redick cracked out a drive that went straight and true down the fairway for nearly 300 yards—a drive that drew the first applause of the day.

Then his playing mate, Raymond J. Daly of the Flossmor Country club, Chicago, drove far and straight—and the first twosome moved down the fairway with a handful of officials at their heels.

At five-minute intervals there came the sounding crack against gutta percha and the twosomes moved off regularly as clock work.

Bob Gardner of Chicago, the first

(Continued on Page 2, Column 1.)

### Weather Forecast

MINNESOTA—Mostly fair today and Wednesday; somewhat warmer Wednesday.

Additional weather on page 9.

## News Index

DOMESTIC.

Lita Grey Chaplin was granted an interculatory decree of divorce from Charles Chaplin, and a property settlement of $625,000. Page 1.

Vice President Dawes declared he was not a candidate for nomination to the presidency. Page 1.

Federal legislation was predicted to prevent fatal stunt flying. Page 1.

Illinois farm leaders gave qualified approval to the adoption of the Canadian wheat pool plan. Page 5.

Officials of an Ohio coal mine were beaten by 100 union labor sympathizers. Page 5.

The political views of Nicola Sacco and Bartolomeo Vanzetti were expressed in prison writings. Page 7.

Disputed points in the trial of Sacco and Vanzetti were again recalled. Page 7.

Eastern railroad executives will reconsider consolidation. Page 9.

LOCAL.

Eugene Homans, with a score of 71, lead the field at the opening round of the National Amateur Golf tournament at Minikahda. Page 1.

St. Paul will give Robert Mead the place of honor beside Lindbergh throughout its reception for the Atlantic flight hero Tuesday. Page 1.

Residents of Penn avenue south held a protest meeting against the extension of the Bryant avenue street car line. Page 2.

The city planning commission started proceedings to widen the repaved section of Lake street six feet. Page 3.

Governor Christianson promised a reply within a few days to the charges of the state livestock sanitary board. Page 3.

State fair officials approved of separate designations for each day of the fair. Page 5.

The council considered recommendations to change the names of both Western and Second avenues south. Page 5.

Three thousand Minneapolis workers attended a meeting of protest in the execution of Sacco and Vanzetti for murder. Page 5.

Aldermen changed the regular committee meeting schedule in order to participate in the welcome to Colonel Lindbergh. Page 8.

The $236,994 Forest Lake paving contract was awarded to a St. Paul firm. Page 8.

Plans were completed for the south side picnic to be held Wednesday. Page 8.

Radio programs. Page 8.

A bill was proposed for the alteration of the city's Elwell work financing system. Page 9.

Members of the board of estimate and taxation were taken on a tour of inspection of the city park system by the park board commissioners. Page 11.

FOREIGN.

The Junkers planes were prepared to attempt an Atlantic flight within a few days. Page 5.

NORTHWEST.

Winona was passed by the first upriver barge tow due in Minneapolis Thursday. Page 1.

President Coolidge, in an unusual jovial mood, jested with Governor Erickson of Montana, on his arrival at Yellowstone. Page [illegible]

Politics became active in South Dakota with President Coolidge absent in Yellowstone park. Page 10.

WOMEN'S ACTIVITIES.

Social and club news. Page 4.

EDITORIALS.

Lindbergh Back in His Home State; A Good Theory—But Will It Work; Tourist Help for South Dakota; Tackling the Water Control Problem. Page 6.

SPORTS.

Eugene V. Homans, a New Jersey youth, is leading the qualifying round in the national amateur golf tournament with the score of 71. Page 12.

Two prep school lads of 19 are taking the spotlight from the champions at Minikahda. Page 12.

National amateur scores. Page 12.

Fine Girl won the grand circuit feature. Page 12.

Babe Ruth hit his fortieth home run but the Indians drubbed the Yankees, 9 to 4. Page 13.

Six Twin Cities players are within qualifying range in the amateur. Page 12.

Cook-Coos. Page 13.

The Mud Hens slugged their way to a 9 to 6 victory over the Millers. Page 13.

The Braves whipped the Cubs again as Hafey's homer won for the Cards. Page 14.

MARKETS.

U. S. Steel and General Motors scored new highs in an irregular stock market. Page 15.

Bond prices were easier and trading light. Page 15.

Bonds and investments. Page 15.

Frost reports from Canada gave a bullish tone to wheat futures and cash prices. Page 16.

Grain futures opened higher in Chicago but lost most of their gains on profit-taking. Page 16.

The South St. Paul cattle market showed little price change with liberal offerings. Page 16.

## Law Predicted to Block Fatal Stunt Flights

### Secretary Wilbur Voices Need for U. S. Action to Cut Loss of Life.

### Admiral Eberle Forecasts Restrictive Legislation Next Session.

### Orders 40 Navy Vessels to Continue Search for Pacific Aviators.

San Francisco, Aug. 22.—(By Associated Press.)—While navy boats and planes searched under an extended "zero hour," Secretary of the Navy Curtis D. Wilbur, visiting in San Francisco, and officials in Washington agreed today that some federal move must be made to prevent a recurrence of the disasters that have befallen the Dole air race entrants, crews of the Golden Eagle, Miss Doran and the Dallas Spirit.

Admiral Eberle, acting secretary of the navy, in Washington, predicted the enactment by congress of a law to prohibit long-distance airplane "stunt flights," except under rigid conditions.

**40 Ships Continue Search.**

At the same time, Admiral Eberle ordered the 40 naval vessels searching the Pacific for the missing fliers to continue their efforts until Thursday. The original plans were that the hunt should terminate officially tomorrow night, a week from the date of the start of the Miss Doran and the Golden Eagle in the Dole race.

Extension was ordered as the result of the disappearance of the Dallas Spirit, piloted by Captain William Erwin of Dallas, Texas, and navigated by A. H. Eichwaldt of Hayward, Calif., which apparently dived into the sea nearly 700 miles west of San Francisco Friday night, after flashing an SOS call on its radio.

**Wilbur Urges Precaution.**

Secretary Wilbur was quoted as agreeing that "some step must be taken by the federal government to prevent future loss of lives in long-distance stunt flights."

He declined to comment on Admiral Eberle's prediction.

The secretary said that the President had some power in this respect,

(Continued on Page 2, Column 1.)

## Story of Lost Cave Explorer Declared Fraud

### Tennessee Mine Inspector Reports Scheme to Get Tourist Trade.

Nashville, Tenn., Aug. 22.—(By Associated Press.)—O. P. Pile, state mine inspector, today reported officially to Governor Austin Peay that Lawrence Ashley's disappearance in Nick-a-Jack cave near Shell Mound, Tenn., was a "fraud perpetrated for the purpose of securing a state highway by the cave."

Mr. Pile's statement charged that Ashley and other inhabitants of the section, including members of the rescue crews which returned with "fabulous stories of wonderful halls in a six-mile-long cave were in the plot, the secondary purpose of which was to give the cave publicity and to attract tourists.

The cave is not over two miles in length, the statement said, is shallow and the roof has fallen in places, making it unattractive to tourists.

Ashley, Pile charged, did not stay in the cave and did not reappear until Sunday. Mr. Pile said he took a crew of 50 miners into the cave to search it and left one stationed at the door. The party had not gone far, he said, when it was recalled to see Ashley appear from the woods and hurry off toward home without walking toward those at the cave mouth.

The geologist, who told of having been cut off by a rock slide and after wandering about in the cave digging his way out, showed no signs of mud on his clothes and boots, Pile asserted, and carried a heavy pack as he walked rapidly away.

### Explorer Declares Charge Ridiculous

Chattanooga, Tenn., Aug. 22.—(By Associated Press.)—"I don't care to make any reply to this ridiculous statement at this time," Lawrence Ashley said, when called by long distance telephone and informed of charges by O. H. Pile, state mine inspector, that his cave episode was a hoax.

**Double Killing at La Crosse.**

La Crosse, Wis., Aug. 22.—Mrs. Mary Bakalars, a widow, was slain here late today by John Oluela, who committed suicide with the gun he used to shoot Mrs. Bakalars.

## Sacco-Vanzetti Case in Brief

Boston, Aug. 22.—(By Associated Press.)—Important dates in the Sacco-Vanzetti case are:

April 15, 1920—Murder of Frederick A. Parmenter, paymaster of Slater & Morrill Co., shoe manufacturers, and his guard, Alexander Berardelli, at South Braintree, Mass.

May 5, 1920—Bartolomeo Vanzetti and Nicolai Sacco arrested in Brocton.

September 11, 1920—Sacco and Vanzetti indicted.

May 31, 1921—Trial starts at Dedham.

July 14, 1921—Both found guilty of first degree murder.

December 24, 1921—Judge Thayer denies new trial motion.

March 27, 1923—Alienists declare Sacco sane.

April 9, 1924 — Vanzetti declared sane.

January 6, 1926—Celestino Madeiros made statement saying "Morelli gang" killed Parmenter and Berardelli.

April 5, 1927—Judge Thayer denies new trial on Madeiros statement and other new evidence.

April 9, 1927—Sacco and Vanzetti sentenced to die week of July 10.

June 29, 1927—Governor Fuller, having begun investigation of case, postpones death of Madeiros, Vanzetti and Sacco to and including August 10.

July 17, 1927—Sacco and Vanzetti begin hunger strike.

July 22, 1927—Governor Fuller interviews Sacco and Vanzetti in prison.

August 3, 1927—Governor Fuller gives decision refusing clemency.

August 8, 1927—Justice Sanderson, Massachusetts supreme court, refuses intervention. Judge Thayer, Massachusetts superior court, refuses intervention.

August 10, 1927—Justice Holmes, United States supreme court, refuses writ of habeas corpus. Governor and council vote further respite to midnight August 22.

August 19-22—Further legal moves fail. Counsel ask governor for further respite.

August 23—Executed.

## Lita Chaplin Gets $625,000 and Divorce

### Interlocutory Decree Is Granted Against Comedian Not in Court.

Los Angeles, Aug. 22.—(By Associated Press)—Lita Grey Chaplin was granted an interlocutory decree of divorce from Charles Spencer Chaplin at a brief court session here today after the film comedian had agreed to pay his wife $625,000 as a property settlement and grant her permanent custody of their two small sons.

Into an hour's session of Judge Walter Guerin's court, at which Mrs. Chaplin played the leading part, were rolled the final gestures to the eight months of marital strife. Chaplin was not present.

A property settlement reached out of court was announced by Edwin E. McMurray, chief of counsel for the suing wife, and Mrs. Chaplin made her own routine case of cruelty from the witness stand. A few corroborative witnesses were sworn, testified briefly and the decree was granted. A year must elapse before the final decree is granted.

The agreement between Chaplin and his wife provides for the creation of a trust fund of $200,000, the

(Continued on Page 2, Column 6.)

## Dawes Denies He Seeks Nomination for President in '28

Cincinnati, Aug. 22.—(By Associated Press.)—Vice President Charles G. Dawes in a letter to Douglas T. Atkinson, judge advocate of the Young America union, secret nonsectarian political organization, relating to the possibility that he might run for president, said:

"I am not a candidate for the nomination."

The Young America union, through Mr. Atkinson, recently pledged its support to Mr. Dawes if he should run for president.

"I want you to accept my thanks for your letter and for the kindly words expressed. They are appreciated. I am, however, not a candidate for the nomination," the letter, dated from the vice president's chambers in Washington and signed by Mr. Dawes, read.

## Three Buried Alive in Building Cave-in

Los Angeles, Aug. 22.—(By Associated Press.)—Three men were reported buried alive and a woman and two men seriously injured here today when a Central avenue two-story rooming house caved in. Dozens of workmen dug into the debris, hoping to save those buried.

## City Will Hail Lindbergh in Parade Today

### 200,000 to Line Route of Minneapolis Procession This Afternoon.

### Police Prepare to Handle Huge Throngs at Wold-Chamberlain Field.

### Loop Gaily Decorated for Reception—Mrs. Lindbergh Coming Here.

Flying in from the southeast, Colonel Charles A. Lindbergh will arrive in Minneapolis at 2 p. m. Tuesday.

The famed trans-Atlantic flier will reach the city in his famous monoplane, The Spirit of St. Louis, and will land at the Wold-Chamberlain field, near Fort Snelling, after a flight from Madison, Wis.

He will then be taken in an open automobile through the heart of the city in order that all who wish can see the intrepid flier. This parade will continue directly to St. Paul, where Colonel Lindbergh will make a public appearance at the St. Paul airport, to be followed later with a dinner at the Saint Paul hotel.

**200,000 Will See Him Here.**

Preparations have been made to handle a crowd upwards of 100,000 persons at the Wold-Chamberlain field, and even larger crowds are expected to line the parade route. In all, 200,000 or more persons will see him in Minneapolis.

Mrs. Evangeline Lindbergh, mother of the young Minnesota flier, will be a guest of the Twin Cities during the visit of her son, at the special invitation of Mayor Leach. She will arrive in Minneapolis from Detroit, where she has made her home.

Colonel Lindbergh will remain in Minneapolis and St. Paul all day Wednesday and until about noon Thursday, but during this time he expects to remain in seclusion to obtain needed rest. His airplane, meanwhile, will be on public exhibition at the Wold-Chamberlain field, until Colonel Lindbergh takes off for Little Falls, his own home town, which is located 100 miles north of Minneapolis.

**Look Profusely Decorated.**

Everything was in readiness Monday for the "Eagle's" visit. Buildings throughout the loop and along the line of the parade have been profusely decorated with flags and pictures of Lindbergh. A further display of colors is expected this morning.

When Mrs. Lindbergh arrives, she will be the guest of Mayor and Mrs. George E. Leach, who will meet her at the station and take her to their home for breakfast. She will be entertained there also at luncheon, before being taken to the airport to meet her illustrious son.

If she so desires, she will be given a place in the same automobile with the flier in the parade, and the rest of her program will be adjusted to suit her desires. She will remain in the city until Thursday noon when it is probable she will fly to Little Falls with her son.

**Will Be Met by Air Circus.**

When Colonel Lindbergh nears the Twin Cities, he will be met by an air circus of 14 planes of the 109th aero squadron, headed by Major Ray S. Miller, who will escort the visitor to the landing field. A salvo from the artillery unit at Fort Snelling will announce the fact that the Spirit of St. Louis has landed, and the entire personnel of Fort Snelling, including 1,000 members of the regular garrison and 2,000 members of the citizens' military training camp, will be on parade to honor the arrival.

When Colonel Lindbergh steps from the cockpit of his plane, he will be placed in a waiting open automobile, with Robert Mead, the 13-year-old boy scout of Excelsior who has been selected for the honor of riding with the colonel. Followed by other automobiles carrying members of the welcoming committee, his car will proceed to Thirty-eighth street and Park avenue, where the official parade will begin.

Motorists planning to drive to the airport to see the landing are advised to take the Thirty-fourth avenue south road out to Sixty-sixth street, where placards will direct the drivers into the field. Automobiles will enter through the driveway used by drivers of racing cars in the days of the speedway, which will take them right into the field. Red flags will guide the drivers to parking spaces, and patrolmen will direct the cars.

**Field Available for Parking.**

St. Paul spectators will use the other side of the airport, although there will be no restrictions. The entire field will be used, if necessary, for the parking of cars, leaving only a long triangular space with its apex at the hangar, in which Colonel Lindbergh will land.

Persons wishing to go to the airport by street car should take the Thirty-fourth avenue line, either on Washington or Cedar avenues, and go to the end of the line. Extra cars will be in service at noon to accommodate persons going to the field, but there will be a walk of several blocks from the end of the line to the airport.

When the official party leaves the

(Continued on Page 2, Column 2.)

## Don't Forget the Little Fellow

Inevitably there will be plenty of scrambling to see Colonel Lindbergh today. The desire to pay honor to the "lone eagle" who flew across the Atlantic is universal. But The Tribune would ask the average Minnesotan on the look-out for the flier not to forget the little fellow who may be near him in the crowd. This little fellow will be small; he will be unable to see well; and he will not have the strength to fight his way through if anybody pushes him back. His small heart, none the less, will be beating with admiration for Lindbergh. The day will be one of the big days of his life—a bigger day than circus day or even the Fourth of July. He will be seeking an opportunity to see the hero of boydom in the flesh. His zeal to see Lindbergh will exceed his zeal to see a circus, Santa Claus, "Babe" Ruth, Jack Dempsey, or Tom Mix. No figure, in either romance or reality, has so captured his imagination as the young knight of the air who flew from New York to Paris.

The Tribune, therefore, would ask the grown-up to aid the little fellow in getting a glimpse of Lindbergh. Give him his chance. Instead of pushing him aside, help him to a place where he can see his hero. The spontaneous admiration which the boys feel for Lindbergh already is one which should be encouraged. In admiring Lindbergh, the boys admire the qualities of fearlessness, determination, modesty, and tact which he symbolizes. These are the qualities which the human race depends upon for its advancement; and they are the qualities which we wish instilled in the coming generation. We need have no worries about the next generation if these young boys of ours all grow up striving to be "like" Lindbergh.

Don't, then, forget the little fellow. Give him a helping hand.

## St. Paul to Give Robert Mead Place of Honor Throughout Lindbergh Celebration There

### Tribune Essay Winner Will Remain at Flier's Side During Every Event on Program — Fellow Scouts Fit Boy Out With New Uniform.

By Frank Murray.

All togged out in a spick-and-span, brand-new scout uniform, the gift of his fellow troopers, Robert Mead, 13-year-old Excelsior boy, is going to ride with Lindbergh in the parade through the streets of Minneapolis Tuesday.

But that's not all. He will be in the parade through the St. Paul loop district. He will occupy a place of honor at the public reception at the St. Paul airport—and he will attend the dinner given in Lindbergh's honor in the Saint Paul hotel Tuesday night.

In short, Robert will be in the center of the Lindbergh celebration from start to finish. The amplification of his day's program came Monday afternoon on invitation from the St. Paul committee handling the Lindbergh reception after the flier leaves the Minneapolis city limits.

The original program called only for the ride in the Minneapolis parade, but there was little difficulty in persuading Robert to fall in with the new plans that have been outlined.

Robert, as representative of all the boys of the northwest, won't miss even the slightest bit of the Lindbergh celebration. He will be right on hand, with a "ring-side" seat in one of the deep cushions of the automobile that Lindbergh will ride in, from Wold-Chamberlain field, when the "Spirit of St. Louis" taxies to a landing.

**Day to Live Forever.**

He will hear Minneapolis roar its first welcome to the flier—and he will listen as that roar swells to a crescendo along the line of march through the loop district. He will be right in the center of the festivities until the business men's dinner for Lindbergh has come to an end and the formal celebration is over.

For Robert Mead, Excelsior Boy Scout, it will be a day to live forever in memory. It will be a day filled with enough thrills to last a lifetime. And Robert is planning not to waste a minute of it.

Ever since he first learned, on Saturday afternoon, that he was the chosen one to ride with Lindbergh, Robert has been doing a lot of

(Continued on Page 2, Column 4.)

## Barges Near City on First Upriver Trip

### S. S. Thorpe and Its Tow Pass Winona on Last Leg of Run.

Winona, Aug. 22.—The S. S. Thorpe, with three barges in tow on the initial trip from St. Louis to the Twin Cities, passed Winona late today full speed ahead, instead of making a stop here to unload a cargo as scheduled.

W. W. Morse of Minneapolis, general operating manager of the upper river barge line service, declared when the fleet stopped at La Crosse this morning that he was particularly anxious to reach the Twin Cities on scheduled time Thursday.

The fleet carried a cargo of soap and automobile tires consigned to this port, and was expected to make a short stop here. The fleet left La Crosse at 9:15 a. m. today for the last leg of its maiden trip inaugurating the upper Mississippi river barge line service.

### Special Train to Meet Barges at Terminal Here

The first barge tow of the Inland Waterways corporation, bearing the Minneapolis welcoming committee and pushing the first cargo of freight sent into the northwest over the new barge line, will be met at terminal port Thursday by a special train which will convey the welcoming party through the yards to the Great Northern station.

The official welcoming party will meet the barges at the high dam and go aboard to ride the seven miles up the river to the new terminal where they will step aboard the first train to be operated in connection with the barge service and ride through the terminal yards into the Great Northern station. The special train is being provided by the Minneapolis & St. Louis railroad.

After riding into the Great Northern station on the train, the party will march to the Nicollet hotel where a celebration dinner will be held. Several hundred reservations for the dinner already have been made, and guests will include General T. Q. Ashburn, head of the Inland Waterways corporation, who is aboard the barge, Congressman Walter H. Newton, Senator Henrik Shipstead, Governor Christianson and Mayor Leach.

## Worker Hurt as Liquid Explodes

Louis Cohen, 1649 Russell avenue north, a cleaner for the Standard Dye House, 1925 Fourth avenue south, was severely burned on the hands Monday afternoon when a quantity of cleaning liquid exploded in a storehouse at the rear of the dye house. Fire followed the explosion and caused approximately $300 damage. Cohen was given first aid treatment by a fire department squad.

## Day's Lindbergh Program Here

Colonel Charles A. Lindberg's program in Minneapolis today will be as follows:

2:00 p. m.—Colonel Lindbergh arrives at the Wold-Chamberlain field in the Spirit of St. Louis.

2:15 p. m.—Parade with Colonel Lindbergh starts at Thirty-eighth street and Park avenue, and traverses the following route: Along Park avenue to Tenth street, along Tenth street to Nicollet avenue, along Nicollet avenue to Second street, along Second street to Third avenue south, along Third avenue and across the Third avenue bridge to University avenue, and along University avenue southeast to the St. Paul city limits.

3:00 p. m.—Parade arrives at University avenue and the city limits, where Colonel Lindbergh is met by a St. Paul committee and escorted to the St. Paul airport.

3:40 p. m.—Colonel Lindbergh makes a three-minute address at the St. Paul airport.

6:30 p. m.—Dinner for the flier begins at the St. Paul hotel, at which Governor Christianson will present Colonel Lindbergh with the Minnesota medal. This is the gold award originally planned by Minneapolis, but the plans were changed to permit the entire state to join in the presentation.

## Electrocuted With Madeiros as Murderers

### Vanzetti Protests Innocence of Braintree Murder to Last.

### 'Long Live Anarchy!' Is Sacco Cry From Death Chair.

### Small Army of Guards Keeps Vigil at Charlestown Prison.

Charlestown State Prison, Boston, Aug. 23.—(Tuesday)—(By Associated Press.)—Nicola Sacco and Bartolomeo Vanzetti, shortly after midnight this morning, paid the penalty of death exacted by the state for murder.

Celestino Madeiros preceded them to the electric chair by a few minutes, the world-known radicals following as rapidly as the execution routine would permit.

Madeiros died at 12:09 a. m., for the murder of a Wrentham bank cashier. Sacco and Vanzetti were executed for the murder of a paymaster and his guard at Braintree, more than seven years ago. Sacco was pronounced dead at 12:19 a. m., and Vanzetti at 12:26 a. m.

**Army of Guards Posted.**

Inside and outside of the high prison wall stood a small army of armed guards. Waiting also were the press wires to inform the world that the long fight to save the men was at an end. The fight in behalf of the men continued up until the last minute.

Both Sacco and Vanzetti made brief speeches in the death chamber before they took their seats in the chair, Vanzetti protesting his innocence to the last.

**Vanzetti Calmest of Three.**

Vanzetti entered the death chamber the calmest of all the three men. Shaking hands with two of the guards as he came through the door of the execution chamber, he walked unassisted to the chair and seated himself.

A moment after the official witnesses entered the death chamber, Madeiros was led in between two guards. The youth, who had won five respites because of his confession that a gang which he was connected with committed the South Braintree murders, was stolid and expressionless. His eyes wandered about the little group of witnesses as he was strapped to the chair, but he said nothing.

Madeiros came in at 12:02:47. At 12:03:37 the shock was applied. He was pronounced dead at 12:09:35.

Then came Sacco. Apart from the prison pallor the little shoeworker who has become an international figure showed no sign of his long hunger strike. He walked erect between the guards, his eyes flashing brightly about the group in the death chamber as he came.

**Shouts 'Long Live Anarchy.'**

He sat down in the chair, and, as the guards began to attach the straps he shouted in a voice that rang strangely through the little white room:

"Viva l'Anarchia," (long live anarchy).

Almost without pause he continued, this time in broken English:

"Farewell my wife and child, and all my friends."

When the work of the guards was almost completed he looked about the group of witnesses again and said:

"Good evening, gentlemen."

Then, just as the head-straps were being applied, came Sacco's last remark. It was:

"Farewell mother!"

**Vanzetti Makes Speech.**

Hardly had Sacco's body been placed beside that of Madeiros behind a screen at the rear of the chamber than the guards appeared again in the doorway leading in from the death cells. This time Vanzetti was in their charge.

He showed no sign of nervousness or hesitation. As he entered the chamber at the rear and to the left of the chair, he shook hands with several guards. Seated in the chair, he launched at once into a brief speech.

"I wish to tell you," he said, "That I am innocent and never committed any crime but sometimes some sin. I thank you, Mr. Warden, for all you have done for me.

"I am innocent of all crime, not only this one but all. I am an innocent man."

**Forgives 'Some People.'**

Vanzetti paused while the guards continued their grim task of attaching the straps and applying the electrodes to his left leg. Then, just before his eyes were covered he continued:

"I wish to forgive some people for what they now are doing here."

Then the current was applied.

In the case of Madeiros the amperage was from nine to 11, and the voltage from 1,400 to 1,900. For Sacco the amperage was from 12 to 15 and the voltage from 1,800 to 2,000. In Vanzetti's execution the amperage was from nine to 11 and the voltage from 1,400 to 1,950. It was explained that the greater voltage in the case of Sacco was made necessary by the fact that he was an unusually rugged and vital type.

The men were dressed in blue

(Continued on Page 7, Column 1.)

# The Minneapolis Morning Tribune

*Sixty-first Year. No. 122.* Thirty-two Pages MINNEAPOLIS, MINN., FRIDAY, SEPTEMBER 23, 1927 *Price Two Cents in Minneapolis*


# TUNNEY RETAINS CHAMPIONSHIP

## Legion Closes Sessions Amid Paris Acclaim

### Resolutions Approve Boy Scouts, Child Welfare and Air Progress.

### Thousands Cheer When American Delegates Visit St. Mihiel.

### Spafford First Veteran of Naval Forces Named National Chief.

Paris, Sept. 22.—(By Associated Press. — The American Legion brought its greatest convention to a glorious close today after the Legionnaires had come again to Paris, seen it with eyes nearly ten years older than when they saw it last, and completely conquered the French capital.

The veterans came with a warning that they would be pelted with rotten eggs and assaulted. They were thrown kisses and embraced.

Doumergue, Poincare, Tardieu, Lygues, Marin and other French statesmen called them brother and a long line of French generals hailed them as comrades.

**Choose Lawyer Commander.**

The Legion chose Edward Elwell Spafford, New York lawyer, as commander and adopted 45 resolutions, many of them designed to improve conditions of American war veterans, their wives and children.

Spafford was commander of the New York department of the American Legion and before that was a lieutenant commander in the navy.

"My title to fame," he told friends, "is that I am the first sailor to be the Legion's commander."

He was nominated and elected without opposition in five minutes.

Jay Ward, 5-year-old citizen of Pennsylvania, shared with Spafford the honors of the closing day of the convention. Jay, the mascot from his state, had been referred to by the commander as a "typical American boy" and was elected national mascot.

**Approve Child Welfare.**

Child welfare, undesirable immigration, approval of the Boy Scout movement and American aviation were matters treated by the convention today.

Before its task was done the convention endeared itself further to thousands of French war veterans by paying tribute to Georges Clemenceau, "Father of Victory." The aged "Tiger" returned to his Paris lair from the country too late to address the convention but told friends: "My heart and soul is in their work." He added, "They are great people."

In addition to the national commander the convention named vice commanders, James Raftis, of Washington; Paul R. Younts, of North Carolina; Ralph T. O'Neill, of Kansas; Dan Spurlock, of Louisianna, and J. M. Henry, of Minnesota. The Rev. Gill Robb Wilson of Trenton, N. J., pastor of the Fourth Presbyterian church there, was elected national chaplain.

**Again Visit Battlefields.**

Outside of the convention proceedings today the Legionnaires devoted themselves to another big day of battlefield pilgrimages, an outstanding visit being to Saint Mihiel, where Premier Poincare received them and they were given the freedom of the city.

There were special ceremonies at Romagne, Thiaucourt, Belleau, Fere-en-Tardenois cemeteries and at Menin gate and Gate Ypres.

A brilliant Lorraine sun flooded the returning ranks of Americans as they passed in review before Premier Poincare at St. Mihiel to the accompaniment of cheers from thousands from all over the province who had gathered to greet them.

**Salute Unknown Warrior.**

In Paris the legionnaires were faithful to their pilgrimage, and delegation after delegation laid wreaths reverently on the tomb of the unknown poilu.

Particularly touching to the French people was the gesture of National Commander Spafford. Only a few minutes after his election he slipped quietly from the convention hall and saluted the flame that burns over the warrior's resting place.

This evening most of the state delegations had their own reunions or dinners preparatory to the big reception at the Hotel de Ville and ball at the opera, two culminating events of the reception of Paris to the honored visitors.

**Pershing Savage Speak.**

One of the most strenuous days of the week for the American Legion closed with a strenuous night. First there was a magnificent reception in Paris city hall, where, after an exchange of cordial speeches by the president of the city council, M. Delsol, Commander Howard P. Savage, General Pershing and others gave talks at a concert.

From this the guests went to a great ball in the operahouse, given by the government, on whose behalf M. Leykues acted as host. Several of the capital's best orchestras played in relays, keeping the legionnaires dancing merrily until daylight.

P. St. George Bissell, New York lawyer, was today unanimously elected chef de chemin de fer of the

(Continued on Page 6, Column 4.)

**Weather Forecast**

MINNESOTA—Mostly fair today and Saturday; not quite so cold today. Rising temperature Saturday.

Additional weather forecast on page 11.

## News Index



## *Marines Again Whip Rebels in Nicaragua*

Managua, Nicaragua, Sept. 22.—(By Associated Press.)—Bandits who again attacked the garrison of United States marines and Nicaraguan constabulary at Telpaneca last night were repulsed after two hours of fighting with the loss of 12 wounded. There were no casualties among the marines or constabulary. Bandits also attacked the ungarrisoned towns of Saklin and Quezalguaque, pillaging and robbing.

**School Dormitory Burns.**

Chicago, Sept. 22.—(By Associated Press.)—Fire caused extensive damage tonight to the interior of Foster hall, the oldest women's dormitory at the University of Chicago. The exact loss is not known.

## Strike Threat Issued by Soo LineTrainmen

### Brotherhood 'Ultimatum' Charges 17 Violations of Rail Contract.

### Settlement Demanded by Noon Today—2,000 Men Affected.

### Company Chiefs Absent From City—Workers to Meet Again.

The Brotherhood of Railroad Trainmen Thursday served notice upon officials of the Soo line railroad demanding, under threat of "drastic measures," a satisfactory settlement before Friday noon of several grievances. The "ultimatum" charges 17 alleged violations of the labor contract with the railroad.

The statement was sent to A. E. Wallace, vice president and general manager of the road, and was signed by A. F. Whitney of Chicago, vice president of the brotherhood, who is in Minneapolis. It was authorized by the general committee of 16 representatives from workers over the entire Soo line railroad and, according to W. A. McDonald of Minneapolis, chairman, had the full backing of practically all the members of the order.

**2,000 Workers Affected.**

Mr. Whitney said the "drastic measures" mean a general strike over the entire Soo line of conductors, brakemen, baggagemen and yardmen. About 2,000 men would be effected.

Mr. Wallace was in Chicago Thursday night and other railroad officials refused to discuss the situation in his absence.

The grievances involved various alleged violations on the part of the Soo line railroad of the labor contract between that road and the brotherhood of railroad trainmen.

**Brotherhood to Meet Today.**

The general committee of the brotherhood will meet at 9 a. m. Friday at the West hotel to discuss the situation and the probable course in case the railroad refuses to accede to their demands.

C. T. Jaffray, president of the road, was in Chicago Thursday with Mr. Wallace.

## 41 Policemen Suspended in Rum 'Pay Off'

### Fifth of Memphis Force Linked With $80,000 Liquor Plot.

Memphis, Tenn., Sept. 22.—(By Associated Press.)—Investigation of an alleged "pay off" book seized by federal agents last March in a raid on a grocery store operated by John Bellomini resulted today in a decision by Thomas H. Allen, commissioner of police, to suspend approximately one-fifth of the Memphis police force.

Forty-one policemen will be affected by the suspension order which is expected to go into effect shortly.

The "pay off" was alleged to have contained names of 51 policemen and four deputy sheriffs. Opposite the names were entered various amounts, ranging from $5 to $20 each, and totaling more than $80,000 over a period of 21 months.

All of the suspended men will have the right to demand trial before a police board.

Bellomini, two of his former clerks and another man have been arrested since seizure of the book on charges of conspiracy to violate the national prohibition law, and their cases will be presented to the federal grand jury next month.

## *Firemen Discover Home Brew Plant in Burning House*

Firemen summoned to a house at 17 North Eleventh street by a fire alarm stumbled through a smoke-filled kitchen and barked their shins on a cache of home-brew equipment and moonshine Thursday afternoon. A stovepipe in the kitchen of the home fell from place and smoke began to pour from the windows. Passersby, noticing the disturbance, summoned the firemen. They discovered five 15-gallon crocks of brewing beer, 400 quarts of beer ready for distribution; 500 empty bottles; 40 pints of moonshine; three five-gallon jugs of "moon." Detective Jack Kaufman and his troop of liquor squad raiders of the police department were notified and paid a flying visit to the house. No one was found in the building.

## *Lindy Pilots Ford Airplane on Coast*

Los Angeles, Calif., Sept. 22.—(INS.)—Piloting an all-metal 12-passenger Ford monoplane from San Diego, Colonel Charles A. Lindbergh landed here at 10:25 a. m. today on a surprise return visit to Los Angeles, bringing a party of officials and aviation enthusiasts from the southern city.

## *Estelle Collapses at News of Jack's Defeat by Tunney*

Chicago, Sept. 22.—(By Associated Press.)—Estelle Taylor, wife of Jack Dempsey, collapsed in her suite at a fashionable North Shore hotel tonight after she heard over the radio that her husband had bene defeated in his comeback attempt against Gene Tunney.

Despite the urging of her private nurse, Miss Violet Watson, "to be brave," Mrs. Dempsey was unable to weather the strain, said the Herald and Examiner's informant.

Everything seemed well until the near end of the eighth round. When the tide of the battle turned to Tunney, Mrs. Dempsey became hysterical, ordered the radio shut off and locked herself in the bathroom, the newspaper said. At the pleadings of the nurse that she "carry hope and believe that Jack will win," Mrs. Dempsey came to the radio again, ordered it turned on until the decision, awarding the contest to Tunney, was announced.

Then, said the newspaper's informant, Mrs. Dempsey collapsed and was not revived for several minutes.

## Three Planes Fail in Flight Across Nation

### Stinson and Schaller Land in Montana on Nonstop Spokane Derby.

Felts Field, Spokane, Wash., Sept. 22.—(By Associated Press.)—Failure tonight met the efforts of Eddie Stinson of Detroit and C. A. (Duke) Schiller of Windsor, in their projected nonstop trans-continental air derby from New York to Spokane.

Stinson was forced down at Missoula, Mont., by a broken rocker arm and a stuck valve. He was persuaded from continuing in the plane by Fred Koehler, his mechanic, who said it would be dangerous. Stinson finished the flight in the plane of R. A. Dake of Pittsburgh, and landed early tonight at the airport.

Schiller was forced to land at Billings, Mont., when his gasoline supply ran low.

**Other Racers Reach Spokane.**

Meanwhile, the Spokane airport received more civilian, marine corps and army planes as contestants in the national air race here.

The last finishers in the class B new York-to-Spokane nonstop cross-country flights came today when five fliers completed the last leg from Missoula.

Frank M. Hawks of Houston, Texas, flying a Ryan brougham, landed at Felts field today. Hawks was entered in the class A New York-Spokane derby.

**Planes Did Not Meet.**

Stinson did not see Schiller from the time he left New York. "I left 15 minutes ahead of him, and didn't fly the same course."

"There was very little trouble flying a straight course by compass," he declared, "and I never had to fly very high. Even at night I was pretty close to the ground.

"I had no motor trouble until I reached Missoula, when I blew an intake valve and was forced down. There was 50 or 60 gallons of gasoline left in the tank when I came down at Missoula."

**Asks for Smoke First.**

Stinson was haggard and weary after his long, sleepless flight across America. He wore a two days' growth of beard.

Stinson's first desire, as he landed at the Spokane airport, was a smoke.

"Who's got a cigaret?" he demanded. Then he was ready to tell how it happened.

"It was good flying all the way," he grinned, "Just a little bit of tough luck."

### Lacey Forced Back After Second Start.

Roosevelt Field, N. Y., Sept. 22.—(By Associated Press.)—Steve Lacey of Lomax, Ill., returned a few minutes after his second take-off for Spokane today.

He was unconscious from gasoline fumes when his plane reached the field.

The plane landed at 2:15 p. m., eastern standard time. Lacey was lifted from the cockpit and after a few minutes was revived and taken from the field by automobile.

L. A. Yancey, Lacey's co-pilot, was not affected by the gasoline fumes. He explained that they were over New York city when motor trouble developed.

**The First News of the Fight**

Minneapolis received its first news of the result of the Tunney-Dempsey fight in

**THE TRIBUNE**

The Tribune extra, containing the round-by-round record of the fight, was on the streets three minutes ahead of any other Minneapolis newspaper.

The Tribune extra gave Minneapolis its first complete and accurate account of the championship match.

## Duvall Found Guilty; Faces Fine and Cell

### Indianapolis Mayor Guilty of Corrupt Act, Says Verdict.

### Finding Disqualifies Defendant From Office for Four Years.

### New Trial Motion or Appeal Considered by Defense Attorneys.

Indianapolis, Sept. 22.—(By Associated Press.)—Mayor John L. Duvall of Indianapolis was found guilty tonight by a jury in criminal court of charges of violating the corrupt practices act. The verdict calls for a fine of $1,000 and a sentence of 30 days in jail.

The jury was out a little more than three hours, but more than one hour was taken for dinner. The jury reached a verdict at 7:49 p. m., and reported to Judge C. C. Shirley at 8:05.

Under the law, Mayor Duval is ineligible to hold public office for four years from the commission of the crime.

"I have nothing to say," Mayor Duvall said. He was pale when the verdict was read.

The jury's verdict was found to be erroneous insofar as it pertained to Duvall's eligibility to hold public office. tI provided that the convicted man should not hold public office from the date of the commission of the crime.

Instructed by Special Judge C. C. Shirley to retire to resume its deliberations, the jury corrected the verdict to make hte time of ineligibility as from November 2, 1925. The correction was made in a few minutes.

**Appeal Considered.**

Duvall was released for the night on his own recognizance with in-

(Continued on Page 6, Column 1.)

## 100,000 Radio Fans Expected at Show Here

### Northwestern Dealers Are Offered Chance to See New Devices.

Nearly 3,000 radio dealers of the northwest are expected to take advantage of the invitation of the managers of the sixth annual Northwest Radio show which opens in the new municipal auditorium Monday night. They have been invited to attend as guests of the management, to give them an opportunity to study every phase of new inventions and improvements in radio reception and broadcasting, which will be fully demonstrated at the show.

It is believed by the managers that fully 100,000 radio enthusiasts will attend during the week, aond preparations have been made for the entertainment and housing of this gathering. If these expectations are realized, the show will break all records for attendance at any radio show ever held in the northwest.

**128 Booths and Exhibits.**

The show will have 128 booths, valued at a half million dollars, and workmen are now busy building and decorating the booths that will hold the displays. Besides the mechanical exhibits, the show will provide entertainment of an unusual character. Scores of artists that most radio fans have heard over their receiving sets in remote control concerts will be present in person.

Community singers will compete at the radio show next week. Two of the contestants were chosen Thursday night, when Katherine Fairweather, 4343 Webber place, and Mrs. Don Gauper, 3535 Thirty-second avenue south, won the semi-final contest for contraltos for community singers in the assembly room of the courthouse. They will compete in the finals, which will be held in the auditorium in connection with the show.

"Minneapolis is the center of the radio industry of the northwest, and we have planned a miniature radio world's fair, both for the entertainment of the thousands of listeners who will attend the exposition, and for the hundreds of dealers who will be our guests," H. H. Reinhard, president of the Northwest Radio Show, Inc., said Thursday. He said that the northwest radio show is patterned after the New York radio show, now under way in Madison Square Gardens.

**Stage Parade Monday.**

A parade will officially open the doors at noon Monday, but the official opening ceremonies will not take place until 8:30 p.m. Monday to permit broadcasting of the event.

The Broadcast Listeners association, at a luncheon meeting held at the Minneapolis Athletic club, Wednesday, voted to participate in the show by having a booth where the "radio hound" will be on exhibition and information will be given radio fans. The "radio hound" or interference detector, loaned by the city, is expected to interest urban fans particularly. The association plans to have one or more members at the booth to record suggestions as to quality of broadcasting, types of sets, interference and program preferences, made by show visitors. Later these suggestions will be investigated. The Listeners' association will also conduct a membership drive.

## Radio Fans of 70 Stations Get Running Blow-by-Blow Narrative of Big Battle

### MacNamee and Carlin Alternate Telling Story Over Wide Hookup.

### Wild Cheering of 150,000 Spectators Drowns Ring Announcements.

*The Tribune presents herewith the report of the Demsey-Tunney fight as it was broadcast from the ringside through the WEAF hookup of 70 broadcasting stations, including WCCO. The announcers were Graham MacNamee and Phillips Carlin.*

Phillips Carlin announcing:

We do not know if the main bout will be put on at this time. We have had four or five preliminaries, and the next one may not be put on until after the Tunney-Dempsey bout and the heavyweight championship is decided. One hundred and fifty thousand people are here, and Tex Rickard has estimated the gate receipts at $2,800,000—a mere bagatel, or a bag of money I should say.

The crowd is beginning to show signs of restlessness. I doubt whether there are many so privileged to be present where the spectators measure 150,000. These things happen only a few times in a lifetime, and it seems that each time the crowd is going to be the biggest, but I know of no place in the country, at least that I have heard of, where they can seat more unless they build a bigger or better arena.

Governor Small is entering the ring with "Big Bill" Thompson, who is wearing his big hat. He is the mayor of Chicago, the much beloved leader of the city's activities. Two boys in blue trousers and white sweaters are putting resin on the ropes.

**Rickard Greets Officials.**

Here comes Tex Rickard in a blue suit and his usual light beige colored Fedora, and he is shaking hands with Mayor Thompson on the other side of the ring and other officials in there. The officials with one exception are men past middle age, all over 45 years of age, and one of them is a man of 60 years.

Tex Rickard is over here in the corner, talking to some of the newspapermen—the gentleman with the Tuxedo on goes over to join them. They are going to get the official list of the officials, and we will give them to you later.

Here comes Jack Dempsey into the ring. Jack is dressed in a white flannel bath robe and is followed by his seconds and Leo Flynn. Jack is wearing a white sweater marked "J. D." on the back. Gene Tunney has not put in his appearance. The ring is full of officials, and the crowd is beginning to get restless. Jack has on his dressing robe a "J. D." in black letters.

**Cheering Drowns Announcements.**

They are tightening up the ropes now and the officials here are endeavoring to shake hands with Jack Dempsey, but as usual, like most great fighters, he sits over by himself and his mind is intent on the encounter.

I will try to find out again the names of the officials. I suppose they will be announced.

The crowd is cheering so much that the announcements cannot be heard at this point.

Dempsey is sitting in the southwest corner of the ring. We are here on the south side right in the middle.

We have a gentleman over here with a green pasteboard box in which is something. I do not know what it is.

**Enthusiasm Increases.**

The enthusiasm is mounting throughout the arena—150,000 people are beginning to get nervous and excited over the coming bout. Jack just shook hands with some friend in a long green coat. Jack is standing in the corner now holding onto the ropes and dancing up and down and he is bowing to various friends of his. Leo Flynn is next to him, his hands in his pockets, looking as much unconcerned as possible, just as though Jack was going into a sparring bout and not the championship battle.

Jim Jeffries is just coming into the ring. We hope to have a speech from him later. Jim is looking great. I suppose he feels quite at home back in the old ring, having been a champion some years back. He came on from the coast to tell the world something of this encounter.

Here comes Jack Sharkey into the ring, the gentleman whom Dempsey defeated some weeks back.

Gene Tunney has not put in his appearance.

The announcer in the ring is asking the crowd to quiet down and

(Continued on Page 2, Column 1.)

## *Dies After Acorn Lodges in Throat*

Milton Mystrom, 8 years old, died in General hospital Thursday afternoon after an operation which was undertaken in an attempt to dislodge an acorn from his throat. Milton, who lived at 2947 Arthur street and was the son of Mr. and Mrs. Donald O. Mystrom, was attending the Thomas Lowry school Thursday morning. At recess time he discovered a tree near the school grounds and helped himself to some of the acorns. One of the nuts lodged in his throat and alarmed by his gasping cries, schoolmates summoned help.

**Government Expects Half Million as Share of Chicago Gate Total**

Washington, Sept. 22.—(By Associated Press.)—Uncle Sam's share of the gate at the Tunney-Dempsey fight tonight, government tax experts figures, will be more than half a million dollars.

They base their carculations on receipts of $3,000,000, but say they won't be able to make accurate computations until they know the exact amount and the exemptions from federal taxes that Tunney, Dempsey and Rickard will claim.

A $3,000,000 gate would yield $300,000 in tax payments on tickets, paid by the buyers.

Without deductions for various items of expense, Tunney, out of his million dollar purse, would owe the government $241,133.

Dempsey, being maried, would get off a bit lighter, and of his $450,000 share of the receipts would have to pay Uncle Sam $103,558, minus alowances for expenses.

The tax Tex Rickard, as promoter, mus pay on his profits cannot be estimated accurately until final figures on gate receipts are obtained along with his deductions and amounts paid in salary to his aides.

## Law Rejects Substitution of Smith Baby

### Judge Weygand Dismisses Action for Production of Boy Child.

Cleveland, Sept. 22.—(By Associated Press.)—Legally the Smith "baby tangle" was solved tonight but in the mind of a heartbroken mother doubt still lurked—undisturbed by the hand of justice.

"I shall accept the baby girl as my child, but doubt as to its parentage will never be dispelled in my mind," Mrs. Sam Smith said tonight through a veil of tears after she had partly recovered from her hysterical reaction to the judge's decision in the courtroom.

Judge Weygandt dismissed the Smith's habeas corpus petition demanding their child "George Smith" after he had heard nurses, doctors, hospital attaches and the Smiths themselves tell their story from the witness stand.

"Mrs. Smith, the only thing you as a mother will do is to accept this baby girl as your very own," Judge Weygandt said in dismissing the petition.

"There is no evidence any place that any other baby might be yours. We will all hope, as the years go on, that if this little girl lives and grows strong, she will make you as happy as though she had been a boy."

**Crowd Hysterical.**

After the judge had finished, pandemonium broke loose in the courtroom. Fathers and mothers, who had crowded the courtroom during the hearing, broke through the railing weeping hysterically to surround the heart-broken mother.

Mrs. Smith was unable to speak for some time while deputies hastened to restore order.

Miss Ruth Meyer, nurse and key witness in the "baby tangle," testified upon cross-examination as the first witness that she was positive the baby girl Mrs. Sam Smith nurses is her child.

Dr. William Glendinning, who followed Miss Meyer on the stand, testified that his examinations had revealed certain dominant characteristics in the baby girl common in other members of the Sam Smith family.

Mr. and Mrs. Smith followed the doctor to the stand and told the court of the doubt in their minds as to the parentage of the baby girl they have been given.

**Clerical Error Explained.**

Nurses, who assisted at the delivery of the child, collaborated Miss Meyer's testimony that a clerical error had been made as the result of Miss Meyer's telling the doctor the baby was a boy when in reality it was a girl. Miss Meyer had said she gained the notion the baby was a boy from casual observance and did not examine the child.

The habeas corpus action was instituted by Sam Smith after he had been dissatisfied with the hospital's explanation of a "clerical error." The mother had been told that she gave birth to a baby boy and discovered nine days later that the child she nursed was a girl.

Mr. Smith, tears streaming down his face, said: "There is always going to be that doubt in my mind. But we will take the baby and do for it like we would any of our other four children."

## *Bull Moose Butts Cave, Breaks Neck*

Hibbing, Minn., Sept. 22.—A big bull moose tried to butt an automobile off the Maple Hill road near here today and was killed. The moose charged the car of Milton Manning, farmer of Maple Hill, and hit the car which was traveling fast, headon. The king of the north woods broke his neck, three legs, and suffered other injuries.

## Wins Decisive Victory From Jack Dempsey

### 150,000 See Spectacular 10-Round Title Battle at Chicago Field.

### Challenger Wobbly When Gong Sounds End of Colorful Contest.

### Gene Goes Down for Count of Nine—Keeps Head as He Comes Up.

By George A. Barton.
Sports Editor of The Tribune.

Ringside, Soldier Field, Chicago, Sept. 22.—Gene Tunney, the fighting marine, successfully defended his title of world's heavyweight champion by decisively defeating Jack Dempsey in a spectacular 10-round contest before 150,000 spectators here tonight.

There was no question regarding the winner at the final gong and the decision in favor of Tunney was unanimous on behalf of Referee Dave Barry and Judges George Lytton and Sheldon Clark, all of Chicago.

Barry is a former lightweight boxer of note who has officiated in many bouts in Illinois and other states of the middle west.

The judges, Lytton and Clark, are prominent business and sportsmen.

**Commission Indorses Decision.**

The verdict handed down by these three men was well received by the crowd, although Dempsey's handlers, Leo P. Flynn and Bill Duffy made a protest to members of the Illinois commission who were seated at the ringside. heirT protest didn't ge them anything, however, for the commissioners were in hearty accord with the decision.

Tunney fought like a real champion tonight and he clearly outboxed, out-speeded and at times outslugged Dempsey. Gene also outfinished the Manassa mauler in the tenth round which found Dempsey wobbly although willing to carry on.

Realizing that he would have to register a knockout to win when the gong started them on their way in the tenth round, Dempsey tore in savagely and whaled away with both fists to Tunney's face and body. He rocked Gene several times during the first minute, but just as Depsey's adherents were shouting for him to put over a haymaker, Tunney suddenly got into action and drove Jack into the ropes near the champion's corner. Gene fairly showered lefts and rights to Dempsey's face and had him virtually out on his feet. The old champion gamely kept his feet and tried to fight back desperately but Tunney slugged away with both fists and Dempsey could not get started.

**Dempsey's Face Battered.**

Dempsey's face was a gory sight in the tenth round and he was a badly whipped fighter when the bell sounded. Blood streamed down Dempsey's countenance from deep cuts over both eyes. He was weak and wobbly but he still possessed the spirit to carry on and won the admiration of the crowd with his exhibition of rare courage.

Tunney, on the other hand, was unmarked and was much stronger and fresher than Dempsey as hostilities closed.

Judging from the glassy expression in Dempsey's eyes and the way his legs were sagging under him in the tenth round I doubt very much whether he could have staved off a knockout much longer.

The fight was sensational and provided the fans with plenty of thrills for the $2,800,000 which they paid to witness the spectacle. The crowd's first big thrills came in the fourth round in which Tunney nearly knocked out the former champion.

**Dempsey Driven to Ropes.**

In this round, Gene drove Dempsey to the ropes under a volley of vicious left hooks and right swings to the face and body. The crowd arose as one man and Tunney battered the Manassa mauler against the ropes, Dempsey's head rocking backward and forward under the terrific beating being meted out to him. It seemed that Tunney had Dempsey ready for a knockout punch when the gong came to his rescue. The old boy staggered to his corner, where his seconds worked frantically over him during the minute's rest.

Thrill number two came in the seventh round when Dempsey whipped a murderous left hook and a crushing right swing to Tunney's jaw. Both punches landed flush on the point of the chin and Tunney dropped to the floor in a sitting position near Dempsey's corner. Although Tunney was badly hurt his brain was clear enough for him to follow the count of Referee Dave Barry and that of the timekeeper and he got up as the referee reached the count of nine.

**Tunney Keeps Head.**

Tunney knew what he was doing when he regained his feet for he immediately went on the defensive and danced around the ring with Dempsey following him with tiger-like ferocity and making every effort to corner Gene and put over a finishing punch. Tunney was too smart, however, and refused to be trapped. He continued to break ground until his addled brain had completely cleared, and then brought a mighty cheer by trading punches with Dempsey just before the bell ended the round.

Dempsey's chances of winning the fight and regaining the championship which he loved so dearly while he had it, and for which he would gladly have given the $450,000 that he received for to-

(Continued on Page 19, Column 1.)

# The Minneapolis Morning Tribune

Sixty-second Year. No. 25. Sixteen Pages MINNEAPOLIS, MINN., MONDAY, JUNE 18, 1928. Price Two Cents in Minneapolis.

# EARHART PLANE TAKES OFF

## 7,000 Rotary Members Due in City Today

### 80 Typewriters Clatter Into Night on Registration Lists.

### Delegates From Northwest States First to Arrive for Convention.

### Gaily-Decorated Loop District Greets Guests at World Congress.

A long row of typewriters, 80 in all, stretching the length of one of the corridors of the municipal auditorium, noisily ground out names and addresses all day Sunday. Behind the machines, ranged like a ballet, were a like number of stenographers, too busy to chew gum.

The names were those of 5,000 Rotary delegates from virtually every state in the union and some from foreign countries. Addresses corresponded to the home towns of the delegates. Registration lists were being prepared.

The vanguard of the 12,000 or more service club men to attend the International Rotary convention this week made their presence known early Sunday morning. The auditorium headquarters was ready for them. The steady stream of visitors started shortly after 6 a. m. at the registration tables and continued throughout the day and night.

**7,000 Due Today.**

Before midnight there were 5,000 names in the convention files. Early arrivals, for the most part, were from Minnesota, North Dakota and South Dakota cities, but during the course of the day nine special trains from far eastern and western points augmented the ever-growing numbers. More than 7,000 delegates will arrive Monday.

A gayly decorated city greeted the throngs of visitors Sunday. From the business houses on all loop streets are flying hundreds of flags, the national colors of 44 nations and the blue and gold flags emblematic of Rotary International. In addition there are hundreds of yards of bunting, many colorful window displays, electric lighting effects and Minneapolis' "Hanging gardens" of flowers and vines. The city seldom has been decorated on such a scale.

**Auditorium Ready.**

In the municipal auditorium, the convention hall which will hold the thousand of visitors during their sessions this week, innumerable changes have taken place over the week-end.

Every available seat that can be squeezed into the large arena and its balconies is in place. Along the balcony railings have been placed rows of flower boxes with their posies and greens. There are no other decorations in the arena, for Rotary officials felt that the auditorium in itself was beautiful to a degree which precluded any extensive decoration schemes.

The exhibition hall, below the arena, however, has undergone a transformation into what is described as the "hall of friendship." Here will be the place where Rotarians will gather to chat, to dance, and to keep appointments. Several hundred wicker chairs and settees have been spread over the area for the comfort and convenience of the delegates and their families. There are writing desks and stationery supplies.

**Outdoor Garden.**

From the walls of the exhibition hall extend canopies and awnings of green and white. In the center of the hall are arbors and around the entire interior are evergreen trees, giving the whole the effect of an outdoor garden. Many oil paintings by Minnesotans, depicting scenes in and about Minneapolis, have been placed on the walls.

At one end of the "hall of friendship" a floor has been laid down for dancing. Rotarians and their friends inclined toward dancing as a recreation, need only turn on the large phonograph supplied to furnish the "orchestra."

At another end of the hall is the postoffice. All mail addressed to delegates is received here. On Sunday there were three bushels of letters and postcards in the auditorium mail clearing house. They bore postmarks from all over the world.

**Telegraph Station Installed.**

To further accommodate the 12,000 or more persons who will crowd the big building this week, a complete telegraph station has been istalled. Telegrams received for the delegates are listed on a big blackboard. Another service feature is a first aid station and hospital.

A fleet of 2,700 autos has been mobilized to transport the visitors to any destination in the city. An auto headquarters has been established at the auditorium and between 200 and 400 cars make the building a base. Groups of 50 and 75 of the machines are dispatched to meet incoming trains, while others are used to take the delegates on sight-seeing tours.

(Continued on Page 5, Column 1.)

### Weather Forecast

MINNEAPOLIS AND VICINITY—Mostly cloudy today and Tuesday; not much change in temperature.

Additional weather on page 7.

## News Index



## E. T. Meredith, Iowa Political Leader, Dead

### Served as Secretary of Agriculture Under President Wilson.

### Published Three Farm Magazines—Had Been Ill Four Months.

### Considered as Democratic Presidential Nominee in Two Campaigns.

Des Moines, June 17.—(By Associated Press.)—Edwin T. Meredith, local publisher and secretary of agriculture in President Wilson's cabinet, died at his home here tonight at 6 o'clock.

Heart disease caused by high blood pressure was ascribed as the cause of Mr. Meredith's death. The former cabinet member, who published three farm magazines here, had been ill for about four months.

His condition became serious a month ago, after Mr. Meredith had been returned to his home from the Johns Hopkin hospital at Baltimore, where he had been under observation.

Death came while the publisher was sleeping. At his bedside was Mrs. Meredith, his mother, a son and a daughter, four brothers and a sister. Plans for the funeral had not been completed tonight.

**Inherited Love of Soil.**

An inherited love of the soil and general interest in the welfare of farmers lifted Edwin T. Meredith from youthful obscurity to national prominence and a place in President Wilson's cabinet.

He started in boyhood as a real "dirt" farmer, the occupation of his father and his grandfather. A high school education and one year at college weaned him away from actual work on the farm, but tended to increase his interest in the lot of those who till the soil.

**Grandfather Publisher.**

Mr. Meredith's grandfather, in addition to his agricultural interests, was the publisher of a farm weekly, The Farmers' Tribune. It was devoted to Populism and met with financial difficulties when that movement died out.

Having completed a year in Highland Park college, Des Moines, young Meredith, then 20 years of age, borrowed $1,800 with which he purchased his grandfather's publication. Through six years it brought him much hard work and little success. The Farmers' Tribune was discontinued and in its place Mr. Meredith established Successful Farming as a monthly periodical.

That proved the foundation of the successful Meredith Publications, the name of Mr. Meredith's business, to which eventually were added "Better Homes and Gardens" and "The Dairy Farmer," the three having a combined monthly circulation of more than 2,000,000.

Through his publications and recognition as a business leader in Des Moines, the growth of Mr. Meredith's influence was a natural sequence, and led him into politics. In 1914 he was the Democratic candidate for United States senator from Iowa and two years later was his party's candidate for governor of that state. He was defeated on both occasions.

**Made Agriculture Secretary.**

In 1917, William G. McAdoo, then secretary of the treasury, appointed Mr. Meredith to the board of excessive profits advisers. Two years later President Wilson named him a member of the industrial conference commission and in January, 1920, selected him for the post of secretary of agriculture to succeed David F. Houston.

Continuing his interest in public affairs, Mr. Meredith became one of the leaders of the "progressive dry" element of the Democratic party. Although not an active candidate for the Democratic nomination for president in 1924, his name was presented to the convention and he received 130 votes on the one hundred and first ballot to rank third behind John W. Davis and Oscar W. Underwood.

He was again in the race for the nomination in 1928, being put forth as Iowa's favorite son candidate in an effort to win delegates in the pre-convention campaign from Governor Alfred E. Smith of New York. The ticket favoring the New York governor, however, was successful in the Iowa primary election.

Edwin Thomas Meredith was born at Avoca, Iowa, December 23, 1876, the son of Thomas Oliver and Minnie Minerva Marsh Meredith. He married Miss Edna C. Elliott of Des Moines in 1896. They had two children.

**Worked for $8 a Week.**

The early interest of the former secretary in agriculture was kindled when, as a boy, he worked after school and during vacations on his father's farm. He got his first taste of the publishing business while he was in college, working during his spare time in the shop of his grandfather. It was during that time also that he conceived the idea of aiding farmers generally through farm papers and when he left college he

(Continued on Page 2, Column 5.)

## Pacific Fliers Get Air Force Medal

Sydney, Australia, June 17.—(By Associated Press.)—The air force cross has been awarded by King George to Captain Kingsford-Smith and Lieutenant Ulm in consequence of their successful trans-Pacific flight recently completed.

**Former Secretary of Agriculture Dies**

E. T. Meredith.

## W. M. Butler on Way to Brule, Declares Hoover Victory Sure

William M. Butler, chairman of the Republican national committee and temporary chairman of the convention at Kansas City, arrived in St. Paul Sunday night on his way to visit President Coolidge, either at the summer capitol at Superior or the lodge at Brule.

Mr. Butler was noncommital on all sujects except that of a Republican victory in November.

"I can comment on that," he said. "I am sure that we will win. I should wait until I learn whom the Democrats nominate, but it will make no difference. We will win no matter whom they nominate."

Mr. Butler repeated' declined to discuss farm relief, t. Republican platform, the party candidates, and controversial issue..

"Let the candidates speak for themselves," was all he would say.

## Payment Refused in Blackmail Plot; Window Smashed

Milwaukee, June 17.—(By Associated Press.)—Bricks were hurled through plate glass windows of the Yale pharmacy here today as the first acts of violence in a fantastic blackmail plot to extort money from the proprietors for an alleged "protective association." Damage was estimated at $500. Alvin Shapiro, store manager, refused a week ago to pay $150 yearly for himself and a similar amount for each employe, though threatened with property damage and personal attacks by a stranger.

## John Coolidge Class Lists 3 Teetotalers

Amherst, Mass., June 17.—(By Associated Press.)—Only three members of the Amherst college graduating class do not drink, according to the "senior statistics" published in the "Amherst Student" during commencement. Those who do drink are numbered 1?0, the statistics indicate. John Coolidge, the President's son, is a member of the class.

President Arthur Stanley Pease of the college is voted the "most boring chapel speaker."

## Oklahoma Twister Death Toll Now 8

Kansas City, June 17.—(By Associated Press.)—Eight persons dead, upward of 100 injured and damage passing the million dollar mark was the toll of tornadic winds that struck southwestern Oklahoma and southern Kansas late Saturday and today.

Two tornadoes, neither of which took any lives, were reported in Kansas, one near Hutchinson last night and the other near Emporia this afternoon.

## Match Fight Stirs Hungary Parliament

Budapest, Hungary, June 17.—(By Associated Press.) — Tumultuous scenes marked the parliamentary session yesterday when Count Bethlen, the premier, presented the government bill vesting the match monopoly in the Swedish-American Match Co. in return for a loan of $36,000,000. Gendarmes with drawn swords were called in immediately after an opposition deputy had called the premier vile names and accused him of being a "dictator who flouts parliament and public opinion."

## Missing Farmer, Children Hunted

Birmingham, Ala., June 17.—(By Associated Press.) — Posses were searching the hills of Blount county tonight for a farmer who disappeared with his two small children Friday, after announcing that he intended to spend "40 days and 40 nights in the wilderness." When he drove away from home in his car, the farmer, Elmer T. Martin, told his wife he was going to Brooksville, Ala., about 20 miles away, to obtain food.

## Minnesota Voters Will Choose Party Slates at Primary Today

### 353 Minneapolis Polling Places to Be Open Until 9 P. M.

### 158,784 Registration in City Is Largest on Record.

Minnesota's state-wide primary election of 1928 will get under way Monday morning, with the voters of the state facing the task of picking candidates for the United States senate, congress, state and county offices, supreme and district benches and house of representatives of the state legislature.

In Minneapolis, the polls in the 253 voting precincts will be open from 6 a. m. to 9 p. m. Indications Sunday were that more than 100,000 of the 158,784 registered voters of Minneapolis will cast ballots at the primary polls Monday. The registration is the largest ever recorded for a primary in the city.

On the party ballots, the voters will name candidates for the United States senate, congress in the 10 districts, governor, lieutenant governor, secretary of state, treasurer, attorney general and state railroad and warehouse commissioner.

**Amendments Face Test.**

Marking their non-party ballots, the voters in Minneapolis and over the state will choose their nominees for one associate justice of the supreme court, for the district bench and for county commissionerships and other county offices.

In Minneapolis, still another ballot will be offered to the citizens and, in marking them, the voters will express their approval or disapproval of the proposed amendments to the city charter. One of these amendments would redistrict the city in 19 wards instead of the present 13 and the second would centralize all street maintenance work in a single department, under supervision of the city engineer, in place of the present 13 ward street systems.

**Three Judges' Terms Expire.**

There are contests for a majority of the public offices, both on the party and non-party tickets. In only a few cases do any candidates gain their nominations automatically, as result of lack of enough candidates to make a contest. An example is the district judgeship nomination in Hennepin county. Terms of three present judges expire this year. They have filed for re-election and three candidates are opposing them for the nomination. As six are to be nominated, there is no contest for the district bench listed on the primary ballots for Monday.

Winners at the Monday primary polls will fight it out at the general election November 6. At that time, the voters will choose between the presidential nominees, named at party conventions, in addition to naming office holders from the candidates who win nominations Monday.

## 5,000 Park Singers Open Trophy Race

### Minnehaha Tops Loring in Initial Songfest of Tribune Contest.

Five thousand persons turned out en masse at two Minneapolis parks Sunday in the opening concerts of the annual community singing contest sponsored by The Minneapolis Tribune and the board of park commissioners.

Despite the light rain 3,000 songsters gathered around the bandstand at Minnehaha Falls park in the opening sing Sunday afternoon, and by virtue of their enthusiasm and attendance gained first place for the day in the community contest, which will be continued nightly and twice Sundays up to the middle of August.

**Concert Held at Loring Park.**

Loring park was the scene of the evening concert, and expected showers held the attendance down to 2,000 persons. Under the direction of Harry Anderson, community sing director, the audience gradually warmed up to a high pitch of enthusiasm as they sang the last number on the program, "Together."

Monday night the lead established Sunday by Minnehaha Falls park will be challenged by the Powderhorn singers defending the community sing trophy won last year.

At Minnehaha Falls Sunday afternoon, the 2,000 grandstand seats were taken an hour before the concert opened. By the time that the neighborhood band under the direction of Jean Koch had begun the first number on the program, the adjoining pavilions were filled to capacity with the arrival of 1,000 more.

**Rules Not Changed.**

The concert was given by the neighborhood band, with Russell Murphy, baritone, and Paul Hundredmark, trumpeter, as soloists. Mr. Murphy sang two popular numbers, "Together," and "Without You Sweetheart."

The contest this year is being conducted under the same set of rules which has governed the community sing contests in the past few years. The scores compiled by Mr. Anderson which give Minnehaha Falls park a temporary lead, are:

Standings of the parks:

**First Round.**

| | Att. | Pep. | Dep't. | Total. |
|---|---|---|---|---|
| Minnehaha ... | 32 | 31 | 16 | 79 |
| Loring ........ | 30 | 32 | 14 | 76 |

## 3,000 Toil in Vain as Wall of Water Breaks Levee and Inundates Missouri Farms

### 21 Americans Sandino Captives, Says Radical After Visiting at Camp

Tegucigalpa, Honduras, June 17.—(By Associated Press.)—Esteban Pavlevitch, a Jugo-Slavian Peruvian, who represents radical associations of Mexico, arrived here today and said that he came from Sandino's headquarters in Nicaragua.

Pavlevitch said that Sandino holds 21 prisoners including George B. Marshall of New York, manager of the La Luz mine which was raided late in April. The other prisoners, according to Pavlevitch are 18 marines and two other American mine workers. He said all were in good health and were being well treated.

He said Sandino had issued a decree saying that he would no longer respect foreign properties except those owned by Spaniards and Latin-Americans. By this action, Pavlevitch said, Sandino expects to prove that the protection enjoyed heretofore by foreign interests was due to him and not to the presence of United States marines in Nicaragua.

## Coolidge Hears Blind Pastor in Church at Brule

### President Makes First Public Appearance Since His Arrival.

By Frank Murray.

Superior, Wis., June 17.—In the tiny, clapboard church at Brule, John Taylor, blind, itinerant "lay-preacher" of Duluth, preached his first sermon to the president of the United States Sunday, and after the services were over, heard from his lips a few words of greeting.

For Calvin Coolidge, it was the first public appearance of any kind since his arrival at Superior on Friday. Throughout the simple worship service he sat alone in a pew reserved for him, third row from the front. Mrs. Coolidge did not venture out of the lodge. The day was dreary with an occasional spatter of rain, and it was deemed advisable for her to remain on the estate.

**Church Is Crowded.**

The little frame church was crowded as it has never been crowded before, in spite of the fact that visitors from out of the district were not encouraged. It has a congregation that fluctuates with the season and the condition of the roads, from 10 or 12 to sometimes as many as 60.

Sunday there were more than 150 persons in the church. The seven rows of pews on each side of the main aisle, ordinarily more than enough to accommodate the devout, were hopelessly inadequate today. Six rows of chairs placed behind them, were filled.

**Visitors Not Encouraged.**

The services at Brule were set for 11 a. m. Long before that time, the church had begun to fill, and a small knot of villagers waited curiously outside, two ushers, one of them Alden Golder, chairman of the church board of trustees, village banker, and leader of the town board, beamed graciously on their parishioners, but offered little encouragement to visitors from Superior. The citizens of Brule were jealous of their distinction in playing host to the President at worship. They felt they didn't need any help.

About 15 minutes before the hour the pillars of the church were all on hand, hair neatly slicked, clothes pressed, faces shining. A predominance of gray hair was sprinkled

(Continued on Page 13, Column 3.)

## 'Most Fun in Year,' Says Lindy After 'Banquet' on Floor

Madison, Wis., June 17.—(By Associated Press.)—Charles Lindbergh, private citizen, sat on a floor early this morning with 30 former classmates and ate waffles.

Aviation topics were taboo and the flying colonel received no more attention than others of the class of 1924, University of Wisconsin. As a result Lindbergh had two and a half solid hours of "The most fun I've enjoyed in a year."

Colonel Lindbergh is the house guest of President Glenn Frank of the university and Mrs. Frank, pending commencement tomorrow when he will become a doctor of laws by special dispensation of school authorities.

**Marine Planes Bomb Rebels.**

Managua, Nicaragua, June 17.—(By Associated Press.)—The brigade headquarters announced today that American marine planes had bombed a group of rebels in northwestern Nicaragua yesterday.

### Crops in Wide Area Ruined as St. Francis River Overflows.

### 1,000 Families Homeless—Damage Is Estimated at $2,000,000.

Kennett, Mo., June 17.—(By Associated Press.)—Unceasing efforts of 3,000 workers to save tehir homes and crops from floods, again went to naught when the second big break in the St. Francis river levee occurred early today and inundating 75,000 additional acres of land and leaving 1,000 families homeless.

Opening a 275-foot gap three and one half miles north of Browns Ferry, and 15 miles above the 400-foot crevase which occured early yesterday the river swept in upon a new area bringing the total area of submerged land to approximately 75,000 acres.

**Crops Total Loss.**

With the flood approaching the proportions of the inundation which occurred in Dunklin county last year, it was estimated that the damage would run from between $1,500,000 to $2,000,000.

Crops of the region are a total loss, an excellent crop, almost ready to harvest.

The new crevasse was the third in two days. The first occurred about 1:30 a. m. Saurday, allowing the river to flood 25,000 acres through a crevasse which grew to be 400 feet wide. The second, about 40 feet wide, broke out shortly after the first.

**Third Crest Causes Break.**

The break today came at 3:30 a. m. on the third crest of the stream, which was estimated to be about a foot and a half higher than that of Saturday. Workers, composed of farmers, merchants and professional men of the surrounding country had been making a vain effort to bolster up the weakening dyke against the rise. Every available man was on hand, but the river was too powerful and a wall of water, eight feet high, brushed aside efforts. With the country around indundated from 10 to 15 feet in depth the weary workers tonight turned to the task of giving aid to the stricken families. It was estimated that 5,000 persons were affected directly by the floods.

## Party Leaders to Visit Hoover

### Interviews With Campaign Advisers Crowd Week's Calendar.

Washington, June 17.—(By Associated Press.)—Sunday enforced a welcome interlude in the task of campaign planning for Secretary Hoover, Republican presidential nominee, but semi-political calls notwithstanding broke repeatedly through the quiet hours of an otherwise restful holiday.

Convention leaders began arriving early today from Kansas City, and Hoover found moments to give brief welcomes and thanks to Secretary Work, his cabinet associate, and to Walter F. Brown, assistant secretary of commerce.

Once this was out of the way, the whole Hoover family, including Mrs. Hoover, two sons and a daughter-in-law, attended the Sabbath gathering in the little Quaker meeting house in downtown Washington.

The candidate's week from Monday promises to be full enough, as tentative plans were laid out today. He is going to see and talk with every important politician, who attended the convention, with the avowed purpose of seeking advice and aid upon campaign organization and methods. James W. Good, who managed his pre-convention organization, is expected to arrive early Monday, and in the next three days, there will be many others.

By Thursday, when he meets the 24 representatives of the Republican national committee who will consult him formally on the subject, it was said today that decisions would be ready on most important points.

## Hungary Urged to Leave League

Budapest, June 17.—(By Associated Press.)—A petition asking that Hungary withdraw from the League of Nations was presented to the government today by the National Political association, the most powerful political body in the country.

## Veteran Attempts Flight Across U.S.

Los Angeles, June 17.—(By Associated Press.)—In an attempt at a non-stop flight to New York, Frank Tomick, World war aviator, took off from a field near Van Nuys, a suburb, at 10:10 o'clock this morning in a De Haviland biplane.

## Fights Winds on Long Flight Over Atlantic

### Steamers Report Hearing Signal From Craft 700 Miles Out.

### Everything O. K. Aboard, Is Message—Mabel Boll Delays Takeoff.

### Social Worker Fifth of Sex to Try Trip—Three Have Lost Lives.

New York, June 17.—(By Associated Press.)—The monoplane Friendship had covered approximately 1,200 miles of its 1,900-mile overwater course if all was well aboard the plane at midnight tonight, flight observers here estimated.

Trepassey, N. F., June 17.—(By Associated Press.)—Carrying a stout hearted young woman as co-pilot, the monoplane Friendship hopped off from here at 12:21 p. m. Newfour land time, (8:51 a. m. Minneapolis time) for a trans-Atlantic flight. The destination is Ireland, with a strong possibility the plane will land at Valencia.

Amelia Earhart.

Miss Amelia Earhart, Boston social worker, is the woman member of the crew. Wilmer Stultz is the pilot and Lou Gordon is the mechanic.

**Plane 700 Miles Out.**

Late tonight the plane was hundreds of miles from Newfoundland, radio reports from the Friendship, picked by ocean liners, indicated. These signals from the airplane indicated that all was well aboard. A message picked up by the steamship Rexmore gave the position of the plane as approximately 700 miles east of the coast of Newfoundland.

Later the Radio Marine corporation announced receipt of a second message from the steamship Rexmore reporting it has been in communication with the Friendship which asked that it be reported to New York.

"Further signals received from Friendship at 22.3 Greenwich meantime (5:30 p. m. eastern standard time), apparently still going strong," the message said. "Signals good. Plane said could not see us nor seen by us."

The United States lines announced tonight receipt of a radio message from the liner President Roosevelt, stating that it had picked up a message from the steamer Elmworth which reported signals from the monoplane Friendship, said "all's well."

The monoplane faced the prospect of encountering headwinds during most of its voyage through the darkness tonight.

At the time of the hop-off, weather bureau reports indicated the fliers would have little better than possible flying weather at least over the first half of their course which is laid along the great circle. Should weather conditions threaten success of a safe passage to Ireland, Stultz said before the start he would alter his course and head for the Azores.

**Fifth Woman to Try.**

If the flight is accomplished, Miss Earhart will have achieved the honor of being the first woman to fly across the Atlantic. Three women have lost their lives and another was forced down at sea and picked up by a ship in attempts to be the first of their sex to make the hazardous crossing.

The Friendship is a tri-motored Fokker monoplane, equipped with pontoons for taking off from and landing on water. The ship carried approximately 700 gallons of gasoline. Two radio sets, one operating on a 600 meter wave length and the other a low wave length emergency set were installed in the plane. The call letters are WOX.

Preparations for the attempt were made in secret and it was not until two weeks ago today, when the monoplane arrived here from Boston, that it became known Miss Earhart and Stultz contemplated a trans-Atlantic flight.

**Women Vie for Honor.**

Interest in the flight has been heightened by the fact that while Miss Earhart and her companions were awaiting a break in the weather for their hop-off, another woman, Miss Mabel Boll, with two pilots, also was poised to go in an attempt to win the honor of being the first woman to cross. Miss Boll and her crew have the trans-Atlantic monoplane Columbia, owned by Charles Levine, at Harbor Brace, N. F., where they have been awaiting fair flying weather.

The monoplane Friendship was tested by pilots for Commander Richard E. Byrd with a view to use in Byrd's proposed south pole flight. After Stultz had been making tests with the plane in the vicinity of Boston for some time, its sale by Byrd was announced, although the identity of the purchaser was not made known. After the ship left Boston it became known that it had been acquired by George Putnam, publisher, and a group of associates for Miss Earhart's trans-Atlantic flight attempt.

**Stultz Drops Gasoline.**

Five unsuccessful attempts were made before the take off. Stultz then dropped all gas in tins, amount-

The Minneapolis Morning Tribune

Sixty-second Year. No. 167. Twenty Pages MINNEAPOLIS, MINN., WEDNESDAY, NOVEMBER 7, 1928 Price Three Cents in Minneapolis.

# LANDSLIDE ELECTS HOOVER; SHIPSTEAD SWEEPS STATE

## Everybody's Business

### Hoover 'Economy.' Noise Elimination. Iceland's Festival. Air Mail Savings.

By John F. Sinclair.



In the days when federal government economies were receiving particular attention, I was discussing the problem with Herbert Hoover, then secretary of commerce.

"There is one place where it is not wise for the government to cut expenditures," he declared. "That is in the department of research. We are spending $100,000,000 a year in government research work now, and the amount should be increased, if anything, not decreased."

Recently the question concerning how much industrial research work the government should do has come to the front.

Dr. Harris E. Howe, member of the national research council, believes that the tendency to expect the federal government to carry on research work rather than to have it largely supported by the industries benefited, tends to create objectionable bureaucracy and actually weaken the industry.

• • •

Professor W. A. Spooner of Oxford university, wants the League of Nations to attack noise as a world problem. "Civilization," he says, "has never before been confronted with such a malignant plague."

What can cities do about the problem of noise? America, with 86 cities of 100,000 population and over, probably suffers more from noises of all kinds than the people of any other country. Transportation is blamed for 85 per cent of New York's noise. How much the productivity of the worker is affected by the amount of noise which consciously or unconsciously he endures is a grave question.

A special investigation in New York shows that the motor trucks furnish 40 per cent of the noise of its streets. The elevated ranks second, with 25 per cent, and the surface cars next with 20 per cent. All the rest of the street noises including factory horns, fire engine gongs, riveting machines, steam shovels, garbage and milk cans, about which there is far more complaint, together make up only 15 per cent of the total.

• • •

Iceland, the little island in the north Atlantic ocean, smaller in area than Ohio, treeless, possessed of many geysers and hot springs, but no railroads, with a smaller population than Utica, expects to celebrate in 1930 the thousandth anniversary of the founding of the Icelandic parliament.

Three hundred years before the English "mother of parliaments" was founded, this little nation had a parliament. As a matter of fact, Iceland was an independent republic from 930 to 1263, finally joining with Norway. About a hundred years later, when Norway was taken over by the Danes, it became Danish territory, and it has now been a part of the Danish possessions for more then 600 years.

Iceland produces hay, potatoes and turnips mostly, although last year valuable aluminum clay and iron ore were found at Mt. Sodarnaes.

Its financial condition is excellent, taxes small, receipts always more than expenditures—usually twice as much. Its public debt is less than $3,000,000.

Its taxes are low because its financial needs are simple. It has neither army, navy nor fortifications. About one-fourth as many natives of Iceland live in the United States and Canada as live in the mother country.

Dr. B. J. Brandson of Winnipeg, chairman of the celebration committee in America, hopes that every Icelander—Canadian or American—returning to Iceland in 1930 will take back trees from the Hudson Bay region of Canada to aid in the new reforestation plans of the little island.

Plain living and high thinking characterizes the people of Iceland. The little, bleak, barren island lends itself to contemplation. It was from Iceland that Lief Ericsson, the Norwegian, left for America in the year 1000, discovered the American mainland and started a colony, near what is now New Bedford, Mass.

In recent times Iceland was the first to extend suffrage to women.

• • •

New York banks save $60,000 a year by using the air mail in clearing checks with Chicago, says the Federal Reserve bank.

It happens this way: If checks are mailed from New York by ordinary mail at the close of the business day, they do not arrive in Chicago until the following afternoon, when the clearings have already been closed. The money represented by these checks is thus idle two days.

But place the checks in the air mail in New York before 6:30 p. m. and they reach Chicago early the following morning in time for that day's clearings, and a day is saved.

## Weather Forecast

MINNESOTA — Somewhat unsettled today, rain probably in south and extreme east portions; somewhat colder in south portion; fair, rising temperature.

Additional weather on page 11.

## News Index



## *Gas Tax Amendment Is Losing in City*

Minneapolis was defeating the proposed constitutional amendment No. 1, which seeks to divert part of the gas tax to county roads, by more than a two-to-one vote, on the basis of early returns. In 76 of the 353 precincts the vote against the amendment totaled 24,384, and in favor of it, 9,810. Returns early this morning had not been tabulated from statewide points on that amendment. The plan offered in the amendment would provide that one-third of the state's gasoline tax would be used on county roads. At present the gas tax goes entirely to the state trunk highway fund. On proposed constitutional amendment No. 2, 76 precincts in Minneapolis gave a vote of 19,934 in favor and 9,546 against. This amendment would remove the double liability from stockholders in all manufacturing corporations.

## Hoover to Get 35,000 Lead in City Vote

### Wins by 78,948 to 52,678, With 251 Precincts Reporting.

### Eighth and Thirteenth Wards Strongholds of Party Chief.

### Smith Leading Rival in First, Third and Sixth Wards.

When 268 of the 353 Minneapolis precincts had been tabulated, the Hoover lead was 29,211. The vote was Hoover 84,987, Smith 55,776.

Minneapolis gave Herbert Hoover a plurality over Governor Smith Tuesday which will probably exceed 35,000 when the final returns are in.

In 251 of the city's 353 precincts Hoover had a lead over Smith of 26,470.

The vote was: Hoover 78,948; Smith 52,478.

Hoover forces carried 10 wards of the city, the partially complete unofficial returns show.

The Hoover wards were the second, fourth, fifth, seventh, eighth, ninth, tenth, eleventh, twelfth and thirteenth. Smith was ahead in the first, third and sixth wards.

**Bears Out Forecast.**

The Hoover vote in Minneapolis in all respects bore out predictions of political observers. Even before Mr. Hoover won the Republican nomination at the Kansas City convention, Minneapolis was marked down as a "Hoover city." The fifth congressional district sent two Hoover delegates to Kansas City. After the nomination the Republican organization in the county, headed by Fred A. Dickey, chairman of the county committee, set to work to build up a Hoover lead that might hold him in good stead in case he failed to get a strong vote in the rural sections of the state.

The eighth and thirteenth wards were the particular Hoover strongholds of the city and they more than made good on the heavy Hoover vote. The eighth ward tabulations show a two-to-one lead over Smith and the thirteenth ward, on partial returns, was going approximately three-to-one. The second ward was two-to-one for Hoover.

## Newton Wins by 8,000 Votes

### Early Returns Favor Godfrey Goodwin in Tenth District.

Congressman Walter H. Newton, Republican, of the fifth district was returned to office for the sixth consecutive term by his Minneapolis constituents, and early returns gave Congressman Godfrey G. Goodwin of the tenth district a lead over his opponents. The fifth district consists of 10 wards in Minneapolis, while the tenth district embraces three city wards, rural Hennepin county and several other counties north of Hennepin.

In 53 precincts Congressman Newton polled 12,857 votes, Ferdinand Johnson, Farmer-Labor, 5,752; James Robertson, Democrat, 5,951, and O. R. Votaw, Workers party, 139.

In 23 Minneapolis precincts, Congressman Goodwin, also Republican, led with 4,405 votes; C. R. Hedlund, Farmer-Labor, 2,935, and Ernest W. Erickson, Democrat, 3,309.

## *M'Knight Leads Lyle in State Senate Race*

In the special election conducted in the thirty-first legislative district to fill the vacancy created by the death of State Senator William F. Brooks, Sumner T. McKnight maintained a lead over his opponent, Donald Lyle, on the face of early returns. Eight election districts out of the 33 precincts reported: McKnight, 1,723; Lyle, 1,556. Mr. McKnight served in the house for two terms.

## The Winners

PRESIDENT.
Herbert Hoover, Republican.

United States Senator.
Henrik Shipstead, Farmer-Labor.

Governor.
Theodore Christianson, Republican.

Lieutenant Governor.
W. I. Nolan, Republican.

Secretary of State.
Mike Holm, Republican.

Treasurer.
Julius Schmahl, Republican.

Attorney General.
G. A. Youngquist, Republican.

Railroad and Warehouse Commissioner.
Christian J. Laurisch, Republican.

Returned to Senate By Heavy Majority

Henrik Shipstead.

## Hoover Smiles as He Learns of N. Y. Lead

### Statement Will Be Withheld Until Today, Akerson Announces.

Hoover Home, Palo Alto, Calif., Nov. 26.—(By Associated Press)—Herbert Hoover received a plurality of 360 over his Democratic opponent in his own voting precinct today at Stanford university. The Republican candidate received 410 votes, the Democratic candidate 50 votes and the Socialist candidate, Thomas, eight votes.

At 7:30 p. m. New York state was added to the column of "Hoover won" states by the tabulations.

Meantime, the nominee had retired to his study, where he read returns occasionally and chatted with friends who dropped in upon him.

**Withholds Statement.**

While Hoover was reported by those about him as feeling confident that he had won, it was stated by George Akerson, his assistant in the campaign, that he would make no statement for publication tonight.

When the news came that he had wiped out the lead of his Democratic opponent, Alfred E. Smith, in New York state, a broad smile wreathed his face and he retired to the privacy of his study where occasionally one or two of the many friends who crowded the living room of his home dropped in upon him.

It was announced that the Republican nominee would have no statement to make for publication tonight. It was indicated, however, that he would issue a brief one sometime tomorrow when returns from over the country in the record-smashing election of today would be far more complete.

**Focuses Interest on South.**

Hoover's interest in the returns centered very largely upon the home state of his opponent and the Solid South. He read with avidity the returns as they came in from Virginia, Florida and Texas, states in which he took an early lead over the Democratic candidate. He appeared to have little concern about the result in the great agricultural west and was confident that the Pacific coast states were in his column even before the first returns began to trickle to him.

After New York had been added by the tabulators to the list of states in the "Hoover Won" column, they put on Tennessee, Iowa and Wisconsin, making the total of the claim 289.

There was applause from the onlookers in the living room when Florida was added. Delaware, Idaho and Wisconsin then were claimed as safe and the friends of the candidate began asking each other how great the vote in the electoral college would be.

**Mingles With Friends.**

The nominee himself left his study to mingle with his friends who stood around in groups extending from the living room into the reception hall.

A flood of telegrams poured in upon Hoover from all sections of the country during the early night hours. A staff of clerks was kept busy opening them.

Interest in the tabulating of the returns slowly lagged as the night wore on, and a complete set of news reels showing all of Hoover's campaigning from the time he left Washington last July to come here for his notification until he came home Wednesday to vote, were exhibited in the dining room of the home where about 40 neighbors gathered.

## *Etna Lava Starts Destroying Village*

Cantania, Sicily, Nov. 7.—(By Associated Press.)—The main stream of lava pouring out of Mount Etna early this morning reached the village of Mascali and began to destroy the houses from which the populace fled yesterday. A smaller lava stream now is advancing toward Nunziata.

## Senator Piles Up Big Lead Over Nelson

### Christianson and State G. O. P. Ticket Returned Victor.

### Hennepin County Gives Coolidge Majority to Hoover.

### Walter Newton 3 to 1 Favorite in Fifth District.

Returns from 620 out of 3,762 precincts in Minnesota give, for president: Hoover (Republican) 131,963; Smith (Democratic) 108,697.

Herbert Hoover, the nation's choice for president of the United States, will come out of Minnesota with approximately 100,000 plurality on the face of scattered returns from all sections of the state. So pronounced was the Republican impression on the electorate of Minnesota that Hoover dug into what had been conceded earlier in the campaign to be strongholds of his Democratic opponent Governor Al Smith, and emerged with the long end of the total vote cast.

**Clean Sweep Expected.**

By the same token Governor Theodore Christianson, the Republican candidate for re-election, has been returned for the third time: Indications point to a clean sweep in Minnesota which means the election of W. I. Nolan, lieutenant governor; Mike Holm, secretary of state, Julius A. Schmall, treasurer; G. A. Youngquist, attorney general, and Christian J. Laurisch railroad warehouse commissioner.

Despite a belated effort which brought the United States senatorial fight in Minnesota into the foreground of the campaign during the last three weeks, Arthur E. Nelson, the Republican nominee appears on the face of returns from more than half of the precincts in the state to be trailing his Farmer-Labor party opponent, Senator Henrik Shipstead, by several thousand votes. In Hennepin county where Nelson was believed to have gained a strong foothold in the last two weeks Senator Shipstead is leading him by better than 2 to 1 in 133 out of 403 precincts. The same ratio holds in the country where Senator Shipstead seems to have a comfortable plurality.

In Ramsey county, Nelson's home, Senator Shipstead is leading Nelson by more than 2 to 1.

In Ramsey county, where a concentrated effort was made by the Democrats from the beginning of the campaign to entrench Governor Smith, the Hoover offensive is making itself felt. With 120 precincts in, the vote stood Smith 26,486 and Hoover 26,095, a neck and neck contest with 391 votes separating the contestants. In Benton and Stearns counties, conceded Smith strongholds, the Democratic nominee was leading Hoover by only a small margin in early returns. With these two exceptions Hoover romped through the state behind the perfect organization machine which was built up for him by the Republicans during the past two months.

**Nears Coolidge Record.**

In Hennepin county the returns from nearly two-thirds of the precincts indicate that Hoover's plurality will approach that of Calvin Coolidge four years ago when the Republican president carried the county by more than 40,000. Before midnight the precincts in which Smith was presumed to be the stronger of the two candidates were accounted for and on the face of these Hoover's lead was indicative of a grand total of more than 35,000 in Minneapolis.

Congressman Walter Newton was leading his nearest opponent by better than 3 to 1 when more than half of the total precincts in the fifth congressional district were accounted for. His election is assured by an overwhelming majority.

Scattered returns from all parts of the state indicate that Judge Clifford L. Hilton will be elected associate justice of the supreme court by a comfortable plurality over his opponent E. J. Lee.

## *Farmers Don't Want Relief, Wolf Asserts*

Joseph Wolf, national Democratic committeeman for Minnesota, conceded the election to Herbert Hoover at midnight and also conceded the state of Minnesota to the Republican candidate. "The victory of Mr. Hoover only proves that the farmers do not want relief." Mr. Wolf stated at the Democratic state headquarters in Hotel Lowry.

## *Dawes Felicitates Hoover and Curtis*

Evanston, Ill., Nov. 6.—(By Associated Press)—Vice President Charles Dawes tonight sent telegrams to Herbert Hoover and Senator Charles Curtis, congratulating them on "a great victory."

Nation's Next President

HERBERT HOOVER.

## N. Y. Rolling Up Gains for Hoover Lead

### Increase of 52,000 Majority Indicated in Late Returns.

New York, Nov. 7.—(By Associated Press)—Herbert Hoover carried the home state of Governor Alfred E. Smith, and with it the rich prize of 45 votes in the electoral college in yesterday's election.

With only 863 districts missing at 12:35 a. m. today, Hoover's majority was 52,000 and there was every indication that it would mount much higher, because the missing districts are normally overwhelmingly Republican.

The election of Franklin D. Roosevelt, Democrat, over Attorney General Albert Ottinger, Republican, for Governor was indicated. United States Senator Royal S. Copeland, Democrat, running for re-election, apparently defeated Alanson B. Houghton, Republican, former ambassador to Great Britain.

The presidential vote, from 7,404 districts out of 8,267 was: Hoover 1,926,693; Smith, 1,874,618.

Roosevelt's lead over Ottinger was nearly 80,000 at 1:45 a. m. today with 879 districts missing.

The vote from 7,388 districts out of 8,267: Roosevelt 1,964,655; Ottinger 1,884,772.

Outside of New York City 4,088 districts out of 4,774 gave: Ottinger, 1,201,020; Roosevelt 891,128, while 3,300 districts out of 3,493 in New York city gave Roosevelt, 1,070,527; Ottinger, 683,552.

Copeland, had a lead of more than 100,000 over Houghton at 2 a. m. today with 1,797 districts missing. The vote from 6,470 districts out of 8,267 was: Copeland 1,671,574; Houghton 1,568,163.

## *Boy Killed When Struck by Auto*

Walter Bashwood, Jr., 3206 Washington avenue north, was fatally injured when he was struck by a car driven by Arthur Baker, 4133 Unity avenue, Robbinsdale, near the intersection of Lowry and Washington avenues north Tuesday about 6 p. m. The boy died three hours later in General hospital as the result of a fractured skull received in the accident. Walter was the son of Mr. and Mrs. Walter Bashwood.

## Curtis Leading 2 to 1 in Area Where He Gave 'Too Damn Dumb' Talk

Des Moines, Nov. 6.—(By Associated Press)—Clay county, Iowa, where Senator Charles Curtis, Republican vice presidential nominee, made his now noted "too damn dumb" statement, gave the Hoover-Curtis ticket a two to one lead for the first 20 of 23 precincts. The Republican vote was 2,659 to 1,878 for Smith.

During a campaign speech at Spencer, Clay county seat, Curtis told a farmer heckler that he was "too damn dumb to understand" an explanation of Republican taxation policies.

During the day Senator Curtis made the remark that returns from this district would prove interesting.

## North Dakota Gives Hoover 12,784 Lead

### George Shafer Appears Certain as Next Governor.

Fargo, N. D., Nov. 6.—(By Associated Press)—Herbert Hoover apparently had carried North Dakota on the basis of returns of 285 of 2,197 precincts in the state. The reported votes came from 33 of the 53 counties in the state, although counties with the most precincts reported were generally in the eastern part of the state. The figures were Hoover 34,645 and Smith 21,851.

At that time scattering returns from the western part of the state, however, apparently failed to show the Smith sentiment which the Democratic managers had predicted. With Hoover 12,794 votes ahead it appeared possible that his lead would increase rather than decrease as additional returns were received.

The returns showed Smith leading in only five of the counties from which returns had been received and of these all but one are counties in which the Nonpartisan league is strong. Smith had Nonpartisan support in his campaign, although many of the Nonpartisan leaders endorsed Hoover.

With 227 precincts reported, the election of George F. Shafer, Republican, as governor appeared certain. The vote was Shafer 24,951; Maddock, Democrat 12,213. Maddock was leading only in Bottineau, McLean and Sargent counties.

Only five districts had reported on the contest for congressman in the second district. These gave Thomas Hall, Republican incumbent, 271 to 148 for J. L. Page, Democrat. Returns on all contests were coming in slowly because of difficulty by precinct election officials in counting the huge vote. The total vote cast in the state apparently exceeded all previous records.

It took returns from only a few precincts to show that the constitutional amendment to bond the state to pay the losses of depositors in closed state banks had been badly beaten. In 22 precincts the vote was yes, 673; no, 7,386.

In 17 precincts on candidates for state office below governor the Republican candidates had commanding leads.

### State Bank Bonds Running Way Behind

Fargo, N. D., Nov. 6.—(By Associated Press)—Incomplete and scattering returns from today's election indicate that the proposal to bond the state for $25,000,000 to pay the losses of depositors in closed state banks, was overwhelmingly defeated.

## *Crowd in Hoover's Home Sings 'America'*

Hoover home, Standford university campus, California, Nov. 6.—(By Associated Press)—The election of Herbert Hoover to the presidency was celebrated in his home here tonight by the singing of "America" by a half a hundred or more friends and neighbors, gathered in the living room of the massive stucco house on the side of San Juan hill.

## Smith Loses New York to G.O.P. Rival

### Republican Ticket Also Cuts Wide Swath Into Solid South.

### Pennsylvania, Bay State Add to Huge Total for Victor.

### Border Vote Helps Swell Tremendous Vote for Winning Party.

By Associated Press.

With east and west and even a part of the solid south rolling in majorities for Herbert Hoover, his election to the presidency was conceded today by Chairman Raskob of the Democratic national committee. At the same time Governor Alfred E. Smith made public a congratulatory message to his Republican opponent, your victory." Governor Smith said, your victory." Governor Smith said" "and extend to my sincere good wishes for your health and happiness and for the success of your administration."

The Democratic concession of victory was announced shortly before 1 a. m. At that hour the returns showed Hoover leading in every eastern, western and border state, except Massachusetts, and in Virginia, Florida and Texas. Should these majorities be sustained until the count is completed, Smith would have less than 100 electoral votes out of a total of 531.

Although throughout the night, Smith had faced the loss of Virginia and Florida, the Democratic crisis gained first importance when Hoover swept out of the upper New York counties with so great a lead that it overrode Smith's New York city advantage.

Having listened to the returns at his home in Palo Alto, Calif., through the earlier hours of the evening, Mr. Hoover had retired, satisfied that he had been elected by one of the largest electoral college pluralities ever given a presidntial nominee.

### Massachusetts Shifts to Smith by 18,000

Boston, Nov. 6. — (By Associated Press.) — An early Hoover lead in Massachusetts was changed into a margin of 18,000 for Smith on returns from 512 of the state's 1,605 precincts, including 255 of the 339 Boston precincts. Smith's lead in these Boston precincts was 83,000 while Hoover led in 317 precincts outside Boston by 65,000.

### 540,000 Lead Given Hoover in Pennsylvania

Philadelphia, Nov. 6.—(By Associated Press.)—A lead of more than 540,000 was rolled up for Herbert Hoover in Pennsylvania in returns from 4,094 out of 8,571 districts in the commonwealth. These districts gave Hoover 1,046,297; Smith, 544,305.

The Republican standard-bearer carried with him the Republican candidates for state-wide offices.

## *Ohio Investigates Vote Sale Rumor*

Columbus, Ohio, Nov. 6.—(By Associated Press.)—Investigation of alleged vote buying in Pike county was being made tonight by observers for Secretary of State Clarence J. Brown. Reports to Brown said from $5 to $10 had been paid for votes. Observers were sent to the county recently by Brown following investigation of alleged fraud in casting absent voters' ballots.

## *Wisconsin Votes 8 to 1 for La Follette*

Milwaukee, Nov. 6.—(By Associated Press.)—The election of United States Senator Robert M. LaFollette of Wisconsin, Progressive Republican, was conceded tonight by his independent Republican opponent, State Senator William H. Markham. Markham conceded his defeat when returns from only one-ninth of the state gave LaFollette an 8 to 1 vote.

## *Wayzata Votes to Be City of Fourth Class*

The village of Wayzata, in a special election held in connection with the state and national election, Tuesday voted by 393 to 84 to become a city of the fourth class. The vote means that the village will become a city within 30 days from the time of election.

## *Hoover Carries Tammany District*

New York, Nov. 6.—(By Associated Press.)—Herbert Hoover carried the district of George Olvany, leader of Tammany Hall. The vote was: Smith 153; Hoover 380.

# The Minneapolis Morning Tribune

Sixty-third Year. No. 100. Thirty-six Pages MINNEAPOLIS, MINN., SATURDAY, AUGUST 31, 1929 ** Price Three Cents in Minneapolis.


# RUSS, CHINESE AGREE ON PEACE

## Everybody's Business

### W. B. Foshay's Start. A Horse for Work. Stock Gyrations. Al Smith's New Job.

By John F. Sinclair

Copyright, 1929, by the North American Newspaper Alliance.

Herbert Fleischhacker, well-known San Francisco banker, probably has his eyes turned towards Minneapolis today when the northwest makes ready to celebrate the dedication of its now world famous building—the Foshay tower.

For it was Fleischhacker who loaned W. B. Foshay the $200 which he needed for transportation to Minneapolis to start anew in business.

Mr. Foshay landed in Minneapolis but his pocketbook was not inflated. He didn't have enough to get his furniture released from the railroad. So he gave a chattel mortgage on his furniture, which he paid in monthly instalments over the next two years.

He still lives in the house in Minneapolis which in those days of adversity, just 15 years ago, he rented for $45 a month.

Today the 32-story Foshay tower is being dedicated by James W. Good, United States secretary of war.

Probably no commercial building in the United States has received more attention during the year of its construction than has this tower. This building is patterned after the beautiful Washington monument at the capital.

Mr. Foshay, the dreamer of dreams and the man responsible for the building of this tower, is inherently an artist. Before entering business, he spent several years at the Columbia university art school as well as at the Art Students' league of New York city.

"I never was interested in making a lot of money for myself. I am not a rich man today," this Minneapolis public utility operator said to me. "But to horde money—to keep it locked up—to take it out of use—is inconceivable to my nature."

Mr. Foshay, now 47 years old, is the dynamic type—short, powerfully built, remarkably agile, full of energy which seems to recreate itself constantly. He crowds four or five days' work into one.

Not long ago I stopped in Minneapolis. I saw him late in the afternoon. He was at his desk with correspondence piled two feet high. He had risen at 4 o'clock that morning, taken a dip in the lake, driven his car to the office and had been at work ever since. His lunch had been brought to him.

A horse for work—his 10 secretaries, who are kept on their toes, attest that fact.

When Mr. Foshay travels, he usually takes three secretaries with him, portable typewriters, personal files and other office conveniences—no interruption in business.

His own offices in this new building occupy two complete floors, and include, in addition to the executive offices, an art gallery, two bedroom suites and a kitchenet and dining room. It has been arranged to combine living with work.

A natural born showman—no business man has done more, in recent years, to advertise the northwest than this unique individual, who today sees his life dream realized in the dedication of the Foshay tower as a "monument to peace" to George Washington.

When I asked a Wall Street broker, a heavy dealer in stocks, his opinion of the present market, he replied as follows: "This market is a strong arm proposition to the nth degree."

Then he went on to explain that the development of specialty buying, which started months ago, has continued. That of the 1,200 listed stocks on the big board, only a few are active. Many of them are unknown to the public.

That when a stock is decided upon to be pushed, pools, that would stagger in strength the old operators, start work and before long—presto—the price rises in a skyrocketing manner. That is why on dull days recently some stocks have gone up 10 to 15 points.

Should a stock sell for 10, 12 or 15, or 20 times its value?

Many meritorious stocks are selling at 10 to 15 times their value now. Others, with pool drive and steam behind them have been pushed up to 20, 30, 40, 50 times their earnings. Some stocks even more.

So when a small investor enters such a market, he must be a wise man indeed to know if, in the final washout, he is to be a joyful winner or a sad loser. United States is filled with both classes.

When former Governor Al Smith of New York announced that he had started business as the head of a corporation which will build the highest building in the world on the site of the old Waldorf-Astoria hotel in New York, he centered the eyes of the nation again on the great sums of money now being spent for modern skyscrapers.

For this new Empire State building, as it will be called, will cost, including the $16,000,000 paid for the site, more than $60,000,000.

## Weather Forecast

MINNESOTA — Partly cloudy today and Sunday, possibly scattered thundershowers; somewhat warmer today along Lake Superior.

Additional weather forecasts on page 18.

## News Index



## Casualty Toll Placed at 68 in Shipwreck

### Rescue Vessels Still Hunt for Survivors of Pacific Disaster.

### 42 Out of 110 on Ill-fated Ship Are Saved From Death in Sea.

### Passenger Boat Collides With Oil Tanker of San Francisco.

San Francisco, Aug. 30.—(By Associated Press.)—Sixty-eight of the 119 passengers and crew of the San Francisco-Los Angeles liner San Juan probably met death early today in the fog obscured waters off the cost of Santa Cruz county after a collision between the San Juan and the Standard Oil tanker S. C. T. Dodd.

The number of missing was cut by two names tonight with the finding of two men not included in the list of survivors prepared by the Standard Oil Co. as the tanker, her bow plates dented and ripped, reached here this afternoon under her own power. The recheck credited the tanker with rescuing one woman, one child, and 29 men, of whom 19 were from the San Juan's crew. Three of the latter and three San Juan passengers were taken to hospitals suffering from injuries or exposure.

**Eleven Survivors Arrive.**

Two additional names were those of Theodore Granstedt and Robert Winston, who tonight gave newspaper interviews saying they were survivors who were aboard the Dodd. Apparently in the confusion aboard the Dodd and at the dock their names were not obtained.

Eleven survivors of the shipwreck, all of them passengers or members of the crew of the San Juan, were brought here tonight by the U. S. coast guard cutter, Shawnee.

The San Juan took 65 passengers and carried 45 in her crew when she sailed last night for Los Angeles. Fog checked visibility outside of the Golden Gate, but the weather was clearing as she swung down the coast for her first stop, Santa Barbara.

**Tells of Crash.**

Captain H. O. Bleumchen of the Dodd declared he was proceeding northward from San Pedro on the regular course when he sighted the San Juan's lights.

"The vessels were proceeding on passing courses when the San Juan apparently changed its direction to cross the path of the Dodd," said Captain Bleumchen. "I then ordered the vessel full speed astern in the hope that the San Juan would main-

(Continued on Page 2, Column 1.)

## Police Rescue 2 Young Girls, Jail Assailant

### 65-Year-Old Man, Said to Have Admitted Assault Charges.

A 65-year-old northeast Minneapolis man, the father of grown children, is alleged to have lured two young girls, one 12 and the other 13 years old, to his rooms Friday night, plied them with liquor, and assaulted them.

The noise made by the children fighting him attracted the attention of neighbors. They saw the melee through a window and called the police. When Detective J. T. Ryan of the east side station entered the room, he said the man was lying across the bed and the two girls were under the bed.

The girls, both of whom live in northeast Minneapolis, said they were returning from a show when the man accosted them and invited them to his rooms. One girl said she had been to his room before with other girls but that on such occasions he had conducted himself as a gentleman.

They said he gave them liquor and later attacked them by tearing off their clothes.

The man is said to have admitted all of the charges made against him.

Ryan said early Saturday morning that he did not know whether parents of the children had filed charges against the prisoner, but that if they do not, he will file charges himself.

Police headquarters indicated that the prisoner will be grilled Saturday about the murder of 12-year-old Dorothy Aune.

Captain of Detectives H. A. Paradeau announced Friday night that he had obtained a signed confession from a south Minneapolis man who admitted he had attacked a 12-year-old Minneapolis girl Thursday.

The confession, police authorities said, came with startling suddenness while Detective Adam Smith was grilling the suspect on the slaywas grilling the suspect on the Aune slaying.

This development occurred while Minneapolis and Hennepin and Anoka county officers were scouring the country for two men who attacked a 14-year-old Minneapolis girl at Onaway park in Anoka county Thursday night.

The girl was lured into an automobile at Main street and East Hennepin about 9 p. m., Thursday by two men.

## Puny Sheriff Tries Vainly to Attach Graf for $125,000 Damages

Naval Air Station, Lakehurst, N. J., Aug. 30.—(By Associated Press.)—A very small under-sheriff of Ocean county tried in vain today to attach a very large Graf Zeppelin.

Otto Hillig, Liberty, N. Y., photographer, had brought suit against the operators of the Graf for $125,000 damages because they refused to carry him around the world. He booked passage with the Hamburg-American line, the Zeppelin's accredited agents. At the last moment he was informed he could not go. Owing to a misunderstanding the Hamburg-American officials had counted on three places and in the final shakeup were allotted only two.

The court at Tom's River ordered the under-sheriff to attach the Zeppelin. Commander Maurice R. Pierce, in charge at Lakehurst, refused to accept the writ on the ground that the airship was on government property.

## Fair Ground Gates Swing Open Today

### Exhibitors Toil Far Into Night Preparing for Opening.

**SATURDAY PROGRAM AT THE STATE FAIR.**

**Auto Race and Children's Day.**

8 a. m.—Admission gates and exhibit buildings open to the public.

9 a. m.—Judging begins in poultry, agriculture, horticulture and bee culture. Contests open in Boys' and Girls' club building. Demonstrations begin in Woman's building.

11 a. m.—Gallery tours open in art galleries.

2 p. m.—Complete entertainment program before grandstand, featuring auto races, aviation stunts, open-air circus acts and 225-piece Minnesota State fair high school band.

6:45 p. m.—Concert in front of grandstand by state fair high school band.

7:30 p. m.—Complete entertainment program featuring open-air circus acts, drill by St. Paul post No. 8 American Legion bugle and drum corps, and gigantic fireworks spectacle, "Last Days of Pompeii."

With its thousands of educational exhibits in place, and every feature of its Saturday afternoon and evening grandstand program completed, the seventieth Minnesota State fair and Northwest Livestock show will open Saturday morning with the biggest exhibition in all its history.

**Toil Far Into Night.**

Thousand of exhibitors and concessionaires worked not only all day Friday but far into the night to put displays and stands in shape for the vanguard of fair visitors expected at 8 a. m. Saturday. In the horticultural and agricultural buildings exhibitors here and there still were hard at work at 2 a. m.

In nearly every instance, record-breaking exhibits of livestock, women's work, boys' and girls' club work, art objects, farm machinery, butter and cheese, poultry, honey, flowers, fruits, vegetables, county exhibits, farm crops, school exhibits, automobiles, state exhibits, fish and game, airplanes, and industrial products have been assembled for visitors Saturday. Educational displays not only from every county in Minnesota but every part of the United States and Canada will be presented.

**Auto Races on Program.**

The grandstand program of Saturday afternoon and evening will be complete, presenting all the events and entertainment on the state fair list. These will include automobile races, a dozen open-air circus acts, an aviation program of stunt and exhibition flying and the initial appearance of the Minnesota State fair high school band. Twenty-one well known auto racers, veterans of both dirt track and speedway contests, will compete Saturday on the state fair track.

Saturday evening there will be the first presentation of "The Last Days of Pompeii," the big fireworks spectacle booked for the 1929 state fair. Supplementing the fireworks will be the program of circus acts, including trained animal, acrobatic, dancing and aerial stunts.

**Carnival on 'Whoopee Way.'**

The music will be furnished by the State Fair High School band of 225 musicians, believed to be the largest band ever booked for the Minnesota fair. The Morris & Castle Shows organization and equipment will reach St. Paul early Saturday, from the Iowa State Fair at Des Moines and will open for business on the "Whooppee Way" as soon as the 40-car train can be unloaded.

Judging of poultry, agriculture, horticulture, and bee exhibits is to begin at 9 a. m. Contest work in baking, canning, calf club and other club projects will open in the boys' and girls' club building and continue until the end of next week. More than 1,100 boy and girl contestants will take part in these contests. Demonstrations featuring the making of women's garments, house furnishings, costume designing, and scores of other things of particular interest to women will be put on in the women's building. Observation balloon flights on machinery hill will begin early in the morning.

"Gallery tours will begin in the

(Continued on Page 2, Column 5.)

## Shells Burst Over City in Foshay Fete

### Hundreds of Bombs Shower Loop District in Fireworks Display.

### Huge Throngs Assemble in Streets to Watch Exhibitions.

### Sousa's Band Concert Is Broadcast From Top of Arcade.

Minneapolis literally was bombed from the air Friday night as hundreds of bursting, scintillating shells showered the business district, each a salute in the dedication exercises for the Foshay tower. It was one of the most pretentious fireworks exhibitions in the city's history.

Scarcely any of the city's nearly 500,000 population missed the spectacle. There were vantage points for everyone, for the fireworks were exploded from the top of the 32-story skyscraper. One after another in quick succession the bombs roared and burst, sending huge showers of vari-colored lights floating earthward while loop buildings trembled and reverberated with the detonations. The sounds echoed and re-echoed, multiplying every explosion many times. The taller buildings caught the shocks and sent them rolling and thundering until persons in downtown buildings were given the impression that nearby structures actually were giving forth the disturbances.

**Exhibit Lasts Hour.**

The celebration lasted for an hour, starting after the evening concert by John Philip Sousa's band. The band played from the roof of the two-story arcade at the tower and the music was carried through loud-speakers to thousands of persons who assembled in the general vicinity of the building. The fireworks were scheduled for 9 p. m., but it took fully 20 minutes to clear the building of the milling thousands who came to hear the band and view the building during the afternoon program.

Many thousands of people gathered in the loop district to watch the display, and all over the city were crowds, of varying sizes, gathered to watch the fireworks. Downtown sidewalks were thronged with persons, and many watched even from parked automobiles. Roofs and windows held more thousands, while in private homes people gathered on porches and lawns. In the lake district, everyone seemed to be out to watch the exhibition. The west shore of Lake Calhoun was lined with people and automobiles.

**Loop Choked By Throngs.**

The entire loop district was choked with automobiles and milling throngs for the duration of the display, and vehicle traffic was almost at a standstill as people parked their cars to see the vari-colored flares. Not all the spectators crowded downtown, however, as many viewed the spectacle from outlying parks. Loring park was the gathering place for one of the largest crowds of the summer.

Later the tower lights were extinguished. Hardly had the semi-darkness settled when many brilliant flares were set off on the roof of the two-story section and in the pit adjoining the tower, throwing the structure into brilliant relief against the sky.

The second chapter of the fireworks display started with the shooting of a burst of flare bombs. After each explosion, before the detonation died down, colored flares burst high above the peak of the skyscraper and settled slowly earthward.

Officials from every section of the

(Continued on Page 6, Column 1.)



## Walsh Says Passage of Hawley Bill Means Disaster for Farmers

### Declares West Would Be Far Better Off If Act Was Scrapped.

### Senator Enlists Support to Fight for Defeat of Tariff Plan.

By J. H. Cleland.

American farmers and the people of the western states whose welfare depends on that of agriculture would be far better off if the Hawley tariff bill, with all its unjust discriminations against agriculture, were scrapped, and the old Fordney-McCumber act of 1922 continued in effect, Senator Thomas J. Walsh of Montana, Democratic leader and champion of the cause of tariff equality for the farmers, said in Minneapolis Friday. Enactment of the Hawley bill, in fact, would be nothing short of a disaster to the farmers and would add to, rather than relieve, the burden on agriculture, he declared.

**Presents Law Better.**

"The present tariff law is far from adequate to give agriculture the protection to which it is entitled but it is vastly better than the Hawley bill can be, even with all the tinkering that has been done on it," Senator Walsh said. "The best thing congress can do is to beat the Hawley bill and start in again to draft a measure on sound, fair and constructive lines. If that can't be done right away, the farmers and the entire agricultural section of the country would be better off with the Fordney-McCumber act continued in force than to try to struggle along under the Hawley measure, with all the advantage it gives to industry.

"In my opinion, it is more important to defeat the Hawley bill than to adopt the Borah resolution, which provides that tariff adjustments for the present shall be limited to agriculture and that the schedules on industrial products shall be left where they are. That is the big job of everyone who has the welfare of the farmer at heart—to help beat the Hawley bill."

**Praises Tribune.**

Senator Walsh took occasion to voice high praise for the work which The Minneapolis Tribune and other agencies and organizations in the northwest are doing to enlist support for an equitable tariff for agriculture.

"It is a great job that The Tribune is doing, and one that should be commended by every friend of American agriculture," the senator said. "The incontrovertable facts that have been collected and published by The Tribune, in support

(Continued on Page 2, Column 3.)

**Assails Hawley Bill as Burden to Farmer**

Senator Walsh.

## Says He Stole to Get Outfit for Wedding

### Suspect Admits Robbing Eight Oil Stations of $518 Loot.

A suspect who told police that he held up oil station attendants to obtain cash with which to buy clothes for his wedding confessed late Friday that he had stolen a total of $518 from eight filling stations during the past summer. His sweetheart, when questioned by police, said she didn't know the prospective bridegroom was a thief but she knew he had "some racket that got him the dough."

The county attorney will ask the grand jury to indict the bandit on a charge of first degree burglary which carries a penalty of five to 40 years on conviction.

The suspect had been questioned at length by police Thursday night without result but when he stood in the lineup at headquarters with other suspects Friday, Eugene Forsland, 2943 Washburn avenue north, an attendant at the John Hancock filling station at Nineteenth and Penn avenues north, pointed him out as the man who robbed him. Then the man wilted and confessed that he had robbed Forsland and seven other persons, detectives said.

When police asked him why he found it necessary to rob so many places to obtain enough money to purchase his wedding garments, he said he had repeatedly lost at gambling the stolen cash which he planned to make the purchases. The suspect was arrested by Detectives Walter Hansford and Al Marxen while visiting the bride-elect at her home Thursday night.

## *Man Dies Within Day of End Set by Doctors*

Paris, Ill., Aug. 30.—(By Associated Press.)—George Steidel, merchant died of heart disease today. He was told at Rochester, Minn., by clinic doctors, that he had 240 days to live, and he died on the two hundred and thirty-ninth day.

**Rum Plane Seized.**

Detroit, Aug. 30.—(By Associated Press.)—An airplane containing 15 cases of assorted liquors was captured by U. S. border patrol officers at Rochester, Mich., near Detroit, late today.

## Tariff Makers Woo Support of Democrats

### Duties on Sectional Products Offered as Bait for Votes.

By George F. Authier.

The Tribune's Washington Correspondent.

Washington, Aug. 30.—While it is still doubtful if any tariff bill will be passed in the present session, the chances are one will be enacted before the short session closes. There is enough opposition to any kind of a bill that could be worked out by the conference committee to kill off the legislation proposed and because of this sentiment it is felt it would be better to have no bill than the one that seems likely.

However, the Democratic opposition is not iron clad, while even among the western group of Republicans there is weasening.

The Democratic opposition to the proposed tariff legislation is honest enough, but there are reservations in it. In the first place, the Democratic party, as an organization, looks upon the passage of the proposed bill especially in its house form, as an unmixed blessing for themselves. The fact they do so regard it, ought to be a warning to the Republican leaders and some of them are in a doubtful state of mind.

However, there are always those who play their own game, and the Democratic party is not solidly aligned on the tariff issue. The party is going through a process of rehabilitation on this issue and there is a wide difference for example between the position of Representative Garner, Democratic floor leader of Texas and Representative Cordell Hull, Democratic member of the ways and means committee of Tennessee. Garner is a protectionist, while Hull, although not standing for the old Democratic idea of a tariff believes the policy should be one of constantly reduced rates.

In the senate there are even more varieties of Democratic opinion than in the house. Senator Simmons of North Carolina, is ageing fast and besides he has the back ground of the fight he put up against the Democratic national ticket in the last campaign. This has left some sore spots in the Democratic minds.

(Continued on Page 2, Column 6.)

## Graf Poised to Fly Home

### Huge Air Liner Will Start Journey Over Atlantic at Midnight.

Naval Air Station, Lakehurst, N. J., Aug. 30.—(By Associated Press.)—Poised in the hangar on the reservation here beside its American-owned sister-ship, the Los Angeles, the Giant German air liner Graf Zeppelin tonight was ready for its return tomorrow at midnight to its homeland.

Although it is scheduled to depart in little more than 24 hours there was little activity around the mammoth bird of the skies tonight. Several members of the crew were overhauling the motors which have carried the craft around the world. The work will be completed tonight.

So efficient has the crew become in the work of stocking the dirigible with foodstuff and other provisions that the store needed for the hop across the Atlantic will not be taken aboard until some time tomorrow, a few hours before the passengers are ordered on board.

Early tomorrow morning the refueling of the tanks of the ship will be started.

## Reds Accept Proposals in Rail Dispute

### Soviet Abandons Demand for Reinstatement of General Manager.

### Acceptance Follows Report of Four Russians Executed in East.

### China Asked to Replace Chairman as Lead to Declaration.

Moscow, U. S. S. R., Aug. 30.—(By Associated Press.)—The Soviet government tonight accepted proposals of China for conclusion of a joint declaration for settlement of all questions arising out of the bitter dispute over control of the Chinese Eastern railway in Manchuria.

The foreign commissariat expressed willingness to abandon the Russian demand for reinstatement of the same Russian general manager of the railroad as a preliminary to discussions. It offered to seek approval of the Soviet government for appointment of a new manager if China would replace the old chairman of the railroad directorate, whom the Soviet holds directly responsible for the present trouble.

The acceptance came just when reports of execution yesterday by Chinese of four Soviet citizens seemed to indicate that drastic measures of retaliation would be taken by Russia.

**Loyal to Kellogg Pact.**

Russia proposed that all pending questions be settled in conformity with the agreement of 1924.

Soviet diplomatic circles tonight declared that this action in the face of continued provocative acts on the part of the Chinese was another evidence of the loyal adherence by Russia to the principles of the Kellogg pact.

The agreement of 1924 provided for the operation of the Chinese eastern railway by a board of 10 directors, five of whom, including the chairman, were to be appointed by China and five including the vice-chairman by Russia. It was also provided that the manager of the railroad should be a Russian and should have one Russian and one Chinese as assistant managers.

**Reinstatement Demanded.**

Early in July China removed the Russian general manager, M. Yemshanov, and his Russian assistant and replaced them by Chinese officials. It declared that evidence had been found that they carried on communist propaganda and had diverted railway funds to that end. Russia demanded their reinstatement and return to the status quo before opening negotiations. China replied that while she was willing to negotiate she could not agree to reinstatement of officials whom she accused of working against the security of the Nationalist government.

Preliminary conversations undertaken near the Siberian-Manchurian border failed to settle this point. Meanwhile the armies of both countries massed on the frontiers and there were well substantiated reports of several clashes involving loss of life.

## German Influence Rumored in Agreement

London, Aug. 30.—(By Associated Press.)—A Reuter's dispatch from Moscow tonight said that, with some modifications, the Soviet government had agreed to the Chinese proposal to sign a joint declaration settling the dispute between them.

Rumors that the Chinese and Soviet governments were attempting to come to an agreement in their dispute over the Chinese Eastern railway in Manchuria had been current for a week. It was reported they were begun by the representatives of the two governments in Berlin.

## *Christianson Host to Dedication Group*

Dignitaries from nearly every state in the union, including governors and lieutenant governors, together with their wives, in Minneapolis as official representatives to the dedication of the Foshay tower as a Washington monument, were entertained Friday by Governor Theodore Christianson at a dinner at the Minikahda club. Among the honor guests was George E. Akerson, secretary to President Hoover. No addresses were given, but Governor Christianson welcomed his guests to the state and invited them to visit the lakeland vacation areas of Minnesota. After the dinner, the gathering moved to the porches of the club to view the fireworks at the Foshay tower. Mr. Foshay was one of the guests at the dinner.

## *Arabs Slay 22 Jews in New Massacre*

Cairo, Aug. 31.—(Saturday)—(By Associated Press.)—Reports to the Jewish Telegraphic agency from Jerusalem early today said that 22 Jews were killed and scores wounded in a massacre perpetrated by Moslem Arabs Thursday night and Friday morning on the Jewish population at the ancient city of Safed. Jewish settlements in the Jordan valley and in south Sharon were said to face grave danger of attack.

# The Minneapolis Morning Tribune

Sixty-third Year. No. 155. | Forty Pages. | MINNEAPOLIS, MINN., FRIDAY, OCTOBER 25, 1929 | ** | Price Three Cents in Minneapolis.

# STOCKS PLUNGE FIVE BILLIONS

## Everybody's Business

Stocks Crash.
Not Alarmed.
Waterway Plans.
Seaman Will.

By John F. Sinclair.



The continued demoralization on the New York stock exchange yesterday occurred in the greatest turnover in the history of that exchange.

Prices melted so fast that even old established houses could not tell the condition of some of their biggest clients.

But that cannot be laid at the door of high money. For money yesterday and the two preceding days, when market losses were the greatest in history, maintained itself around five per cent.

Telegrams from business leaders replying to telegrams which the Minneapolis Tribune and the North American Newspaper alliance sent asking whether in their opinion the stock market drop reflected business conditions, continue to arrive. Here are two just received:

George M. Verity, president of the American Roller Mills, Middletown, Ohio,—"Business moves along in the even tenor of its way with seasonal fluctuations and shows steady progress in every two-year period.

"Industry is just as valuable today as it was 10 days ago and it is the backbone of the nation's business market. The fluctuations neither increase nor decrease its basic values."

Paul Shoup, president of the Southern Pacific railroad, San Francisco,—"On the Pacific coast there are no new conditions controlling business which were not foreseen so far as I know when stock prices were much higher than they are now.

"I do not believe business conditions responsible in any material way for the stock market decline."

The views of such men as Mr. Verity and Mr. Shoup and the like opinions of others which were published in The Tribune yesterday, may not mean anything to those thousands of speculators, large and small, who have lost everything during the past 10 days. But to the public at large such messages mean a lot.

---

Save on battleships and spend on waterways.

This is the advice which President Hoover gave the American people in his Louisville speech.

This speech, the most comprehensive ever made on the subject of inland waterways, will bring cheer to the hearts of millions of people who live in states bordering the Mississippi and its tributaries. The president declared his unequivocal support of a broad and sweeping policy for the "modernizing of every part of our highways which will show economic justification in aid of our farmers and industries."

His program is a five-year one. He wants the Mississippi and its tributaries modernized within that time. Today only 2,000 miles out of 7,200 have been modernized. The practical expansion of inland commerce will demand a channel nine feet deep throughout the entire trunk system of the Mississippi, and from six to seven feet deep in the tributaries. Already the Ohio from Pittsburgh to Cairo has completed the nine-foot channel.

The whole program is a comprehensive one, including not only the Mississippi but the St. Lawrence-Great Lakes route, tying up with certain canal developments to complete the picture.

It is significant that part of the President's speech which got the greatest applause was the reference to his desire to take the millions he expects to save on battleships for the improvement of these great waterways.

The program is ambitious. It will require more than $1,000,000,000 in the next four years. It will link east and west and north and south for the cheap water transportation of heavy goods. It will restore to economic parity what one writer calls the "dislocated commercial geography of the west."

To give the interior states a chance to compete in the development of industries on a fair and much more even basis with those favored by cheaper water rates on the seaboard is worth the effort—whatever the cost.

For, after all, what is $1,000,000,000 here when the stockmarket shows a drop of $5,000,000,000 in one day?

---

Four years ago, a short, stocky, gray-haired man, crossing the street at Broadway and Seventy-ninth street, New York, was run down by a street car. An emergency call was made to the Roosevelt hospital. The then unidentified man was taken to the hospital where his leg was amputated.

The efficient way the case was handled made a great appeal to him, but he kept his own thoughts about it. But when this man—Lloyd W. Seaman—died last Sunday, it was found he had left $1,000,000 to the Roosevelt hospital.

That was not all. He left another $1,000,000 to the Salvation Army, although Commander E. N. Holz, head of the New York area, had never met him. It was the largest gift ever received by the army.

### Weather Forecast

MINNESOTA—Fair in south, increasing cloudiness in north portion. Warmer today. Saturday somewhat unsettled.

Additional weather on page **

## News Index



## One Arrested in Kunze War on Gambling

### Mayor Orders Cleanup of City Dives After Quiz by Grand Jury.

### Denies Police Shakeup Impending—'Functions Efficiently,' He Says.

### Punchboard Is Seized in First Raid of New Campaign.

Less than 24 hours after his appearance before the grand jury, Mayor Kunze Thursday ordered his police department to undertake an immediate investigation and clean-up of gambling and bootlegging dives in the city.

Declaring that he was satisfied in his own mind that the police department has "functioned as efficiently as any the city ever had," Mayor Kunze denied that any shake-up was impending.

Thursday afternoon police made their first move. George Chagaloskis was arrested in the Poppy shop at the Curtis hotel and a punchboard was confiscated. Chagaloskis was charged with having a gambling device in his possession and will be arraigned in municipal court Friday.

The grand jury is scheduled to go back into session Friday and more witnesses may be called in its investigation into reports of "outside interference" with the police department.

The mayor's action in ordering police to be on the alert for gambling and vice violations, he said, was to "set at rest unfounded rumors of widespread law violation."

"There has been no let up in the policy of strict law enforcement announced when I assumed office July 1," the mayor said.

"However, there have been rumors of violations and I am directing the police department to make a special effort to set them at rest. All I am interested in is the facts, and if there is anything wrong, I want it straightened out.

"I wish to reiterate my confidence in Harry Lindholm, the chief of police. If I didn't think he was efficient, I wouldn't have him here. I'd get another chief in five minutes. There will be no changes in the department. We are going to continue our efforts to keep the city clean."

Regarding information of bootlegging and gambling operations reported to have reached the grand jury,

(Continued on Page 2, Column 5.)

## Board Starts Big Livestock Co-op on Way

### National Sales Association Has Backing of 28 Groups.

B. J. H. Cleland.
Tribune Staff Correspondent.

Chicago, Oct. 24.—The federal farm board Thursday took a big step toward stabilization of another branch of American agriculture, the marketing of livestock, when it joined with 66 representatives of the 28 largest co-operative livestock sales agencies in the country to form the National Livestock Marketing association as a nation-wide organization to co-ordinate the activities of the local and district co-operatives and to finance their operations. This action took place at the close of a two-day conference between five farm board members, headed by Alexander Legge, chairman, and the co-operative unit leaders.

The livestock industry now is added to the list of major divisions of agriculture for whose stabilization the farm board has taken definite action. Last July, the board established a national corporation to finance and market grain for the local co-operative groups and to be owned and controlled by them. Next, in September, the board formed a similar organization for the wool growers and their co-operative agencies.

Friday morning, five board members will open an executive conference with members of the committee in charge of the details of organizing the Farmers National Grain corporation, the great co-operative organization formed three months ago. The job at this meeting will be to put the finishing touches to the articles of incorporation and the by-laws of the company, as the last step before it is set to work as the marketing agency for the wheat and grain "co-ops" throughout the country.

In connection with this conference, the farm board will make public the details of the system through which it will make loans to the local groups for financing the grain markets of their farmer members, Chairman Legge said Thursday. It has been indicated that the new grain corporation's program of credit advances to the co-operative groups will be more liberal in its provisions than originally was planned. The announcement of details, therefore, is awaited with keen interest by co-operative marketing leaders throughout the northwest and other grain growing sections.

Samuel R. McKelvie of Lincoln,

(Continued on Page 2, Column 1.)

## Constans Fate Put in Hands of U. S. Jurors

### Voluminous Records of Consumers' Company Being Perused.

### Judge Cant Warns Panel Mails Must Be Involved in Fraud to Council.

### Talesmen Fail to Reach Verdict—Locked Up for Night.

The fate of Nicholas M. Constans, whose trial on charges of using the mails to defraud has been in progress in United States district court for more than two weeks, was placed in the hands of the jury Thursday at 5:30 p. m.

No verdict was reached Thursday night and the jurors were locked up for the night at 10 p. m.

With final arguments of both government and defense counsel concluded late Thursday afternoon, the case was given to the jury following the charge of Judge William A. Cant, who has presided throughout the trial.

The charge of the court to the jurors was direct and explicit. They were told to determine whether a scheme to defraud Esch & Co., place in question existed, whether there was a scheme to do anything wrong, and whether there was a scheme to defraud Esch & Co., through the medium of a false audit.

The existence of the scheme is not enough, the jurors were told, providing it is not established that it was furthered through the use of the United States mails. It is the use of the mails, the court pointed out, that makes the offense one that comes within the jurisdiction of the federal courts.

"Obviously," the court said, "if there is no scheme to defraud there is no guilt, but if a scheme is established it becomes necessary to determine if it was carried out through the use of the mails.

"The defendant is not called upon to prove his innocence and is presumed so until he is proven guilty beyond a reasonable doubt. In criminal matters the rule is stronger than a fair preponderance of the evidence. The charge must be proved beyond a reasonable doubt. If you are not able to decide that, your verdict should be in favor of the defendant; if you are able to do so, then your verdict should favor the government. This is not a personal matter. It is a duty."

The jurors took with them into the jury room a huge stock of books and records of the Consumers Wholesale Supply Co., which were entered as evidence by both the defense and the government.

The jury has been "locked up" by order of the court since the opening of the trial.

## *Five Convict Leaders Sentenced to Hang*

Sacramento, Calif., Oct. 24.—(By Associated Press.)—Five of the six convicts who acted as leaders in the attempted Thanksgiving day break in 1927 at Folsom state prison were sentenced today to hang in January. Anthony Brown and Roy E. Stokes will go to the gallows on January 3, Walter E. Burke and James H. Gregg on January 10 and Eugene Crosby on January 17.

## *Aimee Before Jury; Surrenders Books*

Los Angeles, Oct. 24.—(By Associated Press.)—Aimee Semple McPherson, evangelist, appeared before the county grand jury today to answer questions on asserted manipulations of the financial affairs of her church, Angelus temple.

Mrs. McPherson left the grand jury room after a short time. The district attorney's office announced she had "turned over the books of Angelus temple."

## *Doody Declared Guilty; Must Die*

Chicago, Oct. 24.—(By Associated Press.)—Willie "Baby Face" Doody was convicted by a jury early today for the murder last May of Chief of Police Charles Levy of Berwin. The verdict, returned at 12:55 a. m., fixes the punishment at death.

## *Channel Airplane Disappears in Gale*

London, Oct. 24.—(By Associated Press.)—A great gale, accompanied by rain, which swept Great Britain today, swallowed up an airplane which left Croydon for Nairobi, Kenya colony, Africa, with five persons aboard.

## *Moorfield Storey, Author, Is Dead*

Lincoln, Mass., Oct. 24.—(By Associated Press.)—Moorfield Storey, lawyer and author, died here at his home tonight after a long illness. He was president of the American Bar association in 1896. He was 84 years old.

## Senate Votes 5½-Cent Casein Tariff on Proposal by Blaine; Rate Boost Is Termed Failure

### 3-Cent Increase Held by Dairymen to Be Only Compromise.

### 8 Cents Declared Lowest Figure That Would Do Any Good.

The five and one-half cent tariff rate on casein voted by the Senate Wednesday afternoon is a compromise at the expense of agriculture, and fails to fulfill campaign pledges of the Republican party, in the opinion of officials of the Twin City Milk Producers' association and Land O'Lakes Creameries, Inc.

John Brandt, president of Land O'Lakes, and W. S. Moscrip, president of the milk producers' group, both emphatically declared that the 8-cent rate which the dairy industry is demanding is the lowest figure at which American casein producers can meet foreign competition.

American manufacturers using casein are pursuing a very short-sighted policy when they fight to keep the tariff rate down, Mr. Moscrip contended. Guaranteeing the agricultural industry a healthy purchasing power means more to the manufacturers than does any saving they can effect as the result of a low tariff, he said.

"News of the senate's failure to approve the 8-cent rate came as a great disappointment to me," Mr. Moscrip declared. "That is the lowest figure at which American producers can compete with producers in the Argentine, and also is, in my opinion, the minimum rate that will fulfill the Republican party's campaign promises. This action is an indication that the Republican party has failed signally in its duty to agriculture.

"The casein-using manufacturers certainly are not profiting by a lower rate. The prosperity of the farmers ought to be more important than getting imported raw materials cheaply, and surely means more than any other one thing in the pattern of national prosperity."

While the senate action leaves little hope that the 8-cent rate will eventually be granted, Mr. Moscrip said, the dairy interests "are not through fighting by any means." The one remaining hope is that the desired rate will be approved at the coming house and senate committee conferences, he said.

Voting of the five and one-half

(Continued on Page 2, Column 8.)

## Mrs. Coolidge's Mother Is Dead

Mrs. Elmira Goodhue.

## Illness Fatal to Mother of Mrs. Coolidge

### Parent of Former President's Wife Dies at Northampton.

Northampton, Mass., Oct. 24.—(By Associated Press.)—Mrs. Elmira Goodhue, mother of Mrs. Calvin Coolidge, wife of the former president, died at the Cooley-Dickinson hospital here tonight.

Mrs. Goodhue had been a patient at the hospital since December 11, 1927, on that date she suffered an attack of influenza from which she later rallied. Subsequently she relapsed due to the infirmities of old age and had several sinking spells, two of which brought Mrs. Coolidge from the White House to her mother's bedside.

Since her return to Northampton, Mrs. Coolidge had spent two hours daily with her mother. Mr. Coolidge also was a frequent visitor at the hospital.

Mrs. Coolidge was at the bedside when her mother died, having been at the hospital since the afternoon. The former President was also at the hospital.

Mrs. Goodhue was the widow of Captain Andrew W. Goodhue, a Lake Champlain steamboat inspector and had lived in Burlington, Vt., many years. Although she was 78 years old she was mentally alert almost until her death.

When Calvin Coolidge was inaugurated in 1924 she went to Washington to attend the ceremonies and spent two months at the White House. She returned here with John Coolidge, the former president's son, who was then a student at Amherst college.

She took much interest in preparations for the wedding of John and the former Florence Trumbull.

In addition to Mrs. Coolidge, Mrs. Goodhue leaves one other near relative, a sister, Mrs. John R. Hasel of Roxbury.

## Four Bodies Point to Fate of 50 Sailors

### Mute Evidence of Wreck Picked Up 10 Miles Out on Lake.

Chicago, Oct. 25.—(By Associated Press.)—Captain John O. Anderson of the coast guard, early today was notified by the Kenosha coast guard that four more bodies, believed from the car ferry Milwaukee, were recovered there.

---

Milwaukee, Oct. 24.—(By Associated Press.)—Mute evidence of the fate which befell between 50 and 57 of their mates, the lifebelted bodies of four of the crew of the Grand Trunk car ferry, Milwaukee, which sank in Lake Michigan probably Tuesday night, were taken from the lake about 10 miles off Kenosha this afternoon.

A wireless message from the motor ship Steel Chemist to the U.S.S. Hyacinth, lighthouse tender here, and relayed to Captain Charles H. Hubbard of the lighthouse service, told of the Steel Chemist picking up two bodies and five miles farther out in the lake the white pilot house with "Milwaukee" printed on it. The life belts on the bodies bore the name Milwaukee.

The other two bodies from the ill-fated car ferry were recovered about 10 miles off shore from Kenosha, tonight by coast guardsmen. Neither could be identified. In the pocket of one was a bank book of the Grand Haven, Mich., State bank.

A watch on one of the bodies picked up by the Steel Chemist had stopped at 9:35, indicating that the ferry went down Tuesday night, six hours after it steamed out of the Kinnickinnic river with 27 loaded freight cars aboard, bound for Grand Haven, Mich.

Captain Robert McKay of Grand Haven, veteran skipper of the Grand Trunk fleet, was in command.

The Milwaukee sailed in the face of a violent gale, the worst some marine men here said in the last 16 years.

An investigation into the disaster, the worst on Lake Michigan in 49 years, will be made immediately, Captain W. A. Collins, federal steamboat inspector here, said tonight. In 1880 the Alpena sank in mid-lake with loss of more than 100 lives.

Exactly what happened to the Milwaukee will probably never be known. The ferries are built with the stern end open above the main deck. There is an "apron," which opens and closes, thus permitting railroad cars to be switched onto

(Continued on Page 2, Column 2.)

## Lock Up Jury in Fall Trial

### Eight Men and Four Women Can Not Now Report Until 10 A. M.

Washington, Oct. 24.—(By Associated Press.)—The jury charged with determining Albert B. Fall's guilt or innocence of bribery was locked up for the night at 11:08 p. m., after deliberating almost 12 hours without returning a verdict.

The eight men and four women, who have been held in seclusion since the trial began October 7, slept tonight in the District of Columbia courthouse. They could not report before 10 o'clock tomorrow morning at the earliest.

If any decision is reached by the jury in the meantime it will be sealed until Justice William Hitz opens court in the morning.

Since 11:30 a. m., today the jury had been going over the case, but no information was forthcoming whether any progress had been made.

All the while the former interior secretary was waiting with Mrs. Fall at his hotel for word to proceed to court.

#### Hunter Is Killed.

Burlington, Colo., Oct. 24.—(By Associated Press.)—Joseph M. Swenson, former mayor here, wealthy attorney and real estate man, was found dead with a gunshot wound in his heart near here late today. He was hunting and had attempted to climb over a fence when the gun he was carrying exploded.

### Spokesman of Great Dairying State Blamed for Inadequate Duty.

### Rate of 8 Cents Lost in Senate Because of His Attitude.

By George F. Authier.
The Tribune's Washington Correspondent.

Washington, D. C., Oct. 24.—The senate today voted a 5½-cent duty on casein. It did so because a senator from a northwestern dairy state, Senator Blaine of Wisconsin, insisted this was a sufficient duty. It was a viewpoint in opposition to the dairy interests of the country as represented here, who demanded an 8-cent duty. The 8-cent duty would have been voted, in all probability, had not Senator Blaine opposed the proposal. With a senator from one of the leading dairy states of the northwest opposing the 8-cent duty, there was little chance of getting more than the representative of the Wisconsin dairy state demanded. Accordingly Senator Blaine assumes full responsibility for obtaining, in the senate bill, a duty on casein of 5½ cents per pound instead of 8 cents.

In any event this is an increase over the house of 2½ cents and over the finance committee rate of 3½ cents.

#### Still Chance for Increase.

There still is a chance to raise the rate when the senate comes to the point of voting on the entire bill as a whole. An amendment then can be offered to raise or reduce the rate.

The roll call on this issue showed a mixed-up congeries of motives. Some voted against the Blaine proposal because they thought the rate was too high and others voted against it because they thought the rate too low. Nye and Frazier of North Dakota, McMaster of South Dakota, Brookhart of Iowa and Schall of Minnesota, also Howell of Nebraska, voted against the proposal because they thought the rate not high enough. Blaine and La Follette of Wisconsin and Norbeck of South Dakota voted for the 5½-cent rate.

The viewpoint of those who voted for the Blaine proposal did so on the ground that a rate lower than 8 cents was in the interest of the dairy farmer. They took the position that with an 8-cent duty, the users of coated paper would resort to super calendered paper, which does not utilize casein as does coated paper.

#### Some for Reduction.

Another viewpoint is that this group holds that the general level of tariff rates should be lowered and that agriculture should not demand anything beyond what can be easily justified. They hold that the prime object of the tariff bill should be to reduce the general level of rates and that in order to bring this about, industrial rates should be reduced, and that increases in farm rates should be in line with the reductions proposed in industrial rates.

So far as the benefits to farmers is concerned this group points out that dairy production is nearing the point of saturation and that an embargo upon importations of dairy products might result in placing dairy production on an export basis.

Senator Blaine insisted that shutting off Canadian importations had resulted in Canadians going into the cheese business with the result they were shipping cheese into Wisconsin.

However the issue is not settled. The farm groups are in arms over the result, still claiming they should have an 8-cent duty and hoping to obtain it in the final bill.

## Wheat Drops 12 Cents Here

### Downturn in Stock Market Reverberates in Minneapolis Pit.

The smash of selling orders that hit the stock market Thursday reverberated heavily through the wheat pit of the Chamber of Commerce building, and traders experienced their wildest morning since the war days. Wheat collapsed 12½ cents within a few hours after the market opened, and then struggled back seven cents at the close. May closings were $1.29¾, and December finals, $1.21¼.

The pit was a maelstrom of gesticulating traders during that flurry. Prices fell as much as four cents without a trade. Drops of two or three cents were common. The pace was too fast to execute stop losses and traders fell from two to three cents behind. Excitement and uproar of trading in the pit attracted dealers from the cash wheat floor and hundreds of spectators filled the gallery as news of the break in the market was bruited about.

By noon the avalanche had spent its force, and a steady reintegration of prices began. The upheaval in the pit was attributed directly to the crash on the stock market. Grain men considered the sharp drop was caused by eastern traders, who held blocks of stock and began dumping wheat in an effort to obtain the means to cover their stock margins. Similar conditions were experienced at Chicago and Winnipeg.

## Sales Exceed 12,000,000 as Terror Reigns

### Market Regains Half of Losses in Closing Hour of Trade.

### Scores of Issues Tumble From $15 to $70 Per Share.

### Lamont Feels Reassured After Meeting With Bank Chiefs.

New York, Oct. 24.—(By Associated Press.)—The remarkable era of avid public speculation in stocks which has swept over the country during the past five years came to a climax today in the most terrifying stampede of selling ever experienced on the New York stock exchange and other leading security markets.

Four hours and 8 minutes after the close of the exchange today the ticker recorded the final sale of the most frantic day of stock trading in history. This last quotation on the tape appearing at 7:08 p. m. was a final clarification of the confusion that hung over the wild course of prices at the record total of 12,894,650 shares was traded. Loss in quoted values for the day was estimated at approximately five billion dollars.

#### Hundreds Reach Lows.

Closing prices presented a picture of havoc among quoted values, hundreds of shares selling at or near low levels for the year, and from $20 to more than $100 below the record prices reached in recent months. Nevertheless, the price level at the time the closing gong sounded at 3 o'clock was found to be substantially above the bottom levels of the day, approximately half of the losses of the terrifying early hours of the day having been regained.

Although the ticker tape came to a halt shortly after 7 p. m., the stock clearing corporation directed that all members of the exchange retain their office forces until the day's transactions are completed, which promised an all night vigil in most offices.

Not since the war panic which resulted in closing the exchange for 17 weeks in 1914 has Wall Street seen such a dark and trying day, and never in financial history have security markets been thrown into such a tumult.

It appeared for a time that the stock markets would be unable to face the situation and that trading would have to be suspended, but the leading exchanges saw the ordeal through, although a few floor traders collapsed and had to be aided from the trading floors.

#### Lamont Issues Statement.

By early afternoon, the situation became so grave that a hurried meeting of leading bankers was called at the offices of J. P. Morgan & Co., and a reassuring statement issued from the conference by Thomas W. Lamont, one of the Morgan partners, finally checked the sickening drop of stock prices and saved the market from a complete impasse.

Scores of important stocks tumbled from $15 to $70 a share, paper values vanishing at the rate of tens of millions of dollars a minute, until mid-afternoon, when the bankers' statement prompted large operators who were reaping millions in selling the market short, to cover their commitments, and prices of many issues rebounded substantially.

Total sales on the stock exchange reached the amazing figure of 12,894,650 shares, surpassing by more than 50 per cent the previous record of 8,246,740 reached on March 26. The ticker quotation service fell hours behind transactions, and traders who were unable to get quotations from the floor through their brokers proceeded blindly, save at intervals when a few stock quotations were sent out through the bond market tickers.

Standard dividend paying stocks were thrown overboard along with the more speculative issues. Stocks were sold for what they would bring in blocks of from 1,000 to 150,000 shares. Traders on the floor of the stock exchange shrieked and howled their offers for desperate minutes before they found takers.

Such a roar arose from the stock exchange floor that it could be heard for blocks up and down Broad and Wall streets. Speculators and sightseers poured in Wall street in such volume that extra traffic police were required to handle them, and the stock exchange gallery, to which speculators are admitted only upon recommendation of a partner in a member brokerage firm, was closed to the public.

#### Wires Congested.

The torrent of selling orders poured into the market over the congested private wire systems of commission houses from all cities of the country, over telephone and telegraph wires, and came from abroad by cable, radio and trans-Atlantic telephone. Foreign security markets and domestic and foreign commodity markets broke sharply in sympathy with the stock exchange, and intensified the terror of speculators.

The turning point of the day came soon after the heads of the three largest banks of the country were observed, singly, hastening up the steps of the sober, gray stone house of Morgan, at the corner of Broad and Wall streets, during the early afternoon.

Shortly Thomas W. Lamont, senior [illegible] Morgan partner, consented to see reporters. He stated that the

(Continued on Page 34, Column 1.)

The Minneapolis Morning Tribune

Sixty-third Year. No. 159. | Twenty-two Pages | MINNEAPOLIS, MINN., TUESDAY, OCTOBER 29, 1929 | ** | Price Three Cents in Minneapolis.

# BANKERS ACT ON STOCK CRASH

## Everybody's Business

Stocks Again
A Rational State.
$75,000 a Year.
Tariff and S. A.

By John F. Sinclair.



The violent decline of the stock market Monday has left speculators bewildered—cold. At the opening of the market, even the bears were inclined to think that the drop in prices was over, but the continued decline after the first hour of trading proved they were mistaken, and the lowest prices of the day were recorded at the close.

What is needed at this particular moment is leadership of an outstanding nature to bring order out of chaos. Up to the present time, that leadership has not yet fully developed.

"The business of buying stocks on tape prices or basing investments in American common stocks for a few days or a few weeks' experience—the business of taking fliers and buying for a "turn"— is dangerous and should cease," is the advice of one of the large investment services in its first report after the "big break."

Then how should it be done?

"Build up an investment program and use always therein a substantial investment in common stocks. This is sound practice and will continue to be sound practice during our lifetime," is the reply.

This investment service, followed by thousands throughout the nation, does not advocate switching blindly all one's stocks to bonds and "betting on interest rates rather than capital earnings." It says this is unnecessary and unsound. It would use high grade bonds and short term notes for some investment programs, particularly those of the small investors, and not overlook the fact that many of the best corporations in the land are comparatively free of debt, and their common stocks offer large opportunities, which are denied in an executive bond account.

Again the break in the stock market has brought an opportunity for the first time this year not only to participate in the growth of these companies, but to share a fair rate of return from the start.

The day of borrowing money at 6 to a per cent to buy stocks earning 1 and 2 per cent has gone. A more rational state of affairs has arrived. It should be with us for some time, too.

* * *

The highest paid public official in Canada today is Sir Henry Thornton, head of the Canadian National railways.

He was the highest paid even before signing his latest contract with the Canadian government.

Sir Henry, born in Logansport, Ind., 57 years ago, was one of Pennsylvania's football players in the early '90s. After his graduation from college he entered railroad work, and rose from one position to another until in 1911 he became general superintendent of the Long Island railroad, handling its immense traffic in and out of New York.

In 1917 the Great Eastern railroad of England asked him to become its general manager. He accepted. Before the war was over he became inspector general of transportation for the Allied armies.

Then when Canada found itself in difficulties with the Canadian Northern, Grand Trunk Pacific, Grand Trunk and a dozen smaller lines, all more or less exploited, the government found it necessary to take them all over, unify them and get a master strategist to direct the enterprise.

Sir Henry Thornton was offered the position at a salary of $50,000 a year by McKenzie King, then prime minister.

Under his direction the road has moved ahead and he has turned the net from a deficit to a surplus.

The government increased his salary later to $65,000, and he has just signed a contract for another five years, dating from October, 1928, calling for $75,000 a year.

The financial set-up of the Canadian National, as it is today, is top heavy. It groans under the weight of its bonds and stocks outstanding.

* * *

Paul R. Mahoney, executive vice president of the B. F. Goodrich corporation, back from a business trip to Chile, Brazil, Peru, Cuba, Panama, Uruguay and Argentina, says his company will build a factory to employ at least 1,000 persons on a 60-acre site near Buenos Aires.

When asked how the people of South America felt about increasing tariff duties, he replied:

"Everywhere officials, merchants and business men generally are looking with greatest anxiety at the development of the United States tariff policy on the general principle that foreign commerce cannot be a one way street. Obviously, the ability to buy depends to a considerable degree on the ability to sell, and it is significant that under the present scheme of reciprocity, our foreign trade with the Argentine alone has increased more than 200 per cent in the last 10 years. This applies both to our exports and to our imports."

### Weather Forecast

MINNESOTA—Rain or snow today with strong east and northeast winds; Wednesday partly cloudy, probably snow in east portion, continued cold.

Additional weather on page 11.

## News Index



## Norris to Ask Censure Vote for Bingham

### Nebraskan Announces He Will Present Resolution Today.

### Will Be First Time in 27 Years Senate Is Asked to Act.

### Move Result of Activities Growing Out of Tariff Lobby Activities.

Washington, Oct. 28.—(By Associated Press.)—The dire promise of a resolution proposing censure for Senator Bingham of Connecticut, stilled a savage verbal exchange in the senate today between the Connecticut senator and his accusers of the lobby investigating committee.

An expectant quiet came over the stormy scene when Senator Norris of Nebraska, one of those who came under Bingham's assault, announced he intended to offer a resolution tomorrow. It would be the first time in 27 years that the senate would be called upon to censure a member.

The resolution had not been drafted tonight but it was indicated that it would ask the senate to denounce the use by Senator Bingham of a salaried employe of the Connecticut Manufacturers' association to assist him in helping to frame the tariff bill.

Smarting under the condemnation heaped upon him last Saturday by Chairman Caraway of the lobby investigators, Senator Bingham took the floor at the outset of today's session to strike back. He charged that the lobby committee was "framed" against any friend of the administration and had been unfair to him.

The tall senator who once taught at Yale, was white of face as he pounded his desk in conclusion and said:

"The purpose of this committee has been to befoul me with political slime by the twisting and torturing of flimsy evidence and I resent and I shall resent it until the end of my life."

One by one, four of the members of the lobby committee answered in language as severe. Finally Senator Robinson of Indiana, who had been referred to by Bingham as the lone friend of the administration upon the committee, arose and pronounced his own condemnation upon the Connecticut senator for his relations with the Connecticut manufacturers.

"I don't approve of the transaction," said Senator Robinson. "The Republican party does not approve

(Continued on Page 4, Column 3.)

## Senator Reed Visions Death of Tariff Bill

### Aroused, Faction Leaders Seek Hoover Views on Measure.

Washington, Oct. 28.—(By Associated Press.)—A pronouncement of ultimate death was read over the tariff bill in the senate today by one of its sponsors, Senator Reed, Republican, Pennsylvania, and the post mortems that quickly ensued found leaders of all factions passing the blame around.

The assertion, a repetition of a statement by Senator Reed in a speech in Philadelphia over the week-end, led to a free-for-all political discussion which saw Republican regulars and independents quarrelling over the attitude of President Hoover; Democrats and Republicans demanding that the President state his position on the bill, and all finally agreeing that the senate must get down to serious business and pass some sort of measure.

**Smoot Is Optimistic.**

Although Reed predicted the bill would die in conference with the house, Senator Smoot, Republican, Utah, in charge of the measure for the finance committee, assured the senate that no effort was to be made to kill the legislation in conference and that it would be handled as any other bill when it reaches that stage.

Senator Johnson, California, started the debate by calling attention to conflicting newspaper accounts, one to the effect that the coalition of Democrats and western Republicans was succeeding in writing the type of bill the President wanted, and the other quoting Senator Reed as saying the bill was dead.

"We ought to be advised whether the President stands for this bill as reported by the finance committee or is desirous of what the coalition is attempting to do with it," asserted the Californian.

**Used 'Party Lash.'**

Adverting by inference to the President's statement urging retention of the flexible provisions, Johnson said members of the executive department had used the "party lash" to whip senators into line on the proposition, yet no one knew how Mr. Hoover stood on rates.

The Californian said it was "up to the executive to say whether he wants one kind of a bill or another."

Senator Reed said he had been quoted correctly about the bill being dead and still was of that opinion.

(Continued on Page 2, Column 3.)

Lucrezia in Title Role of Gala Night

Lucrezia Bori.

## Gotham's Opera Opens to Return of Longer Skirts

### Golden Horseshoe Glows as Season Starts With 'Manon Lescaut.'

By Lorena A. Hickok.
Associated Press Staff Writer.

New York, Oct. 28.—In the grim and proud old edifice, the Metropolitan Opera house, whose soot-stained embattlements frown darkly down upon the encroachments of a new society, with its jazz and motor cars and night clubs, the social season was officially opened in New York tonight.

Officially, too, it was the opening of the grand opera season of 1929.

But opera, on the opening night of the season in New York, is ever a matter of secondary importance. It is society's gala night. Society in satins and velvets, jewels and furs that make even the most gorgeous costumes of bygone days worn by the prima donna look almost commonplace, sweeps up the grand staircase, there to see and be seen.

So once again tonight, Lucrezia Bori sang the lovely wistful arias of "Manon Lescaut," the golden horseshoe softly glowed, unable to subdue even in a darkened house its regal magnificence. And as the curtain lowered, and the lights came on, all eyes turned upward and swept around that dazzling curve.

Society came late. Society, ever since there was a Metropolitan Opera house, always has arrived late on the opening night.

One thing that made tonight's opening even more exciting than usual was the return of long skirts and waistlines. Fashionable New York has not taken particularly kindly to long skirts for street wear. In the crowds one sees along Fifth avenue there is no great change. Skirts may be an inch or two longer, but that's all.

## Burton, Ohio Senator, Dies

### Word of Veteran Legislator's Death Grieves Capitol From Hoover Down.

Washington, Oct. 28.—(By Associated Press.)—Senator Theodore E. Burton of Ohio died tonight after an illness of several months.

Word of Burton's death grieved official Washington from President Hoover down. From time to time, the President had called on the 77-year-old legislator to keep in close personal touch with his condition.

Among the last visitors to the bedside were Senator Fess of Ohio and Bishop William T. MacDowell of the Methodist Episcopal church. Miss Grace Burton, a niece of the senator and a nephew, William Burton, were with him through the last hours. He had been unable to take nourishment through the day.

Ever since Mr. Burton suffered a relapse in his long standing illness last week, messages of friendship had been reaching his home from Ohio and elsewhere. One today was from Prime Minister MacDonald of Great Britain, through the British embassy. Mr. MacDonald expressed appreciation for the work the Ohio senator had long done in the cause of peace, and expressed a devout wish for his recovery.

Death came shortly before 10 o'clock. It followed a sinking spell which swept him into unconsciousness from which he did not recover.

## Section Hand Steps Wrong Way; Killed

Obeying the warning of his fellow workmen, but stepping onto the wrong track, John Johnson, 54 years old, a section hand, was instantly killed Monday afternoon when he was struck by an incoming Great Northern passenger train two miles west of Long Lake. Johnson was working between two tracks with his back turned when his fellow workers shouted their warning.

## Schall Decides on A. J. Schunk as Postmaster

### Formal Announcement of Appointment to Be Made Shortly.

### Candidate, Now in Washington, Likely to Return With Job.

### Merits of Others in Race Conceded by Senator in Explaining Choice.

From the Washington Bureau of The Minneapolis Tribune.

Washington, D. C., Oct. 28.—Announcement of the appointment of A. J. Schunk as postmaster in Minneapolis will be made with a short time, it was indicated today. Senator Thomas D. Schall has reached a decision on the matter and will make the recommendation to Postmaster General Brown. It will be acted upon today. Schunk has the best of it in a political way and his standing before the department as a result of the civil service examination placed him on an equal footing with the other candidates. Senator Schall has given a careful consideration to the situation and believes it would be better to close the matter immediately.

Mr. Schunk is in Washington and this morning was a caller at the office of Senator Schall. He is making no statement concerning the situation but it is understood that he was assured by Senator Schall this morning that his appointment would be satisfactory.

In recommending Mr. Schunk, Senator Schall is fully cognizant of the merits of the other candidates but says a choice has to be made and all three cannot be appointed. It is understood the department objects to naming someone already connected in another capacity with the service, which bars George H. Drake, acting postmaster, who is a postoffice inspector.

So, when Mr. Schunk returns to Minneapolis, he likely will return as postmaster.

## County Committee Majority Backs Caswell

A majority of the members of the Hennepin county Republican committee, meeting in the offices of I. W. Lamb, state representative from the thirty-first district, Monday night unanimously indorsed Alexis Caswell as their choice for Minneapolis postmaster. Fifteen members were present at the caucus. During Monday afternoon, the rural members of the committee, by a majority vote in a caucus, also indorsed Caswell. Members of the committee, who favored Clyde Weaver until he withdrew as a candidate Saturday, gave their support to Caswell.

## Teller Confesses $100,000 Theft

Chicago, Oct. 28.—(By Associated Press.)—On the heels of the discovery of a small discrepancy in his accounts, Frank Culliton, collections teller of the Madison-Kedzie State bank, confessed today that he had embezzled more than $100,000 from the bank since last February and implicated a trio of bookmakers to whom he said he had lost the money betting on horse races.

## Capone Files Plea for Prison Release

Philadelphia, Oct. 28.—(By Associated Press.)—Briefs were filed in the supreme court today in the habeas corpus proceedings seeking the early release of Alphonse "Scarface" Capone, Chicago gang leader, and Frank Cline, his body guard, who are serving a one-year sentence for carrying loaded pistols.

## Air Liner Lost With 5 Aboard

Albuquerque, N. M., Oct. 28.—(By Associated Press.)—An eastbound Western Air Mail passenger liner with two passengers, two pilots and a steward aboard, bound from its western terminus at Alhambra, Calif., to Kansas City, was lost somewhere in eastern Arizona or western New Mexico tonight.

## Woman, Two Men Die in Air Crash

Eugene, Ore., Oct. 28.—(By Associated Press.)—Miss Edyth Rose, Portland aviatrix, and two men fliers were killed late today when their large monoplane crashed near Cottage grove and burned. The men killed were Captain F. O. Mercer and Lieutenant W. B. Clark of Portland.

## Diver Recovers Purse for Thea

New York, Oct. 28.—(By Associated Press.)—A diver today recovered from the bottom of the North river a purse which Thea Rasche, German aviatrix, lost overboard last Wednesday when she sailed for Europe aboard the liner Resolute.

## Snow Flurry, Brisk Winds Hint Winter

### First White Flakes of Season Presage Chilly Days to Come.

### Need of Overcoats Felt as Breath of the North Hits City.

### Lake Superior Gale Holds Up Shipping at Duluth Harbor.

Flurries of white flakes, carried on a brisk wind, came Monday night as a gentle reminder that Christmas is only 57 days in the offing. It was the first snowfall of the year for Minneapolis. Other cities in the state reported snowfall with temperatures hovering about the freezing point.

Loop theatergoers, homeward bent, came to the sharp realization that the balmy days of autumn, with their haze and color, had suddenly terminated. Overcoats and galoshes seemed to become pressing needs. It was not hard to conjure thoughts of snowbanks, frozen radiators, frosted noses and slips on icy pavements. As the snow settled on the roofs of automobiles and stuck, there was left not much of a shadow of a doubt but that winter is imminent.

Solace for some, were happier visions of skiing and skating, not unpopular in this clime, but, as a whole, the general picture of what is to come in the frigid months of December, January and February elicited no great glee. The prospect of white-blanketed football fields brought no small amount of apprehension to the gridiron fans. Then, too, is that matter of Christmas shopping, crowds, scurrying and depleted bank balances.

The snow started to fall in Minneapolis shortly after 9 p. m., when the temperature was down to 34, just a little above freezing. As the flakes struck the pavement they melted, but on lawns and automobile tops they stuck. Late in the evening, the snow stayed on the streets.

The Twin Cities area was swept by a cold wind all Monday and the temperature was held to a maximum of 42 degrees. During most of the afternoon the reading remained at 38 degrees, but when the snow started in the evening the mercury started downward. Colder is forecast for Tuesday.

All shipping was stopped out of Duluth and Superior harbors Monday as a 40-mile wind blew in from Lake Superior.

## City Detective Admits He Got Rent for Hotel

### Policeman on Stand Tells of His Arrangements With Negress.

A Minneapolis detective, Frank Nelson of the south side station, took the witness stand in district court Monday and admitted that he had arranged with Effie Carter, Negress, to operate for him the Midland hotel, 246 Fourth avenue south, and that he called around at the hotel two or three times a week to collect the receipts.

She is being tried on a charge of keeping a house of ill fame at that address, and Detective Nelson was summoned by the defense. Mrs. Carter was arrested when two white girls were found in the hotel. The two girls have since been in custody and have told their stories to the grand jury. The detective denied knowing that the girls were staying there.

**Continued Old Arrangement.**

Detective Nelson said he had arranged with Effie to manage the hotel, on which his father has a lease expiring on November 1, after Ed Ball, a Negro, who had been managing the place for himself with the idea of taking over the lease, had left town. He testified that when he went to look for Ball at the hotel on September 7 he found Ball had gone and had left her in charge.

He said he continued the arrangement, which Ball had with Effie and told her to pay no more rental money to Ball.

"Did you know Effie Carter before you entered into this arrangement with her?" Detective Nelson was asked by Arthur Markve, assistant county attorney, on cross-examination.

**Saw Nothing Wrong.**

"No, I had not been acquainted with her before that day," Nelson replied. "She had been running the place for Ball, and as he had left, I told her to continue the same arrangement with me. The place was in a mess and the rent was several months behind, and my father had told me to get after Ball and have him close the deal to take over the lease, or pay the rent which was due."

"How much money did Effie Carter turn over to you?"

"During the month of September she turned over an average of little more than $3 a day, and during October, up to the time of this trouble,

(Continued on Page 2, Column 5.)

## Pledge Buying Aid After Many Issues Plunge $10 to $60

### Several Leaders Fall Below Record Low Levels Set Thursday—9,212,000 Shares Change Hands—Investment Leaders Announce They Will Purchase Best Grade Stocks—Margin Accounts Wrecked.

New York, Oct. 28.—(By Associated Press.)—A further collapse in stock prices, exceeding in intensity last Thursday's demoralizing session, took place today as Wall street continued to weed out its weakened speculative accounts, and place its house in order after the wild orgy of speculation for the advance which has taken place in the last five years. Net declines in many of the active issues ran from $10 to $60 a share, with the market closing practically at the bottom.

Total sales were 9,212,000 shares, which have been exceeded only by the record-breaking total of 12,894,600 shares last Thursday.

A spokesman for New York's leading bankers, following a meeting late today in the offices of J. P. Morgan & Co., said that important investment groups were preparing to enter the market immediately as large buyers of the best grade stocks.

The bankers attending the conference were William C. Potter, president of the Guaranty Trust; Albert H. Wiggin, president of the Chase National bank; several Morgan partners including Thomas Lamont and George Whitney; George F. Baker, Jr., of the First National bank; Charles E. Mitchell, chairman of the National City bank, and Seward Prosser, president of the Bankers Trust Co.

The meeting began shortly before 5 o'clock and was over before 6. The same group met twice last Thursday in an effort to stem the hurricane of selling which broke over the stock market at that time.

**Optimistic.**

No formal statement was issued after today's conference. The bankers, interviewed as they were leaving the Morgan offices, expressed an optimistic viewpoint. They said they had heard nothing to substantiate reports that certain stock exchange houses were in difficulties. They added that it was possible they would not be the first to hear of such cases if they existed.

It was stated that the purpose of all bankers present at the meeting was to co-operate in providing a steadying influence. One spokesman specifically contradicted the frequent statement that the banks would try to prevent a decline. Their only object, it was emphasized, was to assure that a decline should be orderly and not perpendicular.

"In any kind of a decline, whether in commodities or stocks," said one of the conferees, "if the public becomes panicky, the situation is not good. As far as we can determine the market is now behaving in an orderly fashion.

**Weak Market Predicted.**

"Many well informed persons were predicting last Saturday that we would have a weak market on Monday. They based this belief on the fact that many large investors would need the week-end to find out whether their positions were sound. It was widely forseen that many of these would find that they had to liquidate their holdings further."

He emphasized the fact that there was little of the hysteria present in today's market of the kind that made Thursday's debacle memorable. He said that in certain quarters bankers had heard of preparations by people with ample funds to buy stocks on a large scale, believing them to have reached, in many instances, sound investment levels.

Special pains were taken to dismiss reports widely circulated today that the leading bankers of the city were holding aloof from the stock market. It was stated that the bankers were not speaking much about their attitude but that this did not imply indifference to the stock market outlook.

**Alarming Break.**

In the absence of any adverse news developments over the week-end, and in the face of the optimistic comments on business forthcoming in the closing days of last week from President Hoover and leading industrial and banking executives, Wall street's only explanation of today's decline was that a careful checking up of accounts over the week-end disclosed numerous weak spots, which had been overlooked in the hectic sessions of last week, and that brokers immediately proceeded to clean these up. There undoubtedly was a renewal of "bear" attacks against some of the high priced issues, judging from the demand for stocks in the loan crowd after the close, and also some selling of stock temporarily bought for supporting purposes last week.

While today's decline lacked some of the hysteria, which accompanied last Thursday's break, it was viewed with even greater alarm in some quarters. Wall street generally believed that strong buying support would be supplied over the week-end, and that the low prices reached last Thursday probably would hold, at least for a time.

**Selling Increases.**

Instead, the market started to plunge downward from the opening gong, and closed practically at the bottom. A slight rally occurred around 1 p. m. when reports, which later proved to be unfounded, were circulated around the financial district that Morgan brokers were heavy buyers of stock, and that another conference of bankers was being held in the Morgan offices.

The selling increased in intensity when financial news tickers printed a statement quoting Thomas W. Lamont of the Morgan firm as stating that no statement would be forth-

## How 50 Leading Stocks Fared in New Price Crash

New York, Oct. 28.—(By Associated Press.)—Final prices on 50 leading issues traded today on the New York Stock exchange together with the net change compared with Saturday's closing quotations, are given below. When the market closed the stock ticker was approximately two hours behind in printing transactions.

| Stock. | Close. | Net Change. |
|---|---|---|
| Am. Can | 136 | — 7½ |
| Am. & F. P. | 77½ | —11⅝ |
| Am. Smelting | 90 | — 7⅝ |
| Am. T. & T. | 232 | —34 |
| Anaconda Copper | 92½ | — 9 |
| Andes Copper | 40¾ | — 4¼ |
| Atlantic Refin. | 40⅝ | — 9½ |
| B. & O. | 115 | —13⅝ |
| Barnsdall A. | 22½ | — 5½ |
| Bethlehem Steel | 94⅛ | — 9⅜ |
| Briggs Mfg. | 15⅝ | — 2⅝ |
| Can. Pac. | 203 | — 9 |
| Cerro de Pasco | 77½ | — 5 |
| Chrysler | 40 | — 5 |
| Col. G. & E. | 70⅝ | —23½ |
| Columbia Graph | 26⅝ | — 5½ |
| Com. & Southern | 15 | — 3⅛ |
| Consol. Gas | 97¼ | —20 |
| Erie R. R. | 55 | —11¼ |
| Gen. Elec. | 250 | —47½ |
| Gen. Foods | 48¼ | — 6⅜ |
| Gen. Motors | 47½ | — 6¾ |
| Gold Dust | 40 | —12 |
| Hudson Motors | 60 | — 3 |
| Johns-Manville | 132 | —23½ |
| Kennecott | 70⅝ | — 6⅝ |
| M., K. & T. | 25 | —16 |
| Montgomery Ward | 78½ | —15⅝ |
| Nat. Cash Reg. A. | 75 | —13 |
| Nat. Dairy Prod. | 50¼ | — 9¼ |
| N. Y. Central | 186 | —22⅝ |
| Packard Motor | 18½ | — 3⅛ |
| Pan. Amer. Pet. B. | 58 | — 6⅝ |
| Par. Fam. Lasky | 49¼ | —10⅝ |
| Radio Corp. | 40¼ | —18⅝ |
| Sears Roebuck | 111¼ | —16 |
| Sinclair Con. Oil | 27⅞ | — 3⅝ |
| Stand. Oil N. J. | 54⅝ | — 8 |
| Studebaker | 53 | — 6 |
| Texas Corp. | 53 | — 2¾ |
| Tex. Gulf Sulphur | 55⅝ | — 7⅜ |
| Union Carb. | 84 | —20 |
| Union Pacific | 240 | —16 |
| United Aircraft | 60⅛ | —14¼ |
| United Corp. | 33½ | — 8⅝ |
| U. S. Steel | 186 | —17½ |
| Vanadium | 61 | —10¼ |
| Warner Pictures | 44 | — 6¼ |
| Westing El. & Mfg. | 145 | —34¼ |
| Woolworth | 80 | — 7 |

## St. Paul Schoolboy Struck, Killed by Car

Darting out into the street, Alfred Bonn, Jr., 1878 West Seventh street, St. Paul, was struck by an automobile Monday afternoon while on his way to school and died as a result of his injuries.

The boy had been walking with two companions and suggested that they try to "beat" a fourth boy, riding a bicycle, to the schoolhouse. Alfred ran into the street to begin the race, and the automobile driven by Frank Stirzl, 2325 Benson avenue, St. Paul, struck him and passed over his body.

## Baker Bid Accepted for St. Paul City Hall

The Ramsey board of county commissioners, by a vote of 5 to 2, Monday accepted the $700,000 bid of Morris T. Baker, Minneapolis financier, for the St. Paul courthouse and city hall. It was expected that the city council would take similar action Tuesday morning.

## Red Leader Dies on Hunger Strike

Budapest, Hungary, Oct. 28.—(By Associated Press.)—Alexander Loewe, a Communist, died today from a hunger strike despite artificial feeding. Ten others in Hungarian prisons are continuing their strike which began last week.

# THE MINNEAPOLIS JOURNAL

Associated Press—United Press—New York Times, New York Herald-Tribune and Chicago Tribune Foreign News Services

40 PAGES—HOME EDITION. * * WEATHER Fair tonight and Saturday; rising temperature Saturday. FRIDAY EVENING, NOVEMBER 29, 1929. PRICE TWO CENTS IN MINNEAPOLIS

# BYRD FLIES TO SOUTH POLE; RADIO FADES

## MERCURY TO RISE AFTER DROPPING TO 7 BELOW HERE

### Seven Die From Exposure as Frigid Wave Grips U. S. and Canada

### THANKSGIVING IN CITY COLDEST IN 20 YEARS

### Snowstorms Reported in Many States—Motor Line Delayed

Cold which sent the mercury tumbling to 7 below zero at 7 a.m. today will be dispelled tomorrow, the weather bureau promised.

"Fair tonight and Saturday; rising temperatures Saturday," is the official forecast for Minneapolis.

Severe snowstorms accompanied the cold in many parts of the country. Seven men are reported to have died as a result of the cold and storms. They are:

**Nick Smolinski, 45 years old, Racine, Wis., lost in field and died from exposure.**

**Jacob Schmidt, Winnipeg fisherman, caught in storm while mending nets, died of exposure.**

**John Hanson, Harold Johnson and a man known as "Black Pete," believed lost in Lake Superior storm while making way in small boat from Bayfield, Wis., to Manitou Island.**

**Two fishermen, frozen to death in cabin, Lake Winnipeg.**

The coldest place in the United States today was Thief River Falls, Minn., with 26 degrees below zero. Duluth was the coldest yesterday with 14 below.

Although the city and northwest was not caught as suddenly by the cold as it was a week ago, still

**Garages were unable to fill all the calls for assistance from drivers unable to start their cars, and service rooms were filled with cars being thawed out.**

**The Automobile Club received 80 calls from members for service between 7:30 and 8:30 a.m.**

**Streetcars were packed and slightly delayed by excess passengers, hundreds having abandoned driving or walking to work.**

**Missions were filled with homeless men seeking relief from the cold.**

The city had one of its coldest Thanksgiving days in history yesterday and today's mark was the lowest of the 1929-30 winter season. Thanksgiving started with a temperature of 10 degrees above zero.

Continued on Page 19

## *Morocco Grasshopper Swarm Blots Out Sun*

New York Herald-Tribune-Minneapolis Journal Cable

Paris, Nov. 29.—Swarms of grasshoppers have invaded the south part of western Morocco, the French possession in Northern Africa, and threaten to destroy the crops. The insects are moving in clouds that eclipse the sun. A swarm nine miles long and three miles wide was seen moving north toward Casa Blanca. Airplanes may be used to fight the insects with poison gas.—Copyright 1929.

## *Liquor Violators Get Jail and Fine*

Henry Schreiber, transient, arrested when Detective Frank Rickman's educated toe booted open a suitcase containing 16 pints of moonshine at Washington and Marquette avenues, was given 90 days in the workhouse by Judge Manley L. Fosseen in Municipal Court today. He was convicted of transporting liquor. H. J. Hartfield, convicted of maintaining a nuisance at 2733 Penn avenue N., was fined $100.

## ANOTHER $500,000 ALLOTTED LOCK

### Repairs at Dam to Cost $1,300,000, Washington Dispatches Indicate

That it is going to cost $1,300,000 to rebuild the lock at the government high dam here as a result of collapse of the lock last summer was indicated today when an Associated Press dispatch from Washington announced the war department has alloted $500,000 more for the work. It had previously set aside $500,000.

Bids will be opened in December on the project. The new lock will be deeper and narrower, planned to fit into the nine foot channel which some day will be provided in the upper river. It will be planned so a second lock can be installed later.

Colonel Wildurr Willing, United States army engineer in charge, said the new lock probably will not be completed until September 1, although efforts will be made to rush it. It means there will be no navigation to the Minneapolis terminal during a large part of next season, requiring trucking between the Twin Cities.

The higher appropriation was necessary, Colonel Willing said, because of provision for a wall for the second lock to be built later, and because plans were worked out to make the construction without encroaching on the dam itself.

Mrs. Oscar Hellestad

## Bandits Free Minneapolis Missionary

### Demands of American Consul Win Release of Mrs. Oscar Hellestad, Kidnaped From Home in China

Mrs. Oscar Hellestad, American missionary at Sinyeh, southwest Honan province, China, and a graduate of St. Olaf College, Northfield, Minn., was free today, following her kidnaping yesterday by Chinese bandits.

Word of her release was contained in a cablegram received today by Rev. Helge Hoverstad, secretary of the board of foreign missions of the Norwegian Lutheran Church of America, 425 Fourth street S.

The release of Mrs. Hellestad followed demands by the American consul that the Nationalist government take immediate action.

**Second Missionary Held**

Another American missionary, Rev. Ulrich Kreutzen of Calumet, Mich., was kidnaped a few days ago near Wuchang, according to an Associated Press dispatch. In a letter to authorities, Mr. Kreutzen said he was being held south of Tayeh, Hupeh province, for $5,000 ransom. He said his death was threatened if rescue was attempted.

Mrs. Hellestad has been in missionary work in China the last 20 years. She makes Minneapolis her headquarters whenever she returns to this country on a furlough, which is once every seven years.

**Last Visit Here in 1923**

Her last visit was in 1923 and she returned to China the same year. Mr. Hellestad also is in missionary work in China and formerly was treasurer of the Lutheran United Mission in China.

The field in which Mrs. Hellestad works is in the heart of the bandit-infested section of China and beset with danger at all times, according to Mr. Hoverstad.

"Kidnaping of missionaries in China," Mr. Hoverstad said, "is the work of Chinese soldier-bandits—men who have been discharged from the army and who have turned to banditry for a living. There virtually is no other way for them to make a living, once they are kicked out of the army. They rarely kill their captives and usually when they do, it is accidental, their main purpose for holding them being for ransom."

**Made 300-Mile Trip**

A letter dated October 13 was received recently by Mr. Hoverstad from Mrs. Hellestad in which she told of a trip from Kikungshan to Tenechow, a distance of approximately 300 miles.

The journey, made overland by truck, required about three weeks, Mrs. Hellestad reported. She was accompanied by another American woman, also a missionary.

Mrs. Hellestad was born in Trysil, Norway, in 1876. She came to the United States in 1882, going to Lebanon, S. D., where she attended high school. She taught school in South Dakota from 1897 until 1903, when she entered Augustana Academy at Canton, S. D., then went to St. Olaf. After her graduation from St. Olaf College in 1910, she entered missionary work, going directly to China.

## *Dog Steps on Trigger; Rabbit Hunter Shot*

Bay Shore, L. I., Nov. 29.—William Leach, 45 years old, was seriously wounded while hunting rabbits when his dog pounced on the trigger of a shotgun.

## STATE FARMERS LEAD DISTRICT IN BILLION INCOME

### Federal Reserve Report Shows State Earned $394,982,000 of 1928 Return

### MORTGAGES DECREASE FROM 1925 FIGURES

### Minneapolis Center of Great Farm Industry, Bank Statement Reveals

Estimated cash income from farm production in the ninth federal reserve district, of which Minneapolis is the financial center, aveerages more than $1,000,000,000 annually.

Of that total, Minnesota produces the largest share, reaching $394,983,000 in 1928. Three-fifths of all the farm income in the entire ninth district is obtained from animals and animal products and two fifths from crops.

**Revealed in Report**

These estimates of farm income in the northwest, the most comprehensive ever prepered, were compiled by the Federal Reserve bank of Minneapolis, the federal reserve board's statistical division and the department of agriculture. They were revealed today in the monthly report of the Federal Reserve bank of Minneapolis.

The ninth district includes northern Michigan, Minnesota, Montana, North and South Dakota and northern Wisconsin.

At the same time, the total farm mortgage debt of Minnesota, North and South Dakota and Montana was estimated at $1,255,711,000, as of Jan. 1, 1928. This represents a decrease of about $7,000,000 over Jan. 1, 1925, but an increase of $98,000,000 as compared with the estimate for Jan. 1, 1920.

**Mortgages on Increase**

In that eight-year period, farm mortgage indebtedness increased in Minnesota and South Dakota and decreased in North Dakota and Montana.

In 1928 the total farm income of Minnesota was estimated at $394,983,000, of which $296,876,000 was derived from animals and animal

Continued on Page 30

## *Holiday Burglar Gets Lowry Hill Gems*

It was Thanksgiving for Mrs. C. S. Boyce, 1986 Hennepin avenue, who observed the day with friends, but it was only a better day to loot for a burglar who ransacked her apartment, obtaining jewels valued at more than $200.

Mrs. Boyce returned to find two dresser drawers pulled from their places, the contents strewn on the floor. A trunk in a closet had been opened and crystal and pearl necklaces and a ruby ring taken.

A package of rare old coins was broken open, but left spilled on the floor.

## AMUSE WIFE OR 90 DAYS, BARBER TOLD

### "Take Her to Movies," Judge Advises in Settling Domestic Squabble

Roy Hand, barber at 818 Glenwood avenue, must install a bookkeeping system in his shop. A fair portion of his income he must spend upon his wife, and he must take her to the movies or some other place of entertainment at least once each week. Otherwise he must go to the workhouse for 90 days.

This program or its alternative was arranged for Mr. Hand today by Judge Manley L. Fosseen in Municipal Court.

Mr. and Mrs. Hand told Judge Fosseen today that theirs was a stormy domesticity.

"One day last week he beat and choked me," said Mrs. Hand.

"I never struck her in my life," denied Hand, "although I did choke her a little bit."

"He hasn't bought me a winter coat. I am cold in this one," said she.

"She said she preferred a radio and ran me in debt $180 for one," replied the husband.

## Grocer Oils Revolver to Prepare for Next Bandit Raider After Losing $197

### Isadore Z. Silver, Held Up by Ear-lapped Gunman, Chases Thief Despite Warning

Isadore Z. Silver, Minneapolis grocer and World war veteran, cited for bravery, today was preparing to go into action on a new front—the Bandit front in the Holdup sector.

His new resolve for action came after an earlapped bandit had entered his shop at 831 Third avenue S., as Silver opened the place today, forced him against a wall with a revolver, then escaped with $197 in currency, after a chase for two blocks by Silver and a bread truck driver.

An old army pistol was being carefully cleaned and oiled by Silver today—to provide a warm reception for the next gunman who attempts a holdup at the store.

Silver opened the store at 7:30 a.m., took the money from his pockets and placed it in the cash register.

Then the gunman, heavily dressed and muffled, entered. He asked for snuff. As the proprietor turned to fill the order, the pseudo-customer yanked a gun from his pocket, drove Silver against a wall, took the cash from the register and turned to leave.

He bumped into Alfred Iverson, 804 Fourteenth avenue N., the bread truck driver. The latest arrival also was backed up with the gun, and a command of "Don't move. Don't try to follow me or I'll shoot you."

As the holdup man fled, Silver and Iverson darted from the store in pursuit. They chased the fleeing man for two blocks, but lost him when he disappeared in an alley.

Silver described the gunman as 24 years old, wearing a cap with earlaps pulled low on his face, serving as a mask. He wore a short coat.

ROUTE OF BYRD'S GREAT ADVENTURE TO SOUTH POLE

CAPTAIN A. C. McKINLEY — BERNT BALCHEN — HAROLD JUNE — COMMANDER R. E. BYRD

## Hillbilly "Barons" Whip, Beat and Kill to Enforce Demands, Make Peons of Workers

### HOOVER MAGICIAN—WILL

By WILL ROGERS

Santa Monica, Calif., Nov. 29.

ONE thing we have always heard of our President, Mr. Hoover, that while he may not be a political spellbinder and able to sway a vast audience, but that he could take a small bunch of men, talk to 'em, and explain what he was after, and he could have them coming out of the conference promising to cut off a leg, quit smoking, or give up golf. Well lately he has certainly proven it.

He gathers 'em in, a little gang at a time, and when they come out you would suspect that they had something, for they immediately start announcing the spending of not only millions but billions.

Let's hope they don't sober up till the spending is over. We give medals for men laying down their lives for bravery, but this is more, they are promising to lay down their money. So Hoover is not only a great general, He is a magician. Yours, —Will Rogers.

### State and County Officials, Investigating Murder of War Veteran, Uncover Reign of Lawlessness in Arkansas Mountain Community

Special to The Journal

Kansas City, Nov. 29.—The reign of hillbilly "barons," who rule a community in the mountain fastnesses of northern Arkansas, enforcing their demands with the whip and squirrel rifle, making peons of the poor and illiterate, lashing men, women and children to work on their "estates," even committing murder to enforce their demands, has been revealed in the aftermath of the beating and burning of Connie Franklin, 32 years old, a World war veteran, last March.

The Kansas City Journal Post, in a copyrighted story from a staff correspondent under date of Mountain View, Ark., scene of the Franklin murder, where five men are accused of slaying the war veteran, says:

"There are a few persons in the little Ozark community of St. James, 13 miles from here, who are thanking their Maker for intervention of officials of Stone county and the state which promises to lift them from lives of bondage.

"For in the little community hidden in the hills of northern Arkansas live 'barons' who reap wealth much in the fashion of the European barons of the middle ages. The Ozark men have made peons of the poor and the illiterate, after the

Continued on Page 2

## Chapman Files Report as Foshay Company Receiver

### Firm's Ventures Reach Into Alaska, Canada, Mexico, Honduras and Nicaragua

A story of involved business transactions that extended far into Central America, to the southeast and the southwest, to Alaska and into Canada, was revealed today in the preliminary report of Joseph Chapman, receiver for the Public Utilities Consolidated Corporation, filed today in Federal District Court.

Properties of the corporation, a W. B. Foshay interest now in the hands of the receiver, extend over the North American continent. A substantial group of utilities, directly owned by the Public Utilities Consolidated Corporation, are in good financial condition and well managed, the report said. On the other hand, several properties on which contracts of purchase had not been completed hold an involved status at the present time.

Highlights of the report show that

**Books, furniture and paintings from W. B. Foshay's private office, which he claimed as personal property, have been garnisheed to secure payment of $11,000 he is alleged to owe the W. B. Foshay Company.**

**The W. B. Foshay Company owes approximately $6,000,000 to Public Utilities Consolidated Corporation, but the value of the indebtedness to the utilities group is in doubt.**

**The company owns certain utility properties in the state of Sonora, Mexico, and because a foreign corporation cannot**

Continued on Page 19

TANNER AND NAGURSKI WIN PLACES ON ASSOCIATED PRESS' ALL-CONFERENCE TEAM — Full page of news pictures today on Page 16.

## *Kellogg, Returning, Has Hopes for Peace*

Southampton, Eng., Nov. 29.—(AP)—Prior to sailing on the Leviathan today for New York, Frank B. Kellogg, former secretary of state said: "I have great hopes of world peace and for the five power naval conference to be held in London. Such things, however, cannot be accomplished in a hurry; they must evolve gradually."

## Sino-Russian Negotiations Bring Dispute

### War of Words Over Status of Moves for Settlement Replaces Military Hostilities in Manchuria

By Associated Press

The Russo-Chinese controversy over the Chinese Eastern Railway for the present has shifted from warlike activities in Manchuria, to a verbal bombardment between Moscow and Nanking as to the exact status of negotiations looking toward a settlement.

Out of the confusion of denials, counterdenials, charge and countercharges, the following facts emerged:

Nanking emphatically denied that Manchuria was negotiating independently for a settlement with the soviet government.

The Nationalist foreign office insisted that it had sent a note to Moscow containing proposals for a Sino-Russian joint commission to investigate border conditions and for withdrawal of troops by both sides to at least 30 miles from the frontier.

In event of rejection "the Nationalist government will be prepared to meet soviet moves accordingly."

Moscow insisted that negotiations with Mukden were going forward and charged that Nanking, to thwart these, was seeking intervention by the powers.

## *Man Dies When Hit By Auto in St. Paul*

Daniel Dunn, 65 years old, died today in St. Paul following injuries received when he was hit by an automobile driven by H. P. Arneson of Newport, Minn., at Summit avenue and Fourth street, St. Paul. Dunn received a fractured skull and internal injuries. He was rushed to a hospital by Mr. Arneson.

## Liquor in Home Next Year Means Workhouse for 'Mama' Doll Owner

### And Police May Search House for "Evidence" Any Time in Year, Judge Fosseen Rules

Picture on Page 21

Police department officials were given authority to enter and search the home of Mrs. Pearl Yahr, 2439 Cedar avenue, at any reasonable hour day or night during the next year by Judge Manley L. Fosseen in Municipal Court today.

And if on any visit so much as a thimble full of intoxicating liquor should be found on the premises, Mrs. Yahr may be taken forthwith to the workhouse to begin serving a 90-day sentence.

Mrs. Yahr, at whose home the police found liquor hidden in a baby carriage guarded by a "mamma" doll, was found guilty today of having liquor in her possession although a charge of selling against her was dismissed.

As punishment for having liquor in her possession Judge Fosseen sentenced the woman to 90 days in the workhouse but extended probation for a year on condition that she never in that length of time allow a drop of liquor in her home.

The police were instructed to exercise a strict surveillance to see that the probation terms were kept.

## EXPLORERS SOAR OVER MOUNTAINS 10,000 FEET HIGH

### Commander Sends Messages Telling All Well With Four on Adventure

### FLIGHT WILL COVER 1,600-MILE DISTANCE

### Group Expected Back in Camp in 24 Hours—Many Dangers Along Route

**By RICHARD E. BYRD**

**Aboard Airplane Floyd Bennett, Nov. 29.—(By Radio)—We are flying well. Motors fine. Headed south in vicinity of South Pole. To the New Zealand contingent of our expedition I send best greetings. I want you all to know that you are playing just as important a part as any one of us down here.**

**FLIERS DARE MOUNTAINS ON DASH TO SOUTH POLE**



Little America, Antarctica, Nov. 29.—Commander Richard E. Byrd and three companions in the trimotor airplane Floyd Bennett have reached the vicinity of the south pole on their adventurous 1,600-mile dash to the pole and return, radio reports from the airmen received here today indicate.

Daring a mountain range and a vast plateau 10,000 feet high, soaring over a vast ice cap 2,000 feet thick and marked with gapping crevasses, the intrepid fliers set out on their polar flight at 9:29 p.m. (Minneapolis time) yesterday. They expected to be back at the base here in 24 hours.

**Sends Note 90 Miles From Pole**

The latest report from Commander Byrd, received here at 7 a.m. (Minneapolis time) read: "Flying well. Motors fine. Headed south in vicinity of South Pole."

An hour earlier Commander Byrd had reported the craft was functioning perfectly and that the airmen were 90 miles from the pole.

**Report Progress o Flight**

As the flight progressed, frequent reports o the plane's progress were radioed to Little America.

At 4 p.m. a message from June said: "On trail flying well past 45 mile depot. Motors fine."

At times, messages from the plane faded out and at one time, for an hour, nothing was heard from the adventurers. The plane had to climb over the Queen Maud range of mountains, where the elevation ranges from 10,000 to 12,000 feet. When daylight came there was a fading of signals.

The plane was equipped to photograph the region traversed so that an aerial map of the route to the pole could be recorded.

Aboard the plane were Commander Byrd, Bernt Balchen as pilot, Harold June as radio operator, and Captain Ashley C. McKinley as photographer.

**Byrd Starts Flight**

The huge gray plane slipped over the dappled Barrier today, the sun gleaming on its sides, reflecting in bright flashes from its metal wing

Continued on Page 19

## *Milk Deliveries to Be Made Hour Later*

Beginning Sunday morning, milk in Minneapolis will be delivered in most cases about an hour and a half later than at present. This action has been taken by the Milk Drivers and Dairy Employees Union of Minneapolis, and the Minneapolis Milk Dealers Association, following a general trend throughout the northern states of the country, in an effort to eliminate possibilities of frozen milk, and traffic accidents in the dark hours of early morning, and to make less arduous the work of the milkman during the cold-weather months. When milk is pasteurized, it need not necessarily be delivered as soon as milk which is not pasteurized, officials said.

## 7TH STREET SHOW HOUSE TO REOPEN

### Theater to Feature Vaudeville and Motion Pictures After December 21

Workmen today were redecorating and remodeling the interior of the Seventh Street theater, to be reopened about December 21 for vaudeville and motion pictures, representatives of Radio-Keith-Orpheum announced here today.

The work will cost approximately $90,000, it was said, and will include rebuilding of the stage, a new heating plant, new wiring, refurnishing and recarpeting, installation of modern sound equipment and complete redecoration.

A new Neon canopy will be constructed at the front of the theater on Seventh street. The house has been closed for more than a year.

The Hennepin-Orpheum theater, owned by the same interests, will continue as an exclusive motion picture house, it was said.

# 1930~1939

General News Section

# THE MINNEAPOLIS JOURNAL





WEATHER Cloudy north portion today; cloudy, possibly showers south portion Monday. | SUNDAY, OCTOBER 18, 1931. | 76 PAGES—PRICE 6 CENTS IN MINNEAPOLIS

# Al Capone Convicted, May Get 17-Year Prison Term

## Laugh That Off, Says U. S.

Al Capone grinned in court at the opening of his trial. Last night the jury found him guilty.

Picture of Capone Jury on Page 13

### Gang Chief Found Guilty on Five Counts

**TAX EVASION FOR 5 YEARS PROVEN**

**Jury Returns Verdict in 8½ Hours—Liable to $50,000 Fine**

By United Press

Federal Building, Chicago, Oct. 17.—Al Capone, gangster chieftain, was found guilty tonight of income tax evasion by a jury in United States district court.

The verdict was returned at 11:13 p.m.

Capone was found guilty of five counts — three felony counts and two misdemeanor counts—on the second indictment charging tax evasion from 1925 to 1929.

**May Get 17 Years**

The jury found him not guilty on the first indictment which charged income tax evasion in 1924.

The jury was out eight hours and 20 minutes.

The felony counts carry a maximum penalty of five years in the penitentiary and a fine of $10,000 on each count and the misdemeanor counts a year each in prison and $10,000 fine, making Capone subject to 17 years in prison and a fine of $50,000.

Judge Wilkerson deferred sentencing Capone until 10 a.m., Tuesday, and announced he would hear arguments on a motion for arrest of judgment at that time.

Capone had been rushed from his headquarters to the courtroom. The big gangster walked into the Federal building with Defense Attorney Michael Ahern to the boom of news photographers' flashlights.

He was biting his lower lip as he strode up the corridor leading to the courtroom.

Three of the five counts charged tax evasion and were punishable as felonies. Two of the counts charged failure to make return on the income tax and were misdemeanor counts.

The felony counts cover the years 1925, 1926 and 1927. The misdemeanor counts are for years 1928 and 1929.

**Gangster Squirms**

Capone squirmed in his chair as the verdict was read. His eyes filled with tears as the clerk of court read the verdict.

"I'm not through fighting yet," Capone declared.

"My feeling through the whole trial was that I was up to bat with two strikes on me. But I'm not going to admit defeat until the higher court rules against me.

"I guess a guy can't try to do the right thing without getting into a mess. I was a good smoke screen.

"The newspapers built me up into a myth and gave me a lot of raps. Now I'm paying for them."

**Defense Puzzled**

As his attorneys started legal arguments Capone lounged back as if resigned to a bad situation and craned his neck.

Attorney Fink had not decided just what he wanted to do. Judge Wilkerson prompted him several times but the defense attorney took his time.

Finally Judge Wilkerson asked, "Is there a motion before me?"

"No, do you want me to move for a new trial?" asked Fink.

"Do you want me to pass judgment on this defendant now?" the judge inquired.

"No," said Fink. "I want to ask you to arrest judgment in this case.

Continued on Page 4

## Foshay Case Jurors Clash In Hot Debate

**Lengthy Deliberations Hinted in Plan to Continue With Study**

**GROUP OUT 28 HOURS, ADJOURNS FOR NIGHT**

**Jury Room Crowded With 500 Exhibits—Foshay Waits at Home**

Heated arguments were reported emanating from the jury room in the federal building late Saturday where a jury is deliberating on the case of Wilbur B. Foshay and six associates charged with mail fraud.

Intimations in the federal building that differences of opinion are splitting the jury furnished the first definite evidence that the 11 men and one woman left the courtroom Friday with their decisions undetermined.

**Outcome in Doubt**

The fact that the jurors started their work by meeting only two hours Friday and five hours Saturday led to the belief they thought their task was simple. But the disclosures Saturday night dispelled that idea and left the outcome in great doubt.

That the lone woman juror is having a substantial part in deliberations leading to a verdict was the intimation growing out of corridor reports.

**Will Return This Morning**

That no immediate decision was in prospect was further suggested by the jury's agreement to cease work at 5:10 p.m., not to return until Sunday at 9:30 a.m. When they quit the jury room for the day, the jurors appeared tired.

At the time they quit for the day, they had had the case for 28 hours. Had they been near a verdict it was believed they would have gone on into the evening so that they could have ended their part in this difficult case on which they have devoted full time for seven weeks.

Their agreement to work Sunday may have been influenced by intimations from the court that they should put in more time in deliberations. It was believed they continued informal discussion of the issues during the evening before their usual early retirement.

**Defendants Fail to Appear**

None of the defendants in the case was at the federal building yesterday. Fred Horowitz, special assistant attorney general who had charge of the prosecution, and the postal inspectors who worked on the case, waited until nearly 4 p.m. expecting a verdict.

Foshay, according to friends, spent the day at his home. He had made arrangements to be called in case the jury came to a decision.

The small jury room was crowded to capacity by the more than 500 government exhibits and charts introduced at the trial.

**Believed of Little Aid**

Although all of these books and records were carted into the room when the jury took the case, it was said they would be of little assistance to the jury.

The government had placed colored book marks at the pages which were referred to in government testimony and argument, but before the exhibits were given to the jury, all of these markers were removed.

**Difficult to Find**

Observers said it would be difficult for the jurors to locate any of the various figures used in the case without the aid of these markers.

E. G. Hinebaugh and Mrs. Ann Henderson, bailiffs, have charge of the jury. They sit outside the jury room during deliberations.

The jury will not be allowed to leave the hotel where they are making headquarters at times when they are not in the federal building, until they have reached a verdict, except for meals.

## 3rd Degree on 56 Charged

**Attorney General Turns Evidence Over to District of Columbia Officials**

Washington, Oct. 17 — Charges that Washington police used the third degree on prisoners in 56 cases were turned over to District of Columbia officials today by Attorney General Mitchell.

The charges are made in evidence which the department considers insufficient to justify an attempt to secure indictments.

Indictments were returned yesterday against 18 policemen in other cases investigated by the justice investigators.

District officials said the 56 additional cases will be investigated further by their own investigators to see if action is justified. It is understood that many of the charges of police brutality date back several years, whereas most of the indictments dealt with cases which occurred in recent months, some of them since the Wickersham commission's denunciation of third degree methods by police.

## *Son of Lindbergh Quits Summer Home*

By United Press

North Haven, Me., Oct. 17.—One-year-old Charles A. Lindbergh, Jr., left for the Morrow home at Englewood, N. J., late today after spending the summer at the family's summer residence in this island town. With him when he left for Rockland aboard the yacht Mouette were his grandmother, Mrs. Dwight L. Morrow, widow of the senator; her daughter Elizabeth and three maids.

## *Unarmed Policeman, Off Duty, Downs Bandit Who Confesses to 13 Holdups*

**Patrolman H. J. Wilson of Minneapolis, Convalescing From Illness, Bluffs Man Fleeing From Crash and Chased by St. Paul Gun Squad**

Pictures of captor on Page 2; pictures of wrecked cars on Page 11.

A Minneapolis man, captured by an off-duty motorcycle patrolman while St. Paul police pursued him at a 60-mile-an-hour clip following a filling station holdup in St. Paul yesterday, confessed to 13 holdups when questioned last night, police reported.

The capture followed a smashup in which the bandit's car, a St. Paul police car and a private car were involved. Two St. Paul police were injured when their radio car rolled over three times at Forty-fourth street and Nokomis avenue.

**Carries Only Blackjack**

Patrolman H. J. Wilson, recently convalescent from a pneumonia attack, unarmed save for a police blackjack, made the capture singlehanded while the St. Paul police were extricating themselves from the wreck of their machine.

Arthur Klose, 5440 Second avenue S., turned over to St. Paul police, after he was questioned at headquarters here, confessed 13 holdups in St. Paul, according to Frank Cullen, St. Paul assistant chief. Klose confessed, Cullen said, to being the "early morning bandit" who robbed stores shortly after they opened for business.

Shortly before noon yesterday, a filling station at Smith avenue and West Seventh street was held up by a lone bandit. The attendant was robbed of $3.15 by the bandit who fled down an alley to a car parked nearby.

**Police Pick Up Trail**

Police received the alarm and picked up the trail of the fleeing car at an intercity bridge. The bandit was headed for Minneapolis. Two squad cars were manned by Patrolmen A. J. Curran and Louis Berg in one and Sergeants Edward Allen and Clinton Hackert in the other.

They caught sight of the bandit car as it sped across the bridge. They started in pursuit. Roaring through the streets at 60 miles an hour, the police cars began to gain. They finally swung onto Forty-fourth street, the bandit leading by a scant block.

They approached Nokomis avenue. Wilson not due for duty until 4 p.m. was approaching Forty-fourth street. He saw them roar past an intersection. He joined the chase in his own car.

A motorist, Don Craigie, 3428 Oakland avenue, entered the intersection going south on Nokomis avenue. The bandit car struck,

Continued on Page 4

### *Heir and Actress In Twin Flights; Romance Denied*

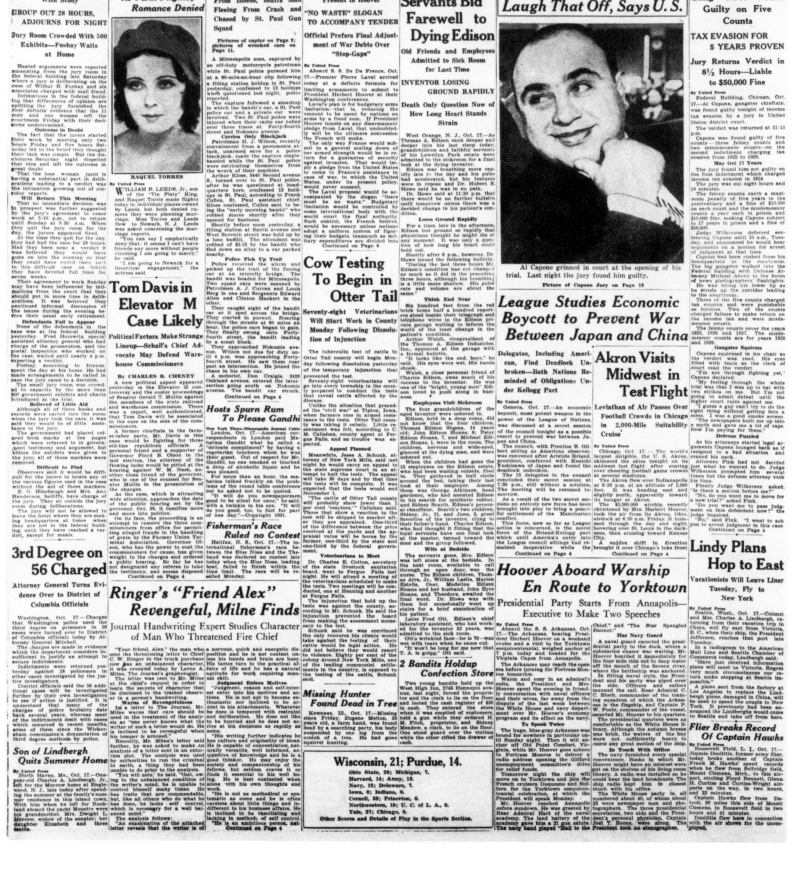

RAQUEL TORRES

By United Press

WILLIAM B. LEEDS, Jr., son of the "Tin Plate" King, and Raquel Torris made flights today in individual planes owned by Leeds, but both denied rumors they were planning marriage. Miss Torres and Leeds flew to Newark, N. J. Leeds was asked concerning the marriage reports.

"You can say I emphatically deny that; it seems I can't have friends any more without people claiming I am going to marry," he said.

"I am going to Newark for a theatrical engagement," the actress said.

## Tom Davis in Elevator M Case Likely

**Political Factors Make Strange Lineup—Schall's Chief Advocate May Defend Warehouse Commissioners**

By CHARLES B. CHENEY

A new political aspect appeared yesterday in the Elevator M controversy and the ouster proceedings of Senator Gerald T. Mullin against the members of the state railroad and warehouse commission. There was a report, well authenticated, that Tom Davis will be associated in the case on the side of the commissioners.

A former chieftain in the farmer-labor party, Mr. Davis in this case would be fighting for three old-line republican officials. A personal friend and a supporter of Governor Floyd B. Olson in the last election, the attorney of the flowing locks would be pitted at the hearing against W. M. Nash, another close friend of the governor, who is one of the counsel for Senator Mullin in the prosecution of the charges.

As the case, which is attracting wide attention, approaches the date of the public hearing set by the governor, Oct. 26, it ramifies more and more into politics.

On its face, the proceeding is an attempt to remove the three commissioners from office for permitting alleged frauds in the handling of grain by the Farmer Union Terminal Association. Governor Olson, who has the power to oust the commissioners for cause, has given weight to the charges and ordered a public hearing. So far he has not designated any referee to take the testimony, and seems disposed

Continued on Page 4

## *Hosts Spurn Rum To Please Gandhi*

New York Times-Minneapolis Journal Cable

London, Oct. 17.—American correspondents in London paid Mahatma Gandhi what he called a "delicate compliment" by having a vegetarian luncheon when he was their guest. Out of respect for Mr. Gandhi, no one smoked or touched a drop of alcoholic liquor and he was pleased.

For more than an hour, the mahatma talked frankly on the problems of the round table conference but he asked not to be quoted.

"It will do you newspapermen good to be silent for once," he said, with a twinkle in his eye. "It will do you good, too, to fast for part of one day."—Copyright 1931.

## *Fisherman's Race Ruled no Contest*

Halifax, N. S., Oct. 17.—The international fisherman's race between the Blue Nose and the Thebaud was declared no contest late today when the Blue Nose, leading boat, failed to finish within the time limit. The race will be re-sailed Monday.

## *Ringer's "Friend Alex" Revengeful, Milne Finds*

**Journal Handwriting Expert Studies Character of Man Who Threatened Fire Chief**

"Your friend, Alex," the man who sent the threatening letter to Chief C. W. Ringer in the truck purchase row has an unbalanced character, it was revealed today by Lorne A. Milne, The Journal's graphologist.

The letter was sent to Mr. Milne at the chief's request in order to learn the secrets of character that lie disclosed to the trained observer in a person's handwriting.

**Warns of Revengefulness**

In a letter to The Journal, Mr. Milne warns that care should be used in the treatment of the analysis as "one never knows what the writer of such a letter would do. He is inclined to be revengeful when his temper is aroused."

Recently, Mr. Milne's letter said further, he was asked to make an analysis of a letter sent in an extortion plot. The analysis was used by authorities to run the criminal to earth, a thing they had been unable to do prior to the analysis.

"You will note,' he said, "that, owing to the unbalanced condition of the writer's mind, he is unable to control himself many times. He has traits that are commendable, but, like all others who do what he has done, he lacks self control, which is necessary for a well balanced mind."

The analysis follows:

"An examination of the attached letter reveals that the writer is of a nervous, quick and energetic disposition and he is not content unless his hands and brain are busy. His tastes turn to the practical affairs of life and he has a natural aptitude for work requiring manual skill.

**Judgment Enters Motives**

"Judgment, reason and self-interest enter into his motives and actions. He is not apt to become enthusiastic nor inclined to be ardent in his attachments. Whatever he does is tempered with restraint and deliberation. He does not like to be hurried and he does not arrive at his decisions as rapidly as some.

"His writing further indicates he has culture and originality of ideas. He is capable of concentration, naturally versatile, well informed, acquisitive of knowledge and he is a good thinker. He may enjoy the society and companionship of his fellows, but seldom craves it or finds it essential to his well being. He is best contented when alone with his own thoughts and work.

"He is not as methodical or systematic as some and he is often careless about little things and indifferent to his business affairs. He is inclined to be vacillating and lacking in methods of self control.

"He is an ambitious person, nat-

Continued on Page 4

## Laval Aims At Budgetary Arms Limit

**French Premier Sailing for U. S. Maps Formula to Present to Hoover**

**"NO WASTE" SLOGAN TO ACCOMPANY TENDER**

**Official Prefers Final Adjustment of War Debts Over "Stop-Gaps"**

By United Press

Aboard S. S. Ile De France, Oct. 17.—Premier Pierre Laval arrived today at a definite formula for limiting armaments to submit to President Herbert Hoover at their Washington conferences.

Laval's plan is for budgetary arms limitation—that is, reducing the amount to be spent by nations on arms by a fixed sum. If President Hoover insists on any disarmament pledge from Laval, that undoubtedly will be the ultimate concession the French will make.

The only way France would submit to a general scaling down of her armed strength would be in return for a guarantee of security against invasion. That would imply a pledge from the United States to come to France's assistance in case of war, to which the United States, under its present policy, would never consent.

The Laval proposal would be accompanied by the slogan "there must be no waste." Budgetary limitation would be controlled by some international body with the world court the final authority. Such control, the French believe, would be necessary unless nations adopt a uniform system of figuring their budgets, inasmuch as military expenditures are divided into

Continued on Page 6

## Cow Testing To Begin in Otter Tail

**Seventy-eight Veterinarians Will Start Work in County Monday Following Dissolution of Injunction**

The tuberculin test of cattle in Otter Tail county will begin Monday following dissolution yesterday of the temporary injunction that prevented the test.

Seventy-eight veterinarians will go into every township in the county prepared to conduct the tests that reveal cattle affected by the disease.

Unlike the situation that preceded the "civil war" at Tipton, Iowa, when farmers rose in armed resistance to the tests, Otter Tail county was taking it calmly. Little resentment was felt, according to C. M. Callahan, county agent at Fergus Falls, and no trouble was expected.

**Appeal Planned**

Meanwhile, Jesse A. Schunk, attorney of New York Mills, said last night he would carry an appeal to the state supreme court in an attempt to halt the tests. The appeal will take 30 days and by that time the tests will be complete. It was expected that the tests would end November 1.

"The cattle of Otter Tail county will probably show fewer than 1 per cent 'reactors,'" Callahan said. Those that show a reaction to the test will be shipped to market after they are appraised. One-third of the difference between the price received at the yards and the appraisal value will be borne by the farmer, one-third by the state and one-third by the federal government.

**Veterinarians to Meet**

Dr. Charles E. Cotton, secretary of the state livestock sanitation board, went to Fergus Falls last night. He will attend a meeting of the veterinarians scheduled to make the tests. Two meetings will be conducted, one at Henning and another at Fergus Falls.

The injunction that held up the tests was against the county, according to Mr. Schunk. He said the injunction prevented the board from making the assessment necessary to the test.

Schunk said he was convinced the only recourse his clients would take against the testing of their cattle would be legal action. He did not believe they would resort to violence. Eighty per cent of the colony around New York Mills, one of the leading communist settlements in the country, is opposed to the testing of the cattle, Schunk said.

## *Missing Hunter Found Dead in Tree*

Kewanee, Ill., Oct. 17.—Missing since Friday, Eugene Melton, 38 years old, a farm hand, was found dead by a searching party, his body suspended by one leg from the crotch of a tree. He had gone squirrel hunting.

## Servants Bid Farewell to Dying Edison

**Old Friends and Employees Admitted to Sick Room for Last Time**

**INVENTOR LOSING GROUND RAPIDLY**

**Death Only Question Now of How Long Heart Stands Strain**

West Orange, N. J., Oct. 17.—As Thomas A. Edison sank deeper and deeper into his last sleep today, grandchildren and faithful servants of his Lewellyn Park estate were admitted to the sickroom for a final look at the dying inventor.

Edison was breathing more rapidly late in the day and his pulse had accelerated, but his features were in repose and Dr. Hubert S. Howe said he was in no pain.

Dr. Howe said at 11:30 p.m. that there would be no further bulletin until tomorrow unless there was a decided change in his patient's condition.

**Loses Ground Rapidly**

For a time, late in the afternoon, Edison lost ground so rapidly that physicians thought he might die at any moment. It was only a question of how long his heart could hold out.

Shortly after 6 p.m., however, Dr Howe issued the following bulletin:

"During the last three hours Mr. Edison's condition has not changed as much as it did in the preceding three hours, although his breathing is a little more shallow. His pulse rate and volume are about the same."

**Think End Near**

Six hundred feet from the red brick home half a hundred reporters stood beside their telegraph and telephone wires in the Edison private garage waiting to inform the world of the least change in the patient's condition.

Arthur Walsh, vicepresident of the Thomas A. Edison Industries, Inc., appeared at the garage with a formal bulletin.

"It looks like the end, boys," he said. His eyes were wet. His hands shook.

Walsh, a close personal friend of Charles Edison, owes much of his success to the inventor. He was one of the "bright, young men" Edison loved to push along in business.

**Employees Visit Sickroom**

The four grandchildren of the aged inventor were ushered in.

Edison, held in a deep coma, did not know that the four children, Thomas Edison Sloane, 14 years old; John Edison Sloane, 9; Peter Edison Sloane, 7, and Michael Edison Sloane, 1, were in the room. The children, nervous and wide-eyed, glanced at the dying man, and were ushered out.

When the children had gone the 15 employees on the Edison estate, who had been waiting outside, filed in. They gathered in half circle around the bed, taking their last look at their employer. Among them was George Atkinson, head gardener, who had assisted Edison in his search for synthetic rubber, and Sidney Scarth, Edison's personal chauffeur. Scarth's two children, Sidney, Jr., 11, and June, 5, great favorites of the inventor, clung to their father's hand. Charles Edison, who had thought it fitting that the loyal servants have one final look at the master, turned toward the door and the group followed.

**Wife at Bedside**

The servants gone, Mrs. Edison was left alone at the bedside. In the next room, available to call through an open door, was the nurse. The Edison children, Thomas Alva, Jr., William Leslie, Marion Estelle, Oser, Madeline Edison Sloane and her husband, John Eyre Sloane, and Theodore, awaited the final word. Dr. Howe was with them but occasionally went up stairs for a brief examination of his patient.

Later Fred Ott, Edison's chief laboratory assistant, who had worked for the inventor 52 years, was admitted to the sick room.

Ott's wrinkled face—he is 70—was wet with tears when he came out.

"It won't be long for me now that T. A. is going," Ott said.

## *2 Bandits Holdup Confection Store*

Two young bandits held up the West High Inn, 2748 Hennepin avenue, last night, forced the proprietor and the clerk to lie on the floor and looted the cash register of $20 in cash. They entered the store when it was emptied of customers, held a gun while they ordered H. M. Fitch, proprietor, and Sidney Meadow, a clerk, to lie on the floor. One stood guard over the victims while the other rifled the drawer of cash.

## Wisconsin, 21; Purdue, 14.

**Ohio State, 20; Michigan, 7.**
**Harvard, 14; Army, 13.**
**Navy, 12; Delaware, 7.**
**Iowa, 0; Indiana, 0.**
**Cornell, 33; Princeton, 0.**
**Northwestern, 19; U. C. of L. A., 0.**
**Yale, 27; Chicago, 0.**

Other Scores and Details of Play in the Sports Section.

## *League Studies Economic Boycott to Prevent War Between Japan and China*

**Delegates, Including American, Find Deadlock Unbroken—Both Nations Reminded of Obligations Under Kellogg Pact**

By United Press

Geneva, Oct. 17.—An economic boycott, most potent weapon in the power of the League of Nations, was discussed at a secret session of the council tonight as a possible resort to prevent war between Japan and China.

The council, with Prentiss B. Gilbert sitting as American observer, was convened after Aristide Briand, president, conferred with Kenichi Yoshizawa of Japan and found the deadlock unbroken.

The 15 delegates to the council concluded their secret session at 7:30 p.m., still without a solution. The meeting will be resumed tomorrow.

As a result of the two secret sessions an entirely new force has been brought into play to bring a peaceful settlement of the Manchurian conflict.

This force, new so far as League action is concerned, is the moral force of the Briand-Kellogg pact which until America's entry into the League council sittings had remained inoperative while the

Continued on Page 4

## Akron Visits Midwest in Test Flight

**Leviathan of Air Passes Over Football Crowds in Chicago in 2,000-Mile Suitability Cruise**

By United Press

Chicago, Oct. 17. — The world's largest dirigible, the U. S. Akron, skimmed the skies tonight on its midwest test flight after soaring over cheering football game crowds at several stadiums.

The Akron flew over Indianapolis at 6:26 p.m. at an altitude of 2,500 feet. It was heading east and slightly north, apparently toward its hangar at Akron.

The $5,500,000 airship, recently christened by Mrs. Herbert Hoover, took the air from its Akron, Ohio, airdock at 6:50 a.m. Friday. It hummed through the day and night, hovering over St. Louis in the darkness, then cruising toward Kansas City.

A sudden shift in direction brought it over Chicago's lake front

Continued on Page 4

## *Hoover Aboard Warship En Route to Yorktown*

**Presidential Party Starts From Annapolis—Executive to Make Two Speeches**

By United Press

Aboard the S. S. Arkansas, Oct. 17.—The Arkansas, bearing President Herbert Hoover on a weekend cruise and a visit to the Yorktown sesquicentennial, weighed anchor at 7 p.m. today and headed for the Virginia Capes from Annapolis.

The Arkansas may reach the open sea before turning for Fortress Monroe tomorrow.

Warm and cozy in an admiral's suite, the President and Mrs. Hoover spent the evening in friendly conversation with naval officers and their wives, far away from the dispute of the last week between the White House and navy department over Mr. Hoover's economy program and its effect on the navy.

**To Speak Twice**

The huge, blue-gray Arkansas was bound for nowhere in particular until Sunday night. Then it will anchor off Old Point Comfort, Virginia, while Mr. Hoover goes ashore to Fortress Monroe to deliver a radio address opening the Gifford unemployment committee's drive for relief funds.

Tomorrow night the ship will move on to Yorktown and join the French cruisers Duquesne and Suffern for the Yorktown sesquicentennial celebration, at which the President will speak Monday.

Mr. Hoover reached Annapolis before sundown. He was greeted by Rear Admiral Hart of the naval academy. The land battery of the academy gave him a 21 gun salute. The navy band played "Hail to the Chief," and "The Star Spangled Banner."

**Has Navy Guard**

A naval guard escorted the presidential party to the dock, where a submarine chaser was waiting. Mr. Hoover boarded it immediately for the four mile ride out to deep water off the mouth of the Severn river, where the battleship was anchored.

In fitting naval style, the President and his party was piped over the side. Officers and sailors manned the rail. Rear Admiral C. C. Bloch, commander of the training squadron of which the Arkansas is the flagship, and Captain P. W. Foote, commander of the vessel, escorted Mr. Hoover to his quarters.

The presidential quarters were as comfortable as the White House library. Although the autumn breeze was brisk, the waters of the bay were not sufficiently heavy to cause any great motion of the ship.

**In Touch With Office**

The navy furnished every special convenience. Books in which Mr. Hoover might have an interest were put on the shelves of his living room library. A radio was installed so he could hear the land broadcasts. The ship radio kept him in closest touch with his office.

The White House party in all numbered about 40, of whom about 25 were newspaper men and photographers. The three presidential secretaries, two aids and the President's personal physician, Captain Joel T. Boone, were along. The President took no stenographer.

## Lindy Plans Hop to East

**Vacationists Will Leave Liner Tuesday, Fly to New York**

By United Press

Seattle, Wash., Oct. 17.—Colonel and Mrs. Charles A. Lindbergh, returning from their vacation trip in China, will fly east from Victoria, B. C., when their ship, the President Jefferson, reaches that port late Tuesday.

In a radiogram to the American Mail Line and Seattle Chamber of Commerce today, Lindbergh said:

"Have just received information plane will meet us Victoria. Regret very much circumstances our return make stopping at Seattle impossible."

A plane sent from the factory at Los Angeles to replace the Lindbergh plane, damaged in China, will be used to speed the couple to New York. It previously had been announced the Lindberghs would come to Seattle and take off from here.

## *Flier Breaks Record Of Captain Hawks*

By United Press

Roosevelt Field, L. I., Oct. 17.—Jimmie Doolittle, former army flier, today broke another of Captain Frank M. Hawks' speed records when he flew from Selfridge field, Mount Clemens, Mich., to this airport, circling Floyd Bennett, Glenn H. Curtiss and Curtiss-Wright airports on the way, in two hours, and 32 minutes.

Captain Hawks flew from Detroit, 20 miles this side of Mount Clemens, to Roosevelt field in two hours and 41 minutes.

Doolittle flew here in connection with the air shows for the unemployed.

**THE WEATHER**
Snow Wednesday; Thursday cloudy with local snows; not much change in temperature. Additional weather on Page 9.

# The Minneapolis Tribune

**MORNING EDITION**
*Three Cents in Minneapolis*

*Sixty-fifth Year. No. 283.* MINNEAPOLIS, MINN., WEDNESDAY, MARCH 2, 1932. • • • *Eighteen Pages*

# LINDBERGHS' BABY KIDNAPED; RANSOM DEMANDED IN NOTE

## COURT REFUSES TO LET HENLEY PASS ON VALUES

### Co-Defendant Fails to Qualify as Accounting and Valuation Expert.

### Fraud Trial Defense Given Setback by Rejection of Testimony.

The defense in the mail fraud trial of W. B. Foshay and H. H. Henley suffered a series of setbacks Tuesday, when Judge Joseph W. Molyneaux sustained the government's objections to various phases of the case concerning which Mr. Henley expected to testify.

The witness could not qualify as an expert on valuations, and was not permitted to give the values of the delivered and undelivered properties of PUCC at the time of receivership. The court ruled that Mr. Henley could give his opinion as to certain values, but that this would not be considered evidence of the values.

Mr. Henley also failed to qualify as an expert accountant and was barred from giving summaries taken from the books of the Foshay company. One of these summaries was intended to show that the Foshay company could at the time of receivership meet all its obligations.

**Calls Writeups Justified.**

After Mr. Henley had admitted that the conclusion to be drawn from the summary was based on a valuation of securities fixed by himself and not the valuation carried on the books, the court held this line of testimony was not admissable.

The government had contended in presenting its case that the majority of the writeups occurred at times when the company anticipated a deficit and were for the purpose of getting funds to prevent deficits.

"Do you believe the writeups were written on the books at a fair value" Josiah Bill, defense attorney, asked Mr. Henley.

"I do," the witness replied.

Mr. Henley admitted a writeup in excess of $511,000 on leaseholds of property occupied by the Foshay building. He said this writeup was based on increasing values of the district and the fact that the leaseholds covered so much property. This appreciation was made to the appraisal by E. J. O'Brien, realtor, he said, and added that there was "an adjustment downward" following this appraisal.

**Explains Dedication Expense.**

The witness also told of some writedowns on the books. He admitted that the dedication expense of the Foshay tower was carried on the books as a deferred asset. It was his contention that the dedication cost was considerably less than the value of publicity obtained. He said it was carried as a deferred asset at the time of receivership, because a plan for writing it off had not been devised at the time. For a similar reason the expense of bringing securities salesmen here to attend the dedication also was carried as a deferred asset, but this was to be written off within a year, he said.

He described the use of rubber stamp initials in the various departments of the Foshay company, and declared that because the rubber stamp imprint of initials of a department head appeared on a document it did not necessarily mean that the department head had seen the document.

The witness said the company's attorneys in Minneapolis had prepared the contract under which PUCC stock was pledged as collateral for a loan from E. C. Warner.

## Volunteers Mobilize to Release Money

Volunteer forces organized to help revive business by bringing idle money out of hiding and putting it to work mobilized in Minneapolis and 35 other Minnesota communities Tuesday. Wednesday 75 more cities and villages in the state will marshall their committees in preparation for the opening of the sale of government baby bonds beginning March 7.

**WELSH DESTROY BRITISH FLAG**

Carnarvon, Wales, March 1.—(AP)—Welsh nationalist students Tuesday hauled down the Union Jack from historic Carnarvon castle and tore it to shreds in the market place. Their action was a reprisal for the government's refusal to accede to the Welsh Nationalist request that the red dragon flag of Wales should fly over the castle St. David's day.

## TRAFFIC VICTIMS

*Death Record in Minneapolis*

1930—Total Killed.....94
1931—Total Killed.....89
1931—To This Date ...17
1932—To This Date....10

**THE DEAD.**

PETER DAVIS, 60, of 927 Sixteenth avenue south, fatally injured when run down at Sixteenth avenue south and Franklin Monday evening by Loren Griswold, 3917 Twenty-seventh avenue south. Died in the General hospital at 10 p. m.

**THE INJURED.**

MRS. DONALD A. WILLIAMS, 3326 Richfield avenue, taken to St. Mary's hospital Tuesday night suffering arm injuries as the result of an automobile accident.

## Japanese Seek Victory Before Peace Parley; Force Chinese Retreat

### 12,000 Fresh Nippon Troops Land on Defenders' Flank.

### Invaders Steadily Advance—Whole Front in Big Battle.

Shanghai, March 2.—(AP)—The Chinese retreat became general at 1:30 p. m. Wednesday when soldiers holding the front lines of Chapei began withdrawing from the vicinity of Liuying road, the official Japanese army report said. Foreign military observers at the boundaries of the international settlement verified the report.

**By Morris J. Harris.**

Shanghai, March 2. — Japanese forces hammered through Chinese defenses on the Kiangwan front Wednesday in a fierce attack that carried them toward Tachang, four miles to the west.

The assault on the Kiangwan lines grew into a thundering duel of heavy artillery over the entire front into Shanghai, jarring the whole city, while reports of a new battle came from Liuho, 20 miles away.

**Chinese Retreat in Night.**

Thousands of newly-landed Japanese troops were fighting their way from Liuho on the south bank of the Yangtze through Chinese fire to join the left flank of their comrades on the Kiangwan line in the drive on Tachang, apparently authentic reports said.

The Japanese, the superiority of their war machines felt more strongly with every onslaught, said they had crushed the Chinese defenses. At 10 a. m. headquarters said their men were within a mile of Tachang, with the right wing closing in from the north in a similar advance.

The Chinese retreated during the night from around Kiangwan, the Japanese said. Observations bore out the claims of Japanese advances.

Toward Chapei, however, the Japanese line bent eastward as the Chinese continued to hold that devastated battle ground of the conflicts beginning more than a month ago.

**12,000 Troops at Liuho.**

Six Japanese airplanes bombed the Shanghai-Nanking railway near Kunshan, sometimes called Quinsan, 35 miles west of Shanghai, Wednesday morning, carrying out a Japanese threat to wreck the line if the Chinese continued to transport troops into Shanghai. It was understood the line was severed under the rain of great explosives.

The Japanese fliers also bombed

(Continued on Page 2, Column 2.)

### Tokio Accepts League Shanghai Conference Plan.

### Believes Decisive Triumph Must Precede Pact.

**By Glenn Babb.**
Copyright, 1932, by Associated Press.

Tokio, March 2.—(AP)—Acceptance of the League of Nations proposal for an international conference at Shanghai to end the conflict with China was announced by the Japanese government, but truce negotiations at Shanghai made no further progress, the foreign office said Wednesday.

Vice Admiral Sir Howard Kelly, commander of the British Asiatic fleet, presented Japanese negotiators with armistice terms Monday. Dispatches said the Chinese previously had assured Admiral Kelly that the terms were acceptable to them.

**Want Decisive Victory.**

The Japanese found them unacceptable, however, and presented counter proposals. The Chinese had not yet replied to the Japanese terms, the foreign office indicated, and there the matter rested while the Japanese forces hurled increased strength against the Chinese lines.

Various government spokesmen made it clear that Japan believes a decisive victory in the field will be necessary to pave the way for the conference.

The league proposal, made by Joseph Paul-Boncour, French delegate to the league council at Geneva, called for negotiations in which the United States, Great Britain, France and Italy would participate, as well as Japan and China.

It was understood the Japanese government interpreted the suggestion as meaning that the conference probably would cover a long period and would seek a permanent solution of the Shanghai problem.

**Tells of Negotiations.**

In official quarters it was said that a decisive Japanese victory was expected to result in bringing the fighting to an early close, thereby producing the conditions under which the proposed conference would be held.

Government officials said that negotiations now being conducted at Shanghai to arrange a cessation of hostilities appeared to be making little progress.

The Paul-Boncour proposal was accepted by Admiral Minea Osumi and Lieutenant General Sodao Araki, ministers of navy and war, at a

(Continued on Page 2, Column 5.)

## NEWS INDEX



## BEVANS' COACH FOUND; BARES SLAYING CLUES

### Empty Shells of Same Type Used in Slaying Discovered in Machine.

### Blood-Stained Car Abandoned at Thirty-First and Cedar Avenue.

Police early Wednesday found the automobile in which Mrs. Jack Bevans rode away from a party at 827 Third avenue south with her husband a few hours before her body was found in a gravel pit on Superior boulevard near Thomas avenue.

The car was picked up on Thirty-first street between Cedar and Longfellow avenues. Residents said it had been parked there since Monday night.

In the car were found two empty shells of the same caliber as the bullets which dealt death to Mrs. Bevans. There was a hat, brown and white, the one she had on when she started her last ride. There were a pair of brown gloves and a blood-soaked blanket, half covering a pool of blood on the seat of the coach. In the back of the machine were scattered the remains of the candy bar, parts of which were found on Mrs. Bevans' body.

**Hunt Spurred for Bevans.**

The car was parked west on Thirty-first street, headed toward the railroad yards two blocks away. Police first noticed it Monday night, but a casual inspection revealed nothing amiss. Early Wednesday, traversing the same spot, they found the car still there, locked. They broke in the door and found the blood-spattered clothes and the empty shells.

Finding of the machine spurred the hunt for the missing husband, wanted for questioning in the case.

Search of the Twin Cities and of haunts in Wisconsin which he had been known to frequent revealed no trace of him Tuesday. The finding of the car was the first tangible clue.

It was established Tuesday, however, that there had been a violent quarrel between Bevans and his wife early Monday in the rooming house she conducted at 827 Third avenue south.

Questioning of three women who had attended a party there, elicited the information that Mr. and Mrs. Bevans had been engaged in a verbal encounter during most of Sunday night and early Monday. The witnesses said the two were still quarreling when they left the place.

**Reported in St. Paul.**

Bevans, it was said, had a taxicab called at about 4 a. m. When it had not arrived 10 minutes later, he followed his wife outside and got into the coach she was driving. The two drove off.

Bevans was believed to have spent Monday night somewhere in St. Paul. Captain Frank Brunskill of the north side station received a report that the man sought was seen on the north side early in the evening. When detectives reached the place named they were told Bevans hod driven to St. Paul.

The former co-publisher of the Twin City Reporter, weekly suppressed by the so-called Minnesota "gag" law, was said to have had little money of his own during the past

(Continued on Page 2, Column 3.)

## HOOVER TO FILE IN OHIO PRIMARY

### Formal Consent Will Be First Step in Campaign for Renomination.

Washington, March 1.—(AP)—President Hoover's first formal bid for renomination will be made in the next few days.

He will consent to the use of his name in the Ohio preferential primary May 10 as soon as he receives formal notification of the selection of one additional candidate for alternate delegate from that state.

When this notice is given, Mr. Hoover will send appropriate letters to all election districts in the state where the law requires the consent of the candidate for whom the delegates are running.

Former Senator Joseph I. France of Maryland, the only candidate in the field against Mr. Hoover, already has entered the Ohio primary, but the President's supporters are confident of winning the state's 55 votes.

Postmaster General Brown has been in Ohio lining up the delegation for the President. He returned to Washington Tuesday and reported on the situation to administration leaders at the capitol, including Senators Watson of Indiana and Moses of New Hampshire.

Brown's appearance on the floor with Senator Fess of Ohio, chairman of the Republican national committee, and former Senator William M. Butler of Massachusetts, chairman of the committee under President Coolidge, started a round of speculation, but the principals said it was just a coincidence.

There were no outstanding preconvention developments on the Democratic side here Tuesday.

Alfred E. Smith's consent to the use of his name in the Massachusetts primary April 26, came as no surprise.

### BRITISH CONTINUE RUSH TO SELL ART, GOLD, AID NATION

London, March 1.—(AP)—Thousands of Englishmen today were tossing goldsmith's masterpieces of centuries past into the melting pot as sacrifices on the altar of patriotism and profit.

There was no esimate as to the amount of gold that has come out of ancestral jewel boxes, but one authority estimated that Englishmen owned a grand total of 1,000,000,000 pounds of gold in all forms including gold sovereigns.

The seller of gold now realizes a profit of 7 shillings on enough gold to make a sovereign, and the whole country appears to have been seized with the selling "fever." The announcement that a slight reduction in the price of the gold sovereign might come and that the price of fine gold had dropped only served to increase the rush.

## REJECTS MILK LAW CHANGES

### Council Group Turns Down Ordinance Provisions in First Test Vote.

In the first test vote before the committee on ordinances and legislation since the controversy started, the proposed new milk ordinance Monday afternoon failed to win aldermanic approval.

By a vote of 2 to 2 the council group rejected motions by Alderman Irwin Hudson to adopt the two chief features of the ordinance as follows:

That all pasteurized milk sold in the city shall be pasteurized within the Minneapolis city limits except that pasteurized by milk producers on their own farms.

That the health department shall inspect the producing farms.

Joining with Alderman Hudson in voting aye was Alderman Ole A. Pearson of the ninth ward. Opposing were Aldermen Frank Cullen and Maxil D. Robb, committee chairman. Alderman Frank Gustafson, fifth member of the committee, was absent.

**Harrington Explains Plan.**

Dr. F. E. Harrington, health commissioner, told the committee that his own ordinance, drafted about a year ago and referred to the council committee on health and hospitals, would permit no pasteurization whatever outside the city and would also exclude all raw milk except the certified. The measure now before the committee would admit all raw milk scoring 85 points or more on the basis of 100.

Dr. Harrington pointed out that of some 16,000,000 gallons of milk sold annually in the city only 3 per cent is raw, that of all the pasteurized milk sold here only six-tenths of one per cent is pasteurized outside.

"Well," remarked Chairman Robb, "it's that very six-tenths of 1 per cent that can give a monopoly."

"We're not concerned with monopoly," was Dr. Harrington's reply. "We're concerned with the health of this city."

**Hopes for Agreement.**

The committee finally voted to adjourn to 2 p. m. Friday and to invite to the Friday session representatives of the state dairy and food department and of opposing factions from the milk organizations.

The councilmen expressed hope that this conference may be able to reach some compromise satisfactory to all as basis for committee action and final council decision.

Objection to the proposed milk ordinance was withdrawn Tuesday by the Robbinsdale Business Men's association. The group sent a communication to Charles C. Swanson, city clerk. It said that "we withdraw our objection to the proposed ordinance regulating the pasteurization of milk provided that an amendment be made to the proposed ordinance so as to include and to allow pasteurization of milk sold in the city of Minneapolis, in municipalities contiguous to Minneapolis."

## Dr. W. B. Riley Honored on 35th Year at Church

### 600 Attend Testimonial Dinner—Religious Leaders Praise Pastor.

Praised as the "dean of all Minnesota Baptist ministers in point of time," Dr. W. B. Riley, pastor of First Baptist church, was the guest of honor Tuesday night at a dinner observing the thirty-fifth anniversary of his pastorate in the churh.

More than 600 members of the church, friends and representatives of other Baptist churches of the city attended the dinner in Dayton's tea rooms.

Greetings were extended to the veteran pastor by representatives of the Minnesota Baptist convention, the Twin City Baptist union and the Northwest Bible school which Dr. Riley aided in developing. Pastors of a number of Baptist churches gave short addresses of greeting, while speakers included Mayor Anderson, George M. Palmer, president of the Baptist convention; Mrs. Frank Ashcroft, who has had the longest membership in Dr. Riley's pastorate; Frank Nelson, former president of Minnesota college; the Rev. Gust F. Johnson, pastor of Swedish Tabernacle; the Rev. C. G.

(Continued on Page 2, Column 6.)

## SNOW BLANKETS N.W. AS STORMS USHER IN MARCH

### Winter Returns—Low Temperatures Expected to Continue Today.

### Flood Drives Families From Homes Near Luverne and in Sioux Falls.

March roared into the 1932 setting in its best lion role Tuesday. Virtually every section of the northwest felt the sting of wind-driven sleet that turned into snow and wiped out all traces of February's mild weather finish.

Temperatures generally were near the freezing point. The snow that whipped across the Dakotas, Minnesota and into Wisconsin will continue into Wednesday, according to the weather bureau forecast. Temperatures are expected to stay down to Tuesday's levels.

Starting as sleet, the snow thickened as the mercury dropped, and by evening the flakes, which lay from one to six inches deep, were piling into drifts as the wind swept across open places.

In the lakes district of Minneapolis, snow plows were kept busy clearing tracks, and throughout the city motormen had their difficulties with switches filed with freezing slush.

**Minnesotans Flee Floods.**

In southwestern Minnesota, and in adjoining areas of South Dakota and Iowa, floods resulting from the rapid thaws of late February added to the discomfiture caused by the weather.

Near Luverne, Minn., several families were forced to flee their homes, and some farmers lost livestock when the Rock river overflowed its banks. Charges of dynamite were used to blast the ice floes that dammed the river.

Acres of farm lands were flooded in the vicinity of Sioux Falls, S. D., and a number of houses were partly inundated when the Big Sioux river bed was unable to handle the sudden rush of water.

A similar situation prevailed at Sioux City, Iowa, where the Floyd river was out of its banks. Several families were rescued by police boats.

At Grand Forks N. D., a north wind drove the mercury down to 28 as the ground was covered with snow. The temperature continued to drop Tuesday night. At Fargo a light fall of snow was whipped by a strong wind. More snow was forecast for Wednesday.

**Mercury Drops 12 Degrees.**

The snow that started early in the day, had piled to a dept of five inches early Tuesday night in Minneapolis, and more was falling. Temperatures dropped 12 degrees, from a maximum of 36 early in the morning, by nightfall.

February weather in Minneapolis showed a range from cold to warm, records at the local weather bureau show. The earlier part of the month was cold, there being seven days in which the mercury dropped below zero. Final days were warm, the temperature climbing to 57 degrees Sunday. The mean temperature for the month was 19.4 degrees, compared with the average February mean of 16.1. But it was short of the February, 1931, mean of 32 degrees. Since 1924, with the exception of 1929, the February mean has been above the normal.

## HOUSE TO VOTE ON LIQUOR BILL

### Wets Obtain 145 Signatures to Force Record Action by Membership.

Washington, March 1.—(AP) — A house vote on considering a bill to give control of liquor to the states was assured Tuesday.

The wet bloc obtained 145 signatures upon a petition to withdraw from the judiciary committee a resolution to bring this about. As a result a vote will be taken automatically on March 14 on the question whether the measure will be placed upon the calendar of the house for its consideration.

In previous congresses 218 petitioners, one more than a majority, have been necessary to discharge a committee from consideration of a bill. At the outset of this session the number was reduced to 145.

Immediately after a sufficient number had signed, Representatives Linthicum of Maryland and Beck of Pennsylvania, leaders of the Democratic and Republican wet organizations, respectively, issued a statement saying the vote March 14 will show "the American people exactly how every representative stands on the vital question." They added:

"We are naturally gratified with the speedy success of our movement to bring the matter of the repeal of the eighteenth amendment before the house of representatives for submission to the people.... We believe that a new chapter was opened today in the history of this controversy and that the success of our efforts is assured."

They called their wet groups to meet Wednesday to consider a bill to increase federal revenues by $500,000,000 through an excise tax on beer and other malted beverages of non-intoxicating alcoholic content. If necessary to force action on it, they

(Continued on Page 4, Column 5.)

## Child Stolen From Crib in Nursery at New Jersey Home

*THE FIRST PICTURE OF KIDNAPED BABY*

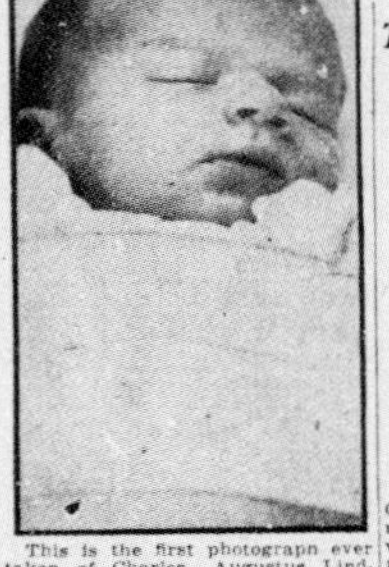

This is the first photograph ever taken of Charles Augustus Lindbergh, Jr. It was eagerly awaited by the entire nation. The baby was a few weeks old at the time.

### 20-Month-Old Boy Is Put to Sleep at 7:30 and Bed Is Empty at 10—Anne Expecting Another Child.

### Two Men in Green Sedan Who Asked Way to Lindbergh Home in Hills Are Hunted—All Roads Barred.

Newark, N. J., March 2.—(AP)—Police at Hillside reported the finding of a blue sedan early today at route 29 and Field Place. The rear seat yielded an odor resembling chloroform. While the spot where it was found is not on the direct route from Princeton, police expressed the belief the car might have been the one used by the kidnapers of the Lindbergh baby.

Copyright, 1932, by Associated Press.

Hopewell, N. J., March 2.—(AP)—Charles Augustus Lindbergh, Jr., 20-months-old son of the flying colonel, was kidnaped Tuesday night from his nursery in the Lindbergh country home near here.

Police said he apparently was spirited away in an automobile, which they have not yet identified. Two men in a dark green sedan stopped at least two persons prior to the kidnaping and asked directions to the isolated Lindbergh home.

Possibility that a woman figured in the kidnaping developed, police said, when a minute examination of the grounds around the home revealed feminine footprints, along with those of a man.

Within an hour after Colonel Lindbergh himself telephoned the first alarm, police squad cars blockaded every Jersey road for miles. They had orders to stop any suspicious persons or cars.

The child, clad in a blue sleeping robe, was put to bed at the usual hour, 7:30 p. m. At about 10 p. m. his nurse peered into the nursery. The crib was empty.

The nursery, filled with every possible device for childish joy, is in the right-hand corner of the second floor of the big house.

**Ransom Note Found.**

The window near his crib, which was open when his nurse went into the room, is 30 feet from the ground.

On the window sill, police said, a note was found and, though they would not divulge its contents, it was indicated that it contained a demand for ransom.

A three-piece ladder was found a hundred feet from the house, as if it had been dropped in a hurry, and police believe this was used to reach the window.

The first newspaperman to reach the home was an Associated Press reporter, who ran a mile over muddy, rut-cut roads to reach a phone to send the first direct news from the residence.

Colonel Lindbergh, bare-headed as usual, was pacing the grounds, while troopers and detectives went over the place with flashlights, seeking clues.

Mrs. Lindbergh, who telephoned the news to her mother, Mrs. Dwight W. Morrow, at the Morrow home in Englewood, N. J., was inside the house, but was shielded carefully from newspapermen. A close friend of Mrs. Lindbergh said she was expecting another child within three months.

The house glowed with lights, a butler appeared at the door, obviously distraught, but he, like his employers, refused to make a statement.

**Mud Delays Police.**

The police, dashing pell-mell to the place, were delayed by the mud-soaked roads. It was an hour before they reached the house, which is perched amidst the Sourland hills, on the second highest eminence in New Jersey.

At the Morrow home in Englewood, it was said Mrs. Morrow had not decided whether to leave at once to be with her daughter.

The first police news of the crime came in the following blunt teletype message:

"Colonel Lindbergh's baby kidnaped from Lindbergh home at Hopewell, between 7:30 and 10 p. m. Boy, 19 months (his age actually is 20 months), dressed in sleeping suit. Search all cars."

For the next hour it was virtually impossible to get telephonic communication with the Lindberghs. One call brought the response—"No one has time to talk!"—and finally the chief operator said she had orders to refer all inquiries to the police, who had no announcement to make.

As news of the kidnaping filtered through the friendly countryside—all Lindbergh's neighbors are farmers—lights began to glow in the hills and many came to the place to volunteer aid in the search.

The Lindbergh baby, probably the most famous infant in the world, is described as a golden-haired replica of his famous father. He is chubby, with blue eyes and curly hair.

He was of about normal stature for his age, had begun to toddle about and was learning to talk. Members of the family stressed the resemblance to his father.

**Lindy Makes Search.**

The window of his nursery looks out on the private road which links the estate with the outside world.

Near the house is a private landing field, and behind it are dense woods, though open country is at the front and on both sides.

Searching the ground about a mile

## Lindberghs Kept Close Guard on Son From First

### 'World's' Most Famous Baby Taken to Country to Escape Publicity.

New York, March 1.—(UP)—The birth of Charles Augustus Lindbergh, Jr., at the Dwight Morrow home in Englewood, N. J., at 3:15 p. m., June 22, 1930, attracted world-wide attention similar to that paid the flying exploits of his famous father.

For weeks newspaper reporters and photographers had waited outside the Morrow estate for the announcement of the birth of an heir to the nation's best known young couple. The announcement came quietly through "a friend of the family," a few hours after the actual birth.

The child was born at the home of the maternal grandparents, where Lindbergh and Miss Anne Morrow had been married May 27, 1929. His birthday is the same as that of his mother.

Last summer the baby was taken to the Maine estate of the late Senator Dwight Morrow while Mr. and Mrs. Lindbergh went on an airplane trip to the orient, flying across the wilds of Canada to Japan and China. While the Lindberghs were in China, Senator Morrow died suddenly at his Englewood home.

**Baby Carefully Guarded.**

The baby had been most carefully guarded. The first pictures taken of the child were made by Lindbergh himself and then distributed to newspapers and press associations. He would not permit other pictures to be taken.

One object in taking him to the Morrow summer home on an island, five miles out of North Haven, Maine, was to keep him away from the infantile paralysis epidemic sweeping New York and environs. Colonel and Mrs. Lindbergh were frank in expressing aversion to publicity for the child. They said they were trying to rear him in a normal, healthy manner. Publicity, they said, would injure him when he grew older.

The baby has never been taken for a ride in an airplane. In the summer of 1930, Lindbergh was reported considering taking the child in an airplane to the Morrow summer home, but physicians decided against this. The roar of the motor might impair the baby's hearing, they said.

The description, "most famous baby in the world," was fittingly applied to Charles, Jr., at the time of his birth. World-wide interest had centered for three years on Lindbergh—through his first exploit in making a non-stop flight from New York to Paris, his subsequent flights and romance with Anne Spencer Morrow in Mexico City, where her father was United States ambassador, their marriage, secretive honeymoon and flights together after that.

**Thousands of Gifts.**

Thousands of messages from all parts of the world poured in to the Morrow home at Englewood, when the birth was announced. Gifts by the hundreds, from the high and the humble, were sent to the son of the most famous aviator.

So many articles of clothing, toys and unclassified gifts were received from well-wishers that the colonel's own collection of gifts and trophies was seriously rivaled. There were manufactured articles and home-made gifts — commonplace and exotic, from next-door neighbors and from foreign lands.

The naming of the baby was reported to have caused as much commotion within the family circle as the anticipated birth did outside. Colonel Lindbergh wanted to name his son after his father-in-law, but Mrs. Lindbergh demurred and finally won her point.

THE WEATHER
Fair Friday and probably Saturday.
Additional weather on page 20.

# The Minneapolis Tribune

MORNING EDITION
Three Cents in Minneapolis

Sixty-fifth Year. No. 355. MINNEAPOLIS, MINN., FRIDAY, MAY 13, 1932. Thirty Pages

# Lindberghs' Baby Killed by Blows; Body, Long Dead, Found in Woods

## Aerial Map Shows Where Body Was Found

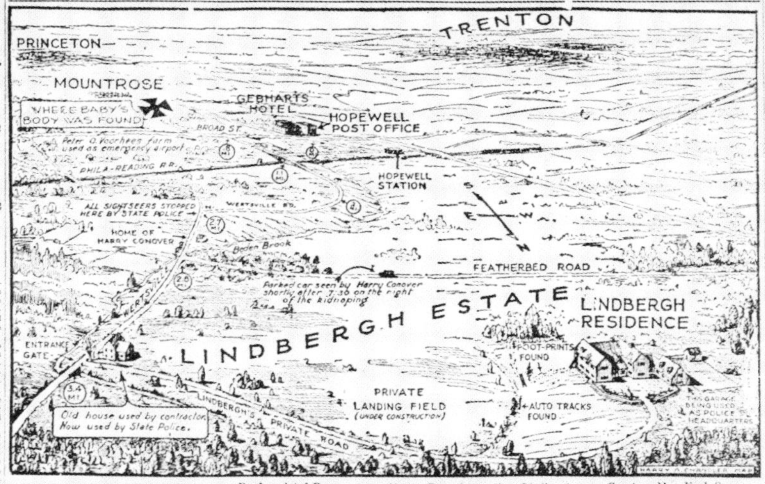


Courtesy New York Sun.

By Associated Press.

Mount Rose, near which the body of Colonel Charles A. Lindbergh's son was found, is a hamlet of half a dozen houses and a general store, on the road connecting Princeton with Hopewell and about a mile and a half from the latter.

The village of Hopewell lies between the Lindbergh home and the scene where the body was found. The dirt road leading from the house crosses the paved highway, which is also the main street of Hopewell, within the limits of the town but about eight blocks from the center of habitation. This road leads into Mount Rose, but it is virtually untraveled.

Coming from the Lindbergh home, the kidnapers could have gone into Mount Rose along that road, turning there onto the asphalt road leading on into Princeton, about seven miles away. The only other manner in which they could have reached Mount Rose from the Lindbergh home, without taking the circuitous route through Stousburg and doubling on their tracks for the greater part of a mile, was to pass through Hopewell.

The road to Princeton turns off Hopewell's main thoroughfare one block from the postoffice and center of the town. Along that road, within the city limits, the kidnapers would have had to pass several blocks of residences.

Mount Rose lies near the top of a long slopping hill, from which, Colonel Lindbergh's home, about four miles away, is visible along parts of the route, which is asphalt. At that point, fairly thick woods come within 10 to 15 yards of the road. The woods in this vicinity were not combed at the time that Colonel Lindbergh and the New Jersey state police searched through the underbrush immediately after the kidnaping.

## Believed Slain Soon After He Was Kidnaped

### Discovery Made by Truckmen Near Lonely Road Five Miles From Colonel's Home---Clothing Aids in Identification by Betty, Nurse of Victim.

### Police Promise Strenuous Efforts to Capture Culprits---Mother Bearing Up Well---Father Is Hurrying Home From Futile Hunt Outside of New Jersey.

By Francis A. Jamieson.
Copyright, 1932, by Associated Press.

Hopewell, N. J., May 12.—The stolen baby son of Colonel Charles A. Lindbergh was found dead Thursday in the stubbly Sourland hills of New Jersey.

The child had been murdered.

Blows on the head, inflicted probably on the same March night he was kidnaped from the home of his famous father, caused the infant's death.

The body, lying face down in a depression and partly covered by leaves and wind-blown debris, was discovered by a Negro truckman in a patch of woods less than five miles from the Lindbergh estate.

The baby had been struck once on the top of the head on the left side, and once on the right below the ear, either blow so violently delivered that it would have caused instant death.

It lay within 75 feet of where linemen had strung special circuits to carry on world-wide communications in the long, unsuccessful effort to get back the curly-haired infant.

So badly was the body decomposed it had to be identified by pieces of clothing, bone structures and teeth, and it was impossible to give the police the slightest clue as to exactly what kind of instrument had brought death.

To the Trenton establishment of a country physician came Betty Gow, nursemaid to the child and the last person to see him alive on the night he was stolen 72 days ago, to forge the final link in the identification. She made her identification both from the appearance of the body and the fragments of the child's garments.

The tragic news found the child's mother, in the words of an intimate friend, bearing up with her "usual equanimity." His flying father was absent from Hopewell, presumably pursuing a private search to which he has devoted all his energies.

He was communicated with, however, and hastened toward Hopewell from an undisclosed place.

The state's law enforcement agencies sprang to the task of trapping the kidnapers with renewed vigor, Colonel H. Norman Schwarzkopf, state police head, announcing that he already had a gang under suspicion, and Governor A. Harry Moore contributing the statement that "every attempt should be made now to find the murderers of the Lindbergh baby."

**Prosecutor Called.**

Significance was attached to a hurried telephone call which summoned County Prosecutor Irwin E. Marshall to the Lindbergh home for a conference late Thursday night.

The skull bore a hole the size of a 25-cent piece above the forehead. An attempt had been made to bury the body. A coroner said death was due to a compound fracture of the skull, caused by two tremendous blows.

The hair of the dead child tallied with the shade of the blond, curly-haired Lindbergh heir, 20 months old when he was stolen.

An undershirt and flannel band furnished a more positive link. Similar articles of clothing from the Lindbergh baby's wardrobe were brought to the spot from the home. They matched closely enough to convince the authorities they had found the body of the famous baby for whom hundreds of thousands of policemen in every part of the globe had searched.

Then as police worked feverishly to be sure of their identification, telephones rang in the state house at Trenton, N. J.

Reporters were summoned to the Lindbergh estate for an important announcement.

The telephone rang again. It was Colonel H. Norman Schwarzkopf, state police head, who has been the field marshal of the official investigation, calling his superior, Governor A. Harry Moore.

"Colonel Schwarzkopf tells me the Lindbergh baby has been found dead," the governor informed the Associated Press correspondent.

**Body Partly Concealed.**

Three hours before (about 3:15 p. m.) a truck bearing four men had stopped on a steep grade between Hopewell and the hamlet of Mount Rose. The vehicle halted opposite a wood separated from the road by a small ditch. William Allen, a Negro, went into the woods and saw the body.

"The body was pretty well concealed by leaves, dirt and bush," the subsequent formal statement by Schwarzkopf explained. "Going under the bush he (Allen) lowered his head and as he raised a branch he saw a skeleton on the ground."

"It was in a bad state of decomposition," was the way Schwarzkopf summarized the gruesome details of the condition of the child.

Physicians later theorized the compound fracture was caused either by a terrific blow on the head with a blunt instrument or from the effects

## Charles Augustus Lindbergh, Jr.

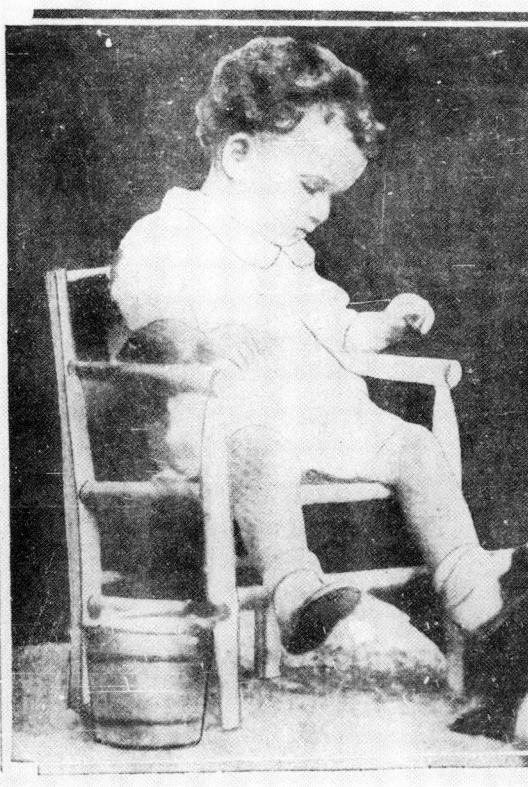

## JAFSIE, CURTIS FACING QUIZ BY JERSEY POLICE

### Schwarzkopf Announces Men Will Be Turned Over to Prosecuting Authorities.

### Hopewell Authorities Assembling Information for Grand Jury Action.

Hopewell, N. J., May 12.—(AP)—Colonel Schwarzkopf early today stated that Dr. John F. Condon and John Hughes Curtis, Lindbergh intermediaries, "are being questioned now and will be questioned later in the day by the prosecutor. They are not under arrest."

Hopewell, N. J., May 13.—(AP)—An automobile believed to have been occupied by Colonel Charles A. Lindbergh, John Hughes Curtis and Edwin B. Bruce of Elmira, N. Y., a friend of Mr. Curtis's, entered the flier's estate early Friday.

*Lindbergh news Pages 10-11.*

Hopewell, N. J., May 13.—(AP)—Colonel H. Norman Schwarzkopf announced early Friday that John F. (Jafsie) Condon, of New York, and John Hughes Curtis, of Norfolk, Va., "will be at these headquarters in a few minutes for questioning in connection with this case and they will be turned over by the police authorities at this point to the prosecuting authorities."

Colonel Schwarzkopf apparently was acting in conjunction with county prosecuting authorities in an effort to assemble all pertinent information regarding the kidnaping which might be made the basis for grand jury action.

It was pointed out early in the case that prosecution of the kidnapers, when and if they were apprehended, might be facilitated by obtaining John Doe indictments in advance.

Several hours before Colonel Schwarzkopf spoke regarding Condon and Curtis it was known that he had summoned the county prosecutor to his headquarters at the Lindbergh home.

The intermediaries in the case had been permitted the widest latitude by officials.

Thus it was regarded likely that the intermediaries might have in their possession certain confidential information which was automatically made privileged by the finding of the baby's body.

Condon, retired educator, and Curtis figured in the case as inter-

(Continued on Page 11, Column 6.)

## MRS. LINDBERGH BEARS UP WELL

### News of Baby's Death Is Received With Her 'Usual Equanimity.'

Hopewell, N. J., May 12.—(AP)—An intimate friend who visited Mrs. Charles A. Lindbergh late Thursday described her as bearing up with her "usual equanimity," upon hearing her son had been found dead.

On the day following the kidnaping Mrs. Lindbergh quietly and quickly prepared and made public a diet which was widely circulated in the hope it might be followed by the kidnapers of her son.

Mrs. Lindbergh, who is expecting a child within several months, has had her mother, Mrs. Dwight Morrow, as her constant companion.

## GIANT FEDERAL FUND PLANNED FOR JOB RELIEF

### $1,500,000,000 to Be Made Available for Loans to States and for Construction.

### Increasing of Reconstruction Corporation Finance Power Would Be Means.

Washington, May 12.—(AP)—Administration and Democratic leaders Thursday night took counsel with their forces upon a gigantic compromise relief plan designed to aid the unemployed and speed up the wheels of construction work.

The proposal, suddenly brought to the fore again as congress works toward adjournment next month, involves doubling the borrowing power of the Reconstruction Finance corporation to a total of $3,000,000,000, the additional $1,500,000,000 to be loaned to states for helping the needy and promoting public and private construction.

President Hoover went over the scheme Thursday night with Republican members of the senate banking committee which direct the new legislation necessary. They were called to the White House for the late consultation.

**Democrats Confer.**

Senator Robinson of Arkansas, the Democratic leader, meanwhile put the various relief propositions up to members of the Democratic steering and policy committees.

No conclusions were reached at the Democratic parley on Capitol hill pending further conferences Friday.

An early solution looking toward a federal unemployment and construction program is in prospect.

"It is proposed," said President Hoover in an announcement after Thursday night's conference, "to use the instrumentality of the Reconstruction Finance corporation, which has a nation-wide organization, by authorizing the corporation either to underwrite or make loans for income producing and self-sustaining enterprises which will increase employment whether undertaken by public bodies or by private enterprises."

Aside from the $300,000,000 loans to states, the remainder of the additional fund would be used to finance this public and private construction.

**Ample Margin Provided.**

"It is not proposed," said the President, "to issue government bonds. It is proposed to provide the necessary funds as they are required by the sale of securities of the Reconstruction Finance corporation and its total borrowing powers to be increased up to $3,000,000,000.

"It is hoped that this further process of speeding up the economic machine will not involve any such sum. But in view of the early adjournment of congress it is desirable to provide an ample margin."

There was every indication of harmony at the Republican conference at the White House, although Senator Couzens of Michigan, who was the first to leave, remarked, "I do my own thinking, that's all."

Copyright, 1932, by Associated Press.

## Farm Board's Wheat Sale Policy Unchanged

Washington, May 12.—(AP)—Chairman Stone of the farm board Thursday denied midwestern reports that the board had been unable to refinance its stabilization wheat holdings and would liquidate them immediately. "Those reports are absolutely untrue," the chairman said. "All loans on the stabilization wheat were renewed by banks this spring. The board has repeatedly said that it would follow rigidly its policy of selling 5,000,000 bushels monthly."

## Permit Is Issued for $124,460 School

A permit for erection of a school building for the Holy Rosary Catholic church at 2426-34 Eighteenth avenue south at a cost of $124,460 was issued Thursday by Building Inspector Louis Clousing. The structure is to be of stone, brick and reinforced concrete. McGough Bros. of St. Paul are the contractors. The structure is to be completed by September 1, 1932.

## TRAFFIC VICTIMS

*Death Record in Minneapolis*

1930—Total Killed.....94
1931—Total Killed.....89
1931—To This Date....41
1932—To This Date....19

**THE DEAD.**

WILLIAM FRIETAG, 28, of Warren, Ohio, died in Midway hospital, St. Paul, from injuries he suffered May 5, at Grand and Fairview avenues, St. Paul. His death is the nineteenth traffic fatality of the year in St. Paul, and the first one in May there.

**THE INJURED.**

HARRY SKILBECK, 40, of 3045 Cedar avenue, injured Thursday when the automobile he was driving collided with a machine driven by G. C. Murray, 3132 Clinton avenue. Taken to St. Mary's hospital. The accident occurred at Twenty-ninth street and Clinton avenue.

MR. AND MRS. J. R. CRANDALL, 2314 Twenty-third avenue south, injured in the same accident.

## N. W. DROUTH WORK FINISHED

### Rains Assure N. D. and Montana Districts of Crops—Red Cross Relief Ends.

Those drouth stricken counties up in northwestern North Dakota and across the border in Montana are coming back.

After a year and a half spent in distributing aid to thousands of families impoverished by continued drouth, the American Red Cross Thursday declared its work complete in the area. Through their own efforts and assistance of bountiful rains this spring, residents of the area are no longer dependent upon outside aid.

Decision by the Red Cross to close its relief offices in North Dakota and Montana was made public in Minneapolis by Howard Bonham of St. Louis, publicity director. Mr. Bonham passed through the city on his way to Chicago.

"We are closing our offices operated since the fall of 1930 in northwestern North Dakota and northeastern Montana," Mr. Bonham said. "The final food orders, garden seeds,

(Continued on Page 11, Column 4.)

## Tragedy Just 5 Years After St. Louis Hopoff

St. Louis, May 12.—(AP)—Revelation of the death of his child came to Colonel Charles A. Lindbergh exactly five years after he hopped off here in the Spirit of St. Louis for New York to make the ocean flight that won him fame. It was May 12, 1927, that he left St. Louis after having flown from San Diego, Calif., the previous day.

**JORDAN JUDGE APPOINTED.**

Theodore F. Pekarna was appointed special municipal judge at Jordan Thursday by Governor Olson. Mr. Pekarna is a nephew of Lieutenant Governor Henry Arens of Jordan.

## GAYETY 'DARK' AFTER SUNDAY

### Theater Seeks to Withdraw License Application and Will Close Doors.

Faced with apparently insurmountable opposition in the city council as aftermath of the victory by the committee of One Thousand before the council license committee, the Gayety theater management Thursday asked permission to withdraw its license application and retrieve its $100 license fee.

Announcement of this was made by Harry D. Hirsch, manager, after formally submitting the withdrawal request to Russell S. Ackerman, superintendent of licenses, weights and measures. The theater, he said, will close Sunday night.

This action brought a statement from Mrs. Robbins Gilman, secretary of the Committee of One Thousand and head of the organization group which appeared against the Gayety license before the license committee Wednesday.

"I'm sorry to see this happen," she said, referring to the move to withdraw the license. "I should like to see the matter tried out on its merits. This appears to be a means of just slipping out from under and gives the theater opportunity to come in again next fall when nobody's looking."

Asked whether she or the Committee of One Thousand would urge the city council to determine the issue on its merits, she said that an effort would be made toward this end.

General sentiment among members of the city council Thursday night, on the eve of the council session, was that Hirsch will be permitted to withdraw his application for license without opposition, unless some definite move is launched on the council floor for a formal denial of the license itself.

## City Life Saving Car to Be Kept on Guard

Because "something might happen in its absence," the fire department life-saving squad car will not be sent to St. Paul for an exhibition before the Minnesota State Medical association next week. The council fire committee so decided Thursday. However, if the physicians are willing to come here and witness an exhibition the fire department will be glad to demonstrate.

## Strange As It Seems--

*A downtown office building is often clearly reflected in Lake Calhoun, more than two miles away.*

* * *

(Submitted by Hall Thompson, 3306 Fifteenth avenue south, and given honorary award in The Minneapolis Tribune "Strange As It Seems" contest.)

## NEWS INDEX

7 A. M. ELECTION EXTRA

# The Minneapolis Tribune

WEATHER
U. S. Bureau Forecast
Rain or snow, colder Wednesday; Thursday mostly cloudy. Additional weather on page 24.

MORNING EDITION
Three Cents in Minneapolis

Sixty-sixth Year. No. 169. MINNEAPOLIS, MINN., WEDNESDAY, NOVEMBER 9, 1932. • • • Twenty-six Pages

# Democrats Win Congress Control; F.-L. Leading House Race in State; Roosevelt, Olson Leads Mounting

## MINNEAPOLIS VOTE PILED UP FOR GOVERNOR

**City, Usually G.O.P. Stronghold, Indicates Strong Lead for Incumbent.**

**Regan Far Behind—Victor's Strength Uniform Over Whole State.**

By Orlin Folwick.

Minnesota turned again to Governor Olson for the direction of its state affairs Tuesday, granting him a second term in the governorship by a decisive majority of votes.

While the extent of his lead was still undetermined at 5 a. m., Wednesday, he had outdistanced his two opponents, Earle Brown, Republican, and John E. Regan, Democrat, to the point where he was in no danger off being overtaken, his lead being 25,000. Regan ran a poor third, falling far short of the votes his backers had anticipated.

When 528 precincts out of 3,716 in the state had reported, the vote on the governorship stood as follows:

Olson, 100,922.
Brown, 75,648.
Regan, 24,724.

Of these, Minneapolis gave the three candidates the following vote in 181 precincts out of 354:

Olson, 56,141.
Brown, 45,090.
Regan, 8,548.

Governor Olson, while winning re-election, failed to amass the total he did in

(Continued on Page 8, Column 4.)

## 'First Lady' Won't Give Statement

***Says She Can't Say Anything Until Franklin Does.***

By Lorena Hickok.

New York, Nov. 9.—(AP)—Mrs. Franklin D. Roosevelt left the Biltmore hotel early Wednesday, declining to make any statement concerning her husband's election until he himself had done so.

The President-elect had gone home a few minutes before without having yet publicly acknowledged his election.

"I'm sorry," Mrs. Roosevelt said, "but you can see that I can't say anything until Franklin does."

"You've been pretty confident right along, haven't you?" she was asked.

"Why—I honestly don't think I've thought about it a great deal," Mrs. Roosevelt replied. She was silent for a moment and then continued:

"It was just one of those things—if it was going to be, it was going to be, and if it was not going to be, it wasn't. And that was that."

"Aren't you pleased?" some one asked.

"If it's true, of course I shall be pleased," she answered. Then she added:

"You can't really look at an election this year quite that way, can you?" "It's a very serious thing, a terrible responsibility. It's not something you can just be pleased about."

Mrs. Roosevelt revealed in the interview that she will continue to teach in the private school of which she is part owner "at least until March 1."

The wife of the President-elect was just Mrs. Roosevelt as earlier Tuesday she taught the class in modern history at the Todhunter school for girls.

The subject was the dawn of the nationalistic spirit in the world and the teacher led the discussion. One of the questions she asked was "What is patriotism?"

It was not the first time during the years she has been teaching that Mrs. Roosevelt had led a class discussing this subject, and she knew what to expect.

"They'll tell me," she said, "that patriotism means 'doing something for your country.' Then I'll ask 'Well, what does a patriot do for his country?' Someone else will say 'Patriotism means hanging up the flag on Memorial day.' And so the discussion will go on."

## Latest Returns

**3,716 precincts in the state; 406 precincts in county; 354 precincts in Minneapolis; 52 precincts Hennepin. xDenotes present holder of office. Principal party designations: R. (Republican), D. (Democrat), S. (Socialist), F-L (Farmer-Labor), C. (Communist), I. (Industrialist). Presidential, state and congressional tickets are elected under party designation. The county and legislative and associate justices of the state supreme court are without party designation. Where not otherwise designated, one candidate is elected.**

### Minneapolis

FOR PRESIDENT.
(226 precincts reported.)

| | |
|---|---|
| *Hoover-Curtis (R) | 51,906 |
| Roosevelt-Garner (D) | 65,096 |
| Foster-Ford (C) | 541 |
| Reynolds-Aiken (I) | 107 |
| Thomas-Maurer (S) | 3,014 |
| Coxey-Reiter (F-L) | 213 |

FOR GOVERNOR.
(207 precincts reported.)

| | |
|---|---|
| Earle Brown (R) | 45,090 |
| *Floyd B. Olson (F-L) | 56,141 |
| John E. Regan (D) | 8,584 |
| Wm. Schneiderman (C) | 314 |
| John P. Johnson (I) | 81 |

FOR CONGRESSMEN-AT-LARGE.
(9 precincts reported.)
Nine to be elected.)

| | |
|---|---|
| *August H. Andresen (R) | 1,420 |
| J. A. A. Burnquist (R) | 1,433 |
| Ray P. Chase (R) | 1,469 |
| Theodore Christianson (R) | 1,50[illegible] |
| N. J. Holmberg (R) | 1,272 |
| *Harold Knutson (R) | 1,415 |
| * W. I. Nolan (R) | 1,406 |
| *W. A. Pittenger (R) | 1,454 |
| *Conrad G. Selvig (R) | 1,206 |
| Henry Arens (F-L) | 1,223 |
| C. F. Gaarenstroom (F-L) | 958 |
| Magnus Johnson (F-L) | 1,392 |
| *Paul J. Kvale (F-L) | 1,414 |
| Ernest Lundeen (F-L) | 1,219 |
| J. L. Peterson (F-L) | 1,030 |
| F. H. Shoemaker (F-L) | 1,105 |
| Henry G. Teigan (F-L) | 989 |
| A. C. Townley (F-L) | 859 |
| Robert C. Bell (D) | 750 |
| James R. Bennett (D) | 638 |
| John Bowe (D) | 619 |
| Silas M. Bryan (D) | 901 |
| Donald A. Chapman (D) | 679 |
| John P. Coughlin (D) | 706 |
| Einar Hoidale (D) | 1,321 |
| Emil E. Holmes (D) | 66[illegible] |
| Hugh T. Kennedy (D) | 595 |
| J. W. Anderson (C) | 31 |
| M. Karson (C) | 19 |
| Fred LeQuier (C) | 15 |
| Christgau | 57 |

LIEUTENANT GOVERNOR.
(142 precincts reported.)

| | |
|---|---|
| T. O. Streissguth (R) | 28,166 |
| K. K. Solberg (F-L) | 29,495 |
| Ruth H. Carpenter (D) | 9,596 |
| John Lindman (C) | 331 |

SECRETARY OF STATE.
(132 Precincts reported.)

| | |
|---|---|
| xMike Holm (R) | 34,782 |
| John T. Lyons (F-L) | 20,916 |
| Jerry A. Harri (D) | 9,096 |
| Robert Turner (C) | 118 |

STATE TREASURER.
(112 Precincts reported.)

| | |
|---|---|
| xJulius A. Schmahl (R) | 24,261 |
| A. H. Kleffman (F-L) | 18,436 |
| Timothy J. Doyle (D) | 10,601 |

ATTORNEY GENERAL.
(98 precincts reported.)

| | |
|---|---|
| xHenry N. Benson (R) | 20,502 |
| Harry H. Peterson (F-L) | 17,554 |
| Ray G. Moonan (D) | 8,857 |
| Tom Foley (C) | 580 |

R. R. & WAREHOUSE COMM'R.
(84 precincts reported.)

| | |
|---|---|
| Oscar A. Swenson (R) | 16,381 |
| Knud Wefald (F-L) | 14,099 |
| Mathew N. Kraus (D) | 8,052 |
| Emil Nygard (C) | 386 |

ASSOC. JUSTICE SUPREME COURT.
(39 precincts reported.)
Three to be elected.

| | |
|---|---|
| xHomer B. Dibell | 9,983 |
| Edward J. Lee | 7,343 |
| xCharles Loring | 11,222 |
| xI. M. Olsen | 8,542 |
| Wm. H. Vanderburgh | 5,819 |

CONSTITUTIONAL AMENDMENT
CONSTITUTIONAL AMENDMENTS.

No. 1—40 precincts reported. (State taxation of incomes and national banks). Yes, 6,375; No, 9,122.

No. 2—37 precincts reported. (Permitting state to tax motor vehicles of public utilities corporations now exempt because of gross earnings tax law). Yes, 9,140; No, 4,119.

No. 3—34 precincts reported. (Permitting state to exchange some of its lands for federal lands to further reforestation program). Yes, 7,262; No, 4,134.

No. 4—34 precincts reported. (Permitting local governments to tax the state on farm lands now held by the state through rural credits mortgage foreclosures) Yes, 6,880; No, 4,680.

JUDGE OF DISTRICT COURT.
(40 precincts reported.)
Four to be elected.

| | |
|---|---|
| Lloyd Ahlstrom | 3,032 |
| *Levi M. Hall | 10,913 |
| Thomas E. Latimer | 8,660 |
| E. Luther Melin | 4,143 |
| *E. A. Montgomery | 9,459 |
| John A. Nordin | 6,216 |
| *Lars O. Rue | 8,083 |
| *Arthur W. Selover | 7,944 |

JUDGE OF PROBATE.
(48 precincts reported.)

| | |
|---|---|
| *Manley L. Fosseen | 10,575 |
| George R. Smith | 10,277 |

COUNTY COMMISSIONERS.

First Dist. (25 precincts reported out of 54.) *Arthur R. Ferrin, 7,584; Olaf A. Pearson, 4,898.

Third Dist. (7 precincts reported out of 137.) *W. W. Heffelfinger, 1,279; Arthur E. Johnson, 553.

Fifth Dist. ( .. precincts reported out of 55.) Kenneth M. Bollum ..; *Herbert A. Morse ..

STATE REPRESENTATIVE IN LEGISLATURE.
Two to be elected.

28th Dist. (14 precincts reported out of 18.) Myrtle Cain, 3,273; Raymond J. Julkowski, 3,235; *Joseph A. Kozlak, 3,667; *John J. McNulty, 3,838.

29th Dist. (3 precincts reported out of 42.) Gust E. Johnson, 604; *Henry A. Johnson, 623; *Burt L. Kingsley, 558; Roy W. Wier, 614.

30th Dist. (6 precincts reported out of 29.) Mrs. Philip Erickson, 525; Paige, 1,637; *Donald O. Wright, 1,663.

31st Dist. (1 precinct reported out of 29.) Howard H. Beck, 157; *Will S. Collins, 203; *Dewey W. Johnson, 357; William McGrath, 163.

32nd Dist. (2 precincts reported out of 49.) Harry S. Alm, 161; *Otto D. Nellermoe, 305; Roy E. Rendahl, 239; *S. A. Stockwell, 335.

33rd Dist. (3 precincts reported out of 96.) Arnon N. Benson, 396; *Walter H. Campbell, 408; Owen Cunningham, 487; *W. I. Norton, 395.

34th Dist. (2 precincts reported out of 43.) *L. E. Brophey, 470; Edwin L. MacLean, 136; Fred J. Pierce, 292; *John A. Weeks, 356.

35th Dist. (6 precincts reported out of 58.) W. F. Bennett, 987; *Harry A. Montgomery, 1,004; Harry L. Scott, 665; *Emil Youngdahl, 1,424.

CITY CHARTER AMENDMENT.
(77 precincts reported out of 354.)

Giving board of estimate and taxation additional powers to borrow money for current expectations. Yes, 22,459; No, 14,852.

### Minnesota

FOR PRESIDENT.
(647 precincts reported.)

| | |
|---|---|
| *Hoover-Curtis (R) | 102,342 |
| Roosevelt-Garner (D) | 149,293 |
| Foster-Ford (C) | — |
| Reynolds-Aiken (I) | — |
| Thomas-Maurer (S) | 3,551 |
| Coxey-Reiter (F-L) | — |

FOR GOVERNOR.
(438 precincts reported.)

| | |
|---|---|
| Earle Brown (R) | 66,472 |
| *Floyd B. Olson (F-L) | 88,352 |
| John E. Regan (D) | 20,658 |
| Wm. Schneiderman (C) | — |
| John P. Johnson (I) | — |

FOR CONGRESSMEN-AT-LARGE.
( 63 precincts reported.)
(Nine to be elected.)

| | |
|---|---|
| *August H. Andresen (R) | 4,227 |
| J. A. A. Burnquist (R) | 6,304 |
| Ray P. Chase (R) | 3,851 |
| Theodore Christianson (R) | 3,914 |
| N. J. Holmberg (R) | 3,331 |
| *Harold Knutson (R) | 3,881 |
| *W. I. Nolan (R) | 3,656 |
| *W. A. Pittenger (R) | 3,696 |
| *Conrad G. Selvig (R) | 3,253 |
| Henry Arens (F-L) | 4,377 |
| C. F. Gaarenstroom (F-L) | 3,331 |
| Magnus Johnson (F-L) | 4,803 |
| *Paul J. Kvale (F-L) | 4,580 |
| Ernest Lundeen (F-L) | 4,081 |
| J. L. Peterson (F-L) | 3,659 |
| F. H. Shoemaker (F-L) | 3,879 |
| Henry G. Teigan (F-L) | 3,398 |
| A. C. Townley (F-L) | 3,.261 |
| Robert C. Bell (D) | 3,178 |
| James R. Bennett (D) | 2,805 |
| John Bowe (D) | 2,480 |
| Silas M. Bryan (D) | 3,003 |
| Donald A. Chapman (D) | 2,654 |
| John P. Coughlin (D) | 2,768 |
| Einar Hoidale (D) | 4,589 |
| Emil E. Holmes (D) | 2,720 |
| Hugh T. Kennedy (D) | 2,677 |
| J. W. Anderson (C) | 66 |
| M. Karson (C) | 28 |
| Fred LeQuier (C) | 31 |
| Victor Christgau (sticker) | 372 |

LIEUTENANT GOVERNOR.
(184 precincts reported.)

| | |
|---|---|
| T. O. Streissgüth (R) | 29,766 |
| K. K. Solberg (F-L) | 31,546 |
| Ruth H. Carpenter (D) | 10,607 |
| John Lindman (C) | 359 |

SECRETARY OF STATE.
(174 precincts reported.)

| | |
|---|---|
| xMike Holm (R) | 37,250 |
| John T. Lyons (F-L) | 22,531 |
| Jerry A. Harri (D) | 9,903 |
| Robert Turner (C) | 138 |

STATE TREASURER.
(152 precincts reported.)

| | |
|---|---|
| xJulius A. Schmahl (R) | 22,264 |
| A. H. Kleffman (F-L) | 20,164 |
| Timothy J. Doyle (D) | 11,707 |

ATTORNEY GENERAL.
(643 precincts reported.)

| | |
|---|---|
| xHenry N. Benson (R) | 22,302 |
| Harry H. Peterson (F-L) | 19,435 |
| Ray G. Moonan (D) | 9,966 |
| Tom Foley (C) | 599 |

R. R. & WAREHOUSE COMM'R.
(126 precincts reported.)

| | |
|---|---|
| Oscar A. Swenson (R) | 18,143 |
| Knud Wefald (F-L) | 15,834 |
| Mathew N. Kraus (D) | 9,108 |
| Emil Nygard (C) | 417 |

ASSOCIATE JUSTICE SUPREME COURT.
(75 precincts reported.)
Three to be elected.

| | |
|---|---|
| Homer B. Dibell | 8,691 |
| Edward J. Lee | 8,691 |
| Charles Loring | 12,750 |
| O. M. Olsen | 10,181 |
| Wm. H. Vanderburgh | 6,830 |

## Three Brooklyn Boys Get Roosevelt Name

New York, Nov. 9.—(AP)—Three baby boys were born at the Menorah maternity hospital in Brooklyn early Wednesday and their parents, thinking about names, all got the same idea. So the babies are Franklin Delano Mayblum, Franklin Delano Ragin and Franklin Delano Finkelstein.

## Youngman Concedes Election of Ely

Boston, Nov. 8.—(AP)—Lieutenant Governor William S. Youngman, Republican candidate for governor, late Tuesday night conceded his defeat and sent his congratulations to his Democratic opponent, Governor Joseph B. Ely.

MAINE'S FIRST REPORT.

Portland, Maine, Nov. 8.—(AP)—The little Somerset county town of Mayfield, first to report in Tuesday's presidential election in Maine, gave four votes to Hoover, none to Roosevelt.

## STATE LEAVES G.O.P. COLUMN FOR FIRST TIME

**Roosevelt Holding 50,000 Majority With 100,000 Indicated.**

**North and South Dakota Also Going Democratic Along With Montana.**

Minnesota's first at-large race for nine congressional seats headed into a mad scramble early Wednesday as first returns from Tuesday's election were tabulated.

Except that the men whose names were best known throughout the state had found favor, as was the case in the primaries, no definite trends were indicated by the few returns. Representatives of each of the three major parties were among the nine leaders, and the others were running not far behind.

The returns included a few from Minneapolis, and from Ramsey county, and a small number of precincts from other parts of the state.

Congressman Victor Christgau, "sticker" candidate, polled a good vote in the few precincts reporting from Mower county, his home county, but got only a negligible amount elsewhere.

Because of the heavy vote and the interest in the presidential and gubernatorial campaigns, election officials did not begin tabulating congressional ballots until late.

Scattering returns from over the state gave Farmer-Labor candidates the edge in the fight for the nine seats. Magnus Johnson, former United States senator, led the list, with Einar Hoidale, Democrat and candidate for the senate against Thomas D. Schall two years ago, in second place.

John Paul Kvale, present Farmer-Labor congressman, was in third place, and Henry Arens, Farmer-Labor lieutenant governor, was fourth. Other Farmer-Laborites among the first ten were Ernest Lundeen, former congressman, and Francis Shoemaker.

Republicans among the leaders were Congressman Harold Knutson of St. Cloud, Theodore Christianson, former governor, August Andresen, present congressman, and Ray P. Chase, former state auditor. Hoidale was the only Democrat near the top of the list.

### STATE DEMOCRATIC ON PRESIDENT

For theh first time in its political history Tuesday, Minneapolis swung its 11 electoral votes to a Democratic presidential candidate, joining the nation-wide landslide that elected Franklin D. Roosevelt president of the United States.

And like most of its sister states, Minnesota gave the Democratic candidate an overwhelming lead. That lead neared 50,000 with less than a sixth of the state's 3,716 precincts reporting and gave indication that it would mount to better than 100,000 when the votes are finally in.

**Carries City by 15,000.**

Nor was the Roosevelt majority confined to a rural "protest vote," which many of the Republican leaders discerned in the offing as the campaign went down the home stretch. The Democratic nominee carried Minneapolis by better than 15,000, winning in all the wards but the eighth and thirteenth. He carried St. Paul by nearly two to one and he was leading in the scattered outstate returns by nearly a two to one margin. It was anticipated that the later returns, from the more isolated rural sections, would increase the lead rather than curtail it.

Returns from 647 precincts in Minnesota gave:

Roosevelt, 149,293.
*Hoover, 102,342.
Thomas, 3,551.

These returns included 226 of the 354 precincts in Minneapolis which gave Roosevelt 65,096 and Hoover 51,908 and 167 St. Paul precincts which gave Roosevelt 42,910 and Hoover 23,051.

**Dakotas in Column.**

That swing toward Roosevelt in Minnesota was matched by her sister states of the northwest. North and South Dakota gave the Democrats strong majorities, while Roosevelt was safely in the lead in Montana.

Out in the state, Roosevelt piled up his total steadily, the strong Farmer-Labor section in the western part of the state, adding impressively to his total, and the Democratic counties in the southern part of the state, swinging in behind him.

Early returns from outstate gave Hoover a lead in only one county, Lake, in the extreme northwestern portion of the state.

The first seven precincts in Freeborn county to report gave Hoover a lead. His vote was 1,190, with Roosevelt receiving 966 and Thomas 9.

Four Stearns county precincts, all within St. Cloud, placed Roosevelt in front with 1,284 to 898 for Hoover.

Olmsted county's first precinct to report was Viola township, which gave Roosevelt a lead of more than

(Continued on Page 2, Column 5.)

## Election Results Summary Shows Democratic Sweep

**PRESIDENT**—Governor Franklin D. Roosevelt of New York, the Democratic nominee, was elected president of the United States, in a landslide victory over President Hoover. Governor Roosevelt swept New York, New Jersey and Massachusetts in the east and won the entire block of northwest states, carrying Minnesota into the Democratic column for the first time in its political history. President Hoover was sure of only five—Maine, New Hampshire, Pennsylvania, Connecticut and Vermont.

**CONGRESS**—The Democratic landslide extended into both houses of congress, indicating strong Democratic working majorities in each branch, and upsetting many of the old Republican leaders. Six Democratic candidates were leading Republican incumbents in senate races, with the Democrats needing only the overturn of two seats to give them a clear majority. One of the casualties was Senator James Watson of Indiana, administration leader. Senator Reed Smoot of Utah, a fixture in the upper house for years, and George H. Moses of New Hampshire appeared doomed to defeat. Senator Hiram Bingham of Connecticut was losing and Senator Oddie of Nevada appeared to be defeated. In California, William G. McAdoo was leading the senate race. Senator Nye was winning in North Dakota. In the house, the Democrats had won seven seats from Republicans, with the possibility that their gains would be greater. In Minnesota the fate of the nine Republican candidates was still veiled by slow counting of ballots.

**GOVERNOR**—Floyd B. Olson, Minnesota's Farmer-Labor governor, swept to an easy victory over Earle Brown, Republican candidate, carrying Minneapolis and St. Paul. His plurality was expected to exceed 75,000. In the other northwest states Republican candidates were being defeated. Walter J. Kohler, former governor of Wisconsin and the Republican candidate, was trailing A. G. Schiedeman by nearly 50,000 votes. In North Dakota, H. C. DuPuy, Democrat, was leading William Langer, Republican. In South Dakota, Tom Berry, Democrat, was ahead of Governor Warren Green, Republican, and in Montana, Governor Erickson, Democrat, held a small lead over Habelbaker. Governor Dan Turner of Iowa was defeated by Clyde Herring, a Democrat.

**STATE TICKET**—Despite the victory of Floyd B. Olson in the governorship race, Republican candidates on the rest of the state ticket held leads over their opponents on scattered returns early Wednesday. T. O. Streissguth, Republican, was leading for lieutenant-governor; Mike Holm, veteran state officer, was leading for re-election as secretary of state; Julius Schmahl, Republican veteran, was well ahead for state treasurer; Henry N. Benson was leading for re-election as attorney general, and Oscar A. Swanson, Republican, was out in front in the race for railroad and warehouse commissioner. Three of the supreme court incumbents were running safely, but a new man, Edward J. Lee, present civil service commissioner, was running in second place on scattered early returns, too incomplete to give any picture of the result.

**CONSTITUTIONAL AMENDMENTS**—The state income tax proposal was losing consistently in early Hennepin county returns. Amendment No. 2, to require companies on gross earnings basis to pay motor vehicle taxes on trucks and cars, was rolling up a 2 to 1 vote of approval. Amendment No. 3, authorizing legislature to exchange state-owned lands for federal lands, was receiving a 7 to 4 favorable vote. Amendment No. 4, to tax lands acquired by state through foreclosure, was receiving a 3 to 2 vote of approval.

**DISTRICT JUDGES**—On the basis of scattered returns, Manley L. Fosseen, judge of Hennepin county probate court was trailing his opponent, George R. Smith in a neck and neck fight. On similarly meager returns, Levi M. Hall and Edmund A. Montgomery, incumbent judges in district court had assumed a substantial lead. Two other incumbents, Lars O. Rue and Arthur W. Selover were in a neck and neck fight to retain their positions, trailing Thomas E. Latimer. Four district judges are to be elected.

**COUNTY TICKET**—With only widely scattered returns tabulated, Arthur R. Ferrin, incumbent, had piled up a substantial lead over his opponent, Olaf A. Pearson, for county commissioner from the first district. In the third district, W. W. Heffelfinger similarly was making a strong fight to retain his position, holding a good lead over his opponent, Arthur E. Johnson.

**STATE LEGISLATURE**—Incumbents in the race for state legislature for the most part started off with early leads on the basis of scattered returns. W. I. Norton, veteran representative from the thirty-third district, was behind on the returns from scattered precincts, being led by Owen Cunningham. Burt L. Kingsley, incumbent in the twenty-ninth district, had also fallen behind in early returns. Other incumbents were enjoying safe leads as precincts slowly reported.

**CHARTER AMENDMENT**—The city charter amendment No. 8, to authorize borrowing by the city in anticipation of collection of current taxes, was running well short of the three-fifths majority necessary for passage.

## How States Voted on President

### Roosevelt

| | | | | | |
|---|---|---|---|---|---|
| Alabama | 11 | Maryland | 8 | Ohio | 26 |
| Arkansas | 9 | Massachusetts | 17 | Oklahoma | 11 |
| Arizona | 3 | Minnesota | 11 | Rhode Island | 4 |
| California | 22 | Mississippi | 9 | S. Carolina | 8 |
| Florida | 7 | Missouri | 15 | S. Dakota | 4 |
| Georgia | 12 | Montana | 4 | Tennessee | 11 |
| Idaho | 4 | Nebraska | 7 | Texas | 23 |
| Illinois | 29 | Nevada | 3 | Virginia | 11 |
| Iowa | 11 | New Jersey | 16 | W. Virginia | 8 |
| Indiana | 14 | New Mexico | 3 | Wisconsin | 12 |
| Kansas | 9 | New York | 47 | Total | 427 |
| Kentucky | 11 | North Carolina | 13 | | |
| Louisiana | 10 | North Dakota | 4 | Needed to Elect | 266 |

### Hoover

| | | | | | |
|---|---|---|---|---|---|
| Connecticut | 8 | Maine | 5 | Pennsylvania | 36 |
| Delaware | 3 | New Hampshire | 4 | Vermont | 3 |
| | | | | Total | 59 |

### Doubtful

| | | | | | |
|---|---|---|---|---|---|
| Colorado | 6 | Oregon | 5 | Washington | 8 |
| Michigan | 19 | Utah | 4 | Wyoming | 3 |
| | | | | Total | 45 |

## Mrs. Roosevelt Second Mother to See Son Elected President

New York, Nov. 9.—(AP)—Some one told Mrs. James Roosevelt, the 78-year-old mother of Franklin D. Roosevelt, Tuesday night that she was the first woman since Mary Washington to see her son elected president of the United States.

Her rejoinder was:

"You know, Franklin is only 50. He looks older tonight, but that's because he's tired."

After it became apparent that her son had been elected, Mrs. Roosevelt bade him goodnight.

"I never thought particularly about my son being president," she said, "but, if he's going to be president, I hope he'll be a great one."

## Negro Congressman Defeated in Chicago

Chicago, Nov. 9.—(AP)—The nation's only sitting Negro congressman, Oscar De Priest, apparently was smothered in Tuesday's Democratic landslide as he sought re-election from the first Illinois district. De Priest, a Republican and Illinois' first and only Negro congressman, was defeated by at least 20,000 votes by Harry Baker, white Democrat, who never before has held office, on the basis of incomplete returns.

## WATSON, SMOOT, BINGHAM AND MOSES BEATEN

**Democratic Host Marches Triumphantly to Victory in All But Few of States.**

**Dozen Republican Representatives Retired in Barrage of Votes.**

Washington, Nov. 9.—(AP)—The Democrats have captured the new senate and house with a sweep that retires to private life some of the most colorful figures on the Republican old guard.

Senators Watson of Indiana, Smoot of Utah, Moses of New Hampshire, and Bingham of Connecticut, all were beaten in Tuesday's election. Jones of Washington was trailing on returns early today.

In all nine Republican senate seats had been definitely seized by the Democrats, and Democrats were leading in four other contests for seats now held by their opponents.

More than a score of Republican seats in the house likewise had been taken over by the Democrats to give them a workable majority after March 4.

William G. McAdoo, treasury secretary under Wilson, was conceded victory in California by his Republican opponent, Tallant Tubbs in a three cornered race with the Rev. Robert P. Shuler, Prohibition candidate.

The nine states taken by the Democrats were Indiana, New Hampshire, Illinois, Connecticut, California, Utah, Iowa, Wisconsin and New Jersey.

By Associated Press.

The people have voted for a change at Washington.

By a popular and electoral plurality that may establish a new high record, they have elevated Franklin D. Roosevelt to the presidency.

The Roosevelt sweep, carrying him to the White House as the third Democrat to sit there since the Civil war, carried to victory many a minor candidate for state and congressional office and rocked some of the principal Republican strongholds in the country.

Senator James E. Watson of Indiana was one of those who, like President Hoover, conceded defeat by his Democratic opponent long before all the votes had been counted.

The Roosevelt-Garner ticket was acclaimed on a platform advocating repeal of the eighteenth amendment and immediate modification of the Volstead law to legalize the manufacture of beer and wine. How completely or how soon this program might be put into effect, if at all, hung however on the congressional and senatorial elections.

The returns showed a large number of candidates whom wet or dry organizations had classified as for repeal or revision had been elected to the new house, which meets 13 months hence. Five of

### HOOVER SENDS HIS CONGRATULATIONS

By Associated Press.

President Hoover, watching the mounting returns with increasing favor to his opponent in 40 states, sent to Governor Roosevelt, shortly after 11 p. m. Minneapolis time, this telegram:

"I congratulate you on the opportunity that has come to you to be of service to the country."

WEATHER
U. S. Bureau Forecast.
Increasing cloudiness, possibly snow Tuesday night; Wednesday generally fair, no decided change in temperature.
Additional weather on first want ad page.

# The Minneapolis Tribune

Sixty-sixth Year. No. 252. MINNEAPOLIS, MINN., TUESDAY, JANUARY 31, 1933. • • • Twenty-two Pages

MORNING EDITION
Three Cents in Minneapolis

# HOUSE VOTES BILL EASING DEBT

## TWO IDENTIFY HANKINS IN HIS MURDER TRIAL

### Witness of East Side Bank Holdup and Deputy Give Opening Testimony.

### A. M. Cary, Advisor of Defense Counsel, Leaves After Argument With Court.

Leonard Hankins, alias Owen Lewis, on trial for the murder of Patrolman Ira L. Evans during the robbery of the Third Northwestern National bank, was identified Monday by two state's witnesses as having been a participant in the robbery of the bank.

Testimony began Monday afternoon after the jury had been completed and W. G. Compton, assistant county attorney, had made his opening statement to the jury, briefly outlining the state's case. The prosecutor said the state would call other witnesses who would identify the defendant, among them a St. Paul man who will testify that he saw a group of men transfer a large sack from a large sedan to a smaller car near Como park shortly after the robbery.

Mr. Compton said this St. Paul witness would testify that the defendant and Robert Newbern, also under indictment for the robbery and murders of Patrolmen Evans and Leo Gorski, were among the men transferring the sack.

**Identified as Machine Gunner.**

Lawrence Barton, alias Barker and Devol, who pleaded guilty to slaying Patrolman Evans and was sentenced two weeks ago to a life term in the Stillwater penitentiary, was brought over from Stillwater Monday afternoon by three prison guards as a defense witness. He was identified by the first witness called by the state as the machine gun operator who stood outside the bank during the raid and opened fire when the two patrolmen stopped their car near the bank.

Barton carried his left hand in a sling, a bullet having been removed from it since he was taken to prison. Barton remained in the courtroom until 4:30 p. m., when the guards took him back to Stillwater. It was understood that Warden Sullivan of the state prison telephoned Sheriff Wall and requested that Barton be returned to the prison before dark. He will be brought back daily for the trial.

**Cary in Argument.**

The jury was completed Monday morning, when Elmer B. Lindstrom, 4140 Forty-third avenue south, a welder, was accepted as the twelfth juror. He was the ninety-first talesman examined during the three and

(Continued on Page 2, Column 5.)

## MAYOR CALLED IN CREDIT TAX

### State Commission Asks for Evidence Increase Should Be $150,000,000.

The Minnesota tax commission Monday, at the request of the chairman, J. G. Armson, called for a "showdown" with Mayor Anderson of Minneapolis as to the total valuation of money and credits in that city.

As a result Mayor Anderson will appear before the commission at a special meeting to be held in the county commissioner's room in the Hennepin county courthouse at 10:30 a. m. Tuesday.

**Newspaper Statements Quoted.**

Ready to act on the report of G. C. Rasmussen, special assessor, on a reassessment of money and credits in Minneapolis, which raised the total $54,834,450, Commissioner Armson called the attention of the other members of the commission to newspaper statements attributed to Mayor Anderson quoting him as saying the increase should be $150,000,000.

"It is time to call for a showdown," Mr. Armson told Commissioners G. B. Bjornson and George C. Wallace. "If Mayor Anderson has any reliable evidence in his possession to show the increase should be $150,000,000 let him come before us and produce it. I desire to subpena him accordingly."

**Assessment Termed Thorough.**

"The reassessment is the most thorough ever made in any district of the state and the mayor in my opinion has no reliable evidence which would indicate the increase allowed should have been in excess of that amount," Mr. Armson said. "If Mayor Anderson has any evidence that is conclusive, we want to know it. We do not want him to say later he was not given an opportunity to be heard."

Unless concrete evidence is produced to show the returns as found by Mr. Rasmussen are incorrect, the commission will accept the $54,834,450 increase which would make the total of money and credits for Minneapolis $167,689,770 as compared with the city assessor's total of $112,855,320, Mr. Armson said.

Although he had not been notified of the hearing Monday night, Mayor Anderson indicated that "he would be glad" to appear before the commission Tuesday morning.

## Chinese Celebrate Arrival of the Year 4875; Forgive Their Enemies, Pay Debts, Eat Much

### Joss Sticks Burn Before Altar—14-Course Dinner Served—But Shark's Fin Soup Is Omitted in Deference to the Depression.

By Earl N. Pomeroy.

*Be but virtuous, in small things as in large, and the myriad regions will rejoice.*
*—From the Shu King, Book of Records.*

So there must have been great rejoicing in the Cosmos Monday if what spake Confucius, Teacher of Ten Thousand Ages, be true.

The year 4875 was dawning. A new year of hopes, pleasures and sorrows. With such advent, the Minneapolis Chinese had paid their debts of the last 12 months, owed not a soul. Likewise, the kindnesses of the year past had been repaid in kind. If there had been any enmities incurred, they were forgotten. The Chinese were content. In the small things and in the large, they were virtuous.

Out of time's corridors there then emerged custom, which decreed that, despite the edict of the Nationalist government which instituted the Gregorian calendar, there must be a celebration for the new Confucian year. Custom cannot be changed in so short a time as a decade or two. In this case custom is nearly as old as China itself.

There was a celebration. In deference to the changing order, the Chinese called it an observance of the anniversary of the founding of the Chinese republic, but behind it all there stood the shadow of something more antique and venerable, dominating, with the other thing merely a screen.

The Hip Sing headquarters, three flights up at 222 Eighth street south, was the scene. At the altar, the scented wisps of smoke curling lazily upward, burned the joss sticks. Before them were two rows of teacups, a trinity of large ones and three that were small. In between were chop sticks. The whole was a symbol: Peace and many blessings come unto you in the new year.

The tables were burdened with food during the early morning hours, but this year there was no pick lan guy chee, shark's fin soup. The fins are too expensive, and the times none too generous. They had to be foregone.

But the Hip Sings did manage to confect a 14-course dinner, even if they did have to resort just a bit to some low hon chai, or "holy man's food."

Your Chinese cook is an alchemist of a high order. With the guidance of Tsao Wang, the god of the hearth, and his own ingenuity, he can transmute a piece of pork into a noble thought. Of a duck he can make a generous sentiment, and under his ministrations an item of sea food becomes redolent of tolerance, and under his ministrations

(Continued on Page 2, Column 2.)

## FREIGHT RATES HIT FARM, MILL

### N. W. Grain and Flour Producers Need Revision Downward, I.C.C. Told.

The urgent need of freight rate adjustments that will retain for Minnesota and the northwest the flour milling industry that still exists here and check further transfer of milling activity to eastern states was stressed at the Monday afternoon session of the interstate commerce commission hearing on rates on grain and grain products. The hearing opened Monday morning and will continue for about three weeks at the Nicollet hotel in Minneapolis.

Facts and figures showing the extent of the decline of milling in the northwest, not only in Minneapolis, but in smaller towns of Minnesota and the Dakotas, were brought out in testimony by E. M. Hendricks, rate expert of the North Dakota railroad commission. His first evidence was in support of a plea by the North Dakota state mill at Grand

(Continued on Page 6, Column 6.)

## NAME RECEIVER FOR THEATERS

### William Hamm, Jr., Selected in Action Affecting 70 Houses in N. W.

Because of failure to pay rent and interest on a mortgage, the Minnesota Amusement Co., the northwest corporate name of the Paramount-Publix interests, was thrown into a receivership Monday.

William Hamm, Jr., was named receiver by Judge M. M. Joyce in federal court on petition of the Hamm Building corporation, which, according to the petition, also represented the other creditors.

The chain controlled by the Minnesota Amusement Co. totals 70 theaters. Fifty-one are in Minnesota, five in North Dakota, nine in South Dakota and five in Wisconsin.

Thirty-five are subject to mortgage by the Publix-Northwest Theaters, Inc., the predecessor of the Minnesota Amusement Co. The mortgage is payable to the Theodore Hamm Brewing Co. and is in excess of $500,000, according to the petition.

## NEWS INDEX



*CAN'T MAKE FILMS; SUES FOR $10,000*

Francis X. Bushman.

## *Actor Says Career Paid 9 Millions*

### *Francis X. Bushman Testifies in Suit Over Auto Injury.*

London, Ont., Jan. 30.—(AP)—With a crowded courtroom as his audience, Francis X. Bushman, an actor well known in the days of the silent movies, made a personal appearance Monday in his $10,000 law suit against Albert E. Hamilton, Windsor business man. He was on the witness stand for two hours.

Bushman declared that because of a disablement, allegedly the result of a motor accident over which he is suing, he cannot engage in making motion pictures.

Bushman testified that during the 22 years he has been in the theatrical business he had made between six million and nine million dollars. Then he told how since 1928 his annual income had dwindled to $7,900 which he said he made last year.

## OLSON ISSUES ULTIMATUMS

### Will Veto Repeal Lacking Control Clause—Opposes Revival of Drainage Act.

Making the most sweeping pronouncement of policy since the beginning of his second term as governor, Governor Floyd B. Olson Monday night handed out two ultimatums.

First he reiterated his declaration that he would veto any repeal of the state enforcement act unless it is accompanied with complete provisions for state control of liquor traffic, on grounds that "no soda fountain will ever sell 3.05 per cent beer to children in this state while I am governor."

Then he declared he would veto any bill which strives to re-enact the Metropolitan drainage act of 1931, which the governor vetoed and which has since been revived by opponents of the bill worked out by the joint council committees of St. Paul and Minneapolis.

**Holds Conferences.**

The governor, holding his first of three conferences with a group of Minnesota state senators at the St. Paul Athletic club Monday night, chose for his first meeting the senate members of his own party.

Governor Olson refrained from any disciplining and disclaimed any desire to "punish anyone," even for the opposition which some of his own party's senators have aroused against Harry E. Boyle of Duluth for state tax commissioner.

He expressed confidence, according to the meager reports from the conference wrich was executive, that his appointment would be confirmed Tuesday by a large majority. He did not discuss the issue before the dinner meeting, however, only privately.

**Wet Takes Issue.**

Earlier in the day, Representative John J. McDonough, leader of the wets in the house had taken issue with the governor on the necessity for state regulation of the sale of 3.05 per cent beer. He asked that the senate approve repeal of the state enforcement act in the form that it passed the house last week.

Representative McDonough declared that whatever action is necessary to control the sale of liquor can be taken later in a separate bill, and that in view of the fact that 3.05 per cent beer will be regarded as "non-intoxicating," the state will have no more control over it than the usual run of soft drinks.

He added that he felt proposals to amend the repeal bill with control clauses would be illegal, and that it would be impossible for the legislature to act intelligently upon a control bill, until Congress had first taken action on its beer measure.

## BERLIN MASSES SALUTE HITLER, HINDENBURG

### Nationalist Germany Jubilant, Expects Two Will Pull Fatherland From Mire.

### Former Austrian Corporal Assumes Highest Political Office in Reich.

Berlin, Jan. 30.—(AP)—Adolf Hitler, Austrian born former interior decorator, reached the zenith—or maybe the near zenith—of his career Monday night when he received the acclaim of thousands of frenzied admirers on being appointed chancellor of the German reich.

The stocky ex-corporal, at one window of the chancellory, was the object of thunderous hails from the multitude—no less vociferous than the hochs for the monumental Field Marshal von Hindenburg at another window where Bismarck often stood. Aged 43 and 85 respectively, they are the two biggest men in Germany today.

Nationalist Germany was thrown into a paroxysm of joy at the union of President von Hindenburg and the Nazi leader in a common effort to pull the fatherland out of the mire.

Hitler, having at last attained the coveted goal, must now show whether the hopes of 13,000,000 Germans in his statesmanship are justified.

**Brings Parties Together.**

The efforts of the Hitlerlites as well as of the Nationalist followers of Dr. Alfred Hugenberg at last triumphed in bringing the three great movements of the right—the Nazis, the Nationalists and the members of the Steel Helmet War Veterans association—together after many ups and downs since they met for common effort at Harzburg in October, 1931.

President von Hindenburg placed the highest political office of the reich in the hands of the former Austrian corporal and at the same time appointed Dr. Wilhelm Frick and Herman Goering (Nazi lieutenants). Nationalist Leader Hugenberg and Steel Helmet Leader Franz Seldte to the cabinet.

Presiding over the first session of his cabinet of "national concentration," Chancellor Hitler at night put through unanimous motions against all policies of suppression, economic adventures or financial experimentation.

He adjured his fellow cabinet members "under no circumstances to disappoint the manifestation of faith and trust which today found spontaneous expression among the rank and file of the German people."

**Works Years to Triumph.**

Later in a press conference the chancellor through Dr. Frick, the new interior minister, assured German and foreign correspondents that "the new governments seek to live in peace and friendship with all the world."

Starting his National Socialist

(Continued on Page 2, Column 4.)

## *Jobless Opens Bible Finds $80.63 Check*

Etowah, Tenn., Jan. 30.—(AP)—Temporarily unemployed, Amos Carson, a boilermaker, turned the pages of the family Bible to carry out a New Year's resolution to read it more. From its pages dropped an uncashed check for $80.63, dated September 3, 1928, made out to his widowed sister and representing the savings of her son, who when it was drawn was employed by an automobile company in Detroit.

## *Three Convicts Killed in Quarry Slide*

Folsom Prison, Calif., Jan. 30.—(AP)—Three convicts were killed and one was injured when they were caught in the prison quarry Monday by two landslides of approximately 400 tons of huge rocks and earth.

## JOIN OPPOSITION TO SEWAGE BILL

The board of directors of the Midway club, St. Paul, joined with the bureau of municipal research and other organizations in opposing the Metropolitan sewage bill now before the city councils of Minneapolis and St. Paul.

**Exercises for Women**

Frederick A. Henckel presents the first specific exercise in the series appearing daily on the woman's page. Illustrated. Turn to page 13, then follow the series each day in

**The Tribune**

## *Payment of Auto Tax Is Postponed by House*

### *Deferring Final Date to April 1 Taken to Indicate Probable Rate Slash.*

Strong indication that the minimum tax on automobiles would be reduced this year was seen Monday when the Minnesota house passed under suspension of the rules a bill postponing the dates for registration and the time when new license plates must be placed on vehicles.

Deferring the date was approved to permit motorists to postpone paying license fees until the new minimums and new rates have been fixed.

The house voted, 109 to 0, to defer the date from February 15 to April 1 and fixing the date when new plates must be attached to cars from April 1 to May 15 with the understanding a bill reducing present licenses will be introduced soon.

The bill, drafted by the motor vehicle committee of the house, will be sent to the senate Tuesday where its passage has been predicted by Representative H. H. Barker, Elbow Lake, committee chairman in the house.

The consensus is, Barker revealed, that the minimum on both class A and class B cars will be cut 50 per cent in line with the recommendation of Mike Holm, secretary of state. This would bring the minimum on class A from $10 to $5 and the tax on class B from $12.50 to $6.25.

A hearing on the proposed reduction in the minimum taxes on motor vehicles will be conducted by the motor vehicles committee of the house Wednesday at 9 a. m., Representative Barker announced Monday.

## CABINET IS SET UP BY DALADIER

### Paul Boncour Made Foreign Minister — Socialists Accept Lineup.

Paris, Jan. 31.—(AP)—Edouard Daladier announced shortly after midnight that he had formed a new French cabinet with himself as premier and minister of war.

Joseph Paul-Boncour, whose government was overthrown Saturday, was designated minister of foreign affairs. George Bonnet, president of the Radical Federation of the Seine, will hold the important post of minister of finance. Lucien Lamoureux, one time minister of public instruction, was named minister of the budget and Camille Chautemps, who unsuccessfully tried to form a cabinet after Edouard Herriot quit on the war debt issue, becomes minister of the interior.

Announcement of other appointees was expected later.

As soon as Socialist participation in the cabinet was declared impossible, M. Daladier, who regained leadership of the Radical Socialist party after the downfall of Premier Herriot, set to work.

Like the two previous cabinets, which had to contend with war debts and budget problems, the new cabinet will be at the mercy of the Socialists, but it is considered unlikely that the latter will be hostile.

The new premier started early Monday to confer with associates and first sounded out M. Paul-Boncour and M. Chautemps, whose short lived cabinet two years ago included Daladier. Daladier was asked by President Lebrun on Sunday to attempt to form a new cabinet.

In so doing, Daladier's first problem was to find support for a plan to halt the daily deficits of $1,250,000, while the budget was unbalanced. Of great, but secondary importance, was the matter of the debts owed the United States.

## BOARD TO ACT ON FARM SALES

### Arbitration Group to Decide on Foreclosures in Lac Qui Parle County.

Madison, Minn., Jan. 30.—(AP)—Farm mortgage foreclosures in Lac qui Parle county hereafter will be referred to a board of arbitration composed of three farmers in an effort to forestall sales in "justifiable" cases, it was decided late Monday at a mass meeting here of 600 farmers.

Selected as the intermediaries were A. J. Windingstad, Walter Erickson and Thom Thorson, all residing in Lac qui Parle county. They were chosen after the protesting farmers, who filled the opera house to capacity, following the prevention of a sale earlier in the day adopted resolutions urging congress to pass the Frazier re-financing bill, Swank-Thomas cost of production bill, and Wheeler bill pertaining to remonetization of silver.

The three farmers will act on farm mortgage foreclosures only in cases where the mortgagor feels he has a "just case and is entitled to remain on his farm." Whenever foreclosure proceedings are instituted, the farmer will place his case before the "committee of three" which will attempt to arbitrate with the mortgagee.

"No force will be used in stopping sales unless all other methods fail," Windingstad said.

Preparations meanwhile are being made for a mass meeting here next Monday afternoon when Milo Reno, Des Moines, Iowa, president of the National Farmers' Holiday association, will be the principal speaker. Farmers from Lac qui Parle and adjacent counties have been asked to attend.

Protestors who surrounded the courthouse to prevent the sale of a 200-acre farm owned by Lanford Hauge, near here Monday. Fifteen minutes after the scheduled time of the sale, Sheriff A. G. Smaagaard announced postponement until February 18 following a telephone con-

(Continued on Page 6, Column 2.)

## *Teacher Will Retire After Four Decades*

### *Mrs. Emma W. Abt of Logan School Corrects Last Spelling Papers.*

Mrs. Emma W. Abt sat at a small table in her living room Monday night. Before her lay a small pile of spelling papers, and a little stack of report sheets.

The spelling papers, written by 2A and 3B pupils of Logan school, were the last she will have to correct. The report sheets, showing the progress of her pupils during the semester which ends Friday, were the last she will have to fill out.

After 40 years as a teacher in the Minneapolis public school system, Mrs. Abt will retire when classes are dismissed Friday. Her resignation already has been handed to the board of education.

The parting is not going to be easy, she admitted.

**Came from Le Sueur.**

"I love those children, and they love me," she said. "That is why I didn't want them to know about it until I had gone. Really, I'm a little bit put out about this. Couldn't you just as well have waited until next week—until I had finished my work?"

But the suggestion that the many persons who had been her pupils during her years of teaching would be interested brought a hesitant agreement that, perhaps, her retirement wasn't just a matter that concerned her alone. So she related, briefly, some of the incidents of her career.

From her home in Le Sueur, Minn., she went to the Mankato normal school. After taking some post graduate work at Winona, she came to Minneapolis in 1893 and began teaching in the Douglas school on Lowry hill. Ever since she has been teaching children in the lower grades.

**Always Lived Near School.**

Thirty-four years ago she transferred to the Logan school, and every year since then she has been helping children of the primary grades advance to the higher grades.

Almost all of that time she has lived near the school in which she taught. For 22 years she has lived near the school in which she taught. For 23 years she has lived in the house at 1618 Girard avenue north, which had just been completed when she moved in.

And now, in addition to hundreds of her former pupils, her list of friends and acquaintances includes most of the residents of that section of town.

"I know almost everyone around here," she said. "You see, the population in this part of town is not transient. Most of the families have lived here for years."

**N. Y. and California Call.**

Now that the end of her teaching is nearing an end, Mrs. Abt and her sister, Mrs. Bertha Chasteen, who has lived with her the last few years, are beginning to think about the time when she will be free to do as she chooses.

"I haven't been thinking much about what I will do after Friday," Mrs. Abt said. "But I suppose sister and I will take a trip. I want to go to New York. Sister wants to go to California."

The result probably will be that they will visit both states next summer, she said. But whether the sister in New York, who is an attorney, or the brother in Los Angeles, also an attorney, will be visited first still remains to be decided.

## AUTOIST KIDNAPED, ROBBED BY PAIR

Two bandits kidnaped a St. Paul man as he was putting a car in his garage Monday night, forced him to drive to a secluded spot in the country and there robbed him of $2, a $50 wrist watch, and his car. The victim, A. G. Granow, 838 Ottawa avenue, was accosted by the men at the rear of his home.

## DENIES ENGAGEMENT TO J. J. ASTOR, 3RD

Miami, Fla., Jan. 30.—(AP)—Mrs. Elsie Moore Torlonia of New York and Rome Monday denied the reported engagement of her daughter, Donna Christiana Torlonia, to John Jacob Astor, third. "I cannot understand how such a rumor could get started," she said. "It is the most absurd thing I ever heard of."

## CREDIT REFORM PROPOSAL HAS SENATE FAVOR

### Measure Aimed Especially at Relief for Farmers and Railroads.

### Shipstead Submits Plan for Refinancing Agricultural Obligations.

By Cecil B. Dickson.
Associated Press Staff Writer.

Washington, Jan. 30.—House response to the debtor's increasing cry for relief Monday was passage of an unprecedented measure drawn to ease in particular the strain on the farmers and the railroads.

Other individual debtors and corporations were included also in the wide scope of the bankruptcy reform measure which was rushed to the senate by a 201 to 43 vote. There is strong sentiment for it there, but a determined attempt will be made to modify it along lines recommended by Solicitor General Thacher.

The overwhelming approval under rigid suspension of the rules climaxed a day of action during which the Democratic leadership drove through legislation extending the federal gasoline tax and provisions of the Glass-Steagall currency bill for another year. The latter measure went to the White House. President Hoover is expected to sign it.

The one cent gasoline tax, which otherwise would expire on June 30, would be in effect to June 30, 1934, if the senate and White House agree with house action. Its estimated yield is $137,000,000 yearly.

**Foes Occupy Two Hours.**

Opponents of the emergency bankruptcy bill lambasted it during two hours of debate, but sentiment was so strong for it that leaders of the opposition accepted a standing ballot and did not ask for a rollcall.

"Members of this house have shed many crocodile tears over the plight of the farmer," Representative Tarver, Democrat, Georgia, said during debate. "Let us see what you will do now. This is the only bill that may be put through at this session to relieve the farmer."

Assailing the measure, Representative Dyer, Republican, Missouri, said it established a debtor's moratorium.

"This is to do the same thing that is being done by force in some farm states," he said.

In brief, the bill enables individuals to put into effect through federal courts a plan under which they may get more time to pay or have their debts slashed down until they can meet them. The courts would have power to prevent the foreclosure of farms pending the arrangement.

The extension of time and reduction of indebtedness apply to corporations, but the latter can reorganize their capital structure and issue new securities which may find the value of holdings by stockholders and bondholders far less than they were before the plan was put into effect.

**Cites Milwaukee Road Case.**

Railroad reorganization would be worked out under the supervision of the interstate commerce commission, but the courts would have the power of approval or disapproval.

Representative LaGuardia, Republican, New York, who drafted the provisions affecting railroads, said it was vital that the carriers be dealt with by someone who was familiar with railroad matters.

He said the Chicago, Milwaukee, St. Paul and Pacific was a reason for this bill, asserting that while that road was in equity receivership it had been "mulcted, there being $3,000,000 in attorneys' fees."

Chairman Sumners of the house judiciary committee, which reported the bill, and Representative Rayburn, chairman of the house interstate commerce committee, said railroads were in distress and that many of them must be reorganized.

"I believe it will result in a fair reorganization of the financial structure of many railroad companies," Rayburn said. "I believe it will better protect bondholders and other preferred claimants in their rights than in past receiverships."

**Sees No Value to Farmer.**

"What this bill does," Representative Dies, Democrat, Texas, said, "is to permit corporations to merge and combine in the face of the Sherman and Clayton anti-trust laws. I don't think it will be of value to the farmer."

"You can't get 12 lawyers to agree on any measure as technical as this one, much less about 400," Representative McKeown, Democrat, Oklahoma, one of the authors of the bill, said. "This is something to relieve an emergency situation, to prevent foreclosures and to save homes. Quick action is badly needed."

Both President Hoover and President-elect Roosevelt have approved the principles of the bill. Administration objections to some of its

**WEATHER**
U. S. Bureau Forecast.
Snow Monday; Tuesday unsettled, not much change in temperature. Additional weather on Page 15.

# The Minneapolis Tribune

**MORNING EDITION**
Three Cents in Minneapolis

Sixty-sixth Year. No. 286. 3 MINNEAPOLIS, MINN., MONDAY, MARCH 6, 1933. • • • Sixteen Pages

# Roosevelt Orders Banks Closed Until Friday; Summons Congress; State Plans for Early Reopening

ROOSEVELT TAKES OVER HELM OF UNITED STATES

Chief Justice Charles Evans Hughes is shown administering the oath of office to President Roosevelt on the inauguration ceremony rostrum before the capitol Saturday.

## *Sweeping Proclamation Puts U.S. in Control of Currency, Provides for Exchange Scrip*

### *Olson Proposes Application for Limited Operation — Plans Under Way to Resume Service.*

By J. H. Cleland.
Tribune Financial Editor.

On the heels of President Roosevelt's proclaamtion, continuing the nation-wide bank holiday through Thursday, and while Twin City bankers late Sunday night were shaping plans to resume business at the earliest possible moment, the possibility developed of reopening the banks for limited services to customers, in advance of Friday morning.

This possibility was explained in a statement by Governor Olson, which pointed out that a national bank, under terms of the presidential order, may apply to the comptroller of the currency for permission to resume partial operations. Legislation to allow state banks to take similar action can be passed by the legislature Monday, the governor said.

The situation, however, was thrown into new confusion by re-

(Continued on Page 2, Column 3.)

### Clearing House Certificates Are to Be Utilized As Medium During Holiday — Limited Operation Included in Provisions.

Washington, March 6.—(AP)—Dramatically clothing himself with war time authority, President Roosevelt Sunday night proclaimed a four-day modified bank holiday and took full command of the nation's currency.

In a sweeping proclamation finding precedent only when the nation has been threatened by a foreign foe, the new chief executive ordered an embargo on exports of gold and silver and prohibited the earmarking of American gold for foreign account.

In addition, the proclamation authorized the issuance of clearing house certificates to provide a medium of exchange with which business can function during the holiday.

Hardly had Mr. Roosevelt's proclamation been issued than the question arose whether the nation has departed from the gold standard, and the proclamation was widely interpreted as having that effect.

Secretary Woodin, however, was quick and emphatic in denying such was the case. He indicated that the cash windows of the treasury would be closed throughout the holiday and with the Federal Reserve banks closed, too, all redemption of currency in gold would be stopped completely.

Mr. Roosevelt issued his proclamation less than 36 hours after he had stood before a great inaugural throng and pledged himself to seek war time dictatorial powers of congress if and when the situation justified such a step.

He did not wait to ask congressional permission.

Returning from worship early in the afternoon, he summoned his cabinet into its first meeting and then called congressional leaders of both parties and senate and house into consultation. There followed a proclamation convening congress into special session on Thursday at noon.

Thus the holiday proclaimed Sunday night overlaps the convening of congress by a few hours. Meanwhile Mr. Roosevelt plans to perfect a program of legislative action to meet the situation, and, if it cannot be enacted by Friday morning, the holiday can be extended. It was indicated the proclamation and reconstruction steps have been under consideration for weeks.

The modifications placed upon the holiday would permit any bank that can gain the permission of the government to stay open to conduct its business as usual and accept new deposits to be placed in trust accounts subject to full withdrawal.

While momentous events were happening at the White House, banking leaders from the great centers of commerce were meeting with the Federal Reserve board and Secretary Woodin at the treasury. Ogden Mills, former President Hoover's treasury head, also was present.

**Work Out Certificate Plan.**

The purpose of the gathering was to prepare machinery for the issuance of the clearing house certificates. Woodin Sunday night said plans were still in an early stage but would be perfected and in operation by morning.

The President's proclamation began with a summary of present conditions in the banks, noting "heavy and widespread withdrawals of gold and currency from our banking institutions for the purpose of hoarding" and "increasingly speculative activity abroad in foreign exchange" which he added has resulted "in severe drains on the nation's stock of gold."

After stating that "it is in the best interfests of all depositors that a period of respite be provided with a view to preventing further hoarding of coin, bullion or currency or speculation in freign exchange," he cited his authority for the action.

**Cites War Time Law.**

To back his power to place a rigid embargo on gold, he cited the trading with the enemy act made law in 1917, during the World war.

"Now therefore, I, Franklin D. Roosevelt, president of the United States of America, in view of such national emergency and by virtue of the authority vested in me by said act and in order to prevent the export, hoarding, or earmarking of gold or silver coin or bullion or currency, do hereby proclaim, order, direct and declare that from Monday, the sixth day of March, to Thursday, the ninth day of March, nineteen hundred and thirty-three, both dates inclusive, there shall be maintained and observed by all banking institutions and all branches thereof located in the United States of America, including the territories and insular possessions, a bank holiday, and that during said period

## Text of Proclamation

*The full text of President Roosevelt's proclamation on the banking situation follows:*

WHEREAS there have been heavy and unwarranted withdrawals of gold and currency from our banking institutions for the purpose of hoarding; and

WHEREAS continuous and increasingly extensive speculative activity abroad in foreign exchange has resulted in severe drains on the nation's stocks of gold; and

WHEREAS these conditions have created a national emergency; and

WHEREAS it is in the best interests of all bank depositors that a period of respite be provided with a view to preventing further hoarding of coin, bullion or currency or speculation in foreign exchange and permitting the application of appropriate measures to protect the interests of our people; and

WHEREAS it is provided in section 5 (B) of the act of October 6, 1917, (RO Stat. L. 411) as amended, "that the President may investigate, regulate, or prohibit, under such rules and regulations as he may prescribe, by means of licenses or otherwise, any transactions in foreign exchange and the export, hoarding, melting, or earmarking of gold or silver coin or bullion or currency...."; and

WHEREAS it is provided in section 16 of the said act "that whoever shall wilfully violate any of the provisions of this act or of any license, rule, or regulation issued thereunder, and whoever shall wilfully violate, neglect, or refuse to comply with any order of the President issued in compliance with the provisions of this act, shall, upon conviction, be fined no more than $10,000, or, if a natural person, imprisoned for not more than 10 years, or both....;"

NOW, THEREFORE, I, Franklin D. Roosevelt, President of the United States of America in view of such national emergency and by virtue of the authority vested in me by said act and in order to prevent the export, hoarding, or earmarking of gold or silver coin or bullion or currency, do hereby proclaim, order, direct and declare that from Monday, the sixth day of March, to Thursday, the ninth day of March, nineteen hundred and thirty-three, both dates inclusive, there shall be maintained and observed by all banking institutions and all branches thereof located in the United States of America, including the territories and insular possessions, a bank holiday, and that during said period all banking transactions shall be suspended. During such holiday, excepting as hereinafter provided, no such banking institution or branch shall pay out, expert, earmark, or permit the withdrawal or transfer in any manner or by any device whatsoever, of any gold or silver coin or bullion or currency or take any other action which might facilitate the hoarding thereof; nor shall any such banking institution or branch pay out deposits, make loans or discounts, deal in foreign exchange, transfer credits from the United States to any place abroad, or transact any other banking business whatsoever. During such holiday, the secretary of the treasury, with the approval of the President under such regulations as he may prescribe, is authorized and empowered (a) to permit any or all of such banking institutions to perform any or all of the usual banking functions, (b) to direct, require or permit the issuance of clearing house certificates or other evidences of claims against assets of banking institutions, and (c) to authorize and direct the creation in such banking institutions of special trust accounts for the receipt of new deposits which shall be subject to withdrawal on demand without any restriction or limitation and shall be kept separately in cash or on deposit in Federal Reserve banks or invested in obligations of the United States.

AS USED in this order the term "banking institutions" shall include all Federal Reserve banks, national banking associations, banks, trust companies, savings banks, building and loan associations, credit unions, or other corporations, partnerships, associations or persons, engaged in the business of receiving deposits, making loans, discounting business paper, or transacting any other form of banking business.

## *Patrons Short of Cash; Symphony Plays Free*

Music lovers of the Twin Cities got a lucky break Sunday as a direct result of the banking holidays. Because of a shortage of ready cash they were able to hear an afternoon "pop" concert by the Minneapolis Symphony orchestra free of charge.

They crammed all available space in the Northrop Memorial auditorium at the University of Minnesota a short time after the decision to play the free concert was announced.

The rush for seats began around noon after word of the free concert was sent out in a radio message by Mrs. Carlyle Scott, manager of the orchestra. The announcement followed a hasty conference with E. L. Carpenter, representing the Minneapolis Orchestral association, and President Lotus D. Coffman of the university.

There had been only a small advance sale for the afternoon concert to begin with. Then came quite a few cancellations. Regular patrons were unable to attend because they were caught without change, and were unable to cash checks.

"The public has stood back of the orchestra," Mrs. Scott said, "and the gracious thing to do is throw the doors open free of charge."

Her announcement was made at 11:30 a. m. A short time later parties were scurrying across the campus from fraternity and sorority houses. From Minneapolis and St. Paul sped automobiles. Others came on street cars.

At 2 p. m. there were four long lines of men and women. At 2:30 p. m. when the director raised his baton more than 5,000 persons were

(Continued on Page 2, Column 4.)



# Cermak Is Dying; Doctors Give Up Hope for His Life

### Mayor Unconscious—Third Blood Transfusion Futile.

Miami, Fla., March 6.—(AP)—Physicians attending Mayor Anton Cermak early Monday morning relinquished hope for his life.

In a bulletin issued at 12:30 a. m., the physicians said that Mayor Cermak was in a condition of coma and that he probably would live only a few hours.

The bulletin said Mr. Cermak was "failing rapidly."

The bulletin was issued to newspapermen standing outside the mayor's combination oxygen room and sun porch several hours after a third blood transfusion had been administered in an attempt to save his life.

The mayor's right lung, punctured on the night of February 15 by a bullet from the pistol of the assassin, Giuseppe Zangara, was aspirated Sunday as physicians sought further information on his condition.

They said they found a gangrenous condition, basing their findings on the presence in the lung of "foul gas." They said they found no pus in the lung cavity.

Members of the family, summoned to the bedside, emerged weeping.

Joe Cermak, a brother, his wife and Mrs. John Kallal, a sister, came from the sun porch at 12:35 a. m. Mrs. Cermak and Mrs. Kallal took their seats on the lawn before the sun porch door and wept.

Vivian Graham, a granddaughter, emerged shortly and joined the group. Daughters of the mayor had been at his side a short time before.

## GENEROUS CITY GIVES CLOTHES

### Tons Donated in 'Share' Drive —Emergency Warehouse Is Opened.

Minneapolis shared its clothes with neighbors Sunday—tons upon tons of them.

From small delivery trucks, a sprinkling of private cars, and trains of big moving vans, clothing and household furnishings were dumped all afternoon upon the sidewalk in front of 1106 Harmon place.

By 4 p. m. Minneapolis had contributed twice as much for the needy as during the 10-day campaign last September. By 5 p. m., the warehouse was piled high with clothing, tables and chairs, kitchen utensils, stoves. They came too fast for the crews trucking goods into the building. They were poured upon the walks.

**Second Warehouse Opened.**

At 5:30 p. m., emergency arrangements opened a new warehouse at 6 East Grant street. Five more huge trucks loaded with furniture rumbled to another storage place at 413 Third street south.

At both the Harmon place and Grant warehouses, night crews of 25 took up the work of carrying in the material evidences of the concern of Minneapolis citizens for their neighbors' welfare. They worked until after midnight. The sidewalks, piled 15 feet high with contributions, required that time for clearing.

It was estimated that 250,000 pounds of clothing and 25 tons of furniture had been collected.

The spirit shown in the first intensive rush of the campaign was considered by Wever Dobson, Share-Your-Clothes chairman, as evidence that Minneapolis would meet further needs.

**Many Homes Missed.**

"Because trucks had to be loaded too quickly," he said, "many homes were missed, and during the coming week we want to reach every home that we overlooked. If a collector failed to reach your home on Sunday, phone Main 5275 and give your address. A truck will pick up your donation.

"The response to the appeal for the city's needy was a demonstration of civic spirit of which we should be proud. And the executive clothing committee of the Minneapolis Council of Social Agencies is grateful for that support."

Distribution of the material will be conducted through the department of public relief of the city and through the Council of Social Agencies supported by the Community fund.

### *Texas Guinan Pays; Gets Furs, Gems Back*

Chicago, March 5.—(AP)—Texas Guinan, night club entertainer, Sunday night reported to police her stolen jewelry, ermine coat and ermine scarf, which she valued in excess of $40,000 had been returned. She was robbed near her hotel early Saturday. A package containing the jewelry and clothing was left at the check room of the cafe where she entertained patrons early Sunday, she said. Later Texas added she had paid cash for its return through her manager, Edward Berman.

### POLICE CAR KNOCKED INTO DOUBLE CRASH

Being chased by a squad car in St. Paul Sunday, a speeder veered to the left and swung into the police machine. With the loss of only a bumper, the quarry sped on, but the squad car smashed against a safety isle at Pascal avenue and University avenues. Then another car hit the damaged police machine, ricocheting on into a second squad car parked at the curb. Fred Bolden, 1694 Brand street, riding in the first squad car, suffered lacerations on head and face.

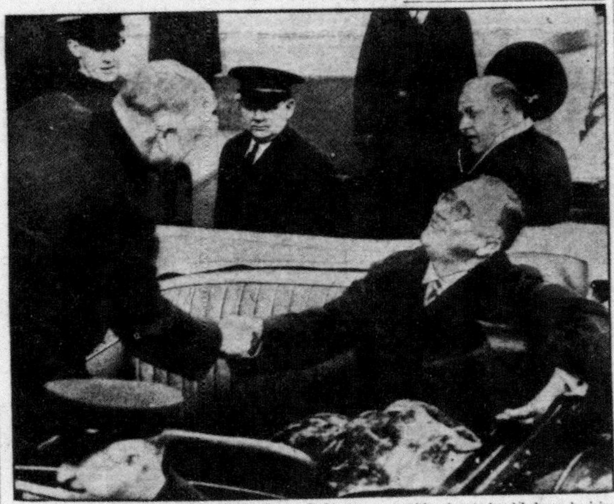

Former President Hoover greeted Mr. Roosevelt, his successor, with a hearty handshake as he joined him to drive to the inauguration.

## NEWS INDEX



## HITLER FORCES WIN ELECTION

### Nazis Make Surprising Gains in Germany and Will Control Reichstag.

Berlin, March 6.—(AP)—More than 17,000,000 voters out of 39,290,000 manifested their confidence in Chancellor Adolf Hitler in Sunday's reichstag election, and demonstrated to President von Hindenburg that he sensed the desires of the German people rightly when he asked the chief of the Nazi brown shirts to take the helm of the ship of state.

Germany now is well on the way to Fascist dictatorship.

Chancellor Hitler, by the vote of the people, has been given the legal tools to annihilate the last vestiges of the democracy which he considers a failure.

The Nazis alone will command nearly 44 per cent of the votes in the new reichstag and can dictate to their Nationalist co-workers in the government what must be done to shape a new Germany in accordance with Nazi ideals.

As the Nazis in their pre-election campaign left no doubt that the Communist deputies would never be allowed to take their seats, the followers of Chancellor Hitler will in fact command a majority in the new reichstag.

The Wolff News agency said the total number of seats in the diet

(Continued on Page 2, Column 2.)

WEATHER
U. S. Bureau Forecast.
Mostly cloudy Monday; Tuesday some rain or snow and colder. Additional weather on Page 13.

# The Minneapolis Tribune

MORNING EDITION
Three Cents in Minneapolis

Sixty-sixth Year. No. 293. 3 MINNEAPOLIS, MINN., MONDAY, MARCH 13, 1933. * * * Fourteen Pages

# SENATE LINES UP FOR ECONOMY

## PERMITS ARRIVE FOR REOPENING BANKS IN CITY

**Complete Service to Be Resumed Under Authority of Federal Government.**

**Institutions Prepared to Issue Currency for All Legitimate Requirements.**

Banks of Minneapolis will reopen Monday morning to resume complete banking service just where it was halted when the bank holiday went into effect March 4.

From the secretary of the treasury in Washington, through the Minneapolis Federal Reserve bank, came permission Sunday night for the reopening of all national banks in the city.

Minneapolis' one exclusive savings institution, the Farmers & Mechanics Savings bank, and the Minnesota Loan & Trust Co., which are among the institutions under the jurisdiction of the state commissioner of banks, also will be among those to open.

A complete list of the state banks which will be open was not available early Monday from J. N. Peyton, state commissioner of banks.

**Prepared to Issue Cash.**

The banks to reopen Monday, which before the holiday provided nearly all of the city's banking service, will be prepared to issue cash for all legitimate requirements of business, and the status of deposits which were impounded or "frozen" during the holiday will be just what it was before the holiday. The only restriction will be that no cash will be released for hoarding.

The list of national banks which will open under the permission of the treasury department includes the First National Bank & Trust Co., the Northwestern National bank, Midland National Bank & Trust Co., Marquette National bank, Third Northwestern National bank, Fourth Northwestern National bank, Fifth Northwestern National bank, Central National bank, Bloomington-Lake National bank and the Minnehaha National bank.

**Affiliates to Resume.**

All branch offices and all affiliates, state and national, of the First National and Northwestern National banks, will be among those reopening.

The order of the secretary of the treasury for the reopening of the national banks in Minneapolis was accompanied by an order for the reopening of all federal land banks, federal intermediate credit banks, joint stock land banks, federal home loan banks, regional agricultural credit corporation agencies, and regional offices of the Reconstruction Finance corporation throughout the country.

Minneapolis has the R.F.C. and agricultural credit corporation offices for this district. The federal land bank and the federal intermediate credit bank are located in St. Paul, and the federal home loan bank is in Des Moines, Iowa.

**St. Paul Opening Delayed.**

Because St. Paul has no federal reserve bank, the banks of that city would not be permitted to open until Tuesday, but bankers of Minneapolis and St. Paul, united in the hope that the close relationship of the two cities might provide grounds for an exception to the general rule, have sought a special dispensation to allow St. Paul banks to open with those in Minneapolis.

An application to the treasury department was made through the Minneapolis Federal Reserve bank, but no answer had been received early Monday.

The fact that a majority of the nation's banks will not be permitted to open until Tuesday or Wednesday is no reflection on the banks. To open as many banks as possible as speedily as possible, the federal government set up the method whereby banks in the 12 federal reserve cities will open Monday, banks in the 250 cities having recognized clearing houses, of which 250 St. Paul is one, will reopen Tuesday, and banks in other cities will reopen Wednesday.

## *Milwaukee Church Damaged by Blast*

Milwaukee, March 12.—(AP)—A violent blast, believed to have been an explosion of dynamite, early Sunday blew a wall from the boiler room of the St. Frederick's Catholic church in Cudahy. A fire followed. Bricks crashed through windows of rooms of nuns in a building adjoining the church, but none was hurt. Firemen estimated damage at $15,000. Investigation established that the blast was not due to explosion of heating system or of gas.

## FIRE WIPES OUT SIX BUILDINGS

Somersworth, N. H., March 12.—(AP)—The worst fire in Somersworth's history swept through an entire business square early Sunday destroying six buildings and doing damage at $200,000. Fifteen business establishments and four families lost everything.

**1866 BILL IS ACCEPTED.**

Denver, March 12.—(AP)—"All the cash I have," said the customer who handed B. C. Reeves, a barber, a tattered bill in payment for a haircut. It was a 50 cent note printed in 1866. Reeves accepted it.

## *Banks Given Order to Bar Drawing of Cash for Hoarding*

Washington, March 12.—(AP)—The treasury Sunday night denied the right of any banking institution to permit withdrawals for hoarding.

The bank is made the judge by the treasury as to whether withdrawals are intended for hoarding. The provision declared that banks, before permitting huge withdrawals, may require from depositors a full statement under oath as to the purpose for which the currency will be used.

At the same time, all banking institutions were authorized to cash official drafts drawn by the various secretaries of state for payment of salaries and for other purposes and to remit the amounts thereof to banks from which the drafts are received. No gold or gold certificates shall be paid out under this ruling.

## *Banks Will Meet Needs, F.R. Assures*

***Promises Salvation for Even Some of the Sorely-Pressed.***

**BANKING SITUATION.**
**By Associated Press.**

"The banks will take care of all needs."

That assurance of financial recovery was given by President Roosevelt on the eve of the first reopenings of banks after a week long national moratorium.

In 12 major cities, the centers of the federal reserve districts, approved institutions will open their doors permanently and unrestrictedly this morning.

Release of cash and credit was expected to bring the early reopening of the security and commodity exchanges.

*Text on President Roosevelt's address on page 4.*

Washington, March 12.—(AP)—President Roosevelt told the nation Sunday night that the banking system was ready for reopening Monday on a progressive basis and asked for renewed confidence and faith by the people.

"Let me make it clear that the banks will take care of all needs," he assured.

Catching a spare moment almost for the first time in his eight busy days in the White House, the President used the press and the radio to tell the people in his own words of what was done and what he intends to do.

He promised the assistance of the Reconstruction Finance corporation

(Continued on Page 2, Column 1.)

# NEWS INDEX



**HOOVER LUNCHEON GUEST.**

New York, March 12.—(AP)—Former President Hoover was a luncheon guest Sunday of Mrs. Theodore Roosevelt, widow of former President Roosevelt at her home at Oyster Bay, Long Island. Mr. Hoover left his hotel here at 11:15 to motor to Oyster Bay and returned in midafternoon.

## Quake Area Relief Starts; New Shocks

**Food Supply, Protection Against Disease Organized.**

Los Angeles, March 12.—(AP)—Fear of disease getting a foothold in the earthquake torn area of the metropolitan district through water pollution or unregulated sanitation added more woe Sunday to the predicament of homeless thousands.

United relief agencies went into action on a wide front and first aid, hospitalization, food distribution and even reconstruction work gathered momentum while the earth was still shaking.

The thirty-fifth major shock occurred about 4 a. m. Sunday, approximately 34 hours after the first at 5:55 p. m., Friday, which wrought the greatest damage.

Another quake of moderate intensity was felt here at 8:33 p. m. Sunday night. It apparently was not strong enough to do further damage.

The continuing shocks did little damage except to shake down more bricks, glass and masonry, but they kept the populace on edge.

Long Beach, center of the greatest destruction, discontinued the use of city water because authorities suspected sewage from broken pipes might have seeped into the water mains where breakage might have occurred. Precautions against typhoid and smallpox was taken immediately.

All waters drunk in the ruined

(Continued on Page 2, Column 4.)

**HAVOC LEFT BY CALIFORNIA QUAKE**

Huntington Park, small town on the outskirts of Los Angeles, was especially hard hit by the earthquakes which began Friday night. In the upper picture firemen and volunteer rescue workers are shown searching for bodies in the ruins of a Huntington Park office building. Quake havoc on Main street in Compton, Calif., is shown in the lower picture, an area in which 12 persons were killed.

*Additional pictures on page 5.*

## *Spirit of Southern California Triumphant in 'Quake Wreckage*

***Grantland Rice Tells of People Undaunted as Disaster Breaks.***

**By Grantland Rice.**

Los Angeles, Calif., March 12.—(NANA)—As the restless earth settles gradually and more solidly into a fixed place, only faint and occasional tremors remain to remind one again of Southern California's famous quake. Every now and then you may still see the window curtains sway as the paper you are reading quivers just a trifle and there is a slight deck-rolling sensation under foot.

It is the zephyr now after the storm that has partially wrecked 20 California cities, towns and hamlets where several thousands of sailors, soldiers and marines enforce martial law.

Although the death toll has passed well beyond the 100 mark with more than 4,000 injured with Long Beach, Compton and Huntington the chief sufferers, the main topic of conversation in Los Angeles now is each one's personal experience when the first main shock arrived with its terrifying thrust out of the gathering darkness.

Those who happened to be above the eighth floor in various hotels saw 13 seconds turn into the border mark of eternity, the longest 13 sec-

(Continued on Page 2, Column 3.)

## *Hoarder Deadline Advanced to Friday*

New York, March 12.—(AP)—Gold hoarders Sunday were given four more days in which to restore their metal to the nation's reserves. Federal reserve banks received word that the date on which the lists of names of persons who had withdrawn gold must be forwarded to Washington had been postponed from Monday to March 17. Last week the amount returned was estimated at well over $200,000,000.

## *Defeat of Bolivian Division Is Claimed*

Asuncion, Paraguay, March 12.—(AP)—The Paraguan war office in a bulletin Sunday said the third Bolivian division had been overwhelmingly defeated after a 32-hour battle with Paraguayan forces in the Gran Chaco.

## SENATOR DAVIS' RECOVERY DELAYED

Pittsburgh, March 12.—(AP)—United States Senator James J. Davis, who underwent an emergency operation Saturday for appendicitis, passed an uncomfortable day, his physician reported Sunday night. "A diabetic condition is upsetting normal recovery, but his condition is satisfactory, everything considered," a report said.

## *MERCURY CLIMBS TO 54; SPRING MAY GET UPSET TODAY*

Hikers and motorists turned out to make the most of the spring-like weather Sunday afternoon, when a mild east wind boosted temperatures to a maximum of 54 degrees in Minneapolis and to similar levels in other sections of the northwest. The mild weather, according to government weather bureau forecasts, will give way to somewhat lowered temperatures and some snow or rain Monday or Tuesday.

## CHARITY LAUDED BY ARCHBISHOP

**John Gregory Murray Delivers Two Addresses on Relief of Needy.**

The stability of the republic rests on the disposition of its citizens to vie with each other in their endeavor to give rather than to receive, said Archbishop John Gregory Murray of St. Paul in two addresses broadcast from that city Sunday.

Archbishop Murray spoke over KSTP at 6 p. m., and WCCO at 9 p. m. on behalf of American Red Cross relief work, with particular stress on the Ramsey county chapter's campaign for collecting clothing for the unemployed.

"The American Red Cross," said Archbishop Murray in his first talk, "is an exemplification of the dictum of the greatest Teacher of all time, Who declared that 'it is more blessed to give than to receive.'

"Such a fundamental and universal principle is at the source of all existence. It was the basis on which the founder of Christianity established his kingdom, declaring: 'by this shall all men know that you are My disciples, that you love one another;' 'greater love than this no

(Continued on Page 2, Column 7.)



### *Ode of Praise Written by Nina Wilcox Putnam to Populace.*

**By Nina Wilcox Putnam.**

Long Beach, Calif., March 12.—(NANA)—Forbidden to re-enter their homes lest the remaining walls crash down about their already overburdened shoulders; with no cooking possible, no light, no coverings to shelter the children and aged from the bitter cold of a heavy sea fog, the women of southern California nevertheless are reacting magnificently to the privations and horror of the earthquake that struck this region.

High tragedy is still active all about them hours after the first crashing disaster. The populace still blanches to the endless scenes of ambulances with their pitiful burdens, and white-faced but courageous and quiet women stare after the fateful vehicles wondering what friend or relative may lie within.

**People Calm, Undaunted.**

The broadcasting station is still calling endlessly the names of missing persons. The streets are filled with the homeless. Yet the calm and bravery of the people are remarkable.

On every side one hears jokes. Humorous incidents are many and never fail to bring a laugh. Despite the wreckage of homes, the ruination of the business center and the million and one privations and inconceivable inconveniences, the stricken area incredibly had an almost holiday air.

Were it not for the property destruction, everywhere apparent, and the knowledge that death has taken a heavy toll, one might almost mistake the crowds gathered at the food tents for members of a picnic party.

**Writes as Chimney Tumbles.**

I am writing this in the home of Harvey Fremming, stabilization commissioner for Los Angeles county. The pictures on the walls are askew.

(Continued on Page 2, Column 3.)

## *Dick Ferris Succumbs in Los Angeles*

***Minneapolis Actor, Theater Manager, Promoter, Had Colorful Career.***

Dick Ferris, old-time Minneapolis actor and theater manager, who promoted everything from horse races and religious revivals to bull fights and revolutions, is dead.

The former manager of the Dick Ferris Co. which played years ago in the old Lyceum theater at 718 Hennepin avenue, died late Saturday at Los Angeles, according to word reaching Minneapolis Sunday night.

In his tempestuous career, Ferris acted as manager for Jim Jefferies when the former ring champion was expounding the gospel; promoted one of the first aviation meets ever held; was reputed to have made and lost a fortune in the Texas oil fields; promoted a scheme to establish a "New Jerusalem" in California; put on bull fights in Mexico, and jumped into the spotlight as head of an independent fillibustering plot to set himself up as ruler of an independent government in lower California.

**U. S. Government Intervenes.**

Developments in that last expedition pyramided to such proportions that the United States government was forced to step in, finally ironing out threatened international complications without imposing serious penalty on its conceiver.

The first wife of Dick Ferris was Grace Hayward, herself known for success as both a playwright and actress. After their divorce, she brought suit against him for royalties of $51,200 that she claimed due for the production of the play, "Graustark," in which both had originally appeared.

That suit kept Minneapolis interested for weeks. Among its spec-

**Keeps Minneapolis Interested.**

tacular elements were armed sheriffs who camped on Ferris' bedroom doorstep at a loop hotel, changing guard in six-hour shifts, while Ferris kept to his bed.

That was in late November, 1919. He was hesitant about putting up $3,000 to guarantee his appearance in the court. He had been ordered to appear in explanation of the amount of his personal property and its whereabouts, and to show cause why he should not pay the default

(Continued on Page 2, Column 2.)

## *French Strother Dies at Capital*

Washington, March 12.—(AP)—French Strother, 49, former administrative assistant to President Hoover and once managing editor of World's work, died unexpectedly here Sunday night in Garfield hospital. He was admitted to the hospital late Saturday for observation, and although a complete diagnosis of his illness had not been completed, attendants said pneumonia apparently was the cause of death.

## *Fritzi Scheff Is Broke But Not Fretting in Adversity*

**By Roger Batchelder.**

New York, March 12.—(NANA)—"Fritzi Scheff is destitute in Connecticut."

The diva of 30 years ago, the toast of the elite of Vienna and of New York's "400," read the item in a newspaper column as she sat in her room in a moderately-priced hotel in the forties.

The windows looked down on the Broadway and Times Square that had been hers for the asking and the taking. A venerable "pom," constant companion of the last 12 years, a rubber ball between his paws, crouched before the wardrobe trunk that bore the large, faded letters "Fritzi Scheff."

The little woman, svelte in a simple afternoon dress, raised clear, sparkling eyes from the paper, and her full mouth pursed in a smile.

"Connecticut," she pondered. "Unhappily, I am not there, at my old summer home near Waterbury. They have just taken that away from me. And 'destitute'—just what does it mean? What is the nuance in English? If it means penniless and friendless—a thousand times no. There are a few pennies, and some silver change besides, and there is still a host of friends.

"If it means 'broke'"—and she tossed back her head with a laugh

(Continued on Page 3, Column 6.)

## BILL'S PASSAGE TO BE VICTORY FOR ROOSEVELT

**Measure Scheduled for Approval on Tuesday or Wednesday Without Change.**

**Grant of Broad Powers to President, Passed by House, to Come Up Today.**

Washington, March 12.—(AP)—A smashing victory for President Roosevelt in his first major tilt with congress was forecast Sunday even by senatorial opponents of his demand that congress give him unprecedented powers to shear $500,000,000 or more from governmental costs.

Approval Tuesday or Wednesday in the senate without change was seen for the measure, already passed by the house, which would permit the chief executive to slash veterans' benefits and federal salaries.

This development Sunday heartened Democratic leaders who are demanding that the President's second request for broad authority to cope with the depression be met promptly to get the government on a balanced financial level.

**Bill Comes Up Today.**

Senator Harrison, Democrat, Mississippi, who as chairman of the finance committee, will be in charge of the legislation, will call up the measure Monday. Before the senate convenes the Republicans will hold a party conference to discuss the legislation but not to bind the minority one way or the other.

"Republican and Democratic votes will pass this bipartisan measure," Harrison said. His prophecy was echoed by Senator Robinson of Arkansas, the Democratic leader, who introduced the bill on behalf of the administration.

Senator McNary of Oregon, the Republican leader, is inclined to favor the measure. There will be many Republican votes for it. In the house Saturday 69 Republicans contributed to the 266 votes cast for the measure as it swept to victory over 138 opposing votes.

**Walsh Expects Passage.**

Senator Connally, Democrat, Texas, one of the two senators in the finance committee who voted against favorably reporting the bill, conceded the bill would pass in its present form. So did Senator Walsh, Democrat, Massachusetts, who is a member of the special committee appointed to study veterans' economies, but which was not consulted in the framing of the legislation.

"In my judgment," Walsh said, "the sentiment of a majority of the senate is heartily in favor of supporting the President regardless of individual views on some of the bill's provisions."

Senator Clark, Democrat, Missouri, the other senator who opposed it in committee, would make no predictions but indicated nothing could stop final passage.

"I think the economy program should be enacted by congress rather than give blanket power to the President," he said. "I am not against the principle proposed, but I don't like to see congress abdicate its power and cause a revolutionary change in our system of government."

**Amendments in Sight.**

Several amendments may be offered on the floor.

One change proposed may be similar to that rejected in the house, which would limit any veteran pension or compensation cut to 25 per cent.

Veterans' organizations, including the American Legion, have said they would be willing to accept a one year flat reduction of 10 per cent in payments to veterans of all wars pending the preparation of recommendations by the congressional committees studying the question.

But since this program would involve less than $100,000,000 in savings as compared with about $400,000,000 in the pending bill's veterans section, there is little likelihood that this modification will be made.

The measure proposes about $120,000,000 savings by federal pay cuts limited to 15 per cent.

**THOUSANDS OF WIRES SENT TO SCHALL, SHIPSTEAD**

Thousands of telegrams were forwarded to Washington from the Twin Cities Sunday, expressing the attitude of individuals and organizations for and against President Roosevelt's economy bill. The messages, which came from Minneapolis, St. Paul and other parts of Minnesota, were sent to United States Senators Thomas D. Schall and Henrik Shipstead.

## *Japanese Victorious in Battle at Pass*

Tokio, March 13.—(AP)—A Rengo (Japanese) news agency dispatch from Chinchow, Manchuria, Monday, said that after an all-day battle Sunday at Haifengkou pass in the great wall, Major General Hattori's fourteenth brigade of Japanese infantrymen had repulsed a desperate Chinese attack. The Chinese troops, the dispatch said, had brought up reinforcements in an effort to recapture the pass, which was taken by the Japanese last week after their victorious march across Jehol province. Japanese machine guns mowed down large numbers of the attackers, the Rengo correspondent said, who had massed inside the pass.

**WEATHER**
U. S. Bureau Forecast.
Generally fair; Sunday possibly local thunderstorms with cooler in south and west portions. Additional weather on page 22.

# The Minneapolis Tribune

Sixty-seventh Year. No. 24. 3 MINNEAPOLIS, MINN., SATURDAY, JUNE 17, 1933. *** Twenty-four Pages

**MORNING EDITION**
Three Cents in Minneapolis

# WALLACE INITIATES FARM AID

## CITY MERCURY AT 97 WITH NO RELIEF TODAY

**Temperatures Over 90 General in N. W.—Many Points Report 100 or Higher.**

**Fair Weather Forecast Expected to Make Saturday Even Hotter.**

June's third measure of excessive heat was spread over most of Minnesota Friday, and it appeared that it was destined to remain for at least another day. Generally fair weather was forecast for Saturday. The weather bureau made no prediction concerning temperatures, but with a reappearance of the blazing sun of Friday it was deemed possible that even higher temperatures might be expected for the weekend.

The mercury soared into the high nineties and even beyond the century mark in the state Friday, while in the Dakotas the maximum readings in nearly every instance were 100 degrees or more.

In Minneapolis a new record for the year was established when the temperature reached 97 degrees at 5 p. m. This surpassed by almost two degrees the year's previous high of 95.3, marked last Saturday. The day was not as uncomfortable as it might have been, since the humidity remained comparatively low at 27 per cent. The beaches gave relief to thousands of persons during the late afternoon and early evening.

**110 at Aberdeen.**

The highest northwest reading reported was 110 degrees at Aberdeen, S. D. It broke all previous records for early June in that locality. At Fargo, N. D., where the mercury touched an even 100 to establish a seasonal new high, there was no prospect of a cooler day Saturday. At Grand Forks, N. D., the all-time heat mark for any June was equalled by the mark of 100. The only other 100-degree June reading on record in that city was set June 12, 1921.

Redwood Falls, in southwestern Minnesota, had an unofficial reading of 105 Friday. Fergus Falls, in the western part of the state, recorded an even 100. Other Minnesota temperatures reported included 98 Little Falls, Hastings and St. Paul, and 100 at Moorhead. Duluth, aided by Lake Superior breezes, had a maximum of but 76.

Bismarck, N. D., had 102; Williston, 94. Other high readings in the state included: Oakes, 103; Hankinson and Napoleon, 102; Max, 101; Jamestown and Minot, 100.

**Damage to Small Grains.**

Serious damage to small grains in sections of the northwest particularly in North Dakota where moisture has been none too plentiful, was forecast Friday by Dr. P. F. Trowbridge, director of the experimental station at Fargo. Continued hot weather for a few days would make the damage widespread, he said. Wheat, barley and oats, he said, are in most danger, with corn and flax better able to withstand the heat.

Other crops experts stated that considerable damage already has been done to crops in the Grand Forks area, while near Aberdeen, S. D., small grains are beyond redemption.

Montana was still oppressed by heat Friday. Havre had a maximum of 104, while Helena had 94. Even in the Canadian provinces there were high readings. Medicine Hat had 104; Minnedosa, 94.

**Heat Moving Southward.**

Des Moines, Iowa, reported 94; Omaha, 94. Sioux City, Iowa, 96; Kansas City, 88.

Outside of the northwest states, the remainder of the country was enjoying moderate temperatures. There were few temperatures above 84 recorded in the midwest, eastern and southern states during the day. The heat wave apparently was moving southward and eastward from Minnesota, the Dakotas and Montana.

## Gandhi's Son Weds High Caste Girl

Poona, India, June 16.—(AP)—The youngest son of the Mahatma Gandhi, Devi Das Gandhi, was married Friday to the beautiful 20-year-old daughter of Raja Gopal Achariar, a high caste Brahmin and former president of the Indian nationalist congress. Before the ceremony, the handsome young son of the Mahatma underwent purification, virtually becoming a Brahmin.

## Business Rush Sets Cash Register Afire

Chicago, June 16.—(AP)—Business was so rushing at a Chicago department store Friday that an overworked cash register burned up. The store had a sale. Women jammed into the hosiery department. The cashier rang up sales all day on the electric cash register. The motor got hot. It started to smoke. Then it burst into flames.

## Davis Lottery Trial Delayed Until Fall

New York, June 16.—(AP)—Because of inability to get a federal judge to try the case earlier, the lottery trial of United States Senator James J. Davis was postponed by agreement today until September 18.

## WALKER 'COVERS' PARLEY

Former Mayor James J. "Jimmy" Walker of New York is covering the world economic conference for a news agency. Photo shows Mr. and Mrs. Walker, on their arrival at Victoria on the boat train from Paris.

## HIT-RUN AUTO PURSUIT TOLD

**Patrolman Tells of Chase at 60 Miles an Hour—Saw Car Strike Something.**

The driver of the hit-run car which fatally injured Miss Dorothy Fredrickson as she was waiting to board a street car, was speeding faster than 60 miles an hour just before the accident, a state's witness testified Friday in the trial of Walter Johnson on a manslaughter charge.

This witness, Joseph La Croix, plainclothes patrolman and driver of a police radio car, testified he pursued the car from Cedar avenue and Fifty-second street north on Cedar avenue to Thirty-eighth street, and that although he was driving the police car from 60 to 62 miles an hour he was unable to overtake the hit-run car.

"The closest I got to the car was about 50 feet," La Croix said. "This was in the vicinity of Forty-fourth street. He began pulling away from me again, and I figured I could not catch him, so I wrote the number of his car with my finger in the dust on the inside of my windshield."

La Croix testified that the speeding car ignored the stop signals as he crossed Minnehaha parkway and also at Fortieth street. He said he continued to follow it at from 60 to

(Continued on Page 5, Column 1.)

## STATE TO GET 10 MILLIONS

**Amount From Public Works Fund to Be Spent on Trunk and Secondary Roads.**

Minnesota's share of the $400,000,000 provided in the public works bill for highway purposes will be approximately $10,000,000, N. W. Elsberg, state highway commissioner said Friday.

Definite plans for the use of the funds during the next two years cannot be made until highway officials in this state learn more about federal regulations as to how it must be spent.

A certain portion of the money, said Mr. Elsberg, will be spent on trunk highways, while certain amounts must be expended on secondary routes and new roads. The federal fund will be augmented by approximately $12,000,000 from the sale of automobile and truck license plates and the gasoline tax.

## Volcano Showers Ashes on Town

San Jose, Costa Rica, June 16.—(AP)—The population was alarmed Friday as showers of fine ashes, sand and soil fell upon San Jose and the entire central plateau from the volcano Irazu.

## NEWS INDEX



## APPROVAL WON FOR CURRENCY STABILIZATION

**Agreement on Fixing Ratios Is Sole Remaining Major Obstacle at London.**

**Roosevelt Has Heard Nothing About It, White House Statement Says.**

London, June 16.—(AP)—An agreement for the stabilization of American and British currencies, which the French government insists is the first essential for any progress in the world economic conference, was said in American delegation quarters Friday night to be fairly complete save for the vital matter as to the rates at which control should begin.

(At the White House in Washington Friday it was emphasized that President Roosevelt had heard nothing from the London conference in the way of a suggestion for currency stabilization and that the conference neither would nor could do anything about stabilization unless the action was approved by the President, the secretary of state and the secretary of the treasury.

It was explained in well-informed quarters that the level of $4.05 at which it was rumored in financial and conference circles that stabilization was likely to start had been used merely hypothetically by experts for the purpose of discussion, but that no agreement had yet been reached, as to the level.

**M. Bonnet Surprised.**

Earlier Friday, George Bonnet, French finance minister, indicated he had considered that the American delegation had agreed to dollar stabilization when he acceded to the election of James M. Cox as chairman of the monetary commission.

The pound closed here Friday at $4.05⅝, up one half cent from Thursday's final quotation.

If the pound and the dollar should be stabilized with relation to each other somewhat above $4, it was explained, this would represent considerable concession by the British who had first insisted that sterling

(Continued on Page 4, Column 1.)

## U. S. THREATENS WHEAT RELEASE

**Surplus Dumping Threat Used to Push for World Crop Restriction.**

London, June 16.—(AP)—Pressing for adoption of its program of restriction of production, the American delegation to the four-power wheat conference Friday significantly called attention to the effect on the world market if the United States released upon it her surplus stocks of the cereal.

The American position, presented by Henry Morgenthau, Sr., was supported by Prime Minister Bennett of Canada, who announced that three of the great wheat-growing western provinces of the dominion were ready to co-operate in a move for limiting production. This permitted him, he said, to promise the support of the entire dominion for the American scheme.

The leader of the Argentine delegation, Dr. Thomas A. le Breton, was disturbed by the American suggestion with its implication that unless an international agreement for control of production could be reached, the huge American surplus might be released, thus driving the price of wheat to a still lower level.

Dr. Le Breton called attention to the fact that the policy of the Argentine senate might tie his hands to prevent his agreeing to any restriction plan.

Stanley Bruce of Australia was extremely doubtful that his country would find it advantageous to participate in such a plan and he insisted as at least temporarily America agree to limit her exports.

The Argentine and the Australian delegates held a second meeting, but were unable to reach any decision.

## Member of Notorious Family Fatally Shot

Chicago, June 16—(AP)—Two gunmen hunted down Joe Petitti today, shot him dead as he played cards on a doorstep and wounded two others. The random shots imperiled a number of girls working in a factory a bullet piercing the dress of one. Learning Petitti's identity, police immediately assumed he was the quarry of the assassins. He was one of a notorious family. A brother, Angelo, is serving 25 years in Joliet prison for the kidnaping of young Billy Ranieri several years ago. Another brother, Fred, was found shot to death in February in a West side pool room. Angelo Petitti's father-in-law, Thomas Tiritilli, was slain in December, 1929, as an aftermath of the Ranieri abduction and Ole Scully, a key witness of the prosecution of the kidnaper, was beaten to death on the eve of the trial.

## Roosevelt Puts Recovery Machinery in High Gear

**National Movement Back to Work Set for July 1.**

**Calls Cabinet and Aid to Start Vigorous Action.**

Washington, June 16.—(AP)—President Roosevelt, with full power from congress, opened a sweeping offensive on the economic emergency Friday on all fronts and designated July as "the beginning of our great national movement back to work."

In a day of almost unparalleled activity at the White House, he ordered into immediate operation the vast public works, industrial stimulation and railroad reorganization programs and designated the field marshals to administer them. Earlier he had signed the bills authorizing these all-inclusive powers.

He signalled Secretary Wallace also to begin the active campaign for improved agricultural prices and orders were issued for acreage reduction and the levying of a processing tax to provide the estimated benefits of $150,000,000 to wheat growers. Cotton comes next.

**Sawyer and Johnson.**

Two special cabinet boards were appointed to work with the administrators of public works and industrial supervision who were designated formally as Colonel Donald H. Sawyer and Hugh S. Johnson, respectively.

A fund of $400,000,000 was made immediately available for highway construction in co-operation with the states. An immediate start on the $238,000,000 naval construction program was ordered with its goal of 32 new ships under the London limitations treaty.

Mr. Roosevelt appointed Joseph B. Eastman of the interstate commerce commission as the newly created railroad co-ordinator. Eastman announced an intention for early exploration of the possibilities of reorganizing the carriers in the interest of economy.

Waking up Friday to find the last of his emergency bills received from the adjourned congress, Mr. Roosevelt went eagerly and confidently to the task he has placed upon himself to guide the nation to better days.

**Veterans' Aid Signed.**

Jubilantly he received congressional leaders to witness the signing of the final batch of measures they had guided through. In rapid order he affixed his signature to the Glass-Steagall banking reform, the public works-industrial control and the railroad reorganization measures.

President Roosevelt later in the day completed signature of all the major bills sent to him by the extra session of congress, by affixing his name to the $3,600,000,000 appropriation

(Continued on Page 2, Column 7.)

## Vaccination for Whooping Cough Found

**Vaccine Treatment Also Is Reported Helpful in Scarlet Fever.**

By F. B. Colton.
Associated Press Science Editor.

Milwaukee, Wis., June 16.—New developments in treatment of two diseases of children, scarlet fever and whooping cough, holding promise of lessening their seriousness, were reported Friday to the American Medical association.

There now is hope that it will be possible to immunize infants against whooping cough just as they are protected from diphtheria by treating them with a vaccine, said Dr. Louis W. Sauer of Evanston, Ill. The vaccine is only a preventive, and does not cure the disease once it has been contracted, he emphasized.

Dr. Sauer reported on a five-year trial of whooping cough vaccine which heretofore had been disappointing in its power to combat the disease. He tried giving larger doses and more of them and obtained more successful results. Three injections are given a week apart, the last two a third larger than the first.

It takes at least four months for the vaccine to take effect, Dr. Sauer said, and it is well to begin injecting it early, preferably during the sec-

(Continued on Page 5, Column 2.)

**What Does It Mean? John Smith Asks.**

The extra session of congress enacted a record and gigantic program, mostly to revive business and cure the farmer's ills. "But what," asks Mr. John American Smith, "Does that mean to me?"

J. R. Brackett, Associated Press business writer, analyzes these new laws and their effect on the average citizen in a series of four articles, the first of which appears on page 11.

## President Starts Vacation After Strenuous 3 Months

***Enthusiastic as Boy on Leaving for a Two-Week Cruise Up Atlantic Coast.***

En route with President Roosevelt to Boston, June 16.—(AP)—With boyish enthusiasm, President Roosevelt sped Friday night toward the Massachusetts coast for his first vacation from a strenuous three months in the White House.

Boarding a special train at 8:30 p. m. Friday after one of his busiest days, which saw his emergency recovery program ordered into full operation, the President went early to bed.

Saturday, after a call at Groton school in Massachusetts, which his younger sons, Franklin, Jr., and John, are attending, he will board the trim schooner, Amberjack II, for two weeks to be spent almost continuously at sea.

Campobello Island, just over the Canadian border from Maine, is his destination. It was here in 1921 that Mr. Roosevelt was stricken with infantile paralysis. This is his first visit since then.

A cruise of from 40 to 70 miles a day, depending upon the wind and weather, along the New England coast with stops at nights in convenient harbors, is the vacation program.

Motoring from Boston to Groton Saturday, he will continue by automobile later in the day to Marion, where he boards the Amberjack.

At Portland, Maine, next Friday, Franklin and John will join the crew. James, the eldest son, will be with him from the start.

Mr. Roosevelt was accompanied Friday night only by members of his staff, Stephen T. Early, a secretary; Miss Marguerite Lehand, his personal secretary; and Henry Kannee of his office.

## FISH CONTRACT INQUIRY AIDED

**Conservation Commission Orders Department Employes to Give All Evidence.**

All employes of the department of conservation Friday were instructed to aid in the investigation of commercial fishing contracts now being conducted by Attorney General Harry H. Peterson.

The Minnesota conservation commission gave the order in unanimously adopting a resolution instructing every person on the department payroll to furnish the attorney general's office with "such information and evidence, if any, pertaining to any irregularities in the issuance of contracts or permits for the removal of so-called rough fish."

This co-operation was desired, the resolution said, "to the end that the public interest may at all times be protected and for the further purpose of bringing to light any irregularity or mistake of the past so that such occurrences may not be repeated, and for the further purpose of aiding the attorney general's office in the full enforcement of the laws of this state."

**Will Do Own Seining.**

The resolution was offered by J. R. Foley of Wabasha, commission chairman, who Thursday successfully offered a new policy under which the department will do its own rough fish seining instead of awarding the jobs to commercial fishermen.

While no detailed plans for disposal of the fish to be seined by the department have been made, E. V. Willard, acting conservation commissioner, Friday said the commission probably will "do as the fishermen do—sell them when there is a market, and give them away when there isn't."

"Our principal purpose is to rid Minnesota waters of predatory fish," Mr. Willard said.

Another action of the commission was acceptance of a plan under which portions of the north shore streams emptying into Lake Superior will be preserved. As soon as funds are available, portions of land along these streams best adapted to hunting and fishing will be acquired by the state and set aside for the public.

**Lake to Be Restored.**

The commission also ordered the restoration of Lake Calhoun in Kandiyohi county, near Green lake and Willmar. This country formerly abounded in wild ducks and was a feeding ground for game before the marshes were drained.

Commissioner Frank Yetka of Carlton was named chairman of a subcommittee which will hold a series of conferences with large land owners in northern Minnesota, with the purpose of working out to better advantage the auxiliary [illegible] forest laws.

Problems relating to land exchange will be taken up at the commission's next meeting June 30 at Bemidji.

## Inventor Convicted on 50-Year Duel Law

Los Angeles, June 16.—(AP)—A superior court jury decided Friday that a 50-year old state statute prohibiting duel challenges was as good now as when it was written and convicted W. P. Blake, 55, an inventor, of challenging a patent attorney to meet him on the field of honor. Blake faces a year imprisonment.

## 150 TO MAKE LOOP SURVEY

**Volunteers to Check Traffic Today Between 7 A. M. and 1 P. M.**

A general traffic survey of the section of the loop district bounded by Fourth and Eighth streets and First avenue north and Second avenue south will be made Saturday from 7 a. m. to 1 p. m. by 150 volunteer workers under auspices of the city planning commission.

Because only 50 per cent of the men and boys who had volunteered their services for the survey showed up for instructions at the mayor's reception Friday afternoon, it was necessary to begin the survey with only one six-hour shift, although it was planned originally to have a second shift work from 1 to 7 p. m. It also was necessary to curtail the size of the district in which the survey will be made.

One group of workers will check the number of cars, trucks, bicycles, motorcycles and other vehicles coming in and going out of the district, while a second group will check the turnover in parking space within the district. The first group also will check on the number of passengers coming into and going out of the city, while the second group will check the number of passengers in vehicles which are parked and also the time each parking space is occupied. Reports will be made on double-parking of cars and trucks.

H. E. Olson, city planning engineer, instructed the workers in their duties Friday. Forms will be provided on which to make the reports, and supervisors are provided for the five crews. Mr. Olson said a second traffic check planned for next Wednesday will depend on the outcome of Saturday's survey. The purpose of the survey is to obtain data on which to base legislation designed to solve the traffic and parking problems in the loop district.

## Boy Drowns; Brother Says Nothing of It

***Mother Overhears Boys Talking—Body Is Recovered.***

When Louis Shand, 14, returned to his home after a swim at Lake Nokomis Friday afternoon without his 10-year-old brother, Joseph, his mother didn't think anything of it.

Joseph, Louis and Donald Bush, 11, of 2305 Twenty-second avenue south, had gone swimming together earlier in the day. Louis and Donald returned to their homes after staying at the beach for several hours.

A short time later, Donald came over to the Shand home at 2119 Twenty-second avenue south. He talked with Louis, whose mother, Mrs. Cecilia Harrington, overheard their conversation. She questioned the boys.

Louis revealed that at the beach he had seen his younger brother disappear in the water. Louis dived into the water several times but could not reach Joseph's body. Frightened, he had hurried home where he had not mentioned the accident to his mother.

Early Friday evening Donald showed park police and life guards where Joseph had disappeared. A life guard recovered the boy's body in five feet of water, approximately 150 feet north of the ropes. Life guards attempted to revive the boy but a physician pronounced him dead.

Joseph is survived by his mother; three brothers, Louis, James and Thomas, and a sister, Patricia.

## WORK TO START ON WATER MAIN

Work of laying the 16-inch water main on Nicollet avenue between Washington avenue and Twelfth street is expected to begin Tuesday. The water department has 2,000 feet of 16-inch water pipe on hand, and bids on 2,000 additional feet were opened Friday by Fred S. Gram, city purchasing agent. The American Cast Iron Pipe Co. was the lowest of four bidders, its bid price being $2.62 a foot. The bids will be referred to the council waterworks committee for speedy action on the contract.

## 30 CENTS IS SET AS PROCESSING TAX ON WHEAT

**Farmers to Get $150,000,000 This Year on Promise of 1934 Acreage Cut.**

**Reduction Program Is Not to Apply to Grain Crop Now in Ground.**

By George F. Authier.
Tribune Washington Correspondent.

Washington, June 16.—Secretary Wallace Friday initiated the Roosevelt farm program with the announcement that a 30 cents a bushel tax on wheat will be levied on wheat processors beginning soon after July 1, to pay farmers $150,000,000 this year for agreements to reduce acreage.

Wallace disclosed that the money would be distributed to farmers under the domestic allotment plan this year for agreements to reduce acreage during the next two years.

He estimated that the tax would be 30 cents on the basis of the formula prescribed in the farm marketing act.

**Purpose to Cut Production.**

The general purpose of the program is to reduce production, and by doing so, to raise prices to a pre-war parity. While making no definite commitments on the world situation, it is evident, Wallace has in mind world agreements to limit wheat production growing out of the initial Geneva conference and of the London conference now in progress.

Without such world agreements, American plans for curtailment will be nullified and new plans to meet the situation will have to be entertained.

The processors' tax, destined to raise $150,000,000 on an estimated milling of 500,000,000 bushels of wheat, will start with the crop year which will be about July 8. The tax is fixed now but the date when it will apply will be determined by the secretary of agriculture. The benefits to be derived will start during the present year, and no distinction will be made as to wheat carried over, or wheat grown this year. The first two thirds of the benefits will be paid about September 15 and the other third will be given the farmer when it is demonstrated he has undertaken to cut his acreage.

Wallace's wheat program took into consideration acreage reduction resulting from natural factors this year and no attempt will be made to reduce the growing crop.

**Payments by September 15.**

Farmers will be offered contracts to reduce the acreages for harvest next year and the following year and two-thirds of bonuses to be raised by the processing taxes will be paid them as a consideration when they sign these agreements.

Wallace said these payments would be made for the most part by September 15 and that this distribution of cash would aid in business recovery. By paying parts of the bonuses this summer, he believes farmers whose acreage has been sharply cut by winter-kill and bad weather in the last nine months will realize a form of crop insurance.

He said the maximum acreage cut would be 20 per cent. The exact reduction will not be determined until the world wheat conference at London has explored fully the possibilities of an international reduction program for Canada, Argentina, Australia and this country.

**Five-Year Average Taken.**

Under allotment provisions, production records for each state will be examined and the average for the last five years fixed as the state's allotment.

Then an allotment will be fixed for each county, also on the basis of average production for the last five years.

Proceeding farther, an allotment will be fixed for each farmer on the basis of his average production for the last three years.

County organizations will be established. The farmer who agrees to reduce his production up to 20 per cent—at whatever specific figure Wallace later proclaims—will be entitled to a benefit payment.

The price of wheat for the state of Minnesota, for example, will be based on a five year basis, for the county within the state also on a five year basis and for the individual farmer on a three-year average.

Frederick C. Howe, former immigration commissioner of New York, has been placed in charge of the trade agreements section. This section will make all necessary agreements with processors and others. Mr. Howe will have under his department all trade agreements growing out of wheat.

**Price of Bread to Go Up.**

The department admits that the application of the new plan will raise the price of bread to the consumer. Secretary Wallace said it probably would raise it one cent a

WEATHER
U. S. Weather Bureau Forecast.
Partly cloudy with rising temperature Thursday; Friday generally fair.
Additional weather on page 10.

# The Minneapolis Tribune

NRA MORNING EDITION

Sixty-seventh Year. No. 239. 3 MINNEAPOLIS, MINN., THURSDAY, JANUARY 18, 1934. Twenty Pages. Three Cents in Minneapolis

# Glass Forces F. R. Gold Bill Revision

## $2,014,250 SCHOOL PROGRAM IS APPROVED

### Washington

By PAUL MALLON

Copyright 1934, by Paul Mallon.

DRIVE ON BRITAIN; ROOSEVELT HAPPY; FAST LEGISLATION

PURPOSE.

THE big thing behind the new money policy is our secret drive for an international currency agreement with Great Britain.

That is the real reason Mr. Roosevelt asked congress for $2,000,000,000 from the gold profits to dabble in foreign exchange. He clouded his purpose by saying he also intended to use the $2,000,000,000 for gold buying, purchase of government securities and maintenance of credit.

Naturally the drive must be conducted under cover. We want to force as good a bargain as we can.

There is every reason to expect that we will.

Mr. Roosevelt can play a lot of poker with $2,000,000,000.

FUNDAMENTALS.

SOME of the inner authorities believe the agreement will not be long in coming. At least they hope it will not be.

Then they expect Mr. Roosevelt to stabilize definitely on a gold basis without any such tricks as the Warren commodity dollar. Some phases of the Warren theory will be adapted to the final agreement, but the original Warren commodity dollar is already out of the window. That is, the idea of tying the dollar to a fluctuating gold base, variable with the labor department's commodity price index, is now dead, done and finished.

If Mr. Roosevelt cared to disclose his whole hand, he would say of his new money message:

"It means 80 per cent stabilization now and the other 20 per cent as soon as I can get an agreement with Britain."

At least that is what his right hand men are whispering. It sounds sincere.

CONGRATS.

MR. ROOSEVELT'S associates thought he was happier last Tuesday morning than they had seen him since October 22, the date of his radio speech.

The reason for his exuberance was the reaction of the country to his gold message. Even such thoroughly sound business and political men as former Governor Cox of Ohio congratulated him.

SPEED.

THE progress we have made in the science of legislation is clearly shown by the inside fight between the banking and the coinage committees of the house as to which committee should handle the President's money bill.

Both committee leaders waylaid Speaker Rainey. They talked like high pressure salesmen, each stressing his own ability to handle the bill better than the other one.

Finally one chairman told Rainey he would promise to report the bill favorably to the house within a single day.

When the other chairman heard about that he said he would pass on the bill in less than a day, which would hardly give his committee members opportunity to read the bill, much less to digest it.

However, that is probably just as well.

ADVICE.

THE latest story about Senator Carter Glass is so well pointed that it makes no difference whether it is true. At least it is being told around the inner governmental circles, and it is accepted there as true.

It seems that the senator received a letter from a constituent telling him that Mr. Roosevelt was going to separate the sheep from the goats in his congressional household, and urged the senator to get right with the White House and not be found among the goats.

The senator took his pen in hand and responded in effect:

"I will take care of my own classification when the separation of the sheep and goats takes place, but I know, sir, that you will be in neither classification, for your advice discloses you to

(Continued on Page 2, Column 8.)



## STATE LIQUOR ACT RULES WITH CITY LAW DEAD

Selling Illegal Despite Decision Declaring Prohibition Ordinances Void.

Police Ordered to Keep 'Lid Clamped' — Drug Clerks Face New Complaints.

Although by court ruling the city's prohibition ordinances are declared void, Minneapolis is not "wide open," and will not be. Chief of Police John Hart issued istructions to such effect to the police force late Wednesday.

To sell liquor the vendor must have a license, and since the city council has not drawn up a new regulatory ordinance and adopted it, no retailers' licenses have been issued. The sale of liquor therefore is still illegal in Minneapolis.

**State Law to Apply.**

Michael Johannes, head of the police morals squad, said violators will be charged under the new state liquor control act until such time as the new ordinance is passed. No offenders will be charged under the old prohibition ordinance.

It was two cases brought under the old ordinances which Wednesday brought a verbal decision from the bench by Municipal Judge Fred B. Wright that the state liquor control act automatically had nullified the ordinances. After leaving the bench he stated that the city ordinances had been based on the old state laws relating to liquor, laws which were repealed in their entirety at the recent special legislative session.

**Draws New Complaints.**

Millard Hoar and John Iglehart, clerks in loop drugstores, had been charged with possession of liquor for sale. Their attorney, Vernon S. Welch, demurred to the charges, contending that the ordinances were voided. Judge Wright upheld the demurrer.

Detective Johannes then drew up complaints charging the clerks with selling liquor without a license, under the state law. As under the old ordinances, guilt under the charge is a misdemeanor, punishable by a fine of $100 or 90 days in jail. The charge under the ordinances carried similar punishment.

### FACTOR AT TOUHY TRIAL

John Factor, center, Chicago speculator, is shown with the Cook county prosecutors who are leading the state's case against the Touhy gangsters on trial in Chicago for the kidnaping of Factor last year. At the left is Wilbur Crowley, assistant state's attorney. At the right is Thomas J. Courtney, state's attorney of Cook county.

## 7 TOUHY TRIAL JURORS PICKED

One, Already Accepted, Found to Have Police Record—Faces Charge.

Chicago, Jan. 17.—(AP)—Seven of the 12 jurors who will try Roger Touhy, Chicago gang leader, for the capital offense of kidnaping John (Jake) Factor, were in the box Wednesday night as the trial moved forward in a sudden burst of courtroom speed.

An eighth juror, however, was in custody.

Two panels—totaling eight jurors—had been selected, when it was discovered that one of the eight had a brief police record, having been arrested once for disorderly conduct and once on suspicion. Judge Michael Feinberg, after considerable excitement in the court-

(Continued on Page 2, Column 7)

## Ghent Sheds No Tears for Late Liquor

*Town Enjoys Itself Drinking Beer With Kick, Awaits Whisky.*

Ghent, Minn., Jan. 17.—Ghent, one of the wetter points in this part of the state, continued on a straight beer diet Wednesday night when its hard liquor cargo encountered further delays.

Original plans were for a grand opening Tuesday night, but a car bearing the strong drinks, authorized by the village council under the new state liquor law, collided with a street car in St. Paul Tuesday.

A. J. Engel, proprietor of the Ghent hotel, climbed out of the wreckage unhurt, took a night train home and announced on his arrival Wednesday that the car would be repaired and should arrive late Wednesday.

But it had not arrived at 11 p. m., and the village's chances of being the first place in Minnesota to serve hard liquor legally since prohibition began to fade.

A truck load of the new six per cent beer did arrive from St. Paul late Wednesday, though, and the throngs, augmented by visitors from distant places, had to be satisfied with the new brew.

"Yes, we were all disappointed," Engel said, "but we have been having a fine time. There has been a splendid crowd, and all are enjoying themselves and keeping good order."

### Twin Cities Milk Pact Terminated

Washington, Jan. 17.—(AP)—Existing milk marketing agreements in 13 markets of the country were terminated Wednesday in a blanket order issued by Secretary Wallace.

Cities affected by the order are: Philadelphia, Detroit, St. Paul, Minneapolis, Evansville, Ind., Baltimore, Knoxvile, Tenn., Los Angeles, San Diego, Oakland, Calif., Richmond, Va., St. Louis, Des Moines and Boston. St. Paul and Minneapolis are covered in one agreement.

Licenses for distributors in each city will remain in effect until further notice, Wallace said, and will be replaced by new licenses conforming to the new milk policy of guaranteeing producers' prices only as soon as new agreements are drawn.

### Hoover Suggested as Iowa 'U' Prexy

Iowa City, Jan. 17.—(AP)—The Iowa City Press-Citizen Wednesday added the name of former President Herbert Hoover to a list of possible successors to Dr. Walter A. Jessup as president of the University of Iowa. The newspapers said that the state board of education would meet at Council Bluffs January 23 and "that former President Hoover's name might be brought into the list of candidates."

### Many Die as Blazing Train Is Derailed

Harbin, Manchukuo, Jan. 18.—(AP)—Reports reached here Thursday that bandits had derailed a burning train on the trans-Siberian railway, killing many persons. Details were lacking.

### R.F.C. AUTHORIZES $390,000,000 LOANS

Washington, Jan. 17.—(AP)—The reconstruction corporation reported to the house Wednesday it had authorized loans totaling $390,567,353 in November.

## NEWS INDEX



## BOARD VOTES FOR PAINTING, REPAIR WORK

Action Would Give Employment to Nearly 4,000 by July 1.

Request to Be Made to Estimate Body for Issuance of $500,000 Bonds.

Plans for a school painting and repair program which will have cost $2,014,250 and will have given employment to nearly 4,000 skilled and unskilled laborers by July 1 were approved by the board of education Wednesday. At the same time the board took steps to finance an additional school rehabilitation after July 1 if the federal CWA program is extended beyond that date. Nearly 2,000 additional laborers would be employed under this program.

The board voted unanimously to request the board of estimate and taxation to authorize the issuance of $500,000 of bonds to finance the repair program. Of this total, the sale of only $300,000 of bonds is requested for the present. The remaining $200,000 would be needed if an additional CWA program is feasible after July 1.

George F. Womrath, business superintendent, said the $300,000 bond issue would be sufficient to pay the school board's share for materials and overhead to keep the CWA projects in operation until July 1, and that this amount of bonds would round out the program of $2,014,250.

The school board now has in operation CWA repair projects for which the total cost will be $719,345.94. More than 1,900 laborers are now employed. If the $300,000 bond issue is authorized the labor force would be doubled. Of the total program of $2,014,250, the board by July 1 would have expended only $450,000 of bond money and $75,000 from its repair and improvement fund or a total of $525,000, while the federal government through CWA would have spent $1,489,250.

Several large business firms of

(Continued on Page 2, Column 5)

## A. B. FRIZZELL RITES FRIDAY

Complications Following Siege of Pneumonia Fatal to Publisher.

Funeral services for Albert Burnett Frizzell, 43, co-publisher of the Minneapolis Star, who died Wednesday at his home, 20 Elmwood place, will be at the Church of the Annunciation, Garfield avenue and West Fifty-fourth street, at 9 a. m. Friday. Burial will be in St. May's cemetery.

Active pallbearers will be Cyrus Hegstrom, Clinton Holmes, John McHardy, W. N. Johnson, H. Stanley Hanson and John Hogan.

Death of Mr. Frizzell resulted from a complication of ailments following a severe attack of pneumonia a year ago. For many years he was an outstanding figure in the Twin Cities advertising and journalistic fields.

**Born in Minneapolis.**

Mr. Frizzell was born in Minneapolis January 16, 1891, the son of the late Charles W. Frizzell and Annie Sweeney Frizzell, pioneer residents of south Minneapolis. He attended Garfield grade school and South high school, later taking a course at the Johnson office school. His first work was in the publicity and advertising department of the old Orpheum theater.

In 1912 he was employed in the advertising department of the Minneapolis Daily News. In 1919 he and Miss Anna Johnston of Minneapolis were married. In the same year he purchased the L. K. Lee advertising agency of St. Paul, operating it in that ctiy until 1928 as the Frizzell advertising agency. Then he moved the business to Minneapolis, where it has been conducted since by his brother, Frederick L. Frizzell.

**Buys Farm Paper.**

In 1923 Mr. Frizzell purchased Farm Stock & Home, widely known farm publication. In 1925, he combined this publication with the Northwest Farmstead, the joint publication being known as Farm Stock & Home and Northwest Farmstead. In 1929 he sold this to the Webb Publishing Co. of St. Paul.

In May, 1924, Mr. Frizzell became associated in purchase of the Minnesota Star. Later this was reorganized as the Minneapolis Star, with Mr. Frizzell as co-publisher and treasurer.

Mr. Frizzell is survived by his wife, a daughter, Marilyn Ann; two brothers, Sydney H. Frizzell and Frederick L. Frizzell, and two sisters, Mrs. A. R. Leonard and Mrs. C. H. Gunderson.

## Mendieta Agrees to Take Over Presidency of Cuba

Hevia, Ruler for 3 Days, Gives Up in Favor of Nationalist Chief.

Havana, Jan. 17.—(AP)—Carlos Mendieta, 60-year-old Nationalist and veteran of nearly four decades of political battling, Wednesday night accepted the presidency of Cuba.

He will head the sixth government Cuba has had in a little more than five months, taking over office from the youthful Carlos Hevia under outward conditions of the utmost possible confusion.

A general strike was impending and military conditions appeared unsettled, but Mendieta's supporters assured him of united backing of the army and navy and of the strongest political factions.

**Will Take Post Today.**

Hevia last Monday maneuvered himself into the presidency when it appeared that Mendieta was sure of the office.

The actual swearing in of Mendieta was scheduled for noon Thursday.

After having held office only since Monday, 33-year-old Hevia resigned as president late Wednesday night, thus clearing the way for the veteran Nationalist leader to enter the office Thursday.

The original directing body of the ABC society visited Medieta shortly after 9 p. m. and assured him of support, issuing a call to all Cubans to observe January 21 as "Mendieta day."

**Victory for Batista.**

Observers considered the navy's pledge of support most significant of all, inasmuch as in the last few days the army and navy have been split wide apart, with former Minister of War Antonio Guiteras controlling the navy and Colonel Fulgencio Batista the army.

Carlos Mendieta.

The Mendieta selection was an important victory for Batista who refused to stay down after Guiteras had outmaneuvered him Monday to help place Hevia in the presidency.

In view of the fast-growing strike which earlier in the day had threatened to paralyze all government activities, Colonel Batista named three army officers to government posts, prepared to install others in like positions, and proclaimed that malcontents would not be permitted to provoke anarchy and disorder. He later explained that the officers were merely emergency appointees.

## Dr. Alice in Death's Shadow, Lawyer Says

*May Die Any Minute From Heart Attack — Insurance Saleswoman Tells of Policy Taken on Rheta.*

Chicago, Jan. 17.—(AP)—Dr. Alice L. Wynekoop was reported in danger of death at any moment Wednesday as the state's star witnesses paraded to the stand in criminal court and gave testimony in her trial for murder.

Defense Attorney W. W. Smith said the 62-year-old defendant's physicians had informed him she "might die any minute" of heart disease. Dr. Catherine Wynekoop, daughter of the elderly woman, said she was "very much afraid mother won't be able to go through the trial."

Details of how Dr. Alice applied for a $10,000 double indemnity life insurance policy on her daughter-in-law, Rheta, a month before the girl was slain; statements made by Dr. Wynekoop to police; and the detailed testimony of Thomas J. Ahern, undertaker, came forth Wednesday as the prosecution built its case.

Prosecutors indicated they believed some of their most important evidence was placed in the records through Miss Julia McCormick, spinster saleswoman of life insurance.

She recalled being summoned to the Wynekoop home by telephone last October 23, told how Dr. Alice furnished the information needed to apply for the $10,000 policy, took it outside Miss McCormick's presence for Rheta's signature, and finally paid the first premium on the policy—reduced to $5,000 by the company because Rheta was under weight—on November 11, just 10 days before Rheta's tragic death.

Dr. Alice's appearance as she slouched in her chair at counsel's table bore out her daughter's statement that her condition was the poorest since the trial began five days ago. At times she closed her eyes, buried her head in her hands on the table, or gazed morosely at the operating table, bundles of bloody garments, a wall chart of the Wynekoop home, a .32 caliber pistol, and other state evidence.

Smith, who would not disclose what physicians told him Dr. Alice was in danger of death, said the de-

(Continued on Page 2, Column 3)

## Moscrip Asks Curb on Fats, Oils Imports

*Must Keep Home Market for American Farmer, He Tells Session.*

Satisfactory results from any production control program cannot be attained "until something is done to assure the American producer of the home market," members of the Minnesota Farm Bureau federation were told Wednesday night at their annual dinner in St. Paul.

Importance of protection of American farmers in their home markets was stressed by W. S. Moscrip of Lake Elmo, president of the Twin City Milk Producers association, who addressed several hundred persons at the dinner in the ballroom of the Lowry hotel.

Touching on the problem of competition from other countries producing farm products and products which are placed on the market to compete with American-grown products, Mr. Moscrip declared "the importation of fats and oils duty free from the Philippine islands is decreasing the demand for fats and oils produced in this country."

"In July, August and September of 1932, we imported from the Philippines 152,000,000 pounds of co-

(Continued on Page 2, Column 4)

## John S. Johnson, World Famous Skater, Is Dead

John S. Johnson.

Minneapolis Man Also Former Champion Bicycle Racer.

John S. (Johnny) Johnson, former world's champion bicycle racer and speed skater—titles he held at the same time—died suddenly shortly before midnight Wednesday.

He suffered a heart attack at his home at 2821 Girard avenue south at 11:45 p. m., five minutes after he returned from the Arena, Twenty-ninth street and Dupont avenue south. He was 60.

He had gone to the Arena to make some arrangements for the national championship skating races to be held Saturday at Powderhorn park next Saturday and Sunday. He had not complained of

(Continued on Page 2, Column 2)

## LIMITS PLACED ON TREASURY'S BANKING POWER

Roosevelt Plan to Take Over Reserve System's Gold Is Ruled Legal.

House Coinage Committee Left in Lurch as Another Reports Bill.

Washington, Jan. 17.—(AP)—Conservative Democratic opponents of the Roosevelt monetary legislation Wednesday gained a revision of the administration bill to guard against treasury invasion of the private banking field.

At the insistence of Senator Glass of Virginia, the wide variety of commercial paper in which the measure would have authorized the treasury to deal, using the proposed $2,000,000,000 stabilization fund, was limited to such items as might be necessary to stabilize the foreign exchange value of the dollar.

Attorney General Cummings went before the senate banking committee to assure Glass and Senator McAdoo, Democrat of California of the constitutionality of President Roosevelt's proposal that the treasury be given title to the federal reserve system's gold stocks.

**Fletcher Introduces Bill.**

A written opinion on this question had been requested by the two, each of whom served as secretary of the treasury under Woodrow Wilson.

Chairman Fletcher of the senate banking committee introduced the bill at the outset of the day's session after making the stabilization fund changes.

Governor Black of the federal reserve board and Adolph Miller, a board member, headed the short list of witnesses summoned.

In the house, where the banking and coinage committees have been disputing over which should have charge of the bill, the banking committee stepped ahead of the coinage committee, substituted the language of President Roosevelt's gold devaluation bill into another measure before it and formally reported the bill to the house.

**Hearings Planned.**

Upshot of the mixup remained to be determined. The bill had been assigned to the coinage committee by the speaker, and Chairman Somers was preparing to hold hearings on it.

"It it my hope to ask the secretary of the treasury to discuss the bill with us at his convenience," Somers said earlier. "Then we shall have, I expect, some further and open hearings. The Republicans have been urging adequate hearings. It is my intention to let them give us a list of persons they think we should hear—and then hear them."

President Roosevelt had told reporters the attorney general upheld the constitutionality of seizing the reserve system's gold last April.

**Fletcher Makes Change.**

As proposed by the administration, the section of the bill dealing with the $2,000,000,000 fund would have authorized the secretary of the treasury "to purchase, sell, discount, or negotiate at home or abroad, with or without indorsement or guarnaty, drafts, checks, bills of exchange, acceptances, including bankers' acceptances, coin, bullion, cable transfers, foreign exchange, bonds, notes, evidences of indebtedness, including the obligations of the United States or any foreign government, and any obligation or securities in whatever currency payable, to establish credits therefor and generally to exercise such powers as are incidental to the powers conferred by this section."

In place of this provision, the bill as introduced by Fletcher would authorize the secretary of the treasury "to deal in gold and foreign exchange, and such other instruments of credit or security as he may deem necessary to carry out the purpose of this section," previously stated to be that of "stabilizing the exchange value of the dollar."

**Annual Audit Ordered.**

The administration text stipulated that the secretary's decisions on the administration of the fund should be "final and not be subject to review by any other officer of the United States." The Fletcher bill omitted this provision, and simply said "an annual audit of such fund shall be made and a report thereof submitted to the President."

Glass' succinct comment on the

### GOLD CAN STILL BE SOLD TO U. S.

Washington, Jan. 17. — (AP) — Secretary Morgenthau Wednesday night authorized federal reserve banks, the treasurer of the United States, mints and assay offices to continue "until further notice" to receive gold coins and gold certificates and pay for them in other currency at their face value.

The new order modifies the previous order setting midnight Wednesday as the deadline for turning gold into the treasury.

Gold hoarding penalties, however, were not lifted if, in the opinion of the secretary of the treasury, the gold paid in had been hoarded.

New York Market Quotations

# THE MINNEAPOLIS JOURNAL

24 PAGES—HOME EDITION. • • WEATHER Partly cloudy tonight and Friday; somewhat colder Friday. THURSDAY EVENING, JANUARY 18, 1934. PRICE TWO CENTS IN MINNEAPOLIS

# Kidnapers Seize Edward Bremer; Ask $200,000 for St. Paul Banker

## Schools Get $108,000 Pay Cut Rebates

### Teachers and Other Employees to Receive Refund on 1933 Slash

### WILL EQUAL FOURTH OF MONTH'S SALARY

### Settlement of Delinquent Taxes Creates Balance to Keep Board Pledge

School teachers and other employees will receive rebates, totaling about $108,000, to make up part of the severe salary reductions levied against them in 1933 to balance the school budget, board officials announced today. The refund will be big enough to give each worker one-fourth of a month's salary, calculated on pay rates in effect in December. This will not mean one-fourth of the basic monthly salary to which the employee theoretically was entitled in 1933, but one-fourth of the reduced pay rate in effect the last four months, which is about 55 per cent of the normal rate.

The arrangement has been approved by the board on recommendation of Superintendent Carroll R. Reed, in fulfillment of a promise made by the board late in 1932, that part of 1933 pay losses would be restored if funds were available.

**Refunds Up to $80,000**

The refund will be made up of $80,000 in delinquent tax payments made in November and December, $15,000 cash balance remaining in the general school fund at the end of 1933, and $10,000 of 1934 current funds.

The normal procedure is to credit collections in November and December of any year to revenue of the following year, but the board agreed to Mr. Reeds' argument that it is justified in using part of the revenue from this source in November and December, 1933, for 1933 purposes, because of abnormal circumstances resulting from recent legislation.

Early in 1933 the legislature provided for the payment of 1931 taxes, collectible in 1932, and delinquent after November 1 of that year, without penalty, if paid one-half before January 1, 1934, and one-half before January 1, 1935," Mr. Reed said in a letter to the board on the subject. "Part of these taxes probably would have been paid before Nov. 1, 1933, if there had been no legislative interference with the normal situation."

**Collections Doubled**

Delinquent tax collections in November and December, 1933, ran $230,000, as compared to $95,000 in the same months in 1932, he said. He argued part of the large increase from 1932 to 1933 was the result of legislation that encouraged persons to delay payment of taxes who otherwise would have paid them before Nov. 1, 1933, which payments may be credited to 1933 revenues.

"In view of the fact the employees of the board took such a drastic cut during the fall of 1933, amounting to approximately 45 per

Continued on page 6

## Order by U. S. Halts Zoo Sale

### Longfellow Property Placed in Federal Court by Debtors Petition

Taking advantage of the recently enacted amendments to the federal bankruptcy laws, Marion C. Rowell today filed a debtors petition with the clerk of United States District Court thereby placing the property of Longfellow zoo under the jurisdiction of the Federal Courts.

Although brought under the bankruptcy laws, the action does not constitute a bankruptcy, it was explained. A debtors' petition asks only for an extension of time in which to effect settlement with creditors who may, ultimately, receive payment in full. The petition, however, forestalls all foreclosures, sheriffs' sales, garnishments or any other legal action designed to acquire the property of the petitioner.

**Halts Sale of Animals**

Mrs. Rowell's action halted a sale of the animals at the zoo, scheduled for 10 a.m. today, to satisfy a chattel mortgage held by Edith Jones, another beneficiary under the will of Richard F. Jones.

The petition declares "that she is insolvent or unable to meet her debts as they mature and that she desires to effect a composition or an extension of time to pay her debts." Among the debts are listed $9,892 in wages of which $7,459 is due H. C. Rowell; $9,500 under the chattel mortgage; $3,622 under a real estate mortgage, and $9,577 of unsecured claims.

**Creditors to Be Called**

The petition will go to Alexander McCune, referee in bankruptcy, and creditors will be called in in an attemtp to reach a settlement, court attaches explained.

At no time, before the discharge of the petition, however, may creditors take any of the property by legal action. The property remains, technically, in custody and under the control of Federal Court.

C. J. WINTON

## Second House Group Backs Dollar Slash

### Coinage Committee Amends Bill to Require Reports to Congress

**Washington, Jan. 18.—(U.P.)—Administration leaders decided today to push the dollar revaluation bill through the house this week in the belief that the foreign exchange situation necessitates early use of the proposed $2,000,000,000 stabilization fund.**

Washington, Jan. 18.—(AP)—The house coinage committee today approved the President's dollar devaluation bill, adding an amendment requiring the secretary of the treasury to report to congress on operations of the stabilization fund.

Meanwhile, Secretary H. L. Morgenthau said at his press conference that the federal reserve bank of New York, acting for the treasury, was purchasing gold abroad as well as domestically.

Members of the house awaited solution of a row between its banking and coinage commitees over possession of the currency legislation. Speaker H. T. Rainey referred it to the coinage committee, but the other group yesterday reported it favorably.

Chairman A. L. Somers said of the 16 members of the coinage committee present all but one voted for the bill with the amendment. That one, he added, withheld his vote for the time being.

The committee, however, did not instruct the chairman to seek imme-

Continued on page 2

## *Byrd Expedition Reaches Base at Little America*

Little America (via Mackay Radio), Jan. 18.—(AP)—Admiral Richard E. Byrd and his Antarctic expedition arrived here at 12:30 a.m. today.

Unusual static interference made it difficult for the Byrd flagship to communicate with civilization.

The flagship was forced to travel at a reduced speed Tuesday night owing to a blizzard. But yesterday the sky cleared slowly and the waters of the Ross sea became deep blue.

The expedition intended to determine the state of the old camp at Little America, which Byrd left four years ago, immediately.

## C. J. Winton, Civic Leader, Dies, Aged 71

### Prominent Lumberman With Wide Interests Succumbs in Hospital

### KNOWN FOR WELFARE WORK IN MINNEAPOLIS

### Played Football on Princeton Eleven More Than Half Century Ago

Charles J. Winton, prominent in the lumber industry of the country and a civic leader in Minneapolis for many years, died early today in Abbott hospital, following a heart attack.

Mr. Winton had been prominently identified in welfare work in the city and was well known for his support and personal interest in charitable activities.

He had been in good health until a few weeks ago, when he contracted a cold which reacted unfavorably on his heart.

Mr. Winton was born Aug. 23, 1862, in Chicago. His family moved to Addison, N. Y., where he spent his boyhood. He was graduated from the Williston Seminary at Easthampton, Massachusetts and then attended Princeton University, in the class of 1884.

**Played Football at Princeton**

He played in the first intercollegiate football games as a halfback on the Princeton team in 1880 and 1881, in contests with Yale and Harvard universities. He also was a member of the Princeton baseball team and in his senior year was director of the Princeton football association.

Following his graduation from university, Mr. Winton came west and entered the lumber business at Wausau, Wis., which was his headquarters for a number of years.

In 1909 Mr. Winton moved to Minneapolis, where the offices of his expanding lumber business were established. He immediately took an active interest in the city's many welfare projects. He was president of the Infant Welfare Association for a number of years, a trustee of the Westminster Presbyterian church and a trustee of Abbott hospital.

**Traveled Extensively**

He continued his college relationship with the presidency of the Princeton Association of the Northwest. He was a member of the Minneapolis, Minikahda and Woodhill Clubs.

Although he had been relinquishing his active direction in his lumber businesses in favor of his sons, at the time of his death he was president of the Winton Lumber Company, Winton Oregon Timber Company, chairman of the board of The Pas Lumber Company, Ltd., and a director of several companies.

**Bank Director for Many Years**

He was a director of the Northwestern National Bank for many years.

Mr. Winton is survived by his wife; a daughter, Mrs. Carl W. Jones; two sons, David Winton and Charles J. Winton, Jr., and a sister, Mrs. S. H. McVitty, Salem, Va. The family home was at 1324 Mount Curve avenue.

**City Leaders Mourn**

Friends and business acquaintances of Mr. Winton were much shocked at his unexpected death.

"I was greatly shocked to hear of his death," E. M. Case said. "I had known him for many years. He was a warm hearted man, big and generous. He was always ready to help the under dog and a square shooter in every way. He was active in welfare projects in the city for many years.

"I can't speak too highly of Mr.

Continued on page 6

## *Three Women Tossed Like Sacks From Sinking Ship*

### Men Leap to Rescue Lifeboat as Adventure Cruise Ends in Atlantic

New York, Jan. 18.—(AP)—Three women survivors of the yacht Alamyth were thrown like sacks of wheat from the deck of the sinking craft to the arms of sailors in a wave-tossed lifeboat.

The story of their rescue, along with that of 11 men, in a sea so rough that no boat could tie to the Alamyth, was related today as soon as they arrived on the coastguard cutter Thetis shortly after 8 a.m.

The Alamyth, a two-masted auxiliary schooner 86 feet long, was abandoned by its small company yesterday, when water was pouring into its hull so fast that pumps could no longer save it.

Rescue of the survivors was effected by the tanker Gulfland, 75 miles south of Barnegat, N. J.

George E. Conklin of Teaneck, N. J., organizer of the cruise which was to take the yacht through the south seas on a share-the-cost basis, said a sudden veering of the wind yesterday brought disaster to the craft.

Conklin said the wind carried away the peak halyard and brought down the foresail.

The yacht began to ship water and two pumps were started.

They drifted through a rough sea and bitter cold with the wind lashing the yacht and the leak ever widening.

At 11 a.m. they sighted the Gulfland. The yacht had no radio.

The ensign was run up, top side down. The Gulfland indicated understanding the signal. The men threw buckets of water over the side of the craft as sign language for "we are shipping water."

Medora Gehben completed the message, "three women on board," by standing atop the tossing cabin and raising her arms high above her head three times.

The Gulfland put out a boat too small to buck the great waves, and had to return. A 36-passenger lifeboat was lowered.

So rough was the sea the lifeboat could make no contact with the Alamyth. It tossed several feet away. The sailors in it braced themselves, held out their arms nad to them were hurled the three women, one at a time.

HELD FOR $200,000 RANSOM

EDWARD G. BREMER, St. Paul, a member of one of the Northwest's wealthiest families, is reported held today by kidnapers who demand $200,000 for his release. The police have not been officially notified and the family refuses to discuss it.

## *Murder Confession Battle Starts at Wynekoop Trial*

### Jury Excused as Defense Opens Fight—Insurance Agents Tell of Policies

**Chicago, Jan. 18.—(U.P.)—The major battle of the Rheta Wynekoop murder case was fought today over Dr. Alice Lindsay Wynekoop's so-called "confession" of the mysterious crime. The jury was excluded immediately after Police Captain John Stege took the stand and the fight started. Judge Joseph B. David interrupted the start of arguments to order bailiffs to maintain more order.**

Chicago, Jan. 18.—(AP)—More insurance agents were paraded to the stand today by the state in its effort to prove that Dr. Alice Lindsay Wynekoop murdered her daughter-in-law Rheta and that the chief motive for the crime was a desire to benefit by policies issued on the girl's life.

The 62-year-old defendant appeared in better physical condition than yesterday as she started the second week of her ordeal. She declared she had a good night's sleep and that a severe headache had left her.

Continuing the line of attack begun the preceding day, the state called to the stand Miss Esther A. English, an agent for a life insurance company. Miss English testified that October 30, 1933, three weeks before Rheta Gardner Wynekoop was found slain on an operating table in the basement office of her mother-in-law's home, she had gone to the Wynekoop home.

"I asked for Rheta and talked to her briefly. Then Dr. Wynekoop came forward and told me she would discuss the matter with me. Rheta left the room. I asked Dr. Wynekoop the questions and filled in the blanks myself. Then Dr. Wynekoop left the room and returned with Rheta's signature."

"Who was the beneficiary?" ask-

Continued on page 6

## Touhy Jury Picking Tense

### Arrest of One Selection for Perjury Tightens Up Atmosphere

Chicago, Jan. 18.—(U.P.)—Selection of a jury for the trial of Roger Touhy and three gangster associates on charges of kidnaping John (Jake the Barber) Factor continued today in an atmosphere of tension.

Prospective jurors faced stiff questioning on whether they will feel free to bring in a death penalty verdict against the accused men as provided under the state laws. William Scott Stewart, defense attorney, meanwhile was concerned with their attitude toward "the beer business before repeal."

The drama of picking this jury was brought to a climax late yesterday when one juror, already accepted by defense and prosecution, was brought back before the court, and perjury and contempt of court charges were placed against him.

The juror, Russell H. Brownell, was charged with having concealed a police record from the court. His removal from the panel left seven jurors accepted.

Touhy, together with Gus Schaeffer, Eddie McFadden and Albert Kator, are charged with having abducted Factor. The latter, expected to be the state's star witness, faces deportation to England, where he must face swindling charges.

## CWA Orders Halt On All Purchases

Washington, Jan. 18.—(AP)—Preparing for possible stoppage of the civil works program on February 10 because of funds running out, the federal civil works administration today halted purchase of materials and supplies for use on projects throughout the country.

The order, issued by Audrey Williams, assistant administrator, on direction of Harry L. Hopkins, represented, it was said, "a stock taking."

## *Hoover Mentioned For President of Iowa University*

Iowa City, Jan. 18.—Former President Herbert Hoover's name today was included in an unofficial list of possible successors to President Walter A. Jessup of the state University of Iowa.

The former president's name was advanced by an Iowa City newspaper, which said that he had been mentioned in connection with the position.

Advices from Palo Alto, Calif., declared that Mr. Hoover "has heard nothing of it." Paul Sexson, his secretary, made the statement.

Discussion of a successor to Dr. Jessup, who resigned to become head of the Carnegie Foundation for the Advancement of Teaching in New York, is to be undertaken at a meeting of the state board of education January 23.



## MOLYNEAUX HALTS NORTHWEST BANCO INQUIRY BY STATE

**Federal Judge Joseph W. Molyneaux of Minneapolis today signed an order temporarily restraining the Minnesota commerce commission from proceeding with its investigation of sale of stock o fthe Northwest Bancorporation.**

## Norling Joins Staff to Raise Level of Lakes

### Appointed by Olson to Aid Zimmerman in Statewide CWA Projects

### TONKA TO BE FIRST ON SURVEY PROGRAM

### Chisago Chains Next in $5,000,000 to $7,500,000 Restoration Scheme

Sven A. Norling, Minneapolis hydraulic engineer and prominently identified in recent years in movements relating to restoration of the level of Lake Minnetonka, today joined the staff of L. P. Zimmerman, state engineer, to take charge of civil works administration projects relating to restoration of the lake levels in Minnesota.

The appointment was made by Governor Floyd B. Olson yesterday and was confirmed today by Mr. Zimmerman.

Mr. Norling will co-operate with the state conservation department in its lake restoration program, and it was reported between $5,000,000 and $7,250,000 will be available for the work.

**Tonka to Come First**

One of the first projects contemplated is a survey of Lake Minnetonka and sources of water diversion for restoring its level. After that, the chain of Chisago lakes will be surveyed in connection with a similar project of restoration.

Mr. Norling said he expected to start Lake Minnetonka surveys "as soon as possible" and indicated that 40 or more skilled workmen would be put to work.

Several sources of water supply for Minnetonka will be studied, among them use of wells, Mississippi, Crow and other waters, and out of the group one will be recommended after all data is compiled.

**Will Cost Around $500,000**

Former surveys, Mr. Norling indicated, had placed the estimated cost of water diversion to Lake Minnetonka around a half million dollars.

Recommendations of the state conservation department for restoring levels of other lakes will be considered first in other projects to be covered under the office in charge of Mr. Norling.

Diversion of water for Lake Minnetonka has been a public subject for several years but cost of the project, reflected upon the taxpayers, was an outstanding factor in blocking definite programs.

**Included in CWA Program**

Mr. Norling emphasized today that diversion of water for Minnetonka and for any other lakes that might be included in the program would be borne now by CWA funds.

Several times bills were presented to the legislature to assure lake-level raising projects directly affecting Lake Minnetonka.

Among the most carefully considered sources of diversion for the lake was the Crow river, which engineers have maintained might be able to supply sufficient water from its surplus flow to raise the lake's level.

**Would Affect Minnehaha**

Raising the level of Minnetonka would have a direct bearing on Minnehaha creek which has its source at the lake. More water in the lake would, it has been pointed out, assure a steady flow of water in the picturesque Minnehaha creek bed and Minnehaha falls, long identified with the beauty spots of the northwest.

The normal high water level of Lake Minnetonka with its 22½ square mile area is 930 feet above mean sea level. In recent years it has been as low as four feet below this mark.

## Son of Adolph Bremer Vanishes After Taking Daughter to School —Friend Receives Phone Call

### VOICE THREATENS DEATH IF POLICE ARE CALLED IN

### Attempt to Trace Call Fails—Note Found Outside Office—Money Instructions Given

Snatched by kidnapers when he took his eight-year-old daughter to school, Edward G. Bremer, son of Adolph Bremer of St. Paul, and a member of a wealthy family, is being held for $200,000 ransom.

Two contacts have already been made with the kidnapers, it is understood, although the police have received no official notification of the crime and the family refused to discuss it.

Bremer, who is president of the Commercial State Bank in St. Paul, left his home at 92 East River Road at 8:15 a.m. Wednesday. As was his custom, he took his small daughter as far as Summit school on his way to the bank. The child arrived safely at the school. Mr. Bremer's failure to arrive at the bank caused little anxiety, as associates assumed he had stopped on some business call.

***Walter Magee First to Get Call From Abductors; Death Warning Given***

Near noon Walter Magee, St. Paul contractor and a close friend of the kidnaped man, as well as a close business associate of the Bremer family, received the first word from the kidnapers, according to reports. Mr. Magee said today he "knew nothing of the affair" and all information came from outside sources.

Answering the telephone in his office, according to information, he heard a deep voice, evidently lowered in an attempt at disguise, say, "Well, we've got your friend Bremer, and if you are not damn careful we'll get you, too."

He was warned, it was reported, that any attempt to communicate with police or newspapers would result in the immediate death of Bremer. He also was informed that a note would be found on the steps at the rear entrance to his office building.

Although Mr. Magee had not been aware that Mr. Bremer had disappeared, he hurriedly dispatched an office assistant to another telephone in an effort to trace the telephone call. He stalled the conversation as much as possible but the kidnapers hung up before the call could be traced.

***Note Signed by Bremer Found Under Mat on Steps at Magee Office***

Under a mat on the back steps of Mr. Magee's office was found a typewritten note signed by Edward Bremer. The note apparently had been written and then folded and Mr. Bremer forced to sign it, probably without knowing its content.

The note, it is reported, said Mr. Bremer had been taken captive by the kidnap gang and that he was held in a safe place and was unharmed. A demand for $200,000 for his safe return was made. Again a threat of death for their victim was made unless the demands were met or in case police and newspapers were notified.

The demand for ransom was that the money be in $5, $10 and $20 bills of used currency and not of consecutive serial numbers as in the Hamm case, according to unofficial report. The note, it is said, specified the money was to be placed in a cardboard box and tied in a specified way.

***Victim Born and Reared in St. Paul—Progress in Bank Career Steady***

Mr. Bremer was born and reared in St. Paul, attending the public schools there until he was graduated and went to Washington where he completed his university education. He returned to St. Paul from school in 1918 and started work in the bank as a messenger. Successive promotions carried him through the various departments and positions until he was elected president of the institution. He is married and has one daughter.

The Bremer family is one of the oldest and most influential in St. Paul. For years their brewery holdings, banking interests and real estate holdings have made them leaders in the city's activities.

Otto Bremer, uncle of the kidnaped man, is Minnesota manager of the home owners loan board, to which position he was appointed by President Roosevelt in recognition of years of service in democratic circles in the state and northwest.

***Bremer's Auto Found Mile From Place Designated in Phone Message***

Mr. Bremer's automobile was not found at the Highland Park water tower, where the telephoner said it had been left, but was located near the home of Martin Thornton, 1910 Edgcombe road, president of Thornton Brothers Contracting Company, more than a mile away.

Bremer was married about 10 years ago to Miss Emily Erswein of Minneapolis. The couple have one child, Betty. In addition to his father, he has one brother, Adolph, Jr., 855 West Seventh street, and three sisters, Louise, 855 West Seventh, whose engagement to George Benz of St. Paul recently was announced; Mrs. Franklyn Holloway Matson (Katherine Bremer), 881 Fairmount avenue, and Mrs. Victor Philip Heim (Marie Bremer), of New Ulm, Minn. His mother is dead.

***Second Big Abduction in Seven Months In Brewery Circles of St. Paul***

It was the second big abduction in seven months of a member of a St. Paul brewing family. William Hamm, Jr., president of the Hamm Brewing Company, paid $100,000 for his release last June.

Bremer is the son of Adolph Bremer, 855 West Seventh street, part owner of the Jacob Schmidt Brewing Company.

Police have not been officially notified by members of the family who refuse to talk.

St. Paul has been the scene of four other major kidnapings in the last 2½ years. From their four victims, the abductors obtained

Continued on page 2

# THE MINNEAPOLIS JOURNAL

Copyright 1934 by The Journal Printing Company

WEATHER Possibly thunderstorms today; not so warm in south portion. | MINNEAPOLIS, MINN., SUNDAY, JULY 22, 1934. | 84 PAGES—PRICE 6 CENTS IN MINNEAPOLIS


# Strikers Given Work Ultimatum; Parleys Halt With No Agreement

## Mercury Hits 105; Hundred Die in Nation

### Forecast for Minneapolis Promises Little Relief, Possible Showers

### HUMIDITY DROPS 37 DEGREES IN HALF DAY

### Farmers Quit Fields Fearing Sunstroke—Girl Collapses in Loop Street

The nation roasted under a merciless sun that sent the thermometer boiling to 105 degrees in Minneapolis at 3 p. m. yesterday and left a train of at least 100 dead and thousands prostrated throughout the nation in its burning wake.

The local weather bureau forecast promised some relief. It read: "Unsettled; possibly some local showers or thunder storms. Not so warm Sunday."

No deaths occurred in Minneapolis, although one person was taken to General hospital overcome with the heat. Florence Bruins, 22 years old, 2322 Pierce street NE., collapsed from the heat at Sixth street and Third avenue N. Her condition was reported not serious.

Another victim of the heat in Minneapolis today was Fred Morgan, 45 years old, 54 Twelfth street N. Mr. Morgan collapsed in his home today and was taken to General hospital, where his condition was said to be serious.

**Humidity Drops to 28**

The humidity dropped from 65 at 7 a.m. to 28 at noon. Had it not been for this, weather bureau officials reported, several deaths and prostrations probably would have occurred.

Weather bureau temperature readings for Minneapolis were:

| | | | |
|---|---|---|---|
| 7 a.m. | 78 | 1 p.m. | 101 |
| 8 a.m. | 85 | 2 p.m. | 104 |
| 9 a.m. | 87 | 3 p.m. | 105 |
| 10 a.m. | 93 | 4 p.m. | 104 |
| 11 a.m. | 96 | 5 p.m. | 104 |
| 12 m. | 99 | 6 p.m. | 102 |
| | | 7 p.m. | 100 |

The three-day total of deaths from the heat was more than 200. The heat wave held the middle west in record breaking temperatures. There was scant prospect of a letup, government forecasters said, for at least another week. Weather books contain no parallel this side of 1901, they said, of a greater heat wave in the drouth-blighted middle west.

**Farmers Quit Fields**

Temperatures soared to record figures. In some sections farmers abandoned their fields in fear of sunstroke. Panting cattle were left to die unheeded in the fields.

Missouri, which has had less rain than any other state in the midwest, reported a total of 29 deaths. Few cities had temperatures reading under 105.

The temperature jumped 10 degrees in an hour at Eau Claire, Wis., yesterday to send the mercury to the 103 mark.

At Dallas, Texas, 2,500 pounds of dynamite was prepared by James A. Baze, chemist, who was reported planning to bomb clouds.

**Steel Workers Collapse**

At steel mills in Ohio and Indiana, scores of workers, accustomed as they are to the searing furnace blasts, collapsed and were treated at hospitals. Prisoners at the Joliet, Ill., state prison were relieved of work as the thermometer showed 115 degrees.

A hazy weather condition prevented the take-off of the U. S. Army-National Geographic Society's stratosphere flight from Rapid City, S. D.

The day intensified the water famine in the great plains states and farmers frantically sank new wells to keep their stock alive.

**BLAST FURNACE HEAT SWEEPS EAST COAST**

Special to The Journal

New York, July 21.—Blast furnace heat today gave the east a return of some of the most torrid weather of the long wave of high temperatures and humidity.

Although along the Atlantic seaboard there was no thermometer reading to match those record maximum temperatures of the midwest, the mugginess was much greater and more general and this, together with heat in the mid-nineties even up in New England, caused widespread discomfort, more than a dozen deaths, four of which were in New York City, and a fresh exodus for lakeside and seashore resorts.

In New York City a high of 94 was reached at 4 p.m., five degrees lower than the record of 99 for July 21, established in 1930.

New England faced another weekend of heat and high humidity, with drouth conditions hourly becoming more serious. The hay crop in Maine withered with a loss of thousands of dollars and farms over the whole area were stricken.

New York and New Jersey truck farms also were heavy sufferers from the burning sun and continued drouth.

GUARDS MAKE BARRACKS AT STATE FAIR GROUNDS—The Minnesota National Guard lost little time Saturday in billeting at the State Fair Grounds, where troopers were called for possible duty in the Minneapolis truck drivers strike. The troops were called out from their annual encampment at Camp Ripley. Above, the quarters of the Ninety Second Infantry Brigade in the vast dairy building. More than 2,000 infantry men as well as mess quarters, first aid stations, ammunition dumps and headquarters offices, are housed here. The men spent Saturday brushing up from their hurried trip and polishing up rifles and machine guns.

## *Frisco Employers, 9 Unions Agree to Arbitrate Strike*

### End of Maritime Walkout Now Up to 4,000 Longshoremen—Quick Vote Ordered

By United Press

San Francisco, July 21.—The fate of San Francisco's million-dollar-a-day maritime strike rested with 4,000 longshoremen tonight.

The other nine union groups concerned in the walkout and all employers were agreed on submitting to arbitration.

Official of the longshoremen's union at a meeting tonight decided to submit to a vote of longshoremen in all ports of the Pacific coast the matter of arbitration in the strike.

The decision was reached after the longshoremen officials had conferred with Senator Robert Wagner of New York, White House emissary, and members of President Roosevelt's national longshoremen's mediation board.

**Longshoremen To Vote**

Ballots were to be printed immediately and sent out tonight by air to all coast ports.

The ballots will contain the following single question:

"Will the International Longshoremen's association agree to submit to arbitration by the national longshoremen's board the issues in dispute in the longshore strike and to be govered by the decision of the board?"

This put the issue directly to the striking men, a majority of whom were reported to favor arbitration. The vote should be returned early next week.

San Franciscans looked eagerly to an early settlement.

**Troop Withdrawals Start**

As an indication that the maritime strike, which precipitated San Francisco's four day general strike, was believed near settlement was the action of Governor Frank Merriam in ordering all but 1,200 national guardsmen withdrawn from the San Francisco and Oakland waterfront.

At the height of the strike 4,200 troopers were on duty.

The situation was very quiet along the waterfront with com-

Continued on page 4

## Raids on Red Hangouts on Coast Pushed

### 550 Under Arrest in Many Cities—U. S. Agents to Deport Aliens

By United Press

San Francisco, July 21.—Raids on alleged communists continued today in various parts of California. More than 550 are under arrest. Federal agents are checking their records, looking for deportable aliens.

In San Francisco 65 more suspects were arrested and held on vagrancy charges.

In Stockton, 75 miles away, 500 citizens wrecked a communist headquarters. One arrest was made there.

The Stockton raiding party originally numbered about 70 and formed at the Civic Memorial auditorium, prepared to break up a communist meeting in the courthouse square. Each of the 70 members of the crowd carried two-foot clubs.

**Two Raiding Parties Clash**

Police spoiled the plan to raid the meeting, however, when they arrived first and broke it up.

The raiding party then moved toward communist headquarters, its numbers growing each block until 500 were in the crowd.

The communists fled. The party wrecked the meeting place, which formerly was a United Brethren church. The windows were broken and furniture demolished.

**13 "Deported" by Committee**

At Sacramento a large crowd of alleged communists was rounded up by police but when officers questioned them for possible deportation they found only two aliens in the group, both Chinese.

Meantime a party of 13 alleged communists, rounded up by a "citizens committee" in San Jose and vicinity yesterday and "deported" continued its enforced wanderings southward.

## Rats Reveal Prison Break

### Rodents Rout Five Convicts From Sewer—Three Recaptured

By United Press

Philadelphia, July 21.—An elaborate prison break at the Pennsylvania eastern penitentiary was foiled tonight when rats drove five convicts from a sewer after they had fled the jail.

Three of the convicts in the desperate attempt to escape were captured. Two others eluded police.

The prisoners jumped down a sewer drain in the prison yard while two convict teams were playing basketball. They followed the sewer line for five blocks before hordes of rats attacked them.

Unable to keep their footing in the slippery sewer the men sought a manhole cover and hurried to the street.

Pedestrians seeing five partially clad men, their clothing having been bitten an torn by the rats, emerging from a sewer, gave the alarm. The convicts fled toward a railroad yard.

## *Bank That Caused Debt Moratorium Sound Once More*

By United Press

Vienna, July 21.—The Credit Anstall, whose imminent collapse in 1931 precipitated the German crisis, the Hoover debt moratorium, the jettisoning of the German reparations demands and finally the Allied debt defaults to the United States, was back on its feet today. A brief statement was issued that, at the request of the bank and with the approval of its big depositors, the government had withdrawn the guarantee to depositors and the bank's other creditors against loss in May 1931. The bank now is stable itself and had absorbed two other banks.

## U. S. Putting Soft Pedal on Debt Relief

Special to The Journal

Washington, July 21.—The administration appeared today to have undertaken a deliberate campaign to soft-pedal the debt reduction opportunities opened to farmers under the drastic Frazier-Lemke mortgage moratorium bill passed by the last congress.

Fearful of the consequences, should the farmers of the country join in a concerted movement to scale down the present $81,000,000,000 farm mortgage debt through voluntary bankruptcy, the federal farm credit administration, it was indicated, is seeking by indirect methods to dissuade farmers from taking advantage of the bill.

Officials of the administration were understood to be watching with some concern a recently-developed downward trend of emergency appeals for government financial aid from farmers throughout the country. Early in July, it was understood, such emergency appeals totaled about 540 a week, whereas they had dropped to 367 a week by the middle of the month.

Farm credit experts were inclined to attribute much of this falling off in farm aid requests to the fact more than $1,000,000,000 now has been advanced to farmers in mort-

Continued on page 4

## Farley Snubs Shipstead and Backs Hoidale

### Pledges Support of National Democratic Committee to Congressman

By LEIF GILSTAD

All the facilities of the democratic national committee Saturday were thrown to the aid of Congressman Einar Hoidale in his race for United States Senator, off-setting reports that the administration is for Senator Henrik Shipstead.

While a letter from James A. Farley, national chairman, pledging his aid to Mr. Hoidale, provided the major contribution to the political situation, attacks on two party platforms were made Saturday as other campaign developments. The democratic state platform was assailed in some particulars by John R. Foley, a democrat, who is chairman of the state conservation commission.

The farmer-labor platform was attacked by A. B. Gilbert, republican candidate for governor in the primary.

**Farley Commends Hoidale**

Mr. Farley wrote Mr. Hoidale for information on the political situation, then added:

"Your loyal and unwavering support of President Roosevelt's program during the seventy-third congress is very much appreciated by everyone connected with the administration. In your devotion to the ideals of the democratic party, in your steadfast adherence to the aims and purposes of the New Deal, I can count no member of the congress with a more genuine record for loyalty than you have.

"I would be remiss in my duty as national chairman of the party if I did not offer you the facilities and services of the national committee in your campaign. Please feel entirely at liberty in calling on me."

**Farley Demands Proof of Charge**

In a letter to Joseph Moonan democratic state chairman, Mr. Farley demanded that his fellow democrats submit proof at a meeting of the conservation commission August 9 to support charges of "extravagant dissipation of game and

Continued on page 4

## *Bills Unpaid, Water Shut Off; 12 Critically Ill of Typhoid*

By United Press

Decatur, Ala., July 21.—Twelve persons receiving federal relief, critically ill from typhoid fever, became ill when they were forced to drink from a stagnant well when their water was shut off because of unpaid bills, it was revealed today.

The sufferers, all neighbors, attracted the attention of city health authorities today when it was discovered they lived within a radius of a few blocks of an old well.

An investigation revealed that those stricken were members of six families. They were unemployed and unable to meet long past due water bills.

City authorities ordered an examination of the well and an analysis of the water, which all admitted drinking, revealed it contained typhoid germs.

At a hospital, where the sufferers were taken, it was reported the patients were critically ill.

## Few of Pickets Wounded in Riot Are Union Drivers, Police Learn

### Several Shot by Johannes' Men Admit Being Communists

### SOME OTHERS FOUND JOBLESS SYMPATHIZERS

### St. Paul Youth Describes Battle in Statement to Detectives

Statements to police and to members of the county attorney's staff indicate that only a minority of the men wounded or arrested in the riot in the wholesale district Friday were legitimate members of the truck drivers union.

Several admitted being members of the communist party or unemployed men who were acting as pickets either through sympathy or through promises of payment from the communists.

Police and the county attorney's office are checking over each case and from those statements, where it is definitely established that the men are communists, consideration is being given to bringing charges of criminal syndicalism under the state law.

**Men Under Guard**

The men were under police guard in hospitals and they will be jailed as their condition permits.

The names of the communists were being withheld until formal charges can be made. At least two men told of being approached in the Gateway district by communists and of being offered high wages to act as strike pickets.

From police investigation the men involved were mostly unemployed men seeking action; which they got. They range from a known communist strong-arm man to a university student "parlor pink."

Following is one statement of a St. Paul youth who did not belong to the union but who belongs to the "M. C. C. W.," although he did not know what that stood for, who came to Minneapolis and slept at strike headquarters and went out on the call for pickets in the wholesale district.

**Detectives Quiz Youth**

The statement was taken in the presence of Detectives Miller and Coskran and Stenographer Feeney at Eitel hospital.

Q—What is your name?

A—David Eugene Crocker.

Q—How old are you?

A—19.

Q—Where do you live?

A—4125 Grand avenue, St. Paul.

Q—Do you belong to the truck drivers' union?

A—No, I belong to the M. C. C. W.

Q—What does that stand for?

A—I don't know.

Q—Then you don't belong to the truck drivers' union?

A—Oh, it's under the union.

Q—Tell how you happened to get down at the strike where the trouble started; were you at strike headquarters first?

A—Yes, that's where I started from.

Q—You got news there that a truck was being loaded?

A—Yes, with groceries to be delivered to the grocery stores. We loaded up quite a few cars and three trucks. I went down there and I was on one of the trucks.

**Says Committee Sent Him**

Q—Who asked you to go down

Continued on page 2

## U. S. to Start 75 Million Job

### Wallace Announces Forest Shelter Belt Will Be Built at Once

Special to The Journal

Washington, July 21.—Immediate start will be made on a $75,000,000 project—a forest shelter belt 100 miles wide extending from the Canadian border to Texas—according the announcement made late today by Secretary Henry A. Wallace. Announcement of the proposed project was made some time ago.

Funds to begin the work have been provided in an executive order signed July 11 and released today. A fund of $15,000,000 is set aside for starting the project.

The shelter belt which will be planted, will extend more than 1,000 miles through North and South Dakota, Nebraska, Kansas, Oklahoma and into Texas. It will be designed to give permanent relief to drouth conditions throughout the midwest.

More than 20,000,000 acres are in the area to be immediately affected. About 1,820,000 acres will be planted to trees. Windbreaks seven rods wide and running north and south will be planted one mile apart. This will make about 100 parallel windbreaks across the 100-mile shelter belt.

### Unofficial Truce in Effect Over Weekend—Mediators Delay Effort to Bring About Settlement

### DRIVERS NOTIFIED TO RETURN TO WORK MONDAY TO SAVE JOBS

### Three Thousand Guardsmen Under Arms at Fair Grounds—Conciliators in Consultation With Capital

Efforts on the part of federal mediators to end the truck drivers strike which has been in progress in Minneapolis since midnight Monday are reported to have ended without accomplishment last night and negotiations will not be resumed until 9:30 a.m. Monday.

In the meantime a virtual truce exists, Mayor A. G. Bainbridge having ordered police to furnish no convoys for trucks late Saturday and Sunday and employers having made no requests for protection during this period.

Employers of the city who have workers on strike have notified them to report for work tomorrow in order to protect their jobs.

Strike developments last night were:

**Conferences between Rev. Francis J. Haas and E. H. Dunnigan, federal mediators, were adjourned unexpectedly last night and, it was reported, without accomplishment in efforts to reach agreement to end strike.**

**Answers have been received on nine points on a tentative agreement from both strikers and employers. Father Haas reports that on some points there is accord and he will attempt to reach agreement on those now disputed.**

**Mayor A. G. Bainbridge had ordered police to furnish no convoys to trucks late Saturday and Sunday. Chief of Police Michael Johannes said he had had no requests for convoys.**

**Mayor Bainbridge made no statement relative to police protection Monday and it was expected that firms of the city would resume the movement of necessities.**

**Twenty-six truck loads of necessities were moved Saturday with police escorts. Several were followed by picket cars. Three arrests of pickets were made, but there were no disorders.**

**Henry B. Ness and John Belor, who were injured in the Friday strike riot, still were in a serious condition. Others injured were reported recovering.**

**The Central Labor Union and the Building Trades Council asked Mayor Bainbridge to dismiss Chief Johannes.**

**More than 3,000 members of the Minnesota National Guard were under arms at the State Fair grounds, including infantry and field artillery, waiting orders from Governor Floyd B. Olson, who had threatened martial law.**

Althought no reports were made by employers following a conference with Father Haas and Mr. Dunnigan shortly after the dinner hour yesterday, and Father Haas declined to say anything more than that "everyone was so hot and tired that they didn't want to go on with the conference and we thought it better to adjourn," it is understood the union has insisted that it be given contracts with the employers of truck drivers to represent not only the drivers, helpers and platform men but also the inside workers,, and these without being required to furnish proof of authority to represent them.

It is also understood the employers insist that section 7A of the national recovery act, which provides that a union may represent employees in collective bargaining when it has in its membership a majority of the employees,, be followed and that the union show the employers its position to represent the inside workers in plants employing truck drivers.

**Failure in Conciliation Leaves No Hope For Early Conclusion of Strike**

It appeared when last night's conference broke up that the conclusion of the strike was not near. From earlier statements made by Father Haas, it was felt he would have insisted on further conferences last night and today had he felt an agreement could bereached through them. He said last night he did not plan to have a conference with the union today.

Father Haas and Mr. Dunnigan were in conference with representatives of employers throughout the morning Saturday. Shortly after he left the conference he was given in writing the employers' stand on nine points which he had proposed for a settlement.

Later in the day the mediators were in conference with representatives of the strikers at the Athletic Club. He left this conference to go again into session with the employers.

Father Haas said that on some of the nine points both strikers and employers were in agreement but on several there were differences. He declined to point out what these were. He said the next step would be to iron out the points in disagreement.

**Men Warned to Return Monday Or Their Jobs Will Be Filled**

"We are going to keep right on," he said at that time. "We will work throughout Sunday if necessary. We have statements in writing from both sides. I am endeavoring at the earliest possible moment to bring both sides together in a common conference in the hope of obtaining agreement on now disputed points."

Both Father Haas and Mr. Dunnigan yesterday were in long distance telephone conversation with authorities in Washington about the situation in Minneapolis.

In a letter which was sent out by employers to their men who are on strike it was stated that "if you care to return to work you may do so by reporting for duty on or before Monday, July 23. After that date any other qualified applicants will be considered for employment on a permanent basis."

The letter stated that the employers had lived up to the labor board order of May and that they believed the employees who had had been misled into doing so.

Governor Olson has threatened to declare martial law if there

Continued on Page 2.

## The Law, the Governor and The State Troops

Article V, Section 4, of the Constitution of Minnesota says:

"The Governor . . . shall be Commander-in-Chief of the military and naval forces, and may call out such forces to execute the laws, suppress insurrection and repel invasion."

Mason's Statutes, 1927, Section 2407, says:

"The Governor shall be Commander-in-Chief of the military forces, except so much thereof as may be in the actual service of the United States, and may employ the same for the defense or relief of the State, the enforcement of its laws, and the protection of life and property therein."

**WEATHER**
U. S. Weather Bureau Forecast. Fair and cooler Friday; Saturday increasing cloudiness and warmer.
Additional weather on page 6.

# The Minneapolis Tribune

NRA MORNING EDITION

Sixty-eighth Year. No. 70. 3 MINNEAPOLIS, MINN., FRIDAY, AUGUST 3, 1934. Twenty-four Pages — Three Cents in Minneapolis

# Mediators Ask Owners Alter Peace Plan; Loop Parking Ban Is Modified

## Washington

By PAUL MALLON

Copyright, 1934, by Paul Mallon.

HULL'S DIPLOMACY; RUSSIA SQUEEZED; BUSINESS PROFITS

### SQUEEZE.

THE Hull school of diplomacy is developing some artful new tricks. The one worked on Russia this week was a gem. It was really only the old-fashioned squeeze play, but it was dressed up with some novel innovations so no one would recognize it.

George Peek staged it. He announced with an innocent look on his face that his second import bank was ready for bigger things. It would, he said, expand its operations beyond Cuba to finance the sale of American goods for all the world—this is, all the world except Russia. The red trade problem was to be handled by the first bank.

That stunned the Russians. They are almost as sensitive diplomatically as the Japanese. Such discrimination against them would ordinarily be considered an affront. They came into the state department on the run.

There, State Secretary Hull greeted them with his best poker face. He said and repeated twice, that he had not read Mr. Peek's announcement either before or after it was written.

He left the impression that he was, perhaps, angry that Mr. Peek had acted without informing him.

### PINCERS.

MR. HULL probably never told a fib in his life, and he did not this time. But, if the Russians had looked on his, or a nearby desk, they might have been able to find, under a pile of papers, a copy of the Peek report. It had been there for some time. Apparently, Mr. Hull had not got around to reading it. You know how those things are. A man should read only what is good for him to read.

It stumped the Russians. They knew darned well they were being affronted, but it was all so indirect, and the state secretary denied any connection with it.

Before long, they caught on to the fact that they had better get busy immediately and resume negotiations about settlement of the czarist and Kerensky debts if they wanted any of Mr. Peek's financial help.

The very next day the Russians resumed debt negotiations.

### PLAN.

THE way the play was worked out was like this:

Mr. Hull's good friend and assistant, Walton Moore, is a director of Mr. Peek's bank. Likewise, Mr. Moore is in charge of Russian debt negotiations. In that second capacity, he has not had much to do lately. The Russians have been slothful on debt negotiations for many months.

Those debts were contracted by previous Russian governments which used the money to fight against the very men controlling Russia today. You could hardly expect the reds to be eager about paying for guns and bullets which shot them down. They have repudiated similar debts to France.

Consequently they have been ducking the payment issue for weeks by insisting that they get a cash loan as a price for settling the debt. They asserted M. Litvinoff got the impression from Mr. Roosevelt that Russia would be given a cash loan.

Our boys have always insisted Mr. Roosevelt never gave Litvinoff such an impression. Early negotiations in Moscow broke down on that point, and were transferred here. Mr. Hull is supposed to have informed the Russian ambassador, Troyanovsky, that, if negotiations were to continue, Russia would have to stop asking impossible things, chief of which was the cash loan. Furthermore, Hull said, the export-import bank would not function for Russia until there was a debt settlement. Mr. Troyanovsky said he would have to ask his government about that.

It was while Mr. Troyanovsky was asking his government that Mr. Peek made his announcement with the double meaning.

It helped the Russians to make up their minds in a hurry.

### PROFITS.

THE secret of the Wall street blues can be found in the General Motors statement for the second quarter. The General Motors people did nearly 58 per

(Continued on Page 2, Column 4)

## Hitler Gets Power as Reichspresident But Rejects Title

### *Obtains Army Oath of Fealty as Hindenburg Dies.*

### *Quick Action Virtually Coup d'Etat—Plebiscite Called.*

By Louis P. Lochner.
Copyright, 1934, by Associated Press.

Berlin, Aug. 2.—Adolf Hitler in a series of lightning-like moves made himself absolute dictator of Germany Thursday.

He concentrated in his own hands the functions of president and of chancellor as soon as the aged president and patriot, Paul von Hindenburg, died at Neudeck early Thursday.

Then he called for and received an oath of personal allegience from officers and soldiers of the reichswehr (regular army).

After these moves, amounting to a virtual coup d'etat, the former lance corporal, who succeeded a field marshal, called for a plebiscite on August 19.

**Hitler Declines Title.**

Although desiring the functions of the presidency, Hitler declined Thursday night to accept the title, holding that the "greatness of the deceased has given to the title of reichspresident unique and non-recurring significance."

In a letter to Wilhelm Frick, minister of the interior, Hitler outlined his plans to assume the office without the title, saying he desired henceforth to be known as before as "fuehrer and reichschancellor."

He directed that a "free secret election" be held at which the centralization of power in his hands and such other matters as may be necessary be held.

The rapidity of the action which concentrated authority over 65,000,000 Germans in the hands of one man recalled the speed with which the Nazis first came to power on the morning of January 30, 1933.

Once again the Germans showed they are a disciplined people, trained to obedience. The change from a country governed at least theoretically by constitution to abso-

(Continued on Page 9, Column 1)

## STORM KILLS 8 IN MICHIGAN

### Excursion Steamer Is Driven Ashore, Property Damage Set at Above $1,000,000.

Detroit, Aug. 2.—(AP)—At least eight persons were killed, a crowded excursion steamer was driven ashore and property damage unofficially estimated at more than $1,000,000 was done by a heavy wind and rainstorm which swept eastern Michigan late Thursday.

The storm, sweeping southward from Flint, unroofed or demolished buildings, uprooted trees and disrupted communication and power services in four counties.

The steamer Tashmoo, en route to Detroit with 250 excursionists aboard, was driven ashore on the Canadian side of the St. Clair river near Algonac. Both paddle wheels of the vessel were smashed. Coast guards took off 150 of the passengers. The 100 remaining aboard were believed to be in no danger.

Flint suffered most, at least 10 injuries and one death being reported there. In Cass lake, in Oakland county, a Detroit man and his son drowned when the storm upset a rowboat.

Reports from Flushing, a village six miles northwest of Flint, stated that scarcely a house in the town was undamaged. The storm swept southward into the Detroit area shortly after 5 p. m., uprooting trees and blowing in windows in many parts of the city. The weather bureau estimated that the wind attained a velocity of more than 100 miles an hour.

**BOAT TIPS; THREE DROWN.**

Windsor, Ont., Aug. 2.—(AP)—Mrs. O. W. Pickard, her daughter, Lucille, 11, and son, Jerry 6, of Detroit, were drowned at Belle River Thursday when their boat was upset by a storm.

## STRIKERS' LEADERS FREED BY MILITARY

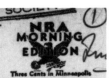

Three leaders of the striking truck drivers' union were released from the military stockade at the fair grounds Thursday afternoon when it was learned that the union had obtained a permit from a national guardsman for the mass meeting held Tuesday night at The Parade. Grant Dunne, at the left above, met the three on their release. Next to him, left to right, are William Brown, president of Local No. 574; Miles Dunne, V. R. Dunne, who spent more than 24 hours in the stockade, and their attorney, Albert Goldman of Chicago.

## NEWS INDEX

| | Page. | | Page. |
|---|---|---|---|
| Bridge | 10 | Society | 16 |
| Editorials | 14 | Sports | 18 |
| Feg Murray | 10 | Winchell | 10 |
| Markets | 20 | Want Ads | 22 |
| Radio | 6 | Weather | 6 |
| Serial | 16 | Women's News | 17 |

DOMESTIC.

Wind and rain storm kills eight in Michigan. Page 1.

Court order for demobilizing troops served on Long. Page 3.

Dillinger's brain destroyed in microscopic examinations. Page 4.

Roosevelt fishes at mouth of Columbia river. Page 5.

Commission men will attempt to open Chicago stockyards. Page 8.

Will of Marie Dressler leaves $50,000 to two servants. Page 10.

Tornado injures dozen in Maryland; rain and hail cause damage in Illinois. Page 15.

WOMAN'S PAGE.

Jessie Marie deBoth writes tempting new ice cream recipes. Page 17.

Louise Bennett Weaver gives two person menus. Page 17.

The August bride receives tips from Helen Rowland. Page 17.

Madame Que Vive gives tips, received from dentist, on good grooming. Page 17.

Change shampoo medium often, advises Helen Follett. Page 17.

Teach children personal rights are important. Page 17.

Marian Martin describes versatile frock. Page 17.

Eleanor Ross tells how to make garden attractive. Page 17.

Evon Nollette describes latest Parisian hats. Page 17.

MARKETS.

Stocks steady; mild rallies lift prices of some favorites. Page 20.

Bonds continue quiet with narrow price changes. Page 20.

New September wheat futures dip a fraction in Minneapolis. Page 21.

Profit-taking holds down the prices of grains in Chicago. Page 21.

Hogs steady to 10 cents higher; steers weaker. Page 21.

Miscellaneous markets. Page 22.

*WALTER WINCHELL has a column of gags today. Page 10.*

*Mark Barron finds the Reds amusing, and writes amusingly about them. Page 14.*

*Popeye shows he can take it. The back page.*

LOCAL.

Twenty-six arrested in truck strike picketing plead not guilty before provost court. Page 2.

Alexander G. Jamie blames 'excess of industrialism' as modern crime cause. Page 5.

London speaker at U sees no serious threat to democracy in United States. Page 6.

Park board standing committees named. Page 6.

Trucks to be available for pushmobile derby racers' cars. Page 8.

Farmer-Labor legislative control drive planned. Page 8.

Cora Belle Price, teacher at Clinton school, dies. Page 8.

Whistling peanut wagon gives guard hard nut to crack. Page 11.

C. C. Webber, Upper Mississippi Waterway association president, extends valley welcome to President Roosevelt. Page 11.

Archie N. Wilcox, Walton league president, dies. Page 11.

Park board playground swimming champions are crowned at Camden park. Page 13.

NORTHWEST.

Winona plans welcome for President Roosevelt. Page 3.

Two hundred fifty cattle drop dead in Albert Lea yards. Page 15.

SPORTS.

Toledo pounds four Miller pitchers to win again, 11 to 2. Page 18.

Yankees trounce Red Sox, 12 to 4. Page 18.

New Ulm wins state Legion baseball championship. Page 18.

Elden Auker of Detroit shuts out Cleveland with four hits. Page 18.

Walter Johnson taken ill and Willie Kamm is appointed temporary Cleveland manager. Page 18.

Charley Retzlaff knocks out Ace Clark. Page 18.

Joe Coria enters semi-finals of national public links. Page 18.

Brandt of Braves blanks Giants with two hits, 8 to 0. Page 19.

Charley Grimm feels his crippled Cubs will have an excellent chance for pennant. Page 19.

Robert Page Lincoln: "Binoculars." Page 19.

## *Tonight Is the Night:*

WHEN the fourth of a series of historical broadcasts will be presented by The Minneapolis Tribune in "The Epic of the Northwest." Tonight you will hear dramatic events in the early days of Fort Snelling. Tune in on WTCN (formerly WRHM) at 8:30. You'll enjoy this highly interesting and educational program.

## STRATOSPHERE FILMS SAVED

### Much Important Information About South Dakota Expedition Salvaged.

Washington, Aug. 2.—(AP)—Much important information, including further facts about the mysterious cosmic ray, was found Thursday by Captain Albert W. Stevens to have been salvaged from the near-tragic stratosphere balloon flight of last week.

Dr. John Oliver La Gorce, vice president of the National Geographic society which backed the flight, disclosed that Stevens, one of the three crew members who had to take to parachutes to save themselves when the gondola crashed into a Nebraska cornfield, had been able to save much of the film he picked from the wreckage.

Numerous cameras clicked away throughout the 60,613-foot near-record ascension and the record they made apparently saved the trip from being fruitless.

In addition to a film from one of the cosmic ray detectors, which La Gorce said Stevens found "sharp, clear and complete," there was a roll developed at the bureau of standards which gave a running record for the flight of temperature both inside and outside the gondola, in addition to sun and sky brightness, the time of each record and the tilt of the gondola.

## *Poderjay Indicted on Perjury Charges*

New York, Aug. 2.—(AP)—Captain Ivan Poderjay, sought for questioning in the disappearance of his bride, Agnes C. Tufverson, was indicted Thursday on perjury charges. The dashing Yugoslav, now detained by Vienna police on suspicion, was accused of swearing falsely that he was unmarried when he obtained a license to wed the woman lawyer 16 days before she disappeared on December 20, 1933. Regarded by police as the key figure in the baffling Tufverson case, Poderjay's indictment was the first step toward bringing him to New York under extradition proceedings. Miss Tufverson, 43-year-old counsel for a utility company, was last seen at her New York apartment the night of December 20, when she and Poderjay returned from the Hudson river pier, from which they were to have sailed for Europe on a honeymoon.

## *Al Smith Quits N. Y. Charter Commission*

New York, Aug. 2.—(AP)—Alfred E. Smith announced Thursday night that he had resigned as chairman of the New York city charter commission. Smith said that he decided to resign after he was convinced that it would be impossible to prepare a proposed charter 60 days before the date of the election as required by law. Shortly afterwards Samuel Seabury announced that he, too, had resigned.

## *Johnson Lambasts Foes of NRA and Cites Gains*

### *Measure 'Stopped Slaughter' Among Little Fellows of Business, General Says.*

Chicago, Aug. 2.—(AP)—Banging away at foes of the recovery act, its administrator, General Hugh S. Johnson, in an adress climaxing celebration of NRA day at the fair, Thursday night asserted the measure "had stopped the slaughter among the little fellows of business" and had spurred this country in a greater advance from depression than had occurred elsewhere. He pledged the full powers of the NRA to aid the small business man.

The general, speaking to thousands at the exposition and to the nation at large over a radio chain, gave a spirited defense of the blue eagle and lambasted its critics.

"Some earnest and sincere critics such as Senator Borah say we could do all that NRA has done and still have anti-trust acts," he said. "The great Idaho senator has observed our work at too great a distance."

**'NRA Stopped Slaughter.'**

"It was under the anti-trust acts that, during the depression, there occurred the greatest mortality among the little fellows in this or any other country—and it was because of these acts."

"The slaughter stopped under NRA and it stopped because of NRA. Monopoly is created by cut-throat price cutting and harsh trade practices. The anti-trust acts permitted both. The NRA forbids both."

In his second address of the day here, the general asserted that it was "ridiculous" to charge the present administration with debasement of the currency, violation of the constitution, usurping congress, and plunging the nation "toward destruction of American institutions."

**Dollar Best on Earth.**

The Roosevelt dollar, he asserted, "will be by all odds the best and strongest dollar on earth."

"The charged debasement of the currency is a joke," he added, "and nobody knows what makes the value of money. A gold reserve has something to do with it and we have the largest in the world and the largest in our history. The resources of a country have something to do with it and ours are the greatest in the world."

**Upshoot in Wages.**

Wages, he said, had taken a decided upshoot from the time President Roosevelt took office and as for the critics, stated it was "easy for an arm-chair economist to make a case that this would not happen."

It was not the so-called "brain trust" that was to be feared, General Johnson said.

"It is not the professors and doctors in government that we have to fear," he said, "they are devoting their lives to public service with no hope of reward save contumely. It is the scum of intellectual prostitutes—the academic mercenaries who write for a controlled and dominated press the thing that is not—in utter disregard of the welfare of this country."

**Comparisons in Recovery.**

"It was said some time ago that recovery in other countries has been more rapid than here. But a study by the wholly impartial London Economist exploded that. It concerned real wages—that is, the purchasing power of workers' wages—it covered France, England, Germany and Italy. The showing was astonishing. It proved that in all other industrial countries the trend remained slowly downward, but in our country from the very day of the passage of the recovery act, the curve started upward and has never declined."

Business has advanced, he claimed "some 44 per cent from its extreme lows."

## *New Pastor to Preach at St. Mark's Sunday*

Recently elected to St. Mark's, Dr. Charles P. Deems has entered upon his duties as rector and will preach for the first time at 11 a. m. Sunday, August 5. Holy Communion will be celebrated. There also will be a celebration of the Holy Communion at 8 a. m. Dr. Deems will be formally instituted by bishops of the diocese in September.

## *Legislation to Curb Crime in State Urged*

Recommendations for legislative action tending to curb crime will be submitted to the state crime commission by November 1, Chief Justice Davaney of the state supreme court, chairman of the commission, said Thursday at the first statewide meeting of directors of the Minnesota Law and Order League at the St. Paul Athletic club.

## *U.S. Adopts New Plan to Crush Bootlegging*

Washington, Aug. 2.—(AP)—The government plans to put locks on the bottling tanks of whisky rectifiers to help crush bootlegging. Guy T. Helvering, commissioner of internal revenue, announced this plan as one of a number of new regulations effective September 1. At the same time, Secretary Morgenthau authorized the use of wood alcohol as a denaturant in the formula for completely denatured alcohol. Wood alcohol was banned from the denatured formula in January, 1931, after several deaths were attributed to its presence in bootleg liquor. Helvering did not go into detail in explaining how locks on rectifiers tanks would check illicit diversion but it was understood that liquor remaining after some of the blend in the tanks had been bottled would be checked against the amount of alcohol and other spirits in the formula submitted by the rectifier.

## LANGER SPIKES NYE RECALL IDEA

### Plan Is Dropped by G.O.P. as Senator Says He Will Back Democrat.

Bismarck, N. D., Aug. 2.—(AP)—North Dakota's deposed governor Thursday forced the rejection of plans to attempt recall of Senator Gerald P. Nye, North Dakota Republican, who less than a year ago turned against him after they had fought political battles shoulder to shoulder.

State Senator A. F. Bonzer, Jr., presented the objections of William Langer, removed recently as governor, to the Republican state central committee executive group shortly after it had announced the recall attempt was under way.

Afterward he announced: "There will be no recall; Langer doesn't want it."

Langer and Nye were elected on the same ticket two years ago. This spring Nye broke with Langer, joining the Nonpartisan league faction opposed to him. He campaigned before the June primary for those aligned with acting Governor Ole H. Olson, and has repeatedly criticized Langer's administration. Recently he declared he believed there was an "untold amount of graft" in state departments.

Plans had already been completed for circulation of petitions in an effort to obtain the number of signatures necessary to place the recall on the ballot in the November general election, when Langer objections were presented. The plans were immediately abandoned.

The proposal was heard by the same committee which Wednesday indorsed Mrs. William Langer for the Republican nomination for governor after her husband had withdrawn. Langer was removed as governor by the state supreme court which held his conviction of conspiracy to defraud the United States government disqualified him. He has appealed.

Mrs. Langer plans a three-week rest preparatory to her fall campaign against the Democrats. Chosen by acclaim Wednesday at the Republican state central committee meeting, to fill the vacancy created by resignation of her husband, Mrs. Langer will go to her summer home at Spiritwood lake near Jamestown.

**NYE WILL SUPPORT MOODIE FOR GOVERNOR**

Washington, Aug. 2.—(AP)—Senator Nye said today he would support the Democratic nominee for governor of North Dakota rather than Mrs. William Langer, wife of the deposed governor.

"I consider it my duty in the light of the principles involved to work for the election of Tom Moodie," Nye said. Moodie is the Democratic nominee.

## IOWA LIQUOR STORE EMPLOYMENT CUT

Des Moines, Aug. 2.—(AP)—Chairman Harold M. Cooper of the state liquor control commission Thursday announced a reduction of nearly one-fourth in the annual pay roll of Iowa retail liquor stores through the reduction of employes.

## NEW PROPOSAL GIVEN STUDY AT NIGHT SESSION

### Announcement Expected to Be Made Today—Strike Leaders Enter Objections.

### Parking Allowed in Loop Except for Restricted Areas in Market District.

*Text of employer's strike settlement proposal on page 2.*

Plans for settlement of the truck drivers' strike began to go forward Thursday night as the two federal mediators, the Rev. Francis J. Haas and E. H. Dunnigan, took up consideration of the plan presented to them by the employers' advisory committee.

After a study of the plan and a series of conferences, the two mediators suggested several changes in one section and their requests were submitted to a meeting of the employers' committee at 7 p. m.

Employers debated the proposed changes until 11 p. m. and then announced that no action would be taken Thursday night, but that a new statement would be issued Friday morning.

**Suggestions Kept Secret.**

Just what revision the mediators suggested was not made public.

Strike leaders had not formally received the peace plan Thursday night. The mediators indicated that they preferred to obtain the plan in its revised form before forwarding it to the union.

Individual strike leaders however informally objected to two sections in the peace terms submitted by the employers. One of these had to do with the section referring to the rehiring of the men on strike, and the other concerned the issuance of a new order by the regional labor board.

**New Committee At Work.**

Thursday night a new committee entered the mediation proceedings. It was composed of officials of the Central Labor union and had been appointed Wednesday night at a meeting of that group.

On the committee were Pat Corcoran of the milk drivers' union; Roy Wier, organizer for the Central Labor union; Carl Heglund of the building trades council, Alderman E. I. Hudson of the carpenters' union, and A. H. Urtubees, president of the Central Labor union.

This committee met Thursday night with strike leaders and went into informal discussion of the plan as originally proposed by the employers.

The purpose of the new committee is to assist in direct negotiation with the employers, who have expressed their unwillingness to meet directly with strike leaders, and it was indicated that the Central labor group would act as a liaison and advisory committee in seeking settlement of the strike that has been running since July 16.

Meanwhile, Adjutant General Walsh, troop commander under martial law, took steps to ease restrictions which have hedged loop shoppers since the declaration of martial law.

**Parking Ban Lifted.**

General Walsh late in the day issued an order which lifted the parking ban on loop streets, and regular parking rules of the city police went into effect at 7 p. m.

Beginning Friday morning all loop streets will be open to regular parking, except restricted areas in the market district, which are still closed.

This district embraces the area bounded by Fifth street and Seventh street and by Second and Third avenues north. Parking also is still forbidden, during the restricted hours, between Third avenue north and the northwest ends of the viaducts crossing the railroad yards at Fifth, Sixth and Seventh streets.

**Pickets Continue Fight.**

While peace plans were under way, guardsmen were still active in rounding up roaming pickets who were tipping over trucks and beating drivers in outlying sections of the city. By 7 p. m. guardsmen had answered nearly 100 calls.

The employers' new peace plan provides that each business concern which has workers on strike shall prepare a preferential list of employes who were on its pay roll July 16, when the strike started, and hire no workers not on this list until all those listed are given jobs. It is stipulated, however, that

WEATHER
U. S. Weather Bureau Forecast.
Rain Thursday; possibly some snow in north portion; mostly cloudy and colder Friday.
Additional weather on page 18.

# The Minneapolis Tribune

Sixty-eighth Year. No. 265. 3 MINNEAPOLIS, MINN., THURSDAY, FEBRUARY 14, 1935. • • • Twenty-six Pages

NRA MORNING EDITION
Three Cents in Minneapolis



# Hauptmann Guilty—Death

JURY LEAVING COURT LAST NIGHT AFTER VERDICT

—Tribune-(AP) WIREPHOTO.

Flemington, N. J., Feb. 14.—Hemmed in on all sides by huge crowds, the jury that convicted Bruno Hauptmann of slaying the Lindbergh baby is shown leaving courtroom last night just after bringing in verdict.

AFTER THE VERDICT

—Tribune-AP WIREPHOTO.

Flemington, N. J., Feb. 13.—Eyes downcast, his arms tightly gripped by officers, Bruno Richard Hauptmann is shown being led back to his cell after the jury found him guilty of slaying the Lindbergh baby.

## Bruno Totters as Verdict Is Read in Court

### Jury Deliberates 11 Hours and 6 Minutes—Week of March 18 Set for Execution—Appeal Believed Certain.

By John Ferris.

Flemington, N. J., Feb. 13.—(AP)—Bruno Richard Hauptmann was condemned to the electric chair Wednesday night by the jury that tried him for the kidnap-murder of baby Lindbergh.

Pale and erect, he heard the sentence of the jury that "we find the defendant guilty of murder in the first degree" and he swayed almost imperceptibly as Justice Thomas W. Trenchard sentenced him to die in the electric chair at Trenton penitentiary "the week beginning Monday, the 18th day of March, 1935."

But he crouched at midnight on the edge of the cot in his guarded cell and wept.

He had not a word for the men who watched him.

Shortly after the jury climaxed 32 days of tragic, dramatic testimony and frenzied pleading with its verdict, Edward J. Reilly, big chief of the defense counsel, announced an appeal would be carried "to the highest court of the country, the United States supreme court, if necessary."

"We believe that we shall be able to secure an ultimate reversal of the judgment," Reilly said.

The first higher court to pass on the appeal is expected to be the court of errors and appeals of the state of New Jersey, and the case probably will not reach that tribunal before the latter part of May.

**Anne Hauptmann Weeps; 'Nothing Left for Me.'**

The jury of eight men and four women spent 11 hours and six minutes in a bare room of the courthouse where Hauptmann had been on trial since January 2 before they reached their verdict.

"We find the defendant, Bruno Richard Hauptmann, guilty of murder in the first degree," intoned foreman Charles Walton, Sr., in the deathly quiet of the littered, smoke-filled courtroom.

Anna Hauptmann, tears rolling down her cheeks as her husband went silently back to his cell, cried "there is nothing left for me."

But she dried her eyes as she pushed through the thronged courtroom and left by a rear door.

"I am not afraid," she said. "I still hope."

Polled individually at the insistence of Edward J. Reilly, chief of the defense counsel, the jurors affirmed the verdict in quavering voices.

**Courtroom Grows Tense As Scene Is Set for Verdict**

Sheriff John H. Curtiss heralded the return of the jury, shouting from the library door of the century-old courtroom.

Under the five garish lights, newspapermen and lawyers had waited for hours in the littered little room, almost unbearably hot and stuffy.

Court crier Elmer Hann, tall and bald, suddenly appeared, rising behind the bench, and adjusted the jurist's chair.

Attorney General David T. Wilentz, pale, his voice tense with emotion, stiffened his shoulders.

He spoke to Colonel H. Norman Schwarzkopf, superintendent of the state police, and Schwarzkopf moved down the aisle, ordering his troopers to close the doors.

The florid Reilly, subdued in manner, stood up right in the space before the bench.

Troopers stood at the alert about the little room, bright-figured in their sky-blue uniforms.

Trooper Lewis J. Bornmann, one of the men who found and handled the kidnap ladder down which baby Lindbergh was carried to his death on the night of March 1, 1932, stood near the jury box.

The minutes dragged.

**Jurors Take Places in Box; White Faced Wife Comes In**

Dolefully, the bell high above began to toll. There was a stir at the library door. The time was 10:31 p. m. (E.S.T.)

Six state troopers entered. Then came Hauptmann, between Deputy Sheriff Hovey Low and a state trooper, handcuffed to each, his face pale, his manner calm.

A tenseness gripped the courtroom.

A constable shouted "quiet, please."

Out in the street, where a massed throng waited, someone set up a shout. It swelled into a prolonged yell.

The jury filed in, took the seats occupied for 32 days,

## Jury Still Under Guard; Verdict on Fifth Ballot

Flemington, N. J., Feb. 13.—(AP)—The Hauptmann trial jury, it was reported Wednesday night, reached its verdict of death on the fifth ballot.

All communication with the jurors who had been sitting in the trial of Hauptmann for nearly six weeks was denied as they returned, under guard of state troopers, to their third-floor quarters in the hotel across the street from the court house.

The members of the jury filed slowly out of the court house and passed through the lane made in the packed crowd on the street and sidewalk. State troopers followed them and stood guard on the stairs and in the entrance of the hotel.

Arrangements were made with the state authorities for the jury to remain under guard Wednesday night and to return to their homes Thursday. Previous orders to Sheriff John H. Curtiss, who provided for the hotel quarters during the trial, were that when the jurors left for the court house Wednesday they would not return except to pick up their belongings and depart for home.

Spectators crowded about the lobby of the hotel and at the foot of the stairs to the jury quarters but none was permitted to pass the line of big blue-coated troopers.

How the jurors stood on the various ballots before reaching their verdict was not disclosed. Reports circulating in the court room before the jury filed in were that they had been deadlocked through the afternoon and evening at 10-2 for a death verdict.

From authoritative sources, it was learned that two of the women jurors had opposed the death penalty throughout the deliberations.

## Washington

By PAUL MALLON
Copyright, 1935, by Paul Mallon.

AUTO PRODUCTION; RECOVERY PUZZLE; MUSSOLINI'S PLANS

EXPEDIENCY.

TWO dressed-up formal statements were all that came out publicly from President Roosevelt's recent meeting with the labor leaders. They were merely for show window purposes.

William Green, president of the A. F. of L. compressed his grievances against the auto code into 1,500 words, and sugared them with a broad promise of co-operation. Mr. Roosevelt had heard in advance about the Green statement and said: "I've got one, too. Let's exchange." He sang his prepared praises of labor objectives in 500 words. It made the gathering quite a sociable affair. But that is not all that happened.

What was not given out was Mr. Roosevelt's private explanation why he renewed the objectionable (to labor) auto code for four months more. He said the strong production of autos is the main driving force behind the encouraging industrial activity now under way, and he did not care or dare to interfere with it.

This reason had never been mentioned before, but it is sound, and it made an impression on the labor leaders. Auto production is now at peak. During the past 60 days it has brought improvement in steel, glass, rubber and all its related industries. In four months more, this situation will have passed.

BOARDS.

ANOTHER thing Mr. Roosevelt let the labor leaders in on privately was his view about NRA. He did not tell them what he was going to do, but did say something like this: "The NRA is creaking. You know it and I know it, because we can hear the squeaks. We are going to take the squeaks out of it very soon."

The President did not directly say so, but he is supposed to have lost patience with the five-man board control over NRA, and in fact with all board control, including the proposed relief board idea. He leans toward a plan placing one man at the top of the NRA and at the top of the new relief set-up, and then instituting boards under these top men.

It is likely that Mr. Roosevelt has come to this view because of all the grief unloaded in his lap by boards (particularly NRA recently) unable to agree. He cannot spend all his time settling the differences of temperamental boards. A top man could settle them, with the President acting as a court of final appeal in the important cases.

MYSTERIES.

THERE are many mysteries in the current industrial revival. No one seems to know, for instance, what is causing steel to be operating at 55 per cent of capacity. Autos are responsible for perhaps 20 per cent of production, but that does not ac-

(Continued on Page 6, Column 5.)

## Macon Skipper Tells How Craft Ran Wild

### Wiley Describes Crazy Veering After Jolt—Reaction Against Cost of Dirigible Voiced.

Pictures on Page 10.

Copyright, 1935, by Associated Press.

San Francisco, Feb. 13.—A strenuous attempt to learn exactly what caused the dirigible Macon to run wild in midair for 35 minutes, then to plunge into the Pacific was begun Wednesday night by her skipper, Lieutenant Commander H. V. Wiley.

He sought the answer among the 80 other survivors of the 83 men who were aboard.

"I have some ideas as to the reason," said the young but gray-haired veteran a few hours after having been brought safely home from his second dirigible crash. "But I want to talk to the officers and men before I draw any conclusions. I may have something to say tomorrow."

At the same time a naval court of inquiry was ordered to start investigating the spectacular end of the navy's third big fighting airship.

**Veers and Plunges.**

For a start Wiley had the fact that the Macon gave a sudden, short lurch, warning her crew that something critical had happened.

Her crazy plunging and veering through the skies for 35 minutes thereafter attested to the seriousness of the shudder felt by those aboard.

Wiley's shipless crew, rescued by

(Continued on Page 10, Column 1)

## NEWS INDEX



## SENATORS ACT TO CUT CAR FEE

### Senate Committee Votes in Favor of Permanent Slash in License Rates.

The senate committee on motor vehicle taxation Wednesday went on record as favoring permanent reduction of car license fees to the temporary basis authorized for 1933 and 1934.

The action followed a prolonged and warmly waged debate. There was no record of the vote but it appeared to be 8 to 5 with Senator Donald Wright, Minneapolis, and Charles E. Adams, Duluth, who led the fight against the bill voting in the negative.

Senator Wright, a first termer in the senate, insisted on having the record show that he voted against faborably reporting the measure after Senator Charles N. Orr, St. Paul, moved that the members not be compelled to vote for the record since "they may want to change their minds before the bill comes to a vote on the floor."

**Companion Bill in House.**

A companion bill still is in committee in the house but Senator Roepke, chairman of the senate committee, declared early in the debate he had been assured the house group would report the bill out this week, perhaps Thursday.

Governor Olson already has signed a bill, also sponsored by Senator Roepke, changing from February 15 to March 15 the deadline for paying 1935 motor vehicle license fees without penalty.

Emphasis was made by opponents of the measure that restoration of the higher rate is needed to guarantee highway department revenue sufficient to enable Minnesota to match approximately $7,000,000 in federal aid in the next two years.

**Politics Involved.**

Sponsors of the bill, charging the highway department carries a surplus of help, some of which devoted time wholly to political purposes, contended that if proper economies are practiced the state could qualify for federal aid without raising motor car license fees.

A highlight of the session was a fiery speech by Senator James A. Carley, Plainview, during which he charged the department had hired men for purely political duties and that the department could have saved a good many hundred thousand dollars during recent years had the proper economies been effected.

## Removal of Officials in Crime Area Urged

Frankfort, Ky., Feb. 13.—(AP)—Recommendations that Sheriff T. C. McDaniel of Clay county be removed from office "under proper showing," and that impeachment proceedings be instituted against certain other Clay county officials and police officials in Corbin, was made Wednesday by Adjutant General Henry H. Denhardt. General Denhardt's report was based on an investigation made in Corbin and in Clay county by state troops and state police sent into the area in a surprise move last month to break up an alleged crime ring.

## Tears Stream Down Face of Bruno's Wife

### First Words: 'Nothing Left for Me'; Then, 'I Still Hope.'

Flemington, N. J., Feb. 13.—(AP)—Mrs. Anna Hauptmann Wednesday night heard her husband sentenced to die in the electric chair, and said, "There is nothing left for me."

Lloyd Fisher, of Bruno Hauptmann's defense counsel, put an arm around her shoulders as tears rolled down her cheeks for the first time since his trial began.

"See here," said Fisher gently, "you be brave. Don't show any emotion here. Don't show anything."

**"I Am Not Afraid."**

Mrs. Hauptmann fought to regain her composure, but her chin still quivered. Then Fisher said, "Mrs. Hauptmann, we'll see this thing through."

She had dried her tears when she made her way through the crowd and left through the courthouse back door. Her words as she left were, "I am not afraid. I still hope."

She had come to court smiling when the courthouse bell began to toll the signal the jury had reached a verdict. It was obvious that she hoped for acquittal.

Her first tears fell when Justice Thomas W. Trenchard uttered the sentence.

**Dazed by Verdict.**

"The sentence of the court is—" then came a long pause—"that you, the said Bruno Richard Hauptmann, suffer death."

She had looked at her husband after the jury poll, but now her eyes returned to the justice, with a dull, dazed expression. She seemed unable to believe it.

Hauptmann was more alert than she. After each of the 12 jurors repeated, "Guilty of murder in the first degree," he looked at his wife, closed his eyes and shook his head.

"Quiet, quiet, quiet, please!" the bailiffs shouted. The justice had given permission for those who wished to leave; and spectators were scrambling out.

As they left, Mrs. Hauptmann seemed to realize for the first time that the trial was over. Tears came to her eyes then, but did not fall.

## BRUNO WILL BE GUARDED WELL

### Death House Guard to Be Doubled—Five Others Await Chair.

Trenton, N. J., Feb. 13.—(AP)—Governor Harold G. Hoffman and William J. Ellis, commissioner of institutions and agencies, announced Wednesday night "every precaution will be taken" to guard Bruno Richard Hauptmann when he is transferred to the death house at the New Jersey state prison to die for the murder of the Lindbergh baby.

Hauptmann will occupy a cell on the first tier of the two-tier brick building where five other prisoners wait death. The present guard of three officers, who work in eight hour shifts, will be doubled, and the lights in Hauptmann's cell and in the corridor will burn night and day as they did at Flemington, Ellis said.

Hauptmann will occupy a cell away from the other prisoners—all five of whom were convicted of slayings committed during robberies or holdups. His cell mates will be Michael Mule, George de Stefano and Connie Scarpone, all of Trenton; Kurt Barth, a Clifton youth, and James Williams, Newark Negro.

The cells in the death house are 8 by 12, slightly larger than those in other parts of the prison. Each cell is equipped with a bed instead of a cot, a chair, table, and toilet facilities.

As Hauptmann enters the death house, he will face a long corridor, at the end of which is the 18x10 death chamber, ironically referred to as the "throne room."

Since installation of the electric chair in 1907, the state has electrocuted 110 men. Hauptmann will be the fifth man to go to the chair from Hunterdon county.

## RETURN FRECHETTE TO SCENE OF CRIME

Nevada City, Calif., Feb. 13.—(AP)—Clarence Frechette, charged with the murder in Howell, Mich., of Robert Brown, his trucking employer, left Wednesday in custody of three Michigan officers for the scene of his alleged crime. Frechette signed a waiver of extradition.

THE MINNEAPOLIS JOURNAL

WEATHER Fair tonight and Tuesday; little change in temperature. MONDAY EVENING, MAY 27, 1935. 36 PAGES—2 CENTS IN MINNEAPOLIS

# Weyerhaeuser Ready to Pay $200,000; Text of Ransom Letter Made Public

## Bandits Take $6,000 in Loop Gunfight

### Policeman Guarding Witts' Messenger Clubbed; Fires On Bandit Grabbing Money

**Three Outlaws Open Fire as They Escape—One Believed Wounded**

**HOLDUP TAKES PLACE ON SEVENTH STREET**

**Theater Cashier Relates Bandits Knocked Down Messenger to Get Loot**

Three bandits armed with sawed-off shotguns seized a $6,000 bank deposit shortly before noon today after fighting a gun battle with police on Seventh street between First avenue N. and Hennepin.

The bandits fled in a small car and one of them is believed to be wounded.

The bank deposit was being taken from Witts market house, Seventh street and Hennepin avenue, to the Produce State Bank a block away. It was carried by Joseph Miller, Negro porter, and Patrolman Wenzel F. Bienafle, detailed to the duty of guarding Miller.

**Bandit Clubs Policeman**

In front of the Alvin theater, a man stepped out from behind a parked car.

"All right copper, stick 'em up," he snapped. Bienafle raised his hands but as he did so he drew his gun. The bandit struck him on the head with a shotgun.

**Policeman Shoots Bandit**

Miller dropped the canvas bag containing the bank deposit, estimated at between $5,000 and $6,000.

Two other men, companions of the bandit, rushed on the policeman and messenger. One of the men stooped to pick up the bag, and as he did so Patrolman Bienafle fired directly at him. The man slumped to the pavement.

His companions picked him up with the money bag, and hurried to the small car parked in front of the Alvin theater. One of the men had beaten Bienafle over the head severely and fired at him with a pistol. The policeman, however, was not wounded, but there were two bullet holes in his coat.

**Gunmen Fire Over Crowd**

A crowd gathered and the bandits fired over their heads as they drove away.

The machine sped toward First avenue N. It had been parked directly in front of the Alvin theater. Later, a car was found abandoned at Fifteenth street and Linden avenue N. It is believed to be the bandit machine.

Helen Borg, cashier at the Alvin, witnessed the holdup. She told police two men got out of the car and accosted the payroll messenger. She beieves a third man sat at the wheel of the car.

Miss Borg said the gunman fired over the heads of spectators as they turned to leave.

She gave police the number "340-704" as the license of the bandit machine, but she was not sure whether it was a 1934 or 35 tag.

**Sure Bandit Was Wounded**

Bienafle reported at headquarters after the holdup that he was sure he wounded one of the bandits.

"I fired at him point blank," the patrolman said. "And he went flop. Then one of his companions ran to him and loaded him in the getaway car."

Police found a .38 caliber pistol on the sidewalk near the place where the bandit fell.

**Second Car Used**

Witnesses told police that a second car was probably used in the robbery. The second car was parked behind the first and used as protective screen. This led police to believe that four men may have engineered the robbery.

The car abandoned on Linden avenue was left with its motor running. It was apparent the bandits had another means of escape.

### TIRED CLERK SHOOS BANDIT OUT OF STORE

PHIL BENDER, clerk in the Rodriguez drug store, 1731 Chicago avenue, was just too tired to be held up last night.

A bandit walked into the place, drew a pistol and demanded money.

"Go away," Bender told him.

"I mean this," the bandit argued, pointing his pistol at Bender's head. "I'm sticking you up."

"If you don't go away and leave me alone, I'm going to call a policeman," Bender, greatly annoyed, threatened.

"Oh, all right," the bandit grumbled, "but you're going to be sorry for this some day."

The gunman left. Bender leaned over on the counter again.

### Patrol Limits Face Voters' Test June 10

**Separate Ballot in City Election to Decide Outside Bars Fate**

Out of a long winter's tangle over liquor licenses in Minneapolis, the patrol limits issue will come to a final verdict two weeks from today as one of the important features of the city election.

Representatives of hotels and restaurants directly concerned declared today it affects the livelihood of 2,000 employees and their 7,500 dependents.

Before the voters on a separate ballot will be the question, "Shall the council continue to grant liquor licenses authorized by Chapter 78, Laws of 1935?"

Lengthy battles were waged in the city council, in the courts, and in the legislature over patrol limits—an ancient charter provision that liquor cannot be sold south of Sixth street or in other areas outside the patrol limits. All efforts failed until the legislature agreed to a measure which permitted the council to continue 37 licenses, which had been issued under a 1933 act, but which expired by limitation.

By the terms of that act, however, the council power to continue those licenses expires, if a majority of citizens voting on the issue decide the power shall be taken away. Then the licenses expire in 60 days.

### F. R. Begins Work on Transport Message

Washington, May 27.—(AP)—President Roosevelt today began writing a message to congress recommending unification of all federal agencies dealing with transport. Arrangements were made for his regular Monday luncheon with Secretary Henry Morgenthau. Herman Oliphant, treasury counsel, and other treasury experts, were invited to join later in what was called "a general financial discussion."

### Frazier Farm Moratorium Is Ruled Invalid

**New Deal Measure Declared Unconstitutional by Supreme Court**

**UNANIMOUS DECISION IS GIVEN BY COURT**

**Justice Starts Reading of Decision on Legality of NRA**

Washington, May 27.—(U.P.)—The Supreme Court today held the Frazier-Lemke farm mortgage moratorium act invalid as a violation of the federal constitution.

The decision of the court was unanimous.

The court immediately began reading its decision on the constitutionality of the national industrial recovery act.

**Billions Affected by Law**

Potentially affecting billions of dollars of indebtedness, the Frazier-Lemke law extended to farmers a five-year moratorium on mortgages.

It provided that if efforts to scale down a farmer's debt to a figure he could pay should fail, the property could not be foreclosed on during five years if a "reasonable rental" was paid by the owner.

Also, the act enabled a farmer to obtain full title to his property by payment of its appraised value at the end of the five-year period, regardless of the amount fixed in the mortgage.

Like the railroad retirement act which the court declared unconstitutional in a five to four decision, the Frazier-Lemke law was forced through closing hours of the last congressional session by use of filibustering tactics. Also like the railway law, President Roosevelt in signing the measure termed it loosely drawn.

**Case Brought by Kentuckian**

The case presented to the high court was brought by William W. Radford, Sr., a Kentucky farmer. After defaulting on payments on a $9,000 mortgage held by the Louisville Joint Stock Land Bank, Radford refused an offer of $9,500 for his property when the bank tried to buy it in. By paying $325 annually, he invoked the Frazier-Lemke act to retain his property with an option to clear his indebtedness by repurchasing for $4,445, the priced fixed by appraisers.

The law was upheld by the federal District Court of Western Kentucky and the Sixth Circuit Court of Appeals. The Louisville bank contended the act took property without due process of law and was not a bankruptcy measure. On these grounds it appealed to the high tribunal. Supporters of the act contended the measure was justified by the financial distress of farmers.

### 9-Month NRA Useless, Says Emily Newell Blair

**Consumers' Board Head Tells St. Paul Meet Brief Period Would Unsettle Industry**

The national consumers advisory board is opposed to only a nine-month extension of the NRA as proposed by the senate and would rather see the recovery act die, June 16, than be extended for such a short period, Mrs. Emily Newell Blair of Washington, chairman of the board, said today in St. Paul.

"The board favors an extension of the act for two years," she said. "An extension of only nine months would merely unsettle industry and accomplish little or nothing. Revising the codes would take at least 90 days and most industries would hesitate to undertake the work involved if the new code were to last only a few months."

Mrs. Blair, former vicechairman of the democratic national committee was to confer with members of the Ramsey county consumers council and will speak at a dinner meeting of the Women's Democratic club of Minnesota, at 6:30 p.m. today in the Hotel Lowry, St. Paul. She will return to Washington tonight.

**Different Now, She Says**

The NRA today is a vastly different agency from the one organized by General Hugh Johnson, Mrs. Blair said. Price fixing, opposed from the start by the consumers board, has been abandoned, she said, partly because it was unworkable and partly because of the board's efforts.

"I believe the great majority of business men are in favor of the NRA," she said. "If it has done nothing else, it has taught them to

MRS. EMILY NEWELL BLAIR

think their own businesses through as they have never done before. We have had wholesalers and processors who hitherto have been classed with manufacturers, come to us and tell us the NRA had shown them for the first time that so far as manufacturers are con-

Continued on page 2

### Life of Weyerhaeuser Heir in Hands of Kidnapers

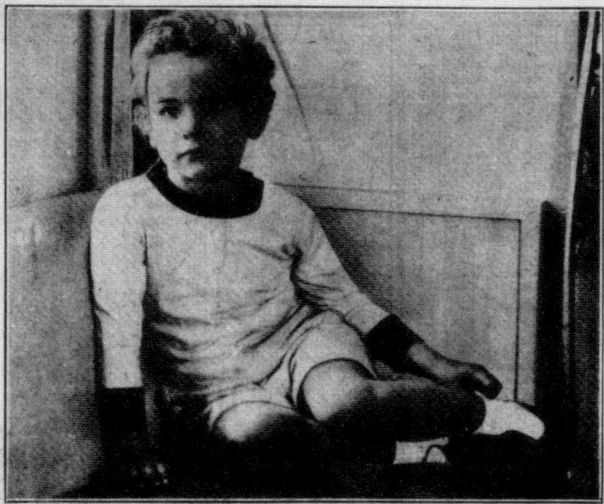

HERE IS GEORGE PHILIP WEYERHAEUSER, member of the Weyerhaeuser family, of Tacoma, Wash., who is threatened with death by kidnapers, who demand $200,000 ransom.

### Old Political Party Chiefs Back Keyes

**GOP and Democratic Leaders to Speak—Latimer Hits Strike Story**

By LEIF H. GILSTAD

Although emphasizing that he is "an independent, nonpartisan candidate and tied up with no party group or faction," Charles F. Keyes, candidate for mayor, today was assured support from leaders in both democratic and republican ranks.

The first of these party leaders to speak up for the Keyes campaign is George F. Williamson, state president of the Younger Democrats, who will talk over WCCO tomorrow at 8:30 p.m. Others from both republican and democratic ranks will follow.

Mr. Keyes made it clear that he "welcomes support from members of all parties who believe in a sane, sensible business administration." But he added that he is "under no obligation to any party groups and shall be free to act according to my best judgment in all matters."

**Latimer Denies Strike Story**

From Thomas E. Latimer, the farmer-labor candidate for mayor, came the statement that a rumor that labor unions are plotting a general strike in the event of his election is "malicious falsehood."

"From several authentic sources I have heard this canard," Mr. Latimer said, "which is going around in

Continued on page 5

### U. S. Hunts for Tinplate Heir

**F. R. Orders Navy and Coast Guard to Hunt Missing Leeds Launch**

Washington, May 27.—(AP)—President Roosevelt today ordered the navy and coast guard to start search for William B. Leeds, heir to the tinplate millions, who is reported missing since 6 p.m., yesterday in a 26-foot fishing launch en route from Miami to Bimini.

The President acted on receipt of the following message from Captain Fox of the yacht Moana:

William B. Leeds missing in 26-foot fishing launch since 6 p.m., yesterday en route from Miami to Bimini.

"Please do your utmost to start immediately systematic search."

Stephen Early, a secretary to the President, immediately notified the navy and coast guard.

**COAST GUARD PLANE BEGINS HUNT FOR LEEDS**

Miami, Fla., May 27.—(AP)—A coast-guard seaplane today searched for the 26-foot launch in which William Leeds, Jr., left Miami yesterday for Bimini.

### Ransom Note Warns 'Slip' Will Be 'Too Bad'

**Seattle, May 27.—(AP)—In a copyright story, the Seattle Post-Intelligencer today printed what is said was the tevt of the kidnap note received by the Weyerhaeuser family in Tacoma on May 25, after disappearance of their 9-year-old son, George.**

**The text, as printed, follows:**

To whom it may concern:

1. 200,000 dollars in cash.
2. 100,000 dollars in $20 bills.
3. 50,000 dollars in $10 bills.
4. 50,000 dollars in $5 bills.
5. All of this money must be in federal reserve notes and unmarked.
6. You are not to take the number of these bills. If they are taken and the bills are marked, it will be all off.
7. You are not to notify the police, department of justice or any private detective agentcy.
8. If you do it will be all off.
9. Keep it out of the papers.
10. This is business be business like.
11. You have got five (5) days to raise the money. Better have it.
12. In five days or as soon as you have the money: advertise in the Seattle P-I personal column. Say 'we are ready, and sign it: Percy Minnie.
13. Remember the money will be gone over before the release so don't mark it.
14. The police can't catch us so be very, very careful to follow the rules.
15. These bills must have been in circulation. Be careful.
16. Remember and don't try to slip any gold certificated notes on us.
17. You will be notified where to go when the time comes. Be sure there is no one following you, as you will be watched from the time you leave.
18. We won't be sitting behind any mail boxes either.
19. Just follow the rules and we will get along fine. Don't follow them and it will be sorrowful. For you, not for us.
20. Any questions ask them in personal column signed as above.
21. Remember to follow the rules of them. A slip on your part will be just too bad for someone else.

We know what we are doing. We have it all planned.

It has been all planned for three years. In the meantime we have looked for places where we might slip and have found none. We are educated and pride says we are fairly intelligent. So if you just stop and reason for a minute you'll see that it is best to follow our rlues.

We don't want to hurt anyone if we can get out of it. So if you just follow the rules as they are lain down by us you will have the one you love back home in a week's time if you care about them $200,000 worth.

So just remember a slip on your part is a slip by us. Don't do it.

Egoist. Egoist.

### 28 Children Drown as Excursion Boat Sinks

Kharkov, U. S. S. R., May 27.—(AP)—The chairman of the soviet of Gadiach and six others were sentenced to prison today for criminal negligence in the drowning of 28 children when a leaky excursion boat sank in the river Psiol early today. Only one adult accompanied the children on the excursion and the boat previously had been abandoned as unsafe.

### French Cabinet Asks Control of Finances

Paris, May 28.—(U.P.)—The cabinet agreed today to ask full powers from parliament to deal with the most serious financial situation since the late Raymond Poincare saved the franc in 1926.

It was decided, at a nearly four-hour meeting, to demand full powers to protect the currency and balance the budget. Members of the coalition cabinet were reported in full agreement.

### Parents Get Small Bills as Demanded; Await New Contact

**Justice Agents Keep Hands Off Until Money Is Paid—Search for Mysterious Tan Sedan Proves Futile**

**DEMAND NOTE GIVES DETAILED INSTRUCTIONS, WARNS OF SLIP**

**Only 48 Hours Remain of Time Limit Set by Abductors—Officials Fear Publicity May Hinder Negotiations**

Tacoma, Wash., May 27.—(LP)—With only 48 hours remaining of the "five days" in which 9-year-old George Weyerhaeuser may be ransomed, his parents today held $200,000 in small bills and waited for the next move of the kidnapers.

The money is ready, the boy's uncle, F. R. Titcomb, revealed, and will be paid as soon as the kidnapers arrange a method and a rendezvous.

Justice officials today expressed the fear that publicity given the kidnap note, which was made public today, may hamper negotiations for safe return of the boy and all law enforcement agencies decided to give the abductors every opportunity to return the captive unharmed.

"Our first concern," a spokesman for the department of justice squad said, "is the safety of the Weyerhaeuser boy. When he is safe at home, we will move into action."

An unsuccessful search for a mysterious tan sedan with California license plates was made all over western Washington by road and by air Sunday. The car was reported seen parked near Lowell school, which George attended, several times last week by L. H. Burnett, Tacoma jeweler, and was seen near the school Friday, the day the lad was seized, by Jean Comfort, 16 years old.

**"Just Too Bad" If Ransom Isn't Paid by Wednesday, Kidnapers Say in Demand Note**

Although there were no announcements from the Weyerhaeuser home, it was apparent first efforts to contact the kidnapers had failed. After inserting the first personal advertisement in the Seattle Post-Intelligencer, the parents inserted a second, asking new instructions. That these instructions will be delivered to the Weyerhaeusers by mail was indicated when the kidnapers did not answer the ad in today's paper.

Unless the curly-haired boy is ransomed by Wednesday, it will be "just too bad," the ransom letter, received at the Weyerhaeuser home by special delivery Friday night, warned. The note did not threaten the boy's life directly, but was replete with inferences that death would be the penalty of failure to carry out instructions.

What purported to be a copy of the ransom letter was published by a Seattle newspaper today. It gave the most detailed instructions and was filed with admonitions against any sort of a "slip." It ended ominously: "So just remember a slip on your part is a slip by us. Don't do it."

**Kidnapers Demand Ransom in Small Bills, Warn Against Including Gold Certificates**

The kidnaper wanted $100,000 in $20 federal reserve notes, $50,000 in $10 notes, and $50,000 in $10 notes, and $50,000 in $5 notes. Apparently aware gold certificates trapped Bruno Richard Hauptmann, kidnaper of the Lindbergh baby, the kidnaper stern warned against their inclusion.

Authorities, more and more convinced they dealth with an educated, clever man, partly and perhaps wholly mad, withdrew completely, wishing to give the family every opportunity to save the child. They feared the man who stole George Friday might carry out his threat.

John P. Weyerhaeuser, father of the child and grandson of the founder of the vast Weyerhaeuser lumber dynasty, waited at the Weyerhaeuser home atop a hill overlooking Puget sound. With him were the young mother—who was reported bearing up well, although she collapsed soon after the ransom note arrived—and other relatives.

It was believed the ransom note had ordered signals displayed from the house in such a way as they could be seen from the sound. A bedsheet was displayed Saturday and part of Sunday from an upstairs window. Later it was replaced with a blue sweater. This was the means that was believed to have failed, explaining this ad in the Seattle Post Intelligencer:

**"Due to publicity beyond our control, please indicate another method of reaching you. Hurry—relieve anguished mother."**

The ransom note had been submitted to the best brains of the department of pustice, whose agents, more than a score in number, waited in Tacoma and Seattle and up and down the Pacific coast for the signal from the parents that would set them on the trail of the kidnaper.

**Believe Kidnaper Educated**

The note, it was surmised, was the work of an educated person, probably a person who had attended college. Agents pointed out the "egoist," the pseudonym of the abductor, was not a word in the vocabulary of uneducated persons. Ordinary criminals and known kidnapers, with one conspicuous exception, would have used "swellhead" to describe the same state.

Only a minimum of activity by police and federal agents was evident.

Police kept strictly away from the big hill-top house and prevented

Continued on page 2

### Fair Weather Due in N. W.

**Rains Benefit Crops, With La Crosse Reporting Fall of 1.76 Inches**

Fair and warm weather was predicted for tonight and tomorrow in the northwest following a beneficial rain which covered most of Minnesota and parts of North and South Dakota yesterday.

Yesterday's rain came at a time when it was highly beneficial to small grain crops and pasturage, agricultural experts said. The rain ranged from .02 of an inch at Campbell, Minn., to 1.31 inches at Grand Meadow. La Crosse, Wis., had a downpour of 1.76 inches.

Rainfall in Minneapolis totaled .51 of an inch. Argyle, Minn., reported .56; Crookston, .28; Duluth, .20; Moorhead, .12; New Ulm, .53; Winnebago, .67.

Lemmon, S. D., had .28 of an inch and Sioux Falls reported .32, Yankton, .12, and Mobridge, .04.

Only light, scattered showers fell in North Dakota.

### Bank Bandits Get $1,000 in S. D. Raid

Freeman, S. D., May 27.—(AP)—Three men held up and robbed the First National Bank of Freeman early today, escaping with approximately $1,000.

SHOWERS, COOLER TONIGHT, SATURDAY

Temperatures Midnight to Noon

| H. | 12 | 1 | 2 | 3 | 4 | 5 | 6 | 7 | 8 | 9 | 10 | 11 | 12 |
|---|---|---|---|---|---|---|---|---|---|---|---|---|---|
| T. | 72 | 71 | 70 | 70 | 69 | 68 | 69 | 71 | 74 | 78 | 83 | 85 | 88 |

Highest year ago, 89; lowest, 64.

# THE MINNEAPOLIS STAR

HOME — In Minneapolis, It's The Star

Vol. 28, No. 154 ★ (U.P.)—UNITED PRESS ASSOCIATION MINNEAPOLIS, MINN., FRIDAY, AUGUST 16, 1935 (INS)—INTERNATIONAL NEWS SERVICE Price Two Cents in Minneapolis

# ROGERS, POST KILLED; PLANE CRASHES IN ALASKA FOG

## PUBLIC'S FURY RUSHES TO AID BOB LA FOLLETTE

### Forces Finance Committee to Vote Out Tax on Lower Incomes

### TRAP PROVES TO BE BOOMERANG

### Hugh Johnson Is Now Being Dated for Lectures at $1,000 Per

By Drew Pearson and Robert S. Allen

Authors of "Washington Merry-Go-Round"

WASHINGTON, AUG. 16. — TO those who sat on the inside the proceedings of the senate finance committee when it broadened income taxes down to $800 brackets were one of the weirdest performances of the present session.

To young Bob LaFollette they were a crazy-quilt nightmare.

He had consistently hammered home the idea of broadening the income tax base down to the lower figures on the theory that if more people paid income taxes they would take more interest in how the money was spent.

At no time, however, did he advocate elimination or decrease of the proposed heavier taxes on wealth.

But there developed in committee a violent drive against the house bill provision for a heavy inheritance tax. This aroused the resentment of old guard Republicans and Democrats alike.

**OPPOSITION LED BY RICH MAN GERRY**

Leader of the opposition was Peter Goelet Gerry, descendant of Elbridge Gerry, a signer of the Declaration of Independence and the man who first evolved the system of cutting up electoral districts for the benefit of one political party — or "gerrymandering."

Peter Gerry, who inherited the wealth of his prosperous ancestors, and shares the wealth of his wife, Edith Stuyvesant Vanderbilt, was elected to the senate from Rhode Island in the Roosevelt landslide. Since then he has been vigorously anti-Roosevelt.

He threw all his strength against the high inheritance tax. And when

(Continued on page four)

## PUBLISHER WINS JUSTICE FIGHT

### Wayzata Official Allows Notes to Be Made of Records

Palmer Holman, publisher of the Minnetonka Herald, today won his fight to force Justice of the Peace L. E. Christ of Wayzata to permit notes to be made of court records for publication. It was announced that Christ has instructed City Clerk E. L. Johnson to permit anyone to make notations from the docket.

The justice's action followed a two-month campaign which reached a climax Tuesday when Holman filed a peition for a writ of mandamum with Judge H. D. Dickinson of Hennepin county district court ordering Christ to show cause at a hearing Aug. 28 why he should not be compelled to permit notes to be made from the docket.

Previously, the Herald has presented the justice with opinions secured from County Attorney Ed J. Goff and Attorney General Harry H. Peterson advising Christ that his records were open to the public. To this the justice replied that publication of the sentences would serve no useful purpose.

Holman then sought the aid of Gov. Floyd B. Olson in an attempt to force the justice to heed the legal opinions, and finally started court action. He indicated the court action would be dropped.

## CRASH DRIVER IS HELD FOR JURY

Leon Warner, 19, Hopkins, driver in a fatal head-on crash Sunday noon on Excelsior boulevard, today was bound over to the Hennepin county grand jury on a reckless driving charge.

Harry Williams, 3764 Yosemite avenue, St. Louis park, driver of the other car, was killed in the accident.

The charge against Warner was filed upon complaint of Oscar Schwartz, 3723 W. Twenty-first street, who with his wife is recovering in Swedish hospital from injuries. They were riding with Williams.

Bail for Warner was set at $5,000 by Judge Fred B. Wright. He waived examination. Warner served 30 days in the workhouse in 1922 on a drunken driving charge.

## Revolt Against Bachelor King

KING ZOG OF ALBANIA

Athens, Aug. 16.—(INS)—Revolution against King Zog has broken out in Albania, according to unconfirmed reports reaching here, and 60 men were killed when rebels marching on Jirana, the capital, clashed with government troops.

The reported uprising followed the fatal shooting yesterday of General Leon de Ghilardi, inspector-general of the Albanian army and friend of King Zog, near Avlona.

The reports mentioned Sefket Virlatsi, a strong tribal leader who once hoped to marry his daughter to King Zog, a bachelor, as leader of the revolt.

## JAIL FREDLUND, NEILSON'S ORDER IN DEATH CASE

### Busch, Father and Husband of Victims, Confirms Report of Crash

Walter Busch, lying near death at Swedish hospital, today corroborated statements of conditions leading up to the crash Sunday on the Shakopee road in which his wife and 7-year-old son were killed and he and an infant daughter seriously injured.

In the first interview with Busch since the crash, Assistant County Attorney Peter S. Neilson outlined reports of the accident and reported that Busch stated they were correct. Neilson refused to give out details of the interview.

**Will Jail Fredlund**

Neilson saw Busch when he went to Swedish hospital to gather further details in connection with the crash. He interviewed three doctors and two nurses, all of whom said the odor of liquor on the breath of Carl H. Fredlund, Minneapolis, the driver of the car that hit Busch, was strong when he was brought to the

(Continued on page four)

## *Jon Lindbergh Is 3 Years Old Today; Dog Guest at Party*

North Haven, Maine, Aug. 16.—(U.P.)—Jon Lindbergh had a birthday party today. He was three years old.

The secrecy that has surrounded domestic affairs of the Lindberghs since Charles A. Lindbergh, Jr., was kidnaped and killed prevailed, but it was assumed Jon would have a cake with three candles and perhaps a small guest or two. One of the principal guests was expected to be the German shepherd dog that is Jon's inseparable companion.

Colonel and Mrs. Lindbergh have been at the summer cottage of Mrs. Lindbergh's mother, Mrs. Dwight Morrow, most of the last month. They have made several cruises along the coast in the yacht used on their honeymoon.

## WESTINGHOUSE CO. RAISES HOUR WAGE

East Pittsburgh, Pa., Aug. 16.—(U.P.)—The Westinghouse Electric and Manufacturing company announced today it was adjusting all hourly wages to result in an average 5 per cent increase.

The adjustment, which will be only for workers on an hourly basis, will affect 25,000 employes in 14 plants throughout the country.

The company said it was unable to estimate the total amount of the increase in dollars and cents.

## ROCKEFELLER HEIR ESTATE IS ROBBED

Greenwich, Conn., Aug. 16.—(U.P.)—Avery Rockefeller, grand-nephew of the Standard Oil magnate, reported to police today that during the night his home had been robbed of jewels and cash.

Rockefeller, a son of the late Percy A. Rockefeller, an incorporator of Standard Oil company, who left a Connecticut estate valued at more than $9,000,000, said the cash loss was no more than $50.

## BOARD TO HAVE SHOWDOWN ON RELIEF INCREASE

### Welfare Body to Ask More Funds From Estimate Group

### 254 MORE WPA PROJECTS SENT IN

### Christgau Forwards Big Batch for Expenditure of $8,327,273

Christgau puts o.k. on more city, county WPA jobs, page 10.

A showdown on the question of Minneapolis relief allowances was scheduled to take place at a special meeting of the board of public welfare late today.

With available funds expected to be exhausted within 10 days if allowances are continued on the basis of the increases voted into effect by the welfare board last week, the board today was expected to request the board of estimate and taxation to issue an additional $500,000 of relief bonds and also to permit expenditures at a rate greater than $100,000 per month.

On the assumption that this request would be made, Mayor Latimer today called a special meeting of the city council Monday at 10 a.m. to pass on the bond request and a special meeting of the board of estimate and taxation at 11 a.m.

**No Help From State**

Funds with which to pay the increased allowances must be provided by the city, it was conceded today. Mayor Thomas E. Latimer and members of the welfare board relief committee appealed to L. P. Zimmerman, acting SERA administrator, for additional funds at a conference late Thursday but, according to reports, received little satisfaction.

As a preliminary to the special welfare board session, Mayor Latimer called a meeting of Farmer-Labor members of the welfare board, city council and board of estimate and taxation in his office today. The officials met in executive session, but it was understood some of those present urged the necessity of preparing a definite budget of relief needs and to get the matter of family allowances "down to a sound basis."

**254 Projects Sent In**

Other relief developments today included:

Announcement by Victor A. Christgau, state WPA administrator, that he had sent a record-breaking batch of 254 projects, totaling $8,327,273, to Washington for final approval, making a grand total of 644 projects, amounting to $23,009,353 approved and pending in Washington.

A dispatch from THE STAR'S Washington bureau announcing an additional federal relief allotment of $1,250,000 has been sent to Minnesota for August needs.

Consideration by the Minneapolis civil service commission of an application by the welfare board for 60-day permits for six persons to organize a relief complaint department, with I. S. Joseph, conservative member of the welfare board, contending the department is not needed and was approved only to provide patronage jobs.

## BAKER SHOT DOWN IN GANG FASHION

Kenosha, Wis., Aug. 16.—(U.P.)—Achille (Kelly) Mango, 41, operator of a bakery shop here, was shot down in gangland fashion today as he stood in front of his place of business.

Just before he died, the man gasped the name of a relative charging him with the fatal shooting.

Police went to the home of the man De Rango named, Sam Covelli, and apprehended him and his son.

## TWO FAMED VICTIMS OF THE TRAGEDY

WILL ROGERS

WILEY POST

## 1,100 IDLE AT STRUTWEAR CO.

### Office Employe Injured in Clash With Union Pickets

Approximately 1,100 workers at the Strutwear Knitting Company, 1015 Sixth street S., today were idle after representatives of the Amalgamated Garment Workers union and others picketed the plant as employes attempted to go to work.

One office employe of the Strutwear company received slight eye injuries in a scuffle with pickets early today. He is Myron Parsons, 2414 Thomas avenue N. He was treated at St. Barnabas hospital. No other violence of injuries were reported by Detective Inspector Fritz Ohman, who sent a squad of police to the plant.

Between 30 and 40 pickets, some of them reported to be wearing buttons of General Drivers union No. 574, appeared at the plant shortly after 7 a.m. today. Speakers addressed arriving employes from automobiles in an attempt to keep them from entering the plant.

Roy Weir, business agent of the Amalgamated union, said that the picketing action was taken in protest against discharge of eight union employes by company officials. Company officials said that no representative of the union has approached them with any proposal or protest.

## Tax Rich Changes Refused in House

Senate passes bill, Page 2

**Washington, Aug. 16.—(U.P.)—The house sent the tax-the-rich bill to conference with the senate today, refusing to accept senate changes in the original measure as it passed the house.**

**The actio nwas along the line congressional leaders expected.**

**Differnces between the house and senate bills will be adjusted in conference and it is expected that the ultimate final draft of the bill will be on its way to the White House within three or four days.**

## *3 Youths, Treated to Lunch, Return to Loot Restaurant*

### $50 in Food and Cash Taken After Proprietor Closes Up

Figuratively biting the hand that fed them, three hungry youths, bound for California, ate sandwiches early today in the Polka Dot inn, 318 Sixth avenue S., and then waited until the place was locked to come back and burglarize it.

Piecing the details of three burglaries together, police believe the trio worked up the block on Sixth avenue, and broke into two filling stations and the restaurant. Food and cash obtained from the cafe was estimated at $50.

A few minutes before 1 a.m. the three youths entered the restaurant and ordered rolls and coffee, which they paid for with pennies.

Noting the hungry look on their faces, a customer in the cafe offered to buy them some sandwiches. According to Leonard Nelson, cafe proprietor, the boys said they were "bumming" their way to Calofirnia.

Nelson locked up and the trio left. At 2:30 the policeman on the beat discovered the restaurant had been broken into and the front door left open.

Further investigation uncovered an additional attempted entry into the Standard Oil station at 530 S. Fourth street. The intruders left tools behind that had been taken from the cafe.

## DERN TO DEDICATE DAM AT ALMA, WIS.

Secretary of War George H. Dern will dedicate the newly constructed Mississippi river dam at Alma, Wis., seven miles south of Wabasha on Sept. 2, officials of the Upper Mississippi Waterway association were informed today.

A group of prominent Minneapolis and St. Paul business men, mayors of both cities and officials from nearby towns and communities will attend. The Third infantry band from Fort Snelling will participate and a regatta of privately-owned pleasure boats, two government vessels, naval reserve boats and a squadron of planes from the national guard and naval reserve will take part.

## CANADIAN REGIONS SWEPT BY FLOODS

Edmonton, Alta., Aug. 16.—(U.P.)—Completing the destruction of waterfront buildings at Slave Lake town, and threatening complete devastation for the settlement, wiping out the repair work of weeks along flooded sections of the northern Alberta railways and striking new terror to the hearts of residents of Slave Lake and Peace River, new strong and fresh flooding occurred in the north country Wednesday night. The new floods occurred a few hours after the first train since July had completed the round trip from Edmonton to the end of the steel in Peace River district.

## KING FAILS TO ASK ABOUT DIONNES

Montreal, Que., Aug. 16.—(U.P.)—Although King George of England is the supreme guardian of the Dionne quintuplets, he didn't even ask about them when he entertained their Canadian guardian, David Croll, minister of welfare and labor, said today on his return from London.

## Subpoenaed Witnesses Must Come Back

## NEW WRINKLE IN JUSTICE

### Defendant Asks Plaintiff Be Satisfied

Picture on page 18

A new wrinkle had been introduced in trials today when a defendant, on trial before Justice of the Peace L. E. Christ of Wayzata, urged the court to grant the complaining witness' plea for a continuance so the complainant would be assured the trial was fair.

The defendant was Allan L. Johnson, Deephaven justice of the peace, who was arrested at the request of J. E. Lewis, president of the Deephaven village council, after Johnson defended himself at a council meeting against charges made by a councilman that he had torn down a fence belonging to Dr. Don Fitzgerald of Robinson's bay. Johnson is charged with breaking up a public meeting.

He was haled before Justice Christ, but was prevented from making his pre-announced defense that political animosity was the real reason for his arrest when Lewis secured a continuance.

A request from Dr. Fitzgerald that he be excused "as he did not see what good his presence would do," provoked Johnson to exclaim that "this whole thing is a ridiculous farce."

Then Lewis asked a continuance.

Calling Justice Christ's attention to the packed courtroom, Johnson explained that most of the spectators were present at the stormy council meeting which ended in Johnson's arrest and had been subpoenaed to testify as to his conduct. He said he hesitated to ask them to return, although he wanted Lewis to feel sure the trial had been fair.

"Well," the justice ruled, "I'm sorry to inconvenience any of you, but as long as the defendant feels the plaintiff is in need of an attorney, I am inclined to think the trial should be continued. Will the witnesses please return at 5 p.m. Friday?"

## CHLORINATION OF WATER TO BE CUT

### TASTE TO BE UNPLEASANT FOR SOME TIME, SAYS OFFICIAL

Harrington and Jensen flayed for water stand, page 7.

Believing purity of Minneapolis city water has been established through heavy chlorination and that dangers of a typhoid epidemic have passed, Dr. F. E. Harrington, health commissioner, today declared chlorination will be reduced "within a few days."

"The only trouble with our city water right now is its taste," Dr. Harrington said. "If typhoid is under control, as we believe it is, our problem is chiefly to keep people away from suspicious places likely to contain contamination and restore the water to its natural taste."

Enough chlorination will be maintained to eliminate possibility of typhoid infection, Dr. Harrington stated, and it will be some time before taste of the city water will be pleasant. Rigid inspection of all public and private wells in the city will continue until the health department and the state board of health definitely determine the source of typhoid contamination.

## GOVERNOR PLANS WASHINGTON TRIP

Governor Olson probably will leave for Washington Monday night, according to information obtained from the governor's office today. According to tentative plans, the governor will go to Red Wing late Monday to spend a few hours at the convention of the Minnesota State Federation of Labor, and will board a train for Chicago about 11 p.m. It was expected the governor would spend about a week in Washington, conferring with federal officials on questions of relief, federal aid for state water conservation projects and the additional legislation, if any, that may be needed to enable Minnesota to participate in the benefits of the social security act.

**TRAIN RIDER INJURED**

Robbert Harris, 22, 508 Sixth avenue N., was injured near the Cedar Lake roundhouse when he was knocked from the top of a box car when a freight train passed under a low bridge.

## Fashion Flashes

Now that all the hubbub over the openings has subsided fashions for fall simmer down to a handful of highlights . . . skirts are definitely shorter . . . Renaissance and military are the themes most heavily drawn on for ideas . . . flares and fullness are the two "musts" for skirts . . . drapery is the most difficult to wear, most difficult to achieve, most sought after dress detail of all . . . dark green will surpass every color for clear, sheer popularity in spite of the noise about all others . . . gold will glitter everywhere on everything . . . the casual line carries on in coats, suits, furs.

—Frances.

## Craft Plows Into Marsh Near Barrow

### Famed Air Duo Forced Down Earlier in Eskimo Village by Missing Engine — Take Off Again Despite Thick Weather—Both Die Instantly

### MOTOR FORCED INTO CABIN OF SPEEDY CRAFT BY IMPACT OF FALL

### Pilot's Body Is Found Crushed in Craft—Cowboy-Humorist Is Thrown Clear of Wreckage—Scene of Accident Is Set Afire by Spilled Gasoline

**Washington, Aug. 16.—(INS)—Col. Charles A. Lindbergh today was believed ready to make an air dash across the continent to Alaska to return the bodies of the ill-starred Will Rogers and Wiley Post to their homes, the coast guard announced today.**

**A sister of Mrs. Will Rogers, who is in Showhegan, Me., communicated with coast guard headquarters and said Col. Lindbergh, who is in North Haven, Me., had "taken charge" of arrangements concerning return of the bodies.**

Other details and pictures page 13.

By United Press

Point Barrow, Alaska, Aug. 16.—Wiley Post and Will Rogers, famous air duo, were killed late Thursday when their plane crashed 15 miles south of here.

Lost in a fog and with the engine missing, Post nosed the plane into the tundra, striking frozen hummocks of moss. Its right wing broken, its nose and engine driven into the cabin, the crash instantly killed both occupants.

### *Engine of Plane Had Been Missing Badly*

They became lost in the fog about 5 p.m. and landed their Lockheed Orion low winged monoplane at Walkpi, an Eskimo village. Post made repairs to the plane's engine which had been missing badly and asked natives the way to Point Barrow.

The fog was lying almost to the tundra and they decided to wait for it to rise. Post and Rogers ate dinner with Eskimos camped on a river bank and after the meal decided to take off despite the fog.

Natives said the engine appeared to be running smoother as the big ship lifted from the river and took off in the blinding mantle which overhung the country.

It was not long after that the ship plumeted into the tundra. The motor being driven into the cabin by the force of the crash, killing Post, who made two successful trips around the world. Rogers was thrown clear of the plane which ground looped over onto its back. Rogers' death was also instantaneous, however.

Post's watch stopped at 8:18 p.m. Point Barrow time. The humorist's was still running when Sergeant Stanley Morgan of the U. S. Signal Corps Point Barrow station, and a newspaperman reached the scene.

Morgan was notified in Point Barrow by excited natives and the vicinity of the crash was reached in a whale boat, manned by natives.

### *Both Bodies Badly Crushed; Speedy Craft Demolished*

Post's body was pulled from the wreckage where it had been smashed among the controls and cabin.

Rogers' body was placed with that of Post in the whale boat and returned to Point Barrow. Here the bodies were turned over to Dr. Henry Griest, superintendent of the Presbyterian Mission hospital, where they were taken to await the arrival of the coast guard cutter Northland.

Both bodies were badly crushed. The plane was demolished. Gasoline spewed over the water between the moss hummocks, caught fire and blazed for several minutes.

Post, round-the-world record holder, and Rogers, the humorist, movie actor and famous air traveler, were on a leisurely trip around Alaska.

Originally intending to visit Point Barrow several days ago, instead they flew from Aklavik, N. W. T., to Fairbanks and spent the interval visiting central Alaskan points. They took off yesterday from Fairbanks and their arrival had been awaited at this farthest north outpost of civilization with keen anticipation by the few white persons here.

### *Plane Partially Submerged in Two Feet of Water*

The report of the accident was filed to the war department to Wasihngton by Sergeant Morgan, who operates the signal corps station at Point Barrow.

His full report said:

"At 10 p.m., a native runner reported a plane has crashed 15 miles south of Barrow. I immediately hired a fast launch and proceeded to the scene. I found the plane a complete wreck and partially submerged in two feet of water.

"I recovered the body of Rogers and then found it necessary to tear the plane apart to extract the body of Post from the water.

"Brought the bodies to Barrow and turned them over to Dr. Greist. Also salvaged the personal effects, which I am holding.

"Advise relatives and instruct this station fully as to procedure.

"Natives camping on the small river 15 miles south of here, Claim Post and Rogers landed, asked their way to Barrow and, on taking off, the engine misfired on a right bank while only 50 feet over the water. The plane out of control, crashed, tearing right wing off and toppling over, forcing the engine back through the body of the plane.

"Both apparently were killed instantly. Both bodies were bruised. Post's wrist watch was broken and stopped at 8:18 p.m."

While natives and whites struggled to breach the boat carrying the

(Continued on page two)

## Roosevelt Voices Regret

**Hyde Park, N. Y., Aug. 16.—(INS)—The tragic crash of Will Rogers and Wiley Post evoked an expression of deepest regret today from President Roosevelt.**

**"I was shocked to hear of the tragedy which has taken Will Rogers and Wiley Post from us," the president said. "Will was an old friend of mine, a humorist and philosopher beloved by all. I had the pleasure of greeting Mr. Post on his return from his round-the-world flight. He leaves behind a splendid contribution to the science of aviation. Both were outstanding Americans and will be greatly missed."**

**WEATHER**
U. S. Weather Bureau Forecast.
Fair, not so cold Friday; Saturday rain, slightly warmer.
Additional weather on page 14.

# The Minneapolis Tribune

MORNING EDITION
Three Cents in Minneapolis

Sixty-ninth Year. No. 133. 3 MINNEAPOLIS, MINN., FRIDAY, OCTOBER 4, 1935. Thirty-six Pages



# Britain, France Plan Ethiopian Aid; Italians Invade Neutral Territory

## Hall on Witness Stand Is Vague About Details in Shakopee Smashup

### Washington

By PAUL MALLON
Copyright, 1935, by Paul Mallon.

EPICUREAN SINCLAIR; HUEY LONG'S SHOES; FLAW IN EPIC PLAN

EPICUREAN.

PASADENA, Calif.—Upton Sinclair's home is a hideout here on a street that even the taxi drivers do not know. They will charge you $5 to find out. The Rockefeller and the Busch family (Anheuser) mansions, a mile away, are easily accessible, but interviewers with the political Epicurean are available only by appointment.

The street rumor reason for this around Los Angeles is that the man who polled 800,000 votes for governor last year is now in retirement, or semi-retirement. The active leader of his bloc of votes is supposed to be State Senator Colbert L. Olson. At least Mr. Olson is running the state EPIC movement, which now controls most of the state governmental offices except that of the governor.

But if you foregather with Mr. Sinclair, you will find that he has grander notions than retirement.

SELLING CAMPAIGN.

THE real reason for the shift of EPIC burdens appears to be that this smart politician has turned his mind to the national scene since the death of Huey Long. Mr. Sinclair will start out on a lecture tour in about 10 days, and hit every large city and section of the country, selling the EPIC doctrines.

His organization, he says, is now in 12 states. He has no idea that this outfit can play any important political role in the next elections. In fact, he is setting up autonomous state groups, permitting them to do whatever they like in their state politics.

Mr. Sinclair's game apparently is one of waiting until President Roosevelt has failed. He will prepare while waiting. He appears to have no presidential aspirations for himself. He knows too much for that. But he certainly is scheming to put his "production for use" unemployment relief scheme into operation nationally through Mr. Roosevelt or any other political agency which happens to be available.

REACHING.

THEREIN lies a full understanding of the political enigma, Sinclair, who has been using the Democratic party to advance his ideas in this state. He is for Mr. Roosevelt. He will be for Mr. Roosevelt up to the 1936 Democratic convention. You may quote him on that. (In fact, you may quote him on anything. He does not talk off-the-record, professing to have no secrets.)

Frankly, he will say his support of Mr. Roosevelt is not because he likes the new dealer. In fact, he believes 90 per cent of the new deal has failed or is about to fail. The only Roosevelt policy he supports is TVA. However, Mr. Roosevelt is the only national figure he can be for, so he is for Mr. Roosevelt.

His EPICS will put their own slate of delegates in the Democratic primary here next year, despite all you may have heard to the contrary. They will contest against the Farley-McAdoo delegates, not on the question of Mr. Roosevelt's renomination but solely to get an EPIC plank in the Democratic national platform.

Thus, further, you can see where Mr. Sinclair is reaching for the shoes that were Huey Long's.

FAULT.

THERE is one grave technical weakness in the proposed national EPIC expansion. For the benefit of people who may have come in late, it may be related that his plan is to make the unemployed earn their own way by self-supporting production for use. Mr. Roosevelt's way is to pay the unemployed from the federal treasury and let them spend the money wherever they choose.

Thus the new deal's money goes into business; Mr. Sinclair would deprive business of that income.

Mr. Sinclair's answer to this is that the business man would not have to pay unemployment relief taxes under his plan, but it is doubtful whether he will be able

(Continued on Page 8, Column 4.)

*Admits Fredlund Was Across Center Line Before Collision.*

*Makes Partial Retraction of First Statement to Prosecutor.*

An unwilling witness, hesitant and often vague in his answers to both prosecution and defense questions, Arthur B. Hall took the stand for the first time Thursday at the trial of Carl H. Fredlund.

It was Hall who sat beside Fredlund in the front seat of the young haberdashery clerk's borrowed sedan when he rounded a turn in the Shakopee road the morning of August 11 and crashed into a machine driven by Walter P. Busch, killing Mrs. Busch and their 7-year-old son, Perry.

**Partial Retraction.**

The state called him as a rebuttal witness and drew from him the reluctant admission that "a few seconds before the crash" Fredlung's big sedan was traveling 'just a little bit over the center line of the paving." Just before that, Hall said, he had looked at the speedometer and it was registering "about 50."

And although Assistant County Attorney William G. Compton, prosecution chief, confronted him with three signed statements he previously had made in which he was quoted as saying the Fredlund car "decidedly was on the wrong side of the road—a car's width over the center line," Hall on the stand would place the sedan no more than "just a little over the center line."

**Stories Tally.**

As Hall testified, Fredlund, held his eyes steadily upon him. A few days ago Hall had remarked Fredlund was his best friend. Just back of the defendant, who is being tried for third degree murder, his parents, Mr. and Mrs. John Fredlund, who have missed not a day of the trial, listened intently. So also did the injured Busch, just now beginning to regain his strength, who had been on the stand earlier in the day.

Except in some detail, Hall's recital of events leading up to the crash tallied with the story told on the stand by Fredlund. One divergence was that Fredlund had come to his barber shop at Twenty-sixth street and Nicollet avenue

(Continued on Page 2, Column 3)

## WELFARE BOARD POLICIES UNDER F.-L. ATTACKED

I. S. Joseph Urges Creation of Citizens' Committee to Study Program.

Conservative Presents Criticisms Before Grain Shippers Association.

Denouncing policies of the Farmer-Labor controlled board of public welfare, I. S. Joseph, only remaining conservative member of the board and its former president, Thursday night urged creation of a citizens' committee which would sit in on board meetings and analyze the procedures.

In his talk, made at a dinner meeting of the Minneapolis Grain Shippers' association, at the Nicollet hotel, Mr. Joseph suggested the proposed committee should be composed of representatives of the Civic & Commerce association, the League of Women Voters, Council of Social Agencies, American Federation of Labor and the Ministerial association. These representatives would pass information gained at board meetings to their respective organizations, he said.

**Raps Political Juggling.**

"We should permit these people to speak for all Minneapolis citizenry and not allow politicians to juggle the important function of the board of public welfare, with expenditures of $8,500,000 annually, to suit their own pleasure and convenience,'" declared Mr. Joseph.

Mr. Joseph charged that demands for a 35 per cent increase in relief allowance, granted by the board early in August, were the result of threats and intimidation by a group consisting of relief clients and a local union. This union, he declared, had charged a membership of 25 cents per family in return for promises that it would represent them before the board and press demands for the increase.

**Blames Scott and Hudson.**

"Both Aldermen I. G. Scott and Edwin I. Hudson encouraged these increases, knowing well that there were no local resources with which to meet these increases and that if

(Continued on Page 11, Column 1.)

## NEWS INDEX



## Suitor Threatened Co-ed, Friend Insists

Colorado Springs, Colo., Oct. 3.—(AP)—A coroner's jury investigating the mysterious death of Margaret Wilm, 21-year-old college beauty, was told Thursday night her suitor, Kenneth Garrett, 22, once threatened to "beat her head in." Frances Stevenson, 20, a business college student, testified Miss Wilm told her of the purported threat. Garrett and his brother-in-law, George Sleppy, 32, both of whom had been held in technical custody, were released in the care of their parents as the jury adjourned its inquest until next Wednesday. Coroner J. Thomas Coghlan announced the jury would seek "further evidence" meanwhile,

### HAS ITALY DOOMED THIS VILLAGE, TOO?

(PICTURE WIRED TO TRIBUNE EXCLUSIVELY IN NORTHWEST.)

Harar, Ogaden, Ethiopia, Oct. 3.—(Wirephoto)—The street of this provincial capital represents a scene typical of such towns as Aduwa and Adigrat, which were bombed Thursday by Italian planes. Harar is in the region of Aussa, to which Emperor Haile Selassie dispatched 50,000 troops Thursday in expectation of an attack. Harar lies south of Aussa and the latter town is near the southern tip of Italian Eritrea. Harar will be in the jaws of a military squeeze if Italy brings troops into Ethiopia. from Italian Somaliland in the south as well as from southern Eritrea. The strolling natives shown here are undoubtedly under arms at the front as a result of the general Ethiopian mobilization called Thursday. See map on page 2.

## Tigers Cool Off Hot Cubs in Second Game, 8 to 3

*Bengals Turn Into Polar Bears, Claw Cubs in Arctic Gale.*

By GRANTLAND RICE.
Copyright, 1935, by NANA., Inc.

Detroit, Oct. 3.—The sixth glacial period moved in on top of the world series, and the Tigers pulled the smartest trick of the year. They turned into polar bears, clawed the hide off the frozen Cubs and moved into Chicago on even terms. Their main job now will be stopping the Cubs on their own turf, where they haven't lost a ball game for a month.

The Cubs were smoking hot until the Arctic circle fell on their necks in the second battle, and the wind that roared in from the barren lands removed all the steam from their systems in about 10 minutes.

It might be suggested here that Tiger bats and a young fellow by the name of Tommy Bridges, from Gordonsville, Tenn., also figured in the day's results.

Outside of the bitter, blasting gale that blew fly balls all over the lot and slipped incipient pneumonia to 47,000 customers, the second contest had one distinct feature. This feature has a direct connection with the punching power of Tiger bats. In the first game, if you care to go back that far, Lon Warneke turned these famous bats into cheese straws. But in the second game, the same set of bats won the ball game before a man was out. This may be a world series record. At least it should be. Bats or bludgeons that were as silent as the grave only a day ago suddenly turned on the expected thunder at the expense of Charley Root, a veteran, who had no liking at all for a winter wind that apparently turned his right arm into an icicle.

Before Root started for the warmth and shelter of the club house, the first four Tigers moving up to the plate had nailed him for four hits and four runs.

White singled and Cochrane doubled. Gehringer singled and lank Hank Greenberg fired a home run into the left field bleachers. There was the ball game. Four runs in,

(Continued on Page 26, Column 3)

## ANNA DICKIE OLESEN HURT IN AUTO UPSET

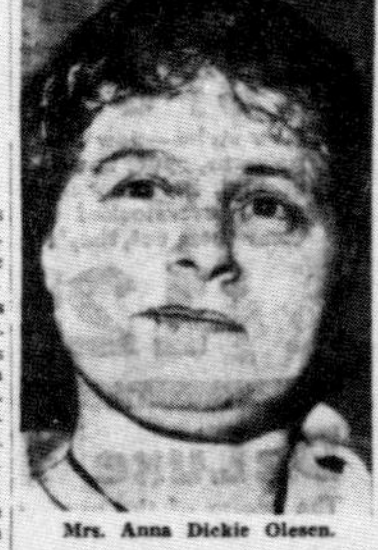

Mrs. Anna Dickie Olesen.

Bemidji, Minn., Oct. 3.—Mrs. Anna Dickie Olesen, state director of the national emergency council and Minnesota's first Democratic national committeewoman, was brought to a Bemidji hospital late Thursday following an automobile accident between Cass Lake and Bemidji. Her car turned over four times when a tire blew out.

Roland Hill of Duluth, secretary to Mrs. Olesen, who was accompanying her to Bemidji where she was to speak at a Democratic meeting Thursday night, was cut, bruised and in the hospital but his condition is not serious.

An X-ray examination disclosed Mrs. Olesen did not suffer any fractures and physicians did not regard her condition as serious.

She had expected to leave Bemidji Thursday night, and go by airplane to Washington Friday. She had been scheduled to deliver an address at a "Prosperity festival" sponsored by Democrats of Bemidji and the ninth district here Thursday night.

## Wounded Wife Near Death in Triple Slaying

Daughter Who Escaped Bullets Suffers From Shock—Son Recovering.

(Pictures on page 10.)

A frightened little girl, a wounded boy, and their mother, who lay near death from a bullet wound in her neck, were all that remained Thursday night of the William Holler family of seven.

Their home at 4518 Fifteenth avenue south, where until just before dawn Thursday the family had lived quietly, was empty. Blood stains on the floor, a broken window and disarranged furniture gave evidence of the tragedy that had struck the small home.

Scores of persons came to look at that house during the day. Some kept their distance. Others, bolder, stood on tiptoe to peer through windows at what remained of the shambles created when the 41-year-old father killed three of his children, critically wounded his wife, wounded his eldest son, and then killed himself.

Like relatives who always had regarded Holler as a hard working, model family man, neighbors who had known the family intimately during the 12 years the Hollers lived there were stunned.

Dudley Williams, 4904 Fourteenth

(Continued on Page 8, Column 1.)

### Stallings Says Ethiopians Have Valor of Ignorance

The Ethiopians are confident that guerrila warfare will give them victory over the Italian invaders, Laurence Stallings says in his dispatch from the headquarters of the Ethiopian armies in the field. They "have the valor of ignorance," he says in telling of their plans.

Turn to Page 21.

## Laval and Eden Hint at Munition Supply for Haile

Casualties 1,700 as Duce's Planes Bomb 2 Towns—Battle Reported—New Roman Advance Ordered.

### *Italian-Ethiopian Situation*

By Associated Press.

**PARIS**—France and Great Britain agreed on a program before the League of Nations which included not only possible economic and munitions shipment boycott of Italy but also consideration of economic assistance for Ethiopia. A pact of mutual naval assistance against Italian aggression in the Mediterranean was in the making.

**ASMARA, ERITREA**—Italian colonial force commandes announces Italian troops had crossed the Mareb river, boundary between Eritrea and Ethiopia for the "defense" of Eritrean tribesmen against Ethiopia. All Eritrea and Italian Somaliland were placed under full martial law.

**ADDIS ABABA**—A battle between Italian and Ethiopian troops was reported under way between Eritrea and Aduwa. The Ethiopian government announced Italian fliers Thursday bombed historic Aduwa and Adigrat, destroying 115 houses with 1,700 casualties. The emperor proclaimed a general mobilization and sent 50,000 troops to Aussa where an Italian attack was expected.

**ROME**—Italian official sources Thursday admitted their planes had dropped bombs on Ethiopian soil but charged firing at the squadron from the ground was the cause. Advance of Italian troops into Ethiopia was announced without any official mention of fighting.

**GENEVA**—League of Nations representatives discuss economic action against Italy, with urgent session of league council called for Saturday. French-British agreement expected to furnish basis for attempt to halt war league failed to prevent.

**WASHINGTON**—Secretary of State Hull drew up plans for an arms embargo to keep the United States free of entanglement in the Italo-Ethiopian conflict. Action awaiting formal word through U. S. diplomatic channels that a state of war exists.

## Britain and France Agree on Steps Against Italy

Paris, Oct. 3.—(AP)—Great Britain and France Thursday agreed on a joint program before the League of Nations which calls for the immediate severance by league members of financial and economical relations with Italy and possible financial help to Ethiopia.

The third of the three points of the agreement, French officials announced, favors prohibition of purchase of Italian goods by league members or sale of goods to Mussolini's nation, including war munitions and their transportation.

Premier Pierre Laval after an hour's conference with Anthony Eden, British minister of League of Nations affairs, which preceded the agreement stated:

"Mr. Eden and I talked over the order of the day for council of the league. We have considered various methods of procedure. We will continue in close collaboration in Geneva."

Under the second provision of the accord, which hints at financial help to Emperor Haile Selassie for national defense, is included also the lifting of the arms embargo against the African empire.

Eden, it was authoritatively stated, disposed of the suggestion for the closing of the Suez canal—through which Italy's troops reach th ezone of war—by reporting the British cabinet thought such an act too risky.

Britain's request fro French assistance if Italy attacks the British Mediterranean fleet will receive the official affirmative of the cabinet Friday, officials said.

Laval promised Eden such a reply, officials continued, in return for the same guarantees from Britain in case France is attacked.

Laval will leave for Geneva after Friday's cabinet session where he will rejoin Eden.

The Italian ambassador, Vittorio Cerruti, called on Laval Thursday, presumably to explain Italy's advance into Ethiopia.

The Havas news agency reported Thursday night it had learned that Premier Mussolini informed the French and British governments definitely that Italy will accept economic and financial sanctions without protest. Such sanctions, however, would have to be applied by the countries concerned as individuals and must be subject to no international supervision, the agency reported.

A clash between a group demonstrating against Italy and police at Toulouse injured several persons. The occasion was the departure of 50 Italians for military service in Italy. After fighting on the station platform, the demonstrators were dispersed and none of the Italians was injured.

### *HAILE EMPTIES JAILS AS DRUMS BEAT WAR CALL*

Addis Ababa, Oct. 3.—(NANA) Emperor Haile Selassie promised the "conquered lands" of Eritrea and Italian Somaliland to a crowd of wildly cheering warriors as a reward for Ethiopian victory in the struggle with Italy.

On receipt of news of the bombing of Aduwa, the emperor ordered that the jails be opened and the prisoners released. It was reported that 7,000 gained their freedom.

As the Menelik war-drum beat a call to arms, signaling nation-wide mobilization, old men drew swords and staged a previously rehearsed demonstration in the palace yards.

The emperor appeared on his balcony only after repeated demands had been shouted by the throngs surging on the terrace below. He concluded a brief address with the pledge that "we will fight to the last drop of blood."

The streets of Addis Ababa are tranquil.



## Italians 12 Miles From Aduwa; Press Advance

*Map of territory involved Page 2.*

Asmara, Eritrea, Oct. 4.—(AP)—Italy's strengthened military arms began reaching into Ethiopia Thursday as cavalry detachments and infantrymen with tank and artillery reinforcements moved forward across the frontier shortly after a proclamation declared both Eritrea and Italian Somaliland under martial law.

In Rome the Fascist newspaper Il Messagero said Italian troops reached Daro Tacle, 20 kilometers beyond the Eritrean frontier and only 20 kilometers (roughly 12 miles) from Aduwa in operations Thursday.

Unofficial reports from the front said the Italian forces, led by Eritrean cavalry, had virtually taken possession of the so-called neutral strip which Ethiopia had announced it was leaving open pending the outcome of conciliation negotiations.

In a proclamation to tribesmen of Eritrea a few hours earlier, General Emilio de Bono, who is commanding the Italian colonial

SOCIETY

EXCLUSIVE ASSOCIATED PRESS DISPATCHES AND WIREPHOTO IN THIS EDITION

# The Minneapolis Sunday Tribune

FIRST in City Circulation—FIRST in TOTAL Circulation—Daily and Sunday

Sixty-ninth Year. No. 282. | One Hundred Four Pages 4 | MINNEAPOLIS, MINN., SUNDAY, MARCH 8, 1936. | *** | (11) | Price Ten Cents

# French Rush Troops to Border as Nazi Soldiers Cross Rhine

## *Wirephoto Flashes Historic Scenes in European Crisis*

GERMAN CAVALRY RETURNS TO RHINE

Cologne, Germany, March 7.—(AP—Wirephoto)—German cavalry returned to the Rhine country Saturday as a consequence of Chancellor Hitler's renunciation of the Locarno pact. Not for 18 years have government troops been seen in this city demilitarized by the Versailles treaty.

'NO LONGER A CONQUERED NATION'

Berlin, Germany, March 7.—(AP—Wirephoto)—"We are no longer a conquered nation," said Chancellor Adolf Hitler Saturday as he addressed the reichstag in a speech announcing the military occupation of the Rhineland and the termination of the Locarno pact. Goering sits beside Hitler.

*(These pictures were taken in Berlin and Cologne Saturday. They are presented herewith exclusively in the northwest by The Minneapolis Tribune. Telephoto to London, radiophoto to New York and Wirephoto to Minneapolis makes possible this service of bringing the pictures with the news.)*

## *Paris Calls Out Full War Power on 150-Mile Front*

***Will Fight If Forced To, Declares Paris in Appeal to Locarno Signers.***

***Soviets and Czechs Pledge Unlimited Backing Against the Germans.***

*Other stories and Wirephotos on German crisis, page 14.*

By John Evans.
Associated Press Foreign Staff.

Paris, March 7. — France's military authorities ordered Saturday night that all fortifications along the northeast frontier be garrisoned immediately with their full quotas of troops.

The order was issued shortly after the French government decided to do its "utmost" under the League of Nations' covenant to compel Germany to take its troops out of the Rhineland.

Officials declared France would ask the league to vote economic and financial sanctions against Germany. Remilitarization of the Rhineland violates the Treaty of Versailles, the pact by which the League of Nations also was created.

**Russia Promises Help.**

In authoritative quarters it was stated France would ask Great Britain, Italy and Belgium, co-signatories of the Locarno pact, which Hitler denounced, to demand immediate evacuation of the Rhineland.

This request will be made, it was said, after the league acts on the violation of the Versailles and Locarno treaties.

Russia and Czechoslovakia, it was stated by French officials, have promised France their unlimited backing against Germany's abrogation of the Locarno pact.

**Army Leaves Cancelled.**

The ambassadors of the two nations, officials declared, told French foreign Minister Pierre-Etienne Flandin that their governments were with France "to the limit" in any action against the Reich.

Authorities said that despite the

## 'Iron Ring Endangers Us'--Hitler

**Reichsfuehrer Asks Vote to Uphold Policies.**

By Louis P. Lochner.
Copyright, 1936, by Associated Press.

Berlin, March 7.—Germany re-established the "watch on the Rhine" Saturday.

By command of Reichsfuehrer Hitler, her troops crossed the famous little river, regiment by regiment, to take up the posts once held by the kaiser's armies on the frontiers of France.

Hitler called the action a precaution against Communism and France's "iron ring around the reich." It smashed the Locarno pact and the remnants of the military clauses of the Versailles treaty.

**Calls for Election.**

Der Fuehrer declared that Germany, reborn as a world power, was ready to re-enter the League of Nations, but as a comrade rather than as a conquered nation.

Then, in an effort to prove that his act was the will of the German people, he dissolved the nation's parliament, the reichstag, and ordered elections for March 29. It is the composition of the reichstag which determines the government of Germany.

Hitler called his action a move for peace. He offered to sign a 25-year nonaggression pact with France and Belgium, with Great Britain and Italy as guarantors.

He offered friendship to Lithuania and Czechoslovakia.

He assured Poland that Germany had no designs on Pomorze, the Polish corridor to the Baltic sea.

**Dramatic Swiftness.**

The German government's action was delivered with the suddenness so characteristic of Hitler. He called the members of the diplomatic corps, including William E. Dodd, United States ambassador, to his chancellery and delivered to them a memorandum setting forth what he intended to do.

He told the diplomats that Germany was alarmed by the recently concluded treaty of military alli-

(Continued on Page 13, Column 4)

## New Deal Taxes to Grow, Hoover Says

**Warns Against Future Costs in Speech Before Colorado Young Republicans.**

*Text of former President Hoover's speech appears on page 6 of second news section.*

By Associated Press.

Colorado Springs, Colo., March 7.—Former President Herbert Hoover asserted Saturday night the new deal had laid the groundwork for an ever-increasing tax burden, yet failed in the "outstanding" governmental job of re-employing the jobless.

Addressing the Young Republican league of Colorado, he said the American system of liberty was endangered and told his young listeners "your freedom and your opportunities in life are being mortgaged."

**Big Crowd Applauds.**

The capacity crowd of over 3,000 in the Colorado Springs auditorium applauded Mr. Hoover repeatedly as he made his points emphatically.

One item of administration legislation came in for favorable comment:

"The new deal regulations of stocks and security promotion in various aspects have the right objectives. They were hastily and poorly formed without proper consideration by congress. But they point right."

After indicting the administration's "planned economy" as endangering the constitution, charging it with waste and ill-founded financial policies, the former president asked:

"What of the taxes that will ooze from this spending and debt all your lives?

**Jobless Still Jobless.**

"Do not mistake. The new taxes of today are but part of them. More of them are as inevitable as the first of the month. The only alternatives are repudiation or inflation. No matter what nonsense you are told about corporations and the rich paying the bill, there will be two-thirds of it for the common man to pay after the corporations and the rich are sucked dry."

He said that election day, 1932, the American Federation of Labor reported 11,600,000 unemployed.

"Today, after three years of the

(Continued on Page 4, Column 1)

**WEATHER FORECAST**

**U. S. Weather Bureau Forecast.** Partly cloudy to cloudy Sunday and Monday, possible snow in northeast portion; rising temperature in east Monday. 24 hour high, 34, at 6 p. m. Saturday; low, 22, at 6 a. m. Saturday. Additional weather in another section.

## *N. Y. Strike Spreads to Big Hotels*

***Building Service Employes Go Out Amid Heavy Week-end Business.***

By Associated Press.

New York, March 7. — Timing their drive to hit the week-end transient business, building service strikers Saturday night strove to disrupt Gotham's hotel and theatrical centers.

By ordering walkouts at half a hundred hotels they created a situation that was called serious, as it affected heavy week-end business.

At the same time the striking elevator operators, porters and other building workers tightened their picket lines at hold-out apartment houses. A definite falling off of week-end reservations was reported by theaters and night clubs. While most managers discounted the effect of the hotel walkout, one official said that the usual week-end influx of guests had changed to a general exodus.

Chris Houlihan, head of the union's hotel division, said 45 members of the United Mine Workers of America, here to negotiate a new anthracite coal contract, had shifted their quarters from the Hotel Commodore to another hostelry "approved" by the union.

Brooklyn and Queens building owners awaited week end developments, wondering whether threats to carry the strike into those boroughs would materialize.

Energizing his drive against

(Continued on Page 13, Column 7)

## REED SURVEYS JUNIOR HIGHS

**Scrapping of Set-up Would Impair $9,000,000 Investment, He Reports.**

Abandonment of Minneapolis' 20-year-old junior high school system would seriously impair an investment in buildings and equipment which, Superintendent Carroll R. Reed revealed Saturday, is fast approaching the $10,000,000 mark.

As the first phase of a survey ordered by the board of education Monday following the appearance of an east side delegation urging a return to the old eight-year grade and four-year high school program, Mr. Reed has compiled figures for subsequent presentation to the board showing the cost of the city's 12 junior high school buildings to be $7,233,000.

Added to these construction expenses in order to arrive at the approximate amount invested in the 12 plants must be the cost of special equipment and fixtures necessary to the junior high school course of study. Mr. Reed estimated the cost of such equipment and fixtures at $1,500,000.

These two figures foot up to $8,733,000. Including an additional $410,000 which the board proposes to spend for annexes to Patrick Henry Junior high school to convert it into a combination junior and senior high school and to Folwell Junior high school to relieve congestion, the total amount involved reaches well over $9,000,000.

"It should be born in mind," Mr. Reed said, "that during the time we have been building up our junior high school system we have built 18 elementary schools on a simplified plan which precludes their use for junior high studies. By that I mean they are not equipped with shops, laboratories, libraries or gymnasiums. We have

(Continued on Page 2, Column 6)



## F.-L. Session Today Plans Judge Drive

**County Convention to Seek Six Court Posts for Members of the Party.**

By Orlin Folwick.
Tribune Staff Writer.

Farmer-Laborites, facing this year the biggest crisis their party has experienced since it took control of the state administration, are planning nevertheless an ambitious program that they hope will add the courts to their political possessions.

That they are headed toward an inter-party controversy that may lose them the statehouse next fall does not concern party leaders in the desire to extend Farmer-Labor influence to the courtrooms, nor will they be deterred by the fact that judicial elections are nonpartisan.

The initial move for a concerted drive on the courts is expected to be made Sunday by the Hennepin county Farmer-Labor convention, which meets at Central Labor Union headquarters, 24 Eighth street north, to select 109 delegates to the state convention in St. Paul March 27 and 28 and to prepare the party slate for county and congressional offices.

**Admit Vigorous Campaign.**

Party leaders admitted openly Saturday that they plan a vigorous campaign to elect six Farmer-Labor judges in Hennepin county, hoping to select indorsees at Sunday's session. Five of these will be for district court positions and the sixth for probate court.

Basis for their action is founded on party dissatisfaction with the present judicial system. It finds numerous faults with the courts and is particularly exercised over the method of choosing grand jurors. A long standing complaint has been the contention that not enough jurors are chosen from the laboring classes.

None of the incumbent judges will receive approval of the Farmer-Laborites, leaders declared Saturday. The five district judges against whom the campaign will be waged are Judges E. F. Waite, W. C. Leary, W. W. Bardwell, Frank E. Reed and Paul W. Guilford. The probate fight involves the tenancy of Judge Manley L. Fosseen. Terms of these six expire this year.

**No Governorship Action.**

Although the Farmer-Laborites in the past have indorsed judgeship candidates who have sought it, this will be the first time the party is moving to install its candidates in all the open judgeships. Should it be successful in replacing the incumbents, it would come within one of controlling the county's ju-

(Continued on Page 11, Column 1)

## *Purse Snatch Gang Broken Up by Arrest*

***Three Boys Confess to 20 Car Thefts and to Stripping Autos.***

A chance arrest a week ago resulted Saturday in the breakup of one youthful purse-snatching gang that "doubled" also in automobile thefts and burglaries from parked cars.

Driving through an alley the evening of March 2, Patrolmen Joe Kolars and Tom Flaherty arrested a 17-year-old boy as he fled after being seen siphoning gasoline from a parked car. The boy admitted taking part in several car thefts and purse snatchings with two older companions.

Detectives obtained the names of his companions, Christy Judge, 19, of 513 Fifteenth avenue south, and Leroy Tuween, 9 Xerxes avenue south. Judge admitted he drove the other two boys on purse-snatching forays.

All three admitted taking purses from Mrs. Teresa Hellum, 1816 Twenty-fifth avenue north; Amanda Ganz, 1815 La Salle avenue, and Mrs. A. C. Sherry, 2216 Twenty-ninth avenue south.

Judge and the 17-year-old youth admitted about 20 car thefts and countless prowls of automobiles. They said they stripped cars of anything they found loose.

In Tuween's home, police found nine pairs of trousers stolen from the parked car of Joe Mirviss, 1000 Newton avenue north. Judge and Tuween were arraigned Saturday on grand larceny charges. Their companion was sent to Red Wing.

## *Engine, 8 Cars Pass Over Boy—He Lives*

By Associated Press.

Washington, March 7.—Jimmy Seis, 2½ years old, had two small cuts on his head and a puffed cheek Saturday after being run over by a locomotive and eight freight cars. He strayed into the Baltimore & Ohio railroad yards and was struck by the train, throwing him between the rails. Unconscious, he lay still as the cars ran over him. Jimmy's mother had come out to look for him when a trainman brought the unconscious lad to her. He was rushed to the hospital, apparently near death, but when the blood was washed from his head, the two cuts and the bruised cheek were found to be the extent of his injuries.

## Fairbanks, Lady Ashley Wed in Paris

**WIREPHOTO OF NEWLYWEDS**

(PICTURE WIRED TO TRIBUNE EXCLUSIVELY IN NORTHWEST.)

**Paris, March 7.—(AP—Wirephoto)—Douglas Fairbanks and Lady Ashley were married in Paris Saturday. This picture, sent from London to New York by radiophoto and from there to The Tribune by Wirephoto Saturday, shows the couple signing the marriage register after the ceremony. The wedding was held in the marriage salon of city hall, a gold-leafed room with a ceiling adorned by floating pink cupids.**

### Mayor Reads Civil Service—Straus Is Witness.

By Associated Press.

Paris, March 7.—Douglas Fairbanks and his bride, the former Lady Ashley, were honeymooning Saturday night after a civil wedding ceremony had culminated their hectic efforts to have the French marriage laws suspended.

The couple planned to leave on a motor trip to Belgium and Holland and then sail for China where Fairbanks plans to produce a motion picture based on the life of Marco Polo.

**Mayor Reads Service.**

Their marriage was performed earlier in the day by Mayor Gaston Drucker in the gold marriage salon of the eighth ward city hall under a ceiling gaily decorated with pink cupids.

Miss Elizabeth Govet of London attended Lady Ashley and American Ambassador Jesse Isidor Straus arrived at the last minute to sign the register as Fairbanks' witness.

Their wedding brought to a climax several days of concerted effort to win suspension of the French marriage regulations of a 30-day residence and 1-day publication of banns.

**Doug Keeps Coat On.**

Mayor Drucker closed the ceremony with the traditional phrase —"I hope that your love marriage will be very happy"—and wished the newlyweds a pleasant voyage to China.

Fairbanks and Straus kept their overcoats on during the ceremony and all the wedding party were seated on red plush benches before the mayor's desk during the short legal ritual.

THE WIREPHOTO NEWSPAPER -- PICTURES BY WIRE

**WEATHER**
U. S. Weather Bureau Forecast. Local showers in east and south, cooler in south Monday; Tuesday fair. 24 hours high, 86, at 5 p. m. Sunday: low, 64, at 5:30 a. m. Sunday.
Additional weather on page 4.

# The Minneapolis Tribune

FIRST in City Circulation—FIRST in TOTAL Circulation—Daily and Sunday

MORNING EDITION
Three Cents in Minneapolis

Seventieth Year. No. 57. 3 MINNEAPOLIS, MINN., MONDAY, JULY 20, 1936. • • • Eighteen Pages

# Spanish Rebels Move on Madrid

## TOWNSENDITES HEAR LEMKE IN PLEA FOR VOTE

**Union Party Nominee Supports Pension Plan, Views New Deal as Lunacy.**

**Townsend, Gerald Smith Exhort Convention to Give Support to North Dakotan.**

Cleveland, July 19.—(AP)—Representative William Lemke, Dr. Francis E. Townsend and the Rev. Gerald K. Smith joined on the same platform here late Sunday in advocating old age pensions and Lemke's candidacy for president.

They addressed the closing session of the national convention of Townsend clubs in Cleveland stadium.

Lemke, the Union party candidate for president, aligned himself "four square behind the old age pension movement" and called the present administration "national lunacy."

**Townsend Hunts 'Big Game.'**

Townsend, head of the pension organization, exhorted his followers to "elect loyal congressmen and senators. They are your meat. I am going after bigger game."

Smith, leader of the Share-the-Wealth clubs, roused the 8,000 listeners to standing cheers with a fiery speech in which he said "the only presidential candidate for your plans is Lemke."

Lemke issued a statement in which he said that, as president, the White House doors would be open to Townsend and "to any other leader of a great and humane cause."

"I am 100 per cent for an old age revolving pension. The details of such legislation must of course be worked out by your organization and congress.

"As president, I will sign any bill that congress enacts which will give an honest and fair compensation to old people who have helped create the wealth of this nation.

**Favors Currency Expansion.**

He said honest and intelligent expansion of currency to save the homes of the farmers—as proposed under the Frazier-Lemke measure—should be provided and added:

"The administration ganged up

(Continued on Page 2, Column 3)

## CROWNING RASPBERRY QUEEN

—Tribune Staff Photographer.

Crowning the queen of the Raspberry festival at Hopkins Sunday climaxed the afternoon's program. Miss Helen Kvetensky, queen, is shown as she received the regal diadem from Frank Madden, who presided at the coronation ceremonies.

## HEAT IS BROKEN BY N. W. RAINS

**City Temperature Stays Below 85—Showers Lessen Damage to Crops.**

With the long heat wave definitely broken by showers that fell over the week-end in many northwest communities, Minneapolis settled back Sunday to enjoy cooler weather.

During the early morning hours the mercury dropped to a low of 65 and at no time during the day did it get above 86 in the city.

As the showers fell in farming sections they lessened to some extent the damage done to crops by the blistering sun and hot winds during the torrid spell. A survey

(Continued on Pafe 2, Column 3.)

## Raspberry Is King for Day at Hopkins

***Thousands Attend Annual Festival at 'America's Raspberry Capital.'***

The raspberry had its day in the limelight Sunday as thousands jammed the gaily decorated streets of Hopkins for its second annual Raspberry festival.

Despite record heat and prolonged drouth which seriously threatened for a time to curtail the yield of berries, Hopkins proved its boast of "America's Raspberry Capital" by providing a portion of sugared berries for each of the visitors who thronged the town.

**Thousands of Visitors.**

Normal activities of the town were suspended early in the morning with the first onrush of visitors. Perfect weather for the celebration, with light clouds shading the sun during the hottest hours of the day helped draw out the thousands of visitors.

Although the entertainment varied widely throughout each hour of the day and night, the theme of the festival never wavered very far from the prime motive—the raspberry. In floats, street decorations, eulogistic speeches, and finally by eating the berries, visitors were continually reminded of the excellence of the fruit produced in Hopkins.

**25,000 Served.**

For the festival had its serious side in addition to the entertainment, and the purpose was to con-

(Continued on Page 2, Column 5)

## NEWS INDEX



## Washington

**By PAUL MALLON**

*Mr. Mallon left Saturday on his annual vacation. His daily column will be resumed here Monday, August 3.*

## Olson Is Reported Resting Comfortably

Rochester, Minn., July 19. — Governor Olson, convalescing from an operation in St. Mary's hospital, was resting comfortably Sunday listening to the radio and writing letters to his friends, according to the official bulletin issued by the Mayo clinic. The bulletin, issued at 5 p. m., said: "The governor has had a comfortable Sunday and spent the day listening to the radio and writing letters. His 4 p. m. temperature was 99.2; pulse and respiration were normal. "His tube feedings were well taken and are being increased to make up a complete adequate nourishment by Monday."



## SEE A SHORTAGE OF ARTISANS IN BUILDING TRADE

**FHA Chiefs Say Skilled Workman Will Be Too Few in State This Fall.**

**Situation National, Statistics Show—Contractors Report Need at Present.**

**By William P. Helm.**
Tribune Washington Correspondent.

Washington, July 19.—(Special)—The federal employment agency reported Sunday that "skilled building mechanics are being called back to work in Minnesota and there probably will be a shortage of building artisans there during the fall."

And the condition in Minnesota is typical of a nation-wide outlook, it was announced Sunday by the federal housing administration. The prospect "of a general shortage of skilled building artisans in the near future" is regarded as a likelihood by FHA. The forecast was made after a survey of conditions on a national scale and after consulting "thoughtful members of the building industry who have been watching the trends in the expanding building industry," FHA announced.

**Cites Reports.**

"That serious consideration must be given this eventuality is borne out by reports from many sections of the country of a present insufficiency of skilled building labor," FHA announced. "Various offices of FHA, newspapers, local employment agencies, contractors and labor organizations in certain cities and towns in 36 states and territories have reported contractors experiencing difficulty in obtaining skilled labor to complete or start home and other building projects.

"In some localities in several of the states it has been necessary to import skilled building mechanics in order, that work could be completed. Such were the conditions are the time reported. Whether they become chronic or not depends upon future developments.

"If a threatened shortage of skilled building labor becomes an actuality it will be due not only to a very material increase in residence building, but also to the fact that apprentices have not entered the building trades during the past few years.

**Shortage for Four Months.**

Building contractors whose national trade organization has headquarters here are far more outspoken than FHA. Some of these contractors assert that there have been local shortages of skilled labor in the building trades for the past four months, and that the general shortage is not prospective but actual in virtually every section of the United States at the present time.

While building has revived somewhat during the year, as compared with the depression era, it is still far behind normal, these contractors say, and the real revival may not begin until next year.

## Bill Schommer, 3 Others Injured as Car Hits Tree

### SMASHED AUTO AND INJURED

THE DRIVER FELL ASLEEP, AND FOUR WERE HURT.

William Schommer.

Evelyn Elwell.

***Driver Dozes on Way Home From Hoidale Girl's Wedding.***

***Granddaughter of Elwell Law Author Among Injured.***

Two University of Minnesota fraternity members, one of them William Schommer, 25, former Big Ten tennis champion, and two sorority girls were injured in an automobile crash two miles west of Excelsior early Sunday.

Schommer, with his partner Charles Britzius, twice won the national public parks doubles tennis championship and for several years dominated the play in the northwest lawn tennis tournament at Deephaven.

The car went off the Victoria road when the driver, Dr. Chester Sitz, 25, of Byron, Minn., fell asleep. The car hit a tree.

In the car with Sitz and Schommer were Evelyn Elwell, 21, of 1815 Como avenue southeast, a member of Alpha Gamma Delta sorority, and Della Jane Brenden, 21, of Sloan, Iowa, member of Pi Beta Phi sorority, who was staying at 2006 Fremont avenue south.

**Suffers Jaw Fracture.**

Miss Brenden suffered a double jaw fracture, and at Eitel hospital Sunday night her condition was described as critical. Miss Elwell was at St. Andrew's hospital for treatment of scalp wounds and a shoulder injury. Her condition was reported generally good.

She is the grand-daughter of the late State Senator James T. Elwell, father of the Elwell law, which was designed to spur road improvements throughout the state.

Dr. Sitz escaped with minor lacerations. Schommer's right leg and chest were hurt, but it was indicated the injuries were not serious, and would have no permanent effect on his tennis playing ability.

**Had Attended Wedding.**

Schommer and Dr. Sitz, a dentist, were graduated from the university last spring, and were staying at the Phi Delta Theta fraternity house, 1027 University avenue southeast.

In the afternoon they attended the wedding of a fraternity brother, Everett Johnson of Spring Valley, to Elsa Hoidale, daughter of former Congressman and Mrs. Einar Hoidale. After leaving the wedding party, with the two co-eds they went for a drive. The car went off the road as they were returning home.

**Truck Driver Loses Arm.**

Martin Fox, 26, a truck driver for the Al W. Page dairy farm near Excelsior, lost his left arm in a collision on the Yellowstone trail about two miles west of Excelsior.

Fox was driving with his left arm dangling out of the window. It was crushed, the large bone being broken in six places, when his car and one driven by L. L. McGladrey of Hollywood, Ill., collided on a curve. The arm was amputated in Eitel hospital, where Fox' condition was described as serious.

McGladrey, who told deputy sheriffs Fox was straddling the center of the highway, escaped with minor injuries, as did his wife, and 6-year-old daughter, and Mrs. F. R. Linner of 1298 Raymond ave-

(Continued on Page 2, Column 7)

## CCC Fire Fighters Tipped From Barge

**24 Youths, 10 From Twin Cities, Are Dumped Into Lake Near Tofte.**

**By Tribune Staff Correspondent.**

Tofte, Minn., July 19.—Twenty-four CCC camp youths, 10 of them from the Twin Cities, were thrown into the middle of Sawbill lake Sunday as their barge, propelled by an outboard motor, overturned as they were returning from a shift of forest fire fighting.

One boy, Otto Webber of St. Paul, was injured when a board struck his leg.

A life preserver was the instrument that almost caused drowning of Ray Thompson of Grand Marais, a woodsman with the party. As the barge turned over, Thompson's feet became entangled in the life preserver. As he struggled to free himself his head was submerged repeatedly.

**Returning from Fire Fighting.**

The boys were on their way back to camp No. 716, 18 miles north of this Cook county town, after fighting fires 24 miles north of Tofte, in the northeastern corner of the state.

Too many of the boys got on one side of the barge and it overturned, dumping the fully-clad youths into the water. They fought their way out of their water-weighted clothing, and most of them struck out for shore. A few clung to the barge, which floated awash and upside down, and were rescued by a boat.

Minneapolis boys in the group were F. Alderman, J. Foley, W. Barnes, R. Berry and W. J. Graham. Those from St. Paul, besides Webber, were J. Kessler, S. O'Neil, L. Doyle and E. McCoy.

**Superintendent's Body Found.**

Other camp youths were W. Arcand, White Bear; L. Mason, Mankato; K. B. Allex, Wabasso; J. Ling, Lamberton; S. Swenson, Duluth; G. Galloway, New Ulm, and H. K. Barber, North St. Paul.

William McKay, Jr., of Duluth, was pilot of the boat. The fire fighting party also included C. Moe, a woodsman from Duluth.

A few hours later a searching party found the body of G. H. McDonald of Grand Marais, camp superintendent, who had been missing two days.

McDonald disappeared while on duty with the fire fighting patrol. Sunday his outboard motor driven canoe was found washed up on the shore of Sitka lake, 32 miles north of Tofte. A little later his body was found in the water.

## PEIFER TRIAL MAY BARE MORE SECRETS

The second week of the trial of Jack Peifer on charges of conspiracy in the William Hamm, Jr., kidnaping will open Monday with the government ready to introduce additional testimony to show police department secrets were sold for part of the ransom money.

Testimony by Byron Bolton, confessed member of the kidnap gang, that $25,000 was set aside for Tom Brown, former St. Paul police chief, climaxed the first week's final session of the trial in federal court in St. Paul.

Bolton said that Peifer, a night club operator, received $10,000 for his part in the crime.

What action may be taken as a result of the accusation against Brown was undetermined Sunday. George F. Sullivan, United States district attorney, said there was no direct evidence on which to prosecute Brown.

## Long's Widow May Seek Re-election as Independent

***Slur on Huey Reported Cast by Senatorial Nominee Rouses Fight.***

New Orleans, La., July 19.—(Universal) — Louisiana political leaders speculated Sunday on reports Senator Rose Long, widow of the slain senator, is considering becoming an independent candidate for re-election.

Should she enter the contest, Mrs. Long will run on a platform of "vindication" of her slain husband, it was learned.

This development comes as an aftermath of remarks attributed to the Democratic senatorial nominee, Allen Ellender at the Democratic national convention at Philadelphia. At the time Ellender was quoted as saying the dead dictator was motivated more by personal ambition than by desire to serve his people.

Publication of the interview created a furore in the legislature at the time, and a number of legislators said they would favor defeating Ellender at the polls. However, Ellender wired the legislature a vigorous denial, and he was given a vote of confidence.

Rose Long.

## PLANES BOMB CITIES SEIZED BY INSURGENTS

**Three Warships Desert—Morocco and Gibraltar Area Held by Fascists.**

**Bloody Street Fighting Marks Battle for Restoration of Monarchy.**

**REVOLT AT A GLANCE.**

**TANGIER**—Rebels in Spanish Morocco claimed complete control of the area and asserted they had won important successes in Spain itself. Loyal aviators bombed the palace of the high commissioner at Tetuan, capital of Spanish Morocco, and were said to have killed 20 persons.

**MADRID**—The Spanish government declared it was in control of the revolt in the peninsula and that workers were supporting it. Jose Giral Pereira organized a cabinet to succeed that of Diego Martinez Barrio, who quit after becoming premier only a few hours earlier.

**ALGIERS**—Reliable reports said 40 were killed and 150 wounded in battles in Spanish Morocco.

**GIBRALTAR**—Rebels were reported to have crossed the strait from Morocco and to be marching on Seville and Cadiz. Heavy casualties were stated to have occurred at La Linea.

**RABAT**—Three Spanish warships sent to oppose the revolters were said to have joined the insurrection.

**LONDON**—Telephone communication with Madrid from London, Paris, Lisbon and Gibraltar was cut off.

Paris, July 20.—(AP)—Reports filtering through a strict Spanish censorship early Monday said the rebels, who claimed control of Spanish Morocco, also held a large part of southern Spain itself.

The revolters were reported to have the upper hand in some other sections of the mainland, and the government was said to be arming civilians to repulse an expected march on Madrid.

**Barcelona Bombed.**

The Havas News agency reported earlier from Gibraltar that the entire region north of that British-owned rock had surrendered to the insurgents.

News of aerial bombardments, desertion of warships, street fighting and widespread bloodshed also filtered through to the outside world from reliable sources. These were in sharp contrast to censored government dispatches from Madrid which claimed control of the peninsula.

Air bombardment of Barcelona, largest city of the five-year-old republic was reported by travelers. Government planes also were attacking Morocco cities, while the rebels, claiming control of all Spanish Morocco as well as the Canary and Balearic islands, were reported landing troops in south Spain to aid allies already rising up in many cities.

**Malaga in Flames.**

In Spain itself, the Fascists appeared to have a strong grip on Seville, metropolis of the south,

### SCENES OF SPAIN'S REVOLTS

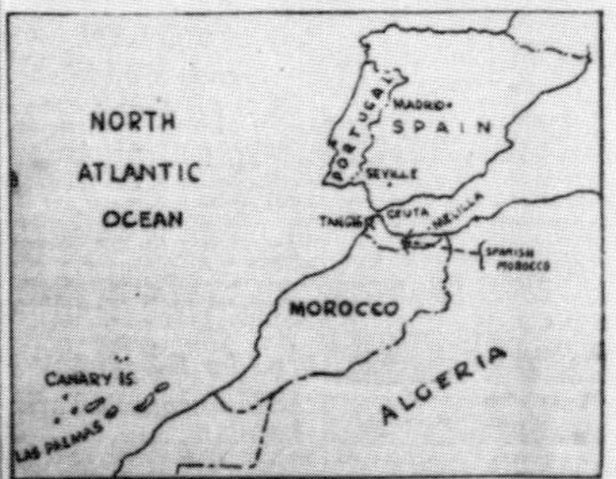


(PICTURE WIRED TO TRIBUNE EXCLUSIVELY IN NORTHWEST.)

Madrid, July 19.—(AP—Wirephoto)—This map shows Spanish Morocco, the Canary islands, and the Spanish mainland, scenes of the widespread military uprisings against the Spanish republic.

THE WIREPHOTO NEWSPAPER -- PICTURES BY WIRE

WEATHER
U. S. Weather Bureau Forecast.
Increasing cloudiness with rising temperature Tuesday; Wednesday unsettled and colder. 24 hour high, 36, at 4 p. m. Monday; low, 18, at 7 a. m. Monday. Additional weather news on page 18.

# The Minneapolis Tribune

FIRST in City Circulation—FIRST in TOTAL Circulation—Daily and Sunday

2ND COPY
MORNING EDITION
Three Cents in Minneapolis

Seventieth Year. No. 156. 3 MINNEAPOLIS, MINN., TUESDAY, OCTOBER 27, 1936. • • • Twenty-eight Pages

# Landon Appeals to Taxpayers

## PUBLIC'S FUNDS USED TO COERCE VOTES, HE SAYS

### Republican Nominee Calls New Deal Political Setup Most Sinister in History.

### Summons Citizens to 'Take New Liberty Oath' in Philadelphia Talk.

*Texts of Landon Speeches, Page 4.*

Philadelphia, Oct. 26.—(AP)—Summoning taxpayers to defeat President Roosevelt, Governor Landon told a Pennsylvania throng Monday night "the little fellow" must pay for new deal "waste and extravagance" which "violates the constitution."

The Republican nominee named, in the constitution's birthplace, "preservation of the constitution" and "a free and popular government" the fundamental issue of the presidential campaign.

**Urges Liberty Oath.**

"This administration," Landon shouted to an audience which jammed 15,000 convention hall seats, packed all available standing room and overflowed into the streets outside, "wields the same axe which has destroyed the liberties of much of the old world; an unbalanced budget, inflation of the currency, delegation of power to the chief executive, destruction of local self-government.

"Let us then, here in Philadelphia, where the charter of our liberty was born, take this high resolve. Let us take an oath that the bell which rang here 160 years shall not have rung in vain."

**Gets Six-Minute Ovation.**

A burst of cheering and waving of thousands of American flags swept the big oval hall as the Kansan's closing words echoed within the same walls where assembled Democrats nominated President Roosevelt four months ago.

A six-minute ovation welcomed Landon to the spot-lighted stage. After waving and smiling a greeting, he was forced to begin several times before the crowd quieted. His first words prompted new outbursts of applause.

Still hoarse from his cold, but speaking forcefully and loudly, Landon was cheered when he said he was going to discus waste and "this administration's open and impudent use of public money for political purposes."

**Can't Shift Responsibility.**

"Go after him, Alf," shouted a voice from the gallery as Landon laid responsibility for using the "people's money....to create the most sinister political machine of our history" rested upon President Roosevelt.

"No words of idealism, no claims of good intentions, can shift the responsibility for the machine," the Kansan said. "The responsibility

## Washington

By PAUL MALLON.



### ITALO-GERMAN PACT; BOTH SUSPICIOUS; F. R. BUYING STAMPS.

SCREENING.

THIS week, Mussolini is holding out the olive branch. Last week, it was the bayonet. Next week it will probably be both. His talk is indicative only of the fact that world statesmen alternately talk peace and war with no real intention of having either.

Mr. Mussolini's current olives are stuffed with the usual pimento. His son-in-law was simultaneously at Berghof, the Hitler hideout in Bavaria, flattering the German leader. The son-in-law and the Fuehrer approved what was advertised as "an accord with Rome," although their anti-Fascist opponents are calling it an incipient Italo-German alliance in preparation for the next war.

The pith of Mussolini's purpose was thus apparent to all.

PALS.

THE Mussolini-Hitler persiflage resolves itself down to the most important question confronting world peace. How far are Messrs. Mussolini and Hitler going together? The answer may be more encouraging to peace than you would surmise offhand.

At least official peace promoters around here think so. They count on two things to keep Mussolini and Hitler from becoming too clubby. For one thing, no German of the present generation will be able to forget that Germany had an alliance with Italy once before, but Italy ran out on it and joined the Allies in the World war.

(Continued on Page 12, Column 3.)

## BELGIANS PLAN FORTRESSES ON FRENCH BORDER

### Traditional Pro-French Foreign Policy May Be Replaced With New Neutrality.

### Hitler Envoy Warns Britain of Soviet Menace—Madrid Strafed From Air.

Brussels, Oct. 26.—(AP)—The possibility that the Belgian government, which until recently has had a strongly pro-French foreign policy, will ask parliament Tuesday to fortify the French frontier as it has the German border was debated in parliamentary circles Monday night.

Such a radical departure from Belgium's traditional stand, it was asserted in some quarters, will be brought forward as part of Belgium's new modified neutrality plans which the government intends to define at a special parliamentary session opening Tuesday afternoon.

Other sources forecast, however, the cabinet pronouncement probably will affirm the government's desire to stand by its existing accords together with an equal wish to keep out of any new alliances.

The government's statement was expected to be an "interpretation of King Leopold's interpretation" of Belgium's foreign policy, made in a speech October 15.

A proposal for fortification of the French frontier, informed persons said, would be a concession to the Fleming people, whose land lies along the German border and whose sympathies are more pro-German than those of Belgium's other residents.

The special parliamentary ses-

(Continued on Page 12, Column 1.)

## NEWS INDEX



**PLAN NORTHFIELD FETE.**

Northfield, Minn., Oct. 26.—Characters from the early roaring west will take over the Northfield armory Tuesday and Wednesday nights in "The Days of '49 Jubilee."

## 12 Persons Injured On Liner Queen Mary

London, Oct. 26.—(AP)—Eight passengers and four sailors aboard the liner Queen Mary were injured slightly as the giant ship was buffeted in a terrific storm, it was disclosed Monday when the vessel arrived at Southampton.

*Hit-Run Victim*

Mrs. Mary Lahoud.

## Speeder Hits, Kills Woman, Flees Scene

### *Stops But Moment to See Mangled Body—Police Launch Search.*

Traveling at a speed estimated at a mile a minute, an automobile shortly after 7 p. m. Monday struck and killed Mrs. Mary Lahoud, 47, of 328 Fifth street northeast, at the intersection of Third avenue northeast and Fourth street. In the impact her body was hurled almost 150 feet.

Before the motorist could stop his car he was a block away. He backed up, looked at the victim's mangled body lying in the street, swung his car around, drove his car over a curbing and then sped away.

**Several Clues Obtained.**

Witnesses said the bumper, right fender and right headlight of the automobile had been smashed, and that part of the cowling had been staved in by the impact.

The police accident squad ordered all garagemen and their attendants to notify police immediately as soon as a car is brought in for repairs. Witnesses identified the car as to its make.

Police were able to obtain several clues with which they hope to track down the hit-run driver—glass from the shattered headlight, and most of the numbers of the license plates on the car. Witnesses were certain of at least the first three of the license numbers.

**One Leg Severed.**

Mrs. Lahoud had been walking eastward on Third avenue, carrying a bottle of milk. She apparently was half way across Fourth street when she was struck by the car, which was traveling southward on Fourth street, toward Central avenue. One leg was completely severed from Mrs. Lahoud's body. The bottle of milk was found about 100 feet away.

## ROOSEVELT SAYS ADEQUATE NAVY IS AID TO PEACE

### Emphasizes Defense Force as Compatible With Good Neighbor Policy.

### Asserts His Determination to Avoid War—'No Imperial Designs,' He Declares.

Washington, Oct. 26.—(AP)—Asserting America's determination to avoid war, President Roosevelt Monday night wrote Secretary Swanson that an efficient navy, "adequate in men and material, is entirely compatible with the good neighbor policy enunciated by this administration."

In a navy day letter, President Roosevelt, congratulating the navy "on its splendid efficiency," said:

"I desire to emphasize the fact that an adequate defensive force is, at the same time, an instrument of peace and good will.

"We, as a people, seek no conquest. We have no imperial designs. We are actuated by a stern determination to avoid armed conflict by every honorable means."

**Navy 'At Home' Today.**

The service's annual "at home" day for the public will be celebrated throughout the country Tuesday, coinciding with the birthday anniversary of the late President Theodore Roosevelt.

The President's letter to Swanson follows:

"It gives me peculiar pleasure again to commend to the service and to all of our countrymen the annual observance of navy day, which in accordance with custom will be celebrated on October 27, Theodore Roosevelt's birthday. The yearly recurrence of navy day is to me personally a happy reminder of my delightful association with the naval service.

"Although happily we are on terms of peace and unanimity with all nations, we cannot close our eyes to the fact that in many parts of the world conditions are disquieting and signs are portentous. An efficient navy, adequate in men and material, is entirely compatible with the good neighbor policy enunciated by this administration as the keystone of its foreign relations. We rejoice that we are at peace with all mankind.

**Message Sent to Vessels.**

"In congratulating the navy on its splendid efficiency, I desire to emphasize the fact that an adequate defensive force is, at the same time, an instrument of peace and good will. We, as a people, seek no conquest. We have no imperial designs. We are actuated by a stern determination to avoid conflict by every honorable means.

"I salute the American navy and believe the American people share a common pride in its purposes and its traditions."

## Request for Bible Reading In City Schools Rejected

### *Council of Federated Church Women Is Told That Proposal Is Undesirable Since Religious Differences Might Be Fostered.*

Confirming action taken last week as a committee of the whole, the board of education Monday rejected a long-standing request by the Council of Federated Church Women that a chapter of the Bible be read each morning in the city schools.

The request was turned down because, in the language of a special committee which had been considering the matter a year, "it should be evident to any fair-minded citizen that a classroom procedure which might lead to a sifting of the children on the basis of religious belief or any activity which might develop a consciousness of religious differences would be undesirable in a public school system."

Discussion of the issue was limited to the committee of the whole session at which this policy was formulated. There was no further comment when the report drawn by the special committee was submitted Monday by Superintendent Carroll R. Reed, who with Directors Henry J. Bessesen and Dr. Charles R. Drake made up the committee.

"This report," President Bessesen remarked, "merely puts into writing the thought expressed at our committee of the whole meeting."

Director Arthur LeSueur's motion that the report be adopted was passed unanimously.

In full, the report reads:

"The board of education is sympathetic with the motives of the Council of Federated Church Women, which requests that one chapter of the Bible be read every morning in every schoolroom. Doubtless, the purpose of the request is to improve the characters of the young people in the schools. The aim of the public schools is, and always has

(Continued on Page 12, Column 5)



## N. W. DIGNITARIES GREET CARDINAL PACELLI

—Tribune Staff Photographer.

Dignitaries of the Catholic church in the northwest late Monday greeted the highest Catholic official ever to visit in the United States, Eugenio Cardinal Pacelli, papal secretary of state. Among those included in the reception committee were, left to right, Archbishop Francis J. L. Beckman, Dubuque, Iowa; Archbishop Samuel A. Stritch, Milwaukee; Cardinal Pacelli; Bishop Joseph C. Plagens, Detroit, and Archbishop John Gregory Murray, St. Paul.

Eugenio Cardinal Pacelli.

## Papal Envoy Is Welcomed To Northwest

### *Cardinal Pacelli Greeted by Dignitaries—To Say Mass Today.*

High dignitaries of the Roman Catholic church from throughout the northwest greeted Eugenio Cardinal Pacelli, papal secretary of state, on his arrival at the St. Paul airport late Monday.

Heading the party that welcomed the cardinal, the highest official of the Catholic church ever to visit this country, was Archbishop John Gregory Murray of St. Paul, to whose residence at 226 Summit avenue the prelate was taken.

An hour before the arrival of the special plane in which the cardinal is traveling, groups of the devout from Catholic parishes in St. Paul began to arrive at the airport. Included in their numbers were dozens of children from parochial schools.

Archbishop Samuel Stritch of Milwaukee and Archbishop Francis Beckman of Dubuque were members of the reception committee. A motorcycle escort took the cardinal and his party directly to Archbishop Murray's residence.

Monday night Cardinal Pacelli was guest of honor at a dinner at the archbishop's home. Guests at the dinner included Archbishop Stritch, Archbishop Beckman, Bishop Alexander McGavick of La Crosse, Bishop John J. Lawler of Rapid City, Bishop Edmond Heelan of Sioux City, Bishop Bernard Mahoney of Sioux Falls, Bishop Joseph C. Plagens of Marquette, Bishop Thomas A. Welch of Duluth, Bishop Francis M. Kelly of Winona, Bishop Theodore Reverman of Superior, Bishop Henry P. Rohlman of Davenport, Auxiliary Bishop Francis J. Spellman of Boston, Bishop James H. Ryan of Omaha, Bishop Gerald T. Bergan of Des Moines, Auxiliary Bishop William R. Griffin of LaCrosse, Bishop A. J. Muench of Fargo and Bishop Joseph Busch of St. Cloud.

Tuesday at 7:45 a. m. the cardinal will celebrate low mass at the Cathedral of St. Paul. Archbishop Murray has arranged for cadets of military academies in the diocese to provide a guard of honor, and has established special seating rules. At other parishes in the diocese masses will be said at the same hour for the intention of the holy father.

Immediately after the mass the cardinal and his party will resume the aerial tour of the United States.

## J. Adam Bede Hurt As Auto Overturns

Duluth, Minn., Oct. 26.—(AP)—J. Adam Bede, 80, former congressman, was in his home here Monday recuperating from bruises received early Sunday morning when an automobile in which he was riding overturned near Atkinson, about 16 miles south of Duluth. Axel Youngstradd, Duluth, driver of the car, and George Grant, Duluth, a passenger, were not injured. Bede was returning from Mora where he had spoken in support of President Roosevelt's re-election. As a result of the accident he cancelled all remaining engagements of a tour in the President's behalf.

J. Adam Bede.

## PEEK ASKS F. R. ABOUT FARMER

### Demands President Give Stand on Cattle, Milk Products Imports, Wheat Prices.

George N. Peek, former supporter of President Roosevelt now campaigning for Governor Alf M. Landon, Republican nominee, in an interview Monday called upon Mr. Roosevelt and Secretary of Agriculture Wallace to answer three questions pertaining to the future of agriculture.

Peek, who asserted the farmers were entitled to an answer to his questions "in the unlikely event this administration is continued in office after November 3," will deliver a campaign speech in Chicago Tuesday night.

"Now that the administration has demonstrated its generosity to our northern neighbors on the cattle weighing over 700 pounds, is it the intention to be equally generous with our neighbors south of us on cattle weighing less than 700 pounds, or in cans?" Peek asked.

The other two questions posed by him were:

"Having settled the tariff and price relationship between different dairy products by the reduction of the tariff on cheese, which dairy farmers were years in establishing, is it the purpose of future trade agreements to re-establish this relationship on a lower price level by reducing the duty on butter, and other dairy products?

"If Secretary Wallace's forecast should prove to be correct, that with favorable crop conditions we should produce on present acreage some 900,000,000 bushels of wheat, and that should happen next year, what is there in your plan to keep prices from dropping to 1932 levels as Secretary Wallace predicts—except to repeat in principle—by your every normal granary plan—the unfortunate experience of the farm board in storing surpluses?

"Farmers should have an answer to these questions before they vote," Peek concluded.

### *Peek Yields Radio To Digest's Poll*

The radio speech from the Twin Cities of George N. Peek, former AAA administrator under President Roosevelt, was cancelled late Monday.

Mr. Peek had come to the Twin Cities to campaign for Governor Alf M. Landon, and his address was to have been broadcast over a nation-wide hook-up at 10 p. m. Late in the day Mr. Peek announced he was yielding his time on the air so that final results of the Literary Digest poll might be broadcast.

The address he had planned to deliver in the Twin Cities will be given Tuesday night over a hook-up from Chicago.

## Weyerhaeuser Bill Passer Pleads Guilty

Seattle, Oct. 26.—(AP)—Edward Fliss, 30-year-old waiter whose confession stated he spent most of his "cut" from exchanging $13,000 in "hot" Weyerhaeuser ransom bills for good times, pleaded guilty Monday to a federal charge of attempting to pass $265 of the money in a Seattle bank last February. He pleaded innocent to another charge—carrying a life imprisonment maximum—of being an accessory after the fact in the $200,000 kidnaping.

## REGAN STRIKES AT F.-L. FUSION

### Calls it 'Betrayal of Honest Democrats'—Urges Election of Nelson.

John E. Regan of Mankato, twice the standard-bearer of the Democratic party in the governorship race, Monday night denounced the Democratic-Farmer-Labor fusion deal as "a betrayal of honest Democrats."

In a radio address over KSTP, he attacked Patrick J. Delaney and Fred Curtis, Democratic candidates for the United States senate and governor, respectively, who withdrew their names from the ticket in favor of Farmer-Laborites.

He quoted parts of the Curtis keynote address delivered at St. Cloud, and challenged him to explain his change in attitude and his withdrawal from the governorship race.

"You said 'we must restore our government in this state to the hands of the people'," Mr. Regan

(Continued on Page 2, Column 4)

## Mrs. Simpson To Get Quick Divorce Today

### *Hearing for King's Friend Expected to Consume Only 3 Minutes.*

*Additional news of Simpson case page 9.*

Ipswich, England, Oct. 26.—(AP)—Mrs. Ernest (Wally) Simpson, King Edward's admired social companion, Monday could look forward to a possible three-minute divorce Tuesday afternoon.

That is customary speed of the judge who will hear her case.

Mr. Justice Sir John Anthony Hawke set 2:15 p. m. (8:15 a. m. Minneapolis time) as the time for hearing of the Ipswich assizes divorce suits which contains the undefended petition of Mrs. Simpson against her broker husband, a former member of the exclusive Coldstream Guards.

While Mrs. Simpson waited with nervously twisting fingers, Mr. Justice Hawke quickly disposed of a short docket of civil and criminal cases Monday.

He indicated that the seven unfended divorce petitions, only cases remaining on the docket, could not be disposed of before Tuesday afternoon.

Court attaches said they did not anticipate a lengthy session on Mrs. Simpson's petition.

Justice Hawke, they pointed out, has a rapid way of dealing with undefended divorce petitions and last week at the Norwich assizes

(Continued on Page 12, Column 2.)

## CONVICT ESCAPES ST. PAUL CITY JAIL

A paroled convict escaped from the St. Paul city jail in the public safety building Monday night after seizing a jailer's gun and locking the two jailers on duty in a vacant cell block.

The convict, George Fortuna, 25, of 175 Lafond street, was being held for investigation of an assault charge. During the evening he was engaged in a cleaning job and was given partial freedom for the cell block. While at work he entered an open locker in which the jailers kept their holstered guns.

Armed, he confronted the two men on duty, William J. Kelley and Ben J. Slater, took the jail keys and forced them into a cell and made good his escape.

Police were ordered to hunt down Fortuna and the two jailers were

A move to reorganize the Col-

WEATHER
U. S. Weather Bureau Forecast: Generally fair with rising temperature Wednesday; Thursday cloudy and snow. 24 hour high, 25, at 2 a. m. Tuesday; low, 17, at 7 p. m. Tuesday.
Additional weather news on page 20.

# The Minneapolis Tribune

FIRST in City Circulation—FIRST in TOTAL Circulation—Daily and Sunday

MORNING EDITION
Three Cents in Minneapolis

Seventieth Year. No. 164. 3 MINNEAPOLIS, MINN., WEDNESDAY, NOVEMBER 4, 1936. • • • Thirty Pages

# ROOSEVELT SWEEPS U. S.

★ ★ ★ ★ ★ ★ ★ ★ ★ ★ ★ ★

## Minnesota in Landslide of 45 States; Benson and Lundeen Build Up Lead

### CITIES, RURAL DISTRICTS GO TO F. R. 2 TO 1

**Lemke Gets Fair Return in Minneapolis But Fails to Prove Threat.**

**Heavy Voting Throughout State Delays Counting of Ballots.**

For the second time in its history, the voters of Minnesota recorded themselves in the Democratic column in a presidential election.

President Roosevelt, running as strongly in the rural districts as he did in the cities, appeared to have clinched the state's 11 electoral votes on the basis of returns that at 2 a. m. were still far from complete. His lead over Governor Alf M. Landon, the Republican nominee was better than two to one, with little prospect that it could be whittled much.

The Roosevelt victory over Hoover in 1932 marked the first time that the state had been won by the Democrats. At 2 a. m. with considerably more than half of the state's 3,734 precincts still to report, his lead was so great that the state had been definitely conceded to him. There was little doubt that the magic of the Roosevelt name (Theodore Roosevelt carried the state for the Bull Moose party in 1912) had not lost any of its potency.

In Minneapolis, with two-thirds of the city's precincts reporting, Roosevelt demonstrated that he would carry the city by a sizeable margin. Out in the rural districts, to the surprise of many, that margin was increased.

Congressman William Lemke, indorsed candidate of the National Union for Social Justice, ran fairly well in Minneapolis but failed to prove the threat that had been anticipated. Out in the rural districts, for the most part his vote was negligible.

**Heavy Vote Delays Count.**

Extremely heavy voting throughout the state delayed returns throughout the evening. It was long after the polls closed at 8 p. m. before the election picture began to shape itself. Even at midnight, only a fragmentary portion of the vote—estimated at about 1,100,000—had been counted, but by that time enough ballots from representative sectors had been counted to assure the President of a victory in Minnesota that would match or exceed his 1932 showing.

Interest in the Minnesota returns was heightened by the situation which developed through the withdrawal of Patrick Delaney, Democratic candidate for the United States senate, and Fred Curtis, candidate for governor, in favor of their Farmer-Labor rivals.

This action caused a split in the Democratic ranks which many thought might react to the detriment of the national ticket, with a number of Democratic leaders avowedly supporting Republican candidates for state offices, while adhering to the President.

### Vote in State

**PRESIDENT.**
610 Pcts. out of 3,734.
Landon-Knox (Rep.) ...... 78,107
*Roosevelt-Garner (Dem.) .. 174,524
Lemke-O'Brien (Union) .... 19,998

**U. S. SENATOR (Long Term).**
264 Pcts. Out of 3,734.
Ernest Lundeen (F.-L.) ..... 59,905
Theo. Christianson (Rep.) ... 35,014

**U. S. SENATOR (Short Term).**
264 Pcts. Out of 3,734.
Guy V. Howard (Rep.) .... 18,064
N. J. Holmberg (Ind.) ..... 10,361
A. O. Devold (Ind.) ....... 11,990
J. G. Alexander (Ind.) ...... 4,844

**GOVERNOR.**
254 Pcts. Out of 3,734.
Elmer A. Benson (F.-L.) .... 49,226
Martin A. Nelson (Rep.) ... 30,135
Earl Stewart (Ind.) ........ 380

**LIEUTENANT GOVERNOR.**
21 Pcts. Out of 3,734.
Gottfrid Lindsten (F.-L.) ... 14,731
Arthur E. Nelson (Rep.) ... 10,620
A. C. Knudson (Dem.) ..... 3,232

**SECRETARY OF STATE.**
82 Pcts. Out of 3,734.
Paul C. Hartig (F.-L.) ..... 10,029
*Mike Holm (Rep.) ......... 10,305
Carl Hennemann (Dem.) .... 1,794
Vincent R. Dunne (Soc.) ... 108

**STATE TREASURER.**
70 Pcts. Out of 3,734.
C. A. Halvorson (F.-L.) .... 7,603
*Julius A. Schmahl (Rep.) .. 6,904
Ray M. King (Dem.) ........ 1,807

**ATTORNEY GENERAL.**
54 Pcts. Out of 3,734.
*Harry H. Peterson (F.-L.) .. 6,473
Oscar F. Youngdahl (Rep.) . 3,433
Thomas Gallagher (Dem.) .. 1,141

**R. R. & WHSE. COMMISSIONER.**
54 Pcts. Out of 3,734.
Hjalmar Petersen (F.-L.) ... 2,590
*Frank W. Matson (Rep.) ... 1,899
Arthur N. Cosgrove (Dem.). 505

**AMENDMENT NO. 1.**
18 Pcts. Out of 3,734.
Lands—Yes, 4,090; No, 3,804.

**SUPREME COURT.**
32 Pcts. Out of 3,734 (Elect Two).
*Andrew Holt ............... 1,053
Edward J. Lee .............. 905
*Royal A. Stone ............ 1,435
Wm. A. Vanderburgh ....... 819

**CONGRESS, 1ST DIST.**
23 Pcts. Out of 390.
Chester Watson (F.-L.) ...... 982
*August Andresen (Rep.) ... 2,452
Richard Morin (Dem.) ...... 1,272

**CONGRESS, 2ND DIST.**
32 Pcts. Out of 413.
Henry Arens (F.-L.) ....... 2,627
Christian Laurisch (Rep.) ... 2,774
*Elmer Ryan (Dem.) ........ 4,005

**CONGRESSMAN, 3RD DIST.**
17 Pcts. Out of 279.
Henry C. Teigan (F.-L.) ..... 5,262
Milton Lindbloom (Rep.) ... 1,645
Martin A. Hogan (Dem.) ... 1,186
Mrs. Frank McConville (Ind.) 937

**CONGRESSMAN, 5TH DIST.**
17 Pcts. Out of 229.
Dewey W. Johnson (F.-L.) ... 3,968
Walter H. Newton (Rep.) ... 4,248
M. J. Dillon (Dem.) ......... 1,131

**CONGRESS, 6TH DIST.**
22 Pcts. Out of 556.
C. A. Ryan (F.-L.) .......... 1,147
*Harold Knutson (Rep.) ..... 2,212
Jos. H. Kowalkowski (Dem.) 534

**CONGRESS, 7TH DIST.**
14 Pcts. Out of 538.
*Paul John Kvale (F.-L.) ... 2,223
H. Carl Andersen (Rep.) .... 812
C. L. Cole (Dem.) .......... 426

**CONGRESS, 8TH DIST.**
4 Pcts. Out of 451.
John T. Bernard (F.-L.) ..... 460
*William Pittenger (Rep.) ... 358

**CONGRESS, 9TH DIST.**
17 Pcts. Out of 627.
*Richard T. Buckler (F.-L.) .. 1,499
Elmer A. Haugen (Rep.) .... 735
Martin O. Brandon (Dem.) . 495

**AMENDMENT NO. 2.**
17 Pcts. Out of 3,734.
Taxes—Yes, 2,759; No, 4,862.

### NEWS INDEX

| | Page. | | Page. |
|---|---|---|---|
| Bridge | 23 | Puzzle | 19 |
| Brisbane | 18 | Radio | 20 |
| Editorials | 18 | Serial | 15 |
| Gopher Tales | 20 | Society | 22-23 |
| Alice Hughes | 19 | Sports | 24-26 |
| Markets | 26-27 | Want Ads | 28-29 |
| Movies | 19 | Weather | 20 |
| Feg Murray | 19 | Winchell | 19 |
| Purvis | 27 | Woman's page | 21 |

ELECTION.
Roosevelt wins sweeping victory. Page 1.
Benson and Lundeen build up leads in Minnesota races. Page 1.
Literary Digest's editor says he is astounded by Roosevelt landslide. Page 1.
County vote table. Page 2.
Minneapolis vote on governor by precincts. Page 3.
Lemke runs thir din North Dakota, his home state. Page 3.
Vote in governor by pre-Presidential vote table. Page 3.

WASHINGTON.
Thirty states voted on amendments in general election. Page 9.
Women believed to have set voting record in this election. Page 12.
Bills for national campaigning continue to rise. Page 15.

FOREIGN.
Madrid citizens atop houses watch battle. Page 16.
Enlargement of Soviet army alarms Germany. Page 19.

DOMESTIC.
Three slain and eight wounded in election disorders. Page 3.
Violence renewed in sailors' strke. Page 6.
Landon jokes with friends as returns come in. Page 8.
Human hibernator wakes up to cast his vote. Page 13.

LOCAL.
Election oddities. Page 7.
Additional committees named to take part in reception of Mrs. Roosevelt. Page 9.
T. K. Kelly dies in Maine while on business trip. Page 10.
Death notices. Page 10.
Dispute of dry cleaners and launderers' factions thrown into court. Page 11.
Sleepy Eye girl wins cow milking contest by a pint. Page 13.
Suspect in two burglaries is jailed. Page 14.
Minnesota Horticultural society holds convention. Page 14.
Four arrested as burglary suspects. Page 19.
"Madame Butterfly" to open San Carlo opera series. Page 19.

NORTHWEST.
French duke gives badlands chateau to North Dakota. Page 1[illegible]

WOMAN'S PAGE.
Evon Nollette learns that Captain Molyneaux, the Paris designer, will visit in America. Page 21.
Don't diet all day and then take your calories all in one meal, Ida Jean Kain warns. Page 21.
Grace McCrea tells her typewriter, Gussie, about a book on how to worry. Page 21.

SPORTS.
Gophers hold practice session in secret. Page 24.
Sport-O-Graphs by George A. Barton. Page 24.
Solem shifts Iowa lineup. Page 24.
Isbell, Drake shame horsemen, says Kizer. Page 24.
"Morning, Sir. Page 25.

MARKETS.
Everybody's Business—Commodity price effect of election is studied. Page 26.
Wheat futures close lower in Winnipeg and Liverpool. Page 27.
Light receipts bring higher prices for livestock. Page 27.

### Digest's Editor Says 'I'm Simply Astounded'

New York, Nov. 3.—(AP)—With a chuckle in his voice, Wilfred J. Funk, editor-in-chief of the Literary Digest, which forecast Governor Landon's election, said Tuesday night, "I'm simply astounded at what is apparently a landslide for Mr. Roosevelt."

The laugh, he said, was to show he could "take it."

"It's beyond comprehension to explain away the Digest poll," he said. "I couldn't possibly do that now. That will take time—and a lot of pencils and paper and figuring."

The Literary Digest, weekly news magazine which predicted the winner in the three previous presidential elections, last week gave Governor Landon 379 electoral votes from 32 states to 161 electoral votes from 16 states for President Roosevelt. It represented a Landon majority of about 54 per cent.

"Don't get me wrong," Funk offered, as an afterthought, "my personal belief was that Roosevelt would win. I thought it would be close.

"But I can't explain that apparent landslide."

### CHRISTIANSON TRAILS 32,000, NELSON 13,000

**Farmer-Laborites' Margin in Cities Greater Than Opponents Expected.**

**G.O.P. Refuses to Concede Defeat—Hopes for Shift in Later Returns.**

By Orlin Folwick.
Tribune Staff Writer.

Farmer-Labor candidates for United States senator and governor kept increasing their leads Tuesday night in the slowly mounting returns from election precincts scattered over the state.

In 384 state precincts, including 145 in Minneapolis, Senator Elmer A. Benson, Farmer-Labor governership candidate, had a 13,000-vote lead over Martin A. Nelson, his Republican opponent.

In 295 precincts, 153 of them in Minneapolis, Congressman Ernest Lundeen was building up a heavy lead over his Republican opponent, Congressman Theodore Christianson, being 32,000 votes ahead.

Republican leaders were unwilling to concede defeat in either contest, maintaining that when the votes from the Republican strongholds come in the picture will be different. So far as the available country votes were concerned, however, their claims were not being borne out.

Should Benson and Lundeen continue their leads in the Minneapolis vote, political observers said, it would be practically impossible to

(Continued on Page 2, Column 2)

### NEWTON RACES NECK AND NECK

**Other Minnesota Congressional Contests See Ryan, Andresen Knutson and Kvale Leading**

The make-up of Minnesota's congressional delegation remained in considerable doubt at 2 a. m. Wednesday as election judges concentrated their efforts on tabulating the state's heavy vote for presidential and state office candidates.

However in most instances, incumbents were ahad on th basis of rturns that rangd from fragmentary t incomplete.

Interest of Minneapolis voters centered in the third and fifth districts, both of which cut into the city.

**Newion Neck and Neck.**

The third district, from which Ernest Lundeen stepped to contest the post of United States senator, the man on whom his toga fell, Henry G. Teigan, was out in front with a lead of more than two to one over the Republican indorsed candidate.

In the fifth district where Walter H. Newton, former secretary to Herbert Hoover, was attempting a political comeback, he was battling on even terms with his Farmer-Labor opponent, Dewey Johnson, former state legislator.

**Andresen Winning&**

In the first district August Andresen, Republican incumbent, led the field by nearly two to one on the basis of scattered returns and appeared headed for re-election.

In the second district, Elmer J. Ryan, sole Democrat in the past congress, was leading Henry Arens, former Farmer-Labor lieutenant governor and Henry J. Laurish, former Republican member of the railroad and warehouse commission.

**IRISH TO FIGHT IN SPAIN.**

Dublin, Nov. 3.—A recruiting office has been opened to enroll volunteers for an Irish brigade to aid Catholic revolutionary forces in Spain.

### Electoral Vote

**Roosevelt Leading**

| | | |
|---|---|---|
| 11—Alabama | 10—Louisiana | 26—Ohio |
| 3—Arizona | 8—Maryland | 11—Oklahoma |
| 9—Arkansas | 17—Massachusetts | 5—Oregon |
| 22—California | 19—Michigan | 36—Pennsylvania |
| 6—Colorado | 11—Minnesota | 4—Rhode Island |
| 8—Connecticut | 9—Mississippi | 8—South Carolina |
| 3—Delaware | 15—Missouri | 4—South Dakota |
| 7—Florida | 4—Montana | 11—Tennessee |
| 12—Georgia | 7—Nebraska | 23—Texas |
| 4—Idaho | 3—Nevada | 4—Utah |
| 29—Illinois | 16—New Jersey | 11—Virginia |
| 14—Indiana | 3—New Mexico | 8—Washington |
| 11—Iowa | 47—New York | 8—West Virginia |
| 9—Kansas | 13—North Carolina | 12—Wisconsin |
| 11—Kentucky | 4—North Dakota | 3—Wyoming |

Total—519.

**Landon Leading**

5—Maine 3—Vermont 4—New Hampshire

Total—12.

**Results in 1932**

Roosevelt—472. Hoover—59.

### Results by States

ELECTION RESULTS.

| State— | Total Dists. | Dists. Reptd. | Popular Vote. Roosevelt. | Popular Vote. Landon. | Indicated Elec. Vote. Rvlt. | Indicated Elec. Vote. Ldn. |
|---|---|---|---|---|---|---|
| Alabama | 2,290 | 333 | 34,572 | 4,513 | 11 | .. |
| Arizona | 443 | 44 | 11,725 | 5,339 | 3 | .. |
| Arkansas | 2,156 | 54 | 3,283 | 560 | 9 | .. |
| California | 11,716 | 2,258 | 311,426 | 143,969 | .. | 22 |
| Colorado | 1,520 | 63 | 6,242 | 5,159 | 6 | .. |
| Connecticut | 169 | 95 | 296,302 | 207,686 | 8 | .. |
| Delaware | 232 | 40 | 6,961 | 5,853 | 3 | .. |
| Florida | 1,322 | 441 | 81,883 | 20,818 | 7 | .. |
| Georgia | 1,766 | 370 | 64,630 | 6,682 | 12 | .. |
| Idaho | 797 | 65 | 7,422 | 4,452 | .. | 4 |
| Illinois | 7,912 | 1,076 | 317,210 | 143,087 | 29 | .. |
| Indiana | 3,840 | 1,193 | 374,924 | 251,089 | 14 | .. |
| Iowa | 2,442 | .... | ...... | ...... | .. | .. |
| Kansas | 2,690 | 584 | 84,808 | 81,309 | 9 | .. |
| Kentucky | 4,299 | 445 | 64,156 | 37,899 | 11 | .. |
| Louisiana | 1,584 | .... | ...... | ...... | .. | .. |
| Maine | 633 | 611 | 124,375 | 166,551 | ... | 5 |
| Maryland | 1,453 | 277 | 82,122 | 37,899 | 8 | .. |
| Massachusetts | 1,765 | 342 | 123,638 | 108,973 | ... | 17 |
| Michigan | 3,470 | 509 | 124,682 | 106,480 | 19 | .. |
| Minnesota | 3,724 | 355 | 110,489 | 50,366 | .. | 11 |
| Mississippi | 1,659 | 147 | 21,683 | 713 | .. | .. |
| Missouri | 4,357 | 1,933 | 400,789 | 231,163 | 15 | .. |
| Montana | 1,237 | 1 | 11 | 12 | .. | 4 |
| Nebraska | 2,031 | 219 | 27,574 | 25,530 | .. | 7 |
| Nevada | 256 | 73 | 4,343 | 1,768 | ... | .. |
| New Hampshire | 295 | 133 | 26,707 | 29,179 | ... | 4 |
| New Jersey | 3,381 | 140 | 37,199 | 13,353 | 16 | .. |
| New Mexico | 904 | 60 | 9,295 | 4,645 | 3 | .. |
| New York | 8,950 | 977 | 412,401 | 209,538 | 47 | .. |
| North Carolina | 1,860 | 123 | 52,868 | 8,068 | 13 | .. |
| North Dakota | 2,245 | 33 | 4,754 | 1,960 | 4 | .. |
| Ohio | 8,600 | 890 | 158,274 | 98,024 | 26 | .. |
| Oklahoma | 3,421 | 1,823 | 255,810 | 113,086 | 11 | .. |
| Oregon | 1,630 | 73 | 7,410 | 4,122 | ... | .. |
| Pennsylvania | 8,010 | 2,889 | 817,117 | 612,378 | 36 | .. |
| Rhode Island | 245 | 130 | 70,181 | 61,797 | ... | 4 |
| South Carolina | 1,272 | 501 | 60,071 | 1,040 | 8 | .. |
| South Dakota | 1,958 | 36 | 4,608 | 4,376 | 4 | .. |
| Tennessee | 2,295 | 825 | 71,148 | 30,864 | 11 | .. |
| Texas | 254 | 80 | 112,471 | 11,224 | 23 | .. |
| Utah | 801 | 33 | 4,229 | 2,028 | 4 | .. |
| Vermont | 248 | 235 | 47,432 | 68,199 | ... | 3 |
| Virginia | 1,704 | 964 | 136,024 | 49,515 | 11 | .. |
| Washington | 2,881 | 25 | 1,941 | 760 | ... | .. |
| West Virginia | 2,347 | 301 | 59,982 | 38,603 | ... | 8 |
| Wisconsin | 2,927 | 633 | 187,934 | 94,619 | 12 | .. |
| Wyoming | 676 | 20 | 746 | 427 | ... | .. |

**MAPPING THE LANDSLIDE**

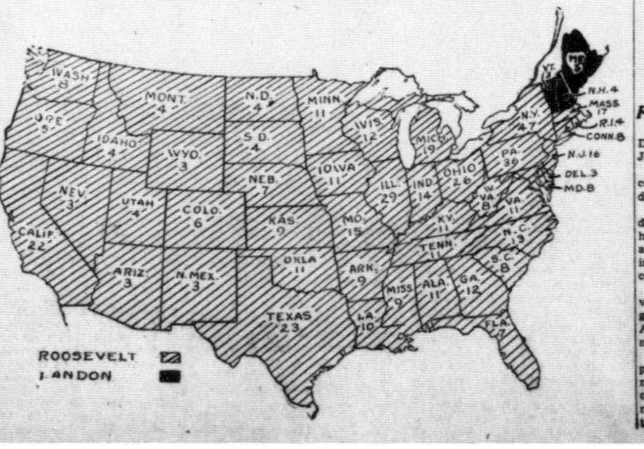

### Electoral Count 519-12; Landon Carries 3 States

**New York, Pennsylvania, Illinois, Ohio, Go to Roosevelt.**

**Kansas Deserts Governor—Landon and Knox Concede.**

By Associated Press.

The election tides were running swift and strong toward Roosevelt early Wednesday.

So impressive was the President's lead — he was ahead in no less than 45 states—that Democratic leaders claimed the most sweeping electoral victory in history.

A tabulatio nof electoral votes gave Roosevelt 519; Landon, 12.

Shortly after midnight Governor Alf M. Landon conceded the election to his opponent.

The great states of New York, Pennsylvania, Illinois and Ohio—a bloc whose weight is usually decisive—were helping pile up the Democratic ticket's impressive margin of leadership. Westward to California, the story was the same.

The totals turned out by busy election tellers were giving Landon the lead in Maine, New Hampshire and Vermont. And even in New Hampshire, the Republican margin was far from conclusive.

Surrounded by friends at his Hyde Park home, the President happily scanned the returns, and told a group of his neighbors that it looked to him like the biggest sweep of all time. At Topeka, Landon in a message, given to the press congratulated Roosevelt as follows:

"The President, Hyde Park, New York: The nation has spoken. Every American will accept the verdict and work for the common cause of the good of our country. That is the spirit of democracy. You have my sincere congratulations. Alf M. Landon."

The eastern industrial states, with the city vote predominating, piled up big totals for Roosevelt. New York state, led by New York

(Continued on Page 2, Column 1)

### How Candidates And Aids Took It

By Associated Press.

The presidential and vice presidential candidates and their campaign managers Tuesday night viewed the flood of election returns with mixed expressions.

***Roosevelt:***

At Hyde Park where with his family he received election returns, President Roosevelt asserted on the basis of the figures before 11 p. m., it "looks as if we are going to have one of the largest sweeps ever heard of in the history of the United States."

A short time later he told a thousand torch-bearing neighbors he couldn't say "anything official," and heard voices cry out from his lawn "four more happy years with Roosevelt."

Said Mrs. Roosevelt:

"I am very happy to feel that a great number of the people seem to wish to have the President carry on the work which he has begun in the last few years."

***Landon:***

Governor Alf M. Landon, Republican presidential candidate, declined comment Tuesday night. He spent the evening entertaining friends in the executive mansion at Topeka and as newspaper photographers poised their cameras, jokingly called to his wife: "Theo, better have our picture taken while we've got a chance."

A red, white and blue frosted "Landon victory cake" remained uncut on the sideboard in the executive mansion.

"However it comes out," said Mrs. Landon, her eyes seeking out her husband, "I'm proud of him. I know he has put up a brave fight."

***Garner:***

Vice-president Garner was without comment.

***Knox:***

Colonel Frank M. Knox, Republican candidate for vice president received the returns in the office of his newspaper, The Chicago Daily News, which, in an election edition, said:

"With fragmentary reports from all but five of the 48 states in the union, President Roosevelt's re-election over the Republican challenge made by Governor Alf M. Landon of Kansas, appears not only to be assured, but his victory has come by a more substantial majority than he had in 1932 over Herbert Hoover."

***Hamilton:***

At Chicago Chairman John D. M. Hamilton of the Republican national committee broadcast a statement shortly before midnight in which he told members of the party they could "go to bed assured that in the morning there would be a totally different outlook."

***Farley:***

In a statement at New York, Democratic National Chairman James A. Farley declared:

"The American people are to be congratulated on the result of today's election.

"President Roosevelt from the day he was inaugurated until this hour has put forth every effort at his command to advance the interests of the people of this country.

"He was given an overwhelming vote of confidence—probably the greatest majority ever given to an American president, when the final results are in.

"Personally I am extremely happy at the effort put forth by the many thousands of people, not only Democrats but women and men in all parties and of no particular political belief."

THE MINNEAPOLIS JOURNAL

WEATHER Fair and colder tonight; cloudy with rising temperature Friday. THURSDAY EVENING, DECEMBER 10, 1936. 36 PAGES—2 CENTS IN MINNEAPOLIS

# KING ABDICATES

★ ★ ★ ★ ★ ★ ★ ★ ★ ★ ★ ★ ★ ★ ★ ★ ★ ★

## *Duke of York Becomes New Ruler*

LEAVING THE THRONE BEHIND

New King and Queen of England

*Duke and Duchess of York*

## Wally's Auto With Baggage Leaves Villa

Cannes, France, Dec. 10.—(U.P.)—At the exact minute that King Edward's abdication was announced in London today Mrs. Wallis Warfield Simpson was in her room atop the Herman L. Rogers' villa. At the same time her famous black limousine, its back seat loaded with baggage, dashed from the garden.

Mrs. Rogers said, as she stood on the porch of her villa, that Mrs. Simpson intended to remain at Cannes through Christmas. She was emphatic and she said positively that former King Edward would not come to Cannes or any other place on the Riviera.

**Abdication Confirmed**

Confirmation of the abdication reached the villa by special telephone call from London.

Inquirers found the villa shrouded in a mystery deeper than ever.

One person was visible in the grounds—a workman who was installing a new telephone line.

Edward will not see the woman

Continued on page 11

**THE REAL MRS. SIMPSON**

The life story of the glamorous Wally, by Adela Rogers St. Johns, famous author and close friend of the Warfield family, starts today on page 2.

## Edward Gives Up Throne For Exile and Marriage To Mrs. Wallis Simpson

### King's Abdication Statement

London, Dec. 10.—(AP)—King Edward's words in renouncing the British throne, were:

"I have determined to renounce the throne.

"After long and anxious consideration I have determined to renounce the throne to which I succeeded on the death of my father and I am now communicating this, my final and irrevocable decision."

"Realizing as I do the gravity of this step, I can only hope that I shall have the understanding of my peoples in the decision I have taken and the reasons which have led me to take it.

"I will not enter now into my private feeling but I would beg that it should be remembered that the burden which constantly rests upon the shoulders of a sovereign is so heavy that it can only be borne in circumstances different from those in which I now find myself."

"I conceive that I am not overlooking the duty that rests on me to place in the forefront of public interest when I declare that I am conscious that I can no longer discharge this heavy task with efficiency or with satisfaction to myself.

"I have accordingly this morning executed an instrument of abdication in the terms following:

"I, Edward VIII, of Great Britain, Ireland and the British dominions beyond the seas, king and emperor of India, do hereby declare my irrevocable determination to renounce the throne for myself and for my descendants and by desire that effect should be given to this instrument of abdication immediately.

"In token whereof I have hereunto set my hand this tenth day of December, 1936, in the presence of the witnesses whose signatures are subscribed.

"Signed, Edward R. I.

"My execution of this instrument has been witnessed by my three brothers, their royal highnesses the Duke of York, the Duke of Gloucester and the Duke of Kent.

"I deeply appreciate the spirit which has actuated the appeals which have been made to me to take a different decision and I have before reaching my final determination, most fully pondered over them.

"But my mind is made up. Moreover, further delay cannot but be most injurious to the peoples whom I have tried to serve as Prince of Wales and as king and whose future happiness and prosperity are the constant wish of my heart.

"I take my leave of them in the confident hope that the course which I have thought it right to follow is that which is best for the stability of the throne and empire and happiness of my people.

"I am deeply sensible of the consideration which they have always extended to me both before and after my accession to the throne and which I know they will extend in full measure to my successor.

"I am most anxious that there should be no delay of any kind in giving effect to the instrument which I have executed and that all necessary steps should be taken immediately so secure that my lawful successor, my brother, his royal highness the Duke of York, should ascend to the throne."

### Decision Irrevocable, Statement Says—Baldwin Explains Entire Crisis—Laws Rushed to Swear In Duke of York as Ruler

By WEBB MILLER

(Copyright 1936 by United Press)

London, Dec. 10—(By Transatlantic telephone)—King Edward VIII abdicated today from the throne of Great Britain, renouncing for love the rulership over the world's greatest empire and one-quarter of the inhabitants of the globe.

He gave up his crown so that he could go into perpetual exile and marry Mrs. Wallis Warfield Simpson, twice-divorced American.

A breathless, stunned house of commons received from the king a historic document giving up the "heavy burden" of kingship because of the difficult personal situation in which he finds himself.

The Duke of York, his brother, will succeed to the throne, it was announced.

The duke's daughter, imperious little 10½-year-old Princess Elizabeth, becomes heir presumptive to the throne, Britain's next queen if her father dies without a son being born to him.

**Edward First King to Give Up Throne Voluntarily**

The scene in the house of commons was one of the most solemn in England's long history. Never before has a king voluntarily given up that mighty throne.

But his majesty's government was determined not to permit a divorcee and commoner to share it with Edward of the House of Windsor.

The king was equally determined to make her queen or marry her in any case. He therefore decided against fighting his ministers and the constitution, a losing struggle.

The historic occasion came after Edward had been on the throne 324 days.

Just before big ben, the voice of the empire, chimed 3:45 p.m., the speaker called on Baldwin.

The prime minister arose from his seat and walked to the bar of the house.

**Decision to Abdicate Is Irrevocable, Statement Says**

In a voice which by a mighty effort of will power he kept steady, the stocky country squire, the very epitome of conservative England, said:

"A message from his majesty the king, sir, signed by his majesty's own hand."

The silence was uncanny, painful. The throng which filled the small, gloomy chamber where centuries of history has been made, seemed to have suspended animation. There was not even the sound of loud breathing.

The speaker read the king's message.

The emotions of the assembly can only be imagined when he came to the solemn words:

"I, Edward VIII of Great Britain, Ireland, the British dominions beyond the seas, king, Emperor of India, do hereby declare my irrevocable determination to renounce the throne for myself and my descendants."

And then:

"I am most anxious that there should be no delay . . . that all necessary steps should be taken immediately to secure that my lawful successor, my brother, his royal highness the Duke of York, should ascend the throne.

(Signed) "Edward R. I."

**King Signs Abdication Papers In Presence of Three Brothers**

Only once more, in all probability, will we write that signature, Edward, king and emperor. That will be when he signs the act of abdication which will be enacted immediately by the house of commons and the house of lords.

The moment his pen leaves the paper, while the ink is still wet, he ceases to rule and at that instant the Duke of York is king.

The king signed the fateful abdication papers today at Fort Belvedere, his country residence, in the presence of his brothers. At

Continued on page 35

# THE MINNEAPOLIS STAR

*The Northwest's Largest Evening Newspaper*

Vol. 32, No. 67 — MINNEAPOLIS, [illegible] FRIDAY, MAY 7, 1937 — Price Two Cents in Minneapolis


Star—Wide World Wired Photo Phoned These Pictures From Scene of Disaster

# 32 DEAD IN ZEP BLAST AND FLAME

## Sabotage Intimated by Dr. Hugo Eckener, Designer of the Hindenburg—Inquiries Seek Cause—Dirigible Captains Among Injured—Destruction Comes Suddenly as Craft Lands at Lakehurst

**By International News Service**

Crashing suddenly to earth, a flaming torch, when stricken by a fatal spark, the proud German airliner Hindenburg lay a mass of smouldering, twisted wreckage at the Lakehurst, N. J., naval air station today.

At least 31 of those who boarded the dirigible at Frankfort-on-Main, Germany, Monday for the airship's first trans-Atlantic crossing of 1937 and a member of the Lakehurst ground crew were dead. Nearly two-score others were injured.

None could say what caused the disaster. A severe electrical storm was playing about the vicinity as the Hindenburg prepared to land and some crew members thought the ship had been struck by lightning.

Commander Charles E. Rosendahl, veteran of the Shenandoah disaster, would not hazard a guess. He witnessed the disaster.

**From Graz, Austria, Dr. Hugo Eckener, grizzled air veteran and designer of the ill-fated ship, claimed sabotage.**

Count O. G. von Zeppelin, now visiting Chicago, concurred and blamed it on "reds," but Berlin officials discredited this theory.

The German government immediately ordered a commission to sail to the United States for an investigation.

Senator Royal S. Copeland, chairman of the senate commerce com-

**Explosion**


*Continued on Page Two*


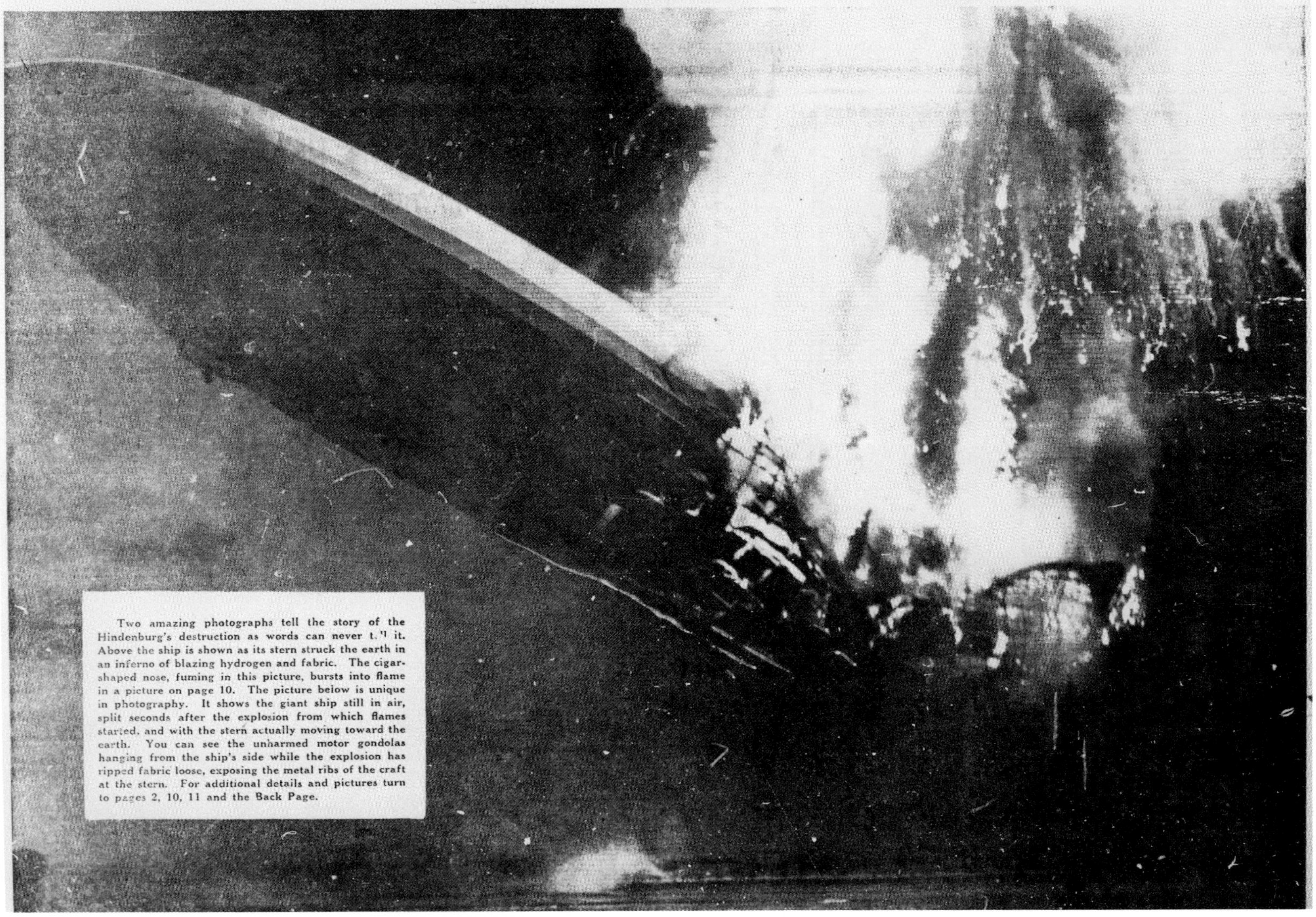

Two amazing photographs tell the story of the Hindenburg's destruction as words can never t. 'l it. Above the ship is shown as its stern struck the earth in an inferno of blazing hydrogen and fabric. The cigar-shaped nose, fuming in this picture, bursts into flame in a picture on page 10. The picture below is unique in photography. It shows the giant ship still in air, split seconds after the explosion from which flames started, and with the stern actually moving toward the earth. You can see the unharmed motor gondolas hanging from the ship's side while the explosion has ripped fabric loose, exposing the metal ribs of the craft at the stern. For additional details and pictures turn to pages 2, 10, 11 and the Back Page.

**WEATHER**
U. S. Weather Bureau Forecast.
Generally fair Friday; Saturday fair, continued warm. 24 hours high, 93, at 3 p. m. Thursday; low, 71, at 6 a. m. Thursday. Additional weather news on page 18.

# The Minneapolis Tribune

FIRST in City Circulation—FIRST in TOTAL Circulation—Daily and Sunday

MORNING EDITION
Three Cents in Minneapolis



*Seventy-First Year. No. 46.* 3 MINNEAPOLIS, MINN., FRIDAY, JULY 9, 1937. • • • *Twenty-eight Pages*

# Bill Doubling Income Tax Passed by Senate, Goes Before Governor

## Benson Expected to Sign Plan Despite Veto Threat.

## HOUSES SPEED ADJOURNMENT

## Chain, Monies Levies and Relief Issues Yet Undecided.

By Orlin Folwick,
Tribune Staff Writer.

The proposed new income tax law, doubling the revenue Minnesota residents must pay into the state treasury, went over its final legislative hurdle Thursday through approval by the senate.

It now goes to Governor Benson for signature or veto, with indications pointing to his acceptance of the act despite reports he is considering a veto and another special session. The governor admitted he is disappointed in the final draft of the law, but indicated he will sign it and declare his position in a statement. Along with it went the inheritance and gift tax bills.

Activities speeded up in the legislature Thursday as leaders looked ahead toward adjournment. The heat wave and reports of good crops from back home have made many lawmakers wish they could leave the capitol. So the senate adopted a resolution fixing Monday as the final day. That will mean that all loose ends of legislation will have to be picked up Friday and Saturday, since no bills can be passed on the final day.

**Goes Through Easily.**

The income tax bill reported out by a conference group from both houses went through without a hitch. It calls for a flat rate of 7 per cent for corporations, with a $1,000 exemption plus deductions up to 10 per cent of their net tax for their Minnesota pay rolls and property. The personal rate runs from 1 per cent on the first $1,000 of income to 10 per cent over $20,000, with single taxpayers allowed a $10 deduction from the net tax and married persons $30. In addition, deductions of $5 each are allowed dependents.

Rates on individual incomes are:

On the first $1,000—1 per cent.

On the second $1,000—2 per cent.

On the third $1,000—3 per cent.

On the fourth $1,000—4 per cent.

On the fifth $1,000—5 per cent.

On the sixth and seventh thousands—6 per cent.

On the eighth and ninth thousands—7 per cent.

From $9,000 to $12,500—8 per cent.

From $12,500 to $20,000—9 per cent.

Over $20,000—10 per cent.

Another change is the elimination of the present exemption of dividends of Minnesota corporations from tax. Taxpayers also would be permitted to deduct only up to $2,000 of capital losses, unless such losses are an offset against capital gains, which are subject to tax.

**Big Inheritances Tax Up.**

The inheritance tax bill increases the rates in brackets above $30,000 from the present 4 per cent to a top of 12 per cent where the recipient is a widow or child of the deceased, with higher rates applying as the degree of kinship of the recipient decreases.

The gift tax bill applies the same rates as the inheritance tax to gifts and is designed primarily to plug loopholes in the inheritance tax. The two together are expected to increase state revenue from these sources about $800,000 a year, beginning in 1938, because inheritance taxes are not payable until 12 months after death.

In the face of the rush to complete the business, a conference group on the new chain store tax disagreed Thursday, leaving the job to another to be appointed Friday. Rates, which the house sought to put at a high figure and the



## Washington

By H. R. Baukhage.
Copyright, 1937, by NANA, Inc.

ROOSEVELT'S SILENCE; CIO INTERPRETATION; POLITICAL PRESSURE.

THE ORACLE.

YOU RECALL how the Delphic oracle answered the soldier who asked what his fate in battle would be?

The oracle hardly paused before he remarked:

"You will go, return, never die in arms."

When, later on, the soldier's widow asked, "how come?" the oracle answered that her late spouse was weak on punctuation. This is the way he should have read the sentence:

"You will go, return never, die in arms."

THE CIO INTERPRETS.

SO IN CIO circles or thereabouts, where they are adept in interpreting oracles, there is an interesting interpretation of the President's refusal to confirm the story of his "break" with John Lewis. It runs this way:

The "break" story emanated from CIO headquarters. It appeared in the papers which were read in Washington just as the President was returning from Hyde Park.

That afternoon occurred the regular semi-weekly White House press conference. When the President was asked if he had any comment on the story, he swept the question back as a friendly mastiff might toss a harmless but yappingly annoying fox terrier from his presence. The story, he said, needed no comment.

To Mr. Lewis' wishful ear, the President's oracular silence was said to be as golden as a silvery speech could have been. In other words, if the President doesn't say there is a split, there isn't any as far as Mr. Lewis is concerned (no matter what Mr. Lewis says).

Some interpreters of the oracle go still further. Even if there is a split, they say, there could be no better strategy for Mr. Lewis than to have the President refuse to admit it.

PROBLEM IN SAVING.

THE President has a hard time when he tries to save a dollar. He's having a harder time saving a certain $900,000 item which the senate stuck into the department of the interior appropriations bill.

The budget bureau had disapproved the item, which covers what is popularly known as the Rocky Mountain park tunnel, officially designated as the Grand Lake trans-mountain waterway diversion project.

The project, if completed, would divert some 44 million dollars. The $900,000 is just for a preliminary survey.

The story behind the project is intriguing. The story, opponents say, of an "inside lobby" that is fighting for the expenditure—inside the department of the interior.

Senator Adams of Colorado naturally would like to see the item go through congress and the hole go through one of his constituent mountains.

But he couldn't have handled it without help. And he has it.

Reclamation Commissioner Page, politically indebted to Mr. Adams, is said to have battled nobly, and he has had the assistance of Rufus Poole, chairman of the legislative committee of the department. In this capacity, Mr. Poole presumably knows what his superiors—or some of them—want. He has been a great help.

The bill, which covers the department's expenditures for the present fiscal year, of course overdue since July 1, is still writhing in conference committee. The administration still has hopes of saving the $900,000 in spite of itself.

BEFORE AND AFTER.

DOWN Pennsylvania way, where the presidential bee has been so busy around the governor's mansion, there has been some large talk which has a very empty ring when it reaches Washington.

Pennsylvania's Attorney General Margiotti announced that he was coming to Washington to "force" Attorney General Cummings to bring about an NLRB election to decide whether CIO holds the majority at the Cambria steel plants in Johnstown. All

(Continued on Page 10, Column 6.)

## STEPSON JOINS AMELIA VIGIL

Oakland, Calif., July 8.—(AP—Wirephoto)—David Putnam, 24-year-old stepson of Amelia Earhart, arrived Thursday from Florida to be with his father, George Palmer Putnam, who is waiting here for word of the lost flier and her navigator. Young Putnam said he was sure Miss Earhart cannot be lost because she is "too smart a flier."

## Search for Amelia Spreads Southward

*Planes and Ships Deploy Fanwise to Sweep Pacific in Area Around Howland Island as Search for Flier Enters Seventh Day.*

Honolulu, July 8.—(AP)—Fighting planes and ships spread fanwise through the Phoenix island region Thursday in a determined search for Amelia Earhart, now missing for six full days.

Three planes catapulted into the air from the battleship Colorado made their second sweep over Winslow reef, southeast of Howland island, which Miss Earhart missed on her attempted world flight, but returned Thursday night without trace of the lost flier and her navigator.

The coast guard cutter Itasca searched islets, reefs and shoals south of Howland and westward of the Phoenix group. The navy minesweeper Swan searched east of Howland.

Although the navy reported no developments in the day's search hopes of friends and relatives persisted.

**Lexington Near Honolulu.**

Nearing Honolulu, the $40,000,000 aircraft carrier Lexington prepared for a quick refueling at Lahaina Roads and a 1,500-mile run to the Howland region to reinforce the search with a great air fleet.

The Colorado's planes first sought a sand bank supposedly lying 45 miles north of Winslow reef, which might have offered a haven for the fliers.

In a two-hour, twenty-minute flight Wednesday the Colorado's planes failed to find the sand bank.

Naval authorities said the search would be extended southward Friday until the entire area of possibility has been covered. Then, if the search proved fruitless, the Lexington's planes would comb the area again.

R. H. Bryan, Jr., of the Bishop museum here, who visited five of the eight Phoenix islands in 1924, said the islands are so small that it would be possible to fly over the entire group without sighting land.

**Had No Water Condenser.**

Such may have been Miss Earhart's predicament when she reported near exhaustion of her gasoline and no island in sight, although she thought her plane was directly over Howland.

Some of the islets, he said, would provide brackish water for drinking and sufficient cocoanuts for food, but that others were barren except for birds and their eggs.

Inquiries developed the information the plane carried no water condenser, as previously reported. Such a condenser would have enabled the fliers to obtain drinking water from the sea. The fliers carried three gallons of water when they left New Guinea and planned to rely in an emergency upon rain squalls to quench their thirst.

## NEWS INDEX



## RESTRICTIONS SET ON COURT BILL DEBATING

### Administration Senators Will Use Technical Rules to Check Filibuster.

### Robinson Calls Wheeler to Order, Gets Rebuke in Disorderly Session.

Washington, July 8.—(AP)—Senate supporters of the Roosevelt court bill angrily fenced the opposition in Thursday with all the technical obstructions to filibustering senate rules permit.

Although the debate was still far from the filibuster stage, Senator Robinson, the majority leader, struck first. Points of order and inquiries to the chair produced a series of rulings to govern the discussion and maneuvering still to come.

**Opponents Protest.**

With opposition leaders irately protesting, but making no appeal to the senate from the dicta of Senator Pittman, Democrat of Nevada, the president pro tempore, it was established that:

From now until the court bill is disposed of, no senator may speak more than twice upon any one subject.

No senator may interrupt a speaker to make a lengthy statement, unless it be a question propounded to the speaker.

**Wheeler Called to Order.**

No business, other than the disposition of the court bill, may be transacted except by unanimous consent.

Without warning, Robinson called Senator Wheeler, Democrat of Montana, to order to a violation of the rule governing interruptions of debate. Obviously taken aback at such procedure so early in the contest, Wheeler angrily leveled a long forefinger at the party leader and laid down an ultimatum.

The opposition will see to it that the rules are scrupulously observed by the proponents of the bill, he

(Continued on Page 2, Column 5)

## JAPS, CHINESE REACH TRUCE

### Both Begin Withdrawal of Troops From Peiping Battle Section.

Shanghai, July 9.—(AP)—A domei (Japanese) news agency dispatch from Peiping Thursday reported that Chinese and Japanese troops began evacuating the zone of conflict west of Peiping at 6:40 a. m. today (4:40 p. m. Minneapolis time Thursday).

Both forces, in conflict since Wednesday night near the Marco Polo bridge, were ordered to cease fire at daybreak, the agency said

The Chinese agreed to withdraw their troops from the vicinity of the bridge to points south of the Peiping-Hangkow railroad and on the right bank of the Yngting river.

The Japanese consented to transfer their forces to points north of the railroad and on the left bank of the river, the reports said.

After the withdrawal, the incident will be placed in the hands of diplomatic negotiators.

**SOVIET THREATENS WAR IF JAPS ENTER SIBERIA**

Moscow, July 9.—(AP)—The Soviet government threatened Japan with open warfare Friday if Japanese troops do not keep out of Siberia.

Maxim Litvinoff, Soviet commissar of foreign affairs, warned the Japanese ambassador, Mamoru Shigemitsu, that Rusian troops along the Siberian-Manchoukuoan border had firm orders "in no case to allow Japanese Manchurian troops to cross Soviet frontiers."

## Devil's Island Fugitive Struggles to New York After Leaving Indian Wife in Panama Jungle

*Rene Belbenoit, the famous fugitive from Devil's island, walked into the New York offices of the North American Newspaper Alliance Thursday and revealed that he had made his way undetected into this country through jungles and across boundary lines. Last August, in a dispatch to The Tribune, Belbenoit, then in Panama, told the thrilling story of his five daring escapes from Devil's island, the French penal colony off the coast of Guiana. Here he tells the story of his subsequent adventures.*

By Rene Belbenoit.

New York, July 8.—I have been a long time coming here—almost a year from Panama—but then it has been a long way. There is a fathomless distance separating a fugitive from Devil's Island and a man walking the city streets.

How many miles, would you say, lie between a man sitting in a Panama jungle with paint on his face and an Indian wife who calls him "Nicatchipou" and a man sitting writing in an easy chair in a New York hotel with ice water on tap and a radio at his elbow and Times Square in his ear? Most of those miles I walked and some I rode on horseback. The rest I sat out as a stowaway on a freighter.

So that is the distance I have come—from the point of view of time, it is even longer. Was it in the year 1936 that I sat in the moist darkness under the green roof before the corpse of one who had

(Continued on Page 4, Column 1.)

## STRIKES LOST, GREEN STATES

### A.F.L. Head Says Steel Industry Tactics of Lewis Have Harmed Labor.

Washington, July 8.—(AP)—William Green, president of the American Federation of Labor, declared Thursday night the steel strikes directed by John L. Lewis have been lost.

"Violent and undemocratic policies pursued by Lewis and his industrial union allies not only defeated the strikers but did great damage to the labor cause generally," he contended.

**Scores Violent Tactics.**

In a statement indicating there is little chance of an early peace between the federation and the Lewis organization, Green added:

"No hostile employer in America has done the cause of organized labor more harm than those who formulated, executed and administered the policies of the Committee for Industrial Organization during the past 18 months."

He continued:

"The violation of agreements, the seizure of public property, violence, riots and uprisings can have no place in the social, economic and industrial life of America.

**'Failure Is Inevitable.'**

"No union of workers who resort to the use of such methods can succeed. Failure for those who pursue such a policy is inevitable. Workers of the United States understand this to be true. They are willing to strike and fight for higher wages and improved conditions of employment, but they will do so as law-abiding people through the exercise of every moral, legal and economic right to which they are entitled, in an orderly way and in conformity with the laws of the land."

Green said at the outset "it now becomes certain" the steel strikes at Chicago, Cleveland, Johnstown, Youngstown, Canton and other cities are lost.

The A. F. of L. leader declared

(Continued on Page 10, Column 1.)

## Crack Train Kills Youth at Newport

Struck by the St. Paul road's streamlined Hiawatha as he walked along railroad tracks near the Oakland tower a short distance from Newport, an unidentified youth about 18 years old was killed Thursday evening. Trainmen said the youth apparenty did not hear or see the train, which hurled him 30 feet from the right of way.

## Taylor of U. S. Steel To Retire, Mentioned As Envoy to London

Myren C. Taylor.

New York, July 8.—(AP)—The New York Herald Tribune said Thursday night Myron C. Taylor has put his associates on notice that he expects to retire as chairman of the board of the U. S. Steel corporation at the end of this year.

The newspaper said this is contingent on the completion of a financing and common stock dividend resumption program. If this program is not carried through by the year end, he has indicated he will continue as chairman until July 1, 1938, at the latest.

The paper said earnings indicate both ends can be achieved and continued, "it is scarcely a secret in Wall street Mr. Taylor would be available for appointment as ambassador to the court of St. James, if the incumbent, Robert W. Bingham, should resign."

Wall street for some time has heard rumors of possible appointment of Taylor to this post.

## F. R. Family Tax Charges To Be Aired

*But Fish Is Ordered to Make No Mention of President.*

Washington, July 8.—(AP)—A congressional inquiry committee gave Representative Fish, Republican, New York, permission Thursday to explain charges that members of the Roosevelt family have used revenue law loopholes to avoid tax payments. It stipulated, however, Fish must not mention the President.

It was on a Republican's motion that the senate-house committee on tax evasion and avoidance voted 7 to 4 to hear Fish Friday, provided he would not bring President Roosevelt into his discussion.

Representative Treadway, Republican, Massachusetts, who made the motion, told reporters the President had filled out his income tax return in proper form and made "proper deductions."

Fish, who represents the congressional district in which Mr. Roosevelt lives, has stated publicly he has proof the chief executive took deductions for "farm losses" and depreciation on his estate at Hyde Park, N. Y., and his Georgia plantation.

Fish told reporters he would name two members of the Roosevelt family Friday, along with a member of the cabinet.

## N. W. MERCURY STAYS OVER 90

### City Reading Hits 93—Bather Drowns at Calhoun—Scant Relief Is Foreseen.

Temperatures of 90 degrees or higher were recorded in most of the northwest Thursday, the fourth consecutive day of the heat wave. Little change was indicated in weather forecasts for the remainder of the week.

In Minneapolis the high for the day was 93 degrees at 4 p. m. Highest temperature reported in Minnesota was 103 at Red Wing, where thunder showers brought relief in the evening.

The heat in Minneapolis again sent crowds to the beaches, and at Lake Calhoun an unidentified man was reported drowned. E. E. Beito, 3815 Upton avenue north, and Donald Cyrtis Matlock, 500 West Lake street, said they saw the man, about 40, enter the water from the west shore about three blocks from the bath house, swim out about 150 feet and disappear under the surface without an outcry or struggle.

**Crews' Dragging Futile.**

Red Cross and park board crews dragged the lake until dark without result. Carl Jensen, bath house manager, said there is a drop-off of about 45 feet at the spot the man was reported to have gone down. Bathing is forbidden at that place.

Several hours later Archie Smith, manager of the Lenox hotel, 403 Washington avenue south, was notified that clothing belonging to S. E. O'Dell, a printer who roomed at the hotel, had been found in a locker at the Calhoun bath house.

Smith said he last saw O'Dell Thursday morning. At that time, Smith said, O'Dell mentioned having been fishing at Lake Calhoun, but said nothing about going swimming. O'Dell had not returned to the hotel early Friday.

**St. Paul Boy Drowns.**

A 6-year-old St. Paul boy, James Fingerholz, son of Mr. and Mrs. Joseph A. Fingerholz, 1171 Jenks street, drowned while wading in White Bear lake. An uncle, John Fingerholz, had taken the boy and his brother, Richard, 10, and sister, Lorraine, 3, to the lake to escape the heat.

After an hour of fishing with his uncle, the boy went wading near the White Bear pumphouse. Shortly afterwards the uncle found the boy in three feet of water. Efforts to revive him failed.

The heat was blamed for the death of John Ballata, 73, at his home at 451 Goodhue street, St. Paul, Thursday. Also in St. Paul, Mrs. James Pullman, 34, of Quincy, Ill., was overcome by the heat at Fifth and St. Peter streets.

**Collapse From Heat.**

In Minneapolis John Riley, 40, of 1413 Third avenue south, collapsed from the heat in a restaurant near his home Thursday noon. Harry Schmitz, 32, of 4345 Thirty-fourth avenue south, was overcome while working in the Ford plant.

Russell Kearn, 27, of 2523 Grand street northeast, was in poor condition at Asbury hospital Thursday night after being overcome by heat. August Piazza, 75, of 624 Morgan avenue north, was overcome at his home. He was treated by a General hospital ambulance doctor.

Some rain fell in North Dakota Thursday. Williston, which had .32 of an inch, stayed cool with a maximum of 74 degrees, but at Bismarck, where the rainfall measured .36 of an inch, the mercury got up to 90 degrees.

## Wallace Refuses $30,000, Asks Half of Mae's Wealth

New York, July 8.—(AP)—Samuel J. Siegel, attorney for Frank Wallace, whom Mae West finally recognized Wednesday as her husband, demanded Thursday a fifty-fifty share of the movie queen's fortune for his client.

Miss West offered Wallace, 47-year-old vaudeville actor, $30,000 to "forget all about the ceremony," Siegel was quoted by the paper, but he will play for higher stakes—half of her reputed $3,000,000.

"Next week we expect to apply for an injunction that will tie up all of Miss West's property in California," said Siegel.

Under California law, he explained, a husband is entitled to half his wife's holdings; all properties are held jointly and business transactions require joint signatures.

Admitting in answer to a suit by Wallace that she married him in 1911, Miss West maintained Wallace remarried without being divorced.

"Her contention that she is an unkissed bride is ridiculous," said Siegel. "We have affidavits to show Miss West and Wallace lived together as man and wife from 1911 to 1915."

Wallace, whose real name is Willities, the lawyer said, will return to New York soon with his dancing partner, Trixie la Mae, from her home in Henderson, Ky.

**WEATHER**
U. S. Forecast: Partly cloudy, warmer in extreme southeast, slightly colder in extreme northwest Sat.; Sun. cloudy, colder; snow in north portion. 24 hour high, 43, at 4 p. m.; low, 27, at 4 p. m. Details on page 16.

# The Minneapolis Tribune

FIRST in City Circulation—FIRST in TOTAL Circulation—Daily and Sunday

MORNING EDITION
Three Cents in Minneapolis

Seventy-First Year. No. 292. 3 MINNEAPOLIS, MINN., SATURDAY, MARCH 12, 1938. • • • Twenty-six Pages

# Austria Surrenders to Hitler; Nazi Government Established

## *Roosevelt Defied By TVA Head at Quarrel Inquiry*

***Dr. Morgan Refuses to Answer Questions as F. R. Seeks to End Row Between Authority's Directors.***

Washington, March 11.—(AP)—Dr. Arthur E. Morgan, chairman of TVA, bluntly defied President Roosevelt Friday and declared himself not a participant in a hearing called by the chief executive to determine "the fact" behind TVA's bitter internal row.

Face-to-face with the President and in the presence of his opponents on the TVA board—Vice Chairman Harcourt A. Morgan and Director David E. Lilienthal—the chairman criticized the inquiry as "an alleged process of fact finding" and repeated his plea for an "impartial, comprehensive and complete" investigation by congress.

Emphatically, he declined to answer Mr. Roosevelt's questions as to what factual basis he might have for the charges of bad faith and malfeasance he has hurled at Harcourt A. Morgan and Lilienthal.

Just before the hearing adjourned at 6 p. m., the President admonished all three directors that they "owed it to the country not to continue longer to jeopardize the public welfare by personal differences."

He said that those who could "not find the way clear" to work in harmony "should resign."

**President Asks 'Facts.'**

At Chairman Morgan's request, the three are to meet the President again next Friday so that he, and they if they choose, may present written statements. Otherwise, a White House aid said, the hearing was over so far as Mr. Roosevelt was concerned.

The fight which has split the TVA for two years was brought to a dramatic climax in the office of the President.

Mr. Roosevelt began the proceedings with a statement that he was preserving an impartial position as between the two factions, that he was not interested in opinions, but wanted facts.

He noted that Chairman Morgan had referred to the claim of Senator George Berry of Tennessee for compensation for marble lands assertedly flooded by Norris dam as an instance of "the difficulty" of obtaining "honesty, openness, decency and fairness in government."

**Says President Ignored Letter.**

"I must, therefore," Mr. Roosevelt continued, "ask you what evidence of dishonesty of malfeasance on the part of your colleagues you have in regard to the so-called Berry marble case."

"During a long period," Morgan replied, "I have repeatedly but unsuccessfully endeavored to secure the President's adequate considera-

(Continued on Page 14, Column 1)

## *City Council Moves to End 'Trade War'*

***Aldermen and C. & C. to Seek 'Truce' in Beer Dispute With St. Paul.***

Steps toward making peace in the "trade war" with St. Paul were taken by the Minneapolis city council Friday, but at the same time the health and hospitals committee informed the council it was ready to reject license renewal applications of all Minneapolis concerns handling St. Paul beer.

The overture for peace was made when the council agreed to a meeting with the Minneapolis Civic & Commerce association Monday out of which it was hoped would come a meeting between governing officials of both cities. Hostilities were precipitated when St. Paul commissioners refused to allow Minneapolis fuel dealers to deliver in St. Paul.

Alderman Harold Kauth, chairman of the health and hospitals committee, told the council that if it is the wish of the council that places handling St. Paul beer be denied licenses, the committee would be glad to be guided.

Action on all license renewal applications for more than 700 taverns in Minneapolis has been delayed by the committee.

## NEWS INDEX



## HOUSE PASSES BUSINESS TAX REVISION BILL

**Administration Forces Lose 2 Attempts to Modify Act —Goes to Senate.**

**Request by Roosevelt for Levy on 'Family Corporations' Goes Unheeded.**

Washington, March 11.—(AP)—The administration suffered two clearcut defeats in the house Friday before the chamber passed the tax revision bill by a vote of 294 to 98.

At one end of Pennsylvania avenue, President Roosevelt told reporters that a proposed tax on closely-held and family-owned corporations was not punitive and that it was designed to erase special privilege existing under the tax laws.

But, at the other end of the avenue, two hours later, the house voted down such a levy in the tax bill.

**Hull Raps Excise Tax.**

Across the street from the White House, Secretary Hull criticized an excise tax on imported pork on the grounds it would be disastrous to the American corn and hog industry. He intimated it would result in retaliation by other countries.

At the capitol, the house refused, 201 to 182, to eliminate the pork tariff-tax from its bill.

There was no angry debate in the chamber—all that had been left behind Thursday. Members merely went through the routine of ratifying their previous tentative decisions, then wrapped up the bill for delivery to the senate.

**Approve Liquor Tax Raise.**

Before the lop-sided vote for passage, they refused to take out an amendment to raise the tax on hard liquors from $2 to $2.25 a gallon.

Balloting along almost rigid party lines, they scuttled a Republican motion to return the bill to the ways and means committee—a motion intended to obtain complete repeal of the undistributed profits tax and imposition of a flat 12½ per cent tax on capital gains instead of the graduated levy the bill provides.

The bill represented the answer of its house sponsors to pleas of business men for the easing of their tax burdens.

## LINDBERGHS SAIL BACK TO ENGLAND

New York, March 12.—(AP)—Colonel and Mrs. Charles A. Lindbergh sailed secretly at 12:30 a. m. E.S.T. Saturday on the Liner Bremen for England to rejoin their two sons.

The famous couple came here December 5 to pass the holidays, arriving unexpectedly on the liner President Harding and listed as "Mr. and Mrs. Gregory" on the passenger lists.

Their departure to resume seclusion they had found in England for more than two years was blanketed with secrecy and it was not until the big ship had eased from her pier into the North river and headed for the sea that the information was made public by the North-German Lloyd line.

## *Plasterer Sues When Union Denies Card*

A damage suit for $25,000 against the Plasterers' union, Local 65, Harry Martin, the local's business agent and the American Federation of Labor was filed Friday by Louis Gedell, plasterer, living at 300 East Fifteenth street. Gedell said he had been unable to get a membership in the union and that because he is a non-union man employers decline to hire him for fear their places would be "picketed, boycotted and harassed."

**NLRB CITES FORD.**

Chicago, March 11.—(AP)—The national labor relations board issued its fourth complaint against the Ford Motor Co. Friday, charging the firm's Chicago plant with five violations of the Wagner act.

## *Last Pictures Before Censorship*

Vienna, March 10.—(AP—Wirephoto)—These pictures, the last sent out of Austria before a tight censorship was established, were taken Friday in Vienna before the Nazis took control.

ABOVE—One of the Schuschnigg propaganda trucks on a downtown Vienna street bannering the resigned chancellor's slogan: "Good Austrian Equals Good German." Note the pictures of Schuschnigg on the rear of the truck with "Fatherland Front" crosses and "Austria" printed below.

BELOW—Truckloads of followers of Schuschnigg circulated through Vienna Friday distributing pamphlets, before his government fell. The pamphlets urged Austrians to support Schuschnigg in the plebiscite scheduled for Sunday, which has since been "postponed."

*These photos were sent to New York by radio and rushed to the Minneapolis Tribune by Wirephoto.*

## NO NEW LIMIT ON N. W. WHEAT

**Anticipated Restriction Dropped; Seeding to Be Based on 1935-37 Acreage.**

There will be no new restrictions on planting spring wheat this year, under the AAA soil conservation program, and farmers of the northwest and other wheat growing areas are limited only to plantings equal to acreage sown in 1935-6-7, Henry Bolstad, member of the Minnesota agricultural conservation committee, said Friday.

At a recent conference in Washington, he explained, officials in charge of the soil conservation program agreed that wheat acreage allotments for 1938 should be made on the basis of wheat plantings in the last three years. This applies only to this year, however.

**Important to N. W.**

There are likely to be acreage restrictions in 1939 and in addition the government probably will assume control over the marketing of this year's wheat harvest, if the crop is so large as to threaten to depress prices.

This removal of new limitations, that were expected to be placed on spring wheat, is of prime importance to the northwest. Soil this month is in uniformly excellent condition.

**Restriction Feared.**

Before the new federal ruling, it had been deemed possible that the spring wheat planting, nearly all of it in Minnesota, the Dakotas and Montana, would be limited to around 5,500,000 acres, less than one-third of the 17,500,000 sown in 1937.

This restriction would have been established by the fact that the government originally proposed to limit the entire wheat planting of the United States to 62,500,000 acres. But some 57,000,000 acres already had been sown to winter wheat last fall, in the wheat belt of Kansas, Nebraska, Oklahoma, Texas and other states of the midwest and southwest.

## RAIL ASSOCIATION TO ASK WAGE CUTS

Washington, March 11.—(AP)—The Association of American Railroads will recommend wage cuts for approximately 1,000,000 workers at a meeting in Chicago March 18. One hundred forty-two rail firms belong to the organization.

The association said the approximately 5 per cent freight rate increase granted by the interstate commerce commission is "entirely inadequate."

"The decision is depressing not only to the railroads but to industry as a whole and to general employment," the association declared, and "it is necessary to reduce operating expenses."

The roads have been pinched between falling income from freight carloadings and rising operating costs, rail men said. They added the downturn in loadings has been "serious" for more than three months.

## HOW NAZIS SEIZED AUSTRIA

***Coup Ousts Anti-Hitler Chancellor***

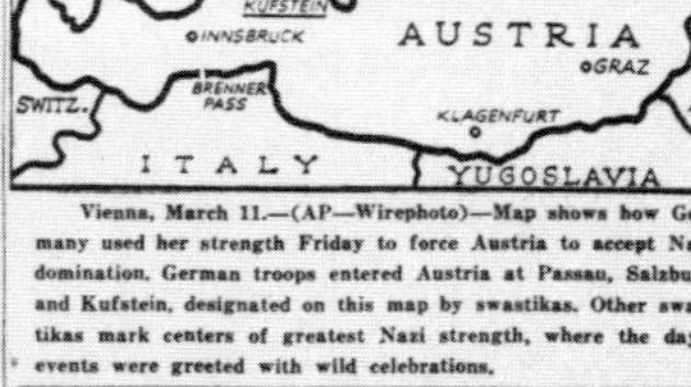

Vienna, March 11.—(AP—Wirephoto)—Map shows how Germany used her strength Friday to force Austria to accept Nazi domination. German troops entered Austria at Passau, Salzburg and Kufstein, designated on this map by swastikas. Other swastikas mark centers of greatest Nazi strength, where the day's events were greeted with wild celebrations.

## *300 Students Strike At Ellsworth, Wis.*

Ellsworth, Wis., March 11.—Three hundred students walked out of the Ellsworth high school Friday afternoon and paraded through town protesting the school board's refusal to renew the contract of Principal C. E. Gluesing.

"No Gluesing, No School," read one banner carried by students who marched the length of town.

## *Suspect Arrested, Admits 3 Holdups*

Arnold Stenvog, 18, arrested late Friday by detectives, admitted in a signed statement that he had held up two street cars and a drugstore in Minneapolis during December, 1937. Stenvog said he left for Seattle December 13, returning to Minneapolis only a few days ago. The three holdups netted $112.

## German Troops Cross Border to Reinforce Coup

### War Threat Moves Schuschnigg to Drop Independence Hope.

Vienna, March 12.—(AP)—Austria capitulated to Adolf Hitler Friday night. Bowing to Germany's war power, the government gave up its five-year fight against domination by the German fuehrer.

German troops, massed on the border, marched into Austria at 10 p. m. (3 p. m. Minneapolis time) at three points, Salzburg, Kufstein, and Passau. Faced with a German ultimatum demanding reorganization of the government, Anti-Nazi Chancellor Kurt Schuschnigg resigned.

**Arthur Seysz-Inquart.** *Nazi Chamber of Austria.*

President Wilhelm Miklas appointed Arthur Seysz-Inquart, Austria's Nazi leader, to succeed him.

Earlier, Seysz-Inquart had sent a telegram to Hitler saying that the "provisional Austrian government" requested Germany to send troops as soon as possible to assist it in "preventing the shedding of blood." The new chancellor was one of five Nazi sympathizers included in the cabinet at Hitler's order February 15.

Friday night's developments came after moves nad counter-moves by Schuschnigg and the Nazi command. There was violence throughout Austria Thursday and Friday.

Early Friday German troops mobilized near the Austrian border. Austria likewise sent troops to danger points. Schuschnigg had his regular army of 70,000, but called out 100,000 reserves and 30,000 guardsmen.

Vienna and many Austrian cities were in turmoil, with Nazis and Schuschnigg supporters clashing over a plebiscite on Austrian independence Schuschnigg had ordered for Sunday.

Then, Schuschnigg announced publicly that, bowing to the German ultimatum, a new government was being formed. He declared that "to prevent the sheddnig of blood" orders had been given for Austrian troops to fall back "in case of invasion."

**Swastika Flags Fly.**

Before midnight the Nazi Swastika flew from the chancellery and the city hall.

Vienna Nazis went wild. Swastikas appeared even on flagpoles about the headquarters of the Fatherland Front, previously the only legal political party in Austria.

While Schuschnigg, President Miklas and Seysz-Inquart were in conference and before the appointment of the new chancellor had been announced, many police and minor officials openly avowed their switch to the Nazi cause.

**New Cabinet Line-up.**

The new cabinet, all but two of whom were Nazis, was announced as follows:

Seysz-Inquart, chancellor and defense minister.

Wilhelm Wolff, foreign affairs.

Franz Hueber, justice. Hueber is a brother-in-law of Germany's No. 2 Nazi, Field Marshal General Hermann Wilhelm Goering.

Oswald Menghin, education.

Dr. Hugo Jury, social welfare.

Rudolf Neumayer, finance.

Anton Rheinthaler, agriculture.

Hans Fitschboeck, commerce.

Michael Skubl, secretary of state.

Ernst Kaltenbrunner, Skubl's assistant.

Hubert Klausner, Nazis' political representative.

**Seysz-Inquart Asks Troops.**

Seven torchlight parades marched into Vienna Jewish quarters. Two Jews were injured. Nazi crowds stormed the Fatherland Front building. Windows were smashed.

Dozens of Nazis hurled torches and tossed them inside. Firemen sprayed the building.

In his telegram to Hitler before his appointment as chancellor was announced, Seysz-Inquart said:

"The provisional Austrian government, which, after the resignation of the Schuschnigg cabinet, considers its task to be that of re-establishing order and quiet in Austria, addresses the urgent request to the German government to assist it in solving this task and preventing the shedding of blood.

"For this reason it requests the German government to send troops as soon as possible."

In a brief talk from the chancellery balcony Friday evening, Seysz-Inquart declared:

"I wish Austria a fortunate, happy return to the German fatherland. Make no disturbance tonight. March home in an orderly manner."

Inside, Schuschnigg made final

(Continued on Page 4, Column 1)

## The Situation

By Associated Press.

VIENNA—Germany nazifies Austria, sending in troops. Seysz-Inquart, Hitler personal friend, made chancellor. Schuschnigg driven from office.

BERLIN—Hitler reported closeted with all members of new Austrian cabinet except Seysz-Inquart as his troops march into Austria.

LONDON—British and French governments protest in "strongest possible terms" against German action.

PARIS—Austrian crisis catches France without cabinet; Premier-Designate Blum expresses confidence he can form new national union government; Italy refuses joint action with France and Britain to save Austria.

ROME—Fascist grand council reconvenes; Italy exercises "diplomatic reserve" on developments.

ZARAGOZA — Insurgents drive to new gains in eastern Spanish offensive designed to divides government territory.

SHANGHAI—Japanese launch offensive in Shensi province, Communist stronghold.

WASHINGTON — Officials studied developments in Austria and central Europe anxiously, but maintained a "hands off" attitude.

PRAHA—The Czechoslovakian cabinet viewed calmly developments in Austria.

# The Minneapolis Tribune

AS OLD AND PROGRESSIVE AS MINNEAPOLIS ITSELF

MORNING EDITION
Three Cents in Minneapolis

*Seventy-Second Year. No. 265.* 8 MINNEAPOLIS, MINN., MONDAY, FEBRUARY 13, 1939. *Fourteen Pages*




**WEATHER**
U. S. BUREAU FORECAST.
Much colder Monday and Tuesday; occasional snow Tuesday. 24 hours high, 39, at 3 p. m. Sunday; low, 8, at 2 a. m. Sunday.
Details on page 8.

# U. S. Will Resist Threat to Interests, Hull Warns; House to Act on Defense

## 35,000 REMAIN IN PYRENEES TO HARASS FRANCO

**Loyalist Band Refuses to Give Up Hamlets as Foe Turns to Central Spain.**

**Negrin Urges New Resistance as Bombs Pound Madrid—Border Town Raided.**

*(Day's News Abroad, page 3.)*

Perpignan, France, Feb. 12.—(AP)—A die-hard government army of 35,000 men, isolated by insurgent conquest of all Catalonia's frontier posts, Sunday resisted Generalissimo Francisco Franco's domination of northeast Spain from among the snowy crags of the Pyrenees.

The government militiamen, forced into the high mountains by insurgent capture of Ripoll, were said still to be holding a group of small hamlets and to be fighting with unexpected strength. The government force was reported to be well armed and supplied with food.

Franco, master now of all but a bare fourth of Spain, meanwhile had turned his powerful military machine toward the central zone which the government still holds.

Madrid, to which government Premier Juan Negrin and his ministers returned Sunday from Valencia, was shelled heavily during the morning. Sixteen inhabitants of the besieged city, again government Spain's capital, were killed and 23 were injured.

A fleet of 12 insurgent warplanes bombed the port of Alicante, killing 20 and wounding 55.

Government dispatches from Madrid gave no indication of the military strategy with which General Jose Miaja intended to defend the area.

**NEGRIN, IN MADRID, PLEADS FOR CONTINUED RESISTANCE**

Madrid, Feb. 12.—(AP)—The Spanish government Sunday night appealed for united resistance against the insurgents "pending the arrival of peace in an atmosphere of independence, safety and liberty." The proclamation was broadcast to all the people in what is left of government territory after Premier Juan Negrin had called his cabinet together for a meeting under the roar of an insurgent shelling of Madrid.

**RAID ON BORDER TOWN KILLS MORE THAN 100**

Perpignan, France, Feb. 12.—(INS)—More than 100 were killed Sunday in an insurgent air raid on the railway junction town of Jativa, according to a Madrid dispatch Sunday night. The town of 16,000 lies 40 miles south of Valencia. Scores were reported wounded.

**BLACKS PATROL BEATEN ARMY IN FRENCH CAMP**

Saint - Cyprien Concentration Camp, near Perpignan, France, Feb. 12.—(AP)—Mounted Algerian Spahis

(Continued on Page 3, Column 4)

## *200,000 Trudge 10 Abreast Past Body of Pius XI*

***Many Disappointed When Unable to Kiss Pope's Slipper—Cardinals Advance Burial to Tuesday Night.***

By Richard G. Massock.

Vatican City, Feb. 12.—(AP)—The first funeral service for Pope Pius XI was sung Sunday in great St. Peter's while thousands of the faithful moved slowly past the body in the Chapel of the Sacrament.

Scenes within the basilica and without, in the vast square, were of stupendous crowds, brilliant colors, simple ceremony and humble reverence.

Vatican City authorities announced that the pope would be buried Tuesday night, instead of Wednesday as had been expected earlier. His body will be placed with elaborate ceremony in three nested coffins—of cypress, zinc and polished elm—and then taken to the final resting place in the grottoes of St. Peter's.

The interment will take place between 5 and 6 p. m. (10 and 11 a. m., Minneapolis time.)

**10 Abreast Passing Bier.**

The throng which assembled to pass before the bier Sunday was estimated to contain more than 200,000. The line of worshipers shuffling slowly toward the great bronze doors of St. Peter's, 12 abreast, extended in the afternoon from the basilica to Castel Saint Angelo, more than half a mile away.

Once inside St. Peter's, the column was narrowed by guards, but sometime the worshipers were 10 abreast in passing the bier.

Crowds began collecting in the early morning in the piazza, until its 15 acres of pavement were black with people.

So enormous was the throng by noon (5 a. m., central time) that 200 regulars of the Italian army in grey-green uniforms and steel helmets joined the carabinieri in their Napoleonic hats in holding the worshipers 75 steps from the basilica.

**Arms Pinned at Sides.**

St. Peter's was opened to the public at 8 a. m.

The original plan had been to close the doors at 5 p. m., but when Eugenio Cardinal Pacelli, camerlengo or administrative head of the church until a new pontiff is elected, heard of the huge influx of people in the parvis, he ordered

(Continued on Page 3, Column 1)

### *Whitney, Duluth Industrialist, Dies*

Duluth, Feb. 12.—(AP)—Gwin A. Whitney, prominent Duluth and New York industrialist, died Sunday night in his home after an illness of several months. He was 45. President of both the Merritt-Chapman & Scott Corp. of New York and the Whitney Corp. of Duluth and Superior, He had resided much of the time in recent years in New York. Surviving are Mrs. Whitney, three young sons and Mr. Whitney's mother, Mrs. H. V. Gard of Superior. Mr. Whitney was a member of the Kitchi Gammi club of Duluth, the Racquet and Tennis, Whitehall and Campfire clubs of New York and the Chicago club.

### *Caretaker, 69, Fights Bandit for Half Hour*

***Robber Gets $100, New Car, Crashes Garage Doors in Escape.***

A 69-year-old night watchman and a young burglar early Sunday fought a furious battle in the C. E. Johnson Motor Sales Co. building at 4204 Lyndale avenue north. After a half-hour, the watchman was bested and slugged unconscious.

The thief made off with approximately $100 and a new car which he rammed through the doors of the garage. The machine later was found in St. Paul, badly damaged.

John Berg of 4443 Aldrich avenue north, the watchman, at 3 a. m. heard a noise in the garage. He found nothing unusual. He then sat down in a salesman's anteroom.

**Confronted by Bandit.**

Some minutes afterward, the burglar confronted Berg. The thief had a hand in a coat pocket, indicating a revolver. He asked for money and threatened to kill the watchman.

Berg said he threw his lunch bucket at the man and tackled him, disregarding the warning. The fight was on. In the battle a chair was broken in the anteroom, papers were scattered, walls were marred and furniture was overturned.

The two carried the fight into an adjoining hallway and into the front office. Here the burglar picked up a pop bottle and hit Berg on the head. Berg said he was hit twice with the bottle, then forced to open drawers as the burglar demanded money.

Berg insisted he did not know the combination of the safe nor how to open the cash register. Finally the burglar forced open the cash register, taking money estimated at $100. The handle of the safe was bent, but the burglar failed to open it. Some change also was taken from Berg, who was slugged again.

**Crashes Through Doors.**

The battered Berg, unconscious, and with no more money to be found, the burglar sought to open the automatic doors at the automobile entrance and apparently pulled the wrong switch. It put the place in darkness and the electric clock stopped at 3:58 a. m.

The thief then got into a new automobile and drove it through the doors, splintering them in springing them open.

The noise attracted attention of William Nevison, 4205 Webber parkway, in his home nearby.

Nevison called C. E. Johnson, 4201 Webber parkway, the owner of the sales company, and the two met in front of the garage. Johnson had called police from his home.

**Watchman Badly Bruised.**

The two found Berg lying part way under a desk in the front office, his feet near the safe. He was slowly regaining consciousness. Berg was taken to General hospital and later to Swedish hospital. His face and body were extensively bruised and lacerated.

Police discovered a broken window. It was believed the breaking glass was what Berg had heard before the battle. There were footprints in the snow at the window.

Another set of footprints were found near the back of the garage, and police believed they might have been made by an accomplice. The accomplice, if there was one, then would have fled when his companion failed to come out of the garage in a reasonable time.

Berg said his assailant was between 20 and 30 years of age, weighing about 170 pounds and was nearly six feet tall. He said he was of dark complexion and wore a dark overcoat and no hat.

**MOONEY TO HAVE OPERATION.**

Los Angeles, Feb. 12.—(AP)—An acute attack of gall bladder trouble Sunday forced Tom Mooney, recently pardoned after 22 years in prison for the San Francisco Preparedness day bombing, to cancel all speaking engagements in preparation for a major surgical operation.

## ARMY REVEALS PLANE NOT AT FAULT IN CRASH

**Officer Hints Pilot of 'Secret' Craft on Cross-U. S. Hop Was to Blame.**

**Flier Kept Secluded and Under Guard as Staff at Air Field Defends Conduct.**

New York, Feb. 12.—(AP)—Possibility that "man failure" caused the crackup of the army's speediest pursuit plane was seen Sunday in a remark by Colonel James Chaney, commanding officer of Mitchell field, where the crash occurred late Saturday after a record transcontinental flight.

He said his preliminary report, sent to Washington, declared that technical defects were not to blame. He did not amplify the remark.

**Pilot Closely Guarded.**

Contributing to the belief the cause of the crash was human was the close guarding of the ship's pilot, Lieutenant Benjamin Kelsey, who suffered only lacerations and shock. After treatment he was kept in seclusion at the residence of Colonel Keith Simpson. Even telephone calls to the home were disallowed.

Officers at the field said the continuous flying that Kelsey did at such speeds was "enough to wear out an iron man." His flight, from March field, Calif., was timed officially by the National Aeronautic association at seven hours, 45 minutes and 36 seconds.

**Fastest on Record.**

The association said that in flying time it was the fastest cross-country dash on record but that his two stops made his elapsed time 17 minutes 11 seconds slower than Howard Hughes' non-stop record of 1937. Kelsey's flying time was seven hours and 36 seconds.

The twin-motored monoplane was severely damaged in the crash, which occurred as Kelsey, its lone occupant, prepared to land.

Field officials said the all-steel cabin saved Kelsey from serious injury.

## ST. PAUL JAILS 42 IN ROUNDUP

**Three Squads Make Raids on Night Clubs, Taverns to Nab Undesirable Characters.**

Forty-two persons, 25 of them men, were arrested by St. Paul detectives early Sunday in a series of raids. They were held pending investigation of charges ranging from gambling and selling liquor without a license to vagrancy and vice.

Charles J. Tierney, assistant chief of police, led the three squads of detectives who made the round of 19 night clubs, taverns and beer parlors, and also raided two private residences.

The purpose, Tierney said, was to round up any undesirable characters who may have been driven from Minneapolis by recent vice raids. Only two of the 42 arrested, however, gave Minneapolis addresses.

All will be questioned Monday, Tierney said, and in cases where the evidence warrants, the prisoners will be arraigned in municipal court.

Eleven arrests were made at Bibeau's tavern, a 3.2 beer place, at 624 Wabasha street. Ten were arrested at the Thirty-Eight club, 38 West Tenth street, and four arrests were made at the Tiger bar, 199 East Seventh street. The other 17 were picked up at the two residences and two taverns.

**Passage of Arms Bill With Little Change Is Seen.**

**FOREIGN POLICY ROW SMOULDERS**

**Measure Includes 300 Million for New Warplanes.**

Washington, Feb. 12.—(AP)—President Roosevelt's rearmament program will come up in congress this week amidst smouldering controversy over the administration's foreign policy.

Even bitter opponents of some of the President's policies admit, however, that there is little likelihood that congress will make any radical changes in the half billion dollar defense program, which calls primarily for expansion of the army's air force to 5,500 planes.

The house will take up on Tuesday an omnibus bill to authorize expenditure of $300,000,000 for new war planes, $23,000,000 on Panama canal defenses and $32,500,000 for "educational" war orders and civilian pilot training.

**Little Senate Opposition.**

By the time the President sets sail on a Carribean trip next week-end, the house may have passed this measure almost intact and have sent it to the senate where there is admittedly little opposition to it.

If the administration forces win approval of this measure, it will be their first major victory of the session.

The bill's advent on the senate floor in a week or two, however, may touch off the pent-up controversy over foreign policy—if something else does not touch it off earlier.

**Controversy Smouldering.**

This controversy has been smouldering since the President called the senate military committee into a secret conference, outlined his foreign policy, and took occasion three days later to denounce as a "deliberate lie" the story that he had said that the frontier of the United States was on the Rhine.

President Roosevelt's foreign policy was assailed as dangerous by Senator Nye, Republican, North Dakota, and praised as a course toward peace by Senator Lee, Democrat, Oklahoma, in a broadcast debate Sunday night.

**Course Defended.**

Nye contended that the administration's "pronounced policy" did not always "square with our actions." He added that such policy is "so dangerous as to convince many that a war now in Europe would quite guarantee our participation in it."

Lee said that Mr. Roosevelt has steered a "straight course toward peace" through one world crisis after another. He said that while the "outrages upon humanity" committed by "gangster" nations had "stirred the blood of every American," President Roosevelt had "controlled his feelings and remonstrated" through courteous notes from the state department.

Both senators are members of the military affairs committee.

Nye pleaded for a "mind-our-own-business" foreign policy, a more mandatory neutrality policy.

**FLEET STARTS DEFENSE OF PANAMA CANAL**

Washington, Feb. 12.—(AP)—With much of the last minute bustle and secrecy of actual war, the

(Continued on Page 5, Column 3.)

### *I'll Catch Up to You!*

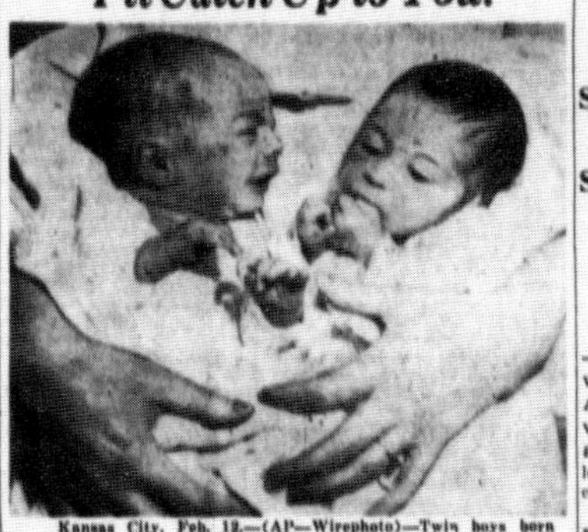

Kansas City, Feb. 12.—(AP—Wirephoto)—Twin boys born six days apart, are shown as they were "introduced" by a nurse, with this result. John Anthony, left, born Friday, and James Charles, six days older, are the twin sons of Mr. and Mrs. Milo C. McDonald. At birth John weighed 5 pounds 12 ounces and James 4 pounds 2 ounces. John seems to resent the head start on life that James has over him.

## Building Collapses On Duluth Crowd

**3,000 Escape With Only Four Injuries as Roof Falls During Hockey Game—Organist Continues Playing to Prevent Panic.**

Duluth, Feb. 12.—The front half of the Duluth Amphitheater roof buckled and crashed Sunday afternoon while a hockey game was in progress. More than 3,000 persons, nearly two-thirds of them children, escaped. Only four were injured.

The roof beams gave way under a heavy weight of snow during the intermission before the third period of a game between the Duluth police and the Virginia fire department teams. The crowd had only five minutes in which to get out after the first warning before the collapse came with a suddenness that blew from the building the stragglers and scattered window glass to injure the four persons already on the outside.

**Organist Plays On.**

Presence of the large number of police and firemen interested in the game helped in making possible the orderly retreat. They, with ushers and hockey players, calmed the spectators and directed them to exits. Organ music also quieted the endangered persons. Leland McEwen remained for three minutes at his organ after the warning had been sounded.

Cracking of the beams first caused a cry of "fire" to be raised. The roof sagged in the northwest portion of the building and then began to fall in progressive sections. The crash, at 4:04 p. m., was heard for blocks. One section of the roof which did not buckle tipped to rest on the bleacher seats.

**Many in Lobby.**

A fortunate circumstance was the fact the crash came between periods. Many of the spectators were in the lobby at this time and the teams were just filing out to resume play. Authorities said that had the crash come during the excitement of the annual contest the death toll probably would have been great.

Snow collected on the roof during a heavy storm last week was blamed for the accident by Fire Chief John Fisher.

Injured were Mrs. O. A. Wendfeldt, wife of one of the Duluth players; Kenneth Erickson, 16; Lloyd Olefson, 20, and Clifford Johnson, 23. All injuries were minor.

**INSPECTORS GUARD CITY FROM SNOW ON ROOFS**

Provisions of the Minneapolis building code guard against the possibility of a roof collapsing under the weight of snow, Jesse Wakeman, administrative assistant in the building inspector's office, said Sunday night. The code requires roofs to be constructed to carry specified loads, and in cases of overloads of snow, the building inspector has power to order the snow removed. No cases of dangerous accumulations of snow from last week's storm have been reported in Minneapolis.

**50 HURT IN PARIS CLASHES.**

Paris, Feb. 12.—(AP)—A dozen persons were injured Sunday and more than 50 arrested when political demonstrators battled in the streets of Paris.

## NEW COLD ON HEELS OF WEEK-END THAW

Thawing weather Sunday came as a sharp contrast to the severe cold of last week, but the weather bureau warned that a new cold wave is on the way. The forecast was for much colder, with the temperature decline to continue through Tuesday.

Minneapolis' highest reading Sunday was 39 degrees above zero at 3 p. m. South Dakota had temperatures even higher in some regions, with the maximum of 48 degrees reported at Huron.

Northern Minnesota and North Dakota also experienced relief from the cold, although the temperature rises were less pronounced.

### *Auto Unionists Fight Over Homer Martin*

Detroit, Feb. 12.—(AP)—Two men were taken to a hospital after fighting broke out between opponents and supporters of Homer Martin at a stormy meeting of the Packard local 190 of the United Automobile Workers Sunday. One of the injured men, Arthur Daniels, 46, told police he was a sergeant-at-arms for the local and that the fighting started when he and seven others who had arrived late attempted to force their way in. A dozen policemen, brandishing night sticks, quelled the disturbance.

### *Pistol Practice Kills FBI School Pupil*

Washington, Feb. 12.—(INS)—John Miller, 40, a Spokane, Wash., policeman attending a federal bureau of investigation police school, was shot and killed Sunday night by a fellow student, Policeman Sidney L. Wade, 38, of Oklahoma City. The shooting was declared by another police school student to have been accidental.

### *Thief Takes Coats Of Guests in Home*

While Abraham Goldfein, 1224 Newton avenue north, chatted with guests in his living room Sunday night, a prowler reached through a bedroom window and dragged out a $35 overcoat and a fur coat valued at $400. Jewelry, clothing and a gun valued at a total of $232 were stolen from the home of Clarence Johnstone, 15 Vincent avenue south.

### *Alaskan Waters Searched For Plane Missing With 5*

Juneau, Alaska, Feb. 12.—(AP)—The coast guard cutter Haida sped through squally weather Sunday night toward a spot in Stephens passage, 15 miles south, where a Marine Airways pontoon plane with five aboard was reported forced down on a flight from Ketchikan to Juneau.

Contact with the plane, piloted by Lon Cope, was lost shortly after 2:15 p. m. Pacific time (4:15 p. m. central time), when Cope reported he was fighting a storm off Grand Island in Taku inlet, only a few miles from Juneau. He took off from Ketchikan at 11 a. m.

The coast guard said icing conditions were bad.

Besides Cope, those aboard the plane were John Chappell, insurance agent; E. E. Eck, Earl Clifford and John Chamberlain, all traveling salesmen.

The Canadian Pacific steamer Norah, en route to Juneau from Skagway, interrupted her trip to cruise around the scene where Cope was reported down.

Pilot Sheldon Simmons, bound with passengers from Ketchikan for Juneau, flew over the Stephens passage area, but reported he had not sighted the plane. Later another pilot, Alex Holden, manager of Marine Airways, searched the area on a scheduled trip from Tulsequah, B. C., to Juneau.

Holden landed his passengers at Juneau and took off again to join an ever widening search.

**Adequate Protection Called Nation's Sacred Duty.**

**SHOULD GUARD PEACE HOPES**

**Secretary Asserts All Americans Abroad Must Be Safe.**

*(Day in Washington, page 11.)*

Washington, Feb. 12.—(AP)—Secretary Hull warned the world Sunday night that the American people will reply with "determined defense and resistance" to any challenge to their "most vital and cherished interests."

Speaking in a broadcast, the secretary of state said: "As long as such a possibility (of challenge or attack) exists, it is the sacred duty of a government worthy of the name to maintain adequate defensive forces."

**Peril to Will for Peace.**

"In times like the present," he continued, "when the specter of a new major armed conflict haunts the world, the issue of war and peace becomes an intensely personal one. It touches every one of us. It is ever present in our homes, in our places of work and recreation, in the cities and on the farms."

He added that this nation is sincerely devoted to the cause of peace and believes there are no international differences that cannot be settled peacefully.

"Yet," he declared, "we also know that circumstances may arise in which a nation's will to remain at peace may be thwarted by the actions of others. Peaceful settlement is possible only if both sides are willing to resort to it.

**'Rights' Must Be Defined.**

"This nation's most vital and cherished interests, however, may be challenged and attacked by another nation, and to such a challenge a free people like ours can offer no other reply but determined defense and resistance."

Hull called for the observance of international law as "the primary basis of civilized relations among nations."

"Such a code of international conduct," he explained, "is essential as an indispensable foundation of all international relationships."

**Aid to Citizens Abroad.**

The secretary said that "an American citizen traveling abroad—whether on business, or pleasure, or in pursuit of cultural aims—must have at least a reasonable expectation that he will sustain no deliberate injury and will not be subjected to arbitrary maltreatment by action of governmental authorities of another country."

He mentioned two duties of the government in this connection—first, "to secure a fair definition of the rights of our citizens abroad," and, second, "to maintain the rights of our citizens thus established and to afford our citizens abroad a full measure of appropriate and legitimate protection."

**Foreign Trade Pushed.**

He said the government is devoting an important part of its conduct of foreign relations to removing and reducing barriers to trade.

"In doing this," he said, "it is actuated by the firm belief that to give private enterprise in international commerce a freer and wider scope of activity will not only enhance the economic well-being—and therefore promote social stability within nations—but also will remove some of the most dangerous causes of international friction, and thus strengthen the foundations of world peace."

**CAR REMOVES MAN'S PANTS.**

Temple, Texas, Feb. 12.—(AP)—Frank Mikska stood on a busy downtown street in long-handled underwear and embarrassment after a car whizzed by and ripped off his pants. The driver bought Mikska a new pair.



## NEWS INDEX

# The Minneapolis Morning Tribune

A MINNEAPOLIS INSTITUTION SINCE 1867

Seventy-Third Year. No. 92. 3 Thirty Pages MINNEAPOLIS, MINN., THURSDAY, AUGUST 24, 1939. Three Cents in Minneapolis.




# Russia Signs 10-Year Nazi Treaty; Soviet Won't Help Hitler's Foes; Britain, France Near War Footing

## DIGEST OF EUROPEAN SITUATION

By the Associated Press.

A Europe mobilized on a virtual war-time basis with 10,000,000 men under arms, looked once more last night to Adolf Hitler for the answer to the fateful question: Will there be war?

The outlook was none too reassuring, for Germany and Russia today signed a non-aggression treaty in Moscow which removed any danger of German armies encountering Soviet troops should an invasion of Poland be attempted, and the Fuehrer held firmly to his demands on Poland.

The pact was signed after two conferences among Joseph Stalin, Soviet Commissar of Foreign Affairs Vyacheslaff Molotoff, and German Foreign Minister Joachim von Ribbentrop.

Hitler's demands on Poland were said by a reliable Berlin informant to include:

**1—Unconditional return of Danzig.**

**2—Cession of those sections of Poland which Germany ruled before the World war, an area embracing 17,811 square miles and population of 3,896,010.**

**3—Acceptance of a protectorate for what would be left of Poland similar to that of Bohemia-Moravia.**

These demands were said to have included two alternatives for Poland:

**Either Poland accepts these terms and permits peaceful German occupation, or Poland fights, with the result that Germany will see to it that her eastern neighbor is partitioned once more as she has been three times in the past.**

Britain's pledge to stand by her independence guarantee to Poland was said to have been conveyed to Hitler. "Too late," was in effect Hitler's reply.

This was the picture in other old world capitals:

Great Britain moved grimly toward a war-time footing.

France ordered partial mobilization, bringing her armed forces on duty to approximately 2,000,000 men. The French had declared conclusion of the German-Russian non-aggression pact would make it virtually impossible to avoid war.

King Leopold of Belgium made a dramatic appeal on behalf of seven small powers of northern Europe, urging the major powers to submit their conflicts "to open negotiations."

President Roosevelt cut short his vacation cruise and sped back to Washington where speculation centered on whether he intended to make another peace appeal to Europe.

**The state department advised that Americans contemplating a trip to Europe stay at home and the American embassies in France and Poland suggested that Americans there leave as soon as possible.**

**Britons and Frenchmen crowded trains leaving Germany.**

Fascist Italy to all appearance stood firmly with her ally, Germany.

Italy stretched anti-submarine chains across the harbor at Naples and other important ports.

Britain was sending reinforcements to the Mediterranean fleet to bring it up to full strength.

The Japanese army and navy were reported in Tokyo to have reached "complete agreement" on steps to take in reply to the German-Soviet negotiations.

## ENGLISH FEAR LAST HOPE OF PEACE FADING

### Gloom Grips Officials—Ships on Way to Baltic Ordered to Return.

### Paris Extends Mobilization—Autos Taken to Rush Troops to Posts.

London, Aug. 24.—(AP)—Already moving to place herself on a wartime footing, Great Britain viewed gloomily but grimly the German-Soviet Russian non-aggression pact signed early Thursday in Moscow.

Diplomatic quarters said the pact was a blow to remaining British hopes that the crisis precipitated by Germany's demands on Poland might be solved peacefully by a firm British-French stand.

In, particular, it was said, Article II, apparently preventing either of the signatories from supporting in any way a third power engaged in war with the other, was regarded as carrying unhappy implications for British-French determination to aid Poland if she goes to war over Germany's demands.

**Black Sea Route Blocked.**

There had been some hope that the British-French front might procure a "benevolent neutrality" from Russia with access to supplies and possibly leeway for troop movements from the Black sea. The Russian-German pact, however, it was said, seemed to remove this possibility.

The British foreign office declined to comment immediately on the pact. It was obvious, however, that the reception was a gloomy one.

In France, partial mobilization was ordered, bringing France's empire forces to approximately 2,000,000 men. Autos were also re-

(Continued on Page 2, Column 3)

## TREATY TERMS

*Moscow, Aug. 24.—(AP)—Following is the text of the 10-year non-aggression pact signed early Thursday by envoys of Germany and Russia:*

"The German reich's government and the Union of the Socialist Soviet Republics, moved by a desire to strengthen the state of peace between Germany and the U.S.S.R. and in the spirit of the provisions of the neutrality treaty of April, 1926, between Germany and the U.S.S.R. decided the following:

"ARTICLE ONE—The two contracting parties obligate themselves to refrain from every act of force, every aggressive action and every attack against one another, including any single action or that taken in conjunction with other powers.

"ARTICLE TWO—In case one of the parties of this treaty should become the object of warlike acts by a third power, the other party will in no way support this third power.

"ARTICLE THREE—The governments of the two contracting parties in the future will constantly remain in consultation with one another in order to inform each other regarding questions of common interests.

"ARTICLE FOUR—Neither of the high contracting parties will associate itself with any other grouping of powers which directly or indirectly is aimed at the other party.

"ARTICLE FIVE—In the event of a conflict between the contracting parties concerning any question, the two parties will adjust this difference or conflict exclusively by friendly exchange of opinions or, if necessary, by an arbitration commission.

"ARTICLE SIX—The present treaty will extend for a period of 10 years with the condition that if neither of the contracting parties announces its abrogation within one year of expiration of this period, it will continue in force automatically for another period of five years.

"ARTICLE SEVEN—The present treaty shall be ratified within the shortest possible time. The exchange of satification documents shall take place in Berlin. The treaty becomes effective immediately upon signature.

*"Drawn up in two languages, German and Russian.*
*"Moscow, 23rd of August, 1939.*
*(Signed) "For the German government, Ribbentrop.*
*"In the name of the government of the U.S.S.R., Molotoff."*

## ACCORD JOLTS EUROPE, SHIFTS POWER LINEUP

### Moscow Agrees to Neutrality If Germany and Poland Clash.

### Reich Coup Seen Death Blow to Tri-Power Staff Talks at Moscow.

Moscow, Aug. 24.—(AP)—Germany and Soviet Russia signed a 10-year non-aggression pact in the presence of Joseph Stalin here early Thursday and remade the military and diplomatic picture of Europe.

In two meetings which Stalin attended, the historic agreement was reached behind the huge walls of the Kremlin.

The principal negotiators were V. Molotoff, Soviet premier and commissar for foreign affairs, and Joachim von Ribbentrop, Nazi foreign minister who flew here only Wednesday in Chancellor Adolf Hitler's private airplane.

**See Tri-Power Talks Doomed.**

This amazing Nazi diplomatic stroke apparently killed military staff talks which had been in progress in Moscow among Britain, France and Russia since August 12 and effected a tremendous shift in Europe's balance of power in one of her most critical times since the World war.

To the average Russian, who tries to adjust himself to the swiftly changing diplomatic picture, the pact seemed to mean this in a nutshell:

*Russia will remain neutral in the event of a European war; If Russia goes to war with Japan, she is promised the tremendous boon of a peaceful western frontier.*

The news was announced in Berlin long before it was in Moscow. Russians, who learned only Wednesday night through a broadcast that Von Ribbentrop had arrived at 1 p. m. Wednesday, read a Tass communique in Thursday morning papers that their country was now pledged not to fight the nation they had been taught to hate.

**Blow to France, Britain.**

Diplomatic circles were convinced that Article IV of the agreement, which pledges either party not to associate itself with any group of powers "which directly or indirectly is aimed at the other party" served a death warrant on the military talks with Britain and France.

The pact did not include the usual escape clause providing for its denunciation in case one of the contracting parties attacked a third power. This provision has been written into most non-aggression agreements signed in the past by Moscow.

Russian official quarters, however, have insisted throughout that a defensive alliance with Britain and France was not incompatible with a non-aggression pact with Germany.

Von Ribbentrop, it was believed, would take off Thursday to make a report to Chancellor Hitler, completing one of the speediest diplomatic flights in world history.

The communique issued here by the official Tass news agency was identical with the one circulated in Berlin.

## 5 MORE JAILED IN WPA STRIKE

### Round-up of Defendants Proceeds Slowly—28 of 103 Now Booked.

The slow round-up of WPA strike defendants continued late yesterday with five more arrests by deputy United States marshals.

The five are:

Simon Barach, 30, of 2605 Fremont avenue south. Barach, held in $5,000 bond, is charged with intimidation of workers on adult education project at 245 Ninth avenue north, July 14.

William F. Greenwald, 33, of 241 Ninth avenue south, Hopkins. He is held in $2,500 bond, charged with depriving WPA of services of worker July 11, at the Hopkins water mains project.

Ralph Block, 25, of 705 Eighth avenue south, Hopkins. Held in $2,500 bond, facing the same charge as Greenwald. Block was taken off WPA bridge project at Deephaven.

Leo Block, 54, of 645 Eighth avenue south, Hopkins, father of Ralph. He is held in $2,500 bond, facing similar charge on Hopkins water mains project.

Leo Lahti, 29, Hopkins, route 2. Held in $2,500 bond, facing similar charge on Hopkins water mains project July 11.

**Arrests Total 28.**

The five arrests brought the number of defendants rounded up to 28. It was Monday that the marshals started the job of rounding up the 103 defendants named in indictments returned by the federal grand jury investigating the WPA strike.

In addition to the 75 warrants still to serve, the marshals yesterday were given the extra task of serving between 50 and 90 subpenas on persons wanted as witnesses to appear before the grand jury when it resumes its work Monday.

The inflow of WPA strike pris-

(Continued on Page 4, Column 4.)

## WEATHER

**Official Weather Forecast.**

Generally fair Thursday and Friday; warmer Thursday and in east portion Friday; cooler in northwest and extreme west portions Friday. 24 hour high, 89 at 3 p. m., low 55 at 5 a. m.

Details on page 18.

## Hitler Warns Demands On Poland Must Be Met

### NEWS INDEX

**THE CRISIS IN EUROPE.**



*IRELAND'S most widely known industry, the sweepstakes, undergoes the scrutiny of an American observer. Thomas Henry, widely known Washington writer, stopped in Dublin and has written a series on the giant lottery. The first appears today on page 15.*

### Partition Threat Seen in the Wording of Russ Pact.

Berlin, Aug. 24.—(AP)—Nazi Germany and Communist Russia, longtime ideological enemies, entered early Thursday upon a 10-year non-aggression pact which smashed what hopes Britain and France may have held to align the Soviet in their bloc.

Hitler also was believed to have told Britain's Prime Minister Neville Chamberlain in detailed memorandum that if Poland resisted Nazi claims and decided to fight it would mean the partition of Poland. In the event of a peaceful settlement, however, Germany would consent to a setup which would put the Polish nation under a German protectorate.

A day of conferences in Moscow in which Joseph Stalin took part, sufficed to reach an understanding which the government said was motivated by a "desire to strengthen the state of peace" between them.

**Burying the Hatchet.**

The agreement, which was even more far reaching than many observers had expected, was signed by Joachim von Ribbentrop, German foreign minister, and Vyacheslaff Molotoff, Soviet foreign commissar, at the Kremlin in the presence of Stalin.

Von Ribbentrop reported the conclusion of the treaty to fuehrer Hitler at Berchtesgaden at once, and made arrangements to leave Moscow Thursday afternoon for the fuehrer's mountain retreat in order to make a personal report.

The understanding in its broadest sense, was felt in political circles here to mean a definite "burying of the hatchet" as far as Nazi diatribes against Communistic Russia are concerned.

**Rules Out New Pact.**

Article four, foreign observers immediately point out, ruled out the possibility of Moscow still joining the London-Paris front by stating that neither Germany nor Russia will associate itself with any other grouping of powers which directly or indirectly is aimed at the other party.

Informed persons considered article three providing for "consultation regarding questions of

(Continued on Page 2, Column 2)

## War Fears Cut Roosevelt Trip

Washington, Aug. 23.—(AP)—President Roosevelt hurried home from a suddenly-curtailed vacation cruise Wednesday while Washington wondered if it was his intention—using his own phrase for it—to "fire another shot for peace" in Europe.

High officials of the state department made arrangements to go into conference with the chief executive immediately upon his return—scheduled for midday Thursday—and also to go over the situation at once with Secretary Hull. The state department chief returned from his vacation Wednesday.

Meanwhile, state and treasury department officers were meeting to discuss America's position in case war actually developed abroad. They were concerned with the grave questions of keeping do-

(Continued on Page 4, Column 5)

## TEN MILLION MEN READY TO FIGHT

—(AP)—WIREPHOTO.

As a new zero hour approched, observers estimated the armies of Europe number nearly 10,000,000 men, excluding naval and air forces. Estimate of French armed strength is based on the mobilization order of Wednesday. War and navy department figures at Washington showed Wednesday Britain leads major world powers in naval strength while Germany has the edge in fighting aircraft. Great Britain has 2,079,863 tons; United States, 1,755,570; France, 815,920; Italy, 717,920, and Germany, 541,023.

The Minneapolis Morning Tribune

A MINNEAPOLIS INSTITUTION SINCE 1867

Seventy-Third Year. No. 100. Thirty-six Pages 3 MINNEAPOLIS, MINN., FRIDAY, SEPTEMBER 1, 1939. • • • Three Cents in Minneapolis.



# HITLER OPENS THE WAR

★ ★ ★ ★ ★ ★ ★ ★ ★ ★ ★ ★

## Commands Army to 'Meet Force With Force'; Gdynia Blockaded, Cities Reported Bombed; Reunion of Danzig With Reich Proclaimed

### German-Polish Trouble Spots

—(P)—WIREPHOTO.

The German official news agency early today reported new border battles between German border police and "Polish insurgents." Seven persons were reported killed in connection with an alleged attack on the German radio station at Gleiwitz in Silesia, while at Pitschen, on the Upper Silesia border, the agency said, three men were killed and many wounded in a skirmish. The agency also reported from Marienwerder that Polish bands had attacked a railway station at Alt Eiche in West Prussia. In addition it was announced that the German navy had blockaded the Polish harbor of Gdynia (shown on map) because "military operations in that region are necessary." Gdynia and Danzig are but a few miles apart.

## NEWS INDEX



### WEATHER

U. S. Weather Bureau Forecast.

Partly cloudy and threatening Friday; slightly warmer Saturday. 24 hour high, 90, at 3 p. m.; low, 64, at 6 a. m. Details on page 24.

## Der Fuehrer's Order To the German Army

Berlin, Sept. 1.—(Friday)—(P)—Adolf Hitler today ordered the German army to meet force with force.

His order of the day to the army read:

"The Polish state has rejected my efforts to establish neighborly relations, and instead has appealed to weapons.

"Germans in Poland are victims of a bloody terror, driven from house and home.

"A series of border violations unbearable for a great power show that the Poles no longer are willing to respect the German border.

"To put an end to these insane incitations, nothing remains but for me to meet force with force from now on.

"The German army will conduct a fight for honor and the right to the life of the resurrected German people with firm determination. I expect that every soldier, mindful of the great traditions of the eternal German military, will do his duty to the last.

"Remember always that you are representatives of the National Socialist Great Germany. Long live our people and our reich!"

## Hitler Aid Proclaims Danzig Part of Reich

Berlin, Sept. 1.—(P)—The German official news agency, DNB, announced Friday that Albert Forster, Nazi chief of state in Danzig, had proclaimed the reunion of the Free City with the reich. Forster notified Adolf Hitler of his action by telegram.

Article one of Forster's decree suspended the constitution of the Free City immediately.

Under the city's League of Nations status its constitution was guaranteed by the league, and changes without its consent were declared illegal.)

Forester's telegram to Hitler read:

"My Fuehrer, I have just signed and then put into effect the following basic law, concerning the reunion of Danzig with the German reich."

"The basic state law of the Free State of Danzig and the reunion of Danzig with the German Reich is effective September 2, 1939.

"To lift the immediate distress of the people and state of the free city of Danzig, I decree the following basic state law.

"Article One: The constitution of the Free City of Danzig has been suspended effective immediately.

"Article Two: All legal and administrative power will be executed exclusively by the head of state (forster).

"Article Three: The Free City of Danzig with its territory and its peoples forms a part of the German Reich, effective immedialeley.

"Article Four: Until a final decision regarding the introduction of German Reich's laws by the fuehrer, the entire laws of the constitution remain in force as they apply at the moment.

Signed at Danzig, September 1, 1939, Albert Forster, Gauleiter (district leader.)"

"I beg you, my fuehrer, in the name of Danzig and its population to consent to this basic state law and to carry out the reunion with the German reich through federal law.

"Obediently, my fuehrer, Danzig pledges to you imperishable thankfulness and eternal loyalty. Haial my fuehrer.

Signed, Albert Forster, Gauleiter."

Forster followed the act with a proclamation to Danzigers that "the hour for which you have longed for 20 years has come.

"Effective today, Danzig has returned to the great German reich. Our Fuehrer, Adolf Hit-

"The swastika flag, the flag of the German reich, waves for the first time today on the public buildings in Danzig. It waves, however, also from former Polish buildings and everywhere in the harbor.

"Church bells peal forth and we thank the Lord for our deliberation and also the fuehrer who has given us the opportunity to get rid of the evils of the Versailles treaty.

"Long live a free Danzig, now returned home, and long live our great fatherland."

In a telegram to Forster, Hitler acknowledged the reception of Forster's proclamation and thanked him for "the loyalty of Danzig to Germans.

## Gdynia Is Blockaded By German Warships

The German radio early today announced a blockade of the Polish harbor of Gdynia.

Neutral ships in the Baltic were warned they entered Danzig harbor or nearby harbors at their own peril.

The radio announced immediately an indefinite closing of all schools of Germany.

Rapid fire orders followed commanding masters of German vessels to get out of the Baltic sea and not to enter the Danzig or Polish harbors.

## Polish Cities Bombed Warsaw Report Says

Warsaw, Sept. 1.—(P)—It was reported here today that Krakow, Katowice, Tczew and Czestocohowa were bombed by German airplanes early this morning.

(Tczew is on the Danzig-Polish border. The other cities are a distance of 25 to 50 miles from the Polish-German border.)

There was no official confirmation of the bombing.

Fighting was reported at Danzig.

Warsaw was awakened at 6:28 a. m. (1:28 p. m., Minneapolis time) by alarming sirens as an air raid was awaited here.

## BRITISH GRAVE ON HEARING OF HITLER ORDER

### Stand Pat on Pledge to Poles—Cabinet to Meet Immediately.

### Evacuation of Three Million Started—Trains on Skeleton Schedule.

*(Although the following report was received from London following Hitler's order to his army to meet force with force, it must be remembered that strict censorship has been in effect in Great Britain since Thursday. No dispatche were sent from France after the order.)*

London, Sept. 1.—(P)—(Passed through British Censorship)—Great Britain, standing pat on her pledge to fight for Poland's independence, received the news of Germany's latest moves in the European crisis with the deepest gravity today as the nation moved swiftly toward a full war footing.

An immediate cabinet meeting was expected to survey the implications both of Germany's eleventh-hour 16-point proposal to Poland and Hitler's early morning order to the Germany army on the Polish border to meet force with force.

Government offices, after a night marked by intense activity, were empty of officials authorized to speak when news of Hitler's instructions to the army was received. But this, together with the radio announcement of the German navy's blockade of the Polish port of Gdynia, created a stir among those on duty.

Attention was attracted particularly by the speed with which the army order and harbor blockade followed the German broadcast which said Hitler had proposed to Poland that Danzig be returned to the reich and that a plebiscite be held to decide whether the Polish corridor should be Polish or German territory.

**Evacuation Started.**

Meanwhile, with the British fleet mobilizing swiftly under the order issued yesterday and the entire army reserve called up, Britain began the evacuation of 3,000,000 women, children and infirm from the danger areas.

Suburban trains ran on skeleton schedules so that the rolling stock would be available to handle the exodus from London. Many of the London underground stations were closed except to those being evacuated.

It was insisted upon that these proposals had been communicated to Poland for the first time last night—presumably by the medium of the German radio.

Because the German radio broadcast was followed by official German reports of a Polish raid on a German radio station at Gleiwitz in which seven persons were said to have been killed, and other border clashes, authoritative British sources expressed concern.

Britain's emergency measures in addition to mobilization and the evacuation order included placing an unexpected censorship on all communications to and from the British Isles, establishing censors at cable offices and telephone exchanges.

**No Solution Sighted**

Furthermore, "all telephone service with countries abroad and ships at sea" was suspended.

The government also announced restrictions on purchases of food and upon flights of civil aircraft.

These moves, coming quickly after the government had dispatch-

(Continued on Page 2, Column 3)

## *Artillery Fire Heard; Attacks On Nazis Cited*

### *England and France Under Censorship---Neutrals Are Warned Poland Is Military Zone.*

By ASSOCIATED PRESS.

Adolf Hitler proclaimed to his army today (Friday) his intention of meeting "force with force," and ordered a blockade of the Polish port of Dydnia.

German sources had reported a number of attacks on Germans by Poles.

Shortly afterward, Albert Forster, chief of state of the Free City of Danzig, declared its reunion with Hitler's reich and dispatches from Gleiwitz on the Polish Silesian border reported the sound of artillery fire in the distance.

Adolf Hitler accepted the Free City Danzig into the reich.

Although Hitler's "orders of the day" to his army did not mention a declaration of war, the German radio warned all foreigners in Poland they were in dangerous territory.

Reports reaching Warsaw said Polish cities, including Krakow, Katowice, Tczew and Czestocohowa, had been bombed by German airplanes early this morning, and Warsaw itself was alarmed by air raid sirens.

**Fighting in Danzig Reported.**

Fighting was reported to have broken out at Danzig.

Little information on these developments were obtainable from London and Paris, where a strict censorship had been set up yesterday. The British cabinet was expected to meet this morning to consider last-minute peace proposals that Hitler had announced late yesterday as well as the new order to meet "force with force."

However, both Britain and France had made plain again yesterday that they would stand by Poland.

**Hitler's 16-Point Peace Plan.**

Only last night the fuehrer had announced a 16-point proposal for settlement of his quarrel with Poland. It included immediate return of Danzig to Germany and a plebiscite in Pomorze, the so-called Polish coridor.

The proposals were announced in Berlin a few hours after Great Britain mobilized her navy, called up her entire regular army reserve, brought th eair force to wartime strength and took other urgent steps in preparation for war, including complete censorship of all communications to and from the British Isles.

Hitler's proposals, starting in that they fell far short of his previous adamantly announced demends, were made public under puzzling circumstances.

Whereas the proposals were announced with the comment that Poland already had "rejected" them by failing to rush to Berlin an emissary prepared to conclude an agreement alang the proposed lines, a German spokesman in London hinted the door still was open for negotiations.

To Berlin's proposal that return of Danzig might be a prerequisite to peace, a Polish government spokesman in Warsaw last night was firm in stating such a term was inacceptable.

Poland, he said, is determined to keep Pomorze and her rights in Danzig.

**Modified Former Demands.**

In addition to return of Danzig and the holding of the plebiscite—under direction of an international commission,—Hitler's proposasls provided for an exchange of populations in case the corridor were awarded to Germayn, demilitarization of both Danzig and the neighboring Polish potr of Gdynia and, in event of acceptance of the proposals, immediate demobilization of both Germany and Poland.

Berlin dispacthes characterized the proposals as "sensational" in that they fell far short of Hitler's previous unconditional demand that both Danzig and the corridor must go to Germany, and because the fuehrer proposed submitting part of this problem to international control by Britain, France, Russia and Italy. Previously the fuehrer always has declared Germany never would submit to such control.

As proposals were announced in Berlin it was stated Hitler had proposed on August 29 that a Polish representative go to Berlin by midnight of the 30th. In authoritative circles in Londo nit was said eary today, however, that Poland did not get the proposals until Thursday night.

Adding further to the confusion, a German spokesman in London said early today that "there is no time limit for acceptance of the 16 points, and they are not a demand; they are merely a basis of negotiation and nothing more."

**Reichstag Session Called.**

In Berlin the press was given to understand that Hitler would address the nation and the world today, possibly at a special session of the reichstag, and observers thought further clarification of the situation might be forthcoming then.

Paris felt the nature of the demands and the tone of the German

# 1940~1949

**NO CHANGE**
U. S. Government Forecast
Partly cloudy today and tomorrow; not much change in temperature. 24 hour high 72 at 4:30 p. m.; low 46 at 4 a. m. Details on page 10.

# Minneapolis Morning Tribune

A MINNEAPOLIS INSTITUTION SINCE 1867

**SURPRISE!**
Wendell Willkie's write-in vote in New Jersey's presidential primary has shocked the GOP politicos, opines Editorial Page Commentator Ray Tucker. Page 4.

Seventy-Fourth Year. No. 6. 3 Twenty-two Pages MINNEAPOLIS, MINN., THURSDAY, MAY 30, 1940 Three Cents in Minneapolis



# Allies Battle to Protect Flight; Open Dunkerque Floodgates

## REFUGEE HORDE STREAMS INTO PARIS

Paris, May 29.—(AP—Wirephoto)—Part of the uncounted thousands of refugees of war who have streamed into France, are shown upon their arrival in Paris, from homes in Belgium, Luxembourg or France, which they may never see again.

## Memorial Day Observance to Stress Tragedy of Battle

A prayer that no more men need die to preserve American independence and the liberties of its people will be raised in Minneapolis today as the city renders Memorial day tribute to its war dead. The day's usual stress on the tragedy of war will be deepened by realization the nation must be ready to resist involvement in Europe's carnage.

After conducting ceremonies at the city's cemeteries, dozens of veterans' organizations and other patriotic groups will unite in the annual Memorial day parade and the city-wide program which will follow.

The parade, with Mayor Leach as marshal, will form at 2 p. m. and will start half an hour later as the courthouse chimes play the national anthem. Parade route will be on Third avenue south from Tenth street to Fourth street, Fourth street to Nicollet avenue, Nicollet to Thirteenth street, and on Thirteenth street to Grant street. Mayor Leach will review the parade at Twelfth street and Nicollet avenue.

The city-wide program, generally held in the municipal auditorium, today will be held in Wesley Methodist church, with Franklin Ellsworth as principal speaker. He will be introduced by Governor Stassen.

The Rev. George Mecklenburg will give the invocation and benediction, and participants in the musical program will include Alice Redlund, organist, the South high school band, the Minneapolis American Legion and Auxiliary chorus, and a corps of Boy Scout buglers.

(Continued on Page 11, Column 1)

### PANAMA SUPPRESSES PRE-ELECTION UNREST

Panama, Panama, May 29.—(AP)—Police announced tonight they had occupied the rebellious town of Laguna and suppressed pre-election unrest. United States Canal Zone authorities denied that a bridge over the Tetas river connecting the zone with the Rio Hato army base was destroyed in the disturbances.

### LONDON ARMY PHONE WIRES REPORTED CUT

New York, May 30—(Thursday).—(AP)—A broadcast heard on the wave length of the Berlin radio this morning by NBC said some of the telephone wires in London, leading to the central command, have been cut in spite of all precautions against fifth column activities.

## NEWS INDEX



## N. W. Reserves Expect Chance at Active Duty

### Defense Moves May Draw Scores Into Air Corps and Navy

Defense measures expected to draw scores of men from Minneapolis and the northwest into active duty with the army air corps and the navy were revealed last night.

The Associated Press reported from Washington that 2,000 army air corps reserve officers have been canvassed to find out how many would accept a year's active duty and that volunteers for active sea training will be sought among the naval reserve.

Although the order to solicit volunteers has not been received here as yet, it is likely the opportunity of active sea duty, offered for periods ranging from two weeks to a year, will attract many members of the ninth naval reserve battalion in Minneapolis, Lieutenant Commander M. A. Heffernan said. A navy drive to obtain ground workers for new air bases, he said, has resulted in transfer of 57 members of the unit, indicating eagerness for active duty.

Enrollment in the air corps reserve is relatively light in this area, because of distance from reserve bases, and army reserve authorities here had not been informed of the move to put men on active duty.

## F. R. Will Ask 750 Millions More for Arms

### Chief of Staff Reports Need for New Guns, Other Material

### AVIATION'S PLACE IN PLANS STRESSED

### New Tax Bill Drafted for Introduction in the House Today

Washington, May 29.—(AP)—Military lessons learned from Germany's blitzkrieg led President Roosevelt today to rush preparation of a request that congress add another large sum—probably $750,000,000—to the $1,182,000,000 extraordinary defense fund.

**New Machine Gun Needed**

General George C. Marshall, army chief of staff, was reported to have told a house appropriations subcommittee that $750,000,000 would be necessary to buy more powerful anti-tank guns, a new type of light machine gun, additional mechanized equipment and other weapons.

**For Dive Bombers**

Committee members said that the general testified the advance of German forces already had demonstrated the comparative ineffectiveness of the 37 millimeter anti-tank guns.

Members said the European war also had demonstrated the need for a light machine gun which soldiers could strap on and fire at any angle. One member mentioned a gun capable of firing 400 shots a minute. They said German parachute troops and other units used such guns with deadly effect.

A new anti-aircraft gun to combat dive bombers also is being developed by the army, members said.

Legislators said the supplemental estimates also would include funds for about 1,800 new airplanes, chiefly training and pursuit types.

**Tax Bill Draft Rushed**

The place of aviation in the defense program was emphasized again during the day when Mr. Roosevelt requested immediate appropriation of $1,200,000 to improve the research laboratory of the national advisory committee for aeronautics at Langley Field, Va.

(Continued on Page 11, Column 3)

### CANADA GIVES HAVEN TO DOLLFUSS' WIDOW

Ottawa, Ont., May 29.—(AP)—Frau Englebert Dollfuss, widow of the chancellor of Austria who was slain in an attempted Nazi putsch in 1934, has been granted permission to enter Canada and intends to take refuge here, it was learned tonight. Informed sources said she is "likely to arrive in Canada shortly." She and her son and daughter went to England in July, 1938, after moving to the Balkans after Adolf Hitler took over Austria in March of that year.

## WAR NEWS IN BRIEF

**LONDON**—RAF blasts Germans in effort to keep Dunkerque outlet open; Americans, other foreigners placed under wartime restrictions; British capture Narvik.

**PARIS**—Main Allied body retreats toward channel, French rearguard battles Germans in Lille streets; Dunkerque only remaining sea escape; French wipe out last German-held bridgeheads on Somme.

**BERLIN** — Germans say Lille, Ostend captured; predict annihilation or surrender of half million trapped Allies within two days.

**ROME** — Italy expected to strike in Mediterranean and southward, rather than directly against France.

**MOSCOW** — Russia cold-shoulders Cripps' trade mission; demands negotiations through ambassador.

## TODAY'S WAR MAP

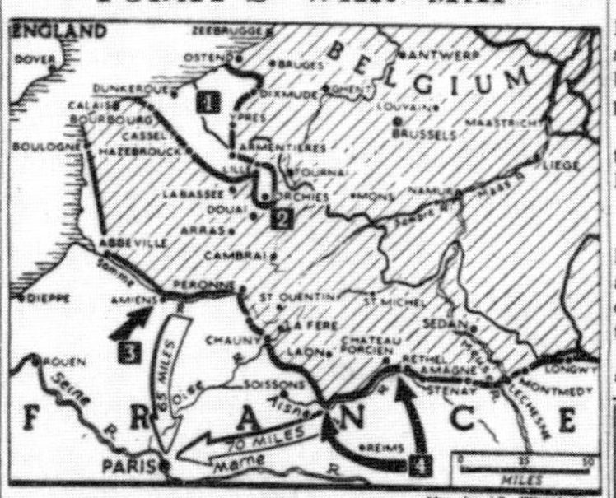


—Map by AP—Wirephoto

With a sharp drive at Lille by the Germans pinching the trapped Allied troops, here is how the Germans said the Western front looked last night. (1) The main bulge of the Flanders pocket was squeezed with the Germans occupying Cassel, Dixmude and Armentieres. Fierce fighting was going on at Ypres. Dunkerque was reported in flames. (2) The tip of the bulge was sheared off trapping French forces within a 12-mile square area below the trapped British. (3) French exerted pressure at Amiens and along the Somme as Germany indicated a swing at Paris (light arrows marking probable routes) before cleaning out the channel ports. (4) Along the Aisne river were two other active fronts where French smashed at the invaders. The shaded area shows the territory in German hands.

## Italo-Soviet Pact to Assure Balkan Status Is Reported

Budapest, May 29.—Italy and the Soviet Union have agreed to guarantee the present situation in the Balkan states, diplomatic quarters in Belgrade understood tonight.

Confirmation is expected soon of reports that Italy is informing all Balkan governments of her peaceful intentions.

For the first time since the Bolshevik revolution of 1917 in Russia, an accredited diplomat of the USSR will visit Belgrade.

The Soviet envoy to Sofia, Bulgaria, M. Lavreniev, will arrive in the Yugoslavian capital Thursday to ratify a Moscow-Belgrade trade treaty. The pact is considered to be the equivalent of Yugoslavian recognition of the Soviet Union.

Meanwhile Italy still teetered on the brink of war.

Many foreign and Italian observers expected her to take the plunge within a few days, but in the Mediterranean and southward rather than directly against France.

In the "event of an act of aggression leading to war in the Mediterranean area," according to the Allied-Turkish treaty of alliance, Turkey, guardian of the Dardanelles, is pledged to enter the war on the side of Britain and France.

### GAMELIN REPORTED DEAD BY OWN HAND

Rome, May 30.—(Thursday)—(AP)—Il Popolo d'Italia's correspondent in Bern, Switzerland, reported today that the French generalissimo, Maurice Gustave Gamelin, is "understood to have killed himself following definite instructions of the French high command." General Corap, who commanded the French ninth army which was overrun in the German breakthrough at Sedan, the correspondent said, had been executed.

## Airfleets and Navies Join Fight to Guard Last Port of Escape

### Germans Bombard Allied Forces in Death Pocket—French Construct New Defense Line on Somme

Paris, May 29.—The Allies gave up as lost, tonight, the Battle of Flanders, and in a great retreat opened the flood sluices around the channel port, Dunkerque, to guard the back door of escape for the last battalions in the "death" pocket.

The bloody conflict in the north was all but over, with the Germans in control of the industrial region of northern France and her northwest coast across from England.

**Rearguard Fight**

It was predicted in Berlin that the 500,000 British and French, crushed into the Flanders' pocket, would be either annihilated or put behind German barbed wire within two days. Germans were reported raining shells and bombs into this sector.

London circles, however, denied a German radio report that Britain and France were conferring on whether to surrender the trapped troops to avert gigantic slaughter. These sources said the troops were putting up a stubborn opposition and would not be a "defeated army" when withdrawn.

But dark as the outlook was in the north, the battle had given the Allies time to build a strong southern front along the Somme and Aisne rivers for 200 miles across France.

The virtual collapse of the Allied cause in Flanders came amid scenes of fire and flood.

Dunkerque, the Germans say, has been burning for three days.

While the waters rose steadily in the vast system of streams around Dunkerque, French divisions fought across the tortured landscape to hold the rear while British troops defended the main points of passage for the main forces seeking the coastline.

The Allies brought on the inundation by opening the locks southwest and northwest of Dunkerque, on the great canal that flows by the city and follows the coast for many miles.

**Admiral Rallies Fight**

In Dunkerque, the last Allied resistance was rallied under Vice Admiral Jean Marie Abrial, 61-year-old commander of the port. The Allied armies, navies and air forces fought together in an effort to save as much as possible from the wreckage of Flanders.

The retreat was harassed by heavy German fire. Some Belgian units, refusing to lay down their arms despite their king's order to capitulate, were reported still fighting beside the British and French.

An single French division tried to hold back the Nazi rush in the Nieuport-Dixmude sector, a World war battlefield on the coast northeast of Dunkerque.

Suicide squads also held out on the eastern and southern sides of the Allied path to the sea. Some Allied units had to fight through German columns.

In the main part of the Allied triangle, pushed against the channel and blazing Dunkerque, are the men of the British expeditionary force which rushed in 19 days ago to resist the invasion of Belgium.

In the broken-off tip of the triangle; south of Lille, stand the Frenchmen who tried to break out of the German trap toward the south, at Valenciennes. Separated from the British, they are reported penned in a segment of 12 square miles. With them are thousands of hapless, homeless refugees.

The German advance sheared off this triangle tip today. Forces fighting from the northeast and southwest met at Lille, taking that city of French industry. The trapped French are below them.

On the sides of the triangle the Germans engulfed the Belgian channel port of Ostend, passed Bruges and reached Dixmude; occupied Langemarck; raised the swastika over Armentieres, near Lille; broke up a fortified French border position near Cassel through a rearguard attack, and stormed Ypres and Kemmel, of tragic World war memory.

The rest of the battlefield was a maelstrom of free-for-all fighting, lighted up by blazing fires.

(Continued on Page 14, Column 1)

### Germany to 'Finish Up' France 'Forever', Berlin Radio Warns

New York, May 30.—(AP)—A broadcast in German on the wave-length of the Berlin radio and picked up here today proclaimed that "Now the German people has started to finish up forever this eternal disturber of its peace"—France. It said "again and again the fuehrer offered the outstretched hand to France" but the latter "has again and again sabotaged this German will for peace." Then it warned:

"Germany's patience is now at an end and France will have to feel the punishment until she has lost all desire for further assaults on Germany."

Germany's press has been taking such a bitter turn toward France in recent days that it is guessed widely that the end of fighting on the northern front will be followed by a giant drive on Paris.

This would take the place of the long-expected assault on the British Isles, for the time being.

### Canadian Fascist Leader Is Sought

Montreal, May 30—(Thursday).—(AP)—The Royal Canadian Mounted police, acting under defense regulations, moved early today to serve warrants for the arrest of Adrien Arcand, head of the national unity party, and seven of his associates. Three members of the Fascist organization had been taken into custody. Arcand was reported in the Laurentian mountains.

### Narvik Nazis Fight Rear-Guard Action

Stockholm, May 30.—(Thursday)—(AP)—German troops today were reported fighting a rear-guard action after withdrawal from the Norwegian ore port of Narvik, but in danger of being trapped by Norwegian forces deployed along the Swedish frontier to bar the Nazis escape into Sweden.

### WINDSORS ARRIVE AT RIVIERA ESTATE

Nice, France, May 29.—(AP)—The Duke and Duchess of Windsor, traveling incognito, have arrived at their La Croe estate on the Riviera. They will stay for an indefinite period.

LETTER TO ROBERT F. PACK RELATES:

## Dutch Battled German Parachute Troops And Spies in Bombed Ruins of Rotterdam

*The lightning thrust of German warfare as it came to Holland—air raid, disguised parachute troops, and mechanized infantry fast advancing on an unbelieving populace—is vividly described in this letter written by Carl Schurmann, a Dutch attorney practicing in Rotterdam and living at The Hague, to his father-in-law, Robert F. Pack, president of the Northern States Power Co. The letter was written May 16 from London, where his Minneapolis wife had gone ahead of him.*

By Carl Schurmann

Having arrived safely in London, I feel that you would like to know something about my experiences during the invasion.

I think you know Anita Bik (an American woman.) She came over to Holland to visit her sister-in-law, Corrie Mollerus, in Eindhoven, on Tuesday, May 7. Corrie met her at the airport of Schiphol and they drove down to Eindhoven together. When they arrived there, they were told that all women and children had to leave at once, so the same evening they came on the train to The Hague, and Anita, having nowhere to go, came to stay with me.

Wednesday and Thursday passed very peacefully, and we were told by our government that there was no reason to be scared nor to expect any attack. On Thursday night Anita and I went to a cinema, and at the time we went to bed we had not the slightest suspicion of what was going to happen to us.

At 4 a. m. Friday, May 10, I was awakened by a terrific noise. I rushed to the window, and in the half-dawn, I saw swarms of ariplanes in the sky, circling and making sudden swoops down till they nearly hit the roofs. Our anti-aircraft guns were going full tilt, and everywhere I saw tracer bullets, clouds of smoke and bursting shells. Two airplanes came down in flames. All around people were standing at the windows and on the roof-tops watching the spectacle. I got Anita and our maid to get up, dress and sit on the ground floor of our house, and telephoned to the chief air raid warden of our district to ask for my orders (being an air raid warden myself.)

He had no instructions as yet, so I went out into the street and tried to persuade the people to go indoors, but most of them remained standing around, waiting to see what was going on. There was not the slightest sign of fright or even nervousness anywhere, and as the morning wore on the tradesmen came to the doors as usual.

I took Anita over to the Witte Brug hotel, where Corrie was staying, and where they have a big air raid shelter in the cellar. Then I went to see my mother, who was in a nursing home. She was quite calm and even refused to be moved down into the cellar, saying she would rather be killed by a bomb outright than be buried in a cellar and have the house come down on top of her.

(Continued on Page 14, Column 2)

# Minneapolis Morning Tribune

A MINNEAPOLIS INSTITUTION SINCE 1867

Seventy-Fourth Year. No. 57. Eighteen Pages 3 MINNEAPOLIS, MINN., SATURDAY, JULY 20, 1940 Three Cents in Minneapolis




MINNEAPOLIS AQUATENNIAL

MINNEAPOLIS AQUATENNIAL

# Britain Scorns Hitler Peace

## City's 9-Day Aquatennial Opens Today

### Vacationers Pour Into City for N. W.'s Greatest Attraction

### PARADE HEADLINES 40 MAJOR EVENTS

### Prevue Held Last Night of Illumined Lagoon of Fountains

With vacationers thronging into the city, Minneapolis today will open its nine-day Aquatennial, the greatest summer festival ever seen in this city of lakes or in the entire northwest.

Its feature attractions have commanded nation-wide attention, and one of these—today's huge five-mile parade that will tour the loop starting at 4:30 p. m.—will headline the Aquatennial's opening bid for the plaudits of spectators.

**Canoe Race Ends at Noon**

A prevue of the coming spectacles and pageantry was given citizens last night when the brilliantly lighted Lagoon of Fountains, stretching for half a mile along the north shore of Lake Calhoun was turned on, with water gushing from 490 fountain heads around the master fountain-pylon 26 feet high. At 8 p. m. today colored lights again will play on the fountains.

The Aquatennial will present 40 major attractions in 187 individual programs during its nine-day run, combining entertainment and sports events of every variety.

Leading into today's events will be a 7 a. m. flag-raising ceremony at three 40-foot flagpoles at the Lagoon of Fountains, with the North Side American Legion post in charge.

The 450-mile Paul Bunyan canoe derby, from Bemidji to Minneapolis, was scheduled to end this noon at the Franklin avenue bridge.

**Plenty of Music**

Today's parade, containing 50 bands and drum corps, novelty marching delegations and 86 decorated floats, will require 40 city blocks for the assembly of marchers.

Its point of entry will be Tenth street and Third avenue south, with marchers passing down Third avenue to Third street, across to Nicollet, up Nicollet avenue to Thirteenth street, and then to Grant street and across to Clinton avenue. Reserved seats accommodating 15,000 persons have been sold along the line of march.

(Continued on Page 9, Column 5)

## TODAY'S PROGRAM

9:30 a. m.—Semi-finals of Women's State Golf tournament, Mipikahda club.
10:00 a. m.—Hennies Brothers' show, Dunwoody Athletic field.
10:30 a. m.—Girls' State Diamondball tournament, Parade grounds.
11:00 a. m.—Aquatennial Hole-in-one tournament, Parade grounds.
12:30 p. m.—Finish of Paul Bunyan Canoe derby, Franklin avenue bridge.
1:00 p. m.—Tribune-Park Board Pushmobile contest, from Minneapolis Art institute.
2:00 p. m.—Girls' State Diamondball tournament, Parade grounds.
2:00 p. m.—Aquatennial Rodeo, featuring Gene Autry, Parade grounds.
2:00 p. m.—Table Tennis championships (women's singles), armory.
3:00 p. m.—Baseball, Minneapolis Millers vs. Louisville, Nicollet park.
3:00 p. m.—Table Tennis championships (men's singles), armory.
4:30 p. m.—Gigantic Aquatennial Opening parade, Loop district.
7:00 p. m.—Hennies Brothers' shows, Dunwoody Athletic field.
7:30 p. m.—"Stars and Moon by Telescope," Powderhorn park.
8:00 p. m.—Table Tennis championships (men's singles, third round and quarter-finals), armory.
8:00 p. m.—Aquatennial Rodeo, featuring Gene Autry, Parade grounds.
8:30 p. m.—Table Tennis championships (men's consolation singles), armory.
Times-Tribune Match Play Bowling championships (all day, evening), all bowling alleys.
9:30 p. m.—Aquatennial "New Year's" Dance, municipal auditorium.

## Canoe Derbyists Ready For Final Dash Today

Racers in the Minneapolis Aquatennial canoe derby will "bear down" for the final day's sprint that is expected to determine winners of the $1,100 in prizes sometime between noon and 1 p. m. today.

They are due to reach the finish line o fthe 450-mile derby at that time under the Franklin avenue bridge.

Competing teams are to leave Anoka—last night's stopping point—about 8 a. m. today.

Although Jesse Goodin and LeRoy Goodin of Minneapolis of team No. 4 made the best time yesterday in the 71-mile stretch from St. Cloud to Anoka, the race leaders remained in the same positions as previously.

Ace and Ed Eliasen, the Hovland team, stayed in first place in elapsed time, however, making the course in 8:55:04 for a total elapsed time of 55:36:35 since the race started. In second place were Bud and Harry Tibbetts of Ball Club, with an elapsed time of 56:00:15.

In third place were Art and Henry Eliasen, brothers of the leaders, with an elapsed time of 56:20:41; in fourth place were Richard and Einar Mattson of Minneapolis, with 56:44:25, and in fifth, Little Wolf and John Wilson of Bemidji, with elapsed time of 57:45:25.

Its trim outlines sharply etched against the night sky by floodlights, this figure of a girl swimmer stood ready last night to set the theme for the Minneapolis Aquatennial, which opens today. The figure is the dominant one of a series set up in the Lagoon of Fountains on the north shore of Lake Calhoun, each one symbolizing a different phase of the recreational opportunities offered in Minneapolis and Minnesota. Fountain sprays will play at the feet of each of the figures in the flag-draped avenue of statuary, which occupies the boulevard strip in the center of the street from East Calhoun boulevard to Calhoun baths. Drive out and see this scenic display.

## 150 Warplanes Clash in 2 Big Coast Battles

### British Reply to Nazis With Bombs, Damage Krupp Works

### CLAIM 11 GERMAN CRAFT SHOT DOWN

### Britons Scoff at Threat to Destroy Empire—Oppose Parley

London, July 20.—(AP)—(Saturday)—Adolf Hitler's "final appeal" for peace with himself as victor drew scornful silence from official Britain today while the press quoted President Roosevelt of the United States in warning against "a false lullaby of appeasement."

The German dictator gave point to his threats last night of total destruction of the British empire by launching one of the widest and heaviest air raids Britain ever has experienced.

**150 Planes in Air Battles**

More than 150 German and British planes fought two bitter air battles over the English channel yesterday in which at least 11 Nazi craft were shot down. Britain listed five of its planes as missing. (Reports in Berlin said 15 British craft had been shot down in the battles.)

The first big battle took place about noon when 70 German raiders attempted to bomb a convoy. In the second battle, in the afternoon, 50 German bombers and fighters attempted to raid a south coast harbor but were driven off. Shore batteries joined in the battling.

**Germans Strike Again**

The Germans came back again today, striking at southeast and southwest Scotland and southwest England. One more German was reported downed in flames.

Britain's reply to Hitler obviously was in the easily-understood language of bomb blast and gunfire.

The royal air force ranged far over Germany and German-subjugated lands to bomb factories and military storage places, including the Krupp plant at Essen, and the royal navy sent to the bottom of the Mediterranean the Italian cruiser Bartolomeo Colleoni, a 40-knot warship rated as one of the world's fastest.

**Scorn Hitler's Offer**

Britons, both of high and low degree, took the attitude that Hitler's latest peace overture had been answered in advance five days ago by Prime Minister Winston Churchill's declaration:

"Be the ordeal sharp or long, or both, we shall seek no terms; we shall tolerate no parley."

The general opinion was that the only surprising thing about it was the lack of anything concrete or even novel.

Of Hitler's threat to destroy the British empire, the ordinary Briton scoffed: "Let him try it."

At the same time the British navy was confronted with the threat of a fresh German sea raider "at large in the Atlantic" when it was announced that two British merchant ships had been sunk near the West Indies.

**Ireland Calls Men**

The Irish government, fearful that she may be in the path of Hitler's projected attack, advertised for "at least 400,000" volunteers for her armed forces which at present number only about 190,000.

(Berlin reported that 15 British pursuit ships and two captive balloons were shot down without a single German loss.) The battles were hailed as proof of the effectiveness of German raids against England. The German high command awaited only Hitler's order to launch the long-awaited blitzkrieg against England. The high command reported successful bombing of airports, docks, piers and troop camps in England as well as ships off the coast of north Scotland and minimized effectiveness of British aerial counter-blows.)

### RAIN STILLS VOICES OF LOGAN SINGERS

Logan park singers were rained out last night as they attempted to hold a third round sing in The Minneapolis Tribune Newspapers-park board community sing contest. The next sing will be tomorrow night at Van Cleve park.

## University Will Be Key Unit in Defense Program

The University of Minnesota emerged last night as one of the nation's key institutions in preparing for national defense, with its staff already participating in the program on half a dozen broad research and defense-training fronts, and martialing facilities to participate on many more.

**Committee Set Up**

President Guy Stanton Ford outlined the role the university is playing in an informal report to the board of regents, commenting that as he served with the committee on public information in Washington during the last war, he has used that experience to try to foresee some of the duties the university will be called on to assume.

Co-ordinating the institution's defense steps, he said, is an all-university committee headed by Dean Harold S. Diehl of the medical school and including Dean Malcolm Willey, assistant to the president; Dean W. C. Coffey of the department of agriculture; and Professors C. A. Koepke, mechanical engineering and T. R. McConnell, associate dean of the arts college and director of the university's committee on educational research. Dean Willey is acting head of the committee in absence of Dean Diehl, who is now on vacation.

**Outline of Work**

All requests for information or aid from public agencies or private sources go to this committee.

Meanwhile, Dr. Ford said, the university is pushing work along these lines:

First—Organizing Base hospital 26, comprising about 40 medical officers.

Second—Training men in the naval ROTC.

Third—Taking part in the CAA flight training program.

Fourth — Pushing two medical school research projects. One headed by Dr. Owen H. Wangensteen,

(Continued on Page 2, Column 4)

## NEWS INDEX



### CLOUDY

U. S. Government Forecast

**Partly cloudy with scattered thundershowers Saturday and Sunday. Not quite so warm in south portion. 24 hour high, 100, at 5 p. m., low, 80, at 6 a. m. Additional details on page 14.**

## Hope of Relief Slight as Heat Wave Spreads

### Northwest Swelters for Second Day—Mercury Hits 109 at Morris

With little hope for relief from a soaring mercury that climbed toward the 100-degree mark in many sections, the northwest sweltered again yesterday under a heat wave.

In Minneapolis the mercury reached 100 degrees at 4:30 p. m. at the airport weather bureau, and the excessive temperatures created "hot spots" in numerous other northwest localities.

Evening showers brought slight temporary relief.

The mercury hit 100 at Sioux City, Iowa; 98 at Sioux Falls, S. D.; 97 at Willmar and Rochester, Minn., and 97 at Frontenac, Wis.

**109 Recorded at Morris**

Morris, Minn., was one of the record hot spots in the midwest Thursday when a temperature of 109 degrees was recorded. The heat wave again yesterday was generally prevalent throughout the midwestern states.

Eau Claire, Wis., with 101, had its hottest day in three years. At New Ulm, Minn., where the temperature dropped to 98 from yesterday's 106, a farm worker, Raymond Orton, was overcome. It was 96 at Pierre, S. D., where temperatures of 106 and 107 were recorded the two previous days, but a humidity rise offset the drop in temperature.

**Tornado in S. D.**

A small tornado near Thomas, S. D., yesterday morning destroyed barns and several small buildings on three farms. No one was injured.

While the heat was the subject of concern among city dwellers, a July rainfall of 2.48 inches brought cheer to farmers in the Wadena area who are assured of good crops. Harvest of rye and barley will start this week. Corn and potatoes are in good shape, and unless an exceptionally bad dry spell hits the area should produce well.

(Continued on Page 2, Column 3)

## Smashup Ends Bandits' Flight; Two Captured

An 85-mile-an-hour chase into Minneapolis during which several shots were fired ended last night with the arrest of two men, 25 and 27, shortly after they held up the Hamline pharmacy at 719 Hamline avenue north, St. Paul.

The bandits, both armed, forced George Paul, proprietor, to hand over $12, then leaped into an automobile at the curb. As the bandits fled, Paul fired a shot at them. A woman motorist jotted down the bandit car license number which was broadcast to police.

The car was sighted at the Lake street bridge by Patrolman Harold Wifall and William Gunderson, St. Paul police. They chased the car 15 blocks, firing several shots. At Thirty-second avenue south the car started to turn off Lake street, struck a pole and went up an embankment.

Patrolmen Leslie Mathews and Walter Helin of Minneapolis captured one of the men as he ran up an alley. The second man was caught by the St. Paul policemen. Both admitted the holdup.

The license plates on the car were stolen May 13 from the car

## Japs in Shanghai Beat U. S. Writer

Shanghai, July 20—(Saturday)—(AP)—Hallet Abend, correspondent for the New York Times, was assaulted in his apartment last night by two Japanese who seized pieces of manuscript after demanding "all his anti-Japanese writings."

### $5 a Snapshot!

The Morning Tribune will pay $5 each for amateur snapshots of Aquatennial events or activities published in the newspaper. Submit your snapshots within 12 hours after they were taken, prints not larger than 8 by 10. Snapshots must be unusual, newsworthy, timely and original.

## Willkie Cause Claims Band Of Democrats

### Former National Chairman and Minneapolis Man Among Converts

Denver, Col., July 19.—(INS)—New converts tonight hit Wendell Willkie's "sawdust trail" as the Republican presidential nominee ended a day of stock yard and beet field inspection, and conferences with stock breeders and sugar growers.

**Wilson Aid Joins**

Converts included Stephen F. Chadwick of Seattle, Wash., former national commander of the American Legion; Irvin S. Cobb, humorist - philosopher, Kirby L. Vedrine, Arizona alternate delegate to the Democratic national convention, and Vance C. McCormick of Pennsylvania, who was national Democratic chairman in President Wilson's second campaign. Lawrence E. Nelson, Utah gubernatorial candidate because he "could not in good conscience run on a ticket" headed by a third term seeker.

**Roland Hill Takes Stand**

Roland Hill, director of the national emergency council in Minnesota in 1936, submitted his resignation as an auditor in the general accounting office at Washington and announced he would campaign for Willkie.

Hill, whose home is in Minneapolis, was president of the junior new dealers' club in Washington in 1935.

"I have been identified with the new deal since it began but I am quitting because I object to breaking a third term precedent and because I do not like the selection of Secretary Wallace as the vice presidential nominee," he said.

In Washington, Senator Arthur Vandenberg in another move toward Republican party unity, announced he would do all he could to help boost his erstwhile rival, Willkie, into the presidency.

The Michigan senator branded the just - concluded Democratic conclave a "totalitarian convention."

CLOUDY
U. S. Weather Bureau Forecast
Partly cloudy Wednesday and Thursday; warmer in northwest Wednesday; thundershowers in southwest. 24 hour high, 87 at 5 p. m.; low, 63 at 6 a. m.
Additional details on page 10.

# Minneapolis Morning Tribune

FOUNDED IN 1867
A HOME-OWNED AND HOME-MANAGED NEWSPAPER

PATRON SAINT
Damon Runyon pays tribute to Stephen Foster, patron saint of "Tin Pan Alley" and has a word to say about present-day leaders in the song-writing profession. On the back page.

Seventy-Fourth Year. No. 103. Twenty-two Pages MINNEAPOLIS, MINN., WEDNESDAY, SEPTEMBER 4, 1940 Three Cents in Minneapolis



## U. S. NAVY RUSHES

# WARSHIPS TO BRITAIN

## Filling Lundeen Post Hinges on A Single Word

### Legal Interpretation of 'Temporary' Will Be Deciding Factor

### HIGH COURT MAY DECIDE QUESTION

### Two Courses Open—Appointing Successor or Holding Election

By ORLIN FOLWICK
Morning Tribune Staff Writer

On the legal interpretation of one word in the federal Constitution will depend whether Governor Stassen appoints a successor to Senator Ernest Lundeen or the vacancy caused by the senator's death goes into a special election.

The word in question is "temporary." It appears in the seventeenth amendment dealing with popular election of United States senators and is a modifier for the word "appointment" relating to the filling of vacancies in the senate.

**Subject of Much Debate**

It was the subject of much debate last night as aspirants gathered in St. Paul or sent delegations to represent them should the governor decide to act after Senator Lundeen's funeral today. There were two distinct versions of the meaning of "temporary appointment" and indications were that solution of the question might find its way into the United States supreme court.

While most Republicans felt the governor should make the appointment, Farmer-Laborites discussed the possibility of going into court to compel the governor to call a spe-

(Continued on Page 14, Column 5)

### Lundeen Honorary Pall Bearers Will Meet Before Rites

Members of Senator Lundeen's family last night requested that all honorary pall bearers at the funeral in the state capitol today meet at 2:30 p. m. in the house chamber.

## SENATOR COMES HOME

—Staff photo

The body of Senator Ernest Lundeen, who died Saturday, with 24 others, in an airplane crash, was brought back to Minneapolis last night. Here the casket is being carried up the steps from the train at the Great Northern station.

## Cortege Through City Honors Sen. Lundeen

To the sound of muffled drums, the body of Senator Ernest Lundeen was borne through the streets of Minneapolis and St. Paul last night as state and nation prepared to pay last respects to the legislator, killed Saturday in an airplane crash.

Taken from a train at the Great Northern station, the sealed casket bearing the body was taken to the state capitol over a route that led on Nicollet avenue to Tenth street, on Tenth street to Third avenue south, and on Third avenue south to University avenue southeast.

Hundreds of the senator's constituents in the two cities where many of his sharpest political battles were fought lined the streets as the cortege passed, headed by a color guard of veterans bearing national standards and flags of the Veterans of Foreign Wars and the United Spanish War Veterans.

The body will lie in state in the capitol until 3 p. m. today, when

(Continued on Page 14, Column 8)

## Attempt to Kill Carol Fails as Coup Is Nipped

### Shots Fired Through Palace Window in Alleged Iron Guard Plot

### YIELDING TO AXIS RESULTS IN CRISIS

### Disorders in Transylvania Area Ceded to Hungary Continue

Bucharest, Sept. 4.—(Wednesday)—(AP)—Gunmen attempted in vain to assassinate King Carol last night in an alleged Iron Guardist plot to seize power and place Prince Mihai on the throne.

While the would-be assassins broke through the palace guard and fired seven shots at a lighted window in Carol's palace, other groups of Iron Guardists attacked the Bucharest radio station and the American-owned telephone company's central office.

Many shots were fired in the palace grounds before the attackers were overcome and hustled away by soldiers in the car in which they had arrived at the palace.

Several men entered the telephone exchange and wrecked some of the switchboards with hatchets. Most local lines were put out of order. The radio station went off the air after a group of men in uniform burst in and tried to destroy the equipment. All were arrested.

(Continued on Page 14, Column 4)

## 25 Arkansas Fugitives Still Free; 4 Dead

### Swamp Area Encircled in Attempt to Save Three Hostages

Columbia, La., Sept. 3.—(AP)—The death toll in Arkansas' sensational Labor day prison farm break stood at four tonight and three high school students were held hostage as armed citizens and peace officers sought other members of the desperate band.

Officers threw a cordon around a 25-mile square swamp area northeast of here tonight—certain they were near capture of five of the convicts who were holding the high school students.

State Police Superintendent Steve Alford said he believed the desperadoes would make a break for freedom during the night or just before daybreak.

**Ringleader Shot Down**

Nine of the 36 convicts who shot their way to freedom yesterday from the Cummins prison farm in Arkansas were recaptured during the night-and-day-long search through two states.

Frank Conley, 34 one of the ringleaders in the massed escape, was shot down by posse bullets on the levee of the Ouachita river here at noon today, only 50 yards from the spot where Frank Gartman, a posseman, was killed last midnight.

The fleeing convicts killed a guard in their break for freedom. The body of an unidentified convict was washed ashore in the Arkansas river near the prison farm today.

**State Police Join Hunt**

One hundred state police were sent here to join nearly 1,000 armed citizens and peace officers who believed they had surrounded Conley's five associates in their frantic efforts to rescue the children.

Two girls and a boy, all about 16, were seized near Rayville, La., last night when the six convicts, fleeing into a forest marsh near here, took their automobile. Using the youngsters as a shield, the convicts escaped one trap last night, fleeing deeper into the swamp, a well-known hideout for desperadoes.

Two of the desperadoes were taken in a gun battle near Texarkana, far from the prison farm, six others were caught without bloodshed, and one was found shot and wounded in a Negro cabin in Arkansas. Twenty-five still were at large, most of them believed hiding near the prison farm.

## British Rejoice Over Transfer Of Destroyers

### Come at Time When Strain on Fleet Is Great, Minister Says

### ENGLAND ADMITS NEED OF VESSELS

### Will Use Warships for Convoys and to Deal With Submarines

London, Sept. 3.—(AP)—The British rejoiced tonight wherever they gathered, from Cheapside pubs to the austere and misty corridors of the foreign office, over the news that 50 over-age U. S. destroyers will fill the gaps of the royal navy in the total German siege of these islands.

First Lord of the Admiralty A. V. Alexander in a statement greeted "with the utmost pleasure and satisfaction" the transfer of destroyers. He added: "They come at a time when the strain upon our destroyer fleet has been very great and will be of inestimable value to us not only for escorting convoys but also for protecting our coasts from the threat of invasion."

**Man in the Street Jubilant**

On the street the little man read President Roosevelt's message, and, despite its assurance that the deal does not in any way affect the United States' status of peace, his usual reaction was something like this:

"It looks like we've got someone with us at last, eh, mate?"

Prime Minister Winston Churchill, who will describe the agreement to the house of commons on Thursday, went tonight to see the king and, undoubtedly, to discuss the arrangements in the light of their significance to the empire.

**Admit Need of Ships**

That agreement in principle had been reached on the air and naval bases was made known here two weeks ago, but the British had waited anxiously for the news of the destroyers; especially so since Churchill told parliament a fortnight back that Britain hoped America would see fit to send these "timely reinforcements" to bridge the gap between the British peacetime flotillas of 1939 and the wartime flotillas they expect to have by 1941.

Officials said it was no secret that Britain needed the destroyers. The Germans have sunk at least 30 of Britain's 185 destroyers and others have been damaged.

### Spirit Called Love Rival

Los Angeles, Sept. 3.—(AP)—Dr. William Boyce testified in the trial of his divorce suit today that he was "in the throes of agony" when he believed his wife to be in love with a spirit, named Sho Sha.

## Nazis Say Destroyer Deal Is Too Late to Aid Britain

Berlin, Sept. 3.—(AP)—German authorized sources displayed extreme caution today in reaction to the United States transfer of 50 over-age destroyers to Great Britain. They declared it involves "a question of conceivable vast import in relation to which the German attitude cannot be defined before a thoroughgoing study of all aspects of international law concerned."

But unofficially some Nazis said they believed the warships were "too late to help Britain."

President Roosevelt's announcement caused no surprise, however.

## Willkie Regrets Ship Transfer Not Debated

### Thinks U. S. Approves F. R. Act—Cites Need of Congress Action

Rushville, Ind., Sept. 3.—Although declaring "the country will undoubtedly approve" of the administration's trade of destroyers for naval base rights in British possessions, Wendell L. Willkie said today it was regrettable President Roosevelt "did not deem it necessary" to obtain prior congressional approval or permit public discussion.

**Expects Approval**

Willkie handed reporters this formal statement at a press conference in his back yard:

"The country will undoubtedly approve of the program to add to our naval and air bases and assistance given to Great Britain. It is regrettable however, that the President did not deem it necessary in connection with this proposal, to secure the approval of congress or permit public discussion prior to adoption.

"The people have a right to know of such important commitments prior to and not after made.

**Threat to Democracy**

"We must be extremely careful in these times when the struggle in the world is between Democracy and totalitarianism not to eliminate or destroy the democratic processes while seeking to preserve democracy.

"It is the contention of the totalitarian rulers that democracy is not effective. We must prove that it is effective by making full use of its process. Congress has constitutional functions as important and sacred as those of the chief executive."

**Says Debate Needed**

Asked if he thought the transfer of war vessels to a belligerent nation constituted an act of war, the Republican presidential nominee replied:

"That is one of the things debate and discussion would have made crystal clear."

## Knudsen Resigns From G. M. Post

New York, Sept. 3.—(INS)—William S. Knudsen, "drafted" from General Motors to become a member of President Roosevelt's national defense advisory commission, today resigned the presidency of the automobile corporation.

THE BOARD OF EDUCATION
MINNEAPOLIS, MINNESOTA

September 3, 1940

Mr. George H. Adams
Executive Editor
The Tribune Newspapers
Minneapolis, Minnesota

Dear Mr. Adams:

I have read the material to be presented in the new patriotic series of articles by famous authors and wish to congratulate the Times-Tribune upon the high quality and the timeliness of these literary gems. They are written by men and women who are masters of the English language and who are imbued with patriotic zeal. I am quite enthusiastic over the opportunity which is being offered to Minneapolis citizens to gain a better understanding of the glorious heritage of America.

Yours sincerely,

C. R. Reed
Superintendent of Schools

### Ship Agreement Hints British May Receive Arms, Too

Washington, Sept. 3.—(AP)—Wording of the United States' agreement with Great Britain aroused speculation today that Britain might receive army equipment, as well as destroyers, in exchange for naval and air base leases.

Lord Lothian's note to Secretary Hull said Britain would make bases available "in exchange for naval and military equipment and material which the United States government will transfer to his majesty's government."

Hull's reply said only that 50 destroyers would be transferred "immediately." No "military equipment" was mentioned. Officials disclaimed any knowledge of additional considerations given to Britain.

## Flares Dropped On Berlin; RAF Hits Nazi Bases

### Germans Bomb 13 British Towns—Turned Back From London

London, Sept. 4.—(Wednesday)—In what was described as the "biggest air bombardment of France to date," huge formations of British planes last night blasted the German-occupied coast from Calais to Boulogne for three solid hours.

After Britain carried large-scale air warfare to German bases, Nazi planes by the hundreds early today bore down on at least 13 towns in every corner of Britain. Yet for the third time in 12 hours the raiders were turned back from central London.

**Drop Flares on Berlin**

(Intensified raids on the continent came as Berlin revealed that two RAF raiders dropped flares on the German capital. The two planes were members of a powerful British bombing armada which was broken up, many of its planes destroyed, long before it reached the capital, officials said.

(Bombs were dropped in the region of Magdeburg, Braunschweig and Halberstadt, authorized sources said, but the main force of the raiders apparently was dispersed by terrific antiaircraft artillery fire and Berlin was declared to have escaped. The capital had a 2½-hour alarm, however.)

**London Has Alarms**

Before midnight London underwent three air raid alarms, bringing the total to 39 for the war. In the morning and afternoon two immense German waves, one involving 300 and the other at least 500 Reich aircraft, swept inland, yet only minor remnants of the formations reached the outskirts of the metropolis.

**Alarm Lasts 14 Minutes**

Britain's antiaircraft defenses proved still more effective in the night alarm, which started at 11:35 p. m. (5:35 p. m. Minneapolis time) and lasted only 14 minutes—one of the shortest "alerts" since the Reich began its mass air attacks.

Nazi aircraft over the Thames estuary caused the alarm, but the planes (this time in comparatively small force) quickly were driven off by antiaircraft fire. None was heard over the London area.

### Gallagher to Talk

Thomas Gallagher, former Democratic candidate for governor, will speak over WCCO at 8:15 p. m. today.

## 8 Destroyers To Leave for Canada Friday

### U. S. Crews to Deliver Vessels to Britons Already En Route

### AMERICA GETS AIR, NAVAL BASE SITES

### Action Is Assailed and Defended in Washington

*(Congress Reaction to Sale of "Over-Age" U. S. Destroyers to England. Page 7.)*

Washington, Sept. 3.—While congressmen split sharply tonight on President Roosevelt's action in turning over 50 "over-age" American destroyers to Great Britain, in return for air and navy base cites, navy department officials prepared to go through with the deal as quickly as possible.

Navy spokesmen said eight destroyers tied up at Boston will start probably Friday with their own crews for Canada, there to be manned by British crews already en route to claim them.

Unofficial sources close to navy affairs said late tonight that the number of reconditioned vessels already at the Boston navy yard awaiting transfer had mounted to 12 with the arrival of several additions during the day.

**Six Destroyers En Route**

An additional six destroyers were disclosed to have left Norfolk, Va., Monday for Boston.

Officers said 11 other destroyers from Brooklyn navy yard will follow as soon as the British admiralty rushes personnel to man them.

In the interest of their safety, the names of the ships to be transferred to Britain was not disclosed, but all were on the eastern seaboard, it was said, and many of them had been in service as part of the "neutrality patrol."

**All 'Over-Age'**

The navy department announced that the destroyers involved were of the 1,200-ton type, carrying four-inch guns and 21-inch torpedo tubes—the exact size used by Britain.

All were completed in 1922 or prior to that time, the navy said, and thus were "over-age." The navy figures that a destroyer no longer retains maximum effectiveness after it is 16 years old.

In announcing his decision to send the warships to aid beleaguered Britain, the President disclosed that the United States is to receive, in turn, the right to construct a string of outlaying naval and air bases extending from Newfoundland to South America. Their chief value, Mr. Roosevelt declared, would be in keeping an overseas enemy away from America's front door.

**Pledge 'No Surrender'**

The state department announced it had received also a British pledge that in no event would the British fleet be sunk or surrendered to Germany. If driven out of European waters, it was said, the English ships of war would be sent abroad for the "defense of other parts of the empire."

The whole transaction, which Attorney General Jackson ruled did not require congressional action, was described by President Roosevelt, in a brief message notifying congress of what was being done, as "an epochal and far-reaching act of preparation for continental defense in the face of grave danger."

"This is the most important action in the reinforcement of our national defense that has been taken since the Louisiana Purchase," Mr. Roosevelt added.

(Continued on Page 14, Column 2)



## YOUR NATIONAL GUARD

*Since Minnesota units are certain to be affected by the President's calling out of the national guard, The Minneapolis Morning Tribune has assembled available rosters of Minnesota units, as of August 1. Believing this information to be of paramount importance at this time, The Morning Tribune will publish these lists together with pictures of local armories from day to day. Watch for yours.*

JACKSON ARMORY

### JACKSON

Company E

Company E, 135th (Rifle) Rgt., 68th Bgd, 34th Division

Captain, Albert A. Svoboda.

First Lieutenant, William G. Kreger; second lieutenant, Walter F. Musegades.

First sergeant, grade II, Joseph J. Vacek; sergeants grade IV, Bert V. Bellows, Clifford L. Dunlavey, Raymond E. Herrick, Robert B. Hunt, William E. Martin, Edward E. Skalincky, Harold J. Vacura.

Corporals, grade V, Donald V. Crowe, Lawrence E. Dunlavey, Van Jensen, Francis J. Jerousek, Glen A. Larsen, Harry E. Perkins, Gordon J. Prokes, Warren F. Ruskell.

Privates, first class, grade VI, William G. Berryman, Glen O. Dunlavey, Orville K. Dunlavey, Winston C. Dunlavey, Lyall W. Guritz, Lowell H. Jensen, Cecil M. Larsen, Frank N. Macek, Farrell D. Peterson, Albert J. Steiner, Orville T. Strube, Claude I. Wedebrand, Edward C. Willis, Dale Worshek.

Privates, grade VII, John F. Babcock, Byron O. Benjamin, Benjamin B. Bezdicek, Robert G. Bramstedt, Irvin A. Christensen, John J. Cirhan, Everett Cook, Kenneth M. Davies, Darwin D. Gee, Victor Gerbracht, Palmer I. Hammer, Bernard G. Hanson, Jerald Hranicka, Edwin Huemoeller, Galen B. Johnson, Duane D. Kime, Harlan O. Knutson, John J. Leonard, Robert W. Matson, Melvin H. Mix, Francis R. Motl, William M. Musegades, Edmund A. Otterson, Jerome C. Otterson, Richard Otterson, Roger J. Partlow, Wallace R. Peterson, William O. Peterson, Richard Polz, Adrian Prokes, Raymond R. Rowley, Edwin H. Schluter, Keith C. Shepard, Wayne W. Snyder, Ralph F. Splinter, Charles D. Stewart, Lynn D. Sullivan, Fred L. Theilhorn, Emanuel J. Voda, John A. Wahl, George T. Winter.

**CLOUDY**

U. S. Weather Bureau Forecast

Partly cloudy in south and west, cloudy with occasional light snow in northeast Tues. Wed. fair; continued cold; 24 hour high, 38, at 3 a. m.; low, 14, at 6 p. m. Mon. Additional details on page 16.

# Minneapolis Morning Tribune

*FOUNDED IN 1867*

A HOME-OWNED AND HOME-MANAGED NEWSPAPER

**WOOLIES**

Damon Runyon goes into the matter of wearing woolen underwear in his column today on Page 20.

*Seventy-Fourth Year. No. 172.* *Twenty Pages* MINNEAPOLIS, MINN., TUESDAY, NOVEMBER 12, 1940 *Three Cents in Minneapolis*



# 7 Known Dead as Blizzard Drives Zero Wave Into N.W.; Drifts Pile Up; Hunters Marooned; Towns Isolated

## *'Loyal Opposition' Needed In Democracy, Willkie Says*

### *Defeated GOP Candidate Lists 5 Steps to Aid U.S. Economy---Recalls F. R. Pledge to Keep Peace*

*(Text on Page 4)*

New York, Nov. 11.—Asserting that a "strong, alert and watchful opposition," was a vital element in the balanced operation of a democracy, Wendell L. Willkie tonight told his followers that "your function during the next four years is that of the loyal opposition."

He spoke of President Roosevelt as "your President" and "my President" and said "we will support him with our best efforts for our country."

**Cites Inflation Evil**

Willkie said he knew President Roosevelt would keep the "solemn pledge" made by both candidates during the election campaign to keep this country out of war unless attacked. Departing from his prepared address, he said:

"Mr. Roosevelt and I both promised the people in the course of the campaign that if we were elected we would keep this country out of war unless attacked. Mr. Roosevelt was re-elected and this solemn pledge for him, I know will be fulfilled and I know the American people desire him to keep it sacred."

Willkie spoke from his personal headquarters in the Hotel Commodore and was in excellent voice, having recovered completely from the hoarseness that marked his last speeches of the campaign.

**Refers to Debt Boost Plan**

In a nation-wide broadcast, the defeated Republican presidential candidate suggested "five steps for our government to take immediately" to "counteract the threat of inflation and to correct some of our economic errors."

Referring to an administration proposal to increase the national debt limit from 49 billion to 65 billion dollars, Willkie said:

(Continued on Page 12, Column 3)

## Berlin Ready For Molotoff Arrival Today

### U.S.-Russ Relations Expected to Cool as Commissar Opens Axis Parley

Berlin, Nov. 11.—(AP)—Soviet Russia's Premier-Foreign Commissar Molotoff arrived in German territory tonight en route to Berlin for conferences with Adolf Hitler and German leaders. It was the first time he had ever left Russian territory.

The first German point reached by his special train was Malkinia, a border town in what last year was Poland. He is due in Berlin tomorrow morning.

Molotoff and German officials will open conferences for the purpose of discussing and agreeing on policies of worldwide scope, informed sources said today, with the Rome-Berlin-Tokyo axis and British-guaranteed Turkey high on the agenda.

In Washington it was believed the slow-moving talks between the United States and Soviet Russia toward a better understanding were in danger of being broken off, as a result of Molotoff's visit to Germany. The visit was interpreted generally here as an indication that Russia was prepared to collaborate even more closely with the axis powers and that efforts of the United States and Great Britain to improve their relations with Moscow were all but futile.

## Gen. Weygand Ignores Vichy Call to Return

### Germany Irritated by Officer's Conduct in North Africa

By Associated Press

General Maxime Weygand's failure to return from Africa to Vichy has aroused speculation in foreign circles who profess to see therein evidence of a stiffening attitude toward France's German and Italian conquerors.

Rear Admiral Rene Platon, French minister of colonies, returned to Vichy from a surprise plane trip to north Africa which informed persons said was for the primary purpose of bringing Weygand back. But Weygand remained in Africa.

**Empowered by Petain**

He has been there since October 10, empowered by Marshal Petain, chief of the French state, to take charge of all political and military matters in France's huge African territories.

There was speculation here as to whether this means that a showdown between Weygand, one-time allied generalissimo, and the French north African army on the one hand, and the Rome-Berlin axis on the other may be at hand.

The Germans were said to have shown disapproval over Weygand's speech in north Africa—where his popularity is great—in which he said France would not cede an inch of territory there.

**Goering Order Reported**

Reports are current here that Reichsmarshal Goering, the No. 2 Nazi, told French Vice Premier Laval in Paris this weekend that the Germans could not continue to deal with the Vichy government unless Vichy brought Weygand back.

It was asserted that Weygand, however, had taken matters into his own hands and refused Vichy's official instructions to return.

The surrender of Libreville, principal port of the Gabon colony of French equatorial Africa, to the "free French" forces of General Charles de Gaulle was announced by the De Gaulle headquarters in London.

Domei, Japanese news agency, at Tokyo, reported Rear Admiral Jean Decoux had resigend as governor general of French Indo-China because of increasing difficulties created by a strong group favoring the "free French" movement.

## NEWS INDEX



Science plays an important role in the main portion of your Thanksgiving dinner . . the turkey! The scientific advances that have been made—improving the looks as well as the taste of the bird are described on

Page 1—Section 2 This Afternoon

THE TIMES-TRIBUNE

### *Too Much Weather So Weather Bureau Forecast Is Delayed*

The weather was almost too much for the weather bureau last night. At 9:55 p. m., the Associated Press sent out the following message:

"Note to editors—

"Chicago weather bureau advises forecasts and temperatures will be delayed because of unusual weather conditions."

Then at 10:32 p. m., the bureau got the weather under control. It came through with the official forecast—"Minnesota: Partly cloudy in south and west, cloudy with occasional light snow in northeast Tuesday; Wednesday, fair, continued cold."

## *GALE BLOWS IN UNEXPECTED GUESTS*

Staff photo.

Busier than on homecoming or during fair week were hotels last night as persons unable to get home asked for rooms. Many were unable to find accommodations. Here is the scene at the Radisson hotel registration desk early in the evening.

## 18 Killed and Scores Injured By Storms in Nearby States

### Illinois, Michigan and Iowa Pounded—Lake Ferry Aground

By International News Service

Eighteen persons were believed dead last night and several score injured as a gale, accompanied by snow, sleet, hail and near zero temperatures swept the north central states.

The toll of property damaged mounted into tens of thousands of dollars. Buildings were wrecked, wires were downed, trees uprooted and windows smashed. Practically all plane traffic was suspended and rail and bus traffic disrupted in the face of probably the worst gale to strike the midwest in 40 years.

**16 Dead in Illinois**

Illinois felt the full force of the storm's fury where 16 were probably killed as a wind, at times reaching 65 miles an hour, swept the Chicago area.

Eight duck hunters, swept into the swirling waters of the Illinois river near Mossville, were believed drowned as deputy sheriffs refused to continue a search on the storm tossed waters. Two more hunters were drowned at Liverpool, Ill. At least 10 hunters were rescued earlier.

Great lakes shipping fled toward shelter. The Coast guard station at St. Joseph, Mich., reported a southwest wind between 75 and 80 miles an hour.

**Lake Ferry Aground**

The 390-foot carferry City of Fint, flagship of the Pere Marquette fleet plying between Michigan and Wisconsin ports, was aground north of Ludington, Mich., and being pounded by heavy seas. The all-steel ship, with its crew and an unknown number of passengers, was not believed to be in immediate danger, though its radio was out of order and it had little communication with watchers on the beach 800 feet away.

(Continued on Page 2, Column 1)

## *Students Stay Overnight In School Near Hibbing*

Hibbing, Minn., Nov. 11.—Urban bus services in Hibbing, and interurban service on the iron range was at a standstill tonight, after one of the worst snowstorms in range history. Hundreds of autos stalled on highways. Schools of the district were closed, and pupils of Cherry school, east of Hibbing, had to stay overnight in the school. Visibility was down to 10 feet at 6:30 p. m., as a wind whipped up the heavy snow, and the temperature was 14 above.

**11 ABOVE AT ROCHESTER**

Rochester, Minn., Nov. 11.—Highway patrolmen warned traffic off the roads in this district tonight, as a 35-mile wind whipped snow into deep drifts. It was 11 above zero at 8 p. m., and getting colder.

**TURKEY LOSSES HIGH**

Worthington, Minn., Nov. 11.—Today's unexpected storm raised havoc with this area's turkey industry, losses of birds running as high as 4,000 per farm. Many western lambs also died on the ranges.

**TRAFFIC AT STANDSTILL**

Grand Rapids, Minn., Nov. 11.—Traffic was at a standstill here tonight, as a 12-inch snow drifted into cuts as rapidly as plows opened them. Schools in this area closed at noon. It was 13 above zero at 6 p. m., and getting colder.

**STUDENTS ACCOUNTED FOR**

Floodwood, Minn., Nov. 11.—Scores of Floodwood high school pupils, lost for several hours in stalled school buses on nearby rural roads, were all accounted for late tonight. Five buses became stuck in huge drifts and until 9 p. m. three had been unaccounted for. The last was found on the Prairie Lake road after a radio appeal for residents of the districts to assist in locating the vehicle. Meanwhile, about 75 persons were marooned in the village overnight. The high school building was opened to provide shelter as all other facilities were taxed.

**MAROONED PUPILS RESCUED**

Verndale, Minn., Nov. 11.—A group of 16 school children, marooned in a snowdrift when their bus stalled, were rescued today when another bus fought its way to the scene, and returned them to Verndale. All busses in this area were cancelled. It was still snowing tonight, and the wind continued unabated. It was eight above zero.

**TRAIN IS DELAYED**

Montevideo, Minn., Nov. 11.—Today's storm forced the Milwaukee railroad to lay over its westbound passenger train No. 15 here until the storm cleared. The train was headed for Aberdeen, S. D., from Minneapolis.

**TRAFFIC AT STANDSTILL**

International Falls, Minn., Nov. 11.—Traffic in this area came to a standstill tonight as 10 inches of snow drifted in front of a 35-mile wind. A barometer reading of 27.97, lowest in local weather bureau history, indicated more stormy weather.

**TRAINS RUNNING LATE**

Fergus Falls, Minn., Nov. 11.—Raging winds whipped 10 inches of snow into drifts that halted motor traffic in this area today, with some trains coming through but running late. The mercury has remained at 7 and 8 degrees above all day.

## *Blocked Streets Force Hundreds To Loop Hotels*

### *Car Mishaps Trap 100 Near New Brighton*

### *Battle to Reopen Trolly Lines by Morning*

An Armistice day storm which passed through rain, sleet and snow flurries into the fury of a blizzard as temperatures fell and winds rose hour by hour, clamped an icy blockade over the northwest last night.

Transportation was tied up almost completely, telephone and telegraph services were hard hit, and most communities were isolated.

The full extent of casualties will not be known until communications are opened up again, but deaths fo six men, three of them hunters, and one woman, were reported last night.

The dead:

**Walter Strom, 1700 Hawthorne Av., Soo Line fireman, killed in wreck at Watkins.**

**Mrs. E. Y. Arnold, 2124 Ann Arbor St., St. Paul, traffic victim.**

**John C. Johnson, 55, 222 Tenth Av. N.E., died of exhaustion.**

**Harry S. Mason, 75, 329 South Warwick St., St. Paul, died of exhaustion.**

**Herbert Junneman, Wabasha, Minn., a hunter.**

**Theodore H. Geiger, Eau Claire, Wis., a hunter.**

**Clyde J. Detra, Eau Claire, Wis., a hunter.**

Thousands of persons stranded in the loop crowded downtown hotels, taking every available room and overflowing into dining rooms and lobbies. It was the busiest night hotel men could recall.

The forecast was for partly cloudy conditions in the south and west parts of Minnesota, with occasional light snow in the northeast portion; Wednesday, fair and continued cold.

**Wind Reaches 60 M P H**

During the storm, winds reached a velocity of 60 miles an hour, drifts piled up as high as five feet, and there was a temperature drop to sub-zero depths, Williston and Minot, N. D., and Hot Springs, S. D., reporting 10 below.

(Continued on Page 12, Column 8)

## 5 Get Rides To Homes in Ambulances

Fifteen persons, stymied in efforts to get rides, thought of a novel solution to their problem. They went to the General hospital receiving station to await ambulance calls which might send an ambulance to their section of town. Five rides were obtained this way.

**CHIP OF WOOD HITS EYE**

At the peak of the storm Claus Johnson, 57, who lives in a small cottage at Twenty-seventh avenue north and the river, was chopping wood to replenish low fuel stock. A chip hit him in the eye, perforating his eye-ball. He was in fair condition in General hospital.

**TREATED BY CITIZENS CLUB**

Passengers in a stalled streetcar in front of the Citizen club at Minnehaha and Twentieth avenues were treated to coffee and sandwiches prepared by officials of the club.

**GO A STEP FARTHER**

A banner on the Minneapolis House Furnishing Co. invited any stranded person to spend the night in the store. A large number accepted the invitation, but the management decided to go a step farther. A bus was chartered and the entire group taken to their homes.

**HARRIET TRAFFIC STALLED**

Traffic on Lake Harriet lines was stalled for nearly two hours when a tree was blown down across tracks near the Lake Harriet platform. Two other bad tieups occurred at Fifth St. and First Av. N., and at Washington and Fourth Avs. S., when large trailer-trucks got stalled on the tracks.

### *Expect Schools Will Be Opened*

Superintendent Carroll R. Reed is expected to make a radio announcement about 7 a. m. today as to whether public schools will be closed because of the weather. So far as determined last night, they are to be open. In special circumstances, however, parents may keep their children home if, in their judgment, attendance would endanger their health.

## *JAIL IS STORM HAVEN*

—Staff photo

Among more than 100 persons who came into the city hall last night seeking either a way home or a place to spend the night was Junior Cybyske, 8, of 1734 Fillmore street northeast. Junior, who was stranded along with his father, Al, was willing to bed right down on the headquarter's desk. Police took many persons home and provided sleeping quarters for others. Thirty women accepted cots in the women's portion of the city jail.

**FAIR**
U. S. Weather Bureau Forecast
Fair Saturday and Sunday; warmer Saturday and in extreme east Sunday. 24 hour high, 22, at 5 p. m.; low, 1, at 2 a. m. Friday.
Additional details on page 11.

# Minneapolis Morning Tribune

FOUNDED IN 1867
A HOME-OWNED AND HOME-MANAGED NEWSPAPER

Seventy-Fourth Year. No. 176. Twenty-two Pages MINNEAPOLIS, MINN., SATURDAY, NOVEMBER 16, 1940 Three Cents in Minneapolis

**GREEN GRASS**
It keeps right on growing all around, even when wintry winds blow. The Early Bird spreads the news in his column on page 6.



# Hamburg, Berlin, London Battered; Axis Mediterranean Drive Expected

## OLD GANG GOES ADVENTURING AGAIN

Staff photo.
"One for all, and all for one"—and in that spirit, this trio, who persuaded officials to raise their draft board's quota so they could volunteer, are heading for the army. Left to right, Harold S. Kempainen, Eugene Hill, Earl W. Auvinen.

## Plea Ups Draft Quota, 4 Pals Serve Together

The old gang will try another adventure—together.

They've known each other a dozen years, have these four youths. They've gone to school together, played football, hung out on the same corner, all in a friendly, carefree way. And now that things have taken a more serious turn, they are going to be companions still—in the army.

**Takes Persuasion**

But it took some persuasion, and some change of regulations to bring this about.

Frank Hajder

The four are Eugene Hill, 21, of 214 Logan Av. N., Harold S. Kampainen, 23, of 1801 Third Av. N. Earl W. Auvinen, 22 of 1821 Second Av. N., and Frank J. Hajder, 25, of 227 Fremont Av. N.

**All Physically Fit**

All registered with draft board No. 5. All volunteered for service ahead of their turns, and all proved, on examination, to be physically fit. They expected to go into service as a sort of unit—a kind of corporal's guard of close pals. Then they learned the board's quota for November would be only two men. Furthermore, another volunteer, Rodney C. Hanson, 25, of 820 Hawthorn Av., had been a few minutes ahead of them.

There was only one way they could go in together—the board's quota would have to be raised.

**Bar Is Lowered**

They talked to George Murphy, local board chairman; he, in turn, talked to Governor Stassen.

And yesterday, the board's quota was raised to five, which made it the largest in Hennepin county, even though it had one of the smallest registrations. That will take care of the four musketeers.

Hill and Auvinen had an impromptu reunion last night with Kampainen who is employed at radio station WCCO. Hajder was missing—tied up with his truck somewhere along the snow-drifted highways of Wisconsin. But the three musketeers are hoping the fourth will show up today.

## NEWS INDEX



## State Highways About Cleared, Still Not Safe

### One-Way Lanes Make Travel Precarious—Loss From Storm Mounts

Although they have succeeded in cutting through single lane passages on practically all major roads, state highway officials last night still were confronted with the problem of making traffic safe on a large portion of the highways hit in last Monday's blizzard.

With a round up of storm damage yesterday producing bodies of two more victims and property losses running into many millions, highway officials recommended that motorists stay off highways except for most urgent reasons.

**Going Precarious**

Travel, explained R. E. Nelson, maintenance division executive, is possible on all major highways and most secondary roads. The going, however, is still precarious in all sections and travelers must exercise the utmost caution.

Aside from the loss of life, which yesterdays' discovery of the bodies of John and Charles Garrison of Little Falls in a swamp near Sauk Centre brought to a total of 47 in the state, the heaviest damage of the storm was wrought on Minnesota's turkey crop.

**Turkey Loss Heavy**

Minnesota and northwest turkey raisers lost an estimated $12,000,000 in the storm. Approximately 2,500,000 turkeys ready for the Christmas market perished. At least 1,000,000 of them were in Minnesota. Estimators said the birds were worth about $3 each or about $7,500,000 for the crop that was killed. Equipment razed by the storm was estimated at $5,000,000.

With many persons still unheard from, public officials feared that the death toll will go considerably higher than the figure so far recorded. The bodies of the Garrison youths were found after a 24-

(Continued on Page 14, Column 1)

## Italo-German Generals Meet to Map Attack

### Hitler Expected to Send Troops to Aid Duce in Greek War

### BRITISH AT SUEZ TO FACE ASSAULT

### Russia Is Counted Upon to Bring Pressure, Curb Turkey

Rome, Nov. 15.— (AP) —A big offensive in the Mediterranean and new impetus for Italy's campaign in Greece were expected in foreign cihcles tonight to result from the conference of the chiefs of the German and Italian high commands.

The meeting between German Marshal General Wilhelm Keitel and Italian Marshal Pietro Badoglio totday at Innsbruck was described officially ni a communique as "military conversations on joint conduct of the war." (This paralleled a similar, cryptic announcement in Berlin.)

**Pressure on Turks**

Some usually - well - informed sources predicted that pressure would be made on Turkey to allow German troops to spread their occupation from Rumania to the Dardanelles in a drive against the British at Suez and, beyond, in the oil-rich near east.

Others said German troops might aid the Italians against Greece through Yugoslavia or Bulgaria, or both.

Newspapers indicated that Soviet Russia probably would help put pressure on Turkey to prevent her opposing Geermans plans.

It was considerd significant that the military conference came on thehecls of talks in Berlin between Soviet Premier Vyacheslaff Molotoff and Adolph Hitler and those here between Rumanian Premier General Ion Antonescu and Premier Mussolini.

**Serano Suner Active**

Almost coincidentally, it was announced that Ramon Serrano Suner, the Spanish foreign minister, would arrive in Germany shortly on the invitation of German Foreign Minister Joachim von Ribbentrop. Suner had a talk with Hitler on September 29 and that conference led to speculation that in the eventual lineup which the axis expects to enforce Spain had been promised Gibraltar.

The Italian high command, summing up Thursday's operations, reported 13 Greek warplanes shot down in violent air action on the Greek battle-front.

It also claimed to have verified the torpedoing of a 3,500 ton battleship of the Ramillies class a week ago off Sicily. The battleship was reported to have been escorting the aircraft carrier Illustrious.

## Bandits Get $103 In Store Holdup

Max Dunaevsky was waiting on a woman customer in his grocery store at 901 Fourth Av. N. last night when two men came in. One ordered a package of cigarets. The other, pulling a pistol, ordered the woman to "keep quiet," then instructed the grocer to "lie on the floor, and keep quiet, too." The bandits then took $103 from a cash register and departed.

## G-Men Guard 2 Ships After Sabotage Tip-Off

New York, Nov. 15.—(AP)—Acting on a tip that an attempt would be made to blow up two United States government transport ships being reconditioned in a private shipyard, police and federal agents closed off a Brooklyn waterfront area tonight and set up special patrols on and around the two vessels.

Fifty Brooklyn police officers were sent to the oTdd Shipyard Corp. drydocks to join federal bureau of investigation agents guarding the U. S. Laramie, an army troop ship, and the U. S. Wharton, a navy vessel assign as an army transport.

Officials said police were assigned to patrol the entire waterfront area around the shipyard, which is near the U. S. navy yard, and that 11 officers had been assigned to search each ship and to stand guard aboard each until further notice.

Two police launches and a coastguard cutter were assigned to patrol the waters off the dryrock he said.

Several weeks ago a mattress fire of undetermined origin blazed on the Wharton.

## Bomb-Razed Coventry Digging Out

### Evacuation Caravan Persuaded to Return

By ALFRED E. WALL

Coventry, England, Nov. 15.—(AP)—Coventry, chosen by the German high command for the most concentrated aerial bombardment of the Batlle of Britain, emerged today from that scourge with at least 1,000 dead and wounded, not counting unknown numbers trapped in her smoking wreckage.

Britain dispatches quoting the high command represented the assault as vengence for the British bombardment of Munich, birthplace of Nazism. The British raided Munich November 8 when Adolf Hitler was addressing a party rally.

Last night it was Coventry's turn and German bombing planes, busy from dusk to dawn, smashed the heart out of this industrially important city in Britain's smoky Midlands.

**CLAIM MILITARY TARGETS NOT HIT**

The British Press association declared, however, that the Germans "failed lamentably" to hit military targets.

Coventry, with a normal population of 190,000, now is known more for her place in midland industry than for her legendary past. It is 95 miles northwest of London.

But it was streets through which Lady Godiva rode nearly 900 years ago which were churned by incendiary and high explosive bombs during last night.

It was here that men strove in a thundering hell against growing piles of stone and smoking timbers to bring out the dead and injured.

Herbert Morrison
*Stops Fleeing Citizens*

Stories of heroism, of rescue workers dying in the debris they were trying to move, of first aid workers killed while trying to save lives, of narrow escapes and sudden, wholesale death piled one on another in an overpowering array.

**STRICKEN DUMB BY BOMB SHOCK**

Cases of bomb shock were reported in which the victims, otherwise unscathed, were found stricken dumb and powerless to help themselves after the night of terror.

Herbert Morrison, minister of home security, here on a tour of the midlands, found in Coventry an example for his urging, earlier in Birmingham, that industrial workers under bombardment "must not be shocked off the job." That, he said, would be "a major disaster."

When Morrison and his wife drove into the city this afternoon their limousine was confronted by a caravan of white-faced people seeking safety in the country. He prevailed upon them to go back.

According to the German version Coventry was attacked by more than 500 planes which dropped 30,000 incendiary bombs and more than 1,000,000 pounds of explosives. As home of the Morris, Bristol, Rover and Napier motor works as well as the General Electric plant, Coventry is regarded by the Germans as a prime military target.

**CATHEDRAL NOW A MASS OF RUBBLE**

At 3 o'clock this afternoon the clock in the main spire of St. Michael's cathedral struck the hour for the first time since a bomb smashed into the building last night. The Fourteenth century brownstone cathedral, save for its 303-foot spire, was a jumble of stone and dusty mortar.

Aside from the cathedral and countless homes, these places were damaged by the raiders: two hospitals, two churches, public baths, two clubs, a school, a hotel, four public shelters, movie theaters, the police station, the postoffice and two first aid posts.

## Spectators, Not Grid Title, Go on Ice Today

### Workmen Buck Stadium Drifts toGet Seats Cleared for Purdue Clash—Final Home Game for Gophers

By MILT DAVIS

Although the weather may not be auspicious for working up a good glowing heart-warmth, there will be several touches of sentimentality to the game between Minnesota and Purdue in Memorial stadium today. More than 33,000 spectators—unless another storm blows up unexpectedly—will turn out.

On tis heart-throb side, the game will wind up the 1940 home seaeson.

It will bid farewell to a group of players—including the Gophers' all-American hope, George Franck.

It will be played before a special section of old-timers—dads of university students.

**Buck Stadium Drifts**

In a sportive way, the game will mark another severe test for Minnesota, as it moves along toward the Big Ten championship and national top-ranking.

Meanwhile, as game time neared, crews of workmen continued yesterday to move drifts out of the stadium to get the field in shape by kickoff. The huge tarpaulins which cover the turf will be kept on until shortly after the contest gets under way. Seats in occupied sections of the stands will be cleared of snow.

Indications were that temperatures around the freezing mark will prevail during most of the afternoon.

**1,000 Dads on Hand**

The game will be the big treat for some 1,000 fathers who will be honored guests in Dad's day ceremonies. They will register on the campus in the morning, visit classes, and then, after the game, have their annual dinner in Coffman Memorial Union. Speakers will be President Guy Stanton Ford; Deans E. E. Nicholson and Anne Dudley Blitz; Edward F. Flynn, St. Paul attorney, who is president of the Minnesota Dads' association, and Victor Jung, president of the All-University council, who will welcome the old-timers.

Purdue's team arrived yesterday, and then went into retirement after a brief unlimbering.

## Name University Head

Norman, Okla., Nov. 15.—(AP)—Joseph A. Brandt, director of the Princeton University press, was elected president of the University of Oklahoma at a meeting of the board of regents today.

## Twin City Concern To Build War Plant

Kansas City, Mo., Nov. 15.—It was reported here today that Foley Bros., Inc., St. Paul contractor, has been selected by the war department as one of the co-contractors for construction of an $18,000,000 plant ni Kansas City for manufacture of small arms ammunition. The factory is to be operated by Remington Arms Co. Work is to start at once and be completed in a year. The other co-contractor is the Walbridge Alinger Co. Detroit. More than 3,000 men are to be employed.

## Britain Adopts New Plane Type

London, Nov. 15.—(AP)—Named for a seabird, the Fulmar, a two-seater low-wing monoplane, has been adopted by the admiralty for service on aircraft carriers as a fighter and dive bomber. It was officially disclosed today they are the fastest planes operating with the navy.

## Archbishop Has Minor Operation

Rochester, Minn., Nov. 15.—Archbishop John Gregory Murray of St. Paul is recovering today in St. Mary's hospital following a minor operation. The Archbishop's condition was described by his physician as "excellent." He will be confined to the hospital about 10 days.

## Russians Ignore New British Offer

London, Nov. 15.—(AP)—Russia has ignored for nearly three months British proposals which included an offer of assurance that Britain would not be associated in any attack on Russia, authoritative sources said tonight.

## Greeks Press On, Claim 700 New Prisoners

### 10 Heavy Guns Also Taken in Intense Battles

Athens, Greece, Nov. 16.—(Saturday) — (AP) — The capture of 700 Italian soldiers and 10 heavy guns in a continuing Greek advance along the 100-mile Albanian battlefront was reported by the high command early today. Both artillery and air actions were described as "intense."

Greek pilots were declared to have bombed Italian columns in action and to have shot down three Fascist planes against two Greek losses.

**Retreat Is Near Rout**

A government spokesman said the Italians were retreating all along the front, although "quite serious battles" were raging.

In the sector near the coast the Greeks declared the Italians had been pushed back against the Albanian frontier in a retreat described as reaching the proportions of a rout. This is one of the few remaining points where the Italians still are on Greek soil after 19 days of fighting.

Above this area in the Pindus mountains, where the Greeks are fighting on Albanian soil, advices from the front said Greek mountain fighters had planted their artillery along the few good routes of invasion which had been open to the Fascists.

**Yugoslav Town Raided**

In Yugoslavia, it was reported that three unidentified foreign planes staged a raid on the town of Bitolj. It was the second time this town had been raided, and marked the first time Yugoslav antiaircraft guns went into action against foreign planes.

From Alexandria, Egypt, came the report antiaircraft guns of Britain's Mediterranean fleet and shore batteries blunted an Italian air attack on that British naval base. A heavy barrage forced the raiders to fly high. It was the fifth air raid on the harbor within 12 hours.

## Nazis and RAF Trade Terrific Punches in Air

### Reich Claims 12 British Craft Shot Down Over Two Cities

### 100 CRAFT STRIKE EMPIRE'S CAPITAL

### Britain Suffers One of Worst Nights—18 of Invaders Downed

By ASSOCIATED PRESS

The Reich and English air forces traded terrific punches in mass bombardments over Germany and England Friday night.

Waves of British bombers attacked Hamburg and Berlin. The German radio in a broadcast heard by NBC in New York said twelve RAF machines were shot down, six in the Berlin area and six near the English channel.

**12 Planes Reach Berlin**

Only 12 of the raiders reached Berlin, the broadcast said. "Insignificant fires" were started and "some damage caused to private houses." Two of the planes reported shot down over Berlin were said to have crashed into houses.

The official German news agency, DNB, said antiaircraft batteries and night-flying German pursuit planes broke up the British effort to carry out a mass raid on Hamburg.

The raiders swept in from the sea, DNB said, only to run into such a fierce barrage that most of them turned back. A few planes, it was acknowledged, reached the heart of the city but damage was reportedly confined to private houses and a hospital. Two British raiders were declared downed in flames.

**100 Planes Over London**

Meanwhile German bombers were devoting their attention once more to London and more than 100 warplanes dropped explosives and fire bombs on the British capital.

Scores of fires were started, apartment buildings were leveled, and casualties were admittedly heavy.

"This is the worst night yet—at least in numbers," one air raid warden said. "I just counted 80 heavy bombers flying low in formation."

**18 Nazi Planes Down**

The attack grew more intense near midnight when the raiders found gaps in the low-hanging clouds curtaining the city. Several hours later the clouds again obscured the city, but hundreds of fire bombs, explosives and bright flares whistled down.

At least 18 Nazi planes were shot down during the day and another early last night to make a total bag of 19, the British said.

Still raging fires at Coventry served as beacons to guide other raiders back to the Midlands, and a southwest sector also was under attack.

## 2 British Ships Reported Sunk

Berlin, Nov. 15.—(AP)—Informed persons said tonight that German bombers in an attack on a British convoy 500 miles off Ireland were believed to have sunk two merchantmen of 9,300 and 1,600 tons, respectively. Six destroyers defending the convoy—which aggregated 20 ships—were said to have answered with heavy salvos.

## Weather 'Fixers' Win

Washington, Nov. 15.—(AP)— A four-day rain in Washington stopped just in time for the dedication this morning of a new building to house the weather bureau.

**Charlie's On the Spot!**

Cash prizes, easy questions and fun highlight the brand-new "Charlie-on-the-Spot" radio program tonight on WTCN! You are invited to attend—admission is by ticket only, and you can clip your ticket from today's Morning Tribune, on the radio page! Or tune in WTCN tonight at 5:30!

WARMER
U. S. Weather Bureau Forecast
Fair and warmer Monday, Tuesday partly cloudy. High, 82 at 3 p.m. Low, 66 at 5:30 a.m.
Additional details on page 15.

# Minneapolis Morning Tribune

FOUNDED IN 1867



Seventy-Fifth Year. No. 30. 18 PAGES MINNEAPOLIS, MINN., MONDAY, JUNE 23, 1941 ★★★★ Price 3 Cents In Twin City Area 5 Cents Elsewhere

# BOMBERS RAID RUSS CITIES; THREE BORDER TOWNS FALL

*THEY DID EACH OTHER A FAVOR*

## When Blind Leads Blind, Whew!

NEWARK, N. J.—(AP)—Michael Laciopa, blind city hall refreshment concessionaire, heard a voice ask "Going across?" at a busy downtown intersection during rush hour.

Laciopa replied in the affirmative, and the pair made their way across the avenue amid screeching brakes and whizzing traffic. Safe on the other side, his anonymous companion said, "Thanks."

When Laciopa, puzzled, asked, "What for?" the other replied:

"I'm blind."

## Eucharistic Congress to Open Today

### Over 125,000 Catholics Go to Communion in Twin Cities

More than 125,000 Twin Cities Catholics went to the Communion tables in their parishes yesterday in the first of a series of outpourings of devotion marking the ninth National Eucharistic Congress.

Not only in the cities, but throughout the Archdiocese of St. Paul, the faithful joined in spiritual preparation for the Congress, which opens today, swelling the ranks of communicants to a higher level than even at the great church festivals of Christmas and Easter.

**Archbishop Is Pleased**

Prior to yesterday's masses and reception of The Holy Eucharist, priests throughout the archdiocese spent long hours in confessionals Saturday.

Highly gratifying was the demonstration of faith to the Most Rev. John Gregory Murray, archbishop of St. Paul, at whose request the faithful had approached the Communion table.

"Symbolic of the spirit of the great Eucharistic Congress was the manifestation today of the nearness to Christ of the faithful of this archdiocese, where thousands upon thousands received the Holy Eucharist—the Bread of Life," he declared.

(Concluded on Page 6)

## News Summary

***FOREIGN***

Germans make smashing air raids on Soviet Russia's Sebastopol and Odessa....Churchill promises British aid to Russia, urges U. S. to do so....Japanese cabinet, tied by treaties to both Germany and Russia, faces critical decision....Turkey officially proclaims neutrality....Foreign Commissar Molotov broadcasts confidence Russia will deal Nazi army crushing blow. ....Rumanian army ordered to win back land lost to Soviet.. . Finland still technically at peace with Soviet but raided by Russ planes....Russia claims biggest air force in world....British silent on Nazi report of London-Moscow pact.

***LOCAL***

125,000 in Twin Cities take communion in preparation for Eucharistic Congress opening today . . . CIO-544 awaits ruling on plea for representation ballot among truckers . . . NLRB enters Worthington produce case . . . Runaway coal barge endangers houseboats . . . St. Paul "Robin Hood" bandits sought in Minneapolis . . . Two more deaths raise toll of Sauk Centre crash to four . . . Minneapolis Finns confused by developments in homeland . . . Nye calls for end to unfounded fears at Svithiod picnic.

***DOMESTIC***

Close economic co-operation of Britain and U. S. with Soviet expected in Washington . . . Senator Pat Harrison dies . . . U. S. naval sources rate Soviet fleet low . . . Senator Pepper urges neutrality act repeal . . . Paul Block, publisher of many newspapers, dies lisher of many newspapers, dies.

***WHERE TO FIND IT***



## *Merry Robin Hoods Want Only 'Rich Men's Money'*

***Commandeer Cab But Don't Rob Driver — Trio Attempts Foray on Cafe Block From St. Paul Police Headquarters***

Search for three "Robin Hood" bandits, who shot a St. Paul cafe employe and kidnaped a cab driver in an abortive holdup attempt, extended to Minneapolis Sunday night, as St. Paul police smarted under the fact that the climax of the exploit took place only a block from police headquarters.

The three made no attempt to rob the cab driver, and told him: "We're only after rich men's money."

**Cab Driver Bound**

Shortly after midnight, the driver, George Twells, 394 Dayton avenue, St. Paul, was approached by the three men as he sat in his cab at Twelfth and Jackson streets. They ordered him to drive to a residential address, but after riding several blocks, pulled guns, forced Twells from the car and tied him.

**Throwing Twells in the back seat, they drove the cab to the Produce cafe at Tenth and Jackson streets, about a block from police headquarters.**

Donning masks, they entered the place through a side door, waving pistols at the 20 patrons and employes in the place.

**Bandit 'Wings' Employe**

While two stood guard, the third went behind the bar, toward the cash register. An employe, George True, 43, 232 E. Tenth street, St. Paul, dived at the man, but the bandit "winged" him with a shot which lodged in True's hip, then bludgeoned him with the pistol.

The bandits fled without loot, leaped into the cab, and drove out on Arcade street, where they freed Twell.

**Cab Abandoned**

Police later found the cab a few blocks away from the point where Twell was freed.

Aside from a superficial bullet wound, True suffered a slight concussion. His condition was not serious.

## Bride Looks on as Mate Drowns

WINDOM, MINN.—(AP)—While his bride of only a few weeks looked on, Allen Liepold, young farmer near Heron lake, drowned in Cottonwood lake here Sunday. Liepold, witnesses said, dived off a tower some distance from the bathing beach, came to the surface, and then disappeared after shouting something unintelligible to the other bathers. Firemen recovered the body after about an hour's search, but their efforts at resuscitation failed.

## Russia Given Pledge of Aid by Churchill

### Prime Minister Urges U. S. to Aid New Hitler Foe

*Text of Churchill Address Page 5*

LONDON — Prime Minister Churchill promised British aid to Russia in her fight against Germany Sunday night and strongly suggested that the United States do likewise.

In a ringing 20-minute radio address to the world, Churchill declared Britain "will give whatever help we can to Russia" and will appeal "to all our friends and allies" to take the same course.

"Russia's danger is our danger, and the danger of the United States," he cried.

**"Any man or state that fights against Hitler will have our aid."**

He offered to the USSR "any technical and economic assistance" within Britain's power.

**"It is not for me to speak of the action of the United States," Churchill said, "but I will say if Hitler imagines that his attack on Soviet Russia will cause the slightest division of aid or slackening of effort in the great democracies who are resolved upon his doom, he is woefully mistaken."**

The prime minister asserted:

"No one has been a more consistent opponent of Communism than I have for the last 25 years.

"I will unsay no words that I have spoken about it. But all this fades away before the spectacle which is now unfolding. The past, with its crimes, its follies and its tragedies, flashes away."

## *Sen. Pat Harrison Dies After Relapse*

WASHINGTON—(AP)—Pat Harrison, the senate's president pro tempore, chairman of its finance committee and beloved by all his colleagues, died Sunday in Emergency hospital.

The tall, genial 59-year-old Mississippi Democrat, a colorful and influential figure during 30 years in congress, had undergone an operation for an intestinal obstruction last Monday. He rallied well after this ordeal, but in mid-week took a turn for the worse.

Harrison

**F. R. Expresses Regret**

When word of his death spread, there was an immediate outpouring of expressions of grief from administration officials and members of congress.

**President Roosevelt said his passing "is a great sorrow to all of us who were his close friends. It is a loss to the nation and to the state of Mississippi....He will be sadly missed in this hour of grave emergency."**

**Funeral Wednesday**

The entire senate membership was invited to accompany the body to Gulfport, Miss., the senator's home, where funeral services will be held at 2:30 p.m. Wednesday.

Elected unanimously as president pro tem of the senate early this year, Harrison also was chairman of the important and powerful senate finance committee. He had much to do with drafting tax legislation to finance the defense program and as ranking member of the foreign relation committee he played a large part in senate passage of the lease-lend bill to give Britain all aid short of war. He spent 30 years in congress, entering the house in 1910 and the senate in 1918. A member of the "economy block," he did not always agree with new deal methods although favoring humanitarian objectives.

## Lease-Lend Aid to Reds Is Forecast

### Washington Studies Possibility of Exporting War Supplies

### Neutrality Proclamation by Roosevelt Is Awaited

WASHINGTON — (AP) — Establishment of close economic co-operation among the United States, Great Britain and Russia was envisaged Sunday as a result of the German invasion of the Soviet union.

**Striking with bombshell effect comparable to the surprise Russian - German nonaggression pact of 1939, Germany's sudden war move eastward caused intense diplomatic activities.**

The American government withheld formal statement of its views but state department sources described the German action as convincing proof that Adolf Hitler was bent on domination of the entire world.

**The state department reaction clearly branded Germany as the aggressor and thus raised the question of possible American aid—lease-lend or otherwise—to Russia.**

Officials would not indicate the American course, pending study of developments.

One high diplomatic source, however, said he expected close economic co-operation at least to develop now between Great Britain and Russia with the United States probably adopting a more liberal policy on exports of vital defense materials to the Soviet Union.

**Viscount Halifax, the British ambassador, made an unusual Sunday call at the state department and was in conference nearly two hours with Undersecretary Sumner Welles.**

A neutrality proclamation by President Roosevelt recognizing existence of a state of war between Germany and Russia was expected in a day or two.

## Turkey Remains Officially Neutral

ANKARA— (AP) —Turkey officially proclaimed her neutrality Sunday in the new war between Russia and Germany, but disclosed new friendship ties with Germany.

Foreign Minister Sukru Saracoglu announced a commercial treaty with Germany would be concluded quickly as an aftermath of the non-aggression pact the two countries signed June 18. Turkey already had a friendship treaty with Russia and a non-belligerent alliance with Britain.

## Finns Not at War, Europe Asserts

WASHINGTON — (INS) — "Finland is not at war," Hjalmar Procope Finnish minister to the United States, declared late Sunday after a trans-Atlantic telephone conversation with Heisinki, Finnish capital.

## Sweden Neutral, Cabinet Decides

By The Associated Press

The Swedish cabinet at an extraordinary session in Stockholm decided on a policy of strict neutrality, the British radio reported.

## London Has First Air Raid in Week

LONDON — (AP) — An air raid alarm sounded in London early today. It was the first since June 14. No gunfire was heard.

**160 JAILED IN RED RAID**

BUENOS AIRES, ARGENTINA —(AP)—One hundred and sixty men were arrested Sunday night at offices of the Leftist newspaper La Hora, where they held a meeting after being dispersed from the waterfront.

## *Nazis Report 40 Enemy Planes Brought Down; Reds Claim 65*

THE CHAMPIONS MEET—

## Russ Long Have Boasted 'Chute Skill; Nazis Proved Selves in Victory at Crete

Russia for years has boasted of her powerful, skilled army of parachutists. Long before the Germans struck out so successfully with this new military arm, Russian publications, including "Red Star," the official army paper, were printing stories and pictures of these soldiers of the sky.

Germany gave much less publicity to her parachutists until they attacked with such paralyzing power in the campaign against the lo wcountries and Crete.

The theory of parachute troops is not new; in the World war the American war department gave some consideration to their use, but dropped the proposal. These soldiers dropping out of the sky serve two purposes; disorganize communication lines and seize airports where troop transports can be landed.

Russian Parachute Troops in Air

German 'Chutists Taking Off

## Japanese Face Vital War Decision; Must Choose Between Its Two Allies

### Cabinet to Confer Today on This New Emergency

TOKYO — (AP) — An emergency joint meeting of the Japanese cabinet with army and navy commanders was ordered for Monday to chart Japan's course in the war between her axis partner Germany and Russia, with whom she has a new friendship treaty.

The session was called after Foreign Minister Yosuke Matsuoka conferred with Emperor Hirohito.

**A government spokesman said Japanese action, or neutral inaction, would not be decided upon probably for two weeks yet.**

Maintaining a discreet silence, the Japanese may stand aside from the new conflict and respect their obligations under both the tripartite pact, with Germany and Italy and the non-aggression pact with Russia, observers said.

**The most significant fact to this empire, however, was that pressure seemingly had been removed from Britain and the United States, thus permitting the United States fleet to remain in the Pacific.**

It was believed that Germany's declaration of war could mean that Hitler was abandoning the idea of early conclusion of his war against Britain, which could not be to the liking of the Japanese with the United States getting several months leeway to prepare.

**Japan was reported to have tried unsuccessfully to intervene in the German-Russian crisis, and the United States was said to have been informed of the Japanese efforts.**

The Japanese-Russian friendship treaty, signed April 13, provides that "should one of the contracting parties become the object of hostilities on the part of one or several third powers, the other contracting party will observe neutrality throughout the duration of the conflict."

## *Gulf to Winnipeg; That's Length of Soviet Front*

BERLIN—(AP)—Adolf Hitler has sent his divisions into battle against Russia along a front exceeding the air-line distance from Brownsville at the southern tip of Texas to Winnipeg, Canada.

Military commentators emphasized that the troops were deployed in three main sections:

1 **The northern segment from the Arctic ocean to the Finnish Bight, covering 700 airline miles, where German sources claimed Finnish soldiers as allies.**

2 **The middle sector from Memel, on the Baltic sea, to the Carpathian mountains on Russia's Rumanian frontier. This 700-mile front is manned only by Germans.**

3 The southern section, covering 300 miles along the Russian-Rumanian border from the Carpathians to the mouth of the Danube. Here Rumanians are fighting beside Germans.

It was said the connection between the northern and middle sectors was maintained through mines to protect that flank and naval patrols.

### *Air Offense Centers on Black Sea Bases*

### *Moscow Holds Black Out---Reserves Called Up*

By AP, UP and INS.

Smashing air assaults on the Russian Black Sea bases of Sebastopol and Odessa and destruction of at least 40 Soviet bombers trying counter-raids against German positions were claimed by Germany today as notable first thrusts of the great new war Adolf Hitler declared at dawn Sunday against Russia.

**A report from Ankara, Turkey, said the Germans attacked Odessa, great Russian grain and oil port on the Black sea, on the same devastating scale as they raided Rotterdam and Belgrade last year.**

Bolstered by Finland and Rumania, the might of the German army was loosed against the Soviet union on a 2,000-mile front ranging from the Black sea to the wastes of the Arctic north—a battle zone which the Germans said at the outset was the most extensive continuous line in the history of warfare.

**Nazis Take 3 Towns**

Moscow radio early today broadcast the first Russian war communique which admitted the enemy had occupied Kalveria, Stoyanov and Tschecanovez in the districts of Grodno and Kiristinopol (towns in former Poland and Lithuania.) The towns taken are 10 to 15 miles east of the border.

**The communique, which called these gains "slight tactical successes," claimed, however, that the Red army held Adolf Hitler's panzer legions at bay at every point along the front.**

The communique revealed gigantic aerial activity, claiming 65 German planes had been shot down during attacks on soviet airdromes.

**Air News Stressed**

First news out of Berlin, delivered by DNB, official German news agency, dealt almost entirely with war in the air.

**In less than 24 hours, DNB said, the luftwaffe smashed hard at Sebastopol, which was occupied by German troops May 1, 1918, near the close of the World war; destroyed numerous Russian airports, hangars and barracks all along the lines; destroyed unnumbered Russian planes on the ground, and smashed columns of Red army tanks, railroads and munitions stores with bombs of all calibers.**

The Russians tried at least twice to raid the Germans, DNB said. The first attempt, directed against East Prussia, cost them seven out of nine attacking bombers, while the second, in the general government area of former Poland, saw 33 of 35 Soviet bombers destroyed, DNB claimed. The full Soviet losses are not determined, it added.

**First Communique**

The first military communique was issued from the German-Rumanian front in the south, stating these allies had joined battle with the Russians from the mountains of Bucovina to the shores of the Black sea.

This indicates a 250-mile battle front in that region alone.

**Information received by military circles in Vichy, France, indicated the main German thrust probably was being made in that area, directed towards Kharkov, about 500**

(Concluded on Page 6)

### *Russ Freighter Torpedoed, Sunk*

BERLIN — (AP) — German speed boats operating in Russian waters torpedoed and sank a 4,000-ton Russian freighter and blew up a fishing boat, the official German news agency announced Sunday night.

THE WEATHER
Showers tonight; Friday partly cloudy; seasonable temperature.
Temperatures Midnight to Noon

| H | 12 | 1 | 2 | 3 | 4 | 5 | 6 | 7 | 8 | 9 | 10 | 11 | 12 |
|---|---|---|---|---|---|---|---|---|---|---|---|---|---|
| T | 67 | 67 | 65 | 64 | 63 | 62 | 61 | 61 | 62 | 63 | 63 | 64 | 64 |

Highest year ago 89; lowest, 70.

# MINNEAPOLIS STAR JOURNAL

Vol. LXIII—No. 247 ★★ MINNEAPOLIS, MINN., THURSDAY, AUGUST 14, 1941 32 PAGES Price 3 Cents in Twin City Area 5 Cents Elsewhere



# F.D.R., CHURCHILL REVEAL AIMS AFTER PARLEY AT SEA

★ ★ ★ ★

## British See Joint Link With Russ

### Think Accord Reached for Action in Pacific

By Associated Press

LONDON — (AP) — The United States is now pledged to the reconstruction of post-war Europe and support of the Russian-British cause on every front, informed British sources said today in reviewing the jointly-issued Roosevelt-Churchill statement.

Things left unsaid in the statement are regarded as fully as important as those of the eight-point joint declaration.

**Omission of reference to Japan "implies Japan was one of the main points of discussion," a Japanese diplomat admitted.**

British informant said the meeting was at Mr. Roosevelt's invitation.

The Japanese source said the tempo of the Japanese advance in South Asia was slowed even as rumors of the historic meeting between the British and American leaders sped around the warring world.

* * *

The Roosevelt-Churchill conferences, which were attended by ranking officials and military naval and air experts of both countries, WERE RELIABLY REPORTED TO HAVE LASTED AT LEAST TWO OR THREE DAYS.

But neither the time nor the place of the meeting was disclosed here immediately.

* * *

Now there would be no surprise in London if a further announcement were made that Roosevelt and Churchill had sent personal assurances to Josef Stalin and the Russian people that Britain and the United States will give the USSR the fullest industrial co-operation in arming and supplying the Red army, air force and navy.

**News of the meeting was broadcast by radio to Britain by Lord Privy Seal Clement Attlee, who has been acting as Churchill's deputy in his absence.**

With the entire nation warned a day ahead of time to stand by

Attlee
Continued on Page Six

★ ★ ★ ★

CHURCHILL
*Met at sea with F. R.*

## Short Voices Fear of New British Ties

### Apparent an Alliance Has Been Formed, He Charges

WASHINGTON — (AP) — High praise came today from administration supporters for the meeting and declaration of policy by President Roosevelt and Prime Minister Churchill but Representative Short (R., Mo.) said it was "quite apparent that some sort of alliance has been formed."

"I don't like these secret, undercover agreements," Short told newsmen. "The president has no authority to form such an alliance. He shouldn't gamble with the destiny of 130,000,000 people and keep them in the dark about it."

Administration lieutenants, on the other hand, called the principles enunciated "noble" and expressed belief they would be well-received in all anti-Axis quarters.

Representative Shafer (R., Mich.), like Short an opponent of administration foreign policy, said the Roosevelt - Churchill statement "sounds to me like the same old sales talk with a little more sugar on it this time."

**One highly placed Republican, Senator Austin (R., Vt.), assistant minority leader, on**

Comment
Continued on Page Eight

## 8 Points of F. R., Churchill Aims

*THE JOINT DECLARATION agreed upon by President Roosevelt and Prime Minister Churchill follows:*

Joint declaration of the president of the United States of America and the prime minister, Mr. Churchill, representing his majesty's government in the United Kingdom, being met together, deem it right to make known certain common principles in the national policies of their respective countries on which they base their hopes for a better future for the world.

* * *

**FIRST**, their countries seek no aggrandizement, territorial or other;

**SECOND**, they desire to see no territorial changes that do not accord with the freely expressed wishes of the peoples concerned;

**THIRD**, they respect the right of all peoples to choose the form of government under which they will live; and they wish to see sovereign rights and self government restored to those who have been forcibly deprived of them;

**FOURTH**, they will endeavor, with due respect for their existing obligations, to further the enjoyment by all states, great or small, victor or vanquished, of access, on equal terms, to the trade and to the raw materials of the world which are needed for their economic prosperity;

**FIFTH**, they desire to bring about the fullest collaboration between all nations in the economic field with the object of securing, for all, improved labor standards, economic advancement and social security;

**SIXTH**, after the final destruction of the Nazi tyranny, they hope to see established a peace which will afford to all nations the means of dwelling in safety within their own boundaries, and which will afford assurance that all the men in all the lands may live out their lives in freedom from fear and want;

**SEVENTH**, such a peace should enable all men to traverse the high seas and oceans without hindrance;

**EIGHTH**, they believe that all of the nations of the world, for realistic as well as spiritual reasons, must come to the abandonment of the use of force. Since no future peace can be maintained if land, sea or air armaments continue to be employed by nations which threaten, or may threaten, aggression outside of their frontiers, they believe, pending the establishment of a wider and permanent system of general security, that the disarmament of such nations is essential. They will likewise aid and encourage all other practicable measures which will lighten for peace-loving peoples the crushing burden of armaments.

## Police Chief Will Return in 3 Weeks

Mayor Marvin L. Kline today announced Police Chief Edward B. Hansen would be back on the job in three weeks, probably sooner.

The announcement followed a visit of Kline with Hansen in Hansen's room in St. Mary's hospital in Duluth late yesterday, two weeks to the day after the mayor's first meeting with his police chief following Hansen's attack of encephalitis.

* * *

Dr. Harry Klein, Hansen's physician, said the chief may be discharged from the hospital by Sunday, and agreed he should be able to return to the job within three weeks.

**Hansen will complete his rest in a north woods retreat before returning to Minneapolis, the mayor said.**

The mayor said Hansen was even faster in his answers and spoke more incisively than before he became ill, and conjectured that in view of the hesitation the chief sometimes had displayed in conversation the illness may have been upon him some time before it was suspected.

He said he was "considerably encouraged" by Hansen's freshness and enthusiasm.

"Of course," the mayor said, he will have to take it easy to start with, but "he has made a truly remarkable recovery since I saw him last.

**"His interest has returned fully and he has been busy the past several days making plans to carry out upon his return.**

"We talked for more than an hour, chiefly upon plans for the training school he has in mind as soon as he is able to take up his duties where he left off.

"We will announce details of the school as soon as he has them in shape."

## Tells of Historic Meeting

While reporters crowd close to his desk, Stephen Early (pipe in mouth), White House secretary, distributes copies of the release telling of the momentous meeting at sea by President Roosevelt and Winston Churchill.—AP Wirephoto.

## Churchill and F. R. Bluffing, Say Germans

BERLIN —(AP)— The first authorized German reaction to the war aims statement of President Roosevelt and Prime Minister Churchill was that the whole declaration was a "propaganda bluff."

**"Churchill and Roosevelt are unfortunate in their declaration being made at a time when every hour brings new reports of impressive successes for German arms in the Ukraine," one spokesman asserted.**

Previously, there had been only DNB's brief, factual report that the United States president and British prime minister had met.

* * *

DNB later said Roosevelt and Churchill had agreed on an eight-point war aim statement, but it did not give the points. It said the high spot was "disarmament of the Axis powers."

* * *

Another objective, the agency told German readers, is that after "final destruction of Nazi tyranny" a permanent system of general security should be established.

It mentioned economic co-operation but gave no details.

★ ★ ★ ★

ROOSEVELT
*Still at rendezvous?*

## Final OK Is Put on Long Draft Term

### Solons Adopt House Version, Send It to F.R.

WASHINGTON — (UP) — Final senate approval today sent to President Roosevelt, legislation extending the service periods of all army enlisted personnel for 18 months.

Final action came in senate acceptance of the house version of the legislation.

* * *

The measure, passed by the single vote margin of 203 to 202 in the house Tuesday, WOULD AUTHORIZE THE PRESIDENT TO RETAIN SELECTEES, NATIONAL GUARDSMN AND RESERVISTS FOR A TOTAL OF TWO AND A HALF YEAR. Regular enlisted men, who signed up for a three-year period, could be held for four and a half years.

* * *

Under the legislation, all men who had served 12 months would receive a $10 monthly pay increase.

* * *

Congress could terminate the president's authority to hold men beyond their original service periods at any time through the adoption of a concurrent resolution. CONGRESS ALSO COULD PERMIT THE PRESIDENT TO HOLD MEN FOR AN UNSPECIFIED PERIOD BEYOND AN ADDITIONAL 18 months by approving a resolution stating further extension was "in the interests of national defense."

★ ★ ★ ★

## Say 'Nazi Tyranny' Must End

### Discuss Aid to Axis Foes, Set 'Future World' Program

WASHINGTON — (UP) — The White House announced today President Roosevelt and British Prime Minister Winston Churchill had met on the high seas and agreed on a joint U. S.-British declaration of peace aims "after the final destruction of the Nazi tyranny."

The White House statement confirmed officially for the first time that the two leaders had met at sea and "had several conferences."

**THEIR EXACT MEETING PLACE WAS NOT DISCLOSED.**

Mr. Roosevelt and Churchill were accompanied by their ranking military, naval and air advisers.

**Lord Beaverbrook was one of the British conferees and proceeded to Washington for further talks on American war aid for his homeland and Russia.**

Their joint declaration of policy embodied eight separate points, including the "disarmament" of the Axis powers after the war.

**The joint declaration, spurning by implication any future Axis peace offer which does not entail complete capitulation to Britain and her allies, contained no mention of any American military action or of strategy which might be followed by the United States in the battle of the Atlantic or on other fronts.**

The White House announcement on the meeting of President Roosevent and Churchill said:

"The president of the United States and the prime minister, Mr. Churchill, representing his majesty's government in the United Kingdom, have met at sea.

* * *

"They have been accompanied by officials of their two governments, including high ranking officers of their military, naval and air services.

**"The whole problem of the supply of munitions of war, as provided by the lease-lend act, for the armed forces of the United States and for those countries actively engaged in resisting aggression has been further examined.**

"Lord Beaverbrook, the minister of supply of the British government, has joined in these conferences. He is going to proceed to Washington to discuss further details with appropriate officials of the United States government.

"These conferences will also cover the supply problems of the Soviet Union.

* * *

"The president and the prime minister have had several confer-

Roosevelt
Continued on Page Six

## Encephalitis Slackens, Federal Officials Note

### Woman Killed When Car Fails at Curve

SPIRIT LAKE, IOWA — (UP) — Mrs. Edward Cook, 23, Worthington, Minn., died today of a skull fracture suffered when the car in which she was riding failed to make a turn near the Iowa-Minnesota line.

Her husband, 25, suffered minor injuries.

### Attlee, Darlan Talks to Be Rebroadcast

WTCN at 6 p.m. today will rebroadcast radio talks by Maj. Clement Attlee, British lord privy seal, and Adm. Jean Darlan, French vice premier.



### No New Deaths Recorded in State; One in N. D.

A pronounced slackening in the Northwest's encephalitis epidemic was noted today by federal and state health officials, and hopeful predictions were voiced the disease had reached its climax.

Dr. F. J. Hill of the North Dakota state health department said the epidemic appeared "slackening off" in the vicinity of Fargo.

**In Minnesota the death toll stood at 34. No new deaths were reported up to noon today.**

One new death in North Dakota and three in Manitoba boosted the Northwest fatality total to 92.

Mrs. Ward Congdon, 52, of Enderlin, N. D., died in a Fargo hospital last night.

* * *

Two new patients, both men in their 50's, a Fargoan and a resident of Sutton, N. D., were admitted to Fargo hospitals.

Estimates today placed the total cases in the epidemic area at

Encephalitis
Continued on Page Six

### Pollen Count

**Ragweed 77 granules per cubic yard of air.**
**Total count 106 granules.**
**Count taken from 8 a.m. yesterday to 8 a.m. today.**

## Newsboy (on Foot) Sued for Breaking Automobile Window

B. B. Gislason, 504 University avenue SE., middle-aged newspaper vendor, ran into the side of an automobile July 29, broke a ventilation window in the car, was stunned, but went about his business.

Gislason today was sued in conciliation court for breaking the window.

The driver, Walter Beasley, 2746 Clinton avenue, is suing for $4.50. The case was set for Sept. 25.

## On the Inside



## Marines in Nevada Rope and 'Break' Own Mounts

HAWTHORNE, NEV.—Add another talent to the others exhibited by the versatile United States marines.

They rope and train their own horses which they use for mounts at the naval ammunition depot here.

Wild horses roam the foothills here and when the marines pitch camp near water holes the leathernecks lariats are put to use and the range is turned into a wild west rodeo.

**The captured horses are brought back to the depot to be "broke," and they are then used for recreation purposes as well as for patrol duty on the reservation.**

Racing, jumping and riding contests are held by the marines.

* * *

When they sent a team to the Yerington, Nev., horses show recently, they won all the prizes in the jumping contests.

## BULLETINS

### F. R., CHURCHILL PRAISE RUSS

**LONDON—(UP)—President Roosevelt and Prime Minister Churchill were reliably reported today to have sent a joint letter to Josef V. Stalin, premier of the Soviet Union, expressing admiration for the Russian fight against German aggression and determination to continue all possible aid to Russia.**

* * *

### WON'T STOP US, AXIS REACTION

**ROME—(AP)—Fascist circles said the joint American-British declaration would fail to run the Axis or Japan off their courses.**

* * *

### 'NIPS HITLER PEACE DRIVE'

**LONDON—(INS)—Observers predicted that the eight-point Anglo-American program would nip any new Hitler "peace offensive" in the bud.**

* * *

### SOVIET ENVOYS PLEASED

**LONDON —INS— The Anglo-American declaration was warmly welcomed by the Soviet embassy in London. References of aid to the Soviet Union are chiefly appreciated, a spokesman said.**

* * *

### PACIFIC THREAT CHIEF REASON?

**LONDON—(By Telephone)—(UP)—Threats of war in the Pacific are believed to have been one of the chief reasons for the meeting of President Roosevelt and Prime Minister Churchill.**

## Youth Admits Speed Charge, Faked Report

A cloud of dust and a burst of speed kept Donald J. Farr, 244 Virginia avenue, St. Paul, from the hands of the law last Sunday . . . but a tell-tale license number caught up with him today.

**St. Paul police chased a speeding car at 60 miles an hour through the south side of St. Paul Sunday, but lost it in the dst.**

A check on the license brought Farr into custody. At first he denied driving the car and made out a report it had been stolen.

* * *

Today he pleaded guilty to reckless driving and makin gout a false report, and was sentenced to 15 day son each charge to serve concurrently.

## Beaverbrook at Capital

WASHINGTON — (UP) — Lord Beaverbrook arrived here by airplane today and proceeded at once to the British embassy.

Beaverbrook

He arrived in Washington in a large American built bomber with British markings.

Secrecy prevailed at army and navy air fields here, and it was not known immediately whether anyone accompanied him. He was expected to hold a press conference later in the day.

## GAS FOR RUSS LEAVES TODAY

WASHINGTON—(AP)—Petroleum co-ordinator Ickes announced today the first shipment of aviation gasoline to Russia aboard an American tanker would leave Los Angeles today for Vladivostok, flying the United States flag.

The co-ordinator told newsmen also priorities had been obtained for the manufacture of 10,000 drums for shipment of petroleum to Russia aboard merchantmen.

## No Axis-Style Fanfare Staged at Meeting on 'Calm Blue Sea'

LONDON—(UP)—President Roosevelt and Prime Minister Churchill met on "the calm blue sea" of the Atlantic for three days last week-end, it was disclosed today, upon the express personal invitation of the chief executive of the United States.

* * *

**The meeting was in dramatic contrast to the fanfare of meetings of Axis leaders in the past.**

* * *

Unlike most Brenner meetings, there was no fanfare, no lines of steel helmeted guards, no swarms of generals, no little girls with posies. There was just the empty Atlantic, which the British and American navies still control. On it Roosevelt and Churchill talked.

The Brenner meetings have ended with sharp action by Germany or Italy or both. Potentialities for action in the meeting of American and British statesmen embraced five continents and all the seas of the globes.

**But the world is apt to be kept guessing for a while at least, on just what was said and done.**

For days uncertainty about just what was happening on the Atlantic seemed to have frozen Axis diplomacy and to have put the brakes on Japanese expansion in the Far East.

**CLOUDY**
U. S. Weather Bureau Forecasts
Partly cloudy Tuesday and Wednesday, continued mild.
High temperature Monday 43 at 3:30 a.m.
Low 34 at 7 p.m.
Humidity 89% at 7 p.m.
Precipitation—trace.
*Details on Page 11.*

# Minneapolis Morning Tribune

FOUNDED IN 1867

Vol. LXXV—No. 192. 18 Pages MINNEAPOLIS, MINN., TUESDAY, DECEMBER 2, 1941 ★★★ Price 3 Cents in Twin City Area, 5 Cents Elsewhere



**MOSCOW**

No one in Washington is especially worried over the likelihood of Moscow's fall, says Paul Mallon in his column on page 4 today. He tells what Russia has done to minimize loss of its capital city.

# 18 GIULTY IN SWP CASE

## RAIL LABOR ROW SETTLED

### Artist Jailed for WPA Fraud

**Syd Fossum, Minneapolis Painter, Charged With Collecting Pay While Absent in N. Y.**

**SYD FOSSUM**
*from a self-portrait*

Charged with presenting a fraudulent claim for $49 WPA wages covering time when he was not working, Sydney G. Fossum, WPA artist, 309 Fifth avenue N.E., surrendered to the United States marshal late Monday.

He was released on $1,000 bond, pending arraignment in federal court here next Monday.

The federal grand jury indicted Fossum last week after the United States district attorney had presented evidence the artist was in New York, instead of working on an art project, last January during the period for which he collected wages.

Fossum is ranked by critics as one of the outstanding artists in the Twin Cities.

His oil paintings, many of them reflecting a liberal philosophy applied to modern social problems, rated high in shows at Minneapolis Institute of Arts, where one of them won first prize in 1939 and another ranked second in the show held last month. He also had been represented in many other art shows here.

He was working on the WPA art project at Walker Art center at time of his indictment.

### Jap Crisis Grows Ominous

PAGE 2

### Reds Repel Moscow Thrust

PAGE 2

### Nazis Battle Against Libya Trap

PAGE 2

### Active Axis Role for Vichy Hinted

PAGE 2

### Priorities Cost 3,000 Jobs in State

PAGE 9

### Wage Boost Ends Threat of Walkout

**Worker and Management Negotiators Agree After 2-Day and 2-Night Session**

WASHINGTON — (AP) — Railroad labor and management representatives settled their wage and vacations dispute Monday night on terms which were understood to add $300,000,000 to $325,000,000 a year to the carriers' payrolls.

The effort of the settlement, worked out by President Roosevelt's emergency fact-finding board after two days and nights of almost continuous negotiations, is that a strike set for Dec. 7 will be called off.

**The board had been sitting as a mediation agency since Saturday night.**

Chairman Wayne L. Morse, who announced the settlement, declined to make public the terms of the settlement until after they had been submitted to President Roosevelt Tuesday.

**30 MILLION MORE THAN FIRST PLAN**

Other sources, however, said the pay increase recommendations totalled about $30,000,000 to $35,000,000 a year more than those suggested by the board in a previous report.

**In the earlier report, the board recommended over-all wage increases of approximately $270,000,000. The unions rejected the recommendations.**

The first report recommended a 7½ per cent increase for the operating brotherhoods and 13⅓ per cent or 9 cents an hour for the non-operating men for the period from Sept. 1, 1941, to Dec. 31, 1942.

**76-CENT BOOST FOR 8-HOUR DAY**

Sources outside the board said that Monday night's recommendations called for payments of 7½ per cent increases for the operating men until Dec. 1, 1941, and 9½ cent-an-hour increases thereafter. This 9½ cent increase would not be in addition to the 7½ per cent increase but would replace it.

(Concluded on Page 5)

### *Baby Kills Mother*

**GUN WAS 'UNLOADED'**

SLAYTON, MINN.— (AP) — While Mrs. Arthur Van de Velde, 31, sat in the kitchen of her parents' home coddling a six-months-old nephew, her own son, Billy, 3, found a fascinating toy to play with Monday.

It was a .22 caliber rifle, supposedly unloaded, that had been left standing in the corner since Mrs. Van de Velde's younger brothers returned from a rabbit hunt Sunday.

Billy's baby fingers grasped the gun.

The weapon discharged and the bullet struck Mrs. Van de Velde in the left temple, killing her instantly.

As she fell from her chair, her body crashed upon that of the nephew and he was slightly injured.

Mrs. Van de Velde's husband, parents and five brothers survive her.

### U. S.-Owned Ship Feared Torpedoed

NEW YORK— (AP) —The United States maritime commission freighter Macbeth, flying the Panamanian flag, is missing in the North Atlantic and unofficial reports said Monday that she had been torpedoed.

One report said the Macbeth, formerly the 4,935-ton Italian ship Ida Z.O., had been towed into a Canadian port.

(Authoritative sources in Washington said the ship had not been torpedoed but would make no other comment).

The freighter, operated by United States lines which chartered her from the maritime commission was ferrying American supplies to England.

The government seized her at Mobile, Ala., last March 30 when all German, Italian and Danish ships in this country were taken under protective custody to prevent sabotage.

### FBI Grabs Third Man in Film Plot

CHICAGO — (UP) — FBI agents Monday seized Nick Dean, Chicago night club operator who has been under indictment since Sept. 29 as an alleged accomplice of Willie Bioff and George Browne in extortion of money from Hollywood motion picture executives.

Dean waived extradition and was taken by airplane to New York for arraignment.

### Miles Dunne and 4 Others Win Liberty

**Vincent Convicted; All Cleared of Conspiracy Charges—Appeal Planned**

Eighteen of 23 defendants in the federal sedition trial growing out of activities of the Socialist Workers party, including V. R. Dunne, prime mover in organization of the old General Drivers union, were found guilty Monday night of "advocating the desirability of overthrowing the government by force and violence."

All 23 defendants were found not guilty on the indictment's first count, which alleged a conspiracy to overthrow the government.

Among five acquitted was Miles Dunne, brother of V. R. Dunne, who also was a leader in the old drivers union.

**LENIENCY IS RECOMMENDED**

In returning its verdict after 56 hours of deliberation, the jury recommended leniency.

Sentence will be imposed by Judge M. M. Joyce at 10 a.m. next Monday.

**The charge on which the 18 were convicted carries a possible penalty of a $10,000 fine, up to 10 years in prison or both.**

The charge on which they were acquitted carried a possible penalty of $5,000 fine, or a term up to six years in prison, or both.

Judge Joyce told defense attorneys he would consider motions for new trials at 10 a. m. Saturday.

Meanwhile, on recommendation of Assistant United States Attorney General Henry A. Schweinhaut, the 18 defendants were allowed their freedom on present bonds.

**DEFENSE PLANS TO APPEAL**

Albert Goldman of New York, defense attorney and himself one of the 18 found guilty, said he would appeal, declaring he would "carry the case to the American people."

"That the government has succeeded in winning a verdict of guilty against 18 members of Socialist Workers party," the statement said, "does not in the least prove they are guilty of the charges leveled against them by the government.

"It still remains a fact that the conspirators are Dan Tobin (president of the international teamsters' union), President Roosevelt and Attorney General Biddle, who have initiated this frame-up for the purpose of violating the will of the truck drivers of Minneapolis and of stilling the voice of the revolutionary opposition to the second world war.

**FREE SPEECH HELD IMPERILED**

"We intend to exhaust every step and every resource for appeal purposes. Above all, we shall appeal to the American people in an attempt to convince them the rights of free speech, free press and free assembly are in real danger."

Prior to the trial various groups protested that freedom of speech and other American rights were nullified by the accusations.

**Most of the defendants denied membership in SWP and others declared they had no thought of violent overthrow of the government.**

At time of the raids, Acting Attorney General Francis Biddle said the action was being taken against "persons who have been engaged in criminal seditious activities . . . and have gained control of a legitimate labor union to use it for illegal purposes."

**NONE APPEAR DOWNHEARTED**

Fifteen of the indicted persons were officers and members of General Drivers Union No. 544, which had bolted from AFL affiliation to CIO shortly before the raids.

Goldman said he would move for a new trial Saturday and, following that, if it is denied, would

(Concluded on Page 3)

## *CONVICTED*

Eighteen of the 23 defendants in the federal court sedition trial were found guilty on one count of a two-count indictment Monday night.

The eighteen were:

**VINCENT R. DUNNE**, organizer, local 544-CIO.

**JAMES P. CANNON**, New York, national secretary of SWP.

Dunne Skoglund Cannon Goldman

**CARL SKOGLUND**, former president of 544.

**ALBERT GOLDMAN**, New York, attorney for SWP.

**FARRELL DOBBS**, national labor secretary of SWP.

**CARLOS HUDSON**, former editor of the Northwest Organizer.

Dobbs Carlson Hudson Hamel

**GRACE HOLMES CARLSON**, St. Paul, state organizer for SWP.

**CLARENCE HAMEL**, organizer 544-CIO.

**FELIX MORROW**, New York, editor of The Militant and Fourth Internationale.

**EDWARD PALMQUIST**, chairman federal workers' section, 544-CIO.

Morrow Kuehn Palmquist Geldman

**KARL KUEHN**, secretary federal workers' section.

**MAX GELDMAN**, formerly with federal workers' section.

**OSCAR COOVER**, secretary SWP.

**HARRY DE BOER**, organizer 544-CIO.

Coover Cooper De Boer Russell

**JAKE COOPER**, truck driver.

**ALFRED RUSSELL**, former teamsters' organizer of Omaha.

Schoenfeld

**OSCAR SCHOENFELD**, New York.

**EMIL HANSON**, organizer 544-CIO.

Hanson

## *ACQUITTED*

Five defendants in the federal court sedition trial were found not guilty of charges contained in the two-count indictment.

They were:

**MILES B. DUNNE**, president 544-CIO.

**RAY RAINBOLT**, organizer 544-CIO.

Dunne Orgon Rainbolt Swanson

**ROY ORGON**, truck driver.

**HAROLD SWANSON.**

**KELLY POSTAL**, secretary - treasurer 544-CIO.

Postal

### Indictment Voted in Assault Case

Phillip Thompson, 26, 3516 Twenty-eighth avenue S., jailed as the man who criminally assaulted a married woman employed as cook in a hospital while she was on her way to work early Thanksgiving morning, was indicted by Hennepin county grand jury late Monday.

### America First to Carry Fight on F.R. to Polls

CHICAGO — (UP) — The America First committee announced Monday night that it will "go into the 1942 national elections" with support for candidates opposing the administration's foreign policy.

The announcement was made by Gen. Robert E. Wood, acting national chairman.

**The committee's statement condemned the administration's policy as a "trend toward Fascism in America" and demanded a "return to congress" of only those members who "faithfully execute the people's trust."**

"Accordingly," the statement said, "the America First committee, which has not yet sought to influence the election of any candidate for public office, now believes that in due time and in proper compliance with the law this policy must be changed.

"Efforts must be directed toward the renomination and re-election in 1942 of those senators and representatives in congress who have kept faith with the people's mandate to avoid participation in the war."

**CARDINAL PRINCIPLE, SAYS LOCAL GROUP**

Officials of the Minneapolis America First committee Monday night explained that support for candidates who believe in keeping this nation out of foreign wars has been a cardinal principle of the organization from its beginning and was stated specifically in resolutions at a Washington conference of leaders a month ago.

The Minnesota and Minneapolis units, however, have taken no definite action along that line and have considered no slate of possible candidates to be supported.

***WHERE TO FIND IT***



### *SCHOOL JANITORS TO GET BOARD 'NO'*

School board members were preapred Monday night to tell representatives of the janitor-engineers union Tuesday that it will be impossible to grant 1942 pay increases to janitors until money has been found to pay in full present scheduled salaries of all school employes.

At the same session, it was said, the board will appeal to the city council for help in obtaining a $660,000 emergency loan to tide the schools over until a long-range budget balancing program can be worked out.

Rejection of the pay raise, said to have been agreed to by the board's majority group, will put squarely up to union leaders the question of calling a strike, which union members already have authorized.

**BOARD CONFIDENT APPEAL WILL WIN**

Board members were confident the loan appeal will convince the union every effort is being made to clear up the financial shortage, and that the janitors will be willing to put off a strike for that reason.

**The board also was relying on a civil service rule, forbidding unexcused absences from work for more than three days, to deter janitors from striking.**

The conference, a session of the board's committee of the whole and representatives of the union, will take place at 4 p.m., with the public excluded. Actions taken by the board will be subject to confirmation at its regular meeting Dec. 9.

**REPAIR BUDGET WOULD BE CUT**

At the Tuesday session, the board also is expected to propose that the janitorial pay budget for 1942 be increased $75,000 by cutting a similar amount from the appropriation for repair and improvement of buildings.

Thus, although it would not be able to grant increases the janitors ask, it would be able to come closer than at present to paying them their present scheduled salaries.

### 'Servant of Fascism'

LOS ANGELES— (UP) —The United Automobile Workers (CIO) Monday night described a proposed new union which would oppose the CIO and the AFL as "obviously predicated upon the serving of the interests of Hitler and Fascism."

SILENT SLUGGER PICKS HIS VICTIMS

### *Clouts Girl, 16, and Man, 70*

A 34-year-old man was jailed on a drunk charge late Monday after he allegedly attacked and slugged two pedestrians with no apparent provocation, near Eighteenth street and First avenue S.

E. F. Carlston, 70, 3951 Pleasant avenue, told police he was approaching his car, parked near the intersection, when the man struck him between the eyes. Carlston said no words were spoken before he was hit.

When he recovered, Carlston said, he followed his assailant and, a short distance away, saw him knock down a young girl.

**Girl Knocked Down**

The second victim was Muriel Peterson, 16, 130 E. Eighteenth street, who was on her way to a neighborhood store on an errand for her mother.

Miss Peterson, who said she never had seen the man before, and had no warning the attack was coming, told police the man struck her full in the face below the right eye with his fist. He knocked her to the sidewalk. Both her knees were skinned and her left elbow bruised.

A crowd gathered quickly, Carlston said, and he urged somebody to follow the man or call a policeman.

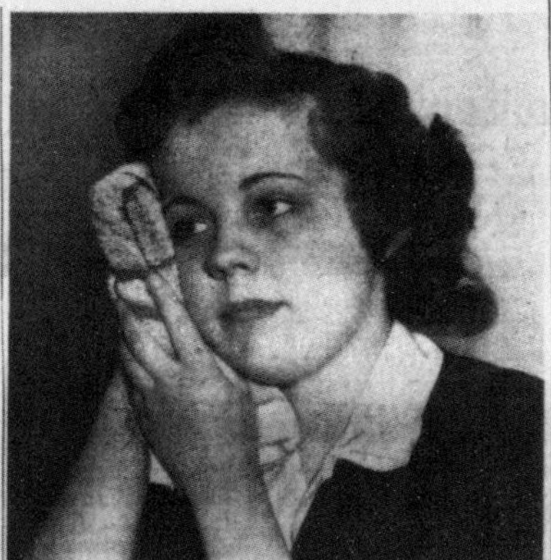

**MURIEL PETERSON**
*Knocked down by blow on face from stranger*

Meanwhile, several calls were received at police headquarters, and the man was picked up near First and Franklin avenues by Patrolman Joe Kolors and H. T. Selvers.

In the city jail, the man gave his name as William Craven. Police charged him with drunkenness, but said they had urged Miss Peterson and Carlston to bring additional charges.

# THE SIXTH WAR EXTRA

**MUCH COLDER**
U. S. Weather Bureau Forecast
Much colder Monday; fair to partly cloudy, continued cold Tuesday.
High temperature Sunday 40 at 11:45 a.m.
Low 28 at 3:30 a.m.
Humidity 90% at 7 p.m.
Precipitation—.03-inch.
*Details on Page 6.*

# Minneapolis Morning Tribune

FOUNDED IN 1867

*Vol. LXXV—No. 198.* | 20 Pages | MINNEAPOLIS, MINN., MONDAY, DECEMBER 8, 1941 | ★★★★ | Price 3 Cents in Twin City Area, 5 Cents Elsewhere



# JAPS OPEN WAR ON U. S.!

## *Attack Hawaii, Guam, Singapore; U. S. Army, Navy Losses Heavy*

By THE ASSOCIATED PRESS

Japan assaulted every main United States and British possession in the central and western Pacific and invaded Thailand Monday in a hasty but evidently shrewdly-planned prosecution of a war she began Sunday without warning.

Her formal declaration of war against both the United States and Britain came two hours and 55 minutes after Japanese planes spread death and terrific destruction in Honolulu and Pearl Harbor at 7:35 a.m., Hawaiian time (12:05 p.m., Minneapolis time) Sunday.

The claimed successes for this fell swoop included sinking of the U. S. battleship West Virginia and setting afire of the battleship Oklahoma.

From that moment, each tense tick of the clock brought new and flaming accounts of Japanese aggression in her secretly launched war of conquest or death for the land of the Rising Sun.

The government officially reported "heavy" naval and "large" army losses.

As compiled from official and unofficial accounts from all affected countries, the record ran like this:

Honolulu bombed a second time.

### WAKE ISLAND REPORTED CAPTURED

Lumber-laden U. S. army transport torpedoed 1,300 miles west of San Francisco and another transport in distress.

NBC reported the U. S. transport General Hugh L. Scott, formerly an American President lines, had been sunk about 1,600 miles from Manila.

It also relayed a report that the former President Harrison, now a transport which has been sent to China to evacuate Americans, "had been either seized or sunk in the Yangtze river, just south of Shanghai."

Shanghai's international settlement seized; U. S. gunboat Wake captured there and British gunboat Peterel destroyed;

Capture of the U. S. island of Wake;

Bombing of the U. S. island of Guam;

Bombing of many points throughout the Philippine islands;

Invasion of Northern Malaya and bombing of Singapore;

Invasion of Thailand (Siam) and bombing of Bangkok.

The first U. S. official casualty report listed 104 dead and more than 300 injured in the army at Hickam field, alone, near Honolulu.

An NBC observer in Honolulu reported the death toll at Hickam was 300.

There was heavy damage in Honolulu residential districts, and the death list among civilians was large but uncounted.

### NAZIS CLAIM THIRD BATTLESHIP HIT

The German radio reported that a sea battle between the Japanese navy on one side and the British and U. S. on the other was in progress in the western Pacific, with a third U. S. warship hit in addition to the West Virginia and Oklahoma.

The British command at Singapore announced the Japanese invasion and said empire forces were engaging the foe.

The White House announced that during President Roosevelt's conference with legislative leaders and members of the cabinet he received word from General Douglas MacArthur that "enemy planes were over central Luzon in the Philippines about 7 p.m., Minneapolis time; that a bombing attack has been made on Davao at the southern end of the southern island of Mindanoa, and that another attack has been made on Camp John Hayes at Baguio in the northern mountains of Luzon.

"So far," the White House announcement said, "No essential damage had been reported."

The navy clamped a tight censorship on news out of Hawaii so there was little news of U. S. defensive actions, except the report that a number of the attacking planes at Honolulu had been shot down in dog-fights over the city; an unconfirmed report that a Japanese aircraft carrier had been sunk off Hawaii; and announcement that U. S. army and navy forces had started carrying out secret instructions long since issued to them in event of just such an emergency.

### WAR DECLARATIONS COME SWIFTLY

A formal U. S. declaration of war could not come until Monday at the earliest, and British summoned her parliament to meet Monday for similar action. President Roosevelt, the cabinet and congressional leaders met Sunday night and a joint session of congress was set on Monday.

The Dutch government in London, the Dutch East Indies, Canada, and the central American nations of Costa Rica and Nacaragua, near the blacked-out canal zone, quickly declared war on Japan.

At the exact moment Japan was irrevocably embarking on her course of "conquer or die," her emissaries in Washington were seeking still another appointment to continue the peace talks with which they have consumed the time since last August, with every protestation of good faith.

Finally, when they saw Secretary of State Hull and gave him the latest statement of Japan's position, he told them he never had seen a document "so crowded with falsehoods and distortions."

With embarrassed smiles, the Japanese left.

### TOKYO PREDICTS GERMAN ACTION

A Tokyo radio broadcast said informed Japanese sources believed Germany would declare war on the United States within 24 hours, but the Germans left this point entirely open since their alliance with Japan calls for aid only in case Japan is attacked.

Details of Japan's explosive rupture of the peace of the Pacific came from many sources.

Singapore reported the Japanese landed in northern Malaya, 300 miles north of there and bombed the great British naval stronghold, causing small loss of life among civilians and property damage.

The Singapore raiders met a vigorous anti-aircraft fire.

The landing in the north was made shortly after a first attempt had been repulsed with small arms fire. British forces were engaged.

Latest reports said the Japanese were filtering inland toward the Kotabahru airdrome.

The first landing attempt was made at Kotabahru, on the northern tip of Malaya near the Thailand border.

After being repulsed, the Japanese were successful at Sabak, 13 miles southward.

They then proceeded overland toward Kotabahru, fighting with British air and land forces as they went.

The British said that Bangkok, capital of Thailand, had been bombed and that Japanese troops have invaded Thailand.

Radio Tokyo said that "in order to maintain the independence of Thailand, Japan has entered the southern portion of the tiny country to combat British troops which have entered from the Malayan border.

(The NBC correspondent in Manila reported that the Pan-American airways base on the Island of Guam had been bombed by the Japanese.

Radio Tokyo reported that Japanese naval ships have surrounded the island of Guam and that an oil reservoir and hotel have been set afire.

### JAP AIRCRAFT CARRIER SUNK

A Reuter (British news agency) dispatch from Shanghai quoted unconfirmed reports saying the Japanese had occupied U. S.-owned Wake island, between Guam and Hawaii.

(A Japanese aircraft carrier was sunk off Hanalulu Sunday, according to United Press reporting a broadcast by the Panama radio heard in New York.)

Early reports from Honolulu said that a direct bomb hit on Hickamn airfield, out of Honolulu, had killed 350 men. The war department's first official estimate of deaths was much lower.

Army chiefs told the White House that there were 104 known dead and more than 300 wounded in the army forces. These figures did not include civilian casualties.

(The Tokyo correspondent of the Japanese newspaper Osaka Mainichi in Shanghai reported that a Japanese-American naval battle was in progress "in the western Pacific.")

(The United Press reported the United States fleet steamed out of Pearl Harbor Sunday night. Shortly afterward sound of gunfire was heard off Oahu and gunflashes were seen. Reliable Washington quarters said anti-aircraft fire and naval action had bagged six Japanese planes and four submarines.)

President Roosevelt, as soon as he heard of the bombing, ordered

(Concluded on Page 6)

# CONGRESS TO HEAR F. R. TODAY

(1) Occupation of Indo-China by Japan drew severe economic reprisals from U. S who saw threat to vital rubber and tin stocks in East Indies. Now Nippon forces are poised over Thailand and Burma Road despite warning against further expansion.

(2) Japan wants to end Chinese war free of "foreign interference"

(3) Russian bombers could reach flimsy cities of Axis Japan easily from Vladivostok base. Both nations have big armies on Manchukuo-Siberia frontier

(4) British fortress city of Singapore is defense keystone of entire Far East Japan could not take over resources of Indies without first reducing it.

—alm

## Roosevelt Will Tell Joint Session of War Status

RICHARD WILSON
Chief of Washington Tribune Bureau

WASHINGTON—An extraordinary joint session of congress to convene at 12:30 p.m. Monday (11:30 a.m., Minneapolis time) will hear from the lips of President Roosevelt that America is at war with Japan.

Decision to call the joint session was reached at an unprecedented meeting of legislative leaders and the cabinet with the president at the White House Sunday night a few hours after Japan had launched an attack on American naval positions in the Pacific.

A state of war exists between the United States and all the Axis powers. This was evident here, whatever may be the form of this belligerency which will come after Mr. Roosevelt addresses congress.

There was little doubt the president will ask congress to recognize a condition that already exists, but the legislative leaders and members of the cabinet, on leaving the White House, refused to say what the president plans to say.

### ITALY, GERMANY MAY ALSO DECLARE WAR

They declared they were not advised of the nature of the president's address, but Attorney General Francis Biddle revealed that "the chief asked us not to discuss it".

Receipts during the night or Monday by the American government of declarations that a state of war exists from Germany and Italy as well as from Japan would occasion little surprise in the state department.

Senator Thomas Connally (D., Texas) chairman of the senate committee on foreign relations announced that the extraordinary joint session will be held.

This was all that can be said, he declared.

Attorney General Biddle pointed out that the existence of a state of war and its recognition by congress, would bring into effect a number of emergency powers which could not otherwise be invoked.

### NO OFFICIAL WORD OF STATE OF WAR

Speaker Sam Rayburn confirming Connally's announcement, gave emphasis to the fact that the United States does not yet have any official word that Japan has declared war on the United States, as reported by the Tokyo radio.

The discussion at the meeting of

(Concluded on Page 6)

### *Network Stations to Carry F.R. Talk*

President Roosevelt's massage to congress will be carried by all three major radio networks at 11:30 a.m. Minneapolis time, Monday. It will be carried locally by WCCO, WTCN, KSTP and WLOL.

### WHERE TO FIND IT



## BULLETINS

### *Casualties Unknown*

WASHINGTON — (AP) — The war and navy departments announced Sunday night that no information has been received about casualties in the Hawaiian area.

"Families will be notified promptly as soon as definite word regarding casualties becomes available. Both departments request individual inquiries be not sent," the announcement said.

### *Nicaragua on U. S. Side*

MANAGUA, NICARAGUA—(AP)—President General Anastasio Somoza announced Sunday night Nicaragua would declare war on Japan concurrently with the United States.

### *Lindbergh Silent*

WEST TISBURY, MASS.—(AP)—Charles A. Lindbergh, visiting in this Martha's Vineyard island village, refused Sunday night to see newspapermen or accept any message.

### *Alaska Calls Banned*

SEATTLE — (UP) —The army Sunday cancelled all commercial telephone calls to Alaska. The army signal corps operates all commercial communications between the United States and Alaska.

### *Here's Your Time Table for Pacific*

With the outbreak of hostilities in the Pacific, you should know the difference in times between Minneapolis and the various "fronts" involved.

This is an easy way to figure the difference. All times are given in the same 24-hour period.

WHEN IT IS 6 A.M. MONDAY IN MINNEAPOLIS:

It is 1:30 a.m. Monday in Hawaii.

It is 8 p.m. Monday in the Philippines.

It is 9 p.m. Monday in Japan.

It is 7 p.m. Monday in French Indo-China and Thailand.

The great difference in time between Hawaii and the other Far Eastern stations is due to the international dateline which runs between them.

**RAIN**

U. S. Weather Bureau Forecast
Light rain entire state; moderately strong winds.

TEMPERATURES SUNDAY

| | | | | | |
|---|---|---|---|---|---|
| 2 a.m. | 31 | 10 a.m. | 32 | 6 p.m. | 45 |
| 3 a.m. | 31 | 11 a.m. | 35 | 7 p.m. | 44 |
| 4 a.m. | 30 | Noon | 38 | 8 p.m. | 44 |
| 5 a.m. | 30 | 1 p.m. | 45 | 9 p.m. | 43 |
| 6 a.m. | 30 | 2 p.m. | 46 | 10 p.m. | 43 |
| 7 a.m. | 30 | 3 p.m. | 49 | 11 p.m. | 44 |
| 8 a.m. | 31 | 4 p.m. | 48 | Midnight | 44 |
| 9 a.m. | 31 | 5 p.m. | 48 | 1 a. m. | 44 |
| | | | | 2 a. m. | 44 |

Details on Page 11

# Minneapolis Morning Tribune

FOUNDED IN 1867

BOTH the MINNEAPOLIS MORNING and SUNDAY TRIBUNE, and the EVENING STAR-JOURNAL are published in this modern newspaper plant, Fifth Street and Sixth Avenue South.

Vol. LXXVI—No. 169. 18 Pages MINNEAPOLIS, MINN., MONDAY, NOVEMBER 9, 1942 ★★★ Price 3 Cents in Twin City Area 5 Cents Elsewhere

# FRENCH SURRENDER ALGIERS

## Americans Occupy Naval Base; Darlan OK's Terms of Armistice

## HITLER VOWS BLOW ON U.S. AFRICA ARMY

### Caught Off Guard by Invasion

LONDON — (AP) — Adolf Hitler declared Sunday night that Germany would strike a counter blow "in due time" against the United States army landings in North Africa.

"Wherever the fronts may be, again and again Germany will parry and go over to the attack," he said in a world broadcast speech delivered to his party stewarts at the Loewenbraeu beer cellar in Munich on the eve of the anniversary of the Munich putsch of 1923. He spoke for 85 minutes.

"The decisive last word will certainly not be spoken by Mr. Roosevelt," he asserted, and then added in an implication that Germany was caught unprepared for immediate action:

"We will prepare counterblows as thoroughly as always, and they will come in due time."

At one point in his speech Hitler promised, terrible reprisals against his foes, whom he accused of attacks on non-military targets in Germany.

"The moment will come," he said when the enemy will find out that Germany's inventive genius has not been asleep. The enemy will receive such a reply that he will be overwhelmed and stupefied."

**Although Hitler did not explain his threat, some listeners believed he was hinting at the use of a new weapon—perhaps gas.**

**PROMISES TO STICK**

The end of the war seemed much on the Nazi fuehrer's mind as he assured his followers again and again that his confidence was unshaken—that he would not desert them and flee the country, but would stay and fight to the bitter end.

In this unusual tone, Hitler saw fit to recall the conditions of Germany's crack-up in the last World war. He told his followers that he foresaw no repetition of Germany's collapse of 1918.

"The kaiser," he said, "was a man who did not have the strength to see things through.

"In me they (the Allies) have an opponent now who doesn't even think of the word capitulation."

He declared that he would offer peace no more.

**DISCOUNTS AFRICAN ROUT**

Hitler sought to gloss over the sharp setback of his armies in North Africa by saying: "The British are trying to pretend that their advance of a few kilometers in the desert sand is a victory. Those who deal out the last blow will win the war. The Germans will do that."

**He urged his followers to have "full confidence" in the German leadership and army, but at the same time struck a peculiar note by declaring that he would not leave his country and "go abroad if things go wrong" as the kaiser did.**

Other notes of doubt and uncertainty crept into the speech of the man who protested repetitiously his confidence in ultimate victory.

**COUNTER BLOWS PROMISED**

"When Roosevelt launches an attack against North Africa we need not waste words about his lies," Hitler said. "We will prepare all counter-blows, as thoroughly as always, and they will come in due time.

**"There was a triumphant shouting when the first British troops landed at Boulogne and advanced, and six months later this triumphant shouting was over. It turned out to be different. It will be different again in this case."**

Hitler started speaking at 6:08

*Concluded on Page 6*

## THE SITUATION

***Action in Africa:***

Greatest Allied armada in military history lands American troops on both sides of three key French Africa points—Casablanca, Oran and Algiers; Vichy radio announces Algiers fighting ended, with city surrendered to Americans; naval battles reported in progress off both Atlantic and Mediterranean coasts of North Africa.

***Vichy Breaks With U. S.:***

Vichy France breaks relations with the United States, after Washington indicates U. S. indifference to Vichy's course; Marshal Petain sorrowfully orders his men to fight, Vichy admits situation is grave, reports DeGaullist uprisings in colonies smashed.

***Britain Assures Spain:***

Britain announces firm stand beside United States in North Africa venture; British Foreign Secretary Eden assures Spain and Portugal their territory and interests will not be harmed.

***Broad Strategy:***

North Africa thrust at present involves only French Morocco and Algeria on Atlantic and Mediterranean coasts but Allied quarters see ultimate junction with British eighth army and smashing of Axis power in Africa.

***Berlin Scornful:***

Germans scornful of American landings; Hitler tells Munich audience the Allied action "would no more win the war than the British landings in France early in the conflict;" Berlin radio screams that attack "veils the imperialist aims of the United States."

## RAIN FORECAST IN CITY TODAY

### Snow and Colder for Rest of State

Weather bureau Sunday night forecast occasional rain and little change in temperature for the Minneapolis area for Monday, but the rest of the state was due for a mixture of rain and snow and colder weather late in the afternoon.

Moderately strong winds were predicted for the western and northern parts of the state Monday.

Lowest temperatures Sunday night centered over northeastern part of the state with temperature at Duluth down to 32 degrees at 6:30 p.m.

Other temperatures at 6:30 p.m. Sunday were: St. Cloud, 43; Alexandria, 42; Grand Forks, N. D., 37; Rochester, 43; and Willmar, 46.

## *Young Wife Kills Herself With Shotgun*

Curiosity about the hereafter was believed to have been the motivating mental force which led a 20-year-old Minneapolis woman to end her life Sunday with a shotgun.

Near the body of Mrs. E. L. Emmons, whose head had been blown off by the blast, were found the words, "I've often wondered, now I'll know," written with a mascara pencil on the side of a washstand in the bathroom of the home, 116 Groveland avenue, where the shooting occurred.

**AUNT FINDS BODY**

Books treating with life after death were found in Mrs. Emmons' room.

Mrs. Mae Wood of Chicago, aunt of Mrs. Emmons, who had been sleeping in a front room, said she was awakened by a sound like a body falling in the hallway.

"I looked into my niece's bedroom where I discovered she had left the bed where she had been sleeping with her husband, who still was asleep," Mrs. Wood recounted. "I then found her body in the bathroom."

**SHOT IN MOUTH**

Neither Mrs. Wood or Mrs. Emmons' husband heard the shot, they said.

J. W. Olson, deputy coroner, said the shot was not heard because Mrs. Emmons had placed the muzzle of the shotgun in her mouth.

## *Yanks Beat Nazi Record at Invasion*

by WES GALLAGHER

FRENCH NORTH AFRICA—(AP)—The American advance in North Africa was going better than planned but reports were too meager to give an overall picture of the entire operation.

The lightning American air move in straffing the captured fields faster than the Germans ever were able to do at the height of their advance into Norway greatly strengthened the ground forces.

Field reports revealed no heavy French air activity while Axis air attacks were described as not intense.

**This was taken as an indication that the giant swift Allied move had caught the Nazi air force by surprise or it was too heavily entangled in the bitter middle east fighting to attack the convoy.**

The scanty communications characteristic of all first days of fighting hid many tales of heroism in the widespread fighting. But the feat of one battle-anxious combat force in sailing 120 miles in their tiny assault boats to the attack after their ship was torpedoed drew the acclaim of the fighting chiefs.

**These tiny, flat-bottomed craft were built only for short forays to landing beaches.**

The bouncing craft undoubtedly had the men seasick at the start of the voyage but the courageous soldiers stuck to their posts and landed at one of the many beachheads after a dangerous voyage.

## SOLDIER SLAIN BY GIRL OF 12

### Alaska Child Shoots Intruder

ANCHORAGE, ALASKA—(AP)—Pvt. Robert H. McNulty, 21, a soldier from Kearney, Neb., was found dead on a doorstep Saturday night. A 12-year-old girl said she had shot him with a .22 rifle when he disregarded her warning to get away from the bolted front door.

The girl was caring for the baby son of Mr. and Mrs. Joseph Boedecker. Mrs. Boedecker discovered the soldier's body when she returned home.

The Boedeckers said McNulty had come to their home with three soldiers who had been invited to dinner Saturday night. They said the other three took him away. The girl said he came back after all the adults had left.

"I told him to go away or I would shoot," she recounted. "He continued to try to get in, and I fired once to scare him. I had to shoot again, and after the second shot he quit trying to get in."

## —PETAIN TO DARLAN:—

### I'm Glad You're on the Spot

LONDON—(AP)—The Vichy radio broadcast Sunday night this message from Marshal Petain to Admiral Jean Darlan, commander of French armed forces, in Algiers:

"I am glad you are on the spot. You can act. Keep me informed."

## VICHY BREAKS U.S. TIES AND REPROVES F.R.

### Hull, President Outline Views

*Text of F. R.'s letter and Petain's reply together with Hull's defense of previous policy toward Vichy appear on Page 6.*

WASHINGTON — (AP) — The Vichy regime of France severed diplomatic relations with the United States Sunday as Chief of State Petain rejected a call from President Roosevelt for co-operation in the African drive against the Axis.

First news of the rupture came from Vichy itself when pro-Nazi Pierre Laval, chief of government, handed formal notice to S. Pinkney Tuck, United State charge d' affaires.

**NO OFFICIAL NOTICE**

No official word of the action had been received at the state department here. It was understood, however, that the official American attitude toward a formal rupture would be one of indifference.

**After news of the break by Vichy and after the French radio had reported Petain reproaching Mr. Roosevelt for the military move against the African colonies, the White House disclosed that the President sent a personal message to Petain.**

"As an old friend of France and the people of France," the President expressed to Petain his "anger and smypathy" over the suffering inflicted on France by the Germans and declared that the ultimate aim of the African campaign was "the liberation of France and its empire from the Axis yoke.

**TERMS IT AGGRESSION**

He explained that he was calling on French authorities in North Africa for "co-operation in repelling Axis threats" and re-affirmed that America sought no territories for itself.

Petain replied that he learned of the American "aggression" with "bewilderment and sadness" and that Mr. Roosevelt in his message "invoked a pretext which nothing justifies."

Secretary of State Hull, in an unusual Sunday afternoon press conference, had declared earlier that diplomatic relations had been maintained with the collaborationist Frenchmen at Vichy chiefly to pave the way and prepare the background for the current military operations.

**That purpose how has been achieved, the secretary declared, noting that those who previously questioned the government's Vichy policy should be able to see clearly and fully now the justification for it.**

A special guard of 10 policemen was thrown around the French embassy Saturday night immediately after announcement of the African landings by American troops.

Ambassador Gaston Henry-Haye could not be reached for comment, the embassy reporting he was not there and disclaiming any knowledge of his whereabouts or of any intention he might have of issuing a statement later.

## PARIS STUNNED BY U.S. ATTACK

### Invaders Repulsed, Say Pro-Nazis

BERLIN—A German dispatch from Paris said the invasion news created a sensation in that city.

The "Paris Midi" (pro-Nazi) was the first French paper in Paris to publish the news and copies literally were torn out of the hands of newsboys by the people.

**"Anglo-Saxons have attacked our North African possessions" read a flaring six-column headline.**

The paper then gave elaborate display to the French reports that the attacking forces had so far been repulsed.

### *Invasion Background*

A history and description of the peoples of the second front area appears on page 7 together with a map and discussion of communications, climate and topography.

Other material prepared by The Tribune war desk and the news services includes:

**ON PAGE 2**—DeGaulle and Giraud lead French revolt. British hail secrecy of invasion preparations.

**ON PAGE 3**—Doolittle is leading U. S. air support in invasion. British navy screens yank landings. Chronology of U. S.-Vichy relations.

**ON PAGE 5**—Large scale map of Mediterranean area. U. professor says Yanks face fight before reaching Egypt army.

**ON PAGE 6**—How home folks feel about opening of second front.

**ON PAGE 7**—Second Front army can move swiftly over good North African highways and railways. How strong is the French Fleet?

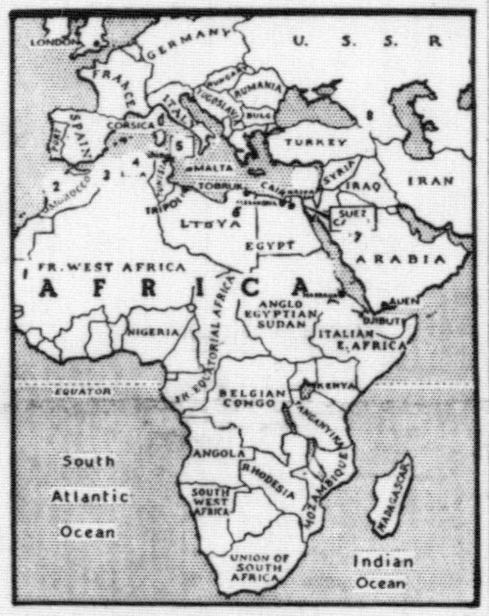

Dakar (1), springboard for a Nazi attack on the Americas, was rendered impotent by Yank landings at Casablanca (2), Oran (3) and Algiers (4). Algiers surrendered and was occupied by American soldiers. There was likelihood that the Americans would cross Tunisia (5) to form a western pincer to crush the remnants of Rommel's forces (6) fleeing General Montgomery's army. Once Africa is cleared of the Axis armies the Suez canal (7) can be used again, cutting thousands of miles off the supply routes to India and the South Pacific. In the Caucasus (8) the Russians were still holding off the Nazis.

*Large Scale Map of Mediterranean Area on Page 5.*

## HORIZON BLACK, FASCIST ADMITS

### Rome Radio Puts Blame on U. S.

LONDON—(AP)—A Fascist commentator on the Rome radio said Sunday night "the horizon is black for Italy—we must expect attacks from any quarter" and, he added, the United States is to blame for it all.

"It was Flying Fortresses that took a big part in the raids on Genoa," the commentator, Aldo Valori, told his audience.

(There has been no Allied reports that Fortresses took part in these RAF attacks.)

"It was American ships which brought troops across the Atlantic.

"It was American factories that poured forth the tanks that now are battling in Egypt.

"Italy's war effort is [illegible] bad position."

## *Yank Hanged for 3 Slayings*

MELBOURNE — (UP) — Pvt. Edward J. Leonski, former New York city grocery clerk, was hanged Monday for the blackout murders of three women in Melbourne. He was convicted by an American court martial last summer.

### *WHERE TO FIND IT*

| | | | |
|---|---|---|---|
| Editorial | 4 | Radio | 10 |
| Women's | 6 | Comics | 16 |
| Theaters | 7 | Serial | 16 |

## Other Fronts

**RUSSIA** — Nazi attacks in Caucasus, Stalingrad and Tuapse repelled.

*Story on Page 8*

**SOLOMONS**—Jap cruiser and destroyer believed sunk by torpedo boats. Yank land forces push east of Koli point.

*Story on Page 8*

**EGYPT**—Allies pursue remnants of Rommel's army. Italians abandoned by Nazis.

*Story on Page 8*

**NEW GUINEA** — Air-borne American troops land in Buna area.

*Story on Page 8*

## Communique

*The war department issued communique No. 234, Sunday night as follows:*

NORTH AFRICA:

1 Landings by United States forces on the Atlantic and Mediterranean coast are proceeding according to plans.

2 Several important airfields have been occupied by the United States army air forces and the Royal Air Force. Ranger units are participating in the operation.

3 The lack of resistance encountered at most of the beaches indicated that the French armed forces in North Africa had no desire to oppose the entry of American troops into this territory.

4 The forces that landed during the night and early hours Sunday morning are advancing rapidly, and other landings continue. Resistance appears to have been confined mainly to navy and coast defense artillery. Owing to the confused nature of the fighting, precise results are not known.

5 Our naval forces are in control and suffered no losses, except for two small ships which entered Oran harbor.

6 During Saturday, one of our transports was torpedoed and disabled. Our troops aboard, under a commander who refused to be idle during the operation, took to their light landing craft and continued toward their objective 120 miles away, landing there this morning.

## *Yanks Push Inland From Eight Beachheads*

*Text of F. R.'s letter to Petain and Hull's defense of previous policy towards Vichy on Page 11.*

By Associated Press

The city of Algiers surrendered at 7 p.m. (2 p.m. Minneapolis time) Sunday night to the attacking American forces, paving the way for occupation of the surrounding defense area.

Before capitulation of the important French naval base, American combat teams had captured two airfields in the vicinity and a third near Oran.

Other U. S. troops were reported to be penetrating "swiftly into the interior" from several beachheads.

The armistice at Algiers was negotiated by the French garrison commander and U. S. Maj. Gen. Charles W. Ryder.

It provides for American occupation of the city at dawn tomorrow.

Maj. Gen. Mark Clark, deputy commander-in-chief of the American forces, stressed that the capitulation applied only to the Algiers area.

He also told how the armistice was delayed by a message garbled in transmission.

**BROKEN BY RANGERS**

The first time the Algiers authorities requested negotiations for the cessation of hostilities the American commanders thought he was merely asking for a truce.

The French garrison, however, sent another wireless message in which the capitulation was announced. All firing then ceased.

While these vast operations were unfolding in western and northern Africa the German Field Marshal Erwin Rommel was being chased out to Libya.

Resistance at Algiers was broken by Rangers who stormed ashore in the face of fire from coastal batteries, by swarms of American planes and by a powerful naval force which lay off the harbor.

**APPROVED BY DARLAN**

The capitulation, approved by Admiral Darlan, came at 7 p.m. Greenwich time (2 p.m. Minneapolis time), and American soldiers Sunday night were patrolling the streets of the ancient city.

**The fate of Darlan, who for a time at least might have been a prisoner, was not clear.**

At the end of the day United States forces dominated many miles of the Mediterranean coast facing the Axis.

Americans seized and were soon operating from at least three French airports, while at sea a powerful fleet was covering land operations.

**BRISK FIGHTING**

There were several instances of brisk fighting against troops which had been ordered by the unreconciled French government to stand up against the invasion.

**But a communique issued simultaneously in London and Washington said that the resistance apparently was confined almost entirely to French naval units and coastal artillery.**

Algiers surrendered after hostilities were suspended, by agreement with French authorities including Admiral Jean Darlan himself, less than 24 hours after fighting began.

American troops, this report said, began policing the city at 11 p.m. while French troops were ordered by their commander, General Juin, to remain in barracks. They were not disarmed.

(Concluded on Page 7)

## BULLETINS

**NORTH AFRICAN HEADQUARTERS—(UP)— Major-Gen. Mark W. Clark, deputy commander-in-chief of the Allied forces here, is leaving for the front to establish advance headquarters, is was announced early Monday.**

By Associated Press

**The Vichy radio estimated Sunday that the United States had thrown 140,000 men into landing operations in French North and West Africa. It added that supporting British divisions were en route.**

By Associated Press

**The German radio said British naval forces sailed Sunday from Gibraltar, apparently escorting transports, and that 55 planes also had left.**

**The report said the British battleship Nelson and some destroyers still remained in Gibraltar harbor.**

**LONDON — (UP) — The 6th Italian division, trapped in the Egyptian desert, has been captured with its complete equipment, it was announced Monday.**

**VICHY—(UP)—All commercial sea traffic between France and North Africa has been suspended.**

By Associated Press

**Radio Morocco (Spanish) announced Sunday night that "for military reasons" the French air base at Rabat, capital of French Morocco, had been evacuated. At the same time the broadcast appealed to members of the French Foreign Legion to report to their respective induction centers.**

**MELBOURNE, AUSTRALIA (INS)—Allied bombers raided a Japanese airdrome and installations on New Britain a communique announced Monday.**

## ALLIES BLAST FRENCH SHIPS

### Heavy Fighting Off Morocco Reported

LONDON—(AP)—The new 35,000-ton French battleship Jean Bart and four French submarines have been hit by Allied dive bombers and two Allied destroyers have been sunk in air and naval fighting still raging off the coast of French Morocco, a Vichy report broadcast by the Berlin radio said Sunday night.

The French ships were reported hit in the initial rounds of aerial fighting. The Nazi-relayed French account said the Allied vessels subsequently were sunk by retaliating French defenses.

The naval action was reported to have started after the French fleet, according to Axis broadcasts, left Toulon, French Mediterranean base, to engage British naval units.

A French Morocco broadcast said the action was still in progress late Sunday night after starting early in the afternoon.

**(A Vichy dispatch broadcast by German news agency DNB said the naval engagement off Casablanca was broken off by the American naval squadron.**

The Jean Bart had been in port at Casablanca since the German-French armistice in 1940.

LIGHT SNOW
U. S. Weather Bureau Forecast
Little change in temperature.

TEMPERATURES MONDAY

| | | | | | |
|---|---|---|---|---|---|
| 2 a.m. | 8 | 10 a.m. | 14 | 6 p.m. | 22 |
| 3 a.m. | 9 | 11 a.m. | 16 | 7 p.m. | 22 |
| 4 a.m. | 8 | Noon | 18 | 8 p.m. | 22 |
| 5 a.m. | 6 | 1 p.m. | 20 | 9 p.m. | 21 |
| 6 a.m. | 6 | 2 p.m. | 23 | 10 p.m. | 21 |
| 7 a.m. | 8 | 3 p.m. | 23 | 11 p.m. | 20 |
| 8 a.m. | 8 | 4 p.m. | 23 | Midnight | 20 |
| 9 a.m. | 12 | 5 p.m. | 23 | 1 a.m. | 19 |
| | | | | z 2 a.m. | 18 |

Details on Page 5 zUnofficial.

# Minneapolis Morning Tribune

FOUNDED IN 1867

Vol. LXXVI—No. 191. 18 Pages MINNEAPOLIS, MINN., TUESDAY, DECEMBER 1, 1942 ★★★ Price 3 Cents in Twin City Area 5 Cents Elsewhere

BOTH the MINNEAPOLIS MORNING and SUNDAY TRIBUNE, and the EVENING STAR-JOURNAL are published in this modern newspaper plant, Fifth Street and Sixth Avenue S.



# FRANCE: THE INSIDE STORY!

## NAZI ATTACKS FAIL AS RUSS DRIVE AHEAD

### German Losses Soar on Twin Fronts

MOSCOW—(AP)—The Red army killed 7,500 more Germans and knocked out 75 tanks on the blizzard-swept central front west of Moscow, and gained as much as six miles near Stalingrad Monday, the Russians announced early Tuesday.

Another special communique — they have been issued almost daily for more than a week—telling of operations in the Rzhev-Vyazma-Velikie Luki triangle of the central front said:

"Our troops, overcoming enemy resistance and repulsing counter-attacks of his infantry and tanks, successfully continued their offensive and occupied several places. During one day's battle, 17 tanks, 37 guns, 40 machine guns and 12 stores (of supplies) were captured and 58 tanks destroyed. The enemy left on the battlefield 7,500 dead officers and men."

NO MOVE TO ESCAPE

On the Stalingrad front where Russian armies were trying to throttle the remnants of the Nazi siege army which originally numbered about 300,000, there appeared to be no German disposition to try to break out of a slowly closing Russian trap.

The special communique did not deal with the greater arms of this movement, but merely with the situation in the immediate Stalingrad area.

**The communique said 20,000 Germans had been slain in four days "near Stalingrad." On the basis of previous special bulletins, the toll of Nazis for the Stalingrad area alone now stands at 67,000 dead and 66,000 captured, or a total of 133,000.**

On the same basis, the total of Nazis on the central front is 22,300 dead and 400 captured, so the grand total for both fronts is 155,700 dead and captured.

GAIN AT STALINGRAD

Of the situation at Stalingrad, the special bulletin said:

"The offensive of our troops continues in the Stalingrad area. Our troops near Stalingrad, overcoming enemy resistance, advanced from 6 to 10 kilometers (from 3.7 to 6.2 miles) and occupied several fortified places."

With many of the Nazi rear supply lines snapped by the Russians at Stalingrad, the German high command was reported trying to fly in food and munitions to the Nazis and Rumanians caught between the Don and Volga rivers by the Soviet encirclement.

PICTURE OF SUCCESS

The regular midnight communique, issued after the special bulletin, gave this picture of Russian successes on both widely separated fronts:

**Central front west and northwest of Moscow — Continued Russian advance.**

**Stalingrad — Artillery duels raged in the northern factory district, but in the southern outskirts German troops were thrown out of several blockhouses.**

Thirty miles northwest of Stalingrad the Red army occupied Vertychy on the eastern bank of the Don loop.

Vertychy is only 25 miles northeast of Kalach, which also is on the Don and previously had been reported taken. The Russians also hold numerous other points on both the northern and southern arms of the river loop, indicating the gravity of the enemy's pocketed position between the Don and Volga rivers.

FIGHT EAST OF DON

"Our troops engaged the enemy deep in the enemy's defenses on the eastern bank of the Don," the communique said of this fight to trap the Nazi Stalingrad army.

Southwest of Stalingrad, presumably in the direction of Kotelnikovski, the communique said the Russians also "successfully continued their offensive." Despite strong German counter-attacks, the Red army was reported to have killed 1,500 Nazis and smashed 12 tanks, 16 guns, 26 blockhouses and other equipment.

## *Every Streetcar on Job Today As Gas Rations Curb Driving*

### *130 Extra Trips Scheduled Into Loop for Rush Periods*

Every Minneapolis streetcar in running order will go into service Tuesday morning to replace automobiles garaged by gasoline rationing which began at midnight Monday.

Officials of Minneapolis Street Railway Co. said Monday night there would be 130 additional trips into the loop between 6:30 a.m. and 9:30 a.m., and that the same number would be added during the evening rush hours.

10 PCT. INCREASE

That will make a total of 1,066 trips during each rush period, an increase of about 10 per cent over present operating schedules.

Streetcar men admitted they didn't know exactly how the gasoline restrictions would affect the trolley business, but they were ready to send all rolling stock on hand onto the streets in an effort to get workers to their jobs on time.

### *It's Not Too Late to Register Today*

Motorists who have not registered for gasoline "A" ration books can do so Tuesday at 125 Fourth street S., Minneapolis, or 460 Robert street, St. Paul, Theodore G. Driscoll, state rationing director, announced late Monday night.

The Minneapolis office will be open from 8:45 a.m. to 5:30 p.m., the St. Paul office from 9 a.m. to 5 p.m.

Monday had been announced previously as the deadline for "A" card registration.

MOTORISTS FILL UP

While these plans were moving forward, motorists were making last-minute mass advances on gasoline service stations to get tanks filled before the rationing deadline.

Starting Tuesday, holders of the basic "A" ration books will be able to buy only four gallons of gasoline a week.

LATE-COMERS REGISTER

Late-comers for ration books jammed registration headquarters at 125 Fourth street S. all day Monday and waited in a line nearly a block long before the door. They also may register for the books Tuesday at the same place.

**Those who have not registered by then must sign up at their local ration boards, or go without gasoline.**

These boards, however, are swamped at present with applications for supplemental "B" and "C" allotments, with problems involving fuel oil rations and sugar and coffee books, as well as with their regular automobile and tire rationing duties, OPA officials said, and those who failed to sign up for the "A" books during regular registrations were urged to hold off until at least next Friday.

TROLLEY SURVEY MADE

Attempting to size up the transportation problem, streetcar officials said their latest survey showed that during October, 73,000 persons moved into the loop between 6:30 a.m. and 9:30 a.m. each working day, 42,000 of them by streetcar, most of the remainder by automobile.

They expect about 30 to 35 per cent of motorists would continue to drive to work, leaving between 20,000 and 22,000 persons to be added to the streetcar load.

CHANGE NOT ABRUPT

However, one of the officials said, "the increase probably will not be as abrupt as that, because Minneapolis people have been ahead of the rest of the country in the tire-saving program, and a good many of them switched to streetcars during November."

GOV. HEIL'S BROTHER DIES

MILWAUKEE—(AP)—Frank Heil, 80, brother of Gov. Julius P. Heil, died Monday at his home. He was chief engineer of a brewing company here for 25 years until his retirement about 15 years ago.

## BOSTON FIRE CLAIMS BUCK JONES

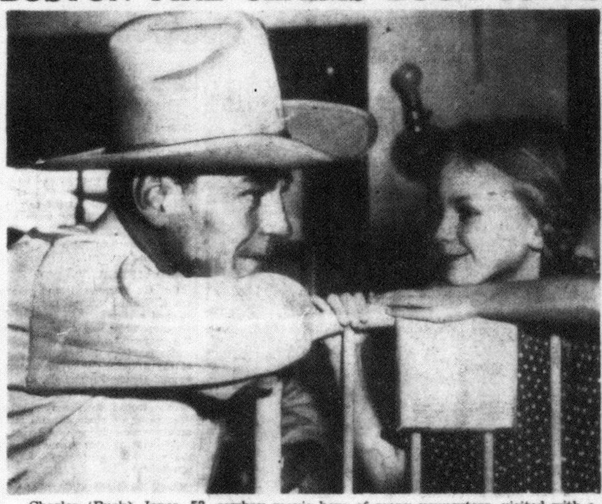

Charles (Buck) Jones, 53, cowboy movie hero of many youngsters, visited with a little girl in Boston Children's hospital only a few hours before he was caught in the fire Saturday night that took the lives of nearly 500 patrons of Cocoanut Grove night club.

This picture was Jones' last. He died late Monday at Massachusetts General hospital "from smoke inhalation and burned lungs, and from second degree burns on the face and neck." His wife was on her way to his bedside when death came.

Jones was honor guest at a party in progress at the night club when fire broke out. Of about two dozen guests at the testimonial dinner, 13 were known dead, seven were missing and presumed dead, and the others were in hospitals, seriously burned.—AP-Wirephoto. (Stories on Page 10).

## CHUTISTS SEIZE TUNIS AIRFIELD

### Allies Push Through Axis Mines

Late News Cables

British parachute troops seized without opposition an airfield in the environ's of Tunis well in advance of U. S. and British armored units nearing the Axis-held Tunisian capital, a dispatch from Allied headquarters in North Africa said Monday night.

Allied ground forces were said to be picking their way cautiously through German minefields. Axis airmen swept over them in strafing attacks, but the Allied pace continued methodically.

COMMUNICATIONS PERILED

German radio quoted dispatches acknowledging that the Allies were menacing communication links between Axis forces in Tunis and Bizerte.

As a result of the Allied advance, the Germans retained control of only one highway between Tunis and Bizerte and this was only 10 miles from a parallel road controlled by the British.

It was considered likely Axis communications soon would be cut, preventing possibility of a withdrawal from Bizerte.

STAND AT BIZERTE

French sources predicted the Germans would make their most determined stand before the big naval base of Bizerte, grouping their heavy forces there.

Berlin radio said Allied batteries had begun shelling Bizerte. Lt. Gen. Dwight Eisenhower's headquarters said in a communique Monday that Allied forces had seized and were holding Djedeida, a rail junction 12 miles northwest of Tunis, which would place Tunis within range of Allied artillery.

(Concluded on Page 2)

### *Roach Powder Cook Held for Grand Jury*

SILVERTON, ORE. — (UP) — Abraham B. McKillop, 64-year-old assistant cook held on an information charging manslaughter in the poison deaths of 47 state hospital inmates, was bound over to the grand jury Monday.

### —YANKS SEE HORSE RACE—

## *Sub Calls on Japs and Sinks 8 Ships*

PEARL HARBOR, HAWAII — (UP) — Lieutenant Commander Thomas Burton Klakring, taking his submarine into Japanese coastal waters and harbors, has sunk eight Japanese ships and damaged and possibly sunk four more, it was announced Monday.

The submarine, which now holds the record for enemy tonnage destroyed by the U. S. Pacific fleet, sank four ships totaling about 34,000 tons within an hour.

It sank two more in a 10-minute engagement during which a half dozen enemy surface ships and airplanes were dropping depth charges.

(The navy department in Washington said it had no information Monday night to show whether the sinkings have been announced previously. This point was not clarified in the Pearl Harbor dispatch either.)

Klakring, who said he is 37 years old "with a big plus" because his next birthday comes soon, is from Annapolis. His wife lives at San Mateo, Calif. He has been with submarines since 1929 and is to receive the navy cross from Adm. Chester W. Nimitz, commander of the U. S. Pacific fleet.

Describing the feats of his submarine in enemy home waters, Klakring said that one Sunday he approached within a few miles of the Japanese shoreline, stopped awhile and watched some horse races on land.

### *Skipper Tells of Four-Ship Coup*

Then he told newspapermen of his four-ship coup.

"While on the surface about dawn one morning in Japanese home waters we sighted a six-ship convoy with three or four escorts. First we saw the masts of a couple of ships appear on the horizon, so we got between them and the shore, maneuvered ahead of them, and then submerged."

The stalking process required most of the day to complete, he continued, but it was worth it.

"When the convoy came up we waited until we were right in the middle of it, and then we let them have it.

"We fired torpedoes at two ships and were lucky enough to hit both. They broke up and sank almost immediately, although a couple of coarloads of survivors got away. We fired at about 500 or 1,000 yards at the ships.

The remaining four went in different directions, and we chased two of them into a harbor—where they couldn't get away."

Asked whether the Japs weren't doing something about all this Yankee impudence, Klakring admitted "They were sort of popping away at us, and all ships were dropping depth charges, but not close enough to bother us."

### *Fleeing Vessel Hides Behind an Island*

One of the ships which ran into the harbor got behind an island where the submarine couldn't reach it.

"The other dropped anchor," Klakring said. "When he halted we fired a torpedo from extreme long range and got him under the stack. He broke in two and sank in about 45 seconds. There were no survivors.

"We really didn't care whether we hit the ship—because if we had missed we would have hit a power plant at the water's edge behind him, where there was a tank of illuminating gas.

"After the hit we did not stay around long. By this time we had an 'escort' of Jap patrol vessels firing guns and depth charges, but we escaped the harbor and managed to head off one of the remaining ships from the convoy and hit him with two torpedoes. He broke up and sank."

(Concluded on Page 5)

## TWO FRENCH SUBS REACH ALLIED PORT

### Third on Way, Fourth Interned by Spain

LONDON — (AP) — Four French submarines were reported Monday night to have escaped German capture at Toulon by a hairbreadth and two of them were in Allied hands at Algiers and another was believed to be on the way there.

The fourth, the little 597-ton Iris, was forced to put in at Barcelona Saturday and Monday its crew of 21 officers and men was interned by the Spaniards.

OTHERS ALL LOST

These were believed to have been the only units of the once-proud fleet of 62 or more warships to have escaped self-destruction or German capture at Toulon.

Algiers radio reported arrival there of the ocean-ranging 1,379-ton Casabianca, formerly the Casablanca, and the 974-ton Marsquin, after escaping aerial-sown mines and Axis air and naval units sent out to cut off their escape.

LEAVES SPANISH PORT

Madrid dispatches Monday night said another large submarine, the 1,379-ton Le Glorieux had put in at Valencia, Spain, and then departed in less than 24 hours for an unannounced destination, presumably North Africa.

**Failure of the Iris also to depart within the 24 hours allowed a belligerent warship in a neutral port under international law may have been due to damage.**

Both Vichy and Axis broadcasts said four submarines attempted to get away, but that one struck a mine. Claims that this one was sunk may have been an error. Madrid dispatches have mentioned no damage to the Iris, but observers were not allowed to examine her.

JOINS DARLAN FORCES

The captain of the Casabianca, was quoted by Algiers radio as saying "we placed ourselves under the order of Admiral Darlan" who is co-operating with the Allies.

Le Glorieux which put in at Valencia was of the Redoutable class, same as the Casabianca, and was completed in 1932. She carried a normal crew of 67 and had a great cruising range.

The Casabianca was completed in 1935 and was designed to carry a crew of 67. The Marsquin, of the Requin class, was somewhat older, having been completed in 1924, and normally carried a crew of 51.

The Casabianca has a wide cruising radius of 30 days, the Marsouin something less.

### *Body of Former Actress Is Found*

NEW YORK — (AP) — Brenda H. Lane, 32-year-old former actress, was found dead Monday night in her small furnished room and police immediately ordered an autopsy after discovering a bruise and scratch on her throat.

Landlord of the building, who discovered her body, told police that she recently had been writing and said her stories had appeared in several well-known magazines.

### Admits Slaying, Dives to Death

LOS ANGELES— (AP) —Francis Edwin O'Toole, alias Frank White, chose his own sentence Monday after pleading guilty to the murder of his wife Lillian.

Breaking from the grasp of officers, O'Toole plunged through a sixth-floor window. He was dead when officers reached him.

### Death Mars Record of 'Safest' Town

MT. VERNON, N. Y. — (AP) — Within an hour after the National Safety Council cited Mt. Vernon as the largest city in the nation having no traffic deaths in the past 10 months, Lewis J. Smith, 7, was killed Monday by a truck. The last traffic death here occurred December 24, 1941.

### *WHERE TO FIND IT*



## *War on Allies Voted Down by Cabinet, 8 to 6*

### *Berlin 'Caught Short' by African Raid, Vichy Diplomat Reveals*



When Anglo-American forces landed in North Africa, Germany demanded that France declare war on the Allies and unite with the Axis, but the French cabinet by the close vote of 8 to 6 refused, it was learned Monday.

A French diplomat who was in the active service of the Vichy regime until the French fleet scuttled itself at Toulon, gave the Associated Press, somewhere in Europe, a first-hand account of events in France following the American move into French North Africa.

CAUGHT BY SURPRISE

The Allied landing caught both Vichy and Berlin by complete surprise and, in the Vichy negotiations with Berlin up to the occupation of Toulon; German authorities gave the French the definite impression they did not know what to do in France, this informant said.

**The Laval regime likewise was at a loss for a plan of action.**

This French diplomat described a turbulent, bewildering, 48-hour Vichy cabinet meeting where the German demand for war was rejected despite urgings of Government Chief Pierre Laval while even then German hordes were swirling around the former unoccupied zone.

NAZIS FEARED REVOLT

Previously, he said, German authorities had seemed reluctant to occupy the rest of France, lacking sufficient troops and fearing the reaction of the people. Orders to proceed, however, came from Adolf Hitler himself.

Upset by this sudden and unexpected Allied thrust to the south and undecided how to meet the new and unforeseen threat, the Germans wavered for days. They appeared particularly nervous about Toulon, he said.

HITLER GAVE ORDERS

Final decision to occupy the Mediterranean port and seize the French fleet appeared to have come likewise exclusively from Hitler himself because of the fuehrer's fear that the Allies, at the invitation of the French commander at Toulon, might attempt to make a landing there.

When Laval went to Munich to confer with German authorities as a result of the Anglo-American move into Africa, he found Joachim von Ribbentrop, German foreign minister, trying to check Count Ciano, Italian foreign minister, this diplomat recounted.

DIPLOMAT'S STORY

His story continues:

Ciano had brought an order from Mussolini to get German approval for immediate occupation of Nice and the island of Corsica by Italian troops.

During discussion of this question, it became obvious to Laval and his aid that Ribbentrop was not anxious to occupy the Vichy zone because the few regular troops kept on the demarcation line between the two zones were all the Germans had available to execute such an operation.

RIBBENTROP ANXIOUS

Ribbentrop appeared anxious to get opinions of the Frenchmen on what would be the reaction of occupants of the Vichy zone in event the Germans came in.

**He seemed most anxious to know if the French in the unoccupied zone would resist.**

In the midst of these discussions came the blunt order from Hitler to proceed with occupation. Hitler also sent along his personal letter to Marshal Petain, informing the aged soldier of the advent of Nazi troops into Vichy territory.

PETAIN PROTESTED

Laval brought the letter to Petain back to Vichy, where the marshal drafted his protest against Hitler's violation of the 1940 armistice agreement.

Following dispatch of the protest, the Vichy cabinet met for 48 hours Nov. 11 and Nov. 12 debating its answer to Berlin's demand for a declaration of war against

(Concluded on Page 5)

## Allies Smash at Japs' Hold Upon Guinea

MELBOURNE, AUSTRALIA — (AP)—Fighting in Buna-Gona area of New Guinea, where American and Australian ground forces are pressing slowly forward is growing more intense, the high command reported Tuesday.

Allied air forces were actively supporting the ground troops.

SEVEN JAPS DOWNED

An enemy flight of 12 Zeros was engaged by a similar force of our fighters, the communique said, and seven of the Japs were shot down.

Two Allied planes also were downed but the pilots were saved.

Another flight of Japanese planes attempted a raid on Port Moresby. The attack was ineffective.

At Darwin an enemy reconnaissance plane was shot down by anti-aircraft fire.

Several hundred of Lt. Gen. Tomatore Horiils fighting men were believed cut off within Gona, a coastal village which Australians once penetrated a week ago.

JAP FLANK THERE

The Japanese right flank is anchored there against the Allied offensive; the whole enemy line is hinged at Buna, down the coast.

U. S. Flying Fortresses loosed many 1,000-pound bombs on the Gona area. Fires were started. A Japanese ammunition dump was hit and when the explosions abated only two small native huts were left standing in the neighborhood.

Other Flying Fortresses, daring storm clouds above the sea, sped north of Vitiaz straits off Japanese-occupied New Britain to rout four enemy destroyers with 500-pounders.

Two destroyers were definitely hit and the others turned northward at full steam, returning pilots said. One destroyer when last seen was burning and listing heavily.

## TWO FOUND NEAR DEATH IN HOMES

### Victims of Sleeping Powder, Gas

Two persons found near death in their homes were in critical condition at General hospital Monday night.

Mrs. Catherine Brown, 55, 149 Bedford street SE., was overcome by gas.

Donald Larson, 25, 16 E. Fifteenth street, took an overdose of sleeping powder, police reported.

## ENGINEER GUILTY IN TRAIN WRECK

ROCKVILLE, MD. — (AP) — Raymond Rufus McClelland, 59, Baltimore & Ohio railroad engineer, was convicted on a manslaughter charge early Monday in connection with a passenger freight train collision near Dickerson, Md., last September which took 14 lives.

McClelland testified that a red warning signal through which he passed had been obscured by smoke and fog and he thought it was changing to green.

A 10 year prison term is the maximum penalty possible.

STRIKE ENDS SPEEDILY

CLEVELAND— (AP) —Agreement to end a work stoppage at the Chase Brass & Copper Co.'s mill in suburban Euclid was reached late Monday after speedy intervention by the war labor board. The controversy was over seniority rights.

**WARMER**

U. S. Weather Bureau Forecast

Continued cool Thursday forenoon. Warmer in afternoon.

TEMPERATURES

| | | | | | |
|---|---|---|---|---|---|
| 2 a.m. | 51 | 10 a.m. | 47 | 6 p.m. | 55 |
| 3 a.m. | 49 | 11 a.m. | 47 | 7 p.m. | 54 |
| 4 a.m. | 50 | Noon | 50 | 8 p.m. | 53 |
| 5 a.m. | 49 | 1 p.m. | 53 | 9 p.m. | 52 |
| 6 a.m. | 46 | 2 p.m. | 56 | 10 p.m. | 51 |
| 7 a.m. | 45 | 3 p.m. | 57 | 11 p.m. | 50 |
| 8 a.m. | 45 | 4 p.m. | 57 | Midnight | 51 |
| 9 a.m. | 46 | 5 p.m. | 57 | 1 a.m. | 50 |
| | | | | z 2 a.m. | 49 |

*Details on page 7.* zUnofficial.

# Minneapolis Morning Tribune

*FOUNDED IN 1867*

*Vol. LXXVII—No. 108.* MINNEAPOLIS, MINN., THURSDAY, SEPTEMBER 9, 1943 ★★★ Price 3 Cents In Twin City Area, 5 Cents Elsewhere

**$800 Food Contest**

You may win one of the 150 prizes offered in the HOW TO SAVE FOOD CONTEST. All you have to do is to write your food-saving idea, in 50 words or less, on the back of a penny postal and mail it to HOW TO SAVE FOOD CONTEST, Minneapolis Star Journal and Tribune.



# ALLIED FORCES LAND AT NAPLES

## U.S. Raid Wrecks Jap Marcus Base

### Navy Reveals Bombers Blasted Isle in Dawn to Dusk Assault

PEARL HARBOR—(UP)—The American task force that raided Jap-held Marcus island Sept. 1 hurled waves of carrier-based bombers against the island in a furious assault that literally wrecked the enemy stronghold and set great fires that still raged unchecked 24 hours later, Adm. Chester W. Nimitz, commander-in-chief of the Pacific fleet, revealed Wednesday night.

Boldly challenging Japanese sea power within 1,200 miles of Tokyo, the American force caught the island's defenders completely by surprise and destroyed 80 per cent of their military installations.

* * *

Nimitz, breaking the official silence that has shrouded the operation since last week when the Japanese radio revealed its Pacific outpost was under attack, disclosed the carrier planes raided the island at dawn and continued to fly over in waves throughout the day.

**Two fighter planes and one torpedo bomber were the only American losses in the smashing blow.**

All three apparently fell at the start of the attack, for Nimitz reported that the bombers blasted the island's anti-aircraft batteries out of action and that not a single enemy plane rose to challenge the attackers.

* * *

"Fires started throughout the island still were burning the day following the attack," Nimitz's communique said, indicating that the task force had lingered in the vicinity for almost 48 hours, even though Marcus is only four hours flying time from the Japanese mainland.

**Seven twin-engined Japanese bombers caught aground were destroyed by machine gun fire from American fighter planes that accompanied the bombers.**

Heavy bombs wiped out hangars, troop barracks and fuel and ammunition dumps, and severely damaged two landing strips on the island. A Jap trawler was sunk.

* * *

Nimitz revealed the task force was commanded by Rear Adm. Charles A. Pownall.

The navy had held up information on the raid, stating that the task force had not broken radio silence to give full details in the attack. Nimitz' communique was interpreted as meaning the warships had returned to a base or to a "safe" zone.

### *Chief Jumps Gun, Signs for $20,000*

Police Chief Joe Jonas jumped the gun on the bond drive Wednesday when he signed an order for $20,000 worth of war bonds for the city pension fund.

To clinch it, he promptly mailed the order to bond headquarters so it could be the first to be recorded Thursday morning.

★ ★ ★ ★

## BOND KICKOFF IS SET TODAY

### Italy's Surrender Spurs Drive

Sparked by President Roosevelt's talk and by surrender of Italy, third nationwide war bond drive will start rolling Thursday morning.

O. J. Arnold, state war finance committee chairman, said fall of Italy "will be a tremendous stimulant to the bond drive, both by encouraging solicitors to work harder, and buyers to buy more."

And Secretary of Treasury Henry Morgenthau, Jr., in a message to state bond headquarters, likewise predicted the surrender "would give the bond drive the greatest possible kickoff."

"The war bonds you have bought have paid for our victory over Italy, in part," Morgenthau said. "Now, more than ever before, we need the help of every American."

* * *

Minnesotans were ready to give their help, to make up the state's $216,000,000 quota for the drive. Quota for Hennepin county is $74,213,800.

**First Minnesota community to push its local bond sale drive over the top was Clara City which, with a $43,000 quota, announced Wednesday night that actual sales of $43,975 already had been cleared through its bank. C. J. Weffen is chairman of the village drive.**

The state campaign will get a shot in the arm Saturday night at a rally of Hennepin and Ramsey county bond workers in Northrop auditorium when Brig. Gen. A. J. Browning, director of purchases for the army service forces, Washington, will speak.

* * *

General Browning has direct charge of spending a large part of the federal money used to buy equipment for the army, and is in a position to know and tell how money from war bond sales is used to speed the war effort.

He recently returned from England and a study of performance of American troops and equipment in action, reporting that "as result of superior training and equipment, loss of life by American troops has been much lower than was expected—so much lower that some hospital supply contracts have been cancelled."

**Bond Drive**
*Continued on Page Seven*

## GERMANY CALLS IT 'TREACHERY'

### Nazi Leaders Ready, Berlin Says

LONDON—(UP)—Berlin broadcast the news of Italy's surrender Wednesday night and denounced it angrily as "open treason" and "a treacherous outrage against the defenders of Europe."

In its first broadcasts on the Italian surrender Berlin pretended that Germany had not been taken by surprise.

But Wednesday night DNB agency said Italy had surrendered "after the king and Marshal Badoglio had refuted such an idea as calumny as late as Sept. 6."

**"German leadership was prepared for this open treason by the Italian government and therefore had taken all necessary military measures," DNB said.**

"This treacherous outrage against the defenders of Europe will fail in the end just as all similar undertakings."

## FERGUS FALLS HAS FIRST SNOW

Let other communities claim those seasonal sooners, first robin of spring or first sunstroke of summer—Fergus Falls Wednesday insisted on having the earliest harbinger of winter, snow.

In that area, it reported, snow flurries that coated windshields followed in the wake of a cold rain.

No other snow was reported officially in the state, the weather bureau disclosed.

Meanwhile Minneapolis, which had another chilly day Wednesday with the mercury dropping to 45, was promised a break in the cold wave Thursday afternoon.

### *WHERE TO FIND IT*



## WE MUST HIT NAZIS ON OWN SOIL, SAYS F.R.

### Appeals for Support in Bond Drive

*Text of speech on Page 15*

WASHINGTON—(AP)—President Roosevelt declared Wednesday night the armistice with Italy was "a great victory" for the United Nations but that "we must drive the Germans out of Italy."

Speaking in a radio program launching a third war loan campaign for $15,000,000,000, he asserted the Nazis also must be driven out of France and all other captive countries and that "we must strike them on their own soil from all directions."

**Ultimate objectives in the war, the President said, continue to be Berlin and Tokyo.**

"I ask you," he said, "to bear these objectives constantly in mind—and do not forget that we still have a long way to go before attaining them.

* * *

Appealing for support of the loan drive, the President said it is now up to American citizens to prove to the soldiers that "you are contributing your share and more than your share."

"We must not delude ourselves" that the Italian armistice means the end of the war in the Mediterranean, he said, because the Germans still must be driven from Italy, from France and all other captive countries.

* * *

"And we must strike them on their own soil from all directions," he said.

"The great news you have heard today from General Eisenhower does not give you license to settle back in your rocking chairs, and say, 'well, that does it. We've got 'em on the run. Now we can start the celebration.'"

**The time has not come for celebration, the chief executive declared, and the war must not stop for a single instant.**

The President referred to the conferences which he and Prime Minister Churchill have been holding in the past few weeks and said they had made "new, extensive plans for the future."

* * *

But they never lost sight of the fact, he said, that the war will become bigger and tougher, rather than easier, during the months to come.

"Today, an armistice with Italy was concluded," he said.

"This was a great victory for the United Nations—but it was also a great victory for the Italian people. After years of war and suffering and degradation, the Italian people are at last coming to the day of liberation from their real enemies, the Nazis.

**"But let us not delude ourselves that this armistice means the end of the war in the Mediterranean.**

"We must drive the Germans out of Italy as we have driven them out of Tunisia and Sicily; we must drive them out of France and all other captive countries; and we must strike them on their own soil from all directions."

Mr. Roosevelt told his vast radio audience it was up to them to prove to their fellow Americans on the fighting fronts that they were contributing more than their share to the cause.

Associated Press Wirephoto

NEW YORKERS CELEBRATE SURRENDER OF ITALY

## HEATER BURNS OUT TWO LIVES

### Couple Found Dead—Girl Overcome

A St. Paul couple met death and a young girl visitor at their home was overcome Wednesday night when a gas water heater burned oxygen from the air in their rooms.

Discovery of the double fatality was made after Frank M. Jelacic, 411 Sinnen street, St. Paul, an insurance collector, stopped at the home of Mr. and Mrs. Frank Le Jeune, 1738 Munster avenue, at 9 p.m., to make a collection.

* * *

As he rapped on the back door, Jelacic heard a groan from inside.

**He pushed open the unlocked door and found Delores Morrison, 10, 703 Bedford street, St. Paul, a friend of the couple, lying unconscious on the floor.**

He carried her to the home of neighbors, who called police.

Le Jeune, who was 50, and his wife, who was 59, were found fully dressed, lying across their bed.

Efforts of a fire department inhalator squad worked more than an hour in a vain effort to revive them.

* * *

Delores was taken to Ancker hospital, where she was in too serious condition to tell what had happened.

In the basement, police found the water heater turned on. Windows of the house had been closed to keep out the cold.

## WFA SETS UP MILK CONTROLS

### Quotas Ordered in Sales Areas

WASHINGTON—(AP)—The war food administration announced Wednesday that sales of fluid milk will be controlled under a system of dealer quotas designed to limit civilian consumption to levels of recent months in order to maintain production of essential manufactured dairy products.

* * *

Milk sales areas will be established and distributors will be assigned quotas which will represent the maximum sales and deliveries of fluid milk, cream, and fluid milk products they may make.

* * *

Separate quotas also may be applied to deliveries to various classes of purchasers such as wholesale outlets, retail stores, restaurants, homes, etc.

Details will vary in each area in accordance with the local supply situation.

### ARMY TO CLEVELAND

COLUMBUS, OHIO—(INS)—Colonel John S. Gullet, commandant of Lockbourne army air base, where Flying Fortress crews are trained, Wednesday announced the army is taking over part of the Cleveland municipal airport.

★ ★ ★ ★

## *U.S. Greets News With Wild Cheers*

By United Press

Americans celebrated their first armistice of the second World war Wednesday by wild cheering and some street demonstrations although in most of the nation's war plants, workers heard the good news and kept right on working.

In New York city Italians danced in the streets of "Little Italy," showers of ticker tape and shredded paper rained from skyscraper windows.

**Thousands of office workers, at a bond sales rally in Times Square, broke into a roar when Newbold Morris, president of the city council, announced the surrender.**

At the same time a snow storm of shredded paper descended on the square and throughout mid-Manhattan from the windows of towering buildings.

A soldier in Times Square was overheard telling the girl on his arm that he would "miss the big show if they don't hurry me over."

In "Little Italy," one of the largest concentrations of Italians outside the mainland of Italy, response to the news ranged all the way from overturning pushcarts to prayers for absent sons.

Spontaneous dancing occurred in the narrow streets of the crowded sector as radios blared the news from stores and flats.

### Yanks and Britons Celebrate in London

LONDON—(UP)—Countless thousands of Britons and Americans milled through Piccadilly circus Wednesday night—some laughing, some crying—but everyone determined to celebrate Italy's surrender like an old-fashioned American New Year's eve.

"It's a leg up," said a grizzled old Welshman who was a machine gunner in the last war.

London newspaper vendors who never shout their wares like American newsboys could not contain their enthusiasm and joined in the general uproar with yells of:

"Italy gives in! Italy gives in!"

## Draft Quota Cut Likely, Says Hershey

AUGUSTA, ME.—(AP)—Almost simultaneous with the announcement of Italy's unconditional surrender was the assertion here Wednesday by the nation's selective service director, Maj. Gen. Lewis B. Hershey, that "we probably won't have to mobilize as many men for the remainder of the war as we have in the past."

"It has been remarkable," Hershey said, "that we have obtained so many men for the armed forces and still have the present number to carry on production on the home front in various fields."

### SOLON'S SON KILLED

PHOENIX, ARIZ.—(AP)—Rep. John R. Murdock (D., Ariz.) was advised Wednesday by the war department that his son, Lt. David N. Murdock, 29-year-old infantryman, was killed in action in the Mediterranean area Aug. 11.

## PLEADS GUILTY AS JAP AGENT

### College Teacher Is Freed on Bond

NEW YORK—(AP)—John C. LeClair, 41, former instructor in New York and New Jersey colleges, pleaded guilty late Wednesday to a federal grand jury indictment charging him with action as an unregistered agent of the Japanese government.

* * *

He was released in $5,000 bail pending imposition of sentence Sept. 22.

**The indictment charged LeClair wrote pro-Japanese articles and procured publication of them in magazines.**

LeClair was employed from July, 1938, to March, 1941, by the Japanese. E. E. Conroy, agent in charge of the FBI in New York said.

* * *

Conroy said LeClair was paid $500 a month by the Japanese consulate in New York from July, 1938, to December, 1939, for writing a syndicated column entitled "comments and forecasts" which contained two pro-Japanese articles a month.

## *Colonel's Insanity Plea Is Rejected*

SELFRIDGE FIELD, MICH.—(AP)—A general court martial, having denied a defense motion for dismissal of assault and drunkenness charges against Col. William T. Colman, former commandant of the army base here, proceeded Wednesday to call additional witnesses in the trial of the officer on 29 counts charging violations of the articles of war.

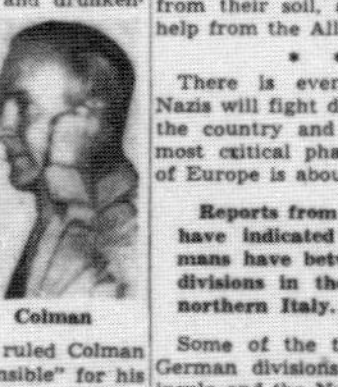

Colman

The court martial ruled Colman was "sane and responsible" for his actions at the time of the shooting last May of Pvt. William R. McRae, Negro chauffeur at the base.

## 7th Army Takes Part in Thrust to Cut Off Germans

### *Other Landings on Italian Coast Reported by Neutrals*

By Associated Press

Allied troops landed early Thursday in the Naples area, a third of the way up the Italian boot, a few hours after the surrender of Italy was announced.

Occupation of the bomb-battered area presumably places Allied forces behind at least some of the German troops retreating from southern Italy.

**The Allied announcement said merely that "further operations have started on the Italian mainland in the vicinity of Naples."**

Gen. Dwight D. Eisenhower granted Italy a military armistice on terms of unconditional surrender Tuesday and Premier Badoglio read the announcement to his people on the Rome radio.

**The announcement did not indicate makeup of the landing parties. A Tunis radio broadcast, however, said powerful British, American and Canadian armies participated.**

Merrill Mueller, NBC correspondent, reported in a broadcast from Allied headquarters, North Africa, that the American Seventh army has landed at Naples.

Naples, in peacetime a city of almost 1,000,000 population, is a vital link in Italy's north-south railway communications and a major supply port.

It has been pounded long and hard by Allied bombers seeking to check its use for military purposes of the Axis.

**The one-sentence announcement of the new operations came just 12 hours after that of the Italian surrender.**

Some 200 miles separate the zone of operations in Calabria, where the British Eighth army is pushing ahead, and the new battlefield created by the invasion in the Naples area.

From Naples it is approximately 83 airline miles in a northeasterly direction across the Italian mainland to the Adriatic sea.

* * *

The Swedish papers reported Allied landings at Naples, Genoa, Gaeta and Civitavecchio as well as on the Island of Sardinia. The Stockholm Dagens Nyheter said there were rumors that parachute troops had dropped at Pizzo, on the instep of the Italian boot.

The Tunis radio said "powerful British, American and Canadian armies are landing at various points in the heart of Italy."

The war between the United Nations and Italy officially ended early Wednesday night.

Eisenhower's announcement was coupled with an appeal to the Italian people to drive the Germans from their soil, and a promise of help from the Allies in doing so.

* * *

There is every likelihood the Nazis will fight desperately to hold the country and that one of the most critical phases of the battle of Europe is about to begin.

**Reports from neutral sources have indicated that the Germans have between 12 and 18 divisions in the Po region in northern Italy.**

Some of the toughest and best German divisions are on the peninsula and the Nazis are solidly en-

**Naples Invaded**
*Continued on Page Seven*

### F. R. Tips Off Landing

For those who were able to "read between the lines" President Roosevelt gave an advance announcement of the Allied landings at Naples.

The tip came in his speech launching the third war loan campaign Wednesday night when he referred to new invasion thrusts and fighting men in landing barges moving against enemy coasts "at this moment."

The phrase "at this moment" was the key. It was interpolated in his prepared text.

## Italians Ordered to Take Dodecanese From Nazis

CAIRO—(UP)—Gen. Sir Henry Maitland Wilson, Allied commander-in-chief in the Middle East, ordered the surrendered Italian army Wednesday night to take by force all points in the Dodecanese islands, between Turkey and Greece, which were in German hands.

In a special order of the day, broadcast repeatedly in the Italian language, Wilson said, also:

**"Italian troops in the Balkans must not obey German orders—they must obey my orders."**

He gave detailed orders for all units of the Italina navy, merchant marine and air force to proceed to designated points.

* * *

Greeks and Yugoslavs were warned by Wilson not to be tricked into a premature outbreak, but to "await our signal for a general uprising."

He declared "the hour of liberation is near, but has not yet arrived."

Regarding the Italian Dodecanese islands, a stepping stone to Greece and Crete at the southeastern corner of the Aegean sea, Wilson said:

"Italian forces in the Dodecanese will take over by force all points now in possession of the Germans."

Cairo radio broadcast a similar message from Wilson to the Greek people, informing them that if the Italians there do not carry out the armistice conditions they are liable to punishment.

## BULLETINS

### British, Nazis in Battle

**NEW YORK—(UP)—The London radio late Wednesday said a British correspondent reported "bitter fighting now in progress" between the British Eighth army and German infantry units on the Gioia plain north of Palmi. The fighting marked the first time since the landings in Italy that the Eighth army had caught up with German infantry.**

### Nazis Usurp Key Posts

**BERN—(UP)—Italian reports reaching here Thursday asserted that German forces in northern Italy had taken over key positions in industrial cities from civilian authorities. A large number of arrests along the lines of "military precautions" were also reported.**

### Milan Set to Fight

**LONDON—(INS)—Reuters reported Thursday from Stockholm that Italian troops have taken up positions in and around the northern Italian industrial city of Milan, to forestall any German attempt to occupy it.**

### Nazis Bolster Riviera

**MADRID—(AP)—A French report said Wednesday rail lines along the Riviera were being sabotaged as German reinforcements from Bordeaux, Toulouse and Avignon were moving in to strengthen its garrisons.**

### Corsica Nazis Seized

**LONDON—(AP)—Reuters quoted Stockholm reports Thursday that the Italian garrison on the island of Corsica had overpowered German troops stationed with them.**

### Bulgaria Gets Warning

**ISTANBUL—(AP)—Allied planes in repeated flights over Bulgaria are dropping leaflets warning Bulgarians that the zero hour is near, reports reaching here Wednesday said.**

### Ban Nazi Movements

**LONDON—(UP)—Radio Algiers said Thursday the Italian government ordered all ships, trains and trucks carrying German troops in Italy to be held.**

### Italian Cities Jubilant

**LONDON—(INS)—Wild demonstrations of joy broke out in the streets of all Italian cities Wednesday night at the news of Italy's surrender, a Swiss radio broadcast said.**

## Pershing Sees No Need for Comment

WASHINGTON—(INS)—Unconditional surrender of Italy does not call for comment in the opinion of Gen. John J. Pershing.

The commander of the American expeditionary forces in World war I, from his Washington home at Walter Reed hospital, Wednesday night made this succinct statement:

"That's what we have been fighting for. The bare fact is there and what need is there for comment?"

CLOUDY
U. S. Weather Bureau Forecast
Cloudy; continued cool.
TEMPERATURES
Details on Page 5

# Minneapolis Morning Tribune

FOUNDED IN 1867

Vol. LXXVIII—No. 13. MINNEAPOLIS, MINN., TUESDAY, JUNE 6, 1944 ★★★ Price 3 Cents In Twin City Area 5 Cents Elsewhere





# NAZIS CLAIM INVASION IS ON

## Report Chutists Landed, LeHavre Shelled

## Germany's Power to Start War Will Be Crushed--F.R.

*COMPLETE TEXT of President Roosevelt's address—Page 16*

WASHINGTON—(AP)—Hailing capture of Rome with the jubilant phrase "one up and two to go," President Roosevelt declared Monday night that the aim now is to drive Germany "to the point where she will be unable to recommence world conquest a generation hence."

Mr. Roosevelt, in a nation-wide radio broadcast, cautioned that this struggle with the Nazis would be tough and costly and that the day of Germany's surrender "lies some distance ahead."

Whether his reaffirmation that the fight would be pressed until Germany surrenders was a reply to the recent speech of Pope Pius XII was not stated. The pope asserted last week that the idea that the war must end either in complete victory or complete destruction is a stimulant toward prolonging the conflict and expressed hope for an early peace.

**Speaking of Rome as the great symbol of Christianity, the President declared "it will be a source of deep satisfaction that the freedom of the Pope and of Vatican City is assured by the armies of the United Nations."**

But he declared that no thanks are due Hitler and his generals "if Rome was spared the devastation which the Germans wreaked on Naples and other Italian cities."

"The Allied generals maneuvered so skillfully," he said, "that the Nazis could only have stayed long enough to damage Rome at the risk of losing their armies."

"Our victory," Mr. Roosevelt asserted, "comes at an excellent time, while our Allied forces are poised for another strike at western Europe—and while armies of other Nazi soldiers nervously await our assault. And our gallant Russian allies continue to make their power felt more and more."

The President extended to Italy the invitation to help in establishing a lasting peace and said, "all the other nations opposed to fascism and nazism should help give Italy a chance.

* * *

"The Germans, after years of domination in Rome, left the people in the Eternal City on the verge of starvation.

**"We and the British will do everything we can to bring them relief. We have already begun to save the lives of the men, women and children of Rome."**

The Italian people "are capable of self-government," Mr. Roosevelt continued. "We do not lose sight of their virtues as a peace loving nation."

* * *

Speaking of the military operations still to come in Europe, the President said:

"We shall have to push through a long period of greater effort and fiercer fighting before we get into Germany itself. The Germans have retreated thousands of miles, all the way from the gates of Cairo, through Libya and Tunisia and Sicily and southern Italy.

"They have suffered heavy losses, but not great enough yet to cause collapse."

* * *

In Italy, the President said, the people had lived so long "under the corrupt rule of Mussolini that, in spite of the tinsel at the top, their economic condition had grown steadily worse. Our troops have found starvation, malnutrition, disease, a deteriorating education and

Roosevelt
*Continued on Page Five*

### ★ ★ ★ HIGHLIGHTS OF F. R.'S SPEECH

WASHINGTON — (AP) — Highlights of President Roosevelt's speech on the fall of Rome:

Our victory comes at an excellent time, while our Allied forces are poised for another strike at western Europe—and while armies of other Nazi soldiers nervously await our assault.

* * *

It would be unwise to inflate in our minds the military importance of the capture of Rome. The victory still lies some distance ahead.

**The United nations are determined that in the future no one city and no one race will be able to control the whole of the world.**

No thanks are due to them (Hitler and his generals) if Rome was spared the devastation which the Germans wreaked on Naples and other Italian cities.

* * *

We want and expect the help of the future Italy toward lasting peace. All the other nations opposed to fascism and nazism should help give Italy a chance.

### Churchill Slated to Speak on Rome

LONDON—(AP)—Prime Minister Churchill is expected to tell the story of the fall of Rome to the house of commons Tuesday.

## BLAZES MARK FLIGHT ROUTE OUT OF ROME

### Rail Yards Bombed to Cut Off Help

ROME—(AP)—Allied armor and motorized infantry roared through the Eternal City Monday—not pausing to sight-see—crossed the Tiber, and proceeded with the grim task of destroying two battered German armies fleeing to the north.

**Flashing forces of Allied fighter-bombers spearheaded the pursuit, jamming the escape highways northward with burning enemy transport and littering the fields with dead and wounded Nazis.**

The enemy was tired, disorganized and bewildered by the slashing character of the Allied assault, which in 25 days had inflicted a major catastrophe on German forces in Italy and liberated Rome almost without damage to the historic city.

* * *

Joining the relentless program of destruction, 500 American heavy bombers blasted rail yards at five points in northern Italy between Venice and Rimini along which the Germans might attempt to move reinforcements and equipment to bolster Marshal Albert Kesselring's beaten armies.

Lt. Gen. Mark W. Clark, tall commander of the victorious Fifth army, entered Rome in a jeep and drove to the city hall, where he formally proclaimed the Allied occupation and praised the valor of his troops.

Addressing his corps commanders and looking out over thousands of cheering Italians, Clark declared that both the Tenth and Fourteenth German armies had been destroyed at least partially, more than 20,000 prisoners taken and untold quantities of Nazi equipment captured.

* * *

He lauded individually the French, British and American troops of the Fifth army and paid tribute to the "gallant men and women who made the supreme sacrifice" that made occupation possible. Mussolini's famous balcony in the Palazzo Venezia, a few blocks from where Clark spoke, looked empty and deserted.

**Pope Pius XII, addressing an enormous crowd including many Fifth army soldiers in St. Peter's square, expressed thanks to God that Rome had not been destroyed by war.**

(In Naples, it was announced that King Victor Emmanuel III had signed a retirement decree conferring his powers upon his son, Crown Prince Umberto, whom he named lieutenant general of the realm. However, the monarch retained the title as head of the House of Savoy, thus remaining a king without power.)

The inhabitants' reception to the troops approached hysteria as the

Italy
*Continued on Page Five*

★ ★ ★ ★   ★ ★ ★ ★   ★ ★ ★ ★

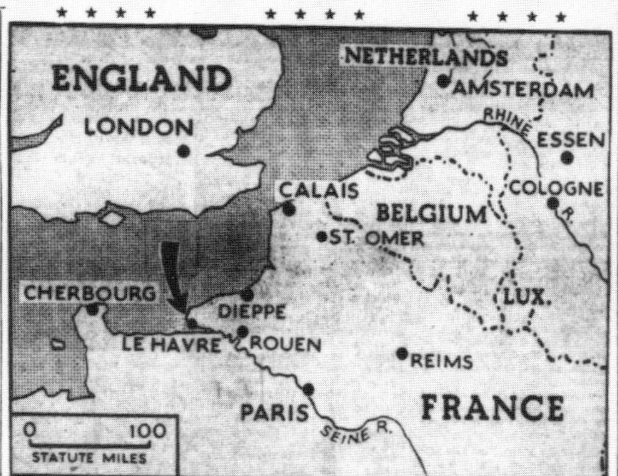


GERMANS REPORT INVASION BEGUN AT LE HAVRE

## RAF FOLLOWS UP HEAVY U.S. RAIDS

### Non-stop Blows Top 90-Hour Mark

LONDON — (UP) — Allied aerial battering of Hitler's European holdings roared past the 90-hour mark Tuesday.

Without giving German coastal defenders a chance to come up for air, RAF heavyweights set out early Monday night in great strength to take up where United States daylight raiders left off.

Axis radios reported "nuisance raiders"—their usual term for Mosquito bombers—over the reich. This suggested main targets were in France or The Lowlands.

American bombers, numbering up to 750, in flying their eighth daylight mission in four days to break all records for heavy bombers, dropped 2,200 tons of bombs on the coastal strip from Calais to Boulogne and boosted the total dumped on the invasion coast since Friday to 15,000 tons.

* * *

A United States strategic air forces communique announced that six American bombers and two fighters were missing from the operation. Apparently they were downed by flak, since no enemy aircraft was encountered.

**Four bombers previously reported missing in Sunday's operations have returned to their bases, the communique said.**

Monday's assault was followed in the afternoon by attacks on bridges, intersections, locomotives, and other rail targets in northern France and Belgium by Thunderbolt fighter-bombers of the United States Ninth air force. Factories and a radio station in northern France also were blasted.

These daylight blows followed quickly the third straight night attack by the RAF on the so-called "mystery emplacements" across the channel in the Pas-de-Calais area.

## Mercury Due for Drop to 40 in City

The mercury is expected to drop 40 to 45 degrees Tuesday in Minneapolis, the weather bureau predicted Monday night, adding that near-freezing weather will prevail in northern areas of Minnesota.

**Temperatures were expected to range from 35 to 40 degrees in some sections.**

Cold here and elsewhere will be attended by fresh to strong winds, with prevailing velocity in the city about 25 miles an hour. In all parts of the state but northern Minnesota, where showers are forecast, relief from the heavy week-end rains is promised.

* * *

After dropping 40 to 45 degrees Tuesday morning, the mercury here was not expected to get above 60 during the day. All-time June low for the city is 36, recorded June 6, 1897.

The mercury was taking a steadily downward course in Minneapolis Monday. From a high of 67 at 2 a.m. it had dropped into the forties by night.

Street crews were busy in Minneapolis Monday shoveling out approaches to sewer drains clogged with sand, cinders and twigs. Repairs were made to streets where holes had been scooped out by water.

## BLUE WINNING IN IOWA VOTE

DES MOINES—(U.P.)—Lt. Gov. Robert D. Blue, Eagle Grove farmer and attorney, was coasting to an easy victory early Tuesday over Henry W. Burma, speaker of the Iowa house of representatives, for the Republican nomination for governor.

Returns from 1,258 precincts out of 2,464 in the state gave: Blue, 55,352; Burma, 32,708.

Milton W. Strickler, Des Moines attorney and former state representative, was trailing badly with 5,032 votes.

In one of the few other contested primary races, State Sen. K. A. Evans of Emerson was building up a substantial lead over state senators G. W. Hunt and Hugh Lundy for the Republican nomination for lieutenant governor.

Returns from 1,252 precincts gave: Evans, 33,804; Hunt, 18,780; Lundy, 25,041.

## Victory Just Ahead, Declares Marshall

WASHINGTON — (AP) — Gen. George C. Marshall, United States army chief of staff, said Monday night "the final action in this terrible European war is now focused on a single battle in which every Allied force will be represented."

"It is to be a battle to the death for the Nazis and a battle to victory for the Allies," he told an audience at the Russian embassy where he was decorated with the Order of Suvorov, first degree, highest honor of the Union of Soviet Socialist republics.

The decoration was presented by Ambassador Andrei A. Gromyko.

## BULLETINS

### War Department Mum

**WASHINGTON— (UP) — The war department said early Tuesday it had no information on reports by the German radio that invasion operations had begun on the French channel coast.**

### Planes Wake London

**LONDON, JUNE 6 — (INS) — London was awakened at an unusually early hour Tuesday morning as a procession of Allied aircraft swept out toward the continent. Observers reported the largest force of bombers and fighters ever seen crossing the channel.**

### D-Day Music

**LONDON—(AP)—The German-controlled Calais radio early Tuesday said in English: "This is D-day. We shall now bring music for the invasion forces."**

### London Radio Off

**NEW YORK—(INS)—An International News service listening post reported at 12:50 a.m. Minneapolis war time that the London radio had gone off the air.**

### Davis Awaits Word

**WASHINGTON—OWI Director Elmer Davis, questioned on the German broadcast of the invasion, said: "We have no more information than you have. I'll stay here until I find out whether the story is true." By 1:45 a.m. EWT almost the entire public relations staff at the war department had reported for duty.**

## KSTP MUSICIANS OPPOSE STRIKE

Strike of staff musicians at KSTP was forestalled Monday when the musicians voted 8 to 6 against "permitting a labor dispute to interrupt war production," in an election conducted by Minneapolis regional office of national labor relations board.

* * *

The strike vote was taken at request of the Minneapolis Musicians association, AFL, which has protested the company's refusal to sign an agreement guaranteeing permanent employment to at least eight musicians at a weekly salary of $52.50.

* * *

The musicians so employed would have to be members of the Minneapolis union, with membership in the St. Paul Musicians association being optional. At present, KSTP musicians are members of both Twin Cities unions.

A three-man panel from the regional war labor board in Chicago recently held a hearing on points at issue in the dispute and a decision on its findings is pending.

### WHERE TO FIND IT



## Allied Leaders Silent But BBC Cautions Dutch

**LONDON — AP — A spokesman for Gen. Dwight D. Eisenhower, in a London broadcast, told the people living on Europe's invasion coast Tuesday that "a new phase of the Allied air offensive has started" and warned them to move inland to a depth of 35 kilometers (about 22 miles).**

**LONDON — UP — Shortly before 7 a.m. British daylight time (midnight Minneapolis time), the BBC broadcast urgent instructions from the Allied high command to Holland advising all people living within 35 kilometers (about 18 miles) of the coast to leave their homes immediately and also keep off roads, railways and bridges.**

LONDON—AP—Three German news agencies Tuesday flashed word to the world that an Allied invasion of western France had begun with Allied parachute troops spilling out of the dawn skies over the Normandy peninsula and seaborne forces landing in the Le Havre area.

**There was no Allied confirmation.**

The Germans also said Allied warships were furiously bombarding the big German-held French port of Le Havre at the mouth of the Seine river, 100 miles west of Paris.

German shock troops also were hurled against Allied troops rushing ashore from landing barges, the broadcasts said.

Le Havre lies 80 miles across the channel from the British coast.

**Dunkerque and Calais, just across the channel coast from Britain, were under attack by strong formations of bombers, DNB said.**

"The long-expected invasion by the British and Americans was begun in the first hours of the morning of June 6 by the landing of parachute troops in the area of the mouth of the Seine," declared the Transocean broadcast.

The German DNB agency said Le Havre was being "violently bombarded at the present moment" (7 a.m. German time, or 12 p.m. Minneapolis war time).

**"German naval forces are engaged in fighting with enemy landing craft off the coast."**

Calais and Dunkerque, which Berlin said were under heavy air attack, also are important French ports along the invasion coast 150 miles northeast of Le Havre.

An hour and a half after the first German bulletin there was no confirmation from Gen. Eisenhower's supreme headquarters.

DNB added that "no enemy landings were made yet," at Calais and Dunkerque, obviously an indication that the Germans were expecting Allied assaults all along the intervening 150 miles separating Dunkerque and Le Havre.

### *Nazi 'Invasion' Broadcasts Relayed to America*

The German broadcasts on the "long-expected invasion" by the Allies were relayed both to North America and to Germans in the homeland. The latter were told by DNB's domestic broadcasts at dawn.

(CBS in New York said after a recheck of recordings of a German broadcast that "there can be no mistaking" that the Germans reported "a landing in the area of the Somme estuary."

**("Thus it appears," said CBS, "that the LeHavre bombardments and the paratroop landings to which the German announcement refer are two separate operations.")**

But half an hour after the first German broadcast announcing the landings, the Nazi-controlled Paris radio spokesman, Robert Debeauplay, declared of the war situation:

"It appears we have been given another month of grace before the invasion will start. A press report from Washington says Roosevelt will come to London at the end of June. Surely this indicates the event will not start before then."

The Germans, however, had run a string of announcements over their Berlin transmitters announcing the big military operation.

"It is believed that these paratroops," said a German broadcast, "have been given the task of capturing airfields in order to facilitate landing of further paratroops.

"The harbor of Le Havre is at the moment being bombarded. German naval forces have engaged enemy landing craft off the coast," Transoceon continued.

Le Havre, one of the great French ports on the Atlantic, is only 100 miles northwest of Paris on the main rail line leading from the French capital through Rouen.

### *Biggest Military Armadas in History Gathered*

The biggest military armadas in history have been gathered in British ports for the fateful summer of 1944.

Huge stockpiles of equipment and vast concentrations of men—Americans, Britons, Canadians, Poles, Dutch and others—have been centered in British invasion bases.

**Allied broadcasts have warned for months past that the Germans might launch a false announcement of Allied invasion operations in an effort to bring patriot French forces out into the open for annihilation.**

There also was the possibility that if the announcement were true, it was only a diversion, or large-scale raid.

After the Transocean and DNB German agencies had announced the "invasion," one of DNB subsidiaries, the Interinf (international information bureau) took to the air with this announcement:

"Anglo-American parachute troops are bailing out on the northern tip of the Normandy peninsula to capture several airfields in order to make room for further landings of parachute troops."

Nazis Report Invasion
*Continued on Page Five*

## Roman Beauty Parade Greets Happy GI Joe

By JAMES E. ROPER

ROME— (UP) —The biggest beauty parade the American army has seen in this war has turned out to welcome GI Joe into Rome. The girls act as if the Americans are the finest men they ever had seen. Everybody is happy.

Tens of thousands of girls swarm the streets. It seemed that the prettiest ones were always in the front lines, ready to pelt the GI's with flowers or kiss their hands. They didn't mind that the soldiers were tired, sweaty and unshaven.

The girls pile onto the jeeps and trucks indiscriminately—three girls to a man or one girl to three men.

**I saw one jeep carrying two soldiers, two girls and two priests.**

The pretty freshness of the Roman girls symbolized a new era for the doughboys who had been battering through scores of towns in southern Italy—all inevitably dirty with their buildings smashed and their people living a slumlike existence in ragged clothes.

* * *

Rome is virtually undamaged by war. Its people are well-dressed and clean.

During the first few hours in Rome the doughboys were more impressed by the good conditions here than by Rome's fabulous cultural and religious treasures. Despite their enthusiastic welcome, the doughboys behaved perfectly and got as many kisses from the parents as they did from the girls themselves.

**FIGHTERS DIG IN—TO FOOD**—American infantrymen are shown surrounding their objective and digging in—the objective being plates of food supplied by women suburbanites of Rome.—AP-Wirephoto from Signal Corps Radiophoto.

CLOUDY
U. S. Weather Bureau Forecast
Occasional rain and cooler.
TEMPERATURES
Details on Page 6

# Minneapolis Morning Tribune

Damon RUNYON Looks at Life ON PAGE 4

Vol. LXXVIII—No. 168. MINNEAPOLIS, MINN., WEDNESDAY, NOVEMBER 8, 1944 ★★★ Price 3 Cents In Twin City Area 5 Cents Elsewhere



# ROOSEVELT IS RE-ELECTED

## *Starkey Defeats Maas; Gale Trailing Gallagher*

## DEMOCRATS TO GAIN EDGE IN CONGRESS

### May Add 20 Seats to Control House

By A STAFF CORRESPONDENT of The Minneapolis Morning Tribune

WASHINGTON — President Roosevelt will have a small majority in both the house of representatives and a control of the treaty-ratifying senate, it appeared at 3:30 a.m. Wednesday.

**Returns on senate races showed: Democrats elected 9, holdovers 36, total 45; Republicans, elected 3, holdovers 24, total 27; contests in doubt 23.**

**Returns on house races showed: Democrats elected 110, Republicans elected 17; contests in doubt 306.**

Washington speculation, based on these trends, was that the Democrats might emerge with a gain of 20 seats in the house, where the parties' strength is now almost even: 214 Democrats, 212 Republicans and 5 vacancies.

**SPECTACULAR RACE**

Three Democratic victories in house races were spectacular: in New York, Augustus Bennett, an Independent Republican running on the Democratic ticket, won over Rep. Hamilton Fish, condemned by both Gov. Dewey and President Roosevelt; in Minnesota, Frank Starkey, DFL candidate topped Rep. Melvin Maas of St. Paul; in Maryland, George H. Fallon ousted incumbent Reg. Daniel Ellison.

For several hours, it appeared that Rep. Clare Booth Luce has lost her Connecticut seat in the house, but as rural precincts came in 29-year-old Margaret E. Connors conceded defeat.

**MOSES LEADING NYE**

In North Dakota, Gov. John Moses, Democrat, was leading isolationist Senator Gerald K. Nye, whose Republican following was split by the independent candidacy of Lynn Stambaugh who filed after losing the Republican nomination to Nye by a narrow margin in the primary election.

Among Democratic senators returned were Majority Leader Barkley of Kentucky and Senator Millard Tydings of Maryland. The solid south sent up six Democratic senators early in the count, and in equally short order rock-ribbed Vermont returned Republican Senator George D. Aiken. Alabama, Arkansas, Georgia, Louisiana, North Carolina and South Carolina were solidly in the Democratic fold.

**NIP AND TUCK**

Democratic nominees were pressing Republican senatorial incumbents in Connecticut and Pennsylvania on the basis of incomplete returns, while Republicans grasped for seats now held by Democrats in Iowa, Missouri and New Jersey.

**Brien McMahon (D) was ahead of Senator John A. Danaher (R) in Connecticut; and Democrat Francis J. Myers had a sizeable margin over Republican "Puddler Jim" Davis in Pennsylvania.**

Iowa's Republican Gov. Bourke B. Hickenlooper led Senator Guy M. Gillette, Democrat; Forrest C. Donnell, Republican, was atop Roy McKittrick in the contest for the seat now held by Democrat Bennett C. Clark in Missouri, and Republican H. Alexander Smith outdistanced Elmer H. Wene in New Jersey with returns incomplete.

Other turnovers in favor of the Democrats retired William J. Miller (R., Conn.) and Thomas B. Miller (R., Pa.) from the house.

The Democrats also picked up seats in the 1st, 2nd, 5th and 6th Pennsylvania district.

### Puerto Rico Rail Disaster Kills 11

SAN JUAN, P. R. —(UP)— At least 11 persons were killed and 40 injured by derailment of the San Juan-Ponce passenger train near Aguadilla early Tuesday. Unofficial reports put the death toll at 41.

THE VICTORY SMILE — President Roosevelt, flashing a broad smile after an evening of listening to election returns that appeared to assure him a fourth term, came out of his Hyde Park study Tuesday to greet neighbors as they formed a torchlight parade terminating at the Roosevelt home.—AP Wirephoto.

## *F. R. Boosts Margin In State to 54,357*

**President Roosevelt's lead over Gov. Dewey in Minnesota was cut to 37,277 with 922 precincts reporting, 230,031 for the President and 192,754 for Dewey. The total included 549 out-state precincts which gave Dewey 89,141 to 82,786 for Roosevelt.**

By WILBUR ELSTON
State Capitol Correspondent of the Minneapolis Morning Tribune

President Roosevelt boosted his Minnesota lead over Gov. Thomas E. Dewey to 54,357 votes on the basis of returns from 854 of 3,703 precincts at 1:30 a.m. Wednesday. Roosevelt had 225,768 and Dewey 171,411.

Roosevelt moved ahead in the rural areas as well as in the Twin Cities and Duluth on the basis of late returns, after first trailing the Republican nominee in Minnesota's rural counties.

The 854 precincts included 191 in Hennepin county which gave Dewey 51,505 and Roosevelt 70,156, and 150 in Ramsey county which reported 44,872 for Dewey and 67,168 for Roosevelt and 50 in St. Louis county which gave the President 19,957 and Dewey 7,962.

The 463 rural precincts showed Roosevelt with a slight lead of 69,387 to 67,072. Earlier returns indicated that rural areas might offset the President's lead in the three metropolitan counties.

**Gov. Edward J. Thye, Republican, maintained his lead over Byron Allen, his Democratic-Farmer-Labor opponent.**

C. Elmer Anderson, former lieutenant governor seeking return to that office, moved ahead of Frank Murphy, DFL, on the basis of early morning returns, after trailing in earlier reports.

Mrs. Viena Johnson, former Farmer-Labor leader who earlier led the incumbent Republican, Frank Matson, for the railroad and warehouse commission long term, finally dropped behind on basis of late returns, but Arthur N. Cosgrove, D-F-L, was ahead of Ray P. Chase for the short term.

Secretary of State Mike Holm, State Treasurer Julius Schmal and Attorney General J. A. A. Burnquist, all Republicans, were building up leads over their D-F-L opponents.

Associate Justice Harry H. Peterson continued to lead the six-man field running for the three associate justice posts, with Associate Justice C. R. Magney and LeRoy Matson running second and third.

**Scattered out-state returns showed Roosevelt running surprisingly well in some of the smaller cities.**

Seven precincts in Rochester and Olmsted county gave Roosevelt 1,196 and Dewey 1,056, while St. Cloud's 17 precincts reported 4,269 for Dewey and 4,075 for Roosevelt.

Albany and St. Joseph, small towns near St. Cloud, went for

State for F. R.
Continued on Page Six

### HAMILTON FISH ADMITS DEFEAT

ALBANY, N. Y.—(AP)—Republican Representative Hamilton Fish conceded Tuesday night that Augustus W. Bennet had won his seat in the 29th congressional district, to which Fish was seeking re-election for a 13th term. Bennet is the candidate of the Democratic, American Labor, Liberal and Good Government parties.

Fish

### Owosso Gives Dewey Favorite-Son Vote

OWOSSO, MICH.—(AP)—Complete returns from this central Michigan city in which Gov. Thomas E. Dewey was born gave him 3,787 votes to 1,947 for President Roosevelt. In 1940 the complete Owosso figures were Roosevelt 2,178, Willkie 3,040.

## JUDD AHEAD; HAGEN HOLDS MEAGER LEAD

### Other Congressmen Appear Elected

*Picture of Starkey on Page Six*

By EARL ALMQUIST
Staff Writer of The Minneapolis Morning Tribune

Frank T. Starkey of St. Paul, the Democratic-Farmer-Labor candidate for congress from the fourth district whose most ardent supporters felt he had but "a little better than an outside chance to win," Tuesday sprang the prize upset of the 1944 general election in Minnesota.

Rep. Maas

He decisively defeated Rep. Melvin J. Maas, Republican incumbent elected in 1926 and who had served continuously since, with the exception of the 1934-35 session.

**JUDD IN LEAD**

In other congressional races in the state, Dr. Walter H. Judd of Minneapolis, fifth district congressman was leading his DFL opponent, Edgar T. Buckley, by 1,704 votes, with approximately 10 per cent of the district's 229 precincts reported.

Possibility of another Republican congressman being unseated loomed in the third district, with William Gallagher, DFL nominee, holding a lead of better than 3,000 votes over Rep. Richard P. Gale, with 1? precincts out of 293 reported.

**HAGEN LEAD SLIM**

This remained but a possibility, however, because the first precincts reporting were heavily anti-Republican districts, while none of the numerous rural districts, which ordinarily give Gale his greatest support, had been heard from at a late hour.

In the other six of the state's nine congressional districts, Republican incumbents appeared to have a safe lead, with the exception of the ninth, where Rep. Harold C. Hagen, who switched from the Farmer-Labor to the Republican party last spring, had but a precarious lead in early returns over Halvor Langslet, the DFL candidate.

**'BEAT HIMSELF'**

Ramsey county political observers hailed Starkey's Fourth district congressional victory as a repudiation of Rep. Maas for his denunciations of President Roosevelt in regard to the Japanese attack on Pearl Harbor, and when reminded that they hadn't even ventured to expect Starkey to win, came back with:

"Maas beat himself."

Starkey, active for many years in the AFL, served in the state

Voting Heavy
Continued on Page Six

### *WHERE TO FIND IT*



### CLARE LUCE IS VICTOR FOR SEAT IN CONGRESS

BRIDGEPORT, CONN.—(AP)—Late reporting rural towns put U.S. Representative Clare Boothe Luce (R) in the lead Tuesday night by 94,505 votes to 85,825 for Miss Margaret E. Connors (D) in returns from 16 out of 23 towns in Connecticut's Fourth congressional district. Mrs. Luce's re-election was conceded by Miss Connors.

Connors

Luce

Mrs. Luce, assailed throughout the campaign by Miss Connors particularly for her views on foreign policy, and singled out by Vice-President Henry Wallace for a full day's tour of her district on the eve of election, had trailed early in the night.

The blond playwright made a strong campaign charging among other things that the Roosevelt administration had been "years of humiliating failure" and attacking Wallace as a "carpet bagger," "repudiated" by his own party.

## How Nation Voted for President

| Electoral Votes | States | No. units | Number Precincts Reported | Roosevelt | Dewey | SOLDIER BALLOTS: States | Estimated Sent | Returned | If not counted Tuesday will be on |
|---|---|---|---|---|---|---|---|---|---|
| 11 | Alabama | 2,300 | 1,088 | 115,094 | 25,403 | Alabama | 6,000 | 3,000 | ....... |
| 4 | Arizona | 438 | 89 | 10,039 | 7,561 | Arizona | 11,128 | 9,000 | ....... |
| 9 | Arkansas | 2,087 | 506 | 31,959 | 11,337 | Arkansas | 35,000 | 17,500 | ....... |
| 25 | California | 14,841 | 4,622 | 409,780 | 307,770 | Calif. | 500,000 | 300,000 | Nov. 24 |
| 6 | Colorado | 1,663 | 171 | 17,003 | 25,431 | Colorado | 36,500 | 25,000 | Nov. 22 |
| 8 | Connecticut | 169 | 149 | 421,112 | 372,438 | Conn. | 70,000 | 40,000 | ....... |
| 3 | Delaware | 250 | 45 | 9,193 | 5,961 | Delaware | 9,035 | 4,350 | ....... |
| 8 | Florida | 1,472 | 600 | 148,354 | 67,597 | Florida | 42,000 | 35,000 | Nov. 8 |
| 12 | Georgia | 1,735 | 587 | 172,276 | 29,499 | Georgia | 50,000 | 20,000 | ....... |
| 4 | Idaho | 845 | 214 | 27,566 | 25,401 | Idaho | 18,000 | 13,500 | ....... |
| 28 | Illinois | 8,748 | 4,519 | 1,138,516 | 876,200 | Illinois | 200,000 | 200,000 | ....... |
| 13 | Indiana | 4,016 | 957 | 244,881 | 246,271 | Indiana | 117,264 | 100,000 | ....... |
| 10 | Iowa | 2,466 | 982 | 179,051 | 189,659 | Iowa | 70,000 | 55,000 | ....... |
| 8 | Kansas | 2,742 | 745 | 52,620 | 94,651 | Kansas | 40,000 | 28,000 | ....... |
| 11 | Kentucky | 4,299 | 2,219 | 256,499 | 200,091 | Kentucky | 60,035 | 40,000 | ....... |
| 10 | Louisiana | 1,871 | 489 | 109,134 | 25,395 | Louisiana | 35,000 | 12,000 | ....... |
| 5 | Maine | 627 | 610 | 138,988 | 153,734 | Maine | 55,000 | 25,000 | ....... |
| 8 | Maryland | 1,327 | 1,076 | 251,309 | 226,757 | Maryland | 55,000 | 40,000 | Nov. 9 |
| 16 | Massachusetts | 1,852 | 731 | 347,993 | 288,709 | Mass. | 136,000 | 100,000 | ....... |
| 19 | Michigan | 3,843 | 675 | 136,900 | 207,098 | Michigan | 146,307 | 125,000 | ....... |
| 11 | Minnesota | 3,703 | 531 | 149,078 | 115,231 | Minnesota | 83,000 | 65,000 | ....... |
| 9 | Mississippi | 1,683 | 695 | 77,150 | 5,488 | Missis'ppi | 50,000 | 30,000 | ....... |
| 15 | Missouri | 4,519 | 2,646 | 363,513 | 369,145 | Missouri | 80,000 | 60,000 | Nov. 10 |
| 4 | Montana | 1,175 | 41 | 6,166 | 5,529 | Montana | 12,561 | 9,500 | ....... |
| 6 | Nebraska | 2,026 | 532 | 43,145 | 72,010 | Nebraska | 31,000 | 25,000 | Dec. 1 |
| 3 | Nevada | 299 | 215 | 11,346 | 11,313 | Nevada | 6,000 | 3,000 | ....... |
| 4 | New Hampshire | 296 | 190 | 49,361 | 51,469 | N. Hamp. | 22,581 | 10,000 | ....... |
| 16 | New Jersey | 3,658 | 1,249 | 307,625 | 350,582 | N. Jersey | 380,000 | 170,000 | ....... |
| 4 | New Mexico | 892 | 176 | 22,488 | 17,229 | N. Mexico | 9,618 | 7,000 | ....... |
| 47 | New York | 9,121 | 3,610 | 1,103,677 | 1,129,008 | N. York | 650,000 | 410,000 | ....... |
| 14 | North Carolina | 1,921 | 1,291 | 382,029 | 158,379 | N. C'lina | 100,000 | 35,000 | ....... |
| 4 | North Dakota | 2,251 | 152 | 13,609 | 12,671 | N. Dak. | 17,800 | 7,500 | Dec. 5 |
| 25 | Ohio | 9,306 | 5,517 | 849,302 | 948,596 | Ohio | 250,000 | 150,000 | ....... |
| 10 | Oklahoma | 3,672 | 2,735 | 283,462 | 219,865 | Oklahoma | 50,000 | 35,000 | ....... |
| 6 | Oregon | 1,829 | 585 | 43,644 | 45,025 | Oregon | 41,000 | 30,000 | ....... |
| 35 | Pennsylvania | 8,197 | 5,350 | 1,207,387 | 1,160,035 | Pennsyl. | 648,974 | 210,000 | Nov. 22 |
| 4 | Rhode Island | 261 | 260 | 158,814 | 114,108 | Rh. Island | 39,532 | 20,000 | Dec. 5 |
| 8 | South Carolina | 1,282 | 663 | 65,770 | 3,648 | S. C'lina | 25,000 | 15,000 | ....... |
| 4 | South Dakota | 1,949 | 803 | 38,906 | 54,840 | S. Dak. | 16,000 | 10,000 | ....... |
| 12 | Tennessee | 2,300 | 1,880 | 213,562 | 141,551 | Tennessee | 48,789 | 35,000 | ....... |
| 23 | Texas | 254 | 197 | 412,227 | 87,172 | Texas | 120,000 | 85,000 | ....... |
| 4 | Utah | 870 | 42 | 8,225 | 5,595 | Utah | 18,000 | 16,500 | Nov. 12 |
| 3 | Vermont | 280 | 245 | 53,916 | 71,428 | Vermont | 15,000 | 7,500 | ....... |
| 11 | Virginia | 1,714 | 1,480 | 201,688 | 126,620 | Virginia | 70,101 | 35,515 | ....... |
| 8 | Washington | 3,163 | 171 | 23,519 | 17,120 | Wash'ton | 60,000 | 45,000 | Dec. 5 |
| 8 | West Virginia | 2,793 | 637 | 89,488 | 72,518 | W. Virg. | 42,000 | 27,000 | ....... |
| 12 | Wisconsin | 3,095 | 1,283 | 261,505 | 265,170 | Wisc'sin | 200,000 | 100,000 | ....... |
| 3 | Wyoming | 673 | 185 | 5,683 | 5,930 | Wyoming | 15,000 | 10,000 | ....... |
| 531 | | 130,773 | | | | Totals | 4,894,225 | 2,855,865 | |

## HOW STATE AND HENNEPIN COUNTY VOTED

### State Vote

**PRESIDENT**
**854 precincts out of 3,703**
Thomas E. Dewey (R) .. 171,411
*Franklin D. Roosevelt (D) 225,768

**GOVERNOR**
**542 precincts out of 3,703**
*Edward J. Thye (R) .... 132,354
Byron G. Allen (DFL) ... 98,397

**LIEUT. GOVERNOR**
**339 precincts out of 3,703**
C. Elmer Anderson (R) ... 75,534
Frank Murphy (DFL) ... 70,837

**SECRETARY OF STATE**
**71 precincts out of 3,703**
*Mike Holm (R).......... 4,463
Emily KneuBuhl (DFL)... 2,653

**STATE TREASURER**
**273 precincts out of 3,703**
*Julius A. Schmahl (R) .. 67,633
A. H. Kleffman (DFL) ... 51,365

**ATTORNEY GENERAL**
**257 precincts out of 3,703**
*J. A. A. Burnquist (R) .. 59,791
Erling Swenson (DFL) ... 50,861

**RAILROAD AND WAREHOUSE COMMISSIONER**
**(Long Term)**
**285 precincts out of 3,703**
*Frank W. Matson (R) ... 50,265
Viena Johnson (DFL) .... 45,461

**RAILROAD AND WAREHOUSE COMMISSIONER**
**(Short Term)**
**285 precincts out of 3,703**
Ray P. Chase (R) ........ 42,015
Arthur N. Cosgrove (DFL) 45,355

**CHIEF JUSTICE OF SUPREME COURT**
**(Elected without opposition)**
Charles Loring ..........

**ASSOCIATED JUSTICE OF SUPREME COURT**
**16 precincts out of 3,703**
**(Three to be elected)**
Clifford E. Enger.......... 1,979
Allan L. Johnson ......... 2,264
*C. R. Magney............ 2,750
Leroy E. Matson.......... 3,055
*Harry H. Peterson....... 3,570
J. Norman Peterson....... 3,602

**AVIATION AMENDMENT**
**4 precincts out of 3,703**
Yes ...................... 1,383
No ....................... 495

*Denotes incumbent.

### Hennepin Vote

**PRESIDENT**
**287 precincts out of 427**
Thomas E. Dewey (R)......64,843
*Franklin D. Roosevelt (D).85,370

**GOVERNOR**
**182 precincts out of 427**
*Edward J. Thye (R)......51,427
Byron G. Allen (DFL)......44,262
Gerald M. York............ 448

**LIEUT. GOVERNOR**
**125 precincts out of 427**
C. Elmer Anderson (R)....39,371
Frank Murphy (DFL)......36,347

**SECRETARY OF STATE**
**107 precincts out of 427**
*Mike Holm (R)............40,599
Emily KneuBuhl (DFL)....23,667

**STATE TREASURER**
**90 precincts out of 427**
*Julius A. Schmahl (R)....28,913
A. H. Kleffman (DFL).....22,377

**ATTORNEY GENERAL**
**91 precincts out of 427**
*J. A. A. Burnquist (R)......27,783
Erling Swenson (DFL).....23,881

**RAILROAD AND WAREHOUSE COMMISSIONER**
**(Long Term)**
**74 precincts out of 427**
*Frank W. Matson (R)....20,760
Viena Johnson (DFL).....15,199

**RAILROAD AND WAREHOUSE COMMISSIONER**
**(Short Term)**
**74 precincts out of 427**
Ray P. Chase (R)..........18,420
Arthur N. Cosgrove (DFL).15,780

**CHIEF JUSTICE OF SUPREME COURT**
**(Elected without opposition)**
Charles Loring ............22,220

**ASSOCIATE JUSTICE OF SUPREME COURT**
**25 precincts out of 427**
**(Three to be elected)**
Clifford E. Enger ..........3,820
Allan L. Johnson...........4,429
*C. R. Magney..............5,223
Leroy E. Matson............5,509
*Harry H. Peterson.........7,003
J. Norman Peterson.........4,024

**AVIATION AMENDMENT**
**85 precincts out of 427**
Yes ......................39,086
No .......................10,774

**JUDGE OF DISTRICT COURT**
**(Five to be elected)**
**11 precincts out of 427**
Alfred W. Anderson ....... 1,625
Tom Bergin ............... 876
*Vince A. Day ............ 3,702
*Levi M. Hall ............ 3,624
*E. A. Montgomery ........ 3,211
W. C. Preus .............. 872
*Lars O. Rue ............. 3,305
*Arthur W. Selover........ 2,927
John A. Weeks ............ 2,894

**JUDGE OF PROBATE COURT**
**(Elected without opposition)**
*Manley L. Fosseen ........ 8,845

**COUNTY COMMISSIONER**
**First District**
**12 precincts out of 71**
*Ralph E. Dickman ....... 3015
Arthur R. Ferrin .......... 2,691

**COUNTY COMMISSIONER**
**Third District**
**(Elected without opposition)**
*W. W. Heffelfinger ....... 2,128

**COUNTY COMMISSIONER**
**Fifth District**
(No report)

**REPRESENTATIVE**
**28th District**
**(Two to be elected)**
**5 precincts out of 18**
*Joseph M. Connors ....... 1,649
*John J. McNulty ......... 1,789
John Joseph O'Brien ...... 998
Art J. Shasky ............ 1,426

**STATE SENATOR**
**29th District**
**4 precincts out of 42**
Emmett L. Duemke ....... 1,712
John F. Shaughnessy ...... 747

**REPRESENTATIVE**
**29th District**
**(Two to be elected)**
**2 precincts out of 42**
Chester G. W. Gustafson ... 486
George Murk .............. 715
James A. Murphy .......... 636
*Carl O. Wegner .......... 578

**REPRESENTATIVE**
**30th District**
**(Two to be elected)**
**2 Precincts out of 29**
Alf L. Bergerud..............429
*William E. Honeycutt........426
Arthur P. Smith..............274
Mrs. Nellie Sperry...........260

**REPRESENTATIVE**
**31st District**
**(Two to be elected)**
**1 Precinct out of 29**
*Carl G. Hagland............202
*Carl L. Lyse...............277
Edward S. Torkelson.........260
Walter P. Wolfe.............274

**REPRESENTATIVE**
**32nd District**
**(Two to be elected)**
**1 Precinct out of 46**
George W. Barker............202
*Harold R. Lundeen..........277
Charles S. Ryberg...........260
*Edward J. Volstad..........274

Vote of State
Continued on Page Six

## LEAD MOUNTS TO 329 VOTES IN 31 STATES

### Defeat Is Conceded by Dewey

**NEW YORK —(AP)— Gov. Thomas E. Dewey told a press conference early Wednesday, that "it's clear that Mr. Roosevelt has been re-elected for a fourth term."**

By Associated Press

Franklin Delano Roosevelt amassed such a lead over Thomas E. Dewey early Wednesday that claims of fourth term victory came from the Democratic camp—and concessions from some Dewey supporters.

Aids reported shortly after midnight that Dewey would not concede. Two of the Republican candidate's staunchest newspaper supporters did, however — the New York Daily News and the New York Herald Tribune. Earlier, the New York Times had proclaimed Mr. Roosevelt, whom it supported, elected.

**31 STATES FOR FR**

At 1 a.m. (Minneapolis time), with some states still see-sawing and the figures subject to change, the electoral votes shaped up:

**Roosevelt 329; Dewey 202; needed to win 266.**

At this hour the popular vote total of 19,418,425 was divided: Roosevelt 10,529,482; Dewey 8,888,943.

The returns showed Roosevelt leading in 31 states having a total of 329 electoral votes, as follows:

Alabama, Arizona, Arkansas, California, Connecticut, Delaware, Florida, Georgia, Idaho, Illinois, Kentucky, Louisiana, Maryland, Massachusetts, Minnesota, Mississippi, Montana, Nevada, New Mexico, North Carolina, North Dakota, Oklahoma, Pennsylvania, Rhode Island, South Carolina, Tennessee, Texas, Utah, Virginia, Washington, and West Virginia.

**'BIG TEN' FOR DEWEY**

Dewey was leading in 17 states with an aggregate electoral vote of 202, as follows:

Colorado, Indiana, Iowa, Kansas, Maine, Michigan, Missouri, Nebraska, New Hampshire, New Jersey, New York, Ohio, Oregon, South Dakota, Vermont, Wisconsin, and Wyoming.

The "Big Ten" electoral vote states outside the solid south gave Dewey the edge six to four in incomplete tabulations, but Roosevelt was out in front in four of the five "border" states.

**Mr. Roosevelt himself told his neighbors at Hyde Park, N. Y., "It looks very much like I'll have to be coming up here on the train from Washington for another four years."**

He had piled up a popular vote majority by midnight of 5,256,743 to 4,346,873 in 26,759 out of 130,834 precincts in a nation which apparently had recorded the biggest ballot in history.

**VICTORY 'OVERWHELMING'**

Democratic National Chairman Robert E. Hannegan said in New York that Roosevelt had won an "overwhelming victory" that meant "national unity on a program of international collaboration for permanent peace."

**The midnight word from Republican headquarters in New York was that the early returns had looked "very encouraging."**

Early this morning, Roosevelt held large leads in the solid south and in most of the far west.

**New England was mostly Dewey's and he held a lead in a number of corn belt states. The mountain area was split.**

New York, home state of both candidates, see-sawed, but the

F. R.-Dewey
Continued on Page Six

## WAR NEWS

*Yanks Repel Nazis* PAGE TWO
*Russ Plan New Drive* PAGE TWO
*Nips Shuffle Generals* PAGE TWO
*440 Jap Planes Shot Down by Yanks* PAGE THREE

SNOW
U. S. Weather Bureau Forecast
Light snow, little change.
TEMPERATURES
[illegible]
Details on Page 8

# Minneapolis Morning Tribune

Vol. LXXVIII—No. 265. MINNEAPOLIS, MINN., TUESDAY, FEBRUARY 13, 1945 ★★★ Price 3 Cents

FROM Washington TOM STOKES on editorial page



# DESTROY NAZIS, BIG 3 AGREE

## RUSS STORM 16 MILES IN GIANT DRIVE

### Dresden 74 Miles Away as Soviets Keep up Plunge

*Russian Map on Page Eight*

LONDON— (LP) —Russian troops, opening the second month of their "win the war" winter offensive, swept 16 miles across Silesia Monday in a giant outflanking drive south of Berlin and reached to within 74 miles of Dresden, seventh city of Germany.

Charging 64 miles west of the upper Oder river at almost-encircled Breslau, the First Ukrainian army seized the Bober river fortress city of Bunzlau, 114 miles southeast of Berlin, reaching the Nazis' second river defense line inside the Reich border.

The Bober flows northward into the big bend of the Oder at Crossen, 31 miles southeast of Frankfurt-on-the-Oder, and it appeared the Russians were intending to outflank Berlin from the south.

**RIVER FORCED**

Berlin said the Russians already had forced the Bober at two points between Bunzlau and Sprottau, 20 miles to the north, and set a tank column plunging up the west bank to within 19 miles south of Crossen.

**At Bunzlau, a pottery center of 16,500 persons, the Russians were 74 miles east of Dresden and 28 miles northeast of Saxony province.**

The Moscow war bulletin announced the First Ukrainian army also overran 100 other German towns in their newest advances west of the Oder. It also disclosed the First White Russian army, charging northward across the Polish corridor, captured 100 places, including Swiecic, 62 miles south of Danzig.

The German encirclement at Torun, on the Vistula river, cost the enemy 13,000 killed and more than 15,000 captured, Moscow said. Torun fell Feb. 1 after a six-day battle.

**BUDAPEST TOTTERS**

The bulletin said the 49-day siege of Budapest was near an end. The Russians captured more than 200 blocks, including the royal palace in Buda.

**More than 30,000 Germans have been taken in Buda and "battles for the liquidation of the final remnants of the garrison" have started, Moscow said.**

On the basis of previous Moscow announcements, the Budapest action, coupled with the Germans captured at Torun, brought enemy losses in the first month of the Soviet offensive to approximately 614,000 killed and 214,000 captured.

Berlin said another wing of the First Ukranian army had swept 12 miles north of Sagan, to reach within 31 miles of the First White Russian army's main forces battling along the Oder in the Frankfurt and Kuestrin areas due east of Berlin.

Berlin had reported the First White Russian army across the Oder on the short road to the capital at several points in the Kues-

Russians
*Continued on Page Eight*

**ROOSEVELT ARRIVES AT YALTA**—President Franklin D. Roosevelt (center, hat over heart) is greeted at the airport at Yalta, in Russia's Crimea, with playing of the Russian anthem after he is met by Prime Minister Churchill (in uniform beside President) and Russian Foreign Secretary Vyacheslav Molotov (left of Churchill). U. S. Secretary of State Edward R. Stettinius, Jr., is at left of Molotov. The welcoming ceremony marked President Roosevelt's arrival for the Big Three conference.—AP Wirephoto. **(Additional pictures on Page 5.)**

## *Allies Loose Three Westwall Anchors*

PARIS—(LP)—Troops of the Canadian First and U. S. Third armies Monday ripped loose the three main anchors of the Siegfried line at both ends of a 110-mile front, capturing Kleve, Gennep and Pruem and setting the stage for an imminent drive to the Rhine.

The U. S. First army was poised along the center of the sagging Westwall in readiness to join the swelling assault and was sending patrols across the flooded Roer river south of Dueren to test powerful enemy defenses on the opposite shore.

Field Marshal Sir Bernard L. Montgomery's Canadian First army crashed completely through original Siegfried defenses by overrunning Kleve in 36 hours of street fighting and then driving a mile east and a mile and half southeast of the town.

**FOE QUITS GENNEP**

Gennep, nine miles southwest of Kleve and the southern anchor of the Gennep-Kleve defense line, was taken when the Germans withdrew their main forces to avoid being encircled and pinned against the Maas (Meuse) river.

The fourth division of Lt. Gen. George S. Patton's Third army cleared all organized resistance from Pruem, a central pivot and road center of the Westwall, after an artillery barrage broke the back of German defense.

**Montgomery was quoted in London reports as saying that "the battle is going very nicely" after viewing the conquered fortress of Kleve.**

Two-thirds of the Reich's forest south of Kleve is in Allied hands as were more than 4,000 prisoners. Front reports said that the German Eighty-fourth division at Kleve was eliminated as a fighting unit and that a huge toll had been taken of enemy reinforcements rushed up to plug the breach.

**COLLAPSE IS SUDDEN**

Pruem fell just 15 days after Patton's Third army jumped off from Belgian soil Jan. 29. German resistance within the fiercely defended road hub collapsed suddenly after thunderous "timed crashes" of artillery dazed the defenders.

Patton's doughboys found only moderate resistance when they rushed through streets fogged with the dust of blasted buildings. Most defenders were too groggy for battle and there was little street fighting.

Resistance in Kleve also collapsed suddenly as the bayonets of Montgomery's troops thinned the ranks of Nazi paratroopers making

West Front
*Continued on Page Eight*

## TORNADO HITS SOUTH, 38 DIE

### Train in Alabama Blown From Tracks

By Associated Press

Tornadoes skipping across Alabama and Mississippi Monday killed at least 38 persons and injured more than 150.

Property damage, unestimated, was expected to run into thousands of dollars.

Alabama counted 33 dead, 23 at Montgomery, nine at Livingston, 125 miles west of Montgomery, and one at York, nine miles from Livingston.

**The dead at Livingston included two members of the crew of a 39-car freight train that was blown from the tracks.**

Gov. Chauncey Sparks called out the state guard for duty in the devastated Alabama areas and Red Cross set up temporary shelter for the homeless.

The Alabama injured numbered more than 100.

Five were known dead and 50 injured after the storm struck several points within a seven-mile radius of Meridian, Miss.

## *ELLIOTT'S A GENERAL DESPITE 'BLAZE'S' TRIP*

WASHINGTON—(UP)—Col. Elliott Roosevelt, second son of the President, won senate confirmation of his promotion to brigadier general Monday after bitter bi-partisan debate in which his conduct in "the affair Blaze" was denounced as unbecoming to an officer.

The vote to confirm was 53 to 11, with all the dissents cast by Republicans who had protested his rise from a captaincy in less than four years had been too rapid.

Before voting, the chamber agreed to separate the nomination from those of 77 other colonels up for promotion.

It later approved them all unanimously.

Sen. Harlan J. Bushfield of South Dakota led the attack on the Blaze incident.

Blaze, Elliott's English bull mastiff, was flown across the country on an "A" priority to Actress Faye Emerson, Elliott's third wife, in Hollywood.

**Gen. Roosevelt**

Three service men were bumped off the plane at Memphis to make room for him.

**Democrats defended Elliott's military record.**

They emphasized that the recommendation for his promotions came from the war department and not from the White House.

The 78 promotions came up in the senate a week ago.

**Elliott's promotion, as well as the others, are temporary.**

"Gen. Marshall was in the army 35 years before he became a brigadier general; Gen. Eisenhower reached that rank in 30 years, and Gen. MacArthur was a soldier for 21 years before he reached one-star rank," Bushfield said.

## JAP PEERS DIG 'GRAVE' SITUATION

WASHINGTON—(UP)—**The Japanese house of peers adopted a resolution urging the government to carry on "all necessary measures for the speedy mobilization of the entire nation in order to bring the war to a successful conclusion."**

The Japanese news agency Domei broadcast quoted observers as saying this resolution and one passed by the house of representatives were "taken to indicate a strong demand on the part of the public for effective and powerful administrative measures to overcome the difficult situation now confronting the country."

## EARLY PRISONER RETURN PLEDGED

### Conference Plans for Repatriation

WASHINGTON— (AP) —Speedy repatriation of American, British and Russian war prisoners and civilians liberated in the conquest of Germany was pledged by the Big Three meeting in the Crimea.

A supplement to the final communique on the conference released Monday reported "a comprehensive agreement" was reached at the parley providing arrangements for the protection and maintenance as well as repatriation of those who fell into Nazi hands.

**"Under these arrangements," the statement said, "each ally will provide food, clothing, medical attention, and other needs for the nationals of the others until transport is available for their repatriation.**

Soviet officers will assist British and American authorities in their task of caring for Soviet citizens liberated by the British and American forces during such time as they on the continent of Europe or in the United Kingdom awaiting transport to take them home.

"We are pledged to give every assistance consistent with operational requirements to help to insure that all these prisoners of war and civilians are speedy repatriated."

## U. S. UNITS MAKE MANILA JUNCTION

### Luzon Split by Gain After Heavy Bombing

MANILA—(UP)—American cavalrymen, infantrymen and airborne troops joined forces in southern Manila Tuesday as Gen. Douglas MacArthur announced shattering aerial bombardments on the tip of Bataan and Corregidor, controlling the entrance to Manila bay.

Tokyo radio asserted Monday that Gen. MacArthur has landed 12 divisions in Luzon, including nine infantry units, two tank forces and one airborne division. The broadcast claimed that American casualties in the Luzon campaign now total 30,000.

To the north, tsoops of the First army corps split Luzon in half from west to east when armored units of the Eighth division hacked through to Dingalan bay on the east coast.

**YANK DIVISIONS JOINED**

The First cavalry and Thirty-seventh divisions south of the Pasig river which divides Manila joined in force near the Paco railroad station.

First cavalrymen and troop of the Eleventh airborne division made contact near the Polo club near the shore of Manila bay.

**"The enemy remnant, now closely enclosed is gradually being compressed into extinction."**

Manila
*Continued on Page Eight*

## *Polish Frontier Fixed, Frisco Parley Called*

By RICHAD WILSON
Chief of Washington Bureau of the Minneapolis Morning Tribune

WASHINGTON—Agreements have been reached between President Roosevelt, Prime Minister Churchill and Marshal Stalin to crush Germany, occupy the nation by zones, destroy German militarism and Nazism and reconstruct liberated Europe on democratic principles.

In a communique issued in Washington, London and Moscow, it was announced that the three leaders meeting for eight days in the summer palace of Czar Nicholas II at Yalta, the Crimea, came to agreement on many of the vexing problems which have caused turmoil in Allied affairs for the past six months.

**To place the capstone on plans for world organization and co-operation the three heads of state agreed to a full-scale international conference to implement the Dumbarton Oaks agreement on April 25 at San Francisco.**

A new agreement was reached on the Polish problem.

Plans were made for occupation of Germany by zones under the direction of a central control commission; reparations will be demanded from Germany; principles of the Atlantic charter were strongly reaffirmed; the basis was laid for Germany's surrender.

These detailed international arrangements were highlighted also by a new approach toward Germany's unconditional surrender more exactly in line with the Russian approach to this problem than to any previously adopted by Churchill and Roosevelt.

**There was nothing in the statements on Germany to indicate whether the Big Three hope for a long or a short period of control.**

Officials here found a clue, however, in the statements that the Germans would find no place in the family of nations until Nazism and militarism have been wiped out.

Few American officials, if any, believe that that can be accomplished in less than a full generation—30 years or more.

Sharp distinction now is made by the three leaders between the German people as a whole and the Nazis and militarists or "Hitlerites," as the Russians usually call them.

**This was considered to be an open promise to the German people that there still is a way of life left for them in the world after Nazism and militarism has been ruthlessly stamped out.**

The scope of the agreements publicly announced led toward the belief among observers in Washington that the question of Japan had not been avoided, though there was no specific mention of Japan in the joint communique.

**F.R. WANTS STALIN'S IDEA**

It is believed here that President Roosevelt would be unlikely to allow this meeting to pass without gaining some impression from Stalin of future Russian moves when Germany is beaten.

The date of the forthcoming United Nations conference in San

Big Three
*Continued on Page Eight*

## SOVIET MUSIC HAILS PARLEY

MOSCOW—(UP)—The Moscow radio broadcast the full text of the Big Three communique Monday night without comment, ending the program by playing the Soviet national anthem, "God Save the King," and "The Star Spangled Banner."

## *Jap Medicine Made by F. R. and Churchill*

By Associated Press

Plans for stepping up the war against Japan as well as finishing off the conflict in Europe were discussed on Malta, war-torn Mediterranean island, by President Roosevelt and Prime Minister Churchill.

They and members of their staffs then flew to their Crimea meeting with Premier Stalin.

This information came from a high-ranking United States officer and constituted the only mention of Japan in connection with the "Big Three" meetings.

Choice of San Francisco as the site for the United Nations security conference April 25 focused attention on the Pacific as an area of prime importance in international collaboration after the war.

**Only explanation for the choice immediately available was that San Francisco was a convenient place for many of the delegates who would be from South America and the distant regions of the Pacific.**

One other explanation which cropped up in speculation was that

*Continued on Page Eight*
Jap Angle

## *Stettinius Arrives for Moscow Visit*

MOSCOW—(AP)—U. S. Secretary of State Stettinius has arrived in Moscow for a short visit.

An official announcement said Monday:

"At the invitation of (Foreign Commissar) Molotov, Mr. Stettinius arrived in Moscow this afternoon by plane from the Crimea. He was accompanied by (W. Averell) Harriman, the American ambassador. His visit will be a brief one."

## *Paul Dana Killed*

NEW YORK—(AP)—Lt. Paul Dana, great grandson of the late Charles A. Dana, editor of the New York Sun, has been killed in action in the Pacific area when the plane in which he was flying as rear gunner and radar man was shot down over Saipan.

## BIG 3 STAND WINS FAVOR IN CONGRESS

### Representatives of Both Parties Hold Cheery Peace Views

WASHINGTON— (AP) —The Big Three statement won bi-partisan applause Monday in congress.

**Both Democrats and Republicans said it held out high hope for future peace.**

Minority Leader White (Maine) praised its "forthright terms" and told his colleagues "I feel a great work has been done." Majority Leader Barkley (Ky.), who also addressed the chamber, said:

"It is a source of great gratification to me, and I am sure to all the peace-loving peoples of the world, that these heads of three great governments have been able to go so far in composing differences growing out of the war and the occupation of liberated territories."

**BLOOM PLEASED**

Chairman Bloom (D., N. Y.) of house foreign affairs committee said "There is a reaffirmation (in the statement) of the Atlantic Charter and if we are falling back again on the Atlantic Charter we've got a pretty good basis to work from."

Hardly had the session recessed until Thursday before Sen. Vandenberg (R., Mich.), a foremost foreign policy spokesman for his party, issued a statement saying the joint announcement "is by far the best that has issued from any major conference."

**Other comment:**

Sen. Kilgore (D., W. Va.): "As I interpret it, we are getting what I have hoped for all the way through, the power of self determination for the smaller nations, mination for the smaller nations."

Calling the agreements "in the main highly satisfactory," foreign relations committee chairman Connally (D., Texas) said that "on the whole, the work of the conference will be very helpful and reassuring."

Destruction of German military strength, said Chairman May (D., Ky.) of the house military committee, "is the only thing that will meet demands of the people throughout the world."

**HOOVER PRAISE**

Former President Hoover indorsed the agreement reached at Yalta, called it a "strong foundation on which to rebuild the world. It is fitting it should have been issued to the world on the birthday of Abraham Lincoln."

Sen. Guffey (D., Pa.): "The agreements represent a much greater achievement than anyone expected."

Sen. Hatch (D., N. M.): "People of the enemy countries who truly hate war ought to take courage from this agreement and instantly repudiate the leadership that is forcing them to remain in the war."

Sen. Chandler (D., Ky.): "People of the world will be en-

Solons Pleased
*Continued on Page Eight*

## *Wife, 73, Charged in Death of Mate*

WINCHESTER, IND.— (UP) —**Mrs. Maggie Deeds, 73, Monday was charged with assault and battery with intent to commit a felony, accused of beating fatally her 83-year-old mate of nearly 50 years.**

The husband, Millard Deeds, wealthy Randolph county farmer and a cripple, died of head wounds officials said were inflicted by a club wielded by Mrs. Deeds during an argument Sunday night.

They would have celebrated their golden wedding anniversary next month.

Mrs. Deeds was free on $10,000 bond.

## *F. R. Settles Family Problem By Taking Anna to Yalta*

WASHINGTON — (AP) —President Roosevelt settled a family problem by taking his daughter, Mrs. John Boettiger, with him to this Big Three meeting.

The President fixed everything to suit himself, and his daughter got her way too.

He has wanted her to be with him much of the time during the past two years, but until now he hadn't taken her along to international conferences.

**GAVE UP COAST HOME**

The chief executive has grown to depend more and more upon her for confidential secretarial work since she gave up her Seattle home to return to the White House in 1943.

**But Anna Roosevelt Boettiger has been showing signs of restlessness these last few months.**

When another Big Three meeting between her father, Britain's

F.R.'s Family
*Continued on Page Eight*

**ROOSEVELT CHATS WITH DAUGHTER**—President Roosevelt and his daughter, Mrs. Anna Boettiger, aboard an unidentified warship at Malta on Feb. 2 while en route to the "Big Three" conference in Yalta, Russian Crimea.—AP Wirephoto from Signal Corps.

## *Snow Is Forecast For City Today*

Light snow and not much change in temperature was the weather bureau's forecast for the Twin Cities Tuesday. A high of 30 was predicted for the day.

Temperature at midnight Monday was 32.

Snow and warmer Tuesday was expected to be general through the state with a slight decline in temperature due Wednesday in the southern portion.

## WHERE TO FIND IT

COLD
U. S. Weather Bureau Forecast:
Fair, continued cold
Details on Page 5

# Minneapolis Morning Tribune

Vol. LXXVIII—No. 271. MINNEAPOLIS, MINN., MONDAY, FEBRUARY 19, 1945 ★★★ Price 3 Cents

Chuckles... POPEYE on Today's Comic Page



# MARINES INVADE IWO JIMA

FACING SMOKE-BLACKENED skies Yank troops move into Manila along a suburban road in their re-occupation of the Philippine capital. The fires were set by Jap soldiers fleeing before the American advance.—AP Wirephoto.

THE ROAD BACK—Forced to leave Manila when Japs still were there, Filipinos march through the town of Polo on their way back after Yank recapture of the city. They carry their own supply of food, picked up as they could find it.

## *Exultant Nimitz Says Tokyo Raid Decisive Victory*

**U. S. PACIFIC FLEET HDQ., GUAM—(AP)—American Marines, their path cleared by the most intensive neutralization campaign of the Pacific war, have landed on strategic little Iwo Jima, one of the Volcano islands 675 statute miles south of the Japanese homeland.**

From Late Dispatches

American troops coming ashore in 100 landing boats made a successful landing on Iwo Jima, Japanese home front bastion 750 miles from Tokyo, beginning at 8 a.m. Monday, Tokyo radio announced Monday.

The enemy broadcast was the first to admit that a successful assault had been carried out by troops supported by a heavy force of battleships, cruisers and destroyers.

Previously Tokyo had reported three "unsuccessful attempts to land on Saturday."

**The Japanese report, which remained unconfirmed from any Allied source, said the landing had been made under heavy naval fire on the southeast coast of the eight-square-mile island of the Volcano group.**

Text of the enemy broadcast:

"Following a series of abortive landing attempts a part of the enemy forces have finally started landings on Iwo Jima since 8 o'clock this Monday morning.

"The landing is being made on the southeast coast of the island. The Japanese garrison immediately pushing the enemy invaders back to the shore is now engaged in fierce counter-attack against the enemy.

**"The landing was preceded by persistent naval and air attacks since early last Wednesday morning."**

"Two enemy battleships and four or five cruisers started a bombardment at six o'clock Sunday morning from the surface one or two kilometers off the southern coast of the island and intense shell fire was exchanged between the Japanese coastal guns and the enemy fleet until 10 o'clock.

**"Simultaneously with this naval bombardment the enemy conducted a reconnaissance along the northeastern shore with a small group of surface vessels.**

"At eight o'clock this Monday morning the enemy started landing on the southeast coastal area with 100 landing boats."

"Enemy forces were reinforcing the first group with troops that are approaching the beach in two separate groups.

"At the waterline fierce engagements are now in progress between the invaders and the Japanese garrison forces who are effectively counter attacking the enemy in close unison with the coastal batteries and our air forces."

American carrier planes scored a "decisive" victory over the Japanese in the mighty 1,500-plane raids on the Tokyo-Yokohama area of the Japanese homeland Friday and Saturday, Adm. Chester W. Nimitz announced Monday.

**509 PLANES BAGGED**

Admiral Nimitz announced the Americans, scoring a "complete tactical surprise," destroyed 332 Japanese aircraft in the air and 177 on the ground.

He said one Japanese escort car-

Iwo Jima
*Continued on Page Six*

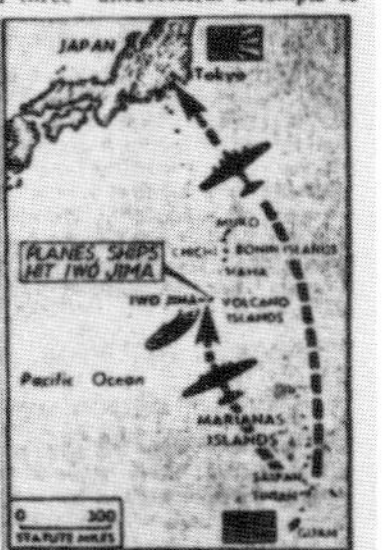


IWO INVADED, JAPS SAY
*Vital Island Protects Tokyo*

## *OPA SCANDAL BARES 'RETREAD MONOPOLY'*

By MILTON KAPLAN
Staff Writer of The Minneapolis Morning Tribune

Details of how a Minneapolis tire dealer "obtained a virtual monoply on retreadable tires in the state" were revealed by Rae E. Walters, Chicago, regional administrator of the OPA, when he arrived in the city Sunday night for conference with the U. S. district attorney.

Walters revealed the contents of an official telegram summarizing the findings of OPA investigators who have probed a tire rationing scandal in the Twin Cities district of the OPA.

**Seven persons were named in the telegram which was signed by William H. Strong, special assistant to the administrator in the OPA, and director of the OPA's investigative unit.**

**No charges have been filed in the case.**

Three officials of the Twin Cities office of OPA have resigned. They are: Harold J. Slawik, acting Twin Cities district director of the OPA; Norman F. Phelps, district rationing executive; Wilcke J. Hicks, district tire rationing officer.

**SLAWIK'S POSITION**

Slawik called for a federal grand jury investigation of the "whole affair" and said he resigned voluntarily "because Chicago's (OPA) approach to the problem was different than mine." He claimed to have known of some irregularities.

Phelps said, "Any irregularities which existed were unknown to me," and Hicks added: "I got my first information about what was going on at the tire inspection station at the same time Slawik did—when the investigator came and told us early in January."

**The telegram from Strong stated that government agents had obtained evidence indicating "serious irregularities existed in the operation of the central truck tire inspection bureau at St. Paul" with the knowledge of certain OPA employes.**

"These irregularities centered around an operation which en-

OPA Scandal
*Continued on Page Six*

## 4 TWIN CITIES INTERNEES FREE

*Prisoner List on Page Seven*

One former Minneapolis resident, and three from St. Paul, were included in the partial list of civilian prisoners of war rescued by American forces from internment camps in the Philippines announced Sunday by the war department.

**Daniel Beebe, uncle of Franklin B. Knoblauch, 1705 Morgan avenue S., was among those rescued from Santo Tomas.**

Those from St. Paul were **Harry N. Salet**, son of Mr. and Mrs. Leon Salet, 1134 Summit avenue; his wife, **Phyllis B.**, and daughter, **Jean J. Salet**. Two other children, Betty and Phillip Salet, were not included in the first list given out.

**BEEBE BORN HERE**

Beebe, 70, was born in Minneapolis. He attended University of Minnesota and following graduation from the medical school, was made an assistant surgeon in the United States navy in 1899. After four years in the navy he returned to Minneapolis for several years, then went to the Philippines where he has since made his home.

**He visited his nephew in Minneapolis in the summer of 1941, Knoblauch said Sunday night, as he retained some business interests here. He was a plantation owner near Davao near the southern end of Luzon. The last direct word from him was received shortly before Pearl Harbor.**

**SALET BUSINESSMAN**

Mr. and Mrs. Leon Salet left St. Paul a week ago to spend the winter in California. A son, Louis, reached in Mankato, Minn., was visibly affected by the news of the release of his brother and family, and said he would communicate with his parents immediately to let them know.

Harry Salet took his family to Manila in 1919, Louis said, where he was in the importing and exporting business. The entire family came to visit in St. Paul in 1937.

The war department said that publication of lists would follow notification of next-of-kin and that further lists will be announced upon receipt of messages from American forces in the Philippines.

## *7,700 Germans Die as Transport Sinks*

LONDON—(AP)—The Finnish radio reported Sunday night the sinking of the 25,000-ton German liner Wilhelm Gustloff with loss of 7,700 persons while she was evacuating refugees and sailors from Danzig.

**The broadcast did not state how or when the German ship was sunk, but said of the 3,700 naval personnel and 5,000 refugees aboard only 1,000 were saved.**

(The Wilhelm Gustloff, a passenger liner before the war, had been converted into a troop transport.)

## *Pass It, Says Stimson of Work Bill*

WASHINGTON—(AP)—Secretary of War Stimson, in words "blunt and plain," warned Sunday night "we dare not delay longer" enacting the war work law.

Voluntary means have failed to keep trained men at their essential jobs and national service legislation is the only remedy, he said. He lauded house passage Feb. 1 of the work-or-jail bill for men.

With the bill now pending for days in the senate military affairs committee, Stimson argued against "prolonged consideration of comparatively trivial details." He told his listeners:

**"I have read that some are troubled lest, under the bill passed by the house, civilian workers may be sent too far from their homes to work in munition plants.**

"Does this seem a very weighty objection to you fathers and mothers, you wives and sweethearts of our fighting men, whose loved ones have been bravely and willingly fighting in the torrid jungles of New Guinea or the frozen hillsides of the Rhine?"

He concluded with these words: "Let us speed the victory by treating this crisis of the war in the true spirit of American democracy."

## *Monetary Measure Off to Good Start*

PHILADELPHIA—(AP)—Legislation legalizing the Bretton Woods international monetary agreement was off to a good start in congress, Secretary of the Treasury Henry F. Morgenthau, Jr., said Sunday.

"The Bretton Woods bill was drafted at the capitol by congressional drafting experts," he said, "with the treasury and state departments assisting, and a good job was done. The fact that the two departments helped means technicalities which might have crept in had there been no cooperation will not be encountered later."

## *Pressing Collector Says He Was Ironed*

When he "dunned" Mrs. Clara Selby, 381 Carroll avenue, St. Paul, for $13 he claims she owes him Mrs. Selby picked up an electric iron in her kitchen and hit him on the head with it, cutting a four inch gash over his left eye, Jay Riley, 50, 444½ St. Peter street, St. Paul, told police Sunday. Police are seeking Mrs. Selby.

## SHOOT HITLER, SAYS SEN. BALL

### Solon Wants Nazis to Rebuild Europe

WASHINGTON—(AP)—The execution of Adolf Hitler and "his immediate war criminals" after the European war ends and the assignment of "several millions of Germans" to "rebuild the Europe they have destroyed" was advocated Sunday by Sen. Joseph H. Ball (R., Minn.)

"Germany must be looked upon as an aggressor and not a normal belligerent in the old sense of the word," he said on the University of Chicago roundtable broadcast.

**"Hitler and his immediate war criminals must be shot, rather than allowed to live out their lives on a tropical isle."**

The Minnesota Republican also commended the decision of the Yalta conference to transfer to a central organization sovereignty over such areas as the Ruhr, Saar and upper Silesia, maintaining such a policy would "prevent a nation from becoming nationalistic."

## NAZIS READY TO ABANDON RUHR BASTION

### Canadians Smash Ahead as Yanks Pierce Reich Frontier

PARIS—(AP)—The Canadian First army smashed through outer defenses to within 1,000 yards of Goch Sunday amid indications that the Germans were preparing to abandon this outflanked bastion at the threshold to the Ruhr industrial basin.

The U. S. Third and Seventh armies invaded Germany at two new points from the west and south as the feeling grew the great Allied storm was gathering in the west.

**Field Marshal Montgomery sent a message to his troops declaring that "we now come to the last and final round" in which knockout blows will be aimed "from more than one direction."**

The German radio, saying an all-out offensive was near, declared that Montgomery had thrown his British Second army into battle alongside the Canadian First army at the approaches to the Ruhr.

British infantry who cut the Goch-Calcar highway fought into the northeastern perimeter of Goch's defenses, and other forces were battling through anti-tank ditches and other obstacles little farther away on the north and northwest.

Patrols returning from the enemy lines before Goch said opposition was lighter than expected, the city of 11,000 was under ceaseless artillery and mortar fire, and all roads but one on the south were in Allied hands.

**YANKS HACK OUT GAINS**

The U. S. Third army broadened its front in western Germany's Eifel hills to 32 miles, hacked out gains of nearly two miles, deepened a new breach in the westwall, and forced a crossing of the Enz river seven miles south of the big enemy base at Bitburg.

**Five German towns were captured as the third plunged five miles or more into Germany.**

Ten miles northwest of the fighting here, mechanized cavalry

West Front
*Continued on Page Six*

## *It'll Warm Up, But Not Much*

Some relief from the cold wave was promised for Monday afternoon by the weather bureau Sunday night with the prediction that increasing cloudiness Monday would be accompanied by a slight mercury rise.

A high reading of 15 degrees above zero will be reached Monday afternoon contrasting with Sunday's high of eight above. Sunday's low was —11.

### WHERE TO FIND IT



## JAP ROCKETS FIZZLE—OUT

LONDON—(AP)—Tokyo broadcast Sunday a propaganda story reporting "panic in the central and western parts of the United States caused by a novel type of Japanese weapon described as a kind of rocket bomb." It said incendiaries and high explosives made in Japan were reported to have caused forest and other fires in several parts of the United States.

## *Jap 'House of Cards' to Get New Deal*

By Associated Press

Tokyo radio says a new political party soon will arise in Japan sponsored by the Imperial Rule Assistance Political Society, (IRAPS), parliamentary wing of Nippon's powerful totalitarian party, which has been severely critical of premier Kuniaki Koiso's government.

Koiso

A broadcast Sunday reported IRAPS president, Adm. Seizo Kobayashi, had conferred with Koiso and in "the next two or three days" the IRAPS will select a committee to form the new party.

**The broadcast gave no hint as to how this political move would affect Koiso's government.**

Members of the IRAPS committee to form the new party will include former members of the both houses of the Japanese diet, representatives of all societies and leaders of the central and district areas, the broadcast said.

Radio reports from Tokyo later said the IRAPS had announced Koiso's support of a proposal to form a new totalitarian party competent to "really meet the demands for the times."

## WOMAN HANGS SELF IN JAIL

A woman, identified by St. Paul police as Jeanette Watson, 25, Malta, Mont., committed suicide by hanging herself with a bed sheet in Ramsey county jail Sunday night. The body was discovered by Mrs. Gladys James, matron.

Donald G. Smith, 20, Brainerd, Minn., is held by St. Paul police for questioning. He was said to have been with the woman in a tavern at 2513 University avenue, St. Paul, Saturday night. She was taken to Ancker hospital after complaining of severe pain.

When she became abusive to hospital attendants, she was taken to the county jail.

## *Gripsholm Due*

NEW YORK—(AP)—The largest group of merchant seamen prisoners of war to be repatriated and the first from Germany will arrive on the exchange ship Gripsholm, scheduled to dock at Jersey City Wednesday, the war shipping administration said Sunday.

## RUSS CIRCLE BASTION CITY

### Konev Army Takes Railroad Center

LONDON—(AP)—Russian troops encircled and broke into the outskirts of the Vistula river stronghold of Grudziadz Sunday in their drive toward Danzig, 57 miles north, while other Soviet forces toppled the Queis river bastion of Naumburg, only 16 miles northeast of Goerlitz, Silesia's second city.

**A violent struggle raged on the muddy southeastern approaches to Berlin, where Marshal Ivan S. Konev's First Ukraine army captured the big rail center of Sagan, 86 miles southeast of the reich capital.**

**Several prisoner of war camps, one of which held Allied airmen shot down over Germany, were located around Sagan.**

The fate of these prisoners has not been determined, but it is likely the Germans moved them westward. Berlin had reported the fall of the town of 18,000 on Saturday.

Berlin reports acknowledged other Soviet forces had crossed the Bober farther north in their effort to turn Berlin's eastern defenses along the central Oder river.

Moscow's communique gave no details of the struggle in this area, but Soviet front dispatches said Russian troops were menacing Cottbus and Guben, 47 and 51 miles southeast of Berlin, and that those two targets were being raided heavily by Soviet bombers.

**Russian infantry was reported within 10 miles east of Cottbus after crossing the Neisse river north of Forst.**

Berlin claimed that these spearheads, including one that thrust

Russ Drive
*Continued on Page Six*

## *Russ Gen. Cherniakhovsky Dies of Battle Wounds*

LONDON—(AP)—Gen. Ivan D. Cherniakhovsky, brilliant 37-year-old Jewish tank commander whose Third White Russian army was the first to invade Germany, died Sunday of wounds suffered on the battlefield in East Prussia, Moscow announced early Monday.

**WAS YOUNGEST GENERAL**

The conqueror of Minsk, Wilno, Kaunas and most of East Prussia died "from a heavy wound received on the battlefield of East Prussia," said the official announcement.

**Cherniakhovsky was the youngest general in the Red army, the youngest army group commander, and one of the nation's outstanding strategists.**

Three days ago he was the subject of an order of the day by Premier Marshal Stalin for his troops' gallantry in the battle of East Prussia.

Cherniakhovsky will be given a hero's funeral in Wilno, capital of the Lithuanian Soviet republic, where a monument will be erected in his honor.

**Cherniakhovsky died as his troops were on the verge of completing the task assigned him by the Soviet high command.**

His army has conquered all except about 550 square miles of

Russ General
*Continued on Page Six*

GEN. CHERNIAKHOVSKY
*Jewish tank expert dies hero's death*

## LUZON YANKS RESCUE 7,000

### Guns Make Tomb of Corregidor

MANILA—(AP)—American troops battled on the rocky slopes and tunnels of Corregidor Monday to mop up Japanese pockets as Gen. Douglas MacArthur disclosed a new dramatic chapter of liberation in the freeing of 7,000 enemy hostages, 100 of them Americans, in Manila.

**Friday's landings on Corregidor opened the entrance of Manila bay to American warships.**

(The Allied broadcasting station in Europe, quoting a late dispatch from Luzon, said U. S. Seventh fleet units already had steamed into Manila bay "without incident.")

**HOSPITAL TAKEN**

Americans fighting street by street in war-wrecked Manila battled into the huge Philippine general hospital and wrested the thousands of Filipinos, Americans and other nationals from under Japanese gunfire.

The building for three days had been the scene of some of the bitterest fighting of the battle for Manila.

A prime Japanese strongpoint, the enemy had big guns mounted in the upper floors.

At least one British subject and several other Europeans subsequently were found among the patients, refugees, doctors and nurses who had been huddled in the building for three terrifying days of fighting.

**A HEROIC BATTLE**

In the communique, which also disclosed capture of Malinta hill, an artillery position on Corregidor, MacArthur took occasion to praise the American-Filipino defense of the fortress and Bataan in 1942 as "one of the decisive battles of the world."

**"Our triumphs of today belongs equally to that dead army," he declared.**

The hungry, exhausted and terrified men, women and children rescued from the hospital building were quickly taken by the troops from the battle zone. It may be several days before a check of names can be completed.

With the clean-up of Corregidor rapidly becoming a dirty business of digging or blowing Japanese from the caves and tunnels, the old walled city south of the Pasig river in Manila again became the center of interest.

**As soon as mines can be cleared, warships are expected to help blast the Japanese out of their last holds in the city.**

Associated Press Correspondent Fred Hampson reported from the

Philippines
*Continued on Page Six*

**RAIN**

U. S. Weather Bureau Forecast

**Rain and cooler.**

TEMPERATURES

| | | | | | |
|---|---|---|---|---|---|
| 2 a.m. | 38 | 10 a.m. | 46 | 6 p.m. | 62 |
| 3 a.m. | 37 | 11 a.m. | 52 | 7 p.m. | 60 |
| 4 a.m. | 36 | Noon | 55 | 8 p.m. | 58 |
| 5 a.m. | 35 | 1 p.m. | 58 | 9 p.m. | 55 |
| 6 a.m. | 35 | 2 p.m. | 59 | 10 p.m. | 55 |
| 7 a.m. | 34 | 3 p.m. | 62 | 11 p.m. | 53 |
| 8 a.m. | 38 | 4 p.m. | 61 | z Midnight | 50 |
| 9 a.m. | 40 | 5 p.m. | 63 | z—Unofficial | |

# Minneapolis Morning Tribune

Vol. LXXVIII—No. 324. MINNEAPOLIS, MINN., FRIDAY, APRIL 13, 1945 ★★ Price 3 Cents In Twin Cities Area, 5 Cents Elsewhere




# FRANKLIN ROOSEVELT DIES; TRUMAN PRESIDENT OF U. S.

★ ★ ★ ★ ★ ★ ★ ★ ★ ★ ★ ★ ★ ★ ★ ★ ★ ★ ★ ★

**TRUMAN SWORN IN**—Harry S. Truman is sworn in by Chief Justice Harlan Stone as President of the United States in the cabinet room of the executive offices of the White House following the death of Franklin D. Roosevelt. Looking on were, left to right, Secretary of War James E. Forrestal and Attorney General Francis Biddle. Between the new president and Mrs. Truman is Secretary of State Edward R. Stettinius.—AP Wirephoto.

WASHINGTON — (UP)—President Roosevelt died of cerebral hemorrhage Thursday at Warm Springs, Ga., and Vice President Harry S. Truman was sworn in here to succeed him, becoming the 32nd president of the United States.

**Mr. Roosevelt died at 3:45 p.m., Minneapolis time. The new president was sworn at 6:08 p.m., Minneapolis time.**

Mr. Roosevelt had served 12 years, one month and eight days of the unprecedented four terms to which he had been elected. Mr. Truman served as vice president since a few moments after noon last Jan. 20.

Mr. Roosevelt was 63 years old, tired by the burdens of a war presidency. Mr. Truman will be 61 years old May 8.

**The White House said Thursday night President Truman had authorized Secretary of State Edward R. Stettinius, Jr., to hold the San Francisco security conference on April 25 "as scheduled."**

The oath was administered to Mr. Truman by Chief Justice Harlan F. Stone in a brief ceremony in the cabinet room of the White House.

Witnesses included the cabinet, whom the new president asked to remain in office, and other top ranking government officials.

Truman picked up a Bible resting on the end of the big conference table, held it with one hand, and placed his right hand on top while Justice Stone pronounced the oath from memory.

Truman repeated the oath after him. Then Justice Stone pressed his hand.

Members of the cabinet were flanked around Truman and the justice during the ceremony, which took no more than a minute.

**Standing behind Truman was his wife, whose eyes were tear stained and who occasionally dabbed at them with a handkerchief.**

The new president wore a grey striped double breasted suit, white shirt and blue and white polka dot bow tie.

Prior to the oath taking, Truman sat in one of the overstuffed leather chairs in the cabinet room, conversing with various members of the cabinet and other officials.

The ceremony was held up for about 10 minutes pending arrival of Mrs. Truman at the White House.

Members of the White House staff—secretaries and stenographers—some of them with tear-stained eyes, stood silently in the three doorways of the cabinet room and watched President Roosevelt's successor sworn in.

There will be no successor as vice president to Mr. Truman. In the event of his death a statute provides that he would be succeeded by the secretary of state, in this instance Stettinius.

Truman made the following statement through White House Secretary Stephen T. Early:

**"For the time being I prefer not to hold a press conference. It will be my effort to carry on**

F. R. Dead
*Continued on Page Three*

★ ★ ★ ★

## TRUMAN GOES INTO OFFICE

### Chief Justice Stone Administers Oath

By WILLIAM H. MYLANDER
Staff Correspondent of The Minneapolis Morning Tribune

WASHINGTON—Since eight minutes past seven Thursday night Harry S. Truman has been President of the United States.

He was sworn into office to succeed Franklin Delano Roosevelt by Chief Justice Harlan F. Stone of the United States supreme court in the White House cabinet room in the presence of his wife, the Roosevelt cabinet, and leaders of the house of representatives.

Just before he was sworn in, Truman pledged himself to carry on as he believes the President would have done, and he asked that the Roosevelt cabinet stay on with him.

In disclosing Truman had said he had asked the cabinet to stay on, Stephen Early, former presidential secretary who in the emergency acted for Truman, first used the word "until," then withdrew it and asked correspondents to simply

Truman
*Continued on Page Two*

## RACING ARMIES 'REDUCE' MAP

PARIS—(AP)—Supreme headquarters changed its wall battle map Thursday in an effort to keep pace with its fast armies.

The huge 1 to 100,000th scale German map was shifted over and bent around the corner of the briefing room.

The new strip showed Berlin and Leipzig.

## STASSEN URGES 'PEACE FORCES'

Comm. Harold E. Stassen, delegate to the San Francisco peace conference, urged the assignment of military "peace forces" to any permanent United Nations organization as deterrents to small disorders which "are often the forerunners of war," in an article in the current issue of Collier's weekly.

Stassen also called for the establishment of an international civil aeronautics commission to "supervise international airways in much the same manner as our own civil aeronautics board supervises airways within our country."

The former governor of Minnesota declared that he favors the Dumbarton Oaks proposal as a "beginning of postwar world cooperation," but claimed that without direct control of any armed forces, the United Nations organization would be about as effective in preventing wars as "a citizens' posse is a deterrent to crime."

## *President's Death Unexpected and Painless, Says His Physician*

By D. HAROLD OLIVER

WARM SPRINGS, GA.—(AP)—President Franklin Delano Roosevelt unexpectedly died in the little white house on top of Pine mountain where he had come for a three-week rest.

Commander Howard Bruenn, navy physician, said he saw the President Thursday morning and he was in excellent spirits at 9:30 a.m.

"At 1 o'clock, Bruenn added, "he was sitting in a chair while sketches were being made of him by an artist. He suddenly complained of a very severe occipital headache (back of the head).

"Within a very few minutes he lost consciousness. He was seen by me at 1:30 p.m., fifteen minutes after the episode had started.

"He did not regain consciousness and he died at 3:35 p.m."

Only others present in the cottage were Comm. George Fox, White House pharmacist and long an attendant on the President; Hassett, Miss Grace Tully, confidential secretary; and two cousins, Miss Laura Delano and Miss Margaret Suckley.

**DIES WITHOUT PAIN**

Bruenn said he called vice Admiral Ross T. McIntyre Navy surgeon general and White House physician in Washington and that McIntyre in turn called Dr. James E. Paullin, of Atlanta, an internal medicine practicioner and honorary consultant to the Navy surgeon general.

**Paullin was present when Bruenn gave the statement of the cause of death to reporters.**

In response to a question, Dr. Bruenn said the President died without pain.

News of the President's death spread quickly and caused many a tear among 125 infantile paralysis patients at the foundation here.

Mayor Frank W. Allcorn of

Warm Springs
*Continued on Page Two*

### *Nazis Sink Low, Goebbels Admits*

LONDON — (AP) — Nazi Propaganda Minister Paul Joseph Goebbels declared Thursday "the war cannot last much longer in my opinion," a German broadcast said.

In an article in his weekly Das Reich, Goebbels said "we have sunk very low."

### A PRESIDENT DIES EVERY 20 YEARS

NEW YORK — (AP) — President Roosevelt's death Thursday carried on an American tradition that presidents elected at 20-year intervals die in office.

The list includes:

1840—William Henry Harrison.
1860—Abraham Lincoln.
1880—James A. Garfield.
1900—William McKinley.
1920—Warren G. Harding.
1940—Franklin D. Roosevelt.

EXCLUSIVE

## *Hopkins Says Just Peace Was F. R.'s Last Wish*

By KENNETH SCHOLES
Staff Writer of the Minneapolis Morning Tribune
(Copyright 1945 by the Minneapolis Morning Tribune)

From a Rochester hospital room where he is convalescing from a stomach operation, Harry Hopkins, President Roosevelt's closest friend and adviser, said Thursday night of his late leader:

"I know that he had more than anybody else in the world to do with the defeat of Germany."

Hopkins paused in his preparations to fly Friday to Washington for the funeral, to make a simple, halting statement to the Minneapolis Morning Tribune by telephone on the President's death.

**"I know he had on his mind, apart from winning the war, a just peace for all the people of the world," Hopkins said.**

"Few people realize how the great masses all over the world felt about him," he continued, "and looked to him for just protection of minority groups and those people who have lived in poverty all their lives.

"The general impression I've

Scholes
*Continued on Page Nine*

## NEW PRESIDENT A HOMEY MAN

### Friends Expect Him to Rely Upon Byrnes

By RICHARD WILSON
Chief of Washington Bureau of The Minneapolis Morning Tribune

WASHINGTON — "A common-sense liberal."

That is what Harry H. Truman of Missouri called himself when, only a few days ago in conversation with friends, he considered the possibility he might become President of the United States.

Truman did not allow himself to consider the possibility often. He merely assumed that he would always be vice president.

**"The job I liked best," he said, "was United States senator from Missouri."**

But the vice president's friends would not allow him to erase from his mind the possibility of Mr. Roosevlt's death.

In intimate sessions in his own office in the senate office building, or in the little room off the senate chamber where he was trying to make friends for Mr. Roosevelt the subject invariably came up.

Indirect, and sometimes direct, references were made to the possibility, none of them ever initiated by President Truman.

**This was because observers in Washington were noting the**

Richard Wilson
*Continued on Page Nine*

**PRESIDENTIAL LIMIT**

WASHINGTON — (UP) — Representative William Lemke (R., N. D.) Thursday introduced a resolution proposing a constitutional amendment to abolish the electoral college.

**LAST PHOTO OF NATION'S LEADER IN PEACE AND WAR**—Franklin Delano Roosevelt, thirty-second President of the United States, was photographed for the last time on March 29, 1945, at the White House. He had led the nation in a precedent shattering era covering the most devastating depression in U. S. history and the greatest war ever faced by mankind.

## *McQuarrie Heads Soviet Medical Unit*

Election of Dr. Irvine McQuarrie, professor and head of the department of pediatrics at University of Minnesota medical school, as president of the Minnesota chapter of American Soviet Medical society was announced Thursday.

Other new officers are Dr. R. F. Hedin, Red Wing, vice-president; Dr. Leo Rigler, head of the department of radiology at University hospitals, treasurer, and Dr. S. A. Corson, instructor in physiology at the University, secretary.

Drs. Owen E. Wangensteen, Maurice Visscher, Moses Barron, E. T. Hermann and J. A. Lepak were elected to the executive board.

SHOWS NO SELF PITY

## *Public Chief Loser, Mrs. Roosevelt Says*

WASHINGTON—(AP)—Mrs. Eleanor Roosevelt said, when informed of the death of the President:

"I am more sorry for the people of the country and the world than I am for us."

The First Lady received Vice President Truman in her second floor sitting room which adjoins the President's bedroom.

She told Truman "The President has just passed away."

"What can I do?" Truman asked.

**"Tell us what we can do," Mrs. Roosevelt replied. "Is there any way we can help you?"**

This version was made public by Presidential Secretary Stephen Early.

Mrs. Roosevelt left the White House at 7:15 to fly to Warm Springs.

As she came out of the White House door she kissed her daughter Anna, Mrs. John Boettiger, goodbye.

Mrs. Boettiger remained at the White House.

Mrs. Roosevelt was accompanied by Stephen Early, presidential secretary and Adm. Ross T. McIntyre, the president's personal physician.

**COOL**
U. S. Weather Bureau Forecast
Continued cold, partly cloudy.
TEMPERATURES

# Minneapolis Morning Tribune

Vol. LXXVIII—No. 337. MINNEAPOLIS, MINN., THURSDAY, APRIL 26, 1945 ★★ Price 3 Cents In Twin Cities Area 5 Cents Elsewhere



# 'NEW WORLD,' TRUMAN S. F. PLEA

## THIRD ARMY TANKS DRIVE FOR AUSTRIA

### Munich Threatened as Yanks, French Race Over Reich

PARIS—(AP)—U. S. Third army tanks punched within 15 miles of the German-Austrian border Wednesday night as other American and French forces raced almost unchecked across southern Germany, threatening Munich and Hitler's Berchtesgaden retreat, which the RAF attacked Wednesday with 12,000-pound "earthquake" bombs.

The Third army spearhead, already east of Berlin although 250 miles to the south, cut the last direct route to the Nazis' so-called national redoubt by mopping up the rail and highway center of Regen and then drove straight for the frontier of Austria at Passau. This column was 76 miles north of Berchtesgaden.

**NAZI VETERANS SMASHED**

To the west the American Seventh army broke through German positions and fanned out on an 80 mile front along or across the Danube river within 45 miles of Munich, and the French First army completely smashed Germany's veteran Nineteenth army in the Black forest.

The Allied armies—estimated at nearly 400,000 men and thousands of tanks—were charging into the Alpine foothills along a 200-mile front in a determined effort to crush any last-ditch Nazi stand in the southern redoubt before it could get well started.

**Resistance at most points was extremely light, bearing out an official announcement from Gen. Eisenhower's headquarters that "the German army has ceased to exist as an integrated fighting force."**

An Associated Press field dispatch declared the encirclement of Munich, birthplace of the Nazi party, was shaping up swiftly.

Leading the rapid surge of Allied forces Wednesday was the Eleventh armored division of Gen. George S. Patton's Third army, which stabbed 18 miles southeast beyond captured Regen to a point only 15 miles from the Austrian border and 79 miles due north of Berchtesgaden.

**THE GERMANS PURSUED**

Joining in the giant squeeze on the enemy's vaguely defined southern redoubt were Russian forces hammering westward across Austria, last reported within 90 miles of Berchtesgaden, and two Allied armies pursuing broken German troops beyond the Po river in northern Italy. The latter Allied force was within 96 miles of the Brenner pass through the Alps, southern gateway to the Nazi "fortress."

Closest to Munich was the Twelfth armored division of Lt. Gen. Alexander Patch's Seventh

West Front
*Continued on Page Three*

★ ★ ★ ★

AMONG AMERICAN DELEGATES welcoming British Foreign Minister Anthony Eden to the San Francisco United Nations conference was former Minnesota governor Harold R. Stassen. Here, talking with Eden are left to right, Rep. Sol Bloom (D., N.Y.), Rep. C. A. Eaton (R., N.J.), Comm. Stassen and Dean Virginia Gildersleeve. At Eden's right is Clement Attlee, British delegate.—AP Wirephoto.

## RUSSIANS CLAW BERLIN'S HEART

LONDON—(AP)—Two mighty Russian armies completely encircled half-conquered and doomed Berlin Wednesday and southwest of the crumbling German capital swarmed across the Elbe river on a 24-mile front, slashing westward toward an imminent link-up with American forces 17 miles away.

As Marshal Stalin announced the encirclement of Berlin in a historic order of the day, the German radio admitted Russian storm troops had smashed through jungles of twisted steel and stone to the blazing heart of the wrecked Nazi capital.

**Moscow's nightly war bulletin disclosed that Marshal Ivan S. Konev's First Ukrainian army had crossed the Elbe river between Torgau and Riesa, northwest of Dresden.**

The Soviet high command also said Russian troops far to the south were fighting on the outskirts of the great Czecho-Slovak war arsenal city of Bruenn (Brno), one of Hitler's last remaining war production centers.

**NAZI STRONGHOLD FALLS**

Stalin, in a second order of the day, announced capture of the East Prussian port of Pillau, last Nazi stronghold on the East Prussian mainland. The port fell to Marshal Alexander M. Vasilevsky's Third White Russian army.

Smashing toward Berlin's center from the north, east, southeast and southwest, Red army tommygunners overran the city districts of Lichtenfelde, Zehlendorf, Treptow and Britz, the latter only a mile from Templehof airdrome, Moscow revealed. In the encirclement of the city, the western suburbs of Falkenseem Falkenhagen and Doeberitz were captured.

**Perhaps 500,000 German troops were trapped in the encirclement of Berlin and these forces rapidly were being overwhelmed in a fantastic, incredible battle that raged with increasing fury above and below ground.**

There was a possibility Adolf Hitler and his propaganda minister, Paul Joseph Goebbels also had been caught in the Red army trap.

Throughout the evening the Hamburg radio—principal Nazi station remaining in operation—began every news item with the slogan: "the fuehrer is in Berlin."

**AS THE REICH DIES**

The broadcast said Red army forces which reached Berlin's cen-

Russians
*Continued on Page Eight*

## 'KILL NO YANKS, ONLY RUSSIANS'

### Captured German Quotes Day's Order

KOSSERN, GERMANY—(AP)—Thousands of German troops and terrified civilians frantically tried to get through American lines on the Mulde river Wednesday to escape the advancing Russians, nearing a junction with the U. S. First army.

**The troops surrendered at every opportunity without firing a shot.**

"Our order of the day this morning was not to fire on American troops but only to fire east toward the Russians," said one German soldier.

The civilians trudged along the roads in straggling groups, but there was no escape for them, as orders came down German civilians are not to be permitted to pass through the American front.

### TURN THE PAGES TO:

RUSSIAN TROOPS Wednesday joined up west of Berlin, completing encirclement of the German capital. To the south American forces driving southwest pushed to within 18 miles of the Austrian border. Solid arrows indicate Allied drives. Broken arrow is enemy report of Russian gain to Eisenerz. Shaded area is German-held.—AP Wirephoto map.

## KISSIN' PARTY WORRIES RUSSIANS

MOSCOW—(AP)—While the world awaited an announcement of a link-up of American and Red army forces, Muscovites worried a little about a Russian custom — of kissing one another at a meeting.

An engineer questioned near Red square said no matter where the link-up takes place "it will be one of the greatest moments of our epoch."

"The only thing that worries me," he said, "is that we Russians usually kiss one another. This may seem strange to Americans, but I suppose everything will be all right on such an occasion."

## RAF DESTROYS HITLER NEST

### Super Bomb Ruins Berchtesgaden Fort

LONDON—(AP)—Adolf Hitler's chalet near Berchtesgaden was obliterated and the adjoining weird "eagle's nest" fortress was damaged Wednesday by more than 350 RAF heavy Lancasters which raided the mountain retreat for the first time in an apparent attempt on the fuehrer's life.

The big barracks of Hitler's bodyguard, munitions stores, and the whole fabulous establishment from which the Nazi overlord once ruled German Europe were smashed by the six-ton British bombs while American Eighth and Ninth air force planes by the hundreds ravaged selected targets throughout the the Berchtesgaden area.

**SKODA WORKS HIT**

Simultaneously the Eighth air force hurled more than 300 flying fortresses at the Skoda munitions works at Pilsen, Czecho-Slovakia.

Whether Hitler was at the sumptuous Berghof Chalet or inside the almost-impregnable Kehlstein fortress, or in Berlin as Nazi propagandists claimed, was not known.

**Returning fliers left no doubt that the two-story chalet had been wiped out by a direct hit of a 12,000-pound bomb.**

Delayed-action bombs of the same great weight buried themselves deep in the Kehlstein (hollow-Stone) mountain of the eagle's nest.

**CALLED NAZI 'CAPITAL'**

Why such a shining target had never been bombed before remained officially without explanation, but an RAF staff officer said unofficially Thursday "With the fall of Berlin near, Berchtesgaden is locked upon as a sort of Nazi capital—the last spot over which the Swastika will fly.

**The bombing has a psychological effect, and it also can be assumed that the Germans are gathering there for a last stand."**

Reaction of the men who did the bombing was summed up by an RAF flier:

"This was the mission we have been waiting for all through the war. I saw one terrific flash right on Hitler's house. It was a 12,000-pounder all right."

## Nazis Free Only U.S. General Captured

WASHINGTON—(UP)—Reports an American U. S. army general had entered Switzerland from Germany after being held there as prisoner of war indicated Wednesday Maj. Gen. Arthur W. Vanaman of the air corps had been liberated.

Gen. Vanaman

Vanaman, former commanding general of materiel center, Wright Field, Ohio, and later of the Oklahoma City air service command, was captured in June, 1944. He was the only U. S. army general captured by the Nazis.

## SILENT PRAYER OPENS S.F. PARLEY

SAN FRANCISCO—(AP)—The United Nations conference was opened, at Secretary Stettinius' request, with "one minute of silent, solemn meditation."

Thus was compromised what had threatened to become somewhat of an issue—whether there should be an opening prayer.

Michael J. McDermott, state department press chief, told inquiring reporters that the official journal of the day said "nothing about prayer."

The questions were prompted by a complaint from the Rt. Rev. Malcolm E. Peabody, Episcopal bishop of Central New York, about what he called the "alleged non-religious procedure" of the conference.

The multitude of religions represented by the attending delegates—and the fact some have no religion—would have posed a difficult problem in settling on any set prayer.

## SUPERFORTS RAID JAP HOME ISLES

### 'Very Large Force,' Washington Says

WASHINGTON—(INS)—American Superfortresses were out on a new mission Wednesday, striking airfields in the homeland islands of Kyushu and Shikoka.

A communique from Twentieth air force headquarters in Washington said "a very large force" of B-29s participated in this attack and that at least 10 installations on the southern islands were the targets.

The planes flew from the Marianas base of Maj. Gen. Curtis E. Lemay's Twenty-first bomber command, but no mention was given in the Twentieth air force communique as to the results of the raid.

## 46 Nations Spurred to 'Permanent Peace'

By RICHARD WILSON
Staff Correspondent of the Minneapolis Morning Tribune

SAN FRANCISCO—In a brilliant ceremonial Wednesday afternoon representatives of 46 nations met in solemn session to dedicate themselves to the lofty ideals of world organization.

President Harry S. Truman and Secretary of State Edward R. Stettinius, Jr., opened the first plenary session of the United Nations conference on international organization. President Truman spoke from Washington to members of the delegations met in the San Francisco Municipal Opera house. Stettinius acted as temporary president of the conference.

In the last flaming days of the European war, delegates of the assembled United Nations heard themselves dedicated by Pres. Truman to building "a new world—a far better world—one in which the eternal dignity of man is respected."

**SPEAKS CALMLY**

In measured tones, his voice coming from Washington over the loudspeaker warned "if we should pay merely lip service to inspiring ideals, and later do violence to simple justice, we would draw down upon us the bitter wrath of generations unborn."

Said Secretary Stettinius, "now the deepest hope and highest purpose of ALL mankind—enduring peace—is here committed to our hands.

"We...are pioneers on a new road. There will be many obstacles and many dangers. We, too must call upon the courage and faith of those who come to California before us — across a wilderness to the shores of this great ocean named for peace."

**The delegates were welcomed in San Francisco by Gov. Earl Warren and Mayor Roger D. Lapham.**

Delegates sat in the famed, pillar-less opera house before a brilliantly lighted speakers stand silhouetted against four great square pylons linked together by heavy cord. The pylons stood for the four freedoms and towered above the draped flags of the 46 nations, each on a separate staff.

The speakers stand itself was as perfect as a movie set, each modernistic line blending to make an impressive spectacle in powder-blue. Four gold chairs stood on the huge stage for the secretary of state, the secretary general of the conference, the mayor of San Francisco and the governor of California.

**GUARD OF HONOR**

Just before the entrance of the secretary of state, 17 members of all branches of the armed services, both women and men, marched in and took their places at attention before the massed flags of the United Nations.

Beribboned American veterans of the wars in Europe and the Pacific remained stiffly at attention. Secretary Stettinius banged the gavel to open the session and asked for one minute of silence and meditation. The great theatre holding 3,200 persons, rustled

Parley
*Continued on Page Three*

## RUSS RELATIONS EYED BY TRUMAN

By NAT FINNEY
Staff Correspondent of the Minneapolis Morning Tribune

WASHINGTON—What President Harry S. Truman has done is to tell Marshall Stalin he is anxious about Russian observance of the Yalta declaration not on the narrow grounds of the Polish issue but in broad terms of future Russo-American relations.

This is the gist of a clearer picture of current discussions with Russia which is becoming known through congress because President Truman is carefully keeping Democratic leaders informed.

Mr. Truman is reported on capitol hill to have brushed aside detailed discussion of the fine points of the Polish issue and to have put the whole hand of American cards on the diplomatic table with Foreign Commissar Molotov with a friendly but firm insistence that the American President must know where he stands.

**FIRM ON POLES**

At the same time President Truman is reported to have been as explicit as he was at his first press conference in letting Molotov know that there is not the slightest chance the United States will recognize a Polish provisional government until it has been reorganized according to the Yalta declaration.

**He is reported to have firmly declined to discuss any misunderstanding about what the Polish section of the Yalta declaration means. Congressional sources report that Mr. Truman's position is that it means what is says.**

Mr. Truman's presentation of the long view of Russo-American relations involved questions of lend lease settlements, aid to Russia in reconstruction and cooperation in handling defeated Germany. He is said to have intimated that any atmosphere of continual disagreement over interpretation of firm agreements would not suit him.

The stand taken by Mr. Truman at his conference with Commissar Molotov is reported to have been friendly and he is said to have expressly told Molotov he did not believe Marshal Stalin desires to do anything less than fulfill the understandings he had with the late President Roosevelt at Yalta.

**SIDELIGHTS**

From British and congressional sources two interesting side lights on the conference between President Truman and Molotov, Stettinius and Eden have developed.

British Foreign Minister Anthony Eden is reported to have been very favorably impressed by Mr. Truman's presentation of the American position. British circles here are openly pleased about it.

**It is a matter of comment that Mr. Truman left it entirely clear that he, like President Roosevelt, intends to be his own secretary of state where the direction of fundamental policy is concerned.**

It was President Truman and not Secretary of State Edward R. Stettinius, Jr., who stated the American position to Molotov.

Because Commissar Molotov did not have plenipotentiary powers he presumably reported his discussions with President Truman and the British and American foreign officers to Stalin in Moscow.

## WAR LEADERS SEE TRUMAN

### Conference Causes Rumor of Big Events

WASHINGTON—(UP)—President Truman and top army and navy leaders spent more than an hour and a half in a closely guarded conference at the army's Pentagon building headquarters Wednesday, leading to speculation momentous events may be at hand.

Present in addition to Mr. Truman were Chief of Staff Gen. George C. Marshall, Secretary of War Henry L. Stimson, Adm. Ernest J. King, commander-in-chief of the U. S. fleet; Adm. William D. Leahy, the President's chief of staff, and Acting Secretary of State Joseph C. Grew.

**It was the second such conference since last Monday when the President summoned all the leaders to a surprise White House conference.**

The fact Wednesday's meeting took place at the huge Pentagon brought into focus the fact the war department maintains direct communication facilities to Gen. Dwight D. Eisenhower, supreme Allied commander in Europe, and to other war theaters.

It was speculated that Mr. Truman and the other conferees might have been in communication with these areas but no confirmation was available immediately.

## Big New Carrier Renamed for F.R.

WASHINGTON—(AP)—A giant aircraft carrier to be launched at the New York navy yard Sunday has been renamed "Franklin Delano Roosevelt."

Congressional sources said Mrs. Roosevelt would sponsor the 45,000-ton vessel.

RAF GOES GUNNING FOR HITLER—Circled section of three buildings is identified by army air forces as Hitler's chalet at Berchtesgaden which Wednesday was the target for British Lancasters' six-ton "earthquake" bombs. Returning fliers said direct hits were scored on the chalet. This photo was made by the Mediterranean Allied air forces.—AP Wirephoto from U. S. army air forces.

## Ol' Man Weather Remains as Cool as a Cucumber

Mark Twain's sage remark about everybody talking about the weather but doing nothing about it, had even the weather man shaking his head Wednesday night.

Even the weather man admitted he couldn't do much about the weather—except point out that it isn't going to be very warm for a few days.

**Partly cloudy, continued cool Wednesday night and Thursday, was the forecast for the Twin Cities area.**

The mercury climbed to a high of 50 Wednesday, but showed no indication of zooming to greater heights. Even the mercury couldn't do anything about it.

WARMER
U. S. Weather Bureau Forecast
Partly cloudy, warmer.
TEMPERATURES

# Minneapolis Morning Tribune

Vol. LXXVIII—No. 343. MINNEAPOLIS, MINN., WEDNESDAY, MAY 2, 1945 ★★ Price 3 Cents In Twin Cities Area, 5 Cents Elsewhere



## German Radio Reports:

# ADOLF HITLER DIES AT POST

## 'We Must See the Body!' Allies Insist

## PATTON RIPS NORTH LINE OF REDOUBT

PARIS—(U.P.)—Gen. George S. Patton's Third army broke the northern face of the Nazi Alpine redoubt wide open Tuesday in a 25-mile power drive that carried within 18 miles of the great communications center of Linz and within 40 miles of slicing off the redoubt forces from Czecho-Slovakia.

Lt. Gen. Alexander M. Patch's Seventh army, smashing into the redoubt on the northern side, reached within nine miles of Innsbruck, entrance to the Brenner pass and was only 96 miles from the Allies in Italy.

**18 MILES FROM LUEBECK**

British troops at the northern end of the front were less than 18 miles from the Baltic port of Luebeck where they would cut off the Schleswig-Holstein Isthmus and Denmark, and were 80 miles from the Russian Baltic forces advancing from the east.

**Patton's and Patch's men were running wild. The Seventh army found Adm. Nicholas Horthy, former regent of Hungary, and captured retired German Field Marshals Wilhelm Ritter von Leeb and Wilhelm List, once dominant army figures.**

They were among an assortment of active generals taken.

The Thirteenth armored plunged 25 miles into Hitler's birthplace at Braunau on the Austro-German border and within 43 miles of Hitler's bomb-blasted headquarters at Berchtesgaden. Opposition was light.

**4-WAY SPLIT DUE**

Remnants of the German main forces were in imminent danger

Patton
*Continued on Page Six*

## Soviets Storm Last Barriers in Berlin

From Late Dispatches

LONDON—(AP)—German resistance in the heart of ruined Berlin neared total collapse Wednesday as 14,000 fanatical Nazi die-hards surrendered to the Red army Tuesday after reportedly losing their leader, Adolf Hitler.

Moscow's nightly war bulletin announced Soviet troops had overrun more than 100 blocks of buildings in the city's administrative core as they smashed toward the Reichschancellery and the Germans' underground fortress in the Tiergarten.

**RUSS CLEAR DISTRICTS**

The Soviet high command did not announce the capture of any specific buildings in Berlin's center and it was not known whether the Russians had reached the Reichschancellery.

Soviet assault troops also cleared the city districts of Charlottenburg and Schoeneberg.

Some days ago the Russians said they believed that Hitler had fled Berlin, probably leaving a double who would die "heroically" and be found amid the ruins of the Nazi capital.

**Earlier, the Nazi high command had said that fanatical last-ditch defenders were huddled around Hitler in the underground fortress in the Tiergarten, which reportedly is linked to the Reichschancellery.**

Premier Stalin, who issued three orders of the day, did not announce any new developments in the savage 11-day battle for Berlin, but his third order told of the capture of Bohumin, Velka-Bytca, Cadca, Grystat and Skocov in the Carpathian zone of Czecho-Slovakia by Gen. Andrei I. Yeremenko's Fourth Ukrainian army.

**Premier Stalin meanwhile announced that Soviet tanks, maintaining a powerful 20-mile a day sweep across Germany's northern redoubt had captured the Baltic port of Stralsund.**

Stralsund is terminus for the main railroad ferry service to Malmo, Sweden.

**NEAR ROSTOCK**

The Russ then surged within 33 miles of Rostock in a drive that won five major communications centers north of Berlin.

Marshal Konstantin K. Rokossovsky's Second White Russian army tanks and cavalry, plunging across the Mecklenburg plains captured Demmin, Grimmen, Malchin, Waren and Wessenberg in a drive that knifed within 63 miles of Field Marshal Bernard Montgomery's British Second army on the lower Elbe.

### *Merle Oberon Set for Mexico Divorce*

HOLLYWOOD—(INS)—Actress Merle Oberon arrived in Mexico City Tuesday, according to word received in Hollywood by friends, where she intends to obtain a divorce from Sir Alexander Korda, producer from whom she has been estranged for some time.

★ ★ ★ ★

## U. S. FEARS TRICKERY ON HITLER DEATH

### Silent Officials Ponder Effect on Surrender Moves

By WILLIAM H. MYLANDER AND MARK McGAFFIN
Staff Correspondents of the Minneapolis Morning Tribune

WASHINGTON—Official sources were silent on the Hamburg radio report of Hitler's death.

Neither the White House nor the war department would comment. Neither has received confirmation of the report, and trickery at this stage of the war has always been considered possible.

One source suggested any change in the German government would increase the chances for a formal surrender. Adm. Doenitz, however, is a member of the Nazi military clique.

**PESSIMISM REIGNS**

Meanwhile informed military experts stuck to their pessimistic views of the possibility of an early unconditional surrender by the Germans late Tuesday afternoon.

**Until factual proof is produced that Hitler is dead and that some one with real authority over the fanatic Nazi elements has succeeded him, they are skeptical that an actual end of resistance can be brought about.**

This is in sharp contrast with the views held by these same observers last Thursday and Friday. At that time they believed the critical moment had arrived when word from a responsible German military leader could have brought about a sudden end to the fighting.

**HOPE WANING**

When that didn't come about, these observers began losing hope rapidly that anyone less than Hitler, himself, could bring it about.

Now they believe that more than a broadcast report of Hitler's death will be necessary to convince Allied leaders that anyone else can deliver on a surrender agreement.

**This does not mean that they believe the moves of the past two days have delayed the final breakdown of resistance.**

On the contrary they consider them as additional proof that the crack up is increasing in momentum.

**TRUMAN CONFERS**

Before the report of Hitler's death was received, President Truman conferred for 45 minutes with Gen. George Marshall. The meeting had been scheduled in advance, and Gen. Marshall declined to say what it was about.

Through Jonathan Daniels, his

U. S. Fears
*Continued on Page Six*

HERE'S HITLER, the monarch fallen at long last, shown with Adm. Karl Doenitz, commandant of the Germany navy, who has succeeded Hitler as the leader of the prostrate reich, having been appointed Monday by the now-dead dictator. Doenitz said "My first task will be to save the German people from the advance of the Bolshevist enemy."

## *Doenitz, U-Boat Master, Leads Nazis' Swan Song*

By LEWIS U. MUENZ
Staff Writer of the Minneapolis Morning Tribune

In Hitler's death, history's gong has sounded to make Adm. Karl Doenitz the possible last reverberation of a Nazi swan song.

British-hating (seamy-faced Doenitz, creator and commander of Germany's U-boat fleet,) has the dubious distinction of laying the groundwork for the greatest submarine fleet in history after he defied the Versailles treaty under the noses of an Allied investigating committee.

**Doenitz, 53, master of U-boat technique, has devoted half his life to the study of underwater warfare.**

Years before the Nazis came into power he had a plan to rebuild the Reich's U-boat fleet. In 1936 the Nazis made him the official commander of their submarine units.

**TRAINS SUB CREWS**

Then, he perfected a liaison system between planes and submarines and evolved a system of training U-boat crews in order to avoid the difficulty with mutinous officer-baited crews which shattered the German U-boat service in World war I.

In an eerie but appropriate sidelight to the new fuehrer's background it can be told that Doenitz, like his compatriot, Hermann Goering, has spent some time in an insane asylum.

As a youth in World war I he commanded a submarine which he scuttled and abandoned in the Mediterranean, off Malta. A British boat fished him from the sea and he was taken, a prisoner, to a Manchester madhouse for treatment.

Two years ago Doenitz said "it makes no difference to the present German submarine fleet whether British ships sail alone or are convoyed. The truth is that neutral ships have an increased danger when they are members of a British convoy."

However, when U.S. strength appeared within British convoys, Doenitz withdrew a large part of his U-boat fleet into the Baltic and created the now famous "wolf-

Doenitz
*Continued on Page Seven*



★ ★ ★ ★

### WHERE ARE THEY?

By Associated Press

Emergence of Adm. Doenitz at the helm of sinking Germany revives the question of the whereabouts of other more famous Nazi leaders.

Heinrich Himmler, Gestapo chief, was not mentioned in Tuesday's German broadcasts. He had been considered mostly likely to assume control.

Goebbels, propaganda chief, although never considered a fuehrer type, likewise was ignored in press dispatches.

Herman Goering, whom Hitler once designated as his first alternate, was reported to have resigned because of heart trouble last week.

Rudolf Hess, Hitler's No. 2 choice, as his successor, remains in an English prison camp.

### TURN THE PAGES TO:



## *ADM. DOENITZ TAKES OVER AS NEW FUEHRER*

*Hitler's Life—Page Nine. Pictures on Page Eight*

LONDON—(AP)—The Nazi radio at Hamburg said Tuesday night Adolf Hitler died Tuesday afternoon at his command post in Berlin and had been succeeded by Adm. Karl Doenitz.

The broadcast, recorded by the Associated Press listening post in London, said:

"From the Fuehrer's headquarters it is reported that our Fuehrer, Adolf Hitler, has fallen this afternoon in his command post at the Reich's chancellery, fighting up to his last breath against bolshevism."

Doenitz, commander of the German navy, then was introduced by the announcer as "our new Fuehrer," and declared Hitler had died "a hero's death."

**'Lie!' Shouts Ghost Voice**

A ghost voice immediately interrupted, shouting, "this is a lie!"

(The British broadcasting company subsequently carried a report that Hitler actually died of a stroke, rather than in battle against the Russians, NBC in New York said.)

A Stockholm message received by Reuter quoted unconfirmed reports as saying Adolf Hitler died at noon on Sunday in his underground headquarters in the Tiergarten, Berlin's Central park.

Hitler was raving during his last days and he spent last week drawing up "a new town plan of London" and addressing imaginary audiences, the message said.

**The Allies will demand that Hitler's body be produced after the surrender of Germany in order to remove all doubt as to the truth of Tuesday's German radio report of his death, it was said Tuesday night at the British foreign office.**

The foreign office said it believes Hitler is dead, but declined to comment on the accuracy of the Hamburg radio's report of how he died.

High official quarters reserved decision as to what implications the report of Hitler's death would have on German peace overtures previously credited to Heinrich Himmler.

**Doenitz Choice Is Puzzle**

The reason for appointment of Adm. Doenitz as Hitler's successor was not immediately apparent to official quarters.

One responsible but unofficial source said it was possible Himmler realized he himself was unpopular in Germany and that Doenitz might be more successful in carrying out surrender terms, particularly as to their acceptance by the German armed forces.

Doenitz said that Hitler personally had appointed him as successor Monday.

The 53-year-old admiral vowed to continue the war "to save the German people from the advance of the Bolshevist enemy," while "against the English and Americans I have to continue the struggle as far and as long as they hinder me in the prosecution of the struggle against bolshevism."

Hitler, who was 56 years old on April 20, was lauded by Doenitz as "one of the greatest heroes in German history."

Here the ghost voice broke in:

**"The greatest of all Fascists!"**

"Filled with proud respect and mourning, we lower the banners before him," Doenitz continued.

"His death calls upon us to act," the ghost voice interrupted. "Strike now!"

**Pep Talk Spoiled**

Doenitz launched into a pep talk to the German people and troops, only to be interrupted again by the ghost voice, crying,

Hitler Dead
*Continued on Page Seven*

### FINAL OUTPOST OF THE FUEHRER-TYRANT

HITLER'S LAST STAND—The Berlin command post, the Reichschancellery, was claimed by the Hamburg radio to have been the scene of Adolf Hitler's reported death.—AP Wirephoto.

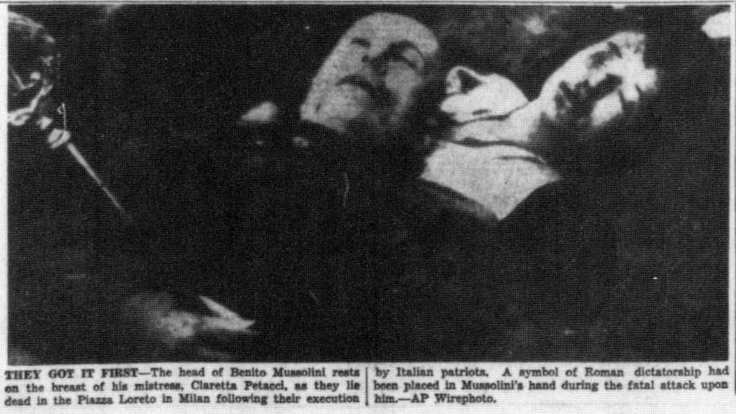

THEY GOT IT FIRST—The head of Benito Mussolini rests on the breast of his mistress, Claretta Petacci, as they lie dead in the Piazza Loreto in Milan following their execution by Italian patriots. A symbol of Roman dictatorship had been placed in Mussolini's hand during the fatal attack upon him.—AP Wirephoto.

**COOLER**
U. S. Weather Bureau Forecast
Partly cloudy, cooler, diminishing winds.

TEMPERATURES

# Minneapolis Morning Tribune

Vol. LXXVIII—No. 349. MINNEAPOLIS, MINN, TUESDAY, MAY 8, 1945 ★★ Price 3 Cents In Twin Cities Area, 5 Cents Elsewhere



## *Announcement Due at 8 A. M.:*

# TODAY WILL BE 'VE-DAY'

## *PATTON TANKS HIT PRAGUE IN LAST CLEANUP*

By the Associated Press

Men still were dying Monday night in Czecho-Slovakia, where the Nazi commander ignored his country's unconditional surrender to the Allies and was fighting on against American and Russian troops and Czech Partisans.

The Partisans, engaging the Germans in bloody street fighting in the capital city of Prague, sent out desperate appeals for assistance. Prague was being burned and sacked by the beaten Nazis in a final orgy of destruction.

**THIRD IN OUTSKIRTS**

Gen. Patton's Third army tanks and infantry drove to the outskirts of the Czech capital, and the German-controlled radio station in Prague said Soviet forces had entered Bohemia at a point 60 to 65 miles north of the city.

**Patton was using nearly 250,000 American troops in the final mop-up.**

His forces already had overrun the great beer and munitions center of Pilsen. Breslau fell to Russian forces after a long siege, and only two German cities, Dresden and Chemnitz, remained in Nazi hands. They apparently were being defended against the Russians in defiance of the surrender at Reims.

A British armored spearhead, occupying Holland, pushed 30 miles through shell-smashed, deserted villages to Utrecht.

**ALPINE TROOPS GIVE UP**

Two more German Alpine groups, who had only just heard of the capitulation in the south, surrendered to the Sixth army group. An estimated 40,000 additional prisoners were taken by the Third army Sunday. The Seventh and Fifth armies made another contact in an Alpine pass 25 miles south of Landeck.

**Supreme headquarters noted that 398,630 Germans surrendered Saturday for a three-day total of 987,573 and an aggregate since June 6 of 3,874,771 on the western front.**

The Allies apparently no longer considered the hold-out Germans a legal army under the rules of warfare. A Czech official in London said they would be treated as guerrillas and that the fight would go one until the last one was "rendered harmless, disarmed or killed."

**BRESLAU SURRENDERS**

In southeastern Germany, meanwhile, the Red army captured the German hold-out garrison in the lower Silesian capital of Breslau after the Germans, headed by the commandant, infantry Gen. Vonneihoff, and his staff "laid down their arms and surrendered."

Thus the German garrison ended an 80-day siege, and the only remaining German pockets on the eastern front, from which there was no word, were in the Courland peninsula of Latvia and on the Vistula delta near Danzig. The Germans said heavy fighting raged near Danzig on the Frische Nehrung Sandspit, but the Nazi command said there were no reports of fighting in Latvia.

Fighting also continued in northern Yugoslavia, where the German high command admitted Nazi forces were withdrawing before the blows of Marshal Tito's Yugoslav freedom fighters.

★ ★ ★ ★

## FLEET ON WAY TO TAKE OVER IN NORWAY

### 300,000 Nazis Are Surrendered Unconditionally

From Late Dispatches

A fleet of 48 Allied warships entered Oslo fjord enroute to Oslo, presumably to accept the German surrender of Norway, the Swedish news agency reported Monday night.

"It is expected troops will be landed at any moment," the agency said as the war brought these developments from the Scandinavian countries:

● **The 10,000-ton German cruisers Prinz Eugen and Seydlitz together with 160,000 tons of merchant shipping surrendered to the Allies at Copenhagen.**

● Sweden severed all diplomatic relations with Germany.

● German military forces in Norway, an estimated 300,000 soldiers, sailors and airmen, surrendered unconditionally. The surrender also included between 200 and 300 U-boats and between 300 and 400 planes.

● The Norwegian garrison surrendered at the order of Gen. Franz Boehm, who said capitulation "hits us very hard because we are unbeaten and in full possession of our strength in Norway and no enemy has dared to attack us."

● Under terms of the capitulation, the Germans will march across the border into internment in Sweden, it was said.

## 'SUMMER' GOING BACK TO HIDING

### No 'Hot Time' for VE-Day, Is Forecast

VE-day Tuesday is going to be slightly cooler with temperatures ranging in the low 50's, the weather man said Monday night.

Official Twin Cities forecast was for partly cloudy and cool Monday night and Tuesday, with the wind diminishing Tuesday night.

**That wind was much in evidence Monday as the temperature reached a high of 55 degrees late in the afternoon. Tuesday's low is expected to be about 35.**

Temperature in Minneapolis at 11 p.m. Monday was 41.

Temperatures in the 50's were prevalent throughout Minnesota Monday, while the Dakotas were slightly cooler.

## *Wild Life President Re-elected in N. D.*

DEVILS LAKE, N. D. —(UP)— L. C. Moore, Devils Lake, Monday returned to his duties as president of the North Dakota wild life federation, following his re-election Sunday.

## SURRENDER ENDS WORLD'S MOST COSTLY, DEADLY WAR

WASHINGTON—(UP)—The victory in Europe cost the United States about 800,000 casualties and more than $185,000,000,000.

These are the best conservative estimates available now. It will be a long time before the final figures are worked out.

A United Press survey showed Monday this country's share of the cost of crushing the Nazi bid for world domination will exceed by three or four times the cost of World war I and its aftermath — whether the measuring standard is casualties or dollars.

**The cost in money will be increased in future years by many billions of dollars through interest on government borrowings and benefits to veterans. The cost in broken lives, too, will be paid over a long period.**

The cost estimate includes not only guns, bullets, planes and tanks, plus the plants to make them, but also such items as lend-lease expenditures, training costs, merchant ships, transportation, subsistence and literally thousands of articles and services that never appeared on the field of battle but were vital to victory.

FIRST ARMY VET BEAMS—His face framed in a newspaper announcing surrender of Germany, Pvt. Henry S. Blaine, 29, Atlantic City, N. Y., who was wounded at Aachen, Germany, grins broadly at Penn station, New York. Blaine was overseas two and a half years and was in six campaigns. He wears the purple heart and bronze star.—AP Wirephoto.

**DEATH AFTER SURRENDER**

## *Nazi 'Beasts' Flee Russ to Die Without Honor*

*(The following dispatch discloses fighting between Russian and German forces along the Elbe continued after unauthorized reports declared the entire Nazi military machine already had been surrendered unconditionally.)*

By FRANK CONNIFF

ON THE ELBE—(INS)—American Ninth army men on the west bank of the Elbe watched panic stricken German soldiers and civilians fight like animals to cross the Elbe ahead of the Russians Monday night.

Some 30,000 pocketed Nazis clawed and fought to get over a single footbridge at Tangermunde while Russian tanks and machine-gunners raked the milling mob with point-blank fire.

**YANKS WATCH**

American spectators watched fascinated while soldiers and civilians, men and women, stripped and attempted to swim the river to escape the Soviet troops.

**Many became exhausted and drowned as they swam, and many others were killed by deadly Russian crossfire.**

More than once Russian shrapnel lashed the American bank of the river as the action raged. At one point, four Russian tanks dashed out of the woods and opened fire into a Nazi traffic jam.

The shells ripped great gaps in the stream of traffic, but the pressure of the fleeing mob was so great that these gaps were immediately filled. Dead and dying were trampled underfoot.

**SOVIETS AMBUSHED**

Some German soldiers hiding behind a bridge let the Russians approach, and then opened up on them at close range. Most of the Soviet column was killed or wounded.

The infuriated Russians retaliated with a terrific mortar and tank barrage which took a murderous toll of Nazis.

**It was one of the most unbelievable encounters ever seen on a modern battlefield.**

All the German soldiers who managed to make their way across the Elbe immediately threw down their weapons and surrendered to the Americans.

The vaunted honor of the Wehrmacht was completely gone. Escaping soldiers were no more than animals, frightened animals scurrying for safety.

## *Catholic Group Elects Minot Regent*

MINOT, N. D. —(UP)— The Catholic Daughters of America elected Mrs. Frank Webb, Grand Forks, as state regent at the biennial conference which closed Sunday.

**TURN THE PAGES TO:**



## VETS' HOSPITAL ADDITION SOUGHT

Plans to increase size of Fort Snelling Veterans hospital by nearly 50 per cent were announced in Washington Monday by Brig. Gen. Frank T. Hines, national veterans administrator.

Hines

Hines said he will recommend to President Truman construction of a 300-bed addition to the hospital. The regular capacity is 666 beds.

Carl D. Hibbard, manager of the hospital, said he had received no information on the proposed construction but that there is ample room on the grounds for an addition. The hospital is now functioning with more than 100 beds above regular capacity.

**HUNTER'S PARADISE**

BATH, MAINE—Here's a hunter's paradise. Following the northward flight of geese this spring, state officials estimate 25,000 birds congregated in the Merrymeeting Bay area near here.

## *Big Three Join to Proclaim End of Nazi Resistance*

By WILLIAM H. MYLANDER
Staff Correspondent of the Minneapolis Morning Tribune

WASHINGTON—President Truman will join Prime Minister Churchill and Marshal Stalin in a simultaneous proclamation of Germany's unconditional surrender at 8 a.m. Tuesday (CWT).

The White House, after maintaining an official silence until 6:25 p.m. Monday on the VE-day tangle, finally announced the President "confidently expects to make an announcement to the nation by radio at that time.

Jonathan Daniels, acting press secretary, added unless "unforeseen developments" caused the President to change his mind, the press and broadcasters would be given the advance text of Mr. Truman's statement at a press conference called for 7:30 a.m.

Although Daniels declined to reply directly to a question whether the announcement to be made on Mr. Truman's 61st birthday, would be the European victory proclamation, the White House permitted that inference to be drawn from other developments which included:

1. Disclosure by Mr. Truman that he has agreed to simultaneous statement by the three Allied governments.

2. Official announcement by the British ministry of information that the hour will be 8 a.m. Tuesday.

**SECOND PROCLAMATION**

Three hours after the first proclamation, it was learned, another will be issued. The nature of the second statement was not disclosed.

**For all practical purposes, the European war was over.**

The President was ready to proclaim it Monday, but was prevented from doing so by his agreement with Moscow and London.

Mr. Truman remained at his desk for lunch. Microphones through which his message will be carried to the country were set up. A crowd assembled outside the White House gate. Inside, reporters and photographers jammed the executive office lobby.

Shortly after 2 p.m., Jonathan Daniels called in correspondents and dictated a statement by the President addressed to the press and radio.

**TRUMAN STATEMENT**

"I have agreed with the London and Moscow governments that I will make no announcement with reference to surrender of the enemy forces in Europe or elsewhere until a simultaneous statement can be made by the three governments. Until then, there is nothing I can or will say to you."

**Daniels was asked to confirm the British announcement. He**

Surrender
*Continued on Page Eight*

## WORLD GOES WILD WITH VICTORY JOY

### Church Bells Ring as Allied Nations Proclaim Holidays

*PICTURES—PAGE FIVE*

By Associated Press

The great bells of St. Peter's basilica rang out over Rome Monday soon after the report peace had come to Europe while several Allied capitals proclaimed VE holidays for Tuesday and Tokyo announced continuation of "this sacred war."

Many of the world's cities went wild at the news, and even neutral capitals were bedecked with flags and filled with celebrating crowds.

Masses of people gathered in front of loudspeakers and newspaper offices.

**CALM ON THE FRONTS**

Only in the unnatural calm of the European fronts was the news reported to have been taken soberly by soldiers who had seen the fighting taper off in one sector after another for the past two weeks.

In bomb-damaged London, only Allied capital which fought its way successfully through the European war from the start, crowds exploded all over the downtown areas after a week of tense expectancy.

An official holiday was proclaimed for Tuesday in Britain.

**King George VI of England Monday night congratulated Gen. Eisenhower and his armies on their "complete and crushing victory" in Europe.**

In Paris, which lived through four years of German occupation

Victory Joy
*Continued on Page Five*

## VE-DAY SCOOP CAUSES RIFT

### Protests Heard After AP Suspension

Newsmen who have said "There aren't any 'scoops' any more" took it all back Monday. The Associated Press, at 8:35 a.m., delivered an exclusive story describing the final German surrender in Europe. As this goes to press, the AP still has a "scoop."

Neither of the AP's principal competitors—the United Press and the International News Service—nor any of the other news agencies in the world had the story from General Eisenhower's headquarters at Reims.

Edward Kennedy, chief of AP staff on the western front and a veteran reporter who has covered the war since its beginning, wrote the story telling the first news from the Allied side of the German capitulation.

All news agencies had distributed 58 minutes earlier a broadcast on the wavelength of the Flensburg radio, used for several days for German announcements. This broadcast, in the name of the German foreign minister, Count Ludwig Schwerin von Krosgk declared Grand Admiral

Scoop
*Continued on Page Eight*

★ ★ ★ ★

## *How the News Came to a Waiting World*

*Following is the Associated Press dispatch which revealed the end of hostilities in advance of the official VE-day announcement:*

By EDWARD KENNEDY

Germany surrendered unconditionally to the western Allies and Russia at 2:41 a.m. French time today. (This was at 8:41 p.m., eastern war time Sunday, 7:41 p.m. Minneapolis time).

The surrender took place at a little red school house which is the headquarters of Gen. Eisenhower.

The surrender which brought the war in Europe to a formal end after five years, eight months and six days of bloodshed and destruction was signed for Germany by Col. Gen. Gustav Jodl.

Jodl is the new chief of staff of the German army.

**It was signed for the supreme Allied command by Lt. Gen. Walter Bedell Smith, chief of staff for Gen. Eisenhower.**

It was also signed by Gen. Ivan Susloparoff for Russia and by Gen. Francois Sevez for France.

Gen. Eisenhower was not present at the signing, but immediately afterward Jodl and his fellow delegate, Gen. Adm. Hans Georg Friedeburg, were received by the supreme commander.

**They were asked sternly if they understood the surrender terms imposed upon Germany and if they would be carried out by Germany.**

They answered yes.

Germany, which began the war with a ruthless attack upon Poland, followed by successive aggressions and brutality in internment camps, surrendered with an appeal to the victors for mercy toward the German people and armed forces.

**After signing the full surrender, Jodl said he wanted to speak and was given leave to do so.**

"With this signature," he said in soft-spoken German, "The German people and armed forces are for better or worse delivered into the victors' hands.

"In this war, which has lasted more than five years, both have achieved and suffered more than perhaps any other people in the world."

## *Monty Meets Russ Marshal at Front*

NEW YORK—The British Broadcasting Corp., in a broadcast heard Monday night said that Field Marshal Sir Bernard L. Montgomery and Marshal Konstantin K. Rokossovsky had met Monday for the first time at Grabow, scene of the junction of the British Second and Soviet Second White Russian armies.

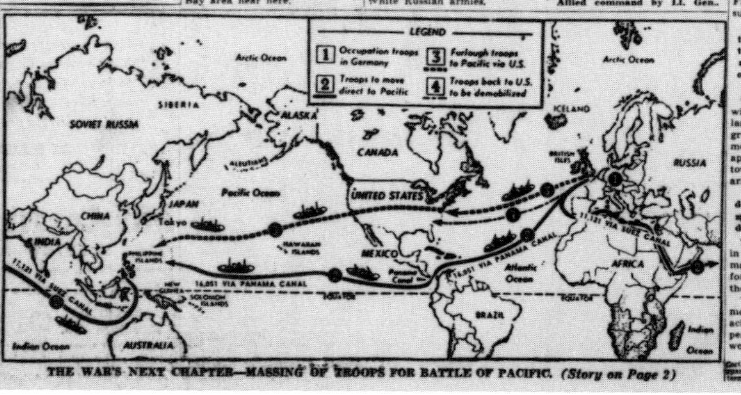


THE WAR'S NEXT CHAPTER—MASSING OF TROOPS FOR BATTLE OF PACIFIC. *(Story on Page 2)*

THE WEATHER
MINNESOTA—Warmer.
NORTH DAKOTA—Fair.
SOUTH DAKOTA—Stormy.
WISCONSIN—Clear.

# Minneapolis Sunday Tribune

YOU'LL FIND .....
EDITORIALS—Page 10, General News
MUSIC, BOOKS—Page 11, General News
CROSSWORD—Magazine section
RADIO—Page 4, Sports section
MARKETS—Classified Adv. section
BUSINESS—Classified Adv. section
THEATERS—Woman's section

Vol. LXXIX—No. 66 MINNEAPOLIS, MINN., SUNDAY, JULY 29, 1945 .... Price 10 Cents in Twin City Area 12 Cents Elsewhere

# SENATE PASSES S. F. CHARTER, 89-2

★ ★ ★ ★ ★ ★ ★ ★ ★ ★ ★ ★ ★ ★ ★ ★ ★ ★ ★ ★ ★ ★

# *2,000 Planes Rip Scraps of Jap Navy*

## FLEET MAY BE TOTALLY DESTROYED

### Waters Off Kure Left Littered With Ships; 3 Battlewagons Hit

From Late Dispatches

GUAM—U. S. Third fleet carrier planes ruling the skies over Japan sank or damaged 15 more ships, including [illegible] warships, destroyed or damaged 150 planes and heaped new disaster on the enemy's shattered navy in Saturday's third day of destructive attacks on the Inland sea.

The figures for the Saturday assault, still incomplete, raised Japanese losses to 1,078 planes destroyed or damaged and 740 ships sunk or damaged, including 47 warships, since Adm. William F. Halsey's mightiest fleet in history opened its bold air-sea bombardments of Japan on July 10.

A few hours before Adm. Chester W. Nimitz announced the results of the third strike against the Inland sea in five days by more than 1,000 American and British carrier planes, Twentieth air force headquarters disclosed that 550 to 600 Superfortresses heaped 3,500 tons of bombs on six Japanese cities early Sunday. All of the cities were on the 11-city "death list" issued by the American commanders less than 24 hours previously.

**OTHER BLOWS REVEALED**

As the carrier planes and Superfortresses worked over the Japanese homeland in a continuation of a 20-day assault that has seen almost 40,000 tons of bombs and shells dropped, Gen. Douglas MacArthur announced a crushing blow against the enemy's ocean supply lanes.

MacArthur's bombers caught three convoys near enemy shores on Thursday, sending nine ships to the bottom and sinking or damaging 62 others, half of them laden with troops. One entire seven-ship convoy was wiped out in the Tsushima strait between Korea and Japan. Other convoys were blasted southwest of Korea and in the Shimonoseki strait between Honshu and Kyushu.

**Nimitz listed damage inflicted only by American fliers in Saturday's Inland sea attacks. Reports from the British fleet still were not available.**

Completing the neutralization of Japan's main battle fleet in the third attack on its inland sea hideout in five days, the Americans sank three submarines, and damaged four destroyers, two destroyer escorts, two medium freighter-transports, three small freighters and an unidentified vessel.

**BATTLESHIP SUNK**

The battleships Haruna and Ise, damaged in last Tuesday's and Wednesday's attacks, were hit anew and left burning. Reconnaissance reports showed that the battleship Hyuga, heavily damaged on Tuesday, was now resting at the bottom of the Inland sea, its decks under water. A fourth Japanese battleship, the Nagato, was damaged heavily at Yokosuka on July 18 and thus Japan, as far as was known, had no seaworthy battleships left.

**The cruisers Aoba and Oyodo, also previously damaged, were left burning and the escort carrier Kaiyo was hit again.**

The newest additions to the list made a total of 35 Japanese warships sunk or damaged in the Inland sea. During the entire 20-day attack 47 Japanese warships have been sunk or damaged—four battleships, seven carriers, four cruisers, 13 destroyers, three submarines and 16 miscellaneous light warships.

**PLANES DESTROYED**

In attacks one Japanese plane attempting to seek out the gigantic battle fleet was shot down. Another 18 were shot down over the target area, 75 were destroyed on the ground and 56 were damaged aground.

Fleet dispatches said that to all intents and purposes the Japanese fleet no longer existed. One United Press correspondent reported from a warship that "if the Japanese don't give up soon they will not have enough ships to carry their envoys to the peace conference."

AFTER THE HOLOCAUST—A gaping hole in the wall of the Empire State building indicates the force with which an army B25 bomber crashed into the structure. Firemen examine the wreckage and debris after extinguishing the fire which followed the crash. Imbedded propeller of plane at left (arrow).—AP Wirephoto.

## JAP SURRENDER URGED AT ONCE

### U. S. Promises Enemy a New Freedom

WASHINGTON—(UP)—The United States told the Japanese people Saturday night if they surrender now they will win "freedom they have never enjoyed under the domination of their military oppressors."

Navy Capt. E. M. Zacharias, official spokesman of the U. S. government, said in an office of war information broadcast "one simple decision" by the Japanese people will save their homeland for "a sovereign existence under a peacefully inclined and responsible government."

**LIFE OR DEATH**

Zacharias said the recent Potsdam proclamation gave Japan choice between life and death. He addressed his remarks to the people as well as "their self-willed militaristic leaders."

Under the "mounting fury of combined sea and air bombardment, he said, "no longer can the leaders of Japan keep the truth of Japan's defeat from their people."

**But what the Japanese people have felt thus far, he continued, is "only the prologue to the great drama of total war."**

The proclamation by President Truman, Winston Churchill, and Chiang Kai-shek, Zacharias said, was drafted "amid the ruins of a nation which foolishly chose the road to destruction."

**QUOTES F.D.R.**

Beholding this "vast monument to German stupidity," he said, "they decided to give Japan an opportunity to escape a similar fate."

But "if the Japanese people are forced by their self-willed militaristic leaders to choose the alternative of ruin," he said, "centuries of sweat and toil will be brought to naught in a catelysmic end of a tragic war."

**He concluded by quoting from the late President Roosevelt's address to congress on Dec. 8, 1941.**

The late President said then the United States was fighting "not for conquest nor for vengeance," but for a peaceful world.

"We Americans," Mr. Roosevelt said, "are not destroyers—we are builders."

## ONE WEEK OLD, SHE LOSES HER 2 TEETH

HAMILTON, ONT.—(AP)—Linda Ann Davis had dental trouble at the age of one week.

Born with two normal lower teeth last Saturday, Linda Ann lost them this Saturday. The dentist explained they had loosened and interferred with the baby's eating.

★ ★ ★ ★ ★ ★

## *13 Now Dead in B25 Empire State Crash*

*PAGE OF PICTURES back page of Second News Section; other stories on Empire State crash on Page Four and Page 12 this section.*

NEW YORK—(UP)—A B25 Billy Mitchell bomber rammed into the 78th story of the Empire State building at 9:52 a.m. Saturday exploding in a cone of flames that turned the world's tallest skyscraper into a pillar of horror and brought death to at least 13 persons and injury to 20.

It was the most spectacular disaster to strike the New York metropolitan area since the burning of the Zeppelin, Hindenburg.

The plane began its flight from the Sioux Falls army air field Thursday morning with a crew of nine, but only two of the crew which left Sioux Falls was with the plane when it crashed, a field spokesman said.

**LEFT FOR NEWARK**

Maj. H. A. Patterson, public relations officer for the field, said the plane left the base at 7:29 a.m. Thursday, for Newark, N. J., by way of Cleveland, with Col. Harris E. Rogner as pilot in charge for the Sioux Falls to Newark trip.

Col. Smith

Col. Rogner and six members of the original crew left the plane at Newark before it continued on to New Bedford, Mass., for an overnight stop.

Men of the original crew who continued with the plane after it left Newark were Lt. Col. William Franklin Smith, Jr., 27, Watertown, Mass., who was at the controls when it hit, and the crew chief, Tech. Sgt. Christopher Domitrovich, 30, Granite City, Ill., Major Patterson reported. Both were killed.

Sgt. Domitrovich

Name of a navy enlisted man reported aboard the plane as a "hitch-hiker" and among the dead, was not disclosed pending notification of next of kin.

Gen. Hugh A. Drum, chairman of Empire State, Inc., declared 10

B25 Crash
*Continued on Page Four*

## IWO SERVES B29S AS REFUELING BASE

GUAM—(AP)—Sixty of the American Superforts which Saturday blasted the first of 11 Japanese cities doomed to destruction unless Japan immediately surrenders, refuelled at Iwo Jima on the outward-bound run for the multiple-target raid. This innovation put all of Japan within reach of the B29s for the first time. Some 750 miles north of the Marianas, Iwo allows Superforts to strike the farthest-north sectors of the Japanese empire.

## *Clear Skies, More Heat Seen Today*

Clearing skies accompanied by a sharp rise in temperature readings were promised for Minnesota Sunday by the weather bureau.

Temperatures in Minneapolis Sunday will reach approximately 85 degrees, after Saturday's high of 70. Official forecast was fair and warmer. Greatest precipitation in Minnesota Saturday was at Frontenac where 1.88 inches of rain fell.

Minneapolis temperature at midnight Saturday was 66.

## *Cuban Mob Cries 'Death to Franco'*

HAVANA—(AP)—The Spanish embassy was stoned and splattered with eggs Saturday by some 1,000 youth carrying banners proclaiming "Death to Franco." The Spanish flag was ripped from its standard and two embassy limousines were overturned. The demonstration began shortly after Manuel Aznar, new Spanish minister to the United States, arrived aboard the Spanish ship Marques de Comillas.

## *Truman's Cruiser on Secret Journey*

ANTWERP—(UP)—The presidential cruiser Augusta and the escort cruiser Philadelphia sailed from Antwerp Friday night for a secret destination, it was learned Saturday.

The Augusta's departure from its downtown berth in the Antwerp harbor could not be kept secret, but dockworkers who might have learned the ship's destination were pledged to secrecy.

## WHAT! NO YAWNS? AFTER 113 HOURS

PASADENA, CALIF.—(AP)—They didn't even sleep around the clock!

After nine hours sleep, the 12 young men who stayed awake 113 hours in a California Institute of Technology experiment arose this morning from their beds and said they felt fine.

The men, from the conscientious objectors camp near Glendora, volunteered for the experiment, conducted for the armed forces.

PHOTO-DIAGRAM OF TRAGIC AIR CRASH
*Key areas involved are shown in this view*
AP Wirephoto

## GOERING STILL MUST FACE TRIAL

### His Heart Attacks Won't Get Him Off

MONDORF-LES-BAINS, LUXEMBOURG—(AP)—Reichsmarshal Herman Goering, who collapsed from a heart attack during an electrical storm two days ago, will face trial when his time comes if he has to be brought into the court room on a stretcher, an authoritative source said Saturday.

This policy will apply to all persons listed as war criminals, the informant said.

**Goering, who told army doctors his terror of thunder and lightning brought on the attack, was still in a highly nervous condition but was in no real danger.**

Capt. Clint L. Miller, Lee's Summit, Mo., listed other Nazi leaders now being treated:

Foreign Minister Joachim von Ribbentrop—"Neuritis of the left side of his head."

**Hans Frank, reichminister without portfolio and Nazi administrator of Poland—"Arrived with self-inflicted wounds and in a serious condition. The wounds have practically healed now."**

Field Marshal Albert Kesselring—"Chronic gall bladder condition. Also a severe heart lesion."

Dr. Robert Ley, leader of the labor front—"Being treated for post gonorrheal stricture."

Alfred Rosenberg, reichminister for occupied territories in the East—"Has a sprained ankle."

Field Marshal Wilhelm Keitel—"Severe carbuncle on neck."

**ART LOOT DISCOVERED**

HEIDENHEIM, GERMANY—(UP)—A valuable collection of looted art objects has been found in the castle residence of Karl Haberstock, Adolf Hitler's personal art agent, the Seventh army announced Saturday night.

## *Pigeon Food, No Pigeons: U. S. Sings Song of India*

By PRESTON GROVER

NEW DELHI—(AP)—The U. S. army procurement division in Asia has tons and tons of pigeon food on its hands—and no pigeons.

Two years ago American troops began filtering into the Assam-Burma jungles with radio listening posts and scouting parties. They intended to keep contact with fancy new radio gadgets the army had rigged up for the purpose.

**"Radio isn't dependable in Assam," British officers told them. "You must have pigeons. The radio blacks out. Get pigeons."**

"Pooh, pooh," said the Americans, and set up their radio system. It worked beautifully for a couple of weeks. Then it blacked out, just as the British said it would.

**THOUSANDS CONTRIBUTED**

In war you can't take chances with communication. So the humbled Americans sent to the United States for pigeons. Owners of messenger pigeons in America contributed thousands of fine birds with names and records and long pedigrees. Automatically, pigeon food began to be shipped for them.

"Pigeons propagate," says Lt. Col. G. W. Power, head of procurement. "When we took inventory, 25,000 pigeons had become 30,000. They loved India. They were kept under ideal conditions. Doctors looked after their health, and soldiers cleaned out their cages. And how they ate! We kept on ordering more and more pigeon food.

**"Then the signal corps beat the radio problem. Their radios didn't black out any more. The pigeons were not needed. But there they were, thousands of them.**

"I used to lie awake nights wondering what the pigeon inventory would be by next morning, and wondering what to do with them."

It would have been easy to sell them in India, but they couldn't be sold for security reasons. If enemy agents had got hold of a fine flock of messenger pigeons, it would have made their work in India and Burma much easier.

**BOXED, SENT HOME**

Finally some of the pigeons were boxed up and sent home. Soldiers returning to America on leave were appointed "pigeon chauffeurs." The rest—well, they just disappeared. (Pigeons are good to eat.)

But in the India theater the army must order supplies for eight months ahead. And long after the pigeons were dead, pigeon food continued to pour into India ports—tons and tons of it.

## SHIPSTEAD, LANGER CAST 'NO' VOTES

### Program to Insure World Peace Wins Speedy Approval

*CHARTER SUMMARY, pictures, other stories on Page Seven of Second News Section.*

By JACK WILSON
Staff Correspondent of The Minneapolis Sunday Tribune

WASHINGTON—The United States senate Saturday ratified the United Nations charter for establishment of a permanent organization to preserve peace.

The final vote for ratification was 89 to 2.

Sen. Henrik Shipstead of Minnesota and Sen. William Langer of North Dakota cast the only votes against ratification.

Sen. Hiram Johnson of California, one of the leaders in the fight against the League of Nations in 1919, was absent when the vote was taken but he sent in word from Bethesda, Md., naval hospital that if present he again would have voted "no."

**OTHERS ABSENT**

The other senators who were unable to be present—Josiah Bailey of North Carolina, Carter Glass of Virginia, Clyde Reed of Kansas and John Thomas of Idaho, sent word that they would have voted for ratification of the charter.

**Shipstead's decision to vote against the charter was not made until shortly before the roll call began. As late as Friday night, after he had delivered a speech seriously questioning the effectiveness of the peace plan, Shipstead told reporters "I might vote for it."**

Saturday, after the roll call, he declined to comment on the reasons for his final decision beyond saying that "I never really made up my mind until after hearing all the testimony and reading all the speeches."

**LANGER STAND CLEAR**

Langer made his stand clear in the last speech before the roll call. "If I voted for it," he said, "I would feel that I had betrayed my trust. If I could feel that it offered even the tiniest hope of preserving peace, I would vote for it, but I feel its adoption will mean perpetual war and the enslavement of millions of poor people all over the world.

"I feel that it is one step more toward compulsory peacetime conscription, and all that goes with it.

"Five years ago when I was elected I pledged in my campaign that I never would vote to send our boys to be slaughtered on the battlefields of Europe. I have kept that pledge. I was not elected to create an organization that would have authority to send our boys all over the earth. We ought not to have voted on this charter in the absence of 11,000,000 fighting men and women. We are blissfully ignorant of what they may be thinking. There is no such hurry that some steps could not have been taken to refer this matter to the people, including the veterans.

"I can not, and God help me, I will not, vote for a measure that

S. F. Charter
*Continued on Page Seven*

★ ★ ★ ★

## SENATE VOTE ON CHARTER

*WASHINGTON—(AP)—Here is the roll call vote by which the senate ratified the United Nations charter:*

For ratification (89).

Democrats for—

Andrews, Bankhead, Barkley, Bilbo, Briggs, Byrd, Carville, Chandler, Chavez, Connally, Downey, Eastland, Ellender, Fulbright, George, Gerry, Green, Guffey, Hatch, Hayden, Hill, Hoey, Johnson (Colo.), Johnston (S.C.), Kilgore, Lucas, Magnuson, Maybank, McCarran, McClellan, McFarland, McKellar, McMahon, Mead, Mitchell, Murdock, Murray, Myers, O'Daniel, O'Mahoney, Overton, Pepper, Radcliffe, Russell, Stewart, Taylor, Thomas (Okla.), Thomas (Utah), Tunnell, Tydings, Wagner, Walsh, Wheeler—(53).

Republicans for—

Aiken, Austin, Ball, Brewster, Bridges, Brooks, Buck, Burton, Bushfield, Butler, Capehart, Capper, Cordon, Donnell, Ferguson, Gurney, Hart, Hawkes, Hickenlooper, Millikin, Moore, Morse, Revercomb, Robertson, Saltonstall, Smith, Taft, Tobey, Vandenberg, Wherry, White, Wiley, Willis, Wilson, Young—(35).

Progressive for—

La Follette—1.

Against ratification—(2).

Republicans against—

Langer, Shipstead—2.

The following pair was announced: Johnson (Calif.), against and Reed and Thomas (Idaho), for. (Pairs on a treaty require two for to one against.)

Announced as unavoidably absent but voting "aye" if present: Bailey, Glass.

WARMER
U. S. Weather Bureau Forecast
Partly cloudy, warmer.

# Minneapolis Morning Tribune

Vol. LXXIX—No. 76 MINNEAPOLIS, MINN., WEDNESDAY, AUGUST 8, 1945 ... Price 3 Cents In Twin Cities Area 5 Cents Elsewhere



# 'HIROSHIMA WENT UP IN ONE PUFF,' RETURNING 'ATOM-BOMBERS' TELL

**GUAM—(INS)—Official reconnaissance photographs of the prostrate city of Hiroshima disclosed Wednesday four and one-tenth square miles of the city's six and nine-tenths sqûre mile area were "completely destroyed" in the atomic bomb attack.**

By MURLIN SPENCER

GUAM—(AP)—There is reason Tuesday night to believe that the Japanese city of Hiroshima, hit by a single American atomic bomb, no longer exists.

This is despite the fact that men who participated in the actual first use of the new weapon, could give no estimate of damage other than that it "must have been extensive."

But they did relate that the lone bomb struck squarely in the center of the industrial-military city of 343,000 on southern Honshu in the Japanese mainland Aug. 6 (Pacific time) with a flash and concussion that brought an exclamation of "My God" from a battle-hardened Superfortress crew 10 miles away.

*Hiroshima, a city of 343,000 is (or was) considerably larger than St. Paul.*

For following up on other enemy targets, there are more B29s ready to carry more of the same awesome bombs. This was announced here by Gen. Carl S. Spaatz, commander of the U. S. army strategic air force.

Crewmen who carried the awful new bomb which is declared to have an explosive power the equivalent of bombs that 2,000 Superfortresses would have had to carry previously although they were far away, felt the concussion like a close explosion of anti-aircraft fire.

Col. Paul W. Tibbets, Jr., of Miami, Fla., who piloted the Superfortress and Navy Capt. William S. Parsons, of Santa Fe., N. M., navy ordnance expert, described the explosions as "tremendous and awe-inspiring."

### Bomb Run Described

CAPT. PARSONS
*'Awe-inspiring,' he says*

"It was 0915 (9:15 a.m.) when we dropped our bomb and we turned the plane broadside to get the best view," said Capt. Parson. "Then we made as much distance from the ball of fire as we could.

"We were at least 10 miles away and there was a visual impact even though every man wore colored glasses for protection. We had braced ourselves when the bomb was gone for the shock and Tibbets said 'close flak' and it was just like that—a close burst of anti-aircraft fire.

**The crew said 'My God' and couldn't believe what had happened.**

"A mountain of smoke was going up in a mushroom with the stem coming down. At the top was white smoke but up to 1,000 feet from the ground there was swirling, boiling dust. Soon afterward small fires sprang up on the edge of town but the town was entirely obscured. We stayed around two or three minutes and by that time the smoke had risen to 40,000 feet. As we watched the top of the white cloud broke off and another soon formed."

### Spaatz Praises New Weapon

Details of the bombing were disclosed at a press conference attended by Gen. Carl Spaatz, who termed the new bomb the "most revolutionary development in the history of the world."

Spaatz was obviously highly elated at the new bombing weapon. He said if he had had it in Europe "it would have shortened the war six to eight months." Maj. Gen. Curtis Lemay said if this bomb had been available there would have been "no need to have had D-day in Europe."

MAJ. FEREBEE
*First to drop bomb*

**Just what damage was done to Hiroshima was not known. Photographs taken at the time of bombing showed only smoke. Photographs taken four hours later showed smoke still obscuring the city and rising to 40,000 feet.**

The Superfortress which carried the bomb took off from a Marianas base, and only three men knew what they carried—Col. Tibbets, Capt. Parsons, and the bombardier, Maj. Thomas W. Ferebee, Mocksville, N. C. Other crewmen knew only that it was a highly secret, important mission.

Tibbets had been trained specially for this mission, which Gen. Spaatz considered so vital he awarded Tibbets the distinguished service cross as he stepped from his plane after the flight. The plane was named "Enola Gay" after Tibbets' mother in Miami.

### Whole Mission Secret

There were many secrets about the flight and the bombing which followed. One secret was the selection of Hiroshima as the target. It was believed probable, however, that it was selected not because of its great importance but partly because the weather was clear there and visibility was such as to permit a close watch of the bomb explosion.

**No difficulty was encountered in reaching the target.**

Many months ago, a special unit was organized to do this special work.

"When we went out we had the best of facilities made available to us," Tibbets said.

Speaking matter-of-factly, he said, "The bomb run up to the target was uneventful, and there were no disturbing elements in the bomb run when the release was made.

"We saw a flash, felt the concussions and it reminded me of a close burst of flak. We stayed in the target area looking at the scene below and the towering column of smoke. I have never seen anything like it."

### Handling Is Dangerous

Capt. Parsons said he had been assigned by the Navy to work on this weapon with the view to making it safe to handle. When one of the correspondents asked "if there was danger in handling this thing," Gen. Spaatz interrupted him with, "what do you think?"

Parsons has carried a number of atomic bomb facsimiles in practice in the Alamagordo bombing range in New Mexico. This was just like carrying another facsimile in this raid, he said. Asked what he thought about dropping such a lethal weapon in the midst of a big city, he said there was no reaction.

**Discusion of the size or other features of the atomic bomb wasn't permitted, but it is carried by a single Superfortress.**

Spaatz, Lemay and other general officers discussed guardedly the possible effectiveness of the new bomb which was described as giving off intense heat for some distance around it. In experiments in New Mexico, the heat was said to have been felt 20 miles away.

One officer described it as essentially an air weapon when asked if it would be possible to be used by the fleet. Parsons was asked whether a bomb was capable of starting tidal waves. He said if it were dropped in the sea, there would be a lot of waves and high geysers, but expressed doubt that it would start a tidal wave.

## Northwest Will Pay Bong Homage

Two funeral services for Maj. Richard Ira Bong, Poplar, Wis., farm boy who became America's ace of aces, will be held with military honors Wednesday.

Bong was killed when a jet-propelled P80 he was testing exploded and crashed at Burbank, Calif., Monday.

At Superior, Wis., church services will be held at 2 p.m. in Concordia Lutheran church where six months ago the 24-year-old major was married. A second service will be read in a shady hillside cemetery 20 miles away at Poplar where Bong is to be buried.

FLIERS TO HONOR HIM

A fighter-plane formation from near-by army bases will fly over Poplar during services.

The Rev. Arvid Hoorn, pastor of Bethany Lutheran church at Poplar, boyhood advisor of Bong and family minister will officiate at church services. He will be assisted by the Rev. Paul Boe who married Maj. Bong last February.

**In the farm home of Mr. and Mrs. Carl Bong, the parents, the family Tuesday quietly went about their daily tasks still too stunned by the news to make comment.**

Mrs. Carl Bong, who had been shopping when she heard the news of her son's death over the radio, recovered slowly from the initial shock.

Nelda Bong, 23, oldest sister of the flier, had arrived from Washington, D. C. Monday for a holiday at home and it was she who first received official news of her brother's death.

FLAGS AT HALF MAST

At the Bong farm also when the tragic news reached there were four sisters and two brothers, Geraldine, 21; Joyce, 17; Barbara, 15; Sue, 13; Carl Jr., 18, and James 8.

Flags in Superior and Poplar were at half mast Tuesday and also will be Wednesday. Poplar business places will close Wednesday out of respect to their famous native son.

**The flier's body, accompanied by a military guard and the flier's 21-year-old widow, was scheduled to be flown east in a C-54 transport piloted by Lt. K. C. McGregor, commanding officer of the Sixth ferrying group.**

The plane was scheduled to take off at 10 p.m. Tuesday from Long Beach Municipal airport and to arrive in Duluth at 8 a.m.

Maj. Earl Kingsley, a friend of Bong since his training days, will be official military escort on the flight east. With Mrs. Bong will also be her brother, Jerome Vattendahl, 27-year-old ex-soldier, and Mrs. Clarence Toy, personal friend.

A military escort brought the body to Long Beach from Burbank, Calif., and a guard of honor was posted at the airport until take-off time. The guard was ordered by Gen. H. H. Arnold because Bong was a congressional medal of honor holder.

ATOMIC HARI-KIRI

## 'Superman' Piker, Says Scientist

*In the following dramatic, exclusive article, Dr. Harold Jacobson, Chicago U. graduate who worked for two years on the Manhattan project—the atomic bomb—reveals that areas struck by the bomb remain saturated with death for years.*

By DR. HAROLD JACOBSON

NEW YORK—(INS)—Any Japanese who try to ascertain the extent of damage caused by the atomic bomb in Hiroshima are committing suicide.

The terrific force of the explosion irradiates every piece of matter in the area. Investigators will become infected with secondary radiation which breaks up the red corpuscles in the blood. This prevents the body from assimilating oxygen which means those so exposed will die in the same way victims of Leukemia die.

**Actually, tests have shown that the radiation in an area exposed to the force of an atomic bomb will not be dissipated for approximately 70 years. Hence, Hiroshima will be a devastated area not unlike our conception of the moon for nearly three quarters of a century.**

Furthermore, rain falling on the area will pick up the lethal rays and will carry them down to the rivers and the sea. And animal life in these waters will die.

I cite these facts to illustrate the awesome force contained in the atomic bomb. It defies the imagination. Flash Gordon looks like a piker compared to it.

## British Chiefs Meet in Special Parley

LONDON—(AP)—Military chiefs closest to Winston Churchill in the direction of the British war effort were summoned by Prime Minister Clement Attlee Tuesday to an almost unprecedented cabinet meeting — the second of the day. The meeting lasted three hours. The meeting was believed connected with the atomic bomb dropped on Japan.

Gen. Sir Hastings Ismay, at Churchill's elbow at the Big Three conferences and remained with Attlee at Potsdam after the change in British leadership; Air Marshal Sir Charles Portal, Field Marshal Sir Alan Brooke and others were at the meeting.

★ ★ ★ ★

## BOMB PERIL PROMPTS JAP CABINET CALL

### Leaders Summoned as Radio Babbles of 'Diabolic Weapon'

SAN FRANCISCO — (AP) — The Japanese cabinet was reported assembled in special session Tuesday, presumably to discuss drastic events prompted by the loosing of an atomic bomb on the homeland.

As enemy broadcasts warned the people to brace for renewed attacks, NBC in New York picked up a BBC broadcast quoting the Tokyo radio as saying the cabinet had been called together.

BBC said wording of the broadcast implied Premier Suzuki had summoned his advisers to discuss the atomic bomb raid on the military base of Hiroshima Monday.

'DESTROYER OF MANKIND'

Throughout the day the Japanese broadcast accounts of the new bomb, refraining from using the word "atomic" but branding it a "diabolic weapon."

**Another broadcast beamed to the United States declared the use of the atomic bomb branded "the enemy for ages to come as a destroyer of justice and mankind."**

All train travel into Hiroshima—which the Japanese conceded was "considerably damaged"—was forbidden.

"The destructive power of the new weapon cannot be slighted," warned Domei agency, which said "a few" of the annihilating bombs floated in over the military city by parachute and burst "before reaching the ground."

CAN'T BELIEVE IT

Apparently the Japanese could not believe that a single atomic bomb, which President Truman disclosed had hit Japan for the first time Monday (Tokyo time), could cause all that violence.

Both Domei and an imperial headquarters communique recorded by the federal communications commission said more than one bomb struck.

The communique, first to acknowledge a new weapon had been unleashed, said "considerable damage" was reported in Hiroshima.

## U. S. Frees Reich Prison Inmates

FRANKFURT, GERMANY—(AP)—American military authorities said Tuesday they have freed more than 15,000 inmates of German prisons after a review of cases disclosed they were unjustly sentenced.

Capt. John J. Reyman, Ann Arbor, Mich., said so many releases have been approved many of the 40 prisons in the American zone are finding it difficult to operate gardens and do other chores formerly performed by inmates.

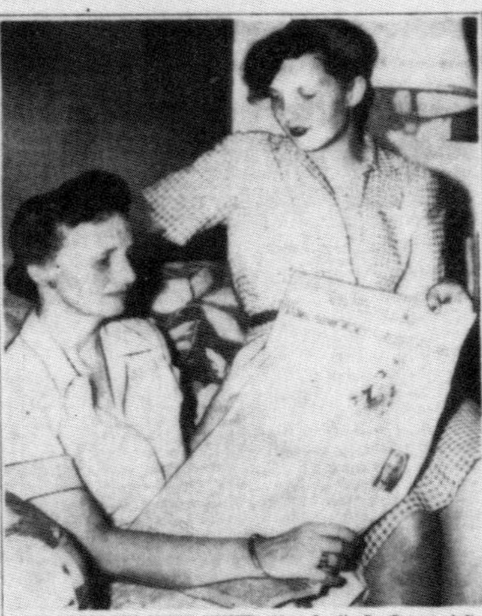

NOT EVEN HIS WIFE KNEW—Mrs. Leslie R. Groves, left, wife of the major general who directed development of the atomic bomb, reads the story of her husband's work in a newspaper at her Washington home with her daughter, Gwen, 16. She said her husband kept the bomb secret from her as well as the public.—AP Wirephoto.

## NIPS MAY TAKE LOT OF ATOM PERSUASION

WASHINGTON—(INS)— The navy said Tuesday night four or five Japanese cities may have to be destroyed with atomic bombs before the Japanese will believe such a weapon exists.

Further proof will soon be forthcoming of the atomic bomb's existence, the navy said, adding:

"We will bring them the proof. With destruction from this new type of bomb, and with continued damage from Adm. Halsey's carrier planes and ships, the Japanese fighting strength—and perhaps even their will to fight—will rapidly weaken."

## HALSEY WARNS JAPS HE'S COMING

WASHINGTON — (AP) — The navy told the Japanese Tuesday Adm. William F. Halsey's third fleet is again off their homeland and will soon "let loose more and more destruction on vital coastal installations."

Explaining the silence from Halsey's fleet for a week, it said the Third had been avoiding a threatening typhoon.

"Adm. Halsey had been caught in one destructive typhoon on June 5. He was going to make sure it didn't happen again so the Third fleet moved into safe waters," the navy added.

## 300 PLANES HIT KYUSHU

### Two Cities Blasted by Fires, Explosion

MANILA — (AP) — More than 300 Liberators, Mitchells and Invaders of the Far East air forces struck heavily at two southern Kyushu cities Monday with fire bombs and jellied gasoline, producing great fires and explosions throughout the target area.

The manufacturing city of Kagoshima took the hardest impact as more than 200 Liberators and Mitchells of the Fifth and Seventh AAF'S, escorted by Thunderbolt fighters, bombed its submarine assembly yards, oil storage depots and iron and sheet metal works.

After bombing by instrument because of heavy undercast, the low flying Mitchells dived through smoke and clouds for treetop strafing of the city of 180,000.

**Pilots reported they saw many fires in the wake of their bombing.**

The rail center of Miyakonojo was hit simultaneously by more than 100 Seventh invaders and Thunderbolts. Rockets and jellied gasoline bombs and strafing bullets swept railroad installations and factories on this fourth largest city on Kyushu.

Logging installations proved particularly vulnerable to the jellied gasoline treatment.

A night flying Liberator sank a 3,000-ton transport-freighter and damaged another Sunday in Tsushima straits, where less than 24 hours earlier a 10,000-ton transport and a 3,000-ton freighter had been destroyed.

### TURN THE PAGES TO:



JAPAN AT CROSSROADS

## WILL NIPPON'S PEOPLE QUIT?

By WILLIAM H. MYLANDER
Tribune Staff Correspondent

WASHINGTON—Only question remaining in the Pacific war is when the Japanese people will force their military rulers to quit.

Defeat of Japan was considered a certainty here before the atomic bomb was perfected, but use of the devastating new weapon is expected to spur the people into earlier action to overthrow the government.

Military sources gave assurance Tuesday enough of the new bombs are on hand to continue the bombardment of targets vital to the war.

If the war is prolonged, however, even the selection of remote installations for atomic destruction is certain to take the lives of millions of civilians in the densely populated Japanese homeland.

YANKS INVOLVED

American lives are at stake, too, for the state department disclosed only last week Japan is following a deliberate policy of moving prisoners and civilian internees into bombardment areas.

The United States government has said repeatedly it does not want to wipe out Japan or the entire Japanese race. It also does not want to kill civilians if this can be avoided without prolonging the war and costing American lives.

In view of these factors, it seems reasonable to assume every effort will be made by the American high command to so utilize atomic bombing as to press home to the people of Japan the suicidal folly and futility of continuing resistance.

**Hope the present military clique ruling Japan would ac-**

Mylander
*Continued on Page Four*

## TRUMAN BACK AT WHITE HOUSE

WASHINGTON—(AP)—President Truman returned to the White House Tuesday night from the Big Three conference at Potsdam. His special train reached here at 9:50 p.m., Minneapolis time.

The USS Augusta, bearing President Truman and his party docked at Hampton Roads port of embarkation at Newport News, Va., Tuesday at 5:25 p.m.

The President and his party left immediately by special train for Washington.

**Mr. Truman, looking physically fit and smiling, came down the gang plank immediately behind George Dresher, head of the secret service detail.**

Behind him came Adm. William Leahy, naval chief of staff to the President; Judge Samuel Rosenman, Secretary of State James W. Byrnes, and other members of the presidential party including Adm. Jonas H. Ingram, commander in chief, Atlantic fleet, who went from Philadelphia to meet the Augusta.

**Mr. Truman will report to the nation by radio within the next few days on the Big Three conference.**

No date has been set for the address.

## Atom Test Awakens Flier, Blast Mistaken for Meteor

Fliers thought a giant meteor had struck the ground when they saw the experimental explosion of an atomic bomb in New Mexico, according to Lt. Don Peterson, 20, now home on leave in Milaca, Minn.

"We saw a big orange ball of fire which lit up the camp as if it were day," Peterson said.

The navigator, brother of Jim Peterson of the Morning Tribune sports staff, was undergoing B29 training at Alamagordo field, N. M., when the bomb was set off 15 miles from camp.

Lt. Peterson

Peterson and all other officers in his quarters, unaware of the experiment, were awakened at 5 a.m. July 16 by the loud blast.

**"Rumors about what caused the explosion floated around camp for days," Peterson said. "We finally decided it was either a meteor or a bomber crash.**

"All planes were grounded immediately after the explosion. A brush fire started and lasted quite awhile before it burned out."

Service men at Alamagordo later were informed the blast was caused by a secret experiment, he said. Most of the men later decided they had seen the tryout of a flying bomb.



## 'JoJo' Finds Bird Is Dog's Best Friend

By BARBARA MAURIN
Tribune Staff Writer

If a dog is man's best friend, then who is a dog's best friend?

In the case of one dog at least, the answer is Peewee, pet robin of Mrs. Frances Malecki, 1218 Fifth street NE.

Peewee's pal is JoJo, a plump, slow-moving little fox terrier who wouldn't harm anything but a flea.

Like most robins who chance to link their destinies with those of humankind, Peewee is an orphan, tossed from his nest when he was tiny and helpless and raised to a husky seven weeks old by Mrs. Malecki.

He lives on nothing but the best. No angel food cake is too good for Peewee, who disdains worms because he once got very sick from eating too many.

**Peewee has a private boudoir in a wooden box beneath the kitchen stove, and not-so-private bath in an old pie tin on the back porch.**

He has the run of the house, and would be a much more outstanding bird, his owner wryly admits, if his talents for screaming to get out of the house were as prominently developed as those he uses to get in.

**But Peewee's favorite diversion is playing with his pal, JoJo. Shunning his fellow birds, and being "given the bird" by them in turn, Peewee tours the neighborhood astride JoJo's broad back.**

Like two children, JoJo and Peewee play at fighting one another—the dog baring her teeth, and, growling, the bird pecking and squawking, and neither meaning a bit of it.

Mrs. Malecki is worried, though, about what will become of Peewee when winter comes.

CAROL MALECKI, 9, WITH PEEWEE AND JOJO
*Robin and fox terrier close pals*

FAIR
U. S. Weather Bureau Forecast
Fair and cool.

TEMPERATURES

| | | | | | |
|---|---|---|---|---|---|
| 2 a.m. | 69 | 10 a.m. | 67 | 6 p.m. | 74 |
| 3 a.m. | 67 | 11 a.m. | 70 | 7 p.m. | 72 |
| 4 a.m. | 66 | Noon | 71 | 8 p.m. | 72 |
| 5 a.m. | 65 | 1 p.m. | 72 | 9 p.m. | 69 |
| 6 a.m. | 64 | 2 p.m. | 72 | 10 p.m. | 66 |
| 7 a.m. | 63 | 3 p.m. | 73 | 11 p.m. | 63 |
| 8 a.m. | 62 | 4 p.m. | 74 | xMidnight | 62 |
| 9 a.m. | 64 | 5 p.m. | 74 | x Unofficial | |

Minneapolis Morning Tribune

Vol. LXXIX—No. 83 MINNEAPOLIS, MINN., WEDNESDAY, AUGUST 15, 1945 Price 3 Cents in Twin Cities Area, 5 Cents Elsewhere



# WAR OVER! SAYS TRUMAN; MacARTHUR TO RULE JAPS

## Radar Tipped Scales, Allies Reveal as Victory Comes

Pictures Page 20; Stories Page 10

★ ★ ★ ★ ★ ★

By MARR McGAFFIN
Minneapolis Tribune Staff Correspondent

WASHINGTON—During the three most difficult years of war, it was radar that gave the United Nations the thin margin of victory that finally brought the defeat of our enemies.

The atomic bomb, the jet propelled plane and the rockets have been the sensations of this war, but the dial-covered black box with its "whirling dish-pan" has been the secret weapon that actually tipped the balance.

In its crude and experimental stages, it enabled the RAF to stop the Nazi air blitz in 1940 and kept Britain in the war.

**IMPORTANT IN PACIFIC**

During the early days of the war in the Pacific it made it possible for our thinly scattered navy to drive the Jap fleet out of the Solomons, choke off the enemy supply lines and beat back enemy air attacks on our scattered bases.

**In 1943, it was radar that finally provided the answer to the submarine menace and opened the supply lines to Britain. If those shipping lanes had not been kept open there might have been no D-day.**

Again, it was radar that finally opened the way for the daily bombing of Nazi factories, railroad center, airfields in the winter months of 1943-44, regardless of cloud-covered skies over Germany.

On D-day, it was radar that made it possible for our bombers to lay down a barrage ahead of our landing troops. It kept enemy submarines and what was left of the Luftwaffe in hiding.

**FOUND ROBOT BOMBS**

Radar pointed out the launching sites of Hitler's robot bombs and aimed the guns that shot down those bombs by the hundreds.

Finally, it was this same miracle weapon that helped smother the enemy in the desperate "battle of the bulge" and led our fleets of B29s on their devastating raids on Tokyo and other Japanese cities.

**Those are only a few of the highlights that illustrate the**

Radar Margin
*Continued on Page Two*

★ ★ ★ ★

## MINNESOTAN AIDS RADAR

### Dr. Robert Page Termed 'Genius'

By MARR McGAFFIN
Minneapolis Tribune Staff Correspondent

WASHINGTON—Credit for a major part of the work that kept the development of radar equipment and use a couple of jumps ahead of the enemy is given to a Minnesotan, Dr. Robert M. Page.

The 42-year-old scientist was born in St. Paul, Minn., graduated from West high school in Minneapolis, and received his bachelor's degree in physics from Hamline university in 1927.

Dr. A. Hoyt Taylor, chief consultant for electronics at the naval research laboratory here, describes Dr. Page as "a great genius."

"He has produced more brilliant ideas and has made more contributions to modern radar than any other man," he declared Tuesday.

**WAS AT PEARL HARBOR**

Long range radar air warning equipment, developed largely as a result of Dr. Page's work at the naval research laboratory, had been installed at Pearl Harbor before the Japs' sneak attack.

**Other sets also had been installed on a number of key vessels of the fleet.**

Had they been in operation at the time, or had the warning received on one set, which according to reports at the time was being used for practice, been properly observed, at least some of the damage suffered might have been prevented.

Dec. 7, 1941, it can well be imagined, was a day of most bitter disappointment for Dr. Page and his associates who had spent endless hours rushing this warning equipment to completion for just such an emergency.

**MADE FIRST DISCOVERIES**

Dr. Taylor is credited with having made the original discoveries that led to the first experiments in radio detection.

With his assistant, Leo C. Young, he was experimenting with a radio direction finder in 1922 when he noticed the signals

Dr. Page
*Continued on Page Five*

★ ★ ★ ★

DR. ROBERT M. PAGE

WHOOPEE—WE'VE WON, said Teresa Gobrysh, Minneapolis girl who was plenty happy when she heard the news of the Japanese surrender.

## HOLIDAYS ORDERED BY TRUMAN

### Today and Thursday Proclaimed for Victory Celebration

By MARR McGAFFIN
Minneapolis Tribune Staff Correspondent

WASHINGTON — Wednesday and Thursday are legal holidays for everyone.

After first declaring the two days a special holiday for federal government workers only, on ground that they had been deprived of a chance to celebrate the victory in Europe, President Truman changed his mind and made the holiday universal.

**He did so, his statement said, because making the two days a legal holiday would provide time and one-half pay for those who must work, despite the urge to let down and celebrate.**

The President declared this was necessary in order to get absolutely essential government work done.

He said the war labor board, in a special ruling, has permitted straight time wages for workers taking the holiday, but that many employers had requested that employes who do work through the victory jubilee receive premium compensation.

**The amendment to WLB's regulations provides the holidays, whether or not work is performed by a war worker, must be counted as days of work in determining whether an employe has worked seven consecutive days in a work week.**

The days must also be computed in determining whether a sixth day has been worked. Under the executive order issued by President Truman Victory day becomes a holiday subject to all rulings and interpretations issued by the secretary of labor with respect to the other six holidays previously specified.

### Humphrey Urges Two-Day Holiday

Mayor Hubert H. Humphrey Tuesday night urged all Minneapolis residents and business organizations to observe Wednesday and Thursday as legal holidays.

**"Since the President has designated Wednesday and Thursday as legal holidays for all Americans in celebration of the end of the war, I ask that the citizens of Minneapolis and all business institutions in the city observe the victory holiday."**

Humphrey suggested that Minneapolis citizens devote the two days to "thanksgiving for the end of the war, rest and recreation," pointing out that park facilities will be open both days.

### DIP IN POOL KEEPS TRUMAN COOL

WASHINGTON —(INS)— In the midst of great tension in Washington and all over the Allied world, President Truman was calm and unexcited Tuesday.

Late in the afternoon he left his office and went swimming in the White Touse pool.

## 5,000,000 GIs to Get Release In 18 Months

By RICHARD WILSON
Chief of the Washington Bureau of the Minneapolis Morning Tribune

WASHINGTON—President Harry S. Truman announced at 6 p.m. Tuesday (Minneapolis time) the Japanese imperial government has accepted the terms of unconditional surrender to the Allies. Similar announcements were made in other Allied capitals.

The war is over.

Allied armed forces have been ordered, Mr. Truman announced, to suspend offensive action.

**Gen. Douglas MacArthur has been appointed supreme Allied commander to receive the Japanese surrender.**

Proclamation of VJ-day will await formal signing of surrender terms by Japan.

This much was officially announced.

### Large Army to Occupy Japan

It is also expected Japan and her Asiatic spheres of influence will be occupied by an army of 500,000 to 1,000,000 troops, mostly American.

The surrender will be to the United States, probably aboard the battleship Missouri.

**President Truman Tuesday night forecast 5,000,000 to 5,500,000 men now in the army may be returned to civilian life within the next 12 to 18 months.**

Furthermore, he said, only the lowest age groups will now be drafted into the army.

### Truman Recommends Draft Cut

His recommendation was that selective service reduce inductions immediately from 80,000 a month to 50 000.

**Selective Service Director Lewis B. Hershey, following Mr. Truman's instructions, Tuesday night telegraphed all state directors ordering them to stop at once the induction of all registrants 26 years of age or older.**

"It is too early to propose a definite figure for the occupation forces which will be required in the Pacific 12 months from now, or what reduction it may be possible to make in the strength of the army force now allotted to occupation duties in Europe," the President said in a statement.

**"It is apparent, however, we can release as many men as can be brought home by the means available during the next year."**

Army releases will be speeded by air and sea transportation in an effort to attain that 5,000,000, to 5,500,000 figure, he said.

Mr. Truman said that in justice to millions of men who have given "long and faithful service under the difficult and hazardous conditions of the Pacific war and elsewhere overseas, a constant flow of replacements to the occupational forces is thought to be imperative."

### Japan's Aggression Leads to Ruin

Japan's 14-years war of ruthless aggression has been brought to an end in her complete defeat, her shipping destroyed, her cities ruined, her military forces beaten.

Defeat of the eastern totalitarian power brings to an end a 6-years conflict in which three nations, Germany, Italy and Japan,

War Over, Says Truman
*Continued on Page Five*

★ ★ ★ ★ ★ ★

## Hirohito Lays Defeat to 'Cruel' Atom Bomb

From Late Dispatches

A Domei dispatch broadcast by the Tokyo radio said Tuesday night Emperor Hirohito had told the Japanese people by radio "the enemy has begun to employ a new and most cruel bomb" and should Japan continue to fight, "it would lead to the total extinction of human civilization."

**The broadcast shattered imperial precedent. A Domei dispatch said "it is the first time in Japan's history that the emporer spoke to the nation over the radio.**

*SAN FRANCISCO — (UP) — Japanese Premier Adm. Kantaro Suzuki, following the emperor in a broadcast speech, told the Japanese people Japan's "war aim" was lost "by the enemy's use of the new type bomb."*

Emperor Hirohito went on the air at noon Wednesday, Japanese time (10 p.m. Tuesday, Minneapolis time) to tell his vanquished Japanese subjects of the acceptance of the Potsdam declaration and of Japan's surrender to the Allies.

**TEXT OF MESSAGE**

The text of the imperial rescript follows:

"To our good and loyal subjects:

"Pondering deeply the general trends of the world and the actual conditions of the world and the actual conditions in our empire today, we have decided to effect a settlement of the present situation by resorting to an extraordinary measure.

**"We have ordered our government to communicate to the governments of the United States, Great Britain, China and the Soviet Union that our emperor accepts the provisions of the Potsdam declaration.**

"To strive for the common prosperity and happiness of all nations as well as the security and well-being of our subjects is the solemn obligation which has been handed down by our imperial ancestors, and which we lay close to our heart.

**'SELF-PRESERVATION'**

"Indeed, we declared war on America and Britain out of our sincere desire to insure Japan's self-preservation and the establishment of East Asia, it being far from our thought either to infringe upon the sovereignty of other nations or to embark upon territorial aggrandizement.

"But now the war has lasted for nearly four years. Despite the best that has been done by everyone—the gallant fighting of the military and naval forces, the diligence and assiduity of our servants of the state and the devoted service of our 100,000,000 people, the war situation has developed not necessarily to Japan's advantage, while the general trends of the world have all turned against her interest."

## Minneapolis Goes Wild With VJ Joy

A few words from President Truman Tuesday night sent Minneapolis on an emotional "binge" in which all the misery and waiting and expectation of four long years were suddenly changed in a few minutes into the joy of the war's end.

The reaction to the President's announcement came as tearful relief for some people on loop streets. For others it was wild yelling. For others the unexplainable, odd things that people do when they're intensely happy.

**EXTRAS CARRY NEWS**

At 6 p.m., Minneapolis streets were quiet. Then the announcement reached the streets in newspaper "extras."

On Fifth street and Marquette avenue, a half dozen women were talking—waiting.

The news was brought to them by a Negro man about 50 years old, who came racing down the street aimlessly, tears streaming down his face, crying to everyone:

"My God! My boys are coming home safe!"

Then the siren atop the Northwestern National bank building started to scream out the news—at 6:08 p.m.—and the automobile horns took up the victorious chant, just a few at first because some drivers were afraid the news might be a false report.

**Then the honking spread and the display increased in intensity and wildness.**

A navy chief petty officer with campaign ribbons and battle stars

*Continued on Page Two*
Celebration

### BULLETINS

GUAM—(AP)—Orders have been issued to the U. S. Pacific fleet and to other forces under command of Adm. Nimitz to cease offensive operations against the Japanese, it was announced Wednesday night.

**NEW YORK—(AP)—The New York Stock Exchange will be closed Wednesday and Thursday.**

WASHINGTON — (AP) — Newspaper, radio and mail censorship all are due to die with the coming of VJ-day. Elmer Davis, director of the office of war information, announced also the life of his agency "soon will be over."

**WASHINGTON— (AP) —Japanese surrender came on the Fourth anniversary of the Atlantic charter framed by President Roosevelt and Prime Minister Churchill.**

OTTAWA—(AP)—Prime Minister Mackenzie King said Wednesday will be VJ-day in Canada and next Sunday will be a day of prayer and solemn thanksgiving.



## NAVY CALLS OFF PROGRAM

### Truman Swings U. S. Into Peace Path

WASHINGTON — (AP) — The navy announced Tuesday night it is cancelling nearly $6,000,000,000 in prime contracts.

This is in addition to a recently announced $1,200,000,000 cut in the shipbuilding program.

The cancellations were ordered, the navy said, to bring production into line with requirements of the postwar navy, and to free men, materials and productive capacity for manufacture of civilian goods.

**At the same time, President Truman turned the whole machinery of government loose to try to carry the nation swiftly—and smoothly—into the broad path of peace.**

The magnitude of the job ahead—getting industry back on a peacetime basis and getting people into jobs—was vividly revealed by the President when he declared shortly after announcing the Japanese surrender:

**"The emergency is as great as it was on Dec. 7, 1941."**

All controls over the nation's manpower were ended abruptly in a nationwide order by the war manpower commission.

The end of gasoline rationing—expected very shortly—will be another sharp demonstration that the war is over.

### TURN THE PAGES TO:



## NEWS GIVEN BY TRUMAN

### Message Ends Nation's Long Wait

By WILLIAM H. MYLANDER
Minneapolis Tribune Staff Correspondent

WASHINGTON — The man from Missouri in the modest blue suit was smiling when he arose.

He had been informed by the customary shout, "All in," that 200 reporters and radio newsgatherers representing a war-weary, impatient world were assembled before him.

The clock was inching toward 7 p.m.

**"I have received this afternoon a message from the Japanese government," President Truman said in calm, clear tones.**

With his usual thoughtfulness, he added:

"What I'm about to read has been incorporated in a release

*Continued on Page Two*
Truman

**FAIR AND MILD**
U. S. Weather Bureau Forecast
High 85

TEMPERATURES

| | | | | | |
|---|---|---|---|---|---|
| 2 a.m. | 64 | 10 a.m. | 71 | 6 p.m. | 79 |
| 3 a.m. | 62 | 11 a.m. | 74 | 7 p.m. | 74 |
| 4 a.m. | 60 | Noon | 76 | 8 p.m. | 73 |
| 5 a.m. | 58 | 1 p.m. | 75 | 9 p.m. | 71 |
| 6 a.m. | 60 | 2 p.m. | 79 | 10 p.m. | 69 |
| 7 a.m. | 65 | 3 p.m. | 80 | 11 p.m. | 67 |
| 8 a.m. | 68 | 4 p.m. | 80 | zMidnight | 65 |
| 9 a.m. | 69 | 5 p.m. | 79 | zUnofficial | |

# Minneapolis Morning Tribune

Vol. LXXXI—No. 83 MINNEAPOLIS, MINN., FRIDAY, AUGUST 15, 1947 Price 5 Cents


# U. S. CUTS ITALY DEBT BY BILLION

## INDIA FETES FREEDOM AS RIOTS FLAME

### Hindustan, Pakistan Become Independent British Dominions

NEW DELHI, INDIA—(AP)—India's 400,000,000 shed their hated role of subject peoples at the clock stroke of a new day today. They began a new chapter of two independent dominions—India (Hindustan) and Pakistan—with celebrations marred by bloodshed, death and terror in wide sections of the country.

In the constituent assembly, Hindu India's legislators took over their responsibility promptly at the first minute after midnight, and waited impatiently for Lord Mountbatten to appear at 8 a.m., to relinquish his office of Britain's last viceroy and assume the duties of India's first governor general.

At Karachi, Thursday, he rode by flag-waving thousands at a formal farewell in that dusty new capital of Moslem Pakistan.

**HOIST NEW FLAG**

Old Delhi whooped it up on Independence day, a Fourth of July and Bastille day rolled into one. In Bombay the provincial premier, B. G. Kher, hoisted the new Indian national flag and recited a prayer in Sanskrit.

**In Washington, President Truman welcomed the new British dominions into the family of nations last night with assurances of the firm friendship of the United States.**

Charles W. Lewis, Jr., Carlsbad, N. M., American consul general at Karachi, was designated as counselor of the new American embassy to be set up in the Pakistan capital. He will serve as the top American diplomatic representative until an ambassador is named.

**153 DIE IN LAHORE**

In embattled Punjab, the province that is to be split between Pakistan and India, wide sections of the city of Lahore and five Sikh temples were aflame and the dead were counted at 153 in rioting between Moslems and non-Moslems since dawn Wednesday. The injured were listed at 136.

The disorders were set off by fears of Moslem and non-Moslem communities that they would be left on the "wrong side" of the line—in Pakistan or India—when a boundary commission makes its expected report. Eastern part of the province is to go to India and the western part to Pakistan.

**FREE TO SECEDE**

The dominion status of India and Pakistan is only temporary. Each dominion is free to cut its strings entirely with the British empire, and Hindu India's leaders declare they mean to go all the way ultimately to complete independence from Britain.

**The deep-toned chimes announcing midnight in New Delhi made Jawaharlal Nehru, leading Congress party minister, the prime minister of the new dominion.**

Mahomed Ali Jinnah, Moslem league leader who fathered Pakistan, takes the oath as governor general of that dominion later in the day.

## *Big Drop Seen in Corn*

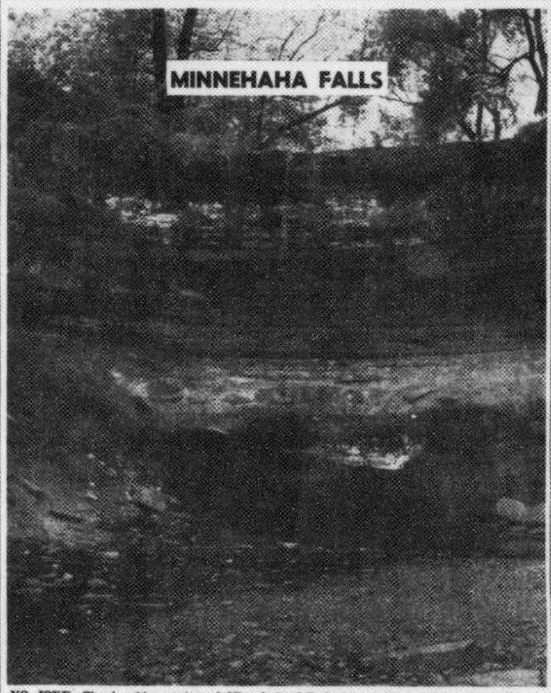


**NO JOKE**—The laughing water of Minnehaha falls had turned into a faint giggle Thursday as the summer's long rainless spell took its toll. The dry rocks recalled to Charles E. Doell, superintendent of parks, the many years when "we only turned on the falls for important people like the crown prince of Sweden." For 18 years in the '20 and '30s the falls were operated by a dam which released water from a lagoon between Hiawatha avenue and Minnehaha parkway.

## AREA SURVEY PUTS CROP AT 50 PER CENT

### Even Worse Feared Unless Rain Falls, Elevator Man Says

By GEORGE HELLICKSON
Minneapolis Tribune Business Editor

Minnesota and South Dakota corn crops will be 50 per cent of normal—with good luck, Paul F. Scheunemann, assistant general manager, Peavey Elevators, reported Thursday.

Scheunemann's report, based on survey of 225 country elevators in the two states, was made at the annual meeting of Minnesota Retail Furniture association in Nicollet hotel.

He said the two states will be fortunate to harvest a 50 per cent corn crop "even if adequate rainfall comes within the next few days."

**U.S. REPORT 'OUTDATED'**

The government's optimistic crop report issued Tuesday, he said, was "outdated by 12 days." His was a spot check with managers of elevators operated by the Peavey company.

**In predicting one of the smallest corn crops in years for Minnesota and South Dakota, he cited figures showing normal production and the peak production reached in 1944.**

Normally, Minnesota averages around 200,000,000 bushels of corn. In 1944 the crop was 253,399,000 bushels.

The normal South Dakota crop is 75,000,000 bushels, but during war years its production jumped to more than 100,000,000 bushels, hitting 140,292,000 in 1944.

**MOST SMALL GRAINS IN**

North Dakota raises comparatively little corn and, for the most part, uses its production for stock feed.

Scheuremann said, "In the main, the small grain crop was 'made' before the last heat wave started, but there has been some damage to the late-seeded small grain."

He told the furniture men the huge government exports of cereal grains—"200 times greater last year than in 1944"—have created market conditions that make it impossible to guess what will happen in price trends.

**Need for relief of the boxcar shortage is made more urgent**

50 Pct. Corn Dip
*Continued on Page 12*

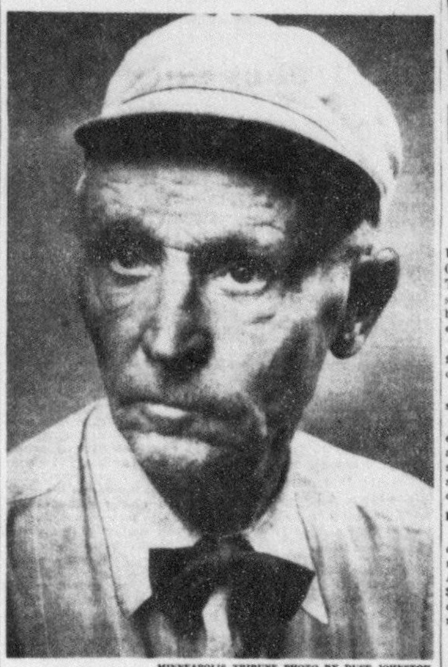

MINNEAPOLIS TRIBUNE PHOTO BY DUFF JOHNSTON
HIRAM AWDE ENDS HIKE OF 1,155 MILES
*"Nobody mistreated me—they just didn't pick me up"*

## *MAN, 72, ENDS 1,155-MILE HIKE*

By ED CRANE
Minneapolis Tribune Staff Writer

The little white-haired man, who has spent most of his 72 years peddling ice cream sandwiches at baseball games, tried not to fidget Thursday.

"Will the picture take long?" he asked. "See, these are just cheap 10-cent sun glasses. If I can get to the Five and Ten before it closes, they have good 50-cent ones. Then maybe I can get some work."

The man's name was Hiram H. Awde. His picture was going to be taken because he'd just walked to Minneapolis from San Antonio, Texas.

"Well, almost," he cautioned. "I did get a ride at Sioux City, Iowa."

**NOT SURE HOW FAR**

He wasn't quite sure just how far it was between San Antonio and Sioux City, but a map put the distance at 1,155 miles.

Awde wasn't sure, either, just when he'd started.

**"My memory's not as good as it used to be," he said, "but it was right after I got out of the hospital. That must be about 42 days ago."**

Awde was peddling ice cream last spring when a careless driver knocked him into a pile of stones. When he went into the hospital he weighed 155 pounds. When he came out nine weeks later, he weighed 91 and had lost the sight of one eye. The other was half covered by a cataract.

**REJECTED PENSION**

He tried to get help in Texas. "But on Friday they told me to come back Monday, and on Monday they said they'd have to talk it over," Awde said. "So I told them, 'Just forget it. I'll go up where my friends are and where I know people.'"

Awde has always been like that—independent.

When they offered him an old

1,155-Mile Hike
*Continued on Page 12*

## WIPING OUT WAR COSTS EASES PEACE

### Pact Bolsters Rule by Non-Communists; Rome Gets 23 Ships

WASHINGTON—(AP)—The United States wiped out a $1,000,000,000 debt owed by Italy Thursday in a stroke aimed at softening the peace treaty and bolstering the non-Communist government there.

The action waived all claims for payment of relief costs and occupation expenses.

It also provides Italy with 23 ships and makes other concessions.

Acting Secretary of State Robert Lovett signed a comprehensive accord for the United States but specified it is not to be considered a precedent for similar treatment of Germany and Japan.

**DE GASPERI BENEFITS**

The American government cancelled $523,000,000 Italy owes for relief supplies furnished by the American government along with $305,000,000 due for occupation costs and $175,000,000 for other miscellaneous claims.

**Government officials said that although no money changes hands in the transaction, it represents major help to the De Gasperi government in its long range battle to curb inflation and restore the country's war-wrecked economy.**

The other main points of the Italian-American agreement are:

- Transfer to the Italian government of 23 merchant ships, 15 of these American Liberty vessels designed to replace Italian ships seized by the United States and later lost in the war.
- Unfreezing of about $60,000,000 in locked Italian assets and invested properties once the Italian government certifies each owner as non-fascist.
- Announcement that Italy and the United States will begin detailed negotiations of a treaty of friendship, commerce and navigation in Rome early this autumn.
- Disclosure that the American government will redeem $10,000,000 to $15,000,000 in script issued to Italian prisoners for work done while held in the United States.
- Payment by the Italian government to the United States of $5,000,000 this year in order to settle claims of American nationals.

**CO-OPERATION PLEDGED**

In an agreement released simultaneously, Italy promised the United States, France and Britain it will co-operate in liquidating German assets in Italy.

**It will turn over the proceeds to a special account to be disposed of later as determined by these three powers.**

The state department said the Italian government had agreed to return to American owners their property in Italy "in good order" or to pay for damage under the formula laid down in the peace treaty.

## RENT CONTROL DATA SOUGHT

### 100 Groups to Get Plea to Back Law

More than 100 Minneapolis civic service, veterans', and fraternal organizations will be asked to submit evidence of the need for a city rent control and eviction-staying ordinance.

This was announced Thursday by William C. Simms, assistant to Mayor Hubert H. Humphrey, after the city council had taken a double short-cut to put into effect the ordinance drafted at Humphrey's request.

The council:

- Eliminated one preliminary step by giving unanimous consent to the introduction of the ordinance, sponsored by Aldermen Henry H. Bank and Harold Kauth. The proposed law was referred to the council committee on ordinances and legislation.
- Approved holding a public hearing on the ordinance at 10 a.m.

Rent Control
*Continued on Page 12*

**CAPITAL 'HET UP'? TOOK FED UP**

## *This Heat Business Can Get Pretty Dry*

By MARTIN TOOK
Minneapolis Tribune Staff Correspondent

WASHINGTON—The natives along the Potomac have been pretty amused the last few days about the complaints that the weather has been somewhat warm in the midwest.

Anybody in Washington knows that you do not mind having it get up to 100 in the shade in Minnesota because it is such a dry heat.

I have it on the authority of a cab driver who once traveled as far west as Baltimore that you can not even work up a sweat when it is 100 in the shade out in your country. This is because it is such dry heat.

I told the cab driver that once when I came into a small inheritance we had a piece of beefsteak at our house and we broiled it under a very dry flame and it came out quite well cooked. He said the beefsteak did not sweat, did it?

Martin Took

This subject is of great interest here right now, because Washington is having some heat, too, and it is not at all dry.

**DRY SUBJECT**

It is a little like living in the bottom of a soup kettle, except that no one in his right mind would make soup out of swamp water.

As soon as anybody finds out you are from the midwest they immediately tell you how you must be suffering here because you are used to such dry heat. They also tell you that you don't mind the cold winters out there because it is such dry cold.

**And if you try to argue with them about it they say what is all this talk about the corn drying up then?**

There are some advantages in being in Washington in hot weather, though, even if we do not have nice dry heat.

For one thing you do not have to wear any clothes. The city attorney has just been checking up on the laws about this, and he has discovered that as long as you are wearing a G-string or a fig leaf you cannot be thrown in the can for indecent exposure.

Another advantage is that there is almost always some interesting stuff going on when the weather is good and hot. Like for instance the other hot night when the cops were chasing a speeder and their car heated up and they lost him. The next thing they knew there he was, driving back to see what had happened to them. They got him that time.

### WEATHERMEN CAN'T TAKE IT ANY LONGER

WASHINGTON—(UP)—The mercury hit 96 degrees here Thursday, the highest mark since July 20, 1946, and guess who were among the first federal employes to be dismissed early.

A group of 150 weather bureau workers!

### Weatherman Says 'Continued Cool'

Temperatures will remain in comfortable ranges in the Upper Midwest today, the weather bureau predicted.

High for Minneapolis is expected to be 85, skies will be fair and light southerly winds will blow. Yesterday's maximum was 81 after an early-morning low of 58.

Minnesota's forecast is "fair and warmer." The Dakotas will be clear to partly cloudy with widely scattered showers in the afternoon. Temperatures will run from 80 to 90.

Temperature in Minneapolis at 11 p.m. yesterday was 67.



## RUSS THREATEN GREEK RUPTURE

### Diplomatic Break Near, Radio Warns

LONDON—(UP)—Russia has threatened to break off diplomatic relations with Greece unless "illegal actions by Greek police" are ended, Radio Moscow announced today.

**The broadcast accused Greek authorities of arresting and torturing persons connected with the Soviet embassy and other Russian establishments in Greece.**

The Russian commentator said the Soviet charge d'affaires in Athens had told the Greek foreign minister that such actions must end, adding that they were incompatible with the maintenance of diplomatic relations between Greece and Russia.

The broadcast, quoting Tass (official Soviet) news agency dispatches from Athens, claimed that persons having commercial ties with the Russian trade delegation had been "subjected to repressions."

**"Police authorities detain, question and sometimes arrest citizens simply because they visited the Soviet embassy," Moscow said.**

The broadcast repeated Tass' previous charge that Soviet officials in Greece are under police surveillance.

These actions, "obviously directed toward hindering the embassy," constitute "an attempt to prevent the maintenance of any economic, cultural, or other ties between the Soviet Union and Greece," the Russian commentator charged.

**TURN THE PAGES TO:**

## SEX CRIME PERIL CITED

### Lack of Decrease Worries Officials

By FRANCIS HATCH, JR.
Minneapolis Tribune Staff Writer

Sex offenses in Hennepin county still are being committed at the same high rate as they were during World war II, a survey conducted by the Minneapolis Tribune revealed Thursday.

County officials are extremely concerned, because they feel there should be a marked decrease in sex crimes noted at this time instead of a levelling off.

"I am particularly concerned about the number of young girls getting in trouble," Howard Hush, chief probation officer of Hennepin county, said.

"Young girls are running around with men 20 or 25 years old. It's not a healthy situation."

Hush attributed the moral letdown partly to the fact that young people are much more sophisticated and more informed on sex now than they used to be.

He said the only immediate remedy for the situation was to increase the number of police and police women.

"Our laws are more than adequate but enforcement isn't good; it can't be with so few members on the police force," he declared.

**Of the 11 persons charged with sex crimes in 1947 by the county attorney's office and found guilty by district court, only three were confined to prison.**

"District judges were given authority to grant probation in all cases up to capital punishment by the 1947 Minnesota state legislature, and that has changed our handling of cases somewhat," Judge John A. Weeks declared.

"Before, we used to get sex offenders out of circulation, but now we have started to allow probation when adequate medical reasons are given by accredited doctors.

"The district judges are alarmed about the continued high rate of sex cases and we are trying to help the matter all we can."

Similar concern was expressed by Michael J. Dillon, Hennepin county attorney.

He said that the number of

Sex Offenses
*Continued on Page 12*

## 25 HURT AS FIRE RAGES AT RESORT

### Ohio Blaze Levels Seven Concessions

BUCKEYE LAKE, OHIO—(UP)—An early morning fire roared through this central Ohio resort Thursday, leveling seven concessions with damage estimated at $200,000.

**Twenty-five persons were treated after inhaling smoke fumes from the blaze.**

Volunteer firemen in the area rushed to battle the flames until fire companies arrived from the nearby towns of Newark, Pataskala, Millersport, Hebron and Granville.

A restaurant waitress discovered the blaze in the wall between the restaurant and the bingo concession about 10 minutes after that part of the park closed at midnight. The fire spread rapidly to other wooden concession buildings in the immediate vicinity.

State highway patrolmen said 22 persons were given first aid at the scene, while three others were taken to Newark city hospital after they were overcome by smoke.



## U. S. CENSUS HITS 141,228,693; POPULATION SHIFTS WESTWARD

WASHINGTON—(AP)—The nation's population was swelled to 141,228,693 on the basis of latest estimates—a gain of about 9,160,000 since 1940—the census bureau reported Thursday night.

The figure, which includes American troops overseas, compares with estimates of approximately 430,000,000 for China, 414,000,000 for India and 193,000,000 for Russia.

The census bureau estimates, as of July 1, 1946, noted that a "great westward movement" has increased the civilian population of Pacific coast states by more than one-third since 1940.

The westward trek gave California the greatest numerical gain—2,485,000. Michigan was next with 797,000.

Although in the six-year period births exceeded deaths by about 9,160,000 over the country, 17 states lost civilian population.

"Large relative losses," were reported for North Dakota, down 16.3 per cent; South Dakota, down 14.9 per cent, and Montana, down 14.7 per cent.

The new estimate places California in third place among the states with an estimated 9,342,036 population, behind New York's 13,693,244 and Pennsylvania's 10,004,220.

The bureau's estimates of population, exclusive of armed forces overseas as of July 1, 1946, and changes from census figures of 1940, include:

Minnesota, 2,821,442, increase 29,142; Wisconsin, 3,168,158, increase 30,751; Iowa, 2,543,502, increase 5,234; North Dakota, 537,084, decrease 104,851; South Dakota, 547,664, decrease 95,297; Montana, 478,477, decrease 80,979.

THE WEATHER FORECAST
Cloudy tonight, Saturday. Colder Saturday
TEMPERATURES
Midnight 13 5 a.m. ...10 *10 a.m. ..13
1 a.m. ...10 6 a.m. ...10 *11 a.m. ..14
2 a.m. ... 9 7 a.m. ... 9 *Noon ...15
3 a.m. ... 9 8 a.m. ...10 *unofficial
4 a.m. ...10 9 a.m. ...12
Highest year ago, 22; lowest, 15.

# THE MINNEAPOLIS STAR



Vol. LXX—No. 56 MINNEAPOLIS, MINN., FRIDAY, JANUARY 30, 1948 Price 5 Cents



# Gandhi Slain While Praying

## Rochester Walkout Is Averted

### Kahler Corp., Union Heads OK 7-cent Pay Hike

ROCHESTER, MINN. — A strike which would have affected the Mayo clinic here was averted today when Kahler Corp. and CIO United Public Workers union negotiators agreed on a wage increase of 7 cents an hour.

Four hospitals, three hotels, a diet kitchen and a laundry would have been crippled by the walkout, which had been scheduled for midnight Sunday.

The clinic has no hospitals of its own. After examinations, it sends patients to St. Mary's or the Kahler institutions.

**"Mayo clinic will continue on normal schedule to examine patients and use hospitals as in the past," said H. J. Harwick, general manager.**

He said the clinic had not been affected by the strike threat except as it made arrangements to change examination schedules for persons who might require hospital care.

Agreement came at 3:45 a.m., after Kahler Corp. and union spokesmen spent the night conferring with Leonard W. Johnson, state labor conciliator, and his assistant, Harry Hanson.

**The 670 members of the Public Workers local must yet approve the agreement Gunhild Bjorklund, 28-year-old business agent said she expects the membership to approve.**

Increases would bring the wages of workers, including waiters, bus boys, cleaners, kitchen helpers and similar service workers, to a minimum of 73½ cents an hour. The increase goes back to Nov. 16, when the old contract expired.

The union had asked a 15-cent hourly boost. A 6½-cent compromise suggested by a state fact-finding commission, was rejected. The company's original offer was a 3½-cent raise.

**A strike would have forced the Kahler company to take emergency measures for caring for 420 patients in the Kahler, Worrall, Colonial and Currie hospitals operated by the firm.**

Officials had planned to start moving some patients to St. Mary's hospital today.

Sixteen AFL unions had promised to respect the CIO picket lines. The AFL unions represented 400 barbers, foodstuff drivers, plumbers and electricians who deal daily with the Kahler enterprises.

## 4 Feared Dead as Fire Sweeps Vermont Hotel

ST. ALBANS, VT.—(AP)—Four persons were feared dead and at least 12 others were injured today in a fire which swept the 136-year-old Jesse Welden Inn.

Damage was estimated at more than $200,000.

Firemen as yet have been unable to enter the ruins for a search, but four persons were listed as missing.

**Several of the nearly 100 guests in the five-story hotel escaped by beating their way through flames or leaping from windows into 16-below-zero temperatures. Two were seriously injured in leaps.**

The fire was discovered by Owner George E. St. Lorent, who ran through the hotel arousing guests before fleeing with his wife and daughter.

The hotel's register book was destroyed and a radio appeal was issued for guests to notify police and give their names.

## Pershing's Health Reported Unchanged

WASHINGTON — (UP) — An army spokesman said there was no basis to rumors that the condition of Gen. John J. Pershing, commander of United States forces in World War I, had taken a sudden turn for the worse.

His health was described as about the "same as usual" by his personal physicial, Maj. Gen. S. U. Marietta.

## Orville Wright's Condition Worse

DAYTON, OHIO — (AP) — Miami Valley hospital today announced that the condition of Orville Wright, 76-year-old co-inventor of the airplane, had taken a turn for the worse during the night and now was critical.

Wright suffered a heart attack Tuesday and lung congestion developed Thursday.

**LOCATION of a point 450 miles east, northeast of Bermuda where a British four-engine aircraft last radioed its base is indicated on this map. The plane, en route to Bermuda from the Azores, is believed lost.**

★ ★ ★ ★

## British Air Marshal on Lost Plane

LONDON—(UP)—Air Marshal Sir Arthur Coningham, wartime Allied air leader, and 28 others were missing today aboard a trans-Atlantic plane believed down about 400 miles east of Bermuda.

The British South American Airways Corp., operators of the Tudor transport, said Coningham was among the 23 passengers and six crewmen aboard the plane.

Coningham

It was last heard from at 11 p.m. (4 p.m. Minneapolis time) Thursday. It was less than two hours out from Bermuda at that time.

The passenger complement was made up of 16 Britons, one Swiss, two Czechs and four "stateless" persons, according to records of the line.

The transport, named the Star Tiger, was piloted by Capt. D. Colby.

**Ten American Superfortresses from Bermuda were searching over the area east of the island.**

Numerous ships in the area were diverted to join in the search, operators of the plane reported.

The plane was flying from the Azores to Bermuda. Some passengers may have remained in the Azores, the British Airway said.

**WRECKAGE OF U. S. PLANE BELIEVED SIGHTED IN ALPS**

By Associated Press

United States air force headquarters in Germany today reported wreckage of a plane was spotted in the lower French Alps, and feared another plane, presumably from the search party, had crashed nearby.

The first plane was believed to be a DC3 transport which disappeared Tuesday while en route from France to Italy.

**It carried three American women and five children, dependents of United States soldiers in the Trieste area.**

The air force said the crew chief of the missing DC3 was Sgt. Donald L. Cimmers, Dumont, Iowa.

Searchers said no signs of life were noticed around the wreckage of the DC3.

## Acrobat Held as 'Human Fly'

The "human fly" element in several recent burglaries was explained to police today after the arrest of a professional acrobat.

In custody with four other suspects is John Edward Gage, 22, 1151 Stevens avenue, who has been the man on the flying trapeze in many county fairs and carnivals.

**Police said Gage has confessed he scaled a fire escape to reach the roof, then dropped through a skylight at the American Legion club at 603 Second avenue S.....**

He and four companions split $565 in loot, he said.

Another suspect also professed some acrobatic ability in taking part in burglary of four business places in which radios were the loot.

He is Leonard Edwards, 25, who has been in jail in connection with holdups of a taxicab driver and of a South St. Paul tavern.

**Places robbed, detectives said, were the LaSalle Co., 1309 Nicollet avenue; Frank's Finer Furniture, 8 Fifth street N.; Turner Radio shop, 1200 Nicollet, and Cardozo Furniture Co., 26 Fifth street N.**

Continued questioning of Edwards resulted in the arrest of the other four suspects, said Detective Charles Wetherille and Art Olson of the robbery detail.

## On the Inside.



## CLU Calls School Huddle

### Union Instructors Approve Taking of Strike Vote

*Text of Teachers' Resolution: Page 16.*

A strategy meeting of representatives of two Minneapolis Federations of Teachers and of business agents for other union school employes has been set for 9 a.m. Tuesday at Central Labor temple.

The meeting was called today by George P. Phillips, president of Central Labor union, after union teachers voted unanimously Thursday night for a strike vote Monday at the labor temple.

**Approximately 750 of the 1,200 members of the men's local 238 and women's local 59 unanimously approved a resolution which protested shortening of spring and fall school terms by two weeks each.**

The action opposes policy adopted by the board of education Dec. 30 calling for a shortened school term and other economies to effect a cut of approximately $1,500,000 in the $13,000,000 school budget.

**Further attempts to reverse this action initiated by Roy Wier, labor-supported board member, were defeated by a tie vote at a board meeting Tuesday.**

While union teachers will cast their strike vote between 3 and 8 p.m. on Monday, union officials emphasized that a strike will not immediately go into effect.

* * *

Representatives from school unions are again expected to negotiate with school board members for a settlement. However, if these negotiations break down, then the unions are expected to put into effect the provisions of the resolution, they said.

## Paris Fire Burns 2,000 Tons of Friendship Food

PARIS —(UP)— Fire sweeping though a warehouse today destroyed 2,000 tons of food from the American Friendship Train.

The French government opened an inguiry into suspected sabotage.

The food was destined for the Paris area. It was stored in a warehouse of the French Welfare organization Entre'aide Francais.

**Loss was estimated at more than $5,000,000.**

Fire started shortly after midnight and whipped through the warehouse despite efforts of 400 firemen to extinguish it.

The newspaper France - Soir quoted the warehouse watchman as saying explosions preceded the fire, and telephone wires were cut.

## Case Against Jap War Leaders Ends

TOKYO—(AP)—Japan's conquerors concluded their case against Hideki Tojo and 24 other Japanese wartime leaders today, but the international tribunal decided to permit the defense to offer rebuttal testimony.

The prolonged trial began June 3, 1946.

Sir William Webb, tribunal president, denied a defense request for a 10-day recess for preparation of rebuttal testimony. Then, of 16 defense documents offered, the court accepted only two.

**STRAUSS MUSIC BANNED**

WARSAW, POLAND—(AP)—Poland barred the music of Richard Strauss today on grounds he embraced "the same ideology as Hitler."

★ ★ ★ ★

## RIOTING STARTS IN BOMBAY

BOMBAY, INDIA—(UP)—Riots started in Bombay tonight the moment the news arrived of the assassination of Mohandas Gandhi.

The riots broke out within a matter of minutes after the news of Gandhi's death was flashed to this teeming Indian metropolis.

**The riots started in three areas —all of them long festering crisis districts and strongholds of the Hindu extremist movement, the Hindu Mahasava group.**

The riots started in the Golpitha, Nagpada and Girgaum areas.

It was not immediately ascertained whether the trouble was launched by pre-arrangement, with the assassination of Gandhi being the signal for attacks by the Hindu extremist groups.

## Carnival Joys Tingle Into St. Paul

WINTER CARNIVAL MERRIMENT tingled throughout St. Paul today as King Boreas XI prepared to open the curtain tonight on the nine-day ice and snow extravaganza.

Before Vulcan and his cohorts storm the glistening ice palace in Como park Feb. 8, tens of thousands of winter sports lovers will see parades, beauty contests, sports events and mythical characters galore.

King Boreas, who is Edward C. Hampe until 8:15 p.m. today, will ascend his ice palace throne amid fireworks, bands and cheering throngs.

**In a brief ceremony, he will receive the royal scepter from his predecessor, Boreas Rex X, Robert Albrecht, and enjoin his subjects to observe winter carnival days in fun and merrymaking.**

Joining uniformed marching units at the ceremony will be princess of the four winds, snow princesses, visiting snow queens and supporting court attendants.

While St. Paul became the nation's fun capital today, it also captured a corner on the beauty market, as close to 100 visiting snow and fire queens arrived in the city by bus, train, plane and automobile.

Snow queens from 36 cities in Minnesota, North and South Dakota, Iowa, Wisconsin and Canada, will be guests of the carnival Saturday through Wednesday.

**The girls will ride on floats in the grand parade Saturday afternoon and will play a prominent part in other events.**

The queens are:

**FROM MINNESOTA** — Esther Lee Holt, Alexandria; Alice Larson, Anoka; Ardis Jennie, Bemidji, Patricia Maghan, Brainerd; Rosita Ellingson, Crookston; June May, Crosby-Ironton; Eleanor Beck, Detroit Lakes; Bonny Lou Jones, Duluth; Gloria Schuller, Faribault; Joyce Hagge, Fergus Falls; Marge Wildes, Hastings; Nancy Jo Jenkins, Hibbing; Phyllis Sullivan, International Falls; Ione Hall, Little Falls.

Others from Minnesota are Gail Bundy, Mankato; Patty McLane, Minneapolis; Patricia Reinhart, New Ulm; Elaine Florine, Red Wing; Carol Jean Dugstad, Rochester; Joyce Rosenberger, St. Cloud; Mary Lynch, Stillwater; Elizabeth Dwyer, Virginia; Joan Hathaway, Willmar, and Phyllis Wunderlich, Winona.

**FROM WISCONSIN** — Donna Snow, Ashland; Rosemary Greenwood, Chippewa Falls; Verity Ann Konitek, LaCrosse; Adele Bryan, Menomonie, and Marjorie Tillung, Rice Lake.

Others are Laurel Hubbard, Dubuque, Iowa; Corene Billings, Fargo, N. D.; Ilene Graff, Grand Forks, N. D.; Darlene Rose De Cory, Aberdeen, S. D.; Joyce Bannister, Seattle, Wash.; Carol Jean

Carnival
*Continued on Page 16*

★ ★ ★ ★

**MOHANDAS K. GANDHI, 78, SPIRITUAL LEADER OF HINDUS**
*Assassinated at prayer meeting in New Delhi*

## Streamliner Derailed; 25 Are Hurt

OGALLALA, NEB. — (AP)— All 18 cars and one of three power units of the crack Union Pacific City of Francisco streamliner were derailed 12 miles east of here early today.

Twenty-five persons were injured, seven seriously enough to require hospitalization here. A hospital spokesman said none of the injured was in critical condition.

The train was eastbound to Chicago.

**Five of the cars—two Pullmans, a diner, and two coaches—were on their sides or leaning.**

Apparently a broken wheel on one of the power units was the cause of the accident, a railroad spokesman said.

**14 HURT IN CRASH OF L. & N. TRAIN**

MITCHELLVILLE, TENN.—(AP)—Fourteen persons were injured early today when the Louisville & Nashville railroad's streamlined train Hummingbird, involved in its fourth accident in recent days, was in collision with a freight train on a siding near this town on the Tennessee-Kentucky border.

## Anne and Michael to Marry in Style

ST. MORITZ — (UP) — Prince Rene of Bourbon Parma said today that his daughter, Princess Anne, will be married to former King Michael of Romania in style in May and not in a winter resort "tourist entertainment" ceremony.

The prince said the marriage would take place either in Copenhagen, Paris, or Villefranche on the French Riviera.

Anne's father would not say whether he intends to see Pope Pius XII concerning the wedding. Vatican dispatches said that special dispensation must be obtained for the marriage because Michael is a Romanian Orthodox Catholic and Anne is a Roman Catholic.

**ASK ART GIFT DEFINITION**

NEW YORK—(AP)—Trustees of the Frick art collection, who have been offered six paintings and two busts owned by John D. Rockefeller, Jr., have asked the state supreme court to define their "rights and powers" to accept gifts.

## GANDHI RITES SATURDAY

NEW YORK—India's prime minister, Jawaharlal Nehru, describes the assasination of Mohandas K. Gandhi as a "great disaster," the all India radio said today. NBC monitored the broadcast.

The dominion leader announced the body will be cremated in accordance with Gandhi's wish, the broadcast said. The body will be taken from Birla house Saturday at 11:30 a.m. and cremation will be at 4 p.m. Nehru designated Saturday as a day of fasting and prayer for all India.

## Democrats Work on Substitute Tax Cut Bill

WASHINGTON — (AP)— Democrats hatched a plan today to use the GOP tax cut bill as the model for a substitute containing a $3,200,000,000 corporation tax.

Debate wa sin its second day with Republicans confident their bill, with its $6,500,000,000 in tax reductions, will pass unchanged on Monday. The Republican bill does not provide any new taxes.

**The Democratic leadership had just about given up any idea of putting President Truman's $40-a-head tax-cutting proposal before the house. Instead ,the search was on for a compromise.**

It was reported that one version considered would:

**IMPOSE a new $3,200,000,000 tax on corporations, as proposed by Mr. Truman.**

**INCREASE** individual exemptions from $500 to $600 (same as Knutson bill).

**APPLY** to all states the community property principle by which married couples may split their income for tax reporting purposes (same as Knutson bill).

**GRANT** percentage cuts ranging from 15 per cent for the lowest income to 5 per cent in the upper brackets (compared with Knutson's 30 to 15 per cent).

## Truman Calls Death of Gandhi Tragic

WASHINGTON—(AP)—President Truman, grieved over the assassination of Mohandas K. Ghandi, today was said to regard the Indian leader's death as "a tragic loss to the whole world."

Presidential Secretary Charles G. Ross thus described Mr. Truman's feelings upon hearing news of Gandhi's death.

Ross said the President will make a statement later in the day.

## Governor of S. D. to Seek Re-election

PIERRE, S. D. — (UP) — Gov. George T. Mickelson said today he will seek re-election to a second term as the state's chief executive.

The governor loosed a flurry of speculation last week when he announced he was reappraising the political situation as a result of the withdrawal of Senator Harlan J. Bushfield from the senatorial race.

## Hindu Assassin Fires Two Shots, Seized by Mob

From The Star's Wire Services

NEW DELHI, INDIA — Mohandas K. Gandhi was shot to death tonight by one of the Hindus he led to independence.

The frail and wizened little political and spiritual leader was the target of two bullets fired at close range at his prayer meeting on the lawn of the sumptuous Birla mansion, the estate of an Indian industrialist who long had supported Gandhi. Gandhi was 78.

**Gandhi was shot by a man giving the name of Ram Naturam.**

The assassin fired two shots from a revolver at Gandhi and then turned his gun on himself, firing a third shot which grazed his head.

The killer, a man about 32 years of age, was seized by Gandhi's hysterical followers who pummelled him severely before he was reached by police who drove the crowd back with rifles and fixed bayonets.

**It appeared that the assassin was a Hindu extremist—one of a group which has attacked Gandhi's policies of moderation and has called for a blood war of extermination against the Moslems.**

Only two weeks ago a bomb was exploded outside Birla house by a member of this group and Gandhi's followers long had feared for his life because of the threats of these extremists.

Eye-witnesses said that just before Gandhi fell he raised both his hands and folded them in a salute to his congregation.

The assassin was held incommunicado at police headquarters.

Sobbing bitterly, Gandhi's personal secretary, S. Kalyanam, told newsmen:

**"Bapu is dead."**

Bapu is the affectionate name for Gandhi. It means father. To millions of his followers, he was known as Mahatma, or great-souled one. His full name was Mohandas Karamchand Gandhi.

**Bystanders said Gandhi slumped forward as the third sot rang out. He seemed unconscious as he was carried to his quarters in Birla house. The secretary said death followed within a half hour.**

A crowd of several hundred persons formed about Birla house, ← many of them weeping.

**Bystanders said the assassin had mingled with the crowd at the prayer meeting. He was inconspicuous in khaki clothing which might have come from army surplus stores. Suddenly, it was said, he drew a pistol and fired.**

Death came less than a year after Gandhi achieved his life's main goal of independence from Great Britain for the teeming subcontinent of India.

However, Gandhi considered his triumph a failure because India and her 400,000,000 people were divided into separate dominions of India (Hindu) and Pakistan (Moslem).

**The partition resulted in bloody, destructive communal warfare between Moslems on one side and Hindus and Sikhs on the other.**

It was in an effort to end the bloodshed that Gandhi undertook this month the last of his many fasts.

After five days in which he threatened to starve himself to death, Gandhi broke his fast Jan. 18 on the "pledge and counsel" of friends in both dominions.

He said they had assured him of "complete unbroken friendship" between all communities.

During the tense days of his fast, some of the more militant shouted bitterly in the streets and before his living quarters:

"Let Gandhi die."

But there was every indication that this was the view of a tiny minority, embittered by the communal warfare.

**Shortly after the fast, a bomb exploded near Gandhi during a prayer meeting, also in the Birla mansion estate, but did no harm. A Hindu was arrested.**

Gandhi after the bomb incident, asked police to be lenient with the young Hindu who threw it.

"We should not harbor hatred," he said. "I will request the police not to trouble him but to have compassion toward him and make him see the righteous path."

Even as he spoke, the spiritual leader was too weak to walk from the effects of his long fast.

Gandhi
*Continued on Page 16*

★ ★ ★ ★

### Other stories and pictures on life of Gandhi:

**Gandhi, Hated by Many, a Saint to Millions, Page 4.**
**Record of Fasts, Page 4.**
**Highlights of Career, Page 7.**
**"Dangerous to be Good," says Shaw, Page 7.**
**Death shocks Hindu students at "U," First page, second section.**
**Pictures on Pages 4 and 7 and on back page.**

## Denham Says Labor Law a 'Balance'

The administrator for much of the Taft-Hartley law said in Minneapolis today that he is "tremendously encouraged by the attitude of employers and labor."

Robert Denham, general counsel of national labor relations board, said in an interview that "both sides are recognizing they are much better off when they find a meeting ground for frank discussions."

**Denham said the new federal labor-management relations law helped provide that meeting ground.**

"The reaction of employers indicates to me that they are taking this law as a new tool in the conduct of their businesses," Denham said as he prepared to address the state meeting of Minnesota Employers association at Radisson hotel.

"The parties are forgetting their old fights," Denham said. "Employers see this law as a balance wheel. It is an equalizer for employers and employes."

**Meanwhile, the man who is selling the "Voice with a Smile" was to tell Minnesota employers today some secrets of the Bell telephone system's success in public relations.**

He is Keith S. McHugh, New York, vice president in charge of public relations for American Telephone & Telegraph Co.

McHugh, a speaker at the Minnesota Employers association meeting, said in an interview:

**"First, business and the public must understand each other.**

"Second, a business must do things the public likes.

"Doing what people like every time we have the chance is the foundation of good public relations and we cannot shut our eyes to it."

**He said that the courtesy of telephone operators "is no substitute for efficiency" but it "can add enormously to it."**

McHugh advocated that employers adopt "overtones of service" as extra benefits and courtesies to their customers and clients.

Licensing electrical contractors and electricians restricts free enterprise, one conference was told by W. J. Donald, director of the National Electrical Manufacturers' association.

**Minnesota is one of eight states which has a license system to which objected.**

"Such licensing is inherently restrictive and is too often conceived and administered with the objective of limiting free enterprise," he said.

## Delaware Papers to Increase Price

WILMINGTON, DEL. — (AP) — The News-Journal Co. today announced it will increase the price of the Wilmington Morning News and the Journal Every Evening from three to four cents, effective Monday, Feb. 2.

The company said the step was taken "to help meet the greatly increased cost of publication."



**NO BAR TO ARREST, SAYS COURT**

## *No Private Roads for Drunks*

A drunken driver is prohibited by state law from driving a motor vehicle "anywhere" within the state—even on a private road.

The Minnesota supreme court, in a unanimous decision written by Justice Frank T. Gallagher, so ruled today in sustaining conviction of Robert F. Carroll of Fergus Falls.

Carroll, sentenced to pay a $75 fine or serve 30 days in jail, contended that application of the statute is limited to operation of vehicles on public highways.

**Justice Gallagher said "it was clearly the intention of the legislature to make it a crime for any habitual user of narcotic drugs or any person under the influence of intoxicating liquor or narcotic drugs to drive or operate any vehicle 'anywhere' within the state."**

"The constitutionality of such legislation in this state has been approved by this court, which also has recognized the menace and hazard to society caused by a person driving an automobile while intoxicated," the decision said.

"A motor vehicle can be a dangerous instrumentality when operated by a drunken person, not only because of the jeopardy to life and safety of the driver himself, but, more important, because of the hazard to the public at large."

**Showers and Mild**
U. S. Weather Bureau Forecast
Cloudy, High of 70
TEMPERATURES
Details on Page 15

# Minneapolis Morning Tribune

Vol. LXXXI—No. 357 Copyright, 1948, Minneapolis Star and Tribune Company. MINNEAPOLIS, MINN., SATURDAY, MAY 15, 1948 Price 5 Cents

**PICTURE STORY**
*Mammoth Band to Perform Sunday*
**SEE PAGE 8**

# GUARDS MOVE INTO STRIKE AREA

## *Truman Recognizes New Jewish State*

### *Zionists Elated, Arabs Stunned as U.S. Power Backs Israel*

By JOHN HIGHTOWER

WASHINGTON—(UP)—President Truman, in a move that surprised the world, Friday night recognized the new Jewish state of Israel in Palestine a few minutes after it was proclaimed.

The news caused intense elation among the Zionists, stunned the Arabs and threw the United Nations into turmoil.

The action placed the great weight of American prestige behind the claim of the Jews to govern the homeland they have carved out for themselves in the Holy Land.

**42-WORD STATEMENT**

In 42 fateful words, Mr. Truman proclaimed:

"This government has been informed that a Jewish state has been proclaimed in Palestine and recognition has been requested by the provisional government thereof.

**"The United States recognizes the provisional government as the de facto authority of the new state of Israel."**

(The use of the legalistic term "de facto authority" is common in such instances where a new government is in process of creation but is still provisional. It means simply that the United States recognizes that the government of Israel is in fact the ruling authority of the territory in question.

("De jure" recognition means recognition of a government as the legally constituted authority.)

**'PRAYER ANSWERED'**

The news of recognition created a sensation in the United Nations assembly hall in New York. It came while the U.N. was rejecting a United States proposal to set up a trusteeship type regime for Jerusalem.

Dr. A. H. Silver, chairman of the American section of the Jewish agency, threw up his hands in elation at the word from Washington.

**"This is what we have been praying for—marvelous!" he exulted.**

Soviet delegate Andrei Gromyko lashed the United States for a Palestine policy "devoid of principle and directed against the United Nations as a whole."

**BRITISH SILENT**

Britain's U.N. representative, Sir Alexander Cadogan, had no comment. His government has ended its mandate in Palestine and is pulling out its troops from the country.

On Capitol Hill in Washington, Sen. George (D., Ga.), former chairman of the senate foreign relations committee, told a reporter:

**"I suppose the step is an advisable one. I can conceive of no valid reason why the President should not recognize the new Jewish nation as a de facto state."**

A short time later, Guatemala's United Nations delegate announced that Guatemala formally recognizes the new Jewish state of Israel.

Mr. Truman's action came while several hundred persons—some cheering, some crying—watched the first official raising of the flag of Israel in Washington.

The ceremony was at the graystone building in the capital's embassy district where the Jewish

U. S. Recognition
*Continued on Page Five*

AP Wirephoto
FR. EDWARD J. FLANAGAN
*Famed priest dies*

## FR. FLANAGAN DIES IN BERLIN

### Heart Attack Kills Boys Town Founder

BERLIN—(UP)—Msgr. Edward J. Flanagan, 61, the priest who founded Boys Town, Neb., died today of a heart attack at an army station hospital.

The tall, amiable priest collapsed of a heart attack at Harnach house, a Berlin dinner club, Thursday night. He was rushed to the 279th station hospital in serious condition.

With him when he died were Patrick Nerton, his assistant at Boys Town; Patrick J. Moriarity, Shakopee, Minn., the European command's top German youth organizer, and several doctors and nurses.

**Fr. Flanagan arrived here May 9 to make a two-week study of conditions among young people in the American zone of Germany. Before that, he made a month's study of Austrian youth problems.**

Born July 13, 1886, in Roscommon, Ireland, Fr. Flanagan was educated in the United States, Austria and Italy. He was ordained in the Catholic priesthood in 1912, and was sent to St. Patrick's church, O'Neill, Neb., the same year.

**A year later he was transferred to Omaha. In 1914, he started the Workingmen's hotel, where he worked with jobless and destitute men.**

But Fr. Flanagan was not satisfied with working with men who had become gamblers, dope addicts and drunkards. He wanted to prevent men from sinking to these depths by training them in their youth. Boys were the answer to his problem.

He borrowed $90 to pay a month's rent on a two-story building. He took two boys from the juvenile court and three other homeless lads from the streets. That was the start of what later became Boys Town, a city for little men.

The project grew as funds increased. Buildings were constructed and more and more boys were taken in. They were boys of every race, creed and color.

He was honored by the Catholic church for his work. He was named a monsignor in 1937, but he remained "Father Flanagan," the name he liked best.

### *Bombers Attack Jewish Port; Arab Armies Begin March*

FROM LATE DISPATCHES

TEL AVIV, ISRAEL — Air raiders bomber this all-Jewish city at about dawn today.

Some 10 bombs were dropped on Tel Aviv by two aircraft described as bombers and accompanied by two small fighters.

One Jew was killed and three were hospitalized.

Jewish army aircraft took to the skies a few minutes after the enemy planes whizzed over the rooftops at an estimated altitude of 300 feet.

**GUNS OPEN UP**

Anti-aircraft guns opened up throughout the port area and in Sarona, the Tel Aviv suburb which will be the capital of Israel. The bombing planes disappeared toward the sea after the raid.

**Meanwhile Arab armies moved from Trans-Jordan to "liberate the Holy Land from Zionism," an official Trans-Jordan communique announced.**

Earlier the Egyptian government announced it had ordered its armed forces to enter Palestine. Haganah, the Jewish army, said its forces have captured the strategic north Palestine port city of Acre.

These developments came as Britain ended its mandate over the Holy Land and Jewish leaders proclaimed a new state.

**CUNINGHAM LEAVES**

The death of the British mandate was signalized by the departure of Sir Alan Cunningham, high commissioner, from Haifa in the royal navy cruiser Euryalus.

**The chief function of the British now in Palestine is to complete the evacuation of their troops. This has been ordered by Aug. 1, as directed by parliament.**

An Egyptian newspaper report said two columns of regular Egyptian forces crossed into the Holy Land at dawn yesterday.

**'TO RESTORE SECURITY'**

Premier Mahmoud Fahmy-Nokrashy Pasha said in a statement to be broadcast to the nation that the invasion was ordered to "restore security and order" in Palestine and end "the massacres perpetrated by terrorist Zionist gangs."

**Syrian and Lebanese troops also are poised on the northern border of the Holy Land, apparently awaiting an invasion zero hour, a Damascus dispatch said.**

Haganah reported that Syrian armored forces already were in-

Egypt Force
*Continued on Page Five*

### *'Accused' Official Resigns U. S. Post*

WASHINGTON — (Special) — Herbert W. Parisius, recently accused in congress of approving shipments of potential war materials to Russia, resigned Friday as a director in the commerce department's international trade office.

The official said he is leaving the government post because he is tired. He said he plans to enter private business after a vacation in his native Wisconsin. He has denied charges made against him on the house floor.

## STASSEN, DEWEY SET DEBATE DATE

### Candidates to Air Views on Communism on Network Monday

By WILLIAM H. MYLANDER
Minneapolis Tribune Staff Correspondent

PORTLAND, ORE. — Presidential aspirants Harold E. Stassen of Minnesota and Gov. Thomas E. Dewey of New York agreed Friday to air their views on communism in a nationwide radio debate Monday night.

Details of the first debate between two top presidential candidates were announced last night by the Mutual Broadcasting system. MBS said that Dewey and Stassen will be on the air from 8 p.m. to 9 p.m. (Minneapolis time).

The broadcast will originate in Portland, Ore., where both men are seeking the state's 12 delegates to the GOP convention.

All four major networks are expected to carry the debate.

The debaters will occupy separate rooms. There will be no platform and no audience, and the terms finally agreed to provide the debate will be in the privacy of the broadcasting studio.

The issue will be: "Shall communism be outlawed?" It has been a point of heated controversy, with Stassen taking the affirmative, Dewey the negative.

Agreement on the debate was finally reached by representatives of the two candidates after Dewey had ducked and run earlier yesterday when he met Stassen on the old Oregon trail.

**FUNNY INCIDENT**

It was one of the funniest incidents in political history, and could prove costly to Dewey in the Oregon primary next Friday.

**There was little doubt that it would cost him the votes of the 738 inhabitants of Cascade Locks, four miles above Bonneville dam on the Columbia river highway.**

What happened was this:

Stassen, who has been badgering Dewey to appear with him in joint debate, left Portland at 8 a.m. for a 90-mile campaign swing by bus to the Dalles, where his chartered plane waited to fly him here 248 miles for an evening speech.

Dewey, also traveling by bus, was en route to Portland after a morning rally in Hood River. (Stassen spoke there at noon, being introduced by the mayor who said, "Earlier this morning we listened to a candidate. Now we are about to hear the candidate.")

**HOLIDAY DECLARED**

Russell H. Nichols, mayor of Cascade Locks, had breakfast with Dewey at Hood River, and on Dewey's promise to make a brief stop, declared a school holiday in his own hamlet.

**When Stassen's bus encountered the crowd of school children and adults at Cascade Locks, the candidate ordered an unscheduled stop.**

After spending 10 minutes signing autographs and joking with the crowd, Stassen re-boarded his bus and was about to proceed when the town's fire engine, escorting the Dewey bus, appeared from the opposite direction.

**DRIVER SPEEDS AWAY**

"Here comes Dewey," someone yelled.

With a big grin, Stassen and the score of correspondents piled out of the bus again and the candidate resumed his autographing.

Newsreel cameramen jumped

Stassen, Dewey
*Continued on Page Five*

MINNEAPOLIS TRIBUNE AERIAL PHOTO BY D. H. JEWETT
SCENE OF THURSDAY'S PICKET-POLICE MEAT STRIKE CLASHES WAS ALMOST DESERTED FRIDAY
*Stock pens were vacant, streets were nearly empty at Swift & Co. South St. Paul plant; circled area is Concord street and Grand avenue, where pickets battled law officers Thursday*

BAYONET CHARGE
*Guardsman in drill*

### *Tavern Owner Sues Village in Shooting*

DULUTH — (AP) — Ralph Grytness, 47, Proctor, Minn., tavern operator who was wounded by bandits during a robbery Jan. 24, is suing the village of Proctor for $20,000.

Grytness blames the village for the robbery, charging that it was caused by the village selling liquor to his minor assailants.

## HOUSE CALLS STRIKE PROBE

### Dieter to Testify at Chicago Hearing

WASHINGTON—(UP)—Chairman Hoffman (R., Mich.) of the house expenditures committee announced Friday that Reps. Harvey (R., Ind.) and Manasco (D., Ala.) will go to Chicago with him May 20 to investigate the packing house strike.

**Among witnesses to be called, Hoffman said, are Captain George Barnes, head of the Chicago police department's labor detail; Sheriff Norman Dieter of South St. Paul, and acting police chief Henry Boesen of Omaha, Neb.**

He listed others as Ralph Helstein, national president of the CIO United Packinghouse Workers of America, and representatives of the packing houses and of the American Legion.

Hoffman told the house yesterday that Republican presidential candidate Harold E. Stassen might well look into labor troubles in his own state of Minnesota.

Citing violence in the packing house strike at South St. Paul, Hoffman said that workers' appeals to Gov. Luther W. Youngdahl for protection were unavailing.

**Hoffman said Stassen has been critical of the Taft-Hartley labor act and suggested "he go home and talk a little to his own governor about law enforcement and violence, the destruction of property and labor relations generally."**

Later Rep. MacKinnon (R., Minn.) told the house that Minnesota has "an enviable record" in labor relations and has done "a much better job" than Michigan in this respect.

**GLAMOR GALORE**

### *'Mr. Minnesota' Wins Title for Big Arms, Back*

"Mr. Minnesota" has the best-developed back and arms in the state. He is also the best-developed medium-sized male in the state.

Ralph Krasky, 1335 Fifth street NE., won all the above honors in a muscle-flexing competition for the "Mr. Minnesota" title, held Friday night at Minneapolis YMCA.

**But there were plenty of other "best" titles for the trunk clad young men.**

Robert Battershell, 656 Short street, St. Paul, took honors for the best-developed short man and the best-developed abdominal muscles.

Best-legs title went to Miles Sackett, 4139 Sixteenth avenue S., who also won the best-chest competition.

Manley Kiefer, 1654 Xerxes avenue N., was named best-developed tall man, and Michael Hibben, 2217 Seventeenth avenue S., swept the field for "most muscular" honors.

## *UNION SEEKS STRIFE HALT*

National guard troops moved into the strike-bound areas of South St. Paul and Newport early today.

**At the same time, leaders of the CIO United Packinghouse Workers union sent out orders aimed at avoiding further violence in the meat strike, and new attempts at settlement of the two-month dispute reportedly were scheduled for Chicago today.**

One guard battalion was dispatched from the Minnesota State fairgrounds to each of the struck meat plants—Swift and Armour in South St. Paul and Cudahy at Newport.

Guard officials refused to divulge how many men are involved, but it was unofficially estimated that some 2,000 were deployed from the fairgrounds. Each of the three battalions had about 30 motorized units.

First troops arrived in South St. Paul at 12:50 a.m today. At the entrance to the Swift plant, at Concord street and Grand avenue, pickets booed, but there was no other disturbance.

**CALLED AFTER RAID**

The guard was called out yesterday by Gov. Luther W. Youngdahl after two days of strike violence culminating in a raid by more than 200 men on the Cudahy plant shortly before midnight Thursday.

Before the movement of guard ground forces started, five P51 Mustang planes bearing national guard insignia flew low over the packing plants. The 109th guard air squadron is based at Holman field, St. Paul.

Guard units also were on their way to the fairgrounds staging area last night from Brainerd and Moorhead.

**Commander of all the guard troops is Col. Lester A. Hancock, Appleton, a veteran of both World wars.**

But under terms of Youngdahl's order—which did NOT call for martial law—the troops will be under immediate direction of Sheriffs Reuben Granquist of Washington county and Norman Dieter of Dakota county. The purpose of the guard call was to "give aid and assistance to civil authority."

Youngdahl also reported late yesterday that he will order the guard to duty at the Albert Lea, Minn., Wilson Co. plant, where a new outbreak of violence occurred.

**The guard will be sent to Albert Lea as soon as the Freeborn county sheriff signs a statement requesting aid to enforce the law.**

About 1,000 members of the CIO United Packinghouse Workers union are on strike there, and Mayor Lyle J. Ostrander said yesterday pickets had overturned a car near the Wilson plant and threw eggs at policemen who attempted to halt them.

**SHERIFF ILL**

Ostrander, who came to St. Paul yesterday to ask the governor's aid, said the formal request will be signed by Sheriff Hjalmer B. Wulff, who is confined to his home by illness.

Similar statements were signed yesterday by Sheriff Dieter of Dakota county, scene of the South St. Paul violence, and Sheriff Granquist of Washington county, in which Newport is located.

**After a meeting yesterday afternoon with Ralph Helstein of Chicago, international president of the UPW, Glenn Chinander, UPW field representative here, announced that pickets have been directed to obey all court orders and picket peacefully.**

Chinander issued a statement in South St. Paul saying "the union regards the calling of the nation-

Troops Move
*Continued on Page Five*

### PLANE LANDS IN RIVER, PAIR SWIMS ASHORE

A small airplane made a forced landing in the Mississippi river near St. Paul Friday afternoon, forcing the pilot and passenger to swim ashore. They were uninjured.

Harold Bradshaw, 21, 355 Maria avenue, St. Paul, and Robert Moody, 23, 140 E. Jenks avenue, St. Paul, were returning from a flight to Superior, Wis. Bradshaw is a pilot instructor for McFadden Flying Service, and Moody is a student pilot.

The plane sank quickly but the two men climbed out and swam to shore.

## MINNESOTA BEDLAM Attendants Hoe Hard Row

*This is the third of a series of articles describing conditions in Minnesota mental hospitals. Geri Hoffner, Tribune writer, and Arthur Hager, Tribune photographer, visited all of the seven state hospitals.*

By GERI HOFFNER
Minneapolis Tribune Staff Writer

To the patient in any of Minnesota's seven mental hospitals, the attendant is the most important person in the world.

What the attendant does or doesn't do can mean the difference between recovery and a lifetime in a state institution. Of all the members of the hospitals' staffs, he is closest to the patient.

**He is with the patient constantly every day; he supervises every activity.**

But few jobs give a worker less job satisfaction than that of an attendant in the state institutions.

The pay is low, working conditions are unpleasant and living facilities are poor.

For example, an attendant in the lowest civil service classification earns $130 a month. (As of July 1, a cost-of-living increase will raise him to $140.)

If he lives on the hospital grounds, $30 is deducted from that amount. In addition, 5 per cent is subtracted for his state retirement fund. After other deductions are made, he takes home about $90 a month.

**Many superintendents point out bitterly that even prison guards earn more than attendants. Starting wage for a guard is $177. Certainly an attendant, on whose skill and understanding the patient's mental health may depend, should be paid as much as a guard, the superintendents reason.**

"We take a chance on every attendant we hire," one superintendent admitted. "Unwillingly we have hired inebriates, dope fiends, drifters and people who could get no other employment."

**MUST SUPPLEMENT PAY**

A superintendent of nurses said, "Some of the attendants here are so far below par mentally that they literally cannot understand directions given to them."

There are attendants, however, whose loyalty and devotion to their work is far above what their salary indicates.

**A supervisor of male wards told us about one promising young attendant, a former service man, who had to pay $60 a month rent from his meager salary.**

"He has another job which

Mental Patients
*Continued on Page Eight*

## Late News on Inside Pages

- Stocks leaped upward $1 to $7 in the fastest trading in eight years. Market value of listed stocks rose $1,700,000,000 in New York....Page 2
- Rep. Blatnik charges bill perils unions....Page 3
- President Truman's recognition of the new Jewish state throws United Nations assembly into turmoil....Page 5
- DFL county conventions deal stiff jolts to third party hopes of capturing DFL machinery for Henry A. Wallace....Page 9
- University of Minnesota regents name Maynard E. Pirsig, 'U' law professor, as new dean of the law school Page 9

**OTHER FEATURES, STORIES INSIDE**

*PICTURE STORY:* Bands .... 8 Bjornson ....6 Your Mind ... 7
Washington 2, 3 Amusements ..4 *JUST ASK* .... 7
Labor ....3 Foreign ....4 Comics ....10 Sports ....11-12
*MINNESOTA MEMO* .... 6 Radio ....10 Markets ..13, 14
Editorials ....6 'Round World 7 *GRIN* .... 9 *JONES* ....10

HIGH 65
U.S. Weather Bureau Forecasts
Partly Cloudy
TEMPERATURES
Details on Page 20

# Minneapolis Morning Tribune

Vol. LXXXII—No. 163 Copyright, 1948, Minneapolis Star and Tribune Company. MINNEAPOLIS, MINN., WEDNESDAY, NOVEMBER 3, 1948 Price 5 Cents



# TRUMAN TAKES SLIM LEAD IN CLOSE U.S. BALLOT FIGHT

## Democrats Win Senate

### CANDIDATES LEAD IN 10 HOT BATTLES

**Seven Victories Are Held Certain; Three Others Close**

By WILLIAM P. STEVEN
Managing Editor of The Minneapolis Tribune

The Democratic party quite probably has won control of the United States senate for the next two years.

Through a long distance telephone conference call, the Minneapolis Tribune talked with editors in 10 states where—like Minnesota—there were hotly contested senate races.

In seven of them—Illinois, Colorado, Iowa, New Mexico, Oklahoma, Tennessee, and West Virginia—editors with whom the Tribune talked interpreted the partial returns as meaning a victory for the Democratic candidate.

In three other states—Wyoming, Kentucky, and Montana—the races were closer, but the Democratic candidates were ahead.

In Minnesota, Democrat Hubert H. Humphrey was the winner.

**The trends indicate that the Democrats may have a majority as high as 53 to 43 in the senate. The Republicans now have a majority—51 Republicans and 45 Democrats.**

Returns at a.m. indicate these men are elected:

**Democrats—17**

Sparkman of Alabama.
McClellan of Arkansas.
Johnson of Colorado.
Russell of Georgia.
Gillette of Iowa.
Ellender of Louisiana.
Long of Louisiana.
Humphrey of Minnesota.
Eastland of Mississippi.
Broughton of North Carolina.
Kerr of Oklahoma.
Green of Rhode Island.
Maybank of South Carolina.
Kefauver of Tennessee.
Johnson of Texas.
Robertson of Virginia.
Neely of West Virginia.

**Republicans—3**

Smith of Maine (elected Sept. 13).
Dworshak of Idaho.
Saltonstall of Massachusetts.

Returns too fragmentary to indicate: Delaware, Kansas, Michigan, Nebraska, New Hampshire, New Jersey, Oregon, South Dakota, Wyoming, Montana.

In the other races, editors in those states told the Tribune:

**ILLINOIS:** Paul H. Douglas, Democratic candidate for senate, will have a projected majority of 509,000 in Cook county, and on previous performance this will be large enough to overcome the normal downstate Republican majorities. Adlai Stevenson, Democrat, has a projected majority of 589,000 in Cook county, and presumably will defeat Governor Dwight H. Green, Republican.

**IOWA:** Guy Gillette, Democrat, former senator, has a wide margin over Sen. George H. Wilson, Republican. The state will be close for Dewey.

**KENTUCKY:** Democrat Virgil Chapman had a 19,000 majority over Sen. John Sherman Cooper, Republican, but Cooper is expected to gain 15,000 votes when as much of the ninth congressional district is reported as has been reported in areas where Chapman had a lead. If Truman's majority is more than 50,000 (it was 77,000 at the time of Chapman's 19,000 majority) Cooper's defeat is regarded as likely.

**NEW MEXICO:** Former secretary of agriculture Clinton Anderson had a three-to-two lead over former secretary of war Partick J. Hurley, Republican, on one-fourth of the precincts. The selection of precincts was regarded as adequately selective by the local editor to fix a trend.

LUTHER YOUNGDAHL
*Holds wide margin*

HUBERT HUMPHREY
*Race narrows*

## HUMPHREY LEAD CALLED DECISIVE

By WALLACE MITCHELL
Minneapolis Tribune Staff Writer

Hubert H. Humphrey appeared early today to have won the state's senate seat from Joseph H. Ball.

The youthful Minneapolis mayor, on the basis of scattered and far from complete returns, stormed into a lead in his fight for the post held by Ball since 1940. The seat is considered vital for continued senate control in congress.

Early returns, heavily weighted in favor of Humphrey by the speedy tabulation of St. Paul's vote-machines, showed in 499 of Minnesota's 3,738 precincts:

| | |
|---|---|
| Humphrey | 158,104 |
| Ball | 91,098 |

Humphrey's strenuous barnstorming through the state's traditional Republican rural areas appeared, however, to have paid winning dividends. The Democratic-Farmer-Labor party standard was riding a strong two-to-one edge over Ball in the farm belt.

BALL HOPES FADE

Ball had pinned his victory hopes on holding down Humphrey's margin in the three big industrial vote cinters of Minneapolis, St. Paul and Duluth and overcoming that lead in the country precincts.

The scattered, early returns showed him falling on both counts.

Labor's opposition to Ball for his Taft-Hartley act support gave Ball a heavy handicap.

**The rural vote virtually sealed his defeat and assured Humphrey of becoming the first "big-city" mayor ever to win a higher Minnesota office.**

In addition to drawing a heavy vote to himself, Humphrey appeared to be drawing support to President Truman.

CAMPAIGN BITTER

The Ball-Humphrey battle was one of the fiercest in Minnesota senatorial history. Wrapped within it was most of the campaigning for and against President Truman and Thomas E. Dewey.

Humphrey based his campaign on flogging the record of Ball and the Republicans on farm legislation and foreign policy. The Minneapolis mayor backed flexible price supports, expanded soil conservation appropriations and less restriction on the rural electrification administration's use of funds. He urged no changes in present laws on taxation of farm co-operatives.

## YOUNGDAHL'S VOTE CLIMBS

**Schmahl, Burnquist Lag in Early Count**

Republican incumbents early today narrowed the leads compiled in initial returns by Democratic-Farmer-Labor candidates for Minnesota constitutional offices.

More than four hours after the polls closed, Gov. Luther W. Youngdahl, Republican, pulled within 8,000 votes of his DFL opponent, Charles L. Halsted. Halsted's early margin was built up chiefly on Ramsey county votes.

Orville E. Olson, Progressive, was a poor third.

SCHMAHL BEHIND

There were two surprises in early returns. Two DFL candidates with Progressive party backing were ahead in their races.

George W. MacDonald, 36, led his 81-year-old Republican opponent, Julius A. Schmahl, by 7,000 votes in the state treasurer contest. Schmahl is seeking his 11th term.

**Francis M. Smith held a 500-vote edge over J. A. A. Burnquist, Republican, the incumbent attorney general.**

Republican Mike Holm, who has been secretary of state since 1920, strengthened his bid for re-election with an early 8,000-vote margin over Koscie H. Marsh.

In the lieutenant governor race, C. Elmer Anderson, Republican incumbent, led John T. McDonough, DFL, by 13,000 votes. The Progressive party candidate, Robert W. Duel, trailed far behind.

Rollin G. Johnson, Republican incumbent, trailed Clifford C. Peterson, DFL, in the state railroad and warehouse commission balloting by 27,000 votes.

Johnson was appointed by Gov. Youngdahl to fill a vacancy on the commission caused by the death of Ray P. Chase a few days after Chase had defeated Johnson in the Republican primary.

Incumbents Oscar R. Knutson and Thomas F. Gallagher took early leads over E. Luther Melin and John S. McGrath for two associate justice seats in the state supreme court.

### Second Victim Dies

DETROIT LAKES, MINN.—(AP)—John Guttu, Detroit Lakes, second victim of a Friday automobile accident, died in a hospital here Tuesday. Ralph Morken, 23, who suffered a broken neck in the same accident, died Monday.

## DEWEY STILL CONFIDENT OF VICTORY

**GOP Nervous at Truman's Lead in First Returns**

By RICHARD WILSON
Chief of Minneapolis Tribune Washington Bureau

NEW YORK—Confident of victory, Thomas E. Dewey waited for the election returns Tuesday night in his suite at the Roosevelt hotel, surrounded by friends.

In various parts of the hotel old associates of the New York governor had taken suites to await the outcome, and the personal staff of the Republican nominee also was gathered together.

ANXIETY GROWS

Anxiety spread in the Dewey headquarters as election reports showed the Republican trailing in states like Connecticut and Massachusetts, so important to a GOP victory.

In anticipation of a Dewey victory, huge radio and television installations were set up in headquarters in the Roosevelt hotel.

**But the early returns failed to show, as the Deweyites expected, an early victory.**

The television and radio setups were mainly to carry the voice and face of a new president-elect, but at midnight in New York there still was doubt of a considerable nature.

Dewey was in his hotel suite, listening to the returns. A victory statement had been prepared. But everyone held off with the unexpected closeness of the early vote.

DINE WITH STRAUS

Two blocks away in the Biltmore hotel, Democratic headquarters, there was jubiliation over resident Truman's good early showing. The crowds of $500 contributors to the Truman campaign cheered as each surprising

Dewey
*Continued on Page Eight*

## TRUMAN GETS STATE LEAD

**Race Is Close in Minneapolis**

President Truman had a 55,000 vote lead with less than a sixth of Minnesota's precincts reporting early today.

The President appeared to have carried St. Paul by about 35,000 votes.

In Minneapolis, where returns were slower coming in (St. Paul has voting machines), the President's lead over Thomas E. Dewey was less than 8,000 votes with more than a fourth of the precincts reporting.

State returns from 607 precincts out of 3,738:

**President Truman 177,671, Thomas E. Dewey 122,289.**

The Progressive candidate, Henry Wallace, was hardly in the running with less than 6,000 votes over the entire state.

In Hennepin county, 146 precincts out of 430 gave the President 50,014 votes to Dewey's 42,412. In Ramsey county, 154 precincts out of 173 gave Mr. Truman 77,943 to Dewey's 42,195.

In the rural areas, 307 precincts gave the President 49,714 votes to Dewey's 37,682. There were indications the President might break into, or at least hold even, in the strongly Republican farm areas of southern Minnesota, carried by Dewey in 1944.

### CAMPAIGN CRAVAT TIES POLLS IN KNOT

NEW YORK—(UP)—Brooklyn voters complained to police Tuesday that a Democrat poll watcher was electioneering. He was wearing a necktie with a picture of President Truman painted on it.

The watcher refused to remove the tie. He told police it was wearing apparel.

After a heated argument with the cops he compromised, however. He turned over his lapel to cover the President's face.

## Election Bulletins

**Associated Press returns at 1:25 a.m. (E. S. T.) Wednesday from 59,327 of the country's 135,868 voting units showed the popular vote:**

**Dewey 9,250,744, Truman 11,260,144, Wallace 618,705, and Thurmond 552,417.**

**Total 21, 682,010.**

**Dewey led in 18 states having a total of 172 electoral votes, as follows:**

**Arizona, California, Connecticut, Delaware, Kansas, Maine, Michigan, Nebraska, Nevada, New Hampshire, North Dakota, Ohio, Oregon, Pennsylvania, South Dakota, Vermont, Washington and Wyoming.**

**Truman was leading in 26 states with an aggregate electoral vote of 320, as follows:**

**Arkansas, Colorado, Florida, Georgia, Idaho, Illinois, Indiana, Iowa, Kentucky, Maryland, Massachusetts, Minnesota, Missouri, Montana, New Jersey, New Mexico, New York, North Carolina, Oklahoma, Rhode Island, Tennessee, Texas, Utah, Virginia, West Virginia, and Wisconsin.**

**Thurmond was in front in four states having a total of 38 electoral votes, winning Alabama and South Carolina and leading in Louisiana and Mississippi.**

**Needed to elect, 266.**

**SAN FRANCISCO—(AP)—California, home state of Republican vice presidential candidate Earl Warren, gave him and his presidential running mate Tom Dewey a mounting lead late Tuesday night. Results compiled from 3,149 out of 16,802 precincts were: Truman 195,138, Dewey 210,058, and Wallace 21,665.**

**NEW YORK—(UP)—Henry A. Wallace, running a poor fourth in the presidential race, said Tuesday night his Progressive party will fight on and organize in every state, city an district in the nation.**

**OKLAHOMA CITY, OKLA.—(AP)—President Truman captured Oklahoma's 10 electoral votes. Returns from 2,263 precincts gave Truman 237,523, Dewey 118,901.**

**BALTIMORE, MD.—(AP)—Jacob France, Republican national committeeman from Maryland, claimed the state's eight electorial votes for Dewey. He said Maryland's 23 counties would return a "majority of about 35,000" for Dewey. This would be more than enough to overcome the 25,427 margin Uresident Truman held over Dewey in Baltimore city.**

## HOW MINNESOTA VOTED

*Denotes incumbent.

**President**
607 Districts of 3,738

| | |
|---|---|
| Dewey and Warren (R) | 122,289 |
| *Truman & Barkley (DFL) | 177,671 |
| Wallace and Taylor (P) | 5,938 |

**United States Senator**
499 Districts of 3,738

| | |
|---|---|
| *Joseph H. Ball (R) | 91,098 |
| Hubert Humphrey (DFL) | 158,104 |

**Governor**
420 Districts of 3,738

| | |
|---|---|
| *Luther W. Youngdahl (R) | 98,001 |
| Charles L. Halsted (DFL) | 105,987 |
| Orville E. Olson | 1,877 |

**Lt. Governor**
273 Districts of 3,738

| | |
|---|---|
| *C. Elmer Anderson (R) | 61,708 |
| John T. McDonough (DFL) | 48,508 |
| Robert W. Duel (P) | 1,456 |

**Secretary of State**
275 Districts of 3,738

| | |
|---|---|
| *Mike Holm (R) | 77,507 |
| Koscie H. Marsh (DFL) | 69,638 |

**State Treasurer**
250 Districts of 3,738

| | |
|---|---|
| *Julius A. Schmahl (R) | 61,195 |
| George MacDonald (DFL) | 68,662 |

**Attorney General**
269 Districts of 3,738

| | |
|---|---|
| *J. A. A. Burnquist (R) | 66,070 |
| Francis M. Smith (DFL) | 66,474 |

**R. R. and Warehouse Commissioner**
264 Districts of 3,738

| | |
|---|---|
| *Rollin G. Johnson (R) | 53,547 |
| Clifford C. Peterson (DFL) | 80,357 |

**Associate Justice Supreme Court**
(Two to be elected)
224 Districts of 3,738

| | |
|---|---|
| *Oscar R. Knutson | 50,206 |
| John S. McGrath | 48,409 |
| E. Luther Melin | 39,442 |
| *Thos. F. Gallagher | 58,392 |

**Rep. in Congress, First District**
42 Districts of 407

| | |
|---|---|
| *August H. Andresen (R) | 6,896 |
| Karl F. Rolvaag (DFL) | 4,491 |

**Rep. in Congress, Second District**
21 Districts of 428

| | |
|---|---|
| *Joseph P. O'Hara (R) | 2,717 |
| Milton F. Maxwell (DFL) | 1,745 |

**Rep. in Congress, Third District**
12 Districts of 294

| | |
|---|---|
| *George MacKinnon (R) | 1,952 |
| Roy Wier (DFL) | 2,580 |

**Rep. in Congress, Fourth District**
153 Districts of 173

| | |
|---|---|
| *Edward J. Devitt (R) | 45,018 |
| Eugene J. McCarthy (DFL) | 64,604 |

**Rep. in Congress, Fifth District**
6 Districts of 231

| | |
|---|---|
| *Walter H. Judd (R) | 2,339 |
| Marcella F. Killen (DFL) | 1,367 |

**Rep. in Congress, Sixth District**
16 Districts of 573

| | |
|---|---|
| *Harold Knutson (R) | 1,084 |
| Fred Marshall (DFL) | 1,962 |

**Rep. in Congress, Seventh District**
62 Districts of 550

| | |
|---|---|
| *H. Carl Anderson (R) | 6,278 |
| James M. Youngdale (DFL) | 4,786 |

**Rep. in Congress, Eighth District**
57 Districts of 457

| | |
|---|---|
| *John A. Blatnik (DFL) | 13,292 |
| William A. Berlin (R) | 9,004 |

**Rep. in Congress, Ninth District**
1 District of 626

| | |
|---|---|
| *Harold C. Hagen (R) | 1,199 |
| Oscar A. Johnson DFL) | 1,094 |

**Judge of Dist. Court**
(Five to be elected)
4 Districts of 430

| | |
|---|---|
| *William A. Anderson | 541 |
| Tom Bergin | 396 |
| *Paul S. Carroll | 821 |
| John P. Good | 243 |
| *Paul W. Guilford | 673 |
| *D. E. LaBelle | 761 |
| William C. Larson | 520 |
| Wesley McMahon | 393 |
| *Frank E. Reed | 736 |

**Judge of Dist. Court, Juvenile**
9 Districts of 430

| | |
|---|---|
| *Earl J. Lyons | 4,045 |

**Judge of Probate Court**
7 Districts of 430

| | |
|---|---|
| Carl J. Benson | 1,159 |
| *James G. Kehoe | 2,108 |

**Co. Commissioner First District**
9 Districts of 53

| | |
|---|---|
| *Richard O. "Dick" Hanson | 2,935 |
| George . hillips | 2,844 |

**Co. Commissioner Third District**
District of 138

| | |
|---|---|
| Jens Christensen | 335 |
| *W. W. Heffelfinger | 273 |

**Co. Commissioner Fifth District**
2 Districts of 82

| | |
|---|---|
| *S. Earl Ainsworth | 690 |
| Einar Jeppesen | 231 |

## HOLDS EDGE IN WISCONSIN, MINNESOTA

By ASSOCIATED PRESS

Fighting Harry S. Truman made a close, hot scrap today of his presidential race with Republican Thomas E. Dewey.

Mr. Truman piled up expected strength in Democratic city strong points to run ahead of his Republican rival in both popular and indicated electoral votes.

As the ballot count pushed past the 11,500,000 mark, the man from Missouri was leading Dewey in the presidential contest 5,819,230 to 5,162,451.

Henry A. Wallace, the Progressive party entry, had picked up 338,575 votes. J. Strom Thurmond, the States' Rights Democratic nominee, tallied 325,877.

But Thurmond had succeeded in grabbing off 19 electoral votes in South Carolina and Alabama, and reached for more in Mississippi and Louisiana.

In vital New York state alone, with its prized total of 47 electoral ballots, the lead switched six times by midnight. At that moment Truman was out in front by a squeaky margin.

The Democratic and Republican high commands were trading claims of capturing around 300 electoral votes. Needed to win: 266.

Herbert Brownell, Jr., Dewey's campaign manager, repeated that the election of the Republican ticket was "assured."

The way he sized it up, the Democrats were merely running true to form in the early count, with big cities amassing the usual Democratic majorities and coming in with the early reports. In nearly all cases, he said, the Democratic margins weren't up to winning size.

Yet Brownell had trimmed from 32 to 24 the number of states he had predicted Dewey would surely take.

RACE VERY CLOSE

Democratic chiefs stood pat on an expression of "great confidence" in Truman. National chairman J. Howard McGrath said his mood was one of "expanding optimism."

These were some of the significant developments:

**Truman at midnight led in Indiana, Iowa and Wisconsin—states that went to Dewey in 1944. He wasn't far behind in Ohio, Wyoming, South Dakota, Kansas and Colorado—more of Dewey's 1944 collection.**

The Dallas News, backing Dewey, conceded Truman had carried Texas.

Virginia upset some advance predictions by moving safely into the Truman column.

Maine, to nobody's surprise, was a Dewey prize. The Democratic state chairman gave up there.

WINS HOME STATE

The key states of New Jersey, California and Pennsylvania were close. The lead teetered back and forth, but Dewey was out ahead most of the time.

The Providence Journal said a Democratic sweep of Rhode Island was apparent in early returns.

**The President picked up a comfortable edge in his home state of Missouri.**

President Truman put up a battle in northern cities, but generally speaking his margins there appeared smaller than Franklin D. Roosevelt's in 1944. Truman needed a big vote in the labor centers to offset Dewey strength elsewhere.

A significant straw in the wind was the situation in Philadelphia. With the returns almost complete, Truman had a thin lead there. Four years ago F.D.R. carried the city by 150,000 and that is how he captured the key-

Truman Leads
*Continued on Page Eight*

## TRUMAN HOPE INCREASES

**Staff Shouts, Laughs as Returns Pour In**

By WILLIAM H. MYLANDER
Minneapolis Tribune Staff Correspondent

KANSAS CITY, MO.—Aids of President Truman were fired with hope and jubilance here late Tuesday night as he continued to hold a popular vote lead.

The President himself was spending the night behind shaded windows at his home in nearby Independence, Mo. He had indicated he would retire early, but the lights remained on late.

As the count indicated that Mr. Truman's vigorous campaign has made a close race out of the predicted Republican landslide, a steady procession of automobiles cruised slowly by his home.

But Charles G. Ross, White House press secretary, said the President wouldn't come to his staff's election headquarters here. He added:

**"There will be no statement tonight unless it comes through here, and I doubt very much whether any will be issued."**

The view at the Hotel Muehlebach penthouse headquarters was that the outcome couldn't be definitely determined until sometime Wednesday.

LAUGHS AND SHOUTS

Friends and aids of the President, however, hung over news teletypes, greeting each bulletin showing him ahead with laughter and elated shouts.

Their optimism was increased by telephone reports from Democratic leaders such as Paul Fitzpatrick, New York chairman, and Jake Arvey, Cook county chairman, claiming positively that early returns showed vital New York and Illinois would cast their electoral votes for Mr. Truman.

Earlier, Mr. Truman had viewed the election in terms of his primary race for senator in 1940. Then, as now, nobody thought he could win except Mr Truman. And in 1940 he emerged the victor.

At a country club luncheon yesterday noon, given for the President and 30 close friends by Mayor Roger T. Sermon of Independence, Mr. Truman recalled the 1940 campaign and its outcome in a brief talk.

Then he went back to his big, old-fashioned white frame home in Independence to spend election night with his family.

At 10 a.m. Mr. Truman drove three blocks through the rain with Mrs. Truman and Margaret to cast their votes in the seventh precinct of the first ward of Blue

Truman
*Continued on Page Eight*

TURN THE PAGES TO:

FAIR
U. S. Weather Bureau Forecasts
High 55
Details on Page 22

# Minneapolis Morning Tribune

Vol. LXXXII—No. 316 | MINNEAPOLIS, MINN., TUESDAY, APRIL 5, 1949 | Price 5 Cents



BONUS
Support Among State Voters Dips, Reports the MINNESOTA POLL
ON PAGE 6

# TRUMAN: PACT IS PEACE BULWARK

Associated Press Wirephoto

**PRIME MINISTER SPAAK OF BELGIUM PUTS THE FIRST SIGNATURE ON THE NORTH ATLANTIC PACT AS OTHER SIGNERS LOOK ON**

*Belgian ambassador Silvercruys stands at left; interpreter at far right. Seated in first row are, left to right, Bevin (Great Britain), Lange (Norway), Bech (Luxembourg), Benediktsson (Iceland), Rasmussen (Denmark), President Truman, Acheson, Pearson (Canada), Schuman (France), Sforza Italy), Stikker (The Netherlands) and Da Matta (Portugal). Behind them are am-bassadors.*

U. S. 'HEALTHIEST,' THEY SAY

## Doctors Defend Private Practice

*Congress is preparing to discuss various plans under which the federal government (and the taxpayers ultimately) would pay part or all of your doctor bills. Victor Cohn, Tribune science and medical reporter, has spent several months gathering the information about these many proposals, how they would affect you, and what they would cost you. The third article is below. The fourth will be published Wednesday in the Minneapolis Morning Tribune.*

### III—THE NATION'S HEALTH

By VICTOR COHN
Minneapolis Tribune Staff Writer

Is John Patient, average American, bursting with health, or is he likely to keel over at any second, the harborer of some evil and unsuspected disease?

The Truman administration, seeking national compulsory health insurance, contends that John and most of us could be a lot healthier.

The American Medical association, defending private medical practice and private medical payment, replies that we are the healthiest people on earth.

Both the administration and the AMA agree that improving health is far more than a matter of providing insurance.

They agree that you must consider doctors, dentists, hospitals, nurses, public health services, medical research and many non-medical factors like food, housing and education.

**They agree that federal aid will be necessary in many fields.**

The AMA favors grants-in-aid to the states, with local control free from federal "strings." The AMA does not favor spending as much as the administration suggests.

Yet the area of agreement is significant.

It means almost certainly that federal, state and local government activity in health and medicine—completely apart from health insurance—will be doubled or trebled in the next 20 years. It means federal subsidies will range from tuition for medical students to grants for building sewerage systems.

A paper-bound green book, available for $1 from the United States government printing office, contains the Truman administration program on health and medicine.

It is a 10-year program, compiled for the President by Oscar R. Ewing, federal security administrator.

**Much of it—though not the finding for national health insurance—is the result of a national health assembly held in Washington last May.**

More than 800 leaders in health and national affairs joined to talk about doctor bills and doctoring and what a nation must do to keep well.

On the assembly's executive committee were the heads of organizations like the American Medical association, American Dental association, Co-operative Health Federation of America, National Association of Manufacturers, CIO, AFL, National Grange and Farmers union.

Three Minnesotans were among the 38 on the executive committee—Katherine Densford, head of the

Nation's Health
Continued on Page Eight



## HUMPHREY'S 'DEAL' BALKED

### Pinball 'Political Debt' Slapped Down

A resolution introduced by St. Paul's mayor, which he said was designed to pay a political debt of Sen. Hubert Humphrey, former mayor of Minneapolis, was slapped down in the metropolitan airports commission Monday.

The resolution provided that on Jan. 1, 1950, the contract for seven pinball machines at Wold-Chamberlain field, now held by a St. Paul concern, should be given to Fred Gates, of Minneapolis.

Mayor Edward K. Delaney of St. Paul introduced the resolution, which met immediate opposition from Harry P. Burgum, conservative Minneapolis alderman and MAC member.

**"If you want to advertise for bids, okay," he said. "But you ought not start passing this around to different fellows. You'll get into quite a mess if you do."**

Burgum added that he didn't want to see the business passed around to pay any debts.

"Who wants to pay any debts?" Delaney demanded.

Burgum replied: "Shove me far enough and you'll get a frank answer."

Delaney then said: "As you know, my good friend, Hubert

Humphrey
Continued on Page Eight

## MAYOR HONORS TWO BOYS FOR SAVING CHILD FROM TRAIN

Two school patrol boys who saved the life of a 3-year-old girl were presented distinguished service awards Monday by Mayor Eric G. Hoyer.

Winners of the awards are Ralph Fuerst, 11, 3647 Polk street, and Edward Sanford, 13, 3547 Central avenue. The child they saved is Carol Rosenthal, daughter of Mrs. Alice Rosenthal, 3670 Polk street.

**Last Dec. 10, the two boys were on school patrol duty at the Soo Line crossing, two blocks north of Cavell school. They had escorted the last group of school children across the tracks when they heard a locomotive approaching.**

Turning, the boys saw Carol standing in the middle of the tracks. They immediately dashed back and pulled the child off the tracks just before the train reached the crossing.

No publicity was given the incident at the time, but Patrolman Ralph Stirratt of the police department learned of it while checking patrol activities at Cavell school recently.

## Four Die in Crash Near Albert Lea

By TRYGVE AGER
Minneapolis Tribune Staff Writer

ALBERT LEA, MINN.—Four persons were killed and one critically injured Monday night when two cars crashed head-on about two and one half miles east of here.

The dead were identified as Elmer H. Gugel, 32, Albert Lea; Willie E. Beckman, 60, and his nephew, Robert Beckman, 19, both of Strool, S. D., and Grace Knapp, about 27, Ipswich, S. D.

Taken to Naeve hospital here with a possible skull fracture was Arthur Bushman, 24, Albert Lea. Late last night he had not regained consciousness.

Sheriff Carl Lindahl of Freeborn county said the cars collided on highway 16 at the top of a hill in a no-passing zone.

**The three persons from South Dakota were traveling east. Gugel and Bushman were returning from a trip to Austin, Minn., where they both went to seek employment.**

Sheriff's deputies and the state highway patrolmen worked with wrenches for close to two hours before the three bodies in the South Dakota car could be removed from the twisted wreckage.

Both the Albert Lea men were sprawled several yards apart on the highway where they were thrown by the impact.

Religious pamphlets, Bibles and letters bearing the inscription "Dakota Conference of Wesleyan Methodist church" were found in the car registered in Robert Beckman's name.

Miss Knapp was the daughter of the Rev. L. L. Knapp, a Methodist minister at Ipswich. She was a representative of the American Sunday School association.

**Last night, Mr. Knapp said young Beckman picked up his daughter early yesterday to take her to Marion, Ind., to visit friends.**

The elder Beckman was riding along as far as Waterloo, Iowa, to attend a missionary convention.

For close to an hour, highway traffic was blocked as workmen attempted to remove the cars, both of which remained on the highway.

Authorities said the Beckmans were wedged in the front seat and Miss Knapp's body was pinned between a caved-in side and the back seat.

Gugel, who was a cousin to Bushman, served six years in the army, most of the time during World war II.

PHOTO BY DICK LEPIRD VIA MINNEAPOLIS TRIBUNE TELEPHOTO

**CRASH SCENE WHERE FOUR WERE KILLED NEAR ALBERT LEA**

*Body of Elmer Gugel lies on pavement, others in car*

## ENVOYS HEAR DEFENSE TALK

### Alliance Called Bar to Aggression

WASHINGTON—(UP)—President Truman hailed the signing of the North Atlantic pact Monday as "a shield against aggression" behind which the free world can build a lasting peace.

In a solemn address just before the foreign ministers of the 12 Atlantic powers put their signatures to the treaty, Mr. Truman told the world that the new grand alliance is intended only to prevent a third great war.

**DENIES CHARGE**

He echoed the theme of peaceful purpose and resolute will set at the opening of the historic ceremony by American Secretary of State Dean Acheson and the 11 other signers representing Canada and western Europe.

**The President coldly brushed aside Moscow's charge that the pact is aimed at banding the western nations together for aggression against Russia.**

"This is absolutely untrue," he declared in a 10-minute speech broadcast to the world by radio and television from the signing table in the government auditorium here.

**'NO AGGRESSION'**

"Twice in recent years, nations have felt the sickening blow of unprovoked aggression," he said. "Our peoples, to whom our governments are responsible, demand that these things shall not happen again.

"We are determined that they shall not happen again.

**"In taking steps to prevent aggression against our own peoples," he added, "we have no purpose of aggression against others.**

"To suggest the contrary is to slander our institutions and defame our ideals and our aspirations."

**'NEIGHBORLY' ACT**

The President reaffirmed American support of the United Nations and he pointed out that

Atlantic Pact
Continued on Page Eight

**PACT FEATURES ON INSIDE PAGES:**



## 12 NATIONS SIGN TREATY

FROM LATE DISPATCHES

WASHINGTON—Twelve men took 11 minutes Monday to sign a document they hope will secure the peace of the world.

The North Atlantic security pact officially came into being at 4:51 p.m. (3:51 Minneapolis time) in an atmosphere of gravity and restraint.

The 12 North Atlantic nations signed the pact in the great gray government building where the World war II draft lottery took place.

After hearing President Truman hail it as a "shield against aggression," the foreign ministers stepped up one by one to put their names to the historic, 1,040-word pact.

Previously they, like Mr. Truman, had proclaimed to Russia and all the world that their only purpose was peace and security.

Several of them added blunt warnings to any nation contemplating violence. Britain's foreign minister, Ernest Bevin, declared:

"Our peoples do not want war and do not glorify war, but they will not shrink from it if aggression is threatened."

Secretary of State Dean Acheson drew on the Bible. "For those who set their feet upon the path of aggression," he said, "it (the pact) is a warning that if it must needs be that offenses come, then woe unto them by whom the offense cometh."

**Acheson's signing of the pact meant that the United States had abandoned its 173-year-old tradition of isolationism and had signed a peacetime military alliance with Europe.**

Acheson presented in alphabetical order the foreign ministers of Belgium, Canada, Denmark, France, Iceland, Italy, Luxemburg, The Netherlands, Norway, Portugal and the United Kingdom. Each briefly addressed the select audience of dignitaries.

Many members of the senate which must favor the treaty with a two-thirds vote before it can go into effect, witnessed the signing.

### Russians Absent

A crowd of 1,500 which jammed the government's gray and gold departmental auditorium also included representatives of most of the nations with envoys in Washington.

But there were several notable exceptions. These were the representatives of Russia and the Soviet bloc. They did not ask for tickets, the state department explained.

The ceremonies began promptly at 3 p.m. (2 p.m., Minneapolis time), when the foreign ministers went to the small semi-circular stage in the front of the blue and gold columned auditorium. They sat in armchairs of dull golden hue framed by a backdrop of banked ferns, azaleas and the flags of the 12 nations.

**The treaty rested on a small mahogany desk. Typewritten of gold-edged rag paper, its only trimming was a red, white and blue ribbon holding together its 12 sheets.**

The ministers squinted in the blare of television and newsreel klieg lights. Britain's Bevin glowered at the spotlights but then decided to try to ignore them.

By the time it was President Truman's turn to speak, many of the foreign ministers and ambassadors were perspiring.

Mr. Truman spoke after each of the visiting foreign ministers and Secretary Acheson completed their brief addresses.

The pre-signing ceremonies ended at 4:38 p.m. when President Truman finished his address.

### Signing of Pact Begins

Acheson then stepped forward and announced that the treaty would then be signed.

Belgium's foreign minister, Paul-Henri Spaak was first in line.

Under the blazing television lights, he fixed his signature to the red-white-and-blue trimmed document at 4:40 p.m. The Belgian ambassador, Baron Silvercruys, signed his name below Spaak's.

The same procedure was followed by each of the 10 other foreign delegations, the ambassador signing below the name of his country's foreign minister. That was necessitated because the ambassadors are the official representatives of their governments here.

**Each foreign minister used a different pen. All were provided by the state department.**

When Secretary of State Dean Acheson prepared to sign, the President went to the front of the stage and asked Vice President Alben Barkley to come up from the audience. Barkley and Mr. Truman watched as Acheson signed in behalf of the United States.

The treaty itself was not read. The diplomats knew every

12 Nations Sign Pact
Continued on Page Four

**Read the Penalty Diet on Page 13**

# 1950~1959

FORECAST
Little change in temperature
TEMPERATURES

| | | | | | |
|---|---|---|---|---|---|
| Midnight | 66 | 5 a.m. | 61 | 10 a.m. | 65 |
| 1 a.m. | 64 | 6 a.m. | 60 | 11 a.m. | ..66 |
| 2 a.m. | 62 | 7 a.m. | 61 | Noon | ....68 |
| 3 a.m. | 62 | 8 a.m. | 62 | *1 p.m. | ..70 |
| 4 a.m. | 60 | 9 a.m. | 64 | *Unofficial | |

Highest year ago, 86; lowest, 62.

# THE MINNEAPOLIS STAR

Vol. LXXII—No. 184 ★ MINNEAPOLIS, MINN., WEDNESDAY, JUNE 28, 1950 Price 5 Cents

# Seoul Falls to Communist Troops

★ ★ ★ ★ ★ ★ ★ ★

EVERYBODY WOULD BE IN NEXT WAR

## *United States Ready for Total Mobilization*

By EDWIN A. LAHEY
Special to the Minneapolis Star

*Washington, D. C.*

EVERYBODY WOULD BE IN the next war, from the very start.

Once the shooting started, the people of the United States would be converted by law overnight into 150 million cogs of an integrated war machine.

**An emergency war powers act has already been drafted by the the national security resources board, headed by W. Stuart Symington.**

The President would send it to capitol hill immediately in the event of war, and in a few hours every aspect of civilian life would be under government controls.

In World War II the government fumbled along gradually toward all-out mobilization.

**In World War III we would start with total mobilization and then have such decontrols as appeared feasible later.**

Complete federal control of labor-management relations, prices, wages, job, transportation, materials, profits, public expression, production, would be the curtain raiser for a new war.

Here is one graphic example of the planning already done by the national security resources board:

There are today, in the locked files of the machine tool manufacturing companies, 900 million dollars in "phantom orders" for big machine tools, gauges, and cutting tools.

**Specifications of these "phantom orders" have been changed from time to time, to keep them up to the minute.**

Telegrams at the opening of a war would change these "phantom orders" into real orders, and the machine tools would start rolling to war contractors as fast as the orders for war material came to these contractors.

The time lag for the production of machine tools was one of the great bottlenecks at the beginning of World War II.

**The first act of total mobilization in the national security resources board blueprint would be the freezing of prices, wages, jobs, and profits. A rationing system would blossom overnight.**

In orderly succession would follow transportation controls, material controls and priorities, censorship, and production controls.

The right to strike would probably go out the window. One of the five major objectives of the emergency war powers act, according to the NSRB prospectus, would be to maintain labor standards and the rights of workers "without interruption to production on essential orders."

Other objectives listed by the NSRB follow:

**MAXIMUM** utilization of the productive potential of industry.

**MAXIMUM** utilization of materials, through conservation, substittuion, and the elimination of hoarding.

**PREVENTION** of excessive profits and speculation in essential materials.

**MAINTENANCE** of a sound civilian economy and the equitable distribution of essential civilian goods.

The only major area in the total mobilization plan not yet worked out in detail is that of civilian defense. This aspect of the overall war plan has remained unsettled because it has not yet been decided whether the federal government or the state and local governments should bear the cost of civilian defense.

**The NSRB planners have not overlooked the probability that a war full of atomic implications might panic the populations of big cities, and start a mass exodus from centers of industry.**

Plans have been perfected to control population movements in the event of war. These plans would be enforced through job controls, food controls, and transportation controls.

Although nothing would be left untouched in total mobilization, the war powers act would state it to be the intent of congress that the vast powers vested in the president would be used "with all possible regard to the ultimate preservation of our form of government, our personal liberties, and our way of life."

The NSRB has even assembled a list of citizens who would be "drafted" to administer the host of war agencies that would spring into being almost instantly, once the nation was enveloped in war.

## GN Lays Off Additional Employes

The Great Northern railroad laid off 1,100 to 1,200 additional employes in Minneapolis and St. Paul today while it attempted "very limited service" in the fourth day of a strike by the switchmen's union.

About 3,500 seasonal track maintenance men had been laid off previously, and more employes will be made idle Thursday, the road reported.

**If the strike continues, only 5,000 employes will be working after Friday out of a total of 28,000 on the Great Northern system, the road said.**

The line has annulled 31 passenger and mixed passenger and freight trains over its routes. Normally it serves about 1,500 cities and towns from Chicago to the Pacific coast.

About half those 1,500 places were without rail service today.

Supervisors who once did the work are operating locomotives and handling switches where regular train crews refuse to cross switchmen's picket lines. But only a few trains are operating.

**Service is being attempted again today on the Empire Builder, the road's fast streamliner. A fast mail train from St. Paul to Seattle is running with a combination of equipment from the Oriental Limited.**

Some service is being attempted on the St. Paul, Minneapolis, Duluth run. The new Red River special, which was inaugurated just a week ago as a fast train between the Twin Cities and Grand Forks, N. D., did not leave St. Paul Tuesday night.

Substitute service is being attempted to Grand Forks and

GN
*Continued on Page 22*

## Dr. Sander Regains Medical License

CONCORD, N. H.—(UP)—Dr. Hermann Sander today regained the medical license that was revoked after his acquittal in the mercy murder of a cancer-doomed woman patient.

Sander

Sander's immediate reinstatement was voted unanimously at a meeting of all five members of the state board of registration in medicine.

Sander's license was revoked by the board April 19 because he did not satisfactorily explain why he injected air into the veins of Mrs. Abbie C. Borroto, 59, last December.

## On the Inside . .

REFUGEES REACH JAPAN — American women and children disembark from an American transport plane at Itazuki air-base, Kyushu, Japan, after a flight from Seoul, Korea. People in the picture were not identified. — AP Wirephoto from the United States army via army radiophoto in Tokyo, Japan.

## HQ IN JAPAN ON WAR BASIS

TOKYO, JAPAN — Gen. Douglas MacArthur's headquarters here has taken on the appearance of wartime. High officers are in continuous conference. All information is being screened for security angles.

**Air bases in Japan are operating with all the precautions of wartime.**

**Anti-aircraft guns, fully manned, point to the sky. Pilots, ground crews and all officers are on wartime alerts.**

## British Put Warships at U.S. Disposal

LONDON, ENGLAND—(AP)—Prime Minister Attlee announced today Britain has decided to place its naval forces in Japanese waters at the immediate disposal of the United States to support American action in South Korea.

Attlee made the announcement in the house of commons.

Winston Churchill, leader of the Conservative opposition, declared: "We shall do our best to give him any support he needs in what seems to me an inescapable duty."

Attlee said British forces around Japan "are almost the same as those of the United States naval forces."

The whole house cheered.

Attlee said it is "certain that this country will carry out its obligations to the United Nations."

(At The Hague a Dutch spokesman said The Netherlands was willing to consider furnishing a token naval force for use in Korea from units now stationed in Indonesia. The spokesman said no definite action would be taken until it was known what contributions were expected from U. N. members. Other Dutch sources said Holland would give the fullest possible support to carrying out the security council resolution.)

## Senate Votes Extension of Draft

WASHINGTON, D. C. — (AP) — A top-heavy senate vote today gave final congressional approval to a one-year extension of the draft act.

The measure puts in President Truman's hands the power to call up thousands of draftees, national guardsmen or reserves, if necessary to keep the strength of the army, navy and air force above the 2,000,000 mark.

**A 315 to 4 margin for the bill was rolled up Tuesday in the house.**

The measure not only allows the President to start actual drafting but also allows him to order army, navy, marine, air force and coast guard reserves to duty.

### Indo-China to Get Eight Aid Planes

SAIGON, INDO-CHINA—(AP)—United States air force pilots will fly eight C47 transport planes to Saigon in the first delivery of military aid to bolster French forces in their fight against the Communist-led Vietminh. They will be formally accepted Saturday.

The twin-engine transports are scheduled to be flown from Clark field in the Philippines on the last leg of their trip from the United States.

The C47 was the workhorse transport of the American air force during World War II. They will be followed by navy Hellcat fighters.

### Truman Had No Choice, Ike Says

NEW YORK, N. Y.—(AP)—Gen. Dwight D. Eisenhower in commenting on the Korean situation said today:

"The best chance for sustaining world peace was to take a firm stand, and when our government guaranteed the government of South Korea, there was no recourse but to do what President Truman said and did."

## Draft Extension Estimates Show 600,000 Increase

WASHINGTON, D. C.—(AP)—Congressional authorities estimated today that the one-year draft extension would allow President Truman to call up well over 600,000 additional men for duty if he finds it necessary.

They based the estimate on a top limit of 2,005,882 listed by the senate-house conference committee in granting authority to call for draftees, national guardsmen and other reserves.

A report by the senate armed services committee listed present strength for the army, navy and air force at 1,370,000 or 635,882 below authorized strength of the three major services:

**Here Are the Totals:**

| Service | Present | Authorized | Increase |
|---|---|---|---|
| Army .................. | 593,000 | 837,000 | 244,000 |
| Navy and Marines ...... | 427,000 | 666,882 | 239,882 |
| Air Force ............. | 350,000 | 502,000 | 152,000 |
| **TOTALS** ............ | 1,370,000 | 2,005,882 | 635,882 |

There have been no inductions in 18 months under the 1948 peacetime selective service act because voluntary enlistments have provided manpower near the levels authorized in congressional appropriations.

Some senators said a draft may be necessary later this year if the army enlistments continued to lag as they have recently.

# *Truman Hopes for Peace in Communism Challenge*

— TRUMAN —

## Situation Serious, He Says

### President Talks Before Reserve Officers Group

WASHINGTON, D. C.—(AP)—President Truman said today he hopes the United States decision to challenge the onward march of Communism will mean "peace in the world."

The President addressed the Reserve Officers association whose members stood and cheered when he came before them at the Mayflower hotel.

**Smilingly acknowledging their demonstration, Mr. Truman then solemnly told them: "We face a serious situation."**

He went on to say he hopes his decision would serve the cause of our country and a peaceful world.

Before Mr. Truman spoke, Louis Johnson, secretary of defense, described the Sunday night White House decision to send planes and warships to the aid of South Korea as "the finest hour in American history."

Top officials here were following reports from Korea closely, but Mr. Truman had put his daily schedule largely back on the usual routine after three days devoted almost exclusively to the far Pacific situation.

However, the President reserved a major spot on his afternoon conference schedule for a talk with W. Stuart Symington, chairman of the national resources security board.

**That board has the duty of preparing detailed plans for civilian defense and industrial mobilization in time of war.**

Mr. Truman's talk to the Reserve association was off the cuff, without benefit of prepared manuscript.

Then, in a light vein, he said he still has a commission although "I am somewhat beyond the age limit."

"But," he added, "I don't believe they are going to retire me."

When he concluded, the presiding officer asked the reserve members for a demonstration of their support for "the commander in chief" for his "dramatic decision" Tuesday.

The audience stood and applauded as one man. Many yelled "Yes."

Acknowledging the demonstration, Mr. Truman said he took the historic action on the advice "of all the best brains I could muster."

Solemnly he added:

**"We face a serious situation, we hope in the cause of peace."**

He said the decision was taken "in the hope we can finally arrive" at the peace for which the United Nations was founded.

Secretary Johnson said it is the prayer of every American that the President "by grasping the nettle yesterday will have plucked safety and peace for the world."

This was a paraphrase from a line in Shakespeare's Henry IV, "Out of this nettle, danger, we pluck this flower, safety."

Johnson also referred to two newspaper comments on Mr. Truman's action.

**He said Arthur Krock wrote in the New York Times that the President and his organization were determined from the outset to adopt the forceful policy which was announced yesterday.**

"That is a true statement as delineated by the President Sunday night," the secretary said.

Johnson said the Washington Post had called this a time for steady nerves, keeping your eye on the ball and a renewed determination to be faithful to America's purposes. He quoted the Post as adding:

"The occasion has found the man in Harry Truman."

### GERMANS WORRIED

BONN, GERMANY — (AP) — Worried by events in Korea, Chancellor Konrad Adenauer will ask the Allies for security guarantees against the possibility of attack from the east, an informed Allied source said today.

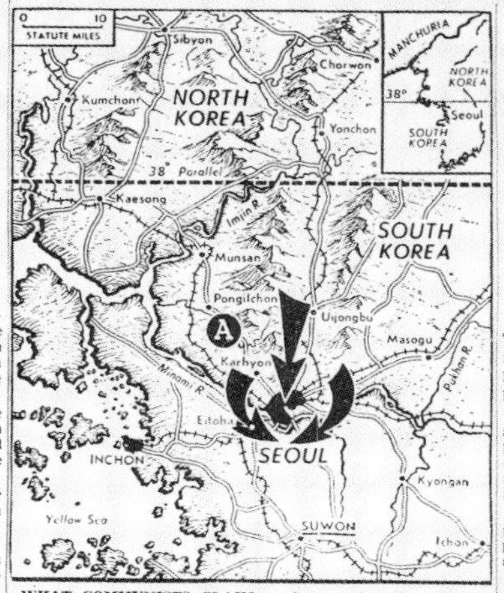



WHAT COMMUNISTS CLAIM — Arrows show how North Korean Communist forces have entered an encircled Seoul, capital of South Korea, according to a broadcast over the Communist radio today. The Communists claimed the encirclement took place Tuesday and that another force had penetrated into the city today. A report from Suwon (underlined) by Associated Press correspondent O. H. P. King said Kimpo airport (A), 16 miles west and slightly north of Seoul, had been captured by the invaders.—AP Wirephoto map.

## U. N. Calls for Arms to Back South Korea

NEW YORK, N. Y.—(AP)—The United Nations embarked upon an historic venture today by calling upon its members to use military force to back up a cease-fire order defied by Communist North Korea.

The decision was taken late Tuesday night by the Russian-boycotted security council, a few hours after President Truman announced the United States already was ordering planes and ships to support the invaded Republic of (South) Korea.

**The vote was 7 to 1, the minimum number of affirmative votes required. India and Egypt asked to be recorded as not participating because they had not received instructions. Yugoslavia cast the negative vote.**

The council's action was momentous in several ways:

**IT GAVE ITS STAMP** of approval to Mr. Truman's bold plan of direct action to stop Communist aggression. This was the first time in its history that the council had authorized the military sanctions provided by the U. N. charter.

**IT WAS A CLEAR** warning to Russia, although Russia was not mentioned in the United States resolution, that the U. N. would not permit the seizure of countries by force.

**IT MAY HAVE MADE** the Russians angry enough that they will decide to make permanent their boycott which they started last Jan. 10 in protest over the presence of Chinese Nationalist delegates. The Russians have insisted they would not return until representatives of Communist China are seated.

**Apart from the council's action, there is another factor which may prolong the China representation deadlock indefinitely. That is President Truman's new policy on Formosa.**

The President announced Tuesday that he had ordered the Seventh fleet to prevent any attack on Formosa and said the future status of Formosa will await restoration of security in the Pacific, a peace settlement with Japan, or consideration by the United Nations.

**All this aroused unusual interest in the projected departure of the Soviet deputy foreign minister, Jakob A. Malik, head of the Russian delegation. Ostensibly Malik is returning to Russia for a vacation, but it was recalled here that Andrei A. Gromyko also went home on vacation in 1948 and never came back as the regular delegate.**

Regardless of the effect the council's Korean decision may have on the Soviet boycott, most delegates agree there was little else they could have done without completely undermining public faith in the U.N.

### MINERS RESCUED

SALTILLO, MEXICO — (AP) — Two miners, buried for 102 hours, were rescued today from the Las Palomas pit.

## Stocks Rally, Prices Gain

NEW YORK, N. Y. — (AP) — The stock market plowed through strong opposition for a decisive rally today.

Prices moved up in a rush at the opening, faltered for a while, and then showed new strength. Gainse ranged to an extreme of around $4 a share.

**The rally followed a spectacular two-day plunge.**

Within 15 minutes after trading started gains running to $3 a share had been scored.

Buying was so aggressive that the high-speed ticker tape quickly dropped behind in reporting transactions from the floor of the exchange.

Aircraft, steel, motor, chemical and railroad issues were outstanding favorites.

— FIGHTING —

## 100 Tanks Spearhead Capture

### Pentagon Says South Koreans' Morale Still High

WASHINGTON, D. C.—(AP)—The defense department confirmed today that the South Korea capital of Seoul has fallen.

An army report here also stated that nearby Kimpo airport is in North Korean hands, and that Inchon (formerly Jinsen) seaport is probably untenable.

**But the report added that dispite loss of these three key points, morale of the South Korean forces remains high.**

An army spokesman said that there had been "no sabotage, no subversive action and no guerrilla warfare" against South Korean forces.

The North Korean invaders apparently have more and heavier tanks than was originally reported, the army said.

A Pentagon spokesman said Seoul apparently was captured by two North Korean thrusts spearheaded by about 100 tanks.

**Late reports identified some of these tanks as Russian-manufactured T34s—identified as 35-ton tanks mounting 76MM or 88MM guns.**

Other North Korean armor has been identified as Russian-built T70s—12-ton tanks mounting lighter guns.

The air force said that United States fighters operating from Japanese bases had destroyed eight North Korean planes, and that another was knocked down by a South Korean Mustang pilot.

The air force announcement said also there had been no United States losses throughout last midnight, Korean time.

(Presumably the air force referred to combat losses. Tokyo dispatches mentioned loss of two United States B26s through crashes.)

**U. S. PLANES BLAST 6 RUSS-MADE TANKS**

TOKYO, JAPAN—(AP)—The first American foot soldiers went into the South Korean shooting war tonight as United States airmen blasted six heavy Russian-built tanks and lost two planes in crashes.

Two B26s returning from combat flights were reported to

Fighting
*Continued on Page 22*

## KOREA AT A GLANCE

WASHINGTON, D. C.—The defense department confirmed that Seoul, capital of South Korea, has fallen to invading Communist troops. **Page One.**

WASHINGTON, D. C.—United States pours arms into pipelines to Pacific. **Page One.**

NEW YORK, N. Y. — The United Nations security council called on all U. N. members to use military force to back up its cease-fire order defied by Communist North Korea. **Page One.**

WASHINGTON, D. C.—The senate unanimously passed a one-year draft extension and sent the bill to President Truman. **Page One.**

LONDON, ENGLAND—Prime Minister Attlee announced Britain has decided to put its naval forces in Japanese waters at the disposal of the United States. **Page One.**

MOSCOW, USSR—Pravda (official Communist party organ) in a front page editorial asked if American ruling circles have not gone too far in Truman's action in the Far East. **Page 2.**

TAIPEI, FORMOSA—Chinese Nationalists, given assurance of protection from the seventh United States fleet, ordered a halt in their raids on the Communists on the mainland. **Page 4.**

PEARL HARBOR, HAWAII—A second task force is being put together by the navy to strengthen United States positions in the Far East.—**Page 4.**

WASHINGTON, D. C.—President Truman declared he hopes the decision of the United States to challenge the onward march of communism will mean "peace to the world." **Page One.**

WASHINGTON, D. C.—Senator Lucas, Democratic leader, in an expression of confidence that the United States and Russia are not going to war over Korea, said the goal of a July 31 adjournment of congress still stands. **Page 7.**

WASHINGTON, D. C.—Long laid plans for tightening up security inside the United States have been put into action by J. Edgar Hoover, FBI chief. **Page 8.**

SUWON, KOREA—Foreign Correspondent Keyes Beech sees United States plane burning after strafing attack, fears he has seen the beginning of World War III. **Page 9.**

**The Weather**
MINNESOTA: Much cooler.
IOWA: Partly cloudy, humid.
WISCONSIN: Little change.
UPPER MICHIGAN: Warmer.
NORTH DAKOTA: Cloudy.
SOUTH DAKOTA: Scattered showers.

# Minneapolis Sunday Tribune

Vol. LXXXIV—No. 130 | MINNEAPOLIS, MINN., SUNDAY, OCTOBER 1, 1950 | PRICE 15 CENTS — 20 cents on farm service and resort routes





# MacArthur Orders Reds to Surrender, Hints Allied Troops May Cross Border; 38th Parallel 'Illegal,' U. S. Tells U. N.

## Korean Gains Held Blow to GOP Hopes

By RICHARD WILSON
Chief of Minneapolis Tribune Washington Bureau

WASHINGTON, D. C.—The victory in Korea, months ahead of schedule, has dropped a bomb in the plans of politicians and government officials.

It has drastically changed the outlook for the congressional elections.

It has raised the question whether the administration can get away with its determination to go forward with economic controls and the military expansion program, in full.

President Truman is considered certain now to get into the fall election campaign just as he planned to do in the first place, but with new and powerful ammunition.

**THE FULL EXTENT** of the drastic change which has come is best illustrated by the fact the President's highest military advisors told him victory in Korea would not come before mid winter.

The most optimistic forecast which came to him from the top echelon was Dec. 1. Members of the joint chiefs of staff warned officials they were only indulging in the most dangerous type of wishful thinking to believe that victory might come before Thanksgiving.

As for a victory before election day, this was considered absolutely unthinkable.

Yet, for all practical purposes, victory has come more than a month before election day. The President has time to make trips across the country and engage in his "give 'em hell" technique without being convicted of politicking while the nation is in danger.

**MANY REPUBLICANS** were far less optimistic than the military leaders. They even doubted the bridgehead at Pusan would be held.

Even if it were held they looked forward to many months of organized fighting. They thought the far eastern question would be a flaming issue at the time of the election. They did not think there was any possibility of a victory before election day.

Thus, the entire Republican campaign, outside of local issues, has centered on the far eastern issue and communism in government. Now it becomes difficult to burden the administration with the far eastern problem while most of the voters sigh in relief over the victory in Korea.

**TO THIS EXTENT** the Republicans have a dead issue. While the facts about the administration's far eastern policy remain unchanged, the Republican attack loses a good deal of its force.

It has been common talk in Washington for several weeks that Republican prospects were greatly heightened by the Korean war.

But William Boyle, chairman

Plans
*Continued on Page 23*

## FOOTBALL SCORES

**Washington 28, Minnesota 13**
Texas 34, Purdue 26
Indiana 20, Nebraska 20
Northwestern 23, Iowa State 13
Wisconsin 28, Marquette 6
Illinois 28, Ohio 2
Southern Methodist 32, Ohio State 27
Michigan State 14, Michigan 7
Notre Dame 14, North Carolina 7
Army 28, Colgate 0
Maryland 35, Navy 21
California 28, Oregon 7

*Details in Peach Sports Section*

## *Huskies Hand Bierman First Loss in Opener*

By HALSEY HALL
Minneapolis Tribune Staff Correspondent

EN ROUTE HOME WITH MINNESOTA FOOTBALL TEAM—Bernie Bierman joined the ranks of mere mortals Saturday afternoon.

His Minnesota football team was beaten by the University of Washington, 28-13, and it was the first time in his career the Gray Eagle lost an opening football game.

Of the game there is merely one simple statement to make: the Washington team deserved the victory over its comparatively green Gopher opponents.

**MINNESOTA ROOTERS**, of whom there were around 1,000 in the stands, were quick to recognize this and there were no bitter feelings.

That was not the immediate reaction of the boys themselves, who naturally were blue when they headed for their special train to start the long ride home.

But that long ride wasn't going to be such a downcast affair, after all, for the kids started rallying early and looking ahead to the Nebraska game at Memorial stadium in Minneapolis next Saturday.

Minnesota fans saw such an accomplished artist of the rapier that they still are talking about him: Don Heinrich, the Huskies' quarterback. Short passes, long passes were mixed with audacity and skill.

Audacity? There was the time Washington, with only a one-touchdown lead, had the ball on its own 10-yard line in the first quarter. Throwing a pass in this position is comparable to stealing third base with two men out in a baseball brawl.

**SO MR. HEINRICH** calmly called a pass and it was completed for about 30 yards—and the Huskies were out of the hole.

The Washingtons had another edge on the Minnesota delegation. School has been in session for a week at Seattle and the

Gophers
*Continued on Page 23*

## Germans Nab 181 Reds to Nip Disorders

FRANKFURT, GERMANY.—(UP)—Police struck at Communist cells all over west Germany Saturday and arrested 181 Reds, in an effort to weaken the anti-west demonstrations which the Communists have scheduled for today in defiance of Allied bans.

German police at Luebeck seized 121 youths and several east zone "people's police," who had slipped over the border disguised as a "culture group." Twenty-one Communists were arrested in Dortmund, which the Reds have boasted will be the site of their biggest "show of strength"; 15 were picked up in Essen, and 24 in other key cities.

Carbines, tear gas bombs and steel helmets were being passed out in Munich, Hamburg, Duesseldorf and other cities as 36,000 police went on full alert, prepared to enforce "without indulgence" the Allied ban against the demonstrations.

The worst trouble was expected in the Ruhr. British and United States officials have informed British zone police they can call on occupation troops if necessary to curb violence.

Leaders of the militant, Soviet-trained "Free German youth" were believed to have set up secret headquarters in west Germany to direct the Red demonstrations. Youth headquarters in Berlin admitted that Erick Honnecker, chief of the movement, and his deputies have been "absent from Berlin for a few days."

German officials estimated that 40,000 Communists in the Soviet zone have been smuggled across the east-west border for the display. The same sources estimated that 100,000 Reds in west Germany would take part in defiance of the ban.

## Plane Too Small for $150,000 Girl

NEW YORK, N. Y.—(AP)—She was insured for $150,000, and was too big to get on passenger or ordinary cargo planes.

So LaGuardia field officials Saturday sent her to Newark, N. J., airport to go out on a larger air-freight plane Monday.

She is a transparent plastic figure of a woman being shipped from a German museum to the Cleveland, Ohio, health museum for use in a medical exhibit.

## Crime Unit Ends Kansas City Probe

KANSAS CITY, MO.—(INS)—The senate crime investigating committee concluded public hearings in Kansas City Saturday. It stated there was no evidence that underworld forces had succeeded in influencing Gov. Forrest Smith's office.

Sen. Estes Kefauver (D., Tenn.) chairman, said he believed Charles Binaggio, political boss and gangster, was murdered because he was unable to fulfill promises to the underworld to open up Missouri to gambling and other rackets.

(Editor's Note: Double slaying sets stage for Chicago investigation—Story on Page 14.)



## Must Remove Korea Threat, Austin Says

By A. M. ROSENTHAL
Special From the New York Times

LAKE SUCCESS, N. Y.—The United States warned the United Nations Saturday night that the North Korean Communists must not be allowed to retire behind the 38th parallel to pose a new threat to world peace.

Informed sources also said the statement of United States delegate Warren R. Austin could be interpreted as notice that this country considers General MacArthur has the right to cross the parallel, though the political future of the country remains in United Nations hands.

Austin told the general assembly political and security committee that the 38th parallel is an "imaginary line" with no basis for existence in law or logic.

**THE 60 COUNTRIES** belonging to the committee heard Austin say the United Nations' goal of restoring peace to war-torn Korea demands taking "appropriate steps" to eliminate ability of North Koreans to launch new attacks.

United Nations delegates took Austin's speech as plain indication that the United States, while it might give the Communists the chance to avoid a forcing of the parallel by the United Nations, is determined to make sure that North Korean troops are disarmed.

Austin's statement was delivered several hours after the committee vote to give priority to the Korea case. The committee decision was taken after Soviet delaying tactics touched off a hectic table pounding uproar that went down in the records as the wildest scene in the organization's history.

Soviet Foreign Minister Andrei Y. Vishinsky fought hard to put debate on death sentences in Greece before the Korea debate. But once he was defeated, he moved in immediately with a motion to hear representatives from both North and South Korea. The committee voted him down, 46 to 6 with 7 abstenations, and instead decided to extend an invitation only to South Korea.

Sometime this week, early delegates hope the committee will vote on an eight-power resolution calling for a new and strong United Nations commission to help Korea on the road to postwar unity and freedom.

The resolution, drafted last week, carries indirect authoriza-

U.N.
*Continued on Page 23*

## Who'll Ransom the Transom?

PHILADELPHIA, PA.—(AP)—Thieves squeezed through a transom Saturday to rob a tap room.

They stole several bottles of liquor, $200, a revolver and the transom.

## *Famine and Disease Peril Seoul*

By ALEX VALENTINE

SEOUL, SOUTH KOREA—(Reuters)—Famine and disease Saturday night faced Seoul's one million inhabitants. Food stocks in the war-battered South Korean capital are exhausted, the new crop of rice will not be harvested for several weeks.

One hundred and fifty tons of rice are being rushed to Seoul from Japan, United Nations officials said last night. It was doubtful, however, if the food could be distributed for several days.

Meanwhile, pitiful groups of civilians cluster around American soldiers in the streets of Seoul. They can say only one word over and over again "chop chop" (food). They stare piteously at the cans of meat and fruit, and crowd around when rations are opened.

Most soldiers, uncomfortably conscious of the hunger-pinched faces, give away most of their rations. But their generosity does nothing to solve the widespread lack of food.

Hunger-weakened people of Seoul are easy prey for disease.

The accumulated filth and garbage of almost a week lies in heaps on the roads, in the muddy alleys between rows of crowded shacks, and in the houses themselves.

The people, already dirty, grew filthier as drains choked and water supplies ran out.

Over all hangs the sickly smell of hundreds of dead bodies lying on the sidewalks. Some of them have been there for four or five days.

Filthy blood-stained pieces of rice matting cover some of the corpses. Others lie just as they fell during the fierce three day battle for the city.

City officials said that gangs of laborers are being recruited to bury the dead, to restore sanitation services, and to clean up.

They added an emergency request had been made to the United Nations forces to spray the entire city with disinfectant. Marine spray trucks have already used all their available stocks of DDT to disinfect their own camps.

The blazing buildings that lighted the city during the three-day battle of Seoul were replaced last night by a thousand camp fires.

People in rags, camping out on heaps of rubble where their homes had once been, tried vainly to warm themselves by these fires as they huddled together in the chill wind.

Hundreds of the South Korean flags and "Welcome United Nations Forces" manners which bedecked Seoul when the battle was finally won vanished. The shivering people had made clothes of them.

**Wed** Mary Rogers, 33, only daughter of the late Will Rogers, and her husband, Walter Brooks, 3rd, are honeymooning in Las Vegas, Nev. They were married in the Little Church of the West in Las Vegas. Brooks is the son of the former Mrs. Louise Cromwell Brooks, first wife of Gen. Douglas MacArthur.—AP Wirephoto.

## South Koreans Await Word to Cross Line

By Associated Press

An eager South Korean army pressed on the 38th parallel border of Red North Korea Sunday to back up General MacArthur's demand that North Korean Communists surrender or take a total beating.

Unofficial reports to United States Eighth army headquarters said the South Korean Third division crossed the 38th parallel Sunday on the east coast of Korea.

These reports could not be confirmed.

The unconfirmed reports said elements of the Third division had penetrated North Korean territory for one-fourth mile.

There was general feeling in Tokyo, Japan, that if the Reds ignore the surrender demand, four South Korean divisions lined up along or near the 38th parallel will get the order to drive into North Korea and smash the remnants of the routed Red invasion army. They are being held in check only by an order from their own Korean high command.

**SPEARHEADS** of the Third have reached the 38th parallel at the east coast village of Ingu.

Three other South Korean divisions rolling north on the Third's left were moving so fast that they were ahead of official reports. Their advance elements probably reached the line Saturday, forming a front a little less than halfway across the country.

West of the massed South Korean troops, the United States 10th corps sent steel-tipped spearheads toward the 38th parallel.

United States marines took off from Seoul for Uijongbu, road hub 12 miles north of the capital and 18 miles south of the Red border. Marine planes smashed Uijongbu flat in their heaviest strike of the war.

The fliers used 1,000-pound "Tiny Tim" rockets to crush the Red-held town.

The road north from Uijongbu, one of the main north-south highways, leads to Chorwon, 48 miles north of Seoul, reportedly headquarters for the retreating North Korean army.

A South Korean army spokesman has estimated that 100,000 Communists have massed in Chorwon. But, he said, most were believed to be poorly and lightly-armed conscripts rounded up in haste.

**UNITED STATES** planes also bombed Chorwon.

(Editor's note: Allied planes over North Korean territory Saturday ran into the "most determined resistance in some time," an air force spokesman said Sunday.

(Anti-aircraft fire was heavier than usual and American planes ran into flak where none had been reported previously, the spokesman said.

(Eight American planes were damaged and one was lost during the day. Four North Korean fighters were damaged or destroyed on the ground.)

Northwest of Seoul, the United States 187th airborne regimental combat team rambled out of Kimpo airfield to within 24 miles of the 38th parallel. They were still south of the Han river.

The immediate objective of the 187th was to clear Reds from the Inchon peninsula, extending northwest of Seoul between the Han river and the Yellow sea.

In Seoul itself the only action was the mopping up of small Red groups in the west and southwest. The old capital was officially restored as the republic's seat of government by Gen. MacArthur Friday, but it was in bad shape.

South of Seoul, the United States Seventh division ad-

Troops
*Continued on Page 16*

## 915 Casualties Reported in Korea

WASHINGTON, D. C.—(AP)—The largest casualty list of the Korean war, containing 915 names, was released by the defense department Saturday.

TOKYO, JAPAN—AP—General MacArthur Sunday called on North Koreans to surrender "in whatever part of Korea situated."

In a broadcast to the enemy, he declared that "complete destruction of your armed forces and war-making potential is inevitable."

MacArthur demanded surrender "at once" under "such military supervision as I may direct."

The supreme commander for the United Nations also demanded immediate release of "all United Nations prisoners of war and civilian internees."

and civilian internees."

The last casualty report issued by the defense department in Washington listed 3,959 American soldiers as missing through Sept. 22.

MacArthur made no mention of any decision by United Nations forces to cross the 38th parallel into North Korea.

(Editors note: But South Korean premier and defense minister Sihn Sung Mo indicated Sunday the South Korean army would sweep across the 38th parallel today or Monday, United Press reported.

("The 38th parallel boundary no longer exists," he said. "The Communist armies themselves destroyed it when they invaded South Korea."

(Regardless of American policy it was doubtful whether the South Koreans could be restrained from at least pushing across the border.)

**HIS DEMAND** that the enemy lay down his arms, whether in North or South Korea, seemed to indicate that his forces would cross the border if necessary.

Following is the text of MacArthur's broadcast:

"To the commander-in-chief, North Korean forces: The early and total defeat and complete destruction of your armed forces and war making potential is now inevitable.

"In order that the decisions of the United Nations may be carried out with a minimum of further loss of life and destruction of property, I, as the United Nations commander-in-chief, call upon you and the forces under your command, in whatever part of Korea situated, forthwith to lay down your arms and cease hostilities under such military supervision as I may direct. I call upon you at once to liberate all United Nations prisoners of war and civilian internees under your control and to make adequate provision for their protection, care, maintenance and immediate transportation to such places as I indicate.

"North Korean forces, including prisoners of war in the hands of the United Nations command, will continue to be given the care dictated by civilized custom and practice and permitted to return to their homes as soon as practicable. I shall anticipate your early decision upon this opportunity to avoid the further useless shedding of blood and destruction of property.

"DOUGLAS MacARTHUR."

**A RESOLUTION**, meanwhile, was adopted by the South Korean national assembly in Pusan Saturday night urging that United Nations forces spear on across the 38th.

MacArthur's broadcast was a

Terms
*Continued on Page 23*

## We're Losing, Korea Reds Say

LONDON, ENGLAND—(UP)—The North Korean army Saturday admitted for the first time that it was being pushed back on all fronts.

The admission was made in a broadcast from Moscow, USSR, of the evening communique issued by the North Korean army. As monitored here the communique said the Communists were waging defensive battles "against numerically superior enemy forces."

The North Koreans said their forces were waging fierce battles against the enemy after withdrawing from Seoul, but acknowledged that American troops were making "fierce attacks."

## China Reds Say U.S. Is Worst Foe

By HENRY R. LIEBERMAN
Special From the New York Times

HONG KONG—Chou En Lai, premier and foreign minister of the Chinese people's republic, denounced the United States Saturday. He termed it his government's "most dangerous enemy" in a speech on the eve of Communist China's first anniversary as a state.

**"THE UNITED STATES** government has stood all along on the side of the enemy of the Chinese people in our war of liberation, using all its might to help Kuomintang Reactionaries attack the Chinese people," he asserted. "Since establishment of the people's republic of China the hostile attitude of the American government has become intensified."

The address was made to the national committee of the people's political consultative conference in Peiping. It was broadcast over a nation-wide hookup.

He did not mention the security council's decision to permit the Peiping regime to participate in discussion of Formosa at Lake Success. But Chou declared that the Chinese Communists were still determined to "liberate" the island. He listed Tibet, too, as an area remaining on the Communists' "liberation" schedule.

**HE PRAISED** the "bravery and determination" of Kim Il Sung's North Korean forces. He also expressed confidence that the North Koreans would overcome "many difficulties" for a "final victory."

(Editor's note: The Associated Press quoted Chou as saying that the Chinese Communists will not "supinely tolerate seeing their neighbors being savagely invaded by imperialists."

(He mentioned no country. Besides Korea, the United States also is committed to sending military aid to the French in Indo-China, another neighbor of China.

(Referring directly to the Korean war, Chou said the Korean Reds would win on the principle of "persistent long-term resistance."

(This sounded like advice to the North Koreans to continue fighting on a guerrilla basis as the Chinese Reds did for years before dislodging the Nationalists.)

## Police Combat Football Mobs

EAST LANSING, MICH.—(UP)—Police padlocked bars in half of neighboring Lansing further mob disturbances by Saturday as a precaution against football-happy Michigan State college students.

Four students were arrested in minor disturbances as the student body drifted back from Michigan State's 14-to-7 upset over the University of Michigan at Ann Arbor yesterday.

## *He Collects Own Life Insurance*

GLENS FALLS, N. Y.—(UP)—A 96-year-old physician has collected his own life insurance.

The Mutual Life Insurance Co., New York, N. Y. said Saturday it sent Dr. Frederick B. Streeter a $5,141 check because he has outlived the life span covered in the insurance mortality table.

Dr. Streeter took out the policy 63 years ago.

Brief Showers
Minneapolis High 40-45
TUESDAY TEMPERATURES
Details on Page 14

# Minneapolis Morning Tribune

Vol. LXXXIV—No. 322 · Copyright 1951 Minneapolis Star and Tribune Company · MINNEAPOLIS, MINN., WEDNESDAY, APRIL 11, 1951 · Price 5 Cents



# MAC ARTHUR FIRED BY TRUMAN
# Ridgway Gets U.N. Far East Command

## *Truman's Threats to Hush RFC Probe Charged by Tobey*

WASHINGTON—(AP)—Sen. Charles Tobey (R., N. H.) was quoted Tuesday as saying President Truman called him up and tried to intimidate him by saying the White House "had the goods" on various members of congress in connection with RFC loans.

Later, however, the President is reported to have talked to Tobey a second time and to have withdrawn the charges he had made against the legislators.

Congressional sources said Tobey told a senate subcommittee Monday he had made recordings of both conversations with Mr. Truman.

Tobey

The New Hampshire senator, it was reported, told his story to a senate banking subcommittee headed by Sen. J. William Fulbright (D., Ark.). It is this subcommittee which has charged that an influence clique extending into the White House has exercised undue influence on lending operations of the Reconstruction Finance Corp.

**THE SUBCOMMITTEE,** it was learned, treated Tobey's remarks about his conversations with the President as "off-the-record" and did not include them in the official session records.

Several Capitol Hill sources gave this version of Tobey's testimony:

The President telephoned the senator and charged that certain members of congress had taken fees for exerting improper influence on the RFC in connection with the granting of government loans.

The President said he "had the goods" on the legislators because he had copies of letters they had written to the RFC.

The time of the conversation was not given exactly, but it presumably was about the time Mr. Truman was in vigorous controversy with the Fulbright committee, whose report he had called "asinine."

One source said Tobey telephoned Mr. Truman some time later—again recording the conversation—and that this time the President told him he had found there was no basis for the charges of congressional influence on RFC loans.

**THERE WAS NO** immediate indication whether the subcommittee planned to take any further action concerning Tobey's report.

The subcommittee was stirred

RFC
*Continued on Page 12*

## Woman Tells of 'Selling' Postal Jobs

JACKSON, MISS. — (AP) —A witness told a senate committee investigating sale of federal jobs in Mississippi Tuesday she had been "afraid to tell all I knew" for fear "we'd probably all go to the pen."

The witness was Mrs. Claude V. Murphy of Winona, Miss., a member of the pro-Truman Mississippi Democratic committee and identified by previous witnesses as their contact with the committee in buying postoffice department jobs.

Mrs. Murphy and her husband, a rural mail carrier, were sworn in together.

**SHE TOLD** the senate committee Curtis Rodgers, secretary of the committee and Forrest Jackson, an attorney at Jackson, "told us we could accept contributions up to $5,000. I understood that if the contributions were made and I recommended them the people would get the jobs."

She said Rodgers would not accept any checks other than her own, and that "he told me he couldn't run the office on hot air."

She said she had collected $2,630 in contributions for the committee. "I've been afraid to tell all I knew," she testified. "Mr. Rodgers told me that if we told everything we knew we'd probably all go to the pen."

**HER HUSBAND** said he had contributed $700 to the pro-Truman group and $600 to the campaign of Rep. Thomas Abernethy of the fourth Mississippi district.

Archie Watson, a navy veteran, testified he was supposed to pay $2,000 for an appointment as rural mail carrier at Stewart, Miss. He said he did pay $350, but did not get the job though he later got $200 of the $350 back.

Ralph Perkins of Calhoun City, low man on the examination got the job and he testified he made a voluntary contribution of $500.

## Almanac
### Tenstrike Has Nothing to Do With Bowling

*Wednesday, April 11, 1951*

Sunrise 5:38 a.m.; sunset 6:52 p.m.

How did Tenstrike, Minn., get its name? the Almanac asked Sunday.

(1) Carl Erlandson of Blackduck, Minn., says when the 10 men working at the sawmill there went out on strike . . .

(2) Louis Gothge, 2418 Columbus avenue, whose brother-in-law lives in Tenstrike, says years ago a meeting over a name for the village was deadlocked when the clock struck ten and . . .

(3) Dave Zaffke, 8525 Fourteenth avenue S., Bloomington, there, says lumberjacks gave the village the name of a popular fiddlers' tune called . . .

(4) E. E. Wagner, 233 SE. Bedford street, says two men once got into a fight in the village and one of the men was knocked down 10 times so . . .

•

The season now is officially declared open on explanations of how Embarrass, Minn., got its name.

•

The weatherman hasn't yet decided whether skis or umbrellas will be the style in the Twin Cities today, but it will be one or the other for a brief period. High of 40-45.

## 100 Chaska Families Flee Flood Peril

More than 100 families in Chaska fled from the rapidly rising waters of the Minnesota river Tuesday. The major flood danger moved downstream from St. Peter, Minn. and North Mankato, Minn.

High water reached Shakopee, washing over highway 169 there and threating the "One Mile" bridge a mile north of the town.

Workmen were trying to reinforce the bridge late last night. The bridge carries highway 169 over a creek, which was boiling with overflow from the Minnesota river.

**THE HIGHWAY** department said only highways 65 and 101 were open into Shakopee. The Minnesota river flooded an athletic field and a dance hall in Shakopee but only a few homes appeared to be in immediate danger.

Pat Thielen, Shakopee police chief, said the Minnesota was rising two inches an hour. A half foot of water covered the highway between the creek bridge and the main bridge.

Another 200 Chaska families were preparing to abandon their homes if the river climbs four feet more as predicted by army engineers.

An area 10 blocks long in the southeast portion of Chaska was under water last night. Width of the area was as much as three blocks in some places.

The first national guard unit to be called into flood duty was dispatched to Chaska.

**BATTERY D** of the 257th antiaircraft automatic weapons battalion from White Bear, Minn., was called up at 6 p.m. Two hours later, 30 men and two officers were on their way to Chaska. The unit is commanded by Lt. Ray Stickler.

Several state guard units have been called up for duty in Mankato and the surrounding area.

Army engineers predicted the river will crest Thursday at about 29 feet. Yesterday it had climbed to 24.4. There is

Chaska
*Continued on Page 11*

•

### *Profits Unsacked*

SYDNEY, AUSTRALIA—(Reuters)—Henry Hale, a dealer in old sacks who can neither read nor write, was fined $2,240 Tuesday for evading income taxes totaling $48,000. Hale made his money by buying up old used sacks, washing them and storing them until they could be sold at a profit.

AP Wirephoto

**Happy Couple** Industrialist Henry J. Kaiser, 68, and his bride smile happily following their wedding at Santa Barbara, Calif., Tuesday. Kaiser was a half-hour late arriving for his wedding. The bride, Alyce Chester, 34, was a nurse to his wife, who died last month. The couple will honeymoon in Jamaica.

## School Board to Appear on TV

The next meeting of the Minneapolis board of education, April 24, will be televised.

The board Tuesday voted to allow WTCN to telecast the meeting on an experimental basis. Rufus A. Putnam, school superintendent, said that such a telecast would be "the first of its kind," as far as he knew.

Putnam indicated that he would have ready for the next meeting his report on school rehabilitation in 1950. In that case, he added, he would use a seven-foot wall map of the city to help outline his presentation.

## Barge May Be Sunk to Clear Dam

The 1,400-ton coal barge hanging over the lip of the Ford dam on the Mississippi river may have to be sunk, Col. L. G. Yoder, army district engineer, said Tuesday.

Central Barge Co., owners, said the barge is valued at $35,000 to $40,000 and the coal $7,000.

"We're afraid the water may get high enough to take the barge over the dam before we can get equipment strong enough to pull it off," Yoder said.

Earlier he had ordered the dredge William A. Thompson, now docked at Fountain City, Wis., to travel upstream and do the job. He said it would take the Thompson at least three days to get manned and make the trip.

Yoder said he is not certain how much damage the barge would do if it went over the dam. "And I'm not interested in finding out," he added.

If the barge is to be sunk, he said, water will be pumped into it. Yoder said it will not be decided until today what will be done.

The barge, 200 feet long, was dislodged from its moorings under the Washington avenue bridge Monday. Blamed was ice and water swirling downstream from Coon Rapids dam where an ice jam was broken.

The barge moved untouched downstream until it struck the Ford dam.

While officials were deciding what to do, a houseboat broke from its moorings near University of Minnesota, flowed downstream and crashed over the Ford dam. It broke into small pieces.

•



## Hit-Run Death Suspect Found in Burning Car

Special to Minneapolis Tribune

DULUTH, MINN.—Nine-year-old James Krajewski was killed Tuesday and his brother, Walter, 10, was injured by a hit-run driver who stopped to look at his victims before he drove off.

About an hour after the accident police found the automobile involved in the death blazing on a seldom-used side street about two miles from the scene.

**RAY NEWMAN,** 45, found slumped over the wheel of the flaming car, was held for police at St. Luke's hospital here where he was suffering from the effects of smoke.

Newman may have been attempting suicide, police said.

Dr. John W. Ekblad said Newman admitted driving the car when it struck the boys.

Formal charges probably will be placed against Newman today, following the outcome of a coroner's inquest, police said.

The two boys were struck late yesterday afternoon as they came through a west end alley on the way home from school.

Walter suffered a broken leg. Witnesses said the driver of the car stopped, got out, looked at the two boys lying in the street, made a second pass at the boys and then drove off.

**A WITNESS** supplied the license number of the 1939 car and a description and an immediate citywide search started.

About 5 p.m., firemen were called to the side street where neighbors reported an auto afire. Firemen recognized it immediately from the broadcast description.

Dr. Ekblad said Newman was revived at the scene and later taken to the hospital.

The two boys are the sons of Mr. and Mrs. Joseph Krajewski.

•

## Cigaret Lighter Starts Home Fire

A fire believed caused by three small boys playing with a cigaret lighter caused $700 damage to a bedroom of the Edmond B. Peterson home, 3817 Forty-first avenue S.

Mrs. Peterson said she was doing the laundry when the fire apparently was started by Edmond, Jr., 3, and two of his playmates who were playing with a table cigaret lighter in the bedroom closet.

Most of the family's clothes were lost in the fire, Mrs. Peterson said.

## Zzzz or Not to Zzzz
### HUBBY GETS 30 DAYS TO QUIET DOWN

CHICAGO — (AP) — If Richard Michalak wants his wife back, he must cure himself of snoring within 30 days.

Mrs. Florence Michalak, 20, told Judge Rudolph F. Desort of superior court Tuesday she would go back to her husband if he could learn to snooze quietly in that time.

Mrs. Michalak is suing for separate maintenance on grounds Michalak's snoring wrecked her health.

Her attorney, Charles C. Colley, gave Michalak a number of suggestions for curing snoring he said he had received from "several hundred" persons.

Some of the snore lore included suggestions that he take a blood test for possible sleeping sickness, take a "brain wave test" from a psychiatrist, or place a rubber tube around his neck.

One person suggested he train himself to keep his mouth closed at night by keeping it closed during the day.

Another wrote that Michalak's head "is too flat on the pillow. Get a higher pillow." Another suggested he sprinkle salt on his tongue. Someone else thought he had anemia and favored a few blood transfusions.

Mrs. McBurney of Chicago advised Michalak to eat an onion sandwich on buttered bread, seasoned with plenty of salt and to drink a cup of tea just before retiring. Then, she said, he should rinse his mouth with lemon juice. Mrs. McBurney assured Michalak it cured her grandfather who "whistled and puffed like an old steam engine."

Judge Desort urged Michalak to try everything to cure himself. Michalak took the list home to start trying.

RICHARD MICHALAK, WIFE
*He seeks snoring cure*

## Senate Kills Family Courts Bill
### Move to 'Postpone' Ends Plan's Chances for This Session

By ROLF FELSTAD
Minneapolis Tribune Staff Writer

The Minnesota senate sentenced the family courts bill to death Tuesday.

It adopted a motion by Sen. Magnus Wefald, Hawley, "to indefinitely postpone," effectively killing the proposal for this session. Vote was 37 to kill, with no "nay" call taken.

Wefald

Senate opponents, in a half day of debate, charged the bill with being expensive, unconstitutional and likely to clutter up the courts with "trivial" matters.

The bill was a product of an interim committee on domestic relations which drafted nine bills relating to divorce, dependency and adoption. Eight have received tentative approval.

**MOST IMPORTANT** of the nine, the family bill would have permitted establishment of domestic relations courts or conciliators, and would require a 90-day "cooling-off" period before an actual divorce action could be started.

The senate yesterday first struck out of the bill a provision enabling Hennepin county to designate its juvenile judge as the domestic relations specialist.

Sen. Daniel S. Feidt, Minneapolis, offered an amendment placing Hennepin county on the same basis as the rest of the state—with district judges authorized to designate one or more of their number as domestic relations judges.

Sen. Wendell Ledin, Bethel, who was acting as chairman, broke an 18-18 tie on the amendment by voting for it. Sen. Gerald T. Mullin, Minneapolis, backer of the bill, asked for another vote and this time the amendment was adopted, 23-22.

Leading off for the "prosecution," Sen. A. O. Sletvold, Detroit Lakes, warned that the conciliation procedure required before a divorce action would waste the time of district judges.

**"THE SHIP** of matrimony doesn't always sail a calm sea," said Sletvold. "When a controversy arose, husband or wife would run right down to the court and also, by that very action, make the other party resentful."

Sletvold said he also believed the measure expensive and unconstitutional.

"You can't conciliate," Sen. Gordon Rosenmeier, Little Falls, pointed out, "such things as impotence, imprisonment, desertion and incurable insanity."

•

## Burglars Develop Weather Quirks

The whims of Minnesota weather apparently have made a strong impression on some Minneapolis burglars.

Sometime Monday night, thieves took 11 steam radiators—weighing about 300 pounds each—from a house being redecorated at 1345 First avenue S.

The radiators, with a scrap value of about $175 and a replacement value of about $500, had been placed alongside the house during the redecoration.

### TURN THE PAGES TO:



## GEN VAN FLEET NAMED TO HEAD EIGHTH ARMY

WASHINGTON—(AP)—President Truman early today forced Gen. Douglas MacArthur from all his commands.

The President said he had concluded that MacArthur "is unable to give his wholehearted support" to United States and United Nations policies.

Mr. Truman immediately designated Lt. Gen. Matthew B. Ridgway as MacArthur's successor as supreme commander, allied powers, commander in chief, United Nations command, commander in chief, far east; and commanding general, United States army, far east.

In a statement, Mr. Truman asserted that "military commanders must be governed" by policies and directives of the government and "in time of crisis, this consideration is particularly compelling."

The President appointed Lt. Gen. James A. Van Fleet to succeed Ridgeway to take over active command of of the eighth army.

**ANNOUNCEMENT** of the almost unprecedented dismissal of the hero-general was made at a rare news conference at the White House at 1 a.m. (EST).

The time was fixed to coincide as nearly as possible with the delivery to MacArthur at Tokyo of the order relieving him of his commands, "effective at once."

The White House released, with the President's statement, a memorandum purporting to show differences between MacArthur's statements and action and presidential policy.

The President's order, telegraphed to MacArthur over the army network, was brief.

"I deeply regret that it becomes my duty as President and commander in chief of the United States military forces to replace you as supreme commander, Allied powers, commander in chief, United Nations command; commander in chief, far east, commanding general, United States army far east.

GEN. MacARTHUR
*Relieved of command*

**"YOU WILL** turn over your commands, effective at once, to Lt. Gen. Matthew B. Ridgway. You are authorized to have issued such orders as are necessary to complete desired travel to such places as you select.

"My reasons for your replacement will be made public concurrently with the delivery to you of the foregoing order, and are contained in the next following message." (This referred to the President's statement.)

The President's action came as the aftermath of a series of differences with MacArthur over policy in the far east and raised prospects that MacArthur might return to this country to deliver a series of blasts against the administration, probably under auspices of Republican supporters of the general.

GEN. RIDGWAY
*New U.N. commander*

The President's statement asserted that MacArthur's place in history "as one of our greatest commanders" is fully established.

**"THE NATION** owes him a debt of gratitude for the distinguished and exceptional service which he has rendered his country in posts of great responsibility," the President's statement said.

"For that reason I repeat my refret at the necessity for the action I feel compelled to take in his case."

Van Fleet

Aware of political reverberations certain to follow in the wake of his action, the President made public a series of heretofore secret directives tending to show how MacArthur failed to follow administrative foreign policy.

**THESE INCLUDED** one from the joint chiefs of staff to MacArthur and other commanders on Dec. 6, 1950, embracing a presidential order that "no speeches, press releases, or other public statement concerning military policy should be released until it has received clearance from the department of defense."

To this was attached another memo from the joint chiefs of staff to MacArthur March 20, 1951, asserting that the state department was planning an announcement shortly that "with clearing of bulk of South Korea aggressors, United Nations now prepared to discuss conditions of settlement in Korea" and adding:

"Strong U.N. feling persists that further diplomatic efforts towards settlement should be made before any advance with major forces north of 38th parallel.

"Time will be required to determine diplomatic reactions and permit new negotiations that may develop."

## Army Plane Burns; 8 Die

FAIRBANKS, ALASKA—(AP)—Eight airmen perished Tuesday in the crash of an air force C54 in a glider pick-up attempt.

Witnesses said the big four-engine transport exploded and burst into flames after striking the south runway of Ladd air force base. There was no chance for any of the men aboard to escape.

Capt. Joe Worthington, base information officer, said the C54 was trying to pick up the glider on a routine flight. Witnesses said flames engulfed the shattered plane from tail to engines within a minute after the blast.

It was a 10th rescue squadron airplane. Names of the victims were withheld pending notification of their families.

•

### *Esther's Flip Nicks Red's Lips*

HOLLYWOOD, CALIF.—(AP)—Film and radio comedian Red Skelton nursed a badly-cut lip Tuesday in the aftermath to a film scene with Esther Williams. Esther threw a tin can at the actor as per script. The blow cut Skelton's lip, necessitating several stitches.

•

### Pastor to Be Installed

FAIRFAX, MINN.—(AP)—The Rev. W. F. Vatthauer of Gillet, Ark., will be installed as pastor of St. John's Lutheran church here Sunday. He succeeds the Rev. I. F. Albricht who resigned after 51 years in the pulpit in Fairfax.

**Partly Cloudy**
Minneapolis High 75
FRIDAY TEMPERATURES
*Details on Page 10*

# Minneapolis Morning Tribune

Vol. LXXXV—No. 107 | Copyright, 1951, Minneapolis Star and Tribune Company | MINNEAPOLIS, MINN., SATURDAY, SEPTEMBER 8, 1951 | Price 5 Cents



# Gromyko Squelched Again

# JAPS APOLOGIZE FOR PEARL HARBOR

## Postage Hikes Pass in Senate

### 4-Cent Letters, 2-Cent Post Cards Included in Boost

WASHINGTON — (AP) — The senate passed a bill Friday night increasing the postage of ordinary letters from three cents to four and calling for other hikes to boost postal revenues a total of nearly 400 million dollars.

The measure would increase postage on postal cards from one cent to two cents.

It raises the postage for air-mail letters from six to eight cents.

Passage came by a voice vote.

The measure, intended to wipe out part of the postoffice department's annual deficit, now goes to the house.

**OTHER INCREASES** would boost the rates on newspapers 30 per cent over a three-year period and on magazines 60 per cent over a like period.

Charges for third and fourth class mail, and such special services as special delivery, also would be hiked by the legislation.

"Here is a chance to save one of the last things the American citizen can spend a penny on," pleaded Senator Long (D., La.), sponsor of an amendment to keep the one-cent rate on cards written by individuals and charitable tax-exempt organizations.

**ON A ROLL-CALL** vote, the senate defeated the amendment, 56 to 10.

The postoffice department hopes to increase its revenue by more than 44 million dollars a year with two-cent postal cards.

The bill also provides that the 500,000 postal workers have the same annual vacations as other government workers. Their new vacations would range from 13 to 26 days a year, depending on length of service.

A separate bill to give 201 million dollars a year in pay increases to postal workers is scheduled to be taken up later.

Earlier the senate refused, for the second time, to order the department to restore twice-a-day mail deliveries in residential areas.

In favor of reconsidering previous senate action were Senators Humphrey (D., Minn.), Langer (R., N. D.) and McCarthy (R., Wis.). Against reconsideration were Senators Case (R., S. D.), Mundt (R., S. D.), and Young (R., N. D.).

Long Langer
*Their pleas go unheeded*

## Almanac

### Does the Commission Get Split?

*Saturday, September 8, 1951*
Sunrise 5:42 a.m.; sunset 6:39 p.m.

A housewife we know called a company for service on a very old dishwasher. Repair man came out, took a look and said it couldn't be fixed.

Thirty-six hours later her phone rang. It was the same company, a different department: "I hear you're in the market for a new dishwasher. . . ."

*On this day 1906, Minnesota's brown beauty, Dan Patch, paced the mile in 1:55 at the Minnesota State fairgrounds, setting a new world's pacing record. The famous horse died in 1916.*

Leonard Lampert, Jr., president of the Lampert Lumber Co., is 59 today.

The Twin Cities weather outlook for the next five days:

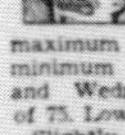

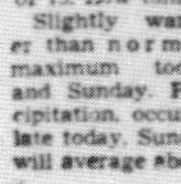

Temperatures will average two to six degrees below the normal maximum of 74 and normal minimum of 54. Cool Tuesday and Wednesday. High today of 75. Low tonight: 55.

Slightly warmer than normal maximum today and Sunday. Precipitation, occurring as showers late today, Sunday and Monday, will average about one-half inch.

**YANKS TAKE FIRST AS INDIANS SPLIT**
•
**Millers Divide Twin-Bill**
•
**DODGERS, GIANTS WIN**
•
*DETAILS in Sports section.*

## Oil Drillers Hit 2nd Well Near Tioga

Special to Minneapolis Tribune

TIOGA, N. D.—Another oil strike near Tioga was reported Friday.

Amerada Petroleum Co. announced it had hit oil and gas in a well about three miles northeast of here at a depth of 8,360 feet.

(*MAP—page 7.*)

The strike is North Dakota's second major one this year and the third in the so-called Williston basin area of western North Dakota and eastern Montana.

**OILMEN AT TULSA,** Okla., where Amerada has headquarters, called it a "second-rank" well, but Amerada said the oil flow was "fairly substantial" and a "fair amount" of gas accompanied it.

The oil showed 40 per cent gravity, considered high grade although not as good as Amerada's original discovery well at Tioga.

Yesterday's discovery was on farmland owned by Harry Bakken in Williams county, section 12, township 157 north, range 95 west.

The Bakken well is 12 miles north of the North Dakota discovery well, the Clarence Iverson No. 1, brought in by Amerada April 4. Company officials said flow of the Bakken well had not been gauged. It was shut off after a 40-minute test. Officials added that drilling will continue.

**OIL FEVER** was running high in this little village of fewer than 400 people and in the two cities nearest here — Minot and Williston. Telephone lines into the area were clogged. Amerada officials, tight-lipped except for the brief verification of the strike, were reported heading for the well.

At Tulsa, Amerada's assistant chief geologist, Charles Agey, denied widespread reports that the discovery was a "gusher" which blew 90 feet into the air.

Rumors of the strike sent Amerada stock on the New York exchange up $6.25 a share even before the official announcement.

Agey said the most important thing about the strike is that it is at a shallower—and thus more economical—depth than the Iverson discovery well.

**HE REFUSED** to confirm the Bakken strike is in the Madison formation, but North Dakota geologists said that depth almost certainly would be in the Madison. There also were reports that it was in the Mississippian formation.

(Madison and Mississippian are names of underground geological layers.)

Some oilmen said that discoveries in the Madison usually represent seepage from other levels and may not sustain production over a long period.

Agey said the oil was about the same quality as that now being produced in the Iverson well at its present level, but not quite so good as the first that came out of the discovery hole.

Drilling has stopped at the Iverson well and it is in regular production. Oil from that well is being refined at Northwestern Refining Co., St. Paul Park, Minn.

**THE SECOND** Tioga strike raised hopes for a major oil field in the Williston basin area. Early in July, Shell Oil Co. brought in a promising well near Richey, Mont., about 50

N. D. Oil
*Continued on Page Seven*

## LILIBET HAS EARS PIERCED

LONDON — (Reuters) — Princess Elizabeth had her ears pierced this week.

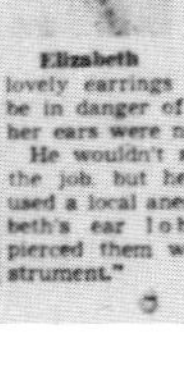

Elizabeth

Cyril Wilkinson said the princess summoned him to her home at Clarence house a few days ago. She wanted him to prick her ears, he said, because "she had some lovely earrings and she would be in danger of losing them if her ears were not pierced."

He wouldn't say how he did the job, but he did reveal he used a local anesthetic on Elizabeth's ear lobes before he pierced them with "a gold instrument."

## Japan: From Vast Asiatic Empire to 4 Home Islands

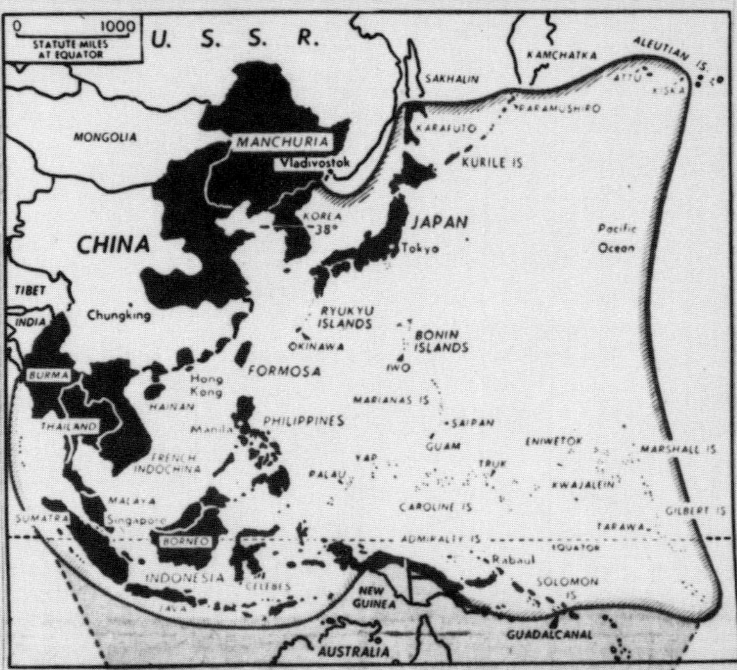



The Japanese empire at its peak of expansion during World War II in 1942 spread far out into the Pacific (map above). It included an area of 3,045,300 square miles with a population of 625 million. By the signing of the San Francisco treaty the Japanese nation shrinks to a nation of four main islands (map below) with an area of 136,000 square miles and a population of 84 million.

1942: PREMIER TOJO
*His empire . . .*

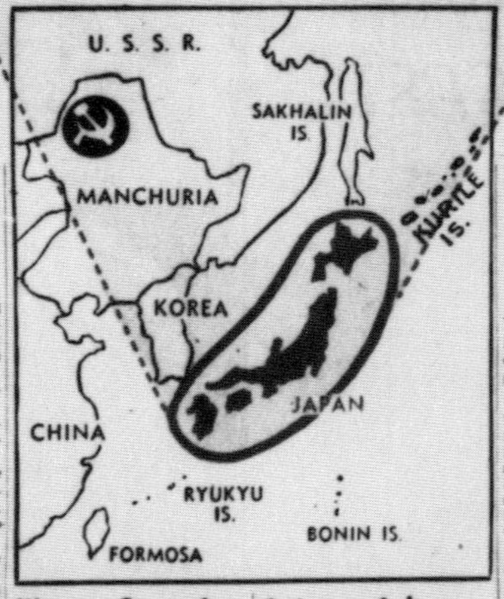

1951: PREMIER YOSHIDA
*. . . has dwindled*

## Record Arms Fund Gains

WASHINGTON — (AP)—A senate committee Friday approved a $61,103,856,030 military spending bill amid new talk of secret and devastating weapons "in a high state of development."

The huge sum would be divided this way:

ARMY — $20,026,170,030, compared with $20,113,524,200 approved by the house.

NAVY — $15,544,881,000, the amount approved by the house.

AIR FORCE — $20,001,585,000, compared with $19,846,985,000 approved by the house.

Reports that "some of the funds" for the new weapons are in the big bill, were confirmed by Senator O'Mahoney (D., Wyo.).

There are also relatively small sums for the national security council and the secretary of defense.

The senate appropriations committee, in addition, set up a five-billion-dollar national emergency fund to be used essentially for development of air power.

Senators Mundt (R., S.D.), and Young (R., N.D.), gave additional but meager information about the mystery weapons, which President Truman referred to earlier this week as "fantastic."

Young told reporters of their "high state of development" and said they probably could be used if an all-out war broke suddenly.

•

**CHURCHES CURBED**

VATICAN CITY — (Reuters) —Vatican radio said Friday the Hungarian government that ordered punishment of persons taking part in Budapest church services if Communist authorities have not been notified of the time of their commencement.

## Woman Strangles Son, 7 Months

A Minneapolis mother strangled her 7-month-old son Friday night, police reported.

Dead is Christopher Max Dean, son of Mr. and Mrs. H. Alexander Dean, 4912 Emerson avenue S.

The mother, Mrs. Marjorie Dean, 34, had to be taken to St. Mary's hospital under restraint, Dr. Russell R. Heim, Hennepin county coroner, said.

In a statement to police, Mrs. Dean said: "The baby died of strangulation because I did it."

Heim said the boy apparently was strangled with a bathrobe cord. The baby's father found the body when he came home about 6 p.m., Heim said.

Mrs. Dean has been in poor mental health the past two months, Heim said, but didn't seek the aid of a physician because of religious beliefs.

Heim said three other children, one son and two daughters, were not harmed.

## Stripper Asks Body Repairs in Crash Lawsuit

MIAMI, FLA. — (Special) — Rosita Royce, a fan dancer who uses doves instead of fans, filed suit Friday against a yacht captain for $50,000 damages, including $3,000 for body repairs.

Rosita charged that Orrie Lafayette Davis, the yachtsman, navigated his automobile, in which both were riding, into a collision while watching her instead of the road.

The strip dancer suffered a cut high on her right thigh and another on her right eyelid.

**TURN THE PAGES TO:**



## Gromyko Walks Out, Walks In

SAN FRANCISCO, CALIF. — (AP) — Andrei Gromyko walked out on the Japanese peace conference Friday night and promptly walked back in.

*PICTURE—page 6.*

At a high point in final debate as the conference raced toward conclusion, Gromyko got up and strode rapidly out while the British delegate was speaking.

It looked like a put-up job as Soviet chauffeurs at the carriage entrance of the opera house here had kept the motors running for a half hour previously.

Suddenly Gromyko turned back and resumed his seat while the audience was in an uproar.

British delegate Kenneth Younger kept right on talking all through all the noise.

During his brief sortie to the lobby, Gromyko was accompanied by two aids. He talked briefly in the front of the lobby with the Czech delegate, Dr. Gertrude Sekaninova. They spoke in low voices.

Then Gromyko slowly turned and stalked back to his seat. If he was amused by his dramatic maneuver, he failed to show it until he reached his seat, when he smiled.

The Czech woman also returned to her seat.

## Bandit, Girl Seized After Long Chase

William Earl Miller, 35, captured in Minneapolis Friday by a detective who tracked him 7,000 miles, admitted robbing a Canadian bank.

He said he made his initial escape by rowing a boat across the Niagara river, two miles below the famous honeymoon falls.

Also being held in city jail is Miller's girl friend, Kathleen Mary Jordan, 18, Toronto, Canada, a plump brunette.

Tong

Both were arrested at the main postoffice by Detective Sergeant Edmund Tong, of Toronto police, assisted by Minneapolis Detectives Craig Mattice and Mike Michaelson.

Tong said he got a tip Miller was to call for a letter yesterday at the general delivery window. He declined to state the nature of the letter.

**MILLER IS WANTED** for the $8,000 holdup of the Bank of Ontario at St. David's, Canada, Aug. 16. Tong said the stickup was staged by two bandits, but Miller refused to name his accomplice.

The detectives waited near the general delivery window yesterday from 8:20 a.m. until Miller and Miss Jordan arrived about noon. Miller, who carried a .32 caliber pistol and a pocketful of bullets, gave up without a struggle.

It was "old home week" for Miller when he spotted Detective Tong. Twice before, the police officer had arrested Miller for armed robbery. Miller, an ex-

Capture
*Continued on Page Eight*

## 4 Injured in Head-on Crash

Special to Minneapolis Tribune

ST. CLOUD, MINN. — Four Twin Cities persons were injured, one seriously, in a head-on collision Friday on highway 152 near Clearwater, Minn.

Taken to St. Cloud hospital were Glen Nelson, 56, 3700 Longfellow avenue, Minneapolis; Alfred J. Bryant, 40, 7710 Harold avenue, Golden Valley; Mrs. Edgar Haugen, 49, 682 Kenneth street, St. Paul, and her daughter, Connie, 19. Mrs. Haugen was in serious condition.

State highway police said the accident apparently resulted when Mrs. Haugen started a left turn in front of the oncoming car driven by Nelson. Bryant was a passenger in Nelson's car and Mrs. Haugen and her daughter were riding together on their way home from Fergus Falls, Minn.

## $79.20 FOR TIP? NO, COURT SAYS

R. F. Ferguson, justice of the peace, decided Friday in St. Paul that $79.20 was more than a "reasonable" tip on an 80-cent taxicab fare.

The Checker Cab Co. agreed, but a former driver for the company, Alton Mabry, 19, 444½ St. Peter street, didn't.

The cab company said Mabry got a check from a woman two months ago for an 80-cent fare, but it was made out by mistake for $80.

When the woman discovered her error, she told the cab firm and was repaid. The company brought the court action against Mabry to get the money, and won.

## 49 Nations to Sign Pact Today

By JAMES RESTON
Special From the New York Times

SAN FRANCISCO, CALIF.—The Japanese peace conference business sessions ended Friday night with Russia fighting all the way.

Reston

The treaty will be signed by 49 nations, including Japan, at 10 a.m. today.

These were the major developments yesterday:

1. Russia's Andrei Gromyko failed in a move to open debate on a series of treaty amendments he proposed Wednesday.

2. Premier Shigeru Yoshida of Japan stood before the 52-nation conference and apologized for his nation's World War II aggression that started with Pearl Harbor.

3. At one point last night, Gromyko walked out, climaxing the implied threat that has hung over the conference from the start. The Russian delegate returned, however. (See story in adjoining column.)

4. The conference imposed a 30-minute rule on debate.

**THE ALLIED GESTURE** of letting the opposition talk again was a good-humored one and, in its way, sort of a put up job.

Ceylon proposed, Cuba seconded it, and it was voted favorably, 41 to 1, with the Czech delegate surprisingly voting "no."

The Allies showed their strength again by voting, 46 to 3, not to consider the Soviet amendments of Wednesday which Gromyko immediately proposed again.

The non-Communist nations were so clearly in control of the conference that an air of jollity was evident.

The annoyed, persistent sallies of Gromyko and other satellite delegates drew good-humored, sarcastic responses from United States Secretary of State Acheson, United States Ambassador John Foster Dulles and others.

**THE DELIGHTED** audience repeatedly roared with laughter as Acheson slapped down the Iron Curtain forces on points of order and Dulles told them they already had been given 11 months to talk and HAD talked 11 months.

Gromyko used up most of his last hour in a tortured rephrasing of his old arguments against the treaty.

It appeared to listeners that Gromyko, recognizing his resounding defeat on the treaty

Treaty
*Continued on Page Eight*

**RUSS READY WITH RAIL RESERVATIONS**

SAN FRANCISCO, CALIF.—(UP)—Southern Pacific railroad officials reported Friday that the Soviet delegation had made reservations to leave San Francisco next Monday. The Russians will travel aboard the Overland Limited in the same two cars which brought them to the conference.

KATHLEEN MARY JORDAN
*Bandit's girl friend*

WILLIAM EARL MILLER
*Admits $8,000 bank robbery*

**Little Change**
Minneapolis High 28

# Minneapolis Morning Tribune

Vol. LXXXV—No. 259 · MINNEAPOLIS, MINN., THURSDAY, FEBRUARY 7, 1952 · Price 5 Cents


# Elizabeth, Queen at 25, Flies Home to Take Over Rule

## U.S. Links 22 Aids to Grain Scandal

By WILBUR ELSTON
Minneapolis Tribune Staff Correspondent

WASHINGTON—At least 22 employes of the department of agriculture have reaped a harvest of gifts from firms dealing with the department, it was learned Wednesday.

They got Stetson hats, cigaret lighters, week-end outings, tickets to baseball and football games, baskets of fruit, kegs of shrimp, boxes of cigars and $100 gift certificates.

**FOUR EMPLOYES** received Holy Bibles (King James version) from an Oklahoma grain company.

The production and marketing administration (PMA) disclosed that three of these employes now have been fired, one has resigned, two have been reprimanded and given 30-day suspensions and three have been "cautioned."

Latest to get the ax were Latham White and Harry J. Solomon, top officials of the Dallas, Texas, PMA office who were fired yesterday.

White has been with the agriculture department since 1936, Solomon since 1933.

They were accused of neglect of duty and conduct "prejudicial to the service," which included receiving gifts themselves and condoning the acceptance of similar gifts by 13 employes under their supervision.

White said in Dallas he did not think the charges justified his or Solomon's dismissal.

**"I REGRET** that the house agricultural subcommittee that met last week did not call us to Washington to testify," White said, "but I have hopes the senate committee will call me up to tell my side of the story."

Solomon could not be reached immediately for comment.

Several storage concerns in the Dallas area have been accused of converting more than 2½ million dollars worth of government grain stored with them to their own use, mainly for speculative purposes.

Brannan announced that White and Solomon were taken off duty more than a month ago pending further investigation and now have been discharged effective Friday.

A spokesman said their answers to department charges of inefficiency were deemed "unsatisfactory" by Brannan. The answers were not made public.

Brannan said none of the gifts were from firms involved in the grain shortages.

Meanwhile, a survey showed the government has gone to court against 35 storage concerns in various parts of the country in an effort to collect $4,875,000 in shortages of farm

Gifts
Continued on Page 11

## Son Born to Child-Slayer Serving Life Term

McALESTER, OKLA.—(AP)—A woman child-slayer serving life in the state penitentiary Wednesday gave birth to a son, who immediately became the center of a custody fight.

The father, Roy J. Dial, Lawton, Okla., cab driver, filed a writ in district court to prevent the child from being turned over to the state child welfare department.

"I do not want to see the baby after it is born," Mrs. Dial, 24, said.

She was convicted of beating her 30-month old daughter to death and was committed last Nov. 14.

## Aldermen Defer Action on Curly's Bar

Aldremanic action on a liquor law violation involving Meyer (Makey) Gordon and Curly's Theater cafe was delayed Wednesday until Feb. 27, but not until the case was discussed at length.

The discussion touched upon questions involving willfulness of the violation and ownership of the cafe at 20 S. Fifth street.

**GORDON WAS FINED** $100 Jan. 23 by Municipal Judge Tom Bergin on a charge of keeping the place open after the 1 a.m. legal hour on Jan. 15.

Gordon is ineligible to hold a liquor license because of a previous liquor law violation.

The city council health and hospitals committee, which makes recommendations to the full council, met to consider whether the liquor license for Curly's should be suspended or revoked.

With Alderman Stanley Anderson absent because of illness and Frank Wolinski absent on

Curly's
Continued on Page 11

## Almanac

### Are They Talking About the Sermons?

*Thursday, February 7, 1952*

There are advertisements scattered throughout the yellow pages of the Minneapolis telephone directory, encouraging people to shop through the yellow pages. Even in the church section.

The advertisement in the church section reads: "For the brand you want look in the Yellow Pages."

•

*One of our northeast side Almanackers spotted a "Rooms for Rent" ad in a Minneapolis weekly newspaper. The ad offers "SLEEPING rooms on streetcar line."*

•

***Another weather reprieve for Twin Cities residents today. Little change in temperature, high of 28.***

•

Bad Pun Department: An Associated Press man reports his wife was touching up some picture frames with gold paint and when she finished, she put the bottle of gold paint in the medicine cabinet.

The other morning he reached into the cabinet to get some mouth wash. He mistakenly grabbed the gold paint and took a healthy slug.

"As soon as I swallowed it, I knew it was wrong," he said, "I felt gilty inside."

•

Summery Item: The Minneapolis park board has accepted bids for 100,000 popcorn boxes, 200,000 paper cups and 50,000 hot drink paper cups. Total cost: $3,921.



## Farm Outgo, Income Set Records

### Receipts in State Rise 14 Per Cent; Costs Up 12 Per Cent

Minnesota farmers took in more money last year than ever before but they also paid out more.

Cash receipts from sale of farm products reached a new peak of 1,391,000,000 in 1951, while expenses rose nearly 12 per cent above the previous high mark set in 1950.

Rex W. Cox, associate professor of agricultural economics at the University of Minnesota, said that the new highs in both receipts and expenses counterbalanced each other and the actual increase in net cash income over last year was only slight.

The billion-dollar cash receipts topped 1950 by 14 per cent and the previous record in 1948 by 4 per cent.

**CASH RECEIVED** from crops dropped sharply but those from livestock, livestock products and dairy products made up for the loss.

Crops brought in 337 million dollars in 1950 but fell to 304 million in 1951. Livestock and dairy incomes rose from 517 million dollars in 1950 to 646 million in 1951.

For the second consecutive year, receipts from sales of cattle and calves exceeded those of hogs.

Marketings of cattle were down, but with prices of cattle and calves averaging 31 and 25 per cent higher, total cash receipts from cattle and calves were larger than in any previous year, Cox reported.

Farmers took in 323 million dollars from cattle and calves in 1951 compared with 257 million in 1950.

Receipts from hogs in 1951 were 304 million dollars as against 246 million in 1950. Sheep and lamb receipts rose from 14 million in 1950 to 19 million dollars in 1951.

**DAIRY PRODUCT** receipts in 1951 were 238 million dollars compared with 207 million in 1950 and a 260-million-dollar high in 1948.

Egg income reached a new high of 137 million dollars in 1951, as did turkeys which brought in 32 million dollars.

Livestock accounted for about half the total 1951 receipts, crops about one-fifth and dairy products less than one-fifth.

## GOP Candidate Slain in Chicago

CHICAGO—(UP)—Charles Gross, 50, a Republican candidate for committeeman of Chicago's 31st ward, was shot and killed in front of his home by gunmen who escaped in a black sedan.

Gross, a soft drink manufacturer, was cut down by six blasts from a shotgun as he left his home on Chicago's west side.

Gross was making his first bid for office. He had been active in Republican politics for many years. Police said there was no apparent motive for his murder.

## Pardon Proposed for Philippine Reds

MANILA, PHILIPPINES—(AP)—A bill authorizing President Elpidio Quirino to grant full amnesty to Communist Huks and their leaders was introduced in the Philippines congress Wednesday.

Hundreds of Huks surrendered under previous grants of amnesty.

## Man Buys Rifle, Kills Self Outside Store

LAWRENCE, KAN.—(AP)—A 64-year-old retired farmer bought a rifle in a Lawrence hardware store, was told how to load it, then shot himself to death in front of the shop.

Police identified him as Roy E. Steffey of Ozawki, Kan.

## $$$ The Big Business of Sports $$$

## The Fans Demand Entertainment

***Sports must amuse these days, and if they do it well they make money, says Joe Hendrickson, Tribune sports editor, in today's installment of his "Big Business of Sports" series. Wrestling, ice and sports men's shows and roller derbies are cited as examples.***

Hendrickson

By JOE HENDRICKSON

The sports fan today wants to be entertained even though he still cares who wins and roots for favorites.

Besides field goals and touchdowns, the fan wants laughs, spectacular daring, grace, beauty and showmanship.

Entertainment is the word.

Wrestling fits the formula. While many sports are fighting a business recession, wrestling enjoys record prosperity, with national attendance 164 per cent above 1946 and gate receipts 180 per cent higher.

**THE ICE SHOW** business, especially the Shipstad and Johnson Ice Follies, is enjoying its biggest season financially.

Auto racing is attracting more spectators than ever. Outdoor or sportsman's shows click. The roller derby draws large crowds.

Oscar Johnson, one of the owners of the Ice Follies, reports his show is surpassing any previous year in attendance. The Follies always draw large crowds—2,250,000 a year at $2 per ticket.

Since 1936 the Follies have played before 30 million with a gate of 60 million dollars. This show proves the ticket buyer will come if he is entertained.

**ABOUT 13 MILLION** persons paid 16 million dollars to see wrestling matches in 1951. From Gorgeous George to Lovable Lou to Hateful Hans, the wrestlers are making money—some $50,000 to $75,000 a year.

Hendrickson
Continued on Page 21

## 2nd Twin, Born in Ambulance, Is Surprise

PITTSBURGH, PA.—(AP)—A doctor took a new baby, born in a speeding ambulance, in his arms and congratulated the police officer who delivered the infant.

Then he gasped. In the blanket covering the new mother he found another baby.

The policeman stared blankly at the infant and the labor weary mother let out a short cry of amazement.

Unknown to Mrs. Thelma Kedzierski she had given birth to twins. The second child came a few seconds after the first during the rapid ambulance ride. Baby No. 1 weighed in at four pounds 13 ounces, baby No. 2 at two pounds two ounces.

## Taft Lead Not Too Big, Ike Forces Say

By RICHARD WILSON
Chief of the Minneapolis Tribune Washington Bureau

WASHINGTON—A secret Eisenhower estimate of delegate strength for the presidential nomination shows Senator Robert A. Taft of Ohio currently in the lead, but not commandingly so.

This estimate is being shown to prospective contributors to the Eisenhower campaign fund as an inducement.

**THE ESTIMATE** coincides with what many political observers in Washington believe, and so some attention is being paid to it now.

According to these figures the delegate strength is divided up about as follows:

Senator Robert A. Taft ..392
Gen. Dwight Eisenhower 326
Governor Earl Warren .. 77
Harold E. Stassen ....... 67

Stassen certainly would contest this estimate of his delegate strength. Taft contends he has the more than the 600 required for his nomination.

According to this compilation, Eisenhower would get all the New Hampshire delegates; Wisconsin would be divided 24 for Taft, 6 for Stassen; New York, 20 for Taft, 96 for Eisenhower; Indiana, 20 for Taft, 12 for Eisenhower; Texas, 27 for Taft, 9 for Eisenhower, 1 for Stassen; Massachusetts, 20 for Taft, 18 for Eisenhower.

Taft people would claim that Eisenhower strength is overestimated in New York, Indiana and Texas. They also believe Eisenhower will not win all the delegates in New Hampshire.

**THEY MIGHT NOT**, however, contest the estimate that at the present time 40 Pennsylvania delegates are being held by Governor John S. Fine for Gen. Douglas MacArthur.

According to the Eisenhower sources, however, the estimate is a conservative one.

What it clearly illustrates is that the Eisenhower backers now believe they do have a real fight on their hands. They will do everything they can to get their candidate back to the United States and out of uniform to conduct a campaign.

They seem to agree that their interests would be best served if Eisenhower were to return to the United States some time in April. This is the target date they are shooting for.

**IT IS USEFUL** to recall that Senator Frank Carlson of Kansas, one of Eisenhower's main backers, was insisting that the general make his statement in January.

Now, it is to be seen whether his backers can prevail upon him again to make a campaign at the time they think a campaign will be necessary.

## National Primary Bill Introduced

By Staff Correspondent of the Minneapolis Tribune

WASHINGTON—Representative Henry O. Talle (R., Iowa) introduced legislation to provide for a federal presidential primary "to take the selection of candidates out of smoked-filled rooms."

Talle said the primary election law issue should not be partisan, and that 18 other representatives—both Democrats and Republicans—have agreed to co-sponsor the bill. He said it will be necessary to get a constitutional amendment to establish a binding presidential primary system.

## Czechs Execute Five

LONDON—(AP)—Czechoslovakia has executed five Czechs convicted of treason and espionage on behalf of the United States, Moscow radio said Wednesday. Three others got life terms.

## Elizabeth's Story—First of a Series

***What kind of queen will Elizabeth be? A correspondent long associated with doings of the British royal family helps provide an answer in the following article, first of several telling about Elizabeth, the person.***

By JOHN E. CARLOVA

LONDON—(INS)—The new Queen Elizabeth was 10 years old when she first gave evidence that she was learning to behave like a queen.

The occasion was a morning in the nursery of the little princesses, Elizabeth and Margaret. Elizabeth had been naughty and her exasperated nurse refused to speak to her.

The child princess—then called "Lilibet" as she still is by some of her intimates—was infuriated, stamped her foot and stormed:

"I say, you must answer me! This is royalty speaking!"

**ONE DAY** during the same period, Elizabeth gave another example of her childlike self-importance. She had accompanied the dowager Queen Mary to an exhibition of goods made by the blind.

An attendant, flustered by the appearance of the queen mother and the solemn-faced little princess, picked up an object he thought would amuse the child and said to Queen Mary:

"Your Majesty, I think this will interest the little lady."

Elizabeth's face froze. "I'm not a little lady," she announced. "I'm a princess!"

The dowager queen flicked a glance downward and stopped with a regal look anything more Elizabeth might have said. She then turned graciously to the attendant and remarked:

"She's quite right, the princess is not a little lady—but we're trying to make her one."

**THAT WAS LONG** ago. The child princess now has become a reigning queen—but only after vigorous, unrelenting and sometimes gruelling training for the job ever since she became heiress apparent.

Neither such temperamental outbursts as those cited nor any graver lapses went unchallenged in the stern, tradition-bound and protocol-ruled schooling of a queen-to-be.

Now, at 25, Elizabeth has come face to face with her destiny.

The high-strung, strong-willed, temperamental little girl has become a serious-minded, intelligent, hard-working young woman with a tremendous pride in her family, in the British empire and in her determination to serve it well.

Like Victoria—who spearheaded the trade and colonization drive that put Victoria on top of the world at the turn of the century—Elizabeth has shown

Elizabeth
Continued on Page Nine

## ELIZABETH 7TH QUEEN TO RULE

LONDON—(Reuters)—With the death Wednesday of her father, King George VI, Princess Elizabeth of the royal House of Windsor became the seventh woman of English history to occupy the throne as ruling queen.

Her predecessors:

**Jane** (Lady Jane Grey) of the House of Tudor ruled for 14 days in 1553 and was beheaded less than a year later at the age of 17.

**Mary I** of the House of Tudor, born in 1516, ruled from 1553 to 1558.

**Elizabeth** of the House of Tudor, born in 1533, ruled from 1558 to 1603.

**Mary II** of the restored House of Stuart, born in 1662, ruled from 1689 to 1694.

**Anne** of the restored House of Stuart, born in 1665, ruled from 1702 until 1714.

**Victoria** of the House of Hanover, born in 1819, ruled from 1837 to 1901.

PICTURE PAGE: *The New Queen*
PAGE 10

HER KING IS DEAD
*London news vendor sells papers telling of death of George VI*

## Philip Takes Difficult Role

LONDON—(AP)—Prince Philip, the duke of Edinburgh, is assuming a new and delicate role—that of consort to a sovereign queen.

The death of King George VI brought this change to the handsome, 30-year-old British naval officer.

Constitutionally Elizabeth's duty is clearly defined. That cannot be said for the obligations of the duke. Britain has not had a male consort to a sovereign for 91 years, and in that time much has changed.

**THE LAST MALE** consort was Prince Albert, German-born husband of Queen Victoria. He died in 1861. Precedents set up in his lifetime do not give the answer to all the questions that arise today.

The duke has no authority over the realm. He is the head of the household. He is socially the first gentleman of the empire. But the queen rules.

Not only have times and usage changed, but the temperaments of Elizabeth and the duke are far from those of Victoria and Albert.

In Victoria's day, the sovereign still kept close watch over administrative matters, kept in daily contact with the prime minister, the home office and the foreign secretary. The sovereign on occasion still initiated policies.

**NOW RELATIONS** between the sovereign and ministers are polite, formal and constitutional. The monarchy allows parliament to assume the blame or credit for any governmental policies.

Queen Victoria took a hand in affairs. It is inconceivable that Queen Elizabeth will attempt to do so.

Prince Albert often was accused of exercising undue influence over Victoria, in effect trying to share her responsibilities.

The duke of Edinburgh is unlikely ever to face similar charges. There would be no point in influencing a queen who wouldn't in any event try to impose her ideas on politicians.

Being without legal authority, the duke, it was said in court circles, is in a better position to voice personal opinions than the queen. Hers cannot be separated from the authority of the crown.

**IT IS EXPECTED** that the duke may take some advantage of his freer position to boost causes which appeal to him.

But—as the price of being a consort—it is also believed that his days as an active sailor are over.

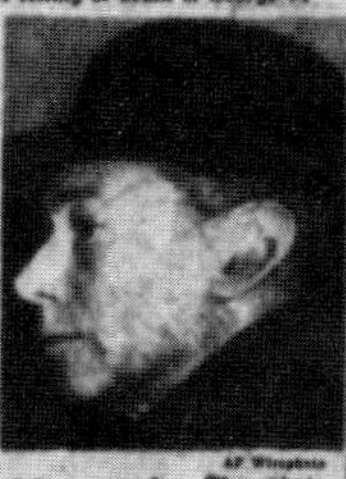

AP Wirephoto

**Monarchs** The photo of King George VI (above) is believed to be the last one taken of the monarch before his death Wednesday. It was taken Feb. 1 while he was en route to the royal estate at Sandringham where he died. Below, Britain's new queen, Elizabeth, is shown at Nairobi, Kenya, during the African part of a world tour she started Jan. 31 from London.

UP Telephoto

## Membership Peak

NEW YORK—(AP)—The Boy Scouts of America reached record membership last year with 2,942,779 youngsters and adult leaders enrolled as of Dec. 31.

## World Tour Canceled on King's Death

LONDON—(UP)—Britain's Princess Elizabeth today was proclaimed Queen Elizabeth II.

The proclamation was drafted by the privy council in the tradition-steeped, crimson and gilt salons of St. James palace.

As the council acted, the grief-stricken, 25-year-old daughter of King George VI, who died Wednesday, was flying over Africa en route home from a tragically interrupted holiday near Nairobi, Kenya.

Approximately 250 notables were present in the banqueting hall of St. James palace—where the first Queen Elizabeth often dined—when the accession council was convened. After the proclamation was read to the members, each signed.

**IT WAS DIRECTED** that the proclamation should be read Friday morning, first from the balcony of St. James palace, then at Charing Cross.

The colorful procession of heralds and messengers from the college of arms, escorted by household cavalry with burnished breastplates and helmets, then will proceed to Temple Bar, the boundary of London proper.

There the heralds will ask the traditional permission of the lord mayor to enter the city and will read the proclamation from the steps of the royal exchange.

Meanwhile it will be read or published in cities, towns, territories, protectorates, islands—everywhere the Union Jack flies.

**OBSERVERS NOTED** what appeared to be one significant addition to the descriptions of the British ruler:

"Head of the commonwealth."

This was in apparent recognition of the importance of the crown in linking the 613,000,000 people who live in countries and territories which comprise the British commonwealth of nations.

Shortly after her return (her plane is due in London at 10:30 Minneapolis time today) Queen Elizabeth will hold her first council of state and make her sovereign declaration.

The death of Elizabeth's father so dismayed Britons that Prime Minister Winston Churchill feared spontaneous outpour-

New Queen
Continued on Page 19

## Text of Proclamation

LONDON—(AP)—A proclamation proclaiming Princess Elizabeth as Queen Elizabeth II was signed by the accession council Wednesday.

The proclamation will be read publicly Friday morning. The text follows:

"Whereas it hath pleased almighty God to call at his mercy our late sovereign lord King George VI of blessed and glorious memory, by whose decease the crown is solely and rightfully come to the high and mighty Princess Elizabeth Alexandra Mary;

"We, therefore, the lords spiritual and temporal of this realm being here, assisted with these His Late Majesty's Privy Council, with representatives of other members of the commonwealth, with other principal gentlemen of quality, with the lord mayor, alderman and citizens of London, do now hereby with one voice and consent of tongue and heart publish and proclaim that the high and mighty Princess Elizabeth Alexandra Mary is now by the death of our late sovereign of happy memory become Queen Elizabeth II by grace of God, queen of this realm and of her other realms and territories, head of the commonwealth, defender of the faith, to whom her lieges acknowledge all faith and constant obedience with hearty and humble affection, beseeching God, by whom kings and queens do reign, to bless the royal princess, Elizabeth II, with long and happy years to reign over us.

"God save the queen."

Colder
Minneapolis High 45
Tuesday Temperatures

# Minneapolis Morning Tribune

Vol. LXXXVI—No. 165 Copyright, 1952, Minneapolis Star and Tribune Company MINNEAPOLIS, MINN., WEDNESDAY, NOVEMBER 5, 1952 Price 5 Cents



# IKE BEATS ADLAI IN LANDSLIDE

## *Minnesota Goes to Ike; Thye and Anderson Races Close; Control of U. S. Senate Remains in Doubt*

—MINNESOTA—

## General Beats Pace of Dewey

By ROLF FELSTAD
Minneapolis Tribune Staff Writer

**Gov. C. Elmer Anderson, Republican incumbent, trailed slightly in his race for reelection shortly after midnight. Sen. Edward J. Thye, also a Republican, took a slight lead at the same time over William E. Carlson. Heavy margins for the DFL nominees in Ramsey county began to dwindle as returns from Hennepin county began coming in.**

Victory for Eisenhower in Minnesota was indicated early today on the basis of mounting returns in the state's vote for president.

Eisenhower trailed in the early hours, largely because of the Democratic vote from St. Paul, where voting machines are used.

But the Republican nominee shortly grabbed the lead and widened it.

**THE TREND** even in the early stages indicated Ike would take Minnesota's 11 electoral votes and put the state in the Republican column for the first time since 1928.

In Ramsey county Eisenhower was polling 41.8 per cent of the vote compared with Dewey's 34.6 per cent in 1948.

Other precincts around the state also showed Ike running well ahead of the pace set by Dewey four years ago.

The first two precincts in Stearns county which, in 1948, polled the same percentage of Democratic votes as the state, showed Eisenhower 797, Stevenson 287.

Both precincts are in St. Cloud. One, in 1948, was narrowly Republican; the other was heavily for Mr. Truman.

Five representative precincts in Freeborn county, which in 1948 cast the same percentage of Democratic votes as the state, showed Eisenhower 733, Stevenson 623.

**INCLUDED** was one Albert Lea precinct, carried by Stevenson 238 to 198, the village of Alden and three rural precincts.

Freeborn county is due south of Minneapolis on the Iowa state line.

Nine other precincts in Stearns county, eight of them in St. Cloud, showed a startling reversal of the 1948 result. Four years ago Mr. Truman had a 1,452 vote margin. This time Eisenhower carried the nine precincts by 1,216.

Madison township, in rural Lac qui Parle county, gave Ike 108 and Stevenson 93, with 95 per cent of the electorate voting.

**THE SAME** township gave Mr. Truman 119 and Dewey 55 four years ago.

The first Kandiyohi county precinct report gave Ike 24, Stevenson 8. This was in a county where Mr. Truman carried every precinct four years ago. Kandiyohi is west of Minneapolis, in the liberal seventh district.

The Republican nominee ran substantially stronger in Hennepin county and in Minneapolis than four years ago.

Ike got 51.9 per cent of the vote in eight precincts of the Minneapolis second ward — a labor ward. In these same pre-

Minnesota
Continued on Page 1B

### *Lawyer Seeks to Reunite Aly, Rita*

NEW YORK—(P)—Rita Hayworth's attorney flew to Paris Tuesday night to try to settle her differences with Prince Aly Khan.

Asked about chances for a reconciliation between the movie star and her wealthy husband, Attorney C. Bartley Crum said: "I honestly won't know until I get there."

UP Telephoto

**Ike Grins** There was a big grin on the face of Dwight D. Eisenhower, GOP presidential candidate, as he watched the returns come in at his election headquarters in the Commodore hotel, New York, Tuesday night.

## KOHLER WINS IN WISCONSIN; McCARTHY, IKE FAR AHEAD

**MADISON, WIS. — (UP) — James E. Doyle, state Democratic chairman, early Wednesday conceded Wisconsin's 12 electoral votes to Republican Dwight Eisenhower.**

**However, Doyle refused to concede that Sen. Joseph McCarthy, leading three to two, had defeated Democrat Thomas E. Fairchild.**

From the Tribune Wire Services

MILWAUKEE, WIS. — A Republican sweep appeared certain in Wisconsin early today as Dwight Eisenhower piled up a lead that virtually assured him the state's 12 electoral votes.

Gov. Walter Kohler was reelected, with his opponent, William Proxmire, conceding before midnight.

Proxmire said Kohler probably would win with "the largest vote any governor ever has received."

**JOSEPH McCARTHY,** controversial Republican senator, also appeared on the way to victory over Thomas E. Fairchild, although he was running poorer than either Kohler or Eisenhower.

With 1,247 of 3,225 precincts reporting, McCarthy had 267,441 votes to 169,157 for Fairchild.

Few returns were in from large cities, where Fairchild was expected to run strong, and Fairchild had not conceded. McCarthy refused to claim victory on the basis of returns received.

Kohler apparently was leading his entire state slate to victory, which the Democrats have sought unsuccessfully in the state for 18 years.

Republicans won in four congressional districts and appeared on the way to victory in five others.

**ELECTED** were Gardner R. Withrow, La Crosse, in the third district; Melvin R. Laird, Marshfield, in the seventh district; William Van Pelt in the sixth district and Alvin E. O'Konski in the 10th district.

Rep. Clement Zablocki, Milwaukee, Wisconsin's lone Democratic house member, appeared to be his party's only chance for victory in the 10 house contests.

With 1,784 of the 3,225 precincts reporting, Eisenhower had 484,675 votes to 315,742 for Stevenson.

Kohler held more than a two to one lead over Proxmire with

Wisconsin
Continued on Page 1B

## KEY RACES

* Denotes incumbent

**ARIZONA**
Senator
169 districts of 755
*McFarland (D) ........ 43,320
Goldwater (R) ........ 58,296

**COLORADO**
Governor
168 districts of 1,650
*Thornton (R) ........ 31,994
Metzger (D) ........ 21,245

**CONNECTICUT**
Senator
169 districts of 169
*Benton (D) ........ 485,159
*Purtell (R) ........ 575,445
(Elected)
Kellems (Ind. Rep) ..... 21,357

Senator
Ribicoff (D) ........ 529,213
Bush (R) ........ 559,586

**DELAWARE**
Senator
174 districts of 276
*Williams (R) ........ 37,037
du Pont Bayard (D) .... 34,351

**ILLINOIS**
Governor
4,099 districts of 9,680
Dixon (D) ........ 1,054,979
Stratton (R) ........ 994,730

**INDIANA**
Senator
1,354 sis'ricts of 4,202
*Jenner (R) ........ 416,376
Schricker (D) ........ 397,824

**IOWA**
746 districts of 2,481
Governor
Beardsley (R) ........ 165,014
Loveless (D) ........ 160,107

**KENTUCKY**
1,502 districts of 4,126
Senator
*Underwood (D) ........ 210,502
Cooper (R) ........ 225,342

**MARYLAND**
Senator
1,291 districts of 1,401
Mahoney (D) ........ 377,056
Beall (R) ........ 408,131
(Elected)

**MASSACHUSETTS**
Senator
546 districts of 1,967
*Lodge (R) ........ 231,758
Kennedy (D) ........ 298,581

Governor
544 districts of 1,967
*Dever (D) ........ 299,076
Herter (R) ........ 239,655

Key Races
Continued on Page 1B

—SENATE-HOUSE—

## Connecticut Picks 2 GOP Senators

By WILBUR ELSTON
Minneapolis Tribune Staff Correspondent

WASHINGTON—The Republicans Tuesday night stood a good chance of capturing control of the 83rd congress along with the presidency.

Republicans captured two important senatorial seats in Connecticut, and were leading in Ohio, Indiana, Arizona, Nevada, Kentucky, New Mexico, Missouri, Nebraska and Wyoming.

**OTHER REPUBLICAN** senatorial candidates were trailing in tight contests in Massachusetts, Missouri, Michigan and Delaware but the prospects were that the GOP might at least tie up the senate at 48 to 48.

With the present split 49 to 47 in favor of the Democrats, the Republicans need only a net gain of one seat to capture control in event of the election of a Republican vice president. He would vote for his party in the organization election.

Returns were still meager from the western states.

Even Democratic senate majority leader Ernest W. McFarland was trailing in Arizona.

**CONTROL** of the house traditionally has gone to the party winning the presidency. With Eisenhower building up his strong margin, there was a strong likelihood that he would sweep in the house with him.

Republicans were making small progress in their bid to recapture control of the house, where they need a gain of 16 seats for the required 218 majority.

Late last night they had unseated six incumbent Democrats, including one in Virginia. However, in Pennsylvania the Democrats defeated an incumbent Republican.

Democrats picked up three of the 14 new house seats created by redistricting. These were one each in Florida, Maryland and Texas. The new Texas seat went to Martin Dies, former chairman of the house un-American activities committee.

Democratic Sen. William Benton of Connecticut was upset by Republican Sen. William Purtell, who had been appointed to the short term vacancy created by the death of Sen. Brien McMahon.

Republican Prescot Bush, who lost to Benton by a narrow margin in 1950, won the four-year term in Connecticut by defeating Rep. A. A. Ribicoff, Democratic house member.

As expected, Sen. Irving Ives, Republican, was re-elected in New York. Sen. Ralph Flanders, Republican, had no trouble in Vermont.

Other Republicans elected to the senate were William Langer in North Dakota, Hugh Butler in Nebraska, William Knowland in California, and J. Glenn Beall in Maryland.

**DEMOCRATS** apparently elected late last night included incumbent Senators Stennis (Miss.), Pastore (Rhode Island), Holland (Fla.) and Byrd (Va.). Rep. Albert Gore of Tennessee and Gov. Price Daniel of Texas, both Democrats, also were apparently sent to the senate.

In Indiana, Sen. William Jenner, Republican, was leading Gov. Henry F. Schricker, Democrat. Sen. Dennis Chavez (D) was trailing Republican Pat Hurley.

Sen. Edward Martin, Republican, was behind in a tight race in Pennsylvania with Democrat Guy Bard, while former Senator John Sherman Cooper, Republican, was leading Sen. Thomas Underwood, Democrat, in an apparent Kentucky upset.

Sen. Henry Cabot Lodge, Republican, close friend and early backer of Eisenhower, was trailing in Massachusetts, however.

**ALSO TRAILING** were incumbent Republican senators James Kem of Missouri and John Williams of Delaware, while Rep. Charles Potter, Republican, was trailing in his attempt to win Sen. Blair Moody's Democratic seat in Michigan.

## RETURNS

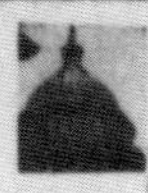

### *Popular Vote:*

**Eisenhower—17,067,455 Stevenson—14,636,366**

### *Electoral Vote Trend:*

**Eisenhower 442** **Stevenson—89**

| State | Voting Units | Units Reporting | Popular Vote Eisenhower | Popular Vote Stevenson | Electoral Vote Trend Eisenhower | Electoral Vote Trend Stevenson |
|---|---|---|---|---|---|---|
| Ala. | 2,505 | 1,907 | 121,055 | 209,610 | x | 1 |
| Ariz. | 505 | 160 | 64,687 | 38,572 | 4 | x |
| Ark. | 2,783 | 854 | 35,622 | 53,323 | x | 8 |
| Calif. | 20,746 | 5,159 | 364,995 | 304,928 | 32 | x |
| Colo. | 1,650 | 168 | 35,744 | 21,200 | 6 | x |
| Conn. | 169 | 169 | 610,989 | 481,482 | 8 | x |
| Del. | 276 | 174 | 36,027 | 35,969 | 3 | x |
| Fla. | 1,682 | 1,203 | 459,831 | 354,795 | 10 | x |
| Ga. | 1,752 | 698 | 104,934 | 223,263 | x | 12 |
| Idaho | 865 | 87 | 19,950 | 8,587 | 4 | x |
| Ill. | 9,680 | 5,716 | 994,475 | 982,627 | 27 | x |
| Ind. | 4,202 | 1,647 | 536,133 | 412,871 | 13 | x |
| Iowa | 2,481 | 889 | 262,055 | 155,197 | 10 | x |
| Kans. | 2,851 | 879 | 154,582 | 69,967 | 8 | x |
| Ky. | 4,126 | 2,057 | 275,134 | 277,808 | x | 10 |
| La. | 2,118 | 606 | 118,450 | 121,988 | x | 10 |
| Maine | 625 | 617 | 232,622 | 118,545 | 5 | x |
| Md. | 1,428 | 1,158 | 406,469 | 334,223 | 9 | x |
| Mass. | 1,967 | 732 | 409,920 | 394,409 | 16 | x |
| Mich. | 4,480 | 186 | 49,205 | 51,246 | x | 20 |
| Minn. | 3,793 | 701 | 216,771 | 204,176 | 11 | x |
| Miss. | 1,790 | 1,337 | 92,447 | 134,667 | x | 8 |
| Mo. | 4,771 | 2,400 | 357,142 | 314,081 | 13 | x |
| Mont. | 1,137 | 105 | 17,399 | 17,027 | 4 | x |
| Neb. | 2,067 | 194 | 32,386 | 12,328 | 6 | x |
| Nev. | 344 | 111 | 65,044 | 39,065 | 3 | x |
| N. H. | 297 | 243 | 109,497 | 65,752 | 4 | x |
| N. J. | 3,840 | 2,743 | 973,447 | 769,790 | 16 | x |
| N. M. | 894 | 115 | 20,232 | 16,671 | 4 | x |
| N. Y. | 10,348 | 7,985 | 2,865,457 | 2,456,600 | 45 | x |
| N. C. | 2,036 | 1,589 | 389,324 | 506,428 | x | 14 |
| N. D. | 2,300 | 300 | 28,849 | 11,624 | 4 | x |
| Ohio | 10,877 | 3,591 | 473,008 | 379,416 | 25 | x |
| Okla. | 3,880 | 2,873 | 315,598 | 272,379 | 8 | x |
| Ore. | 2,269 | 205 | 19,566 | 10,454 | 6 | x |
| Pa. | 8,472 | 6,004 | 1,627,234 | 1,309,240 | 32 | x |
| R. I. | 294 | 290 | 196,125 | 190,590 | 4 | x |
| S. C. | 1,557 | 1,392 | 151,300 | 158,549 | x | 8 |
| S. D. | 1,950 | 935 | 80,238 | 34,482 | 4 | x |
| Tenn. | 2,402 | 1,883 | 212,532 | 206,023 | 11 | x |
| Texas | 254 | 213 | 573,308 | 501,554 | 24 | x |
| Utah | 969 | 1 | 185 | 26 | 4 | x |
| Vt. | 246 | 216 | 76,074 | 27,895 | 3 | x |
| Va. | 1,793 | 1,636 | 297,994 | 227,514 | 12 | x |
| Wash. | 4,381 | 14 | 1,573 | 1,306 | 9 | x |
| W. Va. | 2,841 | 1,096 | 165,654 | 177,393 | x | 8 |
| Wis. | 3,226 | 1,545 | 407,656 | 256,936 | 12 | x |
| Wyo. | 677 | 29 | 514 | 362 | 3 | x |

## How Minnesota Voted

One to be elected for each office
Asterisk (*) identifies incumbent

**PRESIDENT**
735 districts of 3,793
Eisenhower (R) ........ 243,139
Stevenson (D) ........ 226,176

**U. S. SENATE**
483 districts of 3,793
*Edward J. Thye (R) ... 118,925
William Carlson (DFL) . 124,425

**GOVERNOR**
384 districts of 3,793
*C. E. Anderson (R) ... 110,761
O. L. Freeman (DFL) .. 121,127

**CONGRESS**
First District
29 districts of 495
*August Andresen (R). 10,095
George Alfson (DFL) .. 4,169

Second District
11 districts of 439
*Joseph P. O'Hara (R).. 2,334
R. T. Malone (DFL) .... 927

Third District
17 districts of 330
*Roy Wier (DFL) ..... 3,654
Ed Willow (R)........ 3,321

Fourth District
144 districts of 175
*E. J. McCarthy (DFL) . 77,158
Roger Kennedy (R) .... 44,678

Fifth District
12 districts of 243
*Walter Judd (R) ...... 4,904
Karl Rolvaag (DFL) .... 3,362

Sixth District
13 districts of 573
*Fred Marshall (DFL).. 1,134
J. Arthur Bensen (R) ... 1,267

Seventh District
23 districts of 555
*H. Carl Andersen (R) .. 3,683
James Youngdale (DFL). 1,997

Eighth District
30 districts of 451
*John Blatnik (DFL) ... 9,776
Ernest Orchard (R) .... 6,204

Ninth District
18 districts of 633
*Harold Hagen (R) ..... 1,233
Curtiss Olson (DFL) .... 841

**AMENDMENT NO. 5**
(License Plate Fees)
136 districts of 3,793
Yes ................ 11,040
No ................ 74,412
(Passage requires majority of total votes cast in this election.)

## Election Bulletins

By United Press

COLUMBUS, OHIO—(UP)—Ohio was conceded to Eisenhower shortly before midnight Tuesday night. A Volunteers for Stevenson spokesman in Cleveland conceded shortly after Republican State Chairman Ray Bliss claimed Ohio's 25 electoral votes by a margin in excess of 200,000.

*NEWARK, N. J.—(UP)—New Jersey Democratic officials conceded the state to Dwight Eisenhower Tuesday night and said he would have a plurality of at least 800,000 votes.*

NEW YORK—(UP)—James Farley, elder statesman of the Democratic party, virtually conceded victory for Dwight D. Eisenhower in an interview over NBC radio shortly before midnight.

NEW YORK—(UP) The New York Times announced the election of Dwight Eisenhower in its first post-midnight edition today.

**NEW YORK—(UP)—Brooklyn's Democratic borough president, John Cashmore, Tuesday night conceded his defeat by incumbent Republican Sen. Irving Ives in the United States senate race.**

—NATIONAL—

## Stevenson Concedes

**SPRINGFIELD, ILL. — (P) — Adlai Stevenson today conceded victory in the election to Dwight D. Eisenhower.**

**He said, "Our fellow citizens have made their choice. It is Gen. Eisenhower."**

**The Leland hotel ballroom was crowded when Stevenson entered at 12:40 a.m. and the room burst into cheers. The people set up a chant of "we want Stevenson."**

**Stevenson was smiling and he laughed when the crowd started to chant. He wore a dark blue double-breasted suit and a red tie. He appeared relaxed and completely at ease.**

**Stevenson was accompanied by his two youngest sons, his sister, Mrs. Elizabeth Ives, and his brother-in-law, Ernest L. Ives.**

**"It is traditional for Americans to fight hard before an election.**

**"It is traditional also to close ranks after an election."**

By RICHARD WILSON
Chief of the Minneapolis Tribune Washington Bureau

WASHINGTON—Election of Dwight D. Eisenhower as the 34th president of the United States in a victory of landslide proportions was indicated in mounting returns from Tuesday's election.

The hero of World War II, sought as a candidate by both parties, was overwhelming his lesser known opponent, Adlai E. Stevenson, in returns from most states.

A commanding lead came to Ike with sensational breaks in the solid south, a return of much of the farm vote to the GOP and large scale defections in minorities which have cemented Democratic strength for 20 years.

Republican leaders declared the sweep was similar to that which placed Herbert Hoover in the White House in 1928, with a similar break in the south.

New York's 45 and Illinois' 27 electoral votes were conceded to Eisenhower by state chairman Paul Fitzpatrick and Col. Jacob Arvey after it became clear the Republican nominee had won Virginia and was leading in Texas and Florida as well as registering a far better than normal strength in usually Republican states.

**AT THE SAME TIME** early returns from the west coast were rolling up majorities in such areas as normally Democratic Los Angeles county.

A compilation just before midnight showed Eisenhower leading in 35 states with a total of 397 electoral votes and Stevenson leading in 13 states with 134 electoral votes. (266 are required to elect).

At 9:47 p.m., Minneapolis time, Republican Chairman Arthur E. Summerfield in New York claimed Eisenhower was the winner.

"Eisenhower has been elected president of the United States," Summerfield told a cheering crowd at the general's headquarters in the Commodore hotel.

"It is a landslide," Summerfield declared, as the ballroom crowd cut loose with a roar of applause.

"It is obviously a sweep from coast to coast despite the fact that we do not have returns from the far west."

Stephen Mitchell, chairman of the Democratic national committee, said in New York he wasn't conceding anything at this point.

But at 11:25 p.m., one of Stevenson's top aids said in Springfield, Ill.:

"It's all over but the concession to Ike." This adviser said there was no doubt that Eisenhower had won and there wasn't much use in "hanging on" to the outside possibility that Stevenson still had a chance for enough electoral votes to win.

"It's all over. There's no doubt about that, and there really isn't much use of making a concession except for the formality of the thing."

He declined to permit use of his name.

Eisenhower was ahead in Texas and Oklahoma and trailing by 2,500 votes in South Carolina.

The Republican nominee also was leading in normally Democratic Rhode Island. He was ahead in California.

Ike had won his home state of Kansas, 2 to 1, compared to a 10 per cent margin by Thomas E. Dewey four years ago.

**WITH A SMALL NUMBER** of votes in he was ahead in Montana, Arizona and New Mexico, not counted Ike territory in pre-election calculations.

A measure of the Eisenhower sweep in the east was provided by Connecticut, which handed Ike its 8 electoral votes in the greatest GOP victory in that state in 28 years. Eisenhower won by more than 128,000, whereas Dewey in 1948 polled 14,000 over President Truman.

The Connecticut result was seen by top political leaders as a weathervane of what would happen elsewhere. They thought if Ike won big there, he would sweep the country.

A defection of Irish-American Catholic votes was considered to be an important factor in the big Connecticut vote, as it was in other states in the east.

**IT WAS EVIDENT** that three factors had taken heavy toll of Democratic strength. One was the bitterness toward President Truman in the south and other parts of the country which reflected on Stevenson.

Another was the communism issue which had caused many voters to desert the Democratic party. And the third was the prolonged war in Korea. These factors plainly had their effect in the big cities.

States of the Mississippi valley which had gone for Truman in 1948, or had given the Republicans reduced majorities, underwent a sharp change. Included among these were Iowa, Minnesota, Kansas and Missouri.

### Boat Tips, 3 Die

NEW YORK — (Special) — Three men were believed to have drowned Tuesday when their rowboat overturned in the choppy, wind-lashed waters of Long Island sound. Only one body was recovered, that of Henry Schaaf, 54.

### Fit to Be Tried

The race between Eisenhower and Stevenson in Richfield's second precinct wound up Tuesday night exactly where it started. The votes were split—401 to 401.

ANSWER THE CALL

# Minneapolis Morning Tribune

Vol. LXXXVI—No. 286 MINNEAPOLIS, MINN., FRIDAY, MARCH 6, 1953 .... MINNESOTA HISTORICAL SOCIETY 2nd COPY Price 5 Cents

# JOSEF STALIN IS DEAD AT 73

## Party Pleads for Russians to Remain United

### Ike Acts to Unfreeze Top Jobs

#### Order Will End Civil Service Rights for 'Super Grades'

By RICHARD WILSON
Chief of the Minneapolis Tribune Washington Bureau

WASHINGTON — President Eisenhower acted Thursday to clear out hundreds of top government policy-makers and administrators frozen into the civil service system in Democratic administrations so they may be replaced by Republicans.

A drastic shake-out of top civil service levels was recommended to the President by Attorney General Brownell in order that new cabinet members and administrators might surround themselves with associates of their own choosing.

Mr. Eisenhower directed that an executive order be drafted to divest hundreds of top officials of their civil service ratings given them during Democratic administrations to protect them in their jobs.

**MANY OF THE JOBS** at which the order will aim are in the $12,000 to $17,000 class, the so-called "super grades" of the merit system. It is contended that the jobs were given out without adequate civil service examination and on a political basis.

Validity of the "super grade" system has been in considerable question. Other abuses of the civil service system are being revealed in a congressional hearing on the job held by Donald S. Tydings, a nephew of the former Maryland senator, Millard E. Tydings, Democrat.

The White House contends these officials were blanketed into the merit system when they should have been kept on what is called "schedule A," a category of policy-making officials or those who enjoy a close personal and confidential relationship with the head of an agency, who are exempt from protection.

Some cabinet members feared

Civil Service
Continued on Page 15

**Pictorial Debut** Michael Howard Wilding, son of actress Elizabeth Taylor and actor Michael Wilding, posed for his first pictures Thursday with his mother. The boy was born Jan. 6 at the Santa Monica hospital in Hollywood, Calif. He weighed 7 pounds, 3 ounces at birth. (AP Wirephoto)

### Green-Haired Woman Sues for Bleach of Promise

CLEVELAND, OHIO —(AP)— Silver threads among the gold in milady's hair-do may be all right, but Mrs. Margaret Bleaser draws the line at green threads.

Mrs. Bleaser said in a $10,000 damage suit filed here that an oil bleach she bought to tint her hair blond made it green and unmanageable instead.

She asked the damages from a druggist on grounds the bleach caused "permanent impairment of her beauty and attractiveness."

### 2 Die, One Saved When Mine Wall Buries Workmen

VIRGINIA, MINN.—(AP)—The wall of a large ore mine caved in Thursday, dumping rocks and clay onto workmen at the bottom of the open pit.

David Roskrance, 25, Biwabik, and Joe Skerjance, about 29, McKinley, were killed.

The stone and earth deluge almost covered Frank Alexander, 24, Eveleth, but workmen quickly dug him out.

Roskrance's body was uncovered about 45 minutes later. Volunteer searchers and heavy equipment worked four hours to move the tons of heavy rubble covering Skerjance's body.

Ben Tangas, Virginia, St. Louis county mine safety inspector, said it appeared water had loosened the wall to cause the collapse.

### Quake Kills 55 in China Satellite

HONG KONG — (Reuters) — First details of a Tibet earthquake, said to have killed 55 persons and destroyed 870 buildings, came out of the "forbidden land" Thursday, six months after it happened.

The Communist New China news agency reported Communist China sent relief to the victims, and the destroyed buildings have been rebuilt.

#### Radar May Be Used to Detect Speeders

The Minnesota legislature was asked Thursday to approve use of radar for detecting speeding motorists.

Rep. William O. Legvold, St. James, introduced a bill to permit local governments to rent radar equipment to enforce speed laws.

#### 68 Blind Boys Led to Safety in Fire

SHREWSBURY, ENGLAND —(Reuters)— Sixty-eight blind boys were led to safety by their teachers when fire broke out in their school before dawn Thursday.

### Child Says 'U' Should Rehire Weinberg

By CARL T. ROWAN
Minneapolis Tribune Staff Writer

Fay George Child, the state senator who spearheaded a 1951 legislative effort to force the University of Minnesota to suspend Dr. Joseph Weinberg, has said the school should rehire the physicist "if he's needed."

Child made this remark to reporters Wednesday, a day before a Washington jury found Weinberg innocent of charges that he lied in saying he never was a Communist.

"If they acquit him, the law says he's innocent and the university ought to rehire him if he's needed," Child said.

**"I BELIEVE** in staying within our democratic framework in fighting Communists."

*(ANOTHER STORY AND PICTURE—page 17.)*

The university said Thursday, however, that "the case is closed," and that it would not rehire Weinberg.

There was no indication from Weinberg as to whether he would seek to regain his job at the university.

His close friends on the university faculty said, however, "his chances of ever getting an academic job are very poor unless the university offers to rehire him, even if he turns it down."

"And he might have to turn down an academic job," said Dr. Cyrus P. Barnum, Jr., associate professor of physiological chemistry.

"Joe is $12,000 in debt, broke and out of work. He might have to take an industrial job because it pays more."

Dr. J. William Buchta, head

Weinberg
Continued on Page 15

#### State Woman, 100, Dies

BROWNTON, MINN.—(AP)— Mrs. Justine Molls, who observed her 100th birthday last Oct. 18, died here.

### Will Jones at Rassles

Gagne Could Be in Films— See Radio Page

Gagne



IN KOREA
*'Mighty Mo' Shelled by Red Shore Guns — page 9*

### Ike Sends Official Regrets

WASHINGTON —(AP)— President Eisenhower Thursday night instructed Secretary of State Dulles to transmit "official condolences" of the United States government on the death of Premier Stalin of Russia.

The President directed Dulles to send this message to the American embassy in Moscow for transmission to the Russian government:

"The government of the United States tenders its official condolences to the government of the Union of Soviet Socialist Republics on the death of Generalissimo Josef Stalin, prime minister of the Soviet Union."

It was noted immediately the message, which spoke only of "official condolences," omitted the usual words of sympathetic tribute which are almost a part of protocol when the leader of any other nation dies.

The terse Eisenhower statement was a sign of the strained relations which have grown up from Russia's aggressive career under Stalin.

Mr. Eisenhower was informed of Stalin's death at 7:25 p.m. (Minneapolis time) by James C. Hagerty, his press secretary. Hagerty said the President and Mrs. Eisenhower had just finished their dinner.

Hagerty said he relayed the message of condolence to Dulles, who was at the British embassy.

"The message has been sent," Hagerty said. It was sent directly to Jacob D. Beam, charge d'affaires at the American embassy in Russia.

#### Stalin Stories on the Inside



### Malenkov-- Can He Hold the Reins?

#### Beria and Zhukov Believed to Be Top Opponents

By GEORGE WELLER
Chicago Daily News Foreign Service

UNITED NATIONS, N. Y.— The future of Georgi M. Malenkov, leading candidate to succeed Stalin, will be decided by the way he handles two adversaries: police boss Lavrenti P. Beria and Marshal Georgi Zhukov of the Red army.

That is the view of Russian observers here, who possess pipelines to the Soviet political reservoirs.

Pravda's last comment on Stalin, just before the premier's death Thurday, concluded that any changes in the Soviet will be in accordance with Stalin's wishes and with the laws of the nation.

**THE STATEMENT** was credited to Malenkov. No other top personality was mentioned.

Now, all the stubby, moon-faced former secretary of Stalin needs is time and a free hand. He possesses the capacity to wipe out his enemies as neatly as Stalin wiped out his equals, Leon Kamenev and Gregory Zinoviev.

Vyacheslav M. Molotov, spectacled senior vice premier to Stalin, is useful to Malenkov. He is in little danger. Malenkov can use him as senior front man, giving him the empty post of the premiership.

Malenkov, at 51, lacks "staj," a Russian word meaning something between prestige and seniority. He was too young to have more than a rah-rah role in the revolution and his war record was only adequate, not spectacular.

**IT WAS BECAUSE** of Malenkov's lack of staj that he had to engineer, as is generally believed, the murder of the Leningrad fighting hero, Gen. Andrei Zhdanov.

Zhdanov died in 1948, and nine doctors, seven of them Jewish, now are taking the rap for his killing. Zhdanov was Malenkov's only rival to boss the all-powerful Communist party.

Molotov is a useful bridge with the heroic past, a link between Malenkov, the newcomer,

Malenkov
Continued on Page 21

### TEXT OF ANNOUNCEMENT REVEALING STALIN'S DEATH

By Associated Press

*Text of the announcement of Josef Stalin's death follows:*

Dear comrades and friends. The central committee of the Communist party of the Soviet Union, the USSR council of ministers and the presidium of the USSR supreme council announce with profound sorrow to the party and all workers of the Soviet Union that on the fifth of March at 9:50 p.m., after a grave illness, the chairman of the USSR council of ministers and the secretary of the central committee of the Communist party of the Soviet Union, Josef Vissarionovitch Stalin, died.

The heart of the comrade and inspired continuer of Lenin's will, the wise leader and teacher of the Communist party and the Soviet people — Josef Vissarionovitch Stalin — has stopped beating.

Stalin's name is boundlessly dear to our party, to the Soviet people, to the workers of the world.

Together with Lenin, Comrade Stalin created the mighty party of Communists, reared and forged that party.

Together with Lenin, Comrade Stalin was the inspirer and leader of the great October Socialist revolution, founder of the world's first socialist state.

Continuing Lenin's immortal cause, Comrade Stalin led the Soviet people to a world-historic victory of Socialism in our land.

Comrade Stalin led our country to victory over Fascism in the second world war which wrought a radical change in the entire international scene.

Comrade Stalin's death—the man who devoted all his life to the unselfish service of Communist cause—is a tremendous loss to the party, to the workers of the Soviet Union and to the whole world.

Comrade Stalin armed the party and all the people with a great and lucid program of building communism in the USSR.

**THE NEWS** of Comrade Stalin's death will bring profound pain to the hearts of the workers, the collective farmers, the intelligentsia and all the workers of our motherland, to the hearts of the warriors of our glorious army and navy, to the hearts of millions of workers in all countries of the world.

In these sorrowful days all the peoples of our country are rallying even closer in a great fraternal family under the tested leadership of the Communist party, created and reared by Lenin and Stalin.

The Soviet people have boundless faith in and are permeated with deep love for their Communist party, for they know that the supreme law governing all the activity of the party is service in the interests of the people.

The workers, collective farm-

Text
Continued on Page 21

### The Man Stalin

In 1910

In 1924

In 1930

In 1941

In 1949

In 1952

### 7 to Organize State Funeral

LONDON—(AP)—Josef Stalin died Thursday night. He died, aged 73, behind the 12-foot-thick walls of Moscow's Kremlin from which he dominated one-third of the world's peoples as the most powerful dictator in history. He ruled one-sixth of the earth's surface—from the Baltic sea to Bering strait.

The prime minister of the Soviet Union and the supreme chief of the Communist party died at 9:50 p.m. (12:50 p.m. Minneapolis time), four days after suffering a brain hemorrhage.

He had been in coma since the stroke Sunday night and his condition grew progressively worse. Yesterday his 10 physicians said his heart was faltering.

**ANNOUNCEMENT OF HIS DEATH** was broadcast from Moscow at 4:07 a.m. today, Moscow time, more than six hours after he died. The Russian people waited two hours more for the news.

As the news of Stalin's death became known, lights went on all over Moscow in the pre-dawn darkness. Black-bordered flags were put up on almost all public and many private buildings. All entertainment programs were cancelled.

The official announcement said:

"The heart of the comrade and inspired continuer of Lenin's will, the wise leader and teacher of the Communist party and the Soviet people—Josef Vissarionovitch Stalin—has stopped beating."

There was no immediate indication from Moscow who was taking over control of the country.

The announcement was issued in the name of the Communist party's central committee, the council of ministers and the presidium of the supreme council, all organs which Stalin dominated.

Names of none of the men mentioned as Stalin's successors appeared on the document. Nor did the name of Russia's nominal leader, Nikolai Mikhailovich Shvernik, since 1946 president of the nation's parliament.

**APPOINTMENT OF A SEVEN-MAN** committee to organize the funeral was reported by Radio Moscow.

Nikita Krushchev, secretary of the central committee, was named chairman. Other members include Lazar Kaganovich, a member of the presidium and Stalin's brother-in-law; the war minister, Marshal A. M. Vassilevsky; M. A. Yasnov, mayor of Moscow; N. M. Pegov, another secretary of the central committee; Gen. P. A. Artemyev, commander of the Moscow garrison, and Shvernik.

Stalin's body will lie in state in the hall of columns of the House of Unions—the great trade union center in the heart of Moscow, a short distance from Red square and the Kremlin.

The last Soviet leader to lie in the hall was Col. Gen. Lev Z. Mekhlis, a Jew and close associate of Stalin. Former minister of state control, he died Feb. 13.

The hall, built in 1874, can accommodate at least 2,000 persons.

**AS IF APPEALING FOR UNITY,** the official statement said:

"In these sorrowful days all the peoples of our country are rallying even closer in a great fraternal family under the tested leadership of the Communist party, created and reared by Lenin and Stalin.

"'The Soviet people have boundless faith in and are permeated with a deep love for their Communist party, for they know that the supreme law governing all the activity of the party is service in the interests of the people,'" the announcement said.

It concluded:

"The immortal name of Stalin will live forever in the hearts of the Soviet people and all progressive mankind.

"Long live the great and all-conquering teachings of Marx, Engels, Lenin and Stalin! Long live our mighty socialist motherland!

**"LONG LIVE OUR HEROIC SOVIET** people! Long live the great Communist party of the Soviet Union!"

The statement was signed by "the central committee of the Communist party of the USSR; the USSR council of ministers; the USSR supreme council presidium."

Stalin's fatal illness became known Tuesday night, more than two days after he was stricken in his Kremlin apartment.

An official announcement issued from the ministry of health and signed by the 10 physicians said Stalin "had a sudden hemorrhage of the brain" the night of March 1. This "affected vitally important parts of the brain" and paralyzed his right leg and arm. He lost consciousness and the power to speak.

Three more bulletins were issued—one yesterday morning. Another last night only an hour and a half before Stalin died revealed—for the first time—that Stalin had suffered two failures of the heart itself.

**THEN CAME SILENCE,** broken hours later by announcement that death had occurred.

The final bulletin of the physicians was brief. It said:

"At 21:50 hours, with cardiac failure growing, J. V. Stalin died."

Stalin had ruled Russia as undisputed dictator for nearly 30 years. His sway extended beyond the Soviet Union's 200 million people to encompass another half billion people.

He reached the height of his power when he led the Soviet Union against the Nazis of Adolf Hitler as an ally of the United States and Great Britain. He was one of the "big three" of the world—with Britain's Winston Churchill and America's Franklin D. Roosevelt.

Stalin made a deal with Hitler in 1939 which shocked the rest of the world. It unleashed World War II, but gained Stalin time. When the Nazis struck at him, he was ready.

**AT STALINGRAD,** 10 years ago, the Russians fought for a city, block by block, house by house and room by room. They smashed a great German army.

But when the war ended, wartime co-operation with the allies ended as Communists brought Poland, Romania, Bulgaria, Albania and Yugoslavia under Russian domination. Czechoslovakia toppled and Greece rocked before the revolutionists directed from the Kremlin. China became Red. There was blood in Malaya and in Indochina. The Communists tried to pinch off Berlin with a blockade.

Aroused, the west fended off the Communist drive in Finland and whipped the Red rebels in Greece. An airlift beat the Berlin blockade. Soldiers and police stood fast in Indochina and Malaya.

And then the United Nations took up arms to fight Communist invaders of South Korea.

#### Iron Curtain Victims Warned: Be Cautious

MUNICH, GERMANY — (AP) —Radio Free Europe turned on the full power of its 20 transmitters Thursday to tell Iron Curtain listeners Stalin's death will not mean their immediate liberation. It urged them to "remain calm and act with caution."

### Almanac

#### Tax Men Don't Care Who Wears Pants in Family

*Friday, March 6, 1953*
Sunrise 6:43 a.m.; sunset 6:07 p.m.

For some reason or other, a lot of Minnesota married people are causing trouble at the St. Paul internal revenue office by incorrectly using "head of household rates" in figuring their 1952 income tax. We suppose there are some husbands who still think they are head of the household, but that tax rate is available only to unmarried persons who qualify under the terms set out in the form 1040 instruction book.

The rector says that a Minnesota beverage firm using its name three times in its slogan would be more accurate to change it to "Hic, hic, hic."

*No sounds of spring in the Twin Cities forecast today. Occasional cloudiness, high of 15 and a drop to zero tonight.*

Colleague of ours rushed his wife to the hospital last week for a first-time delivery. As the unmistakable signs appeared, they dashed out of the house, only to find the family car had a flat tire. The prospective father called a cab, ordered a garage to repair the tire, and rushed his wife to the hospital just in time for her to have the baby—the next afternoon.

#### Little Change

Minneapolis High 15

THURSDAY TEMPERATURES

| | | | | | |
|---|---|---|---|---|---|
| [illegible] a.m. | [illegible] | 10 a.m. | [illegible] | [illegible] p.m. | [illegible] |
| [illegible] a.m. | [illegible] | 11 a.m. | 14 | [illegible] p.m. | [illegible] |
| [illegible] a.m. | [illegible] | Noon | [illegible] | [illegible] p.m. | [illegible] |
| [illegible] a.m. | [illegible] | 1 p.m. | [illegible] | [illegible] p.m. | [illegible] |
| [illegible] a.m. | [illegible] | [illegible] p.m. | [illegible] | 10 p.m. | [illegible] |
| [illegible] a.m. | [illegible] | [illegible] p.m. | [illegible] | 11 p.m. | [illegible] |
| [illegible] a.m. | [illegible] | 4 p.m. | [illegible] | Midnight | [illegible] |
| 9 a.m. | [illegible] | 5 p.m. | [illegible] | FRIDAY | |
| | | | | 1 a.m. | [illegible] |
| | | | | [illegible] a.m. | [illegible] |

Details on Page 18

Warmer
Minneapolis High 80
TEMPERATURES
Details on Page 14

# Minneapolis Morning Tribune

Vol. LXXXVII—No. 9 MINNEAPOLIS, MINN., TUESDAY, JUNE 2, 1953 Price 5 Cents



Millers Beaten Seventh Time in Row, 4-3

(DETAILS in Sports Section.)

# British Scale Everest as Coronation Present

## Team of 2 First to Climb World's Highest Peak

LONDON, ENGLAND — (UP) — Buckingham palace announced Monday night that a British expedition has conquered Mount Everest, the world's highest mountain.

Two climbers planted the British flag on the peak, 29,002 feet high, as a coronation "gift" to Queen Elizabeth II.

E. P. Hillary, 34, a bee keeper from New Zealand, and Tensing Bhutia, a native guide, were the first men in history to reach the top and return to talk about it.

Bhutia had made nine previous expeditions up Everest. He and Raymond Lambert of last year's Swiss expedition got to within 1,000 feet of the summit, highest point reached by any surviving mountaineer until now.

A radio message to Khatmandu, Nepal, said the peak was topped Friday on the third attempt. Each attempt was made by a team of two men from a 13-man expedition led by Col. H. J. C. Hunt—the 11th organized attack on the mountain and the first to succeed.

The first team to try—Tom Bourdillon and Dr. R. C. Evans—failed a week ago, on Monday, May 25.

The 13 climbers left Khatmandu 80 days ago with 362 porters and 20 guides. Among their five tons of baggage was oxygen equipment and an avalanche gun, resembling a two-inch mortar, to dislode loose snow.

In London, the queen was awakened a few hours before she was to arise for her coronation and told of the feat. Then she went back to sleep. One reason for the delay in the news was that climbers forgot their radio transmitter, and had to depend on runners to take news to the outside world.

New Zealand's prime minister, Sidney Holland, in London for the coronation, said:

"What a grand achievement! A terrific example of tenacity, spirit, endurance and fortitude! A symbol that there are no heights and no difficulties, which the British people cannot overcome!

"Although a New Zealander was the first to conquer Everest, this triumph was made possible by the combined efforts of a great number of people, including other members of the team, and the lessons learned in previous attempts."

For days, weather had been favorable. Everest's summit lacked its customary "plume"—small particles of ice driven by winds of hurricane force which looked, from below, like a cloud streaming from the peak.

**CLIMBERS WORE** outer suits of cotton windproof material double-lined with nylon. Each suit weighed three and three-fourths pounds, including a hood with a visor to give protection against wind and snow.

Inside the suits, climbers wore two-piece suits of down with a second hood. They also were equipped with two lightweight jersey sweaters and one heavy pullover.

The men also wore special hand coverings, made of windproof cotton, wool, and silk. Tents and sleeping bags also were

Everest
*Continued on Page Five*

HIGHEST POINT IN THE WORLD
29,002 Feet

MOUNT EVEREST — A 'GIFT' TO THE QUEEN

## Officials Modify Cut in Air Force

### Talbott Announces Billion Increase in Spending

By RICHARD WILSON
Chief of Minneapolis Tribune Washington Bureau

WASHINGTON — The Eisenhower administration has modified its cutback of the air force and will boost spending in the coming year 1 billion dollars or more over first estimates.

Air Secretary Harold E. Talbott advised Rep. Samuel W. Yorty (D., Calif.), leader of congressional opposition to air force cuts, at the Pentagon Monday that a $15,100,000,000 spending ceiling has been lifted. Talbott insisted that he could not operate under that limitation.

However, the administration is not backing down on its recommendation for a $5,090,000,000 reduction in former president Truman's request for appropriations for the 1953-54 fiscal year.

**NOR IS IT MOVING** away from the reduction in planned air force maximum strength from 143 to 120 groups.

However, Pentagon officials place strong emphasis on a review of American military plans to be made by the new joint chiefs of staff as determining the final size of the air force.

Talbott said Yorty's figures were not correct and that he would announce the air force program Wednesday.

"I got the idea," said Yorty, "that they are edging back toward the 143-wing air force program.

**"THIS MEANS** that the administration is not going to carry out its program because they found it was too drastic. They don't dare carry it out."

Yorty also said that most of the new spending would be for airplane purchases, permitting the delivery of planes on the same schedule as that provided in the Truman program.

However, Pentagon officials previously have insisted that the new Eisenhower program would not reduce the delivery of combat planes.

They insist that the number of combat planes scheduled for delivery to the air force in the 30-month period ending December 1955 will be higher than in the Truman budget.

**IT WAS INSISTED** the cuts would be primarily in support type planes (transports, trainers, helicopters).

Navy Secretary Robert B. Anderson pledged his "loyal support" to President Eisenhower's pared-down defense budget and said it will provide for an increase in navy air combat strength.

Adm. D. B. Duncan, vice chief of naval operations, said the 1,300 new navy planes provided in the budget were about half what the navy wanted to maintain a 10,000-plane force.

## 2-Bus Crash Kills 10

MEXICO CITY, MEXICO — (AP)— At least 10 persons were killed and 27 injured Monday in a two-bus collision on the major tourist highway leading into Mexico City.

## Dulles to Seek Friendship of Arabs, Israelis

WASHINGTON—(AP)— Secretary of State Dulles said Monday the United States will pursue an "impartial" policy aimed at winning friendship of both Arabs and Israelis.

He told a nationwide radio-TV audience that his 20-day tour of Asia and the middle east has convinced him the Arabs are "more fearful of Zionism than of communism."

(Zionism is the movement, launched 50 years ago, to establish a Jewish state. It has members throughout the world but has no voice in Israel's government.)

**ARAB HOSTILITY,** said Dulles, has made the proposed middle east defense organization "a future rather than an immediate possibility."

(The proposal has been stalled by troubles between Arabs and Israel, between Britain and Iran over oil and between Britain and Egypt over the Suez canal and the Sudan.)

"We cannot afford to be distrusted by millions who could be sturdy friends of freedom," he said. "They must not further swell the ranks of Communist dictators."

Dulles expressed confidence that Britain and Egypt can settle their bitter quarrel over the Suez canal. He promised

Dulles
*Continued on Page Five*

## Children Saved as Blasts Wreck Hospital Room

COLUMBUS, OHIO — (AP) — Nurses and parents carried scores of children to safety Monday night after explosions in the oxygen room of Childrens' hospital. An attendant was injured critically.

There were 230 children in the hospital.

A worker in the hospital's oxygen room sensed an explosion was about to take place and warned doctors, nurses and others to clear the area.

One oxygen tank, ripped apart like a huge cartridge shell, was found one block away from the hospital. The first explosion set off several others.

## Palmer: 25 Charges; Police: 25 Denials

By CHARLES E. BENSON
Minneapolis Tribune Staff Writer

The mayoralty campaign scrap over whether Minneapolis is crime-ridden resulted in a stand-off Monday.

Stephen Palmer, Republican-endorsed candidate for mayor, appeared before the mayor's committee on law enforcement at an open meeting. He charged that law enforcement has been lax, circulated pictures of places where he said gamblers have operated and handed over a number of issue squares which he said were policy numbers sold on the North Side.

Top police officials then went into a huddle over Palmer's long, prepared statement and a list of 25 questions, and then came up with a complete denial of the charges.

Representatives of federal law enforcement agencies who had been asked to appear sent their regrets but said regulations forbid their participation in local politics, and anyway their files were confidential.

Members of the committee drew praise from chairman Ed Ryan, Hennepin county sheriff, for their calmness and objectivity in questioning of Palmer.

The proceedings were enlivened a bit when Ed Gates, a furniture broker named by Palmer as a man of influence in the mayor's office, stormed into the meeting and demanded to be given a lie detector test "along with that two-bit, chiseling - - - - who gave Palmer that stuff."

After hearing the police officials, the committee . . . which had been convened by Mayor Eric Hoyer to probe Palmer's charges . . . adjourned until 9:30 a.m. today when it will hear from Gates "and anyone else who has any information for us."

### — TEXT —

*Following is a condensation of the statement read by Palmer to the mayor's committee on law enforcement yesterday:*

Let's start right out with two ideas. The mayor of Minneapolis appoints the chief of police. The mayor is the chief executive and as such establishes the law enforcement policy for the community.

Secondly, the mayor created this committee to advise him on problems of law enforcement. I believe that if we keep this dual premise in mind we can best understand each other in considering law enforcement problems for the community.

I believe Mayor Eric G. Hoyer, as the head of the city government and Minneapolis police force, has been derelict in his duty to establish effectively a policy of rigid law enforcement.

But before I go into the picture of crime, vice, gambling, and prostitution in Minneapolis, I want to read to you a statement by J. Edgar Hoover, head of the FBI.

Here are J. Edgar Hoover's words:

"Gambling, bookmaking, vice and prostitution cannot exist on a day-after-day basis in any community without being known to law enforcement authorities. A bookie or prostitute can operate for a day or so and their operation not be detected, but you can be certain that any organized vice or gambling is

Text
*Continued on Page Eight*

### — QUESTIONS —

Following is a condensation of the questions submitted to the mayor's law enforcement committee by Palmer, and the answers made by these representatives of the Minneapolis police department: Chief Thomas R. Jones, Inspector E. I. (Pat) Walling, Jake Sullivan, head of the morals squad, and Charles Wetherille, inspector of detectives.

**Q. Why didn't Hoyer avail** himself of the services of the telephone company in having telephones removed from the following locations when police records showed the administration was aware these spots were gambling and bookmaking establishments: Pantages Recreation; Fourth Street cigar store; Helberg's Cigar store; 709 Second avenue S. cigar store; 510 E. Hennepin cigar store; The Paddock; 1319 Nicollet avenue cigar store; Lincoln recreation parlor; Hennepin recreation parlor; 112 Washington avenue S.?

**A. (JONES) We have an ar**rangement with the telephone company to remove phones but they state that because of a lawsuit in Missouri we must have irrevocable evidence. Five months ago we had an instance at the Buckingham hotel where a bookmaker was operating and they asked for a conviction first.

**A. (WALLING) We made ar**rests at both the Brunswick (306 Hennepin) and 510 E. Hennepin. I appeared before the health and hospitals committee of the council and asked for revocation of the Brunswick licenses (food, cigarets, etc.). The committee saw fit to suspend for 10 days. In 1951 another arrest was made at the Brunswick and again the defendant was fined $100. Again I made the recommendation to revoke and again the licenses were suspended for 10 days. An arrest was made at 510 E. Hennepin and again the health and hospitals committee recom-

Questions
*Continued on Page Nine*

Minneapolis Tribune Staff photo by Duff Johnston
MORALS SQUAD CHIEF SULLIVAN, CHIEF JONES, INSPECTOR WALLING
*Top Minneapolis police department officials answer crime charges*

### TURN THE PAGES TO:



## Senator Says Truce Looms Short of Honor

WASHINGTON —(UP)— Sen. William F. Knowland (R., Calif.) said Monday night the United Nations Korean truce proposal falls short of "a truce with honor."

He added that if truce negotiations with the Communists collapsed, the United States should expand the Korean fighting and take the "calculated risk" of war with Russia.

**SUPPORTING** proposals made by Sen. Taft (R., Ohio) and rejected by President Eisenhower, Knowland said he does not believe the Allied armistice offer to the Communists will produce a "truce with honor" because it would leave Korea divided.

In his appearance on the Mutual Broadcasting system's radio show, Reporters' Roundup, the chairman of the Republican policy committee said he supports a proposed rider to the money bill for the state, commerce and justice departments which would cut off United States contributions to the United Nations if Red China were seated on the security council.

Knowland was the first GOP leader to break openly with the truce proposal now being considered by the Communist negotiators at Panmunjom.

**KNOWLAND SAID** he is "certain" that acceptance of the

Truce
*Continued on Page Five*

## Almanac

### Fumble! But Car Hop Is on the Ball

*Tuesday, June 2, 1953*
Sunrise 4:29 a.m.; sunset 7:52 p.m.

Couple of Edina couples stopped at a drive-in for a snack. After the male car hop delivered their food, the two men engaged in one of those embarrassing out-fumbling contests.

The car hop, who undoubtedly has seen thousands of these situations, tired of their little game, tapped the driver on the arm and settled it: "Look, let him pay," he demanded, "you drove."

•

Sign outside the entrance to operations office of the naval air station at Wold-Chamberlain field:

"Fly High and Avoid Mink Farms — Wheiping Season Is Here!"

•

*Warmer, the man says, for the Twin Cities today. Warmer means a high near 80 and a low tonight of 60. Partly cloudy.*

•

Minneapolis police will begin tagging lane straddlers today. Laning of streets has been completed. Particular attention will be paid to motorists who make improper turns from one-way streets.

•

Crew was cleaning exterior of one of the downtown department stores. Agent of ours walked by just as one workman up on a scaffold called down the intelligence to a colleague on the ground: "Hey, have you noticed? Everytime you clean it, it gets smaller."

## Raiders Find 400 Minors Drinking Beer

Hennepin county deputy sheriffs raided the Lake Sarah dance hall near Loretto and reported they found 400 teenagers drinking beer while the local constable was present.

Jack Whitney, sheriff's office tavern inspector, said Mrs. Otto Arens, 50, Loretto, was charged Monday with selling beer to a minor and fined $100 by Virgil Schabel, justice of the peace.

Whitney

Whitney said the raid was made Sunday night after several complaints from parents.

He said the teen-agers were mainly from Minneapolis, Robbinsdale, Osseo and the Minnetonka area.

The constable, Glen Cozet, of Greenwood township, was there and was not doing anything to stop the minors from drinking, Whitney said. Cozet could not be reached for comment.

The proprietor, James Mitchell, 58, who lives at the dance hall, appeared in court with Mrs. Arens yesterday and said he would have to close down if he could not sell to minors. He said they were a large percentage of his trade.

Schabel told Mitchell if he were caught again he would serve a workhouse term.

Whitney said there were two gang fights outside the dance hall while he was there.

## 23 Escape as Bus Skids Into River

TOWSON, MD. —(UP) — A school bus skidded off a narrow road and plunged into rain-swollen Patapsco river Monday, but all 23 passengers escaped, including two girls who were swept down-stream.

James M. Gaines, the driver, rescued the two girls who opened the emergency door where the water was six feet deep and then lost their footing as they scrambled out.

The other passengers also left the almost submerged vehicle by the emergency exit. Three were injured slightly.

## TV's Mrs. North Gives Birth to Boy Republican

HOLLYWOOD, CALIF.—(AP)—Television's Mrs. North gave birth to a son Monday and immediately disclosed her politics.

Miss Britton

The 5-pound, 4-ounce son of actress Barbara Britton and Dr. Eugene Czukor was named Dwight Timothy.

"Naturally, we'll call him Ike for short," the mother said. It is the third child for the couple. They have another son, 6, and a daughter, 2.

## Traffic Sergeant Tagged for Going Past Red Light

A Minneapolis police traffic sergeant was tagged for driving through a flashing red signal after a two-car collision Monday in which he and his wife were injured.

Tagged was Lloyd Berg, 37, 3027 Fremont avenue N.

Police said he was driving his private automobile about 1:40 a.m. when he went through the stop light at Lowry and Fremont avenues N. His car collided with another car driven by Laurence L. Baker, 42, 5217 S. Sixth street, and was demolished.

## Millions Jam London for Event

### Elizabeth Ready for Long Ordeal in Westminster

By BOB CONSIDINE

LONDON — (INS) — Britain's youthful, radiant Queen Elizabeth II rose in the predawn darkness of a rainy London morning today to accept the crown of her ancestors in a coronation setting of unparalleled splendor and jubilation.

The great oaken doors of Westminster abbey swung open and through them streamed the first of the 6,000 guests invited from all over the world and from every walk of life.

As the queen awakened in gray old Buckingham palace and knelt in private prayer for divine guidance on this greatest day of her 27 years, hundreds of thousands of her devoted subjects clogged the windswept streets of the historic city.

**UNMINDFUL** of the rain and chill in the air, they battled—not always good-naturedly—for places that would give them a glimpse of the pageantry.

In the scramble to beat a deadline decreed by police, the thousands who lined the processional route posed an ever-increasing problem for London's bobbies.

Many spectators who were sleeping full length on the curbs angrily refused to give way to a continuing surge of new arrivals who stood out in the streets, hoping the police would push them in front of those already on the sidewalks.

(PICTURE—page 4.)

The crowds, expected to swell to three million today along the procession route, cheered and shouted every time they saw a member of the royal family or a visiting dignitary.

Not even the forecast of chilly weather, possibly hail and thunder during the ceremony, could dim their exuberance. They had waited too long for this moment of glory for nation and commonwealth.

**THE MALL,** a fashionable promenade in St. James' park, was transformed into a huge outdoor night club and revelers jitterbugged to such tunes as "Side by Side," "Irish Eyes Are Smiling" and "Doggy in the Window." Harmonicas and accordions provided accompaniment.

Crowds 10 deep lined the sidewalks at many vantage points. Hundreds slept at the foot of the statue of Eros. Water supply officials placed fire hoses, with enamel cups, at many points along the decorated route to permit the crowds to slake their thirst.

A huge bonfire illuminated

Elizabeth
*Continued on Page 10*

### Color Picture of Elizabeth on Page 12

### Coronation Features



## CORONATION TIMETABLE

LONDON—(UP)—Timetable for major events in the coronation of Queen Elizabeth II today (Minneapolis time in parentheses):

| | | |
|---|---|---|
| 11:00 a.m. | (4:00 a.m.) | Queen Elizabeth and the Duke of Edinburgh arrive at Westminster abbey. |
| 11:20 a.m. | (4:20 a.m.) | Coronation ceremony begins. |
| 12:34 p.m. | (5:34 a.m.) | Elizabeth is crowned. |
| 1:53 p.m. | (6:53 a.m.) | Coronation ceremony ends. |
| 2:55 p.m. | (7:55 a.m.) | Elizabeth and the Duke begin drive through London. |
| 4:30 p.m. | (9:30 a.m.) | Queen returns to Buckingham palace. |
| 5:15 p.m. | (10:15 a.m.) | Royal air force jet planes will fly past the palace while the queen takes the salute from the balcony. |
| 8:50 p.m. | (1:50 p.m.) | Prime Minister Winston Churchill broadcasts to the commonwealth. |
| 9:00 p.m. | (2:00 p.m.) | Queen Elizabeth broadcasts to the commonwealth. |

*For detailed schedule of television and radio reporting of the coronation, turn to page 31.*

**Fair and Cool**
Minneapolis High 65
MONDAY TEMPERATURES
*Details on Page 14*

# Minneapolis Morning Tribune

Vol. LXXXVII—No. 359 MINNEAPOLIS, MINN., TUESDAY, MAY 18, 1954 • • • • Price 5 Cents



# High Court Ban on Segregation in Schools Gives States Time to Comply; Hearings Set in Fall

By RICHARD WILSON
Chief of the Minneapolis Tribune Washington Bureau

WASHINGTON—Racial segregation in the public schools was unanimously ruled invalid Monday by the United States supreme court. Now the problem is how to enforce its abolition in 17 states.

There was every indication of peaceful acceptance of this historic reversal in American practice. Previous acts of the court breaking down racial segregation in restaurants, on public conveyances and at the higher-education level have been accepted.

In this more far-reaching action, however, the court yesterday conceded the immense problem involved in making an adjustment from legal segregation to its present illegal and unconstitutional status.

Hearings were ordered by the high court for next fall to determine just how the new order shall be put into effect. The cases, from the District of Columbia, Virginia, South Carolina, Delaware and Kansas, were restored to the docket of the supreme court for this purpose.

### Major Questions Remain

The questions to be considered are these:

"WOULD A DECREE necessarily follow providing that, within the limits set by normal geographic school districting, Negro children should forthwith be admitted to schools of their choice, or may the court, in the exercise of its equity powers, permit an effective gradual adjustment to be brought about from existing segregated systems to a system not based on color distinctions?

"SHOULD THE COURT FORMULATE detailed decrees; if so, what specific issues should the decrees reach; should the court appoint a special master to hear evidence with a view to recommending specific terms for such decrees?

"SHOULD THE COURT SEND the cases back to the lower courts with "directions to frame" such decrees, and if so, what instructions should the lower courts be given?"

These questions were all posed when the court ordered new arguments in the segregation cases early last December.

Many questions were raised on ways of ending segregation at the hearings last December. The principal inquiries then on methods were raised by Associate Justice Robert Jackson, who was back on the bench Monday after recovering from what was described as a mild heart attack.

The court ordered that briefs on the points still unsettled shall be submitted by Oct. 1 by all interested parties, including the attorney general.

### D. C. Negroes in Majority

Integration of the public schools is recognized as a very large administrative problem. In the District of Columbia, for example, it is estimated the Negro enrollment in the public schools, presently segregated in different buildings and with different teaching staffs, will be 64,462 next fall. The white pupils at that time, it is estimated, will number 44,199.

There will be 1,914 Negro teachers, compared to 1,781 white teachers; and there will be 942 Negro classrooms and 892 white classrooms.

Integration brings with it many administrative problems in addition to social problems. One of the greatest, according to school officials in Washington, is the problem of retaining teachers for integrated classes. There are both white and Negro teachers who do not wish to cope with problems they think may be involved.

Two states where great concern is felt over integration are South Carolina and Georgia. The Georgia legislature has approved standby legislation for the abolition of public schools to take effect if the supreme court ruling applies. The state school superintendent, M. D. Collins, said he is "not certain" the decision affects Georgia.

### Will States Close Public Schools?

If it does apply, Georgia would have nothing but private education, possibly subsidized by the state.

Thus would be raised a new question whether it is possible in this way to circumvent the United States supreme court.

The same procedure is under consideration in South Carolina by Gov. James F. Byrnes.

But, for the present, it would appear that since the cases are still on the supreme court docket, the final determination is not to be made on the method of ending segregation until next fall or later. In this case, except where state governments are able to work out their own system of integration, the court's ruling may not take practical effect.

In many areas problems will be raised because Negro schools to which white pupils may be assigned would not be considered "adequate" for the white pupils. This may cause an additional financial burden in some of the states.

In Maryland, no such problem is likely to arise. A new school construction program has provided, in some instances,

Segregation
*Continued on Page Five*

## Guatemala Gets Arms From Reds

### State Department Says Shipment Came From Poland

By DANA ADAMS SCHMIDT


WASHINGTON — The state department said Monday it has reliable information that an important shipment of arms has been sent from Communist-controlled territory to Guatemala.

It said the arms, now being unloaded at Puerto Barrios, Guatemala, were shipped from Stettin. That former German Baltic seaport has been occupied by Communist Poland since World War II.

"Because of the origin of these arms, the point of their embarkation, their destination and the quantity of arms involved, the department of state considers this a development of gravity," the announcement said.

**THE ALFHELM,** believed to be under charter, docked at Puerto Barrios last Saturday, the state department reported, carrying a large shipment of armament.

The state department did not reveal the exact quantity of the arms, their nature or where they were manufactured.

Other sources said, however, that 10 freight-car loads of goods listed in the manifest of the ship as "hardware," had been unloaded from this ship and sent to Guatemala City since Sunday.

A Guatemalan embassy spokesman said he had no doubt the state department's information was accurate.

"But what is 'grave' about it?" he asked. "Guatemala is free to buy its arms where it can."

**DIPLOMATS HERE** are alarmed over the arms shipment because the Guatemalan government has been heavily infiltrated by Communists. There was some question as to destination of the weapons, since the Guatemalan army is generally considered the main limiting influence of the Communists.

At the 10th Inter-American conference in March at Caracas, Venezuela, Guatemala cast the only vote against a resolution declaring that communism was a "threat to the sovereignty and political independence of the American states, endanger the American states."

MAP LOCATES GUATEMALA

## UPS AND DOWNS OF WEATHER ELSEWHERE

**Hottest city in the nation:**
*Yuma, Ariz., 98*

**Coolest place in Minnesota:**
(Reporting to U.S. weather bureau)
*Bemidji, high 57; low 22*

*MIDWEST TEMPERATURES*

| | High | Low | Precipitation |
|---|---|---|---|
| Chicago | [illegible] | [illegible] | |
| Madison, Wis. | [illegible] | [illegible] | |
| Des Moines, Iowa | [illegible] | [illegible] | |
| Dubuque, Iowa | [illegible] | [illegible] | |
| Kansas City, Mo. | [illegible] | [illegible] | |
| St. Louis, Mo. | [illegible] | [illegible] | [illegible] |
| Oklahoma City | [illegible] | [illegible] | [illegible] |
| Omaha, Neb. | [illegible] | [illegible] | |

*Temperature maps on Page 14*

## McCarthy Begins 'Vacation' With a Smile

SEN. McCARTHY (R., WIS.) LEAVES HEARINGS FOR A WEEK'S RECESS
*Army-McCarthy row investigation to get vacation after presidential order upsets order of business*
UP Telephoto

## Both Praise, Defiance Greet Court Decision

By United Press

The supreme court's historic decision outlawing school segregation brought swift — and mixed — reaction across the nation Monday.

From the southland there were cries of defiance and bitter attacks upon the court.

From the north there was praise and an assertion that the ruling "gives the lie to Communist propaganda about what can be done in America."

**DEMANDS** for "patience and moderation" were heard, too. Some southern states and cities announced immediately that they would move immediately to end segregation.

Gov. Johnston Murray of Oklahoma said "Oklahoma has always followed the law, whatever it is."

Missouri's state education commissioner, Hubert Wheeler, said at Jefferson City that the ruling was expected and that he had received no reports of violent opposition.

Headquarters of the Texas Council of Churches in Dallas issued a series of statements by churchmen, among them Methodist Bishops William C. Martin and A. Frank Smith. The two bishops expressed belief the people would accept the ruling of the high court.

**SEN. RUSSELL** (D., Ga.), however, called the decision "a flagrant abuse of judicial power."

Russell, long a states' rights Democrat, said, "Ways must be found to check the tendency of the court to disregard the Constitution and the precedents of able and unbiased judges to decide cases solely on the basis of the personal predilections of some of its members as to political, economic and social questions."

But Sen. Holland (D., Fla.), while calling the ruling "revolutionary," expressed hope that "patience and moderation" will be used in putting it into effect. He said the court was

Reaction
*Continued on Page Five*

## On Inside Pages



## West Proposes Quick Peace in Indochina

GENEVA, SWITZERLAND—(UP)—France laid a western proposal for a quick peace in Indochina before the Geneva conference Monday, but most of the secret session was devoted to a wrangle over evacuation of Dienbienphu's wounded.

The western proposal was reported to outline detailed steps for ending hostilities, leaving political decisions for later. However, details of the plan were not made public. It was presented less than an hour before the session ended, and little debate was possible.

The question of evacuating the wounded from Dienbienphu was unsettled as the nine delegations ended their session. A reliable source said the Communists, headed by Foreign Minister V. M. Molotov of Russia and Red China's Chou En-lai, again tried to bring the French and Viet Minh into direct negotiations on the question here.

Although sentiment among some members of the French delegation for entering such negotiations was reported, Foreign Minister Georges Bidault has consistently rejected this course. He rejected it again yesterday, the informant said.

A communique issued by the American delegation after the meeting said only that statements were heard on evacuation of the wounded and that peace in Indochina also was discussed.

*(FRENCH OFFER TO AID REBEL WOUNDED—page 2.)*

HAMMARSKJOLD SAYS:

## 'U.N. Holds Hope of World Without Fear'

By MIRIAM ALBURN
Minneapolis Tribune Staff Writer

The United Nations remains the main source of hope that a world without fear may be possible, the top spokesman of the U.N. said in Minneapolis Monday.

Dag Hammarskjold, U.N. secretary-general, said he considers this fact "a vote of confidence that reflects a refusal to allow disappointments over lack of spectacular results to cause despair."

Hammarskjold spoke at the awards dinner of the Minneapolis Star program of Information on World Affairs in Nicollet hotel.

*(The text of his address is printed on Page 7. His picture appears on Page 17. A broadcast of his address will be heard over Station WCCO at 9:30 p.m. today.)*

**THE SWEDISH** official, who presides over the representatives of all the member nations, said there is a growing understanding that the U.N. is not a separate authority over member states. Rather, he said, it is "a great association of fully independent nations where all action, or inaction, is determined by the policies of the participating governments."

"The frequent display of clashing ideologies and fundamental differences between some of the most powerful members of this association is in itself a demonstration of this fact," he said.

"But we have also seen that the conflicts, and the lack of agreement, have failed to break up the association or even to cause any of the participants to suggest such a step.

"Surely this shared preference to stay on the road mapped out by the U.N. charter

Hammarskjold
*Continued on Page Seven*

## Millers Win in 10 Innings

•

**BOSTON BEATS DETROIT**

•

*(DETAILS in Sports Section.)*

## 600-Pound Bear Slain by Duluth Farmer

DULUTH, MINN.—(UP)—Alfred Korby, rural Duluth farmer, shot and killed a 600-pound bear he found stalking grazing cattle on his farm.

## Almanac

### Does He Ever Taxi Patience of Passengers?

*Tuesday, May 18, 1954*
Sunrise 5:41 a.m.; sunset 7:38 p.m.

One St. Louis Park bus line driver, a jocular sort, probably has the best-humored busload of passengers in town—a tribute to the running line of chatter he produces. His prize offering is a one-word question he asks—most often of women—as he opens the bus doors to let them in:

"Taxi?"

•

We are in receipt of a postcard from a Minneapolis organization, announcing an important change in dates for an upcoming program. The program has been moved from a Thursday to a Monday.

Says the postcard: "We hope this unavoidable change will not effect your attendance."

•

*Fair and "cool" again today in the Twin Cities. High of 65 and low tonight of 45.*

•

Sign on a barber shop near Thirty-sixth and Bryant avenue S.:

*"There is no place*
*Just like this place*
*Anywhere near this place,*
*So this must be the place."*

## Army-McCarthy Probe Delayed for One Week

WASHINGTON—(AP)—President Eisenhower brought the McCarthy-army hearings to an unexpected halt Monday—for a week at least, and maybe forever.

Taking a personal hand, the President issued an order forbidding army witnesses to testify about the role of White House and other high officials in the controversy between Sen. McCarthy (R., Wis.) and civilian Pentagon chiefs.

**McCARTHY CRIED** "Iron Curtain!" Democrats raised a protest of "whitewash." And in the end the senate investigating subcommittee voted to recess the public inquiry until next Monday to see if Mr. Eisenhower would withdraw or modify his secrecy clampdown.

Acting chairman Mundt (R., S.D.) declared there is nothing about the recess which "even remotely implies a discontinuation of these hearings" for good.

The Democrats, however, said it looked to them as if the hearings may well have blown sky high—unless the President should change his mind. The chances of Mr. Eisenhower doing this appeared pretty slim.

The President said in yesterday's secrecy order, issued to Secretary of Defense Wilson, that his stand was taken "to maintain the proper separation of powers between the executive and legislative branches of government."

"This principle must be maintained regardless of who would

McCarthy
*Continued on Page Five*

## Farmer Killed; Traffic Toll: 221

Death of a Hawley, Minn., bachelor farmer Monday pushed Minnesota's 1954 traffic toll to 221, 53 more than at this time a year ago.

Art Korline, about 45, was killed about 4 p.m. when a car rammed into the trailer he was pulling with a tractor.

Korline apparently had started to turn into a gravel pit off U.S. highway 10 when he saw a car, driven by Martin Michelson, Fort Dodge, Iowa.

Korline pulled back into the road, police said, and Michelson's car struck the trailer, flipping the tractor over.

## Youths in Stolen Auto Flee Into $1,200 Four-Car Pile-up

Two teen-agers, fleeing from police in a stolen car, crashed through a stop sign at Eleventh avenue S. and Twenty-second street Monday and caused a four-car collision.

Nobody was reported seriously injured.

The youths, one 16 and the other 15, were driving a 1952 four-door sedan west on Twenty-second about 8:30 p.m.

First they hit a car being driven north on Eleventh avenue by Garland Hudson, 29, 1206½ Sixth street N. Hudson was alone.

**HUDSON'S CAR** flipped over lengthwise, bouncing off the front of a car being driven south on Eleventh avenue by Richard Norwick, 41, 3116 Twelfth avenue S.

With Norwick were his wife Lorraine, 32, and their sons Bobby, 5, and Tommy, five months.

The stolen car, after hitting Hudson's car, bounced into the side of another car traveling south on Eleventh avenue.

This car, driven by Rueben O. Thompson, 43, 3844 Nineteenth avenue S., spun around and ended on the opposite curb. Thompson was alone.

**THE STOLEN CAR** ended on its side, its front smashed into a telephone pole.

The two teen-agers were arrested and turned over to the crime prevention bureau.

Police estimated total damage to all four cars at $1,200.

## TURN THE PAGES TO:

• • •

Father Divine

**Father Divine, Holy Husband . . . Page 7**



**Food and Women's Section Begins on Page 9**

## High Court Decision Opens Way to End of All Segregation in U.S.

By CARL T. ROWAN
Minneapolis Tribune Staff Writer

*EDITOR'S NOTE: Monday's momentous decision by the United States supreme court outlawing racial segregation in schools is perhaps the most important on race relations in American history.*

*In the accompanying article, Carl T. Rowan, Tribune staff writer, explains just what the ruling means and how it is likely to apply to other areas of race relations in this country.*

*Rowan and Bonham Cross, Tribune staff photographer, visited the areas involved in the lawsuit last November and wrote a series of articles, "Jim Crow's Last Stand?", which won Rowan the Sigma Delta Chi award for general reporting.*

Rowan

The United States supreme court changed the entire course of race relations — and possibly the history of American democracy — Monday when it cast aside the 58-year-old separate but equal doctrine.

With its long-awaited ruling on racial segregation in public schools, the court set the stage for a decade of lawsuits that are certain to come before every school is open to every American.

But amid the anger and glee, the defiance and jubilation, that followed the ruling, the following points stood out:

**THE RULING** opened the door for an attack on segregation in many areas outside public education.

**The greatest** immediate effect of the ruling may be its use in combatting Communist propaganda in Asia and Africa.

**The bitter,** headline-getting comment from the southland was almost entirely by politicians. But in the background were southern leaders—editors and churchmen — who said the south would adjust to the change.

**The troublesome** part of the school segregation issue — how to end Jim Crow and how soon — still was to be dealt with.

In striking down Jim Crow schools, the court gave the National Association for the Advancement of Colored People (NAACP) a smashing victory by going all the way and declaring that segregation, of itself, is a form of discrimination.

**The sentences** in which the supreme court justices state that there is no such thing as

Equality
*Continued on Page 14*

Fair
Minneapolis High 80
MONDAY TEMPERATURES

| | | | | | |
|---|---|---|---|---|---|
| [illegible] | [illegible] | [illegible] | [illegible] | [illegible] | [illegible] |

Details on Page 12

# Minneapolis Morning Tribune

Vol. LXXXVIII—No. 71 MINNEAPOLIS, MINN., TUESDAY, AUGUST 3, 1954 Price 5 Cents



# Senate Votes to Send McCarthy Censure Bid to Special Committee

BISHOP STEPHEN E. KEELER GREETS ARCHBISHOP OF CANTERBURY, RIGHT
*The Most Rev. Geoffrey F. Fisher arrives for Anglican congress*

## Guatemala Army Rises in Revolt

### Castillo Armas Forced to Disband Liberation Forces

GUATEMALA CITY —(AP)— Disgruntled Guatemalan army regulars rushed to the aid of brawling military cadets with mortars and tanks Monday and forced President Castillo Armas' ruling council to disband his revolutionary "liberation army" in a day-long revolt.

An official casualty list said 12 persons were killed. Hospitals listed 42 as wounded. Unofficial reports placed the dead at 100 and the wounded at more than 200.

**FIGHTING** centered around Roosevelt hospital outside the capital near an encampment of the liberation army which spearheaded Castillo Armas' anti-Communist revolt against the regime of former president Jacobo Arbenz Guzman.

Starting with a brawl at dawn between 120 military cadets and the liberation army, the fighting soon was joined by regular army forces.

The regulars brought up mortars and tanks and the firing became very heavy in the hospital zone.

Late yesterday afternoon the army ordered a truce and announced an agreement had been signed with the government junta for disbanding liberation forces.

United States Ambassador John E. Peurifoy was active in bringing about the peaceful settlement. (Roman Catholic Archbishop Mariano Rossell Arellano of Guatemala headed the group of negotiators, dispatches from San Salvador said.)

**A SPOKESMAN** for the American embassy reported late last night that "very great tension" continued in the capital and there was a possibility of a popular uprising.

He said civilian supporters of Castillo Armas resented the army's forcing the president to disband the liberation army.

Planes controlled by the government were sent up early in the fight but were ordered grounded, apparently before they went into action. There was no more aerial action until late afternoon when air force planes circled the capital on patrol.

**THE CEASE-FIRE** became effective when about 700 liberation army soldiers surrendered their arms to regular army officers at Roosevelt hospital. The irregulars will be returned to their homes today.

Meanwhile, hundreds of Guatemalans, mostly women, gathered in front of the National palace and demonstrated in support of Castillo Armas. Most of the speakers lauded the liberation army and criti

Guatemala
*Continued on Page 10*

## Dodgers End Braves' Streak in 13 Innings

MILLERS DOWN SAINTS, 7-6, IN 11 INNINGS

*(DETAILS in Sports Section.)*

## First Picture of State POW Behind 'Bamboo Curtain'

RICHARD TENNESON, 21, AT TIAYUAN, CHINA
*Picture taken in front of studio backdrop (another picture—page 8)*

## Hearings May Delay Adjournment

By CHARLES BAILEY
Minneapolis Tribune Staff Correspondent

WASHINGTON — A compromise proposal by senate "moderates" brought a temporary halt Monday night in the senate debate over censuring Sen. McCarthy (R., Wis.).

By a vote of 75 to 12, the senate sent the censure resolution of Sen. Flanders (R., Vt.) to a special bipartisan six-man committee.

The vote was the wind-up of a day of violent debate culminating with attacks by McCarthy himself on the senators who have proposed to censure him.

*(FLANDERS SAYS Ike Praised Milder Attack; McCARTHY STILL Senate 'Biggie,' Debate Proving—page 3.)*

**THE COMMITTEE** plan, a combination of suggestions by Senators Knowland (R., Calif.), Ives (R., N. Y.) and Jackson (D., Wash.), grew out of the efforts of a group of Republicans and Democrats who said they wanted to make sure that no one would be able to say the senate acted hastily in the censure fight.

By the time it was voted on, the plan had picked up support from the senate leaders of both parties — Knowland and Sen. Johnson (D., Texas).

It was backed by such others as veteran Sen. George (D., Ga.), one of two senators now sitting who took part in the last censure vote over 20 years ago, and Sen. McClellan (D., Ark.), senior Democrat on the committee that aired the McCarthy-army charges.

The plan would do this to the hot Flanders resolution:

**Send it** to the committee, which will presumably be named at once, for study.

**Give the committee power,** under an amendment by Jackson, to hold hearings, subpena witnesses and documents and meet at any time.

**Instruct the committee** to report back before the present senate session adjourns "sine die" (permanently).

Knowland suggested the senate may remain in session—while the house goes home—to hear the committee's report.

Opponents of the plan argued strongly that it would be of no use except to prevent a vote by the full senate.

"You will be unable to make this investigation satisfactory to (McCarthy) unless you turn it over to him," Sen. Monroney (D., Okla.) said. "You will be

McCarthy
*Continued on Page 10*

## Boy, 9, Hit by Truck, Dies 5 Hours Later

David Scofield, 9, 3438 Elliot avenue, died in Swedish hospital Monday, about five hours after he was reported struck by a truck in an alley near his home.

David was the son of Mr. and Mrs. George Scofield. Scofield is a captain in the Salvation Army. The accident occurred about 10:30 a.m., police were told.

Police did not hear of the accident until the coroner was informed of the boy's death.

**NEIGHBORS SAID** the mishap was at the rear of 3418 Elliot avenue. They said the driver of the truck, who was collecting rubbish, waited at the scene until an ambulance arrived.

Police had not learned his identity last night. They said they believe the man may not have been aware of his responsibility to report the accident. They urge him to report today.

Neighbors called a private physician who in turn contacted Swedish hospital. The hospital called a Smith ambulance.

Besides his parents, David is survived by a brother, Jonathan, 5. Funeral arrangements are being made at Gill Brothers mortuary.

**THE BOY'S** death raised the traffic toll in Minnesota to 359 for 1954, a figure 24 higher than at this time a year ago.

William C. Bathurst, 64, 5940 Twelfth avenue S., died in a Detroit Lakes, Minn., hospital of injuries suffered Thursday when his car left highway 34 near Detroit Lakes.

Bathurst was a salesman for the Lehigh Sewer Pipe and Tile Co.

Otto F. Erickson, 60, Kennedy, Minn., was killed yesterday in a two-car crash at the intersection of highways 220 and 1, east of Oslo, Minn., northwest of Crookston.

### Ice Cream Cone Causes Crash; Youth, Man Hurt

An ice cream cone was blamed Monday for an automobile accident in which a youth and a man were injured seriously.

Henry R. Coppock, 17, of rural Ramsey county told New Brighton police he was eating an ice cream cone about 3 p.m. while driving north on highway 8 near Eighth avenue NW. in New Brighton.

When he attempted to put the cone down, he told police, his car swerved, colliding with a south-bound car driven by Donald A. Lundin, 25, Pine City, Minn. Lundin is believed to be staying in St. Paul.

Both were taken to Ancker hospital in St. Paul.

## Archbishop of Canterbury Arrives in Minneapolis

By MIRIAM ALBURN
Minneapolis Tribune Staff Writer

His Grace, the 99th archbishop of Canterbury, stepped off a train in Great Northern depot Monday night, wearing traditional black gaiters, black frock coat, black hat and the gold pectoral cross of his office.

The Most Rev. and Rt. Hon. Geoffrey Francis Fisher, primate of all England and metropolitan, and Mrs. Fisher had come for the meetings of the Anglican congress, which will open at 8 p.m., Wednesday in Minneapolis auditorium.

The archbishop was in jolly mood when he arrived at the station with the Rt. Rev. Stephen E. Keeler, bishop of Minnesota, who had gone to St. Paul to meet him.

He greeted the group who went down to the tracks to welcome him, including the Rt. Rev. Hamilton H. Kellogg, bishop coadjutor of Minnesota, and Mrs. Kellogg; Percival North, British consul for the Twin Cities, and Mrs. Keeler.

**HE JOKED** with photographers and made jaunty gestures with hands and with hat, and he also had a few serious words to say about the coming congress.

As leader of the oldest Episcopal church of the 15 national churches in the Anglican communion, the clergyman who crowned the queen of England is the highest dignitary of this church family.

"All of us will gain by having the congress in Minneapolis," he said, "and we hope that the American Episcopal church also will gain."

The discussions will help to remind members of the churches of the "central contribution the Anglican congress can make in the deliverance of the Gospel," the archbishop said.

**HE SPOKE** of the value of having laymen participate as delegates, along with the bishops and clergymen.

Both the archbishop and the Rt. Rev. Henry K. Sherrill, New York, presiding bishop of the Protestant Episcopal church in the United States, will speak at the services tomorrow night.

The program will begin with a procession of bishops in colorful vestments outside the auditorium.

Tickets have been given to members of Episcopal churches in the diocese, but about 3,000 additional seats are expected to be available to the public. Persons not holding tickets will be admitted after 7:30 p.m.

### ON VACATION IN MINNESOTA?

**Hottest city in the nation:**
*Yuma, Ariz., 104*

**Coolest place in Minnesota:**
(Reporting to U.S. weather bureau)
*International Falls, high 72, low 53*

**MIDWEST TEMPERATURES**
(In 24 hours to 7 a.m. Monday)

| | High | Low | Precipitation |
|---|---|---|---|
| Chicago | [illegible] | [illegible] | [illegible] |
| Madison, Wis. | [illegible] | [illegible] | [illegible] |
| Des Moines, Iowa | [illegible] | [illegible] | [illegible] |
| Dubuque, Iowa | [illegible] | [illegible] | Trace |
| Kansas City, Mo. | [illegible] | [illegible] | [illegible] |
| St. Louis, Mo. | [illegible] | [illegible] | [illegible] |
| Oklahoma City | [illegible] | [illegible] | [illegible] |
| Omaha, Neb. | [illegible] | [illegible] | [illegible] |
| Minneapolis | [illegible] | [illegible] | [illegible] |

*Weather and temperature maps on page 12*

### Marlene Gilds Her Good Foot With Gold Shoe

LONDON —(AP)— Marlene Dietrich left London for Paris Monday with one shoe black and the other shoe gold.

**This way?**

She wouldn't say why. But she was limping heavily and an inch-wide strip of plaster peeped through the toe of the black shoe.

She has just completed appearing at a London night club for a salary in excess of $20,000 a week.

Her original four-week contract was extended to eight weeks after the first four weeks were sold out before opening night.

### Head of Firm Dies in 200-Foot Fall

CHILTON, WIS. —(UP)— William H. Dean, 50, Waukegan, Ill., was killed Monday in a 200-foot fall from a radio tower here. Dean, head of William H. Dean Co., and Edward Weyhe, Waukegan, were changing a rigging on the tower of the state radio station they were painting. A rope broke and the rigging slipped.

## Haymes, Ordered Deported Again, to Appeal Again

LOS ANGELES, CALIF.—(AP)—Crooner Dick Haymes Monday was ordered deported for the second time in an order issued by Ralph Farb, special hearing officer of the immigration service here.

**Haymes**

Farb was sent here a month ago to hear Haymes' appeal after the board of immigration appeals in Washington ordered the case reopened.

The government originally ordered Argentina-born Haymes deported on the ground he illegally re-entered the continental United States after a trip to Hawaii to visit actress Rita Hayworth, whom he later married.

In his decision yesterday Farb cleared Herman R. Landon, district officer of the immigration service, of charges by Haymes' attorneys that Landon helped arrange an "entrapment" of Haymes.

Farb held there is no evidence Landon ordered a subordinate not to warn Haymes he might lose his residential rights if he went to Hawaii.

The first deportation order was issued March 23.

The government contends the singer obtained exemption from military service in World War II as a neutral alien, thus becoming forever ineligible for American citizenship.

Farb said Haymes has 10 days to appeal the order back to the board of immigration appeals in Washington. Immigration service spokesmen said such appeals usually take from 30 to 60 days before they are heard.

In New York Bartley Crum, Haymes' attorney, said an appeal of the order would be filed at once.

"We think the evidence does confirm our view that Mr. Haymes was entrapped by the Los Angeles office," Crum said.

## County Funds to Aid 4 City Road Projects

By WILL HERTZ
Minneapolis Tribune Staff Writer

Four major Minneapolis traffic improvements moved a step nearer realization Monday when $905,000 in Hennepin county funds were approved for use on city streets in 1955.

The $905,000 was part of a $2,612,800 county road and bridge budget approved by the county board's budget committee. The board is expected to vote final approval today.

Hugo Erickson, city engineer, said he will recommend the city council use the county funds for the following projects:

**An underpass** for the East River road under the east end of the Franklin avenue bridge. A similar underpass now is under construction at the west end.

**Conversion** of Humboldt avenue N. into a main traffic artery from Forty-fourth avenue N. to the Minneapolis-Brooklyn Center boundary.

**The long-discussed** east-west crosstown artery on Sixty-second street along the south edge of the city.

**Removal of peat** from under Park and Portland avenues around Forty-third street. The peat has created paving problems on the two thoroughfares.

**COUNTY FUNDS** would only start these projects, Erickson said. The city would have to contribute substantially, and federal aid might be available for the Franklin avenue bridge and Sixty-second street projects, he said.

A small part of the county money, Erickson said, might be used to study the abandoned Como-Harriet streetcar right-of-way from Thirty-sixth street southwest to France avenue and Forty-fourth street.

The total county road and bridge budget of $2,612,800 will call for a five-mill tax levy. (A mill is one-tenth of one cent.) It compares with the 1954 budget of $1,713,951.

**THE 1954 BUDGET** calls for spending $467,000 for construction work outside of Minneapolis. Largest item is paving Excelsior boulevard from highway 100 to county highway 18.

Also approved was a lake improvement budget of $94,280. This will require a tax levy of about two-tenths of a mill.

All county budget proposals must be submitted to the county tax levy board for final approval. The tax levy board cannot cut individual budgets, but may trim the over-all total.

## Fan Blade Kills Litchfield Man

LITCHFIELD, MINN.—(UP)—Ed Hoeff, 59, rural Litchfield, died of loss of blood in a freak accident in his home.

Authorities said Hoeff took his automobile heater into the house to repair it. He plugged it into the electrical circuit and it blew up with such force one of the blades on the heater's fan smashed through the ceiling.

Another of the blades struck him in the face and a third cut his leg so severely that he bled to death before he could reach a hospital.

### Keel Laid on Carrier

NEWPORK NEWS, VA. —(AP)— The keel was laid Monday on the Ranger, third of four 60,000-ton aircraft carriers of the Forrestal class.

TENNESON WRITES MOTHER:

## 'Makes Me Sad We Can't Be Together'

Special to the Minneapolis Tribune

ALDEN, MINN. — Strong love for his mother and other deep emotions were expressed by Richard Tenneson, former American prisoner of war who embraced communism, in letters home.

The letters indicate no change in his attitude toward the United States, but for the first time they are not crowded with lengthy reports on his travels in China.

Tenneson, 21, former army private who elected to remain in Communist China after being held as a POW in Korea, wrote both letters from Tiayuan, China.

The first letter, to his mother, Mrs. Portia Howe, Alden, was dated July 9. It reads, in part:

"It's hard to explain how I felt when I saw your picture. I can truthfully say it raised a lump in my throat.

"The things I thought of were the many times I have caused you undue heartache. I know that you are suffering now, but it is one of those things that can't be helped.

"We couldn't have stayed together if I had gone home with the rest of the POWs. What I believe in would make me move from place to place.

"I couldn't come home from the neutral zone because they (United States government) would have done the same to me as they did to Dickenson and Batchelor.

(In May, an army court-martial in Washington convicted Cpl. Edward S. Dickenson of collaborating with the Chinese Communists while a prisoner of war in Korea. He was sentenced to 10 years at hard labor. His sentence is now before an army review board.

(The fourth army in June announced that Cpl. Claude Batchelor, 23, San Antonio, Texas, will be court-martialed soon on similar charges.)

"I want you to know that I have come to love my mother much more now than I ever did in the past and it makes me sad at times to think we can't be together now.

"But the time will come when we can be together and

Tenneson
*Continued on Page 10*

## Almanac

### Deer Puts His Dear Into a Fine Stew

*Tuesday, Aug. 3, 1954*
Sunrise [illegible] a.m.; sunset [illegible] p.m.

A Faribault man, driving home from Minneapolis early one morning, hit a deer at considerable damage to his car, but none to him.

While waiting for a game warden to claim the deer, he called an undertaker friend and asked him to call his wife. His reason for calling the undertaker: "He was the only friend I had who wouldn't get mad at being awakened at that hour of the night."

The only thing he hadn't given much thought to was his wife's reaction when—at 3 a.m.—she had a call from the undertaker, saying, "Your husband has just been in an accident."

*Fair skies, high temperature of 80 in the Twin Cities today. Low tonight, 60.*

A Garrison, N. D., man, vacationing in Arizona, sends a tribute to a 13-year-old Minnesota boy down there who showed the local cowhands a thing or two.

A story in the Arizona Republic says the boy, Joe Strahan, "lassoed a coyote, tossed another rope around its legs, bound its jaws, and dragged it home." In case local cowboys don't believe it, the newspaper says, "He now has it in a cage for all to see."

Says the North Dakota man: "I don't know Minnesota was cattle country."

## Sore Throat Nips Miss Universe

WINNSBORO, S. C.—(UP)—Miriam Stevenson, who won the Miss U.S.A. and Miss Universe beauty titles 12 days ago, was ordered by her doctor Monday to "stay in bed and not see anyone."

**Miss Stevenson**

Her parents, Mr. and Mrs. L. O. Stevenson, said she was a "pretty sick little girl." Her mother said she had a temperature and a sore throat.

## TURN THE PAGES TO:

### George Grim

*Tribune columnist tells what happened when Minneapolis motorman and conductor took over a streetcar in Norway—PAGE 11.*



### Down the Volga

*New Stalingrad rises from the rubble—Page 9*

### Science Looks at the Cold War

*Scientists tell Asians why U.S. lags in human relations*

Page 9

Cloudy
Minneapolis High, 30
THURSDAY TEMPERATURES
Details on Page 22

# Minneapolis Morning Tribune

Vol. LXXXVIII—No. 193 Copyright 1954 Minneapolis Star and Tribune Company MINNEAPOLIS, MINN., FRIDAY, DECEMBER 3, 1954 Price 5 Cents



Lowly Hawks Tumble Lakers, 117 to 108
(DETAILS in Sports Section.)

# Senate Votes to Condemn McCarthy, 67 to 22

## POPE PIUS FIGHTS FOR LIFE; DOCTORS PONDER OPERATION

VATICAN CITY—(P)—Pope Pius XII has suffered a severe collapse, with a weakening of the gallant heart that has stood him through 55 years of priesthood. Early today there was grave anxiety as he fought for his life.

Through the night troubled Romans gathered in spacious St. Peter's square and knelt on the cobblestones to pray for recovery of their pope and bishop.

Late last night police ringed the square to keep automobiles from disturbing the pope's sleep. Some 200 persons still praying for the pope's recovery were asked to leave the square at the same time.

**THE VATICAN'S** vicar general, Clement Cardinal Micara, urged the world's 425 million Roman Catholics to join in the prayers.

A member of the pope's family, Prince Carlo Pacelli, a nephew, was near the pope's bed in his simple white-walled bedroom. The pope's name is Eugenio Pacelli.

Dr. Riccardo Galeazzi-Lisi, physician to the 78-year-old pontiff, was constantly at his side. He had made emergency X-rays and called in a surgeon for consultation.

The doctor was reported considering an operation on the pope, to be made within 48 hours. The operation would be to relieve what were described as abdominal complications caused by a swelling of the pope's stomach.

A medical authority close to Dr. Pietro Valdoni, noted surgeon called in yesterday, said that an elementary operation known as a cholsystom (an opening of the bowels) might be the only one practicable at the age of the pope.

**THE POPE** has suffered from a stomach ailment and recurring hiccups for the last year. He had been ill before in the nearly 16 years he has headed the church, but never so gravely.

This illness—starting as a recurrence of the gastritis and hiccuping that sapped the pope's strength last winter—became serious last week-end. His collapse Thursday weakened his heart, and there also was an indication that his condition was aggravated by an ulcer.

He was extremely weak and had been unable to take any food by mouth for several days. His physician yesterday described the pope as conscious and completely lucid. But apparently he was unconscious for four hours after his collapse.

One Rome newspaper said he had asked for extreme unction, the sacrament administered to Catholics in danger of death. But the Vatican press office denied that Pius had asked for the last sacrament.

One of the prelates summoned yesterday to the papal apartment was the pope's sacristan, Bishop Pieter Ganisius Van Lierde. The sacristan

AP Wirephoto
**POPE PIUS XII**
*Picture taken Nov. 26*

Pope
*Continued on Page 12*

## U.S. Seeks U.N. Action to Free GIs

### Red China Blockade Would Be Act of War, Ike Says

UNITED NATIONS, N. Y.—(P)—Henry Cabot Lodge, Jr., announced Thursday the United States will request the U.N. to move for the release of 11 American aviators sentenced to jail as spies in Red China.

Lodge said he is confident the United States will get support here.

At the same time, President Eisenhower told a press conference the United States would not consider a blockade of Red China to free the fliers without consultation with congress.

**THE PRESIDENT** said such a blockade would be an act of war.

*(U.S. SIGNS Pact to Aid Formosa If Reds Attack—page 4.)*

Lodge rushed from conferences at the state department to a meeting of the 16 U.N. members who fought the Reds in Korea and then told newsmen:

"Great concern was expressed by all present at the fate of the 11 aviators, and no doubt action will be taken by the U.N.

"The United States is going to request action, and we are confident we will be supported both for the sake of our prisoners and others.

"We are going to act to do everything we can to keep faith with these men. They are

Airmen
*Continued on Page 13*

## WHAT McCARTHY DECISION MEANS

By RICHARD WILSON
Chief of the Minneapolis Tribune Washington Bureau

WASHINGTON — The senate has ended its long travail with Sen. McCarthy (R., Wis.) without condemning or criticizing him for his Communist investigations or any act directly connected with them.

Neither his methods nor his aims are condemned officially or censured by the senate insofar as the Communist investigations are concerned.

Wilson

He is not held accountable for browbeating witnesses, nor for making false or unfounded accusations, nor for stretching guilt by association to the breaking point, nor for any of the practices which have been the main subject of criticism for the past two years.

Senate action against McCarthy has not come near to central point that he has failed to disclose any significant Communist activity, but has instead built up cases without substance and has wrongly maligned the guiltless.

The senate has made no finding of fact whether McCarthy used for his own purposes funds contributed to him to fight communism; it has only held him offensive because he would not of his free will go before a senate committee to explain these transactions.

And, even in that incident, the point most often complained of was that he had maligned a fellow senator, Hendrickson of New Jersey, as without "guts or brains." Many believe that if McCarthy had apologized for his references to Hendrickson the senate would not have voted to condemn McCarthy on any count.

This is not to say that the senate did not "deplore" and "disapprove" of the free-swinging activities of its chief investigator.

The record of senate debate is replete with senatorial expressions of repugnance and horror, even from the majority leader, Sen. Knowland, even from some of the senator's staunchest defenders.

But the senate would not take the final step of officially condemning him for any direct act in his Communist investigations. It did not meet the issue head on and failed to do so with elaborate deliberation.

### Senate Backed Away From One Charge

In the closing hours of this political sideshow of nearly a year's duration, the senate backed away from censuring one of its members for being very rough with an army officer in a public hearing. New facts were said to have been adduced giving provocation for McCarthy's treatment of Brig. Gen. Ralph W. Zwicker.

But it has been evident for weeks that many members of the senate felt an inner compulsion against taking action against a fellow senator for verbally manhandling an army officer. It came out only on the last day that Sen. Russell, an influential southern Democrat who will be chairman of the armed services committee next year, wanted to go slow on this count.

The senatorial prerogative was seen rising to the surface:

**What senator** wished to sacrifice his own right to vent his spleen on the military?

**What senator** was ignorant of the general evasiveness of military officials when giving an accounting to the congress of their stewardship of the national security?

**What senator** had not at some time been rubbed raw by the lofty withdrawal of the top military brass behind their curtains of secrecy?

### Nothing Aimed at Disapproval of Methods

In short, nothing has happened yet which would force McCarthy or any future Red investigator to conclude that the methods of these investigations is disapproved specifically.

He could only conclude that the senate did not like the way the investigations were going, but for political reasons would not meet the issue head on. It chose instead to belabor McCarthy, not because he offended the public or the guiltless, but because he spit in the eye of the senate.

McCarthy is like a boy who has been spared blame for stealing the watermelons but punished lightly for remaining out after 9 p.m. Hereafter it might be presumed that he could steal watermelons if he got home early.

The action taken is a far march from the bold presentation made by a half dozen senators early this year. They presented 33 different charges and ever since then the senate or its select committee has been winnowing them out.

Nothing is said now of McCarthy's $10,000 Lustron Corp. fee, nothing of his classification of Gen. George C. Marshall as doing the work of traitors, nothing of his use of classified government information or possible violation of the espionage act, nothing of his "false" claims of routing out Communists, nothing of his "distortions and innuendo."

The senator takes this to mean, as he has said publicly, that he can resume his Communist investigations Monday morning just as if nothing had happened.

## 'Censure' Cut From Resolution

### Charge of Abusing Army General Also Is Dropped Out

By Staff Correspondent of the Minneapolis Tribune

WASHINGTON—Sen. Joseph R. McCarthy (R., Wis.) was officially "condemned" Thursday by the senate for his defiance and abuse of two senate committees.

The senate voted, 67 to 22, a resolution disapproving his failure to appear before a subcommittee which investigated his finances in 1951-52 and for his recent castigation of the Watkins censure committee as an "unwitting handmaiden" of the Communist movement.

Then the special session of the senate adjourned at 7:10 p.m. and will reconvene Jan. 5, 1955.

*(OTHER McCARTHY STORIES—pages 3 and 4.)*

But the controversial Communist investigator from Wisconsin was not officially "censured," at least by word.

**THE WORD** "censure" was dropped from the resolution before it was adopted.

Sen. Watkins (R., Utah) argued that previous resolutions of censure in the senate had not carried that word but still were resolutions of censure.

The senate did not hold McCarthy officially accountable for his treatment of Brig. Gen. Ralph W. Zwicker as a witness before the senate investigating subcommittee last winter.

This count in the resolution condemning him was displaced by a section criticizing him for attacking the Watkins committee, which had drawn up the charges against him.

The 1952 subcommittee looked into charges that McCarthy used for personal purposes money that was given him for his anti-Communist fight and that he improperly used his position to obtain funds. McCarthy refused to testify before the subcommittee.

Last February McCarthy questioned Zwicker in connection with the honorable discharge of Maj. Irving Peress, army dentist whom McCarthy called a "Fifth amendment Communist."

**McCARTHY CALLED** the general an unco-operative witness and told him he wasn't fit to wear his uniform.

The final outcome of the six-month fight to chastise and restrain the senate's chief investigator and Red hunter was an awkward compromise.

It was far from the wrathful denunciation McCarthy's critics and enemies wanted and was subject to many different interpretations.

There was no sign that the senate action would restrain McCarthy in the slightest and he emerges from the contest

McCarthy
*Continued on Page 17*

## Two Students Hurt by $25,000 Explosion in 'U' Chemical Lab

An explosion and fire injured two students and caused heavy damage to a research laboratory at the University of Minnesota Thursday.

The first blast occurred about 2:45 p.m. while five graduate students were working in the fourth-floor organic chemistry laboratory.

The explosion set off a flash fire that spread through about half of the laboratory. Two more explosions occurred before the fire was brought under control.

Injured were Peter Throckmorton, 27, 292 Arundel street, St. Paul, and Charles Wright, 24, 1523 Brook avenue SE. They were treated at University health service for minor cuts and burns.

Other students in the room at the time were Jack Swenson, 24, 322 Oak street SE.; John Franz, 25, Springfield, Ill., and Robert Brotherton, Dixon, Ill.

University officials said the first explosion was at a bench near where Throckmorton was working.

The blast shook the chemistry building and was heard over most of the campus.

Roy V. Lund, supervising engineer at the university, said damage would amount to approximately $25,000.

*(PICTURE—page 19.)*

## Girl, 16, Swallows Fork; Surgery Removes It

MUSKEGON, MICH.—(P)—Wilma Herman's parents laughed when their 16-year-old daughter told them she had just swallowed a dinner fork.

Then Wilma started to cry and they knew it was no laughing matter. They rushed her to Hackley hospital, where surgeons removed a full-sized dinner fork from her abdomen.

Doctors say she "is recovering nicely."

## James Hilton, 54, Author, in Grave Condition

LONG BEACH, CALIF.—(UP)—Novelist James Hilton, 54, famed English-born writer, was reported in "grave" condition Thursday suffering from an undiagnosed ailment at Seaside Memorial hospital.

Hilton

Disclosure that the author had been hospitalized here since Nov. 21 also revealed that for 10 years Hilton had lived here quietly — about 35 miles from the film studios of Hollywood which brought him even wider fame with adaptations of his books.

Hospital spokesmen refused to give any details of the illness. Specialists were called in to examine Hilton Thursday.

## Spanked Pupil Wins $325 by Suing Teacher

By Associated Press

FERGUS FALLS, MINN.—A 10-year-old boy who was spanked by his teacher because he couldn't pronounce "wizard" was awarded $325 damages Thursday by an Otter Tail county district court jury.

The jury returned the verdict against Mrs. Dorothy Temanson, a Parkers Prairie, Minn., teacher, after deliberating six hours and five minutes.

**IN THE SUIT,** Fred Moske, father of the pupil, David Moske, asked $7,500 damages for his son. A $110 suit in the father's own behalf was dismissed by Judge R. E. Barron.

The suit was directed against Mrs. Temanson and her husband, E. K. Temanson, superintendent of Parkers Prairie schools. The verdict, however, was against Mrs. Temanson only. Judge Barron had ruled the teacher solely responsible for acts of punishment.

The Moske attorney said that on April 26 David and two or three other students were in a group that was not quite as good at reading as the rest of the class.

The attorney said when David was unable to pronounce "wizard," Mrs. Temanson took hold of his shoulder and struck him with a stick on the side of a leg between the knee and thigh.

**THE ATTORNEY** told the court the boy was taken to an Alexandria, Minn., doctor and later remained at home a week while his mother applied hot packs to black and blue marks on his legs.

According to the attorney, the boy is now nervous, cries out in his sleep—making it difficult for an older brother to sleep with him — and has a limp.

The teacher testified she felt the punishment was proper and just and said she didn't mean to cause black and blue marks.

The teacher said the boy's failure to pronounce "wizard," was the immediate cause for punishment but that he had been defiant and guilty of bad conduct for eight months.

## 4 YEARS' LOST

## Imprisoned by Error, He's Not Bitter

By ED MAGNUSON
Minneapolis Tribune Staff Writer
Copyright 1954 Minneapolis Star and Tribune Company

"Well, I guess anyone can make a mistake."

That was the resigned attitude Thursday of Arnold Skogen, 58, a man who served a four-year sentence in Stillwater prison and then was told it was all a mistake.

Skogen, now in Rochester, Minn., admitted he's made a number of mistakes himself.

He said he has no bitter feelings toward authorities who apparently had charged him illegally with grand larceny for passing bad checks in Roseau county in October 1950. Skogen is from Roseau.

"Feeling that way just doesn't do anyone any good," he said.

**HE MADE IT** clear, however, he feels the four years, less 4½ months off for good behavior, spent in the prison "were a complete waste of time for me."

He said he feels so good at being free he hasn't had time to think much about seeking damages for false imprisonment.

He said he's considering it and will talk it over with his lawyer, James Deauville of Stillwater.

Skogen, a divorced father of five grown children, said excessive drinking has been the cause of his troubles with the law.

He concedes that these problems were brought on by himself but hints authorities have put a few unnecessary temptations before him.

He said he passed three bad checks, each for $10, in Warroad, Minn., in 1950, "because I needed the money to get liquor."

**THE CHARGE** of grand larceny brought against him "seemed fishy from the start," he said.

He said he didn't think the

Mistake
*Continued on Page 10*

## INDIAN ARMY SAYS:

## 'Playing With Reds Is a Slow Road to Suicide'

*Carl Rowan, award-winning staff member of the Minneapolis Tribune, presents today the fifth in his series of articles on India. This was written after the experience of nearly four months in India, where he was sent by the United States department of state.*

Rowan

By CARL T. ROWAN
Minneapolis Tribune Staff Writer
Copyright 1954 Minneapolis Star and Tribune Company

NEW DELHI, INDIA—More people than say so publicly believe today that India has a lot to fear from world communism.

Some important army people—who asked me not to name them—told me the Communists can paralyze the heart of India in an invasion, just by using college students.

These army people pointed out what already is known among many Indian civic leaders: there is significant dissension between the army and the ruling Congress party.

On three different occasions, in widely separated parts of India, I heard army men speak with contempt of "those damned dhotiwallahs in the Congress party. (A "dhotiwallah" is a term of derision. Literally, it means one who weaves or sells cloth.)

***A significant portion of the army seems to believe that "by playing with the Reds and pretending they have scruples when it is obvious they do not, we are being led down the slow road to suicide," one air force man said.***

The military men express confidence that the army of roughly a quarter-million men can handle any solely internal situation. But this is what one western-educated, western-trained military man told me:

"People generally talk about a Communist invasion from Tibet, moving down through Assam. Others write about the very true fact that Russia could throw her might against Afghanistan and move through the Khyber pass to Pakistan and India frontiers in two days. All these things may be part of the action.

"But I would wager that the big push would come from the east Bengal-Calcutta area (Calcutta is in the Indian state of Bengal). It seems to me that, following their moderate election successes in the south, the Reds have begun a pretty shrewd softening-up campaign right across the northern part

This Is India
*Continued on Page 10*

## Almanac

### Driveway Was Labeled 'Theirs'

*Friday, Dec. 3, 1954*
Sunrise 7:31 a.m.; sunset 4:32 p.m.

This is a report on swank in Richfield from our R'field man: "Passed the 7200 block on Knox avenue S. Noticed one Richfielder with a two-car garage, one door labeled 'His' and the other, of course, labeled 'Hers.'"

•

Victor Rotering, senior vice president of First National bank, is 65 today.

•

*Cloudy with a high of 30 in the Twin Cities today. Low tonight about 15.*

•

J. T. says this Christmas he is giving his friends books full of trading stamps and letting them pick out their own presents.

•

Long line of cars waited patiently at an Adams school intersection. Young girl was playing ball on the sidewalk and her ball rolled into the street. The driver in truck license Y65-216 halted traffic, stopped, got out, retrieved the ball, threw the girl a perfect strike and she dropped it.

## New Camera Can Photograph Ball at 1,000 Miles

NEW YORK—(INS)—The army has developed a super-camera that is capable of photographing a V2 rocket at the moon's distance from the earth or a tennis ball from 1,000 miles.

Dr. Clyde Tombaugh, astronomer who discovered the planet Pluto in 1930, disclosed Thursday the telescope-camera was developed for the satellite research program he supervises for army ordnance at White Sands proving ground in New Mexico.

He told the annual convention of the American Rocket society a potential "instrumented satellite" could be used in precisely measuring distances on the earth's surface.

## Vote Hardly Cold When Senator Asks If McCarthy Was 'Censured'

WASHINGTON—(P)—The senate had scarcely adopted its resolution condemning Sen. McCarthy's conduct Thursday before a question was raised as to whether McCarthy had been "censured."

Vice President Nixon, to whom the question was addressed, said every senator will have to make his own interpretation.

Sen. Bridges (R., N.H.), saying he had "a parliamentary inquiry," asked if the word "censure" were mentioned in the resolution.

Bridges was grinning as he waited for an answer. Other McCarthy supporters broke into chuckles and laughter.

Nixon said "the word censure does not appear" in the resolution adopted by the senate. He added the title of the resolution would be appropriately amended so that it would be described as one relating to the conduct of the junior senator from Wisconsin.

"Then it is not a censure resolution?" asked Bridges.

Nixon told him that was not a parliamentary inquiry. Bridges then asked if the resolution does censure McCarthy since the word censure, Bridges said, did not appear in the title or the body of the resolution.

Nixon said the resolution relates to the conduct of McCarthy and senators could place their own interpretation on it.

After the final vote, a reporter asked McCarthy if he thought he had been censured.

"I wouldn't say it was a vote of confidence," McCarthy replied.

Sen. Watkins (R., Utah), chairman of the censure committee, has taken the position all along that there was no difference between the meaning of the words censure and condemn.

In the last censure action taken by the senate, in 1929, the resolution also did not use the word "censure."

Instead, like the one adopted today, it condemned the conduct of Sen. Hiram Bingham, a Connecticut Republican, for permitting a lobbyist to attend a closed committee session.

Thus the resolution adopted yesterday condemning McCarthy's conduct is in line with the most recent precedent for a censure case.

In the only other censure case in the senate's history, occurring in 1902, the senate did use the word "censure" in the resolution it adopted. That case involved two South Carolina senators who engaged in an altercation on the senate floor—John McLaurin and Benjamin Tillman.

### 'Censure' and 'Condemn'

*From Webster's New International Dictionary (Unabridged):*

"**censure**—To find fault with or condemn as wrong; to blame; to express disapprobation of; to criticize adversely."

"**condemn**—To pronounce to be wrong; to disapprove of."

### TURN THE PAGES TO:

Light Snow
Minneapolis High 20
Details on Page 14

# Minneapolis Morning Tribune

Vol. LXXXVIII—No. 261 MINNEAPOLIS, MINN., WEDNESDAY, FEBRUARY 9, 1955 Price 5 Cents



# Kremlin Shakeup Forecast as Malenkov Quits; U.S. Expects Tough Policy From New Rulers

**Hierarchy Depleted** In December 1949, a "festive meeting" was held in Moscow's Bolshoi theater to celebrate the 70th birthday of Premier Josef Stalin. World leaders of the Communist movement and top bosses of the Kremlin were assembled for the occasion. Above is shown a section of the speaker's platform at that meeting, revealing the changes that have taken place in the Soviet hierarchy in five years. Those not labeled in the picture are (to right of Stalin) Marshal A. M. Vasilevsky, Red army chief of staff, and (to right of Khrushchev) Dolores Ibarruri, secretary general of the Spanish Communist party; Gheorghe Gheorghiu-Dej, secretary general of the Romanian Communist party, and (at microphones) Nikolai Shvernik, president of the Soviet Union.

## Grading to Start for Ball Park

### Board Orders Architects to Draw Up Plans

By WILL HERTZ
Minneapolis Tribune Staff Writer

The Bloomington major league baseball stadium moved a long step toward reality Tuesday as the metropolitan sports area commission took these two actions:

ADOPTED a revolutionary type of construction for the grandstands, and directed architects and engineers to proceed with detailed plans.

DECIDED TO start grading preparatory to construction between March 15 and April 15, as soon as weather permits.

Target date for completing the stadium in the spring of 1956—in time for the 1956 baseball season.

**THE COMMISSION** will meet again Feb. 17 with its architects, Thorshov and Cerny, and engineers, Toltz, King and Day, to draw up a construction time-table.

The commission talked in terms of a $4,500,000 stadium with 23,250 grandstand seats and 16,750 bleacher seats.

Seating capacity will be set later, however, since it is largely a matter of determining the number of stadium sections to be built.

The stadium, Cedar avenue and highway 100, will be unique because of its four tiers and its cantilever construction.

**THE LOWER THREE** tiers will be used for spectators' seats. The top tier, which will be covered, will house press facilities and club facilities for buyers of stadium bonds.

Cantilever construction means that the upper tiers will jut out from and be supported by a rigid "backbone" framework around the stadium's outside edge.

This will eliminate view-obstructing pillars, and bring seats much closer to the playing field than in any other baseball stadium.

**THE FURTHEST** seat will be 41 feet closer to the playing field than its counterpart in the Milwaukee, Wis., stadium.

Cantilever construction will cost about $5 a seat more than conventional design, but the commission said the expense was justified by improving visibility for spectators.

The commission abandoned the idea of "tilting" the stands 20 degrees toward the playing field because of the much greater construction cost.

Seats in upper sections of the 90-degree vertical stands will be 10 to 15 feet farther from the field than if the stands were tilted, but the upper decks will be closer to the ground.

•

## Quarter Quickly Turns Into Gold, But Try to Find It

CLANTON, ALA. —(UP)— Workmen found a 25-cent piece on land once owned by John Higgins and word of the incident spread.

By the time the story made the rounds of the courthouse for the third time the quarter had grown to $440,000, part of it in gold, and the internal revenue bureau was reported interested in Higgins.

"Not only did I not get any $440,000, I didn't even get the quarter," Higgins said.

HOCKEY
Gophers Lose
GOLDEN GLOVES
14 KNOCKED OUT IN 32 FIGHTS
•
*(DETAILS in Sports Section.)*

## Poor Briefing in NWA Case Annoys Ike

By CHARLES BAILEY
Minneapolis Tribune Staff Correspondent

WASHINGTON — President Eisenhower made his first order in the Northwest Airlines Seattle-Hawaii route case without consulting the civil aeronautics board chairman, it was learned Tuesday.

After conferring with a Minnesota senator and representative, he was reportedly annoyed because staff reports on which his original decision was based lacked facts showing all sides of the dispute.

The President Monday consequently reversed his order to cut NWA out of the Hawaii route, which would have given Pan American World Airways (PAA) a monopoly on the route.

**HIS REVERSAL** allows both NWA and PAA to fly the route, as they do at present, for three years.

The President's order cancelling NWA's route from the Twin Cities to Tokyo via Alaska still stands.

In the Hawaii route case, the President made his first order four days before he consulted Chan Gurney, CAB chairman. The first order, which overturned an unanimous CAB recommendation, brought a storm of protest.

*(NWA STOCK Rides Out Hawaii Storm—page 21.)*

Gurney said the first time he was consulted by the President was last Saturday morning, when he was called into a meeting of the President with Sen. Thye (R., Minn.) and Rep. Walter Judd (R., Minn.).

Gurney said that to the best of his knowledge no other CAB member had been consulted by the President before Mr. Eisenhower reversed the CAB recommendation.

**GURNEY SAID** yesterday the CAB was queried on the case by the bureau of the budget, which he said handled the matter at the White House level, but the President himself did not seek advice or explanation from him before reversing the board.

Also present when Thye and Judd put their case before the

NWA
*Continued on Page 12*

### How's the Legislature Doing?

### 1955 Legislative Progress Report:

- *Some say gas taxes needn't be raised. Others say they should be. And a new division of road-user funds seems certain ....Back Page*

### 49% Object to Old-Age Lien Law, 46% Approve

*A Minnesota Poll report on state issues ..........Page 12*

### Also Turn the Pages To:

• • • •



## Snow, Sleet, Freezing Rain Mar Highways

Freezing rain, snow and sleet mixed over southern Minnesota late Tuesday, making highways treacherous.

The precipitation came as a part of a Canadian storm that was whirling just across Minnesota's Canadian border yesterday.

Worst effects of the storm appeared to be confined to Canada, however.

Today's high temperature here is foreseen as about 25 in contrast with yesterday's thawing 32. A drop to 5 above is due tonight.

Snow flurries will continue today. The weather bureau said Minneapolis might have an additional 2 inches of snow.

Rochester, Minn., had rain last night.

•

## Reds Fire on U.S. Plane Off Tachens

TAIPEI, FORMOSA —(UP)— An American pilot crash-landed his propeller-driven plane into the Pacific ocean today after reporting he was fired upon by Chinese Communist anti-aircraft guns during the evacuation of Tachen island.

The pilot was covering the evacuation as a part of the American protective umbrella of planes when the incident occurred.

*(SEE EARLIER Story—page 2.)*

## Almanac

### She Wants Action for Her Nickel

*Wednesday, Feb. 9, 1955*
Sunrise 7:13 a.m.; sunset 5:28 p.m.

Clerk at a Minneapolis department store was surprised to see a woman walk up to an empty shopping bag dispenser and drop a nickel in the slot provided.

He was even more surprised when, after a reasonable wait for the machine age to produce, she walked over and asked him, "Say, how long do you have to wait before one of those shopping bags comes out of there?"

•

*Cloudy with occasional light snow in the Twin Cities today. High 25, low tonight 5 above.*

•

"There seems to be a little talk around this place," an inmate at Stillwater state prison wrote the editor of the prison newspaper, "about the man running the radio during the noon hour. The fellow that switches from a well-liked musical program to the cattle market report from South St. Paul. I don't think there is anyone in here dealing in livestock at the present time, so how about leaving the music on?"

## Khrushchev, Zhukov Called Key Figures in Russ Power Fight

***EDITOR'S NOTE:** Harrison Salisbury, Minneapolis native, returned last September from Moscow after serving five years as New York Times correspondent there.*

By HARRISON E. SALISBURY
Special from the New York Times

NEW YORK—Marshal Nikolai A. Bulganin almost certainly is a compromise choice as Soviet premier.

He apparently represents a coalition of the party forces of Nikita S. Khrushchev and the army group headed by Marshal Georgi K. Zhukov.

The heralded showdown between Khrushchev and Georgi M. Malenkov, former premier, occurred sooner than this observer had expected. Apparently the army threw its backing to Khrushchev.

### Russ Power to Remain Weakened

Regardless of the fire and vigor of Foreign Minister V. M. Molotov's address, Russia's power in the international arena will remain weakened for a considerable time.

The crisis that resulted in the execution of Lavrenti P. Beria, deputy premier, left little outward signs of cracks in the Kremlin wall. However, it seemed certain the Soviet government would be a longer time in overcoming the effects of the latest transfer to power.

The essentials of the present power transfer seem to foreshadow an almost inevitable power struggle of possibly even greater significance.

With the elimination of Beria, who also was minister of internal affairs, the Soviet secret police were eliminated from the hierarchy. There then remained three power sources:

**The government bureaucracy** controlled by Malenkov.

**The party,** in which control quickly became vested in Khrushchev.

**The army,** headed by an imposing group of military men led by Zhukov.

Now two power groups remain: Khrushchev and his party apparatus and the generals with their military forces. It would seem that unless Khrushchev could split the army group, the military might ultimately gain the whip hand since the army holds the only real weapons of power.

The Russians presumably are aware of the disastrous effect the latest shift will have upon their prestige outside the country. It was mentioned by Malenkov. The fire and aggressive tone of Molotov's speech seem to have been designed to mask the weakness under a screen of belligernt words.

### What Policy Changes Can Be Expected?

What changes may be expected in Soviet policy?

At first, the Soviet Union may seek to talk big but move softly, at least until things settle a bit. The principal Soviet concern for the moment may well be the effect on the Chinese Reds.

There have been signs the Russians are concerned about the growing independence of the Red Chinese.

The Kremlin may well fear that the newest move will encourage further boldness on the part of their Chinese allies. However, it is extremely likely the Soviet military will exert its influence to quiet the Chinese Reds.

Zhukov and his associates do not impress foreigners as men eager to engage in new foreign adventures. On the con-

Power Fight
*Continued on Page 11*

He's in

NIKOLAI BULGANIN

He's out

GEORGI MALENKOV

The Real Ruler?

NIKITA KHRUSHCHEV

—POLICY—

## East-West Tension May Increase

By RICHARD WILSON
Chief of the Minneapolis Tribune Washington Bureau

WASHINGTON —Emergence of Nikita S. Khrushchev, secretary of the Communist party, as the strong man of the Soviet Union causes great concern here over the future of Soviet-American relations.

Members of the United States national security council are forecasting a continuing shakeup in the Soviet ruling group until it meets Khrushchev's requirements.

These are the outstanding reactions from the resignation of Premier Georgi Malenkov and his replacement by Nikolai Bulganin, minister of defense.

Secretary of State Dulles said after appearing at a congressional hearing, "we have been expecting something like this. There have been signs of internal trouble."

(United Press, quoting an unnamed congressional source, reported Dulles told a secret house appropriations subcommittee hearing that the Kremlin shakeup may mean a new get-tough policy toward the free world.)

Vice President Nixon, a close student of intelligence estimates submitted to the national security council, said in Havana, Cuba, that he expects additional changes in the Soviet ruling group.

Little is known of Bulganin here except that he is a military administrator and not himself a professional military man.

But Khrushchev is better understood as he shifts from ominous bluster to reassurance in his contacts with the outside world. He has expressed often his hostility toward the United States.

But he is regarded as wishing to accomplish Communist expansion short of war while nibbling away at the fringes of the western world's sphere of influence.

Last September in Peiping.

Policy
*Continued on Page 11*

—RUSSIA—

## Khrushchev Emerges as Top Leader

By RICHARD KASISCHKE

MOSCOW —(AP)— Georgi Malenkov's resignation as Russian premier likely will mean a substantial reshuffle of the whole Soviet government under the eye of Nikita S. Khrushchev, westerners here said Tuesday night.

Malenkov stepped down yesterday with a confession of failure to do his job.

**TO SUCCEED** him, Khrushchev nominated Nikolai Bulganin, white-haired defense minister and an army marshal, as the choice of the Communist party's central committee which Khrushchev heads. The supreme Soviet (parliament) voted in Bulganin by acclamation.

The day's developments underlined the Soviet Union's renewed emphasis on production of heavy goods, including armament—a policy exemplified by Khrushchev.

The first change in the premiership since Malenkov took it over when Josef Stalin died 23 months ago was followed swiftly by a tough foreign policy statement.

Foreign Minister V. M. Molotov told the supreme soviet (or parliament) that Russia now had superiority over the United States in hydrogen bombs.

**HE DENOUNCED** the United States as an aggressor, particularly in the Formosa dispute, heading toward a third world war. Soviet-American relations could be improved, he said, but only if the United States "demonstrates the desire to do so."

Now what's going to happen?

Today's meeting of the supreme soviet may get an announcement of a reshuffle in the government. It is expected that Bulganin will relinquish the defense ministry.

Will it go to Marshal Zhukov, the Soviet Union's No. 1 soldier who has come strongly to the fore again since Stalin's death?

Will Khrushchev enter the government as a deputy premier or continue as chief of the Communist party and general expediter of everything from livestock and grain through expanding the populations to huge building programs?

And what new duties will be assigned to Malenkov?

Does Bulganin's appointment as premier mean that the army is coming further to the fore and taking over in the Soviet Union?

One of the west's leading ambassadors cautioned last night against accepting such a conclusion. He pointed out that Bulganin is an experienced and able administrator.

**THE EXPANSION** of heavy industry, of course, favors army needs, and the Soviet Union is committed to give aid to its seven Communist east European allies under a joint

Russia
*Continued on Page 11*

## Baby Falls, Mother Jumps Into Furnace; Both Saved

HORNELL, N. Y. —(AP)— A young mother Tuesday jumped down a heat duct into the hot air chamber of a furnace to try to save her baby. The baby, rescued by firemen, was not hurt. The mother, also rescued, was burned.

Mrs. Virginia Shaver, 29, wife of a state police corporal, telephoned the fire department and turned off the heat in her home before she dropped down the pipe after her 19-month-old daughter, Terri.

Mrs. Shaver had removed a cover to clean the dust from it. Terri tumbled into the opening, about two feet in diameter.

Firemen found the child in a cold-air intake at the level of the cellar floor. Three feet away from her Mrs. Shaver, wedged into the hot-air chamber of the furnace, was touching the outside of the seering hot fire box.

Firemen ripped off the side of the air jacket to pull the two out.

First-degree burns covered about 10 per cent of the mother's body. Hospital attaches said her condition was fair.

AP Wirephoto
TERRI SHAVER
*After being 'de-ducted'*

## Switch Called Sign of Weakness, Not Strength

***EDITOR'S NOTE:** James Reston, chief Washington correspondent of the New York Times and writer of the accompanying article, will present the first Gideon Seymour Memorial lecture Feb. 22 in Northrop auditorium at the University of Minnesota. The lecture series is sponsored by the university as a tribute to Mr. Seymour, late executive editor of the Minneapolis Star and Tribune.*

By JAMES RESTON
Special From the New York Times

WASHINGTON—Experts on Russia here Tuesday drew the following conclusions from yesterday's shakeup in top Russian leadership:

**There is trouble** in Russia. Former premier Georgi Malenkov was not dismissed because everything was going well. The dramatic news was a sign of weakness; not of Communist strength.

**It is too early** to reach any conclusions about the effect of the changes on Soviet foreign policy. There undoubtedly will be more tough talk out of Moscow, but Molotov remains as foreign minister. And his tough talk probably will be designed to cover failures of Soviet agricultural and industrial production.

**Nikita S. Khrushchev,** the Communist party boss, probably is the most powerful figure for the moment, but the fierce struggle over succession, always a problem in Russia even in the time of the czars, is far from over.

Every diplomat in town who ever served in the Soviet Union was sought out and questioned. They seemed to agree on the following thesis:

Malenkov started slipping soon after Josef Stalin's death. He had been groomed as Stalin's successor ever since the 19th Communist party congress in 1952. But March 14, 1953, less than a week after Stalin's death, he was relieved of his post as party secretary.

**IN SEPTEMBER** 1953 Khrushchev was named first secretary of the party and began a series of speeches, leading to widespread speculation in western capitals that he was rising and Malenkov was declining.

Instead of placing emphasis on Malenkov personally and on his program of more consumer goods for the Soviet people, the official Soviet press be-

Diplomats
*Continued on Page 11*

## Russ Shakeup Stories Inside

FORECAST
Thursday: Cold.
TEMPERATURES

| | | |
|---|---|---|
| Midnight 30 | 5 a.m. ...26 | 10 a.m. ..23 |
| 1 a.m. ...29 | 6 a.m. ...26 | 11 a.m. ..23 |
| 2 a.m. ...28 | 7 a.m. ...25 | Noon ....21 |
| 3 a.m. ...27 | 8 a.m. ...24 | *1 p.m. ..20 |
| 4 a.m. ...27 | 9 a.m. ...23 | *Unofficial |

Highest year ago, 48; lowest, 23.


# THE MINNEAPOLIS STAR

Vol. LXXVII—No. 65 ★ MINNEAPOLIS, MINN., WEDNESDAY, FEBRUARY 9, 1955 Price 5 Cents


# Zhukov Named Russ Defense Chief

# *Merger Pact for AFL, CIO Is Approved by Negotiators*

## Nehru Advises Peking Against Formosa Grab

LONDON—(AP)—India's Premier Jawaharlal Nehru today advised Red China against any attempt to grab Formosa by force and asked for time to work out a peaceful settlement.

Nehru told a news conference the great powers, including Russia and India, were secretly exchanging ideas on how to bring about a cease-fire in the Formosa strait. But he said no definite approach has yet been agreed upon.

Asked to comment upon Peking radio's recent assertion that Red China intended to take Formosa as soon as possible, Nehru said:

"Personally, I always think force of this type should be avoided. Settlement should be peaceful even if it takes time."

The Indian leader, who has been in contact with Peking during the Formosa crisis, said various suggestions for a Formosa solution—including that of a Geneva-type conference—have been made during the secret diplomatic exchanges.

"Diplomatic representatives are in touch to find out how the minds of governments are working. But there is nothing definite," he said.

★ ★ ★ ★

## Reds Down U.S. Plane; Crew Saved

TAIPEI, FORMOSA—(AP)—Communist anti-aircraft fire today shot down a United States navy attack bomber but an American officer said that was not considered a hostile act. He explained the pilot apparently wandered off course and may have flown over the Red Chinese mainland while on patrol in the Tachens evacuation area.

**The pilot and his two crew members were rescued.**

An officer aboard the amphibious flagship USS Estes said the navy did not consider the shooting a "hostile act" because "the plane apparently made too wide a turn and was off-limits."

The pilot was identified as Lt. (j.g.) W. J. O'Heren, 32, Coronado, Calif.

The crewmen were identified as electronics technician A. J. Chelewski, 37, Imperial Beach, Calif., and aviation machinist's mate 1/c R. E. Drennen, 31, San Diego, Calif.

**The pilot reported he flew for about eight minutes after being hit before the plane's engine stopped. He said that due to low visibility he could not tell the source of the anti-aircraft fire.**

Earlier, a navy patrol plane pilot reported he had been fired on by Communist shore batteries but said he was not hit. On later inspection, however, it was found his P2V Neptune plane had received three hits in the wing section.

The navy said this plane was repaired and ready for another flight in a few hours.

Meanwhile, 3,753 Tachen islanders debarked at Keelung, a north Formosan port. They are the first evacuees to reach Formosa from the threatened islands 200 miles north since the seventh fleet moved in to cover the operation.

## On the Inside . .



## Weather to Dish Out New Cold Spell

The weather dished up a ragout of mist and rain to complicate traffic in southern Minnesota during the night, and a spell of colder temperatures was on the way today.

Rain and mist left a thin film of ice on highways south of highway 12 in the state, creating dangerous slipperiness. Today some of the incrustation had broken off, and other sections were being sanded, but the state highway department said the situation still calls for extreme caution.

**The Twin Cities forecast is for partly cloudy, much colder tonight, continued cold Thursday.**

A low of about zero is expected tonight, a high of 10 above Thursday. The high Tuesday was 31, the mercury declining early today to 24 at 8 a.m.

The state prospect is for cloudy and much colder tonight, except clearing in the northwest, light snow over most of the southeast and extreme south, Thursday partly cloudy and cold, snow in the extreme southeast in the morning.

## Shot-down MIGs 'North Korean'

PANMUNJON, KOREA—(UP)—The Communists disclosed today that the two Russian-built MIG15s shot down by American Sabrejets over the Yellow sea last week were North Korean warcraft. They accused the United States of provoking the aerial battle "to increase tension in the Far East created by United States interference in Formosa."

Eight of the Soviet-made jet fighters attacked a jet reconnaissance bomber and 12 escorting F86 Sabrejets off the west coast of North Korea Saturday. Two MIGs were claimed destroyed in the five-minute dogfight.

## IKE GETS GI BENEFITS BILL

**WASHINGTON—(AP)—Congress sent to President Eisenhower today legislation continuing full GI education benefits for all service people who went into uniform before Feb. 1.**

**Senate passage by voice vote and without debate completed congressional action. The house approved it 366-0 last month.**

## Ike Says U.S. Basic Policy Is Unchanged

WASHINGTON—(AP)—President Eisenhower said today the shakeup in the Soviet high command reflects internal dissatisfaction in Russia.

The President told a news conference the shakeup will bring no change in basic United States policy aimed at achieving a just and lasting peace.

**And, the President said, he does not believe the developments necessarily mean that Russia has launched on a calculated tougher policy toward the United States.**

But, he added, the Russians will say anything which suits their purposes and the United States must remain alert.

Mr. Eisenhower recalled that he became acquainted with Marshal Georgi K. Zhukov during World War II and knew him as a competent soldier—a well-trained military leader.

But Mr. Eisenhower said he could scarcely interpret what the appointment of Zhukov as Soviet defense minister means so far as the possibility of world peace is concerned.

Most of the questions at the President's well attended news conference—there were 230 newsmen present—dealt with the reshuffle in the Soviet government.

The questions on that matter and other subjects developed these points:

**ATOMIC WEAPONS**—Mr. Eisenhower said there certainly is no proof Russia has surpassed the United States in development of the hydrogen bomb and other atomic weapons.

This was in response to a request for comment on Soviet Foreign Minister Molotov's assertion yesterday that hydrogen bomb development by Russia has been so successful that it could make the United States appear backward in that field.

Mr. Eisenhower said it would be a remarkable feat if the Soviets have achieved superiority after starting behind the United States. He added the matter was not worth speculation.

**FORMOSA**—The chief executive said it would be idle to speculate on the possibility of a cease-fire in the Formosa strait inasmuch as Red China rejected a United Nations bid to discuss the matter and instead issued a very bellicose statement.

As for evacuation of the Chinese Nationalist Tachen islands under protection of the United


Ike
*Continued on Page 12*

IKE, ZHUKOV IN 1945—This picture of President Eisenhower and Georgi Zhukov, the new Russian minister of defense, was made in Frankfurt, Germany, in 1945 when Mr. Eisenhower was the Allied commander and Zhukov was head of the Soviet army which took Berlin. Occasion was a victory celebration at which they toasted their triumph over Nazi Germany.—UP Telephoto.

★ ★ ★ ★ ★ ★

*FRIENDSHIP RECALLED*

## May Invite Zhukov to U.S., Ike Hints

WASHINGTON—(AP)—President Eisenhower recalled today pleasant relations with Marshal Georgi Zhukov, new Soviet defense minister, during World War II—and held open the possibility that he might invite Zhukov to visit the United States.

A reporter came out with the idea of such an invitation at the President's news conference. Mr. Eisenhower seemed momentarily taken aback. But he did not close the door against it.

The President, appearing to catch his breath, said he wasn't so sure. It was the first time the idea had been put to him in his present job, he said, but it was a remarkable thing to consider and he certainly wanted to talk it over with his aides.

**Leading up to this, Mr. Eisenhower had related under questioning that while Allied commander in World War II he came to knew and admire Zhukov, who led the Red armies into Berlin.**

Mr. Eisenhower said he invited the Russian soldier to visit America in 1945—even placed his own plane at Zhukov's disposal for the trip and suggested that his son, Maj. John Eisenhower, accompany the Russian as an aide.

A newsman said Zhukov stated recently that he dreams of visiting America. The reporter asked whether Mr. Eisenhower's 1945 invitation was still open.

It was then the President said he would want to talk it over with his aides.

**Mr. Eisenhower warmly recalled his friendship with the Russian military hero. He said he last heard directly from Zhukov in April 1946. It was a letter, Mr. Eisenhower said, and he also received a present—a**


Visit
*Continued on Page 12*


## Pinay Reported Quitting Task of Forming Cabinet

PARIS—(AP)—An informed source said today Antoine Pinay has given up his effort to form a new French government.

The information came on the heels of a decision of the Catholic Popular Republican Movement (MRP) to refuse to take posts in a cabinet headed by Pinay.

**Pinay is a Conservative, while the MRP is a left-of-center party competing with the Socialists for Leftist votes.**

The Socialists announced Tuesday they could not support a Conservative such as Pinay.

The announcement about Pinay's decision, yet to be made official, would throw back on President Rene Coty the job of finding somebody else who might round up enough votes.

## 'Open Shot' A-blast Planned in April

WASHINGTON—(INS)—The atomic energy commission announced today that the spring test series of nuclear explosions in the Nevada desert will include an "open shot" in mid-April which will be witnessed by "hundreds" of invited civilian observers.

The series, expected to include more than a dozen blasts testing the latest types of atomic weapons, is scheduled to begin this month and may get under way next week, depending on weather conditions.

## Stock Market Shows Recovery

NEW YORK—(AP)—The stock market recovered briskly today from Tuesday's decline, which followed news of the political shakeup in Russia.

Advances of $1 to $2 a share were posted in many sections of the list. Up $1 or more were U.S. Steel, Bethlehem, Woolworth, Chance-Vought, Lockheed, Solar, American Telephone, Anaconda, Texas Co. and Du Pont. Western Union was ahead $4.37 on news of a stock split. American Machine & Foundry gained $2 on atomic developments.

## Wind Tips Boxcars

CHEYENNE, WYO.—(UP)—Winds ranging between 75 and 100 miles per hour blew 13 Union Pacific freight cars off the tracks 20 miles west of here Tuesday, disrupting traffic on the line for several hours.

No one was injured.

## Subgroups Hammer Out Terms

### Final OK Would Be Up to Ratifying Conventions

MIAMI BEACH, FLA.—(AP)—Negotiating committees for the AFL and CIO today agreed to a historic merger of their rival labor union groups into a single powerful federation.

The agreement to end the 20-year-old split within organized labor was reached by two three-member subcommittees representing the American Federation of Labor and the Congress of Industrial Organizations.

The merger pact is due to be ratified this afternoon by 10-member committees of each organization.

**The AFL's executive council will pass on the amalgamation at a meeting here Thursday.**

Ratifying conventions of both the AFL and CIO unions will be required to put the merger into effect, but the agreement reached by AFL President George Meany and CIO President Walter Reuther seems sure to win approval of their organizations.

Welding of the 10-million-member AFL and the 5-million-member CIO would represent culmination of two years of effort by Meany and Reuther since they became top men in their respective groups in late 1952.

Details of the merger agreement were not made public immediately but were to be announced later in the day after the expected ratification by the larger merger committees.

## Man Accused of Kidnaping Found in City

A Georgia man accused of kidnaping a 15-year-old girl was located with the girl in Minneapolis today and jailed for Sheriff J. T. Plunkett of Augusta, Ga.

The suspect is John Quincy Williams, 24, Augusta, and the girl is Joan Kitchens, Augusta. In their company was James Hobbs, 21, Augusta, who apparently accompanied the couple on a drive to Minneapolis.

**Plunkett said the couple had been sought for a month. A break in the case came when Williams, according to Plunkett, telephoned a friend in Augusta and gave his Minneapolis telephone number.**

Police traced the call to a ground floor apartment at 3524 Nicollet avenue, where Detectives Wayne Sherman and Thomas Cosgrove found the trio.

Plunkett said he is sending officers to get Williams on a kidnaping warrant and to return the girl. He asked police to hold Hobbs for questioning.

## 2 Die, 18 Hurt in B36 Explosion

FORT WORTH, TEXAS—(AP)—An air force B36 bomber exploded and burned Tuesday night, killing two men and injuring 18, four seriously.

The plane burst into flames soon after its landing gear touched soft earth at the end of a Carswell air force base runway.

The dead were identified by the air force as Sgt. Gerry Nichols, Malvern, Ark., and Airman Dean Grandquist, Ogden, Utah.

## DO YOU AGREE?

A truth that's told with bad intent beats all the lies you can invent.

GEORGI ZHUKOV
*Soviet defense minister*

★ ★ ★ ★

## Speakers Rap U.S. as 'Warlike'

MOSCOW—(UP)—Soviet Marshal Ivan Konev warned today that a Red army more powerful than in World War II would crush any western attack on Russia with "all types of modern weapons."

"We are not alone," Konev said. "The great nation of (Red) China . . . and the Soviet Union now form one camp and a powerful army for peace."

He attacked what he charged was the "continual provocation against China—our great friend."

The Soviet military leader addressed the supreme Soviet (parliament) during debate on the foreign policy speech made Tuesday by Foreign Minister V. M. Molotov, who said the United States—not the Soviet Union—lagged in hydrogen bomb production.

**Georgi Malenkov, who resigned as premier yesterday, attended today's supreme Soviet session and heard speaker after speaker attack the "warlike policy" of the United States.**

Konev, defender of the Soviet Ukrainian front in World War II, spelled out the army's backing just 24 hours after Marshal Nikolai A. Bulganin took over as premier.

Konev, now commander of the western Ukrainian military district, charged with the defense of the southwestern Soviet frontier, is one of the leading combat generals.

**Konev also criticized recent decisions on atomic weapons by the North Atlantic Treaty Organization (NATO).**

He said he believed that if these were added to similar statements by certain American leaders and generals, "it should be clear that it is a campaign of intimidation for those with weak nerves."

"But the Soviet people are not afraid, because their de-


Speeches
*Continued on Page 18*


## EXTRAS *in Today's Star*



## Malenkov Is Minister of Power Stations

### Changes Carry Out Emphasis on Arms Buildup


*Zhukov Is Hero to Red Masses: Page 6; Khrushchev Rise Disturbs U.N. Observers: Page 7.*


By RICHARD KASISCHKE

MOSCOW—(AP)—Georgi K. Zhukov, top Soviet military hero and a warm wartime acquaintance of President Eisenhower, was appointed the new defense minister of the Soviet Union today.

Immediately after the announcement, the supreme soviet (parliament) was informed that Georgi K. Malenkov, who resigned Tuesday as premier, has been named a deputy premier and minister of power stations.

**Both nominations were made by the new premier, Nikolai A. Bulganin, until yesterday the defense minister. A marshal of the Soviet Union, Bulganin still wore his army uniform at today's meeting of the supreme soviet.**

Bulganin, in his first speech as premier, pledged his government to work unswervingly to expand the Soviet Union's heavy industry in order to build up Soviet armed might and raise the country's living standards.

Bulganin proclaimed the idea of Soviet devotion to peace and a determination to thwart what he called aggressive American designs.

"During the last war," said Bulganin, "there was close collaboration between England, the United States and the Soviet Union. It could have been prolonged after the war and up to now, and it is not our fault that it has not been.

**"It is because the government of the United States is trying to build its policy toward the Soviet Union from the so-called 'position of strength.'"**

This was a repetition of previous post-Stalin Soviet statements which have made some slight acknowledgement of the United States part in World War II.

In the days of Stalin, the Soviet people always were told that the Soviet Union alone was responsible for the defeat of Germany and Japan.

With regard to the Far East situation, in which Foreign Minister V. M. Molotov yesterday appeared to back Red China to the hilt, Bulganin said:

**"The American government has undertaken a dangerous task in trying to conquer Taiwan (Formosa).**

"We are surprised at the position of the United Nations, which up to now has not con-


Zhukov
*Continued on Page 12*


## 2 Food Chains in City Cut Price on Own Brand Coffee

Two big food chains serving this area today cut retail coffee prices from 10 to 12 cents a pound, on their own brands.

A & P Food Stores put the price cut into effect today, and National Tea will lower prices to the consumer on its own brands starting Thursday.

**"One official said the price drop was a retail adjustment to lessened costs resulting from a Brazilian currency reform.**

He said he expected to see the decrease reflected within a week by national brands, perhaps with a cut of around 8 cents a pound. But no cuts have yet been announced by national brands, and several coffee men were not as convinced that such brands would follow suit.

A & P dropped the retail price 10 cents on two of its bag coffees; 12 cents on another bag coffee (Bokar) and 10 cents on A & P vacuum-pack can. The change brought 8 O'Clock to 79 cents; Red Circle to 83 cents; Bokar to 85 cents and A & P to 89 cents.

National Tea, with some 60 stores in the Twin Cities, put 10 cent retail drops into effect. It went to 79 cents on Top Taste bag coffee; 89 cents on Natco drip or regular in cans.

Red Owl also is reducing coffee prices, and this afternoon cut its Dependon bag coffee by 10 cents, bringing it to 79 cents a pound.

**The observation of one coffee man was that popular brands which had gone to a high of $1.31 and today are selling at $1.09 will drop a dime in less than a week.**

Others, however, saw the situation on coffee as still too fluid to indicate any definite downturn of price. Among the many factors, for instance, is the recent news out of Russia. Any national brand price reductions, if any, may be made in small steps as a hedge against tightened conditions, according to one authority.

## WIFE'S PLEA SPARED MALENKOV, PAPER SAYS

By ERNIE HILL
Chicago Daily News Foreign Service

**LONDON—The London Daily Sketch claims that Georgi M. Malenkov was saved from liquidation by his wife, Elena.**

**The Sketch claims that Elena, a former actress, is the sister of Russia's new tough boss, Nikita S. Khrushchev, first party secretary. Says the Sketch:**

**"Elena, it is thought, interceded with her brother to spare her husband's life."**

**The Daily Sketch, part of the associated newspaper organization controlled by Lord Rothermere, states that Khrushchev may yet have to place Malenkov on public trial and execute him if Malenkov's closest friends give the new regime any trouble.**

## STAR BEAMS

**The government is criticized for its duplication of advisory agencies, and yet many an average family has both a grandmother and a pediatrician.**

• • •

***One solution for the fellow who is self-conscious about his pink shirt is to stay outside these cold days until his face gets red enough so the shirt will look white by comparison.***
***—Bill Vaughan.***

FORECAST
Thursday: Little change.
TEMPERATURES
Midnight 50 5 a.m.....48 10 a.m. ..48
1 a.m.....50 6 a.m.....47 11 a.m. ..50
2 a.m.....50 7 a.m.....47 Noon ....51
3 a.m.....49 8 a.m.....46 *1 p.m. ..52
4 a.m.....48 9 a.m.....46 *Unofficial.
Highest year ago, 77; lowest, 48.

# THE MINNEAPOLIS STAR

Vol. LXXVII—No. 119 ★ MINNEAPOLIS, MINN., WEDNESDAY, APRIL 13, 1955 Price 5 Cents

KENSINGTON RUNE STONE
*Hoax or History?*

## *Where Could Ohman Learn Old Swedish?*

*EDITOR'S NOTE: Several months ago the Minneapolis Star decided to explore the controversy concerning the Kensington rune stone. The reporter assigned to the job was George Rice, who had been interested in the stone ever since the publication of Hjalmar Holand's "Westward from Vinland." Prior to the time of his assignment Rice had been convinced the rune stone was authentic. The investigation and research which he carried out now has him equally convinced that the stone is not authentic. This is the third of six articles he has written.*

By GEORGE RICE
Minneapolis Star Staff Writer

One of the most unusual of the many unusual things about the Kensington rune stone controversy is the lack of basic investigation. "Experts" for years have been basing opinions, pro and con, on incomplete facts.

One man, at last, has done the necessary spade work. It is nothing less than amazing that it was not done 56 years ago, when Olof Ohman announced to the villagers of Kensington, Minn., that he had found a 200-pound slab of stone, under the roots of a tree, on which was inscribed in runes the story of Norsemen in mid-America in 1362.

But the sadly unscientific fact remains that it was not done. Now, however, we can point to the researches of Prof. J. A. Holvik of Moorhead, Minn., for a great body of evidence.

Holvik has long been a rune stone dissenter. For many years professor of Norse language and literature at Concordia college in Moorhead, he has thrown the weight of his learning into the argument.

But there have been greater runic scholars who have dissented, and perhaps some of the experts who have leaned toward acceptance of the stone have been more versed in the old Scandinavian writing form, too. And no one will deny that Hjalmar R. Holand, of Ephraim, Wis., who has been the outstanding champion of the stone, also is a learned man.

**Holvik's contribution has not been from his sound runic scholarship, but rather from his curiosity. He went to the scene and uncovered basic material that had been there for years.**

The stone came to light in 1898. Since 1908 Hjalmar Holand had been devoting most of his time to proving its authenticity. In 1938 Holvik paid a visit to the Ohman farm.

Ohman had died in 1935, but his widow still lived. Holvik asked her if there was on the place anything that had belonged to Sven Fogelblad, a onetime minister of the state church of Sweden, before his death a resident of the Kensington area, and once thought by many (including Holvik) to have been the author of the stone's inscription.

When Holvik had told her what he wanted and that it was in connection with the rune stone, Mrs. Ohman said: "But it was not Fogelblad who had anything to do with the rune stone."

**Had Holvik pursued the point, to find out just who DID have something to do with the stone, perhaps its mystery would have been cleared up then and there.**

Mrs. Ohman gave Holvik two things: the Montelius volume of Swedish history, the one her husband had clipped, page by page, from the Swedish-language newspaper published in Minneapolis, Svenska Amerikanska Posten, and a scrapbook that had belonged to her husband. Both the history and the scrapbook contained clues to the Kensington rune stone.

In 1949 or 1950, Holvik made another trip to the Ohman farm. Mrs. Ohman had died some time previously, and Holvik sought information from her daughter, Amanda. Amanda reached into the glass-doored bookcase in the parlor and handed him a rather hefty book, "Den Kunskapsrike Skolmastaren" (The Well-informed Schoolmaster), another book that had belonged to her father. This book, too, held clues to the origin of the inscription on the stone.

**All of these books had been in the Ohman bookcase from the time the stone was found in the late summer or fall of 1898.**

Ohman had had the Montelius volume bound by the Kensington shoemaker. Ohman's

Stone
*Continued on Page 10*

## SEXTUPLETS REPORTED

**BELGRADE, YUGOSLAVIA —(P)— The Zagreb weekly newspaper "Vjesnik U Srijedu" reported today that a 19-year-old woman gave birth to sextuplets in the village of Todorovo, Yugoslavia.**

**The paper said all six of the babies — two girls and four boys — died, the boys upon delivery and the girls three days later. The mother was reported in a critical condition.**

## Ike Approves A-weapon Pact

AUGUSTA, GA.—(P)—President Eisenhower today approved a proposed international agreement on exchange of atomic weapons information among the 14 North Atlantic Treaty nations.

The agreement, still to be formally signed by the NATO nations, provides for exchange of data dealing with:

**DEVELOPMENT** of defense plans.

**TRAINING** of personnel in the use of and defense against atomic weapons.

**EVALUATION** of the capabilities of potential enemies in the use of atomic weapons.

Announcement of the President's approval of the proposed agreement was made at his vacation headquarters here.

The agreement provides specifically that under its terms there will be no transfer of atomic weapons or special nuclear material.

## Quemoy Chief Sees Impending Attack

QUEMOY ISLAND—(UP)—A spokesman for the Quemoy commander said today there were indications of an impending Communist attack against this Nationalist-held island.

Col. Tien Shu-sin said the Communists had massed 200,000 troops which could be hurled against Quemoy and that the Reds had built up gun emplacements and assembled 2,000 junks.

## STAR BEAMS

**The author who finds autograph parties too wearing can publicize his new book just as well by getting himself called before a senatorial committee.**

• • •

***Alarmists complain that television has ruined the old-time family dinner-table conversation. Surely you remember the old-time family dinner-table conversation: "What happened in school today?" "Nothin'."—Bill Vaughan.***

## 2 MILLION IN EXILE

**What does the future hold for two million mainland Chinese now on Formosa? Color photo and picture story by Walter Johnson, Minneapolis Star staff writer, are on the Back Page today.**

HONEYMOONERS—Rep. John Blatnik (D., Minn.) and his German bride, the former Gisela Hager, 30, head for a plane at Copenhagen, Denmark, on their way to Hamburg, Germany, where they will board the liner United States for a voyage to New York. The 43-year-old congressman met his bride 18 months ago while on a trip to Germany. She was working at that time as a secretary for a motion picture firm. Last August she visited Blatnik and his mother, Mrs. John Blatnik, Sr., at their home in Chisholm, Minn. The marriage took place Saturday in a Catholic church in Hamburg. The bride's brother and sister-in-law were their attendants.—AP Wirephoto by radio from London.

## Promise of Rain Fades Into Fog

The promise of rain over much of this area during the night simmered down into fog which covered parts of Minnesota, Iowa and Wisconsin early today.

The eastward movement of a high pressure system is expected to clear skies, although some rains may be recorded during the day.

**The forecast in the Twin Cities is for fair and cooler tonight, Thursday fair with little change in temperature.**

A high of about 60 degrees is expected Thursday, a low of 35 tonight.

The state prospect is for partly cloudy with little change in temperature tonight and Thursday, fair and warmer in the northeast.

Lows down to 25 expected tonight may produce frosts touching new vegetation, especially in the northern part of the state.

**Winds of 10 to 15 miles an hour are expected here, northerly today and shifting to southerly Thursday.**

Meanwhile large sections of Minnesota remained in need of a thorough wetting to reduce forest fire dangers arising from light winter snows and a dry spring thus far.

Showers are expected in Wisconsin, Iowa and North Dakota in the next 24 hours.

**SPRING BLIZZARD STRANDS MOTORISTS**

CLAYTON, N. M.—(P)—Snow carried on brisk winds was piled on highways up to eight feet deep here today, isolating the town and stranding hundreds of motorists.

The spring blizzard extended from Wyoming to Nebraska and south into the Texas panhandle. Skies cleared over the area today and snowplows churned in towards the isolated towns.

## Population Put at Over 164 Million

WASHINGTON —(INS)— The census bureau today estimated the total population of the United States, including armed forces overseas, at 164,367,000 on March 1.

The figure represented an increase of 13,235,000 or 8.8 per cent since April 1, 1950—the date of the last census, and an increase of 2,825,000 or 1.7 per cent during the past year.

## France to Stress Peace Use of Atom

PARIS—(INS)—Premier Edgar Faure announced today that France has given up any plans to produce nuclear weapons.

He told a news conference that the government intends to become "a peaceful atomic power" by concentrating its research exclusively toward peaceful uses of atomic energy.

## On the Inside . .



## *Pinball Payoff, Split Told in U.S. Court*

**Mildred R. Varnado, former bookkeeper for the Harmony Music Co., was recalled to the witness stand today and admitted that her earlier testimony concerning the firm's financial activities and bookkeeping between August 1953 and August 1954 were false. She said she did not begin to work there until August of last year.**

By AL WOODRUFF
Minneapolis Star Staff Writer

A Lake street tavern operator testified in federal court today that she had been paying off winners on pinball machines since 1952.

She testified further that she split the profits on the machines with the Harmony Music Co.

The machines she used in the tavern were put there under instructions of the individual who holds the mortgage on the tavern, she said.

*These points were part of the testimony of Nora Louise Davidson, 1501½ E. Lake street. She is a co-partner in and operator of the Lake Street Mug, 1412 E. Lake.*

Her co-partner in the business is Loren R. Downs, she said.

**Miss Davidson stated she had two pinball machines and a jukebox from which weekly collections were taken by Martin Kantar. He previously had been identified as a co-partner in the Harmony Music Co., 1426 Washington avenue S.**

Miss Davidson testified that as a part of a $5,000 mortgage which she took on the business in 1952, she had to let the mortgagee name the type and make of coin-operated machines used in the establishment.

The mortgage, introduced in evidence, listed Lulu Cohen, 5120 Logan avenue S., as the mortgagee.

Miss Davidson, who said she had never taken out a federal gambling occupational stamp, testified she had paid off regularly to winners on the two pinball machines at a rate of five cents for each game won.

The machines were so constructed, she said, that "free" games which were not played off by the winner could be recorded and "erased" from the tally mechanisms.

**This recording enabled Kantar to determine how much money she was to be reimbursed for payouts to winners, she said.**

Kantar made his collections weekly, she testified. After she was reimbursed for payouts, the balance of the money in the machine was divided evenly between her and Kantar.

She testified that last Thurs-

Pinball
*Continued on Page Seven*

## Senate Group Rejects Hike in School Aid

By JOHN COWLES, JR.
Minneapolis Star Staff Writer

Continuance of state basic aids at the present $80 per pupil unit for the next two years was approved today by the education committee of the Minnesota senate.

Defeated in committee voting were motions to set the aid figure at $92, $85, $84 and $82.

**An $85 level has been voted by the education committee of the house, so the matter probably will be resolved around $82 or $83 by a senate-house conference committee.**

Gov. Freeman, who originally asked for $92 aids, recently indicated he would accept the $85 house figure provided other parts of his fiscal program were enacted.

Before voting today on the aid figure, the senate committee heard two proposals from Senators Arthur Gillen, South St. Paul, and Elmer Anderson, St. Paul.

Gillen proposed $80 be retained as the basic aid figure because, he said, such an aid level could be maintained indefinitely by the state despite school population and cost increases.

**The $80 figure would be possible for many years, he said, either through diversion of iron ore tax receipts from the school trust fund to current school expenses, or through use of veterans bonus taxes for education purposes after the World War II and proposed Korean bonuses have been paid for.**

Anderson said the $84 level could be paid this biennium and still leave a surplus, if three million dollars now spent for youth conservation and institutional programs not strictly educational were returned to educational use.

# First Salk Polio Vaccine Arrives in Minneapolis

## 9 Quarts Will Go to Doctors

### Consignment Flown in by Air Freight

By WENDELL WEED
Minneapolis Star Staff Writer

The first shipment of Salk polio vaccine arrived in Minneapolis today by air freight.

It was delivered to the Minneapolis branch of Parke Davis Co., pharmaceutical house, for distribution to doctors.

There were 9,000 cubic centimeters of vaccine in the six cartons. The material was packaged in 3 c.c. vials, the amount needed for immunizing one person in a series of three injections. There are about 500 c.c. in a pint, so the total shipment would be about nine quarts.

There is no indication as to arrival time of another shipment of vaccine, to be distributed by the state health department for inoculation of first and second graders in school clinics.

Minneapolis Star and Tribune trucks, drivers from Teamsters Miscellaneous Drivers union local 638 and contract relay drivers *will speed the vaccine for school clinics to major Minnesota* communities as a volunteer service as soon as it is available.

**Following the polio vaccine evaluation report Tuesday at University of Michigan, Dr. Jonas Salk, University of Pittsburgh, who developed the vaccine, made some recommendations that upset the carefully-planned time schedule worked out in Minnesota.**

He said that instead of giving three shots in a five-week period, greater effectiveness could be obtained by giving two shots now over a two to four-week period and then waiting at least seven months for the third shot.

The Hennepin county polio vaccine subcommittee headed by Dr. W. W. Rieke, Wayzata, immediately shifted its timetable to follow Salk's suggestion.

Minneapolis and Hennepin county first and second graders will receive their first shots at school clinics scheduled for next week, if the vaccine arrives in time. Second shots will be given during the week of May 16.

The final injections probably would be given next December, although the committee has not set a definite time.

Dr. Dean Fleming, head of epidemiology with the state health department, said he plans to recommend to all health officers in the state that Salk's suggested time schedule for vaccination be followed.

The health department will receive enough vaccine for 145,000 children, but will allocate it to local communities only on the basis of actual requests signed by parents.

The Parke Davis consignment will be held in the local branch's cooler until specific

Polio
*Continued on Page Six*

★ ★ ★ ★

## Parents Deluge Schools With Shot Requests

Parents who held back on requesting that their first and second graders receive the Salk polio vaccine in school clinics were so impressed with Tuesday's favorable report on its safety and effectiveness that they now want their children to be included in the program.

Schools and health officials were deluged with phone calls today from parents.

**Thomas P. Cook, executive secretary of the Hennepin County Medical society, announced that all eligible children who bring the signed request cards to the school clinics next week will be vaccinated.**

He said a fee of 50 cents will be collected at the time of each vaccination and urged that no one make advance payments for the entire series.

Cook also emphasized that each eligible child with a signed request card will be vaccinated whether or not the 50-cent fee is paid. The fee covers cost of material, but the vaccine will be supplied without charge by the National Foundation for Infantile Paralysis.

Doctors and nurses will volunteer their services.

## SEATO Treaty Filed With U.N.

UNITED NATIONS, N. Y.—(INS)—The eight SEATO Allies formally notified the United Nations today of their common defense arrangements against Communist aggression in Southeast Asia.

A copy of the Pacific charter and SEATO defense treaty signed at Manila were registered with the U.N. at a brief ceremony attended by representatives of the signatory states.

## STUDENT SEEKS TO REJECT $350,000 TRUST FUND

**NEW YORK—(P)—Eugene F. Suter, Jr., a Yale university senior, is seeking to renounce a $350,000 trust fund and says he prefers to rely on "two hands and a head of my own."**

**The student's petition, filed in surrogate's court, is opposed by the fund trustees. They told Surrogate William T. Collins that under his father's will Suter may not receive the principal of the trust until 1963.**

**By that time, they added, the young man, now 23, may have "a change of mind."**

**Collins has reserved decision on Suter's request.**

**The trust was left to Suter when his father died in 1943. Papers filed in connection with the petition showed that Suter received accumulated income of $35,000 two years ago when he became 21 but that "within a few days gave most of it, if not all, to various charitable and political organizations."**

**It was reported he gave $11,000 to the American Friends Service committee, $5,000 to the Socialist party, $1,500 to the United States Grant School for Negroes, and the remainder to his mother.**

## Freeman Appeals to 'People's Lobby' for Support of Program

By WALLACE MITCHELL
Minneapolis Star Staff Writer

Gov. Freeman pleaded today for public support of his key legislative proposals, which he charged are being fought by high pressure, special interest lobbyists.

With the session deadline but a week away, Freeman issued a statement calling for help in "getting a program which will be of the greatest benefit, not to a handful of special interests but to all Minnesotans."

"For many decades, *the lobbyists who represent special* interest groups have counted on this final week of confusion to help them get the kind of special legislation they want," he charged.

**"The capitol these days has taken on something of the atmosphere of a beehive invaded by a swarm of hornets.**

"The corridors are filled with pressureboys, many of them paid fantastic salaries and given unlimited expense accounts by the special interests they represent.

"Legislators are flattered and entertained and dined — and occasionally wined."

Ordinary voters and taxpayers must "speak clearly and directly for yourselves" on legislation pending before the house and senate, he declared.

**Sketching the key planks of his legislative program, he said the No. 1 item is what he called his "hold-the-line" budget of $167,400,000 in appropriations for the next two years.**

In the closing week, he charged, legislators and the public will "be subjected to a barrage of misrepresentation and calculated confusion from the special interest groups who will be trying to avoid paying their fair share of taxes by forcing tax increases on to the average wage earner and farmer."

He called "absolutely essential" the proposed $5 increase in present $60 maximum old age assistance grants and the jump from $80 to $85 per pupil for public school support.

"Let your senators and representatives know how you feel about it," he appealed.

**He charged that "special interest groups who want tax favors" seek enactment of a general sales tax or an increase in property taxes to balance the budget, both of which he said he is fighting.**

"The administration's tax proposals in effect call for across-the-board tax increases shared equally by everyone," he declared.

"Here are some of the tax increases which have been proposed: A tax increase of not more than 10 cents a month on telephones, a modest increase on insurance annuity premiums, a small tax increase on beer, a tax on tobacco other

Mitchell
*Continued on Page Seven*

## TEAMWORK BRINGS VICTORY NEAR

# *Men, Money, Parents Kayo Polio*

*Other polio vaccine stories: Page 3.*

By ALTON L. BLAKESLEE
Associated Press Science Reporter

ANN ARBOR, MICH.—(P)—Men, money and angry parents delivered the technical knockout to polio through the Salk vaccine.

THE MEN—Many scientists making discoveries step by step paving the way to a vaccine.

THE MONEY—Ten million dollars or more in March of Dimes funds from the public support this research. To this extent the vaccine is something the American people created.

THE PARENTS—Angry at the stealthy invisible killer and despoiler of children, determined to extinguish its nerve-consuming fire.

Today the victory is within grasp with a successful vaccine, developed by the quiet, dark-haired Dr. Jonas E. Salk of Pittsburgh, Pa., a dedicated scientist with an incisive mind.

Today the first batches of an improved Salk vaccine are moving from pharmaceutical houses to public health officials and doctors' offices to begin inoculations of some 30 million or more children this spring and summer.

**Within hours after the official verdict that the vaccine is up to 90 per cent effective in preventing paralysis, it was licensed by the National Institutes of Health for public use.**

Dimes contributed to the National Foundation for Infantile Paralysis will pay for enough vaccine for free inoculations of nine million children in all first and second grades and some in third grades. The rest will be administered by doctors to patients, with high priority urged for children of pregnant women.

Polio, the disease that puts the haunt of fear in human minds at last is on the way to defeat, control, eradication.

The victory did not come easily nor the answer spring forth fullborn. As with most great achievements of medical science it built from the minds of many men.

In 1909 Dr. Karl Landsteiner

Salk
*Continued on Page Seven*

## DO YOU AGREE?

The best way to kill time is to work it to death.

• • •

**(Send your favorite thought to "DO YOU AGREE?" The Minneapolis Star, Minneapolis 15, Minn.)**

Warmer
Minneapolis High 90
Details on Page 18

# Minneapolis Morning Tribune

Vol. XC—No. 63 Copyright 1956 Minneapolis Star and Tribune Company MINNEAPOLIS, MINN., THURSDAY, JULY 26, 1956 Price 5 Cents



# Two Big Liners Collide in Atlantic; 1,700 Abandon Italian Luxury Ship

## Final Action Due Today on Aid Bill

### Conferees Agree, Limit Yugoslav Help for 1957

By Staff Correspondent of Minneapolis Tribune

WASHINGTON — A joint senate-house committee Wednesday agreed on a compromise foreign aid money bill that would provide just under $4,100,000,000 for the program this year.

The conference compromise, expected to have clear sailing when it is called up for final approval in both houses today, also retains a provision added by the senate to limit future aid to Yugoslavia.

The joint committee, working out differences between the senate and house appropriations, provided for new appropriations of $3,766,000,000, and for use of $330,800,000 in previously approved but unused funds.

**THIS COMPROMISE** figure is about one billion dollars below the original request by President Eisenhower. It almost exactly "split the difference" between the senate and house appropriations figures.

The house had approved new appropriations of about $3,400,000,000, while the senate bill, passed Tuesday night, called for $4,110,000,000 in new money.

The anti-Yugoslavia provision was so watered down before its adoption in the senate, however, that it is expected to have little effect on the program planned for this year.

**IT FORBIDS** shipment of any new military equipment, but allows shipments of spare parts, maintenance equipment, replacements, military machinery and economic aid already promised.

The compromise bill provides these general major items of new money:

**Military Aid:** $2,017,000,000. This compares with the pres-

Foreign Aid
Continued on Page 15

## House Passes Bill for Jet Crash Claims

By Staff Correspondent of the Minneapolis Tribune

WASHINGTON—The house Wednesday completed congressional action on a bill to allow the navy and air force to pay about $250,000 worth of claims arising from two jet plane crashes in Minneapolis in June.

The house accepted senate amendments to the bill, which it passed earlier, and by unanimous consent voted final approval and sent it to the White House for signature.

As introduced in the house by Rep. Judd (R., Minn.), the bill would have covered only the June 9 navy jet crash. In the senate, it was amended by Sen. Humphrey (D., Minn.) to add the June 5 air force accident. A similar bill was introduced by Sen. Thye (R., Minn.).

The new law will allow services to exceed the general $1,000 limit on claims that can be paid without a special congressional action, thus allowing full payment without waiting for passage of a number of "private bills" in congress next year.

The services estimate claims from the June 9 crash, which resulted in 11 deaths and destruction of several houses, will total about $200,000. The June 5 crash, in which a jet hit an automobile, killing three persons, resulted in about $50,000 in claims, the air force said.

THE ANDREA DORIA, ITALIAN LUXURY LINER IN COLLISION

THE STOCKHOLM, SWEDISH-AMERICAN LINE MOTOR SHIP

## Swedish Liner Stockholm, Bow Crushed, Trying to Make Port

**BULLETIN**

**BOSTON, Mass. —(AP)— The vessel Cape Ann early today radioed the coast guard that it had picked up 200 survivors from the Italian liner Andrea Doria.**

Special From the New York Times

NEW YORK — The transatlantic liners Andrea Doria and Stockholm collided in a heavy fog at 1:20 a.m. today (11:20 p.m. Wednesday, Minneapolis time) about 45 miles south of Nantucket island.

The Andrea Doria ordered 1,134 passengers and a crew of 575 to abandon ship shortly after as it lay helpless at sea.

It was listing so badly it could not launch any of its 16 lifeboats. Normally they could have carried 2,000 persons.

Running lights and radio on emergency power, the Andrea Doria said it did not know how much longer it could keep in touch.

Fourteen coast guard and private ships were converging on the scene. Not until 2:24 a.m. (12:24 a.m., Minneapolis time), however, was the first boatload of survivors taken aboard the freighter Cape Ann.

The Cape Ann promptly joined the Andrea Doria in appealing for medical assistance for survivors, but there was no indication how many persons were injured.

**THE STOCKHOLM,** capable of carrying 586 persons and manned by a crew of at least 150, apparently was in less danger. It reported its bow was crushed and the number one hold flooded.

At 3:02 a.m. (1:02 a.m., Minneapolis time) the Stockholm radioed that otherwise the ship was tight. It said it would try to proceed to port with slow speed and requested an escort vessel.

The Stockholm reportedly had lowered its lifeboats to pick up passengers from the Andrea Doria. It was not immediately known how many the Stockholm had taken off.

**The FRENCH LINER ILE DE FRANCE** was the first large ship at the scene. It radioed at 2:46 a.m. (12:46 a.m., Minneapolis time) that it would return to New York at full speed "when all are rescued."

There was no concrete word on how long the Andrea Doria expected to remain afloat.

Its radio was so weak that Stockholm had to relay all messages after 1:30 a.m. (11:30 p.m., Minneapolis time).

Repeatedly through the night the Andrea Doria pleaded for lifeboats.

***"Here danger immediate . . . Need lifeboats . . . as many as possible . . . can't use our lifeboats," it said at 1:26 a.m. (11:26 p.m. Minneapolis time) and again at 1:43 a.m. (11:43 p.m., Minneapolis time).***

All it said about its condition was:

"Listing very badly."

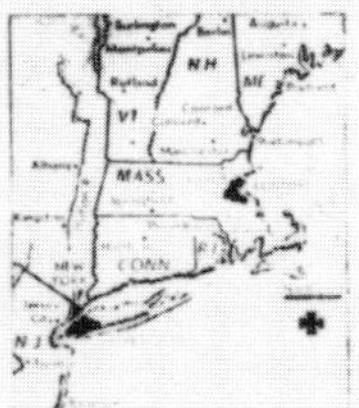


AP WIREPHOTO MAP
WHERE LINERS COLLIDED
*Cross marks sea crash scene*

The coast guard said the Atlantic seas at the scene of the disaster were "not rough." At the time of the collision, however, the weather bureau estimated that visibility there was probably less than one mile.

**IN BOSTON,** Mass., from where the coast guard had wanted to send rescue planes, the visibility was said to be "nil."

But at 2:30 a.m. (12:30 a.m., Minneapolis time) the Stockholm told an approaching rescue vessel that the fog was "not so bad."

The freighter Cape Ann, first vessel to reach the ships, had two lifeboats available. It began receiving passengers from the Andrea Doria.

The coast guard said it did not need to send special medical aid because of medical facilities and doctors aboard most of the vessels it already had dispatched to the scene.

The request for medical assistance was the first indication there may be injuries as a result of the collision.

There were no reports of deaths.

Two navy destroyers were being readied at Boston to rush for the scene. Two more destroyers and two fleet tugs were being dispatched from Newport, R. I.

## Prober: 'Why Did You Take Money?' Hodge: 'Got No Payroll Kickbacks'

Special to the Minneapolis Tribune

SPRINGFIELD, Ill. — Orville E. Hodge's own words confessing guilt in a million-dollar looting of state funds were disclosed Wednesday by George P. Coutrakon, state attorney.

Highlights of the ousted state auditor's admission were read in a 2½-hour session with reporters.

Hodge

Coutrakon read steadily, relating details of the one-time high living political figure's disclosures during nine hours of questioning last week.

Hodge's admissions resulted in his indictment Tuesday on 276 counts of embezzlement, forgery and confidence game.

Hodge's words covered 170 typewritten pages. The prosecutor said the statement, unsigned by Hodge, was incomplete but a full confession of guilt.

Here are some of the highlights of Hodge's statement in which he estimated he had swindled the state out of $500,000 to $550,000 in fraudulent state checks to pay political expenses and cover bad investments:

Coutrakon — Isn't it true you had so many warrants you can't remember them?

Hodge — I was very busy trying to do a good job in the auditor's office and this particular part has always been hazy to me. My mind does not function when it comes to this angle.

Q. Why did you need this money?

A. I talked to Epping (Hodge's former office manager) in May 1955 about a program to get some money for my political campaign. I needed some because I never got any kickbacks from payrollers.

Hodge said he then was considering bucking Gov. William Stratton for the nomination for governor.

Q. How did it first start?

A. One day Epping came in and said he had some warrants he thought we could cash that were payments on services rendered and material purchased. I didn't pay much attention to it and I didn't see the vouchers.

**UNDER** questioning, Hodge finally admitted it was his handwriting on forged indorsements found in 10 warrants totaling $165,260. The warrants were cashed at the Southmoor Bank & Trust Co., Chicago.

Hodge identified all 46 forged warrants cashed at the bank and totaling about $650,000, but said he didn't know who made the typewritten indorsements on the rest of them.

Q. Why didn't you ask Epping for details on how

Hodge
Continued on Page 10

## Many Notables on Andrea Doria Passenger List

Ruth Roman Dilworth
*Aboard stricken liner*

BOSTON, Mass. — (AP) — Among prominent passengers reported aboard the Italian liner Andrea Doria in collision with the liner Stockholm Wednesday night were:

Mayor Richardson Dilworth of Philadelphia, Pa., and his wife and screen actress Ruth Roman and her son, Richard Hall.

Camille Cianfarra, New York Times correspondent in Spain, and F. M. Thierot, circulation manager of the San Francisco Chronicle — both accompanied by their families.

Morris Novak, president of Radio station WOV, New York, and his wife; George P. Kerr, European manager of Procter and Gamble, and family; Robert T. Young, principal surveyor for the American bureau of shipping, and family;

Istzan Rabovsky and his wife, Nora Kovach, internationally known dancers; Vittorio Bifulco, chief inspector, technical services, Italian ministry of foreign affairs, and his wife; Stewart Coleman, a director of the Standard Oil Co. of New Jersey, and family; Marion W. Boyer, also a director of Standard, and his wife.

## Two Minneapolis Men on Italian Liner in Collision

Two Minneapolis men who were returning from a four-months tour of Europe were on board the ill-fated Andrea Doria.

George Staidohar, 65, 5909 Newton avenue S., a Minneapolis barber, was traveling with Robert Tysk, 59, 243 Twentieth avenue S. Tysk is a real estate dealer and owns several apartment buildings.

Relatives said the men had sailed for Europe last March and had toured the continent, including Yugoslavia.

**TOLL RATE CONSIDERED**

ST. IGNACE, Mich.—(AP)— A flat toll rate of $3 a car is being considered for the Mackinac straits bridge linking Michigan's upper and lower peninsulas.

## Minnesota Residents Aboard the Stockholm

Booked aboard the Stockholm were the following Minnesota residents:

Carl O. Carlsson, 25, St. Peter, Minn., a student at Gustavus Adolphus college.

John H. Hermanson, 69, Route 1, Princeton, Minn.

Mr. and Mrs. Gustaf A. Larson, 3234 Twenty-fifth avenue S. Larson was 77 and Mrs. Larson 78.

Hakan Hakanson, 17, 1811 Minnehaha avenue.

Mrs. Engeborg Troswick, 53, and her son, Alf G. Pearson, 22, both of 2115 E. Thirty-first street.

Rune Petterson, 27, 3703 Toledo avenue N., Robbinsdale.

The Larsons were going to visit Stockholm, the city where they were born, to visit relatives. They were to return in November.

Larson is a retired machinist. The Larsons have one daughter, Mrs. Shirley Betcher, who lives in the family residence.

Rune Petterson, a native of Sweden, had spent a year in the United States. He lived with Mr. and Mrs. Seth Anderson.

Petterson had worked for a jewelry firm during his stay. He was en route home to visit his parents in Stockholm, Sweden.

## Almanac

### Blue Suede Shoes Hide Under a Pillow

*Thursday, July 26, 1956*

Things were quiet on the third floor of St. John's hospital, St. Paul. It had been announced a short Lutheran service would originate in the hospital's own chapel and the patients were tuning their under-the-pillow speakers which carry such things and also (at other times) radio programs.

Something was wrong, however. The service wasn't coming through. Listeners kept jerking their cords to change the station. Then a deep-voiced complaint drifted down the hall from one of the rooms:

"All I can hear is Elvis Presley!"

•

*Partly cloudy with occasional showers in the Twin Cities today. High will be 90 with a low of 65.*

•

A mother we know, when asked the age of her typical teen-age son, replied: "Jerry? Oh, he's 15, going on 21."

## Clerk Foils Loop Holdup, Police Capture Suspect

A would-be holdup man was captured by Minneapolis police Wednesday minutes after he attempted to rob a Fanny Farmer candy shop at 501 Hennepin avenue.

The man, who gave his name as Wayne Griffith, 31, Phoenix, Ariz., entered the shop at 4:50 p.m., police said, and ordered a clerk, Lee Ellen Todd, 3237 Irving avenue S., to open the cash register.

**POLICE SAID** he told Miss Todd he was "desperate."

The employe refused to open the cash drawer and while he waited a customer entered the shop.

Griffith "became nervous," Miss Todd said, and left the shop. While the clerk called police the unidentified customer followed Griffith and stopped him in the Loeb arcade.

**THE CUSTOMER** engaged Griffith in conversation for several minutes before the "robber" fled.

Police captured him a few moments later in an alley behind 500 Nicollet avenue.

## Mike Has Two 'Eyes' Again; He Wants to Go Swimming

ORLANDO, Fla. — (UP) — Little Mike Sibole endured without a whimper Wednesday the fitting of a second plastic eye, then asked: "Do I look pretty again, Daddy?"

The plucky youngster was fitted with a light brown plastic eye just a week after surgeons removed his remaining eye to prevent the spread of cancer. The fitting was another step in the adjustment 4-year-old Mike is making in his new world of permanent blindness.

Mike's eye socket was still swollen and sore, and he sat through the painful fitting with his hands clenched but without letting out a cry.

**"HE SEEMED** so pleased that he has two eyes again," the Rev. Sibole said. "And he's glad to get the bandages off."

The operation, doctors said, was necessary to save his life. Mike had his right eye removed when only 2 years old because of cancer and within two years the disease had spread to his left eye.

Mr. Sibole said the family should know within a week or two whether the cancer had spread to other parts of Mike's body before the eye was removed last Wednesday.

"We can only pray it hasn't," Mr. Sibole said. "Mike has made a marvelous adjustment. We just can't believe our own eyes. It's surprising how he gets around now, and he has such enthusiasm."

**MIKE QUICKLY** learned to catch onto his 2-year-old brother's hand or shoulder and use him for his "eyes."

He swings, climbs ladders and romps in the backyard as any normal 4-year-old boy would. His main concern right now is when he can go swimming.

The doctor promised to let him know Friday.



## Tattooer Sounds Taps on Lost Art

Tattooing apparently has fallen on bad times.

"Only work I get now is cover-ups," Joe Marvello told the Minneapolis city council licenses committee Wednesday.

The committee laid over Marvello's application for a tattooing license pending health department O.K.

Marvello, 70, has his shop at 2329 Minnehaha avenue. He told the committee he's "the only tattooer this side of Chicago."

Explaining his reference to "cover-ups," Marvello said, "You know, men who have girls' names tattooed on their arms—only now they're married to somebody else."

## Other Disasters at Sea

By Associated Press

The outstanding peacetime ship disaster in recent history was the sinking of the Titanic in 1912.

The sinking of the Titanic on its maiden voyage after striking an iceberg took a toll of 1,517, many of them prominent.

The same year the Titanic went down, 1,000 lost their lives when the Japanese steamship Kickermaru sank off the coast of Japan.

Two years later 1,024 were lost when the Canadian Pacific steamship Empress of Ireland sank after colliding with a Danish collier in the St. Lawrence river. Another 1,000 lives were lost in 1916 when the Chinese steamer Hain Yu sank off the China coast.

Some of the biggest disasters have been off the China coast. The steamer Hongkong hit a rock near Swaton, China, in 1921 and 1,200 died.

Six thousand Chinese, including government troops, died when a crowded evacuation ship sank off southern Manchuria in November 1948.

Since World War II, the greatest loss of life, some 1,300, was when a Japanese ferry capsized during a typhoon. Another 200 to 300 were lost early this year as the result of the sinking of a coastal steamer during a storm in the Bay of Bengal, East Pakistan.

**Cooler**
Minneapolis High, 80
THURSDAY TEMPERATURES
Details on Page 10

# Minneapolis Morning Tribune

Vol. XC—No. 64 Copyright 1956 Minneapolis Star and Tribune Company MINNEAPOLIS, MINN., FRIDAY, JULY 27, 1956 Price 5 Cents



**Millers Fall to Louisville, 6-5**

Braves Rap Giants, 11-0; Yankees, Indians Win

(DETAILS in Sports Section.)

# Egypt Seizes Suez Canal to Get Aswan Funds

## *St. Paul Woman Tells of Terror on Sinking Ship*

—SURVIVORS—

## N. Y. Roars Welcome to Rescuers

### Tales of Heroism, Tragedy Told as Survivors Arrive

NEW YORK —(AP)— Rescue ships that snatched 1,700 persons from the grip of death at sea began arriving in New York Thursday, scarcely 12 hours after the greatest marine rescue in history.

First into New York harbor was the liner Ile de France with 758 survivors of the sunken Andrea Doria aboard.

**THOSE WHO** were able lined the rails, some of them crying at the sight of land.

Most were shoeless because only by using their bare feet were they able to cling to the decks of the listing Doria in the three hours most of them waited for rescue.

Next into port was the freighter Cape Ann with 175 survivors.

Then came the navy transport Pvt. William H. Thomas with 158 survivors, followed by the destroyer escort Edward R. Allen with 76 rescued crewmen of the Doria aboard.

**WITH THE RESCUE** ships came tales of heroism and stark tragedy in the dead of night after the midnight, fog-shrouded collision between the Doria and the Swedish liner Stockholm.

With them, too, came an accusation. Ninety survivors aboard the Cape Ann charged in a typewritten statement that the Doria's crew was guilty of "complete negligence" at the time of the crash.

This view conflicted with the opinions expressed by other passengers of the vessel, some of whom spoke in glow-

Survivors
Continued on Page Five

Mrs. Widseth Mr. Thompson
*Board Candidates*

## Mrs. Widseth Backed for School Board

By RUSSELL HURST
Minneapolis Tribune Staff Writer

The progressive caucus of the Minneapolis city council Thursday unanimously endorsed Mrs. Edwin C. Widseth for the school board post vacated by the resignation of George Jensen.

The council votes today on Jensen's successor.

With the five progressive votes committed on the first ballot, it appeared the contest would be between Mrs. Widseth and the Rev. Tenner Thompson.

Mr. Thompson, endorsed by the Central Labor union (CLU) and a screening committee of the CIO Hennepin county council, has strong support among the eight council liberals who could decide the election.

Alderman Frank Moulton, progressive caucus leader, said Mrs. Widseth is "uniquely qualified through her active role in governmental and school affairs."

She is assistant chairman for local government of the League of Women Voters. She has been the league's observer of city council activities for two years.

Mrs. Widseth is a member of the schools task force of CLIC, the city's capital long-range improvements committee. She is chairman of the

School Board
Continued on Page Seven

—ST. PAUL WOMAN—

## In Crisis, She Thought of the Titanic

### 'We Just Prayed,' Young Survivor of Italian Liner Says

By CLARK MOLLENHOFF
Minneapolis Tribune Staff Correspondent



ABOARD THE ILE DE FRANCE—Through two hours of quiet terror early Thursday morning a 26-year-old St. Paul woman clung to the rail of the sinking Andrea Doria.

Pretty, blond Mrs. June Swanson, 968 Goodrich avenue, was in the ballroom on the promenade deck of the Italian luxury liner when the 29,000-ton ship was rammed by the Swedish motor ship Stockholm.

Mrs. Swanson

Mrs. Swanson said she and Juliane McLean, a Wichita, Kan., friend, had just finished dancing and were seated at a table with some friends when the bow of the Swedish vessel smashed into the starboard side of the Andrea Doria.

**"COUPLES DANCING** were thrown to the floor and tables were overturned," she said. "I knew it was either an explosion or a collision, but I didn't know which.

*(PICTURE of Mrs. Swanson after rescue—Page 6.)*

"Everyone looked alarmed. I looked out the window of the ballroom and saw sparks and timbers falling. I was stunned for a moment and then the ship's officers came through telling us to be calm and to report on deck.

"I went down one deck to my cabin and got my life preserver. I didn't bother about my coat or anything else because I was sure we were going down with the ship.

**"BY THE TIME** I got back on deck from my cabin we were rolling over and within 15 minutes it was nearly a 50-degree list. There were no long-time friends there with me—just a few people I met on the ship.

"We stayed there together in the middle of the ship, hanging onto the railing."

Most of the passengers took off their shoes so they could maintain a footing on the moist tilted deck. One mother threw her baby toward a lifeboat—and missed.

"I'd just read a story about

St. Paul Woman
Continued on Page Five

AP WIREPHOTO

PROPELLERS SHOW AS LINER ANDREA DORIA STARTS ITS PLUNGE TO THE BOTTOM

AP WIREPHOTO

WATER BOILS AROUND THE STRICKEN LINER AS IT BEGINS TO SLIDE UNDER

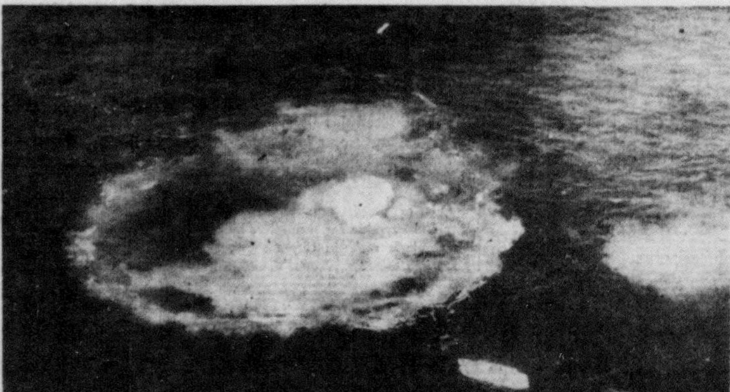

AP WIREPHOTO

ONLY SWIRLING SEA AND AN OIL SLICK, DOTTED WITH DEBRIS, MARK SHIP'S GRAVE

*(PAGE OF PICTURES on Ship Collision Survivors—page 6.)*

## Nasser: 'We Don't Need U.S. Aid'

### Strong Man Reveals Arms Purchase From Russia, Not Czechs

ALEXANDRIA, Egypt —(AP)—Egypt is seizing the Suez canal under a nationalization decree, President Gamal Abdel Nasser announced Thursday.

Its revenues will be used to build the Aswan dam, he said.

Nasser

Nasser said his government could receive 100 million dollars a year in revenue by taking over the canal.

"We don't have to seek American and British aid for building our dam," he said. "We'll build the dam ourselves and with our own money."

**THE DAM'S** cost has been estimated at $1,130,000,000.

"Egypt now is heading toward national economy," Nasser said.

"We shall build the high dam on the skulls of 120,000 Egyptian workmen who died in building the Suez canal.

"We shall industrialize Egypt and compete with the west. We are marching from strength to strength."

Nasser made his announcement after disclosing Egypt's arms-for-cotton deal last September was with the Soviet Union, not Czechoslovakia.

To wildly cheering thousands packed into Alexandria's liberation square, Nasser read this decree:

"In the name of the nation we hereby declare International Suez Canal Co. be nationalized. The company with its assets and liabilities will be transferred to the Egyptian state.

**"THE PRESENT** management will be liquidated. Shareholders will be compensated according to closing prices in the stock exchange.

"The company will be annexed to the Egyptian ministry of commerce. The company will have its own budget. All company money in Egypt and abroad will be frozen.

"Banks and individuals are forbidden to dispose of this money except with permission from the new Egyptian management. All employes will remain in service. No resignations will be accepted."

Egyptian officials seized the offices of Suez Canal Co. in Cairo, Ismailia, Port Said and Suez immediately after Nasser announced nationalization of the company.

**IN LONDON,** Prime Minister Anthony Eden held emer-

Aswan Dam
Continued on Page Seven

## Head of Lakes to Get Taconite Castings Unit

By LEONARD INSKIP
Minneapolis Tribune Staff Writer



The board of directors of National Malleable and Steel Castings Co., Cleveland, Ohio, has approved construction of a multi-million-dollar plant to serve Minnesota's new taconite industry, the company announced Thursday.

The plant will produce grinding balls used in pulverizing iron ore so it can be converted to taconite pellets.

**EARLIER** the company had said it was considering a plant but had not reached a decision.

The company's announcement yesterday, however, indicated a site still remains to be selected. Likeliest locations are Superior, Wis., where the company has an option on a tract, and Duluth, Minn.

The announcement said only that the plant "is expected to be located at the head of the Great Lakes near large taconite iron ore and copper ore processing plants."

"Several important details have yet to be resolved before actual construction can begin," the company said.

**"THE COMPANY** must be assured that utility and other costs in the area (Duluth-Superior) will permit an economically practical operation," it said. "The product must be sold at prices competitive with others in the field."

The company has held discussions with power companies on rates to be charged. A spokesman indicated the statement was not referring to labor or tax costs.

The plant, to be built in five stages, eventually would represent an investment of 10 million dollars if continued expansion proves justified by increased business.

**THE SPOKESMAN** said the company presently has no contracts to supply taconite plants.

Initial employment would be about 200 or 300 workers, later increasing to 800, he said.

Construction is expected to begin later this year.

## Slightly Cooler Air in Store for Upper Midwest

Upper Midwest temperatures will drop a little today, providing good driving weather for week-end vacationers who get an early start.

Partly cloudy and cooler is the general forecast. Minnesota highs will be in the 60s north and the lower 80s south.

Twin Cities high will be 80, the low tonight 60.

North Dakota will have highs ranging from 65 to 72 north and in the 70s south, with scattered rains.

South Dakota may get a thundershower in the west. Highs will be 75 to 80 north and 78 to 85 south.



## TURN THE PAGES TO:



## Almanac

### Young Sirens Sound Off at Night, Too

*Friday, July 27, 1956*
Sunrise 4:52 a.m.; sunset 7:48 p.m.

A siren sounded near a house just off W. Lake street at about 6 a.m. Awakened, a father overheard the following conversation between his two daughters, 5 and 10, who share a bedroom:

Five: "Do police and ambulances have sirens in the daytime, too?"

Ten: "They have sirens in the daytime and the nighttime."

Five: "Great Scott!"

*Partly cloudy and cooler today in the Twin Cities. High will be 80, low tonight 60.*

A philosopher is a fellow who doesn't care whether a thing is right or wrong as long as he can prove it.

**Rain, Cooler**
**Minneapolis High 65**

MONDAY TEMPERATURES

| | | | | | |
|---|---|---|---|---|---|
| 2 a.m. | 57 | 10 a.m. | 60 | 6 p.m. | 59 |
| 3 a.m. | 56 | 11 a.m. | 62 | 7 p.m. | 59 |
| 4 a.m. | 56 | Noon | 63 | 8 p.m. | 60 |
| 5 a.m. | 55 | 1 p.m. | 64 | 9 p.m. | 60 |
| 6 a.m. | 54 | 2 p.m. | 65 | 10 p.m. | 60 |
| 7 a.m. | 55 | 3 p.m. | 65 | 11 p.m. | 60 |
| 8 a.m. | 57 | 4 p.m. | 61 | Midnight | 59 |
| 9 a.m. | 58 | 5 p.m. | 60 | 1 a.m. | 58 |
| | | | | *2 a.m. | 58 |

*Details on Page 22* — *Unofficial


# Minneapolis Morning Tribune

Vol. XC—No. 159 MINNEAPOLIS, MINN., TUESDAY, OCTOBER 30, 1956 Price 5 Cents




# Israel Invades Egypt, Troops Near Suez; U.S. Pledges to Aid Any Aggression Victim

## Adlai Changes Plans, Makes Minnesota His Final Campaign Stop

Adlai Stevenson altered his final campaign plans Monday to make Minnesota his last stop before election day, Sen. Hubert Humphrey announced last night.

Stevenson will come to Minneapolis for a "Breakfast with Adlai" next Monday morning, Humphrey said. Tentatively, it has been scheduled for the Leamington hotel.

Thus both Democratic ticket toppers will close out their campaigns in Minnesota.

**A WHISTLE-STOP** tour through six congressional districts will be made Saturday by Sen. Estes Kefauver.

*(IKE DELUDED U. S. on Mid-East, Adlai Says—page 2.)*

Humphrey said Stevenson's visit will be aimed primarily at counteracting "the money being spent to re-elect Rep. Judd (R., Minn.)."

Joseph Robbie, Judd's DFL opponent in the fifth district, will be honorary chairman of the breakfast.

**DFL CAMPAIGN** workers distributing literature this week also will distribute invitations to the public "Breakfast with Adlai," Humphrey said.

He said Stevenson will fly to Minneapolis Sunday night and return to his farm home in Libertyville, Ill., Monday for a nationwide telecast on election eve.

## Ike Holds Edge in Minnesota, Resurvey Finds

*(Editor's Note: Teams of New York Times reporters have surveyed political trends in 27 closely contested states. Following is a resurvey of Minnesota, dispatched to New York from Minneapolis.)*

By DONALD JANSON
Special From the New York Times

President Eisenhower appears to hold a tenuous lead in the race for Minnesota's 11 electoral votes.

A month ago New York Times reporters found the President and Adlai E. Stevenson running neck and neck in this state. The Eisenhower victory margin of four years ago—155,000 out of 1,379,000 votes cast—had buckled under the impact of defections by farmers who were caught in a cost-price vise.

**ELECTION RESURVEY OF MINNESOTA**

**THE FARM** revolt remains strong today in some areas. Small farmers, despite good crops, have been hard hit by high costs.

But the farm vote in Minnesota is only 19 per cent of the total. It includes a core of stable Republican sentiment, most evident in the southern and southeastern dairy sections of the state.

To work farm discontent for all it is worth Sen. Estes Kefauver is scheduled to make a last-stand tour of rural Minnesota next weekend. The Democratic vice presidential candidate is well liked by Minnesotans, who gave him a solid primary victory over Stevenson in March. He is especially popular with farmers.

**BECAUSE** of rural losses and the normal Democratic majorities in the labor centers of St. Paul and Duluth, it is of vital importance to the Republicans to hold their traditional advantage in the small towns. This they apparently

Survey
Continued on Page 15

## Hold Your Hat, (Umbrella, Too); Winds, Rain Due

More of the same is on tap today for the Twin Cities:

Occasional showers or thunderstorms this morning, cooler temperatures this afternoon, with a high of 65 and a low of 35 to 40.

Despite dark skies and a long-drawn-out drizzle Monday, the Twin Cities weather bureau recorded only .03 inch of precipitation. High temperature was 65.

Only damage reported near Minneapolis was at Anoka, where lightning struck the antenna coils of radio station WCCO at 6:20 p.m., cutting the station off the air for 40 minutes.

Elsewhere in Minnesota the prediction is for scattered showers and thunderstorms. Showers or snow flurries are expected in the extreme northwest corner. Highs will be 50 to 55 north, 55 to 65 south.

## Stassen to Cast His Ballot in Pennsylvania

By Staff Correspondent of Minneapolis Tribune

WASHINGTON — Harold Stassen, former governor of Minnesota, will cast his ballot next Tuesday in a Philadelphia, Pa., suburb.

His office said Monday Stassen will vote in Chestnut Hill, where he lived while president of the University of Pennsylvania.

An aid said Stassen would vote there under federal regulations which permit a government employe working here to vote in the place where he last lived before coming to Washington, whether or not he still owns property there.

Stassen is a property-holder in South St. Paul, but is not now a registered voter there.

## Almanac

### You Hurry Up, But Please Don't Rush ME!

*Tuesday, Oct. 30, 1956*
Sunrise 6:47 a.m.; sunset 5:05 p.m.

Overheard at the state capitol desk where they issue 1957 automobile license tabs:

Cashier: "I wonder why people can't get their tabs earlier . . . only seven weeks 'til Christmas."

Auto Owner: "I suppose you've got all your Christmas shopping done?"

Cashier: "Ha! You know when I do my Christmas shopping? At the very last half-minute!"

*Occasional showers and thunderstorms this morning in the Twin Cities, cooler tonight. High will be 65, low tonight 35 to 40.*

Friend of ours wonders why, with "The Bold and the Brave," "The Proud and the Profane" and all that, they don't call that movie at Radio City theater "The War and the Peace."

AP WIREPHOTO

PRESIDENT SOBERLY HEARS OF ISRAELI DRIVE INTO EGYPT
*Press secretary James Hagerty, left, tells Ike the news at Jacksonville, Fla.*

## Soviet Troops Hold Budapest as Rebels Fight

By ELIE ABEL
Special From the New York Times

VIENNA, Austria — Soviet troops remained in control of Budapest Monday night while the government of Imre Nagy pleaded with the stubborn revolutionaries to lay down their arms.

But the rebels refused to give up the fight until Nagy made good on his promise that Soviet forces would evacuate the battered capital.

The Russians were not budging until the resistance had ceased as Foreign Minister Shepilov made clear in Moscow. The result was a total impasse.

**OUTSIDE** the capital, however, the rebel forces controlled a wide swath of western and southern Hungary. In these areas for the most part Soviet troops were standing without firing.

Western journalists who visited such towns as Gyor and Veszprem in which the revolutionary forces were not being challenged for the moment by Soviet garrison troops, reported lack of a common program among the Hungarians. At least two revolutionary factions had formed, they said.

One wanted to support Nagy's new national front government in the hope the Russians could be persuaded to evacuate if they were persuaded that an independent Hungary would not sway from the Communist path.

**THE SECOND** group was said to be demanding repudiation of Communism and all its works.

During the hours of darkness, sporadic gunfire was heard in the capital from time to time but there was no large scale fighting. Radio Budapest announced at 9 p.m. Hungarian army units had begun to relieve Soviet troops in the capital.

The official statement that the Russians were about to evacuate Budapest met with widespread skepticism in the light of the false reports to the same effect at daybreak. Step-by-step evacuation was agreed to by the Soviet commanders, the radio said, and will get under way about 9 a.m.

**THE PLAN** outlined by the radio, official voice of the Nagy regime, was that withdrawal should proceed sector by sector as local insurgent commanders agreed to end the shooting.

The defense ministry appealed to the Budapest populace to support the changeover by maintaining order.

According to Hungarian Red Cross workers who

Hungary
Continued on Page 15

## Americans Flee Syria, Jordan in War Threat

By ROBERT HEWETT
Minneapolis Tribune Foreign Correspondent

**SPECIAL REPORT From MID-EAST**

BEIRUT, Lebanon — Chartered planes and motor convoys whisked some 400 Americans out of Jordan and Syria in less than 12 hours Monday.

The action was prompted by state department fears that the new outbreak of Arab-Israeli warfare might be very near.

The first planeload of 41 persons from Amman, Jordan, mostly women and children of embassy and Point Four officials, had only two hours' notice to pack before they were taken to the airport.

All were somewhat bewildered by the rapid transfer. They said the situation was normal in Amman when they left.

**EVACUATION** planes have been ready for weeks as the Arab-Israeli tension mounted.

"We just got orders from Washington to leave at once," one embassy official said on condition his name not be used.

Hewett

"There is no question but what the situation is grave," he added.

"But it is my belief that the state department ordered the evacuation to emphasize to Israelis that President Eisenhower meant business when he warned that the United States does not want war in the Middle East. The United States is pledged to act against any aggressor and this shows we are clearing the

Evacuation
Continued on Page 13

—UNITED STATES—

## Will Take Case Before U.N. Today

### Ike Says Special Congress Session May Be Necessary

By CLARK MOLLENHOFF
Minneapolis Tribune Staff Correspondent

WASHINGTON — President Eisenhower held an emergency conference Monday night on Israel's invasion of Egypt and the White House announced "we shall honor our pledge" to aid the victim of any Middle East aggression.

The President and his top diplomatic and military aids met for 90 minutes and agreed to take the situation before the United Nations today.

The U.N. security council agreed to take up the matter at 11 a.m. today.

Following the meeting, press secretary James Hagerty declared a decision on whether to call a special session of congress will be determined "in the light of the unfolding situation."

**PRESENT** at the emergency meeting were Secretary of State John Foster Dulles; Secretary of Defense Charles E. Wilson; Adm. Arthur Radford, chairman of the joint chiefs of staff; Allen W. Dulles, director of central intelligence; undersecretary of state Herbert Hoover, Jr.; Sherman Adams, presidential assistant, and Gen. Wilton B. Persons, white house liaison officer with congress.

Hagerty's full statement is as follows:

"At the meeting the President recalled that the United States under this and prior administration has pledged itself to assist the victims of any aggression in the Middle East. We shall honor that pledge.

"The United States is in

United States
Continued on Page 19

ARROW POINTS IN DIRECTION OF ISRAELI INVASION

—ISRAEL—

## Egypt Says It Has No Troops in Area

JERUSALEM—(AP)—Israeli forces made a big lunge across Egypt's Sinai desert Monday and today were reported advancing only 18½ miles short of the Suez canal.

All indications were that no armed clash had occurred yet between Israel and Egypt in the barren peninsula.

Egyptian army headquarters in Cairo, apparently stunned by the audacity of the blow, acknowledged that Egypt had been invaded.

But the Egyptians said in an official communique, the second within an hour, that no clash had taken place up to midnight.

Cairo's big United States-built international airport was closed suddenly to commercial planes. It can handle the jet planes of Egypt's air force.

United States women and children, trying to flee, were stranded by the airport closedown.

The scare spread around the world.

Cairo's government-backed newspaper Al Gumhurriya bannered:

"Israel Begins War." Other Cairo newspapers carried similar headlines.

Both Al Gumhurriya and army headquarters insisted the Israelis struck at a relatively unimportant point.

The newspaper said no Egyptian troops were stationed there. The army said the point "is a barren desert region where there is only one frontier check post."

An Egyptian army communique said frontier forces reported the Israeli forces reached the road junction of El Kuntilla, four miles inside Egypt.

The communique made no mention of deeper penetrations reported by Israeli sources.

An Israeli spokesman said "I just don't know" when asked if the operation was aimed at the Suez canal.

The unofficial reports would indicate that the Israelis were dashing across the desert peninsula straight for the international waterway.

**FIGHTING** flared up along Egypt's Gaza strip, about 80 miles north of where the northernmost of two Israeli prongs crossed into Egypt.

Egypt said Israeli artillery opened fire on the Gaza strip.

Israeli quarters said Egyptian forces attacked an Israeli patrol with small arms and mortars, but there were no casualties.

*(EAGER But Untested, Egypt's Army Is Beset With Disease, Illiteracy—Page 11.)*

A high Israeli government source commenting on the thrust into the Sinai desert said: "It's too big for a reprisal and too small for a war."

He said the main object of the operation is to wipe out Fedayeen (commando or guerrilla) bases in the Sinai peninsula. The Fedayeen have been operating recently like ordinary Egyptian military units, he said.

**THE ISRAELI** part of Jerusalem maintained an appearance of calm despite the rising tension. Amman, Jordan's capital, also was reported calm.

A Jordan military source said "the Arab legion (national army) is braced on the west bank of the Jordan and is ready for anything. All units are on the alert and watching for anything that can happen."

An Israeli foreign ministry statement blamed Egypt and

Israel
Continued on Page 13

## Britain Ready to Send Forces to Aid Egypt

LONDON — (AP) — Britain early today was reported ready to force Israeli troops out of Egypt if their thrust is proved to be an all-out invasion designed to seize some of Egypt's territory.

An authoritative source said the government is in a position to strike at Israel, or any aggressor in the Middle East, within 24 hours with air, land and sea forces now assembled in the eastern Mediterranean.

**THE INFORMANT** said Britain fully stands by the letter and spirit of the 1950 American-British-French declaration on the Middle East and is prepared to join the United States and France in implementing it.

The declaration binds the western Big Three immediately to "take action both within and without the United Nations" to prevent any Israeli or Arab violation of Middle East frontiers or armistice lines.

Prime Minister Anthony Eden late Monday night summoned an emergency meeting of senior British ministers to discuss the Israeli army's lunge toward the Suez canal.

**IT EMERGED** after the talks that the British government's line of action will be determined finally—probably within the next 12 hours—after it has carefully studied:

**The full reports** on the nature and intention of the Israeli attack from British envoys in Middle East capitals.

**The recommendations** of senior American, British and French diplomats who have met twice in Washington since President Eisenhower's week-end appeal to Israel to avoid endangering the peace.

**The reaction** of Britain's parliament, which later today is expected to debate the situation.

Under Egypt's 1954 agreement with Britain for evacuation of the Suez canal zone, Britain has the right to reoccupy its former zone bases in case the waterway and Egypt itself are threatened by attack.

## Stocks Drop After Israeli Attack

NEW YORK — (UP) — The stock market, enjoying its best gain in more than a month at mid-day, suddenly plunged in a final 30-minute break Monday when news hit the floor of the Israeli invasion of Egypt.

Only the gong closing operations at 3:30 p.m. saved the market from an all-out break. Ironically, yesterday marked the 27th anniversary of the historic 1929 market crash.

The industrial average, riding up to 494.11 high during the day, dipped 10 points following announcement of the Israeli attack.

*(STOCKS TABLE — Page 24.)*

## 18 Lost at Sea on Egypt Plane

CAIRO, Egypt — (UP) — An Egyptian military plane with 18 persons aboard crashed in the Mediterranean sea near Lebanon Monday, it was reported here.

The Weather
MINNESOTA: Cloudy.
WISCONSIN: Cloudy.
SOUTH DAKOTA: Rain.
NORTH DAKOTA: Warmer.
IOWA: Mostly Cloudy.

# Minneapolis Sunday Tribune

General News Section

Vol. XC—No. 164

MINNEAPOLIS, MINN., SUNDAY, NOVEMBER 4, 1956

Price 15c in Twin Cities Area 20c Elsewhere

# Russ Forces Launch All-Out Attack on Hungary

# Israel Agrees to U.N. Demand for Cease-Fire

## We Need More Than One Page One for the News

*With major stories developing at home and abroad, the Minneapolis Sunday Tribune finds itself with more page one news than page one will hold. Here are capsule summaries of important news you will find elsewhere in the newspaper:*

### Politics

**Minnesota Poll** finds President Eisenhower has moved ahead slightly in his lead over Adlai Stevenson. The figures: Ike-Nixon 52½ per cent, Adlai-Kefauver 47½ per cent. In the governor race, the figures are: Gov. Freeman 52 per cent, Ancher Nelsen 48 per cent.—Page One, Upper Midwest Section.

**Estes Kefauver,** barnstorming in Minnesota, says Tuesday's results will be 1948 all over again — an upset victory for the Democratic slate.—Page One, Upper Midwest Section.

**Gallup Poll** discusses major shifts in voting preference of population groups.—Page 15A.

### Middle East

**Soviet Union** offers Syria "every assistance" in regaining complete independence.—Page 5A.

**Jordan faces** the crucial question: will Israeli troops try to seize the Arab section of divided Jerusalem? A story by Robert Hewett from Amman, Jordan.—Page 5A.

### Weather

**Deadwood, S. D.,** is buried under 40 inches of snow.—Page One, Upper Midwest Section.

### Football

**Minnesota "scuttles"** Pittsburgh, 9 to 6, before 63,579 soggy spectators.—Page One, Upper Midwest Section and Sports Peach.

## Campaign Nears End With Ike Big Favorite

By RICHARD WILSON
Chief of the Minneapolis Tribune Washington Bureau

WASHINGTON—A 141,000-mile airborne presidential campaign comes to its end with President Eisenhower a strong favorite for re-election.

Uniform opinion among political writers, observers and poll-takers is that the president will win again with a minimum of 270 of the necessary 266 electoral votes and a possible maximum of 460. But few think the President will win such a great victory.

**A FEW** of the experts dissent altogether, saying Stevenson has a chance to win by a narrow margin as President Harry S. Truman did in 1948.

But the majority believe Mr. Eisenhower will win, but by a smaller margin and with fewer electoral votes than in 1952. In that year the President won with 442 electoral votes to 89 for Stevenson and a popular majority of 6,620,260 over Stevenson.

Mr. Eisenhower received 55.01 per cent of the total popular vote in 1952.

*(SURVEYS GIVE Ike Minimum of 285 Electoral Votes—Page 9A.)*

A consensus of the experts now seems to be that the President's popularity will fall off by 1½ million to two million and that his electoral

Campaign
Continued on page 12A

## Adlai Says Ike Lacks Energy to Do His Job

By FLETCHER KNEBEL
Minneapolis Tribune Staff Correspondent

CHICAGO — Adlai Stevenson Saturday night charged that President Eisenhower "lacks the energy for full-time work at the world's toughest job" in a time of global crisis.

Stevenson made the charge before 20,000 persons in Chicago stadium after a thrilling parade from the heart of the loop three miles away.

Stevenson said that the President's age and the two-term constitutional limit means that President Eisenhower will "inevitably recede more and more from the picture" in the next four years.

**THIS, SAID** Stevenson, destroys the Republican campaign argument of "trust Ike" and replaces it with the issue of whether the nation trusts Vice President Richard M. Nixon.

"Every consideration" — he said in his big campaign climax speech before roaring thousands in Chicago stadium — "the President's age, his constitutional position under the 22nd amendment, make it inevitable that the dominant figure in the Republican party under a second Eisenhower term would be Richard Nixon."

*(ADLAI'S Resources Program — Page 8A.)*

Thus in the final night rally of his long, 32-state second bid for the White House, Stevenson returned to the central issue that has occupied the Democrats for more than a year — the age and health of the President.

**"THE CHIEF** executive," he said, "has never had the inclination and now lacks the energy for full-time work at the world's toughest job."

He again accused the Eisenhower team of ignoring his suggestion of last year that U.N. border patrols be established to keep the peace be-

Adlai
Continued on page 16A

—U.N.—

## Says Egypt Must Also Halt War

### Ambassador Says Israel 'Ready to Negotiate'

By CARL T. ROWAN
Minneapolis Tribune Staff Writer

UNITED NATIONS, N. Y.—Israel agreed to comply with the general assembly demand for an immediate end to Middle East warfare Saturday.

Israeli Delegate Abba S. Eban told the general assembly, locked in its second night of dramatic emergency debate, that Israel will cease fire immediately if Egypt makes a similar commitment.

Eban said Israel is ready to negotiate directly with Egypt and other Arab states to achieve a permanent solution to their dispute.

**THE ARAB** countries have steadfastly refused to negotiate directly with Israel.

Weary, sleepy delegates from 76 nations went on toward almost certain approval of:

**An Indian** resolution again appealing to France and Britain to cease-fire in Egypt within 12 hours.

**A Canadian** resolution calling for establishment of an emergency U.N. police force to keep the peace in the Middle East.

**Preliminary work** leading to approval at a subsequent session of two United States resolutions pledging the U.N. to new, dramatic efforts to work out lasting solutions to both the Israeli-Arab dispute and Suez canal crisis.

Even as Israel agreed to the cease fire, Eban pointed out that Israel regards the old armistice as "a state of war."

**THIS ARMISTICE,** he said, "is a fiction to which Egypt occasionally pays lip service."

But in reality, he said, it has meant military raids and threats from the Arab world and economic efforts to strangle to death his Jewish homeland.

Eban later told correspondents that his government had made no commitments on the portion of the assembly's resolution calling for withdrawal of Israeli troops behind the old armistice line.

Eban said he had no instructions from his govern-

U.N.
Continued on page 17A

## Dulles in 'Fine Shape' After Surgery to Remove Section of Intestine

WASHINGTON — Secretary of State John Foster Dulles underwent a successful operation Saturday for removal of a perforated section of his upper colon.

Dulles

Dulles, 68, was reported "in fine shape" after the 2½-hour operation. He was expected to be able to return to work in about six weeks.

**HE WAS TAKEN** ill early yesterday morning, and the attack was at first tentatively diagnosed as acute appendicitis. The operation, however, disclosed the large intestine was the source of the trouble. The appendix was not removed.

A state department spokesman announced shortly after 9 p.m. (8 p.m. Minneapolis time) that Dulles was in "satisfactory" condition following his operation.

Lincolon White, state department spokesman, was asked whether there was a possibility that the removed section of Dulles' large intestine may have been cancerous.

"The tissue (removed from Dulles' colon) is being subjected to pathological studies, which is routine," White said. "I am unable to state at this time when the results will be known."

White read this statement to reporters after the operation:

"The secretary of state underwent an operation which involved the removal of a portion of the large intestine which had perforated. The operation took 2½ hours and the secretary left the operating table in good condition.

"It is contemplated that the secretary will be in the hospital for a period of two to three weeks.

**"THE DOCTORS** think he should be able to return to his desk in approximately six weeks.

"He is resting comfortably and is in good condition. His pulse is 76. His blood pressure is 126/75.

"The operating team was Maj. Gen. Leonard D. Heaton, commanding officer of Walter Reed, assisted by Washington surgeon Dr. John H. Lyon, Col. Robert Gants and Col.

Dulles
Continued on Page 16A

## Eden Says U.S. Will Approve Mid-East Acts

LONDON — (AP) — Prime Minister Eden declared Saturday night Britain and France acted to prevent a Middle East explosion. He said he will make certain Israeli troops quit Egypt when Britain and French forces take over key positions on the Suez canal.

Eden told the nation he was confident the United States will come around to the conclusion that its two western allies acted only to prevent the Middle East from becoming inflamed in war.

The Prime Minister made clear, however, that British and French forces intend to move into the Suez canal zone and bring about the withdrawal of Israeli forces.

His strongarm tactics sharply divided Britons.

Anthony Nutting resigned as Britain's minister of state for foreign affairs in protest against the British-French attack on Egypt.

**EDEN APPEARED** on a nationwide TV program seeking support for a policy that has rocked Britain with threats of strikes for "no war." The program also was broadcast to Europe.

Just before Eden went on the air Sir Winston Chunchill

Eden
Continued on page 17A

Churchill Nutting
*Growing Disagreement*

## Planes Continue Battering Egypt

By Associated Press

British and French air power hammered at Egyptian communications and troop concentrations Saturday as the two western nations spurned U.N. appeal for a cease-fire. Their military chieftains appeared set for landing of troops in an attempt to seize the closed Suez canal.

More Mid-East Background, News—pages 5,6A

As the British-French planes hammered at Egyptian installations there were these other developments in the Middle East crisis:

1 Damascus radio broadcast an Egyptian claim — not confirmed elsewhere — that coastal artillery already had foiled a landing attempt by sinking a British troop carrier and another vessel off Suez, southern terminus of the canal.

2 Reports from Beirut, Lebanon, said zero hour was approaching on the Israeli-Jordan frontier. Convoys of white ambulances were seen forming in the Israeli section of Jerusalem. Jordanian leaders said an Israeli attack was imminent.

3 Arab saboteurs blasted the Iraq Petroleum Co. pipeline at three points in Syria to stop the flow of oil from Iraq to the Mediterranean coast, company employes reported. The Iraqui government confirmed that the flow of oil had stopped.

Arabian-American Oil Co. (Aramco) said it had reports its big oil pipeline from Saudi Arabia had been "blown up." The line runs from Saudi Arabian oil fields near the Persian gulf through Jordan and Syria to the Mediterranean coast of Lebanon.

An Egyptian embassy source in Washington said in other parts of the Middle East the flow of oil was "coming to a halt." The source said that, in the British protectorate of Bahrein, oil installations were being shut down or put out of commission and that in British-controlled Qatar, a peninsula of Arâbia in the Persian gulf, oil wells were being damaged.

4 Prime Minister Anthony Eden of Britain announced in an emergency session of the house of commons that Britain and France would not comply with the U.N. general assembly request to end the attack on Egypt.

5 In Washington, the navy announced evacuation of Americans from the Middle East war zone "is now complete." A total of 2,500 have been removed. The announcement reported no casualties among civilians during the evacuation.

An official Israeli spokesman said forward patrols of Israeli forces reached the east bank of the Suez canal but later pulled back.

**THE CHIEF** army spokesman, Lt. Col. Moshe Pearlman, said the main body of the Israeli forces was about nine miles from the east bank.

Pearlman said he did not now know whether Israeli forces intended to move to the banks of the canal but said:

"If we want to go to the banks, we can do so."

Egypt's air force was declared virtually destroyed.

There were indications the landing would be made by paratroopers and seaborne invasion units within 48 hours.

**BRITISH** bombers, protected by French and British fighters, turned their heaviest attack from airfields in Egypt to ammunition dumps, barracks and armored - weapons depots of the Egyptian army.

While the effort to cripple the army, as the air force had been crippled, continued through the day, reports indicated the Egyptians were trying to assemble in strength at the canal.

They were said to be with-

Egypt
Continued on page 17A

## U.S. Requests U.N. Meeting on Hungary

By CARL T. ROWAN
Minneapolis Tribune Staff Writer

UNITED NATIONS, N.Y.—The United States early today asked for a special Sunday meeting of the U.N. security council to take up the new Soviet attacks in Hungary.

The request was made by Ambassador Henry Cabot Lodge, Jr., within less than an hour after news dispatches told of widespread attacks by Soviet forces throughout Hungary.

The security council last night had debated the Hungarian question for more than three hours and had adjourned its debate until Monday morning. Lodge, however, told the council president that he would ask for an earlier meeting if the situation worsened.

**AT THE COUNCIL** meeting Lodge had submitted a resolution calling on the U.N. to order an immediate end to Soviet intervention in the internal affairs of Hungary.

Earlier, one of the big mysteries of the current U.N. crisis involved western reluctance to condemn Russian activity in Hungary when it clearly had the support for such a move in the security council.

The 11 council members sat through three verbose hours Saturday, with the west acting like a district attorney who knows the culprit but fears he cannot convict him.

**THE SECOND** day of urgent deliberations by the council were highlighted by a United States resolution to "deplore the use of Soviet military force" in Hungary and demand withdrawal of Russian troops from the satellite.

But the United States clearly was unwilling to press for a vote — a fact that revealed still-significant difference be-

Council
Continued on page 17A

—HUNGARY—

## Budapest Radio Cries 'Betrayal'

### Premier Nagy Calls to World for Assistance

VIENNA, Austria — (AP) — Powerful Russian forces launched a general attack on Hungary and its capital today without warning.

"Russian gangsters have betrayed us," said a Hungarian news agency (MTI) message from Budapest to the Associated Press in Vienna.

"The Russian troops suddenly attacked Budapest and the whole country. They opened fire on everybody in Hungary. It is a general attack."

MTI said Janos Kadar, Hungarian Communist party secretary, formed a new government, sided with the Russians and has begun to "annihilate the counter-revolution."

Imre Nagy, the nationalist Communist who was elevated to the premiership by the anti-Russian revolution, appealed to the world for help.

**ONLY A FEW** hours earlier Nagy's government had announced an "encouraging start" in negotiations to get all Russian troops to leave Hungary.

But while Hungarian and Soviet military negotiators talked, Russian troops and tanks fanned out across Hungary.

The border with Austria on the west was firmly sealed off. The Russians seized railway stations at key points throughout the country.

Hungarian revolutionary headquarters estimated more than 1,000 Russian tanks encircled the Hungarian capital. Then the Russians struck.

**THE HUNGARIAN** news agency said several hundred tanks battered their way into Budapest against Hungarian forces.

Fierce fighting broke out for control of the bridges over the Danube between Buda and Pest.

The Hungarian news agency said the parliament building not far from the United States and British embassies was under heavy Soviet fire.

The agency sent an appeal to the Associated Press in behalf of Nagy. The message said:

"I speak in the name of Imre Nagy. He asks help . . . Nagy and the government and the whole people ask for help."

**"IF YOU HAVE** anything from the Austrian government, tell me," MTI said. "Urgent, urgent, urgent."

MTI said the entire Hun-

Hungary
Continued on Page 17A

*2 DAYS WITHOUT FOOD, THEY LIVED ON HOPE*

## Saved Miners Tell of 42-Hour Ordeal

SPRINGHILL, Canada—(UP)—The first 59 of 115 coal miners trapped for 42 hours in a black hell more than a mile underground were found alive Saturday after hope for them had been all but abandoned. Forty-five survivors have been brought to the surface.

Survivors indicated another 30 to 40 men still were below waiting to be brought up and that oxygen was running dangerously low. Oxygen tanks were rushed to the mine by navy helicopter, truck and automobile.

Total number of known dead is 14.

**THE 59 MEN** were at the 5,400-foot level when an explosion wrecked the Cumberland Railway Coal company's No. 4 pit Thursday. Men caught at other levels by the explosion had not been accounted for.

Charles Burton was one of the first men to reach the surface after nearly two days without food or water. He said men in his group owed their lives to their mine leader,

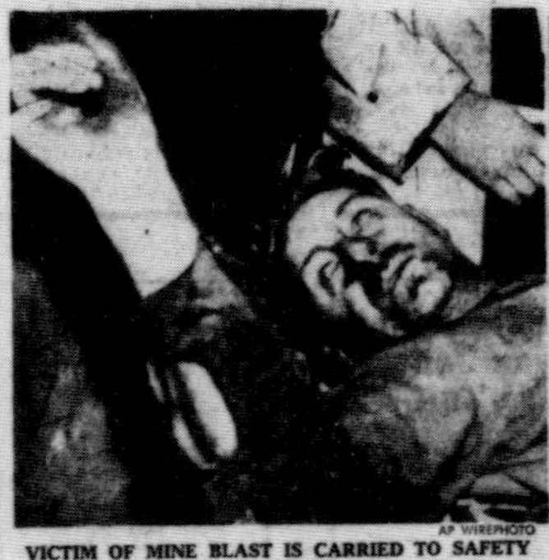

AP WIREPHOTO
VICTIM OF MINE BLAST IS CARRIED TO SAFETY
*Charles Burton was among first to reach surface*

who led them to an air valve, cut a hole in the air tube for each man to suck on and directed the men to tie rags soaked with mine water over their faces while moving about in the gas-filled shaft.

The work of bringing the men to the surface was slow. Some were on stretchers, but most managed to stumble out after the ordeal that lasted for 42 hours and 30 minutes.

Burton said the explosion sounded like a "muffled bang." Smoke poured down the shaft, he said. He said he passed out and when he came to, Conrad Embree, his group leader, had taken charge.

**HE SAID** that after sitting around for nearly two days, Embree decided to send Burton and two others up a 70-degree mine slope to seek a way out. They met rescuers at the 3,200-foot level.

"We ate our lunches on Thursday. We had nothing to eat on Friday or this morning (Saturday). We didn't drink any of the mine water. But the draggermen (rescuers) had some with them when we were rescued."

Burton said it was cold and wet in the mine.

"None of the fellows gave up hope," he said. "We didn't talk too much. We were all determined to get out."

## Girls Barely Escape Mice Freed on Stage

ROTHERHAM, England — (Reuters)—Police were called to a theater here Friday when students turned some mice loose on the stage in the middle of a nudist act.

A girl clad only in three sequins and another posing in the nude screamed and ran off the stage.

No arrests were made. "It was just a practical joke," a student said.

## IN TODAY'S TRIBUNE



*There are three magazine-size sections in your Minneapolis Sunday Tribune today, instead of the usual two. They are PICTURE magazine, the Sunday Tribune's own locally edited magazine designed for Upper Midwest readers; THIS WEEK magazine and the "CHRISTMAS DAYTONIAN," a 76-page rotogravure section presenting gift merchandise.*

**Sample Ballots for Tuesday Election—Page 10B**

**Colder, Rain**
Minneapolis High 42
TUESDAY TEMPERATURES
[illegible]
Details on Page 23

# Minneapolis Morning Tribune

Vol. XC—No. 167 MINNEAPOLIS, MINN., WEDNESDAY, NOVEMBER 7, 1956 Price 5 Cents



# IKE WINS BY LANDSLIDE

## *Senate Control in Doubt; Ike Leads in Minnesota; Freeman Far Ahead; Wier and Judd Near Victory*

## British Seize Suez, Halt Firing

### Egypt Accepts U.N. Cease-Fire Request, Lists Conditions

From the Tribune Wire Services

French and British forces seized effective control of the Suez canal Tuesday and declared a cease-fire.

Just before the deadline they announced the capture of Ismailia, midway control point on the 103-mile canal. (The time was 2 a.m. in Egypt, midnight in London, 6 p.m. Minneapolis.)

Egypt announced it would accept the U.N. request for a cease-fire if all foreign troops withdraw from Egyptian soil and if other conditions are met.

The capture of Ismailia gave British and French forces the northern half of the waterway after two days of battle.

Port Said, the northern terminal, was overrun Monday.

**THE FRENCH** said the cease-fire was possible because the British and French have achieved their main objective of restoring the canal to international control.

The next step is to turn control of the waterway over to a U. N. police force now being organized swiftly.

Cairo radio interrupted a program to read the U. N. announcement that Britain and France agreed to a cease-fire.

*(FIRE, SMOKE, Smell of Blood Identify War-Torn Port Said—page 12; INDIA OFFERS Troops to Police Mid-East—page 6.)*

Then the radio announcement laid down these conditions of acceptance previously insisted upon by Egypt:

**The cease-fire** must be immediate.

**All foreign troops** must be withdrawn from Egypt.

**Combat forces** must withdraw behind the (1948-49) armistice lines.

**There must be no** outside help to combatants.

**Free safety** of passage through the Suez canal must be assured.

Britain and France announced they would be willing to pull out once U.N. police forces can take control in the canal zone.

Israel has announced it agrees to a cease-fire. It has said nothing about giving up any of the Sinai peninsula wrested from Egypt last week.

Egypt gave indications of

Egypt
Continued on Page Nine

—MINNESOTA GOVERNOR—

## Freeman Lead Is 34,000 With Fourth of Votes Counted

By JOHN C. McDONALD
Minneapolis Tribune Staff Writer

Gov. Orville L. Freeman piled up a 34,000-vote lead over his Republican opponent, Ancher Nelsen, with about one-fourth of the votes counted Tuesday night.

Thomas R. Hughes, Freeman's secretary, reported from DFL election headquarters in the Dyckman hotel that spot comparisons showed the governor was running "better than in 1954."

GOV. ORVILLE FREEMAN
*Heads for re-election*

Freeman won his first term two years ago by a 68,000-vote margin.

Hughes said the DFL chief executive carried Duluth by 12,392 votes yesterday. This was a gain of 3,000 over his 1954 plurality in the eighth congressional district's largest city.

McDonald

DFL leaders predicted the governor would come out of the district with a margin of 50,000 votes.

Freeman picked up a 21,000-vote bulge in Ramsey county. Ramsey's fourth district, like the eighth, is a DFL stronghold.

**WITH 310** of 486 voting precincts reported from Hennepin county, Freeman was leading Nelsen by 5,000 votes. His Hennepin edge in 1954 was 11,000 votes.

"But with the Eisenhower vote running the way it is, we'll be happy to break even in Hennepin county," Hughes observed.

Apparently Freeman would do better than break even.

Hughes said reports telephoned to the governor's headquarters from Willmar, Marshall, Triumph, Rochester and other points in southern and western Minnesota indicated he was outdoing his 1952 record.

**HE WAS SAID** to be running 20 per cent ahead of Nelsen in normally-Republican Olmsted county.

Freeman was leading by larger margins than in 1954 in a pair of Lyon county townships. He lost that county two years ago by only 93 votes.

The DFL governor was running 6 to 8 per cent ahead of the Democratic presidential ticket.

**FOR EXAMPLE,** in one Minneapolis Negro district—the 20th precinct in the fifth ward—Freeman received 404 votes, as compared with Nelsen's 151.

This was 72.8 per cent of the total vote, or 3 per cent more than Adlai Stevenson and Estes Kefauver received in the same precinct.

## Ike's Margin in State Falls Below 1952

President Eisenhower was running ahead of Adlai Stevenson with 25 per cent of Minnesota's 3,859 voting precincts reported early today.

But the margin, percentage-wise, was considerably short of the 155,000-vote edge racked up by Mr. Eisenhower in Minnesota four years ago.

Perhaps one straw in the wind was that in pro-Republican Faribault county, which in 1952 witnessed all its precincts voting for the winner, two rural townships went for Stevenson yesterday.

**SEELY TOWNSHIP** gave Stevenson only 40 per cent of its total vote in 1952. This year it boosted his percentage to 54.

Kiester township raised the Stevenson vote from 34.5 per cent four years ago to 53.1 in 1956.

These totals were the only indications of the expected "farm revolt" to be gleaned from early returns.

Returns from a dozen key precincts in Minnesota early last night indicated President Eisenhower was a favorite to win the state's 11 electoral votes.

Mr. Eisenhower appeared to

Minnesota President
Continued on Page 15

—SENATE—

## Even Split Possible in Senate

### Nixon Could Hold Key Tie-Breaking Vote in Congress

WASHINGTON —(AP)— A nip-and-tuck battle developed Tuesday night for control of the senate in the 85th congress.

The lineup now is 49 to 47—Democratic. A net Republican gain of one would give the GOP control, since Vice President Nixon remains to cast his tie-breaking vote.

Ten Democrats and seven Republicans won senate seats in the early returns. All the Democrats were from southern or border states. Five had no opposition.

**EARLY RETURNS** found Republicans leading in fights to take these seats now held by Democrats: two in Kentucky, and one each in Nevada, New York and West Virginia.

Democrats held margins in these states now represented by Republicans: Pennsylvania, South Dakota, Ohio, Idaho, Oregon and Illinois.

Few of these races appeared conclusive, however and the 50-46 Democratic edge they indicate seemed likely to fade.

Returns from Nevada, Oregon and South Dakota were far from complete. In Pennsylvania and Illinois, the Democratic candidates piled up early margins in the traditionally Democratic big cities, but these were in danger of being wiped out by votes from outstate.

**In New York** state, Mayor Robert F. Wagner (D) conceded that Republican Jacob Javits had won the seat being vacated by Democratic Sen. Herbert Lehman.

Republicans re-elected were in Vermont, Connecticut, Maryland and Indiana.

**DEMOCRATS** had hoped to knock off Sen. Prescott Bush in Connecticut and Sen. John M. Butler in Maryland, but both rode the Eisenhower bandwagon to easy victories.

In addition to races already decided, Republican incumbents appeared to be safe in Wisconsin, New Hampshire and North Dakota. Sen. Bourke B. Hickenlooper (R) led in Iowa.

Democratic senators were re-elected in Arizona and North Carolina. Sen. Thomas Hennings (D.) was running well ahead in Missouri.

PRESIDENT EISENHOWER RE-ELECTED

## Presidential Returns

| State | Voting Districts | Districts Reporting | Popular Vote: Eisenhower | Popular Vote: Stevenson | Electoral Vote Trend: Eisenhower | Electoral Vote Trend: Stevenson |
|---|---|---|---|---|---|---|
| Ala. | 2,756 | 2,152 | 155,829 | 214,453 | x | 11 |
| Ariz. | 521 | 243 | 96,861 | 57,000 | 4 | x |
| Ark. | 2,396 | 892 | 35,123 | 48,991 | x | 8 |
| Calif. | 24,984 | 6,396 | 431,260 | 353,813 | 32 | x |
| Colo. | 1,780 | 393 | 86,526 | 56,201 | 6 | x |
| Conn. | 169 | 169 | 709,395 | 404,209 | 8 | x |
| Del. | 336 | 315 | 92,328 | 75,162 | 3 | x |
| Fla. | 1,781 | 1,269 | 546,984 | 388,915 | 10 | x |
| Ga. | 1,780 | 794 | 159,654 | 279,587 | x | 12 |
| Idaho | 893 | 281 | 47,328 | 32,217 | 4 | x |
| Ill. | 9,588 | 3,730 | 832,388 | 728,272 | 27 | x |
| Ind. | 4,384 | 1,975 | 628,643 | 429,713 | 13 | x |
| Iowa | 2,488 | 863 | 207,833 | 157,856 | 10 | x |
| Kan. | 2,976 | 1,102 | 161,115 | 84,074 | 8 | x |
| Ky. | 4,056 | 1,667 | 300,875 | 240,807 | 10 | x |
| La. | 2,040 | 1,002 | 147,536 | 119,100 | 10 | x |
| Maine. | 630 | 627 | 249,024 | 101,979 | 5 | x |
| Md. | 1,289 | 1,278 | 548,737 | 367,132 | 9 | x |
| Mass. | 1,963 | 842 | 524,350 | 402,756 | 16 | x |
| Mich. | 5,171 | 1,499 | 539,398 | 395,378 | 20 | x |
| Minn. | 3,859 | 901 | 240,893 | 223,673 | 11 | x |
| Miss. | 1,820 | 1,335 | 49,383 | 112,809 | x | 8 |
| Mo. | 4,560 | 3,318 | 551,144 | 544,875 | 13 | x |
| Mont. | 1,081 | 67 | 6,778 | 4,810 | 4 | x |
| Neb. | 2,103 | 616 | 81,809 | 42,018 | 6 | x |
| Nev. | 390 | 80 | 15,090 | 9,282 | 3 | x |
| N. H. | 297 | 240 | 113,228 | 53,955 | 4 | x |
| N. J. | 4,155 | 3,046 | 1,166,155 | 628,289 | 16 | x |
| N. M. | 915 | 454 | 87,446 | 63,195 | 4 | x |
| N. Y. | 11,132 | 9,010 | 3,322,907 | 2,241,928 | 45 | x |
| N. C. | 2,055 | 1,544 | 392,003 | 436,235 | x | 14 |
| N. D. | 2,316 | 436 | 24,519 | 16,351 | 4 | x |
| Ohio | 12,097 | 2,482 | 430,112 | 249,675 | 25 | x |
| Okla. | 3,212 | 2,754 | 350,740 | 309,833 | 8 | x |
| Ore. | 2,532 | 995 | 92,848 | 68,824 | 6 | x |
| Pa. | 8,808 | 6,361 | 1,780,205 | 1,457,575 | 32 | x |
| R. I. | 293 | 293 | 220,962 | 160,507 | 4 | x |
| S. C. | 1,580 | 1,470 | 74,455 | 130,335 | x | 8 |
| S. D. | 1,968 | 318 | 15,689 | 14,293 | 4 | x |
| Tenn. | 2,500 | 2,501 | 434,566 | 428,825 | 11 | x |
| Texas | 254 | 233 | 671,514 | 546,239 | 24 | x |
| Utah | 1,029 | 443 | 101,708 | 52,122 | 4 | x |
| Vt. | 246 | 219 | 77,354 | 26,890 | 3 | x |
| Va. | 1,876 | 1,726 | 338,020 | 228,420 | 12 | x |
| Wash. | 4,782 | 284 | 27,253 | 21,604 | 9 | x |
| W. Va. | 2,810 | 1,244 | 188,369 | 165,582 | 8 | x |
| Wis. | 3,349 | 2,206 | 591,618 | 380,609 | 12 | x |
| Wyo. | 683 | 190 | 8,263 | 4,815 | 3 | x |

—ELECTION—

## Adlai Concedes as President Piles Up Huge Vote Margin

By RICHARD WILSON
Chief of the Minneapolis Tribune Washington Bureau

WASHINGTON—President Eisenhower Tuesday won re-election by a landslide.

Adlai E. Stevenson, his Democratic opponent, early today conceded after the President had piled up an overwhelming lead.

Wilson

With a little more than one-half of the nation's 154,744 precincts reporting, the popular vote was:

**Mr. Eisenhower:** 17,201,077.

**Stevenson:** 13,010,764.

In electoral votes, Mr. Eisenhower led in 42 states with 470 votes; Stevenson in six with 61.

In 1952, Mr. Eisenhower's electoral vote victory was 442 to 89.

The Republican sweep may have carried also the house and the senate by relatively narrow margins. Incomplete returns left this outcome in doubt.

Mr. Eisenhower was receiving approximately 57 per cent of the vote on the basis of early returns. At the same stage in 1952 he had just under 53 per cent of the popular vote.

After the mounting Eisenhower lead reached landslide proportions, Stevenson issued his concession at 12:20 a.m. today.

Stevenson told a crowd of supporters in the grand ballroom of the Conrad Hilton hotel in Chicago he had sent the following telegram to President Eisenhower:

"You have won not only the election but also an expression of the great confidence of the American people.

"I send you my warm congratulations.

"Tonight we are not Republicans and Democrats, but Americans.

"We appreciate the grave difficulties your administration faces, and, as Americans, join in wishing you all success in the years that lie ahead."

The Democratic presidential candidate, defeated for the second time by President Eisenhower, thanked his supporters and his "gallant partner" Sen. Estes Kefauver, the vice presidential candidate.

"To you who are disappointed tonight, let me confess that I am, too," Stevenson said. "But we must not be downhearted, for 'there is radiance and glory in the darkness, could we but see and to see, we have only to look.'"

But, he said, "even more urgent is the hope that our leaders will recognize that America wants to face up squarely to the facts of today's world."

Stevenson said the people had made their choice "in a vigorous partisan contest that has affirmed again the vitality of the democratic process."

"And, I say God bless partisanship, for this is democracy's life blood," Stevenson said.

Stevenson cautioned his lesteners to "bear in mind" that in much of the world "partisan controversy is forbidden and dissent suppressed."

"So, I say to you, all of you everywhere, my dear and loyal friends, take heart—there are things more precious than political victory; there is the right to political contest," he said.

Stevenson said he had tried in his campaign to "chart the road to a new and better America." He said he was "supremely confident that our cause will ultimately prevail, for America can only go forward."

"We don't want to draw back from them," he said, "we can't. We are ready for the test we know history has set for us."

Stevenson ended his statement with this quotation from "A Wise Man"—"A merry hearth doeth good like a medicine, but a broken spirit drieth the bones."

"Although I lost the election, I won a grandson," he said in conclusion.

Shortly after Stevenson conceded, Mr. Eisenhower told a cheering Republican crowd at the Sheraton Park hotel here that he thanked "you Republicans, friendly Democrats and independents for this day."

He said he is going to work for 168 million Americans here at home and for peace in the world.

Mr. Eisenhower, smiling from ear to ear in response to a thunderous ovation, went before a Republican victory cele-

Election
Continued on Page Two

## *McCarthy Wins; Wier, Judd Lead in State Congress Race*

By ED GOODPASTER
Minneapolis Tribune Staff Writer

Roy Wier, third district Democratic-Farmer-Labor congressman, and Walter Judd, fifth district Republican, held leads early today in their attempts for re-election.

Goodpaster

But there still was an outside possibility for change in the outcome of both races.

In the other Twin Cities area congressional race, DFL Rep. Eugene McCarthy of the fourth district (Ramsey county) easily licked his Republican opponent, Edward Slettedahl.

Wier, 68, a house member since 1948, held about a 4-to-3 lead over Republican George Mikan with slightly less than one-quarter of the district's precincts reported.

Many of the districts were from north and northeast Minneapolis, where Wier traditionally has had strong support in labor wards.

Mikan, 32, attorney and former player-hero of the Minneapolis Lakers basketball team, was counting on suburban Hennepin county for much of his strength.

Judd, who has held the fifth district seat since 1943, topped the vote total of DFL candidate Joseph Robbie by about 14-to-9 with more than one-fifth of the precincts in.

McCarthy, a house member since 1948, was an easy winner.

With all but 30 of the district's 196 precincts totaled, he had a whopping 47,000-vote lead over Slettedahl, who in the past has been considered a member of the right-wing element of the GOP.

There were no immediate signs that other races would see any upset of the present lineup of five DFL congressmen and four Republicans.

In some cases, incumbents

Minnesota Congress
Continued on Page 15

## Almanac

### *This Girl's Not So Smart--She Didn't Register*

*Wednesday, Nov. 7, 1956*
Sunrise 6:59 a.m.; sunset 4:54 p.m.

One of our agents has a daughter, 6, who more or less by force of circumstances has been hearing considerable election talk, on and off television.

The family had guests the other evening, and when they were leaving the 6-year-old called:

"Goodnight! See you at the polls!"

•

The Turkish information office (an agent of the Turkish government) sends all editors the following on a note of patience worn thin:

"Although cartoonists almost always depict Turks as wearing fezes, it is illegal for anyone in Turkey to wear one—and has been since 1925."

## How Minnesota Voted

(*) Asterisk indicates incumbent

**PRESIDENT**
901 precincts of 3,859
*Eisenhower-Nixon (R) ..............240,893
Stevenson-Kefauver (D) ..............223,673

**GOVERNOR**
855 precincts of 3,859
*Orville L. Freeman (DFL) ............239,712
Ancher Nelsen (R) ...205,156

**LIEUTENANT GOVERNOR**
751 precincts of 3,859
*Karl F. Rolvaag (DFL) ............209,647
Leonard R. Dickinson (R) ..............171,246

**SECRETARY OF STATE**
734 precincts of 3,859
*Joseph L. Donovan (DFL) ............204,630
C. Elmer Anderson (R) ..............171,178

**STATE TREASURER**
706 precincts of 3,859
*Arthur Hansen (DFL) ............183,177
Val Bjornson (R) ....168,683

**ATTORNEY GENERAL**
680 precincts of 3,859
*Miles Lord (DFL) ...177,223
Keith Kennedy (D) ..164,778

**RAILROAD & WAREHOUSE COMMISSIONER**
657 precincts of 3,859
*Paul A. Rasmussen (DFL) ............181,724
W. Victor Lindquist (R) ..............139,982

**ASSOCIATE JUSTICE OF THE SUPREME COURT**
(Nominated without party designation)
For the post of Associate Jus-

How State Voted
Continued on Page 14

## Boy, 13, Stabs Self Critically

William Sederstrom, 13, son of Mr. and Mrs. William S. Sederstrom, 426 SE. Eighth street, was reported in critical condition Tuesday night with a self-inflicted stab wound in his left thigh.

Police said William accidentally stabbed himself with a small hunting knife at 6:40 p.m. while fighting with his brother, Denny, 12.

•

**ROOSEVELT RE-ELECTED**

LOS ANGELES, Calif.—(UP)—Rep. James Roosevelt (D., Calif.) was re-elected in the 26th district Tuesday.



## Election News Inside

MINNEAPOLIS TEMPERATURES

| | | |
|---|---|---|
| Midnight ..75 | 5 a.m. ....72 | 10 a.m. ...72 |
| 1 a.m. ....75 | 6 a.m. ....71 | 11 a.m. ...73 |
| 2 a.m. ....73 | 7 a.m. ....73 | Noon .....73 |
| 3 a.m. ....73 | 8 a.m. ....75 | *1 p.m. ...73 |
| 4 a.m. ....73 | 9 a.m. ....73 | *Unofficial |

1956 high, 78; low, 62. Precip. 12 a.m. to noon, 0.

# THE MINNEAPOLIS STAR

Thursday, July 4, 1957 LXXIX—NO. 190 Two Sections 54 PAGES ★

Single Copy Price 5c In Twin Cities Area 7c Elsewhere



# Kremlin Purge May Spread to Satellites

## Romanian Reds Oust 2 Leaders

*'Big K'—How Much Power Does he Seek? Page 4A*

From the Star Wire Services

An indication that the Kremlin purge announced Wednesday may have touched off a chain reaction in the satellites was given by Romania today.

Romania's ruling Communist party announced the ouster of two leading members of its politburo.

They are Iosif Chisinevsky, also fired from the post of secretary of the party central committee, and Miron Constantinescu, one of four first deputy premiers.

**The dismissals were announced in a communique of the Romanian party's central committee published simultaneously with the communique from Moscow announcing the removal of four top men from the Soviet party hierarchy.**

In Russia Nikita Khrushchev and his policies of peaceful coexistence abroad and government decentralization at home emerged victorious.

These policies and everything else the pudgy Communist party secretary stands for won the overwhelming approval of the Communist party central committee that ousted his bitterest, diehard Stalinist opponents for opposing the softer line Khrushchev laid down at the 20th party congress in February 1956.

The sweeping reshuffle of the party leadership also left Khrushchev surrounded by men — and one woman — identified as supporters of his policies.

Five men were dropped from the party's ruling presidium.

**Nine new faces, most of them previously of minor importance, were added, and the membership was expanded from 11 to 15.**

Specific charges against those ousted indicated a renewal of the Soviet drive for better relations with Yugoslavia and the West.

Moscow radio said their removal "constitutes a further major victory in the cause of peace and co-operation between nations" because they had "impeded the stronger affirmation of a policy of peace and active co-existence."

But Pravda, in an editorial just before announcement of

SHUFFLE
Turn to Page 6A

### -- BULLETIN --

**LONDON —(AP)— Russia followed up its Communist party purge of four top Kremlin leaders today by firing them from their government jobs.**

**Moscow radio said these men were dismissed from government posts: Georgi Malenkov, V. M. Molotov, L. M. Kagonovich and Dmitri Shepilov.**

FIRST WOMAN ever to be a full member of the ruling body in Russia -- the presidium of the central committee of the Communist party — is Ekaterina Furtseva. Mrs. Furtseva, in her late 40s, is regarded as a protege of Khrushchev. — AP Wirephoto.

From a print, Minneapolis Public Library

**Sign Here . . .** "When in the course of human events, it becomes necessary . . ." So reads the opening sentence of the Declaration of Independence—the historical document we are celebrating today. How some of the committee members discussed the document 181 years ago is shown in this detail from the famous painting by the American historical and portrait painter, John Trumbull. John Hancock, president of the continental congress, and Charles Thompson, secretary, signed the document on July 4, 1776. The idea that July 4 was the date of the signing by all the members of the congress arose from a mistake in the 1776 journals. It was not until Aug. 2 that it was ready for signing by all members of congress. (See Letters to Editor, Page 16A.)

★ ★ ★ ★ ★ ★ ★ ★

## Officers Save Car Rider From Bleeding to Death

Two Minneapolis policemen teamed up to save a man from bleeding to death after he suffered a deep cut in the throat in an accident at Twenty-seventh and Sheridan avenues N. at 2:15 a.m. today.

The injured man, Gary Olson, 22, 3006 Queen avenue N., was taken to General hospital in critical condition.

Four quarts of blood were administered to Olson to replace what he lost before Officers Thomas Seawell and Leonard Kuffel stopped the bleeding with hand pressure.

Sewell, on patrol alone, reached the scene first. He said Olson and his wife, Darlene, 19, had been to a party and that she, a novice driver, had taken the wheel for practice driving because there was little traffic.

Mrs. Olson turned from Sheridan onto Twenty-seventh and had trouble straightening out. Seawell said the machine made almost a "U" turn, jumped the curb and hit a pole.

Seawell

Olson's head crashed through the wind shield. From the broken glass he suffered a cut running from his left eye down the left side of his face to his throat.

**The glass cut deeply alongside his jugular vein, exposing the vein, Seawell said.**

Olson managed to get out of the car and staggered 20 feet to the sidewalk, then collapsed. Mrs. Olson became panicky.

Seawell, answering a call from neighbors, found Olson bleeding on the sidewalk. He called for an ambulance, then tried to stop the bleeding with finger pressure.

But Olson, becoming restless and panicky, was "jumpy" and Seawell said he couldn't keep him still to apply the pressure.

Patrolman Kuffel, off duty and returning with his wife from an outing, had seen Seawell speeding to the accident and turned around to follow and see if his fellow officer needed help.

He pulled up in time to assist Seawell, holding Olson while Seawell applied the pressure. A General hospital doctor arrived a moment later to clamp the cut.

Seawell said he charged Mrs. Olson with driving without a license.

JULY 4, 1776

## *New Nation Is Born and Gets No Mention*

PHILADELPHIA—(AP)—Thomas Jefferson noted in his account book that at 6 a.m. July 4, 1776, it was a "pleasant morning."

The temperature was 68 degrees. The wind was from the southeast. It was a nice summer day and Philadelphians thought little more about the date than that.

John Marie, a Paris tailor newly moved to Philadelphia, promised in the papers he could clean clothes without "the unnecessary trouble of ripping and washing."

**The Pennsylvania Evening Post considered the most important news of the day plans for the upcoming county election. Its four pages didn't even mention that the Continental congress was in session here.**

"Surgeon - dentist" Dr. L. Butte wrote he could clean false teeth "so radically that in half an hour they look white as snow."

A young boy was offered for sale as a slave in an ad that said he was "about four or five years of age and has had the smallpox and measles."

John Thompson advertised his lost two-year-old black mare colt with "a long black tail."

**It was such a quiet day that the Pennsylvania hospital did not make a single entry for a death, birth, admission or discharge.**

And what about Jefferson's day, after he entered the "pleasant morning" in his accounts book which that week included the price of a doll for his daughter and the payment for a "barometer, a thermometer, and one violin string"?

As usual he ate breakfast at the city tavern, "the most

NATION
Turn to Page 6A

## Pair to Tell Judge About Their 'Race'

Two young motorists were jailed on careless driving charges after Patrolman Earle T. Anderson caught up to both in what appeared to be a race along Minnehaha parkway at 1:30 a.m. today.

But one of the youths, Peter C. Metzer, 18, 2007 Aldrich avenue S., claimed he was trying to escape from the other driver and companions who, he said, "were trying to pick a fight."

Metzger and the other driver, Gordon W. Becker, 20, 1808 Fourteenth avenue S., will have a chance to tell their stories in traffic court Friday.

**Anderson said both cars were loaded with teen-agers. When he spotted the machines, on Minnehaha parkway at Cedar avenue, he said he clocked them at 70 miles an hour.**

The officer said both cars went through the stop signal at Chicago avenue. He stopped the cars at Portland avenue. Metzger's car was ahead of the other, he said.

• • •

Airman 1/c Howard McGivern, 21, 3878 Idaho avenue N., Crystal, was taken to Hennepin county jail on a drunken driving charge after a chase by New Hope police.

A. D. McLean, police chief, said McGivern's speed got up to 110 miles an hour over a three-mile course ending at Rockford road and Xenia avenue N., Robbinsdale.

McGivern, according to McLean, said his fast drive was the result of an argument with a girl friend.

## Senate Group OKs Federal Pay Raise

WASHINGTON — (UP) — A senate postoffice and civil service subcommittee today approved a bill to raise the pay of the federal government's 750,000 classified employes and 500,000 postal workers by 7½ per cent.

Under the bill, a majority of the postal employes also would receive temporary cost-of-living increases ranging from $80 to $240 a year.

### TWO *Exclusive Series*

• **ROBERT HEWETT**, concluding his articles about Germany Today, finds many Germans complaining that Americans in that country are acting "superior and standoffish." Page 20A.

• **JACK WILSON** reports that possible military uses of the space satellite are being studied. Such uses would include steering guided missiles from the satellite. Page 21A. Full page of satellite pictures and drawings in color on Page 1B.

## Tornado Damages 25 Houses in Iowa

DES MOINES, Iowa — (AP) — Two tornado funnels dropped out of a line of violent thunderstorms that crossed Iowa early today and caused widespread property damage.

Three persons were injured and an estimated 25 houses damaged at Lake City in west central Iowa. A second tornado swept across seven farms in the Odebolt area of Sac county.

## China Jet Crashes; Downed by Reds?

TAIPEI, Formosa — (AP) — The Chinese Nationalist air force said an F84 Thunderjet crashed into the sea today while on a patrol mission off the Red China coast.

Nationalist air force planes and naval ships rushed to the scene, in the Quemoy area, but found no trace of the pilot or the plane.

## Bus Flips; 20 Hurt

ORANGEBURG, S. C.—(AP)—A Queen City Trailways bus, en route from Augusta, Ga., to Fayetteville, N. C., overturned near here today, and 20 persons were reported injured. Five were hospitalized.

## Best Wishes to Ike

MOSCOW — (INS) — Kliment Voroshilov, Russian chief of state, telegraphed congratulations and best wishes today to President Eisenhower on the occasion of American Independence day.

## Hi, High -- Welcome, Fair Weather Friend

A high-pressure system, a rather rare event in these parts of late, promised today to clear it up and cool it off. Both are welcome.

The high this morning was moving east at a fairly rapid rate on the heels of a low which early today lay in a trough down western Minnesota. The rear-end collision of the two weather system developed showers and thunderstorms over a large portion of the area.

The shower belt appeared headed for eastern Wisconsin by tonight.

**A high, however, is the sign of fair weather, and that seemed to be next event on the program.**

The Twin Cities forecast is for fair and cooler tonight, Friday fair and little change.

The mercury, in the uncomfortable range the last couple of nights, is expected to drop to 58 tonight, and a high of about 80 is foreseen for Friday.

**The state prospect is for clearing and cooler this afternoon and tonight, Friday fair and mild.**

Winds which were running westerly at 20 to 30 miles an hour today were scheduled to diminish tonight.

The cooler and drier air brought in by the high pressure area is expected to bathe the entire five-state region by Friday.

## Car Runs Down Road Flagman

Matt Klingelhut, 65, St. Bonifacius, a flagman for a road construction crew, suffered fractures and cuts when he was struck by a car on highway 56 about eight miles north of Anoka at 1:45 p.m. Wednesday.

The driver, George Magnuson, 40, Anoka, drove over a hill and swerved in an effort to avoid the flagman. The car went into a ditch and rolled over, but Magnuson escaped injury. Klingelhut was taken to University hospitals.

## Woman Recluse Dies; Had $37,455

NEW YORK — (INS) — A woman about 70 who died on a New York street was found to have in her possession $11 in cash and bank books showing deposits of $37,455.70.

The woman was identified as Mrs. Margaret Baker.

## 2 Boys Die, One in Lake, 2nd in Pool

Two boys, an 8-year-old from Fergus Falls and a 7-year-old from near South Haven, Minn., drowned in swimming accidents Wednesday.

Gerald Wayne Frappier, the 7-year-old, drowned in Lake Augusta, near Annandale.

**He became panic-stricken while in swimming with his 13-year-old brother, who tried to rescue him.**

Their parents are Mr. and Mrs. Oliver Frappier, of near South Haven, on the west shore of Lake Augusta.

Gerald's body was recovered two hours later in water 30 feet deep.

Gerald, his brothers, Lauren, 13, and Richard, 10, and a neighbor, James Lobb, 13, were playing on a raft about 150 feet from shore when they decided to swim to land.

**Gerald was not a good swimmer and Lauren said he attempted to carry him piggyback.**

About 10 feet from the raft, Lauren said, he decided the distance was too great and turned back. Gerald became frightened and began to struggle, dragging Lauren under twice. The younger boy finally slipped from Lauren's grasp.

• • •

In the second drowning, pals of Eugene Vallevand, Fergus Falls were ready to go home from the Legion pool about 9 p.m. Wednesday when they missed Eugene.

His body was recovered from about eight feet of water.

Firemen worked in vain to revive the lad, son of Mr. and Mrs. Bernard Vallevand.

## TODAY'S ★ NEWS

Sprague

**KHRUSHCHEV**—Observers in Washington and in western Europe agree that the expulsion of four top Soviet officials from the Communist party leadership has made Nikita Khrushchev a far more powerful figure than he has ever been. They suggest that he now has the opportunity to build himself into a dictator. London newspapers warn, however, that the Communist party boss the West must now face will be tougher than the smiling Khrushchev who appeared on American TV screens recently. ★ Page 4A.

**ALGERIA**—Pentagon officials charge that France has used some American-supplied arms in Algeria despite an agreement that the weapons are to be used only in defense of the NATO area. Mansfield D. Sprague, assistant secretary of defense, says the United States is not "financing the civil war in Algeria." ★ Page 4A.

Knowland

**H-BOMBS**—Sen. Knowland (R., Calif.) says he doubts congress would readily agree to furnish Russia with information on how to make a "clean" hydrogen bomb. Democratic Sen. Mansfield of Montana declares, "I would be careful about giving our formula away." The senators commented on President Eisenhower's statement that some top nuclear scientists favor telling Russia and other nations how to make a "clean" bomb as soon as the United States proves it knows how to produce one. ★ Page 11A.

**NORWEGIAN SYNOD**—The Norwegian synod of the American Evangelical Lutheran church has submitted a referendum on a change of name to its congregations. Some delegates to the church's convention at Mankato claim that the Norwegian label in the name has been a handicap in mission fields. They suggest a change to "the Evangelical Lutheran synod." ★Page 18A.

Mansfield

**MIDDLE EAST**—York Langton describes the development of the United Nations police force in the Middle East as an important step toward world peace and suggests that the program be made permanent. Langton, regional vice president for the Upper Midwest of the American Association of the United Nations, told a Good Templars forum that it is vital for Americans to be well

• •

*Turn to Page 4A*

### INDEX



FORECAST
Fair and mild

Complete WEATHER NEWS on Page...... 6A

Television and Radio Logs on Page 27A

Fair
Minneapolis High, 65
TUESDAY TEMPERATURES

| | | | | | |
|---|---|---|---|---|---|
| 2 a.m. | 47 | 11 a.m. | 60 | 8 p.m. | 63 |
| 3 a.m. | 48 | Noon | 65 | 9 p.m. | 60 |
| 4 a.m. | 50 | 1 p.m. | 66 | 10 p.m. | 60 |
| 5 a.m. | 51 | 2 p.m. | 68 | 11 p.m. | 55 |
| 6 a.m. | 52 | 3 p.m. | 71 | 12M | 54 |
| 7 a.m. | 53 | 4 p.m. | 72 | 1 a.m. | 57 |
| 8 a.m. | 53 | 5 p.m. | 71 | *2 a.m. | 51 |
| 9 a.m. | 56 | 6 p.m. | 70 | *Unofficial | |
| 10 a.m. | 58 | 7 p.m. | 67 | | |

# Minneapolis Morning Tribune

Vol. XCI—No. 124



MINNEAPOLIS, MINN., WEDNESDAY, SEPTEMBER 25, 1957

Copy 5c In Twin Cities Area 7c Elsewhere



# U.S. Paratroopers Guard Little Rock School

## SEVEN MODERN MIRACLES

## Medicine Writes New Story of Hope

By VICTOR COHN
Minneapolis Tribune Staff Writer



In the medical city of Rochester, Minn., a Minnesota family doctor rose and addressed the fellow members of his state medical society.

He was Dr. Rolland Wilson of Winona, Minn., 45 miles east of Rochester, and he was making his presidential address as head of this group.

Rolland Wilson is a plain, unimposing-looking man who stands a bit bent behind plain, rimless glasses.

But the story he told was a very thrilling one.

"A number of years ago," he said, "while tramping through the woods with my two older sons, we came upon an old abandoned cemetery. About 50 per cent of the tombstones were dated 1904, and most of these were children. You knew there had been an epidemic of smallpox or diphtheria there that year."

And at least one death, probably, in almost every family.

Dr. Wilson's story was a story of old days of thousands and thousands of tiny white markers in America's cemeteries, and of how these days have passed. Conquered by medicine.

And in this story, at least to this listener, there seemed to be a modern miracle.

**"MIRACLE"** is a big word. Many people of course believe that only God works miracles, and perhaps this is true. It is certainly not the purpose of these articles to claim God's qualities for man.

But the total achievements of modern medicine show that in the human body and human abilities there are many miracles, just awaiting discovery — and my subject is to be how man has discovered some of them.

Take the story that Dr. Wilson told, which he told largely in terms of another doctor's practice—his father's.

"Yes," he said, "I knew medicine of 50 years ago, because I was brought up in a doctor's family. My father was born near a little village of 250 people in Winona county — one of 13 children.

"He grew up as a farm boy, learned the stone mason's trade, worked at that during the summer and in the north woods as a lumberjack during the winter. He had only an eighth grade education, married young and raised a family of six children.

"But he wanted to be a doctor, so for quite some time, at night, he read all the medical books he could get. He then started a sort of hang-around apprenticeship with a nearby country doctor."

**AFTER SOME** time this doctor suggested that Dr.

Miracles
Continued on Page Eight

## Senators Call Hoffa Parley Seat 'Illegal'

By CLARK MOLLENHOFF
Minneapolis Tribune Staff Correspondent

WASHINGTON — The McClellan labor racket committee Tuesday heard evidence challenging the "legality" of the election of a number of Detroit, Mich., delegates—including James R. Hoffa—to the Teamsters convention.

Chairman John L. McClellan (D., Ark.) and Sen. Karl Mundt (R., S. D.), declared the evidence showed a disregard for the Teamsters constitution in selection of delegates by Detroit Teamsters locals 299 and 337.

**THE FACTS** were developed as the chief counsel, Robert F. Kennedy, questioned two witnesses who said they are delegates to the Teamsters convention which will select a successor to Dave Beck, general president.

*(PUBLIC wants Hoffa out; ULTIMATUM Given Textile Union—Page 3).*

James Clift, a business agent for local 337, admitted there had been a meeting of a Teamsters executive board in February that "elected" seven delegates to the Teamsters convention.

However, he said that a general membership meeting is scheduled for tonight in Detroit for the purpose of "reconfirming" the election of the delegates.

**CHIEF COUNSEL** Kennedy then read from the Teamsters constitution which provides that the general membership meeting to elect delegates must be "at least 30 days

Hoffa
Continued on Page Six

## Ike Urges Arkansas to Obey Law

### Says Troops Will Be Withdrawn When Peace Is Restored

By RICHARD WILSON
Chief of the Minneapolis Tribune Washington Bureau

WASHINGTON — President Eisenhower broadcast an appeal to citizens of Arkansas to end the defiance of integration decrees.

"If resistance to the federal court orders ceases at once," he said, "the further presence of federal troops will be unnecessary and the city of Little Rock will return to its normal habits of peace and order and a blot upon the fair name and high honor of our nation in the world will be removed."

The President said our enemies are "gloating" over the Little Rock incident and portraying the United States as a violator of the standards we proclaim and subscribe to in the United Nations charter.

**AFTER** ordering Defense Secretary Charles E. Wilson to federalize the Arkansas national guard and send United States troops into Little Rock, the President flew to Washington from his vacation place at Newport, R. I.

He went to the White House and there addressed the nation.

The President said he had ordered in federal troops because a mob had gathered again at Central high school in Little Rock yesterday morning in another attempt to prevent carrying out the federal court desegregation order.

In these circumstances, he said, the president's responsibility "is inescapable." He said he had hoped that the "localized situation" would be brought under control by the city and state authorities, but this was not the case. Both the law and the national interest, he said, demanded that he take action.

**THE PRESIDENT** reviewed the Little Rock case, and he interpolated that in several other Arkansas communities integration has been carried out without trouble.

The President blamed "certain misguided persons, many of them imported into Little Rock by agitators" for defying the law.

He said that therefore the "very basis of our individual rights and freedoms is the certainty that the president and the executive branch of government will support and insure the carrying out of the decision of the federal courts, even when necessary with all the means at the president's command."

**HE ADDED:** "Unless the president did so anarchy would result.

"Mob rule cannot be allowed to override the decisions of our courts."

Mr. Eisenhower said the troops were sent in solely to prevent interference with orders of the court.

He credited most citizens of Arkansas with deploring "the call of extremists to violence. They do not sympathize with mob rule," he said.

If the defiance in Little Rock, he said, comes to an end "thus will be restored the image of America and of all its parts as one nation, indivisible, with liberty and justice for all."

TROOPS OF THE 101st AIRBORNE DIVISION ARRIVE IN LITTLE ROCK
*Regular army troops, they were sent to Arkansas from Fort Campbell, Ky.*

## All State Guards Called to Service

LITTLE ROCK, Ark. — (AP) — Paratroopers from the famed 101st airborne division took up stations around central high school Tuesday night while hundreds of Little Rock people looked on.

There was no immediate reaction from the crowd.

The troops rolled in convoy from Little Rock air force base shortly after dark.

The planes landed at midafternoon from Fort Campbell, Ky. An officer called the city hall and asked for, and got, permission to enter the city and for a police escort to handle the traffic.

Late last night a second 500 paratroopers arrived.

The new arrivals also separated into two groups and proceeded to the school and the armory.

An army officer said he did not know whether any more troops would be sent.

President Eisenhower took decisive action after racial violence and riots swept small parts of the city Monday and Monday night.

**THE PRESIDENT** ordered Defense Secretary Wilson to send in the troops and also to federalize the Arkansas national guard and call all the state's 9,900 guardsmen to duty.

Army Secretary Brucker said all Arkansas guardsmen were being ordered to report to their armories. He said probably only selected guard units will be needed for immediate duty in Little Rock.

Meanwhile, Mrs. L. C. Bates, president of the Arkansas branch of the National Association for the Advancement of Colored People, said: "If federal troops are there to protect the children, the Negro children will go to school tomorrow."

**THE ORDERS** to the troops will be: to insure enforcement of the federal court orders for racial integration at the 2,000-student high school.

Men on the street in Little Rock as well as state officials were shocked by the action federalizing the guard and sending in troops.

The total force, said to be 1,000, split—one group going to the high school and the other to the national guard armory.

The high school's handsome, stone facade was lighted and the lights from the jeeps and the 2½-ton trucks, carrying the paratroopers, gave the scene almost a wartime look.

A number of Negro paratroopers were seen in the trucks. As the units assigned to the armory drove away, it appeared that most of the Negroes went in those trucks.

**A TRAILER,** marked "explosives," and a weapons carrier came with the paratroopers.

All the troops are under the command of Maj. Gen. Edwin A. Walker, decorated combat soldier, who is commander of the Arkansas military district.

Walker

Walker served in the Pacific in World War II and in the Korean war.

Walker said: "I have been directed by the secretary of the army to assume command of the federalized Arkansas national guard and elements of the active army."

### Little Rock Stories Inside

*TEXT of President Eisenhower's Speech—Page 5.*
*BUTLER Calls South Third Party Possible—Page 7.*
*IKE ACTS to Show South He Will Enforce Integration—Page 13.*
*SOUTHERN Governors, Senators Assail Ike's Use of Troops—Page 13.*
*NO PRECEDENT Found for Ike's Guard Call—Page 14.*

## 4 Killed as Plane Crashes Into 3 Homes

DAYTON, Ohio —(AP)— An air force B26 twin-engine bomber, coming in for an emergency landing at Wright Patterson air force base here, Plunged 70 feet into a suburban housing development Tuesday, killing four persons and injuring at least one.

The plane ripped sections from two houses and demolished a third.

*(PICTURE—page 12.)*

Air force officials said the medium-sized bomber developed engine trouble immediately after takeoff and was returning to the base. Flying at 70 feet, officials said, the B26 suddenly veered to miss a high steel tower, but got its landing gear tangled in a high tension wire and crashed.

The plane's pilot and copilot and two occupants of the demolished house were killed.

The air force withheld names of the crew members pending notification of next of kin, but the other dead were identified as Mrs. Mildred Van Zant, about 40, and Walter Joseph Geisler, reported to be Mrs. Van Zant's brother-in-law.

### 2 Crewmen Die as Plane Hits 2 Homes

VAN NUYS, Calif. —(UP) — The pilot and co-pilot of an air national guard training jet plane were killed late Tuesday and a housewife narrowly escaped death when the plane crashed into two homes near Van Nuys airport.

The two victims were members of the 115th fighter squadron of the California national guard who had just taken off on a routine training mission. They were ejected from the plane but were still strapped in their seats when rescue crews reached them. Names were withheld pending notification of next of kin.

## Senate Probers Call 4 City Witnesses

By CLARK MOLLENHOFF
Minneapolis Tribune Staff Correspondent

WASHINGTON—Although the key witness, Benjamin Dranow, is ill there are four Minneapolis witnesses scheduled to testify today on the relationship of the store executive and James R. Hoffa, central states Teamster boss.

Dranow, chairman of the board of John W. Thomas and Co., entered Mount Sinai hospital, Minneapolis, last week-end.

**CHIEF COUNSEL** Robert F. Kennedy stated Dranow is the key witness in the exploration of loans of more than a million dollars which were made by the Michigan Conference of Teamsters and the Central Conference of Teamsters to the store.

Chairman John W. McClellan (D., Ark.) has arranged for a government doctor to examine Dranow to determine if he is in good enough physical shape to be forced to comply with a subpena this week.

(In Minneapolis Tuesday, Dranow's doctor said that consulation and examination with a government doctor "not only would not be resisted, but would be desirable.")

**IN THE TEMPORARY** absence of Dranow, the committee has subpenaed Jack L. Hudson, listed as president of John W. Thomas and Co., to testify on the details of the loans from the Teamsters union.

The other three Minneapolis witnesses are:

**Arthur Morgan,** former Teamsters union member, who was one of the key figures in efforts to oust labor racketeer Gerald P. Connelly from his position as secretary-treasurer of Teamsters local 548.

**Irving Nemerov,** a Minneapolis attorney who represented Gerald P. Connelly in February 1956, before Connelly's indictment on charges of bombing the home of one Teamster official and the automobile of another.

**Harold Sandahl,** a certified public accountant from Minneapolis who has done some accounting work for John W. Thomas and Co.

## Stock Market Regains Some of Monday's Losses

NEW YORK — (UP) — Stocks scored substantial improvement Tuesday.

The market regained about one-quarter of the $4,700,000 000 slashed from values in Monday's break which pushed industrial prices close to the Feb. 19 lows and cut rail prices back to the levels of November 1954.

Bargain hunters boosted prices sharply in the opening rush, then turned selective.

*(TABLES—Page 22.)*

## Woman Dies After Collision of Truck, Car

Mrs. Eileen Hopkins, 49, 3735 Rhode Island avenue, St. Louis Park, was injured fatally in a car-truck collision at 3:15 p.m. Tuesday at Excelsior avenue and highway 100 in St. Louis Park.

**SHE WAS** a passenger in a car driven by John Whale, 25, a houseguest at her home. He was uninjured.

The truck driver, Harold W. Gunter, 27, 2550 Dakota avenue, St. Louis Park, was treated for knee injuries at a clinic and released.

St. Louis Park police said an examination of the truck's brakes after the accident indicated they were not functioning properly.

**IMPACT** of the collision drove the car into another car driven by Fay Hamre, 60, Tyrol Hills. He was not injured.

Mrs. Hopkins died at Northwestern hospital soon after the accident. Police were investigating the cause of the collision.

Oscar Wendlandt, 60, died on a Blue Earth county road yesterday when his car skidded about 300 feet and tipped over into a ditch, Associated Press said.

The accident occurred a half mile east of Amboy, Minn., about 20 miles south of Mankato.

The Associated Press yesterday reported the death of Mrs. Dorothy E. Myers, 53, Annandale, Minn., in a traffic accident on highway 240, 2½ miles northeast of Annandale.

### AEC Reports Russ H-Blast

WASHINGTON—(AP)—The atomic energy commission (AEC) announced Tuesday night the Soviet Union has set off another nuclear explosion in its current series of weapons tests.

An AEC spokesman indicated the blast was that of a hydrogen bomb with an explosive force equivalent to a million tons of TNT.

## Witness Says Girard Left After Shooting

CAMP WEIR, Japan—(UP) — One of the key prosecution witnesses testified today William S. Girard, 22, disappeared shortly after he shot and killed a Japanese woman shell scavenger Jan. 30.

A new tempest was caused before the trial opened this morning when Judge Yuzo Kawachi, senior jurist of the three-man Meabashi district court, indicated to Japanese reporters present that the Ottawa, Ill., soldier may be let off with a light sentence.

**"I DON'T** think it was deliberate murder," Kawachi said.

Today's star witness was Hidetsugu Onozeki, 29, a farmer who was with Mrs. Naka Sakai, the victim of Girard's fire, at the time of the shooting. A first shot fired by Girard — he claims it was a warning shot — barely missed Onozeki.

Bareheaded and humble, Onozeki testified Girard ran to Mrs. Sakai when she fell, shook her and yelled, "Mama-San, Mama-San." But, he said, by the time a medic arrived to find her dead, Girard was nowhere to be seen.

**TUESDAY,** an American soldier who witnessed the shooting testified Girard beckoned to Mrs. Sakai, took careful aim and fired from a distance of approximately 13 yards.

The witness was Sgt. Victor N. Nickel, Inkster, Mich., who was assigned with Girard to guard United States army equipment on the firing range at Camp Weir last Jan. 30. He gave his testimony to a three - judge Japanese court which is trying Girard on a charge of causing bodily injury that resulted in the death of Mrs. Sakai.

Nickel

**THE COURT** session took place on the firing range. It was here Mrs. Sakai, 46, was shot fatally with an empty shell fired from a grenade launcher. She was picking up scrap metal at the time.

Girard, who denies he beckoned to Mrs. Sakai, told the court earlier yesterday that he held the rifle against his hip and fired into the air to frighten the metal pickers away from a machine gun.

Nickel said Girard placed the gun against his shoulder and aimed directly at the woman.

Nickel said he and Girard were in a foxhole near the machine gun. At Girard's suggestion he threw some spent shells out of the foxhole to entice the Japanese metal pickers closer.

Nickel said he stopped throwing the shells after Girard fired at a Japanese man, missing him.

Then, he said, Mrs. Sakai came near and Girard beckoned her toward the scattered shells saying, "Mama-san daijobu. Takusan, ne. (Mother, it's all right. There are plenty, aren't there?")

## 2 Youths Drink Antifreeze; In Critical Condition

BALATON, Minn. — (AP) — Two Balaton youths were in critical condition Tuesday after drinking what doctors said apparently was an antifreeze solution found in a wine bottle at a deserted farm.

The two, Richard Beert, 15, and Wayne Johnson, 16, became ill late Sunday and were hospitalized Monday. Authorities said a check with the owner of the farm revealed the solution had been used in a car radiator and was about three years old.

The youths had been in the company of three other youths, one of whom had tasted the liquid and spat it out. The other two did not touch it.

Beert was described as semi-conscious and unable to respond to conversation.

The Johnson youth, at Tyler, Minn., was said to be conscious, but suffering "very severe" kidney damage and double vision. Neither youth was able to retain anything in his stomach.

## Frost Flag Goes Up as Mercury Goes Down

The weather bureau color guard hoisted the frost and freezing flags for northern Minnesota Tuesday night.

Overnight lows were expected to hit 28 to 36 in the north and 36 to 45 in southern Minnesota.

Light frost was likely in western Wisconsin

The Upper Midwest will be generally fair and mild today.

Twin Cities high will be 65, low tonight 40. High Tuesday was 72.

### TURN THE PAGES TO:



## Almanac

### Space Man Will Have Safe Landing

*Wednesday, Sept. 25, 1957*
Sunrise 7:03 a.m.; sunset 7:05 p.m.

An accident-prone 18-months-old drove his mother frantic by falling over furniture, tumbling downstairs and generally bending himself out of shape.

On one of her many visits to the doctor to have the youngster's head stitched together again, the mother got some medical advice: Buy him a plastic space helmet."

She did. The kid falls just as frequently now, but hasn't sustained a scratch.

*Fair today in the Twin Cities. High will be 65, low tonight 40.*

Wilderness scene reported by a colleague just back from Bay lake near Deerwood, Minn.: A citizen laying sod in front of his lonely cabin.

Fair and Mild
Minneapolis High 70
FRIDAY TEMPERATURES
2 a.m. 51 10 a.m. 59 6 p.m. 63
3 a.m. 49 11 a.m. 62 7 p.m. 60
4 a.m. 47 Noon 65 8 p.m. 58
5 a.m. 45 1 p.m. 66 9 p.m. 57
6 a.m. 45 2 p.m. 66 10 p.m. 56
7 a.m. 45 3 p.m. 68 11 p.m. 54
8 a.m. 49 4 p.m. 68 12 M. 53
9 a.m. 54 5 p.m. 67 1 a.m. 52
*2 a.m. 51
*Unofficial
Details Page 6

# Minneapolis Morning Tribune

Vol. XCI—No. 134  MINNEAPOLIS, MINN., SATURDAY, OCTOBER 5, 1957 Single Copy Price 5c In Twin Cities Area 7c Elsewhere



# Russ Launch First Earth Satellite

## Bohn Found Guilty of Tax Evasion

### Sentenced on One of Two Counts in Gambling Case

By PEG JOHNSON
Minneapolis Tribune Staff Writer

David Bohn, alleged head of a big-time Minneapolis gambling syndicate, Friday was found guilty by a United States district court jury on two counts of gambling tax evasion.

The 41-year-old confessed gambler was charged with willful failure to pay some $15,000 in federal gambling excise taxes between July 1, 1955, and Feb. 27, 1957.

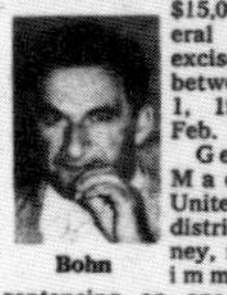
Bohn

George E. MacKinnon, United States district attorney, requested immediate sentencing on one count, charging Bohn has been taking wagers "up to and including the present time, even during his own trial."

**HE ALSO** charged Bohn "has been operating high, wide and handsome in this town for many years, and in very close association with higher-ups in the police department."

MacKinnon declared the circumstances of Bohn's arrest on a local gambling charge in July were "pretty phony, and would lead any reasonable person to conclude it (the arrest) was a framed-up deal to get some credit for the local police department."

The arrest by Minneapolis police morals squad officers led by Jake Sullivan, former head of the squad, came well after Bohn's indictment on the federal charge April 5, MacKinnon pointed out.

**BOHN WAS** fined $100 in municipal court on the local offense.

Federal Judge Edward J. Devitt, acting on the first count of the federal indictment, suspended imposition of sentence and placed Bohn on five years' probation.

Bohn, who lives at 3429 Major avenue N., Crystal, will continue to be free on $2 000 bond, but if he violates any local, state or federal law during that period, he may be sentenced to up to five years in prison and a $10,000 fine, Devitt specified.

**THUS,** even though Bohn now has a $50 federal occupational gambling stamp and says he pays the 10 per cent excise tax on all wagers, he cannot gamble in Minneapolis, where there is a municipal anti-gambling ordinance.

Devitt said he will sentence

Bohn
Continued on Page Eight

## Robbinsdale 70, Bloomington 0!

Roosevelt, Washburn and West Triumph

Buhl Faces Turley in 3rd Series Game

(DETAILS in Sports Peach)

## City Employes Cleared in Vaccine Case

Two suspended Minneapolis city employes Friday were cleared of charges that they helped drug salesman Edward W. Johnson divert public polio vaccine to private sources.

They are L. E. Belair, 2623 NE. Arthur street, city purchasing department employe, and Arnold Hillestad, 28, 1801 Irving avenue S., chief pharmacist at General hospital. Both were charged with malfeasance.

Belair was freed on a directed verdict of not guilty by Judge Harold N. Rogers following presentation of the state's evidence against him in Hennepin county district court.

**THE JUDGE** then dismissed the charge against Hillestad on the motion of County Attorney George M. Scott.

Rogers said he did not condone Belair's alleged act of giving city purchasing order blanks to Johnson so he could order vaccine at cheaper rates.

But he said the state's evidence did not indicate any injury to the city or intention of willful wrongdoing on Belair's part, and therefore a criminal charge was not warranted.

He meant no criticism of the grand jury which indicted Belair, the state public examiner's office or the county attorney's office, Rogers said. These agencies acted in good faith, he said, but he differed with them on the point of law involved.

**THE SAME** evidence and points of law were involved in the Hillestad case, Scott told Rogers.

Hillestad was to have been tried after Belair for allegedly accepting polio vaccine deliveries at General hospital pharmacy and transferring them to Johnson.

George Arneson, city purchasing agent, said Belair will be back on his job Monday. Donald Smith, General hospital superintendent, was out of town and unavailable for comment, but hospital officials had said previously

Vaccine
Continued on Page Six

UP FACSIMILE

**Satellite Talk** With the announcement that Russia has launched the first earth satellite, top Russian and United States satellite experts talked over the launching at a Russian embassy reception in Washington. Left to right are: A. A. Blagonravov, Russian academic commission; Dr. Joseph Kaplan, head of the United States Geophysical year program; V. V. Belovsov, vice chairman for the national commission in Russia, and Dr. Richard Porter, a member of the United States committee for the International Geophysical year.

## Flight of 'Moon' Beats U.S. by Many Months

By WILLIAM J. JORDEN
Special from the New York Times

MOSCOW—The Soviet Union announced Friday night (Minneapolis time) it had launched the first man-made satellite designed to circle the earth.

Moscow claimed it had won the race to be the first country to put such a scientific instrument into the outer reaches of space from which it will be possible to explore the earth, the atmosphere and the heavens.

The Soviet success in sending the tiny man-made device into outer space doubtless will be an embarrassment to American scientists who have been working on this problem. Not long ago the United States disclosed it had run into technical complications in its efforts to launch a man-made sphere and that our satellite would not be sent into space until next year.

The Soviet satellite is said to carry two radio transmitters which emit regular signals that can be heard on the earth.

The Soviet government said in an official announcement the satellite was launched yesterday.

The rocket that carried the satellite into space sped from the earth at a rate of five miles a second, the government news agency, Tass, said.

**(IN WASHINGTON** the defense department said last night the naval research laboratory had recorded three passes of the Russian satellite over the United States.

(The department said the laboratory, with its radio-tracking equipment, reported one pass seemed to be in the vicinity of Washington and two further west.

(In New York a Columbia university astronomer said the object should be visible to the naked eye at certain times of the day if the observer knew exactly where to look to spot the tiny object.)

**THE SATELLITE** is said to be circling the earth once every 95 minutes at a height of about 560 miles. The tiny globe is about 23 inches in diameter and the Soviet government said it should be visible with ordinary binoculars or telescopes when it reflects the rays of the rising or setting sun.

The man-made globe is reported to be moving in an elliptical course at a speed of about 17,000 miles an hour. Nothing was revealed concerning the material of which the Soviet earth satellite is made, but its over-all weight is reported to be about 180 pounds.

The Soviet government said its successful launching of the satellite was "a mighty contribution to world science and culture." It said the new device would have "huge significance for the knowledge of the nature of the cosmos and the study of the earth as a planet in our solar system."

**THE SOVIETS** said they would launch "several additional artificial earth satellites" during the International Geophysical year (IGY)

Satellite
Continued on Page Six

## 'U' Dean Says Russ Violated Spirit of IGY

By VICTOR COHN
Minneapolis Tribune Staff Writer



Russia has violated the spirit of the International Geophysical year (IGY) by refusing to give world scientists advance information on satellite plans, Dr. Athelstan Spilhaus of the University of Minnesota charged Friday night.

Spilhaus

Spilhaus, Minnesota technology dean, is a member of both the executive committee and the satellite panel of the United States IGY committee.

Here is how he detailed his charge:

"Four Russian participants are now at an international IGY conference in Washington, a conference called for the special purpose of co-ordinating rocket and satellite programs.

"I was there earlier this week, and we tried to get information from them on their plans, as we have tried before. And they wouldn't say a thing.

**"SO WHEN** they say they've sent up a satellite in accordance with international IGY agreements, that's not true at all—because the IGY agreement was that any nation launching a satellite would give others full advance information, for the fullest scientific benefit.

"It appears that the whole thing was done under cover by them just to beat the gun."

Spilhaus specifically accused the Russians of unwar-

Spilhaus
Continued on Page Six

## 20,000 Poles Riot, Ask for Ouster of Gomulka

WARSAW, Poland — (UP) —An estimated 20,000 Poles battled club-swinging police and militiamen Friday night in central Warsaw. Many of the rioters shouted for the downfall of Communist party chief Wladyslaw Gomulka.

Two separate clashes left a number of persons injured, including some women. It was the second straight night of rioting in the tense Polish capital.

**AN ESTIMATED** 1,000 steel-helmeted police and "workers militia" charged with clubs and fired tear gas bombs to try to break up the rioting. The mobs fought back with their fists, rocks and paving blocks.

Rioting flared viciously for three hours. Students surged into the streets and were joined by adults.

Pent-up fury burst after police moved to break up a student protest rally called at Polytechnic high school. The rally was called to condemn police treatment of students who demonstrated Thursday night against the closing of the anti-Stalinist student weekly, Po Prostu (Plain Speaking). The newspaper has been harsh in criticizing recent Communist party and government policy.

**THE FIRST** wave of students leaving Polytechnic auditorium last night was chased into side streets. Steel-helmeted riot police went in after them with clubs.

A new wave of students massed on the steps of the auditorium. A truck with Russian markings went by. The crowd whistled in derision.

The police moved in again, swinging clubs and throwing tear gas and noise bombs. Students kept up their taunting cry of "Gestapo, Gestapo."

Several students collapsed in the road.

**(WARSAW** radio announced last night that Poland's Communist party has ordered party penalties for card-carrying Communists on the banned newspaper's staff. The radio as heard in London quoted a communique saying the weekly was suspended for printing articles harmful to the regime but did not mention student protest demonstrations.

(The communique said the press censor's decision to ban Po Prostu was correct because it "presented the actual political and economic situation in the country in a false light and in many matters proclaimed bourgeois conceptions.")

As police charged with clubs to head off the demonstration, another crowd swiftly formed and marched to the central committee headquarters of the Polish Communist party.

Government forces tried vainly to stop the march on the headquarters. Fistfights broke out. Whistles and catcalls against the government spread.

## 400,000 Strike in Argentine Labor Crisis

BUENOS AIRES, Argentina—(INS)—A state of seige was proclaimed in Argentina Friday night after more than 400,000 workers went out on strike in a major labor crisis.

The government announcement followed reports the cabinet split over the extensive labor unrest surrounding the rising cost of living.

The latest to leave their jobs in support of pay raise demands were employes of Standard Oil and Shell Petroleum companies.



## Russ Satellite May Be Visible in Minnesota

Some of us may see the Russian satellite from Minnesota, but we may have to be lucky.

It will pass over much of the earth—traveling on a nearly north-south path, with the earth revolving beneath it.

The most favorable time for trying to see it will be at dawn and twilight, when the earth is semi-dark and the sun still shines on the

Sighting
Continued on Page Eight

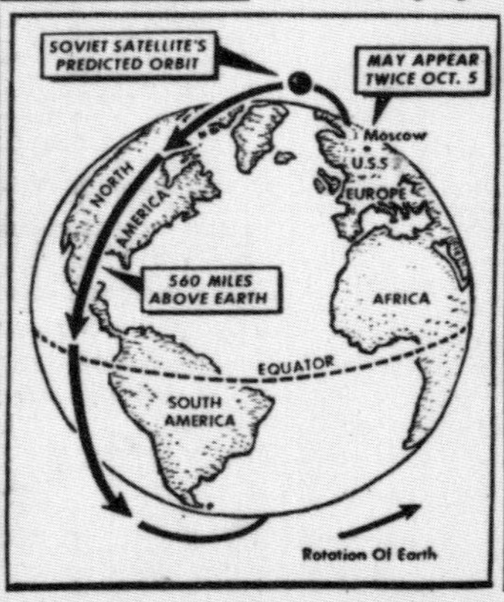


## Ideal Day Is Promised Ducks and Gopher Fans

The weatherman says it's going to be a good day for the Gophers and a bad one for the duck hunters.

Minnesota football fans sitting in Memorial stadium watching their favorites tangle with Purdue university today are assured of the same perfect weather that supported last week's triumph over University of Washington.

And the ducks—they will undoubtedly fly Minnesota air lanes at high altitudes when state hunters open fire at noon today.

It may be slightly cloudy in western portions of the state today, the weatherman reports. But with that possible exception our Indian summer will continue as is.

Fair and mild is the report for the Twin Cities today. High temperature will be 70, low 45.

Fair with little change in temperature is the report for Wisconsin.

Those headed in the direction of Milwaukee for the third game of the World Series can expect the same good play-ball weather.

## —Almanac—

### Penalize Him for 'Illegal Procedure'

*Saturday, Oct. 5, 1957*
Sunrise 6:16 a.m.; sunset 5:47 p.m.

Men attending a Red Cross meeting last Saturday were grumbling to themselves about missing the Minnesota-Washington football game.

Actually, the man scheduling the meeting had sought to avoid such a conflict. He consulted the Big 10 schedule and thought the game was in Seattle. Regrettably, he used the 1956 schedule.

*Continued fair and mild today in the Twin Cities. High will be 70, low 45.*

We don't know if this is a straw in the political wind or not. A teletype machine at the Tribune was pecking off the standard test line, "The quick brown fox, etc.," then paused and launched a new one: "William Jex quickly caught five dozen Republicans."

## Senate to Probe 'Abuses' in State Farm Elections

By Staff Correspondent of the Minneapolis Tribune

WASHINGTON — Senate agriculture committee investigators have been ordered to Minnesota to check on alleged abuses in recent farmer-committee elections.

Ellender

Sen. Ellender (D., La.), now on a trip in eastern Russia, cabled instructions for Harker Stanton, committee counsel, and staff member Henry Casso to look into charges made by Gov. Orville Freeman.

**THE GOVERNOR** charged last week-end that the Sept. 12 election of township agricultural stabilization and conservation (ASC) committees had been marred by irregularities.

Freeman, in a letter Tuesday to state ASC chairman Floyd Sjolander, Dawson, said the irregularities included more than one ballot being mailed to some farmers, insufficient identification on ballots and mailing of some ballots with only a township number for return identification.

Freeman and Sen. Hubert H. Humphrey (D., Minn.) asked for the senate committee investigation.

**THE FREEMAN** charges brought a reply from George Etzell, state Republican national committmen, who called them "malicious" and said the governor had not furnished evidence to the state ASC committee to back his charges.

Stanton said yesterday he and Casso will go to Minneapolis this week-end and will talk to Freeman, Humphrey and other officials about the charges. He said the first check would be a "preliminary" one to see how much more work, if any, is needed.

Stanton said he also expects to talk to Sen. Edward J. Thye (R., Minn.), like Humphrey a senate agriculture committee member.

## 'Moon' Launching 'Opens New Era'

### 'Let's Be Glad It's Been Done,' Says U.S. Scientist

From the Tribune Wire Services

"This opens a new era in science," one American scientist commented at Washington on hearing the Soviet announcement of the launching of an earth satellite.

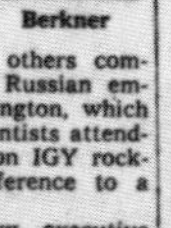
Berkner

L. V. Berkner, vice president for the international Geophysical year (IGY), added: "Let's be glad it has been done."

Berkner and others commented at the Russian embassy at Washington, which had invited scientists attending the 13-nation IGY rocket-satellite conference to a cocktail party.

Hugh Odishaw, executive director of the United States committee for the IGY, termed the launching "of great scientific interest" and urged the Soviets to supply details of their scientific experiments.

Dr. Richard Porter, a member of the United States committee for the IGY, was asked at Washington about the announcement.

"I believe it," he replied. "What other comment is possible?"

Asked when this country plans to launch its satellite, Porter answered: "Who knows? Maybe in two months; maybe a year."

Another member of the United States IGY committee, P. H. Wyckoff, said: "We are all elated that it is up there. They have been very good to us, telling us about the frequencies and other information about tracking the satellite. We are very happy for them."

Dr. Joseph Kaplan, chairman of the United States national committee for IGY, said, "It certainly is the most interesting experience of my life."

He added: "I am amazed that in the short time which they had to plan—obviously not any longer than we had—I think it was a remarkable achievement on their part.

"From the point of view of international co-operation the important thing is that a satellite has been launched. They did it and did it first.

"I hope they give us enough information so our moon watch teams can help learn the scientific benefits."

The chief of Japan's largest meteorological observatory, Dr. Maaji Miyaji, said no observatory in Japan would observe the Russian satellite because it would have no "scientific value."

"I am not observing the satellite," he said, "and I have no plans to do so in the

New Era
Continued on Page Eight

### SATELLITE FACTS AND FIGURES

MOSCOW —(UP)— Here is data on the Soviet satellite:

**Size:** 23 inches in diameter.

**Weight:** 187 pounds.

**Speed:** 17,000 miles an hour.

**Estimated life:** Not more than three weeks.

**Altitude of orbit:** 560 miles high.

**Signals:** Two radio transmitters sending signals at 20.005 and 40.002 megacycles, strong enough to be picked up by ham operators.

**Visibility:** Best at sundown and sunset with naked eye.

**Rotation:** Circles earth once every one hour and 35 minutes.

**Thunderstorms**
**Minneapolis High, 90**
MONDAY TEMPERATURES

| | | | | | |
|---|---|---|---|---|---|
| 2 a.m. | 78 | 10 a.m. | 81 | 6 p.m. | 95 |
| 3 a.m. | 78 | 11 a.m. | 81 | 7 p.m. | 93 |
| 4 a.m. | 76 | Noon | 86 | 8 p.m. | 92 |
| 5 a.m. | 76 | 1 p.m. | 88 | 9 p.m. | 87 |
| 6 a.m. | 75 | 2 p.m. | 88 | 10 p.m. | 85 |
| 7 a.m. | 75 | 3 p.m. | 85 | 11 p.m. | 84 |
| 8 a.m. | 76 | 4 p.m. | 90 | 12M | 83 |
| 9 a.m. | 78 | 5 p.m. | 94 | *1 a.m. | 82 |

*Details Page 12* *Unofficial

# Minneapolis Morning Tribune

Vol. XCII—No. 38  MINNEAPOLIS, MINN., TUESDAY, JULY 1, 1958  3-3111 5c In Twin Cities Area 7c Elsewhere

# Senate Votes Statehood for Alaska; Ike Gets Bill

ALASKA GOV. MIKE STEPOVICH RAISES ARMS IN VICTORY
*Key senate supporters of Alaska statehood bill celebrate with 49-star American flag*

UPI TELEPHOTO

## President May Sign Act Today

**By CHARLES BAILEY**
**Minneapolis Tribune Staff Correspondent**

WASHINGTON—The senate Monday night passed and sent to the White House a bill to admit Alaska as the 49th state of the Union.

The historic vote—paving the way for creation of the first new state since the admission of Arizona and New Mexico in 1912—came on a 64-20 roll call after a week of debate.

In winning the senate floor fight, statehood backers successfully fought off a series of amendments, points of order and other moves that would have tied up or killed the bill.

The measure approved by the senate was identical in language to that passed last month by the house. This action avoided a parliamentary snarl that could have strangled the bill in the few remaining weeks of the session.

**THE BILL,** which will probably be signed by the President today or tomorrow, does not automatically transform Alaska from a territory into the largest of the states.

Alaskans must vote in a special election and approve the provisions of the bill, including a controversial land withdrawal for the defense department.

If this approval is granted, the territory becomes a state, and its citizens will elect two senators and one representative before Dec. 1.

*(MAP, OTHER Stories — Page 8.)*

**APPROVAL** of the bill was a smashing victory for the President, who counted Alaskan statehood high on his list of legislative "musts."

It touched off a riotous celebration that stretched from congress to isolated villages in Alaska's frozen northland. And it sparked prompt demands for similar statehood status for Hawaii.

Alaska Gov. Mike Stepovich, almost overcome with tension, shouted "Thank God for everything that's happend here. We will show the people of the United States they have not made a mistake."

**DELEGATE** E. L. Bartlett, democrat who represents Alaska in the house of representatives predicted Alaskans will accept terms of statehood by possibly as much as 8 to 1 margins.

Thirteen Democrats and seven Republicans voted against passage of the statehood bill. All of the Democrats except Sen. A. S. (Mike) Monroney of Oklahoma were from southern states.

Voting to make Alaska the 49th state were 31 Democrats and 33 Republicans.

Managers of the bill in the senate started work a week

**Alaska**
**Continued on Page Eight**

## How Alaska Can Become a State

Before Alaska can become a state, these procedures must be met:

**The President** must sign the bill. By Thursday, he must inform the Alaska governor that the bill has been enacted.

**Alaskans must** approve provisions of the bill in a special election.

**Alaska voters must** nominate and elect two senators, a representative, governor, secretary of state and state legislators.

**The governor must** certify election and referendum results to the President.

**Then Mr. Eisenhower** can issue his official proclamation making Alaska the 49th state.

# Fox to Sue Adams and Five Others for $6,000,000

**By CLARK MOLLENHOFF**
**Minneapolis Tribune Staff Correspondent**

WASHINGTON—Financier John Fox said Monday he'll file libel and slander suits against Sherman Adams and five other of his "enemies" for one million dollars apiece.

Fox said his lawyers will file the suits today because of "scurrilous" statements concerning the charges he made against presidential assistant Adams and Boston, Mass., financier Bernard Goldfine.

AP WIREPHOTO
**JOHN FOX**
*'How silly can you get?'*

Fox's charges were made during three days of testimony before the house investigating subcommittee.

Besides Adams, Fox said, the suits will be aimed at Roger Robb and Samuel Sears, lawyers for Goldfine; Robert B. Choate, publisher of the Boston Herald-Traveler; William J. Dempsey, attorney for the newspapers, and Boston Herald-Traveler Corp.

**WHITE HOUSE** press secretary James Hagerty said Adams would have no comment. But Hagerty asked: "How silly can you get?"

Meanwhile, speaker Sam Rayburn (D., Texas) rejected a Republican effort to get house action on a resolution to censure and discredit the Harris subcommittee.

A resolution by Rep. Thomas B. Curtis (R., Mo.) was ruled out of order by Rayburn, who declared this attack on the subcommittee was the first he had seen in his 25 years in the house.

**CURTIS HAD** charged that the subcommittee, headed by Rep. Oren B. Harris (D., Ark.), had violated the rules of the house in taking public testimony from Fox which tended to "defame, degrade and incriminate" Adams.

Harris answered that his subcommittee abided by house rules. He said all the testimony given by Fox was direct evidence that would be admissible in a federal court against Goldfine, the Boston textile and real estate millionaire.

Harris also said he had cautioned Fox against going into some of the testimony relative to what Goldfine had allegedly told Fox about paying for securities and a house for Adams.

**HARRIS SAID** he did not approve or condone the fact that Fox had "blurted out" some testimony that he had been cautioned not to give in the open hearing.

Curtis charged the testimony amounted to a "smear" of Adams, which he contended the committee should have avoided by hearing Fox in a closed session.

Although Rayburn rejected the effort by Curtis to get an immediate vote on the censure resolution, Curtis proceded to put the resolution in the house hopper, and it was referred to the rules committee where it is expected to die.

The move by Curtis represented only one of the many prongs of the Republican administration offensive against the Harris subcommittee.

**THE FACT** some of the statements by Fox could not be substantiated gave hope

**Adams**
**Continued on Page Six**

# Russ Agree to Attend Atom Talks

### Reds Switch Stand, Limit Discussions to Test Detection

**Special From the New York Times**

GENEVA, Switzerland — The Soviet Union, in a reversal of its past position, agreed Monday to enter into technical talks with the West on detection of atomic weapons tests.

As a result talks between scientists of four western and four communist nations will begin here today.

The Soviet agreement was announced by Dr. Y. K. Federov, head of the Soviet delegation of scientists, following a two-hour conference with Dr. James B. Fisk, chairman of the western scientific group.

**FEDEROV TOLD** reporters it had been agreed that talks would begin today and that discussions would be limited to technical problems of detecting atomic tests.

The Soviet Union therefore had apparently acceded at least momentarily to the long-held position of the United States that talks should be restricted to technical aspects of detecting atomic tests and not go into the broader political question of an international agreement to suspend atomic tests.

Conflicting Soviet and United States positions on this political issue had left the fate of the talks in doubt until the very eve of the scheduled conference.

Only last Wednesday the Soviet Union had declared the talks would be useless unless the United States agreed in advance that their goal was a cessation of atomic tests. Without such an assurance, the Soviet statement noted, the Soviet Union could not send its delegates to the conferences.

**THIS PAST** Soviet insistence upon prior western commitment to agree to the atomic test ban was not evidenced yesterday by Soviet officials.

Reporters asked if it had been agreed that the talks would be concerned only with technical problems of monitoring a ban on atomic testing.

Fisk, standing alongside Federov, quickly replied, "Yes."

Federov, speaking through an interpreter, replied that,

**Nuclear**
**Continued on Page Six**

U.S. PLANS NEW SCRAP PROBE

# Court Says MacKinnon Erred; Isaacs Conviction Set Aside

**By RUSSELL HURST**
**Minneapolis Tribune Staff Writer**



Clifford Janes, acting United States district attorney, said Monday his office will investigate whether Harry Isaacs, president of American Iron & Supply Co., Minneapolis, had any connection with $99,000 in payments listed by the firm as "business expenses."

Janes' statement came after the United States circuit court of appeals yesterday set aside Isaacs' conviction for contempt in St. Paul federal court for refusing to tell a grand jury who received the money.

The appeals court held that:

**George MacKinnon,** former United States district attorney, erred in telling Isaacs before the grand jury that Isaacs had no right to plead the fifth amendment unless he was guilty of a crime.

**Federal Judge** Dennis F. Donovan had no authority to extend Isaacs immunity from prosecution when he ordered Isaacs to testify in open court regarding the payments.

The court said it was "possible" that Isaacs received part of the $99,000 himself and failed to report it for federal income tax purposes.

**JANES REFERRED** to this phase of the opinion in announcing his office will try "to see if there was any unlawful concealment, and, if so, what connection Isaacs had with it, if any."

The appeals court laid emphasis, however, on MacKinnon's contention that Isaacs waived his privilege of claiming possible self-incrimination by asserting he was not guilty of any federal offense. Judge Donovan also apparenttly held this view, the court said.

"Such an interpretation," the court added, "would unduly abridge and render ineffectual the protection guaranteed by the Constitution, which manifestly protects the innocent as well as the guilty.

**"THE ARGUMENT** implies that testimony will never tend to incriminate an innocent person. Guilt or innocence is usually a question to be determined by a jury, and we may take judicial notice of the fact that many an accused person on trial is found to be not guilty."

On the question of the grant of immunity, the appeals court said such a grant "was not within the judicial power but was an attempted exercise of executive or legislative power."

The $99,000 was paid during a period when Twin City Rapid Transit Co. was converting from streetcars to buses.

Isaacs' firm was a principal buyer of scrap metal and

**Isaacs**
**Continued on Page Six**

## Court Refuses to Intervene in Little Rock

**By RICHARD WILSON**
**Chief of the Minneapolis Tribune Washington Bureau**

WASHINGTON — The supreme court Monday declined to exercise its right to review directly the lower court decision postponing school desegregation in Little Rock, Ark. for 2½ years.

The reason given was that the circuit court of appeals has plenty of time to act on a stay of the federal district court decision before the opening of the school year this fall.

In the event the decision by Judge Harry J. Lemley halting integration is sustained, the petitioners, the National Association for the Advancement of Colored People (NAACP), still could attempt to bring the issue before the court again.

**IT IS POSSIBLE,** however, that enough time might be absorbed so as to make it difficult to change Little Rock school board plans. In any event, this point might be argued if the case does get up to the supreme court.

The high court, in another ruling before its summer adjournment, struck down a $100,000 fine levied against the NAACP by an Alabama judge. The judge imposed the fine on the ground the NAACP was in contempt for failing to comply with an order to produce a list of its members.

The supreme court ruled unanimously that such lists are immune from state scrutiny. However, the NAACP was told to appeal to state courts first from an order barring the organization from operating in Alabama.

**OBSERVERS** here thought the court's refusal to act directly and immediately in the new Little Rock case might have a tendency to impress the judges of the circuit court.

The point involved would be that if the supreme court did not act at once in this case, it might be suggested that the Lemley decision falls within the court's dictum of "deliberate speed" in desegregation.

At least it can be argued that the court saw in the Lemley decision no outrageous wrong which could not be remedied in time enough.

The court, in an unsigned opinion, said, "We have no

**Court**
**Continued on Page Six**

## Russia Favors Meetings With Slavs on Loan

LONDON —(UPI)— The Soviet Union today proposed negotiations with Yugoslavia on 285 million dollars in credits which the Kremlin previously announced were suspended.

The proposal, coming as a surprise to western observers, appeared to be a sudden softening in the Kremlin's attacks on Yugoslavia's Marshal Tito for his determination to follow his own "independent" line of Communism.

Moscow radio said the proposal was contained in a Russian note sent to Yugoslavia June 28 and published today in Moscow newspapers.

Russia pointed out an earlier note to Tito's government had suggested revisions in existing economic agreements, including the postponing of one loan for several years. Russia received no reply to the suggestions, the new note said.

"The Soviet government suggests that talks of representatives of both governments should be held as soon as possible to introduce modifications into the agreement," Moscow radio quoted the note as saying.

## Hot Weather Will Remain in Twin Cities

Monday's damaging storms will give way today to a bit more normal weather in the Upper Midwest.

But it's going to stay hot, and scattered showers and thunderstorms will continue to dapple most of the area.

The Twin Cities and Minnesota can expect to get a little wet now and then. Skies will be variably cloudy.

High temperature will be 90 in the Twin Cities, 75 to 95 in Minnesota. Highest reading in Minneapolis yesterday was 95, for the second consecutive day.

**SCATTERED** rainstorms also threaten South Dakota, North Dakota and northern, western and central Wisconsin today.

Highs will be 80 to 95 in South Dakota, 75 to 85 in North Dakota and 76 to 93 in Wisconsin.

Punishing storms cut a wide path of destruction from eastern North Dakota southeastward through Minnesota Monday, Associated Press reported.

Several tornadoes were reported sighted during a weather bureau alert covering a 120-mile-wide area from Alexandria, Minn., to Eau Claire and Green Bay, Wis.,

**Weather**
**Continued on Page Six**

## Almanac

### She Saved the Best Until Last

***Tuesday, July 1, 1958***
**Sunrise 5:30 a.m.; sunset 9:03 p.m.**

A carload of Sullivan lake folks went to the drive-in movie at Garrison, Minn., and, at half-time, ordered a batch of hot dogs.

One of the women, munching away in the darkness, complained that her sandwich was rather dry. When she finished, she felt something solid in the bottom of the bag.

It was the wiener.

•

***Variable cloudiness and hot today in the Twin Cities, with occasional showers and thunderstorms. High will be 90, low tonight 70.***

•

The Eau Claire, Wis. Daily Telegram received a complaint that curbside mail boxes for motorists are unfair to foreign car owners, who can't reach them without getting out of their eentsy vehicles.

AP WIREPHOTO

**Dig It, Queen** Attired in white coveralls, black rubber boots and a miner's helmet, Queen Elizabeth of England rode an elevator 1,700 feet underground to watch coal miners at work. She splashed through puddles and was pelted by dripping water. Miners cheered the queen and Prince Philip.

**Showers**
Minneapolis High, 65
WEDNESDAY TEMPERATURES

| | | | | | |
|---|---|---|---|---|---|
| 2 a.m. | 53 | 10 a.m. | 53 | 6 p.m. | 57 |
| 3 a.m. | 55 | 11 a.m. | 54 | 7 p.m. | 56 |
| 4 a.m. | 55 | Noon | 56 | 8 p.m. | 56 |
| 5 a.m. | 55 | 1 p.m. | 57 | 9 p.m. | 55 |
| 6 a.m. | 55 | 2 p.m. | 57 | 10 p.m. | 55 |
| 7 a.m. | 55 | 3 p.m. | 58 | 11 p.m. | 53 |
| 8 a.m. | 54 | 4 p.m. | 58 | 12M | 52 |
| 9 a.m. | 53 | 5 p.m. | 57 | *1 a.m. | 51 |

Details Page 18 *Unofficial

# Minneapolis Morning Tribune

MINNESOTA HISTORICAL SOCIETY

Vol. XCII—No. 138 Copyright 1958 Minneapolis Star and Tribune Company MINNEAPOLIS, MINN., THURSDAY, OCTOBER 9, 1958 FE 3-3111 5c In Twin Cities Area 7c Elsewhere

# POPE PIUS XII DIES AT 82

REPORT RECOMMENDS:

## City Must Build Rooms for Men From Skid Row

By FRANK WRIGHT
Minneapolis Tribune Staff Writer

Minneapolis must build at least 1,250 new single room units to house skid row residents displaced by the lower loop redevelopment.

Construction must be completed before demolition of skid row begins, perhaps next spring.

The job probably will require some public financial aid because most of the people of skid row can afford only the cheapest housing.

These are the principal recommendations in the most extensive report to date on characteristics and relocation needs of lower loop residents.

The report is based on a survey made for the city housing and redevelopment authority by the University of Minnesota sociology department and the authority staff, with the assistance of the federal census bureau.

**THE RESEARCHERS** will present the 213-page report formally to the five-man commission which runs the authority at a 10:30 a.m. meeting Friday, according to chairman S. L. Stolte.

Contained in the report, seven months in the making, is a tentative list of six areas suitable for construction of the new housing facilities. The boundaries:

**One**—N. 18th Av., 3rd St., N. 22nd Av. and 2nd St.

**Two**—Northwest corner of the redevelopment project.

**Three**—Nicollet island.

**Four**—S. 14th Av., 4th St., S. 11th Av. and a line between S. Washington Av. and 2nd St.

**Five**—E. Franklin Av., S. Clinton Av., E. 16th St. and S. 5th Av.

**Six**—S. 11th Av., E. 14th St., 10th St., Centennial Pl., Chicago Av. and 8th St.

Lower loop redevelopment plans call for the authority to buy 70 acres of blighted property, clear it and resell it to private builders for office buildings and a variety of other uses.

**COST OF BUYING** and clearing the land is estimated

Loop
Continued on Page 11

### Yanks Tip Braves 4-3 to Tie Series

Weary Spahn Loses in 10th Inning

Spahn

Burdette to Face Larsen or Kucks Today

*(DETAILS in Sports Peach.)*

### Winter's Hint Will Not Be Mild

Colder temperatures and occasional showers are forecast for the Twin Cities tonight. During the day the prospect is for little temperature change and cloudy skies.

The high will be 65, low 38. Wednesday's top reading was 59. Northwesterly winds at 20 to 30 miles an hour are expected tonight.

### The Year of the SPUTNIK

## Despite Price, Russia Leads in A-Power

By VICTOR COHN
Minneapolis Tribune Science Reporter
Copyright 1958 Minneapolis Star and Tribune Company

Russia intends to lead the world in developing power from the atom—electrical power and political power—though the human price may be heavy.

Here are the flamboyant ways Russia is exploiting the atom and a glimpe at the human price:

1 Russia is ahead now with the biggest atomic power station. It is also holding closely to what seems to be the most ambitious A-power program.

This is not what many news reports said during the recent Geneva atomic meetings. It was widely and sometimes gloatingly reported that Russia was "falling far short" of its goals.

The whole story was heard only in a last-day talk after most people had left. The fact is, they still intend to cook with uranium.

2 In scientific development of A-power techniques they are not leading. The United States is. But they are wielding what they have politically and for propaganda with telling effect, and willing to do things we consider "too expensive."

They consider it worthwhile, in other words, to have a grand power program, even if it does not pay for itself—even if it is another drain on the average Russian's standard of living. One reason is to say to the backward and uncommitted world: "We lead in atoms-for-peace."

3 They are moving fast scientifically. Here, too, they mean to catch up.

The setting in which all this is taking place tells of the human price. The setting is backward Russia.

The science city of Dubna—it is a key scientific center—is 74 miles from Moscow. To drive to it you allow at least two hours. The roads are not American roads.

You pass through Moscow quickly, by car. For a city of millions, it is surprisingly small, because

Sputnik
Continued on Page Four

*EDITOR'S NOTE: Victor Cohn, Minneapolis Tribune science writer, has returned from five weeks in Russia as the first American reporter to make an extensive tour of Russian centers of physical science, followed by two weeks at last month's Geneva atomic energy conference. This is his fourth in a series of articles on Russian science.*

Cohn

## Premier of Lebanon Quits Post

### Coalition Rises in Parliament to Foster No-Confidence Vote

BEIRUT, Lebanon — (AP) — Lebanon's Premier Raschid Karami handed his resignation to President Fuad Chehab Wednesday night.

It was not known immediately whether Chehab accepted it. Karami, leader of the rebellion in Tripoli, Lebanon, has been premier only two weeks.

Karami

Karami's action followed refusal of 31 deputies in the Lebanese parliament to give him a vote of confidence.

The deputies signed a petition declaring no-confidence and parliament speaker Adil Osseiran submitted it to President Fuad Chehab.

New disorders have broken out in the capital.

**CHRISTIAN** Phalangist foes of Karami charge that more than 100 of their followers had been kidnaped. Lebanese security forces took up new positions between the Phalangist and Moslem sectors of the city yesterday. It appeared they had the situation in hand.

More than 1,000 Phalangists, demonstrating against Karami's pro-Nasserism, clashed with Lebanese security forces on the road to Damascus, Syria. Seven women were reported shot in the melee that followed, one fatally.

**THE POLITICAL** move against Karami was taken by members of the National Liberal party, headed by ex-President Camille Chamoun, the Bekaa bloc and the Social National party.

The 31 signers represent almost half the deputies in the 66-man parliament.

Karami, a Sunni Moslem holding the premier post traditionally given to a Moslem of his sect, was a rebel leader in Tripoli in last summer's campaign to unseat Chamoun and ex-premier Sami Solh.

### Almanac

#### Tot Fears Mom Won't Have Room for Her

*Thursday, Oct. 9, 1958*
Sunrise 6:21 a.m.; sunset 5:39 p.m.

A Glen Lake woman was named room mother of her daughter's kindergarten class. She assumed the girl would be delighted but instead, got a flood of tears.

"I don't want you to be mother of all those other kids," she wailed. "I want you to stay home with us."

*Colder temperatures and showers are forecast for the Twin Cities tonight. High will be 65, low 38.*

A lad less buffaloed by semantics is the Crystal 5-year-old whose mother said the baby-sitter wouldn't be able to come that night. "You see," mother explained. "Diane turned her ankle."

"Which way?" the kid demanded.



**Will Jones Tries Poetry and Jazz in Greenwich Village**
—Page 34

POPE PIUS XII GIVING BLESSING
*Portrait was made in 1945 during a Vatican audience*

POPE OF PEACE

## Pius XII Sought Justice, Opposed Three Dictators

NEW YORK—Pope Pius XII was known as the "Pope of Peace."

He had taken for his motto "opus justitiae pax"—"the work of justice is peace."

He was a gentle, esthetic Italian of aristocratic birth and intellectual features.

But his reign as spiritual leader of the world's Roman Catholics was marked by continuous struggle toward his goals of world peace and social justice based upon Christian principles.

One after another he opposed Mussolini, Hitler and Stalin and their different forms of totalitarian aggression.

He acted with the wiles of a remarkably skilled diplomat.

**HE WAS A MAN** of great piety who believed in efficacy of work and faith. He spent two hours daily in meditation and prayer.

Many of his innovations led some to refer to him as the "modern" pope.

Tall and very slender, he looked as though the weight of his robes was too much for his frail shoulders. But his bright brown eyes sparkled behind the glasses he habitually wore at his desk.

His day was a long one—from 18 to 19 hours. Seldom did he retire to his plain brass-knobbed bed before 1 or 2 a.m.

The formality of his office required that he eat alone, but his company was a little finch he had rescued from the garden.

It hopped on the table, picking up crumbs.

He was the first pope to use an electric razor, and the finch perched on his wrist as he shaved.

He also was the first to write his speeches and church documents on a typewriter, using a white portable which he operated deftly.

**WHEN HE WAS** papal secretary of state, he was the first future pope to fly in a plane.

In that office, he was instrumental in having installed the Vatican's first broadcasting station, and was the first pope to witness a television demonstration as well as first to use the telephone regularly.

He answered the telephone and announced his own outgoing calls with the same simple formula.

"Pacelli here."

In his early days, Pope Pius enjoyed smoking, but gave it up when he felt it affected his throat and marred the resonance of his voice.

He was reported to have been a violinist of "more than ordinary merit."

**MOST PONTIFFS** merely walked in the garden for exercise, but Pope Pius had a completely fitted gymnasium with rowing machine and electric horse which he used early in his reign.

Later he limited himself to milder exercises.

His audiences were marked with simplicity in contrast with the practice of previous pontiffs.

He spoke fluently in six modern languages — Italian, French, German, Spanish, Portuguese and English, and could exchange greetings with callers in a number of others.

He also spoke Latin and Greek.

**HIS ELECTION** as pope, the 262nd successor to St. Peter as bishop of Rome, took place in March 1939, six months before the Nazi inva-

Biography
Continued on Page 15

## Archbishop: World, Church Lose Leader

Archbishop William O. Brady of the St. Paul archdiocese said Wednesday night the pope's death "will be recorded as a great loss to the world and to the church."

"For 19 years he has been the spiritual leader of the Catholic church," he said. "For much longer he was priest in his native Rome, a friend of youth, a counsellor to religious and, at the same time, developed his character and his skills and language and diplomacy for the international work of peace to which his life and regime were dedicated.

Archbishop Brady

"**WE HAVE** lost a good man and a holy man as well as a good pope and world citizen.

"For me there is a personal loss also. It was Pope Pius XII who appointed me bishop in 1939, the first bishop to be put in charge of a diocese in the United States following his election as pope. He appointed me archbishop of St. Paul, recently granted me the sacred palium, appointed me assistant at his throne and six times received me in private audience.

"**HIS WORK** has been worldwide, but it has also been a personal work the ending of which will bring grief to millions."

Archbishop Brady last saw the pope in August when he and Bishop Leonard Cowley accompanied Mr. and Mrs. I. A. O'Shaughnessy, St. Paul millionaire philanthropists, to Rome to receive high papal awards for their charities.

## 2 Strokes Bring His Death in Summer Home

CASTEL GANDOLFO, Italy—(AP)—Pius XII, for 19 troubled years the "pope of peace," died today in the papal summer castle alongside Lake Albano.

A crucifix lay on his chest and a rosary in his hands in the final hours.

Two strokes, developing into a grave condition of the heart and lungs, carried him away under the weight of his 82 years.

The Vatican radio said death occurred at 8:52 p.m. Wednesday Minneapolis time.

The announcement of death was made by a Jesuit priest, the Rev. Francesco Pellegrino, who had broadcast developments from an ante-chamber of the pope's death room for the past two days.

He said: "With soul profoundly saddened we give you now, at 3:56 a.m. the following announcement: The holy father, Pius XII, is dead. Pius XII, the man most esteemed and venerated in the world, one of the greatest pontiffs of the century, passed away in saintly manner at 3:52 today."

### Funeral to Be at Vatican

Eugene Cardinal Tisserant, dean of the college of cardinals, made the official recognition of the pope's death.

He entered the death chamber, lifted a white cloth that covered the pope's face, and announced to other cardinals present that Pius XII was dead. Then the fisherman's ring, symbol of papal power, was removed from the pope's hand.

Usually the official recognition is made by the papal chamberlain. Pope Pius XII died without appointing a chamberlain.

The body will be borne back to Vatican City, 18 miles from Castel Gandolfo, for the funeral rites.

He was the 261st pope and the first to die outside Rome since the 18th century.

The new pope will be designated by the college of cardinals in an election expected to be held at the Vatican within the next two or three weeks—after a nine-day period of mourning.

All the popes for the last 400 years have come from Italy. The feeling at the Vatican has been that this likely will be the case again, even though Italians no longer command a majority in the college of cardinals.

### Held Audience Last Sunday

His valiant heart, grieved by years of war and the onslaughts of Communist atheism, finally gave way after a period of more than 12 hours in which doctors despaired of saving him.

In 1953 and 1954 his stamina had overcome serious illnesses, but this time his age and the two strokes affecting his circulatory system were too heavy a burden.

He had spent a strenuous summer at this papal summer estate.

Last week he had a recurrence of gastritis and hiccups, accompaniments of the illness that took him to the verge of death in December 1954.

The pope showed some improvement, and last Friday warmly welcomed Francis Cardinal Spellman, heading a pilgrimage of 600 New Yorkers. Doctors continued to urge him to rest, and asked him to conserve his strength by not talking at one audience. He continued active, however, and held an audience Sunday.

That night, while being treated for his stomach ail-

Pope
Continued on Page 15

### Stories and Pictures on Inside



## Prophecy: New Pope Will Be Pastor, Sailor

VATICAN CITY —(AP)— "Pastor et nautus"—shepherd and sailor.

This was St. Malachy's prophecy, made more than 800 years ago, for the next pope.

Several Roman Catholic prelates measure up to it. Among them are:

Gregory Peter Cardinal Agagianian, member of the congregation of the holy office.

Eugene Cardinal Tisserant, dean of the cardinals.

Monsignor Giovanni Battista Montini, archbishop of Milan.

One of them may be the next pope. But the college of cardinals may make a choice not immediately obvious. For once the cardinals retire in solemn conclave to the Sistine chapel, Vatican sources emphasize, it would be foolhardy to try to guess who will emerge as pope. In the past, many ballots often were needed before a new pope was named.

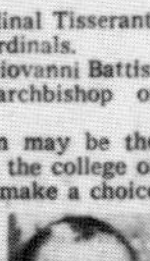

Cardinal Tisserant

Cardinal Agagianian

Monsignor Montini

The new pope must be elected by a majority of one more than two-thirds of the cardinals present.

**ST. MALACHY**—born at Armagh, Ireland, in 1094—journeyed to Rome to prophesy characteristics of the popes to be elected from 1143 onward. Many of the prophetic forecasts he made were apt.

Pius XI, a dauntless mountain climber, was described as fides intrepida—intrepid in the faith.

The description for Pius XII

Successor
Continued on Page 15

**Colder, Snow**
**Minneapolis High, 5**
THURSDAY TEMPERATURES

| | | | | | |
|---|---|---|---|---|---|
| 2 a.m. | 13 | 10 a.m. | 22 | 6 p.m. | 27 |
| 3 a.m. | 15 | 11 a.m. | 23 | 7 p.m. | 26 |
| 4 a.m. | 16 | Noon | 25 | 8 p.m. | 26 |
| 5 a.m. | 18 | 1 p.m. | 27 | 9 p.m. | 25 |
| 6 a.m. | 18 | 2 p.m. | 28 | *10 p.m. | 25 |
| 7 a.m. | 18 | 3 p.m. | 28 | *Unofficial | |
| 8 a.m. | 19 | 4 p.m. | 28 | | |
| 9 a.m. | 21 | 5 p.m. | 28 | | |

*Details Page 10*

# Minneapolis Morning Tribune

Vol. XCII—No. 223 MINNEAPOLIS, MINN., FRIDAY, JANUARY 2, 1959 FE 3-3111 5c In Twin Cities Area 7c Elsewhere



# Castro's Forces Push to Cinch Control of Cuban Government

CUBANS CELEBRATED BATISTA'S DOWNFALL BY TAKING OVER BUS IN HAVANA AP WIREPHOTO

## 3 Policemen Killed, 20 Hurt in Rioting

HAVANA, Cuba—(AP)—The dictatorship of Fulgencio Batista collapsed Thursday and partisans of rebel leader Fidel Castro immediately moved in to seize the reins of government.

President Batista fled into exile before dawn and by nightfall Castro's men held virtual control of this capital. The rebel radio in eastern Cuba announced his forces had entered Santiago de Cuba, the nation's second city.

Reports were current here that Castro would arrive at any hour.

Some of Castro's followers embarked on a wild orgy of celebration, looting, burning and killing in Havana. They killed at least three policemen and wounded 20.

**POLICE SHOT** down at least 10 looters, then other Castro partisans took a hand in restoring order and the violence began to wane.

For the moment, Cuba was without an established government. Justices of the supreme court refused to accept the oath of a provisional president, Justice Carlos Piedra, unless Castro approved.

*(PROFILES of Batista, Castro and Urrutia—Page 5.)*

Castro held out for recognition of Manuel Urrutia, longtime Cuban judge and Castro supporter, as head of government.

In the wake of Batista's flight with hordes of his supporters, Castro's men were racking up victory after victory.

**THE REBEL** radio confidently broadcast pronouncements which virtually set up a provisional government.

Castro named Col. Ramon Barquin, just released from a political prison, as chief of the armed forces as soon as the revolutionary movement takes over officially. He also named rebel leaders to various other commands inside or near Havana.

Barquin, a former Cuban military attache in Washington, had been imprisoned on the Isle of Pines. He was reported to be at Camp Columbia, the army headquarters in Havana, talking with Castro by radio about a nationwide cease-fire.

By nightfall there was virtually no government in Cuba except Castro's.

**A GENERAL** strike ordered by the rebels after Batista's

Cuba
Continued on Page 10

## Six Die in State Traffic

### New Year's Eve Crash at Canby Kills Father, 2 Children

By Associated Press

Traffic deaths in Minnesota's long New Year holiday week-end Thursday stood at six, three of them members of the same family.

Latest death was that of August Ostendorf, 74, Melrose, Minn., killed there at 8:45 p.m. Thursday when he was struck by a hit-and-run auto while crossing a highway in town. There were no witnesses.

Four of the deaths occurred in the waning hours of the old year, bringing the state's 1958 traffic toll to 699, up 14 from the previous record high set in 1957.

Killed in a New Year's eve crash near Canby, Minn., were Raymond DeJong, 42, Montevideo, Minn., a son, Roger, 8, and a 1½-months-old DeJong baby.

**HOSPITALIZED** at Canby were Mrs. DeJong and four other DeJong children, Leonora, 13, Carl, 11, Sheryl, 9, and Darold, 5. Mrs. DeJong was reported in serious condition. The children were listed as fair.

The highway patrol said a car driven by DeJong was struck from behind by a car driven by Ernest B. Erickson, 46, Dawson, Minn.

The collision sent both vehicles into the ditch, causing the DeJong car to roll over several times. Erickson and a passenger, Ezra Knowles of Dawson, were treated at the hospital and released. The accident occurred about 10 p.m.

**KILLED** in a New Year's morning accident was Glenn French, 21, Anoka. His car plunged off highway 169 in Brooklyn Park about 1:35 a.m. and smashed into a tree. French was alone in the car.

John Brandt, 8, of rural Windom, Minn., was killed New Year's eve when he stepped from a car into the path of an oncoming machine on a foggy country road about two miles east of Windom.

## Coya Files Vote Contest But May Not Press It

WASHINGTON —(UPI)— Rep. Coya Knutson (D., Minn.) said Thursday she has filed a notice of contest against Odin Langen, the Republican who won her house seat, but that she does not know yet whether she will press it.

Mrs. Knutson earlier filed an election complaint against Langen, charging that his Republican backers made unfair use of her husband's "come home, Coya" campaign and thus defrauded the voters.

This complaint was rejected by a special house elections committee. However, an election contest, in event Mrs. Knutson decided to press it, would be handled by a different committee and under different procedure.

Mrs. Knutson, packing yesterday in preparation for vacating her congressional office suite, said she filed the notice of contest with Langen some time ago to protect her rights.

Under the law, such a notice must be filed by the loser with the winner within 30 days of the determination of the election outcome.

Under the complicated and time-consuming election challenge procedure, an election contest winds up eventually in the house administration committee. After hearings, that committee can recommend to the house either that the apparent winner be affirmed in his seat or that he be turned out and replaced with the loser.



## Get Ready: First '59 Cold Wave Seen

Another big cold wave will swoop across the Upper Midwest today, putting an abrupt stop to mild weather and replacing it with temperatures far below zero in some sections.

Overnight readings were predicted to slip all the way to 15 below in northwestern Minnesota and 20 below zero in northwestern North Dakota.

**ONLY LIGHT** snow is expected to come with the mercury drop, but the flurries will be carried by winds 30 to 50 miles an hour.

Light snow mixed with rain or freezing drizzle prompted the weather bureau to issue a hazardous driving warning for Wisconsin Thursday night.

Winds 40 to 50 miles an hour whipped snow squalls into blizzard conditions last night in the Red River valley.

Blizzards also are forecast for the Black Hills of South Dakota today.

**WINDS SHOULD** die down by tonight, but temperatures will stay cold.

Highs will be 5 above in the Twin Cities, 5 below to 5 above in Minnesota, zero to 10 below in North Dakota and South Dakota, 10 to 30 in Wisconsin.

## 7 Dead, 28 Injured in Japanese Crash

TOKYO—(Reuters)—Seven persons were killed and 28 injured Thursday when a bus with 43 passengers left the road and plunged into a valley while on a New Year's tour to a shrine near Wakayana prefecture.

## Iowa, Sooners, LSU Win in Bowl Games

*Iowa's Rose Bowl victory was a work of pure football artistry. There was superb team effort, and dazzling individual play, says Dick Cullum.*

**In the Orange Bowl,** Oklahoma coasted to a 21-6 victory over Syracuse.

**In the Sugar Bowl,** Louisiana State had a tougher time than expected but beat Clemson 7-0.

**In the Cotton Bowl,** Air Force academy and Texas Christian University tied 0-0.

*(DETAILS in Sports section.)*

*(ROSE PARADE Is 'Fabulous'—Page 13.)*

SURVEY FINDS

## N.Y. Police Oppose Hoffa Union Drive

Special From the New York Times

NEW YORK—Members of the New York police force appeared Thursday, almost without exception, antagonistic to James R. Hoffa's campaign to bring them into the International Brotherhood of Teamsters.

Of more than 50 policemen questioned in random interviews only one said he was receptive to the idea. A dozen said they might sign up if the organizing drive were conducted by some union other than the racket-ridden Teamsters.

Nearly half of those interviewed expressed resentment at the system by which Police Commissioner Stephen P. Kennedy is the sole arbiter, from whom there is no appeal, of their grievances.

**THEY ENDORSED** the demands of the Patrolmen's Benevolent association (PBA) and other police organizations for a better grievance procedure.

Some said most of the sentiment for unionization would disappear if Mayor Robert Wagner would appoint an impartial arbiter to review the commissioner's labor relations decisions.

Several of the PBA members said that organization might represent them more effectively if it had a civilian head who could "talk up better to the commissioner" than a member of the force might dare to.

A similar sampling showed that policemen throughout the metropolitan area were mostly hostile to the Hoffa drive. There was, however, strong support in Nassau county for some sort of police union that could bargain more effectively than a benevolent association.

**THE BOARD** of governors of the Nassau county PBA will consider Monday offers from four different unions—not yet identified publicly—to organize the police force.

## Almanac

### Trick Ad Puts Family Out on a Limb

*Friday, Jan. 2, 1959*
Sunrise 7:52 a.m.; sunset 4:42 p.m.

An Edina family is victim of one of the most fiendish practical jokes we've heard of in some time. Someone put a want ad in the Edina Courier which said: "Wanted: your old Christmas trees. 65c upon delivery."

The ad then listed the number of the victims' phone, which has been ringing like all the bells of Christendom ever since.

*Cold wave, occasional snow flurries and northerly winds 20 to 40 miles an hour today in the Twin Cities. High will be 5 above, low tonight 10 below.*

And a bachelor friend has wondered what the current crop of kids is coming to ever since he passed the shop on 10th St. with this sign in the window: "We have emotional toys."

## Castro Man Takes Post as Envoy to U.S.

WASHINGTON—(AP)—Collapse of President Fulgencio Batista's government in Cuba forced Ambassador Nicolas Arroyo to resign Thursday and put a rebel-backed career officer in charge of the embassy.

Earlier in the day, rebel supporters in the Washington area made a friendly invasion of the Cuban embassy.

**THEIR LEADER,** Ernesto Betancourt, Washington representative for Fidel Castro, said they wanted Dr. Emilio Pando, embassy economic counselor, put in charge as provisional ambassador.

Pando

Arroyo then telephoned Roy Rubottom, assistant United States secretary of state for inter-American affairs, to tell him he was resigning and putting Pando in charge of the embassy.

Betancourt and half a dozen other rebels sat around one of the embassy offices at the entrance to the building. On the third floor, where Arroyo lived with his wife and young son, servants were busy moving trunks around and piling books onto tables.

Despite the circumstances, there were courteous relations between the rebels and the embassy people being put out of jobs.

**"OUR MAIN** concern here is that everything develops in an orderly manner and all Cubans hope for early restoration of normal conditions in our country," Pando said.

The state department, obviously worried about reports of street rioting in Havana, kept in close communication throughout the day with the United States embassy in Havana, but said it had no plans to remove United States citizens from the island republic.

President Eisenhower, vacationing at his Gettysburg, Pa., farm, was kept advised of developments by telephone. The only official comment from the President's press secretary, James C. Hagerty, was this:

"There is no danger or reports of danger to American citizens in Cuba."

## Batista Says Castro's Guerrilla Tactics, Arms Were Decisive

CIUDAD TRUJILLO, Dominican Republic — (AP) — Fulgencio Batista said Thursday Fidel Castro's guerrilla warfare and superior armament, as Batista called it, forced him to give up the fight in Cuba.

The overthrown Cuban president reached exile here yesterday. This country is ruled by Batista's good friend, dictator Rafael Trujillo.

A reporter asked Batista how it had been possible for a handful of rebels to grow in two years into a force big enough to topple the entrenched Batista regime.

Batista said Castro got the jump on the government by restricting his activities to guerrilla warfare against rural soldiers not trained for that type of fighting.

By the time the rebels moved into the open in eastern Cuba, he said, they had attracted many more adherents and were superior in armament to Batista's army.

The rebels received a continuous flow of arms while government troops could not be supplied, Batista said.

(UNITED STATES arms aid to Batista had been cut off in recent months. But he had obtained supplies elsewhere. Batista did not mention in the interview that his forces, heavily outnumbering Castro's soldiers, were backed by planes and tanks, which the rebels lacked.)

Showing his weariness, Batista stopped for a cup of coffee on arrival before going to a hotel.

Seven of Batista's eight children were accounted for in exile.

He said he was glad to be here but regretted the em-

Batista
Continued on Page Nine

## Cuban Refugees Flee to U.S. by Airliners, Small Boats

By Associated Press

By the score, henchmen of fallen Cuban President Fulgencio Batista followed him into exile Thursday, many of them to this country. Some of the refugees commandeered an airliner to New York at gun point.

Refugee-laden planes from Havana landed in New York, New Orleans, La., and Jacksonville, Fla. Police found guns aboard at least two of the aircraft.

Two planes carrying 66 refugees landed at New Orleans; 54 more landed at Jacksonville.

Other refugees fled to the Florida keys by boat. A dozen persons landed from Batista's yacht, others in a converted PT boat. More than 70 others were reported aboard an auto - passenger ferry that plies between Havana and Key West, Fla.

**THE BIGGEST** furor occurred with the arrival at Idlewild airport in New York of Batista refugees among a planeload of 92 passengers from Havana.

*(PICTURES—Page 8.)*

Police forced back a horde of angry, shouting Castro sympathizers who sought to

Refugees
Continued on Page 10

RIOTERS SMASHED HOTEL CASINO IN HAVANA UPI RADIOPHOTO

**Partly Cloudy**
Minneapolis High, 40

THURSDAY TEMPERATURES

| | | | | | |
|---|---|---|---|---|---|
| 2 a.m. | 30 | 10 a.m. | 31 | 6 p.m. | 36 |
| 3 a.m. | 30 | 11 a.m. | 33 | 7 p.m. | 35 |
| 4 a.m. | 29 | Noon | 34 | 8 p.m. | 33 |
| 5 a.m. | 29 | 1 p.m. | 35 | 9 p.m. | 33 |
| 6 a.m. | 29 | 2 p.m. | 37 | 10 p.m. | 32 |
| 7 a.m. | 29 | 3 p.m. | 38 | 11 p.m. | 32 |
| 8 a.m. | 29 | 4 p.m. | 40 | 12 M | 32 |
| 9 a.m. | 30 | 5 p.m. | 38 | *1 a.m. | 32 |

*Unofficial

Details Page 14

# Minneapolis Morning Tribune

Vol. XCII—No. 293

MINNEAPOLIS, MINN., FRIDAY, MARCH 13, 1959

FE 3-3111 5c In Twin Cities Area 7c Elsewhere





# Hawaii Is Voted Into Union as 50th State

## The Steps Toward Statehood

WASHINGTON—(AP)—Hawaii could be a full-fledged state with two senators and a representative in Washington before congress quits this summer.

It would take some rather fast action. President Eisenhower has 10 legislative days (these don't include Sundays) to sign the bill after it is formally presented to him. He may get the bill today.

The governor of Hawaii, William Quinn, has 30 days after formal notification of the President's approval in which to issue a proclamation of elections.

The primary election could be held no less than 60 days or no more than 90 days after the proclamation.

A general election could be held no later than 40 days after the primary.

Once the results of the election are officially certified to the President, he would issue his proclamation admitting Hawaii as the 50th state.

AP WIREPHOTO

**CHESTER KAHAPEA, 13, SOLD EXTRA OF HONOLULU STAR-BULLETIN**
*The extra was on the streets immediately after congress voted statehood for Hawaii*

## 2 Elections Now Must Be Held

By CHARLES BAILEY
Minneapolis Tribune Staff Correspondent

WASHINGTON—After 40 years of saying "no," congress relaxed Thursday and let the Hawaiian statehood bill ride through to passage as smoothly as an ocean wave rolling into Waikiki beach.

The bill that will make a state out of the Pacific island chain passed the house of representatives on a lopsided roll-call in midafternoon. It had been approved by an even wider margin in the senate Wednesday night.

**ACTUAL FORMAL** admission of Hawaii as the 50th state in the union may not come until summer or fall, since the authorizing law requires holding of two elections before the President can issue his proclamation of admission.

*(PEARL HARBOR RAID Ended Idyllic Life in Hawaii; WILLIAM QUINN, Governor of Hawaii—Page 2.)*

But the step will be taken in 1959, making this year a statehood double - header, since Alaska was admitted formally in January.

The two former territories thus will have entered the union almost together, just as was the case in the last previous addition to the union in 1912, when Arizona and New Mexico were admitted.

On the final house roll-call, the tally was 323 to 89; 203 Democrats and 120 Republicans voted for the bill, with

Hawaii
Continued on Page 11

NOISE, KISSING AND DANCING IN STREETS

## Gay Hawaiians Hula Into Union

From the Tribune Wire Services

HONOLULU, Hawaii — They danced the hula in the streets Thursday night.

Hawaii—a melting pot of many races — celebrated congressional acceptance of statehood.

**JUBILANT** islanders lit bonfires. They set off firecrackers. They whooped it up in a noisy climax to a 40-year quest for admission to the union.

Street dancing began at sunset at 14 places in and around Honolulu.

The acting governor, Edward E. Johnston, called an immediate holiday.

"This is the biggest day in Hawaii history," said Johnston, sitting in for Gov. William Quinn, who is in Washington.

When the roll call vote began in the house, in Washington, Quinn left the gallery and went to the office of Sam Rayburn, speaker of the house.

**QUINN PUT IN** a phone call to Johnston, asking him to hold the line. When the roll call recorded 219 ayes — a majority of the house — Quinn shouted: "Sound the sirens! Close the schools! Get going!"

Within 15 minutes the whole town of Honolulu went crazy. Schools, shops and offices were closed. Traffic was virtually halted by the dancing and kissing in the streets.

Almost all work was suspended except in newspapers, radio stations and a few key spots.

Streets in downtown Honolulu were reminiscent of V-J day in 1945. Girls were hugging and kissing strange men. Everyone was exchanging leis. Confetti and serpentine tape were pouring out of windows. And above all there was noise. Happy noise.

Boat whistles, police sirens and a huge replica of America's Liberty bell joined the clamor made by auto horns, church bells, whistles, noisemakers and just plain shouting by happy islanders.

**AS SOON** as the word was flashed, Honolulu Mayor Neal Blaisdell and his aids went to the historic Hawaiian Kawaiahao church to give solemn prayer of thanksgiving. They then dashed back to the patio of the city hall where the Royal Hawaiian hotel band was assembled and hula dancers — both professional and amateur — began their performances.

In downtown Honolulu and on Waikiki beach the first spontaneous demonstrations ran their course in an hour or so and things settled down to a few degrees above normal.

Among the first of the statehood gags was the informal greeting exchanged between friends and strangers alike on the streets:

"Hello, citizen!"

On the University of Hawaii campus, students finished a 50-star flag just a half hour before congress completed the voting. They rushed from classrooms and raised the flag on the university flagpole. The school band played the national and Hawaii anthems.

**AT NIGHTFALL**, military planes dropped flares for more than an hour off Waikiki beach.

In the territorial legislature, the public address system announced:

"Everyone prepare to become first-class citizens."

The territorial house adopted a resolution making "Aloha State" the official nickname of the islands. Both houses offered prayers of thanksgiving.

**OAHU PRISON** trusties, riding a truck outside the prison walls when the news came, broke out in cheers.

William J. Lederer, author of "The Ugly American," broke open an $18 bottle of champagne.

James Michener, author of South Pacific tales, paraded Waikiki beach in shorts and "the loudest aloha shirt I have."

Michener

The biggest of many bonfires blazed on a small island in Honolulu harbor. It was fed with logs collected from the 49 states and many foreign countries. Boy Scouts on the chain of islands lit other bonfires.

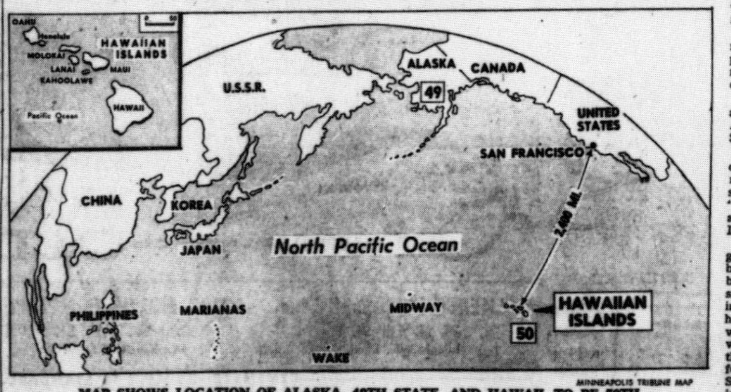

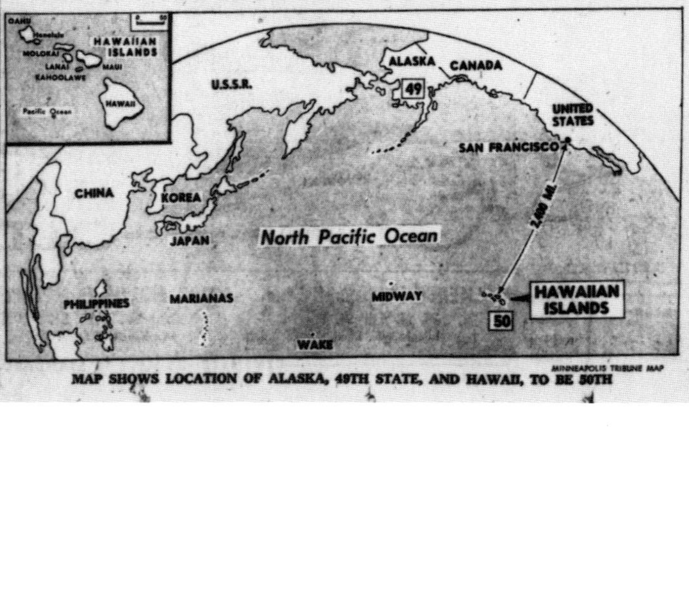

MINNEAPOLIS TRIBUNE MAP

**MAP SHOWS LOCATION OF ALASKA, 49TH STATE, AND HAWAII, TO BE 50TH**

# Macmillan Reported Willing to Negotiate European Arms Cut

From the Tribune Wire Services

British Prime Minister Harold Macmillan told Chancellor Konrad Adenauer Thursday that Britain was willing to negotiate a limitation of armed forces in central Europe without creating a military vacuum in the area.

A spokesman for Macmillan outlined the British position after the prime minister conferred for three and one-half hours with Adenauer in the latter's office in Bonn, West Germany.

Macmillan Adenauer
*Apprehensions eased?*

Informed diplomatic souces indicated Adenauer's apprehension about British intentions in central Europe, particularly marked since Macmillan's trip to Russia, might have been allayed as a result of Macmillan's remarks.

Macmillan and his party arrived in Bonn almost at the moment that Soviet Premier Nikita S. Khrushchev flew back to Moscow from East Berlin after a week-long East German visit that left little change in his basic demand that the western allies leave West Berlin.

**IN A STATEMENT** on his arrival, Macmillan declared the West must stand by its principles in dealing with the Soviets but added, "We must not be inflexible in our methods."

Adenauer told Macmillan that "since your last visit here a couple of months ago, world conditions have once more changed substantially and, I must say, have not improved.

Meanwhile, it was announced in Washington that Macmillan and President Eisenhower will hold their strategy talks on the Berlin crisis at the President's retreat at Camp David, Md. It appeared doubtful that Secretary of State Dulles would play any direct role in the discussions.

Macmillan is scheduled to arrive in Washington next Thursday and he and the President will go to Camp David the next day.

**ANOTHER** development in the Berlin situation was announced in Paris: President Charles deGaulle may spring a surprise proposal later this month for settling the dispute and establishing peaceful coexisitence on a permanent basis.

Informants said deGaulle will reveal his plan at a press

Macmillan
Continued on Page 11

## Ford Foundation Will Sell More Ford Stock

DETROIT, Mich. — (AP) — The Ford foundation announced Thursday it would offer two million shares of Ford Motor Co. common class "A" stock for sale to the general public at the end of this month.

The foundation filed a registration statement covering the sale with the securities and exchange commission.

The foundation said the sale was to be made in order to let it further diversify its investments.

Ford stock owned by the foundation totals 36,132,239 shares. It was acquired through gifts and bequests from Henry and Edsel Ford.

The foundation, a nonprofit corporation organized for scientific, educational and charitable purposes, sold 10,200,000 shares of Ford stock early in 1956, making the Ford stock available to the general public for the first time.

The prospectus outlining plans for the new stock sale said the offering price would depend on the price of Ford stock on the New York Stock exchange just before the block of shares is released. The stock closed on that exchange yesterday at $55.37, up 62 cents on the day.

This compares with the original offering price of $64.50 a share and a low of $35.87 in 1957.

# Probers Told Union Head Spied on Police, Bought Love Nest

By CLARK MOLLENHOFF
Minneapolis Tribune Staff Correspondent

WASHINGTON — A mobster-connected Chicago Teamster boss had spies in the Chicago police department and used union money to buy a love nest, the McClellan committee was told Thursday.

Glimco Pantaleo
*They refuse to testify*

Joseph P. (Joey) Glimco, pal of Teamster President James R. Hoffa, took the fifth amendment on questions about the $44,000 home he bought with union funds for occupancy by himself and Laverne Murray.

Miss Murray, a 26-year-old secretary in the office of Teamster local 777, also took the fifth amendment on questions dealing with a trip to California with Glimco and the purchase of the home.

**THERE** was also testimony from Maurice Adler, a Chicago private detective, that Glimco had informants in the police department who could give accurate information to allow Glimco and the mobsters to keep a surveillance on any honest police.

Glimco, an associate of such Capone mobsters as Tony Accardo, was key figure in a Teamster - gangster group. According to the testimony this group:

**Had the power** to deal itself in on a subcontract on 60 per cent of all the sheet-metal work on defense department subcontracts on Nike missile installations in the Chicago area.

**Looted the union** treasury of hundreds of thousands of dollars for Miami, Fla., Cabana parties, a Caribbean cruise, luxury hotels in California, and just plain cash kickbacks.

**Extorted thousands** of dollars from businessmen for the privilege of doing business peacefully in the Fulton street market, which deals in poultry products.

**Spent $5,000** in union money to send Glimco and a union aid to Chicago to stay at the Woodner hotel to be with Hoffa when Hoffa was on trial on a charge of an attempt to bribe a member of the McClellan committee staff. Hoffa was acquitted by a jury.

The only thing Glimco told the committee was that he is an American citizen, which he barked out in reply to one of the first questions.

**BUT HE TOOK** the fifth amendment when chairman

Probe
Continued on Page 11



*Read Will Jones' Report From Hollywood*

## Hawley Defeats Wheaton, 56-53, to Win Its 22nd Straight Victory

St. Paul Central Upset in Region 4 by North St. Paul

*(DETAILS in Sports Section.)*

# House Adopts Redistricting in Original Form

By JOHN C. McDONALD
Minneapolis Tribune Staff Writer

Minnesota house members Thursday took a second look at the way they amended a reapportionment bill the day before, removed the amendment and gave the bill preliminary approval in essentially its original form.

The measure—which would ask voters to ballot on a constitutional amendment in November 1960—will be up for final action today.

Other Legislative Stories—Page 10

Feature of the two and one-half hour debate was a verbal battle royal between rural members.

Some pleaded for acceptance of the compromise bill as the best they could hope to get, and others sought to load it down with the amendments which have defeated reapportionment many times before.

Leading rural forces in support of the bill sponsored by a citizen-legislator interim commission was Rep. Carl Iverson, Ashby. In the past, he has been an arch-foe of districting both houses according to population as presently prescribed by the constitution.

Iverson

He and others like Burnett Bergeson, Twin Valley; Rod Searle, Waseca, and Alvin Hofstad, Madison, reminded rural colleagues that the bill was a "compromise" which, if approved by the voters, will make area a factor in selection of house members. (Senators would continue to be chosen by population alone, according to the bill.)

**IN THE FRAY** on the other side, time and again, were Everett Battles, Warroad; Harold R. Anderson, North Mankato; Aubrey Dirlam, Redwood Falls, Don McLeod, Lewiston, and others.

They argued that a "sliding-scale" compromise writ-

Reapportion
Continued on Page 10

## Almanac

### This Family Belongs to Who's Who

*Friday, March 13, 1959*
Sunrise 6:30 a.m.; sunset 6:16 p.m.

We are in receipt of a technical paper read before the American Soap and Glycerine Producers association. It is entitled "A New Family of Fatty Based Amphoteric Surfactants" and is only moderately stimulating prose — except for the final sentence:

"We feel that amphoterics have a great future and that some day the word 'amphoteric' will be in just as common usage as cationic, anionic and non-ionic."

*Considerable cloudiness today in the Twin Cities. High today 40, low tonight 20.*

The doctor produced a blood-test needle and said to the small girl: "Let's see what your blood looks like."

"Don't bother," she replied. "It's red."

# Dairy Props to Continue Unchanged

### Benson Establishes Price Supports for Next Year

By CHARLES BAILEY
Minneapolis Tribune Staff Correspondent

WASHINGTON— Agriculture Secretary Benson Thursday ordered dairy price supports continued a. their present levels for the next 12 months.

Benson announced the support for manufacturing milk will be held at $3.06 per hundredweight in the marketing year that starts on April 1. Butterfat supports will stay at 56.6 cents a pound.

Because of the drop in parity prices caused by the revision of the parity index a month ago, the new level will represent 77 per cent of parity, compared with 75 per cent of the old parity in the past marketing year, even though the dollar-and-cents level is unchanged.

Benson

Benson could have used the new lower parity level to drop supports to about $2.96 had he wished to do so. This would have lowered butterfat props to about 55 cents a pound.

The secretary told a news conference he was retaining the present support level because it seemed desirable to "assure an adequate supply," as required by law, "with an adequate margin of safety."

He cited a slight increase in total commercial use of dairy products in 1958 over 1957, due primarily to increased population and a higher per-capita consumption of cheeses. In addition, he said, milk cow numbers were down and total milk output declined so that government surplus purchases were lower.

**HE NOTED** that government stocks of dairy products are below last year in the case of cheese and butter, although "somewhat" higher in the case of dried milk.

On Feb. 28 of this year, the government had uncommitted stocks of 28.5 million pounds of butter, 6.5 million pounds of cheese and 49.3 million

Dairy
Continued on Page 11

## Dreary, Dreary Hangs the Day

The weather forecast today for the Upper Midwest is uniformly dreary — clouds, snow, rain.

The snow and rain, expected to be scattered and light, is predicted for northeast Minnesota, northern and southern Wisconsin, eastern South Dakota and most of North Dakota.

High temperature today in the Twin Cities will be 40 degrees, low tonight 20. Thursday's hight was 40.

Other highs will range from high 20s to 45 in Minnesota, 30s to 40s in Wisconsin, 30s in North Dakota and 34 to 46 in South Dakota.

# 1960~1969

MINNEAPOLIS TEMPERATURES

| | | |
|---|---|---|
| Midnight 48 | 5 a.m. ....49 | 10 a.m. ...52 |
| 1 a.m. ....47 | 6 a.m. ....49 | 11 a.m. ...53 |
| 2 a.m. ....48 | 7 a.m. ....50 | Noon .....54 |
| 3 a.m. ....49 | 8 a.m. ....51 | *1 p.m. ...56 |
| 4 a.m. ....49 | 9 a.m. ....52 | *Unofficial |

Year ago high, 79; low, 52. Precip. 12 a.m. to noon, 0.

# THE MINNEAPOLIS STAR

Thursday, May 5, 1960 LXXXII—NO. 139 Four Sections ★ Telephone FE. 3-3111 5c in Twin Cities Area 7c Elsewhere

# Hennepin County Plans 3 New Parks

The Hennepin county park board is planning to create three new parks of nearly 1,000 acres each and expand the present Baker park at Lake Independence.

Purchase of 300 acres has already been completed near the Hyland lake area in Bloomington. Plans call for eventual purchase of more than 800 acres near the lake and to create a wilderness west of Normandale road and east of the Bush lake road.

In the north end of Hennepin county, said Edwin P. Chapman, vice chairman of the county park commission, the board may buy 1,000 to 1,200 acres between Diamond and Hayden lakes and along Diamond creek.

**This property is located in Dayton township and probably all of it can be purchased without condemnation proceedings, said Chapman.**

The board is also hoping to take over the entire shoreline of Lake Rebecca on the western edge of the county near Rockford.

This site is five miles west of Lake Independence, where the first county-owned park was donated by the late Morris T. Baker.

Baker park also is in for expansion, according to present plans of the county park commissioners in their $1,500,000 land acquisition program.

**The 250-acre site should be enlarged to about 800 acres, said Chapman, and will adjoin the Moon lake and the Spurzem lake areas.**

By creating parks in the northern, southern and western parts of the county, residents will have less than a 30-minute drive to reach any one of them, Chapman said.

## ★ Features



FORECAST
Rain, Cooler

## 2 Missing Girls Found Near Home

TUSTIN, Calif. —(AP)— An overnight search by 300 police, marines and volunteers ended today when two small girls who set out to see the world were found in an all-night laundromat at neighboring Santa Ana.

Jeannette Sharin Sexton, 9, and Michele Marie Miller, 8, found some religious calendars in a trash can and started selling them door-to-door Wednesday in this orange belt town. Apparently they decided to keep going and reached Santa Ana, 7 miles away.

## Dow-Jones Averages

NEW YORK— (Special) — The noon Dow - Jones stock averages Thursday:

| | Noon | Chg. |
|---|---|---|
| 30 Indust. ... | 610.57 | —.42 |
| 20 RRs. ..... | 140.85 | +.47 |
| 15 Utils. ..... | 88.78 | +.04 |
| 65 Stocks ... | 202.41 | +.08 |

Sales: 1,060,000 shares.

Minneapolis Star photo by Wayne Bell

KING AND QUEEN OF NEPAL ARRIVE AT ROCHESTER

*Dr. and Mrs. C. W. Mayo meet guests at airport*

★ ★ ★ ★

# Nepal King Captivates Rochester

By RALPH CLARK
Minneapolis Star Staff Writer

ROCHESTER, Minn.—King Mahendra of Nepal—shy, reticent, regal and much of the time unsmiling — came to Rochester Wednesday and captivated the city.

Town officials said the city turned on the biggest welcome ever given a visitor.

**Mahendra, 39, and his attractive queen, 31, arrived in Rochester at 12:50 p.m. yesterday aboard a military air transport service Constellation.**

The big plane arrived 23 minutes earlier than officials expected, but the airport reception went off without a hitch.

"It's in sight," shouted an official when the plane was spotted coming out of the clouds.

The plane circled slowly, touched its wheels gently to the airstrip and taxied to waiting officials.

Workers rolled out long rolls of colorful Oriental rug for the royal visitors. About 40 men from the 354th military police company, Rochester, their uniforms complete with spotless white gloves, snapped to attention and saluted.

**First to greet Mahendra and Queen Ratna were Dr. and Mrs. C. W. Mayo, hosts to the royal couple.**

Mrs. Mayo presented the queen with a large bouquet of red roses, and Mrs. J. T. Priestley, wife of the chairman of the Mayo clinic board of governors, gave a similar bouquet to Mrs. Subarna S. J. B. Rana, wife of the Nepalese deputy prime minister and minister of finance, planning and development.

The king, dressed in a brown business suit, spoke few words. The queen, wear-

ROYALTY
Turn to Page 3A

'I NEVER WANT TO SEE HIM'

# *Briton Hands Over Her Unwanted Son*

BRIGHTON, England — (AP) — Dry-eyed and unmoved, Mrs. Yvonne Moore Wednesday night handed over her unwanted 11-day-old son to the American wife who hopes to adopt him.

"I know you will look after him and love him more than I ever could," she told 38-year-old Mrs. Gladys Simon, New York, who flew here to collect the baby.

British-born Mrs. Simon will stay six months in this country to complete the legal process of adoption.

**The baby will be christened Francis, after Mrs. Simon's husband.**

She was handed the baby in a hotel room shortly after Mrs. Moore had been released from a Brighton maternity hospital.

When she saw Francis curled in his mother's arms Mrs. Simon cried: "I can't believe it's true, I can't believe it."

In handing over the baby, Mrs. Moore said:

"He's yours now, Mrs. Simon. I promise you after today you will never see me or my husband again."

Mrs. Moore took a final peek at her son and sighed:

**"I don't know why it is, but I no more feel his mother than any woman in the street.**

"I never want to see him again — the farther he goes the better it will be. To me he would just be 24 hours' work a day."

Mrs. Moore, 39 and married 20 years, claims she's too old now to start a family.

Her husband, a bus driver, quit his job because of the neighbors' criticism of their desire to get rid of the baby. The couple have kept their present residence a secret.

# Cave-in Traps Youth in 35-foot Dry Well

IRONTON, Ohio — (AP) — Rescue crews from Ohio and West Virginia have poured into tiny Burlington, Ohio, in an effort to free an 18-year-old boy from his entrapment at the bottom of a 35-foot dry well.

Individual digging efforts were halted this morning because of the well's repeatedly collapsing walls.

A clamshell shovel was brought in to do the work.

**Weight of the hundreds of persons standing near the well site probably was hastening the collapse, a spokesman said.**

Warren Payne was buried under eight feet of sandy soil Wednesday afternoon as he worked at the bottom of the newly dug well. Sides of the pit had not been shored up.

Rescuers have been hampered from the start by the shifting soil. Late last night one of the youth's arms was uncovered but a collapse of the walls quickly buried it.

Contractors and fire rescue teams from Huntington, W. Va., and Proctorville, Ohio, came to the Ohio river community near the Ohio-Kentucky-West Virginia conjunction to help extricate the boy.

**Lt. Z. T. Earls of the Huntington fire department, however, said he never knew of anyone surviving such an entombment for more than two hours.**

Earls said the youth probably has been crushed by weight of the sand.

Officials said they had warned residents about the dangers of digging such dry wells in the area. The amateur diggers usually do not shore up the sides properly if at all, they said. The wells are a type of cesspool.

The trapped youth is one of eight children of Mr. and Mrs. Minor Payne. The well was being dug at the back of their home.

The father, a contractor, said his sons had finished digging the well and Warren had stayed at the bottom to begin building the sides with brick.

His brother David ran screaming for help when the well collapsed.

# Wedding Fever Grips Britain; Meg Cheered

LONDON — (UPI) —Wedding fever gripped Britain today and thousands gathered around the royal palaces and Westminster abbey in a massive rebuke from the common man to critics of the marriage of Princess Margaret to commoner Antony Armstrong-Jones.

Scotland Yard tightened its arrangements to control the crowd that will jam the wedding procession route to Westminster Abbey Friday morning.

**Last night some 50,000 broke through police lines to mob the automobile carrying the princess and her fiance to Buckingham palace.**

Police now estimate that more than 500,000 people—absolute capacity—will pack the three-quarters of a mile from Clarence house and Buckingham palace to the abbey when Queen Elizabeth and her procession and Princess Margaret in her glass coach travel along flower-decorated streets to the wedding.

Despite a relentless campaign of innuendo almost since the engagement was announced 10 weeks ago, the crowds that cheered the prin-

WEDDING
Turn to Page 3A

# Nikita Reports Russ Downed U.S. Plane, Adds Rocket Threat

## Angered by Nixon as Summit Alternate

By STANLEY JOHNSON

MOSCOW — (AP) — Nikita S. Khrushchev told the Russian parliament in a bristling speech today that Soviet armed forces have shot down a plane he described as an American military craft.

He threatened to retaliate with rockets if American bombers appear over Russia.

Khrushchev's speech cast gloom over prospects for the summit conference opening in 11 days.

**He issued an unveiled threat to United States allies, took a hefty slap at Vice President Nixon, and charged that President Eisenhower's freedom of movement at the summit is being restricted by "certain United States circles."**

Khrushchev referred angrily to Eisenhower's suggestion that Nixon might sit in for him at the summit if the President's presence is required in Washington on domestic matters.

Khrushchev said he had met Nixon several times and it was difficult for him not to gain the impression Nixon was the last person to think of stopping the cold war or ending the arms race.

"I am afraid that if Nixon becomes entitled to carry on negotiations at the summit, it would be, as we say in Russia, like sending a goat to take care of the cabbage," the Soviet premier said.

**The supreme soviet (parliament) session burst into a wave of applause as Khrushchev announced the downing of an American plane May 1.**

(A single-engine jet U2 research plane has been missing since May 1 after a takeoff in Turkey, Pentagon officials said.

(It is assumed to have come down near Lake Van, not far from the border of Soviet Armenia. In this general area a United States C130 transport was downed by Soviet forces in 1958. By U.S. reckoning, the Soviets accounted for only 6 of 17 men lost then.

(The U2, a ship assigned to the national aeronautics and space administration is a flying laboratory assigned to make weather observations and check air for radioactivity.)

Khrushchev called the

NIKITA
Turn to Page 3A

★ ★ ★ ★

AP Wirephoto via radio from London

KHRUSHCHEV TELLS SUPREME SOVIET ABOUT PLANE

*He said American craft was shot down May 1*

★ ★ ★ ★ ★ ★ ★ ★ ★ ★ ★ ★

# *Russ May Have Bagged Unarmed Jet, U. S. Says*

WASHINGTON — (AP) — The state department said today Soviet forces may have shot down an unarmed United States research plane with an unconscious pilot rather than a "military craft" as Premier Khrushchev claimed.

Under instruction from President Eisenhower, the department and the national aeronautics and space administration issued reports after the assertion by Khrushchev that an American plane was shot down over the Soviet Union early Sunday.

The state department report said a single-engine, high-altitude jet used in weather research, took off from Adana, Turkey, that day with a civilian pilot and has been missing since.

The disappearance of the plane was announced Tuesday.

**"During the flight of this plane," the report said, "the pilot reported difficulty with his oxygen equipment.**

"Mr. Khrushchev has announced that a United States plane has been shot down over the USSR on that day. It may be that this was the missing plane.

"It is entirely possible that having a failure in the oxygen equipment which could result in the pilot losing consciousness, the plane continued on automatic pilot for a considerable distance and accidentally violated Soviet air space."

Lincoln White, state department press officer, announced United States Ambassador Llewellyn Thompson in Moscow is being instructed to ask the Soviet government for full information on the fate of the pilot.

White said that so far as he knew no other planes were missing in the border area.

**At the capitol, meanwhile, congress members were reacting angrily to word of the downing of another American plane.**

Sen. Johnson (Texas), the senate Democratic leader, speculated Khrushchev may be "simply using this as an incident to apply leverage for the coming summit meeting."

Other comment at the capitol ranged up to suggestions that Khrushchev's announcement, and the truculent tone of other parts of his speech, make it inadvisable for President Eisen-

PLANE
Turn to Page 3A

## TREASURER GETS RID OF HEADACHE FOR 12 CENTS

**MOUNT VERNON, ILL.—(UPI)—Jefferson County Treasurer Walter Randall paid a delinquent landowner's 12-cent tax bill himself Wednesday.**

**The county already had spent $2 for bookkeeping and 8 cents for postage trying to collect. The taxpayer finally sent in a check for 6 cents, promising the second installment later. But the check wasn't signed.**

**"Enough is enough," grumbled Randall. He dug into his pocket and handed over a dime and two pennies.**

## SPEECH IS HINT

# *Nikita Trying to Get Off Policy Hook?*

By WILLIAM L. RYAN
Associated Press News Analyst

Nikita Khrushchev, self-styled champion of world peace, seems to have come to the conclusion that too much peace can be dangerous both for him and for the Communist world movement.

**Behind the Day's News**

The Soviet premier's address to his rubber-stamp parliament dashes already slim hopes for any real progress at the summit in Paris.

**But when the three-hour oration is viewed against the background of a significant shakeup in the Soviet power structure, one gets the impression that Khrushchev had little choice but to pull the rug from under those who invested great hopes in the big power meeting.**

Khrushchev makes much of the shooting down of an American plane — presumed in Washington to be a stray weather observation craft, with one man aboard. Khrushchev calls it a military plane.

There must be more compelling reasons than the surface reasons for Khrushchev to make such an issue of it.

Khrushchev's speech, and

SHAKEUP
Turn to Page 3A

## → INSIDE THE STAR →

Trujillo

Miss Tollefson

Cerf

**U.S. PROTEST**—The state department has again focused its displeasure on the dictatorial rule of Rafael Leonidas Trujillo of the Dominican Republic. The department protested the expulsion of diplomat Carl E. Davis from the country as "unsupported and unjustified." ★ **Page 2A.**

**BUILDING TRADES**—Federal and state labor conciliators resumed sessions with building trades groups today. Some progress was made toward settlement of the dispute Wednesday. ★ **Page 1B.**

**REDEVELOPMENT BILL**—House passage of a 251-million-dollar area redevelopment bill sent the measure back to the senate and put it a step closer to an expected veto. Fate of the bill could become a major political issue in the presidential campaign. ★**Page 6A.**

**TCRT CASE**—Marilyn Tollefson will testify for the government today in the Twin City Rapid Transit Co. fraud case. Testimony of the 27-year-old prostitute reportedly will concern conversations between herself and Isadore (Kid Cann) Blumenfeld regarding the case. ★ **Page 6A.**

**FARMERS' PROBLEMS**—Democrats who are drafting recommendations for the party's campaign platform will sift the problems of the American family farmer Friday. Gov. Freeman will be the first witness to testify on farm issues at the hearing in Minneapolis. ★ **Page 1B.**

**PUBLISHING MERGERS**—Bennett Cerf maintains that the recent rash of mergers in the publishing industry poses no threat to the small, independent firm. "All that is needed for success is a good book," said the president of Random House.

**SENIOR CITIZENS**—A population expert points out that there are more voters over 65 years of age than there are Negro, farm and foreign-born voters combined. "It would be a major problem," said Dr. Kingsley Davis, "if the situation of the aged became so bad that they started voting as a bloc." ★ **Page 1B.**

**MEDICAL CARE**—Congress now has a choice of four

• • *Turn to Page 2A*

B-r-r-r!
TUESDAY TEMPERATURES

| | | | | | |
|---|---|---|---|---|---|
| 2 a.m. | 40 | 10 a.m. | 42 | 6 p.m. | 32 |
| 3 a.m. | 40 | 11 a.m. | 44 | 7 p.m. | 30 |
| 4 a.m. | 41 | Noon | 42 | 8 p.m. | 29 |
| 5 a.m. | 41 | 1 p.m. | 45 | 9 p.m. | 27 |
| 6 a.m. | 41 | 2 p.m. | 44 | 10 p.m. | 28 |
| 7 a.m. | 41 | 3 p.m. | 43 | 11 p.m. | 25 |
| 8 a.m. | 39 | 4 p.m. | 38 | 12 M. | 23 |
| 9 a.m. | 41 | 5 p.m. | 35 | 1 a.m. | 21 |
| | | | | *2 a.m. | 20 |

Details Page 18 *Unofficial

# Minneapolis Morning Tribune

Vol. XCIV—No. 169 Copyright 1960 Minneapolis Star and Tribune Company MINNEAPOLIS, MINN., WEDNESDAY, NOVEMBER 9, 1960 Telephone FE 3-3111 Price 7c



# Kennedy Apparently Elected

## Humphrey, Judd and Karth Win Re-Election; Balance of Major State Races Are Undecided

—MINNESOTA GOVERNOR—

## Freeman, Andersen Are Running Neck-and-Neck

By SAM NEWLAND
Minneapolis Tribune Staff Writer

Gov. Orville L. Freeman and Elmer L. Andersen, his Republican challenger seeking to block his path to an unprecedented fourth term, were locked in a potentially neck-and-neck struggle today on the basis of incomplete returns.

Andersen, a St. Paul businessman who pitched his campaign on the need for a favorable business and tax climate in Minnesota, was trailing the 42-year-old DFL governor as returns trickled in from throughout the state.

But more than two-thirds of the state's 3,766 precincts were yet to be heard from. And on the basis of past elections, Andersen might expect to gain strength as ballot-counting continued into the morning.

Early this morning, Andersen appeared to be narrowing the gap. Previously, Freeman held a margin of about six to five—or slightly less than the margin by which he defeated Republican George MacKinnon two years ago.

In Hennepin county, the two candidates were only 79 votes apart with more than two-thirds of the precincts reporting.

In Austin, Mower county, voters gave Andersen pluralities in three precincts which

Minnesota Governor
Continued on Page Nine

### HOW MINNESOTA VOTED

Asterisk (*) indicates incumbent

**PRESIDENT**
1,362 precincts of 3,766
Kennedy (D) .......361,236
Nixon (R) ..........331,654

**CONGRESS**

**U.S. Senate**
1,353 precincts of 3,766
*Humphrey (DFL) ..400,673
Peterson (R) ........267,425

**HOUSE OF REPRESENTATIVES**

**First District**
100 precincts of 409
Shepherd (DFL) ..... 20,471
*Quie (R) .......... 27,800

**Second District**
72 precincts of 442
Schwandt (DFL) .... 6,137
*Nelsen (R) ........ 8,333

**Third District**
139 precincts of 331
*Wier (DFL) ....... 71,327
MacGregor (R) ..... 79,478
Bergsten (Ind) ...... 2,975

**Fourth District**
178 precincts of 212
*Karth (DFL) ...... 96,644
Mitchell (R) ........ 59,856

**Fifth District**
136 precincts of 138
Matthews (DFL) .... 54,184
*Judd (R) .......... 83,259

**Sixth District**
101 precincts of 581
*Marshall (DFL) .... 11,172
King (R) .......... 7,423

**Seventh District**
210 precincts of 561
Duenow (DFL) ..... 18,953
*Andersen (R) ..... 18,447

**Eighth District**
79 precincts of 453
*Blatnik (DFL) ..... 24,304
Ketola (R) ......... 11,180

**Ninth District**
185 precincts of 642
Knutson (DFL) ..... 12,082
*Langen (R) ....... 11,360

**STATE OFFICES**

**Governor**
1,340 precincts of 3,766
*Freeman (DFL) ....342,191
Andersen (R) .......324,984

**Lieutenant Governor**
1,027 precincts of 3,766
*Rolvaag (DFL) ....314,928
Ogle (R) ..........243,153

**Secretary of State**
1,020 precincts of 3,766
*Donovan (DFL) ....331,953
Joyce (R) ..........242,931

**State Treasurer**
1,035 precincts of 3,766
Hammar (DFL) .....270,037
*Bjornson (R) ......285,758

**Attorney General**
1,029 precincts of 3,766
*Mondale (DFL) ....333,471
Saetre (R) .........218,211

**Railroad and Warehouse Commissioner**
1,001 precincts of 3,766
*Petersen (DFL) ....304,464
Johnson (R) ........222,922

**STATE SUPREME COURT**

**Chief Justice**
(Nominated without party designation)
949 precincts of 3,766
*Dell ............... 89,752
Hansen ............ 71,085

**Associate Justice**
(Nominated without party designation)
965 precincts of 3,766
Dressel ............ 83,248
*Knutson ..........264,913
*Thomas Gallagher and *Martin A. Nelson were re-elected without opposition.

**STATE CONSTITUTIONAL AMENDMENTS**
(Majority of all votes cast in election needed for passage)

**Amendment No. 1**
Length of legislative session and legislators' candidacy for other offices.
879 precincts of 3,766
Yes ...............266,504
No ................186,700

**Amendment No. 2**
Reapportionment of legislature
879 precincts of 3,766
Yes ...............199,537
No ................255,340

**Amendment No. 3**
Succession to governor and continuity of government.
879 precincts of 3,766
Yes ...............323,327
No ................103,215

**Amendment No. 4**
Voting after residence is changed
879 precincts of 3,766
Yes ...............331,229
No ................. 97,430

SENATOR JOHN F. KENNEDY
*He corralled early lead in big states*

## Judd, Karth Re-Elected; Wier Trails

By CHARLES HANNA

Representatives Walter Judd and Joseph Karth were re-elected Tuesday to Minnesota's fifth and fourth congressional seats.

It appeared that DFL Rep. John Blatnik was well on his way to re-election in his eighth district contest with Republican Jerry Ketola.

**REPUBLICAN** Judd had a margin of nearly 30,000 votes over his DFL challenger George Matthews, a Hennepin county commissioner. All but two of the district's 138 precinct totals were reported.

Karth, fourth district DFL incumbent, had better than a 36,500 vote lead over Joseph Mitchell, St. Paul comptroller with 178 of 212 precincts totals counted.

Blatnik held onto a 10,000 vote margin as returns from the northeastern district came in. Less than one fourth of the 453 precincts were reported.

Clark MacGregor, third district Republican challenger, took an 8,000 vote lead with slightly less than half of the precincts recorded. Incumbent Democrat Roy Wier led in early reports. Al Berg-

Minnesota Congress
Continued on Page Nine

LEAD IS 133,000 VOTES

## Humphrey Wins Over Peterson

By CARL T. ROWAN
Minneapolis Tribune Staff Writer

Hubert H. Humphrey was re-elected to his third six-year term in the United States senate.

With more than a third of the state's 3,766 precincts reporting early today, the 49-year-old Democrat had a 133,000 vote lead over his Republican rival, P. Kenneth Peterson.

Humphrey was maintaining a margin of about 5 to 3.

The state's senior senator declined to claim victory, however.

"We prefer to wait until the opposition recognizes defeat," one of his aids said.

Peterson, 45-year-old Minneapolis mayor, would concede only that he had fared worse in Minneapolis and St. Paul than he had anticipated.

**"WE ARE ABOUT** 20,000 votes behind our projections," he said.

But Peterson expressed confidence that out-state areas—particularly the first, second and seventh congressional districts — would give him enough support to wipe out Humphrey's margin.

Humphrey supporters were jubilant, however, for in both Hennepin and Ramsey counties the incumbent was running well ahead of his 1954 pace. At that time he won re-election easily, defeating Val Bjornson by more than 160,000 votes.

In Hennepin county, with 266 of 343 precincts reporting, Humphrey had won 59.4 per cent of the vote, compared with 55.6 per cent in 1954.

**HUMPREY CAME** out of St. Paul with more than a 45,000-vote margin, a substantial increase over 1954.

With 162 of Ramsey county's 212 precincts reporting, Humphrey had about 68 per cent of the votes, a 5 per cent jump over six years ago.

"We're so happy we can hardly talk," said a Humphrey aid, obviously relieved that the contest had not been as close as some Humphrey supporters had feared.

At one point in the campaign, several of his supporters had said privately that the senator had a "safety margin" of only a percentage point or two over his rival.

Peterson had said that the race was "dead even."

The unanswered question up till the vote tallying began last night was whether Humphrey's support of Sen. John Kennedy, a Catholic, had hurt him in predominantly Protestant communities.

William Rivkin, Chicago lawyer and Kennedy's liaison man in Minnesota and Iowa,

Minnesota Senate
Continued on Page Nine

Judd

Karth

Blatnik

Mrs. Knutson

—NATIONWIDE VOTING—

## Youngest Candidate Ever to Win Top Office

By RICHARD WILSON
Chief of the Minneapolis Tribune Washington Bureau

WASHINGTON—John Kennedy, 43-year-old Massachusetts senator, swept big cities and states in Tuesday's election to take a strong lead for the presidency.

If elected, he would be the youngest man and the first Catholic elected president. (Theodore Roosevelt, who succeeded the assassinated William McKinley, also was 43 when he took office.)

But it did not appear to be what is ordinarily known as a landslide victory. The popular vote ran on the order of 52 per cent for Kennedy, 48 per cent for Vice President Richard Nixon.

New York, Pennsylvania, Texas and Illinois gave Kennedy the advantage.

Nixon penetrated the south, winning Florida, Virginia, Tennessee and Kentucky but losing South Carolina. The vice president ran strong also in some farm states and the west. He won Indiana, surprised Democratic leaders with an apparently decisive lead in Ohio, and defeated Kennedy in Oklahoma as well as the mountain states.

**BUT** the crushing effect of the big totals of the electoral votes in the eastern industrial states, plus Texas, the advantage in Illinois, and above all in Pennsylvania gave Kennedy the strength he needed.

The Kennedy victory seemed clinched even before the votes were counted in Nixon's home state of California, where Kennedy also led.

In spite of Kennedy's commanding lead, Nixon at his headquarters in Los Angeles, Calif., gave no sign of conceding.

The Los Angeles Examiner and the San Francisco Chronicle declared on the basis of partial returns that Kennedy had won California, as well as the big states of the east. This would give Kennedy his 334 electoral votes.

**AT HIS** headquarters at Hyannis Port, Mass., Kennedy decided to make no statement until Nixon had conceded.

Some forecasts were upset. Texas went for Kennedy and his running mate, Sen. Lyndon Johnson, also electing Johnson to another senate term, which he will resign.

City after city tumbled to Kennedy, most devastatingly in upstate New York, once the eastern stronghold of the Republican party. Kennedy carried New York city by more than 750,000 and appeared to be winning the state by 400,000.

A huge Philadelphia, Pa., majority for Kennedy of more

Nationwide Voting
Continued on Page Nine

### PRESIDENTIAL VOTE NATIONWIDE

By Associated Press

| State | Voting Units | Units Reporting | POPULAR VOTE Nixon | Kennedy | ELEC. Nixon | TREND Kennedy |
|---|---|---|---|---|---|---|
| Ala. x | 3,293 | 2,488 | 176,288 | 243,369 | .. | 5 |
| Alaska | 300 | 9 | 196 | 185 | 3 | .. |
| Ariz. | 654 | 361 | 144,150 | 111,936 | 4 | .. |
| Ark. | 2,389 | 1,704 | 103,103 | 128,370 | .. | 8 |
| Calif. | 30,682 | 7,422 | 516,909 | 567,412 | .. | 32 |
| Colo. | 1,914 | 1,322 | 285,766 | 242,198 | 6 | .. |
| Conn. | 169 | 169 | 566,497 | 656,494 | .. | 8 |
| Del. | 356 | 351 | 95,555 | 98,354 | .. | 3 |
| Fla. | 1,969 | 1,786 | 745,330 | 695,557 | 10 | .. |
| Ga. | 1,826 | 994 | 198,000 | 318,715 | .. | 12 |
| Hawaii | 240 | 184 | 61,160 | 59,918 | 3 | .. |
| Idaho | 886 | 545 | 85,673 | 76,216 | 4 | .. |
| Ill. | 10,015 | 4,396 | 778,925 | 1,086,928 | .. | 27 |
| Ind. | 4,299 | 2,971 | 876,425 | 743,238 | 13 | .. |
| Iowa | 2,488 | 1,187 | 330,344 | 267,588 | 10 | .. |
| Kan. | 2,961 | 1,647 | 369,816 | 180,912 | 8 | .. |
| Ky. | 3,533 | 2,579 | 478,460 | 443,702 | 10 | .. |
| La. | 2,114 | 1,804 | 168,071 | 344,888 | .. | 10 |
| Maine | 630 | 416 | 157,693 | 119,661 | 5 | .. |
| Md. | 1,338 | 1,336 | 481,697 | 559,971 | .. | 9 |
| Mass. | 1,984 | 780 | 245,207 | 530,438 | .. | 16 |
| Mich. | 5,074 | 2,460 | 754,534 | 895,397 | .. | 20 |
| Minn. | 3,766 | 755 | 217,342 | 259,550 | .. | 11 |
| Miss. x | 1,828 | 1,535 | 51,258 | 82,345 | .. | .. |
| Mo. | 4,371 | 3,706 | 675,679 | 742,051 | .. | 13 |
| Mont. | 1,080 | 280 | 32,383 | 36,960 | .. | 4 |
| Neb. | 2,129 | 573 | 70,877 | 40,736 | 6 | .. |
| Nev. | 451 | 174 | 33,720 | 32,854 | 3 | .. |
| N. H. | 301 | 250 | 112,971 | 93,766 | 4 | .. |
| N. J. | 4,291 | 3,988 | 1,250,355 | 1,297,967 | .. | 16 |
| N. M. | 979 | 452 | 88,473 | 87,558 | 4 | .. |
| N. Y. | 11,793 | 11,283 | 3,282,432 | 3,691,770 | .. | 45 |
| N. C. | 2,089 | 1,848 | 563,775 | 642,287 | .. | 14 |
| N. D. | 2,311 | 844 | 50,388 | 41,821 | 4 | .. |
| Ohio | 14,076 | 8,482 | 1,232,291 | 1,090,979 | 25 | .. |
| Okla. | 3,224 | 8,773 | 1,281,527 | 1,128,943 | 8 | .. |
| Ore. | 2,895 | 1,478 | 125,268 | 109,038 | 6 | .. |
| Pa. | 9,044 | 7,472 | 1,876,560 | 2,078,099 | .. | 32 |
| R. I. | 467 | 467 | 144,953 | 257,158 | .. | 4 |
| S. C. | 1,602 | 1,578 | 183,321 | 193,295 | .. | 8 |
| S. D. | 1,890 | 620 | 38,034 | 28,715 | 4 | .. |
| Tenn. | 2,699 | 2,517 | 509,540 | 436,653 | 11 | .. |
| Tex. | 254 | 246 | 846,750 | 900,010 | .. | 24 |
| Utah | 1,128 | 707 | 127,548 | 102,764 | 4 | .. |
| Vt. | 246 | 246 | 98,157 | 69,382 | 3 | .. |
| Va. | 1,947 | 1,852 | 376,131 | 330,956 | .2 | .. |
| Wash. | 5,200 | 904 | 93,358 | 91,625 | 9 | .. |
| W. Va. | 2,751 | 2,171 | 309,138 | 385,198 | .. | 8 |
| Wis. | 3,476 | 2,489 | 638,845 | 609,709 | 12 | .. |
| Wyo. | 673 | 240 | 12,307 | 8,681 | 3 | .. |
| Total | 166,075 | 102,841 | 21,843,180 | 23,251,317 | 194 | 329 |

x—Alabama—of the 11 leading Democratic electors, 5 are pledged to Kennedy and 6 unpledged. Mississippi—8 unpledged Democratic electors are leading.

IN MINNESOTA

## Kennedy Holds Slender Lead

By JOHN C. McDONALD
Minneapolis Tribune Staff Writer

Sen. John Kennedy, Democratic presidential candidate held a slim lead early today with nearly one-half of the votes counted in Minnesota.

The greater part of his 30,000-vote margin was attributed to returns from the heavily populated Twin Cities metropolitan area and from Duluth and other areas in which his Roman Catholic religion was likely to count in his favor.

Outstate, a trio of bellwether precincts which recently had voted right in eight crucial election contests gave sizable majorities to the Kennedy - Johnson ticket as well.

The three districts were Belle Plaine borough in Scott county and New Market township, both south of Minneapolis, and Barber township in Faribault county in pro-Republican southern Minnesota.

All three gave majorities to Harry Truman in the 1948 presidential election and to Dwight D. Eisenhower in 1952 and 1956. They also gave their support to Orville L. Freeman in his three successful gubernatorial races and to Hubert H. Humphrey and Eugene McCarthy in their 1954 and 1958 senatorial bids.

Four years ago Barber township gave President Eisenhower 54 per cent of

Minnesota President
Continued on Page Nine

## We Didn't Vote Much, Russians Told

LONDON— (Reuters) — Moscow radio Tuesday told Russians that "many millions of American citizens have declared their unwillingness to vote" in the presidential election.

It said they had stayed away from the polls because "a naked eye cannot find any discernible difference" between Vice President Richard Nixon and Sen. John Kennedy.

Nevertheless, it said that "according to early results in many districts, John Kennedy seems to have a slight edge over Nixon.

"The polling," it said, "took place on a beautiful day."



IN STATE RACES

## 5 Incumbents Hold Early Leads

By SAM ROMER
Minneapolis Tribune Staff Writer

Four Democratic-Farmer-Labor Minnesota state officers and one Republican incumbent led their opponents early today in returns from more than one-fourth of the state's 3,766 precincts.

Some of the DFL margins were scored in normally Democratic territories, including Ramsey county, and none of the returns was conclusive.

**IN THE** nonpartisan race for chief justice of the supreme court, Chief Justice Roger L. Dell held a comfortable lead over Clifford F. Hansen, Minneapolis attorney.

Hansen, former assistant United States attorney, ran an unexpectedly strong race against Dell, the state's chief justice since 1953.

In the other supreme court race, Justice Oscar R. Knutson, seeking his third term, led William G. Dressel, Minnetonka, by better than a 3-to-1 margin.

In the party races, Val Bjornson, the veteran Republican state treasurer, ran ahead of the GOP slate to overcome the early DFL margins and led Conrad H. Hammar, Jr., St. James, by a slim majority.

Walter F. Mondale, the young Minneapolis attorney whom Gov. Orville L. Freeman named attorney-general last May, led the other state officers on the DFL ticket.

**MONDALE PILED** up a 6-to-4 margin over Gaylord A. Saetre, Moorhead, his Republican opponent.

A slightly smaller lead was held by Joseph L. Donovan, St. Paul, the DFL secretary of state, in his race for re-election against Kenneth O'Brien Joyce, Morningside advertising man.

Karl F. Rolvaag, Roseville, Freeman's lieutenant - governor during the governor's three terms, ran somewhat behind the DFL leaders al-

State Races
Continued on Page Nine

**Light Snow**

TUESDAY TEMPERATURES

| | | | | | |
|---|---|---|---|---|---|
| 2 a.m. | 36 | 10 a.m. | 46 | 6 p.m. | 42 |
| 3 a.m. | 37 | 11 a.m. | 47 | 7 p.m. | 39 |
| 4 a.m. | 36 | Noon | 48 | 8 p.m. | 39 |
| 5 a.m. | 36 | 1 p.m. | 48 | 9 p.m. | 38 |
| 6 a.m. | 36 | 2 p.m. | 48 | 10 p.m. | 39 |
| 7 a.m. | 37 | 3 p.m. | 45 | 11 p.m. | 37 |
| 8 a.m. | 40 | 4 p.m. | 40 | 12M | 34 |
| 9 a.m. | 43 | 5 p.m. | 42 | *1 a.m. | 33 |

*Details Page 16* *Unofficial

# Minneapolis Morning Tribune

Vol. XCIV—No. 323 MINNEAPOLIS, MINN., WEDNESDAY, APRIL 12, 1961 Telephone FE 3-3111 Price 7c



# Russians Put Astronaut Into Space

## House Passes Tax Program By 66-62 Vote

By JOHN C. McDONALD
Minneapolis Tribune Staff Writer

The Liberal - dominated Minnesota house of representatives passed its late-blooming tax package Tuesday and sent it to the senate without a single vote to spare.

The count on final passage was 66 to 62, with three members absent or not voting. Sixty-six votes is the simple majority necessary to pass a bill.

**THE MAJORITY** leadership beat down a series of five amendments before final action on the program, which is designed to raise $62,700,000 in additional revenue in the two-year fiscal period beginning July 1.

Most of the objections and the proffered amendments came from members who attacked a 3 per cent excise tax proposal on new automobiles and trucks. Rep. D. D. Wozniak, chairman of the house tax committee, said this recommendation, which was contained also in Gov. Andersen's budget message, would raise $24,000,000.

Other features of the bill are:

**A cigaret tax** increase of one cent per pack to 6½ cents.

**A corporate income tax** reduction but removal of the corporate privilege of deducting federal tax payments from state returns.

**Speeded-up corporate tax** payments to a current basis.

**Repeal** of a 10 per cent individual income surtax and a ½ per cent increase in all rate brackets.

Conservative Rep. Fred Schwanke, Deerwood banker, joined 65 members of the majority Liberal caucus to edge the bill over the top. Six Liberals voted with 56 Conservatives to form the minority side.

They were Ernest Beedle, St. Paul; Stanley Fudro and Edward Tomczyk, Minneapolis; Carl Iverson, Ashby; Julian Newhouse, Alexandria, and Richard O'Dea, Mahtomedi.

**LIBERAL** Rep. Peter Popovich, St. Paul, was present in the chamber but did not vote. Absent were Rep. John Kinzer, Cold Spring Conservative, and Rep. Francis La Brosse, Duluth Liberal.

Wozniak, who explained the bill, said he expects the house to cut 10 million dol-

Tax
Continued on Page 12

## Almanac

### Twins Fan Makes Error on Home Run

*Wednesday, April 12, 1961*
Sunrise 5:34 a.m.; sunset 6:54 p.m.

A fourth - grade boy at Wooddale school in Edina had been unusually quiet and alert-looking all Tuesday afternoon.

The reason became apparent when he suddenly forgot himself and yelled excitedly: "It's a home run!"

The teacher found he had a transistor radio concealed upon his person. He was listening, of course, to THE game.

•

*Light snow in the Twin Cities today. High today in the middle 30s, low tonight 20.*

•

A bachelor colleague, planning a candlelight dinner in his apartment, has promised his female guest homemade rolls "like grandma used to make." What he has not told her is that his grandmother, who lives in the other half of his duplex, will be making the rolls.



## He Radios That He Is Feeling Well

MOSCOW —(AP)— The Soviet Union announced today that it has launched a man into orbit around the earth and that he has reported back that he is feeling fine.

The anouncement was made over Moscow radio, after all stations in the country had been called to listen. all stations in the country had been called to listen.

Moscow radio said:

"The launching of the multi-stage rocket was successful and after attaining the first escape velocity and the separation of the last stage of the carrier rocket the space ship went into free flight on a round-the-earth orbit.

"According to preliminary data the period of the evolution of the satellite space ship around the earth is 89.1 minutes.

"The minimum distance from the earth (at perigee) is 175 kilometers (110 miles) and the maximum (at apogee) is 302 kilometers (188 miles).

The broadcast said that the first astronaut is Maj. Yuri Alekseyevich Gagarin and that he was launched today.

The space ship carrying

Space
Continued on Page 12

## Witness Dies on Stand in City Court

A Minneapolis man collapsed on the witness stand and died in Minneapolis municipal court Tuesday.

Floyd A. Johnson, 53, 6516 N. Brentwood Av., Crystal, died shortly before noon after suffering an apparent heart attack. His death caused a mistrial.

Johnson, chief state witness in the trial of Frank K. Seifert, 819 Kenwood Pkwy., on careless and hit-run driving charges, was undergoing cross - examination at the time.

**JOHNSON HAD** just answered a question about an accident March 29 on Franklin Av., near S. 1st Av., witnesses said, when he leaned over in the witness stand and said, "Just a minute."

Presiding Judge Elmer R. Anderson said that it immediately became apparent that Johnson was stricken seriously. The judge excused the jury and ordered the rescue squad called.

Attorneys and police officers tried to aid Johnson, the judge said, but the insurance salesman died within about 10 minutes after being stricken.

**ANDERSON THEN** reconvened the jury of 11 men and one woman in an adjacent courtroom, ordered a mistrial and dismissed them after relating what had occurred.

# Twins Win Opener 6 to 0

AP WIREPHOTO

**TWINS' OUTFIELDERS JIM LEMON, LEFT, LENNY GREEN COLLIDED UNDER FLY BALL**
*Lemon was charged with error when Green dropped the ball in left center field*

## Allison, Bertoia Homer; Ramos Allows 3 Hits

By TOM BRIERE
Minneapolis Tribune Staff Writer

NEW YORK—Pedro Ramos yielded only three hits Tuesday to earn the Minnesota Twins a 6-0 opening-day victory over the New York Yankees, defending champions in the American league.

It was the first regular-season game for the Minnesota Twins, who up to last year were the Washington Senators.

**Other Stories, Opening Day Pictures in Sports Section**

The huge Yankee stadium scoreboard read: "Yankees have won 25 American league pennants, 18 world titles." But for one day, at least, the Twins top the standings with a 1-0 record and the Yankees are on the bottom at 0-1.

Ramos, who has been talking all spring about going home to fight with anti-Castro forces in Cuba, fought the Yankees with a fast ball, curve, slider-type small curve and change of pace. He struck out five, including Mickey Mantle twice.

### 3-Run Seventh Breaks Tie

Ramos ran his opening-day record to 3-0 in besting southpaw Whitey Ford, whom the Twins shelled out in a three-run seventh inning to break a 0-0 stalemate. Ford granted only two hits until the seventh.

Then Bob Allison's 315-foot homer down the left-field line on a one-ball, no-strike pitch started Ford on the way to the showers. Earl Battey doubled into the left-field corner and Reno Bertoia walked. Billy Gardner sacrificed and the switch-hitting Ramos, batting right-handed against Ford, singled into center for two more runs.

That was all for the 32-year-old Yankee, who beat the Washington Senators in 1955 and 1957 openers.

The Yankees lost their home opener after ending their season last year with a string of 15 at-home victories. It also was the first home opening loss in the last eight, stretching back to 1953.

### Berra Is 'the Toughest Yankee'

Ramos yielded a two-out single to Yogi Berra, whom Pedro considers "the toughest Yankee," in the first inning. The Yankees put two men on base in the second on left fielder Jim Lemon's error on Roger Maris' fly and a walk to Tony Kubek. But Ramos retired Clete Boyer on a fly to right and Ford on a grounder to third.

The Yankees got a two-out single by Bill Skowron in the fourth and a one-out infield hit by Ford in the fifth. A double play took care of Ford and Ramos went on to erase the last 14 Yankees in order.

Minnesota tagged Ford, Ralph Terry and Jim Coates for nine hits.

The Twins increased their lead to 5-0 off Terry in the eighth on Allison's single, Battey's fielder's choice and Reno Bertoia's 325-foot homer into the left-field seats. They added one more in the ninth.

Shortstop Zoilo Versalles singled to left, stole second and third after Len Green popped out, and came home on Harmon Killebrew's sacrifice fly.

Moments later Dan Dobbek, who replaced Lemon in left for defensive purposes, was hit by a pitch. He stole second but was stranded there.

### First Six Innings Are Scoreless

It was scoreless through six innings. Killebrew singled to center field to start the fourth and end Ford's no-hit spell. Billy Gardner singled in the fifth and then it was all quiet until the seventh.

"I pitched a one-hitter against Detroit last year," Ramos said after the game, "but to beat the Yankees today gave me a bigger thrill. It was easy for me, really. I felt loose after the first couple of innings, and got better control. I hit, too."

Whitey Ford said he didn't tire in the seventh, "but I suddenly lost it." He added that "Ramos was a tough guy on the mound."

Ramos has blanked the Yankees for 16 innings this year, including seven shutout innings on five hits in an exhibition game at St. Petersburg, Fla., April 1. The Twins won that one 4-0 with Jim Kaat finishing up. In all, yesterday's victory gave the Twins a string of 18 shutout innings against Yankee sluggers this year.

The Twins and Yankees take today off, and then meet again at 2 p.m. Thursday with right hander Camilo Pascual of the Twins slated to pitch against right hander Bob Turley of the Yankees.

UPI TELEPHOTO

**MARILYN MONROE, JOE DiMAGGIO WATCHED**
*Actress, ex-Yankee star saw Twins win*

## $15 Limit Put on Gifts to Kennedys

By FLETCHER KNEBEL
Minneapolis Tribune Staff Correspondent

WASHINGTON — President Kennedy has placed a $15 limit on gifts the White House will accept.

Presents of all shapes, sizes and descriptions are pouring into the White House. More than 2,000 have been sent to the President and about triple that number to his family, Mrs. Jacqueline Kennedy, Caroline and John F. Kennedy, Jr.

The $15 limit, set by the President himself, is not a precise valuation, but a guideline for David F. Powers, the staff assistant in

Gifts
Continued on Page Seven

IN $30,000,000 DEAL

## Cream of Wheat, Nabisco to Merge

Agreement to merge Cream of Wheat Corp., Minneapolis, into National Biscuit Co., New York, has been reached in principle, the two companies announced Tuesday.

Terms of the proposal call for Nabisco to exchange 360,000 shares of common stock for the 600,000 shares of Cream of Wheat common outstanding, or six-tenths of a share to one.

**BASED ON** Nabisco's closing price of $82.25 yesterday, this would put a current market value of about 30 million dollars on the transaction.

Cream of Wheat, which employs 200 persons in its Minneapolis and Winnipeg, Canada, cereal plants, reported record sales of $11,796,880 in 1960. Profits were $1,365,809, or $2.28 per share.

Nabisco, which employs 25,000, reported 1960 sales of $451,800,000. The company makes biscuits, crackers, cereals, dog biscuits, breads and cakes, and cake mixes and processes fruits.

Daniel F. Bull, chairman, and David F. Bull, president of the 64-year-old Minneapolis company, declined to answer questions concerning the future corporate relationship of Cream of Wheat to Nabisco.

**DAVID BULL** declared he was "not prepared to say" whether the Cream of Wheat plant would remain operating in Minneapolis or whether the proposal was subject to approval of Cream of Wheat stockholders.

"The two companies have agreed not to make any

Nabisco
Continued on Page 12

## Israel Argues Right to Try Eichmann

Special to the Minneapolis Tribune

JERUSALEM—Israel's attorney general will open the second day of Adolf Eichmann's trial today with an attempt to hammer home the Jewish nation's right to try the former Nazi leader on mass murder charges.

Attorney General Gideon Hausner spent Tuesday night studying defense attorney Robert Servatius' bulky folder of documents challenging the court's jurisdiction. The challenge was made as the trial got under way yesterday thereby causing postponement of Eichmann's plea of guilty or not guilty.

After the hour-long reading of the 15-count indictment, Dr. Robert Servatius of Cologne, West Germany, Eichmann's attorney, challenged the court's jurisdiction not only on points of law but on the personalities of the three trial judges. There will be no jury.

**"THE FEAR** of possible bias exists with all the judges, stemming generally from the material of the trial," Servatius said.

The new, brilliantly lit auditorium was crowded shortly before 9 a.m. as Eichmann, wearing a new blue-gray suit and accompanied by two blue-uniformed guards, entered his bullet - proof glass cage and walked quickly to his seat.

Eichmann sat erect and half smiling as he looked about at the crowd. A neat man of 55, wearing black horn-rimmed spectacles and growing bald, he seemed quite ordinary. He would never be noticed in a crowd.

A pair of reading glasses lay on a counter in front of him. He touched them and listened as a third police officer explained the workings of the microphone and of the earphones through which

Eichmann
Continued on Page 12

PUTS ROLE OF FIRST LADY SECOND

## Mrs. Kennedy Voices Fear That Caroline May Become 'Spoiled'

WASHINGTON — (UPI) Mrs. Jacqueline Kennedy expressed concern Tuesday that the public attention showered on her 3-year-old daughter Caroline eventually may change her.

Mrs. Kennedy, who stressed that her role as first lady is second to her job as a mother and wife, said it is hard to raise children in the White House because "there is so little privacy."

**THE PRESIDENT'S** 31-year-old wife said her active blond child has not been affected by the White House spotlight so far because she is too small.

"But someday," she added, "she is going to have to go to school, and if she is in the newspapers all the time that will affect her little classmates and they will treat her differently. That is why I am so anxious—we always treat her the same, but it is how other people treat her because they have read about her."

Mrs. Kennedy discussed the matter in a television interview, the first she has granted since becoming first lady. The show was filmed March 24 with commentator Sandor Vanocur sitting beside Mrs. Kennedy by the fireplace in the Green room.

**ASKED** whether the White House was a "very good place to raise children" and whether her life had changed, she replied:

"It is rather hard with children. There is so little privacy. For instance I wanted to take my daughter to the circus last week, and I decided I shouldn't because I would ruin it for her.

"I worked so hard to make her ballet school a private thing we could do together, and there were all the photographers waiting there when we got there. So it is a little hard."

(Mrs. Kennedy finally sent Caroline to the circus with friends.)

She said she planned to send Caroline to school when she reaches kindergarten age, "but I rather hold my breath about that day."

As for herself, Mrs. Kennedy said she believes "every first lady should do something in this position to help the things she cares about."

She said, for example, that when she leaves the White House, she hopes she will have done something to help point up the arts. She said she also hoped to further "anything to do with children."

## Snow Expected in Part of Region

Snow is expected in parts of the Upper Midwest today, with the heaviest fall forecast for a 75-mile-wide strip running from the southwest corner of Minnesota to Duluth.

Accumulation of one to three inches is expected in that area. Light rain or snow is expected in Wisconsin most of the day and in western North Dakota and western South Dakota late today.

Predicted high temperatures today are in the 30s in Minnesota and eastern North Dakota, in the 40s in western North Dakota, 38 to 45 in South Dakota and 34 to 40 in northern Wisconsin.

Light snow, a high in the middle 30s today and a low of 20 tonight are forecast for the Twin Cities.

**Warmer**

MONDAY TEMPERATURES

| | | | | | |
|---|---|---|---|---|---|
| 2 a.m. | 33 | 10 a.m. | 36 | 6 p.m. | 38 |
| 3 a.m. | 33 | 11 a.m. | 37 | 7 p.m. | 37 |
| 4 a.m. | 34 | Noon | 38 | 8 p.m. | 37 |
| 5 a.m. | 35 | 1 p.m. | 38 | 9 p.m. | 36 |
| 6 a.m. | 34 | 2 p.m. | 39 | 10 p.m. | 36 |
| 7 a.m. | 34 | 3 p.m. | 39 | 11 p.m. | 36 |
| 8 a.m. | 35 | 4 p.m. | 39 | 12M | 35 |
| 9 a.m. | 35 | 5 p.m. | 39 | *1 a.m. | 34 |

Details Page 16 *Unofficial

# Minneapolis Morning Tribune

Vol. XCIV—No. 329 Copyright 1961 Minneapolis Star and Tribune Company MINNEAPOLIS, MINN., TUESDAY, APRIL 18, 1961 Telephone FE 3-3111 Price 7¢

# Anti-Castro Forces Report Cuba Invasion Successes

CUBAN WOMEN LINED COMMUNION RAILS IN MIAMI, FLA., TO PRAY FOR INVADERS

UPI TELEPHOTO

*The long-awaited invasion was launched against Castro forces Monday*

## Fidel Says His Troops Keep Up Fight

By Associated Press

Anti-Castro forces struck their long-awaited invasion blow for liberation of Cuba Monday and claimed immediate successes.

Their counter-revolutionary blows went in by air and sea with help from Castro foes rising inside Cuba.

**PREMIER** Fidel Castro announced early today that Cuban government troops are continuing their fight to repel the invasion.

In a communique broadcast over a hastily assembled nationwide radio network Castro said, "The revolutionary troops continue to fight heroically in southwest Las Villas province where mercenaries disembarked with imperialist support."

The two-paragraph statement, heard in Miami, Fla., said, "The successes of the revolutionary army, air force and militia will be announced to the people in the next few hours."

The communique was read by an announcer who said it was signed by "Dr. Fidel Castro, commander in chief and prime minister."

*(REDS SAY They'll Help Castro Cubans; CUBA SAYS U.S. Jets Attack From Carriers—Page Three.)*

**CASTRO'S** Havana radio last night called for students, workers and peasants to go about their business and work as usual. The broadcast may have been aimed at preventing a general strike. It urged vigilance against "counter-revolutionary worms."

Direct communications with Cuba were cut off and few of the rebel claims and reports could be confirmed. Among the reports were these:

The Cuban Revolutionary council in New York said in mid-evening that much of the 400,000-man militia Castro recruited "has already defected from Castro" and that the principal battle would be fought in a few hours.

"Our partisans in every town and village," it added, would receive the coded message "the fish will soon stand," to rise up against Castro and his remaining militiamen. The fish, it was pointed out, was a symbol of Christian resistance.

Anti-Castro sources in Mexico City, Mexico, were quoted as saying the Isle of

Cuba
Continued on Page Six

## Elizabeth Taylor, Burt Lancaster Win Top Oscars.

SANTA MONICA, Calif.—(AP)—Elizabeth Taylor, near death two months ago, reached the peak of her career Monday night by winning the award as best actress of 1960 from the Motion Picture academy.

Lancaster Miss Taylor

Miss Jones Ustinov

*In winning roles*

Burt Lancaster was acclaimed best actor for his role as the shady revivalist of "Elmer Gantry."

**"THE APARTMENT"** won as best picture. Billy Wilder of "The Apartment" was named best director.

Shirley Jones of "Elmer Gantry" and Peter Ustinov of "Spartacus" won the Oscars for supporting roles.

Miss Taylor originally refused the "Butterfield 8" role that won her the Oscar, because it cast her as a call girl.

When she heard her name called as winner by Yul Brynner, she clapped both hands over her mouth and stared in apparent astonishment. Then she turned to husband Eddie Fisher, and he helped her to her feet.

Still weakened by her bout with double pneumonia, she was helped to the stage of civic auditorium, walking slowly and uncertainly.

**SHE STOOD** trembling before the audience of 2,500 and finally said hesitantly in hushed and halting tones:

"I don't really know how to express my gratitude. All I can say is thank you very much."

**THE USUALLY** composed Lancaster also seemed shaken by his award.

He leaned over to kiss his wife, Norma, then proceeded slowly to the stage, still wearing his glasses. He removed them and made a brief acceptance speech, thanking members of the academy who voted for him. He added, grinning:

"Right now I feel so happy I want to thank all the members who didn't vote for me."

This was Lancaster's second Oscar nomination.

## Hoffa Picks 3 to Hear Charges

### Hearing Set on Accusations in City Local 544

By SAM ROMER
Minneapolis Tribune Staff Writer

A three-man panel has been named by President James R. Hoffa of the Teamsters International union to hear charges against Edward Blixt and Fred Snyder, president and secretary-treasurer of Minneapolis local 544.

A spokesman for Hoffa in Washington Monday said the panel will hold a hearing in Minneapolis April 27.

**A TEST** of the standing of both the administration and its foes within the local will take place May 19 and 20 when the membership votes on delegates to the Teamsters convention in July.

Both Snyder and Blixt as well as several of their opponents were nominated Sunday for the 10 vacancies—five delegates and five alternates.

As has been the custom in recent local 544 elections, the membership will ballot by voting machine. Members of the over-the-road local who will be out of the city will vote by absentee ballot.

**THE ELECTION,** however, will not settle the issues involved in the charges made against the two local 544 officers.

These were filed last month by two individual members of the union, both of whom had been active in a "rank-and file" group formed to protest the Snyder administration.

The group no longer exists although it may be revived for election purposes.

Snyder and Blixt have filed countercharges against the two individuals and these presumably will be heard by the same panel which tries the original allegations.

**THE PANEL** consists tentatively of James Konowe, New York, Hoffa's administrative assistant; Frank Fitzsimmons, Detroit, Mich., and Roy Williams, Kansas City, Mo.

Hoffa apparently took jurisdiction under a clause in the Teamsters constitution which empowers him to do so whenever charges "involve or relate to a situation imminently dangerous to the welfare of a local union."

In effect, this procedure bypasses the usual routine of having the charges tried by the local executive board, subject to an appeal to the joint council and then to the international.

Hoffa intervened after all sides agreed that any decision by the local board almost certainly would be appealed by the loser and thus keep the union membership in turmoil until the issue is settled.

**THERE HAS BEEN** no announcement as to the nature of the charges. However, they are believed to be linked to similar charges made in March 1960 against Snyder reportedly alleging excessive expense accounts and salary withdrawals.

At the time, Snyder denied any wrongdoing and called

Teamsters
Continued on Page Six

## Andersen Hails Legislature at Adjournment

By JOHN C. McDONALD
Minneapolis Tribune Staff Writer

Minnesota lawmakers went home for a week Monday following adjournment of the 1961 regular session.

The senate quit at 11:18 a.m. and the house of representatives adjourned at 4:50 p.m.

Gov. Andersen, who summoned them back into an extra session starting next Monday to complete the legislation that remained undone when the bill-passing deadline was reached at midnight Saturday, appeared briefly before each house yesterday.

He complimented members for legislative achievements "far above the average."

**"IT'S A** considerable list and an impressive one," he said to house members in reference to the more than 750 bills enacted into law. "I commend you, congratulate you and hope you have a good week at home."

He said he may speak to them again next Monday to outline his legislative recommendations for the special session.

Meantime the senate rules committee outlined boundaries within which it hopes to limit the scope of the upcoming session.

**THE SENATE'S** decision angered house Liberals, who said that prior to a special session two years ago, leaders of the two houses sat down together and agreed upon joint limitations. They postponed decision upon the limitations they will adopt. If the two bodies decide upon rules that are not alike, they may find one another killing bills from the opposite house

Legislature
Continued on Page Six

## Some Sunshine, Temperature in 50s Predicted

Intermittent sunshine and warmer temperatures are forecast for today in most parts of the Upper Midwest.

The weather bureau said Twin Cities temperatures will reach a high of 50, with tonight's low set at 30.

Other area highs will range from 45 to 55 in Minnesota, the 50s to the 60s in North Dakota and South Dakota and the mid 40s in Wisconsin.

## April Poetry Doesn't Cut Ice Here

By DON MORRISON
Minneapolis Tribune Staff Writer

"April," T. S. Eliot advises us, "is the cruelest month, breeding lilacs out of the dead land, mixing memory and desire, stirring dull roots with spring rain."

Mr. Eliot concludes his poem with the observation: "Datta. Dayadhvam. Damyata. Shantih shantih shantih."

The latter is quoted from the Sanskrit epic, the Upanishad, and means the equivalent of Give. Sympathize. Control. Peace.

Quite the opposite of this April in Minnesota, which has been stirring tempers with snowstorms, not dull roots with rain.

We don't know what other Minnesotans said when they looked out their windows Saturday morning. We said, "Damyata!"

And we didn't mean "peace."

An unusually surly-looking squirrel overheard us and nodded. "Dayadhvam," it muttered, then abandoned the snowdrift in which it had been digging and headed for the neighbor's bird-feeding station.

The weekend snowfall was the heaviest for an April since 1907, when 13 inches fell on April 26 and 27.

We are indebted to Joseph H. Strub, weather bureau climatologist for this datta.

He rehearsed a few April atrocities for us Monday. On April 15 and 16, 1897, for example, 6.5 inches of snow fell.

Other snowfalls were 6.3 inches, April 21-22, 1904; 8.5, April 12, 1928, and 7.4 on April 4-5, 1957.

We won't even mention

April
Continued on Page Six



## Almanac

### Gray Flannel Bonnet Has Bee in It

*Tuesday, April 18, 1961*
Sunrise 5:24 a.m.; sunset 7:02 p.m.

There'll Always Be an Adman's Victim Dept.: In the written test for the Minneapolis Tribune Spelling Bee Saturday, one of the words was "saccharin."

Several of the kids spelled it "Sucaril."

•

***Partly cloudy and warmer today in the Twin Cities. High today 50, low tonight 30.***

•

A Golden Valley mother received a birthday card from her small daughter on which was written the equivocal message: "Happy birthday, Mother. You are younger than you look."

## Kennedy Sends Farm Bill to Congress, Asks Haste

By CHARLES W. BAILEY
Minneapolis Tribune Staff Correspondent

WASHINGTON — A far-reaching farm bill to make possible sweeping changes in the nation's agricultural programs was sent to congress Monday by the Kennedy administration with urgent appeals for speedy action.

The 70-page bill, drafted in the agriculture department but given important finishing touches by congressional farm leaders, offered a framework under which the administration, with the advice and approval of both farmers and congress, would be empowered to write new programs for any or all commodities.

**AMONG THE** mechanisms that would be authorized are 90 per cent of parity price supports; direct production payments to farmers; nationwide marketing orders or marketing quotas for all commodities, and production control through acreage allotments, bushel-bale-pound limits or restrictions on "production units" such as milk cows or hogs.

Agriculture Secretary Orville L. Freeman, calling the proposal "no panacea, but a license for hard work," joined the President in asking for swift approval.

"Delay or postponement now could mean economic disaster. Time is running out," he said.

Mr. Kennedy asked "prompt consideration." Administration officials are hopeful hearings will start within a fortnight.

**SEVERAL** important revisions were made over the weekend at the suggestion of Sen. Allen J. Ellender (D., La.), chairman of the senate agriculture committee, and other legislators. The main result of the changes was to give congress a larger role in shaping proposed new programs.

As finally submitted yesterday, the administration bill would authorize separate programs for each farm commodity. Aim of the programs would be to balance production with demand and to raise farmers' prices and incomes.

The proposal calls for establishment of farmer committees, chosen by the agriculture secretary from nominations made by farmers and farm organizations, to help write commodity programs.

The procedure for writing and putting into effect new supply-control and price-support programs would be this:

**The agriculture** secretary would consult with the commodity advisory committee, then draft a program for the crop.

**This would be** submitted to congress, which would have 60 days in which it could veto the program by majority vote of either house if it did not approve.

**If the program** were not killed by congress, it would be submitted to a referendum vote of the producers

Farm
Continued on Page Six

## General Is Relieved in Birch Controversy

WASHINGTON — (AP) — Maj. Gen. Edwin A. Walker has been relieved of his division command in Germany pending a "complete and impartial" investigation of statements that he exposed his troops to a propaganda barrage about the John Birch society.

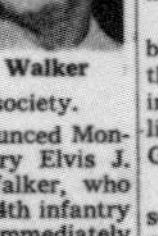

Walker

The army announced Monday that Secretary Elvis J. Stahr ordered Walker, who commanded the 24th infantry division, shifted immediately to United States army in Europe headquarters at Heidelberg, West Germany, pending the outcome of the inquiry.

**SEVERAL** congress members demanded an investigation last week after a privately owned servicemen's newspaper, Overseas Weekly, reported that an information program set up by Walker was distributing material about the philosophy of the controversial John Birch society.

The 51-year-old bachelor general, who commanded the troops at Little Rock, Ark., during the 1957 integration disorders, denied that the program was connected with any organization or society.

"It is designed to develop the understanding of American military and civil heritage, responsibility toward that heritage, and the tactics and objectives of those enemies who would destroy it," Walker said.

**HE ALSO** described as untrue statements attributed to him that former President Harry S. Truman, former Secretary of State Dean Acheson and Mrs. Eleanor Roosevelt are "definitely pink."

The army statement did not mention the Birch society, a militantly conservative anti-Communist organization, but officials said it was the matter involved.

The army said Walker was being transferred "pending the outcome of an official investigation of certain public statements and actions of Gen. Walker."

**AMONG** other things, the servicemen's newspaper quoted him as saying 60 per cent of the American press, radio and TV industry is Communist.

Gen. Bruce Clarke, commander in chief of army forces in Europe, directed Lt. Gen. Frederick J. Brown, commanding general of the V corps at Frankfurt, West Germany, to conduct the investigation.

On April 11, several days before the controversy arose, the army announced that in August Walker would be reassigned as commanding general of the VIII army corps at Austin, Texas. Yesterday the army said there has been no change in this order.



## U.S. Offers Cuban Rebels Its Sympathy

By RICHARD WILSON
Chief of the Minneapolis Tribune Washington Bureau

WASHINGTON—The United States government gave its "sympathy" but carefully refrained Monday from intervention in the rebel attempt to establish a base in Cuba to overthrow the regime of Fidel Castro.

As invaders landed in Cuba by sea and air, the chief question discussed here was whether the attackers could establish and hold pockets of military opposition to Castro's militia.

If so, it is expected that the head of the revolutionary council, Dr. Jose Miro Cardona, will try to establish a headquarters in Cuba and appeal for support from all the American countries in a prolonged guerilla war.

**OFFICIALS** of revolutionary organizations in New York claim that far superior forces of Cuban militiamen find it impossible to mop up guerrillas in the Escambray mountains and Oriente province. The new invaders are expected to further complicate Castro's problem of keeping supplied with food and war material his hastily organized militia estimated at 250,000.

Secretary of State Dean Rusk repeated President Kennedy's declaration of nonintervention yesterday, but went a step further than the President at a press confer-

Sympathy
Continued on Page Six

## Clothing Worth $14,000 Stolen; 3 Men Sought

Police Monday sought three "extremely well-dressed" men wanted on suspicion of breaking into a downtown Minneapolis clothing store and stealing a spring wardrobe valued at $14,000.

Taken from Hubert W. White Co., 611 Marquette Av., were 198 silk neckties with a retail value of $9 each, 8 sport jackets selling at $195 each and 42 suits bearing price tags of about $250 each.

Police said the prime suspects were three "young, good-looking and extremely well-dressed" men who visited the store last week and aroused the suspicion of clerks by examining the layout carefully.

## Highway Official Faces Challenge: His Driver's Test

One of the first challenges for Minnesota's new highway commissioner will be to take written and road tests for a driver's license.

Marshall

James C. Marshall, a retired general who lives in New York state, is expected to arrive in Minnesota Friday.

Sometime next week he will perform at the steering wheel for a state inspector in order to exchange his New York license for a Minnesota permit.

"He'll take the tests just like anyone else," said Holt Warn, secretary to the commissioner.

Marshall, who will replace L. P. Zimmerman, has said he plans an extensive tour of Minnesota highways early in the summer. He has said he will do his own driving—"to get the viewpoint of a motorist."

**Light Rain**

FRIDAY TEMPERATURES

| | | | | | |
|---|---|---|---|---|---|
| 2 a.m. | 51 | 10 a.m. | 52 | 6 p.m. | 60 |
| 3 a.m. | 50 | 11 a.m. | 53 | 7 p.m. | 59 |
| 4 a.m. | 49 | Noon | 55 | 8 p.m. | 58 |
| 5 a.m. | 48 | 1 p.m. | 56 | 9 p.m. | 57 |
| 6 a.m. | 48 | 2 p.m. | 57 | 10 p.m. | 56 |
| 7 a.m. | 48 | 3 p.m. | 60 | 11 p.m. | 55 |
| 8 a.m. | 49 | 4 p.m. | 61 | 12 M. | 53 |
| 9 a.m. | 51 | 5 p.m. | 60 | *1 a.m. | 51 |

*Details Page 28* *Unofficial

# Minneapolis Morning Tribune

Vol. XCIV—No. 347  MINNEAPOLIS, MINN., SATURDAY, MAY 6, 1961 Telephone FE 3-3111 Price 7c

## 115 Miles Up Between Handshakes

AP WIREPHOTO

A GOOD-BYE HANDSHAKE BEFORE ALAN SHEPARD LEFT

AP WIREPHOTO

HE WAS HOISTED TO HELICOPTER AFTER CAPSULE LANDED

UPI TELEPHOTO

A WELCOME BACK HANDSHAKE AS HE LEFT HELICOPTER

**For picture stories on Shepard's day, technical problems involved in the shoot and how a Minneapolis firm helped solve them, see pages 2 and 3.**

# American Hopes Soar Along With Successful Astronaut

## *West Rejoices; Reds Disdainful*

**From the Tribune Wire Services**

Alan Shepard's space flight was hailed by America's allies Friday, but the Communists were disdainful.

Millions of Britons listened to a direct radio report of the feat and British newspapers broke out with banner headlines such as "Heavens above! He's up and down."

**IT TOOK MOSCOW RADIO** just over an hour after the flight to come up with a brief factual report near the end of a regular afternoon news bulletin.

Moscow radio named Shepard as the astronaut and said the flight lasted 15 minutes, attaining a maximum altitude of 115 miles.

Two hours later, Moscow radio dropped the item from its 9 p.m. newscast and the Soviet news agency, Tass, still had not reported the space flight.

The news came too late for the evening newspaper Izvestia. But the paper carried a New York item from Tass saying the aim of American astronauts was to "buy houses, industrial plants and stores" with profits made from writing articles about the space flights.

But Radio Free Europe, an anti-Communist radio station in Munich, West Germany, sponsored by a private American organization, was quick to broadcast the news to Poland, Czechoslovakia, Romania and Bulgaria.

**IN DERRY, N. H.,** the whole town—and more—turned out to help the overjoyed parents of Shepard celebrate.

The astronaut's parents, Mr. and Mrs. Alan B. Shepard, Sr., with their daughter, Pauline, were the stars of the biggest parade Derry has seen, and the biggest gathering of spectators in the town's history.

Gov. Wesley Powell came to Derry to join in the parade, greeting Mrs. Shepard with a hug and a kiss as he said: "This is the greatest day in the history of the state."

The Shepards said they prayed all through the flight for the safety of Alan and for success.

After the flight they got a phone call from Cdr. Shepard's wife, Louise, at Virginia Beach, Va.

The eldest Shepard couldn't remember what she said. "But she was deliriously happy," he added.

**A BEAMING LOUISE SHEPARD** said in Virginia Beach her husband's journey to the fringe of space was "just a baby step" compared to new challenges ahead.

"Would you like to see your husband in orbit around the earth?" she was asked. She hesitated.

"Well," she said, drawing the word out, "it is a hard question. But," she sighed, "yes, since he wants it so very badly."

Here are other comments:

**Sen. Hubert H. Humphrey** (D., Minn.): "If we cannot

**Reaction**
**Continued on Page Two**

## Shepard Gets Presidential Congratulations

WASHINGTON — (AP) — When President Kennedy congratulated Cdr. Alan Shepard by radio-telephone Friday after the Astronaut's space flight, here is what they said as recorded at the White House:

**The President:** "Hello Commander."

**Shepard:** "Yes, sir."

**Mr. Kennedy:** "I want to congratulate you very much."

**Shepard:** "Thank you very much, Mr. President."

**Mr. Kennedy:** "We watched you on TV, of course, and we are awfully pleased and proud of what you did."

**Shepard:** "Well, thank you, sir. As you know by now, everything worked out just about perfectly. And it was a very rewarding experience for me and for the people who made it possible."

**Mr. Kennedy:** "We are looking forward to seeing you up here, commander."

**Shepard:** "Thank you very much. I am looking forward to it, I assure you."

**Mr. Kennedy:** "The members of the national security council are meeting on another matter this morning, and they all want me to give you their congratulations."

**Shepard:** "Thank you very much, sir, and I am looking forward to meeting you in the near future."

**Mr. Kennedy:** "Thank you, commander, and good luck."

## Shepard Calls It 'Whale of a Trip'; Scientists Agree

**By JACK WILSON**
**Minneapolis Tribune Staff Correspondent**

CAPE CANAVERAL, Fla.—Freedom Seven was A-OK Friday and America's space hopes soared again when Alan Shepard calmly climbed out of his space capsule after a 302-mile rocket trip.

It was the most exciting day this capital of excitement had seen. Veteran rocket men who have watched dozens of launchings yelled like tourists when the word came that Shepard's little space capsule was descending on target and that its pilot was safe.

**AN OLD-TIME** reporter, veteran of the police beat and the political campaigns, pulled a rosary out of his pocket and murmured a prayer of hope when the first flames shot out of the big rocket at the moment of launching.

The least excited man in the whole affair was the 37-year-old navy commander who made the 15-minute excursion beyond the fringes of space as casually as though he were driving his white sports car down a familiar street.

And even Shepard showed that he was pleased about it. "A whale of a trip," he exclaimed after he landed and was carried safely aboard the aircraft carrier Lake Champlain, where he was greeted with the news that President Kennedy wanted to talk to him by radiotelephone.

**THE FLIGHT,** even though it was delayed two hours by unfavorable weather, was a marvel of precision. "As nearly perfect as we could ever expect," said Walter C. Williams, the launch director.

"An absolutely perfect flight," said Wernher von Braun, national aeronautics and space administration (NASA) rocket expert.

Said Lt. Col. John Glenn, the back-up astronaut who would have made the trip if Shepard had suddenly become unable to, "Just leave those ships out there and give us another rocket and we'll repeat it this afternoon."

The flight was a sorely needed shot in the arm for America's man in space program. It did not equal the achievement of Russian rocketeers who launched Yuri Gagarin into orbit and brought him back safely three weeks ago.

But it was the first

**Space Flight**
**Continued on Page Four**

Glenn Gilruth
*'We'll repeat it'*

## Twins Beat Red Sox, 5-1

Jack Kralick Yields Only Six Hits in Winning His Second Game

*(DETAILS in Sports Section.)*

## JFK Studies Sending U.S. Forces to Asia

**By RICHARD WILSON**
**Chief of the Minneapolis Tribune Washington Bureau**

WASHINGTON — The United States government is believed to be preparing to use its military forces to prevent further Communist expansion in southeast Asia.

President Kennedy said Friday that he is considering the wisdom of using forces in South Viet Nam but that no firm decision has been reached.

**FROM OTHER** sources, however, comes information that Vice President Johnson has been instructed to tell Viet Nam officials that the United States will fight if guerrilla forces internally and Viet Minh and Pathet Lao forces from the outside threaten the pro-western government.

The United States is reported also prepared to aid the governments of Thailand and Cambodia if they desire it. Thailand is aligned with the West. Cambodia is a neutralist country.

Johnson will leave next week on a world trip that will take him to southeast Asia for the specific purpose of backing up the anti-Communist forces and governments.

**WHAT ACTION** the United States government will take will depend, Mr. Kennedy said, on further consultations with friendly governments in southeast Asia. These consultations evidently now are going on to determine the extent and nature of United States military support.

The action the government now is contemplating is based on the concept that Laos, under the cease-fire, is unavoidably being drawn into the Communist grouping, and may become the base from which future assaults on other southeastern Asian nations will be launched.

**IT IS BELIEVED** that the United States will send not only its own troops but seek forces from other nations in the Southeast Asia Treaty organization (SEATO). The threat to Viet Nam was mentioned in the resolution for possible intervention adopted by SEATO.

But it is now evident that the United States will take the leading part in supplying the forces that would bolster the pro-western forces.

In advancing toward the final decision on the use of

**U.S. Forces**
**Continued on Page Four**

## JFK Warns: Space Efforts Need Money

WASHINGTON — (AP) — President Kennedy publicly and proudly rejoiced Friday at America's launching of a man into space. But he tempered elation with word that more money must be poured into redoubled efforts to explore space.

Minutes after navy Cdr. Alan Shepard returned from flashing 115 miles into the skies, Mr. Kennedy issued a statement saying, "All America rejoices in this successful flight" — but it also should provide an incentive for redoubled efforts "in this vital field."

**AT A LATER** news conference the President spoke with pride of Shepard's accomplishment and again of the challenge that lies ahead.

He said that he is going to ask congress for additional appropriations—"We are going to make a substantially larger effort in space."

After a bow to the human accomplishment and courage demonstrated in Russia's successful effort to put a man into orbit around the earth and bring him back, Mr. Kennedy added:

**"WE HAVE** a long way to go in the field of space. We are behind. But we are working hard and we are going to increase our efforts."

He repeated what he had said earlier, that the United States intends to share with the world the scientific information obtained in yesterday's space flight and will continue to be motivated by the view that "the probe into space should be peaceful."

To his knowledge, Mr. Kennedy said, Russia has not offered to share the facts it developed from its manned space shot.

**THE AMERICAN** shot, covered in minute detail by reporters and cameramen, led

**Kennedy**
**Continued on Page Five**

## *Are the Twins Mudders? Today May Tell*

The Minnesota Twins may find a soggy field for today's game with the Boston Red Sox.

Light rain will spatter the Twin Cities and the rest of the Upper Midwest, the weather bureau predicted.

The Twin Cities will be slightly cooler, with the high 52, the low 42.

Showers are expected throughout Minnesota, South Dakota, North Dakota and Wisconsin. Highs will range from 45 to 55 over the region.

### Launching Viewed by Judge With 'Evidence'

INDIANAPOLIS, Ind. —(AP) — A stolen television set, brought into court as evidence in an Indianapolis trial, did double duty.

While waiting for cases to come up for hearing, Judge Thomas J. Faulconer and his staff turned on the set and watched the astronaut launching.

### Plastic Bag Kills Mock Astronaut

DERBY, England — (AP) — A 23-year-old steelworker, Herbert P. Kennedy, was found dead Friday with a plastic bag over his head.

A neighbor told police: "Herbert had read about the American astronaut and was playing at being a spaceman."

### TURN THE PAGES TO:



## DFL Plans Talks to End Labor Split

**By CHARLES HANNA**
**Minneapolis Tribune Staff Writer**

Minnesota and Hennepin county DFL leaders will try this weekend to patch the labor split in the party before the Minneapolis general election June 13.

A major break occurred Wednesday when the Committee on Political Education (COPE) of the Central Labor union (CLU) council moved to oppose Arthur Naftalin, a DFLer, who won nomination in the primary race for mayor.

**ALTHOUGH** COPE took no formal action opposing Naftalin, its sentiment was clear.

Walter Cramond, CLU president, was asked to appoint a committee to consider ways to stop Naftalin.

Cramond said the possibilities included a write-in vote for Roe, a boycott of the polls or a shift to Mayor P. K. Peterson, a Republican who also was nominated in the primary.

Cramond said labor is disenchanted with Naftalin for his anti-labor attitudes while he was state commissioner of administration under former Gov. Orville Freeman.

**HE SAID** the labor group objects to Naftalin's over-all position and that many of the union members feel that Naftalin is not a true Liberal.

George Farr, chairman of the state DFL central committee, said yesterday he would probably discuss the problem today or Sunday with Steve Nehotte, county DFL chairman.

Farr said chances of a new DFL convention being called to seek harmony in the party are "most unlikely."

"We want to confer with

**Labor**
**Continued on Page Five**

## Almanac

### Versailles Is Lost to Baseball Wars

*Saturday, May 6, 1961*
Sunrise 5:43 a.m.; sunset 6:48 p.m.

A Princeton high school history instructor complains that the boys in his class insist on pronouncing "Versailles," as in the treaty, like Versalles, as in the Minnesota Twins shortstop.

•

***Light rain is expected in the Twin Cities today. High 52, low 42.***

•

On election day in Minneapolis this week, a man showed up at the Fulton school polling place with a 4-year-old boy in tow. Told he couldn't bring his cigar into the polls, he gave it to the boy to hold for him out in the hall. Eyebrows were never higher than those on passers-by for the next few minutes.

Snow

TUESDAY TEMPERATURES

| | | | | | |
|---|---|---|---|---|---|
| 2 a.m. | 4 | 10 a.m. | 4 | 6 p.m. | 11 |
| 3 a.m. | 3 | 11 a.m. | 8 | 7 p.m. | 12 |
| 4 a.m. | 1 | Noon | 10 | 8 p.m. | [illegible] |
| 5 a.m. | -1 | 1 p.m. | 13 | 9 p.m. | 12 |
| 6 a.m. | -3 | 2 p.m. | 13 | 10 p.m. | 12 |
| 7 a.m. | -4 | 3 p.m. | 12 | 11 p.m. | 12 |
| 8 a.m. | -4 | 4 p.m. | 12 | 12M | 12 |
| 9 a.m. | 0 | 5 p.m. | 12 | *1 a.m. | 12 |

Details Page 18 *Unofficial

# Minneapolis Morning Tribune

Vol. XCV—No. 273  MINNEAPOLIS, MINN., WEDNESDAY, FEBRUARY 21, 1962 Telephone FE 3-3111 Price 7c

# 'WE ARE PROUD OF YOU,' PRESIDENT TELLS GLENN

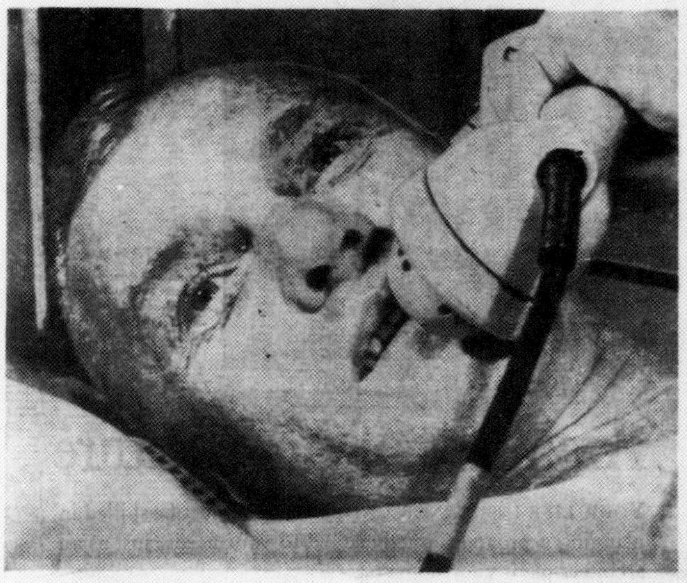

Associated Press

Seasoned astronaut Glenn talked with the President after his recovery

## Other Orbit Stories Inside



## Kennedy Plans to Visit Astronaut in Florida

By JACK WILSON
Minneapolis Tribune Staff Correspondent

CAPE CANAVERAL, Fla.—Astronaut John H. Glenn Jr. soared triumphantly around the world three times Tuesday and had scarcely splashed down safely in the Atlantic when President Kennedy took steps to honor him.

Mr. Kennedy telephoned his congratulations to the freckle-faced, grinning pilot on the destroyer Noa and arranged to fly to Cape Canaveral Friday to tender a grateful nation's thanks.

United Press International

MRS. ANNIE GLENN BEAMED AT NEWSMEN
*She had faith all along*

The President, who anxiously watched the orbital flight over television, told the 40-year-old Marine lieutenant colonel by radio phone:

**"COLONEL,** we are really proud of you and I must say you did a wonderful job."

"Thanks, Mr. President," replied the astronaut with the same composure he had displayed throughout his near 18,000-mile-an-hour circuit of the globe.

The President's announcement that he would make a flying visit to Glenn also disclosed that he would receive the astronaut in Washington, D. C., on Monday or Tuesday. That event is likely to touch off a huge celebration for the national hero.

**GLENN WAS** picked up in the Atlantic by the Noa and, after taking a shower aboard the vessel, talked to his wife and Mr. Kennedy.

At 5:44 p.m., he was transferred by helicopter to the anti-submarine carrier Randolph for a brief physical examination and at 8:04 p.m. was sent by helicopter to Grand Turk Island in the Bahamas, arriving about 9 p.m. There he saw his fourth sunset of the day.

He was to remain at Grand Turk for about 48 hours and undergo a more exhaustive physical examination and questioning about his flight by a team of scientists and doctors.

Vice President Lyndon Johnson will visit him there and will fly with him to meet the President.

There was someone else vitally interested in Glenn's welfare: his wife.

At her Arlington, Va., home, Mrs. Glenn, her face shining with happiness, told reporters, "I'm happy — I feel great."

Glenn parachuted to a safe landing in his space capsule yesterday after three trips around the world.

The Mercury capsule,

Orbit Flight
Continued on Page Eight

## City Goes Into Orbit With Glenn

Minneapolis police went to jail.

Children refused to go to school.

Women went shopping with transistor radios tucked in their purses.

**THE MAYOR** and other city officials went running from a meeting.

The Marines went wild.

For just about every Minneapolis area resident, young or old, no matter where he went Tuesday, he was "go"ing with Astronaut John Glenn.

Early yesterday morning, dozens of city policemen crowded around one of the few television sets in city hall — right smack in the city jail — to watch Glenn's space capsule rise from the launch pad.

**A FEW** minutes later, in southeast Minneapolis, a 4-year-old boy refused to leave for nursery school until his mother guaranteed him he could watch the excitement on TV there.

In mid-morning, as a woman wandered through the notions department of a store, a muffled voice blared from her purse with the information that Glenn was passing over Australia.

Shortly after lunch, just about the time Mayor Arthur Naftalin was telling a meeting about space problems—City Hall variety — someone yelled that Glenn had just splashed into the Atlantic Ocean. The meeting adjourned quickly to a television set in the next room.

**IT WAS** one of thousands of sets tuned in to the space shot. Northern States Power

Minneapolis
Continued on Page Eight

## Snowstorm Begins Howling Into Region

A fresh snowstorm howling in from the Rockies hit South Dakota late Tuesday afternoon and headed for the Twin Cities.

Up to 15 inches of new snow were predicted. By sunset the storm had dropped three inches of snow and edged its way into southern Minnesota, where it was expected to leave 4 inches or more by today.

Light snow and some drifting was predicted for the Twin Cities.

Total accumulation will be two or three inches today.

Heavy snow warnings also were out for northern Iowa and southern Wisconsin.

**WHIRLING** snow cut visibility to 500 feet on some South Dakota roads by late afternoon yesterday.

The State Highway Department advised no auto travel east of Pierre. North-northeast winds up to 35 miles an hour were reported in the area. Western Airlines canceled its Pierre flights.

Public schools in Faulkton, Redfield, Doland and Castelwood closed early, giving pupils a chance to get home before the blizzard began in earnest late in the afternoon.

Gov. Archie Gubbrud canceled a trip to a Student Government Day banquet in Yankton.

The weather bureau said the storm was to spread east

Weather
Continued on Page Seven

## TURN THE PAGES TO:



## Wisconsin Man Slated for Next Trip Into Space

From the Tribune Wire Services

CAPE CANAVERAL, Fla—Now that John Herschel Glenn Jr. has floated weightless in the heavens as the nation's first human satellite, America can rocket toward more space adventures: Man on the moon, man among the planets.

But first things first. Next—perhaps within six to eight weeks — astronaut Donald K. Slayton will travel the Glenn way through the skies; three times around and down.

**WHILE GLENN** was in orbit, workers at the General Dynamics Convair plant in San Diego, Calif., were finishing preparation of the next man-carrying Atlas.

B. G. McNabb, General Dynamics operations officer here, said the rocket had been held at the factory in case any modifications were required as a result of Glenn's shot. It seemed clear, McNabb said, that the launching was so successful that the new rocket could be moved here quickly, without any important changes.

That is the rocket that will carry astronaut Donald Slayton into an orbital flight similar to Glenn's.

**SLAYTON,** 37, an Air Force test pilot from Sparta, Wis., is preparing for a three-orbit ride essentially identical to Glenn's.

(The mother of the second astronaut scheduled for the orbital flight said Tuesday her son has told her he's "anxious to get off the ground.")

(As for herself, Mrs. Charles Slayton said the success of Glenn's flight eases her anxiety about the hours when her son will be in a Mercury space capsule.

(Mrs. Slayton listened with her husband to radio reports of Glenn's flight.)

**BEFORE THE** end of the year, two more thrice-around flights using the Atlas rocket are probable; and hopefully, one trip 18 times around, in an attempt to match Russian cosmonaut Gherman Titov's one-day trip.

In 1963, more 18-orbit missions, all designed to get more information about the mysterious illness suffered by Maj. Titov in his long flight, are planned.

In 1964, two men in a capsule are expected to be whirling around the earth for

Next
Continued on Page Seven

Associated Press

SPACE CAPSULE PULLED OUT OF OCEAN
*Astronaut Glenn was still inside*

*IT WAS A BEAUTIFUL DAY*

## *Clouds Parted, the Rocket Rose*

By VICTOR COHN
Minneapolis Tribune Staff Writer

CAPE CANAVERAL, Fla. — It was a beautiful day at Cape Canaveral, the day that put the first American into orbit.

It started in the glare of powerful searchlights. They shone on a great white rocket inside a brick-red steel frame called a gantry.

**THEIR BEAMS** crisscrossed into the black late night sky, stopping ominously on a low bank of clouds.

Five o'clock, six o'clock, seven o'clock. The clouds widened and spread. They would have prevented a launching.

About a quarter to eight they started disappearing. By eight a bright sun had broken through.

**AT 6:03 A.M.** EST (5:03 a.m. Minneapolis time), John Glenn—looking pleasant but intent, not nervous—entered his spacecraft to begin his day inside its space, about the size of a phone booth.

### Cohn, Wilson at Canaveral

*Jack Wilson of the Minneapolis Tribune Washington Bureau and Victor Cohn, Minneapolis Tribune staff writer, were at Cape Canaveral, Fla., for astronaut John Glenn's orbital flight.*

A radio beacon, essential for tracking, failed in the Atlas rocket. A breathing sensor failed and had to be replaced in Glenn's helmet.

A bolt broke in the spacecraft hatch, and the hatch had to be removed for repair. The count—short here for "countdown" started and stopped, started and stopped.

**BUT AT 8:28 A.M.** EST the 10-story gantry was rolled back on wide rails, and the rocket stood free, tiny capsule and Glenn at the top, and the sun shone beautiful and bright in a nearly cloudless blue sky.

Next came fueling with forced icy liquid oxygen—it must be kept at nearly minus 300 degrees—from a vent at the top of the rocket. Out came its fumes like steam from a tea kettle.

**MORE FUMES** rolled down the missile's stainless steel side and made missile and spacecraft and Glenn vibrate and rattle.

A liquid oxygen loading valve had to be replaced. Electrical power failed in a computer at Bermuda, essential to compute in a wink whether the rocket was putting Glenn in proper orbit, or whether he must be brought right down.

Everything was fixed quickly.

**ONE EAGER** watcher in

Cape
Continued on Page Eight

## *A Friendly Voice From Space*

*CAPE CANAVERAL, Fla. — (UPI) — Here is a voice from space—an edited transcript of what astronaut John H. Glenn Jr. radioed to earth during his three-orbit space flight:*

"5-4-3-2-1. Liftoff. The clock is operating. We are under way.

"It is a little bumpy along about here. Coming into high gear a little bit. A little contrail went by the window, or something.

"Coming out real fine. Flight very smooth now."

**(GLENN REPORTED** a steady flow of technical information on such items as cabin pressure, booster engine cutoff, oscillations, fuel and his own physical condition.)

"Zero G and I feel fine. Capsule is turning around. Oh! That view is tremendous. Capsule turning around, and I can see the booster doing turnarounds just a couple of hundred yards behind. It looks beautiful.

"Can see clear back a big cloud pattern away back across the cape. Beautiful sight.

"Temperature is 60 on the suit. I am very comfortable.

**"THE HORIZON** is a brilliant blue. There I have the mainland in sight at present time coming up on the scope and have the Canaries in sight, through the window and picked them up on the scope just before I saw them out the window." (At this point he was passing over the Canary Islands for the first time.)

Technical communications continued until Glenn came in radio contact with fellow astronaut Gordon Cooper stationed at Muchea, Australia.

**"HELLO COOP,** this is Friendship 7 reading you loud and clear. We are doing real fine up here. Everything is going real well.

". . . The only unusual thing I have noticed was the rather high, what appeared to be a haze layer up some 7 or 8 degrees above the horizon on the night side, the stars I can see through it as they go down toward the real horizon, but it is a very visible single band, or layer or . . . above the normal horizon.

"I had a lot of cloud cover coming off of Africa. It has thinned out considerably now and although I can't definitely see . . . there is a lot of moonlight here that reflects off of what clouds there are.

"That was a short day. That was about the shortest day I have ever run into.

**"JUST** to my right I can see a big pattern of light. Apparently right on the coast (of Australia), I can see . . . and a very bright light just to the south of it.

"I have had no ill ef-

Transcript
Continued on Page Seven

## Almanac

### She's the One Who Needs Their Help

*Wednesday, Feb. 21, 1962*
Sunrise, 7:05 a.m.; sunset, 5:49 p.m.

A Camp Fire Girls' group was meeting and the leader asked if the mothers of some members might not help out with some activities of the troop. Said one child:

"Oh, I'm afraid my mother couldn't do anything for two reasons: She's got a new baby and she seems to hate kids."

•

*Two or three inches of snow and winds up to 25 miles an hour in the Twin Cities today. High 20, low tonight 15.*

•

Letter from one politician to another politician (of dissimilar partisan tastes) wound up with this sweeping stroke of courtesy: "I close wishing you the very best of luck — with the exception of the next election."

**Warmer**

SUNDAY TEMPERATURES

| | | | | | |
|---|---|---|---|---|---|
| 2 a.m. | 46 | 10 a.m. | 47 | 6 p.m. | 46 |
| 3 a.m. | 46 | 11 a.m. | 50 | 7 p.m. | 41 |
| 4 a.m. | 44 | Noon | 50 | 8 p.m. | 39 |
| 5 a.m. | 43 | 1 p.m. | 51 | 9 p.m. | 40 |
| 6 a.m. | 42 | 2 p.m. | 52 | 10 p.m. | 37 |
| 7 a.m. | 41 | 3 p.m. | 51 | 11 p.m. | 38 |
| 8 a.m. | 42 | 4 p.m. | 51 | 12 m. | 36 |
| 9 a.m. | 44 | 5 p.m. | 48 | *1 a.m. | 35 |

Details Page 18 *Unofficial

# Minneapolis Morning Tribune

Vol. XCVI—No. 158 Copyright 1962 Minneapolis Star and Tribune Company MINNEAPOLIS, MINN., MONDAY, OCTOBER 29, 1962 Telephone FE 3-3111 Single Copy Price 10c Lower Price for Carrier Delivery

# KHRUSHCHEV ORDERS SOVIET MISSILES HOME FROM CUBA

## Vikings Beat Eagles in Rough Tilt, 31-21

*Giants End Redskin Streak; Green Bay Edges Baltimore*

*(DETAILS in Sports Section.)*

## U.S. Probes Claim of Improper Work on Road in State

**By DAVID MAZIE**
**Minneapolis Tribune Staff Writer**

The United States Bureau of Public Roads is investigating charges of substandard construction on a stretch of Minnesota interstate highway scheduled to open Thursday.

Rep. John A. Blatnik, D-Minn., said Sunday two investigators from the bureau have been assigned to look into allegations involving a stretch of Interstate 35 near Hinckley.

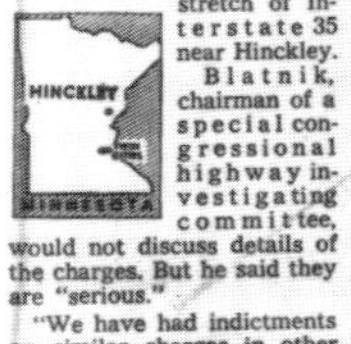


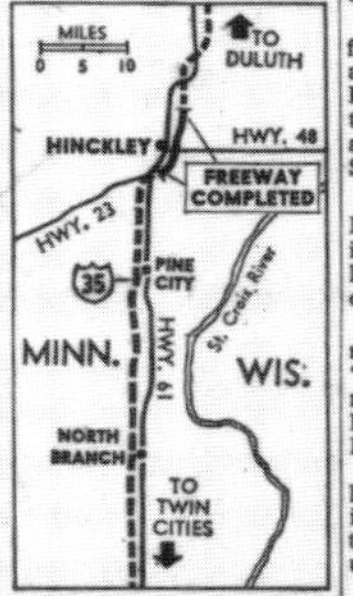


**HIGHWAY UNDER PROBE**
*Black line, completed or near complete; dotted, planned*

Blatnik, chairman of a special congressional highway investigating committee, would not discuss details of the charges. But he said they are "serious."

"We have had indictments on similar charges in other states," he said.

"If the present investigation turns up anything, we will move into it," he said. "If there is anything there, we will find it."

Blatnik's committee has found substandard construction practices, fraud and collusion in the highway program in several states.

Minnesota recently was cited on a national television program as one of the few states with an absolutely clean record.

**IT WAS** learned last night that the charges were made within the last month by an inspector of material in highway construction who has been with the Minnesota Highway Department for five years.

The alleged irregularities involve three instances where road construction specifications or normal procedures were not followed.

The inspector said in a notorized statement that he had heard there was pressure to get the job done by Nov. 1.

**HE SAID** he concluded from what was told him that "we were supposed to overlook some of the specifica-

**Highways**
**Continued on Page Eight**

## Almanac

### Aristophanes Was the Greek With Frogs

Sunrise, 6:47 a.m.; sunset, 5:06 p.m.
*Monday, Oct. 29, 1962*

"You never know what'll happen if you keep your eyes open, kids," said a Minneapolis father. "Newton discovered gravity when an apple hit him on the head. And do you know what Archimedes discovered while sitting in his bathtub?"

"A frog?" asked his daughter.

•

***Mostly fair with occasional cloudiness is forecast for the Twin Cities today. High today 62, low tonight 35.***

•

"What would happen if the Pope were to die during the Ecumenical Council?" asked the priest (as he tells it) of his catechism class.

A little boy raised his hand: "They'd bury him?"

## De Gaulle's Plan Wins Referendum

PARIS, France — (UPI) — President Charles de Gaulle Sunday won a key national referendum on changing the constitution. But his support dropped to its lowest point since his 1958 return to power despite a threat he had made to resign.

Provisional final returns gave De Gaulle nearly 62 per cent of the votes cast, but only about 46 per cent of the total of registered voters. About six million voters stayed home.

**PREMIER** Georges Pompidou said the results gave De Gaulle no cause to resign.

"The president took the stand that the majority in his favor must not be either mediocre or indecisive," he said. "I do not think these adjectives apply in this case."

Any doubts about De Gaulle's intentions were removed early today by Interior Minister Roger Frey, who said:

"Gen. De Gaulle will remain at his post as head of state. He himself agreed that a 60 per cent 'yes' vote would be a success for him, while a 65 per cent vote would be a triumph."

The provisional final returns issued early this morning gave these results:

**Registered voters: 27,579,-859.**

**Votes cast: 21,306, 910.**

**Valid votes: 20,741,247.**

**"Yes" 12,808,848 (46.44 per cent of registered votes; 61.76 per cent of votes cast).**

**"No" 7,932,399 (28.76 per**

**France**
**Continued on Page 12**

## Nehru Will Ask U.S. Arms Aid

### Only American Weapons Can Turn Tide, Aids Say

NEW DELHI, India—(AP)—Prime Minister Jawaharlal Nehru finally has agreed with his generals that only a massive volume of American arms can turn aside the Red Chinese threat to Indian independence, authoritative sources said Sunday, as Communist troops opened a fierce new border attack.

Nehru is no longer worried about compromising his long-cherished nonalignment policy in the Cold War, informants said, and is consulting with top generals on the arms problem and the situation at the front.

Personally directing the Defense Ministry, he has pushed aside Defense Minister V. K. Krishna Menon, who blocked the generals' efforts a year ago to turn to the United States for weapons.

**DESPITE REPORTS** that Menon has resigned, the leftist defense minister still holds his job, but in name only, officials said.

In his first public statement in days, Menon said, "We will procure the equipment from wherever we can. But it is best to depend on India's own efforts."

Menon flew to Leh, army headquarters in Ladakh province, and Srinigar in Kashmir to confer on the military situation in the western sector.

On the frontier, a defense spokesman said a post was lost when overwhelming numbers of Chinese with rapid-firing weapons opened an attack at Demchok in southern Ladakh on the western end of the Himalayan border.

**FIGHTING** was continuing and the Chinese were bringing up more forces.

Demchok, more than 14,-000 feet high, is close to the undefined border of Kashmir itself and the farthest south of any attack point by the Chinese in the western sector.

On the northeastern border, only one clash—in which India suffered two casualties and the Chinese 20—was reported.

But the Chinese have been

**India**
**Continued on Page Eight**

## Day to Be Fair, Forecaster Says

Mostly fair weather with occasional cloudiness is forecast for the Upper Midwest today.

For the Twin Cities, southwesterly winds of 10 to 15 miles an hour are expected to shift to northwesterly during the day. The high today will be 62, the low tonight 35.

Highs throughout the Upper Midwest will be: Minnesota, 48 to 56 in the northeast, 56 to 66 in the west and south; North Dakota 55 to 65; South Dakota, in the 60s, and Wisconsin 53 to 62.

### TURN THE PAGES TO:



## Threat Lifts, But No One Gloats

**By RICHARD WILSON**
**Chief of the Minneapolis Tribune Washington Bureau**

**Analysis: WHAT THE NEWS MEANS**

WASHINGTON, D.C.—On an October Sunday afternoon of rare beauty in the capital, the imminent threat of nuclear war lifted.

Neither gloating nor claims of a Russian capitulation were in order here. The problem of Castro and what is to become of him remains at the top of the American agenda of serious problems.

It is realized that in the Kremlin there must be still serious challenges to Premier Nikita Khrushchev's announcement of withdrawal from and dismantling of the nuclear rocket bases that have jeopardized American security.

**WHAT** Khrushchev gets from this is the American assurance that it will not invade Cuba now; no commitment is made if the security of the hemisphere is endangered in the future or in any other way.

Khrushchev's choice was between the probability of nuclear war and maintaining his Cuban bases. When confronted with the high resolve of American policy, supplemented by Russian intelligence which showed that the United States was prepared to attack, Khrushchev backed away.

For his part, President Kennedy made the deliberate choice of accepting Khrushchev's private letter of Friday, rather than the publicly announced policy for a Turkish base trade-off on Saturday, as the true position.

This paid off yesterday

**Threat**
**Continued on Page Nine**

PREMIER KHRUSHCHEV

PRESIDENT KENNEDY

## Thant Accepts Invitation to Confer with Castro in Cuba

UNITED NATIONS, N.Y.—(AP)—Acting Secretary General U Thant said Sunday he will go to Cuba at Prime Minister Fidel Castro's invitation to seek a solution of the Cuban crisis. A United Nations spokesman said Thant expects to leave Tuesday.

U Thant

Radio Moscow's report that Premier Nikita Khrushchev had agreed to dismantle the missile bases in Cuba under United Nations inspection sent Thant into a new series of conferences.

**BUT THANT** made no public statement on the dismantling order and a United States source said "we still have no information that the missile bases are coming down."

Chief United States delegate Adlai Stevenson conferred twice with Thant. One topic reportedly was Thant's Cuban trip and how the United Nations might carry out inspection of the missile withdrawal.

Stevenson said Thant was "ready for all eventualities" that might arise from Khrushchev's announcement. There was no comment from the United States delegation on Thant's accepting Castro's invitation.

Thant also met during the

**U.N.**
**Continued on Page Nine**

## U.S. Accepts Russ Pledge

**By RICHARD WILSON**
**Chief of the Minneapolis Tribune Washington Bureau**

WASHINGTON, D.C. — Soviet Premier Nikita Khrushchev announced Sunday that he is ordering Russian missiles and other offensive weapons in Cuba crated up and carried home.

In his broadcast message, he accepted in exchange an American pledge not to invade Cuba.

President Kennedy, without waiting to receive the Khrushchev message through official channels, hailed it as "statesmanlike" and joined the Soviet premier in the "step back from danger."

Thus the explosive Cuban crisis, which threatened the world with nuclear war, moved suddenly toward settlement.

Mr. Kennedy Saturday informed Khrushchev that the United States would not attack Cuba if the Soviet bases were dismantled and withdrawn. The dramatic Khrushchev reply was heard yesterday morning in Washington, only a few hours later.

*(KHRUSHCHEV, KENNEDY TEXTS—Pages Two and Three.)*

The details are to be worked out through acting Secretary General U Thant of the United Nations. Khrushchev sent Deputy Foreign Minister V. V. Kuznetsov to New York, N.Y., to make the arrangements with American representatives and United Nations officials.

In a Moscow broadcast the text of a Khrushchev letter to Mr. Kennedy said:

"In order to liquidate with greater speed the dangerous conflict, to serve the cause of peace, to give confidence to all peoples longing for peace, and to calm the people of America, who, I am sure, want peace as much as the peoples of the Soviet Union, the Soviet government, in addition to previously issued instructions for the cessation of further work at the weapons building sites, has issued a new order for the dismantling of the weapons, which you describe as 'offensive', their crating and returning to the Soviet Union."

Mr. Kennedy in a reply made public yesterday afternoon said: "I consider my letter to you of Oct. 27 and your reply of today as firm undertakings on the part of both our governments which should be promptly carried out. I hope that the necessary measures can at once be taken through the United Nations, as your message says, so that the United States in turn will be able to remove the quarantine measures now in effect.

"Perhaps now, as we step back from danger, we can together make real progress in this vital field (of disarmament.)"

Khrushchev coupled his backdown with a new complaint of a U2 plane intrusion last week in Siberia. Mr.

**Crisis**
**Continued on Page Eight**

## U.S. Admits U2 Flew Over Russ Area in 'Error'

WASHINGTON, D.C. — (UPI) — President Kennedy acknowledged Sunday that an American plane had flown over Russian territory in the Far East, but said that this was accidental and that steps would be taken to prevent a recurrence.

He plainly told Soviet Premier Nikita Khrushchev that the craft was in the area to sample air in the vicinity of current Soviet nuclear tests. But he said no arms nor photographic equipment were aboard.

Mr. Kennedy made the statement in reply to a letter from Khrushchev which contained a charge that the plane violated Soviet air space over the Chukotka Peninsula, near Alaska.

Reference to the plane was included in the President's message concerning withdrawal of missiles from Cuba.

The President said:

"I have learned that this plane, without arms or photographic equipment, was engaged in an air sampling mission in connection with your nuclear tests. Its course was direct from Eielson Air Force Base in Alaska to the North Pole and return.

"In turning south, the pilot made a serious navigational error which carried him over Soviet territory. He immediately made an emergency call on an open radio for navigational assistance and was guided back to his home base by the most direct route.

"I regret this incident and will see to it that every precaution is taken to prevent reoccurence."

In his message to Mr. Kennedy, Khrushchev said that repetition of the territory violation "could lead to a fatal step" in view of current world tensions.

The Soviet leader also linked this latest flight with the flight of an American U2 reconnaissance plane over Sakhalin Island in the Soviet Far East Aug. 30.

## Glen Ora Lunch Is Cuba Bonus

MIDDLEBURG, Va. — (UPI) — With the international situation suddenly eased President Kennedy flew here Sunday to have lunch with his wife and children at Glen Ora, their country estate.

Accompanying him by helicopter was a small group including Capt. Tazwell Shepard, White House naval aid, and K. L. Billings, a friend of the President from New York, N.Y.

As the President walked from the helicopter to his residence, Mrs. Kennedy ran to him, and hugged and kissed him. They walked arm-in-arm to the house.

## Argentine Destroyers to Join Quarantine

BUENOS AIRES, Argentina —(AP)— Two Argentine destroyers equipped for prolonged patrol and antisubmarine duty sailed Sunday to join in the United States arms quarantine of Cuba.

The destroyers are the Rosales and Espora. Argentina is the first Latin American nation to take an active part in the blockade.

## Four Venezuela Oil Field Power Stations Sabotaged

CARACAS, Venezuela—(AP)—Saboteurs, believed to be followers of Cuban Prime Minister Fidel Castro, blew up four oil company power stations in Lake Maracaibo, early Sunday, knocking out one-sixth of Venezuela's oil production. Venezuela is the world's leading oil exporter.

The bombs destroyed transformer stations of the Creole Petroleum Co., a subsidiary of Standard Oil of New Jersey. A Creole spokesman said the entire Creole field in the oil-rich lake was rendered inoperable.

Secretary of State Dean Rusk told Latin American diplomats Sunday the United States had detected the Havana Radio code signal instructing local Communists in Venezuela to take action against the Venezuelan oil fields. The problem of coping with Cuban-fomented subversion will be the chief topic of an Organization of American States council meeting today.

**AUTHORITIES** seized two men, believed to be the bombers, swimming in debris in the lake. Police said they believed a third man, the apparent ringleader, was killed when one of the explosions blew up the saboteurs' boat.

Police said they believed one of the bombers was a Creole employe because of the expertness with which the saboteurs knocked out the field.

(Authoritative sources in Washington, D.C., said Castro has signaled for a campaign of general terrorist agitation in Latin America.

(Word of the new Cuban move has been passed to United States embassies in Latin America to caution the governments to expect trouble, the sources said. Secretary of State Dean Rusk met late yesterday with ambassadors of the 19 non-Communist Latin republics at the State Department.)

Eighteen sticks of dynamite failed to explode at one of the power stations in the Tijuana field near Cabimas, a town on the northeast shore of Lake Maracaibo. The lake, about 300 miles west of Caracas, is roughly 75 miles wide and 130 miles long and holds beneath its waters one of the world's richest stores of oil.

**THE CREOLE** spokesman said the blasts came before dawn and knocked out the transformers that convert the voltage powering the company's rigs in the lake, thus

**Sabotage**
**Continued on Page Eight**

## Crisis at a Glance

**Associated Press**

MOSCOW, U.S.S.R.—Premier Nikita Khrushchev says he is ordering Soviet bases in Cuba dismantled and rockets sent home.

WASHINGTON, D.C.—President Kennedy hails Khrushchev's announcement as a contribution to peace. He says that the United States will work with the United Nations to solve the Cuban crisis and that he hopes other East-West tensions can be tackled after the Cuban threat ends.

WASHINGTON, D.C.—Military build-up continues as officials await verification of the Soviet shift in Cuba. The Pentagon says planes reconnoitering the missile sites will be protected.

HAVANA, Cuba—Premier Fidel Castro demands that the United States abandon its naval base at Guantanamo, discontinue the naval quarantine and aerial surveillance and any assistance to anti-Castro elements, and stop any arms build-up in areas close to Cuba.

UNITED NATIONS, N.Y.—Acting Secretary General U Thant accepts Cuban invitation to visit Castro; expects to leave Tuesday.

CARACAS, Venezuela — Saboteurs believed to be Castro followers blew up four power stations on Lake Maracaibo, knocking out about a sixth of Venezuela's heavy oil production. In Washington, the State Department said it had monitored a radio signal from Havana to Caracas ordering the sabotage.

MINNEAPOLIS TEMPERATURES

| | | |
|---|---|---|
| Midnight ..53 | 5 a.m. ....56 | 10 a.m. ...40 |
| 1 a.m. ....55 | 6 a.m. ....56 | 11 a.m. ...39 |
| 2 a.m. ....54 | 7 a.m. ....57 | Noon ....36 |
| 3 a.m. ....54 | 8 a.m. ....52 | *1 p.m. ...34 |
| 4 a.m. ....55 | 9 a.m. ....43 | *Unofficial |

Precipitation Midnight-Noon, .05. Forecast: Colder.

THE MINNEAPOLIS STAR

Friday, Nov. 22, 1963 LXXXV—NO. 311 Two Sections 56 PAGES ★★★★★

Telephone FE. 3-3111 Single Copy Price 10c Lower Price for Carrier Delivery

# PRESIDENT SLAIN

## *Sniper Cuts Down Kennedy, Texas Governor in Dallas*

***BULLETIN***

WASHINGTON, D.C.—(AP)—Government sources said today that President Kennedy is dead.

Two priests who stepped out of Parkland Hospital's emergency ward said President Kennedy died of his bullet wounds.

The priests came out of the ward at approximately 1:37 P.M.

DALLAS, Tex.—(UPI)—President Kennedy and Gov. John B. Connally of Texas were cut down by an assassin's bullets as they toured downtown Dallas in an open automobile today.

The President, his limp body cradled in the arms of his wife, was rushed to Parkland Hospital. The governor also was taken to Parkland.

The shooting occurred just east of the triple underpass facing a park in downtown Dallas.

Reporters about five car lengths behind the chief executive heard what sounded like three bursts of gunfire.

Secret service agents in a follow-up car quickly unlimbered their automatic rifles.

The bubble top of the President's car was down.

They drew their pistols, but the damage was done.

The President was slumped over in the back-seat of the car face down. Connally lay on the floor of the rear seat.

It was impossible to tell at once where Mr. Kennedy was hit, but bullet wounds in Connally's chest were plainly visible, indicating the gunfire might possibly have come from an automatic weapon.

There were three loud bursts.

Dallas motorcycle officers escorting the President quickly leaped from their bikes and raced up a grassy hill.

At the top of the hill, a man and woman appeared huddled on the ground.

In the turmoil, it was impossible to determine at once whether the secret service and Dallas police returned the gunfire that struck down Mr. Kennedy and Connally.

Both Mrs. Kennedy and Mrs. Connally were crouched down in the car over the inert forms of their husbands as the big car raced toward the hospital.

Mrs. Kennedy was on her knees on the floor of the rear seat with her head toward the President.

Vice President Lyndon B. Johnson was in a car behind the President's. There was a report he was wounded slightly.

The President had landed only a short time before at Dallas Love Field and was driving to the trade mart to deliver a luncheon speech sponsored by three Dallas organizations.

The largest turnout of the current Texas tour was on the streets to greet Mr. Kennedy.

An estimated 250,000 people lined the streets.

The motorcade was so strung out as the result of the speedy Secret Service departure from the scene of the shooting that members of the Kennedy staff were from 15 minutes to a half hour behind in reaching the hospital.

Some of the Secret Service agents thought the gunfire was from an automatic weapon fired to the right rear of the Chief Executive's car, probably from the grassy knoll to which motorcycle policemen directed their attention as they raced up the slope.

When the President was taken into the emergency room, a call was sent out immediately for some of the top surgical specialists in Dallas.

A call also was sent for a Roman Catholic priest.

A second priest was escorted in a few moments later.

At the height of the emergency room drama, a weeping Negro woman bearing a small bloody child rushed into the hospital, where a nurse and an intern went quickly to her side.

Mrs. Kennedy apparently was safe. Mrs. Connally also was safe, it appeared. Both women were stunned.

PRESIDENT KENNEDY

Both women disappeared into the emergency section of Parkland Hospital, to wait news of their husbands.

Outside the emergency room, in a hallway, anxious members of the White House staff gathered, including Maj. Gen. Chester V. Clifton, military aide to the President, and Brig. Gen. Godfrey McHugh, Air Force aide.

The President spoke at a breakfast given by the Fort Worth Chamber of Commerce and his wife, clad in a pink wool suit with blue satin collar and a matching pillbox hat, made a stunning entrance.

The breakfast crowd of 2,200 people rose in ovation and a few minutes later the President said he felt like he did in France two years ago when he identified himself as "the man who accompanied Mrs. Kennedy to Paris."

A Father Huber, of Holy Trinity Church in Dallas administered the last sacrament of the church to the President.

Sheriff's officers took a young man into custody at the scene and questioned him behind closed doors.

The sacrament was administered shortly before 1 p.m.

Another priest, who declined to give his name, said the chief executive still was alive at the time.

At 1:12 p.m., a special carton of blood, apparently for transfusion purposes, was rushed into the emergency ward by two Dallas police officers.

The vice president's wife, after a quick check on conditions in the emergency section, said her husband was unharmed.

The vice president was somewhere in the hospital, but it was impossible to determine his precise whereabouts at once.

He was reportedly badly shocked by the shooting. Doctors were trying to keep him as quiet as possible.

He was under heavy secret service and police protection.

Throughout the Texas trip, when Mr. Kennedy and Johnson had been in the same motorcade, as an obvious security measure they have ridden in separate cars. The Johnson car has always been some distance from the Kennedy car, sometimes by as much as 60 yards.

The last shooting incident involving a President occurred in 1950 when President Harry S. Truman was in office and was living in Blair House in Washington. The White House was being renovated at the time.

Two Puerto Rican nationalists tried to gun their way into Blair House and assassinate Truman, who was taking a nap at the time on the second floor. One White House police officer was killed and another seriously wounded.

One of the assassins was killed in a blaze of gunfire on Pennsylvania Avenue.

Bill Stinson, an assistant to Gov. Connally, said he talked to the governor in the hospital operating room. He said the governor was shot just below the shoulder blade in the back.

Stinson said he asked Connally how it happened and he said:

"I don't know, I guess from the back. They got the President, too."

## *Witness Says Phone Was in Thompson's Car*

By LARRY FITZMAURICE
Minneapolis Star Staff Writer

A moveable house telephone was in the back seat of T. Eugene Thompson's automobile, and he had 44 $100 bills in an office brief case the morning his wife, Carol, was stabbed and beaten to death March 6, a prosecution witness testified at Thompson's murder trial today.

R. Donald Kelly, who shared offices with Thompson, told a jury in Judge Rolf Fosseen's Hennepin District Court today he was with Thompson from 8:30 a.m. to about 8 p.m. the day of the slaying.

After Thompson received a telephone call from a neighbor telling him his wife had been stabbed, Kelly testified, he and Thompson drove in his car first to the Thompson home. Later they went to Ancker Hospital, where Mrs. Thompson died four hours after being attacked.

While at the hospital, Kelly testified, Thompson asked him to go to Thompson's parked car to get his brief case.

### Phone in Car

It was at this time, the witness said, that he saw the plug-in type house phone on the floor in the back seat of Thompson's car.

It is the prosecution's contention that Thompson "deliberately" removed the portable telephone from the couple's master bedroom to force Mrs. Thompson to answer an allegedly prearranged telephone call in the kitchen the morning of the slaying.

In outlining the state's case against Thompson three weeks ago, County Attorney William B. Randall contended that Thompson called his residence at 8:30 a.m. the day of the slaying while an intruder lurked on the basement stairs to strike when the woman answered the phone.

A previous state witness, Kathleen Zajac, Thompson's office secretary, testified that Thompson made the call at that hour.

After a neighbor, to whose home Mrs. Thompson staggered after the attack, telephoned Kelly, the witness said, he and Thompson left their offices together.

Sobbing uncontrollably at the hospital, Thompson asked Kelly to make a series of phone calls to "the best doctors and surgeons in town" to come to the hospital immediately, the witness said.

### Breakdown

After Mrs. Thompson died at 12:58 p.m. that day, the witness said, "Gene broke down badly." A doctor gave the defendant some sedatives to quiet him down.

During the afternoon of March 6, the witness testified, Thompson asked Kelly to return to their offices to get him a second brief case.

Thompson opened the brief case and withdrew an envelope containing the $4,400 in cash, the witness said.

Under questioning by Randall, Kelly testified "there was some discussion about bills for remodeling his house."

**Q.** Was that the reason he gave for having the money?
**A.** Yes.

Two days later, after discussing his wife's slaying with St. Paul police, Thompson asked his secretary to make a $5,000 withdrawal from a St. Paul savings and loan association, the witness testified.

When asked what he intended doing with the money, Kelly testified, Thompson told him he intended to hire private investigators to find his wife's slayer.

"I told him the police were working hard and diligently to solve the murder and that he would be throwing his money away," Kelly testified.

Previous witnesses testified that John S. Connolly, a St.

TRIAL
Turn to Page 6A

GOV. JOHN CONNOLLY

## Mayor Asks for Vote in Council

By RODGERS ADAMS
Minneapolis Star Staff Writer

A plan to make the mayor a voting member of the Minneapolis City Council was proposed today by Mayor Arthur Naftalin to "break the deadlock" over charter change.

Naftalin suggested making the mayor the presiding officer of the council. He said the mayor also could retain his veto power and the council could retain its power to override a veto by a two-thirds majority.

The mayor proposed expanding the council to 17 members by adding, in addition to the mayor, three new members elected at large.

The at-large members, he said, could provide some balance to the 13 aldermen elected by wards.

Today's statement was a major policy change for Naftalin, who in the past has advocated a "strong mayor" government with the mayor in charge of all administrative departments.

Naftalin said last spring's defeat of such a plan at the polls has convinced him the voters will not accept either a strong mayor system or sweeping charter change.

But, he added, neither could he support the "strong council" plan now being considered by the aldermen.

That plan would create a finance director appointed by the council, consolidate tax levies under the council and transfer the powers of the Board of Estimate and Taxation to the council.

### Objected

Naftalin objected that this plan does not provide proper

MAYOR
Turn to Page 6A

## Cold Reaches City; Rain, Snow Hit Area

Rain, snow, hail and high winds hit the Upper-Midwest today. Near-zero weather was forecast for the Twin Cities area by Saturday night.

Temperatures were dropping sharply behind a long-awaited cold front that reached the Twin Cities about 7:30 a.m., after a night thunderstorm that left .44 an inch of badly needed precipitation in the area. It was the first substantial moisture in the area since Oct. 24, when .41 of an inch of rain fell.

Temperatures ranged from 9 below zero at Williston, N.D., to a record-shattering 57 in the Twin Cities just before the cold front moved through. The previous high tempeature for Nov. 22 was 53 in 1908.

The drop in temperatures is expected to take Twin Cities readings down to about 12 tonight, the Weather Bureau said, and about 5 above Saturday night.

Wind, gusting to 23 miles an hour from the southeast just ahead of the front, switched to the west and northwest behind the front and was expected to be about 22 miles an hour late in the day.

Compacted snow left highways slippery in some western Minnesota areas, the Minnesota Highway Department reported. Reports to the highway department showed snow running half an inch to an inch west of a line running approximately from Breckenridge to International Falls, Minn., with rains ranging up to downpours east of the line.

Duluth had 1.11 inches of rain, Milaca .87 and Hibbing .73. In southeastern Minnesota, rain ranged up to 1.32 at Caledonia, 1.30 at Harmony and 1.04 at Lanesboro.

Rochester, Minn., reported 1.24 inches of rain, St. Cloud .62 and Alexandria .51.

The rain extended into western Wisconsin, where some areas are exceedingly dry. La Crosse reported .58, Eau Claire .39 and Wausau .10.

Highway engineers said hazardous driving conditions in the Twin Cities area depend to a large extent on continuation of pavement-drying wind before freezing temperatures arrive.

## Council OKs Language Uses

VATICAN CITY—(AP)—The Vatican Ecumenical Council voted final approval today of its first completed schema, providing for modernization of the language used in Roman Catholic worship.

The Roman Catholic cardinals, patriarchs, archbishops and bishops put their final seal of acceptance on the council's liturgy schema by a vote of 2,158-19.

All that is left for the document to become the council's first decree is formal promulgation by Pope Paul in a public council session, expected to be held Nov. 29.

## Three Students Die in Crash

STANTON, Tenn. —(AP)— Three teen-agers were killed today when a tanker truck rammed the rear of a school bus, sending it over a levee and into river backwater.

The dead were identified as J. C. Malone, 16; Joseph Brewer, 17; and Neal May, 18, all from Stanton. Nine students were reported injured.

Police quoted the truck driver, Vincent Abston, as saying his brakes failed.

## Dow Jones Averages

NEW YORK—(Special)—2 p.m. Dow-Jones Stock Averages Friday:

| | | |
|---|---|---|
| 30 Industrials | 730.18 | —2.47 |
| 20 Rails .... | 169.69 | Unch. |
| 15 Utilities . | 136.20 | — .72 |
| 65 Stocks .. | 257.44 | — .77 |

Sales 4,430,000 shares.

## *Christmas Shopping Called Healthy Pursuit*

*Beverly Mindrum's "Medical Scrapbook": Page 1B*

* * *

Bob Murphy Discovers How Not to Read a Book: 1B

* * *

JOHN SHERMAN REVIEWS 'DOCTOR FAUSTUS': PAGE 19A

* * *

MINNEAPOLIS TEMPERATURES

| | | |
|---|---|---|
| Midnight ..33 | 5 a.m. ....34 | 10 a.m. ...35 |
| 1 a.m. ....33 | 6 a.m. ....34 | 11 a.m. ...37 |
| 2 a.m. ....34 | 7 a.m. ....33 | Noon ....38 |
| 3 a.m. ....34 | 8 a.m. ....33 | *1 p.m. ...39 |
| 4 a.m. ....34 | 9 a.m. ....34 | *Unofficial |

Precipitation, Midnight-Noon, T. Forecast: Cooler.

# THE MINNEAPOLIS STAR

Monday, Nov. 25, 1963 LXXXV—NO. 313 Two Sections 46 PAGES ★★★



Telephone FE. 3-3111 Single Copy Price 10c Lower Price for Carrier Delivery

# Mrs. JFK Leads Mournful March to Funeral Rites

WASHINGTON, D.C.—(AP)—John F. Kennedy's body was borne from the White House for funeral rites in solemn pageantry today, mourners walking behind the horse-drawn caisson bearing the casket.

Bells tolled as the slain President's sorrowing widow, Jacqueline, set out on foot heading a procession of the world's great leaders on an eight-block march to St. Matthew's Roman Catholic Cathedral for a funeral mass.

***Atty. Gen. Robert F. Kennedy clutched Mrs. Kennedy's hand as they walked out the northwest gate of the White House.***

President Johnson and Mrs. Johnson walked behind a line of members of the immediate family who followed Mrs. Kennedy.

French President Charles de Gaulle was close behind, leading the foreign leaders.

Chief Justice Earl Warren, former President Dwight E. Eisenhower and others also were in the walking procession.

Senate Democratic leader Mike Mansfield and Senate Republican leader Everett M. Dirksen headed a group from Congress.

Mrs. Kennedy and the two Kennedy brothers, Robert and Sen. Edward, walking behind the caisson, were separated from it only by the sailor carrying the presidential flag and the riderless horse that symbolizes the fallen warrior in a military funeral.

## Family Rides Part Way

The procession from the White House began at 11:40 a.m. (10:40 a.m., Minneapolis time).

The cortege had moved from the Capitol, where Mr. Kennedy's body lay in state this weekend, to the White House. Mrs. Kennedy and members of the family had ridden in the limousines on this trip.

After a brief halt at the White House, the cortege moved on to the cathedral with the mourners walking.

Thousands lined the streets through all areas. For the most part it was a silent crowd, a crowd of bowed heads and tears.

But at one point, as the caisson turned the corner by the Treasury Building a woman broke into a high-pitched, repeated wail, "President Kennedy is gone. Oh, Lord, Lord."

When Mrs. Kennedy stepped out of the limousine at the White House, she stood still for a moment, listening to a hymn sung by the Naval Academy choir.

Then she turned and set out at the head of the procession of walking mourners.

Women along the White House drive wept.

***Mrs. Kennedy stood straight between Robert and Edward Kennedy. Her face, beneath its shear black veil, was composed.***

The Kennedy children—John, who was 3 today, and Caroline, who will be 6 Wednesday—were taken to the cathedral in a limousine. From the back seat, Caroline gazed around at the crowd. She was pale.

The world's notables, here to pay homage to the assassinated President, were a sight of splendor walking in the bright sun of a clear autumn day.

Emperor Haile Selassie of Ethiopia glittered with ribbons and decorations. France's President Charles de Gaulle towered over the man with whom he walked. He stared ahead, his lined face expressionless.

The international figures made no attempt to march, just strode as purposefully as the slow pace would allow behind the cortege of their dead colleague. They were surrounded by security men.

In the march, there was scarlet sashes with gold epaulets. There were top hats and the tall fur hats of the East.

## Viet Nam Veterans March

Rank on rank the military came, representing all the services.

One unit was formed of green-bereted Army Special Forces men, many of whom had seen service in South Viet Nam.

Church bells pealed in the distance and the crowd watched in utter silence.

At 11:55 a.m. the caisson bearing President Kennedy's flag-draped coffin arrived in front of the cathedral and halted.

Ahead marched members of the Joint Chiefs of Staff.

***Mrs. Kennedy, after a pause, took daughter Caroline and son John by their hands and led them to the steps. The children were dressed in blue.***

Richard Cardinal Cushing, archbishop of Boston, in a tall white hat and purple and black robes, came down the steps followed by other churchmen to greet the Kennedy family.

The family filed between the wide open doors of the church.

Meanwhile, the mass of foreign government leaders and diplomats waited in the background.

Finally, with De Gaulle in the front rank in his olive-drab uniform, the great men of all lands filed quietly into the cathedral.

There were Prince Philip of Britain, Queen Frederika of Greece and all the many others who had come from thousands of miles.

Behind the heads of state and representatives of foreign government came the Supreme Court, the cabinet, federal agency officials, White House staff men.

***And far back behind the last rank of male dignitaries walked Mrs. Peter Lawford, sister of the late President.***

An usher spotted her in the rear and took her by the arm to lead her to the cathedral.

The church already was crowded when the procession entered and a choir sang.

Mrs. Kennedy and the Kennedy brothers sat in a front pew. Her children were with her. Caroline rocked back and forth gently as the choir stopped singing and silence fell over the church. Then an organ began playing.

Former Vice President Richard Nixon sat with folded hands, his wife beside him. Both bowed their heads.

## Admission Was by Ticket Only

Because of the cathedral's limited accommodations, admission to the service was only by special card.

Except for those who walked behind the caisson, the invited were in their places when the procession arrived.

There was former President Harry Truman, in gray

★ ★ ★ ★ ★ ★ ★ ★

Associated Press

MRS. KENNEDY IN FINAL CAPITOL TRIBUTE

*Returned today with Robert (left) and Edward Kennedy*

★ ★ ★ ★ ★ ★ ★ ★

coat, hat and suit. With him was his daughter, Margaret, who is Mrs. Clifton Daniel of New York City.

Dr. Billy Graham, noted Protestant evangelist, arrived bareheaded, wearing a gray topcoat.

Rep. John W. McCormack, speaker of the House, walked in by himself.

A group of senators followed, among them Barry Goldwater, R., Ariz.

***Mayor Robert F. Wagner of New York City arrived just ahead of Gov. and Mrs. Nelson Rockefeller of New York.***

Three buses brought members of the House of Representatives generally.

* * *

Just before the casket was carried into the cathedral, Cardinal Cushing sprinkled holy water on it.

Then the cardinal turned and walked into the cathedral, followed by the honor guard carrying the casket with the body of the assassinated President.

The procession down the aisle of the cathedral was led by three priests, one carrying a cross, the other two flanking him with candles.

The cardinal ascended to the altar to recite the first hymn of the mass, pleading for eternal rest for the dead and reminding men that all that is flesh and blood "must come before the throne of God."

As the procession came by the White House on the way to the cathedral, the Marine Band played a dirge. Earlier, the strains of "Onward Christian Soldiers" had filled the air.

The white horses pulling the caisson carrying the coffin plodded along quietly, but the traditional riderless horse was quite restive, keeping its handler busy. It turned, twisted and pranced sidewise.

***Before the casket was placed on the caisson at the Capitol, Mrs. Kennedy had knelt before it and prayed briefly.***

Then, as the coffin was carried from the catafalque that had sustained the remains of another martyr, Abraham Lincoln, there was a roll of ruffles and flourishes.

"O God of Loveliness," a band played, and the procession began, to the measured cadences of muffled drums.

The cortege reached the White House at 11:35 a.m., while church bells tolled mournfully.

* * *

Hours before the procession began from the Capitol to the White House and to the cathedral, there was a mass of humanity packed about the Capitol grounds and along the streets.

Some had been there all night. Other thousands

FUNERAL
Turn to Page 7A

Associated Press

CAISSON BEARING CASKET OF JOHN F. KENNEDY REACHED CAPITOL

*Thousands viewed flag-draped coffin in the rotunda*

★ ★ ★ ★ ★ ★ ★ ★

# World's Mighty Pay Tribute

*Pictures on Page 18A*

WASHINGTON, D.C.—(AP)—A solemn procession of the world's mighty—some of them nearly twice the age of the slain young President of the United States—came to Washington to pay homage to John F. Kennedy.

They arrived, sometimes in twos and threes, somber and unsmiling, expressing the grief of their countrymen and wishing Lyndon B. Johnson, the new President, well.

At modernistic Dulles International Airport in the Virginia countryside, south of the capital, hundreds of Americans stood six deep behind barriers to watch jets deposit their important cargo.

Long after the blue of a chill Sunday afternoon had given way to night, the arrivals continued.

Several dignitaries flew into Washington's other airport, National, and a few motored in by limousine.

Fifty-three countries were represented by a dozen members of ruling families, 26 presidents and heads of state, 30 foreign ministers and five defense ministers.

They were on hand to march behind the caisson carrying Mr. Kennedy's body from the White House to St. Matthew's Roman Catholic Cathedral.

After the burial in Arlington Cemetery, Mrs. Kennedy receives the foreign emissaries at the White House.

In late afternoon, President Johnson greets them at the State Department. The President plans to confer privately with some of them Tuesday.

One of the first to arrive was France's President

WORLD LEADERS
Turn to Page 4A

★ ★ ★ ★

## Spellman Says Requiem Mass

ROME, Italy — (Reuters) — President Antonio Segni today attended a requiem mass for President Kennedy in the patriarchal archbasilica of Saint John Lateran, the world's foremost Roman Catholic Church and the cathedral of the Pope as bishop of Rome.

Francis Cardinal Spellman of New York, senior United States cardinal, officiated. Bishops from all over the world at the Vatican ecumenical council were present.

Cardinal Spellman, in black vestments, conducted the service at the high altar by permission of Pope Paul.

This altar is reserved to the Pope alone and special authorization from him is needed for a cardinal to officiate at it.

* * *

**SENATE RESOLUTION EXPRESSES SORROW**

WASHINGTON, D.C. —(AP) — Members of the Senate met today and adopted a resolution expressing their sorrow over the death of President John F. Kennedy. The resolution extended sympathy to his family.

Democratic Leader Mike Mansfield of Montana and Republican Leader Everett

TRIBUTES
Turn to Page 4A

★ ★ ★ ★

## *Johnson Leads in Mourning*

WASHINGTON, D.C.—(UPI) —President Johnson led his fellow citizens and the mighty of the earth today in mourning a fallen comrade, John Fitzgerald Kennedy.

The new Chief Executive of the United States, ramrod-straight, his face etched with sadness, joined with millions around the world in paying his last respects to the slain President.

But within hours after the last, sad rites for his former chief, President Johnson was to take up anew the great burdens of the office.

He planned a reception for the many foreign heads of state attending the funeral, the greatest number ever to gather in the United States. It was expected that some of the pressing international problems facing the new administration would be touched upon, if only briefly.

### Set Fast Pace

Mr. Johnson, working at a breathtaking pace since his elevation to the presidency in Dallas Friday, goes before

JOHNSON
Turn to Page 7A

★ ★ ★ ★

## France, Spain Sign Financial Aid Pact

PARIS, France — (Reuters) —A Franco-Spanish financial protocol pact was signed today at the French Finance Ministry.

Under the agreement, France will help finance a number of projects within the framework of Spain's economic development program.

The Weather
MINNESOTA: Cooler
WISCONSIN: Warmer
NORTH DAKOTA: Cooler
SOUTH DAKOTA: Cooler
IOWA: Cloudy, cooler

# Minneapolis Sunday Tribune

Vol. XCVII—No. 226 Copyright 1964 Minneapolis Star and Tribune Company MINNEAPOLIS, MINN., SUNDAY, JANUARY 5, 1964 Price 20c In Minnesota, border-ing cities and Western Wisconsin. Price 25c Elsewhere. Mail subscription prices on Opinion Page

# Pope Jostled by Joyful Throngs in Jerusalem

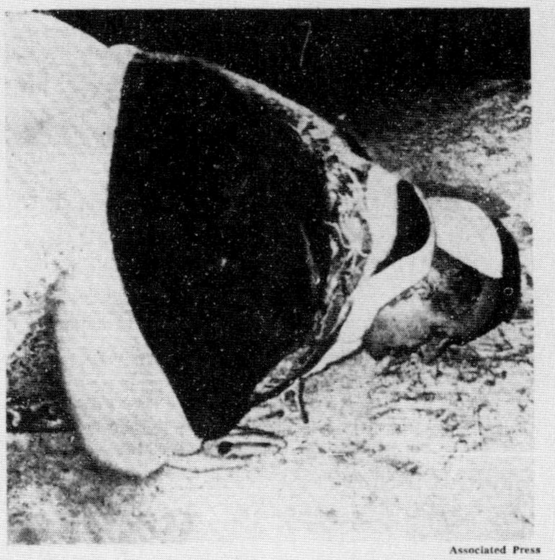

POPE KNELT TO KISS ROCK OF AGONY BY GARDEN OF GETHSEMANE
*Rock is embedded in floor of Church of All Nations*
Associated Press

## Mood Quiet at Gethsemane

JERUSALEM—(Reuters)—Pope Paul Saturday began an historic three-day tour of the Holy Land with near-riotous scenes of affection and jubilation during which police were occasionally called on to use force to quell the milling crowds.

But the day ended on a quieter note when the Pope arrived during the evening at the hushed Garden of Gethsemane, where Christ awaited His crucifixion, to pray at the Franciscan Church of All Nations.

More Pictures—Page 1B

Wearing a red robe, the pontiff blessed the huge crowd waiting for him and knelt in meditation before the altar. A hush fell upon the crowd as the Pope knelt for prayer and a choir sang "Ave Maria."

The Pope also presided at a multilingual vigil ceremony in the basilica adjoining the garden where Christ was arrested.

The pontiff led prayers and scriptural passages in Latin, Greek, Arabic, Armenian and old Russian recalling how Christ asked the apostles to keep watch while He prayed.

**PILGRIMS CARRYING** torchlights waited in the roadway below the Mount of Olives to greet the Pope.

Cheering crowds milled around the Pope as he left the basilica to drive back through the walls of Old Jerusalem.

After celebrating mass earlier at the Church of the Holy Sepulcher, the pontiff moved through a crowd of 1,000 persons to the apostolic delegate's residence and received the Greek Orthodox Patriarch, Benedictos, of Jerusalem.

It was the first contact at this level since formal relations between the two churches broke down in the 15th century.

He spoke to the patriarch about "efforts being made to eliminate points of friction" between "unhappily separated Christians" and appealed to all Christians to "enter with us into the spirit of this pilgrimage."

**"LET US TOGETHER** implore the most desired grace of union among all the disciples of the gospel," he said.

The Pope also received His Beatitude Yeguishe Derderian, American Orthodox patriarch of Jerusalem, in the second such interdenominational meeting in half a millenium.

"Our meeting," said the pontiff, "has a particular significance because of the friendly ties which have developed between us and the Armenian church through the delegated observers who participated in the work of the Second Vatican Council."

From the moment of his arrival here, the 66-year-old pontiff, who followed the footsteps of Christ along the cobbled road to Calvary and visited the spot where Jesus was baptized, never lost his composure as the welcoming crowds swarmed in on him.

He kept spreading his arms in welcome and occasionally blessed the crowds.

The crush was so great at one spot on the route that several persons were later treated for minor injuries.

The pontiff was given an hysterical welcome marked by near rioting when he drove into this ancient biblical city as the first Roman Catholic leader to visit the Holy Land in 2,000 years.

Exuberant crowds mobbed the slight, white-clad figure at every turn and hard-pressed security and police forces

Pope
Continued on Page 12A

Associated Press
POPE'S HONOR GUARD USED STICKS TO BEAT BACK JERUSALEM CROWD
*Pope was visiting Stations of Cross on Via Dolorosa*

# Most Youths to Get Physical, Mental U.S. Exams at 18

JOHNSON CITY, Tex.—(AP)—President Johnson ordered a new effort Saturday to correct physical and mental flaws found among young men eligible for military service.

He directed that most youths reaching 18 be given physical and mental tests, starting July 1. He said those who fail will be allowed to enter new, voluntary rehabilitation programs.

"This will be the most important human salvage program in the history of our country," Secretary of Labor W. Willard Wirtz told reporters.

The President released a report of a task force on manpower conservation with the comment that it revealed "a situation more serious and more extensive than has been our understanding."

Findings included estimates that one-third of all young men in the nation reaching 18 years of age will be found unqualified for induction in the armed forces, about half being rejected for medical reasons and the remainder flunking mental tests.

**THE REPORT** also said the majority of those disqualified appear to be the victims of inadequate education and insufficient health services.

"The findings of the task force are dramatic evidence that poverty is still with us, still exacting its price in spoiled lives and failed examinations," the President said in a statement accompanying the report.

"For entirely too many Americans the promise of American life is not being kept. In a nation as rich and productive as ours this is an intolerable situation."

Mr. Johnson said he will shortly present to Congress a program designed "to attack the roots of poverty in our cities and rural areas."

**MEANWHILE,** he gave two orders, effective July 1, designed to discover job training and education deficiencies as soon as possible and correct many of them.

The Department of Defense and the Selective Service System are directed to give physical and mental examinations to most youths reaching 18, as soon as possible. Most youths eligible for military service are not examined now until they are 22 or 23.

The President stressed that early examination did not mean earlier induction into service.

**SECOND,** he directed the secretaries of labor and health, education and welfare to set up rehabilitation programs to correct the physical and mental defects found in the examinations.

Wirtz told reporters that the rehabilitation programs would not be compulsory, "but we have found in the task force report that most of those with deficiencies want help to correct them."

Wirtz estimated that of the estimated 1.4 million youths reaching 18 next year, only 500,000 to 600,000 would be examined. He said those in school and those married likely will get deferrals. Of those failing the examinations, he estimated that 75,000 to 80,000 would be enlisted in the rehabilitation projects.

▪

## Prophet Mohammed's Hair Is Recovered

SRINAGAR, Kashmir — (AP) — Recovery of a hair that Moslems believe to be a sacred relic of the prophet Mohammed was announced Saturday. Its theft from a nearby shrine week before last touched off rioting that took two lives.

Shams-Uddin, premier of Indian-held part of Kashmir, disputed by India and Pakistan, did not explain in his brief announcement how the hair was recovered.

▪

## East German Escapes

HANNOVER, West Germany — (Reuters) — A 32-year-old East German laborer escaped across the border during the night and reported to West German police officials Saturday.

Brown Eva Gabor
*Thought it was joke*

## Bandits Take Eva Gabor's $25,000 Ring

MIAMI, Fla. — (UPI) — Actress Eva Gabor lost her $25,000 15-carat diamond ring Saturday to two gunmen who knocked "a knot on my head, darling, as big as an egg."

The fiery Hungarian said she had the last word before the hotel room bandits trussed her and her husband, stuffed socks in their mouths and fled.

"I told them it's a helluva way to make a living," Miss Gabor said from her hospital bed where she was recovering from a cerebral concussion, a bruised mouth and the knot on her head.

Doctors said she was progressing nicely.

Miss Gabor also reported one of "those nasty boys hit me, darling, in the mouth, with his fist."

The attack took place at the Racquet Club, an exclusive island hideaway located on the inland waterway at North Bay Village between Miami and Miami Beach.

Miss Gabor's husband, New York stock broker Richard Brown, said the gunmen, two muscular youths in their 20s, were waiting in their room for them when he and his wife came in from the club bar.

"We both thought it was a joke at first," Miss

Gabor
Continued on Page 6A

# Auburn U. Enrolls Its First Negro

### Registration Goes Peacefully for Graduate Student

New York Times Service

AUBURN, Ala. — Auburn University peacefully enrolled its first Negro student Saturday.

Harold A. Franklin, 31, registered for Graduate School after checking into Magnolia Hall, a dormitory where he will live with white male students.

State troopers, who previously had been a symbol of Gov. George C. Wallace's defiance of the Federal Courts, provided massive police protection for the court-ordered registration.

**THE TROOPERS,** wearing felt hats in place of the riot helmets they wore at Birmingham and Tuscaloosa, were stationed at all entrances to the campus and admitted only students, faculty and employes who showed identification cards.

Franklin was driven to the campus by a university official and walked to the glass and concrete library building.

A light rain was falling, and about 200 students lined the sidewalk in front of the building. Many of them were under umbrellas. Troopers stood at all entrances to the building.

**A NUMBER** of the students jeered and laughed as Franklin approached, bareheaded and wearing a dark gray raincoat.

"Boo, nigger!" one of them shouted.

"I bet the nigger won't have to stand in line to register like we do," another said.

Reporters and photographers had been led in a group to the library and were directed inside the building to where Franklin was met by Dr. William Vann Parker, dean of the Graduate School, and Dr. M. C. McMillan, a history professor.

**THEY DIRECTED** Franklin to a table and talked with him about his courses while photographers took pictures.

Franklin appeared nervous and was unable to hear some questions.

Col. Al Lingo, Alabama public safety director, who headed the security guard, ordered reporters and pho-

Auburn
Continued on Page 6A

## IN TODAY'S TRIBUNE

• • • •

*Around and About the News:*

MINNESOTA began its Big Ten basketball season with a 97 to 93 win over Purdue in Williams Arena. Story and pictures on Page One, Sports Peach.

THOSE IN REAL ESTATE and construction fields can look back on 1963 as a good, if not banner, year for the Upper Midwest. Story on Page 11, Editorial-Feature Section.

*Among the Features:*

WHATEVER HAPPENED to Nancy Carroll? The onetime movie star is touring with William Bendix in the play "Never Too Late." Story and Pictures—Page One, Editorial-Feature Section.

WHAT ARE women's rights worth? Some of the recent recommendations from those who served on the President's Commission on the Status of Women, and how Minnesotans have reacted to them, are on Page One, Women's Section.

Nancy Carroll

*Among the Old Friends:*

Ann Landers ..1 Women's Theaters ......6, 7 Feature
George Grim ...1 Feature Will Jones .......7 Feature

BOOKS AND MUSIC—12 and 13, Home and Hobby

***MINNESOTA POLLS — 2 and 3, Editorial-Feature Section, and Page One, Upper Midwest Section***

EDITORIAL, OPINION—2 and 3, Editorial-Feature

***TV for the Week—9, 10, Editorial-Feature***

### STARTING MONDAY
#### NEW TRIBUNE PHONE NUMBERS

| 372-4141 | 372-4242 | 372-4343 |
| --- | --- | --- |
| for general information and for telephone numbers of individuals or departments. | to place want ads. (Outside metropolitan area, call 372-4215 until 5 p.m.) | for the circulation department — to start home delivery and inquire about service. |

**TODAY ONLY, CALL FE 3-3111**

# Goldwater Rejects Debates; Rockefeller Denies 'Me-Tooism'

### GOLDWATER

LOS ANGELES, Calif.—(AP)—Sen. Barry Goldwater said Saturday that New York's Gov. Nelson A. Rockefeller is more Democrat than Republican and added:

"I'd rather take on President Johnson on the weaknesses of his administration."

*(NIXON LEAD Over GOP Rivals Widens—Page 10A.)*

The Arizona conservative, who announced Friday that he'll seek the Republican nomination for president, paused in Los Angeles as he headed for Washington, D.C., to launch his campaign.

In an airport interview, Goldwater said he sees no sense in face-to-face debates proposed by Rockefeller, the only other announced GOP candidate.

Goldwater said Rockefeller advocates policies more in keeping with the Democratic platform than with Republican principles, and:

**"DEBATING** him would be more like debating a member of the New Frontier than like debating another Republican."

If he wins the nomination, the Arizonan said, he wants to meet President Johnson in debate. He said he thinks Mr. Johnson will debate during the presidential race.

"I see no sense in Republicans berating other Republicans," said Goldwater. He added that that seems to be Rockefeller's chosen course.

**"IF I CAN GET** the nomination," Goldwater continued, "I think I can run a stronger race than any other Republican. A strong race, win, lose or draw . . . will strengthen the Republican party."

A strong showing in the presidential election, he said, would carry with it victory for Republicans running for governor, Congress and state legislatures around the nation.

Goldwater said he thinks President John F. Kennedy would have been a stronger opponent for the GOP than will Mr. Johnson.

**"HE HAD** a lot of things that President Johnson doesn't have," Goldwater asserted.

Whether he wins or loses in the presidential primaries he enters, an aide said, Goldwater will stay in the race for the nomination until the GOP convention picks its candidate in July.

### ROCKEFELLER

New York Times Service

CONCORD, N.H. — Gov. Nelson Rockefeller Saturday rejected Sen. Barry Goldwater's charge that he would be politically indistinguishable from the Democratic opposition in the 1964 presidential election.

A reporter asked the governor at a news conference in Concord whether the Arizona senator's contention that Goldwater would offer "a choice, not an echo" as a national candidate was not making Rockefeller out to be a "me-too" nominee.

**"I DON'T** think that 'me-too' label has any application, either to the Democratic party here or on the national level," he replied. "There are fundamental differences between my views and their (the Democrats') views.

"I think that was just a political statement on his part, and I have complete confidence that the American people can understand more subtle differences in policies and programs than those that are presented by the extremists."

Asked for comments on President Johnson's programs, Rockefeller said yesterday that the new President has "talked about his objectives, but the results as yet have not been seen."

**"THE AMERICAN** people," the governor predicted, "are going to withhold judgment to see how effective he (President Johnson) can be."

In contrast, Rockefeller opened up on Goldwater. He said in a preliminary news conference statement that he had discovered that the Arizona conservative planned to campaign in the New Hampshire primary on the issues of "sanity, security and solvency." Then he posed these questions for the senator:

**"How are we going** to preserve the solvency of this great democracy of ours with fiscal integrity and at the same time abolish the progressive income tax?

**"How are we going** to preserve the security of America if we abolish the major source of revenue, which is the source of support for our national defense?

**"How are we going** to preserve security if we withdraw from the United Nations?

**"How are we going** to preserve security and stability in the world if we cut off all foreign aid?"

## Hoffa Assistant Resigns From $35,000 Position

ST. LOUIS, Mo. — (AP) — Harold J. Gibbons has given up his $35,000-a-year job as executive assistant to Teamster Union president James R. Hoffa.

Gibbons

Gibbons, vice president of the independent union, said he would have preferred not to announce his resignation publicly — in a Teamster publication in St. Louis.

"But publicity made it imperative to comment and quell speculation that this international union is beset with dissension," Gibbons said. "This is not so."

He added that his personal relationships with Hoffa "have been excellent in the past, are now, and shall continue to be in the future."

**Showers**
THURSDAY TEMPERATURES
Details Page 14

# Minneapolis Morning Tribune

Vol. XCVIII—No. 40 Copyright 1964 Minneapolis Star and Tribune Company MINNEAPOLIS, MINN., FRIDAY, JULY 3, 1964 Telephone 372-4141 Single Copy Price 10¢ Lower Price for Carrier Delivery

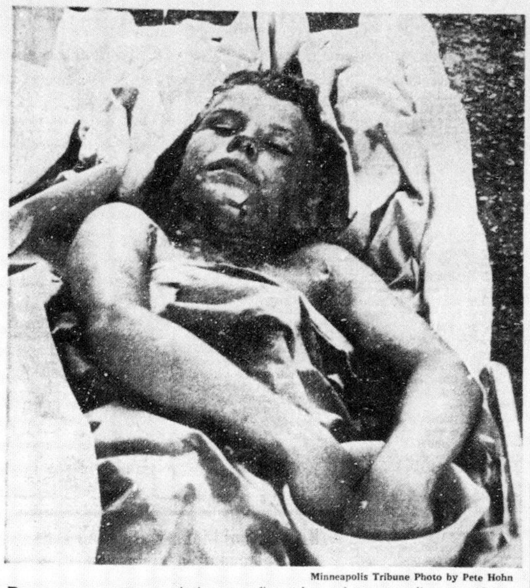

Minneapolis Tribune Photo by Pete Hohn

**Dangerous Toys** A tin can, a firecracker and some gasoline sent 10-year-old Donald Westergaard, above, to General Hospital Thursday in serious condition with second degree burns. Donald, who lives at 4704 36th Av. S., was playing with an 11-year-old companion when he lit the firecracker under the can, moist with gasoline. He was burned from the waist up, including his face.

# Johnson Signs Civil Rights Bill

WASHINGTON, D.C. — (AP) — President Johnson signed the strongest civil rights law in nearly a century Thursday night, only three hours after Congress approved it amid cheers, and called on Americans to "eliminate the last vestiges of injustice in America."

In an historic ceremony in the East Room of the White House, Mr. Johnson pledged himself to "faithful execution" of the statute and announced immediate steps to insure its enforcement.

Mr. Johnson delivered a conciliatory statement to the nation, by radio and television, and to more than 200 lawmakers, civil rights leaders and government officials on the spot who helped bring the sweeping legislation to enactment.

"We have come now to a kind of testing," Mr. Johnson said slowly and solemnly.

"We must not fail.

"Let us close the springs of racial poison. Let us pray for wise and understanding hearts. Let us lay aside irrelevant differences and make our nation whole.

"Let us hasten that day when our unmeasured strength and our unbounded spirit will be free to do the great works ordained for this nation by the just and wise God who is the Father of all."

*(SOUTH VARIES in Reaction to Rights Law—Page Two.)*

Then dignitaries clustered around him, each to claim one of the 72 pens with which he signed the bill delivered from the capital with extraordinary speed after a 289-126 House vote which ended long and bitter congressional debate.

He appealed for voluntary compliance and predicted it would be given "because most Americans are law-abiding citizens who want to do what is right."

All provisions of the bill go into effect immediately except that barring discrimination in employment. That equal opportunities section takes effect in one year.

**IN WHAT** was clearly an effort to calm the indignation of many Southerners and refute the objections of those who have denounced the measure as an invasion of states rights, Mr. Johnson told the country:

"It provides for the national authority to step in only when others cannot and will not do the job."

"I urge every public official, every religious leader, every business and professional man, every working man, every housewife — I urge every American — to join in this effort to bring justice and hope to all our people and peace to our land."

His five-point program of implementation included:

1 Announcement that he was nominating LeRoy Collins, former governor of Florida, to the key post as director of the Community Relations Service.

Collins is stepping out as president of the National Association of Broadcasters to take the position.

2 Disclosed he was appointing an advisory committee of distinguished Americans to assist Collins.

3 Announced he would send Congress a supplemental appropriation request to meet the added costs of administering the law.

4 Directed federal agencies concerned to discharge their new responsibilities "without delay, and to keep me personally informed of their progress."

5 Announced that administration officials would meet with citizens' groups to

Rights
Continued on Page Eight

# ICC Eases Grain Rail Rate Rules

### Ruling Allows Negotiations on Some Shipments

By NICK KOTZ
Minneapolis Tribune Staff Correspondent

WASHINGTON, D.C. — The Interstate Commerce Commission (ICC) ruled Thursday that railroads no longer are required to observe the "absolute rate-break rule" as the exclusive basis of charges in setting rates on grain shipments at points from which proportional rates are applicable.

The ruling makes it possible for grain millers and wholesalers at Minneapolis and elsewhere to negotiate with the railroads for possibly lower freight rates in certain instances. The decision leaves to the railroads the prerogative to submit to the ICC new proposals they deem appropriate.

(Yesterday's ruling does not automatically mean that grain freight rates will be lowered, explained Minneapolis grain interests. But it does open the door for negotiations.)

**THE ICC** ruling involves five cases brought by the grain trade against various railroads. Among the complaints were cases brought by the Minneapolis Grain Exchange against the Atchison, Topeka and Santa Fe Railway Co.; Pillsbury Co. against the Abilene and Southern Railway Co., and the Omaha Grain Exchange against the Abilene Rail Line.

Some of the grain concerns asked the ICC to eliminate the "rate-break rule." The ICC declined to do so in its ruling.

The shippers at major grain centers such as Minneapolis contended that the regulation discriminated against them in rates charged by railroads in comparison with rate costs to smaller millers and shippers at intermediate locations.

The ICC ruling commented that the record in the case "does not substantiate an as-

ICC
Continued on Page Eight

# Thunderstorms Seen for Cities

Increasing cloudiness with scattered thundershowers developing late this afternoon was predicted for the Twin Cities.

Winds will be light and variable, becoming southeasterly 8 to 15 miles an hour late in the afternoon. A high today of 90 and overnight low of 62 are forecast.

Predicted regional highs: Minnesota, 78 to 90; North Dakota, 82 to 92; South Dakota, 82 to 92; Wisconsin, 80s.

# Present, Former Muslims Talk Snakes, Brotherhood

LOUISVILLE, Ky. —(AP)— Cassius Clay, back home after a tour of Africa, said Thursday, "I would feel safer in Mississippi than in New York."

The heavyweight boxing champion slapped at integration with this question:

"Do you fear more the rattlesnake, which warns you before it strikes, or the cobra, which sneaks up before springing?"

Clay said injustice is not limited to the South, and that at least the Southerners' stand is known. "In places like New York, integration is preached but injustice is practiced," he added.

Clay discounted the effectiveness of sit-ins, stand-ins, swim-ins and other methods of civil rights groups. "We look silly doing this."

**THE CHAMP** also criticized the civil rights law enacted yesterday as an inadequate answer to Negroes' problems, and said peace never will be achieved in America using integrationists' methods.

"When you win the right to be employed by a company, then you have to fight discrimination on the job, and when you overcome that, there's something else," he said.

Clay feels the real solution lies in the Black Muslim faith, which teaches complete separation of the races.

Clay disclosed his affiliation with the Muslims after he won the title and, in an interview, referred to himself by his adopted Muslim name, Muhammad Ali.

**EXPLAINING** that Muslim teachings concern a new nation of American Negroes, Clay said the federal government should repay his people for more than "310 years of labor given while in bondage."

He said four or five states of the 50 should be given to American Negroes

Clay
Continued on Page Eight

Clay Malcolm X
*Messages on race issues*

*EDITOR'S NOTE: Malcolm X is perhaps the most violent Negro leader with a large following in the United States today. During recent months, however, he has dropped his battle cry of complete segregation between blacks and whites and a separate Negro state within America and begun preaching a doctrine of equal rights and "brotherhood." He explains why in the following exclusive interview.*

By BRYCE B. MILLER

NEW YORK, N.Y.—(UPI)—Two years ago, when an air crash in Paris, France, killed 121 white citizens of Atlanta, Ga., a Black Muslim leader named Malcolm X exulted in public:

"God really answered our prayers and dropped an airplane out of the sky with more than 120 white people on it. We call on our God—he gets rid of 120 of them in one whop."

That statement, among others, marked Malcolm X as the "angriest Black Muslim" of them all as he went about the country preaching the cult's message of complete segregation—of a separate black state somewhere within the United States.

**IT IS WELL** known that Malcolm X was expelled from the Black Muslims late last year. But what has gone generally unnoticed is that this forceful and eloquent man has done a complete about face on the question of separation of the races and is now preaching to his fellow Negroes a message of "brotherhood" with the whites.

It is still a militant and even violent message that he preaches. But the hate-all-whites doctrine that once marked his every word is no longer there.

"I have done a complete about face and I'm man enough to admit it . . . even if it makes me look ridiculous in the eyes of the world," he said Thursday, and went on to explain why he was rejected the teachings of Black Muslim chief Elijah Muhammad whom he served as a chief lieutenant for 12 years.

**"WHEN I LOST** my confidence in Muhammad as a person, I began to reexamine his philosophy, perhaps objectively for the first time, and his doctrine — his entire organization and behavior pattern.

"He teaches hate, and offers something that is unobtainable. I believe the black man needs something more. I try to show my followers how they can get something more.

"We don't believe in any of Muhammad's philosophy of separation. We believe the Afro-American should have his full part in the entire American experience," Malcolm X said.

"We have made such a great sacrifice to America as slaves and as soldiers. We believe, if America says we are citizens, we should have our rights now, not by degrees as some courts and others say. If they are ours, they are ours, and if we have to fight for them we will fight for them."

**MALCOLM X** made it clear that his followers are being taught not to hate

Malcolm X
Continued on Page Three

# Fight Aboard Forces Airliner to Turn Back

CAIRO, U.A.R. — (AP) — A fist-fight among passengers forced a Kuwaiti Airways plane to return to Cairo Airport, Egypt, Thursday half an hour after it took off for Beirut, Lebanon.

The captain of the Comet, carrying 64 passengers, contacted the airport to report a fight had broken out between Kuawiti and Qatar passengers above Port Said. He said he was unable to control the situation and asked permission to return.

Airport police failed to cool down the hot-tempered Arabs and had to call for reinforcements as the fight raged on within the airport limits.

Eyewitnesses said some persons had their clothes torn and were covered with blood. The plane was held pending an investigation into the fight.

# Senate Approves $556 Million Rise in Federal Pay

WASHINGTON, D.C. —(UPI)— The Senate Thursday approved a $556 million pay increase for almost two million government workers and officials, including a $7,500 annual pay raise for lawmakers themselves.

The broad salary measure is one of the top priority items on President Johnson's election-year program. House and Senate negotiators next will seek to work out a compromise with a $535 million measure passed earlier by the House.

The vote was 58 to 21.

*(PAY BILL Clause to Deny Baker Pension Is Defeated by Senate—Page Three.)*

Despite a flurry of proposed amendments, the bill weathered two days of Senate debate without major change.

**THE FIGHTS** featured rejection of efforts to attach to the bill stiff financial disclosure tests on members and government officials; a partisan wrangle over a "Bobby Baker" amendment; and a GOP move, gleefully supported by Dixie Democrats, resulting in a $5,000 cut in the salary raises for the nine Supreme Court justices.

The proposed "Bobby Baker" change would have taken pension benefits away from any members of Congress or government workers who invoked the Fifth Amendment before congressional investigators.

**IN A SURPRISE** action, the Senate voted 46 to 40 to cut $5,000 from proposed pay increases for each of the nine justices on the Supreme Court.

Sen. Gordon Allott, R-Colo., sponsor of the amendment, argued that there was no justification for paying the justices $42,500. They would now get only a $2,500 increase, which would mean a

Pay
Continued on Page Eight

## Twins Defeat Boston, 15-9

*Oliva, Mincher, Rollins Hit Home Runs*

**Kaat Gets 9th Win, 9th Complete Game**

*(DETAILS in Sports Section)*

# GOP Platform Unit to Hear Whitney

By FRANK WRIGHT
Minneapolis Tribune Staff Writer

Wheelock Whitney, Republican-endorsed candidate for the U. S. Senate from Minnesota, will appear Wednesday before the GOP national convention Platform Committee.

Whitney

He is expected to delineate further his differences with Sen. Barry Goldwater of Arizona, front-runner for the party's presidential nomination, during 30 minutes of testimony in San Francisco, Calif.

Feeling some pressure from Democratic - Farmer - Labor party critics to speak out on his presidential preferences and the civil rights issue, Whitney said Thursday that he had requested and received permission to speak at a committee session before the Republican national convention opens July 13.

**"I WANT** to make clear any differences of opinion I have with all the possible presidential nominees," he said yesterday. "And I want to do it before the convention is over."

"There are a lot more areas where I agree with Goldwater than where I disagree. I may also have some differences with Pennsylvania's (Gov. William) Scranton. I don't know."

Whitney, who carefully avoided intervention in the GOP presidential dispute in Minnesota until he had the Senate endorsement, broke his public silence last week, saying he would feel more comfortable running on a platform of views more moderate than Goldwater's.

**UNLIKE** Goldwater, Whitney said he, for example, would have voted for cloture on the civil rights bill and would have voted for the bill itself.

He said he would be proud to run with any of the potential candidates for president but added that he agreed with some more than others.

His statement brought rapid response from Goldwater backers, he said.

Several returned in the mail their Whitney auto bumper stickers, together with communications saying they no longer would support him for the Senate.

Whitney, who obviously thinks the party's selection of a presidential candidate

Whitney
Continued on Page Eight

# Castro Family Triangle Assists CIA Agents

By BARNARD L. COLLIER
New York Herald Tribune Service

WASHINGTON, D.C. — Premier Fidel Castro's sister, Juana, who defected to Mexico June 20, had been in contact with Central Intelligence Agency (CIA) operatives for nearly four years, the New York Herald Tribune Service learned Thursday.

And Premier Castro's brother, Raul, his trusted No. 2 man in the Communist Cuban regime, had protected Juana from the bearded dictator's wrath for all that time and then paved the way for her flight to Mexico City while Premier Castro was busy away from Havana.

In Havana Wednesday, Premier Castro told reporters that Juana's defection was indeed a blow. "This incident to me personally is very bitter and profoundly painful. But I understand this is the price of being a revolutionary."

It was made all the more galling by confirmation from highly placed intelligence sources yesterday that the CIA had been in contact with Juana since 1960 and that she had been instrumental in spiriting at least 200 Cubans out of the country.

The CIA also made it easy for Juana to enter Mexico when she arrived on a scheduled Cubana Airlines flight from Havana on the afternoon of June 20.

"She came out quite openly," said an intelligence source. "People at the airport in Mexico City saw her getting off the plane." First reaction of the Cubans, who at first were dumbfounded, was to jeer. But she was whisked immediately through the usually scrupulous Mexican customs—with all 21 pieces of luggage—and taken to a secure hideway.

First public knowledge that Juana had defected came 10 days later when the tall brunette appeared at an emotional press conference and condemned her brother's regime as "a dictatorship of fear," and warned Latin nations to "halt the insidious campaign of sabotage and Communist subversion."

The fact that she left Havana's International Airport, always swarming with heavily-armed G2 men, without being stopped confirmed that her defection was approved and planned on the highest level of Cuba's Communist government.

Intelligence sources said Raul Castro, who has shielded openly anti-Fidelista Juana from Premier Castro's retaliation for five years, plotted her escape—mostly out of long-standing brotherly loyalty—before Fidel could do her physical harm. Juana, who just didn't seem

Castro
Continued on Page Eight

Miss Castro

Castro Raul
*'Revolution's price'*

## TURN THE PAGES TO:



**TRIBUNE TELEPHONES**
News, General . . 372-4141
Circulation . . . . . 372-4343
Want Ads . . . . . . 372-4242

## Almanac

### Safety Unit Advises No 5th for 4th

*Friday, July 3, 1964*
185th day, 181 to go this year
Sunrise 5:31 a.m.; sunset 9:03 p.m.

Holiday weekend driving tips from the National Foundation for Highway Safety:

***Buying a 5th on the 3rd for the 4th = a 6-foot hole.***

*Make safe driving a habit; make sober driving a must.*

**Even one drink is too many when you must drive. It just takes one accident for you to lose your life.**

•

Summer consolation prize for harried mothers:

"Of all the animals, the boy is the most unmanageable," said Plato.

Warm

FRIDAY TEMPERATURES

Details Page 16

# Minneapolis Morning Tribune

Vol. XCVIII—No. 69 Copyright 1964 Minneapolis Star and Tribune Company MINNEAPOLIS, MINN., SATURDAY, AUGUST 1, 1964 Telephone 372-4141 Single Copy Price 10c Lower Price for Carrier Delivery

## Ranger Robot Gives You This Closer View of Moon

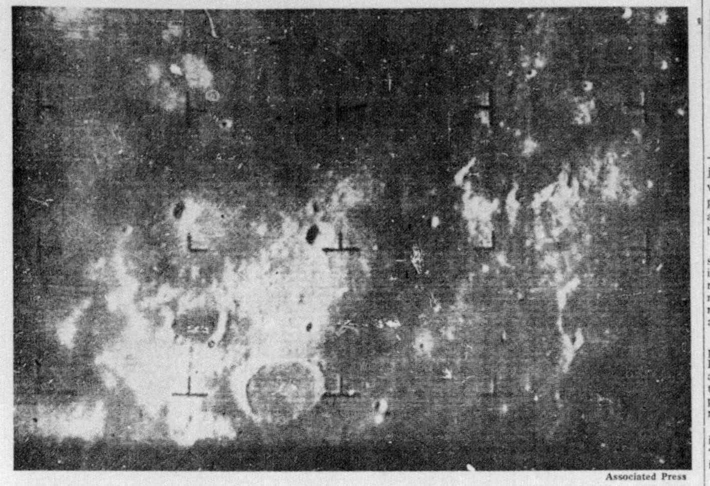

Associated Press

THE MOON PHOTOGRAPHED FROM 480 MILES ABOVE IT, SECONDS BEFORE RANGER'S IMPACT

*One of the first pictures released early Saturday from Pasadena, Calif.*

## Wagner Rejects Negro Demand for New Police Board

NEW YORK, N.Y.—(AP)—Mayor Robert F. Wagner Friday turned down demands of Negro civil rights leaders for an independent nonpolice board to review complaints of police brutality.

The leaders have made the demands almost daily since clashes between Negroes and police in racial riots last week in Harlem and Brooklyn's Bedford-Stuyvesant section.

Negro reaction to the mayor's position was one of disappointment.

**LATER IN** the day, the Police Department lifted the ban on street meetings in Harlem and the Bedford-Stuyvesant section of Brooklyn, saying "in our estimation, the necessity for curtailing street meetings no longer exists."

The action cleared the way for the United African Nationalist movement to go ahead — legally — with a rally in Harlem today.

James Lawson, president of the group, had said earlier the meeting would be held despite police refusal to issue a permit.

He said 17 Black Nationalist groups will participate in the rally, calling for the ouster of the police commissioner and the firing of the white policeman who fatally shot a Negro youth.

**THREE GROUPS** forbidden under a court injunction to hold demonstrations were not affected by the police action lifting the ban. They are the Progressive Labor Movement, the Harlem Defense Council and the Community Council on Housing.

The mayor, in a five-page

New York
Continued on Page Six

Wagner Murphy

*Commissioner backed*

## Oklahoma Primary Is Voided

### U.S. Court Orders Election Based on Population

OKLAHOMA CITY, Okla. — (AP) — A special three-judge federal court Friday wiped out Oklahoma's spring primary legislative elections and ordered new elections based solely on population.

The court ruled membership of Oklahoma's 1965 legislature must comply with recent U.S. Supreme Court rulings requiring apportionment of legislative seats on an equal population formula.

**AFTER** vacating the spring primaries, it directed Gov. Henry Bellmon to proclaim and conduct special legislative elections under a stern population-only reapportionment order it adopted.

The court warned that if its order is not followed, it "stands ready" to implement it by judicial decree.

After conferring with his attorney, Bellmon said he will comply with the decree.

"The finding of the court will become the law in Oklahoma, and as Governor I intend to implement the order of the court without delay," Bellmon said.

The reapportionment plan adopted by the court was prepared by Atty. Gen. Charles Nesbitt and calls for a 48-member senate and 99-member house.

**THE COURT'S** action was a crushing blow to rural legislators who for a half-century have dominated Oklahoma's legislature and successfully resisted attempts to give city residents more representation.

An appeal by rural forces was considered likely, although plans for one were not immediately announced.

In their ruling, the judges fitted Nesbitt's formula into the framework of State Question 416, a rurally slanted constitutional amendment adopted May 26 by Oklahoma voters.

**THE COURT** picked out and used parts of the amendment it considered constitutional, junking the rest. The new formula replaces another population reapportionment plan issued by the court last summer.

The judges explained that last summer's formula was based on constitutional provisions wiped out by passage of Question 416. Last summer's ruling was stayed in February by a U.S. Supreme Court justice, allowing a standby state supreme court formula to go into effect for the primary elections.

The original formula subsequently was affirmed by the U.S. Supreme Court, but only after voters had adopted new constitutional reapportionment provisions.

**IN ITS** 500-word "oral announcement of judgment to be entered," the court enjoined the state election board from conducting legislative elections under any plan other than the one the court issued.

The judges also declared an emergency situation existed and that money in the state emergency fund should be used to pay for the special elections.

The heart of the court's announcement said:

**"IT IS** the judgement and opinion of the court that the primary and run-off elections for legislative offices in

Oklahoma
Continued on Page Six

## Killer's 2-Run Homer Beats Yanks, 4-3

*Worthington Wins in Relief; Allison Also Homers*

*(DETAILS in Sports Section)*

## Sentiment for Humphrey Is Up in Midwest

By FRANK WRIGHT
Minneapolis Tribune Staff Writer

Sentiment among Midwest Democrats was running stronger than ever Friday for selection of Minnesota Sen. Hubert Humphrey as President Johnson's running mate.

Regional support had been evident as early as May at the Midwest Democratic conference in Des Moines, Iowa, where some Democrats, including Gov. Harold Hughes of Iowa, had to be restrained by Minnesotans from launching an open campaign on Humphrey's behalf.

*(RFK WANTS Secretary of State's Job; No. 2 Spot Still Open to Many Despite His Restrictions, LBJ Insists—Page 14.)*

Yesterday, in the wake of Mr. Johnson's announcement eliminating several vice presidential possibilities, a new wave of farm belt enthusiasm for Humphrey apparently was developing, based on reports reaching Minnesota.

**MIDWEST** leaders were indicating that they and their delegations to the Democratic national convention, to be held in Atlantic City, N.J., starting Aug. 24, not only liked Humphrey personally but also enthusiastically believed he would help the ticket in their states.

Democratic governors in states like Missouri and Nebraska have indicated to the White House that, while the choice is of course clearly up to the President, their preference is Humphrey.

Support for Atty. Gen. Robert Kennedy in Wisconsin and Illinois was going to Humphrey, who already was given the edge in those states, according to first indications.

**KENNEDY,** who helped his brother, the late president, defeat Humphrey in Wisconsin's 1960 presidential primary, was on Mr. Johnson's list of those he will not choose. So were United Nations Ambassador Adlai Stevenson and Peace Corps Director Sargent Shriver, both of whom have roots in Illinois.

Humphrey's emergence as the leading candidate for the nomination as a result of Mr. Johnson's announcement, was greeted with joy by Minnesota DFL officials.

Some, aware that Minnesota's junior senator, Eugene McCarthy, also was given a boost by the presidential statement, declined to speak out.

But most made it clear they favor Humphrey, one of the molders of the Democratic-Farmer-Labor party in Minnesota and a veteran foreman in the Congress, where he has risen to the post of assistant majority leader.

**ALTHOUGH** the state party was aquiver yesterday at the increasing prospect of a Minnesotan being on the national ticket, the word went out that no official organized campaign for either Humphrey or McCarthy will be started unless the President indicates it is permissible.

Both Gov. Karl Rolvaag, chairman of the Minnesota delegation, and George Farr, state DFL chairman, said no overt moves will be made.

Humphrey and McCarthy repeatedly have said Presi-

Sentiment
Continued on Page Six

## Five-Year City Public Works Plan Offered

A five-year capital spending program—reflecting costs of around $300 million—was proposed for Minneapolis Friday.

It was submitted to the City Council by Public Works Director Hugo Erickson.

The public works schedule is seen as a possible step toward what many consider to be lacking in City Hall—a detailed, public programming or construction projects or more than a year-to-year basis.

**THE COUNCIL** referred Erickson's construction schedule to various standing committees without discussion.

Except for the Water Works plans, no costs were indicated for the construction program. But Erickson later estimated the total costs—including state, county and even federal funds—would be around $300 million.

One of the most vigorous critics of council budgeting practices, Mayor Arthur Naftalin, said yesterday Erickson's projects schedule "is a good first step."

But in addition, a list of priorities, costs and indicated sources of revenue "are crucially needed," he said.

**"THIS HAS** been fuzzed up for years," he added.

Naftalin and others believe the council's budgeting and spending practices permit excessive balances in capital spending accounts, with the ultimate result that operating programs—such as welfare—are neglected.

Erickson said the anticipated rate of construction in the next five years is basical-

Public Works
Continued on Page 10

## Thaw Is Cool During Day, Warm at Night

NORWICH, Conn. — (AP) — When Dr. B. D. Thaw built his house in an exclusive West Hartford suburb, he had it equipped for comfort.

A $45,000 air conditioner kept him cool as he slept through the summer nights in the huge and expensive dwelling, built on a five-acre plot.

There was only one problem — the air conditioner kept the neighbors awake. Or so said attorney and Mrs. Harry L. Nair, the doctor's neighbors, in testimony in Superior Court.

Judge Joseph S. Longo agreed, and now Dr. Thaw must sleep without the aid of his air conditioner. The court Friday ordered it turned off at night.

## Rusk: Foreign Policy Tough as Necessary

By MAX FRANKEL
New York Times Service

WASHINGTON, D.C.—Secretary of State Dean Rusk, in an oblique jab at Sen. Barry M. Goldwater, said Friday that it was "unrealistic" to think the Soviet Union would "roll over and play dead" if its vital interests were threatened by the United States.

Rusk

In answering several political questions at a news conference, Rusk said the administration had "eminently demonstrated" that it was "just as tough and just as stubborn as is necessary" to protect its vital interests and those of the Western allies.

**BUT HE** cautioned that the Soviet Union, too, would be stubborn in defending its interests. Therefore, he said, conflicts of interest must be approached with care and persistence to find ways in which the Communist and Western parts of the world can live together.

Rusk did not refer to Goldwater, the Republican candidate for president, or his views, but the secretary's questioners did, leaving no doubt about the meaning of their inquiries.

The secretary said he thought the main lines of American foreign policy had been remarkably consistent since the end of World War II with "very strong support throughout the country and on a bipartisan basis."

**HE DID** not say whether he thought Goldwater opposed these policy lines, but said in reference to the coming campaign: "I think that if we were to bend those policies in any significant way, the American people would bend them back in the course of our discussion."

Rusk commented only briefly on other foreign affairs subjects.

He said he could not yet be specific about the projected buildup of American forces in South Viet Nam. It will involve "several thousand" men needed for specific tasks. He said it was perfectly "normal" for that buildup to have been announced by the government of South Viet Nam instead of the United States.

**THE SECRETARY** said past warnings to Communist China and North Viet Nam about the risks of aggression in Southeast Asia had "registered" in Peking and that there should be no misunder-

Rusk
Continued on Page Six

## Close-Up Pictures Reveal Hard, Not Dusty, Lunar Shell

By STUART H. LOORY
New York Herald Tribune Service

WASHINGTON, D.C.—Man explored the moon from close up Friday, using a glistening mechanical emissary named Ranger 7. The robot, whistling merrily along, snapped 4,420 television pictures in the last 16 minutes of its 243,665-mile flight, radioed them back to scientists waiting eagerly on earth and then crashed into oblivion—and history—in the moon's Sea of Clouds.

Ranger's feat becomes a major monument of the space age. Its last pictures, taken and transmitted within a fraction of a second of its crash, showed an area of lunar surface only 60 feet on each side—less than the area of a football field.

The last of those pictures show "a fairly smooth surface with small craterlets," according to Bernard P. Miller, Ranger project manager for RCA Astro-Electronics of Princeton, N.J., which built the six-camera television system that was the heart of the Ranger spacecraft.

Miller was one of about two dozen men who got the first look at preliminary pictures in the monitoring room of the Goldstone Tracking Station, deep in California's Mohave Desert.

**THE ENGINEERS AND** scientists from the Jet Propulsion Laboratory, which built Ranger and conducted its flight, had hooked a small Polaroid camera—the kind commonplace among amateur photographers these days—into the complicated electronics equipment in the room.

Shortly after Ranger's cameras went to full power, one of the engineers snapped the shutter and recorded a view from the whirling television monitor. He waited for the self-developing process to take place and then carefully removed the print.

"It was pandemonium," Miller said of the ensuing scene.

Handed from man to man in the room was a snapshot similar in quality to those taken through the largest telescopes man has on earth.

"It was like a New Year's Eve celebration," Richard Heyser, a JPL engineer, reported later. "It was a very emotional scene."

The emotion was heightened by the fact that four times previously — on Rangers 3, 4, 5 and 6 — many of the same men in that group had sat in that same room and had been frustrated by Ranger failures.

**RANGER 7'S HISTORIC** first close ups of the moon, released last night, showed the surface in its impact area to be a smooth plain pocked with hundreds of small craters, Associated Press reported.

(Scientists at the Jet Propulsion Laboratory, which made and guided the spacecraft, released five pictures

Ranger
Continued on Page Six

## Uptown Art Fair Cleared by Council

By PAT McCARTY
Minneapolis Tribune Staff Writer

The City Council cleared the way Friday for the First Annual Uptown Art Fair to be held on city sidewalks.

By amending an ordinance prohibiting the sale of merchandise on sidewalks, the council authorized the Aug. 7-8 promotion by businessmen of the Lake St. and Hennepin Av. area.

**THE AMENDMENT** permits neighborhood and civic groups to use sidewalks for the sale of goods if they obtain special permits from the council.

No dissents were recorded on the voice vote.

Council President George Martens had earlier expressed opposition to the amendment, saying it would open the door to the wholesale commercial use of sidewalks. H. P. (Red) Christensen, 6th Ward alderman, warned his colleagues that a time limit should be written into the amendment.

**BUT NEITHER** voted against the measure.

The Uptown Commercial Association hopes to stimulate interest in the Hennepin and Lake area with a display and auction of locally produced paintings.

One of the effects of the ordinance amendment would be to legalize the sale of refreshments along the Aquatennial parade route, an activity now conceded by Asst. City Atty. Dabe Shama to be technically illegal.

**THE COUNCIL** yesterday authorized a special sidewalk sale permit to the Northside Commercial Club for its

Art Fair
Continued on Page 10

## Heffelfinger, Wife Differ on Supporting Goldwater

By FRANK WRIGHT
Minneapolis Tribune Staff Writer

F. Peavey Heffelfinger, Minneapolis grain merchant and long-time Republican fund raiser, won't join his wife's disavowal of GOP presidential candidate Sen. Barry Goldwater, it was learned Friday.

Mrs. Heffelfinger, former Republican national committeewoman from Minnesota, and a backer of Gov. William Scranton of Pennsylvania for the presidential nomination, said in an interview Tuesday that she could not vote for Goldwater at the present time.

She said she did not agree with his views on extremism, moderation, civil rights and foreign policy.

Wednesday Heffelfinger, former chairman of the national Republican Finance Committee, attended a luncheon at the Minneapolis Club.

The main purpose of the gathering was to discuss campaign organization, issues and financing with Robert Odegard, Princeton, GOP congressional candidate in the 6th District.

At the conclusion of the meeting, Heffelfinger, according to reliable sources, was given time to speak at his own request.

He said he always had been a Republican because the principles in which he believed and which had been tested by time were consistant with the aims of the GOP and were not to be

Mrs. Heffelfinger F. Peavey Heffelfinger

*A family difference*

found in the goals of the Democratic party.

He reportedly mentioned his years of work for the Republican organization and said he had had differences on issues with party candidates for public office in the past but nevertheless always had supported them in their campaigns.

He said that in the same vein he would support Goldwater for the presidency this year and wanted his position clearly understood by his close associates in the party.

## 95-Degree High Expected Today

Temperature and humidity readings will climb in the Twin Cities this weekend as the sun plays hide-and-seek in partly cloudy skies.

Daytime temperatures both days will reach a high of 95 with an overnight low of 70. Scattered showers and thunderstorms may bring temporary relief from steamy conditions.

Winds will be southeasterly at 10 to 20 miles an hour today.

## Almanac

### Game Mishap Is Bloody But Side Issue

*Saturday Aug. 1, 1964*

214th day, 152 to go this year
Sunrise 5:58 a.m.; sunset 8:40 p.m.

A Prospect Park 6-year-old came home after a hotly-contested ball game and announced that one of the boys on his team had gotten a bloody nose.

He explained, "He was running back from the drinking fountain and fell on the sidewalk."

•

*It's National Sandwich Month. Don't get caught between two slices of bread.*

•

A Hopkins cocktail lounge advertises "THE COLLOSSAL COCKTAIL." A purist says he asked the bartender for one with only one "L" and even that was pretty powerful.

## TURN THE PAGES TO:



TRIBUNE TELEPHONES
News, General ..372-4141
Circulation .....372-4343
Want Ads ......372-4242

Cooler
WEDNESDAY TEMPERATURES
Details Page 22

# Minneapolis Morning Tribune

Vol. XCVIII— No. 74 Copyright 1964 Minneapolis Star and Tribune Company MINNEAPOLIS, MINN. THURSDAY, AUGUST 6, 1964 Telephone 372-4141 Single Copy Price 10c Lower Price for Carrier Delivery

# Guns Silent Off Viet Nam as Crisis Moves to U.N.

## $30,000 Reward May Have Led to Mississippi Bodies

From the Tribune Wire Services

JACKSON, Miss.—With its six weeks' search for the bodies ended, the FBI Wednesday hunted the killers of three civil rights workers.

The relentless, 44-day search ended Tuesday when three decomposed, mangled bodies were dug out of an earthen watershed dam near Philadelphia, Miss. A pathologist said all three were shot to death.

A Birmingham, Ala., newspaper reported that a $30,000 reward was paid for information on the location of the bodies.

Reliable sources said "several arrests" were imminent in the case, but authorities would make no official comment.

The dam is about six miles from Philadelphia in the thickly wooded, often swampy back country of Neshoba County—an area infested with poisonous water moccasins and rattlesnakes.

**AN OFFICIAL,** who asked not to be identified, said bullets were recovered from all three bodies.

Two of the dead, both definitely identified, were white. They were Andy Goodman, 20, and Mickey Schwerner, 24, both of New York City.

They disappeared near Philadelphia June 21, along with a Negro companion, James

Mississippi
Continued on Page 10

## Mississippian Is Dazed, Angry

By DICK CUNNINGHAM
Minneapolis Tribune Staff Writer

PHILADELPHIA, Miss.—He was ashamed of the first thing he said.

What he said was: "Well, what did they expect, coming down here and stirring things up?"

But instantly he realized the remark was no longer acceptable. It might have been all right when the three young civil rights workers were merely missing.

But it was not acceptable Wednesday night. Twenty-four hours earlier, the bodies of the three had been found compacted into the base of an earth dam. The Negro, according to one report, was buried like a dog at the feet of the two young white men.

The speaker was reacting with the dazed anger that seemed typical of people in Philadelphia last night as they faced the fact that the killings did happen here.

The man was a devoted father, 33-years-old, a house builder, a veteran of the Korean War, and a farmer who can still grow cotton without machines.

**"YOU KNOW** why? Because the Nigras will work for me. They know who takes care of them. We don't have to have machines."

The sunburned speaker gripped his thick restaurant coffee cup tightly and massaged the improperly healed fractures and the teeth scars on his right hand.

"My granddaddy didn't think you could grow to be a man

Reaction
Continued on Page 16

## Twins Beat Boston, 6-1

*Pascual Wins 11th; Killebrew Hits 38th; Oliva, Allen Also Homer*

Ford Frick to Retire

*(DETAILS in Sports Section)*

## Gas Station Employe Killed in Robbery

By JOHN SHAVER
Minneapolis Tribune Staff Writer

A young gas station attendant was shot in the back of the head and killed Wednesday night in Eden Prairie by a bandit who stole about $200 from the cash register.

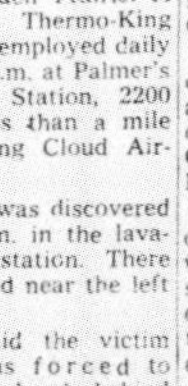

Hardy

The victim was Richard Gingerich, about 22, who lived on Starling Lanes, Eden Prairie. A draftsman at Thermo-King Corp., he was employed daily from 7 to 10 p.m. at Palmer's Big Discount Station, 2200 Hwy. 169, less than a mile north of Flying Cloud Airport.

**HIS BODY** was discovered about 9:45 p.m. in the lavatory of the station. There was one wound near the left ear.

Deputies said the victim apparently was forced to kneel with his hands behind his back—then was shot.

Inspector Eugene Arnold of the Hennepin County sheriff's office said a .25 caliber pistol cartridge was

Shooting
Continued on Page 16

## Red China: 'Won't Sit Idly By'

### Peking Says U.S. Goes Over 'Brink of War'

TOKYO, Japan—(AP)—Red China said today that "aggresion by the United States against the Democratic Republic of (North) Viet Nam means aggression against China." It declared "U.S. imperialism" had gone "over the 'brink of war.'"

In a wordy reaction to the U.S. bombing of torpedo boat bases in North Viet Nam, an official statement broadcast by Peking said:

"The Chinese people will absolutely not sit idly by without lending a helping hand" to prevent North Viet Nam from being "subjected to aggression."

**AN EARLIER** statement by Peking's official New China News Agency (NCNA) charged that President Johnson ordered the bombings "to enhance his position" in the U.S. presidential election and "to spread the flames of war to the northern part of Viet Nam."

The latest official statement was expected, since Red China has been supporting the guerrilla warfare in South Viet Nam by funneling supplies to North Viet Nam by land and via the Gulf of Tonkin.

Red China recently warned foreign ships to stay out of the gulf, where two U.S. destroyers were attacked by North Vietnamese PT boats early this week.

**THE LATEST** statement said "the situation is one of utmost gravity" but there was no reference to what sort of action Peking planned to take, if any.

"The debt of blood incurred by the United States to the Vietnamese people

Red China
Continued on Page 16

## Cochairmen Named for Goldwater

By FRANK PREMACK
Minneapolis Tribune Staff Writer

In an apparent unity effort by Minnesota Republicans, William McFadzean, Barry Goldwater's state coordinator, and George Thiss, party officer and part of its liberal-moderate wing, were named Wednesday to run the conservative Arizona senator's state campaign for the presidency.

Robert Forsythe, state GOP chairman, told a news conference in Minneapolis that McFadzean, director of civic affairs at Archer Daniels Midland Co. (ADM) and Goldwater's preconvention chief in Minnesota, and Thiss, party first vice chairman and administrative officer at Breck School, would act as cochairmen of the Goldwater drive in Minnesota.

**IT WAS** reported, however, that McFadzean will be in charge of the Goldwater machinery, with Thiss acting principally as liaison between the Goldwater people and the party's leadership, which was in the Walter Judd favorite-son camp at the national GOP convention.

Asked if his appointment of the two men reflected an attempt to heal the wounds of the fierce fight between Goldwater and Judd forces in Minnesota, Forsythe replied:

"I am not choosing Thiss or McFadzean because of where they fit in the Minnesota Republican party. I didn't pick them because they were either liberal, moderate or conservative.

**"THE SELECTIONS** reflect my own personal approach to getting the job (of running Goldwater's Minnesota campaign) set up. I simply thought it wise to have two

GOP
Continued on Page 10

## U.S. Attack Called Act of Defense

New York Times Service

UNITED NATIONS, N.Y.—The United States told the Security Council Wednesday that despite "acts of deliberate aggression" by North Viet Nam, it is determined to maintain the "assured and guaranteed independence" of Southeast Asia.

"We are in Southeast Asia," Adlai E. Stevenson declared, "to help our friends preserve their own opportunity to be free of imported terror, alien assassination, managed by the North Viet Nam Communists based in Hanoi and backed by the Chinese Communists from Peking."

The U.S. representative insisted that the United States bombing of North Vietnamese torpedo boats "and their facilities" was an act of self-defense against attacks on U.S. destroyers on the high seas, and was authorized by international law and the United Nations charter.

**HE SAID** this was a "single action designed to make unmistakably clear that the United States cannot be diverted by military attack from its obligations to help its friends establish and protect their independence."

R. W. Jackling, the British representative, supported the United States, holding that the bombing was authorized by Article 51 of the charter, which recognizes the right

U.N.
Continued on Page 10

Associated Press

AMBASSADOR ADLAI STEVENSON AT THE UNITED NATIONS WEDNESDAY
*He reported to the Security Council on events in Viet Nam*

## Negro Voter Drive Launched in City

By IRV LETOFSKY
Minneapolis Tribune Staff Writer

A massive voter registration in Minneapolis' four Negro neighborhoods started Wednesday night with this warning:

"We must, we must get the job done. We must vote because of Goldwater. This is a stop-Goldwater movement, let's face it.

"Any sensible man must realize that he is not only a threat to civil and human rights but he's a threat to the image of the country."

**THE WARNING** was delivered with passion by the Rev. Stanley R. King of Sabathani Baptist Church before 100 persons in Prince Hall Masonic Temple.

He is cochairman of the so-called Community Service Registration Campaign, which is perhaps the first drive uniting the city's often-independent civil rights groups.

The campaign includes the National Association for the Advancement of Colored People, Congress of Racial Equality, Northside Community Action Council, Joint Committee on Equal Opportunity and others, some predominantly Negro groups, some predominantly white.

**MR. KING** said he wanted a 1,000-man army to canvass the Negro precincts house to house beginning Monday through Aug. 18. Another mass meeting is scheduled at 4:30 p.m. Sunday at St. Peter's AME Church.

These neighborhoods will be covered: Area 1—North Side, most of Ward 5, part of Ward 3, headquartered at Zion Baptist Church; Area 2—Ward 6 and parts of Wards 2 and 9, Pillsbury Settlement House; Area 3 — Ward 8 and part of Ward 11, Sabathani Church; Area 4 — Snelling area, parts of Wards 9, 12 and 2, St. James AME Church.

Although organizers first hoped to have a worker on each block, Mr. King said it now appears that each volunteer will have to cover four full blocks, perhaps on a schedule of one block a night.

**PLANS ALSO** were made to obtain notary service for shut-ins who need absentee ballots, free driving service

Voters
Continued on Page 10

## Crisis Blamed on China Aim to Cause U.S.-Russ Clash

By RICHARD WILSON
Chief of the Minneapolis Tribune Washington Bureau

**Analysis: WHAT THE NEWS MEANS**

WASHINGTON, D.C. — Officials here have little doubt that the Red Chinese are behind the Viet Nam attacks in the Gulf of Tonkin and wish to involve the United States and Russia in an intense and explosive crisis of world-wide proportions.

There is no proof of Red Chinese involvement but it has been the conclusion of Defense Secretary Robert S. McNamara and Secretary of State Dean Rusk for some months that the new factor in the Southeast Asia problem is the more apparent aim of Red China to force issues and control the whole area.

**IN A CRISIS** atmosphere, the Red Chinese might be better able to force the adjustments they want, and the purpose of these adjustments is to neutralize the entire area, and get the United States out of this strategically important part of the world.

Reactions to the U.S. air strike on the PT boat bases in the Gulf of Tonkin area is growing sharper, both from Peking and Moscow.

An official Soviet statement warned that further "rash" steps in Viet Nam could lead to "broad armed conflict" and that the situation is "pregnant with dangerous implications."

**ALTHOUGH IT** is recognized that the long-range aims of the Red Chinese may ultimately involve the United States in a full-scale war, still it was decided that there should be a "measured response," one that fit the circumstances, and fell short of a definite commitment to war.

It is reasoned that the choice on expanding the conflict thus rests with the Red Chinese and that if they press

Analysis
Continued on Page 10

## Other Crisis News Inside



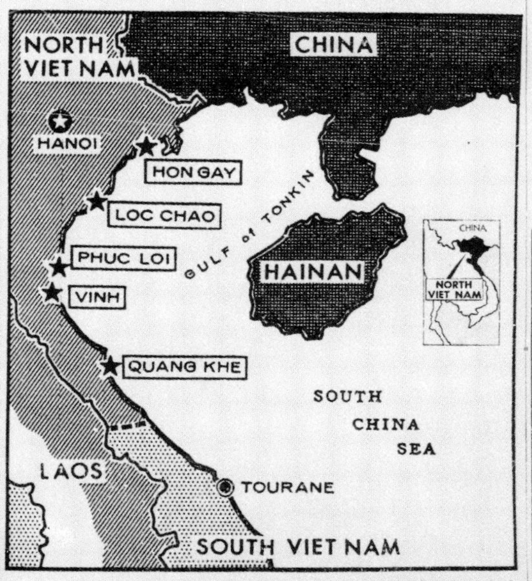


United Press International

NORTH VIET NAM TARGETS FOR U.S. NAVAL AIRCRAFT
*Stars indicate Red PT bases and Vinh oil depot*

## TURN THE PAGES TO:



TRIBUNE TELEPHONES
News, General .. 372-4141
Circulation ..... 372-4343
Want Ads ...... 372-4242

## U.S., Red Charges Echo Around World

By JACK WILSON
Minneapolis Tribune Staff Correspondent

WASHINGTON, D.C. — The guns were silent off the coast of North Viet Nam Wednesday but a barrage of charges and countercharges thundered from the United Nations headquarters to Moscow to Hanoi.

The Pentagon reported no new hostile activity in the Gulf of Tonkin, where two American destroyers fought four hours Tuesday with a flotilla of North Vietnamese torpedo boats.

(Reconnaissance flights have confirmed that the U.S. air strikes against North Vietnamese PT boat bases and supporting facilities were "very successful," Secretary of Defense Robert S. McNamara said last night, Associated Press reported.

(The reconnaissance planes drew no Red antiaircraft fire, McNamara said, and intelligence gleaned from the flights indicates the air strikes Tuesday wiped out two-thirds to three-fourths of North Viet Nam's operational patrol boat fleet, which the Pentagon estimated at about 40.

**(THE IMMEDIATE** crisis in Tonkin Bay is over, McNamara added, and the only military action under way there is the routine patrol of

Viet Nam
Continued on Page 10

## Cooling Trend Due to Linger

Give three cheers for the weatherman for promising a little cooler weather today in the Twin Cities area.

The forecast is for partly cloudy and turning cooler with the chance of an isolated thundershower during the day, then turning fair and even cooler tonight and Friday.

The temperature should top out at 90 degrees today, down about 5 degrees from the steady 95 we've been getting this week—and got yesterday. The low tonight should be 62 with the high Friday 85.

For Minnesota, today's highs will be 78 to 88 in the west and north with 86 to 92 in the southeast. North Dakota will have highs of 75 to 85, and in South Dakota it will be 78 to 88.

High temperature yesterday in Bismarck, N. D., was 104, the hottest in three years.

## Almanac

### Wet Paint Could Be Protective

*Thursday, Aug. 6, 1964*
219th day, 147 to go this year
Sunrise 6:04 a.m.; sunset 8:34 p.m.

Mary, 4-year-old Bloomington menace, has done it again.

Two months ago her father spent two days painting their fence, most of which time (an estimated 40 times a day) was spent fending off neighborhood kids, mostly Mary.

The other day Mary was in the neighbor's yard intently ignoring her fourth summons for dinner.

Confronted by her father, she took on a defiant look and started edging toward Cindy's house on the corner.

Father finally put his hand on the fence as if he were going to leap over it and drag her home.

"Careful, Dad," she said. "The paint might still be wet."

*"Always do right," noted Mark Twain. "This will gratify some people and astonish the rest."*

MINNEAPOLIS TEMPERATURES

| | | |
|---|---|---|
| Midnight ..38 | 5 a.m. ....37 | 10 a.m. ...55 |
| 1 a.m. ....36 | 6 a.m. ....37 | 11 a.m. ...58 |
| 2 a.m. ....38 | 7 a.m. ....39 | Noon .....60 |
| 3 a.m. ....38 | 8 a.m. ....43 | *1 p.m. ...64 |
| 4 a.m. ....37 | 9 a.m. ....50 | *Unofficial |

Precip. Midnight-Noon, 0. Forecast: Cooler.

THE MINNEAPOLIS STAR

Monday, Sept. 28, 1964 LXXXVI—NO. 264 Two Sections 44 PAGES ★



Telephone 372-4141 Single Copy Price 10c Lower Price for Carrier Delivery

# *Did FBI File Mark Oswald as Dangerous Character?*

## -- BULLETINS --

**ATLANTA, Ga. —(UPI)— Lester Maddox, white operator of a cafeteria, shoved four Negro clergymen off his property. Maddox, under federal court injunction not to refuse service to Negroes at his restaurant, now closed, reopened Saturday as a cafeteria at the same location.**

★

**DETROIT, Mich. — (AP)— General Motors threatened court action against the United Auto Workers Union on charges pickets were illegally preventing employes not involved in the AUW strike from entering eight GM plants.**

WASHINGTON, D.C.—(AP)—How much information about Lee Harvey Oswald did the FBI have?

Why didn't the FBI turn the file over to the Secret Service?

These questions are getting more and more attention as the 888-page report of the Warren Commission gains wider circulation.

The report leveled sweeping criticism at both the FBI and the Secret Service for lack of co-ordination.

No investigative agency at that time knew that Oswald had tried to kill former Maj. Gen. Edwin A. Walker. But the FBI knew of Oswald's defection to Russia, his pro-Castro tendencies, his hostility to the United States, his trip to Mexico and the fact that he had a job in a building along the motorcade route.

"All of these (facts), if we had them altogether, would have added up to pointing out a pretty bad individual," Secret Service official Robert I. Bouck told the commission.

"And, I think, that together, had we known he had a vantage point, (it) would have seemed somewhat serious to us."

FBI Director J. Edgar Hoover, however, told the commission, "There was nothing up to the time of the assassination that gave any indication that this man was a dangerous character who might do harm to the President or the vice-president."

The FBI, the Warren Report revealed, first opened a file on Oswald in October, 1959, when he defected to the Soviet Union.

News reports of his defection also caused Oswald file folders to be opened up by the State Department, the Central Intelligence Agency and the Office of Naval Intelligence.

For the next six months the FBI put into the Oswald file information about his relations with the U.S. Embassy in Moscow and background data from other government agencies about his military service.

In April 1960, his mother, Mrs. Marguerite Oswald, and his brother, Robert, were interviewed by FBI agents about the transfer of small sums of money from Mrs. Oswald to her son in Russia.

The FBI continued to keep tabs on Oswald in Russia by periodic checks with the State Department and the Office of Naval Intelligence.

It knew he had attempted to renounce his United States citizenship, had described himself as a Marxist, had said he would turn over to the Soviet Union any useful information garnered as a Marine radar technician and "had displayed an arrogant and aggressive attitude at the U.S. Embassy."

From the passport office, the FBI learned that Oswald had protested his "undesirable" discharge from the Marines in a letter to Gov. John B. Connally of Texas, whom he believed was still secretary of the navy.

This is the letter in which he promised to "employ all means to right this gross mistake or injustice."

Less than two weeks after Oswald returned from Russia, FBI agencs John W. Fain and B. Tom Carter dropped in to see him at his brother's home in Fort Worth.

### Unco-operative

He was unwilling to answer questions about why he went to Russia and denied he had ever renounced his United States citizenship or had any involvement with Soviet intelligence.

Fain interviewed Oswald again on Aug. 16, 1962. Oswald still refused to discuss why he had gone to Russia, protested his Marine discharge and again denied any deal with Russian agents.

Fain concluded Oswald "was not a security risk or potentially dangerous or violent" and recommended the case be put in a closed status—which did not preclude gathering of more information or its being reopened, if further work seemed necessary.

The FBI continued to keep a routine check on the Oswalds. They learned that he "was drinking to excess and beating his wife," that he had moved from Fort Worth to Dallas and had began

FILE
Turn to Page 2A

★ ★ ★ ★ ★ ★ ★ ★ ★ ★ ★ ★

## *WARREN COMMISSION CONVINCED*

# Assassination Guilt Oswald's Only

WASHINGTON, D.C — (AP) — Lee Harvey Oswald, hostile to his world and hungry for fame, assassinated President John F. Kennedy and shot his way to infamy without the help of any conspiracy, the Warren Commission reports.

And Jack Ruby also acted alone when he gunned down Oswald in the Dallas jail two days after the President's death, the commission said in its report to President Johnson, made public Sunday night.

It told Mr. Johnson there were loopholes in the presidential protection system and urged that the murder of a president or vice-president be made a federal crime.

It criticized some operations of the Secret Service, the FBI, Dallas police and news media.

The President promptly named a four-man group to advise him on the commission's recommendations.

And Senate Democratic leader Mike Mansfield said if White House recommendations come, Congress "should stay in session to carry them out."

### Bills in Hopper

The Senate Judiciary Committee will meet Tuesday and may consider several bills to make it a federal crime to kill a president or vice-president.

Also before the committee is a bill introduced by Mansfield and Senate Republican leader Everett M. Dirksen of Illinois to provide Secret Service protection for GOP presidential nominee Barry Goldwater and for the two major party vice-presidential candidates.

The Warren Report pinned down Oswald's guilt, to the commission's own unqualified certainty, under a weight of eyewitness testimony and other evidence far more massive than was believed to exist.

It revealed muddled testimony from Oswald's pretty, Russian-speaking widow, Marina, that her unstable husband seven months earlier had threatened to kill former Vice President Richard M. Nixon with a pistol.

But Oswald might actually have been threatening Mr. Johnson, not Nixon. The commission said it was Mr. Johnson, then vice president, who was in Dallas at the time.

Mr. Johnson's visit—April 23, 1963—was just 13 days after Oswald fired a night-time rifle shot that just missed former Maj. Gen. Edwin A. Walker.

The 888-page report by Chief Justice Earl Warren and six colleagues urged creation of a cabinet committee to assume top responsibility for presidential safety.

This new body, it said, might consider "suggestions" made to the commission — but not specifically endorsed by it—that the duty of protecting presidents be removed from the Secret Service.

The report praised the swift action of individual agents in the November tragedy. The response of some "was in the highest tradition of government service."

But the report called for more funds and personnel immediately, better lines of co-ordination between gov-

WARREN
Turn to Page 4A

**Exhibit** An FBI photographer crouched at a window of the Texas School Book Depository building and aimed the Mannlicher-Carcano rifle at a car in the street below. The rifle was the one found on the sixth floor the day President Kennedy was assassinated. Inset (upper right) shows how a car representing the presidential limousine was viewed in the rifle's telescopic sight. The pictures, made during an FBI re-enactment, are a part of the Warren Commission report released Sunday.

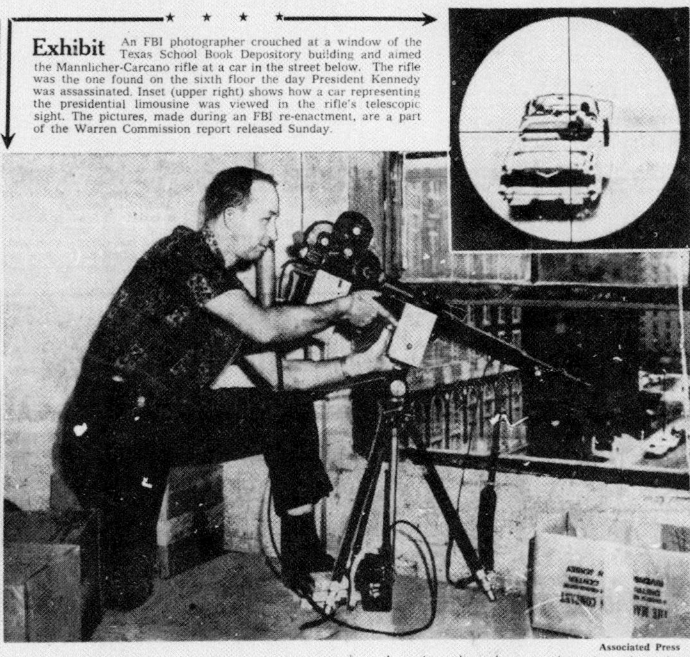

Associated Press

★ ★ ★ ★ ★ ★ ★ ★

## SUMMARY OF WARREN REPORT

*Following is the text of the Summary and Conclusions chapter in the report of the President's Commission on the Assassination of President Kennedy:*

The assassination of John Fitzgerald Kennedy on Nov. 22, 1963, was a cruel and shocking act of violence directed against a man, a family, a nation, and against all mankind. A young and vigorous leader whose years of public and private life stretched before him was the victim of the fourth presidential assassination in the history of a country dedicated to the concepts of reasoned argument and peaceful political change. This commission was created on Nov. 29, 1963, in recognition of the right of people everywhere to full and truthful knowledge concerning these events. This report endeavors to fulfill that right and to appraise this tragedy by the light of reason and the standard of fairness. It has been prepared with a deep awareness of the commission's responsibility to present to the American people an objective report of the facts relating to the assassination.

### Narrative of Events

At 11:40 a.m., CST, on Friday, Nov. 22, 1963, President John F. Kennedy, Mrs. Kennedy, and their party arrived at Love Field, Dallas, Tex. Behind them was the first day of a Texas trip planned five months before by the president, Vice President Lyndon B. Johnson, and John B. Connally Jr., governor of Texas. After leaving the White House on Thursday morning, the president had flown initially to San Antonio where Vice President Lyndon B. Johnson joined the party and the president dedicated new research facilities at the U.S. Air Force School of Aerospace Medicine. Following a testimonial dinner in Houston for U.S. Rep. Albert Thomas, the president flew to Fort Worth where he spent the night and spoke at a large breakfast gathering on Friday.

Planned for later that day were a motorcade through downtown Dallas, a luncheon speech at the Trade Mart, and a flight to Austin where the president would attend a reception and speak at a Democratic fund-raising dinner. From Austin he would proceed to the Texas ranch of the vice president. Evident on this trip were the varied roles which an American president performs—head of state, chief executive, party leader, and, in this instance, prospective candidate for re-election.

The Dallas motorcade, it was hoped, would evoke a demonstration of the president's personal popularity in a city which he had lost in the 1960 election. Once it had been decided that the trip to Texas would span two days, those responsible for planning, primarily Gov. Connally and Kenneth O'Donnell, a special assistant to the president, agreed that a motorcade through Dallas would be desirable. The Secret Service was told on Nov. 8 that 45 minutes had been allotted to a motorcade procession from Love Field to the site of a luncheon planned by Dallas business and civic leaders in honor of the president.

After considering the facilities and security problems of several buildings, the Trade Mart was chosen as the luncheon site. Given this selection, and in accordance with the customary practice of affording the greatest number of people an opportunity to see the president, the

SUMMARY
Turn to Page 10A

## New Thompson Trial on Changes Asked

By LARRY FITZMAURICE
Minneapolis Star Staff Writer

An attorney for T. Eugene Thompson charged today that Dick W. C. Anderson, chief witness of the state in the Thompson and Norman Mastrian trials for Mrs. Thompson's death, has changed his stories "faster than we can get them down in writing."

C. Paul Jones, Minneapolis, who has represented Thompson since he was convicted of instigating the March 6, 1963 slaying of Mrs. Carol Thompson last December, was making a final oral plea for a new trial for Thompson in Hennepin District Court.

Thompson, a St. Paul lawyer, and Mastrian and Anderson are serving life sentences for the $1-million insurance slaying of Mrs. Thompson.

Prior to making his oral argument, Jones filed new affidavits related to evidence in the case.

In one affidavit Jones said he has learned from interviews with "some law enforcement officers" that four prosecution witnesses in the Thompson trial who had been charged with burglaries and other offenses would be given immunity from prosecution "if they assisted authorities in solving the Carol Thompson murder case."

Since the conviction of Thompson in Hennepin District Court last December and the conviction of Mastrian at Duluth earlier this year, the courtroom testimony of Anderson has become a central issue in motions for new trials for each of them.

Anderson last July wrote a letter to the governor and gave an 85-page statement to attorneys for Thompson and Mastrian, repudiating his trial court testimony implicating the pair in Mrs. Thompson's slaying. Anderson wrote that while he personally killed the woman, it occurred during a burglary and that neither Thompson nor Mastrian had anything to do with it.

In today's argument Jones relied heavily on those written repudiations, although Anderson on Sept. 16 testified at a hearing that both repudiations were inspired by threats on his life in Stillwater Prison. Anderson at that time said his courtroom

TRIAL
Turn to Page 3A

### Dow-Jones Averages

NEW YORK — (Special) — The noon Dow-Jones stock averages Monday:

| | Noon | Chg. |
|---|---|---|
| 30 Industrials | 874.39 | — .32 |
| 20 Railroads | 217.98 | — .05 |
| 15 Utilities . | 153.09 | + .89 |
| 65 Stocks .. | 309.76 | + .[illegible]4 |

Sales 2,380,000 shares.

## Car Burns in Johnson's Motorcade

PROVIDENCE, R.I. — (UPI) — President Johnson aroused one of the wildest crowd scenes in his political career today as he arrived at Providence on a campaign swing through five New England states.

As his motorcade crawled through downtown Providence, a car two cars behind the President burst into flames. No one was hurt.

About 25 minutes before, two teen-age youths and a girl were seized as they stood atop the Sheraton-Biltmore Hotel overlooking the motorcade route. Police released the three after determining that they only went to the roof to get a better view of the President.

### Choice Cited

The President carried with him speeches lambasting "the faction that temporarily leads the Republican party," and he said voters face a choice in November of keeping a "responsible government" or changing to one "that is reckless abroad and heartless at home."

Mr. Johnson was mobbed through a seven-mile motorcade from the Theodore F. Green Airport at Hillsgrove to Brown University in Providence — scene of his first speech.

The President made 13 brief stops along the way to talk informally to throngs of

JOHNSON
Turn to Page 3A

★ ★ ★ ★ ★ ★ ★ ★ ★ ★ ★ ★

## *Warren Report Answers Assassination Questions*

WASHINGTON, D.C.—(AP)—The assassination of President John F. Kennedy raised many questions—particularly in Europe, where conspiratorial theories gained wide acceptance.

In its 888-page report on its investigation of the tragedy, the presidential commission headed by Chief Justice Earl Warren devoted a section to answering some of "the various hypotheses, rumors and speculations that have arisen."

Here are some of the questions that have persisted since the assassination. The answers provided are in the words of the Warren report:

**Q. Was Lee Harvey Oswald really the assassin?**

**A.** "The shots which killed President Kennedy and wounded Gov. Connally were fired by Lee Harvey Oswald."

**Q. Did Oswald have accomplices?**

**A.** "Oswald assassinated President Kennedy, acting alone and without advice or assistance. The commission has found no credible evidence that he was a member of a foreign or domestic conspiracy of any kind."

**Q. Was he a Communist agent?**

**A.** "There is no credible evidence that Oswald was an agent of the Soviet government . . .

**Q. Was it a right-wing plot?**

**A.** "The commission has found no evidence that the extreme views expressed toward President Kennedy by some right-wing groups centered in Dallas or any other general atmosphere of hate or right - wing extremism which may have existed in the city of Dallas had any connection with Oswald's actions on Nov. 22."

**Q. Did Jack Ruby know Oswald?**

**A.** "The commission . . . was unable to find any credible evidence to support the rumors linking Oswald and Ruby directly or through others. The commission concluded they were not involved in a conspiratorial relationship with each other or any third parties."

**Q. Do the ballistics tests show that Oswald's rifle was the murder weapon?**

**A.** "The commission has evaluated the evidence tending to show how Lee Harvey Oswald's Mannlicher - Carcano rifle, serial number C2766, was brought into the

ANSWERS
Turn to Page 4A

GOPHER TURNABOUT

## *Explosive Offense, But Porous Defense*

*Dick Gordon: Page 11B*

ENGLAND---CRADLE OF DEMOCRACY: 1B



STAR TELEPHONES

WANT ADS 372-4242
NEWS, GENERAL 372-4141
CIRCULATION 372-4343

Mild

THURSDAY TEMPERATURES

| | | | | | |
|---|---|---|---|---|---|
| 2 a.m. | 52 | 10 a.m. | 65 | 6 p.m. | 64 |
| 3 a.m. | 50 | 11 a.m. | 69 | 7 p.m. | 60 |
| 4 a.m. | 48 | Noon | 71 | 8 p.m. | [illegible] |
| 5 a.m. | 48 | 1 p.m. | 72 | 9 p.m. | [illegible] |
| 6 a.m. | 46 | 2 p.m. | 74 | 10 p.m. | [illegible] |
| 7 a.m. | 47 | 3 p.m. | 74 | 11 p.m. | [illegible] |
| 8 a.m. | 48 | 4 p.m. | 72 | 12M | 54 |
| 9 a.m. | 61 | 5 p.m. | 69 | *1 a.m. | 52 |

Details Page 22 *Unofficial

# Minneapolis Tribune

MORNING

Vol. XCVIII—No. 145  MINNEAPOLIS, MINN., FRIDAY, OCTOBER 16, 1964 Telephone 372-4141 Single Copy Price 10¢ Lower Price for Carrier Delivery

# NIKITA 'RELEASED' FROM JOB

## Labor Apparently Is Victor in Britain

By GRAHAM HOVEY
Minneapolis Tribune European Correspondent

LONDON, England — British voters Thursday apparently turned out Sir Alec Douglas-Home's Conservative (Tory) government and returned the Labor party with a narrow majority.

Harold Wilson, who at 48 will become Britain's youngest prime minister in 134 years, seemed likely to have a majority of 20 or less in a House of Commons of 630 seats.

A strong Labor trend developed early in the counting but the Conservatives rallied later to hold some of the crucial marginal districts and narrow the gap.

**WITH** 428 results in at 4 a.m., Labor had 246 seats, the Conservatives had won 180 and the Liberals 2.

Of the 18 million ballots counted out of an expected 27 million, the popular vote divided this way: Labor 8,364,000, Conservatives 7,843,000 and Liberals 1,881,000.

Labor's lead of 66 is certain to be reduced drastically when counting is completed today for a great majority of the 200 districts still out are heavily Conservative.

Experts agreed that it was still debatable whether Wilson's government would have an effective majority in Commons for putting into effect its extensive economic and social reform program.

**IN ADDITION** to a thin majority, Wilson faced another specific problem in launching the first Labor government since 1951. Patrick Gordon Walker, slated to be foreign secretary in a Labor government, lost the Commons seat in the Birmingham suburb of Smethwick which he had held for 19 years.

Even prominent Conservatives admitted that their Smethwick candidate, Peter Griffiths, had upset Gordon Walker by arousing resentment at the influx of colored immigrants from Commonwealth countries.

Referring to this racial issue, Wilson called the Smethwick result "a disgraceful exception to the trend of British politics for the last hundred years."

**HE MADE** it clear that he still intended to have Walker in his Cabinet, however. This could be accomplished within a few weeks by persuading some labor member to vacate a safe seat to make room for Walker's return to Commons.

Wilson, who was re-elected from his Lancashire constituency of Huyton with a whopping majority of 19,000 declined to claim national victory. He retired to a Liverpool hotel suite saying only that "the results are moderately encouraging."

He also indicated, however,

Britain
Continued on Page Seven

## Cards Beat Yankees, 7-5, to Win World Series

*Gibson Is Top Player, Sets Strikeout Record*

WORLD CHAMPIONSHIP IS FIRST FOR CARDINALS IN 18 YEARS

•

**U.S. Olympians Win 8 Gold Medals**

Bob Hayes Runs 100 Meters in Record 10 Seconds

•

*(DETAILS in Sports Section)*

KHRUSHCHEV, BREZHNEV AND KOSYGIN
*Principals in Soviet government*

Associated Press

## Brezhnev, Kosygin Divide His Duties

New York Times Service

Moscow, U.S.S.R. — Premier Nikita Khrushchev has lost political power in the Soviet Union. He was replaced by Leonid I. Brezhnev, 57, as first secretary of the Communist party, and by Alexei N. Kosygin, 60, as premier.

He even lost his seat in the Presidum of the Central Committee of the party, the third and last position he held in the leadership. This indicated that he had fallen into total disgrace.

The appointment of Brezhnev makes him the No. 1 man in the Soviet Union, with power stemming from his role as party chairman. He was the Soviet president until July 15, when he resigned to become Khrushchev's party assistant as deputy chairman.

Kosygin had been first deputy chairman of the Council of Ministers.

*(BREZHNEV: From Heir Apparent to Red Chief; ECONOMIST Kosygin Has Survived Many Upheavals—Page 12.)*

The changes were announced by Tass, the official press agency, a few minutes after midnight today.

This morning's Pravda, the Communist party newspaper, carried the news of Khrushchev's dismissal and the appointments of Kosygin and Brezhnev under a banner headline that said: "Information About the Plenum of the Central Committee of the Communist Party of the Soviet Union."

The newspaper printed the same bare announcement that had been carried in the English-language version of Tass at midnight. There were one-column pictures of Kosygin and Brezhnev, but no comment and no biographical material.

Alongside its masthead, Pravada printed the following: "The Communist party of the Soviet Union firmly and positively translates into reality the Leninist general line worked out at the 20th and 22nd Congress of the party."

This could be construed as an assurance that there would be no return to Stalin's policies, including the "cult of the personality," which were denounced at these two Congresses.

The Tass statement said:

"A plenary meeting of the Central Committee of the Communist party of the Soviet Union was held on Oct. 14 of this month.

"The plenary meeting

Khrushchev
Continued on Page Seven

### U.S. SURPRISED, NOT ALARMED

## No Major Changes Expected

By MAX FRANKEL
New York Times Service

**Analysis: WHAT THE NEWS MEANS**

WASHINGTON, D.C. — The administration was surprised but not alarmed by the change of leadership in Moscow Thursday.

Analysts of Soviet affairs were almost unanimous in the view that Premier Nikita Khrushchev had been forced to step down by his colleagues for reasons of personality and policy and not merely age and health.

But the survival and promotion of Khrushchev lieutenants, officials said, seemed to preclude any radical policy changes in the near future, at least in East-West relations.

There were many signs that Khrushchev himself was surprised by the sudden change. But the promotion from within his own administration led both the Soviet and U.S. governments to maintain calm as the news became known.

In 1953, the Soviet leaders announced Stalin's death with a plea against panic. They handled the Khrushchev ouster routinely. Neither Soviet nor American military forces were placed on special alert, officials said.

The new leader of the Soviet Communist party, Leonid I. Brezhnev, had to be counted for the time being as the top man in Moscow.

In the expected period of transition, however, Brezhnev, Alexei N. Kosygin, the new premier, and other leaders are expected to share power in a "collective" leadership to an even greater extent than in the closing years of Khrushchev's rule.

Like Khrushchev, the new men are regarded here as prudent custodians of Soviet nuclear power. They are respected as formidable adversaries of the West in many parts of the world, but are also expected to be preoccupied for a long time with economic

Policy
Continued on Page Seven

## CLU Votes to Back Taconite Amendment

The Minneapolis Central Labor Union Council (CLU) has voted to back the taconite amendment, Robert Gomsrud, CLU president, said Thursday.

The CLU assembly, at its regular meeting Wednesday night, first voted to reconsider an earlier vote accepting a tax committee report opposing the amendment.

Then it voted, 62 to 34, to reject the committee report.

**ALTHOUGH** this technically left the CLU without a formal position on the issue, Gomsrud said he regards the action as an endorsement of the amendment.

He said he had so informed the delcgates before they voted on the question.

The vote followed a 90-minute debate on the issue, Gomsrud said.

The action aligns the CLU with the Minnesota AFL-CIO Federation of Labor, the St. Paul Trades and Labor Assembly and other union groups backing the amendment.

**STATE** Sen. Jack Davies, secretary of the Constitution Protection Committee which has been leading the fight against the amendment, charged last night that the CLU reversal is "a power play" by amendment backers.

"The CLU voted on orders from leadership, embarrassed by its independent stand," he asserted.

Davies identified the "leadership" as Robert Hess, executive vice president of the Minnesota AFL-CIO Federation of Labor, and Gomsrud.

**HESS DID** not attend Wednesday's meeting. Gomsrud, who had opposed the Tax Committee report last month, did not participate in the CLU debate Wednesday.

The CLU also voted unanimously to support the school referendum on the November ballot which would give the School Board authority to increase the tax levy.

The proposal would authorize the School Board to increase taxes by 3.4 mills but the board is pledged to limit the raise next year to 2.9 mills.

## Johnson Denies He Knew About Jenkins' Conduct

WASHINGTON, D.C.—(AP)—President Johnson said Thursday night that he had no information or report of any kind until late Wednesday that "had ever raised a question" with respect to the personal conduct of Walter Jenkins.

Flying back from a campaign tour of New York state, Mr. Johnson issued his first statement on the resignation of Jenkins, his long-time friend and key aide, who quit after being arrested on a morals charge.

The President's statement was, in effect, a reply to an allegation by Dean Burch, chairman of the Republican National Committee, that Mr. Johnson had covered up for Jenkins for 5½ years—an allegation based on the fact that Jenkins had been arrested on a morals charge in 1959.

**HERE IS** the text of Mr. Johnson's statement:

"Walter Jenkins has worked with me faithfully for 25 years. No man I know has given more personal dedication, devotion and tireless labor.

"Until late yesterday no information or report of any kind to me had ever raised a question with respect to his personal conduct. Mr. Jenkins is now in the care of his physician and his many friends will join in praying for his early recovery.

"For myself and Mrs. Johnson I want to say that our hearts go out with the deepest compassion for him and for his wife and six children—and they have our love and prayers.

"On this case as on any such case, the public interest comes before all personal feelings. I have requested and received Mr. Jenkins' resignation.

"Within moments after being notified last night, I ordered director J. Edgar Hoover of the FBI to make an immediate and comprehensive inquiry and report promptly to me and the American people."

Mrs. Johnson yesterday issued a statement which said "my heart is aching" for Jenkins."

**"HE IS NOW** receiving the medical attention which he needs," the first lady said. "I know our family and all of his friends and I hope all others pray for his recovery."

Burch had declared that Mr. Johnson must explain "why he covered up for 5½ years" the fact that Jenkins had been arrested in 1959 and was permitted to hold a top White House post.

Former Vice President Richard M. Nixon demanded that Mr. Johnson go before a nationwide audience and tell what he knew of "this sick man."

Barry M. Goldwater, Republican presidential candidate, told reporters while campaigning in Texas that he would not comment on the Jenkins case at "any time." It was learned from high GOP sources that he wants to rule out the Jenkins developments as a campaign issue except as they relate to security matters.

**HOWEVER,** Nixon, appearing in Fort Wayne, Ind., said that the Jenkins disclosure and the Bobby Baker case showed that Mr. Johnson's "two closest associates" turned out to be "bad apples."

The political impact of the charges was on the minds of officials in both parties, but few would make a prediction. Most preferred to wait a few days to measure public reaction.

All were agreed that it was a hard blow to the Democratic campaign, but most seemed to feel that it was not enough to overturn what had been believed to be a wide lead for Mr. Johnson.

The White House an-

Jenkins
Continued on Page Seven

## Three National Candidates to Be in Region Today

Sen. Barry Goldwater and both major party vice presidential candidates will campaign in the Upper Midwest today.

Sen. Goldwater, Republican presidential nominee, will appear this afternoon at the National Cornpicking Contest in Sioux Falls, S.D.

*(MILLER WILL Tour State by Air—Page 43.)*

An hour later, Sen. Hubert Humphrey, Democratic vice presidential hopeful, will speak at the Sioux Falls contest.

Humphrey's opponent for the vice presidency, Rep. William Miller, will campaign in Minnesota, appearing at Duluth, St. Cloud and Collegeville before ending his state visit with a stopover this afternoon in the Twin Cities.

## At 3½, Elise Ericksson Leaves City for New Life in Sweden

At age 3½, Elise Ericksson started life over again Thursday.

But the peppery little girl didn't really realize that she was leaving Minneapolis and the United States and flying to Sweden to meet, for the first time, her new "parents."

Elise skipped around Minneapolis-St. Paul International Airport—her long blonde hair bobbing perpetually — like any other 3½-year-old.

She crawled onto a mechanical horse and squeezed off a few shots (all misses) at some stampeding buffalo. She hopped over to the observation deck railing and watched jets climb into the sky.

And she wanted to rummage in a small bag that had been packed with goodies and games for her long flight from Minneapolis to Chicago, Ill., and then to Stockholm, Sweden. Mrs. O. B. Perry adroitly foiled that plan.

Mrs. Perry has been keeping Elise since the gir''s father allegedly shot and killed her mother in July. Mrs. Perry explained that Elise, who speaks no Swedish, "doesn't really understand what has happened."

Alf Ericksson, 29, gave up his legal rights to Elise two months ago, and arrangements were made with the Swedish Consul in Minneapolis, Olof Landenius, to have her live with her mother's relatives in Sweden.

Both Ericksson and his wife, Anita, 21, were immigrants from Sweden and have no relatives in this country.

Ericksson, who shot him-

Home
Continued on Page Seven

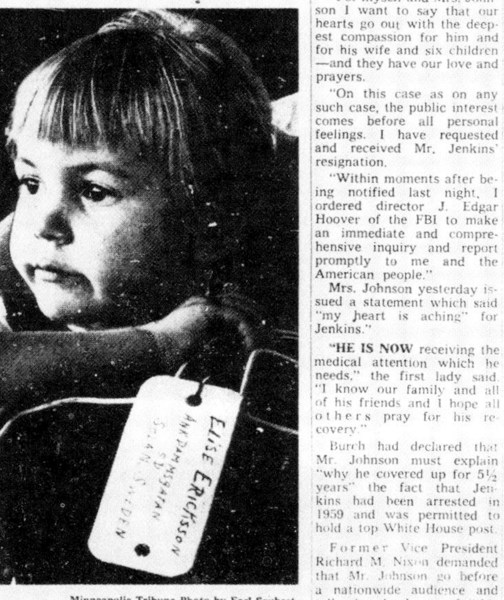


Minneapolis Tribune Photo by Earl Seubert

ELISE ERICKSSON AT THE AIRPORT
*Off to Sweden with her little bag*

## Sen. McCarthy Flies to Ailing Daughter

Sen. Eugene McCarthy, D-Minn., canceled campaign engagements and flew to Washington, D.C., Thursday after learning that his eldest daughter was hospitalized there.

Ellen McCarthy, 17, a junior at Stoneridge Day School, Maclean, Va., became ill at school yesterday and was admitted to Georgetown University Hospital for tests and observation. The nature of her illness was not learned immediately.

Mrs. McCarthy interrupted an Iron Range tour in behalf of her husband's re-election campaign to return to the Twin Cities last night. A spokesman said she plans to go to Washington this morning.

According to a McCarthy aide, the senator's return to his speaking schedule will depend on his daughter's condition.

Earler, it was announced that McCarthy would take time off next week from his campaign against Republican candidate Wheelock Whitney to campaign for the Democratic ticket in other parts of the country.

He is scheduled to speak in Las Vegas, Nev., Sunday; Los Angeles, Calif., Monday, and Westport, Conn., and New York, N.Y., Tuesday. These engagements had not been canceled yesterday.

The McCarthys have three other children, Mary, 15; Michael, 13, and Margaret, 9.

### Almanac

**It Doesn't Take Him Long to Get Fuzzy**

*Friday, Oct. 16, 1964*

290th day. 76 to go this year
Sunrise 6:30 a.m.; sunset 5:27 p.m.

A St. Louis Park family is not permitted to refer to police officers by any derogatory terms—since father is a policeman.

"However," his wife relates, "I came home from Minneapolis the other day lambasting the Police Department for giving me my third parking ticket in less than a year."

Her 11-year-old boy's immediate comment: "Is it all right if we call the cops 'fuzz' from now on, Mom?"

•

*It's National Macaroni Week. Get twisted all out of shape tonight.*

## Mild Weather May Stay on for Weekend

It's likely to be a mild, comfortable weekend in the Twin Cities area.

Today's forecast is for a high temperature of 78, variable winds of 10 miles an hour and mostly fair skies.

After an overnight low of 48, the temperature is expected to warm to 72 on Saturday, with partly cloudy skies likely.

Highs forecast for the Upper Midwest today: Minnesota, 65 to 75 north, 72 to 82 south; North Dakota 60 to 70; South Dakota, 64 to 72 northwest, 70 to 82 southeast; Wisconsin, 74 to 82.

## CORRECTION

The Minneapolis Tribune incorrectly reported Thursday that Kenneth T. Robinson, 2640 Bloomington Av., pleaded guilty to a drunk driving charge after hitting the rear of another vehicle driven by a police officer.

Kenneth T. Robinson was not involved in the incident in any way.

The driver of the car involved in the incident was Harry L. Robinson, 2219 Blaisdell Av.

The Minneapolis Tribune regrets any embarrassment or inconvenience that might have been caused Kenneth T. Robinson.

## TURN THE PAGES TO:



TRIBUNE TELEPHONES

News, General .. 372-4141
Circulation ..... 372-4343
Want Ads ...... 372-4242

Mild

TUESDAY TEMPERATURES

| | | | | | |
|---|---|---|---|---|---|
| 2 a.m. | 56 | 10 a.m. | 59 | 6 p.m. | 54 |
| 3 a.m. | 54 | 11 a.m. | 61 | 7 p.m. | [illegible] |
| 4 a.m. | 53 | Noon | 58 | 8 p.m. | [illegible] |
| 5 a.m. | 52 | 1 p.m. | 58 | 9 p.m. | 52 |
| 6 a.m. | 52 | 2 p.m. | 58 | 10 p.m. | 52 |
| 7 a.m. | 51 | 3 p.m. | 59 | 11 p.m. | 52 |
| 8 a.m. | 54 | 4 p.m. | 59 | 12 M. | 52 |
| 9 a.m. | 58 | 5 p.m. | 56 | 1 a.m. | 48 |
| | | | | *2 a.m. | 46 |

Details Page 18 *Unofficial

Minneapolis Tribune

MORNING

ELECTION FINAL

Vol. XCVIII—No. 164 Copyright 1964 Minneapolis Star and Tribune Company MINNEAPOLIS, MINN., WEDNESDAY, NOVEMBER 4, 1964 . . . . . . Telephone 372-4141 Single Copy Price 10c Lower Price for Carrier Delivery

## A DEMOCRATIC LANDSLIDE

# JOHNSON, HUMPHREY WIN

## McCarthy, Fraser, MacGregor, Karth Are Re-elected

—MINNESOTA SENATE—

## Senator Wins by Big Margin

By DICK YOUNGBLOOD
Minneapolis Tribune Staff Writer

U.S. Sen. Eugene McCarthy Tuesday swept to a second term in an overwhelming victory over his hard-driving opponent, Wheclock Whitney.

With more than 70 per cent of the state's 3,800 precincts tabulated, the 16-year congressional veteran held a commanding 267,000-vote margin over Whitney.

In his winning drive for the Republican-held Senate seat in 1958, McCarthy held a final margin of 73,218 votes.

Whitney, in his election-night headquarters at the Leamington Hotel, announced at 11:30 p.m. that he had conceded his loss.

"I THINK we've made some contributions during this campaign," he later told a cheering crowd at Republican headquarters in the Leamington. "Let's not point the blame (for the loss) at any individual or any issue."

McCarthy, who received a great ovation when he appeared before a DFL rally a. Radisson Hotel, said, "I thank you for your help. Not only do I thank you, I commend you."

Of the Johnson-Humphrey victory, he said: "We demonstrated our political maturity to ourselves and to the people around the world. It must be a great relief to those peoples . . ."

Predictably, a big share of

Minn. Senate
Continued on Page Six

—MINN. CONGRESS—

## 7 Incumbents Are Re-elected; Langen Ahead

By JERRY KIRSHENBAUM
Minneapolis Tribune Staff Writer

Minnesotans returned seven incumbents to the U.S. Congress Tuesday, and the election of the eighth appeared certain.

A trace of doubt lingered this morning only in the 7th District where Republican Odin Langen held a 2,200-vote lead over DFL candidate Ben Wichterman with returns tabulated in 804 of 895 precincts.

All three Twin Cities area congressmen were re-elected handily.

Minneapolis voters gave DFLer Donald M. Fraser of the 5th District about a 55 per cent majority in his race against 13th Ward Alderman John W. Johnson. It was Fraser's first re-election bid.

**RE-ELECTED** with ease in the metropolitan area were Republican Clark MacGregor in the 3rd District and the DFL's Joseph Karth in the 4th.

Elsewhere in Minnesota, 8th District DFLer John Blatnik rolled to an easy win, while Republican incumbents Albert Quie and Ancher Nelsen were returned to Congress in the 1st and 2nd Districts, respectively.

DFL Rep. Alec Olson withstood a strong showing by Republican Robert Odegard to carry the 6th District.

Langen appeared a likely winner on the strength of still unreported precincts in Otter Tail County, where the third-term Republican traditionally amasses 2-to-1 majorities.

In losing to Fraser, the 35-year-old Johnson refused to blame his defeat on the presence of Sen. Barry Goldwater at the head of the Republican ticket.

"IT WASN'T because Barry Goldwater headed the na-

Minn. Congress
Continued on Page Nine

TURN THE PAGES TO:

• • • •



TRIBUNE TELEPHONES
Want Ads ...... 372-4242
News, General .. 372-4141
Circulation ..... 372-4343

Associated Press

LYNDON B. JOHNSON AND HUBERT H. HUMPHREY
*The President and vice president - elect*

## Taconite Proposal Wins Approval

By SAM ROMER
Minneapolis Tribune Staff Writer

Minnesota voters approved two amendments to the state constitution in Tuesday's election, incomplete returns indicated last night.

The amendment tc provide tax equity for the taconite industry was polling more than 75 per cent of all votes cast, with 60 per cent of all precincts reporting.

An amendment to eliminate obsolete provisions from the constitution was scoring better than 60 per cent.

**TO PASS,** an amendment to the Minnesota constitution must receive a majority of all ballots cast in the election, not just on the amendment issue.

Both amendments were given overwhelming approval by the voters who cast ballots on the specific issues—with the taconite amendment's margin almost 7 to 1 and the "obsolete" amendment better than 4 to 1.

As it turned out, there were more "no" votes cast on the "obsolete" amendment—to which there was no open opposition—than on the taconite amendment, which had aroused considerable controversy.

In addition, it was apparent that fewer voters were casting ballots on the second amendment than on the well-publicized taconite proposal.

**THE TWO** amendments were passed by the 1963 legislature.

The proposal to remove obsolete sections from the Minnesota constitution was sponsored by the Minnesota State Bar Association after a study of the constitution.

None of these sections has been obeyed in practice, despite their presence in the constitution. One, for instance, provides for a state census while another limits a woman's right to vote to school and library elections.

It was generally regarded as noncontroversial.

**THE STORY** was different on the taconite amendment.

Yesterday's vote climaxed an intensive campaign on behalf of the amendment, sup-

Taconite
Continued on Page Nine

## HOW MINNESOTA VOTED

Asterisk (*) denotes incumbent

### PRESIDENT
2,730 precincts of 3,800

DeBerry (Soc Wkrs) ...... 391
Goldwater (R) ..... 422,348
Hass (Ind Gov) .... 570
*Johnson (D) ...... 766,340

### U.S. SENATE
2,737 precincts of 3,800

Braatz (Ind Gov) .. 1,066
Luoma (Soc Wkrs).. 546
*McCarthy (DFL) .. 725,834
Whitney (R) ....... 458,506

### CONGRESS

#### 1st District
269 precincts of 449

Daley (DFL) ...... 62,243
*Quie (R) ......... 78,615

#### 2nd District
431 precincts of 519

*Nelsen (R) ....... 74,951
Simpson (DFL) .... 55,886

#### 3rd District
121 precincts of 195

*MacGregor (R) ... 95,521
Parish (DFL) ...... 65,231

#### 4th District
240 precincts of 280

Drexler (R) ........ 45,705
*Karth (DFL) ...... 128,424

#### 5th District
195 precincts of 195

*Fraser (DFL) ..... 127,894
Johnson (R) ....... 105,720

#### 6th District
528 precincts of 667

Odegard (R) ....... 66,188
*Olson (DFL) ...... 73,921

#### 7th District
804 precincts of 895

*Langen (R) ....... 73,665
Wichterman (DFL) . 71,423

#### 8th District
384 precincts of 600

Glossbrenner (R) ... 41,250
*Blatnik (DFL) ..... 91,575

### RAILROAD AND WAREHOUSE COMMISSIONER
2,519 precincts of 3,800

*Anderson (DFL) .. 518,537
Peterson (R) ....... 424,199

### STATE SUPREME COURT
(Nominated without party designation)

#### Chief Judge
2,070 precincts of 3,800

*Knutson ......... 593,162

#### Associate Judge
2,069 precincts of 3,800

*Rogosheske ...... 543,041

#### Associate Judge
2,540 precincts of 3,800

Dressel ........... 274,570
*Sheran ........... 446,073

### STATE CONSTITUTIONAL AMENDMENTS
(Majority of all votes cast in election needed for passage)

#### Amendment No. 1
Taxation of Taconite and Other Metals
2,465 precincts of 3,800

Yes .............. 787,626
No ............... 113,070

#### Amendment No. 2
Removal of Obsolete Provisions from the State Constitution
2,459 precincts of 3,800

Yes .............. 658,347
No ............... 154,463

## Minnesota Gives LBJ 2-to-1 Edge

By FRANK WRIGHT
Minneapolis Tribune Staff Writer

Minnesota voters joined the nation Tuesday in sweeping the Democratic team of President Johnson and Sen. Hubert Humphrey into the White House.

With slightly more than two-thirds of the state's 3,800 precincts reported, the Democratic team was ahead of the Republican duo of Sen. Barry Goldwater and Rep. William Miller by a margin of almost 2-to-1.

Robert Forsythe, state Republican chairman, conceded at 11:35 p.m. that Minnesota had gone to the Democrats.

The state Republican party, he added, however, "has come out of this election strong and vigorous."

The state, which gave its 10 electoral votes to Democrat John F. Kennedy in 1960 by a bare 22,000 popular votes, was doing much better for the Democrats yesterday as returns mounted.

Mr. Johnson and Sen. Humphrey, one of Minnesota's own, were easily headed for the biggest victory by a presidential ticket in the state since Franklin Delano Roosevelt piled up a 65 per cent majority against Alf Landon in 1936.

Results showed the Democratic ticket running much stronger in friendly areas

Minn. President
Continued on Page Six

More Election News, Pages 3, 4, 5, 6, 10

—NATIONWIDE—

## Goldwater Takes 5 Deep South States

By RICHARD WILSON
Chief of the Minneapolis Tribune Washington Bureau

WASHINGTON, D.C. — President Johnson won election Tuesday in a record-setting sweep which carried at least 45 states and gave him the greatest popular majority in history.

It was a Republican rout with Sen. Barry Goldwater carrying only five states in the Deep South and leading in his home state of Arizona.

Coast to coast and North to south, the Johnson majority rolled up to equal and exceed previous landslide records of Warren G. Harding, Franklin D. Roosevelt and Dwight D. Eisenhower.

Returns from 83 per cent of the country early this morning gave the following vote:

**President Johnson,** 61.7 per cent—35,955,007.

**Sen. Goldwater,** 38.3 per cent—22,869,581.

Mr. Johnson won 43 states with 479 electoral votes and was ahead in 2 states with 7 electoral votes for an indicated total of 486.

Sen. Goldwater won 5 states with 47 electoral votes and was ahead in one state with 5 electoral votes for an indicated total of 52.

Mr. Johnson's percentage of the popular vote apparently will set a record exceeding the 60.4 per cent won by Harding in 1920 and the 60.8 per cent in the defeat of Alfred M. Landon by Roosevelt in 1936.

Sen. Goldwater remained at his home in Phoenix, Ariz., without making a concession of the election or a postelection statement. He will do so at 10 a.m. today after he has studied the returns to determine their effect on the conservative cause.

Sen. Goldwater won Alabama, Mississippi, South Carolina, Louisiana and Georgia. But Virginia, Florida, Tennessee, Texas, North Carolina and Arkansas went to Mr. Johnson.

**HEAVY** majorities for Mr. Johnson and Sen. Hubert H. Humphrey in the East and Northeast — even Vermont— and in the industrial Midwest — Ohio, Illinois, Indiana — were rolled up and then repeated as returns gave California and the whole West Coast to the Democratic ticket.

Farm states of Iowa, Minnesota, Kansas, Missouri, North Dakota and South Dakota added to the Democratic total.

Mr. Johnson won as big as he had hoped in his bid for a full four-year term after serving 20 days less than a year since the assassination of President John Kennedy.

The result was a Republi-

Nationwide
Continued on Page Nine

## PRESIDENTIAL VOTE NATIONWIDE

Associated Press

| State | Voting Units | Units Rptng. | Popular Vote Johnson | Popular Vote Goldwater | Electoral Vote Trend Johnson | Electoral Vote Trend Goldwater |
|---|---|---|---|---|---|---|
| Ala. x | 3,672 | 3,097 | | 428,270 | .. | 10 |
| Alaska | 356 | 105 | 9,299 | 4,894 | 3 | .. |
| Ariz. | 741 | 562 | 182,410 | 192,347 | .. | 5 |
| Ark. | 2,543 | 1,704 | 140,416 | 101,662 | 6 | .. |
| Calif. | 31,498 | 21,668 | 2,976,031 | 1,885,153 | 40 | .. |
| Colo. | 1,966 | 1,910 | 459,476 | 289,970 | 6 | .. |
| Conn. | 600 | 600 | 825,205 | 391,685 | 8 | .. |
| Del. | 356 | 356 | 122,562 | 78,203 | 3 | .. |
| D.C. | 91 | 91 | 163,746 | 27,627 | 3 | .. |
| Fla. | 2,279 | 2,274 | 891,284 | 862,026 | 14 | .. |
| Ga. | 1,857 | 1,641 | 438,362 | 513,936 | .. | 12 |
| Hawaii | 242 | 125 | 79,490 | 22,696 | 4 | .. |
| Idaho | 890 | 819 | 129,153 | 122,276 | 4 | .. |
| Ill. | 10,329 | 8,417 | 2,217,851 | 1,484,198 | 26 | .. |
| Ind. | 4,416 | 4,120 | 1,050,016 | 839,098 | 13 | .. |
| Iowa | 2,476 | 2,054 | 607,847 | 370,853 | 9 | .. |
| Kan. | 2,927 | 2,235 | 463,489 | 387,887 | 7 | .. |
| Ky. | 2,994 | 2,966 | 661,778 | 364,011 | 9 | .. |
| La. | 2,224 | 2,217 | 386,287 | 503,077 | .. | 10 |
| Maine | 628 | 583 | 249,866 | 113,445 | 4 | .. |
| Md. | 1,521 | 1,426 | 735,597 | 378,118 | 10 | .. |
| Mass. | 2,024 | 1,251 | 957,884 | 263,866 | 14 | .. |
| Mich. | 5,211 | 4,265 | 1,828,715 | 887,558 | 21 | .. |
| Minn. | 3,800 | 2,545 | 727,449 | 399,146 | 10 | .. |
| Miss. | 1,878 | 1,865 | 52,538 | 354,459 | .. | 7 |
| Mo. | 4,414 | 3,524 | 931,679 | 504,149 | 12 | .. |
| Mont. | 1,065 | 569 | 81,789 | 52,636 | 4 | .. |
| Neb. | 2,158 | 1,622 | 214,124 | 185,905 | 5 | .. |
| Nev. | 615 | 594 | 71,205 | 59,127 | 3 | .. |
| N.H. | 302 | 296 | 172,826 | 98,823 | 4 | .. |
| N.J. | 4,603 | 4,429 | 1,789,504 | 919,112 | 17 | .. |
| N.M. | 1,049 | 934 | 185,947 | 131,283 | 4 | .. |
| N.Y. | 12,439 | 10,902 | 4,077,154 | 1,931,136 | 43 | .. |
| N.C. | 2,164 | 2,147 | 805,731 | 631,855 | 13 | .. |
| N.D. | 2,255 | 1,599 | 97,656 | 68,389 | 4 | .. |
| Ohio | 13,485 | 11,018 | 2,088,457 | 1,302,089 | 26 | .. |
| Okla. | 3,085 | 3,016 | 508,346 | 402,112 | 8 | .. |
| Ore. | 3,256 | 2,374 | 360,236 | 215,261 | 6 | .. |
| Pa. | 9,286 | 8,613 | 2,768,994 | 1,503,505 | 29 | .. |
| R.I. | 469 | 469 | 304,579 | 71,893 | 4 | .. |
| S.C. | 1,611 | 1,603 | 217,520 | 309,2[illegible] | .. | 8 |
| S.D. | 1,771 | 1,443 | 108,275 | 87,486 | 4 | .. |
| Tenn. | 2,742 | 2,666 | 598,864 | 487,770 | 11 | .. |
| Tex. | 5,525 | 4,960 | 1,479,079 | 870,169 | 25 | .. |
| Utah | 1,223 | 1,048 | 181,591 | 150,592 | 4 | .. |
| Vt. | 246 | 246 | 107,963 | 54,841 | 3 | .. |
| Va. | 2,016 | 1,965 | 539,161 | 464,855 | 12 | .. |
| Wash. | 5,659 | 4,100 | 543,184 | 336,820 | 9 | .. |
| W. Va. | 2,668 | 2,402 | 498,171 | 237,747 | 7 | .. |
| Wis. | 3,550 | 2,793 | 809,082 | 489,809 | 12 | .. |
| Wyo. | 621 | 499 | 57,139 | 45,471 | 3 | .. |
| | 175,796 | 145,125 | 35,955,007 | 22,869,581 | 486 | 52 |

x—Alabama Democratic elector slate unpledged. Thus no specific Johnson vote obtainable.

## KEY U.S. RACES

**MASSACHUSETTS**—Sen. Edward Kennedy easily won a smashing victory.

**CALIFORNIA**—Former Hollywood actor George Murphy was leading 2,516,888 to 2,375,566 with 23,958 of 31,498 precincts reporting in the U.S. Senate race.

**OHIO** — Republican Senate candidate Robert Taft Jr. defeated Democrat Stephen M. Young, the incumbent.

**MICHIGAN**—Gov. George Romney cut into normal Democratic strongholds in Detroit to win re-election and national attention as a shining hope for the battered Republican party.

**IOWA** — Democratic Gov. Harold E. Hughes piled up more than a 2-to-1 majority in defeating Atty. Gen. Evan Hultman.

**NEW YORK** — Robert F. Kennedy, brother of the late president and former U.S. attorney general, defeated Republican Sen. Kenneth B. Keating.

**OKLAHOMA** — Fred Harris, the Democratic candidate, beat Bud Wilkinson, former Oklahoma University football coach and a Minnesota star in college days, in a nip-and-tuck race.

**TEXAS** — Sen. Ralph Yarborough defeated his conservative Republican opponent, George Bush.

**PENNSYLVANIA** — Republican Sen. Hugh Scott and Democrat Genevieve Blatt took turns at leading.

**ARKANSAS** — Gov. Orval E. Faubus, running well ahead of the Democratic national ticket, led Republican Winthrop Rockefeller.

**ILLINOIS** — After trailing, Gov. Otto Kerner pushed ahead of Republican Charles H. Percy and won re-election.

## Almanac

### Polling Place Fails to Buoy Their Spirits

*Wednesday, Nov. 4, 1964*
309th day, 57 to go this year
Sunrise 6:55 a.m.; sunset 4:58 p.m.

The scene at Rice Creek School:

A mother leaving the polling place with her angry children was trying to explain to them, "I told you we were going to VOTE, not go on a boat."

•

Seen by a colleague on the car ahead, in huge black letters against a startling pea-green-and-heliotrope background, was a sign the width of the guy's bumper: "BUMPER STICKER."

Snow

SUNDAY TEMPERATURES

| | | | | | |
|---|---|---|---|---|---|
| 2 a.m. | 15 | 10 a.m. | 18 | 6 p.m. | 21 |
| 3 a.m. | 17 | 11 a.m. | 20 | 7 p.m. | 21 |
| 4 a.m. | 16 | Noon | 22 | 8 p.m. | 20 |
| 5 a.m. | 15 | 1 p.m. | [illegible] | 9 p.m. | 20 |
| 6 a.m. | 13 | 2 p.m. | 21 | 10 p.m. | 20 |
| 7 a.m. | 14 | 3 p.m. | 22 | 11 p.m. | 20 |
| 8 a.m. | 12 | 4 p.m. | 22 | 12M. | 21 |
| 9 a.m. | 15 | 5 p.m. | 22 | *1 a.m. | 21 |

*Unofficial

Details Page 20

# Minneapolis Tribune

MORNING

Vol. XCVIII—No. 246 Copyright 1965 Minneapolis Star and Tribune Company MINNEAPOLIS, MINN., MONDAY, JANUARY 25, 1965 Telephone 372-4141 Single Copy Price 10c Lower Price for Carrier Delivery

# Queen Decrees State Funeral for Sir Winston Saturday

## Goldwater Senate Bid Foreseen

### He Is Expected to Run at First Opportunity

New York Times Service

CHICAGO, Ill. — Republican leaders in Arizona and elsewhere are almost certain Barry Goldwater will run for senator from Arizona again at the first opportunity.

Like others who have discussed the subject privately with the defeated presidential nominee, Keith S. Brown, Phoenix, the Arizona Republican chairman, said in an interview that the party people in his state take a future Goldwater candidacy for granted.

**"WE LOOK** forward to it," added Brown. "Barry is our foremost Republican, and he belongs in high public office."

The current term of Democratic Sen. Carl Hayden, 88, dean of the upper house who has been in Congress since Arizona achieved statehood 53 years ago, expires in 1968.

Arizona's other senator is Paul L. Fannin, a Republican and a political protege of Goldwater. He was elected last November to the seat from which Goldwater retired to seek the presidency. His term expires in 1970.

An unusual Arizona law would benefit Goldwater should a vacancy occur before the regularly scheduled elections.

The law requires a special election within 30 to 90 days instead of permitting an interim appointment by the governor, as is the case in nearly every other state. The present governor, Samuel P. Goddard, is a Democrat.

**THE LAW** was enacted three or four years ago by an overwhelmingly Democratic legislature to take the appointive power away from the then Republican governor, Fannin. At the time, it was explained, Hayden had been ailing and was rumored to be considering retirement.

The prospect of the conservative Goldwater's eventual return to Congress was the subject of considerable private conversation when Republicans from the 50 states met in Chicago last week.

Practically none advocated or foresaw another Goldwater nomination for president. But many, including moderates who had fought to terminate control over the national party organization, expressed the hope he would resume public life as a senator.

**"ALTHOUGH** Barry is a maverick and was, perhaps unintentionally, a magnet for far-rightists," said one who seldom had agreed with him, "he is a devoted Republican and has been a constructive senator."

Another political figure said: "The Senate needs a conservative free-wheeler like Goldwater just as it needs a liberal free-wheeler like (onetime Republican senator) Wayne Morse of Oregon."

No, Fido, That Isn't the Way to Track Radiations

Science Reading Series Today on Page 14

Minneapolis Tribune

## 'History's Child' Is Mourned by World's Leaders

From the Tribune Wire Services

LONDON, England — Tributes to a lifetime of mighty accomplishment poured in Sunday for Sir Winston Churchill.

**Queen Elizabeth** wrote to Lady Churchill:

"The news of Sir Winston's death causes inexpressible grief to me and my husband. We send our deepest sympathy to you and your family. The whole world is poorer by the loss of his many-sided genius, while the survival of this country and the sister nations of the Commonwealth, in the race of the greatest danger that has ever threatened them, will be a perpetual memorial to his leadership, his vision and his indomitable courage."

Queen Elizabeth

Pope Paul

**Pope Paul:** "We offer our profound sympathy on the passing of your beloved husband, Sir Winston Churchill, great statesman and indefatigable champion of freedom, independence and peace. We assure you our prayers to God that he comfort you and yours in the painful mourning."

**President Johnson:** "When there was darkness in the world, and hope was low in the hearts of men, a generous providence gave us Winston Churchill.

"As long as men tell about that time of terrible danger and of the men who won the victory, the name of Churchill will live.

"Let us give thanks that we knew him. With our grief let there be gratitude for a life so fully lived, for services so splendid, and for the joys he gave by the joy he took in all he did.

"The people of the United States—his cousins and his fellow-citizens—will pray with his British countrymen for God's eternal blessing on this man, and for comfort to his family.

"He is history's child, and what he said and what he did will never die."

President Johnson

Hubert Humphrey

**Hubert H. Humphrey:** "Democracy has lost one of its greatest champions. With his death an era has come to an end, but he will live in the hearts of the American people just as Lincoln, Jackson, Franklin Roosevelt and John F. Kennedy.

"He had great spiritual re-

Tributes
Continued on Page 10

## LBJ Hopes to Go to London for Funeral

By CHARLES W. BAILEY
Minneapolis Tribune Staff Correspondent

WASHINGTON, D.C. — President Johnson, saying his throat infection is "all over," told reporters from his hospital bed Sunday that he "wants very much" to attend funeral services for Sir Winston Churchill in London, England, Saturday.

The President's cough, which had repeatedly racked him Saturday, was much improved, according to reporters who spent eight minutes with him at midafternoon.

**IN ADDITION,** his voice appeared to have lost most of the hoarseness that was painfully evident Saturday.

Mr. Johnson yesterday issued a statement mourning Churchill's death and also ordered all United States flags flown at half-staff until the Briton's burial in an apparently unprecedented mark of respect for a former foreign leader.

The President's health obviously had improved to the point where his thoughts were again on outside matters — particularly his desire to attend the Churchill funeral.

"I want very much to go," he replied when reporters asked his plans for the ceremony. "It all depends on how I feel in the next day or two."

The White House press office said it did not expect a decision on the trip until at least today.

**IT WAS** clear that the President's physicians would have something to say about it, although it was equally likely that their word would not necessarily be the final one.

Describing his current condition, the President said "it's all right now. I have no discomfort in my throat or chest."

As to how long he will be hospitalized — his doctors have said they hope to keep him in bed four or five days — Mr. Johnson said, "It depends on when the fever is gone . . . It's easier for them to take care of me here than at home."

The White House said the President is still receiving the same medications — antio-

Johnson
Continued on Page Eight

Biography, Pictures--Pages 4, 5

United Press International

SIR WINSTON AND HIS FAMOUS V-FOR-VICTORY SIGN

*This picture was made in 1954*

## She Orders a Week of Mourning

By GRAHAM HOVEY
Minneapolis Tribune European Correspondent

LONDON, England — Sir Winston Churchill died "in peace and without pain" shortly before 8 a.m. Sunday.

Lady Churchill, their three surviving children and other members of the immediate family were at the bedside when the end came for Britain's great World War II leader.

**THEY HAD** kept a 10-day vigil at the Churchill home in London's Kensington Borough in which the entire British nation and much of the world had seemed to participate.

Sir Winston apparently never regained consciousness after it was announced Jan. 15 that he had suffered a stroke. He died at 90 on the 70th anniversary of the death of his father, Lord Randolph Churchill.

By request of Queen Elizabeth Britain became a nation in mourning for a week, and plans shaped up for probably the most elaborate tribute ever given an English commoner.

Sir Winston's body will lie in state Wednesday, Thursday and Friday in the 11th century Westminster Hall adjoining the House of Commons where he served for more than 60 years.

**IT WILL BE** taken by gun carriage through London streets Saturday for a state funeral in St. Paul's Cathedral attended by the queen and many heads of state, possibly including President Johnson.

The body then will be taken by barge up the Thames to Festival Pier near Waterloo Station, then by train to the village of Bladon in Oxfordshire for burial in a cemetery adjoining the Blenheim estate where Sir Winston was born.

Not since William Ewart Gladstone in 1898 has any prime minister or former prime minister been accorded the honor of lying in state at Westminster Hall.

**IF THE QUEEN** attends the service in St. Paul's as expected, it will mark the first time in Britain's long history that any commoner has been so honored by the monarch.

Elizabeth, who is at her

Churchill
Continued on Page Eight

## Cold Expected to Follow Snow in Area

Occasional periods of snow, accompanied by southeasterly winds of eight to 15 miles an hour, are expected in the Twin Cities today.

The forecast calls for a high today of 28, a low tonight of 8 and a high Tuesday of 15.

Snow is also expected in most of the Upper Midwest today, although Wisconsin may get some relief from the weekend blizzard.

North Dakota and South Dakota are expected to have colder temperatures, while Wisconsin's forecast calls for cloudy and a little warmer, with light snow in the north.

Minnesotans may expect occasional snow mixed with freezing drizzle.

**MOST** of the Midwest experienced the worst ice storm in 17 years over the weekend, causing 10 deaths in Wisconsin, four each in Illinois and Kansas, and three each in Michigan and Indiana since Friday.

The storm was particularly devastating in Chicago, Ill., yesterday, where more than 150,000 homes and businesses were left in darkness for hours when city transformers were shorted by ice.

Linemen were called in from Iowa and Indiana to help repair lines felled by trees or snapped by the weight of the ice.

In Elgin, Ill., residents were without power for nearly 24 hours due to the storm.

**MILWAUKEE,** Wis., has had more than 10 inches of snow since Friday.

Predicted highs in the Upper Midwest: North Dakota, 2 to 12 north and 5 to 18 south; South Dakota, 10 to 22 north and 15 to 30 south; Minnesota, 10 to 22 northwest and 15 to 30 east and south, and Wisconsin, 25 to 32 north and 30s south.

## De Gaulle to Attend 'My Friend's' Funeral

New York Times Service

PARIS, France — France mourned Sir Winston Churchill Sunday night as though he had been one of her sons. To the French he was the father of victory in World War II.

President Charles de Gaulle, who will attend the funeral of his old comrade in arms, set the tone for France's sorrow with a stately and moving tribute.

**"FRANCE** feels profoundly the grief which has stricken Britain," the president said in a message to Queen Elizabeth.

To Lady Churchill the general sent a message "from the bottom of the heart" telling her that news of Sir Winston's death had aroused the greatest sorrow in France.

"For myself," De Gaulle said, "I see the departure in the person of so great a man, my wartime companion and my friend."

At De Gaulle's order, the French flag will fly at half staff for 24 hours to honor the memory of Sir Winston.

**FROM EVERY** quarter of France and from every political party, except the Communists, came tributes to this most English of Englishmen who had been France's friend, counsellor and ally in two world wars.

Paul Reynaud, premier of France and ally of Sir Winston in the dark days of 1940, said flatly, "Churchill was the greatest man of our time."

During the terrible hours when the Germans poured into northern France, "the most tragic hours for France, there was never a reproachful word between us," Reynaud recalled.

**FRENCH** radio and television devoted long programs to reviews of Sir Winston's life and to tributes by French leaders. The permanent Council of the North Atlantic Treaty Organization (NATO) will meet today to pay tribute to Sir Winston.

The most spontaneous and moving grief came from the people of Paris, mostly those now in their 40s and older. In the quiet little bars in the side streets this rainy night, they were talking about him as though he could not die.

An elderly lawyer explained it: "Churchill offered us all that was best in the English, fortitude, loyalty, courage, perhaps that touch of ruthlessness that is necessary in war. We always knew he was a friend, a harsh friend at times, but a friend."

BRITISH MAN-IN-STREET REACTION:

## 'I Hate to Think What Would Have Happened Without Him'

LONDON, England — (UPI) — "I hate to think what would have happened to us all without him. I just dread to think of that."

These words from James Crumley, 75, former Scottish international soccer player, typified man-in-the-street reaction Sunday to the death of Sir Winston Churchill.

Crumley, now proprietor of a chain of fish and chip shops in London, went on:

**"HIS DEATH** is a great loss to this country. He has been such a great man. Throughout his life, he proved himself a great battler, a man you just had to respect. There is no doubt about it. During the war he saved this country and saved us all."

The reaction among even the youngest was the same as that of the elderly: a great man to whom all owe so much has gone from their midst.

Mrs. Eve Browne, a young London housewife, told her children, Carolyn, 6, and Ann 5, of the death, and explained to them: "He led our people during the war."

The two children discussed the matter with each other for a few moments, then returned to mother and said: "The robbers will be glad now, won't they?"

Said Mrs. Browne: "I think even the robbers will be sad to see him go. They had just as much respect for him as we had."

**A LONDON** fashion model, Karen Van Laun, 21, said: "I was just born when he was still a very powerful man. His death is the end of a great chapter in British history. I suppose we all knew he was dying, but we did not really want to believe it. It is very sad, especially after he had made such a tremendous fight. But he had a very full life—he did everything he wanted to do."

As the news spread, flags went to half-staff all over London and elsewhere in the country. Men were seen wearing black ties.

Explained Mark Cogley, landlord of the Goat Tavern, in fashionable Mayfair:

"As soon as I heard of Sir Winston's death, my first thought was: Where is my black mourning tie? I have never worn the tie except in mourning for relatives or the monarch."

A London antique dealer, Peter Ritchie, said: "He was the man we all admired, irrespective of politics. I cannot think there will ever be a greater Briton."

Ivor Spencer, secretary of the Guild of Professional Toastmasters, who had introduced Sir Winston Churchill to many dinner guests over the years, said:

"I still have a Churchill cigar I got some years ago. I would never dream of smoking it. It is a relic I will always treasure. You must believe in miracles after the miraculous way that Churchill saved this country from defeat in World War II. He was worth a dozen divisions to the British people and the Allied cause."



Tribune Telephones

| | |
|---|---|
| News, General | 372-4141 |
| Circulation | 372-4343 |
| Want Ads | 372-4242 |

## Almanac

### Party of First Part Is a Spoilsport

*Monday, Jan. 25, 1965*

25th day. 340 to go this year
Sunrise 7:41 a.m.; sunset 5:11 p.m.

A Minneapolis man discovered by accident that his wife was planning a surprise birthday party for him. At the appointed hour, the guests bounced in, yelling, "Surprise!"

The birthday boy calmly unbuttoned his jacket, baring a sign he had taped to his shirt. It read, "WHAT SURPRISE?"

•

*Haggis is a mixture of mincemeat, oatmeal and spices cooked in the lining of a sheep's stomach. Robert Burns, who adored haggis, was born 209 years ago today.*

•

The movie, "My Fair Lady," had been on the screen 90 seconds when the pretty young thing exclaimed: "Oh, I can't wait to see it again."

Cold
SUNDAY TEMPERATURES

| | | | | | |
|---|---|---|---|---|---|
| 2 a.m. | [illegible] | 10 a.m. | [illegible] | 6 p.m. | 0 |
| 3 a.m. | [illegible] | 11 a.m. | [illegible] | 7 p.m. | [illegible] |
| 4 a.m. | [illegible] | Noon | [illegible] | 8 p.m. | [illegible] |
| 5 a.m. | [illegible] | 1 p.m. | 4 | 9 p.m. | [illegible] |
| 6 a.m. | [illegible] | 2 p.m. | [illegible] | 10 p.m. | [illegible] |
| 7 a.m. | [illegible] | 3 p.m. | [illegible] | 11 p.m. | [illegible] |
| 8 a.m. | [illegible] | 4 p.m. | [illegible] | 12M | [illegible] |
| 9 a.m. | 2 | 5 p.m. | 2 | *1 a.m. | [illegible] |

*Unofficial

Details Page 16

# Minneapolis Tribune

MORNING

Vol. XCVIII—No. 274 Copyright 1965 Minneapolis Star and Tribune Company MINNEAPOLIS, MINN., MONDAY, FEBRUARY 22, 1965 Telephone 372-4141 Single Copy Price 10c Lower Price for Carrier Delivery

# Malcolm X Is Slain at New York Rally

Associated Press
MALCOLM X
*Death premonition?*

NEW YORK, N.Y. —(AP)— A fusillade of gunfire cut down the fiery, renegade Negro fanatic, Malcolm X, as he rose to address a rally Sunday in an upper Manhattan ballroom. At least five men were believed to have sprung the ambush, after lurking amid the ranks of 500 of his disciples.

His lawyer claimed that the slim, goateed Malcolm had known he was marked for murder, and was preparing in his speech to disclose "the names of those who were trying to kill him."

**POLICE** blamed the slaying on a feud between Malcolm, 39, and the Black Muslim movement, with which he broke in 1963. The Muslims, however, denied any complicity.

A diversion in the rear of the ballroom drew attention from the stage long enough for the assassins to race down an aisle and pump bullets into Malcolm's chest from three weapons. He had just begun to address his followers, starting, "Brothers and sisters . . ."

Malcolm's wife, Betty, 37, was nearby. She screamed, "They're killing him—they're killing him."

**THE KILLERS** turned around and raced from the second-floor ballroom with a mob shouting at their heels, "Kill them—don't let them get away."

Unlike the Black Muslims, the Malcolm group does not search people for weapons at their meetings. When the shooting started, guns also were pulled by Malcolm X's followers.

Outside the hall, quickly converging police grabbed three Negroes, themselves suffering from gunshot wounds. They were hospitalized under guard for questioning. One of them was identified as Thomas Hagan, 22.

**AS WORD** spread in the area north and west of Harlem, near the George Washington Bridge, a Negro woman ran through the streets shrieking:

"God, oh God, they shot Malcolm X!"

Sanford Garelick, assistant chief police inspector, told reporters:

"This is the result, it would seem, of a long-standing feud between the followers of Elijah Muhammad and the people who broke away from him, headed by Malcolm X."

**HARLEM** remained calm in the immediate aftermath of the murder, although extra uniformed police were sped to the area. There was a rumor that half a dozen of Malcolm's followers had slipped out of town for Chicago, Ill., bent on revenging themselves on Muhammad, the head of the Black Muslims.

Malcolm at one time was the most articulate spokesman of the Muslims. However, he was ousted in 1963 after he called the assassination of President John F. Kennedy an instance of "the chickens coming home to roost."

"Being an old farm boy myself," Malcolm added at the time, "chickens coming home to roost never did make me sad. They always made me glad."

**YESTERDAY,** one Chicago Muslim said of Malcolm, "You might say the chickens have come home to roost."

Later, Malcolm said of Muhammad and the Muslims:

"They had been waiting the past two years to try to find some excuse to get rid of me. So they used the remark I made about President Kennedy . . . I was too militant. I was rocking the boat. I was looked on as an outlaw.

"Muhammad got sick at that time, and some elements within the Muslims thought I was trying to take over."

Malcolm claimed that shortly afterwards he first was marked for death.

**ON HIS OWN,** Malcolm became a caustic critic of the Muslims, seeking meanwhile to build a following for an organization of his own called the Afro American Union. He advocated an eye for an eye in racial confrontations, and

Malcolm X
Continued on Page Five

United Press International
MALCOLM X WAS TAKEN FROM BALLROOM ON A STRETCHER SUNDAY
*After fatal shooting while he was addressing Afro American Union*

# Khanh Formally Announces Resignation as Military Chief

SAIGON, South Viet Nam —(UPI)—Lt. Gen. Nguyen Khanh today formally announced his resignation as commander in chief of the South Vietnamese armed forces. Khanh made the announcement by telephone from a seldom-used mountain airfield where his plane landed after running low on fuel.

There was speculation that he was trying to flee the country when his plane put down at the military airstrip at Dalat, 150 miles northeast of Saigon. The airfield has no refueling facilities.

A spokesman for South Viet Nam's Armed Forces Council said that Khanh telephoned the generals at 6:30 a.m. to say that he was resigning and giving up in his bid to remain in power.

Shortly after receiving the call, the Armed Forces Council sent three members to Dalat to negotiate with Khanh the terms of his surrender.

**EARLIER** today, Khanh refused to accept his ouster as head of the armed forces and called on all nine army division commanders to remain loyal to him. At that time, he reportedly was at the seaside resort of Vung Tau, 40 miles southeast of Saigon.

*(GOLDWATER: Viet Conflict will Engulf SE. Asia—Page Two; Hanoi Claims Blasted by Arms Find —Page Three.)*

Later, U.S. Air Force Brig. Gen. Richard R. Rowland told reporters that Khanh had asked to take part in a press conference in which he would confirm his own overthrow.

It was understood that Khanh was to have flown from Vung Tau to Saigon's Tan Son Nhut Airport, where Vietnamese air force headquarters is located and the Armed Forces Council was meeting.

South Vietnamese military leaders who had deposed Khanh Sunday night had gathered at the air base to prepare for any attempt by the ousted strongman to shoot his way back to power. They declared a general alert at the air base.

Saigon radio last night broadcast a decree announcing that Khanh had been kicked out and replaced temporarily by Maj. Gen. Tran Van Minh, a Catholic who is chief of staff of the armed forces.

**A SPOKESMAN** for the anti-Khanh forces appealed over Saigon Radio this morn-

Viet Nam
Continued on Page Four

# 'You Wrote on Our Hearts' Indelibly

*First of a series*

*EDITOR'S NOTE: When John H. Glenn returned to his Arlington, Va., home following his space flight of Feb. 20, 1962, he found three mailbags in the middle of his living room floor. Later a postman came to the door and told Glenn, the first American to orbit the earth, that the Post Office was holding nearly a truckload of additional bags. More letters continued to arrive. Many are contained in Glenn's recently published book, and several will appear in a five-part series that begins today. "The orbital flight of Friendship 7," Glenn says in his book, "was so well covered by the press and television that many people literally did 'live through' the whole event with us. And when they shared our delays, our disappointments and successes, they felt they just had to let their feelings be known—and we appreciated hearing from these many friends."*

Glenn

By COL. JOHN H. GLENN JR.



**From a mother of three:**

It seems an imposition to write to you as we know how busy and exciting these days must be for you all but still we feel such an affinity to you that even though this letter is never read I feel compelled to put into words what it all meant to me, to mine and to those around us.

Do you have any idea, Colonel, how close we were to you in those last moments of countdown? It was a soul-shattering experience beyond human description. Five minutes before lift-off I asked my 6-year-old Mark if he would pray with me for you and the mission. "Mama," he said quietly, "I already have." Through those last heart-stopping seconds there was an almost holy feeling in the room as we each in our own way beseeched our Lord to take care of you. I've wondered since then, if all the prayers of the people could be printed on a tape and stretched into miles if they, too, might not girdle the earth. Our thoughts were for you, too, Annie; for if we felt this way, how must you be feeling?

This letter is to thank you, John, . . . [illegible]ffering up your life so willingly for your country. I've always loved and been proud of my country. Surely there are bad things and evil deeds here, but they lie in the giant shadow of good, fine and brave deeds that hover over our land. I will always say the same, good or bad, success or failure. Pray that all the adulation a sometimes foolish public can bestow will not change you or your family situation one bit. The first time you get kissed by a devastating movie star I hope it's not on TV because I'll be sick to my stomach! Sometimes I think TV is an X ray of the human soul as it shows so much more than it is supposed to.

Those first seconds of lift-off, the moments before

Heartbeat
Continued on Page Five

# Mother, Son Killed in Collision

**Deaths Raise State Toll to 89, Two Above Year Ago**

The wife of a U.S. Army private and her 22-month-old son were killed Sunday night when their car went out of control on Hwy. 55 five miles south of the Mendota Bridge, jumped a lane divider and crashed headon into another vehicle.

Nancy Karr, 24, Rte. 2, Mound, and her son, Roger, were killed. A four or five year-old daughter, whose first name was not known, was taken to Ancker Hospital, St. Paul, where she was being treated for a broken hip.

(PICTURE — Page 15.)

The occupants of the other car, Allan Fritz, 18, 888 S. Wilder St., and Diana Roth, 18, 1432 Hague St., both of St. Paul, were treated at Ancker for cuts and bruises.

Highway patrolmen said the Karr vehicle was headed south and went out of control about 7 p.m.

The victim's husband, Russell Karr, was stationed at St. Bonifacius.

The deaths raised the Minnesota 1965 highway toll to 89—two more than a year ago.

Two persons were killed in a head-on collision a half mile west of Richmond, Minn., on Hwy. 23 Saturday night.

They were identified as Meredith Lehman, 18, Paynesville, Minn., and Edward George Pryzibylski, 60, St. Cloud.

Injured were a Finnish exchange student at Paynesville High School, Pirkko Nykanen, 18; Pryzibylski's son and the son's girl companion.

A 19-year-old Red Wing, Minn., youth died Sunday of injuries from an accident late Saturday near Bay City, in Pierce County, Wis. Michael Harris was driving a car which left the road south of Bay City and hit a bridge.

# Russia Launches 3-in-1 Satellite

MOSCOW, U.S.S.R. —(UPI) — The Soviet Union Sunday launched three unmanned research satellites into orbit around the earth from a single rocket.

The official news agency Tass, in announcing the launch, said No. 54, 55 and 56 in the Cosmos satellite series were functioning normally.

It was the third time since the Cosmos program was begun in March 1962 that the Russians have launched a triple header.

# Cold to Ease Grip Today

The cold air mass that stole spring from the Twin Cities Sunday will dissipate somewhat today. But it is expected to leave an aftertaste.

Northwest winds will decrease and become southerly by tonight. Under fair skies, a high today of 10 is forecast.

As skies grow cloudy, the mercury will drop to 2 below tonight, then rise to 18 Tuesday, accompanied by snow.

Predicted regional highs: Minnesota, 2 to 10 above north, 8 to 18 south; North Dakota, 10 to 20 east and north, 20 to 35 southwest; South Dakota, 15 to 25 east, 25 to 40 west; Wisconsin, zero to 10 above.

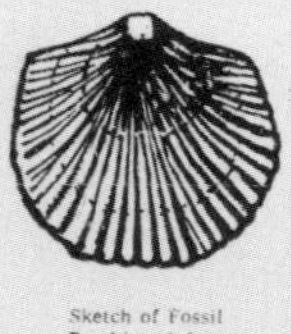

Sketch of Fossil Brachiopod from the Silurian Period

**How to Hunt for Fossils**

Science Reading Series Today on Page 8

Minneapolis Tribune

# Worker Rescued After 79 Hours Under Mine Camp Avalanche Ice

KETCHIKAN, Alaska—(AP) — A Finnish construction worker survived for 79 hours under tons of snow and ice that avalanched onto a mining camp east of here.

Einar Myllyla, about 30, was pulled from the smashed remains of a bunkhouse at the Granduc mining camp Sunday afternoon. He was nearly frozen but conscious and coherent.

Dr. James Wilson, head of a medical team treating Myllyla at Ketchikan, described Myllyla's condition as "very serious." He said more than half of the man's arms and legs were frozen solid and parts probably would have to be removed.

**MYLLYLA,** a bachelor, was pulled from the snowy graveyard where at least 12 other men perished. Rescuers, carefully probing the glacial debris, stumbled across the man and a Canadian helicopter flew Myllyla to Ketchikan.

Wilson said Myllyla told him he slept most of the time while buried. Myllyla said he thought he was in a coma, but he wasn't sure.

"I thought the most wonderful things," Myllyla said. He did not elaborate.

He was one of 130 men in the Granduc camp when the avalanche squashed the area Thursday.

So far rescuers have uncovered a dozen bodies. Fourteen others are missing and feared dead.

Myllyla arrived at the hospital with his arms swathed in bandages. He held them up as he was wheeled into emergency on a stretcher.

Wilson tapped the man's feet with his fingers and asked Myllyla:

"Where do you hurt?"

"I don't know. I don't know. I just don't know where," Myllyla replied.

Myllyla's hands were chalk white, a sure sign of severe frost-bite.

**WILSON SAID** the man would be kept in isolation at room temperature to thaw out. Until then, no surgery will be attempted.

He said Myllyla was fed milk and two slices of toast. He also received intravenous injections of alcohol, dextrose and vitamins.

Myllyla said he thought another man was near him but he didn't know who or how far from where he lay trapped for more than three days.

Wilson said there were no signs of broken bones, and he was amazed that Myllyla had come through as well as he did.



*Tribune Telephones*

| | |
|---|---|
| News, General | 372-4141 |
| Circulation | 372-4343 |
| Want Ads | 372-4242 |

# Moon Photos Stir Dispute on Landing

PASADENA, Calif. — (AP) — Scientists plan to resume study today of the Ranger 8 photographs which touched off a new controversy over whether men could land safely on the moon.

The insect-shaped spacecraft sent back more than 7,000 pictures early Saturday in the final 23 minutes before it crashed into a broad, dusty plain called the Sea of Tranquillity.

**EIGHT** sample photographs released at a Jet Propulsion Laboratory news conference Saturday afternoon showed no surprises. The Sea of Tranquillity was remarkably like the area near the Sea of Clouds 1,000 miles to the west where Ranger 7 crashed July 31. Both are pocked with craters ranging from very large to very small.

Only one of the pictures showed a different type of terrain, a mountainous highlands area over which Ranger 8 streaked for several minutes before its plunge into the western edge of the Sea of Tranquillity.

In this photograph, taken at an altitude of 270 miles, are two wide grooves more than 50 miles long which look like tracks made by two giant worms.

Dr. Gerard P. Kuiper of the University of Arizona, chief of a five-man team assigned to analyze the photographs, said the grooves were rilis, believed created by faults or cracks in the lunar crust which over thousands of years have become partly filled with dust.

**"THEY LOOK** almost like a freeway," Kuiper said.

But these were not the features that caused the controversy.

Kuiper said analysis of the light variations in the black

Ranger
Continued on Page Five

# Hoodlum 'Big Red' Became Malcolm X

New York Times Service

NEW YORK, N.Y.—He was Malcolm Little, alias Big Red, a marijuana-smoking, cocaine-sniffing, zoot-suited, hip-talking hoodlum when he went to prison in 1946.

When he went free seven years later he was Malcolm X, an ascetic, a Black Muslim, a highly articulate man who hated the white world—a world he never made but by whose standards he said he had lived.

Sunday the Black Nationalist leader, who broke away last year from the Black Muslims of Elijah Muhammad, was shot dead as he prepared to speak at a rally in Harlem.

**"CHRISTIANITY** took me to prison and Islam brought me out," Malcolm X used to say; he had no apologies for his criminal record, he said, "because it was all done when I was part of the white man's Christian world."

He was born in Omaha, Neb., on May 19, 1925, the son of the Rev. Earl Little, a 6-foot-4 man who preached the "back to Africa" movement of Marcus Garvey, a Jamaican Negro who died in 1940.

His mother was a West Indian whose father was white. From this "white devil" grandfather Malcolm X got his reddish-brown complexion and reddish-brown hair. "I hate every drop of that white rapist's blood that is in me," Malcolm once wrote.

**THE FAMILY,** including 11 children, moved to Lansing, Mich. Malcolm's earliest vivid memory was seeing, at the age of 4, his house being burned to the ground by white racists. When he was 6 his father was killed under the wheels of a streetcar. Malcolm always believed his father had been murdered — first bludgeoned and then laid across the tracks.

The family broke up and Malcolm was sent to a state institution and was enrolled in the local public school at Mason, Mich. He was the only Negro student, and his

Biography
Continued on Page Five

# Mattress Fire Kills Father of Rolvaag Aide

The father of Gov. Karl Rolvaag's executive secretary died in a mattress fire at his north Minneapolis home Sunday.

Jerome J. Rice, 73, 4606 Camden Av., father of James Rice, was found dead on the floor near his bed by his wife, Edith, about 5 p.m.

Mrs. Rice had been at a neighborhood birthday party when the fire broke out. A relative said it was probably the first time Mr. Rice had been left home alone since he became bedridden with leukemia seven years ago.

**A MINNEAPOLIS** fire official said the only possible cause of the blaze was smoking in bed, although relatives said Mr. Rice smoked very rarely. A pole lamp was found knocked over on the bed, but officials said the lamp did not appear to be the cause.

Damage to the home, mainly due to smoke, was estimated at about $3,000.

Mr. Rice was a retired employe of the state grain division of the Railroad and Warehouse Commission. He was a former clerk of the Minnesota House of Representatives.

**HE WAS** a member of the Rainbow Division in World War 1, past commander of the Russell Gaylord VFW Post

Fire
Continued on Page Five

## Almanac

**Honesty Didn't Keep Lincoln Out of Politics**

*Monday, Feb. 22, 1965*
53rd day, 312 to go this year
Sunrise 7:04 a.m.; sunset 5:51 p.m.

A Robbinsdale second grader, writing a composition in class, praised Abraham Lincoln at some length.

He concluded with these two sentences:

"Lincoln was very honest.

"But he made it to be President."

•

*Thanks to friendly Indians, colonists of the Massachusetts Bay Colony tasted their first "popped corn" 335 years ago today. Then they watched a Cagney thriller.*

•

A southwest Minneapolis 6-year-old on the subject of volcanoes: "Sometimes they interrupt on you."

MINNEAPOLIS TEMPERATURES
Midnight ..61 — 1 a.m. ....61 — 2 a.m. ....62 — 3 a.m. ....62 — 4 a.m. ....62
5 a.m. ....62 — 6 a.m. ....63 — 7 a.m. ....62 — 8 a.m. ....62 — 9 a.m. ....63
10 a.m. ...63 — 11 a.m. ...65 — *Noon ....67 — *Unofficial
TOMORROW: Cooler.

# THE MINNEAPOLIS STAR

Copyright 1965 Minneapolis Star and Tribune Company

Friday, June 4, 1965 — LXXXVII—No. 164 — Four Sections — 52 PAGES ★ — Telephone 372-4141 — Single Copy Price 10c — Lower Price for Carrier Delivery



# Gemini Twins Head for Space Record

★ ★ ★ ★ ★ ★ ★ ★ ★ ★ ★ ★ ★ ★ ★ ★

## TOLD TO GO EASY ON FUEL

By ... B. WEBB JR.

HOUSTON, Tex.—(UPI)—Gemini twins James McDivitt and Edward White, keeping a sharp eye on the "gas gauge" and a growing collection of trash, whizzed through their first full day in orbit and set their sights on the U.S. space endurance record.

Ground controllers told Pilot McDivitt and his spacewalking co-pilot to go easy on the fuel, and cancelled a pair of orbital changes that would have drastically reduced the supply.

As Gemini-4 soared across the northwest coast of Africa and finished its first 24 hours in space, project chiefs assured the pilots their orbit—101 to 179 miles above earth—was enough to keep them aloft 97 hours and 49 minutes.

A fuel supply depleted by a futile chase after another satellite, a collection of "paper and stuff" that began to fill the cabin and continued problems with communications headed a list of minor troubles plaguing the mission one-fourth of the way to its goal.

But flight chiefs at Houston appeared unworried—and White and McDivitt, refreshed by plenty of sleep and a successful return to their original flight plan, took dead aim at the U.S. space mark of slightly more than 34 hours, set two years ago by astronaut Gordon Cooper.

They reached the 24-hour mark in the 16th orbit.

At 24 hours after lift-off, the astronauts had compiled this record of space triumphs and setbacks:

**A 20-minute walk in space** by White using a twin-jet space gun to maneuver. In exhilaration, he frolicked outside the capsule eight minutes longer than assigned —and thereby doubled the 10-minute operation in space by Soviet cosmonaut Alexei Leonov.

**An aborted attempt to rendezvous** with the burned-out second stage of the Titan-2 rocket that hurled the Gemini twins into space. The experiment was taking more fuel than it was worth.

★

**Abandoning the related attempt** to have White approach and possibly touch

**Related Dispatches: Pages 2A, 3A, 6A, 8A**

the tumbling second stage. When he took his walk, the 27-foot-long stage was 65 miles ahead of the capsule.

**An on-the-nose record for** maintaining the flight and performing other experiments despite an abrupt change in flight plans.

**A smooth-working capsule** with all systems "absolutely" functioning as planned.

• • •

At the start of the second day, each pilot alternately had got eight hours of sleep. The first four-hour segments were fairly sporadic for them. The second four-hour segments were deep sleep for both.

John Hobbs, pinchhitting as flight director, said the astronauts probably would not make a pair of fuel-consuming orbital changes that had been planned for early Saturday and again early Sunday. A space agency spokesman said the reason was that "they already have a good enough orbit."

Nevertheless, ground stations were keeping tab on a tight problem created when McDivitt used more control-jet fuel than expected yesterday when he unsuccessfully chased another satellite —the Titan-2 second stage booster that put him in orbit —in America's first attempt at a "rendezvous" in space.

Houston Control, after making sure "we had enough fuel left" for any vital maneuvers, ordered McDivitt and White to "do as much of the experiments as you can without using fuel."

The most important fuel item ahead was a scheduled attempt to lower Gemini-4 into a "fail-safe" orbit just before landing Monday.

When the maneuver is finished, the capsule should be close enough to earth to reenter with the help of atmosphereic friction in case the reverse rockets fail.

The trash problem appar-

GEMINI
Turn to Page 4A

Associated Press

**Short Story** Anne Rowston, 19, hobbled along on crutches at Oswestry Orthopedic Hospital near Hyde, England, Wednesday. Anne, who used to be 6 feet 7, is now 5 feet 11. Too tall to find a boy friend, she underwent surgery which removed four inches of bone from each leg and below each knee. Her first date, when she can leave the hospital, will be a 23-year-old Londoner, who wrote to her while she was awaiting surgery. He is 6 feet, 5 inches.

★ ★ ★ ★ ★ ★ ★ ★

*EXHILARATION--EXCITEMENT--BEAUTY*

# White Falls in Love With Space

By ROBERT BUCKHORN
United Press International

Astronaut Edward H. White seemed almost to be in love with space.

For the moment, it was all his. Like a child, he didn't want to leave.

"Get back in," came the near stern command from his fellow astronaut, James A. McDivitt.

The reply? Laughter could be heard as White dangled 103 miles in space silently coasting through the great void at 17,500 miles an hour.

This was an exhilaration known to only one other man. This was excitement and beauty. This was the reason for being an astronaut.

The schedule called for a stay of only 9 or 10 minutes. But things like that are hard to give up. White seemed to dawdle.

McDivitt cautioned him again: "You still have three and a half more days to go, Buddy."

But McDivitt was strapped in a capsule. That was one thing, but White was floating in space, tied to the capsule only by a 25-foot-long goldplated lifeline.

The planned 10-minute stay was stretching out. White toyed with his space gun in a Buck Rogers-like exercise.

Firing a blast of compressed oxygen, he moved himself around the space capsule. Inside, McDivitt took pictures.

At one point McDivitt had trouble keeping White in sight.

"Move closer," he urged White.

When he did, McDivitt told him, "Smile."

Then the free-wheeling White apparently got too close to McDivitt's windshield with his jet-propulsion gun.

"You're smearing up my windshield, you dirty dog," quipped McDivitt.

It didn't sound dramatic. But it was. It was dangerous, too.

White and McDivitt knew it. While they joked, death in its most fantastic form was there.

A meteorite could puncture White's space suit. Or an oxygen leak could dim his senses, leaving him confused and disoriented.

But now, White was nearing the 20-minute mark in his stroll. He still could not get over the joy of it.

"This is fun," he told McDivitt when the astronaut again urged him to re-enter the capsule.

The "fun" White described could be converted into statistics that boggle the mind of the man in the street.

White had left the capsule as it soared toward the California Coast. He did not re-enter until the space ship was east of the Dominican Republic, having crossed the entire United States.

He had claimed space for his own for a total of 20 minutes—10 more minutes than his Soviet counterpart, Lt. Col. Alexei Leonov, who turned his feat last March 18.

How did White feel?

As if talking to someone other than McDivitt, he said, "I'm very thankful in having the experience to be first."

All the while he still moved about the space ship

'WALK' IN SPACE
Turn to Page 4A

★ ★ ★ ★

## *Astronaut Meal Out of World*

By ROBERT HERGUTH
Chicago Daily News Service

An astronaut's meal looks and tastes like something mother used to make.

Especially if mother was only 2 feet tall, lived on Mars without a stove and did her cooking with distilled water.

That's the conclusion drawn from an astronaut's dinner that strayed into Chicago. It was packed in a plant at Benton Harbor, Mich.

The dice-sized brownies weren't bad, though coated with something resembling chocolate plastic.

The four pieces of cinnamon toast were great, but each tiny slice would fit neatly into the hand of a Barbie doll.

The four apricot cubes —¾ inches on a side—were something else. They needed that extra touch, like a live apricot.

The freeze-dried pot roast looked like an asphalt shingle on a doll house. When you added distilled water to the pot roast, it looked much better. It resembled a dollhouse shingle after a heavy rain.

It tasted good, though, like a pot roast should.

It is the only pot roast in the universe that is filter tipped.

The trouble is, you must virtually take Astronautics 101 before you can safely sip at your diced pot roast via a tube stuck into its vacuum-packed plastic bag.

One false move in your weightless space capsule and pow! — wall-to-wall pot roast.

Mostly, an astronaut's

TASTE
Turn to Page 4A

## Last 2,100 Marines Leave Santo Domingo

SANTO DOMINGO, Dominican Republic — (AP) — The U.S. Marines said goodbye to Santo Domingo today as President Johnson ordered the rest of them out.

Helicopters were airlifting the 2,100 Leathernecks to the carrier Boxer offshore.

There was no indication whether the carrier and her escort would sail once the Marines were aboard.

(Mr. Johnson announced in Chicago Thursday night that Brazilian Gen. Hugo Panasco Alvim, commander of the Inter-American Peace Force in the Dominican Republic, had advised him "that conditions in the Dominican Republic now permit further reduction of our military personnel."

("I have accordingly ordered the withdrawal of all remaining units of the United States Marine Corps totaling approximately 2,100 men," the President said.)

Departure of the Marines leaves 14,200 U.S. paratroopers serving with 1,500 Latin American troops in the Inter-American force.

Peace negotiators of the Organization of American States (OAS) continued talks with rebel and junta leaders.

The stalemate in the capital was reflected in the Cibao Valley, the nation's best farming region and the area in which are located the second and third largest cities, Santiago and San Francisco de Macoris.

Police and army units on the Cibao are loyal to the junta. But even pro-junta officials concede that a majority of the people favor the rebels.

Two members of a U.N. mission met in Santiago last week with 400 representatives of various groups. Seventy-five per cent spoke in favor of the rebels, contending that they stood for antimilitarism, and end to corruption and restoration of constitutional government.

## *Miss Minnesotas Hold Reunion--Pictures: 1C*

• • •

## Mele Adopts Slogan of 'We Can't Stand Pat'

*Max Nichols: Page 1D*

• • •

## 'BACKGROUND BRIEFING' ON CLAY-LISTON FIGHT

*Art Buchwald: Page 4A*

• • •



STAR TELEPHONES
NEWS, GENERAL 372-4141
CIRCULATION 372-4343
WANT ADS 372-4242

## Dow Jones Averages

NEW YORK, N.Y. — (Special) — The Noon Dow Jones Stock Averages Friday:

| | Noon | Chg. |
|---|---|---|
| 30 Industrials | 900.60 | +1.38 |
| 20 Rails .... | 200.01 | — .41 |
| 15 Utilities . | 157.96 | + .15 |
| 65 Stocks .. | 309.83 | + .16 |

Sales 2,070,000 Shares.

## Thornton Burgess Slips Into Coma

HAMPDEN, Mass. —(AP)— Ailing Thornton W. Burgess, who retired five years ago after a lifetime of writing about Peter Rabbit and other denizens of the Old Briar Patch, slipped into a coma today.

Burgess, 91, has been under care in a nursing home in recent months.

He wrote 15,000 stories for children and books which sold more than 7½ million copies.

## JULY DRAFT CALL TOPS SINCE '61 BERLIN CRISIS

**WASHINGTON, D.C.—(AP)—The Defense Department issued today its biggest monthly draft call since the Berlin crisis late in 1961.**

**It asked Selective Service to induct 17,100 men in July for the Army. This is slightly above the June call of 17,000.**

**The call in November 1961, during the Berlin crisis, was for 20,000 men.**

**Draft quotas have been rising in large part because enlistments have fallen off.**

**The Navy, Marine Corps and Air Force do not intend to draw on the draft in July, the Pentagon said.**

## -- BULLETINS --

**SAIGON, South Viet Nam—(AP)—The South Vietnamese cabinet crisis apparently was resolved, with the National Legislative Council in effect giving Premier Phan Huy Quat a vote of confidence.**

★

**SPRINGFIELD, Mass.—(UPI)—Twelve civil rights demonstrators were arrested when they refused to end a sit-in in the office of the superintendent of schools.**

## Mosquitoes Now 'In' for Sections of County Parks

Mosquitoes are "in" and mosquito-killers are "out" in some parts of the Hennepin County park system.

The Park Reserve District has declared parts of its system off-limits to the crews of the Metropolitan Mosquito Control District.

"Some of these areas are natural and we want to keep them that way," said Clifton French, park director. "It is thought that the spraying disrupts the balance of nature."

Albert W. Buzicky, director of the Metropolitan Mosquito Control District, was caught by surprise. His crews normally have had the run of park property, hunting prime breeding grounds.

This season park superintendents have been telling his crews where they can and where they cannot spray fuel oil and DDT, said Buzicky.

"We've been doing it for seven years," he said.

French told the park district board Thursday that Buzicky wants a peace conference. The board agreed and turned the matter over to a committee.

Lawrence Haeg, a member of the park board, indicated the board could get into trouble with its policy.

"I want to be sure we don't put ourselves on record in favor of mosquitoes," said Haeg.

Buzicky says his crews aim at the biting varieties of mosquitoes and do little damage to the other insects.

He was to go to the County Courthouse today, looking for support.

Robert Janes, chairman of the County Board, said he thinks Buzicky and his men ought to be allowed into the parks as soon as possible.

## 'U' Prepares to Offer Atom Smasher Site

By JIM SHOOP
Minneapolis Star Staff Writer

The University of Minnesota is preparing to offer the U.S. Atomic Energy Commission (AEC) part of its 9,000-acre experimental station site at Rosemount as a site for a giant, $280-million atom smasher, it was learned today.

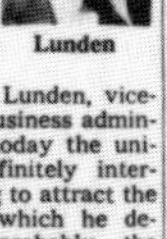

Lunden

Laurence R. Lunden, vice-president for business administration said today the university is "definitely interested" in trying to attract the huge facility, which he described as "probably the most powerful machine of its type ever developed."

AEC requirements for the project are 3,000 acres of land within one hour's commuting distance from a major metropolitan area, and reasonably available housing for 2,000 scientists, engineers and technicians, and 300-man visiting staff.

The atom smasher, capable of delivering a 200-billion-electron-volt charge to break up the atom, would take up to eight years to build.

Lunden said he; Dr. Bryce L. Crawford, graduate school dean and professor of chemistry; Dr. William G. Shepherd, vice-president for academic administration, and Leonard Kaercher, superintendent of the University's Rosemount experiment station, were to meet today to iron out details.

Lunden said this would amount to reviving and bringing up to date engineering and site data prepared several years ago when the university was engaged in a joint effort with other midwestern universities to bring an atom smasher development to the Upper Midwest.

Lunden said power, water and bedrock necessary to support the heavy machine are available at the Rosemount site. He said Rosemount is the only site in Minnesota capable of handling the installation.

Lunden said after details of the university's proposal are worked out, it will be presented to University President O. Meredith Wilson, who will probably present it to the Board of Regents June 12.

The AEC deadline for applications is June 15.

Lunden said university officials would meet next week, possibly Wednesday, with Gov. Karl Rolvaag's Business Advisory Commission to coordinate efforts on the proposal.

The commission had called a meeting for noon today to discuss the possibility of bidding on the project, but it was postponed to allow more time to gather facts and information.

**LBJ TO GIVE TALK**

WASHINGTON, D.C.—(UPI) —President Johnson is scheduled to address the graduating class and guests at Howard University's 97th annual commencement tonight.

**Cloudy**

TUESDAY TEMPERATURES

| | | | | | |
|---|---|---|---|---|---|
| 2 a.m. | 22 | 10 a.m. | 28 | 6 p.m. | 34 |
| 3 a.m. | 22 | 11 a.m. | 31 | 7 p.m. | 33 |
| 4 a.m. | 20 | Noon | 33 | 8 p.m. | 32 |
| 5 a.m. | 19 | 1 p.m. | 35 | 9 p.m. | 33 |
| 6 a.m. | 18 | 2 p.m. | 37 | 10 p.m. | 33 |
| 7 a.m. | 15 | 3 p.m. | 38 | 11 p.m. | 33 |
| 8 a.m. | 20 | 4 p.m. | 37 | 12M | 33 |
| 9 a.m. | 25 | 5 p.m. | 35 | *1 a.m. | 33 |

*Details Page 18* *Unofficial

# Minneapolis Tribune

MORNING

Vol. XCIX—No. 170 Copyright 1965 Minneapolis Star and Tribune Company MINNEAPOLIS, MINN., WEDNESDAY, NOVEMBER 10, 1965 Single Copy Price 10¢ Lower Price for Carrier Delivery



# Power Failure Blacks Out New York, Northeast U.S.

Associated Press

POWER FAILURE CAUSED NEAR TOTAL BLACKNESS ON NEW YORK SKY LINE

*Lights in foreground were from ships lighted by their own power systems*

## 30 Million Are Affected by Blackout

From the Tribune Wire Services

The nation's largest power failure plunged an estimated 30 million persons into darkness Tuesday night in the huge metropolitan areas of the Northeast.

The blackout cut off power in an 80,000-square-mile area, stretching from Pennsylvania deep into Canada. Most of New York's teeming millions appeared to be without power for most of the night.

The blackout came at the worst possible hour. The usually bright lights suddenly dimmed and then went dark about 5:30 p.m., in the heart of the rush hour.

Traffic was choked up, communications were disrupted and emergency orders piled up as the night wore on. National Guard units were ordered out by the governors of New York, Massachusetts and Rhode Island.

**ALL AVAILABLE** police, firemen and Civil Defense workers were called out in most places.

Eight-hundred-thousand commuters were stranded in New York's subways, and and many others were trapped in elevators and on electric trains.

As late as three hours after the power failure hit, the New York Transit Authority estimated 300,000 persons were still stranded in subway tunnels.

President Johnson ordered a sweeping investigation of the power failure and directed the Federal Power Commission to head up the investigation. He ordered all federal facilities mobilized to meet the crisis and kept in close touch with developments.

The White House in Austin, Tex., reported that the President's science adviser, Dr. Donald Hornig, had told the President that the failure started near Syracuse, N.Y., in the area of the Niagara-Mohawk Power Co.

**THE FAILURE,** Hornig said, was created by a "cascading or domino" effect. As the power failed in one area, it created an overload in adjacent areas and these, in turn, blacked out.

The Pentagon in Washington said the nation's defense communications lines remained intact during the power failure because "all defense communications have auxiliary power systems" which can be switched on when needed.

Order was the keyword in most of the blacked out area, but some rioting and looting was reported in Buffalo, N.Y.

At Boston, during the middle of the blackout, prisoners rioted at Walpole State Prison and took over at least one cell block. A spokesman for Gov. John Volpe said that 200 prisoners were in the block and were "tearing the place apart."

Helmeted state troopers finally controlled the rioting with tear gas.

Nowhere was the stunning effect of the blackout more stunning than in New York City. The busiest city in the world suddenly became a candlelit dream world where millions struggled to make do without the necessities of urban life.

Looking up Broadway's "Great White Way" it appeared as though thousands of fireflies were lighting up the area as pedestrians trooped along the street carrying candles and flashlights.

Candles glowed in skyscraper windows, and there was a festive air in much of the city. Bars and restaurants, about the only businesses

New York
Continued on Page Seven

# Magnusson to Take Leave Without Pay

Minnesota Insurance Commissioner Cyrus E. Magnusson agreed Tuesday to take a leave of absence without pay, and his suspension by Gov. Karl F. Rolvaag was lifted.

Magnusson

Atty. Gen. Robert Mattson and Thomas Moore, attorney for Magnusson, announced they had reached this agreement on Magnusson's status pending his federal court trial and removal proceedings brought against him by the governor.

"While this will not determine the ultimate question of removal, it does resolve the question of the commissioner's status during the interim period," the joint announcement said.

**MAGNUSSON AND** 16 other men were indicted Oct. 29 on charges of fraud in the collapse of American Allied Insurance Co., of St. Paul. They are scheduled to be arraigned in U.S. District Court in St. Paul this morning.

U.S. Atty. Miles Lord has indicated he hopes the case can be tried in February or March.

Under yesterday's agreement, the state removal proceedings, originally scheduled for Nov. 17, were continued until after the federal trial.

**ROLVAAG ASKED** Magnusson to resign the day following the federal indictment. Magnusson refused, contending he had done nothing wrong.

The governor then suspended the commissioner last Friday, issuing 11 formal charges against him and ordering a hearing on Magnusson's conduct in office. The governor would then have made a decision on removal of the commissioner, following the hearing.

Magnusson replied Saturday by challenging the legal-

Magnusson
Continued on Page Seven

# U.S. Ends Viet Duty for Lads 17

### McNamara Issues Order After Death of Two Soldiers

WASHINGTON, D.C. — (UPI) — Defense Secretary Robert S. McNamara, acting in the aftermath of two combat deaths, Tuesday ordered all 17-year-old servicemen exempted from duty in South Viet Nam.

The question was brought to top-level attention last month when two 17-year-olds serving with the 1st Cavalry Division in Viet Nam were killed during fighting. They were Pfc. Terry T. Wright of Fort Wayne, Ind., who would have been 18 Dec. 23, and Pfc. James C. Ward of Ft. Bliss, Tex., whose 18th birthday would have been Jan. 26.

Wright died Oct. 10 and Ward on the next day. The Defense Department gave no specific details of the circumstances, but troops of the 1st Cavalry were involved in offensives against the Viet Cong north of Saigon on those dates.

**AFFECTED** by McNamara's order are approximately 1,500 soldiers, sailors and Marines now in South Viet Nam. The directive does not apply to 17-year-olds aboard 7th Fleet vessels off Viet Nam or at other overseas post.

The new policy is effective immediately. The secretary ordered the services to "cancel or modify orders for any 17-year-olds now destined for Viet Nam." In addition the services were given until Feb. 1 to transfer any troops from Viet Nam who still will be 17 after that date.

The Marine Corps said it had 228 youths in the 17-year bracket in Viet Nam, while the Navy said it had only 30 ashore and the Air Force just one. That apparently meant there are about 1,250 in army units there out of the 1,500 total.

**McNAMARA SAID** his order was based on a recognition that 17-year-olds comprise only about 1 per cent of 148,380 U.S. troops in South Viet Nam, and that they were not subject to draft until the age of 18½. The minimum age for servicemen is 17.

"This action is being taken in order to make the assignment policies in all the armed forces uniform," the secretary said.

During the Korean War the Marine Corps withheld 17-year-olds from service there. A Pentagon spokesman said the Marines recommended the new policy to McNamara.

**THE SPOKESMAN** said protests had been received from the public about the use of 17-year-olds, but that they were fewer than those "concerning delays in GI. mail."

The Pentagon spokesman said the armed forces will continue to accept 17-year-olds, partly because this is required by the draft law.

# *Young Pacifist Near Death After Protest by Burning at U.N.*

NEW YORK, N.Y. — (AP) — A young Roman Catholic pacifist, almost every inch of his body burned, lingered on the brink of death Tuesday, after turning himself into a human torch outside the United Nations to protest the Viet Nam War. Later, he apparently repented the deed.

LaPorte

"I'm antiwar, all wars, I did this as a religious action," said Roger LaPorte, 22, the second American in a week to set fire to himself in such a protest.

Taken to Bellevue Hospital with 95 per cent of his body seared, LaPorte showed signs of kidney damage and his breathing was labored. Nevertheless he was conscious and able to talk.

**"I KNOW** of no one who had 95 per cent total body burns surviving," declared Dr. Jay Grosfeld, a member of a medical team working over LaPorte.

The last rites of the Roman Catholic Church were administered to LaPorte after he expressed repentance over his violation of its strict religious credo against suicide.

The Rev. Alexander Busuttil, Catholic chaplain at Bellevue, said:

"It was the most devout act of contrition I've heard. He was clear and expressive when I spoke with him."

LaPorte spoke, the priest said, "of things eternal."

"He was so badly burned," Father Busuttil went on, "that I had a difficult time finding a place on his body upon which to place the holy oil. He was not in pain because, ironically enough, he was so badly burned that pain was not there."

**EVENTUALLY,** the priest annointed LaPorte's right cheek, to fulfill the church's last sacrament of extreme unction.

A hospital spokesman said LaPorte nodded affirmatively when asked by hospital psychiatrists if he wanted to live.

LaPorte's self-immolation followed by a week the suicide of Norman Morrison, 31, who burned himself to death

Protest
Continued on Page Six

## Continued Cold Expected Today

Variable cloudiness and continued cold weather are forecast for the Twin Cities and vicinity today as a weak low pressure area moves across the area.

Winds will be northeasterly at 8 to 15 miles per hour. Today's high temperature will be 40, tonight's low, 25, and Thursday's high, 38.

# State Has Only 'Good Fighting Chance' to Get Atom Smasher

By VICTOR COHN
Minneapolis Tribune Staff Writer

Minnesota has only a "fighting chance but a good fighting chance" to get a $300 million, federal-built atom smasher, a University of Minnesota official estimated Tuesday.

Declining to be named, he commented as an Atomic Energy Commission (AEC) group visited a possible Rosemount site — and made no comment whatsoever.

**FOUR AEC** officials started their day by breakfasting with Gov. Karl Rolvaag and university spokesmen, including President O. Meredith Wilson.

Then they spent the morning at the university's Rosemount Research Center and helicoptered over it.

"I think they were quite impressed with the site's excellent geologic characteristics," Stephen Quigley, state commissioner of administration, commented afterward.

"I think we ought to be one of the finalists from many standpoints," said Dr. William G. Shepherd, the university's academic vice-president. He was not the official who made the above comments.

**"THEY WERE** very interested in our university, in cultural activities here and in many other things in which we are strong," Shepherd said.

Quigley and Shepherd accompanied the group.

David Roe, president of the Minnesota State Building Trades Council, pledged yesterday the Minnesota building workers would engage in no work stoppages if the installation is built here. A similar pledge was made to the taconite industry in 1955.

Rosemount is one of 85 possible sites in 43 states now be-

Site
Continued on Page Six

# Labor Offers Middle Road to Parliament

By ANTHONY LEWIS
New York Times Service

LONDON, England — The socialist government laid out Tuesday a program for the next year containing almost no hint of socialism. Many observers saw it as a move to broaden the Labor party's political appeal in preparation for an early election.

Wilson

The voice that announced the plans was Queen Elizabeth's, in her traditional address at the opening of Parliament. But the hand that wrote the speech was Prime Minister Harold Wilson's.

**THE WORD** steel was not mentioned in the speech—not a word about Labor's commitment to renationalize the industry. Instead, on the economic front, there was emphasis on the need to get people working more efficiently and to stop excessive wage rises.

Wilson promised more houses, new moves to reduce speculative land profits and stronger controls on Commonwealth — mostly colored —immigration. All these are popular measures that the Conservatives can hardly oppose frontally.

Indeed, it was being widely said last night that Wilson would love to lose in the vote that will follow a week's general debate on the speech — and be "forced" to an election. The Conserva-

Britain
Continued on Page Seven

# U.S. Boosts Aluminum Sale 100,000 Tons

WASHINGTON, D.C. — (AP) — The government hiked by 100,000 tons the amount of aluminum it intends to release as surplus from its 2.1-million-ton stockpile.

This makes a total of 300,000 tons and the new figure was revealed as one aluminum company spokesman termed the squabble between the industry and the government "relatively minor differences of agreement."

Another company said it intends to stick by its announced price increase.

**TOP GOVERNMENT** officials announced last Saturday the intention to release 200,000 tons next year. At the same news conference, price boosts by aluminum companies were hit as inflationary and as not justified by Gardner Ackley, chairman of the President's Council of Economic Advisers.

Secretary of the Treasury Henry H. Fowler and Secretary of Defense Robert S. McNamara said repeatedly the decision to release the aluminum was not tied to the price hikes. Republican spokesman and some others say it is.

But McNamara said the reduction is "bound to relieve some of the pressure on prices."

**THE OFFICE** of Emergency Planning (OEP) announced yesterday that the additional 100,000 tons would be sold immediately. The effect of its order is to authorize the General Services Ad-

Aluminum
Continued on Page Seven

# *Indonesians Stage Rally Against Reds*

JAKARTA, Indonesia — (UPI) — Scores of thousands of Indonesians massed Tuesday in Jakarta to demonstrate support for the armed forces and demand the outlawing of the Communist party for its role in the attempt to overthrow President Sukarno.

The hunt went on, meantime, for Communist party boss D. N. Aidit and marauding bands of Red terrorists. Army authorities said terrorists had killed at least 238 persons and burned 1,862 dwellings and other houses in Central Java alone.

Radio Jakarta said 1.5 million persons took part in the rally. More conservative estimates placed the number of demonstrators at about 100,000.

It was the biggest anti-Communist rally ever held in Jakarta, once the headquarters of the Peking-oriented Indonesian Communist party (PKI) which claimed a mem-

Indonesia
Continued on Page Seven

## Almanac

### *This Boy May Wash Blackboards*

*Wednesday, Nov. 10, 1965*

314th day. 51 to go this year
Sunrise 7:04 a.m.; sunset 4:50 p.m.

A Minneapolis grade school teacher was teaching her pupils the use of Roman numerals. "Teacher," a boy inquired, "how much is CXXVII minus XLVIII?"

•

***On this day in 1871 explorer Henry M. Stanley discovered the missing Scottish missionary and explorer, David Livingstone, in a small settlement in deepest Africa. Stanley's first words were, "Dr. Livingstone, I presume. You're two months behind in the payments on your new Jaguar."***

•

On this day in 1919 the American Legion, organized by American war veterans in Paris earlier in the year, held its first national convention in Minneapolis. They found Minneapolis' night life slightly less exciting.

# *Chest Pains Hospitalize Ike; Condition: 'Very Satisfactory'*

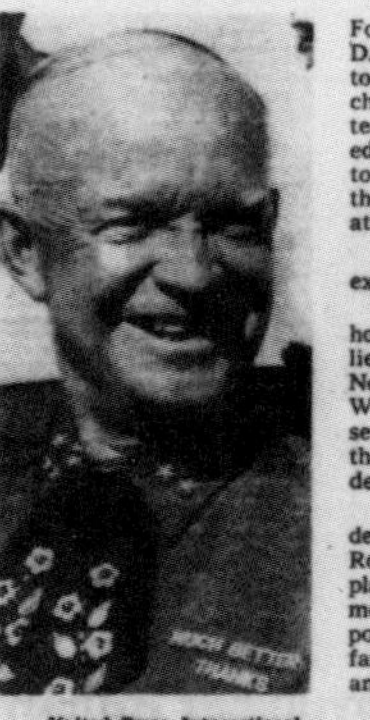

United Press International
DWIGHT D. EISENHOWER
*Photo from 1955 illness*

AUGUSTA, Ga.—(UPI)—Former President Dwight D. Eisenhower was rushed to an Army hospital with chest pains Tuesday, but a team of specialists reported him in "very satisfactory" condition and said that if he suffered a heart attack "it was a mild one."

A definite diagnosis was expected in 24 to 36 hours.

The 75-year-old Eisenhower, who as supreme Allied commander led the Normandy invasion in World War II, suffered a severe heart attack during the third year of his presidency in 1955.

President Johnson ordered Defense Secretary Robert S. McNamara to place any needed government facilities at the disposal of the Eisenhower family, including doctors and planes.

Eisenhower was stricken while vacationing at the Augusta National Golf Club, one of his favorite retreats, where he played 18 holes of golf Monday.

**A HIGHLY** placed source said Eisenhower suffered the pains for about 30 minutes after the onset of the attack shortly after midnight, but that the pains subsided once he was hospitalized and placed under oxygen.

The same source said there had been no recurrence of the pains by late morning.

Flowers, phone calls and telegrams poured in by the hundreds when news of Eisenhower's illness became known. The first flowers to arrive, a bouquet of roses, were sent by 8-year-old Calvin Coolidge, and his brother Harry, 13, sons of a Ft. Gordon Army sergeant.

**A SPOKESMAN** said Eisenhower was "deeply touched."

Dr. Thomas Mattingly,

Eisenhower
Continued on Page Six

## TURN THE PAGES TO:



Tribune Telephones
News, General ....... 372-4141
Circulation .......... 372-4343
Want Ads ........... 372-4242

**Little Change**

WEDNESDAY TEMPERATURES

| | | | | | |
|---|---|---|---|---|---|
| 2 a.m. | 20 | 10 a.m. | 21 | 6 p.m. | 22 |
| 3 a.m. | 20 | 11 a.m. | 22 | 7 p.m. | 22 |
| 4 a.m. | 20 | Noon | 23 | 8 p.m. | 22 |
| 5 a.m. | 20 | 1 p.m. | 23 | 9 p.m. | 21 |
| 6 a.m. | 19 | 2 p.m. | 23 | 10 p.m. | 21 |
| 7 a.m. | 18 | 3 p.m. | 23 | 11 p.m. | 20 |
| 8 a.m. | 19 | 4 p.m. | 24 | 12M. | 17 |
| 9 a.m. | 19 | 5 p.m. | 23 | *1 a.m. | 16 |

Details Page 34 *Unofficial

# Minneapolis Tribune

MORNING

Vol. XCIX—No. 206 Copyright 1965 Minneapolis Star and Tribune Company MINNEAPOLIS, MINN., THURSDAY, DECEMBER 16, 1965

Single Copy Price 10c Lower Price for Carrier Delivery



# SPACE SHIPS RENDEZVOUS

## CCC Wheat Stocks Go on Sale

### Price Stability Seen as Reason for USDA Action

By NICK KOTZ
Minneapolis Tribune Staff Correspondent

WASHINGTON, D.C. — The U.S. Department of Agriculture (USDA) announced Wednesday that its surplus wheat supplies are for sale in a move designed to insure price stability in the face of greatly expanded United States wheat donations overseas.

The Department said all qualities of wheat in Commodity Credit Corp. (CCC) stocks are for sale at market prices or at 108 per cent of the current support price plus carrying charges, whichever is higher.

**THIS MEANS** that little CCC wheat probably will be purchased at present, since the minimum CCC sale price is above market price. Wheat of ordinary protein sold Wednesday in Minneapolis for $1.74 a bushel, compared with the CCC minimum of $1.80.

*(YOUNG URGES Tight Control of Crops—Page 9).*

But the department is saying, in effect, that its sales leverage is available to keep prices from rising above 108 per cent of the support price. The department was concerned that massive United States exports of donated wheat to India and other countries might cause a sharp rise in prices.

Yesterday's action broadened the sales policy announced Nov. 23 when the department offered to sell higher protein wheats from its surplus stocks. This department action immediately was attacked by some grain trade officials and congressmen as an action to deprive farmers of higher grain prices.

**HOWEVER,** department officials pointed out that few CCC sales actually took place, and tnat after a brief drop in prices, price levels returned to their former levels.

In announcing that all CCC stocks were available for sale, the department stated:

"This decision is consistent with the ever-normal-grainery principle of adding to stocks when production exceeded needs and using reserve supplies when demand is strong. The price and income stability that results is

Wheat
Continued on Page 14

BIG PUFF—GEMINI 6 DEPARTED FROM CAPE IN CLOUD OF SMOKE

Associated Press

## Flight Is Flawless; Geminis Continue

By JACK WILSON
Minneapolis Tribune Staff Correspondent

CAPE KENNEDY, Fla. — Two Gemini satellites flew around the world in formation Wednesday night, after achieving the first orbital rendezvous in space history.

"This is the biggest milestone in space since the flight of John Glenn in 1962," said Christopher Kraft, the flight director for the National Aeronautics and Space Administration (NASA).

It was a flawless performance from the moment the Gemini 6 lifted off its launch pad here to the instant it pulled up alongside Gemini 7 and demonstrated that trained astronauts could maneuver space capsules almost like pilots guiding airplanes.

It was, said George Mueller, the program director, a successful completion of the most difficult part of our attempt to reach the place where we can actually operate in space, instead of simply staying alive there.

In the future, as a direct outgrowth of the rendezvous technique, were such operations as sending spacecraft up to inspect unidentified satellites, to carry replacement crews to and from orbiting space laboratories, even to rescue spacemen who might be stranded in orbit and unable to bring their craft down.

Astronaut Walter Schirra was at the controls of Gemini 6 when it pulled up just ahead of Gemini 7 about 1:30 p.m. Minneapolis time. For the next few hours he and his co-pilot, Thomas P. Stafford, took turns jockeying their spacecraft around the target vehicle in which Frank Borman and James Lovell had been flying since a week ago last Saturday.

And at intervals Borman and Lovell took control and maneuvered Gemini 7 around Gemini 6, so that each of the four would get some practice in the new art.

**MORE SPACE DISPATCHES ON PAGES 32 AND 33**

Schirra, who said several weeks ago that he was sure the rendezvous would be "a piece of cake," discovered he was right. After he had flown Gemini 6 clear around the world while staying within a few feet of Gemini 7, Schirra said, "I'm sure there will be no problem in docking (linking two spacecraft (together while in flight). It's easier than in the Gemini docking simulator."

And Kraft said it was evident that the technique of rendezvous was the most difficult part of docking. The crews of Gemini 6 and 7 were under orders not to let their capsules touch, but Kraft said docking would be merely an extension of the formation flying—called station keeping—which seemed to give the crews no trouble at all.

At one point the two spacecraft were within about six feet of each other, Stafford reported. They flew around the world within 20 feet of each other, virtually nose to nose all the way.

Schirra said he could see Lovell's beard through the window, and Stafford said he could see that Borman was chewing gum. They noted long wires trailing from each other's capsule, apparently connections that hadn't sheared off during the launching.

**THE RENDEZVOUS** was begun while both spacecraft were on the night side of the earth, so the pilots could use the stars as a background for guidance.

The rendezvous radar in Gemini 6 locked onto the responding radar in Gemini 7 while the spacecraft were 235 miles apart, flying across the U.S. Schirra was able to see the other vehicle at a distance of about 35 miles, when the sun glinted on it.

All four pilots apparently were upside down during the approaching maneuvers, Kraft said. In the weightless condition they are free to assume whatever position gives them greatest visibility.

**VETERAN** spacemen who have become understandably blase about some aspects of orbital flight stood up and cheered when the word came that Gemini 6 had drawn close to Gemini 7.

Robert Gilruth, director of the space center, said "It all looked easy because it clicked off so perfectly, but this was a day of more tension than any I have seen since Shepard's flight."

After about 5½ hours of close formation flying the two spacecraft opened the formation and were to fly

Gemini
Continued on Page 14

LITTLE PUFF—CIGARS TO CELEBRATE RENDEZVOUS, SPACE CENTER, HOUSTON, TEX.
*Chris Kraft, left, Astronaut Gordon Cooper and Dr. Robert Gilruth*

## Fatal Error Revealed in City Hospital

By VICTOR COHN
Minneapolis Tribune Staff Writer



A fatal mistake in a Minneapolis hospital came to light Wednesday.

At 10:45 p.m. last Feb. 19, Arne Nelson of 6506 Wilryan Av., Edina, died at Swedish Hospital of chemical injury to internal organs — the result of a nurse's error in copying a doctor's order.

"It was just a human error," the hospital's administrator, Lester G. Johnson, said yesterday. "She is an extremely conscientious nurse —one of our best, most careful girls."

**IN COPYING** the doctor's instructions, a decimal point and the word "dilute" were omitted from an order for a stomach wash before intended ulcer surgery.

As a result, according to the doctor, Nelson was given a "6 per cent" mixture instead of a ".6 per cent" mixture of hydrochloric acid solution in water — and the hydrochloric acid used was a strong, 36 per cent solution instead of a "dilute," 6 per cent solution.

The cause of Nelson's death was determined by autopsy Feb. 20.

It was not reported to his widow for two months, she said.

The "immediate cause of death" was left blank on a death certificate signed by Dr. Hamlin Mattson, the attending surgeon, on Feb. 22. Nothing was said on the certificate about chemical injury.

**THE DEATH** was not reported to the Hennepin County medical examiner (former-

Hospital
Continued on Page 16

## Partly Cloudy Skies Forecast

The Twin Cities can expect fair to partly cloudy skies with light snow flurries ending tonight. There will be no important temperature change with light southwesterly winds. Today's high will be 25, tonight's low, 15, and Friday's high, 30.

The Upper Midwest weather picture calls for little change with temperatures slightly above normal for this time of year.

Other parts of the nation are experiencing wintery storms. Parts of New Mexico received up to 14 inches of snow Wednesday causing at least one death and many accidents.

The 30-day outlook calls for temperatures in this area to be slightly below normal until mid-January with moderate to heavy precipitation in Minnesota and parts of eastern North Dakota and South Dakota.

## Story Teller Maugham Dies at His Villa

NICE, France — (AP) — W. Somerset Maugham, a great English story teller and craftsman who roamed the world for material, died early today at his Riviera villa. He was 91 and doctors days ago realized he could not recover from a recent fall.

Mr. Maugham

At the end, however, when all hope was gone, he was taken from the British-American Hospital to die in the Villa, his secretary and companion of years, Alan Searle, said in announcing the death this morning.

The feeble Mr. Maugham suffered the fall last Friday, was taken to the hospital Saturday and given only hours to live after a medical consultation Sunday.

He rallied for a time but weakened yesterday and arrangements were made to let him die at his beloved villa, La Mauresque.

**DOCTORS SAID** the stroke had produced a nervous ailment afflicting blood vessels and a heart specialist told reporters Saturday he believed the condition would lead to death "within two or three days at maximum."

On Sunday, doctors reported Mr. Maugham's condition was aggravated by a rise in temperature and pulmonary congestion. Dr. Georges Rosanoff, the author's physician said then his brain was no longer supplied with blood, "but the heart is still holding out."

One of the most prolific

Mr. Maugham
Continued on Page 14

## U.S. Defense Shifting to Asia, NATO Told

By RICHARD REID
Minneapolis Tribune European Correspondent

PARIS, France — Europe's growing realization that American defense emphasis is shifting to Asia was dramatically reinforced by Secretary of Defense Robert S. McNamara here Wednesday.

In an 18-minute address, McNamara gave the North Atlantic Treaty Organization (NATO) foreign and defense ministers a possible timetable for Red Chinese nuclear capability and urged them to "share the American concern as we look several years in the future and make prudent preparations for the problem confronting us all."

McNamara's statement's were relayed to reporters by an American spokesman.

Coming after Secretary of State Dean Rusk's appeal Tuesday for NATO nations to identify their national interests in the South Viet Nam conflict, the speech was taken as another indication that the United States feels the next major threat to world peace may arise outside Europe.

McNamara said Thailand was the next target for Communist Chinese guerrilla action. And it has been widely reported here that United States bases in South Viet Nam are being built to last.

The American defense secretary made clear that the increasing defense burden borne by the American taxpayer will make it unnecessary to redeploy large combat units from Europe to meet the threat in Asia. But it was considered significant that McNamara saw fit to plant the thought of such action in European minds.

President Lyndon Johnson is expected to explore the British defense commitment "east of Suez" in talks with Prime Minister Harold Wilson in Washington, D.C., today. American defense planners are known to be concerned about Communist intentions in Pakistan, India, Nepal, and other such areas of British influence.

Red Chinese actions have been consistent with their purpose of establishing power in the countryside and moving in on the cities of the world, McNamara said. He emphasized that the cities of North America, Europe, Africa and Latin America

NATO
Continued on Page 16

## U.S. Wins Lead in Two Aspects of Space Race

By JOHN W. FINNEY
New York Times Service

**Analysis: WHAT THE NEWS MEANS**

WASHINGTON, D.C. — With the trail-blazing rendezvous in space and the long-endurance flight of Gemini 7, the United States has taken a commanding lead in two of the most important events in the accelerating space race.

In the eyes of the world, the United States undoubtedly has gained the psychological advantage in a race which is being waged as much for national prestige as technological accomplishments.

This is a distinct reversal of the situation only a few days ago when Russia was riding a propaganda crest on the basis of its accomplishments in space.

**BUT, AS** even jubilant American space officials acknowledged, it would be an oversimplification and misleading to claim that the United States, on the basis of the spectacular Gemini flights this week, has seized the technological lead.

In some events, such as the size of rocket boosters and spacecraft, the Soviet Union is still ahead. Furthermore, it still has the technological capacity for spurting ahead in some events in which it apparently is lagging.

But in other events, the United States is definitely leading and is building up a technological momentum that is going to be difficult for the Soviet Union to overcome.

**ONE OF THE** critical events in which the United

Space Race
Continued on Page 14

## Almanac

### His Diet Is Aimed at Ugly Fat

***Thursday, Dec. 16, 1965***
350th day, 15 to go this year
Sunrise 7:45 a.m.; sunset 4:32 p.m.

From behind his desk came the businessman's solemn announcement, "I'm going to lose 20 pounds, so help me."

His unbelieving secretary, a shapely blonde, replied teasingly, "If you lose 20 pounds, so will I."

All of which was overheard by another fellow sitting across the office. "I'll take your 20," said he, nodding at the secretary.

•

***The Minneapolis Public Library opened on this date in 1889. At 2 cents a day, that's $554.80 ago. Return borrowed books.***

•

A Christmas shopper reports uncovering a record album, "The Voice of Ireland." The jacket says in fine print, "Recorded in Great Britain."

## Justice Douglas' 3rd Wife Asks Divorce, Cites Cruelty

YAKIMA, Wash. —(AP)— The attractive young third wife of Supreme Court Justice William O. Douglas, 67, filed suit for divorce Wednesday. Her complaint accused the jurist of cruel treatment and personal indignities.

Joan Douglas, 25, whom Douglas met at a college lecture in 1961, said in her complaint he agreed to pay $500 a month for eight months beginning Jan. 1 and $400 a month thereafter for the rest of her life or until she remarries.

The suit was filed in Superior (county) Court here because the couple has a summer residence in the Gooseprairie area of western Yakima County.

A Seattle attorney, Dan Reaugh, represented Mrs. Douglas. She asked for restoration of her maiden name, Joan Carol Martin.

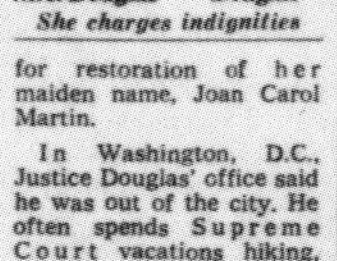

Mrs. Douglas Douglas
*She charges indignities*

In Washington, D.C., Justice Douglas' office said he was out of the city. He often spends Supreme Court vacations hiking, climbing mountains and traveling abroad.

The third Mrs. Douglas,

Douglas
Continued on Page 14



Tribune Telephones

News, General ..... 372-4141
Circulation .......... 372-4343
Want Ads ........... 372-4242

## Tass Is Reserved on Gemini Feat

MOSCOW, U.S.S.R.—(AP)— Tass reported factually and without comment today the space rendezvous of Gemini 6 and 7. It did not mention that this was an historic space first or disclose Soviet plans for a similar feat.

**Little Change**
MONDAY TEMPERATURES

| | | | | | |
|---|---|---|---|---|---|
| 2 a.m. | 55 | 10 a.m. | 69 | 6 p.m. | 71 |
| 3 a.m. | 55 | 11 a.m. | 71 | 7 p.m. | 68 |
| 4 a.m. | 52 | Noon | 73 | 8 p.m. | 67 |
| 5 a.m. | 53 | 1 p.m. | 74 | 9 p.m. | 64 |
| 6 a.m. | 51 | 2 p.m. | 73 | 10 p.m. | 64 |
| 7 a.m. | 56 | 3 p.m. | 76 | 11 p.m. | 60 |
| 8 a.m. | 61 | 4 p.m. | 73 | 12M | 57 |
| 9 a.m. | 65 | 5 p.m. | 75 | *1 a.m. | 55 |

*Details Page 18* *Unofficial

# Minneapolis Tribune

MORNING

Vol. C—No. 21 MINNEAPOLIS, MINN., TUESDAY, JUNE 14, 1966 Single Copy Price 10¢ Lower Price for Carrier Delivery



# Supreme Court Sets Strict Guides for Police Inquiries

From the Tribune Wire Services

WASHINGTON, D. C. — The U.S. Supreme Court Monday laid down a strict set of guidelines for police investigations — including a rule that if a suspect "is alone and indicates in any manner that he does not wish to be interrogated, the police may not question him."

Before questioning begins, the prisoner must be told of his right to remain silent and to have a lawyer at his side, Chief Justice Earl Warren said for a 5 to 4 court. Also, Warren said, the suspect need not request a lawyer in order to have one. And, if he cannot afford one, counsel must be provided "prior to any interrogation."

**IF THESE** "procedural safeguards" are not taken before police questioning, the chief justice declared, confessions or other incriminating statements made by the suspect cannot be used at trial.

"The current practice of incommunicado interrogation is at odds with one of our nation's most cherished principles — that the individual may not be compelled to incriminate himself," the chief justice wrote in a ruling that is of historic importance.

The cases involved in yesterday's decision were a California holdup slaying, robbery cases from California and New York and a kidnap-rape in Arizona.

In the California slaying, the high court upheld the California Supreme Court's

Court
Continued on Page Eight

## Twins Split With A's

*Lose 1st Game, 5-2; Capture Nightcap, 6-1*

•

**Orioles Top N.Y.**

•

*(Details in Sports Section)*

# GOP Unit Proposes Law to End All Housing Bias

By DICK CUNNINGHAM
Minneapolis Tribune Staff Writer

A Minnesota Republican task force Monday recommended a law that would open all housing—including the spare room in Mrs. Murphy's house—to Negroes and other minority renters or buyers.

The task force chairman admitted that a similar law was blocked by a member of the Republican oriented Conservative caucus, Rep. George French, in the 1965 Minnesota Legislature.

Republicans can wipe out French's civil rights image by including the housing recommendation in the party platform at the state convention June 23-25 in Minneapolis, said Mrs. Wright Brooks, chairman of the party's Task Force for Civil and Human Rights.

French, who was accused of bottling up last year's fair housing bill in the House Civil Administration Committee of which he was chairman, will be opposed for reelection by Minneapolis Alderman John W. Johnson, who won endorsement from the 37th District Republican convention last week.

Whether the Platform Committee and the convention adopt the recommendation depends on whether Republicans recognize that there is a "new legislature, that there has been a realignment" as the result of reapportionment, said Mrs. Brooks.

Reapportionment has weakened rural control of the legislature.

"Republican leadership" always has favored civil rights legislation, but "outstate" Republicans "who are not in contact with the problems of minority groups do not feel it as pressing," Mrs. Brooks said at a press conference at the Radisson Hotel. Mrs. Brooks is the former chairman of the Governor's Human Rights Commission.

**THE TASK FORCE** report says specifically that the state fair housing law should be amended to "prohibit discrimination in connection with the sale or rental of single family dwellings, whether owner-occupied or publicly financed."

Mrs. Brooks said the intention was to extend the law to "publicly or privately" financed dwellings.

State and federal fair housing laws now cover only dwellings on which the mortgage is guaranteed by public agencies such as the Federal Housing Agency (FHA) or the Veterans Administration (GI). More than half the single homes in Minneapolis are thus exempted, civil rights spokesman say.

Mrs. Brooks also said the task force's intention was specifically to cover the rental of a room in an owner-occupied single family dwelling, the so-called "Mrs. Murphy's boarding house."

Such rentals now are not covered by state or federal law.

**THE REPORT,** which will be presented to the state convention Platform Committee, calls for a new state department of human relations merging not only the State Commission Against Discrimination (SCAD) and the Governor's Human Rights Commission but the Status of Women Commission, the Indian Affairs Commission and other commissions concerned with minority groups.

The report did not recommend an end to "de facto" school segregation, but it called for "improvement in quality education for all."

The task force also called for improved housing conditions for Indians and enforcement of laws giving Indians rights over the wild rice harvest.

# Buddhist-Led Mob Attacks GIs in Jeep

From the Tribune Wire Services

SAIGON, South Viet Nam — An unruly crowd of 300 Buddhist-led youths burned an American jeep and a Vietnamese military jeep in Saigon today and attacked their occupants.

Riot police, swinging clubs and hurling tear gas grenades, broke up the mob, but a Vietnamese policeman in one of the jeeps was grabbed by the crowd and hustled from the scene.

It was the second day of demonstrations after a two-week lull.

**THERE WAS** no word on whether the Americans, military policemen, were injured. The rioters seized a machine gun from the U.S. MPs before overturning their jeep and setting it aflame.

The fresh rioting occurred after a crowd had gathered at the Buddhist Institute about three blocks from where they attacked the jeeps.

At the same time, the government of Premier Nguyen Cao Ky pushed ahead with reforms it had agreed to earlier under Buddhist pressures, including election of a constituent assembly and appointment of a military-civilian advisory council.

About 500 Buddhist monks, nuns and youths yesterday attempted to march through the streets of Saigon to the U.S. embassy but were dispersed by riot police.

The demonstrations were an indication that Thich Tam Chau, chairman of the Buddhist Institute and the leading moderate among the Buddhists, might be losing the tenuous control he had established over the militant faction.

**TAM CHAU,** while sharing the militants' ultimate objective of bringing down Ky, has sought a compromise with the military junta and has opposed street demonstrations and other forms of violent protest, such as suicides, which the militants favor.

Tam Chau, however, has

Viet Nam
Continued on Page Eight

Associated Press

**Reaction** A woman reacted to a swat by a policeman during a demonstration outside a polling place in Nairobi, Kenya. Members of the Kenya Peoples Union clashed with supporters of the government party, the Kenya African Nationalist Union, during weekend elections. The elections to name new legislators to Parliament, followed the recent walkout of several Parliament members who disagreed with the policies of President Jomo Kenyatta.

# Chicago Riot Flares Again; Two Wounded

CHICAGO, Ill. — (AP) — A policeman was hit by a brick and two Puerto Ricans were shot Monday night as more than 1,000 persons ran through the littered streets of a strife-torn Puerto Rican neighborhood, throwing home-made bombs and shattering windows.

Three hospitals said injured had been admitted. The number could not be determined. The injured policemen and the two who were shot were reported in good condition.

Police arrested jeering bystanders to heed directions, and fired warning shots into the air.

Several hundred persons gathered in a nearby park, and police gave them an ultimatum: break up or be arrested. Most of the group dispersed, but others threw rocks and bottles at police.

Officers then began herding them into police vans.

More than 150 helmeted policemen ordered businesses closed in the northwest side neighborhood, where violence erupted Sunday after a Puerto Rican youth was shot by a policeman.

Some businesses boarded up their windows. Most businesses had only the jagged remains of window panes.

The vandalism and shooting occurred about eight blocks from Sunday night's disturbances in which police clashed with 1,000 persons.

Police Cmdr. William Coesfeld said two Puerto Ricans were shot by police last night when they threw bottles filled with gasoline. (United Press International reported in a late dispatch that six persons had been shot).

General looting was taking place.

An unidentified news photographer was mobbed and beaten.

The violence began suddenly last night after a "peace rally" in a neighborhood park in which commu-

Chicago
Continued on Page Three

# Money-Saving Facts About Medicare

*Second in a series*

By VICTOR COHN
Minneapolis Tribune Staff Writer

***Medicare isn't the world's simplest insurance plan.***

***Everyone who's over 65 or will be soon—and everyone who has to aid an aged parent or relative—ought to know some of its rules.***

***Knowing the following facts may save you time and money. You will probably want to clip and save them.***

First, Medicare may not cover quite half of all health bills. It does not cover prescriptions or other drugs you buy. In several categories, it runs out after 100 days.

You would be wise, say many experts, to buy other insurance, too, if you can manage it.

Two popular plans in Minnesota (judged by past performance) are:

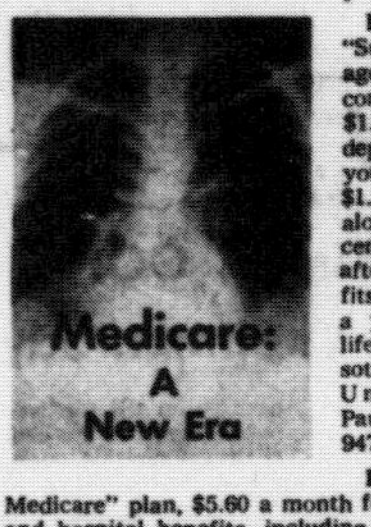


**Blue Cross-MII** "Supplemental Coverage," five plans or combination plans for $1.25 to $8.50 a month depending on what you want to buy. The $1.25-a-month plan alone will pay 80 per cent of hospital costs after Medicare benefits end, up to $5,000 a year or $20,000 a lifetime. Write Minnesota Blue Cross, 2610 University Av., St. Paul, or phone 646-9477 for details.

**Blue Shield** "Major Medicare" plan, $5.60 a month for medical, surgical and hospital benefits, including drugs. Write Minnesota Blue Shield, 2344 Nicollet Av., Minneapolis, or phone 338-8511.

Several other private firms offer widely advertised supplementary plans. Ask your agent.

• • •

Now, Medicare itself.

THE BASIC HOSPITAL PLAN covers almost everyone over 65 starting July 1, no matter whether or not you are working and how much you make. You are covered even if you are in a hospital or under a doctor's care already. Not covered (unless entitled to Social Security or railroad retirement benefits) are certain federal employes (who have their own plan) and aliens who have not been permanent U.S. residents for five years.

You should automatically get your red-white-and-blue Medicare card in the mail on nearing age 65. If you don't, ask your nearest Social Security office. Show this card on entering the hospital. The hospital collects the part of your bill covered by Medicare without bothering you.

IN THE HOSPITAL, you are covered for up to 90 days for each "spell of illness," IF your doctor certifies that your care is medically necessary and recertifies it from time to time. A "spell" starts on the first day you get hospital or extended care (nursing home or chronic disease unit) benefits. It ends when you have not been in any hospital or extended care facility for 60 consecutive days. A new "spell" begins the next time you get such services.

**You must pay** $40 for your first 60 days—Medicare pays the rest. From the 61st to 90th day in each spell, you pay $10 daily.

**Medicare covers** room and board in semiprivate room (two or more beds); nursing; supplies, appliances and equipment (such as splints, casts, wheelchairs, crutches); blood (except for the first three pints); medical social services; treatments like X-ray or radium; operating room costs; hospital-furnished

Medicare
Continued on Page Eight

AWARDED BRONZE STAR

# Soldier With Cancer Fights in Viet Nam

WASHINGTON, D. C. — (UPI) — Special Forces Sgt. 1/C Phillip A. Hesse, 29, of Fayetteville, N. C., won the Bronze Star on President Johnson's orders Monday simply for having served in Viet Nam.

Hesse

He led no heroic assaults against the Communist Viet Cong. He made no dramatic, one-man stands against overwhelming odds.

For Hesse, the war and the odds are personal.

He has cancer.

He knew it last September when he volunteered for Viet Nam. The doctors said he had no more than five years to live, and probably only two.

The tall, blond paratrooper emerged unscathed from mortar attacks on Pleiku and from jungle sorties. Yet on May 16, visibly unmarked to his buddies, Hesse was medically evacuted as a casualty of the private war he carried to Viet Nam.

He now is in Walter Reed Army Medical Center and faces almost certain amputation of his right leg, probably next week. The odds for survival are questionable, but Hesse said he is determined to stay in the Army and return to Viet Nam, even on one leg.

On Monday, Maj. Gen. Philip W. Mallory, commanding general of Walter Reed, pinned the nation's fourth highest military decoration on Hesse in a special hospital ceremony.

Hesse is married and has two children. He joined the Navy in 1955, flew dirigibles at Lakehurst, N.J., joined the Army in 1958, jumped with the 101st Airborne and joined the special forces in 1961.

He served in Laos and in Germany, where in 1964 he contracted a form of cancer, chondrosarcoma. After three operations, he was offered retirement with a 100 per cent medical disability rating. He refused.

With part of a hip gone, he went to Ft. Bragg, N. C., and trained arduously until he could use his right leg again. Then to Viet Nam.

Hesse denies any heroism. "I want to go there," he told anxious friends and relatives.

# Continued Mild, Some Clouds Are Forecast

Fair to partly cloudy skies with no important temperature change are predicted for the Upper Midwest and the Twin Cities today by the Weather Bureau.

Winds in the Twin Cities area will be west to northwesterly at 10 to 18 miles an hour, the Weather Bureau said. The high today should be 75. Skies should be sunny.

Other highs include Minnesota, 64 to 72 north, mostly 70s south; Wisconsin, 62 to 70 north, 70s south; North Dakota, 68 to 75; South Dakota, 72 to 82.

# United Fund Sets Record Goal for 1966 Campaign

A record goal of $6,098,543 was set Monday for this year's United Fund (UF) drive.

The goal, set by fund directors, is $268,877 more than was raised a year ago. The contributions will be divided among 82 health, welfare and recreational agencies.

John Cowles Jr., editor of the Minneapolis Tribune and Minneapolis Star, will head this year's drive. Funds will be collected in Hennepin County and parts of Anoka and Carver Counties.

Solicitation of employes, executives and corporations will begin in mid-September. The door-to-door phase of the campaign will open Oct. 6, with the entire drive ending Oct. 27.

**UF PRESIDENT** Clarence R. Chaney said expanded United Service Organization and Red Cross services to U.S. servicemen overseas were largely responsible for the increased fund drive goal.

An increase in the number of persons being served by UF agencies and a 4 to 5 per cent rise in agency operating expenses also contribute to the stepped-up campaign, according to Alan H. Moore, chairman of the UF admissions and allocations committee.

Increasing UF benefits also were noted by Chaney who cited studies showing that 50 per cent of the families in

United Fund
Continued on Page Eight

■

# 2 West German Fighters Crash

BONN, West Germany — (UPI)—Two more West German air force F104E Starfighters crashed Monday, killing both pilots, the Defense Ministry announced.

The crashes brought to 59 the total of Luftwaffe Starfighters to crash since the West German air force began using the plane in 1961. A total of 33 pilots have been killed.

# President Names Spilhaus to National Science Board

By CHARLES W. BAILEY
Minneapolis Tribune Staff Correspondent

WASHINGTON, D.C. — Athelstan Spilhaus, outgoing dean of the University of Minnesota's Institute of Technology, was nominated Monday by President Johnson for membership on the National Science Board (NSB).

Spilhaus

Spilhaus was one of eight men named to six-year terms on the board, whose 24 members determine over-all national policy for promoting basic research and education in the sciences.

Spilhaus, a native of South Africa, has been dean of technology at the university since 1949. He gained fame for his work in oceanography and is a member of the National Academy of Sciences.

(The university announced Saturday that Spilhaus would step down as dean, effective July 1, to devote his full time to teaching physics).

The others are:

Clifford M. Hardin, president of the University of Nebraska; Charles F. Jones, president of Humble Oil and Refining Co.; Thomas F. Jones Jr., president of the University of South Carolina; Joseph M. Reynolds, vice-president for graduate studies and research development at Louisiana State University; Richard H. Sullivan, president of Reed College; Robert S. Morison, professor of biology and director of the biological sciences division at Cornell University, and E. R. Piore, vice-president and chief scientists of International Business Machines Corp.

Mr. Johnson yesterday also filled eight vacancies on the federal bench, promoting three federal district judges to new posts on the circuit court of appeals and naming five new district judges.

## TURN THE PAGES TO:

• • • •



*Tribune Telephones*
News, General ...372-4141
Want Ads .......372-4242
Circulation ......372-4343

## Almanac

### He Felt Like Joining the Club

*Tuesday, June 14, 1966*
165th day, 200 to go this year
Sunrise 5:26 a.m.; sunset 9:01 p.m.

At Hiawatha Golf Course last Friday, a young golfer put suntan lotion on his hands, picked up his club, stepped to the tee, swung — and his golf club flew into the lake and sank in 30 feet of water.

•

***The most shots recorded for a hole in a professional tournament is 21 for the 17th by the 1927 U.S. Open Champion Tommy Armour in the Shawnee, Del., Open Championship of that year.***

•

The longest hole-in-one ever recorded was one of 427 yards on the par 4 16th at Lake Hefner, Okla., by former major league baseball pitcher Lou Kretlow on March 26, 1961.

Rain
WEDNESDAY'S TEMPERATURES
Details Page 32

# Minneapolis Tribune

MORNING

Vol. CI—No. 15 · Copyright 1967 Minneapolis Star and Tribune Company · MINNEAPOLIS, MINN., THURSDAY, JUNE 8, 1967 · *** · Single Copy Price 10c · Lower Price for Carrier Delivery



# Israel Proclaims Victory in Egypt; U.N. Cease-fire Deadline Passes

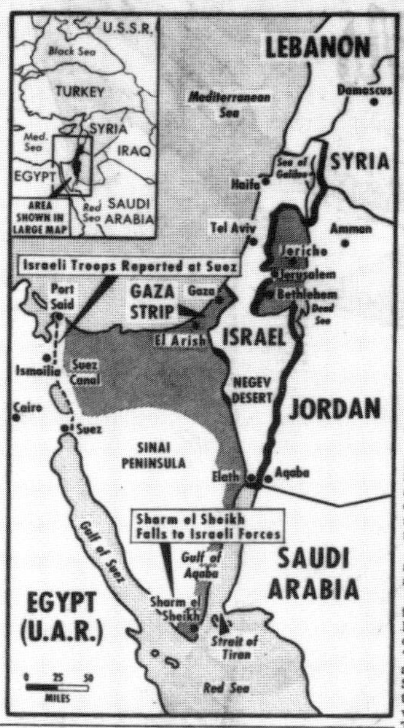


## Campaign for Sinai Reported Won

From the Tribune Wire Services

Israel Wednesday night proclaimed victory in the Sinai Peninsula campaign against Egypt. On the eastern front, both Old Jerusalem and Bethlehem were reported in Israeli hands.

Capture of the Suez Canal seemed to be only hours away.

"The Egyptians are defeated," said Maj. Gen. Itzhak Rabin, the Israeli chief of staff, in Tel Aviv. "All their efforts are aimed at withdrawing behind the Suez Canal and we are taking care of that. The whole area is in our hands. The main effort of the Egyptians is to save themselves."

At the United Nations, a member of the Israeli delegation said last night that Israeli forces have captured the Egyptian town of Ismalia, the nerve center of the Suez Canal. Ismalia is midway between Port Said and Suez.

In Tel Aviv, giving a terse but sweeping description of developments through the third day of the third Arab-Israeli war in 19 years, Rabin declared:

**Sinai,** the Egyptian territory between Israel's Negev Desert and the Suez Canal, is taken.

**Most of** the west bank of the Jordan River, Jordanian territory including Jericho, is in Israeli hands.

**Relative to** what was done, the number of Israeli casualties was "not great."

The general said his men took on Egypt, Jordan, Syria and Iraq, knocked out their air forces and overran their armor and infantry.

**"ALL THIS** the armed forces of Israel did alone," he said. The Arabs have been

Fighting
Continued on Page Seven

Associated Press

ISRAELI FIREPOWER IGNITED JORDANIAN ARMY BARRACKS IN OLD JERUSALEM

*The barracks were near the former Augusta Victoria Hospital, right*

## Council May Meet Again This Morning

From the Tribune Wire Services

The deadline for complying with a United Nations cease-fire in the Middle East was set at 4 p.m. EDT Wednesday in a Security Council resolution voted just 80 minutes before that time.

**More News of Mideast: P. 12, 13**

Israel accepted the deadline but declared it was virtually impossible to put the cease-fire into effect in the face of Egyptian silence.

Foreign Minister Abba Eban communicated the Israeli decision to Secretary General U Thant when they conferred for 55 minutes last night. Thant circulated the news to the members of the Security Council.

A cease-fire already is in effect between Israel and Jordan, Eban told Thant.

**ISRAEL'S** agreement came a few hours after the Security Council had unanimously adopted a resolution submitted by the Soviet Union demanding that the combatants "cease fire and all military activities on 7 June 1967" at 4 p.m. EDT.

A report from Cairo said that soon after the 4 p.m. deadline a senior Egyptian government spokesman declared, "Egypt will fight on."

Although no date was set for the next Security Council meeting on the Middle East, diplomats were advised that one might be called for 11:30 a.m. EDT today.

**THE SOVIET** resolution to set a time on the cease-fire voted Tuesday night by the council was approved unanimously in an emergency session requested by the Soviet Union. Some U.N. diplomats saw the move as an effort by the Russians to rescue the Arabs from total military defeat at the hands of Israel.

Ambassador Arthur J. Goldberg told the council the

Diplomacy
Continued on Page Seven

HE WAS STATE OFFICIAL

## Kroman Indicted on Bribe Charge

By DICK CUNNINGHAM
Minneapolis Tribune Staff Writer

David R. Kroman, former Minnesota official charged with fraud in the American Allied Insurance case, was charged with receiving bribes in a different case Wednesday.

Kroman

Kroman was indicted by the Hennepin County Grand Jury on two counts of bribery and one of conspiracy.

Specifically the jury charged that Kroman:

**Received** $250 in June 1964 from Joseph Haveson, former acting state insurance commissioner.

**Received** $500 at the same time from Harry M. Beyer, Beverly Hills, Calif.

**Conspired** with Haveson starting in the fall of 1963 to receive bribes from Beyer. In return Kroman was to use his influence to have the securities of Equity Funding Corp. of America registered for sale in Minnesota.

Kroman was an attorney with the State Insurance Division at the time.

*(KITZER JR. CLAIMS Fraud by State Insurance Agency—Page 31.)*

Later Kroman became an officer in one of the firms in the American Allied Insurance complex and one of the principal defendants in the American Allied fraud case now being tried in U.S. District Court in Bismarck, N.D.

U.S. District Judge Edward J. Devitt declared a mistrial in Kroman's case and sent him for psychiatric assessment after Kroman claimed he was run off the road by people who wanted to get him for what he knew about the Kennedy assassination.

He was declared sane and was free on $10,000 bond yesterday awaiting a new trial on the federal charge.

Kroman surrendered on the bribery charges yesterday afternoon and told Hennepin District Judge Rolf Fosseen he would move to have the indictment dismissed on the grounds the statute of limitations forbids prosecution of an offense after a certain period of years.

Fosseen continued the case

Kroman
Continued on Page Eight

BIG-POWER ATTITUDE

## Mideast Outbreak Viewed With Relief

By CHARLES W. BAILEY
Minneapolis Tribune Staff Correspondent

Analysis: WHAT THE NEWS MEANS

WASHINGTON, D.C. — The exchanges of invective and gunfire in the Middle East have dominated the headlines for a fortnight. But throughout the crisis, the men who manage the U.S. government have been more deeply concerned with a different problem.

The danger of a direct military confrontation between the United States and the Soviet Union has been a preeminent, sometimes even an overriding consideration in the words and acts of President Johnson and his advisers in the crisis.

Both external evidence and the opinion of expert observers suggest that the same thing has been true of the leaders in Moscow.

**IT IS** a fact, no matter how ironic or cold-blooded it may sound, that the actual outbreak of fighting came almost as a relief to responsible officials here. Many of them would doubtless agree — if only privately — with the Russian here who told an American friend on Monday morning:

"I feel better today. Last week I was afraid our two countries might come to a confrontation. Now that the others are fighting, this will not happen."

He was expressing one of the unpleasant truths of a nuclear-armed world: that the actual fact of a limited and local war is quite likely to be less of a threat to world peace than the mere prospect of a U.S.-Soviet conflict.

**AS LONG** as the Arab-Israeli dispute revolved

Confront
Continued on Page Seven

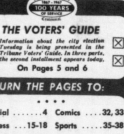

Rivers · Russell

*Lottery eliminated*

## Conferees Agree on Draft Bill

WASHINGTON, D.C. — (UPI) — Senate and House negotiators reached agreement Wednesday on a new military draft bill which rules out, for the present, any lottery-like random selection system to determine the order of induction.

The compromise bill was approved on the basis of differing bills passed by the Senate and House. It would guarantee the continuance of educational deferments for college undergraduates and students enrolled in apprentice and job-training programs.

Sen. Richard B. Russell, D-Ga., chairman of the Senate conferees, said the Senate may act on the four-year draft extension bill today. House action must await Senate approval.

The present draft law expires June 30.

**CONGRESSIONAL** action will clear the way for President Johnson, under current discretionary powers, to reverse the order of induction and take 19-year-olds first rather than the oldest eligibles in the Selective Service pool starting with age 26.

Under the approved compromise bill, however, the President would have to seek congressional approval of a separate bill before instituting the lottery-like Fair And Impartial Random selection system (FAIR) that was proposed by a national commission which studied draft reforms for the president.

Conscientious objectors would continue to have the option of serving two years of non-combat duty in the military or being assigned by their local draft board to a humanitarian civilian job for the same period.

**RUSSELL SAID** testimony before the Senate and House Armed Services Committees indicated that there was "not much clarity" as to how the random selection plan would work. Chairman L. Mendel Rivers, D-S.C., of the House Armed Services Committee agreed there was "no clear-cut plan" for the system and

Draft
Continued on Page Seven

## Steady Rain Boosts State Crops Outlook

Steady rainfall exceeding an inch at most stations over the past two days has improved the outlook for Minnesota farmers, according to reports from county agents Wednesday night.

George Roadfeldt, Hennepin County extension agent, said, "The farmers were very concerned about the hay crop, the germination and survival of corn and soybeans and the wheat control chemicals."

"Without rain the chemicals wouldn't be absorbed into the ground.

**"THE RAIN** came in gradual amounts — 2 or 2½ inches over a several day period so it was absorbed by the ground and there was little runoff and no erosion," Roadfeldt said.

He said the rain would "increase the tonnage of the first cutting of alfalfa which will begin next week."

"It will carry us for awhile," he said.

Sample rainfall for the past two days included 1.2 inches in the Twin Cities area, 1.67 at Alexandria, 1.72 at Crookston, 1.23 at Thief River Falls and 1.11 at Halstad. More than an inch fell yesterday over most of western Minnesota.

Freeborn County Agent Eldon H. Senske, called it "a million - dollar rain."

**"THE CORN** wasn't hurting," he said, "but we did need moisture for plantings

Crops
Continued on Page Seven

## House Rejects Higher Ceiling on Debt Limit

WASHINGTON, D.C. — (AP) — The House rocked President Johnson's administration Wednesday night by refusing to increase the Treasury's borrowing authority by the requested $29 billion.

The 210-197 vote means administration forces will have to try again, with a lower figure, or the government will be unable to pay its bills next month.

The requested increase would have been the biggest single step-up since World War II and would have brought the national debt ceiling to $365 billion.

Unless Congress acts on a new increase by June 30, the debt limit automatically drops to $285 billion, well below the actual debt of $330 billion.

**THE VOTE** saw a new combination — Republicans, conservative Democrats and some liberals apparently opposed to higher spending in Vietnam—overcoming the administration forces.

Not a single Republican voted for the debt limit increase. Voting against it were 176 Republicans and 34 Democrats.

The Republicans had called for rejection of the proposed increase as a way to force Mr. Johnson to revise his budget with cuts in domestic spending.

They attacked what they called a credibility gap in the administration's projections of income and expenditures.

"I'll put it bluntly," said Rep. Thomas B. Curtis, R-Mo., "We don't believe the President's figures. I don't see any reason why we should. They're false on the revenue estimates and false on the expenditure estimates."

**CURTIS SAID** that as long as the administration withholds factual budget estimates from Congress and the public, as he put it, "we have a dictatorship in the United States," and he called for a vote of "no confidence in the

Debt
Continued on Page Seven

## Senate Approves LBJ Plan to Avert Railroad Walkout

WASHINGTON, D.C.—(AP) — The Senate Wednesday passed President Johnson's proposal to avert at least through 1968 a nationwide railroad strike in the dispute involving 137,000 shopcraft union workers.

The roll-call vote was 70 to 15.

The action sent the measure to the House, where a committee completed hearings on a similar measure.

**BEFORE** passing the bill, the Senate beat down efforts by Sens. Ralph Yarborough, D-Tex., and Edward M. Kennedy, D-Mass., to revise the bill more to the unions' liking.

Yarborough, Kennedy and some other Democratic senators argued that the resolution as submitted by the President is weighted too heavily on the side of management.

They pushed unsuccessfully for amendments which they said would "hold the scales down" and put equal pressure on both sides to reach a settlement.

**UNDER** Mr. Johnson's proposal, the strike now threatened by six shopcraft unions for June 19 would be barred for another 90 days to give time for intensive mediation efforts seeking voluntary agreement between the parties.

But if there were no voluntary settlement, the special five-man mediation board set up in the bill could impose its own settlement terms to continue until Jan. 1, 1969,

Rails
Continued on Page Seven

## City Indian Job Office Loses Federal Funds

By SAM NEWLUND
Minneapolis Tribune Staff Writer

Federal funds for an experimental Indian employment center in Minneapolis are being cut off, it was disclosed Wednesday.

The center's Executive Board called the action "shocking to Indians and non-Indians alike."

The American Indian Employment and Guidance Center, 1632 Chicago Av., was billed as the nation's first government - financed employment bureau for city - dwelling Indians.

The federal Bureau of Indian Affairs (BIA), which up to that time concentrated services to reservation-dwelling Indians, awarded a $23,175 contract for operation of the center last August. The contract went to a group of private citizens that operated an Indian employment center intermittently with donated funds.

**CITY-DWELLING** Indians in Minneapolis and other cities had been clamoring for BIA job-finding support, claiming that a move to the cities should not disqualify Indians for help. The Indians won their point and a BIA official in Washington, D.C., called the contract "a milestone in Indian affairs."

The federal contract, beginning in November 1966, was for six months. Later, it was extended to run through June 30, 1967.

Henry E. Allen, co-ordinator of student religious activities at the University of Minnesota, is acting chairman of the center board. Gerald R. Vizenor, part-Indian and member of the Mayor's Commission on Human Relations, is executive director.

On May 29, Glenn R. Landbloom, BIA area director, wrote the board that the BIA in Washington had decided

Indians
Continued on Page Eight

## Light Showers Possible Today

Possible light showers and little temperature change are predicted for the Twin Cities today. Temperatures will range from an expected high of 72 to a low of 58.

Winds will be northeasterly at 10 to 18 miles an hours. Precipitation possibility is 30 per cent.

The entire Upper Midwest area will experience scattered showers today. Warming trends will be noted in portions of South Dakota and in southern Wisconsin.

## Almanac

### Poundwise But Dessert Foolish

*Thursday, June 8, 1967*

159th day. 206 to go this year
Sunrise 5:27 a.m.; sunset 8:58 p.m.

A Minneapolis man, dedicated to losing pounds, went to the supermarket for low-calorie food and came home with:

12 cans of Metrecal

3 packages of no-calorie cookies

1 pumpkin pie with whipped cream

•

*On this date in 68, Emperor Nero fiddled his last tune.*

•

Actor Bob Cummings is 57 today and should know better by now.

Minneapolis Tribune 1867 - 1967 100 YEARS OF SERVICE Centennial

### THE VOTERS' GUIDE

*Information about the city election Tuesday is being presented in the Tribune Voters' Guide. In three parts, the second installment appears today,*

On Pages 5 and 6

### TURN THE PAGES TO:



Tribune Telephones
Circulation ......372-4343
News, General ...372-4141
Want Ads .......372-4242

**Little Change**

TUESDAY TEMPERATURES

| | | | | | |
|---|---|---|---|---|---|
| 2 a.m. | 70 | 10 a.m. | 73 | 6 p.m. | 81 |
| 3 a.m. | 70 | 11 a.m. | 73 | 7 p.m. | 79 |
| 4 a.m. | 70 | Noon | 74 | 8 p.m. | 76 |
| 5 a.m. | 70 | 1 p.m. | 78 | 9 p.m. | 75 |
| 6 a.m. | 64 | 2 p.m. | 80 | 10 p.m. | 75 |
| 7 a.m. | 63 | 3 p.m. | 81 | 11 p.m. | 74 |
| 8 a.m. | 66 | 4 p.m. | 80 | 12 M | 74 |
| 9 a.m. | 69 | 5 p.m. | 82 | *1 a.m. | 74 |

*Details Page 22* *Unofficial

# Minneapolis Tribune

MORNING

Vol. CI—No. 21  MINNEAPOLIS, MINN., WEDNESDAY, JUNE 14, 1967 ★ Single Copy Price 10c Lower Price for Carrier Delivery



# MAYOR NAFTALIN IS RE-ELECTED

## *Liquor Patrol Amendment Defeated for Second Time; Martens, Johnson, Newton, Denny Lose*

Associated Press

THURGOOD MARSHALL, RIGHT, AT NOMINATION

*President Johnson named him to Supreme Court*

## 1st Negro Named to High Court

WASHINGTON, D.C.—(AP)—For the first time in U.S. history, a Negro was chosen Tuesday to sit on the Supreme Court. President Johnson named Solicitor General Thurgood Marshall to succeed Justice Tom C. Clark.

"I believe it is the right thing to do, the right time to do it, the right man and the right place," Mr. Johnson said in personally making the announcement to newsmen summoned to the White House rose garden.

Standing beside Mr. Johnson was Marshall, a former federal circuit judge who served for 23 years as chief legal officer of the National Association for the Advancement of Colored People.

Clark resigned as an associate justice Monday, at the end of the court term, because his son, Ramsey Clark, earlier this year was named attorney general.

The older Clark's departure was prompted by his desire to avoid any possible implication of a conflict of interest.

Marshall, who will be 59, July 2, will be Mr. Johnson's second appointment to the nation's highest tribunal. The first was his close friend and adviser, Abe Fortas, who was confirmed by the Senate Aug. 11, 1965, the day it

Marshall
Continued on Page 12

## Detroit Shells Twins, 15-10

**In 6th, Tigers Get 10 Runs, Minnesota 5, Setting League Scoring Record**

•

**Chicago White Sox Beat Senators, 6-0**

•

*(Details in Sports Section)*

## 2 Villages Vote for Sunday Liquor

Two small villages Tuesday became the first Minnesota communities to approve Sunday liquor sales under the local option law passed by the 1967 Legislature.

Miesville, a Dakota County village 10 miles south of Hastings, voted 65 to 2. Island View, a Rainy Lake resort community 12 miles east of International Falls, voted 24 to 0.

Licenses were issued by the village councils to two establishments in Miesville and three in Island View. Liquor will be served beginning Sunday in both communities.

The new law permits referendums for establishing special Sunday licenses that permit the sale of liquor by the drink from noon to midnight to patrons seated at dining tables.

— LIQUOR —

## Proposal Falls Short 2,072 Votes

BY BERNIE SHELLUM
Minneapolis Tribune Staff Writer

Minneapolis voters Tuesday defeated for the second time in six weeks a charter amendment to abolish the liquor patrol limits.

The proposal, given a second referendum on the assumption that voters were confused by developments preceding the May 2 primary, got only a fraction of a percentage point more support yesterday.

It failed by 2,072 votes to get the 55 per cent required for passage. In the primary it failed by 1,288 votes. Both times it was supported by approximately 53 per cent of those voting on the issue.

The vote yesterday was 54,924 for abolition and 48,706 against.

Three of the city's five dry wards, the 10th, 11th and 13th, favored the amendment, and two, the 4th and 12th, voted against it. The 7th and 13th wards gave the amendment its biggest margins of support.

Voters indicated, however, that they considered the issue apart from the candidates. The 8th Ward went against the amendment by a wide margin while defeating Alderman Elsa Johnson, one of its staunchest opponents. The ward elected Gerard Hegstrom, who had taken a strong stand in favor of the amendment.

Wards 1, 2, 3, 5, 6, 7, 10, 11 and 13 voted for the proposal. Wards 4, 8, 9 and 12 voted against it.

The principal purpose of the amendment was to allow dispersal of some of the 267 liquor licenses now inside the patrol limits. Many outlets already have been removed to make way for urban renewal projects and freeways. Planners estimate that as many as 80 more will be jeopardized in the next few years.

Liquor concentration has been cited as a major cause of blight in the 6th Ward, which has 113 establishments. Dealers say concentration results in high competition and

Liquor
Continued on Page Eight

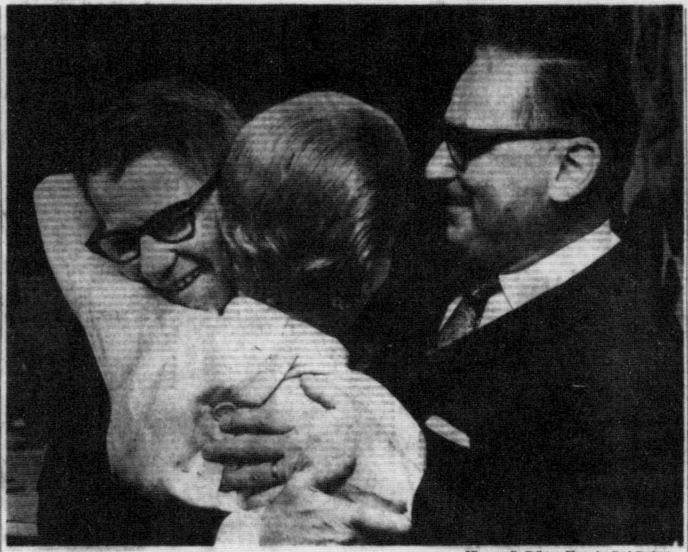

Minneapolis Tribune Photo by Earl Seubert

ORVILLE FREEMAN, LEFT, ARRIVED JUST IN TIME FOR NAFTALIN VICTORY NEWS

*Mayor Arthur Naftalin watched at his headquarters as Freeman hugged Mrs. Naftalin*

— MAYOR —

## Margin Is Slimmest He Ever Got

By DICK CUNNINGHAM
Minneapolis Tribune Staff Writer

Arthur Naftalin defeated Republican Arne Carlson to win re-election for a fourth term as mayor of Minneapolis Tuesday.

His margin of 3,243 votes was the narrowest of any of his victories.

Final unofficial returns gave Naftalin, a Democratic-Farmer-Laborite, 56,888 votes to 53,645 for Carlson.

**NAFTALIN SAID** he was disappointed that he didn't do better and that DFL-oriented Liberals didn't win control of the City Council.

More Election News—Page 17

But he told cheering supporters at the Pick - Nicollet Hotel, "I intend to work with the closest possible harmony with the City Council and with all the boards and commissions."

Carlson conceded defeat at 9:30 p.m., telling several hundred campaign workers gathered at the Sheraton-Ritz Hotel that he had attempted "to conduct a constructive campaign but we were not accepted."

Muttering to himself, Carlson said:

"What does it take to get this guy out of office? Incredible!"

**HIS WIFE,** Barbara, drew loud cheers by promising that "if I have anything to do about it, we'll be back in two years."

A campaign aide said afterwards that Carlson lost because of his small pluralities in Republican wards like the 11th and 13th.

The mayor ran with the support of a Democratic-Farmer-Labor party that was consciously trying to bind up wounds from the split between former Gov. Karl F. Rolvaag and former Lt. Gov. A. M. Keith. Naftalin, for instance, had the support of all the major labor bodies in the city for the first time.

**NAFTALIN BECAME** the fourth mayor to be elected to more than three two-year terms.

The first was James Clark Haynes, who served four terms from 1902 to 1904 and from 1906 to 1912. The second was George Emerson Leach, who served six terms from 1921 to 1929 and from 1937 to 1941.

The third was Eric G. Hoy-

Mayor
Continued on Page Eight

## *More Rain Is Forecast for Today*

Showers and thunderstorms are forecast for the Twin Cities and vicinity again today. There is a 40 percent chance of precipitation today and tonight, according to the Weather Bureau.

Skies will be cloudy. It will be warm and humid. The high today should be 80.

Tornado warnings were in effect for southeast South Dakota, the southwestern corner of Minnesota, eastern Nebraska and northwestern Iowa until 5 a.m. today.

Large hail and damaging winds were also forecast for the area.

A storm that moved in a line from Sioux Falls, S.D., north of Redwood Falls, Minn., to Danbury, Wis., yesterday morning caused damage to a home in Worthington, Minn.

**A SMALL** tornado or a heavy gust of wind tore the roof off a boat house on the north shore of Lake Okabena. The roof was thrown across the road, about 150 feet, and into the Robert DeLoughter home.

Rainfall in Minnesota included .99 of an inch in International Falls, 1.85 in Bemidji, .92 in Detroit Lakes, .27 in Duluth, .51 in Grand Rapids, 1.73 in St. Louis Park, 1.76 in Edina and .79 in the Twin Cities.

The measurements include rainfall from 7 a.m. Monday to 7 p.m. Tuesday.

## Rider, Adams Elected to School Board

By FRED JOHNSON
Minneapolis Tribune Staff Writer

Stuart W. Rider Jr., an incumbent, and Frank E. Adams, a former board member, were elected to the Minneapolis School Board Tuesday in a tight three-way race.

Incumbent Richard S. Larson was defeated narrowly. Verne H. Hansen, the fourth candidate, ran far behind.

Rider and Larson are Republicans. Adams and Hansen are DFLers.

**THE ELECTION** of Adams, 51, a former state senator who served on the board from 1953 to 1962, will even the political balance on the board.

The new board will have three Republicans, three DFLers and one unaffiliated member. The present division is four Republicans, two DFLers and one unaffiliated.

Rider, 48, an attorney who has been board chairman for two years, led the race with an unofficial vote total of 53,483.

Adams had 52,279 votes, Larson 50,508 and Hansen 28,691.

Political ties have had little apparent effect on policies of the present board, and there has been little evidence of bloc voting.

**RIDER SAID** last night that he hopes the board will "continue to work on a fairly nonpolitical basis."

He said he is sorry that Larson lost, but added that he is sure he and Adams will work together effectively.

During the campaign, Adams indicated that he had no complaints with decisions of the present board, but claimed the board was responsible for a "credibility gap" between it and the voters.

The election, he said last night, indicates that the electorate was "not completely pleased with the incumbents."

**THIS IS** the fourth time Adams has been elected to the board. He resigned in 1962 after he was elected to

School Board
Continued on Page Eight

## *Six New Faces in City Council*

By BERNIE SHELLUM
Minneapolis Tribune Staff Writer

Four aldermen, including Independent Elsa Johnson and Liberal George Martens, were defeated in the Minneapolis general election Tuesday as the Republican-oriented Independents retained control of the City Council.

The others defeated were Robert J. Denny, unaffiliated appointee of the present Independent majority, and Jack E. Newton, the DFLer who upset council veteran Frank Moulton two years ago.

Two seats are being vacated voluntarily, so a total of six new faces will appear when the new council convenes after July 1.

**THEY ARE** Albert J. Hofstede, Gerard D. Hegstrom and Byron F. Nelson, DFLers, and Richard T. Curtin, Vern Anderson and Gladys S. Brooks, Republicans.

Hofstede, once an aide to former Gov. Karl F. Rolvaag, defeated Denny in the heavily DFL 3rd Ward. A bachelor, he is 26.

Curtin, a 25-year-old attorney, will become the youngest member of the council. He ran 375 votes ahead of Martens, 58, who has served on the council 18 consecutive years. Martens' DFL rival, Thomas E. McDonald, got 61 write-in votes.

**HEGSTROM, 36,** a lawyer and former FBI agent, defeated Mrs. Johnson, a six-year veteran of the council, by 316 votes. She had won three previous elections by a total of 655 votes.

Vern Anderson, 46, a businessman, defeated Newton by only 50 votes in the closets of all the races. He is a political novice.

Mrs. Brooks, wife of a Minneapolis attorney, has long been active in Republican politics and civic affairs at local and national levels, and her easy victory over Ward L. Canfield, a former policeman, was expected. She will occupy the seat being vacated by Council President Glenn G. C. Olson, a Republican who has served since 1963. She is 52.

Nelson, 58, is an employe of the Minneapolis-St. Paul Sanitary District.

**HE SERVED** as 12th Ward

Council
Continued on Page Eight

## City Election Results

(*Asterisks denote incumbents.)

**MAYOR**
195 precincts of 195

| | |
|---|---|
| *Arthur Naftalin | 56,888 |
| Arne H. Carlson | 53,645 |

**COMPTROLLER**
195 precincts of 195

| | |
|---|---|
| Earl A. Arneson | 56,213 |
| Ron Moir | 45,938 |

**TREASURER**
195 precincts of 195

| | |
|---|---|
| *Rey C. Malmquist | 68,907 |
| Walter S. Hobot | 33,665 |

**PARK BOARD**
**At Large**
195 precincts of 195

| | |
|---|---|
| William Holbrook | 53,038 |
| Richard D. Hall | 42,638 |

**34th District**
22 precincts of 22

| | |
|---|---|
| George W. Bauman | 8,046 |
| Alice N. Felien | 6,145 |

**36th District**
23 precincts of 23

| | |
|---|---|
| Leonard H. Neiman | 6,660 |
| Delwin R. Kruschke | 2,920 |

**38th District**
23 precincts of 23

| | |
|---|---|
| John F. Bergford Jr. | 4,513 |
| Walter W. Thulin | 4,101 |

**40th District**
19 precincts of 19

| | |
|---|---|
| *Stefan Romanowski | 5,419 |
| Ronald E. Corrigan | 2,644 |

**42nd District**
24 precincts of 24

| | |
|---|---|
| David N. Kienitz | 3,490 |
| Zollie Green | 2,744 |

**BOARD OF ESTIMATE AND TAXATION**
195 princincts of 195

| | |
|---|---|
| Douglas Wallace | 52,283 |
| Carl Hafften | 46,765 |

Table
Continued on Page Eight

## Russia Seeks Emergency U.N. Assembly Session on Mideast

From the Tribune Wire Services

The Soviet Union tried to force a showdown Tuesday night in the U.N. Security Council on withdrawal of Israeli forces from occupied Arab territory and to open the way for an emergency session of the 122-nation General Assembly on the Middle East.

There were indications that the Russians were importing high-level reinforcements from Moscow to press their case in the United Nations. Speculation was that Soviet Premier Alexei N. Kosygin might head the Soviet delegation at an emergency session in New York.

**A LETTER** from Soviet Foreign Minister Andrei A. Gromyko caused the speculation with a remark that the Soviet delegation would include "leading statesmen."

In Washington, State Department sources said that the Soviet Union requested through the U.S. Embassy in Moscow Monday a permit for a special Soviet plane landing in New York this week, probably Thursday. The permit was granted.

An announcement that Kosygin would attend the session might lead to quick decisions by other heads of government to gather in New York and turn the emergency session into a sort of summit meeting.

*(ADDITIONAL Middle East News—Page Three.)*

The Soviet Union's bid to get a showdown in the 15-nation Security Council on its resolution for withdrawal of Israeli troops was delayed last night by a vote to adjourn until today.

**SOVIET** Ambassador Nikolai T. Fedorenko had demanded an immediate vote on the Soviet resolution, which appeared to face defeat. Independent surveys indicated that the Soviet resolution will receive no more than six Security Council votes, three short of the required number.

At the same time, Fedorenko announced he would veto a rival U.S. resolution calling for talks aimed at establishing stability and peace in the Middle East.

The Soviet moves came as U.N. legal officials indicated they had decided that failure of the 15-nation council to adopt either the Soviet or the U.S. resolution would create the conditions required for calling the emergency ses-

Mideast
Continued on Page 11

Minneapolis Tribune 1867 - 1967 100 YEARS OF SERVICE Centennial

## *TURN THE PAGES TO:*



*Tribune Telephones*

| | |
|---|---|
| Circulation | 372-4343 |
| News, General | 372-4141 |
| Want Ads | 372-4242 |

## Almanac

### *Lord, Give Me Strength—and Accuracy*

*Wednesday, June 14, 1967*

165th day. 200 to go this year
Sunrise 5:26 a.m.; sunset 9:01 p.m.

The Golden Valley mother was lecturing her 13-year-old daughter on the virtues of enduring constant grief administered by her 14-year-old brother.

"You must ask the good Lord for strength to endure," the mother urged.

The girl replied, "I've got a better idea. I'll ask the Lord for the strength to slug him in the mouth."

•

***On this date in 1949, the Missouri Legislature adopted the "Missouri Waltz" as the official state song and lights burned late in the White House.***

MINNEAPOLIS TEMPERATURES

| | | | | | |
|---|---|---|---|---|---|
| Midnight.. | 4 | 4:30 a.m. | -2 | 9 a.m. .... | 5 |
| 1 a.m. .... | 4 | 5 a.m. .... | -1 | 10 a.m. .. | 11 |
| 2 a.m. .... | 1 | 6 a.m. .... | 0 | 11 a.m. .. | 17 |
| 3 a.m. .... | -1 | 7 a.m. .... | -1 | *Noon ... | 21 |
| 4 a.m. .... | -1 | 8 a.m. .... | 1 | *Unofficial | |

TOMORROW: Warmer.

THE MINNEAPOLIS STAR

Tuesday, Jan. 30, 1968 XC—No. 57 Four Sections ★

Single Copy Price 10c Lower Price for Carrier Delivery



# Cong Attack 8 Cities, 5 Airfields

By GEORGE ESPER

SAIGON, South Vietnam—(AP)—The Viet Cong attacked seven provincial capitals, South Vietnam's second largest city and four American airfields today, ushering in the lunar new year with the biggest co-ordinated assault of the Vietnam war.

By midafternoon, the guerrillas were reported still in control of parts of two coastal cities—Nha Trang, 190 miles northeast of Saigon, and Hoi An, 365 miles northeast of the capital.

Some fighting also was reported still going on at Pleiku, in the central highlands, while the situation was not clear at Kontum and Ban Me Thuot, both in the highlands, and at coastal Tuy Hoa and Qui Nohn.

Associated Press correspondent Robert D. Ohman reported that South Vietnamese Rangers and U.S. Marine MPs had wiped out the last pocket of enemy resistance in Da Nang, South Vietnam's second city, and reported 63 Viet Cong killed.

President Nguyen Van Thieu canceled the rest of the 36-hour truce he had proclaimed for Tet, the new year festival. He had already modified it before it began, to exclude the country's five northernmost provinces and to continue U.S. bombing of the North Vietnamese panhandle for 125 miles above the demilitarized zone, the chief supply area for the thousands of North Vietnamese troops threatening the U.S. Marines at Khe Sanh.

Gen. William C. Westmoreland, commander of U.S. troops in Vietnam, said the seven-day truce the Communists had proclaimed for the lunar new year, Tet, "is clearly revealed as a hoax and a fraud."

The Viet Cong guerrillas and demolition teams caught the South Vietnamese defenders off guard, with many of them celebrating Tet. The guerrillas raced through the streets of Da Nang and the seven provincial capitals, all in the central and northern part of South Vietnam, terrorizing the population and seizing key installations.

The obvious aim was to undermine confidence in the Saigon government, capping a three-month-long Communist campaign of attacks on district capitals throughout South Vietnam.

The attacks on the U.S. airfields destroyed or damaged at least 42 jet fighter-bombers, cargo planes, observation aircraft and helicopters. The loss was estimated at more than $25 million.

WAR
Turn to Page 4A

★ ★ ★ ★

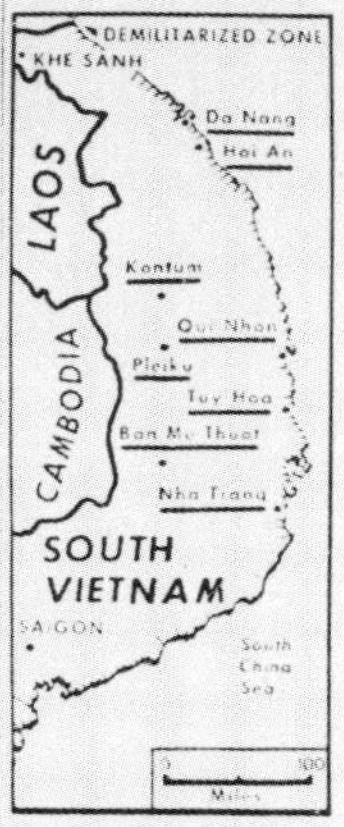


★ ★ ★ ★

## LBJ Asks Increased Veterans' Benefits

WASHINGTON, D.C. — (UPI) — President Johnson asked Congress today to increase benefits and job opportunities for veterans.

In a special message to the House and Senate he urged that the thrust of new veterans programs be aimed at helping them function as "free, upstanding and self-reliant citizens" after returning to civilian life.

To finance his proposals Mr. Johnson included $7.3 billion in the fiscal 1969 budget for services to some 26 million veterans and their families who comprise 46 per cent of the current American population.

Among the President's new recommendations:

**Increasing** the maximum federal guarantee on GI home loans from $7,500 to $10,000. Such mortgage guarantees under the GI bill normally cover about 35 per cent of a loan. (The President said the lower limit, in effect for 18 years, is no longer realistic in today's housing market.)

**Expansion** of vocational rehabilitation for veterans

VETS
Turn to Page 4A

## Youths Sentenced in Rozenberg Case

Two North Minneapolis youths, both 17, pleaded guilty to third-degree murder today in the Sept. 28 shooting of Plymouth Av. shoemaker Paul Rozenberg and were sentenced to not more than 25 years in the St. Cloud, Minn., Reformatory.

Fred Clay Jr., 1336 Knox Av. N., and Roy L. Rodgers, 3235 Girard Av. N., were sentenced by District Court Judge Douglas K. Amdahl.

Associated Press

**Just Too Much** One of the men assigned to shovel part of a block-long parking lot at Portland, Ore., spelled out in large letters why the job wasn't finished. At left, another shoveler continued the job. He got a break later. Rain washed away most of 3 inches of snow that had fallen.

COUNCIL PROPOSAL

## Edwards Compromise May Be Developing

By AL WOODRUFF
Minneapolis Star Staff Writer

A compromise solution to the problem of Mayor Arthur Naftalin's attempts to appoint Ronald A. Elwards to the Minneapolis Human Relations Commission appeared to be developing today.

Curtin

Ironically, the move toward a possible solution was started by an absence of action by the Minneapolis City Council Ordinances and Legislation Committee today on a proposal to increase the number of persons serving on the commission from 15 to 21.

Alderman Richard Curtin, chairman of the powerful committee, expressed "extreme hopefulness" on arriving on a solution by Feb. 9, the date of the next council meeting. All changes in ordinances plus new ordinances must come before the committee.

Technically, the committee took under advisement for further study a proposal by Alderman Gerard Hegstrom to increase the size of the commission.

However, Curtin pointed out, the proposal could be amended further and changed in such a way that the entire section of the existing ordinance pertaining to the composition and make-up of the human relations commission could be changed substantially.

Possible changes could include a commission of 21 members, with the mayor appointing a majority of them and the council the balance.

### One Possibility

Another possibility would be for the council to appoint a majority of the 21 commission members with the mayor appointing the rest.

Included in either of these proposals would be the condition that none of the appointments would require confirmation by the council.

In either proposal, Edwards could take a seat on the commission as a mayor's appointee.

The present ordinance provides appointment of commission members with confirmation by the council required for all.

Curtin pointed out that no matter how the commission composition might be changed, it could not affect the 14 commissioners who already have been confirmed.

"They remain inviolate and are members of the commis-

EDWARDS
Turn to Page 2A

### Dow Jones Averages

| (Noon N.Y.) | Avg. | Chg. |
|---|---|---|
| 30 Industrials | 858.88 | -4.79 |
| 20 Rails .... | 230.82 | -.49 |
| 15 Utilities . | 129.44 | -.48 |
| 65 Stocks .. | 304.86 | -1.28 |

Noon sales, 5,860,000 shares.

## Lost File Leads to GI's Death

A Stewart, Minn., Marine who was assigned to a Marine infantry unit because his records had been lost was one of two corps members from Minnesota killed last week in Vietnam.

The victims were:

**Pfc. Kenneth V. Goodman,** 20, son of Mr. and Mrs. Virgil Goodman, Stewart.

**Pfc. David C. Auge,** 18, son of George J. Auge, 97 E. Orme St., West St. Paul.

Goodman was a rocket specialist but had been given an infantry assignment, his mother said today, because the Marine Corps could not locate his service records when he arrived in Vietnam on Dec. 5.

He died of gunshot wounds suffered at Khe Sanh Valley just below the demilitarized zone last Wednesday, the Defense Department informed his parents.

A graduate of Stewart High School and a graduate in histology of the Medical Institute of Minnesota, Minneapolis, Goodman was interning in a Fergus Falls Hospital when he enlisted in the Marines last June 28.

Auge died of a fragmentation wound in the neck suffered while he was on patrol in Quang Tri Province, his father was informed.

Auge, who had volunteered for the Marines after he graduated from Humboldt High School in St. Paul last June, had been in Vietnam about two weeks, his father said.

## Plan for Hwy. 55 Work Would Take 100 Homes

By ABE ALTROWITZ
Minneapolis Star Staff Writer

A new plan for improvement of Hwy. 55 which would take out about 100 homes instead of about 21 acres of Minnehaha Park has been submitted to the Minnesota Highway Department, it was learned today.

Highway department officials estimated that the cost of removing the homes would be about $2.5 million. Highway department crews were sent into the area today to check the proposed routing.

The proposal, still in preliminary form, was outlined at a meeting of city and highway department officials Monday.

It was prepared by the San Francisco, Calif., firm of consultants—Eckbo, Dean, Austin and Williams — for the Minneapolis Park Board in its court fight to prevent the highway department from taking park land.

★ ★ ★ ★ ★ ★ ★ ★

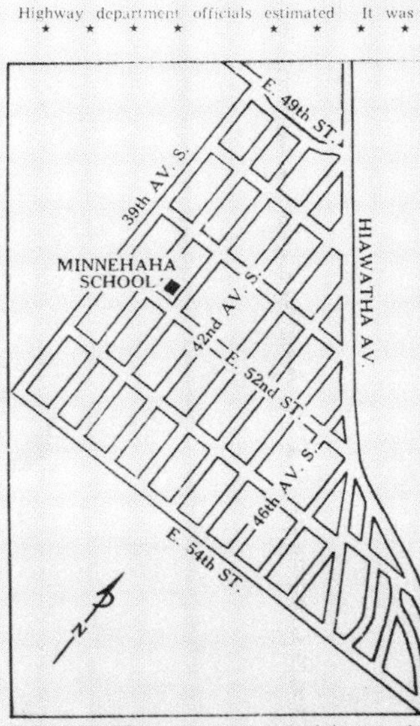


**FREEWAY AREA** — Above is a map of the area where a new routing of the Hiawatha Av. freeway is being offered by the Minneapolis Park Board to avoid taking some 21 acres from Minnehaha Park. The proposed highway would curve westward from Hiawatha Av. to a point equivalent to 37½ Av. S., in order to bypass the park. Park Board officials said they have not completed plans for the route but intend to have a completed proposal ready for a court hearing Monday.

Under provisions of the preliminary plan, houses would be taken out in area roughly bounded by Minnehaha Pkwy. on the north and 54th St. on the south. West of Hiawatha Av., the curved routing would extend to about a half block west of 38th Av. S., but the exact routing probably will not be completed until the end of the week.

The proposal, scheduled for completion this week, is to be presented to Hennepin District Judge John A. Weeks, who has been hearing testimony in the suit brought by the Minneapolis Park Board to prevent the highway department from taking a portion of Minnehaha Park.

Under the highway department plan, Hwy. 55 would cross what is the western edge of the park on an embankment rising from 18 to 25 feet in height.

In opposition to the highway department plan, Park Supt. Robert W. Ruhe has referred to highway programs as having been "for the most part engineered rather than designed."

The initial hearing of the Park Board lawsuit to block the highway department from

PARK
Turn to Page 4A

## Area Warm-up Won't Last Long

A little warmer weather is expected in the Twin Cities area tonight and Wednesday, but colder readings are expected to return late tomorrow.

The weather bureau predicted a high today of 25, a drop to 12 tonight, a high Wednesday of 30 and a low Wednesday night of zero.

Sub-zero readings were common in most of Minnesota today, with 17 below at Duluth the lowest temperature recorded in the contiguous 48 states. The Twin Cities area low was 2 below at 4:30 a.m.

**WORST EPIDEMIC**

SAN JUAN, Puerto Rico—(Reuters)—The Puerto Rican Health Department Monday reported the island's worst influenza epidemic — 35,358 cases since Jan. 1.

## Why the Cease-fire Ceased

### S. VIETS SAY:

SAIGON, South Vietnam—(Reuters)—The South Vietnamese government today released a statement asserting that allied forces were no longer bound by their cease-fire arrangements because of "premeditated and callous violation" by Communist units of their own declared truce.

The statement said: "In view of the premeditated and callous violation by North Vietnamese and Viet Cong units of their own declared cease-fire through wide-spread attacks on the civil popuplation and on South Vietnamese and allied military installations today, the Republic of Vietnam and its allies have instructed their armed forces to undertake all measures necessary to provide protection to both the civilian victims of these attacks and their own forces.

"To this end, the Republic of Vietnam and its allies have been forced to conclude that they are no longer bound by the cease-fire order which was in effect."

### N. VIETS SAY:

HONG KONG — (Reuters) — North Vietnam said the new attack today on Da Nang was launched "to punish the U.S. aggressors and their henchmen for unilaterally canceling their own cease-fire."

The North Vietnam News Agency monitored here said the attacks dealt a telling blow at the U.S. aggressors "who insolently slighted the traditional lunar new year festival of the Vietnamese people."

It said the Viet Cong attacks were also to punish the United States for sending planes from the Da Nang base to attack Vietnamese people in many parts of the country."

"The United States-puppet (South Vietnam government) Tet truce cancellation has laid bare to public opinion at home and abroad the bloodthirsty and obdurate nature of the United States aggressors on the one hand and shown their embarrassment on the other," the agency said in another article attacking the truce cancellation.

## Hippie Employes 'Invade' Post Office

★ ★ ★ ★

BIZARRE IMAGE IS FEARED

By LOUIS CASSELS

WASHINGTON, D.C. — (UPI) — The Post Office Department is drafting new regulations to insure that its swift couriers do not make their appointed rounds in unkempt beards, psychedelic beads and bare feet.

The regulations are necessary, assistant postmaster general Richard Murphy said in an interview, to cope with a hippie invasion of the postal service.

It started in San Francisco and is still centered there. But postal officials fear it may spread and give the whole service a bizarre image.

Murphy, who recently returned from a personal inspection of the San Francisco Post Office, said he was greatly distressed by some of the "fantastic getups" which he saw being worn by letter carriers and postal clerks.

"Some of the men had hair down to their shoulders," he said with a grimace. "They were wearing everything from bearskin coats to dungarees. Some wore sandals, and some simply went barefoot."

"I think it is highly inappropriate for a representative of the United States government to appear before the public in such attire."

Why does the post office hire them for mailmen?

The answer, Murphy said, is that postmasters are hemmed in by numerous laws and regulations de-

POSTAL
Turn to Page 2A

## Vikings Draft Yary as Bonus Selection

*Details: Page 1D*

## Twin Citizens Favor Uniform Teacher Salaries

*Metro-Poll: Page 1B*

## MINNEAPOLIS FAMILIES SMACK LIPS OVER STEAK

*Marcia Black's report: Page 5C*



STAR TELEPHONES
NEWS, GENERAL 372-4141
CIRCULATION 372-4343
WANT ADS 372-4242

Warmer
THURSDAY'S TEMPERATURES
Details Page 16 *Unofficial

# The Minneapolis Tribune

FRIDAY

Vol. CI—No. 317 Copyright 1968 Minneapolis Star and Tribune Company MINNEAPOLIS, MINN., FRIDAY, APRIL 5, 1968 ★★ Single Copy Price 10¢ Lower Price for Carrier Delivery



# MEMPHIS SNIPER KILLS DR. KING

## LBJ Postpones War-Review Trip to Hawaii Until Today

## President Asks End of Violence

By RICHARD P. KLEEMAN and CHARLES W. BAILEY
Minneapolis Tribune Staff Correspondents

WASHINGTON, D.C. — A grim President Johnson appealed for peace and understanding from a nation he called "shocked and saddened" Thursday at the assassination of the Rev. Dr. Martin Luther King Jr.

"I ask every citizen to reject the blind violence that has struck Dr. King, who lived by nonviolence," Mr. Johnson said in a brief statement he delivered in person to newsmen gathered in the White House west wing.

Mr. Johnson postponed until today his departure for Hawaii for a review of the Vietnam war and canceled plans for a breakfast in California this morning with former President Dwight D. Eisenhower.

**THE PRESIDENT** also canceled plans to appear at a Democratic fund-raising dinner here last night, at which Vice-President Hubert H. Humphrey announced the news of Dr. King's death.

The President received the news of the murder in Memphis as he met in his office with Llewellyn E. Thompson, U.S. ambassador to Moscow and one of the two men Mr. Johnson designated Sunday to be ready to negotiate with representatives of North Vietnam.

Less than two hours after word of the assassination was flashed over newswires, Mr. Johnson, striding rapidly and looking straight ahead, stepped to the battery of microphones in the White House press headquarters and delivered the following statement over nationwide television:

"America is shocked and saddened by the brutal slaying tonight of Dr. Martin Luther King. I ask every citizen to reject the blind violence that has struck Dr. King who lived by nonviolence.

**"I PRAY** that his family can find comfort in the memory of all he tried to do for the land he loved so well.

"I have just conveyed the sympathy of Mrs. Johnson and myself to his widow, Mrs. King.

"I know that every American of good will joins me in mourning the death of this outstanding leader and praying for peace and understanding throughout this land.

"We can achieve nothing by lawlessness and divisiveness by the American people. It is only by joining together and only by working together that we can continue to move toward equality and fulfillment for all of our people.

"I hope that all Americans will search their hearts as they ponder this most tragic incident.

"I have canceled my plans for the evening. I am postponing my trip to Hawaii until tomorrow. Thank you."

A White House press spokesman said Mr. Johnson reached Mrs. King by telephone while she was still at her Atlanta, Ga., home.

(At the Washington headquarters of the Poor People's March on Washington, which Dr. King was to have led on April 22, a spokesman said there would be no immediate statement about future plans. "Everything here is confusion tonight," the spokesman said.)

In Hawaii, Mr. Johnson will confer with President Korea as well as U.S. military and diplomatic officials from Vietnam. The meeting with Park will be focused on developments in Korea since

Trip
Continued on Page 12

Associated Press
THE LORRAINE MOTEL IN MEMPHIS WAS FILLED WITH POLICE AFTER ASSASSINATION
*Dr. King was standing on the second-floor balcony when bullet struck him*

## Rights Leader Shot at Motel

New York Times Service

MEMPHIS, Tenn. — The Rev. Dr. Martin Luther King Jr., world-famed Negro civil rights leader, was fatally shot here Thursday night while leaning over a second-floor railing outside his motel room.

DR. KING
*Killed in Memphis*

Four thousand National Guard troops were ordered into Memphis by Gov. Buford Ellington after Dr. King's death. A curfew was imposed on the city of 550,000 inhabitants, about 40 per cent of whom are Negro.

The death of the 39-year-old recipient of the Nobel Peace Prize was reported by Frank Holloman, director of Memphis police and fire departments, after Dr. King had been taken to St. Joseph's Hospital.

**"I AND ALL** the citizens of Memphis," Holloman said, "regret the murder of Dr. King and all resources at our and the state's command will be used to apprehend the person or persons responsible."

Holloman said the assassin might have been a white man who was "50 to 100 yards away in a flophouse."

Police broadcast an alarm for "a young white male, dark-haired, well dressed" who was reported to have rushed out of a building across the street and who might have dropped a Browning automatic rifle with a telescopic sight before leaping into a car.

Later they reported that two persons had been picked up several blocks from the scene of the shooting, but added they still had no definite leads.

In a television broadcast after the curfew was ordered, Holloman said, "Rioting has broken out in parts of the city." He asserted, "Looting is rampent."

Dr. King had been bleeding profusely from what appeared to be a huge wound in the right jaw or neck area as he lay face up on the concrete walkway before he was taken away in a fire department ambulance.

**HIS EYES** appeared first half-closed and then open but staring.

Dr. King had come back to Memphis Wednesday morning to organize support once again for 1,300 sanitation workers who have been on strike since Lincoln's birthday.

Just a week ago he led a march on behalf of the strikers that ended in violence with a 16-year-old Negro killed, 62 persons injured and 200 arrested.

**POLICE POURED** into the area around the Lorraine Mo-

Dr. King
Continued on Page Four

Other Dispatches, Pictures --Pages 4, 5

VOICE DISMAY, ANGER

## Leaders in State Mourn Dr. King

By DICK CUNNINGHAM
Minneapolis Tribune Staff Writer

"How do you answer the people who said nonviolence was no use in the first place?" asked a young Negro advertising man in Minneapolis.

"The last disciple of peace, goodwill and nonviolence is dead," said **Samuel Richardson,** president of the Minneapolis branch of the National Association for the Advancement of Colored People (NAACP).

Richardson was overwhelmed by the news of the murder of the Rev. Dr. Martin Luther King as were other Minneapolitans involved in race relations.

**Lillian Anthony,** director of the city's new Civil Rights Department, wept at the news.

"I can't talk now. I just can't," she said.

The anger with which many Negroes reacted was verbalized by William W. Smith, a community organization consultant now associated with Twin Cities Opportunities Industrialization Center (TCOIC).

"The nonviolent concept evidently cannot succeed in the United States because of the predominance of violence as a means of settling issues.

"Obviously black folks are not supposed to have leaders who can champion causes in an aggressive, militant and honest manner.

"But America should be advised that no longer are we going to sit back and let our leaders commit suicide by daring to represent our causes. We are going to protect them in more meaningful ways."

Two of Minnesota's congressmen heard the news

Local
Continued on Page Four

**Muskies Lose to Pittsburgh, 125 to 117**

•

**Twins Defeat Houston, 3 to 1**

•

**Los Angeles Tips North Stars 2 to 1**

•

*(Details in Sports Section)*

AFTER ASSASSINATION

## Violence, Looting Erupt in North, South

From The Tribune's Wire Services

Violence and looting were reported Thursday night in several cities — both North and South — in apparent reaction to the assassination of the Rev. Dr. Martin Luther King Jr. in Memphis, Tenn.

Two policemen were reported shot in Memphis, and state troopers and National Guardsmen were sent in to help restore order. The soldiers had been released a few days ago after quelling violence that left one dead and 62 injured last week.

**SPORADIC LOOTING** and rock-throwing broke out in Harlem and Bedford - Stuyvesant, New York City's two largest Negro areas, last night as news spread of the assassination. Looters set a fire in a store and battled firemen trying to put it out.

Several other stores in the area were looted.

Mayor John V. Lindsay sped to Harlem to help calm angry youths. Police ordered 7,000 men, due off duty at midnight, to remain on the city's streets.

In Bedford - Stuyvesant, youths stopped a city bus and pelted it with rocks and bottles. None of the 30 passengers, almost all of whom were Negro, appeared hurt.

A crowd of about 100, screaming "Yeah, man!" and "Get whitey!" watched as about 30 youths began pulling merchandise out of John's Bargain Store.

**THEN THEY** set the fire and battled the firemen who, in turn, turned their hoses on the youths.

About 4,000 Tennessee National Guardsmen were ordered to duty in Nashville, Tenn., as scattered violence occurred.

The order was issued after groups of Negroes began

Violence
Continued on Page Five

## Humphrey Cuts Short Party Dinner

By FRANK WRIGHT
Minneapolis Tribune Staff Correspondent

WASHINGTON, D.C. — Vice-President Hubert Humphrey, grim-faced and saddened by the assassination of the Rev. Dr. Martin Luther King Jr., Thursday night cut short a huge Democratic fund-raising dinner out of respect for the fallen Negro leader.

Some 3,000 party people overflowing the ballroom of the Washington Hilton Hotel, had paid $250 a plate to attend the annual affair, which raised an estimated $700,000 for Democratic Congressional campaigns in this fall's elections.

Many of those in the audience had come in the hope of hearing Humphrey, the featured speaker, use the occasion to announce his candidacy for president.

**THERE ALSO** had been hints that President Johnson, who has announced he will not run again, might attend. It would have been his first appearance at a political gathering since his announcement stunned the country Sunday night.

But Mr. Johnson, when he heard of Dr. King's death, canceled out.

And Humphrey confined

Humphrey
Continued on Page 13

## Warm-up Is Predicted for Region

Warmer weather is forecast for the Upper Midwest today and this weekend, following a spring storm which struck large portions of North Dakota, South Dakota and Minnesota.

**Weekend Weather Outlook**

A high today of 45 is predicted for the Twin Cities, with a low tonight of 30. Precipitation probabilities are near zero today. Winds will be from the south at 5 to 12 miles per hour.

Predicted regional highs: Minnesota 34 to 46; Wisconsin, in the 40s; North Dakota, 42 to 54; South Dakota, 42 to 56.

**HIGHWAYS**

A storm which hit the Upper Midwest Wednesday and early Thursday left highways in slippery condition in northwestern Minnesota, northeastern and eastern North Dakota and much of South Dakota.

No highways in the region were reported closed.

All Minnesota roads north and west of a line from Pipestone to Duluth, generally were covered with ice or compacted snow yesterday. A reduction in speed of 10 to 30 miles an hour was recommended in the Pipestone, Brainerd and Duluth areas.

Highways in the southeastern part of Minnesota generally were clear, with scattered slippery spots.

Roads were icy in the northeast corner of North Dakota. Scattered icy spots were reported along the eastern edge of the state in the Fargo area. The rest of North Dakota's highways were in generally good condition.

In South Dakota, slippery

Outlook
Continued on Page 12

**Dr. Martin Luther King Jr. lived with the threat of death for many years. He was not unaware of the threat and, on occasion, commented upon it:**

In 1958, after he was stabbed by a demented woman in Harlem:

***"The pathetic aspect of this experience is not the injury to one individual. It demonstrates that a climate of hatred and bitterness so permeates areas of our nation that inevitably deeds of extreme violence must erupt. Today it was I. Tomorrow it could be another leader or any man, woman or child, who will be the victim of lawlessness and brutality."***

In an Albany, Ga., church in 1962 after shots were fired in nearby houses:

***"It may get me crucified. I may even die. But I want it said even if I die in the struggle that 'He died to make me free.'"***

On the death of black nationalist Malcolm X in 1965:

***"I have learned to face threats on my life philosophically and have prepared myself for anything that might come."***

And, finally, in an impromptu speech to 2,000 persons in Memphis Wednesday night:

***"Like anybody, I would like to live a long life. Longevity has its place, but I'm not concerned about that now. I just want to do God's will and he has allowed me to go up the mountain and I've seen the Promised Land. I may not get there with you but I want you to know tonight that we as a people will get to the Promised Land.***

## Shame Marks Reactions to Death of Rights Leader

From The Tribune's Wire Services

Dismay and shame mingled with anger, and an air of forboding pervaded the reactions across the country Thursday night to the murder of the Rev. Dr. Martin Luther King Jr.

From the high offices of state to the man in the street, news of the moderate civil rights leader's violent death in Memphis, Tenn., drew, for the most part, stunned and sober statements.

Some Negro militants responded angrily, although most major Negro organizations and Negro leaders, lamenting Dr. King's death, expressed hope that it would spur others to carry on in his spirit of nonviolence.

Roy Wilkins, executive director of the National Association for the Advancement of Colored People, said his organization was "shocked and deeply grieved."

"Dr. King was a symbol of the nonviolent civil rights protest movement. He was a man of peace, of dedication, of great courage. His senseless assassination solves nothing. It will not stay the civil rights movement; it will instead spur it to greater activity. It is to be hoped that this tragedy will help move the American people to prompt action to expunge racism from our national life. If such action is taken forthwith, the sacrifice of this great and good man will not have been in vain."

**Sen. Edward Brooke,** R-Mass., declared: "In our anguish and bitterness of this awful event, we must not lose sight of the mean-

Reaction
Continued on Page Five

Associated Press
REV. ANDREW YOUNG SHOWED WHERE SHOT HIT
*Aide of Dr. King was waiting in hospital*

## Rockefeller Still Candidate, His Brother Says

LITTLE ROCK, Ark.—(AP)—Gov. Winthrop Rockefeller of Arkansas said Thursday his brother, New York Gov. Nelson A. Rockefeller, had told him he was still a candidate for the Republican presidential nomination.

Although the New York governor said after the New Hampshire primary that he would enter no primaries to actively seek delegate votes, "He told me he thought he made it clear that he is a candidate," Winthrop Rockefeller told newsmen.

The Arkansas governor said there was confusion over his brother's status because of his post-New Hampshire announcement, but he indicated the New York governor would clarify his position within three days.

"I think you'll find Nelson will be active this summer," Rockefeller said.

The Minneapolis Tribune 1867 - 1967 100 YEARS OF SERVICE Centennial

**Ever Seen an Egg Scale?**

*Hens were once so scarce in Hennepin County that eggs for sale were weighed individually. At the Hennepin Historical Museum there is a scale once used for that purpose, along with much other curiosa from the early days of the county. Ben Kern visited the museum, and shares his discoveries in his 'your weekend' column, on PAGE 19.*

TURN THE PAGES TO:

• • • •



Tribune Telephones: News, General . . .372-4141; Want Ads . . . . . . .372-4242; Circulation . . . . . .372-4343

**Warm**

WEDNESDAY'S TEMPERATURE

| | | | | | |
|---|---|---|---|---|---|
| 2 a.m. | 78 | 10 a.m. | 81 | 6 p.m. | 88 |
| 3 a.m. | 74 | 11 a.m. | 84 | 7 p.m. | 87 |
| 4 a.m. | 73 | Noon | 86 | 8 p.m. | 85 |
| 5 a.m. | 72 | 1 p.m. | 88 | 9 p.m. | 82 |
| 6 a.m. | 70 | 2 p.m. | 87 | 10 p.m. | 81 |
| 7 a.m. | 74 | 3 p.m. | 87 | 11 p.m. | 79 |
| 8 a.m. | 76 | 4 p.m. | 89 | 12 p.m. | 78 |
| 9 a.m. | 79 | 5 p.m. | 90 | 1 a.m. | 77* |

Details Page 10 *Unofficial

# The Minneapolis Tribune

THURSDAY

Vol. CII—No. 13


MINNEAPOLIS, MINN., THURSDAY, JUNE 6, 1968 ★ Single Copy Price 10¢ Lower Price for Carrier Delivery


# Kennedy Remains Near Death From Bullet Wound in Brain

## Other News Inside:



## Jordanian Identified as Suspect

### Mayor Yorty Tells Contents of Notebook

LOS ANGELES, Calif. (AP)—The man who shot Sen. Robert F. Kennedy was identified Wednesday as Sirhan Bishara Sirhan, 24, a Jordanian from Jerusalem who recently has been living in Pasadena, Calif.

Los Angeles Mayor Samuel Yorty and Police Chief Thomas Reddin told a press conference Sirhan lived with a brother, Munir (Joe) Sirhan, Pasadena, a department store employe.

**THEY SAID** identification was made through Joe and another brother, Adel, who were traced through the .22-caliber pistol used in the shooting. It had passed through many hands.

Yorty said a notebook apparently belonging to Sirhan mentions "the necessity to assassinate Sen. Kennedy before June 5, 1968."

Yorty's statements were contained in a copyrighted interview with Radio News International.

"There's much scribbing, repeated phrases, many references to Sen. Robert Kennedy . . . They're not very clear but there's a direct reference to the necessity to assassinate Sen. Kennedy before June 5, 1968," Yorty said.

"I don't know why. He does a lot of writing, pro-Communist and anti-capitalist, anti-United States. Evidently he was quite pro-Arab in the Arab-Israeli matter. He has 'Long live Nasser' written in there. And he said he favors communism of all types, whether Russian, Chinese and so forth," said the mayor.

**OFFICIALS** of the Southern California Chapter of the American Civil Liberties Union (ACLU) said Yorty's revelation was "to be regretted" and could prejudice Sirhan's chance for a fair trial.

A. L. Wirin, chief ACLU counsel, said, "With the exception of the statement attributed to Mayor Yorty, the response of public officials and the press has been commendable."

Sirhan has requested that the ACLU help him secure private counsel of his own choosing, and the ACLU has agreed to do so.

This was disclosed late

Suspect
Continued on Page 11

## Shooting Puts Campaign in Chaotic State

By TOM WICKER
New York Times Service

**Analysis: WHAT THE NEWS MEANS**

WASHINGTON, D.C.—The shooting of Sen. Robert F. Kennedy left the 1968 presidential campaign in a state of uncertainty Wednesday, with nothing sure but that it had been transformed.

The vital political question was the same as the source of the personal suspense at Good Samaritan Hospital. Could Kennedy recover without permanent damage from so extensive an injury to the brain as he apparently suffered?

**IN THE ABSENCE** of any conclusive evidence on that point, all the presidential candidates immediately suspended political activity. Their motive was personal respect for Kennedy and his family; yet, their action reflected the fact that none could be sure how to proceed anyway.

Even if Kennedy were to make a complete recovery, for instance, there appeared to be great doubt that it could be rapid enough for him to return to the 1968 campaign.

If he did recover so quickly, on the other hand, his whole personal and political situation would be something entirely different from what it was before the attempt on his life.

**THUS,** for the third—and most harrowing — time, a shock wave of unexpected events has completely altered the shape of the 1968 campaign.

The first came March 12 when Sen. Eugene McCarthy of Minnesota won 42 per cent of the Democratic vote in the New Hampshire primary, and Kennedy immediately thereafter became an active candidate.

The second transformation occurred March 21, when

Campaign
Continued on Page 12

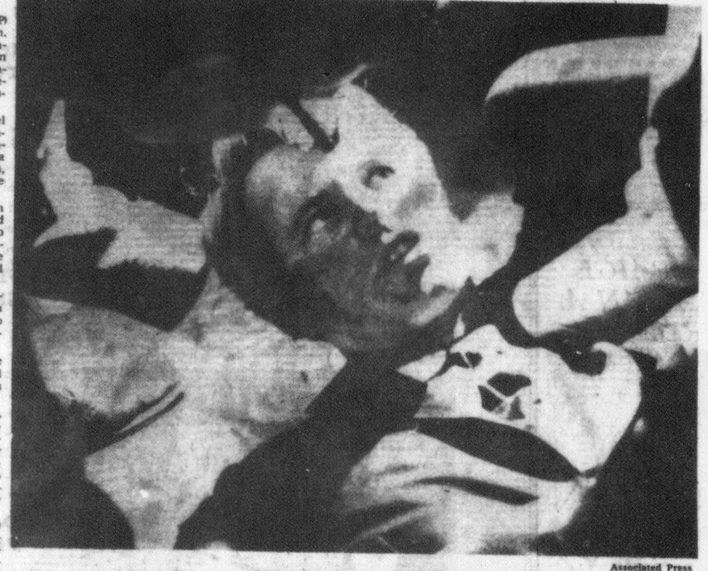

Associated Press

KENNEDY LAY CRITICALLY WOUNDED AFTER BEING SHOT THREE TIMES
*He was wounded near his right ear, in the shoulder and across his forehead*

## Kin on Way to Los Angeles

By CHARLES W. BAILEY
Chief of the Minneapolis Tribune Washington Bureau

LOS ANGELES, Calif. — Sen. Robert F. Kennedy remained at the edge of death Wednesday after an assailant fired a .22-caliber bullet into his brain at close range.

A 24-year-old Los Angeles man, described by officials as a native of Jordan now living permanently in this country, was held by Los Angeles police on six counts of assault with intent to murder.

The suspect, Sirhan Bishara Sirhan, was seized at the scene of the shooting within seconds after the shots were fired.

Surgeons worked for 3 hours and 40 minutes early yesterday to remove bullet fragments from Kennedy's brain after he was shot in a hotel kitchen corridor about 2.15 a.m. (Minneapolis time).

His condition was described by doctors yesterday as "extremely critical as to life." Kennedy, who was shot just after he completed a speech following his victory in the California presidential primary Tuesday, remained in a coma.

A medical bulletin issued at 8 p.m. Minneapolis time said: "The team of physicians attending Sen. Robert Kennedy is concerned over his continuing failure to show improvement over this post-operative period. Sen. Kennedy's condition is still described as extremely critical as to life."

Frank Mankiewicz, Kennedy's press secr''ary, underlined the gravity of the senator's condition by adding that there would be no further "regular" medical bulletins until early morning today.

His emphasis on "regular" made clear his fear that he might have to make some emergency announcement before dawn.

Immediate relatives were converging on Los Angeles from the East Coast and Europe.

Mrs. John F. Kennedy, widow of the president, flew to Los Angeles by private jet to join other members of the Kennedy family. She visited the hospital, where her entrance was slowed by a crowd of about 200 gathered outside.

Mrs. Martin Luther King, widow of another assassinated leader, also paid a short visit to the hospital.

**THE ATTEMPTED** murder threw the nation and its political processes into a state of deep shock.

Sen. Eugene J. McCarthy, D-Minn., Vice-President Hubert H. Humphrey and other presidential candidates immediately suspended all campaign activity and headed for Washington, D.C.

President Johnson, awakened early yesterday to be told of the shooting, immediately ordered the FBI to enter the case under authority of federal voting rights laws. Mr. Johnson also ordered the Secret Service to assign agents to protect all

Kennedy
Continued on Page 11

## LBJ Selects Commission on Violence

By JACK WILSON
Minneapolis Tribune Staff Correspondent

WASHINGTON, D.C. — President Johnson told the nation Wednesday night that he shared its feeling of bafflement and anger at the shooting of Sen. Robert F. Kennedy and the mindless violence and hatred that lay behind it.

*(TEXT—Page 35.)*

In an unannounced nationwide television talk, the President disclosed that he was appointing a commission of prominent persons "to look into the causes and the ways of controlling physical violence across the country."

**THE GROUP** will be headed by Dr. Milton Eisenhower of Johns Hopkins University.

But the creation of the commission was almost an incidental formality.

Mr. Johnson's principal aim was to try to rally the people of the United States to the realization of the degree to which violence has become a major factor of today's life.

"The country faces the consequences of lawlessness and hatred," he said. "It would be wrong to ignore it.

**"IT WOULD** be just as wrong to assume that the country is sick. Two hundred million Americans did not strike down Robert F. Kennedy. But in the climate of extremism and contempt for law, violence may bring down the best among us."

Mr. Johnson did not recommend any course of action to counter the trend, although he did again talk about the "insane traffic in guns" of which he has repeatedly warned in the past.

Significantly, he spoke a few hours after Congress had virtually assured pas-

President
Continued on Page 11

## 'I Looked and My Heart Broke'

### HE ACCOMPANIED VICTIM TO HOSPITAL

By WARREN ROGERS


*EDITOR'S NOTE: Warren Rogers was there when Sen. Robert F. Kennedy was shot. He was the only reporter to stay with the senator and his wife after they left the scene of the shooting. He rode in the ambulance with them to Central Receiving Hospital. Rogers is chief of the Washington Bureau of Look magazine.*

LOS ANGELES, Calif.—It sounded like firecrackers. Why is it that it always sounds like firecrackers?

Other eyewitnesses reported five and six shots, but I heard only four: Pop, a one-second pause, and then pop, pop, pop.

I was in the small conference room with a couple of dozen other newsmen, waiting for Sen. Robert Kennedy to come in for a question-and-answer session.

He was in the nearby Embassy Ballroom of the Ambassador Hotel, making his way through a narrow, cave-like kitchen corridor connecting the two rooms.

We were chatting, writer Budd Schulberg and his wife, Geraldine, and I. Minutes before, the three of us had been talking with Kennedy in the hotel's fifth-floor Royal Suite, the senator's headquarters.

The Schulbergs, who had campaigned hard for Kennedy, were jubilant. We laughed at the howling happy supporters in the ballroom, whooping it up for the senator's victory speech.

We were watching them on TV, but with our eyes cut to the big swinging doors through which we expected him to enter momentarily.

**AT THE SHOTS,** my first thought was that firecrackers were a stupid, tasteless way to celebrate. But in the next second I was running through the doors.

I banged into a wave of people, mostly young girls. They screamed, "He's shot! He's shot! Get a doctor."

And then I stumbled

Scene
Continued on Page Five

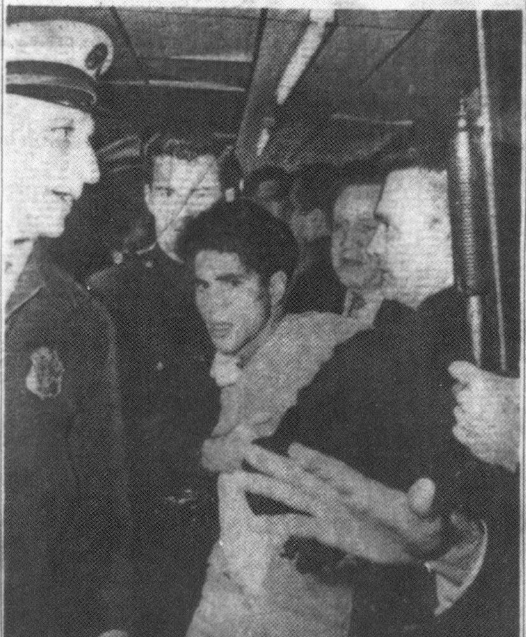

United Press International

POLICE LED SUSPECT AWAY FROM SHOOTING SCENE
*When questioned, he refused to discuss the incident*

## New Anticrime Bill Is Likely to Pass

By JACK WILSON
Minneapolis Tribune Staff Correspondent

WASHINGTON, D.C. — The House of Representatives responded Wednesday to the shooting of Sen. Robert F. Kennedy by virtually assuring passage of an anti-crime bill that has been in the works since last August.

It rejected, by a 60 to 317 vote, a motion by Rep. Emanuel Celler, D-N.Y., to turn down the Senate version and send the bill to a Senate-House conference committee for extensive rewriting.

Celler

Today it will vote on an alternative motion to accept the bill, with the wire tapping and gun control features and the provisions to curb the Supreme Court, which the Senate had attached to the bill that passed the House last August. That bill would merely have authorized federal aid for local police forces.

**IN VIEW** of the decisive vote against Celler's motion, the House appeared almost certain to accept the measure and send it to the White House.

Although President Johnson has urged adoption of a bill to control crime in the streets, and had asked for gun control legislation, there was no assurance that he would accept the revised measure.

In its present form, the bill is designed principally to set aside Supreme Court decisions limiting the authority of police to question suspects and take confessions from them without giving them the right to have a lawyer present. It also would

Crime
Continued on Page 12

## Almanac

### He Probably Won't Stand in Line, Either

*Thursday, June 6, 1968*
158th day. 208 to go this year
Sunrise 5:28 a.m.; sunset 8:56 p.m.

A University of Minnesota student who recently returned from military service in Vietnam had developed the habit of walking into his English class about 20 minutes late.

This practice continued daily for the first couple weeks of the quarter. The instructor finally decided it was time to bring it to the fellow's attention.

"Tell me," the instructor began, as the man's appearance again interrupted the class, "what did they say in the Army when you sauntered into meetings late?"

The student, a former captain, replied, "Most of the time they just stood up and said 'Good Morning, Sir.'"

## TODAY ON THE INSIDE:

### North Side Park Sites

*Low-income and minority race families are getting five new parks on the North Side. Read a Tribune staff writer's report on Wednesday's action by the Minneapolis Park Board in consultation with Pilot City and school officials. It's on*

Page 13

## TURN THE PAGES TO:



Tribune Telephones
News, General ...372-4141
Want Ads .......372-4242
Circulation ......372-4343

## More Warm, Humid Weather Seen for Area

Partly cloudy and continued warm, humid weather is forecast for the Twin Cities today and Friday, with a chance of thundershowers tonight and tomorrow. A high today of 90 and low of 68 are predicted.

Scattered thundershowers and little temperature change are also forecast elsewhere in Minnesota, and in North Dakota and South Dakota into Friday.

Predicted regional highs: Minnesota, 72 north, 90 south; North Dakota, 62, northwest, 82 southeast; South Dakota, 65, northwest to 90 southeast; Wisconsin, northwest 8[illegible] and 88 to 93 elsewhere.

Hot

TUESDAY'S TEMPERATURES

| | | | | | |
|---|---|---|---|---|---|
| 2 a.m. | 65 | 10 a.m. | 74 | 6 p.m. | 88 |
| 3 a.m. | 64 | 11 a.m. | 79 | 7 p.m. | 86 |
| 4 a.m. | 63 | Noon | 84 | 8 p.m. | 82 |
| 5 a.m. | 62 | 1 p.m. | 85 | 9 p.m. | 81 |
| 6 a.m. | 63 | 2 p.m. | 88 | 10 p.m. | 78 |
| 7 a.m. | 61 | 3 p.m. | 89 | 11 p.m. | 78 |
| 8 a.m. | 66 | 4 p.m. | 90 | Midnight | 77 |
| 9 a.m. | 70 | 5 p.m. | 89 | *1 a.m. | 76 |

*Details Page 21* *Unofficial

# The Minneapolis Tribune

WEDNESDAY

Vol. CII—No. 89 Copyright 1968 Minneapolis Star and Tribune Company MINNEAPOLIS, MINN., WEDNESDAY, AUGUST 21, 1968 Single Copy Price 10¢ Lower Price for Carrier Delivery



# Russ Bloc Invades Czechoslovakia

## *Little Fighting Reported as Main Cities Seized*

## LBJ Calls Security Advisers, Orders Talks With Russians

By CHARLES W. BAILEY
Chief of the Minneapolis Tribune Washington Bureau

WASHINGTON, D.C. — President Johnson called the National Security Council (NSC) into emergency session Tuesday night on the latest Soviet - Czechoslovakian crisis and then ordered the State Department to confer at once with the top Russian diplomat in the United States.

The chief executive summoned his advisers only minutes after Anatoly Dobrynin, Soviet ambassador to the United States, had paid a secret personal visit to Mr. Johnson to inform him of the latest Soviet move against the rebellious Czech government.

Dobrynin's back - door White House call—an unprecedented move for a Soviet envoy here in a major international crisis — had given Mr. Johnson his first word of the movement of Russian troops across the Czech border.

**WHITE HOUSE** spokesmen declined to confirm this, but The Minneapolis Tribune learned that Dobrynin was in fact the first to bring word of the situation to the President.

By 10:15 p.m. (Washington time)—little more than an hour after Prague Radio had told the world that Soviet, East German, Polish, Hungarian and Bulgarian troops had crossed the border—the NSC was in its first night crisis session since the Arab-Israeli war early in June 1967.

After the meetings, which lasted a few minutes less than an hour, presidential press secretary George Christian made this brief announcement:

"The President convened a meeting of the National Security Council at 10:15 tonight to consider the situation in Czechoslovakia.

"**THE PRESIDENT** informed the NSC on a message on the subject he had received from Ambassador Dobrynin earlier in the evening."

"After reviewing such information as was available, the President asked the Secretary of State to call in Ambassador Dobrynin tonight and to discuss the matter further.

"That is the only statement I have this evening on the matter."

Christian declined to answer questions on other aspects of the situation. He did not respond to queries about the possibility that American troops stationed in West Germany would be placed on alert.

**THE PRESS** secretary identified those at the meeting, in addition to the President and Vice-President Hubert H. Humphrey as:

Secretary of State Dean Rusk; Defense Secretary Clark Clifford; Richard Helms, director of the Central Intelligence Agency; Gen. Earl G. Wheeler, chairman

Council
Continued on Page Six

## Russian Move Transforms Politics Again

By JAMES RESTON
New York Times Service

**Analysis: WHAT THE NEWS MEANS**

NEW YORK, N.Y. — The Soviet invasion of Czechoslovakia has transformed world and American politics.

It took place in the middle of the American presidential election of 1968, as the Soviet invasion of Hungary took place during the Eisenhower-Stevenson presidential election of 1956. The Russians moved on Prague while the United States was preoccupied in Vietnam, as they moved on Budapest in 1956 while the British and French were preoccupied with the invasion of Suez, and the latest move by Moscow startled Washington just as officials there were convening on new moves to reach an understanding with the Soviet Union on Vietnam.

Washington was prepared for a dramatic move by the Soviet Union against the new liberal regime in Prague, but not for anything quite so bold as an invasion by the Red army. It had been observing closely the increasingly violent attacks on the Czech government in the Soviet press, and Undersecretary of State Charles E. Bohlen, former U.S. ambassador to the Soviet Union and

Analysis
Continued on Page 10

## Prague Issues Denunciation

From The Tribune's Wire Services

PRAGUE, Czechoslovakia—Soviet, Polish, East German, Hungarian and Bulgarian troops, tanks and planes invaded Czechoslovakia Tuesday night

Western travelers fleeing the East bloc nation said the invaders seized control of Prague and other Czechoslovak cities and towns.

The Soviets announced they acted to save communism in Czechoslovakia from "counterrevolutionary forces."

Shots were fired from windows of the Centeral Committee building shortly after dawn today when a crowd of several hundred young Czechoslovaks marched on the building shouting, "Out with the Russians."

**PRAGUE RADIO** said early today that the invaders came without the knowledge or permission of Czechoslovak party or government officials. It broadcast an official Czech denunciation of the invasion, but asked the nation "not to offer resistance."

Travelers reaching West Germany said Soviet bloc tanks and troops quickly occupied not only Prague but such key towns as Cheb and Pilsen. They said invading tanks and troops lined the highways and "great numbers" of Soviet jet fighters landed in Prague airport.

In Moscow, Tass said the Soviets acted "to meet the request for rendering necessary help to the fraternal Czechoslovak people . . . This decision is also in line with vital interests of our countries in safeguarding European peace against forces of militarism, aggression and revanchism which have more than once plunged the people of Europe into wars."

**TASS SAID** the forces of the five invading powers would be "immediately withdrawn" as soon as the threat to communism in Czechoslovakia and the East bloc was eliminated "and the lawful authorities find the further presence of these armed units there is no longer necessary."

It was the same reason Moscow gave for the Soviet crushing of the 1956 Hungarian uprising.

The Soviet bloc forces — acting after three months of vain Kremlin diplomatic pressure against Czechoslovak reforms — moved with lightening speed.

Five hours after Russian tanks first smashed across the Czechoslovak frontier, Prague Radio fell silent.

**THE RADIO** had been broadcasting invasion reports steadily. Then at 4:40 a.m. (10:40 p.m. CDT), after a time check, a Prague Radio

Czech
Continued on Page Six

Minneapolis Tribune Photo by Mike Zerby

WITH A GROUP OF SUPPORTERS AT HIS BACK, JOHN RICHTER SPOKE TO CITY ALDERMEN
*In return for $800,000 per year to support the airport, all the taxpayers get is noise, he said*

AT PLATFORM HEARING

## Czech Invasion Interrupts Rusk

By FRANK WRIGHT
Minneapolis Tribune Staff Correspondent

WASHINGTON, D.C.—The news of the invasion of Czechoslovakia disrupted Secretary of State Dean Rusk's testimony before the Democratic Platform Committee Tuesday night.

The invasion also cast a new pall over the already slender chances of peace forces led by Sen. Eugene McCarthy of Minnesota and Sen. George McGovern of South Dakota to wrest the party's presidential nomination from Vice-President Hubert Humphrey or to influence the party's platform when the Democratic national convention meets in Chicago, Ill., next week.

Word that Russian troops had crossed the Czech border was announced by Chairman Hale Boggs as Rusk completed a 20-minute defense of President Johnson's Vietnam war policies.

**COUNTERING** a mounting pile of testimony from critics, Rusk had urged the administration-controlled committee to draft a Vietnam plank that spoke only in general terms and did not spell out specific terms for settling the war.

As some of those critics on the committee sought to question the secretary, Boggs made his announcement. Rusk excused himself, apologized and left immediately.

"I think I ought to go see what this is all about," he said.

Boggs, House majority whip from Louisiana, had received word of the Czechoslovakian development from reporters just as Rusk was endorsing collective security agreements as a means of

Platform
Continued on Page Six

## Mississippi Delegation Is Barred

By BERNIE SHELLUM
Minneapolis Tribune Staff Writer

CHICAGO, Ill. — The Credentials Committee voted, 84 to 10, Tuesday night to bar the regular Mississippi delegation to the Democratic national convention and to seat a racially balanced delegation elected by a new political coalition.

It was the only one of five challenged delegations whose cases have been reviewed by the 110-member committee to be ousted. Delegations from four other states, including Minnesota, were seated during a 3½-hour closed committee session on the top floor of the Conrad Hilton Hotel here.

Only four members of the committee voted against seating the Minnesota delegation, which favors Vice-President Hubert H. Humphrey by a vote of 38½ to 13½ over Sen. Eugene J. McCarthy.

**THE SIZE** of the margin, the biggest in the five votes, assures that there will be no minority report which could lead to a floor fight over the Minnesota delegation.

The other state delegations seated were from Pennsylvania, Washington and Connecticut. In all of those, there were more than 11 votes cast against seating, which means that they could become the subject of floor fights.

The results were announced at 11:40 p.m. in the basement of the hotel by Gov. Richard J. Hughes of New Jersey, the committee chairman. He told reporters that the seating of the four delegations "doesn't necessarily mean the committee holds all the party rules and all the laws to be perfect instruments" in those states.

**A HALF-HOUR** earlier, Bayard Rustin, director of the A. Philip Randolph Institute, and Walter Davis, national director of the department of education for the AFL-CIO, had leaked word to reporters that the challenging delegation from Mississippi had won.

That delegation, which in-

Delegates
Continued on Page Six

COUNCIL HEARS PROTESTS

## *350 Ask Relief From Jet Noise*

By HOWARD ERICKSON
Minneapolis Tribune Staff Writer

Nearly 350 south Minneapolis residents jammed the Minneapolis City Council chambers Tuesday morning, most of them to voice their objections to the noise from jet aircraft from Minneapolis-St. Paul International Airport.

The subject was a proposed ordinance which would prohibit "unnecessary noise" from planes and ban training flights over the city.

The key provision would bar takeoffs and landings over the city when wind speeds are below 12 knots (13 to 14 miles per hour).

Alderman Richard M. Erdall, 13th Ward Republican, said this provision seeks to force aircraft to use air space over a sparsely-populated industrial zone adjacent to the Minnesota River southeast of the airport.

**THE AIRFIELD'S** longest runway lies in a southeast-northwest direction, and the northwesterly air space is over some of the city's most attractive upper-middle class homes in southwest Minneapolis.

The Council's Ordinance and Legislation Committee took no action after yesterday's 2½-hour hearing, except to refer the measure to

Noise
Continued on Page 12

## Ike Fights On, But Condition Is Still Critical

From The Tribune's Wire Services

WASHINGTON, D. C. — Former President Dwight D. Eisenhower remained in critical condition Tuesday night, and his doctors said in a bulletin he continued to have irregular heart spasms. But his former vice-president, Richard M. Nixon, said after a hospital visit that Eisenhower "has the will to live despite the physical blows he has received."

A late afternoon news bulletin from Walter Reed Army Medical Center said of the former president: "Gen. Eisenhower remains in critical condition and there has been no major change in his status since this morning's bulletin."

GALLUP POLL

## *Nixon Stretches Lead Over HHH*

By GEORGE GALLUP
Director, American Institute of Public Opinion

PRINCETON, N.J. — Republican nominee Richard Nixon has stretched a slim edge over Vice-President Hubert Humphrey in mid-July to a lead of 45 per cent to 29 per cent in a nationwide Gallup survey conducted immediately following the GOP convention in Miami, Fla.

Against Minnesota Sen. Eugene McCarthy—Humphrey's chief rival for the Democratic nomination—Nixon holds a lead of 42 per cent to 37 per cent, almost the same margin he had in the previous test in mid-July.

Nixon's improved advantage over the Vice-President is due more to Humphrey losses than to gains for Nixon. Nixon is five percentage points higher than in the pre-convention survey, while the figure for Humphrey is nine points lower.

*(MINNESOTA POLL—Page 24.)*

Support for independent candidate George Wallace of Alabama has held up. He polled 18 per cent in the Nixon-Humphrey-Wallace test and 16 per cent in the Nixon-McCarthy-Wallace post-convention survey.

The following question was asked of a representative sample of 1,526 adults in personal interviews in more than 320 localities. Interviewing was completed between Aug. 8 and 11.

*"Suppose the Presidential election were being held today. If Hubert Humphrey were the Democratic candidate, running against Richard Nixon, the Republican candidate, and George Wallace of Alabama were the candidate of a third party, which would you like to see win."*

(The same question was then asked, substituting McCarthy's name for Humphrey's.)

The results are based on persons who are currently registered to vote:

**Nixon - HHH - Wallace (National Totals)**

| | Latest % | Mid-July % |
|---|---|---|
| Nixon | 45 | 40 |
| Humphrey | 29 | 38 |
| Wallace | 18 | 16 |
| Undecided | 8 | 6 |

**Nixon - McCarthy - Wallace (National Totals)**

| | Latest % | Mid-July % |
|---|---|---|
| Nixon | 42 | 41 |
| McCarthy | 37 | 36 |
| Wallace | 16 | 16 |
| Undecided | 5 | 7 |

The GOP convention, judged by post-convention survey evidence, achieved these goals:

1 Closed party ranks, bringing most of the GOP voters behind the Nixon candidacy, something that the 1964 convention failed to achieve. At the present time, 84 per cent of all Republicans support Nixon; only 5 per cent support Humphrey. Immediately following the GOP convention of 1964, only 65 per cent of Republicans favored Goldwater, 24 per cent supported President Johnson.

2 Made gains in the South, where Nixon is catching up to Wallace and presently trails the former Alabama governor by

Gallup Poll
Continued on Page Six

## Fair and Humid Day Forecast for Twin Cities

Fair to partly cloudy skies are forecast for the Twin Cities today, with increased humidity but little chance of rain, the Weather Bureau said.

A high of 90 is predicted for the Twin Cities today, with a low tonight of 70. Precipitation probabilities are 5 per cent today and 10 per cent tonight.

Minnesota highs will range from 74 to 86 in the north and from 85 to 95 south. Showers are expected in the northern part of the state by Thursday.

Predicted highs: North Dakota, 70 to 85; South Dakota, 85 to 89, Wisconsin, 80s north, 86 to 92 south.

TODAY ON THE INSIDE:

### A Day in Court

*The drama in criminal court proceedings is low-key and the tension is rather like an iceberg—little of it surfaces. The Tribune's Robert T. Smith visited court in Hastings during preliminary motions in the cases of two men suspected of a slaying. Read his account, describing a typical day in court on PAGE 13.*

TURN THE PAGES TO:



Tribune Telephones: News, General . . . .372-4141; Want Ads . . . . . . . .372-4242; Circulation . . . . . . .372-4343

## Almanac

### *Double Trouble Continues*

*Wednesday, Aug. 21, 1968*
234th day, 132 to go this year
Sunrise 6:22 a.m.; sunset 8:10 a.m.

Persons who know them both say there's a remarkable similarity between a reporter for The Minneapolis Tribune and the husband of a secretary who works in the Minneapolis City Hall-Courthouse. It's so remarkable, in fact, that the secretary has to look twice when the reporter walks into her office.

He came in the other day, and after doing her usual double-take, she said, "I won't have this trouble any more." Her husband, she explained, had just gotten contact lenses and wouldn't be wearing glasses any more.

Our man broke it to her as gently as possible: He'd just made an appointment with his eye doctor — to be fitted for contact lenses.

•

*It has been suggested that the Minnesota Twins start wearing nylon stockings. It's one sure way of getting some runs.*

**Little Change**

WEDNESDAY'S TEMPERATURES

| | | | | | |
|---|---|---|---|---|---|
| 2 a.m. | 34 | 10 a.m. | 36 | 6 p.m. | 36 |
| 3 a.m. | 34 | 11 a.m. | 37 | 7 p.m. | 35 |
| 4 a.m. | 34 | Noon | 38 | 8 p.m. | 35 |
| 5 a.m. | 34 | 1 p.m. | 38 | 9 p.m. | 35 |
| 6 a.m. | 34 | 2 p.m. | 38 | 10 p.m. | 34 |
| 7 a.m. | 34 | 3 p.m. | 38 | 11 p.m. | 34 |
| 8 a.m. | 35 | 4 p.m. | 38 | Midnight | 34 |
| 9 a.m. | 35 | 5 p.m. | 37 | *1 a.m. | 33 |

*Details Page 29* *Unofficial

# The Minneapolis Tribune

THURSDAY

Vol. CII—No. 167 Copyright 1968 Minneapolis Star and Tribune Company MINNEAPOLIS, MINN., THURSDAY, NOVEMBER 7, 1968 ★ Single Copy Price 10¢ Lower Price for Carrier Delivery




# NIXON NARROWLY WINS PRESIDENCY

## Nixon Faces Democratic Congress

By FRANK WRIGHT
Minneapolis Tribune Staff Correspondent

WASHINGTON, D.C. — The newly-elected 91st Congress fails to give Richard Nixon the "overwhelming mandate to govern" that he sought.

The voters have retained the Democratic majorities that now control the Senate and the House, according to Wednesday's nearly complete unofficial returns from Tuesday's national election.

The people rejected Nixon's appeal, made repeatedly in his campaign, for friendly Republican majorities that would help him put his legislative proposals into effect.

The new line-up in the Senate will be 58 Democrats to 42 Republicans, a net gain of 5 for the GOP. The present split is 63 to 37.

**IN THE HOUSE,** the Democrats will wind up with 243 or 244 seats to 191 or 192 for the GOP, a gain of 3 or 4 for the Republicans. The present count is 247 Democrats and 188 Republicans, including two vacant seats that were held by the former and one by the latter.

No one ever gave the Republicans more than an outside chance to take over the Senate; but the GOP had hoped to make more inroads than it did, and the Democrats feared it would.

The House was a greater disappointment for Nixon.

GOP Minority Leader Gerald Ford of Michigan had predicted his party would gain at least enough seats to take control, a net of 31.

**NIXON'S ADVISERS** were less optimistic but did contend last weekend that the GOP would pick up 10 or 12 seats.

In the Senate the Democrats won 18 of the 34 seats at stake and the Republicans 16, although their lead in Oregon was still shaky.

Democrats took two seats held by Republicans:

**Alan Cranston,** former state controller, defeated Max Rafferty, the state superintendent of public instruction, in California. A conservative, Rafferty had ousted liberal Sen. Thomas Kuchel in the GOP primary.

**Gov. Harold Hughes** of Iowa won by a slender 9,800-vote margin the spot being vacated by Sen. Bourke Hickenlooper, who is retiring after four terms.

Republicans won at least six seats held by Democrats.

**Barry Goldwater,** making a comeback to the Senate after his unsuccessful run for the presidency in 1964, easily took the seat of Carl Hayden, who is retiring after having been in Congress since Arizona joined the union in 1912.

**Rep. Edward Gurney** defeated former Gov. Leroy Collins in Florida for the


Congress
Continued on Page 12

Associated Press

NIXON AND WIFE, PAT, JOINED THE REPUBLICANS' VICTORY CELEBRATION IN NEW YORK, N.Y.
*The president-elect thanked his supporters at the Waldorf-Astoria Hotel*

## Nixon Pledges to Seek Unity

By RICHARD P. KLEEMAN
Minneapolis Tribune Staff Correspondent

Richard Milhous Nixon, whose college football coach once advised him to forget about the glories of being a good loser, had no such problem Wednesday.

Before heading for a three-day Florida vacation, the 55-year-old Republican president - elect appeared before some 1,500 campaign workers, backers and newsmen in the grand ballroom of the Waldorf-Astoria Hotel in New York, N.Y.

*(TEXT on Page 10.)*

He pledged an administration of unity, its guiding philosophy to be that of a placard carried by a teen-ager at a campaign rally in Deshler, Ohio.

**"BRING US** together," the sign had said, and candidate Nixon quoted it often on the campaign stump.

"That will be the great objective of this administration at the outset—to bring the American people together," said Nixon, clearly pleased at his victory but not demonstratively emotional.

"We want to bridge the generation gap, we want to bridge the gap between the races.

"I am confident that this task is one which we can undertake and one in which we shall be successful."

**AFTER** accepting his presidential victory, Nixon stopped briefly in Washington, D.C., especially to visit with former President Dwight Eisenhower, confined to Walter Reed Army Medical Center following a series of heart attacks. Nixon was vice-president during Eisenhower's two terms in office.

Nixon arrived in Miami, Fla., at 10 p.m. A crowd of about 250 persons surged onto the runway to greet him as his silver and white Air Force jet pulled to a stop amid numerous security personnel.

Nixon and his wife, Pat,


Nixon
Continued on Page 15


## Margin Is Smallest in Recent Past

By CHARLES W. BAILEY
Chief of the Minneapolis Tribune Washington Bureau

WASHINGTON, D.C. — Richard M. Nixon won the presidency of the United States Wednesday by the narrowest popular margin in modern times.

The 55-year-old Republican finally emerged as the winner over Democrat Hubert Humphrey of Minnesota after an agonizing wait when Illinois, with 26 crucial electoral votes, fell into his column at midday yesterday.

**BUT HUMPHREY'S** closing rush—the climax of a one-man battle that carried him far closer to triumph than had seemed possible—left Nixon with a tenuous mandate. And a surprisingly strong Democratic showing in congressional contests not only denied Republicans control of either Senate or House but left Congress almost as strongly Democratic as before.

Thus the president-elect faces the prospect of trying to govern a deeply divided nation with a tiny popular mandate and a hostile Congress. It appeared that he will have to seek to form some kind of coalition — presumably through Cabinet choices — in order to overcome these problems.

Nixon's victory margin in the popular vote appeared last night to be less than 60,000 votes out of a total of 59 million cast for the two men—about one-tenth of 1 per cent. The closest previous popular-vote margin occurred in 1960, when John F. Kennedy beat Nixon by 118,550 votes.

**ON THE BASIS** of elector-


Election
Continued on Page Eight


## Snow Possible in Cities Today

Snow may make a slight Twin Cities appearance today, a day expected to be cloudy and cold, the Weather Bureau predicted Wednesday. The high should be 35, with a low tonight of 25.

The precipitation chances (and that means snow) are 20 per cent for today and tonight. That cold predicted for the Twin Cities is expected to be general throughout the region.

## *Humphrey Says He'll Stay in Politics*

By JACK WILSON
Minneapolis Tribune Staff Correspondent

Hubert H. Humphrey told his followers to "go have some fun" Wednesday and then went to his Waverly, Minn., home to begin adjusting to a new future.

He planned to leave in a few days for a vacation hideaway in the Virgin Islands, where he will spend a week or longer before returning to Washington, D.C., where he still has a job as Vice-President of the United States.

In his final words to a crowd of staff workers, Democratic party volunteers and friends at his campaign headquarters at the Leamington Hotel, Humphrey made it clear that he expected to continue in politics, in one way or another.

**"I INTEND** to continue my dedication to public service and to the building of a responsive and vital Democratic party," he said. "I shall continue my personal commitment to the cause of human rights, of peace, and to the betterment of man."

*(TEXT of Humphrey's Concession Statement — Page 17.)*

He did not give any sign of how he expected to go about it and his associates insisted he had made no plans beyond Jan. 20, when his term ends.

There will be a seat open in the Senate in two years if Sen. Eugene J. McCarthy carries out his plan not to seek re-election, but Humphrey has given no indication that he would consider running for it. If he were elected to the Senate he would have virtually the same seniority status as any other freshman member, with some


Humphrey
Continued on Page 12


## THE HOW AND WHY OF MINNESOTA'S VOTE

By BERNIE SHELLUM
Minneapolis Tribune Staff Writer

The most noteworthy aspect of Tuesday's presidential election in Minnesota was Richard Nixon's failure to recover normally Republican votes lost to President Johnson in 1964.

The president - elect ran slightly better than Barry Goldwater, the 1964 nominee, in the three major cities and in the suburbs, but achieved a significant improvement only in the rural villages.

Had Nixon improved on the 1964 showing statewide at the rate that he did in those villages, Minnesota's 10 electoral votes would have been in doubt.

**THIS CONCLUSION** was drawn from an analysis of The Tribune's 100 - precinct scale model of the Minnesota electorate. The model was built by a scientific method to achieve a balance among the precincts in numbers of voters, geographic location and party affiliation. Once drawn, the precincts were studied to determine population characteristics such as religion, education, race, income level and labor union activity.

Though comprising less than 3 per cent of the state's 3,806 precincts, the model projected the outcome of state presidential balloting within .5 of a percentage point of the actual result.

Humphrey, who lost the presidency to Nixon, won in Minnesota by a landslide in which he took 56 per cent of the DFL and Republican vote.

**IN DOING** so, he kept Nixon's improvement over Goldwater to 2.4 percentage points in the cities — Minneapolis, St. Paul and Duluth — 4.3 points in the suburbs and 9.7 points in rural farm precincts.

Looked at another way, Nixon gained back one-fifth of the Republican vote lost to Mr. Johnson in the rural villages in 1964, but only 3 per cent of the city voters who fled Goldwater in droves.

In the rural villages tested by the sample, Nixon did 11.1 points better than Goldwater, a rate which, if carried statewide, would have given the former vice-president an additional 90,000 votes, at Humphrey's expense. Nixon had 635,034 votes, to 820,952 for Humphrey, with all but 150 precincts counted.

**IN THE FOUR** heaviest Republican precincts in the sample—those with at least 75 per cent allegiance to the party—Humphrey got 35 per cent of the vote, compared with 20 per cent for former


Model
Continued on Page 12

Minneapolis Tribune Photo by Kent Kobersteen

HUMPHREYS FACE THE FUTURE WITH SMILES
*After Vice-President conceded his loss of presidency*

## Almanac

### *They're Now in Shape for Bargain Day*

*Thursday, Nov. 7, 1968*
312th day, 54 to go this year
Sunrise 6:59 a.m.; sunset 4:54 p.m.

A group of reporters and photographers were trying to top one another's tales about the terrible crush at Democratic National Headquarters Tuesday night.

An editor listened sympathetically and then said, "The trouble is, we sent you in there cold. We should have had you go out to a discount store on three Saturdays running to train for this."

•

***Today is the anniversary of the Bolshevik Revolution in Russia. It is called the October Revolution, quite naturally, because it occurred on Nov. 7-8. If you don't feel like celebrating that, it's also National Tuna Week.***

## TODAY ON THE INSIDE:

### Night of Hope Sours

***Backers of Hubert Humphrey worked hard Tuesday night at believing they were attending a victory celebration at the Leamington Hotel. After the bartenders and musicians stopped, and Richard Nixon's lead lengthened, hope faded. Staff writer Allan Holbert's report and pictures are on PAGE 17.***

## TURN THE PAGES TO:

• • • •



**Tribune Telephones**

| | |
|---|---|
| News, General | 372-4141 |
| Want Ads | 372-4242 |
| Circulation | 372-4343 |

## Rural Voters' Shift Nearly Defeats Langen

By ROBERT FRANKLIN
Minneapolis Tribune Staff Writer

MacGregor Fraser
*Easily re-elected*

A dramatic shift in rural votes nearly unseated Republican Congressman Odin Langen in northwestern Minnesota's 7th District in Tuesday's general election.

But the 55-year-old Langen held enough city strength to win 51 per cent of the vote and defeat DFLer Robert Bergland of Roseau by about 2,500 votes in the state's closest congressional contest.

Langen's victory, not certain until Wednesday, meant all eight of Minnesota's congressmen were re-elected.

**IN THE ONLY** contest for state office, DFL incumbent Paul A. Rusmussen used heavy labor support and surprising strength in the 6th District to beat Republican Lyle Nelson of Moorhead for public service commissioner.

An analysis of 100 precincts throughout Minnesota, a scientific scale model of the state's electorate, indicates where some of the candidates showed strengths and weaknesses.

In the 7th District, Langen won two years ago with 63.2 per cent of the vote, an unusually high figure for the normally marginal district. Langen defeated Keith Davi-


Minnesota
Continued on Page 16


SADDENED COED FOLLOWS HIS ADVICE

## *HHH Inspires Future Citizen*

By DICK CUNNINGHAM
Minneapolis Tribune Staff Writer

Petra Kelly's blue eyes glistened near tears as she pressed against the backs of the Secret Service men in the Hall of States at the Leamington Hotel Wednesday morning.

Hubert H. Humphrey moved past the officers toward a back door leading to a service corridor.

The job was done.

His voice had nearly broken twice as he told supporters and reporters, some of whom had been with him since April:

"Go have some fun."

**HUMPHREY'S** face was set in the familiar jut-jawed smile, but his own eyes seemed bright and somehow unseeing as he moved toward the quiet hall.

But suddenly he saw Petra's blonde head past the shoulders of the men, and the eyes came alive.

He reached out for her hand.

"You look so sad. What's the matter?" he asked.

Then Petra's tears came.

"I don't know what to do anymore," she sobbed.

The Vice - President squeezed her hand.

**"YOU HAVE** to have cheer." He looked squarely into her eyes. Then he was gone.

But it wasn't easy for Petra. She is 20, a German girl in her junior year at American University in Washington, D.C.

In her hotel room Petra had her papers ready to file for U.S. citizenship.

Hubert H. Humphrey was listed as her sponsor.

She had planned to file

PETRA KELLY
*'You have to have cheer'*


Citizenship
Continued on Page 16

MINNEAPOLIS TEMPERATURES

| | | |
|---|---|---|
| Midnight . . 68 | 5 a.m. . . . . 58 | 10 a.m. . . . 55 |
| 1 a.m. . . . . 67 | 6 a.m. . . . . 58 | 11 a.m. . . . 55 |
| 2 a.m. . . . . 63 | 7 a.m. . . . . 58 | *Noon . . . . 55 |
| 3 a.m. . . . . 62 | 8 a.m. . . . . 57 | *Unofficial. |
| 4 a.m. . . . . 60 | 9 a.m. . . . . 56 | |

TOMORROW: COOL


# THE MINNEAPOLIS STAR

Copyright 1969 Minneapolis Star and Tribune Company

Thursday, June 19, 1969 XIC—No. 177 Four Sections ★

Single Copy Price 10c Lower Price for Carrier Delivery


ONE COLOR

Minneapolis Star Photo by Russell Bull

MARGO BOYD CHECKED OIL AT ALMA BEACH

*Paper came out of the water coated with oil*

## *Fish from barge-leak area rejected*

More pictures, Page 1C

By EDWARD SCHAEFER
Minneapolis Star Staff Writer

Fish netted from the Mississippi were rejected Wednesday as unfit for human consumption because of the film of fuel oil that now covers virtually all of the Weaver Bottoms, a few miles downstream from Alma, Wis., on the Minnesota side of the river.

How extensive the duck loss will be in the famed bottomland area cannot be determined until later, said James Everson, Cochrane, Wis., conservation warden, but he said blue herons, egrets and terns have left the area.

"Either the stink of the oil or the absence of food caused the birds to leave," said Everson. "We'll see later how many of them come back. We also won't know until later how much damage was done to foliage and vegetation."

### Catch rejected

Alvin Leitha, one of the last commercial fishermen in the area, had his gill nets in the river when one of three oil-filled barges pushed by the tugboat Jim Hougland hit a submerged wingdam and was punctured, releasing more than 60,000 gallons of fuel into the river.

Leitha retrieved his nets yesterday along with several hundred pounds of buffalo fish and carp, normally shipped daily in season to Chicago. The catch was rejected by the fish-processing plant at Pepin, Wis., which also told Leitha the fishery didn't want any more fish from the area until well after the oil situation has been cleared up.

There were about 25,000 more gallons of fuel oil in the damaged barge. Workmen succeeded late Wednesday in turning around the barge, which had been beached about half a mile above the lock and dam above Alma. The river current then prevented much more oil from draining into the river.

Then the remaining oil was pumped into undamaged compartments in the barge. The compartments were sealed and padlocked by game wardens, who said the padlocks would not be removed until the barge leaves Wisconsin waters. The oil was consigned to St. Paul.

The towing company has been charged by the Wisconsin Department of Natural Resources with polluting the waterway, and the towboat pilot, George Stroube, Godfrey, Ill., was charged with careless operation of a barge.

The charges carry maximum fines of $200 for the company and $50 for the operator. Bond was posted Wednesday and the cases were continued until June 30 in Buffalo County Court.

### Feeding area

Stroube said smoke from the Dairyland Power Cooperative at Alma, Wis., obscured his vision as he was negotiating a turn in the river above Alma about 12:05 a.m. Monday. He said he saw a reflection in the river channel and mistook it for a channel marker.

OIL
Turn to Page 4A

United Press International

FOLLOWED ORDERS — Charles Tinker may have second thoughts now about the old Army saying that "you can't get in trouble for following orders." Tinker, 27, of Highwood, Ill., was refused a hardship discharge from the Army and was told to go home and wait for orders. He did. That was in 1966. He didn't hear from the Army again until 1968, when he got a letter asking what he had been doing for the last two years and inviting him to come in and explain. Now Tinker reports in each day in uniform while his case is pending. The Army reportedly leans toward giving him an honorable discharge.

## Student discontent runs deep, Nixon told

By JOHN BECKLER

WASHINGTON D.C. (AP) — President Nixon has been warned by a group of House Republicans that student dissatisfaction with campus and national life is far deeper than generally realized.

"The critical urgency of the problem cannot be overstated," said the 22 congressmen in a 37-page report to Mr. Nixon based on recent visits they made to more than 50 colleges.

Despite their sense of urgency, the congressmen said it would be a mistake to enact any "rash legislation" that would cut off federal aid to a college caught up in a student revolt.

In their major conclusion, the GOP representatives said the responsibility for dealing with student dissatisfaction rests primarily with the colleges themselves.

"Any action by Congress," they said, "that would penalize innocent and guilty alike by cutting off all aid to any institution which has experienced difficulties would only serve to confirm the cry of the revolutionaries and compound the problem for each university."

The report, delivered to Mr. Nixon Wednesday, thus strengthened the administration's hand in its effort to keep the House Education and Labor Committee from approving legislation that would use the threat of withholding federal funds as a means of trying to control campus disorders.

The committee was about

STUDENTS
Turn to Page 4A

# Reds fight way into provincial capital

By GEORGE ESPER

SAIGON, South Vietnam (AP) — Enemy forces launched six attacks on the city of Tay Ninh 50 miles northwest of Saigon today and about 300 Viet Cong guerrillas and North Vietnamese broke into an outlying district battling allied troops in the streets.

About 1,000 South Vietnamese civilians fled their homes.

The fighting continued into the night.

The outlying district hit hardest by the enemy is three miles from the heart of the city proper. Tay Ninh is 12 miles east of the Cambodian border.

The assault was the biggest so far in the enemy's summer campaign. Initial reports said nearly 200 enemy troops had been killed in the string of fights around the city. Allied casualties were reported light.

Elsewhere, North Vietnamese commandos blasted their way into a U.S. artillery base in the north; 63 rocket attacks hit allied towns and bases overnight and two Viet Cong terrorists assassinated a Saigon city councilman.

The assassination of Councilman Van Dien Quang touched off a gun battle in the heart of Cholon, Saigon's Chinese quarter. A woman bystander and one of the terrorists were killed, and three women and one man were wounded. The second gunman escaped on a motor scooter, but was believed wounded by police gunfire.

Tay Ninh City, capital of Tay Ninh Province, which borders Cambodia, was reported threatened by elements of two North Vietna-

WAR
Turn to Page 6A

## HEAD SAYS HE'LL RUN FOR SENATE

**Minnesota Atty. Gen. Douglas Head today announced he will seek the GOP nomination for the U.S. Senate.**

**Head thus joined Rep. Clark MacGregor, R-Minn., as an announced contestant for the nomination.**

**Their prime DFL target is Sen. Eugene McCarthy, D-Minn., who announced last October he would not be a DFL candidate in 1970. Subsequent statements by McCarthy, however, have led to speculation he may run again.**

**Another possible DFL candidate in the race is former Vice-President Hubert Humphrey.**

**(Details on Pages 10A and 11A.)**

## Battle deaths climb; U.S. toll 335

SAIGON, South Vietnam (AP)—Battle deaths in Vietnam climbed last week as a result of intensified ground fighting and the enemy's continuing rocket and mortar attacks.

The U.S. command said 335 Americans were killed in action, compared with 252 the previous week. South Vietnamese battle losses went up from 457 to 516 men killed.

The two commands said 4,360 enemy were reported killed last week.

The new casualty figures raised to 36,378 the number of Americans killed in action in the Vietnam war since Jan. 1, 1961, and enemy reported dead reached 516,087.

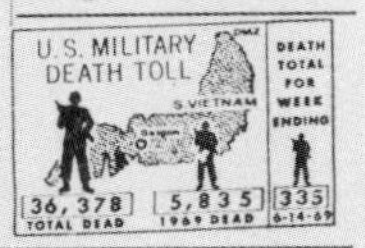


## *Hurried accord cloaked Civic Center differences*

**EDITOR'S NOTE: This is the ninth of 10 articles describing how key decisions are made in St. Paul.**

By DAVID NIMMER
Minneapolis Star Staff Writer

St. Paul Decision Makers

A hasty, last-minute agreement to hush up differences of opinion played a key role in the most recent—and successful—effort to advance plans to build a Civic Center complex in downtown St. Paul.

By the first week in March this year, a split had developed among the members of the Civic Center Commission, the agency charged with building the Civic Center.

Two of the businessmen on the commission had been particularly concerned that a new, round arena, billed as a multi-purpose facility, might not be so multi-purpose after all.

Lloyd Leider and William Price, both bank vice-presidents, felt that the building would be primarily a sports arena — a good hockey stadium that would not provide space for the convention exhibitors the businessmen hoped to attract to their Civic Center complex.

On the other hand, Daniel Gephart and Richard Radman were two commission members who were outspoken in their support of the arena.

In fact, Gephart announced his intention late in February to ask the commission to go on record supporting the plans which, he pointed out, had been under study "for many months."

When word of Gephart's intention reached Leider, vice-president of the First National Bank of St. Paul, Leider took action.

He quietly drafted a statement which raised questions about the feasibility of the round arena and suggested that the commission withhold approval and study the design further.

Leider secured the support of the other businessmen on the commission, and they were in the majority.

DECISION MAKERS
Turn to Page 4A

RICHARD RADMAN

Minneapolis Star Photos by Charles Bjorgen

THOMAS BYRNE

## Committee cuts HUD funds bill by $384 million

WASHINGTON, D.C. (AP) — A 19-per-cent, $384.3-million cut in proposed new funds for the Department of Housing and Urban Development (HUD) was recommended today by the House Approrpiations Committee.

The $1.65 billion earmarked for HUD in an omnibus $14.9 - billion appropriatio nbill sent to the House for consideration next week reflects deep cuts in funds for Model Cities and urban renewal programs.

The overall reduction of $473.1 million represented only a 3 per cent cut from the $15.3 billion requested by President Nixon.

The committee turned down a subcommittee recommendation to include in the bill, financing 19 agencies, $150,000 to start work on an official residence for the vice-president. The project was authorized three years ago at a total cost of $750,000.

In one major area the com-

FUNDS
Turn to Page 4A

Minneapolis Star Photo by Arthur Hager

**In wool pageant** Miss Wool of Minnesota, Claudia Bertramson, 20 W. 102nd St., Bloomington, a University of Minnesota student, left Wednesday for the national Miss Wool of America Pageant at San Angelo, Texas. Miss Bertramson, who also will represent North Dakota, will be one of 20 contestants vying for the crown. The winner will receive a year of travel to major American cities, a college scholarship and a dawn-to-dusk wardrobe of wool and mohair fashions.

SOLD IN AREA

## *FDA calls respirator 'dangerous'*

By GORDON SLOVUT
Minneapolis Star Staff Writer

Three Twin Cities area dealers have handled an emergency respiratory device that the U.S. Food and Drug Administration (FDA) said Wednesday "is dangerous and should not be used," it was announced today.

The device is designed to be used in efforts to revive apparent drowning victims, persons who suffer heart attacks and others with breathing problems.

It has a plastic bellows with an air vent at the top and a mouthpiece with a shield at the bottom.

### Seizure urged

Fermer Adair, enforcement officer for the FDA here, said it is certain that "a number" of the devices — known as Res-Q-Aire— are being used by rescue squads and similar emergency-care units in the region.

He said his office has recomended seizure of 27 of the devices now in stock at a Minneapolis dealership.

The device, distributed by a firm identified as Res-Q-Aire, Inc., Canton, Ohio, is sold to dealers for $5.52 each and probably for about $9.95 to rescue squads, Adair said.

The FDA said an estimated 40,000 of the hand-pumped devices have been distributed across the nation in the past two and a half years.

Adair said it isn't certain who the buyers of the device have been. Hennepin County General Hospital ambulances

DEVICE
Turn to Page 4A

## *Horsemen still ride range . . . in suburbia*

Ralph Thornton: B Section

●

## All this trolley needs is track to rickety-rack

Barbara Flanagan: Page 1C.

●

## HOME RUN REGGIE CHALLENGES THE BABE

Dick Gordon: Page 9C

●




STAR TELEPHONES

| | |
|---|---|
| NEWS, GENERAL | 372-4141 |
| CIRCULATION | 372-4343 |
| WANT ADS | 372-4242 |


## Weatherman sees cool, rain tonight

Cool weather with the prospect of rain tonight is seen for the Twin Cities area.

The Weather Bureau expects a low tonight of 48 with a high Friday of 65. There is a 20 percent chance of rain tonight.

### *Chastity costs*

LONDON, England (UPI) — Anne Hugessen is fighting for her chastity belts, which she contends are safety equipment and not subject to a 13.75 percent tax the British goverament is trying to impose on them. The taxmen say the belts, made by Anne's company as souvenirs, are durable goods.

### Dow Jones Averages

| (Noon N.Y.) | Avg. | Chg. |
|---|---|---|
| 30 Industrials | 882.76 | –4.33 |
| 20 Rails . . . . | 218.42 | – .66 |
| 15 Utilities . | 123.02 | + .03 |
| 65 Stocks . . | 301.25 | –1.06 |

Noon sales, 6,250,000 shares.

MINNEAPOLIS TEMPERATURES

| | | |
|---|---|---|
| Midnight ..54 | 5 a.m. ....53 | 10 a.m. ...57 |
| 1 a.m. ....54 | 6 a.m. ....53 | 11 a.m. ...60 |
| 2 a.m. ....54 | 7 a.m. ....54 | Noon .....61 |
| 3 a.m. ....54 | 8 a.m. ....53 | 1 p.m. ....62 |
| 4 a.m. ....53 | 9 a.m. ....56 | |

TOMORROW: Warmer

# THE MINNEAPOLIS STAR

Monday, June 23, 1969 XIC—No. 180 Two Sections 46 PAGES ★★★★

Single Copy Price 10c Lower Price for Carrier Delivery

Associated Press

CHIEF JUSTICE BURGER HELPED WITH ROBE

*Before he was sworn in at Washington today*

# Burger becomes chief justice

By CHARLOTTE MOULTON

WASHINGTON, D.C. (UPI) — Warren Earl Burger was sworn in as chief justice of the United States today in a ceremony at which President Nixon paid tribute to retiring Earl Warren and his 16-year court leadership.

Warren, in his last act as chief justice, administered two oaths of office to the 61 - year - old Minnesota - born Burger in a ceremony in the Supreme Court.

In a precedent - setting address to the court, Mr. Nixon praised Warren for his "dignity, example and fairness."

"He has helped keep America on the path of continuity and change which is so essential for our progress," the President said. ". . . This nation owes a debt of gratitude to the chief justice for his example."

### Years of change

Mr. Nixon spoke about 10 minutes, terming Warren's tenure on the court "years of greater change in America than any in our history."

In assuming his post as head of the federal judiciary, Burger promised to "bear true faith and allegiance" to the Constitution and to "administer justice without respect to persons." He had taken the same oaths when he became a member of the U.S. Court of Appeals in the District of Columbia in 1956.

Immediately after the swearing in, President and Mrs. Nixon joined members of the court for a reception in a nearby room for Burger, who became the nation's 15th chief justice.

### Warren appreciative

Warren, apparently moved by the unprecedented appearance of the President before the court to pay him tribute, said Mr. Nixon's words were "most generous and I greatly appreciate it."

Mr. Nixon told the justices that he was appearing before them "not as president of the United States but as a member of the bar."

In a light-hearted comment, the President remarked that "there is only one ordeal more challenging than a presidential press conference and that is to appear before the Supreme Court."

### Continuity

In his remarks responding to the President's tribute, Warren also noted the continuity in the court's 180-year history.

Warren said that in one sense at least the court is in a position similar to that of the presidency — "it speaks the last word in government affairs."

He concluded: "We have no constituency. We serve the public interest as we see it — guided only by the Constitution and our consciences."

Warren said the justices do not always agree on great issues that come before them but that fact is inherent in an institution of nine independent individuals.

"If the court ever agrees on all things I am sure its virility will have been sapped," he said.

## Suburb considers 3 percent excise tax

By LARRY FULLER
Minneapolis Star Staff Writer

A plan for a 3 percent municipal hotel, motel and entertainment tax in Bloomington has brought opposition from motel owners and representatives of professional sports teams.

A "first draft" of the ordinance has been prepared by Bloomington City Atty. Adrian Herbst and is to be reviewed tonight by the Bloomington City Council.

If adopted, the tax would apply to admissions to events in Metropolitan Stadium and Metropolitan Sports Arena, where professional sports are played.

Herbst said today that he believes that the Bloomington City Charter gives the city power to adopt the special taxes without special permission from the Minnesota Legislature.

There are indications that up to 24 other cities in the Twin Cities metropolitan area might have the power to follow with similar actions if Bloomington has the power to adopt the special taxes.

The Legislature last month granted permission for cities of the first class—Minneapolis, St. Paul and Duluth—to adopt a 3 percent excise tax on hotel and motel room rentals and amusements. The enabling resolution passed by the Minneapolis City Council last Thursday was vetoed by Mayor Arthur Naftalin.

Stephen Gillette, manager of the Holiday Inn in Bloomington, said the 3 percent city motel tax would bring the total tax on lodging to 6 percent.

"I think a 6 percent tax on a room would be the highest in the country and definitely will hurt us," Gillette said. "I think it's just a shame if they enact it."

Rod Wallace, owner of the Thunderbird Motel, said the proposed tax "puts us in a position where we're hamstrung again." Bloomington already charges among the highest liquor and motel license fees in the state, he said.

Stating that the Bloomington Council would be "singling out an industry" through the motel and hotel tax, Wallace added: "Everything has an affect on how much business you can do. If your taxes and licenses in Bloomington are higher than another municipality—which they are—we're just not going to be placed in a position where we are going to be competitive."

Representatives of the three professional sports teams estimated that the 3 percent admissions tax would give the city between $187,000 and $235,000 a year.

The strongest reaction

TAX
Turn to Page 3A

### Dow Jones Averages

| (1 p.m. N.Y.) | Avg. | Chg. |
|---|---|---|
| 30 Industrials | 867.11 | −9.05 |
| 20 Rails .... | 213.97 | −2.16 |
| 15 Utilities . | 120.72 | − .89 |
| 65 Stocks .. | 259.61 | −2.92 |

1 p.m. sales, 9,690,000 shares.

## *McNAMARA:* ARMS CAN'T BUY SAFETY

**BOSTON, Mass. (UPI) — Congress buys defense items the way women buy perfume—"if it costs more, they conclude it must be better," former Defense Secretary Robert S. McNamara said in an interview published today in the Boston Globe.**

**McNamara added, "No amount of military hardware can buy us security, and that's a fact we have yet to learn."**

**McNamara, president of the World Bank, was defense secretary for seven years under Presidents Kennedy and Johnson.**

## A VIEW OF BURGER'S ROLE

# *What direction for the court?*

**EDITOR'S NOTE: Warren Burger, whose roots are in Minnesota, was sworn in today as chief justice of the United States. A view of what this event may mean is provided in this article by Philip B. Kurland, professor of law at the University of Chicago and editor of the Supreme Court Review. He is recognized as one of America's foremost authorities on constitutional law.**

By PHILIP B. KURLAND
Written for the Chicago Daily News Service

The 1952 Republican presidential nominating convention is now responsible for the appointment of two chief justices of the United States.

Earl Warren translated the California delegation's vote in the credentials battle between Sen. Robert Taft of Ohio and Dwight D. Eisenhower into the nomination for the highest judicial office in the land.

Warren Earl Burger, who had only the Minnesota delegation to deliver, received an appointment as assistant attorney general, in turn converted into a judgeship on the U.S. Court of appeals for the District of Columbia, and now to the center chair of the Supreme Court of the United States.

It is somewhat disheartening to learn that, in President Nixon's opinion, Burger's outstanding qualification for the new post was his "unquestioned personal integrity." Certainly integrity must be a sine qua non for appointment to any governmental post. But if it is a necessary condition, it can hardly be a sufficient one. A chief justice's qualifications must start there, but they cannot end there.

This emphasis, it is said, is the result of a reaction on the part of the President to the actions of Justice Abe Fortas, who resigned from the court under fire. If so, it was a reaction as short - lived as the Senate confirmation hearings on Burger's nomination. The contrast between the hearings on Fortas' nomination to be chief justice and Burger's is sharp.

One might have expected, as the senators promised, that more careful scrutiny would be given future judicial nominations than had been afforded in the past. Despite these promises, Burger's nomination went through the Senate like a hot knife through butter.

For Burger there was no attempt at an extensive catechization on the opinions he had written as a court of appeals judge. Indeed, there was no evidence that any of his opinions had been read by many menbers of the Senate Judiciary Committee.

Burger, too, it turned out, had taken foundation money for dubiously valuable service, but the senators found no need to look into this. Burger, too, rode the circuit making speeches hither and yon, attacking Supreme Court jurisprudence rather than defending it, but the Senate was not interested in whether he got paid for this, how much, or by whom.

Moreover, if there is a new sensitivity about judicial conflicts of interest, neither the Senate Judiciary Committee nor the nominee seemed concerned with the fact that Burger so readily indicated his approval of the validity of legislation being proposed by members of the very committee who were passing on his qualifications for this high judical office.

Justice Robert Jackson and Judge Learned Hand, among others, none of whom was at the time being considered for higher office, thought it improper for a member of the judiciary to comment on the validity of similar bills.

### *Nixon's 'own kind of man'*

It cannot be that the "unquestioned personal integrity" of Judge Burger was essentially what commended him to the President. The answer must lie elsewhere. As one newspaper headline trumped: "Mr. Nixon Picks His Own Kind of Man."

James Reston of the New York Times said the same thing when he described the new chief justice: "Judge Warren Earl Bruger is . . . a perfect symbol of the qualties and values President Nixon is clearly trying to emphasize n his new administration . . . middle-class, middle-age, midde - of - the - road, middle - western. . . No great intellect, no great innovator or speaker, he has somehow climbed the greasy pole like Richard Nixon."

These qualities that recommended him to the President have, for the most part, also brought acclaim, if not wild enthusiasm, from the legal profession in and out of government. Some of the approbation was qualified, wittingly or not, by the proposition that men appointed to the Supreme Court have grown into greatness. Unfortunately, it is not true of most of them.

Earl Warren, it is said, showed none of the qualities prior to his appointment that he demonstrated as chief justice, except his affability. But Earl Warren had never been a judge, so one could not tell what his judicial demeanor was likely to be.

Warren Earl Burger has been a judge for 13 years and his judicial capacities have long since been revealed. The fact is that, in the history of the court, it is hard to find a single lower - court judge who developed into a greater jurist after appointment to the high court, and there have been many of them. Some, notably Oliver

CHIEF JUSTICE
Turn to Page 4A

United Press International

JUDY GARLAND AND MICKEY DEANS

*He told Scotland Yard of her death*

## Autopsy conducted to determine how Judy Garland died

By WILLIAM F. WRIGHT

London, England (UPI) — Scotland Yard pathologists conducted an autopsy today on Judy Garland to determine the cause of death of the singer who found torment, despair and loneliness over the rainbow, and death Sunday on her bathroom floor.

While doctors began their clinical tests today, a solitary fan stood in the rain outside her London home, clutching the sheet music of "Somewhere Over the Rainbow" in a silent tribute to the Dorothy of "The Wizard of Oz" who died at the age of 47.

Scotland Yard already had ruled out foul play — the body was unmarked — and ruled initially the sudden death was from natural causes, possibly brought on from the cirrhosis of the liver from which she suffered.

Miss Garland, who was born in Grand Rapids, Minn., made a comment in 1967 that could serve as her own epitaph:

"When you have lived the life I've lived, when you have loved and suffered and been madly happy and desperately sad — well, that's when you realize that you'll never be able to set it all down . . . Maybe you'd rather die first."

The man with whom she said she had finally found happiness, Mickey Deans, found Miss Garland's body Sunday morning on the floor of their bathroom.

"This is it. For the first

GARLAND
Turn to Page 4A

## AREA LAWNS DRINK DEEP AS RAINS FALL

**Almost three-quarters of an inch of rain fell on parched lawns in the Twin Cities area over the weekend and there is a chance of showers tonight and Tuesday, the U.S. weather bureau said today.**

**Temperatures are expected to rise, with a high of 78 predicted for tomorrow, after a low of 55 tonight.**

**The probability of precipitation is 20 percent tonight and tomorrow.**

## Investment partnership becomes corporation

Related article: Page 12B

By RALPH THORNTON
The Star's Business Editor

Piper, Jaffray & Hopwood (PJH), the state's oldest investment banking institution, announced today that it will become a corporation.

The brokerage firm now is a partnership, as are most such stock and bond houses. Until 1954, in fact, no corporation was allowed to belong to the New York Stock Exchange (NYSE).

Today nearly one-third are incorporated, said Harry C. Piper Jr., chairman of the firm's directing partners and a member of the NYSE board of governors.

He refused to comment when asked whether Piper, Jaffray intended to go public—that is, sell shares of stock to the public.

"All I can say is that the present rules of the exchange prohibit public ownership," Piper said.

The New York brokerage of Donaldson, Lufkin & Jenrette recently caused a stir in investment circles by registering with the U.S. Securities and Exchange Commission (SEC) to sell 800,000 shares of common stock to the public.

Dan Lufkin, a newly elect-

BROKERS
Turn to Page 8A

## The Harris Survey

By LOUIS HARRIS

### Living-cost vexes

Public concern over the high cost of living has reached record proportions and President Nixon is now in the eye of the hurricane on this explosive issue.

Here are the key findings on the inflation issue as they have emerged from the latest Harris Survey:

**President Nixon's rating in** "controlling the cost of living" now is 46 to 32 percent negative.

**Ninety-seven percent of** the public feels that the cost of living has gone up over a year ago.

**A majority of Americans** is convinced, by 56 to 31 percent, that such rises in the cost of living are not inevitable and can be avoided.

**By 79 to 6 percent,** the American people feel the most urgent step to take in curbing inflation is "to cut federal spending."

**The public rejects,** by 3 to 2, putting in a policy of "tight money."

**People also turn down the** proposal, 54 to 14 percent, to substitute a national sales tax for the corporate income tax.

**However, the public does** favor, 50 to 26 percent, instituting a system of "wage and price control.

**The American people oppose** continuation of the 10 percent surcharge tax by 63 to 22 percent.

The basic bind the President is in on the cost of living issue comes down to this: The American people fundamentally have an all-or-nothing view about inflation. The complaint about the rises in the cost of living have

HARRIS SURVEY
Turn to Page 4A

## *Yale football player tackles M.D. training*

Report, pictures: Page 1B

•

## Can Quarry survive Frazier's first flurry?

Bill Hengen's column: Page 8B

•

## 'NIGHT OF FOLLOWING DAY' FILM WORTHY OF ATTENTION

Don Morrison: Page 2B

•



• • •

STAR TELEPHONES

NEWS, GENERAL 372-4141
CIRCULATION 372-4343
WANT ADS 372-4242

Associated Press

CRUSHED — A Pompano Beach, Fla., couple was crushed to death inside this car at Fort Lauderdale when the tanker (background) blew a tire, jackknifed and turned on top of it. Killed were Lawrence, 70, and Elizabeth Dann, 55.

**Showers**
SUNDAY'S TEMPERATURES

| | | | | | |
|---|---|---|---|---|---|
| 2 a.m. | 71 | 10 a.m. | 73 | 6 p.m. | 79 |
| 3 a.m. | 73 | 11 a.m. | 75 | 7 p.m. | 78 |
| 4 a.m. | 69 | Noon | 78 | 8 p.m. | 77 |
| 5 a.m. | 67 | 1 p.m. | 79 | 9 p.m. | 75 |
| 6 a.m. | 66 | 2 p.m. | 80 | 10 p.m. | 73 |
| 7 a.m. | 66 | 3 p.m. | 81 | 11 p.m. | 72 |
| 8 a.m. | 68 | 4 p.m. | 82 | Midnight | 70 |
| 9 a.m. | 71 | 5 p.m. | 80 | *1 a.m. | 68 |

*Details Page 25* *Unofficial

# The Minneapolis Tribune

MONDAY

Vol. CIII—No. 58 MINNEAPOLIS, MINN., MONDAY, JULY 21, 1969 ★ Single Copy Price 10c Lower Price for Carrier Delivery

Once on the surface of the moon, Armstrong and Aldrin read plaque, left, planted U.S. flag, center, then talked to President Nixon

# Two U.S. Astronauts Walk on the Moon After Piloting Craft to a Smooth Landing

## Honeywell Devices Guide Ship

By LEWIS COPE
Minneapolis Tribune Staff Writer

HOUSTON, Texas — The spaceship Eagle swept gracefully down to the moon Sunday but it took a tricky bit of manuevering by its astronauts at the last minute to achieve its smooth landing.

Apollo 11 astronauts Neil Armstrong and Edwin Aldrin had to maneuver around a football-field-sized crater for a final touchdown. They used a pistol-grip hand control, made by Honeywell Inc. workers in the Twin Cities area, to order the final steering commands.

Most of the way down, the ship's guidance computer steered the ship with high accuracy through its required intricate maneuvers.

**THE BIG** engine used in the landing, the ship's right arm, and the many other systems apparently all performed in excellent fashion.

Still, the spacemen had their hands busy monitoring many things and throwing the proper switches during the descent.

One of the astronauts radioed mission control here after the landing, "The auto (automatic guidance) targeting was taking us right into a football-field-size crater, with a large number of big boulders and rocks for about one or two crater diameters around us.

**"AND IT** required . . . flying manually over the rock field to find a reasonably good touchdown area."

They were at about 200 feet altitude at the time.

As the ship finally started settling down, the astronauts reported that it was "picking up some dust," starting at between 40 and 30 feet off the ground. But officials here said this in no way interferred with visibility.

The astronauts' bug-shaped lunar module spaceship, which they named Eagle, landed on its long legs in the Sea of Tranquility, which is actually a plains area on the moon.

**ARMSTRONG'S** first report: "Houston, Tranquillity

Descent
Continued on Page Eight

ON WORLDWIDE TV, NEIL ARMSTRONG STEPPED ONTO THE SURFACE OF THE MOON, LEFT, FOLLOWED BY EDWIN ALDRIN
*A camera housed in an equipment bay in the lunar module transmitted the event to earth as it happened*

WORDS FOR HISTORY

## 'Engines Stopped; Eagle Has Landed'

From The Tribune's Wire Services

HOUSTON, Texas — "Eagle, this is Columbia—they just gave you a 'go' for powered descent."

With those words of Apollo 11—(astronaut Michael Collins alone in the mother ship called Columbia) — the drama of man's descent to a moon landing began unfolding.

"Current altitude about 46,000 feet," reported Mission Control (MC), describing the progress of Neil Armstrong and Edwin Aldrin in the landing craft dubbed Eagle. "Everything's looking good here."

**Eagle:** Our position check downrange shows us to be a little off.

**MC:** You are to continue power descent. It's looking good. Everything's looking good here, over.

**Eagle:** Copy.

**MC:** Two minutes 20 seconds, everything looking good.

**Eagle:** I'm getting a little fluctuation in . . .

**MC:** Looking good.

**Eagle:** . . . Shows us to be a little long.

**MC:** You're go to continue power descent, you're go to continue power de-

Transcript
Continued on Page Nine

## President Talks With Astronauts

From The Tribune's Wire Services

President Nixon, following the flight on television along with millions of others around the world, spoke with the two astronauts Sunday after they planted the American flag

Reaction
Continued on Page Ten

DO-IT-YOURSELF LAUNCH

## Takeoff Today Is Crucial Test

By LEWIS COPE
Minneapolis Tribune Staff Writer

HOUSTON, Texas — The two Americans who Sunday achieved history's first manned moon landing have another space first on their schedule for today. Their lives depend on it.

On earth, hundreds of experts have been required at the launch pad to prepare for every manned space launching.

Yet today, Apollo 11 astronauts Neil Armstrong and Edwin Aldrin must perform the first do-it-yourself manned space launching ever tried. They must take off from the moon and go into orbit without the help of a single person within miles for the countdown of their rocket.

**AND WHILE** it took a mammoth Saturn V rocket with 7.6-million pounds of thrust to start their mission from Cape Kennedy, Fla., last Wednesday, the

Takeoff
Continued on Page Eight

BOULDERS INTEREST SCIENTISTS

## Moon Site May Prove Bonus

By WALTER SULLIVAN
New York Times Service

HOUSTON, Texas — Although the discovery that they were coming down in the middle of a boulder-filled moon crater may have given the two Apollo astronauts a few anxious moments Sunday, it proved a scientific boon.

The area in which they came to rest was still strewn with boulders of many sizes and varieties. Some were presumably blown out of the lunar depth when the crater was formed, and represent rock buried perhaps 100 feet or more below the surface — far beyond the reach of the astronauts' sampling tools.

**OTHER ROCKS** probably were thrown from over the horizon by more massive impact and thus are specimens from other regions of the moon. Since the moon has virtually no air and its gravity is one-sixth as strong as earth gravity, explosive impacts sometimes blow debris half-way around the moon.

Furthermore the boulders may make it possible to place the two scientific packages to be left on the moon so that they will be sheltered from dust thrown up by the blast of the take-off rocket.

Such dust is probably the chief worry of those who have prepared the two packages, one of which is a small but highly sensitive seismic station.

**THOSE WHO** have long debated whether the moon is a dead body with a cool interior and no volcanic activity, or has a turbulent interior like the earth are eagerly awaiting the data from this instrument. They hope, from the four different seismometers inside it, to distinguish between earthquakes generated within the moon, volcanic eruptions at the surface and meteorite impacts.

Operation of the miniature observatory, however, is dependent on its light-gathering panels being free from dust.

**THE OTHER** scientific package, a device to reflect laser beams back to earth, is equally dependent for its success on remaining dust-free.

The third experimental package to be deployed on the moon is a scroll of aluminum foil mounted on a spring loaded bar, similar to a long, narrow window shade. It will be placed on the lunar surface, suspended from a pole driven into the ground so that the foil faces the sun.

The foil will then be brought back for analysis by a Swiss laboratory. It is hoped that nuclei of such inert gases as neon and argon blowing out from the sun will be embedded in the foil. The relative abundance of the various gases would have implications regarding the manner in which the sun and planets originated.

## Apollo Timetable Today

**6:11 A.M.**—Armstrong and Aldrin eat, then rest for four hours and 40 minutes.

**1:53 P.M.**—Astronauts fire ascent engine of lunar lander, a critical step if they are to return to command ship circling overhead.

**2:00 P.M.**—Ascent half of landing craft inserts into intermediate moon orbit.

**2:51 P.M.**—Lander begins series of maneuvers, aiming toward rendezvous and docking with command ship where Collins waits.

**5:30 P.M.**—Command ship and lunar lander dock. Armstrong and Aldrin vacuum-clean their equipment and spacesuits in preparation for entering mother ship.

**9:23 P.M.**—Ascent stage of moon lander jettisoned from command ship and abandoned in moon orbit.

### TV Coverage

**WCCO (Ch. 4)**—Midnight to 5 p.m. today.
**KSTP (Ch. 5)**—Midnight to 5 p.m. today.
**KMSP (Ch. 9)**—Midnight to 5 p.m. today.

**More Apollo News, Photos Page 2, 3, 7, 27**

## Possible Rain Seen for Cities

Variable cloudiness with a chance of an occasional shower or thunderstorm is predicted for the Twin Cities and vicinity today through Tuesday, according to the Weather Bureau.

The high for the Twin Cities will be 82 today with a low tonight of 65. Chance of measurable rainfall is 5 percent today and 30 percent tonight.

## 'Giant Leap for Mankind'

By JACK WILSON and LEWIS COPE
Minneapolis Tribune Staff Writers

HOUSTON, Texas — Neil Armstrong thrust his boot into a thin layer of fine dust beside his spacecraft at 9:55 p.m. (Minneapolis time) Sunday and became the first man ever to set foot on the moon.

Armstrong and Edwin Aldrin had landed their craft gently in the moon's Sea of Tranquillity at 3:17 p.m. after maneuvering at the last minute to avoid a "football-field-size crater with a large number of big boulders and rocks" around it.

Armstrong's first words as he stepped onto the lunar surface were a simple report of what it was like: "The surface is fine and powdery. "I can kick it up with my toe.

"It does adhere like powdered charcoal to my boots. My feet only go in about an eighth of an inch and I can see footprints here where I have walked."

In those few words the Apollo II astronaut ended thousands of years of speculation and guesswork and shattered many scientific theories about the moon.

Aldrin reentered the landing module at midnight, and Armstrong followed at 12:11.

At one time astronomers were fearful that a spaceship would disappear in hundreds

Apollo
Continued on Page Nine

## Luna 15 Dips Nearer Moon

JODRELL BANK, England (AP) — Luna 15 darted dramatically nearer the moon Sunday in a maneuver that Jodrell Bank scientists said could only mean the Soviet unmanned probe was to perform reconnaissance during the Apollo 11 mission or was preparing to land.

Observatory Director Sir Bernard Lovell said Luna's new orbit meant it was possibly on a course over the Apollo landing site in the Sea of Tranquillity.

He said the orbit was so close to the moon that the Russians could not expect to leave Luna in it for a long period.

Associated Press
MICHAEL COLLINS EDWIN ALDRIN NEIL ARMSTRONG
*Apollo 11 astronauts prepared for return*

## TODAY ON THE INSIDE:

### The View From Peking

The familiar picture of Red China is a huge crowd waving little red books while a speaker denounces "U.S. imperialism." Ronald Ross, The Tribune's Far East correspondent, "plugs into Peking's wavelength" to understand why the Chinese think the way they seem to. His report, *the second of a series, is on Page 8.*

## TURN THE PAGES TO:



Tribune Telephones
News, General . . . 372-4141
Want Ads . . . . . . . 372-4242
Circulation . . . . . 372-4343

## Almanac

### Finding Her Song Was a Revelation

**Monday, July 21, 1969**
202nd day. 163 to go this year
Sunrise 5:46 a.m.; sunset 8:52 p.m.

A superior kiddie story:

One day during vacation Bible school in south Minneapolis recently a class of 8-year-olds was asked to turn to the index of the New Testament to find a particular chapter.

Suddenly one young lady shouted, "Oh boy! They've got my favorite song in here!"

"Which one is that?" inquired the teacher.

"Jude."

# 1970~1979

Rain
SUNDAY'S TEMPERATURES

| | | | | | |
|---|---|---|---|---|---|
| 2 a.m. | 40 | 10 a.m. | 40 | 6 p.m. | 39 |
| 3 a.m. | 39 | 11 a.m. | 40 | 7 p.m. | 39 |
| 4 a.m. | 39 | NOON | 40 | 8 p.m. | 39 |
| 5 a.m. | 40 | 1 p.m. | 39 | 9 p.m. | 39 |
| 6 a.m. | 41 | 2 p.m. | 40 | 10 p.m. | 39 |
| 7 a.m. | 42 | 3 p.m. | 40 | 11 p.m. | 38 |
| 8 a.m. | 42 | 4 p.m. | 40 | Midnight | 37 |
| 9 a.m. | 42 | 5 p.m. | 40 | *1 a.m. | 37 |

Details Page 25 *Unofficial

# The Minneapolis Tribune

MONDAY

Vol. CIII—No. 331  MINNEAPOLIS, MINN., MONDAY APRIL 20, 1970 * Price 10¢

## News Digest and Index

### LOCAL

Minneapolis public schools will remain closed today. Negotiators for the school board and teachers met into the night Sunday in an effort to settle the teachers strike which has kept schools shut down for a week. ● Page 1.

An associate professor at the University of Minnesota has proposed a futuristic plan for personalized mass transit in the Twin Cities area. Under the plan, the commuter of tomorrow would step into a 3-by-12-foot, two-seat vehicle and be whisked non-stop to his destination at speeds up to 70 miles an hour. ● Page 20.

An old method of disposing of municipal sewage is rapidly gaining the attention of environmentalists in Minnesota. Spraying the waste water over the land to grow trees, bushes and even farm crops is "so logical," according to one official. ● Page 28.

A deaf-mute Minneapolis couple was instrumental in alerting firemen to a blaze in an apartment-office building next door to them. There were no injuries in the fire, which caused about $75,000 in damage. ● Page 1.

### NATIONAL

President Nixon conferred with Pacific commanders in Honolulu, Hawaii, on the issue of pulling more troops from Vietnam. The President will announce his decision on a fourth round of U.S. troop withdrawals at 8 o'clock tonight Minneapolis time. ● Page 2.

The Apollo 13 astronauts—James A. Lovell Jr., Fred W. Haise Jr. and Jack L. Swigert—flew to the Manned Spacecraft Center in Houston, Texas, to take on the job of analyzing what went wrong during the ill-fated flight around the moon. ● Page 3.

### FOREIGN

Premier Fidel Castro announced that a group of "mercenaries" landed in eastern Cuba Friday and that his troops were still fighting the invaders. The invasion took place in Oriente Province, near the eastern tip of Cuba across from Haiti. Castro said four of his soldiers and two of the invaders were killed. ● Page 1.

The United States secretly stationed air observers in northern Laos in 1966 to help guide the bombing of Pathet Lao and North Vietnamese forces by Royal Laotian and American planes. The operation was described in testimony made public by a secret subcommittee headed by Sen. Stuart Symington, D-Mo. ● Page 1.

Viet Cong troops occupied Saang, only 18 miles south of Phnom Penh, the closest they have moved to the Cambodian capital. A local commander said the Reds took the town without a fight because Camodian forces had been told to withdraw while holding their fire. ● Page 2.

A Cambodian army unit has sought sanctuary and medical help in South Vietnam's Mekong Delta after it engaged in sharp fighting inside Cambodia against the North Vietnamese and Viet Cong. The clash occurred at a Cambodian outpost three miles inside the border. The post was overrun last week. ● Page 2.

Egyptian fighter-bombers attacked Israeli military targets in the Sinai area for the second consecutive day and an Egyptian spokesman said one of his country's planes was shot down. Israel reported gun duels across the Suez Canal and said two of its soldiers were wounded. ● Page 4.

### BUSINESS

The Labor Department predicted that by 1980 the United States would have an economy totaling $1.8 trillion annually, with a younger, better-educated working force of 100 million. ● Page 9.

### SPORTS

The Twins rolled to a 6-3 victory over Oakland. It was the third victory for Jim Perry, without a loss this season. ● Page 29.

Howie Johnson faded over the last five holes and finished in a three-way tie with Bob Charles and Miller Barber in the Greater New Orleans Open golf tournament. Darkness forced a sudden death playoff to be moved to today ● Page 29.

### Features

Mrs. Rosalie Butler, who has won some victories in her joustings with the downtown St. Paul establishment but lost her bid for mayor in 1968, discusses her attempt to win a seat on the St. Paul City Council this year. ● Page 21.

Mrs. Butler

Columnist Will Jones went to see "Gaily, Gaily," and he came away comparing the film to what Walt Disney might have done if he had been willing to admit the existence of such institutions as bordellos. ● Page 26.

### Inside



• • • •

Tribune Telephones
News, General .... 372-4141
Want Ads ........ 372-4242
Circulation ....... 372-4343

## Castro Battling 'Invasion'

### 'Mercenaries' From U.S. Land in Eastern Cuba

New York Times Service

MIAMI, Fla.—Premier Fidel Castro announced Sunday that a group of "mercenaries" landed in eastern Cuba Friday and that government troops were still fighting the rebels.

In a 270-word communique, broadcast by Havana Radio, Castro said that the landing took place some 15 miles east of Baracoa, Oriente Province, near the eastern tip of Cuba across from Haiti.

The communique said that four Cuban soldiers were killed and two seriously wounded in clashes with the "mercenaries," two of whom were killed and three captured.

Castro indicated that the "mercenaries who came from the United States" were Cuban exiles. He said they were equipped with "modern automatic Yankee army weapons."

The fact that the communique was signed by Castro, and that it acknowledged that operations against the rebels were continuing, appeared to indicate that the Cuban government regards the landing as a significant development.

In Miami, Ardres Nazario, secretary general of Alfa 66, an exile "action group," said in a telephone interview that it was "possible" the men who disembarked in Cuba

Cuba
Continued on Page 12

## Deaf Mutes Give Fire Alarm

### All Escape Apartment-Office Blaze

By PAT MARX
Minneapolis Tribune Staff Writer

A deaf-mute couple was instrumental in bringing the Minneapolis Fire Department to a fire Sunday that destroyed an apartment-office building at 2742 Hennepin Av.

Mrs. Thompson — Thompson
*They saw smoke*

Mr. and Mrs. Eugene Thompson, 2736 Hennepin Av., both unable to speak or hear, were eating their Sunday afternoon dinner when they noticed smoke gushing out of the building across the alley.

Mrs. Thompson rushed downstairs to the apartment of Mrs. Mary Bennett, their caretaker and pointed to the fire. Mrs. Bennett called the Fire Department about 2 p.m.

Everyone in the three-story building, which houses three families and the office of the Colony Del-Mar food brokers, escaped without injury.

Fire officials said the fire apparently began in a hallway on the second floor, which was unoccupied.

The building was heavily damaged by fire in 1966.

One of the residents, Mrs. S. R. Speedy, was critically injured in a 1956 fire at 2634 Harriet Av. S. She and her husband were not injured in the blaze yesterday.

The Speedys and another family, Mr. and Mrs. Calix Caldorn and their three children, all living on the third floor, were able to escape through the rear entrance of the building. Caldorn is an instructor at the University of Minnesota.

Mr. and Mrs. David Westerson, the caretaker, were in the only basement apartment when they noticed smoke pouring down the hallway. They tried to get out the flaming front entrance, but were forced out the rear exit.

Firemen fought the blaze for about an hour in a steady rain, which, according to Fire Chief Kenneth Hall, was helpful in quelling the flames.

Fire investigators said the fire caused about $75,000 worth of damage. Cause of the fire was not determined.

Minneapolis Tribune Photo by Powell Krueger

A fire in this three-story apartment-office building at 2742 Hennepin Av. Sunday left three families homeless

## North Gets Snow; More Is Expected

A heavy wet snow that moved eastward over northern North Dakota and Minnesota Sunday left half a foot of snow in some areas.

About 7 inches had fallen at Bemidji between 5 a.m. and 8 p.m. yesterday.

Light snow is forecast again for the northern portions of North Dakota and Minnesota early today, diminishing by late today or tonight.

Cloudy skies are forecast for the Twin Cities today, with a 20-percent chance of rain today and a 10-percent chance tonight. A high of 42 is predicted, with a low tonight of 30.

Predicted area highs: Minnesota, 35 to 45; South Dakota, 38 to 48; North Dakota, 35 to 45; Wisconsin, 40s north, 50s south.

## Blackmun Says He Favors End of Death Penalty

ROCHESTER, Minn. (AP) — Supreme Court nominee Judge Harry A. Blackmun says that he personally is opposed to the death penalty and would not be surprised if it is ruled unconstitutional soon.

But Judge Blackmun, who has upheld the death sentence in past decisions, did not say how he would vote if he is confirmed.

Judge Blackmun could become the tie-breaking member of the court, thought to be deadlocked on whether the death penalty should be banned as cruel and inhuman.

The legal struggle has halted all legal executions in the United States for nearly three years. More than 500 prisoners are waiting on "death rows" across the country.

Judge Blackmun, in an interview, said that repeal of the death penalty is basically a legislative issue. He said that, if he were a lawmaker, he would vote against the death sentence.

But he added:

"I guess I would say it wouldn't surprise me if one day the Supreme Court would say today in 1970 or 1980 that it is cruel and inhuman. Maybe we are progressing in our attitudes . . . toward criminal law."

Judge Blackmun, who sits on the 8th Circuit Court of Appeals, acknowledged that his personal views against the death penalty could plunge his nomination into dispute in the Senate.

"This will be a matter of grave concern to, I suppose, some senators," Judge Blackmun said.

The Senate Judiciary Committee is scheduled to start hearings April 29 on Judge Blackmun, named last week to the court seat by President Nixon after two previous nominees were rejected by the Senate.

Throughout the interview, an earlier news conference, and a review of his 11-year court record, Judge Blackmun gave no firm clue as to whether he will continue to be the

Blackmun
Continued on Page Five

### AS ALTERNATIVE TO CAPTURE

## Lucky Charm Had Fatal Needle

*EDITOR'S NOTE: In 1956, Air Force 1st Lt. Francis Gary Powers accepted a job as a civilian pilot for the Central Intelligence Agency. He and several other Air Force pilots signed 18-month contracts under which they would be paid $2,500 a month. (Before that, Powers and his wife, Barbara, had a combined income of $700 a month.) The pilots manned Operation Overflight, a program for flying the U-2, a new plane capable of higher altitude than any other, along the borders of the Soviet Union and across Soviet territory.*

*Late in 1956, Powers was sent to Incirlik Air Base, near Adana, in southern Turkey. There were about 100 men in his unit, including six other pilots. They flew from Incirlik and, later, from Lahore and Peshawar, Pakistan. Their planes were equipped with a timed destruct mechanism and the pilots received cyanide tablets, which they were free to use if they chose in the event of capture.*

*When the 18-month contracts expired in November, 1957, they were renewed on a 12-month basis by many of the pilots, Powers included. Also during 1957, an ejection seat was added to the plane's equipment. The contracts were renewed again in 1959, and the suspicion began to grow among the pilots that the Russians had developed their radar to the point where it was capable of tracking the high-flying U-2.*

*The only threat that really disturbed the pilots was the SAM, the surface-to-air missile. Eventually, a "granger," a device designed to throw off radar tracking the plane, was installed in the U-2.*

*Operation Overflight was top-secret, and the situation was more critical than ever in early 1960 as the United States and the Soviet Union prepared for a summit meeting.*

*Before the year was half over, Operation Overflight would be on the front pages everywhere and Francis Gary Powers would be world renowned. This is his story of how it happened.*

By FRANCIS GARY POWERS



*Second in a Series*

Not long after the installation of the "granger," the intelligence officer introduced us to another piece of "equipment."

We couldn't figure it out. It looked like a good-luck charm. It seemed to be an ordinary silver dollar with a metal loop at one end so it could be fastened onto a key chain or a chain around the neck.

Obviously enjoying our puzzlement, he unscrewed the loop. Inside the dollar was what appeared to be an ordinary straight needle, but it wasn't. Toward the end there were grooves. Inside the grooves was a sticky brown substance.

Powers

It was curare, the intelligence officer explained. Just one prick would suffice.

From now on, we could carry this, if we wanted to, instead of cyanide.

The majority of pilots had decided against carrying cyanide. I had never carried it.

But we were fascinated with the dollar-pin-needle device. Passing it around, quite carefully, leaving the needle in the sheath, we each examined it. It was ingenious. Who would ever think of looking inside a silver dollar for something like this?

We were champing at the bit. Most of 1958, all of 1959, and thus far in 1960, there had been a drastic reduction in the number of overflights. Months would pass without one. Although never told the reason for the severe cutback, we presumed it was because of the political climate. We were quite capable of making many more flights than was the case, in fact were anxious to do so.

We were not inactive: we continued to make border-surveillance missions and "special" missions, but were definitely restive. The longer the layoff, the greater the tension. The fewer the overflights, the more appre-

Powers
Continued on Page 12

## Schools Closed Today

### Rehiring Policy, Salaries Remain Issues in Strike

By SAM NEWLUND
Minneapolis Tribune Staff Writer

Public schools in Minneapolis will remain closed today.

Negotiators for the School Board and the striking Minneapolis Federation of Teachers (MFT) began meeting at 10 a.m. Sunday in an efforst to break the deadlock that has kept the schools closed for a week.

Negotiations were still going on at 12:30 a.m.

Conflicting reports emerged on how much progress has been made, but MFT President Norman Moen told about 1,000 teachers in a rally at the Minneapolis Auditorium last night that "some hard-core issues remain and the whole package has not been completed."

The major roadblocks to settlement apparently continued to be salaries and the terms of rehiring teachers in the face of the state law prohibiting teachers' strikes. The law requires school boards to fire strikers and to rehire them only after freezing their salaries for a year and denying them tenure for two years.

In other developments announced at the rally:

**Picket lines** will be removed at the schools, in keeping with a temporary injunction issued Friday against the MFT. Instead, rotating shifts of 500 teachers each are scheduled to be-

Teachers
Continued on Page 12

## U.S. Observers Aid Bomb Runs in North Laos

New York Times Service

WASHINGTON, D. C. — The United States, it was disclosed Sunday, secretly stationed air observers in northern Laos in 1966 to help guide the bombing of Pathet Lao and North Vietnamese forces by Royal Laotian and American planes.

The operation, known as Project 404, was declared in testimony on the American involvement in Laos made public yesterday by a secret foreign relations subcommittee headed by Sen. Stuart Symington, D-Mo.

The testimony by State and Defense Department officials represented the first official acknowledgement that American personnel in Laos were at least indirectly engaged in the ground war that has been going on for years in northern Laos between the Royal Laotian government, supported by the United States, and the Communist Pathet Lao faction supported by North Vietnamese troops.

The testimony brought out that since 1962 about 100 American civilian and military personnel have been killed by Communist forces in northern Laos. Of these casualties, about half were stationed in Laos. The remainder were Air Force pi-

Laos
Continued on Page 12

## Almanac

### The Wills Have Ears

*Monday, April 20, 1970*

110th day, 255 to go this year
Sunrise, 5:21 a.m., sunset, 7:05 p.m.

A hearing-aid salesman went to check on a 78-year-old customer last week. He told the woman, "I imagine your family is happy about your new hearing aid."

"They don't know I have it," she said, "and in the last week I've had to change my will three times."

Minneapolis Tribune

Volume CV
Number 259
M



3 Sections
15c Single copy

1A

Monday
February 7
1972



# N. Ireland Catholics defy ban, march peacefully

Associated Press

A group of civil-rights marchers moved down a street in Newry, Northern Ireland, Sunday.

By Bernard Weinraub
New York Times Service

**Newry, Northern Ireland**
Thousands of Roman Catholics surged silently through the streets of Newry Sunday in a mass civil-rights protest against the British and Northern Ireland governments.

The two-hour demonstration — in defiance of a ban on marches in Northern Ireland—avoided the center of the city where hundreds of helmeted British soldiers waited in armored cars behind barbed-wire roadblocks. There were no major incidents.

**(Pope asks prayer for peace in Northern Ireland. Page 6A.)**

"This is a big victory for the civil-rights movement in Northern Ireland," Kevin Boyle, a 28-year-old leader of the march, said excitedly from the speakers' platform in a muddy meadow one mile from the center of Newry.

"We have defied the ban. There has been no violence. We've shown that we will not be intimidated by a government that's unacceptable to us," he added.

Moments later, Rory McShane, a 25-year-old law student who heads the Newry Civil Rights Association, said into a microphone:

"An illegal march has taken place because we reject the law and we reject the repressive government that made the law. We will continue to reject the law until the British army leaves and this government ends."

By the early evening, British army officials were obviously pleased at the outcome of the march. A spokes-

**March** continued on page 11A

Associated Press

Bernadette Devlin, center, marched in Ulster Sunday.

## Prison guards wear new look in Minnesota

By Sam Newlund
Staff Writer

Jim Wilder neither looks nor acts like a prison guard.

You might find him sauntering around Stillwater Prison wearing a bright purple shirt that is open at the neck, sports slacks, a plaid cap pulled low on his forehead and dark glasses with wire rims.

Or, you might find him in sneakers coaching a prison basketball team.

The new look in prison guards? Perhaps, except that Wilder, a 29-year-old black athlete, has a newer look than most. He is reputed to be the sole member of the prison custodial force who declines to wear a uniform.

**(Stillwater inmates confined to cells during shakedown—Page 2B.)**

But he has one thing in common with a growing number of guards in Minnesota correctional institutions. Nearly half of the approximately 725 guards in all the institutions are no longer called by their old official Civil Service title—correctional officers. These officers are now called correctional counselors.

To acquire this title—and with it higher pay—currently employed guards must complete college-level courses in counseling and other social sciences. New job applicants must complete a similar series of courses before they can be hired.

Unlike the days when guards were reprimanded for getting personally involved with inmates and their problems, the push now is to train them for that very kind of involvement.

The days of control of inmates by brute force may be numbered. Reform-minded corrections officials in Minnesota and elsewhere say they don't want that kind of system, and inmates are becoming stronger in resisting it.

"Giving orders to inmates—those days are gone," said one of Wilder's fellow counselors last week.

**Guards** continued on page 11A

## Thuy tells Hanoi terms for release of POWs

By Tad Szulc
New York Times Service

**Washington, D.C.**
North Vietnam says that American prisoners of war will be released only when the United States has withdrawn its support from the administration of President Nguyen Van Thieu and the war has been brought to an end.

**(Jackson scolds critics of Nixon's peace plan. Page 2A.)**

In a major clarification of Hanoi's position, Xuan Thuy, the chief North Vietnamese negotiator in Paris, France, made it clear at the same time that the setting of a specific date by the United States for the total removal of its forces from Vietnam would not longer be sufficient to secure the prisoners freedom.

Answering questions from a panel of reporters on "Face the Nation," a television program of the Col-

**Talks**
Continued on page 12A

Rogers

Thuy

## Senate group plans hearings on amnesty

Associated Press

**Washington, D.C.**
Sen. Edward M. Kennedy, D-Mass., announced Sunday that a Senate subcommittee will hold hearings on Selective Service procedures and on the possibility of granting amnesty to draft evaders through administrative procedures.

Kennedy, who heads the subcommittee on administrative practice and procedures, said the panel will hold three days of hearings beginning Feb. 28.

Kennedy said his panel wanted to examine the actual practices of the 1971 Selective Service Act, which incorporated many of the subcommittee's earlier recommendations to insure greater fairness in administration of the draft law.

## Britain prepares new political program for Northern Ireland

By Anthony Lewis
New York Times Service

**London, England**
The British government has prepared a radical new political plan for North Ireland, ready for release when it thinks the time is right. The peaceful march in Newry Sunday could help clear the way for early action.

No details of the government's thinking have been disclosed. But informed quarters believe the proposal would call for a fixed number of Roman Catholics in the Ulster provincial government.

Since Northern Ireland

Heath

Faulkner

was created by the partition of Ireland 50 years ago, it has been dominated by the Protestant Unionist Party. The Catholic minority has regarded the government as a sectarian and alien one.

The new British plan, if the speculation about it is correct, would try to deal with this by what would amount to communal representation in the Northern Ireland government.

It is understood that the Catholic community would be given a larger share of ministers than its proportion of the Ulster population. That is about one-third.

A difficult question would still be whether Catholics committed to the idea of a united Ireland — as most now are in the north—could serve as Belfast ministers. The Northern Ireland prime minister,

**Policy**
Continued on page 7A

## Indochina bombing called 'total war'

### Former American volunteer in Laos testifies at 'war crimes' session

By Doug Stone
Staff Writer

A former American volunteer and journalist who spent four years in Laos told Sunday how the American bombing in Indochina represented the "third Indochina war."

Fred Branfman, who was a teacher with the International Voluntary Services, said the air bombing in the last seven years is "total war, an automated war and a secret war of which the American people know nothing."

Branfman, 29, who now directs Project Air War in Washington, D.C., was speaking at the opening session of the Honeywell Project's corporate war crimes investigations being held at the University of Minnesota.

The investigations are an attempt to examine the relationship between Honeywell and other weapons makers and American war policies. They were organized by the Honeywell Project, a group of Twin Cities antiwar activists formed four years ago in an effort to get Honeywell to stop manufacturing antipersonnel fragmentation bombs.

The sessions will continue through Sunday at the Newman Center.

**Hearings**
Continued on page 11A

Fred Branfman

## Telephone firm delays Minnesota rate rise

Northwestern Bell Telephone Co. Sunday postponcd its controversial Minnesota rate increase until Feb. 18 because the federal Price Commission has requested additional information on the case.

The new rates were to have gone into effect yesterday. Present phone rates will continue in effect until Feb. 18, Wayne L. Huffman, vice-president of Northwestern Bell's Minnesota operations, said yesterday.

The rate increase, approved by the Minnesota Public Service Commission (PSC) on Jan. 27 but later protested by State Atty. Gen. Warren Spannaus, would give the telephone company about $34 million in new annual revenues.

The average general-rate increase would be 12.5 percent for the company's 960,000 Minnesota customers.

The company originally had requested an average general-rate increase of about 14 percent, which would have generated new revenues of about $38 million.

The PSC held hearings on the rate increase from July to December 1971

**Telephone**
Continued on page 11A

## Inside news

### Foreign

Prime Minister Sheik Mujibur Rahman of Bangladesh told a rally in Calcutta, India, that the United States has turned its back on the sufferings of his people and failed the cause of democracy on the Indian subcontinent. Page 2A.

American troops in helicopters dropped napalm on what appeared to be newly constructed North Vietnamese bunkers 25 miles northeast of the capital of South Vietnam. Thirty Viet Cong soldiers attacked South Vietnamese forces west of Saigon, killing five and wounding five. Page 2A.

### National

Another woman has surfaced in the Clifford Irving-Howard Hughes saga. A woman identified only as Ann Baxter reportedly flew with Irving to St. Croix in the Virgin Islands and gave him scuba diving lessons while he was there trying to contact Hughes. Page 3A.

Llewellyn Thompson, former U.S. ambassador to the Soviet Union, died in Bethesda, Md., at the age of 67. Thompson had entered the National Institute of Health last week for treatment of cancer. Page 3A.

More than 400 firemen from 35 cities and towns fought a $15-million blaze in Wakefield, Mass., that destroyed five buildings and damaged five others in an industrial park. Officials said 1,000 persons would be jobless because of the fire. Page 8A.

### Local

Fifty-three percent of those interviewed by the Minnesota Poll said the renewed bombing of North Vietnam won't make any difference in the war and 23 percent said it will prolong the war. Seventeen percent said the bombing will shorten the war. Page 2A.

Three years ago the University of Minnesota announced plans to deemphasize freshman-sophomore level offerings in order to put more emphasis on upper division and graduate programs. Now, university figures offer proof of the change. Page 1B.

### Business

Financial analysts reported that fourth-quarter earnings of the nation's largest corporations increased 24 percent in 1971 over the previous year's fourth quarter. The First National City Bank of New York surveyed 932 nonfinancial corporations, and found that three out of four increased their earnings. Page 9A.

### Sports

Tony Esposito recorded his seventh shutout of the season as Chicago beat the Minnesota North Stars 5-0 in Chicago. Page 1C.

Mario Andretti and Jackie Ickx shared $12,000 of the $50,000 purse by driving their ailing Ferrari to victory in the Continental Auto Race at Daytona Beach, Fla. Despite the loss of a piston, they averaged 124.716 miles per hour for a Daytona road-race record. Page 1C.

## Index

Ard Schenk

## Features

Ard Schenk of the Netherlands skated to victory in the 1,500 meters at the Winter Olympics, and then he charmed all the girl reporters in the interview room with his blond, blue-eyed, beautiful single status. Page 1C.

More than a million earthquakes that place each year. Some so gentle they are not noticed, others so violent that they cause great destruction and loss of life. To find out how an earthquake comes about, see the Science Reading Series. Page 5A.

Tribune

Telephones
372 4141 News General
372 4242 Classified
372 4343 Circulation

## Almanac

**Monday**
**February 7 1972**
**38th day**
**328 to go this year**
**Sunrise 7:26 a.m.**
**Sunset 5:29 p.m.**

### Today's weather
### Cold

Details Page 9B.

**Sunday's temperatures**

| | | | | | | | | | | | | |
|---|---|---|---|---|---|---|---|---|---|---|---|---|
| am | 1 | 2 | 3 | 4 | 5 | 6 | 7 | 8 | 9 | 10 | 11 | Noon |
| temp | 0 | −1 | −2 | −3 | −3 | −5 | −6 | −6 | −6 | −5 | −3 | −2 |
| pm | 1 | 2 | 3 | 4 | 5 | 6 | 7 | 8 | 9 | 10 | 11 | Midn |
| temp | 0 | 0 | 0 | −1 | −3 | −5 | −7 | −8 | −10 | −11 | −12 | −13 |

Continued cold weather is forecast for the Twin Cities and vicinity today and Tuesday with northwesterly winds from 6 to 12 miles per hour forecast. The high today should be 2 below with a low tonight of 12 below and a high Tuesday of 6 above.

Predicted area highs: Minnesota, 12 below to 4 above; North Dakota, 12 above southwest to 6 below northeast; South Dakota, 0 northeast to 30 above southwest; Wisconsin, 15 to 15 below northwest, 2 above to 10 below southeast.

### Enough glory for all

Italians will not be happy with this news. Because of the new Monday-holiday law, Columbus Day will fall on Oct. 9 this year, instead of the traditional Oct. 12. Oct. 9 is Leif Ericson Day. The Sons of Norway, a fraternal society, brought this to our attention.

THE MINNEAPOLIS STAR



Thursday, February 17, 1972

Single Copy Price 15c


# Nixon off on first leg of China trip

Associated Press

THE NIXONS SAY GOOD-BY TO THEIR DAUGHTERS AT THE WHITE HOUSE

*At left Tricia hugs the First Lady; at right Julie kisses her father*

## *Congressmen briefed on 'peace journey'*

WASHINGTON, D.C. (AP) — President Nixon, his wife and a handful of top aides left today on a "journey for peace" to Communist China, saying he hopes it will reduce the possibility of a future war.

The Presidential jet, the "Spirit of '76," took off from Andrews Air Force Base on the first long leg of the trip at 10:34 a.m.

Before leaving the White House by helicopter for Andrews, Nixon briefed 10 Democratic and Republican leaders of Congress. Then he delivered brief rmarks to a crowd including about 1,000 school children on the South Lawn.

Standing coatless in damp, 35-degree weather, he repeated a prediction he first made July 15 when he stunned the world with his announcement that he would become the first American president ever to visit China. The China trip, he said, "would be a journey for peace."

He said again that he does not expect the trip to erase all difficulties between Washington and Peking, but hopes it will help to avoid any possible future war.

"We of course have no illusions that 20 years of hostility between the United States and China are going to be swept away by one week of talks," he said.

"As we look to the future we must realize that the government of the People's Republic of China and government of the United States have had great differences," he said. "They will continue to have differences. But what we must do is to find a way to see that we can have difference without being enemies in war."

He cited the words on the plaque left on the moon by America's astronauts to underline the purpose of his journey. The words: "We came in peace for all mankind."

Then the President kissed his two daughters, Julie Eisenhower and Tricia Cox, stepped past a special military honor guard and into the presidential helicopter.

A sizable crowd lined the fence encircling the White House on the south side and some were holding up large signs. One of them read: "Nixon's war is escalating;" another said "Withdraw support of Thieu."

A bit of snow began to fall as the presidential jet took off for a 10-hour nonstop flight to Kaneohe Marine Corps Air Station on the northern shore of the Hawaiian island of Oahu.

The Nixons plan to remain there until late Saturday afternoon when they will fly to Guam for an overnight stop before landing on the Chinese mainland next Monday.

They plan to stay in China one week, the longest time any chief executive has devoted to a single country since Woodrow Wilson went to Europe at the end of World War I.

## *Hughes reported to have left Bahamas, may be in Nicaragua*

NASSAU, Bahamas (AP)—Howard Hughes has reportedly left the Bahamas after 15 months of seclusion there. A Bahamaian official indicated today he may have returned to the United States, but a cargo plane loaded with his possessions was headed for Nicaragua.

Hughes

The report that Hughes was returning to his homeland could not be confirmed and so the mystery remains: Where is he?

In Los Angeles, a Hughes spokesman said he understood his boss had left Nassau Tuesday, but insisted that the whereabouts of the 66-year-old recluse billionaire was unknown to him.

The report of Hughes' departure and possible U.S. destination came from a ranking Bahamian government official who refused to be identified.

U.S. Customs in Washington declined to comment on whether Hughes had been processed through customs.

Meantime, an official of Paradise Island Limited said Hughes may have left the island as early as last weekend with a few members of his staff.

Paradise Island Limited owns and operates the Britannia Beach Hotel, where Hughes had been living since leaving Las Vegas on Thanksgiving Eve in 1970.

A spokesman for the hotel said he was in Hughes' suite Wednesday night. "I was up there and ascertained that the rooms are definitely empty," he said.

In Los Angeles, Richard Hannah, publicity chief of Hughes Tool Co., said he inferred from his sources that Hughes left the Britannia Beach Hotel Tuesday.

Hannah said he could not confirm that Hughes was in the United States. He said it appeared that Hughes' whereabouts would not be revealed until he has settled down, wherever he is going.

The C46 cargo plane left Nassau this morning, loaded with furniture and other items removed from Hughes' ninth-floor suite of the Britannia Beach Hotel yesterday. Among the items were a hospital bed, blood plasma stand, many cases of bottled water, easy chairs, refrigerators, two reclining beds, mattresses, reels of film and many pots and pans.

In Miami, a spokesman for the Federal Aviation Administration said the C46 stopped briefly at Fort Lauderdale International Airport before the pilot filed a flight plan for Managua, Nicaragua.

The spokesman said the aircraft left Fort Lauderdale at 9:18 am. EST and was due in Managua at 2:15 p.m.

The flight plan said the aircraft had fuel for eight hours and carried four persons, according to the FAA spokesman.

Ten porters from a local trucking company were seen carrying furniture and other items from the Hughes hideaway yesterday. Among the items were a hospital bed, blood plasma stand, many cases of bottled water, refrigerators, easy chairs, two reclining beds, mattresses, reels of film and many pots and pans.

The goods were then loaded onto three flatbed trucks and taken to Nassau Airport, where they were placed into the C46 aircraft.

Standing by with the C46 at the airport was a Cessna 421, a seven passenger executive-type plane. Nearby was an unmarked 707 passenger jetliner that has been at the airport for several days. An airport spokesman said he knew nothing about the plane.

## Mayor seeks broader law to halt 'smut'

By DEBORAH HOWELL
Minneapolis Star Staff Writer

Mayor Charles Stenvig today proposed a far-reaching city ordinance to license all stores which sell magazines, books and pictures in an attempt to prevent the sale of "obscene" material to anyone and the displaying of such materials to minors.

Stenvig made the proposal after allowing an ordinance passed last week by the Minnespolis City Council to become law without his signature. The ordinance provides for licenses for adults-only bookstores.

Stenvig said the ordinance is "unenforcable" and not strong enough.

"I personally feel stronger laws are needed to control the proliferation of the smut merchant who would make a profit at the expense of our children," Stenvig said today in a letter to Council members.

The new ordinance he proposes was drafted on the advice of Jon Prentice, head of the city police morals squad.

Stenvig's proposal would have the Council license not just adults-only bookstores but also all bookstores or drugstores or grocery stores or any store selling books, magazines and pictures.

Grounds for denying a license would be conviction under any state law, city ordinance or federal law prohibiting the sale of obscene material to any person or the display or sale of obscene or "sexually provocative" material to persons under 18.

Prentice said a license could be de-


STENVIG
Turn to Page 2A


## Briefly

### Variety has 'fun recipes' for children

3-D box can show story of George Washington: Page 4D

### National

**Houston**—A manned space shot after dark, a first, is the plan for Apollo 17, the last of the Apollo probe series. Apollo 17 is to lift off the night of Dec. 6. Astronauts will be looking for the moon's oldest rocks during their stopover. Meanwhile, spacemen continued practicing for the Apollo 16 lunar shot, planned for April 16.

**Anchorage**—An extra $80,000 will be coming out of Russian pocketbooks as a result of three Russian captains' attempt to escape the U.S. Coast Guard in a chase in the Aleutians. The three were also fined $170,000 for illegal fishing off Alaska, bringing the total tab to a record $250,000. They must stay in Anchorage until their fines are paid.

**Washington** — A new Census Bureau survey indicates that most young married women plan to limit their families to fewer than three children. The study of birth expectations indicates that American families will be smaller in the future and that the overall growth rate has turned sharply downward.

### City and state

**Saying** the state can no longer afford single-purpose efforts on behalf of air, rail, water and highway transportation, Gov. Anderson has asked Highway Commissioner Lappegaard to draft a bill establishing a state department of transportation. **Details: Page 17C.**

**Being sentimental** with labor leaders and folksy with senior citizens, Hubert H. Humphrey campaigned in the Twin Cities Wednesday. It became clear that he retains with many the affection and respect he first won in 1945 when he was elected mayor of Minneapolis. **Details: Page 1C.**

**The University** of Minnesota Board of Regents retroactively approved overspending in the entertainment and travel budget of President Malcolm Moos, Regent John Yngve said. The original budget of $3,000 a year was raised July 9, 1971, to $10,000 for 1969 and $12,000 for 1970, he said.

### Weather

**The snow** will end in the Twin Cities area tonight, but the warm weather which boosted the overnight temperature to 33 degrees will disappear and colder weather will move in. The overnight low is expected to be 2 tonight and 18 Friday. About 1½ inches of snow fell overnight in the area. The chance of snow tomorrow is almost zero, but tonight's chance of additional precipitation is 10 percent. Winds should diminish overnight. **Details: F Section.**

**MINNEAPOLIS TEMPERATURES**

| | | | |
|---|---|---|---|
| Midnight | 25 | 6 a.m. | 31 |
| 1 a.m. | 25 | 7 a.m. | 33 |
| 2 a.m. | 26 | 8 a.m. | 33 |
| 3 a.m. | 26 | 9 a.m. | 29 |
| 4 a.m. | 27 | 10 a.m. | 28 |
| 5 a.m. | 27 | 11 a.m. | 26 |

**TOMORROW: Clearing and Colder**

### Southeast Asia

**Paris**—North Vietnam demanded today that the United States and South Vietnam agree to a session of the Vietnam peace talks next Thursday. The anti-Communist side has not decided yet when it will agree to another meeting.

**Phnom Penh** — Cambodian troops have beaten back a fierce Communist attack in the first serious ground fighting of the Laotian government's drive to recapture the ancient temples at Angkor Wat, the military command reported today. The battle raged most of Wednesday on the eastern side of the temple complex, 150 miles northwest of Phnom Penh.

### International

**London** — The Conservative government says it will make further drastic cuts in Britain's power supplies next Wednesday. However, it warned that electricity from coal-fueled generators may be exhausted after next week if the six-week-old coal miners' strike continues. **Details: Page 14C.**

**Belfast** — Northern Ireland's reign of terror continued with the murder of two men, one a British soldier and the other a Catholic member of a mostly Protestant Ulster militia force. The terrorist shootings raised the province's 2½-year toll to at least 245. **Details: Page 7A.**

### Business

**Northern** Natural Gas Co. will spend $30 million beginning in 1974 under an agreement with British Petroleum Co., Ltd., to obtain gas from Alaska's North Slope. Part of the prepayment, to be made in five equal amounts, is for setting up an exploration program. Northern supplies Minneapolis Gas Co., NSP in St. Paul and about 1,000 communities. **Details: Page 7E.**

**Thursday Dow Jones Averages**

| (Noon N.Y.) | Avg. | Chg. |
|---|---|---|
| 30 Industrials | 926.85 | +3.91 |
| 20 Transportations | 256.12 | +1.53 |
| 15 Utilities | 112.47 | +1.05 |
| 65 Stocks | 319.44 | +1.77 |

Noon sales, 9,790,030 shares

### Index



1


6 Sections XCIV—No. 72


** STAR TELEPHONES **

News, General ...... 372-4141
Want Ads ...... 372-4242
Circulation ...... 372-4343

## U.S. admits jets shot down in new DMZ raids

**SAIGON, South Vietnam (UPI)—U.S. jet fighter-bombers struck artillery batteries and other targets in North Vietnam Wednesday and today. Radio Hanoi said seven planes were shot down and several pilots killed and captured.**

**The raids into the north followed a week of record bombing of Communist targets in Indochina aimed at disrupting what U.S. officials have predicted would be a major Communist offensive timed to coincide with the Tet holidays and President Nixon's visit to China.**

**U.S. spokesmen reported only one U.S. plane was shot down, "probably by a missile." They acknowledged that others were lost, but declined to give details pending the completion of search and rescue operations.**

**Military sources said the United States had rushed a fresh squadron of 20 F4 Phantom fighter-bombers to Indochina to boster its air power and to make up for recent losses.**

**The move was the latest in a series of steps to build up American airpower. Recently the command ordered a third aircraft carrier on line in the Tonkin Gulf, adding about 80 warplanes to the fleet, and asked the Strategic Air Command to start flying B52s from Guam.**

## Finally, the copper in her brain was found

### *'IT WAS SO BAD I WAS CRAWLING ON MY BELLY'*

By GORDON SLOVUT
Minneapolis Star Staff Writer

Three years ago Jan Bourgerie began feeling tired all of the time.

She thought it would go away. But within two months she had lost nearly all sensation in her hands. Hot objects would burn her skin before she knew they were hot.

Then she developed a peculiar, twisting, bobbing walk and double vision.

"It was all so strange I thought I must be imagining it all," Mrs. Bourgerie, 28, 2960 Kentucky Av. N., Crystal, recalls.

Mrs. Bourgerie, the mother of three grade-school-age children, stayed in the house most of the time, avoiding people.

"Finally," she said, "I said I'd had enough and would have to go to a doctor."

She presented herself at Hennepin County General Hospital. She was run through numerous tests as doctors sought the cause of her problems. They ruled out a brain tumor. They had blood serum tests performed to check the possibility of rare metabolic diseases.

Finally they decided multiple sclerosis was her problem—an incurable disease of unknown cause which attacks the nerve coverings and mysteriously comes and goes. She was put on ACTH—a steroid drug—and showed some improvement and went home.

"I'd seem to be all right for three months, then I'd have problems

Minneapolis Star Photo by Roy Swan

MRS. JAN BOURGERIE

again, and then I would get worse," she said.

Her condition really worsened last fall. "It reached a peak in October," she said. "It was so bad I was crawling on my belly."

She telephoned Dr. John G. Bradley, a Minneapolis internist, and Dr. Roger E. Farber, a Golden Valley neurologist, and they suggested that she enter Abbott Hospital for some tests.

"I took some steroids so I could go to the hospital in a car instead of an ambulance," she says. "My husband drove me."

Farber and Bradley went over her tests and thought that perhaps the woman didn't have multiple sclerosis. The disease is one selected after ruling out others, but a symptom, sometimes, is a reflex called a "positive" Babinski (checked by stroking the bottom of the foot). Her Babinski was negative.

Farber, whose specialty involves the brain and nervous system, suspected that perhaps she had Wilson's disease, a relatively rare familial disease in which the body stores copper instead of excreting it. There


ILLNESS
Turn to Page 2A

Minneapolis Tribune

Wednesday
September 6
1972

15c Single copy
3 Sections

1A

Volume CVI
Number 105
M

# 9 Israeli Olympians, 4 Arabs die in shootout at German air base

Tribune Wire Service

**Munich, West Germany**
Nine Israeli hostages who were seized more than 20 hours earlier by Arab guerrillas died in a blaze of gunfire and the explosion of a helicopter early today as their captors tried to spirit them out of the country from an airport near Munich.

The hostages were killed after they endured a day of terror in their Olympic Village headquarters, where two of their countrymen had been killed in an early morning raid by the radical Palestinian terrorists.

A West German government informant said four of the Palestinian guerrillas were dead, three were captured and one was unaccounted for following a gun battle with police at Fuerstenfeldbruck air base, 25 miles from Munich. One policeman was reported killed.

It had been reported earlier that the hostages were rescued.

The guerrillas and their hostages had been flown to the base in helicopters, seeking an aircraft for a flight to Tunisia.

Olympic officials said a decision on whether to continue the games would be made after today's memorial service for the dead Israelis.

The guerrilla group, members of an organization called Black September, early Tuesday morning had invaded the quarters of the Israeli men's Olympic team in Munich where they seized the hostages.

They demanded that 200 guerrillas held in Israeli prisons be freed in exchange for the lives of the hostages.

Bavarian Interior Minister Bruno Merck offered no explanation why spokesmen had officially announced that the kidnapped Israelis had been rescued safely. The refusal of the guerrillas to back down on their demands for planes to transport the hostages to an Arab country, and for the Palestinian prisoners release, led German police to concoct a trap with sharpshooters.

They pretended to accede to the Arab demands and late last night three helicopters left an improvised landing pad in the Olympic Village for Fuerstenfeldbruck. The eight guerrillas and their eight blindfolded and bound hostages rode in the first two helicopters. German officials including German Interior Minister Hans-Dietrich Genscher rode in the third.

A Boeing 727 was waiting at the airport and two of the guerrillas went to inspect it. The sharpshooters thought they had the Arabs isolated from the plane and the helicopters and opened fire. But, according to one version, at least one Arab managed to toss a grenade into the helicopter carrying the hostages.

Merck said the hostages had agreed to go with the Arabs on a flight to Cairo. But the German negotiators feared "this would have been a certain death sentence for them. Therefore, we had to take a chance and attempt to free the hostages."

The events began about 4:30 a.m. (10:30 p.m. Monday, Minneapolis time) when some technicians saw a number of men, faces blackened, climbing a wall into the village. Some versions place the number of climbers at nine. The technicians did not report the incident since they thought the men might be athletes breaking training.

Weinberg Berger Shapira

Not long thereafter there was a burst of shooting outside 31 Connolly Strasse, a three-story building in which Israel had the two lower floors. Hong Kong and Uruguay shared the third floor.

Israeli Coach Moshe Weinberg was shot to death when the terrorists burst into his apartment after climbing the fence surrounding the village.

The Israeli Olympic Committee said Yosef Ramano, a weightlifter, also was killed. Olympic officials a little later confirmed this second death.

Some Israelis escaped by leaping out windows or dashing down back stairs.

For a few hours, the games went on. Then they were suspended by Avery Brundage, the Olympic chief, and the German organizing committee. Announcing the memorial service for today, they said, "This service should make clear the Olympic idea is stronger than terror and violence."

The entire Egyptian team flew home after forfeiting a basketball game. "They fear for their lives," a spokesman said.

**Hostages** continued on page 4A

Ramano Spitzer Shorr

United Press International

**A helicopter carrying Arab guerrillas and their Israeli hostages took off from Olympic Village Tuesday.**

United Press International

**Two Munich policemen escorted an unidentified prisoner away from the Israeli team quarters late Tuesday following the departure of a group of Arab guerrillas and their Israeli hostages.**

## German reports on hostages confused

New York Times Service

**New York, N.Y.**
Contradictory reports about the fate of the Israeli hostages seized by Arab terrorists in the Olympic Village threw the public into confusion all over the world Tuesday.

Throughout the day, as the tragedy in Munich, West Germany, unfolded, millions of viewers throughout the world watched the drama on television, which was employing circuits that had been intended for the games. But in the evening, when the events reached their climax, viewers could get no definitive word for hours on how the hostages fared.

At first the German government's official spokesman, Conrad Ahlers, announced that intervention of German police and soldiers at an airport had led to the escape of the hostages unharmed. This was confirmed by Avery Brundage, retiring president of the International Olympic Committee.

Then there was silence, while police reports dealt with the number of terrorists killed or still at large. There was some speculation about how the hostages had escaped.

The next phase was an expression of doubt by the Munich police. A telephone call to Munich police headquarters by the New York Times brought the admission that "everything is confused."

A minor Olympics official said he had received no confirmation of any reports about the hostages and did not know if they were alive or dead.

At this point, what had been a partial news blackout became very strict, touching off rumors that some, perhaps all, of the hostages were dead.

Finally, a complete contradiction of the German government spokesman's first position came from the mayor of Munich, when he told reporters that all of the hostages were dead.

## Almanac / Index

Wednesday
September 6 1972
250th day
116 to go this year
Sunrise: 6:41 am
Sunset: 7:42 pm

**Today's weather**
**Showers**

Details page 9B

**Tuesday's temperatures**

| am | 1 | 2 | 3 | 4 | 5 | 6 | 7 | 8 | 9 | 10 | 11 | Noon |
|---|---|---|---|---|---|---|---|---|---|---|---|---|
| temp | 58 | 57 | 57 | 55 | 53 | 53 | 53 | 53 | 57 | 58 | 62 | 65 |
| pm | 1 | 2 | 3 | 4 | 5 | 6 | 7 | 8 | 9 | 10 | 11 | Midn |
| temp | 66 | 67 | 69 | 70 | 71 | 71 | 68 | 64 | 63 | 62 | 62 | 62 |

Cloudy skies and a 70-percent chance of rain are predicted for the Twin Cities today. Winds from the south will range from 15 to 25 miles per hour, but will be stronger if thunderstorms occur as predicted this afternoon or tonight. High temperatures today will be in the low 70s, lows tonight in the mid 50s.

Other predicted high temperatures: Minnesota, low 60s north, mid 70s south; North Dakota, 60s; South Dakota, near 70 northwest to low 80s southeast; Wisconsin, 68 to 76 north, 75 to 84 south.

### She's not taking any chances

A Mankato woman recently called her regular service station and asked if she should have her car serviced for a long trip. "Where are you going?" asked the the attendant. "Minneapolis," the woman said.



Telephones
372 4141 News General
372 4242 Classified
372 4343 Circulation

## State candidate for House runs on rural-poverty issue

By Steve Dornfeld
Staff Writer

**Detroit Lakes, Minn.**
While his opponents talk about the evils of crime and gun control, Jerry Buckanaga is attempting to make an issue of rural poverty in his campaign for the Minnesota House.

"Year after year our county (Becker) ranks as one of the poorest in the state," Buckanaga says. "Yet, the issue has never been discussed in a legislative race in our district."

Buckanaga, a DFLer from Ponsford, is one of three candidates on the Sept. 12 primary ballot in District 10A, which is located in northwestern Minnesota.

This primary is attracting special attention because Buckanaga, Harvard-educated Chippewa Indian, is attempting to crack the all-white state Legislature, as are eight black candidates in metropolitan districts.

His opponents are Rep. Frank DeGroat, a Conservative from Lake Park who describes himself as "a spokesman for the Indians," and Robert Coalwell, a DFLer from Detroit Lakes who operates a bank within the White Earth Indian Reservation.

In contrast to Buckanaga, Coalwell said "law-and-order is the biggest single issue of this campaign" and DeGroat said his constituents are most concerned about possible gun-control legislation.

Buckanaga, 31, grew up in poverty in Ponsford on the southern edge of the reservation. Unlike many of his Indian friends, he completed high school in Park Rapids.

A Golden Gloves boxer, Buckanaga won the Upper Midwest light heavweight championship and a scholarship that helped him earn a bachelor's degree in education at Moorhead State College.

Buckanaga was principal at an experimental school

**Primary**
Continued on page 4A

Coalwell Buckanaga DeGroat

## Berrigan, nun are sentenced to prison

Tribune Wire Services

**Harrisburg, Pa.**
The Rev. Philip Berrigan — cleared of charges that he led a plot to kidnap presidential adviser Henry A. Kissinger — was sentenced in federal district court here Tuesday to four two-year terms for smuggling letters out of the Lewisburg Penitentiary.

The terms are concurrent, which means they run at the same time.

His purported co-conspirator, Sister Elizabeth McAlister, was sentenced to one year in prison and three years probation on letter smuggling charges.

At the same time, the government said it would not seek new trials for Father Berrigan and other members of the so-called Harrisburg Seven on the conspiracy charges upon

**Berrigan**
Continued on page 15A

## Vote on election delay sought

By Catherine Watson
Staff Writer

The Concerned Citizens of Minneapolis Tuesday handed the city clerk about 850 petitions with an estimated 12,000 signatures calling for a referendum on an ordinance which changes the city's election date.

The petitioners needed only 7,671 signatures of registered Minneapolis voters to put the matter on the general-election ballot in November.

Although the signatures must be reviewed by the city's Voter Registration Bureau, the petitioners are almost certain to have collected the necessary minimum.

This means the City Council must either rescind its ordinance postponing the next city election by six months — or put the election-date change before the people this November.

Either way is fine with the Concerned Citizens. They are confident that a referendum would fail.

The conservative, education-oriented citizens' group mobilized its petition drive in June, before the City Council on June 30 overrode Mayor Charles Stenvig's June 15 veto of the election-date change.

The council's action postpones the next city election from next spring to November 1973 — and extends by six months the terms of aldermen, the mayor and other elected city officials, and members of the School Board, the Library Board and the Park and Recreation Board.

Aldermen said they approved the election-date change, despite the mayor's veto, because a fall election will allow city officials to spend spring months at the State Legislature, lobbying on the city's behalf.

To the people who carried the petitions around the city, that kind of reasoning does not ring true.

"The main thing is that incumbents shouldn't be allowed to extend their own terms," said Chris Flynn, Concerned Citizens member and coordinator of the petition drive.

"The City Council tried to duck that issue," he said. The petitioners "don't object to a uniform (election) date — we're not opposed to a November election at all" — provided it doesn't extend the terms

**Petitions**
Continued on page 7A

## Fischer's timing better as champ

Associated Press

**Reykjavik, Iceland**
Newly crowned world chess champion Bobby Fischer, noted more for his chess skills than for his punctuality, was the first guest to arrive at a reception given Tuesday night by President Kristjan Eldjarn of Iceland.

Fischer arrived at the presidential residence 10 minutes before the time specified on the invitation.

He had kept 1,200 guests waiting for 50 minues Sunday night when he failed to arrive punctually for his formal crowning ceremony.

"This is not a chess game," Fischer said. "It's the president of Iceland."

Boris Spassky, whom Fischer defeated for the title, was also a guest at the reception. He arrived precisely on time.

Minneapolis Tribune

Wednesday
November 8
1972

Volume CVI
Number 168
S

15c Single copy
3 Sections

1A





# NIXON WINS IN A LANDSLIDE

## Democrats, GOP hold even in Senate races; Mondale, 5 congressmen win; 3 races in doubt

### President

By Frank Wright
Staff Correspondent

**Washington, D.C.**
President Nixon and Vice-President Spiro Agnew won reelection to a second term by a smashing and perhaps record margin in Tuesday's 1972 national election.

In state after state the Republican ticket rolled up huge majorities over the Democratic opposition of Sen. George McGovern of South Dakota and his running mate, Sargent Shriver.

McGovern conceded his defeat shortly before midnight, sending Mr. Nixon a congratulatory telegram pledging to support his pursuit of peace abroad and "justice at home."

Moments after the concession Mr. Nixon, in a televised victory appearance from his office in the Oval Room of the White House expressed his "appreciation" to those who voted for him.

As returns mounted, the Associated Press showed Mr. Nixon and Agnew carrying close to 40 states with upwards of 400 electoral votes — far surpassing the 270 electoral college votes necessary to win.

A total of 538 electoral votes were at stake in the 50 states and the District of Columbia, with a simple majority required for victory.

The Republican national ticket was winning almost everywhere—in such usually GOP strongholds as the suburbs; in such usually Democratic strongholds as the blue-collar precincts of the central cities; in the once-solidly Democratic South, where states that went to the now-incapacitated Gov. George Wallace of Alabama in 1968 shifted this year to Mr. Nixon; in the industrial northeast; in border states such as Kentucky and Tennessee, and in the agricultural Midwest, where rising farm prices kept the farmers happy and on the side of the incumbent.

McGovern, in contrast, could claim victory only in the District of Columbia and Massachusetts on the basis of returns counted in the first hours after the voting ended.

Mr. Nixon also was running way ahead in the popular vote, which has no legal meaning but is an excellent measure of the candidate's across-the-board national appeal. His margin over McGovern was holding at almost 2 to 1, which would be the biggest landslide ever if maintained.

It would surpass the best previous mark of 61.1 percent of the votes which Democrat Lyndon Johnson rolled up against Republican Sen. Barry Goldwater of Arizona in 1964.

**President** continued on page 8A

United Press International

**President and Mrs. Nixon appeared happy as they arrived at Andrews Air Force Base near Washington.**

### Senate

By Al McConagha
Staff Correspondent

**Washington, D.C.**
President Nixon's landslide victory Tuesday night appeared to be insufficient in the counting of early returns to propel the GOP into control of the Senate.

According to early reports, both parties won one seat previously controlled by the other. Democrats led in three states with GOP incumbents. Republican candidates were ahead in three states with Democratic incumbents.

This indicated to observers last night that the GOP was unlikely to achieve the net gain of five seats needed to wrest control from the Democrats who now enjoy a 55-45 margin.

Democrat Walter Huddleston, 46, defeated former GOP Gov. Louie B. Nunn, 48, to become the first Democrat elected by Kentucky to the Senate in 18 years. GOP incumbent John Sherman Cooper is retiring.

In New Mexico, Republican Peter V. Domenici clung to the Nixon coattails to defeat Democrat Jack Daniels, former state representative, as the successor to retiring Democratic Sen. Clinton Anderson.

Two other veteran Democrats and committee chairmen were reelected. Sen. James Eastland of Mississippi and Sen. John McClellan of Arkansas were returned in easy contests. In Georgia State Rep. Sam Nunn, 34, Democrat, defeated GOP Rep. Fletcher Thompson, 47, in another close race. Earlier Nunn beat freshman incumbent David Gambrell in a Democratic party runoff.

In one of the evening's most startling races, Rep. William D. Hathaway, Democrat, unexpectedly led GOP Sen. Margaret Chase Smith, who became a Maine institution in her 24 years in the Senate.

In Delaware, Joseph R. Bi-

**Senate**
Continued on page 8A

### Congress

By Howard Erickson
Staff Writer

Minnesotans reelected Sen. Walter F. Mondale and five congressmen Tuesday.

Returned to new terms in the House were Reps. Donald M. Fraser of Minneapolis, Bill Frenzel of Golden Valley, Joseph Karth of St. Paul, Albert Quie of Dennison, and John Blatnik of Chisholm.

Early returns left the status of three other Congressmen unclear:

- Rep. Ancher Nelson of Hutchinson, who faced DFLer Charlie Turnbull, 39, a social agency supervisor in St. Peter. The 67-year-old former lieutenant governor, the ranking Republican on the House District of Columbia Committee, sought his eighth term representing the 2nd District of south central Minnesota.

- Republican Rep. John M. Zwach of Walnut Grove who was running against DFL State Rep. Richard Nolan, 28, a St. Cloud instructor and two-term legislator from a Little Falls district. Zwach, 65, was seeking his fourth term in the 6th Congressional District of central and western Minnesota.

- Rep. Robert Bergland of Roseau who outdid his 1970 performance in many precincts in the northwestern Minnesota 7th District against GOP State Rep. Jon O. Haaven, 38, an Alexandria publisher and former TV news director. The 44-year-old DFL farmer unseated Republican Odin Langen in 1970 by 12,082 votes.

Mondale, 44, defeated Republican Philip Hansen, 45, a Lutheran minister and alcoholics counselor from Roseville, to win his second full term in the Senate.

The Afton DFLer was appointed in 1964 after Hubert Humphrey resigned to become vice-president.

Hansen, a political novice, mounted a vigorous campaign against the former attorney general, but the well-known Mondale was never in serious trouble.

Also running yesterday was Karl Heck, a White Bear Lake school janitor with Socialist Labor Party backing.

Frenzel, 44, a former warehouse president and four-term state representative, had his principal opposition from DFLer James Bell, 40, a Bloomington school consultant. The GOP freshman also beat Donald H. Wright, 36, a St. Louis Park salesman who had T-Party endorsement in the suburban Minneapolis 3rd District.

DFLer Fraser, a lawyer and former state senator, defeated three opponents to win his sixth term in Congress from the 5th Dis-

**Congress**
Continued on page 8A

Frenzel

Fraser

## The How and Why of Minnesota's Vote

**The following analysis of how Minnesotans voted in Tuesday's election is derived from a representative model of the state's 3,900 precincts. Though it comprises less than 3 percent of the precincts, the 101-precinct model accurately reflects the state's political, social and economic complexion.**



By Bernie Shellum
Staff Writer

President Nixon made heavy inroads into the Democratic-Farmer-Labor vote in precincts heavily populated by labor union members. With 54 of the Minneapolis Tribune's 101 sample precincts reported, he was taking as much as 15 percent of the vote that has gone to major DFL candidates in these precincts in recent elections.

These incursions contributed to a slim lead which Mr. Nixon held over Sen. George McGovern, the Democratic nominee. In the 54 sample precincts, Mr. Nixon was winning 49.6 percent of the vote, compared with 48.1 percent for McGovern. Five minor presidential tickets were receiving a total of 2.3 percent of the Minnesota vote.

In those precincts with the heaviest concentration of labor unionists, McGovern was running 11 percentage points behind Sen. Hubert Humphrey's performance as the Democratic nominee in 1968. The McGovern loss was lessened in precincts with lighter union concentration, but still ranged to a substantial 6 percentage points.

Mr. Nixon's share of the vote in the labor precincts ranged from 44, where to concentration is heaviest, to 50 percent in those where it is light to moderate.

These vote losses appeared to cost McGovern most heavily in the 4th, 5th and 8th Congressional Districts. He was running 21 points behind Rep. Joseph Karth in the 4th, 18 points behind Rep. Donald Fraser in the 5th, and 32 points behind Rep. John Blatnik in the 8th.

**Model** continued on page 8A

## Wisconsin vote favors Nixon for 3rd time

By Sam Martino
Staff Writer

**Milwaukee, Wis.**
Wisconsin, which boosted George McGovern into the presidential sweepstakes with his first primary victory, leaned toward President Nixon for the third straight time, early election returns indicated.

Mr. Nixon carried the state in 1960 in his race against John F. Kennedy and again in 1968 against Hubert H. Humphrey.

McGovern had considered Wisconsin a friendly state after it gave him a dramatic primary-election victory on April 4.

Mr. Nixon was running about even with McGovern in normally Democratic areas of the state, which has 11 electoral votes. However, not all was sweet for the GOP.

The outcome was uncertain in the race between Republican Alvin O'Konski, 68, the dean of the state's congressional delegation, and Rep. David Obey, 34, a Democrat.

O'Konski has served in the House since 1942 while Obey won election to Congress in 1969 when he replaced Melvin Laird who vacated his seat to become secretary of defense in the Nixon administration. The districts of the two congressmen were merged in reapportionment.

Another Republican congressman, Vernon Thomson, appeared in trouble in the 3rd Congressional District.

Walter Thoresen, a sociology professor from the University of Wisconsin-Eau Claire, was in a tight race with Thomson, 66, a former two-term Republican governor who has served in the House for six terms. Both Thomson and O'Konski have been

**Wisconsin**
Continued on page 8A

## Democrats' control of House seems safe

By Finlay Lewis
Staff Correspondent

**Washington, D.C.**
Control of the U.S. House of Representatives appeared destined to remain safely in the hands of the Democrats, despite President Nixon's massive sweep of the popular vote at the top of the Republican ticket.

Early returns from Eastern and Midwestern districts indicated that voters were splitting their tickets in massive numbers to prevent the Republican congressional campaign from making significant inroads in the Democratic majority.

At present, the Democrats control 254 seats and the Republicans, 177, with four vacancies. Two of the vacant seats were held most recently by Democrats and two by Republicans. The figures mean that Republicans must pick up 41 seats in order to seize control of House machinery.

Mr. Nixon's coattails, however, were appearing to have only minor effect in early returns which recorded one clear shift of a Democratic seat to a Republican.

That shift occurred in Indianapolis, Ind., where the Rev. William Hudnut III, 39, a Presbyterian minister, defeated the Democratic incumbent, Rep. Andrew Jacobs, 40, a four-term congressman.

In other races, Republicans were leading in races for 20 seats now held by Democrats, while Democrats were leading in contests for seven Republican seats.

In Brooklyn, Elizabeth Holtzman, a 30-year-old lawyer who defeated Emanuel Celler in the Democratic primary, appeared headed for victory in the final election yes-

**House**
Continued on page 8A

## Election at a Glance

Sen. George McGovern conceded defeat as President Nixon won the electoral votes of at least 40 states Tuesday night.

However, the Nixon landslide did not appear to be sweeping large numbers of Republicans into other offices.

- Senate. The Republican Party appeared to be only holding its own, winning a Democratic seat but losing one of its own.

- House. The House appeared destined to remain in the hands of the Democrats. Although the Republicans were leading in several races for Democratic seats, Democrats were also making inroads in Republican territory.

- Minnesota. There were few surprises in legislative races. The reelection of Sen. Jack Davies, proponent of no-fault auto insurance, was one of them. Former Gov. Karl Rolvaag held a slight lead over P. Kenneth Peterson in their contest for a seat on the Public Service Commission.

## McGovern lauds peacemakers in tearless concession speech

By James Parsons
Staff Writer

**Sioux Falls, S.D.**
While two of his daughters wiped away tears, Sen. George McGovern conceded Tuesday's election to President Nixon and told his supporters at a rally in Sioux Falls that they should not "shed any tears" over his defeat.

McGovern told a cheering crowd of 2,000 to 3,000 supporters that he sent a telegram to Mr. Nixon about 10:30 p.m. last night (Minneapolis time) congratulating him on the victory.

McGovern said in the wire that he hopes the next four years will bring peace abroad and in America.

McGovern went to the gaily-decorated Coliseum in Sioux Falls after watching the election returns on television in his suite at the nearby Holiday Inn.

He quoted one of Abraham Lincoln's favorite sayings about the man who said "'it hurts too much to laugh and I'm too old to cry'" to describe his feelings.

"Shed no tears because all our efforts, I'm positive, will bear fruit for years to come. The joy of this campaign for the past two years must be washed away with the tears and regrets of one night.

"There is no question in my mind that we have pushed this country in the direction of peace. I'm sure each one of us loves the title of peacemaker more than any office in this land," he said.

The audience interrupted him with the loudest applause of the evening at that point.

McGovern urged his supporters, many of them in their teens and twenties, to "not despair of the political process in this country."

He said the campaign has helped the nation renew its ideals and become a more humane society.

McGovern then embraced his wife and children before leaving the platform.

The crowd chanted, "'76," "'76," "'76" . . .

Earlier, Judith Dodge, who is 45 and the mother of three, was in the front row along with the teenagers in their hip huggers, waiting for McGovern's return.

Mrs. Dodge thought he looked quite distinguished, even "dynamic."

**McGovern**
Continued on page 8A

## Almanac / Index

**Wednesday
November 8 1972
313th day
53 to go this year
Sunrise: 7:01 am
Sunset: 4:53 pm**

**Today's weather**
**Warmer**

Details page 9B

**Tuesday's temperatures**

| am | 1 | 2 | 3 | 4 | 5 | 6 | 7 | 8 | 9 | 10 | 11 | Noon |
|---|---|---|---|---|---|---|---|---|---|---|---|---|
| temp | 40 | 38 | 38 | 36 | 35 | 34 | 33 | 32 | 32 | 31 | 31 | 33 |
| pm | 1 | 2 | 3 | 4 | 5 | 6 | 7 | 8 | 9 | 10 | 11 | Midn |
| temp | 33 | 34 | 34 | 34 | 33 | 33 | 31 | 31 | 33 | 33 | 34 | 34 |

Partially clearing skies are expected this afternoon in the Twin Cities area, with increasing cloudiness again tonight and a possibility of occasional rain Thursday. Predicted high today, 40; low tonight, about 32, and predicted high Thursday, about 45.

Other predicted highs today: Minnesota, 25 to 35 northeast, 35 to 45 south and west; North Dakota, 32 to 42 east, 42 to 52 west; South Dakota, mid 40s northeast to upper 50s southwest; Wisconsin, 30s.

### Vote for the flag

A northeast Minneapolis mother, about to leave home to vote yesterday, asked her 3½-year-old son who she should vote for, Nixon or McGovern. Her son's reply was to the point. "Vote for the flag, Mommy," he said.



Telephones
372 4141 News General
372 4242 Classified
372 4343 Circulation

Minneapolis Tribune

Wednesday
December 27
1972

Volume CVI
Number 217
M

15¢ Single copy
3 Sections





# Renewed bombing stirs debate over strategy

By David E. Rosenbaum
New York Times Service

**Washington, D.C.**
The resumption of sustained bombing by the United States throughout North Vietnam has revived the debate here and abroad over the efficacy of the bombing strategy.

Does the bombing of military and industrial targets significantly hamper the capacity of North Vietnam to fight the war? Does it prevent the movement of North Vietnamese troops and supplies into South Vietnam? Does it make the Hanoi government more willing to negotiate or concede, or does it strengthen resistance and determination to pursue the war?

If there are military and diplomatic benefits from the bombing, do they justify the civilian casualties? What were the provocations that triggered the latest campaign? Are the current raids different, in magnitude or in terms of the targets assaulted, from those of the past? Is it immoral, in time of war, for a large nation that itself is not under attack to drop bombs on a small nation that has no offensive capacity in the air?

These are the questions that provide the meat of the debate, although, clearly, only the North Vietnamese know precisely how bad the country, its people and its military system have been and are being hurt by the bombing.

In the first year of the Nixon administration, the government acknowledged only occasional incidents of "suppressive fire" by small numbers of planes against antiaircraft installations in North Vietnam that threatened American reconnaissance aircraft.

But in May 1970, following the movement of American troops into Cambodia, the United States conducted a series of heavy raids on supply dumps and other targets north of the demilitarized zone. The raids were described as "protective reaction." Similar attacks continued over the next two years.

In April 1972, in response to a North Vietnamese offensive, the rule of protective reaction was officially lifted and intensive bombing resumed throughout North Vietnam. For the first time B52s were used extensively and, for the first time since 1968, Hanoi and Haiphong

**Strategy** continued on page 11A

# National day of mourning is proclaimed for Truman

Tribune Wire Service

A national day of mourning Thursday for the funeral of Harry S Truman was proclaimed Tuesday by President Nixon.

Mr. Truman died at 7:50 a.m. (Minneapolis time) yesterday at Research Hospital in Kansas City, Mo. He was 88.

He had been a patient there for 22 days, stubbornly struggling against lung congestion, heart irregularity, kidney blockages, failure of his digestive system and the encroachments of old age.

Harry S Truman

A hospital spokesman said death resulted from the "complexity of organic failures causing collapse of the cardio-vascular system." The former president had been in a coma for three days.

A state funeral will be held Thursday in Independence, situated about 10 miles east of Kansas City. Independence is the site of the former president's home and the library that houses the papers and mementos he accumulated during 18 years in Washington as senator, vice-president and president.

Mr. Nixon's proclamation ordered flags flown at half-staff for 30 days and the closing of all but essential government agencies Thursday.

He and Mrs. Nixon will fly to Independence today and will lay a wreath at the Truman Library, where the body will lie in state.

The Nixons plan to return to Washington immediately, indicating that they will not attend the funeral. The reason, it appeared, is the desire of the Truman family to have a private funeral.

**Reaction — 3A**

**Obituary — 4A**

**Pictures — 5A**

In a statement issued an hour after word of Mr. Truman's death reached the vacation White House in Key Biscayne, Fla., Mr. Nixon said:

"Harry S Truman will be remembered as one of the most courageous presidents in our history, who led the nation and the world through a critical period with exceptional vision and determination. Our hopes today for a generation of peace rest in large measure on the firm foundations that he laid.

"He was a fighter, who was at his best when the going was toughest," Mr. Nixon continued. And then, making tacit reference to his own criticisms, Mr. Nixon said, Mr. Truman's friends and opponents alike "recognized and admired him—i. a description he himself might

**Truman** continued on page 11A

United Press International

**Mrs. Bess Truman, right, and Mrs. Margaret Truman Daniel left the Truman home Tuesday for the funeral home where the body of Harry S Truman was taken.**

## Reds: Talks can resume if bombing is halted

New York Times Service

**Paris, France**
North Vietnam, denouncing the resumption of American bombing of Hanoi, indicated Tuesday that it is still ready to resume negotiation if the attacks are halted.

Nguyen Than Le, spokesman for Hanoi's delegation to the peace talks, said in a statement that if the United States really wants to settle the war by serious negotiation, "it must cease immediately the acts of escalation of the war against the Democratic Republic of Vietnam, abandon threats through use of force and, in the first place, return to the situation existing before Dec. 18."

It was on that date that the Nixon administration announced resumption of air attacks above the 20th parallel following an apparent breakdown of the private talks held here between Henry Kissinger, the President's national security adviser, and Le Duc Tho, the North Vietnamese Politburo member.

Yesterday's statement by the North Vietnamese made it apparent that attacks on Hanoi, Haiphong and other heavily populated areas are an obstacle to further talks but that those conducted below the 20th parallel are not.

"Flouting the vigorous denunciations of the Vietnamese people, of world opinion and of large sectors of American opinion," Le said, "the Nixon administration persists in going back on its commitments to cease the bombings of Hanoi, to abstain from bombing above the 20th parallel, and to restrict bombing below the 20th parallel to create a climate favorable for negotiation."

The demilitarized zone, the line of demarcation between North Vietnam and South Vietnam, lies along the 17th parallel. Between the 17th and 20th parallel lies the narrow southern tip of North Vietnam with a large number of towns and villages but nothing of the size and importance of Hanoi and Haiphong.

# U.S. resumes bombing of North Vietnam

Associated Press

**Saigon, South Vietnam**
U.S. planes and warships Tuesday resumed the bombardment of North Vietnam, ending a 36-hour Christmas pause in the war's heaviest raids.

The U.S. command, in its first announcement on the holiday suspension, also said that a 24-hour bombing pause in South Vietnam ended at dusk Monday.

North Vietnam claimed that eight more U.S. B52 Stratofortresses and an F4 fighter-bomber were shot down yesterday after the raids were resumed. A broadcast from Hanoi said "many aggressor pilots" were captured.

The broadcast said five B52s were shot down over Hanoi, two over the port of Haiphong and one north of Hanoi. There was no reaction from the U.S. command. It does not comment on Hanoi claims.

Command spokesmen refused to say why the break over North Vietnam lasted longer than that in South Vietnam.

Other U.S. officials indicated that the northern suspension had been extended hour by hour while President Nixon awaited some indication from Hanoi that it was willing to resume the stalled secret peace talks. In recent years, U.S. holiday truces have applied only to South Vietnam.

Maj. Jere K. Forbus, spokesman for the U.S. command, refused to link the raids on North Vietnam with peace negotiations although he said there were different reasons behind the suspensions in North Vietnam and South Vietnam. Forbus said U.S. military authorities had known from the start how long the pause over North Vietnam would last.

The raids resumed under the same secrecy that masked the suspension and the escalation of bombing to the Hanoi-Haiphong area last week. Forbus said no new limitations had been imposed on the renewed strikes, and refused to comment on the number of raids or their targets.

Asked why the holiday suspensions of attacks were not announced in advance as in the past, Forbus replied: "Given the condition, we believed an advantage would accrue to the enemy by virtue of foreknowledge of the stand-down."

Asked why no word was forthcoming until nearly 24 hours after the southern pause ended, he said the command deemed it reasonable to announce it only after it had terminated as a package."

Other officials said the Hanoi-Haiphong heartland was again being hit. Hanoi Radio claimed that a U.S. F4 Phantom fighter-bomber was shot down northeast of Hanoi shortly after the attacks resumed at 1 p.m. yesterday. It did not mention the two crewmen.

North Vietnam claims that it has shot down 55 U.S. planes — including 18 B52 bombers — since Dec. 18. The U.S. command has acknowledged 18 aircraft lost — including 11 B52s — and 70 fliers missing. The command does not give exact figures on missing fliers in the hope that some may be rescued.

A lull persisted in ground fighting in South Vietnam. The South Vietnamese command reported 63 Communist attacks — about average over recent weeks — during the Communists' announced Christmas truce period from 1 p.m. Sunday to 1 p.m. Monday.

Thirty-two of the attacks resulted in 38 government troops and five civilians killed and 51 South Vietnamese troops and 10 civilians wounded plus 60 Communists killed, the Saigon command said.

The U.S. command said no Americans were killed or wounded in cease-fire violations, but that one U.S. serviceman was wounded in a 35-round rocket attack that hit Da Nang Air Base and nearby residential areas. Two civilians were reported killed and two wounded. A U.S. Army helicopter was reported destroyed.

## City hospital plans to start major mental health effort

By Lewis Cope
Staff Writer

Abbott Hospital announced plans Tuesday to launch a major mental health program, including a walk-in center to make it easier for anyone to get help.

Hospital officials said that assuming they are granted a necessary certificate of need from the Minnesota Board of Health, they plan to:

■ Increase the number of beds for psychiatric patients from the present 52 to almost 100 and, in the process, add specialized units for young children and young adults.

The hospital already has adolescent and regular adult psychiatric units. The expansion to 100 beds would give Abbott one of the largest inpatient psychiatric programs in the Minneapolis area.

■ Open a "neighborhood counseling center" with a professional staff of seven in a building across the street from the hospital. It is to provide quick help or advice about minor mental health concerns, and also extensive outpatient counseling for those who need it.

The center is to be "readily accessible" to anyone from a youngster with a drug problem to "the elderly who are depressed

**Abbott**
Continued on page 12A

## City woman found stabbed to death was 'upper-class call girl'

By Greg Schmidt
Staff Writer

"If she was in trouble," said Jon Prentice, "I just wish she had come to us. It might have been a different story."

Prentice, head of the Minneapolis Police Department's Morals Squad, was talking about Jeanne Henderson, a 22-year-old call girl who was found Sunday after she had been beaten and stabbed to death on the floor of her North Side apartment.

Said one police officer, "She was a good whore.

"She wasn't like a lot of them," he said. "She didn't go in for robbing and rolling her customers, and kept off the streets.

Jeanne Henderson

"And she was one of the prettiest ones there was."

Her body was found by her mother and sister. They had flown in from Salt Lake City for a Christmas visit.

Homicide Capt. Henry Deason said she apparently had been killed last

**Jeanne**
Continued on page 12A

# Law to dampen New Year spirits early

By John Gehrke
Staff Writer

Many New Year's Eve revelers in Minnesota this year may have a headache before the morning after. Why? Because the holiday falls on a Sunday and, under state law, no liquor can be sold after midnight on Sundays and the bars then must close.

Nineteen of Bloomington's nightclub owners have come up with a gimmick to alleviate the problem: They're going to set the clocks ahead a half hour.

"Then when people see the clock says midnight, we'll break out the hats and noisemakers," said Al Baker, general manager of Howard Wong's restaurant, 2701 W. 78th St. "But it will really only be 11:30 and we'll still have 30 minutes to sell liquor."

William Brooks Jr., a member of the state Commission on Alcohol Problems, likes the Bloomington plan.

"If people belt down their booze at the last minute (midnight), they become drunk sooner," he said.

But most bar owners in the Twin Cities surveyed Tuesday looked askance at the plan.

"Who needs another half hour?" said Joe Duffy, owner of Duff's, 21 S. 8th St. "Because people are going to start drinking on Friday they'll be so drunk by midnight Sunday that it doesn't make that much difference."

"If it isn't that time (exactly midnight), it isn't that time," said a bartender at Arthur's Four Seasons, 2300 University Av. NE. "It just won't work. Years ago we even tried celebrating it on a Saturday and it flopped."

Some bar owners said the Bloomington plan is illegal. (It's not, according to the state attorney general's office.) "Well, at least it's wrong," one said.

One St. Paul bar owner said he will lock the doors at midnight and let those customers inside drink until the wee hours of the morning.

**Closing** continued on page 12A

## Almanac / Index

**Wednesday**
**December 27 1972**
**362nd day**
**4 to go this year**
**Sunrise: 7:51 am**
**Sunset: 4:38 pm**

**Today's weather**
**Warmer**

Details page 7B

**Tuesday's temperatures**

| | | | | | | | | | | | | |
|---|---|---|---|---|---|---|---|---|---|---|---|---|
| am | 1 | 2 | 3 | 4 | 5 | 6 | 7 | 8 | 9 | 10 | 11 | Noon |
| **temp** | **9** | **11** | **10** | **10** | **9** | **7** | **4** | **1** | **2** | **3** | **6** | **8** |
| pm | 1 | 2 | 3 | 4 | 5 | 6 | 7 | 8 | 9 | 10 | 11 | Midn |
| **temp** | **12** | **15** | **16** | **14** | **13** | **14** | **14** | **18** | **21** | **22** | **22** | **22** |

Warmer weather is predicted today for the Twin Cities area. There is little chance of precipitation. High temperatures today and Thursday will be in the mid 30s. The low tonight will be in the low 20s.

Other predicted highs: Minnesota, high 20s north, low 40s south; North Dakota, 28 northeast, 44 southwest; South Dakota, 38 to 40 northeast, 48 to 58 southwest; Wisconsin, low to mid 30s.

### Pulling the wool over our eyes?

A former Twin Cities man now raises cattle in Wyoming. He says you can tell the beef men out there by their bumper stickers: "Eat Sheep 100,000 coyotes can't be wrong."



**Telephones**
372 4141 News General
372 4242 Classified
372 4343 Circulation

Minneapolis Tribune

Sunday
January 28
1973

35c Single copy

1A

Volume CVI
Number 249
M



# Cease-fire ends Vietnam War

Associated Press

Secretary of State William P. Rogers reached for a pen to sign the agreement ending the Vietnam War. Behind Rogers was Leon Zinzus, a member of the French Foreign Ministry staff. The man at left, an aide to Rogers, was not identified.

Associated Press

**Paris, France**
The United States and North Vietnam formally called an end to their long undeclared war Saturday and their envoys drank a champagne toast to peace and friendship.

They were joined by the South Vietnamese and the Viet Cong in signing the documents that called for a cease-fire, the exchange of prisoners and a withdrawal of all U.S. forces from Vietnam.

The time for the cease-fire on Vietnam's battlefields was midnight Greenwich Mean Time—6 p.m., Minneapolis time. The exchange of prisoners and the withdrawal of U.S. troops is to take place within 60 days.

To get around the refusal of South Vietnam and the Viet Cong's provisional revolutionary government to recognize each other, Secretary of State William P. Rogers and North Vietnam's foreign minister, Nguyen Duy Trinh signed a separate set of documents later in the day.

The two ceremonies, the first lasting 18 minutes and the other 10 minutes in the ballroom of the former Hotel Majestic, were followed by toasts with champagne.

Witnesses said all the envoys taking part clinked glasses, including Foreign Minister Tran Van Lam of South Vietnam and Mrs. Nguyen Thi Binh, the Viet Cong foreign minister.

All four ministers were silent during the signing ceremonies held under the floodlights of television cameras. But while Lam and the other South Vietnamese officials wore grim expressions throughout, Rogers and Hanoi's Trinh twice exchanged nods and a flicker of a smile.

Lam and Mrs. Binh attended only the first ceremony, which began and ended with a noisy celebration by several hundred Viet Cong and North Vietnamese sympathizers in front of the building.

Lam later called on the French foreign minister, Maurice Schumann, to lodge a formal protest that the demonstration was tolerated by French police. The demonstrators waved hundreds of Viet Cong and North Vietnamese flags and shouted slogans hostile to President Nguyen Van Thieu. South Vietnamese delegation informants said Schumann expressed his regrets.

**Cease-fire** continued on page 10A

Staff Photos by Richard Olsenius

The cemetery in Dexter, Minn.

# Laird ends draft after signing

Associated Press

**Washington, D.C.**
Defense Secretary Melvin R. Laird announced Saturday that "use of the draft has ended."

His action, which places the nation's armed forces on an all-volunteer footing for the first time in nearly 25 years, came five months ahead of President Nixon's goal.

In a message to senior defense officials, Laird said:

"With the signing of the peace agreement in Paris today, and after receiving a report from the secretary of the Army that he foresees no need for further inductions, I wish to inform you that the armed forces henceforth will depend exclusively on volunteer soldiers, sailors, airmen and Marines."

Laird's decision cancels plans to draft about 5,000 men before next June 30, when legal authority to induct men into the armed forces will expire.

(Minnesota's Selective Service director, Col. Robert P. Knight, said Laird's announcement came as no surprise to him because the state has received no draft calls for January, February and March.

(Col. Knight said only 10 or 20 men in Minnesota are affected by the announcement. The men had been ordered for induction last year but were temporarily deferred.)

Pentagon manpower officials said that the flow of volunteers, spurred by a series of military pay raises and improved fringe benefits, has encouraged them to believe that these 5,000 men can be raised by recruiting.

Laird also issued a strong appeal for congressional approval of new bonuses and other legislation designed to make military service more attractive, particularly to National Guardsmen and reservists.

The Nixon administration has set a policy that, in any future war emergency, the roughly one-million National Guardsmen and reservists will be called before the country turns to the draft for the necessary military manpower.

Defense officials said there still is a possibility that a few doctors might be drafted. The Pentagon is pressing for passage of a bill that would give doctors extra pay, in hopes of attracting more medical professionals to military careers.

The special doctor draft has not been used since 1971, when the Pentagon asked for 1,600 physicians and osteopaths.

There are skeptics in the

**Draft**
Continued on page 11A

# Dexter, Minn., paid high price in war

Danny Wilson

Wayne Mees

Stan Gilbert

By James Parsons
Staff Writer

**Dexter, Minn.**
They realized, of course, that the cease-fire was an important moment in history and all of that, but it was little things — sort of disjointed, unconnected little things — that many of the folks in Dexter thought about.

Like the way that carefully groomed forelock of red hair kept drooping across Wayne Mees's forehead as he dashed around the basketball court; or the time Danny Wilson speared a goldfish in science class and threatened to swallow it; or how quiet Stan Gilbert was so strong that he played basketball as if he were afraid of hurting someone.

And remembering again, perhaps for the hundredth time, how close Wayne and Stan were. How they grew up on farms next to each other, how they had ferocious one-on-one battles under the basketball goal in the yard, how they played side by side at tackle and end on the football team, how they both went to Vietnam as machine gunners in infantry units and how Wayne, and then Stan, came home in caskets.

The shock wore off quickly but, five years later, there is still a tinge of bitterness in Dexter.

The two young men were doing their duty, of course, but somehow it seemed unfair for two boys from such a small town (pop. 252) to get killed. After all, no one from Dexter had been killed in the Korean fighting and only one boy died in World War II.

When Danny Wilson was killed three years later while manning a helicopter machine gun, it opened the wound again for many of the people. His parents' farm near Elkton is just 3 or 4 miles away on the other side of Interstate Hwy. 90 that runs west into Austin.

The children from the area go to the same school so the towns live and die with the fate of the same football and basketball teams. Any rivalry between the towns ends abruptly when someone mentions the dead soldiers.

Dexter's mayor, Everett Vermilyea, doesn't hesitate to use the word "bitter" when describing his feelings toward the war. "How come we were over there in the first place?" he asked. "I'm bitter 'cause I think we oughta got out long ago."

"Ja," said his wife, Ann, who says she is "100 percent Dutch." "I don't think this cease-fire will

**Casualties**
Continued on page 8A

A group of boys waged a snowball fight on the main street.

## Peace-related dispatches:



# U.S. gives somber thanks for peace

New York Times Service

**New York, N.Y.**
President Nixon, like millions of other Americans, watched the signing of the Vietnam cease-fire agreement on television Saturday and then, like many others, took part in a modest and somber celebration of the end of a tragic war.

The President, relaxing in his home at Key Biscayne, Fla., had proclaimed 6 p.m. yesterday as a "national moment of prayer and thanksgiving" and the 24-hour period thereafter as a day of prayer.

Throughout the country, in cities and in hamlets, church bells tolled, fire companies sounded their horns, and small, quiet gatherings were held in homes and in public places.

In Elmira, N.Y., Mrs. Lucielle Cesari did not turn on the lights of a Christmas tree in her yard, lights she had lit every night for five years in a "vigil" remembering the war.

In Longmeadow, Mass., a bell forged by Paul Revere, the silversmith and patriot, was sounded in its steeple at the First Church of Christ. The bell was first sounded to signal the end of the War of 1812.

In Key Biscayne, the President made plans to attend church services a mile from his home at the Key Biscayne Presbyterian Church.

The minister, Rev. John A. Huffman Jr., prepared a service he said was designed to emphasize that "the real peace comes only from Jesus Christ."

**Thanksgiving** continued on page 8A

## Almanac / Index

**Sunday**
**January 28, 1973**
**28th day**
**337 to go this year**
**Sunrise: 7:38 a.m.**
**Sunset: 5:15 p.m.**

### Today's weather

**Colder**

Details page 6B

**Saturday's temperatures**

| am | 1 | 2 | 3 | 4 | 5 | 6 | 7 | 8 | 9 | 10 | 11 | Noon |
|---|---|---|---|---|---|---|---|---|---|---|---|---|
| temp | 30 | 30 | 31 | 31 | 31 | 32 | 33 | 34 | 35 | 35 | 35 | 35 |
| pm | 1 | 2 | 3 | 4 | 5 | 6 | 7 | 8 | 9 | 10 | 11 | |
| temp | 34 | 32 | 33 | 32 | 31 | 30 | 30 | 28 | 28 | 27 | 27 | |

Fair and colder weather is predicted for the Twin Cities area today. It is expected to be mostly cloudy and warmer Monday with a chance of light snow by afternoon. A high around 18 is forecast today, with a low near 0 tonight and a high Monday in the mid 20's.

Other predicted highs today: Minnesota, 5 to 10 north, near 20 south; North Dakota, 10 to 20; South Dakota, 20 northeast, 35 southwest; Wisconsin, teens northwest, low 30s southeast.

### Persistence pays off

200 newspaper carriers earned trips to Hawaii by selling new subscriptions. In Hawaii, a woman and her husband from Edina got on the hotel elevator and there was their carrier. "You didn't have to follow me," the woman said. "I know I paid you before I left."



# Fighting goes on after cease-fire

Tribune Wire Services

**Saigon, South Vietnam**
A long-sought cease-fire officially came to Vietnam at 8 a.m. today, but it was marred by reports of continued fighting.

A major battle was reported under way after the cease-fire along Hwy. 1 near the district town of Trang Bang, 30 miles northwest of Saigon.

An Associated Press reporter at the scene of the battle said two South Vietnamese propellor-driven Skyraider planes began bombing a few minutes before 8 a.m. and dropped 25 bombs during the next half hour. They later were joined by South Vietnamese air force jets, which strafed Communist position.

Fighting also was reported continuing after the cease-fire at Tay Ninh, a provincial capital 55 miles northwest of Saigon where Communist troops infiltrated two hamlets on the outskirts of the city at 2 a.m. Saturday.

Reports from South Vietnamese and American officers in the field early this morning said the Communists had been driven from all but two heavily populated hamlets on the southeastern outskirts of Tay Ninh.

The South Vietnamese command reported this morning that in the 24 hours ending at dawn, North Vietnamese and Viet Cong troops initiated 334 incidents throughout the country.

According to government officers, that was the highest number since they

**Fighting**
Continued on page 11A

Minneapolis Tribune

Monday
August 6, 1973

15c Single copy
3 Sections



Volume CVII
Number 74
M

1A

Final

Associated Press

Police escorted two Arab gunmen, center in light-colored shirts, from the Athens airport terminal after they surrendered following a gun and grenade attack on passengers in the lounge.

# Arab terrorist raid kills three, wounds 55 in Athens airport

Associated Press

**Athens, Greece**
Arab terrorists tossed hand grenades and fired pistols into a crowded airport lounge Sunday, killing three persons and wounding more than 55 others before surrendering to police.

At least two of those killed were Americans.

Two terrorists held 35 hostages for two hours while they crouched behind a marble bar at Athens International Airport and negotiated for a plane to the Middle East. The terms of their surrender were not immediately announced.

The terrorists identified themselves to police as Zechod Mohammed, 21, of Palestine, and Palaat Hussam, 21, of Cairo. They reportedly had no passports.

Police said one grenade was thrown from a balcony overlooking the lounge, indicating that more than the two terrorists may have taken part in the attack. Officers questioned two young Arabic-speaking women, who kicked and screamed as police pushed them into a squad car.

Two of those killed were identified as Mrs. Jeannie Salandis, 23, New York, and Albert Kersen, 53, Union, N.J. Police said the third victim was a man of about 50 whose identity was not immediately established.

Officials said initially that the attack seemed to be aimed at passengers about to board two Trans World Airlines (TWA) flights. Flight 881 was bound for New York and flight 806 for Tel Aviv.

Later, Police Chief Nicholas Daskalopoulos said a preliminary investigation indicated that the gunmen had intended to attack passengers boarding a flight operated by El Al, the Israeli airline.

He said the El Al flight left 10 minutes before the grenade attack. The flight was still listed on the information board as not having departed and this may have confused the terrorists, he added.

Daskalopoulos said the two men refused to comment on their actions beyond declaring: "We accomplished what we wanted to do."

Palestinian guerilla groups in Beirut blamed the attack on "enemies of the Palestine revolution" and denied any connection with the incident. The Palestinian news agency Wafa, speaking for the major Palestinian groups, said, "The Athens airport incident proves . . . that there

**Terrorists**
Continued on page 3A

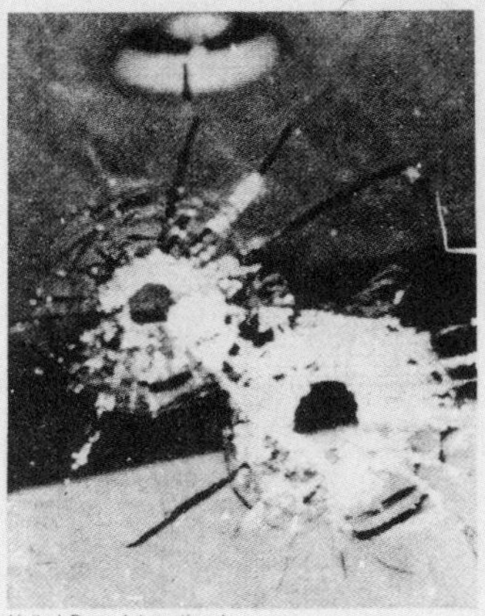

United Press International

Bullets pierced the lounge windows during an attack Sunday at the Athens airport.

## Cambodian troops plan retreat at bombing halt

**By Bernard Gwertzman**
New York Times Service

**Washington, D.C.**
Secretary of State William P. Rogers has revealed that Cambodian troops plan to give up exposed positions and retreat to more secure areas where they can better defend themselves against insurgent pressure once American bombing support ends on Aug. 15.

In an affidavit filed with the Supreme Court Saturday, and released that night, Rogers disclosed that in advance of the bombing halt, "intensive planning" has taken place within the Nixon administration and with the Cambodian government on how to make the best of the situation which will develop when the American combat effort stops as the result of congressional action.

**(Cambodians retake village under U.S. air cover. Page 8A.)**

Rogers's affidavit was filed as part of the government's successful effort to overturn a ruling earlier in the day by Associate Justice William O. Douglas. The ruling called for an immediate halt to all bombing in Cambodia.

By an 8-to-1 decision, the court left further legal action up to the U.S. Court of Appeals for the Second Circuit which will decide on the merits of the bombing issue after taking arguments next Wednesday.

The thrust of Rogers's affidavit was that not allowing the bombing to continue until the agreed cutoff date of Aug. 15, "would cause irreparable harm to

**Rogers**
Continued on page 4A

## Shultz: Beef freeze to go on

Associated Press

**Washington, D.C.**
Treasury Secretary George Shultz said Sunday that the freeze on retail prices of beef will remain in effect until Sept. 12, the date set by President Nixon, despite the growing absence of red meat in supermarkets.

Shultz first said that lifting of the freeze before Sept. 12 "remains to be seen," but then said: "That date stands.

"The last I talked to the President that was the date that had been set," Shultz said. "As far as I know he hasn't shifted his view."

He explained that by saying a decision on the Sept. 12 date "remains to be seen," he reflected a "recognition of the fact that lots of questions have been raised and lots of pressure has been put on."

Shultz spoke yesterday on the American Broadcasting Co. television program "Issues and Answers."

"The evidence, of course, that we have to evaluate is evidence about particularly any long term effects on the production of cattle," he said. "So far as I can determine . . . we do not have any long-term adverse effects.

"The cattle that are being held off the market today are going to have to come on the market at some point in the future," he said. He said he saw no decrease in the production of cattle.

Shultz said predictions that prices would increase by as much as 20 percent when the freeze is lifted were high.

"The more they hold back now the more will come onto the market on Sept. 12 and that will tend to hold prices down in the future," he said.

Shultz said the freeze was a method of letting food prices rise over a period of time, rather than letting them "burst on the consumer at once."

Shultz also said he saw no

**Shultz**
Continued on page 3A

# Kleindienst testimony may back Nixon stand

Associated Press

**Washington, D.C.**
Former Atty. Gen. Richard G. Kleindienst is prepared to testify this week that he gave President Nixon all the facts in the Watergate investigation last April 15 and came away convinced that Mr. Nixon did not know until then about the cover-up.

Richard Kleindienst

Sources close to the investigation said Sunday that Kleindienst will tell the Senate Watergate committee that he first learned all the facts about the June 17, 1972, break-in at Democratic national headquarters and the cover-up the night before he went to see the President.

He was said to have gotten the information from Henry E. Petersen, the assistant attorney general in charge of the inquiry, during a meeting lasting until 5 a.m.

Three hours after the meeting ended, Kleindienst called Mr. Nixon and made an appointment to see the President after Sunday morning church services at the White House, the sources said.

"The President was amazed," Kleindienst was quoted as telling investigators. "The President acted as if he was hearing it for the first time, or if he had heard something, it was just the day before."

There were reports that Petersen would confirm the account offered by Kleindienst, who resigned last April 30, saying he was too close to some of the key figures in the case.

Ousted White House Counsel John W. Dean III has testified that he gave

**Watergate**
Continued on page 4A

## Blackmun tells ABA: Watergate 'pall' is upon us

**By Lesley Oelsner**
New York Times Service

**Washington, D.C.**
Supreme Court Justice Harry Blackmun said Sunday that, under the "pall" of the Watergate scandal, the "very glue of our ship of state seems about to become unstuck."

"There is a resulting fear of consequent grave damage to the democratic process of which we have been so proud, and in which we firmly have believed, and which we have proclaimed to the world," he said in a speech at the American Bar Association convention here.

Justice Blackmun

Justice Blackmun was appointed to the court by President Nixon and is generally counted as part of the court's conservative bloc.

But he gave his audience a perspective on Watergate that was different from the official White House stance that the scandal has been blown out of proportion.

The justice noted that America has often been marked by "adversity," that there have been "other scandals, large and small, that have rocked every administration of recent times." He noted, too, that various public officials were recently implicated in other crimes or improprieties.

"One senses a laxness in public life that 20 years ago, if indulged in, could not be politically surmounted," he told the lawyers and judges and their families, gathered for the association's annual prayer breakfast.

Then he turned to Watergate, and said:

"The pall of the Watergate, with all its revelations of misplaced loyalties, of strange measures of the unethical, of unusual doings in high places, and by lawyer after lawyer after lawyer, is upon us. It is something that necessarily touches us all, irrespective of political inclination.

**ABA** continued on page 3A

Herman Talmadge

## Talmadge: No evidence to impeach Nixon

Associated Press

**Washington, D.C.**
A Democratic member of the Senate Watergate committee said Sunday that there is no evidence now that would justify impeaching President Nixon and that the public would not support such a move.

But Sen. Herman E. Talmadge, D-Ga., said a heavy cloud of doubt and suspicion will be removed from the White House only when the President releases tape recordings of relevant presidential conversations and submits himself to examination.

"I don't think the tape issue ever will be laid to rest until they are made public," Talmadge said. "I think the President is making a great mistake in not making the tapes available to the committee and to the public."

The Watergate committee has subpoenaed those tapes and will go to court this week in an attempt to compel the President to produce them.

Talmadge was interviewed on the Columbia Broadcasting System program "Face the Nation."

The committee today begins what is expected to be the final week of testimony on the June 17, 1972, break-in of Democratic headquarters in the Watergate.

L. Patrick Gray III, former acting FBI director, returns to the witness table for cross-examination. He is to be followed by former U. S. Atty. Gen. Richard Kleindienst.

**(Watergate probe takes toll on L. Patrick Gray. Page 2A.)**

Talmadge said he expects the hearings to conclude Wednesday or Thursday. The committee has then scheduled a three-week recess.

The committee will file a report on the first phase of the hearings, but Talmadge said that eventually the question of who has been lying and who has been telling the truth will

**Talmadge**
Continued on page 3A

## Area bike racers train in obscurity

**By Jack Coffman**
Staff Writer

Bicycle racers put up with a lot.

Like nagging leg pains, weekends away from home and spaghetti for breakfast.

They worry about things like blood sugar levels, tire cost, wind direction and how to shave a few more ounces off an already featherweight bike. If they are successful, they know there won't be much applause because their sport is obscure in the nation once the center of the sport.

Despite these factors, there is a growing number of serious bicycle racers in the Twin Cities area — somewhat over 150. Many of them feel their ranks will contribute at least one of the eight members of the U.S. Olympic bicycle road racing team in 1976.

This effort to be the best and the fastest requires major personal commitment and peak physical condition — the commitment and condition, for example, of James Ballenthin and Chris Kvale.

Ballenthin, 26, a St. Paul attorney, sometimes rides 100 miles before going to court. Kvale, 28, a geographer who became a bike shop manager, rides a $2,000 bicycle made of metals so light they could almost float in the breeze.

Married and the father of two small children, Ballenthin often starts the day at 5:30 a.m. flashing his Raleigh professional across the countryside. By the time he gets to his office, his workout has finely honed his mental condition as well as his physical condition.

"I'm just always pushing myself so I can feel a little pain in my legs," he said. "As the season goes along I will always feel a bit of pain."

Ballenthin recently finished tenth in a five-day, 450-mile race in Quebec, the best showing of the Minnesota racers.

"A real classy race. Very exciting. Totally exhausting," he said.

The tires on Ballenthin's bike are made of rubber-covered silk. They cost up

**Bikes**
Continued on page 4A

Staff Photo by Donald Black

James Ballenthin loosened up his legs for a 30-mile practice run.

## Almanac / Index

Monday
August 6, 1973
218th day
147 to go this year
Sunrise: 6:04 a.m.
Sunset: 8:34 p.m.

**Today's weather: Showers**

Details Page 9B

Sunday's temperatures

| | | | | | | | | | | | | |
|---|---|---|---|---|---|---|---|---|---|---|---|---|
| a.m. | 1 | 2 | 3 | 4 | 5 | 6 | 7 | 8 | 9 | 10 | 11 | Noon |
| temp. | 75 | 75 | 74 | 72 | 72 | 70 | 71 | 73 | 77 | 79 | 82 | 84 |
| p.m. | 1 | 2 | 3 | 4 | 5 | 6 | 7 | 8 | 9 | 10 | 11 | Midn. |
| temp. | 85 | 88 | 88 | 88 | 86 | 84 | 83 | 80 | 78 | 76 | 76 | 76 |

Twin Cities skies will be varied in cloudiness and may contain an occasional thunderstorm today and Tuesday. The National Weather Service predicts continued hot and humid weather, with a high today in the upper 80s, a low tonight in the upper 60s and a high Tuesday in the middle 80s. Probability of rain is 40 percent today and tonight.

Other predicted highs today: Minnesota, upper 70s northeast to mid and upper 80s south; North Dakota, mid 70s northwest to mid 80s southeast; South Dakota, 80s west to low 90s east; Wisconsin, 87 to 95.

### Right to the point

A downtown Minneapolis office worker gazed over at another department that was regularly a bit slow in doing its work and mused aloud: "The only thing that works over there is the pencil sharpener."



Telephones
372 4141 News General
372 4242 Classified
372 4843 Circulation

Minneapolis Tribune

Tuesday
August 7, 1973

15c Single copy
3 Sections

Volume CVII
Number 75
M

1A

Final



# Agnew target of criminal investigation

By R. W. Apple Jr.
New York Times Service

**Washington, D.C.**
Vice-President Spiro T. Agnew announced Monday night that he has been informed that he is under investigation for possible violations of criminal law.

In a terse, late-night statement issued through his press secretary, Marsh Thomson, the Vice-president declared:

"I have been informed that I am under investigation for possible violations of the criminal statutes. I will make no further comment until the investigation has been completed, other than to say that I am innocent of any wrongdoing, that I have confidence in the criminal justice system of the United States and that I am equally confident my innocence will be affirmed."

A spokesman for the Vice-President later confirmed that the investigation is being conducted by the United States attorney in Baltimore, George Beall, the younger brother of Sen. J. Glenn Beall Jr., a Republican.

A Baltimore grand jury has for several months been investigating kickbacks allegedly paid by contractors, architects and engineers to officials of Baltimore County. Agnew served as the county executive there from 1962 until 1967, when he was elected governor of Maryland.

Sources in Baltimore said the investigation of Agnew is related to the alleged kickback scheme, but there was no official confirmation. The Wall Street Journal reported in its editions today that Agnew is suspected of extortion, bribery and tax evasion.

The case apparently has no connection with the Watergate scandal that has bedeviled the Nixon Administration for the last 13 months.

At Camp David, Md., where President Nixon spent the night, a White House spokesman declined comment on the Vice-President's announcement, but he said the White House had been informed shortly before the statement was issued at about 11 o'clock last night.

The Vice-President's spokesman, Thomson, at first refused to comment when asked in a telephone interview whether Agnew

Agnew
Continued on page 11A

Spiro Agnew

# B52 bombs Cambodians by mistake

Associated Press

**Phnom Penh, Cambodia**
An American B52 mistakenly bombed a Cambodian naval base Monday, killing or wounding hundreds of Cambodian servicemen and their famililies, military sources said.

Casualty figures from Phnom Penh hospitals and reports from the bombed Mekong River garrison town of Neak Luong indicated that as many as 100 men, women and children were killed and up to 300 were wounded.

The bombing accident was believed to be the most serious in the history of the Indochina conflict. On March 2, 1967, American jets mistakenly bombed the refugee-crammed village of Lang Vei, South Vietnam, killing 83 villagers and injuring 176, according to U.S. reports.

Pentagon spokesman Jerry W. Friedheim said in Washington that the base was hit when part of the bomb load from an eight-jet B52 fell short of its target "into an area where there were some Cambodian military and dependents."

He declined to speculate on the cause of the accident, saying the Defense Department was still gathering information.

Field reports said that a dozen civilians were killed Sunday in another off-base U.S. bombing attack at a village along Hwy. 1 south of Phnom Penh. There was no official confirmation of this accident.

U.S. military advisers, faced with an Aug. 15 deadline for ending the

Mistake
Continued on page 5A

# $10 million said spent on Nixon's two homes

Associated Press

**Washington, D.C.**
About $10 million in federal funds has been spent since 1969 for security and communications installations and other projects at President Nixon's San Clemente and Key Biscayne compounds, officials said Monday.

As the administration gave its fullest accounting yet of the costs of protecting and supporting the first family's homes and offices outside Washington, the White House promised that Mr. Nixon would reveal within a month all details of his purchase of California and Florida residences.

In an apparent reference to the impact of the Watergate scandal, Arthur Sampson, administrator of the General Services Administration, said the disclosures were made because of "the atmosphere that exists today government-wide."

Sampson said much of the data on the projects was kept secret "because it would compromise the security of the President."

"Putting these figures in front of you is compromising his security," he said, gesturing toward large charts and aerial photographs of the President's California home. "Anyone who wants to go in and do something to the President now has more information than he has had before."

This series of announcements yesterday stripped much of the secrecy from taxpayer-financed projects at Mr. Nixon's out-of-town homes and offices and the residences of his daughters:

■ White House Deputy Press Secretary Gerald L. Warren said more than $2 million had been spent for communications equipment at Key Biscayne, Fla., about $3.7 million for similar equipment at San Clemente, Calif., and $160,000 for communications equipment in the Ba-

Homes
Continued on page 4A

Staff Photo by Earl Seubert

## Cosmic invader? Moon explorer? Underwater treasure hunter?

**No, it's a sandblaster inside the Butler Building at 6th St. and 1st Av. N., which is being restored and remodeled. Because of the sand in the air, the blaster wears a special suit, including a helmet with a hose attachment for fresh air. The building, 71 years old, has been placed in the National Registry of Historical Places and has been designated for heritage preservation by the City Council. The building is being turned into a complex of offices, shops and restaurants, to be called Butler Square. (More pictures on 1B.)**

# Skylab sun shade unfurled on space walk

United Press International

**Houston, Texas**
The Skylab astronauts unfurled a garage-sized sun shade over America's space station in the longest space walk ever Monday as ground engineers prechecked plumbing problems and decided they were not serious.

The astronauts found no signs of a cooling-system leak outside the ship. Engineers said the problem was not as serious as first believed and Skylab would be fit for manned flight the rest of the year.

Like repairmen on telephone poles, astronauts Owen Garriott and Jack Lousma ran up a 22-by-24-foot silver and white shade, flagpole style, to protect Skylab from the searing sun. Skylab 2 Commander Alan Bean, fourth man to walk on the moon, stayed in the station's airlock monitoring vital systems.

Garriott and Lousma put in nearly a full day's work outside the station, doubling the previous space walk record of 3 hours, 28 minutes by the Skylab 1 crew in June. Bean said they were outside 6 hours, 31 minutes.

The walk began at 12:32 p.m. Minneapolis time but flight controllers said they would have to refine the windup time with a further data check. The astronauts were back inside Skylab by 7:20 p.m., when the station came into radio contact again after the last orbit during the space walk.

Asked which tasks they had completed, Lousma replied, "We got it all done."

Working under a half-moon at times, Garriott and Lousma also reloaded film in the battery of sun-watching telescopes, mounted piggy-back on the 100-ton station, and inspected two rocket units that failed on the Apollo ferry ship docked to the nose of Skylab.

Garriott, 42, and Lousma, 37, painstakingly erected the sunshade, taking much longer than planned. They were outside during four orbits 270 miles above earth, traveling at 17,100

Skylab
Continued on page 4A

# Witness says Reserve is source of asbestos in lake

By Dean Rebuffoni
Staff Writer

A government witness testified Monday in U.S. District Court that he is convinced that asbestos-type fibers found in Duluth's water supply could only come from the Reserve Mining Co. taconite plant at Silver Bay, Minn.

"There's absolutely no doubt in my mind they (the fibers) come from Reserve Mining Co." said Phillip Cook, a research chemist. "I have studied the rivers, I have studied the historical samples, the whole pattern of the lake.

"After many years of study," Cook said, he has concluded that the controversial taconite plant "could be the only possible source" of the potentially injurious fibers found in the drinking water Duluth draws unfiltered from Lake Superior.

Cook's testimony yesterday before Judge Miles Lord reaffirmed what he had repeatedly alluded to earlier in the trial: That the Silver Bay plant, which discharges 67,000 tons of taconite wastes daily into Lake Superior, is the sole source of the fibers—and that the materials do not enter the lake by natural means.

His testimony came on the fourth day of the environmental trial in which the federal government is asking that Judge Lord order Reserve to halt its disposal of taconite wastes.

The government alleges that the practice pollutes Lake Superior, hastens its deterioration and violates water-quality laws. Reserve claims the lake is able to assimilate the taconite wastes without any adverse effects on its ecology or on human health.

The mining firm said in court that it will present "concrete evidence" that significant amounts of

Reserve
Continued on page 5A

# NSP Monticello nuclear plant closed because of faulty safety equipment

By Dean Rebuffoni
Staff Writer

The Northern States Power Co. (NSP) nuclear-generating plant at Monticello, Minn., has been shut down since last Tuesday because several of its hydraulic shock absorbers — safety equipment that protects steam pipes from seismic damage — have been found to be defective, it was learned Monday.

NSP said the plant initially was shut down while engineers examined the absorbers in the wake of a bulletin from the U.S. Atomic Energy Commission (AEC). The absorbers were then found to be leaking hydraulic fluid.

The AEC bulletin, dated July 27, notified operators of all 34 nuclear power plants in the nation to inspect any shock absorbers manufactured by Bergen-Patterson Co. of New Jersey and to report on their findings.

An AEC spokesman said yesterday that the shock absorbers — called hydraulic seismic suppressers by engineers — are used to protect steam pipes and other plant equipment from damage from vibrations, including earthquakes. A significant vibration, coupled with failure of the absorbers, could rupture the steam pipes, the AEC said.

The AEC said the Monticello facility is one of 11 nuclear-power plants found to have faulty shock absorbers, out of a total of 20 plants using the Bergen-Patterson product.

Six other plants reported no problems and tests have not been completed at the remaining three, the AEC said.

The federal agency said the bulletin resulted from a report that a New Jersey nuclear power plant had lost hydraulic fluid from its absorbers, apparently through faulty seals.

An NSP spokesman said

Monticello
Continued on page 11A

# Gray says he alerted Nixon about staff three weeks after break-in

By James M. Naughton
New York Times Service

**Washington, D.C.**
L. Patrick Gray III testified Monday that he was mystified when President Nixon paid no heed to a warning three weeks after the Watergate break-in that White House aides were trying to "mortally wound" the President.

Gray, the former acting director of the Federal Bureau of Investigation (FBI), told the Senate Watergate committee yesterday that his warning in a July 6, 1972, telephone conversation with Mr. Nixon should have been "adequate to put him on notice" that members of the White House staff were engaged in something improper.

"Frankly," Gray replied to a question by Sen. Herman E. Talmadge, D-Ga., "I expected the President to ask me some questions."

When the President did not do so, Gray added, he made the assumption that he had been unduly alarmed about efforts to cloud the early stages of the FBI investigation of the Watergate break-in.

Gray's testimony was related to efforts by the FBI last summer to determine whether funds in the Miami bank account of Bernard L. Barker, one of the Watergate conspirators, had come through a Central Intelligence Agency source or a "political money chain" in Mexico City. Eventually, Gray said, the FBI determined that the funds were linked to the Committee to Re-Elect the President.

Underscoring the importance of the Mexico City inquiry last year, Sen. Lowell P. Weicker Jr., R-Conn., asked Gray if the Mexican money had been "one of the few hard pieces of evidence that the FBI had" soon after the Watergate break-in.

"At that early stage, it

Hearing
Continued on page 4A

Associated Press

**L. Patrick Gray III, former acting director of the FBI, checked documents during testimony Monday.**

## Almanac / Index

**Tuesday**
**August 7, 1973**
**219th day**
**146 to go this year**
**Sunrise: 6:05 a.m.**
**Sunset: 8:32 p.m.**

**Today's weather: Cool**

Details Page 5B

**Monday's temperatures**

| a.m. | 1 | 2 | 3 | 4 | 5 | 6 | 7 | 8 | 9 | 10 | 11 | Noon |
|---|---|---|---|---|---|---|---|---|---|---|---|---|
| temp. | 75 | 74 | 71 | 71 | 71 | 70 | 68 | 68 | 69 | 71 | 75 | 78 |
| p.m. | 1 | 2 | 3 | 4 | 5 | 6 | 7 | 8 | 9 | 10 | 11 | Midn. |
| temp. | 80 | 80 | 78 | 79 | 79 | 79 | 80 | 79 | 77 | 75 | 73 | 73 |

Thundershowers may occur this afternoon and tonight in the Twin Cities area. Clearing skies are expected by tonight, however, with fair to partly cloudy skies and cooler weather Wednesday. The high today will be in the lower 80s, the low tonight in the lower 60s and the high Wednesday in the upper 70s. Chance of rain is 40 percent today, 20 percent tonight.

Other predicted highs today: Minnesota, 70s to mid 80s; North Dakota, upper 60s to upper 70s; South Dakota, 70s to low 80s; Wisconsin, upper 70s to upper 80s.

### I love my wife, but oh Euclid

A University of Minnesota graduate student has been getting pressure from his wife to get into shape. The mathematics student now feels that he has come up with a way of combining study and body building. He calls it "isoscelcs exercises."



Telephones
372 4141 News General
372 4242 Classified
372 4343 Circulation

Minneapolis **Tribune**

Saturday
October 13, 1973
15c Single copy
3 Sections
1A
Volume CVII
Number 142
M
Final



# Rep. Ford is Nixon choice

## Consent likely for vice-president nominee

**By Frank Wright**
Staff Correspondent

**Washington, D.C.**
President Nixon, apparently eager to avoid another fight with Congress, Friday night nominated House Republican Leader Gerald Ford to succeed Spiro Agnew as vice-president.

The immediate indication following Mr. Nixon's announcement was that the 25-year congressional veteran from Michigan will have little trouble as he now faces his confirmation test in the Democratically controlled House and Senate.

Ford said after his nomination that he had told Mr. Nixon he would not seek the presidency in 1976. "I have no intentions of running for president or vice-president," he told reporters.

Ford, 60, top man in the GOP minority in the House since 1965, had become the favored candidate of many of his Republican colleagues in the two days since Agnew threw the capital city into turmoil after pleading no contest to a charge of income tax evasion and resigning.

Mr. Nixon, who spent Thursday night pondering his choice of a replacement at the Camp David presidential retreat in the Maryland mountains, said in his announcement that Ford met his criteria:

■ Of being qualified to become president.

■ Of sharing the president's views on foreign policy and national defense.

■ Of being able to work with both parties in Congress, where the Democrats have fought Mr. Nixon for many long months on numerous issues, foreign and domestic, and have spotlighted, with extended hearings, the Watergate affair, the major embarrassment of his tenure.

There are many who would debate the qualifications of Ford, known mainly for his dogged persistence, for the presidency. But there is no doubt that he reflects Mr. Nixon's positions on foreign policy and national defense, having fought for them loyally on the House floor, with little deviation.

And, on the last point about working with both parties, there was a roar of approval from both Republican and Democratic members of Congress in the White House East Room audience when Mr. Nixon disclosed he had chosen Ford, one of their own.

The response would have been considerably different had the president picked, for example, former Treasury Secretary John Connally, whose name had generated an

**Nixon** continued on page 5A

### On the inside:



## GOP lauds choice, Democrats restrained

**By David Kuhn**
Staff Correspondent

**Washington, D.C.**
Minnesota's Republican delegation in Congress Friday night enthusiastically endorsed President Nixon's nomination of Rep. Gerald Ford for vice-president.

The Democrats were more restrained in their support for Ford, but most indicated they would vote for him unless congressional hearings on his nomination produce some unexpected information.

Sen. Walter Mondale said, "President Nixon is to be commended for selecting someone who has a reasonable prospect of a quick confirmation" instead of a controversial figure.

He said, however, that Ford isn't a "strong choice" because he doesn't offer the prospect of a "new strong, creative, important personality" in the office.

Mondale said he would have preferred Sen. Charles Percy, R-Ill.; Sen. Edward Brooke, R-Mass., or Gov. Nelson Rockefeller, R-N.Y. But he said he is inclined to vote for Ford's confirmation, pending the outcome of hearings.

Sen. Hubert Humphrey said he viewed Ford's nomination favorably but would reserve final judg-

**Delegation**
Continued on page 7A

United Press International

**Rep. Gerald Ford, R-Mich., acknowledged the applause of the crowd in the East Room of the White House Friday night after President Nixon nominated him to become vice-president.**

## Heating oil put under controls

**Associated Press**

**Washington, D.C.**
The Nixon administration Friday reluctantly adopted a mandatory allocation program governing the wholesale distribution of home heating oil.

The administration's limited program, which takes effect Nov. 1, requires suppliers to distribute home heating oil, jet fuel, kerosene, diesel fuel, range oil, stove oil and gas oil to customers in proportion to purchases made in the calendar year of 1972.

The administration on Oct. 2 imposed a similar allocation program on propane gas, but so far there is no government control over the distribution of crude oil, gasoline and other petroleum products.

Legislation now in Congress would require mandatory allocation of all petroleum products and crude oil. The House Rules Committee Thursday cleared the bill for a floor vote, over the protests of White House energy adviser John Love.

Love admitted on Oct. 2 that voluntary compliance was not working and that home heating oil and the other "middle distillates" would be placed under a mandatory program.

The allocation regulations issued yesterday set aside 10 percent of available supplies for distribution by each state government to hardship cases.

The regulation does not, however, propose any list of consumers or uses which should get priority consideration.

Violations of the program will be punishable by fines up to $5,000.

# Court rejects Nixon's plea for tapes secrecy

**Tribune News Services**

**Washington, D.C.**
In what it called an "unavoidable" and historic ruling, the U.S. Court of Appeals ruled Friday that President Nixon must turn over to the federal district court here the disputed White House tape recordings bearing on Watergate.

By a 5-to-2 vote, the court of Appeals said that the District Court could then give the Watergate grand jury any relevant material, unless it feels that there is some public interest to be served by withholding "particular" statements or information.

"Though the president is elected by nationwide ballot, and is often said to represent all the people, he does not embody the nation's sovereignty," the court said. "He is not above the law's commands."

The court's ruling substantially upheld the order last August of Federal District Judge John Sirica—though it appeared to take an even tougher stance against the president than Judge Sirica had.

The appellate court made its ruling in response to requests by both Mr. Nixon and Archibald Cox, the special prosecutor in the Watergate case, to reverse Judge Sirica. Cox, who had initiated the proceedings when he had a subpoena issued for the tapes, asked the appeals court to order that the tapes be turned over directly to the grand jury.

The court ruled that the president does not have absolute immunity from the compulsory process of the court; it ruled too that executive privilege is not absolute, and that the president does not have sole and final say in deciding when executive privilege is applicable.

Over and over the court noted its sadness at being forced to make such a ruling. At one point it said: "Here, unfortunately, the court's order must run directly to the president, because he has taken the unusual step of assuming personal custody of the government property sought by subpoena."

"The central question before us is, in essence, whether the president may, in his sole discretion, withhold from a grand jury evidence in his pos-

**Tapes**
Continued on page 7A

## Ford has backed Nixon down the line and been his friend for 25 years

**By Richard D. Lyons**
New York Times Service

**Washington, D.C.**
When Vice-President Spiro Agnew was castigated on the floor of the House of Representatives two years ago as being an "intellectual sadist," "the buffoon of the year," and a "clown," the Republican who rose to his defense was the minority leader, Gerald Rudolph Ford.

In attacking Democratic Rep. William Clay of Missouri, who made the charges, Ford said, "I cannot imagine somebody in this body on either side of the aisle using language of that kind on the floor of the House in reference to the second-ranking member of the United States government."

Friday night Ford himself was nominated for that office after serving eight years as Republican quarterback in the House.

The football analogy with politics makes sense in Ford's case. The broad-shouldered 6-footer was the star center for the University of Michigan teams of 1932-34. He later worked his way through Yale Law School as an assistant football coach.

President Nixon is reported to have told a colleague that "Gerry Ford is a hell of a nice guy — when he was playing football they played with leather helmets."

The president and his 60-year-old vice-presidential nominee have been extremely close over the past quarter century. They first met when they served as young Republican representatives together. Mr. Nixon was elected in 1946. Ford was elected in 1948.

When Mr. Nixon was nominated for the presidency during the 1960 Republican national convention, Ford was mentioned frequently as a vice-presidential nominee. He lost out to Henry Cabot Lodge. But Ford remained in close touch with Mr. Nixon during his eight years out of political office.

**Ford**
Continued on page 5A

**Former Vice-President Spiro T. Agnew will explain the events leading to his resignation in a nationwide address Monday night. His speech will be carried on NBC, CBS and ABC television at 6:30 p.m. Minneapolis time and on CBS radio at 7 p.m.**

## Almanac / Index

**Saturday**
**October 13, 1973**
**286th day**
**79 to go this year**
**Sunrise: 7:26 a.m.**
**Sunset: 6:32 p.m.**

**Today's weather:**
**Fair, windy**

Details Page 7B

**Friday's temperatures**

| a.m. | 1 | 2 | 3 | 4 | 5 | 6 | 7 | 8 | 9 | 10 | 11 | Noon |
|---|---|---|---|---|---|---|---|---|---|---|---|---|
| **temp.** | **55** | **54** | **53** | **52** | **50** | **47** | **46** | **45** | **46** | **46** | **47** | **52** |
| p.m. | 1 | 2 | 3 | 4 | 5 | 6 | 7 | 8 | 9 | 10 | 11 | Midn. |
| **temp.** | **55** | **57** | **59** | **59** | **60** | **58** | **56** | **53** | **54** | **55** | **55** | **52** |

Fair to partly cloudy skies are forecast for the Twin Cities area today, with southwest winds of 12 to 28 miles per hour, turning occasionally cloudy tonight and Sunday. The high today and Sunday is forecast in the mid 60s, the low tonight near 40.

Other predicted highs today: Minnesota, 56 to 71; North Dakota, Mid 50s to low 60s; South Dakota, 70s; Wisconsin, 56 to 66.



**Telephones**
372 4141 News General
372 4242 Classified
372 4343 Circulation

## Stenvig opposes people mover plan

Mayor Charles Stenvig said Friday that he does not support a proposal for an elevated people-mover circulation system in downtown Minneapolis.

Stenvig said he likes the concept of a people mover, but that the area has more pressing transit needs and that there aren't "enough facts and figures in the plan that I could accept it."

"You have to have priorities," Stenvig said in an interview, "and the biggest priority now is to get mass transit for the whole area. You have to worry about getting them into and out of the loop first."

The $53-million circulation proposal calls for 4.5 miles of fixed guideways running above downtown streets at the second and third-story levels. The people-mover system would be designed to circulate persons within downtown from city-operated parking garages on the edges of downtown.

The other two major candidates for mayor in the Nov. 6 election have also criticized the proposal.

DFL candidate Albert Hofstede said Thursday that he opposes the plan because it would benefit suburban commuters more than city residents.

Alderman Gladys Brooks, the Republican candidate, has called the proposal a "visual pollution disaster" and said that other means of transit downtown should be considered first.

# Israelis reportedly advancing into Syria

**Associated Press**

Israeli forces battled their way to within 25 miles of the Syrian capital of Damascus Friday, Israel's state radio said. The Syrians acknowledged some Israeli progress, but claimed their enemies were forced to retreat late in the day.

The Israeli military command has not indicated how far it intends to push into Syria or if Damascus is an objective.

In Moscow, the official Soviet news agency Tass said yesterday that Israeli missiles sank a Soviet cargo ship in a Syrian harbor.

The Egyptian military command claimed its forces sank several Israeli warships in the Gulf of Suez and destroyed a tank column on the Sinai Desert. There was no confirmation of this from the Israeli military command.

Israel's state radio said the Israeli army had advanced 15 miles into Syria from the 1967 war's cease-fire line in the Golan Heights. Damascus is about 40 miles from that line. Military analysts in Tel Aviv said Damascus was almost within range of Israeli field artillery.

The fighting apparently was accompanied by fierce air battles over the Golan Heights. The Israeli command claimed its jets made 29 kills. A Syrian communique said at least 35 Israeli planes were knocked down. U.S. intelligence observers believe

**Mideast**
Continued on page 7A

## Note to readers:

Beginning Monday, the Minneapolis Tribune will discontinue its early evening street-sale edition Monday through Saturday in the Minneapolis area. (An early street-sale edition of the Sunday Tribune will continue to be available.)

Same-day, truck-delivered distribution of the daily Tribune in much of North Dakota and South Dakota also will end starting Monday. The Tribune will be available by mail in the affected areas.

Same-day, home-delivered service for the Tribune will be continued in major population centers of extreme eastern North Dakota and South Dakota.

The circulation cutbacks have been necessary because of rising costs in maintaining and servicing circulation and because of the newsprint shortage.

**Gale W. Freeman**
**Associate Publisher**

## Twin Cities Jews asked to support Israeli cause

**By M. Howard Gelfand**
Staff Writer

Kent Confeld didn't hesitate last Saturday when he heard that the Mideast war had flared anew. He tried to make a reservation for the first flight to Israel.

His parents talked him out of it — "My Dad says I'm nuts" — but after reflecting on it he decided to go through with his plans.

Confeld, 24, St. Louis Park, will be one of about 10 Twin Citians leaving for Israel next week to help harvest the crops while most young Israelis are involved in the war.

About 200 area Jews have indicated an interest in going to Israel to help with efforts unrelated to the war according to Tuvia Abramson, who works through Israeli consulates in Chicago and New York in lining up volunteers.

The volunteers are among many of the 35,000 Twin Cities Jews donating blood, sweat and money for Israel as the war completes its first week. (A blood drive is planned today.)

**Kent Confeld**

The United Jewish Appeal said yesterday it will attempt to collect $100 million nationally in the next five days. The organization stressed that none of the money will go for arms.

Local officials of the agency won't say how much has been collected so far, but during the 1967 war about $1.6 million was do-

**Aid**
Continued on page 7A

# THE MINNEAPOLIS STAR

Wednesday, July 10, 1974

5c




# Panel's version ties Nixon, cover-up

By LOU CANNON and JULES WITCOVER
Washington Post

WASHINGTON, D.C.—President Nixon, nine days after ruling that White House aides not disclose their involvement in the Watergate cover-up, explicitly ordered that the cover-up go on.

He said March 27, 1973, in these tape-recorded words: "I want you alltostonewall it, let them plead the Fifth Amendment, cover-up or anything else, if it'll save it — the plan. That's the whole point."

The quote—omitted in the White House transcript of the conversation of that date—is in transcripts from the actual tapes of eight presidential conversations made by the House Judiciary Committee and released yesterday. The committee obtained the tapes from the Watergate grand jury March 26.

In the same conversation, the Judiciary Committee version shows the President saying former Atty. Gen. John Mitchell was arguing that "we use flexibility . . . in order to get on with the cover-up plan." The White House version has Nixon saying Mitchell was arguing "that now we use flexibility in order to get off the cover-up line."

The new committee versions of the White House tapes —obtained from higher-quality equipment than used by the White House—reveal not only omissions from the White House versions, but significant discrepancies.

They also convey much more the image of a chief executive in charge than do the White House transcripts, and of a president sometimes ambivalent but ultimately moving to support the continuance of the cover-up.

The two references to the "cover-up plan" made by

**Excerpts from Judiciary Committee report and related dispatches: C Section**

Nixon in the March 22 conversation are the only times these words are used by him in the transcripts. They are never defined but are an apparent reference to containing the Watergate scandal within the White House.

The quote in which the President said he wanted his aides to "stonewall it" or "cover up" was part of a 15-minute additional segment to the March 22 conversation as first transcribed by the White House.

According to the Los Angeles Times, Judiciary Commitee lawyers were able to copy it when a Secret Service agent at the White House overseeing the copying inadvertently let the recorder run past the section previously transcribed.

Sen. Sam Ervin, D-N.C., chairman of the Senate Watergate Committee, said the transcripts released by the Judiciary Committee were "in perfect harmony" with testimony his committee received that John Dean, Mitchell, H. R. Haldeman and John Ehrlichman met in February 1972 and "concluded that they would be publicly in favor of the committee's investigation but would do everything they could to impede and obstruct the investigation."

For all the discrepancies in the Judiciary and White House versions, both depict a president frequently contradictory in his discussion of Watergate options. For example, immediately after he had instructed Mitchell, Dean and Haldeman to "stonewall it" in the March 22 conversation, the President said:


REPORT
Turn to Page 7A

EARL WARREN
*Dies at 83*

## *Earl Warren dies; champion of rights era on high court*

WASHINGTON, D.C. (AP) — The death of Earl Warren, a champion of the Bill of Rights in his 16 years as chief justice, removes a figure indelibly linked to landmark decisions of the Supreme Court in one of its most controversial eras.

Warren, 83, died in Georgetown University Hospital last night, a little more than five years after his retirement from the nation's highest judicial post. A hospital spokesman said he died of heart failure. Funeral arrangements were pending.

**Under his leadership, the court struck down segregated schools, laid down the rule of "one man-one vote" and greatly expanded the rights of the accused in criminal cases.**

Tributes came swiftly.

President Nixon, who often was at odds with Warren in their years as California politicians and who criticized many of his court decisions, saluted him as "a partisan for America."

Chief Justice Warren E. Burger, named by Nixon to succeed Warren and steer the court toward "strict construction" of the Constitution, said "his contribution was large indeed."

Rosa Parks, the black seamstress


WARREN
Turn to Page 6A


## Tapes differ on Nixon role in hush money

**Mitchell testifies on 'hush money': C Section**

WASHINGTON, D.C. (AP — On the crucial issue of President Nixon's involvement in the payment of Watergate hush money, there are differences in the versions of presidential transcripts published by the House Judiciary Committee and by the White House.

The committee version, released yesterday, quotes Nixon that payment of hush money would be "worth it." The White House version contains no such statement.

**The committee version quotes Nixon as saying, during a discussion of Watergate conspirator E. Howard Hunt Junior's demand for money, "Well for Christ's sake get it . . ." The White House version deleted the words, "Well for Christ's sake."**

At another point, after Nixon was told that former Atty. Gen. John Mitchell and campaign aide Frederick LaRue knew of Hunt's demands for money, the committee version quotes the President as saying "(unintelligible) do something." The White House version casts Nixon's words as a question: "Do they intend to do something?"

These references to hush money were made in meetings on March 21, 1973, the day Nixon says he rejected the idea of paying for Hunt's silence. Later that night LaRue allegedly delivered a final $75,000 payment to Hunt's lawyer.

**The Watergate grand jury, in naming Nixon an unindicted co-conspirator in the cover-up, focused on this payment. A key element of the Judiciary Committee's impeachment investigation is whether Nixon authorized the payment. The President denies it.**

Both versions of the transcripts quote John Dean telling Nixon that Hunt, who was about to be sentenced to prison after conviction in the Watergate break-in and bugging, was demanding $120,000 for support money and legal fees.

Dean told Nixon that Hunt was threatening to reveal things he had


MONEY
Turn to Page 7A

Minneapolis Star Photo by William Seaman

**Watch out!** This woman cringed yesterday after she was "attacked" by a red-wing blackbird as she walked along the parking lot sidewalk at Methodist Hospital in St. Louis Park. The birds have nests in the Minnehaha Creek marsh near the sidewalk, and apparently consider humans a threat. A hospital official said complaints have been received from people who have been swooped on and pecked by the birds, but nothing has been done about them. The sign behind the woman says "Beware of Birds."

## Freed convict 'set an example'

By MARIETTA SMITH
Minneapolis Star Staff Writer

After serving five years in prison for the first-degree manslaughter of his wife, chiropractor John R. Mitchell is back in practice at his old clinic at 3152 Minnehaha Av.

Mitchell, who spent three of his five years in minimum security at Stillwater State Prison, had to retake his chiropractic exams in March 1972 while still in prison. He was paroled Feb. 22 and began practicing in a clinic in south Minneapolis in May.

Mitchell

Richard Mulcrone, chairman of the Minnesota Corrections Authority, said Mitchell was paroled "primarily because of his exemplary behavior while at Stillwater.

"He had worked in his profession as a chiropractor at the institution and had been a tremendous help to


MITCHELL
Turn to Page 7A


## AT LAST, THEY SAY

**Practically frigid temperatures are predicted for the weekend in the Twin Cities area — although there still are a couple of warm days to come.**

**The highs Sunday are expected to be in the upper 70s, after lows Friday and Saturday in the mid and lower 60s.**

**There's also a 30 percent chance of rain tonight and a chance of thundershowers again Friday.**


3

6 Sections XCVI—No. 194

•• STAR ★


TELEPHONES

| | |
|---|---|
| News, General | 372-4141 |
| Want Ads | 372-4242 |
| Circulation | 372-4343 |
| Column 1 | 372-4444 |

## *Highway study: speeds reduced*

Cars and trucks slowed noticeably this spring according to a study by the Minnesota Highway Department from April 22 to May 16.

On urban freeways, the average car speed went from 66 miles per hour last year to 57 miles per hour, according to preliminary results of the study. Trucks on urban freeways slowed from 60 to 55.

**On rural freeways car speeds dropped from 68 to 58 and truck speeds from 61 to 57. Other state highways in Minnesota had a decrease for cars from 62 to 56 m.p.h. and for trucks from 56 to 54 m.p.h.**

Speeding arrests by the state patrol during April and May rose 42 percent from the same months last year, from 8,855 to 12,537, according to Patrol Chief James Crawford.

The highway department study, made in conjunction with the highway patrol, was based on radar measurements taken at 15 locations throughout the state. Three


SPEED
Turn to Page 6A


## Cuts OKd by 60% of car insurers

Reductions in automobile-insurance premiums required by Minnesota's no-fault insurance law have been agreed to by companies that sell 60 percent of the auto insurance in the state, according to the state insurance commissioner's office.

A 30-percent reduction in liability, medical payment and uninsured-motorist coverage ordered by the Legislature is expected to lower total premiums about 12 percent from 1973 levels when no-fault takes effect next Jan. 1, officials said.

However, some drivers may pay more for automobile insurance because the law requires greater liability coverage than many now carry. Under no-fault, Minnesota motorists must carry at least $25,000-per-person, $50,000-per-accident liability insurance and $10,000 in property-damage insurance.

**The no-fault law passed last year by the Legislature requires insurance companies to compensate their policy-holders for injury up to certain financial limits regardless of who was at fault in an accident.**

Because many smaller insurance companies feel they would suffer financially from the mandated premium reductions, more firms have asked for relief than have promised to reduce liability premiums the full 30 percent.

By yesterday, 146 companies that sell $104 million in automobile in-


NO-FAULT
Turn to Page 6A


## Column 1

*Got a problem? Then so has Column 1. Eight staff members have the sole task of trying to help you. Write to Column 1, The Minneapolis Star, Minneapolis, Minn. 55415 or call 372-4444 Monday through Friday.*

*There's one problem we can't solve — answering all your calls and letters. Each question is read and considered carefully and we'll answer as many as possible. Please send copies of documents, not the originals.*

**We would like to have you check into the Suburban Law Enforcement Association. Is it on the up and up? Someone comes around selling circus tickets. We always buy, but we'd like to know if it's a worthwhile charity.**

*R.S., Bloomington*

It's yes, no and maybe, depending on whom you talk to. The Suburban Law Enforcement Association is a group of individuals from several area law-enforcement agencies. Most of the money it gets from the circus goes for an annual school patrol picnic, said Ronald Markgraf, association president and a Maple Grove police sergeant. It's the amount of money the association has received in the past from the circus promoters which has been controversial. There have been some problems of proper licensing, too. George Morton, the promoter of the George Matthews Great London Circus, told us three days before he was licensed to solicit for tickets sales that he already had been selling tickets by telephone for a week. Charities must file an annual financial report under the law, but professional fund raisers such as Morton aren't required to. The group's 1972 report said the association got $2,098 out of $58,350 raised. Last year, said Harold Adams, director of the Minnesota Charities Review Council, the association got $16,776 out of $88,489 raised. Fund raisers may be asked to file such audits or reports, said Adams. The circus was asked to file in 1972. It didn't, he said. There appears to be enough money on hand already before this year's circus in September to pay for the picnics for the next three years or more, Adams said. He also said that the contract between the circus and the association "is the poorest I've ever read in terms of the benefit to a charity." Adams said also that "the thing that sticks in my craw is: How come this business (the circus) can exploit the idea of a charity and not have to be responsible the way a charity is and not provide an audit?" Ronald Graham, general manager of the Minneapolis Better Business Bureau, recommends that persons think of it more as a circus than a charity. "Based on prior experience," he said, "the money raised primarily benefits the circus." By the way, there can be no solicitation of tickets in Minneapolis by the circus. It does not have a permit for that.

Column 1

**My problem is with a $308.80 down payment on a truck at Art Goebel Ford in Coon Rapids. We were told we would need a larger down payment or a cosigner, but we couldn't afford the larger down payment and we couldn't get a cosigner, and now the company is balking at giving back part of our down payment. We got back $100 we paid in cash, but we used a payroll check to pay the other $208.80, and they say it will take two weeks to get our refund. Could you help us get our money back?**

*J.B., Anoka*

Art Goebel, president of Art Goebel Ford, said it's a company policy to wait two weeks before refunding money paid by check because a customer once accepted a refund and then stopped payment on his check. "You only have to get burned once," Goebel said. But since your check was a payroll check he agreed to make an exception to the policy, and you picked up your refund.

Column 1

**COLUMN 1 POSTSCRIPT:** Thanks to our readers, we were able to identify a couple of close-to-home sources for identification tags for children. Bracelets are available from Vital Products, Rural Rt. 1, Audubon, Minn. 56511. They cost $1 and you should send a self-addressed, stamped envelope and the information you want engraved on the bracelet, we were told by Joan Ellsworth, who owns the company. Allow about two weeks for delivery. Many Mrs. Jaycees groups also are selling the bracelets for fund-raising. The Marine Corps has offered to provide military-type identification tags to persons with mental or physical handicaps. Maj. H. L. Causey told us that six to seven lines of information can be stamped on the tags and that they also have a distinguishing color tag for a medical alert. Persons wanting these tags should apply to Causey, U.S. Marine Air Reserve Training Unit, Naval Air Station, Minneapolis, Minn. 55450. Please include your telephone number. And order blanks for the bracelets and necklaces from the National Identification Co. in Denver that we mentioned in the July 3 column are available at Prescription Shop, 110 S. 7th St., Minneapolis.

## *Index . . .*

Minneapolis **Tribune**

Saturday
July 13, 1974
Volume CVIII
Number 60
M

15c Single copy
3 Sections





1A
Final

# Ehrlichman found guilty on 4 counts

Associated Press

**Washington, D.C.**
John D. Ehrlichman, once one of the ranking members of President Nixon's White House staff, was convicted Friday of conspiracy and perjury in the Ellsberg break-in case.

Ehrlichman, 49, Mr. Nixon's chief domestic adviser until he resigned in April 1973 amid rising Watergate scandals, said after the verdict he had doubted all along he could get a fair trial in Washington and said he would appeal.

The verdict made Ehrlichman one of the most powerful government officials ever convicted of a crime. Interior Secretary Albert B. Fall went to jail for a year in 1931 in the Teapot Dome scandals.

Others of such high rank have been charged in the past but not convicted, including former attorney general and Mr. Nixon's reelection campaign manager, John N. Mitchell, and Mr. Nixon's former commerce secretary and campaign fund-raiser, Maurice Stans, who were acquitted by a jury in the Robert Vesco case in March.

Former Attorney General Richard G. Kleindienst pleaded guilty to a misdemeanor for his inaccurate and incomplete testimony before a Senate committee investigating the ITT case but was given a suspended sentence.

The jury convicted Ehrlichman, G. Gordon Liddy, Bernard L. Barker and Eugenio R. Martinez of a civil rights charge of conspiring to enter the Beverly Hills, Calif., office of Dr. Lewis Fielding and examine his files on Daniel Ellsberg, the man who leaked the Pentagon Papers.

This count carries a maximum prison sentence of 10 years. Ehrlichman also was convicted of three other counts, carrying a potential five years each, and was cleared of a fifth.

This leaves Ehrlichman subject to a possible total sentence of 25 years. U.S. District Judge Gerhard Gesell will pass sentence July 31. The defendants remain free pending sentencing.

Ehrlichman still faces trial in September in the Watergate cover-up case, along with Mitchell, former White House chief of staff H. R. Haldeman, former Assistant Attorney General Robert Mardian and two others.

Liddy, Barker and Martinez, who were convicted last year in connection with the 1972 break-in at Democratic Party headquarters in Washington's Watergate complex, were charged only in the conspiracy count.

Ehrlichman, however, also was convicted of one count of lying to the FBI and two counts of committing perjury before the Watergate grand jury.

Outside the courthouse following the verdict, Ehrlichman said he had met with his lawyers and instructed them to prepare and file an appeal.

"As you know, we have been concerned from the very beginning about our ability to obtain a fair trial in this district," Ehrlichman said.

In pretrial motions, Ehrlichman had asked that the trial

**Plumbers** continued on page 7A

Associated Press

**John Ehrlichman and his wife, Jean, left the District of Columbia Court of Appeals after his conviction.**

## Rapid rise of industrial prices slows during June

By Edwin L. Dale Jr.
New York Times Service

**Washington, D.C.**
The rapid rise of industrial wholesale prices slackened a bit in June while farm and food prices declined for the fourth consecutive month, the Labor Department reported Friday.

The result was that the rise in the wholesale price index for June, at five-tenths of 1 percent, was by far the smallest for any month this year. It was the best performance since October, when there was a small decline.

**(Slimmer grain harvests may lower meat output. Page 8A.)**

There were two important qualifications, however, to this seemingly improved inflation picture:

■ Farm prices have turned upward since the June price figures were collected, and the July index for this sector is sure to show an increase after four months of decline.

■ The rise in the sector of industrial commodities, at 2.2 percent last month, was still very large although it was less than in the three preceding months. The series of big increases in industrial wholesale prices signals future increases in non-food consumer prices.

The wholesale price index for June was 155.7, with prices in 1967 taken as 100. The rise from May was five-tenths of 1 percent both before and after adjustment for normal seasonal changes in some prices.

The index last month was 14.5 percent above a year earlier. Thanks mainly to the drop in farm and food prices, the inflation rate as measured by this indicator has declined substantially in recent months.

For the last three months

**Prices**
Continued on page 4A

# Andreas is found innocent

By Paul Light
Staff Writer

**Dwayne Andreas**

Minneapolis financier Dwayne Andreas was found innocent Friday of charges stemming fom four $25,000 contributions to Hubert Humphrey's 1968 presidential campaign.

Judge Edward J. McManus filed his verdict in U.S. District Court in Minneapolis, finding Andreas and his First Interoceanic Corp. innocent of a total of eight counts in violation of federal statutes.

The government claimed that in October 1968 Andreas illegally withdrew $100,000 from Interoceanic accounts to complete his contributions to Humphrey's campaign.

Andreas and the company had been arraigned under a 1907 federal law prohibiting campaign donations from corporations.

Judge McManus gave no reason for his decision, reached without a jury or witnesses. In his signed order acquitting the defendants, he said. "The court having examined the evidence and considered the briefs and arguments of the parties finds both defendants not guilty of the offenses charged."

Andreas's defense counsel, trial lawyer Edward Bennett Williams, had maintained that the indictments were invalid since the five-year statute had

**Andreas**
Continued on page 7A

## Things and Dave Pence have changed a lot since days of antiwar protests

By M. Howard Gelfand
Staff Writer

**David Pence**

Four summers ago he stood in the packed courtroom and quoted Thomas Jefferson and his words brought cheers, but Friday Dave Pence was nearly alone in another courtroom and his words brought only silence and a guilty verdict.

Things had changed during those four years. No longer was Pence the popular leader of the antiwar movement who talked about love and brotherhood. Now he was the isolated ex-convict who on Memorial Day was arrested for openly carrying a shotgun in downtown Minneapolis.

During those four years Pence, 27, spent nine months in Sandstone Federal Prison for refusing to report for alternative non-military service. As the Vietnam War ended, he began to drift away from the closely knit resistance community, which rallied around Pence and other defendants on trial several years ago. By the time he got out of prison he was talking about forming a male militia to protect the streets.

On May 30 he decided to do something about it. When he was arrested for violating the Minneapolis gun ordinance he was walking down 3rd Av. S. near 2nd St. toting a .20

**Pence**
Continued on page 7A

## Petersen says he found no data linking Nixon, cover-up

Associated Press

**Washington, D.C.**
Assistant Attorney General Henry Petersen told the House Judiciary Committee Friday that he never received any information indicating President Nixon was involved in the Watergate cover-up.

During a closed session of the committee's impeachment inquiry, Petersen was asked by Rep. Charles Sandman, R-N.J., "Have you ever had any information that the president was wrongfully involved?"

Sandman later reported: "Petersen said he had no information or evidence the president was wrongfully involved."

Rep. Don Edwards, D-Calif., confirmed Sandman's version of the exchange and said, "Petersen is testifying point-blank that the president didn't know about the cover-up."

However, Rep. Hamilton Fish Jr., R-N.Y., said that Petersen has not been "on top of the case" for more than a year.

"He doesn't know what we know," Fish said, adding that Petersen had told the committee he had not read all of the edited White House transcripts and was unfamiliar with other developments in the case.

Petersen, head of the criminal division in the Justice Department, supervised the initial investigation of the Watergate break-in.

He told the committee of a series of conversations in April 1973 during which he briefed Mr. Nixon about the progress of the Watergate investigation.

Petersen said he gave the president information about developments in the secret sessions of the Watergate grand jury but had been unaware that the president subsequently relayed what he said to aides.

Fish said Petersen contended it was proper to tell the president what was happening before the

**Committee**
Continued on page 4A

## Stock market makes biggest gain of year

Associated Press

**New York, N.Y.**
The stock market gave its strongest performance of the year Friday. The Dow Jones industrial average rose 27.61 points to 787.23, the biggest daily gain in more than a year, and the sixth largest daily advance on record.

Sales expanded to 17.77 million shares. Good news about inflation and interest rates triggered the rally, brokers said.

The government reported yesterday that wholesale prices in June rose at a 6-percent annual rate, the smallest increase since last October.

**(Details. Page 8A.)**

## Local heroin seizures show 30-fold increase

By Michael Hall
Staff Writer

Nearly four pounds of heroin was seized by Minneapolis police during the first half of the year, a figure almost 30 times the amount seized during the same time period last year.

A report released Friday by the narcotics division indicates that 29,416 dosages of heroin were seized during the first half of the year compared with 1,088 during the first six months of 1973.

Calling the increase an epidemic, Lt. George Bendt, head of the division, said, "The actual figure is probably double what the report shows since much of the heroin seized had not yet been cut for street sale."

The seizure of amphetamines was at a record high with 1,460,440 pills being seized so far this year compared with 52,268 during the first six months of last year. The seizure of hashish was nearly doubled with 2 lbs. 9 oz. confiscated so far this year compared with 1 lb. 7 oz. during the same time period in 1972.

The amount of cocaine seized during the first six months was down to 1,316 dosages compared with 6,074 in 1973.

Bendt said in an interview yesterday, "Our division may get 5 percent of the drugs that come into the area. The fact that we are seizing record amounts only is a hint at how much

**Narcotics**
Continued on page 4A

## Almanac / Index

**Saturday**
**July 13, 1974**
**194th day**
**171 to go this year**
**Sunrise: 5:39 a.m.**
**Sunset: 8:59 p.m.**

**Today's weather: Fair, warm**

Details page 5B

**Friday's temperatures**

| | | | | | | | | | | | | |
|---|---|---|---|---|---|---|---|---|---|---|---|---|
| a.m. | 1 | 2 | 3 | 4 | 5 | 6 | 7 | 8 | 9 | 10 | 11 | Noon |
| **temp.** | 73 | 72 | 72 | 71 | 71 | 71 | 71 | 70 | 71 | 74 | 74 | 75 |
| p.m. | 1 | 2 | 3 | 4 | 5 | 6 | 7 | 8 | 9 | 10 | 11 | Midn. |
| **temp.** | 78 | 82 | 84 | 85 | 84 | 88 | 89 | 86 | 83 | 80 | 78 | 77 |

Fair to partly cloudy skies and continued warm weather are forecast for the Twin Cities area today and Sunday. Today's high is expected to be in the lower 90s and a low near 70 is expected tonight. A high near 90 is expected Sunday. Predicted highs today: Minnesota, 84 to 94; North Dakota, 90s; South Dakota, 90s to low 100s; Wisconsin, 80s.

### The apple of the CBS eye

A Winnipegger visiting in Minneapolis called the Tribune this week to ask for more Canadian news. It's only fair, he said, "because in Canada the media have been carrying nothing but news concerning your Applegate scandal."



**Telephones**
372 4141 News General
372 4242 Classified
372 4343 Circulation

# Puzzling situation clears after 3 itchy summers

By Gerri Williams

Employees in the data-processing department of the Hennepin County Welfare Building were itching.

In fact, they had been itching every summer for the past three years, and nobody knew why. All they knew was that with the advent of warm weather, tiny red welts would appear on arms and legs. No one else in the welfare building had this condition.

Rumors were rife. There was speculation that the unseen pests were lice, mites, bugs, fleas, flies, or all of these.

Officials sought some solution. Boxes of blank cards and papers that might be harboring paper mites were discarded. Clerks and office equipment were moved to other rooms. The department was sprayed and fumigated.

"Although we knew we were getting bitten by something, people began hinting that maybe it was all in our heads," said Keith Nelson, director of data processing.

This summer rolled around and the mysterious situation prevailed.

By now, however, the "bites" had become more than just a nuisance. Several employees required hospitalization due indirectly to the "bites." One woman developed a leg infection. Another had a number of swollen, raised welts on her face.

(One of the employees has since returned, and both received workmen's compensation.)

Then, about 10 days ago, an observant employee whose father works in the fiberglass business noticed an 8-foot-square piece of fiberglass left over from some past construction work lying atop an exposed duct. The duct led to the air conditioning system.

Nelson said that tiny particles of the fiberglass had been carried on the air through the system, causing cuts in the skin. The other departments in the building were not affected because data processing, located in the basement, had a separate system.

The filters have been vacuumed, cleaned and scrubbed, and cheesecloth has been placed over the vents. Since then, there have been no more outbreaks of "bites."

"It seems we've finally come up with an answer that makes sense," Nelson said.

**Gerri Williams is a trainee for the Minneapolis Tribune.**

Minneapolis Tribune

Tuesday
July 16, 1974

Volume CVIII
Number 53
M

15c Single copy
3 Sections

1A

Final



# Panel members differ on Colson testimony

By Finlay Lewis
Staff Correspondent

**Washington, D.C.**
After a full day of testimony from Charles Colson, several members of the House Judiciary Committee said Monday it was apparent that President Nixon was more closely involved with the Ellsberg operation than previously acknowledged.

Colson's appearance before the committees' impeachment inquiry yesterday was the occasion for a marathon session in which the former special counsel to the president ranged over a broad range of topics related to his days on Mr. Nixon's staff.

Once known as Mr. Nixon's political hatchet man, Colson was recently sentenced to one to three years in prison for his activities in 1974 related to the prosecution of Daniel Ellsberg, a codefendant in the Pentagon Papers trial.

Colson pleaded guilty to a charge of having obstructed justice by participating in a conspiracy to discredit Ellsberg, who was accused of stealing a secret government study of the Vietnam War and leaking it to several newspapers.

But beyond that, Colson was the White House contact man with E. Howard Hunt, one of the original Watergate conspirators. He also played an important role in the administration's 1971 decisions to settle an antitrust suit against International Telephone and Telegraph Co. (ITT) and to raise milk price supports.

All are matters being investigated by the committee and, as a result, Colson has long been regarded as possibly the most explosive impeachment witness who might be called before the committee.

However, after about eight hours of questioning committee members had differing perceptions of the impact of his testimony, with some Democrats asserting that Colson had damaged the president while several Republicans thought Mr. Nixon had been helped.

But the most damaging assessment came from a Republican, Rep. Hamilton Fish of New York, who emerged from the closed-door session to say that Colson had "directly implicated the president in ordering the Ellsberg burglary."

Rep. Charles Wiggins, R-

**Committee**
Continued on page 13A

United Press International

Former presidential counsel Charles Colson talked with chairman Peter Rodino before testifying in the House Judiciary Committee's impeachment inquiry.

## Appraisers value Nixon papers at half of tax claim

By Eileen Shanahan
New York Times Service

**Washington, D.C.**
The Internal Revenue Service, as part of its audit of President Nixon's tax returns, employed independent appraisers who valued Mr. Nixon's pre-presidential papers at less than half the $576,000 claimed by the president's own appraiser.

This fact is contained in the agency's full report on the audit of Mr. Nixon's taxes, of which the House Judiciary Committee has copies. It is debating whether to make them public.

According to committee sources, the audit report contains other previously unpublished information concerning defects that the IRS found in the tax returns, as originally filed, for the years 1969 through 1972.

The fact that the agency found the pre-presidential papers greatly overvalued did not affect the amount of additional tax that Mr. Nixon was called upon to pay.

The reason was that Mr. Nixon's entire deduction for the gift of these papers to the National Archives was disallowed on the ground that it had not been made before Congress prohibited such deductions.

The report, according to a committee source, goes into considerable detail about the lack of historical value of many of the donated papers.

For example, Mr. Nixon's appraiser, Ralph Newman of Chicago, declared that there were 15,000 items relating to the 1959 visit to the United States of Soviet Premier Nikita Khrushchev. The auditors found that there were only one-tenth that many and that most were newspaper clippings.

Newman has appraised the papers of many public figures, including those of former President Lyndon Johnson.

A Democratic member of

**Tax**
Continued on page 13A

## Judge says high court may settle Reserve

By Dean Rebuffoni
Staff Writer

There will be no settlement of the Reserve Mining Co. case until the U.S. Supreme Court renders a final decision in the matter, U.S. District Judge Miles Lord predicted Monday.

The judge also said that he does not believe he can legally order the State of Minnesota to issue the permits necessary for Reserve to discharge its taconite tailings on land at Palisade Creek, as the company proposes to do.

However, he stressed that he has not yet decided whether he favors the use of that site for tailings disposal. Also, he does not believe that the state is wrong in strongly opposing Reserve's proposal.

Judge Lord based his prediction on what he termed his "observation of the attitudes" of the mining company and its two parent firms, Armco and Republic Steel Corporations.

He said the companies' efforts to negotiate a private settlement of the case with trial plaintiffs in fact served only to delay a final resolution. He also indicated that Reserve might be using its Palisade Creek proposal to further delay a resolution.

The judge's statement about the nation's high court came yesterday after a day-long hearing in which he and the plaintiffs strongly questioned the Palisade Creek proposal.

Judge Lord obviously was frustrated about the apparent lack of movement in the case when he briefly spoke about the Supreme Court but he did not elaborate.

The nation's high court already has acted once in the Reserve case. On July 9, it denied a request by

**Reserve**
Continued on page 14A

**Found guilty**

**Elmer Wayne Henley, the 18-year-old figure in 27 murders in the Houston area last year, was found guilty of six of the slayings Monday by a jury in San Antonio, Texas. (News report on page 3A.)**

## 2 convicts surrender at capital courthouse

Associated Press

**Washington, D.C.**
Two armed convicts who had held seven hostages in a cellblock at the U.S. District Courthouse for three days surrendered Monday night.

Frank Gorham Jr., 26, and Robert Jones, 24, were driven to nearby Andrews Air Force Base, Md., and put aboard a government jet for a flight to a federal penitentiary in Atlanta, Ga.

Justice Department spokesman John Russell said the men, who at first bargained for a flight to freedom in Africa, would be placed in maximum-security detention.

The surrender came after the men chopped their way into an air vent with axes in an attempt to escape from the basement cellblock. Russell said they were forced back into an enclosed area next to the cellblock after an exchange of gunfire and a burst of tear gas.

They surrendered to the deputy District of Columbia police chief, Maurice Cullinane, after he persuaded the men they would not be shot if they came out.

Norman A. Carlson, director of the Bureau of Prisons, said it was his decision to send the prisoners to Atlanta. He said the prisoners, who earlier attempted to bargain for their choice of federal prisons, had no say about it.

Before the escape attempt and surrender, a federal spokesman said the pair had vacillated repeatedly on a proposal that they surrender peacefully in exchange for an immediate flight to a federal prison hospital in Springfield, Mo.

# Makarios is ousted in Cyprus

Associated Press

The Greek-led Cypriot National Guard forced President Makarios from power Monday, plunging the Mediterranean island republic of Cyprus into civil strife.

Radio Cyprus claimed that Makarios was killed in the coup. But news dispatches from Nicosia, the capital, said the 61-year-old archbishop broadcast an appeal to the Cypriot people "to resist and fight." A United Nations spokesman in New York said late yesterday that the British district commander in the town of Pophos had seen Makarios alive. Fighting was reported in Nicosia, Limassol and other cities between Makarios's national police forces and the national guard.

The reports from Nicosia said the coup had been preceded by a police crackdown on members of EOKA-B, the clandestine Greek Cypriot organization sworn to "enosis," unity of Cyprus with Greece.

Archbishop Makarios

More than 200 suspects were reported detained before the national guard sent tanks into the streets. The national guard is a 6,000-man Cypriot army led by 650 Greek officers.

The national guard announced the coup in an early morning broadcast and said Makarios had been replaced by Nikos Sampson, 39, a former pro-Greek resistance leader. Sampson promised elections within a year, declaring: "Unity and tranquility will now be restored among the Greek-Cypriot people in the army."

Fighting subsided last night, but citizens were warned to stay in their homes. Ambulances and military vehicles raced through empty streets during the night.

In New York the Cyprus ambassador to the United Nations said he received a message through U.N. channels purporting to be a request from Makarios for an urgent session of the Security Council.

At San Clemente, Calif., a spokesman said President Nixon was informed of the Cyprus developments by Secretary of State Henry Kissinger, who telephoned from Washington. Kissinger met with the Cypriot ambassador yesterday morning.

Press Secretary Ronald Ziegler said the State Department reported that the situation in Cyprus was unclear and there were no specific details to provide.

The Soviet Union, through its official news agency, Tass, expressed support for Makarios. Tass said the Soviet government saw the coup as "acts openly violating the U.N. charter," and observers said this could be preparation for a council summons.

One U.N. source explained the apparent lack of movement by the U.N. peacekeeping force on Cyprus, saying

**Cyprus** continued on page 13A

## County group still hopes to vote move for courthouse

By Jack Coffman
Staff Writer

**Warren, Minn.**
From more than five miles out on the flatlands that surround this community drivers can see the little tower that sticks up above the two-story Marshall County Courthouse.

One of the county's higher points of elevation, it also marks one of the most controversial points in the county: the very courthouse itself. A large group of residents want to rip the county seat out of Warren and move it somewhere else.

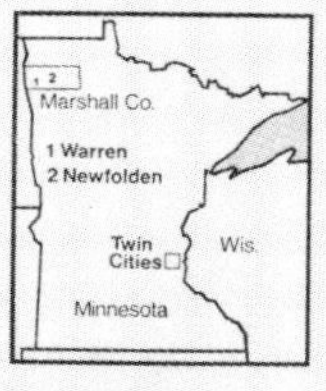


In rural areas like Marshall County, where acres far outnumber people, the courthouse is important for a town. There are public employees pumping their paychecks into local businesses and there is the prestige of having elected officials in town. Moving a courthouse is serious business.

A large segment of Marshall County apparently wants to move the entire county government from Warren, a prosperous community of about 2,000 in the extreme western end of the county, to centrally located Newfolden, a town of just over 300 where the addition of a Dairy Queen, much less a

**Courthouse**
Continued on page 13A

## Three test-tube babies reported born in Europe

Associated Press

**London, England**
Three babies conceived in laboratory test tubes and then implanted in the mother's womb have been born in Europe within the past 18 months, a British gynecologist revealed Monday.

Dr. Douglas Bevis of Leeds University said that he believes the births were the first of their kind in the world.

The babies were conceived in the test tube with eggs taken from the mother's womb and fertilized with male sperm, and then put back in the womb after growing in the laboratory for about a week, Dr. Bevis said.

All three babies are alive and do not have any apparent abnormalities, Dr. Bevis said.

The work could eventually be a boon to women who are infertile because of a blockage of the fallopian tubes leading from the ovaries to the womb, Dr. Bevis indicated. He said that only a few hundred British women fall into this category. When an egg is released each month, it must travel through the fallopian tubes to the point where it

**Babies**
Continued on page 4A

## Almanac / Index

Tuesday
July 16, 1974
197th day
168 to go this year
Sunrise: 5:41 a.m.
Sunset: 8:56 p.m.

**Today's weather:**

**Fair, warmer**

Details page 5B

**Monday's temperatures**

| a.m. | 1 | 2 | 3 | 4 | 5 | 6 | 7 | 8 | 9 | 10 | 11 | Noon |
|---|---|---|---|---|---|---|---|---|---|---|---|---|
| Temp. | 65 | 64 | 62 | 61 | 61 | 60 | 61 | 69 | 73 | 74 | 77 | 80 |
| p.m. | 1 | 2 | 3 | 4 | 5 | 6 | 7 | 8 | 9 | 10 | 11 | Midn. |
| temp. | 81 | 80 | 83 | 84 | 83 | 83 | 84 | 82 | 78 | 74 | 71 | 71 |

Sunny skies and hot weather are forecast for today in the Twin Cities area. There is a slight chance of thundershowers tonight and Wednesday. A high in the upper 80s is forecast for today, with a low tonight in the upper 60s and a high Wednesday around 90.

Other predicted highs today: Minnesota, mid 70s to lower 80s north, mid 80s to lower 90s south; North Dakota, lower 80s northeast to lower 90s west; South Dakota, 90s northeast to around 105 west-central; Wisconsin, upper 80s to mid 90s.

### You mean it's all in the mind?

A Minneapolis man who obviously believes in putting up a good front—even during the recent hot spell—told his coworkers, "I don't have air conditioning, but I always drive with my car windows up, and smile a lot so people will think I do."



# Recent inflation has something for everybody

**Editor's note: This is the third in a series of five articles by Tribune Business Editor Dick Youngblood on inflation in the United States, how it came about and what to expect.**

By Dick Youngblood
Staff Writer

Some economists blame our flight into double-digit inflation on the blackmail of Arab oil producers and the combination of natural disaster and bureaucratic blundering that produced a global food shortage.

Others lean more toward miscalculations in fiscal and monetary policy that flooded the economy with more money and more demand than could be absorbed at a time when economics were booming worldwide.

**(Profits help to balance supply with demand. Page 2B.)**

Some talk of the coincidence of global economic boom, coupled with the distortions of economic controls, and the resulting pressures on raw-material industries that had not expanded for 20 years because of low profit margins.

Others look for the culprit in the unrestrained power of labor and industry to enforce inflationary wage and price patterns.

Still others blame a war that hardly anyone liked and no one wanted to pay for.

That's what's nice about the inflationary pattern of the past eight years — there's a little something for everybody.

All of them are right, in part: the fiscalists can blame the monetarists and the monetarists the fiscalists; the businessman can blame the unions, and vice-versa; the antiwar bloc can blame the Pentagon, Congress can blame the White House and everybody can blame the Agriculture Department because they're accustomed to it.

And we can all blame ourselves, because all of these were merely short-term factors piled on top of a pattern of chronic excess demand that we have been shaping with unrelieved gusto since World War II.

The inflationary spiral began in 1966 with the "guns and butter" policies of President Johnson — policies that provide an almost classic example of the "inflationary bias" built into American society.

In an economy already approaching full capacity, LBJ escalated two wars — against North Vietnam and against domestic poverty.

But he perceived that the public would not accept a tax increase that would pull enough demand out of the private economy to balance the demands of both the Vietnam War and the War on Poverty.

It was 1968 before LBJ's—and Congress's—reluctance

**Inflation** continued on page 4A

Minneapolis Tribune

Sunday
July 28, 1974
40c by carrier
45¢ by motor route
50¢ single copy
Volume CVIII
Number 65
M




# Panel votes for impeachment; Article is sent to House, 27-11

By Finlay Lewis
Staff Correspondent

**Washington, D.C.**
The House Judiciary Committee voted Saturday to recommend the impeachment of President Nixon for obstructing the investigation of the Watergate scandal.

All 21 of the committee Democrats and six Republicans supported the accusation that Mr. Nixon "prevented, obstructed and impeded the administration of justice."

The article was opposed by 11 Republicans on a tense and hushed roll-call vote that capped an eight-month committee investigation into allegations that Mr. Nixon was guilty of high crimes and misdemeanors in the office of the presidency.

Mr. Nixon thus becomes the second president — and the first in this century — to become the object of an impeachment action in the full House of Representatives. The articles voted yesterday will go to the House as a committee recommendation.

The 27 to 11 vote appeared to fulfill the expectations of impeachment's leading proponents, who have acknowledged that they would need bipartisan committee support in order to win the vote in the House and force Mr. Nixon to stand trial in the Senate. Conviction there would force him from office.

Crossing over to vote against the Republican president were Reps. Thomas Railsback of Illinois, Hamilton Fish of New York, Lawrence Hogan of Maryland, Caldwell Butler of Virginia, William Cohen of Maine and Harold Froehlich of Wisconsin.

The drama of the occasion suddenly seemed to fill the committee's modern hearing room as the 38 members began answering the first of two roll calls, one procedural, the other on final acceptance of the article. Many votes were barely audible.

"I was just awfully, awfully tired," Fish recalled later.

The committee will return to work Monday morning to consider a second impeachment article accusing Mr. Nixon of having abused the powers of his office.

Key committee Republicans and Democrats have been negotiating over the article's wording and content in recent days, and a GOP informant reported late yesterday that the measure would also likely enjoy bipartisan support.

The informant said that one of the votes for the article might be cast by Rep. Robert McClory of Illinois. The panel's second ranking Republican voted no yesterday. The article voted yesterday is centered on the burglary and bugging operation against Democratic national offices that ended when Washington police arrested five men in the Watergate office complex at 2 a.m. June 17, 1972.

The article describes the burglars as "agents of the Committee for the Re-Election of the President" and then goes on to declare that:

"Richard M. Nixon, using the powers of his high office, engaged personally and through his close subordinates and agents, in a course of conduct or plan designed to delay, impede and obstruct the investigation of such unlawful entry; to cover up, conceal and protect those responsible; and to conceal the existence and scope of oth-

Committee continued on page 6A

## Ziegler: Nixon sure of support

Tribune Wire Services

**San Clemente, Calif.**
President Nixon "remains confident" that the House will not vote to impeach him, despite the House Judiciary Committee's impeachment recommendation, Press Secretary Ronald Ziegler said Saturday night.

The White House reaction came in a one-paragraph statement issued an hour after the vote that Mr. Nixon should be impeached for allegedly having "prevented, obstructed and impeded administration of justice" in the Watergate cover-up.

The statement said:

"The president remains confident that the full House will recognize that there simply is not the evidence to support this or any other article of impeachment and will not vote to impeach. He is confident because he knows he has committed no impeachable offense."

The committee vote came as no surprise to Mr. Nixon and his staff. Ziegler and other officials had been saying for some time that they expected the committee to vote against the president. But they predict that the House will not vote to impeach after examining the matter, as Ziegler put it, "with an open mind."

Mr. Nixon received the news at his home in San Clemente, where he was ending a 16-day stay.

Ziegler said the president wasn't watching the television broadcast of the impeachment vote but was being kept "very closely" informed by himself and Chief of Staff Alexander Haig Jr. Mr. Nixon was also keeping abreast of the judiciary committee proceedings by reading White House news summaries and the newspapers.

Aides said Mr. Nixon was walking on the beach when he learned of the committee's 27 to 11 vote to recommend his impeachment.

Haig informed him of the vote over a special telephone connection on the beach. The call came about half an hour after the vote was cast in Washington.

"The president was not surprised. He had expected this outcome as you know," Deputy Press Secretary Gerald L. Warren told reporters.

Mr. Nixon does not plan a lobbying effort against impeachment in the House, Ziegler said, adding that "we do have a firm belief that the president has supporters in Congress."

Associated Press

**Chairman Peter Rodino of the House Judiciary Committee was followed by a security agent Saturday after his committee adopted an impeachment article against President Nixon.**

## Rules panel next stop for Nixon impeach bill

By Frank Wright
Staff Correspondent

**Washington, D.C.**
The next stop for the first article of impeachment against President Nixon, approved Saturday by the House Judiciary Committee, will be H 313.

H 313 is the office of the House Rules Committee, a cramped suite on the third floor of the Capitol that belies the importance of the work that is done there.

The suite is small, consisting essentially of one room, dominated by a long, heavy, dark brown table surrounded by 15 chairs for the members of the committee. Desks for the eight staff members are jammed around the fringes, butting against each other and filling every cranny. Less than a score of seats are available for press and members of the public who want to watch the committee.

House Democratic leaders have said they may permit televising of the Rules Committee's processing of the impeachment papers.

About the only way to do that in H 313 would be to hang the cameras from the ceiling or stuff them into the fireplace.

So, if Speaker Carl Albert of Oklahoma and others are serious about televising the committee action, the proceedings likely will be moved to a more spacious spot.

Wherever the action occurs, however, it will

Procedure
Continued on page 18A

## Inside:



## Each panel member felt the drama of his vote

By Finlay Lewis
Staff Correspondent

**Washington, D.C.**
In the end, they seemed haunted by the limelight that they all shared. For nearly 20 hours, the 38 Judiciary Committee members were the main players in a historic drama being enacted in front of a national television audience.

There had been moments of eloquence and passion, of lofty rhetoric and crafty political appeals to the folks back home, of wisdom and cunning demagoguery, of confusion and guile.

But when Associate Counsel Garner J. Cline called their names on the final vote, the dimensions of the impeachment question suddenly appeared to dawn on the members and only a few chose to return the TV camera's gaze as it recorded their decision for posterity.

For Rep. Hamilton Fish, Republican descendant of a Revolutionary War family, the vote could only have been a terrible wrench. Generations before him have served in Congress, including his father, whose name frequently appears prominently in full-page newspaper ads supporting President Nixon.

[redacted]

The father's name has also appeared at the bottom of many personal letters, scrawled in that familiar hand, pleading the president's case with his son.

But when the final moment came, Fish, tall, Harvard-educated aristocrat in tone and manner, voted to accuse the president of one of the most serious constitutional breaches of office —of high crimes and misdemeanors.

No one in the room doubted Fish when he announced moments before the roll call that he had decided to vote for impeachment "with deep reluctance."

"I intend to vote in favor of this, the first article of impeachment. After long deliberation, I can assure you it is not cast lightly," he said.

Afterward, Fish, his eyes red-rimmed with fatigue, recalled the vote: "I just

Mood
Continued on page 14A

## Reinecke found guilty of lying about ITT offer

Associated Press

**Washington, D.C.**
Lt. Gov. Ed Reinecke of California was convicted of perjury Saturday for his testimony about a financial commitment by International Telephone & Telegraph Corp. (ITT) to the 1972 Republican national convention.

Reinecke, 50, described his trial as a gross miscarriage of justice and said he will appeal.

U.S. District Judge Barrington D. Parker directed him to appear at a Washington probation office Monday for a presentencing interview. No date was set for sentencing. The maximum penalty on the single count of the indictment is five years in prison and a fine of $2,000.

Reinecke showed no emotion when the verdict was announced, but Mrs. Reinecke cried out, "Oh, my God, no — no, he's not guilty." She and the three Reinecke children, who had been present throughout the 12 days of the trial, wept over the verdict.

(In Sacramento, Calif., Gov. Ronald Reagan, who had picked Reinecke for the lieutenant governor's job in 1969, said, "This is a tragic event for Ed Reinecke. I personally have always had confidence in his integrity and feel that he did not intentionally do wrong." Reagan said he would have no comment on Reinecke's tenure in office until he has had a

Ed Reinecke

chance to talk to Reinecke and his attorneys.

(Several sections of the California Government Code exclude from office people convicted of certain offenses, but an opinion on Reinecke would probably be required from

Reinecke
Continued on page 18A

## Excellence—the vision may elude university's grasp

By Gregor W. Pinney
Staff Writer

**Analysis**

The drive for excellence at the University of Minnesota is not materializing as planned and probably will not bring any dramatic changes in the forseeable future.

In particular, no significant part of the university is scheduled to be shut down or cut back, even though that has been the key element in the talk about excellence over the past year.

And so far, no formal plans have been made to move certain parts of the university into the "front-ranks" of the competition in American higher education. That, too, was part of the original excellence scenario.

Instead, the excellence movement—for the time being—has dwindled to a familiar activity at the university: trying to get a big increase in money from the next session of the legislature.

The excellence drive began last fall. If it had worked out, it would have been a momentous development in the history of the university. It would have changed the shape and the fundamental character of the institution.

The idea was that the university would abandon its long tradition of trying to provide just about everything. Instead, it would de-emphasize or shut down certain programs (they would be "shucked off," said Vice President Harold S. Chase) and use the money it saved to boost the remaining programs into the "front ranks." There was some talk about emulating Harvard, but most people at the university settled for competing with the best of the Big Ten, particularly the University of Michigan.

Excellence
Continued on page 13A

## Elderly, handicapped square off in St. Cloud

By Jack Coffman
Staff Writer

An unusual civil rights case is coming to a head in St. Cloud.

The opponents are the city housing authority and one of its tenants. Simple enough, so far. But the tenant is a 30-year-old epileptic, Virginia Cox. Virtually all of the other tenants of the building are senior citizens who meet the authority's age requirement to live in the subsidized housing.

According to authority officials, Ms. Cox recently has begun to suffer an increasing number of epileptic seizures, which they say are having a detrimental effect on the elderly residents. They also contend that she does not take her medicine as prescribed and that there is no staff in the project to watch over her.

But Ms. Cox's defenders charge that she is being discriminated against because of her disability and because of friction between the project's 122 elderly residents and Ms. Cox and three other handicapped tenants, all of whom are younger.

"We don't get invited to some of the functions the senior citizens get to go to," one handicapped resident said last week.

"They (the handicapped residents) always say we discriminate against them, but we don't," retorted William Eller, a senior citizen who is a member of the project's tenant council. "We never did anything to hurt them. They just want to take over."

Eller said that since the controversy and the disruptions started, many of the elderly tenants have begun to stay in their rooms more.

"We have a lot of people here in their 70s and 80s who just can't take it," he said. "They can't cope with the seizures," he explained.

Both sides of the dispute

Evict
Continued on page 14A

## Almanac / Index

Sunday
July 28, 1974
209th day
156 to go this year
Sunrise: 5:54 a.m.
Sunset: 8:45 p.m.

**Today's weather: Little change**

Details Page 12B

Saturday's temperatures

| | 1 | 2 | 3 | 4 | 5 | 6 | 7 | 8 | 9 | 10 | 11 | Noon |
|---|---|---|---|---|---|---|---|---|---|---|---|---|
| a.m. temp. | 64 | 62 | 61 | 60 | 58 | 56 | 58 | 66 | 70 | 71 | 77 | 79 |
| p.m. temp. | 82 | 84 | 84 | 85 | 86 | 85 | 84 | 81 | 76 | 69 | 70 | |

Mostly fair skies are forecast for the Twin Cities area through Monday, with continued mild weather. The high today is expected to be in the low 80s, the low tonight near 50 and the high Monday near 80.

Other predicted highs: Minnesota, mid to upper 70s north to mid 80s south; North Dakota, low to mid 80s; South Dakota, mid 80s to low 90s; Wisconsin, upper 70s to low 80s.

### Was she hit by a garbage truck?

A St. Louis Park woman has been put in traction because of an injury, which is causing quite a stir in her neighborhood. The cause of this commotion is her three-year-old daughter, who is going around the neighborhood telling everyone, "My mother is in a trash can."



Telephones
372 4141 News General
372 4242 Classified
372 4343 Circulation

Minneapolis **Tribune**

Friday
August 9, 1974
Volume CVIII
Number 77
M S

15c Single copy
3 Sections

1A
Final

# President resigns

## Ford will be sworn in at noon today; he will continue Nixon's foreign policy

### Nixon

By Frank Wright
Staff Correspondent

**Washington, D.C.**
President Nixon resigned Thursday, driven from office by the irresistible blight of the Watergate scandal less than two years after being reelected by the biggest majority in history.

Mr. Nixon's decision to become the first American chief executive to give up the office voluntarily, and to turn the leadership of the nation over to Vice President Gerald Ford, was announced last night in a 16-minute speech after three days of mounting pressures from Congress, rumors, denials and inner personal turmoil.

His resignation as the 37th president of the United States will be effective at noon today, Mr. Nixon said. Ford will be sworn in as the 38th by Chief Justice Warren Burger in ceremonies beginning at that moment in the White House. Mr. Nixon and his family will have departed for their native California by then and will not attend.

One of Ford's first tasks will be the selection of a new vice president, an act that, for the first time, will give the country both a president and vice president who have not been elected by the voters.

Mr. Nixon's speech allayed fears that he might depart in an angry and divisive farewell appearance. Instead it was apologetic and conciliatory, centering on an appeal to Americans to unite behind Ford, leave the "bitterness" of Watergate behind and "rediscover shared ideals.'

The president spoke from his desk in the Oval Office, the same office in which, on June 23, 1972, six days after the Watergate break-in, he and H. R. Haldeman, then his White House chief of staff, plotted to derail an FBI investigation that was unearthing the link between Mr. Nixon's reelection committee and the burglary. It was the tape recordings of those conversations with Haldeman, released Monday by the president after he had withheld them for more than two years, that triggered Mr. Nixon's downfall.

**Nixon** continued on page 6A

United Press International

**President Nixon announced his resignation in a nationally televised speech Thursday evening.**

Associated Press

**Vice President Gerald Ford, his successor, spoke at a medal-presentation ceremony earlier yesterday.**

### Ford

Tribune News Services

**Washington, D.C.**
Gerald R Ford said Thursday night that Henry Kissinger will remain as secretary of state.

Appearing outside his home shortly after President Nixon's announcement, Ford said he plans to continue Mr. Nixon's foreign policies

"I want Kissinger to be my secretary of state and I'm glad to announce he will be secretary of state," said the man who at noon today will succeed Mr. Nixon as the nation's 38th president.

Ford said he expects "a spirit of cooperation between the new president and the Congress."

"I've been very fortunate in my lifetime in public office to have a great many adversaries in the Congress," he said. "But I don't think I have any enemies in the Congress."

Ford said in praising Mr. Nixon that "I think the president of the United States has made one of the greatest personal sacrifices for the country and one of the finest personal decisions on behalf of all of us as Americans."

Having watched Mr. Nixon's foreign policy the last 5½ years, he said, "Let me say without any hesitation or reservation that the policy that has achieved peace . . . will be

**Ford**
Continued on page 17A

## White House shaken by Nixon step

By Finlay Lewis
Staff Correspondent

**Washington, D.C.**
For the record, let it be known that Ronald Ziegler began his briefing for the White House press corps at 12:20 EDT and ended it at 12:21 EDT. His words were veiled but in that fleeting moment he conveyed one of the most extraordinary messages in the history of the American presidency.

It was the death knell of the Nixon administration.

Ziegler was pale and trembling, and his voice broke as he acknowledged the obvious, saying, "This has, of course, been a difficult time." He concluded with an announcement, innocuous on its face but momentous in import.

"Tonight, at 9 o'clock eastern daylight time, the president of the United States will address the nation on radio and television from his Oval Office."

And so, on a drizzly August day, Richard Milhous Nixon told the world that he was going to become the first chief executive to resign the White House.

One middle-level presidential aide told a reporter about the gloom and heartbreak that shrouded the inner workings yesterday of the White House. He said that some, hopeful and denying the inevitable, volunteere help man the switchboard thinking that the president's mind might be changed if presented with tangible evidence of public support.

The informant said there was also a burst of optimism last night when Mr. Nixon's daughter, Julie, told a member of her mother's staff that she was still fighting resignation — and expecting to win.

The other members of the president's immediate family — Mrs. Nixon and daughter Tricia — shared that feeling and forcefully expressed it during a family dinner Wednesday

**Day**
Continued on page 6A

### Analysis

## Ford likely to follow Nixon's policies

By Alan Ehrenhalt
Congressional Quarterly

**Washington, D.C.**
Gerald R. Ford's record in Congress makes it unlikely he will strike out in major new directions from Nixon administration policies.

Ford favors a strong defense establishment and advocates limiting federal involvement to solve social issues. He was among the first to propose revenue sharing with the states, a key element of Mr. Nixon's "new federalism."

Ford's voting record in Congress was one of close agreement with his predecessor. In 1973, for example, Ford supported Mr. Nixon on 80 percent of the House votes on which Mr. Nixon had taken a position. That put Ford ahead of all but one of his colleagues.

He voted to sustain every Nixon veto the House considered in 1973. About the only serious difference came on mass transit legislation. Ford, from auto-

**Record**
Continued on page 17A

## Resignation speech of Nixon

Associated press

**Washington, D.C.**
Following is the text of President Nixon's resignation address to the nation Thursday night:

Good Evening. This will be the 37th time I will have spoken to you from this office where so many decisions have been made that shaped the history of this nation.

Each time I have done so to discuss with you some matters which I believed affected the national interest. In all the decisions I have made in my public life I have always tried to do what was best for the nation.

Throughout the long and difficult period of Watergate, I have felt it was my duty to persevere, to make every possible effort to complete the kind of office to which you elected me.

In the past few days, however, it has become evident to me that I no longer have a stron , enough political base in the Congress to justify continuing that effort.

As long as there was such a base, I felt strongly that it was necessary to see the constitutional process through to its conclusion; to do otherwise would be unfaithful to the spirit of that deliberately difficult process, and a dangerously destabilizing precedent for the future.

But with the disappearance of that base I now believe that the constitutional purpose has been served and there is no longer a need for the process to be prolonged.

I would have preferred to carry through to the finish no matter the personal agony that would have been involved. And my family unanimously urged me to do so.

But the interest of the nation must always come before any personal consideration.

From the discussions I have had with congressional and other leaders, I have concluded that because of the Watergate matter I might not have the support of the Congress that I would consider necessary to back the very difficult decisions and carry out the duties of this office in the way the interests of the nation will require.

I have never been a quitter. To leave office before my

**Text** continued on page 6A

### Inside the Tribune



## Juvenile justice:

a defective syst

**A key conflict in the juvenile justice system is that between police and probation officers, between the police and the courts. Today's Juvenile Justice report by three Tribune reporters explores this difference of opinion. Page 13A.**

## Sense of relief dominates reactions of Midwest residents to resignation

By Staff Writers

There were the predictable cheers from the bitter few and some gasps from the disbelieving fewer. But mostly it was a sense of relief that dominated the reactions of area residents.

Watergate was finally over.

While some in the University of Minnesota student center cheered, the men and women who had once been part of the president's "silent majority" were quietly hoisting a few at places like the St. Anthony Municipal Bar.

"Now they can get back to running the country," Mike Davis said after the patrons of the workingmen's bar had watched much of the speech in silence.

There was little jubilation anywhere else. "What the hell is there to be happy about?" Ray Harvey, a local DFL officer, wondered as he sipped a beer in a Blooming Prairie, Minn., tavern. "Sure, we got rid of that bum, but what a way to do it," Harvey said.

And Mr. Nixon's last loyalists — when you could find one — were accepting resignation with resignation. "The guy did a hell of a job." Dean Messmer was saying at a Mandan, N.D., restaurant. "I'd vote for him again." But he also said he thought the president should "get the full treatment of the law."

Silence dominated more than the bars and bedrooms in which people heard the last speech of President Nixon. As he spoke there was an eerie emptiness to normally bustling places. At 7th St. and Hennepin Av. in downtown Minneapolis, 8 p.m. found the sidewalks and streets nearly empty save for a few people listening to transistor radios while they waited for a bus or a lone motorist listening to history on a car radio.

Somewhere, though, there were celebrations. Liquor store clerks reported a surge in the sale of champagne. An employee of Kick's Liquor Store said he'd sold 12 bottles of champagne yesterday afternoon; normally, he said, he might have sold one.

And at the University of Minnesota the sound of the president resigning had to compete with cheers in the student union. When he referred to "those who have withheld from me their support," many of the 150 onlookers laughed.

Even some GOP officials were bitter, though their bitterness rarely took the

**Reaction**
Continued on page 17A

### Almanac / Index

**Friday
August 9, 1974
221st day
144 to go this year
Sunrise: 6:07 a.m.
Sunset: 8:29 p.m.**

**Today's weather: Thundershowers**

Details page 7B

**Thursday's temperatures**

| a.m. | 1 | 2 | 3 | 4 | 5 | 6 | 7 | 8 | 9 | 10 | 11 | Noon |
|---|---|---|---|---|---|---|---|---|---|---|---|---|
| **temp.** | 65 | 63 | 62 | 61 | 60 | 60 | 59 | 63 | 66 | 71 | 74 | 75 |
| **p.m.** | 1 | 2 | 3 | 4 | 5 | 6 | 7 | 8 | 9 | 10 | 11 | Midn. |
| **temp.** | 77 | 79 | 79 | 78 | 79 | 77 | 76 | 75 | 73 | 72 | 70 | 68 |

A chance of showers and occasional thundershowers are predicted for the Twin Cities area today through Saturday. Variable cloudiness is expected through Saturday. Highs today and Saturday in the upper 70s, low tonight in the low 60s.

Other predicted highs today: Minnesota, 68 to 80; North Dakota, mid to upper 70s west to mostly low 80s east; South Dakota, mid to upper 70s; Wisconsin, 70s and low 80s.



Telephones
372 4141 News General
372 4242 Classified
372 4343 Circulation

Minneapolis Tribune

Monday
September 9, 1974
Volume CVIII
Number 108
M

15c Single copy
3 Sections



1A
Final

# Ford grants Nixon full pardon

## Action called 'act of mercy'

By John Herbers
New York Times Service

**Washington, D.C.**
President Ford Sunday granted former President Richard Nixon an unconditional pardon for all federal crimes he may have committed during his term of office, an act, Mr. Ford said, that was intended to spare both Nixon and the nation further punishment in the Watergate scandals.

Nixon, in San Clemente, Calif., accepted the pardon, which exempts him from indictment and trial for his role in the cover-up of the Watergate burglary. Nixon issued a statement saying that he can now see he was "wrong in not acting more decisively and more forthrightly in dealing with Watergate."

Philip W. Buchen, the White House counsel who advised Mr. Ford on the legal aspects of the pardon, said the "act of mercy" on the president's part was done without making any demands on Nixon and without asking the advice of the special Watergate prosecutor, Leon Jaworski, who had the legal responsibility to prosecute the case.

### Inside



Buchen said that he had, at the president's request, asked Jaworski how long it would be, in the event Nixon was indicted, before he could be brought to trial. He said that Jaworski replied it would be at least nine months or more, due to the enormous amount of publicity the charges against Nixon had received when the House Judiciary Committee recommended impeachment.

This was one of the reasons Mr. Ford cited for granting the pardon, saying he had concluded that "many months and perhaps more years will have to pass before Richard Nixon could hope to obtain a fair trial by jury in any jurisdiction of the United States under governing decisions of the Supreme Court."

"During this long period of delay and potential litigation, ugly passions would again be aroused, our people would again be polarized in their opinions, and the credibility of our free institutions of government would again be challenged at home and abroad," Mr. Ford said in a statement he read yesterday morning in the Oval Office when he signed the pardon.

Mr. Ford's decision was not unexpected, in light of his previous statements that he thought the former president had suffered enough by being forced out of office. Yet the unconditional nature of the pardon, taken without the recommendation of Jaworski, was more generous

**Ford** continued on page 7A

Associated Press

**President Ford put his signature on a document Sunday at the White House pardoning former President Richard M. Nixon for all "offenses against the United States" during Nixon's presidency.**

## Nixon says he was wrong

By Everett R. Holles
New York Times Service

**San Clemente, Calif.**
President Ford's pardon for Richard M. Nixon Sunday evoked from the former president the most forthright acknowledgement — and apology — that he has yet made of his personal implication in the Watergate scandal and cover-up.

Within 10 minutes after the presidential pardon was announced in Washington, Nixon's statement was released at his Casa Pacifica estate, saying, "No words can express the depth of my regret" for his mistakes in allowing Watergate to become "a national tragedy."

"That the way I tried to deal with Watergate was the wrong way is the burden I shall bear for every day of the life that is left to me," he said.

In a subsequent statement, given in response to reporters' questions, an aide quoted Nixon as saying that, in gratefully accepting the presidential pardon, he hoped Mr. Ford's "compassionate act would contribute to lifting the burdens of Watergate from our country."

When the Nixon statement was released by his adviser and former White House press secretary, Ronald Ziegler, at 8:30 a.m., Pacific time, Nixon and his wife already were en route to a new haven of seclusion away from their heavily guarded estate.

They left at 7 a.m. in a large black limousine accompanied by Secret Service agents and Nixon's military aide, Lt. Col. Jack Brennan, reportedly for the Palm Desert estate of Walter Annenberg, ambassador to Britain.

A close friend of the Nixons said the former president planned to play golf yesterday afternoon on Annenberg's private 18-hole course and "might or might not" return to San Clemente last night.

The presence of the Nixons at the Annenberg estate on the outskirts of Palm Springs could not be confirmed.

Nixon, in his statement following the announcement of the presidential pardon, said:

"Looking back on what is still in my mind a complex and confusing maze of events, decisions, pressures and personalities, one thing I can see clearly now is that I was wrong in not acting more decisively and more forthrightly in dealing with Watergate, particularly when it reached the stage of judicial proceedings and grew from a political scandal into a national tragedy.

"No words can describe the depths of my regret

**Nixon**
Continued on page 7A

## Reaction to pardon split mostly, but not all, by party

Tribune News Service

Reaction was sharply divided Sunday over President Ford's pardon of former President Richard Nixon, but the division was not altogether along party lines.

Most of the Democrats who commented immediately expressed various shades of disapproval and dismay while most Republican comments supported Mr. Ford's decision.

Two Republicans who disagreed with the action were Sens. Jacob Javits of New York and Edward W. Brooke of Massachusetts. Both had been critical of Nixon in recent months, and Brooke was the first Republican senator to call publicly for Nixon's resignation from the presidency.

Brooke issued a statement calling the pardon, without Nixon's full confession of his involvement in the Watergate scandals, a serious mistake.

Javits said he had hoped that Mr. Ford would have waited for the courts to deal with the matter, but he added that the pardoning power was something between the president and his conscience.

A spokesman for Sen. Barry Goldwater, R-Ariz., said the senator believed Nixon has been punished enough. He said Goldwater also thought it would have taken more than a year to get Nixon's case to court.

At the White House, switchboard operators said "angry calls, heavy and constant," began jamming their boards soon after Mr. Ford's announcement.

Mike Mansfield of Montana, the Senate majority leader, said he was disturbed by the circumstance that perhaps as many as 40 to 50 persons either had been indicted or sent to prison in the aftermath of the Watergate and related scandals, while the former president would not even be charged.

**Reaction**
Continued on page 6A

## TWA jet crashes off Greece; 88 feared dead

Associated Press

**Athens, Greece**
A TWA jetliner crashed into the stormy Ionian Sea off Greece Sunday, and Greek aviation officials said all 88 aboard were believed killed.

Airline officials said 17 Americans were aboard the Boeing 707.

The Greek Civil Aviation Authority reported that its rescue pilots saw "remnants of the wreckage and bodies floating on the surface" about 60 miles west of Kefallinia Island and 235 miles west of Athens.

"Only when our ships can get nearer will we be able to finally confirm whether anyone has survived, but their chances are minute," a spokesman for the authority said.

The airplane, on the Athens-to-Rome leg of Flight 841, originating in Tel Aviv and continuing to New York and Los Angeles, went down after an engine apparently failed.

Trans World Airlines officials in Israel said the Americans were among 49 passengers boarding in Tel Aviv for Rome and the United States. Nationalities of others boarding in Tel Aviv included 13 Japanese, four Italians, four French, three Indians, two Iranians, two Israelis, two Ceylonese, an Australian and a Canadian.

The nationalities of 30 passengers who joined the flight in Athens and the nine crew members were not known immediately.

TWA headquarters in New York ruled out sabotage, despite a claim by a telephone caller in Beirut that a Palestinian organization called the Nationalist Youth for the Liberation of Palestine had sabotaged the airplane. In Beirut, the Palestinian news agency reported that a spokesman for the Palestine Liberation Organization, which speaks for the guerrilla organizations, said the call was a hoax and emphatically denied that Arab groups were involved in the disaster.

## Ford's press secretary resigns in pardon protest

Jerald terHorst

Associated Press

**Washington, D.C.**
Jerald F. terHorst, close friend and adviser to President Ford for many years, resigned as Mr. Ford's press secretary Sunday to protest the pardon Mr. Ford granted to former President Richard M. Nixon.

"The president acted in good conscience and I also found it necessary to resign in good conscience," terHorst said.

A few hours later, Mr. Ford issued a statement through a press aide saying "I deeply regret" the resignation but "I understand his position."

"I appreciate the fact that good people will differ with me on this difficult decision," Mr. Ford added. "However, it is my judgment that it is in the best interest of the country. I think Jerry did an outstanding job in a controversial period of transition. I thank him for his service."

Sourses said terHorst told Mr. Ford of his plans to resign a half-hour before the president announced that he had decided to grant a full pardon to the man he succeeded in the nation's highest office Aug. 9.

TerHorst was the first man Mr. Ford hired for his White House staff after Nixon quit, and the press secretary's resignation clearly was a jolt to Mr. Ford's young administration.

Another White House official said he did not expect other Ford aides to join terHorst in resigning, but most of Mr. Ford's close advisers could not be reached for comment last night.

TerHorst himself refused to talk with reporters as word of his resignation swept through a capital still stunned by the suddeness of Mr. Ford's pardon announcement.

TerHorst was not answering a White House telephone that had been in-

**TerHorst**
Continued on page 7A

## Nixon to sell memoirs, agent says

Associated Press

**New York, N.Y.**
Literary agent Irving Lazar said Sunday that former President Nixon has authorized him to negotiate the sale of his memoirs for what will probably be over $2 million in advance payments.

He said Nixon plans one, two or three volumes beginning with the former president's childhood and going through his career "including his accomplishment for peace and the events of Watergate."

Lazar predicted hard-cover sales of at least 500,000 copies, which should bring Nixon over $2 million, he said. "It's customary for the first payment to be made before the author starts writing and the rest in installments."

## Knievel safe after ship fizzles, falls into canyon

By Larry Batson
Staff Writer

**Twin Falls, Idaho**
Almost everything that could go wrong with his steam rocket did go wrong Sunday, but by incredible fortune and his own presence of mind, Evel Knievel lived through an unsuccessful attempt to soar across the Snake River Canyon.

The rocket twisted sharply coming off the ramp. The reason is not known. An explosive charge with which Knievel was supposed to fire the drogue parachute exploded on the ramp—apparently because of a jolt or a short in the electrical system—and the chute blasted out behind the rocket as it streaked up the ramp.

**(Knievel jump awes, stirs Met crowd. Page 1C.)**

The small drogue chute slowed Knievel's start from a planned 400 miles an hour to less than half that. The rocket nosed over about 700 feet above the canyon and began to fall, spinning like a corkscrew.

At that point, Knievel, survivor of 300 motorcycle jumps, of 11 dreadful smash-ups, shoved forward the handle that released the main parachute. It deployed, even though the drogue chute had malfunctioned.

Knievel's action, said the engineer who built the rocket, was the only possible thing that could have saved him, and there was less than two seconds in which to do it.

"I remembered sometime back Bob Truax (engineer who built the rocket ship) told me that if I ever looked out and saw canyon wall instead of sky to let it (the chute handle) go. Thank God I remembered," Knievel said later.

As the main chute popped out of the rocket's tail, red smoke flares in the tailfins began to fire, giving the spectators — about 14,000 by police count — the impression that the craft was on fire. It twisted downward, to the canyon's top before the chute filled about halfway. Knievel could be seen in the cockpit each time the rocket revolved. His hands were moving frantically, but he stayed in place.

"Oh God! Oh God! Oh God!" screamed dozens of people in the press site, where writers, photographers, celebrities and friends of the promoters were segregated. Many said later

**Knievel** continued on page 6A

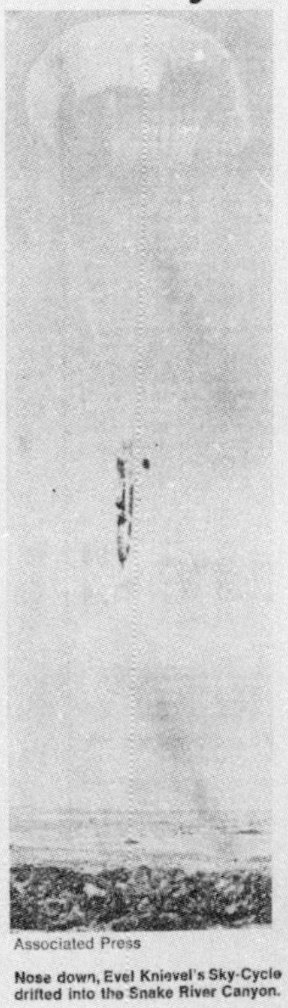

Associated Press

**Nose down, Evel Knievel's Sky-Cycle drifted into the Snake River Canyon.**

## Almanac / Index

**Monday**
**September 9, 1974**
**252nd day**
**113 to go this year**
**Sunrise: 6:44 a.m.**
**Sunset: 7:36 p.m.**

### Today's weather: Cloudy, mild

Details Page 9B

**Sunday's temperatures**

| a.m. | 1 | 2 | 3 | 4 | 5 | 6 | 7 | 8 | 9 | 10 | 11 | Noon |
|---|---|---|---|---|---|---|---|---|---|---|---|---|
| **temp.** | 65 | 64 | 62 | 60 | 60 | 58 | 57 | 59 | 60 | 61 | 63 | 69 |
| p.m. | 1 | 2 | 3 | 4 | 5 | 6 | 7 | 8 | 9 | 10 | 11 | Midn. |
| **temp.** | 71 | 74 | 75 | 75 | 74 | 74 | 71 | 68 | 62 | 61 | 62 | 62 |

Mostly cloudy skies with a chance of occasional showers and thunderstorms are forecast for the Twin Cities area today and Tuesday. Today's high will be in the low 70s with tonight's low in the mid 50s. Tuesday's high will be in the upper 60s.

Other predicted highs: Minnesota mid 50s north to mid 70s south; North Dakota, 70s; South Dakota, mid 70s to low 80s; Wisconsin, 60s and low 70s.

### An argument for cash contributions?

It must be a bad year for politicians and their money. The San Francisco Chronicle reports that South Dakota Sen. James Abourezk tried to check into a San Francisco hotel recently, but that the clerk insisted on payment in advance—and then the clerk wouldn't accept a check.



**Telephones**
372 4141 News General
372 4242 Classified
372 4343 Circulation

Minneapolis Tribune

Wednesday April 30, 1975
15c Single copy
3 Sections
1A
Volume CVIII
Number 341
M
Final



# Saigon surrenders

## U.S. evacuates last Americans

By George Esper
Associated Press

**Saigon, South Vietnam**
The Saigon government surrendered unconditionally to the Viet Cong today (Tuesday night, Minneapolis time), ending 30 years of warfare. Within two hours North Vietnamese and Viet Cong troops began moving into the city.

Columns of South Vietnamese troops pulled out of their defensive positions in the city and marched to central points to turn in their weapons.

President Duong Van (Big) Minh spoke to the nation only hours after an armada of U.S. Marine helicopters had completed an emergency evacuation of nearly 900 Americans and thousands of Vietnamese from the besieged capital. Minh, a retired general and neutralist, was named president Monday in a desperate and unsuccessful attempt to negotiate peace with the Communist leaders.

In a five-minute radio address, Minh said:

"The Republic of Vietnam policy is the policy of peace and reconciliation, aimed at saving the blood of our people. I ask all servicemen to stop firing and stay where you are. I also demand that soldiers of the Provisional Revolutionary Government (Viet Cong) stop firing and stay in place. We are here waiting for the Provisional Revolutionary Government, to hand over authority in order to stop useless bloodshed."

Gen. Nguyen Huu Hanh, deputy chief of staff, then went on the air to order all South Vietnamese troops to carry out Minh's orders. "All commanders must be ready to enter into relations with commanders of the Provisional Revolutionary Government to carry out the cease-fire without bloodshed," he said.

As they spoke, Saigon fell silent and shellfire subsided along the northern rim, where Viet Cong gunners had been bombarding the airport. Saigon police and militiamen remained at their posts, indicating that the Communist-led troops had not yet entered the city.

(In Washington, John Hushen, White House deputy press secretary, said when asked for comment on Minh's announcement: "There will be no statement forthcoming from the White House tonight."

Surrender continued on page 4A

## Copters, marines take out 5,500 S. Vietnamese

By John W. Finney
New York Times Service

**Washington, D.C.**
The United States ended two decades of military involvement in the Vietnam War Tuesday as a fleet of helicopters and combat marines evacuated the last Americans in Saigon and more than 5,500 South Vietnamese.

After the final American retreat from South Vietnam was completed, President Ford, in a statement issued by the White House, said the evacuation "closes a chapter in the American experience." In a plea for national unity in the post-Vietnam period, the president said:

"I ask all Americans to close ranks, to avoid recrimination about the past, to look ahead to the many goals we share and to work together on the great tasks that remain to be accomplished."

The last Americans were removed by 81 helicopters flying from U.S. Navy ships lying off the South Vietnamese coast. Nearly 1,000 marines went ashore to protect the evacuation and overhead air cover was provided by U.S. Navy and Air Force F4 fighter-bombers that for more than eight years were the main bombing force of the United States in Vietnam.

The final withdrawal of Americans was completed at 7:52 a.m. Saigon time (6:52 p.m. Tuesday, Minneapolis time) some two hours after the White House had announced the evacuation was completed — when 11 marines were taken by helicopter from the roof of the American Embassy in Saigon. Officials said that the marines, the last of the security force, were safely removed although small-arms fire had broken out around the deserted embassy.

The evacuation was ordered Monday night by Mr. Ford after the Saigon airport was closed because of Communist rocket and artillery fire. A total of 1,000 Americans — the last contingent of a force that once numbered more than 500,000 — were removed.

Evacuation continued on page 4A

United Press International

**Looking tired, President Ford walked with Secretary of State Henry Kissinger to the White House Tuesday**

### On the inside:



## Kissinger: Surrender to have wide impact

New York Times Service

**Washington, D.C.**
Secretary of State Henry Kissinger said Tuesday the fall of South Vietnam will have repercussions throughout the world.

"There is no question that the outcome in Indochina will have consequences not only in Asia but in many other parts of the world," the secretary said. "To deny these consequences is to miss the possibility of dealing with them."

"We are determined to manage and to progress along the road toward a permanent peace we have sought, even though there is no question there will be consequences," he said.

Kissinger said he is opposed to any aid to North Vietnam. He said the United States will have to wait and see what happens in South Vietnam "and whether there is going to be a South Vietnam" before deciding on aid or diplomatic ties.

Clearly concerned about the world situation he said that the United States

Kissinger
Continued on page 4A

Associated Press

**Vietnamese outside the gates watched a helicopter carry some of the last Americans out of the U.S. Embassy in Saigon Tuesday.**

## Marines' arrival, departure contrasted

By Peter Arnett
Associated Press

**Saigon, South Vietnam**
Ten years ago I watched the first U.S. Marines arrive to help South Vietnam. They were greeted on the beaches by pretty Vietnamese girls in white silken robes who draped flower leis around their necks.

A decade has passed.

And on Tuesday I watched U.S. Marines shepherding the last Americans out of South Vietnam. They were the same, cleancut-looking young men of a decade ago.

But the Vietnamese were different.

Those who didn't have a place on the last helicopters out of Saigon, and there were thousands of them left behind, hooted, booed and scuffled with the U.S. Marines guarding the landing zones.

Some Vietnamese threw themselves over walls and wire fences, only to be thrown back by the marines.

Bloodshed was avoided seemingly only by good

Saigon
Continued on page 4A

## The last exodus: by wit, guile, force

Associated Press

**Aboard the U.S.S. Blue Ridge**
Waves of marine and air force helicopters flew 6,400 evacuees Tuesday from Saigon to a 40-vessel armada waiting 17 to 25 miles off the coast of South Vietnam.

The Americans, Vietnamese and other foreigners were picked up from an American compound near the Tan Son Nhut airport by helicopters flown in from the U.S. carriers Okinawa, Hancock and Midway.

Vice Air Marshal Nguyen Cao Ky, a former South Vietnamese premier, had no comment as he stepped aboard this command and communications vessel in the center of the fleet.

Ky had been flown earlier to the Denver along with Mrs. Graham Martin, wife of the U.S. ambassador to South Vietnam.

Other South Vietnamese, by wit, guile or access to military aircraft, fled Saigon to Thailand, Hong Kong or the Philippines.

Long before the operation by carrier helicopters started, a wave of Air America and Vietnamese air force helicopters descended by surprise on the waiting American vessels.

Aircraft carrying frightened Vietnamese pilots and passengers from Saigon converged on this ship in a race for its single helipad. Seven aircraft appeared in the late morning sky from the westerly direction of Saigon and two of the first to arrive collided on the deck. Later arrivals circled the ship, awaiting their turns.

As one helicopter was about to take off from the rear of the ship, another Vietnamese pilot brought his aircraft down into its whirling blades. He almost toppled

Abandon continued on page 5A

## Legion softballers unfazed by Saigon

By Peg Meier
Staff Writer

Saigon fell, but that wasn't the topic of conversation Tuesday night at American Legion Post 334 in Coon Rapids. The topic was the post's softball practice that was rained out.

The post commander, Robert E. Lee — yes, he said, that's really his name — said post members were sitting around tables ignoring news of Vietnam. "Besides softball, the hockey players are talking hockey and the soccer players are talking soccer," he said.

When pressed for his views on the unconditional surrender to the Viet Cong, Lee said he agrees with Barry Goldwater: "Years ago we should have bombed Hanoi and then it would have been over. Really bombed it, I mean." Because the United States didn't do that, he continued, "we had quite a bit of wasted men and materials."

Lee was an army 1st sergeant north of Saigon for about five months in 1965. "I saw enough. What I

Reaction
Continued on page 4A

## Almanac / Index

**Wednesday**
**April 30, 1975**
**120th day**
**245 to go this year**
**Sunrise: 6:05 a.m.**
**Sunset: 8:17 p.m.**

**Today's weather:**
**Cloudy, cool**
Details page 5B

**Tuesday's Temperatures**

| | | | | | | | | | | | | |
|---|---|---|---|---|---|---|---|---|---|---|---|---|
| a.m. | 1 | 2 | 3 | 4 | 5 | 6 | 7 | 8 | 9 | 10 | 11 | Noon |
| **temp.** | 46 | 45 | 45 | 46 | 46 | 46 | 45 | 45 | 45 | 46 | 47 | 52 |
| p.m. | 1 | 2 | 3 | 4 | 5 | 6 | 7 | 8 | 9 | 10 | 11 | Midn. |
| **temp.** | 52 | 52 | 52 | 52 | 51 | 50 | 50 | 50 | 49 | 47 | 47 | 47 |

Mostly cloudy skies and continued cool weather are predicted for today and Thursday in the Twin Cities area, with a chance of a few sprinkles or light showers. The predicted high today and Thursday is in the low 50s and the low tonight about 40.

### . . . your (Caucasian) tired, your poor

A California congressman reportedly said he's happy that none of the Vietnamese refugees being sent to California will be staying in his district, because "we've got too many Orientals now." A Minneapolis Occidental says the congressman must be exaggerating. "They're can't be that many Orientals there," he says. "At least not enough to swing an election."



## House passes bill spreading indigent medical-care costs across county

By Jack Coffman
Staff Writer

Minneapolis legislators, with the support of many outstate and Ramsey County House members, won final approval Tuesday for legislation shifting much of the cost of medical care for indigents at Hennepin County Medical Center from the city to the suburbs.

The controversial bill has caused bitter divisions among county legislators. It now goes to the Senate where a struggle is under way to reverse a narrow, previous city setback.

After squeaking through a preliminary vote on Monday by only 60 to 54, the bill yesterday won approval on a final roll call by 77 to 51.

Rep. James Rice, DFL-Minneapolis, who left a hospital where he is under treatment for pneumonia to vote on the bill, said the city "simply needs to be treated as every citizen in the other 86 counties is treated." The statement refered to the fact that Hennepin County is the only county where the city and the suburbs pay on a different basis for medical care for the poor at the county hospital.

Under a formula created in 1963 Minneapolis residents pay much more for the care of indigent patients at the hospital than do residents of the suburbs. City dwellers pay

Hospital
Continued on page 4A

## Advertising of drug prices approved

By Lewis Cope
Staff Writer

The Minnesota Board of Pharmacy approved a new regulation Tuesday that would allow price advertising of prescription drugs in Minnesota. But one key question remains about whether consumers seeking such advertising have finally achieved victory.

The board not only unanimously approved the price-advertising proposal yesterday, but it gave in to consumer demands on a number of key points raised at an April 2 hearing.

However, the state attorney general's office now must decide if the way that the board handled this case allows the regulation to go into effect — or if some of the changes mean that new hearings and then a new board vote must be held.

The case developed this way:

Regulations that have been in force for many years prohibit all price advertising of prescription

Pharmacy
Continued on page 5A

THE MINNEAPOLIS STAR



Friday, August 1, 1975

# Heat wave lights fire under beer sales

By RANDY FURST
Minneapolis Star Staff Writer

Minnesotans consumed enough beer and soda pop last month to demoralize a lot of bladders.

It was the third-hottest July on record, with 90-degree temperatures on 15 days, and sales for some companies were sizzling:

**Coca Cola** Bottling Midwest, Inc., Minneapolis, said it may set a record for a single month, with case sales topping one million in July.

**Surdyk's Liquor Store** said it sold more beer last month than any other month in its history. The last two weeks, the store averaged close to 1,000 cases a day.

**Sanitary Ice Co.** in St. Paul last month produced 6½ million pounds of ice, including enough for 14-million drink glasses.

"The last two weeks it's just been unbelievable," said Lawrence Abdo, general manager of Sanitary Ice. "It's been terrific weather for ice."

The hotter it got, the longer the lines have been at the Shore Dairy Queen in Shoreview. "It's the best month I've ever had," said Norm Espersen, who runs the store.

The hotter it got, the more indiscriminate people became.

"The customer doesn't really care what kind of beer it is," says James Surdyk, vice-president of Surdyk's. "They come and grab whatever beer we have that's stacked on the floor."

Sears' Lake St. store sold between 250 and 300 air conditioners in the last week. "People don't care what the model is," a sales clerk said yesterday. "They buy anything we've got."

Area beaches have been thronged. During Aquatennial Sunday, the refreshment stand at Calhoun Beach sold 900 ice cream cones in two hours. Swimmers got belligerent when the pop machine broke down.

"We love it when it gets hot," said Bob Allison, formerly of the Minnesota Twins and now branch manager of Coca-Cola Bottling Midwest, Inc. Added Allison, "We don't want it to rain too often."

Meanwhile, a Coke rival — Pepsi Cola — said it's doing a land-office business. "Things look beautiful," said James Kueppers, sales manager of Pepsi Cola Bottling Co. of Minneapolis and St. Paul.

He said sales have shown "dramatic increases" in vending machines at service stations and factories where people are working "and there isn't any air conditioning."

Cooper's Super Valu supermarket in Chaska said demand for Kool Aid was so high the store couldn't get enough of it. The store sold about 16,000 cans of Elf soda pop in July.

Dayton's said sales of swim suits were "fantastic."

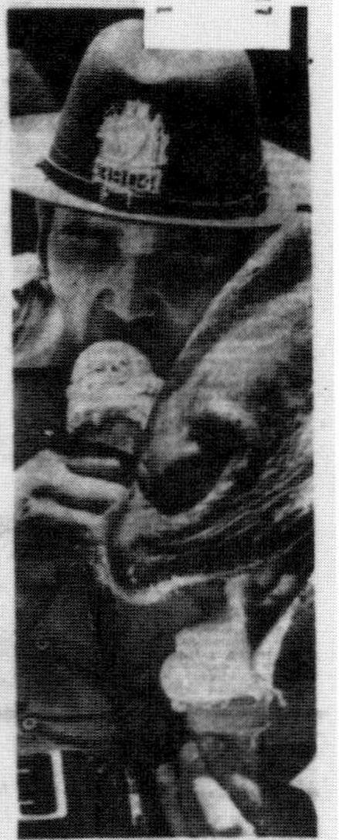

Associated Press

KEEPING COOL — Philadelphia, Pa., mounted patrolman Angelo Mendez and his horse took time out for ice cream treats in an effort to keep cool yesterday.

# House-passed oil-price rules face Ford veto

No sign local gas prices increasing: Page 7A

Washington Post

WASHINGTON, D.C. — The House sent a six-month extension of oil-price controls to President Ford yesterday for an almost certain veto. Congress plans to go home for a month tonight, leaving the future of oil prices unresolved.

The law which holds the price of two-thirds of domestic oil production at $5.25 a barrel, expires Aug. 31, three days before Congress returns. If controls end, the price could increase to the market level of about $12.50 at the discretion of the industry.

The Federal Energy Administration (FEA) has calculated that ending price controls could mean a boost of up to seven cents in the price of a gallon of gasoline at the pump.

**THE FEA SAID CONSUMERS** would feel the impact only gradually in the next six to nine months.

Ford has said he would veto an extension of the control bill if Congress rejected his plan to phase out controls over 39 months. The House killed his plan Wednesday.

FEA Administrator Frank Zarb said yesterday, "There is no doubt in my mind that as things stand today" Ford will veto the extension bill when he returns from Europe.

The House passed the extension bill 303 to 117, which, like the Senate vote, is more than the two-thirds needed to override a veto, but Zarb predicted that Congress would not override.

The White House hopes to get the veto upheld by putting controls on bottled and natural gas, thus assuring the farm states that their allotment of propane, which is a major fuel on many farms, will not be bought up by industry when supplies of natural gas are curtailed this winter.

## Fears mount that Hoffa may be dead

Chicago Daily News

DETROIT, Mich. — Fears mounted today that missing former Teamsters President James Hoffa was kidnapped and killed.

"I know the police suspect foul play," said Oakland County Prosecutor L. Brooks Patterson. "Jimmy never stayed out this long without reporting in."

**HOFFA HASN'T** been seen since Wednesday, when his 1974 auto was abandoned outside a fashionable Bloomfield Twp. restaurant, where Hoffa apparently had a luncheon date.

Michigan Gov. William Milliken said he understood that Hoffa planned to meet a top Detroit hoodlum, Anthony Giacalone, at the Machus Red Fox Restaurant.

But Giacalone, a long-time Hoffa friend, said, "That's absolutely untrue."

Hoffa, 62, was last seen about 2 p.m. Wednesday outside the restaurant, where his auto was later found, unlocked and untampered with.

**THE PERSON HOFFA** was to meet at the restaurant never showed up, and Hoffa called his wife, police said.

"That's the last we've seen or heard of him," said Lt. Curt Grennier of the Bloomfield Twp. police.

Hoffa's disappearance came in the wake of a series of violent incidents involving key figures in Detroit Teamsters Local 299.

The North American Newspaper Alliance quoted a Hoffa family spokesman as saying, "If Jimmy hasn't turned up by now, he's dead. We're praying for a ransom note. But we have to face facts."

Star Photo by Steve Schluter

YOUNGSTERS COOLED OFF IN MINNEAPOLIS' CEDAR LAKE YESTERDAY

*View was achieved by using camera partially under water*

## IF THINGS WORK OUT, HEAT MAY WASH AWAY

Keep your fingers crossed. The heat wave may soon be over.

The National Weather Service said that some rain may fall late this afternoon and tonight and that a cold front may begin to cool off the area tomorrow afternoon.

At the same time, air pollution levels may reach a near-alert stage for the second straight day, the Minnesota Pollution Control Agency (PCA) reported.

**THE PCA ISSUED** an advisory for yesterday urging motorists to cut travel until pollution levels drop. The PCA blamed the conditions on "high temperatures, intense sunlight and southerly winds" which combined to produce "high levels of oxidants" that irritate eyes, nose, throat and lungs.

A 40-percent chance of showers and thunderstorms was forecast for this afternoon and tonight, but the National Weather Service said the rain will be scattered and that not

WEATHER
Turn to Page 8A

*57-STORY TOWER IS IN FINANCIAL HOLE*

# IDS Center casts giant shadow in the loss column

By JOHN GREENWALD
Minneapolis Star Staff Writer

The IDS Center has been good for almost everyone but the company that built it. That firm, Investors Diversified Services, Inc., (IDS), is suffering grievously.

"I am absolutely convinced that if the facts that are known today had been known before the first shovel was in the ground, the building would never have gone up," admits H. Clifton Whiteman, IDS senior vice-president for corporate finance.

The $138-million steel and glass complex, topped by a 57-story tower that dominates the city skyline, attracts tourists and favorable notice throughout the country. But it cost IDS more than $4 million last year.

"For the present there doesn't seem to be any near-term cure for the losses," Whiteman said in an interview.

But the company is petitioning in Hennepin District Court to have the center's property taxes lowered from the $5.4 million the city says is due to about $4.1 million. It also is asking to have the previous year's bill trimmed by about $1 million.

If IDS wins, the city would lose about seven-tenths of 1 percent of this year's total tax revenues, according to an assessment department estimate.

The giant financial services company and the city still are talking in an effort to find a compromise. The petition is scheduled to be heard the week of Oct. 27 before Judge Allen Oleisky.

"I guess we would all prefer not to be in litigation on this subject," Whiteman said in a candid discussion of the center's problems, during which he revealed:

**IDS doesn't expect** the center to stop losing money for at least 10 years.

**IDS Properties, Inc.,** the IDS subsidiary that owns the center, is unlikely to be profitable during the

IDS
Turn to Page 8A

# 14 possible sleeping sickness cases examined in flood area

By GORDON SLOVUT
Minneapolis Star Staff Writer

Doctors have found 14 possible cases of a serious form of sleeping sickness — western equine encephalitis — in the Red River Valley area of Minnesota and North Dakota.

Officials of the U.S. Center for Disease Control, which has assigned personnel to the Fargo, N.D., and Moorhead, Minn., area, said today that blood serum from the patients has been sent to a federal laboratory in Fort Collins, Colo.

**TECHNICIANS** there will check to see whether the serum contains evidence of the presence of the encephalitis virus.

Dr. Barry Levy, Minnesota's epidemiologist, said that of the 14 cases, he considers "four or five very suspicious" of actually being sleeping sickness.

One of the problems in making the diagnosis early is that encephalitis symptoms can be very similar to those of viral meningitis, another potentially serious disease.

**IN ANY EVENT,** the outbreak — no matter what the cause — is fairly large and health authorities are urging people with early encephalitis-like symptoms (headache, fever and nausea in adults) to see their physicians.

Dr. Jack Poland, a federal epidemiologist from Fort Collins, said earlier this week that the aim is to test the serum of almost everyone sick with encephalitis-like symptoms. Encephalitis is an inflammation of the white matter of the brain.

Fear of an outbreak came in the wake of heavy rains and flooding earlier this summer that produced a huge increase in the mosquito population, especially of culex tarsalis, a variety that can transmit western equine encephalitis to humans and horses.

The disease has been diagnosed — at least tentatively — in several dozen horses, but there has been no positive diagnosis in humans.

Poland and others on the scene said in telephone interviews that they suspect that much of the encephalitis-like illness may actually be caused by so-called enteroviruses, a family of germs that includes the polio virus. Enterovirus infections generally are suspected of being contracted through contaminated water or food.

Dr. John Harris, an epidemiologist from the Center for Disease Control at Atlanta, Ga., said 11 of the 14 possible human encephalitis patients are hospitalized.

**ONE OF THE PATIENTS** is the 9-year-old son of a migrant worker. The boy became seriously ill a month ago, and was taken to a Moorhead hospital. He lapsed into a coma, but is out of the coma now

DISEASE
Turn to Page 8A

## Index . . .



2 Sections XCVII—No. 213

STAR TELEPHONES

| | |
|---|---|
| News, General | 372-4141 |
| Want Ads | 372-4242 |
| Circulation | 372-4343 |
| Column 1 | 372-4444 |

# St. Louis drug raid nets 5 state men, 40,000 tablets

By DAVID E. EARLY
Minneapolis Star Staff Writer

Five Minnesota men were charged with manufacturing an illegal drug after federal agents in St. Louis yesterday raided a laboratory they said was producting a sedative.

In Minneapolis, agents seized a pill-making machine, a mixing machine and two 10-pound bags of bicarbonate of soda they said was mixed with the drug to make pills at a north Minneapolis garage.

It is believed the machines already had made 40,000 aspirin-sized tablets, said David Haight, acting special agent in charge of the Minneapolis office of the Federal Drug Enforcement Administration.

**ALMOST ALL** were found in the St. Louis laboratory, Haight said. It is not known whether any of the pills were distributed in the Twin Cities area, Haight added.

Seven men were arrested in St. Louis after agents culminated months of investigation by raiding and dismantling the laboratory at about 2 p.m.

**IDENTIFIED AS** residents of Minneapolis were Kenneth Sherman, 25; Timothty Olson, 26; John Kueffner, 30, and Michael Sorenson, 28. No street addresses were available. Also arrested was Douglas Bartels, Prior Lake, Minn.

Local drug agents and Minneapolis police used a warrant to search the garage at 2700 Penn Av. N. Haight said it was believed the equipment there was to have been moved to St. Louis soon.

The drug involved is a relatively new sedative called Methaqualone. It is a federally controlled substance available only by prescription.

"This is the first major arrest involving this drug," Haight said.

Minneapolis Tribune

Sunday
March 21, 1976
Volume CIX
Number 302
M

1A Final

50c by carrier
55c by motor route
60c by single copy


# Jury finds Miss Hearst guilty

Tribune News Services

**San Francisco, Calif.**
Patricia Hearst was convicted Saturday of armed bank robbery and the use of a gun to commit a felony.

Miss Hearst had testified that she had helped a revolutionary group rob the Sunset branch of the Hibernia Bank April 15, 1974. But she said she had done so only under threat of death.

After hearing 66 witnesses, viewing almost 1,000 exhibits and measuring that evidence against instructions of Federal Judge Oliver J. Carter, the jurors refused to accept Miss Hearst's contention.

**(Hearst verdict pleases Browning, surprises Bailey. Page 6A.)**

Miss Hearst seemed to shrink, and her pale face became ashen as the verdict was read. Her parents, Mr. and Mrs. Randolph A. Hearst, sat 10 feet away. She did not look at them.

Mrs. Hearst, who left the court in tears Friday, dropped her gaze to the floor. Hearst rubbed his forehead and stared into space.

F. Lee Bailey

Judge Carter

James Browning

Their daughter Anne, 20, seated beside them, broke into tears. Two other sisters, Vickie, and Mrs. Virginia Bosworth, were in the courtroom. A fourth, Catherine, was not present.

After the verdict was announced, Miss Hearst leaned toward her chief lawyer, F. Lee Bailey, and said, "I wonder if I ever had a chance."

As the jury filed into its box at 4:27 p.m., Bailey, put his arm around her and leaned his heavy shoulder as if to support her upright, slender form. Bailey's partner, Albert Johnson, sat on the other side of Miss Hearst. The prosecution team, led by U.S. Attorney James L. Browning Jr., sat beyond them at another table.

Bailey asked that the jury be polled. The verdict had to be unanimous in this case. As the court clerk, Gene F. Driscoll, read their names, each of the seven women and five men replied that it was his or her verdict.

The verdict was handed up at 4:30 p.m. by court crier Howard Frank, who had received it in an envelope from William E. Wright, jury foreman. Wright is a retired army colonel, 55, from Hill Valley, Calif., a San Francisco suburb.

Frank handed the verdict to Driscoll, who slit the envelope, withdrew the prepared verdict and extended it open to Judge Carter without looking at it himself. The judge read it, and it seemed that his face muscles sagged before he instructed Driscoll to read it.

Judge Carter set April 19 for sentencing. The maximum sentence for armed bank robbery is 25 years. The maximum sentence for use of a firearm to commit a felony is 10 years.

Turning to the jurors, who were still seated in the jury box, the judge told them of his gratitude for their service. Their verdict, he said, was "well within the evidence in this case and is accepted.

"You have done the best you can under the circumstances of this case as it was presented to you," the judge said. "Don't second-guess yourself. Judgment day is a difficult day," said the judge, who has spent 25 years on the bench. "I know. I have been through it again and again.

"What occurred in the jury room is your collective property. It belongs not only to you but to your fellow jurors. Deal with those experiences with good manners, good sense and good judgment. I am not going to try to tell you not to talk about the case."

The defendant, 22, still faces a number of felony counts in state court in Los Angeles, as a result of an incident May 16, 1974, when she fired an automatic carbine into a street and storefront as she sought to help two members of the revolutionary group, the self-styled Symbionese Liberation Army. The two were about to be seized by store clerks who suspected them of shoplifting. Bailey has said that he will represent Miss Hearst in the state cases.

Miss Hearst will be taken to Los Angeles as soon as possible to face state charges of robbery, assault

**Hearst** continued on page 10A

**Patricia Hearst entered the courthouse to hear the verdict.**

## Elections panel may end tomorrow

By Finlay Lewis and Frank Wright
Staff Correspondents

**Washington, D.C.**
Those handy checks from Uncle Sam for 100 or 200 grand will stop next week unless Providence intervenes, meaning that all of those politicians who want to be president may have to find some fat cats to pinch-hit temporarily for the American taxpayer as bankrollers of their campaigns.

"It's gonna hurt," conceded one campaign operative for Arizona Rep. Morris Udall as she contemplated the imminent demise Monday of the Federal Elections Commission (FEC) as the premier financier of her principal's campaign for the Democratic nomination.

How much it's going to hurt depends on the candidate. For Udall, whose fund-raising is heavily dependent on small private contributions that are matched by federal funds, a cutoff of the federal subsidy could be serious, particularly if the FEC is allowed to remain in legal limbo for many weeks. For President Ford, whose financial trend lines are streaking upward, the interruption in federal payments is likely to be a minor problem at worst, barely worthy of note.

The severity of the problem, obviously, depends on how long the present congressional hiatus over

**Campaign** continued on page 9A

Staff Photo by John Croft

### A couple of happy Cardinals

**Steve Newby (24) leaped with glee toward teammate Ronnie Henderson after their Marshall-University team won the Class A state high school basketball tournament Saturday by beating Mankato Wilson 64-53 in overtime. Bloomington Jefferson won the Class AA crown with a 60-51 victory over Hibbing. (Details in Sports Section).**

## Taxes, other disputes will keep Legislature working

By Steven Dornfeld and Dennis Cassano

Staff Writers

Despite earlier talk about adjourning within the next few days, the Minnesota Senate and House will need another week—and possibly longer—to resolve their differences on taxes and other issues.

DFL leaders in the two houses, who have differed frequently in past sessions on tax issues, are engaged in a staring contest on the Senate's proposal to grant $100 million in income-tax rebates. The House refused Friday to establish a conference committee even to talk about the possibility.

In addition, the two houses have a long list of bills that have not received final action. Among them are bills dealing with catastrophic health insurance, campaign financing, low-cost housing, increased planning powers for the Metropolitan Council and bonds to finance the construction of new state buildings and bridges.

Many of them are likely to emerge from the two houses in different forms and will have to go to conference committee, where representatives of the two houses will have to work out the differences.

Five days ago, House Majority Leader Irvin Anderson, DFL International Falls, told members of his caucus that adjournment might be possible by yesterday or Monday —well ahead of the original April 1 target date for adjournment.

Yesterday, neither house even met and House Speaker Martin Sabo amended that optimistic prediction.

"There are lots of major unresolved issues," the Minneapolis DFLer said in an interview. "I guess I would be surprised if it (adjournment) happened this coming week. If everything falls into place, fine. But I think it would be a mistake to go rushing toward adjournment."

Senate Majority Leader Nicholas Coleman, DFL-St. Paul, who was the first to talk about an early adjournment, said yesterday, "The session could still end this week. I don't know if it will."

The two houses are expected to have little difficulty working out compromises on most of the issues on which they have differences. However, the same cannot be said for the tax issue.

By custom, the leaders of the two houses assign themselves to negotiate in any disputes involving taxes. The leaders tend to have the largest and most easily bruised egos,

**Legislature** continued on page 19A

## Our stadium (burp) is already in debt $185

J.P. Berling of Irving, Texas, is a disinterested party in the Minnesota Legislature's stadium dispute. As far as he's concerned, the Legislature already has an unpaid stadium debt.

It totals $185.81.

To be sure, there's a disagreement here. Berling, vice president of Texas Stadium Corp., claims the Minnesota Senate owes that amount as a result of a visit to the firm's stadium near Dallas last fall by five legislators.

A Senate staff member, who arranged the trip, says most of the bill represents a misunderstanding.

James Pirius, the Senate aide, said Thursday that Texas Stadium officials invited a legislative delegation to use a stadium suite to watch a Dallas Cowboys football game last fall while the legislators were studying sports stadiums around the country.

The Minnesotans were told they would have to pay only for a buffet luncheon, Pirius said, and there was no mention of other charges. They watched the game from a suite — "and I never asked to be put in a suite," Pirius emphasized — supplied with food and liquor.

Then the bill came. In addition to the buffet luncheons, there was a tab of $106.70 for the food and liquor in the suite.

Pirius said he called Bert Rose of the Texas corporation and said the legislators would pay for their luncheons but the state could not pay for the unrequested food and liquor. Pirius said he thought Rose agreed.

"If they wanted to give us a suite with food and liquor, most of which we didn't eat anyway, without telling us we were going to pay for it, that's ridiculous. When the

**Debt** continued on page 19A

## Experts call balanced diet best way to health

How safe is our food?

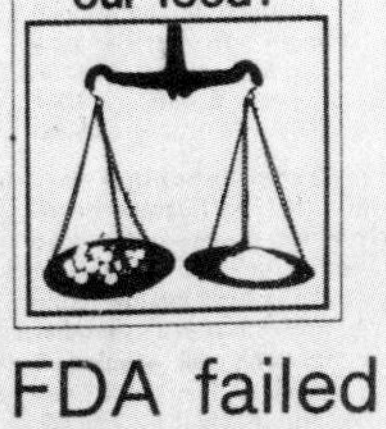

Last in a series

By Joe Rigert
Staff Writer

Some Americans, concerned about the safety of their foods, have given up food additives as though they were giving up sweets on a diet.

Marilyn Silverstein of Willingboro, N.J., is one of them. "I am upset and concerned about the use of sodium nitrate and sodium nitrite," she told the U.S. Agriculture Department, "to the point where I no longer purchase or eat, or allow my family to eat, any preserved meat or fish. We've totally given up hot dogs, corned beef, bologna, smoked fish, salami, processed turkey and chicken and delicatessen (meat) of any kind. (We use no pork products.)"

Other Americans, suffering from a problem overload, toss up their shopping lists and ignore all the warnings.

Mrs. Sam Haroldson of Minneapolis feels that way. "There is so much of it in the paper," she said, "I don't pay much attention to it. You read about all these additives — can't eat this, can't eat that. Pretty soon you can't eat anything."

What should the consumer do? Is it wise or possible to stop eating foods with additives that might be hazardous? Are additives really that much of a problem? Is there a better way?

Experts say that the better way to avoid cancer and other health risks is to eat a prudent or balanced diet.

Don't eat too much fat and meat. Eat more fruits, vegetables and cereals. Eat everything in moderation.

Dr. Gio B. Gori is heading a new $6-million program in the National Cancer Institute to study the relationships between nutrition and cancer. When asked recently about what to advise consumers, he cited the many unknowns of what causes cancer, but added, "When we speak of prudence, of common sense, I think we have enough evidence to start changing, somehow, our diet."

Advises Dr. Gori, "The only thing I can say with confidence to the American people is they should probably eat less. They eat too many calories. They should eat more vegetables and fresh fruit, more fiber, and less packaged food of less value.

"But whether they should eat red meat or chicken or all that, I just say they should eat less and eat a varied diet. We were created to eat a wide variety of things. Primitive peoples eat 50 to 100 varieties a day. We are restricted to six, seven or ten. So we restrict our capacity to vary our diet."

**Additives** continued on page 12A

## FDA failed to recall tainted turkey meat

Associated Press

When the U.S. Department of Agriculture (USDA) found illegal residues of a suspected cancer-causing drug in turkeys last summer, it mistakenly impounded thousands of clean birds while the contaminated meat was processed into turkey rolls and sold to consumers, it was learned Saturday.

But the Food and Drug Administration (FDA), rejecting the recommendation of one of the inspectors, decided not to recall the meat or prosecute the turkey grower because those actions might embarrass the USDA.

The events were outlined in an internal government memo that came out Friday in a hearing before the subcommittee on oversight and investigations of the House Committee on Interstate and Foreign Commerce. The report was fleshed out through interviews with officials from the FDA and the USDA.

The memo, dated July 22, 1975, and signed by Dr. C. D. Van Houweling, director of the FDA's Bureau of Veterinary Medicine, was written after a meeting between the two agencies.

It disclosed that USDA scientists, during routine sampling of turkey flocks, found up to 48 parts of the drug Ipronidazole for each billion parts of turkey tissue in certain birds. Marilyn Perez, special assistant

**Turkeys** continued on page 12A

## Almanac

**Sunday, March 21, 1976**
**81st day; 285 to go this year**
**Sunrise: 6:15. Sunset 6:27.**

Today's weather:

**Colder**

Partly cloudy and colder weather is forecast for the Twin Cities today. Highs today and Monday near 30 and a low tonight of 12 are predicted. Increasing cloudiness is likely Monday. Winds will be from the northwest at 10 to 20 miles per hour today.

**Details on page 12B.**

**Legislative laffs and gaffes**

The Minnesota Senate inadvertently passed an amendment recently authorizing only biennial legislative sessions. This "funny little amendment," as one Senate leader called it, is not expected to survive. It's a good thing: Humor in Minnesota would be cut in half with a return to every-other-year legislative sessions.




| | |
|---|---|
| Tribune telephones | 372-4141 News General<br>372-4242 Classified<br>372-4343 Circulation |

Minneapolis Tribune

Friday
January 21, 1977
Volume CX
Number 242
MN o

1A. Final
3 Sections
20c Single copy
Carrier delivery 70c a week



# Carter takes office, asks unity

## Affirms 'fresh faith in founders' dream'

By Frank Wright
Staff Correspondent

Washington, D.C.
Jimmy Carter Thursday became the 39th president of the United States, two years to the day after beginning his dark-horse election campaign as a little-known former Georgia governor.

He did his best to maintain throughout the long day of ceremony and celebration the populist image that helped carry him from his tiny home town of Plains to the White House.

Both Carter and the new vice president, Minnesota's Walter Mondale, wore business suits to their inaugu.ation instead of more customary formal wear.

Chief Justice Warren Burger of the supreme court swore in the new chief executive as Jimmy, as the man preferred, rather than by his formal name of James Earl Carter Jr.

In his inaugural speech Carter pictured himself as an ag..nt of the citizenry rather than their anointed leader.

He said his inauguration "marks a new beginning, a new dedication within our government and a new spirit among us all." However, he added, while a president "may sense and proclaim that new spirit . . . only :· people can provide it.

"You have," he continued, "given me a great responsibility—to stay close to you, to be worthy of you, and to exemplify what you are. Let us create together a new national spirit of unity and trust. Your strength can compensate for my weakness, and your wisdom can help to minimize my mistakes.

Inauguration continued on 10A

Staff Photo by Kent Kobersteen

President and Mrs. Carter walked from the Capitol to the parade reviewing stand Thursday.

### More inaugural reports inside

- Carter and his family provide a unique, unpretentious inauguration. Page 4A.
- Inauguration photos. Pages 4A, 6C.
- Text of address. Page 5A.
- Many entertainment stars, both black and white, performed at the inaugural events. Page 5B.
- When Carter and his close friends walked into the White House, one found an irreverent warning from a predecessor. Page 3A.
- The Senate confirmed the appointments of eight Cabinet members and two other top administration officials. Page 6A.
- The Minnesota Independent-Republican leader wants the state to make sure it isn't paying for state officials' inauguration trips. Page 6C.

## Ford says proud farewell to capital

By Philip Shabecoff
New York Times Service

Washington, D.C.
The presidency of Gerald R. Ford ended in traditional and dignified fashion Thursday, in marked contrast to the drama a·d crisis with which it began on a humid August day two and a half years ago.

Ford left the White House convinced, as he said when bidding farewell to his Cabinet and staff Thursday morning, that the administration had been a successful one, "which history will treat kindly."

His departure from Washington, where he has lived for nearly three decades as a member of Congress, vice president and finally president, was relatively high-spirited and punctuated by only a few moments of emotion.

One such moment came when President Carter, in the opening sentence of the inaugural address, thanked Ford on behalf of the nation "for all he has done to heal the land." The large crowd gathered below the east front of the Capitol responded with warm applause.

Ford, obviously moved. arose and grasped the hand of the man who defeated him for the presidency last N· vember.

Ford continued on page 10A

## Mondale ends trek to No. 2 office

By Finlay Lewis
Staff Correspondent

Washington, D.C.
Let the record reflect that Walter Frederick Mondale spoke his part almost flawlessly Thursday as he approached the high noon of his political life.

There may have been the slightest hint of a clumsy tongue when Mondale, repeating the oath administered by House Speaker Tip O'Neill, affirmed that he would "be of true faith and allegiance" to the Constitution.

But the newly installed vice president recovered nimbly and finished strong when he promised, in a clear and unwavering voice, to "well and faithfully discharge the duties of the office that I'm about to enter, so help me God."

With those words, the 48-year-old preacher's son from Elmore, Minn., completed the trek that carried him from the ward clubs and county caucuses of Minnesota's Democratic-Farmer-Labor Party to the second highest office in the land.

Some fingers were crossed while O'Neill was leading him through the rites of office, Mondale revealed later.

The nervous one, he said, was his wife, Joan, who has watched her husband over the years build a

Mondale continued on 5A

## Green is acquitted of bribery charge

By Doug Stone
Staff Writer

Minneapolis Alderman Zollie Green was acquitted Thursday of a charge that he accepted a $1,000 bribe from a former bar owner in December 1975.

A Hennepin County District Court jury of six men and six women deliberated about 13 hours Wednesday and yesterday before returning its verdict about 3:30 p.m.

Green, 52, raised his hand and slapped it down on the defense table when the verdict was announced. Then he sobbed for 10 minutes as his son, Tom, 26, and his attorney, Theodore Collins, comforted him.

Many of the approximately 30 spectators, who included friends and three members of the city council, applauded when the verdict was read.

Green, DFL Ninth Ward alderman since 1971, went into seclusion last night and wes not available for comment. Aides said he will be at city hall today.

Green was indicted by a special Hennepin County grand jury on a charge of accepting a bribe from John Edward Paulson to facilitate the transfer of Paulson's liquor license to new owners. Green recommended approval of the license transfer to the city council licenses committee on Dec. 22, 1975, five days after he received the check made out to "cash" from Paulson. On Dec. 30 he recommended the license transfer for the Five Corners Cafe, 501 Cedar Av., to the full council.

Green continued on page 13A

### Almanac

Friday, Jan. 21, 1977
21st day; 344 to go this year
Sunrise: 7:44. Sunset: 5:05

Today's weather:
**Little change**

Mild, occasionally cloudy weather is forecast for the Twin Cities today. A high today in the lower 20s and a low tonight around 10 above are predicted.

Details on page 5B.

**A foresight saga**

In a recent report on the future of the Kansas City metropolitan area, Midwest Research Institute quoted the following ad from the Times of London: "The Tuesday evening meeting of the Clairvoyance Society of Wicksell has been canceled because of unforeseen circumstances."



## Heat survey finds people cooperating

Residents of the Twin Cities area show a strong willingness to cooperate with energy-saving measures, according to a spot-check telephone survey by the Minneapolis Tribune.

(Real test in energy crisis is seen ahead. Page 1B.)

The study shows:

- A majority of the 200 people contacted Wednesday night said they already have set their thermostats to the re ommended levels, 65 degrees during the day and 60 degrees at night.
- Widespread agreement exists that the energy-saving measures are necessary.
- People generally approve of the way Minnesota officials have handled the energy situation.

People were first asked:

*"Minnesota officials have urged that thermostats be set at 65 degrees during the day and 60 degrees at night. Are you planning to turn back your thermostat to those levels or are there reasons why you cannot turn it back?"*

Fifty-one percent said they already have made the change, an answer that was volunteered, not suggested in the question. "We have kept our thermostat at 65 degrees for the past couple of years," a St. Paul man said. Another is a Stillwater resident who said: "The fireplace really helps us keep warm."

An additional 9 perc..nt are planning to adopt the recommended settings. Some, however, sounded

Survey continued on page 13A

# Fans mourn at Elvis' estate after 'the king of rock' dies

By LES SEAGO

Related articles and photos: Pages 20A, 1B

MEMPHIS (AP)—Fans of yesterday and today, old and young, teenyboppers and their middle-aged mothers, gathered today on Elvis Presley's doorstep, not to scream and cheer but to mourn. Their king is dead.

Elvis Aron Presley, the Mississippi truckdriver whose hip-grinding performing style helped launch the sexual revolution as he became America's greatest king of rock 'n' roll, died yesterday of a heart ailment. He was 42.

**A CROWD OF MORE THAN** 200 mourners had gathered by midmorning outside the gates of Graceland mansion, where Presley's body was to be on public view from 3 to 5 p.m. today in a special copper and steel casket.

Jim Stewart, night supervisor at the Memphis Funeral Home where the body was taken after Presley died, said the casket was similar to the one the singer chose for his mother when she died in 1958.

"We don't even keep this casket in stock. They are very expensive," Stewart said, adding it had been flown in from Oklahoma City last night.

Outside the mansion, a special police security detail was assigned to direct traffic and keep watch over the crowd, which ranged from young children and teen-agers to people in their 40s and 50s.

At one point during the night, the gates opened, several cars came out, and the crowd swarmed around taking pictures and trying to get autographs. One of the cars carried Vester Presley, an uncle who was chief of security, and his wife.

Callers swamped the White House switchboard today urging that President Carter declare a national day of mourning for Presley, White House telephone operators said.

A California couple sent a telegram scolding the president for not issuing a statement on the singer's death. "No death has moved the American people so much since that of John Fitzgerald Kennedy," the telegram said.

ONE COLOR

Vester Presley said Elvis' former wife, Priscilla, whom he divorced in 1973, arrived at the mansion at about 3 a.m.

"She is taking it hard. She is in a total state of shock," he said.

Stewart said the switchboard at the funeral home received calls from all 50 states and from as far away as Guam and Johannesburg, South Africa.

**"EVERYBODY WANTED TO KNOW** where to send flowers," Stewart said.

Vester Presley said the decision to open the casket to public view was made by the singer's father, Vernon Presley.

Dr. George Nichopoulos, long-time physician to the swivel-hipped, throaty baritone who appeared in 31 films—including "Love Me Tender," "GI Blues," and "Jailhouse Rock,' said an autopsy revealed a constriction in one of the main arteries to

PRESLEY
Turn to Page 7A

Star Photo by Tom Sweeney

**PRESLEY'S LAST CONCERT IN TWIN CITIES**
*He sang to 16,000 fans on April 30, 1977*

THE MINNEAPOLIS STAR

Wednesday, August 17, 1977

Single copy 20¢
Carrier delivery: 70¢ a week
By motor route: 80¢ a week

Star Photo by William Seaman

**Fire at Four Seasons Estates North apartment complex, Plymouth, hurt five persons, caused extensive damage**

# 5 people hurt in Plymouth predawn fire

By BRENDA INGE.:SOLL
Minneapolis Star Staff Writer

Two children and three fire fighters were injured today in a predawn, extra-alarm fire that routed more than 50 residents from their beds and caused at least $250,000 damage to an apartment complex in Plymouth.

Two women were trapped by smoke and flames on wooden balconies outside the three-story brick building, Four Seasons Estates North, 9610 37th Pl. N.. However, they climbed to safety without injury down a ladder that had been placed by Plymouth fire fighters.

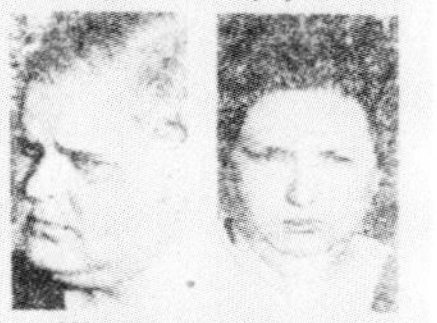

MR. AND MRS. STRABLE

The blaze apparently stemmed from an earlier wastebasket fire in the first-floor apartment of caretaker James Strable, 24. Strable criticized the Plymouth Fire Department for "giving us the all-clear to go back in" after checking the building to determine if the first fire was out.

**STRABLE SAID** a live cigarette ash may have started the fires. He and his wife, Merna, 34, extinguished the wastebasket fire at about 1 a.m., he said.

"We had had some company. They left and we went to bed. We smelled smoke and got up and found the fire in the wastebasket and put it out. We saw that one ashtray had been emptied, I guess by our company.

"The fire department came out and checked around and said it was okay to reenter, but I don't feel it was handled right at all, because an hour and 15 minutes later the whole place went up," Strable said. "Here we lose everything we've got and we're supposed to smile about it."

**PLYMOUTH** Fire Chief Francis Bauer said fire fighters were not careless in checking the building after the wastebasket fire. Bauer said that Plymouth District Fire Chief Ralph Begin "was in the apartment and he made the determination the fire was out. He's a very competent officer and is so very, very thorough.

"In any case, it is standard policy with our department to tell the people to go back in and to watch, and protect their own property," Bauer said.

About a month ago, a fire in the apartment complex garage destroyed 16 automobiles, two motorbikes and a bicycle, Bauer said. The cause of that fire is still undetermined.

The Strables had gone to an apartment next door to discuss the first fire and were leaving when another first floor resident "came

FIRE
Turn to Page 6A

# Stenvig says he will seek 4th term as city mayor

By ROBERT GUENTHER
Minneapolis Star Staff Writer

Flanked by his wife, children and grandchild, Charles Selmer Stenvig announced today that he will seek a fourth two-year term as mayor of Minneapolis.

Stenvig

At a press conference, Stenvig outlined a strategy that in many respects will be similar to the ones he has used in past races. Stenvig said the issues facing voters will be taxes, crime and new construction.

He lost no time in taking a few swings at his DFL-endorsed opponent, Al Hofstede, saying, "I'm very confident the voters of this city will decide they cannot afford another two years of Al Hofstede." He accused Hofstede of trying to conceal his record as mayor from

STENVIG
Turn to Page 6A

# State's male beluga whale just can't stomach traveling

Photos: Page 3A

By DAVID PETERSON
Minneapolis Star Staff Writer

It may have been a protest over being dragged out of a nice cold ocean and sent to the southern climate of Minnesota, or maybe it was just an attempt to put things in perspective.

Whatever, the male beluga whale, recently captured for the Minnesota Zoological Garden, celebrated its first few hours in Minnesota yesterday by losing its breakfast amidst the noise and jet-aircraft fumes at the Minneapolis-St. Paul International Airport.

The whale had been nervous and angry on the trip down, but quietly took to its new home in Apple Valley last night. The female whale companion, caught with the male last week in Churchill, Canada, thrashed and squealed in protest and stuck close to the male in the tank.

The whales were flown to Minneapolis in wooden crates lined with plastic. They were put on thick foam rubber covered with ice and were continually sprayed with water to keep their smooth skin moist. Flat-bed trucks carried them into the Churchill airport and away from the cargo terminal at Minneapolis-St. Paul airport.

"These are the first whales we've ever had," said Marjorie Maki, a U.S. Customs agent at the airport. Only a small group, mostly friends and relatives of staff members, was at the airport for the arrival.

The whales won't be allowed into their eventual home, a gaping 560,000-gallon aquarium, until they're sufficiently trained to come to their trainer at the proper signal and have learned to eat dead fish. The whales have always eaten live fish and so far have had to be force-fed.

The training is likely to take four weeks or more, according to Donald Bridgwater, the zoo's general director. The whales are among the first species to be brought to the zoo, which is expected to be completed this fall for its official opening next May.

The whales don't have official names, although the

WHALES
Turn to Page 6A

# 'Crystal 8' nab suspects in theft of store's cash

By STEVE JOHNSON
Minneapolis Star Staff Writer

Two men who reportedly robbed a Crystal supermarket employee of about $20,000 picked the wrong way to escape yesterday and ran into Thomas Arneson and seven of his friends.

Arneson, 19, was standing in front of a Crystal home with seven of his buddies waiting to go on a camping trip when the two men jumped over a nearby fence with another man close on their heels.

The man chasing them was yelling "Call the police, they just robbed Thrift-Way, stop those guys," Arneson said.

**THE TWO MEN** being chased reportedly had just robbed Joel Saisberg, who was making a night bank deposit for Thrift-Way Supermarket, 5715 W. Broadway, Crystal.

A police report of the theft said Salsberg was robbed of $20,317.86, although Salsberg today said that report was "exaggerated" and would not say how much money was stolen.

Salsberg was beaten and robbed by the two men as he was about to deposit the money at the Crystal State Bank near the market, according to charges filed yesterday.

When the men grabbed his money deposit bag and ran off, Salsberg, bloodied and dizzy from the beating, chased the pair past Arneson and his friends who were standing in front of 5668 Maryland Av. N., Crystal.

Arneson, 5518 Vera Cruz Av., Crystal, and his friends reacted quickly to Saisberg's cries for help, according to police reports attached to the complaint against the two men.

"We lit after them, all of us, and I went after the guy with the long

CHASE
Turn to Page 6A

## Index . . .



4 Sections XCIX—226
G

**STAR TELEPHONES**

News, General..........372-4141
Want Ads..........372-4242
Circulation..........372-4343
Column 1..........372-4444

# CARTER PICKS JUDGE FOR DIRECTOR OF FBI

WASHINGTON (AP)—President Carter plans to nominate Frank Johnson, a southern judge with a strong civil rights record, as the next director of the FBI, according to administration sources.

Carter is expected to announce today that he will send Johnson's name to the Senate, which must confirm the selection. The choice will end a seven-month search for a director.

Johnson

Carter and Atty. Gen. Griffin Bell chose the 58-year-old federal district judge to succeed Clarence Kelley after rejecting four candidates recommended by a presidentially appointed search committee, the sources said.

Johnson's nomination is expected to please civil rights groups, who assailed the bureau in the 1960s for allegedly ignoring beatings of black activists in the south.

That charge came while the late J. Edgar Hoover, then FBI director, was conducting a secret campaign to discredit the movement's chief leader, the Rev. Martin Luther King Jr. Since then, civil rights groups have continued to criticize the FBI for failing to add more than token numbers of blacks and other minorities as agents.

Johnson's record seems to show a quality Bell particularly sought in an FBI director. The attorney general had said he wanted someone strong enough to control "the dominant personalities" in the bureau's hierarchy.

# Perpich challenges all to bocce at fair

By DEBRA STONE
Minneapolis Star Staff Writer

While other politicians will be strolling around the state fairgrounds shaking constituent's hands, Minnesota Gov. Rudy Perpich will be in the bocce court looking for challengers.

Perpich said that if his schedule permits, he will try to play bocce every evening of the 12-day Minnesota State Fair, which begins Aug. 25.

"It's a nice and easy way to meet people," the governor said. Perpich said he has brought his bocce ball to county fairs and has taught people around the state how to play.

"When I go to country fairs, I take my bocce balls with me and people love them," he said.

Last spring, Perpich announced a promotion plan for bocce, an outdoor Italian bowling game, to try to encourage family recreation.

**BECAUSE OF HIS CAMPAIGNING** for the sport, Perpich said, he has been invited to the National Bocce Tournament in Las Vegas in October. However, he said, he probably will not have time to attend.

State Fair officials said they were "surprised and delighted" when a member of the governor's staff called them to say Perpich would like to play bocce at the fair.

Julie Nathanson, fair publicity director, said she thinks the governor wants to play against Grandstand performers. A bocce court has been set up east of the Natural Resources Building.

Ms. Nathanson said she had not heard from the governor's office lately and feared the governor had been frightened away by critics who say he spends too much time playing bocce and not enough time in the office.

To avoid that kind of "Mickey Mouse" criticism, Perpich said, he plays bocce now only at 7 a.m., at noon or in the evening.

Minneapolis Tribune

# Saturday

January 14/1978

Volume I
Number 21
M g
1A

5 Sections
20¢ Single copy
Lower price for home delivery
Final



# Hubert H. Humphrey dies

By Lewis Cope
Staff Writer

Related articles on pages 4A, 5A, 6A and 9A.

Sen. Hubert H. Humphrey died of cancer at 9:25 p.m. Friday.

His death, at age 66, ended a remarkable political career and more than three decades of public service. President Carter recently called him "the greatest American that I know."

President Carter is sending his presidential plane to Minneapolis today to return Humphrey's body to Washington, where it will lie in state in the Capitol. Similar honors in the state capitol in St. Paul will follow. Precise times and dates haven't been set.

Family members had been summoned early in the afternoon yesterday to the senator's bedside at his home near Waverly, Minn., where he died.

David Gartner, Humphrey's chief aide, said the senator had been in a coma for several hours before his death and had "suffered no pain."

He said Humphrey's wife, Muriel, "has accepted this, and she is getting along well, as are the other members of the family."

The first public announcement that the senator's condition had become grave came at 3:25 p.m. It said that he was in "critical condition as a result of a spreading tumor" but was "resting comfortably." It wasn't announced that he was in a coma until several hours later, but sources said he already had slipped into unconsciousness at the time the first announcement was made.

Death apparently came when his cancer-stricken body simply became too weak to sustain life. His aides had said yesterday afternoon that there were no plans to hospitalize the senator, presumably because there was nothing more that doctors could do.

At his bedside yesterday were his wife, Muriel; their three sons, Hubert III (Skip), Robert and Douglas; the sons' wives; their daughter, Nancy Solomonson, and her husband, Bruce. He also is survived by 10 grandchildren.

Until three days ago, when Humphrey became bedridden, he had been living a relatively active life even though he had known for five months that he had cancer too extensive to be removed by surgery.

Humphrey first underwent cancer surgery in October 1976 when a malignant tumor was found in his bladder. It was the return of this cancer, in the form of the inoperable tumor found in his pelvis Aug. 18, 1977, that finally took his life.

Since the surgery, Humphrey, a vice president of the United States who was narrowly defeated for the presidency in 1968 by Richard Nixon, had received a parade of tributes from across the nation. They have come from members of his own Democratic Party and from Republicans as well.

Until yesterday, his aides had continued to insist that they expected him to return to Washington next week for the reconvening of Congress.

The anticancer drugs he had been given over the past three months were designed to control the cancer for as long as possible. But for this type of malignancy, these drugs could offer only the hope of prolonging life, not providing a cure, cancer experts had said from the beginning.

Minnesota Gov. Rudy Perpich announced a 30-day mourning period in the state. He ordered all flags on state facilities to be flown at half-

**Humphrey** continued on page 6A

Sen. Hubert H. Humphrey

## Politics of Joy moved Humphrey to top rungs

By Al McConagha
Staff Correspondent

**Washington, D.C.**
Hubert Horatio Humphrey's ebullient high-energy "politics of joy" propelled him from Dakota prairies to national prominence — but his dream of reaching the presidency remained unfulfilled.

Possessor of singular personal style, Humphrey was one of the most influential national politicians of the past 30 years and the dominant Minnesota political force of the period.

In contrast to the generation of restrained, buttoned-down politicians that followed him, Humphrey on the stump was renowned for his exuberant vibrancy and easy common touch. His mode evoked small-town America. The thrust was evangelical and revivalist. His optimism was occasionally qualified in later years, but he persevered in the conviction that a better world is possible.

A member of the U.S. Senate most of his adult life, Humphrey's views were buttressed by Midwestern progressivism and a nearly romantic celebration of what he saw as the common man. He was one of his generation's most effective and fluent — and sometimes long-winded — public speakers, and many believed he had one of the quickest and best-informed minds in Congress.

From 1965 to 1969, he was vice president. This was his highest post. His stewardship became controversial because of his support of the late President Johnson's escalation of the nation's military intervention in Vietnam.

Humphrey made three formal attempts for the presidency — in 1960, 1968 and 1972.

Only in 1968, however, was he successful in becoming the presidential nominee of the Democratic Party. In that election Humphrey was defeated narrowly by Richard Nixon. The Minnesotan nearly overcame his unpopular identification with the Vietnam War, however, to score a last-minute upset.

"The top rung is never going to be mine," said Humphrey, re-creating that election-night heartbreak. "My fingernails are scraping it, but I don't have a grip. Yet maybe . . ."

After his defeat and two years of teaching in Minnesota, Humphrey returned to the Senate. There he refurbished his reputation as an expert and innovative lawmaker.

Although he was viewed as an orthodox liberal when he began his Senate career in 1949, Humphrey saw himself in later years as a composer of differences rather than an ideologue.

Even though he was the state's foremost figure in the period after World War II, Humphrey was never able fully to control or "boss" the Minnesota DFL, despite widespread views to the contrary. He grew proud of the stout independence of his Minnesota associates. He used to cite with amusement the refusal of fellow state delegates to the 1960 convention to let him make a gesture of unity toward John Kennedy. Nevertheless, his moral authority and persuasiveness had enormous impact on Minnesota politics, and he was unquestionably one of the greatest leaders in the history of the state.

From a tradition of prairie reform politics, Humphrey founded a career that, despite repeated disappointments in seeking the presidency, helped shape the great events of his time.

"I want to believe I've worked hard," he wrote

**Obituary** continued on page 4A

## Mondale praises HHH decency

By Finlay Lewis
Staff Correspondent

**Washington, D.C.**
Vice President Walter Mondale, obviously distraught, stood and waited to pay tribute to a man who had been like a second father.

The vice president, a product of Minnesota's robust Democratic-Farmer-Labor tradition, learned that Hubert H. Humphrey had died moments after Mondale had arrived here from a political fence-mending mission to western states.

Red-eyed, occasionally wringing his hands, Mondale described the man who had launched him into public life as "the most decent man ever to serve" in politics.

Mondale notified President Carter of Humphrey's death. He made the call to the White House seconds after learning from David Gartner, Humphrey's administrative assistant, that the Minnesota senator had died.

In his statement to reporters, Mondale said, "all my public life I've been close

**Mondale** continued on page 6A

## Israel, Egypt recess Sinai talks

New York Times Service

**Cairo, Egypt**
Egypt and Israel recessed their talks Friday in Cairo on military aspects of a Middle East peace solution. There were indications that their joint military committee would not resume work until progress was made by the political committee due to convene Monday in Jerusalem.

Israeli Defense Minister Ezer Weizman flew to Jerusalem after a short session yesterday morning. His Egyptian counterpart, Gen. Mohamed Abdel Ghany Gamassy, said, "We agreed on some principles and disagreed on others and thus we did not reach any specific decision."

Gamassy said they would not proceed until they receive guidelines from the political committee, which will include the United States as well as Israel and Egypt. "The resumption of the talks depends on how much progress the political committee in Jerusalem can achieve," Gamassy said.

When he arrived in Jerusalem, Weizman said the military committee meetings had produced a general understanding on creating three zones in the Sinai but that the road to peace was "long, very long."

The zones would consist of a United Nations or buffer zone, a demilitarized zone and a zone containing some Egyptian troops. But details on how large the zones

**Mideast** continued on page 9A

### Note to readers:

A special magazine, "Hubert H Humphrey, The Happy Warrior", will be published by the Minneapolis Tribune on Sunday, Jan. 22. It will be distributed that day with the Sunday Tribune.

### Almanac

**Saturday, January 14, 1978**
**14th day; 351 to go this year.**
**Sunrise: 7:49. Sunset: 4:56.**

Today's weather

**Partly cloudy**

Slightly colder weather and a chance of snow flurries are forecast for the Twin Cities area today. Partly cloudy skies are expected tonight and Sunday. Highs around 15 today and near 10 Sunday are predicted. A low of 10 below is forecast for tonight.

Other predicted highs today: Minnesota, 5 to 12; North Dakota, 5 to 15 above; South Dakota, 10 northeast to 20 southwest; Wisconsin, 15 below west to zero southeast.

Details on Page 7C.

**For those who keep track**

Voyager 2, launched last August, was 101,102,480 miles from earth on the first day of 1978. It is due to reach Jupiter July 9, 1981, and Saturn a few weeks later.



| Tribune telephones | |
|---|---|
| | 372-4141 News General |
| | 372-4242 Classified |
| | 372-4343 Circulation |

## Five more power-line protesters arrested

By Staff Writers

**Lowry, Minn.**
Five power-line protesters were arrested Friday near surveying sites in Pope County. One of them was arrested for lying down in a field in front of a tripod, and others were taken off to jail after they thumped a surveyor's truck with their fists.

Also yesterday, state officials said most of the 170 members of the Minnesota State Patrol assigned to the protests this week will be sent home for the weekend, and the Pope County attorney said he will resign because he doesn't want to prosecute his "good friends."

The arrests were made during a shoving and name-calling fracas. Demonstrators were more derogatory of state troopers and surveyors yesterday than they had been earlier in the week. They yelled such things as "Redcoats (state patrolmen) are political agitators," "Goddam pigs," "You know when they assassinated Kennedy, they forgot Rudy (Gov. Rudy Perpich)" and "You guys are less than human."

Most of the time, however, the protesters were joking with the troopers and trying to get them to admit they were privately against construction of the high-voltage line. And most of the time the troopers reacted with smiles or self-conscious kicks at the snow. The arrests took place in about half an hour.

**Power line** continued on page 9A

Staff Photo by Darlene Pfister

**Arrested power-line opponent Dean Danielson went limp as state troopers waited for a car to transport him to jail.**

## Special election bill is likely

By Steven Dornfeld
Staff Writer

The DFL majority in the Minnesota Legislature appears likely to pass a bill that would schedule a special election for Hubert Humphrey's Senate seat at the same time as the November general election.

Such legislation, which will be considered when the two houses reconvene Tuesday, would necessitate some provision for the governor to make an interim appointment.

DFL Gov. Rudy Perpich already has filled one U.S. Senate vacancy through appointment since taking office 13 months ago, and sources say he probably would appoint a "caretaker" who would agree not to seek election to the seat.

However, Independent-Republi-

**Successor** continued on page 6A

Today:
The men's movement

THE MINNEAPOLIS STAR SATURDAY MAGAZINE

Minneapolis Tribune

Tuesday
March 27, 1979
Volume CXII
Number 263
M y

1A Final
3 Sections
20¢ Single Copy


# Egypt, Israel sign peace treaty

## Historic event at White House starts new era

By Barry Schweid
Associated Press

**Washington, D.C.**
Egypt and Israel, neighbors but enemies for a generation, signed a treaty Monday to begin a new, fragile era of peace between Arab and Jew.

In a solemn ceremony on the front lawn of the White House, Egyptian President Anwar Sadat and Israeli Prime Minister Menachem Begin put their names to Arabic, Hebrew and English copies of a treaty promising mutual recognition, respect and peace.

"Peace has come!" declared a beaming President Carter, whose personal intervention 19 days ago brought negotiations back to life after they had stalemated on the details.

And last night at a White House state dinner, both Begin and Sadat proposed that Carter receive the 1979 Nobel Peace Prize for his efforts.

Begin, who shared the 1978 prize with Sadat, said he was certain both he and the Egyptian leader would be in Oslo, Norway, next December to see Carter accept the award.

Earlier yesterday, during the signing ceremony, Carter quoted the Bible and the Koran, and he offered a personal prayer that Arabs and Jews may one day be brothers. Sadat, replying, declared, "Let there be no more bloodshed between Arabs and Israelis."

"Let us work together until the day comes when they beat their swords into plowshares and their spears into pruning hooks," the Egyptian said.

Carter quoted the same words from Isaiah.

"No more war," agreed Begin. "No more bloodshed. Peace unto you. Shalom. Salaam. Forever."

"Shalom" means "peace' in Hebrew. "Salaam" means

Treaty continued on page 7A

United Press International

President Sadat, left, President Carter and Prime Minister Begin smiled broadly as they shook hands after the treaty was signed Monday.

## Carter takes center stage at treaty signing

By Finlay Lewis
Staff Correspondent

**Washington, D.C.**
Anwar Sadat called him "Jeemy."

Menachem Begin, mocking his own reputation for diplomatic contentiousness, offered a friendly "amendment" to Sadat's affectionate tribute.

It was unabashed political theater, and Jimmy Carter happily preempted the center of the stage.

The symbolism was so obvious it hardly needed to be stressed: A born-again Christian flanked by an Arab and a Jew with the White House in the background and a freshly signed peace treaty at their fingertips.

Even the glossy, eight-foot-long mahogany table used in the signing was endowed with historic significance. In 1898 President McKinley used it to sign the protocol ending the Spanish-American War. It also was used in the signing of the Kellogg-Briand peace pact in 1928 and the U.S.-Russian arms limitation agreement of 1972.

Now it was President Carter's turn to claim his niche in history as the man who brokered a peace treaty that would — in identical English, Arabic and Hebrew texts — declare an end to a 30-year era of hatred and warfare between Egypt and Israel.

That moment arrived on a blustery March afternoon when Carter strode out the north portico on to the White House's front lawn, where about 1,200 carefully selected guests were waiting to witness the treaty signing. Walking at his elbows were Sadat, who launched the Egyptian armies against Israel in a surprise attack $5\frac{1}{2}$ years ago, and Begin, a one-time Zionist terrorist.

The step they were about to take involved more than reconciling a territorial dispute between two modern nations. Their words made it apparent that both were aware of a Biblical rivalry pitting Jew and Arab in contention over Palestine.

And so it was perhaps inevitable that all three should commemorate their diplomatic accomplishment by quoting Isaiah ("... swords into plowshares ...") and that Begin should conclude by donning a yarmulke before quoting a prayer of thanksgiving — Psalm 126.

But it was also in the nature of things that the moment should be hedged with a lingering and almost ominous sense of uncertainty. Carter, Begin and Sadat individually cautioned that the next steps toward a comprehensive Middle Eastern peace, embracing Israel and its other Arab neighbors, would be more difficult to

Scene continued on page 5A

## Judge blocks H-bomb article

By Doug Stone
Staff Writer

**Milwaukee, Wis.**
A federal judge, citing danger to national security, Monday ordered the Progressive magazine not to print an article on how the hydrogen bomb works.

U.S. District Judge Robert Warren issued a preliminary injunction against the liberal monthly magazine, based in Madison, Wis. The magazine had planned an article entitled "The H-Bomb Secret: How WE Got It, Why We're Telling It," for its May issue.

The injunction will remain in effect until there is a trial or other final resolution of the case, or until there is a decision on any appeal of the injunction.

It was believed to be the first time that a federal judge had issued an injunction for prior restraint against a newspaper or magazine on the grounds that publication would harm national security.

Progressive continued on page 4A

## Solemn children uncertain treaty will halt the killing

By Al McConagha
Staff Correspondent

**Jerusalem**
In the morning, there had been hail and rain.

But in the afternoon, there was only the hard, cold wind, bending the cypress and causing the youngsters to shiver as they dropped the flowers one by one.

As the Egyptian-Israeli peace treaty was glorified in Washington Monday, members of the Gadna Military Youth Organization visited Israel's 300 military cemeteries.

At the national cemetery on the north side of Mount Herzl, high over west Jerusalem, 60 youngsters from the nearby community of Petach Tikva quietly made their rounds. They placed the flowers on graves of officers and enlisted men laid out in terraces of Jerusalem stone under pines and cedars.

They were solemn youngsters. "We realize that because of the people buried here we can live in security and peace," said Schraga Voliner, 16. "We want to show our gratitude with all our heart."

The nation counts five wars with Egypt — the War of Independence in 1948, the Sinai Campaign of 1956, the Six-Day War of 1967, the War of Attrition of 1968-70 and the October War of 1973.

Israel continued on page 6A

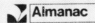

Associated Press

Prime Minister Begin, wearing the Jewish yarmulke, embraced his defense minister, Ezer Weizman, after the signing ceremony.

## Egyptians take first day of new peace in stride

Tribune News Services

**Cairo, Egypt**
Egyptians shrugged off their first day of formal peace with Israel Monday by treating it pretty much like any other workday.

They responded with relief and satisfaction but with none of the euphoria they had shown when President Anwar Sadat went to Israel 16 months ago.

Only last evening did interest perk as families crowded around television sets and transistor sets for the live broadcast of the signing ceremony, which was accompanied by a simultaneous Arabic translation. Cairo's normally crowded downtown streets emptied and some coffee houses filled with passersby who stopped in to watch the event on television.

Otherwise, Cairo was no more frenetic, noisy or exuberant than usual. Children donned school smocks and trudged off to classes. Their fathers jammed into the decrepit city buses and went to work. Farmers hauled their lettuce and tomatoes to market by donkey cart. Merchants haggled with customers. Policemen labored to unsnarl the honking traffic tie-ups.

One reason for the lack of excitement was that the government is planning a public celebration when Sadat comes home. But the people of Egypt have also seen too many premature hopes dashed over the last 16 months to

Egypt continued on page 7A

## Almanac

**Tuesday, March 27, 1979**
**86th day: 279 to go this year**
**Sunrise: 6:04. Sunset: 6:34**

Today's weather

**Partly cloudy**

Increasing cloudiness today with a chance of snow by tonight is predicted for the Twin Cities area. Today's expected high metro temperature will be in the mid to upper 30s.

Other predicted high temperatures: Minnesota, upper 20s to upper 30s; North Dakota, 20s; South Dakota, 20s northeast to 40 southwest; Wisconsin, mid 20s to low 30s.

**Details on Page 5B**



Tribune telephones
372-4141 News General
372-4242 Classified
372-4343 Circulation

## Arab world reacts with threats and anger

By Aly Mahmoud
Associated Press

**Beirut, Lebanon**
Much of the Arab world seethed with hatred and sorrow Monday, the day of peace for Egypt and Israel.

Palestinian leader Yasir Arafat vowed to "chop off the hands" of "the stooge Sadat, the terrorist Begin and the imperialist Carter."

Effigies of President Carter, Israeli Prime Minister Begin and Egyptian President Sadat went up in flames in Palestinian refugee camps in Beirut and elsewhere in Lebanon.

"This is my worst day since I left my home in Palestine in 1948," one Palestinian, tailor Mohammed Khaldi, told a reporter. "I wish I were dead rather than be alive and witness this stigma and disgrace."

Palestinians staged general strikes in the Israeli-occupied West Bank of the Jordan River and Gaza Strip to protest the treaty. General strikes also paralyzed Lebanon's Muslim areas.

In Teheran, Iran, protesters seized the Egyptian Embassy and held four employees as hostages but said they would not be harmed. A mob stormed the Egyptian Embassy in the Persian Gulf state of Kuwait, smashing doors and windows. Protesters occupied the offices of Egypt Air in Damascus, Syria.

In other world capitals, Palestinians, other Arabs and sympathizers paraded, held sit-ins and rallied to denounce a treaty that ends 30 years of war between Israel and Egypt but leaves Israel in control of some occupied Arab lands and does not meet

Arabs continued on page 3A

### Other stories about peace treaty

Minneapolis Tribune

Monday
November 5, 1979
Volume CXIII
Number 141
M y

1A Final
3 Sections
20¢ Single Copy


# U.S. Embassy in Teheran seized

## Staff held hostage for return of shah

By Sajid Rizvi
United Press International

**Teheran, Iran**
Muslim students battled with U.S. Marines for three hours and seized the U.S. Embassy in Teheran on Sunday, taking dozens of staff members hostage to press demands that the deposed shah be extradited to Iran.

About 450 Muslim youths, who said they had tacit approval from Ayatollah Ruhollah Khomeini, stormed the embassy at 10:30 a.m. (1 a.m. Minneapolis time) and "fought with embassy personnel," press reports said.

"We shall not give up the hostages unless the shah is given to us," one of the student spokesman told the few reporters allowed into the compound. "So long as we are here, the embassy will remain closed."

The students seized about 90 American men, women and children and 10 Iranians, the spokesman said. However, other reports put the number of American hostages at 40 to 50.

The protesters told reporters that marines used tear gas to try to prevent the takeover.

He said the students faced the strongest opposition from the marine contingent when they tried to take over what appeared to be a specially guarded room. "Six men guarding the room resisted our students until all documents inside the room were burned. The documents which were destroyed probably belonged to the CIA," said the spokesman.

(The State Department in Washington said there was no indication the Americans were hurt.

(In New York yesterday, park police arrested seven Iranian demonstrators nearly four hours after they handcuffed themselves to the Statue of Liberty's crown and draped a 20-foot banner from the arm demanding that Shah Muhammad Riza Pahlavi be returned to Iran for trial.

(The seven were charged with trespassing and disorderly conduct and released pending later court appearances. Ellen Britton, acting superintendent of Liberty Island, the national park on which the statue is situated, said the island was closed to the public during the demonstration and would remain closed the rest of the day.

(The shah is in a New York hospital recovering from gall bladder surgery and for treatment of cancer. Doctors have said he will need at least 18 months of chemotherapy.)

"The action taken today by a group of our countrymen reflects the natural feelings of the Iranian nation toward the U.S. government's disregard on this issue," the Iranian Foreign Ministry said, referring to the embassy takeover.

**Iran** continued on page 4A

United Press International

A man put up a poster of the Ayatollah Ruhollah Khomeini on the outer wall of the U.S. Embassy in Teheran, Iran, after the compound was seized by students Sunday.

# 50,000 leaflets attack Fraser

By David Phelps and Tom Davies
Staff Writer

Antiabortion forces rallied against Don Fraser's bid for mayor Sunday, distributing up to 50,000 pamphlets claiming that the former congressman supported fetal experimentation.

The literature, which did not endorse any other candidate for mayor, was placed on car windshields near many Minneapolis churches yesterday morning and on parked cars downtown.

It was prepared and financed by an organization known as the Committee for Truth About Fetal Research. The committee's leaders were identified as David N. LaFontaine and William W. McGuire, both of whom used antiabortion issues against Fraser in the DFL primary for U.S. Senate in 1978.

Fraser's major opposition in the mayor's race — independent Charles Stenvig and Independent-Republican Mike Barros — denied any involvement with the group or knowledge of its existence.

LaFontaine said the committee was independent. "This is not a political committee. It's more of an educational kind of thing."

He would not say who he was supporting for mayor but added, "I think if a lot of people are aware of Mr. Fraser's inconsistency in the human rights area, this might sway their vote."

LaFontaine said a network of friends and acquaintances in antiabortion groups helped distribute the pamphlet. He said the one-page pamphlet cost about $1,300 but declined to identify contributors to the committee.

One young family that was seen distributing the literature near Holy Cross Catholic Church, 17th St. and University Av. NE., said that a friend from their church had asked them earlier in the morning to help with distribution.

There were at least two versions of the leaflet distributed yesterday. Most were printed with blue ink and

**Campaign** continued on page 7A

# Iran says it will try to free hostages

By Bernard Gwertzman
New York Times Service

**Washington, D.C.**
The United States said Sunday that it had received assurances from the Iranian government that it would "do its best" to free the Americans being held hostage in the U.S. Embassy in Teheran, but officials here were uncertain that the Iranian government could fulfill its pledge.

The takeover of the embassy by about 450 Iranian students caused a major crisis in Washington. Top officials were roused in the predawn hours by the State Department's Operation Center and a special task force, headed by Harold Saunders, assistant secretary for Near East and South Asian affairs, was set up.

The State Department said later that no Americans had been injured and that the takeover was relatively peaceful. A few tear gas shells had been fired initially by the Marine Corps security contingent of 14 members, but officials denied that there had been "a battle" for the embassy as stated in some reports from Teheran.

Secretary of State Cyrus Vance, who had just returned from South Korea where he attended the funeral of President Park Chung-hee, spent several hours at the State Department and President Carter was kept informed at Camp David, Md. But no high-level meetings were scheduled.

The problem facing the Carter administration — deeply concerned over the safety of the 40 to 50 Americans in the embassy — was that the takeover was another example of the disorder and disunity that has plagued Iran since the fall of Shah Muhammad Riza Pahlavi. There has been no clear center of power in Iran, and thus the uncertainty over who was making major decisions.

The Iranian students claimed in statements issued in Teheran that they had the tacit approval of Ayatollah Ruhollah Khomeini, the spiritual leader of Iran, for the takeover.

The indications in Washington were that neither Iranian Prime Minister Mehdi Barzagan nor Foreign Minister Ibrahim Yazdi had any involvement in the action.

This division at the top has been the pattern throughout the year of turmoil in Iran. The United States, concerned about Iran's political future and with ensuring a continued flow of oil, has been trying to find a way of working in a businesslike way

**Reaction** continued on page 5A

## Anderson, St. Louis rip Minnesota 37-7; Vikings fall to 3rd

**St. Louis, Mo.**
Rookie running back Ottis Anderson scored two touchdowns as the St. Louis Cardinals humiliated the Minnesota Vikings 37-7 Sunday, dropping the Vikings to third place in the National Football Conference's Central Division with a 4-6 record.

Anderson gained 164 yards in 25 carries, bringing his season total to 1,000 yards in 10 games. The Cardinals (3-7) also rushed for a team single-game record of 325 yards in 45 carries, a 7.2-yard average.

**(Details on page 1C.)**

# New Bolivia regime declares martial law, fires on opponents

Col. Alberto Natusch

Tribune News Services

**La Paz, Bolivia**
Bolivia's new military regime stepped up efforts Sunday to impose its authority on the country, declaring martial law and censorship and using planes and tanks in an attempt to disperse opponents.

At noon, two air force T33 combat jets fired machine guns and rockets over several hundred people gathered in front of the headquarters of the Bolivian Workers Confederation. There were no reports of casualties.

The labor headquarters was machine-gunned Saturday night by soldiers in tanks and armored cars trying to break up demonstrations. Hospitals reported six killed and 21 injured, but other reports said that up to 20 civilians had been killed overnight and 50 injured.

Anti-coup civilians building barricades on city streets Saturday night were attacked by troops, who kept up gunfire barrages for about five hours.

The new military ruler, Col. Alberto Natusch, announced over national television during the night that he had imposed martial law and censorship, four days after he overthrew the legally elected president, Walter Guevara. Congress also was suspended. Under martial law, soldiers are authorized to shoot at will anyone moving in the streets after dark.

The military used the radio in an attempt to end a paralyzing general strike, offering workers full pay for last month, including the days on strike, but threatening to dismiss those who did not return to work today.

"The armed forces will save Bolivia from the intrigues of the Communists who want to destroy the work-

**Bolivia** continued on page 5A

## Almanac

**Monday, November 5, 1979**
**309th day; 56 to go this year**
**Sunrise: 6:57. Sunset: 4:56**

### Today's weather

### Cold

Cloudy and cold with a chance of rain or snow is the forecast for the Twin Cities area today. Flurries are likely Tuesday. Highs of about 40 are expected today and Tuesday.

**Details on Page 13B**



Tribune telephones
372-4141 News General
372-4242 Classified
372-4343 Circulation

## 5 more bodies recovered in Texas ship collision

Associated Press

**Galveston, Texas**
The charred remains of five crewmen of the tanker Burmah Agate were recovered Sunday as a team of workers prepared to extinguish the fire on the ship.

The discoveries raised to 10 the number of bodies discovered since the ship, carrying 400,000 barrels of light crude oil, collided with the freighter Mimosa Thursday morning near Galveston. Twenty-two crewmen still are missing and are presumed dead.

# Election analyst Scammon says only issue is what Kennedy will bring U.S.

By Al McConagha
Staff Correspondent

**Washington, D.C.**
As he paused before his quadrennial marathon, Minneapolis's contribution to the highest levels of election analysis defined next year's "real" campaign issue: "What will this prince bring us after coronation day?"

Richard M. Scammon wrestled with that conclusion. There were qualifications. But, finally, there it was: "Yeah, that's it: 'What will this prince bring us after coronation day — and we just don't know."

This reference, of course, is to the expected candidacy (and nomination) of Sen. Edward Kennedy, despite the fact he is what Scammon describes as a "glass jaw candidate," an analysis to which we will return in a moment.

What we do know is that Scammon is regarded as a walking encyclopedia on election behavior and his expertise as statistician and political scientist is again in gigantic demand as the nation gets ready for another political binge.

Indeed, the man who meets that demand is gigantic in his own way. He is 6-foot-5 and weighs 280 pounds. The fact that he is nearly bald only adds to his larger-than-life, computer-like aura.

Among the press and politicians of

**Scammon** continued on page 4A

# County's 'hidden poor' may get help

By Elena O. de la Rosa
Staff Writer

Bertha Jacobson, 74, probably doesn't fit the "image" of a Lake Minnetonka-area resident, although she's lived there 38 years.

In her uninsulated, one-bedroom cottage that once was someone's summer home, which is "very, cold, cold, cold," she saves every coupon she can and spends a lot of time wondering how she'll make it another month on her $321 income.

Jacobson lives in Mound, in an area where such items as private boat docks, two-car garages and double fireplaces are not uncommon. In fact, those very things adorn rambling lakeside houses not far from her little cottage.

"That money goes for everything, and if anything goes wrong with the house it comes out of the same money. That goes for clothes, for haircuts for my husband, for clothes for him," said Jacobson of her husband, Carl, 87, who is now in a nursing home.

After owning a house for 38 years it's not unusual to have things break down. First it was the roof "leaking terrible" and ruining the knotty pine paneling in the living room. Then the basement wall cracked.

Yet Jacobson doesn't complain and she doesn't consider herself poor. "Low income" is what she prefers.

Whatever the label, Jacobson's $321 monthly income places her in the poor or near-poor category set by the federal government.

And she is not alone out there in what some have characterized as the "Golden West." It is not so golden for about 24,000 other people like Jacobson, scattered throughout rural and suburban Hennepin County.

These poor, most of them elderly and on fixed incomes, represent almost one-third of the 76,000 poor people in Hennepin County.

"I think most of the people outside this area feel everybody here is rich, but this whole Lake Minnetonka area, it has real rich people and it has some real poor people," said Tim Lovaasen, mayor of Mound.

Figures on county financial assistance substantiate the claim that there are thousands of poor where most people would least expect them.

Assistance case-load records for December 1978 show that there were 275 cases in Edina, 464 in Golden Valley, 797 in Bloomington, 770 in

**Poor** continued on page 6A

Staff Photo by Donald Black

Bertha Jacobson, 74, stood in front of her uninsulated, one-bedroom home in the Lake Minnetonka-area.

# 1980 ~ 1989

# THE MINNEAPOLIS STAR

ONE COLOR

Monday, February 25, 1980




Single copy 25¢

# For a brief moment, we're together

By JIM KLOBUCHAR
Minneapolis Star Staff Writer

In the storybooks of our childhood, America is painted in good, clean vivid colors. Its voices lift together. Its dreams mingle with its sweat and, at the end, there is a picture where its people are welded into a kind of imperishable congregation of purpose and belief.

That is the storybook.

Life and truth intrude after that. They fuzz and twist the colors and images so that sometimes the pictures are taunting cartoons of themselves and we forget what an incomparable thrill it is to be truly together.

Victory in a world war can do that, or our grief at the death of a president. But how much better the sights and din from an arena where thousands of voices spontaneously recreate the community of our childhood with the rhythm and rising joy of their declaration: "USA! USA! USA! USA!"

The jubilance of the crowd in Lake Placid unites with the country's and somehow gets mixed with the gap-toothed grin of a kid wearing the country's colors on the bench, a hockey stick in his hand and an elfin wink in his eye.

"We're going to win, pals," he is telling us. "Isn't it the nuttiest, the greatest?"

The laughing warrior and the unseen millions nourish each other and, for this indelible moment, and maybe for a lot more in its aftermath, we are together again, and it is a ride to another planet.

Even in the United States of America, with all of its power and, therefore, all of its dilemmas, the people yearn for those magical flights when suddenly everybody is brother and sister and we just want to stand and shout for the exhilaration of it.

USA!

Not in defiance or vindication but just because it is our land, and we are together. Not because we would die for Capitalist Tech or

Klobuchar
Turn to Page 11A

Star Photo by Tom Sweeney

U.S. hockey player Jack O'Callahan, flanked by Soviet and Swedish teams, raised his arms triumphantly at medal ceremony

## Olympic memory lingers

By RALPH THORNTON
Minneapolis Star Staff Writer

LAKE PLACID, N.Y.—The main street of this Adirondack village is empty again, like a carnival midway the morning after the State Fair. Kids kick through the rubbish for something of value.

There's not much. The world is gone.

There are tears mixed with the mud in the streets, amid the shards of plastic cups, torn ticket stubs and receipts for a million junk souvenirs—the tears of those who came seeking gold and found dross.

*Related articles: Page 14C*

The images of the past 13 days flash kaleidoscopically across the memory, like a television set with its vertical hold gone berserk.

Unforgettable scenes: The gentle Finnish giant, Mieto, crying after losing a cross country gold medal by one-hundredth of a second.

Heiden.

The mini-war of the biathlon, those skiers carrying popguns.

The wipe-out that put a Swiss luger in the hospital. Ski jumper Jan Holmlund of Sweden landing on his head. The Canadian bobsled sliding down the chute on its side, four helmeted heads banging into the wall. And Bill Koch, our strongest cross-country skier, quitting a race.

It was a U.S. hockey team that excited the nation, and proved that we can still beat the Europeans at

Olympics
Turn to Page 11A

# Carter on top

## He leads state poll, even with IR voters

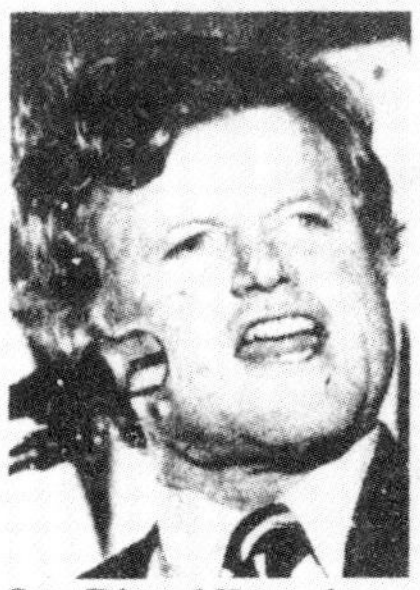

Sen. Edward Kennedy

By BETTY WILSON
Minneapolis Star Staff Writer

President Carter has gained a wide lead over other candidates among Minnesota voters and is drawing surprising support from Republicans and independents, according to a poll completed Friday by Mid-Continent Surveys Inc.

Among DFL voters, Carter is running six-to-one ahead of Sen. Edward Kennedy.

Even among those who identified themselves as Republicans, Carter got slightly more support than any Republican candidate, including George Bush and Ronald Reagan.

Among Twin Cities Republicans, Bush is the two-to-one favorite over Reagan. The two are running neck-and-neck, however, among outstate Republicans.

Forty-four percent of all eligible Minnesota voters interviewed said that if the election were held today, they would vote for Carter.

Bush, who jumped to national prominence following his Iowa victory in January, is the choice of 8.9 percent of the 1,006 persons questioned in personal interviews. The survey was made during the first three weeks in February.

Kennedy appears to be doing little damage to the Carter-Mondale ticket in Vice President Walter Mondale's home state.

Only 7.3 percent of all respondents to the survey said they now would vote for Kennedy. Last summer and fall, before he formally announced his candidacy, Kennedy ran well ahead of Carter in several polls. California Gov. Jerry Brown was favored by fewer than one percent in last week's survey in Minnesota.

About 7 percent said they would vote for Reagan, who is generally considered the front-runner among Republicans.

Fewer than 2 percent said they would vote for any other announced Republican candidate.

Former President Gerald Ford, who is not a candidate, has some support among Republicans in the Twin Cities area, where 7.2 percent said they would vote for him.

One out of four of those interviewed said they didn't know whom they would vote for.

Carter's broad support across party lines indicates that Minnesota voters this year are likely to follow their tradition of voting for the man, not the party.

It also may show how volatile public opinion has become. Last August, the president's popularity was sagging, and the survey firm found that there were more people who thought the president was doing a poor job than thought he was doing a good job.

Those interviewed in the latest poll, a cross section of Minnesota adults, were asked the question:

"If the election for president of

Poll
Turn to Page 12A

President Carter

*New Hampshire*

## Favorite is likely to win presidency

From The Star's News Services

MANCHESTER, N.H.—The nation's first significant direct-vote presidential primary Tuesday looks like this: President Carter well in front on the Democratic side and a cliffhanger between George Bush and Ronald Reagan on the Republican side.

A relatively few New Hampshire voters—moderates and independents who have a penchant for unpredictability—will decide the outcome

And once again, as has happened so often in the past two decades, this tiny state will set the tone for the long string of delegate-selecting primaries yet to come, with political sages reminding us that since 1952, either the Republican or Democratic winner in New Hampshire has gone on to become president.

This fact offends political statisticians and strategists. New Hampshire doesn't look like any kind of representative sample of the United States. It is too rural, too white, too conservative to reflect the nation.

In terms of political impact, the state is minor: 22 of the 1,994 Republican and 19 of the 3,331 Democratic delegates who will nominate presidential candidates this summer will be chosen in New Hampshire's 1980 primary. It simply doesn't justify a major campaign effort.

Yet, New Hampshire (notwithstanding spurts of interest in such

Primary
Turn to Page 12A

Index




Star Telephones

| | |
|---|---|
| Want Ads | 372-4242 |
| Circulation | 372-4343 |
| News | 372-4141 |

Star Illustration by Todd Grande

## A 'how-to' lesson for the caucuses

By DANE SMITH
Minneapolis Star Staff Writer

When he was chairman of the Minnesota Republican Party in the early '70s, Bob Brown needled college audiences by telling them, "If you can't give up two hours once every two years (to attend a precinct caucus), you forfeit your right to complain about politicians."

While this may not be literally true, he had a point. Precinct caucuses are one of the few political events at which one citizen can make a difference.

As the bottom rung of the political ladder, the miniature town-meetings set the agenda for the rest of the state's voters.

But, for the political rookie, the thought of a caucus with party regulars and veteran political workers may seem intimidating.

Here are answers to the most commonly asked questions about caucuses.

**Q. When are the caucuses held?**

A. Tuesday evening. State law requires major political parties to convene a caucus for each precinct at 8 p.m. on the fourth Tuesday in February in every general-election (even-numbered) year.

**Q. Should I attend a DFL, IR or American party caucus?**

A. You should attend the caucus of the party that most closely represents your views or the one affiliated with your favorite candidates. For example, if you favor nationalizing all major industries and confiscating privately-owned handguns, you might feel uncomfortable at the very conservative American Party caucus.

If you consider yourself an independent, you might consider at-

Caucus
Turn to Page 12A

THE MINNEAPOLIS STAR

Copyright 1980 Minneapolis Star and Tribune Company

Monday, May 19, 1980

Associated Press

A Miami policeman, left photo, grabbed a looting suspect; in right photo, a national guardsman stood watch in an area of Miami where rioters had started fires

# Miami just went mad

## Victims' bodies reveal horrors of mob savagery

From The Star's News Services

MIAMI—Some of the deaths were sadistic and deliberate; others were cruelly random:

• Fourteen-year-old Andre Dawson was gunned down as he walked to a neighborhood store. He lay dead in the street for an hour before ambulance crews could reach him.

• A white man jumped from a pickup truck and sprayed gunfire into a crowd in front of the Lakeview Lounge, killing Thomas Reese, 34. The gunman fled.

• A black mob pulled three white males from their car and beat them to death. The victims were identified as Benny Higdon, 21; Charles Barreca, 15, and Robert Owens, 14.

• Emilio Munoz was driving home from his job as a butcher about 3 a.m. Sunday when a crowd of blacks began tossing rocks at the car. He swerved into a wall, about 20 people surrounded the auto, overturned it, jabbed him with sticks and set the car on fire, burning Munoz to death.

• One of the first victims, a white man, still was unidentified. A county morgue spokesman said the body had numerous stab wounds and apparently had been run over by a car.

Those were some of more than a dozen deaths confirmed in Miami today after two days and nights of burning, looting and rioting touched off Saturday night by the acquittal of four white former policemen in the fatal beating of a black man.

By today, a sort of stunned peace seemed to be prevailing.

National guard troops with M-16 rifles diverted thousands of job-bound commuters away from miles and miles of heavily populated devastation.

The acrid smell of burning buildings and debris hung in the humid air on the outskirts of the forbidden areas. A tower of black smoke plumed above Liberty City, a sprawling ghetto area of northwestern Miami.

The smouldering remains of three major night blazes served as visible reminders that the nightmare had been real.

Firefighters, backed by police squads clearing the streets with tear gas, had finally brought hundreds of blazes, including 40 to 50 major fires, under control in the pre-dawn hours.

Dade County Public Safety Director Bobby Jones, put in command by Gov. Bob Graham of all police, 1,100 national guard troops plus scores of state patrolmen and other officers, said the situation was stable this morning.

Was the worst over?

"I would sure as hell hope that it is, but I'm very cautious when it comes to that kind of op-

Riot
Turn to Page 12A

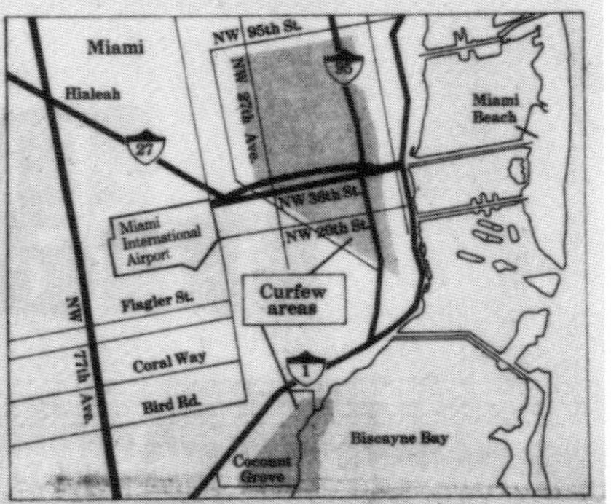


Star Map by Jody Smith / United Press International

Associated Press

Abrasive volcanic ash, smoke and debris rose from Mount St. Helens after a violent eruption Sunday

# Quick, fiery fury stuns Northwest

From The Star's News Services

CASTLE ROCK, Wash.—The once lushly forested flanks of Mount St. Helens resemble the desolate wastes of the moon now that the volcano's violent eruption has altered the landscape.

"There's one helluva big hole up there—a big chunk of the mountain is gone," said Tom Robinson, a state Department of Natural Resources manager who flew over the mountain by helicopter Sunday, only hours after it erupted with a bang felt for 200 miles.

"It looked like someone had literally taken a butter knife and sliced off the top of the mountain," he added.

U.S. Geological Survey scientists agreed with Robinson's observations. By nightfall Sunday, after a full day of volcanic activity, the 9,677-foot mountain was reduced by 1,300 feet, according to U.S. Geological Survey spokesman Worner Gerhard. The crater, spitting ash and hot gases at the sky, was a half-mile across.

Pyroclastic flows—mixtures of gas and superheated rock—sped down all sides of the mountain Sunday.

Before the eruption, the mountain, with its nearly perfect conical shape and pristine snow covering, had been compared to Japan's scenic Mount Fujiyama.

Now, "it kind of looks like the moon—everything is gray," Robinson said.

The volcanic ash, which prompted health warnings, fell half an inch deep on the ground up to 500 miles away after Sunday's convulsion that turned day into night in much of eastern Washington, northern Idaho and western Montana.

Today, a plume of steam and ash was still billowing 14,000 feet high from the crater, but there were no

Volcano
Turn to Page 4A

# *Coalition forms to fight initiative-referendum*

By ROBERT WHEREATT
Minneapolis Star Staff Writer

An unorganized group of union officials, businessmen and individuals who are close to the state legislative process are quietly discussing what they might do to defeat the initiative and referendum amendment in this fall's election.

The question of referendum (and initiative) was grudgingly put on the ballot by the 1980 Legislature.

If the voters approve it, they will have a method of proposing their own laws or vetoing laws passed by the Legislature.

But the concept is not universally accepted in the state, especially among special interest groups.

To many, it is an idea whose time has not come and should never come.

They are exploring the possibility of pooling manpower and resources to convince the rest of the voters that initiative and referendum is not needed in Minnesota.

So far, organized labor has been the most active.

"We're starting to get organized right now," said David Roe, president of the Minnesota AFL-CIO. "We hope by sometime in June we will have put everything together so that by July 1 we will have an umbrella group."

Roe met last week with officials from the Teamsters, United Auto Workers and the Minnesota Farmers Union. He said he also met this week with some businessmen "about some of their proposed activities.

The conversations revolve around putting together a coalition of groups that could secure funding and launch a campaign to explain initiative and referendum, Roe said.

"Once the public understands initiative and referendum, they will want to stay with our existing system. I don't think anyone's ever

Initiative
Turn to Page 8A

# His wife, child missing, he hopes God in control

By KATHERINE SKIBA
Minneapolis Star Staff Writer

The Rev. Irving Stauffer of Arden Hills is a like a steady vessel in tempestuous waters.

His wife and 8-year-old daughter have been missing since Friday afternoon in an apparent abduction.

A 6-year-old Roseville boy was seized about two hours after the Stauffers disappeared, and authorities believe one man is responsible for all three disappearances.

Yet Stauffer, a Baptist missionary, is generally composed and hopeful.

"The doubts creep in," he says, "but I know God is in control and Mary and Beth and this little boy are in his hands."

His strength is not without its limits. Twice during a 30-minute interview, he raised a clenched hand to his face to fight back tears.

Stauffer, 39, was to leave Wednesday with his wife, Mary, 36, and children, Beth, 8, and Steven, 6, for the Philippines.

A barrel and wooden crates—

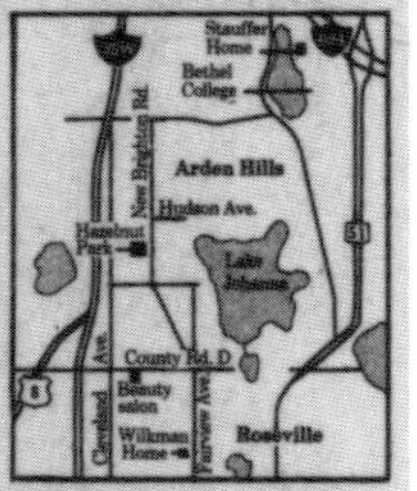


marked for Cebu, the Philippines—already house some of the family's belongings for overseas shipment.

In the Philippines, the family was to begin their second four-year residence as missionaries of the Baptist General Conference

Kidnap
Turn to Page 14A

# THE MINNEAPOLIS STAR

Tuesday, December 9, 1986 — A Section, Part 1 — Single copy 25¢

Star Graphic by Kent MacIntosh

## 'Aspirin' tax may fix fiscal headache

By BETTY WILSON
The Minneapolis Star

How do you spell budget-deficit relief in Minnesota?

R-O-L-A-I-D-S, that's how.

Gov. Al Quie and his financial advisers, in an effort to offset any increases in the state's projected $195 million deficit, are considering taxing headaches, upset stomachs, sore muscles, itches and bad breath—specifically, taxing the non-prescription drugs sold to ease such problems.

Quie, who has long said he wouldn't propose any tax increases in 1981—except possibly on gasoline—hinted Monday that it may now be necessary to propose such actions when the Minnesota Legislature meets in January.

High interest rates and a deeper recession than earlier predicted could mean less money coming into the state coffers—even less money than the dire forecasts of recent months.

As a result, Quie said, his staff, now working on the 1982-1983 budget, is looking at all available options.

Quie refers to the proposals as "adjustments" to correct inequities rather than tax increases.

"I suppose it's all semantics," he acknowledged to reporters.

Some of the options, which could raise as much as $200 million in the next biennium, include:

- Apply the 4-percent state sales tax to non-prescription drugs, which now are exempt along with prescription drugs. That would include aspirin and other pain killers, antacids, rubbing alcohol, cough syrups, skin-care products and even mouthwashes. Such a tax would raise $7.5 million a year,

Taxes
Turn to Page 10A

Associated Press

**Comfort**

**Record producer David Geffen comforted Yoko Ono after the shooting death of her husband John Lennon Monday night.**

## 'Tell me it isn't true,' say Lennon's wife, fans

From The Minneapolis Star's News Services

*Reactions to Lennon's death from former Beatles and Minneapolis' West Bank: Page 1B*

NEW YORK—John Lennon, the singer-songwriter who helped make the Beatles musical superstars and pop-culture legends in the 1960s, was killed in a late-night spray of gunfire outside his luxury apartment building.

Minutes after the shots rang out, police took a suspect, Mark David Chapman, into custody. Chapman, 25, of Honolulu, was taken under heavy guard to the Tombs prison in downtown Manhattan early today to await arraignment on murder charges. No motive was known immediately.

The shooting occurred at 10:50 p.m. (9:50 p.m., Minneapolis time) Monday at the Dakota, a century-old building at the corner of 72nd Street and Central Park West. Police used a squad car to rush the former Beatle to Roosevelt Hospital, about a mile away.

"Tell me it isn't true," said his sobbing wife, Yoko Ono, when doctors pronounced the 40-year-old Lennon dead soon after.

According to police, Lennon was shot five times as he stepped out of his limousine after returning from a recording session. His wife was with him but was not hurt.

Chapman, police said, was waiting in the courtyard, where the Dakota permitted fans of the former Beatle and other celebrity residents to congregate.

As Lennon left his car and walked past the Dakota's iron gate and into the archway, officers said, Chapman approached him, calling out, "Mr. Lennon?" Chapman drew a .38-caliber gun from his coat, crouched down in a combat stance and fired five times, they said.

Lennon staggered to an office at the entrance of the building.

"I'm shot," he moaned, and fell face down.

While the doormen summoned police, witnesses said, Chapman waited calmly. They said he dropped his gun, which a guard kicked aside and saved for police.

"Do you know what you just did?" a doorman asked the gunman.

"I just shot John Lennon," the gunman

Lennon
Turn to Page 4A

## Lennon led life as Beatles' magical mystery man

An essay by Jon Bream
Rock critic

I had the fortune of meeting three of the four Beatles. Maybe it was fitting that I never met John Lennon.

He was the Beatles' mystery man.

Beatlemaniacs may have once thought Paul McCartney was dead, but they know he has been merely writing silly, little love songs. Meanwhile, Ringo Starr has been drumming his way into the movies and George Harrison has been searching for the perfect guru.

But where has John Lennon been? What have he and partner Yoko Ono been doing in seclusion for the past five years? Why has this once-prolific, once-revolutionary artist become an inscrutable, nowhere man for so long?

Whatever he was doing, John Lennon was fueling the mystique surrounding the Beatles' most controversial member.

Remember, he was the one who said the Beatles were more popular than Jesus Christ. He was the one who married his pregnant mistress, posed with her for a nude album cover photo and staged a "bed-in" to record an anti-war song. He was the one who fought deportation from the United States because of a prior European marijuana bust. He was the one tossed out of a Beverly Hills nightclub for heckling Tommy Smothers. And he was the one who, after achieving stardom, slammed the door in the face of his begging father, who had deserted him as a child.

*"The way things are going,*
*They're going to crucify me."*

**—"The Ballad of John and Yoko" 1969**

Sure, Lennon was controversial. But more importantly, he was the Beatles' key member. Not only is he generally blamed for the breakup of the band in 1970, but he reportedly has been the artistic obstacle to any kind of a Beatles reunion. Yet, if it hadn't been for Lennon's guiding artistic and intellectual vision, the Beatles may never have been the musical and cultural force they became. John Lennon certainly rivaled Bob Dylan as the most important pop-music figure of the 1960s.

While McCartney provided the Beatles' tuneful, pop underbelly, it was his songwriting partner Lennon who gave the quartet its rock 'n' roll edge. McCartney admired the vocal harmonies of the Everly Brothers and the toe-tapping pop of Buddy Holly whereas Lennon was affected by the raw music of Elvis Presley, Little Richard and other Ameri-

Bream
Turn to Page 4A

## Housewives are happy—and so's househusband

*One in a series*

By KAY MILLER
The Minneapolis Star

Susan Meyer is stuck in a single-story suburban box with her child and fears she always will be.

Meyer (not her real name), limited by a lack of education and a year out of a job as a switchboard operator, has been cranking up her nerve to return to school. Her husband earns about $25,000—enough that Meyer seldom worries about money—but she has the nagging sense that she's accomplished little so far in life.

Looking back, she'd have done things differently, she says, and it all boils down to one thing: "I would've waited 'til I got my degree to get married and have family."

But for now, Meyer's a housewife. And she hates it.

Michele Markley would gladly change places with her.

Unlike Meyer, Markley (also not her real name) would give anything to be at home with her three children. For now, and perhaps for a very long time to come, Markley is a secretary at the University of Minnesota.

She works because she has no choice. Her husband's income is modest and he lacks the skill and education to land a better job.

She's in a box, too.

The dimensions are just different.

You might expect deep discontent from scores of women doing work where the pay is little and the chances for promotion are nonexistent. But The Star asked and found that the vast majority of people in one such job (a quarter of the Twin Cities residents surveyed) say they love their work.

They're homemakers. And many feel they have the best of all worlds—travel to work is convenient, there are lots of opportunities to make friends, the surroundings are pleasant and they have the opportunity do the things they do best.

In its survey of Twin Cities attitudes, The Star talked with 284 homemakers—including one self-proclaimed male homemaker, a former salesman who tired of peddling products and dropped out.

Housewives were happy, all right.

Happy with their husbands: 48 percent said they were "completely satisfied" with their marriages, compared with 44 percent of "completely satisfied" working wives. Forty-four percent of homemakers said they were somewhat

Survey
Turn to Page 13A

## In the political game of weapons, players use deadly chips

By RUSSELL WARREN HOWE

*Second of five parts*

In our era, the major weapons systems have become more a feature of politics, economics and diplomacy than of the battlefield.

In weapons politics, as in Monopoly, you win according to how rich you become. You win by retaining, not spending, the symbols you acquire.

In their new role as weapons of finance and diplomacy, arms have strangely become even more indispensable than in the past. They are like the cattle that the Bamangwato of Botswana breed, not to eat or sell, but just to have, to keep up with their neighbors in prestige and power.

Today, the rattling saber is the first real line of defense for almost every major nation—including the United States. Yet to give clout to this mythical sword, the United States, Russia, China and many major and lesser powers spend more on defense than on any other single budget item. A world which has all but renounced, overtly, the notion of conquest continues to produce arms as though conquest is still the ultimate objective. The post-imperial age manufactures far more, and more powerful, weapons than imperial eras ever dreamed of.

The simple fact is that *weapons are not what they were.* In past centuries, wars were carefully prepared and judiciously announced. Often it took weeks to translate the declaration to the battlefield. The weapons makers took orders: swords, customed in length and weight to the physiques and battle styles of each officer; crossbows for the small standing armies; longbows for the arrow-fodder shanghaied in the taverns. After the war, the swords went back into ornate scabbards; the bows and arrows rotted; a peacetime terrorist like Robin Hood had to make his own.

In World War I, despite the ex-

Arms
Turn to Page 8A

Star Graphic by Craig MacIntosh, Duane Braley

In the political game of weapons, you win according to how rich you become

☆ NEWS INSIDE



☆ OPINION

**Tough job**

Being an economic adviser to Ronald Reagan would be a thankless task—there are too many problems, says columnist.

Page 6A

☆ SPORTS

**Trading's such a lot of fun**

Baseball general managers are enjoying their winter meetings. There's nothing scientific about this trading session. You want to make a trade, you make a trade.

Page 12B

☆ MARKETPLACE

**Polluted water means profits**

A water-purification project assigned by a college engineering teacher led to a process which turns polluted water into gold—or at least profits—for Osmotics Inc. a Hopkins company

Page 1C

Index

Minneapolis Tribune

Wednesday January 21, 1981 1A
Volume CXIV
Number 197
M o
3 Sections
25¢ Single Copy




# Day 1 of a new life

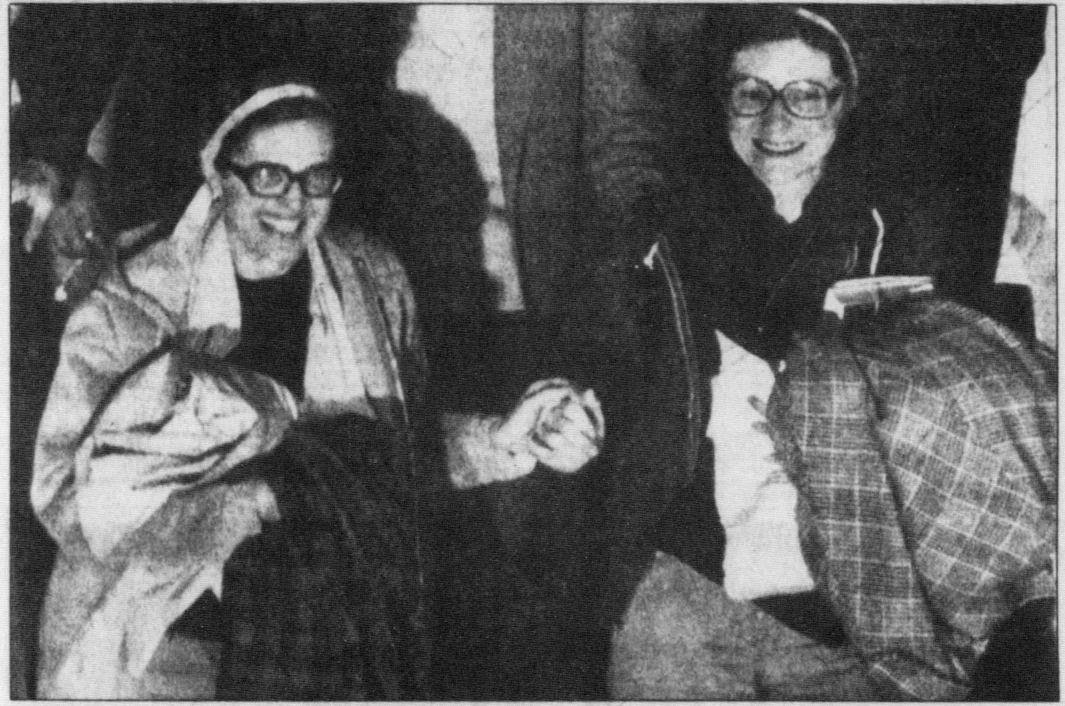

In the end, there was yet another small delay as the plane sat on the tarmac in Algiers.

The television cameras showed the open door, with cabin attendants and Algerian airline officials moving to and fro. Suddenly, L. Bruce Laingen, the Minnesota native who was charge d'affairs in Teheran, emerged with the two broadly smiling women pictured at left: Elizabeth Ann Swift and Kathryn Koob. After 444 days of captivity in Iran, Laingen, Swift, Koob and 49 other Americans were safe on the ground in Algeria.

In a joyous welcome witnessed by millions on television, they were officially transferred to U.S. government control. Ninety minutes later they were on their way to an American military base in Wiesbaden, West Germany, for several days of physical and mental evaluation.

The ribbons in Swift's and Koob's hair were yellow, like the thousands of ribbons that appeared all over the United States during the long wait. The ribbons usually were tied around trees, but also showed up in such unlikely places as the 27th floor of the Foshay Tower in Minneapolis.

The hostages were finally free.

**Hostage release details:**
**2A, 3A, 4A, 1B, 6B, 7B**

# Day 1 for a new leader

Minutes before the hostages' plane left Teheran, Ronald Reagan was sworn in as President of the United States.

After taking the oath of office as the 40th president, Reagan and his wife Nancy turned from the lectern to wave to onlookers, left, on the west front of the Capitol building.

In his inaugural address, the new president called for "an era of national renewal . . . It is time," he said, "to reawaken this industrial giant, to get government back within its means, and to lighten our punitive tax burden. These will be our first priorities, and on these principles, there will be no compromise."

Less than an hour later, Reagan signified the seriousness of his intent by ordering a freeze on the hiring of all federal civilian employees.

Former President Jimmy Carter, who had been without sleep for two nights, went home to Plains, Ga., after the ceremony for a brief rest before leaving today for Wiesbaden, where he will be Reagan's envoy to greet the hostages.

**Inauguration articles:**
**6A, 7A, 8A and 10A**

## Almanac

**Wednesday, Jan. 21 1981**
**21st day; 344 to go this year**
**Sunrise: 7:44. Sunset: 5:05.**

Today's weather

**Balmy**

A high in the low 40s is likely today in the Twin Cities area.



Tribune telephones
372-4141 News General
372-4242 Classified
372-4343 Circulation

Minneapolis Tribune

Tuesday
March 31, 1981
Volume CXIV
Number 256
MN

1A. Final
3 Sections
25¢ Single Copy
Section A / Part I

# Reagan, 3 others shot

## President's prospects 'excellent' after surgery

Associated Press

**President Reagan was shoved into his limousine by Secret Service agents after he was shot outside the Washington Hilton Hotel.**

## Colorado man arrested; press aide 'critical'

**Tribune News Services**

**Washington, D.C.**
President Reagan was wounded Monday in an assassination attempt by a gunman who also shot the White House press secretary and two law officers.

Reagan was hit in the left side of the chest during a rapid series of gunshots at about 1:30 p.m. (Minneapolis time) as he left the Washington Hilton Hotel after addressing a labor union meeting.

The president was described in good and stable condition after a two-hour operation that ended about four hours after the shooting. A hospital official said surgeons removed a single .22 caliber bullet that struck Reagan's seventh rib, penetrating about three inches into the lung and collapsing it.

"He is alert and should be able to make decisions by tomorrow," said Dr. Dennis O'Leary, dean of clinical affairs at George Washington University. Noting that Reagan's lung has been reinflated, O'Leary said that the president "was never in any serious danger" because the bullet did not damage the heart. O'Leary said Reagan probably would be hospitalized for about two weeks.

Authorities arrested a 25-year-old Colorado man, John W. Hinckley Jr., who, eyewitnesses said, fired six shots at the presidential entourage from among the television camera crews and reporters assembled outside a hotel exit.

Press secretary James Brady, 40, was struck above the right eye. Doctors performed a skull operation called an craniotomy and discovered

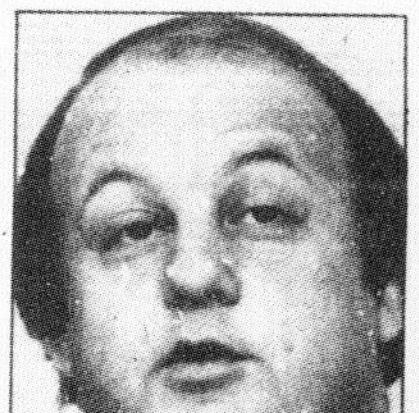

James Brady

a trauma so severe that it probably would cause permanent brain damage should the press secretary survive.

Brady was still in surgery at mid-evening, and medical sources said the part of the brain that was damaged governs the personality. O'Leary described his condition as "critical." "This is not a good injury," he said. "It causes a lot of damage."

Hinckley was booked on charges of attempted assassination of a president and of assault with intent to kill a police officer. He was in FBI custody last night. Roger Young of the FBI described the weapon as a "Saturday night special" and said it was purchased at a Dallas gun shop.

Young said there had been "no problem" with Hinckley's coherence when questioned by authorities.

Hinckley was arrested last Oct. 9 at

**Reagan** continued on page 7A

## Arms arrest, Nazi group in suspect's background

**Tribune News Services**

**Washington, D.C.**
John Warnock Hinckley Jr., arrested Monday in an attempt on the life of President Reagan, recently had been under psychiatric care and had been arrested while carrying handguns in Nashville, Tenn., on a day former President Carter visited the city.

Little was known about Hinckley's activities in the years after high school — except sporadic attendance at Texas Tech University — and hints emerged yesterday of a troubled man and his weapons.

The head of a neo-Nazi group, the National Socialist Party of America, said Hinckley was a party member who quit in 1979 because "he felt that we were not sufficiently militant for him."

"We agreed mutually NSPA was not his cup of tea. He wanted us to go out and commit unlawful acts. We sort of carried on a debate about it," said Harold Covington of Raleigh, N.C.

John W. Hinckley Jr.

The suspect was arrested Oct. 9 in Nashville for possession of concealed weapons, according to Nashville police records.

Nashville police records say Hinckley was arrested at Metropolitan Air-

**Suspect** continued on page 8A

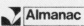

Associated Press

**Secret Service agent Timothy McCarthy, foreground, lay wounded after the assassination attempt outside a Washington hotel Monday. On the ground behind him were Washington police officer Thomas Delahanty, center, and press secretary James Brady, partially covered by Secret Service agents. In left background, Secret Service agents surrounded the suspect.**

### Inside:

■ Two Minnesota medical experts said that President Reagan's age is no reason to doubt that he will make a speedy recovery. **Page 2A.**

■ Television provided graphic documentation of the attack on the president's life, though reports on the condition of Reagan and Brady were confused and conflicting. **Page 5A.**

■ The stock exchanges closed early because of the assassination attempt. **Page 9A.**

■ The latest Minnesota Poll shows that most state adults favor tighter controls on the ownership of pistols. State pistol owners disagree. **Page 1B.**

■ The Academy Awards ceremonies were postponed for 24 hours. **Page 7B.**

### Other news:

■ Leaders of Poland's Solidarity union called off a nationwide strike planned for today after a seven-hour negotiating session with government officials. **Page 6A.**

■ Indonesian commandos stormed a hijacked plane in Bangkok, Thailand, killing four of five hijackers aboard and freeing the captive crew and passengers. **Page 6A.**

■ The body of a young boy was found in a river near Atlanta, raising to 21 the number of black children found slain there in 20 months. **Page 8B.**

■ The U.S. Supreme Court let stand Minnesota rulings that allowed parents to lock up an adult "child" and try to "deprogram" her out of a religious cult. **Page 3B.**

■ Indiana University beat North Carolina 63-50 for the 1981 NCAA basketball championship. **Page 1C.**

### Almanac

**Tuesday, March 31, 1981**
**90th day; 275 to go this year**
**Sunrise: 5:56. Sunset: 6:39.**

Today's weather

**Showers**

Cloudy skies and thunderstorms with a high in the low 60s are likely today in the Twin Cities area.

Other predicted highs: Minnesota, 60s; North Dakota, 40s; South Dakota, 50s; Wisconsin, 60s.

| | | | |
|---|---|---|---|
| **Arts** | 5B | **Obituaries** | 19A |
| **Business** | 9-13A | **Sports** | 1-4C |
| **Comics** | 4B | **Theaters** | 18A |
| **Corrections** | 2A | **TV, Radio** | 7B |
| **Editorial** | 14-15A | **Weather** | 5B |

Tribune telephones
372-4141 News General
372-4242 Classified
372-4343 Circulation

Minneapolis Tribune

Wednesday April 15, 1981 | 1A Final
Volume CXIV Number 269
M r | 3 Sections

25¢ Single Copy | Section A/Part I

# State temporarily unable to pay bills on time



**By Steve Brandt and Lori Sturdevant**
Staff Writers

The state of Minnesota temporarily cannot pay its bills because it doesn't have enough money on hand, the Minneapolis Tribune has learned.

A state accounting official confirmed to the Tribune Tuesday that 6,785 checks written to pay bills totaling $19.1 million cannot currently be mailed by the department because it lacks enough money to cover them.

The Department of Finance began to delay paying state bills April 6. Despite this, Finance Commissioner Wayne Burggraaff as recently as yesterday morning told the House Tax Committee that the state faces no cash flow problems. Burggraaff said last night he was referring to the cash situation at the end of the state's fiscal year in June.

"It's been a little tight in the last two to three weeks," he said. "I don't think it's a serious problem if we hold on to these checks for three or four or five days."

Assistant Commissioner Ed Hunter said state aid payments have been delayed at times since state budget problems developed last fall. However, this period is the first time the state has delayed mailing checks because it couldn't cover them since at least 1973 when the finance department was created.

The checks normally would have been mailed last week, according to Roy Muscatello, state accounting director. However, most will be mailed today, he said, and some will not be mailed until Thursday.

This delay follows the department's withholding of $10.5 million in checks earlier last week. They finally were mailed yesterday, Muscatello said.

This round of delayed payments followed a more severe cash flow problem that occurred in February, according to Muscatello. That situation was never revealed by the administration of Gov. Al Quie.

The governor's press secretary, Robert Anderson, said he believed that Quie has not yet been informed of the situation.

The situation came to light when the Senate DFL staff made a routine check of a veteran's complaint that his benefit check was late. Among examples of the varied state bills left unpaid are agency phone bills or travel expenses. Examples of obligations to individuals Muscatello cited are veterans' benefits or benefits to handicapped people. (The veterans' benefits are a short-term state grant for veterans who are disabled and out of money.) He said the department has let a few checks trickle out if an agency protests.

Muscatello said he anticipates that the state will be able to return to a normal payment schedule late this week. That means state employees should get their paychecks on schedule this Friday, he said.

The problem is an outgrowth of the state's current budgetary problems,

**Cash** continued on page 4A

# Hail, Columbia

Associated Press

The space shuttle Columbia rolled down the runway at Edwards Air Force Base, Calif., after a flawless landing Tuesday. (More pictures, other articles on pages 10A and 11A.)

## Shuttle makes triumphant return

**Tribune News Services**

**Edwards Air Force Base, Calif.**
The space shuttle Columbia rocketed out of orbit and glided to a safe landing Tuesday. Columbia's landing on the California desert concluded a successful demonstration of a bold new approach to extraterrestrial travel.

Heralding its triumphant return with a sharp double sonic boom, Columbia appeared in the clear blue sky, soared over the base, looped back and touched its wheels down on the hard-packed clay of a dry lake bed. Touchdown came at 12:21 p.m., Minneapolis time.

"Welcome home, Columbia!" was the simple message from Mission Control.

Astronauts John W. Young and Navy Capt. Robert L. Crippen brought the 122-foot long, 80-ton gliding vehicle to a smooth landing at a speed of 215 miles an hour, about twice the velocity of a jetliner landing.

After landing, the astronauts fidgeted in their cockpit for about an hour while support crews made sure no dangerous gases lingered.

"If we're going to get this thing operational, this is one of the parts we're

**Columbia** continued on page 11A

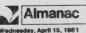

Associated Press

Astronauts John Young, left, and Robert Crippen beamed after they came out of the shuttle yesterday.

## Mission Control celebration is brief

**By Lewis Cope**
Staff Writer

**Houston, Texas**
The landing Tuesday of the world's first reusable spaceship changed even the way that Mission Control workers celebrate.

As Columbia was heading back toward earth, flight director Don Puddy told the 100 controllers on duty that they would have "exactly 15 seconds to whoopee" after touchdown.

As the space shuttle Columbia's wheels were touching down on the runway with two little puffs of black smoke, he gave the controllers the go-ahead.

With that, everyone stood up, cheering and applauding, waving their arms.

But there could be none of the sus-

**Houston** continued on page 11A

## Columbia's success spurs plans for future trips

**By Walter Sullivan**
New York Times Service

**Edwards Air Force Base, Calif.**
After the almost flawless performance of the space shuttle on its first voyage, space agency officials began Tuesday to draw up firmer plans for the future.

Columbia's triumph is expected to lead to flights with countless commercial, scientific and military applications.

One space agency official said an "optimistic" estimate was that the shuttle would fly again under its own power in "less than six months" on a four-day flight, after which it might be able to turn around and return to space four months later. Ultimately, officials envision the shuttle making return trips in a matter of weeks.

Yesterday, officials were uncertain just how quickly the Columbia could be readied for another flight. Specialists must determine the extent of the damage to the tiles that protected the ship from the searing heat of reentry into the atmosphere. There was also some question about the launching pad, which was heavily damaged during liftoff.

If a close inspection of the tiles reveals no fundamental problems, the optimistic estimate of a launching in the fall could prove true, with the third test mission in the spring and the fourth and final test flight late in 1982. The first operational — or non-experimental — flight would take place by the end of 1982.

The payload for that flight, as now planned, will be a TDRS — Tracking and Data Relay Satellite — to be gently released into earth orbit. Three more missions will carry a variety of satellites for communications and other purposes. The fifth operational mission is planned for mid-1983. That mission would carry the first military satellite of undisclosed purpose. The sixth mission is planned for later in 1983. It would involve the European-built Spacelab,

**Future** continued on page 10A

## Quie to request joining of agencies

**By David Phelps and Steve Brandt**
Staff Writers

Gov. Al Quie will propose at least a partial reorganization of state government when he tells Minnesotans tonight how he plans to eliminate a projected $503 million budget deficit.

Quie will ask the Legislature to combine agencies dealing with energy, economic development and planning into a single agency, at a savings estimated from $5 million to $8 million.

But his other recommendations remain known to only a tight circle of advisers and aides.

**(County board votes to adopt hiring freeze. Page 1B.)**

The Independent-Republican governor will outline his revised 1981-83 budget during a 30-minute speech at 8 p.m., carried live by WCCO-AM and Minnesota Public Radio.

In meetings with Independent-Republican legislators and other officials during the past few days Quie has offered few hints about his plan for balancing a state budget of more than $8 billion.

But he has made several things plain, said legislators who attended those meetings. Among the things Quie said he will not do:

■ Substantially increase income taxes. The governor remains steadfast in his support of income tax indexing, which adjusts tax brackets near the rate of inflation. However, he may approve a tax increase by

**Quie** continued on page 12A

## Midnight tonight is the deadline for filing tax returns

If you haven't already filed, your federal and state income tax returns are due today. By midnight, to be precise.

The Internal Revenue Service (IRS) said it expected about 13 million tax returns to be filed in the seven days before the deadline. About 94 million federal returns will be filed this year.

Most large post offices that provide 24-hour service will accept tax returns up to the deadline and affix postmarks so that they meet the deadline, the Postal Service said.

For those who can't meet the deadline, the IRS provides a two-month automatic extension, to June 15, with the filing of Form 4868.

A taxpayer who is granted a federal extension can use a copy of it for Minnesota taxes as well. Those who do not have federal extensions can apply for state extensions by filing Form M-522E.

## Almanac

**Wednesday, April 15, 1981**
**105th day; 260 to go this year**
**Sunrise: 5:29. Sunset: 6:58.**

### Today's weather

**Pleasant**

Fair, sunny weather is on tap today for the Twin Cities area. The predicted high is in the low 60s.



Tribune telephones: 372-4141 News General; 372-4242 Classified; 372-4343 Circulation

# THE MINNEAPOLIS STAR

Friday, September 25, 1981




Single copy 25¢

ONE COLOR

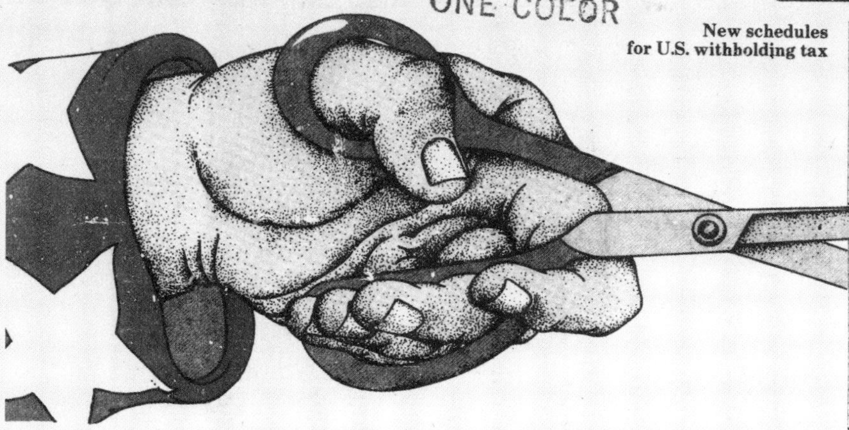

New schedules for U.S. withholding tax

| Biweekly pay | Currently withheld | Oct. 1 | July 1 | Extra take home (est.) |
|---|---|---|---|---|
| **Single** | | | | |
| $300 | $37.20 | $34.90 | $30.30 | $6.90 |
| 400 | 58.20 | 54.40 | 46.80 | 11.40 |
| 500 | 83.10 | 78.40 | 69.00 | 14.10 |
| 600 | 110.20 | 104.10 | 91.90 | 18.30 |
| 700 | 140.60 | 133.40 | 119.00 | 21.60 |
| 800 | 174.60 | 165.40 | 157.00 | 27.60 |
| 900 | 208.90 | 197.70 | 175.30 | 33.60 |
| 1,000 | 247.90 | 234.70 | 208.30 | 39.60 |
| 1,100 | 286.90 | 271.70 | 241.30 | 45.60 |
| 1,200 | 325.90 | 308.70 | 275.30 | 51.60 |
| 1,300 | 364.90 | 345.70 | 307.30 | 57.60 |
| **Married, one child** | | | | |
| $300 | $15.30 | $14.30 | $12.30 | $3.00 |
| 400 | 31.60 | 28.30 | 21.70 | 9.90 |
| 500 | 49.60 | 44.30 | 30.70 | 18.90 |
| 600 | 69.80 | 63.30 | 50.30 | 19.50 |
| 700 | 91.40 | 83.50 | 67.70 | 23.70 |
| 800 | 115.40 | 108.50 | 94.70 | 20.70 |
| 900 | 141.60 | 133.50 | 117.30 | 24.30 |
| 1,000 | 169.60 | 158.50 | 136.30 | 33.30 |
| 1,100 | 201.10 | 189.50 | 163.30 | 37.90 |
| 1,200 | 233.10 | 220.50 | 195.30 | 37.80 |
| 1,300 | 269.20 | 254.00 | 223.60 | 45.60 |
| 1,400 | 306.20 | 288.00 | 251.60 | 54.60 |
| 1,500 | 343.20 | 324.40 | 288.60 | 54.60 |
| 1,600 | 380.20 | 361.40 | 325.60 | 54.60 |
| 1,700 | 413.50 | 398.40 | 368.20 | 45.30 |

Star Graphic by Kent MacIntosh

# Paycheck grows, but it's spoken for

By DAVE ANDERSON
The Minneapolis Star

After Wednesday there will be a little something extra in your paycheck.

But before you begin feeling too prosperous because of the federal income tax cut, be careful. There are more than a few hooks already in that money.

In fact, for the next nine months it appears that most middle-class wage earners in Minnesota will be paying increased taxes.

What has happened is that Congress has cut each wage earner's taxes 5 percent and the IRS has sent your employer a new federal tax withholding schedule. On any paycheck issued after Sept. 30, regardless of the pay period covered, the employer is to deduct about 5 percent less for federal taxes. For instance, if you are paid $300 every two weeks, the federal government will take $2.30 less (from $37.20 to $34.90.)

The theory underlying the tax cut is that you will put at least some of it in a bank, where it can be loaned to others who will use it for purposes that will improve the American economy.

The 5 percent tax cut will last from Oct. 1 through June 30. During that period the single person earning $400 a week and claiming one deduction will take home an extra $179.40. But other government policies and taxes probably will take it all back, plus some.

## State income taxes

The same day that federal withholdings drop 5 percent, Minnesota tax withholding will rise from 1 to 3 percent, depending on your income.

That is because of a number of factors. For one thing, the Legislature rolled back a portion of the indexing it passed in 1980 to keep cost-of-living raises from pushing you into a higher tax bracket. It also lowered the amount you can deduct on your state tax return for medical expenses and gasoline taxes.

And because of the cut in the federal income taxes, which are deductible from state income taxes, you will be left with a higher taxable Minnesota income.

## Social Security

On Jan. 1 the amount of pay withheld for Social Security will rise from 6.65 percent of that portion of your income under $29,700 to 6.7 percent of an even larger amount of your income, probably about $33,000.

So for those earning over $635 a week both now and after the first of the year, Social Security withholding will rise from $1,975 a year to about $2,200 a year.

The ceiling is supposed to be raised proportionate to increases in


Paycheck
Turn to Page 4A

# More cuts

## *Reagan plan may break deals with Congress*

From The Minneapolis Star's News Services

WASHINGTON—In proposing additional "12 percent cuts" in all government programs other than defense and entitlements such as Social Security, President Reagan has broken most of the deals he made on Capitol Hill to win passage of his budget proposals last spring and summer. He also has asked for real cuts that will go much deeper than 12 percent for some big programs.

The White House said the reductions were necessary to help hold the deficit to $43.1 billion for the fiscal year that begins Thursday, Oct. 1—$600 million higher than Reagan had been aiming for.

Reagan pledged that the $13 billion in program reductions and the $3 billion in higher tax revenues for 1982 would help put the economy on a path toward a balanced budget in 1984. But meeting that target depends on further unspecified cuts of $34.7 billion in 1983 and 1984.

When the president spoke Thursday night of 12 percent reductions, he did not spell out that he meant 12 percent below his original budget-cutting proposals of March. Since then, the administration has accepted numerous changes in those proposals, including some that markedly increased spending for education, Amtrak and Conrail, public housing, low-income energy assistance, student loans, highways and others.

Those changes were made to win votes for the overall budget ceilings that Reagan sought. Reneging on them now would mean cutting Amtrak, for example, not by 12 percent but by 46 percent—


Budget
Turn to Page 5A


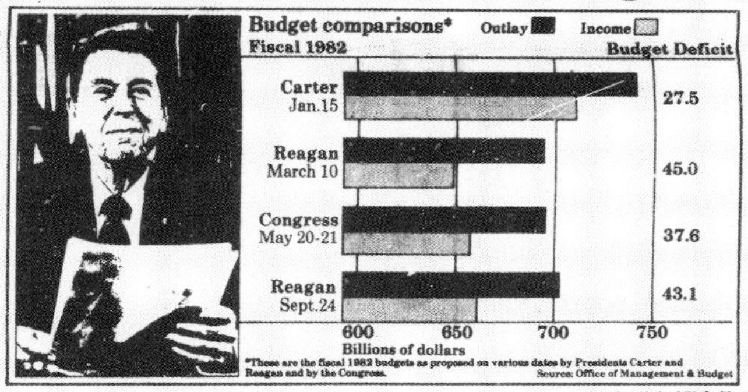


*These are the fiscal 1982 budgets as proposed on various dates by Presidents Carter and Reagan and by the Congress.

Source: Office of Management & Budget

Star Graphic by J.W. Smith

## *President modifies Social Security proposals, but warns of problems*

From The Minneapolis Star's News Services

WASHINGTON—With Congress doing it anyway, President Reagan is shelving his package of long-range Social Security cuts and urging restoration of the minimum benefit eliminated at his behest earlier this year.

Reagan told the nation Thursday night that he now favors mingling the system's three trust funds to keep the main retirement fund from running out of money by the end of next year, and "to give us time to seek a permanent solution."

At the same time, he challenged the Democratic majority in the House to join in a bipartisan effort to restore fiscal integrity to Social Security and remove it "once and for all from politics."

Reagan defended his May 12 proposal to eliminate the $122-a-month minimum benefit, slash early retirement, disability and other benefits and delay July's cost-of-living increase for three months. But he did not urge Congress to adopt any elements of that plan.

He said he never intended to take the minimum away "from those who truly need it," and asked Congress to restore it for "current beneficiaries with low incomes."

He did not elaborate, but a senior aide said the White House envisions an income ceiling of $7,500 a couple to qualify for the minimum benefit. That would cost the Treasury $300 million in 1982 and $500


Benefits
Turn to Page 4A


# Even at shelter, dogs end up in grisly battle

By PAUL McENROE
The Minneapolis Star

The irony overwhelms Virginia Payne. After all, the Humane Society of Ramsey County shelter is a place where animals are supposed to be safe.

But one of the 18 pit bull dogs picked up in May in the state's first raid on a dog-fight convention has died after a dog fight inside the society's kennels. The dogs were apparently released by intruders.

And Payne, the society executive director, says it could happen again as long as the society is required to hold the dogs as evidence for the criminal trials of the people arrested in the Stacy, Minn., raid.

Payne says the dogs are being held there because the dog-fighting law does not say what should be done with dogs taken in a raid.

"Here you have these dogs that fought in the pit arenas and were recovering from their wounds being put here for safekeeping until the trial, and they end up not really being safe at all—what with the break-ins going on here all the time," Payne said Thursday.

Joan Lisi, the shelter worker who discovered the grisly aftermath of the kennel dog fight, said "The dying one was lying there like a prizefighter who had lost—spent and knowing he was dying. The victor greeted me, tail wagging as he walked over the mess, as if to say, 'Hi Joan, look what


Dogs
Turn to Page 2A

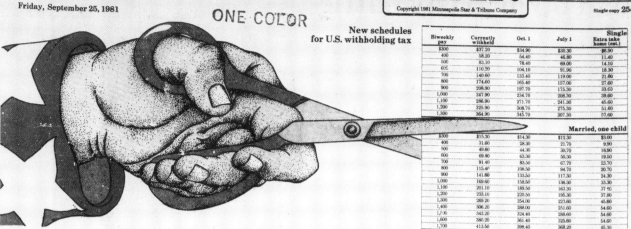

Star Photo by Duane Braley

One of the pit bulls held at the humane society

# Unwinding secrets of body time clocks

By GORDON SLOVUT
The Minneapolis Star

Your body may be harmed by a drug you take at 6 p.m., but helped by it if you take it at 6 a.m.

Sex hormones are at their highest levels in August and September, at their lowest in February.

Your blood pressure is lowest in the morning, so a doctor could miss a diagnosis of borderline high blood pressure if he or she never gets an afternoon reading.

These are some examples of the scores of rhythms and time clocks in the human body, some on hourly cycles, some daily, some monthly, some seasonal.

Because of these rhythms, there are predictable peaks and valleys of everything from the flow of hormones, blood pressure and body temperature to the susceptibility to infection; from nausea and mental ability to the possibility of rapes and other violent crimes occurring.

The study of those biological rhythms is called chronobiology, and the University of Minnesota's Chronobiology Laboratories—on the fifth floor of Lyons Laboratories on the Minneapolis campus—is one of the leading centers for the research in the field.

Scores of chronobiologists from around the world were in Minneapolis last weekfor the 15th international conference of the International Society for Chronobiology. The president is Dr. Franz Hallberg, who also is director of the


Rhythms
Turn to Page 2A

THE MINNEAPOLIS STAR

A Section, Part 1

Single copy 25¢



# A great cry in Egypt

## As nation mourns, Sadat's successor vows to carry on

From The Minneapolis Star's News Services

CAIRO—Vice President Hosni Mubarak declared a one-year state of emergency seven hours after President Anwar Sadat was mortally wounded by a squad of soldiers who sprayed gunfire and hurled grenades at a stand where Sadat, Mubarak and other leaders were reviewing a military parade commemorating the 1973 Arab-Israeli war.

"We will continue in the name of the spirit and soul of our leader and our constitution .... We will abide by all treaties and commitments made," Mubarak said in a broadcast to the shocked nation.

Mubarak, 53, was unhurt in the attack that reportedly killed five other Egyptians in addition to the 62-year-old president and wounded at least 29 men, including the chief of staff, four Americans, Belgian Ambassador Claude Ruelle, Japanese Ambassador Toshio Yamazaki and Irish Defense Minister James Tully.

There were unconfirmed reports that 10 other men on the reviewing stand were wounded.

Army sources said the six assassins who leaped from a truck in the military parade were Egyptian artillerymen, a lieutenant and five enlisted men, with Moslem fundamentalist leanings. The semi-official newspaper Al Ahram reported that police and troops killed one of the assassins and arrested four others, leaving one unaccounted for, but other papers published pictures of the bodies of two dead "traitors."

A state funeral was scheduled for Saturday.

Sadat will be entombed in a mausoleum to be built near the grandstand where he was slain, al-Ahram reported today.

The newspaper said that while driving to the parade grounds Tuesday, Sadat had told Mubarak and Defense Minister Abdel Halim Abu Ghazalla that a mosque and reception pavillion should be built near the grandstand.

Sadat's two partners in the Camp David peace accords, former President Jimmy Carter and Israeli Prime Minister Menachem Begin, announced that they would attend the funeral. U.S. officials in Washington said President Reagan was considering asking Carter and former Presidents Gerald Ford and Richard Nixon to represent the United States.

Sadat
Turn to Page 13A

## Questions of U.S. oil reliance rise again

By ANTHONY P. CARIDEO
The Minneapolis Star

Before the assassination of Anwar Sadat, the United States had three friends in the Middle East: Egypt, Saudi Arabia and Israel. Now it has two, and a big question mark.

A common reaction among diplomatic and world energy experts Tuesday in the wake of the Egyptian president's death was that once again the instability of the Middle East—a region that supplies the non-Communist world with 15 million barrels of oil a day—has been brought into focus. And, in Sadat, said a number of experts, the U.S. lost one of its best friends, an almost singular force in stabilizing a highly volatile region.

"There were two key leaders in the Middle East that we depended on, the shah [of Iran] and Sadat," said Daniel Yergin of the Harvard Business School, author of "Energy Future."

"Now we have neither Sadat nor the shah, and it really shows how fragile our system of oil supply really is.... Sadat's loss emphasizes how irresponsible the talk of an oil glut is. It doesn't immediately portend anything in the supply of oil—we have to wait and see—but it really suggests that we are living on borrowed time," Yergin said.

Egypt is not a significant supplier of oil. The country, which is not a member of the Organization of Petroleum Exporting Countries, produces only 500,000 barrels of oil a day. Of that amount, the U.S. buys about 31,000 barrels, a miniscule portion of its 5.6-million-barrel daily import total.

According to world oil expert Melvin Conant, president of Conant & Associates Ltd., Great Falls, Va., the possible repercussions of Sadat's death center more on Egypt's geographical role in the world oil picture.

"Because of the highly tempo-

Oil
Turn to Page 19A

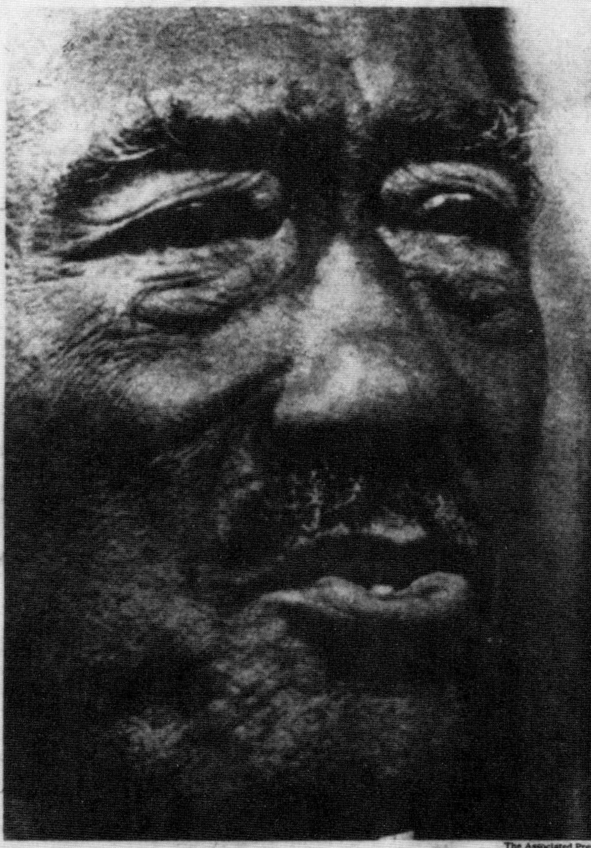

The Associated Press

Anwar Sadat's death leaves the future of peace in the Middle East in question

## Policies on Israel, U.S., appear safe

From The Minneapolis Star's News Services

CAIRO—President Anwar Sadat's twin policies of peace with Israel and close alliance with the United States appear safe in the hands of his protege and Egypt's new leader, Vice President Hosni Mubarak.

Mubarak appears certain to have the crucial help of the armed forces in carrying them on.

Officially nominated Tuesday for the presidency, Mubarak is a former air force commander Sadat personally chose as his successor. He vowed that he would carry on Sadat's policies at home and abroad.

According to the constitution, Sufi Abu Taleb, the speaker of Egypt's Parliament, will be acting president until elections are held within 60 days. But Mubarak, Sadat's right-hand man since the president's stunning trip to Jerusalem in 1977 to negotiate peace with Israel, is expected to be the dominant force in the interim government.

The official Middle East News Agency said the Politburo of the ruling National Democratic Party, formed by Sadat in 1978, met in emergency session hours after Sadat was assassinated Tuesday. They nominated Mubarak as the party's candidate for president in the election within 60 days, and he was expected to be unopposed.

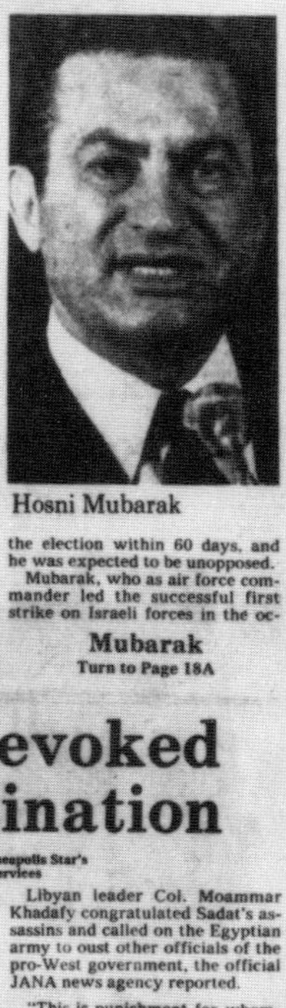

Hosni Mubarak

Mubarak, who as air force commander led the successful first strike on Israeli forces in the oc-

Mubarak
Turn to Page 18A

## Pain, joy evoked by assassination

From The Minneapolis Star's News Services

The assassination of Egyptian President Anwar Sadat plunged Israel into doubt and foreboding Tuesday night about the future of Middle East peace, while hardline Arab states rejoiced and Western leaders warned that the world "is a more dangerous place without him."

Israeli Prime Minister Menachem Begin, ashen-faced and his voice quavering with emotion, emerged Tuesday night from an emergency meeting of his senior Cabinet officials and said that he prayed that the first rapprochement with an Arab world power would not also die at the hands of "the enemies of peace."

Libyan leader Col. Moammar Khadafy congratulated Sadat's assassins and called on the Egyptian army to oust other officials of the pro-West government, the official JANA news agency reported.

"This is punishment for whomever betrays the Egyptian people," JANA quoted Khadafy as saying during a speech broadcast over Libyan television and radio.

Across a broad political spectrum, Israeli leaders expressed shock and outrage over Sadat's assassination, calling it an affront to the spirit of peace that marked

Reaction
Turn to Page 13A

## Sadat may have had inkling of plot

By MICHAEL GETLER
and SCOTT ARMSTRONG
The Washington Post

WASHINGTON—U.S. officials said Tuesday that Anwar Sadat may have had some very recent warning signs that an attempt on his life was being plotted and had reason to fear portions of his own military and assassination squads from Libya.

Nevertheless, a number of U.S. specialists, sifting through bits of information and claims of responsibility for the attack by an Egyptian exile group headquarted in Libya, said they had no hard evidence at the moment nor any conclusions about who killed Sadat and why.

The specialists, however, disclosed these points:

- During a crackdown in recent weeks by Sadat on many domestic foes, including Islamic fundamentalists and such fanatic Islamic revivalist groups as the Moslem Brotherhood, evidence of planning for a coup against the Egyptian president was uncovered. Among the plotters were some military people who had a connection to the Brotherhood.

While some members of the military have been members of fundamentalist groups for many years, sources said they had not been connected before to plots against the government. The information suggested that the Brotherhood and other extremist

Plot
Turn to Page 20A

**Inside:**



# Pupils shift to brown bags as school lunch cuts hit home

By CHRISTINE HUDGINS
The Minneapolis Star

It was like a revolution, with miniature rebels.

Aaron Schultz, 11, stood on a bench and proclaimed that kids should get free lunches. And his friends at Minneapolis' Anderson-A Elementary School raised their chicken patty sandwiches in salute.

Aaron's mother, Linda, agrees. Her family, like many others, is becoming intimately familiar with national school lunch budget cuts that were abstractions only months ago.

Lunch prices in some Twin Cities area school districts have increased as much as 50 percent this year.

For example, senior high school lunches this year cost $1.10 in the Anoka-Hennepin School District, up from 70 cents last year. In Minneapolis the increase is about 12 percent.

For the first time in years the number of students buying lunches has fallen—as much as 38 percent in some districts—and more are bringing their lunches, some filled with snacks and soda pop. Some high school students are splitting the cost of meals—and the meals themselves—with their friends. Others buy only a order of french fries, or don't eat at all.

Among the hardest hit, it seems, are families like Aaron's. Last year Linda Schultz, a housekeeper, qualified for free lunches for both her sons. But because maximum incomes to qualify for free and reduced-priced meals were lowered this year, each of her children now has to pay $2 a week for lunch. That new expense comes as she loses $200 a month because of federal welfare cutbacks.

"I don't think Reagan gives a damn about the poor people," Schultz said. "I work. But I don't have the education to make $15,000 or $20,000 a year. I don't know how I'll make it. I'll exist. That's what I'll do."

Federal budget cuts are coming home. The traditionally sacrosanct National School Lunch Program was cut along with many other social programs this year. In August federal subsidies for many districts

Lunches
Turn to Page 8A

### ☆ News Inside

**Reagan's grip on House falters**

Page 3A

**Acid rain claims draw U.S. attack**

Page 3A

**37 illegal aliens arrested in state**

Page 21A

Index



### ☆ Local Pulse

**Elm program cuts decried by expert**

Proposed Minneapolis Park Board budget cuts for diseased elm tree removal could be disastrous, a national expert says. The number of disease-carrying beetles increased sevenfold in 1980.

Page 11A

### ☆ Variety

**Updike suspects we're all uptight**

Author John Updike says his latest book is an attempt to find out where America and anxious Americans are now. But he's unsure whether he is famous, despite his outpouring of acclaimed works.

Page 1B

### ☆ Sports

**Astros' Ashby is an unlikely hero**

Houston catcher Alan Ashby agreed after his two-run ninth-inning home run gave the Astros a 3-1 victory over Los Angeles that he was hardly the person one would expect to do such a thing.

Page 8B

### ☆ Marketplace

**BN hurts service, jobs, union says**

A rally of union leaders renewed charges that Burlington Northern Inc. is switching its efforts to making more money on non-railroad operations at the expense of Midwest rail service.

Page 1C

THE MINNEAPOLIS STAR
A Section, Part 1
Single copy 25¢

## The Crash of Flight 90

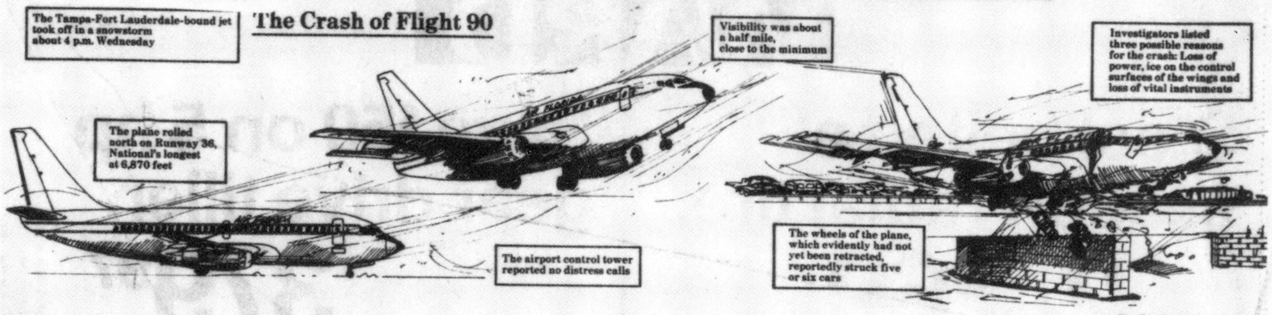
The Tampa-Fort Lauderdale-bound jet took off in a snowstorm about 4 p.m. Wednesday
The plane rolled north on Runway 36, National's longest at 6,870 feet
Visibility was about a half mile, close to the minimum
The airport control tower reported no distress calls
The wheels of the plane, which evidently had not yet been retracted, reportedly struck five or six cars
Investigators listed three possible reasons for the crash: Loss of power, ice on the control surfaces of the wings and loss of vital instruments
Star Graphic by Kent MacIntosh

# Survivor knew plane was in trouble

## *Icy water revived him after crash*

From The Minneapolis Star's News Services

WASHINGTON—Joseph Stiley turned to his secretary in the seat beside him as the Air Florida plane reached the top of its arc and started falling.

"We're not going to make it," he told her. "We're going in."

Stiley said he knew that the Boeing 737 bound from Washington National Airport to Tampa and Fort Lauderdale, Fla., was in trouble even before the plane got into the air.

"I figured I had taken one airplane ride too many," he said. "I had a pretty good indication things weren't going right when we started down the runway. I think it might have been just a little bit heavy from the ice."

Stiley, 42, of Alexandria, Va., and his secretary, Patricia "Nicki" Felch of Herndon, Va., were two of the five persons who survived Wednesday afternoon's crash of Air Florida Flight 90. Seventy-four of the 79 people on the plane were killed, many still strapped in their seats as the plane sank in the Potomac River after striking the 14th Street Bridge.

District of Columbia police said two other people were killed when the plane broadsided cars as they inched across the bridge laden with rush-hour traffic.

Stiley was hospitalized with two broken legs at National Hospital for Orthopaedics and Rehabilitation in Arlington, Va. He also was suffering from hypother-

Crash
Turn to Page 11A

## *Passenger aided others—then died*

From The Minneapolis Star's News Services

WASHINGTON—For rescue workers, it was a race to save lives in bone-chilling cold.

The heroes were many, and will be thanked later. But one, who remained unidentified today, gave his life to help his fellow passengers who were aboard Air Florida Flight 90.

The passenger, hurled into the freezing waters of the Potomac River when the airliner crashed Wednesday afternoon, passed up repeated opportunities to be saved, choosing instead to help others.

Another hero was 28-year-old Lennie Skutnik, who was driving home from work at the Congressional Budget Office. Skutnik got out of his car, jerked off his boots and coat, dived into the Potomac and dramatically rescued a woman when she lost her grip on a life preserver tied to a rope dangling from the rescue helicopter.

Also heroes were helicopter pilot Donald Usher and paramedic Gene Windsor, who rescued others who survived the crash of the jetliner that killed 74 of the 79 people aboard.

Usher and Windsor flew to the crash site from the Anacostia Naval Annex in their seven-seat Bell Jet Ranger helicopter, designated Eagle One by the Park Po-

Rescue
Turn to Page 6A

The Associated Press

Passenger clung to safety ring while being pulled from Potomac

# Half of pupils may switch schools

By NANCY PAULU
The Minneapolis Star

Take one last look at the Minneapolis public school district. It won't be the same when schools reopen next fall.

If the school board goes along with recommendations made Wednesday night school administrators, 18 schools—about one in four—will be closed. Among those scheduled for extinction are three senior high schools: West, Marshall-University and Central.

From there the ripples will spread. About half the city's 39,000 students probably will go to different schools. Every school attendance boundary could change; many will reach into new and different neighborhoods.

When the children get to school, they'll find about half the buildings housing different academic programs—better ones, school officials say. Many will accommodate children of different ages than they do now.

More students will be bused than ever before—24,000, up 6,000 from this year. There will be more "magnet schools," which offer enhanced academic programs to draw white students voluntarily into inner-city schools. The magnet schools will focus on science, vocational classes and the visual and performing arts.

In short, assuming these administrative proposals are accepted by the Minneapolis school board, the impact will be quick and dramatic.

But nothing less will patch up a weakened school district, officials told about 500 students, parents and staff members who gathered in the Minneapolis Auditorium Wednesday night to hear the plans.

The school closings, to be voted on Feb. 23, are expected to save the district $5.5 million a year, they say, and to improve the district's academic quality. The other major reason for the proposed closings is steadily declining enrollment.

Most of those suggested for closing have three common elements:

- They cost too much to operate. Many are expected to need major rehabilitation soon.
- They cannot accommodate the academic programs well.
- They had to be closed to help

Schools
Turn to Page 4A

# Resigned to change, students wonder how they'll fit in

By SHERI VENEMA and ELLEN FOLEY
The Minneapolis Star

Nathan Teske was elected captain of next year's soccer team at Marshall-University High School. But he's afraid that next year, at the next school he attends, he may not even make the team.

Perry Smith, a junior at West High School, says he's so worried about his future that he may cross the suburban boundary and pay tuition at the high school in St. Louis Park. He doesn't want to spend his senior year in a rival Minneapolis school, scorned as one of the outcasts from West.

And Claudia Backstrom, a senior at Marshall-U, isn't looking forward to being an alumnus of a school that no longer exists. Normally, she says, after you graduate, "you can come back and see your teachers and friends, and see your teams play. I'll come back, and there will be nobody here."

But Backstrom, who works on the school's yearbook, says the attitude of the yearbook staff is, "It'll be our last one, so we'll make it a good one."

And so it is with a mixture of resentment, apprehension and nostalgia that students at the three Minneapolis high schools destined for closing—Marshall-University, West and Central—are greeting the news.

Not that it surprised them. Rumors have circulated at all of them for weeks. And most seemed resigned to the news. Said Backstrom: "It seems like it's hopeless now."

But that doesn't mean they like it.

Going to another school "would be kind of depressing," said Teske, a junior who also writes for the school paper. "Most of my loyalty is here. I feel like I should be grad-

Reaction
Turn to Page 10A

Star Photo by Steve Schluter

Marshall-U's Stephanie Davis fears loss of status

Star Photo by Marlin Levison

Sigurd Olson: soul of the conservation movement

# Silence of the forest pays tribute to Olson

Jim Klobuchar
Columnist

A few hours before he died, Sigurd Olson teased a friend whose sociable chatter on the telephone was keeping him indoors.

"I want to get out in the snow on these new snowshoes the kids got for me," he said. "Elizabeth [his wife of 60 years] is all bundled up ready to go."

The old man and his lady strolled the evergreen forest behind their home in Ely, romping and trudging in the snow as they had hundreds of times, feeling the sting of the northern winter but clothed in the easy intimacy of one more day in the woods together.

Not far from his house Sig Olson, 82, collapsed of a heart attack. He died shortly afterward in a hospital in Ely. Funeral arrangements are pending at Kerntz Funeral Home in Ely.

The silence of the forest was a requiem for a man who for more than half a century poured his eloquence, nerve and endurance into the struggle to preserve the earth's dwindling wilderness.

He was the flint and the soul of the conservation movement in America, both warrior and missionary. He was revered by millions who read his works and were lifted by the sensations they evoked of humanity united with the earth and nur-

Olson
Turn to Page 15A

## ☆ News Inside

### FDR recorded talks in office

A secret microphone captured discussions in Franklin D. Roosevelt's office at the White House for 11 weeks in 1940. The Oval Office bugging was disclosed by American Heritage magazine.

Page 25A

### Drunken driving may get riskier

The Minnesota Legislature appears to be ready this session to pass tougher laws to combat drunken driving, probably by providing for canceling the driver's licenses of offenders.

Page 3C

### Thatcher's son reportedly OK

Page 22A

### Index

## ☆ Variety

### Plimpton lives out fantasies

Daring deeds gave George Plimpton his start 35 years ago. Since then, the writer-actor-athlete has lived almost everyone's fantasies, but not all of his own.

Page 1B

## ☆ Marketplace

### Check-writing checkers busy

A company that verifies checks for businesses by telephone received one-third more calls this Christmas season than last, but the rush started later than usual.

Page 1C

## ☆ Sports

### Sonmor steps down—for now

Having tried everything else to end the North Stars' lengthening slump, Coach Glen Sonmor stepped down temporarily after Wednesday night's 2-0 loss to the New York Rangers.

Page 8B

Minneapolis Tr

# Saturday

April 3 / 1982
5 Sections
25¢ Single copy
Volume V
Number 32
1A
Final



# Argentina seizes islands from Britain

Associated Press

**Buenos Aires, Argentina**
Several thousand Argentine troops led by marines seized the Falkland Islands from Britain on Friday.

The Argentine government claimed the islands' governor surrendered unconditionally.

"The Argentine flag flies again in the Malvinas. Mission accomplished," the communique said, using the Argentine term for the island group. Jubilant Argentines cheered, waved flags and sounded sirens.

The military reported one dead and two wounded among its assault forces; there were no official reports of British casualties. Unconfirmed reports in Buenos Aires, however, said there were "lots of casualties," without specifying whether dead or wounded, or on which side.

Britain said it was sending warships to the scene and a task force was being assembled to recapture the archipelago, 250 miles off the Argentine coast.

Britain condemned the takeover, broke diplomatic relations and demanded the invaders withdraw from the islands, which Britain has ruled for 149 years. Prime Minister Margaret Thatcher convened an emergency Cabinet meeting in London.

The attack was the first time in more than 100 years that Argentina has been involved in a conflict outside its borders.

Uruguayan Interior Minister Gen. Yamandu Trinidad said the captured British governor and marines were taken to Montevideo, the Uruguayan capital, to be turned over to the British ambassador there. He said their stay in Uruguay would be brief.

Some reports said the fighting lasted

Falklands continued on page 6A

# Tornadoes kill at least 22

Associated Press

Dozens of tornadoes spawned by an enormous low pressure zone marched through the Midwest and South Friday, killing at least 22 people and injuring hundreds.

The National Weather Service said three dozen twisters touched down in states from the Mississippi Valley to the Great Plains, with deaths in Texas, Missouri and Arkansas.

The wave of tornadoes, and accompanying thunderstorms that triggered flood warnings, were blamed on an intense low pressure zone centered far to the north over Minnesota.

"It's a near record low pressure system," said Dennis Slaughter, a weather service forecaster in Kansas City. "It's as low a pressure as you would ever want to see. It draws the warm air (from the south) and the cold air (from the north) into a collision to spawn [illegible]e tornadoes."

Thunderstorms continued and tornado watches were in effect last night over parts of Texas, Louisiana, Mississippi, Arkansas, Tennessee, Illinois, Missouri, Kentucky and Indiana.

Thirteen people died in tornadoes that swept across Arkansas, includ-

Storms continued on page 7A

# After 61 years, The Star is gone

By Jacqui Banaszynski
Staff Writer

The Minneapolis Star died Friday at 61.

It was a victim of the times, of a sharply declining circulation and of the irony that it was trying to be the newspaper of tomorrow with yesterday's news.

Many of its features and staff writers will be carried in the merged Star and Tribune, which will have morning and afternoon editions, but that didn't lessen the grief for many Star employees yesterday.

"It sure was fun while it lasted," said Star reporter John Oslund. "It was more fun than any other newspaper on earth because nothing was off-limits. I've always considered being a reporter for The Star a lot better than working for a living."

■

The newspaper appeared on the city's doorsteps and newsstands a final time yesterday. The bright yellow logo of years past was emblazoned on the paper's nameplate, a reminder of the days when The Star was the largest-circulation paper in the Twin Cities and the journalistic flagship of the Minneapolis Star & Tribune Company.

"This is it — the final edition," read the paper's main headline, bannered under an illustration of the Star logo sinking behind the Minneapolis skyline. A smaller headline over a column by Jim Klobuchar read: "For those of you who loved us, thank you for years of loyalty."

For many, even the most loyal readers, The Star's passing will not signal a dramatic change today, or next week, or next month. The nameplate on the merged newspaper will be familiar, if more crowded, as the Star logo bumps heads with that of its morning counterpart, the Minneapolis Tribune.

The bylines will be familiar, too, as former journalistic rivals join forces to write for the Minneapolis Star and Tribune, which will begin publication Monday.

But for those reporters and editors who created The Star each day, the change was irrevocable.

"You've just got to reconcile yourself to the fact that things are never going to be the same," said Chris Beringer, 28, the former editor of The Star's Variety and Weekend sections who will be a newsroom supervisor with the merged newspaper. "It's like any other adjustment in life."

Star continued on page 6A

Staff Photo by Art Hager

**Staff members of The Minneapolis Star gathered in the newsroom Friday for some sparkling grape juice to mark the last day of the newspaper's independent publication. From left were Sue Loth (with visor), Robert Ostmann (behind Loth), Diane Osby, Carol Byrne, Editor Steve Isaacs, Zeke Wigglesworth and Steven Poulter (behind Wigglesworth).**

# Nordlund was legally drunk in crash

By Paul Klauda
Staff Writer

Former Minneapolis Police Chief Elmer Nordlund was legally drunk when he crashed into a light post and died in an automobile accident early Thursday, a spokesman for the Hennepin County medical examiner's office said Friday.

Nordlund, 64, captain of the department's Second Precinct, died of abdominal injuries suffered when the impact of the crash apparently threw him into the steering wheel of his mobile home van, the medical examiner's office said. The accident happened about 12:30 a.m. on 3rd Av. S. near 1st St., police said.

The spokesman, who would not identify himself, said Nordlund's exact blood-alcohol level at the time of his death is not public information. But he conceded that it was above .10 percent, the legal limit for drunken

Nordlund continued on page 7A

Charles Lichenstein

# U.S. vetoes U.N. move on Nicaragua

Associated Press

**United Nations, N.Y.**
The United States vetoed a Security Council resolution Friday night calling for nonintervention in Nicaragua.

The United States also vetoed a Jordanian resolution in the council that would have called on Israel to rescind its dismissal of two Arab mayors and a municipal council in the occupied West Bank. U.S. Ambassador Charles Lichenstein said he voted "no" because the resolution "did not, would not, promote the cause of peace" in the Mideast.

In the first action, Lichenstein cast the sole vote against a watered-down resolution instructing all states to "refrain from the direct, indirect, overt or covert use of force against any country of Central America and the Caribbean."

Nicaraguan Foreign Minister Miguel D'Escoto said despite the veto, Nicaragua maintained its "readiness to embark as soon as possible on a fruitful dialogue with the United States."

D'Escoto suggested high-level talks between Managua and Washington could begin in mid-April after his return from a meeting of nonaligned nations in Kuwait.

Lichenstein said "the door to negotiations and conciliation — bilateral, regional, and multilateral — is now open and has always been open."

The absence of Ambassador Jeane Kirkpatrick for the vote underscored U.S. disapproval of U.N. involvement in hemispheric affairs. Lichenstein is her deputy.

Kirkpatrick earlier had complained that the resolution undermined the mediation role of the Organization of American States and "mocks the search for peace."

The final draft of the resolution had

Vetoes continued on page 6A

# Minnesota's tax collections exceed expectations

By Jim Ragsdale
Staff Writer

Minnesota collected almost $37 million more in taxes than expected in March, giving officials hope that the state's budget is at last holding up.

The state took in $336.2 million in March against an estimate of $299.3 million in its major tax categories. The greatest increases came in the corporate income and sales tax categories, according to Revenue Commissioner Clyde Allen.

State officials, who have had to lower their expectations for tax collections three times in the last year because of a weakening state economy, said the latest tax estimate appears to be accurate.

"It's a good indication that the economy is doing as badly as we expected it to," said state economist Hal Lofgreen.

Allen said, "The estimate looks very good."

The state budget is based on estimates of what Minnesota will collect in its various tax categories during the 1981-83 budget period. Each time these estimates have been lowered, the Legislature and Gov. Al Quie have had to raise taxes and cut spending to bring the budget back into balance.

On March 9 Lofgreen lowered the previous tax estimate for the biennium by $228 million because of gloomier predictions about the performance of the national economy. Ten days later the Legislature raised taxes, cut spending and delayed some payments.

The March tax-collection figures are the first test of the new, lower estimates.

The breakdown by tax categories is:

■ Corporate income tax. The state collected $79.6 million, $12.1 million more than Lofgreen predicted. These payments are based on esti-

Taxes continued on page 11A

# Steve Berg / Spring doesn't make things okey-dokey in D.C.

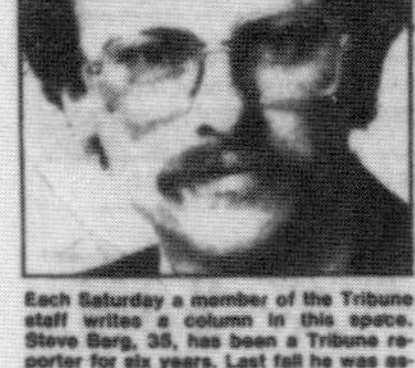

Each Saturday a member of the Tribune staff writes a column in this space. Steve Berg, 35, has been a Tribune reporter for six years. Last fall he was assigned to the newspaper's Washington Bureau, where he writes about politics and national affairs. He, his wife and son live in Chevy Chase, Md.

**Washington, D.C.**
It's about this time of year that the hotshot columnists around Washington feel obliged to pause from heavier matters and write about the splendors of spring in Washington.

One guy from the New York Times is sure to toss out a few lines on cherry blossoms and azaleas, sending a snotty signal to those who live in places where the ice has yet to recede from Lake Calhoun.

Another guy from the Washington Post has already done his obligatory piece on the beloved Chicago Cubs.

Others will be tempted to tap out day-dreamy tales about the sacred rite of baseball and how they are planning clandestine trips to Baltimore or Philadelphia for a glorious afternoon of sunshine, flat beer and bad hot dogs.

But for all the joy that spring should bring to this place, you'd never know it.

Even now, with dozens of vendors selling bouquets of fresh daffodils on the streets, Washingtonians remain a most serious bunch.

This is the city of the furrowed brow.

Spring seemed a bigger occasion back in Minneapolis, when it finally arrived. You could see it in the jauntier movements of those strolling down Nicollet Mall, their eyes glazed over, chocolate ice cream dripping from the corners of their mouths. This was it!

In Washington, the robots of bureaucracy still enter the subway train the same way each morning despite their deliverance from winter, their mouths safely wiped free of toast crumbs, their faces immediately hidden behind the morning papers. Some of them are very young men, 21, maybe 22, dressed in the formal dark business suits designed for men much older.

For them, life is extremely serious. Many of them have been up for hours reading the papers and, once on the train, immerse themselves in government manuals . . . "Uploading efficiencies and response mechanisms to maintain high quality of services delivery standards is desirable in terms of meat."

I am not above reading over peoples' shoulders on crowded trains. It's easy in Washington. This is the only town in which commuters underline key passages with yellow felt-tipped pens.

Washington is a traditionally fashionable city where preppy was never really out. It leads the nation in the wearing of the Burberry raincoat.

Professional women, however, are in the midst of a grave campaign against shoe fashion. They have not given up the designer eye glasses, the Evan Picone business suits, the smart leather briefcases or the nylon stockings. But they have taken to bottoming out their ensembles with, ugh, sneakers.

As one women explained to me the other day, "We carry our high heels

Berg continued on page 11A

## Almanac

**Saturday, April 3, 1982**
**93rd day; 272 to go this year**
**Sunrise: 5:51. Sunset: 6:43**

### Today's weather

**Icky**

High winds, light snow and falling temperatures are predicted today for the Twin Cities. The low tonight will be 5 to 10 above.



Tribune telephones
372-4141 News General
372-4242 Classified
372-4343 Circulation

Minneapolis Tribune

Sunday
April 4, 1982
1A Final
Volume CXV
Number 270
90¢ Single Copy
$1 in coin-operated racks


# British dispatch armada, freeze Argentine assets

Tribune News Services

Britain's Prime Minister Margaret Thatcher said Saturday the Falkland Islands "remain British territory" and ordered a large naval task force to the South Atlantic.

In addition, she said that Argentina's financial assets in Britain would be frozen and other economic sanctions would be imposed.

The armada will sail today, Thatcher said. Prince Andrew, 22, a helicopter pilot, will be aboard a carrier leading the 40-ship fleet, which represents about two-thirds of Britain's naval strength. The 8,000-mile voyage is expected to take more than two weeks.

In Buenos Aires, Argentine President Gen. Leopoldo Galtieri declared early today that his nation was prepared to fight to defend the islands.

"If the Argentine people is attacked by military forces — be they land, naval or air forces, the Argentine nation in arms will present battle with all the means at its disposal," he was quoted by the official Argentine news agency Telam as saying.

Yesterday Defense Minister Amadeo Frugoli had said that "Argentina will not retreat from its position as regards the steps already taken." He added that the rights and property of about 1,800 British sheepherders on the South Atlantic archipelago "will be respected."

At the United Nations, the Security Council voted 10-1 for a British-sponsored resolution calling for Argentina's immediate withdrawal from the territory. The United States was among those voting in favor of the resolution. Panama was the lone dissenter. There were four abstentions.

Argentina's Foreign Minister Nicanor Costa Mendez said the vote showed support for an obsolete colonial situation.

In London, Thatcher was speaking during the first weekend session of Parliament since the Suez crisis of 1956. She declared:

"The Falkland Islands and their dependencies remain British territory; no aggression and no invasion can alter that simple fact. It is the government's object to see the islands are free from occupation."

Despite Thatcher's actions, politicians of both parties called during the tumultuous three-hour session yesterday for the resignations of key ministers.

The prime minister, who canceled her weekend engagements to remain at 10 Downing St., refused to say what action would be taken when the convoy reaches the Falklands.

"I stress I cannot foretell what orders the task force will receive as they proceed," said Thatcher. "That will depend on the situation at the time."

Defense Secretary John Nott said the task force would be led by the 19,500-ton aircraft carrier Invincible. The force will include a second carrier, destroyers, frigates, landing ships, 1,000 marine commandos and a substantial number of other troops, military officials said.

The government has refused to provide military details, but the ships are expected to rendezvous at the mid-Atlantic island of Ascension, which is being restocked with ammunition, fuel and supplies by Royal Air

Falklands continued on page 5A

Staff Photo by Neil McGahee

Twins President Calvin Griffith watched from his private box Saturday night as his team won the first game played in the Hubert H. Humphrey Metrodome. (More reports, pictures in the sports section.)

Staff Photo by Darlene Pfister

Outside, of course, it was wintry in Minnesota yesterday. Cully Anderson bought his Twins tickets and then waited for friends near the Metrodome.

# Domewatching overshadowed baseball for many of the fans

By Nick Coleman
Staff Writer

It was the biggest display of unabashed rubber-necking hereabouts since the mighty Foshay tower sprang from the prairie a half-century ago.

The Hubert Humphrey Metrodome — praised, cursed and fought over for five years — was finally opened to the people in whose name it was built. First a hole in the ground, then a steel and concrete skeleton and finally a brooding presence that had been a mystery for so long, the dome now belonged to the public (or 25,292 paying members of the public, anyway) to roam and enjoy.

Almost as awesome as the stadium itself was the surprising performance of the Minnesota Twins, who pasted the Philadelphia Phillies 5 to 0. Ironically, the Twins were led by hometown boy Kent Hrbek, who grew up in the shadow of the old Met Stadium in Bloomington. The rookie first baseman's two home runs seemed to answer everybody's question as to whether the ball will travel well in the dome and raised hopes for the low-rated Twins.

The first fans to see the inside of what the scoreboard proclaimed as "the Fabulous Metrodome" were, on the whole, won over by it. Many reserved judgment on how well they will enjoy indoor baseball, but most were awed by the size and sheer accomplishment of the building they

Scene continued on page 9A

# Light snow and high winds drive robins back

By Elena O. de la Rosa
Staff Writer

Winter weather made a brief return to Minnesota Saturday, bringing light snow, near-record low pressure and high winds.

No major injuries were reported, but the State Patrol recommended no travel through most of yesterday, as winds of up to 70 m.p.h. caused drifting snow and poor visibility.

"If we could close any highway, we'd close Hwy. 52, but we can't keep the barricades up," said Barb Reiland, dispatcher for the State Patrol office in Rochester, where winds were recorded at between 65 and 70 m.p.h.

Ron Weltzin, dispatcher for the Rochester police, said, "It has been one continual blow here for the last two or three days." He reported that the winds caused minor damage, confined mostly to blown-over stop signs and toppled utility sheds.

"I guess we kind of lucked out," Weltzin said.

Ernie Pelto, meteorologist with the National Weather Service at the Minneapolis-St. Paul International Airport, said the entire area was lucky.

"This low-pressure system was identified by our severe storm center in Kansas as capable of producing many tornadoes," he said.

The low pressure that moved through the state Friday evening was part of the same system that caused at least 79 tornadoes, 31 deaths and hundreds of injuries in a triangle stretching from Texas to Ohio to Georgia.

Minnesota escaped anything that severe, but the pressure level of the storm was unusual. The pressure in Minneapolis fell to within two-tenths of an inch of the previous record, set in January 1975. At midnight Friday the weather service at the airport recorded 28.62 inches of mercury.

Pelto said that very little snow fell over the state, but that high winds made recording the amounts difficult. Snow depth reports ranged from half an inch at the airport to 10 inches reported in Virginia, Minn.

Travel advisories were lifted at 4 p.m. yesterday for all but the northeastern part of Minnesota.

The weather service at the airport reported that the cumulative snowfall for the season reached 90.7 inch-

Weather continued on page 6A

Gallup Poll

# Many believe U.S.S.R. has superiority

By George Gallup
Director, American Institute of Public Opinion

Princeton, N.J.
Whether or not President Reagan was correct in his assertion Wednesday that the Soviet Union had achieved military superiority over the United States, a Gallup Poll indicates that that perception is shared by a plurality of the American people.

Asked which nation is stronger in terms of military power, 43 percent in the latest Gallup survey named the Soviet Union; 22 percent said the United States. The remaining 35 percent thought the two nations were about equal (28 percent) or were uncommitted (7 percent).

At the same time, however, the weight of public opinion has clearly swung to the view that the money budgeted by Washington for defense and military purposes is "too much" or "about the right amount," rather than "too little.". A year ago, at the

Gallup Poll continued on page 5A

# Treatment gone wrong costs man his leg

By Margaret Zack
Staff Writer

Last August, Byron Mallin, an 82-year-old heart patient, was supposed to be going home from the hospital in a few days.

But a heat treatment he received in those final days at Metropolitan Medical Center apparently went terribly wrong, and he did not go home. Now Mallin and his wife contend that the effects of that treatment will keep him in a nursing home the rest of his life.

On Tuesday his left leg is to be removed to stop an infection that began after the treatment burned part of his leg to the bone.

A Hennepin County District Court jury awarded Mallin $150,875 last month for his injuries, and his wife received $50,000 for loss of consortium.

Mallin went into the hospital on June 10, 1981, for heart problems, which had hospitalized him in the past.

He received the heat treatment on Aug. 3. Meanwhile, his wife, Marcella, was meeting with hospital staff members to learn how she would care for him at home.

"I was so anxious to get him home," she said during an interview last week at the couple's home at 5131 Portland Av. S.

When she went to her husband's room after her meeting she was told he was still in therapy. Knowing he would be tired when he returned to the room, she left.

"I went home that same night and emptied out the bedroom to make room for special equipment he'd need," she said. "The next day about 10:30 or 11 I went to the hospital. I shaved Mr. Mallin, combed his hair and fussed over him."

The blanket covering his legs fell off. She went to replace it and saw a large burn covered with plastic on his left knee.

"I think I was speechless. I called his nurse and asked what had happened to Mr. Mallin," she said.

"I can't say I feel bitter about the hospital. I am angry because I wasn't told when it happened, and for the fact that I spent the whole night here (at home) and I was in the hospital when it happened.

"I never did have anyone tell me how it happened."

Her attorney, Alan Nettles, said what did happen to Byron Mallin remains

Mallin continued on page 8A

## Almanac

Sunday, April 4, 1982
94th day; 271 to go this year
Sunrise: 5:49. Sunset: 6:44

Today **January?**

A high of 15 to 22 is forecast for the Twin Cities today.

**Weatherfact — or fiction?**

**Snow in April is manure.**

True, actually and poetically. While a city dweller may call the snow such after being sick of seeing it all winter, to the farmer snow in April is moisture that soak into the thawed soil, increasing his yield.

Bruce Watson, consulting meteorologist

Beaupre blanks Blues 6-0; Stars lead series / 1D
Reagan departs on first leg of China trip / 17A
Twins fall to Reggie Jackson and the Angels / 1D

It's kite-flying time / 1C

Minneapolis STAR and Tribune

1A Metro

Thursday
April 19, 1984
5 Sections
25c Single copy
Section A / Part I

NW1
Volume III / Number 13/ 9



# Committee agrees on bill to cut taxes

By Betty Wilson
Staff Writer

A conference committee agreed Wednesday night on a $359 million tax-cut bill that would give Minnesotans their first tax cut in four years.

The bill would repeal the 10 percent surtax on income taxes retroactive to Jan. 1, and give tax relief to farmers, homeowners and businesses — all financed by a state surplus projected at $900 million, the largest in recent memory.

The measure now goes to the floors of the House and Senate, which are expected to approve it today and send it to Gov. Rudy Perpich to be signed into law.

"This has been one of the most pleasant and easiest tax conference committees we have had for a few years, being able to provide tax relief for Minnesotans which they so much deserve," said Senate Tax Committee Chairman, Douglas Johnson, DFL-Cook.

The bill also provides for a three-months' tax "amnesty" period, when delinquent taxpayers could pay up and be forgiven 20 percent of the penalties on their back taxes, up to $2,000.

The amnesty plan, expected to bring in $5 million in delinquent taxes, also would deny licenses to businesses that owe the state more than $1,000 in sales taxes or withheld income taxes.

The bill also would increase the state budget reserve by $250 million, to $375 million, and would provide an additional $114 million in tax relief in the 1986-87 biennium.

The bill, reached in five days of mostly private negotiations, is a compromise between House and Senate approaches that differed on the amnesty provisions and other features, but had unanimous support of their respective chambers.

Among the provisions added in conference committee was one that would have the state take over the regulation of bingo and other gambling now under local control. The 6 percent tax on gross profits would be replaced by a 10 percent state tax on the net profits (after prizes), which would bring in $5.6 million a year. A 13-member board would administer the operations, with revenues going to arts programs and a new high school emphasizing the arts.

One of the largest business tax breaks in the bill is a $22 million, three-year, tax-cut package for the taconite industry in northeastern Minnesota. That would cost the state general revenue fund $12.5 million in the next biennium.

Johnson said taconite companies have agreed to drop court suits challenging taconite tax laws. He called the plan "very important for people of the Iron Range" and said it would

Taxes continued on page 9A

Staff Photo by Bruce Bisping

Rep. James Rice, DFL-Minneapolis, spoke against the lottery bill Wednesday afternoon in the House.

# Lottery's chances this year grow dim

By Robert Whereatt
Staff Writer

An unusual alliance of Independent-Republicans and liberal DFLers joined forces in the Minnesota House Wednesday to virtually kill the state lottery bill.

Chief sponsor Tom Osthoff, DFL-St. Paul, said he planned no heroics to breathe new life into the bill in the final hours of the session.

"The author is convinced he has run out of time," Osthoff said. "It's disappointing. I knew that coalition was there from the beginning."

Gov. Rudy Perpich, an active lobbyist for the lottery, said he has given up on the idea of getting the proposed constitutional amendment before Minnesota voters this fall.

"We tried," he said. "We lost. We go on to something else. It'll be on the ballot in '86."

Sixty-eight House members, the barest majority for this type of vote, supported sending the amendment to committee — a move Osthoff said effectively concludes debate on the issue this session.

"I don't expect to do anything (more) unless the Senate does something," he said. "I would guess this vote would discourage the Senate."

The Senate sponsor, DFLer Clarence Purfeerst of Faribault, was not willing to concede defeat. "The session hasn't stopped yet," he said.

But while it is not impossible for the

Lottery continued on page 8A

- A school aids bill approved by a conference committee will trim slightly the local property tax requirement. Page 1B.
- A bill approved by the Senate would allow many bars to stay open until 3 a.m. Page 1B.
- The unemployment compensation debt bill has been sent to a conference committee. Page 6B.
- A $179 million bonding and appropriations bill has been sent to the governor for his signature. Page 6B.

# Libyans let 25 leave embassy in Tripoli

By R.W. Apple Jr.
New York Times

London, England
Troops and demonstrators ringing the British Embassy in Tripoli held 25 people captive for most of Wednesday, but allowed the group to go home early yesterday evening, the Foreign Office announced. It said it welcomed the move.

In London, police still held the Libyan Embassy under siege early today, nearly two days after the fatal shooting of a British policewoman. Intensive negotiations with the occupants of the building produced only slight signs of progress.

Under the terms of the end of the siege at the British Embassy in Tripoli, the Libyan capital, members of the group, including women and children, were allowed to go home and to move freely within the city, the Foreign Office said.

Earlier, Ambassador Oliver Miles was allowed to leave the embassy briefly, surrounded by more than 60 uniformed policemen, to visit his wife and the Libyan Foreign Ministry.

British police surrounded the Libyan Embassy Tuesday morning in London after policewoman Yvonne Fletcher, 25, was killed and Libyan dissidents were wounded by gunfire that police said came from the embassy. The shooting occurred as protesters demonstrated against the Libyan government.

Libyan troops and demonstrators surrounded the embassy in Tripoli Tuesday in what British officials said was an apparent response to events in London.

British officials said three unidentified Britons had been arrested in Libya, apparently in retaliation for the detention Tuesday of three Libyans at Heathrow Airport. The Libyans were freed yesterday. One of the Britons was believed to be an employee of British Caledonian Airways, which flies regularly between London and Tripoli.

The government of Prime Minister Margaret Thatcher, who is in Portugal on an official visit, appeared disinclined to force the issue. Its caution reflected not only the situation in Tripoli and the presence of some 8,000 British subjects in Libya but also the strictures of the international laws governing diplomatic immunity. "We have little choice but to play it long," one minister said.

Richard Luce, a junior minister with special responsibility for the Middle East, declared in a radio interview that the police were in regular tele-

Libya continued on page 5A

- 2 professors answer questions on rising tensions among Libyan communities. Page 6A.

# Shots down helicopter carrying U.S. senators

By Freddy Cuevas
Associated Press

Tegucigalpa, Honduras
A U.S. Army helicopter with two U.S. senators aboard was struck by gunfire and forced down Wednesday in Honduras near the El Salvador border, U.S. officials said. No one was injured.

Sen. J. Bennett Johnston, D-La., said the UH1 helicopter carrying him and Sen. Lawton Chiles, D-Fla., was struck three times by .50-caliber slugs that came "presumably from Salvadoran guerrillas."

A second UH1, carrying Diana Negroponte, wife of U.S. Ambassador John Negroponte, also was fired on. U.S. Embassy officials in Tegucigalpa and Pentagon officials in Washington agreed that the second helicopter was not hit. No injuries were reported in the second helicopter either.

The mountainous area where the helicopters were fired on is 55 miles west of Tegucigalpa and 10 miles from the Salvadoran province of Morazan, a stronghold of guerrillas who are fighting the U.S.-supported government in El Salvador.

The two senators, accompanied by aides, were on an inspection trip from Palmerola Air Base in central Honduras to a U.N. refugee camp at Colomoncagua. The Palmerola base houses about 1,000 U.S. servicemen and is headquarters for U.S. military exercises in Honduras. Many residents of the camp, Colomoncagua, are considered sympathetic to the Salvadoran guerrillas.

Johnston, speaking at a Tegucigalpa airport press conference yesterday, said he had no idea what was happening aboard the small helicopter until he felt air coming up from the

Helicopter continued on page 7A

- A House Intelligence Committee member says the panel learned in October about the CIA's direct supervision of a commando raid on the Nicaraguan port of Corinto. Page 4A.
- Two years after breaking with his former Sandinista comrades, Nicaraguan rebel commander Eden Pastora has gained a badly needed propaganda victory. Page 4A.

## Almanac

Thursday, April 19, 1984
110th day; 256 to go this year
Sunrise: 5:22. Sunset: 7:03

### Today's weather /

Best in the Midwest

Clouds in the Dakotas are waiting to move into Minnesota, but they won't ruin the shine in the Twin Cities area. Partly sunny skies and a high near 60 are expected, and the wind will be a moderate 10 to 15 m.p.h. Friday has just as much to offer.

### Index /



### Telephones /

| | |
|---|---|
| News general | 372-4141 |
| Classified | 372-4242 |
| Circulation | 372-4343 |

**Big profits for Chrysler**
Chrysler Corp. earned $705.8 million in the first quarter of 1984 — a larger profit than for any full year in history — and Chairman Lee Iacocca said Wednesday it was "the payoff" for the company's sacrifices and improvements. Chrysler earned $701 million in all of 1983. Page 9B.

**Office complex planned**
A major office complex is planned for the block south of Hennepin County Government Center. Page 9B.

# Director of Children's Theatre charged with sexually abusing 3 boys

By Paul McEnroe
Staff Writer

John Clark Donahue, founder and artistic director of the nationally renowned Children's Theatre Company, was arrested Wednesday on charges of sexually abusing three boys.

Hennepin County Attorney Tom Johnson said the incidents occurred between 1981 and 1983 and involved students or former students of the school that is run by the theater company. Each was younger than 16 at the time, he said.

Donahue, 45, was arrested yesterday afternoon at the theater complex, 2400 3rd Av. S., by agents of the Minnesota Bureau of Criminal Apprehension. He was taken to Hennepin County Jail and booked on six counts of criminal sexual conduct. He is being held in lieu of $150,000 bail and is expected to appear in court this morning.

The crime bureau had been investigating the case for two years, Johnson said. Authorities said that only in the past six weeks has sufficient evidence been gathered to justify the charges.

After Donahue was arrested, the theater's board of directors suspended him until the case is resolved. Donahue has run the theater for about 20 years and is a member of the board.

The criminal complaints allege that Donahue:

- Supplied liquor to a boy and then had sex with him in his office, which overlooks the theater's stage.
- Had sex with a boy after telling him that he should have sex with men and that the young man's parents didn't care.
- May have used his position as artistic director to gain sexual favors from a boy.

John Donahue

Donahue continued on page 11A

# New charges against Winton being studied

By Dennis Cassano
Staff Writer

The Minnesota Board on Judicial Standards is investigating an allegation that Hennepin County District Judge Crane Winton has recently been engaged in homosexual activity with a male prostitute.

Winton admitted in 1982 that he had used male prostitutes, and the Minnesota Supreme Court is considering the board's recommendation that as a result, the judge should be removed from the bench. An attorney for Winton has said that Winton now considers the use of prostitutes unacceptable.

In an interview Wednesday, another of Winton's attorneys, Joseph Friedberg, described the new allegation as "the most obvious frameup I've

Winton continued on page 11A

Minneapolis STAR and Tribune

1A Metro

Wednesday
November 7, 1984
5 Sections
25c Single copy

Volume III/Number 204/

Section A/Part I



# Reagan sweeps nation

## Mondale leads in state; Democrats hold House

By Finlay Lewis
Staff Correspondent

President Reagan buried Walter Mondale, a native son of Elmore, Minn., in a popular and electoral vote landslide Tuesday, becoming the first president since 1972 to win a mandate for a second term.

With 48 percent of the nation's precincts counted, Reagan had 58 percent of the popular vote, versus Mondale's 41 percent, placing the president slightly behind the pace of Lyndon Johnson who, in 1964, won the largest popular vote landslide in history with 61.05 percent of the vote.

Reagan won 46 states with 505 electoral votes, led in two more with 17. Mondale won the District of Columbia with 3 electoral votes, and was leading in Minnesota, which has 10 electoral votes.

Republicans, however, were struggling to translate Reagan's apparent landslide into significant gains in Congress.

In Senate races, with 33 seats at stake and 51 needed to forge a majority, Republicans won in 16, led in one and had 36 holdovers. Democrats won 14, led for one and had 31 holdovers. The pre-election count was 55 Republicans and 45 Democrats.

In the 435 House races, Democrats won 201 and led for 44 more, while Republicans had captured 152 and led for 33. It takes 218 for a majority. The old House lineup was 266 Democrats, 167 Republicans, and two vacancies in seats that had been held by one Democrat and one Republican.

Reagan, appearing before a victory rally in Los Angeles, declared, "Our work isn't finished. There is much more to be done."

Reagan said his second-term goals would center on achieving "strong economic growth without inflation" and on maintaining U.S. military strength as a bargaining lever to reduce nuclear weaponry and "ultimately ban them from the Earth entirely."

Mondale, a DFL activist since his student days at Macalester College 37 years ago, called the president to offer his congratulations and then conceded defeat at an election-watch gathering of partisans and supporters at the St. Paul Civic Center shortly after 10 p.m. Minneapolis time.

Speaking slowly and with obvious emotion, Mondale told his backers, "He has won. We are all Americans; he is our president and we honor him tonight."

Flanked by his family, Mondale said of his campaign that began 20 months ago when he officially declared his candidacy a few miles away in the State Capitol: "This fight didn't end tonight. It begins tonight. I've been around for awhile and I have noticed in the seeds of every victory are to be found the seeds of defeat and in every defeat are to be found the seeds of victory . . .

"I'm at peace with the knowledge that I gave it everything I've got . . . I am confident that history will judge me fairly."

Reagan, at 73 the oldest president in U.S. history, displayed strength across the board. By midnight Minneapolis time, Reagan was projected as the winner in 37 states with 381 votes in the electoral college, 111 more than required for victory. The president was ahead in seven more states with 89 electoral votes, while Mondale won the three electoral votes of the District of Columbia and claimed victory in Minnesota with 10 electoral votes.

Those returns made it apparent that Mondale, 56, would join his mentor, the late Hubert Humphrey, the only

Elect continued on page 7A

Associated Press

President Reagan gave a triumphant thumbs-up signal Tuesday night during his victory celebration at the Century Plaza Hotel in Los Angeles.

## Mondale shifted campaign to focus on political legacy

By Finlay Lewis
Staff Correspondent

*"He taught us how to hope and how to love; how to win and how to lose . . ."* — **Walter Mondale's eulogy to Hubert Humphrey.**

It started 20 months ago with a simple declaration — "I am ready to be president" — and ended Tuesday when the nation shrugged its shoulders.

Before it was over, Walter Frederick Mondale's long campaign changed character — from an effort to win the presidency to a quest for respectability and a favorable historical verdict about the nature of his candidacy.

Even during his bitter, up and down struggle to win the Democratic nomination, Mondale worried about what type of legacy he would leave as a defeated politician. A hapless loser? A paper tiger? A gutless political hitchhiker who advanced himself by currying favor and then collapsed

**Mondale** continued on page 7A

Staff Photo by Darlene Pfister

Eleanor Mondale hugged her father, Walter, Tuesday night on the stage at the St. Paul Civic Center.

## Flushed with victory, Jerry Falwell looks beyond the campaign to his own crusade

Larry Batson's
**America**

**Lynchburg, Va.**
It all came together Tuesday night for the Rev. Jerry Falwell: His personal crusade, the mood of the country, his candidate.

Even the massive turnout.

"Wonderful for us. For the first time a big turnout is good for the Republicans and it's going to be that way from now on.

"The country is becoming more conservative; the youth of America is now the great conservative base and conservatives will keep on out-registering the Democrats."

Falwell, 51-year-old evangelist and creator and driving force of Moral Majority, watched returns in his office. Across a courtyard, a revival was underway. Down the hall, cameras were set up and interviewers from three networks and cable news waited for him.

"Ronald Reagan will be Ronald Reagan for the next four years, I think. He will be more aggressive about his interests, the moral issues.

"I think his most meaningful appointments will be two to five appointments to the Supreme Court. Contrary to what Mr. Mondale has said, he (Reagan) will make the appointments, not I."

**Falwell** continued on page 6A

## Election '84

### Reagan won on charm, strength of economy

See story, page 4A.

### Republicans pick up 3 governors' seats

See story, page 9A.

### Helms wins costly N.C. battle over Hunt

Republican Sen. Jesse Helms defeated Democratic Gov. Jim Hunt Tuesday for the North Carolina Senate in a race that attracted national attention. The confrontation between the moderate Hunt and the arch-conservative Helms was considered as much a referendum on a pillar of the New Right as a battle over issues.

Helms, 63, and Hunt, 47, broke national records by spending \$21.8 million on the race by Oct. 17. Helms outdistanced Hunt in both spending and fund-raising by an almost 2-1 ratio in seeking his third term.

Jesse Helms

See story, page 10A.

### GOP gains in House, but is short of control

See story, page 9A.

**Minnesota House races**

### Sikorski is apparent winner

DFL Rep. Gerry Sikorski was the apparent winner in the fiercely fought Sixth District congressional contest with Independent-Republican Patrick Trueman. With 19 percent of the precincts reporting, Sikorski had almost 62 percent of the vote and apparently was heading for a victory shortly before midnight Tuesday. Sikorski was running as much as 15 percent ahead of his 1982 mark in some precincts. **See story, page 8A.**



**Key Minnesota races**



**Key national races**



**Other election news**

■ The voting in his home town yesterday showed what Walter Mondale was up against. "People will vote for Mondale on account of where he's from," said Joe Ingebritson, a farmer near Elmore, a Republican town where some of the 549 registered voters openly stood firm for the GOP. **See story, page 5A.**

■ North Oaks residents openly welcome the transformation from Walter Mondale, presidential candidate, to Walter Mondale, private citizen. Politics aside — although the St. Paul suburb voted overwhelmingly for Ronald Reagan in 1980, the town will be glad for the return of its highly prized privacy and tranquility. **See story, page 5A.**

## Boschwitz handily defeats Growe

By Lori Sturdevant
Staff Writer

Sen. Rudy Boschwitz romped to a second term Tuesday, handily defeating his DFL challenger, Secretary of State Joan Growe.

With votes counted in more than half of the state's precincts, the Republican senator enjoyed a solid 11-percentage-point lead. TV network projections, based on interviews with Minnesota voters leaving the polls, had Boschwitz winning by a ratio of nearly 3 to 2.

Growe conceded defeat at 9:45 p.m., saying she had sent the Republican senator a telegram congratulating him on a "clear-cut victory" and wishing him "continued wisdom and courage" in the next six years.

In a voice that sometimes quavered with emotion, she defended her campaign as one of "issues, not images," and added, "I have no regrets . . . . We set out to make a difference, and we have, and we will."

The senator acknowledged her concession 30 minutes later, amid a sea of smiley face signs waved by cheering supporters. He said his victory indicates the acceptance of the Re-

**Senate** continued on page 7A

## Almanac

**Wednesday, November 7, 1984**
**311th day; 55 to go this year**
**Sunrise: 6:58. Sunset: 4:55**

### Today's weather/

No nonsense

Hard as the wind might try, today's clouds won't be moved. A high in the 50s is expected in the Twin Cities, but there's a chance of a shower.

### Inside/

**Robert Naegele dies**
Robert O. Naegele, 69, the hard-charging businessman whose billboard company spread advertising across the Twin Cities and in 18 states over 48 years, died Tuesday. **Page 3B.**

**Jets to Nicaragua**
A Soviet freighter is on its way to Nicaragua and may be carrying advanced jet fighters, CBS News reported Tuesday, quoting U.S. intelligence officials. **Page 32A.**

### Index/

Minneapolis **STAR and Tribune** 1A Metro
Wednesday January 29, 1986
6 Sections
25¢ Single copy
Volume IV / Number 300

# Fireball engulfs shuttle; nation mourns 7 aboard

## Teacher among disaster victims

From News Services

**Cape Canaveral, Fla.**
The space shuttle Challenger exploded in a mid-air flash of fire and smoke moments after launch Tuesday, killing all seven astronauts in the worst disaster in the history of manned space flight.

The spectacle occurred at 11:39 a.m. EST, 74 seconds after liftoff from the Kennedy Space Center.

The explosion was witnessed by thousands of spectators and millions more Americans watching on television. Extraordinary attention was focused on the mission because of the presence onboard of Christa McAuliffe, a 37-year-old high school teacher from New Hampshire and a mother of two children.

Other crew members were Francis R. Scobee, 46, the commander; pilot Michael J. Smith, 40; mission specialist Ellison S. Onizuka, an Air Force lieutenant colonel, 39; Ronald E. McNair, 35; Judith Resnik, 36, and Gregory B. Jarvis, a 41-year-old payload specialist who works for Hughes Aircraft Co.

"This was truly a national loss," said President Reagan, who last year declared an educator should be the first everyday American to ride on a shuttle mission.

After the explosion, helicopters and ships converged on an offshore point 18 miles downrange from where the Challenger disappeared from monitors. By nightfall, the searchers had found only "a small amount" of debris and no signs of survivors. All aboard were presumed dead.

National Aeronautics and Space Administration officials said they did not know what triggered the fireball. An immediate internal investigation was ordered and all shuttle activity was suspended. In his statement, Reagan vowed there would be future shuttle flights.

On board Challenger was the world's largest privately owned communication satellite, the $100 million Tracking and Data Relay Satellite. The crew also was to have deployed a a smaller $10 million payload that was to have studied Halley's comet and McAuliffe was to have broadcast two lessons from space to millions of students around the country.

The explosion came at one of the most critical points in the launch. One minute into the blastoff, Scobee received pre-planned instructions to restore shuttle engines to full power.

The engines had been slowed to decrease air pressure on the spacecraft, as well as on the expendable, auxiliary fuel tank and booster rockets needed to propel the shuttle into orbit. Pushing the engines back to full power would subject the spacecraft to the most extreme pressure during the entire procedure.

"Go with throttle up," a controller in

**Shuttle** continued on page 8A

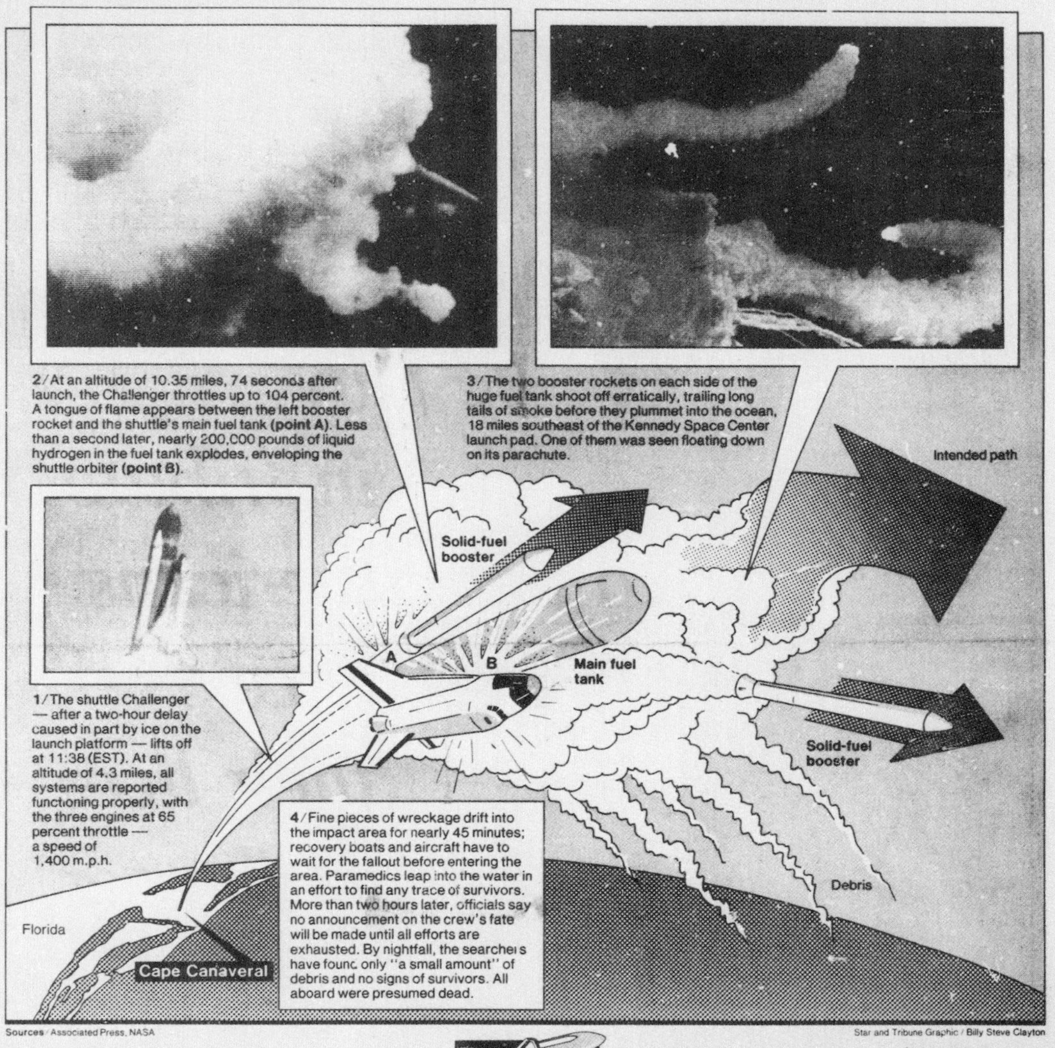
2 / At an altitude of 10.35 miles, 74 seconds after launch, the Challenger throttles up to 104 percent. A tongue of flame appears between the left booster rocket and the shuttle's main fuel tank (point A). Less than a second later, nearly 200,000 pounds of liquid hydrogen in the fuel tank explodes, enveloping the shuttle orbiter (point B).
3 / The two booster rockets on each side of the huge fuel tank shoot off erratically, trailing long tails of smoke before they plummet into the ocean, 18 miles southeast of the Kennedy Space Center launch pad. One of them was seen floating down on its parachute.
Intended path
Solid-fuel booster
A
B
Main fuel tank
Solid-fuel booster
1 / The shuttle Challenger — after a two-hour delay caused in part by ice on the launch platform — lifts off at 11:38 (EST). At an altitude of 4.3 miles, all systems are reported functioning properly, with the three engines at 65 percent throttle — a speed of 1,400 m.p.h.
4 / Fine pieces of wreckage drift into the impact area for nearly 45 minutes; recovery boats and aircraft have to wait for the fallout before entering the area. Paramedics leap into the water in an effort to find any trace of survivors. More than two hours later, officials say no announcement on the crew's fate will be made until all efforts are exhausted. By nightfall, the searchers have found only "a small amount" of debris and no signs of survivors. All aboard were presumed dead.
Debris
Florida
Cape Canaveral

Sources / Associated Press, NASA

Star and Tribune Graphic / Billy Steve Clayton

## Speculation on cause centers on fuel tanks

By Thomas H. Maugh II
Los Angeles Times

A little more than a minute after the shuttle Challenger lifted off from pad 39B at the Kennedy Space Center Tuesday morning, a thin tongue of flame appeared between the left booster rocket and the shuttle's main fuel tank. The flame was not seen by observers on the ground, but slow-motion videotapes of the launch show it clearly.

Less than a second later, nearly 200,000 pounds of liquid hydrogen remaining in the main fuel tank exploded in a massive fireball that enveloped the shuttle orbiter and sent both solid rocket boosters flying in nearly opposite directions.

The explosion destroyed the orbiter, killed its passengers, and seriously damaged the future of the U.S. space program.

**Explosion** continued on page 11A

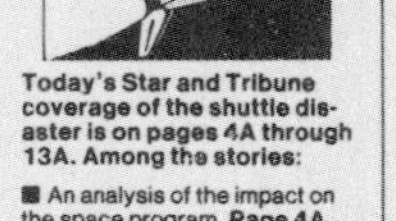

## Reagan vows 'quest in space' will continue

From News Services

**Washington, D.C.**
President Reagan, stunned by America's first in-flight space disaster, postponed his State of the Union address Tuesday to praise the lost Challenger astronauts as heroes and vow the nation's manned space flight program will continue.

"The future doesn't belong to the fainthearted," he said. "It belongs to the brave."

In brief, nationally televised remarks from the Oval Office late yesterday afternoon, Reagan, who was described by aides as shaken by the disaster, promised "to continue our quest in space."

"I'd planned to speak to you tonight to report on the state of the union," he said. But he explained he was putting off for a week what aides had described as an upbeat, forward-

**Reagan** continued on page 8A

## Inside/

### Tarkenton named

Fran Tarkenton, who scrambled to prominence as quarterback of the Minnesota Vikings, was named Tuesday to the National Football League Hall of Fame.

Tarkenton, who also played for the New York Giants during his 18 years in the NFL, is No. 1 in the record books for passing yardage and touchdown passes.

Paul Hornung, the Green Bay Packers' running back and kicker, was among four others elected. **Page 1D.**

Fran Tarkenton

### Hormel developments

At the annual meeting of Geo. A. Hormel & Co. yesterday in Houston, Texas, the company said that it might not reopen its 350-person hog-slaughtering operation in Austin, Minn., which has been barely profitable at best in recent years.

In St. Paul last night, Gov. Perpich said he was ordering National Guard members to leave the Austin plant at 7 a.m. today and withdraw to the Austin Armory, where they will remain in a "supporting role." **Page 1M.**

### Angry Fraser talks taxes

An increase of 12 to 18 percent in the Minneapolis property tax rate would be necessary next year to offset the loss of $12 million in state and federal aid, an angry Mayor Don Fraser said yesterday.

He blasted Gov. Rudy Perpich in his remarks at a City Council committee meeting yesterday after the committee recommended a freeze on hiring, nonessential travel and furniture purchases as a temporary solution to the projected $6.8 million reduction in state aid. **Page 1B.**

## Almanac

**Wednesday, January 29, 1986**
**29th day; 336 to go this year**
**Sunrise: 7:37. Sunset: 5:17**

### Today's weather/

No breaks

The Twin Cities won't see a break in the clouds today and the temperature won't be a record-breaker, either. A high near 10 is expected. Wind will be from the northwest at 10 to 15 miles per hour.

### Index/

### Telephones/

| | |
|---|---|
| News general | 372-4141 |
| Want Ads | 372-4242 |
| Circulation | 372-4343 |

**'We Are the World' dominates Grammys/**
Phil Collins' 'No Jacket Required' wins best album / 16D

**Gorbachev ties 2nd summit to arms progress / 3A**

**MPLS. VICE** — **Chic fits our local police** / 1C


Minneapolis **STAR and Tribune**

1A Metro

Wednesday
February 26, 1986
6 Sections
25¢ Single copy

Volume IV/Number 328




# Marcos flees the Philippines

## 'People power' carries Aquino to presidency

Associated Press

**Manila, Philippines**
Ferdinand Marcos fled the Philippines Wednesday after 20 years in power, and Corazon Aquino, the new president, promised her nation that an era of hope would follow "the long agony."

The Aquino government received immediate recognition from the United States.

Marcos, 68, who was driven from office by a military and civil rebellion in support of Aquino, left the presidential palace Tuesday night. He was taken with his family and a group of supporters in U.S. helicopters to Clark Air Base, 50 miles northwest of Manila. There they boarded two U.S. Air Force planes and flew to Guam, a U.S. territory. Marcos' next destination was said to be Hawaii.

The U.S. Defense Department issued a statement in Washington saying a C9 transport jet carrying Marcos, his wife, Imelda, and the ousted armed forces chief, Gen. Fabian Ver, and his wife landed at Guam's Andersen Air Force Base. It said a C141 Starlifter followed with others in the Marcos group, adding, "The total Filipino party aboard both aircraft was 55."

Marcos was taken off the plane on a stretcher. The Reuter news agency said the base commander ordered that Marcos be carried off because he appeared tired and physically frail.

"Mr. Marcos will receive a medical checkup at the U.S. Naval Hospital in Agana, Guam," the statement said. "The period of time (Marcos will be) on Guam and further destinations

**Philippines** continued on page 5A

**Inside/**

A view of private palace quarters gave indications of the Marcos family's lavish life style, including a room filled with hundreds of silk dresses and dozens of quart and gallon bottles of French perfume.

- President Reagan's handling of the Philippine must be scored as a triumph in policy.
- The Reagan administration moved quickly to recognize the government of Corazon Aquino and praised the peaceful way Marcos relinquished rule.

**Details, related articles on pages 6,7A.**

## Phone call to U.S. led Marcos to quit

**By Bernard Gwertzman**
New York Times

**Washington, D.C.**
It was about 3 a.m. Tuesday in Manila, and President Ferdinand Marcos was telephoning to find out whether the message he had received from Washington calling for "a peaceful transition" to a new government actually meant he should quit.

Sen. Paul Laxalt, who received the call in Washington, where it was 2 p.m. Monday, said later that Marcos was "a desperate man, clutching at straws," even though he would be sworn in as president in about nine hours.

Marcos seemed to trust Laxalt as a confidant of President Reagan. It was Laxalt, a Republican from Nevada, who last year went to the Philippines as Reagan's emissary to voice U.S. concerns directly to Marcos.

During yesterday's call, Marcos told Laxalt that he did not want to resign

**Laxalt** continued on page 5A

Reuter

**The official portrait of Imelda Marcos was trashed and burned Tuesday in Manila after it was taken from the presidential palace by Filipinos celebrating the departure of President Ferdinand Marcos.**

## Aquino facing huge political obstacles

**By Frank Wright**
Foreign Correspondent

**Frank Wright**
**Analysis**

This is a day of celebration and fulfillment for Corazon Aquino.

In a little more than two years, she has gone from being just a housewife, by her own description, to tragic widow, to reluctant and insecure candidate, to a charismatic campaigner drawing crowds of hundreds of thousands of the hopeful.

And now to the presidency — the presidency that might have been her husband's had he not been assassinated — in one of the most inspiring human and political stories of modern times.

But while she enjoys the present, it also is the beginning of a new time for Aquino, the time in which she must face the realities of turning her hopes and those of hundreds of thousands of Filipinos into a better day.

When Emil Ong, one of Aquino's regional campaign chairmen, was speaking during the election on the

**Wright** continued on page 8A

## Engineers say booster firm overruled them, approved flight

Associated Press

**Washington, D.C.**
An engineer for Morton Thiokol testified Tuesday that he did "all I could to stop the launch" of Challenger, but that company managers overruled his fears and those of other engineers concerned that a cold-weather liftoff might doom the space shuttle.

The testimony came as sources revealed that investigators have uncovered a pre-launch protest from the manufacturer of the shuttle.

The protest, from Rocco Petrone, president of the space division of Rockwell International, was issued the day before the launch and expressed fears that ice might fall from the external fuel tank and damage Challenger's fragile tiles, the sources said.

Petrone is a former NASA launch director and his involvement was to be disclosed today or Thursday as the presidential commission sum-

**Shuttle** continued on page 4A

- NASA administrator resigns. Reagan plans to name successor soon. **Page 4A.**

### Session '86

- Gov. Rudy Perpich should stay at the Capitol and show more leadership on legislative issues, instead of being on the road so much, his chief legislative ally, Sen. Roger Moe, said Tuesday.

**Details on Page 1B.**

### Almanac

**Wednesday, February 26, 1986**
**57th day; 308 to go this year**
**Sunrise: 6:57. Sunset: 5:56**

**Today's weather/**

Snow it is

Rather have snow than freezing rain? All right, then! There's a chance of light snow in the afternoon. A high in the low 30s is expected in the Twin Cities. Wind will be from the north at 10 to 20 miles per hour.

**Index/**



## Victory for 'duck lady'

Staff Photo by Art Hager

**CBS correspondent Charles Kuralt congratulated Leila Nicol, 85, of New Brighton, Tuesday after a judge dropped charges that she was creating a public nuisance by feeding ducks and geese on Long Lake. (Details on page 1B.)**

## Arbitrator rescinds 18 police transfers in Second Precinct

**By Larry Oakes**
Staff Writer

An arbitrator has rescinded the transfer of 18 Minneapolis patrol officers who were removed from the Second Precinct after three fellow officers were caught playing cards while on duty.

Arbitrator George Jacobs of Minnetonka ruled Tuesday that Police Chief Tony Bouza violated the officers' contract by using transfers as a disciplinary measure without proving any wrongdoing on the part of the officers.

The transfers were ordered last November after three veteran officers were secretly videotaped playing cards at a southeast Minneapolis fire station while on duty. Those officers eventually were suspended five days each and transferred.

**Police** continued on page 12A

## Judge cites ruling, throws out 150 truancy cases

**By Dan Oberdorfer**
Staff Writer

A juvenile judge Tuesday dismissed all 150 truancy complaints pending against students in Hennepin County, saying that a recent appeals court decision essentially wiped out the state's truancy laws.

District Judge Allen Oleisky acted after prosecutors argued that a decision this month by the Minnesota Court of Appeals made it all but impossible for them to win contested truancy cases in court.

The appeals court decision "puts us in the position of not having any legal recourse to ensure that students stay in school," said Keith Kromer, director of special education for the Minneapolis public schools. "In effect there are no teeth in the (state's) compulsory attendance law."

He said Minneapolis schools plan to

**Truancy** continued on page 4A

# Vikings draft for defense first

No.1 pick is Auburn lineman; they also trade for rights to USFL tackle / 1D

**David Stockman: storm, fury before the quiet / 11A**

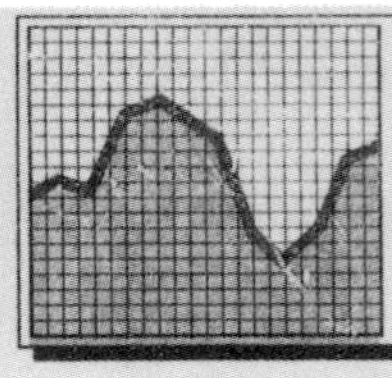

**'The economy and you': New financial strategies / 1M**


Minneapolis **STAR and Tribune**

1A. Metro

Wednesday
April 30, 1986
6 Sections
25¢ Single copy

Volume V / Number 26




Section A / Part I

# Soviets seek aid in reactor fire

## Only two killed, Kremlin says; evacuation affects thousands

**Associated Press**

**Moscow, U.S.S.R.**
The Soviet Union appealed Tuesday for Swedish and West German help to fight a nuclear reactor fire and evacuated thousands of people imperiled by one of history's worst nuclear disasters.

In its first report on casualties, the Soviet government said the nuclear plant disaster near the Ukrainian capital of Kiev killed two people, and a Soviet official visiting Washington said fewer than 100 had been injured.

U.S. arms control administrator Kenneth Adelman, asked in a U.S. Senate hearing about the Soviet report of two deaths, described it as "frankly preposterous in terms of an accident of this magnitude."

U.S. Sen. Patrick Leahy said after a CIA briefing in Washington, "I've seen nothing that indicated that huge numbers of people are dead. It could be two, 12 or two dozen." Leahy, D-Vt., vice chairman of the Senate Intelligence Committee, said he had heard nothing to support a report that as many as 2,000 people were killed.

The U.S. State Department said the U.S. Embassy in Moscow was in contact with registered Americans known to be in the Kiev area and there was no indication any had been injured. It did not say how many Americans were in Kiev, a city of 2.4 million people 60 miles southeast of the Chernobyl plant site.

**Chernobyl** continued on page 16A

**Inside /**



## U.S. cites evidence of blast, meltdown

**From News Services**

**Washington, D.C.**
The accident at a Soviet nuclear power plant involved "quite an explosion," apparently followed by a meltdown in the reactor, Reagan administration sources said Tuesday.

Administration officials, who declined to be named or to disclose the sources of their information, said intelligence data showed a roof blown away, walls at least partly crumbled and evidence of continuing fire three days after the explosion, which is believed to have occurred Saturday.

The officials who studied the information concluded that there was no equivalent accident in the history of the U.S. nuclear power industry.

"There was quite an explosion," said one official, adding that the site of the blast, the Chernobyl power com-

**Explosion** continued on page 17A

## With credit limit reached, FHA halts loan applications

**By James Rowley**
**Associated Press**

**Washington, D.C.**
The boom in home sales and the rush of homeowners to refinance mortgages to the lowest rates in eight years have depleted the Federal Housing Administration's $57.4 billion credit program, forcing the agency Tuesday to stop processing of applications for new government-insured mortgages.

"The game's over, we're out of business," at least temporarily, said Silvio DeBartolomeis, FHA's acting administrator. He ordered FHA's regional offices to suspend the mortgage-insurance program at close of business yesterday.

Home buyers and builders who have received financing commitments won't be affected, but no new applications will be accepted for now.

The action means more delays for the more than 22,000 Minnesotans who have applied for appraisals for FHA-insured mortgages since early March, said Patricia Mack, special assistant to the manager of the Minneapolis-St. Paul office of the U.S. Department of Housing and Urban Development (HUD), which administers the mortgage program.

Because of the record number of appraisal requests the past two months in Minnesota, it has been taking about eight weeks to complete appraisals, Mack said. Although appraisals for those whose requests were received by HUD by late yesterday will be made, none of those loans can be closed until and unless Congress raises the credit ceiling.

"This means that however many thousands of people who aren't already in line to get appraisals are going to get backed up," said Mike George, executive vice president of the Mortgage Bankers Association of Minnesota. "Even if there's only a week's gap before the program gets started again, it's going to exacerbate the problem because as soon as HUD is back in business, everyone will be knocking on the door wanting an appraisal. The backlog is going to get worse because of this."

Said DeBartolomeis, "This means that the public will have to rely on the private sector" for mortgage insurance until Congress completes action on pending legislation to raise FHA's credit ceiling."

**Home loans** continued on page 6A

Associated Press

**Remains of astronauts flown to mortuary**

**One of seven flag-draped coffins holding the remains of astronauts killed three months ago in the explosion of the space shuttle Challenger was carried to a jet by an honor guard Tuesday at Kennedy Space Center in Florida. The remains were flown to Dover (Del.) Air Force Base, where some of the bodies were turned over to families. Others will buried in Arlington National Cemetery. (Article, page 3A.)**

## 34 miles to go and the path looks passable

**By Sharon Schmickle**
**Staff Writer**

**Resolute Bay, Northwest Territories**
Just 34 miles from the North Pole Tuesday afternoon, the Steger expedition expected to be on top of the world sometime tonight.

A Canadian military reconnaissance airplane made several passes over the six team members at 4 p.m. yesterday and reported their position as 89 degrees, 30 minutes, 41 seconds north and 53 degrees, 5 minutes, 1 second west.

There was no open water in the Arctic Ocean ice that could stop the march that began March 8 about 480 miles from the pole.

"There are some small cracks, but they are passable," the radio operator said. "Anywhere from 50 to 100 feet. There are extensive pressure ridges up to 30 feet high."

The weather was clear and sunny with southwest wind, he said.

Team members want to reach the pole without outside help, and that has made the trip a constant struggle with heavy loads and with the question of what to keep and what to jettison.

One of those key decisions was detailed in a team member's diary obtained this week by the Star and Tribune.

In the diary, Geoff Carroll tells about an overload crisis the team faced April 11. He said he felt that the expedition was moving too slowly and was conserving too much food and that he became convinced that "At this rate we don't have a chance."

The result, described in Carroll's words below, was a decision to throw some of their own food to the dogs and to abandon hundreds of dollars worth of gear to get sleds moving faster.

Team leaders Paul Schurke and Will Steger of Ely, Minn., had requested an airplane check of their position

**Expedition** continued on page 8A

Journey to the top of the world

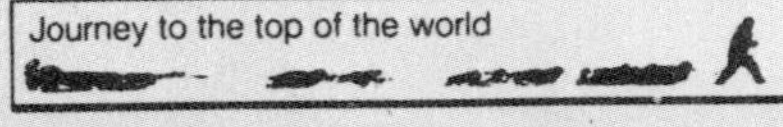

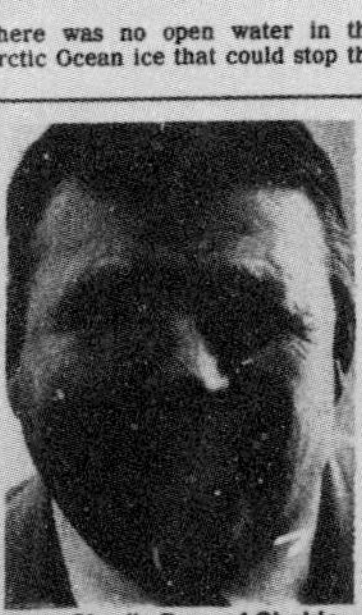

**Sen. Charlie Berg of Chokio accepted the DFL label Tuesday. (Article, page 3B.)**

## From roaming buffalo to rotating crops, Capitol mall designers cover the range

**By Randy Furst**
**Staff Writer**

The State Capitol Mall would be transformed into a reflecting pool such as the one at the Lincoln Memorial in Washington, D.C., under one design proposal submitted to a competition to be judged tomorrow and Friday.

A laser beam stretching from the Capitol dome to downtown St. Paul would "catch the sparkle of falling snow" under another design.

Buffalo grazing in a pasture in front of the Capitol alongside a glass-tube walkway running the length of the mall is a third proposal.

A total of 173 designs from across the United States and several foreign countries had been submitted by midafternoon yesterday, formal deadline for the competition. About 12 late entries were expected and will be accepted if postmarked by last Friday. Most designs are very elaborate and serious.

Contest consultant Ken Paolini of Boston, Mass., estimated that the value of the architectural services used in each submission was about $10,000, making the total value about $1.8 million. Designers were told to make proposals that will cost between $5 million and $15 million to build.

The number of contestants will be narrowed to five, probably Friday. More detailed drawings and models will be required of finalists and the winner is to be chosen Aug. 8, said Gary Grefenberg, executive secretary of the state Capitol Area Architectural and Planning Board, which is running the competition.

The Legislature will be asked to fund a portion of the proposal next year, under a plan that would be phased in over several years. Some money has

**Capitol** continued on page 9A

## Almanac

**Wednesday, April 30, 1986**
**120th day; 245 to go this year**
**Sunrise: 6:05. Sunset: 8:17**

### Today's weather /

Rain

There are only so many ways to say it, and with our record rainfall this month, we've run out. So, simply put, it's expected to rain this morning and clear this afternoon. The high will be in lower 70s.

### Inside /

**Economic index up 0.5 pct.**
The government's main economic forecasting gauge posted a 0.5 percent increase in March that analysts viewed as further evidence that economic growth will rebound in the second half of the year. **Page 1M.**

**Strikeout record**
Roger Clemens set a major-league record for a nine-inning game Tuesday night by striking out 20 Seattle batters in a 3-1 Boston win over Seattle. Clemens, with four wins and no losses, allowed three hits and walked none. **Page 1D.**

### Index /



## Hummels are hot items in series of state thefts

**By Ellen Foley**
**Staff Writer**

Collectors ooh and ahh at the image of a rosy-cheeked Hummel child wearing the look of innocence.

Many do not realize that the sweet-faced figurine could be "hot."

Police say a black market for Hummels and other valuable collectible figurines has emerged in Minnesota the past year.

Sixteen stores in 12 cities have recently had thefts of the German-made figurines and other collectibles worth between $7 and $2,000.

Police officials say they suspect that many other stores have been victimized but have failed to report their losses.

Some merchants report losing up to $10,000 in merchandise to slick teams of shoplifters who case the shops, then return in pairs to steal the porcelain or hand-painted ceramic statues, often from locked cabinets.

Thefts of collectibles have been reported to police or confirmed by shopkeepers in Wayzata, Prior Lake,

**Hummels** continued on page 8A

**Sports**

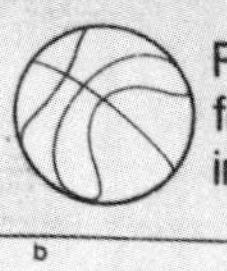

Park Center qualifies for its first state tournament berth in a really big way/**1D**

**Variety**

Noel Holston looks at businesses' role as the heavy on TV/**1C**

**Variety**

Spring break: The tough ride down /**1C**


Minneapolis

# STAR and Tribune

1A. Metro

Tuesday
March 24/1987
4 Sections
35¢ Single copy

Volume V/Number 354

John Mariucci

## Father of U.S. hockey John Mariucci dies at age 70

**Doug Grow**

■ John Mariucci was an All-America player at the 'U,' coach of the 1956 U.S. Olympic team and an NHL Hall of Famer. **Page 1D.**

It should be cold out today and there should be a strong north wind blowing across the state.

There should be snow. A lot of snow, banked up around skating rinks. And standing in the snow there should be shivering mothers and fathers watching little kids pursue a puck.

That's the sort of day it should be because John Mariucci is dead and kids pursuing a hockey puck are his legacy.

Mariucci, 70, died Monday night at University of Minnesota Hospital in Minneapolis after a bout with prostate cancer.

To be sure, there was hockey before Mariucci. But it was Mariucci who made hockey a game for more than Canadians. It was Mariucci, who by force of his play and his personality, made the game a Minnesota game, and then a U.S. game, as well.

Pee Wee leagues and summer camps and a state high school hockey tournament and Brotens and Herbies and gold medals. . . . All those things, which have become so much a part of Minnesota's culture, can be traced to the toughest member of the Hay Street gang, John Mariucci.

The Hay Street gang grew up in Eveleth, Minn., in the 1920s and '30s.

"Hay Street was also known as Incubator Street," recalled John Brimsek, a member of the gang and the big brother of Frank Brimsek, who would become a Hall of Fame National Hockey League goalie. "See, there must have been about 25 different nationalities living on Hay Street, but it got to be known as Incubator Street 'cause just about every family had eight or nine kids."

And in the winter, those kids would pour out of the little houses and into the street with tree branches for hockey sticks and overshoes instead of skates and they'd imitate the Canadian players who were imported into town for the entertainment of the miners.

Back a couple of years ago, when another of the legendary Hay Street gang, NHL goalie Sam LoPresti, died, Mariucci recalled how Communists would help sneak kids like Mariucci and LoPresti into those games. Members of the Communist Party, who were trying to organize the miners, would tell the kids to loiter near the main gate. Then, the Communists would create a ruckus. While arena security people subdued the Communists, the kids would rush into the building.

"The next day," said Mariucci, "we

**Mariucci** continued on page 9A

## U.S. offers naval escorts in gulf

**New York Times**

**Washington, D.C.**
The United States has offered to extend military protection to Kuwaiti-owned vessels traveling through the Persian Gulf to meet possible threats from Iran, administration officials said Monday.

The protection, which the officials said was requested by Kuwait about a month ago, could include escorts for ships as they enter and leave Kuwaiti oil terminals and as they pass through the Strait of Hormuz. This is the first time any of the gulf countries has specifically asked for U.S. military escorts and, if such escorts are provided, it would represent an escalation of U.S. military activity in the region.

Kuwait, however, was reported to have asked for both U.S. and Soviet naval escorts. The U.S. desire to be the only protecting force might lead the Kuwaitis to decline the offer, as they have turned down U.S. protection in the past. But U.S. officials yesterday said they expected Kuwait to accept the U.S. plan.

Tension in the region has increased over Iran's deployment of Chinese-made antiship missiles at the Strait of Hormuz, the narrow southern entrance to the Persian Gulf. Fear has grown that the Iranians might try to close the strait.

Beyond the offer of military protection, the U.S. move was seen as an important diplomatic step, reinforcing its position with the pro-Western Arab countries of the Persian Gulf. Since the revelations last November of secret U.S. sales of military equipment to Iran, several Arab countries have raised questions about U.S. intentions in the region.

One State Department official said that if Kuwait goes through with the protection arrangement, it would send a significant signal to other Arab countries. In the past, Kuwait has been reluctant to accept U.S. mil-

**Gulf war** continued on page 7A

## Kidnappers offer trade of ill hostage for Arabs

**From News Services**

**Beirut, Lebanon**
Muslim kidnappers said Monday a captive American professor is so ill he may die in 10 days and offered to trade him for 100 Arab prisoners held in Israel.

In Tel Aviv, the chief aide to Prime Minister Yitzhak Shamir said Israel would not consider the kidnappers' demand. "Israel does not negotiate with terrorists," Avi Pazner said.

In other developments, another terrorist group said it had canceled plans to kill a French hostage.

Iran's official radio said the group had kidnapped Anglican Church envoy Terry Waite but reported later that the group denied it.

A statement delivered to the Beirut newspaper An-Nahar said Alann Steen, 47, of Boston "may die within 10 days" and demanded the United States persuade Israel to make the exchange.

It was signed by Islamic Jihad for the Liberation of Palestine, which holds Steen, two other Americans and an Indian. All were teachers at Beirut University College when they were abducted from the school's west Beirut campus in January.

The group warned that Steen's condition could deteriorate, "exposing him to the danger of death in 10 days.

"The advice of doctors counseling care for his state of health and humanitarian motives compel us to free the sick spy in exchange for 100 prisoners from the jails of (Israeli) occupation," the statement said. A photograph of one of Steen's missing colleagues, Robert Polhill, 53, was enclosed with the letter as proof of authenticity.

The statement said the United States and Israel would be responsible for "the dangers he will be exposed to after this period" and promised to release a videotape within 72 hours

**Hostages** continued on page 7A

## Durenberger admits to quotes on Reagan

### But says they're 'out of context'

**By David Phelps**
Staff Correspondent

**Washington, D.C.**
Sen. Dave Durenberger, R-Minn., reversed himself Monday and acknowledged that he said last week that President Reagan "doesn't know what the hell is going on" in the Iran-contra affair. But Durenberger said that the quote, which has caused strong negative reactions among Minnesota Republicans, was taken out of context.

Durenberger had told a Minnesota church audience Sunday that reports about his Reagan statement were "patently not true."

The Star and Tribune obtained a tape recording of Durenberger's breakfast interview with a dozen Washington reporters Thursday and questioned the senator yesterday on his remarks about the president.

After reviewing another tape recording of the interview, Durenberger said yesterday, "I can't argue that I found those same eight words in a 50-word sentence."

**Durenberger** continued on page 9A

Staff Photo by Steven Zerby

**Waldorf warehouse heavily damaged**

**Firefighters poured water onto burning bales of paper Monday at the Waldorf Corp. warehouse just off Interstate Hwy. 94 in St. Paul. The bales could smolder for days, said officials, who said the fire was started by a faulty light fixture. The fire at the former Champion International building was well underway when firefighters first arrived early yesterday morning. Details on page 1B.**

## Sales tax on services seems a likely source of budget-balancing cash

**By Betty Wilson**
Staff Writer

Extending the sales tax to cover services appears likely if more money is needed to balance the budget, Gov. Rudy Perpich and some legislative leaders said Monday.

"That's where it looks like, yes," Perpich told reporters yesterday, opening the door the widest he's done yet to tax increases above his budget proposals. While hinting that he might look at extending the state's 6 percent sales tax to now-exempt items, he said, however, he would not agree to broadening the sales tax to food, drugs and clothing.

House Speaker Fred Norton said earlier that Perpich's proposal to tax purchases of local governments "doesn't make much sense" because it would only be passed on in higher property taxes. Norton said he would consider broadening the sales tax to include services, but he, too, ruled out food, clothing and drugs.

Perpich said, too, that he "wouldn't mind" if legislators laid over until next year his complex property tax revision plan, which has run into strong opposition in the Legislature.

He made the remarks after private

**Sales tax** continued on page 8A

### Almanac

**Tuesday, March 24, 1987**
**83rd day; 282 to go this year.**
**Sunrise: 6:10. Sunset: 6:30**

**Today's weather/**

Wind, maybe rain

Today will probably be windy and wet, with a 40 percent chance of thunderstorms. A high of 55 is expected, with winds out of the east from 10 to 20 miles per hour.

**Index/**

**Martin missing**

**Dean Paul Martin, son of entertainer Dean Martin, piloted a jet that is missing. 16D.**

## Triple Five is among five potential suitors for Donaldsons Stores

**By Neal St. Anthony**
Staff Writer

Triple Five Corp. of Canada, which is developing the giant Mall of the Americas in Bloomington, is interested in buying Donaldsons Department Stores, Twin Cities real estate and retail sources said Monday.

Triple Five is one of five prospective buyers, including the nation's largest department store operator, that have reviewed a prospectus of Donaldsons.

Acquiring the Minneapolis-based 15-store chain would give Triple Five, the company owned by the Ghermezian brothers, "a captive anchor (store) at the new mall," said Dick Guidera, a local shopping center consultant.

Triple Five, which has yet to name tenants, needs big department stores to serve as anchors for its $500 million project on the former Met Stadium site.

It is not known whether Triple Five or any other companies have submitted bids for Donaldsons, which is being sold following a takeover of its parent company, Allied Stores Corp. of New York, by another Canadian

**Donaldsons** continued on page 6A

Twin Cities DFL legislators criticize Perpich /1B
Milwaukee fans already have pennant fever /1D
Humphrey moves toward Senate candidacy /1B

Variety
Richard Harris loves being lured back to 'Camelot' /1C

Minneapolis STAR and Tribune

1A. Metro
Friday
April 17 / 1987
4 Sections
35¢ Single copy

Volume VI/Number 13



# Winter free to sell his Vikings stock

## Pohlad, Jacobs win round in bid for control

**By Margaret Zack**
Staff Writer

The Minnesota Supreme Court has cleared the way for Max Winter to sell his Minnesota Vikings stock to Carl Pohlad, Irwin Jacobs and former Vikings quarterback Fran Tarkenton.

In a 4-3 decision to be filed today, the court said Vikings president Winter and his three daughters did not have to offer their stock to other shareholders before selling to outsiders.

Winter owned one-third of the team's voting stock and 46 percent of its equity, which he sold for $25 million to Pohlad, Jacobs and Tarkenton.

Shareholders John Skoglund and the E.W. Boyer estate, who each hold a third of the voting stock, claimed that agreements signed in 1977 and 1984 gave them right of first refusal to Winter's shares.

But the Supreme Court said the agreements had not been properly

**Vikings** continued on page 10A

## FCC broadens its definition of indecency

The Federal Communications Commission asked Thursday for the possible prosecution of a California radio station on obscenity charges, serving notice that it will impose a broader definition of indecency over the airwaves.

The prosecution request to the Justice Department, as well as warnings to two other companies and an amateur broadcaster, came as the FCC said it no longer would limit its definition of indecency to the famous "seven dirty words." It also said broadcasting after 10 p.m. no longer was safe harbor. **Page 3A.**

# Concerns voiced as Shultz briefs allies on Soviet proposal

**From News Services**

**Brussels, Belgium**
Secretary of State George Shultz briefed NATO allies Thursday on his talks with Soviet leaders in Moscow, and several expressed concern about a Soviet proposal to eliminate both short-range and medium-range nuclear missiles in Europe.

Shultz appeared more accepting of the Soviet package than were representatives of several European countries, raising the possibility that the issue could become a source of contention between the United States and its allies.

Arriving in California later yesterday to brief President Reagan on his trip, Shultz said he expected a prompt response by the NATO allies on the missile proposal.

Shultz flew to Point Mugu Naval Air Station and was taken by helicopter to brief Reagan, who is vacationing at his mountaintop ranch near Santa Barbara. On his way back from Brussels, Shultz stopped at Pease Air Force Base in New Hampshire.

**Shultz** continued on page 7A

# St. Paul playwright wins Pulitzer for drama

**By Peter Vaughan**
Staff Writer

St. Paul playwright August Wilson received the 1986-87 Pulitzer Prize for Drama Thursday for "Fences," a taut family drama that opened on Broadway in March, with James Earl Jones in the leading role.

The Pulitzer is the country's highest playwriting honor, and its recipients have included Eugene O'Neill, Thornton Wilder, Tennessee Williams, Edward Albee, David Mamet and Sam Shepard. Wilson is the first Minnesota playwright to win the award, which honors the best new play staged in the United States during the previous year.

Wilson, 42, came to St. Paul from Pittsburgh in 1977 and began writing plays soon after. His first break came in 1980 when he was named a fellow of the Playwrights Center in Minneapolis for a play called "Jitney," which was staged in the Twin Cities in 1984 by Penumbra Theatre. The only other Twin Cities productions of Wilson plays were Penumbra's stagings of "Black Bart and the Sacred Hills" and "Malcolm," a one-man play about Black Muslim leader Malcolm X. "Ma Rainey's Black Bottom," Wilson's first Broadway play, will open May 7 at Penumbra.

The Pulitzer for biography also went to a work addressing the black experience in America, "Bearing the Cross: Martin Luther King Jr. and the Southern Christian Leadership Conference," by David J. Garrow, an associate professor at City College of New York. The fiction prize went to Peter Taylor for the novel "A Summons to Memphis," which

**Pulitzer** continued on page 10A

■ The Philadelphia Inquirer wins 3 Pulitzers. Page 15A.

Staff Photo by Tom Sweeney

**St. Paul playwright August Wilson: "It's always pleasing when people see value in your work and go as far as giving you a prize for it."**

# Senate debates sales tax on services

## Called preferable to the alternatives

**By Betty Wilson**
Staff Writer

If your car needs a tuneup or a muffler, it might pay to get done right away.

If your refrigerator needs fixing, this might be a good idea to call the repairman.

Getting your winter clothes drycleaned before putting them away?

After July 1 you may have to pay a 6 percent sales tax on those services, and others.

A state Senate panel, looking for new taxes to balance the 1987-89 budget, is considering a bill that would extend the 6 percent sales tax to about 100 business and personal services.

It has been called "the yuppie tax" because it would fall on fees charged by attorneys, accountants, architects, engineers and other professional people whose services are often bought by well-heeled Minnesotans.

Though a similar bill isn't moving in the House, a sales tax on services is likely to be more palatable than many revenue-raising options to conferees who will assemble the tax bill next month.

Whether to tax what one critic calls "all that Mickey Mouse stuff" is shaping up as a major test of whether Senate DFL leaders can keep their

**Sales tax** continued on page 8A

# Drug raids net 19 on Wall Street

## Cocaine used in trading, agents say

**Washington Post**

**New York, N.Y.**
Federal drug agents conducted raids in the Wall Street financial district Thursday, breaking up what they described as a ring of young stockbrokers who traded stocks, customer lists and tips for cocaine.

Drug Enforcement Administration (DEA) agents swept through four brokerage firms at 10 a.m. in simultaneous raids, creating traffic jams and drawing crowds of curious bystanders as they took 15 brokers and other employees into custody.

Later, they were marched — chain-gang style — about 100 yards from Manhattan's federal building to U.S. District Court for arraignment. Ranging in age from 20 to 35 and dressed mostly in business suits, many walked with their heads ducked to avoid photographers.

Robert M. Stutman, special agent in charge of the New York DEA office, said 19 people have been arrested — 16 of them employees of securities firms — in what has been named Operation Closing Bell. All are being charged with possession and distribution of cocaine. He said he expects the investigation to continue, with special attention from the Securities and Exchange Commission and the Internal Revenue Service.

**Cocaine** continued on page 10A

United Press International

**Wall Street employees, arrested on drug charges, were marched from the federal building in New York City.**

# U.S. clears way for patents on new forms of animal life

**New York Times**

**Washington, D.C.**
The federal government, in a decision with broad moral and ethical implications, said Thursday that it was clearing the way for inventors to patent new forms of animal life created through gene splicing.

The policy also will allow the patenting of animals with new traits produced by a host of new reproductive technologies, including genetic engineering.

The policy, adopted by the Commerce Department's Patent and Trademark Office and scheduled to be published early next week, makes the United States the first country to patent animals.

The policy specifically bars the patenting of new genetic characteristics in humans, but one official of the U.S. Patent and Trademark Office acknowledged that the decision could eventually lead to commercial pro-

**Genetics** continued on page 8A

## Almanac

**Friday, April 17, 1987**
**107th day; 258 to go this year**
**Sunrise: 6:26. Sunset: 8:01**

### Today's weather/

Get out!

There's no point in being indoors today. It's going to be sunny and in the high 70s.

### Index/

**Sports**

4 homers help Tigers beat Twins 15-7/**1D**

**Variety**

Corinne Chilstrom: She'll leave parish to aid a bishop/**1C**

**Shelter**

At $1.45 million, this estate near Winona could be a bargain/**25S**

Minneapolis **STAR and Tribune** 1A Metro

Saturday May 30/1987
5 Sections
35¢ Single copy

Volume VI/Number 56

Section A/Part I

# Jurgens guilty of murder

## Sanity phase will decide her fate

By Dan Oberdorfer
Staff Writer

More than 22 years after Dennis Jurgens' death, a jury Friday convicted his adoptive mother of murder, deliberating only 3½ hours.

The jury in the oldest homicide case ever tried in Minnesota found that Lois Jurgens, 61, unintentionally killed her adopted son through a brutal pattern of abuse that culminated in his death in April of 1965.

Jurgens was acquitted of a charge of intending to kill the 3½-year-old boy.

Jerry Sherwood, Dennis' birth mother, let out a loud sigh of relief when the guilty verdict was read in a St. Paul courtroom late yesterday afternoon. She and her other children cheered, burst into tears and hugged. "The baby can rest in peace now," Sherwood said.

The verdict means that on Monday a second phase of the trial will begin to determine if Jurgens was insane when she caused Dennis' bowel to rupture, which killed him in a matter of days.

Jurgens, a Washington County homemaker, sat and stared straight ahead for 15 minutes after the verdict was read. Her husband, Harold, came to her side to comfort her.

**Jurgens** continued on page 8A

Staff Photo by Donald Black

**Lois Jurgens left the Ramsey County Courthouse in St. Paul Friday after being convicted of third-degree murder.**

## Pilot's stunt has Soviets red-faced

By William Tuohy
Los Angeles Times

Moscow, U.S.S.R.
The young West German pilot who put his light plane down Thursday night in Red Square, apparently as a lark, was interrogated Friday by distressed Soviet authorities.

Officials said that although the pilot, 19-year-old Mathias Rust of Hamburg, may look on the flight as a stunt, it is no laughing matter to the Soviet government and may have serious military and political ramifications.

Soviet officials were described as anxious to learn how Rust managed to penetrate Soviet airspace and proceed, in daylight, for 560 miles or so from Helsinki to Moscow through what is reputed to be the world's finest air defense system, made up of jet fighters, armed helicopters, missiles and antiaircraft guns.

Further, they would like to know how Rust, flying a single-engine, four-seat Cessna, could circle the Soviet capital, over which all flights are prohibited, and put down next to the Kremlin, the seat of Soviet power. "The implications for Soviet defenses, and for the whole debate on how a war could start by mistake, are astounding," a military analyst said.

The Soviet government was believed to be highly embarrassed by the incident.

Some observers said it might be seized on by opponents of Soviet

**Flight** continued on page 7A

## Five 'Twilight Zone' defendants acquitted

Associated Press

Los Angeles, Calif.
A jury found "Twilight Zone" director John Landis and four associates not guilty of involuntary manslaughter Friday in the movie set deaths of actor Vic Morrow and two children nearly five years ago.

The Superior Court jury deliberated for nine days after the 10-month trial of Landis, associate producer George Folsey Jr., production manager Dan Allingham, special effects coordinator Paul Stewart and Dorcey Wingo, pilot of the helicopter that crashed in a firestorm.

It was Hollywood's first criminal trial resulting from deaths on a movie set and the case was watched anxiously in the film community, where it was viewed as an indictment of safety standards.

"This was all an unforeseeable accident and you don't prosecute people for unforeseeable accidents," said jury forewoman Lois Rogers.

Landis said he was "very grateful to

**Verdict** continued on page 10A

### Lynn group buys Vikings stock

Minnesota Vikings general manager Mike Lynn and local businessmen Wheelock Whitney and Jaye Dyer on Friday bought most of the one-third Vikings voting stock owned by the Boyer estate.

The announcement of the sale came shortly after the state Supreme Court denied an appeal from the Boyer family and one-third stock owner John Skoglund asking for a rehearing on an earlier decision that permitted Max Winter to sell his one-third stock to Irwin Jacobs and Carl Pohlad. **Page 1D.**

## Perpich's choice for judge has history of mental problems

By Jim Parsons and Joe Kimball
Staff Writers

Sean Rice, a Minneapolis attorney with a history of mental illness, was named a Hennepin County district judge Friday by Gov. Rudy Perpich, who said he believed people who have overcome mental illness should not be denied opportunities.

Perpich said that he has assurances from doctors that Rice's disorder will not affect his performance as a judge.

Rice, the 35-year-old son of veteran DFL state Rep. Jim Rice, said that he has been hospitalized seven times for his disorder, most recently in 1985.

His doctor told Perpich that Rice's illness is commonly known as manic depression and that Rice is "psychiatrically stable" as long as he takes medication.

"Given Sean's willingness to continue (lithium carbonate) therapy, his future mental health status should continue to be satisfactory" and he can "perform at the effective, responsible level he has in the past," wrote Dr. John Kelly, a professor of psychiatry at the University of Minnesota and associate head of the Department of Family Practice and Community Health.

Sources who know Rice said yesterday that his illness has occasionally manifested itself in inappropriate and illogical comments. However, several judges said that Rice has always behaved appropriately in their courts.

In discussing the appointment yesterday, Perpich said he has long been concerned that people who have

**Rice** continued on page 10A

## Medicare benefits plan approved by Senate panel

Associated Press

Washington, D.C.
The Senate Finance Committee unanimously approved a catastrophic-illness Medicare benefit Friday that would cover all hospital and most doctor bills for the elderly after a $1,700 annual deductible is met.

Medicare now pays full hospital bills for only 59 days a year and only 80 percent of covered doctor bills, no matter how high they are.

The Senate bill is similar to a House version already approved by the Ways and Means Committee, including a tax-based progressive mechanism to finance the bulk of the program.

The striking similarity between both the benefits and financing scheme outlined in the Senate and House bills is a strong indication of the final shape of legislation almost certain to

**Medicare** continued on page 9A

## A tearful tribute to a fallen president

Associated Press

**Sen. Edward Kennedy, left, and Massachusetts Gov. Michael Dukakis wiped away tears Friday while former First Lady Jacqueline Kennedy Onassis looked on during the dedication of the John Fitzgerald Kennedy Park on the Harvard campus in Cambridge, Mass. It occurred on what would have been Kennedy's 70th birthday. A report on what JFK's life after the presidency might have been: Page 3A.**

## Loan-disclosure law puzzles some lenders

By Ingrid Sundstrom
Staff Writer

Minnesotans seeking mortgages to buy or refinance their homes next week could find lenders unwilling to guarantee interest rates until just before closing.

Many mortgage lenders said Friday they can't risk offering long-term interest rate commitments until the dust settles on new legislation that lenders call ambiguous, too restrictive and puts them under threat of what they called "extreme penalties."

If Gov. Rudy Perpich signs the legislation Monday as expected, it will take effect Tuesday.

The legislation, passed in the session that ended May 18, requires mortgage lenders to disclose to borrowers — in writing — all of the terms and costs of the loan, and all of the steps that would be required to process, approve and close the loan. It calls for penalties of $500 to be paid to the borrower if a lender fails to make these disclosures or if the lender creates "unreasonable" delays in processing a loan application. Also, the lender would be liable for all addi-

**Mortgages** continued on page 6A

## Almanac

**Saturday, May 30, 1987**
**150th day; 215 to go this year.**
**Sunrise: 5:31. Sunset: 8:51.**

### Stormy possibilities

There will be variable clouds today with a 40 percent chance of thunderstorms. The high will be around 85.

### Index/

**Sports**

- **Twins sweep White Sox**/Double victory makes win streak 7
- **Willmar 5, Hopkins 4**/A last-gasp 5-run rally wins Class AA championship
- **Seahawks pick Bosworth**/Oklahoma linebacker claims he'll sit out a year

**PTL seeks Chapter 11 bankruptcy protection**/3A

**Shelter**

Prize-winning design for 'A New American House' finally will be built/**23S**

Minneapolis **STAR and Tribune**

1A.. Metro

Saturday June 13/1987
5 Sections
35¢ Single copy

Volume VI/Number 70



Section A/Part I

# Night falls on Lake Wobegon, but Keillor leaves a legacy

**By Kim Ode**
Staff Writer

**■ Keillor was a throwback to time before TV. Page 1C.**

> "It's real easy for me to say I think it was the best show in broadcasting. And to see it develop from the morning show to the Saturday show, well, it was quite the deal, no doubt about it."
> **Writer Howard Mohr**

Writer Howard Mohr has known Garrison Keillor for years, yet there never was a more revealing moment in their relationship than one Saturday evening about seven years ago.

"We were sitting around his kitchen table talking, and we were drinking a little whiskey, too," Mohr said. "We were talking and talking and the main subject was religion, which was a common subject.

"Well, it must have been 1:30, 2 in the morning when he told me that Powdermilk Biscuits were the grace of God. And I tell you what, I believed it. . . . Then I could see why he often started the show with a Powdermilk Biscuits Spot — 'Nice to know something so plain can be so good.' 'Heavens! they're tasty.' 'Has your family tried 'em?' — It all fit. I really believe he thought he had a kind of mission there."

The mission changed, of course, as the Powdermilk Biscuit logo started appearing on T-shirts and coffee mugs, as the cast started traveling in jets instead of buses, as it finally appeared on TV. At 5 p.m. today, the mission as people have come to know it will end when "A Prairie Home Companion" is broadcast for the last time.

The Saturday-evening institution grew out of a free-wheeling morning show Keillor hosted in the early 1970s, but it owes allegiance to the Grand Ole Opry, which Keillor once wrote about for the New Yorker magazine. In 13 years, the audience for "A Prairie Home Companion" has grown to 4 million people who tune in on 279 stations of the American Public Radio network. Based on the characters and settings of his radio monologues, Keillor's first novel, "Lake Wobegon Days," sold 1.2 million copies in hardcover, and 2.3 million paperback copies have been printed.

Ironically, the show that celebrated the worth of shy people turned Keillor into a celebrity, and led to some disquieting weeks in Lake Wobegon.

**Keillor** continued on page 9A

# Marines drop Bracy spy charge

## Prosecutors cite inability to corroborate confession

**New York Times**

**Washington, D.C.**
Charges were dropped Friday against a second Marine guard accused of spying at the U.S. Embassy in Moscow, in what amounted to the collapse of the case brought against him by military prosecutors.

Cpl. Arnold Bracy, 21, New York City, was freed from the Marine brig in Quantico, Va. At a press conference he accused investigators of coercing his confession and misusing the results of a lie-detector test.

Similar charges were dismissed last month against another Marine guard, Sgt. Clayton J. Lonetree, although he still faces a court-martial on other espionage counts.

Lonetree, who set off the spying investigation last year when he confessed to an affair with a Soviet woman, is accused of providing Soviet agents with secret U.S. documents, including embassy blueprints and the names of U.S. intelligence officers.

The two guards, who worked as a team, originally were charged with allowing Soviet agents to roam through the U.S. Embassy.

The Marine Corps said it had dropped the case against Bracy be-

**Marine guard** continued on page 11A

Associated Press

**A spectator jumped up and applauded Friday while President Reagan gave a thumbs-up sign at the end of his speech in front of the Brandenburg Gate in West Berlin. At right is West German Chancellor Helmut Kohl.**

# Met Council finds no harm in new NBA arena

## But report criticizes plan as unnecessary

**By Laurie Blake**
Staff Writer

A new Minneapolis basketball arena would not drain enough business from the Metropolitan Sports Center and the St. Paul Civic Center to warrant Metropolitan Council action delaying its construction, the council staff advised Friday.

But the staff criticized the proposed $54 million home of the Timberwolves as an unnecessary public investment. It recommended that Minneapolis reconsider its $19 million backing for the National Basketball Association (NBA) arena. It also urged Timberwolves' owners Harvey Ratner and Marv Wolfenson to reopen negotiations with Bloomington's Met Center, the St. Paul Civic Center, or consider sharing facilities with the University of Minnesota.

The Metropolitan Council cannot force Minneapolis to reconsider the project, however, unless the council disagrees with its staff and concludes that the arena would seriously threaten the others. In that case, the council could suspend the arena's construction for up to a year.

The staff's recommendations, while not binding on the council, are typically adopted. The council will hold a public hearing on the report June 24 and decide on the recommendations in July.

The council staff's somewhat contradictory recommendation — to allow the project to proceed while advising that it not be built — gave both sides in the arena debate reason to claim to have scored points yesterday.

The staff explained its position by

**Arena** continued on page 8A

# Case against Lonetree appearing to crumble

**Analysis**

**By Paul McEnroe**
Staff Writer

The unraveling of the Marine spy scandal, namely the release of Marine Cpl. Arnold Bracy in Quantico, Va., means it will be much harder to prosecute Sgt. Clayton Lonetree of St. Paul on espionage charges.

Attorneys and legal experts said Friday that Lonetree's chances for acquittal are growing because the case against Bracy, the defendant prosecutors had wanted to use to testify against Lonetree, was too weak, and therefore evidence against Lonetree is more suspect.

What is happening — first with the dropping of a serious charge last month against Lonetree that he let Soviet agents roam the U.S. Embassy in Moscow and now with Bracy's release — is the crumbling of an investigation. The latest development raises questions about why the military appears to be botching what once was believed to be a sound case involving one of the country's most damaging spy cases.

A legal expert in espionage law ventured her opinion in an interview yesterday with the Star and Tribune, saying the weakened case indicates

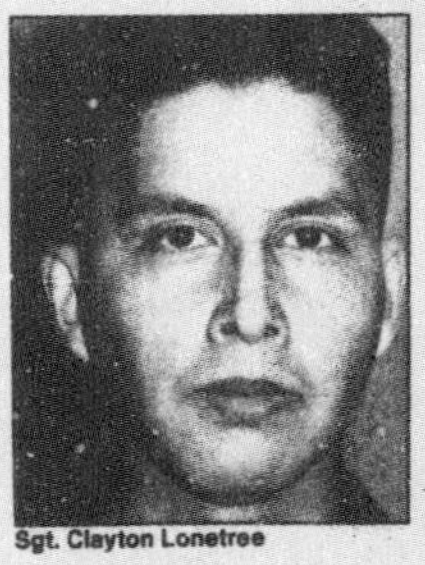

**Sgt. Clayton Lonetree**

**Investigation** continued on page 5A

# Reagan stands before Berlin Wall, challenges Gorbachev to tear it down

**From News Services**

**Berlin**
President Reagan stood Friday before the Brandenburg Gate, the symbol of the divided city of Berlin, and challenged Soviet leader Mikhail Gorbachev to tear down the Berlin Wall.

"General Secretary Gorbachev, if you seek peace, if you seek prosperity for the Soviet Union and Eastern Europe, if you seek liberalization: Come here, to this gate," Reagan said. "Mr. Gorbachev, open this gate. Mr. Gorbachev, tear down this wall.

"This wall will fall," Reagan declared in the speech, carried by loudspeakers to several hundred East Berliners trying to listen from beyond the gate. "For it cannot withstand faith. It cannot withstand truth. The wall cannot withstand freedom."

The speech was intended as a dramatic capstone of Reagan's trip to Europe, and the setting was stark, with East German sentries watching through binoculars from atop the Brandenburg Gate.

Accompanied by West German Chancellor Helmut Kohl, Reagan stood behind a bulletproof glass shield on a raised platform and gazed over the wall at the Brandenburg Gate and the Reichstag, the former German parliament building. The

**Reagan** continued on page 6A

## Almanac

**Saturday, June 13, 1987**
**164th day; 201 to go this year**
**Sunrise: 5:26. Sunset: 9:01**

### Today's weather/

Pool it

Head for the nearest body of water. It'll be sunny with a high in the lower 90s.

### Inside/

**Cut in jet noise forecast**
Negotiated voluntary agreements with airlines will reduce airport noise up to 14 percent from last August's peak levels, the chairman of the Metropolitan Airports Commission predicts. **Page 1B.**

### Index/



| | |
|---|---|
| News general | 372-4141 |
| Want Ads | 372-4242 |
| Circulation | 372-4343 |

## U.S. deficit falls; prices up slightly

The U.S. trade deficit narrowed for the second consecutive month, while wholesale prices, posting their smallest increase in three months, eased fears about runaway inflation.

The better-than-expected statistics were greeted enthusiastically on Wall Street, where stock prices jumped 17.60 points for a gain of 51.58 for the week. **Page 7B.**

# Jurgens was told in '65 she wouldn't be prosecuted

**By Dan Oberdorfer**
Staff Writer

An assistant Ramsey County attorney told Lois Jurgens in 1965 that prosecutors had no intention of bringing criminal charges against her at that time for the death of her adopted son, Dennis, it was disclosed Friday.

A year after Dennis died, then-Ramsey County Juvenile Judge Archie Gingold reassured Jurgens that no charges would be brought, telling her lawyer that the threat of prosecution "is way by the boards now."

Jurgens, who was convicted of murder last week, operated for the next 21 years under the assumption that prosecution of her case had been ruled out, her attorney, Douglas Thomson, said yesterday. It wasn't until last year, when Dennis' birth mother, Jerry Sherwood, began raising questions that old reports in the case were re-examined, and charges were finally initiated.

Thomson said yesterday that the statements assuring Jurgens that she would not be prosecuted will form a cornerstone of his appeal of her conviction for unintentional murder. He said they amount to a contract not to bring charges, a contention with which prosecutors vehemently disagree.

Yesterday's development was the latest twist in the oldest homicide case ever prosecuted in Minnesota. Both reassuring statements were made in open court and recorded in a dusty old transcript of juvenile proceedings that was accidentally found last month just as jurors were being selected for Jurgens' murder trial. The transcript does not explain why prosecutors decided not to bring charges against Jurgens, who is now 61.

According to the transcript, then-Assistant County Attorney Bertrand Poritsky said in October 1965 that his office was "not interested in prosecution of these parents at this time."

Poritsky, now a Ramsey County district judge, made the comments during a juvenile court hearing before

**Jurgens** continued on page 10A

**Senate OKs trillion-dollar federal budget plan/3A**

**Twins romp past Indians, open up 4-game lead/1D**

**Richfield roof falls, killing construction worker/1B**

**Variety**

Longest-running broadcast show is 50 years old/1C

Minneapolis STAR and Tribune

1A. Metro

Thursday June 25/1987

6 Sections

35¢ Single copy

Volume VI/Number 82




# Anti-takeover session is today

By Gregor W. Pinney and Josephine Marcotty
Staff Writers

Gov. Rudy Perpich Wednesday night called the Minnesota Legislature into a special session today to enact a law designed to prevent a hostile takeover of the Dayton Hudson Corp.

The move came just seven days after Dayton's asked for help in fighting off a threatened takeover from the Dart Group Corp. of Landover, Md. And it came minutes after leaders of the Senate and House agreed on details of the bill.

That was about 10:25 p.m. — just in time to catch the end of the nightly television news and just 45 minutes after the two sides had parted company in apparent irritation over tactics. House members went to their offices across the street in the State Office Building, but eventually cleaned up the last items of disagreement by telephone.

Before the breakup, they had met for nearly two hours in an informal and closed-door conference committee meeting, attended by Dayton Hudson attorneys, to hash over their differing versions of the proposed legislation.

The legislators are to convene at 2 p.m. today and get the new law on the books before Friday, reputedly the favorite day of the week for a strike by corporate raiders.

Committees in both houses had spent the day preparing to negotiate and they met with Perpich at suppertime when, it was expected, he would announce a call of a special session. But the governor refused to call a special session until the legislative leaders reached an agreement.

One of the final sticking points was the Senate's proposal that the entire law go out of existence next year, which would force the Legislature to reexamine the hastily enacted law. House members balked at the idea. But they finally struck a compromise saying that the law will affect all companies for the next two years, but after that only those electing coverage.

The two sides also compromised on a plan for discouraging "greenmail" buyouts of corporate raiders that was stiffer than the House wanted but less than the Senate proposed.

**Dayton Hudson** continued on 15A

## One man raised question about bogus bid

By Maura Lerner and Josephine Marcotty
Staff Writers

**Cincinnati, Ohio**
Even before a bogus takeover attempt of Dayton Hudson Corp. was announced Tuesday, at least one man in a position to know was raising questions about its validity.

Richard Miller, president of Capital Management Corp., said he called the Dow Jones News Service and asked a reporter to cancel the press release "three or four minutes" after he heard his employee, P. David Herrlinger, phoning it in.

The press release ultimately touched off a trading fury on Wall Street, briefly raising the paper value of Dayton Hudson by almost $1 billion before it was revealed as the "mistake" of a troubled man who since has been hospitalized for psychiatric evaluation.

Miller, in an interview Wednesday, said he tried to cancel the release because he feared that he and his company had been falsely implicated in the deal and he did not believe there was any validity to the offer. "It was not an offer that I had any knowledge of," he said. "I asked them to cancel the wire."

Dow Jones officials tell the story

**Hoax** continued on page 12A

**Inside/**

As they prepare to enact anti-takeover legislation, state lawmakers are trying hard to make it appear they are not merely rubber-stamping legislation designed to help Dayton Hudson, the state's leading retailer.

**Analysis, Page 16A.**

**Other stories, pages 12, 13A.**

## Opposition regroups after talks fail in Seoul

### More protests are threatened

From News Services

**Seoul, South Korea**
Opposition leader Kim Young-sam and his newly freed ally, Kim Dae-jung, discussed South Korea's political crisis Thursday after calling for massive new demonstrations when talks with President Chun Doo-hwan collapsed.

Opposition politicians had denounced political concessions offered by Chun yesterday, and suggested they would encourage a redoubling of a two-week-old campaign of protests against the government.

But government spokesmen played down the rejection as posturing, and said the government and opposition were still headed toward a "grand compromise."

Kim Young-sam went to Kim Dae-jung's home early today for their second meeting in two days, then met with U.S. envoy Gaston Sigur, an assistant secretary of state. No details were released on the meeting between the two opposition leaders.

Kim Young-sam quoted Sigur as saying the United States was opposed to "any military move" by the government, such as the imposition of martial law.

Chun presented his concessions to Kim Young-sam, head of the Reunification Democratic Party, in a three-hour meeting yesterday. It was the first time the two had met.

**Korea** continued on page 10A

Staff Photo by David Brewster

**Officer Mike McKenzie examined the slippery mayfly mess Tuesday night on the Interstate Hwy. 494 bridge in South St. Paul.**

## Some shiver, others rejoice at mayfly blizzard

By Ellen Foley
Staff Writer

The state dusted off its snowplows and dispatched them to an Interstate Hwy. 494 bridge in South St. Paul Tuesday night, where a slippery mess had piled up on the road, causing two accidents and forcing the State Patrol to close the highway for a short time.

Millions of mayflies attracted by the lights swarmed above the bridge over the Mississippi River about 11:30 p.m., then died after their frantic annual mating ritual.

Their bodies formed up to a foot of slippery goo on the highway, which had to be plowed and then sanded before it was reopened.

Experts forecast that the snowplows will have to stand ready because another enormous batch of adult flies is expected to emerge during the week of July 5 for their day of life.

While the mess might send shivers down some people's spines, biologists and federal officials said people in the Twin Cities should rejoice that the mayflies are back.

Their return in the past two years after a 10-year hiatus signals that the Mississippi River is getting healthier — slowly being transformed from an open sewer back into a natural wonder, experts said.

**Mayflies** continued on page 10A

Jackie Gleason

## Jackie Gleason dies of cancer

Associated Press

**Lauderhill, Fla.**
Jackie Gleason, the rotund "Great One" who got laughs and riches as a blustering bus driver in "The Honeymooners" and an Academy Award nomination as a pool shark in "The Hustler," died Wednesday.

Gleason, 71, died of cancer at his home at 7:20 p.m., said his wife, Marilyn.

He was released June 18 from Imperial Point Medical Center in Fort Lauderdale after spending about a month there. Lauderhill is a suburb of Ford Lauderdale.

Gleason, creator of the Poor Soul, Reggie van Gleason III and Joe the Bartender, was one of television's biggest draws in the 1950s. Millions of viewers shouted along when bus driver Ralph Kramden turned to his wife, shaking his fist and threatening, "One of these days, Alice."

**Gleason** continued on 8A

## U.S. accuses Chrysler of altering odometers in sales of 'new' cars

From News Services

**Detroit, Mich.**
Chrysler Corp. was indicted Wednesday on charges that it committed fraud by disconnecting the odometers on as many as 60,000 new cars that were driven by its executives and later sold as new cars.

Some of the cars were involved in accidents, repaired and then sold, said the 16-count indictment by a federal grand jury in St. Louis. Two Chrysler officials also were indicted.

Chrysler denied that it had done anything illegal and said the cars were part of a "legitimate quality assurance program." It did not deny the tampering, however, and said that in the future it would keep the odometers connected during testing.

The odometer practice came to light when Missouri state highway patrolmen stopped Chrysler executives for speeding, according to a Justice Department spokesman. The drivers gave the excuse that they did not know how fast they were going because disconnecting the odometer, which records miles driven, also had turned off the speedometer.

It is a common practice in the auto

**Chrysler** continued on page 9A

**Business news inside/**

■ A federal judge in Minneapolis approved a $5.7 million settlement of a class action lawsuit against Burlington Northern that is believed to be one of Minnesota's biggest sex-discrimination suits. The action covered 13,700 employees, though only about 2,800 filed claims.

■ Thanks to the dollar's prolonged decline, the United States has seen the worst of its trade deficits, economists, businessmen and other experts say. The shrinking deficits could blunt efforts in Congress to impede imports, they say. Nevertheless deficits are expected to remain huge at least into the 1990s.

**Details on Page 1M.**

## Religious organizations may favor workers of their faith, court rules

From News Services

**Washington, D.C.**
The Supreme Court ruled unanimously Wednesday that religious organizations may practice employment discrimination by favoring members of their faith even for non-religious jobs.

The justices, in a case involving the Mormon Church, said 1972 legislation that exempts religious groups from a federal antibias law does not violate separation of church and state.

In another decision, the court ruled that a Houston police secretary could not be fired for having said on the day President Reagan was shot in 1981, "If they go for him again, I hope they get him."

Justice Thurgood Marshall, writing for a 5-4 majority in Rankin vs. McPherson, said the employee's free-speech right must be balanced against police department's need for efficient operations.

**Ruling** continued on page 17A

■ Officials cannot be convicted of mail fraud unless the public loses money. **Page 7A.**

## Almanac

**Thursday, June 25, 1987.
176th day; 189 to go this year.
Sunrise: 5:27. Sunset: 9:04.**

**Today's weather/**

The Twin Cities will be partly cloudy and cooler today with a high of 78.

**Index/**

**Sports**

Twins hold on to win /1D

**Variety**

A summer festival guide to help cover the circuit of fun /1C

**Taste**

Food for glorious eating on the Fourth /1T

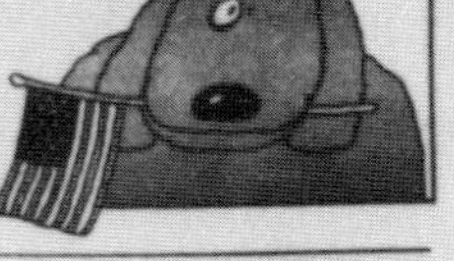

Minneapolis

STAR and Tribune

1A. Metro

Wednesday
July 1/1987
6 Sections
35¢ Single copy

Volume VI/Number 88



# Chun OKs elections

## He calls on South Korea to 'work miracle'

New York Times

**Seoul, South Korea**
President Chun Doo-hwan approved sweeping democratic changes today, including direct presidential elections, and said he hopes they will usher in "a new era of democratic development and mature politics."

"Let us work another miracle by developing Korea into a model of political development deserving to be so recorded in world history," Chun said in a nationally broadcast address. "We must not be content with having newly become a model of economic development."

Chun's acceptance of change, recommended unexpectedly Monday by his designated successor, sealed one of the most dramatic and sudden reversals of policy in South Korea's 39-year history.

It was an action Chun clearly did not seek, but instead had forced upon him by a mixture of street protests, U.S. pressure and concern about the long-range consequences for the South Korean economy and the 1988 Olympic Games in Seoul.

In his speech, Chun referred to the recent civil unrest in Seoul and other major cities, and in the process extended a rare olive branch to college students who have been in the vanguard of antigovernment protest.

"I believe that everyone — the students who have participated in demonstrations, the policemen who have labored to quell them, the citizens who have been tormented by the clouds of tear gas — has the same desire to defend and promote free-

Korea continued on page 17A

Associated Press

**South Koreans filled a shop in downtown Seoul to watch President Chun Doo-hwan's nationally televised speech today. Chun approved sweeping democratic changes, including direct presidential elections.**

A LETTER FROM THE PUBLISHER

## To our readers/

For the past two decades, the people of the Twin Cities have been growing closer together. It started when Interstate Hwy. 94 cut travel time between downtown Minneapolis and downtown St. Paul from nearly an hour to less than 15 minutes, and it's been evolving since.

There's no doubt about it: The Twin Cities today is a single metropolitan area, embracing not only Minneapolis and St. Paul but other cities and suburban communities as well. It looks like one metro area when you fly over it. And increasingly, it feels that way, as people throughout the area watch the same TV stations, listen to the same radio personalities, go to the same theaters, root for the same sports teams and shop in the same department stores.

The Star and Tribune, since its merger in 1982 from two newspapers into one, has been paying steadily more attention to the whole Twin Cities area, and last fall opened a bureau in downtown St. Paul.

Now this newspaper is ready for the natural next step, a step which we think reflects what is happening in this metro area and enables us to serve our readers better.

Starting August 31, we will become a truly metrowide newspaper.

On that day, we will change our name to Star Tribune: Newspaper of the Twin Cities. And every day, we will publish a Minneapolis edition, a St. Paul edition, and, as before, a state edition for the rest of our readers in Minnesota and surrounding states.

Roger Parkinson

The Minneapolis edition will give more space and prominent display to news that affects people in Minneapolis and western suburbs, while the St. Paul edition will focus more on news that affects people in St. Paul and eastern suburbs.

The Minneapolis edition will go to readers in Minneapolis and the western suburbs, including

Letter continued on page 6A

Star Tribune
NEWSPAPER OF THE TWIN CITIES

# Michigan picked for low-level radioactive waste site

By Dean Rebuffoni
Staff Writer

**Dearborn, Mich.**
Michigan was chosen overwhelmingly Tuesday as the host state for a $250 million repository for the low-level radioactive waste generated by seven Midwest states, including Minnesota.

An interstate commission also selected Ohio as the first alternate host state in the event Michigan decides to withdraw from the commission, as some of its residents said yesterday that it should, citing environmental and public-health concerns. Minnesota was chosen as the second alternate.

Michigan's selection was widely expected, largely because it generates by far the largest amount of waste — more than one-third of the total — of the states in the Midwest Interstate Low-Level Radioactive Waste Commission. Ohio is the second-largest generator; Minnesota is third. The other commission members are Wisconsin, Iowa, Missouri and Indiana.

Michigan officials said yesterday that they will begin searching for a safe repository site within the state. But they stressed that, before Michigan might accept low-level waste from the other states, it needs firm assurances that federal waste-disposal laws and policies adequately protect Michigan's interests. Existing laws and policies do not, said David Hales, Michigan's representative on the commission.

"Michigan will not site . . . a waste facility that would compromise its public safety, health or environment," he said. Speaking for his boss, Michigan Gov. James Blanchard, Hales called upon all 50 states to examine closely the potential ramifications of the 1980 federal law that requires the states, rather than the federal government, to assume responsibility for disposal of their low-level wastes.

Hales said one of Michigan's major arguments is that Congress has not ensured that there will be adequate liability insurance to protect a host state against claims resulting from

Dump site continued on page 14A

# Bryn Mawr struggle against I-394 wanes

By Mike Kaszuba
Staff Writer

The fight to save a neighborhood in Minneapolis ended, on this particular evening, in the back bedroom of David Gross' home. From a cluttered bookcase behind a door, Gross seized a 400-page government report and began talking of broken promises and highway interchanges all over again.

All in all, it had not been a good night. Only six people, including Gross, had attended the latest neighborhood meeting earlier in the evening. "Frankly, I was disappointed," Gross said later, in a rare acknowledgment that the fight may be waning. For 15 years and something close to 200 meetings, the issue in the Bryn Mawr neighborhood of Minneapolis and four western suburbs has been the $400 million transformation of Hwy. 12 into Interstate Hwy. 394. Throughout that time, Bryn Mawr has had the misfortune of being one of two residential neighborhoods along the 11-mile stretch of highway that, by late 1992, will carry six lanes of traffic from downtown Minneapolis to Wayzata.

But while the cities along I-394 gradually have dropped their opposition to the freeway and now push state highway officials to build it as quickly as possible, the Bryn Mawr neighborhood is still waging a lonely and decidedly uphill campaign against the project.

"Minnetonka, Wayzata, they can't wait. They're pushing

Highway continued on 13A

# Disputed report says U.S. hostages in Iran

Associated Press

**Beirut, Lebanon**
Iranian Revolutionary Guards smuggled two U.S. hostages from Lebanon to Iran a month ago, concealing them in coffins part of the way, a Shiite Muslim source said Tuesday.

A top U.S. official expressed skepticism about the report, and Iran's foreign minister denied it.

The source said the hostages probably were Terry Anderson and Thomas Sutherland, who were seized separately more than two years ago by Shiite extremists loyal to Iran. The source has been reliable in the past on information regarding foreign hostages.

Britain's Independent Television network reported last night that Anderson, Sutherland and Anglican Church negotiator Terry Waite were taken to the Iranian holy city of Qom. Waite dropped from sight after leaving his west Beirut hotel Jan. 20 to meet with hostage holders. The television network also quoted Shiite sources.

It said the hostages were moved by different routes, with the Americans smuggled overland, part of the way in coffins, and Waite by ship, via the Suez Canal and Arabian Sea or, more probably, by ship to Turkey and overland to Iran.

The Associated Press source said the two Americans were taken from Lebanon to the Iranian Embassy in Damascus, the Syrian capital, late in

Hostages continued on page 15A

Terry Anderson

Thomas Sutherland

## Reagan rejects Gulf plan delay

President Reagan rejected Democrats' demands that he delay the planned reflagging of Kuwaiti oil tankers in the Persian Gulf, and Democratic congressional leaders predicted Congress won't block the increased U.S. military presence in the region.

Meanwhile, an Iranian gunboat fired a rocket into a Kuwaiti cargo ship in the Persian Gulf before dawn Tuesday. The attack came near where Iranian missiles hit two Scandinavian supertankers four days ago.

Articles on page 4A.

## Almanac

**Wednesday, July 1, 1987**
**182nd day; 183 to go this year**
**Sunrise: 5:30. Sunset: 9:04**

### Today's weather/

Sunny skies this morning will turn partly cloudy in the afternoon and a thunderstorm is possible in the Twin Cities. High will be in the low 80s.



### Inside/

**Dozier signing reported**

D.J. Dozier reportedly has signed a three-year, $1 million contract with the Minnesota Vikings. **Page 1D.**

**Connors beats Pernfors**

Jimmy Connors won a five-set victory over Mikael Pernfors Tuesday at Wimbledon. Connors, 34, beat Pernfors, 11 years his junior, in a 1-6, 1-6, 7-5, 6-4, 6-2 decision that took three hours, 40 minutes. **Page 1D.**

# Northwest starts campaign against brokering of 'frequent flier' tickets

By John J. Oslund
Staff Writer

Nestled among the "business personals" in the classified section of the Minneapolis Star and Tribune Sunday were eight announcements from ticket brokers eager to buy bonus airline tickets earned by frequent fliers.

Also among those ads, however, was one from Twin Cities-based Northwest Airlines that carried a warning to bargain hunters: People who buy frequent flier tickets from brokers risk having those tickets confiscated and their wallets lightened by the cost of the full fare.

Northwest spokesman Red Tyler said the carrier has placed similar warnings in newspapers in its major markets across the country, pointing out that the bonus tickets become "void if sold."

"We want the frequent flier to utilize the (bonus) ticket for the intended purpose — that is the enjoyment of travel on Northwest Airlines. We are not providing the tickets for any other use."

Tyler said Northwest has asked the Minnesota attorney general to look into what the carrier contends is an illegal use of the bonus awards. The

Coupons continued on page 16A

- Twins methodically conquer Seattle, 5-1/1D
- Faithful gather for 'harmonic convergence'/8A
- Reagan, Congress near accord on contra aid/3A

**Variety**
Seed collectors keep plants from extinction
/1C

Minneapolis STAR and Tribune

1A . Metro

Monday
August 17/1987
4 Sections
35¢ Single copy

Volume VI/Number 135



# 153 die in Northwest crash

## Plane hits overpass on takeoff from Detroit

From News Services

**Romulus, Mich.**
A Northwest Airlines plane crashed in a ball of fire Sunday night shortly after it took off from Detroit Metropolitan Airport, killing all 153 people aboard.

The crash of Flight 255, bound for Phoenix, Ariz., and then Orang County, Calif., scattered wreckage and pieces of bodies over half a square mile of ground.

At least five people on the ground were reported injured, including a 4-year-old girl with serious burns.

Witnesses said the plane hit a freeway overpass shortly before 7:45 p.m. Twin Cities time near a car-rental agency and may have been on fire before it crashed.

Ed Jarvis, an attendant at Airlines Parking, about a mile west of the crash site, said he saw the crash just as night fell. "I saw three fireballs, then lots of smoke. I was inside, and I didn't hear anything, but one of the guys who was outside said it sounded like a bomb going off."

Jarvis said a customer coming to get her car from his lot had told him she saw the plane when it was taking off. "She said there were sparks coming out of the bottom, like a car dragging a muffler."

FBI agents were sent to the scene because of reports that there might have been an explosion before the crash, said FBI spokesman John Anthony in Detroit.

He said the agents would check for any indication that an explosive device had been on the jet.

"There's a great deal of bedlam," said Wayne County Executive Ed McNamara. "Burning metal. Blankets covering what appear to be the remains. It's just total destruction. It just looks like a large bomb fell."

Yesterday's crash was the first since February 1963 in which Northwest passengers died. In that crash, a Northwest Boeing 720 was knocked from the sky by a thunderstorm after it took off from Miami. All 43 people aboard were killed. In 1974, three Northwest crew members were killed when their plane crashed on its way from New York City to Buffalo.

**Crash** continued on page 6A

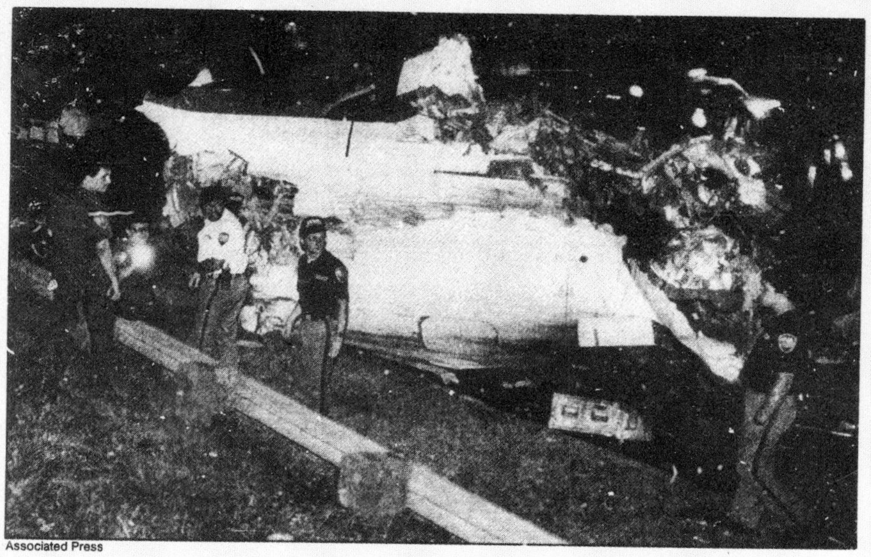

Associated Press

**Emergency officials examined a piece of the fuselage of a Northwest Airlines jet that crashed Sunday north of Detroit Metropolitan Airport.**

### Inside/

- Sunday's crash was the first time in 24 years that passengers died in an accident involving a Northwest Airlines plane. The last occurred in 1963 when 43 people died in a crash in Miami. **Page 7A.**
- Canceled flights, lost baggage and long delays have plagued Northwest Airlines at Detroit Metropolitan Airport since its $884 million merger with Republic Airlines in May 1986. **Page 18D.**

## Couple watched in disbelief

**Romulus, Mich.**
Richard Webb and his wife, Diana, escaped by seconds.

They were driving north on Middle Belt Rd. when Northwest Airlines Flight 255 crashed and killed the 153 passengers and crew on board, injured at least five people on the ground and may have killed others in automobiles.

"If we'd been just a few seconds earlier, we would have been killed when it hit the intersection," Richard Webb said. "When I saw that Thunderbird crushed like someone had stepped on it, I thought God must be looking over my shoulder."

Webb, 37, an electrician, said the crash occurred right in front of the couple.

"The plane was just taking off and heading north. It was on fire. The plane was turned on its side with its wings almost perpendicular to the ground. It struck an airport two-story building with the wing tip, traveled about 200 yards and then hit an Avis rental car agency.

"The plane crashed in flames, stretching from the Avis parking lot to the middle of Wick and Middle Belt Rd. It hit cars that were stopped at the traffic light. I saw at least two hit by the burning plane."

The wings and various airplane parts were scattered from the parking lot to the intersection, he said.

"The main fuselage of the plane slid

**Witness** continued on page 7A

## Iranians threaten to escalate mining of Persian Gulf

From News Services

**Manama, Bahrain**
Iran warned Sunday that it would "plant mines like seeds" throughout the Persian Gulf unless the United States and other Western powers withdraw their naval forces from the region.

The warning, one of several bellicose statements made by members of the Iranian leadership yesterday, came amid reports that the amphibious U.S. assault ship Guadalcanal had arrived in the gulf with eight minesweeping helicopters to help protect convoys of Kuwaiti tankers the U.S. Navy is escorting through the waterway.

Iran's Parliament Speaker Hashemi Rafsanjani said that if Iraq attacks Iranian oil tankers and interrupts Iranian oil shipments out of the gulf, Iran would retaliate by disrupting all oil exports from the region, "even through pipelines."

Iraq sent warplanes deep into Iranian territory yesterday, bombing two oil fields in Ahvaz in southwest Iran, according to a military communique from Baghdad.

The threats and counterthreats underlined the dangers of what is seen by diplomatic observers as a critical moment in the Persian Gulf crisis. Although Iran is seeking to avoid a confrontation, they said, resumed Iraqi air strikes on Iranian shipping, unauthorized raids by Iranian Revolutionary Guards or miscalculation could lead to hostilities involving the U.S. naval forces deployed in the gulf.

The Guadalcanal, which had been making its way to the gulf from the Indian Ocean island of Diego Garcia, where it picked up eight mine-sweeping Sea Stallion helicopters, was spotted 30 miles off Bahrain in the gulf by a British television journalist. The helicopters flew what appeared to be practice drills over the Persian Gulf yesterday, a witness said.

The reported arrival of the Guadalcanal and the Sea Stallions means the U.S. Navy probably is planning to include the mine-damaged supertanker Bridgeton in its next convoy out of the gulf, shipping sources in Kuwait said. They said departure of the convoy is imminent.

The 401,382-ton Bridgeton, the largest Kuwaiti vessel flying the U.S. flag, hit a mine July 24 during the first U.S.-escorted convoy to Kuwait. Shipping officials said the Bridgeton, temporarily patched up and partially loaded with oil, was kept in Kuwait pending arrival of the mine-sweeping Sea Stallions.

Smaller vessels, such as the Gas Prince, which was escorted in and out of the gulf, and the three ships

**Arms** continued on page 9A

**President Reagan**

## White House to seek $1 billion sale of jets, missiles to Saudi Arabia

Washington Post

**Washington, D.C.**
The Reagan administration, arguing that Saudi Arabia's ability to defend Persian Gulf oil supplies must be strengthened because of the Iran-Iraq war, is planning a $1 billion arms sale to the Saudis.

Congressional sources, noting that the proposed sale includes 1,600 Maverick antitank missiles and up to 14 of the latest F15 jet fighter planes, predicted that the move will touch off a new test of strength between the White House and the Democratic-controlled Congress.

These sources warned that the administration can expect pro-Israeli members and others disenchanted with Saudi Arabia to fight the plan with the same ferocity that forced the White House just two months ago to withdraw a proposed sale of $360 million worth of Mavericks to the Saudis.

The administration is expected to notify Congress of the new sale proposal shortly after legislators return from their summer recess Sept. 9. Administration officials denied that they were trying to gain "the advantage of surprise" by moving immediately after the recess. One senior official said the timing was dictated by the Persian Gulf situation and by the need for sufficient time for the required consultations with Congress before the end of its current session, which could come as early as October.

The same official also said there are "no surprises" in the proposed sale because its components have been discussed in informal contacts with key members of Congress, leaders of American Jewish organizations and the Israeli government.

The senior official said the administration believes that Iran's increased threats, which led to U.S. escorts of reflagged Kuwaiti tankers, will strengthen Reagan's arguments that a militarily strong Saudi Arabia can be an effective deterrent to the Iranians and might alleviate the need for further increases in U.S. forces in the region.

## Lake tornado approached cabins with little warning

By Norman Draper
Staff Writer

**Battle Lake, Minn.**
It came across the lake at the end of a muggy Saturday, a harmless-looking white cloud without the fanfare of hail or blustery winds.

Linda Mertens, a 38-year-old registered nurse from Algonquin, Ill., saw what looked like a water spout moving across the middle of the lake. She called to her two children to look at the "whirling dervish."

The danger didn't dawn on her; in the 27 years she had come to her parents' cabin on Eagle Lake she had seen similar white clouds bearing down on the cabin many times. Usually they just brought rain.

This one was different.

It hit about 7:30 p.m. with an explosion that sounded like a bomb going off. The cabin blew apart, but Mertens, her husband, their two children

**Tornado** continued on page 9A

## McMartin trial puts child witnesses in spotlight

By Carol Byrne
Staff Writer

**Los Angeles, Calif.**
It was her fourth day on the witness stand, and the 12-year-old girl with the long blond hair and the horrifying story was tiring visibly.

Calmly and matter-of-factly, she had identified defendant Raymond Buckey as the man at her nursery school who had made her play the game called "Naked Movie Star" and watch while he mutilated a dead cat.

> ■ Dean Gits, a defense attorney in the McMartin sex abuse case in suburban Los Angeles, is a Minneapolis native and 1970 graduate of the William Mitchell College of Law in St. Paul/**5A.**

But now, as defense attorney Danny Davis cross-examined her, probing for inconsistencies, she kept saying, "I don't remember" and "I don't understand."

After an hour and a half, Superior Court Judge William Pounders called a halt.

"I'm determined to get her off the stand today," he told Davis. "This is obviously wearing her out. ... We need to finish so she can put this out of her mind."

"Do you feel I'm harassing the witness?" Davis asked.

"I feel the process is harassing her," the judge replied.

The difficult legal and ethical problems inherent in prosecuting child sexual-abuse cases are apparent as the 14 child witnesses start taking the stand at the McMartin Preschool trial. The 12-year-old girl was the first.

The basic dilemma is the same one that arose in Minnesota at the Jordan

**Trial** continued on page 4A

## Almanac

**Monday, August 17, 1987**
**229th day; 136 to go this year**
**Sunrise: 6:17. Sunset: 8:17**

### Today's weather/

Comfortable

Partly cloudy with a 40 percent chance of showers and thunderstorms. High in the upper 70s, low in the mid 50s.

### Inside/

Metro and state news that usually appears in the B section is included in today's A section because of production considerations.

Twins' skid continues with 11-3 loss in Boston/1D

Contras accept Central American peace plan/3A

Lamaur Inc. takes steps to avoid a takeover/5B

**Sports**

**Puttin' on the hits**

Paul Molitor extends his streak to 36 games/**1D**

Minneapolis STAR and Tribune

1A Metro

Saturday August 22/1987

5 Sections

35¢ Single copy

Volume VI/Number 140



Section A/Part 1

# Lonetree convicted of spying

## Sentencing hearing set Monday; appeal planned

Sgt. Clayton Lonetree

**By David Phelps**
Staff Correspondent

**Quantico, Va.**
Marine Sgt. Clayton Lonetree was convicted Friday of spying against his country in a historic case that raised questions about the way the United States guards its embassies in Communist countries.

A jury of eight Marine officers deliberated less than four hours before finding Lonetree guilty of all 13 counts, which included giving classified information to Soviet agents, identifying U.S. intelligence officials and fraternizing with a Soviet woman.

Lonetree, whose sentencing hearing is scheduled for Monday, is the first Marine in the corps' 212-year history to be convicted of espionage. He faces a maximum sentence of life imprisonment.

Lonetree, 25, of St. Paul, remained impassive as he stood and listened to the jury president read the verdict. He then turned and embraced his mother and aunt and hugged defense counselor William Kunstler.

"I put my arms around him and he was shaking," Kunstler said. "But he took it like a Marine."

Lonetree's mother, Sally Tsosie, vowed to appeal the conviction. Carrying an eagle's feather for good luck during a press conference, Tsosie was impassioned as she told how she raised her son "to be an honest, law-abiding citizen." When he was led out of the courthouse by armed guards, she shouted, "Innocent!"

Lonetree's father, Spencer Lonetree, was not present.

The Marine's aunt, Kathy Lone Tree, said she had sent a message to her parents, Clayton Lonetree's paternal grandparents, in Aurora, Colo. "Clayton sends his love. He's fine. ... If the government wants a fight on their hands, we'll give it to them," she said with tears in her eyes.

Defense attorneys, saying they were handcuffed by a judge who "clearly wanted a conviction," said they would appeal the case to the Court of Military Review.

"This judge violated his oath of office to administer fairly," Kunstler said. "He is a disgrace.

"The jury, with the best of intentions, could not surmount the fact that this is a Marine charged with espionage," he said. "I think corps pride and corps prejudice had a lot to do with the conviction."

Earlier, Lonetree's attorneys rested their case without calling any witnesses; they said their hands had been tied by the judge's rulings in the court-martial.

Prosecution attorneys declined to comment on the verdict.

**Lonetree** continued on page 5A

## Price rise in July lowest for year

**Associated Press**

**Washington, D.C.**
A dip in food costs and moderating energy prices held inflation at the retail level to a tame 0.2 percent increase in July, its best performance this year, the government reported Friday.

The rise in the Labor Department's consumer price index (CPI) was half the 0.4 percent increase posted in June. Analysts cited the report as further evidence that inflation is calming again, at least temporarily, after a spurt in the first half of the year.

It was the lowest one-month rate since a 0.2 percent increase in December.

Food and beverage prices, which had increased 0.7 percent in June, did a turnaround and fell 0.2 percent in July, paced by a 0.5 percent drop in grocery prices. Energy prices were up a moderate 0.5 percent after rising 1.5 percent in June.

Donald Straszheim, chief economist for Merrill Lynch, said the July figure was "good news, but I don't think it is time to do much celebrating." He said a further weakening of the dollar on foreign-exchange markets will inevitably contribute to higher import prices and more inflation in the months to come.

In a separate release Thursday, the Labor Department said consumer prices in the Twin Cities rose 1.3 percent in the first half of 1987 from

**Prices** continued on page 6A

Staff Photo by Stormi Greener

**Admirers outnumbered buyers Friday at the sale of wild horses and burros in St. Cloud.**

## Buyers take wild horses, burros from their home on the range

**By Bob von Sternberg**
Staff Writer

**St. Cloud, Minn.**
Three large men strained and pulled while two more pushed. In between them was a wild burro, recently transplanted from the grasslands of California and none too enthusiastic about being dragged into a livestock trailer and hauled to her new home on a dairy farm.

Trish Gleiter, the burro's new owner, watched and asked one of the wranglers, "They that stubborn all the time?" He just grinned.

"If nothing else, she may be good to chase the cows with," Gleiter said. "Never had a burro before — I just wanted to see if I can train it."

It took five minutes, but the burro was finally hauled into the trailer, along with the wild mare Gleiter bought Friday. "That's it for us -- thank God," she said as she left for her home in Alma, Wis.

That scene was repeated, usually without the low comedy, all day yesterday at a St. Cloud livestock yard, where the federal government came to unload 100 wild horses and 61 wild burros into the care of farmers, country residents and animal lovers. Horses went for the bargain price of $125, burros for an even cheaper $75.

The sale, a first for Minnesota, was a booming success for federal officials, who expect all 161 animals to be sold by the time the sale ends Sunday. But politics managed to cast its shadow over the horse-trading.

As appealingly symbolic of the Old West as the mustangs and burros are, they're about as welcome in Western rangelands as stray pit bulls in a city neighborhood.

Periodic sales like yesterday's are designed to thin the population of horses and burros from public lands, as an alternative to killing them. In the 15 years the sales have been held, about 60,000 animals have found homes.

**Sale** continued on page 6A

## Mine owners fire 4,000 black strikers in South Africa; 1 miner killed in clash

**From News Services**

**Johannesburg, South Africa**
Mine owners fired 4,000 striking black workers Friday and one miner was killed in a clash at a mine in the first reported death of a striker since the miners' walkout began 12 days ago.

Also yesterday, a bus carrying home striking black mineworkers crashed into a cliff face, killing at least 20 people and injuring 49, the South African Broadcasting Corp. said.

The National Union of Mineworkers said one striker was killed and at least 20 strikers were seriously injured in a clash with security personnel at the Libanon gold mine, about 40 miles southwest of Johannesburg.

According to Richmond Mdange, a union organizer based near Libanon, only about 10 percent of the mine's 7,000-man work force had been participating in the strike until Thursday, when virtually all the others decided to join. He said management tried to force the night shift to work, provoking the clash.

Gold Fields of South Africa, which operates the mine, confirmed the death, but disputed the union's account.

**South Africa** continued on page 14A

## Attorney Grose dies at age 63

Clinton Grose, a prominent Minneapolis civil attorney who was a former head of the Minnesota Trial Lawyers Association, died Thursday night. He was 63.

Grose was himself a defendant in 1985 when he was indicted and subsequently cleared of perjury charges brought by a Scott County grand jury. **Page 1B.**

## Shakopee amphitheater OK'd – with restrictions

**By Conrad deFiebre**
Staff Writer

A proposed 17,000-seat outdoor music amphitheater next door to Canterbury Downs won approval Friday from the Shakopee Planning Commission, but with such severe restrictions on noise, traffic and other matters that it may never be built.

Developers of the Starwood Music Center said they will not decide the future of their $9 million project before reviewing in writing the restrictions, which were drafted during a stormy six-hour commission meeting that ended at 1:30 a.m. yesterday.

But opponents of the amphitheater, who say it would bring noise, congestion and crime to Shakopee, were claiming apparent victory in their fight against the developers.

**Amphitheater** continued on 4A

## Girl, 6, believed kidnapped from East Bethel home

**By Kevin Diaz**
Staff Writer

More than 25 Anoka County sheriff reserves and deputies searched the East Bethel area Friday, looking for a 6-year-old girl believed kidnapped from her parents' home early in the morning.

Nichole Mau, a kindergartner at East Bethel Community School, was abducted from her bed between 2 and 4 a.m., said Sheriff Ken Wilkinson. But her disappearance was not noticed until 9 a.m., he said, when the girl telephoned her mother and said, "Hello, Ma. This is Nicky. I'm fine."

The telephone went dead, Wilkinson said, but not before Nichole also said she was with a man whom she identified only by first name.

Using the name, sheriff's deputies arrested a suspect at 1:20 p.m. while he was driving a car in East Bethel, Wilkinson said. "The only man known to the family by that name is one with whom they had a verbal altercation the night before," Wilkinson said.

However, the 41-year-old suspect denied any knowledge of the girl's whereabouts, the sheriff said. "He's saying he knows nothing about it and we're really short of leads," he said as the search was called off at nightfall.

The man was being held last night in the Anoka County Jail. The search,

**Missing** continued on page 4A

## Almanac

**Saturday, August 22, 1987**
**234th day; 131 days to go**
**Sunrise: 6:23. Sunset: 8:09**

**Today's weather/**

Fresh

Sunshine, a breeze from the northwest and a high temperature in the low 70s are expected in the Twin Cities area.



**Telephones/**

| | |
|---|---|
| Circulation | 372-4343 |

**Goetz gets six-month jail term, $5,000 fine/3A**

1987 World Series

# Star Tribune

MINNESOTA HISTORICAL SOCIETY

ST. PAUL EDITION

TUESDAY/October 20/1987 NEWSPAPER OF THE TWIN CITIES 35¢

■ St. Paul begins working on plans for arts high school/**1B**

# Dow plummets 508 points on a wave of panic selling

## 22% drop exceeds worst day in 1929

By Bill Sing
Los Angeles Times

Fear and panic of historic proportions overwhelmed the stock market Monday, forcing the Dow Jones industrial average to a stunning decline of 508.00 points, by far its biggest one-day plunge in history.

The Dow Jones average lost nearly a quarter of its value, nearly doubling the percentage drop on Oct. 28, 1929, a crash that preceded the Great Depression. With yesterday's plunge, the Dow has lost half the ground it has gained since the bull market got under way on Aug. 12, 1982, when the Dow stood at 776.92.

The unprecedented dive in the Dow, to a close of 1,738.74, immediately triggered fears of an international economic crisis and a recession in the United States. Mutual funds, pension funds, stock brokerages, individual investors and others together lost hundreds of billions of dollars in wealth, and the impact could reverberate throughout the U.S. economy.

Yesterday's debacle alone wiped out $503 billion in the market value of all stocks. A total of about $1 trillion in stock market wealth has been erased since the market peaked on Aug. 25, as measured by Wilshire Associates of Los Angeles.

"I think everyone is a little puzzled," President Reagan told reporters when asked to explain the plunge. "I don't know what meaning it might have because all the business indices are up. There is nothing wrong with the

**Stocks** continued on page 6A

### Psychological effect could be most harmful

■ Unless the market bounces back quickly, most Americans are likely to be hurt by Monday's decline — even those who own no stock — because of reactions that can cause an economic slowdown. **6A.**

■ There was pandemonium Monday for area brokers, money managers and investors. **7A.**

■ Gold prices rose to their highest level in more than four years as investors sought a haven for their money. **11B.**

**Related stories, 6A, 7A, 11B.**

## Economy far stronger than it was during October '29 debacle

By Paul Richter
Los Angeles Times

**New York, N.Y.**
The stock market's plunge has evoked memories of the stock market crash of October 1929, which burst the euphoria of a decade-long speculative bubble and foreshadowed the Great Depression.

Although the parallels seem to grow daily, economists and other analysts say the differences far outweigh the similarities between the current decline and the debacle of 1929. Since the Great Crash, limits have been placed on borrowing for stock purchases, government has assumed an active role in regulating the markets and the economy, and nations have made greater efforts to minimize international economic disruptions.

Today's economy is far stronger than the one that succumbed to depression within three years of the 1929 market dive.

To be sure, Monday's drop in the Dow Jones industrial average has overshadowed the losses suffered on Black Monday — Oct. 28, 1929 — when the Dow lost 12.82 percent of its value. The index fell 508.00 points yesterday, to 1,738.74, for a 22.62 percent loss.

**Crash of '29** continued on page 6A

## A downer of historic proportions

Monday's plunge in the stock market drained more than $500 billion from the nation's wealth. That drop in stock value, some economists say, could shake confidence in the economy and even bring a recession, as consumers buy fewer goods and services, and businesses are forced to cut spending and lay off workers.

### The Dow's losses hour by hour

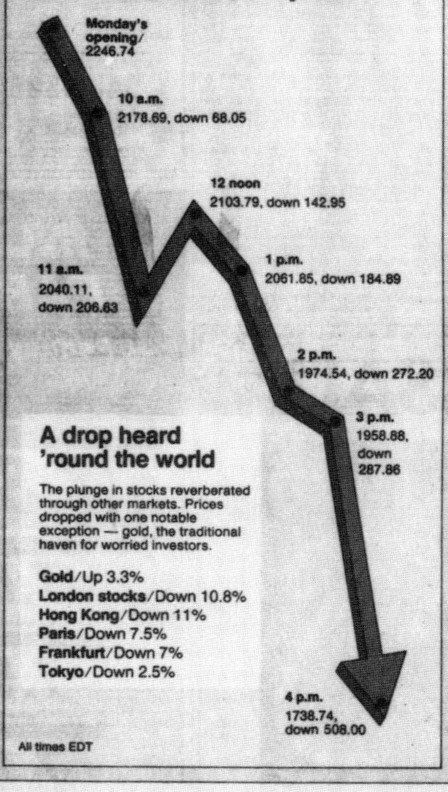


All times EDT

### A drop heard 'round the world

The plunge in stocks reverberated through other markets. Prices dropped with one notable exception — gold, the traditional haven for worried investors.

**Gold**/Up 3.3%
**London stocks**/Down 10.8%
**Hong Kong**/Down 11%
**Paris**/Down 7.5%
**Frankfurt**/Down 7%
**Tokyo**/Down 2.5%

### 10 days in October

This month's declines rival those in the 1929 market crash.

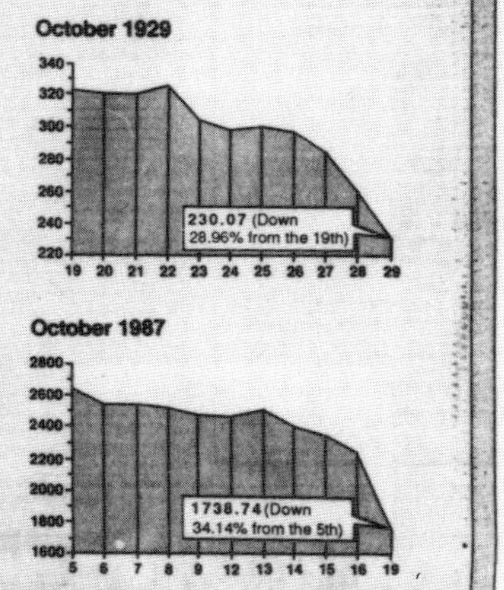


### Handing back its winnings

The "October Massacre" has erased the market's gains over the past year.

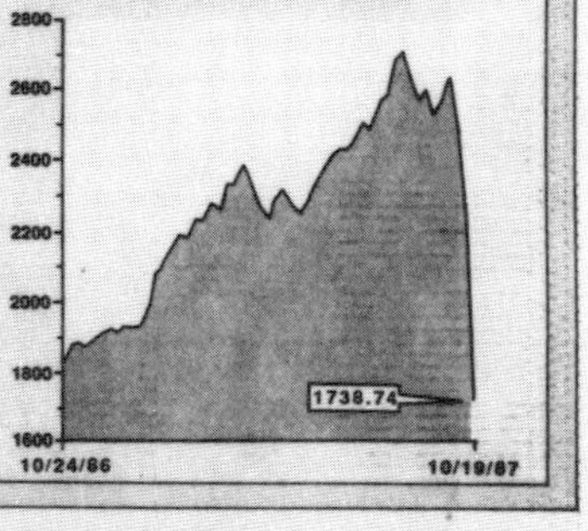


# U.S. attacks Iranian oil platforms

## Iran vows 'crushing response'

From News Services

**Manama, Bahrain**
Four U.S. warships destroyed two Iranian oil platforms in the Persian Gulf Monday, and Navy commandos raided a third.

President Reagan called the 85-minute attack, in which Iranian crews on the platforms were given time to flee, "a prudent yet restrained response" to Iran's missile strike Friday on a U.S.-flagged tanker off Kuwait. The missile was believed to have been fired from the nearby Faw Peninsula, which Iran captured from Iraq in their seven-year war.

Iran said the Americans had begun a "full-fledged war" to which it promised "a crushing response."

Reagan, speaking briefly with reporters as he left the White House to visit his hospitalized wife, Nancy, was asked if the attack meant the two nations were at war.

"No, we're not going to have a war with Iran; they're not that stupid," he said.

In a similar vein, Defense Secretary Caspar Weinberger said, "We do not seek further confrontation with Iran, but will be prepared to meet any

**Gulf** continued on page 12A

## Reagan's reaction is cautious

From News Services

**Washington, D.C.**
President Reagan, in ordering a U.S. attack on Iranian oil platforms, was seeking a low-risk response that would appeal to many factions in government in his push for support for U.S. policy in the Persian Gulf, analysts and U.S. officials said Monday.

Yesterday's attack, an 85-minute naval bombardment of Iranian offshore oil drilling platforms used as a base for attacks on gulf shipping, was in retaliation for an Iranian missile strike on a U.S. reflagged tanker last week.

The oil platform attack won praise on Capitol Hill but may not have satisfied U.S. military commanders and some in the Reagan administration who wanted stronger action.

At the same time, analysts said, the action left the United States in the same uncomfortable position it has occupied since it began escorting reflagged Kuwaiti tankers through the gulf in July: waiting for the next Iranian move and trying to strike a convincing deterrent stance.

The limited scale of the U.S. attack and the 20-minute warning given to

**Decision** continued on page 12A

## Twins obviously have yet to earn Herzog's respect

By Mark Vancil
Staff Writer

**St. Louis, Mo.**
You got the feeling St. Louis manager Whitey Herzog talked before he thought and that the words left his mouth but never passed through his ears.

Either way, one thing had become clear to most observers long before Herzog's Monday afternoon smear in Busch Stadium. Millions of witnesses have watched a mugging, and he has no one to blame in this World Series but the Twins.

Following the Twins' 8-4 victory in Game 2 Sunday, Herzog told reporters, "If they're (Twins) so damn good, why have they only won nine (road) games since the All-Star break? Why have they only won 85 games all season?"

Yesterday, before the Twins worked out in preparation for Game 3 tonight at 7:30, Herzog offered another jab in what has been a one-sided fight on the field. He complained about the day off and implied the Twins weren't good enough to beat St. Louis over an entire season. He also doesn't seem to think a whole lot of Les Straker, who will start against Cardinals

**World Series** continued on page 4A

### Martin to manage Yankees fifth time

Billy Martin was named manager of the New York Yankees for the fifth time Monday after Lou Piniella, who some thought would be fired, instead was promoted to general manager. **1D.**

## Almanac

**Tuesday, October 20, 1987**
**293rd day; 72 to go this year**
**Sunrise: 7:35. Sunset: 6:20**

### Flurries maybe

Flurries possible. Winds out of the northwest winds at 10-20 miles per hour. High 39.

### Index/




Volume VI/Number 199 4 sections

Minnesota loses bid for US West research lab/15A

MINNEAPOLIS EDITION

City Council votes to buy historic Grain Belt Brewery/1B

1987 World Series

Star Tribune

SATURDAY/October 24/1987 NEWSPAPER OF THE TWIN CITIES .35¢

# Gorbachev won't set summit

## He wants compromise on 'Star Wars' before meeting with Reagan

By William Beecher
Washington Bureau Chief

Moscow, U.S.S.R.
Soviet General Secretary Mikhail Gorbachev declined Friday to set a date for a summit with President Reagan unless a compromise can be struck in curbing the U.S. "Stars Wars" program.

A disappointed George Shultz reported the unexpected development as he told of major progress toward finalizing a medium-range missile treaty, previously believed to be key to holding a summit in Washington this fall.

Reagan said he would not agree to strict limits on the Strategic Defense Initiative (SDI) testing program. "I cannot make that a bargaining chip," he told foreign journalists.

White House officials suggested that Gorbachev was deliberately raising an obstacle to a summit meeting by linking such a meeting with progress on SDI. "The issue seems to be whether or not Gorbachev wants to come to the United States for a summit," said Marlin Fitzwater, the White House spokesman.

Shultz said Gorbachev does not yet feel "comfortable" about coming to the United States, but the Soviet leader assured him he still wants and hopes to meet Reagan this year and soon would send a letter spelling out his feelings.

According to a Tass account, Gorbachev told Shultz that he wanted to be sure a summit meeting also would lead to "an accord on the key provisions" of another treaty, this one limiting long-range weapons and strengthening the 1972 anti-ballistic missile treaty, which restricts space defenses.

"We believe the Soviet proposal linking strategic arms reductions to changes in the ABM (anti-ballistic missile) treaty are not warranted," Shultz told a press conference in Moscow shortly before boarding a plane for Brussels, where he planned to brief NATO allies on the two days of talks in Moscow.

Shultz lamented what he called a shift in attitude between that exhibited by Foreign Minister Eduard Shevardnadze in Washington last month and what he encountered in Moscow, including 4½ hours with Gorbachev yesterday. U.S. negotiators had expected that a summit date would be set if remaining differences over an intermediate-range missile treaty could be resolved.

In the view of some officials in Moscow, the trouble over a crashing

Arms continued on page 6A

# Senate rejects Bork, 58-42

Associated Press

U.S. Circuit Court of Appeals Judge Robert Bork returned to his home Friday after his nomination to the Supreme Court was defeated.

## Reagan is warned against choosing similar nominee

By Cliff Haas
Staff Correspondent

Washington, D.C.
The Senate on Friday rejected the Supreme Court nomination of Robert Bork by a 58-42 vote, with some Bork opponents warning President Reagan that if his next choice for the high court is like Bork "he will be rejected like Judge Bork."

The vote against Bork was the largest the Senate has ever recorded in rejecting a Supreme Court nominee, indicating legislators' reservations about Bork, the strength of the organized campaign against him, White House miscues in the fight and the weakness of Reagan in dealing with Congress as he approaches the end of his presidency.

After the vote, Reagan said he was "saddened and disappointed" by the outcome. He added that the confirmation process had become "a spectacle of misrepresentation and single-issue politics."

He also declared, "My next nominee for the court will share Judge Bork's belief in judicial restraint — that a judge is bound by the Constitution to interpret laws, not make them."

Bork said he was "glad the debate took place" because "there is now a full and permanent record by which the future may judge not only me but the proper nature of a confirmation proceeding."

Six Republicans joined 52 Democrats in rejecting Bork while 40 Republicans and two Democrats voted for confirmation. Minnesota's Republican senators, Rudy Boschwitz and Dave Durenberger, voted for Bork.

Bork continued on page 10A

# Nerveball

## World Series trauma is make-believe drama that makes us feel alive

By Bruce Benidt
Staff Writer

Millions of stomachs are churning over one baseball game.

Anxiety is piling high on both sides before the sixth game of the World Series, which starts at 3 p.m. today in the giant amplifier known as the Metrodome. The Twins are down 3-2 in the Series; if they lose today, the season is over.

But the Cardinals have to be remembering how they blew the 1985 series after leading three games to one. And they certainly recall the rattling noise of the Twins fans from last weekend's two losses here.

As for Minnesotans, they're "incredibly, incredibly, incredibly anxious" in the view of Karal Ann Marling, a professor of American culture at the University of Minnesota and a baseball fan gripped with "desperate optimism that when we get home we can do it." Fans here are asking, "Can our boys do it, or is this going to be another Minneapolis fiasco, another instance of Minnesota folding at the last minute?"

She's hungry. "It's time we come face to face with this unseemly unmidwestern emotion — we want it all, we want to win," she said. "I think if we don't get it, we'll probably just sink into winter and not be seen again till spring."

But the Cardinals and their fans aren't without fear, either.

For starters, even though they see themselves as underdogs, the Cardinal players want to wipe out the memory of the 1985 Series, when they let the underdog Kansas City Royals get away. There are 12 players on their roster from that

Anxiety continued on page 8A

## Welcome back, Cards, to din bin of a Dome

Jim Klobuchar

Strangers in town need and deserve guidance. Since this is a civil place where we live, St. Louis Cardinals, I thought today I would enhance your peace of mind by welcoming you once more to banshee ball.

The rest of the World Series starting today, St. Louis, is new-era baseball. It's Baseball A.D., for Acoustical Daze.

If you're homesick for sensible silence at the ballpark when absolutely nothing is happening, don't come to me for consolation. Baseball in most places today is run by organists and wind-tunnel engineers, not by the commissioner. I also recognize that you're traditionalists, St. Louis, attuned to such fixtures of traditional baseball as Spuds MacKenzie taking a victory lap and draft horses hauling beer wagons into the outfield. Consider what's happening in the Metrodome today just an extension of that tradition. What we have for you this weekend is baseball amplified by the Queen Mary's diesel horn. That part of Baseball A.D. you can call raw suspense: Is the Queen Mary going to hit an iceberg or beach itself in your dugout, about where Red Schoendienst is putting on his voodoo signs?

Baseball A.D. is jet engines coming off the roof to create G4 air pockets. It's the March of the

Klobuchar continued on page 8A

# Economy grows healthy 3.8% while inflation rate is low 0.2%

By Oswald Johnston
Los Angeles Times

Washington, D.C.
The economy grew at a healthy 3.8 percent annual rate last summer, far higher than expected, and consumer price inflation was only 0.2 percent in September.

But economists shaken by the week's huge Wall Street selloff reacted to both government reports Friday by expressing worries about the future.

"If Monday hadn't happened, this would be pretty hot news," said David Levine of Sanford C. Bernstein & Co., a New York investment banking firm.

"Under normal circumstances, this news would have been terrific," said Allen Sinai, chief economist for Shearson Lehman Brothers. "But looking ahead, the economy is very likely to soften more in the fourth quarter and next year because of the severe market decline."

President Reagan hailed the GNP report, the government's first look at how the economy performed last summer, as proof that there is nothing wrong with the underlying economy despite the huge losses suffered on Wall Street.

"All of this is concrete evidence of an economy that is strong and fundamentally sound," Reagan said. "It is an economy, judged in pure economic terms, that has a very bright future before it — a future of growth, low inflation and high employment."

Economy continued on page 4A

### Market closes week with welcome quiet

The stock market, exhausted by its most turbulent week in 30 years, closed two hours early Friday virtually where it began the day. The Dow Jones industrial average rose 0.33, closing at 1,950.76, while broader measures of the market were slightly down. Volume on the New York Stock Exchange was 245.6 million shares, bringing the number of shares traded this week to 1.3 billion. Page 5B.

**DST ends Sunday**
Daylight Savings Time ends at 2 a.m. Sunday. Turn your clocks back one hour tonight and regain the hour of sleep you lost last spring.

## Almanac

**Saturday, October 24, 1987**
**298th day; 67 to go this year**
**Sunrise: 7:40. Sunset: 5:14**

Clouds and a 40 percent chance of snow today. High into the 40s.



Circulation 372-4343



Volume VI/Number 203 5 Sections

# U.S. says Social Security rise is safe despite strife

Associated Press

Washington, D.C.
At a time of financial uncertainty, the government told the nation's 38 million Social Security beneficiaries Friday they can count on a 4.2 percent benefit increase at year's end that will increase the average retired worker's pension by $21 a month.

The increase, the biggest in 5½ years, will raise the typical benefit from $492 to $513 a month. However, the raises will be offset by a $6.90 increase in the monthly Medicare premiums that the elderly and disabled will pay starting in January. The payroll tax also will climb in 1988.

The Social Security Administration said the maximum monthly benefit for a worker retiring in 1987 at age 65 will rise $33, from $789 to $822. For someone who turns 65 in 1988, the maximum benefit will be $838.

The raises became official yesterday when the Labor Department announced a Consumer Price Index of 339.1 for September. The 4.2 percent increase mirrors the inflation rate for urban wage earners and clerical workers from the third quarter of 1986 through the third quarter of 1987.

Social Security spokesman John Trollinger also announced that the so-called wage base — the maximum amount of earnings subject to the payroll tax — will jump from $43,800 to $45,000.

The maximum tax on employees will increase $247.80 next year from

Social Security continued on 4A

# Star Tribune

ST. PAUL EDITION

MONDAY/October 26/1987 NEWSPAPER OF THE TWIN CITIES




# Embracing destiny

## Twins, fans revel in World Series victory

By Doug Grow
Staff Writer

In the end, nobody wanted to leave.

Fans and players stood in the Dome cheering each other. Hugging each other. Instamatics flashed. 10,000 Instamatics. Maybe more. Cops ringed the field knocking down the half-dozen or so people who forgot their Minnesota manners. Players hugged each other. Fans hugged each other.

The Minnesota Twins were World Series champions. And nobody wanted it to end because this whole fall has been so much fun. Unbelievable fun from a team that few believed in not so long ago.

But after last night there wasn't a soul in Minnesota who didn't believe. The Minnesota Twins beat the St. Louis Cardinals 4-2 and believers everywhere hugged and screamed and hoped it wouldn't end.

Long after the game was over, thousands of fans stayed in the Dome. Stayed to see the Boys of a remarkable 1987 Summer come out for one last curtain call.

They did. They finally came back. And once more fans screamed for the Minnesota Twins. The World Series champion Minnesota Twins.

Once more the theme from "Star Wars" boomed over the Dome speaker as the players returned and shouted "We're No. 1" and threw kisses to the crowd. But it was a different sort of welcome when the Twins returned to the field. There were no decibel-meter-busting screams left in Twins fans.

Instead there was exhaustion. Sweet exhaustion. It was over. And nobody wanted to leave but everyone seemed too tired to scream, too.

"They keep talking about Minnesota not being No. 1," Kent Hrbek yelled to the crowd. "That's a

**Grow** continued on page 10A

Staff Photo by Richard Sennott

**The Twins bathed in admiration — and Gatorade — on the Metrodome field after the game.**

## Fantasy and reality meet at the moment of triumph

The Twins' magic carpet took Minnesota to the moon Sunday night.

It was borne by the sound of 55,000 exploding voices in the Metrodome and hundreds of thousands more from border to border in one floor-stomping, chest-pounding declaration:

"We're No. 1."

And the moment Gary Gaetti fired to Kent Hrbek in the ninth inning to retire Willie McGee and beat the St. Louis Cardinals 4-2, The Celebration began.

It cascaded from the playing field where the Twins mobbed themselves in a primeval scream of glory, clutching, laughing and crying, and from the grandstand were the fans erupted in a feast of triumph and vindication. It came rolling out of the upper galleries like the boom of an ocean surf, and it flashed to the world on television in a wild swirl of white bandanas.

The champions of baseball. The World Series. No. 1.

Is that sweet? Run it up the aerials on the IDS and the Foshay Tower in Minneapolis; wrap it around Rice St. in St. Paul and stick it in the cones of a thousand red silos. Plant it in the cornfields and drape it on the snouts of all the canoes on 15,000 lakes.

Play it on your car horn going to work this morning. Da da-da da. We're No. 1. What do you mean you hocked your car for Series tickets? Tell the bus driver to play it.

If you couldn't join the voices in the Metrodome, you were in it. If you lived in this place, and got pelted all those years by the brays of comedians and the wise guys about Also Ran Acres and Losersville, U.S.A., you were there in the Metrodome to howl your deliverance.

It was a baseball game at the Dome last night, all right, but it was something more. It was an odyssey that united a baseball team they called sad sack not so long ago and a public hungry for a day on the pedestal.

**Jim Klobuchar**

And was it a trip? It was wacky and tumultuous. It was a fantasy but it was as real as the tears that blended with the screeches in the stands and on the streets.

Can a baseball team they called ragtag and ragamuffin dine with the royalty? It can, because today it *is* royalty, the best in major league baseball and the winner of the 1987 World Series, a team everybody in Nevada said had once chance in 150 to win the championship.

It was a team that couldn't finish fourth in the National League East or the American League East, Whitey Herzog calculated.

He may have been right. It didn't have to finish anyplace in the

**Klobuchar** continued on page 10A

## Streets outside of Dome explode with fans' joy

By Norman Draper, Maura Lerner and Larry Oakes
Staff Writers

It was Minnesota mayhem.

And the likes of it never have been seen before and may never be again. Thousands of fans were screaming, yelling and high-fiving themselves into a frenzy after the last out of the 1987 World Series.

Jubilant fans took over the streets, throwing streamers and screaming victory cries as more than 55,000 baseball fanatics poured out of the Metrodome Sunday night. And nobody appeared to mind that they brought traffic to a halt. The Twins had won. In Minneapolis last night, everyone was a Twins fan.

As the police and Guardian Angels looked on, people danced in the street, slapping hands with strangers in the buses and cars stuck in traffic.

At 6th St. and Chicago Av. S., two men in gorilla outfits and Twins T-shirts danced. A woman led another decked out in a redbird costume, with a sign reading: "Dead Bird."

"Cheer up!" Sgt. Dennis Haven said with a laugh as he slapped a reveler on the back. "I wouldn't want to be driving through here," he said. But he wasn't worried about the crowd getting out of control. "They've really been nice."

In downtown Minneapolis, celebrations erupted only moments after the final out. Shouting "We're No. 1," people poured into the streets from bars and thousands more flocked down from the Dome. At 6th St. and Hennepin Av. S., several thousand fans clogged the street, blocking it.

About 25 fans climbed aboard an MTC bus and rocked it back and forth. A fan blowing a trumpet played "Hanky Panky" as other fans sang. A police officer watched, giving high fives to fans as they walked by cheering. He said there wasn't much the police could do to control the crowds.

At Sweeney's bar in St. Paul, they could feel it and smell it and taste it by the eighth inning. To celebrate what the crowd decided is certain to be a new winning era, the crowd revived an old song: Na-na-na-na, hey-hey-hey, goodbye.

They kept it up until the last out and then the place exploded. They jumped up and down and screamed.

"I've waited all my life for this," said Paul Heuer, 23, of St. Paul. "We proved the whole world wrong."

At Schwietz Bar on St. Paul's East Side, patrons were moving into the streets drawing staccato honks from passing motorists. Inside, "Celebrations" was on the jukebox and it was one steady, loud party.

For Sally Spreeman and her sister,

**Celebration** continued on page 9A

**Our Constitution/** The myth that binds us

Would a constitutional convention be a blessing or a nightmare? Opposing views appear on page 16A.

## Shultz says delay may cancel summit

Baltimore Sun

**Washington, D.C.**
Secretary of State George Shultz said Sunday that if Soviet leader Mikhail Gorbachev waits too long to fix a date, a superpower summit might not occur at all during the Reagan presidency.

"We'll have it when he's ready or, if he waits too long, maybe we won't be ready," Shultz said.

"This administration ends in January 1989, and as you get into the heat of the election campaign it's no time for a Soviet leader to be here. So there is only a finite amount of time and only a finite amount of patience with all of this," he said on NBC's "Meet the Press."

In a marked change from his tone of disappointment Friday when he announced that no summit date had been set, Shultz played down the importance of a superpower meeting to the Reagan administration.

**Summit** continued on page 6A

## Almanac

**Monday, October 26, 1987**
**300th day; 65 to go this year**
**Sunrise: 6:43. Sunset: 5:11**

### Today's weather/

Windy and warmer with decreasing cloudiness. High near 57. Northwest winds of 15 to 30 miles per hour.





Volume VI/Number 205 5 sections

## Arthritis yields to aquatic therapy

By Anthony Lonetree
Staff Writer

Dorothy Peterson remembers the early battles with rheumatoid arthritis, of trying to walk with rigid knees and trying to grip with hands she says were about as flexible as stone.

And then there was the pain, which she doesn't even try to think about.

"If you're going to have arthritis, rheumatoid arthritis is the sad kind — there's no cause and there's no cure," said Peterson, 71, of Golden Valley. "I was swollen and crippled from rheumatoid arthritis."

Or at least she was until August 1985, when Peterson's physician recommended she take part in an aquatic therapy program at the Courage Center in Golden Valley.

That same program for people afflicted with arthritis will be offered in Stillwater in the fall of 1988 at Courage St. Croix, a new $2.6 million aquatic therapy facility. Courage

**Center** continued on page 7A

**Nicaragua shoots down U.S. pilot/4A**

VARIETY

Picking partywear for the holidays

TASTE

Match your meal, mood with the right dessert

**MINNEAPOLIS EDITION**

- Urban League raises concerns about three murder cases/**1B**
- Minneapolis reaches settlement with former bakery workers/**1B**
- Triple Five Corp. may announce new mall partner today/**1M**


# Star Tribune

**WEDNESDAY**/December 9/1987 — NEWSPAPER OF THE TWIN CITIES — 35¢

Associated Press

**Soviet leader Mikhail Gorbachev, left, and President Reagan signed a treaty to eliminate intermediate- and shorter-range missiles during a ceremony Tuesday in the White House.**

# A historic pledge for peace

## Reagan, Gorbachev sign treaty, seek beginning of a new era

**New York Times**

**Washington, D.C.**
With fervent calls for a new era of peaceful understanding, President Reagan and Soviet leader Mikhail Gorbachev Tuesday signed the first treaty reducing the size of their nations' nuclear arsenals.

Reagan and Gorbachev, beginning three days of summit talks aimed at even broader reductions, pledged to build on the accord by striving toward what Gorbachev called "the more important goal" — reducing long-range nuclear weapons.

In their White House conversations, the leaders were said to have discussed undisclosed proposals to further those negotiations, and they established an arms-control working group of ranking officials to hold parallel sessions.

An immediate mood of warmth was established as the two leaders agreed yesterday morning to call each other by their first names in private work sessions, a White House official said.

The treaty, which provides for the dismantling of all Soviet and U.S. medium- and shorter-range missiles, establishes the most extensive system of weapons inspection ever negotiated by the two countries, including placing technicians at sensitive sites on each other's territory.

The signing, the fruition of years of negotiation, set the mood for 2½ hours of talks between the leaders. The talks were "very serious, substantive discussions," Secretary of State George Shultz said last night before a formal dinner in the White House.

The visit to Washington by Gorbachev was the first by a Soviet leader

**Summit** continued on page 13A

### Inside

- Despite reservations by some conservatives, approval of the treaty is likely. **Page 12A.**
- A 5-1 majority of Americans backs the treaty, according to a Gallup Poll completed Sunday. **Page 9A.**
- The treaty divides the Republicans, but it takes an issue away from the Democrats. **Page 12A.**
- Excerpts of remarks by Reagan and Gorbachev. **Page 10A.**

## Signing may encourage further Soviet offers

**By William Beecher**
Washington Bureau Chief

### Analysis

**Washington, D.C.**
Now that a treaty to eliminate medium-range missiles has been signed, senior U.S. officials say privately they would not be surprised if Mikhail Gorbachev offers President Reagan either an assymetrical cutback of conventional forces in Europe or a unilateral Soviet reduction.

Depending on the size and character of the offer, it could serve one or more of the following purposes:

- Allay concerns in Congress that the destruction of the U.S. missiles would only increase the vulnerability of Western Europe to a Soviet conventional force threat, thereby enhancing the ratification prospects of the INF treaty and building support for conclusion of a Strategic Arms Reduction Treaty (START) by next spring.
- Convince European opinion that Gorbachev is sincere in wanting to move away from confrontation, thus

**Analysis** continued on page 14A

## FBI crash probe centers on fired employee

**From News Services**

**Los Angeles, Calif.**
An FBI investigation into the crash of a jetliner in California focused Tuesday on a recently dismissed airline employee who was believed to have boarded the flight with a handgun, intent on killing the man who fired him.

USAir confirmed that David Burke, who was fired last month, and his former boss were aboard Pacific Southwest Airlines (PSA) Flight 1771, which crashed Monday afternoon. USAir recently bought PSA.

Forty-three people were aboard the British-built, four-engine jet, which had been bound from Los Angeles to San Francisco.

A source close to the investigation described the revenge-murder scenario as "a very, very good theory."

FBI agents and police yesterday converged on the Long Beach condominium where Burke lived, and talked with a woman and teen-aged girl who neighbors believed were his girlfriend and his daughter. The condominium was placed under police guard.

"At this point it does not appear that it was an accident," said Richard Bretzing, agent in charge of the FBI's Los Angeles office. "It appears at this point — and has yet to be substantiated — that it was a criminal act on board that caused the craft to come down."

**Plane** continued on page 6A

### Almanac

**Wednesday, December 9, 1987**
**343rd day; 22 to go this year**
**Sunrise: 7:39. Sunset: 4:32**

### Today's weather/

Clearing

Snow will be diminishing to flurries this morning, and the cloudiness should decrease this afternoon. The high will be in the middle 30s.

### Index/



### Telephones/

| | |
|---|---|
| News general | 372-4141 |
| Want Ads | 372-4242 |
| Circulation | 372-4343 |


Volume VI/Number 249 — 6 sections

## Latimer asks for tougher liquor-license enforcement

**By Chris Ison**
Staff Writer

St. Paul Mayor George Latimer, responding to reports of compromised liquor enforcement practices in the city, called Tuesday for stronger scrutiny of liquor license applications to help "protect the interests of the city and integrity of the system."

Latimer's response comes two weeks after the Star Tribune reported that city License Inspector Joseph Carchedi has accepted favors from bar owners he regulates, failed to report law violations to the City Council and participated in licensing cases involving his close friends.

In a letter to the City Council, the mayor also said that the Police De-

**Liquor** continued on page 8A

### Auditor criticizes state priorities

Minnesota has dropped from fourth to 10th place in spending on education while its rank in welfare spending has increased from 18th to fifth since 1971, according to Auditor Arne Carlson. Carlson said state and local governments spend too much on welfare and sports facilities and not enough on education and highways.
**Page 1B.**

## Stock plunge reveals questionable practices at Minneapolis Drexel office

**By Anthony Carideo**
Staff Writer

A series of questionable stock trading practices at the Minneapolis office of Drexel Burnham Lambert Inc. was unearthed by the stock market's 508-point crash Oct. 19. The practices have resulted in the replacement of Drexel's office manager, the resignation of one broker and censure for three other brokers.

In one of two separate incidents, "Black Monday" produced the collapse of a "partnership" of three young brokers who engaged in what industry sources described as a "very, very aggressive" stock trading strategy. Those trading practices late last month triggered the replacement of the office manager, William Krebs, who founded the 41-person branch several years ago.

A second incident has caused a suit on behalf of a Hastings physician who lost an estimated $74,000 on stock market futures contracts whose purchase he claims he never authorized. A Drexel spokesman said the physician's broker resigned from the firm "for medical reasons" on the day after the crash. The broker, Eugene Pitra, declined to comment.

**Brokerage** continued on page 7A

SUNDAY

**Gophers fall to Wichita St.; Rangers beat Stars 5-3**

**Reagan, Mulroney sign free-trade agreement/3A**

MAGAZINE

A pill that worked a miracle

TASTE

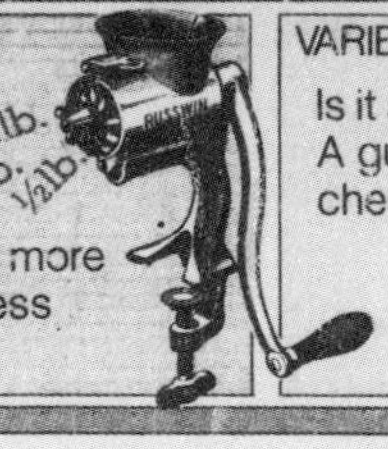


Doing more with less meat

VARIETY

Is it a heart attack? A guide to chest pain

**MINNEAPOLIS EDITION**

■ Panel focuses on the homeless mentally ill/**1B**

■ Snowblower plunges into Lake Harriet/**9B**



# Star Tribune

**SUNDAY**/January 3/1988 — NEWSPAPER OF THE TWIN CITIES — G — $1.25


# Green named chancellor of New York City schools

By **Mary Jane Smetanka**
Staff Writer

Minneapolis school Superintendent Richard Green will become chancellor of the New York City schools, the nation's largest school district.

The announcement was made Saturday in New York. The terms of his contract — his salary and when he starts work — are being negotiated.

Green, 51, called his new job "a great opportunity and a great challenge."

He added, "Are there problems in New York? Yes . . . (Should) we live with these problems? No. If public education can work in New York City, it can work anywhere in this country . . . I'm very excited."

Enormous challenges face Green, who in his eight years as Minneapolis superintendent supervised sweeping changes in the schools that gained national attention. Those successes may be hard to duplicate in New York City, where size, organization and the political turmoil surrounding the district present unique challenges.

As an outsider, Green faces an additional handicap. He has spent his entire career in Minneapolis, a district where both enrollment and problems are minuscule compared with New York. That concerned some New York school board members, and Green will have to prove himself to them as well as to city politicians and the teachers union. Some wanted someone with experience in the New York City schools to get the job.

That didn't bother Green.

Staff Photo by Bruce Bisping

**Richard Green, in his Minneapolis home, called his new job "a great opportunity and a great challenge."**

"I don't believe in failure, but should it turn out that I cannot make an impact on the schools I will be the first to say so to the Board of Education," he said.

Robert F. Wagner Jr., New York City school board president, said Green was the consensus choice of the board, which will vote formally

Green continued on page 16A

■ New York job is another in a series of challenges for Green. Page [illegible].

# St. Paul chief accepted bar owners' pledge

## Donation offered during period when bars were unhappy with police


By **Allen Short, Joe Rigert and Chris Ison**
Staff Writers

St. Paul's police chief accepted a $21,000 fund-raising pledge for his department from a group of St. Paul bar owners last year at a time when the bar owners were complaining about unfair treatment by St. Paul's police and licensing departments.

Weeks after accepting the first installment of $3,000, Chief William McCutcheon set up a meeting at his private club to consider complaints by bar owners about enforcement actions by the licensing department.

Both McCutcheon and the liquor dealers defended the contribution plan, which called for giving $21,000 to the department through the purchase of tickets to a St. Paul horse show. Most of the ticket proceeds from the annual show are passed to the police department.

But the unorthodox fund-raising venture drew criticism from other law enforcement experts and appears to violate the ethics code of the International Association of Chiefs of Police. The code prohibits members from receiving money when it could be inferred that the gift was intended to influence them.

McCutcheon said he thought the contribution complied with the code because the money did not go directly

**Police** continued on page 6A

# New 'morning in America' is the day when country's many debts must be paid

By **Dave Hage**
Staff Writer

Remember the prodigal son?

Like the New Testament youth who wasted his inheritance on "riotous living," America has been on a binge. To buy missiles at home and Sonys abroad, we doubled the pace of federal borrowing, halved the rate of consumer saving and borrowed the difference from foreigners. By 1986 we spent $104 for every $100 we earned.

But this isn't the forgiving world of St. Luke's parable. If there's a message in the stock market crash of Oct. 19 and the dollar's subsequent plunge, it is this: Americans have borrowed too much and the bill is overdue.

Settling up for the 1980s almost certainly will mean living on less into the 1990s.

We will keep less of what we produce, consume less of what others produce and cut into our standard of living to pay off our neighbors. Our

**Outlook** continued on page 5A

## The bill comes due

As the new year begins, America finds itself discovering the modern miseries of indebtedness. The situation could eventually lead to a decline in our standard of living. In today's Marketplace section, New York correspondent Mike Meyers analyzes the burden of being a nation in debt.

Other stories in a report on the 1988 economy:

■ Personal finance reporter Anthony Carideo advises investors on where to put their money in an age of austerity.

■ Agriculture reporter Sharon Schmickle says farmers' greatest hope lies in exports.

Part Two is Monday.

## The debt burden grows heavier

If the total U.S. debt today were divided equally among all Americans, each man, woman and child would face a bill for more than $34,000. That's roughly a 60 percent increase over the past decade.

Per capita debt in constant 1986 dollars

*Borrowing by households, state and local governments and non-financial businesses.

**Source**/President's Council of Economic Advisers; Data Resources Inc.

Star Tribune graphic Jim Freitag

# A DAY OF CRIME

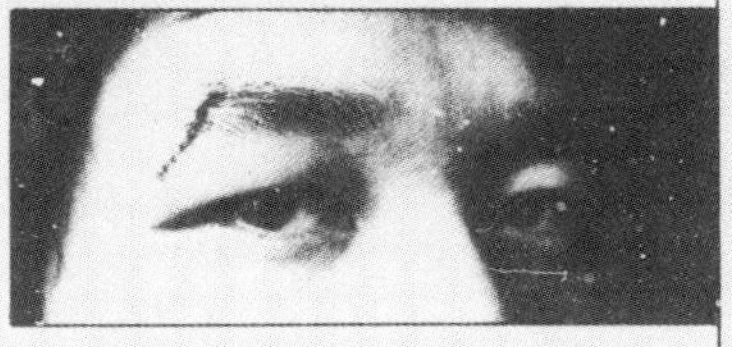

# Victims won't forget Dec. 11 in Twin Cities

**This report was written by staff writers Bruce Benidt, Kurt Chandier, Norman Draper and Chuck Haga.**

MAYBE YOU HEARD THE SIRENS.

At 2 a.m. on Dec. 11, a man struck Thiphakone Sivilay of Brooklyn Park after an argument. Sivilay needed 13 stitches above his eye.

At 2 p.m. that day, John and Barbara Pickering came out of the Ward's parking lot in Bloomington and couldn't find their car. Police found it later in south Minneapolis, wheels stripped off, locks and ignition broken.

And at 10:50 p.m., James Van Hall of north Minneapolis answered a knock at his door. A man said he had struck Hall's car on the street outside. When Hall went to investigate, the man robbed him at gunpoint.

We looked at crime in the metro area over one 24-hour period, Dec. 11, to see how much happens in a day, where, when, how.

But mostly, to whom.

We filtered out such crimes as shoplifting and vandalism done to stores. We skipped white-collar crime. We focused on crimes where we could put names and faces to the victims.

Nobody was murdered Dec. 11. No rapes were reported, either. In 1986, the seven-county area averaged three murders every two weeks, and about five rapes every two days. But we counted 11 aggravated assaults, close to the 1986 average of 13.7 a day.

In all, law enforcement agencies recorded 502 crimes that day — crimes with victims. It was, police said, a somewhat lighter day than usual.

We picked some of those people, victims of crimes ranging from petty theft to aggravated assault, and asked them to tell their stories. For those people, "the crime problem" became a personal problem on Dec. 11. They lost property, got hurt, felt violated; somebody did them wrong.

For some of the victims, the trauma will continue. A month, a year from now, they'll still be victims. For others, the legacy is fear, irritation, inconvenience. The Pickerings' car still doesn't work right, a daily taunt. "It's like a tumbleweed," Barbara Pickering said of the crime's effect on her life. "It just keeps rolling along."

And we counted only the official victims. There were others.

In a south Minneapolis neighborhood on the evening of Dec. 11, police stormed into a house on a tip that a robbery suspect was hiding there. They swept into each room, but the suspect had fled moments earlier. In the kitchen, a woman broke into sobs. Her daughter, 5 or 6 years old, stood wide-eyed in the living room and cried quietly. As the excitement ebbed, the girl returned to her cartoon drawings on a coffee table. Her tears mixed with red crayon on a smiling Mickey Mouse.

We didn't count the woman and her daughter because they don't show up in the statistics. But they, too, were victims of crime on Dec. 11.

So were the people next door who heard the sirens, saw the squad-car lights and worried for their neighborhood, their city, their quality of life.

**The full story of Friday, Dec. 11, begins on Page 12A.**

## Almanac

**Sunday, January 3, 1988**
**3rd day; 363 to go this year**
**Sunrise: 7:52. Sunset: 4:44**

### Today's weather/

Very cold

Partly cloudy with a few flurries then turning much colder. High from 10 to 15 but falling to 2 to 7 by afternoon.

### Index/




Volume VI/Number 274 — 8 sections

**Indiana steamrolls Gophers 92-63/1C**

**Stars shut out 3rd straight game/1C**

**2 Israelis, 1 Palestinian killed in raid/4A**

VARIETY

'Patti Rocks' is a provocative comedy about male chauvinism

**MINNEAPOLIS EDITION**

- Minneapolis wraps up $15 million purchase of Cedar Square West/**1B**
- Hennepin County jury awards $2.3 million to man who lost eye/**1B**
- Front-end loader gives police a boost in another crack raid/**1B**


# Star Tribune

**FRIDAY**/February 5/1988 NEWSPAPER OF THE TWIN CITIES 35¢


# Panama's Noriega indicted by U.S. juries

From News Services

**Miami, Fla.**
Panama's military strongman, Gen. Manuel Antonio Noriega, was indicted Thursday by federal grand juries in Miami and Tampa, Fla., on charges of racketeering, cocaine trafficking and money laundering, law-enforcement sources said.

The indictments, long expected, were sealed by a federal magistrate, but the U.S. attorneys in the two cities scheduled announcements for today.

Noriega's indictment is expected to have serious diplomatic and political ramifications that extend far beyond the specific criminal allegations.

Current and former U.S. officials said that in the short run, the charges are likely to make it more difficult for Noriega to resign and permit a smooth transition to a civilian government.

And, U.S. officials noted, Noriega would be effectively blocked from moving to the United States or to a country where he could be extradited to the United States.

The U.S.-Panama extradition treaty does not require Panama to arrest or extradite Noriega, and the general

**Noriega** continued on page 14A

Gen. Manuel Antonio Noriega

# Senate endorses Reagan's contra-aid plan in symbolic vote

From News Services

**Washington, D.C.**
The Senate, serving notice that the fight over aiding the Nicaraguan contras is far from over, defied House Democratic leaders Thursday and endorsed in a symbolic vote the Reagan administration's plan to give weapons and humanitarian aid to the anti-Sandinista rebels.

Proponents of contra aid conceded that the 51-48 vote was moot because the plan had been defeated by the House Wednesday night, but they said that it would keep the issue alive and vowed to introduce new requests for military aid.

Democratic opponents insisted that the military aid issue was dead for now, and vowed to press ahead with a plan of strictly humanitarian aid

**Contra aid** continued on page 8A

# Dole demands Bush apology for aide's remark

United Press International

"This business doesn't have to be so nasty, so mean, so vindictive. I want to be president, but I want to get there discussing the issues, not groveling in the mud."
– Robert Dole

From News Services

**Washington, D.C.**
Kansas Sen. Robert Dole heatedly confronted Vice President George Bush in the Senate chamber twice Thursday, demanding an apology for a campaign aide's statement and later accusing Bush of reducing the GOP presidential race to "groveling in the mud."

Both candidates had returned from Iowa for a Senate vote on aid to the Nicaraguan contras. At a lull for a procedural vote, Dole strode to podium and angrily shoved a press release issued by the Bush campaign in front of the vice president, who was presiding over the chamber.

The statement, issued Wednesday in Iowa by George Wittgraf, Bush's state campaign chief, accused Dole of "cronyism and mean-spiritedness" and outlined federal investigations of a blind trust held until recently by Elizabeth Harford Dole, the candidate's wife and former Transportation secretary.

Dole, described by aides as "steaming mad" over the charges, said later that the press release was "one of the nastiest things I've seen in politics." He said he confronted Bush because "I wanted the vice president to tell me man to man" whether he had authorized it.

During the five-minute confrontation, which apparently was not heard by others in the chamber, Dole frowned and pounded his fist on the desk. Bush, who looked at the memorandum before quickly putting it away, spoke only a few words.

Still visibly angry in a subsequent meeting with reporters, Dole said he told Bush: "I think you owe my wife an apology. He knew I was coming up there to see him. What kind of

**Campaign** continued on page 8A

Staff Photo by Mike Zerby

## Man, 86, dies in Minneapolis house fire

**Firefighters sought to revive an 86-year-old man outside his smoke-filled house in Minneapolis Thursday morning as a friend of his, Leonard Gunderson, left, watched for the ambulance. Morse Delplain, 5205 39th Av. S., died as a result of the fire. No one else was home at the time. Gunderson, who lives nearby, had come by to check on Delplain when his phone calls went unanswered. Article on page 3B.**

# Perpich's kindergarten plan seems likely to lose

By Dennis J. McGrath and Gregor W. Pinney
Staff Writers

Gov. Rudy Perpich's proposal for all-day kindergarten appears dead for the 1988 Legislature, according to key lawmakers and a Star Tribune survey of legislators.

When the Legislature convenes Tuesday, full-time kindergarten will be considered during a session in which lawmakers will focus on the first and last years that students spend in school.

Early childhood education, the University of Minnesota's Commitment to Focus program and the governance of the state technical institutes and community colleges top the education issues.

But all-day kindergarten will quickly be dropped from that list, according to chairmen of the four House and Senate education-related committees.

"It's dead. It isn't going anywhere," said Robert McEachern, DFL-St. Michael, chairman of the House Education Committee.

McEachern and other education chairmen questioned whether Perpich would propose much funding for voluntary full-time school for 5-year-olds because of the lack of support in both parties and both houses. Interviews with legislators and the Star Tribune survey suggest that the cost — about $75 million — is only one obstacle. There also is philosophical opposition to the concept, despite some studies that show benefits from early schooling.

In the House, 64 of the 96 members surveyed, or 67 percent, opposed the principle of public schools offering a whole day of kindergarten. In the Senate, 28 of the 48 members surveyed, or 58 percent, objected to the

**Education** continued on page 6A

# Schulstad, Carlson top council fund-raisers

By Rob Hotakainen
Staff Writer

Dennis Schulstad and Barbara Carlson, the two independents on the Minneapolis City Council, topped their DFL colleagues in fund-raising in 1987 and may be adding to their coffers to run for mayor in 1989.

In an off-election year, Schulstad outpaced all council members by raising more than $39,000. He raised less than $9,000 in 1986.

Carlson, who raised only $250 in cash contributions in 1986, ranked second last year by receiving more than $32,000.

Walt Dziedzic, a DFLer, was the only other council member to raise more than $30,000 last year. He raised more than $31,000 after bringing in less than $10,000 in 1986.

Schulstad said council members are getting ready for the possibility of a wide-open mayoral race next year by raising money early. "That's clearly why people are doing it," he said Thursday.

Mayor Don Fraser, who raised more than $20,000 in 1987, said again yesterday that he will seek a fourth term. He finished the year with a cash balance of $36,940.

But Schulstad and Carlson said Fraser, an ex-congressman, could be lured away with a presidential appointment if a Democrat succeeds President Reagan.

Fraser said he expects a Democrat in the White House, but added: "The notion that I would find a niche there is not very likely."

**Funds** continued on page 6A

## NYSE tightens rules on trading with computers

The board of the New York Stock Exchange voted unanimously Thursday to restrict a form of computerized stock trading that had been blamed for accelerating the market's October crash. The proposed regulation would ban securities firms from using the exchange's electronic order system to execute so-called index-arbitrage-program trades if the Dow Jones industrial average rose or fell 50 points or more on any day.

The move came against a background of congressional scrutiny into the causes of the crash, as well as growing fear in the securities industry that lawmakers will impose unwanted regulations unless the markets take aggressive steps themselves. **Page 1D.**

# State's tax rank drops to 12th, lowest since '71

By Betty Wilson and Dane Smith
Staff Writers

Minnesota dropped from sixth-highest to 12th-highest among states in total state and local tax collections per capita for the fiscal year ending June 30, 1986, according to the annual report by the Minnesota Taxpayers Association.

But Minnesota's high rate of revenue collection from other sources — fees, charges and interest earnings — maintained the state's fifth-place ranking in total government revenue and spending.

Furthermore, the association's executive director, Don Paterick, predicted that $690 million intax increase passed by the 1987 Legislature would boost Minnesota back into the top 10.

The tax ranking was, nevertheless, Minnesota's lowest since 1971, when it was 13th, the association reported.

"That's a fantastic drop, but it's short-lived," Paterick said.

The main reason for Minnesota's drop in the tax rankings was the $1 billion tax cut passed by the Legislature in 1985, he said. Independent-Republicans made that cut their battle cry in the 1984 election when they won control of the Minnesota House.

Despite the drop in the tax burden, Minnesota's per capita spending rank remains fifth-highest in the nation, the same as in 1984 and 1985. Only Alaska, Wyoming, New York and the District of Columbia outspend Minnesota on a per capita basis, it said.

(A Star Tribune study of state and local government spending published

**Taxes** continued on page 6A

## Almanac

**Friday, February 5, 1988**
**36th day; 330 to go this year**
**Sunrise: 7:29. Sunset: 5:27**

### Today's weather/ Bitter

It will be blustery and very cold today with highs 2 below to 6 below. The wind chill will be 40 to 60 below. The cold weather is expected to continue through Tuesday.



### Telephones/

| | |
|---|---|
| News general | 372-4141 |
| Want Ads | 372-4242 |
| Circulation | 372-4343 |


Volume [illegible] Number 307 [illegible] sections

Strikers lose a tough one at home/1C

SPORTS

**NCAA pairings:**
Top four teams get top tournament seeds

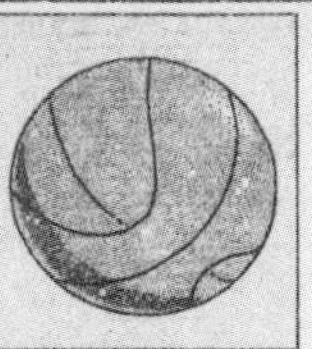

VARIETY

Crankshaft and Iota make their comic debut

**MINNEAPOLIS**
EDITION

■ Legislators considering wage increases for nursing home aides/**1B**

■ Hennepin County is pushing ahead to try to make recycling work/**1B**

B


# Star Tribune

**MONDAY**/March 14/1988 NEWSPAPER OF THE TWIN CITIES 35¢


# Keller resigns as president, hoping to save Focus plan

## He apologizes for Eastcliff mistakes

By Chuck Haga and Betty Wilson
Staff Writers

Kenneth Keller resigned as president of the University of Minnesota Sunday night.

Clearly frustrated by public preoccupation with controversy over renovation of his official residence and office, Keller said he will step down to try to save his Commitment to Focus, an extensive plan to make the university one of the best in the nation.

Reading from a prepared statement shortly after 10 p.m., Keller said the $1.5 million renovation of Eastcliff, the presidential mansion, was a "mismanaged" project that had claimed the public's attention at the expense of more significant and more positive matters.

"I bear a key responsibility for it," he said. "I have said before and I repeat now that I am profoundly embarrassed and profoundly sorry for it."

**Inside**

■ The university is getting a chance to return to substance over style, columnist Doug Grow writes. **9A.**

■ Possible successors to Keller. **9A.**

■ A chronology of the Keller presidency. **8A.**

■ Text of Keller's statement. **9A.**

**Details, Pages 8,9A.**

Senate Majority Leader Roger Moe said that the $23 million funding proposal for Commitment to Focus still should be postponed a year.

"That would allow a cooling-off period and give the university time to regain public confidence," Moe said. Keller's ability to remain as president

**Keller** continued on page 8A

## Keller fought public's perception of elitism

By Bruce Benidt
Staff Writer

Ken Keller rose fast through the forcefulness of his vision and ideas. He fell when people perceived that he liked too well the heights he'd gained.

He was a respected teacher who saw beyond the narrow confines of his own field to a larger university that worked together to advance knowledge and find practical applications to human problems. When he rose to a position where he could propose change that would remake the university, he took such full advantage of it that he was handed the presidency to put his ideas into effect. He was steering major changes through huge inertia-laden institutions, having gotten many people in the Legislature, the university community and the state at large to agree with his aims, when he was snared by an expensive set of details he hadn't paid enough attention to.

Through these last weeks, Keller was burdened with terms such as arrogance and elitism that for many people added up to a feeling he was too impressed with himself — a victim of hubris. Even the name of the rock his ship foundered on had a Shakespearean resonance to it — Eastcliff.

Rutherford Aris, a university regents

**Career** continued on page 9A

Staff Photo by David Brewster

**Kenneth Keller: "I bear a key responsibility for it. I have said before and I repeat now that I am profoundly embarrassed and profoundly sorry for it."**

## Analysis

## Departure may help Focus in long run

By David Peterson
Staff Writer

Commitment to Focus has something in common with the Edina High School hockey team.

Not long ago, Edina lost its leading scorer. And when its coach was asked, after the team became state champion, how it survived such a calamity, he replied that at times such a loss galvanizes the rest of the team.

Kenneth Keller could not have imposed Commitment to Focus upon an unwilling state. The Board of Regents appeared to have chosen him because of it. He was able to raise more than $300 million because the people who have that kind of money supported it. And, presumably, the Capitol remained so patient for the past few weeks precisely because political leaders believed in it.

None of that has changed simply because the team's leading scorer has placed himself on the disabled list. Commitment to Focus — and a decision as to whether to proceed — remains.

"A lot of people were using Eastcliff as a smokescreen because they don't want to come out and say that they're opposed to Commitment to Focus," said Judy Grew, president of the Minnesota Student Association. "That's one positive thing. Now if they don't like Commitment to Focus, they're going to have to say so and they're going to have to say what their alternative will be."

**Focus** continued on page 8A

## Attacks on fuel trucks lead to West Bank delivery cutoff

Associated Press

**Jerusalem**
Israel choked off gasoline supplies to the occupied West Bank Sunday after Palestinian protesters set fire to two fuel trucks and pelted others with stones. Prime Minister Yitzhak Shamir left for Washington today to meet with U.S. officials.

The army confirmed that an Arab died after being shot in the eye in a clash last week but denied reports that a 5-year-old boy died of burns caused by a tear gas grenade. The army said the boy had been playing with a kerosene stove when he was fatally burned. A spokesman said the parents initially blamed soldiers but later retracted the allegation.

A police spokesman said more than half of the 850 Arab policemen in the occupied West Bank and Gaza Strip had resigned in response to a campaign led by the Palestine Liberation Organization.

The United Nations said at least 91 Palestinians have been killed since

**Israel** continued on page 12A

**Deaf dean picked as Gallaudet president**
Gallaudet University chose the dean of its college of arts and sciences to become the first deaf president in the 124-year history of the school for the hearing-impaired.

I. King Jordan was chosen to replace Elisabeth Ann Zinser, a hearing woman who resigned after protests from students seeking a deaf leader virtually paralyzed the Washington, D.C., school. **3A.**

## Dole vows to remain 'active all the way'

From News Services

**Oak Brook, Ill.**
Sen. Robert Dole of Kansas, rejecting the advice of some of his closest aides, vowed Sunday to remain in the Republican presidential race after the Illinois primary Tuesday.

Facing enormous odds in his effort to wrest the Republican nomination from Vice President George Bush, Dole said he would remain "active all the way."

Only three days ago, after being beaten badly by Bush in the Super Tuesday contests, the Dole campaign canceled its TV advertising in Illinois, and some of Dole's top aides urged

**Campaign** continued on page 6B

## Fate of daughter who ran away at 17 still haunts parents 10 years later

By Kurt Chandler
Staff Writer

Seventeen-year-old Jackie Kolstad ran away from her St. Paul home 10 years ago.

In the months after her disappearance, her parents cruised the streets of St. Paul and Minneapolis on weekends, searching for the runaway. They distributed copies of her photograph to Twin Cities taxi drivers. When Jackie called home months later to say she was working at a restaurant in Duluth, her mother drove north to find her.

Jackie was not found.

The teen-ager unexpectedly returned home for one night a year after running away, then left again for good.

Today her parents have no idea of her whereabouts, no clue to her fate. The case of Jacquelyne Ann Kolstad remains the longest-standing missing-person file in the Twin Cities. Her name remains listed with the National Crime Information Center, which forwards information to the Kolstads whenever a body is discovered matching their daughter's description.

Mary and Ralph Kolstad can offer no easy explanation for Jackie's disappearance, and they no longer talk about her. At family picnics

**Missing** continued on page 6B

## Almanac

**Monday, March 14, 1988**
**74th day; 292 to go this year**
**Sunrise: 6:28. Sunset: 6:18**

Variable cloudiness, with a high in the lower 20s and a northwest wind of 10 to 20 miles per hour.




Circulation 372-4343




Volume VI/Number 345 6 sections

## Taxing question of who's exempt again faces state

By Robert Franklin
Staff Writer

■ It is harder to get a property tax break in Hennepin County than in any other Minnesota county. **Page 1B; chart, 5B.**

When the Franciscan sisters of Little Falls, Minn., opened their exercise center to the public, the tax man took notice. It operated like a health club, charging a fee for use of its pool, workout room, racquetball courts, sauna, shower rooms and massage area. It advertised like a health club, and it competed with a health club.

So, reasoned then-assessor Steve Hurni of Morrison County, it should pay taxes like a health club, even if it was run by a bunch of nuns.

The sisters challenged that, citing their tax-exempt status as a religious organization. In January they won a Tax Court decision that as "an institution of purely public charity" they should be free of property taxes.

The patterns of tax exemption in Minnesota resemble a crazy quilt:

**Taxes** continued on page 4A

Reardon's streak broken in 4-3 loss/1C

Palestinians protest holy site digging/3A

Rains delay men's Wimbledon final/1C

SPORTS

The brushback: Throwing caution to the batter

**MINNEAPOLIS EDITION**

■ Flight instructor, student die in plane crash in Ham Lake/**1B**

■ St. Anthony Park is small-town enclave within urban setting/**1B**

■ Poss' big-city skills, savvy are a benefit to small city of Blaine/**1B**


# Star Tribune

MONDAY/July 4/1988 NEWSPAPER OF THE TWIN CITIES 35¢


# 290 die when U.S. warship shoots down Iranian airliner

## Passenger jet mistaken for attacking fighter plane

From News Services

**Manama, Bahrain**
A U.S. Navy ship shot down an Iranian civilian jetliner over the Persian Gulf Sunday, and Iran said all 290 people aboard were killed. The United States said its forces mistook the jet for an F-14 fighter plane.

Iranian Prime Minister Hussein Musavi said the incident showed that the United States had "entered a more direct war with our nation," and he warned that it must face the consequences of "this criminal act." He did not elaborate.

Iran's official Islamic Republic News Agency (IRNA) said the Iran Air jet, an A300 Airbus, was hit by two U.S. missiles minutes after leaving Iran for Dubai in the United Arab Emirates. All the passengers were believed killed after the plane exploded at an altitude of 7,500 feet, IRNA said.

Iranian television showed helicopters shooting flares across the crash area and small motorboats moving in to pick up floating corpses. It said 110 had been recovered.

A camera zeroed in on a rescue ship. On the ship's deck, a rescue worker held up the body of an infant and shook his fist. The report said the victims included 66 children. Iran declared today a day of mourning.

President Reagan said the shooting occurred during "proper defensive action" after the jet headed for the missile cruiser Vincennes as it was engaged in a battle with Iranian gunboats in the Strait of Hormuz, the entryway to the gulf. He promised a full investigation.

"We deeply regret any loss of life," Reagan said from his retreat at Camp David.

Pentagon officials said the civilian

**Gulf** continued on page 4A

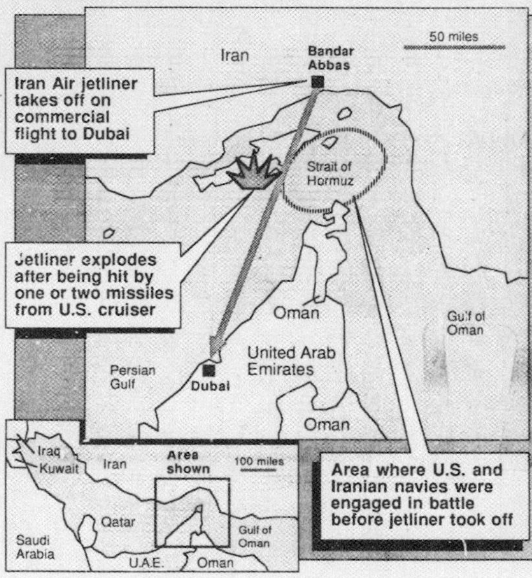


**THE TRAGEDY OF FLIGHT 655/**
Mistake in the Gulf

1/The cruiser Vincennes and frigate Elmer Montgomery encounter and battle Iranian patrol boats in the Straight of Hormuz at 9:40 a.m. (1:10 a.m. Twin Cities time), sinking two patrol boats.

2/Iran Air jet takes off from Bandar Abbas in Iran at 10:15 a.m., headed across the gulf on the 150-mile flight to Dubai in the United Arab Emirates with 290 passengers aboard.

3/The Vincennes, still fighting with the patrol boats, detects an aircraft over Iran at 10:17 a.m. and sends warnings to it. Haze prevents making positive visual identification.

4/About seven minutes after the radar sighting, two Standard surface-to-air missiles are launched at the airliner, which the Vincennes believed was an F-14 fighter plane. It was at 7,500 feet, about six miles from the ship.

5/The plane disintegrated in the air upon being hit at about 10:30 a.m., killing all passengers.

6/Iranian navy frogmen recover bodies and parts of the wreckage.

Source/News services — Star Tribune graphic

## Chance for error grows as decision time shrinks

From News Services

**Washington, D.C.**
The downing of an Iranian jetliner is striking evidence of how split-second decisions in modern warfare have heightened the risk of error.

The U.S. military's steady increase in authority over the past year to confront Iran's aggressive behavior in the Persian Gulf has made the decision about when to shoot even more of a dilemma for U.S. commanders.

U.S. warships are operating in a small, crowded war zone that has become more dangerous because of tough new orders from the Reagan administration to prevent Iran from harassing the growing number of oil tankers and commercial freighters that pass through the Strait of Hormuz.

In doing so, U.S. warship commanders have come under even more pressure to respond on a hair-trigger basis to an array of mine, missile and chemical-weapon threats. The situation produces what has become day-to-day psychological warfare and raises the risk of the kind of catastrophe that occurred Sunday when a U.S. warship downed a civilian Iranian airliner.

After the 1987 Stark incident, in which the commander of a U.S. frigate failed to respond in time to a missile attack by an Iraqi jet and 37 sailors were killed, U.S. commanders have operated under strict instructions to defend against any approaching plane or vessel that demonstrates "hostile intent."

In the busy gulf, where any radar blip could be the seagoing equivalent of a terrorist truck bomber in Beirut, U.S. commanders have challenged both commercial and military traffic in the region, demanding over marine and aviation radios that unidentified

**Procedure** continued on page 4A

## Attack offers comparisons, contrasts to Soviet downing of South Korean jet

Los Angeles Times

**Washington, D.C.**
The downing of an Iran Air passenger plane by U.S. missiles Sunday has prompted comparisons — and contrasts — to the destruction of a South Korean airliner shot down by a Soviet fighter pilot nearly five years ago.

In each instance, hundreds of innocent victims aboard an unarmed commercial airliner were killed. A total of 269 people died aboard Korean Air Lines (KAL) Flight 007. Iran's official news agency said the death toll in the gulf incident was 290.

Likewise in both cases, the United States and the Kremlin insisted they had acted in self-defense and both insisted that the doomed planes ignored warning signals and were out of their assigned air corridors.

Despite advanced radar systems and other missile-age technology, both superpowers said they were unable to tell that the planes were commercial airliners rather than military planes. In the Soviet case, a pilot even saw the plane at close range before shooting it out of the sky.

And U.S. and Soviet leaders implied in their statements that their armed forces might have to shoot down another airliner if the same circumstances occurred again.

"I don't understand the responsibility of a country . . . that flies a commercial airliner over an area where (military) attacks are underway," said Adm. William Crowe, chairman

**KAL** continued on page 4A

**Inside/**
The Navy was trying to determine why electronic equipment aboard its missile cruiser indicated that the jetliner it downed was an F-14 jet fighter. President Reagan decided to stay at Camp David as part of an effort to keep the events from being characterized as a crisis.

Meanwhile, diplomatic progress made in recent months between Iran and the United States seems certain to be damaged by the incident. **All stories on page 5A.**

## For 300 new citizens, July 4th now will be a personal holiday

By Michelle M. Miller
Staff Writer

July 4th means barbecues, fireworks and parades for most Americans, but for 48-year-old Seoun Chunn of Rochester, Minn., and 300 other immigrants in Minnesota today likely will mean much more.

Chunn, a Kampuchean refugee, escaped from his strife-torn country seven years ago. He and the 300 other immigrants will be naturalized as U.S. citizens today at the Taste of Minnesota festival at the Capitol in St. Paul, the second naturalization ceremony at the festival.

The new citizens have come from around the world with dreams of freedom, jobs, education — and even cold weather.

"I had to escape," Chunn said. "In the 1975 Communist occupation, they killed a lot of people. They ordered all of the people to the farm. We had no freedom."

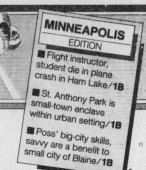

Irene Hellie

He and his family tried to escape in 1979, and lived on the border of Kampuchea and Thailand for two years. They were shifted from several Red Cross camps along the border until they received sponsorship to come to the United States.

"I came to America because I wanted freedom," he said.

He lives in Rochester with his wife and four of his six children, ages 7 to 25. He does laundry for Bethany Samaritan Heights, a nursing home.

"It will be a great day when I become a citizen," Chunn said. "I want to be American, follow the laws of Americans and live in America for the rest of my life."

Irene Hellie was born 41 years ago in Munich, Germany. "I don't think people remember what happened 200 years ago. When they think of the 4th of July, they think, party time. And that's what it will be for me."

Hellie moved to the United States 16 years ago to be with her parents, who immigrated from Canada. She had completed graduate and postgraduate studies at U.S. universities and believed she would have a better chance of

**Immigrants** continued on page 2A

## Almanac

**Monday, July 4, 1988**
**186th day; 180 to go this year**
**Sunrise: 5:32. Sunset: 9:03**

**Today's weather/**
Hot holiday

Mostly sunny and hot weather is forecast for the Twin Cities. High will be in the 90s. An overnight low from 65 to 70 is expected.

**Inside/**
**PHP foe is now friend**
Dr. K. James Ehlen has made his peace with Physicians Health Plan. Now he's the company's interim chief executive officer. **Page 1D.**

**Index/**



| | |
|---|---|
| News general | 372-4141 |
| Classifieds | 372-4242 |
| Circulation | 372-4343 |


Volume VII/Number 91 6 sections

Rethinking the Cold War

## Antagonistic allies

### The big chill between the superpowers was developing well before World War II

**Fifth in a series of articles appearing each Monday.**

By Eric Black
Staff Writer

The Cold War started soon after World War II ended.

Or did it?

According to traditional interpretations, the 40-year-old global staring contest between the United States and the Soviet Union began between 1945 and 1948.

After all, the argument goes, in 1945 the two powers were still cooperating to defeat the Nazis. In 1948, the first Berlin crisis occurred. (That was when the Soviets blockaded West Berlin, the United States airlifted in food and supplies and the world held its breath in case the Soviets shot down an U.S. plane.)

So at first glance it makes sense to assume that something went wrong in that immediate post-war period to turn allies into adversaries.

Lots did go wrong in that period. But one could argue (in fact, one is about to) that World War II created the Cold War.

World War II converted the Soviet Union from the weak, disorganized military power that was almost overrun by Germany in 1941 into one of the world's two military superpowers by 1945, a status the Soviets have maintained since. Without Soviet military might, the Cold War would become the old war.

World War II lured the United States out of the isolationist mood into which it had reverted in the 1920s and '30s. Without an internationalist,

**Cold War** continued on page 8A

Sequential transplants give two patients new organs/1B

MINNEAPOLIS EDITION

■ Minneapolis schools sued over beating death of student/3B


# Star Tribune

WEDNESDAY/November 9/1988 NEWSPAPER OF THE TWIN CITIES 35¢


# Bush cruises to victory

## State goes for Dukakis, Durenberger; Lottery appears headed for approval

By Clift Haas
Staff Correspondent

George Herbert Walker Bush, who shed an image as Ronald Reagan's wealthy, weak-kneed understudy to press a harsh, aggressive campaign against Michael Dukakis, won election Tuesday as the 41st president of the United States.

The Democrats countered with decisive control of both houses of Congress.

With 78 percent of the vote, Bush had a lead of 54 percent to 46 percent for Dukakis. But in the electoral college, Bush was projected to have a lead of 352 to 102, with 270 needed for election. Bush's victory marked the seventh time in the past 10 elections that a Republican has won the presidency.

Minnesota, though, bucked the national trend, backing Dukakis while returning Republican Dave Durenberger to the Senate for another six-year term. Partial results of a Star Tribune election model showed Dukakis leading Bush 53 to 46 percent, with 84 of 100 sample precincts reporting.

In claiming his prize, the president-elect told supporters in his adopted hometown of Houston, "We can now speak the most majestic words a democracy has to offer: the people have spoken.

"With a full heart and great hopes I thank all the people throughout America who have given us this great victory," Bush said, adding that he would seek to win the support of those who did not vote for him.

Bush said he meant to be president of all the people, and expressed his goal for an "America that is strong and resolute in the world, strong and big-hearted at home. And when I said I wanted a kinder, gentler nation, I meant it and I mean it."

Dukakis, in Boston, offered Bush his concession first in a private telephone call, then later at a rally with his supporters. "The nation must work together," Dukakis said, echoing sentiments Bush expressed just minutes later.

Bush received a call of congratulations from President Reagan, as did Vice President-elect Dan Quayle of Indiana.

Bush's victory, built on a strong base of support in the South, Midwest and Rocky Mountain West, makes him the first sitting vice president to be elected to the Oval Office since Martin Van Buren in 1836. With Bush

Election continued on page 5A

## ELECTION '88

### Vote at a glance

78% of precincts reporting nationally, 75% in Minnesota

| Candidate | Pct. of nat'l vote | Pct. of Minn. vote | National pop. vote | States won | Electoral votes |
|---|---|---|---|---|---|
| Dukakis | 46% | 54% | 32,171,924 | 10 | 102 |
| Bush | 54% | 46% | 38,007,921 | 37 | 352 |

Needed to win: 270 electoral votes. May not total 100% because of additional candidates.

### Democrats keep grip, knock off Weicker

Democrats tightened their grip on the Senate Tuesday as they knocked off maverick Republican Sen. Lowell Weicker of Connecticut and engineered wins by two former governors — Virginia's Charles Robb and Nebraska's Robert Kerrey — in GOP territory.

Democrats appeared likely to pad their 54-46 Senate majority by one or two seats. Two incumbent Democratic senators survived strong Republican challenges. Democrats also renewed their comfortable control of the U.S. House. **9A.**

### IR makes gains, but DFL keeps state House

Page 1B

### Democrats pick up 2 governorships

Page 7A

### U.S. House races in Minnesota

#### Seven incumbents are reelected; Stangeland fights strong challenge

Seven of Minnesota's eight congressmen apparently won reelection Tuesday, with the outcome in one race in doubt. Incomplete returns showed IR incumbent Rep. Arlan Stangeland with a small lead over DFLer challenger Marv Hanson in the Seventh District. **8A.**

#### Minneapolis voters reject all four amendments to change City Charter

In a vote that confounded city politicians, Minneapolis residents rejected all four of the City Charter amendments, including one to reduce the size of the City Council and Mayor Don Fraser's proposal for a stronger role for the mayor. The two other amendments that lost were a proposal to eliminate party designations on the ballot and one to stagger the terms of the mayor and the council. **1B.**

### St. Paul rights proposal fails

Page 6B

### Hennepin County commissioner

Jude winning against Clausnitzer

Keefe easily wins a second term

Randy Johnson winning tough race

Page 1B

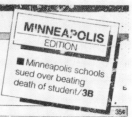

Associated Press

George and Barbara Bush liked what they saw as they watched election returns on TV in Houston with their grandchildren Jenna, left, and Barbara Bush. Later, George Bush said, "With a full heart and great hopes I thank all the people throughout America who have given us this great victory."

## Humphrey fails to win father's former seat

By Betty Wilson
Staff Writer

U.S. Sen. Dave Durenberger rolled to an easy victory Tuesday and a third term in the seat once held by the father of his DFL challenger, Hubert Humphrey III.

Star Tribune projections said Durenberger would win by 13 percentage points, in an election that drew a turnout projected to be slightly larger than the 67 percent forecast by Secretary of State Joan Growe.

With ballots counted in 64 percent of the state's roughly 4,000 precincts when this edition went to press, Durenberger was leading by 13 points.

"I feel very good, and I feel particularly good about the fact that from now on, people won't refer to Minnesota as a Democratic state," an exuberant Durenberger said.

"The size of my victory is really an indication that anybody can run for office and get elected, and you don't have to be a DFLer."

It's also an affirmation that his 1978 election was not a fluke, Durenberger said. That year he won a Senate seat held by DFLers for many years, after a bitter DFL Party split. He bested DFLer Robert Short with a 61-35 percent vote margin, after Short had defeated party-endorsed Don Fraser in the DFL primary.

Senate continued on page 10A

## Voters seem to have opted to give lottery a chance

By Robert Whereatt
Staff Writer

Minnesota voters apparently approved a constitutional amendment clearing the way for a state-operated lottery.

According to the Star Tribune's sample of representative precincts, 57 percent of all voters endorsed the proposition. National Election Service figures show 52.8 percent supporting the proposition, based on 36 percent of the state's precincts.

In addition, voters overwhelmingly approved an amendment that sets up an environmental trust fund to protect and improve the state's natural resources, and approved a third amendment permitting the use of six-member juries in civil and nonfelony court cases.

To pass, each amendment needed a majority of all votes cast in the election. Failure to vote on an amendment counted as a "no" vote.

The lottery was approved by almost 57 percent of the voters in 84 of the Star Tribune's 100 sample precincts.

The lottery amendment was pushed by Proponents of the Lottery Law, an organization that got more than $40,000 from lottery suppliers and

Lottery continued on page 10A

## Bush benefited from voters' optimism, sense that Reagan era has been good

By Steve Berg
Staff Correspondent

**Analysis**

New York, N.Y.
George Bush was propelled to victory Tuesday by voters who feel they benefited from the Reagan years and are optimistic about the future.

The Republican vice president, who campaigned as the candidate of the great American mainstream, won the slice of the electorate he was aiming for, although his victory wasn't as broad as Ronald Reagan's landslide of four years ago.

Bush owes his triumph to a coalition dominated by white, middle-income suburbanites from the Sun Belt who prospered during the Reagan years and hope a new Republican administration will keep moving the country in the same direction.

According to the results of NBC-Wall Street Journal exit polls, those mainstream voters considered Bush more experienced and competent than Dukakis, particularly in handling matters of national security.

But as is so often the case, the econo-

Analysis continued on page 5A

### Almanac

Wednesday, November 9, 1988
314th day; 52 to go this year
Sunrise: 7:02. Sunset: 4:51

Cloudy, high in middle 40s.



Circulation 372-4343



Volume VII/Number 219 7 sections

Vikings' fate remains up in the air/1C

Gophers winless over the weekend/4C

Control Data also betting on lottery/1D

VARIETY

**A comic view**

Joel Hodgson thinks up novel way to watch old movies

**MINNEAPOLIS EDITION**

■ Coon Rapids church in embezzlement case feels betrayed/**1B**

■ Environmental education would expand under new proposal/**1B**

# Star Tribune

MONDAY/December 19/1988 NEWSPAPER OF THE TWIN CITIES 35¢

# Pillsbury agrees to takeover

## $66-a-share deal ends 2-month fight

By Josephine Marcotty
Staff Writer

Pillsbury Co. will be acquired by Grand Metropolitan PLC for $5.7 billion, the companies announced Sunday night, abruptly ending a two-month battle that culminated Saturday when agents for both parties cut a $66-per-share deal in a New York City restaurant.

The agreement means that Pillsbury shareholders will receive $6 more than Grand Met's original Oct. 4 offer of $60 per share and $3 more than its sweetened offer of $63 per share made a week ago.

Since the battle began, the deal has been sweetened by $513.6 million. Grand Met's new tender runs until Jan. 3.

Pillsbury's board of directors, which met for two hours yesterday afternoon, approved the deal. The board has "determined that the terms of the offer and merger are fair to, and in the best interests of, Pillsbury stockholders and recommends that stockholders accept the offer and tender their shares," the announcement said.

Philip Smith, chairman of Pillsbury said: "We are pleased that we have succeeded in protecting the interests of our shareholders, employees, franchisees and communities and that we have reached a negotiated agreement that works to the advantage of everyone."

The joint announcement was terse, and said nothing about the effect of the acquisition on employees. However, Grand Met, the British liquor,

Pillsbury continued on page 12A

Pillsbury's highs and lows
Pillsbury's stock traded nervously in the high $30s and low $40s all summer on reported waves of speculation that the company was going to be taken over. It shot up after Grand Metropolitan PLC made its $60-a-share offer on Oct. 4. After weeks of silence, Pillsbury negotiated secretely with Grand Met but rejected a $65 per share friendly deal Dec. 11. Then Grand Met sweetened its offer to shareholders to $63 and after a court defeat Friday, Pillsbury agreed to sell for $66.
Stock offers
$66 merger price
$37.87
Oct. 1
Oct 4
Dec. 11
Dec. 12
Dec. 18
Star Tribune graphic

## Small stakeholders, charities may have less to gain from deal

To the glint and rustle of golden parachutes, the Pillsbury Co. Sunday abandoned its clearly hopeless struggle to remain free of the clutches of Grand Metropolitan PLC, the British food and liquor conglomerate.

With the company's decision yesterday to accept a $66-a-share offer from Grand Met, Pillsbury lined its stockholders' pockets with upwards of $5.7 billion. The Grand Met price was $6 a share or $513.6 million above the $60-a-share, $5.23 billion offer that was announced Oct. 4.

The Grand Met offer, which is about $18 a share higher than the best price Pillsbury's stock ever had attracted, means that the 15 Pillsbury directors may well collect more than $20 million for their holdings.

And it means senior Pillsbury managers stand to reap as much as $10 million to $12 million more in severance pay if they lose their jobs in the takeover.

Alas, there's a whole passel of other Pillsbury stakeholders — from lower-level headquarters employees to a long list of charities to the communities in which the company operates — that are not similarly blessed.

**Dick Youngblood**

I know, I know, when Grand Met's well-oiled publicity machine rolled into the Twin Cities Oct. 4, its top U.S. officer, Ian Martin, offered soothing pledges that he would maintain Pillsbury's charitable giving, which totaled $8 million in cash and $4 million in food products in fiscal 1988.

There's no reason not to believe Martin, mind you — although he subsequently sent me a letter saying what a pleasure it was to meet me, and I didn't believe *that* for one nanosecond.

Nevertheless, a man who's in a position to know said yesterday that "Ian Martin is a man of integrity." The endorsement came from Walter

Youngblood continued on page 12A

## Takeover tide pulls in yet another company

By Anthony Carideo
Staff Writer

**Analysis**

Farewell, PSY.

No longer will that three-letter symbol for the stock of Pillsbury Co. scuttle across the electronic ticker screens in brokerage houses and investment firms. The loss of the PSY symbol, and the 85.6 million shares that trade under it, is in its own way a symbol of a deepening trend that has taken hundreds of billions of dollars worth of stock off the public market.

Until Sunday's announcement of its merger with Grand Metropolitan PLC, PSY, like other stocks, traded at a price that reflected investors' views of the company's future. For more than two years, that future for various reasons has been dim or subject to investor confusion, and the price they were willing to pay for Pillsbury has steadily deteriorated.

With that future now part of a larger concern, PSY goes to an electronic graveyard that includes the symbols that represented Kraft Inc., Nabisco, General Foods, Beatrice Foods, Macy's, Allied Stores, Federated Stores, Getty Oil, Sterling Drug, Ranier Bancorp., E.F. Hutton and Sperry Corp., to name just a few, and just the biggest.

Stocks continued on page 12A

## PLO official says military attacks on Israel won't stop

From News Services

Washington, D.C.
A top PLO spokesman Sunday signaled intentions to continue military attacks on Israel as Reagan administration officials vowed to closely monitor whether the Palestine Liberation Organization honors its anti-terrorism pledge.

Salah Khalaf, second in command to PLO leader Yasir Arafat in Fatah, the largest PLO group, told a news conference in Abu Dhabi, United Arab Emirates, that Arafat's denunciation of terrorism last week "did not include military attacks against Israel."

"Our struggle will continue until we raise the Palestinian flag over Jerusalem," he said.

■ Israeli troops shot and killed three Palestinians in the occupied territories. Page 9A.

State Department spokesman Dennis Harter said yesterday that he was unfamiliar with Khalaf's statement and that there would be no immediate comment from the department. But U.S. officials said yesterday that they will be checking to ensure that Arafat keeps his word.

"We have our sources — we have

PLO continued on page 9A

**Regent Lebedoff won't run again**

David Lebedoff, chairman of the University of Minnesota Board of Regents, said he won't run for reelection when his term expires at the end of the year. **Page 1B.**

## Almanac

**Monday, December 19, 1988**
**354th day; 12 to go this year**
**Sunrise: 7:47. Sunset: 4:33**

**Today's weather/**

Shades of gray

Partly cloudy and warmer today with southerly winds up to 15 miles per hour. High in the mid-40s. Chance of rain or freezing rain tonight.

**index/**

**Telephones/**

| | |
|---|---|
| News general | 372-4141 |
| Classifieds | 372-4242 |
| Circulation | 37. -4343 |

Volume VII/Number 259 6 sections

Staff Photo by Joey McLeister

**Tim Hayes of Pierz, Minn., looks for a good neighborhood with plenty of chimneys.**

## Firewood sales can be a choppy business

By Norman Draper
Staff Writer

Tim Hayes' first sale was a real fluke. It was at the first house he went up to. A man answered the door, dickered over Hayes' price and bought a half-cord of firewood. Usually Hayes will ring a lot more doorbells before he makes the first sale of the day.

After that the pace turned glacial. Hayes and his neighbor, Jerry Kapus, went to about 40 houses in Bloomington in 90 minutes without another sale. That's not unusual for an afternoon's work.

Usually the pace picks up after 5 p.m., Hayes said.

There's not much market research done in door-to-door firewood sales. Hayes, a bearded man with a ruddy complexion and a tape measure clipped to the back pocket of his well-worn jeans, decides what his target area will be on the drive down from his home town of Pierz, Minn., near Little Falls. Then he crosses his fingers. If the neighborhood he chooses has been blanketed by competitors, it can be a long, unproductive day. As many as several hundred door-to-door firewood sellers descend on the Twin Cities this time of year.

Many are probably legitimate businessmen with good wood to sell at reasonable prices. Others are con men, taking advantage of city slickers' unfamiliarity with firewood types and measurements to cheat them.

Paul Stegmeir, a St. Paul wood energy consultant, estimates that as many as 500 door-to-door firewood

Firewood continued on page 7A

2 Soviets return after year in space/12A
Gophers win 5th, top Detroit 93-69/1C
Kings rally to defeat North Stars/1C

VARIETY
**Plantsitters**
There are places to board your begonias

MINNEAPOLIS EDITION
■ Fire drives back paramedics trying to save 8-year-old girl/1B
■ Cocaine worth $2,700 found in Minneapolis police car's armrest/1B
■ Schiek's to feature Las Vegas-style acts, topless dancers/1B


# Star Tribune

THURSDAY/December 22/1988 — NEWSPAPER OF THE TWIN CITIES


# Hundreds die in Pan Am crash

## Jet with 258 aboard hits village in Scotland

**From News Services**

**Lockerbie, Scotland**
A Pan Am jumbo jet bound for New York with 258 passengers and crew aboard crashed Wednesday night in this Scottish village, exploding into a fireball, destroying 40 houses and spreading wreckage for miles.

No survivors were found from the Boeing 747, said John Boyd, the police chief for the area. Presumed to be dead in the crash were at least 36 students from Syracuse University, the U.N. commissioner for South West Africa and several business executives. An unknown number of military personnel also were reported to be on the flight.

Royal Air Force rescuers said the plane "demolished two rows of houses. There are no survivors from those houses." A gas station also was destroyed. A senior police official in nearby Dumfries said there had been 15 fatalities on the ground. But the toll could rise as the search for victims continues.

Some bodies and wreckage from the plane were found 3 miles from the impact site.

Flight 103 crashed in Lockerbie, 10 miles northeast of Dumfries in southern Scotland, about an hour after leaving London's Heathrow Airport. Wreckage came down in several locations.

A Heathrow spokesman said the plane was carrying 258 people, many laden with Christmas gifts. There were 15 crew members aboard.

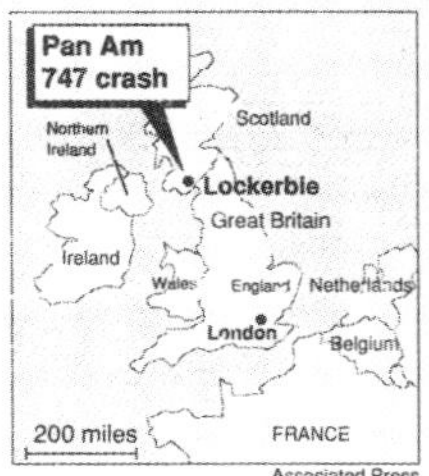


Associated Press

"The aircraft clearly experienced some form of explosion," said Scottish Secretary Malcolm Rifkind, because wreckage was scattered over a wide area. But Rifkind, who arrived early today with U.S. Ambassador Charles Price, refused to speculate on the cause.

**Crash** continued on page 4A

Associated Press

**Buildings in Lockerbie, Scotland, burned Wednesday night after a Pan Am jet crashed into the village. Wreckage of the 747 was in the foreground.**

## Executives, at least 36 Syracuse students on plane

**From News Services**

Among those reported aboard Pan Am Flight 103 when it crashed Wednesday were at least 36 students from Syracuse University, a United Nations official and executives from several corporations.

Pan American executives declined last night to release a passenger list, saying names still had to be compiled and relatives notified. But a spokesman for the airline said "some people of note" were on board.

There were no reports of survivors from the Boeing 747, according to British officials and the airline.

New York's Syracuse University said it confirmed that 36 of its students studying abroad were on the plane and that two others held tickets for the flight, but it was uncertain if they were aboard. The semester's foreign study program ended Saturday.

At the campus in Syracuse, more than 25,000 people attending a basketball game paused for a minute of silence and a brief prayer by the university minister.

Brent Carlsson of Sweden, the U.N. commissioner for South West Africa, was one of the passengers aboard the jet, U.N. officials said. Carlsson, 50, was to have been a witness today when an accord granting South West Africa, also known as Namibia, its independence from South Africa is signed in New York.

In a recent interview, Carlsson had hailed the agreement ending South African occupation of South West Africa, a colony whose affairs he nominally was in charge of even though he never was allowed to set foot there. "My job is to make myself unemployed as soon as possible," Carlsson said.

There were unconfirmed reports that U.S. servicemen were aboard the Pan Am jet. Cable News Network reported there were several State Depart-

**Victims** continued on page 4A

## Public education sharply criticized in state-ordered study

By Mary Jane Smetanka
and Bruce Benidt
Staff Writers

Minnesota's cherished reputation for educational excellence is "overstated and out of date," its educational standards are "lax and permissive" and its high schools are losing their advantage over those in other states, according to a highly critical report by the Office of the Legislative Auditor.

The report, released Wednesday, is one of the most comprehensive ever done on state high schools. It criticizes high school education in Minnesota as inequitable and hints at sweeping school consolidation or restructuring by recommending that about 75 mostly rural school districts — almost 20 percent of those in the state that have high schools — undergo "gradual reorganization" because they have too few students to offer a complete curriculum.

The study, ordered by the Legisla-

**Schools** continued on page 18A

■ Minnesota's educational system has been drawing unvaforable reviews lately. **Page 7B.**

### Highlights of the report

- Minnesota's excellent national reputation is somewhat overstated and out of date.
- Minnesota's education policies and standards need revising.
- Small districts tend to provide the fewest academic opportunities, and those with fewer than 100 high school students should be encouraged to reorganize.
- A statewide uniform student test is needed to ensure minimum reading and math skills, and to check on district performance.
- Graduation requirements should be raised.
- The Legislature should consider requiring a longer school year and district homework policies.
- Twin Cities districts provide an average of 51 courses in core subjects such as math and English; outstate districts provide only 20 to 35 such courses.

Star Tribune graphic

## Drexel agrees to plead guilty, pay penalty of $650 million

By Stephen LaBaton
New York Times

**New York, N.Y.**
In the largest-ever settlement of federal securities-law violations, Drexel Burnham Lambert Inc., the Wall Street powerhouse, agreed in principle Wednesday to plead guilty to six felony counts and pay a $650 million penalty.

If the settlement is approved, it would end an investigation lasting more than two years into Drexel's relationship with Ivan Boesky, the Wall Street speculator who pleaded guilty to insider-trading charges in 1986.

Government lawyers have said that since 1984, the investment firm and Boesky have broken the law by ille-

**Settlement** continued on page 17A

■ At the center of Wall Street's insider-trading scandal is Michael Milken. **Page 1D.**

Lawrence Marlyn Coss

## Green Tree's Coss gets embroiled in conflict

By Allen Short
and David Phelps
Staff Writers

In the spring of 1965, a penniless young businessman moved from South Dakota to the Twin Cities, where he found a job as a used-car salesman.

Today, Lawrence Marlyn Coss, 50, makes more than $1 million a year as chairman, president and chief executive officer of Green Tree Acceptance Inc., the nation's largest financier of mobile home purchases.

But a series of reverses now threatens the success of Green Tree and its self-made captain, and the story of Coss's rise may be about to end.

During the last 18 months it has become a complex tale about declining earnings, gov-

**Coss** continued on page 6A

## Rich traditions commune as Jewish pupils visit Catholic school, church

By Jean Hopfensperger
Staff Writer

A hush fell over the class at Nativity School in St. Paul as its young guests filed through the door.

Twenty-eight pairs of eyes turned to watch the 16 students from the Minneapolis Jewish Day School walk past the crucifix and Advent wreath and put their coats in the back of the third-grade classroom.

"Look at their caps," whispered a few boys, sitting on the floor with the rest of the class Wednesday.

But they didn't look long. In no time at all, the Catholic and Jewish children began talking and playing with the dreidels (tops) brought by the Jewish visitors. As the teachers paired the pupils with their previously unseen pen pals, the room developed an air of excitement.

For many of the Catholic kids, these students were their first Jewish friends. For most of the Jewish students, this was their first chance to visit a Christian school and church. For both, it was a time to ask questions about seemingly strange religious celebrations: Christmas and Hanukkah.

**Exchange** continued on page 8A

Staff Photo by Jeff Wheeler

**Ron Garber, left, got acquainted with John Skinner after giving him a gift of a dreidel and some peanuts at Nativity School in St. Paul.**

## Almanac

**Thursday, December 22, 1988**
**357th day; 9 to go this year**
**Sunrise: 7:49. Sunset: 4:35**

Snow, possibly mixed with rain at times, is forecast to taper off by afternoon.




Volume VII/Number 262 — 7 sections

Twins trade Atherton to Cleveland/1C

Hunt for cyanide source narrows/3A

Begin breaks long public silence/3A

VARIETY

**Eroticism**
Counselor stresses healthy, nurturing aspects

**MINNEAPOLIS EDITION**

■ After 40 years, Medtronic's Wallin can see retirement coming/**1D**

■ Star of North games drawing a major-league volunteer effort/**1B**


# Star Tribune

MONDAY/March 27/1989 NEWSPAPER OF THE TWIN CITIES


# Soviets go to polls; rebel heading for win

**Washington Post**

**Moscow, U.S.S.R.**
The Soviet Union staged the country's first contested elections in 70 years Sunday, with early returns in some key legislative districts showing strong support for independent-minded reformers competing against candidates supported by the Communist Party apparatus.

In Moscow, Kremlin maverick Boris Yeltsin appeared headed for a landslide victory in a citywide contest that has been widely viewed as a crucial test of Soviet public opinion. Yeltsin, who was ousted as Moscow party chief in November 1987, campaigned on a populist platform that included abolition of privileges for the Communist elite.

Liberal and radical-reformist candidates also appeared to be doing well in the Soviet Baltic republics and in cities where they had gotten their names on the ballot despite bureaucratic obstacles. Early results suggested that the revamped national legislature would include a sizable minority of independent deputies committed to wider-ranging political and economic reform. Final official vote totals are not expected until later this week.

Speaking to reporters after he and his wife, Raisa, voted in Moscow, Soviet leader Mikhail Gorbachev described

**Election** continued on page 5A

## Troubled waters

Associated Press

**The smaller Exxon Baton Rouge loaded crude oil from the grounded Exxon Valdez in Prince William Sound off the Alaska coast Sunday. The Exxon Valdez spilled thousands of barrels of oil into the pristine sound.**

## Final Four is set

Staff Photo by Regene Radniecki

**The basketball court at the Metrodome became a celebration site Sunday for the University of Illinois after its victory over Syracuse.**

### Illinois downs Syracuse to join Duke, Michigan and Seton Hall

Illinois became the second Big Ten team to reach the Final Four of the NCAA college basketball tournament Sunday, beating Syracuse 89-86 to win the Midwest Regional before 33,496 at the Metrodome. Duke, the team that ended the Gophers' season, gained the last berth in the Final Four with an 85-77 victory over Georgetown in the East Regional finals in East Rutherford, N.J. Illinois will play Michigan and Duke will face Seton Hall on Saturday in Seattle. **Details in Sports.**

# Farmland values rose 9% in state during year

**By Sharon Schmickle**
Staff Writer

Marking the reversal of a 7-year slump in farm land values, the average estimated value of rural real estate in Minnesota climbed 9 percent during the year ending July 1988, according to a University of Minnesota study.

It was the first increase measured by the continuing university study since 1981, when land values crashed and set off chaos in the agricultural economy as the collateral for billions of dollars in farm loans vanished.

Except for northeastern Minnesota, the average value of rural real estate increased throughout the state during the first half of 1988, said agricultural economist Philip Raup and research assistant Andrew Schwab. The greatest gain, 17 percent, was in the southwestern part of the state, where the average estimated value was $784 per acre, up $113 from a year earlier.

Southeastern Minnesota, excluding Hennepin and Ramsey counties, had a 16 percent increase to $648. West-central Minnesota showed a 6 percent increase to $499. Northwest Minnesota was up 4 percent to $390, and east-central Minnesota increased 3 percent to $268.

Northeastern Minnesota values declined 11 percent to $251.

Statewide, the average stood at $523 per acre in July 1988.

Raup credited the reversal to "stabilizing and positive effects of government support measures" and a rise in grain exports.

The study was based on land value estimates. In 1,077 actual real estate sales measured by the researchers, the average price paid statewide for farm land jumped during the first six months of 1988 by 24 percent over the same period in 1987, to $691 an acre.

The study period ended before the 1988 drought had run its course, but

**Farm land** continued on page 5A

# Northern suburbs see power in population

**By Paul Klauda**
Staff Writer

The southern part of the Twin Cities area includes Minnesota's fastest-growing county, a 100,000-job freeway corridor and an international airport. It also tops the region in commercial development and traffic jams.

So which side of the Twin Cities is more populated?

The north.

Suburbs north of Hwy. 12, from western Hennepin County to eastern Washington County, have 50,000 more residents than those south of the highway, according to 1988 population estimates for the seven-county metropolitan area. The north has held the edge for nearly two decades, despite rapid growth in Dakota County that appears to have trimmed the gap in recent years.

What has changed is that the north is using its people clout to try to catch

**Population** continued on page 2A

# Uncertified third mate was pilot when tanker hit reefs off Alaska

**From News Services**

**Valdez, Alaska**
An uncertified officer was in command when the tanker Exxon Valdez hit an undersea reef and began spilling 240,000 barrels of oil into Prince William Sound, a company official said Sunday.

The official, Frank Iarossi, president of the Exxon Shipping Co., also disclosed that the Valdez had struck a first reef and sustained serious damage to the tanks and hull on the right side before running aground on a second rocky reef about 2 miles away.

Meanwhile, Alaska Gov. Steve Cowper declared Prince William Sound a disaster area as the toll on the waterway's abundant wildlife began to mount. The declaration frees state resources for cleanup and paves the way for a federal disaster declaration.

The Coast Guard said the slick and patches of oil separated from it were spread over 50 square miles. Workers tried to contain the oil with floating booms.

Iarossi said he did not know why Capt. Joseph Hazelwood of Huntington, N.Y., had left the bridge shortly after midnight Friday, just before the crash, or why the third mate, Gregory

**Oil** continued on page 5A

# Board puts Wilder School on a planning roller coaster

**By Rob Hotakainen**
Staff Writer

■ Minneapolis school board members looked at a plan that would give parents more choice of schools for their children. Most of them didn't like what they saw. **Page 1B.**

In a sixth-grade classroom at Laura Ingalls Wilder School in Minneapolis, the calendar announces that the last week of March, or *marzo*, is time for *la vacacion de la primavera*.

That means "spring vacation" for the 243 students enrolled in something called Spanish immersion. Vacation ends April 3 and, by then, the uncertainty over the school's fate should have ended, too.

It has been a roller-coaster week for the most extensive elementary language program in the Minneapolis school district.

The Minneapolis school board provided the first jolt Tuesday when it voted to shift Spanish immersion from Wilder to a reopened Windom School. But Wednesday the board suspended its decision to give Superintendent Robert Ferrera more time to study alternatives. A final decision is expected next week.

The language program is the oldest in Minneapolis and one of only a handful of similar programs in Minnesota. Longfellow Elementary in Minneapolis offers a less extensive program, while St. Paul and Robbinsdale schools have more extensive ones.

Spanish abounds at Wilder. It's on

**Wilder** continued on page 5A

## Almanac

**Monday, March 27, 1989**
**86th day; 279 to go this year**
**Sunrise: 6:04. Sunset: 6:34**

### Today's weather/

High in the mid-60s.



### Telephones/

| | |
|---|---|
| Classifieds | 372-4242 |
| Circulation | 372-4343 |


Volume VII/Number 357 6 sections

# Biotechnology gives rise to debate on food safety

**By Sharon Schmickle**
Staff Writer

**Washington, D. C.**
Scientists have identified the gene that makes tomatoes rot and have manipulated it to curb spoilage.

Fruit from the genetically altered plant looks like tomatoes and should taste better than the rubbery red balls now in produce bins because they can ripen longer on the vine and still hold up en route to market.

But is it a tomato? Or is it a new food with unknown and possibly hazardous traits?

The questions are central to food-safety issues surfacing as a wave of new biotechnology sweeps through the food-production industry. According to the U.S. Food and Drug Administration (FDA), at least 155 companies are working on more than 400 food research projects involving technology that gives scientists powerful tools to combine and manipulate plant and animal species through gene splicing, cloning and other techniques.

That has opened a chasm of disagreement over answers to the food-safety

**Food safety** continued on page 5A

VARIETY
**Just a sip**
Jeremy Iggers tries out several wine-tasting dinners

**Cities urged to take steps against racial violence**/1B

**Twins, Viola lose 3-2**/1C

VARIETY
**Melting pot**
57th Festival of Nations relishes cultural diversity

**MINNEAPOLIS**
EDITION

■ Embassy Suites disorderly conduct case goes to jury/**1B**

■ Retailers group asks for 20 more foot-patrol officers downtown/**1B**

■ Judge throws out suspect's confession in knife assault/**1B**


# Star Tribune

**FRIDAY**/May 5/1989 NEWSPAPER OF THE TWIN CITIES W 35¢


# North is convicted on 3 counts

## Jury acquits him of 9 charges; he could get 10 years in prison

From News Services

**Washington, D.C.**
Oliver North, the Marine who became the Reagan administration's covert guardian of the Nicaraguan rebels, was convicted Thursday of shredding documents and two other crimes but was acquitted of nine charges stemming from his role in the Iran-contra affair.

North, wearing a dark gray suit and striped tie, sat ramrod straight at the defense table as U.S. District Judge


■ An analysis of the jury's verdict. **18A.** ■ John Poindexter's trial is next. **19A.**


Gerhard Gesell read the jury's findings, handed up after 12 days of deliberations.

Indicating his intention to appeal the guilty verdicts, North later said, "We will be fully vindicated."

Gesell set sentencing for June 23, when North, 45, will face a possible maximum punishment of 10 years imprisonment and $750,000 in fines. The judge allowed North to remain free on bond during his appeal, a process that normally takes about 18 months.

The verdict appeared to reject important parts of the government's case. North, who was an aide to the National Security Council, was found not guilty of accusations that he lied


**North** continued on page 19A

Oliver North

## Bush denies involvement in '85 deal to aid contras

Los Angeles Times

**Washington, D.C.**
President Bush, challenging evidence presented in the trial of former Lt. Col. Oliver North, denied Thursday that he took part in any Reagan administration effort in 1985 to offer U.S. aid to Honduras in direct exchange for that country's aid to Nicaragua's rebels.

"The word of the president of the United States, George Bush, is there was no quid pro quo," Bush said in his first public response to evidence presented at the North trial.

"There has been much needless, mindless speculation about my word of honor — and I've answered it, now, definitively," he added as he spoke to reporters just before a jury returned guilty verdicts on three of 12 felony counts against North.

Bush not only denied that he personally discussed a quid pro quo with Honduran President Roberto Suazo Cordova when they met in Honduras


**Bush** continued on page 19A


## Perpich proposes holding line on property taxes

By Dane Smith
Staff Writer

Gov. Rudy Perpich shook up the Minnesota Legislature Thursday with a proposal to hold the state's total property tax collections in 1990 to this year's level. That would be the first time this decade that total property taxes have not increased.

His proposal arrived 18 days before the scheduled adjournment of the legislative session. And it came at a news conference just three days after he said he preferred to work behind the scenes with legislators to extend more state-paid relief, especially for business property.

Most reductions would come through lowering the tax rates that local governments are allowed to levy. The resulting loss in revenue to those units would be mostly compensated through increased state aids. Perpich financial aides would not release details, but said money for the increased aids would be raised by diverting money from a variety of other Perpich initiatives.


**Property tax** continued on page 17A

■ Perpich tax-relief plan marks end of DFL legislative harmony. **Page 16A.**


## Major news inside today/

Associated Press

**100,000 demonstrate in China**/ Legions of students shoved their way through hundreds of unarmed police and marched in Beijing Thursday to mark the 70th anniversary of China's first student movement. In a conciliatory response, Communist Party chief Zhao Ziyang said he planned "extensive consultations and dialogues" with the students. **Page 4A.**

**Atlantis sends probe to Venus**/
The space shuttle Atlantis rocketed into orbit Thursday, then sent the spacecraft Magellan on a 456-day journey to Venus.

Magellan's 15-month mapmaking voyage is the first American planetary expedition in 11 years.

The robot spacecraft slipped from the shuttle's cargo bay at 8:01 p.m. Twin Cities time and drifted into space. An hour later, a rocket attached to Magellan fired, lifting it on a trajectory to Venus. **Page 3A.**

**Korean rally blocked**/ About 8,000 riot police stopped an antigovernment rally in Masan, South Korea, Thursday, arresting 433 workers and students a day after six police were killed in violent protests. Hundreds of other workers were prevented from reaching the rally site. **Page 4A.**

**Budgets approved**/ The House and Senate passed similar versions Thursday of a $1.17 trillion federal budget for next year. Both versions uphold an agreement with President Bush, criticized by many lawmakers, to postpone painful tax and spending decisions. **Page 3A.**

**Pill's risk cited**/ A major British study says that young women who take birth control pills for more than four years run a significantly increased risk of breast cancer. Among women under 36, the study found a 43 percent increase in the risk of breast cancer after four years of use. **Page 4A.**

## Woman retains her scars as man who nearly killed her rises to power on Capitol Hill

By Ken Ringle
Washington Post

**Washington, D.C.**
One evening in 1973, when she was a 20-year-old college student still living with her parents, Pamela Small entered a discount import store in suburban Annandale, Va., to buy some furnishings for her first apartment. It was just before closing time. The manager, a freckle-faced 19-year-old youth she'd never seen before, was the only person in the store.

Small took $31 worth of purchases to the cash register but discovered a flaw in the window blinds she had selected. The manager said he had more in the storeroom and suggested she come along and pick out the ones she wanted.

Once inside, however, he blocked the door and ordered her to lie face down on the floor. When she refused, he grabbed a hammer and slammed it into her skull. She lost consciousness but he continued pounding, exposing the skull in five places. Then he grabbed a steak knife, stabbed her five times in the left breast and shoulder near her heart, and slashed her repeatedly across the throat.

Bundling her limp body into the car she had left parked out front, he drove around for a while, then left the vehicle in an alley behind the store, the keys in the ignition. Then he went to the movies.

"He told the police he thought I was dead," said Small, who, to the astonishment of the doctors who later treated her, was not dead. Regaining consciousness about eight hours later, she managed to start the car and drive a mile to an all-night Exxon station, where an attendant, wide-eyed at the sight of the gory figure in the blood-soaked seat, summoned help.


**Mack** continued on page 12A


## Almanac

**Friday, May 5, 1989**
**125th day; 240 to go this year**
**Sunrise: 5:57. Sunset: 8:23**

### Today's weather/
A nasty turn

The forecast for the metropolitan area today calls for cloudy, windy and colder weather with a 30 percent chance of showers. A high in the upper 40s is expected along with a northwest wind at 25 to 35 miles per hour. A cloudy night with a low of 30 will be followed by variable cloudiness Saturday and another high in the upper 40s.

### Index/



### Telephones/

| | |
|---|---|
| News general | 372-4141 |
| Classifieds | 372-4242 |
| Circulation | 372-4343 |



Volume VIII/Number 31 6 sections


## Koop to resign as surgeon general

From News Services

**Washington, D.C.**
Dr. C. Everett Koop, the surgeon general whose straight talk about smoking, AIDS and abortion made him a lightning rod for critics, said Thursday he will resign after seven years as the nation's top health officer.

During his tenure, Koop lived up to his reputation as a tough-minded professional and made what had been a figurehead position into a pulpit from which he hammered at the ills of smoking and became the nation's No. 1 promoter of condoms in the fight against AIDS.

In a brief letter to President Bush delivered yesterday, Koop said he had told the president in February he would not serve out his full second term, which ends in November. Koop told Bush yesterday that he would leave the job July 13 and retire Oct. 1.

Friends said Koop was leaving with ill feelings. They said he was deeply angered when Bush did not nominate him to be secretary of health and human services or make any effort to keep him in his current job. Koop made no public statement yesterday before leaving for a meeting of the World Health Organization in Geneva.

Senior federal health officials said that Bush advisers believed Koop no longer could play an important role


**Koop** continued on page 18A


## Judge denies bid to limit spearfishing catch

By Bob von Sternberg and Pat Doyle
Staff Writers

Angry rhetoric and political pressure kept building Thursday in Wisconsin's fishing war as a showdown neared between Indian spearfishers and sport anglers.

U.S. District Judge Barbara Crabb rebuffed Gov. Tommy Thompson's request to limit the catch by the state's most-active Indian band, the Lac du Flambeau. But the Madison judge held off until today a decision on whether to grant Thompson's request for an order that would shut down the spearfishing season by the state's six Chippewa bands at midnight tonight.

After almost two weeks of Indian spearfishing in the lakes of northern Wisconsin, the state's fifth spearfishing season could reach a flashpoint at one minute after midnight. That's when the sport fishing season begins, the first time anglers and spearfishers will have been on the water legally at the same time.

Fears of violence prompted Thompson's move in court, as well as a flurry of other actions yesterday:

■ The St. Croix Chippewa band in northwest Wisconsin became the second of the six bands to announce it would not fish during the sport fishing opener. The band's council decided yesterday that no spearing permits would be issued tonight, Saturday or Sunday night and that the status of spearfishing would be reviewed next


**Spearfishing** continued on page 14A

Dollar hits high; White House voices concern/1D

Valdez captain indicted/9A

MARKETPLACE

**'Family friendly'**

Firms try to ease conflict between work, home life

VARIETY

**Still making memories**

Hope celebrates 86th birthday

**MINNEAPOLIS EDITION**

- County attorney to review decision to halt abortion coverage/**1B**
- Summer's first crop of mosquitoes makes its appearance/**3B**
- Drug suspect's trial is near, but police still don't know his name/**3B**


# Star Tribune

TUESDAY/May 23/1989 NEWSPAPER OF THE TWIN CITIES 35¢


# Lottery, state pension bills pass

## Lottery could be running by year-end

**By Robert Whereatt**
Staff Writer

Responding to the voters' directive, the Minnesota Legislature Monday approved legislation that establishes a state-operated lottery.

That means Minnesotans should be buying instant or scratch-off lottery tickets by this December or January and playing the high-stakes, big-jackpot lotto game by July 1990.

The House approved the measure 100-33.

The bill then was sent to the less receptive Senate, where opponents railed against the lottery as a state-sponsored scheme to fleece citizens rather than serve them.

But supporters mustered 39 votes, five more than needed to pass. There were 28 "no" votes.

"For us to have turned it down, the public out there would have gone bananas," said Sen. Bob Lessard, DFL-International Falls, chief sponsor.

The margin was bolstered by Gov. Rudy Perpich, who called four or five senators to his office shortly before the vote and prevailed upon them to support the bill.

The bill has no limit on the amount of prizes and no ban on advertising.

Sen. Allan Spear, a lottery opponent and historian at the University of Minnesota, recalled how another governor, Luther Youngdahl, waged war on gambling in Minnesota in the 1940s.

"When you leave this building tonight and you hear a little rumbling in the ground, that's Gov. Youngdahl turning in his grave," said Spear, DFL-Minneapolis.

There was disenchantment among some senators who felt the Senate had given up too much when it negotiated last week with the House on compromise language.

Sen. Donna Peterson, DFL-Minneapolis, voted for the Senate version earlier this month. Yesterday, though, she switched and voted against the final bill, saying the state is moving too far, too fast in an activity that until last November had been constitutionally prohibited. Voters in the general election lifted the ban and authorized the Legislature to establish a lottery.

**Lottery** continued on page 8A

Staff Photo by Jeff Wheeler

**Rep. Joe Quinn, right, DFL-Coon Rapids, chief sponsor of legislation to establish a state lottery, was congratulated by Rep. Tony Bennett, IR-Shoreview, as they watched the House vote 100-33 to approve the bill. After Senate approval it was sent to the governor.**

## SESSION WRAPUP '89

**Education/** Under bills awaiting Gov. Rudy Perpich's signature, the state would spend $3.47 billion for the state's school districts over the next two years and $1.96 billion for higher-education institutions.

**Public services/** Auto registration fees would rise to help pay for future highway improvements. A provision in the health and human services bill also would begin moving most mentally retarded people to group homes.

**Environment/** The Legislature agreed to spend $17 million over the next two years to protect Minnesota's ground water. About half of that money will come from increased fees from pesticide and ground-water use.

**Justice/** The Legislature has sent to the governor a bill that provides funds for a new prison and longer sentences for murderers, rapists and "career" criminals. Another bill adds three judges to the State Court of Appeals.

**Government/** Public employees, including legislators, won $1 billion in pension improvements from the Legislature. Included in a bonding bill is $157.7 million to make state buildings accessible to the handicapped.

**Politics/** Perpich has said he will sign a bill giving Minnesota its first presidential primary in 36 years. The primary was added as an amendment to a routine election bill in the Senate last week.

## Legislature's last day had large, medium and small frustrations

**By Dennis J. McGrath**
Staff Writer

Sen. Charles Berg knew by 8 a.m. that the last day of the 1989 Legislature was going to be lousy.

The Chokio DFLer had just returned to his rented St. Paul condominium after having been in a particularly long and difficult committee meeting that began at 2 p.m. the day before. There he stood in the shower, exhausted and frustrated.

And still wearing his socks.

"It just added to the frustration," Berg said.

As legislators plunged into a mad rush to finish their business before the constitutional deadline of midnight Monday night, the frustration and the frantic pace at the State Capitol in St. Paul kicked up a few notches.

Baggy-eyed legislators tried to balance the marathon sessions with nature's call for sleep. Some succeeded; others dozed.

Overworked photocopying machines raised the temperature inside the building, but sometimes they didn't work fast enough. An attempt by two senators to offer an amendment that would have provided a pension increase for public employees, but none for legislators, was never made because copies of the amendment didn't arrive in the Senate chamber before the bill was voted on.

As Rep. Howard Orenstein, DFL-St. Paul, said, it was a day in which everything depended on everything else.

**Last day** continued on page 9A

## Legislators' benefits to increase up to 50%

**By Dennis J. McGrath**
Staff Writer

On the last day of the 1989 Legislature, Minnesota lawmakers rewarded themselves with a hefty increase in their pensions.

For a senior legislator, the new pension benefits could be worth about $14,000 a year, an increase of more than 50 percent.

In a separate bill, legislators gave themselves a pay raise of 6 percent each year for two years, beginning Jan. 1, 1991.

Legislators received $25,138 annually this year, not including per diem.

A legislator who serves for 24 years and retires in 1990 would earn a pension of $25,636 under current law. The bill approved yesterday will give that same legislator a pension of $41,725 a year.

The legislative pension improvements were included in a $1 billion pension package for public employees.

Only three days before, the Senate rejected the entire package by a single vote. But pressure from House members, who approved the bill 130-1, and from an unusually united coalition of public employee unions, caused seven senators to change their vote and approve the pension bill. It passed 40-26.

Gov. Rudy Perpich said last night that he would sign the bill.

**Pensions** continued on page 8A

## Inside/

- A bill providing $37 million for waste recycling programs died as the session ended. **Page 1B.**
- The focus of the 1989 Legislature was on politics. An analysis. **Page 8A.**
- Gov Rudy Perpich's veto threat hangs over the 1989 omnibus tax bill. **Page 1B.**
- It's up to the governor to decide it there will be two high school hockey tournaments. **Page 7B.**

## China military leaders oppose using troops to quell Beijing unrest

**From News Services**

**Beijing, China**
In a major blow to the authority of Premier Li Peng, seven senior military figures formally objected Monday to the government's plan to bring troops into the capital and suppress China's democracy movement.

The seven military leaders, who signed a strongly worded letter sent to the leadership and the official People's Daily newspaper, include a former defense minister and a former army chief of staff. They command great prestige and influence, although they no longer are on active duty. Sources said 100 other military and other officials signed the document.

"In view of the extremely serious situation, we as veteran soldiers demand that the People's Liberation Army not confront the population, nor quell the people," the letter said. "The army must absolutely not shoot the people. In order to prevent the situation from worsening, the army must not enter the city of Beijing."

The letter was the clearest indication yet of the opposition within the military to the crackdown begun early Saturday by Li and Deng Xiaoping, China's senior leader.

It was not clear whether the government would be able to muster

**China** continued on page 6A

## Almanac

**Tuesday, May 23, 1989**
**143rd day; 222 to go this year**
**Sunrise: 5:36. Sunset: 8:44**

### Today's weather/

Partly sunny and warm with a 20 percent chance of an afternoon thunderstorm. A high near 83.

### Index/



### Telephones/

| | |
|---|---|
| News general | 372-4141 |
| Classifieds | 372-4242 |
| Circulation | 372-4343 |


Volume VIII/Number 49 6 sections

## Baker urges compromises by Israel, Arabs

Secretary of State James Baker called on Israel to renounce "the unrealistic vision of a greater Israel" that would incorporate the West Bank and Gaza Strip. Speaking in Washington to members of a pro-Israel U.S.lobbying group, Baker urged Israel to "forswear annexation. Stop settlement activity. . . . Reach out to the Palestinians as neighbors who deserve political rights."

At the same time, he made clear that the Arabs must accept Israel's right to exist in peace and, as a first step, should make a "constructive response" to Prime Minister Yitzhak Shamir's proposal for Palestinian elections in the occupied territories. **Page 4A.**

## Zoning ordinance for sex-oriented firms struck down

**By Kevin Diaz**
Staff Writer

A Minneapolis zoning ordinance forcing sex-oriented businesses to move out of residential areas and into a central downtown business district was struck down Monday as an unconstitutional infringement on free speech.

Chief U.S. District Judge Donald Alsop found the recently implemented ordinance unduly vague and restrictive, and barred city officials from enforcing it.

The decision is a victory for Ferris Alexander, a bookstore and theater operator who had filed a constitutional challenge to block enforcement of the ordinance against any of his businesses.

"It means that the city forefathers have to learn to respect the Bill of Rights," said attorney Randall Tigue, who represented Alexander in the suit.

City officials said they had not had time to review the decision yesterday. "I think we put in a good, strong case that it was a method of regulation the court would find acceptable," said City Attorney Bob Alfton. "The same issue is being litigated around the country. We'll have to

**Poruography** continued on 6A

VARIETY: Some places you can see July 4th fireworks tonight

MINNEAPOLIS EDITION

Star Tribune

TUESDAY/July 4/1989

NEWSPAPER OF THE TWIN CITIES

■ Metro population has grown 10.8% since 1980/**1B**

# Court retreats on abortion, allows states to impose limits

## But splintered 5-4 ruling stops short of overturning Roe vs. Wade decision

From News Services

**Washington, D.C.**
A splintered Supreme Court began a historic retreat on abortion rights Monday, limiting — but not discarding — its landmark 1973 ruling while dropping a clear hint that it may go further next year.

The 5-4 ruling upheld a Missouri law that bans abortions in public hospitals and forbids public employees from assisting abortions in any way. Moreover, the court said, Missouri may require all doctors to test women who are at least 20 weeks pregnant to determine if their fetuses are viable.

But the Missouri law does not forbid abortions in private medical facilities, where 90 percent of the state's abortions are performed. And the public employee involvement ban, the only new restriction on abortion in yesterday's ruling, actually extends existing limits rather than breaking with precedent.

While the court stopped just short of overturning Roe vs. Wade, the 1973 decision that established a woman's constitutional right to obtain an abortion, the majority made it clear that they now are prepared to uphold state restrictions on abortion that have been ruled unconstitutional for the past 16 years.

The ruling, on the final day of the court's term, was proclaimed a victory by abortion opponents, while abortion rights advocates described it as a serious setback. Both sides vowed to press their case in state legislatures around the nation.

Although the court's five-member majority agreed that the time had come to approve some restrictions of the right to abortion, it remained split over how far down that path the court should travel.

Only Justice Antonin Scalia said he would overturn Roe vs. Wade, while three other justices in the majority said they favored a position that would at least "modify and narrow" the Roe decision.

By contrast, Justice Sandra Day O'Connor, while accepting the out-

**Ruling** continued on page 16A

### The decision at a glance/

**Public involvement/**
States may ban the use of public funds for abortions, prohibit abortions at public hospitals or clinics, and bar public employees at those institutions from taking any part in abortions.

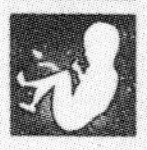

**Viability/**
States may require tests to determine the ability of the fetus to survive outside the womb in cases where the pregnancy is at least 20 weeks old. A plurality of the court also suggested abortions could be regulated before the point of viability

**Beginning of life/**
The court did not rule on the preamble to the Missouri law, which declares that "Life . . . begins at conception," because the wording carried no penalty.

**Outlook/**
The decision will shift the abortion battle to the state legislatures, and probably will lead to restrictions in many states. And because the high court accepted three new abortion cases for next term — from Minnesota, Illinois and Florida — a further narrowing or an outright reversal of Roe vs. Wade is possible next year.

### Six pages of inside coverage

■ Excerpts from yesterday's opinions. **8A.**

■ Harry Blackmun, the justice from Minnesota who wrote the majority opinion in Roe vs. Wade, is troubled by the new ruling. **8A.**

■ Praise and denunciation for the ruling abounded here and around the nation. **9A.**

■ A state-by-state look at current abortion law. **10A.**

■ Why do Minnesota's anti-abortion forces appear to have the upper hand politically in a traditionally liberal state? **10A.**

■ Fewer than 1 percent of abortions are performed after 20 weeks of pregnancy. **11A.**

### What it means:

## Justices may nibble further at abortion rights

By David Lauter
Los Angeles Times

**Washington, D.C.**
Monday's long-awaited Supreme Court abortion decision has changed nothing, legal experts said Monday. And it has changed everything.

**Analysis**

Nothing has changed because the court announced no new principles governing abortion.

Everything has changed because, for the first time since the 1973 Roe vs. Wade decision, five justices are on record as supporting increasingly tough antiabortion regulations.

And so, analysts said, the opinion upholding Missouri's abortion law indicates that the court's conservative majority may handle abortion in much the same way that similar majorities have handled liberal precedents on criminals' rights — not discarding them directly, but nibbling away at them until there is virtually nothing left.

Harvard Law School constitutional law expert Laurence Tribe said the court may never overrule Roe, because it may never have to.

**Analysis** continued on page 13A

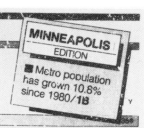

Associated Press

**Darlene Carra of the Coalition Opposing Operation Rescue tried to drown out Michael Hirsh of Operation Rescue at a news conference.**

### A look back:

## The struggle has been long and bitter in Minnesota

By Chuck Haga
Staff Writer

Since 1973, abortion has become the most common of surgical procedures in Minnesota, more frequent than tonsillectomies.

The typical patient is an unmarried white woman, 20 to 24 years old, who wasn't using contraception, state statistics show. She's less than nine weeks pregnant and never had children. It's her first abortion.

One patient in four is a teenager. One in four was using birth control but it failed.

Five percent of the patients are black, 1 percent Indian, 2.4 percent Asian.

Fifteen percent are married. One-third have had abortions before. Nine in 10 women are in their first trimester, the first 12 weeks, when they have their abortions. Five percent are between 16 and 20 weeks.

Since the Supreme Court's decision in Roe vs. Wade made abortion a woman's right, the right has been quietly exercised by a quarter-million Minnesotans and embraced or at least tolerated by many more.

However, for legions of others, abortion remains a crime, an evil worthy of crusade.

The struggle between those factions has divided churches and political parties in Minnesota, strained friendships and families and frustrated a weary majority that won't or can't decide whether abortion is liberating right or callous murder.

**History** continued on page 12A

### What happens next?

## The battle moves to statehouses

By Steve Berg
Staff Correspondent

Monday's Supreme Court decision on abortion did little to resolve the most divisive social issue of these times. Rather, it sounded a call-to-arms for activists on both sides who now promise to carry their emotional fight from the courts to the steps of 50 state legislatures.

In the days and years ahead, politics won't be the same in Tallahassee, Topeka, Sacramento and St. Paul.

There, the shrill voices on both sides will be even more shrill. Few of the 50 governors or 7,461 legislators will find refuge from taking a stand on the explosive issue. And questions about the beginnings of life may overshadow the more common priorities of government: the raising of taxes; the balancing of budgets; the building of highways and schools.

**Issue** continued on page 13A

### What about Minnesota?

## Sentiment for a new law is strong

By Kurt Chandler
and Robert Whereatt
Staff Writers

Minnesota could be one of the first states to revamp its abortion law in a special legislative session likely to be held in September.

Although Gov. Rudy Perpich has said he wants to limit the session's agenda to property taxes, the political influence of the state's antiabortion lobby could persuade legislative loyalists to seize the opportunity to rewrite abortion laws right away.

"It's like the 900-pound gorilla that sleeps anywhere it wants," House Majority Leader Dee Long, a prochoice advocate, said o. the antiabortion lobby.

Monday an ecstatic but cautious Jackie Schwietz, lobbyist and codirector of Minnesota Citizens Concerned for Life, said she was unsure whether the lobby could draft legisla-

**Legislature** continued on page 10A

# Court draws fine line on religious displays

From News Services

**Washington, D.C.**
The Supreme Court drew a very fine distinction Monday between permissible and impermissible government commemorations of religion in two decisions.

The court said the Constitution does not permit Allegheny County, Pa., to display a Nativity scene in its courthouse. But the court upheld the display, a block away, of an 18-foot-tall Hanukkah menorah on the steps of the Pittsburgh City Hall next to a Christmas tree.

The critical distinction in the treatment of the two displays was a matter of context.

In his majority opinion declaring the Nativity scene unconstitutional, Justice Harry Blackmun said that the creche, unadorned by more secular symbols of the Christmas season, gave the impression that the county government was endorsing the display's religious message.

Under the court's precedents, he said, "Government may celebrate Christmas in some manner and form, but not in a way that endorses Christian doctrine." He added, "Here, Al-

**Displays** continued on page 7A

### Almanac

**Tuesday, July 4, 1989**
**185th day; 180 to go this year**
**Sunrise: 5:32. Sunset: 9:03**

**Today's weather/**

Sunny and hot in the Twin Cities today. High around 95.



**Telephones/**

| | |
|---|---|
| News general | 372-4141 |
| Classifieds | 372-4242 |
| Circulation | 372-4343 |


Volume VIII/Number 91 6 sections

### Jim Backus, voice of 'Mr. Magoo,' dies

Jim Backus, 76, the voice of the nearsighted cartoon character "Mr. Magoo" and the millionaire Thurston Howell III on "Gilligan's Island," died Monday of pneumonia. **Page 4B.**

### MTC talks continue; strike plan tested

Negotiations to avert a strike by Metropolitan Transit Commission bus drivers continued last night, but still officials tested an emergency traffic plan in anticipation of a strike Wednesday. **Page 1B.**

# Former Soviet envoy Andrei Gromyko dies

From News Services

**Moscow, U.S.S.R.**
Andrei A. Gromyko, the former foreign minister whose enigmatic scowl was the face of Soviet foreign policy for most of the postwar period, died Sunday, two weeks short of his 80th birthday.

President Mikhail Gorbachev announced the news to the Supreme Soviet Monday morning. A few days earlier the press agency Tass reported that Gromyko had undergone surgery after "a fit of vascular pathology," apparently a stroke.

Beginning with his assignment to Washington, D.C., as a junior diplomat in 1939, Gromyko served every Soviet leader except Lenin, and conferred with every U.S. president since Franklin Roosevelt.

He was foreign minister for 28 years before being moved to the largely ceremonial presidency by Gorbachev in 1985. He also served for periods as ambassador to the United States and Britain and envoy to the United Nations.

He weathered five changes of power in the Kremlin, but was edged gracefully from the stage by age and by

**Gromyko** continued on page 7A

**Two U.S. soldiers freed after Panama standoff**/4A

**Anderson blanks O's**/1C

MARKETPLACE
**Hot cars**
Manufacturers are racing to get blockbuster toy

VARIETY
**Toxic parents:**
How to cleanse the effects of their abuse

**MINNEAPOLIS EDITION**

- One-year moratorium urged for new projects at Hennepin-Lake/**1B**
- Ash storage problem could delay test of new waste incinerator/**1B**
- Hatch alleges loan program run by minister is a pyramid scheme/**1B**

# Star Tribune

**THURSDAY**/August 10/1989 NEWSPAPER OF THE TWIN CITIES 30¢

# Federal rescue of S&L industry set in motion

## Bush signs $148 billion bailout

Los Angeles Times

**Washington, D.C.**
President Bush, signing into law a massive savings-and-loan rescue package, set in motion Wednesday a seven-week crash program to put the sickest thrifts out of their misery and to clear the way for a reshuffling of the nation's lending institutions.

The bailout, the biggest ever undertaken by the federal government, authorizes $20 billion over the next seven weeks and another $30 billion in the following two years to close hundreds of S&Ls and make good on federal insurance of deposits up to $100,000.

The total cost, including interest payments on the bonds that will be sold to raise the up-front cash, will reach an estimated $148 billion over the first 10 years of the rescue effort, according to revised government projections.

Taxpayers will pay about $47 billion of the 10-year cost — about $300 per taxpayer — and the financial industry will pick up the rest, mainly through higher deposit-insurance fees.

At least one-third of the approximately 3,000 S&Ls operating today are expected to disappear within the next few years, and many of the remaining thrifts are likely to be absorbed into large banking institutions.

**S&Ls** continued on page 13A

### Two of state's biggest S&Ls look vulnerable

Federal legislation designed to rescue savings and loans could turn Minnesota's two largest S&Ls into targets for takeovers.

"Overall, I feel like I got hit by a truck and came out only slightly bruised," said Bill Cooper, chairman of TCF Financial Corp., parent of the Twin Cities' largest thrift. "It's far better than it could have been."

TCF, of which banker-investor Carl Pohlad's MEI Diversified Inc. owns 9 percent, is considered a likely acquisition target for Pohlad or a big national bank. **Page 1D.**

# Perpich tax plan criticized by IRs, business leaders

By Dane Smith
Staff Writer

Independent-Republicans and business leaders upstaged Gov. Rudy Perpich Wednesday on the eve of his long-awaited property tax reform proposal, dismissing his plan as too timid, too late or downright deceptive.

Perpich clamped a lid on release of the proposal until 8 a.m. today, but enough details have leaked out in recent days to tempt some critics into passing final judgment.

■ Gov. Perpich will begin trying to sell his long-awaited property tax reform plan today. **Page 17A.**

Perhaps the harshest assessment came from Assistant Senate Minority Leader Fritz Knaak, IR-White Bear Lake, who compared the Perpich proposal to "whitewash over rot." He accused Perpich of "cynically" buying votes with a $274 million state buy-down of property taxes in 1990, while substituting "promises" for long-term reform.

**Report** continued on page 17A

# Colin Powell expected to head Joint Chiefs

From News Services

**Washington, D.C.**
President Bush is expected to nominate Army Gen. Colin Powell to succeed Adm. William Crowe as chairman of the Joint Chiefs of Staff, administration sources said Wednesday night.

Powell, if confirmed by the Senate, would be the first black officer to hold the nation's top military job. He was chosen over more than 30 other four-star generals.

Defense Secretary Dick Cheney informed the Joint Chiefs yesterday that he would recommend Powell to the president for a two-year term as chairman. The White House is expected to make the announcement today.

As commander of the Forces Command in Atlanta, Powell oversees Army units in the United States from headquarters at Fort McPherson, Ga. At 52, he is among the youngest four-star generals in American peacetime history; he was promoted to that rank in April.

As chairman of the Joint Chiefs, Powell will be the principal military adviser to the president, the National Security Council and the secretary of

**Powell** continued on page 14A

Associated Press

### Suicide bomber hits Israeli convoy

**Israeli soldiers examined one of the vehicles in their military convoy that was heavily damaged Wednesday when an explosives-laden truck driven by a Shiite Moslem clergyman exploded, wounding six soldiers. The truck's driver and a passenger died. The bombing occurred as the convoy moved along a road south of the village of Qleiaa in the security zone Israel has designated in Lebanon. In Washington, meanwhile, the Bush administration signaled that it was prepared to deal with terrorists to help secure the return of eight U.S. hostages. Reports on Page 4A.**

# Jet makes emergency stop; engine damaged

## NWA plane headed here

Associated Press

**Denver, Colo.**
A Northwest Airlines DC-10 en route from Los Angeles to Minneapolis on Wednesday made an emergency landing in Denver after the jet's No. 2 engine apparently began breaking up and the pilot shut it down, officials said.

Flight 308, carrying 256 people, landed at Stapleton International Airport about 6:30 p.m. without incident, said Richard Boulware, a spokesman at the airport.

Said Northwest spokesman Kevin Whalen in the Twin Cities: "They experienced a severe vibration from the No. 2 engine," and as a precautionary measure made the unscheduled landing in Denver.

Boulware, who saw the damage to the plane after it landed, said there were "multiple shrapnel-like holes in the outer cowling" of the No. 2 engine, which is mounted in the vertical stabilizer at the tail of the DC-10 aircraft. The plane's other two engines are under the wings.

"One of the holes was big enough I could have stuck my hand through," he said. He said the holes were along the upper side of the engine cowling. "Whatever exited exited upward," he said.

The No. 2 engine of United Airlines Flight 232 is the focus of an investigation into its fatal crash last month. That engine was made by a different manufacturer than the engine in the Northwest DC-10. The United plane was over Iowa when the engine apparently disintegrated.

The shrapnel generated from the en-

**Plane** continued on page 8A

# Steinbrenner pullout leaves Canterbury deal in doubt

By Joe Blade
Staff Writer

New York Yankees owner George Steinbrenner has pulled out of Canterbury Downs racetrack without ever getting in. Steinbrenner has decided it would be too risky to participate in buying the track's $43 million in bank debt at a reduced price.

"We have a backup," said Lawrence Greenberg, a retired Minneapolis accountant who hopes to buy the track.

Greenberg said he would probably be unable to swing the deal unless that backup company joins the Pohlads in buying the debt. But there are other potential buyers still interested. "It ain't dead yet," Greenberg said.

He would identify the new potential investor only as a very large, well-known company.

Greenberg would like to buy both the track and some real estate through a bankruptcy reorganization plan submitted by Scottland Inc. and its chief executive, J. Brooks Hauser. Under the plan, the sons of Twins owner Carl Pohlad would buy the track's debt, which is owed to a consortium of banks, at a discount. Greenberg would pay off the Pohlads with reduced payments from the track's cash flow and other sources.

Steinbrenner was invited in last week by Pohlad, who became concerned about the track's continuing losses and wanted a partner to help defray the deal's risks. Six of Steinbrenner's employees visited the Twin Cities on Sunday and Monday, then returned to Chicago to study the information they had received and to make a recommendation. Steinbrenner owns a Florida racing stable and has been an owner of a Florida racetrack.

Officials said Steinbrenner was not forced out because of a 1974 felony conviction connected with an illegal contribution to President Richard Nixon's 1972 campaign. A presidential pardon last January wiped the conviction off his record and would have allowed him to be licensed, if that proved necessary, according to Ralph Strangis, chairman of the Minnesota Racing Commission.

**Canterbury** continued on page 16A

# State farms larger, and fewer work them

By Sharon Schmickle
Staff Writer

Despite efforts to preserve the cherished small family farm, Minnesota farms swelled in size during the 1980s while the number of people who run them shrank, according to a new five-year census of the nation's farms.

The trends shows that rural Minnesota must continue to diversify its economic base to slow further population declines. Fewer and larger farms mean fewer families to buy everything from shoes to burgers on small-town main streets.

The average Minnesota farm grew by 6 percent to 312 acres between 1982 and 1987, according to findings of the U.S. Bureau of the Census being released today by the State Planning Agency. If hobby farms are ruled out by counting only operations with $10,000 or more in sales, the growth was a significant 9 percent to 407 acres. And in some key crop-growing counties, average farms now exceed 300 acres.

**Farms** continued on page 15A

## Almanac

**Thursday, August 10, 1989**
**222nd day; 143 to go this year**
**Sunrise: 6:08. Sunset: 8:28**

### Today's weather/

Mostly sunny with the high temperature expected to be in the middle 80s. South wind around 10 miles per hour.



### Telephones/

| | |
|---|---|
| News general | 372-4141 |
| Classifieds | 372-4242 |
| Circulation | 372-4343 |


Volume VIII/Number 128 7 sections

# Steger sleds damaged in Antarctic collision; crew forced to improvise

By Bob von Sternberg
Staff Writer

Just a few miles after they passed an icy landmark named Cape Disappointment, members of the International Trans-Antarctica Expedition encountered their first serious disappointment Tuesday: Two of their three dog sleds collided on an icy slope, wrecking one of the sleds.

"We had a very rough day," trek leader Will Steger radioed to the expedition's support crew.

The accident, occurring just two weeks and less than 100 miles into an attempted crossing of Antarctica, was not expected to derail the intricately planned, heavily publicized trek.

"The name of this game is improvisation, so they'll just have to figure out what to do," expedition spokeswoman Jennifer Kimball Gasperini said Wednesday. "It's not going to jeopardize the expedition in any way."

Still, the mishap underscored the difficulties of Antarctic travel — some anticipated, some not — that team members will face during the early portion of the seven-month, 4,000-mile trip.

The accident occurred in what Steger described as "a minefield of crevasses," which had been expected along the Antarctic Peninsula where the trek began. But it happened on a steep slope of hard, blue ice that was more

**Expedition** continued on page 14A

INSIDE: **Jump in trade deficit prompts 18.65-point drop in Dow**/1D

MINNEAPOLIS EDITION

■ 2 dead in apparent kidnapping murder-suicide/**1B**


# Star Tribune

WEDNESDAY/October 18/1989 NEWSPAPER OF THE TWIN CITIES 35¢


# Major quake jolts Bay Area; at least 250 reported killed

## Oakland freeway section collapses

From News Services

**San Francisco, Calif.**
A catastrophic earthquake rocked northern California during Tuesday's evening rush hour, killing more than 250 people and injuring 400, caving in bridges and freeways, igniting fires and causing widespread damage to buildings.

At least 250 people were crushed to death in their cars when a mile-long section of the upper level of Interstate Hwy. 880 in Oakland collapsed onto the lower level, according to the Alameda County public-information office.

A spokesman for the California Office of Emergency Services said at least 400 people had been injured throughout the area.

The earthquake, which was felt as far as 400 miles away, knocked out electrical power, television broadcasts and telephonic communications through large parts of the region. It also forced cancellation of Game 3 of the World Series at Candlestick Park, where 60,000 baseball fans were evacuated from the stadium.

A 30-foot section of the upper level of the San Francisco-Oakland Bay Bridge collapsed onto the lower level, trapping three cars in the wreckage.

The quake, which registered 6.9 on the Richter scale, was centered about 75 miles south of San Francisco on the San Andreas fault. It was the second deadliest in the nation's history, exceeded only by the 1906 San Francisco earthquake that destroyed much of the city and killed more than 700 people.

Three hours after the quake, the magnitude of the disaster began to emerge as reports came in of widespread death and destruction.

At least two bridges in the Santa Cruz area collapsed and other highways leading out of the city suffered significant damage. "All the mountain passes are closed because of major landslides and fissures in the road,"

**Earthquake** continued on page 14A

Associated Press

**Firefighters and rescuers removed an injured motorist from a section of Interstate Hwy. 880 that collapsed in Oakland. Smoke rose from a burning auto trapped between the decks.**

### On the inside/

■ President Bush sent the secretary of transportation to to assess the damage. **18A.**

■ Surprised scientists said the quake occurred on part of the San Andreas Fault where no one had expected a severe earthquake. **19A.**

**Additional coverage on pages 14A, 18A and 19A.**

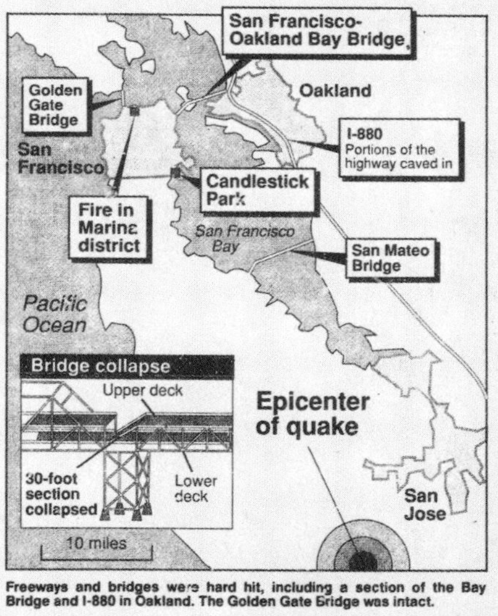


**Freeways and bridges were hard hit, including a section of the Bay Bridge and I-880 in Oakland. The Golden Gate Bridge was intact.**

## Residents calm, but braced for trouble as night approaches

New York Times

**San Francisco, Calif.**
As the initial shock of Tuesday's earthquake struck and in the seconds immediately after, residents, office workers, shop owners, hospital patients and even police officers ran in terror from buildings and homes throughout San Francisco.

But soon, acting out of what must have been instinct, people across the city adopted a calm demeanor and took to helping those who remained stricken with panic.

Night fell with the city black, with only the occasional office building lighted by emergency generators. There was a strange quiet, but residents were braced for a difficult time as reports of looting and assaults filtered in from around the city.

Fire engines and ambulances picked their way through the darkness and over glass-strewn, traffic-clogged streets. A few stars peeked through a layer of smoke from a fire raging in the Marina district.

In the financial district downtown, near the foot of the Bay Bridge, Presbyterian Hospital rumbled with long intense shakes as the quake hit. People from the main building and the surrounding complex ran out shrieking, but soon they calmed down and concentrated on helping others.

**San Francisco** continued on 18A

## Journalistic instinct gave way to survival

**Patrick Reusse**

**San Francisco, Calif.**
The main press box for baseball in Candlestick Park is one of the smallest in the major leagues. That's why more than 300 newspaper reporters were located in an auxiliary working area, high above home plate in the upper deck.

I was sitting in row 12, between Mike Baumann of the Milwaukee Journal and Tom Powers of the St. Paul Pioneer Press Dispatch. At 5 p.m., ABC's pregame show for the third game of the World Series kicked on, and the fans who had portable TV sets cheered.

In a few minutes, the participants — the Oakland Athletics and the San Francisco Giants — would line up along the first- and third-base lines to be introduced. The Giants' fans, considered the rowdiest in the National League, were getting ready to let out a roar that would shake the locals out of the hitting doldrums they had experienced over the weekend in Oakland.

Those of us in the upper deck felt a slight movement in the concrete. At the same time, a jet passed overhead, climbing from nearby San Francisco International Airport and into a brilliant, blue sky.

It had been a marvelous October afternoon in the Bay Area. A couple

**Reusse** continued on page 18A

## Canterbury Downs checks worthless after banks freeze accounts

By David Phelps
Staff Writer

In another financial blow to Canterbury Downs, its cash accounts were frozen by lenders holding $43 million in track debt, making recently written checks worthless and causing the track to miss a $1.5 million property tax payment to Scott County.

Led by the Union Bank of Bavaria, the lenders froze the accounts Thursday with no advance warning to track officials, said marketing director Doug Eichten.

"It did come as a surprise," Eichten said.

Track owner Brooks Fields, general manager Mike Manning and finance director Dave Carlson have been in New York since Monday negotiating with the Bank of Bavaria to get the accounts reopened.

"We very much expect to clear this up by the end of the week," Eichten said late Tuesday. "These are banks we've worked with for five years, so I'm sure we're going to work something out."

**Canterbury** continued on page 17A

### Almanac

**Wednesday, October 18, 1989**
**291th day; 74 to go this year**
**Sunrise: 7:32. Sunset: 6:24**

### Today's weather/

Partly cloudy and cold with light wind. High in the lower 40s. Low tonight in the mid-20s.

### Index/



### Telephones/

| | |
|---|---|
| News general | 372-4141 |
| Classifieds | 372-4242 |
| Circulation | 372-4343 |


Volume VIII/Number 197 7 sections

## Walker Art director will retire next year

By Mary Abbe Martin
Staff Writer

Martin Friedman, director of the Walker Art Center for 28 years, announced Tuesday that he will retire Nov. 1, 1990, shortly after his 65th birthday. During his tenure he has transformed the Minneapolis museum from a modest regional institution into an internationally known contemporary art center.

"He's made the best museum of 20th century art for its size in the world. There's nobody like him in America," said John Walsh, director of the J. Paul Getty Museum in Santa Monica, Calif.

**Martin Friedman**

The international roster of artists and performers who have appeared at the Walker during Friedman's tenure have contributed to the museum's reputation as "one of the most origi-

**Friedman** continued on page 17A

## $9 million OK'd to aid opposition in Nicaragua vote

The Senate approved President Bush's proposal to send $9 million to Nicaragua to boost the chances of the political opposition in February's elections; the House passed the bill earlier, and it now goes to the president for his signature.

The money would be funneled through the National Endowment for Democracy, a quasigovernmental agency that promotes democratic elections around the world. Some funds will go to support nonpartisan efforts, and the Sandinista government will get a chunk under Nicaraguan tax laws. **Page 16A**

Rain, high winds delay efforts/7A

Hungary/4A



VARIETY
**Eye of the beholder**
TV's 'Beauty and the Beast' fosters devoted fans

VARIETY
**Good seats**
Stumpf designs feel as good as they look

**MINNEAPOLIS EDITION**

■ Ogren, Simoneau named to head key House panels/1B
■ 13 private job agencies face charges of discrimination/1B
■ Secretary Cavazos visits to see effects of educational choice/1B

**Star Tribune**

NEWSPAPER OF THE TWIN CITIES

TUESDAY/October 24/1989 — 35¢ — B



# Soviets admit to 2 illegal acts

## Afghan invasion, radar station are cited

New York Times

**Moscow, U.S.S.R.**
Soviet Foreign Minister Eduard Shevardnadze Monday publicly condemned his nation's 1979 invasion of Afghanistan and the construction of a controversial radar station in Siberia, acknowledging that both actions had violated legal conventions.

In a speech to the Soviet legislature that later was broadcast nationally, Shevardnadze said the nine-year Soviet military presence in Afghanistan had violated Soviet law and international norms of behavior.

He also admitted that construction of the radar station near Krasnoyarsk was "an open violation" of the Antiballistic Missile (ABM) Treaty with the United States, and he suggested that the Kremlin had known that for some time.

The Soviet Union agreed last month to dismantle the station.

It was the first time that the Soviet leadership had formally described either action as illegal, and it amounted to a highly unusual national act of contrition.

In Washington, the Bush administration welcomed Shevardnadze's admission. "It reflects a different kind of mindset," a U.S. official said. "It's encouraging. It builds a degree of confidence; it builds a degree of trust."

"The main thing is not to conceal, to acknowledge and correct mistakes," Shevardnadze said in remarks that were broadcast in full last night on Soviet TV.

During a broad, generally rosy overview of foreign policy presented to

**Soviets** continued on page 6A

# St. Joseph boy, 11, kidnapped at gunpoint

By Pat Doyle
Staff Writer

**St. Joseph, Minn.**
A bloodhound, helicopter pilots and scores of college students and firefighters searched cornfields and woods Monday for 11-year-old Jacob Wetterling, who authorities said was abducted at gunpoint Sunday by a masked man on a rural township road.

The athlete and A-student was snatched as he and his younger brother and a friend were returning from a convenience store on their bicycles at about 9:15 p.m. Sunday, said Stearns County Sheriff Charlie Grafft.

No ransom demands have been received and authorities said they knew of no motive for the abduction and had no suspects.

"It could be kidnapping for ransom, could be sex," Grafft said. "We don't know. He could be in the next state by now."

Said Dr. Jerry Wetterling, 41, Jacob's father, "I've never received any threats." Wetterling, a local chiropractor and president of the St. Cloud chapter of the National Association for the Advancement of Colored People (NAACP), said it was impossible his son's disappearance was a prank. "They are really honest boys," he said.

Grafft said an account of the abduction provided by Jacob's brother, Trevor, 10, is credible and authorities assume the boy has been kidnapped. Trevor said that he, Jacob, and Aaron Larson, 11, were returning on bicycles from a convenience store a mile from home where they had rented a videotaped movie. The area is about 5 miles west of St. Cloud.

They were about halfway home when a man wearing dark clothing, black boots and carrying a pistol walked out of a long gravel driveway leading to a farm.

"He had a mask; it looked like pantyhose, on his head," Trevor said. "He told us to get off our bikes or he'd shoot. We did what he said. We laid in a ditch and he asked our ages."

After the boys told their ages, "He looked at Aaron's face and he told me to run to the woods as fast as I could," Trevor said.

Said Aaron, "He told me to run, too, or else he'd shoot."

**Kidnapping** continued on page 8A

Staff Photo by Rita Reed

**Friends and family gathered Monday at the St. Joseph, Minn., home of Jacob Wetterling, 11, son of Jerry Wetterling, standing, and his wife, Patty, holding poster. Shannon Brannan, right, a former foster daughter, and Lisa Overturf, a niece, offered comfort over Jacob's apparent abduction.**

**Doug Grow**

# Friend's at end of his tether

"He's the best," Clifton Miller was saying of his running partner, Ross Mitchell. "Sometimes I worry that he's going to forget to tell me where the trees are, but he never forgets. It works out pretty well."

The buddies, who are teammates on the Minneapolis North High School cross-country team, laughed. Usually, at least, it works out well. Usually they're in physical and mental sync.

Ross, the 16-year-old sophomore, sets a pace that feels right. He yells out to Clifton, the 15-year-old junior who is captain of the team, when they're approaching hills or tricky footing or trees or a group of other runners. When Ross yells, Clifton holds the 3-foot cord that unites them just a little tighter, and then he can go about the business of proving to himself and to his peers that being blind doesn't mean surrendering. Clifton has been blind since he was stricken with glaucoma at age 3.

Usually Clifton and Ross are testimony to the power of selflessness, friendship and teamwork.

But they also are human.

"Third race this year, it didn't go so well," Clifton said. "He cut right in front of me three times. We did some arguing in that race."

And then there was a tree in

**Grow** continued on page 13A

# State cocaine use has risen dramatically, report says

By Donna Halvorsen
Staff Writer

Cocaine use has increased dramatically in Minnesota over the past several years, the State Planning Office said Monday.

The agency's findings appear to be at odds with a national study showing declining cocaine use. But the two studies used different methods, and it's unclear how comparable their results may be.

"We haven't seen any decline in Minnesota," said Stephen Coleman, coauthor of the agency's report. It showed:

■ A near tripling of cocaine and narcotics arrests from 1985 to 1988, from 470 people arrested in 1985 to 1,376 in 1988.

■ A sharp increase in juvenile arrests for various drug offenses — up 38 percent in a single year, from 1986 to 1987.

■ A tripling of reported cocaine use among people seeking help in hospital emergency rooms.

**Cocaine** continued on page 11A

Associated Press

**Flames and intense heat kept rescue workers from getting close to the Phillips plant in Pasadena, Texas. "We're betting there's a lot of fatalities, just because of the nature of the explosion," said Dr. Paul Pepe.**

# 1 dead, 100 injured in Texas blast

Associated Press

**Pasadena, Texas**
Explosions rocked a Phillips Petroleum Co. plastics plant Monday, hurling chunks of metal and other debris miles away and creating a fireball visible for 15 miles.

At least one worker died, more than 100 were injured and 23 were unaccounted for last night.

Flames and intense heat kept rescue workers from getting close enough to investigate, said Dr. Paul Pepe, the director of Houston emergency medical services. "We're betting there's a lot of fatalities, just because of the nature of the explosion and where it happened," he said. "We don't think there's anybody alive in there."

Twenty Phillips employees and at least three contract workers were missing more than eight hours after the explosions, Phillips Petroleum President Glenn Cox said last night.

**Plant** continued on page 12A

# Debt crisis has worsened the world's food supply

Third of six parts.

By Jeremy Iggers
Staff Writer

**Bamako, Mali**
The rainy season has begun and the potholes in the muddy unpaved streets of Mali's squalid, sprawling capital are filling with water. Tiemoko Sangare sits in the semi-darkness of his modest office. He oversees a dozen development projects funded by the Boston-based relief agency Oxfam America, in towns and villages throughout the impoverished West African nation.

There is no electricity this day, reportedly because the government has no money to maintain the local power plant. Mali, with 8 million inhabitants and an annual per capita income of $210, is more than $2 billion in debt to international lending institutions such as the World Bank and the International Monetary Fund, the leading underwriters of Third World development.

The blackout is the least of Mali's problems: Few Malian homes or businesses are wired for electricity. Fewer still have running water.

**Food** continued on page 10A

## Almanac

**Tuesday, October 24, 1989**
**297th day; 68 to go this year**
**Sunrise: 7:40. Sunset: 6:14**

### Today's weather/

Mostly sunny, high around 75.




Volume VIII/Number 203 — 6 sections

Producer prices were up moderately in October/1D

Stars beat Red Wings/1C

MARKETPLACE

**Fish farmer**

Range entrepreneur raises salmon and trout in old ore pits

VARIETY

Music of the Vietnamese

**MINNEAPOLIS EDITION**

- Social-service funds to be tapped to extend downtown patrols/1B
- After election loss, Carlson says it's time for a change in life/1B
- Control Data says it will sell Ticketron to Washington firm/1D

**Star Tribune**

FRIDAY/November 10/1939 NEWSPAPER OF THE TWIN CITIES

# Berlin Wall opens to West

## E. Germany lets citizens pass across all borders

From News Services

**Berlin**
The East German government threw open its borders Thursday and announced that its citizens now may travel freely to West Germany. Late yesterday and early today, exultant East Germans coursed through Berlin Wall checkpoints; others entered West Germany at other border crossings.

In a day rife with signs of continuing turmoil, the Communist Party leadership also announced that it would convene a party conference Dec. 15-17 to discuss "urgent policy questions."

The moves were hailed in Washington and Moscow as positive developments, though there was concern that the changes might be happening too fast.

Confronted by a mounting political crisis that a top East German official said has placed the ruling Communist Party's very existence at stake, the government said authorities had been instructed to grant permission without delay for people to journey abroad or leave the country.

"Today, the decision was taken that makes it possible for all citizens to leave the country through East German border crossing points," media chief Guenter Schabowski told an evening news conference.

As word spread, hundreds of jubilant East Berliners poured into West Berlin on their first visits to the western half of the city, divided for 28 years

**E. Germany** continued on page 14A

Associated Press

**East and West Berliners crowded atop the Berlin Wall in front of the Brandenburg Gate, celebrating the opening of the 28-year-old barrier. Said West Berlin Mayor Walter Momper: "The long-awaited day has arrived. The Berlin Wall no longer divides Berliners."**

## Berliners unite to dance on the Wall

From News Services

**Berlin**
The 28-year-old Berlin Wall opened up Thursday, and by midnight thousands of East Berliners — of all ages, from every way of life — were walking, biking and driving across to the western half of the city, a place they could only gaze at just hours before.

"I can't believe I'm here," an elderly East Berliner told reporters as he crossed into the West. "This is what we have dreamed of all these years."

Cheers, sparkling wine, flowers and applause greeted the new arrivals. On the West Berlin side of the Wall, at the Brandenburg Gate, the most prominent landmark of the city's division, hundreds of people chanted, "Open the gate! Open the gate!" Some West Berliners held impromptu dances atop the Wall and hoisted people up from the other side of the divided city to join them.

Some Germans used hammers to chip away at the Wall for keepsakes or in their own small way to try to destroy a major symbol of East-West division.

Later, revelers waved copies of today's edition of Bild Zeitung, the West Berlin tabloid newspaper. Its banner headline proclaimed, "The Wall is gone! Berlin is again Berlin."

"It's over, it's all over, I can't believe it," said an East German as he ducked to get under the red-and-white barriers at the Bornholmer Strasse crossing, an act that might have cost him his life several months

**Wall** continued on page 14A

## House gaming panel chairman raised gambling money for trip

By Robert Franklin and Joe Rigert
Staff Writers

The chairman of the state House Gaming Subcommittee raised about $66,000 from gambling organizations this year to take a Minnesota hockey team to the World Masters Games in Denmark.

Rep. Joe Quinn, DFL-Coon Rapids, said Thursday that he raised about $40,000 from the Minneapolis Fire Fighters Welfare Association, whose name appeared on the team jerseys, $12,000 from the St. Therese nursing home in New Hope and $14,000 through James H. Adams, a lobbyist and former hockey executive who has been a target of several gambling investigations.

State authorities have accused Adams and a partner of illegally diverting nearly $60,000 from an Arden Hills bingo hall. The $14,000 for the hockey team came from two organizations that have operated at the bingo hall, the Concordia Singing Society and Light Brigade.

Two weeks ago, the Star Tribune reported that the Arden Hills hall paid $17,700 to State Rep. Richard O'Connor, DFL-St. Paul. O'Connor said the money was for him to use to help find softball fields for charitable organizations, but questions were raised about that explanation.

While the hockey donations did not go personally to Quinn, his actions raise questions about how they were solicited, especially the funds he obtained from a lobbyist, and whether they were used for lawful purposes.

**Quinn** continued on page 12A

## Deng gives up last formal job

Deng Xiaoping turned over the leadership of China's armed forces — his last formal leadership post — Thursday to Communist Party chief Jiang Zemin.

It is widely believed, however, that Deng's prestige and residual authority will enable the 85-year-old leader to continue to be the ultimate arbiter of Chinese politics for as long as he is in reasonably good health. One diplomat called yesterday's move the beginning of "a transition phase" in China. **Page 4A.**

## Darville defense says 'U' leaders knew of payments

By Rob Hotakainen
Staff Writer

Luther Darville began giving money to University of Minnesota athletes in 1983 with the "advice and consent and full knowledge of his superiors," his attorney said Thursday.

The defense, which opened its case yesterday, intends to call only two witnesses: Darville and Ron Edwards, ex-president of the Minneapolis Urban League. Edwards testified yesterday that high-ranking university officials, including former President Kenneth Keller and former Vice President Frank Wilderson, knew of Darville's payments to athletes.

Darville testified for two hours, giving a glimpse of his personal background and early years at the university, where he led the office of minority affairs. It was his first testimony in a U.S. court since being extradited from his native Bahamas on Aug. 18.

Darville said he first became involved with the Athletic Department when former football coach Joe Salem asked for help with the "dismal

**Darville** continued on page 12A

## Alzheimer's may be more prevalent than estimated

New York Times

**Washington, D.C.**
Alzheimer's disease, the dementia that robs the elderly of their memory and self-reliance, may be much more common than previously estimated, particularly in the very old, according to a study to be published today.

The federally financed study by Harvard Medical School researchers, one of the largest and most detailed ever attempted on the subject, found that 10.3 percent of people over age 65 had memory impairment or other mental problems for which the most likely cause was Alzheimer's.

The study also found that a startling 47.2 percent of those older than 85 probably had the disease. That finding doubles previous estimates.

Experts said the new figures, if they apply to older people throughout the country, would raise the estimated number of Alzheimer's cases to 4 million from 2.5 million.

If it is confirmed, specialists said, the data suggest that the costs of the disease in treatment, lost productivity and to families could be enormous because the elderly are the fastest increasing segment of the population.

"These estimates might lay the groundwork for developing the most accurate picture of Alzheimer's disease in the U.S. population to date," said Dr. Zaven Khachaturian, associate director of the National Institute on Aging, which sponsored the study.

**Alzheimers's** continued on page 13A

## Almanac

**Friday, November 10, 1989**
**314th day; 51 to go this year**
**Sunrise: 7:04. Sunset: 4:50**

### Today's weather/

More murk

Increasing cloudiness is forecast for the metropolitan area with high temperatures from the upper 30s to lower 40s. The wind will be 10 to 20 mph.

### Index/



### Telephones/

| | |
|---|---|
| News general | 372-4141 |
| Classifieds | 372-4242 |
| Circulation | 372-4343 |


Volume VIII/Number 220 6 sections

## Minnesota mariner's tale gets support

By Donald Woutat
Staff Writer

The New Zealand government has concluded that a Minneapolis man and three others were telling the truth about their improbable four-month odyssey on a capsized yacht in the South Pacific.

The marine growth on the submerged hull of the trimaran Rose-Noelle and a computer analysis of wind and currents in the region supported the sailors' story, the New Zealand Transport Ministry said Thursday.

"They say I was telling the truth!" responded Minneapolis sailor Jim Nalepka, 38, in mock surprise. He was reached by phone at his home in New Zealand, where he is writing a magazine account of the ordeal.

Nalepka, who is on leave from his job as a laborer for the city of Minneapolis, and three fellow sailors spent 119 days adrift in the waters east and north of New Zealand before crashing ashore on Great Barrier Island on Sept. 30.

**Sailors** continued on page 11A

## Minneapolis voters grew tired of Carlson, White

By Dennis J. McGrath
Staff Writer

**Analysis**

The defeat of two veteran City Council members Tuesday probably is not a sign of widespread discontent among Minneapolis voters.

Barbara Carlson and Van White lost because they simply had worn out their welcomes.

White was first elected in 1979, making history as the first black elected to the 13-member council. Carlson assumed office two years after White, and went on to establish a new mark by which to measure flamboyance among local elected officials.

But Carlson's appeal also may have been her downfall. She became the best-known council member and rivaled Mayor Don Fraser, a political legend, for name recognition among city residents. But people didn't feel mildly about her. They either celebrated her spunk and free spirit, or feared that she was a loose cannon.

**Council** continued on page 11A

SPORTS: Timberwolves fall to Bullets; Oilers shut out North Stars

MINNEAPOLIS EDITION

■ Incinerator vapor cloud won't be fixed before spring/1B

# Star Tribune

WEDNESDAY/December 20/1989 NEWSPAPER OF THE TWIN CITIES 35¢

# U.S. moves on Noriega

From News Services

President Bush ordered U.S. troops in Panama "to apprehend Manuel Noriega," White House spokesman Marlin Fitzwater said early today, and U.S. forces were involved in combat in Panama City as he spoke.

U.S. troops and armored personnel carriers surrounded Noriega's headquarters in a blaze of gunfire, and opposition leader Guillermo Endara proclaimed himself the new president of Panama.

Mortar, machine-gun and cannon fire echoed across the capital late Tuesday night as truckloads of American troops headed from U.S. military bases toward the Panamanian Defense Forces headquarters.

The sky was bright with the light of gunfire and a fire appeared to have started near the headquarters. Noriega's whereabouts were unknown.

U.S. soldiers surrounding the main Panamanian military installations yelled over megaphones for the Panamanian troops to surrender, residents living near the installations said.

The government's national radio station said the headquarters had been "cruelly bombarded."

Fitzwater, noting that Noriega was under indictment in the United States for drug trafficking offenses, said that Endara, the opposition presidential candidate, and the vice presidential candidate from last spring's Panamanian elections were "sworn in and assumed their rightful positions."

He said the United States had recognized their government.

Asked whether Noriega had been taken into custody, Fitzwater said, "the situation is such that we are not at liberty to comment" on the details of the military operation.

Fitzwater said the other reasons for moving against Noriega involved the

Panama continued on page 15A

# Cornered at farm, Cole gives up

## Slain police officer is buried

By Chuck Haga, Pat Doyle, Jill Hodges, Kevin Diaz and Mark Brunswick
Staff Writers

Alan Otto heard sirens late Monday night and looked out the window of his McLeod County farmhouse. He saw police cruisers on the highway about 200 yards away, their lights flashing off a car in the ditch.

Then he saw two figures coming toward the house, a man and a woman. Through the noise, he could make out only a few shouted words, but one of the shouts sounded like "Cole."

Otto had heard the name earlier, on the news. He tried to lock his door, then rushed his wife and daughter to an upstairs bathroom. He locked that door, too.

But neither lock helped. Phillip Lewis Cole, 29, wanted for the murder Friday of a police officer in nearby Hutchinson, burst into the farmhouse and then talked the Ottos out of their bathroom, adding them to the 21-year-old Minneapolis woman he had abducted, sexually assaulted and taken hostage earlier, police said.

The Ottos' ordeal lasted 5½ hours, a tense night controlled by a man whose life story is a compendium of fights, flight, jails and halfway houses. Cole has spent most of his life in trouble or on the run.

His latest adventure could have ended in suicide or more homicides, police said, but shortly before dawn Tuesday, after talking with members of his family on the phone, Cole quietly emptied his gun, tossed it out a door and surrendered. The capture ended a frustrating three-day manhunt that left Minneapolis police speculating that an informant had double-crossed them and tipped Cole two or three times on impending stakeouts.

A few hours after Cole's capture, the officer he is accused of shooting in the face was buried. More than 1,000

Manhunt continued on page 10A

The accused gunman

Photo by Clint Wood, McLeod County Chronicle

**Phillip Lewis Cole was escorted into McLeod County District Court Tuesday for arraignment on murder charges.**

2 of the families affected

Staff Photo by Mike Zerby

**Sharon Hogan, wife of the slain Hutchinson police officer, Michael Hogan, received the flag that had covered his casket at Hogan's funeral at Fort Snelling Tuesday. Story on Page 11A.**

Staff Photo by Richard Sennott

**Alan and Sandy Otto and their child, Alaina, were held hostage in their home for more than five hours before the gunman surrendered.**

## Grace Cole says son bad from the start

By Paul McEnroe
Staff Writer

"I'm the mother of the boy who done it," said Grace Cole from the morning shadows.

She sat in a house without hope or light, leaning into the dining room table on one elbow for two hours early Tuesday, talking about a son whom she said had gone bad from the start.

A son whose life was so fouled that by the time he was 17 years old, Phillip Lewis Cole had tried to kill Minneapolis police officers.

"I couldn't handle getting busted; I'd rather get killed than busted," he said after his arrest 12 years ago. "Either the police kill me or I kill them."

Grace Cole, a retired teacher's aide, didn't go into that. Instead she described her son's brain hemorrhage at birth 29 years ago "that made the whites of his eyes turn red for six months." She spoke of his violent-behavior problems, which she said made even him wonder why he did things he didn't want to do.

By 1977 he'd been convicted of aggravated robbery. In 1980 came a conviction for attempted murder.

"He was a time bomb waiting to go off ever since he was a kid," said a law enforcement source familiar with Cole. "Everyone saw it happening over and over again. He was a classic case of the system being unable to do anything for his kind."

And now this: a dead police officer in a small town in central Minnesota, and her son, Phillip, in jail after a three-day manhunt.

She talked behind the closed curtains and over a blaring TV quiz show while her husband, daughter and nephew slept for the first time in days. From inside the house at 36th

Cole continued on page 10A

# Perpich lifestyle no issue; people disagree with Lola

Copyright 1989 Star Tribune
By Lori Sturdevant
Staff Writer

The recent flap over Gov. Rudy Perpich's residence and lifestyle hasn't budged the DFL governor's approval rating in the Star Tribune-KSTP Minnesota Poll, the latest poll shows.

But a separate, metro-only survey conducted for KSTP last weekend found widespread disagreement with the suggestion by Perpich's wife, Lola, that the Governor's Residence be sold.

Moreover, that survey showed that most Twin Cities residents who were aware of the flap think the Perpiches were overreacting to news reports when they proposed the mansion's sale, dropped personal security ser-

MINNESOTA POLL
Star Tribune / KSTP TV

Poll continued on page 15A

# Shooting, fires continue in Romania; reports hint hundreds may have died

Associated Press

Vienna, Austria
Shooting and fires were reported Tuesday in western Romania, where security forces may have killed hundreds of people who protested the harsh Communist regime of President Nicolae Ceausescu, witnesses said.

Greek students who crossed into Yugoslavia from the western Romanian city of Timisoara, site of the greatest unrest over the weekend, said shots were fired indiscriminately, "killing dozens."

They said many children were killed or wounded "because people used them as shields," assuming security forces would hold their fire.

A Romanian doctor who arrived in Austria spoke of protesters stoning armored vehicles. He said that one vehicle drove into the crowd, crushing a woman, and that rows of people were mowed down by gunfire.

Romania continued on page 14A

## Inside today's Star Tribune/

**Another mail bomb/** Police disarmed a mail bomb at the NAACP office in Jacksonville, Fla., the fourth in a series that has killed two. Authorities said "racial motivation" was possible. 18A.

**Award winner/** Cyclist Greg LeMond, the Tour de France winner who lives in Minnesota part of the year, was named Sports Illustrated's "Sportsman of the Year." 1C.

**Brandenburg Gate to open/** The leaders of the two Germanys met and agreed to reopen the Brandenburg Gate and introduce free border crossing for all Germans by Christmas. 4A.

■ The Czech Parliament appeared ready to elect playwright Vaclav Havel, the dissident non-Communist, as president. 4A.

■ An Amtrak train collided with a truck in fog at a grade crossing near Stockton, Calif., killing three people. 7A.

## Almanac

**Wednesday, December 20, 1989**
**354th day; 11 to go this year**
**Sunrise: 7:48. Sunset: 4:34**

Cold
High from zero to 5 below.

| | | | |
|---|---|---|---|
| Comics | 8,9E | Obituaries | 8B |
| Movies | 4,5E | TV, Radio | 10E |
| Complete index | | | 2A |
| Classifieds | | | 372-4242 |
| Circulation | | | 372-4343 |

Volume VIII/Number 260 7 sections

# City leadership passes to new generation today

By Rob Hotakainen
Staff Writer

After weeks of deal-making and head-counting, the Minneapolis City Council will elect new leadership today. The torch passing at City Hall promises to put the council in the control of more liberal, inner-city hands.

Sharon Sayles Belton is expected to emerge as president, while Brian Coyle appears to have enough votes to become vice president. Sayles Belton would become the council's first black president. Coyle is the council's first openly gay member. Both represent inner-city wards.

In another major change, Sandra Hilary is expected to become head of the Community Development Committee, one of the most powerful

Council continued on page 17A

# 1990 ~ 1992

SHELTER

**Home under the Dome**

Two-story house to be erected for Home Show

**Wolves stun Celtics 116-105**

Campbell scores 44 in 3rd straight win/1C

VARIETY

**Best Bette**

Midler is on a Hollywood hot streak

**MINNEAPO!.IS EDITION**

- Violent crime down; property crime up in Twin Cities/**1B**
- City will appeal award to developer of Calhoun high-rise/**3B**
- Oak Park Heights case helps kill local rent-subsidy rule/**3B**


# Star Tribune

SATURDAY/February 3/1990 NEWSPAPER OF THE TWIN CITIES . Y 35¢


# Reform plan stuns S. Africa

## 30-year ban on antiapartheid groups is lifted

Los Angeles Times

**Cape Town, South Africa**
In a landmark speech that shocked black and white South Africans, President Frederik de Klerk on Friday lifted the 30-year ban on the African National Congress and other antiapartheid groups, sharply scaled back the 3½-year-old state of emergency and announced his "firm decision" to release jailed black nationalist Nelson Mandela quickly and unconditionally.

De Klerk's sweeping reform initiatives, the most sudden and significant peace offering to the black majority in decades, went most of the way toward reopening political expression in the country and meeting demands made by the ANC as conditions for black-white negotiations.

"The season of violence is over. The time for reconstruction and reconciliation has arrived," De Klerk said in his 45-minute speech opening Parliament, which was greeted with cheers from supporters and silence from the right-wing opposition.

"The time for talking has arrived, and whoever still makes excuses does not really wish to talk," he declared. "The table is laid for sensible leaders to begin talking" about a new constitution.

Members of the white, Indian and mixed-race Colored chambers of Parliament murmured loudly in surprise as De Klerk ticked off steps to create a climate for negotiation with the voteless black majority, who outnumber whites 5-1.

As De Klerk spoke, several thousand

**South Africa** continued on page 10A

Associated Press

**Anglican Archbishop Desmond Tutu, with Winnie Mandela at his side, said in Cape Town on Friday, "Give him (President De Klerk) credit. I do."**

## Blacks joyfully hail promise of change

Associated Press

As many whites watched silently from the sidelines, black taxi-drivers honked horns and stopped traffic, and other revelers surged into the streets to celebrate President Frederik de Klerk's announcement Friday of watershed political changes.

Blacks in Cape Town, Durban and Johannesburg broke into whistles and shouts of joy at the news that the African National Congress and all other organizations had been legalized and many national emergency restrictions lifted.

They streamed into the dusty roads of townships to cheer, and marched through a Cape Town train station. A thin line of white police in Cape Town silently watched the pulsating throng, and small groups of glum-looking white civilians stood behind the police, staring at the jubilant blacks, waving the organization's black, green and gold flag as they chanted, "ANC! ANC!"

Other whites, eyes cast down, walked quickly past the exuberant blacks. The police, who broke up a peaceful demonstration in central Cape Town on Wednesday, made no move to block the crowd yesterday.

"We are probably seeing history in the making in South Africa," said Anglican Archbishop Desmond Tutu, who smiled throughout a news conference. "We had expected that Mr. De Klerk might deliver something, but what he said has certainly taken my breath away."

Drivers stopped their cars in the street, honking their horns and

**Reaction** continued on page 11A

## New policy will let some illegal aliens stay with 'legal' families

From News Services

**Washington, D.C.**
Thousands of illegal aliens who are children or spouses of legal immigrants will be allowed to stay in the United States under a policy announced Friday by Immigration Commissioner Gene McNary.

Under McNary's order, those aliens will be given permission to stay if they were in the United States on Nov. 6, 1986, the day the Immigration Reform and Control Act took effect.

Immigration and Naturalization Service (INS) officials estimated that more than 100,000 people might be affected by the policy, which takes effect Feb. 14.

The change was hailed as positive by immigrant rights advocates, who used unusually complimentary words to describe the heretofore much-despised immigration agency.

"People were filled with anxiety, just as any family would be when worried about being separated from their spouses and children," said Kip Steinberg, attorney with the National Immigration Project of the National Lawyers Guild. "This is a nice change in direction."

Arnoldo Torres, national political director of the League of United Latin American Citizens, called the order "probably one of the most reasonable positions that INS has taken."

The policy previously enforced by the INS allowed family members who are illegal aliens to stay only if there was a "compelling humanitarian reason" against deportation.

**Aliens** continued on page 2A

### German-unity vote proposed

An international referendum of the issue of German reunification was proposed Friday by Soviet Foreign Minister Eduard Shevardnadze.

He expressed concern over "the revival of sinister shadows of the past. . . . All peoples, especially those of the Soviet Union, must have a guarantee that the war threat will never come from German soil." He proposed an all-European referendum with the participation of the United States and Canada.

**Page 4A.**

## Alleged rent scam victimizes churches

By Kevin Diaz
Staff Writer

It was another hard-luck story, just like a lot of stories that pastors hear from down-and-out supplicants who go to them for help:

A young woman new to town, without enough money to pay her rent. She just needed help getting on her feet, and she could provide the landlord's telephone number. Sometimes she showed up with her small daughter.

"I guess I fell for it," said the Rev. Norman Anderson, pastor of Community of the Cross Lutheran Church in Bloomington, who got fleeced for $99.

Anderson, like the pastors of about 30 other churches that gave the woman money in the last few months, found out too late that his charity check was not likely to go toward anybody's rent.

In fact, it was cashed in the bar at the Prior Lake VFW club the same day he wrote it.

**Churches** continued on page 8A

## Officer owns building that prompts many calls to Minneapolis police

By Randy Furst
and Mark Brunswick
Staff Writers

A Minneapolis apartment building owned by a city police officer has generated some of the highest numbers of police calls of any building in the city.

In 1989 the three-story building at 909 E. 18th St. generated 85 police calls, including reports of shootings, stabbings, fights and assaults. That ranks it in the top .2 percent of the city's 100,000 addresses.

"It's been an outstanding problem for a long time, which neighbors and my office have been complaining about," said City Council Member Brian Coyle, who represents the Sixth Ward, where the building is located.

The owner of the 18-unit building is Robert M. Anderson, a Minneapolis police officer who is assigned to teach crime prevention to school-children. Repeated attempts by the Star Tribune to reach Anderson at work and at his south Minneapolis apartment this

**Policeman** continued on page 6A

### Almanac

**Saturday, February 3, 1990**
**34th day; 331 to go this year**
**Sunrise: 7:31. Sunset: 5:24**

**Today's weather/**

Chance of light snow morning, becoming sunny afternoon. High upper 20s.

**Index/**



**Telephones/**

| | |
|---|---|
| General Information | 673-4000 |
| Classifieds | 673-7000 |
| Circulation | 673-4343 |


Volume VIII/Number 305 7 sections

## 'Time bomb' at FBS?

### Italian businessman holds signed blank checks that pose 'limitless' risk for bank

By Anthony Carideo
Staff Writer

An Italian businessman holds 21 blank, but negotiable, bank drafts issued by First Bank System Inc. that a federal judge Friday called "financial time bombs."

The drafts could conceivably be made out for any sum. At a court hearing yesterday, U.S. District Judge James Rosenbaum characterized the bank's exposure as "literally limitless."

The bank drafts were issued by two officers at First Bank's Hopkins branch in December 1988, ostensibly to provide interim, or "bridge," financing to a group of Minneapolis and European investors. The investors said they would fill out the drafts to secure roughly $30 million worth of permanent financing to buy several businesses and other assets.

Since senior bank officers learned of the drafts, First Bank notified major banks throughout Europe that the checks are not to be accepted if presented for payment.

One such draft, for $5 million, was presented for payment about a month ago, but was not accepted.

The bank disputes the judge's assessment of unlimited exposure to loss, saying that it is confident that its efforts to stop payment of the drafts will be successful. But First Bank is seeking what its lawyers characterized as an "emergency" restraining order to avoid litigation to block each of the drafts.

**FBS** continued on page 12A

SUNDAY

12-year-old girl strangled in Minneapolis home/1B

Jill Trenary wins U.S. title; North Stars clip Hawks/1C

ARTS

Happy birthday, Meridel

MAGAZINE

The war on Drew Av.

TASTE/TRAVEL

Love–at home and abroad

MINNEAPOLIS EDITION

■ Flynn wins special vote in Senate District 61/5B

■ 80-year-old city plan still ignites the imagination/1F


# Star Tribune

SUNDAY/February 11/1990 NEWSPAPER OF THE TWIN CITIES $1.25

$1.50 outside the Twin Cities metro area


# Mandela to be freed today

Nelson Mandela

From News Services

**Cape Town, South Africa**
Nelson Mandela, the symbol of South African blacks' struggle for equality, will be freed today after 27 years in prison for fighting white-minority rule.

President F.W. de Klerk said Saturday that he hoped Mandela's long-awaited release would halt decades of racial conflict and clear the way for negotiations that would extend political rights to the black majority.

The release "will bring us to the end of a long chapter," said De Klerk, who told Mandela of the decision Friday night. "There can no longer be any doubt about the government's sincerity in seeking to create a just dispensation based on negotiations."

De Klerk said he is convinced that Mandela, jailed for helping launch the African National Congress' guerrilla campaign, is "committed to a peaceful solution."

Asked about Mandela's plans after leaving prison, De Klerk said that he preferred not to "answer questions on Mr. Mandela's behalf" and that Mandela could speak for himself today.

De Klerk said the national state of emergency declared in July 1986 could be lifted soon if there is no upsurge of unrest with Mandela's release. He also voiced a willingness to negotiate the possible release of remaining political prisoners.

In recent talks with the government, Mandela has demanded freedom for all political prisoners and an end to the state of emergency.

Mandela's freedom has been a long-standing demand of black leaders in South Africa, as well as governments and human-rights groups abroad. The decision drew immediate international praise.

In Johannesburg and its main black township, Soweto, blacks thronged the streets in celebration.

"Our leader is coming!" shouted a black youth in Johannesburg amidst

**Mandela** continued on page 20A

# Tyson loses crown

By Ed Schuyler Jr.
Associated Press

**Tokyo, Japan**
Mike Tyson lost for the first time when James (Buster) Douglas knocked him out in the 10th round and captured the heavyweight championship today in one of the biggest upsets in boxing history.

Douglas knocked out the heavily favored Tyson with a left-right-left to the head that dropped Tyson in a heap in Douglas' corner. Douglas had narrowly escaped defeat when he struggled up at nine from a one-punch knockdown late in the eighth round. The time of the knockout was 1:23 of the 10th round.

"I was real relaxed," Douglas said. "I wasn't afraid of the man. I'm only afraid of God."

Instead of a third straight heavyweight championship mismatch, which had been predicted, Japanese fans got one of the great shocks in boxing history. Tyson, who was 37-0 with 33 knockouts entering the fight, was such a prohibitive favorite that the sports book in Las Vegas refused to put up a betting line. The betting

**Tyson** continued on page 13A

CHILDREN OF 'CRACK'/**CASUALTIES OF WAR**

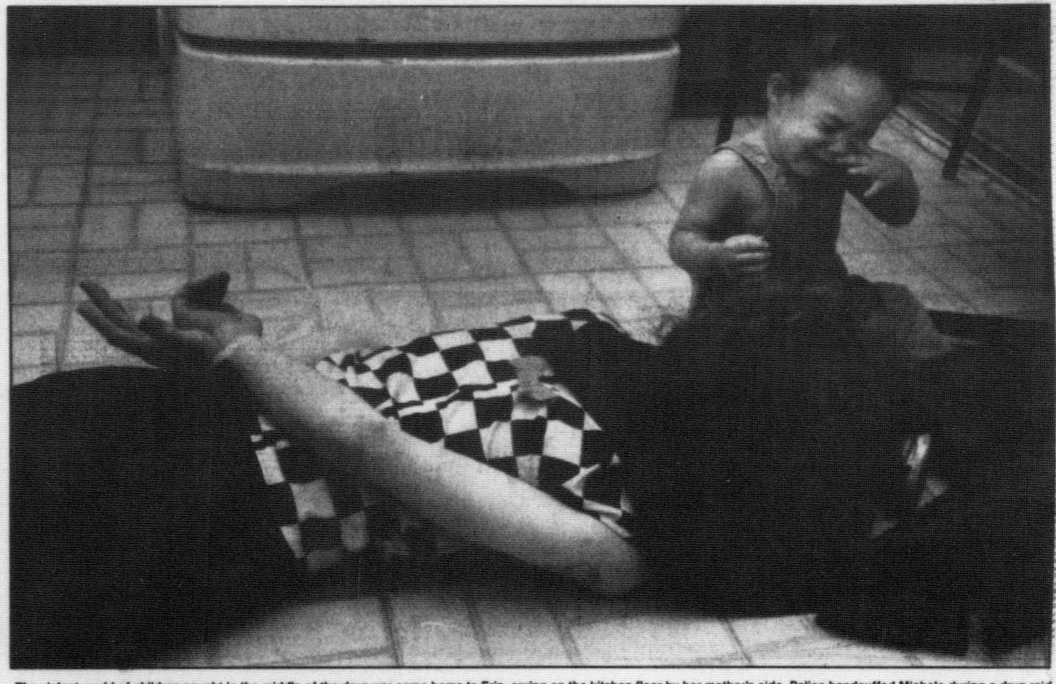

**The violent world of children caught in the middle of the drug war came home to Erin, crying on the kitchen floor by her mother's side. Police handcuffed Michele during a drug raid on the apartment on E. 39th St. No cocaine was found in the apartment and Michele was released.**

# Violence, despair tarnish hope for new generation

*Editor's note: For two months, a Star Tribune reporter and photographer accompanied the narcotics unit of the Minneapolis Police Department on raids of "crack" houses. Out of those raids comes this story of the toll that the crack war is taking on the city's children. The city's black community, outraged at the damage caused by crack, is demanding that police rid the streets of the drug. But authorities say the drug war has been lost in Minneapolis, and the only battles left are for the children's futures.*

Story by Paul McEnroe/ Photos by Richard Sennott

Detronza is off in a world of his own, playing on his Mickey Mouse bedspread full of magic scenes from "Fantasia."

Under the 4-year-old's mattress is a pearl-handled, .22-caliber pistol and five shells.

Outside, off Golden Valley Rd., a group of men bursts silently from a van, one with a machine gun strapped over his arms and two others hauling a battering ram. They run soft as dancers through the night and into the dim hallway, making no sound other than the rush of heavy breathing, a wall of firepower ascending on Apt. 102.

Behind the men carrying the ram comes another with a shield that looks like a "Star Wars" mask. Once at the door they all step aside.

Into the breach races the man with a shotgun aimed at the deadbolt lock. Two muffled blasts from the gun, the rich smell of powder, smoke filling the hallway, two bashes from the ram and the door is down.

Then the screams from inside, high-pitched from the women, bucket-deep bass moans from the men.

"Police! Get your ----ing asses down, down, you ----ers! Get the f--- down now! I want to see your hands behind your back, now, now, now!" The machine gun waves. Fingers a breath away from triggers.

"There's a baby in here!" shouts a cop.

Detronza's 18-year-old mother, Rhonda, is on the floor now, a bedspread dropped over her head so she can't see anybody. "Please don't

**Crack** continued on page 16A

# Not all towns celebrating Minnesota

## Winners and losers in battle for grants

By Donald Woutat
Staff Writer

Not much is missing from the long list of events crowded under the umbrella of "Celebrate Minnesota 1990," Gov. Rudy Perpich's plan for whipping the brainpower state into a yearlong civic frenzy.

All the big ones are there — the Winter Carnival in St. Paul, the Aquatennial in Minneapolis, the Finnish ethnic festival in Embarrass — and there is a new trans-Minnesota bicycle tour that will be just as good as Iowa's.

But there is a gaping hole on the calendar the first Saturday of March. Organizers of the Mud and Bud Gizzard Feed, an annual fund-raiser at Roy's Tavern in Theilman, a hamlet of 71 people in Wabasha County, are having no part of Celebrate Minnesota. Likewise the town's annual Memorial Day street dance.

Turned down on its request for $1,375 from Celebrate Minnesota to salvage and fix up the local park and miffed that bigger, richer Wabasha got an $11,715 grant, the Theilman Sportsmen's Club has little good to say about the governor's celebration.

**Celebration** continued on page 12A

# School 'combinations' ease consolidation woes

By Mary Jane Smetanka
Staff Writer

**Henderson, Minn.**
At Kay's Kitchen, where gray-haired men in feed caps and overalls linger over coffee and the day's news, the regulars shrug when asked how they feel about Henderson high school students going to school in nearby Le Sueur, Minn., next year.

There's no money, they say. It's inevitable. Best for the kids.

Two years from next fall, if things go according to plan, Henderson and Le Sueur schools will be one. This spring's graduating class of 15 students, Henderson's 108th senior class, will be the last.

**Schools** continued on page 5A

**To our readers:** I am pleased to tell you that we will be increasing our use of recycled newsprint to a full 20 percent by 1992. A new source in Thunder Bay, Ontario, can now provide us with a steady supply. We won't stop with 20 percent and are continuing to work with our other suppliers.

More good news is that the new recycling plant will create a demand for used newspapers. It will consume about 90,000 tons of old papers a year, far more than is now collected in Minnesota. We strongly encourage our readers to recycle rather than discard your newspapers.

The dilemma of waste is one that affects all of us. To learn more about how to solve it, write the Star Tribune Public Relations Department. We'll be happy to send you a copy of our new publication, "Reduce, Reuse, Recycle." Write us at 425 Portland Av., Minneapolis, MN. 55488. By working together and sharing our knowledge, we can resolve this complex and challenging issue.

**Roger Parkinson, Publisher and President**

## Almanac

**Sunday, February 11, 1990**
**42nd day; 323 to go this year**
**Sunrise: 7:20. Sunset: 5:35**

Mostly sunny; high in the upper 30s.



**Telephones/**

| | |
|---|---|
| Circulation | 673-4343 |



Volume VIII/Number 313 13 sections

Bellows gets 50th, 51st goals as North Stars rout Red Wings/1C

MINNEAPOLIS EDITION

■ Traffic concerns may delay building of skyscraper/1B

Star Tribune

FRIDAY/March 23/1990 NEWSPAPER OF THE TWIN CITIES 35¢

# Jury: No Hazelwood felony

## Former Exxon captain is convicted of one misdemeanor

From News Services

**Anchorage, Alaska**
Joseph Hazelwood, accused of being drunk, reckless and most responsible for the nation's worst oil spill, was acquitted of all but a minor pollution charge Thursday.

The former skipper of the Exxon Valdez was found not guilty of felony mischief, operating a vessel while under the influence of alcohol and reckless endangerment.

The guilty verdict was for the negligent discharge of oil, a misdemeanor carrying a maximum penalty of 90 days in jail and a $1,000 fine, far less than the 7¼ years and $61,000 fine he faced if convicted on all counts.

The Exxon tanker ran aground and spilled nearly 11 million gallons of oil into Alaska's Prince William Sound on March 24, 1989.

Superior Court Judge Karl Johnstone set sentencing for this afternoon.

There were bursts of applause in the court room as the judge read the three verdicts of "not guilty."

Jurors said they were swayed by defense arguments that the grounding was an accident, not a crime. Some members of the panel said after the verdict that they felt Hazelwood had been negligent, but not criminally reckless, when he left the bridge about 12 to 15 minutes before the accident.

Juror Terrill Smith said he and the others on the panel based their decision on the law and evidence, and "the state just didn't have the evidence."

Hazelwood's New York lawyer, Michael Chalos, a former classmate of his at the New York State University Maritime Academy at Fort Schuyler, N.Y., clapped the skipper on the shoulder and hit the counsel table with his hand at the first "not guilty" verdict.

**Hazelwood** continued on page 12A

# Moscow steps up war of nerves on Lithuania

From News Services

**Moscow, U.S.S.R.**
Soviet President Mikhail Gorbachev's campaign of psychological pressure on Lithuania intensified Thursday as he demanded that the Vilnius government end any plans for a self-defense system and ordered the KGB to reinforce Soviet border posts.

Moscow also reportedly was sending a team of prosecutors to the breakaway Baltic state to halt "extremist misdeeds," while a convoy of personnel carriers and trucks rolled through Vilnius, the Lithuanian capital.

President Bush implored the Soviet Union not to use force to block the secession of Lithuania but acknowledged he was half a world away from "certain realities" governing Moscow's control over the republic.

The Kremlin, continuing to flood state-controlled news outlets with a mood of heightening crisis, announced that Gorbachev had sent a protest to Lithuanian officials over their continuing steps to carry out their declaration of independence from Soviet authority, made 12 days ago. Those steps include forming volunteer detachments to replace KGB

**Lithuania** continued on page 14A

# 18 years later, man charged with murder

By Mark Brunswick
Staff Writer

Eighteen springs ago, Herbert Jahnke of north Minneapolis went out to buy bread and was stabbed to death when someone tried to steal the $1.75 in his pocket and the bike he was riding.

A suspect was arrested and released and then arrested again and released, but no one has ever faced trial for the slaying of the 24-year-old part-time mailroom worker. Wednesday, prompted by information from a witness who came forward three months ago, Minneapolis police arrested the same suspect they jailed and released in 1972 and 1973. Lavertes Burch, now 34, was charged with second-degree murder. He was in the Hennepin County jail last night in lieu of $150,000 bail.

"Nobody likes an unsolved murder, especially a homicide cop," said Inspector Sherman Otto, head of the department's criminal investigation division. "All those years. It's a closure for the family. You can be happy about that."

Police and prosecutors now have another chance to try Burch, who is accused of asking Jahnke for his bike and money and then stabbing him in the chest when he refused. Burch was 16. Jahnke and his wife had moved to Minneapolis from Chicago several months earlier.

"It was a heinous, senseless act," said Capt. Carl Johnson, who was head of the homicide division at the time. "Whether it was out of fear or friendship, 25 people witnessed what went on there and did not come forward."

That was one of the key reasons the case against Burch fell apart several times: one witness was arrested after failing to appear before a grand jury, then left the state and was not available for a later hearing. Several witnesses testified before another grand jury in 1973, but because Burch was only 17, it was believed that a juvenile judge would first have to certify him as an adult before any regular District Court proceedings against him could be initiated. Before that happened, though, he disappeared,

**Arrest** continued on page 14A

## A special victory for the Polars

Staff Photo by Richard Sennott

**North's Lamar Elliot (34) and David Dennis (40) celebrated the Polars' 60-54 victory over Cretin-Derham Hall in Thursday's quarterfinals of the boys' basketball tournament. The Polars (16-8) were led by Dennis' 25 points as they rallied to knock off the No. 2-rated Raiders (21-3).**

| Class AA | Class A |
|---|---|
| **Minneapolis North 60, Cretin-Derham Hall 54** | **De La Salle 66, Russell-Tyler-Ruthton 53** |
| **Fergus Falls 49, Bloomington Jefferson 48** | **Lake City 60, Staples-Motley 47** |
| **Chaska 76, St. Francis 61** | **Mankato Loyola 72, East Central 53** |
| **Owatonna 72, Mounds View 59** | **Fairmont 76, Mahnomen 47** |

# NWA crew charged with flying while intoxicated

By Randy Furst
Staff Writer

The captain of Northwest Flight 650 was so drunk at a Moorhead bar on March 7 that he fell out of his chair and later got lost trying to find his motel a block away, the U.S. attorney's office said Thursday.

Norman Prouse, along with copilot Robert Kirchner and flight engineer Joseph Balzer were charged yesterday with one federal felony count of flying under the influence of alcohol, U.S. Attorney Jerry Arnold announced.

The three are scheduled to surrender to the FBI in Minneapolis next Thursday morning and will be arraigned before U.S. Magistrate J. Earl Cudd. The case will be presented to a federal grand jury within 30 days.

They were arrested at Minneapolis-St. Paul International Airport March 8 after flying their Boeing 727 from Fargo with 91 passengers aboard. Arnold said that if the men are convict-

**Pilots** continued on page 11A

# Idaho Legislature passes strictest state abortion bill

From News Services

**Boise, Idaho**
The Idaho Legislature approved the most restrictive abortion law in any state Thursday after an emotional debate that touched on such subjects as Romanian dictators and pioneer values.

The bill was specifically fashioned by abortion opponents outside of Idaho to give the Supreme Court an opportunity to overturn Roe vs. Wade, the 1973 Supreme Court decision that recognized a legal right to abortion.

Gov. Cecil Andrus has not said whether he will sign the bill, which passed the Senate yesterday by a vote of 25 to 17; it was approved by the House several weeks ago. The measure would take effect July 1.

Andrus, a Democrat in a state dominated by Republicans, has said he does not support abortion except in cases of rape, incest, severe fetal deformity and threats to the physical health of the woman.

**Abortion** continued on page 12A

## Almanac

**Friday, March 23, 1990**
**82nd day; 283 to go this year**
**Sunrise: 6:11. Sunset: 6:29**

Clear and cold weather with a high in the mid-20s is forecast for the Twin Cities today. The wind will be from the west to northwest at 15 to 20 mph.




Volume VIII/Number 353 6 sections

Associated Press

## Art of debate

**Canadians are caught up in a debate on the value of this painting. Page 4A**

# Cost of medical care takes a seat at the head of the bargaining table

By Chuck Haga
Staff Writer

The issue that has 1,400 Ramsey County workers on strike this week — the cost and control of employee health benefits — has become one of the most important and bitterly contested labor issues throughout the country.

"These days, you get to wages only after you deal with health issues," said Peter Benner, a union official who represents Minnesota state employees. "It used to be the other way around."

In fact, Benner said, the issue has become "too emotional for the bargaining table." Unions and employers need to cooperate more before contract time, he said, whether establishing "preferred provider organizations" or jointly demanding accountability.

Virtually everyone agrees that something has to be done about costs.

"We are in a crisis, and we are moving toward an even greater crisis," said Patricia Drury, executive director of the Minnesota Coalition on

**Health care** continued on page 12A

# Princeton gambling take includes load of woes

By Robert Franklin
Staff Writer

**Princeton, Minn.**
This Rum River town, which calls itself the City of Flowers, is also a city of pulltabs.

Its six gambling organizations donate more than $400,000 a year, mostly for youth activities, the food shelf, parks, the library, police equipment and other causes in town. The hockey group alone, sponsoring gambling in nearby towns, has raised about $100,000 a year for its arena mortgage, ice time for more than 200 youngsters and other expenses.

That's welcome cash in any town of 3,400. The gambling has brought misery as well as money, however. Princeton's gambling represents an unusual combination of pulltab problems and broader policy issues that are being discussed at the state level:

■ The Princeton Youth Hockey Association, torn by dissension, has sidestepped some gambling rules, been audited by the state, lost its most lucrative gambling site and has discussed selling the arena. The Internal Revenue Service called the gambling unrelated business income and sent a tax bill for $109,000, but that is being held in abeyance pending an IRS ruling from Washington.

**Princeton** continued on page 15A

**North Stars fall 5-1; Wolves routed 110-77; Twins bow 3-1/1C**

**MINNEAPOLIS EDITION**

■ 2 killed, cop hurt in separate incidents in Minneapolis/**1B**


# Star Tribune

FRIDAY April 13/1990 NEWSPAPER OF THE TWIN CITIES 35¢


# East Germany apologizes

## Begs forgiveness for Nazi atrocities

From News Services

**Berlin**
East Germany's first democratic government began its work Thursday by trying to heal the past and seal the future, asking Jews and the Soviet Union to forgive East Germans for their role in Nazi atrocities and pushing to achieve economic and social unification with West Germany by July 1.

In a rapid-fire series of resolutions, the new parliament assured Poland that its border with East Germany is inviolable, demanded that the new Germany maintain East Germany's constitutional guarantees of work and housing and agreed that a united Germany should join NATO, but only if the alliance changes its nuclear strategy.

The Volkskammer, or People's Chamber, elected Lothar de Maiziere as the country's first non-Communist prime minister The vote was 265-108 for the quiet former musician whose Christian Democratic Union won last month's election.

De Maiziere announced a 24-member Cabinet that emerged from nearly a month of negotiations with four other parties, including the main opposition, the Social Democrats. The resulting grand coalition, a clean sweep of Communist control, gives the new government the two-thirds majority of parliament it needs to make the wholesale constitutional changes necessary to reunite the two Germanys.

"The goal is a united Germany in a united Europe," De Maiziere said. "I hope that the negotiations go quickly and bring good results." The new coalition announced its support for unification "without delay," to be achieved through West German an-


**Germany** continued on page 12A


### President has 'early glaucoma'

President Bush was diagnosed Thursday as having "an early glaucoma" in his left eye, but he said it had not affected his vision.

The glaucoma, which was found during a routine physical examination at Bethesda Naval Hospital, will be treated with prescription eye drops, said press secretary Marlin Fitzwater


Page 7A


# Star Tribune, playwright Wilson win Pulitzers

"I've said for years that prizes in journalism don't mean much. That was before I won. I guess I was wrong."
– Chris Ison

## Investigative reporters honored for fire series

By Chuck Haga
Staff Writer

Star Tribune reporters Lou Kilzer and Chris Ison won the Pulitzer Prize for investigative reporting Thursday for "Fire in St. Paul," a two-part series that exposed a thriving industry that profited from arson and suspicious fires, with the assistance of several key firefighters.

"I've said for years that prizes in journalism don't mean much," Ison told his colleagues, smiling. "That was before I won. I guess I was wrong."

It was the newspaper's first Pulitzer in 31 years, and Executive Editor Joel Kramer told the staff, assembled for a noisy champagne celebration, that everyone could claim a part of the award.

The arson series "was not an easy story," Kramer said. It came from "a combination of old-fashioned gumshoe detective work with modern, computerized, data-base reporting. And then we told it as a gripping tale, and it's clear that the community was gripped."

Kilzer, 39, is a special projects reporter who joined the Star Tribune in 1987. A 1973 graduate of Yale University, he previously worked at the Rocky Mountain News and the Denver Post, where he shared a 1986 Pulitzer Prize for an investigative report on missing children.

"It doesn't get old," he said.

Ison, 32, who covered St. Paul city government before joining the projects office a year ago, came to the Star Tribune in 1986. He previously worked at the Duluth News-Tribune. A native of Crandon, Wis., he graduated in 1983 from the University of Minnesota, where he was editor of the Minnesota Daily.

The two reporters and top editors huddled around a video display terminal in the newsroom and waited for the award results, as the rest of the staff gathered around.

The news came at 2:07 p.m. and was followed by cheers, onfetti and — thanks to a temporary suspension of a company rule prohibiting alcohol on the premises — champagne.

Kramer also saluted "the extraordinary achievement" of Star Tribune photographer Stormi Greener, who for the second time was one of three Pulitzer finalists.

Kramer read from an Academy Awards-style list, thanking editors, reporters, photographers, graphic designers, tape transcribers, library researchers, staff lawyers and others.

The newspaper "has received an incredible amount of national recognition in recent months," he said. "I'm especially proud that these awards are not for one or two pieces of work, but for many, from many parts of the newsroom.

"We all should feel proud because (the Pulitzer) is not a fluke. It's a


**Pulitzer Prize** continued on 15A

Staff Photo by Brian Peterson

**Star Tribune reporters Lou Kilzer, left, and Chris Ison won the Pulitzer Prize for investigative reporting Thursday.**

August Wilson

## St. Paul dramatist's award is his second

By Peter Vaughan
Staff Writer

**New York, N.Y.**
August Wilson was understandably beaming Thursday afternoon after an interview with a reporter in the Hotel Edison coffee shop was interrupted by the news that he had won his second Pulitzer Prize for drama, for "The Piano Lesson."

"It's a surprise. It's great!" said the St. Paul playwright, who won his first Pulitzer in 1987 for "Fences." "Now there's two, and I get to go to the luncheon again. Wow!" he said with almost childlike glee.

In some respects, this Pulitzer is the more important of the two, he said. "I like this play very much. I'm glad it was chosen. In some ways, it's more important, since it deals with larger issues like what to do with your legacy," he said. "There is a larger question here than in 'Fences,' which is about the life of a black man born in 1904."

"The Piano Lesson," which opens on Broadway next week, recounts the


**Wilson** continued on page 14A


# Many taxpayers hoping for refund from state may get unhappy surprise

By Dennis J. McGrath
Staff Writer

■ Waited until the last minute again, huh? Here's a tip: **Story on Page 1D.**

More than 200,000 Minnesotans may be in for a surprise this weekend when they fill out state income-tax forms and end up having to mail a check along with the form.

Because of changes in tax withholding tables, many taxpayers who have always banked on receiving a state refund will find they owe money this year, Minnesota revenue officials said Thursday.

That doesn't mean people will be paying more taxes. They'll just be paying them in a different way. They'll pay now, instead of having had them withheld from paychecks during 1989.

The change results from a new withholding formula put into effect in July 1988, which took full effect for 1989 income. The formula was altered because "For several years the state significantly overwithheld," said Finance Commissioner Peter Hutchinson. "The purpose of chang-


**State taxes** continued on page 14A


### Ex-governor pleads guilty

Arch Moore Jr., the former governor of West Virginia, agreed Thursday to plead guilty to extortion, mail fraud, tax fraud and obstruction of justice, according to a federal prosecutor. Moore had been indicted for illegal acts related to election campaigns in 1984 and 1988 and to his third term in office. He could be sentenced to up to 36 years in prison and fined $1.2 million.


Page 7A


# Estonia parliament votes to end all military service

New York Times

**Moscow, U.S.S.R.**
The Estonian parliament has voted overwhelmingly to end all military service in the republic, a move certain to increase tension between Moscow and the independence-minded Baltic republics, Estonians said Thursday.

After a rambunctious debate, the legislators voted 71-3 late Wednesday night to rescind Soviet constitutional articles governing the draft. Angered by the proposal, 27 pro-Moscow deputies refused to take part in the vote.

Military service has become one of the most contentious issues between Moscow and the Baltic republics of Estonia, Latvia and Lithuania as they seek to regain the independence they lost in 1940, when the Soviet Union


**Baltic** continued on page 14A


# Minneapolis working to avoid growth-caused traffic tangles

By Laurie Blake
Staff Writer

The days of driving alone to work in downtown Minneapolis and finding a parking spot near the office will come slowly but surely to an end for many drivers in the next 20 years.

City officials plan to convert most of the 13,000 spots in city-owned downtown parking garages to spaces reserved for vehicles carrying two or more passengers. Private ramp owners, who control another 44,000 spots, will be encouraged to do the same.

Parking changes will be one of a number of transportation-related side effects of booming downtown development. City officials also are count-


**Downtown** continued on page 8A


## Almanac

**Friday, April 13, 1990**
**103rd day; 262 to go this year**
**Sunrise: 6:33. Sunset: 7:56**

High around 50.






Volume IX/Number 9 6 sections


# Sorry, Charlie! Three U.S. canners won't buy tuna netted with dolphins

Associated Press

**Washington, D.C.**
Three U.S. tuna canners, including the world's largest, said Thursday that they will no longer buy or sell tuna captured along with dolphins. Environmentalists who have long sought to protect dolphins from fishing nets praised the decisions.

The actions were announced by companies selling the StarKist, Bumble Bee and Chicken of the Sea brands.

Environmentalists and lawmakers said they hoped the move would save some of the estimated 100,000 dolphins that die annually in huge nets used to catch schools of tuna.

"StarKist will not purchase any tuna caught in association with dolphins," said Anthony O'Reilly, president of the H.J. Heinz Co., which owns the StarKist Seafood Co. "StarKist will sell only dolphin-free tuna."

The change could cost consumers "a couple or more cents" per can, O'Reilly said, adding that he hoped


**Tuna** continued on page 12A

**SUNDAY**

**Fate of Schmidt brewery dim as talks fold again/1B**

**Gladden's double in 8th delivers Twins to win/1C**

TRAVEL
**Pure wilderness**

MAGAZINE
**Queen of tragedy**

ARTS
**Book a vacation**

**MINNEAPOLIS**
EDITION

■ NWA pilot charged with drunken driving/1B

■ Man, 82, swindled out of life savings/1B

# Star Tribune

SUNDAY/June 3/1990 NEWSPAPER OF THE TWIN CITIES $1.25

$1.50 outside the Twin Cities metro area

# Bush, Gorbachev talk, relax

## Leaders move to Camp David in last day of summit

From News Services

**Camp David, Md.**
President Bush and Soviet President Mikhail Gorbachev withdrew to the relative informality of Camp David Saturday to test whether their growing rapport can narrow differences on unresolved problems.

But Bush's spokesman said the leaders skirted two of the toughest issues that divide them: Germany and Lithuania.

■ Gorbachev left the summit smiling, but at home he faces the most severe test of his five years in power. **Page 17A.**

The final full day of their summit moved from the formal splendor of the White House to the rustic mountainside where the presidents took off their ties for relaxed talks.

The First Ladies, riding in another helicopter, joined the presidents at the 143-acre presidential compound 60 miles from Washington, D.C.

On a brilliant sunny day, Gorbachev and his wife, Raisa, strolled around the paths that lace the compound and stopped to pitch horseshoes.

After several days debate on questions involving arms, economics, Europe and the Baltic secession drives, the Bush-Gorbachev agenda involved discussion of less contentious regional issues, including Nicaragua, the Middle East, Afghanistan, Cambodia, Cuba, El Salvador, India, Pakistan and the Middle East.

According to spokesman Marlin Fitzwater, Bush told Gorbachev that Cuban President Fidel Castro was swimming against the tide of democracy.

Gorbachev's spokesman, Arkady Maslennikov, said there were "not any formal agreements" on the regional issues.

**Summit** continued on page 17A

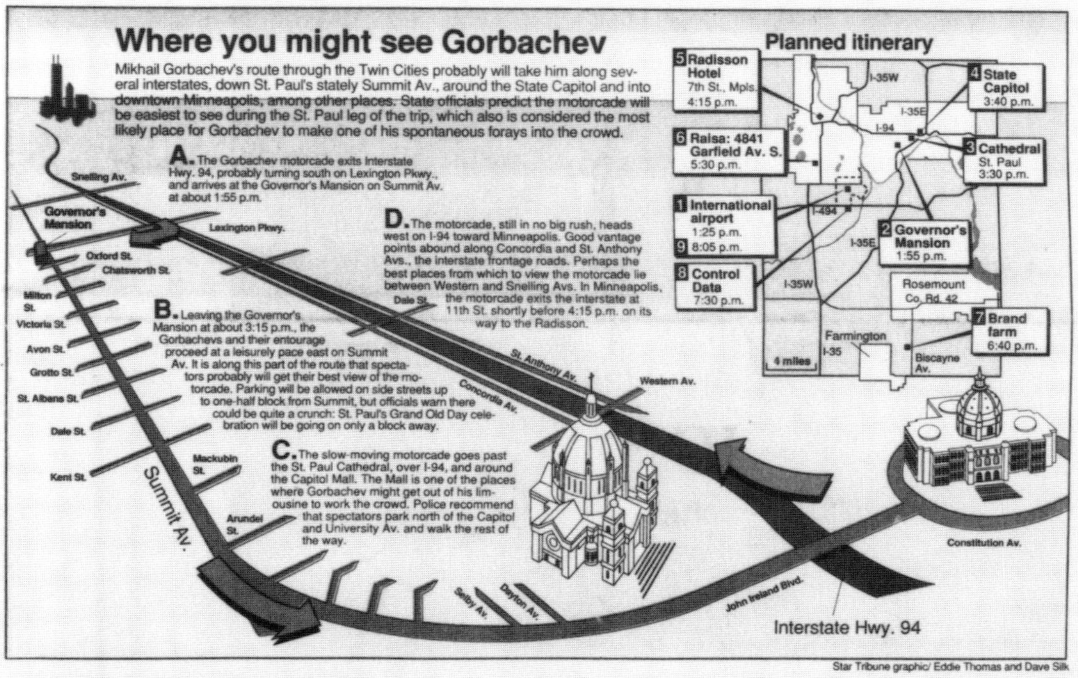

Where you might see Gorbachev
Mikhail Gorbachev's route through the Twin Cities probably will take him along several interstates, down St. Paul's stately Summit Av., around the State Capitol and into downtown Minneapolis, among other places. State officials predict the motorcade will be easiest to see during the St. Paul leg of the trip, which also is considered the most likely place for Gorbachev to make one of his spontaneous forays into the crowd.
A. The Gorbachev motorcade exits Interstate Hwy. 94, probably turning south on Lexington Pkwy., and arrives at the Governor's Mansion on Summit Av. at about 1:55 p.m.
B. Leaving the Governor's Mansion at about 3:15 p.m., the Gorbachevs and their entourage proceed at a leisurely pace east on Summit Av. It is along this part of the route that spectators probably will get their best view of the motorcade. Parking will be allowed on side streets up to one-half block from Summit, but officials warn there could be quite a crunch: St. Paul's Grand Old Day celebration will be going on only a block away.
C. The slow-moving motorcade goes past the St. Paul Cathedral, over I-94, and around the Capitol Mall. The Mall is one of the places where Gorbachev might get out of his limousine to work the crowd. Police recommend that spectators park north of the Capitol and University Av. and walk the rest of the way.
D. The motorcade, still in no big rush, heads west on I-94 toward Minneapolis. Good vantage points abound along Concordia and St. Anthony Avs., the interstate frontage roads. Perhaps the best places from which to view the motorcade lie between Western and Snelling Avs. In Minneapolis, the motorcade exits the interstate at 11th St. shortly before 4:15 p.m. on its way to the Radisson.
Snelling Av.
Governor's Mansion
Lexington Pkwy.
Oxford St.
Chatsworth St.
Milton St.
Victoria St.
Avon St.
Grotto St.
St. Albans St.
Dale St.
Kent St.
Mackubin St.
Arundel St.
Summit Av.
Dale St.
St. Anthony Av.
Concordia Av.
Western Av.
Selby Av.
Dayton Av.
John Ireland Blvd.
Constitution Av.
Interstate Hwy. 94
Planned itinerary
5 Radisson Hotel 7th St., Mpls. 4:15 p.m.
6 Raisa: 4841 Garfield Av. S. 5:30 p.m.
1 International airport 1:25 p.m.
9 8:05 p.m.
8 Control Data 7:30 p.m.
4 State Capitol 3:40 p.m.
3 Cathedral St. Paul 3:30 p.m.
2 Governor's Mansion 1:55 p.m.
7 Brand farm 6:40 p.m.
I-35W
I-35E
I-94
I-494
Rosemount
Co. Rd. 42
Farmington
I-35
Biscayne Av.
4 miles

Star Tribune graphic/ Eddie Thomas and Dave Silk

Mikhail Gorbachev

# Making history

## Time will tell if he will be triumphant

By Eric Black
Staff Writer

Does Mikhail Gorbachev have history by the tail, or is it the other way around?

This year, Time magazine named Gorbachev "Man of the Decade." When Gorbachev's resignation was rumored, world stock markets plummeted. A recent poll found that Western Europeans favor Gorbachev for president of a united Europe. And when Gorbachev lands here today, he will focus more international attention on the Twin Cities than at any time since — well — probably ever.

Since Gorbachev has shaken up the world order, he has held the imagination of the Western World in thrall. Gorby frees Poland. Gorby cuts arms deal. Gorby tells truth about rotten Soviet economy.

And yet his efforts to improve that rotten economy have been an abject failure. Lines are longer for fewer, lousier goods. And perhaps the most dramatic line is that of non-Russian republics waiting to secede.

**Gorbachev** on page 16A

# Summit, Capitol, I-94 frontage roads might be best Gorby-watching spots

By Norman Draper
Staff Writer

You might just see the vehicles — 40 to 60 of them, including long, black limousines with windows darkened so you can't see inside and with no identifying marks to distinguish one from the other.

Then again, you could be the next Kimberly Spartin.

Spartin was part of the lunchtime crowd gathered on a busy Washington, D.C., street corner in 1987 when Soviet President Mikhail Gorbachev popped out of his limo and started shaking hands and talking with the pedestrians. After he shook her hand, the mesmerized Spartin looked at her hand and gushed: "It was like the coming of the second Messiah or something."

Officials are expecting the unexpected when Gorbachev visits the Twin Cities today. Given Gorbachev's penchant for occasional crowd-mingling, nobody will be surprised if he orders his motorcade to halt somewhere along the route so he can schmooze a little with the common folk.

Where that might happen is anybody's guess.

**Visit** continued on page 18A

### If you're going to be outside:

The weather forecast for today indicates that it'll start out windy and wet, but that showers may be ending by the time Soviet President Gorbachev arrives in the afternoon.

The morning will be very windy, with cool temperatures and a high likelihood of rain. The afternoon high might reach the low 60s, and while it will stay cloudy, the chances of rain will diminish.

### If you're going to be inside:

It will be dry and not so windy indoors throughout the metro area, and TV and radio plans plenty of visit coverage.

**TV:** WCCO-TV (Ch. 4) will cover Gorbachev live from 1-7 p.m. KSTP-TV (Ch. 5) will have live coverage from 1-7:30 p.m. KARE-TV (Ch. 11) will have live coverage from 12:45 p.m. until 7 p.m., with a break at 5:30 for local news. **Radio:** WCCO (830 AM) will have live coverage from 11:40 a.m. to 6:45 p.m. and KNOW (1330 AM) will be live from 1-7 p.m.

### Related articles in today's paper:

## Rex Harrison, 82, dies in his sleep

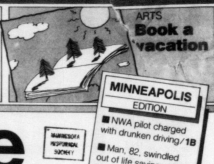

Sir Rex Harrison, who won Tony and Oscar awards for his stage and screen portrayals of Prof. Henry Higgins in "My Fair Lady," died in his sleep Saturday. During his 66-year career he also talked to the animals as the lovable Dr. Dolittle and was knighted last year by Queen Elizabeth.

The 82-year-old actor died of pancreatic cancer at his New York City apartment, three weeks after dropping out of the hit Broadway show "The Circle." **Page 8B.**

# U.S. fertility rate appears to be rising with baby boomlet, but will it all last?

By Paul Klauda
Staff Writer

The baby business is booming.

Just when experts saw a decline coming, 4 million tykes were born nationwide last year, the most since the baby-boom finale of 1964. Perhaps more significantly, the fertility rate of U.S. women continued to inch upward, reaching levels not seen since the early 1970s.

What in Dr. Spock is going on here? Until recently, the birth boomlet has been attributed to the increase in the number of women passing through childbearing years. But now it appears that some groups of women, most certainly those in their 30s and quite possibly those in their 20s, are having more children, too.

The new figures prompted a respected marketing newsletter to cast this year as a significant "fork in the trend road" for childbearing. If the number of births doesn't fall, "then we are looking at something new — or maybe at a return to the old," according to the May issue of Numbers News, published by American Demographics magazine.

The question, and perhaps the key to whether births and fertility will continue to rise, is whether young women will delay childbearing as older women did, or start sooner. The answer will profoundly influence planning for health care, schools, social services and consumer buying.

"We're still kind of keeping an eye out to see what's happening at the

**Births** continued on page 11A

## Almanac

**Sunday, June 3, 1990**
**154th day; 211 to go this year**
**Sunrise: 5:29. Sunset: 8:53**

### Today's weather/

Mostly Gorby, high in 50s.

### Telephones/

| | |
|---|---|
| General Information | 673-4000 |
| Classifieds | 673-7000 |
| Circulation | 673-4343 |

Volume IX/Number 60 13 sections

Nolan Ryan fails to reach 300th victory; Tapani wins his 10th/1C

MINNEAPOLIS EDITION

■ Some say new police promotion test is biased/1B

Star Tribune

THURSDAY/July 26/1990 NEWSPAPER OF THE TWIN CITIES B 35¢

'The evidence of knowing and willful misconduct is clear and convincing . . .'
**Sen. Howell Heflin, D-Ala., ethics committee chairman**

'After this is all over and we denounce him, we still want him to be our friend.'
**Sen. William Armstrong, R-Colo.**

# Senate formally denounces Durenberger for misconduct

## He apologizes, pledges to be a better senator

**By Cliff Haas**
Washington Bureau Correspondent

**Washington, D.C.**
The Senate voted without dissent Wednesday to denounce Sen. Dave Durenberger for "reprehensible" financial conduct that was "clearly and unequivocally unethical" and ordered him to pay up to $123,000 in restitution.

After the punishment was imposed by a 96-0 vote, Durenberger, R-Minn., told a hushed Senate chamber: "To my colleagues here, who know me and work with me, I would just say how deeply sorry I am for the painful, and the necessary, experience we've just been through and . . . for that extra burden that my misconduct has placed on each of you."

He added, "As a result of what I have lived — and it has been a costly education — I have reordered my personal and my professional priorities to be, first, a better man and, then, a better senator. And the proof of that . . . will be my actions over the next four years."

Later, at a brief news conference, Durenberger renewed his vow to serve the remainder of his Senate term, which runs through 1994. He did not say whether he would seek reelection.

The denouncement was a bitter moment for Durenberger, 55, who in his 12 years in the Senate has cultivated the image of a thoughtful, principled man embodying his home state's best political traits. It also was an unpleasant task for the Senate, which

**Durenberger** continued on page 16A

Associated Press

**"Today is an ending and it's a beginning," Sen. Dave Durenberger told his colleagues on Wednesday.**

## Analysis

## He may lose prestige but his power is still intact

**By Tom Hamburger**
Washington Bureau Correspondent

**Washington, D.C.**
Joseph McCarthy was ostracized by his colleagues after formal condemnation by the Senate in 1957. Herman Talmadge was viewed with disdain after senators denounced him in 1979.

Dave Durenberger will fare better.

Although Sen. Durenberger's sanction is the same as former Sen. Talmadge's, the character of the two men and their crimes are viewed differently by their peers.

The editorial-page debate over whether Durenberger should resign often has turned on the question of the Minnesota Republican's continued effectiveness, an imprecise buzz word in electoral politics.

In Washington, Durenberger will lose prestige and for months he will carry a blemish. But in the Capitol such

**Analysis** continued on page 17A

### DAY OF RECKONING

**INSIDE:**

■ Sen. Dave Durenberger's denouncement is one of the darkest chapters in Minnesota's political annals, historians and political scientists said. **16A.**

■ The Senate tried to put on its best face during a painful moment for one of its own. **Analysis, 16A.**

## Dark IR day lightened by senators' praise

**Doug Grow**

Leaders of the Independent-Republican Party couldn't have been more surprised.

They'd come to work Wednesday expecting the worst in the matter of one of their own, Dave Durenberger. They'd expected that when the members of the U.S. Senate got through officially denouncing Durenberger, the entire party would be feeling bruised. After all, in the history of the Senate, precious few senators had stood where Durenberger was standing.

But as the afternoon wore on, the IR leaders weren't sad at all. Why, at times during what was supposed to be Durenberger's darkest hour, they felt almost giddy.

Senator after senator stood up and sang the praises of the man who'd pleaded guilty to breaking rules to benefit himself. An event that was to have been punitive sounded at times like a Durenberger testimonial.

"If he decides to run again, he can just use films of this for his campaign," said Barb Sykora, IR chairwoman.

"You couldn't afford to buy this sort of (television) time," said another

**Grow** continued on page 17A

## Main Hazelwood charges dismissed

### His ship license is suspended

**Associated Press**

**Long Beach, Calif.**
The Coast Guard dismissed charges of drunkenness and misconduct against Exxon Valdez skipper Joseph Hazelwood on Wednesday, but suspended his license as a ship's master.

The defense alleged that Hazelwood's blood alcohol tests were botched and then covered up, but the Coast Guard denied this was why it dismissed the charges.

At an administrative hearing, Hazelwood pleaded no contest to two allegations stemming from the wreck of his tanker, which unleashed the nation's worst oil spill in Alaska's Prince William Sound.

The plea that resulted in a nine-month license suspension covered two allegations: that he violated Coast Guard policy by drinking liquor less than four hours before taking command of the Exxon Valdez, and that he improperly left the vessel's bridge while it was headed for jagged Bligh Reef.

Joseph Hazelwood

**Hazelwood** continued on page 21A

### Iraq, Kuwait schedule talks

Egyptian President Hosni Mubarak said that Iraq and Kuwait will open direct talks this weekend over oil policy and boundary differences.

Meanwhile, diplomatic sources said that Iraq will begin pulling back its troops from the border. The troop withdrawal had been a precondition for talks on Kuwait's part.

**Page 4A.**

## Eastern, some top managers charged with falsifying records

**Associated Press**

**New York, N.Y.**
Eastern Airlines and several top managers were charged Wednesday with falsifying safety and maintenance records in New York and Atlanta in a scheme that allegedly allowed unsafe planes to fly.

The 60-count criminal indictment is unprecedented in the airline industry and adds to Eastern's problems in seeking to regain passengers, rebuild service and reorganize in bankruptcy court after a strike.

The charges, handed up by a federal grand jury in U.S. District Court in New York City, completed a 10-month investigation and plea bargain talks that collapsed when Eastern refused to admit to a conspiracy.

"Thousands of innocent passengers may have been put at risk every day by the criminal actions of these defendants," Attorney General Dick Thornburgh said in a statement.

The indictment charges conspiracy to defraud the government, wire fraud, falsification of documents and obstruction of justice.

**Eastern** continued on page 21A

## Cole says prison system forced him into spot where he had to kill officer

**By Dennis Cassano**
Staff Writer

Phillip Cole testified at his murder trial Wednesday and railed against the prison system that he said pushed him into the situation where he shot a police officer.

"I hate the system with every fiber of my body; I hate 'em," he said.

He testified that he did not intend to kill officer Michael Hogan last Dec. 15 in a J.C. Penney store in Hutchinson, Minn.

Cole, who said he had been taking drugs for days and hadn't gotten much sleep, said that when he pointed his revolver at Hogan, the officer put his hands on top of his head. Cole said that when he glanced away he saw Hogan move and he fired out of panic over the fear of going back to prison and because of the effects of the drugs and lack of sleep.

"My intentions were not to kill officer Hogan. If my intentions were to kill officer Hogan, I would have killed April Brandt," he testified in

**Cole** continued on page 21A

### Almanac

**Thursday, July 26, 1990**
**207th day; 158 to go this year**
**Sunrise: 5:52. Sunset: 8:47**

High around 80.



Circulation 673-4343



Volume IX/Number 113 8 sections

SPORTS: **North Stars bring back Bobby Smith; Twins lose 5-3**/1C

**MINNEAPOLIS** EDITION

# Star Tribune

**WEDNESDAY**/August 8/1990 NEWSPAPER OF THE TWIN CITIES 35¢

■ Residents turn out to reclaim neighborhoods from crime and fear/**1B**

R

# U.S. troops to aid Saudis

## Bush dispatches forces to join multinational effort

**From News Services**

**Washington, D.C.**
President Bush on Tuesday ordered U.S. military aircraft and thousands of troops to Saudi Arabia after King Fahd approved the deployment of a multinational force to defend his nation against a growing Iraqi invasion force in Kuwait, administration officials said.

Capitol Hill sources said Egypt and Morocco are joining the effort to counter the Iraqi troops massed near the Saudi border with Kuwait.

While using an oil embargo in an effort to reverse the Kuwaiti invasion, allied forces hoped the unusual multinational defense would deter Iraqi President Saddam Hussein's million-man army from storming the Saudi oil fields as well.

There was no announcement from the White House of the military moves; word came instead from Pentagon sources and from Capitol Hill. "We're not playing games. There are strategic reasons why I can't tell you," said White House spokesman Marlin Fitzwater. "We believe there is an imminent threat to Saudi Arabia."

While U.S. and Arab forces were mobilizing yesterday, Turkey shut down the Iraqis' vital oil outlet to the Mediterranean Sea, honoring a U.N. trade embargo ordered to punish Iraq for last week's lightning conquest of Kuwait. In Saudi Arabia, the Iraqi oil flow was reported to be slowing to a trickle through another pipeline.

Despite the global pressure, Hussein remained defiant, declaring in a nationwide speech that he would never back down and leave Kuwait.

"We would rather die than be humiliated, and we will pluck out the eyes of those who attack the Arab nation," he said.

The State Department said that 39 Americans are being detained in a Baghdad hotel and 500 others had been blocked from leaving Iraq since the invasion. There were reports that some might be allowed to leave

**Gulf** continued on page 13A

## Cornered Hussein likely to surrender or attack

**By Michael Wines**
New York Times

**Washington, D.C.**
Iraqi President Saddam Hussein, faced with a rapid and menacing global response to his invasion of Kuwait, is being backed into a corner from which his most likely options are to surrender or to lash out militarily, private and government experts on the Middle East said Tuesday.

Those experts said that in the next several days Hussein may well decide whether to choose war, striking at Saudi Arabia in an attempt to capture or destroy oil fields on which the Western economies rely, or withdraw his forces into Iraq, perhaps through a face-saving negotiated agreement.

Hussein also could choose to remain entrenched in Kuwait and hope that an international ban on trade with Iraq, imposed Monday by the United Nations, will crumble. But OPEC members' decision to increase oil production, offsetting some of the shortage of 4

**Iraq** continued on page 12A

### Bush will address nation this morning

President Bush will address the nation at 8 a.m. (Twin Cities time) this morning concerning the Persian Gulf crisis. The speech is expected to be carried live by the TV networks.

**On inside pages:**

■ U.S. troops and planes are intended only to deter an Iraqi move on Saudi Arabia. **14A.**

■ Oil prices rose again, and events jolted securities exchanges. **1D.**

■ Twin Cities grocers and mortgage lenders talk about the effect on prices here. **11A.**

## OPEC to boost output to cover Iraq shortfall

**By Stanley Meisler and Tom Redburn**
Los Angeles Times

**Bogota, Colombia**
OPEC members have agreed to increase oil production to help make up for the shortage caused by the international boycott of Iraq and Kuwait, President Carlos Andres Perez of Venezuela told Vice President Dan Quayle on Tuesday.

White House officials confirmed the disclosure, which was relayed to Quayle by Perez in a meeting shortly before the two attended the inauguration of Cesar Gaviria as president of Colombia, said a senior Bush administration official.

Perez said he had consulted with all members of OPEC except Iraq and Kuwait and that those with spare capacity had agreed to increase production to make up about 4 million barrels of the 4.6 million barrels a day that would be kept from the market by a boycott of Iraq and Iraqi-controlled Kuwait.

**Saudi Arabia** continued on 15A

## Target hits bull's-eye in Wolves' new arena

### Team, chain announce deal

**By Kevin Duchschere**
Staff Writer

The red Target bull's-eye, symbol of the discount store chain, will go up soon on the new Timberwolves arena in downtown Minneapolis.

Officials of Target and the Timberwolves of the NBA announced Tuesday that they have agreed on a multiyear deal to name the arena Target Center.

The agreement will cost Target between $250,000 and $400,000 per year, based on figures provided by John Pellegrene, Target senior vice president of marketing.

That is about 25 to 30 percent per year more than a promotional arrangement between the company and the team during last year's first season, he said. It also is considerably less than the $1 million per year that some had speculated could be the price tag for naming the arena. The agreement will run until 1996, with options to renew at a number of five-year increments.

The agreement also includes Target sponsorship of Timberwolves TV and radio broadcasts, player appearances at Target stores and extensive Target signs in and out of the arena. Pellegrene said a special Target Center logo incorporating the red bull's-eye will be placed on the building, tickets, arena uniforms and skyways. Another logo is being designed for center court, he said.

**Arena** continued on page 11A

## Liberia awaits intervention

U.S. Marines evacuated 21 more foreigners from Liberia Tuesday, including several Americans, as a rebel leader threatened to attack the 237 Marines protecting the U.S. Embassy in Monrovia unless the United States or another country intervenes to halt the civil war there. Meanwhile, five West African countries announced that troops and a naval task force would soon go to Liberia in an effort to end the conflict.

The rebel leader, Prince Johnson, is holding 22 hostages from eight countries. He and a rival rebel leader, Charles Taylor, are trying to oust the government of President Samuel Doe. **Article, page 4A.**

In the turmoil last week, Johnson shot and killed a man (center, in photos at right and below) whom he accused of profiteering from rice sales. The man was handcuffed to a French relief worker, far right, who later was evacuated to safety. **Article, page 4A.**

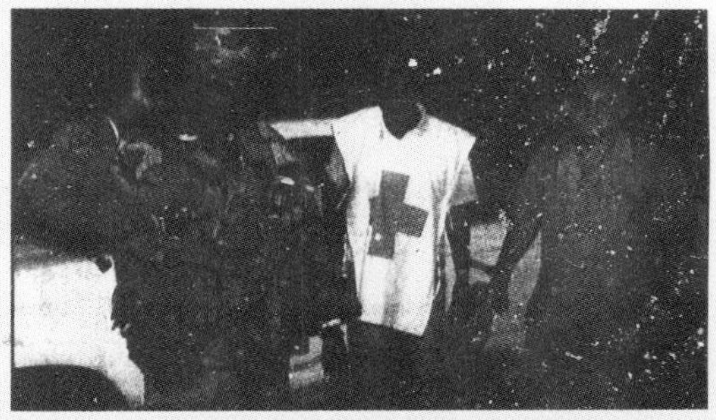

Associated Press photos

## Twin Cities an emerging U.S. 'control center'

### Key national role predicted

**By Paul Klauda**
Staff Writer

The Twin Cities area is one of a handful of emerging "national command and control centers" that are likely to grow in the same fashion as port cities and manufacturing hubs did before the 1970s, according to a new study of metropolitan areas.

The region also scored high as a magnet for baby boomers approaching their most productive and affluent years.

The report, published by the Population Reference Bureau, ranks the Twin Cities wit[illegible] Atlanta and Dallas-Fort Worth as regional hubs that will become "key actors" in the national economy.

"These metropolitan areas tend to be centers of national and regional financial and corporate decision-making activities and also serve as distribution centers for various national consumer products," wrote William Frey, an associate di[illegible]ctor at the University of Michigan's Population Studies Center.

Instead of making cars of steel, these areas produce the "ability to coordinate things" because of their proximity to banking, finance, consulting, specialized legal work, advertising, marketing and sales, Frey said in an interview. "That's what's being produced in successful cities today."

The level of population growth will vary, but these cities could become what Frey calls "world cities," with similarities to New York, Los Angeles, Chicago and San Francisco. Each boasts strong financial and trading roles in the international economy and will become even more dominant as centers of international finance, headquarters for multination-

**Cities** continued on page 10A

### Almanac

**Wednesday, August 8, 1990**
**220th day; 145 to go this year**
**Sunrise: 6:06. Sunset: 8:31**

**Today's weather/**
Plenty of sunshine and warmer with southwest winds at 15-25 miles per hour. High 84.

| | | | |
|---|---|---|---|
| Comics | 6,7E | Obituaries | 4B |
| Movies | 4,5E | TV, Radio | 8E |
| Complete index | 2A | | |

| | |
|---|---|
| General information | 673-4000 |
| Classifieds | 673-7000 |
| Circulation | 673-4343 |

Volume IX/Number 126 7 sections

## Lotto lure has many lined up to learn betting basics

**By Howard Sinker**
Staff Writer

Curious folks and dreamers stood in lines that sometimes reached five and six deep Tuesday in the atrium of St. Paul Center, just to get worthless lottery tickets.

Really worthless ones, since they were being used only to demonstrate the new Lotto Minnesota and Daily 3 games, which will debut around the state next Tuesday.

Lotto Minnesota will be the latest part of the Iowa-based Lotto America game. Players get two shots for $1 and odds of 1 in 12.9 million at winning a jackpot that starts at $2 million and grows until someone wins the twice-weekly drawing.

Daily 3 offers a 500-to-1 payoff for beating the 1,000-to-1 odds of guessing the three-digit number that will be drawn on TV every night.

Scratch-and-win games will continue to be offered, but when people talk about state lotteries, they usually are talking about the longer-odds numbers games that were on display yesterday, said Jim Burleson, executive assistant in the Minnesota State Lottery's marketing division.

The thought of winning millions of dollars has gotten to Jeanne Neubeck, who lives in White Bear Lake. She and her friend, Marilyn Jeukens of Forest Lake, take a lunch-hour walk once a week. Each buys $2 worth of tickets for the scratch-and-win games, the only ones now being offered.

Neither has w[illegible]n more than $5.

"We've promised each other that if we win the $10,000 (top prize), we'll take the rest of the day off and shop," Neubeck said. "So far we've gone back to work each time."

**Lottery** continued on page 10A

SPORTS: Toronto's $375,000 lures Weinke away from college football

MINNEAPOLIS EDITION

■ Five protesters dragged from HUD home, arrested/1B

Star Tribune

TUESDAY/August 21/1990 NEWSPAPER OF THE TWIN CITIES 35¢

# Northwest crew found guilty

## 3 convicted of flying while under influence of alcohol

By Randy Furst
Staff Writer

Three former Northwest Airlines crew members were convicted Monday of flying while under the influence of alcohol after a night of heavy drinking at a bar in Moorhead, Minn.

Norman Prouse, Robert Kirchner and Joseph Balzer showed little emotion as a clerk read the verdict in a quiet, packed courtroom at the federal courthouse in Minneapolis.

Balzer's wife, Deborah, sitting in the front row, turned and wept on the shoulder of Balzer's mother, and there were tears in the eyes of Kirchner's wife, Jane.

The three were accused of flying a Boeing 727 with 91 passengers aboard, from Fargo, N.D., to the Twin Cities on March 8 after having consumed enough alcohol to impair them. It was the first trial and conviction under a 1986 federal law making it a crime to operate common carriers — including commercial airplanes — while under the influence of alcohol.

Ruth Boylan, 43, of Excelsior, the jury forewoman, said in an interview later that jurors were not persuaded by the defense argument that a "perfect" flight was evidence that the crew members were not impaired. "Fortunately, (the flight) went fine," she said. "We felt that they were impaired enough that something could have gone wrong."

Boylan and another juror said the very fact that the three decided to fly the plane indicated that their judgment was impaired by alcohol.

After the verdict, Prouse told reporters, "I came into this expecting the worst, so in that sense, it was no surprise." Prouse, who testified that he drank about 17 rum drinks at the Speak Easy bar, said the jury acted fairly. "Northwest has taken a terrible beating on

Pilots continued on page 8A

Staff Photos by Mike Zerby

Former Northwest Airlines flight engineer Joseph Balzer and his wife, Deborah, left, walked out of the federal courthouse in Minneapolis after Balzer and two others were found guilty of flying while under the influence of alcohol. At right, captain Norman Prouse told reporters that the verdict should not reflect upon other Northwest pilots. "Only three of us were on trial," he said.

# Detainees called hostages

## Bush marks a shift in U.S. policy

From News Services

**Baltimore, Md.**
The United States crossed a threshold in the escalating crisis in th Mideast Monday when President Bush for the first time described Americans and other foreign nationals trapped in Iraq and Kuwait as "hostages" and demanded their immediate release.

Bush's characterization marked a reversal of the administration's policy not to call the detained Americans "hostages" and came after Iraqi President Saddam Hussein said that Americans and other foreign nationals would be kept as a shield against possible U.S. attack and set demands for their release.

The official Iraqi News Agency quoted a spokesman for Baghdad's National Council, or parliament, as saying: "Iraq's foreign guests have been in fact moved to all vital and military installations. They have been provided with all modern facilities and they are all in good physical condition." It did not say how many foreigners were moved or give other details.

Detainees continued on page 8A

Associated Press

Members of the 82nd Airborne Division took a break from patrol in the Saudi desert Monday. The buildup of U.S. forces in the region continued. The United Arab Emirates said it would allow U.S. military cargo planes to operate from its airfields.

# Academic recording

## Parents can keep in touch with touch-tone

By Jim Dawson
Staff Writer

Not sure that Jane got her homework assignment straight? Curious about that class project Johnny only mumbles about over dinner?

Technology might provide a solution early next year at one Minneapolis school in the form of a new voice mail telephone service for parents. It reportedly has had a dramatic impact on schools elsewhere in the country.

The system will allow parents to call the school each day and listen to a one- or two-minute recorded message from their child's teacher about homework, projects, special events — anything the teacher wants to say. The school has not yet been selected.

The impact of the system has been tremendous in other states, said Bob Brancale, coordinator of early childhood family education for the school district. "Between a third and two-thirds of the parents call every day," he said. "There is four to eight times more contact between parents and teachers, and the rate of homework completed increases dramatically. Along with that, student academic levels increase."

Brancale saw the system several years ago and has received a $50,000 grant from the U S West Foundation to install it in one school. The Minneapolis system will be the first in Minnesota, but the St. Paul school district also has expressed interest in the technology.

Andersen, Wilder and Lyndale elementary schools are submitting proposals to the district, Brancale said, and one will be selected by the end of the year. If the voice mail technology is successful, it will be expanded throughout the school district, he said.

The system, known as the "TransParent School," was developed by Jerold Bauch, a professor at Vanderbilt University.

Technology continued on page 6A

# Bush reversal suggests U.S. faces Iraq standoff

Los Angeles Times

**Analysis**

**Washington, D.C.**
By using the previously taboo word "hostages," President Bush has for the first time acknowledged that the United States could face a grim, long-term standoff with Iraq, one that revives unhappy memories of earlier U.S. showdowns in Iran and Lebanon.

But if the 3,000 Americans inside Iraq and Kuwait are in fact all heid hostage, then the scale of this crisis dwarfs that of either of the two previous hostage episodes, which brought down one presidency and threatened another.

Until Monday, the United States had avoided using the word "hostage" in

U.S. options continued on page 11A

## Crisis to renew energy debate

The Middle East crisis is sure to renew debate over the nation's energy policy. But the United States has been in this situation before and there is little reason to believe the outcome will be different this time. **An analysis, page 10A.**

■ The cost of U.S. operations in the Persian Gulf could hit $1 billion a day. **Page 10A.**

■ Gulf crisis causes Northwest Airlines to refine plans. **Page 1D.**

# Another gulf struggle being waged in banks

By Glenn Frankel
Washington Post

**London, England**
Overshadowed by the drama of military confrontation in the Persian Gulf, a second, more hidden conflict is being waged in the world's banks and financial markets — the war over money.

In the shooting war, Iraq's massive army swallowed up tiny Kuwait in less than a day. But in the money war, the two sides are more evenly matched, and analysts say the struggle is just beginning.

Iraq plundered Kuwait's domestic assets like "a thief walking into an unguarded bank," one exiled financier said. It now hopes to use those resources and its own gold and hard currency to bust the U.N. embargo

Money war continued on page 11A

# High court has shifted rightward; where does it go from there?

By Steve Berg
Washington Bureau Correspondent

**Washington, D.C.**
While Washington occupies itself with finding clues to the innermost thoughts of Supreme Court nominee David Souter, a broader realization is taking hold — that the court's long-anticipated shift to the right is suddenly at hand.

By the mid-'90s, it's possible that a string of court rulings could paint a new social landscape for the nation. It might be a landscape in which abortions are crimes in a few states and harder to obtain in many others; where burning a flag or publishing a pornographic magazine might no longer be so easily protected as free speech; where preferential opportunities for women and minority employees might be harder to secure; where religious activities might be more freely allowed in public schools, and where justice for criminal defendants might be more swift and less sure.

All these impacts are highly speculative, of course. Without its leading liberal, William Brennan, the court might move a mile to the right — or it might move only a few inches.

"Apocalyptic visions that we are either on the edge of nirvana or at the

Court continued on page 9A

## Almanac

**Tuesday, August 21, 1990**
**233rd day; 132 to go this year**
**Sunrise: 6:22. Sunset: 8:11**

**Today's weather**

High in the middle 70s, light winds.



| | |
|---|---|
| General Information | 673-4000 |
| Classifieds | 673-7000 |
| Circulation | 673-4343 |


Volume IX/Number 139 6 sections

# Neighbors hope to revive North Side shopping mall

By Jon Jeter
Staff Writer

For years, Plymouth Av. has been unable to recapture the luster of its glory years, when it was a thriving marketplace on Minneapolis' Near North Side.

But residents, merchants and city officials have high hopes for a new proposal to revive the neighborhood — hopes that hinge on the revitalization of a long-struggling shopping center and the man who has been picked to rejuvenate it.

Residents and shopkeepers hope that developer Ray Harris can do for Plymouth Av. what he did for the Uptown area when he built Calhoun Square, turning Lake St. and Hennepin Av. S. into a hub of economic vitality.

"There have been a lot of attempts to

Plymouth Av. continued on 6A

Iraq promises to release another 108 foreign hostages/4A

MINNEAPOLIS EDITION

■ Priest won't take responsibility for all abuse problems/3B

Star Tribune

WEDNESDAY/November 7/1990 NEWSPAPER OF THE TWIN CITIES 35¢

# It looks like a Wellstone upset; Perpich, Carlson in tight race

U.S. Senate

## Underdog projected as winner

By Robert Whereatt and Paul Klauda
Staff Writers

Paul Wellstone, the political science professor who used his underdog status to stalk Sen. Rudy Boschwitz throughout a bitter campaign, was projected as the apparent winner early this morning in a stunning upset, according to exit polls.

The projection was made by Voter Research and Surveys of New York for several major news organizations, including the Star Tribune.

Wellstone apparently gained on the incumbent over the weekend and battled him evenly through a long night of protracted ballot counting, pulling ahead by midnight.

There was no concession by the Boschwitz camp. The two-term incumbent left his headquarters in the Thunderbird Hotel in Bloomington and went to his home in Plymouth.

If Boschwitz loses, he will be the nation's only Senate incumbent to fall. A Wellstone victory would be the biggest political upset in a Minnesota general election in recent history.

With 47 percent of the vote in, Wellstone led 51 to 49 percent. At one point, with 26 percent of all precincts counted, the two were separated by a single vote — 126,719 for Wellstone and 126,720 for Boschwitz.

Senate continued on page 11A

### U.S. Senate

†Denotes incumbent.

1,917 of 4,090 precincts

| | |
|---|---|
| Paul David Wellstone/DFL | 308,891 |
| Rudy Boschwitz/IR† | 295,099 |
| Russell B. Bentley/GRP | 1,681 |

## Peterson leads Stangeland with 34% of vote counted

By Jim Parsons
Staff Writer

Arlan Stangeland, the veteran Minnesota congressman who became embroiled in an ethics controversy, was trailing an old foe as vote counting droned on early today.

DFL challenger Collin Peterson had 54 percent of the vote with 34 percent of the Seventh District's precincts reporting, but he wasn't claiming victory as this edition of the Star Tribune went to press.

"It looks like it is going to hold," said Peterson, "but I'm not making the mistake of predicting anything." He noted that in virtually every one of the reporting precincts, he was doing better than in 1986, when he lost to Stangeland by 121 votes.

Congress continued on page 16A

### Almanac

**Wednesday, November 7, 1990**
**311th day; 54 to go this year**
**Sunrise: 6:59. Sunset: 4:54**

Mostly sunny, high 38.




Volume IX/Number 217 6 sections

Staff Photo by Jeff Wheeler

DFL Senate candidate Paul Wellstone, with his wife, Sheila, was upbeat as he answered reporters' questions early Tuesday evening at the downtown Minneapolis Holiday Inn. He was projected as the apparent upset winner in his race with Sen. Rudy Boschwitz.

ELECTION '90

## Early returns favor Minneapolis school levy

Page 1B

## Helms wins reelection; Bradley survives scare

Page 8A

## Mark Dayton holds lead in race for state auditor

DFLer Mark Dayton was leading IR candidate Bob Heinrich in the race for state auditor, the only state constitutional office in which the incumbent was not seeking reelection.

In the other state constitutional races, Attorney General Hubert Humphrey III and Secretary of State Joan Growe, both DFLers, were capturing more than 60 percent of the vote in their reelection bids. State Treasurer Michael McGrath, another DFLer, led IR challenger John Burger by a lesser margin.

Page 1B

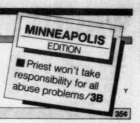

Mark Dayton

### U.S. Senate, House trends

| U.S. Senate | Dem. | GOP | Other |
|---|---|---|---|
| Seats won | 17 | 16 | 0 |
| Leading | 1 | 1 | 0 |
| Holdovers | 38 | 27 | 0 |
| Trend | 56 | 44 | 0 |
| Current | 55 | 45 | 0 |
| **Net change** | **+1** | **−1** | **0** |

| U.S. House | Dem. | GOP | Other |
|---|---|---|---|
| Seats won | 236 | 146 | 1 |
| Leading | 26 | 24 | 0 |
| Trend | 262 | 170 | 1 |
| Current | 259 | 176 | 0 |
| **Net change** | **+4** | **−5** | **+1** |

Newt Gingrich fighting for survival **Page 9A**

IR, DFL trade several Senate seats **Page 1B**

### Election Final to be published this morning

Because local election results were delayed by hand-counting, the Star Tribune will publish an Election Final later this morning with the latest election returns available. This special edition will be available by about 10 a.m. from street vendors and at most news dealers in both downtown Minneapolis and St. Paul. Outside of the downtowns, the Election Final will be available at most Byerly's and Lund's stores, Southdale, Ridgedale and Rosedale and about 60 other locations in the Twin Cities. For additional information on where the Election Final can be purchased, call 673-7600 for a recorded listing.

## Surprising turnout across state could exceed 60 percent

By Norman Draper
Staff Writer

Statewide voter turnout was unexpectedly heavy Tuesday, and election officials predicted that it might surge past 60 percent of Minnesota's registered voters.

That's much higher than the 49 percent that had been predicted by Secretary of State Joan Growe.

In Hennepin County, election supervisor Marge Christianson estimated that 62 percent of the county's voters cast ballots. Hundreds of voters in cities such as Bloomington and Richfield were still in long lines after 8 p.m. when the polls closed. Those in line then were allowed to vote, and some Richfield residents didn't finish voting until 9:30.

"Richfield is inundated with voters," Christianson said. "Wayzata could go as high as 70 percent."

Ramsey County election supervisor Joan Pelzer said that suburbs such as Maplewood and New Brighton reported a heavy turnout, and that New Brighton election officials were worried about running out of ballots.

The small town of Independence in western Hennepin County reported the largest turnout of its voters ever by midafternoon. Residents had to stand in line to vote at City Hall, the town's only polling place, said City Clerk Mary Leintz.

There were plenty of signs that voters might troop to the polls in greater numbers than expected.

In Dakota County, Auditor Norma Marsh said the "phone was ringing off the wall this morning" with calls from people asking where to vote. The picture was the same outside the metropolitan area.

"Turnout is uniformly higher than expected," said Joe Mansky, director of the election division at the secretary of state's office. "The likely culprits are the governor's race, the Senate race and tax elections."

Turnout continued on page 14A

Governor

## Big turnout may help IR challenger

By Betty Wilson and Paul Klauda
Staff Writers

Exit polls in Tuesday's election suggested that Gov. Rudy Perpich was having difficulty in his bid for an unprecedented fourth term, and that a large voter turnout across Minnesota was benefiting his Independent-Republican opponent, Arne Carlson.

Perpich, fighting for his political life, told a crowd of cheering, chanting supporters at the downtown Minneapolis Holiday Inn just before 11 11 p.m. that he was going to win.

"It's going to be a long night," he said. "I have been in these before. This will be my third cliffhanger. It's never decided until those canoe precincts come in," Perpich said, referring to the state's precincts along the Canadian border.

The DFL governor, who was accompanied by his wife, Lola, suggested that the coattails of Paul Wellstone, the DFL candidate for U.S. Senate, might help put him over.

"Lola and I are going to sleep," he said. "I know those canoe precincts are going to retain me as governor for four more years."

The mood in the Carlson campaign, meanwhile, buoyed by the extraordinarily high surge of voting in Twin Cities suburbs and other strong IR areas, was one of growing optimism as the night wore on.

Last night, Carlson and his running mate, Joanell Dyrstad, awaited returns with their families in 24th-floor suites at the Hyatt Regency Hotel in downtown Minneapolis. They went downstairs twice to give pep talks to about 200 supporters in the Greenway Athletic Club gymnasium below.

"We're feeling extraordinarily upbeat," Carlson said. "It looks awfully good for us. . . . Two weeks ago, the voter turnout was projected at 26 percent. Now it's hovering around 65 percent. It speaks well for the restoration of dignity in Minnesota politics."

Carlson also predicted "one whale of a long night" waiting for results, but

Governor continued on page 15A

### Governor

†Denotes incumbent.

1,824 of 4,090 precincts

| | |
|---|---|
| Rudy Perpich/DFL† | 282,161 |
| Carlson/IR | 285,087 |
| Wendy Lyons/SWP | 378 |
| Ross S. Culverhouse/GRP | 972 |
| Heart Warrior (Judith Ann) Chosa/ERP | 836 |

## Democrats win governor's races in Florida, Texas; GOP wins in Ohio

Associated Press

Democrats wrested governorships from the GOP in Texas, Florida and four other states Tuesday in midterm elections that sealed a season of Republican disappointment. Democrats also moved to expand their dominion of Congress, although they lost a hard-fought challenge to Sen. Jesse Helms, R-N.C.

Upsets were hard to find, despite stirrings of voter discontent. House Republican Whip Newt Gingrich was in a Georgia deadlock. Sen. Bill Bradley of New Jersey, a 1992 Democratic presidential contender, narrowly avoided a stunning defeat by a virtual unknown.

Texas elected as governor Democrat Ann Richards, whose late charge was pushed to victory by Republican Clayton Williams' series of blunders.

Democratic National Committee Chairman Ron Brown claimed, "Democrats have done extraordinarily well," but the question of which party could claim victory when the evening was over depended on still-to-be-determined races for governor of California, Michigan and Illinois.

There was little good news for the GOP. The best of it was in Ohio, where George Voinovich won a Democratic governorship, and in Connecticut, where Gary Franks became the first black House Republican since 1935.

Former Sen. Lowell Weicker vexed the GOP, this time as an outsider. He won an independent bid for governor of Connecticut. Vermont sent Socialist Bernie Sanders to the House, in place of a Republican.

In Florida, former Sen. Lawton Chiles won handily over first-term Republican Gov. Bob Martinez. Democrat David Walters grabbed the open Republican governorship in Oklahoma. Bruce Sundlun wrested the governorship from Republicans in hard-times Rhode Island, ousting Edward DiPrete. Former Gov. Bruce King's successful comeback returned New Mexico to the Democratic column, and Joan Finney ousted GOP Gov. Mike Hayden in Kansas.

Democrats easily renewed their majority in the Senate and were headed for the same or more in the House.

WAR COVERAGE INSIDE: **14 pages of news starting on Page 3A**

MINNEAPOLIS EDITION

■ Carlson decides not to deliver State of State speech/**1B**

# Star Tribune

**THURSDAY**/January 17/1991 NEWSPAPER OF THE TWIN CITIES 35¢

# War begins

## U.S., allied planes pound Iraq in massive one-sided strike

**From News Services**

Under cover of darkness, the United States and its allies mounted a sweeping attack against Iraq that pitted their air power against an Arab nation that for five months has held Kuwait in defiance of the rest of the world.

"Tonight the battle has been joined," President Bush said Wednesday night in a nationally televised address from Washington, D.C. His speech came just after 8 p.m. Twin Cities time, about 2½ hours after the predawn assault on Iraq began.

Although there was no official confirmation of the raids' success, sources in Washington said the attacks had inflicted massive damage on targets in the Iraqi capital and elsewhere in Iraq and Kuwait. The sources indicated that U.S. and allied planes successfully took out Iraqi air bases and missile sites, knocked out Iraqi radar and communications facilities in Baghdad and inflicted heavy damage on the elite Iraqi Republican Guard forces and on chemical and nuclear plants.

No ground fighting was reported, and officials expressed surprise at the lack of any effective Iraqi military response in the early hours of hostilities. Defense Secretary Dick Cheney suggested that losses of U.S. aircraft and crews had been minimal.

The bombing paused after several hours. In a private meeting with the United Nations Security Council, U.S. Ambassador Thomas Pickering promised that Iraq could avoid further punishment by beginning a complete, unconditional withdrawal from Kuwait.

But an unbowed Iraqi President Saddam Hussein, in his first remarks after the outbreak of war, called Bush a "hypocritical criminal" and vowed to crush "the evil and satanic intentions of the White House."

Hussein, in a radio address to "the glorious sons of our nation," said the battle was one of "justice against vice, of the believers against the infidels."

Cable News Network reported early today that bombing had resumed in daylight near Baghdad about six hours after the initial 2:30 a.m. attack on the city.

Bush, who won congressional backing Saturday for the use of force, telephoned congressional leaders with his decision to strike shortly before the campaign began.

Gen. Colin Powell, chairman of the Joint Chiefs of Staff, told a Pentagon news conference that "there has been no air resistance" from the Iraqis, although that could change with the arrival of daylight.

Reports from Saudi Arabia indicated that only a few Iraqi airplanes scrambled to battle the allied force. The first waves to return to Saudi bases showed little indication of being in any air fights, according to press pools.

Cheney said the strikes were designed to "destroy Saddam Hussein's offensive military capabilities."

"For the time being," he said, it is strictly an air operation. He declined to speculate on when ground troops might invade Kuwait.

Cheney said the "operation appears to have gone very, very well." Asked about U.S. casualties, he said, "Preliminary reports . . . are very, very encouraging." A senior U.S. general,

**War** continued on page 13A

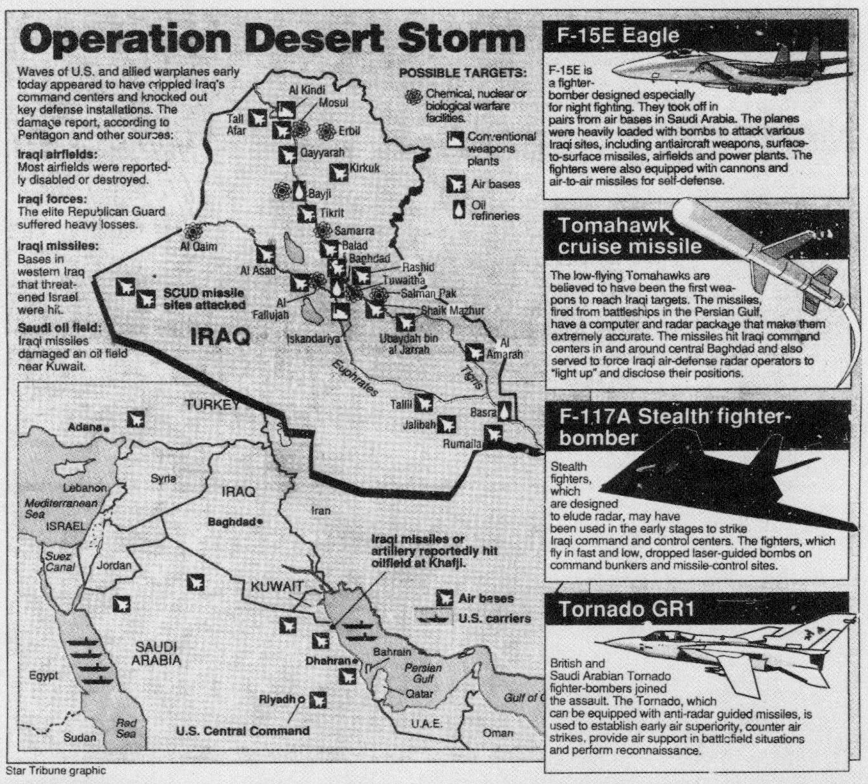

Operation Desert Storm
Waves of U.S. and allied warplanes early today appeared to have crippled Iraq's command centers and knocked out key defense installations. The damage report, according to Pentagon and other sources:
Iraqi airfields: Most airfields were reportedly disabled or destroyed.
Iraqi forces: The elite Republican Guard suffered heavy losses.
Iraqi missiles: Bases in western Iraq that threatened Israel were hit.
Saudi oil field: Iraqi missiles damaged an oil field near Kuwait.
POSSIBLE TARGETS:
Chemical, nuclear or biological warfare facilities.
Conventional weapons plants
Air bases
Oil refineries
Al Kindi
Mosul
Tall Afar
Erbil
Qayyarah
Kirkuk
Bayji
Tikrit
Samarra
Al Qaim
Balad
Baghdad
Al Asad
Rashid
Tuwaitha
Salman Pak
SCUD missile sites attacked
Al Fallujah
Shaik Mazhur
IRAQ
Iskandariya
Ubaydah bin al Jarrah
Al Amarah
Euphrates
Tigris
Tallil
Basra
Jalibah
Rumaila
TURKEY
Adana
Syria
Lebanon
Mediterranean Sea
ISRAEL
IRAQ
Baghdad
Iran
Suez Canal
Jordan
Iraqi missiles or artillery reportedly hit oilfield at Khafji.
KUWAIT
Air bases
U.S. carriers
SAUDI ARABIA
Egypt
Bahrain
Dhahran
Persian Gulf
Qatar
Riyadh
Gulf of O
U.A.E.
Red Sea
Sudan
U.S. Central Command
Oman
F-15E Eagle
F-15E is a fighter-bomber designed especially for night fighting. They took off in pairs from air bases in Saudi Arabia. The planes were heavily loaded with bombs to attack various Iraqi sites, including antiaircraft weapons, surface-to-surface missiles, airfields and power plants. The fighters were also equipped with cannons and air-to-air missiles for self-defense.
Tomahawk cruise missile
The low-flying Tomahawks are believed to have been the first weapons to reach Iraqi targets. The missiles, fired from battleships in the Persian Gulf, have a computer and radar package that make them extremely accurate. The missiles hit Iraqi command centers in and around central Baghdad and also served to force Iraqi air-defense radar operators to "light up" and disclose their positions.
F-117A Stealth fighter-bomber
Stealth fighters, which are designed to elude radar, may have been used in the early stages to strike Iraqi command and control centers. The fighters, which fly in fast and low, dropped laser-guided bombs on command bunkers and missile-control sites.
Tornado GR1
British and Saudi Arabian Tornado fighter-bombers joined the assault. The Tornado, which can be equipped with anti-radar guided missiles, is used to establish early air superiority, counter air strikes, provide air support in battlefield situations and perform reconnaissance.

Star Tribune graphic

**War news inside:**

**Israel declared** a state of emergency when the attack on Iraq was reported, but military officials reassured citizens that the nation had not been attacked. **3A.**

**Word swept** the nation that the war had started in the gulf. In the nation's capital, some seemed to hear the news without surprise, while others protested outside the White House. **5A.**

**The economy** is almost certain to be wounded by war. The prices of stocks and long-term bonds will decline, perhaps precipitously, and a war of more than a few weeks, economists forecast, could prolong the current recession. **1D.**

**Minnesotans reacted** with tears, apprehension and hope as they watched reports of the attack. **6A.**

**Local peace** activists stepped up plans for an antiwar rally this afternoon at Peavy Plaza. **7A.**

## Minnesotans stopped, listened to sound of history being made

It was one of those moments we'll never forget. Everyone will remember where they were and how they reacted when they heard the news.

At dozens of places throughout the Twin Cities area — from a tavern in northeast Minneapolis to a college campus in St. Paul — the reaction was largely the same: subdued, no cheering. For some, a grim eagerness to settle the score with Saddam Hussein; for most, an uncertainty about the future, concerns about a possibly greater war.

Years from now, people will ask: "Where were *you* when the war in the Persian Gulf began?"

This is where some Twin Citians were, and how they reacted, when "Operation Desert Shield" became "Operation Desert Storm."

■

At 6:15 p.m., the intercom broke into the quiet at the downtown Minneapolis Public Library.

"May I have your attention, please?" said library aide Cheryl Pederson, with just a trace of shakiness in her voice. "As of 7 p.m. Eastern time, the White House announced an invasion of Kuwait and Iraq by multinational forces . . . "

**Reaction** continued on page 14A

## U.S. role as dominant power at stake as Bush takes extraordinary gamble

**Analysis**

**By Jim Mann**
Los Angeles Times

**Washington, D.C.**
In ordering U.S. troops into war against Iraq, President Bush has taken one of the biggest gambles any U.S. chief of state has ever taken.

The stakes are, in many ways, much larger than those in the Vietnam War. At that time, a quarter century ago, U.S. troops went into battle in a world in which the relationships among the world's leading powers were relatively static. Now, U.S. forces are going to war at a time in history when the world is in a state of almost-unprecedented flux.

As a result, the president's decision involves an extraordinary gamble. At stake: Washington's position as world leader.

If the president is successful, if he turns back Iraqi aggression under the banner of an international coalition without setting the entire Middle East ablaze, then the "new world order" about which he has spoken so often will be one dominated by the United States and its military power.

No longer constrained by the Soviet Union and the Cold War, Washington is likely to stand unchallenged as

**Analysis** continued on page 19A

### Almanac

**Thursday, January 17, 1991**
**17th day; 348 to go this year**
**Sunrise: 7:46. Sunset: 5:00**

Skies will become partly sunny in the Twin Cities today. Winds will be northwest at 8 to 16 mph. High 28.

Circulation 673-4343

Volume IX/Number 288 7 sections

Erickson wins his 10th straight as Twins win their 12th straight/1C

MINNEAPOLIS EDITION

■ Zubaz creators moving operation to Brooklyn Center/1D


# Star Tribune

FRIDAY/June 14/1991 NEWSPAPER OF THE TWIN CITIES 35¢


# Tragedy strikes U.S. Open

## Lightning kills one spectator, injures 5

By Paul Klauda
Staff Writer

A lightning bolt from a swift-moving thunderstorm killed one spectator and injured five others Thursday during the opening round of what had been described as a "fairy tale" U.S. Open in Chaska.

The victims were standing under a willow tree in one of the most crowded gallery areas of Hazeltine National Golf Club when lightning scorched the tree. The incident occurred at 1:07 p.m. during a driving rainstorm that had caused play to be suspended at 12:49 p.m.

Witnesses said the bolt knocked down six to eight people "like bowling pins" as they stood under or leaned against the tree. William Fadell, 27, of Spring Park, was rushed by ambulance to St. Francis Regional Medical Center in Shakopee, where he was pronounced dead of cardiac arrest at 2:09 p.m.

It is believed to be the first spectator death caused by lightning at any championship golf tournament in the United States.

The speedy development of the storm overwhelmed the tournament's storm-warning plan, which is supposed to alert fans before play is suspended. Many spectators and golfers said they did not hear sirens warning them to seek shelter.

Hale Irwin, who won last year's

Lightning continued on page 18A

Staff Photos by Brian Peterson

Golf fans, above, rushed to the aid of the victims of a lightning strike at the U.S. Open. One man was killed and five others were injured when a bolt of lightning struck the tree in the background. Below, medical personnel helped one of the victims near the 11th tee of the Hazeltine National Golf Club in Chaska.

**1991 U.S. OPEN** Hazeltine National

**THE LEADER BOARD**

| | Score |
|---|---|
| Payne Stewart | 67 |
| Nolan Henke | 67 |
| Tom Byrum | 68 |
| Scott Hoch | 69 |
| Mark Calcavecchia | 69 |
| Jack Nicklaus | 70 |
| Craig Parry | 70 |
| Scott Simpson | 70 |
| Davis Love | 70 |
| Keith Clearwater | 70 |
| Jim Gallagher | 70 |
| Chris Perry | -2 after 14 |
| Brian Kamm | -2 after 13 |
| David Jackson | -2 after 12 |

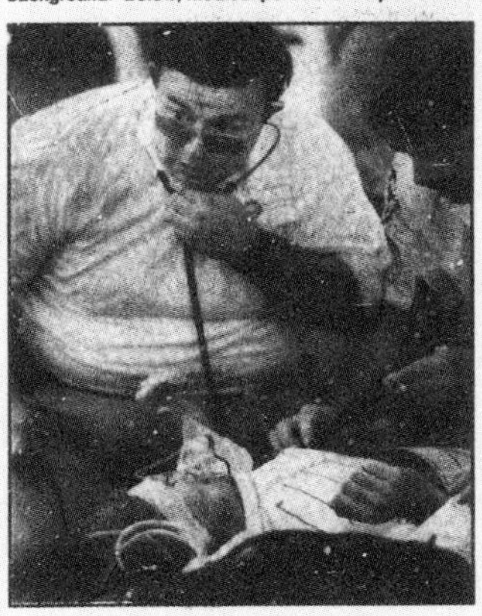

## Hazeltine survivor recalls a bang, then a jolt

By Chuck Haga
Staff Writer

When the rain turned hard Thursday, Glenn Engstrom took shelter beneath a large oak tree near Hazeltine's 11th tee.

But he didn't feel safe there.

"I ran, and I thought I had found a shorter tree that wouldn't get hit," he said.

He and five other men huddled beneath the smaller tree. The lightning struck a few moments later. Engstrom remembers facing the tree to keep the wind and rain at his back, and joking with another man about Minnesota weather.

"All of a sudden, bang!, and I felt this jolt," he said. "My legs went totally numb and I was down. I've never felt anything like that before in my life. I would imagine it was like if you were shot.

"My legs felt like they were 50 feet wide."

Engstrom and three of the other men were taken to Ridgeview Medical Center in Waconia. All four were in stable condition and were being held overnight for observation. The fifth injured man was in serious condition last night at St. Paul-Ramsey Medical Center.

Survivors continued on page 6A

## As storm rolled in, fans had nowhere to hide

By Jay Weiner
Staff Writer

The darkening gray-blue sky rumbled. The hush that normally hangs over the U.S. Open was broken by distant thunder.

It was 12:47 p.m. Thursday. Hazeltine National Golf Club was 20 minutes from a disaster.

The threesome of Corey Pavin, Craig Parry and Ronan Rafferty was on the tee of Hazeltine's "signature" 16th hole; trees to the south, Lake Hazeltine to the north.

"I knew it was just about to rain," said Parry, who was the first up. "I sort of rushed my shot."

The Australian used a 1-iron to lift his ball into the fairway. As he followed through with his swing, a bright, white streak of lightning flashed in the sky over the lake. Parry pointed.

"As soon as I saw the lightning, I was out of there," said Parry. "I knew we were in for a little bit of trouble."

Still, Pavin, then Rafferty executed their tee

Scene continued on page 24A

## Russians elect Yeltsin president in strong mandate for reforms

From News Services

**Moscow, U.S.S.R.**
Boris Yeltsin on Thursday was declared the winner of the first direct election for the presidency of Russia with a nearly 60 percent mandate that carried a powerful message at home and abroad.

Yeltsin's victory is likely to increase pressure on his chief rival, Soviet President Mikhail Gorbachev, to accelerate the pace of reform. And it gave Yeltsin instant credibility elsewhere; the United States responded with an invitation to the White House to meet with President Bush. The meeting is tentatively set for Thursday.

As the first popularly elected president in Russia's 1,000-year history, Yeltsin said he will dedicate his five-year term of office to the creation of democratic political institutions and a Western-style market economy.

The election was a stunning defeat for Communists across the Soviet Union's largest and most powerful republic. Not only did Yeltsin win, but like-minded reformers swept mayoral elections in Moscow and Leningrad. In probably the most emotional of the races, an unexpected 55 percent of the voters in Lenin-

Yeltsin continued on page 16A

**INSIDE/**

### DFLers ask court to act on vetoes

DFL legislative leaders asked the state Supreme Court to settle their dispute with Gov. Arne Carlson over the validity of 14 vetoes that DFLers maintain were returned late. Carlson had no comments on the DFLers' suit. **Page 1B.**

### Were all Iraqi nuclear sites hit?

Secretary of Defense Dick Cheney acknowledged some Iraqi nuclear facilities may have been so well concealed that they escaped destruction during allied bombing raids. **Page 2A.**

### Volcano could keep base on hold

U.S. officials said an erupting volcano may shut down the U.S.-run Clark Air Base in the Philippines for months, if not years. **Page 2A.**

## Test scores show decline at innovative Saturn school

By James Walsh
Staff Writer

St. Paul's Saturn School of Tomorrow, which President Bush hailed three weeks ago as an innovative effort to reinvent education, is showing less-than-stellar results in student achievement tests. In fact, scores have dropped each of the three times Saturn students have taken standardized tests in math, reading and language since the school opened two years ago.

Slight declines were recorded in all areas of the standardized tests, and the biggest plunge was a 10 percent drop in a math concepts test. Over the same period, scores rose for the St. Paul School District as a whole.

While school officials say test scores alone can't measure what children learn, many admit that the school

Saturn continued on page 14A

## What price justice? In St. Paul, it's almost $1,100

**Doug Grow**

Being not guilty in St. Paul can be expensive.

Consider, for example, the costly case of Johnny Koger. Earlier this week he was found not guilty by a jury of his peers on charges that were brought against him by St. Paul authorities. Now that he's been found not guilty, he's being confronted with a bill for almost $1,100 from those same St. Paul authorities.

What in the name of justice is going on?

"Outrageousness," says Koger's attorney, Alan Margoles.

"He can sue if he wants," says a St. Paul city attorney, Paul McCloskey.

Back up to Feb. 8. On that date, Koger, a 37-year-old factory worker, was picked up in one of the city's "john sweeps." St. Paul police said he had tried to buy sex from a St. Paul police decoy.

St. Paul doesn't treat johns gently. Using an ordinance passed by the City Council a year ago, the city confiscates the cars of those charged with soliciting a prostitute if the car is used in the solicitation. The city can keep the car only if the person charged is found guilty.

On Feb. 8, Koger's car, a Ford valued at about $6,000, was confiscated when he was arrested.

But earlier this week, a jury in St. Paul needed only a few minutes to

Grow continued on page 13A

### Almanac

**Friday, June 14, 1991**
**165th day; 200 to go this year**
**Sunrise: 5:26. Sunset: 9:00**

Humid, with high of 91; low, 70.





Volume X/Number 71 6 sections

**13 in a row**
Twins' 7-0 victory sets club record
Details on page 1C

SHELTER
**Mortgage miseries**
New FHA rules will add to costs

VARIETY
**Gardener's corner**
Native plants of Minnesota

**MINNEAPOLIS**
EDITION

■ DFL legislator claims another tardy veto: moratorium on cow hormone/**1B**

■ Burnsville man sues lottery, says scratch-off game was misleading/**3B**

W

**Star Tribune**

SATURDAY/June 15/1991 NEWSPAPER OF THE TWIN CITIES 35¢

# Europe backs terms of U.S.-Soviet treaty

## Bush to seek Senate ratification of pact

New York Times

**Washington, D.C.**
The United States' NATO allies and five Eastern European countries Friday formally approved a U.S.-Soviet compromise to end a dispute over a treaty limiting conventional military forces in Europe.

The Bush administration will send the treaty to the Senate for its approval.

It is not expected to meet much opposition, considering that it will require the Soviets to withdraw thousands of pieces of military equipment from Europe to bring their forces down to levels about equal to those of NATO's and will require the Soviets to destroy about 20,000 tanks, artillery and armored vehicles.

Even without the treaty, the Soviets were withdrawing their forces from Eastern Europe. But the treaty will ensure that they do it in a timely, verifiable fashion.

The treaty on conventional forces in Europe was signed at a Paris summit meeting Nov. 19. But its ratification by the 16 NATO and 6 Warsaw Pact countries covered by the agreement had been held up because of a last-minute Soviet attempt to reinterpret the pact in a way that would enable the Soviet military to spare some of its equipment.

"After months of concern that the Soviet military might be trying to undermine the treaty, President (Mikhail) Gorbachev seems to have reasserted control," said Sen. Joseph Biden, D-Del., who as chairman of the subcommittee on European affairs will manage the ratification hearings and the floor debate.

**Arms** continued on page 6A

## Gigantic Old Glory

Agence France-Presse

**Hundreds of volunteers unfurled the world's biggest flag Friday on the grounds of the Washington Monument in Washington, D.C., as part of Flag Day festivities. The flag measures 210 feet by 411 feet. It was going to be hung from the monument, but engineers feared the 7-ton flag would topple it.**

# BCED says it will return two St. Paul properties to lender

**By Sally Apgar and Bill McAuliffe**
Staff Writers

Troubled Toronto-based BCE Development Corp., once the largest landowner in downtown St. Paul, said Friday that it is walking away from the 27-story North Central Life office tower and the adjacent Town Square retail center.

After the deed is transferred to the lender, Travelers Insurance Co., BCED's only remaining stake in St. Paul will be its 50 percent partnership in the Minnesota World Trade Center, which is held under a new, affiliated entity called Brookfield World Trade Center.

St. Paul officials and business people reacted to BCED's pending departure with relief and optimism after watching the developer's fitful negotiations over the past 18 months with lenders, including the St. Paul Port Authority.

"Perhaps the silver lining that will come out of this for the city is having a new owner who does feel a responsibility beyond their economic interests," said Lisa Clemens, deputy director for economic development for the city's Planning and Economic

**BCED** continued on page 5A

## Making his mark

Staff Photo by Jeff Wheeler

**Leader Payne Stewart marked his ball on the 17th green Friday; moments later he sank his putt for a par 3. He shot a 2-under-par 70 yesterday.**

# End of the road?

## Small town considers municipal suicide

**By Howard Sinker**
Staff Writer

**Island View, Minn.**
This is one of the places where Minnesota ends. The twisting two-lane state highway just stops, an honest-to-goodness end of the road. Go too far and it's a cold plunge into Rainy Lake.

Island View, 12 miles east of International Falls, was incorporated as a city in 1939, mostly so liquor could be sold. There was no city hall, nor anything that passed for a business district. Island View was several resorts, a handful of summer residents and stunning views.

That's changed. Roads were built. Property was bought, sold and subdivided. Folks built summer homes that became places they lived in for most of the year. Property values skyrocketed.

But there's still no city hall, nor anything that passes for a business district. Island View never became *that* kind of city.

On July 2, its 87 eligible voters will decide if it should remain any kind of city. The ballot will pose a simple question: "Should the city of Island View dissolve?"

The issue is being debated seriously, yet politely and with some humor. It took City Clerk Tom Neagbour more than four years after graduating from St. Cloud State, with a degree in public administration, to find a job in his field.

"I went to college to learn about things like economic development and how to build up a city," said Neagbour, whose $275 per month part-time salary makes him the highest-paid city employee. "Then I get into the business

**Island View** continued on page 14A

## New evidence of recession's end

Fresh evidence that the recession has probably ended was provided Friday in government reports showing inflation was moderate and industrial production rose sharply in May. **Page 1D.**

## Presidential poisoning?

A Kentucky coroner will be allowed to test the corpse of former President Zachary Taylor to see if he was poisoned in 1850. **Page 7A**

## CHIP SHOTS

### THE LEADER BOARD

| | Score |
|---|---|
| **Seven under par** | |
| Payne Stewart .... | 67-70—137 |
| **Six under par** | |
| Corey Pavin ........ | 71-67—138 |
| Nolan Henke ...... | 67-71—138 |
| Scott Simpson .... | 70-68—138 |
| **Four under par** | |
| Scott Hoch ......... | 69-71—140 |
| Fred Couples ...... | 70-70—140 |
| Craig Stadler ...... | 71-69—140 |

### BACK SWING

Payne Stewart has a bad back. So he switched beds with his 2-year-old son to get a harder mattress. He now holds a one-shot lead.

### FIELD OF SCREAMS

A highly placed clubhouse source says Kevin Costner will be at Hazeltine this weekend. It was Patrick Swayze earlier in the week.

# Doctor with AIDS virus reportedly limits practice

**By Lewis Cope**
Staff Writer

A 39-year-old Minneapolis-area family physician who is infected with the AIDS virus reportedly has agreed with state medical officials to limit his practice to prevent any risk of spreading the virus to patients.

Some of his patients are expected to be asked to have blood tests to see if they have the virus. But health officials have said that the risk of any doctor-to-patient spread of the virus is extremely small.

WCCO-TV identified the doctor as Philip D. Benson, who practices in Minneapolis and Columbia Heights. He could not be reached for comment Friday night. It is the first time such actions have been taken in Minnesota, although they have been taken in several other states.

Michael Osterholm, state epidemiologist at the Minnesota Department of Health, said there is no known state case of any doctor spreading the AIDS virus to a patient during patient care. But Osterholm said he couldn't comment on the reports that a doctor's practice has been limited, except to say "we are doing an investigation and hope to be able to say more soon."

The doctor reportedly has agreed to forgo doing any surgery, child delivery or other procedure in which the patient's body is entered in a way that risks spread of blood from the doctor to the patient. It is not clear how often a family practitioner might be involved in such proce-

**Doctor** continued on page 11A

## Almanac

**Saturday, June 15, 1991**
**166th day; 199 to go this year**
**Sunrise: 5:26. Sunset: 9:00**

Cloudy, with high of 82 and low of 57



Circulation 673-4343



Volume X/Number 72 7 sections

# Rain muddies Round 2 traffic, parking picture

**By Paul Klauda**
Staff Writer

Thousands of fans at the U.S. Open in Chaska got a taste of city and country Friday, enduring downtown-style traffic gridlock for up to an hour on some roads before slopping their way through muddy alfalfa-field parking lots.

An unexpectedly steady drizzle in the morning rendered much of the parking space unusable and forced Open officials to change parking plans "on the fly." They rerouted about 16,000 fans to lots at the Renaissance Festival in Shakopee, from which shuttle buses brought them to Hazeltine National Golf Club.

The change in plans, which began shortly after 8 a.m., caused traffic tie-ups of 25 minutes to more than an hour on at least three major roads around the course during the morning. The public lots, which drew about 25,000 people, were completely closed about 11 a.m.

The Hazeltine parking lots will be closed today, and all fans and volunteers will be shuttled to the course from the Renaissance lots, 7 miles away. The gates at Renaissance, west of Shakopee on Hwy. 169 (**see map on Page 9A**), will open at 6 a.m. Spectators coming from the metro area should add 30 to 60 minutes to

**Open** continued on page 9A

MARKETPLACE

**PC decade**

IBM unveiled first personal computer just 10 years ago

**Twins rally over Angels 4-3 in happy homecoming/1C**

**NWA loses Pan Am bid/1D**

VARIETY

**Bladerunners**

In-line skating booms in the state where it was born

**MINNEAPOLIS EDITION**

■ Hepatitis scare slows business at Chi-Chi's/**1B**

■ Hmong man sues woman's parents for unreturned dowry/**3B**

■ Garbage firm to pay $625,000 to settle Hennepin case/**3B**

B

# Star Tribune

TUESDAY/August 13/1991 — NEWSPAPER OF THE TWIN CITIES — 35¢

# Chenoweth identified as man slain on beach

## Police investigation focuses on hate crimes against gays

By Mark Brunswick
Staff Writer

John Chenoweth, former state senator and head of the Minneapolis city pension fund, was identified on Monday as the man killed during a weekend shooting at a beach frequented by gays.

Police said the shooting, which left another man seriously wounded, was related to the shooting death two weeks ago of Joel Larson, another gay man, in Loring Park.

Police would not describe the possible connection but said they are investigating the deaths as bias crimes against gays. "Certainly that's the natural assumption," said police chief John Laux. "Whether this is the motive or there are other motives, I'm looking at this as a hate, bias crime."

The Hennepin County medical examiner identified Chenoweth, 48, as the shooting victim yesterday afternoon after examining dental records.

Although investigators say they are not ruling out any possibilities in the Chenoweth shooting, Lt. Brad Johnson, head of the department's homicide unit, said police are focusing more on Chenoweth's gay lifestyle than his previous business dealings as a possible motive.

Chenoweth, a well-connected former DFL state legislator, resigned as head of the city's pension fund in May last year. In the months that followed, his handling of personal and fund investments was questioned and he was named in lawsuits.

"Gay-bashing is only one possibility, several others are being investigated," Johnson said.

The connection in the deaths of Chenoweth and Larson fueled concerns from members of the gay community that police were not doing enough to solve the slayings. Gay activists attended an afternoon news conference and peppered Laux with questions. They also called for a protest outside City Hall in which they denounced inactivity in the cases and also called for putting openly gay police officers on the force.

John Chenoweth

Deputy Police Chief David Dobrotka and several other city officials met with the activists for an hour to try to defuse tensions over what gays characterize as the department's pattern of hostility or indifference toward them.

**Slayings** continued on page 10A

## Ex-pension chief neither hid nor flaunted his lifestyle

By Dennis J. McGrath
and David Phelps
Staff Writers

The news of John Chenoweth's slaying was a shock, but the circumstances in which he died — shot at 5 a.m. on a riverbank beach frequented by gays — weren't totally surprising to his friends and to most people who dealt with him when he headed an $800 million public employee pension fund.

His death drew attention to something that was an open secret at City Hall and the Legislature: He was gay.

Chenoweth, 48, neither broadcast nor tried to conceal his gay lifestyle. He never publicly acknowledged it, but he was seen at gay bars and other gay hang-outs, and parties he threw at his house were attended predominantly by gays, according to his friends and acquaintances.

It was that lifestyle that apparently led him to the gay beach on the east bank of the Mississippi River in Minneapolis, where his partly disrobed body was found Saturday morning. Police said he may have been the victim of a hate crime against gays.

**Chenoweth** continued on page 10A

Staff Photo by Brian Peterson

**Members of the gay community met with Deputy Police Chief David Dobrotka Monday to voice their concern that not enough was being done to solve the recent slayings of two gay men. Said Dobrotka: "The first thing is not to focus on the animosity. . . . We both have the same goal."**

# Letter offers swap for hostages

## Captors seek to free Arabs

Los Angeles Times

**Washington, D.C.**
In a letter derided by President Bush as grist for "the rumor game," an Islamic fundamentalist group has offered to exchange the 10 remaining hostages in Lebanon for "the release of our freedom-fighters from prisons" in Israel and Europe, the United Nations announced Monday.

The emotional letter from Islamic Jihad was carried out of captivity by freed British hostage John McCarthy and turned over to U.N. Secretary-General Javier Perez de Cuellar Sunday. As requested by the group, its contents were made public at U.N. headquarters in Geneva.

Despite Bush's tart comment, White House press secretary Marlin Fitzwater said, "Our preliminary analysis suggests there may be some positive aspects to the letter."

Others found glimmers of hope as well. Perez de Cuellar, who met with a key Israeli official Sunday night and conferred with French Foreign Minister Roland Dumas yesterday, said later that the letter had made him "a little more hopeful than before because we have very concrete evidence that those who hold the hostages are more interested in a solution."

Asked if he thought an end to the

**Hostages** continued on page 10A

## Israel rejects demand to free Arabs, but door open for deal

From News Services

**Jerusalem**
Expressing disappointment with an Islamic terrorist group's letter to the United Nations secretary-general, Israeli officials Monday rejected demands that they free hundreds of Arab prisoners as a good-will gesture to encourage the release of Western hostages believed held in Beirut.

But there were at least some signs from the Israeli government that it retained a measure of optimism about the possibility of striking a deal that would free Israeli soldiers missing in Lebanon as well as the Arab and Western captives in the region.

Two Israeli hostage negotiators returned empty-handed from a meeting in Geneva with U.N. Secretary-General Javier Perez de Cuellar in which they expected information of a possible deal to free as many as seven missing Israeli soldiers. In exchange, Israel is offering to release Lebanese prisoners as well as at least one hostage of its own — a Muslim cleric abducted from Lebanon two years

**Israel** continued on page 11A

# Depression, other demons of war still haunt state's Asian refugees

By Wendy S. Tai
Staff Writer

Pov Srey Kong's cheeks flush bright red with heat and pain. Her vision blurs, and she gets severe headaches.

She lies awake at night, unable to purge the memories: her husband shot to death, a newborn son dying, three other children lost during the chaos of war in Cambodia.

She was beaten, raped and starved, forced to work day and night clearing forests and building dams during the bloody reign of the Khmer Rouge.

It all happened more than a decade ago, but Kong feels the pain every day.

"If I think too much, I get dizzy again," she said last week in her Minneapolis apartment. "When I think about my background, the destruction of my family, my husband, my face gets pain. I cannot sleep for the whole night."

Doctors and mental health workers say Kong's plight is common among Southeast Asian refugees. Serious depression is widespread, experts say, estimating that 50 to 70 percent of the approximately 36,000 Southeast Asian refugees in Minnesota suffer some type of emotional or psychological problem. A 1986-87 study of more than 400 Southeast Asian refugees treated at the Community University Health Care Clinic in Minneapolis found that nearly 75 percent experienced major depression.

**Refugees** continued on page 4A

## Other news inside/

**School near racial waiver**/ A State Board of Education committee voted unanimously Monday to allow the Minneapolis School District to operate a new school for an American Indian and French program with a minority enrollment of more than 83 percent. The issue goes to the full school board today, and already has enough votes to assure passage. **1B.**

**KARE-TV manager resigns**/ Linda Rios Brook, a controversial figure in local broadcasting, has resigned as general manager at Channel 11. **1B.**

**Schmidt labor terms reached**/ Investors trying to buy the Schmidt brewery have reached contract agreements with labor union officials, a major step toward reopening the plant. **5B.**

**Big banks to merge**/ BankAmerica Corp. and Security Pacific Corp. plan to merge, creating the nation's second-biggest bank. **1D.**

## Almanac

**Tuesday, August 13, 1991**
**225th day; 140 to go this year**
**Sunrise: 6:12. Sunset: 8:24**

Hazy, with high of 86. Low, 63.

| | | | |
|---|---|---|---|
| Comics | 4,5E | Obituaries | 4B |
| Movies | 8E | TV, Radio | 6E |
| Complete index | 2A | | |
| Classifieds | 673-7000 | | |
| Circulation | 673-4343 | | |

Volume X/Number 131 6 sections

# The bottled-up dreams of 1924 'modern girls' are unearthed

By Laurie Blake
Staff Writer

'The fortune teller . . . told me that I would be married within two years. I wonder what will really happen.'

It was August 1924 when four young Minneapolis women sat down together to record their hopes and dreams in letters to themselves. They placed the letters in a blue canning jar and buried it, vowing to dig it up five years later to see how their lives compared with their aspirations.

Last week, construction workers unearthed the jar at the base of the old Lake St.-Marshall Av. Bridge, which was demolished on Friday.

The lid had rusted off the jar, and one letter was badly damaged by water and mold. But parts of all four letters were legible, and three are in remarkably good condition.

"The letters give a nice glimpse into the lives and hopes of young working women in Minneapolis," said Mark Greene, chief of manuscript acquisition for the Minnesota Historical Society, which wants to add the letters to the society's collection of manuscripts.

The letters are now in the possession of the state Transportation Department, which is holding them to see if the women or their relatives come forward to claim them.

The letters tell the story of four friends impatient with their post-high-school clerical jobs, and eager to get on with marriages and musical performances. They wrote the letters at the farewell lunch for one of the four, who was going to music school.

"What could be more interesting or unique than to see four perfectly normal modern girls

**Letters** continued on page 8A

INSIDE: **Twins rally to win their third straight over A's 6-4**/1C

**MINNEAPOLIS**
EDITION

■ Noise protesters think time ripe for NWA concessions/**1B**

# Star Tribune

**MONDAY**/August 19/1991 NEWSPAPER OF THE TWIN CITIES 35¢

# Gorbachev ousted by hard-line group

## State of emergency is declared

**From Wire Services**

**Moscow, U.S.S.R.**
Soviet President Mikhail Gorbachev was replaced today while he was on vacation by a ruling committee that includes Vice President Gennady Yanayev, the defense and KGB chiefs and other hard-liners, the Tass news agency said.

An official announcement said Gorbachev could no longer perform his duties for health reasons, but it appeared that he was pushed from power six years into his "perestroika" reform program.

Tass said that a state of emergency had been imposed in parts of the country and that an eight-member "State Committee for the State of Emergency" had been formed to take "decisive measures." It includes Yanayev, Defense Minister Dmitri Yazov and KGB Chairman Vladimir Kryuchkov.

Gorbachev has angered conservatives by making concessions to the United States on arms control, failing to improve the economy and failing to prevent the 15 republics from adhering to national laws.

His apparent removal came three days after a warning of a coup from his closest reform adviser, Aleksandr Yakovlev.

Yanayev, in a statement carried by Tass this morning, declared a state of emergency for six months in "individual localities." It did not say what areas were affected. Neither did he say what health problems prevented the 60-year-old Gorbachev from continuing as president.

"All power in the country is transferred for this period to the state committee for the

**Gorbachev** continued on page 9A

Gennady Yanayev

Mikhail Gorbachev

## Salomon firm is penalized; 3 officers quit

**New York Times**

**New York, N.Y.**
In an extraordinary action Sunday, the Treasury Department suspended Salomon Brothers Inc., one of Wall Street's biggest trading and investment houses, from bidding in Treasury auctions because of a scandal involving the firm's illegal bidding in that market.

But hours later, the department largely reversed itself after a personal appeal to Nicholas Brady, the Treasury secretary, by Warren Buffett, who was appointed chairman and chief executive of the scandal-torn firm at a board meeting yesterday

Buffett's appeal, made during several telephone calls yesterday, did not succeed, however, in stopping the department from limiting Salomon's role in Treasury auctions until the scandal is investigated.

While Salomon will be permitted to bid in the auctions for itself, the firm will not be allowed to place orders for clients, a move that will drive that business to the firm's competitors.

The actions by the Treasury Department came as the scandal at Salomon appeared to widen further. Buffett disclosed yesterday that records of the firm had been altered by some executives in what appeared to be an attempt to cover up the illegal bidding. He also said the firm had committed one additional violation of the bidding rules that had not been previously disclosed.

Previously Salomon had said that it violated government rules by exceeding bidding limits in the Treasury auctions in December, February, April and May.

**Salomon** continued on page 6A

## Rarick wins Northgate Classic

Staff Photo by Marlin Levison

**Cindy Rarick celebrated Sunday after sinking a 7-foot birdie putt on the third hole of a sudden-death playoff to beat Beth Daniel in the Northgate Computer Classic at Edinburgh USA. Details in Sports.**

## Hurricane hits North Carolina islands

### Roads flooded in Outer Banks

**Associated Press**

**Manteo, N.C.**
Hurricane Bob blasted North Carolina's Outer Banks and hurtled northward early today with 115-mile-per-hour winds and gusts to 138 mph. Forecasters said the storm could slam into New England this evening.

The storm's 20-mile-wide eye stayed just offshore of North Carolina's narrow barrier beach islands, said Robert Molleda, a meteorologist at the National Hurricane Center in Coral Gables, Fla.

But the west wall of the eye — the most intense part of a hurricane — did sweep over Cape Hatteras late Sunday, Molleda said.

The wind whipped trees and downed power lines, and a 3- to 5-foot tidal surge churned the surf and combined with torrential rain to flood roads along the resort islands.

It was impossible to get damage reports immediately.

"The wind's blowing so hard right now and it's raining so hard that we're not really going to get any idea of damage assessment until daybreak," said Kill Devil Hills police spokeswoman Mary Quidley.

At midnight, she said, "You could hardly see the streets because the rain's coming down in sheets."

The storm was moving to the north-

**Hurricane** continued on page 6A

## 8 arrested after fights erupt at crowded dance at Convention Center

**By Mark Brunswick**
Staff Writer

Eight people were arrested late Saturday after several fights prompted authorities to close down a dance at the Minneapolis Convention Center.

The arrests followed reports of fights inside a ballroom at the center where a dance for black college-age people had become overcrowded. Following the outbreak of fights, police and promoters decided to shut down the event, which may have caused additional fights to break out, according to police reports.

In what appears to be a separate incident following the fights, two people were arrested in a confrontation with Minneapolis police that one witness described as "a full-blown free-for-all" by police.

One of those arrested, Dennis Cherry, 21, said he and a friend were roughed up by police while they were trying to leave the area. Cherry was treated for facial injuries.

Both Cherry, who lives in Eden Prairie, and a witness who lives near the center said they plan to contact authorities today to complain about what happened.

Minneapolis Deputy Chief Ted Faul said officials will review police reports of the incident today and begin an internal review of the events leading up to the arrests. Police reports

**Dance** continued on page 12A

## Golf means gold for cities that have their own greens

**By Mike Kaszuba**
Staff Writer

At 5:30 in the morning, parents are dropping off 10-year-olds for lessons at Bloomington's municipal golf course.

Over in Inver Grove Heights, the city opens a golf driving range June 1, thinking it'll produce $35,000 in revenues by the end of the summer; it now watches as the figure nears $50,000 in early August.

And in Cottage Grove, the city's new 18-hole golf course projects 20,000 rounds of golf will be played on it this summer. The projection has since been upped to 27,000 rounds.

"Golf is in," said Jack Denzer, a Cottage Grove City Council member.

All across Minnesota, but especially in Twin Cities suburbs, municipal golf courses are good business for City Hall. More than a quarter of the 22 golf courses being developed in Minnesota are being built by cities or counties. A Bloomington official says the city could easi-

**Golf** continued on page 4A

## Almanac

**Monday, August 19, 1991**
**231st day; 134 to go this year**
**Sunrise: 6:19. Sunset: 8:14**

### Today's weather/

Sunny, with a high of 76. Low, 55.

### Index/



### Telephones/

| | |
|---|---|
| General Information | 673-4000 |
| Classifieds | 673-7000 |
| Circulation | 673-4343 |


Volume X/Number 137 6 sections

### America West to get NWA loan

Northwest Airlines has announced a deal to loan $20 million to financially troubled America West Airlines. In exchange, Northwest gets a joint marketing plan and the option to buy a route from Honolulu to Japan for $15 million in two years. **Page 1B.**

## Peers aid elderly women who have little left but pride

**By Warren Wolfe**
Staff Writer

They seek out their targets on city buses, in grocery stores, at banks and in apartment buildings — old women of color in trouble.

"We know they are there. Most of them are almost invisible. They don't know about programs that can help them, they don't trust officials and often they're too proud to ask for assistance," said Margery Chan Goebel, 68.

She and five other women prowl Minneapolis in search of older minority women who need help. Older minority women are twice as likely as older white women to live in poverty and twice as likely not to use community services, organizers say.

Since April 1, the six women have been peer outreach workers hired by the Minneapolis YWCA to find minority women age 55 and older who are in need, helping them make contact with agencies that can help.

The six were chosen in part because they have attributes that make it easier for older women to identify with them. They range in age from 61 to 75 and include a black, American Indian, Hispanic, two Asians and a white woman who uses a wheelchair.

"We look like them. We talk like them. We may be their best bet for getting enough food, heat or medical help — just helping them live the way they deserve to live," Goebel said.

**Women** continued on page 12A

Hurricane Bob smashes trees, power lines in New England/6A

MINNEAPOLIS EDITION

■ Protest calls for end to 'queer bashing' and violence/1B

Star Tribune

TUESDAY/August 20/1991

NEWSPAPER OF THE TWIN CITIES

35¢

# Soviet coup leaders move to impose hard-line controls

## Dissent suppressed as tanks guard Moscow

## Yeltsin tries to rally support for Gorbachev

From News Services

**Moscow, U.S.S.R.**
The group dominated by the military and the KGB that engineered Soviet President Mikhail Gorbachev's ouster moved quickly Monday to reimpose hard-line control across the Soviet Union. The coup leaders banned protest meetings, shut independent newspapers and flooded the capital with troops and tanks.

President Boris Yeltsin of the Russian republic, who often had been at odds with Gorbachev, became one of his strongest supporters yesterday, seeking to rally resistance to Gorbachev's overthrow by climbing atop an armored truck and calling for a general workers strike today to protest the Kremlin move as an unconstitutional coup d'etat.

By nightfall, Yeltsin had some of his own Russian republic troops and armored combat vehicles rallying to his headquarters, and some positive responses were being heard to his call for a strike, notably from coal miners and auto workers in Siberia.

The scene was set for a possible confrontation between troops loyal to Yeltsin and those under the command of the central authorities when some federal troops began rallying to Yeltsin's side, including an airborne battalion from Rayazan, south of Moscow, and tanks from the elite Tamanskaya Guards division.

"We came here for the people's sake, for Russia's sake," a first lieutenant in the airborne battalion said.

President Bush called for the restoration of the deposed Soviet leader and urged those who ousted him not to use force against Gorbachev's supporters.

"This misguided and illegitimate effort bypasses both Soviet law and the will of the Soviet peoples," Bush said in a statement directed at the hard-liners behind the coup. "We call upon the U.S.S.R. to abide by its international treaties and commitments," Bush said, "including its commitments to respect basic human rights and democratic practices."

Bush issued the statement after cutting short a vacation at his Kennebunkport, Maine, compound to return to Washington for 24 hours.

In the Soviet Union, one death was reported, that of an unidentified person said to have been killed in Riga, Latvia.

**Coup** continued on page 14A

KREMLIN COUP

**Takeover builds**/ Hard-liners who deposed Soviet President Mikhail Gorbachev moved to consolidate power by declaring a state of emergency in Moscow and Leningrad, sending troops to storm key sites in the Baltics and reimposing strict censorship.

**Opponents gather**/ Russian President Boris Yeltsin took the lead of internal opposition, denouncing the coup and calling for nonviolent protests. Scattered demonstrations were met by shows of military force, but few violent clashes or casualties were reported.

**Bush blasts coup**/ President Bush also condemned the ouster of his Soviet counterpart, threatening to suspend U.S. aid to Moscow and calling for Gorbachev's immediate restoration to power. The Soviet president's whereabouts were unknown.

**Markets gyrate**/ Events in Moscow brought turmoil to financial markets – stock prices plunged, bond and oil prices rallied, the dollar soared and gold prices went nowhere. Experts disagreed about how much the world economy would suffer from Gorbachev's ouster.

Associated Press

**Russian President Boris Yeltsin, left, read a statement from atop a tank in Moscow Monday, urging the Soviet people to resist the hard-line takeover of central government and appealing to Soviet soldiers not to fire on their countrymen. The soldiers, sent by the newly installed government, made no move to stop him.**

## Soviet crisis news inside

Nine pages of coverage of the Kremlin coup begin inside today on page 7A.



## Muscovites awaken to nightmare, fear for the future

**By Celestine Bohlen**
New York Times

**Moscow, U.S.S.R.**
As a dozen tanks rolled through Mayakovsky Square, kicking up a cloud of exhaust in the moist evening air, Alla Mikhailovna, in the capital for a visit with her 7-year-old son, stood on the sidewalk and cried.

"It is horrible, just horrible," said the 43-year-old geologist from Tashkent. She identified herself with her given name and patronymic, in the Russian fashion, but declined to give her last name. "I am so sad for my country. What will come of this? Where will it end? War? It is just so frightening."

Across this bedraggled city, people struggled through the day, trying to figure out what had happened to them overnight.

They had awakened to find their president mysteriously gone, purportedly for "health reasons," a new State Committee for the State of Emergency in control and military vehicles roaming the city.

As the day wore on, doused by heavy rains, many Muscovites knew no more than they did when they listened to the first terse bulletins on the state-controlled television and radio. But what they knew was enough to make them stiffen with anxiety.

"We woke up to the noise of tanks on the streets," said Slava Ivanov, a 45-year-old driver. "Beyond that, I still don't know anything concretely. Where is Gorbachev? Where is Yeltsin? All I know is nothing good can come from tanks."

**Moscow** continued on page 14A

## New regime must now show its muscle

**By Michael Parks**
Los Angeles Times

**Analysis**

Having seized power to save the Soviet Union from what they see as chaos and collapse, the country's new conservative leaders must now show how ruthless they will be in using that power.

As Russian President Boris Yeltsin called for a nationwide strike in opposition to the putsch, and crowds of Muscovites surrounded tanks deployed in the capital, the self-proclaimed State Emergency Committee faced an immediate challenge Monday.

After deposing Soviet President Mikhail Gorbachev, were they prepared to arrest Yeltsin, the country's most popular politician? Were their soldiers ready to fire on crowds of demonstrators or striking workers? Would a show or even use of force intimidate a nation that recently has taken so ardently to democracy?

Beyond that, however, was the equally tough question of what strategy the conservatives hope to implement with their new power.

Could the conservatives, who have increasingly undermined Gorbachev's reforms, pull the country out of the crisis they had done so much to create? How would the government bureaucrats who mismanaged the Soviet economy for so long now save it?

**Analysis** continued on page 15A

## Almanac

**Tuesday, August 20, 1991**
**232nd day; 133 to go this year**
**Sunrise: 6:20. Sunset: 8:13**
Partly sunny. High 79. Low 63.



Circulation 673-4343



Volume X/Number 138 6 sections

Cuban inmates hold 11 hostages at federal prison in Alabama/2A

MINNEAPOLIS EDITION

■ Mammenga retreats on desegregation of black academy/1B

Star Tribune

THURSDAY/August 22/1991 NEWSPAPER OF THE TWIN CITIES 35¢

# Coup collapses

## Gorbachev returns to power, thanks Yeltsin, Soviet people

**From News Services**

**Moscow, U.S.S.R.**
A coup by hard-line Communists collapsed on Wednesday as abruptly as it began, and President Mikhail Gorbachev returned to Moscow early this morning to reassert control.

Tanks withdrew from Moscow and national legislative leaders invalidated the coup leaders' decrees, including press restrictions. Even the Communist Party belatedly denounced the coup, and a prosecutor announced investigations into the men behind the overthrow.

In a message read on Soviet evening television news — his first words to be made public after three days spent under house arrest — Gorbachev said he was "in full control of the situation" and would resume his full duties within a day.

He also made it clear that the high-level officials who tried to overthrow him, many of them longtime and trusted colleagues, would be made to bear "full responsibility." Within hours, the reckoning may have begun: Russian authorities reported that the chairman of the KGB, one of the plotters, had been arrested.

Gorbachev arrived at 2:15 a.m. at remote Vnukovo Airport from his summer retreat in the Crimea. Smiling broadly and with no visible indication of ill health, he was dressed casually in a loose, tan sportcoat and sweater instead of his usual dark suit and tie.

"This is some serious victory of the perestroika process," he told Soviet television. Speaking in the third person, he said the coup organizers had tried to isolate him.

"What did they do to the president and his family? For 72 hours, they surrounded him with troops, and they wanted to break his willpower, but they lost," Gorbachev said. "And here is my respect to the Soviet people, and specificaly, to Boris Yeltsin, the president of Russia, and to all labor collectives, to all people who stood up in the way of reaction."

Later, he told Moscow Radio that the failure of the plot was a victory for his policies of reform and showed that the Soviet people trusted their leaders. "I congratulate our Soviet people, who have both a sense of responsibility and a sense of dignity and a concern for respecting all those to whom they entrust power," he said in a broadcast monitored by the BBC.

Gorbachev was expected to meet today with Yeltsin, who led the popular resistance that defeated the coup. He had already spoken by telephone with Yeltsin and President Bush, as well as with the acting heads of his Cabinet and Defense Ministry, both of whose leaders participated in the coup.

Tens of thousands of anticoup demonstrators outside the Russian Parliament building, Yeltsin's

**Coup** continued on page 18A

Associated Press

**Soviet President Mikhail Gorbachev arrived in Moscow early this morning from the Crimea, where he reportedly had been held.**

### KREMLIN COUP

**What happened/**
The Kremlin coup attempt is over. The tanks that surrounded the Russian Parliament building are gone. President Mikhail Gorbachev, liberated from posh imprisonment, is back in charge.

**Why it happened/**
To President Bush, it happened because you can't put the genie of freedom back in the bottle. Others attribute the coup's failure to the bungling of its leaders. There's even an intriguing, if far-fetched, theory that it happened because Gorbachev planned it that way.

**What's next?/**
Russian Republic President Boris Yeltsin, after a heroic two nights as resistance leader, might be the leader of the future. Hard-line Communists might disappear as a factor in Soviet politics. The pace of democratic and free-market reforms might accelerate.

**Fourteen pages of coverage of the coup collapse begin on Page 7A.**

## Failed takeover attempt leaves old guard breathing last gasp

**By Bill Keller**
New York Times

**Analysis**

**Moscow, U.S.S.R.**
The bungled takeover of the Soviet government left the incumbents of the Communist past discredited and hastened the demise of the old guard, which long had been whispering caution in the ear of Soviet President Mikhail Gorbachev.

Communism as an ideology already was so moribund that even the conspirators did not wave the Marxist-Leninist flag, claiming instead stability as their cause.

Communism as a political force was Wednesday's casualty, because the coup debunked Gorbachev's rationale for clinging to the Communist Party as his power base, in the hope that by doing so he could keep its diehard partisans in check.

The failed coup legitimized the claim of post-Communist reformers that they are the rightful heirs to power and invigorated them for the mammoth task of civilizing their country.

It also raised the possibility that those who have prevailed may move against those pillars of the KGB and the military who conspired against them.

When the euphoria recedes, however, Gorbachev and the radicals will still face a fundamental problem that the conspirators were banking on to carry their coup: the public's fear of anarchy, ethnic conflict and economic insecurity, which has eroded trust in all politicians.

**Analysis** continued on page 19A

### Almanac

**Thursday, August 22, 1991**
**234th day; 131 to go this year**
**Sunrise: 6:23. Sunset: 8:09**

Sunny. High 83. Northeast wind 5-10.

**Index/**



**Telephones/**

| | |
|---|---|
| General Information | 673-4000 |
| Classifieds | 673-7000 |
| Circulation | 673-4343 |


Volume X/Number 140 7 sections

## Kremlin junta disappears into an inglorious defeat

**By Francis X. Clines**
New York Times

**Moscow, U.S.S.R.**
The Kremlin junta's sense of cliche was unfailing to the end.

Facing defeat, the anxious men of the sagging coup d'etat reportedly fled for the airport on Wednesday to seek sanctuary elsewhere.

One report said some went to distant Kirghizia, while others were off to the Crimea to see their captive, President Mikhail Gorbachev.

A beige Volga limousine with anti-junta policemen from the Russian federation followed in pursuit. The Volga's mission was to catch the junta. But the outer road was crowded with more than 100 tanks, moving as ingloriously in retreat as the junta.

The Volga finally arrived at the locked VIP gates at Vnukovo airport, and a guard rebuffed the pursuing plainclothes police agents.

"Who are you? Where are your papers?" the guard demanded.

Instantly, a large man stepped from

**Moscow** continued on page 16A

**Twins and West top Indians/1C**

VARIETY
**Take me to the river**

SPORTS
**High school football preview**

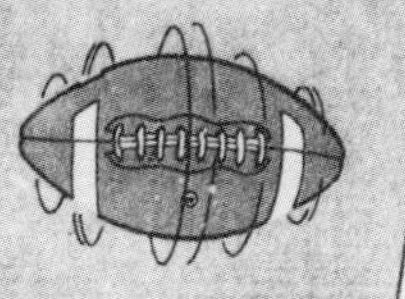

**MINNEAPOLIS EDITION**

- Woman leads coup attempt against drainage pond/**1B**
- New Metro Mobility fares discriminate, state says/**1B**
- Action against Kelley in Durenberger case found unwarranted/**1B**

Star Tribune
THURSDAY/August 29/1991
NEWSPAPER OF THE TWIN CITIES
W
35¢

# Russia, Ukraine form alliance

From News Services

Russia and the Ukraine, the two most populous Soviet republics, agreed early today to form a temporary economic and military alliance and invited other "former subjects of the U.S.S.R." to join them.

The agreement did not mention any significant future role for the Kremlin or for Soviet President Mikhail Gorbachev.

In Moscow, meanwhile, the Russian prosecutor's office charged 13 men accused of leading last week's Kremlin coup with high treason, while Gorbachev carried out a full-scale purge against the KGB and his own government.

The Russian-Ukrainian agreement, announced in the Ukrainian capital of Kiev after a day and night of talks, said the two republics intend "to undertake joint actions with the goal of preventing the uncontrolled disintegration of the union state." However, the wording of the joint communique also indicated that the agreement could form the basis of a new system of states to replace the Soviet Union.

Seven Soviet republics have declared themselves independent. The Ukraine made its declaration on Saturday, followed by its neighbors Byelorussia on Sunday and Moldavia on Tuesday. Russia has declared sovereignty but not outright independence from Kremlin rule.

After Russia, the Ukraine is considered the republic most important to the survival of the Soviet Union, with its agricultural and industrial bounty, its warm-water ports and lengthy border with Central Europe.

The Kiev talks began yesterday afternoon after reports that Ukrainian officials were concerned by Russian officials' suggestions that Russia might seek to alter its borders with certain republics in a post-Communist era.

The talks also focused on the future of Soviet nuclear weapons. Russian Federation President Boris Yeltsin had offered to take into Russia all nuclear weapons now stationed in the Ukraine, which borders Russia on the west and has declared itself a nuclear-free state.

In Moscow, Gorbachev yesterday fired the top leadership body of the KGB and directed the agency's new chief, Vadim Bakatin, to undertake a complete reform of the secret police. In the Supreme Soviet legislature.

**Soviets** continued on page 6A

■ Rep. Les Aspin, chairman of the House Armed Services Committee, proposed that Congress draw $1 billion from the Pentagon budget for humanitarian aid to the Soviet Union this winter. **Page 7A.**

**Other stories on 6A and 7A.**

## Informers find conspirators everywhere

By Carey Goldberg
Los Angeles Times

**Moscow, U.S.S.R.**
A strapping guard stands watch over the damning documents, just in case a guilty official with too much to lose resorts to violence to get at them.

Nearby, the phones ring repeatedly as the calls pour in: neighbors denouncing neighbors, workers denouncing bosses and coworkers. The accusation: showing too much enthusiasm for last week's attempted coup.

"They taught us for so long how to inform on each other," Yuri Khramov, a deputy on the Moscow City Council, said Wednesday. "Now, we're getting a new breed — democratic denunciations."

Khramov is a member of a city commission set up to investigate the coup. It is just one of a rash of investigative panels that have sprouted across the country to pin down and punish the thousands upon thousands of conservatives who backed the failed putsch.

Members of such bodies say they know they must walk a very careful line between justice and revenge.

"This is not a witch hunt, and we don't like to look like bloodthirsty commissars," Moscow deputy Igor Belyaev said. "We take only information that is not anonymous. There are too many informants who have their own personal goals."

Many of the calls to the Moscow

**Informers** continued on page 17A

## 5 killed, more than 130 hurt in N.Y. subway accident

Associated Press

**A tangle of metal remained from part of a subway car that derailed in New York City early Wednesday. Five people were killed and more than 130 hurt after five cars derailed. A motorman was charged with manslaughter after police alleged that he operated the train recklessly and had been drinking before the incident. Page 2A.**

## Got the sniffles?
### Stress could double your risk for colds

From News Services

The stress of such problems as losing a job, breaking off an engagement or simply feeling overwhelmed by life's burdens nearly doubles the risk of catching a cold, a study has found.

In the clearest demonstration yet of the relationship between emotions and infections, researchers in Pittsburgh and Britain found that high levels of psychological stress could nearly double a person's chances of catching a cold by lowering resistance to viral infection.

Results of the study, conducted on more than 400 volunteers at the Medical Research Council's Common Cold Unit in Salisbury, England, were published today in the New England Journal of Medicine.

In an accompanying editorial, Dr. Morton N. Swartz of Massachusetts General Hospital praised the study for avoiding the deficiencies that have marred previous investigations of the relationship between stress and disease.

The study bolstered a growing movement within medicine that contends that state of mind plays a major role in helping the body resist infection and disease.

Many mainstream researchers remain skeptical. Although few health professionals doubt that emotional distress plays a role in many ail-

**Colds** continued on page 18A

## Dayton to sue NWA, airport panel over 'secret' financing

By Laurie Blake
Staff Writer

State Auditor Mark Dayton announced Wednesday that he plans to sue Northwest Airlines and the Metropolitan Airports Commission, saying it is "outrageously wrong" for public officials to keep the airline's finances secret while deciding whether to approve $740 million in financial assistance for the airline.

"The public has the right to know the facts — no secret deals," he said.

Dayton's announcement touched off a day of debate among officials about how open the negotiations between the state and Northwest will be. At issue is the airline's financial condition as the state decides whether to provide it with a $390 million loan and $350 million in construction funds for two maintenance bases.

It's unclear how Dayton will proceed with the suit and whether it will interfere with negotiations for the deal, which Northwest has said must be concluded by Sept. 30. Dayton, who said he supports the deal itself, is expected to meet today with members of the airport commission and state officials to discuss his intentions.

**NWA** continued on page 14A

## Almanac

**Thursday, August 29, 1991**
**241st day; 124 to go this year**
**Sunrise: 6:31. Sunset: 7:57**

### Today's weather/
Sticky, maybe wet

Partly sunny and humid with southwest winds at 10-15 mph and a chance of a thunderstorm in the Twin Cities today. High 87. Tonight, chance of a lingering shower, with skies clearing later. Low 66.



### Telephones/

| | |
|---|---|
| General Information | 673-4000 |
| Classifieds | 673-7000 |
| Circulation | 673-4343 |


Volume X/Number 147 6 sections

## City animal shelter, already in need, fears more pain from Fraser's budget

By Jon Jeter
Staff Writer

At the converted sheet-metal shop that serves as Minneapolis' animal shelter, stray dogs and cats are destroyed on the cold linoleum floor of a tiny storage area. Skunks meet a slow death by drowning in garbage bins.

Kennels are constructed of woven wire, increasing the chances of spreading a fatal disease from one dog to another. Worn fiberglass cages are havens for disease, which infect the cats that stay in them.

The shelter is cramped and outdated, with files stored on index cards rather than in a computer. It is ill-equipped for surgical procedures and dangerous for workers and animals.

But Minneapolis' animal-control program could be one of the biggest casualties of the city's $20 million fiscal crisis. Mayor Don Fraser plans to trim almost $100,000 from its

**Shelter** continued on page 10A

## Family feud over funeral tests state, tribal laws

By Kevin Diaz
Staff Writer

Robert Iron Cloud lived his 29 years quietly, without making trouble for anybody and out of public view. He took care of himself, and nobody had ever made much of a fuss over him.

On Monday, the painter and tree planter from the Pine Ridge Indian Reservation in South Dakota apparently shot himself in the head in a Minneapolis house.

Now his mother and his girlfriend, who is also the mother of his three children, are locked in a legal tug-of-war over what to do with his body: Bury him in Minnesota, according to his girlfriend's wishes, or in Pine Ridge, S.D., according to his mother's wishes.

The case pits the power of Oglala

**Burial** continued on page 10A

Group hopes to bring nightclub smorgasbord to Riverplace/1D

MINNEAPOLIS
EDITION

■ Hennepin County to collect less in property taxes/1B

# Star Tribune

FRIDAY/August 30/1991 NEWSPAPER OF THE TWIN CITIES Y 35¢

# Greenwood, 3 others guilty on 61 of 73 federal charges

By Neal St. Anthony
and David Phelps
Staff Writers

Hal Greenwood Jr. and three other former executives of Midwest Federal Savings and Loan were convicted Thursday on 61 of 73 federal charges that they defrauded investors, fooled regulators and profited personally before its 1989 collapse.

"I'm very, very disappointed," a squinting, ashen-faced Greenwood said in the hot sun outside U.S. District Court in St. Paul. "I've had a lot of victories, some defeats and I guess that's all I can say."

The jurors, mostly avoiding the gaze of the defendants, watched Judge Paul Magnuson as he read a verdict pronouncing Greenwood guilty of 25 of 27 felony charges; former Executive Vice President Charlotte Masica guilty of 13 of 21 counts; former Senior Vice President Robert Mampel guilty of 14 of 15 counts, and Greenwood's daughter, former Vice President Susan Greenwood Olson, guilty of nine of 10 counts.

The verdicts, which included violations of the Racketeer Influenced and Corrupt Organizations Act, mean that the defendants will be required to forfeit approximately $4.2 million in salary, bonuses and other compensation. Greenwood will have to forfeit most of that amount.

They were originally charged in a 49-count indictment that was revised by the end of the trial. All the defendants are expected to appeal.

"The verdict was based on the evidence," said Assistant U.S. Attorney

Midwest continued on page 18A

Staff Photo by Mike Zerby

**Hal Greenwood Jr., left, and his attorney, Doug Olson, answered questions in front of the Federal building in St. Paul after Greenwood's conviction on various fraud charges.**

## The Midwest verdict

Here are the counts against the four former Midwest Federal officials. Each charge carries a maximum five-year prison sentence and maximum fines of $100,000 to $250,000.

**Hal Greenwood Jr.**
Former chairman

**Convicted on 25 of 27 counts,** including one count of conspiracy, seven of securities fraud, one each of misapplication of funds and concealment, six of false accounting entry, five of wire fraud, two of unlawful trading, and two of racketeering. Acquitted on one count of submitting a false report with the Securites and Exchange Commission and one of securities fraud.

**Charlotte Masica**
Former executive vice president

**Convicted on 13 of 21 counts,** including one of conspiracy, seven out of eight counts of securities fraud, one each of misapplication of funds and concealment, one of four counts of false accounting entry, one of five counts of wire fraud and one count of racketeering.

**Robert Mampel**
Former senior vice president

**Convicted on 14 of 15 counts,** including one of conspiracy, three of securities fraud, four of five counts of misapplication of funds, two counts of false accounting entry, and one count each of attempted misapplication of funds, false appraisal, wire fraud and racketeering.

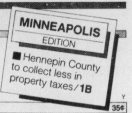

**Susan Greenwood Olson**
Former vice president

**Convicted on nine of 10 counts,** including two of three counts of misapplication of funds and one count each of conspiracy, securities fraud, attempted misapplication of funds, false appraisal, false accounting entry, wire fraud and racketeering.

Star Tribune graphic

### Inside/

■ Hal Greenwood Jr. can share the guilt with politicians who gave Midwest and other S&Ls room to ramble. **Dick Youngblood, page 1D.**

■ Jurors said that they began deliberations believing that they'd return many not-guilty verdicts.

■ On the eve of leaving office, U.S. Attorney Jerome Arnold won his biggest case of a five-year tenure scattered with big cases.

**Stories on page 20A.**

## Defendants' pain was hard to watch, but jurors' hard work served justice

**Doug Grow**

The jury was back. The wait in the trial of Hal Greenwood finally was to be over.

What an excruciating wait it had been. For 27 days, the jury had deliberated the fate of the once-mighty Greenwood, Greenwood's daughter and two other former Midwest Federal officers.

In the moments before the jury filed into the courtroom Thursday, Joe Friedberg, attorney for defendant Charlotte Masica, had talked of how awful the waiting was.

"The amount of suffering they've been through is incredible," he said. "I know how hard the waiting has been for me. Multiply it by 10 for them."

Doug Thomson, defense attorney for Susan Greenwood Olson, who was a Midwest vice president, also talked of the agony of waiting for the jury's decision.

"I think everybody expected a week," Thomson said. "Maybe two weeks. But this! The anxiety keeps building and building. The client wants to know, 'What do you suppose this means?' You don't want to be evasive but you don't know. Five weeks. I've never had a client who had to wait five weeks."

But then, Thomson said, there's never been a trial like the trial of the Midwest Four, not in the Twin Cities, anyway. It lasted for

Grow continued on page 21A

# Soviets suspend party activities

## Funds frozen as coup role probed

From News Services

Moscow, U.S.S.R.
Soviet legislators dealt a potential death blow Thursday to the Communist Party, suspending the crippled and discredited organization and freezing its bank accounts because of the party's leading role in last week's coup.

The Supreme Soviet voted, 283-29 with 52 abstentions, to suspend the party's activities while prosecutors examine its role in the attempt to overthrow Soviet President Mikhail Gorbachev, who resigned as party leader last week after the failed coup.

The vote did not legally dissolve the Soviet Communist Party, which at last word had about 14 million members. But it ordered a halt to all operations of the organization that Vladimir Lenin once called the "mind, honor and conscience of our era."

"The Communist Party is dead already, and this is just its funeral," said Sergei Khrushchev, a historian and son of the former government and Communist Party leader Nikita Khrushchev, after the vote in the Supreme Soviet. "Such a party had to die. It was just a matter of time."

Later, the parliament finished its fourth straight day of furious debate by, in effect, dissolving itself — passing a resolution that called on the Congress of People's Deputies to elect new legislators.

But before doing so, the legislature stripped its former chairman, Anatoly Lukyanov, of his parliamentary immunity so he could be prosecuted for his actions during the coup attempt. Lukyanov, a friend and former law school classmate of Gorbachev, already had resigned his post but denied any guilt.

After making the case against Lukyanov, Nikolai Trubin, the prosecu-

Soviets continued on page 6A

# Chief's vow to enforce sodomy law angers gays

By Mark Brunswick
Staff Writer

The tenuous relationship between Minneapolis' gay community and Police Chief John Laux is strained again, this time by Laux's remarks in a Christian newsletter that the state sodomy law ought to be enforced.

"I'd be extremely disappointed if it were not enforced," said the police chief in a recent edition of Twin Cities Christian. "Sodomy is a serious law violation, and I'd want my officers to take the appropriate enforcement action." He made it clear that he was referring to acts of sodomy in public places "if we observe it."

The subject is particularly touchy because Laux has recently advocated hiring gay police officers, and some gays have expressed an interest in increased police patrols because of the recent death of former state Sen. John Chenoweth on a Mississippi River beach and the shooting death of another gay man in Loring Park.

"The comments, even if they are nothing but pandering to a Christian

Laux continued on page 9A

# Study of brain tissue suggests biological aspect to homosexuality

Washington Post

Are homosexuals born gay and heterosexuals born straight, or is sexual orientation shaped by some combination of upbringing, choice and environment?

Debate on these questions, the source of controversy in science and society for centuries, is about to be sparked anew because evidence has been found that homosexuality may have a biological component.

Neuroscientist Simon LeVay of the Salk Institute in San Diego reports in today's issue of Science that, in at least one critical region, the brain structures of gay and straight men appear to be dramatically different.

The area LeVay examined, part of a deep interior formation called the hypothalamus, is known to be involved in regulating sexual behavior. One tiny node of that organ, LeVay's tissue studies found, is nearly three

Brain continued on page 10A

### Almanac

**Friday, August 30, 1991**
**242nd day; 123 to go this year**
**Sunrise: 6:32. Sunset: 7:55**

### Today's weather/

Mostly sunny. High 88. Low 63.

### Index/



### Telephones/

| | |
|---|---|
| General Information | 673-4000 |
| Classifieds | 673-7000 |
| Circulation | 673-4343 |


Volume X/Number 148 6 sections

# HUD cuts off repair money for Minneapolis housing authority

By Jon Jeter
Staff Writer

The Minneapolis Public Housing Authority, which relies on a federal grant to pay for costly major building repairs each year, will not receive the money this year, jeopardizing the authority's ability to maintain its public housing.

The U.S. Department of Housing and Urban Development rejected the Housing Authority's request for $17.6 million last week. It was the first time that HUD has decided not to provide the city with even a portion of the funds requested from the federal Comprehensive Improvement Assistance Program (CIAP). Last year the Housing Authority received $8.5 million of the $13.9 million requested.

The unexpected decision has stunned city and Housing Authority officials, who planned to use the grant to remove hazardous lead paint from

Housing continued on page 16A

Connors keeps rolling at Open/1C

VARIETY
**'Imaging America'**
A retrospective of Ken Burns' films

SPORTS
**Big Ten preview**
Michigan looms as favorite

MINNEAPOLIS EDITION

- Firefighter candidates file discrimination suit/**1B**
- Nine candidates seek Brian Coyle's seat on City Council/**3B**
- Felony charges are filed in series of attacks with bats, canes/**5B**


**Star Tribune**

FRIDAY/September 6/1991

NEWSPAPER OF THE TWIN CITIES

35¢


# Soviets create a looser union

## Parliament ushers in government that will pass power to republics

From News Services

**Moscow, U.S.S.R.**
Bowing to the reality of a collapsing union and an ultimatum from President Mikhail Gorbachev, the Soviet Union's highest legislative body Thursday grudgingly handed its powers over to the republics, accepting the old empire's demise while laying in its ruins the foundation for a new, far-looser union of sovereign states.

"Communism is dead. This is the end of the Soviet Union in its old Leninist-Stalinist form," exulted Yuri Shcherbak, a deputy from the Ukraine, a 50-million-strong state that plans to restrict its ties to Moscow to defense and economic cooperation.

Gorbachev, jubilant, said his country had given itself a "chance to do everything anew."

It took considerable bullying and cajoling by Gorbachev to persuade a reluctant Congress of People's Deputies, the semifree parliament set up in 1989, to agree to its own demise. During the transitional period leading to the creation of a voluntary union of independent states, the congress will be replaced by a small working legislature largely made up of delegates from individual republics.

Under the formula approved yesterday by the congress, each republic will be allowed to "determine independently the form of its participa-

**Soviet** continued on page 8A

## Gorbachev, Yeltsin go live on TV to field Americans' questions

Associated Press

**Moscow, U.S.S.R.**
Mikhail Gorbachev and Boris Yeltsin spoke to Americans today about the upheaval in the Soviet Union, and the two leaders agreed that communism had failed in their country.

In an unprecedented joint appearance on ABC-TV, they discussed their often stormy relationship and answered questions from people around the United States. One of the more dramatic responses came to a question when they were asked about the Soviet experience with communism.

Yeltsin answered first and said it was a "tragedy for our people. And it was too bad it happened on our territory."

Then Gorbachev said the experience "has allowed us to say in a decisive fashion that the model has failed."

The two men fielded questions on whether Soviets who had left the country could return and discussed the new governmental setup and tried to assure questioners that the Soviet nuclear arsenal was in safe hands.

One American questioner who said he had left the Soviet Union was assured by Yeltsin, "There is no more danger . . . please come back."

The two men also promised questioners that they were working to

**TV** continued on page 24A

### THE NEW UNION

These are the key elements of the interim Soviet government, a confederation of independent states that is supposed to function as a single nation in matters such as foreign policy and defense. The existing Soviet republics can choose whether to join in the new union. And the new parliament is expected to rewrite the Soviet constitution, potentially resulting in yet another organizational structure.

#### Collective executive

**State Council**/ Highest government body, led by Soviet President Mikhail Gorbachev and consisting of the presidents of all participating republics. Will coordinate decisions on domestic and foreign policy affecting "the common interests of the republics." Will run defense, security, law enforcement and foreign affairs. Its decisions are to have "a mandatory character." Roughly speaking, this might be compared to a federal executive branch.

**Economic committee**/ Will coordinate the national economy and implement economic reforms. Members will be chosen by the republics; the committee's chairman will be named by the Soviet president, with agreement of the State Council.

#### Legislature

**Supreme Soviet**/ Highest legislative body, consisting of two chambers that will jointly decide changes in the Soviet constitution, accept states into the union, hear president's reports on major issues, confirm the union budget, declare war and conclude peace.

- **Council of Republics**/ This chamber has at least 20 deputies from each republic, chosen by the republic's leaders. In addition, autonomous areas – the smaller political subdivisions – in each republic c. send one representative. The Russian Federation will have the most deputies, 52, to reflect all of its subdivisions. But no matter how many deputies a republic sends, each republic has only one vote in the chamber. This equality of voting strength is similar to the U.S. Senate.
- **Council of the Union**/ Members are chosen by each republic's legislature, based on the number of lawmakers each now has in the Congress of People's Deputies. Thus, representation will be roughly comparable to population, as in the U.S. House of Representatives.

#### Sovereign republics

Each republic's legislature has the right to suspend in its territory any Soviet laws that contradict its constitution. All republics must approve changes in the Soviet constitution. The republics will have much more power and autonomy than, say, U.S. states or Canadian provinces.

Source: Associated Press

Agence France-Presse

**Soviet President Mikhail Gorbachev said that, with Thursday's actions, the country had given itself a "chance to do everything anew."**

## Humphrey proposes moratorium, new laws to keep gambling clean

By Dennis J. McGrath and Robert Whereatt
Staff Writers

Attorney General Hubert Humphrey III called Thursday for a moratorium on new forms of gambling in Minnesota, saying regulators are already overburdened by the $2-billion-a-year gaming industry.

Humphrey also said that while he has seen no evidence that organized crime has infiltrated the rapidly growing Indian gaming business, he said he fears that "dirty money" will be used to finance new ventures or expansion projects.

To prevent corrupt influences from tainting the business, he said, changes are needed in federal and state laws to give regulators more control over gambling on Indian lands. Humphrey also proposed creation of a state-federal team to step up enforcement.

"I'd like to see us stop the expansion of gambling in this state for at least a while," Humphrey said at a Capitol

**Gambling** continued on page 16A

## State family planning grant may go to group promoting teen abstinence

By Kurt Chandler
Staff Writer

A Grand Rapids group that encourages teenagers to abstain from sex rather than use birth control could become the first such organization to receive state funding in Minnesota.

The Itasca County Abstinence Project has been endorsed by the County Board as the recipient of a $10,000 grant earmarked by the Legislature for family planning services. If approved by a tricounty panel and the state Department of Health this fall, the abstinence program would replace a sex education project run by parents.

County officials said they recommended the change, which has riled advocates of family planning, because of the continuing increase in teenage pregnancies in Itasca County and a feeling that sex education has failed to make a significant difference.

Formed in 1989, the Abstinence Project has been financed mostly

**Birth Control** continued on page 19A

### Almanac

**Friday, September 6, 1991**
**249th day; 116 to go this year**
**Sunrise: 6:41. Sunset: 7:43**

**Today's weather/**
Just a few clouds

Partly cloudy, with light winds and a high of 79. Low tonight of 53, with southerly winds.

**Inside/**

Unisys Corp. has agreed to plead guilty to charges arising from a Pentagon procurement scandal and to pay $190 million in fines and forfeited profits, officials say. **Page 2A.**

**Index/**



**Telephones/**

| | |
|---|---|
| General Information | 673-4000 |
| Classifieds | 673-7000 |
| Circulation | 673-4343 |


Volume X/Number 155 6 sections

## Teen killed by shot from friend's pistol in south Minneapolis

By Kevin Duchschere
Staff Writer

A 15-year-old Minneapolis boy, out for a stroll with a couple of friends after the first day of school, was killed late Thursday afternoon by a shot fired from a pistol carried by one of his companions.

Shawn Haroldson died on the street corner where he was shot at 31st St. and 32nd Av. S., just after 5 p.m. The bullet from the .38-caliber revolver apparently struck him in the upper chest.

Police said last night that they had not determined the nature of the shooting, but that it may well have been accidental.

"We're not sure yet, but there's nothing really to point to" a deliberate shooting, Lt. Brad Johnson said.

Police questioned Haroldson's two friends, a boy and a girl who was identified by some school friends as Haroldson's girlfriend. Johnson said the boy, believed to be 11 and the younger brother of a good friend of Haroldson's, apparently owned the gun and had it when he was approached by police. He was being held last night at the Juvenile Detention Center.

Some of Haroldson's acquaintances said that the gun was shared by Haroldson and the 11-year-old boy's older brother, and that yesterday was Haroldson's day to have it. Other friends of Haroldson's, though, were surprised at the suggestion that he had a gun.

Haroldson's two companions apparently were the only witnesses to the shooting. Several neighbors said they

**Shooting** continued on page 21A

**10 Soviet republics agree to treaty on economic community/2A**

MINNEAPOLIS EDITION

■ Review board's police complaints pile up/**1B**


# Star Tribune

SATURDAY/October 12/1991 — NEWSPAPER OF THE TWIN CITIES — 35¢


# A furious Thomas denies allegations

## Hill tells of sexual advances in vivid detail

From News Services

**Washington, D.C.**
Supreme Court nominee Clarence Thomas denounced and denied the sexual-harassment accusations against him twice Friday, before and after a day of graphic, detailed testimony to the contrary by Anita Hill.

During seven hours before the Senate Judiciary Committee, Hill, a law professor at the University of Oklahoma, leveled lurid, explicit charges against him. Thomas returned to the witness chair last night to tell the committee that its proceedings were "a travesty . . . disgusting."

Hill complained of sexual approaches in vivid detail; Thomas angrily denied the charges.

And, after his angry, 90-minute rebuttal to Hill's charges, the committee was confronted last night with a point-by-point contradiction.

Thomas was to resume his testimony today at 9 a.m. Twin Cities time, followed by witnesses to corroborate each side.

During the 10-hour hearing, Hill insisted that her allegations of sexual harassment, of pressures to date Thomas, of his boasts of his own sexual prowess and repeated remarks about X-rated movies were the truth. "I'm not given to fantasy," she said in the face of Republican efforts to shake her story.

Hill, 37, did not budge in her insistence that Thomas harassed her with demands and explicit talk when she worked for him at the Department of Education and at the Equal Employment Opportunity Commission (EEOC) between 1981 and 1983. When she was done, committee members — particularly Democrats — said they admired her courage in going public, 10 years after the epi-

**Thomas** continued on page 5A

### THE ACCUSATION

**"I felt that implicit in the discussion about sex acts was the offer to have sex with him."**

Anita Hill

"On several occasions Thomas told me graphically of his own sexual prowess."

"My working relationship became even more strained when Judge Thomas began to use work situations to discuss sex. . . . He spoke about acts that he had seen in pornographic films involving such matters as women having sex with animals and films showing group sex or rape scenes."

"I'm not given to fantasy."

"I confess that I am very sorry that I did not do something, say something (earlier). Maybe it was a poor judgment, but it was not a dishonest and not a particularly unreasonable judgment."

"I don't like the attention, and even if I did, I would not lie to get the attention."

### THE DENIAL

**"I categorically deny all of the allegations and deny that I ever attempted to date Anita Hill."**

Clarence Thomas

"This is a circus. It's a national disgrace, and from my standpoint as a black American, as far as I'm concerned, it is a high-tech lynching for uppity blacks. It is a message that unless you kowtow to the old order, this is what will happen to you."

"Though I am by no means a perfect person, no means, I have not done what she has alleged, and I still don't know what I could possibly have done to cause her to make these allegations."

"Enough is enough. I am not going to allow myself to be further humiliated to be confirmed."

"I am proud of my life, proud of what I have done and what I have accomplished, proud of my family, and this process, this process is trying to destroy it all. No job is worth what I have been through, no job. No horror in my life has been so debilitating."

Associated Press photos

# Pags in a pinch!

## His homer in the 10th gives Twins 3-2 win

By Howard Sinker
Staff Writer

**Toronto, Ontario**
Numbers can be nifty benchmarks or nasty buggers. They can explain a whole bunch of stuff or tell you next to nothing. Smart folks can ignore them; fools can rely on them.

Game 3 of the American League Championship Series offered a chance to balance the emotion of the postseason with some of the numbers that were being served up Friday at the SkyDome.

Does it mean much that the AL playoffs had been tied at one game apiece seven times before last night, and that every time but twice, the winner of Game 3 went on to take the pennant?

Hey, with the Twins winning 3-2 in 10 innings last night, that one will play pretty well in Minnesota over morning coffee.

Want some advanced-level numbers? That home run by Mike Pagliarulo, the pinch-hit job to right with one out in the 10th, was only the third one in 23 seasons of AL playoffs. Pat Sheridan hit the last one in 1985, against the Jays.

And what did it mean that, before last night, the Twins and Jays had played 14 times in 1991 — 12 in the regular season and the two bigger games earlier this week — and that the team scoring first had won 13?

**Twins** continued on page 13A

Staff Photo by Brian Peterson

**Mike Pagliarulo celebrated in the dugout at the Toronto SkyDome Friday after smacking a 10th-inning homer that won the game and gave the Twins a 2-1 lead in the playoff series.**

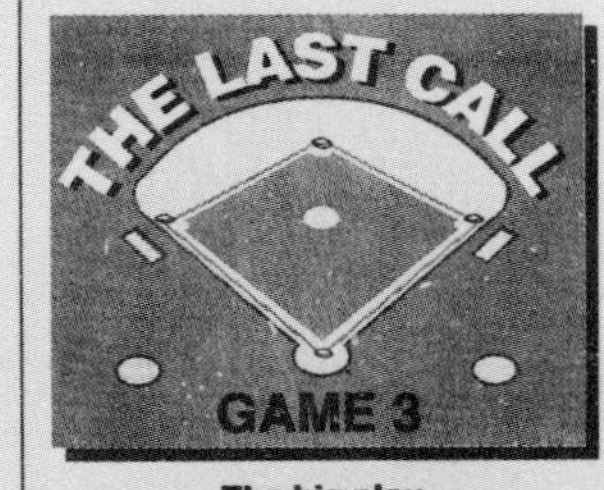


**The big play**

***Top of the 10th, pinch hitter Mike Pagliarulo crushed a Mike Timlin fastball over the right field fence, catapulting the Twins to victory.***

**Heroes**
Relievers David West, Carl Willis, Mark Guthrie and Rick Aguilera shined, blanking the Jays for 6 innings after Scott Erickson faltered.

**Big hit**
Kirby Puckett's single in the sixth scored Chuck Knoblauch, who slid head-first under Pat Borders' tag. That tied the score at 2.

**Changeup**
Joe Carter jammed his ankle climbing the wall trying to catch Shane Mack's fifth-inning triple. Carter's status for Game 4: probable.

**Extra innings**
Pagliarulo's game-winner was only the fourth extra-inning homer in 23 years of playoffs; it was the Twins' first dinger of the series.

**Game 4**

***7:26 tonight at the SkyDome. Starting pitchers: Twins' Jack Morris vs. Jays' Todd Stottlemyre.***

**Analysis**

## Senators face stark choice

By R.W. Apple Jr.
New York Times

**Washington, D.C.**
The choices presented to the Senate by Friday's lurid, gut-wrenching proceedings on Capitol Hill could hardly have been much starker.

By the time Prof. Anita Hill had finished her testimony, filled with vivid and often excruciating sexual detail that few people had anticipated, but delivered with a prim earnestness that seemed to bespeak reserve and reluctance to discuss such subjects, the senators who must vote Tuesday were left with only two options: Either she was telling the truth or she is a sociopath; either these horrifying events took place or she, for some reason, invented

**Analysis** continued on page 7A

**THE THOMAS HEARINGS**

**Today's TV coverage**
ABC, CBS and NBC will provide live coverage when Supreme Court nominee Clarence Thomas resumes his testimony at 9 a.m. today. All three networks have afternoon telecasts of sports events, but said they would break away for the Thomas hearing if events warranted.

CNN plans extensive live coverage, and PBS and C-Span will air the hearings on a gavel-to-gavel basis.

**■ Excerpts of Hill's and Thomas' statements. Page 7A.**

**■ Related articles on pages 6A and 10A.**

## Senate hearing was mesmerizing viewing

By Chuck Haga
Staff Writer

**Twin Cities Journal**

Anita Hill spoke from a dozen television monitors. The movie "Ghost" played soundlessly from banks of sets behind her.

Jerry Brown never took his eyes off Hill — not until she began to detail the offensive behavior that she alleges Clarence Thomas committed 10 years ago.

"His conversations were very vivid," she said. "He spoke about acts that he had seen in pornographic films involving such matters as women having sex with animals and films showing group sex or rape scenes."

Brown winced.

"He talked about pornographic materials depicting individuals with large penises or large breasts involved in various sex acts," Hill said. "On several occasions, Thomas told me graphically of his own sexual prowess."

Brown shut his eyes, dropped his head and turned momentarily from the TVs.

He is 28, a third-year law student at the University of Minnesota. He went to Dayton's in Minneapolis Friday because he was downtown

**Journal** continued on page 7A

**Redd Foxx dies at 68**

Comedian Redd Foxx, who was best known for his role as a crabby junkman on the 1970s TV series "Sanford and Son," died Friday night in Los Angeles. He suffered a heart attack at Paramount Studios while rehearsing his new TV show, "The Royal Family."

**Obituary on page 4B.**

## Bush vetoes extension of benefits for jobless

New York Times

**Washington, D.C.**
President Bush vetoed a $6.5 billion bill Friday that would have provided as many as 20 additional weeks of unemployment benefits for 3 million people who have been out of work more than half a year.

He said the measure would damage the economic recovery by abandoning budget discipline.

Bush's 23rd veto was accompanied by a message intended to blunt the political issue the Democrats have made out of his opposition to this bill and a similar measure that he killed in August.

He said his administration was "deeply concerned about the needs of the unemployed and their families." Bush added that if a "responsible"

**Veto** continued on page 14A

**Almanac**

**Saturday, October 12, 1991**
**285th day; 80 to go this year**
**Sunrise: 7:24. Sunset: 6:34**

**Today's weather/**
Sunny. High, 65; low, 41.




Volume X/Number 191 7 sections

14 pages on the Series in News and Sports

1991 World Series

# Star Tribune

METRO EDITION

For Page 1A and the start of today's paper, turn the page

MONDAY/October 28/1991

NEWSPAPER OF THE TWIN CITIES

35¢

# Twincredible!

## One for the storybooks

Staff Photo by Jeff Wheeler

Dan Gladden was mobbed by teammates as he touched home plate in the 10th inning at the Metrodome Sunday night, scoring the only run of a 1-0 Minnesota victory over Atlanta in Game 7 of the World Series. Jack Morris, at left, pitched all 10 innings and was named the Series' most valuable player.

Wolves drop opener to Utah before 6,973 storm-steeled fans/1C

MINNEAPOLIS EDITION

■ For the caregiver, group offers a few hours of relief/1B

Star Tribune

SATURDAY/November 2/1991 NEWSPAPER OF THE TWIN CITIES 35¢

# It fell and fell and fell. . .

## Twin Cities area bears brunt of deadly blizzard

So much for fall — and so much for most of the snowstorm records in Minnesota history.

The Great Halloween Snowstorm of 1991 buried the Twin Cities and most of Minnesota under an appallingly deep blanket of snow Friday, obliterating October's fallen leaves and the other remnants of autumn.

It shattered at least six records kept by the National Weather Service: The 27 inches of snow that had fallen by 11 p.m. was the greatest single snowfall in the metro area's history. And as much as 8 more inches was expected overnight, as the storm escalated into a blizzard 30 hours after it began.

So much snow has fallen during this megastorm that U.S. Weather Service meteorologists said yesterday that there's no hope that an Indian Summer will melt it — meaning some of it will still be here next spring.

It was lethal: Six people have died — two from heart attacks while removing snow, four in traffic accidents; scores of people suffered hand injuries from snowblowers or non-lethal heart attacks. Treacherous roads and whiteouts caused nearly 1,000 traffic accidents, most of them minor.

It strangled travel on rural highways and city streets, at airports and bus terminals. Metropolitan Transit Commission buses were pulled off the streets at 8 last night, the first time that had happened in a decade. Minneapolis-St. Paul International Airport was forced to shut down for a time late last night.

The snow shut down much of the state: 900 schools and businesses never opened yesterday. Stores struggled to open for a few hours; concerts and most sporting events were postponed. Downtowns became ghost towns.

And it just wouldn't quit. By late yesterday, hours after the snow was supposed

**Snowstorm** continued on page 13A

Staff Photo by Rita Reed

**Dave Brashear of Minneapolis sized up the task of freeing his car, which was buried on 42nd Av. S. by more than 2 feet of snow plus several layers added by snowplows.**

### SUPER STORM

Minnesota and the Twin Cities got more national TV exposure Friday, but for most of us it didn't involve as much pleasure as the World Series.

**The biggest** employers shut down for the day, along with many of the smaller ones, and the school closing list was the longest in WCCO's memory. Some homebound workers stayed on the job, however, through phones and faxes. Details on pages 1B and 3B.

**Friendliness** was rampant, as it often is in such circumstances, from the crowded bus stops to the car-pushing bees in neighborhood streets and alleys. 1B. And some stay-at-homes even had fun. 16A.

**Shovelers** and plow jockeys moved many tons snow that, by one calculation, weighed 12 pounds per square foot. That's what's known as "heart attack" snow, and emergency rooms were filled. Some precautions to take are listed on page 3B.

**More than half** of the metro area's annual average snowfall was recorded during this Great Halloween Storm, a freakish one that has amazed even the meteorologists and etched itself into our memories. 13A.

**Stories and photographs on pages 11A, 12A, 13A, 16A, 1B and 3B.**

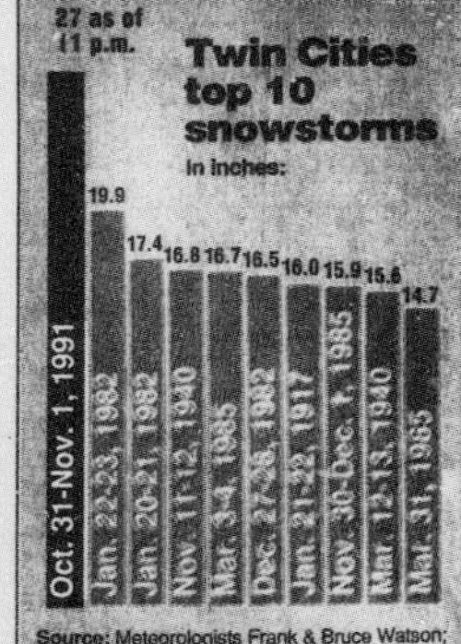


Source: Meteorologists Frank & Bruce Watson; National Weather Service.

## Inch by inch, we were overwhelmed

By Kurt Chandler
Staff Writer

Caught off guard Friday? You weren't the only one. Blindsided by a furious first snowstorm of the season, many of us still hadn't raked leaves, hung storm windows or mounted snow tires. Barbecue grills, picnic tables and birdbaths suddenly were buried in winter. Best-laid plans were thrown totally out of kilter. Fooled again by Mother Nature.

■

Susan Robinson of Crystal had everything under control. Until yesterday.

"I'm getting married Saturday (today) and everything's going wrong with the weather," said the panicky 32-year-old. "All of the relatives live out of state and everyone's coming in and there's only one runway open and I don't know if they'll get in or not.

"One of the groomsmen is driving in from North Carolina, and we haven't even heard from him. The other two are coming in from Boston and L.A. The one from Boston made it to Chicago, and he's stuck there. And the one from L.A., his flight got canceled and he doesn't have another one yet.

"I was supposed to pick up my ring today. I was supposed to have a make-over done. I was supposed to pick up the tuxes and have a final fitting on my dress. We'll have to do it *all* tomorrow. It's supposed to stop snowing, isn't it?"

It took some doing but at least three couples did pull off weddings yesterday in Hennepin County District Court. In Judge Henry McCarr's courtroom, Roger T. Goth, 56, and Kathleen G. Hlavinka, 49, both of New Brighton, exchanged vows in a four-minute ceremony.

**Surprise** continued on page 12A

### To our customers and carriers

I want to thank Star Tribune customers for their patience and understanding during this record snowstorm. And I want to thank our newspaper carriers for their extraordinary efforts to deliver the newspaper, when almost everything else in town came to a halt.

We didn't bat 1.000 with our deliveries Friday, but I can assure you that it wasn't from lack of effort. If we missed you, I'm sorry. We appreciate your patience.

**Jim Midtbo**/Vice President/Circulation

### Almanac

**Saturday, November 2, 1991**
**306th day; 59 to go this year**
**Sunrise: 6:52. Sunset: 5:00**

### Today's weather/

More snow and wind should make roads treacherous. High, 21; low, 4.

### Index/



### Telephones/

| | |
|---|---|
| General information | 673-4000 |
| Classifieds | 673-7000 |
| Circulation | 673-4343 |


Volume X/Number 212 7 sections

## Envoys struggle to bring foes to new round of talks

From News Services

■ Related stories are on pages 8A and 9A.

**Madrid, Spain**
The opening phase of the fragile Mideast peace talks ended in rancor, invective and uncertainty Friday as diplomats struggled to get feuding Arabs and Israelis talking about a settlement of their 43-year conflict.

A second round of face-to-face bilateral negotiations, which are in doubt because of a dispute between Israel and the Arabs over where they should be conducted, could mark the success or failure of the whole peace conference.

After a closing session in which Israeli Prime Minister Yitzhak Shamir and Syrian Foreign Minister Farouk Sharaa hurled charges and personal insults at each other, Secretary of State James Baker and Arab diplomats worked to overcome last-minute Syrian resistance to attending the bilateral talks, which were planned to begin Sunday as a substantive continuation of this week's ceremonial sessions.

The sudden hitch came after a day in which Baker admonished all of the participants that the opening confer-

**Mideast** continued on page 10A

### News inside/

**Energy bill scuttled**

The Senate voted Friday to scuttle a wide-ranging energy bill intended to reduce the nation's dependence on foreign oil. In effect, the vote defeated the Bush administration's plan to open a vast Alaskan wildlife refuge to oil drilling. **Page 7A.**

**Jobless rate rises**

In two bleak reports, the government said that the nation's jobless rate inched up 0.1 points to 6.8 percent in October and that the Index of Leading Economic Indicators, which is designed to predict future economic activity, fell in September. **Page 1D.**

## Student fatally shoots 4, self at University of Iowa

By Greg Smith
Associated Press

**Iowa City, Iowa**
A student upset about not being nominated for an academic honor went on a shooting spree Friday through two buildings at the University of Iowa, killing four people before fatally shooting himself, a school official said.

The dead included faculty members and a student who had won the honor. Two others were critically wounded, authorities said.

The gunman was identified as Gang Lu, a graduate student in physics from China, said Ann Rhodes, vice president of university affairs. He had filed a complaint with the school's academic affairs office because his dissertation wasn't nominated for an academic award, she said.

Lu shot three members of the school's physics and astronomy departments and another graduate student from China in one classroom in Van Allen Hall, then went to Jessup Hall, the administration building, and shot an associate vice president for academic affairs and a staff member, Rhodes said.

Rhodes said Lu apparently had

**Shooting** continued on page 3A

VARIETY

**Size XXXS**

"Pi… put… min…

**Wolves lose to Nuggets 88-77/7C**

VARIETY

**Heavy hitter**

Metallica blossoms from cult band into best-selling act

**MINNEAPOLIS EDITION**




# Star Tribune

FRIDAY/November 8/1991 NEWSPAPER OF THE TWIN CITIES 35¢


"I think sometimes we think, well, only gay people can get it – 'It's not going to happen to me.' And here I am saying that it can happen to anybody, even me, Magic Johnson."

## Magic Johnson has AIDS virus, retires

**New York Times**

**Inglewood, Calif.**
Magic Johnson, one of the most popular and accomplished players in basketball history, said Thursday that he had been infected by the virus that causes AIDS and that he would retire immediately from the Los Angeles Lakers.

Speaking in composed, straightforward terms, Johnson said at a news conference at the Great Western Forum, where he played with the Lakers for 12 seasons, that he learned Wednesday that he was infected with the human immunodeficiency virus.

"Because of the HIV virus I have obtained, I will have to retire from the Lakers today," he said. His doctors said that although Johnson was healthy now, he was leaving the game because the physical stress of pro basketball would not be good for his condition.

- Johnson's illness touches America. Reactions come from players and fans.
- It's news enough to make anyone cry.

**More stories on Page 1C.**

A gifted athlete whose abilities and magnetic personality brought worldwide popularity and success to his team and to the National Basketball Association, Johnson is by far the most famous sports figure to be infected by the AIDS virus.

Johnson did not say how he became infected with the virus, which is usually transmitted through sexual intercourse or intravenous drug use. But he did say that he wanted young people "to understand that safe sex is the way to go."

"I think sometimes we think, well, only gay people can get it — 'It's not going to happen to me.' And here I am saying that it can happen to anybody, even me, Magic Johnson," he said.

Johnson and his trademark smile helped turn a struggling NBA into the biggest sports success story of the 1980s. With Johnson running the fast break, Los Angeles Lakers games were "Showtime." The Lakers won

**Johnson** continued on page 20A

Agence France-Presse

**Superstar Earvin (Magic) Johnson announced his retirement Thursday from the Los Angeles Lakers.**

## High court is asked to review abortion

### Rights groups try strategic move

**From News Services**

**Washington, D.C.**
In a move calculated to intensify the political debate on abortion before the 1992 elections, abortion-rights groups Thursday asked the Supreme Court to take up a case that could overturn Roe vs. Wade.

The groups filed a petition with the court seeking review of a federal appeals-court ruling two weeks ago that upheld most of Pennsylvania's restrictive abortion law. They asked the court to use the opportunity to say definitively whether Roe, the 1973 ruling establishing abortion as a fundamental constitutional right, remains the law of the land.

"This court must now decide whether women's childbearing choices are worthy of the highest level of constitutional protection," lawyers for the American Civil Liberties Union and the Planned Parenthood Federation of America told the court.

Abortion-rights advocates acknowledged that their action risks an outright reversal of Roe by the increasingly conservative court.

But in making their admittedly political request, the organizations made clear that they were looking beyond the Supreme Court and hoping to

**Abortion** continued on page 22A

## Curt Carlson retakes control of his companies

**By David Phelps, Tony Kennedy and Sally Apgar**
Staff Writers

In a top-level shakeup at Carlson Companies, 77-year-old founder Curt Carlson assumed full operating responsibilities for his worldwide conglomerate Thursday while son-in-law and onetime heir apparent Edwin (Skip) Gage stepped aside to pursue private interests.

The move appeared to signal that eventual control of the travel, lodging and marketing giant could go to Carlson's daughter Marilyn Carlson Nelson, who was promoted yesterday to the position of vice chairman of the company's corporate parent. It's also another twist in the story of one of Minnesota's wealthiest and most visible families.

Inside and outside of the company there was speculation that Gage's decision to resign as chief executive and president also was a sign that Carlson wanted to reclaim control of the company from Gage, who was appointed CEO in 1989. Gage remains with the corporation as vice chairman of the holding company, a newly created position he will share with Nelson.

In an interview last night, Nelson said the changes were largely prompt-

**Carlson** continued on page 24A

**News inside**/Bolsheviks have their day

Agence France-Presse

**A pro-Communist demonstrator waved a Soviet flag in front of the Lenin Mausoleum in Moscow on Thursday, the 74th anniversary of the day the Bolsheviks seized power. Story on page 2A.**

### Bush talks tough to NATO members

President Bush threatened Thursday to pull the United States back from its central role in NATO if the other members of the alliance let the military organization wither. Bush's maneuver at the NATO summit conference in Rome was intended not so much to bring about a U.S. withdrawal as to force NATO to commit itself to recognizing the continuation of Washington's preeminent role. Secretary of State James Baker later described Bush's threat as a "complete and total red herring." **Page 2A.**

### Gene Tierney dies

Actress Gene Tierney, who starred as the enigmatic victim in the 1944 murder mystery "Laura" and was nominated for an Academy Award for "Leave Her To Heaven," died Wednesday at her home in Houston. She was 70. **Page 6B.**

## Rich would finance Democratic tax cut

**From News Services**

**Washington, D.C.**
House Democratic leaders lined up Thursday behind a new initiative to top their 1992 election-year agenda: a tax credit of up to $200 a year per worker, paid for by upper-income Americans.

Ninety million couples and individuals would get tax cuts in 1992 and 1993 while the richest 1 million would pay more — permanently.

"It runs to the heart of what Democrats stand for," said Rep. Dan Rostenkowski, D-Ill., chairman of the House Ways and Means Committee and author of the proposal.

The plan was promoted as good medicine for a sluggish economy and as a major effort to make the tax system fairer.

The Democrats, who control Congress, emphasized that no action will be taken on the proposal until early next year, even though they promised that the tax relief would be retroactive to Jan. 1, 1992.

While action must wait, said House Majority Leader Richard Gephardt, D-Mo., the mere fact that the top two

**Tax plans** continued on page 18A

## Seniors facing increase in HMO premiums Jan. 1

**By Gordon Slovut**
Staff Writer

Three of Minnesota's largest health maintenance organizations (HMOs) are announcing increases of up to 25 percent in their Medicare-HMO premiums effective Jan. 1.

HMO officials say the increases are needed because Medicare hasn't increased reimbursements enough to cover the rising cost of health care.

In addition, Group Health Seniors, which hasn't yet announced its rates, has asked the state for permission to drop its coverage of prescription drugs for the elderly.

Pamela Effertz, spokeswoman for Group Health Inc., said the final decision hasn't been made on drug coverage. Kent Peterson, head of the state Department of Health's HMO unit, said he doubts that the request will be denied.

He said Group Health is "the only HMO still offering drug coverage, so

**HMO** continued on page 6A

## Women cite sexy ads in harassment suit against Stroh's

**By Paul McEnroe**
Staff Writer

In what appears to be the first such case in the nation, five women are expected to file suit today alleging that they suffered harassment at the Stroh Brewing Co. plant in St. Paul that was caused partly by the company's sex-oriented advertising.

The case could heighten the debate over whether advertising based on sexual imagery influences how men behave toward women.

Attorney Lori Peterson, representing the women, said the company's advertising helped create a climate at the St. Paul brewery in which sexual harassment was more easily tolerated. The company's marketing campaign ranges from calendars depicting large-breasted women to TV commercials of bikini-clad women

**Stroh** continued on page 23A

### Almanac

**Friday, November 8, 1991**
**312th day; 53 to go this year**
**Sunrise: 7:01. Sunset: 4:52**

Dim sun. SE. winds 10-20. High 29.



**Telephones/**

| | |
|---|---|
| General information | 673-4000 |
| Classifieds | 673-7000 |
| Circulation | 673-4343 |


Volume X/Number 218 6 sections

High-tech shipment for Libya seized/2A

Algeria arrests head of Islamic party/2A

Gopher rally falls short in 72-69 loss/1C

VARIETY

**Still the focus**

Clyde Bellecourt has changed, but remains at the center of AIM

**MINNEAPOLIS EDITION**

- Contempt charges against Starkey lawyers being considered/**1B**
- Scissors in the back cut short actor's role in murder mystery/**1B**
- Man slain in his apartment was random victim of intruders/**2B**


# Star Tribune

THURSDAY/January 23/1992 NEWSPAPER OF THE TWIN CITIES 35¢


# Bush vows aid to ex-Soviet states

## U.S. pledges $645 million; Japan holds off

From News Services

Washington, D.C.
President Bush pledged $645 million in new U.S. assistance to the former Soviet Union on Wednesday, but Japan said it would not provide additional help until it settled a territorial dispute with Russia left over from World War II.

Opening a 47-nation conference on aid to the Commonwealth of Independent States, Bush called on the world community to show the new nations that it "cares about them and supports their hard struggle to build new societies on the ruins of communism."

He said he will ask Congress to approve the $645 million in outright grants for food, medicine and other humanitarian assistance. If approved, the aid would boost the U.S. commitment to more than $5 billion. Most of that is in loans to finance the purchase of U.S. agricultural products, but the new funding would not have to be repaid.

It was not clear yesterday whether Congress, under pressure in an election year to deal with domestic problems, would approve the assistance.

House Majority Leader Richard Gephardt of Missouri said he is inclined to back the additional aid, but only if Bush "will finally take the lead in selling it to the American people, explaining to them why it is in their self-interest and helping them to understand that this is not the end but the beginning if we are to seize this great moment."

**Aid** continued on page 6A

## A magical start for the Winter Carnival

### Fire and ice wow 'em in St. Paul

By James Walsh
Staff Writer

Build a 166-foot-tall palace of ice, splash it in a kaleidoscope of light and explode green, red, white and gold fireworks overhead and what do you get?

One hundred and fifty-thousand people gasping "Ooooooh."

St. Paul's Winter Carnival exploded into action Wednesday night with the illumination of a breathtaking, skyscraping, awe-inspiring ice palace that left an estimated crowd of 150,000 on Harriet Island shrieking with glee.

"It's beautiful," Michelle Primus of Minneapolis shouted over the roar of the crowd as all the colors of the rainbow danced inside the palace's crystal walls. "It's like magic."

For the past year, carnival officials boosted anticipation for what was to be the grandest castle of them all. Built at a cost of about $1 million by professional bricklayers, carpenters, iron workers and electricians working

**Ice palace** continued on page 13A

Sizzling fireworks heralded the lighting of the Pepsi Ice Palace. Brian Peterson captured the moment for a poster page on **20A.**

Staff Photo by Richard Sennott

**Torchbearers lit the parade route for the 1992 Winter Carnival Wednesday along Wabasha St. in St. Paul. The parade continued to Harriet Island, the site of the ice palace. The parade and the lighting of the palace were highlights of last night's opening festivities. "You've Got to Believe" is the theme of the 106th carnival, which will continue through Feb. 2.**

# Efficiency commission draws fire over report

## Critics see lack of effort, ideas

By Dennis J. McGrath
and Dane Smith
Staff Writers

A highly touted panel that Gov. Arne Carlson created a year ago to find ways to reduce the cost of local government produced a thin document Wednesday that local officials and even some commission members criticized as insubstantial and unimaginative.

They said the commission, headed by Lt. Gov. Joanell Dyrstad, was unfocused and failed to address what they considered its primary charge: to answer the governor's call to "fundamentally restructure" the expensive and complex links between state and local governments.

Among the critics was an influential Independent-Republican member of the commission, Morris Lanning of Moorhead, who said he was "not at all happy to have my name on it," referring to the report. Other commission members said they stopped going to meetings because of frustration over the commission's low ambitions.

Although Carlson said last year that the Dyrstad Commission on Local and State Government Relations was among the most important of his cost-cutting commissions, he was unfamiliar with the 14-page report's conclusions even after it was released yesterday.

**Commission** continued on page 8A

## Almanac

**Thursday, January 23, 1992**
**23rd day; 343 to go this year**
**Sunrise: 7:41; Sunset: 5:08**

Blustery, with high of 22. Low, 3.




Volume X/Number 294 7 sections

# Big demand for low-rate mortgages slows process

By Mike Meyers
and Ingrid Sundstrom
Staff Writers

■ New housing construction reached a 46-year low in 1991, the government reported. **Page 1D.**

Mortgage borrowers have learned in the past two weeks that good news has a short shelf life.

In early January, home loan rates declined to a 17-year low and lenders were eager to make deals. Home buyers and people stuck with old, high-interest mortgage rates could count themselves lucky.

How things have changed.

In the past few days, the good news of those low mortgage rates has been frustrating the crowds of anxious home owners and buyers trying to obtain those rates. Meanwhile, mortgage rates have been inching up, adding hundreds or thousands of dollars to the cost of home loans. But some lenders are turning away people seeking to refinance their mortgages. Some hapless callers are waiting days for lenders to return their telephone messages, if they are returned at all.

Paradoxically, the reasons for all the trouble are partly the result of election-year politics. Bond traders have

**Mortgages** continued on page 10A

## Super Bowl XXVI

### THE POINT AFTER

**Some pig/** Danny Garber is driving to Minneapolis from Washington, D.C., with a 700-pound porker named Rootie 2, in honor of the "Hogs" who make up the Redskins' offensive line. Rootie is not featured at the Ahmad Rashad celebrity roast tonight in Bloomington.

**Ease up, buddy/** Nobody's predicting gridlock akin to last year's Halloween storm, but drivers, beware: Heavy traffic and delays are likely in downtown Minneapolis and St. Paul in the days ahead as 60,000 people pour into the Twin Cities.

**Circling the bandwagon/** Four of Minnesota's most prominent politicians agree on one thing: The Redskins should change their nickname. **See page 16A.**

**Fan mail/** A confidential memo describing how Super Bowl visitors can get along with Minnesotans appears in today's **Variety section.**

**Calendar of today's Super Bowl events/** Page 3E.

Star Tribune graphic

### Super Bowl 'videowalls' have downtown skyways covered

**Twin Cities Journal**

By Chuck Haga
Staff Writer

Every half-hour of Shamwattee Gaya's working day this week, eight Mark Rosens talk at once — two big, six little — and to Gaya he makes no sense. None of him.

She sweeps the Pillsbury Center's inner courtyard of butts and muffin bits and glances now and then at the television screen . . . the 24 screens programmed as one, or four, or 24.

All those Rosens talk, and then come commercials, then football: playoff highlights in spectacular slow motion, announcers droning on in that muffled drumbeat tone until Atlanta's final score against New Orleans: "My God, my God, somebody caught the ball!"

Gaya, a Twin Citian for three years, is from Guyana. She could watch Buffalo beat Denver 12 times a day if she wanted, thanks to the Electrosonic Superchannel XXVI, the Super Bowl's skyway network.

"I don't understand it, but I look," she said. "In my country, we play football with the foot, not with the hands. I don't know why they catch

**Journal** continued on page 16A

Staff Photo by David Brewster

**Roe vs. Wade opponents rally**

**Abortion foes rallied at the State Capitol in St. Paul Wednesday on the 19th anniversary of the decision that legalized abortion in the United States. A protest also was held in Washington, D.C. See report, page 7A.**

## Winning start

Knoblauch, Puckett help Twins beat Brewers 4-2 in the season opener

VARIETY

## A perfect time

Kids tell Mindworks how they'd design a day of their own

MINNEAPOLIS EDITION

■ Owner claims cash that man had found in envelope/**1B**

■ Minneapolis police object to plan to trim overtime backlog/**4B**

■ Hennepin County to decide on paving road with ash/**7B**


# Star Tribune

TUESDAY/ April 7/1992 NEWSPAPER OF THE TWIN CITIES Y 35¢


# Minnesotans vote for their favorites today, but eyes are on N.Y.

'92 CAMPAIGN

**Today is Minnesota's first presidential primary in 36 years. Most polls are open from 7 a.m. to 8 p.m. If you don't know where to vote, call your county auditor or city clerk. Remember, you must declare which party primary you're voting in.**

Minnesotans will vote today in the first state presidential primary since 1956, when voters selected Democrat Estes Kefauver and Republican Dwight Eisenhower.

While Minnesotans are casting their ballots, the nation's attention will be focused on New York, where the Democratic primary could give Arkansas Gov. Bill Clinton a big push toward the nomination. The state's 244 delegates are the biggest prize today. Primaries also will be held today in Wisconsin and Kansas.

If Clinton wins in New York, it would be difficult for former California Gov. Jerry Brown or anyone else to catch him. A win by Brown could throw the Democratic contest into turmoil.

There are signs of unrest in both New York and Minnesota that could affect the primary results today. The latest Star Tribune/WCCO-TV Minnesota Poll shows that voters are not happy about their financial situations, are not confident that things will get better and are dissatisfied with the way the country is being run.

In New York, some voters aren't pleased with the choices they have today.


**Details of the Minnesota primary: Page 1B.**
**Details of the New York primary: Page 7A.**


# Peru leader, army seize government

**From News Services**

**Lima, Peru**
Wielding newly seized dictatorial powers Monday, President Alberto Fujimori and the Peruvian armed forces held top congressional leaders prisoner, censored the news media and surrounded key locations with troops and tanks.

Fujimori stunned the nation late Sunday by announcing an emergency government with military support. He closed the Congress and courts and suspended unspecified constitutional guarantees.

The commanders of the armed forces and national police pledged their "decided backing and support" for the move. It was what Latin Americans call an *auto-golpe*, a "self-coup," and it was the first reversal of a democratic trend that has filled the continent with elected governments.

The U.S. government deplored the change as a "regrettable step backwards" and suspended all aid to Peru.

Nations in Latin America joined in the criticism.


**Peru** continued on page 12A


# 'Duke II,' the sequel

## Laettner leads Devils' second-half surge

Staff Photo by Brian Peterson

**Duke coach Mike Krzyzewski looked up Monday night as a jubilant Christian Laettner held up the NCAA championship trophy at the Metrodome after the Blue Devils defeated Michigan, 71-51.**

*1992 Final Four*
TWIN CITIES

**By Paul Levy**
Staff Writer

The 1992 NCAA basketball championship was a classic case of better Laettner than never.

Christian Laettner, college player of the year, who had what his coach called "his worst half of the year," came back with 14 second-half points Monday night to lead Duke to a 71-51 victory over Michigan. It was the Blue Devils' second consecutive NCAA title — they became the first repeat champions since UCLA in 1973.

Duke's Grant Hill contributed 18 points and 10 rebounds and teammate Bobby Hurley was named the tournament's outstanding player, but it was Laettner who brought the 50,379 fans at the Metrodome out of their seats time and again in the second half.

Laettner claimed his team was not "emotionally spent" after Duke trailed 31-30 at halftime. He had struggled with seven turnovers and only five first-half points.

The second half was another matter, with Laettner scoring 10 quick points to give Duke a lead it never surrendered. Even with Chris Webber's 14 points and 11 rebounds, foul-plagued Michigan could do little to postpone the inevitable.

The victory capped a storybook season for the Blue Devils, who won their first 17 regular-season games and were ranked No. 1 in the nation from start to finish this season.

The fans, who were treated to a sloppy but exciting first half, seemed as tense as the players. Even in the second half, as Duke began to pull away, the crowd remained raucous. It was hardly a classic championship game, but few in the crowd seemed to complain. They knew that in watching Duke win, they had witnessed a piece of NCAA history. **Page 1S.**

■ Some tickets for last night's final game were going at *face value.* **Page 8A.**

■ How do the national media like it here? **Page 8A.**

# 2 arrested in death of elderly woman

**By Bill McAuliffe**
Staff Writer

St. Paul and Minneapolis police teamed up Monday to arrest two Minneapolis men in connection with the death of 88-year-old Estelle Flaherty of St. Paul.

Flaherty was apparently abducted March 29 as she sat in an idling car on University Av. in St. Paul's Midway area. The car was found less than four hours later in south Minneapolis; Flaherty's body was found two days later in a broken-down van three blocks from her apparent abduction.

Working on an anonymous tip received Friday, police yesterday matched a fingerprint from the stolen car to Roberto Orta Castillo, 29, and arrested him in south Minneapolis. Based on the tip, they also arrested Mario Rodriguez, 31, while he was walking near E. Franklin Av. and Clinton Av. S. in Minneapolis.

The two men are being held in Ramsey County jail. Police were still interviewing them yesterday and had


**Flaherty** continued on page 6A


# Isaac Asimov, the master of science fiction, dies at age 72

**New York Times**

**New York, N.Y.**
Isaac Asimov, the preeminent popular-science writer of the day and for more than 40 years one of the best and best-known writers of science fiction, died Monday at age 72 of heart and kidney failure.

Asimov wrote nearly 500 books on a wide range of subjects, from works for preschoolers to college textbooks.

He was perhaps best known for his science fiction, but he also wrote many mysteries, as well as books about the Bible, physics, chemistry, biology, astronomy, limericks, humor, Shakespeare, Gilbert and Sullivan, ancient history, modern history and many other subjects.

**Isaac Asimov wrote almost 500 books on a variety of topics.**

In the realm of science fiction, he was a pioneer in elevating the genre from pulp-magazine adventure to a more intellectual level that dealt with sociology, history, mathematics and science.


**Asimov** continued on page 6A


# High court tightens 'sting' rules in pornography case

**New York Times**

**Washington, D.C.**
The Supreme Court overturned a federal pornography conviction Monday on the ground of entrapment, ruling 5-4 that the government had failed to prove that a Nebraska farmer would have violated the law in the absence of an elaborate sting operation that took more than two years to induce him to order child pornography through the mail.

The decision, written by Justice Byron White, was based on earlier Supreme Court rulings on entrapment, requiring the prosecution to show that a person induced by government agents to commit a crime had been "independently predisposed" to the criminal conduct.

The ruling is unlikely to cramp the government's routine use of undercover operations to investigate drug trafficking or the fencing of stolen property. The majority appeared to view this case as an anomaly, an extreme misuse of government power in which an innocent person was led to commit a manufactured crime.

Still, the decision was notable, both


**Court** continued on page 6A


## Almanac

**Tuesday, April 7, 1992**
**98th day; 268 to go this year**
**Sunrise: 6:43. Sunset: 7:47**

### Today's weather/

Partly sunny and breezy. Winds northwest at 10 to 20 miles per hour. High 55. Clearing out tonight. Low 32.






Volume XI/Number 3 7 sections

Boy's reattached hand amputated/1B

Wolves join move to raise prices/1C

Abortion protests in Buffalo on hold/7A

VARIETY

**Cosby glow**

His show revived NBC, changed the face of TV

**MINNEAPOLIS EDITION**

■ End of limits on property taxes unlikely to bring big increases/**1B**

■ Dayton couple is charged in videotaped rape of 15-year-old/**2B**

■ Passenger alleges police brutality after high-speed chase/**2B**


# Star Tribune

THURSDAY/April 30/1992 — NEWSPAPER OF THE TWIN CITIES — 35¢


# King verdicts trigger violence

## Officers acquitted; jury finds no use of excessive force

From News Services

**Simi Valley, Calif.**
Four white Los Angeles police officers were acquitted Wednesday of using excessive force when they beat black motorist Rodney King 13 months ago, a beating captured on videotape and broadcast across the nation and around the world.

Violence and fires erupted in Los Angeles as leaders appealed for calm. One person was killed and at least 72 injured as looting, gunfire, street fignts, vandalism and fires swept across widely scattered parts of the city hours after the verdict. Gov. Pete Wilson said he would send in the National Guard. Mayor Tom Bradley declared a state of emergency.

There were reports of at least 40 fires, although not all could be immediately confirmed, a Fire Department spokesman said.

Daniel Freeman Memorial Hospital spokesman Marv Schnack said one person was killed in the violence and at least 72 were treated for injuries at her hospital alone.

The not guilty verdicts by the Ventura County jury, which included no blacks, were reached on the first day of deliberations last week, the panel's forewoman disclosed in court.

For the rest of the six days of deliberations, she said, the panel focused exclusively on a single count of assault against one of the officers. The jury was unable to reach a consensus, and Judge Stanley Weisberg declared a mistrial on that count.

Jurors apparently were not convinced by a videotape that showed the March 3, 1991, beating of King by Sgt. Stacey Koon and officers Laurence Powell, Theodore Briseno and Timothy Wind.

**Motorist Rodney King is shown after he was beaten by Los Angeles police officers in March 1991.**

The 81-second video, filmed by an amateur photographer, showed the officers delivering repeated baton blows and kicks to King as he lay prone on the ground. Its images have been seared in the minds of viewers the world over who have watched the tape broadcast repeatedly.

"My client and I are just outraged," King's lawyer, Steve Lerman, said after the verdict. "It sends a bad message. It says it's OK to go ahead and beat somebody when they're down and kick the crap out of them."

The acquittals triggered immediate protests and expressions of outrage by shocked community leaders, poli-

**Beating** continued on page 17A

Associated Press

**A motorcyclist watched as flames engulfed a row of businesses in south-central Los Angeles Wednesday night in the worst outbreak of violence. At least two dozen structures were burning throughout the business and residential area. Cars also were set on fire.**

## L.A. is hit by looting, assault and arson

Associated Press

**Los Angeles, Calif.**
Violence erupted Wednesday evening in Los Angeles after the acquittals of four white policemen in a black motorist's beating.

Looters ravaged stores, motorists were beaten, several buildings were set afire and demonstrators rushed police headquarters.

Gov. Pete Wilson agreed to send in National Guard troops at Mayor Tom Bradley's request.

In the worst outbreak of violence, an intersection in predominantly black south-central Los Angeles was plunged into chaos. Looters ran free, and motorists were pulled from cars and attacked. Police and paramedics were ordered to steer clear.

At least two dozen structures were burning throughout the sprawling south-central business and residential area, said Fire Department spokesman Bob Collis. Cars also were on fire.

Pillars of smoke could be seen across a wide area of the city. Fire companies were called in from other cities. Police with shotguns guarded firefighters.

"The fires in many cases have been very difficult for us to get to because of the hostility in the area. We're apparently getting police assistance

**Violence** continued on page 16A

## Tamoxifen to be tested to find if it can prevent breast cancer

By Gordon Slovut
Staff Writer

■ A Red Wing woman has been relieved of the seizures that plagued her three to 12 times a day in pioneering surgery at United Hospital in St. Paul. Dr. Mary E. Dunn put more than 600 shallow cuts on the patient's brain's surface. **Page 1B.**

The National Cancer Institute announced Wednesday the start of a large-scale trial to see if tamoxifen, one of the most benign of anticancer drugs, can prevent breast cancer in women.

The apparent ability of the drug to prevent osteoporosis (thinning of the bones) and heart attacks also will be evaluated.

"Tamoxifen has the potential to decrease breast cancer somewhere in the range of 30 to 50 percent," said Dr. Richard Zera, chief of cancer surgery at Hennepin County Medical Center and one of the principal researchers.

Hennepin County's is one of 270 medical centers around the country that are expected to enroll 16,000 healthy women willing to take one or two tablets a day for five years. Most other Twin Cities hospitals and the Duluth Clinic also will be involved.

Half of the women will get the real drug, half will get a placebo. They won't know which pill they have received until the five years are up.

Even if successful, tamoxifen won't entirely prevent breast cancer. "Clearly, not every woman responds to tamoxifen," Zera said. "So obviously, there is more than one mechanism for the development of breast cancer."

Dr. Bernard Fisher, the National Cancer Institute's chief investigator of the national trial, said there is no doubt that tamoxifen has an anticancer effect in some women who al-

**Treatment** continued on page 12A

### News inside/

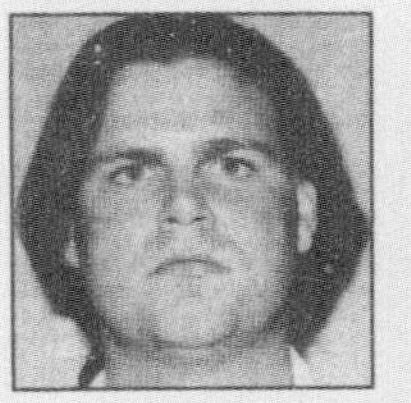

**Jolley tells of killing girl**

John Jolley, accused of killing Margaret Marques, 8, has testified that he suffers from multiple personalities and implied that he may have been acting as another personality during the killing. **Page 1B.**

**Is justice really blind?**

**When two men confess to a killing in court and no one gets convicted, what in the world is going on?**

**Columnists Jim Klobuchar and Doug Grow take a look at the perplexing and frustrating case of the killing of Julie Everson. Klobuchar writes about the prosecution and the jury. Grow remembers the victim.**
**Page 3B.**

**Other stories deal with the reaction to this truly bizarre event in our criminal justice system.**
**Pages 1B and 3B.**

## House votes to comply with subpoena for bank records

New York Times

**Washington, D.C.**
In a resounding defeat for the Democratic leadership, the House voted Wednesday night to comply with a Justice Department subpoena for House bank records.

The move came in two votes. The first, a Democratic proposal to challenge the subpoena in federal court in what was called a politically inspired investigation, was defeated by the Democratic-controlled House by a vote of 284-131; 123 Democrats broke ranks to join a unanimous Republican vote.

That was followed by a second vote on a resolution favored by Republicans, which was intended to do the opposite: give the Justice Department records of every check written on the now-closed House bank from July 1988 to October 1991. The resolution was overwhelmingly approved 347-64, with all the opposing votes cast by Democrats.

In a lawsuit filed last night, two Democratic representatives, Henry Gonzalez of Texas and Sidney Yates of Illinois, asked a U.S. District Court to invalidate the subpoena, arguing that it violated the House's powers as an independent branch of government.

Democratic members said the defeat was particularly damaging for Speaker Thomas Foley, who has consistently appeared to be slow in re-

**Bank** continued on page 13A

## More women showing clout in the political ring

Los Angeles Times

■ Discrimination in her job put Yeakel on career path to oppose Specter. **Page 11A.**

**Washington, D.C**
About midday on Tuesday, when Lynn Yeakel sensed that she had done the amazing and come out of nowhere to win the Democratic nomination for U.S. Senate in Pennsylvania, she called the president of the National Women's Political Caucus.

"I hope the women will get the credit," Yeakel told caucus president Harriett Woods. "I feel that women are standing up and making this possible."

Yeakel was expressing a hope shared by many this election year — that 1992 will become a turning point for women, the year in which they finally begin to significantly increase their numbers in the nation's councils.

Though they constitute more than half the population, though they have been a major factor in the economy for decades and though they boast records of achievement in many fields, women have never constituted

**Women** continued on page 10A

### Almanac

**Thursday, April 30, 1992**
**121st day; 245 to go this year**
**Sunrise: 6:04. Sunset: 8:15**

Some sun with high clouds. East winds at 15-25 mph. High 70.

**Index/**



**Telephones/**

| | |
|---|---|
| General information | 673-4000 |
| Classifieds | 673-7000 |
| Circulation | 673-4343 |


Volume XI/Number 26 — 7 sections

## Man suspected of luring children hurt in 35W chase

By Pat Pheifer
Staff Writer

A 37-year-old Minneapolis man who police said resembled a man who had tried to lure children into his car, was seriously injured Wednesday while fleeing from officers who wanted to question him.

Police said the unidentified man was naked from the waist down when he was removed from his car after it hit at least four cars and a truck on Interstate Hwy. 35W.

No one else was seriously injured, police said.

The accident closed the northbound lanes of I-35W at Diamond Lake Rd. in Minneapolis for nearly two hours yesterday and backed up rush-hour traffic in both directions.

According to reports at the Minneapolis Police Department, here's what happened:

Police officers first spotted the man shortly before 3 p.m. near 32nd St. and 3rd Av. S. in Minneapolis. He apparently fit the description of a man who, about a week ago, had been hanging around a school and trying to lure children into his car.

**Chase** continued on page 6A

Little Al is latest Unser to win Indy/1C

Twins batter Detroit Tigers 15-0/1C

'U' out of NCAA baseball tourney/1C

BUSINESS

**Eggs with low cholesterol**

Twin Cities company rolls out 'Simply Eggs'

**MINNEAPOLIS EDITION**

- Record numbers of women are seeking state office this year/**1B**
- Charles Kuralt names Ely, Minn., as his favorite summer spot/**1B**


# Star Tribune

MONDAY/May 25/1992 NEWSPAPER OF THE TWIN CITIES 35¢


# Baker condemns Serbia

## He calls for sanctions, hints at use of force

From News Services

**Lisbon, Portugal**
Secretary of State James Baker called Sunday for mandatory U.N. sanctions against Serbia for its aggression against Bosnia-Herzegovina, and he pointedly did not rule out U.S. participation in a multinational military force to open channels for humanitarian aid.

He also used his toughest language yet in criticizing European nations for not trying to stop the fighting or punish Belgrade.

"Anyone who is looking for reasons not to act, or arguing somehow that action in the face of this kind of nightmare is not warranted at this time, I think in the view of all of us in the civilized world is on the wrong wavelength," Baker said.

His remarks, made at the conclusion of an international conference on aid to the former Soviet Union, appeared to be directed especially at France and Greece, which seem to be holding up any European decision on sanctions against Serbia in the civil war engulfing Yugoslavia.

U.N. officials said the Security Council is likely to approve mandatory, step-by-step sanctions this week against Serbia and Montenegro, which have banded together as a smaller Yugoslavia as the other republics have declared their independence. U.N. actions are likely to include a ban on civilian air links and then an oil embargo, the officials said.

Baker also raised the specter of the Persian Gulf War, saying discussions had been opened at the United Nations on the possibility of invoking Chapter 7 of the U.N. Charter, which allows collective action, including economic sanctions and military intervention, against a renegade nation.

**Yugoslavia** continued on page 12A

125 YEARS

## On our anniversary, we present our past

Minneapolis Tribune.

Hinckley burns. Lucky Lindy crosses the Atlantic. Dillinger battles St. Paul police. A 350-pound bear is shot in the Hotel Duluth. Since 1867 the Star Tribune has covered it all. Today we celebrate the paper's 125th anniversary with a 32-page special section that highlights memorable moments in our history.

## U.S. to seek global effort to topple Serb leader

By William Beecher
Washington Bureau Chief

**Washington, D.C.**
After sitting on the sidelines during nearly a year of brutal warfare in Yugoslavia, the Bush administration has decided to seek the fall of Serbian President Slobodan Milosevic, who is now seen as the principal obstacle to peace in the Balkans.

Well-placed officials told the Star Tribune that unlike the case of Iraqi President Saddam Hussein, where President Bush has repeatedly called on the Iraqi people to topple him, the effort to oust Milosevic will probably remain undeclared. The strategy is to build a worldwide coalition to so severely isolate the country diplomatically and economically that the Serbian people will themselves decide to replace him through mass demonstrations and work stoppages.

"We have decided that Milosevic and his policies are the problem," one ranking official said.

"We have decided his word cannot be believed. He lies with a straight face to everyone, to Cyrus Vance, to Lord Carrington, to everyone," the official said, referring to two peace envoys who have traveled to the region. "It is his strategy that has caused so much bloodshed in Croatia, in Bosnia. He must go."

Even if Milosevic, in an effort to stave off diplomatic and economic pressures, should offer concessions, officials say there would be enormous skepticism that his word could be taken at face value any longer. "His concessions would have to be demonstrably irreversible," one official said.

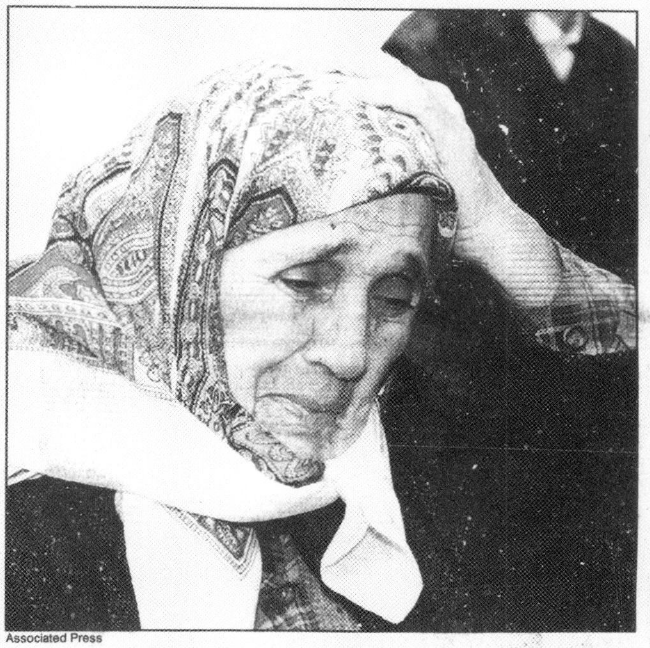
Associated Press

**A Muslim woman wept Sunday after she arrived by ferry at the Croatian port of Rijeka with a group of refugees from Bosnia-Herzegovina. More than 2,000 Muslim and Croatian refugees arrived in Rijeka yesterday.**

Senior planners concede that such an effort could take six to 12 months to have any chance of success. And during that time, more suffering is likely to befall the citizens of Bosnia-Herzegovina, Croatia and perhaps other former republics of Yugoslavia.

Even though Secretary of State James Baker declined to totally rule out military intervention, using force against Serbia would be difficult because no combination of Western nations is currently willing to get bogged down in a long, costly guerrilla war.

In Bosnia, for instance, 40,000 to 50,000 Serb irregulars, backed by regular army troops from Belgrade, and

**Milosevic** continued on page 12A

## Secret admirer believes Hubert H. Humphrey was too good to be forgotten

**Doug Grow**

On Friday, before the rain came, the woman was back at the gravesite of Hubert Humphrey.

She had red geraniums to place on the grave at Lakewood Cemetery in south Minneapolis.

"They really look nice," she said. "There was someone else who was there when I came with the flowers, they had come to see the place where Hubert was buried. They took pictures and commented on how nice the flowers looked."

For 10 years, the woman said, she's been taking flowers to Humphrey's grave for Memorial Day. For 10 years, she's also been taking a wreath with a red bow to the Humphrey grave at Christmas.

She's been taking the flowers and wreaths, she said, because she believed in Humphrey's approach to life and politics — and because she thought everyone else had forgotten him.

"I first noticed it 10 years ago when I was at the cemetery to put flowers on the grave of one of my aunts," she said. "Her grave is near Hubert's. I looked over there. It was day or two before Memorial Day and there weren't flowers there. I couldn't believe it. This man was a great senator. This man had been a vice president. My daughter told me, 'gone and forgotten.' I couldn't let that happen."

**Grow** continued on page 6A

## House vet Sabo caught between activists and the wider electorate

By Cliff Haas
Washington Bureau Correspondent

92 CAMPAIGN

**Washington, D.C.**
This improbable election year is making "Alice's Adventures in Wonderland" look reasonable.

An untested Texas billionaire, not even a declared candidate, is more popular than the Democratic and Republican contenders for the White House; the nation's leaders are debating the lifestyle of a character on a television situation comedy, and Rep. Martin Sabo is under fire for not being liberal enough.

At first glance, there is a comic element to it all. But it indicates how difficult governing has become in a nation of increasing diversity with a restless, angry and disappointed public confronting nervous and frustrated politicians.

Constituents complain that elected officials are aloof and ignoring them. Elected officials, in turn, complain that the public is blaming them for the problems inherent in trying to forge the consensus necessary to do business in a divided government.

Incumbents end up caught between activists, whose support is critical, pushing their individual causes and a wider electorate convinced that the politicians respond only to interest groups.

Sabo, who began winning elections in Minneapolis the same year John Kennedy was elected president, took his turn in the frying pan two weeks ago, when he had to struggle through seven ballots before securing the DFL endorsement at his district convention.

**Election** continued on page 5A

### Prime minister quits in Thailand

Prime Minister Suchinda Kraprayoon resigned over his role in the worst political violence in Thailand's modern history, but tens of thousands of Thais took to the streets demanding further punishment. **Page 2A.**

### Almanac

**Monday, May 25, 1992**
**146th day; 240 to go this year**
**Sunrise: 5:35. Sunset: 8:44**
Mostly cloudy and cool, with lingering showers and light northeast winds at 5 to 10 miles per hour. High of 55.



### Telephones/

| | |
|---|---|
| Circulation | 673-4343 |


Volume XI/Number 51 7 sections

## Coast Guard ordered to repatriate refugees caught fleeing from Haiti

Washington Post

**Kennebunkport, Maine**
President Bush, citing a "dangerous and unmanageable situation," on Sunday ordered the Coast Guard to forcibly repatriate Haitians caught fleeing their country by boat.

Shifting policy for the second time in a week in the face of the new, massive Haitian exodus, Bush signed an executive order that prevents fleeing Haitians from landing at the U.S. Naval Base at Guantanamo Bay, Cuba, to make a claim for political asylum.

Almost a third of the 34,000 Haitians processed at Guantanamo since the Sept. 30 coup in Haiti have been granted asylum or otherwise been approved for entry into the United States.

White House spokeswoman Judy Smith said that as a result of yesterday's executive order, the Coast Guard will process refugees on the high seas only if a captain determines there is an unusual emergency. The point is to deter Haitians from leaving their homeland and to require them to make their claims for asylum there, rather than on U.S. territory at Guantanamo or in Florida.

**Haiti** continued on page 10A

## Crime figures show suburbs are safe

By Norman Draper
Staff Writer

Miles from the central cities, new jails are being built, horrible crimes are being committed, and suburbanites are lining up at gun stores to arm themselves.

Despite this suggestion of a worsening crime problem in suburbia, none of it quite jibes with the most recent statistics from the Minnesota Department of Public Safety. Yet-to-be published figures for 1991 show crime rate decreases in many metro area suburbs, and little change or only modest increases in others.

In Eagan, Burnsville, Shoreview and Eden Prairie, the crime rates have been dropping for several years.

In Bloomington, Plymouth, Burnsville and Golden Valley, for example, crime rates have remained fairly steady, but they are still lower than those of the late 1970s and early to mid-1980s.

A few suburbs have witnessed crime rate hikes. But in terms of the most serious offenses, crime rates for suburbs remain substantially lower than those for Minneapolis and St. Paul.

"The truth is that in most communities here you're basically safe," said Rick DiBello, a Hennepin County planner.

**Crime** continued on page 10A

# INDEX

# INDEX

# iNDEX



## 1930~1939

# iNDEX

# iNDEX

# iNDEX

# *i*NDEX

# iNDEX



## 1990~1992